INFORMATION
PLEASE
ALMANAC®
ATLAS & YEARBOOK

49TH EDITION

HOUGHTON MIFFLIN COMPANY   BOSTON & NEW YORK

1996

Executive Editor
Otto Johnson
Associate Editor
Vera Dailey
Electronic Production Specialist
Christine Frantz
Manuscript Editors
Erik T. Johnson
Robert A.T. Scalza
Contributing Editors
Arthur Reed, Jr. (Current Events)
Thomas Nemeth, Ph.D. (World Countries)
Dennis M. Lyons (Sports)
Maps
Maps copyright ©
Mapping Specialists Ltd.,
Madison, Wisconsin.

The Information Please Almanac invites comments and suggestions from readers. Because of the many letters received, however, it is not possible to respond personally to every correspondent. Nevertheless, all suggestions are most welcome, and the editors will consider them carefully. (Information Please Almanac does not rule on bets or wagers.)

ISBN (Hardcover): 0-395-75525-5
ISBN (Paperback): 0-395-75524-7
ISSN: 0073-7860

Previous editions of INFORMATION PLEASE were published from 1984–1994 by Houghton Mifflin Company, in 1982 by A&W Publishing Company, in 1979–1981 by Simon & Schuster, in 1978 and 1977 by Information Please Publishing, Inc., and from 1947–1976 by Dan Golenpaul Associates.

HOW TO ORDER BY MAIL

Copies of Information Please Almanac may be ordered directly by mail from: Customer Service Department, Houghton Mifflin Company, 181 Ballardvale Road, Wilmington, MA 01887. FAX 800-634-7568. Phone toll-free, (800) 225-3362 for price and shipping information.

INFORMATION PLEASE ALMANAC®
Editorial Office
Houghton Mifflin Company
215 Park Avenue South
New York, N.Y. 10003

QUICK CONTENTS

Also *see* Contents, pages 4–5, and complete Index, pages 6–32.

CONTENTS

SPORTS CONTENTS

(Special Calendar of 1996 Olympic Gold Medal Events on pages 892, 960)

SPECIAL FEATURES

SPECIAL SECTIONS

USING THIS ALMANAC

Information Please Almanac is divided topically into 55 major sections which cover the scope of the *Almanac*. Readers can quickly locate most of the facts they are seeking by turning directly to the appropriate section. For example, the TAXES section will contain the latest data on the Federal Income Tax. Information on Social Security and Medicare can be found in the SOCIAL SECURITY & AGING section. Current postage information can be located in the special POSTAGE section. In addition, the thumb tabs on the front and back covers permit fast access to the information you need.

To find a particular fact, date, or idea in the Comprehensive Index, one should begin by looking under the most specific word. For example, to find the population of Des Moines, one should start by looking for Des Moines. But that city is not listed separately. Therefore, the next step is to look under Iowa or Cities, U.S. Under Iowa, the designated page (757) gives the latest population for Des Moines. Under Cities, U.S., there is a sub-head, Population figures, with two alternatives: Largest (of which Des Moines is not one) and Largest by State (which refers back to Iowa).

For President George Washington, one should look under Washington, before checking President. Where general headings (such as Presidents, U.S.) are given, they refer to a section where the subject is treated at some length.

COMPREHENSIVE INDEX

A

H

M

N

ELECTIONS

The Hundred and Fourth Congress

Composition of 103rd and 104th Congresses

	104th Congress[1]					103rd Congress[1]			
	Dem.	Rep.	Male	Female		Dem.	Rep.	Male	Female
Senate[2]	53	46	92	8		55	45	93	7
House[2]	233	199	386	49		257	178	388	47

1. One independent member in the House. 2. As of October 2, 1995 there is one vacancy in the Senate and two in the House.

The Senate

Senior Senator is listed first. The dates in the first column indicate period of service. The date given in parentheses after the Senator's name is year of birth. All terms are for six years and expire in January. Mailing address of Senators: The Senate, Washington, D.C. 20510.

ALABAMA
1979–97   Howell T. Heflin (D) (1941)
1987–99   Richard Shelby (R) (1934)
ALASKA
1968–97   Ted Stevens (R) (1923)
1981–99   Frank H. Murkowsky (R) (1933)
ARIZONA
1987–99   John McCain (R) (1936)
1995–2001 Jon Kyl (R) (1942)
ARKANSAS
1975–99   Dale Bumpers (D) (1925)
1979–97   David H. Pryor (D)(1934)
CALIFORNIA
1993–2001 Dianne Feinstein (D) (1933)
1993–1999 Barbara Boxer (D) (1940)
COLORADO
1991–97   Hank Brown (R) (1940)
1993–99   Ben Nighthorse Campbell (R) (1933)
CONNECTICUT
1981–99   Christopher J. Dodd (D) (1944)
1989–2001 Joseph I. Lieberman (D) (1942)
DELAWARE
1971–99   William V. Roth, Jr. (R) (1921)
1973–97   Joseph R. Biden, Jr. (D) (1942)
FLORIDA
1987–99   Bob Graham (D) (1936)
1989–2001 Connie Mack III (R) (1940)
GEORGIA
1972–97   Sam Nunn (D) (1938)
1993–99   Paul Cloverdell (R) (1939)
HAWAII
1963–99   Daniel K. Inouye (D) (1924)
1990–2001 Daniel K. Akaka (D) (1924)
IDAHO
1991–97   Larry E. Craig (R) (1945)
1993–99   Dirk Kempthorne (R) (1951)
ILLINOIS
1985–97   Paul Simon (D) (1928)
1993–99   Carol Moseley Braun (D) (1947)
INDIANA
1977–2001 Richard G. Lugar (R) (1932)
1989–99   Dan Coats (R) (1943)
IOWA
1981–99   Charles E. Grassley (R) (1933)
1985–97   Tom Harkin (D) (1939)
KANSAS
1969–99   Robert J. Dole (R) (1923)
1978–97   Nancy Landon Kassebaum (R) (1932)
KENTUCKY
1974–99   Wendell H. Ford (D) (1924)
1985–97   Mitch McConnell (R) (1942)

LOUISIANA
1972–97   J. Bennett Johnson (D) (1932)
1987–99   John B. Breaux (D) (1944)
MAINE
1979–97   William S. Cohen (R) (1940)
1995–2001 Olympia J. Snowe (R) (1947)
MARYLAND
1977–2001 Paul Sarbanes (D) (1933)
1987–99   Barbara A. Mikulski (D) (1936)
MASSACHUSETTS
1962–2001 Edward M. Kennedy (D) (1932)
1985–97   John F. Kerry (D) (1943)
MICHIGAN
1979–97   Carl Levin (D) (1934)
1995–2001 Spencer Abraham (R) (1952)
MINNESOTA
1991–97   Paul Wellstone (R) (1944)
1995–2001 Rod Grams (R) (1948)
MISSISSIPPI
1978–97   Thad Cochran (R) (1937)
1989–2001 Trent Lott (R) (1941)
MISSOURI
1987–99   Christopher S. (Kit) Bond (R) (1939)
1995–2001 John Ashcroft (R) (1942)
MONTANA
1978–97   Max Baucus (D) (1941)
1989–2001 Conrad Burns (R) (1935)
NEBRASKA
1979–97   J. James Exon (D) (1921)
1989–2001 Robert Kerrey (D) (1943)
NEVADA
1987–99   Harry M. Reid (D) (1939)
1989–2001 Dick Bryan (D) (1937)
NEW HAMPSHIRE
1991–97   Robert C. Smith (R) (1941)
1993–99   Judd Gregg (R) (1947)
NEW JERSEY
1979–97   Bill Bradley (D) (1943)
1982–99   Frank R. Lautenberg (D) (1924)
NEW MEXICO
1973–97   Pete V. Domenici (R) (1932)
1983–2001 Jeff Bingaman (D) (1943)
NEW YORK
1977–2001 Daniel P. Moynihan (D) (1927)
1981–99   Alfonse M. D'Amato (R) (1937)
NORTH CAROLINA
1973–97   Jesse Helms (R) (1921)
1993–99   Lauch Faircloth (R) (1928)
NORTH DAKOTA
1993–2001 Kent Conrad (D) (1948)
1987–99   Byron Dorgan (D) (1942)

OHIO
| 1974–99 | John H. Glenn, Jr. (D) (1921) |
| 1995–2001 | Mike DeWine (R) (1947) |

OKLAHOMA
| 1981–99 | Don Nickles (R) (1948) |
| 1995–97 | James M. Inhofe (R) (1934) |

OREGON
| 1967–97 | Mark O. Hatfield (R) (1922) |
| | Vacancy |

PENNSYLVANIA
| 1981–99 | Arlen Specter (R) (1930) |
| 1995–2001 | Rick Santorum (R) (1958) |

RHODE ISLAND
| 1961–97 | Claiborne Pell (D) (1918) |
| 1976–2001 | John H. Chafee (R) (1922) |

SOUTH CAROLINA
| 1956–97 | Strom Thurmond (R) (1902) |
| 1966–99 | Ernest F. Hollings (D) (1922) |

SOUTH DAKOTA
| 1979–97 | Larry Pressley (R) (1942) |
| 1987–99 | Thomas A. Daschle (D) (1947) |

TENNESSEE
| 1995–2001 | Bill Frist (R) (1952) |
| 1995–97 | Fred Thompson (R) (1942) |

TEXAS
| 1095–97 | Phil Gramm (R) (1942) |
| 1995–2001 | Kay Bailey Huchison (R) (1943) |

UTAH
| 1977–2001 | Orrin G. Hatch (R) (1934) |
| 1993–99 | Robert Bennett (R) (1933) |

VERMONT
| 1975–99 | Patrick J. Leahy (D) (1940) |

VIRGINIA
| 1979–97 | John H. Warner (R) (1927) |
| 1989–2001 | Charles Robb (D) (1939) |

WASHINGTON
| 1989–2001 | Slade Gorton (R) (1928) |
| 1993–99 | Patty Murray (D) (1950) |

WEST VIRGINIA
| 1959–2001 | Robert C. Byrd (D) (1918) |
| 1985–97 | John D. (Jay) Rockefeller IV (D) (1937) |

WISCONSIN
| 1989–2001 | Herbert Kohl (D) (1935) |
| 1993–99 | Russell D. Feingold, Jr. (D) (1953) |

WYOMING
| 1979–97 | Alan K. Simpson (R) (1931) |
| 1995–2001 | Craig Thomas (R) (1933) |

The House of Representatives

The numerals indicate the Congressional Districts of the states; the designation AL means At Large. All terms end January 1997. Mailing address of Representatives: House of Representatives, Washington, D.C. 20515.

ALABAMA
(7 Representatives)
1. H.L. (Sonny) Callahan (R)
2. Terry Everett (R)
3. Glen Browder (D)
4. Tom Bevill (D)
5. Bud Cramer (D)
6. Spencer Bachus (R)
7. Earl F. Hilliard (D)

ALASKA
(1 Representative)
AL Don Young (R)

ARIZONA
(6 Representatives)
1. Matt Salmon (R)
2. Ed Pastor (D)
3. Bob Stump (R)
4. John Shadegg (R)
5. Jim Kolbe (R)
6. J.D. Hayworth (R)

ARKANSAS
(4 Representatives)
1. Blanche Lambert (D)
2. Ray Thornton (D)
3. Tim Hutchinson (R)
4. Jay Dickey (R)

CALIFORNIA
(52 Representatives)
1. Frank Riggs (R)
2. Wally Herger (R)
3. Vic Fazio (D)
4. John T. Doolittle (R)
5. Robert T. Matsui (D)
6. Lynn C. Woolsey (D)
7. George Miller (D)
8. Nancy Pelosi (D)
9. Ronald V. Dellums (D)
10. Bill Baker (R)
11. Richard Pombo (R)
12. Tom Lantos (D)
13. Fortney Pete Stark (D)
14. Anna G. Eshoo (D)
15. Vacancy
16. Zoe Lofgren (D)
17. Sam Farr (D)
18. Gary A. Condit (D)
19. George P. Randanovich (R)
20. Cal Dooley (D)
21. Bill Thomas (R)
22. Andres Seastrand (R)
23. Elton Gallegly (R)
24. Anthony C. Beilenson (D)
25. Howard P. (Buck) McKeon (R)
26. Howard L. Berman (D)
27. Carlos J. Moorhead (R)
28. David Dreier (R)
29. Henry Waxman (D)
30. Xavier Becerra (D)
31. Matthew G. Martinez (D)
32. Julian C. Dixon (D)
33. Lucille Roybal-Allard (D)
34. Esteban E. Torres (D)
35. Maxine Waters (D)
36. Jane Harman (D)
37. Walter R. Tucker (D)
38. Steve Horn (R)
39. Ed Royce (R)
40. Jerry Lewis (R)
41. Jay Kim (R)
42. George E. Brown (D)
43. Ken Calvert (R)
44. Sonny Bono (R)
45. Dana Rohrabacher (R)
46. Robert K. Dornan (R)
47. Christopher Cox (R)
48. Ron Packard (R)
49. Brian P. Bilbray (R)
50. Bob Filner (D)
51. Randy (Duke) Cunningham (R)
52. Duncan Hunter (R)

COLORADO
(6 Representatives)
1. Patricia Schroeder (D)
2. David Skaggs (D)
3. Scott McInnis (R)
4. Wayne Allard (R)
5. Joel Hefley (R)
6. Dan Schaefer (R)

CONNECTICUT
(6 Representatives)
1. Barbara Bailey Kennelly (D)
2. Sam Gejdenson (D)
3. Rose L. DeLauro (D)
4. Christopher Shays (R)
5. Gary A. Franks (R)
6. Nancy L. Johnson (R)

DELAWARE
(1 Representative)
AL Michael N. Castle (R)

FLORIDA
(23 Representatives)
1. Joe Scarborough (R)
2. Pete Peterson (D)
3. Corrine Brown (D)
4. Tillie K. Fowler (R)
5. Karen L. Thurman (D)
6. Clifford B. Stearns (R)
7. John L. Mica (R)
8. Bill McCollum (R)
9. Michael Bilirakis (R)
10. C.W. Bill Young (R)
11. Sam M. Gibbons (D)
12. Charles T. Canady (R)
13. Dan Miller (R)
14. Porter J. Goss (R)
15. Dave Weldon (R)
16. Mark Foley (R)
17. Carrie P. Meek (D)
18. Ileane Ros-Lehtineor (R)
19. Harry Johnston (D)
20. Peter Deutsch (D)
21. Lincoln Diaz-Balart (R)
22. Clay Shaw (R)
23. Alcee L. Hastings (D)

GEORGIA
(11 Representatives)
1. Jack Kingston (R)
2. Sanford Bishop (D)
3. Mac Collins (R)
4. John Linder (R)
5. John Lewis (D)
6. Newt Gingrich (R)
7. Bob Barr (R)
8. Saxby Chambliss (R)
9. Nathan Deal (R)
10. Charlie Norwood (R)
11. Cynthia McKinney (D)

HAWAII
(2 Representatives)
1. Neil Abercrombie (D)
2. Patsy Takemoto Mink (D)

IDAHO
(2 Representatives)
1. Helen Chenoweth (R)
2. Mike Crapo (R)

ILLINOIS
(20 Representatives)
1. Bobby L. Rush (D)
2. Vacancy
3. William O. Lipinski (D)
4. Luis V. Gutierrez (D)
5. Michael Patrick Flanagan (R)
6. Henry J. Hyde (R)
7. Cardiss Collins (D)
8. Phillip M. Crane (R)
9. Sidney R. Yates (D)
10. John E. Porter (R)
11. Gerald C. Weller (R)
12. Jerry F. Costello (D)
13. Harris F. Fawell (R)
14. J. Dennis Hastert (R)
15. Thomas W. Ewing (R)
16. Donald Manzullo (R)
17. Lane Evans (D)
18. Ray LaHood (R)
19. Glenn Poshard (D)
20. Richard J. Durbin (D)

INDIANA
(10 Representatives)
1. Peter J. Visclosky (D)
2. David M. McIntosh (R)
3. Tim Roemer (D)
4. Mark Edward Souder (R)
5. Steve Buyer (R)
6. Dan Burton (R)
7. John T. Meyers (R)
8. John Hostettler (R)
9. Lee H. Hamilton (D)
10. Andrew Jacobs, Jr. (D)

IOWA
(5 Representatives)
1. Jim Leach (R)
2. Jim Nussle (R)
3. Jim Ross Lightfoot (R)
4. Greg Ganske (R)
5. Tom Latham (R)

KANSAS
(4 Representatives)
1. Pat Roberts (R)
2. Sam Brownback (R)
3. Jan Meyers (R)
4. Todd Tiahrt (R)

KENTUCKY
(6 Representatives)
1. Edward Whitfield (R)
2. Ron Lewis (R)
3. Mike Ward (D)
4. Jim Bunning (R)
5. Harold Rogers (R)
6. Scotty Baesler (D)

LOUISIANA
(7 Representatives)
1. Robert Livingston, Jr. (R)
2. William J. Jefferson (D)
3. W.J. (Billy) Tauzin (R)
4. Cleo Fields (D)
5. Jim McCrery (R)
6. Richard H. Baker (R)
7. Jimmy Hayes (D)

MAINE
(2 Representatives)
1. James B. Longley, Jr. (R)
2. John Baldacci (D)

MARYLAND
(8 Representatives)
1. Wayne T. Gilchrest (R)
2. Robert L. Ehrlich, Jr. (R)
3. Benjamin L. Cardin (D)
4. Albert R. Wynn (D)
5. Steny H. Hoyer (D)
6. Roscoe G. Bartlett (R)
7. Kweisi Mfume (D)
8. Constance A. Morella (R)

MASSACHUSETTS
(10 Representatives)
1. John W. Olver (D)
2. Richard E. Neal (D)
3. Peter Blute (R)
4. Barney Frank (D)
5. Martin T. Meehan (D)
6. Peter G. Torkildsen (R)
7. Edward J. Markey (D)
8. Joseph P. Kennedy II (D)
9. Joe Moakley (D)
10. Gerry E. Studds (D)

MICHIGAN
(16 Representatives)
1. Bart Stupak (D)
2. Peter Hoekstra (R)
3. Vernon J. Ehlers (R)
4. Dave Camp (R)
5. James A. Barcia (D)
6. Fred Upton (R)
7. Nick Smith (R)
8. Dick Chrysler (R)
9. Dale E. Kildee (D)
10. David E. Bonior (D)
11. Joe Knollenberg (R)
12. Sander Levin (D)
13. Lynn Nancy Rivers (R)
14. John Conyers, Jr. (D)
15. Barbara-Rose Collins (D)
16. John D. Dingell (D)

MINNESOTA
(8 Representatives)
1. Gil Gutknecht (R)
2. David Minge (D)
3. Jim Ramstad (R)
4. Bruce F. Vento (D)
5. Martin Olav Sabo (D)
6. William P. Luther (D)
7. Collin C. Peterson (D)
8. James L. Oberstar (D)

MISSISSIPPI
(5 Representatives)
1. Roger Wicker (R)
2. Bennie G. Thompson (D)
3. G.V. (Sonny) Montgomery (D)
4. Mike Parker (D)
5. Gene Taylor (D)

MISSOURI
(9 Representatives)
1. William Clay, Sr. (D)
2. James M. Talent (R)
3. Richard A. Gephardt (D)
4. Ike Skelton (D)
5. Karen McCarthy (D)
6. Pat (Patsy Ann) Danner (D)
7. Melton D. Hancock (R)
8. Bill Emerson (R)
9. Harold L. Volkmer (D)

MONTANA
(1 Representative)
AL Pat Williams (D)

NEBRASKA
(3 Representatives)
1. Doug Bereuther (R)
2. Jon Christensen (R)
3. Bill Barrett (R)

NEVADA
(2 Representatives)
1. John Ensign (R)
2. Barbara F. Vucanovich (R)

NEW HAMPSHIRE
(2 Representatives)
1. Bill Zeliff (R)
2. Charles Bass (R)

NEW JERSEY
(13 Representatives)
1. Robert E. Andrews (D)
2. Frank A. LoBiondo (R)
3. Jim Saxton (R)
4. Christopher H. Smith (R)
5. Marge Roukema (R)
6. Frank Pallone, Jr. (D)
7. Bob Franks (R)
8. Bill Martini (R)
9. Robert G. Torricelli (D)
10. Donald M. Payne (D)
11. Rodney Frelinghuysen (R)
12. Dick Zimmer (R)
13. Robert Menendez (D)

NEW MEXICO
(3 Representatives)
1. Steven H. Schiff (R)
2. Joseph R. Skeen (R)
3. Bill Richardson (D)

NEW YORK
(31 Representatives)
1. Michael P. Forbes (R)
2. Rick A. Lazio (R)
3. Peter T. King (R)
4. Daniel Frisa (R)
5. Gary L. Ackerman (D)
6. Floyd H. Flake (D)
7. Thomas J. Manton (D)
8. Jerrold L. Nadler (D)
9. Charles E. Schumer (D)
10. Edolphus Towns (D)
11. Major R. Owens (D)
12. Nydia M. Velazquez (D)
13. Susan Molinari (R)
14. Carolyn B. Maloney (D)
15. Charles B. Rangel (D)
16. Jose E. Serrano (D)
17. Eliot L. Engel (D)
18. Nita M. Lowey (D)
19. Sue W. Kelly (R)
20. Benjamin A. Gilman (R)
21. Michael R. McNulty (D)
22. Gerald B.H. Solomon (R)
23. Sherwood L. Boehlert (R)
24. John M. McHugh (R)
25. James T. Walsh (R)
26. Maurice D. Hinchey (D)
27. Bill Paxon (R)
28. Louise M. Slaughter (D)
29. John L. LaFalce (D)
30. Jack Quinn (R)
31. Amo Houghton (R)

NORTH CAROLINA
(12 Representatives)
1. Eve M. Clayton (D)
2. David Funderbunk (R)
3. Walter B. Jones, Jr. (R)
4. Frederick Kenneth Heineman (R)
5. Richard Burr (R)
6. Howard Coble (R)
7. Charles G. Rose III (D)
8. W.G. (Bill) Hefner (D)
9. Sue Myrick (R)
10. T. Cass Ballenger (R)
11. Charles H. Taylor (R)
12. Mel Watt (D)

NORTH DAKOTA
(1 Representative)
AL Earl Pomeroy (D)

OHIO
(19 Representatives)
1. Steve Chabot (R)
2. Rob Portman (R)
3. Tony P. Hall (D)
4. Michael G. Oxley (R)
5. Paul E. Gillmor (R)
6. Frank A. Cremeans (R)
7. David L. Hobson (R)
8. John A. Boehner (R)
9. Marcy Kaptur (D)
10. Martin R. Hoke (R)
11. Louis Stokes (D)
12. John R. Kasich (R)
13. Sherrod Brown (D)
14. Thomas C. Sawyer (D)
15. Deborah Pryce (R)
16. Ralph Regula (R)
17. James A. Traficant, Jr. (D)
18. Bob Ney (R)
19. Steven C. LaTourette (R)

OKLAHOMA
(6 Representatives)
1. Steve Largent (R)
2. Tom Coburn (R)
3. Bill K. Brewster (D)
4. J.C. Watts (R)
5. Ernest Istook (R)
6. Frank Lucas (R)

OREGON
(5 Representatives)
1. Elizabeth Furse (D)
2. Wes Cooley (R)
3. Ron Wyden (D)
4. Peter De Fazio (D)
5. Catherine Webber (D)

PENNSYLVANIA
(21 Representatives)
1. Thomas M. Foglietta (D)
2. Chaka Fattah (D)
3. Robert A. Borski (D)
4. Ron Klink (D)
5. Bill Clinger (R)
6. Tim Holden (D)
7. Curt Weldon (R)
8. Jim Greenwood (R)
9. Bud Shuster (R)
10. Joseph M. McDade (R)
11. Paul E. Kanjorski (D)
12. John P. Murtha (D)
13. Jon D. Fox (R)
14. William J. Coyne (D)
15. Paul McHale (D)
16. Robert S. Walker (R)
17. George W. Gekas (R)
18. Mike Doyle (D)
19. Bill Goodling (R)
20. Rank R. Mascara (D)
21. Phil English (R)

RHODE ISLAND
(2 Representatives)
1. Patrick J. Kennedy (D)
2. John F. Reed (D)

SOUTH CAROLINA
(6 Representatives)
1. Mike Sanford (R)
2. Floyd D. Spence (R)
3. Lindsey Graham (R)
4. Bob Inglis (R)
5. John Spratt (D)

6. James E. Clyburn (D)

SOUTH DAKOTA
(1 Representative)
AL Tim Johnson (D)

TENNESSEE
(9 Representatives)
1. James H. Quillen (R)
2. John J. Duncan Jr. (R)
3. Zech Wamp (R)
4. Van Hilleary (R)
5. Bob Clement (D)
6. Bart Gordon (D)
7. Ed Bryant (R)
8. John Tanner (D)
9. Harold E. Ford (D)

TEXAS
(30 Representatives)
1. Jim Chapman (D)
2. Charles Wilson (D)
3. Sam Johnson (R)
4. Ralph M. Hall (D)
5. John Bryant (D)
6. Joe Barton (R)
7. Bill Archer (R)
8. Jack Fields (R)
9. Steve Stockman (R)
10. Lloyd Doggett (D)
11. Chet Edwards (D)
12. Pete Geren (D)
13. William M. (Mac) Thornberry (R)
14. Greg Laughlin (D)
15. E. (Kika) de la Garza (D)
16. Ronald Coleman (D)
17. Charles W. Stenholm (D)
18. Shelia Jackson Lee (D)
19. Larry Combest (R)
20. Henry B. Gonzalez (D)
21. Lamar Smith (R)
22. Tom DeLay (R)
23. Henry Bonilla (R)
24. Martin Frost (D)
25. Kent Bentsen (D)
26. Dick Armey (R)
27. Solomon P. Ortiz (D)
28. Frank Tejeda (D)
29. Gene Green (D)
30. Eddie Bernice Johnson (D)

UTAH
(3 Representatives)
1. James V. Hansen (R)

2. Enid Greene Waldholtz (R)
3. Bill Orton (D)

VERMONT
(1 Representative)
AL Bernard Sanders (I)

VIRGINIA
(11 Representatives)
1. Herbert H. Bateman (R)
2. Owen B. Pickett (D)
3. Robert C. Scott (D)
4. Norman Sisisky (D)
5. L.F. Payne, Jr. (D)
6. Robert W. Goodlatte (R)
7. Thomas J. Bliley, Jr. (R)
8. James P. Moran (D)
9. Frederick C. (Rich) Boucher (D)
10. Frank R. Wolf (R)
11. Thomas M. Davis III (R)

WASHINGTON
(9 Representatives)
1. Rick White (R)
2. Jack Metcalf (R)
3. Linda Smith (R)
4. Doc Hastings (R)
5. George Nethercutt (R)
6. Norm Dicks (D)
7. Jim McDermott (D)
8. Jennifer Dunn (R)
9. Randy Tate (R)

WEST VIRGINIA
(3 Representatives)
1. Alan B. Mollohan (D)
2. Bob Wise (D)
3. Nick Joe Rahall II (D)

WISCONSIN
(9 Representatives)
1. Mark W. Neumann (R)
2. Scott L. Klug (R)
3. Steve Gunderson (R)
4. Gerald Kleczka (D)
5. Tom Barrett (D)
6. Thomas E. Petri (R)
7. David R. Obey (D)
8. Toby Roth (R)
9. F. James Sensenbrenner, Jr. (R)

WYOMING
(1 Representative)
AL Barbara Cubin (R)

Characteristics of Voters in 1992 Presidential Election

(in thousands)

Characteristic	Persons of voting age	Persons reporting they voted Total	Percent	Persons reporting they did not vote	Characteristic	Persons of voting age	Persons reporting they voted Total	Percent	Persons reporting they did not vote
Male	88,557	53,312	60.2	35,245	Northeast	38,329	23,448	61.2	14,881
Female	97,126	60,554	62.3	36,573	Midwest	44,410	29,830	67.2	14,580
White	157,837	100,405	63.6	57,432	South	63,659	37,590	59.0	26,068
Black	21,039	11,371	54.0	9,668	West	39,286	22,997	58.5	16,289
Hispanic origin[1]	14,688	4,238	28.9	10,450	Education				
Age: 18–20	9,727	3,749	38.5	5,979	8 years or less	15,391	5,406	30.3	9,985
21–24	14,644	6,693	45.7	7,951	9–11 years	20,970	8,638	41.2	12,332
25–34	41,603	22,120	53.2	19,483	12 years	65,281	37,517	57.5	27,765
35–44	39,716	25,269	63.6	14,447	16 or more	37,351	30,236	81.5	7,115
45–54	28,058	19,292	68.8	8,766	Employed	116,290	74,138	63.8	42,152
55–64	21,089	15,107	71.6	5,982	Unemployed	8,263	3,820	46.2	4,444
65–74	18,445	13,607	73.8	4,839	Not in labor force	61,131	35,908	58.7	25,223
75 and over	12,401	8,030	64.8	4,371	**Total**	**185,684**	**113,866**	**61.3**	**71,818**

1. Persons of Hispanic origin may be of any race. *Source:* Department of Commerce, Bureau of Commerce, Bureau of the Census, *Current Population Reports,* April 1993..

Senate and House Standing Committees, 104th Congress

Committees of the Senate

Agriculture, Nutrition, and Forestry (17 members)
Chairman: Richard G. Lugar (Ind.)
Ranking Dem.: Patrick J. Leahy (Vt.)
Appropriations (28 members)
Chairman: Mark O. Hatfield (Ore.)
Ranking Dem.: Robert C. Byrd (W. Va.)
Armed Services (21 members)
Chairman: Strom Thurmond (S.C.)
Ranking Dem.: Sam Nunn (Ga.)
Banking, Housing, and Urban Affairs (16 members)
Chairman: Alfonse D'Amato (N.Y.)
Ranking Dem.: Paul S. Sarbanes (Md.)
Budget (22 members)
Chairman: Pete V. Domenici (N.M.)
Ranking Dem.: Jim Exon (Neb.)
Commerce, Science, and Transportation
(19 members)
Chairman: Larry Pressler (S.D.)
Ranking Dem.: Ernest F. Hollings (S.C.)
Energy and Natural Resources (18 members)
Chairman: Frank H. Murkowski (Alas.)
Ranking Dem.: J. Bennett Johnston (La.)
Environment and Public Works (16 members)
Chairman: John H. Chafee (R.I.)
Ranking Dem.: Max Baucus (Mont.)
Finance (20 members)
Chairman: William V. Roth, Jr. (Del.)
Ranking Dem.: Daniel Patrick Moynihan (N.Y.)
Foreign Relations (18 members)
Chairman: Jesse Helms (N.C.)
Ranking Dem.: Claiborne Pell (R.I.)
Governmental Affairs (15 members)
Chairman: William V. Roth, Jr. (Del.)
Ranking Dem.: John Glenn (Ohio)
Judiciary (18 members)
Chairman: Orrin G. Hatch (Utah)
Ranking Dem.: Joseph R. Biden, Jr. (Del.)
Labor and Human Resources (16 members)
Chairman: Nancy Landon Kassebaum (Kan.)
Ranking Dem.: Edward M. Kennedy (Mass.)
Rules and Administration (16 members)
Chairman: Ted Stevens (Alas.)
Ranking Dem.: Wendell H. Ford (Ky.)
Small Business (19 members)
Chairman: Christopher S. Bond (Mo.)
Ranking Dem.: Dale Bumpers (Ark.)
Veterans' Affairs (11 members)
Chairman: Alan K. Simpson (Wyom.)
Ranking Dem.: John D. Rockefeller IV (W. Va.)

Select and Special Committees

Aging (19 members)
Chairman: William S. Cohen (Maine)
Ranking Dem.: David Pryor (Ark.)
Ethics (6 members)
Chairman: Mitch McConnell (Ky.)
Ranking Dem.: Richard H. Bryan (Nev.)
Indian Affairs (17 members)
Chairman: John McCain (Ariz.)
Ranking Dem.: Daniel K. Inouye (Hawaii)
Intelligence (17 members)
Chairman: Arlen Specter (Pa.)
Ranking Dem.: Bob Kerrey (Neb.)

Committees of the House

Agriculture (49 members)
Chairman: Pat Roberts (Kan.)
Ranking Dem.: E. "Kika" de la Garza (Texas)
Appropriations (56 members)
Chairman: Robert L. Livingston (La.)
Ranking Dem.: David R. Obey (Wis.)
Banking and Financial Services (49 members)
Chairman: Jim Leach (Iowa)
Ranking Dem.: Henry B. Gonzalez (Texas)
Budget (42 members)
Chairman: John R. Kasich (Ohio)
Ranking Dem.: Martin Olav Sabo (Minn.)
Commerce (46 members)
Chairman: Thomas J. Bliley, Jr. (Va.)
Ranking Dem.: John D. Dingell (Mich.)
Economic and Educational Opportunities
(43 members)
Chairman: Bill Goodling (Pa.)
Ranking Dem.: William L. Clay (Mo.)
Government Reform and Oversight (49 members)
Chairman: William F. Clinger, Jr. (Pa.)
Ranking Dem.: Cardiss Collins (Ill.)
House Oversight (12 members)
Chairman: Bill Thomas (Calif.)
Ranking Dem.: Vic Fazio (Calif.)
International Relations (41 members)
Chairman: Benjamin A. Gilman (N.Y.)
Ranking Dem.: Lee H. Hamilton (Ind.)
Judiciary (35 members)
Chairman: Henry J. Hyde (Ill.)
Ranking Dem.: John Conyers, Jr. (Mich.)
National Security (55 members)
Chairman: Floyd D. Spence (S.C.)
Ranking Dem.: Ronald V. Dellums (Calif.)
Resources (45 members)
Chairman: Don Young (Alaska)
Ranking Dem.: George Miller (Calif.)
Rules (13 members)
Chairman: Gerald B.H. Solomon (N.Y.)
Ranking Dem.: John J. Moakley (Mass.)
Science (50 members)
Chairman: Robert S. Walker (Pa.)
Ranking Dem.: George E. Brown, Jr. (Calif.)
Small Business (41 members)
Chairman: Jan Meyers (Kan.)
Ranking Dem.: John J. LaFalce (N.Y.)
Standards of Official Conduct (10 members)
Chairman: Nancy L. Johnson (Conn.)
Ranking Dem.: Jim McDermott (Wash.)
Transportation and Infrastructure (61 members)
Chairman: Bud Shuster (Pa.)
Ranking Dem.: Norman Mineta (Calif.)
Veterans' Affairs (33 members)
Chairman: Bob Stump (Ariz.)
Ranking Dem.: G.V. "Sonny" Montgomery
(Miss.)
Ways and Means (36 members)
Chairman: Bill Archer (Texas)
Ranking Dem.: Sam M. Gibbons (Fla.)

Select Committee

Intelligence (16 members)
Chairman: Larry Combest (Texas)
Ranking Dem.: Norm Dicks (Wash.)

Speakers of the House of Representatives

Dates served	Congress	Name and State	Dates served	Congress	Name and State
1789–1791	1	Frederick A. C. Muhlenberg (Pa.)	1869–1869	40	Theodore M. Pomeroy (N.Y.)[5]
1791–1793	2	Jonathan Trumbull (Conn.)	1869–1875	41–43	James G. Blaine (Me.)
1793–1795	3	Frederick A. C. Muhlenberg (Pa.)	1875–1876	44	Michael C. Kerr (Ind.)[6]
1795–1799	4–5	Jonathan Dayton (N.J.)[1]	1876–1881	44–46	Samuel J. Randall (Pa.)
1799–1801	6	Theodore Sedgwick (Mass.)	1881–1883	47	J. Warren Keifer (Ohio)
1801–1807	7–9	Nathaniel Macon (N.C.)	1883–1889	48–50	John G. Carlisle (Ky.)
1807–1811	10–11	Joseph B. Varnum (Mass.)	1889–1891	51	Thomas B. Reed (Me.)
1811–1814	12–13	Henry Clay (Ky.)[2]	1891–1895	52–53	Charles F. Crisp (Ga.)
1814–1815	13	Langdon Cheves (S.C.)	1895–1899	54–55	Thomas B. Reed (Me.)
1815–1820	14–16	Henry Clay (Ky.)[3]	1899–1903	56–57	David B. Henderson (Iowa)
1820–1821	16	John W. Taylor (N.Y.)	1903–1911	58–61	Joseph G. Cannon (Ill.)
1821–1823	17	Philip P. Barbour (Va.)	1911–1919	62–65	Champ Clark (Mo.)
1823–1825	18	Henry Clay (Ky.)	1919–1925	66–68	Frederick H. Gillett (Mass.)
1825–1827	19	John W. Taylor (N.Y.)	1925–1931	69–71	Nicholas Longworth (Ohio)
1827–1834	20–23	Andrew Stevenson (Va.)[4]	1931–1933	72	John N. Garner (Tex.)
1834–1835	23	John Bell (Tenn.)	1933–1934	73	Henry T. Rainey (Ill.)[7]
1835–1839	24–25	James K. Polk (Tenn.)	1935–1936	74	Joseph W. Byrns (Tenn.)[8]
1839–1841	26	Robert M. T. Hunter (Va.)	1936–1940	74–76	William B. Bankhead (Ala.)[9]
1841–1843	27	John White (Ky.)	1940–1947	76–79	Sam Rayburn (Tex.)
1843–1845	28	John W. Jones (Va.)	1947–1949	80	Joseph W. Martin, Jr. (Mass.)
1845–1847	29	John W. Davis (Ind.)	1949–1953	81–82	Sam Rayburn (Tex.)
1847–1849	30	Robert C. Winthrop (Mass.)	1953–1955	83	Joseph W. Martin, Jr. (Mass.)
1849–1851	31	Howell Cobb (Ga.)	1955–1961	84–87	Sam Rayburn (Tex.)[10]
1851–1855	32–33	Linn Boyd (Ky.)	1962–1971	87–91	John W. McCormack (Mass.)[11]
1855–1857	34	Nathaniel P. Banks (Mass.)	1971–1977	92–94	Carl Albert (Okla.)[12]
1857–1859	35	James L. Orr (S.C.)	1977–1987	95–99	Thomas P. O'Neill, Jr. (Mass.)[13]
1859–1861	36	Wm. Pennington (N.J.)	1987–1989	100–101	James C. Wright, Jr. (Tex.)[14]
1861–1863	37	Galusha A. Grow (Pa.)	1989–1994	101–103	Thomas S. Foley (Wash.)
1863–1869	38–40	Schuyler Colfax (Ind.)	1995–	104–	Newt Gingrich (Ga.)

1. George Dent (Md.) was elected Speaker pro tempore for April 20 and May 28, 1798. 2. Resigned during second session of 13th Congress. 3. Resigned between first and second sessions of 16th Congress. 4. Resigned during first session of 23rd Congress. 5. Elected Speaker and served the day of adjournment. 6. Died between first and second sessions of 44th Congress. During first session, there were two Speakers pro tempore: Samuel S. Cox (N.Y.), appointed for Feb. 17, May 12, and June 19, 1876, and Milton Sayler (Ohio), appointed for June 4, 1876. 7. Died in 1934 after adjournment of second session of 73rd Congress. 8. Died during second session of 74th Congress. 9. Died during third session of 76th Congress. 10. Died between first and second sessions of 87th Congress. 11. Not a candidate in 1970 election. 12. Not a candidate in 1976 election. 13. Not a candidate in 1986 election. 14. Resigned during first session of 101st Congress. *Source: Congressional Directory.*

Floor Leaders of the Senate

Democratic	Republican
Gilbert M. Hitchcock, Neb. (Min. 1919–20)	Charles Curtis, Kan. (Maj. 1925–29)
Oscar W. Underwood, Ala. (Min. 1920–23)	James E. Watson, Ind. (Maj. 1929–33)
Joseph T. Robinson, Ark. (Min. 1923–33, Maj. 1933–37)	Charles L. McNary, Ore. (Min. 1933–44)
Alben W. Barkley, Ky. (Maj. 1937–46, Min. 1947–48)	Wallace H. White, Jr., Me. (Min. 1944–47, Maj. 1947–48)
Scott W. Lucas, Ill. (Maj. 1949–50)	Kenneth S. Wherry, Neb. (Min. 1949–51)
Ernest W. McFarland, Ariz. (Maj. 1951–52)	Styles Bridges, N. H. (Min. 1951–52)
Lyndon B. Johnson, Tex. (Min. 1953–54, Maj. 1955–60)	Robert A. Taft, Ohio (Maj. 1953)
Mike Mansfield, Mont. (Maj. 1961–77)	William F. Knowland, Calif. (Maj. 1953–54, Min. 1955–58)
Robert C. Byrd, W. Va. (Maj. 1977–81, Min. 1981–86, Maj. 1987–88)	Everett M. Dirksen, Ill. (Min. 1959–69)
George John Mitchell, Me. (Maj. 1989–1994)	Hugh Scott, Pa. (Min. 1969–1977)
Thomas A. Daschle, S.D. (Min. 1995–)	Howard H. Baker, Jr., Tenn. (Min. 1977–81, Maj. 1981–84)
	Robert J. Dole, Kan. (Maj. 1985–86, Min. 1987–94, Maj. 1995–)

NOTE: Min. = Minority Leader; Maj. = Majority Leader. *Source:* United States Senate, Secretary for the Majority.

Presidential Election of 1992

Principal Candidates for President and Vice President
Republican: George H. Bush; J. Danforth Quayle
Democratic: William J. Clinton; Albert A. Gore, Jr.
Independent: H. Ross Perot; James B. Stockdale

State	Total	Bush Rep.	Percent	Clinton Dem.	Percent	Perot Ind.	Percent	Plurality	Electoral vote		
									D	R	I
Alabama	1,688,060	804,283	48	690,080	41	183,109	11	114,203R	—	9	—
Alaska	258,506	102,000	39	78,294	30	73,481	28	23,706R	—	3	—
Arizona	1,486,975	572,086	38	543,050	37	353,741	24	29,036R	—	8	—
Arkansas	950,653	337,324	35	505,823	53	99,132	10	168,499D	6	—	—
California	11,131,721	3,630,574	33	5,121,325	46	2,296,006	21	1,490,751D	54	—	—
Colorado	1,569,180	562,850	36	629,681	40	366,010	23	66,831D	8	—	—
Connecticut	1,616,332	578,313	36	682,318	42	348,771	22	104,005D	8	—	—
Delaware	289,735	102,313	35	126,055	44	59,213	20	23,742D	3	—	—
D.C.	227,572	20,698	9	192,619	85	9,681	4	171,921D	3	—	—
Florida	5,314,492	2,173,310	41	2,072,798	39	1,053,067	20	100,512R	—	25	—
Georgia	2,321,125	995,252	43	1,008,966	43	309,657	13	13,714D	13	—	—
Hawaii	372,842	136,822	37	179,310	48	53,003	14	42,488D	4	—	—
Idaho	482,142	202,645	42	137,013	28	130,395	27	65,632R	—	4	—
Illinois	5,050,157	1,734,096	34	2,453,350	49	840,515	17	719,254D	22	—	—
Indiana	2,305,871	989,375	43	848,420	37	455,934	20	140,955R	—	12	—
Iowa	1,354,607	504,891	37	586,353	43	253,468	19	81,462D	7	—	—
Kansas	1,157,236	449,951	39	390,434	34	312,358	27	59,517R	—	6	—
Kentucky	1,492,900	617,178	41	665,104	45	203,944	14	47,926D	8	—	—
Louisiana	1,790,017	733,386	41	815,971	46	211,478	12	82,585D	9	—	—
Maine	679,499	206,504	30	263,420	39	206,820	30	56,600D	4	—	—
Maryland	1,985,046	707,094	36	988,571	50	281,414	14	281,477D	10	—	—
Massachusetts	2,773,664	805,039	29	1,318,639	48	630,731	23	513,600D	12	—	—
Michigan	4,274,673	1,554,940	36	1,871,182	44	824,813	19	316,242D	18	—	—
Minnesota	2,347,947	747,841	32	1,020,997	43	562,506	24	273,156D	10	—	—
Mississippi	981,793	487,793	50	400,258	41	85,626	9	87,535R	—	7	—
Missouri	2,391,565	811,159	34	1,053,873	44	518,741	22	242,714D	11	—	—
Montana	410,611	144,207	35	154,507	38	107,225	26	10,300D	3	—	—
Nebraska	739,283	344,346	47	217,344	29	174,687	24	127,002R	—	5	—
Nevada	506,318	175,828	35	189,148	37	132,580	26	13,320D	4	—	—
New Hampshire	537,945	202,484	38	209,040	39	121,337	23	6,556D	4	—	—
New Jersey	3,343,594	1,356,865	41	1,436,206	43	521,829	16	79,341D	15	—	—
New Mexico	569,986	212,824	37	261,617	46	91,895	16	48,793D	5	—	—
New York[1]	6,926,933	2,346,649	34	3,444,450	50	1,090,721	16	1,097,801D	33	—	—
North Carolina	2,611,850	1,134,661	43	1,114,042	43	357,864	14	20,619R	—	14	—
North Dakota	308,133	136,244	44	99,168	32	71,084	23	37,076R	—	3	—
Ohio	4,939,964	1,894,310	38	1,984,942	40	1,036,426	21	90,632D	21	—	—
Oklahoma	1,390,359	592,929	43	473,066	34	319,878	23	119,863R	—	8	—
Oregon	1,462,643	475,757	33	621,314	42	354,091	24	145,557D	7	—	—
Pennsylvania	4,959,810	1,791,841	36	2,239,164	45	902,667	18	447,323D	23	—	—
Rhode Island	453,478	131,605	29	213,302	47	105,051	23	81,697D	4	—	—
South Carolina	1,202,527	577,507	48	479,514	40	138,872	12	97,993R	—	8	—
South Dakota	336,254	136,718	41	124,888	37	73,295	22	11,830R	—	3	—
Tennessee	1,982,638	841,300	42	933,521	47	199,968	10	92,221D	11	—	—
Texas	6,154,018	2,496,071	41	2,281,815	37	1,354,781	22	214,256R	—	32	—
Utah	743,999	322,632	43	183,429	25	203,400	27	119,232R	—	5	—
Vermont	289,701	88,122	30	133,592	46	65,991	23	45,470D	3	—	—
Virginia	2,558,665	1,150,517	45	1,038,650	41	348,639	14	111,867R	—	13	—
Washington	2,288,228	731,235	32	993,039	43	541,801	24	261,804D	11	—	—
West Virginia	683,711	241,974	35	331,001	48	108,829	16	89,027D	5	—	—
Wisconsin	2,531,114	930,855	37	1,041,066	41	544,479	22	110,211D	11	—	—
Wyoming	200,587	79,347	40	68,160	34	51,263	26	11,187R	—	3	—
Total	104,426,659	39,104,545	37	44,909,899	43	19,742,267	19	5,805,345D	370	168	—

1. Bush figure is combined Republican, Conservative, and Right to Life Party votes; Clinton figure is combined Democratic and Liberal Party votes. NATIONAL TOTALS OF OTHER CANDIDATES FOR PRESIDENT: Andre Marrow, Libertarian, 291,628; James "Bo" Gritz, Populist/America First, 107,002; Lenora Fulani, New Alliance, 73,708; Howard Phillips, U.S. Taxpayers, 43,398; John Hagelin, Natural Law, 39,163; Ron Daniels, Independent, 27,969; Lyndon LaRouche, Independent, 26,334; James Mac Warren, Socialist Workers, 23,091; Drew Bradford, Independent, 4,749; Jack Herer, Grassroots, 3,875; John Quinn Brisben, Socialist, 3,064; Helen Halyard, Workers League, 3,050; John Yiamouyiannis, Independent, 2,199; Delbert Ehlers, Independent, 1,149; Earl Dodge, Prohibition, 961; Jim Boren, Apathy, 956; Eugene Hem, Third Party, 405; Isabelle Masters, Looking Back Group, 339; Robert J. Smith, American, 293; Gloria Estella La Riva, Workers World, 181; None of These Candidates, Nevada, 2,537; write-ins, 13,907. *Source:* Federal Election Commission.

The Governors of the Fifty States

State	Governor	Current term[1]	State	Governor	Current term[1]
Ala.	Fob James, Jr. (R)	1995–99	Mont.	Mark Racinot (R)	1993–97
Alaska	Tony Knowles (D)	1994–98 [2]	Neb.	Ben Nelson (D)	1995–99
Ariz.	Fife Symington (R)	1994–98 [2]	Nev.	Bob Miller (D)	1995–99
Ark.	Jim Guy Tucker (D)	1995–99	N.H.	Steve Merrill (R)	1995–97
Calif.	Pete Wilson (R)	1995–99	N.J.	Christine Todd Whitman (R)	1994–98
Colo.	Roy Romer (D)	1995–99	N.M.	Gary Johnson (R)	1995–99
Conn.	John Rowland (R)	1995–99	N.Y.	George E. Pataki (R)	1995–99
Del.	Tom Carver (D)	1993–97	N.C.	Jim Hunt (D)	1993–97
Fla.	Lawton Chiles (D)	1995–99	N.D.	Ed Schafer (R)	1993–97
Ga.	Zell Miller (D)	1995–99	Ohio	George V. Voinovich (R)	1995–99
Hawaii	Ben Cayetano (D)	1994–98 [2]	Okla.	Frank Keating (R)	1995–99
Idaho	Phil Batt (R)	1995–99	Ore.	John Kitzhaber (D)	1995–99
Ill.	Jim Edgar (R)	1995–99	Pa.	Tom Ridge (R)	1995–99
Ind.	B. Evan Bayh III (D)	1993–97	R.I.	Lincoln C. Almond (R)	1995–99
Iowa	Terry Branstad (R)	1995–99	S.C.	David Beasley (R)	1995–99
Kan.	Bill Graves (R)	1995–99	S.D.	Wlliam J. Janklow (R)	1995–99
Ky.	Brereton C. Jones (D)	1991–95 [2]	Tenn.	Don Sundquist (R)	1995–99
La.	Edwin W. Edwards (D)	1992–96	Texas	George W. Bush (R)	1995–99
Me.	Angus King (Ind.)	1995–99	Utah	Mike Leavitt (R)	1993–97
Md.	Parris N. Glendening (D)	1995–99	Vt.	Howard Dean (D)	1995–97
Mass.	William F. Weld (R)	1995–99	Va.	George Felix Allen (R)	1994–98
Mich.	John Engler (R)	1995–99	Wash.	Mike Lowry (D)	1993–97
Minn.	Arne H. Carlson (R)	1995–99	W. Va.	Gaston Caperton (D)	1993–97
Miss.	Kirk Fordice (R)	1992–96	Wis.	Tommy G. Thompson (R)	1995–99
Mo.	Mel Carnahan (D)	1993–97	Wyo.	Jim Geringer (R)	1995–99

1. Except where indicated, all terms begin in January. 2. December.

Black Elected Officials

Year	U.S. and State Legislatures[1]	City and County Offices[2]	Law Enforcement[3]	Education[4]	Total
1970 (Feb.)	182	715	213	362	1,472
1975 (Apr.)	299	1,878	387	939	3,503
1980 (July)	326	2,832	526	1,206	4,890
1981 (July)	343	2,863	549	1,259	5,014
1982 (July)	342	2,951	563	1,259	5,115
1983 (July)	366	3,197	607	1,369	5,559
1984 (Jan.)	396	3,259	636	1,363	5,654
1985 (Jan.)	407	3,517	661	1,431	6,016 [5]
1986 (Jan.)	420	3,824	676	1,504	6,424 [5]
1987 (Jan.)	440	3,966	728	1,547	6,681
1988 (July)	436	4,105	738	1,550	6,829
1989 (Jan.)	448	4,406	759	1,612	7,225
1990 (Jan.)	447	4,499	769	1,655	7,370
1991 (Jan.)	484	4,508	847	1,638	7,480
1992 (Jan.)	510	4,569	847	1,623	7,549 [6]
1993 (Jan.)	571	4,825	923	1,694	8,016 [6]

1. Includes elected State administrators and governors. 2. County commissioners and councilmen, mayors, vice mayors, aldermen, regional officials, and other. 3. Judges, magistrates, constables, marshals, sheriffs, justices of the peace, and other. 4. Members of State education agencies, college boards, school boards, and other. 5. Includes Black elected officials in the Virgin Islands. 6. Includes two statehood senators and one statehood representative, all non-voting, from the District of Columbia. *Source:* Joint Center for Political and Economic Studies, Washington, D.C., *Black Elected Officials: A National Roster,* Copyright.

1995 Annual Salaries of Federal Officials

President of the U.S.	$200,000 [1]	Senators and Representatives	$133,600
Vice President of the U.S.	171,500 [2]	President Pro Tempore of Senate	148,400
Cabinet members	148,400	Majority and Minority Leader of the Senate	148,400
Deputy Secretaries of State, Defense, Treasury	133,600	Majority and Minority Leader of the House	148,400
Deputy Attorney General	133,600	Speaker of the House	171,500
Secretaries of the Army, Navy, Air Force	133,600	Chief Justice of the United States	171,500
Under secretaries of executive departments	123,100	Associate Justices of the Supreme Court	164,100

1. Plus taxable $50,000 for expenses and a nontaxable sum (not to exceed $100,000 a year) for travel expenses. 2. Plus taxable $10,000 for expenses. NOTE: All salaries shown above are taxable. *Source:* Office of Personnel Management.

Blockbuster Tax Reform

By Robert T. Gray

"My plan would make the tax system so simple that Americans could fill out their taxes on a postcard."

"We've got to tear the income-tax system out by its roots. We have to remove the Internal Revenue Service from the lives of Americans totally."

"[We] need to abolish the income-tax law of this land and substitute . . . an unlimited savings allowance."

Such proposals have generally come from reformers deemed out of touch with political and fiscal reality. But they are being advanced today by top elected officials with major roles in setting tax policy.

The certainty that recommendations for such fundamental change will become the center of a national debate over the next few years—the legislative firepower of their sponsors guarantees that—is an important measure of Washington's changed political environment.

The principal advocate of a flat-rate tax is Rep. Richard K. Armey, R–Texas, majority leader of the House of Representatives, whose plan is geared to a 10-line return for individual taxpayers—the postcard method of filing. He proposes a single rate of 17 percent, with capital gains and returns on savings and investments included from taxable income.

The call for abolishing the present income-tax system comes from Rep. Bill Archer, R–Texas, who as chairman of the House Ways and Means Committee, is one of the most powerful individuals in government when it comes to drafting tax legislation.

The statement on behalf of replacing the current tax system with one that provides for "an unlimited savings allowance" was made by Sen. Pete V. Domenici, R–N.M., chairman of the Senate Budget Committee and one of Congress' most respected authorities on fiscal policy, and his partner in this bipartisan endeavor, Sen. Sam Nunn, D–Ga.

The Armey Plan

"A flat-rate tax," Majority Leader Armey told *Nation's Business*, "does everything that you want a tax code to do. It covers individuals' entire earnings—but only taxes them once. It is simple, direct, and honest. It would lower the tax burden on nearly all Americans, particularly families with children. And it would create a powerful incentive to save and invest."

Income would be determined by subtracting a personal allowance from salary, wage, and pension income. The balance would be taxed at a flat rate of 20 percent for the first two years the new system is in effect and 17 percent thereafter. Currently, the top effective rate is nearly 40 percent, and the average marginal rate is 28 percent.

Interest would be neither deductible nor taxable, resulting in a net increase in revenue collected, Armey says. He notes that more interest is deducted

than taxed under the current system. The exclusion of returns on savings and investments from taxable income would also eliminate the present double taxation of that income, Armey says.

He would abolish the present withholding system, which he calls the most egregious "of all the deceptive government practices." Taxpayers would be expected to file their postcard returns monthly or quarterly to enable them to "measure the true cost of government against the benefits."

The personal allowance would be determined by filing status and the number of dependents. A married couple filing jointly would receive an allowance of $26,200; a single taxpayer, $13,100; and single head of household, $17,200. The personal allowance for each dependent (exclusive of spouse) would be $5,300. Those figures would be indexed to cost-of-living increases.

"Because of the generous exemptions," Armey says of his plan, "millions of taxpayers are taken off the rolls entirely, and middle-income Americans receive a tax-cut."

Businesses would pay the 17 percent rate on the surplus of revenues over expenses. That levy would apply to corporate, partnership, professional, farm, and rental profits as well as to royalties. The tax base would be gross revenue less costs of goods, services, capital equipment, structures, land, and wages paid to employees. No deductions would be permitted for costs of fringe benefits, interest, or payments to owners. The expensing provision—full write-off of capital investments—would eliminate current depreciation schedules.

The majority leader says the initial 20 percent level would provide most Americans with a modest tax cut while limiting revenue losses. The plan would be kept revenue-neutral, he says, through spending cuts that it would also mandate.

Beyond that, the plan relies on the premise that tax cuts provide incentives for work and investments that increase incomes. "By the third year," the Armey plan says, "it will be abundantly clear that a low,

Rep. Armey's Flat-Tax Form

1. Wages, Salary, Pensions . . . . ____
2. Personal Allowance . . . . ____
   a. $26,200 for married filing jointly . . . . ____
   b. $13,100 for single . . . . ____
   c. $17,200 for single head of household . . . . . . ____
3. Number of dependents, not including spouse . ____
4. Personal allowances for dependents
   (line 3 multiplied by $5,300) . . . . ____
5. Total personal allowances (line 2 plus line 4) . ____
6. Taxable wages
   (line 1 less line 5, if positive; otherwise zero) . ____
7. Tax (17 percent of line 6) . . . . ____
8. Tax already paid . . . . ____
9. Tax due (line 7 less line 8, if positive) . . . . ____
10. Refund due (line 8 less line 7, if positive) . . . . ____

simple, and neutral tax code will energize the economy and lead to greater revenue for the Treasury."

But like previous flat-rate proposals, Armey's has encountered the argument that it would be politically impossible to eliminate tax deductions related to home ownership and charitable contributions.

Armey responds that while sharp reductions in tax rates during the Reagan administration lowered the value of such deductions, home ownership and charitable giving grew because of economic growth stimulated by the tax cuts.

The Archer Plan

If he succeeds in his goal of abolishing the present income-tax system, Ways and Means Chairman Archer would replace it with some form of consumption tax. He says the specifics of his plan are being developed and that he is determining "which type of design is best for the United States."

When that is done, Archer adds, he will launch the debate over alternative tax systems at congressional hearings, possibly this year.

But preservation of the present system is not among those options. "I have lost confidence that we can ever fix the income-tax system," Archer says. "We have to find a new concept." Tax-reform goals, he says, should include simplification, incentives for savings and investment, extension of tax compliance to the underground economy, and recognition of the U.S. role in a global economy where the nation "is in a competition that we must win."

"The present system fails on all of those counts," Archer says. "It seems clear to me that the only tax that can succeed in achieving those goals is some type of a broad-based consumer tax that completely and totally replaces the present system." Under the system that he envisions, "there is no tax on savings and investment. You don't pay taxes until you consume."

To aid U.S. competitiveness in world trade, Archer says, the taxes would not apply to U.S. goods being shipped for sale overseas but would affect imports destined for sale in this country. Those steps would be designed to be "GATT-legal," he says, meaning that they would be acceptable under the General Agreement on Tariffs and Trade, which sets international rules—including those involving tax policy—on trade.

While agreeing to consider a flat tax, Archer nevertheless says that he has "sort of matured" beyond that concept. "We are looking at a very different world in the next century," he says of the trade aspects of tax policy. "A flat tax cannot be waived at the border. It cannot be removed. Nor can it be charged to incoming products at the border."

His goal, he says, is a tax code "where the cost of our government can be off-loaded onto incoming foreign products when they enter this country. . . . If we can do that, we can build a margin of 30 to 40 percent differential between our products and foreign products." The result, Archer predicts, will be "better, higher-paying jobs for millions of Americans."

While Archer is not ready to specify what type of consumption taxes he will recommend, the two most frequently discussed are a national sales tax and a value-added tax, or VAT, which is widely used in European countries.

A value-added tax is assessed at each stage of the process by which raw materials are converted into products and then sold. The tax is based on the value added at each point. In computing the tax, companies along the production chain deduct the amount paid for materials from the amount for which the product was sold, paying a tax on the balance, which represents the value added.

Critics of a VAT say that its strong money-raising capability is exact reason it should not be considered. They say that Congress could simply notch up the rate a point or two every time it wanted more money. Archer replies that all taxes need to have limits placed on them.

While Archer does not want to suggest that he is leaning toward a VAT as his preferred consumption tax, he says that his plan will be designed to eliminate excessive compliance costs from the tax system, not add to them.

The Domenici–Nunn Plan

In offering their tax-reform plan, Sens. Domenici and Nunn said in a joint statement that the current tax code "is doing a good job of discouraging savings." As a result, there are investment shortages that result in insufficient growth, stagnating incomes, and a loss of high-wage jobs, they added.

Specifics of their proposal—the Unlimited Savings Account (USA)—are still being drafted, but the sponsors have identified two major components:

Individual Taxes: Income would include wages, salaries, interest, dividends, earnings withdrawn from unincorporated businesses, proceeds from asset sales, and similar cash flow. There would be a "very generous standard deduction," probably in the range of $20,000 to $25,000 for a family of four.

The main feature of the proposal is an additional deduction for income put into savings. "That is the key," the senators say. "You save money, and you would deduct that money before you pay taxes. It is fundamentally different from what we do today."

The savings would be computed on a year-end to year-end basis. There would thus be no advantage to shifting money among various forms of savings and investment or to putting funds into savings accounts and investments with the intention of immediate withdrawal.

Deductions for home-mortgage interest and charitable contributions would also be allowed for postsecondary tuition. The sponsors warn, however, that "there is a trade-off—the higher the number of deductions, the higher the rates."

In addition to the family allowance—the plan's equivalent of the standard deduction—lower-income taxpayers would receive a credit equal to the current Social Security tax, against the amount of income taxes due.

Business taxes: All businesses, regardless of whether they are incorporated, would be taxed alike. After deducting expenses from gross sales, companies could further deduct the full costs of new plant and equipment—but not wages—for the year in which those expenses were incurred.

The balance would be taxed at "a low and flat rate," probably 10 percent or less. Taxing net cash flow rather than profits would be a fundamental change, the plan's sponsors say.

Businesses would also receive the credit against taxes due for their share of Social Security payroll taxes.

Products exported would not be taxed, but imports would be taxed on the same basis as products sold in this country.

Profits earned by U.S. companies overseas would not be included in their tax base, while profits of U.S.-based subsidiaries of foreign companies would be.

Although the Domenici–Nunn plan would eliminate about 75 percent of the current tax code's 700 sections, Domenici and Nunn point out that "in the final analysis, everybody pays taxes. That is not going to change. We are not offering a tax cut or tax increase. We are proposing a change in the way our democracy raises revenue."

They describe the principle message of their plan in these terms: "If you choose to defer some of your current consumption in favor of savings income for your future and the future of your children, the tax code will not penalize you for doing so."

And to business: "If you choose to invest your profits in a new machine or a new process that will help you grow and put more people to work, the tax code will help make this feasible."

Excerpted by permission, *Nation's Business*, April 1995. Copyright 1995, U.S. Chamber of Commerce.

History of the Income Tax in the United States

Source: Deloitte & Touche LLP

The nation had few taxes in its early history. From 1791 to 1802, the United States Government was supported by internal taxes on distilled spirits, carriages, refined sugar, tobacco and snuff, property sold at auction, corporate bonds, and slaves. The high cost of the War of 1812 brought about the nation's first sales taxes on gold, silverware, jewelry, and watches. In 1817, however, Congress did away with all internal taxes, relying on tariffs on imported goods to provide sufficient funds for running the Government.

In 1862, in order to support the Civil War effort, Congress enacted the nation's first income tax law. It was a forerunner of our modern income tax in that it was based on the principles of graduated, or progressive, taxation and of withholding income at the source. During the Civil War, a person earning from $600 to $10,000 per year paid tax at the rate of 3%. Those with incomes of more than $10,000 paid taxes at a higher rate. Additional sales and excise taxes were added, and an "inheritance" tax also made its debut. In 1866, internal revenue collections reached their highest point in the nation's 90-year history—more than $310 million, an amount not reached again until 1911.

The Act of 1862 established the office of Commissioner of Internal Revenue. The Commissioner was given the power to assess, levy, and collect taxes, and the right to enforce the tax laws through seizure of property and income and through prosecution. His powers and authority remain very much the same today.

In 1868, Congress again focused its taxation efforts on tobacco and distilled spirits and eliminated the income tax in 1872. It had a short-lived revival in 1894 and 1895. In the latter year, the U.S. Supreme Court decided that the income tax was unconstitutional because it was not apportioned among the states in conformity with the Constitution.

In 1913, the 16th Amendment to the Constitution made the income tax a permanent fixture in the U.S. tax system. The amendment gave Congress legal authority to tax income and resulted in a revenue law that taxed incomes of both individuals and corporations. In fiscal year 1918, annual internal revenue collections for the first time passed the billion-dollar mark, rising to $5.4 billion by 1920. With the advent of World War II, employment increased, as did tax collections—to $7.3 billion. The withholding tax on wages was introduced in 1943 and was instrumental in increasing the number of taxpayers to 60 million and tax collections to $43 billion by 1945.

In 1981, Congress enacted the largest tax cut in U.S. history, approximately $750 billion over six years. The tax reduction, however, was partially offset by two tax acts, in 1982 and 1984, which attempted to raise approximately $265 billion.

On October 22, 1986, President Reagan signed into law The Tax Reform Act of 1986, one of the most far reaching reforms of the United States tax system since the adoption of the income tax. In an attempt to remain revenue neutral, the Act called for a $120 billion increase in business taxation and a corresponding decrease in individual taxation over a five-year period.

Following what seemed to be a yearly tradition of new tax acts which began in 1986, the Revenue Reconciliation Act of 1990 was signed into law on November 5, 1990. As with the '87, '88, and '89 acts, the 1990 act, while providing a number of substantive provisions, was small in comparison with the 1986 act. The emphasis of the 1990 act was increased taxes on the wealthy.

On August 10, 1993, President Clinton signed the Revenue Reconciliation Act of 1993 into law. The Act's purpose was to reduce by approximately $496 billion the Federal deficit that would otherwise accumulate in fiscal years 1994 through 1998. Approximately $241 billion of the deficit reduction will be accomplished through tax increases.

In recent years, the tax system has come under increased scrutiny leading to proposals for tax reform. Many policy makers in Washington have advocated some form of flat tax, a value added tax, or a retail sales tax—or a combination of these. Because any new tax law would have to be considered and passed by the Presidential administration and both branches of Congress before a transition would take place, it is unlikely that a radically changed tax system would become fully effective prior to the year 2000.

Internal Revenue Service

The Internal Revenue Service (IRS), a bureau of the U.S. Treasury Department, is the federal agency charged with the administration of the tax laws passed by Congress. The IRS functions through a national office in Washington, 7 regional offices, 63 district offices, and 10 service centers.

Operations involving most taxpayers are carried out in the district offices and service centers. District offices are organized into Resources Management, Examination, Collection, Taxpayer Service, Employee Plans and Exempt Organizations, and Criminal Investigation. All tax returns are filed with the service centers, where the IRS computer operations are located.

IRS service centers are processing an ever increasing number of returns and documents. In 1994 the number of returns and supplemental documents processed totaled 204.97 million.

Prior to 1987, all tax return processing was performed by hand. This process was time consuming and costly. In an attempt to improve the speed and

Internal Revenue Service

	1994	1993	1992	1991	1990	1970
U.S. population (in thousands)	261,698	259,015	256,219	252,901	251,329	204,878
Number of IRS employees	110,665	113,352	116,673	115,628	111,858	68,683
Cost to govt. of collecting $100 in taxes	$.58	$0.60	$0.58	$0.56	$0.52	$0.45
Tax per capita	$4,878.00	$4,543.33	$4,374.38	$4,343.84	$4,203.12	$955.31
Collections by principal sources (in thousands of dollars)						
Total IRS collections	$1,276,466,776	$1,176,685,625	$1,120,799,558	$1,086,851,401	$1,056,365,652	$195,722,096
Income and profits taxes						
Individual	$619,819,153	585,774,159	557,723,156	546,876,876	540,228,408	103,651,585
Corporation	$154,204,684	131,547,509	117,950,796	113,598,569	110,016,539	35,036,983
Employment taxes	$443,831,352	411,510,516	400,080,904	384,451,220	367,219,321	37,449,188
Estate and gift taxes	$15,606,793	12,890,965	11,479,116	11,473,141	11,761,93	3,680,076
Alcohol taxes	NOTE 4	NOTE 4	NOTE 4	NOTE 4	NOTE 4	4,746,382
Tobacco taxes	NOTE 4	NOTE 4	NOTE 4	NOTE 4	NOTE 4	2,094,212
Manufacturers' excise taxes	NOTE 3	NOTE 3	NOTE 3	NOTE 3	NOTE 3	6,683,061
All other taxes	$43,004,794	34,962,476	33,565,587	30,451,596	27,139,445	2,380,609

NOTE: For fiscal year ending September 30th. NOTE 2: Alcohol and tobacco tax collections are included in the "All other taxes" amount. NOTE 3: Manufacturers' excise taxes are included in the "All other taxes" amount. NOTE 4: Alcohol and tobacco tax collections are now collected and reported by the Bureau of Alcohol, Tobacco, and Firearms. *Source:* IRS 1994 Annual Report.

efficiency of the manual processing procedure, the IRS began testing an electronic return filing system beginning with the filing of 1985 returns.

The two most significant results of the test were that refunds for the electronically filed returns were issued more quickly and the tax processing error rate was significantly lower when compared to paper returns.

Electronic filing of individual income tax returns with refunds became an operational program in selected areas for the 1987 processing year. This program is continually expanding. In 1993 12,342,000 individual returns were filed electronically. In 1994 13,510,000 individual returns were filed electronically.

In addition to expanding the program for the electronic filing of individual returns, the IRS has also implemented programs for the electronic filing of partnership, fiduciary, and employee benefit plan returns.

Auditing Tax Returns

Most taxpayers' contacts with the IRS arise through the auditing of their tax returns. The Service has been empowered by Congress to inquire about all persons who may be liable for any tax and to obtain for review the books and/or records pertinent to those taxpayers' returns. A wide-ranging audit operation is carried out in the 63 district offices by 15,409 revenue agents and 2,587 tax auditors.

Selecting Individual Returns for Audit

The primary method used by the IRS in selecting returns for audits is a computer program that measures the probability of tax error in each return. The higher the score, the greater the tax change potential. Other returns are selected for examination on the basis of claims for refund, multi-year audits, related return audits, and other audits initiated by the IRS as a result of informants' information, special compliance programs, and the information document matching program.

In 1994, the IRS recommended additional tax and penalties on 1,225,707 individual returns, totaling $6.2 billion.

The Appeals Process

The IRS attempts to resolve tax disputes through an administrative appeals system. Taxpayers who, after audit of their tax returns, disagree with a proposed change in their tax liabilities are entitled to an independent review of their cases. Taxpayers are able to seek an immediate, informal appeal with the Appeals Office. If, however, the dispute arises from a field audit and the amount in question exceeds $10,000, a taxpayer must submit a written protest. Alternatively, the taxpayer can wait for the examiner's report and then request consideration by the Appeals Office and file a protest if necessary. Taxpayers may represent themselves or be represented by an attorney, accountant, or any other advisor authorized to practice before the IRS. Taxpayers can forego their right to the above process and await receipt of a deficiency notice. At this juncture, taxpayers can either (1) not pay the deficiency and petition the Tax Court by a required deadline or (2) pay the deficiency and file a claim for refund with the District Director's office. If the claim is not allowed, a suit for refund may be brought either in the District Court or the Claims Court within a specified period.

Federal Individual Income Tax

The Federal individual income tax is levied on the world-wide income of U.S. citizens and resident aliens and on certain types of U.S. source income of non-residents. For a non-itemizer, "tax table income" is adjusted gross income (*see* below) less $2,500 for each personal exemption and the standard deduction (*see* below). If a taxpayer itemizes, tax table income is adjusted gross income minus total itemized deductions and personal exemptions. In addition, individuals may also be subject to the alternative minimum tax.

Tax Brackets—1995
Taxable Income

Joint return	Single Taxpayer	Rate
$0–$39,000	$0–$23,350	15%
39,001–94,250	23,351–56,550	28%
94,251–143,600	56,551–117,950	31%[2]
143,601–256,500	117,951–256,500	36%[2]
256,501 and up[1]	256,501 and up[1]	39.6%[2]

1. The deduction for personal exemptions is phased out as the taxpayer's gross income exceeds $172,050 for a joint return and $114,700 for single taxpayers. 2. The tax rate is effectively increased because total otherwise allowable itemized deductions are reduced by 3% of the taxpayer's adjusted gross income in excess of $114,700.

Who Must File a Return[1]

You must file a return if you are:	and your gross income is at least:
Single (legally separated, divorced, or married living apart from spouse with dependent child) and are under 65	$6,400
Single (legally separated, divorced, or married living apart from spouse with dependent child) and are 65 or older	$7,350
A person who can be claimed as a dependent on your parent's return, and who has taxable dividends, interest, or other unearned income	$650
Head of household under age 65	$8,250
Head of household over age 65	$9,200
Married, filing jointly, living together at end of year (or at date of death of spouse), and both are under 65	$11,550
Married, filing jointly, living together at end of year (or at date of death of spouse), and one is 65 or older	$12,300
Married, filing jointly, living together at end of year (or at date of death of spouse), and both are 65 or older	$13,050
Married, filing separate return, or married but not living together at end of year over age 65	$2,500

1. In 1995.

Adjusted Gross Income

Gross income consists of wages and salaries, unemployment compensation, tips and gratuities, interest, dividends, annuities, rents and royalties, up to 85% of Social Security Benefits if the recipient's income exceeds a base amount, and certain other types of income. Among the items excluded from gross income, and thus not subject to tax, are public assistance benefits and interest on exempt securities (mostly state and local bonds).

Adjusted gross income is determined by subtracting from gross income: alimony paid, penalties on early withdrawal of savings, payments to an I.R.A. (reduced proportionately based upon adjusted gross income levels if taxpayer is an active participant in an employer maintained retirement plan), payments to a Keogh retirement plan, and self-employed health insurance payments. Employee business expenses and job related moving expenses are treated as itemized deductions.

Itemized Deductions

Taxpayers may itemize deductions or take the standard deduction. The standard deduction amounts for 1995 are as follows: Married filing jointly and surviving spouses, $6,550; Heads of household, $5,750; Single, $3,900; and Married filing separate returns, $3,275. Taxpayers who are age 65 or over or are blind are entitled to an additional standard deduction of $950 for single taxpayers and $750 for a married taxpayer.

In itemizing deductions, the following are major items that may be deducted in 1995: state and local income and property taxes, charitable contributions, employee moving expenses, medical expenses (exceeding 7.5% of adjusted gross income), casualty losses (only the amount over the $100 floor which exceeds 10% of adjusted gross income), mortgage interest, and miscellaneous deductions (deductible only to the extent by which cumulatively they exceed 2% of adjusted gross income).

Personal Exemptions

Personal exemptions are available to the taxpayer for himself, his spouse, and his dependents. The 1995 amount is $2,500 for each individual. No exemption is allowed to a taxpayer who can be claimed as a dependent on another taxpayer's return.

Credits

Taxpayers can reduce their income tax liability by claiming the benefit of certain tax credits. Each dollar of tax credit offsets a dollar of tax liability. The following are a few of the available tax credits:

Certain low-income households may claim an Earned Income Credit. The maximum Earned Income Credit is $314 for taxpayers with no qualifying children, $2,094 for taxpayers with one qualifying child and $3,110 for taxpayers with two or more qualifying children. This maximum credit will be reduced if earned income or adjusted gross income exceeds $11,290, or $5,130 for taxpayers with no qualifying children. For families with one qualifying child, the credit will be zero if earned income or adjusted gross income exceeds $24,396; for families with two or more qualifying children the credit will be zero if income exceeds $26,673, and for families with no qualifying children, the credit will be zero if income exceeds $9,230. The earned income credit is a refundable credit.

A credit for Child and Dependent Care Expenses is available for amounts paid to care for a child or other dependent so that the taxpayer can work. The credit is between 20% and 30% (depending on adjusted gross income) of up to $2,400 of employment-related expenses for one qualifying child or dependent and up to $4,800 of expenses for two or more qualifying individuals.

The elderly and those under 65 who are retired under total disability may be entitled to a credit of up to $750 (if single) or $1,125 (if married and filing jointly). No credit is available if the taxpayer is single and has adjusted gross income of $17,500 or more. Similarly, the credit is unavailable to a married couple filing jointly if their adjusted gross income exceeds $25,000.

Federal Income Tax Comparisons

Taxes at Selected Rate Brackets After Standard Deductions and Personal Exemptions[1]

Adjusted gross income	Single return listing no dependents				Joint return listing two dependents			
	1995	1994	1993	1975	1995	1994	1993	1975
$ 10,000	$ 540	$ 563	$ 593	$ 1,506	$ -3,110[2]	$ -2,527[2]	$-1,511[2]	$ 829
20,000	2,040	2,063	2,093	4,153	-773	-358	236	2,860
30,000	3,573	3,693	3,833	8,018	2,018	2,078	2,160	5,804
40,000	6,373	6,493	6,633	12,765	3,518	3,578	3,660	9,668
50,000	9,173	9,293	9,433	18,360	5,018	5,078	5,160	14,260

1. For comparison purposes, tax rate schedules were used. 2. Refund based on a basic earned income credit for families with dependent children.

Federal Corporation Taxes

Corporations are taxed under a graduated tax rate structure as shown in the chart. If a corporation has taxable income in excess of $100,000, the amount of tax shall be increased by the lesser of five percent of such excess or $11,750. When a corporation has taxable income in excess of $15,000,000 the amount of tax shall be increased by an additional amount equal to the lesser of three percent of such excess or $100,000.

If the corporation qualifies, it may elect to be an S corporation. If it makes this election, the corporation will not (with certain exceptions) pay corporate tax on its income. Its income is instead passed through and taxed to its shareholders. There are several requirements a corporation must meet to qualify as an S corporation including having 35 or fewer share-holders, and having only one class of stock.

Tax Brackets—1995

Taxable income	Tax rate
$0–$50,000	15%
$50,001–$75,000	25%
$75,001–$100,000	34%
$101,000–$335,000	39%
$335,001–$10,000,000	34%
10m–15m	35%
15m–18.3m	38%
18.3m and up	35%

State Corporation Income and Franchise Taxes

All states except Texas, Nevada, South Dakota, Washington, and Wyoming impose a tax on corporation net income. The majority of states impose the tax at flat rates ranging from 2.35% to approximately 12.5%. Several states have adopted a graduated basis of rates for corporations.

Nearly all states follow the federal law in defining net income. However, many states provide for varying exclusions and adjustments.

A state is empowered to tax all of the net income of its domestic corporations. With regard to non-resi-dent corporations, however, it may only tax the net income on business carried on within its boundaries. Corporations are, therefore, required to apportion their incomes among the states where they do business and pay a tax to each of these states. Nearly all states provide an apportionment to their domestic corporations, too, in order that they not be unduly burdened.

Several states tax unincorporated businesses separately.

Federal Estate and Gift Taxes

A Federal Estate Tax Return must generally be filed for the estate of every U.S. citizen or resident whose gross estate, adjusted taxable gifts, and specific exemption exceed $600,000. An estate tax return must also generally be filed for the estate of a non-resident, if the value of his gross estate in the U.S. is more than $60,000 at the date of death. The estate tax return is due nine months after the date of death of the decedent, but a reasonable extension of time to file may be obtained for good reason.

Under the unified federal estate and gift tax structure, individuals who made taxable gifts during the calendar year are required to file a gift tax return by April 15 of the following year.

A unified credit of $192,800 is available to offset both estate and gift taxes. Any part of the credit used to offset gift taxes is not available to offset estate taxes. As a result, although they are still taxable as gifts, lifetime transfers no longer cushion the impact of progressive estate tax rates. Lifetime transfers and transfers made at death are combined for estate tax rate purposes.

Gift taxes are computed by applying the uniform rate schedule to lifetime taxable transfers (after deducting the unified credit) and subtracting the taxes payable for prior taxable periods. In general, estate taxes are computed by applying the uniform rate schedule to cumulative transfers and subtracting the gift taxes paid. An appropriate adjustment is made for taxes on lifetime transfers—such as certain gifts within three years of death—in a decedent's estate.

Among the deductions allowed in computing the amount of the estate subject to tax are funeral expenditures, administrative costs, claims and bequests to religious, charitable, and fraternal organizations or government welfare agencies, and state inheritance taxes. For transfers made after 1981 during life or death, there is an unlimited marital deduction.

An annual gift tax exclusion is provided that permits tax-free gifts to each donee of $10,000 for each year. A husband and wife who agree to treat gifts to third persons as joint gifts can exclude up to $20,000 a year to each donee. An unlimited exclusion for medical expenses and school tuition paid for the benefit of any donee is also available.

Federal Estate and Gift Taxes

Unified Transfer Tax Rate Schedule, 1995[1]

| If the net amount is: | | Tentative tax is: | | |
From	To	Tax +	%	On excess over
$ 0	$ 10,000	$ 0	18	$ 0
10,001	20,000	1,800	20	10,000
20,001	40,000	3,800	22	20,000
40,001	60,000	8,200	24	40,000
60,001	80,000	13,000	26	60,000
80,001	100,000	18,200	28	80,000
100,001	150,000	23,800	30	100,000
150,001	250,000	38,800	32	150,000
250,001	500,000	70,800	34	250,000
500,001	750,000	155,800	37	500,000
750,001	1,000,000	248,300	39	750,000
1,000,001	1,250,000	345,800	41	1,000,000
1,250,001	1,500,000	448,300	43	1,250,000
1,500,001	2,000,000	555,800	45	1,500,000
2,000,001	2,500,000	780,800	49	2,000,000
2,500,001	3,000,000	1,025,800	53	2,500,000
3,000,001 and up	—	1,290,800	55	3,000,000

1. The estate and gift tax rates are combined in the single rate schedule effective for the estates of decedents dying, and for gifts made, after Dec. 31, 1976. 2. The tentative tax determined above is increased by an amount equal to 5% with respect to cumulative taxable transfers between $10,000,000 and $21,040,000.

Tax Freedom Day

Tax Freedom Day is the day on which the American taxpayer will have earned enough money to pay all federal, state, and local taxes, assuming every dollar earned from the start of the year went to pay taxes. Tax Freedom Day in 1994 fell on May 6, three days later than the 1993 date. The three-day jump was primarily due to the tax increases passed in the 1993 federal budget.

According to a special report by Tax Foundation economist, Patrick Fleenor, Tax Freedom Day 1995 arrived on May 6. This means that the average American had to work the first 126 days of the year in order to pay his total tax bill of $8,303. Approximately 83 of these days were spent working to pay

the $5,461 federal portion of this bill. The balance of the days were spent working to pay state and local taxes toaling $2,841.

The residents of Connecticut and New York bore the nation's highest average tax burdens in 1995. The average resident of Connecticut worked 97 days to pay his $8,464 federal tax bill. The balance of the 144 days were spent working to pay his state and local taxes, which were expected to total $4,120. New Yorkers, on average, had to work 85 days to pay their federal tax bill of $6,754. The remaining 59 days were spent working to pay their state and local taxes which were expected to total $4,618. ☐

State General Sales and Use Taxes[1]

State	Percent rate	State	Percent rate	State	Percent rate
Alabama	4	Louisiana	4	Ohio	5
Arizona	5	Maine	6	Oklahoma	4.5
Arkansas	4.5	Maryland	5	Pennsylvania	6
California	6	Massachusetts	5	Rhode Island	7
Colorado	3	Michigan	6	South Carolina	5
Connecticut	6	Minnesota	6.5	South Dakota	4
D.C.	5.75	Mississippi	7	Tennessee	6
Florida	6	Missouri[2]	4.225	Texas	6.25
Georgia	4	Nebraska	5	Utah	4.875
Hawaii	4	Nevada	6.5	Vermont	5
Idaho	5	New Jersey	6	Virginia[4]	3.5
Illinois	6.25	New Mexico	5	Washington	6.5
Indiana	5	New York[3]	4	West Virginia	6
Iowa	5	North Carolina	4	Wisconsin	5
Kansas	4.9	North Dakota	5	Wyoming	4
Kentucky	6				

1. Local and county taxes, if any, are additional. 2. State use tax 5.725% in areas where local tax and state meet or exceed 5.725%. In areas that do not meet or exceed 5.725%, the use tax rate is 4.225%. 3. New York City, 8.25%. 4. Local rate 1%. NOTE: Alaska, Delaware, Montana, New Hampshire, and Oregon have no state-wide sales and use taxes. *Source: Information Please Almanac questionnaires to the states.*

FY 1995 Federal Tax Burden Per Capita and
FY 1994 Federal Expenditures Per Dollar of Taxes

	1995 Federal tax burden per capita	Rank	1994 Federal expenditures per dollar of taxes[1]	Rank
United States	**$4,996**	—	**$1.00**	—
Alabama	3,922	41	1.37	6
Alaska	5,797	6	1.32	11
Arizona	3,981	40	1.17	19
Arkansas	3,751	46	1.26	14
California	5,130	17	0.97	34
Colorado	5,182	15	1.01	30
Connecticut	7,769	1	0.66	50
Delaware	5,969	5	0.71	48
Florida	4,974	20	1.03	28
Georgia	4,414	31	1.04	27
Hawaii	5,370	12	1.21	18
Idaho	3,986	39	1.11	22
Illinois	5,739	8	0.75	47
Indiana	4,518	28	0.87	40
Iowa	4,287	33	1.09	23
Kansas	4,773	24	1.04	25
Kentucky	3,836	44	1.21	17
Louisiana	3,848	43	1.33	10
Maine	4,094	36	1.34	8
Maryland	5,777	7	1.28	13
Massachusetts	6,113	4	0.97	33
Michigan	5,072	19	0.82	41
Minnesota	5,220	14	0.80	44
Mississippi	3,170	50	1.69	2
Missouri	4,585	25	1.33	9
Montana	4,060	37	1.36	7
Nebraska	4,583	27	1.02	29
Nevada	5,401	10	0.77	45
New Hampshire	5,441	9	0.76	46
New Jersey	6,889	2	0.70	49
New Mexico	3,654	47	1.88	1
New York	6,185	3	0.82	43
North Carolina	4,220	34	0.98	32
North Dakota	4,026	38	1.55	3
Ohio	4,836	22	0.91	39
Oklahoma	3,908	42	1.26	15
Oregon	4,585	26	0.93	38
Pennsylvania	5,173	16	1.00	31
Rhode Island	5,279	13	1.05	24
South Carolina	3,788	45	1.25	16
South Dakota	4,181	35	1.29	12
Tennessee	4,391	32	1.12	21
Texas	4,501	29	0.97	35
Utah	3,574	48	1.12	20
Vermont	4,493	30	0.94	36
Virginia	5,090	18	1.39	5
Washington	5,374	11	0.93	37
West Virginia	3,547	49	1.51	4
Wisconsin	4,783	23	0.82	42
Wyoming	4,844	21	1.04	26
Wash., D.C.	7,396	—	5.27	—

1. When calculating this ratio, expenditures by state were adjusted downward to account for deficit spending. As might be expected, states with either low federal tax burdens and/or high federal expenditures tend to benefit most, on net, from federal fiscal operations. The most obvious example of this is New Mexico, the state with the higest federal expenditure/tax ratio of 1.88 (or $1.88 federal spending for every $1 of federal taxes). *Source:* Tax Foundation; Census Bureau.

A Small-Business Nation

By Bruce Bartlett

Only 14,000 of the 21 million U.S. businesses have more than 500 workers.

Almost every day one reads in the press about another large corporation "downsizing" or "restructuring" its operations. To many workers, however, these terms are merely code words for layoffs. Yet despite such layoffs, the U.S. unemployment rate has declined steadily over the last two years.

How can it be that employment has expanded even as layoffs continue? The answer lies in the vibrant small-business sector, which has expanded to compensate for the loss of jobs in large corporations.

The fact is that fewer and fewer American workers are employed by large companies. Employment in the Fortune 500 companies, for example, fell from over 20 percent of the labor force in 1973 to just over 10 percent in 1991. And this trend is continuing. Between 1991 and 1992, industries dominated by large firms lost 400,000 jobs, whereas those dominated by small firms gained 178,000 jobs. Between 1987 and 1992, firms with fewer than 100 employees created 5.9 million net new jobs, while large firms lost 2.3 million net jobs, according to Cognetics, an economic research firm.

This is because small firms dominate many of the fastest-growing industries in the United States today, such as health, child care, recreation, public relations, social services, job training, and food service. By contrast, many of the industries losing employment are those dominated by large firms, such as department stores, aircraft manufacturing, grocery stores, telephone communications, and commercial banks.

Of course, the United States has always been a nation of small businesses. In 1992, there were approximately 21.3 million active businesses in the country. However, in only 5.7 million of these does the owner employ any workers. And of these, only 14,000 have more than 500 employees. In fact, close to half of all workers employed in private business work in establishments employing fewer than 100 workers. Thus, the vast bulk of businesses in the United States are small, most employing no one other than their owner.

Historically, small firms have tended to increase their employment faster than large firms do during economic up-turns. However, they also tend to reduce employment more quickly during downturns. About 50,000 businesses fail in the United States each year, and the vast bulk of these are small firms. Thus the gross number of jobs created by small businesses is much greater than the net number.

As a result of this faster turnover among small businesses, their work forces tend to be younger and consist of fewer full-time, full-year workers. However, for this very reason they are more likely to create employment opportunities for the unskilled, unemployed, or those just entering the labor force for the first time.

Because small companies tend to hire younger, less-skilled workers, pay and benefits also tend to be lower with such firms. Small-business wages in 1992 average $10.75 per hour, with an additional $3.81 for benefits, while large firms averaged $12.88 in wages and $5.64 in benefits. Also, the range of benefits tends to be narrower in small firms. For example, fewer small firms than large companies offer pensions or life insurance to their employees, and the range of health benefits is narrower.

For these reasons, government policy has historically tilted in favor of large firms. It was believed that workers were better off in such firms, where pay and benefits were higher and where job stability was much greater. Moreover, large companies can more easily afford Washington offices and lobbyists to press for policies favorable to them, features that are often unavailable or of no value to small companies.

At the same time, many of the government's polices are inherently more damaging to small businesses than large ones. Environmental, health, and safety regulations, for example, are like an overhead cost. Large firms can spread this cost over a larger production base and minimize the impact, whereas many small companies are forced under by such regulations.

For example, recent environmental regulations on dry-cleaning establishments have increased the start-up cost for such firms by $15,530 and annual operating expenses by $4,100, according to Rep. Dick Armey (R–Texas). However, such firms typically have just five employees and net just $10,000 per year for their owner. Similar examples could be given for recent regulations in other small-business-dominated industries.

Nevertheless, the small-business sector remains healthy, despite the risks and the costs. A major reason is because many Americans still deeply yearn to be their own boss. Also, the restructuring of American industry away from heavy manufacturing, with its high start-up costs, to service industries, where start-up costs are low, has created more opportunities for individual entrepreneurs.

This is especially so for women and minorities, who still often suffer discrimination in the workplace. For them, owning and running their own business is the ultimate means of overcoming such discrimination.

Women, in particular, have been aggressive in starting new companies in recent years. Between 1979 and 1990 the number of women-owned businesses increased by more than 8 percent per year, rising from 25.1 percent of all nonfarm sole proprietorships to 32.2 percent. Over this same period, receipts per firm increased by 36 percent for those owned by women, but only 5.3 percent for those owned by men.

Minorities are also a growing element in small-business ownership. In 1987, the most recent period for which there is data, minorities owned about 9 percent of all businesses in the United States and about 7 percent of those with employees. Of the latter, about a third were owned by Hispanics, 28 percent were owned by blacks, and the balance owned by other minorities.

In conclusion, small businesses remain a vibrant and vital part of the U.S. economy. They are an especially important source of jobs for younger, less-skilled workers, and the owners of such firms are increasingly becoming minority and female. As the U.S. economy becomes more decentralized, with technology creating more opportunities for people to work at home or on their own, it is likely that small businesses will only continue to increase their role.☐

This article appeared in the *March 1995* issue and is reprinted with permission from *The World & I*, a publication of *The Washington Times Corporation*, copyright © 1995.

Bruce Bartlett is a senior fellow at the Alexis de Tocqueville Institution. He was formerly deputy assistant secretary of the treasury for economic policy.

Fastest Growing Occupations, 1992–2005

Employment will continue to shift from the goods-producing to the service sector of the economy, but the shift will be less pronounced than during past years. The bulk of employment growth will be in three industries: Health services; Retail trade, including eating and drinking places; and Business services, including temporary help services, computer and data processing services, and services to buildings.

Americans will find the best employment opportunities in the major occupational groups that require the most education and training. They also pay higher than average earnings. Service and professional occupations, particularly in the health and educational fields will dominate as shown in the table.

Occupation	Growth, %
Paralegals	86
Teachers, special education	74
Medical assistants	71
Corrections officers	70
Detectives except public	70
Travel agents	66
Childcare workers	66
Radiologic technologists and technicians	63
Nursery workers	62
Medical records technicians	61
Operations research analysts	61
Occupational therapists	60
Legal secretaries	57
Manicurists	54
Producers, directors, actors and entertainers	54
Teachers, preschool and kindergarten	54
Flight attendants	51
Speech-language pathologists and audiologists	51
Guards	51

Occupation	Growth, %
Home health aides	138
Human services workers	136
Personal and home care aides	130
Computer engineers and scientists	112
Systems analysts	110
Physical and corrective therapy assistants and aides	93
Physical therapists	88

Source: Occupational Outlook Quarterly, U.S. Department of Labor. Latest data

The General Agreement on Tariffs and Trade (GATT)

GATT was formally signed on April 15, 1994, in Marrakesh, Morocco, by representatives from 124 member countries. GATT was known as the Uruguay Round of talks because the wide-ranging trade liberalization negotiations began in the Uruguayan resort of Punta del Este in 1986.

The sweeping trade pact opens global markets between member countries for goods and services and projects a worldwide reduction of tariffs of up to 40% and a $235-billion increase in annual global income.

The U.S. House of Representatives approved the legislation on November 29, 1994, and the Senate ratified the accord on December 1. President Clinton signed the bill on December 8.

The treaty established a successor to GATT, the World Trade Organization (WTO), and it replaced GATT on January 1, 1995. Because of U.S. concerns that some future decisions by the organization may be unacceptable under U.S. laws, a provision in the treaty allows any member to withdraw from the WTO six months after giving notice. ☐

North American Free Trade Agreement (NAFTA)

In three separate ceremonies in the three capitals on Dec. 17, 1992, President Bush, Mexican President Salinas, and Canadian Prime Minister Mulroney signed the historic North American Free Trade Agreement (NAFTA). The framework agreement proposed to eliminate restrictions on the flow of goods, services, and investment in North America. The House of Representatives approved NAFTA, by a vote of 234 to 200 on November 17, 1993, and the Senate voted 60 to 38 for approval on November 20. It was signed into law by President Clinton on December 8, 1993, and took effect on January 1, 1994.

Under NAFTA, the United States, Canada, and Mexico become a single, giant, integrated market of almost 400 million people with $6.5 trillion worth of goods and services annually. Mexico is the world's second largest importer of U.S. manufactured goods and the third largest importer of U.S. agricultural products.

Prior to NAFTA, Mexican tariffs averaged about 250% as compared to U.S. duties. After the pact, about half of the tariffs on trade between Mexico and the United States were eliminated, and the remaining tariffs and restrictions on service and investment (as far as it is possible) will be phased out over a 15-year period. The United States and Canada have had a free-trade agreement since 1989.

The treaty provides full protection of intellectual property rights (patents, copyrights, and trademarks) and also includes provisions covering trade rules and dispute settlement and establishes trilateral commissions to administer them. NAFTA also marks the first time in the history of U.S. trade policy that environmental concerns have been directly addressed. ☐

Poverty and Income in the United States

Source: Current Population Reports, "Consumer Income," Bureau of the Census, issued February 1995.

Poverty Thresholds

The poverty thresholds in 1993 were as follows: One person under 65: $7,518; age 65 and over: $6,930; two persons: householder under 65, $9,728; householder 65 and over, $8,740; three persons: $11,522; four persons, $14,763; five persons, $17,449; six persons, $19,718; seven persons, $22,383; eight persons, $24,838; and nine or more persons, $29,529.

The number of persons below the official government poverty level was 39.3 million in 1993, representing 15.1% of the Nation's population. While the number of poor showed a statistically significant rise from the corresponding 1992 figure of 38.0 million poor, the percentage of the population below the poverty level was unchanged.

Age

In 1993, the poverty rate for all children under 18 was 22.7%, 12.4% for persons 18 to 64 years of age, and a similar percentage (12.2%) for the elderly. Half of the Nation's poor in 1993 were either children under 18 years or elderly.

The elderly are underrepresented in the poverty population. Persons 65 and over are approximately 11.9% of the total population but make up only 9.6% of the poor. However, a higher proportion of elderly (7.5%) than nonelderly (4.5%) were concentrated just over their respective poverty thresholds (between 100% and 125% of their thresholds), 18.5% of the Nation's 12.5 million "near poor" persons were elderly.

Children represent a very large segment of the poor (40.1%) even though they are only a little more than one-fourth of the total population. Between 1992 and 1993, the poverty rate for children did not change significantly. Children under 6 have been particularly vulnerable to poverty. In 1993, the overall poverty rate for related children under 6 years of age was 25.6%. Of children under 6 living in families with a female householder, no spouse present, 63.7% were poor, compared to 13.4% of such young children in married-couple families.

Race and Hispanic Origin

In 1993, the poverty rate was 12.2% for non-Hispanic Whites, and 33.1% for Blacks. For persons of Hispanic origin (who may be of any race) the poverty rate was 30.6%. For Asians and Pacific Islanders, the largest component of persons of other races, the poverty rate was 15.3% in 1993. Even though the poverty rate for Whites was lower than that for the other racial and ethnic groups, the majority of poor persons in 1993 were White (66.8%) and 48.1% were non-Hispanic White.

Blacks showed no significant increase in poverty between 1992 and 1993. Whites and persons of Hispanic origin showed an increase only in the number living in poverty, not in the rate. Poverty rates for Whites, Blacks, and persons of Hispanic origin did increase from 1989 levels. The poverty rate for Asians and Pacific Islanders was not significantly different from their poverty rate in 1992 or in 1989.

Families

There was no significant change in either the number of poor families or their poverty rate between 1992 and 1993. The poverty rate for families was 12.3% in 1993. For families with a female householder, no spouse present, the poverty rate was 35.6%. Married-couple families had a poverty rate of 6.5%.

Female-householder families were over-represented among the poor. White 52.7% of all poor families had a female householder, with no spouse present, only 18.1% of all families in the U.S. had a female householder. Neither of these figures was statistically different from their respective 1992 estimates. Those persons not in families (the 38.0 million unrelated individuals—persons living alone or with nonrelatives only) had a poverty rate of 22.1 in 1993, not significantly different from the 1992 rate. The number of poor unrelated individuals rose to 8.4 million in 1993. Unrelated individuals accounted for 21.4% of the poverty population, compared with only 14.7 percent of the entire U.S. population.[1]

---

1. Persons who are homeless and not living in shelters are not included in these poverty statistics.

Persons Below the Poverty Level, 1974–1993

(in thousands)

Year	All persons	White	Black	Hispanic origin[1]	Year	All persons	White	Black	Hispanic origin[1]
1974	23,370	15,736	7,182	2,575	1984	33,700	22,955	9,490	4,806
1975	25,877	17,770	7,545	2,991	1985	33,064	22,860	8,926	5,236
1976	24,975	16,713	7,595	2,783	1986	32,370	22,183	8,983	5,117
1977	24,720	16,416	7,726	2,700	1987	32,221	21,195	9,520	5,422
1978	24,497	16,259	7,625	2,607	1988	31,745	20,715	9,356	5,357
1979	26,072	17,214	8,050	2,921	1989	31,528	20,785	9,302	5,430
1980	29,272	19,699	8,579	3,491	1990	33,585	22,326	9,837	6,006
1981	31,822	21,553	9,173	3,713	1991	35,708	23,747	10,242	6,339
1982	34,398	23,517	9,697	4,301	1992[2]	38,014	25,259	10,827	7,592
1983	35,303	23,984	9,882	4,633	1993	39,265	26,226	10,877	8,126

1. Persons of Hispanic origin may be of any race. 2. Revised. *Source:* U.S. Department of Commerce, Bureau of the Census.

INCOME

The median income of households in the United States declined by 1.0% in real terms between 1992 and 1993. The median household income in 1993 was $31,241 compared with an inflation-adjusted 1992 median of $31,553. Although the most recent recessionary period ended in March 1991, household income has not yet recovered to its 1989 pre-recessionary peak of $33,585 (in 1993 dollars). Real median household income has declined 7.0% since 1989.

Race and Hispanic Origin

Median household income by race and Hispanic origin remained unchanged in real terms between 1992 and 1993. In 1993, the median household income of White households was $32,960, for Black households it was $19,532, for Asian and Pacific Islander households it was $38,347, and for households maintained by a householder of Hispanic origin the median income was $22,886. (Persons of Hispanic origin may be of any race.) The median income of households maintained by White, not Hispanic-origin persons, $34,173, also remained unchanged.[2]

The real median household incomes for all the race and Hispanic-origin groups remain lower in 1993 than in 1989. The median income of White households remains 6.7% lower; Black households 8.0% lower; Asian and Pacific Islander households 8.6% lower; Hispanic-origin households 9.8% lower; and White, not Hispanic households 5.5% lower.[3]

2. Detailed tabulations on the income characteristics of the White, not Hispanic population can be obtained by contacting the Income Statistics Branch, Housing and Household Economic Division, U.S. Census Bureau.
3. Except for the difference between the changes in the median incomes of Hispanic and White, not Hispanic households, the differences between the changes are not statistically significant.

Year-Round, Full-Time Workers

The real median earnings of year-round, full-time workers 15 years old and over declined for males and females alike between 1992 and 1993. The median earnings of males declined by 2.2% from $31,101 in 1992 to $30,407 in 1993; the decline in earnings for females was 1.2% from $22,015 in 1992 to $21,747 in 1993.[4] The female-to-male earnings ratio in 1993 was unchanged at .72, remaining comparable with the all-time high reached in 1990.

Per Capita Income

The per capita income for all persons increased by 1.8% between 1992 and 1993, after adjusting for inflation, to $15,574. A similar change was evident for the per capita income of the White population, increasing by 2.0% to $16,576 in 1993. The per capita income of the Black and Hispanic origin populations, however, remained unchanged. The 1993 per capita income of the Black population was $9.806, for Hispanics it was $8,771.[5]

Between 1989 and 1993, the real per capita income of the overall population and the White and Hispanic origin populations declined. The per capita income of the Black population remained unchanged. The per capita income of the overall population declined by 3.9%, for Whites by 3.5%, and for Hispanics the decline was 8.1%. (The difference between the total and White declines is not statistically significant.) ☐

4. The difference was not statistically significantly between the percent decline in the earnings of males and females.
5. The difference between the change in per capita income for the total and White populations was not statistically significant.

Percent of Persons in Poverty, by State: 1991–1993

State	1993 Percent	1992[r] Percent	1991[1] Percent	State	1993 Percent	1992[r] Percent	1991[1] Percent
Alabama	17.4	17.3	19.0	Montana	14.9	13.8	15.5
Alaska	9.1	10.2	12.0	Nebraska	10.3	10.6	9.8
Arizona	15.4	15.8	15.5	Nevada	9.8	14.7	11.6
Arkansas	20.0	17.5	17.4	New Hampshire	9.9	8.7	7.4
California	18.2	16.4	16.3	New Jersey	10.9	10.3	10.0
Colorado	9.9	10.8	10.6	New Mexico	17.4	21.6	23.0
Connecticut	8.5	9.8	9.0	New York	16.4	15.7	15.7
Delaware	10.2	7.8	7.7	North Carolina	14.4	15.8	14.6
D.C.	26.4	20.3	18.6	North Dakota	11.2	12.1	14.7
Florida	17.8	15.6	15.7	Ohio	13.0	12.5	13.5
Georgia	13.5	17.7	17.1	Oklahoma	19.9	18.6	17.2
Hawaii	8.0	11.2	7.8	Oregon	11.8	11.4	13.6
Idaho	13.1	15.2	14.1	Pennsylvania	13.2	11.9	11.2
Illinois	13.6	15.6	13.8	Rhode Island	11.2	12.4	10.7
Indiana	12.2	11.8	15.8	South Carolina	18.7	19.0	16.5
Iowa	10.3	11.5	9.8	South Dakota	14.2	15.1	14.3
Kansas	13.1	11.1	12.4	Tennessee	19.6	17.0	15.5
Kentucky	20.4	19.7	18.8	Texas	17.4	18.3	18.0
Louisiana	26.4	24.5	19.2	Utah	10.7	9.4	13.0
Maine	15.4	13.5	14.2	Vermont	10.0	10.5	12.7
Maryland	9.7	11.8	9.3	Virginia	9.7	9.5	10.0
Massachusetts	10.7	10.3	11.3	Washington	12.1	11.2	9.7
Michigan	15.4	13.6	14.2	West Virginia	22.2	22.3	17.9
Minnesota	11.6	13.0	13.1	Wisconsin	12.6	10.9	10.0
Mississippi	24.7	24.6	23.8	Wyoming	13.3	10.3	9.9
Missouri	16.1	15.7	14.9				

r. Revised, based on 1990 census population controls. 1. 1991 poverty estimates were adjusted using a ratio of 1992 estimates with 1980 and 1990 census population controls. *Source:* "Income, Poverty, and Valuation of Noncash BenefitsL 1993," *Current Population Reports,* U.S. Bureau of the Census, published February 1995, latest data.

Consumer Price Indexes

(1982–84 = 100)

Year	All items	Energy	Food	Shelter	Apparel[1]	Transportation	Medical care	Fuel oil	Electricity	Utility (gas)	Telephone	Commodities
1960	29.6	22.4	30.0	25.2	45.7	29.8	22.3	13.5	29.9	17.6	58.3	33.6
1970	38.8	25.5	39.2	35.5	59.2	37.5	34.0	16.5	31.8	19.6	58.7	41.7
1980	82.4	86.0	86.8	81.0	90.9	83.1	74.9	87.7	75.8	65.7	77.7	86.0
1990	130.7	104.5	132.4	140.0	124.1	120.5	162.8	n.a.	n.a.	n.a.	n.a.	122.8
1992	140.3	108.1	137.9	151.2	131.9	126.5	190.1	n.a.	n.a.	n.a.	n.a.	129.1
1993	144.5	111.2	140.9	155.7	133.7	130.4	201.4	n.a.	n.a.	n.a.	n.a.	131.5
1994	148.2	111.7	144.3	160.5	133.4	134.3	211.0	n.a.	n.a.	n.a.	n.a.	133.4

1. Includes upkeep. n.a. = not available. *Source: Monthly Labor Review, July 1995.*

Consumer Price Index for All Urban Consumers

(1982–84 = 100)

Group	March 1995	March 1994	Group	March 1995	March 1994
All items	151.4	147.2	Fuel oil, coal, bottled gas	89.0	92.5
Food	147.4	143.2	House operation[1]	122.6	120.6
Alcoholic beverages	153.1	151.4	House furnishings	111.2	110.5
Apparel and upkeep	134.4	136.1	Transportation	138.0	132.2
Men's and boys' apparel	127.2	125.6	Medical care	218.4	208.3
Women's and girls' apparel	131.5	137.2	Personal care	146.0	143.0
Footwear	125.9	127.0	Tobacco products	222.5	217.7
Housing, total	147.4	144.1	Entertainment	152.6	149.6
Rent	156.7	153.2	Personal and educational		
Gas and electricity	117.1	118.1	expenses	232.0	219.1

1. Combines house furnishings and operation. *Source: Monthly Labor Review, May 1995.*

Per Capita Personal Income

Year	Amount	Year	Amount	Year	Amount	Year	Amount	Year	Amount
1935	$474	1965	$2,773	1980	$9,910	1985	$13,896	1990	$18,635
1945	1,223	1970	3,893	1981	10,949	1986	14,597	1991	19,091
1950	1,501	1975	5,851	1982	11,480	1987	15,638	1992	20,105
1955	1,881	1978	7,729	1983	12,098	1988	16,615	1993	20,800
1960	2,219	1979	8,638	1984	13,114	1989	17,696	1994[1]	21,809

1. Preliminary. *Source:* Department of Commerce, Bureau of Economic Analysis.

Per Capita Income and Personal Consumption Expenditures

(In current dollars)

Year	Gross national product	Personal income	Disposable personal income	Personal Consumption Expenditures Durable goods	Nondurable goods	Services	Total
1950	$1,900	$1,504	$1,368	$203	$648	$416	$1,267
1955	2,456	1,901	1,687	235	755	570	1,560
1960	2,851	2,265	1,986	240	847	741	1,829
1965	3,268	2,840	2,505	327	987	954	2,268
1970	4,951	4,056	3,489	418	1,318	1,385	3,121
1975	7,401	6,081	5,291	627	1,927	2,135	4,689
1980	11,985	9,916	8,421	963	2,992	3,653	7,607
1985	16,776	13,895	11,861	1,555	3,807	5,622	10,985
1990	21,737	18,477	15,695	1,910	4,748	7,888	14,547
1991	22,500	19,100	16,700	1,800	5,000	8,700	15,400
1992	23,340	19,802	17,346	1,881	5,053	9,101	16,035
1993	24,576	20,810	18,153	2,083	5,185	9,683	16,951
1994	25,774	21,846	19,003	2,266	5,342	10,126	17,734

Source: U.S. Department of Commerce, *Survey of Current Business, June 1995.*

Total Family Income in 1992 CPI-U–XI Adjusted Dollars
(figures in percent)

Income range	White			Black			Hispanic[1]		
	1992	1990	1985	1992	1990	1985	1992	1990	1985
Families (thousands)[2]	57,858	56,803	54,991	7,888	7,471	6,921	5,318	4,981	4,206
Under $5,000	2.7	2.5	2.9	11.3	11.5	10.1	6.0	6.3	5.9
$5,000 to $9,999	4.5	4.7	5.6	15.0	14.1	15.7	11.7	12.3	13.6
$10,000 to $14,999	6.6	7.0	7.3	11.8	11.3	12.4	12.6	12.6	13.7
$15,000 to $24,999	15.2	16.0	17.0	18.8	19.5	21.2	21.7	21.7	20.9
$25,000 to $34,999	15.3	16.5	16.7	13.0	14.0	14.2	16.2	16.6	17.0
$35,000 to $49,999	20.0	20.8	21.1	14.0	15.0	14.2	15.1	15.7	15.1
$50,000 to $74,999	20.8	19.3	18.5	10.8	9.8	9.3	11.3	10.0	10.3
$75,000 to $99,999	8.2	7.3	6.3	3.4	3.4	2.1	3.4	2.9	2.4
$100,000 and over	6.7	5.9	4.5	1.8	1.3	0.9	2.0	1.9	1.2
Median income	$38,909	$36,915	$35,410	$21,161	$21,423	$20,390	$23,901	$23,431	$23,112

1. Persons of Hispanic origin may be of any race. 2. As of March 1993. *Source:* Department of Commerce, Bureau of the Census, *Current Population Reports, Consumer Income, Series P–60, No. 184.* NOTE: Data are latest available.

Median Weekly Earnings of Full-Time Workers by Occupation and Sex

Occupation	Men		Women		Total	
	Number of workers (in thousands)	Median weekly earnings	Number of workers (in thousands)	Median weekly earnings	Number of workers (in thousands)	Median weekly earnings
Managerial and prof. specialty	13,021	$803	12,187	$592	25,208	$683
Executive, admin, and managerial	6,785	797	5,548	541	12,333	658
Professional specialty	6,236	809	6,639	623	12,875	705
Technical, sales, and admin. support	9,764	548	15,954	376	25,718	420
Technicians and related support	1,638	622	1,536	466	3,174	534
Sales occupations	4,836	575	3,633	324	8,470	450
Administrative support, incl. clerical	3,289	482	10,785	374	14,074	392
Service occupations	4,784	350	4,702	257	9,486	294
Private household	14	([1])	311	166	324	179
Protective service	1,674	538	277	430	1,951	517
Service, except private household and protective	3,096	293	4,115	256	7,211	271
Precision production, craft, and repair	9,824	515	970	370	10,795	504
Mechanics and repairers	3,593	519	160	520	3,753	519
Construction trades	3,407	492	52	408	3,460	491
Operators, fabricators, and laborers	11,333	406	3,412	293	14,745	373
Machine operators, assemblers, and inspectors	4,469	415	2,563	292	7,032	361
Transportation and material moving occupations	3,854	469	242	361	4,096	461
Handlers, equipment cleaners, helpers, and laborers	3,010	319	608	279	3,617	311
Farming, forestry, and fishing	1,265	290	161	234	1,426	282

1. Data not shown where base is less than 100,000. NOTE: Figures are for the year 1994. *Source:* U.S. Department of Labor, Bureau of Labor Statistics, "Employment and Earnings," January 1995.

Consumer Credit
(installment credit outstanding; in billions of dollars, not seasonally adjusted)

Holder	1994	1993	1992	1991	1990	1985	1980	1975
Commercial banks	427.8	367.1	331.9	340.7	347.	245.1	147.0	82.9
Finance companies	134.8	117.0	117.1	121.9	133.3	111.7	62.3	32.7
Credit unions	119.5	114.4	97.6	92.7	93.1	72.7	44.0	25.7
Retailers[1]	38.4	47.4	42.1	39.8	43.5	43.0	28.7	18.2
Other[2]	60.9	37.5	47.8	50.3	57.0	53.8	20.1	9.2
Pools[3]	143.3	123.6	120.4	99.6	77.9	—	—	—
Total	**925.0**	**807.1**	**756.9**	**745.0**	**751.9**	**526.3**	**302.1**	**168.7**

1. For 1994, Source includes retailers and gasoline companies in nonfinancial business category. 2. Includes mutual savings banks, savings and loan associations, and gasoline companies. For 1994, gasoline companies not included. 3. Beginning 1989, outstanding balances of pools upon which securities have been issued; these balances are no longer on the balance sheets for the loan originators. Data are *not* available historically. *Source:* Federal Reserve Board.

The Public Debt

Year	Gross debt Amount (in millions)	Per capita	Year	Gross debt Amount (in millions)	Per capita
1800 (Jan. 1)	$ 83	$ 15.87	1950	$256,087[1]	$1,688.30
1860 (June 30)	65	2.06	1955	272,807[1]	1,650.63
1865	2,678	75.01	1960	284,093[1]	1,572.31
1900	1,263	16.60	1965	313,819[1]	1,612.70
1920	24,299	228.23	1970	370,094[1]	1,807.09
1925	20,516	177.12	1975	533,189	2,496.90
1930	16,185	131.51	1980	907,701	3,969.55
1935	28,701	225.55	1985	1,823,103	7,598.51
1940	42,968	325.23	1990	3,233,313	12,823,28
1945	258,682	1,848.60	1994	4,643,711	17,805.64

1. Adjusted to exclude issues to the International Monetary Fund and other international lending institutions to conform to the budget presentation. *Source:* Department of the Treasury, Financial Management Service.

Gross Domestic Product or Expenditure[1]

(in billions)

Item	1994	1993	1992	1991	1990	1989	1987	1980	1970
Gross domestic product	6,736.1	6,343.3	6,038.5	5,667.5	5,513.8	5,244.0	4,539.9	2,708.0	1,010.7
GDP in constant (1987) dollars	5,342.4	5,134.5	4,986.3	4,821.0	4,884.9	4,836.9	4,540.0	3,776.3	2,875.8
Personal consumption expenditures	4,628.0	4,378.2	4,139.9	3,887.7	3,742.6	3,517.9	3,052.2	1,748.1	646.5
Durable goods	591.4	538.0	497.3	446.1	465.9	459.8	403.0	212.5	85.3
Nondurable goods	1,394.4	1,339.2	1,300.9	1,251.5	1,217.7	1,146.9	1,011.1	682.9	270.4
Services	2,642.1	2,501.0	2,341.6	2,190.1	2,059.0	1,911.2	1,637.4	852.7	290.8
Gross private domestic investment	1,031.6	882.0	796.5	721.1	802.6	837.6	749.3	467.6	150.3
Residential	282.8	250.6	223.6	190.3	215.7	230.9	225.2	123.3	41.4
Nonresidential	696.9	616.1	565.5	541.1	587.0	570.7	497.8	353.8	106.7
Change in business inventories	51.9	15.4	7.3	−10.2	0	36.0	26.3	−9.5	2.3
Net export of goods and services	−98.6	−65.3	−29.6	−21.8	−74.4	−82.9	−143.1	−14.7	1.2
Government purchases	1,175.2	1,148.4	1,131.8	1,090.5	1,042.9	971.4	881.5	507.1	212.7
Federal	437.3	443.6	448.8	447.3	424.9	401.4	384.9	209.1	100.1
State and local	737.9	704.7	683.0	643.2	618.0	570.0	496.6	298.0	112.6

1. Current dollars except as noted. *Source:* Department of Commerce, Bureau of Economic Analysis, *Survey of Current Business,* Vol. 74, No. 2, February 1995.

Producer Price Indexes by Major Commodity Groups

(1982 = 100)

Commodity	1994	1990	1985	1980	1975	1970
All commodities	120.4	116.3	103.2	89.8	58.4	38.1
Farm products	106.3	112.2	95.1	102.9	77.0	45.8
Processed foods and feeds	125.5	121.9	103.5	95.9	72.6	44.6
Textile products and apparel	118.3	114.9	102.9	89.7	67.4	52.4
Hides, skins, and leather products	148.5	141.7	108.9	94.7	56.5	42.0
Fuels and related products and power	77.8	82.2	91.4	82.8	35.4	15.3
Chemicals and allied products	132.1	123.6	103.7	89.0	62.0	35.0
Rubber and plastic products	117.6	113.6	101.9	90.1	62.2	44.9
Lumber and wood products	180.0	129.7	106.6	101.5	62.1	39.9
Pulp, paper, and allied products	152.5	141.3	113.3	86.3	59.0	37.5
Metals and metal products	124.8	123.0	104.4	95.0	61.5	38.7
Machinery and equipment	125.1	120.7	107.2	86.0	57.9	40.0
Furniture and household durables	126.1	119.1	107.1	90.7	67.5	51.9
Nonmetallic mineral products	124.2	114.7	108.6	88.4	54.4	35.3
Transportation equipment	137.2	121.5	107.9	82.9	56.7	41.9

Source: U.S. Department of Labor, Bureau of Labor Statistics, Division of Industrial Prices and Price Indexes.

Weekly Earnings[1] of Full-Time Women Workers

Major occupation group	1994 weekly earnings	% Men's weekly earnings
Managerial and professional specialty	$592	73.7
Executive, administrative, and managerial	541	67.9
Professional specialty	623	77.0
Technical, sales, and administrative support	376	68.6
Technicians and related support	466	74.9
Sales occupations	324	56.3
Administrative support, including clerical	374	77.6
Service occupations	257	73.4
Precision production, craft, and repair	370	71.8
Operators, fabricators, and laborers	293	72.2
Machine operators, assemblers, and inspectors	292	70.4
Transportation and material moving	361	77.0
Handlers, equipment cleaners, helpers, and laborers	279	87.5
Farming, forestry, and fishing	234	80.7
All occupations	**$399**	**76.4**

1. Median usual weekly earnings. Half the workers earn more and half the workers usually earn less each week. *Source:* U.S. Department of Labor, Bureau of Labor Statistics.

Median Family Income[1]

(in current dollars)

Year	Income	Percent change	Year	Income	Percent change
1980	$21,023	—	1987	$30,970	5.1
1981	22,388	6.5	1988	32,191	3.9
1982	23,433	4.7	1989	34,213	6.3
1983	24,580	4.9	1990	35,353	3.3
1984	26,433	7.5	1991	35,939	1.7
1985	27,735	4.9	1992	36,573	1.8
1986	29,458	6.2	1993	36,950	1.0

1. Table has been revised. *Source:* U.S. Department of Commerce, Bureau of the Census, *Income, Poverty, and Valuation of Noncash Benefits: 1993,* Series P60–188, February 1995.

Expenditures for New Plant and Equipment[1]

(in billions of dollars)

Year	Manufacturing	Transportation[2]	Total nonmanufacturing	Total
1950	$7.73	$2.87	$18.08	$25.81
1955	12.50	3.10	24.58	37.08
1960	16.36	3.54	32.63	48.99
1965	25.41	5.66	45.39	70.79
1970	36.99	7.17	69.16	106.15
1975	53.66	9.95	108.95	162.60
1980	112.60	13.56	205.48	318.08
1985	152.88	14.57	302.05	454.93
1988	163.45	16.63	344.77	508.22
1989	183.80	18.84	380.13	563.93
1990	192.61	21.47	399.34	591.96
1991	182.81	22.66	405.12	587.93
1992	174.02	22.64	433.69	607.71
1993	179.47	21.77	470.95	650.41
1994	144.14	32.32	412.14	556.29

1. Data exclude agriculture. 2. Transportation is included in total nonmanufacturing. NOTE: This series was revised in April 1993. *Source:* Department of Commerce, Bureau of the Census.

New Housing Starts[1] and Mobile Homes Shipped

(in thousands)

Year	No. of units started	Year	No. of units started	Year	Mobile homes shipped
1900	189	1970	1,469	1965	216
1910	387	1975	1,171	1970	401
1920	247	1980	1,313	1975	213
1925	937	1985	1,745	1980	222
1930	330	1987	1,623	1985	284
1935	221	1988[2]	1,488	1988	218
1940	603	1989	1,376	1989	198
1945	326	1990	1,193	1990	188
1950	1,952	1991	1,014	1991	171
1955	1,646	1992	1,200	1992	211
1960[1]	1,296	1993	1,288	1993	254
1965	1,510	1994	1,457	1994	304

1. Prior to 1960, starts limited to nonfarm housing; from 1960 on, figures include farm housing. 2. As of 1988 data for housing starts no longer include public housing starts and only include private housing starts. *Sources:* Department of Commerce, Housing Construction Statistics, 1900–1965, and Construction Reports, Housing Starts, 1970–to present, Manufactured Housing Institute, 1965–to present.

Life Insurance in Force

(in millions of dollars)

As of Dec. 31	Ordinary	Group	Industrial	Credit	Total
1915	$16,650	$100	$4,279	—	$21,029
1930	78,576	9,801	17,963	$73	106,413
1945	101,550	22,172	27,675	365	151,762
1950	149,116	47,793	33,415	3,844	234,168
1955	216,812	101,345	39,682	14,493	372,332
1960	341,881	175,903	39,563	29,101	586,448
1965	499,638	308,078	39,818	53,020	900,554
1970	734,730	551,357	38,644	77,392	1,402,123
1980	1,760,474	1,579,355	35,994	165,215	3,541,038
1985	3,247,289	2,561,595	28,250	215,973	6,053,107
1990	5,366,982	3,753,506	24,071	248,038	9,392,597
1994	6,835,239	4,608,746	20,145	209,491	11,673,621

Source: American Council of Life Insurance.

Farm Indexes

(1990–92 = 100)

Year	Prices paid by farmers[1]	Prices rec'd by farmers[2]	Ratio
1975	47	73	155
1980	75	98	137
1985	86	91	106
1990	99	104	105
1991	100	100	99
1992	101	98	98
1993	103	101	98
1994	106	100	94

1. Commodities, interest, and taxes and wage rates. 2. All crops and livestock. *Source:* Department of Agriculture, National Agricultural Statistics Service.

Estimated Annual Retail and Wholesale Sales by Kind of Business
(in millions of dollars)

Kind of business	1994	1993	Kind of business	1994	1993
Retail trade, total	$2,236,966	$2,074,499	Electrical goods	$147,440	$131,893
Building materials, hardware, garden			Hardware, plumbing, heating, and		
supplies, and mobile home dealers	122,533	109,604	supplies	63,238	55,531
Automotive dealers	526,319	456,890	Machinery, equipment, supplies	180,017	160,622
Furniture, home furnishings,			Professional and commercial		
and equipment stores	119,626	105,728	equipment and supplies	165,020	159,167
General merchandise group stores	282,541	264,617	Metals and minerals except petroleum	95,331	80,216
Food stores	397,800	385,386	Miscellaneous durable goods	124,095	113,775
Gasoline service stations	142,193	138,299	Nondurable goods, total	981,345	953,263
Apparel and accessory stores	109,603	107,184	Paper and paper products	64,828	59,216
Eating and drinking places	228,351	213,663	Drugs, drug proprietaries, and		
Drug and proprietary stores	81,538	79,645	druggists' sundries	78,207	72,240
Liquor stores	21,823	21,567	Apparel, piece goods, & notions	73,252	70,351
Merchant wholesale trade, total	2,070,248	1,940,175	Groceries and related products	286,073	285,336
Durable goods, total	1,088,903	986,912	Beer, wine, distilled alcoholic		
Motor vehicles and automotive			beverages	53,018	51,325
parts and supplies	201,045	179,327	Farm-product raw materials	95,512	96,112
Furniture and home furnishings	35,998	34,910	Chemical and allied products	42,146	39,129
Lumber and other construction			Petroleum and petroleum products	138,033	139,266
materials	76,719	71,471	Miscellaneous nondurable goods	150,276	140,388

Source: Department of Commerce, Bureau of the Census.

Shareholders in Public Corporations

Characteristic	1990	1985	1983	1981	1980	1975	1970
Individual shareholders (thousands)	51,440	47,040	42,360	32,260	30,200	25,270	30,850
Adult shareowner incidence in population	1 in 4	1 in 4	1 in 4	1 in 5	1 in 5	1 in 6	1 in 4
Median household income	$43,800	$36,800	$33,200	$29,200	$27,750	$19,000	$13,500
Adult shareowners with household							
income: under $10,000 (thousands)	n.a.	2,151	1,460	2,164	1,742	3,420	8,170
$10,000 and over (thousands)	n.a.	40,999	36,261	26,913	25,715	19,970	20,130
$15,000 and over (thousands)	42,920	39,806	33,665	24,376	22,535	15,420	12,709
$25,000 and over (thousands)	38,230	32,690	25,086	17,547	15,605	6,642	4,114
$50,000 and over (thousands)	17,910	11,321	7,918	5,457	3,982	1,216	n.a.
Adult female shareowners (thousands)	17,750	17,547[1]	20,385	14,154	13,696	11,750	14,290
Adult male shareowners (thousands)	30,220	27,446[1]	19,226	15,785	14,196	11,630	14,340
Median age	43	44	45	46	46	53	48

NOTE: 1990 results are not strictly comparable with previous studies because of differences in methodologies. 1. Revised to correspond to 1990 methodology. n.a. = not available. *Source:* New York Stock Exchange. Data are latest available as of April 1995 publication.

50 Most Active Stocks in 1994

Stock	Share volume	Stock	Share volume	Stock	Share volume
Telefonos de Mexico (4)	937,012,100	K mart Corp. (22)	283,442,000	ADS (42)	235,993,300
General Motors (6)	574,748,500	Glaxo Holdings (11)	279,631,200	Abbott Laboratories (23)	233,968,500
RJR Nabisco Holdings (5)	565,884,700	EMC Corporation	278,614,400	Eastman Kodak (12)	233,355,200
Merck & Co., Inc. (2)	521,695,900	WMX Technologies Inc. (24)	270,159,500	Home Depot Inc. (25)	229,629,100
Wal–Mart Stores (3)	496,447,300	American Barrick (30)	258,453,900	Limited, Inc. (28)	227,863,600
Int'l Business Machines (7)	492,335,600	Disney (Walt) Company (17)	257,092,300	Blockbuster Entertainment	
Ford Motor (14)	480,090,600	Exxon Corp. (33)	255,603,900	Corp.[1]	223,651,200
Philip Morris (1)	479,286,300	GTE Corp. (39)	254,528,300	Digital Equipment Corp.	233,492,600
Chrysler Corporation (8)	443,742,600	Johnson & Johnson (18)	250,140,900	Merrill, Lynch & Co., Inc.	219,279,400
Hanson PLC (31)	439,791,300	Columbia/HCA Healthcare		Advanced Micro Devices (32)	215,199,900
AT&T Corp. (10)	434,747,100	Corp.	245,188,200	Chemical Banking Corp. (36)	212,866,900
COMPAQ Computer (37)	428,344,700	McDonald's Corp.	244,254,600	Time Warner Inc. (35)	212,648,000
General Electric (40)	390,148,500	BankAmerica		Sears Roebuck & Co. (38)	205,442,600
Motorola Inc. (27)	380,790,800	Corporation (26)	242,805,200	Int'l Game Technology	204,498,200
Citicorp (9)	380,495,200	duPont de Nemours (50)	240,467,500	Westinghouse Electric (43)	202,326,500
American Express (13)	342,415,175	National Semiconductor		Sara Lee Corp.	196,914,400
PepsiCo., Inc. (16)	337,068,800	Corp.	237,665,200	Placer Dome Inc. (44)	195,206,600
Coca–Cola Company (19)	329,141,200	VPF Sociedad Anonima		Sprint Corp.	194,823,300
Micron Technology Inc.	323,999,200				

1. Suspended as of September 30, 1994. NOTE: 1993 ranking in parentheses, if among top 50. *Source:* New York Stock Exchange.

Geographic Distribution of Shareowners of Public Corporations (1990)

Metropolitan Area	Individuals	Households	Metropolitan area	Individuals	Households
New York	2,470,000	1,630,000	Pittsburgh	450,000	300,000
Los Angeles	1,850,000	1,230,000	Denver	440,000	290,000
Chicago	1,610,000	1,070,000	San Jose	420,000	280,000
Detroit	1,240,000	820,000	Cincinnati	410,000	270,000
Philadelphia	1,100,000	720,000	Riverside-San Bernardino	410,000	270,000
Washington D.C.	1,000,000	670,000	Bergan-Passaic, N.J.	400,000	270,000
Boston	940,000	620,000	Milwaukee	400,000	270,000
Houston	880,000	580,000	Kansas City	390,000	260,000
Nassau-Suffolk, N.Y.	750,000	500,000	Seattle	380,000	260,000
Dallas	670,000	440,000	Fort Worth	370,000	240,000
Phoenix	650,000	430,000	Fort Lauderdale	360,000	240,000
St. Louis	640,000	420,000	Columbus	330,000	220,000
Anaheim	630,000	420,000	Portland	310,000	210,000
Atlanta	630,000	410,000	Sacramento	310,000	210,000
Minneapolis	620,000	410,000	Hartford	310,000	210,000
Newark	600,000	400,000	Indianapolis	280,000	190,000
Cleveland	540,000	360,000	Norfolk	280,000	180,000
Baltimore	520,000	350,000	New Orleans	270,000	180,000
San Francisco	490,000	330,000	Orlando	270,000	180,000
Oakland	490,000	320,000	Charlotte	240,000	160,000
Tampa	480,000	320,000	Middlesex, N.J.	230,000	150,000
Miami	470,000	310,000	San Antonio	230,000	150,000
San Diego	450,000	300,000			

Source: New York Stock Exchange. Data are latest available as of April 1995 publication.

New York Stock Exchange Seat Sales for Cash, 1994

Month	Price High	Low	Number	Month	Price High	Low	Number
January	—	—	0	July	—	—	0
February	—	—	0	August	—	—	0
March	$830,000	—	1	September	—	—	0
April	—	—	0	October	$825,000	—	1
May	—	—	0	November	—	—	0
June	830,000	—	1	December	760,000	—	1

NOTE: In addition, there were 9 private seat sales, ranging from a high of $830,000 and a low of $760,000 and one EX–OTR sale at $740,000. *Source:* New York Stock Exchange.

Largest Businesses, 1994

(in millions of dollars)

Source: FORTUNE 500 © 1995 Time Inc. All rights reserved.

	Revenues	Assets		Revenues	Assets
General Motors	$154,951.2	$198,598.7	Chevron	$31,064.0[18]	$34,407.0
Ford Motor	128,439.0	219,354.0	Procter & Gamble[5]	30,296.0	25,535.0
Exxon	101,459.0[18]	87,862.0	PepsiCo	28,472.4	24,792.0
Wall–Mart Stores[1]	83,412.4	32,819.0	Amoco	26,953.0[18]	29,316.0
AT&T[2,3]	75,094.0	79,262.0	Hewlett–Packard[6]	24,991.0	19,567.0
General Electric	64,687.0	194,484.0	ITT	23,767.0	100,854.0
Intl. Business Machines	64,052.0	81,091.0	Conagra[7]	23,512.2	10,721.8
Mobil	59,621.0[18]	41,542.0	Kroger	22,959.1	4,707.7
Sears Roebuck	54,559.0	91,896.0	American International Group	22,385.7	114,346.1
Philip Morris	53,776.0[18]	52,649.0	Metropolitan Life Insurance	22,257.9	136,125.3
Chrysler	52,224.0	49,539.0	Motorola	22,245.0	17,536.0
State Farm Group[4]	38,850.1	76,670.0	Boeing	21,924.0	21,463.0
Prudential Ins. Co. of America[4]	36,945.7	211,902.0	Dayton Hudson[1]	21,311.0	11,697.0
E.I. du Pont de Nemours	34,968.0[18]	36,892.0	United Technologies	21,197.0	15,624.0
K mart[1]	34,313.0	17,029.0	J.C. Penney[1]	21,082.0	16,202.0
Texaco	33,768.0[18]	25,505.0	Dow Chemical	20,015.0	26,545.0
Citicorp	31,650.0	250,489.0	GTE	19,944.3	42,499.8

	Revenues	Assets		Revenues	Assets
United Parcel Service	$19,575.7	$11,182.4	Tenneco	$13,222.0	$12,542.0
Fed. Natl. Mortgage Assn.	18,572.4	272,508.3	McDonnell Douglas	13,176.0	12,216.0
Travelers Inc.	18,465.0	115,297.0	Lockheed[12]	13,130.0	9,113.0
Cigna	18,392.0	86,102.0	Nationsbank Corp.	13,126.0	169,604.0
American Stores[1]	18,355.1	7,031.6	AlliedSignal	12,817.0	11,321.0
Merrill Lynch	18,233.1	163,749.3	Georgia–Pacific	12,738.0	10,728.0
Xerox	17,837.0	38,585.0	Chemical Banking Corp.	12,685.0	171,423.0
Aetna Life & Casualty	17,524.7	94,172.5	Sprint	12,661.8	14,936.3
Eastman Kodak	16,862.0[19]	14,968.0	Ameritech	12,569.5	19,946.8
Bellsouth	16,844.5	34,397.0	Home Depot[1]	12,476.7	5,778.0
USX	16,799.0[18]	17,517.0	McKesson[14]	12,428.2	3,192.7
BankAmerica Corp.[3]	16,531.0	215,475.0	Phillips Petroleum	12,367.0[18]	11,436.0
Price/Costco[9, 10]	16,480.6	4,235.7	Delta Air Lines[5]	12,359.0	11,896.0
Coca–Cola	16,172.0	13,873.0	Goodyear Tire & Rubber	12,288.2	9,123.3
AMR	16,137.0	19,486.0	May Department Stores[1]	12,223.0	9,472.0
Supervalu[11]	15,936.9	4,042.4	IBP	12,075.4	1,865.0
Fleming	15,753.5	4,608.3	New York Life Insurance[4]	12,066.6	68,925.7
Johnson & Johnson	15,734.0	15,668.0	Anheuser–Busch	12,053.8[18]	11,045.4
Atlantic Richfield	15,682.0[18]	24,563.0	Bristol–Myers Squibb	11,983.6	12,910.0
Safeway	15,626.6	5,022.1	J.P. Morgan & Co.	11,915.0	154,917.0
American Express	15,593.0	97,006.0	Albertson's[1]	11,894.6	3,621.7
Sara Lee[5]	15,536.0	11,665.0	SBC Communications[15]	11,618.5	26,005.3
RJR Nabisco Holdings	15,366.0	31,408.0	Intel	11,521.0	13,816.0
Minnesota Mining & Mfg.	15,079.0	13,496.0	US West	11,506.0	23,204.0
Merck	14,969.8	21,856.6	Archer Daniels Midland	11,374.4	8,746.9
International Paper	14,966.0	17,836.0	Melville	11,285.6	4,735.5
Caterpillar	14,328.0	16,250.0	Rockwell International[16]	11,204.7	9,860.8
UAL	13,950.0	11,764.0	Chase Manhattan Corp.	11,187.0	114,038.0
Bell Atlantic	13,791.4	24,271.8	Nationwidelns. Enterprise[4]	11,183.1	47,696.0
Loews	13,515.2	50,336.0	Columbia/HCA Healthcare[17]	11,132.0	12,339.0
Digital Equipment[5]	13,450.8	10,579.8	Winn–Dixie Stores[5]	11,082.2	2,146.6
MCI Communications	13,338.0	16,336.0	Sysco[5]	10,942.5	2,811.7
NYNEX	13,306.6	30,068.0	COMPAQ Computer	10,866.0	6,166.0

All figures are for the year ended December 31, 1994, unless otherwise indicated. 1. Figures are for fiscal year ended January 31, 1995. 2. Acquired McCaw Cellular Communications Sept. 19, 1994. 3. Name changed from American Telephone & Telegraph, April 20, 1994. 4. Financial data are based on statutory accounting. 5. Figures are for fiscal year ended June 30, 1994. 6. Figures are for fiscal year ended October 31, 1994. 7. Figures are for fiscal year ended May 31, 1994. 8. Acquired Continental Bank Corp. Sept. 1, 1994. 9. Figures are for fiscal year ended Aug. 31, 1994. 10. Figures reflect merger with Costco Wholesale Oct. 21, 1993. 11. Figures are for fiscal year ended February 28, 1994. 12. Figures do not reflect merger between Lockheed and Martin Marietta, March 15, 1995. 13. Figure as of December 31, 1994. 14. Figures are for fiscal year ended March 31, 1994. 15. Name changed from Southwestern Bell, October 3, 1994. 16. Figures are for fiscal year ended Sept. 30, 1994. 17. Figures reflect merger with Hospital Corp. of America, Feb. 10, 1994. 18. Excise taxes have been deducted. 19. Includes sales of discontinued operations of at least 10%.

New Business Concerns and Business Failures

Formations and failures	1993[1]	1992	1991	1990	1989	1988	1985	1980
Business formations								
Index, net formations (1967 = 100)	120.8	116.3	115.3	120.7	124.7	124.1	120.	129.9
New incorporations (1,000)	n.a.	667	629	647	677	685	663	534
Failures, number (1,000)	86.0	97.0	88.1	60.0	50.4	57.1	57.1	11.7
Rate per 10,000 concerns	90	109	107	75	65	98	115	42

1. Preliminary. n.a. = not available. *Sources:* U.S. Bureau of Economic Analysis and Dun & Bradstreet Corporation. From *Statistical Abstract of the United States 1994.* NOTE: Data are most recent available.

Borrowing on Home Equity

Single-family home owners with home equity lines of credit (HEL's) in 1991 were generally white and lived in the Northeast, in a metro area, and in a suburb, according to the Bureau of the Census. Most were couples in their mid-40s who had purchased their home before 1980. They comprise one-third (35 percent) of owners with HEL's although the region contains only 20 percent of the nation's single-family homeowners. The remainder were divided among the South (24 per-

cent), Midwest (23 percent), and the West (18 percent).

The number one reason for taking out a HEL was to make additions, improvements, or repair to the property (54 percent). The next most important reason was to consolidate debts (21 percent). Other reasons were to buy consumer products (10 percent), pay for education or medical expenses (6 percent), or make other types of investments (4 percent) or invest in other real estate (3 percent).

50 Leading Stocks in Market Value

Stock	Market value (millions)	Listed shares (millions)	Stock	Market value (millions)	Listed shares (millions)
Exxon Corp.	$110,129	1,813	Minnesota Mining & Manufacturing	$25,194	472
General Electric Co.	94,706	1,857	Southwestern Bell	24,470	606
Coca–Cola Co.	87,895	1,707	McDonald's Corp.	24,287	830
AT&T Corp.	78,525	1,563	Ameritech Corp.	23,725	588
Merck & Co.	56,536	1,483	Royal Dutch Petroleum	23,066	215
Morris (Philip) Co.	53,781	935	Hewlett–Packard Co.	22,502	225
Wal–Mart Stores	48,876	2,300	American Home Products	22,303	355
Procter & Gamble	45,271	730	Dow Chemical	21,999	327
International Business Machines	43,157	587	Bell Atlantic	21,708	436
Johnson & Johnson	42,015	767	Gillette Company	20,856	279
du Pont de Nemours	38,297	681	Home Depot	20,798	452
Mobil Corp.	37,251	442	Federal National Mortgage Association	20,565	282
Motorola, Inc.	34,144	590	Lilly (Eli)	19,216	293
American International Group	33,063	337	Schering–Plough	18,609	251
General Motors	31,841	754	Sears, Roebuck	18,043	392
Chevron Corp.	31,795	712	Kellogg Co.	18,021	310
PepsiCo. Inc.	31,268	863	Eastman Kodak	17,842	374
Bristol–Myers Squibb	30,817	532	Chrysler	17,837	364
Amoco Corp.	29,379	497	US West	17,575	493
GTE Corp.	29,131	959	Anheuser–Busch	17,487	344
Berkshire Hathaway	28,179	1.4	Texaco	16,423	274
Bellsouth Corporation	27,198	502	Atlantic Richfield	16,356	161
Abbott Laboratories	26,524	813	Boeing Company	16,328	349
Disney (Walt) Company	26,154	567	NYNEX Corp.	16,097	438
Pfizer Inc.	25,679	332	**Total**	**$1,628,326**	**32,341**
Ford Motor	25,408	907			

NOTE: As of Dec. 30, 1994. *Source:* New York Stock Exchange.

Top 50 Banks in the World

(in millions of dollars)

Bank	Country	Assets (U.S. dollars)	Bank	Country	Assets (U.S. dollars)
Sanwa Bank Ltd. Osaka	Japan	$588,349	Compagnie Financiere de Paribas, Paris	France	$242,146
Dai–ichi Kangyo Bank Ltd., Tokyo	Japan	587,773	Westdeutsche Landesbank Girozentrale, Duesseldorf	Germany	237,292
Fuji Bank, Ltd., Tokyo	Japan	577,107	Toyo Trust & Banking Co., Ltd., Tokyo	Japan	236,612
Sumitomo Bank Ltd., Osaka	Japan	571,942	Union Bank of Switzerland, Zurich	Switzerland	226,966
Sakura Bank, Ltd., Tokyo	Japan	565,381	Commerzbank, Frankfurt	Germany	220,478
Mitsubishi Bank, Ltd., Tokyo	Japan	553,515	BankAmerica Corp., San Francisco	United States	214,406
Norinchukin Bank, Tokyo	Japan	500,434	Bayerische Vereinsbank, Munich	Germany	204,214
Industrial Bank of Japan, Ltd., Tokyo	Japan	437,853	Shoko Chukin Bank, Tokyo	Japan	186,800
Mitsubishi Trust & Banking Corp, Tokyo	Japan	394,001	Nippon Credit Bank, Ltd., Tokyo	Japan	183,862
Long-Term Credit Bank of Japan Ltd. Tokyo	Japan	375,515	Bayerische Hypotheken-und Wechsel-Bank, Munich	Germany	177,354
Deutsche Bank, AG, Frankfurt	Germany	367,883	Credit Suisse, Zurich	Switzerland	176,910
Sumitomo Trust & Banking Co., Ltd. Osaka[1]	Japan	355,984	Zenshinren Bank, Tokyo	Japan	175,190
Tokai Bank Ltd., Nagoya	Japan	351,637	Bayerische Landesbank Girozentrale, Munich	Germany	171,640
Mitsui Trust & Banking Co., Ltd., Tokyo	Japan	331,209	Chemical Banking Corp., New York	United States	170,319
Credit Agricole Mutuel, Paris	France	328,054	NationsBank Corp., Charlotte, N.C.	United States	168,920
Credit Lyonnais, Paris	France	327,806	Swiss Bank Corp., Basel	Switzerland	162,128
Asahi Bank, Ltd., Tokyo	Japan	317,472	Bankgesellschaft Berlin, AG, Berlin[2]	Germany	158,769
HSBC Holdings, Plc., London	United Kingdom	314,368	Deutsche Genossenschaftsbank, Frankfurt	Germany	158,065
Daiwa Bank, Ltd., Osaka	Japan	304,716	Rabobank Nederland, Utrecht	Netherlands	154,992
ABN–AMRO Bank, N.V., Amsterdam	Netherlands	290,666	J.P. Morgan & Co., New York	United States	154,331
Societe Generale, Paris	France	277,923	Istituto Bancario San Paolo di Torino, Turin	Italy	153,711
Bank of Tokyo, Ltd.	Japan	274,075	Abbey National Plc, London	United Kingdom	147,138
Yasuda Trust & Banking Co., Ltd. Tokyo	Japan	271,580			
Banque Nationale de Paris	France	271,561			
Dresdner Bank, Frankfurt	Germany	258,079			
Citicorp, New York	United States	249,049			
Barclays Bank Plc, London	United Kingdom	248,606			
National Westminster Bank Plc. London	United Kingdom	244,753			

1. The data for 1994 (published June 29) have been revised to exclude certain trust assets. Furthermore the 1994 data are consolidated. 2. Holding company formed on Jan. 1, 1994, by three Berlin-based institutions: Landesbank Berlin–Girozentrale, Berliner Hypotheken-und Pfandbrebank, and Berliner Bank. NOTE: As of Dec. 31, 1994. Exception: Japanese bank data are for fiscal yearend March 31, 1995. *Source: American Banker, July 28, 1995.* Reprinted with permission from American Banker/Bond Buyer.

National Labor Organizations With Membership Over 100,000

Members[1]	Union
747,936	Automobile, Aerospace and Agricultural Implement Workers of America; International Union, United[2]
125,000	Bakery, Confectionery, and Tobacco Workers International Union
91,500	Bricklayers and Allied Craftsmen, International Union of
140,000	Bridge, Structural and Ornamental Iron Workers, International Association of
510,000	Carpenters and Joiners of America, United Brotherhood of
650,000	Communications Workers of America
2,238,435	Education Association, National (Ind.)
750,000	Electrical Workers, International Brotherhood of
150,000	Electronic, Electrical, Salaried, Machine and Furniture Workers, International Union of
200,000	Fire Fighters, International Association of
1,350,000	Food and Commercial Workers International Union, United
210,000	Government Employees, American Federation of
175,000	Graphic Communications International Union
300,000	Hotel Employees and Restaurant Employees International Union
700,000	Laborers' International Union of North America
315,000	Letter Carriers, National Association of
600,000	Machinists and Aerospace Workers, International Association of[2]
200,000	Mine Workers of America, United
355,000	Needletrades, Industrial and Textile Employees, Union of[3]
209,000	Nurses Association, American (Ind.)
110,614	Office and Professional Employees International Union
100,000	Oil, Chemical and Atomic Workers International Union
375,000	Operating Engineers, International Union of
135,000	Painters and Allied Trades, International Brotherhood of
260,300	Paper Workers International Union, United
300,000	Plumbing and Pipe Fitting Industry of the United States and Canada, United Association of Journeymen and Apprentices of the
365,000	Postal Workers Union, American
100,000	Retail, Wholesale, and Department Store Union
100,000	Rubber, Cork, Linoleum, and Plastic Workers of America, United[4]
1,100,000	Service Employees International Union
140,000	Sheet Metal Workers' International Association
1,300,000	State, County and Municipal Employees, American Federation of
700,000	Steelworkers of America, United[2]
875,000	Teachers, American Federation of
1,500,000	Teamsters, International Brotherhood of
160,000	Transit Union, Amalgamated
125,000	Transportation • Communications International Union
135,000	Transportation Union, United

1. Data are for 1995. Unless otherwise noted, unions are ALF-CIO affiliated. 2. These three unions announced on July 27, 1995 they will merge over a five year period. 3. Merger of the International Ladies Garment Workers' Union and the Amalgamated Clothing and Textile Workers Union. 4. Merged with the United Steelworkers of America.

Persons in the Labor Force

Year	Labor force[1] Number (thousands)	% Working-age population	Percent in labor force in[2] Farm occupation	Nonfarm occupation	Year	Labor force[1] Number (thousands)	% Working-age population	Percent in labor force in[2] Farm occupation	Nonfarm occupation
1840	5,420	46.6	68.6	31.4	1920	42,434	51.3	27.0	73.0
1850	7,697	46.8	63.7	36.3	1930	48,830	49.5	21.4	78.6
1860	10,533	47.0	58.9	41.1	1940	52,789	52.2	17.4	82.6
1870	12,925	45.8	53.0	47.0	1950	60,054	53.5	11.6	88.4
1880	17,392	47.3	49.4	50.6	1960	69,877	55.3	6.0	94.0
1890	23,318	49.2	42.6	57.4	1970	82,049	58.2	3.1	96.9
1900	29,073	50.2	37.5	62.5	1980	106,085	62.0	2.2	97.8
1910	37,371	52.2	31.0	69.0	1990	125,182	65.3	1.6	98.4

1. For 1830 to 1930, the data relate to the population and gainful workers at ages 10 and over. For 1940 to 1960, the data relate to the population and labor force at ages 14 and over; for 1970 and 1980, the data relate to the population and labor force at age 16 and over. For 1940 to 1980, the data include the Armed Forces. 2. The farm and nonfarm percentages relate only to the experienced civilian labor force. *Source:* Department of Commerce, Bureau of the Census.

Corporate Profits[1]

(in billions of dollars)

Item	1995[2]	1994	1993	1990	1985	1980	1975	1970
Domestic industries	462.9	444.6	383.6	236.4	190.8	161.9	107.6	62.4
Financial	115.2	104.0	99.0	18.7	21.0	26.9	11.8	12.1
Nonfinancial	347.7	340.6	284.6	217.7	169.7	134.9	95.8	50.2
Manufacturing	143.9	145.6	131.7	88.8	73.0	72.9	52.6	26.6
Wholesale and retail trade	66.7	67.6	54.4	41.5	49.7	23.6	21.3	9.5
Other	59.5	55.1	98.4	87.5	47.0	38.4	21.9	14.1
Rest of world	68.7	60.5	58.7	56.9	31.8	29.9	13.0	6.5
Total	**531.6**	**505.1**	**442.3**	**293.3**	**222.6**	**191.7**	**120.6**	**68.9**

1. Corporate profits before tax with inventory valuation adjustment. 2. First quarter (seasonally adjusted at annual rates). *Source:* U.S. Bureau of Economic Analysis, *Survey of Current Business,* June 1995.

National Income by Type

(in billions of dollars)

Type of share	1994	1993	1990	1985	1980	1975	1970	1965	1960
National income	$5,458.4	$5,131.4	$4,459.6	$3,222.3	$2,121.4	$1,215.0	$800.5	$564.3	$414.5
Compensation of employees	4,004.6	3,780.4	3,290.3	2,368.2	1,596.5	931.1	603.9	393.8	294.2
Wages and salaries	3,279,0	3,100.8	2,738.9	1,965.8	1,343.6	805.9	542.0	358.9	270.8
Supplements to wages and salaries	725.6	679.8	551.4	402.4	252.9	125.2	61.9	35.0	23.4
Proprietors' income[1,2]	473.7	441.6	373.2	254.4	130.6	87.0	66.9	57.3	46.2
Business and professional	434.2	404.3	330.7	225.2	107.2	63.5	50.0	42.4	34.2
Farm	39.5	37.3	42.5	29.2	23.4	23.5	16.9	14.8	12.0
Rental income of persons[1]	27.7	24.1	−12.9	7.6[1]	31.8	22.4	23.9	19.0	15.8
Corporate profits[1,2]	542.7	485.8	319.0	280.7	182.7	95.9	69.4	76.1	49.9
Net interest	409.7	399.5	490.1	311.4	179.8	78.6	36.4	18.2	8.4

1. Includes capital consumption adjustment. 2. Includes inventory valuation adjustment. *Source:* Department of Commerce, Bureau of Economic Analysis.

Per Capita Personal Income by States

State	1994[1]	1993	1990	1980	State	1994[1]	1993	1990	1980
Alabama	$18,010	$17,129	$14,899	$7,465	Montana	$17,865	$17,316	$14,743	$8,342
Alaska	23,788	23,070	20,887	13,007	Nebraska	20,488	19,672	17,379	8,895
Arizona	19,001	18,085	16,262	8,854	Nevada	24,023	22,894	20,248	10,848
Arkansas	16,986	15,995	13,779	7,113	New Hampshire	23,434	22,357	20,231	9,150
California	22,492	21,895	20,656	11,021	New Jersey	28,038	26,876	24,182	10,966
Colorado	22,333	21,498	18,818	10,143	New Mexico	17,106	16,346	14,213	7,940
Connecticut	29,402	28,151	25,426	11,532	New York	25,999	24,824	22,322	10,179
Delaware	22,828	21,852	19,719	10,059	North Carolina	19,669	18,670	16,284	7,780
D.C.	31,136	29,500	24,643	12,251	North Dakota	18,546	17,072	15,320	8,642
Florida	21,677	20,650	18,785	9,246	Ohio	20,928	19,696	17,547	9,399
Georgia	20,251	19,249	17,121	8,021	Oklahoma	17,744	17,026	15,117	9,018
Hawaii	24,057	23,504	20,905	10,129	Oregon	20,419	19,437	17,201	9,309
Idaho	18,231	17,512	15,304	8,105	Pennsylvania	22,324	21,281	18,884	9,353
Illinois	23,784	22,560	20,159	10,454	Rhode Island	22,251	21,244	19,035	9,227
Indiana	20,378	19,213	16,815	8,914	South Carolina	17,695	16,861	15,101	7,392
Iowa	20,265	18,275	16,683	9,226	South Dakota	19,577	17,879	15,628	7,800
Kansas	20,896	19,849	17,639	9,880	Tennessee	19,482	18,439	15,903	7,711
Kentucky	17,807	16,889	14,751	7,679	Texas	19,857	19,145	16,747	9,439
Louisiana	17,651	16,612	14,279	8,412	Utah	17,043	16,136	14,063	7,671
Maine	19,663	18,780	17,041	7,760	Vermont	20,224	19,437	17,444	7,957
Maryland	24,933	23,908	22,088	10,394	Virginia	22,594	21,653	19,543	9,413
Massachusetts	25,616	24,410	22,248	10,103	Washington	22,610	21,774	19,268	10,256
Michigan	22,333	20,584	18,239	9,801	West Virginia	17,208	16,169	13,964	7,764
Minnesota	22,453	29,979	18,784	9,673	Wisconsin	21,019	19,806	17,399	9,364
Mississippi	15,838	14,745	12,578	6,573	Wyoming	20,436	19,719	16,905	11,018
Missouri	20,717	19,557	17,407	8,812	**United States**	**21,809**	**20,800**	**18,667**	**9,494**

1. Preliminary. *Source:* U.S. Department of Commerce, Bureau of Economic Analysis, *Survey of Current Business.*

The Federal Budget—Receipts and Outlays

(in billions of dollars)

Description	1996[1]	1995[1]	1994	Description	1996[1]	1995[1]	1994
RECEIPTS BY SOURCE				Commerce & housing credit	−7.6	−12.0	−5.1
Individual income taxes	623.4	588.5	543.1	Transportation	38.6	39.2	38.1
Corporate income taxes	157.4	150.9	140.4	Community development	12.8	12.6	10.5
Social insurance taxes				Education	57.2	56.1	46.3
and contributions	509.3	484.4	461.5	Health	124.0	115.1	107.1
Excise taxes	57.2	57.6	55.2	Medicare	177.8	157.3	144.7
Estate and gift taxes	16.8	15.6	15.2	Income security	233.2	223.0	214.0
Customs duties	22.3	20.9	20.1	Social security	354.5	336.1	319.6
Miscellaneous receipts	29.0	28.6	22.3	Veterans benefits	38.1	38.4	37.6
Total budget receipts	**1,415.5**	**1,346.4**	**1,257.7**	Administration of justice	19.7	17.6	15.3
OUTLAYS BY FUNCTION				General government	14.6	14.5	11.3
National Defense	261.4	271.6	281.6	Net interest	257.0	234.2	203.0
International affairs	16.7	18.7	17.1	Allowances	−0.2	—	—
Gen. science	16.9	17.0	16.2	Undistributed receipts	−42.4	−41.4	−37.8
Energy	4.4	4.6	5.2	**Total outlays**	**1,612.1**	**1,538.9**	**1,460.9**
Natural resources	21.8	21.9	21.1	**Total deficit**	**−196.6**	**−192.5**	**−203.2**
Agriculture	13.6	14.4	15.1				

1. Estimated. NOTE: The fiscal year is from Oct. 1 to Sept. 30. *Source:* Budget of the United States Government, Fiscal Year 1996.

Foreign Assistance

(in millions of dollars)

	Non-military programs			Military programs		
Calendar years tance[1]	Net new grants	Net new credits	Net other assistance	Net grants	Net credits	Total net assis-
1945–1950[2]	$18,413	$8,086	—	$ 1,525	—	$28,023
1951–60	18,750	2,012	2,767	26,555	49	50,132
1961–70	18,192	14,776	12	21,591	176	54,747
1971–80	27,216	16,519	−1,144	22,601	9,004	74,196
1981–90[3]	69,012	5,467	−120	30,596	1,605	106,561
1991[3]	−32,764	−3,842	23	4,622	−1,556	−33,517
1992[3]	8,824	205	(4)	7,017	−23	15,623
1993[3]	10,498	−817	−3	6,085	−257	15,506
1994	10,680	−1,293	−13	5,133	41	14,548
Total postwar period	**148,421**	**41,112**	**1,522**	**125,725**	**9,039**	**325,819**

1. Excludes investment in international nonmonetary financial institutions of $23,840 million. 2. Includes transactions after V-J Day (Sept. 2, 1945). 3. Includes contributions received from coalition partners for Persian Gulf operations. 4. Less than $500,000. NOTE: Detail may not add to total due to rounding. *Source:* Department of Commerce, Bureau of Economic Analysis.

Women in the Civilian Labor Force

(16 years of age and over; in thousands)

Labor force status	1994	1993	1992	1991	1990	1989
In the labor force:	60,239	58,407	57,798	56,893	56,554	56,030
16 to 19 years of age	3,585	3,261	3,204	3,330	3,544	3,818
20 years and over	56,655	55,146	54,594	53,563	53,010	52,212
Employed	56,610	54,606	53,793	53,284	53,479	53,027
16 to 19 years of age	3,005	2,694	2,613	2,749	3,024	3,282
20 years and over	53,606	51,912	51,180	50,535	50,455	49,745
Unemployed	3,629	3,801	4,005	3,609	3,075	3,003
16 to 19 years of age	580	568	591	581	519	536
20 years and over	3,049	3,233	3,414	3,028	2,555	2,467
Not in the labor force:	42,221	42,522	42,237	42,321	41,845	41,601
Women as percent of labor force	46.0	45.6	45.5	45.4	45.3	45.2
Total civilian noninstitutional population	102,460	100,930	100,035	99,214	98,399	97,630

Source: Department of Labor, Bureau of Labor Statistics, annual averages.

Employed Persons 16 Years and Over, by Race and Major Occupational Groups

(number in thousands)

Race and occupational group	1994[1] Number	1994[1] Percent distribution	1993 Number	1993 Percent distribution
WHITE				
Managerial and professional specialty	30,045	28.6	28,859	28.1
Executive, administrative, & managerial	14,605	13.9	13,888	13.5
Professional specialty	15,439	14.7	14,971	14.6
Technical, sales, & administrative support	32,232	30.6	32,082	31.2
Technicians & related support	3,301	3.1	3,437	3.3
Sales occupations	13,235	12.6	12,809	12.5
Administrative support, including clerical	15,696	14.9	15,836	15.4
Service occupations	13,207	12.6	12,969	12.6
Precision production, craft, and repair	11,974	11.4	11,955	11.6
Operators, fabricators, and laborers	14,416	13.7	13,910	13.5
Farming, forestry, fishing	3,315	3.2	3,037	3.0
Total	**105,190**	**100.0**	**102,812**	**100.0**
BLACK				
Managerial and professional specialty	2,405	18.7	2,140	17.6
Executive, administrative, & managerial	1,103	8.6	959	7.9
Professional specialty	1,302	10.1	1,181	9.7
Technical, sales, & administrative support	3,637	28.3	3,416	28.1
Technicians & related support	376	2.9	387	3.2
Sales occupations	1,056	8.2	948	7.8
Administrative support, including clerical	2,205	17.2	2,081	17.1
Service occupations	2,890	22.5	2,859	23.5
Precision production, craft, and repair	1,040	8.1	985	8.1
Operators, fabricators, and laborers	2,677	20.9	2,535	20.9
Farming, forestry, and fishing	187	1.5	211	1.7
Total	**12,835**	**100.0**	**12,146**	**100.0**

1. Data for 1994 are not directly comparable with data for 1993 and earlier years because of the introduction of a major redesign of the Current Population Survey (household survey) questionnaire and collection methodology and the introduction of 1990 census-based population controls adjusted for the estimated undercount. *Source:* Department of Labor, Bureau of Labor Statistics.

Mothers Participating in Labor Force

(figures in percentage)

Year	Mother with children Under 18 years	Mother with children 6 to 17 years	Mother with children Under 6 years[1]
1955	27.0	38.4	18.2
1965	35.0	45.7	25.3
1975	47.4	54.8	38.9
1980	56.6	64.4	46.6
1985	62.1	69.9	53.5
1986	62.8	70.4	54.4
1987	64.7	72.0	56.7
1988	65.0	73.3	56.1
1989	n.a.	n.a.	n.a.
1990	66.7	74.7	58.2
1991	66.6	74.4	58.4
1992	67.2	75.9	58.0
1993	66.9	75.4	57.9
1994	68.4	76.0	60.3

1. May also have older children. NOTE: For 1955 data are for April; for 1965 and 1975–94, data are for March. *Source:* Department of Labor, Bureau of Labor Statistics. NOTE: Data are most recent available.

Women in the Civilian Labor Force

Year	Number[1] (thousands)	% Female population aged 16 and over[1]	% of Labor force population aged 16 and over[1]
1900	5,319	18.8	18.3
1910	7,445	21.5	19.9
1920	8,637	21.4	20.4
1930	10,752	22.0	22.0
1940	12,845	25.4	24.3
1950	18,389	33.9	29.6
1960[2]	23,240	37.7	33.4
1970	31,543	43.3	38.1
1980	45,487	51.5	42.5
1990	56,554	57.5	45.3
1993	58,407	57.9	45.6
1994[3]	60,239	58.8	46.0

1. For 1900–1930, data relate to population and labor force aged 10 and over; for 1940, to population and labor force aged 14 and over; beginning 1950, to civilian population and labor force aged 16 and over. 2. Beginning in 1960, figures include Alaska and Hawaii. 3. Data for 1994 are not directly comparable with data of 1993 and earlier years because of the introduction of a major redesign of the Current Population Survey (household survey) questionnaire and collection methodology and the introduction of 1990 census-based population controls, adjusted for the estimated undercount. *Sources:* Department of Commerce, Bureau of the Census, and Department of Labor, Bureau of Labor Statistics.

Manufacturing Industries—Gross Average Weekly Earnings and Hours Worked

Industry	1994 Earnings	1994 Hours worked	1990 Earnings	1990 Hours worked	1985 Earnings	1985 Hours worked	1980 Earnings	1980 Hours worked	1975 Earnings	1975 Hours worked	1970 Earnings	1970 Hours worked
All manufacturing	$506.52	42.0	$442.27	40.8	$385.56	40.5	$288.62	39.7	$189.51	39.4	$133.73	39.8
Durable goods	542.28	42.8	468.76	41.3	415.71	41.2	310.78	40.1	205.09	39.9	143.07	40.3
Lumber and wood products	405.00	41.2	365.82	40.2	326.36	39.8	252.18	38.5	167.35	39.1	117.51	39.7
Furniture and fixtures	385.82	40.4	333.52	39.1	283.29	39.4	209.17	38.1	142.13	37.9	108.58	39.2
Primary metal industries	639.66	44.7	550.83	42.7	484.72	41.5	391.78	40.1	246.80	40.0	159.17	40.5
Iron and steel foundries	605.07	45.7	484.99	42.1	429.62	40.8	328.00	40.0	220.99	40.4	151.03	40.6
Nonferrous foundries	486.92	42.9	413.48	40.3	388.74	41.8	291.27	39.9	190.03	39.1	138.16	39.7
Fabricated metal products	510.60	42.8	447.28	41.3	398.96	41.3	300.98	40.4	201.60	40.0	143.67	40.7
Hardware, cutlery, hand tools	506.18	42.5	440.08	40.9	396.42	40.7	275.89	39.3	187.07	39.3	132.33	40.1
Hardware	505.83	42.4	448.63	40.6	385.40	41.3	195.42	39.4	133.46	40.2		
Structural metal products	462.42	42.0	416.56	41.0	369.00	41.0	291.85	40.2	202.61	40.2	142.61	40.4
Electric and electronic equipment	485.72	42.2	420.65	40.8	384.48	40.6	276.21	39.8	180.91	39.5	130.54	39.8
Machinery, except electrical	567.23	43.7	494.34	42.0	427.04	41.5	328.00	41.0	219.22	40.9	154.95	41.1
Transportation equipment	730.51	44.3	592.20	42.0	542.72	42.7	379.61	40.6	242.61	40.3	163.22	40.3
Motor vehicles and equipment	780.62	46.0	619.46	42.4	584.64	43.5	394.00	40.0	262.68	40.6	170.07	40.3
Nondurable goods	460.13	40.9	405.60	40.0	342.86	39.5	255.45	39.0	168.78	38.8	120.43	39.1
Textile mill products	380.22	41.6	320.40	40.0	266.39	39.7	203.31	40.1	133.28	39.2	97.76	39.9
Apparel and other textile products	274.88	37.5	239.88	36.4	208.00	36.3	161.42	35.4	111.97	35.1	84.37	35.3
Leather and leather products	306.85	38.5	258.43	37.4	217.09	37.3	169.09	36.7	120.80	37.4	92.63	37.2
Food and kindred products	440.67	41.3	392.90	40.8	341.60	40.0	271.95	39.7	184.17	40.3	127.98	40.5
Tobacco manufactures	735.39	39.2	645.23	39.2	448.26	37.2	294.89	38.1	171.38	38.0	110.00	37.8
Paper and allied products	604.06	43.9	532.59	43.3	466.34	43.1	330.85	42.2	207.58	41.6	144.14	41.9
Printing and publishing	468.22	38.6	426.38	37.9	365.31	37.7	279.36	37.1	198.32	37.0	147.78	37.7
Chemicals and allied products	655.78	43.2	576.80	42.6	484.78	41.9	344.45	41.5	219.63	40.9	153.50	41.6
Petroleum and allied products	848.48	44.4	723.86	44.6	603.72	43.0	422.18	41.8	267.07	41.6	182.76	42.7

Source: Department of Labor, Bureau of Labor Statistics *Employment & Earnings, March 1995.*

Scam Alert

The FDIC wants people to be aware of a variety of frauds turning up around the country. One involves phony "certified money orders," usually sold as part of $200–$600 kits that con artists say you can use to pay off all your mortgage or other debts. The so-called "certified" money order is bogus.

Another scheme involves "prime bank notes" that promise an unrealistic interest rate of 30 percent or more for investing in financial instruments of elite (thus "prime") foreign banks. Even if you receive an interest payment or two, the notes are worthless.

Yet in another growing scam, fake companies try to pass themselves off as legitimate banks, even claiming to be FDIC-insured, just so they can solicit funds from the public.

Finally, the U.S. and Nigeria are warning about letters from fictitious Nigerian government officials or businesses offering lucrative contracts or other opportunities if you first send money or bank account information. Such letters, which have been widely distributed in the U.S. are totally fraudulent.

If you encounter any one of these scams, call the local office of the Federal Bureau of Investigation listed in your phone book.

Nonmanufacturing Industries—Gross Average Weekly Earnings and Hours Worked

Industry	1994 Earn-ings	1994 Hours worked	1990 Earn-ings	1990 Hours worked	1985 Earn-ings	1985 Hours worked	1975 Earn-ings	1975 Hours worked	1970 Earn-ings	1970 Hours worked
Bituminous coal and lignite mining	$812.68	45.3	$740.52	44.0	$630.77	41.4	$284.53	39.2	$186.41	40.8
Metal mining	703.27	43.6	602.07	42.7	547.24	40.9	250.72	42.3	165.68	42.7
Nonmetallic minerals	608.22	46.5	524.12	45.3	451.68	44.5	213.09	43.4	155.11	44.7
Telephone communications	656.73	41.2	578.74	40.9	512.52	41.1	221.18	38.4	131.60	39.4
Radio and TV broadcasting	513.81	34.6	438.61	34.7	381.39	37.1	214.50	39.0	147.45	38.2
Electric, gas, and sanitary services	734.79	42.4	636.76	41.7	534.59	41.7	246.79	41.2	172.64	41.5
Local and suburban transportation	410.40	38.0	376.65	38.2	309.85	38.3	196.89	40.1	142.30	42.1
Wholesale trade	459.98	38.3	411.48	38.1	358.36	38.7	188.75	38.6	137.60	40.0
Retail trade	216.46	28.9	195.26	28.8	177.31	29.7	108.22	32.4	82.47	33.8
Hotels, tourist courts, motels	239.32	31.0	214.68	30.8	176.90	30.5	89.64	31.9	68.16	34.6
Laundries and dry cleaning plants	247.02	33.7	232.22	34.0	198.70	34.2	106.05	35.0	77.47	35.7
General building contracting	531.50	38.1	487.08	37.7	414.78	37.1	254.88	36.0	184.40	36.3

Source: Department of Labor, Bureau of Labor Statistics, *Employment & Earnings, March 1995.*

Median Income Comparisons of Year-Round Workers by Educational Attainment and Sex, 1992
(persons 25 years and over)

Years of school completed	Median income Women	Median income Men	Income gap in dollars	Women's income as a percent of men's	Percent men's income exceeded women's
Less than 9th grade	$7,942	$12,206	$4,264	65	54
High school:					
9th to 12th grade (no diploma)	9,784	15,928	6,144	61	63
Graduate (includes equivalency)	13,266	22,765	9,499	58	72
College:					
Some, no degree	16,611	26,873	10,262	62	62
Bachelor's degree	24,126	36,691	12,565	66	52

Source: Department of Commerce, Bureau of the Census. NOTE: Data are latest available.

Money Income of Households with Female Householder, 1992
(No husband present)

Income bracket	Number of Households All	Number of Households White	Number of Households Black	Number of Households Hispanic[1]
Less than $5,000	1,648,000	851,000	744,000	188,000
$5,000 to $9,999	2,057,000	1,126,000	862,000	295,000
$10,000 to $14,999	1,631,000	1,009,000	577,000	211,000
$15,000 to $19,999	1,335,000	918,000	373,000	144,000
$20,000 to $24,999	1,132,000	787,000	305,000	121,000
$25,000 to $29,999	926,000	675,000	220,000	91,000
$30,000 to $34,999	791,000	600,000	163,000	53,000
$35,000 to $39,999	534,000	404,000	115,000	33,000
$40,000 to $44,999	496,000	371,000	101,000	28,000
$45,000 to $49,999	340,000	262,000	66,000	12,000
$50,000 to $54,999	284,000	224,000	51,000	16,000
$55,000 to $59,999	197,000	151,000	34,000	11,000
$60,000 to $64,999	137,000	105,000	26,000	7,000
$65,000 to $69,999	108,000	99,000	4,000	11,000
$70,000 to $74,999	62,000	52,000	6,000	3,000
$75,000 to $79,999	35,000	30,000	5,000	3,000
$80,000 to $84,999	32,000	26,000	2,000	2,000
$85,000 to $89,999	45,000	35,000	5,000	2,000
$90,000 to $94,999	39,000	31,000	5,000	2,000
$95,000 to $99,999	23,000	20,000	—	1,000
$100,000 and over	95,000	70,000	17,000	3,000
Median income	$17,221	$20,130	$11,956	$12,894
Mean income	$22,656	$25,119	$16,836	$17,552

1. Persons of Hispanic origin may be of any race. *Source:* Department of Commerce, Bureau of the Census, *Current Population Reports, Consumer Income, Series P-60, No. 184.* NOTE: Data are latest available.

Unemployment by Marital Status, Sex, and Race[1]

Marital status and race	Men		Women	
	Number	Unemployment rate	Number	Unemployment rate
White, 16 years and over	3,275,000	5.4	2,617,000	5.2
Married, spouse present	1,288,000	3.4	1,129,000	3.9
Widowed, divorced, or separated	451,000	6.8	569,000	6.0
Single (never married)	1,535,000	9.6	920,000	7.8
Black, 16 years and over	848,000	12.0	818,000	11.0
Married, spouse present	195,000	6.0	133,000	5.4
Widowed, divorced, or separated	114,000	10.6	185,000	8.9
Single (never married)	540,000	19.4	499,000	17.3
Total, 16 years and over	4,367,000	6.2	3,629,000	6.0
Married, spouse present	1,592,000	3.7	1,352,000	4.1
Widowed, divorced, or separated	594,000	7.4	791,000	6.6
Single (never married)	2,181,000	11.0	1,486,000	9.7

1. 1994 Annual Averages. *Source: Employment and Earnings,* January 1995, U.S. Department of Labor, Bureau of Labor Statistics.

Earnings Distribution of Year-Round, Full-Time Workers, by Sex, 1993

(persons 15 years old and over as of March 1994)

Earnings group	Number		Distribution (percent)		Likelihood of a woman in each earnings group (percent)[1]
	Women	Men	Women	Men	
$2,499 or less	562,000	746,000	1.7	1.5	1.1
$2,500 to $4,999	360,000	231,000	1.1	0.5	2.2
$5,000 to $7,499	880,000	718,000	2.6	1.4	1.9
$7,500 to $9,999	1,493,000	1,071,000	4.5	2.1	2.1
$10,000 to $14,999	5,107,000	4,534,000	15.2	9.1	1.7
$15,000 to $19,999	5,849,000	5,688,000	17.4	11.4	1.5
$20,000 to $24,999	5,656,000	5,979,000	16.9	12.0	1.4
$25,000 to $49,999	11,588,000	20,619,000	34.6	41.4	0.8
$50,000 and over	2,028,000	10,231,000	6.0	20.5	0.3
Total	**33,524,000**	**49,818,000**	**100.0**	**100.0**	**(X)**

1. Figures obtained by dividing percentages for women by percentages for men. Percentages may not add to totals because of rounding. (X) not applicable. *Source:* Department of Commerce, Bureau of the Census.

Comparison of Median Earnings of Year-Round, Full-Time Workers 15 Years and Over, by Sex, 1960 to 1993

Year	Median earnings		Earnings gap in current dollars	Women's earnings as a percent of men's	Percent men's earnings exceeded women's	Earnings gap in constant 1993 CPI-U-xl adjusted dollars
	Women	Men				
1960	$3,257	$5,368	$2,111	60.7	64.8	$9,473
1970	5,323	8,966	3,643	59.4	68.4	12,746
1980	11,197	18,612	7,415	60.2	66.2	13,019
1984	14,780	23,218	8,438	63.7	57.1	11,735
1985	15,624	24,195	8,571	64.6	54.9	11,510
1986	16,232	25,256	9,024	64.3	55.6	11,898
1987	16,911	25,946	9,035	65.2	53.4	11,493
1988	17,606	26,656	9,050	66.0	51.4	11,054
1989	18,769	27,331	8,562	68.7	45.6	9,977
1990	19,822	27,678	7,856	71.6	39.6	8,685
1991	20,553	29,421	8,868	69.9	43.1	9,408
1992r	21,375	30,197	8,822	70.8	41.3	9,086
1993	21,747	30,407	8,660	71.5	39.8	8,660

r = based on implementation of 1990 census population controls. *Source:* Department of Commerce, Bureau of the Census.

Occupations of Employed Women[1]

(16 years of age and over. Figures are percentage)

Occupations	1994	1993	1992	1991	1990	1989	1988
Managerial and professional	28.7	28.3	27.4	26.9	26.2	25.9	25.2
Technical, sales, administrative support	42.4	43.0	43.8	43.8	44.4	44.2	44.6
Service occupations	17.8	18.0	17.9	17.9	17.7	17.7	17.9
Precision production, craft and repair	2.2	2.1	2.1	2.1	2.2	2.2	2.3
Operators, fabricators, laborers	7.7	7.6	7.9	8.1	8.5	8.9	8.9
Farming, forestry, fishing	1.2	0.9	1.0	1.0	1.0	1.1	1.1

1. Annual averages. NOTE: Details may not add up to totals because of rounding. *Source:* Department of Labor.

Employed and Unemployed Workers by Full- and Part-Time Status, Sex, and Age: 1970 to 1994

(In thousands)

	1994[1]	1993	1992	1990	1985	1980	1975	1970
Total 16 yr and over								
Employed	123,060	119,306	117,598	117,914	107,150	99,303	85,846	78,678
Full time	99,772	98,439	97,026	97,994	88,535	82,564	71,585	66,752
Part time	23,288	20,868	20,572	19,920	18,615	16,742	14,260	11,924
Unemployed	7,996	8,734	9,384	6,874	8,312	7,637	7,929	4,093
Full time	6,513	7,146	7,746	5,541	6,793	6,269	6,523	3,206
Part time	1,483	1,588	1,638	1,332	1,519	1,369	1,408	889
Men, 20 yr and over								
Employed	63,294	61,865	61,019	61,198	56,562	53,101	48,018	45,581
Full time	57,707	56,602	55,878	56,640	52,425	49,699	45,051	43,138
Part time	5,587	5,265	5,141	4,558	4,137	3,403	2,966	2,444
Unemployed	3,627	4,204	4,619	3,170	3,715	3,353	3,476	1,638
Full time	3,359	3,934	4,339	2,936	3,479	3,167	3,255	1,502
Part time	269	270	280	234	236	186	223	137
Women, 20 yr. and over								
Employed	53,606	51,912	51,181	50,455	44,154	38,492	30,726	26,952
Full time	40,183	40,051	39,409	39,036	33,604	29,391	23,242	20,654
Part time	13,423	11,861	11,772	11,419	10,550	9,102	7,484	6,297
Unemployed	3,049	3,234	3,413	2,555	3,129	2,615	2,684	1,349
Full time	2,506	2,623	2,794	2,044	2,536	2,135	2,210	1,077
Part time	543	611	620	511	593	480	474	271
Both sexes 16–19 yr.								
Employed	6,161	5,530	5,398	6,261	6,434	7,710	7,104	6,144
Full time	1,883	1,786	1,739	2,318	2,507	3,474	3,292	2,960
Part time	4,278	3,744	3,659	3,943	3,927	4,237	3,810	3,183
Unemployed	1,320	1,296	1,352	1,149	1,468	1,669	1,767	1,106
Full time	648	589	614	561	777	966	1,057	626
Part time	672	707	739	587	690	701	709	480

1. Data for 1994 are not directly comparable with data for 1993 and earlier years because of the introduction of a major redesign of the Current Population Survey (household survey) questionnaire and collection methodology and the introduction of 1990 census-based population controls, adjusted for the estimated undercount. *Source:* U.S. Dept. of Labor, Bureau of Labor Statistics.

Work Stoppages Involving 1,000 Workers or More[1]

Year	Work stoppages	Workers involved (thousands)	Man-days idle (thousands)	Year	Work stoppages	Workers involved (thousands)	Man-days idle (thousands)
1950	424	1,698	30,390	1986	72	900	11,861
1960	222	896	13,260	1987	46	174	4,456
1970	381	2,468	52,761	1988	40	118	4,381
1975	235	965	17,563	1989	51	452	16,996
1980	187	795	20,844	1990	44	185	5,926
1982	96	656	9,061	1991	40	392	4,584
1983	81	909	17,461	1992	35	364	3,989
1984	68	391	8,499	1993	35	184	3,981
1985	61	584	7,079	1994	45	322	5,020

1. The number of stoppages and workers relate to stoppages that began in the year. Days of idleness include all stoppages in effect. Workers are counted more than once if they were involved in more than one stoppage during the year. *Source:* U.S. Department of Labor. Bureau of Labor Statistics, *Monthly Labor Review. June 1995.*

Leading Advertising Agencies in Worldwide Billings

(in thousands of dollars)

Agency	1994	1993
McCann–Erickson	$7,177,554[1]	$6,594,159[2]
Foote, Cone & Belding	6,500,000[1]	6,226,207
J. Walter Thompson	6,133,000[1]	5,811,800
BBDO Worldwide	5,883,576[1]	5,376,675
Young & Rubicam	5,657,480	5,313,673
Ogilvy & Mather Worldwide	5,302,582	4,749,884
Bates Worldwide	5,048,216	4,673,491[2]
Saatchi & Saatchi Advertising	5,007,200	5,566,100
Lintas: Worldwide	5,006,000[1]	4,700,000[2]
Grey Advertising	4,817,200	4,564,500

1. Estimated. 2. Restated to reflect acquisition or merger. *Source: Adweek Magazine,* Top 20 Worldwide Agencies, March 20, 1995 edition. © 1995 Adweek. Used with permission from *Adweek.*

Unemployment Rate, 1994

Race and age	Women[1]	Men[1]
All races:	6.0	6.2
16 to 19 years	16.2	19.0
20 years and over	5.4	5.4
White	5.2	5.4
16 to 19 years	13.8	16.3
20 years and over	4.6	4.8
Minority races:	10.9	10.7
16 to 19 years	27.9	31.8
20 years and over	9.8	9.3

1: Annual averages. *Source:* Bureau of Labor Statistics, Department of Labor.

Unemployment Rate in the Civilian Labor Force

Year	Unemployment rate	Year	Unemployment rate
1920	5.2	1984	7.5
1928	4.2	1985	7.2
1930	8.7	1986	7.0
1932	23.6	1987	6.2
1934	21.7	1988	5.4
1936	16.9	1989	5.3
1938	19.0	1990	5.5
1940	14.6	1991	6.7
1942	4.7	1992	7.4
1944	1.2	1993	6.8
1946	3.9	1994	6.1
1948	3.8	Jan.	6.7
1950	5.3	Feb.	6.5
1952	3.0	March	6.5
1954	5.5	April	6.4
1956	4.1	May	6.1
1958	6.8	June	6.1
1960	5.5	July	6.1
1962	5.5	Aug.	6.0
1964	5.2	Sept.	5.8
1966	3.8	Oct.	5.7
1968	3.6	Nov.	5.6
1970	4.9	Dec.	5.4
1972	5.6	1995	
1974	5.6	Jan.	5.7
1976	7.7	Feb.	5.4
1978	6.0	March	5.5
1980	7.1	April	5.8
1982	9.7		

NOTE: Estimates prior to 1940 are based on sources other than direct enumeration. *Source:* Department of Labor, Bureau of Labor Statistics.

Employment and Unemployment

(in millions of persons)

Category	1994	1993	1990	1985	1980	1975	1970	1950	1945	1932	1929
EMPLOYMENT STATUS[1]											
Civilian noninstitutional population	196.8	193.6	188.0	178.2	167.7	153.2	137.1	105.0	94.1	—	—
Civilian labor force	131.1	128.0	124.8	115.5	106.9	93.8	82.8	62.2	53.9	—	—
Civilian labor force participation rate	66.6	66.2	66.4	64.8	63.8	61.2	60.4	59.2	57.2	—	—
Employed	123.1	119.3	117.9	107.2	99.3	85.8	78.7	58.9	52.8	38.9	47.6
Employment-population ratio	62.5	61.6	62.7	60.1	59.2	56.1	57.4	56.1	56.1	—	—
Agriculture	3.4	3.1	3.2	3.2	3.4	3.4	3.5	7.2	8.6	10.2	10.5
Nonagricultural industries	119.7	116.2	114.7	104.0	95.9	82.4	75.2	51.8	44.2	28.8	37.2
Unemployed	8.0	8.7	6.9	8.3	7.6	7.9	4.1	3.3	1.0	12.1	1.6
Unemployment rate	6.1	6.8	5.5	7.2	7.1	8.5	4.9	5.3	1.9	23.6	3.2
Not in labor force	65.8	65.5	63.3	62.7	60.8	59.4	54.3	42.8	40.2		
INDUSTRY[2]											
Total nonfarm employment	114.0	110.7	109.4	97.4	90.4	76.9	70.9	45.2	40.4	23.6	31.3
Goods-producing industries	23.9	23.4	24.9	24.8	25.7	22.6	23.6	18.5	17.5	8.6	13.3
Mining	0.6	0.6	0.7	0.9	1.0	0.8	0.6	0.9	0.8	0.7	1.1
Construction	5.0	4.7	5.1	4.7	4.3	3.5	3.6	2.4	1.1	1.0	1.5
Manufacturing: Durable goods	10.4	10.2	11.1	11.5	12.2	10.7	11.2	8.1	9.1	—	—
Nondurable goods	7.9	7.9	8.0	7.8	8.1	7.7	8.2	7.2	6.4	—	—
Services-producing industries	90.1	87.4	84.5	72.5	64.7	54.3	47.3	26.7	22.9	15.0	18.0
Transportation and public utilities	6.0	5.8	5.8	5.2	5.1	4.5	4.5	4.0	3.9	2.8	3.9
Trade, Wholesale	6.1	6.0	6.2	5.7	5.3	4.4	4.0	2.6	2.0	—	—
Retail	20.4	19.8	19.6	17.3	15.0	12.6	11.0	6.7	5.4	—	—
Finance, insurance, and real estate	6.9	6.8	6.7	5.9	5.2	4.2	3.6	1.9	1.5	—	—
Services	31.5	30.2	27.9	21.9	17.9	13.9	11.5	5.4	4.2	—	—
Federal government	2.9	2.9	3.1	2.9	2.9	2.7	2.7	1.9	2.8	—	—
State and local government	16.2	15.9	15.2	13.5	13.4	11.9	9.8	4.1	3.1	2.7	2.5

1. For 1929–45, figures on employment status relate to persons 14 years and over; beginning in 1950, 16 years and over.
2. Data for 1993 have been revised. Data for 1994 are not directly comparable with data for 1993 and earlier years because of the introduction of a major redesign of the Current Population Survey (household survey) questionnaire and collection methodology and the introduction of 1990 census-based population controls, adjusted for the estimated undercount. *Source:* U.S. Department of Labor, Bureau of Labor Statistics.

Livestock on Farms (in thousands)

Type	1995	1994	1993	1992	1990	1985	1980	1975	1970	1965
Cattle[1]	103,265	101,749	100,892	100,110	98,162	109,582	111,242	132,028	112,369	109,000
Dairy cows[1]	9,532	9,638	9,844	9,904	10,153	10,311	10,758	11,220	13,303	16,981
Sheep[1]	8,895	9,079	10,191	10,850	11,363	10,716	12,699	14,515	20,423	25,127
Swine[2]	58,415	55,630	58,340	56,974	51,150	54,073	67,318	54,693	57,046	56,106
Chickens[3]	3,489,881	3,397,818	6,753,170	6,499,971	5,873,923	4,689,973	4,201,706	3,173,820	3,220,085	2,535,141
Turkeys[4]	289,025	291,750	288,980	285,110	261,280	185,427	165,243	124,165	116,139	105,914

1. As of Jan. 1. 2. As of Dec. 1 of the previous year for 1965–85 and 1992; as of March 1 for 1990, 1991, 1993–95. 3. Layers as of Dec. of the previous year for 1965–93. 4. 1975–85 as of Dec. of previous year, 1990–94 total for previous calendar year. *Source:* Department of Agriculture, Statistical Reporting Service, Economic Research Service.

Agricultural Output by States, 1994 Crops

State	Corn (1,000 bu)	Wheat (1,000 bu)	Cotton (1,000 ba[1])	Potatoes (1,000 cwt)	Tobacco (1,000 lb)	Cattle[2] (1,000 head)	Swine[3] (1,000 head)
Alabama	24,960	4,560	740.0	1,628	—	1,780	—
Alaska	—	—	—	—	—	9.8	—
Arizona	2,550	11,186	870.0	1,670	—	830	—
Arkansas	10,800	40,480	1,760.0	—	—	2,010	—
California	28,050	44,365	2,910.0	15,267	—	4,700	—
Colorado	133,500	79,734	—	28,720	—	2,950	—
Connecticut	—	—	—	—	2,625	75	—
Delaware	18,750	3,780	—	816	—	29	—
Florida	6,800	630	100.0	9,992	16,575	2,020	—
Georgia	57,240	20,400	1,550.0	—	80,660	1,560	1,000
Hawaii	—	—	—	—	—	175	—
Idaho	4,900	100,280	—	134,340	—	1,780	—
Illinois	1,786,200	50,400	—	1,450	—	1,820	5,600
Indiana	858,240	38,430	—	1,148	15,265	1,170	4,200
Iowa	1,930,400	2,115	—	328	—	4,250	14,600
Kansas	304,590	433,200	1.7	—	—	6,300	1,350
Kentucky	156,160	25,200	—	—	458,075	2,650	810
Louisiana	35,190	2,590	1,500.0	—	—	960	—
Maine	—	—	—	17,250	—	113	—
Maryland	46,020	12,100	—	250	12,750	315	—
Massachusetts	—	—	—	775	803	68	—
Michigan	260,910	30,740	—	14,910	—	1,200	1,120
Minnesota	915,900	71,948	—	20,035	—	2,800	4,750
Mississippi	30,500	6,400	2,150.0	—	—	1,340	—
Missouri	273,700	49,500	595.0	1,734	8,190	4,500	2,850
Montana	2,700	170,590	—	3,200	—	2,700	—
Nebraska	1,153,700	71,400	—	5,296	—	6,000	4,200
Nevada	—	670	—	2,760	—	500	—
New Hampshire	—	—	—	—	—	48	—
New Jersey	9,639	1,344	—	588	—	65	—
New Mexico	12,750	5,520	90.0	4,238	—	1,500	—
New York	68,440	6,095	—	7,805	—	1,450	—
North Carolina	81,900	30,380	820.0	3,186	597,525	1,130	5,700
North Dakota	54,000	356,404	—	28,200	—	1,920	—
Ohio	486,500	68,440	—	1,348	19,295	1,490	1,580
Oklahoma	16,500	143,100	240.0	—	—	5,700	—
Oregon	3,400	58,580	—	25,784	—	1,470	—
Pennsylvania	123,600	7,920	—	3,780	18,360	1,750	1,040
Rhode Island	—	—	—	253	—	7.5	—
South Carolina	29,325	18,000	380.0	—	110,450	500	—
South Dakota	367,200	95,278	—	1,540	—	4,000	1,680
Tennessee	66,120	15,000	890.0	—	134,672	2,550	500
Texas	238,680	75,400	5,052.0	2,900	—	15,100	—
Utah	2,860	7,012	—	1,590	—	890	—
Vermont	—	—	—	—	—	290	—
Virginia	34,300	14,000	79.2	1,425	108,752	1,750	—
Washington	19,425	134,000	—	88,920	—	1,310	—
West Virginia	3,675	550	—	—	3,600	500	—
Wisconsin	437,100	7,940	—	25,740	5,800	3,850	1,170
Wyoming	5,856	4,949	—	476	—	1,390	—
U.S. Total	10,103,030	2,320,610	19,727.9	459,342	1,593,397	103,265.5	57,350

1. 480-lb net-weight bales. 2. Number on farms as of Jan. 1, 1995. 3. Number on farms as of March 4, 1994. Totals include states for which individual estimates are not available. *Source:* Department of Agriculture, Statistical Reporting Service.

Farm Income
(in millions of dollars)

Year	Cash receipts from marketings		Government payments	Total cash income[1]
	Crops	Livestock, livestock products		
1930	$3,868	$5,187	—	$9,055
1935	2,977	4,143	$573	7,693
1940	3,469	4,913	723	9,105
1945	9,655	12,008	742	22,405
1950	12,356	16,105	283	28,764
1955	13,523	15,967	229	29,842
1960	15,023	18,989	703	34,958
1965	17,479	21,886	2,463	42,215
1970	20,977	29,532	3,717	54,768
1975	45,813	43,089	807	90,707
1980	71,746	67,991	1,285	143,295
1985	74,293	69,822	7,705	157,854
1988	71,720	79,434	14,480	172,902
1989	77,020	84,122	10,887	179,845
1990	80,131	89,843	9,298	186,824
1991	82,060	86,735	8,214	184,858
1992	84,853	86,350	9,169	188,160
1993	84,497	90,555	13,402	197,215

1. Includes items not listed. 2. Preliminary. *Source:* Department of Agriculture, Economic Research Service. NOTE: Data are latest available.

Per Capita Consumption of Principal Foods[1]

Food	1993	1992	1991
Red meat[2]	111.9	114.1	111.9
Poultry[2]	61.1	60.0	58.0
Fish and shellfish[2]	14.9	14.7	14.8
Eggs	30.1	30.2	30.0
Fluid milk and cream[3]	226.7	230.8	233.1
Ice cream	16.1	16.3	16.3
Cheese (excluding cottage)	26.2	26.0	25.0
Butter (actual weight)	4.5	4.2	4.2
Margarine (actual weight)	10.8	11.0	10.6
Total fats and oils[4]	65.0	65.6	63.8
Fruits (farm weight)[5]	308.7	291.7	289.5
Peanuts (shelled)	6.0	6.6	6.5
Vegetables (farm weight)	396.6	391.7	388.5
Sugar (refined)	64.2	64.5	63.7
Corn sweeteners (dry weight)	81.5	77.9	75.4
Flour and cereal products	189.2	187.0	185.4
Soft drinks (gal)	46.6	45.4	44.9
Coffee bean equivalent	10.0	10.3	10.4
Cocoa (chocolate liquor equivalent)	4.6	4.6	4.6

1. As of August 1994. Except where noted, consumption is from commercial sources and is in pounds retail weight. 2. Boneless, trimmed equivalent. 3. Includes milk and cream produced and consumed on farms. 4. Fat-content basis. 5. Excludes wine grapes. NOTE: Data are latest available.

Government Employment and Payrolls

Year and function	Employees (in thousands)				October payrolls (in millions)			
	Total	Federal[1]	State	Local	Total	Federal[1]	State	Local
1940	4,474	1,128		3,346	$566	177		$389
1945	6,556	3,375		3,181	1,110	642		468
1950	6,402	2,117	1,057	3,228	1,528	613	218	696
1955	7,432	2,378	1,199	3,855	2,265	846	326	1,093
1960	8,808	2,421	1,527	4,860	3,333	1,118	524	1,691
1965	10,589	2,588	2,028	5,973	4,884	1,484	849	2,551
1970	13,028	2,881	2,755	7,392	8,334	2,428	1,612	4,294
1975	14,973	2,890	3,271	8,813	13,224	3,584	2,653	6,987
1980	16,213	2,898	3,753	9,562	19,935	5,205	4,285	10,445
1982	15,841	2,848	3,744	9,249	23,173	5,959	5,022	12,192
1983	16,034	2,875	3,816	9,344	24,525	6,302	5,346	12,878
1984	16,436	2,942	3,898	9,595	26,904	7,137	5,815	13,952
1985	16,690	3,021	3,984	9,685	28,945	7,580	6,329	15,036
1986	16,933	3,019	4,068	9,846	30,670	7,561	6,810	16,298
1987	17,212	3,091	4,116	10,005	32,669	7,924	7,263	17,482
1988	17,588	3,112	4,236	10,240	34,203	7,976	7,842	18,385
1990	18,369	3,105	4,503	10,760	39,228	8,999	9,083	21,146
1991, total	18,554	3,103	4,521	10,934	41,237	9,687	9,437	22,117
National defense and international relations	1,019	1,019	(2)	(2)	3,294	3,294	(2)	(2)
Postal service	803	803	(2)	(2)	2,359	2,359	(2)	(2)
Education	8,086	14	1,999	6,074	15,724	41	3,551	12,132
Instructional employees	4,618	n.a.	624	3,995	11,057	n.a.	1,632	9,425
Highways	568	4	259	305	1,238	18	613	607
Health and hospitals	1,817	303	724	793	4,048	876	1,585	1,588
Police protection	844	83	87	674	2,253	304	205	1,699
Fire protection	341	(2)	(2)	341	771	(2)	(2)	771
Sewerage & solid waste management	241	(2)	3	238	518	(2)	7	510
Parks & recreation	342	26	44	271	489	66	69	353
Natural resources	433	233	162	39	1,150	732	349	70
Financial administration	508	147	149	212	1,119	400	343	376
All other	3,552	467	1,094	1,988	8,278	1,597	2,671	4,010

1. Civilians only. 2. Not applicable. NOTE: n.a. = not available. Detail may not add to totals because of rounding. Data are most recent available. *Source:* Department of Commerce, Bureau of the Census. NOTE: Data are latest available.

Receipts and Outlays of the Federal Government
(in millions of dollars)

From 1789 to 1842, the federal fiscal year ended Dec. 31; from 1844 to 1976, on June 30; and beginning 1977, on Sept. 30.

Year	Customs (including tonnage tax)[1]	Receipts Internal revenue Income and profits tax	Other	Miscellaneous taxes and receipts	Total receipts	Net receipts[2]
1789–1791	$ 4	—	—	—	$ 4	$ 4
1800	9	—	$ −1	$ 1	11	11
1810	9	—	—	1	9	9
1820	15	—	—	3	18	18
1830	22	—	—	3	25	25
1840	14	—	—	6	20	20
1850	40	—	—	4	44	44
1860	53	—	—	3	56	56
1870	195	—	185	32	411	411
1880	187	—	124	23	334	334
1890	230	—	143	31	403	403
1900	233	—	295	39	567	567
1910	334	—	290	52	675	675
1915	210	$ 80	335	72	698	683
1929	602	2,331	607	493	4,033	3,862
1939	319	2,189	2,972	188	5,668	4,979
1944	431	34,655	7,030	3,325	45,441	43,563
1945	355	35,173	8,729	3,494	47,750	44,362
1950	423	28,263	11,186	1,439	41,311	36,422
1956[4]	705	56,639	20,564	389	78,297	74,547
1960	1,123	67,151	28,266	1,190	97,730	92,492
1965	1,478	79,792	39,996	1,598	122,863	116,833
1970	2,494	138,689	65,276	3,424	209,883	193,743
1975	3,782	202,146	108,371	6,711	321,010	280,997
1980	7,482	359,927	192,436	12,797	572,641	520,050
1985	12,079	474,074	311,092	18,576	815,821	733,996
1988	16,198	495,376	377,469	19,909	(5)	908,953
1989	16,334	549,273	402,200	22,800	(5)	990,691
1990	16,707	560,391	426,893	27,470	(5)	1,031,462
1991	15,949	565,913	449,577	22,846	(5)	1,054,265
1992	17,359	576,234	470,401	26,459	(5)	1,090,453
1993	18,802	627,200	488,934	18,290	(5)	1,153,226
1994	20,099	683,123	531,924	22,041	(5)	1,257,187

Year	Outlays Department of Defense (Army, 1789–1950)	Department of the Navy	Interest on public debt	All other	Net outlays[3]	Surplus (+) or deficit (−)
1789–1791	$ 1	—	$ 2	$ 1	$ 4	—
1800	3	$ 3	3	1	11	—
1810	2	2	3	1	8	$ +1
1820	3	4	5	6	18	—
1830	5	3	2	5	15	+10
1840	7	6	—	11	24	−4
1850	9	8	4	18	40	+4
1860	16	12	3	32	63	−7
1870	58	22	129	101	310	+101
1880	38	14	96	120	268	+66
1890	45	22	36	215	318	+85
1900	135	56	40	290	521	+46
1910	190	123	21	359	694	−19
1915	202	142	23	379	746	−63
1929	426	365	678	1,658	3,127	+734
1939	695	673	941	6,533	8,841	−3,862
1944	49,438	26,538	2,609	16,401	94,986	−51,423
1945	50,490	30,047	3,617	14,149	98,303	−53,941
1950	5,789	4,130	5,750	23,875	39,544	−3,122
1956[4]	35,693	—	6,787	27,981	70,460	+4,087

			Outlays			
Year	Department of Defense (Army, 1789–1950)	Department of the Navy	Interest on public debt	All other	Net outlays[3]	Surplus (+) or deficit (–)
1960	43,969	—	9,180	39,075	92,223	+269
1965	47,179	—	11,346	59,904	118,430	–1,596
1970	78,360	—	19,304	98,924	196,588	–2,845
1975	87,471	—	32,665	205,969	326,105	–45,108
1980	136.138	—	74,860	368,013	579,011	–58,961
1985	244,054	—	178,945	513,810	936,809	–202,813
1988	290,349	—	151,711	621,995	1,064,055	–155,102
1989	303,600	—	169,100	649,943	1,142,643	–123,785
1990	299,355	—	183,790	768,725	1,251,850	–220,388
1991	273,292	—	194,541	855,924	1,323,757	–269,492
1992	298,350	—	199,439	883,005	1,380,794	–290,340
1993	291,086	—	198,811	918,635	1,408,532	–255,306
1994	281,451	—	202,957	976,149	1,460,557	–203,370

1. Beginning 1933, tonnage tax is included in "Other receipts." 2. Net receipts equal total receipts less (a) appropriations to federal old-age and survivors' insurance trust fund beginning fiscal year 1939 and (b) refunds of receipts beginning fiscal year 1933. 3. Includes Air Force 1950–65 (in millions): 1950—$3,521; 1956—$16,750; 1960—$19,065; 1965—$18,471. 4. Beginning 1956, computed on unified budget concepts; not strictly comparable with preceding figures. 5. Net receipts are now the total receipts. Public Law 99–177 moved two social security trust funds off-budget. *Source:* Department of the Treasury, Financial Management Service. NOTE: Totals figures may not add to totals because of rounding of some items.

Contributions to International Organizations
(for fiscal year 1994 thousands of dollars)

Organization	Amount	Organization	Amount
United Nations and Specialized Agencies		Cooperation	11
Food and Agriculture Organization	$79,662	North Atlantic Assembly	698
International Atomic Energy Agency	50,755	North Atlantic Treaty Organization	32,849
International Civic Aviation Organization	12,450	Organization for Economic Cooperation and Development	50,366
International Labor Organization	53,292		
International Maritime Organization	1,242	South Pacific Commission	1,149
International Telecommunications Union	6,604	Other International Organizations	
United Nations	315,362	Bureau of International Expositions	31
United Nations Industrial Development Organization	24,069	Customs Cooperation Council	3,336
		General Agreement on Tariffs and Trade	8,845
Universal Postal Union	1,185	Hague Conference on Private International Law	93
World Health Organization	92,515	International Agency for Research on Cancer	1,541
World Intellectual Property Organization	511	International Bureau of the Permanent Court of Arbitration	18
World Meteorological Organization	9,264		
Peacekeeping Forces		International Bureau for the Publication of Custom Tariffs	95
U.N. Disengagement Observer Force	6,258		
U.N. Interim Force in Lebanon	42,950	International Bureau of Weights and Measures	802
U.N. Angola Verification Mission II/III	16,273	International Center for the Study of Cultural Property	725
U.N. Iran–Kuwait Observer Mission	3,343		
U.N. Observer Mission in El Salvador	5,934	International Cotton Advisory Committee	234
U.N. Transitional Authority in Cambodia	26,148	International Hydrographic Organization	103
U.N. Protection Force in Yugoslavia	459,722	International Institute for the Unification of Private Law	102
U.N. Observer Mission in Somalia	330,883		
U.N. Observer Mission in Mozambique	110,724	International Jute Organization	69
U.N. Uganda/Rwanda Observer Mission	1,107	International Lead and Zinc Study Group	47
U.N. Observer Mission in Georgia	1,784	International Natural Rubber Organization	323
U.N. Mission in Haiti	464	International Office of Epizootics	82
U.N. Observer Mission in Liberia	12,251	International Organization for Legal Metrology	106
U.N. Assistance Mission for Rwanda	32,874	International Office of the Vine and Wine	48
Inter-American Organizations		International Rubber Study Group	72
Inter-American Indian Institute	120	International Seed Testing Association	8
Inter-American Institute for Cooperation on Agriculture	15,980	International Tropical Timber Organization	149
		International Union for the Conservation of Nature and Natural Resources	223
Organization of American States	45,802		
Pan American Health Organization	47,413	International Wheat Council	348
Pan American Institute on Geography and History	402	Interparliamentary Union	954
		Permanent International Association of Road Congresses	20
Pan American Railway Congress Association	25		
Regional Organizations		World Tourism Organization	385
Asia-Pacific Economic Cooperation	360	**Total U.S. Contribution**	**1,911,600**
Colombo Plan Council for Technical			

Source: Budget of the United States Government Fiscal Year 1996.

Social Welfare Expenditures Under Public Programs

(in millions of dollars)

Year and source of funds	Social insur- ance	Public aid	Health and medical pro- grams[1]	Veter- ans' pro- grams	Edu- cation	Hous- ing	Other social welfare	All health and medical care[2]	Total social welfare	Total social welfare as: Percent of gross domestic product	Percent of total gov't outlays
FEDERAL											
1982	250,551	52,485	14,598	24,463	11,917	7,176	6,500	90,776	367,691	11.8	52.5
1983	274,212	55,895	15,594	25,561	12,397	8,087	7,046	100,274	398,792	12.1	51.9
1984	288,743	58,480	16,622	25,970	13,010	10,226	7,349	103,927	420,399	11.4	50.2
1985	313,108	61,985	18,630	26,704	13,796	11,088	7,548	118,955	452,860	11.4	47.8
1986	326,588	65,615	19,926	27,072	15,022	10,164	7,977	125,730	472,364	11.2	47.6
1987	345,082	69,233	22,219	27,641	16,054	11,110	8,504	143,020	499,844	11.2	50.4
1988	358,412	74,137	22,681	28,845	16,952	14,006	8,112	149,102	523,144	11.0	49.1
1989	387,291	81,731	21,148	29,638	18,660	15,184	8,492	166,056	565,143	10.9	49.5
1990	422,257	92,858	27,204	30,428	18,374	16,612	8,905	190,616	616,639	11.2	51.4
1991	453,534	113,235	29,668	32,331	19,084	18,696	9,831	213,811	676,380	11.9	52.8
1992	495,710	138,704	31,872	34,212	20,188	17,950	10,677	249,499	749,312	12.6	57.1
STATE AND LOCAL											
1982	52,481	28,367	19,195	245	121,957	778	5,154	40,738	228,178	7.4	62.6
1983	56,846	29,935	20,382	265	129,416	1,003	5,438	42,854	243,285	7.4	60.1
1984	52,378	32,206	20,383	301	139,046	1,306	5,946	44,540	251,569	7.0	58.9
1985	59,420	34,792	22,430	338	152,622	1,540	6,398	48,587	277,540	7.1	59.0
1986	63,816	37,464	24,408	373	163,495	1,872	6,728	53,884	298,158	7.3	58.2
1987	69,941	41,462	25,400	410	188,486	2,129	6,773	60,566	344,601	7.5	59.6
1988	73,783	46,237	29,859	409	202,416	2,550	7,368	70,511	362,622	7.5	60.1
1989	80,765	47,352	32,468	466	220,111	2,943	8,117	75,224	392,222	7.6	68.0
1990	91,565	53,953	36,263	488	240,011	2,856	9,012	85,775	434,148	7.9	68.0
1991	107,641	68,104	38,504	526	258,063	2,826	9,949	102,715	485,613	8.6	70.4
1992	121,266	69,241	39,163	555	272,011	2,668	10,855	104,559	515,758	8.7	70.6
TOTAL											
1982	303,033	80,852	33,793	24,708	133,874	7,954	11,654	131,514	595,869	19.2	55.7
1983	331,058	85,830	35,976	25,826	141,813	9,090	12,484	143,128	642,077	19.6	54.5
1984	341,120	90,685	37,006	26,275	152,056	11,532	13,295	148,467	671,969	18.3	52.8
1985	372,529	96,777	41,060	27,042	166,418	12,627	13,946	167,542	730,399	18.4	51.2
1986	390,404	103,079	44,334	27,445	178,518	12,036	14,705	179,614	770,522	18.5	47.9
1987	415,023	110,695	47,619	28,051	204,540	13,240	15,278	203,586	834,446	18.7	53.5
1988	432,195	120,375	52,540	29,254	219,368	16,556	15,480	219,613	885,766	18.5	52.8
1989	468,056	129,083	56,616	30,104	238,771	18,127	16,609	241,280	957,365	18.5	55.2
1990	513,823	146,811	63,467	30,916	258,385	19,468	17,918	276,391	1,050,788	19.2	56.7
1991	561,175	181,339	68,172	32,857	277,147	21,523	19,780	316,526	1,161,993	20.5	58.6
1992	616,975	207,945	71,035	34,767	292,198	20,617	21,532	354,058	1,265,070	21.3	61.6
PERCENT OF TOTAL, BY TYPE											
1985	51.0	13.2	5.6	3.7	22.8	1.7	1.9	22.9	100.0	(3)	(3)
1986	50.7	13.4	5.8	3.6	23.2	1.6	1.9	23.3	100.0	(3)	(3)
1987	49.7	13.3	5.7	3.4	24.5	1.6	1.8	24.4	100.0	(3)	(3)
1988	48.8	13.6	5.9	3.3	24.8	1.9	1.7	24.8	100.0	(3)	(3)
1989	49.0	14.0	6.0	3.0	25.0	2.0	1.0	25.0	100.0	(3)	(3)
1990	49.0	14.0	6.0	3.0	25.0	2.0	1.0	26.0	100.0	(3)	(3)
1991	48.0	16.0	6.0	3.0	24.0	2.0	1.0	27.0	100.0	(3)	(3)
1992	49.0	16.0	5.0	3.0	23.0	2.0	2.0	28.0	100.0	(3)	(3)
FEDERAL PERCENT OF TOTAL											
1985	84.0	64.0	45.4	98.8	8.3	87.8	54.1	71.0	62.0	(3)	(3)
1986	83.6	63.7	44.9	98.6	8.4	84.4	54.2	70.0	61.3	(3)	(3)
1987	83.1	62.5	46.7	98.5	7.8	83.9	55.7	70.3	59.9	(3)	(3)
1988	82.9	61.6	43.2	98.6	7.7	84.6	52.4	67.9	59.1	(3)	(3)
1989	83.0	63.0	43.0	98.0	8.0	84.0	51.0	69.0	59.0	(3)	(3)
1990	82.0	63.0	43.0	98.0	7.0	85.0	50.0	69.0	59.0	(3)	(3)
1991	81.0	62.0	44.0	98.0	7.0	87.0	50.0	68.0	58.0	(3)	(3)
1992	80.0	67.0	45.0	98.0	7.0	87.0	50.0	70.0	59.0	(3)	(3)

1. Excludes program parts of social insurance, public aid, veterans, and other social welfare. 2. Combines health and medical programs with medical services provided in connection with social insurance, public aid, veterans, and other social welfare programs. 3. Not applicable. NOTE: Figures are latest available. *Source:* Department of Health and Human Services, Social Security Administration.

Distribution of Federal Funds by State and Territory: FY 1994

Million dollars. Detail may not add to total because of rounding.

State and Territory	Total	Grants to state and local governments	Salaries and wages	Direct payments for individuals	Procurement	Other programs
United States, total	$1,320,132	$214,239	$168,951	$691,666	$197,959	$47,317
Alabama	22,280	3,209	3,125	11,996	3,364	585
Alaska	4,640	1,063	1,367	924	1,007	278
Arizona	19,011	2,996	2,269	10,558	2,679	510
Arkansas	11,376	1,966	1,020	7,298	596	496
California	155,391	26,219	18,830	75,466	30,416	4,460
Colorado	18,899	2,102	3,540	7,987	4,472	888
Connecticut	16,591	3,028	1,405	8,902	2,751	506
Delaware	2,950	472	455	1,784	167	72
District of Columbia	21,766	2,222	11,415	2,523	4,103	1,503
Florida	71,092	8,018	7,263	46,381	8,306	1,124
Georgia	32,067	5,028	5,945	15,486	4,799	809
Hawaii	7,603	1,088	2,498	2,898	905	213
Idaho	4,965	778	611	2,520	844	212
Illinois	49,936	8,506	5,402	31,367	3,222	1,440
Indiana	22,104	3,553	2,101	13,804	1,674	971
Iowa	12,979	2,015	954	7,590	637	1,783
Kansas	12,506	1,666	1,892	6,914	1,151	883
Kentucky	17,504	3,096	2,608	10,068	1,322	410
Louisiana	21,672	5,233	2,136	10,656	3,037	611
Maine	6,708	1,269	773	3,518	1,023	125
Maryland	36,576	3,637	7,414	13,600	8,228	3,695
Massachusetts	35,374	6,261	3,112	17,672	6,609	1,720
Michigan	38,975	7,117	2,887	25,535	2,479	956
Minnesota	18,797	3,515	1,617	10,113	1,798	1,753
Missisippi	14,072	2,507	1,539	7,308	2,295	424
Missouri	31,766	3,971	3,332	14,889	7,455	2,119
Montana	4,638	906	611	2,250	204	666
Nebraska	7,439	1,114	971	4,178	561	615
Nevada	6,104	797	763	3,409	1,045	90
New Hampshire	4,636	956	432	2,648	487	113
New Jersey	37,328	6,163	3,739	22,685	4,218	524
New Mexico	11,274	1,714	1,590	4,041	3,596	333
New York	90,346	22,445	7,428	51,909	6,142	2,422
North Carolina	28,858	4,862	4,833	16,481	1,897	786
North Dakota	3,909	702	566	1,704	210	727
Ohio	48,023	8,366	4,467	29,488	4,775	926
Oklahoma	15,718	2,359	2,627	8,943	1,142	648
Oregon	13,057	2,355	1,419	8,275	493	516
Pennsylvania	61,025	9,705	5,802	39,193	4,525	1,800
Rhode Island	5,473	1,100	641	3,109	499	123
South Carolina	17,097	2,726	2,503	8,839	2,721	308
South Dakota	3,814	724	541	1,848	197	503
Tennessee	25,056	3,940	2,669	13,461	4,478	508
Texas	79,308	12,669	9,999	41,079	12,842	2,719
Utah	7,594	1,209	1,479	3,444	1,190	271
Vermont	2,411	546	268	1,435	109	53
Virginia	45,890	3,180	12,147	17,168	11,689	1,705
Washington	26,644	3,924	4,187	13,381	4,086	1,065
West Virginia	9,550	2,166	788	6,003	445	148
Wisconsin	19,670	3,450	1,396	12,616	1,282	925
Wyoming	2,344	714	358	1,070	121	81
American Samoa	111	67	3	31	11	—
Guam	1,048	154	457	139	276	22
Northern Marianas	61	52	2	4	3	—
Puerto Rico	9,315	3,388	695	4,744	316	172
Virgin Islands	385	191	35	137	17	4
Undistributed	24,318	1,059	23	193	23,043	

— Represents zero. *Source: Federal Expenditures by State for Fiscal Year 1994.*

Domestic Freight Traffic by Major Carriers

(in millions of ton-miles)[1]

Year	Railroads		Inland waterways[2]		Motor trucks		Oil pipelines		Air carriers	
	Ton-miles	% of total	Ton-miles	% of total	Ton-miles	% of total	Ton-miles	% of total	Ton-miles	% of total
1940	379,201	61.3	118,057	19.1	62,043	10.0	59,277	9.6	14	—
1945	690,809	67.3	142,737	13.9	66,948	6.5	126,530	12.3	91	—
1950	596,940	56.2	163,344	15.4	172,860	16.3	129,175	12.1	318	—
1955	631,385	49.5	216,508	17.0	223,254	17.5	203,244	16.0	481	—
1960	579,130	44.1	220,253	16.8	285,483	21.7	228,626	17.4	778	—
1965	708,700	43.3	262,421	16.0	359,218	21.9	306,393	18.7	1,910	0.1
1970	771,168	39.8	318,560	16.4	412,000	21.3	431,000	22.3	3,274	0.2
1975	759,000	36.7	342,210	16.5	454,000	22.0	507,300	24.6	3,732	0.2
1980	932,000	37.2	420,000	16.9	567,000	22.6	588,000	23.1	4,528	0.2
1985	895,000	36.4	382,000	15.6	610,000	24.9	564,000	22.9	6,080	0.2
1988	1,028,000	37.0	438,000	15.8	700,000	25.2	601,000	21.6	9,330	0.3
1989	1,048,000	37.3	449,000	16.0	716,000	25.5	584,000	20.8	10,210	0.4
1990	1,071,000	37.4	460,000	16.1	735,000	25.7	584,000	20.4	10,420	0.4
1991	1,077,000	37.6	443,000	15.5	758,000	26.4	579,000	20.2	9,980	0.3
1992	1,107,000	37.4	454,000	15.3	815,000	27.5	573,000	19.4	10,990	0.4
1993[3]	1,146,000	37.8	457,448	14.9	879,836	28.7	574,719	18.7	11,540	0.4

1. Mail and express included, except railroads for 1970. 2. Rivers, canals, and domestic traffic on Great Lakes. 3. Preliminary. *Source: Transportation in America,* Eno Foundation for Transportation (latest figures from 12th Edition, 1994). NOTE: Data are latest available.

Tonnage Handled by Principal U.S. Ports

(Over 10 million U.S. short tons (2,000 lbs per ton) annually)

Port	1993	1992	Port	1993	1992
Port of South Louisiana	193,796,104	199,665,010	Chicago, Ill.	25,048,025	22,153,979
Houston, Texass	141,476,979	137,663,612	Richmond, Calif.	24,570,112	21,042,244
New York, N.Y. & N.J.	116,735,760	115,310,756	Huntington, W. Va.	22,833,285	21,833,428
Valdez, Alaska	85,722,337	93,736,659	Paulsboro, N.J.	22,614,762	20,254,199
Baton Rouge, La.	85,078,863	84,699,463	Seattle, Wash.	21,693,410	21,883,200
New Orleans, La.	67,037,285	66,441,189	Boston, Mass.	19,447,857	19,207,776
Corpus Christi, Texas	59,649,751	60,866,092	Jacksonville, Fla.	18,849,849	17,208,707
Long Beach, Calif.	54,320,932	52,048,625	Tacoma, Wash.	18,651,709	20,116,344
Texas City, Texas	53,652,781	43,104,101	Detroit, Mich.	17,421,533	16,303,234
Port of Plaquemine, La.	53,110,120	58,473,474	Newport News, Va.	16,734,878	24,450,445
Norfolk Harbor, Va.	45,543,792	53,496,276	Port Everglades, Fla.	16,297,269	14,507,888
Lake Charles, La.	45,436,380	44,038,688	Indiana Harbor, Ind.	15,546,403	15,325,931
Tampa, Fla.	44,992,777	46,434,233	Savannah, Ga.	14,962,844	13,988,735
Pittsburgh, Pa.	44,490,094	34,320,725	New Castle, Del.	14,242,529	11,831,119
Mobile, Ala.	43,959,704	40,482,387	San Juan, P.R.	14,153,403	14,330,502
Los Angeles, Calif.	43,622,807	40,103,692	Cleveland, Ohio	14,083,014	13,653,652
Philadelphia, Pa.	42,707,684	39,667,259	Freeport, Texas	14,024,604	14,952,599
Port Arthur, Texas	38,326,902	33,524,964	Lorain, Ohio	13,676,686	13,282,176
Duluth–Superior, Minn./Wis.	37,679,398	39,303,709	Cincinnati, Ohio	13,648,255	11,852,263
Baltimore, Md.	37,170,223	37,655,691	Memphis, Tenn.	13,332,165	13,281,285
Marcus Hook, Pa.	30,907,303	26,569,805	Anacortes, Wash.	13,123,794	15,259,637
Portland, Ore.	29,804,208	28,226,591	Oakland, Calif.	12,733,691	13,211,391
St. Louis, Mo./Ill.	27,551,350	31,947,230	Toledo, Ohio	12,149,760	12,721,759
Pascagoula, Miss.	27,020,433	29,245,347	Portland, Maine	11,171,097	12,511,340
Beaumont, Texas	25,409,757	22,701,500	Two Harbors, Minn.	10,711,059	12,500,967

Source: Department of the Army, Corps of Engineers.

Annual Railroad Carloadings[1]

Year	Total	Year	Total	Year	Total	Year	Total
1940	36,358,000	1965	28,344,381	1985	19,501,242	1990	21,401,246
1945	41,918,000	1970	27,015,020	1986	19,588,666	1991	20,868,297
1950	38,903,000	1975	22,929,843	1987	20,602,204	1992	21,205,530
1955	32,761,707	1980	22,223,000	1988	22,599,993	1993	21,682,874
1960	27,886,950	1984	20,945,536	1989	21,226,015	1994[2]	22,983,846

1. Only Class 1 railroads after 1950. 2. Estimated. *Source:* Association of American Railroads.

Estimated Motor Vehicle Registration, 1994

(in thousands; including publicly owned vehicles)

State	Autos[1]	Trucks and buses	Motor-cycles	Total	State	Autos[1]	Trucks and buses	Motor-cycles	Total
Alabama	2,112	1,272	38	3,384	Montana	556	390	21	946
Alaska	314	182	12	496	Nebraska	963	508	19	1,471
Arizona	2,078	829	73	2,907	Nevada	642	321	20	963
Arkansas	1,000	547	13	1,547	New Hampshire	759	218	36	977
California	17,414	5,548	556	22,962	New Jersey	5,193	470	89	5,663
Colorado	2,268	788	88	3,056	New Mexico	867	572	33	1,439
Connecticut	2,468	133	37	2,601	New York	8,813	1,420	195	10,233
Delaware	435	123	10	558	North Carolina	3,897	1,501	64	5,398
Dist. of Col.	255	13	2	268	North Dakota	402	268	17	670
Florida	7,883	2,060	189	9,943	Ohio	7,570	1,844	233	9,414
Georgia	3,846	1,737	55	5,583	Oklahoma	1,773	1,036	54	2,809
Hawaii	656	101	24	757	Oregon	2,051	637	60	2,688
Idaho	640	390	32	1,030	Pennsylvania	6,674	1,711	172	8,385
Illinois	6,704	1,426	201	8,130	Rhode Island	601	108	19	709
Indiana	3,469	1,285	96	4,754	South Carolina	2,026	703	35	2,729
Iowa	1,977	803	149	2,780	South Dakota	492	327	26	819
Kansas	1,276	636	53	1,912	Tennessee	4,077	988	85	5,065
Kentucky	1,694	889	32	2,583	Texas	8,902	4,253	132	13,155
Louisiana	2,017	1,189	36	3,206	Utah	850	509	22	1,359
Maine	799	239	33	1,038	Vermont	364	123	15	487
Maryland	2,903	600	40	3,503	Virginia	4,200	1,331	62	5,531
Massachusetts	3,376	512	68	3,888	Washington	3,217	1,328	109	4,545
Michigan	5,774	1,688	137	7,462	West Virginia	832	523	20	1,355
Minnesota	2,927	816	126	3,743	Wisconsin	2,440	1,406	198	3,846
Mississippi	1,546	482	28	2,028	Wyoming	290	282	11	572
Missouri	2,889	1,233	57	4,122	**Total**	**147,171**	**48,298**	**3,932**	**195,469**

1. Includes taxicabs. NOTE: Figures are latest available. *Source:* Department of Transportation, Federal Highway Administration.

Passenger Car Production by Make

Companies and models	1994	1990	1985	1980	1975	1970
American Motors Corporation	—	—	109,919	164,725	323,704	276,127
Chrysler Corporation						
Plymouth	169,637	212,354	369,487	293,342	443,550	699,031
Dodge	303,678	361,769	482,388	263,169	354,482	405,699
Chrysler	77,993	136,339	414,193	82,463	102,940	158,614
Imperial	—	16,280	—	—	1,930	10,111
Total	**551,308**	**726,742**	**1,266,068**	**638,974**	**902,902**	**1,273,455**
Ford Motor Company						
Ford	1,220,512	933,466	1,098,627	929,627	1,301,414	1,647,918
Mercury	260,251	221,436	374,446	324,528	405,104	310,463
Lincoln	180,587	222,449	163,077	52,793	101,520	58,771
Total	**1,661,350**	**1,377,351**	**1,636,150**	**1,306,948**	**1,808,038**	**2,017,152**
General Motors Corporation						
Chevrolet	651,647	1,025,379	1,691,254	1,737,336	1,687,091	1,504,614
Pontiac	597,137	649,255	702,617	556,429	523,469	422,212
Oldsmobile	481,452	418,742	1,168,982	783,225	654,342	439,632
Buick	483,029	405,123	1,001,461	783,575	535,820	459,931
Cadillac	226,136	252,540	322,765	203,991	278,404	152,859
Saturn	280,363	4,245	—	—	—	—
Total	**2,719,764**	**2,755,284**	**4,887,079**	**4,064,556**	**3,679,126**	**2,979,248**
Volkswagen of America	—	—	96,458	197,106	—	—
Honda	498,710	435,437	238,159	145,337	—	—
Mazda	246,991	184,428	—	—	—	—
Nissan	312,675	95,844	43,810	—	—	—
Toyota	399,341	321,523	—	—	—	—
Diamond Star	169,829	148,379	—	—	—	—
Subaru Legacy	54,002	32,461	—	—	—	—
Industry total	**6,613,970**	**6,077,449**	**8,184,821**	**6,375,506**	**6,716,951**	**6,550,128**

Source: American Automobile Manufacturers Association.

Motor Vehicle Data

	1993	1990	1980	1970	1960
U.S. passenger cars and taxis registered (thousands)	146,314	143,550	121,724	89,280	61,671
Total mileage of U.S. passenger cars (millions)	1,623,972	1,513,184	1,111,596	916,700	588,083
Total fuel consumption of U.S. passenger cars (millions of gallons)	75,059	71,989	71,883	67,820	41,169
World registration of cars, trucks, and buses (thousands)	610,103	582,982	411,113	246,368	126,955
U.S. registration of cars, trucks, and buses (thousands)	194,036	188,655	155,796	108,418	73,858
U.S. share of world registration of cars, trucks, and buses	32.0%	32.4%	37.9%	44.0%	58.2%

Source: American Automobile Manufacturers Association.

Domestic Motor Vehicles Sales

(in thousands)

Type of Vehicle	1992	1991	1990	1989	1988	1987	1985	1980
Passenger Cars								
Passenger car factory sales	5,684	5,407	6,050	6,807	7,105	7,085	8,002	6,400
Passenger car (new) retail sales[1]	8,214	8,175	9,300	9,772	10,530	10,277	11,042	8,979
Domestic[2]	6,277	6,137	6,897	7,073	7,526	7,081	8,205	6,581
Imports[3]	1,938	2,038	2,403	2,699	3,004	3,196	2,838	2,398
Trucks								
Truck and bus factory sales	4,042	3,375	3,719	4,062	4,121	3,821	3,357	1,667
Truck and bus retail sales[4]	4,513	3,842	4,261	4,483	4,608	4,174	3,984	2,232
Light duty (up to 14,000 GVW)[5]	4,264	3,621	3,984	4,171	4,273	3,885	3,700	1,964
Med. duty (14,000–26,000 GVW)[5]	57	50	71	73	83	55	53	92
Heavy duty (over 26,000 GVW)[5]	192	171	207	239	251	234	231	176
Under 6,000 pounds	3,217	2,724	2,866	2,854	2,926	2,696	2,408	985
Utility	666	549	490	447	445	403	429	51
Van	21	17	31	43	47	89	115	79
Mini van (cargo)	63	66	83	97	105	101	103	(X)
Station wagon (truck chassis)	201	110	112	138	138	108	86	(X)
Mini passenger carrier	840	706	750	688	692	546	301	(X)
6,000 to 10,000 pounds[6]	1,021	876	1,097	1,297	1,333	1,175	1,280	975
Utility	51	37	68	93	90	91	108	108
Van	241	203	254	289	302	254	261	172
Pickup conventional	524	476	568	663	666	569	628	546
Station wagon (truck chassis)	80	55	85	100	104	91	95	39
10,001 pounds and over	275	242	298	331	349	302	295	271

1. Based on data from U.S. Dept. of Commerce. 2. Includes domestic models produced in Canada and Mexico. 3. Excludes domestic models produced in Canada. 4. Excludes motorcoaches and light-duty imports from foreign manufacturers. Includes imports sold by franchised dealers of U.S. manufacturers. Starting in 1987 includes sales of trucks over 10,000 lbs. GVW by foreign manufacturers. 5. Gross vehicle weight (fully loaded vehicles). 6. Includes vehicles not shown separately. NOTE: X = not applicable. *Source: Statistical Abstract of the United States 1994.* NOTE: Data are most recent available.

Domestic and Export Factory Sales of Motor Vehicles

(in thousands)

	From plants in United States								
	Passenger cars			Motor trucks and buses			Total motor vehicles		
Year	Total	Domestic	Exports	Total	Domestic	Exports	Total	Domestic	Exports
1970	6,547	6,187	360	1,692	1,566	126	8,239	7,753	486
1975	6,713	6,073	640	2,272	2,003	269	8,985	8,076	909
1980	6,400	5,840	560	1,667	1,464	203	8,067	7,304	763
1985	8,002	7,337	665	3,464	3,234	231	11,467	10,571	896
1990	6,050	5,502	548	3,719	3,448	271	9,769	8,950	819
1991	5,407	4,874	533	3,375	3,038	338	8,783	7,912	871
1992	5,684	5,164	520	4,042	3,683	360	9,727	8,846	880
1993	5,960	5,471	489	4,786	4,362	424	10,746	9,833	913
1994	6,551	5,967	585	5,633	5,131	502	12,184	11,098	1,087

Source: American Automobile Manufacturers Association.

U.S. Direct Investment in EU Countries, 1994

(in millions of dollars)

Countries	All indus-tries	Petro-leum	Manu-factur-ing	Whole-sale	Banking	Finance & insur-ance	Serv-ices	Other indus-tries
Belgium	$13,966	$318	$7,108	$1,816	$245	$3,175	$1,260	$43
Denmark	1,993	(1)	298	190	(1)	380	533	14
France	27,894	1,177	14,521	4,810	387	4,724	1,407	867
Germany	39,886	2,020	22,131	4,049	2,283	6,716	946	1,741
Greece	446	(1)	124	(1)	(1)	32	(1)	0
Ireland	10,337	(1)	5,766	273	(1)	3,729	487	54
Italy	14,998	422	8,572	2,034	315	2,263	1,180	203
Luxembourg	5,730	24	1,374	(1)	232	3,956	(1)	(1)
Netherlands	24,150	1,484	8,908	3,494	149	7,959	1,291	866
Portugal	1,458	(1)	438	361	(1)	126	190	(1)
Spain	8,048	135	4,512	824	1,349	665	413	149
United Kingdom	102,244	14,320	27,247	5,564	4,983	42,494	5,034	2,602
Total	**$251,149**	**$20,574**	**$101,009**	**$23,584**	**$10,375**	**$76,220**	**$12,825**	**$6,561**

1. Suppressed to avoid disclosure of data of individual companies. *Source: Survey of Current Business,* June 1995.

Balance of International Payments

(in billions of dollars)

Item	1994	1993	1990	1985	1980	1975	1970	1965	1960
Exports of goods, services, and income	$838.8	$763.8	$652.9	$366.0	$343.2	$157.9	$68.4	$42.7	$30.5
Merchandise, adjusted, excluding military	502.5	456.8	389.5	214.4	224.0	107.1	42.5	26.5	19.7
Transfers under U.S. military agency sales contracts	12.4	12.6	9.8	9.0	8.2	3.9	1.5	0.8	0.3
Receipts of income on U.S. investments abroad	137.6	119.2	130.0	90.0	75.9	25.4	11.8	7.4	4.6
Other services	186.3	175.1	123.3	45.0	36.5	19.3	9.9	6.4	4.3
Imports of goods and services	−954.3	−829.7	−722.7	−461.2	−333.9	−132.6	−60.0	−32.8	−23.7
Merchandise, adjusted, excluding military	−668.6	−589.4	−497.6	−339.0	−249.3	−98.0	−39.9	−21.5	−14.8
Direct defense expenditures	−10.3	−12.2	−17.1	−12.0	−10.7	−4.8	4.9	−3.0	−3.1
Payments of income on foreign assets in U.S.	−147.0	−110.2	−118.1	−65.0	−43.2	−12.6	−5.5	−2.1	−1.2
Other services	−129.0	−118.0	−89.8	−46.0	−30.7	−17.2	−9.8	−6.2	−4.6
Unilateral transfers, excluding military grants, net	−36.0	−34.0	−22.3	−15.0	−7.0	−4.6	−3.3	−2.9	−2.3
U.S. Government assets abroad, net	−0.3	−0.3	2.9	−2.8	−5.2	−3.5	−1.6	−1.6	−1.1
U.S. private assets abroad, net	−131.0	−183.0	−58.5	−26.0	−71.5	−35.4	−10.2	−5.3	−5.1
U.S. assets abroad, net	−126.0	−185.0	−57.7	−27.7	−86.1	−39.7	−9.3	−5.7	−4.1
Foreign assets in U.S., net	291.3	248.5	86.3	127.1	50.3	15.6	6.4	0.7	2.3
Statistical discrepancy	−14.2	36.0	63.5	23.0	29.6	5.5	−0.2	−0.5	−1.0
Balance on goods, services, and income	−115.4	−66.0	−69.7	−106.8	9.5	25.2	8.5	10.0	6.9
Balance on current account	−151.2	−100.0	−92.1	−118.0	3.7	18.4	2.4	5.4	2.8

NOTE: — denotes debits. *Source:* Department of Commerce, Bureau of Economic Analysis.

Foreign Investors in U.S. Business Enterprises

	Number				Investment outlays (millions of dollars)			
	1994[1]	1993	1992	1991	1994[1]	1993	1992	1991
Investments, total	1,025	980	941	1,091	$47,244	$26,229	$15,333	$25,538
Acquisitions	753	554	463	561	43,095	21,761	10,616	17,806
Establishments	272	426	478	530	4,149	4,468	4,718	7,732
Investors, total	1,194	1,094	1,019	1,220	47,244	28,229	15,333	25,538
Foreign direct investors	360	368	350	438	14,640	6,720	4,058	8,885
U.S. affilates	834	726	669	782	32,604	19,509	11,275	16,653

1. Figures are preliminary. *Source:* U.S. Department of Commerce, *Survey of Current Business,* May 1995.

Employment and Wages in Foreign-Owned Businesses in the United States

Fourth Quarter 1991

Employment in foreign-owned business establishments in the United States averaged 4.8 million, or 5.4 percent of total private employment, in the fourth quarter of 1991, according to preliminary data released December 1994 by the Bureau of Labor Statistics of the U.S. Department of Labor. Workers in foreign-owned U.S. establishments earned about $2,700 per month on average, 23% more than workers in all U.S. establishments in the private sector in fourth quarter 1991.

Average Monthly Employment

Employment in foreign-owned U.S. establishments as a percentage of employment in all U.S. establishments varied among industries. In fourth quarter 1991, the major industry divisions with the highest percentage of employment in foreign-owned establishments were mining (15.8%) and manufacturing (10.4%). In absolute numbers, three industries in other divisions had the highest levels of employment in foreign-owned establishments—grocery stores and eating and drinking places in retail trade and hotels and motels in services.

At least half of the employment in foreign-owned establishments was in businesses owned by British, Japanese, or Canadian investors.

Among states, the proportion of employment in foreign-owned establishments ranged from highs of 14.6% in Delaware and 12.1% in Hawaii to lows of 1.6% in North Dakota and 2.1% in South Dakota.

The five counties with the most employment in foreign-owned U.S. establishments were Los Angeles County, Calif.; New York County, N.Y.; Cook County, Ill.; Harris County, Tex.; and Dallas County,

Tex. (These five counties had the highest levels of employment for all U.S. counties.)

Average Monthly Wages

In all industry divisions except services, employees in foreign-owned establishments earned higher wages than their counterparts in all U.S. establishments. This pattern reflects many factors, including possible differences in occupational mix and industry concentration. The largest wage differences occurred in agriculture; finance, insurance, and real estate; and construction. Foreign-owned establishments paid 43, 42, and 39% more, respectively, than the average monthly wage for workers in all U.S. establishments in those divisions. The only industry division where workers in foreign-owned establishments earned lower wages was services, where wages paid by foreign-owned establishments were 3% less than in all U.S. establishments. In addition to salaries, wages include bonuses, the cash value of lodging and meals when supplied, tips and other gratuities, and, in some states, employer contributions to 401(k) plans.

In each state, wages were higher for workers in foreign-owned establishments than for workers as a whole. (They were lower in the District of Columbia.) The ratio of wages in foreign-owned establishments to wages in all establishments ranged from 102.2% in New Hampshire to 166.9% in Wyoming. (The ratio of wages in foreign-owned establishments to wages in all establishments for the District of Columbia was 83.0%.)

Among the 50 counties with the highest levels of employment in foreign-owned establishments, New Castle, Del., had the highest wage ratio (152.8%) and Nassau County, N.Y., the lowest (89.3%).

Private Industry by Major Industry Division: Employment and Wages, All U.S. and Foreign-Owned U.S. Establishments, Fourth Quarter 1991

Industry	All United States establishments				Foreign-owned U.S. establishments			
	1991		Percentage change from 1990		1991		Percentage change from 1990	
	Average employment	Average monthly wages	Average monthly employment	Average monthly wages	Average monthly employment	Average monthly wages	Average monthly employment	Average monthly wages
Total[1]	89,539,583	$2,172	−1.9	4.2	4,824,461	$2,672	1.9	5.1
Agriculture, forestry, and fishing	1,454,470	1,320	1.1	2.3	23,320	1,891	−3.7	11.5
Mining	674,321	3,514	−6.7	6.5	106,614	4,153	−5.9	9.4
Construction	4,635,186	2,411	−7.6	1.3	92,859	3,359	8.8	6.6
Manufacturing	18,366,678	2,662	−3.1	5.1	1,914,392	2,933	2.2	3.9
Transportation and public utilities	5,507,841	2,689	−1.0	4.5	225,644	2,865	−1.5	7.3
Wholesale trade	6,075,156	2,857	−2.6	3.8	495,387	3,570	.0	6.9
Retail trade	19,611,490	1,143	−1.7	3.7	928,994	1,305	1.9	4.8
Finance, insurance, and real estate	6,490,043	2,801	−1.1	6.2	360,993	3,963	10.6	6.8
Services	26,585,024	2,145	−.4	4.1	673,312	2,089	.0	1.0

1. Includes data for nonclassifiable establishments, not shown separately.

Imports of Leading Commodities
(value in millions of dollars)

Commodity	1994	1993
Food and agricultural commodities	**$23,769**	**$21,867**
Animal feeds	436	368
Cocoa	698	739
Coffee	2,270	1,383
Corn	85	61
Cotton, raw	21	12
Dairy products, eggs	583	544
Fish and preparations	6,593	5,820
Furskins, undressed	78	59
Hides and skins, undressed	126	119
Live animals	1,392	1,536
Meat and preparations	2,629	2,792
Oils and fats, animal	22	21
Oils and fats, vegetable	1,051	859
Rice	130	106
Soybeans	46	22
Sugar	551	606
Tobacco, unmanufactured	698	942
Vegetables and fruits	6,074	5,665
Wheat	286	213
Machinery and transport equipment	**194,968**	**166,520**
ADP equip.; office machinery	52,118	43,193
Airplanes	3,805	3,805
Airplane parts	2,743	2,613
Cars and trucks	70,961	61,366
Parts	19,610	17,653
Spacecraft	219	0
General industrial machinery	21,337	17,082
Metalworking machinery	4,614	3,683
Power generating machinery	19,561	17,125
Manufactured goods	**163,938**	**146,244**
Artwork and antiques	2,427	2,673
Chemicals—fertilizers	1,296	1,136
Chemicals—medicinal	4,680	4,135
Chemicals-organic and inorganic	14,904	12,563
Clothing and footwear	48,460	44,953
Gem diamonds	5,740	5,103
Glass	1,351	1,004
Iron and steel mill products	12,876	9,027
Metal manufactures	8,848	7,647
Paper and paperboard	9,065	8,640
Photographic equipment	4,678	4,267
Plastic articles	4,513	3,937
Pottery	1,556	1,436
Printed matter	2,232	2,026
Rubber articles	1,251	1,014
Scientific instruments	9,964	8,457
Textile yarns, fabric	9,208	8,438
Tires and tubes, automotive	3,035	2,736
Toys, games, sporting goods	11,824	11,637
Watches, clocks and parts	2,643	2,546
Wood manufactures	3,387	2,869
Mineral fuels and related products	**53,366**	**53,450**
Coal	646	514
Natural gas	4,014	3,678
Petroleum and petroleum products	48,706	49,258
Crude materials excluding agricultural products	**12,251**	**10,549**
Cork, wood and lumber	6,683	5,633
Pulp and waste paper	2,315	1,886
Metal ores, scrap	3,253	3,030
Tobacco excluding agricultural, beverages	**1,897**	**2,228**
Cigarettes	71	491
Distilled alcoholic beverages	1,826	1,737
All others	**213,579**	**179,801**
Total	**663,768**	**580,659**

Exports of Leading Commodities
(value in millions of dollars)

Commodity	1994	1993
Food and agricultural commodities	**$40,356**	**$38,146**
Animal feeds	3,348	3,464
Cocoa	34	39
Coffee	53	32
Corn	4,187	4,504
Cotton, raw	2,676	1,575
Dairy products, eggs	717	820
Fish and preparations	3,033	2,991
Furskins, undressed	131	98
Hides and skins, undressed	1,392	1,187
Live animals	587	519
Meat and preparations	5,191	4,353
Oils and fats, animal	567	472
Oils and fats, vegetable	962	734
Rice	1,008	791
Soybeans	4,353	4,580
Sugar	5	1
Tobacco, unmanufactured	1,303	1,299
Vegetables and fruits	6,752	6,008
Wheat	4,057	4,679
Machinery and transport equipment	**146,660**	**135,962**
ADP equip.; office machinery	30,879	27,177
Airplanes	18,824	21,270
Airplane parts	9,841	9,487
Cars and trucks	19,557	16,390
Parts	21,163	19,307
Spacecraft	444	393
General industrial machinery	21,783	19,515
Metalworking machinery	3,899	3,256
Power generating machinery	20,270	19,167
Manufactured goods	**93,499**	**83,773**
Artwork and antiques	1,185	951
Chemicals—fertilizers	2,699	1,798
Chemicals—medicinal	6,093	5,751
Chemicals—organic and inorganic	16,894	14,886
Clothing and footwear	6,111	5,420
Gem diamonds	183	153
Glass	1,459	1,341
Iron and steel milll products	3,548	3,330
Metal manufactures	7,012	5,975
Paper and paperboard	7,450	6,463
Photographic equipment	3,017	2,932
Plastic articles	3,573	2,988
Pottery	105	110
Printed matter	3,973	3,995
Rubber articles	785	679
Scientific instruments and parts	16,463	15,223
Textile yarns, fabric	6,429	5,895
Tires and tubes, automotive	1,614	1,465
Toys, games and sporting goods	3,086	2,707
Watches, clocks and parts	277	236
Wood manufactures	1,543	1,475
Mineral fuels and related products	**6,421**	**7,378**
Coal	2,962	3,197
Natural gas	254	241
Petroleum and petroleum products	3,205	3,940
Crude material excluding agricultural products	**13,081**	**11,991**
Cork, wood, lumber	5,554	5,786
Pulp and waste paper	3,793	2,978
Metal ores, scrap	3,734	3,227
Tobacco, excluding agricultural, beverages	**5,321**	**4,262**
Cigarettes	4,965	3,919
Distilled alcoholic beverages	356	343
All other	**207,332**	**183,579**
Total	**512,670**	**465,091**

Source: Department of Commerce, Bureau of the Census, Foreign Trade Division.

FIRST AID

Information Please Almanac is not responsible and assumes no responsibility for any action undertaken by anyone utilizing the first aid procedures which follow.

The Heimlich Maneuver[1]

Food-Choking

What to look for: Victim cannot speak or breathe; turns blue; collapses.

To perform the Heimlich Maneuver when the victim is standing or sitting:

1. Stand behind the victim and wrap your arms around his waist.

2. Place the thumb side of your fist against the victim's abdomen, slightly above the navel and below the rib cage.

3. Grasp your fist with the other hand and press your fist into the victim's abdomen with a quick upward thrust. Repeat as often as necessary.

4. If the victim is sitting, stand behind the victim's chair and perform the maneuver in the same manner.

5. After the food is dislodged, have the victim seen by a doctor.

When the victim has collapsed and cannot be lifted:

1. Lay the victim on his back.

2. Face the victim and kneel astride his hips.

3. With one hand on top of the other, place the heel of your bottom hand on the abdomen slightly above the navel and below the rib cage.

4. Press into the victim's abdomen with a quick upward thrust. Repeat as often as necessary.

5. Should the victim vomit, quickly place him on his side and wipe out his mouth to prevent aspiration (drawing of vomit into the throat).

6. After the food is dislodged, have the victim seen by a doctor.

NOTE: If you start to choke when alone and help is not available, an attempt should be made to self-administer this maneuver.

Burns[2]

First Degree: Signs/Symptoms—reddened skin. **Treatment**—Immerse quickly in cold water or apply ice until pain stops.

Second Degree: Signs/Symptoms—reddened skin, blisters. **Treatment**—(1) Cut away loose clothing. (2) Cover with several layers of cold moist dressings or, if limb is involved, immerse in cold water for relief of pain. (3) Treat for shock.

Third Degree: Signs/Symtoms—skin destroyed, tissues damaged, charring. **Treatment**—(1) Cut away loose clothing (do not remove clothing adhered to skin). (2) Cover with several layers of sterile, cold, moist dressings for relief of pain and to stop burning action. (3) Treat for shock.

Poisons[2]

Treatment—(1) Dilute by drinking large quantities of water. (2) Induce vomiting except when poison is corrosive or a petroleum product. (3) Call the poison control center or a doctor.

Shock[2]

Shock may accompany any serious injury: blood loss, breathing impairment, heart failure, burns. Shock can kill—treat as soon as possible and continue until medical aid is available.

Signs/Symptoms—(1) Shallow breathing. (2) Rapid and weak pulse. (3) Nausea, collapse, vomiting. (4) Shivering. (5) Pale, moist skin. (6) Mental confusion. (7) Drooping eyelids, dilated pupils.

The Heimlich Maneuver

Courtesy of New York City Department of Health

Treatment—(1) Establish and maintain an open airway. (2) Control bleeding. (3) Keep victim lying down. Exception: Head and chest injuries, heart attack, stroke, sun stroke. If no spine injury, victim may be more comfortable and breathe better in a semi-reclining position. If in doubt, keep the victim flat. Elevate the feet unless injury would be aggravated. Maintain normal body temperature. Place blankets under and over victim.

Nosebleed[2]

Nosebleeds are more often annoying than life threatening. They are more common during cold weather, when heated air dries out nasal passages.
Treatment—(1) Keep the victim quietly seated, leaning forward if possible. (2) Gently pinch the nostrils closed. (3) Apply cold compresses to the victim's nose and face. (4) If the person is conscious, it may be helpful to apply pressure beneath the nostril above the lip. (5) Instruct victim not to blow his/her nose for several hours after the bleeding has stopped, or clots could be dislodged and start the bleeding again.

Frostbite[2]

Most frequently frostbitten: toes, fingers, nose, and ears. It is caused by exposure to cold.
Signs/Symptoms—(1) Skin becomes pale or a grayish-yellow color. (2) Parts feel cold and numb. (3) Frozen parts feel doughy.
Treatment—(1) Until victim can be brought inside, he should be wrapped in woolen cloth and kept dry. (2) Do not rub, chafe, or manipulate frostbitten parts. (3) Bring victim indoors. (4) Place in warm water (102° to 105°) and make sure it remains warm. Test water by pouring on inner surface of your forearm. Never thaw if the victim has to go back out into the cold which may cause the affected area to be refrozen. (5) Do not use hot water bottles or a heat lamp, and do not place victim near a hot stove. (6) Do not allow victim to walk if feet are affected. (7) Once thawed, have victim gently exercise parts. (8) For serious frostbite, seek medical aid for thawing because pain will be intense and tissue damage extensive.

Heat Cramps[2]

Affects people who work or do strenuous exercises in a hot environment. To prevent it, such people should drink large amounts of cool water and add a pinch of salt to each glass of water
Signs/Symptoms—(1) Painful muscle cramps in legs and abdomen. (2) Faintness. (3) Profuse perspiration.
Treatment—(1) Move victim to a cool place. (2) Give him sips of salted drinking water (one teaspoon of salt to one quart of water). (3) Apply manual pressure to the cramped muscle.

Heat Exhaustion[2]

Signs/Symptoms—(1) Pale and clammy skin. (2) Profuse perspiration. (3) Rapid and shallow breathing. (4) Weakness, dizziness, and headache.
Treatment—(1) Care for victim as if he were in shock. (2) Remove victim to a cool area, do not allow chilling. (3) If body gets too cold, cover victim.

Heat Stroke[2]

Signs/Symptoms—(1) Face is red and flushed. (2) Victim becomes rapidly unconscious. (3) Skin is hot and dry with no perspiration.
Treatment—(1) Lay victim down with head and shoulders raised. (2) Reduce the high body temperature

as quickly as possible. (3) Apply cold applications to the body and head. (4) Use ice and fan if available. (5) Watch for signs of shock and treat accordingly. (6) Get medical aid as soon as possible.

Artificial Respiration[3]

(Mouth-to-Mouth Breathing—In Cases Like Drowning, Electric Shock or Smoke Inhalation.)
There is need for help in breathing when breathing movements stop or lips, tongue, and fingernails become blue. When in doubt, apply artificial respiration until you get medical help. No harm can result from its use and delay may cost the patient his life. Start immediately. Seconds count. Clear mouth and throat of any obstructions with your fingers.
For Adults: Place patient on back with face up.
Lift the chin and tilt the head back. If air passage is still closed, pull chin up by placing fingers behind the angles of the lower jaw and pushing forward.
Take deep breath, place you mouth over patient's mouth, making leak-proof seal.
Pinch patient's nostrils closed.
Blow into patient's mouth until you see his chest rise.
—OR—
Take deep breath, place your mouth over patient's nose, making leak-proof seal.
Seal patient's mouth with your hand.
Blow into patient's nose until you see his chest rise.
Remove your mouth and let patient exhale.
Repeat about 12 times a minute. (If the patient's stomach rises markedly, exert moderate hand pressure on the stomach just below the rib cage to keep it from inflating.)
For Infants and Small Children: Place your mouth over patient's mouth and nose. Blow into mouth and nose until you see patient's chest rise normally.
Repeat 20 to 30 times per minute. (Don't exaggerate the tilted position of an infant's head.)
NOTE: For emergency treatment of heart attack, cardiopulmonary resuscitation (CPR) is recommended. Instruction in CPR can be obtained through local health organizations or schools.

Sources: 1. New York City Department of Health. NOTE: Heimlich Maneuver, T.M. Pending. 2. *First Aid*, Mining Enforcement and Safety Administration, U.S. Department of the Interior. 3. *Health Emergency Chart*, Council on Family Health.

NUTRITION & HEALTH

The Global AIDS Situation

Source: World Health Organization (WHO).

Fig. 1—Estimated Total Adult HIV Infections From Late 1970s/Early 1980s Until Mid-1995

Western Europe 600,000

Eastern Europe & Central Asia 50,000 +

North America 1.1 Million

North Africa & the Middle East 150,000

East Asia & the Pacific 50,000 +

Latin America & the Caribbean 2 Million

Sub-Saharan Africa 11 Million +

South & Southeast Asia 3.5 Million

Australasia 25,000 +

Global Total: 18.5 million

Fig. 2—Estimated HIV-Infected Adults Alive as of Mid-1995

Western Europe 450,000

Eastern Europe & Central Asia 50,000 +

North America 750,000 +

North Africa & the Middle East 100,000 +

East Asia & the Pacific 50,000 +

Latin America & the Caribbean 1.5 Million +

Sub-Saharan Africa 8.5 Million

South & Southeast Asia 3 Million

Australasia 20,000

Global Total: 14–15 Million

The AIDS Pandemic

Source: World Health Organization (WHO).

As of June 30, 1995, 1,169,811 cumulative AIDS cases in adults and children have been reported to the World Health Organization Global Programme on AIDS since the onset of the pandemic. This represents a 19% increase from the 985,119 cases reported in the July 1, 1994, Report.

Allowing for under-diagnosis, incomplete reporting, and reporting delay, and based on the available data on HIV infections around the world, it is estimated that over 4.5 million AIDS cases in adults and children have occurred worldwide since the pandemic began.

As of mid-1995, it is estimated that around 18.5 million adults, and more than 1.5 million children, have been infected with HIV since the beginning of the pandemic (late 1970s to early 1980s). Figure 1 presents the estimated regional distribution of total HIV infections in adults to date. The continued increase in HIV infections, particularly in southern and central Africa and South Asia, will accentuate the disproportionate impact of HIV/AIDS on the developing world.

Figure 2 shows the estimated regional distribution of HIV-infected adults (including AIDS cases) alive as of mid-1995. ☐

Understanding AIDS

The Acquired Immune Deficiency Syndrome, or AIDS, was first reported in the United States in mid-1981. The cumulative number of AIDS cases in the United States as of Dec. 31, 1994, that were reported to the Center for Disease Control and Prevention was 441,528. Adult and adolescent AIDS cases totaled 435,319 with 376,889 cases in males and 58,428 cases in females. There were 6,209 cases reported in children under age 13 at the time of diagnosis. Total AIDS deaths reported for that period were 270,870, including 3,391 children.

AIDS is characterized by a defect in natural immunity against disease. People who have AIDS are vulnerable to serious illnesses which would not be a threat to anyone whose immune system was functioning normally. These illnesses are referred to as "opportunistic" infections or diseases: in AIDS patients the most common of these are Pneumocystis carinii pneumonia (PCP), a parasitic infection of the lungs; and a type of cancer known as Kaposi's sarcoma (KS). Other opportunistic infections include unusually severe infections with yeast, cytomegalovirus, herpes virus, and parasites such as Toxoplasma or Cryptosporidia. Milder infections with these organisms do not suggest immune deficiency.

AIDS is caused by a virus usually known as human immunodeficiency virus, or HIV. Symptoms of full-blown AIDS include a persistent cough, fever, and difficulty in breathing. Multiple purplish blotches and bumps on the skin may indicate Kaposi's sarcoma. The virus can also cause brain damage.

The credit for discovering the AIDS virus is jointly shared by Dr. Robert Gallo, a researcher at the National Cancer Institute, and Luc Montagnier of the Pasteur Institute, France.

People infected with the virus can have a wide range of symptoms—from none to mild to severe. At least a fourth to a half of those infected will develop AIDS within four to ten years. Many experts think the percentage will be much higher.

The national Centers for Disease Control and Prevention changed its AIDS surveillance case definition for adolescents and adults in 1992 to include HIV-infected people who have a CD4 T-lymphocyte (a white blood cell) count less than 200 cells per microliter (a millionth of a liter), or a CD4 percent less than 14. A normal adult has 800 to 1,200 CD4 cells in a microliter of blood. People with HIV infection lose all of the CD4 cells over time as their ability to produce them diminishes.

Also, CDC added recurrent pneumonia, pulmonary tuberculosis, and invasive cervical cancer in HIV-infected people to the 23 clinical conditions in the case definition published in 1987. According to CDC, the addition of these conditions reflects their documented or potential importance in the HIV epidemic. CDC reports, for instance, that cities with large numbers of AIDS cases have had parallel increases in TB rates, with the racial, ethnic, and age groups most affected by HIV having the greatest increase in TB incidence.

AIDS is spread by sexual contact, needle sharing, or less commonly through transfused blood or its components. The risk of infection with the virus is increased by having multiple sexual partners, either homosexual or heterosexual, and sharing of needles among those using illicit drugs. The occurrence of the syndrome in hemophilia patients and persons receiving transfusions provides evidence for transmission through blood. It may be transmitted from infected mother to infant before, during, or shortly after birth (probably through breast milk).

The AIDS virus can be spread by sexual intercourse whether you are male or female, heterosexual, bisexual, or homosexual. This happens because a person infected with the AIDS virus may have the virus in semen or vaginal fluids. The virus can enter the body through the vagina, penis, rectum or mouth. Anal intercourse, with or without a condom, is risky. The rectum is easily injured during anal intercourse.

Remember, AIDS is sexually transmitted, and the AIDS virus is not the only infection that is passed through intimate sexual contact.

Other sexually transmitted diseases, such as gonorrhea, syphilis, herpes, and chlamydia, can also be contracted through oral, anal, and vaginal intercourse.

Scientists have discovered how AIDS infects brain cells and have identified genes that affect the AIDS virus. But efforts to devise a treatment or vaccine are complicated by the fact that AIDS is caused by two, perhaps three, similar viruses, and that the virus mutates frequently.

With no cure in sight, prudence could save thousands of people in the U.S. who have yet to be exposed to the virus. Their fate will depend less on science than on the ability of large numbers of human beings to change their behavior in the face of growing danger. Experts believe that couples who have had a totally monogamous relationship for the past decade are safe. A negative blood test would be near-certain evidence of safety.

People who should be tested for AIDS include gay men and intravenous drug users, their sex partners, and anyone who has had several sex partners, if their sexual history is unknown, during any one of the last five years. Anyone who tests positive should see a physician immediately for a medical evaluation. Persons testing positive should inform their sex partners and should use a condom[1] during sex. (NOTE: According to the U.S. Food and Drug Administration, natural membrane condoms made from lambskin may not protect against the AIDS virus.) They should not donate blood, body organs, other tissue or sperm, nor should they share toothbrushes, razors, or other implements that could become contaminated with blood.

Toll-Free AIDS Information

The government's HIV–AIDS Treatment Information Service toll-free phone line provides the latest research and treatment information in Spanish and English to people with AIDS, their families, and home care providers. The number is (800) HIV–0440, 9:00 a.m. to 7:00 p.m., EST, Monday through Friday.

Access for the deaf is included and all calls are confidential.

It takes an average of ten years for an HIV-infected person to fully develop AIDS and afterwards most people die within eighteen months. However, some HIV-infected persons' immune systems seem to be able to resist AIDS-type infections better than others. An intense study of a small number of gay and bisexual men who have remained relatively healthy although they were infected with the HIV virus for a long time is under way at several major medical centers.

If AIDS researchers can understand what causes these atypical subjects to keep from becoming ill, they might be able to develop a vaccine to help other HIV-infected persons do the same. Researchers believe that less than five percent of people infected with teh AIDS virus are among these long-term survivors.

Information about where to go for confidential testing for the presence of the AIDS virus is provided by local and state health departments. There is a National AIDS Hot Line: (800) 342-2437 for recorded information about AIDS, or (800) 433-0366 for specific questions. □

Helping a Person With AIDS

No one will require more support and more love than your friend with AIDS. Feel free to offer what you can, without fear of becoming infected. You need to take precautions such as wearing rubber gloves only when blood is present.

If you don't know anyone with AIDS, but you'd still like to offer a helping hand, become a volunteer. You can be sure your help will be appreciated by a person with AIDS.

This might mean dropping by a supermarket to pick up groceries or just being there to talk. Above all, keep an upbeat attitude. It will help you and everyone face the disease more comfortably. □

Other Sexually Transmitted Diseases (STD)

Reliable data on the worldwide incidence of STD are not available. The World Health Organization's minimal estimates for the four major bacterial STD are: gonorrhoea, 25 million cases; genital chlamydial infections, 50 million cases; infectious syphilis, 3.5 million cases; and chancroid, 2 million cases. Rough estimates of genital herpes, a viral STD, is 20 million cases. □

1. Although condoms greatly reduce the risk of getting an AIDS infection, they are not guaranteed to be 100% effective. Considering that there is a 16% chance of failing when condoms are used as contraceptives it could also happen that a condom could fail in protecting against AIDS. The human sperm is many times larger than the AIDS virus. One sperm measures about 3,000 nanometers (a nanometer is one-billionth of a meter) and the AIDS virus is only 100 nanometers.—Ed.

Cancer Risks You Can Avoid

Source: National Cancer Institute, National Institutes of Health.

What is Cancer?

Cancer is really a group of diseases. There are more than 100 different types of cancer, but they all are a disease of some of the body's cells.

Healthy cells that make up the body's tissues grow, divide, and replace themselves in an orderly way. This process keeps the body in good repair. Sometimes, however, normal cells lose their ability to limit and direct their growth. They divide too rapidly and grow without any order. Too much tissue is produced and *tumors* begin to form. Tumors can be either *benign* or *malignant.*

Benign tumors are not cancer. They do not spread to other parts of the body and they are seldom a threat to life. Often, benign tumors can be removed by surgery, and they are not likely to return.

Malignant tumors are cancer. They can invade and destroy nearby tissue and organs. Cancer cells also can spread, or *metastasize,* to other parts of the body, and form new tumors.

Because cancer can spread, it is important for the doctor to find out as early as possible if a tumor is present and if it is cancer. As soon as a diagnosis is made, treatment can begin.

Signs and Symptoms of Cancer

Cancer and other illnesses often cause a number of problems you can watch for. The most common warning signs of cancer are:

Change in bowel or bladder habits;

A sore that does not heal;

Unusual bleeding or discharge;

Thickening or lump in the breast or elsewhere;

Indigestion or difficulty swallowing;

Obvious change in a wart or mole;

Nagging cough or hoarseness.

These signs and symptoms can be caused by cancer or by a number of other problems. They are *not* a sure sign of cancer. However, it is important to see a doctor if any problem lasts as long as 2 weeks. Don't wait for symptoms to become painful; pain is not an early sign of cancer.

Preventing Cancer

By choosing a lifestyle that avoids certain risks, you can help protect yourself from developing cancer. Many cancers are linked to factors that you can control.

Tobacco—Smoking and using tobacco in any form has been directly linked to cancer. Overall, smoking causes 30 percent of all cancer deaths. The risk of developing lung cancer is 10 times greater for smokers than for nonsmokers. The amount of risk from smoking depends on the number and type of cigarettes you smoke, how long you have been smoking, and how deeply you inhale. Smokers are also more likely to develop cancers of the mouth, throat, esophagus, pancreas, and bladder. And now there is emerging evidence that smoking can also cause cancer of the stomach and cervix.

The use of "smokeless" tobacco (chewing tobacco and oral snuff) increases the risk of cancer of the mouth and pharynx. Once you quit smoking or using smokeless tobacco, your risk of developing cancer begins to decrease right away.

Diet—What you eat may affect your chances of developing cancer. Scientists think there is a link between a high-fat diet and some cancers, particularly those of the breast, colon, endometrium, and prostate. Obesity is thought to be linked with increased death rates for cancers of the prostate, pancreas, breast, and ovary. Still other studies point to an increased risk of getting stomach cancer for those who frequently eat pickled, cured, and smoked foods. The National Cancer Institute believes that eating a well-balanced diet can reduce the risk of getting cancer. Americans should eat more high-fiber foods (such as whole-grain cereals and fruits and vegetables) and less fatty foods.

Sunlight—Repeated exposure to sunlight increases the risk of skin cancer, especially if you have fair skin or freckle easily. In fact, ultraviolet radiation from the sun is the main cause of skin cancer, which is the most common cancer in the United States. Ultraviolet rays are strongest from 11 a.m. to 2 p.m. during the summer, so that is when risk is greatest. Protective clothing, such as a hat and long sleeves, can help block out the sun's harmful rays. You can also use sunscreens to help protect yourself. Sunscreens with a number 15 on the label means most of the sun's harmful rays will be blocked out.

Alcohol—Drinking large amounts of alcohol (one or two drinks a day is considered moderate) is associated with cancers of the mouth, throat, esophagus, and liver. People who smoke cigarettes and drink alcohol have an especially high risk of getting cancers of the mouth and esophagus.

X-rays—Large doses of radiation increase cancer risk. Although individual x-rays expose you to very little radiation, repeated exposure can be harmful. Therefore, it is a good idea to avoid unnecessary x-rays. It's best to talk about the need for each x-ray with your doctor or dentist. If you do need an x-ray, ask if shields can be used to protect other parts of your body.

Industrial Agents and Chemicals—Being exposed to some industrial agents or chemicals increases cancer risk. Industrial agents cause damage by acting alone or together with another cancer-causing agent found in the workplace or with cigarette smoke. For example, inhaling asbestos fibers increases the risk of lung disease and cancer. This risk is especially high for workers who smoke. You should follow work and safety rules to avoid coming in contact with such dangerous materials.

Being exposed to large amounts of household solvent cleaners, cleaning fluids, and paint thinners should be avoided. Some chemicals are especially dangerous if inhaled in high concentrations, particularly in areas that are not well ventilated. In addition, inhaling or swallowing lawn and garden chemicals increases cancer risk. Follow label instructions carefully when using pesticides, fungicides, and other chemicals. Such chemicals should not come in contact with toys or other household items.

Hormones—Taking estrogen to relieve menopausal symptoms (such as hot flashes) has been associated with higher-than-average rates of cancer of the uterus. Numerous studies also have examined the relationship between oral contraceptives (the pill) and a variety of female cancers. Recent studies report that taking the pill does not increase a woman's chance of getting breast cancer. Also, pill users appear to have a lower-than-average risk of cancers of the endometrium and ovary. However, some researchers believe that there may be a higher risk of cancer of the cervix among pill users. Women taking hormones (either estrogens or oral contraceptives) should discuss the benefits and risks with their doctor.

Unavoidable Risks

Certain risk factors for cancer cannot be controlled, but people at high risk can help protect themselves by getting regular checkups. Some groups that have a higher-than-average risk of developing cancer are described below.

(1) Individuals who have close relatives with melanoma or cancer of the breast or colon. A small number of these cancers tend to occur more often in some families. If a close relative has been affected by one of these cancers, you should tell your doctor and be sure to have regular checkups to detect early problems.

(2) Persons who have had x-ray treatment to the head or neck when they were children or young adults. Exposure to these x-ray treatments may result in thyroid tumors, which have been associated with radiation given for an enlarged thymus gland, enlarged tonsils and adenoids, whooping cough, ringworm of the scalp, acne, and other head and neck conditions. Most thyroid tumors are not cancer. If thyroid cancer does develop, it usually can be cured. If you have had such x-rays, you should have a doctor examine your throat and neck every 1 or 2 years.

(3) Daughters and sons whose mothers took a drug called diethylstilbestrol (DES) to prevent miscarriages while they were pregnant with them. DES and some similar drugs given to mothers during pregnancy have been linked to certain unusual tissue formations in the vagina and cervix of their daughters. DES also has caused a rare type of vaginal and cervical cancer in a small number of exposed daughters. Women who took DES and DES-type drugs during pregnancy may themselves have a moderately increased risk of developing breast cancer. DES-exposed daughters and mothers should have examinations at least once a year that include pelvic and breast exams and Pap tests.

No link with cancer due to DES exposure before birth has been found in boys and men. However, there may be an increase in certain reproductive and urinary system problems in DES-exposed sons, who should also be examined regularly by a doctor.

Dietary Guidelines for Americans

Source: U.S. Dept. of Agriculture, U.S. Dept. of Health and Human Services

Eat a Variety of Foods

You need more than 40 different nutrients for good health. Essential nutrients include vitamins, minerals, amino acids from protein, certain fatty acids from fat, and sources of calories (protein, carbohydrates, and fat).

These nutrients should come from a variety of foods, not from a few highly fortified foods or supplements. Any food that supplies calories and nutrients can be part of a nutritious diet. The content of the total diet over a day or more is what counts.

No single food can supply all nutrients in the amounts you need. For example, milk supplies calcium but little iron; meat supplies iron but little calcium. To have a nutritious diet, you must eat a variety of foods.

One way to assure variety—and with it, an enjoyable and nutritious diet—is to choose foods each day from the five major food groups.

Use Sugars Only in Moderation

Sugars and many foods that contain them in large amounts supply calories but are limited in nutrients. Thus, they should be used in moderation by most healthy people and sparingly by people with low calorie needs. For very active people with high calorie needs, sugars can be an additional source of calories.

Both sugars and starches—which break down into sugars—can contribute to tooth decay. Sugars and starches are in many foods that also supply nutrients—milk; fruits; some vegetables; and breads, cereals and other foods with sugars and starches as ingredients. The more often these foods—even small amounts—are eaten and the longer they are in the mouth before teeth are brushed, the greater the risk for tooth decay. Thus, eating such foods as frequent

Suggested Weights for Adults

Height[1]	Weight in pounds[2]	
	19 to 34 years	35 years and over
5'0"	[3]97—128	108—138
5'1"	101—132	111—143
5'2"	104—137	115—148
5'3"	107—141	119—152
5'4"	111—146	122—157
5'5"	114—150	126—162
5'6"	118—155	130—167
5'7"	121—160	134—172
5'8"	125—164	138—178
5'9"	129—169	142—183
5'10"	132—174	146—188
5'11	136—179	151—194
6'0"	140—184	155—199
6'1"	144—189	159—205
6'2"	148—195	164—210
6'3"	152—200	168—216
6'4"	156—205	173—222
6'5"	160—211	177—228
6'6"	164—216	182—234

1. Without shoes. 2. Without clothes. 3. The higher weights in the ranges generally apply to men, who tend to have more muscle and bone; the lower weights more often apply to women, who have less muscle and bone.
Source: Derived from National Research Council, 1989.

between-meal snacks may be more harmful to teeth than having them at meals.

Regular daily brushing with a fluoride toothpaste helps reduce tooth decay by getting fluoride to the teeth. Fluoridated water or other sources of fluoride that a doctor or dentist suggest are especially important for children whose unerupted teeth are forming and growing.

Use Salt and Sodium Only in Moderation

Table salt contains sodium and chloride—both are essential in the diet. However, most Americans eat more salt and sodium than they need. Food and beverages containing salt provide most of the sodium in our diets, much of it added during processing and manufacturing.

Drink Alcohol in Moderation

Alcoholic beverages supply calories but little or no nutrients. Drinking them has no net health benefit, is linked with many health problems, is the cause of many accidents, and can lead to addiction. Their consumption is not recommended. If adults elect to drink alcoholic beverages, they should consume them in moderate amounts.

Choose a Diet Low in Fat, Saturated Fat, and Cholesterol

Most health authorities recommend an American diet with less fat, saturated fat, and cholesterol. The higher levels of saturated fat and cholesterol in our diets are linked to our increased risk for heart disease.

A diet low in fat makes it easier for you to include the variety of foods you need for nutrients without exceeding your calorie needs because fat contains over twice the calories of an equal amount of carbohydrates or protein.

A diet low in saturated fat and cholesterol can help maintain a desirable level of blood cholesterol. For adults this level is below 200 mg/dl. As blood cholesterol increases above this level, greater risk for heart disease occurs. Risk can also be increased by high blood pressure, cigarette smoking, diabetes, a family history of premature heart disease, obesity, and being a male.

The way diet affects blood cholesterol varies among individuals. However, blood cholesterol does increase in most people when they eat a diet high in saturated fat and cholesterol and excessive in calories. Of these, dietary saturated fat has the greatest effect; dietary cholesterol has less.

Choose a Diet with Plenty of Vegetables, Fruits, Grain Products

This guideline recommends that adults eat at least three servings of vegetables and two servings of fruit daily. It recommends at least six servings of grain products, such as breads, cereals, pasta, and rice, with an emphasis on whole grains. Children should also be encouraged to eat plenty of these foods.

Vegetables, fruits, and grain products are emphasized in this guideline especially for their complex carbohydrates, dietary fiber, and other food components linked to good health.

These foods are generally low in fats. By choosing the suggested amounts of them, you are likely to increase carbohydrates and decrease fats in your diet, as health authorities suggest. You will also get more dietary fiber.

Maintain Healthy Weight

If you are too fat or too thin, your chances of developing health problems are increased.

Being too fat is common in the United States. It is linked with high blood pressure, heart disease, stroke, the most common type of diabetes, certain cancers, and other types of illness.

Being too thin is a less common problem. It occurs with anorexia nervosa and is linked with osteoporosis in women and greater risk of illness.

Whether your weight is "healthy" depends on how much of your weight is fat, where in your body the fat is located, and whether you have weight-related medical problems, such as high blood pressure, or a family history of such problems. □

Two Myths About Heart Disease

Source: Reproduced with permission. "Heart and Stroke Facts: 1995 Statistical Supplement." 1994 © Copyright American Heart Association.

Heart disease no longer is a serious threat.—Medical scientists have made tremendous progress in fighting cardiovascular diseases. Even so, every 34 seconds an American dies of CVD. That's more than 925,000 deaths annually; more than 42 percent of all deaths every year. In fact, the No. 1 killer in the United States *in every year but one (1918) since 1900* has been CVD.

Deaths don't tell the whole story, either. Of the current U.S. population of about 255 million, nearly 59 million people have some form of these diseases. And as the population ages, these diseases may have an even greater human and economic impact. Heart failure, for example, is becoming much more prevalent.

Cancer, AIDS, and other diseases deserve research and attention. But it's important to remember that CVD ranks far ahead of them as a cause of death.

Finally, according to the most recent computations done by the National Center for Health Statistics, if all forms of major cardiovascular disease were eliminated, total life expectancy would rise by 9.78 years. If all forms of cancer were eliminated, the gain would be three years.

If a heart attack doesn't kill you, you'll recover and be fine.—People who survive the acute stage of a heart attack have a chance of illness and death two to nine times higher than the general population. The rates of another heart attack, sudden death, angina pectoris, heart failure, and stroke—for both men and women—are all substantial. Within six years after a heart attack,

- 23 percent of men and 31 percent of women will have another heart attack;
- 41 percent of men and 34 percent of women will develop angina;
- about 20 percent will be disabled with heart failure;
- nine percent of men and 18 percent of women will have a stroke; and
- 13 percent of men and six percent of women will experience sudden death.

About two-thirds of heart attack patients don't make a complete recovery, but 88 percent of those under age 65 are able to return to work.

Prevalence.—58,920,000 Americans—about one in four—have one or more forms of cardiovascular disease (CVD) according to current estimates.

Leading Causes of Death for Total Males, Females
United States: 1991 Final Mortality

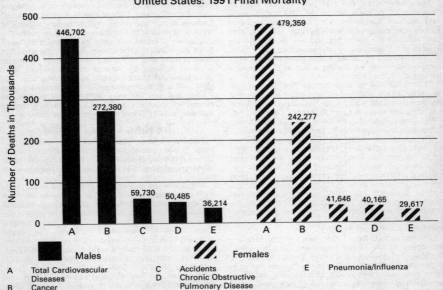

A Total Cardiovascular Diseases
B Cancer
C Accidents
D Chronic Obstructive Pulmonary Disease
E Pneumonia/Influenza

Source: National Center for Health Statistics and the American Heart Association.

- High blood pressure—50,000,000.
- Coronary heart disease—11,200,000.
- Stroke—3,080,000.
- Rheumatic heart disease—1,350,000.
- One in six men and one in eight women age 45 and over have had a heart attack or stroke.

Mortality—Cardiovascular diseases claimed 925,079 lives in the United States in 1992. This is 42.5 percent of all deaths or 1 of every 2.4 deaths.

- More than 2,500 Americans die each day from cardiovascular diseases.
- More than one-sixth of all people killed by CVD are under age 65.
- At all ages CVD is the leading cause of death for blacks.
- 1991 final mortality: male deaths—446,702 (48.2 percent); female deaths—479,359 (51.8 percent).
- In 1991 death rates from CVD were 237.0 for white males and 347.9 for black males (46.8 percent higher); for white females 131.2 and for black females 221.6 (68.9 percent higher).
- From 1982 to 1992 death rates from CVD declined 24.5 percent. despite this decline in the death rate, in the same 10-year period the actual number of deaths declined only 5.5 percent.
- In 1950 the death rate from cardiovascular disease was 424.2; in 1991 it had dropped to 186.0.

Facing Real Fears in Virtual Worlds

By Mark Hodges

The student donned a head-mounted display and plunged into a computer-animated world in which she found herself inside a glass elevator in the open atrium of a multistory hotel. At the prompting of her instructor's voice, she pushed a button, then rode upward in the elevator while the atrium floor receded visibly beneath her.

This trip was no joyride into virtual reality. The student, a victim of acrophobia, was trying to face her fear of heights in a controlled experiment of virtual-reality-assisted therapy. Even though the animated scenes viewed were cartoonlike in detail, the student—and nine other acrophobic volunteers—showed actual manifestations of distress, including pounding hearts, weak knees, sweating palms, and verbalizations of fear.

As unpleasant as these symptoms undoubtedly were, they achieved the desired therapeutic effect. Indeed, researchers from Emory University and the Georgia Institute of Technology report that the acrophobic students experienced a significant reduction in discomfort after seven exposures to virtual environments.

More important, most of the subjects showed "meaningful" progress outside the laboratory as well, says Barbara Rothbaum, a clinical psychologist at Emory and the project's co-director. She explains that, although the researchers did not ask the students to seek out frightening situations in their daily lives, 7 of the 10 did so, riding a real glass elevator up a hotel's outer wall or driving a car to the top of a parking deck, for example.

"Our goal was to demonstrate first that people would be afraid in virtual environments and then that the therapy would work," adds Rothbaum's collaborator, computer scientist Larry Hodges of Georgia Tech. "We haven't shown that virtual-reality treatment works better than other approaches, just that it's successful."

Though virtual-reality-assisted therapy makes use of innovative technology, it builds on standard therapeutic approaches. Psychologists have long believed that exposure to the source of one's anxieties can produce a tolerance of fear and a lasting reduction of phobic symptoms. When treating acrophobia, for example, clinicians have used two basic techniques: they ask acrophobes to imagine frightening heights and then encourage them to relax (systematic desensitization), or they guide patients in climbs to ever-higher places (in-vivo therapy).

The researchers from Emory and Georgia Tech are attempting to use virtual reality to treat acrophobia, Rothbaum says, because it offers several advantages over established treatment methods. Patients can confront their fears more vividly in immersive, animated worlds than when simply imagining they are at great heights, while clinicians may find virtual reality more convenient than trips out of the clinic and can tailor treatment to individual cases—for example, by exposing patients to the specific kinds of situations that alarm them most.

After an initial orientation, individuals in the treatment group came to a Georgia Tech computer science laboratory once a week for seven weeks, undergoing 40-minute sessions of virtual-reality-assisted therapy. There, they wore head-mounted displays that immersed them in computer-generated scenes of an elevator in a hotel atrium, a series of balconies, and several open-air bridges strung across a canyon. Under the supervision of a doctoral student in clinical psychology, the subjects progressed at their own pace from one situation to the next.

This study is the first peer-reviewed experiment in which virtual reality has been used to desensitize victims of acrophobia. But last year [1994], psychologist Ralph Lamson of the Kaiser Permanente health-maintenance organization in San Rafael, Calif., reported in the popular press that a group of approximately 40 acrophobes attained significant physiological and cognitive relief after a single exposure to heights in a virtual environment. "We're still looking at the data," Lamson says, "but virtual-reality therapy appears to work well enough to become a standard treatment."

Lamson's group not only experienced elevated heart rates and blood pressure during treatment, but most of them also "felt shaky" during their 50-minute sessions, he says. By the end of the treatment, their heart rates and blood pressure had lowered considerably, and a high percentage of the patients reported feeling less fear, he says. Within three months, 90 percent of these subjects fulfilled Lamson's request that they ride 15 floors in an open, glass elevator.

Treating Other Phobias

Lamson plans to build on his initial research in a study of 300 patients at several Kaiser Permanente facilities this year, exposing subjects to a broader range of virtual environments and testing its effectiveness in treating acrophobia, agoraphobia, and claustrophobia.

Rothbaum and Hodges also plan to test virtual reality's effectiveness in easing the symptoms of other anxiety disorders such as fear of flying. In multiple sessions at a Georgia Tech laboratory, a phobic patient will wear a head-mounted display that projects a visualization of commercial jet flight. The patient will first look at the exterior of the animated airliner on a runway, then "take a seat" inside the jet. There, he or she will hear the sound of the hatch closing, ride in the plane as it taxis across the runway, experience takeoff, fly through good and bad weather, and finally land. Hodges hopes to arrange an actual commercial airline flight at the end of the experiment to assess any changes in the patient's behavior.

Rothbaum and Hodges are also hoping to conduct a pilot study of the effectiveness of virtual-reality-assisted therapy in treating military veterans with post-traumatic stress disorder. The animated environment used in such an experiment will include the sights and sounds of battle, such as the chopping noise of helicopters.

Evidence of virtual reality's effectiveness in treating anxiety disorders would be largely academic if the costs of equipment and software remained out of reach. But in fact they are shrinking, spurred by the growing popularity of virtual reality in the game industry. Hardy Dunn, a program manager at Division, Inc., says that his company's virtual-reality workstations are priced from $40,000 to $80,000—well below the typical $500,000 of five years ago.

Among the challenges to be resolved in future studies is the degree of realism required for virtual environments to trigger a patient's phobic response. "Our goal," Hodges says, "is to figure out the least realistic environment that allows us to have effective therapy." He hopes that minimizing system demands will cut costs.

Aside from questions of economics, technical limitations with virtual-reality-assisted therapy remain. One problem is that as users turn their heads, they experience a slight delay as the computer updates the animated scene to reflect changes in visual perspective. This mismatch between "where you are and where you feel you are," Hodges says, caused some patients in the Emory–Georgia Tech experiment to experience simulator sickness, especially in extended treatment sessions. Subjects in the experiment were able to ward off most of these symptoms by moving their heads more slowly, either on their own initiative or at the suggestion of the research staff.

Physiological barriers may also limit the use of virtual environments in therapy. For example, some people have trouble perceiving the illusion of three dimensions in computer visualizations. Other patients with weakly developed neck muscles, such as young children and bedridden patients, may lack the strength to wear head-mounted displays, which normally weigh from one to five pounds. And some claustrophobia sufferers may not feel comfortable covering their faces with head-mounted displays.

But the most decisive factor in the new treatment's acceptance will probably be the simple willingness of patients and clinicians to give virtual reality a try. Some victims of phobic disorders may shy away from such all-involving encounters with their fears, but Rothbaum believes that the novelty and intrinsic interest of the therapy will attract many others. As for therapists, the virtual-reality approach is meeting some resistance, largely because it is a radically new medium, she says. Still, she hopes that as the technology becomes more commonplace, clinicians will come to accept virtual environments as a "natural extension" of the exposure therapy many already embrace. □

Mark Hodges is a science writer based in Atlanta, Georgia. This article first appeared in *Technology Review,* May/June 1995.

World Health Report Highlights, 1995

The World Health Organization (WHO) noted in its first annual global survey, entitled "The World Health Report, 1995: Bridging the Gaps," that many of the world's population die needlessly from preventable illnesses due to lack of access to proper health care. Some of the report's alarming findings are summarized below:

Biggest Killers

Ischemic heart disease (blood flow obstruction) is the deadliest disease in the world, killing 4.3 million people in 1993. The next deadliest is acute lower respiratory infections, mainly pneumonia, in children under age five, which killed 4.1 million. These are followed by cerebrovascular disease, which killed 3.9 million; diarrhea, including dysentery, under age five, 3 million deaths; chronic obstructive pulmonary disease, 2.9 million; tuberculosis, 2.7 million; malaria, 2 million; measles, 1.2 million; and other heart diseases, which killed 1.1 million people. Falls, fires, drownings, and other accidents killed 1.8 million people. Such diseases accounted for around 50 percent of the 51 million deaths globally in 1993, many of which could have been prevented.

Disabling Diseases

The report estimated the cumulative total of people disabled on a permanent and long-term basis. In 1993, some of the long-term disabled included: lymphatic filariasis, 43 million; hearing loss in children over age 3 (41 decibels and above), 42 million; mental retardation (all types), 41 million; cataract-related blindness, 16 million; epilepsy, 15 million; dementia, 11 million; poliomyelitis, 10 million; and schizophrenia, 8 million.

Infants and Children Under Five

Infants often come into the world with little chance to survive. About 200 million children under five in the world suffered from malnutrition in 1990—about 40% were in Asia, 25% in Africa, and about 10% in Latin America. Of the 12.2 million children under five that die yearly in the developing world, more than four million are killed by acute respiratory infections, particularly pneumonia. Diarrheal diseases, resulting from unsafe water and poor sanitation, coupled with poor food-handling practices, kill 3 million children.

School-Age Children and Adolescents

The highest rates for sexually transmitted diseases (STDs) generally occur in the 20–24 age group, followed by 15–19 and 25–29. In many countries, more than 60% of all new HIV infections are among the 15–24 age group globally, half the HIV infections have been in people under 25—with 60% of infections in females occurring by the age of 20.

Adolescents are at risk from tobacco, alcohol, and other drug use and from exploitation as cheap and often illegal labor. Another is the growth in the numbers of street children, to some 100 million, at a high risk of malnutrition, infectious diseases and criminal and sexual exploitation. The rise in accidents, violence and suicides involving young people is also a cause of concern.

Adults

Of total deaths in 1993, some 20 million died from communicable diseases, including 3.7 million from maternal, perinatal, and neonatal causes, and 19 million died from non-communicable diseases such as cancer and heart disease, the overwhelming majority of whom are adults. More than 75% of all deaths occurred in the developing world. Accidents and violence accounted for about 4 million deaths in 1993, most of them adults.

Sexually transmitted diseases impose a huge health burden. Some 236 million people suffer from trichomoniasis, with 94 million new cases a year. Chlamydial infections affect 162 million people, with 97 million new cases annually; and each year, there are 32 million new cases of genital warts; 78 million of gonorrhea; 21 million of genital herpes; 19 million of syphilis; and 9 million of chancroid. □

Guidelines in Choosing an HMO or PPO

Source: U.S. Department of Health and Human Services.

Health Maintenance Organizations (HMOs)—Health maintenance organizations are prepaid health plans. As an HMO member, you pay a monthly premium. In exchange, the HMO provides comprehensive care for you and your family, including doctors' visits, hospital stays, emergency care, surgery, lab tests, X-rays, and therapy.

The HMO arranges for this care either directly in its own group practice and/or through doctors and other health care professionals under contract. Usually, your choices of doctors and hospitals are limited to those that have agreements with the HMO to provide care. However, exceptions are made in emergencies or when medically necessary.

There may be a small **copayment** for each office visit, such as $5 for a doctor's visit or $25 for hospital emergency room treatment. Your total medical costs will likely be lower and more predictable in an HMO than with fee-for-service insurance.

Because HMOs receive a fixed fee for your covered medical care, it is in their interest to make sure you get basic health care for problems before they become serious. HMOs typically provide *preventive care*—office visits, immunizations, well-baby checkups, mammograms, and physicals. The range of services covered vary in HMOs, so it is important to compare available plans. Some services, such as outpatient mental health care, often are provided only on a limited basis.

Many people like HMOs because they do not require claim forms for office visits or hospital stays. Instead, members present a card, like a credit card, at the doctor's office or hospital. However, in an HMO you may have to wait longer for an appointment than you would with a fee-for-service plan.

In some HMOs, doctors are salaried and they all have offices in an HMO building at one or more locations in your community as part of a prepaid group practice.

In others, independent groups of doctors contract with the HMO to take care of patients. These are called individual practice associations (IPAs) and they are made up of private physicians in private offices who agree to care for HMO members. You select a doctor from a list of participating physicians that make up the IPA network. If you are thinking of switching into an IPA-type of HMO, ask your doctor if he or she participates in the plan.

In almost all HMOs, you either are assigned or you choose one doctor to serve as your **primary care doctor.** This doctor monitors your health and provides most of your medical care, referring you to specialists and other health care professionals as needed. You usually cannot see a specialist without a referral from your primary care doctor who is expected to manage the care you receive. This is one way that HMOs can limit your choice.

Before choosing an HMO, it is a good idea to talk to people you know who are enrolled in it. Ask them how they like the services and care given.

Questions to Ask About an HMO

• **Are there many doctors to choose from?** Do you select from a list of contract physicians or from the available staff of a group practice? Which doctors are accepting new patients? How hard is it to change doctors if you decide you want someone else? How are referrals to specialists handled?

• **Is it easy to get appointments?** How far in advance must routine visits be scheduled? What arrangements does the HMO have for handling emergency care?

• **Does the HMO offer the services I want?** What preventive services are provided? Are there limits on medical tests, surgery, mental health care, home care, or other support offered? What if you need a special service not provided by the HMO?

• **What is the service area of the HMO?** Where are the facilities located in your community that serve HMO members? How convenient to your home and workplace are the doctors, hospitals, and emergency care centers that make up the HMO network? What happens if you or a family member are out of town and need medical treatment?

• **What will the HMO plan cost?** What is the yearly total for monthly fees? In addition, are there co-payments for office visits, emergency care, prescribed drugs, or other services? How Much?

Preferred Provider Organizations (PPOs)— The preferred provider organization is a combination of traditional fee-for-service and an HMO. Like an HMO, there are a limited number of doctors and hospitals to choose from. When you use those providers (sometimes called "preferred" providers, other times called "network" providers), most of your medical bills are covered. When you go to doctors in the PPO, you present a card and do not have to fill out forms. Usually there is a small copayment for each visit. For some services, you may have to pay a deductible and coinsurance.

As with an HMO, most PPOs require that you choose a primary care doctor. That doctor monitors your health and refers you to specialists.

Most PPOs cover preventive care. This usually includes visits to the doctor, well-baby care, immunizations, and mammograms.

In a PPO, you can use doctors who are not part of the plan and still receive some coverage. At these times, you will pay a larger portion of the bill yourself (and also fill out the claims forms). Some people like this option because even if their doctor is not a part of the network, it means they don't have to change doctors to join a PPO.

Questions to Ask About a PPO

• **Are there many doctors to choose from?** Who are the doctors in the PPO network? Where are they located? Which ones are accepting new patients? How are referrals to specialists handled?

• **What hospitals are available through the PPO?** Where is the nearest hospital in the PPO network? What arrangements does the PPO have for handling emergency care?

• **What services are covered?** What preventive services are offered? Are there limits on medical tests, out-of-hospital care, mental health care, prescription drugs, or other services that are important to you?

• **What will the PPO plan cost?** How much is the premium? Is there a per-visit cost for seeing PPO doctors or other types of copayments for services? What is the difference in cost between using doctors in the PPO network and those outside it? What is the deductible and coinsurance rate for care outside of the PPO? Is there a limit to the maximum you would pay out of pocket? □

HEADLINE HISTORY

In any broad overview of history, arbitrary compartmentalization of facts is self-defeating (and makes locating interrelated people, places, and things that much harder). Therefore, Headline History is designed as a "timeline"—a chronology that highlights both the march of time and interesting, sometimes surprising, juxtapositions.

Also see related sections of *Information Please,* particularly Inventions and Discoveries, Countries of the World, etc.

B.C.

Before Christ or Before Common Era (B.C.E.)

4.5 billion B.C.   Planet Earth formed.

3 billion B.C.   First signs of primeval life (bacteria and blue-green algae) appear in oceans.

600 million B.C.   Earliest date to which fossils can be traced.

4.4 million B.C.   Earliest known hominid fossils (*Ardipithecus ramidus*) found in Aramis, Ethiopia, 1994.

4.2 million B.C.   *Australopithecus anamensis* found in Lake Turkana, Kenya, 1995.

3.2 million B.C.   *Australopithecus afarenis* (nicknamed *"Lucy"*) found in Ethiopia, 1974.

2.5 million B.C.   *Homo Habilis* ("Handy Man"), first brain expansion and first chipped stones.

1.8 million B.C.   *Homo Erectus* ("Upright Man"). Brain size twice that of *Australopithecine* species.

1.7 million B.C.   *Homo Erectus* leaves Africa.

100,000 B.C.   First modern *Homo Sapiens* in South Africa.

70,000 B.C.   Neanderthal man (use of fire and advanced tools).

35,000 B.C.   Neanderthal man being replaced by later groups of *Homo sapiens* (i.e. Cro-Magnon man, etc.).

18,000 B.C.   Cro-Magnons being replaced by later cultures.

15,000 B.C.   Migrations across Bering Straits into the Americas.

10,000 B.C.   Semi-permanent agricultural settlements in Old World.

10,000–4,000 B.C.   Development of settlements into cities and development of skills such as the wheel, pottery and improved methods of cultivation in Mesopatamia and elsewhere.

NOTE: For futher information on the geographic development in Earth's prehistory, see the Science section.

4500–3000 B.C.   Sumerians in the Tigris and Euphrates valleys develop a city-state civilization; first phonetic writing **(c.3500 B.C.)**. Egyptian agriculture develops. Western Europe is neolithic, without metals or written records. Earliest recorded date in Egyptian calendar **(4241 B.C.)**. First year of Jewish calendar **(3760 B.C.)**. Copper used by Egyptians and Sumerians.

3000–2000 B.C.   Pharaonic rule begins in Egypt. Cheops, 4th dynasty **(2700–2675 B.C.)**. The Great Sphinx of Giza. Earliest Egyptian mummies. Papyrus. Phoenician settlements on coast of what is now Syria and Lebanon. Semitic tribes settle in Assyria. Sargon, first Akkadian king, builds Mesopotamian empire. The Gilgamesh epic **(c.3000 B.C.)**. Abraham leaves Ur **(c.2000 B.C.)**. Systematic astronomy in Egypt, Babylon, India, China.

3000–1500 B.C.   The most ancient civilization on the Indian subcontinent, the sophisticated and extensive Indus Valley civilization, flourishes in what is today Pakistan.

2000–1500 B.C.   Hyksos invaders drive Egyptians from Lower Egypt **(17th century B.C.)**. Amosis I frees Egypt from Hyksos **(c.1600 B.C.)**. Assyrians rise to power—cities of Ashur and Nineveh. Twenty-four-character alphabet in Egypt. Israelites enslaved in Egypt. Cuneiform inscriptions used by Hittites. Peak of Minoan culture on Isle of Crete—earliest form of written Greek. Hammurabi, king of Babylon, develops oldest existing code of laws **(18th century B.C.)**. In Britain, Stonehenge erected on some unknown astronomical rationale.

1500–1000 B.C.   Ikhnaton develops monotheistic religion in Egypt **(c.1375 B.C.)**. His successor, Tutankhamen, returns to earlier gods. Moses leads Israelites out of Egypt into Canaàn—Ten Commandments. Greeks destroy Troy **(c.1193 B.C.)**. End of Greek civilization in Mycenae with invasion of Dorians. Chinese civilization develops under Shang dynasty. Olmec civilization in Mexico—stone monuments; picture writing.

·1000–900 B.C.   Solomon succeeds King David, builds Jerusalem temple. After Solomon's death, kingdom divided into Israel and Judah. Hebrew elders begin to write Old Testament books of Bible. Phoenicians colonize Spain with settlement at Cadiz.

Brontosaur

Moses

**Egyptian chariots
(1500 B.C.)**

ANCIENT EMPIRES

The Egyptian Empire (1400 BC)
Alexander's Empire (323 BC)
The Roman Empire (120 AD)
Path of the Crusaders (1000-1200 AD)

Some Ancient Civilizations

Name	Approximate dates	Location	Major cities
Akkadian	2350–2230 B.C.	Mesopotamia, parts of Syria, Asia Minor, Iran	Akkad, Ur, Erich
Assyrian	1800–889 B.C.	Mesopotamia, Syria	Assur, Nineveh, Calah
Babylonian	1728–1686 B.C. (old) 625–539 B.C. (new)	Mesopotamia, Syria, Palestine	Babylon
Cimmerian	750–500 B.C.	Caucasus, northern Asia Minor	—
Egyptian	2850–715 B.C.	Nile valley	Thebes, Memphis, Tanis
Etruscan	900–396 B.C.	Northern Italy	—
Greek	900–200 B.C.	Greece	Athens, Sparta, Thebes, Mycenae, Corinth
Hittite	1640–1200 B.C.	Asia Minor, Syria	Hattusas, Nesa
Indus Valley	3000–1500 B.C.	Pakistan, Northwestern India	—
Lydian	700–547 B.C.	Western Asia Minor	Sardis, Miletus
Mede	835–550 B.C.	Iran	Media
Minoan	3000–1100 B.C.	Crete	Knossos
Persian	559–330 B.C.	Iran, Asia Minor, Syria	Persepolis, Pasargadae
Phoenician	1100–332 B.C.	Palestine (colonies: Gibraltar, Carthage Sardinia)	Tyre, Sidon, Byblos
Phrygian	1000–547 B.C.	Central Asia Minor	Gordion
Roman	500 B.C.–A.D. 300	Italy, Mediterranean region, Asia Minor, western Europe	Rome, Byzantium
Scythian	800–300 B.C.	Caucasus	—
Sumerian	3200–2360 B.C.	Mesopotamia	Ur, Nippur

900–800 B.C. Phoenicians establish Carthage (**c.810** B.C.). The *Iliad* and the *Odyssey*, perhaps composed by Greek poet Homer.

800–700 B.C. Prophets Amos, Hosea, Isaiah. First recorded Olympic games (**776** B.C.). Legendary founding of Rome by Romulus (**753** B.C.). Assyrian king Sargon II conquers Hittites, Chaldeans, Samaria (end of Kingdom of Israel). Earliest written music. Chariots introduced into Italy by Etruscans.

700–600 B.C. End of Assyrian Empire (**616** B.C.)—Nineveh destroyed by Chaldeans (Neo-Babylonians) and Medes (**612** B.C.). Founding of Byzantium by Greeks (**c.660** B.C.). Building of the Acropolis in Athens. Solon, Greek lawgiver (**640–560** B.C.). Sappho of Lesbos, Greek poetess, Lao-Tse, Chinese philosopher and founder of Taoism (born **c.604** B.C.).

600–500 B.C. Babylonian king Nebuchadnezzar builds empire, destroys Jerusalem (**586** B.C.). Babylonian Captivity of the Jews (starting **587** B.C.). Hanging Gardens of Babylon. Cyrus the Great of Persia creates great empire, conquers Babylon (**539** B.C.), frees the Jews. Athenian democracy develops. Aeschylus, Greek dramatist (**525–465** B.C.). Confucius (**551–479** B.C.) develops philosophy-religion in China. Buddha (**563–483** B.C.) founds Buddhism in India.

500–400 B.C. Greeks defeat Persians: battles of Marathon (**490** B.C.), Thermopylae (**480** B.C.), Salamis (**480** B.C.). Peloponnesian Wars between Athens and Sparta (**431–404** B.C.)—Sparta victorious. Pericles comes to power in Athens (**462** B.C.). Flowering of Greek culture during the Age of Pericles (**450–400** B.C.). Sophocles, Greek dramatist (**496–c.406** B.C.). Hippocrates, Greek "Father of Medicine" (born **460** B.C.). Xerxes I, king of Persia (rules **485–465** B.C.).

400–300 B.C. Pentateuch—first five books of the Old Testament evolve in final form. Philip of Macedon assassinated (**336** B.C.) after conquering Greece; succeeded by son, Alexander the Great (**356–323** B.C.), who destroys Thebes (**335** B.C.), conquers Tyre and Jerusalem (**332** B.C.), occupies Babylon (**330** B.C.), invades India, and dies in Babylon. His empire is divided among his generals; one of them, Seleucis I, establishes Middle East empire with capitals at Antioch (Syria) and Seleucia (in Iraq). Trial and execution of Greek philosopher Socrates (**399** B.C.). Dialogues recorded by his student, Plato. Euclid's work on geometry (**323** B.C.). Aristotle, Greek philosopher (**384–322** B.C.). Demosthenes, Greek orator (**384–322** B.C.). Praxiteles, Greek sculptor (**400–330** B.C.).

300–251 B.C. First Punic War (**264–241** B.C.): Rome defeats the Carthaginians and

Confucius (551-479 B.C.)

Plato (427?-347 B.C.)

**Archimedes
(287-212 B.C.)**

begins its domination of the Mediterranean. Temple of the Sun at Teotihua-can, Mexico (**c.300** B.C.). Invention of Mayan calendar in Yucatán—more exact than older calendars. First Roman gladiatorial games (**264** B.C.). Archimedes, Greek mathematician (**287–212** B.C.).

250–201 B.C. Second Punic War (**219–201** B.C.): Hannibal, Carthaginian general (**246–142** B.C.), crosses the Alps (**218** B.C.), reaches gates of Rome (**211** B.C.), retreats, and is defeated by Scipio Africanus at Zama (**202** B.C.). Great Wall of China built (**c.215** B.C.).

200–151 B.C. Romans defeat Seleucid King Antiochus III at Thermopylae (**191** B.C.)—beginning of Roman world domination. Maccabean revolt against Seleucids (**167** B.C.).

150–101 B.C. Third Punic War (**149–146** B.C.): Rome destroys Carthage, killing 450,000 and enslaving the remaining 50,000 inhabitants. Roman armies conquer Macedonia, Greece, Anatolia, Balearic Islands, and southern France. Venus de Milo (**c.140** B.C.). Cicero, Roman orator (**106–43** B.C.).

100–51 B.C. Julius Caesar (**100–44** B.C.) invades Britain (**55** B.C.) and conquers Gaul (France) (**c.50** B.C.). Spartacus leads slave revolt against Rome (**71** B.C.). Romans conquer Seleucid empire. Roman general Pompey conquers Jerusalem (**63** B.C.). Cleopatra on Egyptian throne (**51–31** B.C.). Chinese develop use of paper (**c.100** B.C.). Virgil, Roman poet (**70–19** B.C.). Horace, Roman poet (**65–8** B.C.).

50–1 B.C. Caesar crosses Rubicon to fight Pompey (**50** B.C.). Herod made Roman governor of Judea (**47** B.C.). Caesar murdered (**44** B.C.). Caesar's nephew, Octavian, defeats Mark Antony and Cleopatra at Battle of Actium (**31** B.C.), and establishes Roman empire as Emperor Augustus—rules 27 B.C.—A.D. 14. Birth of Jesus Christ (variously given from **4** B.C. to A.D. 7). Ovid, Roman poet (**43** B.C.—A.D. 18).

A.D.

The Christian or Common Era (C.E.)

**Jesus Christ
(4? B.C.-29? A.D.)**

1–49 After Augustus, Tiberius becomes emperor (dies, **37**), succeeded by Caligula (assassinated, **41**), who is followed by Claudius. Crucifixion of Jesus (probably **30**). Han dynasty in China founded by Emperor Kuang Wu Ti. Buddhism introduced to China.

50–99 Claudius poisoned (**54**), succeeded by Nero (commits suicide, **68**). Missionary journeys of Paul the Apostle (**34–60**). Jews revolt against Rome; Jerusalem destroyed (**70**). Roman persecutions of Christians begin (**64**). Colosseum built in Rome (**71–80**). Trajan (rules **98–116**); Roman empire extends to Mesopotamia, Arabia, Balkans. First Gospels of St. Mark, St. John, St. Matthew.

100–149 Hadrian rules Rome (**117–138**); codifies Roman law, establishes postal system, builds wall between England and Scotland. Jews revolt under Bar Kokhba (**122–135**); final *Diaspora* (dispersion) of Jews begins.

150–199 Marcus Aurelius (rules Rome **161–180**). Oldest Mayan temples in Central America (**c.200**)., Mayan civilization develops writing, astronomy, mathematics.

200–249 Goths invade Asia Minor (**c.220**). Roman persecutions of Christians increase. Persian (Sassanid) empire re-established. End of Chinese Han dynasty.

250–299 Increasing invasions of the Roman empire by Franks and Goths. Buddhism spreads in China.

300–349 Constantine the Great (rules **312–337**) reunites eastern and western Roman empires, with new capital (Constantinople) on site of Byzantium (**330**); issues Edict of Milan legalizing Christianity (**313**); becomes a Christian on his deathbed (**337**). Council of Nicaea (**325**) defines orthodox Christian doctrine. First Gupta dynasty in India (**c.320**).

350–399 Huns (Mongols) invade Europe (**c.360**). Theodosius the Great (rules **392–395**)—last emperor of a united Roman empire. Roman empire permanently divided in **395**: western empire ruled from Rome; eastern empire ruled from Constantinople.

400–449 Western Roman empire disintegrates under weak emperors. Alaric, king of the Visigoths, sacks Rome (**410**). Attila, Hun chieftain, attacks Roman provinces (**433**). St. Patrick returns to Ireland (**432**). St. Augustine's *City of God* (**411**).

450–499 Vandals destroy Rome (**455**). Western Roman empire ends as Odoacer, German chieftain, overthrows last Roman emperor, Romulus Augustulus, and becomes king of Italy (**476**). Ostrogothic kingdom of Italy established by Theodoric the Great (**493**). Clovis, ruler of the Franks, is converted to Christianity (**496**). First schism between western and eastern churches (**484**). Peak of Mayan culture in Mexico (**c.460**).

500–549 Eastern and western churches reconciled (**519**). Justinian I, the Great

(483–565), becomes Byzantine emperor (527), issues his first code of civil laws (529), conquers North Africa, Italy, and part of Spain. Plague spreads through Europe (from 542). Arthur, semi-legendary king of the Britons (killed, c.537). Boëthius, Roman scholar (executed, 524).

550–599 Beginnings of European silk industry after Justinian's missionaries smuggle silkworms out of China (553). Mohammed, founder of Islam (570–632). Buddhism in Japan (c.560). St. Augustine of Canterbury brings Christianity to Britain (597). After killing about half the population, plague in Europe subsides (594).

600–649 Mohammed flees from Mecca to Medina (the *Hegira*); first year of the Muslim calendar (622). Muslim empire grows (634). Arabs conquer Jerusalem (637), destroy Alexandrian library (641), conquer Persians (641). Fatima, Mohammed's daughter (606–632).

650–699 Arabs attack North Africa (670), destroy Carthage (697). Venerable Bede, English monk (672–735).

700–749 Arab empire extends from Lisbon to China (by 716). Charles Martel, Frankish leader, defeats Arabs at Tours/Poitiers, halting Arab advance in Europe (732). Charlemagne (742–814).

750–799 Caliph Harun al-Rashid rules Arab empire (786–809): the "golden age" of Arab culture. Vikings begin attacks on Britain (790), land in Ireland (795). Charlemagne becomes king of the Franks (771). City of Machu Picchu flourishes in Peru.

800–849 Charlemagne (Charles the Great) crowned first Holy Roman Emperor in Rome (800). Arabs conquer Crete, Sicily, and Sardinia (826–827). Charlemagne dies (814), succeeded by his son, Louis the Pious, who divides France among his sons (817).

850–899 Norsemen attack as far south as the Mediterranean but are repulsed (859), discover Iceland (861). Alfred the Great becomes king of Britain (871), defeats Danish invaders (878). Russian nation founded by Vikings under Prince Rurik, establishing capital at Novgorod (855–879).

900–949 Vikings discover Greenland (c.900). Arab Spain under Abd ar-Rahman III becomes center of learning (912–961).

950–999 Eric the Red establishes first Viking colony in Greenland (982). Mieczyslaw I becomes first ruler of Poland (960). Hugh Capet elected King of France in 987; Capetian dynasty to rule until 1328. Musical notation systematized (c.990). Vikings and Danes attack Britain (988–999). Holy Roman Empire founded by Otto I, King of Germany since 936, crowned by Pope John XII in 962.

11th century A.D.

c.1000 Hungary and Scandinavia converted to Christianity. Viking raider Leif Ericson discovers North America, calls it *Vinland*. Chinese invent gunpowder. *Beowulf*, Old English epic.

1009 Moslems destroy Holy Sepulchre in Jerusalem.

1013 Danes control England. Canute takes throne (1016), conquers Norway (1028), dies (1035); kingdom divided among his sons: Harold Harefoot (England), Sweyn (Norway), Hardecanute (Denmark).

1040 Macbeth murders Duncan, king of Scotland.

1053 Robert Guiscard, Norman invader, establishes kingdom in Italy, conquers Sicily (1072).

1054 Final separation between Eastern (Orthodox) and Western (Roman) churches.

1055 Seljuk Turks, Asian nomads, move west, capture Baghdad, Armenia (1064), Syria, and Palestine (1075).

1066 William of Normandy invades England, defeats last Saxon king, Harold II, at Battle of Hastings, crowned William I of England ("the Conqueror").

1073 Emergence of strong papacy when Gregory VII is elected. Conflict with English and French kings and German emperors will continue throughout medieval period.

1095 (*See* special material on "The Crusades.")

12th century A.D.

1150–67 Universities of Paris and Oxford founded in France and England.

1162 Thomas à Becket named Archbishop of Canterbury, murdered by Henry II's men (1170). Troubadours (wandering minstrels) glorify romantic concepts of feudalism.

1189 Richard I ("the Lionhearted") succeeds Henry II in England, killed in France (1199), succeeded by King John.

13th century A.D.

1211 Genghis Khan invades China, captures Peking (1214), conquers Persia (1218), invades Russia (1223), dies (1227).

Viking Discovery of Greenland (c.900)

The
MOSLEM WORLD
about 732

Territory overrun by Moslems
The Byzantine Empire

Scale of Miles
0   300   600   900

1215 King John forced by barons to sign Magna Carta at Runneymede, limiting royal power.
1233 The Inquisition begins as Pope Gregory IX assigns Dominicans responsibility for combatting heresy. Torture used (**1252**). Ferdinand and Isabella establish Spanish Inquisition (**1478**). Tourquemada, Grand Inquisitor, forces conversion or expulsion of Spanish Jews (**1492**). Forced conversion of Moors (**1499**). Inquisition in Portugal (**1531**). First Protestants burned at the stake in Spain (**1543**). Spanish Inquisition abolished (**1834**).
1241 Mongols defeat Germans in Silesia, invade Poland and Hungary, withdraw from Europe after Ughetai, Mongol leader, dies.
1251 Kublai Khan governs China, becomes ruler of Mongols (1259), establishes Yuan dynasty in China (1280), invades Burma (1287), dies (1294).
1271 Marco Polo of Venice travels to China, in court of Kublai Khan (1275–1292), returns to Genoa (1295) and writes *Travels*.
1295 English King Edward I summons the Model Parliament.

14th century A.D.

1312–37 Mali Empire reaches its height in Africa under King Mansa Musa.
1337–1453 Hundred Years' War—English and French kings fight for control of France.
c.1325 The beginning of the Renaissance in Italy: writers Dante, Petrarch, Boccaccio; painter Giotto. Development of *No* drama in Japan. Aztecs establish capital on site of modern Mexico City. Peak of Moslem culture in Spain. Small cannon in use.
1347–1351 At least 25 million people die in Europe's "Black Death" (bubonic plague).
1368 Ming dynasty begins in China.
1376–82 John Wycliffe, pre-Reformation religious reformer and followers translate Latin Bible into English.
1378 The Great Schism (to 1417)—rival popes in Rome and Avignon, France, fight for control of Roman Catholic Church.
c.1387 Chaucer's *Canterbury Tales*.

15th century A.D.

1415 Henry V defeats French at Agincourt. Jan Hus, Bohemian preacher and follower of Wycliffe, burned at stake in Constance as heretic.
1418–60 Portugal's Prince Henry the Navigator sponsors exploration of Africa's coast.
1428 Joan of Arc leads French against English, captured by Burgundians (1430) and turned over to the English, burned at the stake as a witch after ecclesiastical trial (1431).
1438 Inca rule in Peru.
1450 Florence becomes center of Renaissance arts and learning under the Medicis.
1453 Turks conquer Constantinople, end of the Byzantine empire. Hundred Years' War between France and England ends.
1455 The Wars of the Roses, civil wars between rival noble factions, begin in England (to 1485). Having invented printing with movable type at Mainz, Germany, Johann Gutenberg completes first Bible.
1462 Ivan the Great rules Russia until 1505 as first czar; ends payment of tribute to Mongols.
1492 Moors conquered in Spain by troops of Ferdinand and Isabella. Columbus discovers Caribbean islands, returns to Spain (1493). Second voyage to Dominica, Jamaica, Puerto Rico (1493–1496). Third voyage to Orinoco (1498). Fourth voyage to Honduras and Panama (1502–1504).
1497 Vasco da Gama sails around Africa and discovers sea route to India (1498). Establishes Portuguese colony in India (1502). John Cabot, employed by England, reaches and explores Canadian coast. Michelangelo's *Bacchus* sculpture.

**John Wycliffe
(1320-1384)**

**Joan of Arc
(1412-1431)**

**Christopher Columbus
(1451-1506)**

THE CRUSADES (1096–1291)

In 1095 at Council of Clermont, Pope Urban II calls for war to rescue Holy Land from Moslem infidels. *First Crusade* (1096)—about 500,000 peasants led by Peter the Hermit prove so troublesome that Byzantine Emperor Alexius ships them to Asia Minor; only 25,000 survive return after massacre by Seljuk Turks. Followed by organized army, led by nobility, which reaches Constantinople (1097), conquers Jerusalem (1099), Acre (1104), establishes Latin Kingdom protected by Knights of St. John the Hospitalier (1100), and Knights Templar (1123). Seljuk Turks start series of counterattacks (1144). *Second Crusade* (1146) led by King Louis VIII of France and Emperor Conrad III. Crusaders perish in Asia Minor (1147).

Saladin controls Egypt (1171), unites Islam in Holy War (*Jihad*) against Christians, recaptures Jerusalem (1187). *Third Crusade* (1189) under kings of France, England, and Germany fails to reduce Saladin's power. *Fourth Crusade* (1200–1204)—French knights sack Greek Christian Constantinople, establish Latin empire in Byzantium. Greeks re-establish Orthodox faith (1262).

Children's Crusade (1212)—Only 1 of 30,000 French children and about 200 of 20,000 German children survive to return home. Other Crusades—against Egypt (1217), *Sixth* (1228), *Seventh* (1248), *Eighth* (1270). Mamelukes conquer Acre; end of the Crusades (1291).

16th century A.D.

**Michelangelo Buonarroti
(1475-1564)**

**Martin Luther
(1483-1546)**

**Anthony Van Dyck
(1559-1641)**

1501 First black slaves in America brought to Spanish colony of Santo Domingo.

c.1503 Leonardo da Vinci paints the *Mona Lisa.*

1506 St. Peter's Church started in Rome; designed and decorated by such artists and architects as Bramante, Michelangelo, da Vinci, Raphael, and Bernini before its completion in **1626.**

1509 Henry VIII ascends English throne. Michelangelo paints the ceiling of the Sistine Chapel.

1517 Turks conquer Egypt, control Arabia. Martin Luther posts his 95 theses denouncing church abuses on church door in Wittenberg—start of the Reformation in Germany.

1519 Ulrich Zwingli begins Reformation in Switzerland. Hernando Cortes conquers Mexico for Spain. Charles I of Spain is chosen Holy Roman Emperor Charles V. Portuguese explorer Fernando Magellan sets out to circumnavigate the globe.

1520 Luther excommunicated by Pope Leo X. Suleiman I ("the Magnificent") becomes Sultan of Turkey, invades Hungary **(1521)**, Rhodes **(1522)**, attacks Austria **(1529)**, annexes Hungary **(1541)**, Tripoli **(1551)**, makes peace with Persia **(1553)**, destroys Spanish fleet **(1560)**, dies **(1566)**. Magellan reaches the Pacific, is killed by Philippine natives **(1521)**. One of his ships under Juan Sebastián del Cano continues around the world, reaches Spain **(1522)**.

1524 Verrazano, sailing under the French flag, explores the New England coast and New York Bay.

1527 Troops of the Holy Roman Empire attack Rome, imprison Pope Clement VII—the end of the Italian Renaissance. Castiglione writes *The Courtier.* The Medici expelled from Florence.

1532 Pizarro marches from Panama to Peru, kills the Inca chieftain, Atahualpa, of Peru **(1533)**. Machiavelli's *Prince* published posthumously.

1535 Reformation begins as Henry VIII makes himself head of English Church after being excommunicated by Pope. Sir Thomas More executed as traitor for refusal to acknowledge king's religious authority. Jacques Cartier sails up the St. Lawrence River, basis of French claims to Canada.

1536 Henry VIII executes second wife, Anne Boleyn. John Calvin establishes Presbyterian form of Protestantism in Switzerland, writes *Institutes of the Christian Religion.* Danish and Norwegian Reformations. Michelangelo's *Last Judgment.*

1541 John Knox leads Reformation in Scotland, establishes Presbyterian church **(1560)**.

1543 Publication of *On the Revolution of Heavenly Bodies* by Polish scholar Nicolaus Copernicus—giving his theory that the earth revolves around the sun.

1545 Council of Trent to meet intermittently until **1563** to define Catholic dogma and doctrine, reiterate papal authority.

1547 Ivan IV ("the Terrible") crowned as Czar of Russia, begins conquest of Astrakhan and Kazan **(1552)**, battles nobles (boyars) for power **(1564)**, kills his son **(1580)**, dies, and is succeeded by a son who gives power to Boris Godunov **(1584)**.

1553 Roman Catholicism restored in England by Queen Mary I, who rules until **1558.** Religious radical Michael Servetus burned as heretic in Geneva by order of John Calvin.

1554 Benvenuto Cellini completes the bronze *Perseus.*

1556 Akbar the Great becomes Mogul emperor of India, conquers Afghanistan **(1581)**, continues wars of conquest (until **1605)**.

1558 Queen Elizabeth I ascends the throne (rules to **1603)**. Restores Protestantism, establishes state Church of England (Anglicanism). Renaissance will reach height in England—Shakespeare, Marlowe, Spenser.

1561 Persecution of Huguenots in France stopped by Edict of Orleans. French religious wars begin again with massacre of Huguenots at Vassy. St. Bartholomew's Day Massacre—thousands of Huguenots murdered **(1572)**. Amnesty granted **(1573)**. Persecution continues periodically until Edict of Nantes **(1598)** gives Huguenots religious freedom (until **1685)**.

1568 Protestant Netherlands revolts against Catholic Spain; independence will be acknowledged by Spain in **1648.** High point of Dutch Renaissance—painters Rubens, Van Dyck, Hals, and Rembrandt.

1570 Japan permits visits of foreign ships. Queen Elizabeth I excommunicated by Pope. Turks attack Cyprus and war on Venice. Turkish fleet defeated at Battle of Lepanto by Spanish and Italian fleets **(1571)**. Peace of Constantinople **(1572)** ends Turkish attacks on Europe.

1580 Francis Drake returns to England after circumnavigating the globe. Knighted by Queen Elizabeth I (**1581**). Montaigne's *Essays* published.
1583 William of Orange rules The Netherlands; assassinated on orders of Philip II of Spain (**1584**).
1587 Mary, Queen of Scots, executed for treason by order of Queen Elizabeth I. Monteverdi's *First Book of Madrigals.*
1588 Defeat of the Spanish Armada by English. Henry, King of Navarre and Protestant leader, recognized as Henry IV, first Bourbon king of France. Converts to Roman Catholicism in **1593** in attempt to end religious wars.
1590 Henry IV enters Paris, wars on Spain (**1595**), marries Marie de Medici (**1600**), assassinated (**1610**). Spenser's *The Faerie Queen,* El Greco's *St. Jerome.* Galileo's experiments with falling objects.
1598 Boris Godunov becomes Russian Czar. Tycho Brahe describes his astronomical experiments.

Francis Bacon
(1561-1626)

17th century A.D.

1600 Giordano Bruno burned as a heretic. Ieyasu rules Japan, moves capital to Edo (Tokyo). Shakespeare's *Hamlet* begins his most productive decade. English East India Company established to develop overseas trade.
1607 Jamestown, Virginia, established—first permanent English colony on American mainland.
1609 Samuel de Champlain establishes French colony of Quebec.
1611 Gustavus Adolphus elected King of Sweden. King James Version of the Bible published in England. Rubens paints his *Descent from the Cross.*
1614 John Napier discovers logarithms.
1618 Start of the Thirty Years' War (to **1648**)—Protestant revolt against Catholic oppression; Denmark, Sweden, and France will invade Germany in later phases of war. Kepler proposes his Third Law of planetary motion.
1620 Pilgrims, after three-month voyage in *Mayflower,* land at Plymouth Rock. Francis Bacon's *Novum Organum.*
1633 Inquisition forces Galileo to recant his belief in Copernican theory.
1642 English Civil War. Cavaliers, supporters of Charles I, against Roundheads, parliamentary forces. Oliver Cromwell defeats Royalists (**1646**). Parliament demands reforms. Charles I offers concessions, brought to trial (**1648**), beheaded (**1649**). Cromwell becomes Lord Protector (**1653**). Rembrandt paints his *Night Watch.*
1644 End of Ming Dynasty in China—Manchus come to power. Descartes' *Principles of Philosophy.* John Milton's *Areopagitica* on the freedom of the press.
1648 End of the Thirty Years' War. German population about half of what it was in **1618** because of war and pestilence.
1658 Cromwell dies; his son, Richard, resigns and Puritan government collapses.
1660 English Parliament calls for the restoration of the monarchy; invites Charles II to return from France.
1661 Charles II is crowned King of England. Louis XIV begins personal rule as absolute monarch; starts to build Versailles.

Giordano Bruno
(1548-1600)

George Washington
(1732-1799)

THE FOUNDING OF THE AMERICAN NATION

Colonization of America begins: Jamestown, Va. (**1607**); Pilgrims in Plymouth (**1620**); Massachusetts Bay Colony (**1630**) New Netherland founded by Dutch West India Company (**1623**), captured by English (**1664**). Delaware established by Swedish trading company (**1638**), absorbed later by Penn family. Proprietorships by royal grants to Lord Baltimore (Maryland, **1632**); Captain John Mason (New Hampshire, **1635**); Sir William Berkeley and Sir George Carteret (New Jersey, **1663**); friends of Charles II (the Carolinas, **1663**); William Penn (Pennsylvania, **1682**); James Oglethorpe and others (Georgia, **1732**).

Increasing conflict between colonists and Britain on western frontier because of royal edict limiting western expansion (**1763**), and regulation of colonial trade and increased taxation of colonies (Writs of Assistance allow search for illegal shipments, **1761**; Sugar Act, **1764**; Currency Act, **1764**; Stamp Act, **1765**; Quartering Act, **1765**; Duty Act, **1767**.) Boston Massacre (**1770**). Lord North attempts conciliation (**1770**). Boston Tea Party (**1773**), followed by punitive measures passed by Parliament—the "Intolerable Acts."

First Continental Congress (**1774**) sends "Declaration of Rights and Grievances" to king, urges colonies to form Continental Association. Paul Revere's Ride and Lexington and Concord battle between Massachusetts minutemen and British (**1775**).

Second Continental Congress (**1775**), while sending "olive branch" to the king, begins to raise army, appoints Washington commander-in-chief, and seeks alliance with France. Some colonial legislatures urge their delegates to vote for independence. Declaration of Independence (July 4, **1776**).

Major Battles of the Revolutionary War: *Long Island:* Howe defeats Putnam's division of Washington's Army in Brooklyn Heights, but Americans escape across East River (**1776**). *Trenton and Princeton:* Washington defeats Hessians at Trenton. British at Princeton, winters at Morristown (**1776–77**). Howe winters in Philadelphia; Washington at Valley Forge (**1777–78**). Burgoyne surrenders British army to General Gates at *Saratoga* (**1777**).

France recognizes American independence (**1778**). The War moves south: Savannah captured by British (**1778**); Charleston occupied (**1780**); Americans fight successful guerrilla actions under Marion, Pickens, and Sumter. In the West, George Rogers Clark attacks Forts Kaskaskia and Vincennes (**1778–1779**), defeating British in the region. Cornwallis surrenders at *Yorktown,* Virginia (Oct. 19, **1781**). By **1782**, Britain is eager for peace because of conflicts with European nations. *Peace of Paris* (**1783**): Britain recognizes American independence.

The
UNITED STATES
during the
REVOLUTION

1664 British take New Amsterdam from the Dutch. English limit "Nonconformity" with re-established Anglican Church. Isaac Newton's experiments with gravity.

1665 Great Plague in London kills 75,000.

1666 Great Fire of London. Molière's *Misanthrope*.

1683 War of European powers against the Turks (to **1699**). Vienna withstands three-month Turkish siege; high point of Turkish advance in Europe.

1685 James II succeeds Charles II in England, calls for freedom of conscience **(1687)**. Protestants fear restoration of Catholicism and demand "Glorious Revolution." William of Orange invited to England and James II escapes to France **(1688)**. William III and his wife, Mary, crowned. In France, Edict of Nantes of **1598**, granting freedom of worship to Huguenots (French Protestants), is revoked by Louis XIV; thousands of Protestants flee.

1689 Peter the Great becomes Czar of Russia—attempts to westernize nation and build Russia as a military power. Defeats Charles XII of Sweden at Poltava **(1709)**. Beginning of the French and Indian Wars (to **1763**), campaigns in America linked to a series of wars between France and England for domination of Europe.

1690 William III of England defeats former King James II and Irish rebels at Battle of the Boyne in Ireland. John Locke's *Human Understanding*.

John Locke
(1632-1704)

18th century A.D.

1701 War of the Spanish Succession begins—the last of Louis XIV's wars for domination of the continent. The Peace of Utrecht **(1714)** will end the conflict and mark the rise of the British Empire. Called Queen Anne's War in America, it ends with the British taking New Foundland, Acadia, and Hudson's Bay Territory from France, and Gibraltar and Minorca from Spain.

1704 Deerfield (Mass.) Massacre of English colonists by French and Indians. Bach's first cantata. Jonathan Swift's *Tale of a Tub*. *Boston News Letter*—first newspaper in America.

1707 United Kingdom of Great Britain formed—England, Wales, and Scotland joined by parliamentary Act of Union.

1729 J. S. Bach's *St. Matthew Passion*. Isaac Newton's *Principia* translated from Latin into English.

1735 John Peter Zenger, New York editor, acquitted of libel in New York, establishing press freedom.

1740 Capt. Vitus Bering, Dane employed by Russia, discovers Alaska.

1746 British defeat Scots under Stuart Pretender Prince Charles at Culloden Moor. Last battle fought on British soil.

1751 Publication of the *Encyclopédie* begins in France, the "bible" of the Enlightenment.

1755 Samuel Johnson's *Dictionary* first published. Great earthquake in Lisbon, Portugal—over 60,000 die. U.S. postal service established.

1756 Seven Years' War (French and Indian War in America) (to **1763**), in which Britain and Prussia defeat France, Spain, Austria, and Russia. France loses North American colonies; Spain cedes Florida to Britain in exchange for Cuba. In India, over 100 British prisoners die in "Black Hole of Calcutta."

1757 Beginning of British Empire in India as Robert Clive, British commander, defeats Nawab of Bengal at Plassey.

1759 British capture Quebec from French. Voltaire's *Candide*. Haydn's *Symphony No. 1*.

1762 Catherine II ("the Great") becomes Czarina of Russia. J. J. Rousseau's *Social Contract*. Mozart tours Europe as six-year-old prodigy.

1765 James Watt invents the steam engine.

1769 Sir William Arkwright patents a spinning machine—an early step in the Industrial Revolution.

1772 Joseph Priestley and Daniel Rutherford independently discover nitrogen. Partition of Poland—in **1772**, **1793**, and **1795**, Austria, Prussia, and Russia divide land and people of Poland, end its independence.

1775 The American Revolution (*see* "The Founding of the American Nation"). Priestley discovers hydrochloric and sulfuric acids.

1776 Adam Smith's *Wealth of Nations*. Edward Gibbon's *Decline and Fall of the Roman Empire*. Thomas Paine's *Common Sense*. Fragonard's *Washerwoman*. Mozart's *Haffner Serenade*.

1778 Capt. James Cook discovers Hawaii. Franz Mesmer uses hypnotism.

1781 Immanuel Kant's *Critique of Pure Reason*. Herschel discovers Uranus.

1783 End of Revolutionary War (*see* special material on "The Founding of the

Catherine II
(1729-1796)

Napoleon Bonaparte (1769-1821)

American Nation"). William Blake's poems. Beethoven's first printed works.

1784 Crimea annexed by Russia. John Wesley's *Deed of Declaration*, the basic work of Methodism.

1785 Russians settle Aleutian Islands.

1787 The Constitution of the United States signed. Lavoisier's work on chemical nomenclature. Mozart's *Don Giovanni*.

1788 French *Parlement* presents grievances to Louis XVI who agrees to convening of Estates-General in **1789**—not called since **1613**. Goethe's *Egmont*. Laplace's *Laws of the Planetary System*.

1789 French Revolution (*see* special material on the "French Revolution"). In U.S., George Washington elected President with all 69 votes of the Electoral College, takes oath of office in New York City. Vice President: John Adams. Secretary of State: Thomas Jefferson. Secretary of Treasury: Alexander Hamilton.

1790 H.M.S. *Bounty* mutineers settle on Pitcairn Island. Aloisio Galvani experiments on electrical stimulation of the muscles. Philadelphia temporary capital of U.S. as Congress votes to establish new capital on Potomac. U.S. population about 3,929,000, including 698,000 slaves. Lavoisier formulates *Table of 31 chemical elements*.

1791 U.S. Bill of Rights ratified. Boswell's *Life of Johnson*.

1794 Kosciusko's uprising in Poland quelled by the Russians. In U.S., Whiskey Rebellion in Pennsylvania as farmers object to liquor taxes.

1796 Napoleon Bonaparte, French general, defeats Austrians. In the U.S., Washington's Farewell Address **(Sept. 17)**; John Adams elected President; Thomas Jefferson, Vice President. Edward Jenner introduces smallpox vaccination.

1798 Napoleon extends French conquests to Rome and Egypt. U.S. Navy Department established.

1799 Napoleon leads coup that overthrows Directory, becomes First Consul—one of three who rule France.

19th century A.D.

1800 Napoleon conquers Italy, firmly establishes himself as First Consul in France. In the U.S., Federal Government moves to Washington. Robert Owen's social reforms in England. William Herschel discovers infrared rays. Alessandro Volta produces electricity.

1801 Austria makes temporary peace with France. United Kingdom of Great Britain and Ireland established with one monarch and one parliament; Catholics excluded from voting.

1803 U.S. negotiates Louisiana Purchase from France: For $15 million, U.S. doubles its domain, increasing its territory by 827,000 sq. mi. (2,144,500 sq km), from Mississippi River to Rockies and from Gulf of Mexico to British North America.

1804 Haiti declares independence from France; first black nation to gain freedom from European colonial rule. Napoleon proclaims himself emperor of France, systematizes French law under *Code Napoleon*. In the U.S., Alexander Hamilton is mortally wounded in duel with Aaron Burr. Lewis and Clark expedition begins exploration of what is now northwestern U.S.

1805 Lord Nelson defeats the French-Spanish fleets in the Battle of Trafalgar. Napoleon victorious over Austrian and Russian forces at the Battle of Austerlitz.

1807 Robert Fulton makes first successful steamboat trip on *Clermont* between New York City and Albany.

1808 French armies occupy Rome and Spain, extending Napoleon's empire. Britain begins aiding Spanish guerrillas against Napoleon in Peninsular War. In the U.S., Congress bars importation of slaves. Beethoven's *Fifth* and *Sixth Symphonies* performed.

1812 Napoleon's Grand Army invades Russia in June. Forced to retreat in winter, most of Napoleon's 600,000 men are lost. In the U.S., war with Britain

Thomas Jefferson (1743-1826)

Alexander Hamilton (1755-1804)

FRENCH REVOLUTION (1789–1799)

Revolution begins when Third Estate (Commons) delegates swear not to disband until France has a constitution. Paris mob storms Bastille, symbol of royal power **(July 14, 1789)**. National Assembly votes for Constitution, Declaration of the Rights of Man, a limited monarchy, and other reforms **(1789–90)**. Legislative Assembly elected, Revolutionary Commune formed, and French Republic proclaimed **(1792)**. War of the First Coalition—Austria, Prussia, Britain, Netherlands, and Spain fight to restore French nobility **(1792–97)**. Start of series of wars between France and European powers that will last, almost without interruption, for 23 years. Louis XVI and Marie Antoinette executed. Committee of Public Safety begins Reign of Terror as political control measure. Interfactional rivalry leads to mass killings. Danton and Robespierre executed. Third French Constitution sets up Directory government **(1795)**.

declared over freedom of the seas for U.S. vessels. U.S.S. *Constitution* sinks British frigate. (*See* special material on the "War of 1812.")

1814 French defeated by allies (Britain, Austria, Russia, Prussia, Sweden, and Portugal) in War of Liberation. Napoleon exiled to Elba, off Italian coast. Bourbon King Louis XVIII takes French throne. George Stephenson builds first practical steam locomotive.

1815 Napoleon returns: "Hundred Days" begin. Napoleon defeated by Wellington at Waterloo, banished again to St. Helena in South Atlantic. Congress of Vienna: victorious allies change the map of Europe.

1817 Simón Bolívar establishes independent Venezuela, as Spain loses hold on South American countries. Bolívar named President of Colombia **(1819)**. Peru, Guatemala, Panama, and Santo Domingo proclaim independence from Spain **(1821)**.

1820 Missouri Compromise—Missouri admitted as slave state but slavery barred in rest of Louisiana Purchase north of 36°30′ N.

1822 Greeks proclaim a republic and independence from Turkey. Turks invade Greece. Russia declares war on Turkey **(1828)**. Greece also aided by France and Britain. War ends and Turks recognize Greek independence **(1829)**. Brazil becomes independent of Portugal. Schubert's *Eighth Symphony* ("The Unfinished").

1823 U.S. Monroe Doctrine warns European nations not to interfere in Western Hemisphere.

1824 Mexico becomes a republic, three years after declaring independence from Spain. Beethoven's *Ninth Symphony.*

1825 First passenger-carrying railroad in England.

1830 French invade Algeria. Louis Philippe becomes "Citizen King" as revolution forces Charles X to abdicate. Mormon church formed in U.S. by Joseph Smith.

1831 Polish revolt against Russia fails. Belgium separates from the Netherlands. In U.S., Nat Turner leads unsuccessful slave rebellion.

1833 Slavery abolished in British Empire.

1834 Charles Babbage invents "analytical engine," precursor of computer. McCormick patents reaper.

1836 Boer farmers start "Great Trek"—Natal, Transvaal, and Orange Free State founded in South Africa. Mexican army besieges Texans in Alamo. Entire garrison, including Davy Crockett and Jim Bowie, wiped out. Texans gain independence from Mexico after winning Battle of San Jacinto. Dicken's *Pickwick Papers.*

1837 Victoria becomes Queen of Great Britain. Mob kills Elijah P. Lovejoy, Illinois abolitionist publisher.

1839 First Opium War (to **1842**) between Britain and China, over importation of drug into China.

1840 Lower and Upper Canada united.

1841 U.S. President Harrison dies **(April 4)** one month after inauguration; John Tyler becomes first Vice President to succeed to Presidency.

1844 Democratic convention calls for annexation of Texas and acquisition of Oregon ("Fifty-four-forty-or-fight"). Five Chinese ports opened to U.S. ships. Samuel F. B. Morse patents telegraph.

1845 Congress adopts joint resolution for annexation of Texas.

1846 Failure of potato crop causes famine in Ireland. U.S. declares war on Mexico. California and New Mexico annexed by U.S. Brigham Young leads Mormons to Great Salt Lake. W.T. Morton uses ether as anesthetic. Sewing machine patented by Elias Howe.

1848 Revolt in Paris: Louis Philippe abdicates; Louis Napoleon elected President of French Republic. Revolutions in Vienna, Venice, Berlin, Milan, Rome, and Warsaw. Put down by royal troops in **1848–49**. U.S.-Mexico War ends; Mexico cedes claims to Texas, California, Arizona, New Mexico, Utah, Nevada. U.S. treaty with Britain sets Oregon Territory boundary at 49th parallel. Karl Marx and Friedrich Engels' *Communist Manifesto.*

1849 California gold rush begins.

1850 Henry Clay opens great debate on slavery, warns South against secession.

1851 Herman Melville's *Moby Dick.* Harriet Beecher Stowe's *Uncle Tom's Cabin.*

1852 South African Republic established. Louis Napoleon proclaims himself Napoleon III ("Second Empire").

Charles Dickens
(1812-1870)

Henry Clay
(1777-1852)

WAR OF 1812

British interference with American trade, impressment of American seamen, and "War Hawks" drive for western expansion lead to war. American attacks on Canada foiled; U.S. Commodore Perry wins battle of Lake Erie **(1813)**. British capture and burn Washington **(1814)** but fail to take Fort McHenry at Baltimore. Andrew Jackson repulses assault on New Orleans after treaty of Ghent ends war **(1815)**. War settles little but strengthens U.S. as independent nation.

**Dred Scott
(1795?-1858)**

**Abraham Lincoln
(1809-1865)**

**Ulysses S. Grant
(1822-1885)**

1853 Crimean War begins as Turkey declares war on Russia. Commodore Perry reaches Tokyo.

1854 Britain and France join Turkey in war on Russia. In U.S., Kansas-Nebraska Act permits local option on slavery; rioting and bloodshed. Japanese allow American trade. Antislavery men in Michigan form Republican Party. Tennyson's *Charge of the Light Brigade*. Thoreau's *Walden*.

1855 Armed clashes in Kansas between pro- and anti-slavery forces. Florence Nightingale nurses wounded in Crimea. Walt Whitman's *Leaves of Grass*.

1856 Flaubert's *Madame Bovary*.

1857 Supreme Court, in Dred Scott decision, rules that a slave is not a citizen. Financial crisis in Europe and U.S. Great Mutiny (Sepoy Rebellion) begins in India. India placed under crown rule as a result.

1858 Pro-slavery constitution rejected in Kansas. Abraham Lincoln makes strong antislavery speech in Springfield, Ill.: ". . . this Government cannot endure permanently half slave and half free." Lincoln-Douglas debates. First trans-Atlantic telegraph cable completed by Cyrus W. Field.

1859 John Brown raids Harpers Ferry; is captured and hanged. Work begins on Suez Canal. Unification of Italy starts under leadership of Count Cavour, Sardinian premier. Joined by France in war against Austria. Edward Fitzgerald's *Rubaiyat of Omar Khayyam*. Charles Darwin's *Origin of Species*. J. S. Mill's *On Liberty*.

1861 U.S. Civil War begins as attempts at compromise fail (*see* special material on "The Civil War"). Congress creates Colorado, Dakota, and Nevada territories; adopts income tax; Lincoln inaugurated. Serfs emancipated in Russia. Pasteur's theory of germs. Independent Kingdom of Italy proclaimed under Sardinian King Victor Emmanuel II.

1863 French capture Mexico City; proclaim Archduke Maximilian of Austria emperor.

1865 Lincoln fatally shot at Ford's Theater by John Wilkes Booth. Vice President Johnson sworn as successor. Booth caught and dies of gunshot wounds; four conspirators are hanged. Joseph Lister begins antiseptic surgery. Gregor Mendel's Law of Heredity. Lewis Carroll's *Alice's Adventures in Wonderland*.

1866 Alfred Nobel invents dynamite (patented in Britain 1867). Seven Weeks' War: Austria defeated by Prussia and Italy.

1867 Austria-Hungary Dual Monarchy established. French leave Mexico; Maximilian executed. Dominion of Canada established. U.S. buys Alaska from Russia for $7,200,000. South African diamond field discovered. Volume I of Marx's *Das Kapital*. Strauss's *Blue Danube*.

1868 Revolution in Spain; Queen Isabella deposed, flees to France. In U.S., Fourteenth Amendment giving civil rights to blacks is ratified. Georgia under military government after legislature expels blacks.

1869 First U.S. transcontinental rail route completed. James Fisk and Jay Gould attempt to control gold market causes Black Friday panic. Suez Canal opened. Mendeleev's periodic table of elements.

1870 Franco-Prussian War (to **1871**): Napoleon III capitulates at Sedan. Revolt in Paris; Third Republic proclaimed.

THE CIVIL WAR
(The War Between the States or the War of the Rebellion)

Apart from the matter of slavery, the Civil War arose out of both the economic and political rivalry between an agrarian South and an industrial North and the issue of the right of states to secede from the Union.

1861 After South Carolina secedes (**Dec. 20, 1860**), Mississippi, Florida, Alabama, Georgia, Louisiana, and Texas follow, forming the Confederate States of America, with Jefferson Davis as president (**Jan.–March**). War begins as Confederates fire on Fort Sumter (**April 12**). Lincoln calls for 75,000 volunteers. Southern ports blockaded by superior Union naval forces. Virginia, Arkansas, Tennessee, and North Carolina secede to complete 11-state Confederacy. Union army advancing on Richmond repulsed at first Battle of Bull Run (**July**).

1862 Edwin M. Stanton named Secretary of War (**Jan.**). Grant wins first important Union victory in West, at Fort Donelson; Nashville falls (**Feb.**). Ironclads, Union's *Monitor* and Confederate's *Virginia* (*Merrimac*) duel at Hampton Roads (**March**). New Orleans falls to Union fleet under Farragut; city occupied (**April**). Grant's army escapes defeat at Shiloh. Memphis falls as Union gunboats control upper Mississippi (**June**). Confederate general Robert E. Lee victorious at second Battle of Bull Run (**Aug.**). Union

army under McClellan halts Lee's attack on Washington in the Battle of Antietam (**Sept.**). Lincoln removes McClellan for lack of aggressiveness. Burnside's drive on Richmond fails at Fredericksburg (**Dec.**). Union forces under Rosecrans chase Bragg through Tennessee; battle of Murfreesboro (**Oct.–Jan. 1863**).

1863 Lee defeats Hooker at Chancellorsville; "Stonewall" Jackson, Confederate general, dies (**May**). Confederate invasion of Pennsylvania stopped at Gettysburg by George Meade—Lee loses 20,000 men—the greatest battle of the War (**July**). It and the Union victory at Vicksburg mark the War's turning point. Union general George H. Thomas, the "Rock of Chickamauga," holds Bragg's forces on Georgia-Tennessee border (**Sept.**). Sherman, Hooker, and Thomas drive Bragg back to Georgia. Tennessee restored to the Union (**Nov.**).

1864 Ulysses S. Grant named commander-in-chief of Union forces (**March**). In the Wilderness campaign, Grant forces Lee's Army of Northern Virginia back toward Richmond (**May–June**). Sherman's Atlanta campaign and "march to the sea" (**May–Sept.**). Farragut's victory at Mobile Bay (**Aug.**). Hood's Confederate army defeated at Nashville. Sherman takes Savannah (**Dec.**).

1865 Sheridan defeats Confederates at Five Forks; Confederates evacuate Richmond (**April**). On **April 9**, Lee surrenders to Grant at Appomattox.

1871 France surrenders Alsace-Lorraine to Germany; war ends. German Empire proclaimed with Prussian King as Kaiser Wilhelm I. Fighting with Apaches begins in American West. Boss Tweed corruption exposed in New York. The Chicago Fire, with 250 deaths and $196-million damage. Stanley meets Livingston in Africa.

1872 Congress gives amnesty to most Confederates. Jules Verne's *Around the World in 80 Days.*

1873 Economic crisis in Europe. U.S. establishes gold standard.

1875 First Kentucky Derby.

1876 Sioux kill Gen. George A. Custer and 264 troopers at Little Big Horn River. Alexander Graham Bell patents the telephone.

1877 After Presidential election of **1876,** Electoral Commission gives disputed Electoral College votes to Rutherford B. Hayes despite Tilden's popular majority. Russo-Turkish war (ends in **1878** with power of Turkey in Europe broken). Reconstruction ends in the American South. Thomas Edison patents phonograph.

1878 Congress of Berlin revises Treaty of San Stefano ending Russo-Turkish War; makes extensive redivision of southeastern Europe. First commercial telephone exchange opened in New Haven, Conn.

1880 U.S.-China treaty allows U.S. to restrict immigration of Chinese labor.

1881 President Garfield fatally shot by assassin; Vice President Arthur succeeds him. Charles J. Guiteau convicted and executed (in **1882**).

Geronimo
(1829-1909)

1882 Terrorism in Ireland after land evictions. Britain invades and conquers Egypt. Germany, Austria, and Italy form Triple Alliance. In U.S., Congress adopts Chinese Exclusion Act. Rockefeller's Standard Oil Trust is first industrial monopoly. In Berlin, Robert Koch announces discovery of tuberculosis germ.

1883 Congress creates Civil Service Commission. Brooklyn Bridge and Metropolitan Opera House completed.

1885 British Gen. Charles G. "Chinese" Gordon killed at Khartoum in Egyptian Sudan.

1886 Bombing at Haymarket Square, Chicago, kills seven policemen and injures many others. Eight alleged anarchists accused—three imprisoned, one commits suicide, four hanged. (In **1893,** Illinois Governor Altgeld, critical of trial, pardons three survivors.) Statue of Liberty dedicated. Geronimo, Apache Indian chief, surrenders.

1887 Queen Victoria's Golden Jubilee. Sir Arthur Conan Doyle's first Sherlock Holmes story, "A Study in Scarlet."

1888 Historic March blizzard in Northeast U.S.—many perish, property damage exceeds $25 million. George Eastman's box camera (the Kodak). J.B. Dunlop invents pneumatic tire. Jack the Ripper murders in London.

Samuel Clemens
(Mark Twain)
(1835-1910)

1889 Second (Socialist) International founded in Paris. Indian Territory in Oklahoma opened to settlement. Thousands die in Johnstown, Pa., flood. Mark Twain's *A Connecticut Yankee in King Arthur's Court.*

1890 Congress votes Sherman Antitrust Act. Sitting Bull killed in Sioux uprising.

1892 Battle between steel strikers and Pinkerton guards at Homestead, Pa.; union defeated after militia intervenes. Silver mine strikers in Idaho fight non-union workers; U.S. troops dispatched. Diesel engine patented.

1894 Sino-Japanese War begins (ends in **1895** with China's defeat). In France, Capt. Alfred Dreyfus convicted on false treason charge (pardoned in **1906**). In U.S., Jacob S. Coxey of Ohio leads "Coxey's Army" of unemployed on Washington. Eugene V. Debs calls general strike of rail workers to support Pullman Company strikers; strike broken, Debs jailed for six months. Thomas A. Edison's kinetoscope given first public showing in New York City.

1895 X-rays discovered by German physicist, Wilhelm Roentgen.

1896 Supreme Court's *Plessy v. Ferguson* decision—"separate but equal" doctrine. Alfred Nobel's will establishes prizes for peace, science, and literature. Marconi receives first wireless patent in Britain. William Jennings Bryan delivers "Cross of Gold" speech at Democratic Convention in

Thomas A. Edison
(1847-1931)

SPANISH-AMERICAN WAR (1898–1899)

War fires stoked by "jingo journalism" as American people support Cuban rebels against Spain. American business sees economic gain in Cuban trade and resources and American power zones in Latin America. Outstanding events: Submarine mine explodes U.S. battleship *Maine* in Havana Harbor **(Feb. 15)**; 260 killed; responsibility never fixed. Congress declares independence of Cuba **(April 19).** Spain declares war on U.S. **(Apr. 24);** Congress **(Apr. 25)** formally declares nation has been at war with Spain since Apr. 21. Commodore George Dewey wins seven-hour battle of Manila Bay **(May 1).** Spanish fleet destroyed off Santiago, Cuba **(July 3);** city surrenders **(July 7).** Treaty of Paris (ratified by Senate **1899**) ends war. U.S. given Guam and Puerto Rico and agrees to pay Spain $20 million for Philippines. Cuba independent of Spain; under U.S. military control for three years until **May 20, 1902.** Yellow fever is eradicated and political reforms achieved.

Marie Curie
(1867-1934)

Theodore Roosevelt
(1858-1919)

Albert Einstein
(1879-1955)

Chicago. First modern Olympic games held in Athens, Greece.

1898 Chinese "Boxers," anti-foreign organization, established. They stage uprisings against Europeans in **1900**; U.S. and other Western troops relieve Peking legations. Spanish-American War (*see* special material on the "Spanish-American War"). Pierre and Marie Curie discover radium and polonium.

1899 Boer War (or South African War). Conflict between British and Boers (descendants of Dutch settlers of South Africa). Causes rooted in longstanding territorial disputes and in friction over political rights for English and other "uitlanders" following 1886 discovery of vast gold deposits in Transvaal. (British victorious as war ends in **1902**.) Casualties: 5,774 British dead, about 4,000 Boers. Union of South Africa established in **1908** as confederation of colonies; becomes British dominion in **1910**.

20th century A.D.

1900 Hurricane ravages Galveston, Tex.; 6,000 drown. Sigmund Freud's *The Interpretation of Dreams*.

1901 Queen Victoria dies; succeeded by son, Edward VII. As President McKinley begins second term, he is shot fatally by anarchist Leon Czolgosz. Theodore Roosevelt sworn in as successor.

1902 Enrico Caruso's first gramophone recording.

1903 Wright brothers, Orville and Wilbur, fly first powered, controlled, heavier-than-air plane at Kitty Hawk, N.C. Henry Ford organizes Ford Motor Company.

1904 Russo-Japanese War—competition for Korea and Manchuria: In **1905**, Port Arthur surrenders to Japanese and Russia suffers other defeats; President Roosevelt mediates Treaty of Portsmouth, N.H., ending war with concessions for Japan. *Entente Cordiale:* Britain and France settle their international differences. General theory of radioactivity by Rutherford and Soddy. New York City subway opened.

1905 General strike in Russia; first workers' soviet set up in St. Petersburg. Sailors on battleship *Potemkin* mutiny; reforms including first Duma (parliament) established by Czar's "October Manifesto." Albert Einstein's special theory of relativity and other key theories in physics. Franz Lehar's *Merry Widow*.

1906 San Francisco earthquake and three-day fire; 500 dead. Roald Amundsen, Norwegian explorer, fixes magnetic North Pole.

1907 Second Hague Peace Conference, of 46 nations, adopts 10 conventions on rules of war. Financial panic of **1907** in U.S.

1908 Earthquake kills 150,000 in southern Italy and Sicily. U.S. Supreme Court, in Danbury Hatters' case, outlaws secondary union boycotts.

1909 North Pole reached by American explorers Robert E. Peary and Matthew Henson.

1910 Boy Scouts of America incorporated.

1911 First use of aircraft as offensive weapon in Turkish-Italian War. Italy defeats Turks and annexes Tripoli and Libya. Chinese Republic proclaimed after revolution overthrows Manchu dynasty. Sun Yat-sen named president. Mexican Revolution: Porfirio Diaz, president since 1877, replaced by Francisco Madero. Triangle Shirtwaist Company fire in New York; 145 killed. Richard Strauss's *Der Rosenkavalier*. Irving Berlin's *Alexander's Ragtime Band*. Amundsen reaches South Pole.

1912 Balkan Wars (**1912–13**) resulting from territorial disputes: Turkey defeated by alliance of Bulgaria, Serbia, Greece, and Montenegro; London peace treaty (**1913**) partitions most of European Turkey among the victors. In second war (**1913**), Bulgaria attacks Serbia and Greece and is defeated after Romania intervenes and Turks recapture Adrianople. *Titanic* sinks on maiden voyage; over 1,500 drown.

1913 Suffragettes demonstrate in London. Garment workers strike in New York and Boston; win pay raise and shorter hours. Sixteenth Amendment (income tax) and 17th (popular election of U.S. senators) adopted. Bill creating U.S. Federal Reserve System becomes law. Stravinsky's *The Rite of Spring*.

1914 World War I begins (*see* special material on "World War I"). Panama Canal officially opened. Congress sets up Federal Trade Commission, passes Clayton Antitrust Act. U.S. Marines occupy Veracruz, Mexico, intervening in civil war to protect American interests.

1915 U.S. protests German submarine actions and British blockade of Germany. U.S. banks lend $500 million to France and Britain. D. W. Griffith's film *Birth of a Nation*. Albert Einstein's *General Theory of Relativity*.

1916 Congress expands armed forces. Tom Mooney arrested for San Francisco bombing (pardoned in **1939**). Pershing fails in raid into Mexico in quest of

The Partition of Africa ~ 1914

EUROPE

TANGIER (Sp.)
Casablanca
MADEIRA IS. (Port.)
Algiers
TUNISIA
Tripoli
Suez Canal
CANARY IS. (Spain)
RIO DE ORO
MOROCCO
ALGERIA
LIBYA
EGYPT (Br. Protect)
Cairo
ARABIA
SAHARA
Red Sea
ERITREA
Massawa
FRENCH WEST AFRICA
ANGLO EGYPTIAN SUDAN
Khartum
Blue Nile
Adua
FR. SOMALILAND
Lake Chad
GAMBIA (Br.)
Senegal
Niger
PORT. GUINEA
NIGERIA (Br.)
FRENCH EQUATORIAL AFRICA
BR. SOMALILAND
SIERRA LEONE (Br.)
IVORY COAST
CAMEROONS (Ger.)
ETHIOPIA
ITAL. SOMALILAND
LIBERIA
GOLD COAST (Br.)
TOGOLAND (Ger.)
RIO MUNI (Sp.)
Congo R.
BELGIAN
UGANDA
BRITISH EAST AFRICA
EQUATOR
CONGO
L. Victoria Nyanza
KENYA
Mombasa
Lake Tanganyika
GERMAN EAST AFRICA
ZANZIBAR (Br.)
ANGOLA (Port.)
NYASALAND
RHODESIA
PORT. EAST AFRICA
MADAGASCAR (Fr.)
GERMAN SOUTHWEST AFRICA
BECHUANALAND
UNION OF SOUTH AFRICA
TRANSVAAL
ORANGE FREE STATE
NATAL
Capetown
CAPE COLONY

European Colonies in Africa ~ 1878

ALGERIA
SENEGAL
GAMBIA
ANGOLA
MOZAMBIQUE
CAPE COLONY

KEY

British	Italian
French	Portuguese
German	Belgian
Spanish	

Vladimir Lenin
(1870-1924)

Woodrow Wilson
(1856-1924)

rebel Pancho Villa. U.S. buys Virgin Islands from Denmark for $25 million. President Wilson re-elected with "he kept us out of war" slogan. "Black Tom" explosion at munitions dock in Jersey City, N.J., $40,000,000 damages; traced to German saboteurs. Margaret Sanger opens first birth control clinic. Easter Rebellion in Ireland put down by British troops.

1917 First U.S. combat troops in France as U.S. declares war **(April 6)**. Russian Revolution—climax of long unrest under czars. February Revolution— Czar forced to abdicate, liberal government created. Kerensky becomes prime minister and forms provisional government **(July)**. In October Revolution, Bolsheviks seize power in armed coup d'état led by Lenin and Trotsky. Kerensky flees. Revolutionaries execute the czar and his family **(1918)**. Reds set up Third International in Moscow **(1919)**. Balfour Declaration promises Jewish homeland in Palestine. Sigmund Freud's *Introduction to Psychoanalysis*.

1918 Russian Civil War between Reds (Bolsheviks) and Whites (anti-Bolsheviks); Reds win in **1920**. Allied troops (U.S., British, French) intervene **(March)**; leave in **1919**. Japanese hold Vladivostok until **1922**. World-wide influenza epidemic strikes; by **1920**, nearly 20 million are dead. In U.S. alone, 500,000 perish.

1919 Third International (Comintern) establishes Soviet control over international Communist movements. Paris peace conference. Versailles Treaty, incorporating Wilson's draft Covenant of League of Nations, signed by Allies and Germany; rejected by U.S. Senate. Congress formally ends war in **1921**. Eighteenth (Prohibition) Amendment adopted. Alcock and Brown make first trans-Atlantic non-stop flight.

1920 League of Nations holds first meeting at Geneva, Switzerland. U.S. Dept. of Justice "red hunt" nets thousands of radicals; aliens deported. Women's suffrage (19th) amendment ratified. First Agatha Christie mystery. Sinclair Lewis's *Main Street*.

1921 Reparations Commission fixes German liability at 132 billion gold marks. German inflation begins. Major treaties signed at Washington Disarmament Conference limit naval tonnage and pledge to respect territorial integrity of China. Irish Free State formed in southern Ireland as self-governing dominion of British Empire. In U.S., Nicola Sacco and Bartolomeo Vanzetti, Italian-born anarchists, convicted of armed robbery murder; case stirs world-wide protests; they are executed in **1927.**

1922 Mussolini marches on Rome; forms Fascist government. Irish Free State officially proclaimed.

1923 Adolf Hitler's "Beer Hall Putsch" in Munich fails; in **1924** he is sentenced to five years in prison where he writes *Mein Kampf;* released after eight months. Occupation of Ruhr by French and Belgian troops to enforce reparations payments. Widespread Ku Klux Klan violence in U.S. George Gershwin's *Rhapsody in Blue.*

WORLD WAR I (1914–1918)

Imperial, territorial, and economic rivalries lead to the "Great War" between the Central Powers (Austria-Hungary, Germany, Bulgaria, and Turkey) and the Allies (U.S., Britain, France, Russia, Belgium, Serbia, Greece, Rumania, Montenegro, Portugal, Italy, Japan). About 10 million combatants killed, 20 million wounded.
1914 Austrian Archduke Francis Ferdinand and wife assassinated in Sarajevo by Serbian nationalist, Gavrilo Princip **(June 28)**. Austria declares war on Serbia **(July 28)**. Germany declares war on Russia **(Aug. 1)**, on France **(Aug. 3)**, invades Belgium **(Aug. 4)**. Britain declares war on Germany **(Aug. 4)**. Germans defeat Russians in Battle of Tannenberg on Eastern Front **(Aug.)**. First Battle of the Marne **(Sept.)**. German drive stopped 25 miles from Paris. By end of year, war on the Western Front is "positional" in the trenches.
1915 German submarine blockade of Great Britain begins **(Feb.)**. Dardanelles Campaign—British land in Turkey **(April)**, withdraw from Gallipoli **(Dec. to Jan. 1916)**. Germans use gas at second Battle of Ypres **(April–May)**. *Lusitania* sunk by German submarine—1,198 lost, including 128 Americans **(May 7)**. On Eastern Front, German and Austrian "great offensive" conquers all of Poland and Lithuania; Russians lose 1 million men (by **Sept. 6**). "Great Fall Offensive" by Allies results in little change from 1914 **(Sept.–Oct.)**. Britain and France declare war on Bulgaria **(Oct. 14)**.

1916 Battle of Verdun—Germans and French each lose about 350,000 men **(Feb.)**. Extended submarine warfare begins **(March)**. British-German sea battle of Jutland **(May)**; British lose more ships, but German fleet never ventures forth again. On Eastern front, the Brusilov offensive demoralizes Russians, costs them 1 million men **(June–Sept.)**. Battle of the Somme—British lose over 400,000; French, 200,000; Germans, about 450,000; all with no strategic results **(July–Nov.)**. Romania declares war on Austria-Hungary **(Aug. 27)**. Bucharest captured **(Dec.)**.
1917 U.S. declares war on Germany **(April 6)**. Submarine warfare at peak **(April)**. On Italian Front, Battle of Caporetto—Italians retreat, losing 600,000 prisoners and deserters **(Oct.–Dec.)**. On Western Front, Battles of Arras, Champagne, Ypres (third battle), etc. First large British tank attack **(Nov.)**. U.S. declares war on Austria-Hungary **(Dec. 7)**. Armistice between new Russian Bolshevik government and Germans **(Dec. 15)**.
1918 Great offensive by Germans **(March–June)**. Americans' first important battle role at Château-Thierry—as they and French stop German advance **(June)**. Second Battle of the Marne **(July–Aug.)**—start of Allied offensive at Amiens, St. Mihiel, etc. Battles of the Argonne and Ypres panic German leadership **(Sept.–Oct.)**. British offensive in Palestine **(Sept.)**. Germans ask for armistice **(Oct. 4)**. British armistice with Turkey **(Oct.)**. German Kaiser abdicates **(Nov.)**. Hostilities cease on Western Front **(Nov. 11)**.

TERRITORIAL CHANGES
following WORLD WAR I

Territory lost
by Germany   by Russia
by Bulgaria   by Austria-Hungary

1924 Death of Lenin; Stalin wins power struggle, rules as Soviet dictator until death in **1953.** Italian Fascists murder Socialist leader Giacomo Matteotti. Interior Secretary Albert B. Fall and oilmen Harry Sinclair and Edward L. Doheny are charged with conspiracy and bribery in the Teapot Dome scandal, involving fraudulent leases of naval oil reserves. In **1931,** Fall is sentenced to year in prison; Doheny and Sinclair acquitted of bribery. Nathan

**Charles A. Linbergh
(1902-1974)**

**Herbert Hoover
(1874-1964)**

Leopold and Richard Loeb convicted in "thrill killing" of Bobby Franks in Chicago; defended by Clarence Darrow; sentenced to life imprisonment. (Loeb killed by fellow convict in **1936;** Leopold paroled in **1958,** dies in **1971.**)

1925 Nellie Tayloe Ross elected governor of Wyoming; first woman governor elected in U.S. Locarno conferences seek to secure European peace by mutual guarantees. John T. Scopes convicted and fined for teaching evolution in a public school in Tennessee "Monkey Trial"; sentence set aside. John Logie Baird, Scottish inventor, transmits human features by television. Adolf Hitler publishes Volume I of *Mein Kampf.*

1926 General strike in Britain brings nation's activities to standstill. U.S. marines dispatched to Nicaragua during revolt; they remain until **1933.** Gertrude Ederle of U.S. is first woman to swim English Channel.

1927 German economy collapses. Socialists riot in Vienna; general strike follows acquittal of Nazis for political murder. Trotsky expelled from Russian Communist Party. Charles A. Lindbergh flies first successful solo non-stop flight from New York to Paris. Ruth Snyder and Judd Gray convicted of murder of Albert Snyder; they are executed at Sing Sing prison in **1928.** *The Jazz Singer,* with Al Jolson, first part-talking motion picture.

1928 Kellogg-Briand Pact, outlawing war, signed in Paris by 65 nations. Alexander Fleming discovers penicillin. Richard E. Byrd starts expedition to Antarctic; returns in **1930.**

1929 Trotsky expelled from U.S.S.R. Lateran Treaty establishes independent Vatican City. In U.S., stock market prices collapse, with U.S. securities losing $26 billion—first phase of Depression and world economic crisis. St. Valentine's Day gangland massacre in Chicago.

1930 Britain, U.S., Japan, France, and Italy sign naval disarmament treaty. Nazis gain in German elections. Cyclotron developed by Ernest O. Lawrence, U.S. physicist.

1931 Spain becomes a republic with overthrow of King Alfonso XIII. German industrialists finance 800,000-strong Nazi party. British parliament enacts statute of Westminster, legalizing dominion equality with Britain. Mukden Incident begins Japanese occupation of Manchuria. In U.S., Hoover proposes one-year moratorium on war debts. Harold C. Urey discovers heavy hydrogen. Gangster Al Capone sentenced to 11 years in prison for tax evasion (freed in **1939;** dies in **1947).**

1932 Nazis lead in German elections with 230 Reichstag seats. Famine in U.S.S.R. In U.S., Congress sets up Reconstruction Finance Corporation to stimulate economy. Veterans march on Washington—most leave after Senate rejects payment of cash bonuses; others removed by troops under Douglas MacArthur. U.S. protests Japanese aggression in Manchuria. Amelia Earhart is first woman to fly Atlantic solo. Charles A. Lindbergh's baby son kidnapped, killed. (Bruno Richard Hauptmann arrested in **1934,** convicted in **1935,** executed in **1936.)**

1933 Hitler appointed German chancellor, gets dictatorial powers. Reichstag fire in Berlin; Nazi terror begins. (*See* special material on "The Holocaust.") Germany and Japan withdraw from League of Nations. Giuseppe Zangara executed for attempted assassination of President-elect Roosevelt in which

---

THE HOLOCAUST (1933–1945)

"Holocaust" is the term describing the Nazi annihilation of about 6 million Jews (two thirds of the pre-World War II European Jewish population), including 4,500,000 from Russia, Poland, and the Baltic; 750,000 from Hungary and Romania; 290,000 from Germany and Austria; 105,000 from The Netherlands; 90,000 from France; 54,000 from Greece, etc.

The Holocaust was unique in its being *genocide*—the systematic destruction of a people solely because of religion, race, ethnicity, nationality, or homosexuality—on an unmatched scale. Along with the Jews, another 9 to 10 million people—Gypsies, Slavs (Poles, Ukrainians, and Belorussians)—were exterminated.

The only comparable act of genocide in modern times was launched in April 1915, when an estimated 600,000 Armenians were massacred by the Turks.

1933 Hitler named German Chancellor (**Jan.**). Dachau, first concentration camp, established (**March**). Boycotts against Jews begin (**April**).
1935 Anti-Semitic Nuremberg Laws passed by Reichstag (**Sept.**).

1937 Buchenwald concentration camp opens (**July**).
1938 Extension of anti-Semitic laws to Austria after annexation (**March**). *Kristallnacht* (Night of Broken Glass)—anti-Semitic riots in Germany and Austria (**Nov. 9**). 26,000 Jews sent to concentration camps; Jewish children expelled from schools (**Nov.**). Expropriation of Jewish property and businesses (**Dec.**).
1940 As war continues, Nazi acts against Jews extended to German-conquered areas.
1941 Deportation of German Jews begins; massacres of Jews in Odessa and Kiev—68,000 killed (**Nov.**); in Riga and Vilna—almost 60,000 killed (**Dec.**).
1942 Unified Jewish resistance in ghettos begins (**Jan.**). 300,000 Jews from Warsaw Ghetto deported to Treblinka death camp (**July**).
1943 Warsaw Ghetto uprisings (**Jan. and April**); Ghetto exterminated (**May**).
1944 476,000 Hungarian Jews sent to Auschwitz (**May–June**). D-day (**June 6**). Soviet Army liberates Maidanek death camp (**July**). Nazis try to hide evidence of death camps (**Nov.**).
1945 Americans liberate Buchenwald and British liberate Bergen-Belsen camps (**April**). Nuremberg War Crimes Trial (**Nov. 1945 to Oct. 1946**).

The German Attack on Soviet Russia, 1941-1943

Axis occupied areas and Finland, June 22, 41
Russian areas held by Axis-Apr. 15, '43
Retaken by Russia after Nov. 19, '42
(185,300 sq. miles)

Arctic Ocean

Murmansk

SWEDEN

FINLAND

White Sea

Archangel

Vieuru

Lake Ladoga

Leningrad

Vologda

Sverdlovsk

Baltic Sea

ESTONIA

Novgorod

L. Ilmen

Kalinin

Dmitrov

Gorki

Kazan

Ufa

Riga

LATVIA

Velikiye Luki

Mozhaisk

MOSCOW

LITHUANIA

Vilna

Vitebsk

Vyazma

Ryazan

Kuibyshev

Minsk

Smolensk

Bialystok

BATTLE LINE as of APRIL 15, 1943

Tula

Michurinsk

POLAND

Brest-Litovsk

Dnieper

Orel

Kursk

Voronezh

Saratov

Volga

BATTLE LINE as of NOV. 19, 1942

Zhitomir

Kiev

Kharkov

Tarnopol

RETAKEN by AXIS

Stalingrad

Dniepropetrovsk

Stalino

Taganrog

Rostov

Astrakhan

Odessa

Kerch

CRIMEA

Sevastopol

Novorossiisk

Maikop

Grozny

Tuapse

Makhach Kala

ROUMANIA

Black Sea

Caspian Sea

BULGARIA

Istanbul

Batum

Tiflis

Baku

DARDANELLES

TURKEY

IRAN

The Pacific Theater of War 1941~1945

Japanese territory 1942

Area retained by Japan after World War II

Allied drives, 1942–45

Chicago Mayor Cermak is fatally shot. Roosevelt inaugurated ("the only thing we have to fear is fear itself"); launches New Deal. Prohibition repealed. U.S.S.R. recognized by U.S.

1934 Chancellor Dollfuss of Austria assassinated by Nazis. Hitler becomes Führer. U.S.S.R. admitted to League of Nations. Dionne sisters, first quintuplets to survive beyond infancy, born in Canada.

1935 Saar incorporated into Germany after plebiscite. Nazis repudiate Versailles Treaty, introduce compulsory military service. Mussolini invades Ethiopia; League of Nations invokes sanctions. Roosevelt opens second phase of New Deal in U.S., calling for social security, better housing, equitable taxation, and farm assistance. Huey Long assassinated in Louisiana

1936 Germans occupy Rhineland. Italy annexes Ethiopia. Rome-Berlin Axis proclaimed (Japan to join in **1940**). Trotsky exiled to Mexico. King George V dies; succeeded by son, Edward VIII, who soon abdicated to marry American-born divorcée, and is succeeded by brother, George VI. Spanish civil war begins. (Franco's fascist forces defeat Loyalist forces by **1939**, when Madrid falls.) War between China and Japan begins, to continue through World War II. Japan and Germany sign anti-Comintern pact; joined by Italy in **1937**.

**Amelia Earhart
(1898-1937)**

1937 Hitler repudiates war guilt clause of Versailles Treaty; continues to build German power. Italy withdraws from League of Nations. U.S. gunboat *Panay* sunk by Japanese in Yangtze River. Japan invades China, conquers most of coastal area. Amelia Earhart lost somewhere in Pacific on round-the-world flight.

1938 Hitler marches into Austria; political and geographical union of Germany and Austria proclaimed. Munich Pact—Britain, France, and Italy agree to let Germany partition Czechoslovakia. Douglas "Wrong-Way" Corrigan flies from New York to Dublin.

1939 Germany occupies Bohemia and Moravia; renounces pacts with Poland and England and concludes 10-year non-aggression pact with U.S.S.R. Russo-Finnish War begins; Finns to lose one-tenth of territory in **1940** peace treaty. World War II begins (*see* special material on "World War II"). In U.S., Roosevelt submits $1,319-million defense budget, proclaims U.S. neutrality, and declares limited emergency. Einstein writes FDR about feasibility of atomic bomb. New York World's Fair opens.

1940 Trotsky assassinated in Mexico. Estonia, Latvia, and Lithuania annexed by U.S.S.R. U.S. trades 50 destroyers for leases on British bases in Western Hemisphere. Selective Service Act signed.

WORLD WAR II (1939–1945)

Axis powers (Germany, Italy, Japan, Hungary, Romania, Bulgaria) vs. Allies (U.S., Britain, France, U.S.S.R., Australia, Belgium, Brazil, Canada, China, Denmark, Greece, Netherlands, New Zealand, Norway, Poland, South Africa, Yugoslavia).

1939 Germany invades Poland and annexes Danzig; Britain and France give Hitler ultimatum **(Sept. 1)**, declare war **(Sept. 3)**. Disabled German pocket battleship *Admiral Graf Spee* blown up off Montevideo, Uruguay, on Hitler's orders **(Dec. 17)**. Limited activity ("Sitzkrieg") on Western Front.

1940 Nazis invade Netherlands, Belgium, and Luxembourg **(May 10)**. Chamberlain resigns as Prime Minister; Churchill takes over **(May 10)**. Germans cross French frontier **(May 12)** using air/tank/infantry "Blitzkrieg" tactics. Dunkerque evacuation—about 335,000 out of 400,000 Allied soldiers rescued from Belgium by British civilian and naval craft **(May 26–June 3)**. Italy declares war on France and Britain; invades France **(June 10)**. Germans enter Paris; city undefended **(June 14)**. France and Germany sign armistice at Compiègne **(June 22)**. Nazis bomb Coventry, England **(Nov. 14)**.

1941 Germans launch attacks in Balkans. Yugoslavia surrenders—General Mihajlovic continues guerrilla warfare; Tito leads left-wing guerrillas **(April 17)**. Nazi tanks enter Athens; remnants of British Army quit Greece **(April 27)**. Hitler attacks Russia **(June 22)**. Atlantic Charter—FDR and Churchill agree on war aims **(Aug. 14)**. Japanese attacks on Pearl Harbor, Philippines, Guam force U.S. into war; U.S. Pacific fleet crippled **(Dec. 7)**. U.S. and Britain declare war on Japan. Germany and Italy declare war on U.S.; Congress declares war on those countries **(Dec. 11)**.

1942 British surrender Singapore to Japanese **(Feb. 15)**. U.S. forces on Bataan peninsula in Philippines surrender **(April 9)**. U.S. and Filipino troops on Corregidor island in Manila Bay surrender to Japanese **(May 6)**. Village of Lidice in Czechoslovakia razed by Nazis **(June 10)**. U.S. and

Britain land in French North Africa **(Nov. 8)**.

1943 Casablanca Conference—Churchill and FDR agree on unconditional surrender goal **(Jan. 14–24)**. German 6th Army surrenders at Stalingrad—turning point of war in Russia **(Feb. 1–2)**. Remnants of Nazis trapped on Cape Bon, ending war in Africa **(May 12)**. Mussolini deposed; Badoglio named premier **(July 25)**. Allied troops land on Italian mainland after conquest of Sicily **(Sept. 3)**. Italy surrenders **(Sept. 8)**. Nazis seize Rome **(Sept. 10)**. Cairo Conference: FDR, Churchill, Chiang Kai-shek pledge defeat of Japan, free Korea **(Nov. 22–26)**. Teheran Conference: FDR, Churchill, Stalin agree on invasion plans **(Nov. 28–Dec. 1)**.

1944 U.S. and British troops land at Anzio on west Italian coast and hold beachhead **(Jan. 22)**. U.S. and British troops enter Rome **(June 4)**. D-Day—Allies launch Normandy invasion **(June 6)**. Hitler wounded in bomb plot **(July 20)**. Paris liberated **(Aug. 25)**. Athens freed by Allies **(Oct. 13)**. Americans invade Philippines **(Oct. 20)**. Germans launch counteroffensive in Belgium—Battle of Bulge **(Dec. 16)**.

1945 Yalta Agreement signed by FDR, Churchill, Stalin—establishes basis for occupation of Germany, returns to Soviet Union lands taken by Germany and Japan; U.S.S.R. agrees to friendship pact with China **(Feb. 11)**. Mussolini killed at Lake Como **(April 28)**. Admiral Doenitz takes command in Germany; suicide of Hitler announced **(May 1)**. Berlin falls **(May 2)**. V-E Day—Germany signs unconditional surrender terms at Rheims **(May 7)**. Potsdam Conference—Truman, Churchill, Atlee (after July 28), Stalin establish council of foreign ministers to prepare peace treaties; plan German postwar government and reparations **(July 17–Aug. 2)**. A-bomb blasts Hiroshima **(Aug. 6)**. U.S.S.R. declares war on Japan **(Aug. 8)**. Nagasaki hit by A-bomb **(Aug. 9)**. Japan surrenders **(Aug. 14)**. V-J Day—Japanese sign surrender terms aboard battleship *Missouri* **(Sept. 2)**.

D-Day, June 6, 1944

**Winston Churchill,
Franklin D. Roosevelt,
and Joseph V. Stalin
at Yalta**

**Harry S. Truman
(1884-1972)**

1941 Japanese surprise attack on U.S. fleet at Pearl Harbor brings U.S. into World War II. Manhattan Project (atomic bomb research) begins. Roosevelt enunciates "four freedoms," signs lend-lease act, declares national emergency, promises aid to U.S.S.R.

1942 Declaration of United Nations signed in Washington. Women's military services established. Enrico Fermi achieves nuclear chain reaction. Japanese and persons of Japanese ancestry moved inland from Pacific Coast. Coconut Grove nightclub fire in Boston kills 491.

1943 President freezes prices, salaries, and wages to prevent inflation. Income tax withholding introduced.

1944 G.I. Bill of Rights enacted. Bretton Woods Conference creates International Monetary Fund and World Bank. Dumbarton Oaks Conference—U.S., British Commonwealth, and U.S.S.R. propose establishment of United Nations.

1945 Yalta Conference (Roosevelt, Churchill, Stalin) plans final defeat of Germany **(Feb.)**. Germany surrenders **(May 7)**. San Francisco Conference establishes U.N. **(April–June)**. FDR dies (April 12). Potsdam Conference (Truman, Churchill, Stalin) establishes basis of German reconstruction **(July–Aug)**. Japan signs surrender **(Sept. 2)**.

1946 First meeting of U.N. General Assembly opens in London **(Jan. 10)**. League of Nations dissolved **(April)**. Italy abolishes monarchy **(June)**. Verdict in Nuremberg war trial: 12 Nazi leaders (including 1 tried in absentia) sentenced to hang; 7 imprisoned; 3 acquitted **(Oct. 1)**. Goering commits suicide a few hours before 10 other Nazis are executed **(Oct. 15)**. Winston Churchill's "Iron Curtain" speech warns of Soviet expansion.

1947 Britain nationalizes coal mines **(Jan. 1)**. Peace treaties for Italy, Romania, Bulgaria, Hungary, Finland signed in Paris **(Feb. 10)**. Soviet Union rejects U.S. plan for U.N. atomic-energy control **(March 4)**. Truman Doctrine proposed—the first significant U.S. attempt to "contain" communist expansion **(March 12)**. Marshall Plan for European recovery proposed—a coordinated program to help European nations recover from ravages of war **(June)**. (By **1951**, this "European Recovery Program" had cost $11 billion.) India and Pakistan gain independence from Britain **(Aug. 15)**. Cominform (Communist Information Bureau) founded under Soviet auspices to rebuild contacts among European Communist parties, missing since dissolution of Comintern in **1943 (Sept.)**. (Yugoslav party expelled in **1948** and Cominform disbanded in **1956**.)

1948 Gandhi assassinated in New Delhi by Hindu fanatic **(Jan. 30)**. Communists seize power in Czechoslovakia **(Feb. 23–25)**. Burma and Ceylon granted independence by Britain. Organization of American States (OAS) Charter signed at Bogotá, Colombia **(April 30)**. Nation of Israel proclaimed; British end Mandate at midnight; Arab armies attack **(May 14)**. Berlin airlift begins **(June 21)**; ends **May 12, 1949**. Stalin and Tito break **(June 28)**. Independent Republic of Korea is proclaimed, following election supervised by U.N. **(Aug. 15)**. Verdict in Japanese war trial: Tojo and six others sentenced to hang (hanged Dec. 23); 18 imprisoned **(Nov. 12)**. United States of Indonesia established as Dutch and Indonesians settled conflict **(Dec. 27)**. Alger Hiss, former U.S. State Department official, indicted on perjury charges after denying passing secret documents to communist spy ring. Convicted in second trial **(1950)** and sentenced to five-year prison term.

1949 Cease-fire in Palestine **(Jan. 7)**. Truman proposes Point Four Program to help world's backward areas **(Jan. 20)**. Israel signs armistice with Egypt **(Feb. 24)**. Start of North Atlantic Treaty Organization (NATO)—treaty signed by 12 nations **(April 4)**. German Federal Republic (West Germany) established **(Sept. 21)**. Truman discloses Soviet Union has set off atomic explosion **(Sept. 23)**. Communist People's Republic of China formally proclaimed by Chairman Mao Zedong. **(Oct. 1)**.

1950 Truman orders development of hydrogen bomb **(Jan. 31)**. Korean War (*see special material on the "Korean War"*). Assassination attempt on President Truman by Puerto Rican nationalists **(Nov. 1)**. Brink's robbery in Boston; almost $3 million stolen **(Jan. 17)**.

KOREAN WAR (1950–1953)

1950 North Korean Communist forces invade South Korea (June 25). U.N. calls for cease-fire and asks U.N. members to assist South Korea (June 27). Truman orders U.S. forces into Korea (June 27). North Koreans capture Seoul (June 28). Gen. Douglas MacArthur designated commander of unified U.N. forces (July 8). Pusan Beachhead—U.N. forces counterattack and capture Seoul (Aug.–Sept.), capture Pyongyang, North Korean capital (Oct.). Chinese Communists enter war (Oct. 26), force U.N. retreat toward 39th parallel (Dec.).

1951 Gen. Matthew B. Ridgeway replaces MacArthur after he threatens Chinese with massive retaliation (April 11). Armistice negotiations (July) continue with interruptions until June 1953.

1953 Armistice signed (June 26). Chinese troops withdraw from North Korea (Oct. 26, 1958), but over 200 violations of armistice noted to 1959.

1951 Six nations agree to Schuman Plan to pool European coal and steel **(March 19)**—in effect **Feb. 10, 1953.** Julius and Ethel Rosenberg sentenced to death for passing atomic secrets to Russians **(March).** Japanese peace treaty signed in San Francisco by 49 nations **(Sept. 8).** Color television introduced in U.S.

1952 George VI dies; his daughter becomes Elizabeth II **(Feb. 6).** NATO conference approves European army **(Feb.).** AEC announces "satisfactory" experiments in hydrogen-weapons research; eyewitnesses tell of blasts near Enewetak **(Nov.).**

1953 Gen. Dwight D. Eisenhower inaugurated President of United States **(Jan. 20).** Stalin dies **(March 5).** Malenkov becomes Soviet Premier; Beria, Minister of Interior; Molotov, Foreign Minister **(March 6).** Dag Hammarskjold begins term as U.N. Secretary-General **(April 10).** Edmund Hillary, of New Zealand, and Tenzing Norkay, of Nepal, reach top of Mt. Everest **(May 29).** East Berliners rise against Communist rule; quelled by tanks **(June 17).** Egypt becomes republic ruled by military junta **(June 18).** Julius and Ethel Rosenberg executed in Sing Sing prison **(June 19).** Korean armistice signed **(July 27).** Moscow announces explosion of hydrogen bomb **(Aug. 20).**

1954 First atomic submarine *Nautilus,* launched **(Jan. 21).** Five U.S. Congressmen shot on floor of House as Puerto Rican nationalists fire from spectators' gallery; all five recover **(March 1).** Army *vs.* McCarthy inquiry—Senate subcommittee report blames both sides **(Apr. 22–June 17).** Dien Bien Phu, French military outpost in Vietnam, falls to Vietminh army **(May 7).** (*see* special material on the "Vietnam War.") U.S. Supreme Court (in *Brown* v. *Board of Education of Topeka*) unanimously bans racial segregation in public schools **(May 17).** Eisenhower launches world atomic pool without Soviet Union **(Sept. 6).** Eight-nation Southeast Asia defense treaty (SEATO) signed at Manila **(Sept. 8).** West Germany is granted sovereignty, admitted to NATO and Western European Union **(Oct. 23).** Dr. Jonas Salk starts innoculating children against polio. Algerian War of Independence against France begins **(Nov.)**; France struggles to maintain colonial rule until 1962 when it agrees to Algeria's independence.

1955 Nikolai A. Bulganin becomes Soviet Premier, replacing Malenkov **(Feb. 8).** Churchill resigns; Anthony Eden succeeds him **(April 6).** Federal Republic of West Germany becomes a sovereign state **(May 5).** Warsaw Pact,

Dwight D. Eisenhower
(1890-1969)

Joseph Stalin
(1879-1953)

VIETNAM WAR (1950–1975)

U.S., South Vietnam, and Allies versus North Vietnam and National Liberation Front (Viet Cong). Outstanding events:

1950 President Truman sends 35-man military advisory group to aid French fighting to maintain colonial power in Vietnam.

1954 After defeat of French at Dienbienphu, Geneva Agreements **(July)** provide for withdrawal of French and Vietminh to either side of demarcation zone (DMZ) pending reunification elections, which are never held. Presidents Eisenhower and Kennedy (from **1954** onward) send civilian advisors and, later, military personnel to train South Vietnamese.

1960 Communists from National Liberation Front in South.

1963 Ngo Dinh Diem, South Vietnam's premier, slain in coup **(Nov. 1).**

1961–1963 U.S. military advisors rise from 2,000 to 15,000.

1964 North Vietnamese torpedo boats reportedly attack U.S. destroyers in Gulf of Tonkin **(Aug. 2).** President Johnson orders retaliatory air strikes. Congress approves Gulf of Tonkin resolution **(Aug. 7)** authorizing President to take necessary steps to "maintain peace."

1965 U.S. planes begin combat missions over South Vietnam. In area, 23,000 American advisors committed to combat. By end of year over 184,000 U.S. troops in area.

1966 B-52s bomb DMZ, reportedly used by North Vietnam for entry into South **(July 31).**

1967 South Vietnam National Assembly approves election of Nguyen Van Thieu as President **(Oct. 21).**

1968 U.S. has almost 525,000 men in Vietnam. In Tet offensive **(Jan.–Feb.),** Viet Cong guerrillas attack Saigon, Hue, and some provincial capitals. President Johnson orders halt to U.S. bombardment of North Vietnam **(Oct. 31).** Saigon and N.L.F. join U.S. and North Vietnam in Paris peace talks.

1969 President Nixon announces Vietnam peace offer

(May 14)—begins troop withdrawals **(June).** Viet Cong forms Provisional Revolutionary Government. U.S. Senate calls for curb on commitments **(June 25).** Ho Chi Minh, 79, North Vietnam president, dies **(Sept. 3);** collective leadership chosen. Some 6,000 U.S. troops pulled back from Thailand and 1,000 marines from Vietnam (announced **Sept. 30).** Massive demonstrations in U.S. protest or support war policies **(Oct. 15).**

1970 Nixon announces sending of troops to Cambodia **(April 30).** Last U.S. troops removed from Cambodia **(June 29).**

1971 Congress bars use of combat troops, but not air power, in Laos and Cambodia **(Jan. 1).** South Vietnamese troops, with U.S. air cover, fail in Laos thrust. Many American ground forces withdrawn from Vietnam combat. *New York Times* publishes Pentagon papers, classified material on expansion of war **(June).**

1972 Nixon responds to North Vietnamese drive across DMZ by ordering mining of North Vietnam ports and heavy bombing of Hanoi-Haiphong area **(April 1).** Nixon orders "Christmas bombing" of north to get North Vietnamese back to conference table **(Dec.).**

1973 President orders halt to offensive operations in North Vietnam **(Jan. 15).** Representatives of North and South Vietnam, U.S., and N.L.F. sign peace pacts in Paris, ending longest war in U.S. history **(Jan. 27).** Last American troops departed in their entirety **(March 29).**

1974 Both sides accuse each other of frequent violations of cease-fire agreement.

1975 Full-scale warfare resumes. Communists victorious **(April 30).** South Vietnam Premier Nguyen Van Thieu resigns **(April 21).** U.S. Marine Embassy guards and U.S. civilians and dependents evacuated **(April 30).** More than 140,000 Vietnamese refugees leave by air and sea, many to settle in U.S. Provisional Revolutionary Government takes control **(June 6).**

1976 Election of National Assembly paves way for reunification of North and South.

**Yuri A. Gagarin
(1934-1968)**

**Fidel Castro
(Aug. 13, 1926)**

east European mutual defense agreement, signed **(May 14).** Argentina ousts Perón **(Sept. 19).** President Eisenhower suffers coronary thrombosis in Denver **(Sept. 24).** Martin Luther King, Jr., leads black boycott of Montgomery, Ala., bus system **(Dec. 1);** desegregated service begun **(Dec. 21).** AFL and CIO become one organization—AFL-CIO **(Dec. 5).**

1956 Nikita Khrushchev, First Secretary of U.S.S.R. Communist Party, denounces Stalin's excesses **(Feb. 24).** First aerial H-bomb tested over Namu islet, Bikini Atoll—10 million tons TNT equivalent **(May 21).** Worker's uprising against Communist rule in Poznan, Poland, is crushed **(June 28–30).** Egypt takes control of Suez Canal **(July 26).** Israel launches attack on Egypt's Sinai peninsula and drives toward Suez Canal **(Oct. 29).** British and French invade Egypt at Port Said **(Nov. 5).** Cease-fire forced by U.S. pressure stops British, French, and Israeli advance **(Nov. 6).** Revolt starts in Hungary—Soviet troops and tanks crush anti-Communist rebellion **(Nov.).**

1957 Eisenhower Doctrine calls for aid to Mideast countries which resist armed aggression from Communist-controlled nations **(Jan. 5).** Eisenhower sends troops to Little Rock, Ark., to quell mob and protect school integration **(Sept. 24).** Russians launch *Sputnik I,* first earth-orbiting satellite—the Space Age begins **(Oct. 4).**

1958 Army's Jupiter-C rocket fires first U.S. earth satellite, *Explorer I,* into orbit **(Jan. 31).** Egypt and Syria merge into United Arab Republic **(Feb. 1).** European Economic Community (Common Market) established by Rome Treaty becomes effective **Jan. 1, 1958.** Khrushchev becomes Premier of Soviet Union as Bulganin resigns **(Mar. 27).** Gen. Charles de Gaulle becomes French premier **(June 1),** remaining in power until **1969.** New French constitution adopted **(Sept. 28),** de Gaulle elected president of 5th Republic **(Dec. 21).** Eisenhower orders U.S. Marines into Lebanon at request of President Chamoun, who fears overthrow **(July 15).**

1959 Cuban President Batista resigns and flees—Castro takes over **(Jan. 1).** Tibet's Dalai Lama escapes to India **(Mar. 31).** St. Lawrence Seaway opens, allowing ocean ships to reach Midwest **(April 25).**

1960 American U-2 spy plane, piloted by Francis Gary Powers, shot down over Russia **(May 1).** Khrushchev kills Paris summit conference because of U-2 **(May 16).** Powers sentenced to prison for 10 years **(Aug. 19)**—freed in **February 1962** in exchange for Soviet spy. Top Nazi murderer of Jews, Adolf Eichmann, captured by Israelis in Argentina **(May 23)**—executed in Israel in **1962.** Communist China and Soviet Union split in conflict over Communist ideology. Belgium starts to break up its African colonial empire, gives independence to Belgian Congo (Zaire) on **June 30.** Cuba begins confiscation of $770 million of U.S. property **(Aug. 7).**

1961 U.S. breaks diplomatic relations with Cuba **(Jan. 3).** John F. Kennedy inaugurated President of U.S. **(Jan. 20).** Kennedy proposes Alliance for Progress—10-year plan to raise Latin American living standards **(Mar. 13).** Moscow announces putting first man in orbit around earth, Maj. Yuri A. Gagarin **(April 12).** Cuba invaded at Bay of Pigs by an estimated 1,200 anti-Castro exiles aided by U.S.; invasion crushed **(April 17).** First U.S. spaceman, Navy Cmdr. Alan B. Shepard, Jr., rockets 116.5 miles up in 302-mile trip **(May 5).** Virgil Grissom becomes second American astronaut, making 118-mile-high, 303-mile-long rocket flight over Atlantic **(July 21).** Gherman Stepanovich Titov is launched in Soviet spaceship *Vostok II:* makes 17 1/2 orbits in 25 hours, covering 434,960 miles before landing safely **(Aug. 6).** East Germans erect Berlin Wall between East and West Berlin to halt flood of refugees **(Aug. 13).** U.S.S.R. fires 50-megaton hydrogen bomb, biggest explosion in history **(Oct. 29).**

1962 Lt. Col. John H. Glenn, Jr., is first American to orbit earth—three times in 4 hr 55 min **(Feb. 20).** Adolf Eichmann hanged in Israel for his part in Nazi extermination of six million Jews **(May 31).** France transfers sovereignty to new republic of Algeria **(July 3).** Cuban missile crisis—U.S.S.R. to build missile bases in Cuba; Kennedy orders Cuban blockade, lifts blockade after Russians back down **(Aug.-Nov.).** James H. Meredith, escorted by Federal marshals, registers in University of Mississippi **(Oct. 1).** Pope John XXIII opens Second Vatican Council (Oct. 11)—Council holds four sessions, finally closing Dec. 8, 1965. Cuba releases 1,113 prisoners of 1961 invasion attempt **(Dec. 24).**

1963 France and West Germany sign treaty of cooperation ending four centuries of conflict **(Jan. 22).** Pope John XXIII dies **(June 3)**—succeeded June 21 by Cardinal Montini, who becomes Paul VI. U.S. Supreme Court rules no locality may require recitation of Lord's Prayer or Bible verses in public schools **(June 17).** Civil rights rally held by 200,000 blacks and whites in Washington, D.C. **(Aug. 28).** Washington-to-Moscow "hot line" communications link opens, designed to reduce risk of accidental war **(Aug. 30).** President Kennedy shot and killed by sniper in Dallas, Tex. Lyndon B.

Johnson becomes President same day **(Nov. 22)**. Lee Harvey Oswald, accused assassin of President Kennedy, is shot and killed by Jack Ruby, Dallas nightclub owner **(Nov. 24)**.

1964 U.S. Supreme Court rules that Congressional districts should be roughly equal in population **(Feb. 17)**. Jack Ruby convicted of murder in slaying of Lee Harvey Oswald; sentenced to death by Dallas jury **(March 14)**—conviction reversed **Oct. 5, 1966;** Ruby dies **Jan. 3, 1967,** before second trial can be held. Three civil rights workers—Schwerner, Goodman, and Cheney—murdered in Mississippi **(June)**. Twenty-one arrests result in trial and conviction of seven by Federal jury. President's Commission on the Assassination of President Kennedy issues Warren Report concluding that Lee Harvey Oswald acted alone.

1965 Rev. Dr. Martin Luther King, Jr., and more than 2,600 other blacks arrested in Selma, Ala., during three-day demonstrations against voter-registration rules **(Feb. 1)**. Malcolm X, black-nationalist leader, shot to death at Harlem rally in New York City **(Feb. 21)**. U.S. Marines land in Dominican Republic as fighting persists between rebels and Dominican army **(April 28)**. Medicare, senior citizens' government medical assistance program, begins **(July 1)**. Blacks riot for six days in Watts section of Los Angeles: 34 dead, over 1,000 injured, nearly 4,000 arrested, fire damage put at $175 million **(Aug. 11-16)**. Power failure in Ontario plant blacks out parts of eight northeastern states of U.S. and two provinces of southeastern Canada **(Nov. 9)**.

1966 Black teen-agers riot in Watts, Los Angeles; two men killed and at least 25 injured **(March 15)**. Michael E. De Bakey implants artificial heart in human for first time at Houston hospital; plastic device functions and patient lives **(April 21)**.

1967 Three Apollo astronauts—Col. Virgil I. Grissom, Col. Edward White II, and Lt. Cmdr. Roger B. Chaffee—killed in spacecraft fire during simulated launch **(Jan. 27)**. Israeli and Arab forces battle; six-day war ends with Israel occupying Sinai Peninsula, Golan Heights, Gaza Strip, and east bank of Suez Canal **(June 5)**. Red China announces explosion of its first hydrogen bomb **(June 17)**. Racial violence in Detroit; 7,000 National Guardsmen aid police after night of rioting. Similar outbreaks occur in New York City's Spanish Harlem, Rochester, N.Y., Birmingham, Ala., and New Britain, Conn. **(July 23)**. Thurgood Marshall sworn in as first black U.S. Supreme Court justice **(Oct. 2)**. Dr. Christiaan N. Barnard and team of South African surgeons perform world's first successful human heart transplant **(Dec. 3)**—patient dies 18 days later.

1968 North Korea seizes U.S. Navy ship *Pueblo;* holds 83 on board as spies **(Jan. 23)**. President Johnson announces he will not seek or accept presidential renomination **(March 31)**. Martin Luther King, Jr., civil rights leader, is slain in Memphis **(April 4)**—James Earl Ray, indicted in murder, captured in London on **June 8. In 1969** Ray pleads guilty and is sentenced to 99 years. Sen. Robert F. Kennedy is shot and critically wounded in Los Angeles hotel after winning California primary **(June 5)**—dies **June 6.** Sirhan B. Sirhan convicted **1969.** Czechoslovakia is invaded by Russians and Warsaw Pact forces to crush liberal regime **(Aug. 20)**.

1969 Richard M. Nixon is inaugurated 37th President of the U.S. **(Jan. 20)**. Apollo 11 astronauts—Neil A. Armstrong, Edwin E. Aldrin, Jr., and Michael Collins—take man's first walk on moon **(July 20)**. Sen. Edward M. Kennedy pleads guilty to leaving scene of fatal accident at Chappaquiddick, Mass. **(July 18)** in which Mary Jo Kopechne was drowned—gets two-month suspended sentence **(July 25)**.

1970 Biafra surrenders after 32-month fight for independence from Nigeria **(Jan. 12)**. Rhodesia severs last tie with British Crown and declares itself a racially segregated republic **(March 1)**. Four students at Kent State University in Ohio slain by National Guardsmen at demonstration protesting April 30 incursion into Cambodia **(May 4)**. Senate repeals Gulf of Tonkin resolution **(June 24)**.

1971 Supreme Court rules unanimously that busing of students may be ordered to achieve racial desegregation **(April 20)**. Anti-war militants attempt to disrupt government business in Washington **(May 3)**—police and military units arrest as many as 12,000; most are later released. Twenty-sixth Amendment to U.S. Constitution lowers voting age to 18. U.N. seats Communist China and expels Nationalist China **(Oct. 25)**.

1972 President Nixon makes unprecedented eight-day visit to Communist China **(Feb.)**. Britain takes over direct rule of Northern Ireland in bid for peace **(March 24)**. Gov. George C. Wallace of Alabama is shot by Arthur H. Bremer at Laurel, Md., political rally **(May 15)**. Five men are apprehended by police in attempt to bug Democratic National Committee headquarters in Washington D.C.'s Watergate complex—start of the Watergate scandal **(June 17)**. Supreme Court rules that death penalty is unconstitutional

John F. Kennedy
(1917-1963)

Lyndon B. Johnson
(1908-1973)

Richard M. Nixon
(1913–1994)

(**June 29**). Eleven Israeli athletes at Olympic Games in Munich are killed after eight members of an Arab terrorist group invade Olympic Village; five guerrillas and one policeman are also killed (**Sept. 5**).

1973 Great Britain, Ireland, and Denmark enter European Common Market (**Jan. 1**). Nixon, on national TV, accepts responsibility, but not blame, for Watergate; accepts resignations of advisers H. R. Haldeman and John D. Ehrlichman, fires John W. Dean III as counsel. (**April 30**). Greek military junta abolishes monarchy and proclaims republic (**June 1**). U.S. bombing of Cambodia ends, marking official halt to 12 years of combat activity in Southeast Asia (**Aug. 15**). Fourth and biggest Arab-Israeli War begins as Egyptian and Syrian forces attack Israel as Jews mark Yom Kippur, holiest day in their calendar. (**Oct. 6**). Spiro T. Agnew resigns as Vice President and then, in Federal Court in Baltimore, pleads no contest to charges of evasion of income taxes on $29,500 he received in 1967, while Governor of Maryland. He is fined $10,000 and put on three years' probation (**Oct. 10**). In the "Saturday Night Massacre," Nixon fires special Watergate prosecutor Archibald Cox and Deputy Attorney General William D. Ruckelshaus; Attorney General Elliot L. Richardson resigns (**Oct. 20**). Egypt and Israel sign U.S.-sponsored cease-fire accord (**Nov. 11**).

1974 Patricia Hearst, 19-year-old daughter of publisher Randolph Hearst, kidnapped by Symbionese Liberation Army. (**Feb. 5**). House Judiciary Committee adopts three articles of impeachment charging President Nixon with obstruction of justice, failure to uphold laws, and refusal to produce material subpoenaed by the committee (**July 30**). Richard M. Nixon announces he will resign the next day, the first President to do so (**Aug. 8**). Vice President Gerald R. Ford of Michigan is sworn in as 38th President of the U.S. (**Aug. 9**). Ford grants "full, free, and absolute pardon" to ex-President Nixon (**Sept. 8**).

1975 John N. Mitchell, H. R. Haldeman, John D. Ehrlichman, and Robert C. Mardian found guilty of Watergate cover-up. Mitchell, Haldeman, and Ehrlichman are sentenced on Feb. 21 to 30 months-8 years in jail and Mardian to 10 months-3 years (**Jan. 1**). American merchant ship *Mayaguez*, seized by Cambodian forces, is rescued in operation by U.S. Navy and Marines, 38 of whom are killed (**May 15**). *Apollo* and *Soyuz* spacecraft take off for U.S.-Soviet link-up in space (**July 15**). President Ford escapes assassination attempt in Sacramento, Calif., (**Sept. 5**). President Ford escapes second assassination attempt in 17 days. (**Sept. 22**).

1976 Supreme Court rules that blacks and other minorities are entitled to retroactive job seniority (**March 24**). Ford signs Federal Election Campaign Act (**May 11**). Supreme Court rules that death penalty is not inherently cruel or unusual and is a constitutionally acceptable form of punishment (**July 3**). Nation celebrates Bicentennial (**July 4**). Israeli airborne commandos attack Uganda's Entebbe Airport and free 103 hostages held by pro-Palestinian hijackers of Air France plane; one Israeli and several Ugandan soldiers killed in raid (**July 4**). Mysterious disease that eventually claims 29 lives strikes American Legion convention in Philadelphia (**Aug. 4**). Jimmy Carter elected U.S. President (**Nov. 2**).

Viking I and II
(Launched 1975)

1977 First woman Episcopal priest ordained (**Jan. 1**). Scientists identify previously unknown bacterium as cause of mysterious "legionnaire's disease" (**Jan. 18**). Carter pardons Vietnam draft evaders (**Jan. 21**). Scientists report using bacteria in lab to make insulin (**May 23**). Supreme Court rules that states are not required to spend Medicaid funds on elective abortions (**June 20**). Deng Xiaoping, purged Chinese leader, restored to power as "Gang of Four" is expelled from Communist Party (**July 22**). Nuclear–proliferation pact, curbing spread of nuclear weapons, signed by 15 countries, including U.S. and U.S.S.R. (**Sept. 21**).

1978 President chooses Federal Appeals Court Judge William H. Webster as F.B.I. Director (**Jan. 19**). Rhodesia's Prime Minister Ian D. Smith and three black leaders agree on transfer to black majority rule (**Feb. 15**). Former Italian Premier Aldo Moro kidnapped by leftwing terrorists, who kill five bodyguards (**March 16**); he is found slain (**May 9**). U.S. Senate approves Panama Canal neutrality treaty (**March 16**); votes treaty to turn canal over to Panama by year 2000 (**April 18**). Californians in referendum approve Proposition 13 for nearly 60% slash in property tax revenues (**June 6**). Supreme Court, in Bakke case, bars quota systems in college admissions but affirms constitutionality of programs giving advantage to minorities (**June 28**). Pope Paul VI, dead at 80, mourned (**Aug. 6**); new Pope, John Paul I, 65, dies unexpectedly after 34 days in office (**Sept. 28**); succeeded by Karol Cardinal Wojtyla of Poland as John Paul II (**Oct. 16**). "Framework for Peace" in Middle East signed by Egypt's President Anwar el-Sadat and Israel Premier Menachem Begin after 13-day conference at Camp David led by President Carter (**Sept. 17**).

1979 Oil spills pollute ocean waters in Atlantic and Gulf of Mexico (**Jan. 1,**

Voyager I and II
(Launched 1977)

June 8, July 21). Ohio agrees to pay $675,000 to families of dead and injured in Kent State University shootings (**Jan. 4**). Vietnam and Cambodian insurgents it backs announce fall of Phnom Penh, Cambodian capital, and collapse of Pol Pot regime (**Jan. 7**). Shah leaves Iran after year of turmoil (**Jan. 16**); revolutionary forces under Moslem leader, Ayatollah Ruhollah Khomeini, take over (**Feb. 1** et seq.). Conservatives win British election; Margaret Thatcher new Prime Minister (**March 28**). Nuclear power plant accident at Three Mile Island, Pa., releases radioactivity (**March 28**). Carter and Brezhnev sign SALT II agreement (**June 14**). Nicaraguan President Gen. Anastasio Somoza Debayle resigns and flees to Miami (**July 17**); Sandinistas form government (**July 19**). Earl Mountbatten of Burma, 79, British World War II hero, and three others killed by blast on fishing boat off Irish coast (**Aug. 27**); two I.R.A. members accused (**Aug. 30**). Iranian militants seize U.S. Embassy in Teheran and hold hostages (**Nov. 4**). Soviet invasion of Afghanistan stirs world protests (**Dec. 27**).

Margaret Thatcher
(Oct. 13, 1925)

1980 Six U.S. Embassy aides escape from Iran with Canadian help (**Jan. 29**). F.B.I.'s undercover operation "Abscam" (for Arab scam) implicates public officials (**Feb. 2**). U.S. breaks diplomatic ties with Iran (**April 7**). Eight U.S. servicemen are killed and five are injured as helicopter and cargo plane collide in abortive desert raid to rescue American hostages in Teheran (**April 25**). Supreme Court upholds limits on Federal aid for abortions (**June 30**). Shah of Iran dies at 60 (**July 27**). Anastasio Somoza Debayle, ousted Nicaraguan ruler, and two aides assassinated in Asunción, Paraguay capital (**Sept. 17**). Iraq troops hold 90 square miles of Iran after invasion (**Sept. 19**). Ronald Reagan elected President in Republican sweep (**Nov. 4**). Three U.S. nuns and lay worker found shot in El Salvador (**Dec. 4**). John Lennon of Beatles shot dead in New York City (**Dec. 8**).

1981 U.S.-Iran agreement frees 52 hostages held in Teheran since Nov. 4, 1979 (**Jan. 18**); hostages welcomed back in U.S. (**Jan. 25**). Ronald Reagan takes oath as 40th President (**Jan. 20**). President Reagan wounded by gunman, with press secretary and two law-enforcement officers (**March 30**). Pope John Paul II wounded by gunman (**May 14**). Supreme Court rules, 4-4, that former President Nixon and three top aides may be required to pay monetary damages for unconstitutional wiretap of home telephone of former national security aide (**June 22**). Reagan nominates Judge Sandra Day O'Connor, 51, of Arizona, as first woman on Supreme Court (**July 7**). More than 110 die in collapse of aerial walkways in lobby of Hyatt Regency Hotel in Kansas City; 188 injured (**July 18**). Air controllers strike, disrupting flights (**Aug. 3**); Government dismisses strikers (**Aug. 11**).

Sally K. Ride
(May 26, 1951)

1982 British overcome Argentina in Falklands war (**April 2-June 15**). Israel invades Lebanon in attack on P.L.O. (**June 4**). John W. Hinckley, Jr. found not guilty because of insanity in shooting of President Reagan (**June 21**). Alexander M. Haig, Jr. resigns as Secretary of State (**June 25**). Equal rights amendment fails ratification (**June 30**). Lebanese Christian Phalangists kill hundreds of people in two Palestinian refugee camps in West Beirut (**Sept. 15**). Princess Grace, 52, dies of injuries when car plunges off mountain road; daughter, Stephanie, 17, suffers serious injuries (**Sept. 14**). Leonid I. Brezhnev, Soviet leader, dies at 75 (**Nov. 10**). Yuri V. Andropov, 68, chosen as successor (**Nov. 15**). Artificial heart implanted for first time in Dr. Barney B. Clark, 61, at University of Utah Medical Center in Salt Lake City (**Dec. 2**); Barney Clark dies (**March 23, 1983**).

1983 Pope John Paul II signs new Roman Catholic code incorporating changes brought about by Second Vatican Council (**Jan. 25**). Second space shuttle, *Challenger*, makes successful maiden voyage, which includes the first U.S. space walk in nine years (**April 4**). U.S. Supreme Court declares many local abortion restrictions unconstitutional (**June 15**). Sally K. Ride, 32, first U.S. woman astronaut in space as a crew member aboard space shuttle *Challenger* (**June 18**). U.S. admits shielding former Nazi Gestapo chief, Klaus Barbie, 69, the "butcher of Lyons," wanted in France for war crimes (**Aug. 15**). Benigno S. Aquino, Jr., 50, political rival of Philippines President Marcos, slain in Manila (**Aug. 21**). South Korean Boeing 747 jetliner bound for Seoul apparently strays into Soviet airspace and is shot down by a Soviet SU-15 fighter after it had tracked the airliner for two hours; all 269 aboard are killed, including 61 Americans (**Aug. 30**). Terrorist explosion kills 237 U.S. Marines in Beirut (**Oct. 23**). U.S. and Caribbean allies invade Grenada (**Oct. 25**).

Space Shuttle Columbia
(Launched April 12, 1981)

1984 Bell System broken up (**Jan. 1**). France gets first deliveries of Soviet natural gas (**Jan. 1**). Syria frees captured U.S. Navy pilot, Lieut. Robert C. Goodman, Jr. (**Jan. 3**). U.S. and Vatican exchange diplomats after 116-year hiatus (**Jan. 10**). Reagan orders U.S. Marines withdrawn from Beirut international peacekeeping force (**Feb. 7**). Yuri V. Andropov dies at 69; Konstantin U. Chernenko, 72, named Soviet Union leader (**Feb. 9**). Italy and Vatican agree to end Roman Catholicism as state religion (**Feb. 18**). Reagan ends U.S. role in Beirut by relieving Sixth Fleet from peacekeeping force (**March 30**). Con-

**Indira Gandhi
(1917-1984)**

**Ronald W. Reagan
(Feb. 6, 1911)**

**Mikhail S. Gorbachev
(March 2, 1931)**

gress rebukes President Reagan on use of federal funds for mining Nicaraguan harbors **(April 10).** Soviet Union withdraws from summer Olympic games in U.S., and other bloc nations follow **(May 7** et seq.**).** José Napoleón Duarte, moderate, elected president of El Salvador **(May 11).** Three hundred slain as Indian Army occupies Sikh Golden Temple in Amritsar **(June 6).** Thirty-ninth Democratic National Convention, in San Francisco, nominates Walter F. Mondale and Geraldine A. Ferraro **(July 16-19).** Thirty-third Republican National Convention, at Dallas, renominates President Reagan and Vice President Bush **(Aug. 20-25).** Brian Mulroney and Conservative party win Canadian election in landslide **(Sept. 4).** Indian Prime Minister Indira Gandhi assassinated by two Sikh bodyguards; 1,000 killed in anti-Sikh riots; son Rajiv succeeds her **(Oct. 31).** President Reagan re-elected in landslide with 59% of vote **(Nov. 7).** Toxic gas leaks from Union Carbide plant in Bhopal, India, killing 2,000 and injuring 150,000 **(Dec. 3).**

1985 Ronald Reagan, 73, takes oath for second term as 40th President **(Jan. 20).** General Westmoreland settles libel action against CBS **(Feb. 18).** Prime Minister Margaret Thatcher addresses Congress, endorsing Reagan's policies **(Feb. 20).** U.S.S.R. leader Chernenko dies at 73 and is replaced by Mikhail Gorbachev, 54 **(March 11).** Two Shiite Moslem gunmen capture TWA airliner with 133 aboard, 104 of them Americans **(June 14);** 39 remaining hostages freed in Beirut **(June 30).** Supreme Court, 5-4, bars public school teachers from parochial schools **(July 1).** Arthur James Walker, 50, retired naval officer, convicted by federal judge of participating in Soviet spy ring **(Aug. 9).** P.L.O. terrorists hijack *Achille Lauro,* Italian cruise ship, with 80 passengers, plus crew **(Oct. 7);** American, Leon Klinghoffer, killed **(Oct. 8).** Italian government toppled by political crisis over hijacking of *Achille Lauro* **(Oct. 16).** John A. Walker and son, Michael I. Walker, 22, sentenced in Navy espionage case **(Oct. 28).** Reagan and Gorbachev meet at summit **(Nov. 19);** agree to step up arms control talks and renew cultural contacts **(Nov. 21).** Terrorists seize Egyptian Boeing 737 airliner after takeoff from Athens **(Nov. 23);** 59 dead as Egyptian forces storm plane on Malta **(Nov. 24).** U.S. budget-balancing bill enacted **(Dec. 12).**

1986 Spain and Portugal join Common Market **(Jan. 1).** President freezes Libyan assets in U.S. **(Jan. 8).** Supreme Court bars racial bias in trial jury selection **(Jan. 14).** *Voyager 2* spacecraft reports secrets of Uranus **(Jan. 26).** Space shuttle *Challenger* explodes after launch at Cape Canaveral, Fla., killing all seven aboard **(Jan. 28).** Haiti President Jean-Claude Duvalier flees to France **(Feb. 7).** President Marcos flees Philippines after ruling 20 years, as newly elected Corazon Aquino succeeds him **(Feb. 26).** Prime Minister Olaf Palme of Sweden shot dead **(Feb. 28).** Kurt Waldheim service as Nazi army officer revealed **(March 3).** Union Carbide agrees to settlement with victims of Bhopal gas leak in India **(March 22).** Halley's Comet yields information on return visit **(April 10).** U.S. planes attack Libyan "terrorist centers" **(April 14).** Desmond Tutu elected Archbishop in South Africa **(April 14).** Major nuclear accident at Soviet Union's Chernobyl power station alarms world **(April 26** et seq.**).** Ex-Navy analyst, Jonathan Jay Pollard, 31, guilty as spy for Israel **(June 4).** Supreme Court reaffirms abortion rights **(June 11).** World Court rules U.S. broke international law in mining Nicaraguan waters **(June 27).** Supreme Court voids automatic provisions of budget-balancing law **(July 7).** Jerry A. Whitworth, ex-Navy radioman, convicted as spy **(July 24).** Moslem captors release Rev. Lawrence Martin Jenco **(July 26).** Senate Judiciary Committee approves William H. Rehnquist to be Chief Justice of U.S. **(Aug. 14).** House votes arms appropriations bill rejecting Administration's "star wars" policy **(Aug. 15).** Three Lutheran church groups in U.S. set to merge **(Aug. 29).** Congress overrides Reagan veto of stiff sanctions against South Africa **(Sept. 29 and Oct. 2).** Congress approves immigration bill barring hiring of illegal aliens, with amnesty provision **(Oct. 17).** Reagan signs $11.7-billion budget reduction measure **(Oct. 21).** He approves sweeping revision of U.S. tax code **(Oct. 22).** Democrats triumph in elections, gaining eight seats to win Senate majority **(Nov. 4).** Secret initiative to send arms to Iran revealed **(Nov. 6** et seq.**);** Reagan denies exchanging arms for hostages and halts arms sales **(Nov. 19);** diversion of funds from arms sales to Nicaraguan contras revealed **(Nov. 25).** Walkers, father and son, sentenced in naval spy ring **(Nov. 6).** Soviet lifts ban on Andrei D. Sakharov, rights activist **(Dec. 19).**

1987 William Buckley, U.S. hostage in Lebanon, reported slain **(Jan. 20).** U.S. puts Austrian President Kurt Waldheim on list of those banned from country **(April 27).** Quebec accepts Canadian Constitution as "distinct society" **(May 1).** Supreme Court rules Rotary Clubs must admit women **(May 4).** Iraqi missiles kill 37 in attack on U.S. frigate *Stark* in Persian Gulf **(May 17);** Iraqi president apologizes **(May 18).** Prime Minister Thatcher wins rare third term in Britain **(June 11).** Supreme Court Justice Lewis F. Powell, Jr., retires **(June 26).** Klaus Barbie, 73, Gestapo wartime chief in

Lyons, sentenced to life by French court for war crimes (**July 4**). Marine Lieut. Col. Oliver North, Jr., tells Congressional inquiry higher officials approved his secret Iran-Contra operations (**July 7–10**). Admiral John M. Poindexter, former National Security Adviser, testifies he authorized use of Iran arms sale profits to aid Contras (**July 15–22**). George P. Shultz testifies he was deceived repeatedly on Iran-Contra affair (**July 23–24**). Defense Secretary Caspar W. Weinberger tells inquiry of official deception and intrigue (**July 31, Aug. 3**). Reagan says Iran arms-Contra policy went astray and accepts responsibility (**Aug 12**). Severe earthquake strikes Los Angeles, leaving 100 injured and six dead (**Oct. 1**). Senate, 58–42, rejects Robert H. Bork as Supreme Court Justice (**Oct. 23**)

1988　U.S. and Canada reach free trade agreement (**Jan. 2**). Supreme Court, 5–3, backs public school officials' power to censor student activities (**Jan. 13**). Marine Lieut. Col. William H. Higgins abducted in Lebanon (**Feb. 17**). Robert C. McFarlane, former National Security Adviser, pleads guilty in Iran–Contra case (**March 11**). Israel court dooms John Demjanjuk, 68, "Ivan the Terrible," for Nazi war crimes (**April 25**). Supreme Court rules against private-club membership restrictions (**June 20**). U.S. Navy ship shoots down Iranian airliner in Persian Gulf, mistaking it for jet fighter; 290 killed (**July 3**). Terrorists kill nine tourists on Aegean cruise (**July 11**). Democratic convention nominates Gov. Michael Dukakis of Massachusetts for President and Texas Senator Lloyd Bentsen for Vice President (**July 17** et seq.). Republicans nominate George Bush for President and Indiana Senator Dan Quayle for Vice President (**Aug. 15** et seq.). Plane blast kills Pakistani President Mohammad Zia ul-Haq (**Aug. 17**). Republicans sweep 40 states in election. Vice President Bush beats Gov. Dukakis (**Nov. 8**). Soviet legislature approves political restructuring and new national legislature (**Dec. 1**). Benazir Bhutto, first Islamic woman prime minister, chosen to lead Pakistan's government (**Dec. 1**). Pan-Am 747 explodes from terrorist bomb and crashes in Lockerbie, Scotland, killing all 259 aboard and 11 on ground (**Dec. 21**).

1989　U.S. planes shoot down two Libyan fighters over international waters in Mediterranean (**Jan. 4**). Emperor Hirohito of Japan dead at 87 (**Jan. 7**). George Herbert Walker Bush inaugurated as 41st U.S. President (**Jan. 20**). Iran's Ayatollah Khomeini declares author Salman Rushdie's book "The Satanic Verses" offensive and sentences him and his publishers to death (**Feb. 14**). Ruptured tanker *Exxon Valdez* sends 11 million gallons of crude oil into Alaska's Prince William Sound (**March 24**). Tens of thousands of Chinese students take over Beijing's central square in rally for democracy (**April 19** et seq.). More than one million in Beijing demonstrate for democracy; chaos spreads across nation (**mid-May** et seq.). Mikhail S. Gorbachev named Soviet President (**May 25**). U.S. jury convicts Oliver L. North in Iran-Contra affair (**May 4**). Thousands killed as Chinese leaders take hard line toward demonstrators (**June 4** et seq.). Army Gen. Colin R. Powell is first black to become Chairman of Joint Chiefs of Staff (**Aug. 9**). P.W. Botha quits as South Africa's President (**Aug. 14**). *Voyager 2* spacecraft speeds by Neptune after making startling discoveries about the planet and its moons (**Aug. 29**). L. Douglas Wilder, Democrat, is elected as first black governor of Virginia (**Nov. 7**). Deng Xiaoping resigns from China's leadership (**Nov. 9**). After 28 years, Berlin Wall is open to West (**Nov. 11**). Czech Parliament ends Communists' dominant role (**Nov. 30**). Romanian uprising overthrows Communist government (**Dec. 15** et seq.); President Ceausescu and wife executed (**Dec. 25**). U.S. troops invade Panama, seeking capture of Gen. Manuel Noriega (**Dec. 20**); resistance to U.S. collapses (**Dec. 24**).

1990　Gen. Manuel Noriega surrenders in Panama (**Jan. 3**). Yugoslav Communists end 45-year monopoly of power (**Jan. 22**). Soviet Communists relinquish sole power (**Feb. 7**). South Africa frees Nelson Mandela, imprisoned 27 1/2 years (**Feb. 11**). Violeta Barrios de Chamorro inaugurated as Nicaraguan President (**April 25**). U.S.–Soviet summit reaches accord on armaments (**June 1**). South Africa lifts emergency decrees (**June 7**). Supreme Court upsets law banning flag burning (**June 11**). President Bush breaks with no-new-tax pledge in budget agreement (**June 26**). Imelda Marcos acquitted in New York of raiding Philippine Treasury (**July 2**). Western Alliance ends cold war and proposes joint action with Soviet Union and Eastern Europe (**July 6**). U.S. Appeals Court overturns Oliver North's Iran–Contra conviction (**July 20**). Iraqi troops invade Kuwait and seize petroleum reserves, setting off Persian Gulf War (**Aug. 2** et seq.). East and West Germany reunited (**Aug. 31** et seq.). Republicans set back in midterm elections (**Nov. 8**). Gorbachev assumes emergency powers (**Nov. 17**). Leaders of 34 nations in Europe and North America proclaim a united Europe (**Nov. 21**). Margaret Thatcher resigns as British Prime Minister (**Nov. 22**); John Major succeeds her (**Nov. 28**). Lech Walesa wins Poland's runoff Presidential election (**Dec. 9**). Haiti elects leftist priest as President in first democratic election (**Dec. 17**).

Corazon C. Aquino
(Jan. 25, 1933)

Kurt Waldheim
(Dec. 21, 1918)

George H. Bush
(June 12, 1924)

**L. Douglas Wilder
(Jan. 17, 1931)**

**Neptune seen from
Voyager 2**

1991 Lithuania Government resigns **(Jan. 8)**. U.S. and Allies at war with Iraq **(Jan. 15)**. U.N. forces win Persian Gulf war **(Feb. 4 et seq.)**. Liberal priest becomes Haiti president **(Feb. 7)**. Warsaw Pact dissolves military alliance **(Feb 25)**. Supreme Court limits race in trial jury selection **(April 1)**. Cease-fire ends Persian Gulf war **(April 3)**. Europeans end sanctions on South Africa **(April 15)**. Supreme Court limits death row appeals **(April 16)**. Winnie Mandela sentenced in kidnapping **(May 13)**. William H. Webster retires as Director of Central Intelligence; Robert H. Gates succeeds him **(May 14)**. France agrees to sign 1968 treaty banning spread of atomic weapons **(June 3)**. Communist Government of Albania resigns **(June 4)**. Jiang Qing, widow of Mao, commits suicide **(June 4)**. South African Parliament repeals apartheid laws **(June 5)**. Berlin again becomes German capital **(June 20)**. Warsaw Pact dissolved **(July 1)**. Boris N. Yeltsin inaugurated as first freely elected president of Russian Republic **(July 10)**. Bush-Gorbachev summit negotiates strategic arms reduction treaty **(July 31)**. China accepts nuclear nonproliferation treaty **(Aug. 10)**. Coup fails to unseat Gorbachev after Soviet hardliners seize him; he credits Yeltsin for rescue **(Aug. 18 et seq.)**. Gorbachev seals Communist Party doom, resigns as secretary-general **(Aug. 24)**.Three Baltic republics win independence **(Aug. 25)**; Bush recognizes them **(Sept. 2)**. New Soviet ruling council recognizes independence of Lithuania,Estonia, and Latvia **(Sept. 6)**. Charges against Oliver North dropped **(Sept. 15)**. Haitian troops seize president in uprising **(Sept. 30)**. U.S. suspends assistance to Haiti **(Oct. 1)**. Woman professor accuses Judge Clarence Thomas of sexual harassment **(Oct. 6)**; Senate, 52–48, confirms Thomas for Supreme Court after stormy hearings **(Oct. 15)**. Israel and Soviet resume relations after 24 years **(Oct. 18)**. First photo ever taken of an asteroid in space, *Gaspara* **(Oct. 29)**. European Community imposes economic sanctions on Yugoslavia **(Nov. 8)**. U.S. indicts two Libyans in 1988 bombing of Pan Am Flight 103 over Lockerbie, Scotland **(Nov. 15)**. Anglican envoy Terry Waite and U.S. Prof. Thomas M. Sutherland freed by Lebanese **(Nov. 18)**. U.N. Security Council names Egyptian Deputy Prime Minister Boutros Boutros-Ghali as sixth Secretary-General **(Nov. 21)**. Charles H. Keating, Jr., convicted of fraud in savings and loan crisis **(Dec. 4)**. Last three U.S. hostages freed in Lebanon **(Dec. 2–4)**. Soviet Union breaks up after President Gorbachev's resignation; constituent republics form Commonwealth of Independent States, which U.S. and other nations move to recognize **(Dec. 25)**.

1992 Yugoslav Federation broken up **(Jan. 15)**. Bush and Yeltsin proclaim formal end to Cold War **(Feb. 1)**. U.S. lifts trade sanctions against China **(Feb. 21)**. U.S. recognizes three former Yugoslav republics **(April 7)**. Gen. Noriega, former Panama leader, convicted in U.S. court **(April 9)**. F.D.A. restricts use of silicone breast implants **(April 16)**. Small new Yugoslavia proclaimed **(April 27)**. Four officers acquitted in Los Angeles beating; violence erupts in Los Angeles **(April 29 et seq.)**. Caspar W. Weinberger indicted in Iran-Contra affair **(June 16)**. Last Western hostages freed in Lebanon **(June 17)**. Supreme Court reaffirms right to abortion **(June 29)**. Gen. Noriega sentenced to 40 years on drug charges **(July 10)**. Court clears *Exxon Valdez* skipper **(July 10)**. Democrats nominate Bill Clinton and Al

---

THE PERSIAN GULF WAR (Aug. 2, 1990–April 6, 1991)

1990: Iraq invades its tiny neighbor, Kuwait, after talks break down over oil production and debt repayment. Iraqi Pres. Saddam Hussein later annexes Kuwait and declares it a 19th province of Iraq **(Aug. 2)**. President Bush believes that Iraq intends to invade Saudi Arabia and take control of the region's oil supplies. He begins organizing a multinational coalition to seek Kuwait's freedom and restoration of its legitimate government. The U.N. Security Council authorizes economic sanctions against Iraq. Pres. Bush orders U.S. troops to protect Saudi Arabia at the Saudis' request and "Operation Desert Shield" begins **(Aug. 6)**. 230,000 American troops arrive in Saudi Arabia to take defensive action, but when Iraq continues a huge military buildup in Kuwait, the President orders an additional 200,000 troops deployed to prepare for a possible offensive action by the U.S.-led coalition forces. He subsequently obtains a U.N. Security Council resolution setting a Jan. 15, 1991, deadline for Iraq to withdraw unconditionally from Kuwait **(Nov. 8)**.
1991: Pres. Bush wins Congressional approval for his position with the most devastating air assault in history against military targets in Iraq and Kuwait **(Jan. 16)**. He rejects a Soviet-Iraq peace plan for a gradual withdrawal that does not comply with all the U.N. resolutions and

gives Iraq an ultimatum to withdraw from Kuwait by noon February 23 **(Feb. 22)**. In a brilliant and lightning-fast campaign, U.S. and coalition forces smash through Iraq's defenses and defeat Saddam Hussein's troops in only four days of combat. Allies enter Kuwait City **(Feb. 26)**. Iraqi army sets fire to over 500 of Kuwait's oil wells as final act of destruction to Kuwait's infrastructure. Pres. Bush orders a unilateral cease-fire 100 hours after the ground offensive started **(Feb. 27)**. Allied and Iraq military leaders meet on battlefield to discuss terms for a formal cease-fire to end the Gulf War. Iraq agrees to abide by all of the U.N. resolutions **(Mar. 3)**. The first Allied prisoners of war are released **(Mar. 4)**. Official cease-fire accepted and signed **(April 6)**. 532,000 U.S. forces served in Operation Desert Storm. There were a total of 148 battle deaths during the Gulf War, 145 nonbattle deaths, and 467 wounded in action. Battle deaths by branch of service were: Army, 98; Navy, 6; Marines, 24; Air Force, 20. Nonbattle deaths: Army, 105; Navy, 8; Marines, 26; and Air Force, 6. The United States estimated that Iraqi military casualties werre 100,000 killed, 300,000 wounded, and over 88,000 captured.

Gore **(July 1)**. Israeli Parliament approves Yitzhak Rabin's coalition government, dominated by Labor Party **(July 13)**. Supreme Court upholds return of Haitians **(Aug. 1)**. U.S. indicts four police officers in Los Angeles beating **(Aug. 5)**. North American trade compact announced **(Aug. 12)**. Republicans renominate Bush and Quayle **(Aug. 20)**. U.N. expels Serbian-dominated Yugoslavia **(Sept. 22)**. Senate ratifies second Strategic Arms Limitation Treaty **(Oct. 1)**. U.N. council creates Bosnian "no-fly" zone **(Oct. 9)**. Top Japanese leader, Shin Kanemaru, resigns in scandal **(Oct. 14)**. Bill Clinton elected President, Al Gore Vice President; Democrats keep control of Congress **(Nov. 3)**. Russian Parliament approves START treaty **(Nov. 4)**. U.S. forces leave Philippines, ending nearly a century of American military presence **(Nov. 24)**. Czechoslovak Parliament approves separation into two nations **(Nov. 25)**. U.N. approves U.S.-led force to guard food for Somalia **(Dec. 3)**. Prince and Princess of Wales agree to separate **(Dec. 9)**. Bush pardons former Reagan Administration officials involved in Iran-Contra affair **(Dec. 24)**.

1993 Clinton withdraws Zoe Baird nomination as Attorney General **(Jan. 22)**. Vaclav Havel elected Czech President **(Jan. 26)**. Clinton agrees to compromise on military's ban on homosexuals **(Jan. 29)**. Judge Kimba M. Wood withdraws as Clinton's second choice for Attorney General **(Feb. 5)**; President names Janet Reno to post **(Feb. 11)**. U.S. begins airdrop of supplies to besieged Bosnian towns **(Feb. 28)**. Law agents besiege Texas Davidian religious cult after six are killed in raid **(March 1 et seq.)**. Senate, 98–0, confirms Janet Reno as Attorney General **(March 11)**. Five arrested, sixth sought in bombing of World Trade Center in New York **(March 29)**. Russian Congress accepts Yeltsin call for national referendum **(March 29)**. Seven industrial nations agree on aid to Russia **(April 15)**. Two police officers convicted in Los Angeles on rights charges in Rodney King beating **(April 17)**. Fire kills 72 as cult standoff in Texas ends with Federal assault **(April 19)**. President of Sri Lanka assassinated **(May 1)**. British Commons approves European unity pact **(May 20)**. Twenty-two U.N. troops killed in Somalia **(June 5)**. Ruth Bader Ginsburg, rights advocate, appointed to Supreme Court **(June 14)**. Iraq accepts U.N. weapons monitoring **(July 19)**. President dismisses F.B.I. Director William S. Sessions **(July 19)**; names Judge Louis J. Freeh as successor **(July 20)**. Vincent W. Foster, Jr., senior White House lawyer, is apparent suicide **(July 22)**. Midwest flood damage expected to exceed $10 billion **(July 24)**. Two Los Angeles police officers sentenced in Rodney King beating **(Aug. 4)**. Israeli-Palestinian accord reached **(Aug. 28)**. South Africa agrees to share transition powers **(Sept. 7)**. Yeltsin dissolves Russian Parliament **(Sept. 21)**. U.S. agents blamed in Waco, Tex., siege **(Oct. 1)**. Yeltsin's forces crush revolt in Russian Parliament **(Oct. 4 et seq.)**. China breaks nuclear test moratorium **(Oct. 5)**. NATO offers "peace partnership" to Eastern European nations **(Oct. 20–21)**. Canada's opposition Liberal Party regains power in landslide **(Oct. 25)**. Europe's Maastricht Treaty takes effect, creating European Union **(Nov. 1)**. Jean Chretien sworn in as Canada's 20th Prime Minister **(Nov. 4)**. Yeltsin approves new draft constitution for Russia **(Nov. 8)**. House of Representatives approves North American Free Trade Agreement **(Nov. 17)**; Senate follows **(Nov. 21)**. South Africa adopts majority rule constitution **(Nov. 18)**. Clinton signs Brady bill regulating firearms purchases **(Nov. 30)**. Space shuttle repairs orbiting Hubble telescope **(Dec. 2–13)**. C.I.A. reports North Korea has atomic bomb **(Dec. 25)**. U.S. radiation tests on humans disclosed **(Dec. 28)**.

1994 Serbs heavy weapons pound Sarajevo **(Jan. 5–6)**. Olympic figure skater Nancy Kerrigan attacked **(Jan. 6)**; three arrested in attack **(Jan. 13)**. Ukraine agrees to scrap atomic weapons **(Jan. 10)**. Major earthquake jolts Los Angeles; 51 dead **(Jan. 17 et seq.)**. Deep cold wave paralyzes Northeast **(Jan. 20 et seq.)**. Tonya Harding's ex-husband pleads guilty to Kerrigan attack **(Feb. 1)**. White supremacist convicted in 1964 killing **(Feb. 5)**. Pact resolves Palestinian self-rule issues **(Feb. 9)**. Clinton ends trade embargo on Vietnam **(Feb. 9)**. Aldrich Ames, high C.I.A. official, charged with spying for Soviet **(Feb. 22)**. Ukraine Russian Parliament frees Yeltsin opponents **(Feb. 2#)**. Ukraine figure skater wins Olympic gold medal **(Feb. 25)**. Four convicted in World Trade Center bombing **(March 4)**. Killer of abortion doctor found guilty **(March 5)**. President appoints special counsel **(March 8)**. Four women complain of sex harassment in military **(March 9)**. Chinese rebuff Christopher warning **(March 10)**. Israel outlaws Jewish terrorists **(March 13)**. Tonya Harding gets plea bargain **(March 16)**. I.M.F. approves $1.5-billion loan for Russia **(March 22)**. Mexican Presidential candidate assassinated **(March 23)**. Gun battles kill 31 in Johannesburg **(March 28)**. Thousands dead in Rwanda tribal warfare **(April 6)**. Strike halts 22 major trucking companies **(April 6)**. Accord reached to end tie-up **(April 28)**. U.S. planes bomb Serbian targets **(April 10)**. Zulu nationalists

Asteroid *Gaspra*
(Oct. 29, 1991)

**William J. Clinton
(Aug. 19, 1946)**

end election boycott (**April 19**). South Africa holds first interracial national election (**April 29**). V.M.I. upheld on exclusion of women (**May 1**). Israel and Palestinians sign accord (**May 4**). American youth caned in Singapore (**May 5**). Clinton accused of sexual harassment while Governor (**May 6**). Congress votes protection for abortion clinics (**May 12**). Russia joins West in Bosnia peace move (**May 13**). Jacqueline Kennedy Onassis dies of cancer (**May 20**). Thousands dead in Rwanda tribal warfare (**May 31 et seq.**). Wartime allies mark D-Day after 50 years (**June 2**). U.S. jury finds Exxon reckless in Alaska oil spill (**June 13**). O.J. Simpson arrested in two killings (**June 18**). Carter reports end to North Korea crisis (**June 19**). F.D.A. head charges nicotine manipulation (**June 21**). Russia and NATO agree on close military ties (**June 22**). Japanese conservatives back in power (**June 29**). Supreme Court approves limit on abortion protests (**June 30**). Kim Il Sung, North Korea's Communist leader, dies (**July 6**). Floods wreak havoc in Georgia (**July 6 et seq.**). Senate confirms Stephen G. Breyer for Supreme Court seat (**July 29**). Abortion doctor shot dead outside Florida clinic (**July 29**). Serbia severs link with allies in Bosnia (**Aug. 4**). Congress finally passes anti-crime bill (**Aug. 11**). U.S. indicts accused Florida abortion clinic killer (**Aug. 12**). Major league baseball players strike (**Aug. 13**). Carlos, international terrorist, captured (**Aug. 15**). U.S. halts Cubans fleeing by sea (**Aug. 19**). Mexican voters keep governing party (**Aug. 22**). I.R.A. declares cease-fire in Northern Ireland (**Aug. 31**). Small plane crashes against White House (**Sept. 12**). Baseball owners end season and cancel World Series (**Sept. 14**). U.S. and Russia agree on arms reduction (**Sept. 29**). Agriculture Secretary Mike Espy quits under fire (**Oct. 3**). Powerful earthquake strikes Japan (**Oct. 4**). Aristide returns to a joyous Haiti (**Oct. 4**). Abortion protester guilty in clinic killings (**Oct. 5**). U.S. sends forces to Persian Gulf (**Oct. 7**). Ulster Protestants declare cease-fire (**Oct. 13**). Israel and Jordan sign peace treaty (**Oct. 17**). U.S. and North Korea settle nuclear dispute (**Oct. 21**). Assaulted naval women awarded $1.7 million (**Oct. 28**). Gunman fires at White House (**Oct. 29**). Abortion foe guilty of killing two at clinic (**Nov. 2**); Florida jury recommends death penalty (**Nov. 3**). Reagan, 83, reveals Alzheimer's disease (**Nov. 6**). Serbian official charged with war crimes (**Nov. 7**). G.O.P. wins control of House and Senate (**Nov. 8**). Aristide forms Haitian Government with Prime Minister and full Cabinet (**Nov. 9**). Clinton orders Bosnian arms embargo ended (**Nov. 10**). Sweden votes to join European Union (**Nov. 13**). Hurricane kills more than 400 in Caribbean (**Nov. 17**). NATO retaliates against Serb bombing attack in Bosnia (**Nov. 19**). Italian premier target in corruption inquiry (**Nov. 22**). Norway rejects link to European Union (**Nov. 29**). Mexico inaugurates new President, pledged to fight poverty (**Dec. 1**). Congress votes for global trade alliance, GATT (**Dec. 1**). Killer of abortion doctor sentenced twice (**Dec. 2**). Newt Gingrich named House Speaker (**Dec. 5**). Bentsen resigns as Treasury Secretary (**Dec. 6**). Simpson jury selection completed (**Dec. 8**). Surgeon General Joycelyn Elders resigns under pressure (**Dec. 9**). Russians attack secessionist Republic of Chechnya (**Dec. 11 et seq.**). U.S. orders safety review of all airlines (**Dec. 14**). Bullet strikes White House (**Dec. 15**). Centrist named Irish Prime Minister (**Dec. 15**). One U.S. pilot killed over North Korea; another survives (**Dec. 18**). Mexican currency plummets (**Dec. 22**). James Woolsey, Jr., resigns as Director of Central Intelligence (**Dec. 28**). Gunman kills two at Massachusetts abortion clinic (**Dec. 30**). Gingrich gives up $4.5-million advance on book (**Dec. 30**). Leaders agree to four-month Bosnia truce (**Dec. 31**).

WORLD STATISTICS

A PROFILE OF THE WORLD

Source: The World Factbook, 1994.

GEOGRAPHY

Total area: 510.072 million sq km (196.93 million sq mi.).
Land area: 148.94 million sq km (57.50 sq mi.). **Water area:** 361.132 million sq km (139.43 sq mi.). **Comparative area:** land area about 16 times the size of the United States. **Note:** 70.8% of the world is water, 29.2% is land

Land boundaries: The land boundaries in the world total 250,883.64 km (155,891.81 mi.) (not counting shared boundaries twice)

Maritime claims:
Contiguous zone: 24 nm (nautical miles) claimed by most but can vary. *Continental shelf:* 200-m (656 ft) depth claimed by most or to the depth of exploitation, others claim 200 nm or to the edge of the continental margin. *Exclusive fishing zone:* 200 nm claimed by most but can vary. *Exclusive economic zone:* 200 nm claimed by most but can vary. *Territorial sea:* 12 nm claimed by most but can vary

Note: Boundary situations with neighboring states prevent many countries from extending their fishing or economic zones to a full 200 nm; 42 nations and other areas that are landlocked include Afghanistan, Andorra, Armenia, Austria, Azerbaijan, Belarus, Bhutan, Bolivia, Botswana, Burkina Faso, Burundi, Central African Republic, Chad, Czech Republic, Ethiopia, Holy See (Vatican City), Hungary, Kazakhstan, Kyrgyzstan, Laos, Lesotho, Liechtenstein, Luxembourg, Macedonia, Malawi, Mali, Moldova, Mongolia, Nepal, Niger, Paraguay, Rwanda, San Marino, Slovakia, Swaziland, Switzerland, Tajikistan, Turkmenistan, Uganda, Uzbekistan, West Bank, Zambia, Zimbabwe

Climate: Two large areas of polar climates separated by two rather narrow temperate zones from a wide equatorial band of tropical to subtropical climates

Terrain: Highest elevation is Mt. Everest at 8,848 meters (29,028 ft) and lowest depression is the Dead Sea at 392 meters (1,286 ft) below sea level; greatest ocean depth is the Marianas Trench at 10,924 meters (35,840 ft)

Natural resources: The rapid using up of nonrenewable mineral resources, the depletion of forest areas and wetlands, the extinction of animal and plant species, and the deterioration in air and water quality (especially in Eastern Europe and the former USSR) pose serious long-term problems that governments and people are only beginning to address

Land use:
Arable land: 10%. *Permanent crops:* 1%. *Meadows and pastures:* 24%. *Forest and woodland:* 31%. *Other:* 34%. *Irrigated land:* N.A. square kilometers

Environment: Large areas subject to severe weather (tropical cyclones), natural disasters (earthquakes, landslides, tsunamis, volcanic eruptions), overpopulation, industrial disasters, pollution (air, water, acid rain, toxic substances), loss of vegetation (overgrazing, deforestation, desertification), loss of wildlife resources, soil degradation, soil depletion, erosion

PEOPLE

Population: 5,643,289,771 (July 1994 est.); **Growth rate:** 1.5% (1994 est.)
Birth rate: 25 births/1,000 population (1994 est.)
Death rate: 9 deaths/1,000 live births (1994 est.)
Infant mortality rate: 65 deaths/1,000 live births (1994 est.)
Life expectancy at birth:
Total population: 62 years. *Male:* 61 years. *Female:* 64 years (1994 est.)
Total fertility rate: 3.1 children born/woman (1994 est.)
Literacy: age 15 and over can read and write (1994 est.)
Combined: 82%. *Male:* 68%. *Female:* 75%.
Labor force: 2.24 billion (1992)

GOVERNMENT

Administrative divisions: 265 sovereign nations, dependent areas, other, and miscellaneous entries
Legal system: Varies by individual country; 182 are parties to the United Nations International Court of Justice (ICJ or World Court)

ECONOMY

Overview: Real global output—gross world product (GWP)—rose roughly 2% in 1993, with results varying widely among regions and countries. Average growth of 1% in the GDP of industrialized countries (57% of GWP in 1993) and average growth of 6% in the GDP of less developed countries (37% of GWP) were partly offset by a further 10% drop in the GDP of the former U.S.S.R./Eastern Europe area (now only 6% of GWP). Within the industrialized world the U.S. posted a 3% growth rate whereas both Japan and the 12-member European Union (formerly the European Community)[1] had zero growth. With the notable exception of Japan at 2.5%, unemployment was typically 6–11% in the industrial world. The U.S. accounted for 22% of GWP in 1993; Western Europe accounted for 22.5%; and Japan accounted for 9%. These are the three "economic superpowers" which are presumably destined to compete for mastery in international markets on into the 21st century. As for the less developed countries, China, India, and the Four Dragons—South Korea, Taiwan, Hong Kong, and Singapore—once again posted good records; however, many other countries, especially in Africa, continued to suffer from drought, rapid population growth, inflation, and civil strife. Central Europe, especially Poland, Hungary, and the Czech Republic, made considerable progress in moving toward "market-friendly" economies, whereas the 15 ex-Soviet countries typically experienced further declines in output of 10–15%. The addition of nearly 100 million people each year to an already overcrowded globe is exacerbating the problems of pollution, desertification, underemployment, epidemics, and famine. Because of their own internal problems, the industrialized countries have inadequate resources to deal effectively with the poorer areas of the world, which, at least from the economic point of view, are becoming further marginalized.

1. 12 full members: Belgium, Denmark, France, Germany, Greece, Ireland, Italy, Luxembourg, Netherlands, Portugal, Spain, UK.

National product: GWP (gross world product)—purchasing power equivalent—$29 trillion (1993 est.)
National product real growth rate: 2% (1993 est.)
National product per capita: $5,200 (1993 est.)
Inflation rate (consumer prices):
Developed countries: 5% (1993 est.). *Developing countries:* 50% (1993 est.).
Note: these figures vary widely in individual cases
Unemployment rate: developed countries typically 6–11%; developing countries, extensive unemployment and underemployment (1993)
Exports: $3.64 trillion (f.o.b. 1992 est.) *Commodities:* the whole range of industrial and agricultural goods and services. *Partners:* in value, about 75% of exports from the developed countries.
Imports: $3.82 trillion (c.i.f., 1992 est.) *Commodities:* the whole range of industrial and agricultural goods and services. *Partners:* in value, about 75% of imports by the developed countries
External debt: $1 trillion for less developed countries (1993 est.)
Industrial production: growth rate −1% (1992 est.)
Electricity: 2,864,000,000 kW capacity; 11,450,000 million kWh produced, 2,150 kWh per capita (1990)
Industries: industry worldwide is dominated by the onrush of technology, especially in computers, robotics, telecommunications, and medicines and medical equipment; most of these advances take place in Organization for Economic Cooperation and Development[2] (OECD) nations; only a small portion of non-OECD countries have succeeded in rapidly adjusting to these technological forces, and the technological gap between the industrial nations and the less-developed countries continues to widen; the rapid development of new industrial (and agricultural) technology is complicating already grim environmental problems.

---

2. 24 full members: Australia, Austria, Belgium, Canada, Denmark, Finland, France, Germany, Greece, Iceland, Ireland, Italy, Japan, Luxembourg, Netherlands, New Zealand, Norway, Portugal, Spain, Sweden, Switzerland, Turkey, UK, US.

Agriculture: The production of major food crops has increased substantially in the last 20 years; the annual production of cereals, for instance, has risen by 50%, from about 1.2 billion metric tons to about 1.8 billion metric tons; production increases have resulted mainly from increased yields rather than increases in planted areas; while global production is sufficient for aggregate demand, about one-fifth of the world's population remains malnourished, primarily because local production cannot adequately provide for large and rapidly growing populations, which are too poor to pay for food imports; conditions are especially bad in Africa where drought in recent years has intensified the consequences of overpopulation

COMMUNICATIONS

Railroads: 148,775 mi. (239,430 km) of narrow gauge track; 441,642 mi. (710,754 km) of standard gauge track; 156,059 mi. (251,153 km) of broad gauge track; includes about 118,060 to 121,167 mi. (190,000 to 195,000 km) of electrified routes of which 91,814 mi. (147,760 km) are in Europe, 15,229 mi. (24,509 km) in the Far East, 6,866 mi. (11,050 km) in Africa, 2,624 mi. (4,223 km) in South America, and only 2,585 mi. (4,160 km) in North America; fastest speed in daily service is 186 mph (300 km/hr) attained by France's SNCF TGV-Atlantique line
Ports: Mina al Ahmadi (Kuwait), Chiba, Houston, Kawasaki, Kobe, Marseille, New Orleans, New York, Rotterdam, Yokohama
Merchant marine: 23,943 ships (1,000 GRT [gross register ton] or over) totaling 397,225,000 GRT/652,025,000 DWT (dead weight ton); includes 347 passenger-cargo, 12,581 freighters, 5,473 bulk carriers, and 5,542 tankers (January 1992)

DEFENSE FORCES

Branches: ground, maritime, and air forces at all levels of technology
Defense expenditures: Somewhat less than $1.0 trillion, 3% of total world output; decline of 5–10% (1993 est.)

Area and Population by Country

Mid-1994 Estimates

Country	Area[1]	Population	Country	Area[1]	Population
Afghanistan	250,000	21,252,000	Brunei	2,226	292,000
Albania	11,100	3,414,000	Bulgaria	42,823	8,775,000
Algeria	919,595	28,539,000	Burkina Faso	105,870	10,423,000
Andorra	175	66,000	Burundi	10,747	6,262,000
Angola	481,350	10,070,000	Cambodia	69,884	10,561,000
Antigua and Barbuda	171	65,000	Cameroon	183,569	13,521,000
Argentina	1,072,067	34,293,000	Canada	3,851,809	28,435,000
Armenia	11,500	3,557,000	Cape Verde	1,557	436,000
Australia	2,966,150	18,322,000	Central African Republic	241,313	3,210,000
Austria	32,375	7,987,000	Chad	495,752	5,587,000
Azerbaijan	33,400	7,790,000	Chile	292,132	14,161,000
Bahamas	5,380	257,000	China, People's Republic of	3,691,521	1,203,097,000
Bahrain	240	576,000	Colombia	439,735	36,200,000
Bangladesh	55,598	128,095,000	Comoros	690	549,000
Barbados	166	256,000	Congo	132,046	2,505,000
Belarus	80,200	10,437,000	Costa Rica	19,652	3,419,000
Belgium	11,781	10,082,000	Côte d'Ivoire	124,502	14,791,000
Belize	8,867	214,000	Croatia	21,829	4,666,000
Benin	43,483	5,523,000	Cuba	44,218	10,938,000
Bhutan	18,000	1,781,000	Cyprus	3,572	737,000
Bolivia	424,162	7,896,000	Czech Republic	30,464	10,433,000
Bosnia–Herzegovina	19,741	3,202,000	Denmark	16,631	5,199,000
Botswana	231,800	1,392,000	Djibouti	8,490	421,000
Brazil	3,286,470	160,737,000	Dominica	290	83,000

Country	Area[1]	Population	Country	Area[1]	Population
Dominican Republic	18,704	7,948,000	Namibia	318,261	1,652,000
Ecuador	106,927	10,891,000	Nepal	54,463	21,561,000
Egypt	386,900	62,360,000	Netherlands	16,041	15,453,000
El Salvador	8,260	5,870,000	New Zealand	103,884	3,407,000
Equatorial Guinea	10,830	420,000	Nicaragua	50,180	4,206,000
Eritrea	45,754	3,579,000	Niger	489,206	9,280,000
Estonia	18,370	1,625,000	Nigeria	356,700	101,232,000
Ethiopia	446,952	55,979,000	Norway	125,049	4,331,000
Fiji	7,078	773,000	Oman	82,030	2,125,000
Finland	130,119	5,085,000	Pakistan	310,400	131,542,000
France	212,918	58,109,000	Panama	29,761	2,681,000
Gabon	103,346	1,156,000	Papua New Guinea	178,704	4,295,000
Gambia	4,093	989,000	Paraguay	157,047	5,358,000
Georgia	26,900	5,726,000	Peru	496,222	24,087,000
Germany	137,838	81,338,000	Philippines	115,830	73,266,000
Ghana	92,100	17,763,000	Poland	120,727	38,792,000
Greece	50,961	10,648,000	Portugal	35,550	10,562,000
Grenada	133	94,000	Qatar	4,000	534,000
Guatemala	42,042	10,999,000	Romania	91,700	23,198,000
Guinea	94,925	6,549,000	Russia	6,592,800	149,909,000
Guinea–Bissau	13,948	1,125,000	Rwanda	10,169	8,605,000
Guyana	83,000	724,000	St. Kitts and Nevis	100	41,000
Haiti	10,714	6,518,000	St. Lucia	238	156,000
Honduras	43,277	5,460,000	St. Vincent and the Grenadines	150	118,000
Hungary	35,919	10,319,000	São Tomé and Príncipe	370	140,000
Iceland	39,709	266,000	Saudi Arabia	865,000	18,730,000
India	1,229,737	936,546,000	Senegal	75,954	9,007,000
Indonesia	735,268	203,584,000	Seychelles	175	73,000
Iran	636,293	64,625,000	Sierra Leone	27,700	4,753,000
Iraq	167,920	20,644,000	Singapore	246	2,890,000
Ireland	27,136	3,550,000	Slovakia	18,917	5,432,000
Israel	8,020	5,143,000	Slovenia	7,819	2,052,000
Italy	116,500	58,262,000	Solomon Islands	11,500	399,000
Jamaica	4,411	2,574,000	Somalia	246,199	7,348,000
Japan	145,874	125,506,000	South Africa	471,440	45,095,000
Jordan	34,573	4,101,000	Spain	194,884	39,404,000
Kazakhstan	1,049,000	17,377,000	Sri Lanka	25,332	18,343,000
Kenya	244,960	28,817,000	Sudan	967,491	30,120,000
Kiribati	280	79,000	Suriname	63,251	430,000
Korea, North	46,768	23,487,000	Swaziland	6,704	967,000
Korea, South	38,031	45,554,000	Sweden	173,800	8,822,000
Kuwait	6,880	1,817,000	Switzerland	15,941	7,085,000
Kyrgyzstan	76,000	4,770,000	Syria	71,498	15,452,000
Laos	91,429	4,837,000	Taiwan	13,895	21,501,000
Latvia	25,400	2,763,000	Tajikistan	55,300	6,155,000
Lebanon	4,015	3,696,000	Tanzania	364,879	28,701,000
Lesotho	11,720	1,993,000	Thailand	198,455	60,271,000
Liberia	43,000	3,073,000	Togo	21,925	4,410,000
Libya	679,536	5,248,000	Tonga	290	106,000
Liechtenstein	61	31,000	Trinidad and Tobago	1,980	1,271,000
Lithuania	25,174	3,876,000	Tunisia	63,379	8,880,000
Luxembourg	999	405,000	Turkey	300,947	63,406,000
Macedonia	9,928	2,160,000	Turkmenistan	188,500	4,075,000
Madagascar	226,660	13,862,000	Uganda	91,459	19,573,000
Malawi	45,747	9,808,000	Ukraine	233,000	51,868,000
Malaysia	128,328	19,724,000	United Arab Emirates	32,000	2,925,000
Maldives	115	261,000	United Kingdom	94,247	58,295,000
Mali	478,819	9,375,000	United States	3,536,341	263,814,000
Malta	122	370,000	Uruguay	68,040	3,223,000
Marshall Islands	70	56,000	Uzbekistan	172,700	23,089,000
Mauritania	397,953	2,263,000	Vanuatu	5,700	174,000
Mauritius	787	1,127,000	Venezuela	352,143	21,005,000
Mexico	761,600	93,986,000	Vietnam	127,246	74,393,000
Micronesia	271	123,000	Western Samoa	1,093	209,000
Moldova	13,000	4,490,000	Yemen	203,850	14,728,000
Mongolia	604,250	2,494,000	Yugoslavia[2]	39,449	11,102,000
Morocco	172,413	29,169,000	Zaire	905,365	44,061,000
Mozambique	303,073	18,115,000	Zambia	290,586	9,446,000
Myanmar	261,220	45,104,000	Zimbabwe	150,698	11,140,000

1. Square miles. 2. On April 27, 1992, Serbia and Montenegro formed a new state, the Federal Republic of Yugoslavia.
Source: U.S. Bureau of the Census, International Data Base.

World's Largest Cities by Rank
(Estimated Mid-Year Population in Thousands)

Rank in 1992	City	1992	1995	2000	Average Annual Growth Rate (%) 1992–95	Area (square miles)
1.	Tokyo–Yokohama, Japan	27,540	28,447	29,971	1.1	1,089
2.	Mexico City, Mexico	21,615	23,913	27,872	3.4	522
3.	Sao Paulo, Brazil	19,373	21,539	25,354	3.5	451
4.	Seoul, South Korea	17,334	19,065	21,976	3.2	342
5.	New York, United States	14,628	14,638	14,648	(Z)	1,274
6.	Osaka–Kobe–Kyoto, Japan	13,919	14,060	14,287	0.3	495
7.	Bombay, India	12,450	13,532	15,357	2.8	95
8.	Calcutta, India	12,137	12,885	14,088	2.0	209
9.	Rio de Janeiro, Brazil	12,009	12,788	14,169	2.1	260
10.	Buenos Aires, Argentina	11,743	12,232	12,911	1.4	535
11.	Manila, Philippines	10,554	11,342	12,846	2.4	188
12.	Moscow, Russia	10,526	10,769	11,121	0.8	379
13.	Cairo, Egypt	10,372	11,155	12,512	2.4	104
14.	Jakarta, Indonesia	10,185	11,151	12,804	3.0	76
15.	Tehran, Iran	10,102	11,681	14,251	4.8	112
16.	Los Angeles, United States	10,072	10,414	10,714	1.1	1,110
17.	Delhi, India	9,243	10,105	11,849	3.0	138
18.	London, United Kingdom	9,168	8,897	8,574	−1.0	874
19.	Paris, France	8,589	8,764	8,803	0.7	432
20.	Lagos, Nigeria	8,487	9,799	12,528	4.8	56
21.	Karachi, Pakistan	8,174	9,350	11,299	4.5	190
22.	Essen, Germany	7,506	7,364	7,239	−0.6	704
23.	Lima, Peru	7,028	7,853	9,241	3.7	120
24.	Shanghai, China	7,000	7,194	7,540	0.9	78
25.	Istanbul, Turkey	6,937	7,624	8,875	3.2	165
26.	Taipei, Taiwan	6,924	7,477	8,516	2.6	138
27.	Chicago, United States	6,493	6,541	6,568	0.2	762
28.	Bogota, Colombia	6,176	6,801	7,935	3.2	79
29.	Bangkok, Thailand	6,088	6,657	7,587	3.0	102
30.	Madras, India	5,998	6,550	7,384	2.9	115
31.	Beijing, China	5,791	5,865	5,993	0.4	151
32.	Hong Kong, Hong Kong	5,762	5,841	5,956	0.5	23
33.	Santiago, Chile	5,484	5,812	6,294	1.9	128
34.	Pusan, South Korea	5,161	5,748	6,700	3.6	54
35.	Bangalore, India	5,080	5,644	6,764	3.5	50
36.	Nagoya, Japan	4,909	5,017	5,303	0.7	307
37.	Tianjin, China	4,857	5,041	5,298	1.2	49
38.	Milan, Italy	4,718	4,795	4,839	0.5	344
39.	St. Petersburg, Russia	4,645	4,694	4,738	0.4	139
40.	Dhaka, Bangladesh	4,640	5,296	6,492	4.4	32
41.	Madrid, Spain	4,577	4,772	5,104	1.4	66
42.	Lahore, Pakistan	4,475	4,986	5,864	3.6	57
43.	Baghdad, Iraq	4,358	4,566	5,239	1.6	97
44.	Shenyang, China	4,323	4,457	4,684	1.0	39
45.	Barcelona, Spain	4,221	4,492	4,834	2.1	87
46.	San Francisco, United States	4,005	4,104	4,214	0.8	428
47.	Kinshasa, Zaire	3,997	4,520	5,646	4.1	57
48.	Manchester, United Kingdom	3,984	3,949	3,827	−0.3	357
49.	Philadelphia, United States	3,970	3,988	3,979	0.2	471
50.	Belo Horizonte, Brazil	3,920	4,373	5,125	3.6	79
51.	Ahmadabad, India	3,826	4,200	4,837	3.1	32
52.	Hyderabad, India	3,787	4,149	4,765	3.0	88
53.	Ho Chi Minh City, Vietnam	3,725	4,064	4,481	2.9	31
54.	Athens, Greece	3,613	3,670	3,866	0.5	116
55.	Sydney, Australia	3,528	3,619	3,708	0.9	338
56.	Guadalajara, Mexico	3,525	3,839	4,451	2.8	78
57.	Miami, United States	3,522	3,679	3,894	1.5	448
58.	Surabaya, Indonesia	3,327	3,428	3,632	1.0	43
59.	Guangzhou, China	3,314	3,485	3,652	1.7	79
60.	Caracas, Venezuela	3,247	3,338	3,435	0.9	54
61.	Wuhan, China	3,231	3,325	3,495	1.0	65
62.	Porto Alegre, Brazil	3,220	3,541	4,109	3.2	231
63.	Toronto, Canada	3,182	3,296	3,296	1.2	154
64.	Casablanca, Morocco	3,136	3,327	3,795	2.0	35

Rank in 1992	City	1992	1995	2000	Average Annual Growth Rate (%) 1992–95	Area (square miles)
65.	Monterrey, Mexico	3,084	3,385	3,974	3.1	77
66.	Rome, Italy	3,028	3,079	3,129	0.6	69
67.	Greater Berlin, Germany	3,020	3,018	3,006	(Z)	274
68.	Ankara, Turkey	3,000	3,263	3,777	2.8	55
69.	Naples, Italy	2,996	3,051	3,134	0.6	62
70.	Alexandria, Egypt	2,981	3,114	3,304	1.5	35
71.	Montreal, Canada	2,933	2,996	3,071	0.7	164
72.	Detroit, United States	2,890	2,865	2,735	−0.3	468
73.	Rangoon, Burma	2,876	3,075	3,332	2.2	47
74.	Melbourne, Australia	2,865	2,946	2,968	0.9	327
75.	Dallas, United States	2,856	2,972	3,257	1.3	419
76.	Taegu, South Korea	2,837	3,201	4,051	4.0	(n.a.)
77.	Kiev, Ukraine	2,837	2,983	3,237	1.7	62
78.	Singapore, Singapore	2,743	2,816	2,913	0.9	78
79.	Harbin, China	2,625	2,747	2,887	1.5	30
80.	Poona, India	2,617	2,987	3,647	4.4	(n.a.)
81.	Washington, D.C., United States	2,572	2,637	2,707	0.8	357
82.	Lisbon, Portugal	2,505	2,551	2,717	0.6	(n.a.)
83.	Chongqing, China	2,468	2,632	2,961	2.1	(n.a.)
84.	Tashkent, Uzbekistan	2,461	2,640	2,947	2.3	(n.a.)
85.	Boston, United States	2,460	2,480	2,485	0.3	303
86.	Vienna, Austria	2,392	2,474	2,647	1.1	(n.a.)
87.	Houston, United States	2,369	2,456	2,651	1.2	310
88.	Salvador, Brazil	2,366	2,694	3,286	4.3	(n.a.)
89.	Chengdu, China	2,365	2,465	2,591	1.4	25
90.	Budapest, Hungary	2,304	2,313	2,335	0.1	138
91.	Kanpur, India	2,184	2,356	2,673	2.5	(n.a.)
92.	Birmingham, United Kingdom	2,177	2,130	2,078	−0.7	223
93.	Bucharest, Romania	2,175	2,214	2,271	0.6	52
94.	Havana, Cuba	2,152	2,218	2,333	1.0	(n.a.)

Source: U.S. Bureau of the Census International Data Base. NOTE: For this table cities are defined as population clusters of continuous built-up area with a population density of at least 5,000 persons per square mile. The boundary of the city was determined by examining detailed maps of each city in conjunction with the most recent official population statistics. Exclaves of areas exceeding the minimum population density were added to the city if the intervening gap was less than one mile. To the extent practical, nonresidential areas such as parks, airports, industrial complexes, and water excluded from the area reported for each city, thus making the population density reflective of the concentrations in the residential portions of the city. By using a consistent definition for the city, it is possible to make comparisons of the cities on the basis of total population, area, and population density.

Political and administrative boundaries were disregarded in determining the population of a city. Detroit includes Windsor, Canada.

The population of each city was projected based on the proportion each city was of its country total at the time of the last two censuses and projected country populations.

Population figures for the nine cities with (n.a.) in the area column were derived by a less precise method, not involving the use of detailed maps. Thirty-four other cities are projected to have at least 2,000,000 inhabitants by midyear 2000. These population figures may not agree with those in the Countries of the World section as the source is different, and the basis for these figures is spelled out above. Z less than .05.

Crude Marriage Rates for Selected Countries
(per 1,000 population)

Country	1993	1992	1991	1990	1989	1988	Country	1993	1992	1991	1990	1989	1988
Australia	6.4	6.6	6.6	6.9	7.0	7.1	Japan	6.4	6.1	6.0	5.8	5.8	5.8
Austria	5.6	5.8	5.6	5.8	5.6	4.7	Luxembourg	6.0	6.4	6.7	6.2	5.8	5.5
Belgium	5.4	5.8	6.2	6.6	6.4	6.0	Netherlands	5.8	6.4	6.3	6.4	6.1	6.0
Bulgaria	4.9	5.0	5.4	6.7	7.0	7.0	New Zealand	6.4	6.5	6.8	7.0	6.9	7.1
Czech Republic[1]	6.4	n.a.	6.7	8.4	7.5	7.6	Norway	n.a.	4.5	4.7	5.2	4.9	5.2
Denmark	6.1	6.2	6.0	6.1	6.0	6.3	Poland	5.4	5.7	6.0	6.7	6.8	6.5
Finland	4.9	4.6	4.7	4.8	5.1	5.3	Portugal	6.9	7.1	6.8	7.3	7.4	6.9
France	4.4	4.7	4.9	5.1	5.0	4.9	Romania	7.1	7.7	7.9	8.3	7.7	7.5
Germany[2]	5.4	5.7	6.3	6.5	6.7	6.8	Russia	n.a.	7.1	8.5	8.9	9.4	9.5
Greece	5.9	4.7	6.0	5.8	6.0	5.2	Sweden	3.9	4.3	4.6	4.7	12.8	5.2
Hungary	5.3	5.5	5.9	6.4	6.3	6.2	Switzerland	6.2	6.6	7.0	6.9	6.8	6.9
Ireland	4.5	4.5	4.8	5.0	5.2	5.1	United Kingdom	n.a.	6.1	6.1	6.8	6.8	6.9
Israel	6.2	6.5	6.5	7.0	7.0	6.9	United States	9.0	9.2	9.4	9.8	9.7	9.7
Italy	4.8	5.4	5.5	5.4	5.4	5.5	Yugoslavia[3]	5.8	6.0	n.a.	6.2	6.7	6.8

1. Data prior to 1993 pertain to the former Czechoslovakia. 2. All data pertaining to Germany prior to 1990 are for West Germany. 3. Beginning January 1992, data refer to the Federal Republic of Yugoslavia. Prior to that date, data refer to the Socialist Federal Republic of Yugoslavia. NOTE: n.a. = not available. *Source:* United Nations, *Monthly Bulletin of Statistics, June 1995.*

World Population by Country, 1995–2020

(Covers countries with 10 million or more population in 1995)

Country	1995	2000	2010	2020
Afghanistan	21,252,000	25,725,000	32,889,000	41,518,000
Algeria	28,539,000	31,743,000	38,186,000	44,096,000
Angola	10,070,000	11,513,000	14,982,000	19,272,000
Argentina	34,293,000	36,202,000	39,947,000	43,190,000
Australia	18,322,000	19,386,000	21,151,000	22,724,000
Bangladesh	128,095,000	143,548,000	176,902,000	210,248,000
Belarus	10,437,000	10,576,000	10,864,000	11,047,000
Belgium	10,082,000	10,144,000	10,135,000	10,015,000
Brazil	160,737,000	169,543,000	183,742,000	197,466,000
Burkina Faso	10,423,000	11,871,000	14,478,000	18,123,000
Cambodia	10,561,000	12,098,000	15,679,000	20,208,000
Cameroon	13,521,000	15,677,000	21,165,000	28,329,000
Canada	28,435,000	29,867,000	32,265,000	34,347,000
Chile	14,161,000	15,207,000	17,266,000	19,225,000
China				
Mainland	1,203,097,000	1,260,154,000	1,348,429,000	1,424,725,000
Taiwan	21,501,000	22,448,000	24,092,000	25,122,000
Colombia	36,200,000	39,172,000	44,504,000	49,266,000
Côte d'Ivoire	14,791,000	17,371,000	22,924,000	29,705,000
Cuba	10,938,000	11,617,000	12,274,000	12,755,000
Czech Republic	10,433,000	10,607,000	10,892,000	10,991,000
Ecuador	10,891,000	11,945,000	13,990,000	15,894,000
Egypt	62,360,000	67,542,000	82,478,000	97,434,000
Ethiopia	55,979,000	70,340,000	94,496,000	124,294,000
France	58,109,000	59,354,000	61,001,000	61,793,000
Germany	81,338,000	82,239,000	82,837,000	82,385,000
Ghana	17,763,000	20,608,000	27,305,000	35,877,000
Greece	10,648,000	10,878,000	10,920,000	10,689,000
Guatemala	10,999,000	12,408,000	15,284,000	18,131,000
Hungary	10,319,000	10,372,000	10,477,000	10,449,000
India	936,546,000	1,018,105,000	1,173,621,000	1,320,746,000
Indonesia	203,584,000	219,496,000	250,033,000	276,474,000
Iran	64,625,000	78,347,000	107,676,000	143,624,000
Iraq	20,644,000	24,731,000	34,545,000	46,260,000
Italy	58,262,000	58,865,000	59,089,000	57,844,000
Japan	125,506,000	127,554,000	129,361,000	126,062,000
Kazakhstan	17,377,000	17,886,000	18,794,000	19,404,000
Kenya	28,817,000	32,479,000	37,990,000	44,240,000
Madagascar	13,862,000	16,232,000	22,064,000	29,362,000
Malaysia	19,724,000	21,953,000	26,589,000	31,681,000
Mexico	93,986,000	102,912,000	120,115,000	136,096,000
Morocco	29,169,000	32,189,000	38,112,000	43,701,000
Mozambique	18,115,000	20,868,000	27,381,000	35,240,000
Myanmar	45,104,000	49,300,000	57,720,000	65,914,000
Nepal	21,561,000	24,364,000	30,783,000	37,767,000
Netherlands	15,453,000	15,801,000	16,140,000	16,222,000
Nigeria	101,232,000	118,620,000	161,969,000	215,893,000
North Korea	23,487,000	25,491,000	28,491,000	30,969,000
Pakistan	131,542,000	148,540,000	195,108,000	251,330,000
Peru	24,087,000	26,258,000	30,483,000	34,340,000
Philippines	73,266,000	77,747,000	90,316,000	101,530,000
Poland	38,792,000	39,531,000	41,332,000	42,474,000
Portugal	10,562,000	10,744,000	10,997,000	11,038,000
Romania	23,198,000	23,383,000	23,950,000	24,337,000
Russia	149,909,000	151,460,000	155,933,000	159,263,000
Saudi Arabia	18,730,000	22,070,000	30,494,000	42,085,000
Serbia & Montenegro	11,102,000	11,121,000	11,625,000	11,881,000
South Africa	45,095,000	51,334,000	65,850,000	82,502,000
South Korea	45,554,000	47,861,000	51,677,000	54,014,000
Spain	39,404,000	39,972,000	40,682,000	40,241,000
Sri Lanka	18,343,000	19,146,000	20,972,000	22,463,000
Sudan	30,120,000	35,236,000	46,167,000	58,090,000
Syria	15,452,000	18,519,000	25,768,000	34,309,000
Tanzania	28,701,000	32,254,000	38,651,000	48,526,000
Thailand	60,271,000	63,620,000	64,181,000	62,941,000

Country	1995	2000	2010	2020
Turkey	63,406,000	69,624,000	81,790,000	93,362,000
Uganda	19,573,000	22,748,000	26,997,000	34,106,000
Ukraine	51,868,000	51,931,000	52,280,000	52,337,000
United Kingdom	58,295,000	58,951,000	59,617,000	60,042,000
United Statees	263,814,000	275,327,000	298,621,000	323,113,000
Uzbekistan	23,089,000	25,467,000	30,380,000	35,422,000
Venezuela	21,005,000	23,196,000	27,407,000	31,312,000
Vietnam	74,393,000	80,533,000	91,729,000	102,359,000
Yemen	14,728,000	13,603,000	18,985,000	25,907,000
Zaire	44,061,000	51,413,000	69,079,000	92,860,000
Zimbabwe	11,140,000	12,013,000	12,990,000	14,620,000

Source: U.S. Department of Commerce, Bureau of the Census.

Estimates of World Population by Regions

Year	North America[1]	Latin America[2]	Europe[3]	Former U.S.S.R.	Asia[4]	Africa	Oceania	World total
			Estimated population in millions					
1650	1	7	103	(5)	257	100	2	470
1750	1	10	144	(5)	437	100	2	694
1850	26	33	274	(5)	656	100	2	1,091
1900	81	63	423	(5)	857	141	6	1,571
1950	166	164	392	180	1,380	219	13	2,513
1960	199	215	425	214	1,683	275	16	3,027
1970	226	283	460	244	2,091	354	19	3,678
1980	252	365	484	266	2,618	472	23	4,478
1985	264	410	492	278	2,831	566	24	4,865
1990	276	442	501	289	3,130	625	26	5,292
1995	292	481	509	297	3,403	721	28	5,734

1. U.S. (including Alaska and Hawaii), Bermuda, Canada, Greenland, and St. Pierre and Miquelon. 2. Mexico, Central and South America, and Caribbean Islands. 3. Includes Russia 1650-1900. 4. Excludes Russia (U.S.S.R.). 5. Included in Europe. NOTE: From 1930 on European Turkey included in Asia not Europe. *Sources:* W.F. Willcox, 1650-1900; United Nations, 1930-70. United States Department of Commerce, Bureau of the Census, 1980–95.

World's 20 Most Populous Countries: 1995 and 2020

	1995			2020	
Rank	Country	Population	Rank	Country	Population
1.	China	1,203,097,000	1.	China	1,424,725,000
2.	India	936,546,000	2.	India	1,320,746,000
3.	United States	263,814,000	3.	United States	323,113,000
4.	Indonesia	203,584,000	4.	Indonesia	276,474,000
5.	Brazil	160,737,000	5.	Pakistan	251,330,000
6.	Russia	149,909,000	6.	Nigeria	215,893,000
7.	Pakistan	131,542,000	7.	Bangladesh	210,248,000
8.	Bangladesh	128,095,000	8.	Brazil	197,466,000
9.	Japan	125,506,000	9.	Russia	159,263,000
10.	Nigeria	101,232,000	10.	Iran	143,624,000
11.	Mexico	93,986,000	11.	Mexico	136,096,000
12.	Germany	81,338,000	12.	Japan	126,062,000
13.	Vietnam	74,393,000	13.	Ethiopia	124,294,000
14.	Philippines	73,266,000	14.	Vietnam	102,359,000
15.	Iran	64,625,000	15.	Philippines	101,530,000
16.	Turkey	63,406,000	16.	Egypt	97,434,000
17.	Egypt	62,360,000	17.	Turkey	93,362,000
18.	Thailand	60,271,000	18.	Zaire	92,860,000
19.	United Kingdom	58,295,000	19.	South Africa	82,502,000
20.	Italy	58,262,000	20.	Germany	82,385,000

Source: U.S. Department of Commerce, Bureau of the Ceusus.

Infant Mortality Rates and Life Expectancy at Birth by Sex for Selected Countries, 1994

Country	Infant deaths per 1,000 live births			Life expectancy at birth (years)		
	Both sexes	Male	Female	Both sexes	Male	Female
NORTH AMERICA						
Canada	7	8	6	78	75	82
United States	8	9	7	76	73	79
Mexico	27	33	22	73	69	77
CENTRAL AND SOUTH AMERICA						
Brazil	60	64	55	62	57	67
Chile	15	17	14	75	72	78
Costa Rica	11	11	11	78	76	80
Ecuador	39	44	34	70	67	73
Guatemala	54	58	50	64	62	67
Panama	17	18	15	75	72	78
Peru	54	59	49	66	63	68
Trinidad and Tobago	17	19	14	71	68	73
Uruguay	17	19	15	74	71	77
Venezuela	28	31	25	73	70	76
EUROPE						
Austria	7	8	6	77	73	80
Belgium	7	8	6	77	74	80
Cyprus	9	10	8	76	74	79
Czech Republic	9	11	8	73	69	77
Denmark	7	8	6	76	73	79
Finland	5	5	5	76	72	80
France	7	8	6	78	74	82
Germany	7	7	6	76	73	80
Greece	9	9	8	78	75	80
Hungary	13	14	11	71	67	76
Ireland	7	8	7	76	73	79
Italy	8	8	7	78	74	81
Netherlands	6	7	5	78	75	81
Norway	6	7	6	77	74	81
Poland	13	15	11	73	69	77
Portugal	10	11	8	75	72	79
Russia	27	31	23	69	64	74
Slovakia	10	12	9	73	69	77
Spain	7	8	6	78	74	81
Sweden	6	6	5	78	75	81
Switzerland	7	7	6	78	75	82
United Kingdom	7	8	6	77	74	80
Yugoslavia	21	22	20	74	71	76
ASIA						
Bangladesh	107	115	99	55	55	55
India	78	78	79	59	58	59
Iran	60	61	60	66	65	67
Israel	9	10	8	78	76	80
Japan	4	5	4	79	76	82
Pakistan	102	103	100	57	57	58
South Korea	22	20	24	71	67	74
Sri Lanka	22	24	20	72	69	74
Syria	43	43	42	66	65	68
AFRICA						
Egypt	76	78	75	61	59	63
Kenya	74	78	71	53	51	55
South Africa	47	45	49	65	62	68
OCEANIA						
Australia	7	8	6	78	74	81
New Zealand	9	9	8	76	73	80

Source: U.S. Bureau of the Census, International Data Base.

Fourth World Conference on Women

Draft Platform for Action
12 Critical Areas of Concern

Source: UN Chronicle, June 1995.

Prior to the Beijing Conference held from September 4 to 15, 1995, the U.N. Commission on the Status of Women issued a draft Platform for Action, focusing on 12 "critical areas of concern" that have been identified as obstacles to the advancement of women. Related to these concerns, the draft proposed to:

1. Poverty

• Create social security systems wherever they do not exist.
• Develop gender-sensitive national and international policies, including those related to structural adjustment.
• Provide poor women with economic opportunities and equal access to affordable housing, land, natural resources, credit, and other services.
• Devise statistical means to recognize and make visible the work—including unpaid and domestic—of women and their contribution to national economies.

2. Education

• Closing the gender gap in primary and secondary school education by the year 2005.
• Eradicate illiteracy of women worldwide by 2000 or another target date to be agreed at the Conference.
• Improve women's access to and provide funding for vocational training, science and technology.
• Develop curricula, textbooks, and teaching aids free of gender stereotypes.

3. Health

• Strengthen and reorient health services in order to reduce maternal mortality by at least 50 percent of the 1990 levels by the year 2000.
• Strengthen preventive programs that address threats to women's health.
• Make efforts to combat HIV/AIDS and other sexually transmitted diseases, and recognize the impact of those diseases on women.
• Promote research on and increase funding for women's health issues and services.

4. Violence

• Take integrated legal and social measures to prevent violence and protect women.
• Adopt measures to eliminate trafficking in women and eradicate violence against women who are vulnerable, such as those with disabilities and migrant workers.
• Study the causes of violence against women and effective measures of prevention.

5. Armed Conflicts

• Increase and strengthen women's participation in conflict resolution.
• Promote women's contribution to fostering a culture of peace.
• Reduce the incidence of human rights abuses in conflict situations, protect refugee and displaced women, and provide assistance to women of the colonies.

6. Economic Disparity

• Enact laws to guarantee the rights of women and men to equal pay for equal work, and adjust work patterns to promote the sharing of family responsibilities.
• Provide women with equal access to resources, employment, markets and trade, as well as to information and technology.
• Eliminate sexual harassment and other forms of discrimination in the workplace.

7. Power-Sharing

• Ensure women's full and equal participation in power structures and decision-making.
• Develop education and training to increase women's capacity to participate in decision-making and leadership.
• Aim at gender balance in government bodies and the composition of delegations to the U.N.

8. Institutions

• Ensure that responsibility for the advancement of women is invested at the highest level of government.
• Integrate gender perspectives in all legislation, public policies, programs and projects.
• Collect and disseminate statistics showing gender impact of policies and programs.

9. Human Rights

• Encourage ratification of international human rights treaties and promote their implementation.
• Provide gender-sensitive human rights training to public officials.
• Improve access to legal services and literacy through information campaigns and national training programs.

10. Mass Media

• Take steps to ensure women's access to information and the media on an equal basis.
• Encourage elimination of gender stereotyping in the media through studies, campaigns, and various forms of self-regulation by media organizations.

11. Environment

• Involve women in environmental decision-making and integrate gender concerns in policies for sustainable development.
• Assess the impact of development and environmental policies on women.

12. Girl Child

• Eliminate all forms of discrimination, as well as negative cultural attitudes and practices, against girls.
• Ensure that girls develop a positive self-image and have equal access to education and health care.
• Protect girls from economic exploitation and eliminate violence against them.

Crude Birth and Death Rates for Selected Countries
(per 1,000 population)

Country	Birth rates					Death rates				
	1993	1990	1985	1980	1975	1993	1990	1985	1980	1975
Australia	14.7	15.4	15.7	15.3	16.9	6.9	7.0	7.5	7.4	7.9
Austria	11.8	11.6	11.6	12.0	12.5	10.3	10.6	11.9	12.2	12.8
Belgium	12.1	12.6	11.5	12.7	12.2	10.8	10.6	11.2	11.6	12.2
Czech Republic[1]	11.7	13.4	14.5	16.4	19.6	11.5	11.7	11.8	12.1	11.5
Denmark	13.0	12.4	10.6	11.2	14.2	12.1	11.9	11.4	10.9	10.1
Finland	12.8	13.2	12.8	13.1	13.9	10.1	10.0	9.8	9.3	9.3
France	12.3	13.5	13.9	14.8	14.1	9.2	9.3	10.1	10.2	10.6
Germany[2]	9.8	11.4	9.6	10.0	9.7	11.1	11.2	11.5	11.6	12.1
Greece	10.0	10.2	11.7	15.4	15.7	9.4	9.3	9.4	9.1	8.9
Hong Kong	11.9	11.7	14.0	16.9	n.a.	5.3	4.9	4.6	5.1	n.a.
Hungary	11.4	12.1	12.2	13.9	18.4	14.6	14.1	13.9	13.6	12.4
Ireland	14.0	15.1	17.6	21.9	21.5	8.6	9.1	9.4	9.7	10.6
Israel	21.4	22.2	23.5	24.1	28.2	6.3	6.2	6.6	6.7	7.1
Italy	9.4	9.8	10.1	11.2	14.8	9.5	9.4	9.5	9.7	9.9
Japan	9.5	9.9	11.9	13.7	17.2	7.0	6.7	6.2	6.2	6.4
Luxembourg	13.4	13.3	11.2	11.5	11.2	9.8	10.1	11.0	11.5	12.2
Mauritius	20.9	21.0	18.8	27.0	25.1	6.8	6.5	6.8	7.2	8.1
Netherlands	12.8	13.3	12.3	12.8	13.0	9.0	8.6	8.5	8.1	8.3
New Zealand	17.0	18.0	15.6	n.a.	18.4	7.9	7.9	8.4	n.a.	8.1
Norway	14.1	14.3	12.3	12.5	14.1	11.0	10.7	10.7	10.1	9.9
Panama	22.8	23.9	26.6	26.8	32.3	n.a.	n.a.	n.a.	n.a.	n.a.
Poland	12.8	14.3	18.2	19.5	18.9	10.2	10.2	10.3	9.8	8.7
Portugal	11.5	11.8	12.8	16.4	19.1	10.8	10.4	9.6	9.9	10.4
Romania	11.0	13.6	15.8	n.a.	n.a.	11.6	10.6	10.9	n.a.	n.a.
Singapore	17.6	17.0	16.6	17.3	17.8	5.0	n.a.	5.2	5.2	5.1
Sweden	13.5	14.5	11.8	11.7	12.6	11.1	11.	11.3	11.0	10.8
Switzerland	12.1	12.5	11.6	11.3	12.3	9.0	9.5	9.2	9.2	8.7
Tunisia	n.a.	25.8	31.3	35.2	36.6	n.a.	n.a.	n.a.	n.a.	n.a.
United Kingdom	13.1	13.9	13.3	13.5	12.5	n.a.	11.2	11.8	11.8	11.9
United States	15.6	16.7	15.7	16.2	14.0	8.8	8.6	8.7	8.9	8.9
Yugoslavia[3]	13.4	14.0	15.9	17.0	18.2	10.0	9.0	9.1	9.0	8.7

1. Data prior to 1993 pertain to the former Czechoslovakia 2. All data pertaining to Germany prior to 1990 are for West Germany. 3. Beginning January 1992, data refer to the Federal Republic of Yugoslavia. Prior to that date, data refer to the Socialist Federal Republic of Yugoslavia. NOTE: n.a. = not available. *Source:* United Nations, *Monthly Bulletin of Statistics,* May 1995.

Legal Abortions in Selected Countries, 1983–1991

Country	1983	1984	1985	1986	1987	1988	1989	1990	1991
Bulgaria	134,165	131,140	132,041	134,686	133,815	—	132,021	144,644	—
Canada	61,750	62,291	60,956	62,406	63,585	—	70,705	71,092	—
Cuba	116,956	139,588	138,671	160,926	152,704	155,325	151,146	147,530	—
Former Czechoslovakia	108,662	113,802	119,325	124,188	158,451	164,730	160,285	159,705	—
Denmark	20,791	20,742	19,919	20,067	20,830	21,199	21,456	20,589	19,729
Finland	13,360	13,645	13,832	13,310	13,000[1]	12,995	12,658	12,232	—
France	182,862	180,789	173,335	166,797	161,036	163,000	165,199	161,646	—
Former Germany, West	86,529	86,298	83,538	84,274	88,540	83,784	75,297	78,808	74,571
Greece	220	193	180[1]	—	—	—	—	—	—
Hungary	78,599	82,191	81,970	83,586	84,547	87,106	90,508	90,394	89,931
Iceland	687	745	705	684	691	673	670	714	—
India	492,696	561,033	583,704	—	—	534,870	582,161	596,345	—
Israel	15,593	18,948	18,406	17,469	15,290	16,181	15,216	18,000	15,800[1]
Italy	231,061	228,377	210,192	196,969	187,618	175,541	166,290	161,285	—
Netherlands	19,700	18,700[1]	17,300[1]	—	17,760	18,014	17,996	18,384	—
New Zealand	7,198	7,275	7,130	8,056	8,789	10,000[1]	10,200[1]	—	—
Norway	13,646	14,070	14,599	15,474	15,422	15,852	16,208	15,551	15,528
Poland	130,980	132,844	135,564	129,720	122,536	105,333	80,127	59,417	30,878
Singapore	19,100	22,190	23,512	21,374	21,226	20,135	20,619	18,654	17,798
Sweden	31,014	30,755	30,838	33,090	34,707	37,585	37,920	37,489	35,788
United Kingdom	170,620	179,102	180,983	157,168	165,542	178,426	180,622	184,092	184,092
United States	1,575,000	1,577,200	1,588,600	1,574,000	1,559,000	1,590,800	—	—	—

1. Provisional. NOTE: Data latest available. *Source:* United Nations, *Demographic Yearbook, 1992.*

Cost of Living of United Nations Personnel in Selected Cities as Reflected by Index of Retail Prices, 1994

(New York City, December 1994 = 100)

City	Index	City	Index	City	Index
Abu Dhabi	89	Guatemala City	82	Nassau	112
Addis Ababa	80[1]	The Hague	102	New Delhi	85
Algiers	95	Helsinki	99	Panama City	90
Amman	81	Islamabad	81	Paris	108
Ankara	88	Jakarta	93	Port-au-Prince	87
Athens	89	Kabul	71	Quito	85
Bangkok	91	Kathmandu	80	Rabat	89
Beirut	107	Kiev	91	Rome	93
Bogata	98	Kingston	91	Roseau	100
Bonn	113	La Paz	84	San Salvador	79
Bratislava	92	Lagos	134[1]	Santiago	95
Brazzaville	105[1]	Lima	93	Seoul	107
Brussels	112	London	99	Sofia	83
Bucharest	92[1]	Madrid	97	Sydney	85
Budapest	94	Managua	86	Tallin	92
Buenos Aires	119	Manila	100	Tokyo	183
Cairo	95	Mexico City	96	Tripoli	131[1]
Caracas	85	Minsk	90	Tunis	89
Copenhagen	107	Montevideo	110	Valetta	85
Dhaka	84	Montreal	76	Vienna	116
Dakar	90	Moscow	98	Warsaw	88
Geneva	133	Nairobi	103	Washington, D.C.	90

1. Calculated on the basis of cost of Government or subsidized housing which is normally lower than prevailing rentals.
Source: United Nations, *Monthly Bulletin of Statistics, March 1995.*

Consumer Price Indexes for All Items for Selected Countries, 1994

(1980 = 100)

Country	Index	Country	Index	Country	Index
Australia	225.8	Greece	1,002.1	Philippines	194.3[3]
Austria	162.1	Hong Kong	311.9	Singapore	140.2
Canada	194.3	Indonesia	157.4[2]	Slovakia	153.7[1]
Chile	1,122.3	Italy	304.5	South Africa	615.7
Cyprus	197.6	Japan	131.1	Spain	298.9
Czech Republic	147.7[1]	Jordan	243.2	Sri Lanka	480.0
Denmark	191.6	Korea, South	237.2	Sweden	248.5
Egypt	787.2	Mexico	25,046.3	Turkey	4,395.9[4]
Finland	212.5	Morocco	135.1[2]	United Kingdom	215.6
France	201.8	Netherlands	112.2	United States	179.9
Germany	149.5	Norway	228.8	Uruguay	86,679.2

1. Base: 1991 = 100. 2. Base: 1989 = 100. 3. Base: 1988 = 100. 4. Base: 1987 = 100. *Source:* International Labour Office from *Monthly Bulletin of Statistics, July 1995.*

Labor Force Participation Rates by Sex[1]

Country	Females				Males				Females as percent of total labor force			
	1992	1990	1985	1980	1992	1990	1985	1980	1992	1990	1985	1980
Australia	47.7	49.3	42.9	41.9	66.6	71.3	70.4	75.1	42.1	41.3	38.4	36.4
Canada	51.6	53.7	48.8	46.2	65.0	69.8	68.7	73.0	45.5	44.7	42.7	39.7
France	41.7[2]	41.5	39.6	40.1	59.6[2]	61.3	62.3	68.5	43.8[2]	43.0	41.4	39.5
Germany[3]	41.9[2]	40.9[2]	37.1	37.7	65.3[2]	65.6[2]	66.4	70.9	42.0[2]	41.2[2]	39.0	38.0
Italy	n.a.	29.2[2]	27.8	27.9	n.a.	60.1[2]	62.5	66.0	n.a.	34.7[2]	32.8	31.7
Japan	48.7	48.0	46.3	45.7	76.1	75.4	75.9	77.9	40.5	40.3	39.4	38.4
Netherlands	n.a.	n.a.	33.4	31.0	n.a.	n.a.	67.6	74.1	n.a.	n.a.	34.0	30.2
Sweden	59.4[2]	62.7[2,4]	59.7	58.0	66.8[2]	71.7[2,4]	70.5	73.6	48.3[2]	47.8[2,4]	47.2	45.2
United Kingdom	48.8[2]	49.7[2]	44.3	44.8	65.0[2]	70.1[2]	67.1	72.8	44.9[2]	43.5[2]	42.0	40.4
United States	53.8	54.4	50.4	47.7	69.7	71.9	70.9	72.0	45.7	45.4	44.1	42.4

1. Civilian employment as a percent of the civilian working age population. 2. Preliminary. 3. Former West Germany. 4. Break in series. *Source:* U.S. Bureau of Labor Statistics, *Comparative Labor Force Statistics for Ten Countries, 1959–1992, August 1993.* From *Statistical Abstract of the United States 1994.* NOTE: n.a. = not available. Data are most recent available.

Unemployment Figures for Selected Countries: 1989–1994

(In thousands except for percentages)

Country	1994 No.	1994 %	1993 No.	1993 %	1992 No.	1992 %	1991 No.	1991 %	1990 No.	1990 %	1989 No.	1989 %
Australia	855.5	9.7	939.2	10.9	933.1	10.8	821.0	9.6	587.1	6.9	509.1	6.2
Austria[1]	214.9	6.5	222.3	6.8	193.1	5.9	185.0	5.8	165.8	5.4	149.2	5.0
Barbados	28.2	21.8	31.0	24.7	28.8	23.0	20.9	17.2	18.6	15.0	19.8	16.5
Belgium[1]	588.7	13.9	549.7	13.1	472.9	11.2	429.5	10.4	402.8	9.8	419.3	10.1
Canada	1,458.0	10.3	1,562.0	11.2	1,556.0	11.3	1,417.0	10.3	1,109.0	8.1	1,018.0	7.5
Chile[2]	311.3	5.9	223.6	4.5	n.a.	n.a.	253.7	5.3	281.3	5.6	249.8	n.a.
Denmark[1]	340.4	12.1	348.8	12.4	314.7	11.3	293.9	10.5	269.1	9.6	264.9	9.4
Finland	456.0	18.4	444.0	17.9	328.0	13.1	193.0	7.6	88.0	3.4	89.0	3.5
Germany[1, 3]	2,556.0	9.2	2,270.9	8.2	1,820.6	6.7	1,689.4	6.3	1,872.0	7.2	2,032.0	7.9
Hong-Kong	57.2	1.9	56.9	2.0	54.7	2.0	50.3	1.8	37.0	1.3	30.0	1.1
Ireland[4, 5]	282.4	n.a.	294.0	n.a.	283.1	n.a.	253.9	19.1	224.7	17.4	231.6	17.9
Israel	158.5	7.8	2,360.0	10.4	207.5	11.2	187.4	10.6	157.9	9.6	142.5	n.a.
Italy	2,586.0	11.5	2,360.0	10.4	2,799.0	11.5	2,653.0	10.9	2,621.0	11.0	2,865.0	12.0
Japan	1,920.0	2.9	1,655.8	2.5	1,420.8	2.1	1,370.0	2.1	1,340.0	2.1	1,420.0	2.3
Korea, South	488.8	2.4	551.1	2.8	463.4	2.4	436.0	2.3	451.0	2.5	459.0	2.6
Netherlands[1, 6]	486.0	7.6	415.0	6.5	303.0	4.2	319.0	4.5	346.0	4.9	390.0	5.8
New Zealand[1]	183.5	n.a.	212.7	n.a.	216.9	n.a.	195.1	n.a.	164.0	7.7	153.6	n.a.
Norway	116.5	5.4	127.0	6.0	126.0	5.9	116.0	5.5	112.0	4.3	106.0	3.8
Portugal	312.2	6.9	248.3	5.6	186.9	4.1	198.6	4.1	220.1	4.7	232.8	5.0
Sweden	340.0	8.0	326.1	8.7	214.0	4.8	122.0	2.7	69.0	1.6	61.0	1.4
Switzerland[1]	171.0	4.7	163.1	4.5	92.3	n.a.	39.2	1.3	18.1	0.6	17.5	0.6
Turkey[1]	n.a.	n.a.	682.6	n.a.	840.1	n.a.	859.0	n.a.	979.5	n.a.	1,076.2	n.a.
United Kingdom[1, 7]	2,636.5	9.4	2,919.2	10.4	2,778.6	9.8	2,291.9	8.1	1,664.5	5.9	1,800.5	6.4
United States[8]	7,996.0	6.1	8,734.0	6.8	9,384.0	7.4	8,426.0	6.7	6,874.0	5.5	6,528.0	5.3

1. Employment office statistics. All others labor force sample surveys unless otherwise indicated. 2. Average of less than 12 months. 3. Data prior to October 3, 1990, are for West Germany. 4. Excluding agriculture, fishing and private domestic services. 5. Compulsory unemployment insurance statistics. 6. Based on labor force sample surveys beginning 1988 and scope of series revised. 7. Excluding persons temporarily laid off. Excluding adult students registered for vacation employment. 8. Scope of series revised. NOTE: n.a.= not available. *Source:* United Nations, *Monthly Bulletin of Statistics, July 1995.*

Non-Agricultural Employment for Selected Countries, 1988–1994

(in thousands)

Country	1994	1993	1992	1991	1990	1989	1988
Australia[1, 2, 3]	7,483.2	7,299.6	7,262.9	7,284.0	7,413.7	7,299.8	6,907.3
Canada[3, 4]	—	—	11,674.6	11,556.0	12,040.0	11,949.0	11,804.0
Chile[3]	4,179.4	4,160.4	3,913.2	3,674.2	3,574.6	3,568.0	3,401.2
Finland[3]	1,857.0	1,867.0	1,987.0	2,154.0	2,260.0	2,252.0	2,193.0
Germany[4, 6]	27,113.0	27,405.0	27,805.0	27,589.0	26,985.0	26,133.0	25,740.0
Hungary[5]	2,704.8	2,614.0	1,585.7	1,916.1	2,249.9	2,483.3	2,614.9
Israel	1,883.7	1,750.6	1,659.8	1,551.9	1,415.5	1,263.3	1,259.3
Italy[3]	18,464.0	18,919.0	19,710.0	19,769.0	19,409.0	19,058.0	19,045.0
Japan[3, 4]	60,797.5	60,663.3	60,249.2	59,410.0	57,990.0	56,650.0	55,360.0
Korea, South[4]	17,138.0	16,358.2	15,896.0	15,473.0	14,744.0	14,094.0	13,386.0
New Caledonia	48.3	47.2	46.4	45.9	44.4	42.2	38.0
New Zealand[7]	1,397.8	1,338.1	1,307.5	1,294.6	1,315.9	1,310.8	1,346.7
Norway[3, 8]	1,928.0	1,893.0	1,894.0	1,894.0	1,901.0	1,917.0	1,980.0
Poland	8,290.0	8,272.5	8,465.0	9,064.0	9,669.0	10,565.0	10,715.0
Portugal[3]	3,761.3	3,772.9	3,850.6	3,831.8	3,700.7	3,566.0	3,413.8
Spain[3]	10,579.2	—	10,933.5	11,264.3	11,093.3	10,660.4	10,078.4
Sweden[4]	3,793.0	3,827.3	—	4,287.0	4,358.0	4,307.0	4,231.0
Switzerland[9]	—	99.7	102.3	104.7	106.4	105.1	103.7
United States[3, 4, 10]	119,651.0[8]	116,232.0	114,391.0	113,644.0	114,728.0	114,142.0	111,800.0
U.S. Virgin Islands	—	48.6	44.8	43.8	43.1	42.0	41.5

1. Annual averages: one month of each year. 2. Excluding armed forces. 3. Persons aged 15 years and over (Finland: 15–74; Italy: 14; Norway and Sweden: 16–74, Spain, and U.S.A.: 16 years; Portugal: 12 years). 4. Civilian labor force. 5. Socialized sector. 6. All data shown for Germany prior to October 3 are based on its territories as West Germany at the time indicated. 7. Annual averages: average of less than 12 months. 8. Revised scope. 9. Base: third quarter 1985 = 100. 10. Including forestry and fishing. *Source:* United Nations, *Monthly Bulletin of Statistics, July 1995.*

Energy, Petroleum, and Coal, by Country

Country	Energy consumed[1] (coal equiv.) Total (mil. metric tons) 1991	1980	Per capita (kilograms) 1991	1980	Electric energy production[2] (bil. kwh) 1991	1980	Crude petroleum production[3] (mil. metric tons) 1991	1980	Coal production[4] (mil. metric tons) 1991	1980
Algeria	27	25	1,044	993	16	7	37	47	(Z)	(Z)[6]
Argentina	65	50	1,977	1,537	51	40	25	25	(Z)	(Z)
Austria	32	31	4,195	4,051	50	42	1	1	—	—
Bahrain	8	4	15,608	8,728	4	2	2	2	(n.a.)	(n.a.)
Bangladesh[7]	9	4	77	35	8	3	(Z)[6]	(Z)	(X)	(X)
Belgium	69	65	6,900	6,560	71	53	(X)	(X)	1[8]	
Brazil	121	92	797	619	223	139	33	9	5	(n.a.)[6]
Bulgaria	29	34	3,270	3,771	41	35	(Z)	(Z)[6]	(Z)[6]	(Z)
Canada	294	259	10,903	9,725	482	378	76	70	38	20
Chile	16	11	1,182	864	18	12	1	2	2	1
China	933	545	811	481	621	301	138	106	1,080[10]	596
Colombia	28	20	848	627	35	21	22	7	21	4
Cuba	13	14	1,208	1,288	16	10	1[6]	(X)	(X)	(X)
Czechoslovakia	89	99	5,666	6,317	89	73	(Z)	(Z)	23[6,8]	28[8]
Denmark	26	28	5,084	5,381	26	27	6	(Z)	(X)	(X)
Ecuador	8	6	757	539	6	3	15	10	(n.a.)	(n.a.)
Egypt	38	21	713	399	39	19	44	29	(X)	(X)
Ethiopia	1	1	29	16	1	1	(X)	(X)	(n.a.)	(n.a.)
Finland	34	27	6,845	5,497	54[5]	39[5]	(X)	(X)	(X)	(X)
France[23]	311	257	5,457	4,535	420[5]	246[5]	3	1	11[8]	20[8]
Germany[13]	509	382	6,375	6,237	455	368	4[14]	5[14]	76[6]	94
Greece	32	20	3,169	1,998	35	23	1[14]		(X)	(X)
Hong Kong	11	7	1,920	1,277	29	13	(n.a.)	(n.a.)	(X)	(X)
Hungary	38	39	3,574	3,730	28	24	2	2	2[8]	3[8]
India[9]	290	140	336	165	286	119	33	9	202	109
Indonesia	65	36	348	196	44	14	70	78	7	(Z)
Iran[15]	99	46	1,654	784	56	22	159	73	1[6]	1[6]
Iraq	18	11	970	589	29	11	101	130	(n.a.)	(n.a.)
Ireland	14	11	4,143	3,264	15	11	(X)	(X)	(Z)	(Z)
Israel	15	9	2,999	1,895	21	13	(Z)	(Z)	(X)	(X)
Italy[16]	231	192	3,998	3,335	217	183	5	2	(Z)	(Z)
Japan	590	455	4,754	3,684	857	578	1	(Z)	8	18
Korea, North	96	49	4,308	2,230	54	35	(X)	(X)	41[6]	36[6]
Korea, South	130	52	2,977	1,206	119	40	(X)	(X)	17	19
Kuwait[17]	4	12	1,925	5,605	21	9	60	84	(n.a.)	(n.a.)
Libya	20	7	4,328	1,607	19	5	67	88	(X)	(X)
Malaysia	28	11	1,534	632	23	10	30	13	(Z)	(X)
Mexico	162	116	1,879	1,376	122[5]	67[5]	133	100	10[6]	7
Morocco	10	7	384	260	10	5	(Z)	(Z)	1	1
Myanmar[9]	2	2	55	48	3	1	1[6]	2	(Z)[6]	(Z)
Netherlands	109	100	7,248	6,695	72	65	4	1	—	—
New Zealand[18]	20	11	5,838	3,338	30	22	2	(Z)	2	2
Nigeria	24	12	210	110	10	7	86	104	(Z)[6]	(Z)
Norway[19]	29	26	6,818	6,217	122	84	80	25	(Z)	(Z)
Pakistan[7]	35	17	290	141	44	15	3	(Z)	3	2
Peru	10	11	476	512	14	10	7	10	(Z)[6]	(Z)
Philippines	26	18	405	292	26	18	(Z)	1	1	(Z)
Poland	121	177	3,167	4,630	136	122	(Z)	(Z)	147[6]	193
Portugal	19	13	1,960	1,268	29	15	(X)	(X)	(Z)	(Z)
Romania	70	99	3,025	4,254	64	67	8	12	5[6]	8
Saudi Arabia[17]	107	25	6,922	1,704	47	19	320	496	(n.a.)	(n.a.)
South Africa[20]	107	84	2,431	1,955	167	90	(X)	(X)	176	117
Soviet Union (former)	1,867	1,592	6,415	5,502	1,726	1,294	566	603	543	493
Spain	120	88	3,065	2,270	152	109	1	2	15[8]	13[8]
Sudan	2	2	62	60	1	1	(X)	(X)	(n.a.)	(n.a.)
Sweden	59	51	6,892	5,941	146	96	(Z)	(Z)	(Z)	(Z)
Switzerland[21]	32	28	4,698	4,114	56	47[5]	(X)	(X)	(X)	(X)
Syria	14	9	1,100	699	12	4	23	9	(X)	(X)
Taiwan[11]	76	39	3,645	2,126	(n.a.)	(n.a.)	(Z)	(Z)	1	3
Tanzania	1	1	8	33	1	1	(X)	(X)	(Z)[6]	(Z)
Thailand	46	17	833	317	46	15	1	(Z)	—	—
Trinidad and Tobago	11	7	8,400	6,041	4	2	8	11	(n.a.)	(n.a.)
Tunisia	7	4	839	510	6	3	5	6	(X)	(X)
Turkey	59	31	1,036	555	58	23	4	2	3	4

Country	Energy consumed[1] (coal equiv.) Total (mil. metric tons)		Per capita (kilograms)		Electric energy production[2] (bil. kwh)		Crude petroleum production[3] (mil. metric tons)		Coal production[4] (mil. metric tons)	
	1991	1980	1991	1980	1991	1980	1991	1980	1991	1980
United Arab Emirates	36	10	22,379	6,233	14	6	102	83	(n.a.)	(n.a.)
United Kingdom	309	281	5,353	4,877	319	284	88	79	94[8]	130[8]
United States	2,727	2,391	10,798	9,566	3,041[5]	2,354[5]	371	424	854	710
Venezuela	68	49	3,429	2,549	56	36	112	115	2	(Z)
Vietnam	8	7	116	103	9	4	3	(Z)	5	5
Yugoslavia	41	46	1,731	1,927	86	59	4	4	(Z)	(Z)
Zaire	2	2	65	52	6	4	1[6]	1	(Z)	(Z)
Zambia	2	2	205	279	8	9[5]	(X)	(X)	(Z)	1
World, total	**10,950**	**8,783**	**2,026**	**1,626**	**11,771**	**8,237**	**3,019**	**2,982**	**3,561**	**2,728**

— Represents or rounds to zero. n.a. = not available. X = Not applicable. Z = Less than 50,000 metric tons. 1. Based on apparent consumption of coal, lignite, petroleum products, natural gas, and hydro, nuclear, and geothermal electricity. 2. Comprises production by utilities generating primarily for public use, and production by industrial establishments generating primarily for own use. Relates to production at generating centers, including station use and transmission losses. 3. Includes shale oil, but excludes natural gasoline. 4. Excludes lignite and brown coal, except as noted. 5. Net production, i.e., excluding station use. 6. Provisional. 7. For year ending June of year shown. 8. Includes recovered slurries. 9. For year ending April of year shown. 10. Includes lignite. 11. *Source:* U.S. Bureau of Census. Data from Republic of China publications. 1992 data shown for 1991. 12. Includes Monaco. 13. Prior to 1991, data for former West Germany. 14. Includese inputs other than crude petroleum and natural gas liquids. 15. For year ending March 20 for year shown. 16. Includes San Marino. 17. Includes share of production and consumption in the Neutral Zone. 18. For year ending March 31 for year shown. 19. Includes Svalbard and Jan Mayen Islands. 20. Includes Botswana, Lesotho, Namibia, and Swaziland. 20. Includes Liechtenstein. *Source:* Except as noted, Statistical Office of the United Nations, New York, N.Y., *Energy Statistics Yearbook,* annual (copyright). From: *Statistical Abstract of the United States, 1994.* NOTE: Data are most recent available.

Wheat, Rice, and Corn—Production for Selected Countries

(in thousands of metric tons)

Country	Wheat			Rice			Corn		
	1992	1991	1990	1992	1991	1990	1992	1991	1990
Argentina	9,685	9,000	11,014	695	347	428	10,699	7,768	5,047
Australia	16,184	9,633	15,066	1,128	726	846	210	159	219
Belgium[1]	1,428	1,620	1,347	(X)	(X)	(X)	86	62	56
Brazil	2,796	3,077	3,094	9,962	9,503	7,421	30,557	22,604	21,348
Canada	29,871	32,822	32,098	(X)	(X)	(X)	4,883	7,319	7,066
China: Mainland	101,594	95,003	98,232	188,290	187,450	191,589	95,760	93,350	97,158
Egypt	4,618	4,483	4,268	3,910	3,152	3,167	5,069	5,270	4,799
France	1,428	34,483	1,347	122	109	125	14,886	12,787	9,291
Germany[2]	15,542	11,948	15,242	(X)	(X)	(X)	2,139	1,809	1,552
Greece	2,385	2,750	1,938	101	127	99	2,048	1,700	2,131
Hungary	3,444	5,954	6,198	15	38	39	4,417	7,509	4,500
India	101,594	54,522	98,232	108,011	110,945	111,517	10,400	8,200	8,962
Indonesia	(X)	(X)	(X)	47,700	44,321	45,179	7,996	6,409	6,734
Iran	10,350	8,900	8,012	2,500	2,100	1,981	200	7	130
Iraq	1,006	525	1,196	180	125	229	260	74	172
Italy	8,943	9,289	8,109	1,284	1,236	1,291	7,679	6,208	5,864
Japan	759	860	952	13,216	12,005	13,124	1	1	1
Korea, South	1	1	1	7,835	7,478	7,722	92	75	120
Mexico	3,626	4,115	3,935	361	354	394	17,003	13,527	14,640
Myanmar	143	123	124	14,915	13,201	13,969	206	190	187
Pakistan	15,684	14,505	14,316	4,674	4,903	4,891	1,178	1,190	1,185
Soviet Union (former)	90,037	80,000	101,891	1,969	2,200	2,166	7,319	8,500	9,886
Sweden	1,411	1,524	2,243	(X)	(X)	(X)	(X)	(X)	(X)
Thailand	1	0	0	19,935	20,040	17,193	3,672	3,990	3,722
United Kingdom	14,092	14,300	14,033	(X)	(X)	(X)	n.a.	n.a.	n.a.
United States	66,920	53,915	74,473	8,123	7,006	7,080	240,774	189,867	201,532
Yugoslavia	4,100	6,530	6,359	43	32	59	7,025	8,800	6,724
World, total	**566,282**	**550,993**	**592,811**	**526,360**	**519,869**	**520,549**	**530,067**	**478,775**	**479,008**

1. Includes Luxembourg. 2. Former West Germany (prior to unification). NOTES: Rice data cover rough and paddy. Data for each country pertain to the calendar year in which all or most of the crop was harvested. X = Not applicable. n.a. = not available. *Source:* U.S. Department of Agriculture, Economic Research Service, *World Agriculture—Trends and Indicators.* From: *Statistical Abstract of the United States, 1994.* NOTE: Data are most recent available.

Wheat, Rice and Corn Exports and Imports, 1980–1991

(In millions of dollars. Countries listed are the 10 leading exporters or importers in 1991)

Exporters	1991	1990	1980	Importers	1991	1990	1980
WHEAT				**WHEAT**			
United States	3,350	3,887	6,376	USSR (former)	2,553	2,490	2,891
Canada	3,315	2,863	3,302	Italy	1,685	1,217	773
France	2,793	3,296	2,110	China, Mainland	1,460	2,157	2,436
Australia	1,338	1,971	2,425	Japan	920	1,019	1,236
United Kingdom	758	760	260	Egypt	620	853	620
Argentina	479	871	816	South Korea	577	419	367
Germany	463	504	198	Brazil	550	331	1,051
Greece	311	156	27	Belgium–Luxembourg	501	384	360
Denmark	211	229	23	Spain	454	162	71
Turkey	204	4	52	Indonesia	366	282	162
RICE				**RICE**			
Thailand	1,196	1,086	953	Brazil	372	144	99
United States	756	804	1,285	Iran	236	225	209
Italy	361	357	289	France	231	216	154
Pakistan	345	242	422	United Kingdom	205	209	98
India	339	258	173	Saudi Arabia	147	153	230
Vietnam	188	305	10	USSR (former)	145	119	265
Spain	171	108	22	Malaysia	127	100	60
Belgium–Luxembourg	152	168	91	South Africa	117	87	58
China, Mainland	152	84	450	Belgium–Luxembourg	108	106	80
Australia	140	143	145	Netherlands	104	112	93
CORN				**CORN**			
United States	5,147	6,206	8,571	Japan	2,242	2,295	2,011
France	1,420	1,854	869	USSR (former)	1,536	1,690	1,508
China, Mainland	864	404	17	Taiwan	736	704	437
Argentina	410	329	513	South Korea	697	837	376
Thailand	153	162	352	Netherlands	532	538	626
Hungary	120	51	27	United Kingdom	398	396	547
Greece	94	32	—	Germany	392	486	996
Canada	93	28	113	Belgium–Luxembourg	323	298	473
Germany	88	71	39	Italy	291	363	450
Spain	86	41	1	Spain	255	307	668

— Represents or rounds to zero. *Source:* U.S. Dept. of Agriculture, Economic Research Service, *World Agriculture—Trends and Indicators.* From *Statistical Abstract of the United States 1994.* NOTE: Data are most recent available.

Passenger Car Production[1]

(in thousands, monthly averages)

Country	1993	1992	1991	1990	1989	1988	1987
Argentina[2]	27.6	21.0	11.1	9.5	9.5	10.4	13.0
Australia[2]	23.8	22.5	25.9	30.1	27.7	26.2	25.2
Austria	—	—	1.2	1.2	0.6	0.6	0.6
Brazil[2]	—	27.6	24.4	22.3	26.1	32.9	33.1
Canada	97.1	75.1	74.2	78.4	82.0	84.0	67.5
Former Czechoslovakia	—	—	14.7	15.9	15.7	13.7	14.5
France	243.4	301.3	260.1	246.9	284.5	261.5	248.5
Germany, East[3]	—	—	—	—	18.2	18.2	18.1
Germany, West[3]	327.2	405.5	355.8	384.9	378.6	359.1	361.7
India	19.1	15.2	16.1	17.8	14.8	14.5	12.9
Italy	—	122.9	135.6	156.1	164.2	157.0	142.7
Japan	723.5	781.2	813.0	829.0	697.5	683.3	657.6
Korea, South[2]	127.3	107.8	94.3	79.8	70.6	72.3	64.8
Mexico[2]	70.7	65.7	61.1	51.2	37.9	29.0	19.0
Netherlands	—	8.6	7.1	10.3	11.2	10.0	10.4
Poland	27.8	18.3	13.9	22.2	23.8	24.5	24.5
Romania	7.8	—	6.2	—	10.0	10.0	10.8
Spain	125.5	149.6	152.5	144.7	141.3	131.3	119.3
Sweden	—	—	—	28.0[4]	32.0[4]	—	34.7
Former U.S.S.R.	—	—	98.7	104.9	101.4	105.1	108.3
United Kingdom	114.6	107.6	106.5	108.0	108.3	102.2	95.2
United States[5]	496.3	473.7	450.6	504.3	567.3	592.1	590.4
Yugoslavia[6]	0.6	2.2	18.2	24.3[2]	26.0[2]	25.8[2]	25.8

1. Vehicles built on imported chassis or assembled from imported parts are excluded except for those countries marked. 2. Including assembly. 3. Unification of Germany occurred on October 3, 1990. All data which pertain to Germany prior to that date are indicated separately for East and West Germany. 4. Provisional, preliminary or estimated figure. 5. Factory sales. 6. Beginning January 1992, data refer to the Federal Republic of Yugoslavia. Prior to that date, data refer to the Socialist Federal Republic of Yugoslavia. *Source:* United Nations, *Monthly Bulletin of Statistics, July 1995.*

Meat—Production by Country
(in thousands of metric tons)

Country	1993	1990	1980	Country	1993	1990	1980
Argentina	3,617	3,383	3,622	Mexico	3,628	3,478	2,540
Brazil	7,545	6,439	4,550	USSR (former)	15,566	19,996	15,072
France	6,085	5,765	5,455	Spain	3,701	3,466	2,648
Germany	5,947	7,292	6,972	United Kingdom	2,340	3,357	3,070
India	3,992	3,723	2,675	United States	31,350	28,632	24,599
Italy	3,936	3,950	3,564	**World**	**185,917**	**178,169**	**135,940**
Japan	3,378	3,503	3,046				

NOTE: Covers beef and veal (incl. buffalo meat), pork (incl. bacon and ham), and mutton and lamb (incl. goat meat), horsemeat and poultry. Refers to meat from animals slaughtered within the national boundaries irrespective of origin of animals, and relates to commercial and farm slaughter. Excludes lard, tallow, and edible offals. NOTE: Data are most recent available. *Source:* U.S. Department of Agriculture, Economic Research Service, *World Agriculture—Trends and Indicators* and Food and Agriculture Organization of the United Nations, Rome, Italy. *FAO Production Yearbook, 1992.* From: *Statistical Abstract of the United States 1994.*

Crude Steel Production
(in thousands of metric tons)

Country	1993	1992	1991	Country	1993	1992	1991
Argentina	236	223	248	Korea, South	2,752	2,338	2,234
Australia[1]	567	538	518	Luxembourg	274	256	282
Austria	346	328	367	Mexico	n.a.	696[4]	643
Belgium	843	861	941	Netherlands	499	453	431
Brazil	2,101	1,992	1,884	Norway	41	38	37
Bulgaria	162	129	135	Poland	828	822	870
Canada	2,079	2,166	1,987	Portugal	62	62	48
China	7,384	6,670	5,880	Romania	454	441	593
Czechoslovakia, former[2]	564	612	1,006	South Africa	n.a.	755	745
Finland	271	257	241	Spain	1,080	1,050	1,047
France	1,426	1,502	1,536	Sweden	383	363	353
Germany[3]	3,135	3,073	3,232	Turkey	959	862	775
Greece	82	77	82	USSR, former	n.a.	n.a.	11,660
Hungary	146	130	155	United Kingdom	1,372	1,334	1,386
India[4]	1,138	1,083	1,366[4]	United States	7,250	7,633	7,287
Italy	2,152	2,062	2,086	Venezuela	214	204	259
Japan	8,302	8,178	9,137	Yugoslavia[5]	n.a.	7	n.a.

1. Annual figures: averages of 12 months ending June 30 of year started. 2. From 1992 data for Czech Republic. 3. Prior to October 1990 West Germany. 4. Provisional, preliminary, or estimated figures. 5. Beginning January 1992, data refer to the Federal Republic of Yugoslavia. NOTE: Production data cover ingots and steel for casting. Wrought (puddled) iron is included. n.a. = not available. *Source:* United Nations, *Monthly Bulletin of Statistics, July 1995.*

Railway Freight Traffic for Selected Countries
(Net ton-kilometers in millions)

Country	1993	1992	1991	Country	1993	1992	1991
Austria[1,2]	983	1,017	1,072	Korea, South	1,220	1,175	1,208
Belgium	631	679	679	Latvia	819	843	1,395
Bulgaria[3]	624	647	724	Luxembourg	54	56	59
Chile	211	222	225	Mexico	2,992	2,800	2,749
China	n.a.	96,172	91,433	Netherlands	225	233	252
Colombia	38	20	25	Norway[8]	238	184	223
Czech Republic[4]	2,137	3,998	4,161	Poland	5,338	4,814	5,429
Finland	772	654	636	Portugal	149	149	149
France	3,822	4,198	4,299	Romania	2,098	n.a.	3,154
Germany	5,349	5,849	6,719	Spain	n.a.	780	876
Greece	44	n.a.	50	Sweden	1,376	1,462	1,524
Hong Kong	4	5	5	Turkey	700	678	n.a.
Hungary	622	835	995	USSR, former[9]	133,979	163,925	275,978
India[3,5,6]	20,819	21,146	20,440	United Kingdom[10]	1,141	1,271	1,289
Ireland	n.a.	49	47	United States[11]	134,280	129,596	127,173
Italy[7]	1,686	1,848	1,796	Venezuela	n.a.	n.a.	4
Japan	2,135	2,222	2,279	Zimbabwe[1,7]	n.a.	n.a.	909

1. Federal railroads only. 2. Full carloads only (Austria: monthly data). 3. Including service traffic. 4. Data prior to January 1993 pertain to the former Czechoslovakia. 5. Government railways: broad meter and narrow gauges only. 6. Annual figures: 12 months beginning April 1. 7. Excluding livestock. 8. Average of two months. 9. 1992 and 1993 data are for Russian Federation. 10. British railways only. Excluding Northern Ireland. 11. Class I railways only. n.a. = not available. *Source:* United Nations, *Monthly Bulletin of Statistics, July 1995.*

COUNTRIES OF THE WORLD

Major sources: *Information Please Almanac* questionnaires to the individual countries and
C.I.A. *World Factbook.* Most 1995 data on country populations, birth rates, natural increase,
and infant mortality rates are taken from *1995 World Population Data Sheet* by the
Population Reference Bureau.
(As of August 1, 1995. For later reports, *see* Current Events of 1995.)

Definitions: Gross domestic product (GDP): The value of all goods and services produced domestically; Gross national product (GNP): the value of all goods and services produced domestically plus income earned abroad, minus income earned by foreigners from domestic production; c.i.f.: cost, insurance, and freight; f.o.b.: free on board; inflation: based on consumer prices; literacy: There are no universal definitions and standards of literacy. Literacy rates are those supplied by the individual countries or else taken from the World Fact Book. The standards that each country uses to assess the ability to read and write is beyond the scope of this almanac.

AFGHANISTAN

Islamic State of Afghanistan
President: Burhanuddin Rabbani (1992)
Area: 250,000 sq mi. (647,500 sq km).
Population (est. mid-1995): 18,400,000 (Average annual rate of natural increase: 2.8%); birth rate: 50/1000; infant mortality rate: 163/1000; density per square mile: 73.6
Capital: Kabul; **Largest cities (est. 1993):** Kabul, 1,424,400; Kandahar, 225,500; Herat, 177,300; Mazare-Sharif, 131,000.**Monetary unit:** Afghani; **Languages:** Pushtu, Dari Persian, other Turkic and minor languages; **Religion:** Islam (Sunni, 84%; Shiite, 15%; other 1%); **National name:** Dawlat Islami Afghanistan; **Literacy rate:** 29%
Economic summary: Gross domestic product (1989): $3 billion, $200 per capita. Average annual growth rate (1989 est.): .0%. Inflation (est. 1991): over 90%. Arable land: 12%; labor force: 4,980,000. Principal products: wheat, corn, barley, rice, cotton, fruit, nuts, karakul pelts, wool. Labor force in industry: 10.2%. Major industrial products: carpets, rugs, textiles, furniture, shoes, fertilizer, cement. Natural resources: natural gas, oil, coal, copper, sulfur, lead, zinc, iron, salt, precious and semi-precious stones. Exports: $1 billion (1992 est.): fresh and dried fruits, nuts, natural gas, carpets, karakul. Imports: $1.7 billion (est. 1992): petroleum products, sugar, manufactured goods, tea. Major trading partners: Europe, Central Asian republics, Japan, Singapore, Malaysia, India, and Pakistan.

Geography. Afghanistan, approximately the size of Texas, is bordered on the north by Turkmenistan, Uzbekistan, and Tajikistan, on the extreme northeast by China, on the east and south by Pakistan, and Iran in the west. The country is split east to west by the Hindu Kush mountain range, rising in the east to heights of 24,000 feet (7,315 m). With the exception of the southwest, most of the country is covered by high snow-capped mountains and is traversed by deep valleys.

Government. With the fall of the Marxist Najibullah regime in April 1992 the victorious insurgents established a 50-member ruling council of guerrillas, religious leaders and intellectuals, who announced the creation of an Islamic republic and promised free elections.

History. Darius I and Alexander the Great were the first conquerors to use Afghanistan as the gateway to India. Islamic conquerors arrived in the 7th century and Genghis Khan and Tamerlane followed in the 13th and 14th centuries.

In the 19th century, Afghanistan became a battleground in the rivalry of imperial Britain and Czarist Russia for the control of Central Asia. The Afghan Wars (1838–42 and 1878–81) fought against the British by Dost Mohammed and his son and grandson ended in defeat.

Afghanistan regained autonomy by the Anglo-Russian agreement of 1907 and full independence by the Treaty of Rawalpindi in 1919. Emir Amanullah founded the kingdom in 1926.

After a coup in 1978, Noor Taraki's attempts to create a Marxist state with Soviet aid brought armed resistance from conservative Muslim opposition.

Taraki was eventually succeeded by Babrak Karmal, who called for Soviet troops under a mutual defense treaty.

The Soviet invasion was met with unanticipated fierce resistance from the Afghan population, resulting in a bloody war. Soviet troops had to fight Afghan tribesmen who called themselves "mujahedeen," or "holy warriors." In the early fighting, many of the guerrillas were armed only with flintlock rifles, but later they acquired more modern weapons, including rockets that they used to attack Soviet installations.

In April 1988, the U.S.S.R., U.S.A., Afghanistan, and Pakistan signed accords calling for an end to outside aid to the warring factions, in return for Soviet withdrawal by 1989. This took place in February of that year.

An agreement signed in September 1991 between the U.S.S.R. and the U.S.A. called for an end to all outside military assistance to the warring factions. By mid-April 1992 then-President Najibullah was ousted as Islamic rebels advanced on the capital. Almost immediately the various rebel groups began fighting each other for control.

Factional battles resumed in Kabul on January 1, 1994, between forces loyal to the president and numerous other groups. In February 1995 the U.N. announced a peace plan calling for a multiparty governing commission. A government military victory in the Kabul area in March led the president to refuse to resign as called for in the peace plan.

ALBANIA

The Republic of Albania
President: Sali Berisha (1992)
Prime Minister: Alesander Meksi (1992)
Area: 11,100 sq mi. (28,748 sq km)
Population (est. mid-1995): 3,500,000 (average annual rate of natural increase: 1.8%); birth rate: 23/1000; infant mortality rate: 32.9/1000; density per square mile: 315.3
Capital and largest city (1990): Tirana, 243,100; **Monetary unit:** Lek; **Language:** Albanian, Greek; **Religions:** Muslim, 70%; Greek Orthodox, 20%; Roman Catholic, 10%; **National name:** Rupublika e Shqiperise; **Literacy rate** 75%

Economic summary: Gross domestic product (1993 est.): $3.3 billion; per capita, $1,100; real growth rate, 11%; inflation, 31%; unemployment, 18%. Arable land: 21%; labor force: 1,500,000 (1987). Principal agricultural products: wheat, corn, potatoes, sugar beets, cotton, tobacco. Labor force in industry and commerce: 40%. Major products: textiles, timber, construction materials, fuels, semi-processed minerals. Exports: $70 million (f.o.b., 1992): asphalt, petroleum products, metals and metallic ores, electricity, crude oil, vegetables, fruits, and tobacco. Imports: $524 million (f.o.b., 1992): machinery, consumer goods, grains. Major trading partners: Italy, Macedonia, Germany, Czechoslovakia, Romania, Poland, Hungary, Bulgaria, Greece.

Geography. Albania is situated on the eastern shore of the Adriatic Sea, with Yugoslavia to the north and east and Greece to the south. Slightly larger than Maryland, it is a mountainous country, mostly over 3,000 feet (914 m) above sea level, with a narrow, marshy coastal plain crossed by several rivers. The centers of population are contained in the interior mountain plateaus and basins.

Government. A multi-party system was installed in March 1991. Elections in March 1992 gave the Democratic Party 92 of the 140 parliamentary seats, thus assuring it the two-thirds majority for enacting constitutional reform. Election of the president is by parliamentary majority.

History. Albania proclaimed its independence on Nov. 28, 1912, after a history of Roman, Byzantine, and Turkish domination.

Largely agricultural, Albania is one of the poorest countries in Europe. A battlefield in World War I, after the war it became a republic in which a conservative Moslem landlord, Ahmed Zogu, proclaimed himself President in 1925, and then proclaimed himself King Zog I in a monarchy in 1928. He ruled until Italy annexed Albania in 1939. Communist guerrillas under Enver Hoxha seized power in 1944, near the end of World War II.

Hoxha was succeeded by Ramiz Alia, 59, who had been President since 1982.

The elections in March 1991 gave the Communists a decisive majority. But a general strike and street demonstrations soon forced the all-Communist cabinet to resign. In June 1991 the Communist Party of Labor renamed itself the Socialist Party and renounced its past ideology. The opposition Democratic Party won a landslide victory in 1992 elections.

The expulsion of seven prominent party members in August 1992, however, resulted in their formation of a new Democratic Alliance party. Another split from the Democratic party occurred in mid-1993 and led to the founding of the Democratic Party of the Right, albeit with little popular support.

ALGERIA

Democratic and Popular Republic of Algeria
President: Liamine Zeroual (1994)
Prime Minister: Mokdad Sifi
Area: 919,595 sq mi. (2,381,751 sq km)
Population (est. mid-1995): 28,400,000 (average annual rate of natural increase: 2.4%); birth rate: 30/1000; infant mortality rate: 55/1000; density per square mile: 30.8
Capital: Algiers; **Largest cities (1987):** Algiers, 1,507,241; Oran, 628,558; Constantine, 440,842; Annaba, 305,526;
Monetary unit: Dinar; **Languages:** Arabic (official),

French, Berber dialects; **Religion:** 99% Islam (Sunni); **National name:** République Algérienne Democratique et Populaire—El Djemhouria El Djazaïria Demokratia Echaabia; **Literacy rate** (1990): 57%
Economic summary: Gross national product (1994): $47 billion; $1,750 per capita; real growth rate, 0.3%; inflation, 26%; unemployment (1993 est.), 22%. Arable land: 3%; labor force: 6.2 million (1992 est.). Principal agricultural products: wheat, barley, oats, wine, citrus fruits, olives, livestock. Labor force in industry: 40%. Major industrial products: petroleum, gas, petrochemicals, fertilizers, iron and steel, textiles, transport equipment. Natural resources: petroleum, natural gas, iron ore, phosphates, lead, zinc, mercury, uranium. Exports: $11.4 billion (f.o.b., 1993 est.): petroleum and natural gas, 97%. Imports: $9 billion (f.o.b., 1993 est.): capital goods, 39.7%; food and beverages, 2.7%; consumer goods, 11.8% (1990). Major trading partners: France, Germany, Italy, Spain, U.S., Japan.

Geography. Nearly four times the size of Texas, Algeria is bordered on the west by Morocco and Western Sahara, and on the east by Tunisia and Libya. To the south are Mauritania, Mali, and Niger. Low plains cover small areas near the Mediterranean coast, with 68% of the country a plateau between 2,625 and 5,250 feet (800 and 1,600 m) above sea level. The highest point is Mount Tahat in the Sahara, which rises 9,850 feet (3,000 m).

Government. Headed by a Prime Minister since 1994 for a transitional period to a new presidential election to take place at the end of 1995.

History. As ancient Numidia, Algeria became a Roman colony at the close of the Punic Wars (145 B.C.). Conquered by the Vandals about A.D. 440, it fell from a high state of civilization to virtual barbarism, from which it partly recovered after invasion by the Moslems about 650.

In 1492 the Moors and Jews, who had been expelled from Spain, settled in Algeria. Falling under Turkish control in 1518, Algiers served for three centuries as the headquarters of the Barbary pirates. The French took Algeria in 1830 and made it a part of France in 1848.

On July 5, 1962, Algeria was proclaimed independent. In October 1963, Ahmed Ben Bella was elected President. He began to nationalize foreign holdings and aroused opposition. He was overthrown in a military coup on June 19, 1965, by Col. Houari Boumediène, who suspended the Constitution and sought to restore financial stability.

Boumediène died in December 1978 after a long illness. Chadli Bendjedid, Secretary-General of the National Liberation Front, took the presidency in a smooth transition of power.

Nationwide riots in 1988 led the government to introduce democratic reforms. In December 1991 in the first parliamentary elections ever held in Algeria a militant Islamic fundamentalist party won. In an apparent effort to thwart the electoral results senior army commanders arranged the resignation of President Benjedid. The government then canceled the continuation of the electoral process. In late June President Boudiaf was assassinated.

Since January 1992 the country has been torn between Islamic militants and the security forces that appears increasingly like a civil war.

In early 1995 government forces attempted a major offensive to combat the rebels. The latter in turn stepped up their pace of assassinations.

ANDORRA

Principality of Andorra
Head of Government: Oscar Ribas Reig (1991)
Area: 175 sq mi. (453 sq km)
Population (est. mid-1994): 63,930 (average annual growth rate: 2.99%); birth rate: 13.3/1000; infant mortality rate: 7.9/1000; density per square mile: 365
Capital (1990): Andorra la Vella, 20,437; **Monetary units:** French franc and Spanish peseta; **Languages:** Catalán (official); French, Spanish; **Religion:** Roman Catholic; **National names:** Les Vallées d'Andorre-Valls d'Andorra; **Literacy rate** 100%
Economic summary: Gross domestic product (1992 est): $760 million; per capita, $14,000. Arable land: 2%; labor force: NA. Principal agricultural products: oats, barley, cattle, sheep. Major industrial products: tobacco products and electric power; tourism. Natural resources: water power, mineral water. Exports: $23 million (f.o.b., 1989): electricity, tobacco products, furniture. Imports: $888.7 million (f.o.b., 1989): consumer goods, food. Major trading partners: Spain and France.

Geography. Andorra lies high in the Pyrenees Mountains on the French-Spanish border. The country is drained by the Valira River.

Government. A new constitution, their first, was approved on March 14, 1993 which redefined Andorra as a parliamentary co-principality and sharply differentiated the three branches of government.

History. An autonomous and semi-independent co-principality, Andorra has been under the joint suzerainty of the French state and the Spanish bishops of Urgel since 1278.

In 1990 Andorra approved a customs union treaty with the E.C. permitting free movement of industrial goods between the two, but Andorra would apply the E.C.'s external tariffs to third countries. This treaty went into effect on July 1, 1991.

In elections of December 1993 the chief executive's party won a plurality of the parliamentary seats.

The government in 1994 announced consideration of allowing, under strict guidelines, foreign ownership of residential property.

ANGOLA

People's Republic of Angola
President: José Eduardo dos Santos (1979)
Area: 481,350 sq mi. (1,246,700 sq km)
Population (est. mid-1995): 11,500,000 (average annual rate of natural increase: 2.7); birth rate: 47/1000; infant mortality rate: 137/1000; density per square mile: 23.9
Capital and largest city (est. 1990): Luanda, 1,544,000; **Monetary unit:** Kwanza; **Languages:** Bantu, Portuguese (official); **Religions:** 47% Indigenous, 38% Roman Catholic, 15% Protestant (est.); **Literacy rate:** 42%
Economic summary: Gross domestic product (1993 est.): $5.7 billion, $600 per capita; real growth rate –22.6%; inflation (1993 est), 1,840%; unemployment (1993 est.), 15%. Arable land: 2%. Labor force: 2,783,000; Labor force in agriculture: 85%. Principal agricultural products: coffee, sisal, corn, cotton, sugar, tobacco, bananas, cassava. Major industrial products: oil, diamonds, processed fish, tobacco, textiles, cement, processed food and sugar, brewing. Natural resources: diamonds, gold, iron, oil. Exports: $3 billion (f.o.b., 1993 est.): oil, coffee, diamonds, fish and fish products, iron ore, timber, corn. Imports: $1.6 billion (f.o.b., 1992 est.): machinery and electrical equipment, bulk iron, steel and metals, textiles, clothing, food, substantial military deliveries. Major trading partners: U.S., France, Germany, Netherlands, Brazil, Portugal, Spain.

Geography. Angola, more than three times the size of California, extends for more than 1,000 miles (1,609 km) along the South Atlantic in southwestern Africa. Zaire is to the north and east, Zambia to the east, and South-West Africa (Namibia) to the south. A plateau averaging 6,000 feet (1,829 m) above sea level rises abruptly from the coastal lowlands. Nearly all the land is desert or savanna, with hardwood forests in the northeast.

Government. President José Eduardo dos Santos, head of the Popular Movement for the Liberation of Angola–Workers Party, won a U.N. certified election in September 1992 against the guerilla organization UNITA led by Jonas Savimbi. The U.S. recognized the new democratic Angolan administration on May 8, 1993.

History. Discovered by the Portuguese navigator Diego Cao in 1482, Angola became a link in trade with India and the Far East. Later it was a major source of slaves for Portugal's New World colony of Brazil. Development of the interior began after the Treaty of Berlin in 1885 fixed the colony's borders, and British and Portuguese investment pushed mining, railways, and agriculture.

Following World War II, independence movements began but were sternly suppressed by military force. The April revolution of 1974 brought about a reversal of Portugal's policy, and the next year President Francisco da Costa Gomes signed an agreement to grant independence to Angola. The plan called for election of a constituent assembly and a settlement of differences by the MPLA and the National Front for the Liberation of Angola (FNLA) and the National Union for the Total Independence of Angola (UNITA).

The Organization of African Unity recognized the MPLA government led by Agostinho Neto on Feb. 11, 1976, and the People's Republic of Angola became the 47th member of the organization.

In March 1977 and May 1978, Zairean refugees in Angola invaded Zaire's Shaba Province, bringing charges by Zairean President Mobutu Sese Seko that the unsucessful invasions were Soviet-backed with Angolan help. Angola, the U.S.S.R., and Cuba denied complicity.

Neto died in Moscow of cancer on Sept. 10, 1979. The Planning Minister, José Eduardo dos Santos, was named President.

The South-West Africa People's Organization, or Swapo, the guerrillas fighting for the independence of the disputed territory south of Angola also known as Namibia, fought from bases in Angola and the South African armed forces also maintained troops there both to fight the SWAPO guerrillas and to assist the UNITA guerrillas against Angolan and Cuban troops.

In December 1988, Angola, Cuba, and South Africa signed agreements calling for Cuban withdrawal from Angola and South African withdrawal from Namibia by July 1991 and independence for Namibia.

Elections in late September 1992 gave the MPLA the most votes with UNITA second. A runoff was set when UNITA's Savimbi withdrew charging the election was unfair. Fighting resumed between the government and UNITA in October.

Fighting between the government and UNITA continued throughout 1993 punctuated with on-and-off-again peace talks at various locales throughout the year.

Government bombing of a UNITA stronghold in August 1994 saw the withdrawal of UNITA's negotiating team from peace talks in Lusaka for an unspecified period.

ANTIGUA AND BARBUDA

Sovereign: Queen Elizabeth II (1952)
Governor-General: Sir James Beethoven Carlisle (1993)
Prime Minister: Hon. Lester Bryant Bird
Land area: 171 sq mi. (442 sq km)
Population (est. mid-1994): 64,762 (average annual growth rate: 1.2%); birth rate: 18/1000; infant mortality rate: 18/1000; density per square mile: 378.7
Capital and largest city (est. 1986): St. John's, 36,000. Capital of Barbuda is the village of Cordrington, est. pop. 1,000; **Monetary unit:** East Caribbean dollar; **Language:** English; **Religions:** Anglican and Roman Catholic; **Literacy rate:** 90%
Member of Commonwealth of Nations
Economic summary: Gross domestic product (1993 est.): $368.5 million, per capita $5,800; real growth rate n.a.; inflation rate 7% (1993); unemployment rate (est. 1989) 3.0%. Arable land: 18%; Labor force: 30,000; Labor force in industry (1990) 19.7%; principal product: cotton, bananas, coconuts, cucumbers, mangoes. Major industry: tourism which accounts for 60% of economic activity and over half of the GNP. Exports: $32 billion (f.o.b., 1991): petroleum products, manufactures, machinery and transport equipment. Imports: $317.5 million (c.i.f., 1991): fuel, food, machinery. Major trading partners: U.K., U.S., Canada, Caribbean community and Common Market members.

Geography. Antigua, the larger of the two main islands located 295 miles (420 km) south-southeast of San Juan, P.R., is low-lying except for a range of hills in the south that rise to their highest point at Boggy Peak (1,330 ft; 405 m). As a result of its relative flatness, Antigua suffers from cyclical drought, despite a mean annual rainfall of 44 inches. Barbuda (formally known as Dulcina) is a coral island, well-wooded.

Antigua is 108 sq. miles (280 sq km), and the island dependencies of Redonda (an uninhabited rocky islet) and Barbuda are 0.5 sq miles (1.30 sq km) and 62 sq miles (161 sq km), respectively.

Government. Executive power is held by the Cabinet, presided over by Prime Minister Lester B. Bird. A 17-member Parliament is elected by universal suffrage. The Antigua Labour Party, led by Prime Minister Bird, holds 11 seats.

History. Antigua was discovered by Christopher Columbus in 1493 and named for the Church of Santa Maria la Antigua in Seville. Colonized by Britain in 1632, it joined the West Indies Federation in 1958. With the breakup of the Federation, it became one of the West Indies Associated States in 1967, self-governing in internal affairs. Full independence was granted Nov. 1, 1981.

The opposition in 1992 continued its attacks on the prime minister alleging a scandal. The three chief opposition parties merged under the name United Progressive Party. Bird has said he would step down by the time of the next general election in 1994. The Labour Party elected Lester Bird, son of Vere Bird, as

its leader. He had led the party in its successful parliamentary campaign in March 1994.

ARGENTINA

Argentine Republic
President: Carlos S. Menem (1989)
Area: 1,072,067 sq mi. (2,776,654 sq km)
Population (est. mid-1995): 34,600,000 (average annual rate of natural increase: 1.3%); birth rate: 21/1000; infant mortality rate: 23.6/1000; density per square mile: 32.2
Capital: Buenos Aires (plans to move to Viedma by 1990 indefinitely postponed); **Largest cities (est. 1991):** Buenos Aires, 2,961,000; Córdoba, 1,180,000; La Matanza, 1,121,164; General Sarmiento, 646,900; Morón, 641,540 (1983); Rosario, 908,000 (1983). **Monetary unit:** Peso; **Language:** Spanish, English, Italian, German, French; **Religion:** Predominantly Roman Catholic (nominally); **National name:** República Argentina; **Literacy rate** 95%
Economic summary: Gross domestic product (1993 est.): $185 billion; $5,500 per capita; real growth rate (1993) 6%; inflation (1993) 7.4%; unemployment (1993) 10%. Arable land: 9%; labor force: est. 10,900,000. Principal products: grains, oilseeds, livestock products. Labor force in industry: 31%. Major products: processed foods, motor vehicles, consumer durables, textiles, chemicals. Natural resources: minerals, lead, zinc, tin, copper, iron, manganese, oil, uranium. Exports: $12.7 billion (f.o.b., 1993 est.): meat, wheat, corn, oilseed, hides, wool. Imports: $16 billion (c.i.f., 1993, est.): machinery and equipment, chemicals, fuels and lubricants, agricultural products. Major trading partners: U.S., Brazil, Bolivia, Germany, Japan, Italy, Netherlands.

Geography. With an area slightly less than one third of the United States and second in South America only to its eastern neighbor, Brazil, in size and population, Argentina is a plain, rising from the Atlantic to the Chilean border and the towering Andes peaks. Aconcagua (23,034 ft.; 7,021 m) is the highest peak in the world outside Asia. It is bordered also by Bolivia and Paraguay on the north, and by Uruguay on the east.

The northern area is the swampy and partly wooded Gran Chaco, bordering on Bolivia and Paraguay. South of that are the rolling, fertile pampas, rich for agriculture and grazing and supporting most of the population. Next southward is Patagonia, a region of cool, arid steppes with some wooded and fertile sections.

Government. Argentina is a federal union of 23 provinces, and the Federal District. Under the Constitution of 1853 the President and Vice President are elected every six years by popular vote through an electoral college. The President appoints his Cabinet. The Vice President presides over the Senate but has no other powers. The Congress consists of two houses: a 46-member Senate and a 254-member Chamber of Deputies.

History. Discovered in 1516 by Juan Díaz de Solis, Argentina developed slowly under Spanish colonial rule. Buenos Aires was settled in 1580; the cattle industry was thriving as early as 1600.

Invading British forces were expelled in 1806–07, and when Napoleon conquered Spain, the Argentinians set up their own government in the name of the Spanish King in 1810. On July 9, 1816, independence was formally declared.

As in World War I, Argentina proclaimed neutrality at the outbreak of World War II, but in the closing phase declared war on the Axis on March 27, 1945, and became a founding member of the United Nations. Juan D. Perón, an army colonel, emerged as the strongman of the postwar era, winning the Presidential elections of 1946 and 1951.

Opposition to Perón's increasing authoritarianism, led to a coup by the armed forces that sent Perón into exile in 1955. Argentina entered a long period of military dictatorships with brief intervals of constitutional government.

The former dictator returned to power in 1973 and his wife was elected Vice-President.

After Peron's death in 1974, his widow became the hemisphere's first woman chief of state, but was deposed in 1976 by a military junta.

In December 1981. Lt. Gen. Leopoldo Galtieri, commander of the army, was named president.

On April 2, 1982, Galtieri landed thousands of troops on the Falkland Islands and reclaimed the Malvinas, their Spanish name, as national territory. By May 21, 5,000 British marines and paratroops landed from the British armada, and regained control of the islands.

Galtieri resigned three days after the surrender of the island garrison on June 14. Maj. Gen. Reynaldo Bignone, took office as President on July 1.

In the presidential election of October 1983, Raúl Alfonsín, leader of the middle-class Radical Civic Union, handed the Peronist Party its first defeat since its founding.

Twin economic problems of growing unemployment and quadruple-digit inflation led to a Peronist victory in the elections of May 1989. Inflation of food prices led to riots that induced Alfonsin to step down in June 1989, six months early, in favor of the Peronist, Carlos Menem.

A group of army leaders and their followers attempted an uprising on December 3, 1990. Most commanders, however, stood by the legitimate government, and the insurrection was suppressed in less than 24 hours.

In 1991 President Menem hammered out a vast deregulation of the economy designed to reverse decades of state intervention and protectionism.

The May 1995 presidential election saw the re-election of Menem, which was widely interpreted as an endorsement of his market reforms. Menem's party also won in both houses of Congress, leading to some concern about the concentration of power in too few hands.

ARMENIA

President: Levon A. Ter-Petrossian (1990)
Prime Minister: Hrant Bagratyan (1993)
Vice President: Gaguik G. Haroutunian
Area: 11,500 sq mi. (29,800 sq km)
Population (est. mid-1995): 3,700,000 (average annual rate of increase: 0.8%) (Armenian, 93%; others, Kurds, Ukrainians, and Russians); birth rate: 16/1000; infant mortality rate: 17/1000, density per square mile: 321.7
Capital and largest city (1992): Yerevan, 1,400,000; other large cities (est. 1992): Gyumri (Leninakan), 120,000; Vanadzor, 169,000; **Money:** Dram; **Language:** Armenian; **Religion:** Armenian Orthodox, 94%; **Literacy rate:** 100% (1970)
Economic summary: Per capita GNP (1993): $660; 5% real growth rate (1994); inflation under 1% (1994); unemployment 7%. Labor force: 1.53 million. Agriculture:

49% of GDP; arable land, 29%; dairy farming, vineyards. Exports: $209.2 million (1994): to outside the successor states of the former USSR: machinery and transport equipment, light industrial products, processed food. Imports: $401.3 million (19944): from outside the successor states of the former USSR: machinery, energy, consumer goods.

Geography. Armenia is located in the southern Caucasus and is the smallest of the former Soviet republics. It is bounded by Georgia on the north, Azerbaijan on the east, Iran on the south, and Turkey on the west. It is a land of rugged mountains and extinct volcanoes. Mt. Aragats, 13,435 ft (4,095 m) is the highest point. Although the terrain is rugged and dry with few trees, it has excellent pastures. The largest lake, Sevan, 541 sq mi, is the main source of the republic's vast irrigation system and hydroelectric power.

Government: A presidential republic.

History: Armenia has been the scene of struggle throughout its long history with the Greeks, Romans, Persians, Mongols, and Turks. Russia acquired the present day Armenia S.S.R. from Persia in 1828. Armenia joined Azerbaijan and Georgia in 1917 to form the anti-Bolshevik Transcaucasian Federation, but it was dissolved in 1918. Armenia's independence was short-lived and it was annexed by the Red Army in 1920. On March 12, 1922, the Soviets joined Georgia, Armenia, and Azerbaijan to form the Transcaucasian Soviet Socialist Republic which became part of the U.S.S.R. In 1936, after a reorganization, Armenia became a separate constituent republic of the U.S.S.R.

Since 1983, Armenia has been involved in a territorial dispute with Azerbaijan over the enclave of Nagorno-Karabakh which both republics lay claim to. The autonomous region of Nagorno-Karabahk lies entirely within Azerbaijan. The majority population of the enclave are Armenian Christians who want to secede from Azerbaijan and join with Armenia.

The political disruption in Azerbaijan in June 1993 led to significant military advances for the Armenian forces, leaving them in control of much of the disputed region as well as a corridor to Armenia proper.

A number of opposition parties in September 1994 formed an alliance with the intent of applying political pressure on the government. In December the government banned an opposition party, claiming it had terrorist ties.

Although the economy showed signs of improvement in 1994, living standards remained quite low. In October the country joined the NATO Partnership in Peace program.

AUSTRALIA

Commonwealth of Australia
Sovereign: Queen Elizabeth II (1952)
Governor-General: William Hayden (1989)
Prime Minister: Paul Keating (1991)
Area: 2,966,150 sq mi. (7,682,300 sq km)
Population (est. mid-1995): 18,000,000 (average annual rate of natural increase: 0.8%); birth rate: 15/1000; infant mortality rate: 6.1/1000; density per square mile: 6
Capital (est. 1990): Canberra, 310,100; **Largest cities (1990):** Sydney, 3,656,500; Melbourne, 3,080,000; Brisbane, 1,301,700; Adelaide, 1,049,100; Perth,

1,193,100; **Monetary unit:** Australian dollar; **Language:** English; **Religions:** 26.1% Anglican, 26.0% Roman Catholic, 24.3% other Christian; **Literacy rate:** 100%
Member of Commonwealth of Nations
Economic summary: Gross domestic product (1993): $339.7 billion; per capita $19,100; real growth rate 4%; inflation 1.1%; unemployment (Dec. '93): 10%. Arable land: 6%. Principal products: wool, meat, cereals, sugar, sheep, cattle, dairy products. Labor force (1992–93): 8,646,500; finance and services, 33.8%; public and community services, 22.3%; wholesale and retail trade, 20.1%; manufacturing, 16.2%. Natural resources: iron ore, bauxite, zinc, lead, tin, coal, oil, gas, copper, nickel, uranium. Exports: $44.1 billion (1992): coal, gold, meat, wool, alumina, wheat, machinery and transport equipment. Imports: $43.6 billion (1992): machinery and transport equipment, computers and office machines, crude oil and petroleum products. Major trading partners: Japan, U.S., U.K., New Zealand, Germany, South Korea, Singapore, Germany.

Geography. The continent of Australia, with the island state of Tasmania, is approximately equal in area to the United States (excluding Alaska and Hawaii), and is nearly 50% larger than Europe (excluding the U.S.S.R.).

Mountain ranges run from north to south along the east coast, reaching their highest point in Mount Kosciusko (7,308 ft; 2,228 m). The western half of the continent is occupied by a desert plateau that rises into barren, rolling hills near the west coast. It includes the Great Victoria Desert to the south and the Great Sandy Desert to the north. The Great Barrier Reef, extending about 1,245 miles (2,000 km), lies along the northeast coast.

The island of Tasmania (26,178 sq mi.; 67,800 sq km) is off the southeastern coast.

Government. The Federal Parliament consists of a bicameral legislature. The House of Representatives has 146 members elected for three years by popular vote. The Senate has 76 members elected by popular vote for six years. One half of the Senate is elected every three years. Voting is compulsory at 18. Supreme federal judicial power is vested in the High Court of Australia in the Federal Courts, and in the State Courts invested by Parliament with Federal jurisdiction. The High Court consists of seven justices, appointed by the Governor-General in Council. Each of the states has its own judicial system.

History. Dutch, Portuguese, and Spanish ships sighted Australia in the 17th century; the Dutch landed at the Gulf of Carpentaria in 1606. Australia was called New Holland, Botany Bay, and New South Wales until about 1820.

Captain James Cook, in 1770, claimed possession for Great Britain. A British penal colony was set up at what is now Sydney, then Port Jackson, in 1788, and about 161,000 transported English convicts were settled there until the system was suspended in 1839.

Free settlers established six colonies: New South Wales (1786), Tasmania (then Van Diemen's Land) (1825), Western Australia (1829), South Australia (1834), Victoria (1851), and Queensland (1859).

The six colonies became states and in 1901 federated into the Commonwealth of Australia with a Constitution that incorporated British parliamentary tradition and U.S. federal experience. Australia became known for liberal legislation: free compulsory educa-

tion, protected trade unionism with industrial conciliation and arbitration, the "Australian" ballot facilitating selection, the secret ballot, women's suffrage, maternity allowances, and sickness and old age pensions.

In the election of 1983, Robert Hawke, head of the Labor Party, became Prime Minister. The Labor government was reelected in a Federal election in December 1984.

Amid a deep recession Hawke was ousted by Paul Keating in 1991—the first time an Australian prime minister was removed from office by his own party.

March 1993 general elections returned Prime Minister Keating and his Labour Party to power. Mr. Keating successfully campaigned for the 2000 Olympics to be held in Sydney, but his efforts to transform the country into a republic continued to arouse controversy. Even within the opposition Liberal Party disagreements emerged over support for the monarchy with the Liberals' new leader, Alexander Downer, favoring it.

Australian External Territories

Norfolk Island (13 sq mi.; 36.3 sq km) was placed under Australian administration in 1914. Population, 2,620 (July 1992); growth rate, 1.7%.

The Ashmore and Cartier Islands (.8 sq mi.), situated in the Indian Ocean off the northwest coast of Australia, came under Australian administration in 1934. In 1938 the islands were annexed to the Northern Territory. On the attainment of self-government by the Northern Territory in 1978, the islands which are uninhabited were retained as Commonwealth Territory.

The Australian Antarctic Territory (2,360,000 sq mi.; 6,112,400 sq km), comprises all the islands and territories, other than Adélie Land, situated south of lat. 60°S and lying between long. 160° to 45°E. It came under Australian administration in 1936.

Heard Island and the McDonald Islands (158 sq mi.; 409.2 sq km), lying in the sub-Antarctic, were placed under Australian administration in 1947. The islands are uninhabited.

Christmas Island (52 sq mi.; 134.7 sq km) is situated in the Indian Ocean. It came under Australian administration in 1958. Population 929 (July 92).

Coral Sea Islands (400,000 sq mi.; 1,036,000 sq km, but only a few sq mi. of land) became a territory of Australia in 1969. There is no permanent population on the islands.

Cocos (Keeling) Islands. The territory of the Cocos comprises a group of 27 small coral islands in two separate atolls in the Indian Ocean, 1,721 miles (2,768 kilometers) northwest of Perth. West Island is the largest, about 6.2 miles (10 kilometers) long. The islands became an Australian territory in 1955. Population 597 (July 92); growth rate –0.5%.

AUSTRIA

Republic of Austria
President: Thomas Klestil (1992)
Chancellor: Franz Vranitzky (1986)
Area: 32,375 sq mi. (83,851 sq km)
Population (est. mid-1995): 8,100,000 (average annual rate of natural increase: 0.1%); birth rate: 12/1000; infant mortality rate: 6.2/1000; density per square mile: 250.2

Capital and largest city (1991): Vienna, 1,700,000; **Other large cities (est. 1991):** Graz, 232,150; Linz, 203,000; Salzburg, 144,000; Innsbruck, 115,000; **Monetary unit:** Schilling; **Languages:** German. Slovene, Croatian, Hungarian; **Religion:** Roman Catholic, 89%; **Literacy rate:** 98%
National name: Republik Österreich
Economic summary: Gross domestic product (1994): $149.8 billion; per capita $19,000; real growth rate: 1.2%; inflation rate: 2.9%; unemployment: 4.3%. Arable land: 17%. Labor force: 3,037,000; 56.4% in services; principal agricultural products: livestock, forest products, grains, sugar beets, potatoes. Principal products: iron and steel, chemicals, machinery, paper and pulp. Natural resources: iron ore, petroleum, timber, magnesite, aluminum, coal, lignite, cement, copper, hydropower. Exports: $47 billion (1994 est.): iron and steel products, timber, paper, textiles, chemical products. Illicit drugs: transshipment point for southwest heroin transiting the Balkan route. Imports: $57 billion (1994 est.): machinery, chemicals, foodstuffs, textiles and clothing, petroleum. Major trading partners: Germany and European Community (EC), Eastern Europe, U.S., Japan, EU countries.

Geography. Slightly smaller than Maine, Austria includes much of the mountainous territory of the eastern Alps (about 75% of the area). The country contains many snowfields, glaciers, and snowcapped peaks, the highest being the Grossglockner (12,530 ft; 3,819 m). The Danube is the principal river. Forests and woodlands cover about 40% of the land area.

Almost at the heart of Europe, Austria has as its neighbors Italy, Switzerland, Germany, Czech Republic, Hungary, Slovenia, and Liechtenstein.

Government. Austria is a federal republic composed of nine provinces (Bundesländer), including Vienna. The President is elected by the people for a term of six years. The bicameral legislature consists of the Bundesrat, with 58 members chosen by the provincial assemblies, and the Nationalrat, with 183 members popularly elected for four years. Presidency of the Bundesrat revolves every six months, going to the provinces in alphabetical order.

History. Settled in prehistoric times, the Central European land that is now Austria was overrun in pre-Roman times by various tribes, including the Celts. Charlemagne conquered the area in 788 and encouraged colonization and Christianity. In 1252, Ottokar, King of Bohemia, gained possession, only to lose the territories to Rudolf of Hapsburg in 1278. Thereafter, until World War I, Austria's history was largely that of its ruling house, the Hapsburgs.

Austria emerged from the Congress of Vienna in 1815 as the Continent's dominant power. The *Ausgleich* of 1867 provided for a dual sovereignty, the empire of Austria and the kingdom of Hungary, under Francis Joseph I, who ruled until his death on Nov. 21, 1916. He was succeeded by his grandnephew, Charles I.

During World War I, Austria-Hungary was one of the Central Powers with Germany, Bulgaria, and Turkey, and the conflict left the country in political chaos and economic ruin. Austria, shorn of Hungary, was proclaimed a republic in 1918, and the monarchy was dissolved in 1919.

A parliamentary democracy was set up by the Constitution of Nov. 10, 1920. To check the power of Nazis advocating union with Germany, Chancellor Engelbert Dolfuss in 1933 established a dictatorship, but was assassinated by the Nazis on July 25, 1934.

Kurt von Schuschnigg, his successor, struggled to keep Austria independent but on March 12, 1938, German troops occupied the country, and Hitler proclaimed an *Anschluss* (union) with Germany, annexing it to the Third Reich.

After World War II, the U.S. and Britain declared the Austrians a "liberated" people. But the Russians prolonged the occupation. Finally Austria concluded a state treaty with the U.S.S.R. and the other occupying powers and regained its independence on May 15, 1955. The second Austrian republic, established Dec. 19, 1945, on the basis of the 1920 Constitution (amended in 1929), was declared by the federal parliament to be permanently neutral.

On June 8, 1986, former UN Secretary-General Kurt Waldheim was elected to the ceremonial office of President in a campaign marked by controversy over his alleged links to Nazi war-crimes in Yugoslavia.

The chief of Austria's diplomatic corps. Thomas Klestil, handily won election to the Presidency, paving the way for a normalization of relations strained during Waldheim's term.

Voters in June 1994 emphatically endorsed membership in the European Union, which took effect on January 1, 1995. Despite the membership Austria retained its strict constitutional neutrality and forbade the stationing of foreign troops on its soil.

The right-wing Austrian Freedom Party realized gains in parliamentary elections in October 1994 at the expense of the two largest parties.

AZERBAIJAN

Republic of Azerbaijan
President: Heydor Aliyev (1993)
Prime Minister: Fuad Guliyev (1994)
Area: 33,400 sq mi. (86,600 sq km)
Population (est. mid-1995): 7,300,000 (average annual rate of natural increase: 1.6%); (Azerbaijanis, 83%; major minorities, Russians, and Armenians). The republic is noted for the longevity of its population. Forty-eight out of every 100,000 residents are over 100 years old. Birth rate: 23/1000; infant mortality rate: 26/1000; density per square mile: 218.5
Capital and largest city (1991): Baku, 1,713,300, a port on the Caspian Sea. Other large cities: Ganja (1989), 278,000; Sumgait, 231,000. **Monetary unit:** Manat.
Languages: Azerbaijani Turkic, 82%; Russian, 7%; Armenian, 2%. **Religion:** Moslem, 87%; Russian Orthodox, 5.6%; Armenian Orthodox, 2%
Economic summary: Gross domestic product (1993 U.N. World Bank data est.): $15.5 billion; $2,040 per capita; –13.3% real growth rate; inflation: 20% (per mo., avg. 1993); unemployment: 0.7% (Dec. '93). Azerbaijan's Apsheron peninsula is an oil-rich area and is now being developed under a $7.4 billion contract with western oil companies. Industries: petroleum and natural gas, petroleum products, oilfield equipment, steel, iron ore, cement, chemicals and petrochemicals and textiles. Agricultural production includes cotton, wheat, tobacco, fruit, wine grapes, potatoes, sheep and other livestock. Labor force: 2,789,000 (1990): agriculture and forestry, 32%; industry and construction, 26%. Exports: $821 million (f.o.b., 1992 to outside the successor states of the former U.S.S.R: oil and gas, chemicals, textiles, cotton (1991). Imports: $300 million (c.i.f., 1992 est.) from outside the successor states of the former USSR: machinery and parts, consumer durables, foodstuffs, textiles (1991). Major trading partners: Mostly CIS and European countries.

Geography: Azerbaijan is located on the western shore of the Caspian Sea at the southeastern extremity of the Caucasus. The region is a mountainous country. About 7% of it is arable land. The Kura River Valley is the area's major agricultural zone. The republic is bounded on the north by Russia, by the Caspian Sea in the east, by Iran in the south, and by Georgia and Armenia in the west. Azerbaijan has about a 10-mile border with Turkey.

Government: A constitutional republic in transition.

History: Azerbaijan was known in ancient times as Albania. The area was the site of many conflicts involving Arabs, Kazars, and the Turks. After the 11th century, the territory became dominated by the Turks and eventually became a stronghold of the Shi'ite Muslim religion and Islamic culture.

The territory of Soviet Azerbaijan was acquired by Russia from Persia through the Treaty of Gulistan in 1813 and the Treaty of Turkamanchai in 1828.

After the Bolshevik Revolution, Azerbaijan declared its independence from Russia in May 1918. The republic was reconquered by the Red Army in 1920, and was annexed into the Transcaucasian Soviet Federated Socialist Republic in 1922. It was later reestablished as a separate Soviet Republic on Dec. 5, 1936.

Since 1983, the rival republics of Azerbaijan and Armenia have been feuding over the enclave of Nagorno-Karabakh located within Azerbaijan. Both nations claim this autonomous region. The majority of the enclave's residents are both Armenians and Christians and they are agitating to secede from the predominantly Muslim Azerbaijan and join with Armenia.

Campaigning on a platform calling for the country to break from the CIS and retain Nagorno-Karabakh, Popular Front leader Elchibey won the 1992 vote.

A power struggle in June 1993 sent Elchibey fleeing when rebel forces advanced on the capital. These events were set against a worsening of the economy and major reverses in the war with Armenia.

In November 1993 Aliyev received almost 99% of the vote in a presidential election.

Forces loyal to then-prime minister Husseynov seized several cities but where overwhelmed by those loyal to the president. Although claiming innocence Husseynov was fired and charged with treason, whereupon he fled to Russia.

In February 1994 Aliyev signed a 10-year treaty of friendship and cooperation with Turkey. In May the country joined NATO's Partnership in Peace program.

BAHAMAS

Commonwealth of the Bahamas
Sovereign: Queen Elizabeth II (1952)
Governor-General: Sir Clifford Darling (1992)
Prime Minister: Hubert Ingraham (1992)
Area: 5,380 sq mi. (13,939 sq km)
Population (est. mid-1995): 300,000 (average annual rate of natural increase: 1.5%); birth rate: 20/1000; infant mortality rate: 23.8/1000; density per square mile: 55.7
Capital and largest city (1991 census): Nassau, 171,542;
  Monetary unit: Bahamian dollar; **Language:** English;
  Religions: Baptist, 29%; Anglican, 23%; Roman Catholic, 22%, others; **Literacy rate:** 95%
Member of Commonwealth of Nations
Economic summary: Gross domestic product (1993 est.): $4.4 billion; $16,500 per capita; real growth rate 2% (1991); inflation rate: 6.5% (1991); unemployment: 5.7%

(1992 est.). Labor force: 127,400; Principal agricultural products: fruits, vegetables. Major industrial products: fish, refined petroleum, pharmaceutical products, banking, rum, cement, salt production, spiral welded steel pipe; tourism. Natural resources: salt, aragonite, timber. Exports: $310 million (f.o.b., 1992) rum, crawfish, pharmaceuticals, cement, rum. Imports: $1.2 billion (f.o.b., 1992): foodstuffs, manufactured goods, fuels. Major trading partners: U.S., U.K., Nigeria, Canada, Iran, Japan, Norway, France, Denmark.

Geography. The Bahamas are an archipelago of about 700 islands and 2,400 uninhabited islets and cays lying 50 miles off the east coast of Florida. They extend from northwest to southeast for about 760 miles (1,223 km). Only 22 of the islands are inhabited; the most important is New Providence (80 sq mi.; 207 sq km), on which Nassau is situated. Other islands include Grand Bahama, Abaco, Eleuthera, Andros, Cat Island, San Salvador (or Watling's Island), Exuma, Long Island, Crooked Island, Acklins Island, Mayaguana, and Inagua.

The islands are mainly flat, few rising above 200 feet (61 m). There are no fresh water streams. There are several large brackish lakes on several islands including Inagua and New Providence.

Government. The Bahamas moved toward greater autonomy in 1968 after the overwhelming victory in general elections of the Progressive Liberal Party, led by Prime Minister Lynden O. Pindling. The black leader's party won 29 seats in the House of Assembly to only 7 for the predominantly white United Bahamians, who had controlled the islands for decades before Pindling became Premier in 1967.

With its new mandate from the 85%-black population, Pindling's government negotiated a new Constitution with Britain under which the colony became the Commonwealth of the Bahama Islands in 1969. On July 10, 1973, The Bahamas became an independent nation as the Commonwealth of the Bahamas. The islands established diplomatic relations with Cuba in 1974.

In the 1992 election, the Free National Movement won 32 of 49 seats in Parliament; the Progressive Liberal Party, 17. Hubert A. Ingraham was sworn in as Prime Minister on Aug. 20, 1992, ending 25 years of rule by the Progressive Liberal Party.

History. The islands were reached by Columbus in October 1492, and were a favorite pirate area in the early 18th century. The Bahamas were a crown colony from 1717 until they were granted internal self-government in 1964.

Illegal Haitian immigration posed a major problem for the government in 1993.

BAHRAIN

State of Bahrain
Emir: Sheik Isa bin-Sulman al-Khalifa (1961)
Prime Minister: Sheik Khalifa bin Sulman al-Khalifa (1970)
Area: 240 sq mi. (620 sq km)
Population (est. mid-1995): 600,000 (average annual rate of natural increase: 2.5%); birth rate: 29/1000; infant mortality rate: 25/1000; density per square mile: 2,500
Capital (1991): Al-Manámah, 120,937; **Monetary unit:** Bahrain dinar; **Languages:** Arabic (official), English, Farsi, Urdu; **Religions:** Shi'a Muslim, 70%; Sunni Muslim, 30%. **Literacy rate:** 80%

Economic summary: Gross domestic product (1993 est.): $6.8 billion, $12,000 per capita; real growth rate: 4%; inflation: 2%; unemployment: 8–10%. Labor force (1982): 140,000; labor force in industry and commerce: 85%. Principal agricultural products: eggs, vegetables, fruits. Major industries: petroleum processing and refining, aluminum smelting, offshore banking, ship repairing. Natural resources: oil, fish. Exports: $3.5 billion (f.o.b., 1993 est.): petroleum and petroleum products, 80%; aluminum, 7%. Imports: $3.7 billion (f.o.b., 1993 est.): machinery, oil-industry equipment, motor vehicles, foodstuffs. Major trading partners: Saudi Arabia, U.S., U.K., Japan, India, Pakistan, Singapore, Germany.

Geography. Bahrain is an archipelago in the Persian Gulf off the coast of Saudi Arabia. The islands for the most part are level expanses of sand and rock.

Government. Traditional monarchy. Political parties prohibited.

History. A sheikdom that passed from the Persians to the al-Khalifa family from Arabia in 1782, Bahrain became, by treaty, a British protectorate in 1820. It has become a major Middle Eastern oil center and, through use of oil revenues, is one of the most developed of the Persian Gulf sheikdoms. The Emir, Sheik Isa bin-Sulman al-Khalifa, who succeeded to the post in 1961, is a member of the original ruling family. Bahrain announced its independence on Aug. 14, 1971.

The country's territorial dispute with Qatar was taken to the International Court of Justice in 1992 with the latter saying it would seek ICJ arbitration.

Protests by groups opposed to the monarchy occurred in December 1994 leading to violent clashes with government forces. Nine died and hundreds were arrested as a result of the protests.

BANGLADESH

People's Republic of Bangladesh
President: Abdur Rahman Biswas
Prime Minister: Begum Khaleda Zia (1991)
Area: 55,598 sq. mi. (143,998 sq km)
Population (est. mid-1995): 119,200,000 (average annual rate of natural increase: 2.4%); birth rate: 36/1000; infant mortality rate: 88/1000 (1992); density per square mile: 2,144
Capital and largest city (mid-1994 est.): Dhaka, 7,000,000+; other large cities (est. mid-1994): Chittagong, 3,000,000; Khulna, 2,000,000; **Monetary unit:** Taka; **Principal languages:** Bangla (official), English; **Religions:** Islam, (official) 88.30%; Hindu, 10.51%; **Literacy rate:** 36%
Member of Commonwealth of Nations
Economic summary: Gross domestic product (Feb. 1994): per capita $224; real growth rate: 4.6% (1993–94); inflation: 1.8% (1993–94); unemployment rate (est. FY90): 30%. Arable land: 67%. Agriculture accounts for 40% of GDP and 70% of employment. Principal agricultural products: rice, jute, tea, sugar, potatoes, beef. Labor force: 50.7 million est., 11% in industry and commerce. Major industrial products: jute goods, textiles, sugar, fertilizer, paper, processed foods. Natural resources: natural gas, uranium, timber. Exports: $2.534 billion (FY93/94): garments, jute and jute goods, leather and leather goods, seafood, tea, paper, fertilizer. Imports: $4.191 billion (FY93/94): capital goods, petroleum, food, textiles. Major trading partners: U.S., EU, Japan, China, South Korea, India.

Geography. Bangladesh, on the northern coast of the Bay of Bengal, is surrounded by India, with a small common border with Burma in the southeast. It is approximately the size of Wisconsin. The country is low-lying riverine land traversed by the many branches and tributaries of the Ganges and Brahmaputra rivers. Elevations averages less than 600 feet (183 m) above sea level. Tropical monsoons and frequent floods and cyclones inflict heavy damage in the delta region.

Government. Khaleda Zia, widow of assassinated President Ziaur Rahman, and her Bangladesh Nationalist Party won the election of late-February 1991. P.M. Zia returned Bangladesh to the parliamentary system. In a referendum in September 1991 the electorate voted to reduce the president to a figurehead.

History. The former East Pakistan was part of imperial British India until Britain withdrew in 1947. The two Pakistans were united by religion (Islam), but their peoples were separated by culture, physical features, and 1,000 miles of Indian territory. Bangladesh consists primarily of East Bengal (West Bengal is part of India and its people are primarily Hindu) plus the Sylhet district of the Indian state of Assam. For almost 25 years after independence from Britain, its history was as part of Pakistan (*see* Pakistan).

The East Pakistanis unsuccessfully sought greater autonomy from West Pakistan. The first general elections in Pakistani history, in December 1970, saw virtually all 171 seats of the region (out of 300 for both East and West Pakistan) go to Sheik Mujibur Rahman's Awami League.

Attempts to write an all-Pakistan Constitution to replace the military regime of Gen. Yahya Khan failed. Yahya put down a revolt in March 1971. An estimated one million Bengalis were killed in the fighting or later slaughtered. Ten million more took refuge in India.

In December 1971, India invaded East Pakistan, routed the West Pakistani occupation forces, and created Bangladesh. In February 1974, Pakistan agreed to recognize the independence of Bangladesh.

On March 24, 1982, Gen. Hossain Mohammad Ershad, army chief of staff, took control in a bloodless coup. Ershad assumed the office of President in 1983.

Gen. Ershad resigned on December 6, 1990 amidst protests and numerous allegations of corruption.

A general strike calling for the resignation of the government halted most activity in the capital and four other cities for several days in 1994. To no avail opposition parties called for new elections even though not required until March 1996. Opposition legislators boycotted parliament for much of the year as a result.

BARBADOS

Sovereign: Queen Elizabeth II
Governor-General: Dame Nita Barrow (June 1990)
Prime Minister: Owen Arthur (1994)
Area: 166 sq. mi. (431 sq km)
Population (est. mid-1995): 300,000; growth rate: 0.7%.; birth rate: 16/1000 infant mortality rate: 9.1/1000; density per square mile: 1,807
Capital and largest city (1990): Bridgetown, 6,700; **Monetary unit:** Barbados dollar; **Language:** English; **Religions:** Anglican, 40%; Methodist, 7%; Pentecostal, 8%; Roman Catholic, 4%; **Literacy rate:** 99%

Member of Commonwealth of Nations
Economic summary: Gross domestic product (1993 est.): $2.2 billion; per capita $8,700; real growth rate 1.0%; inflation, 3.7%; unemployment, 24.5%. Arable land: 77%. Principal products: sugar cane, subsistence foods. Labor force (1991): 120,900; 37% services and government. Major industrial products: light manufactures, sugar milling, tourism. Tourism industry is major employer of labor force. Exports: $158 million (f.o.b., 1992): sugar and molasses, chemicals, electrical components, clothing, rum, machinery and transport equipment. Imports: $465 million (f.o.b., 1992): foodstuffs, consumer durables, raw materials, machinery, crude oil, construction materials, chemicals. Major trading partners: U.S., Caribbean nations, U.K., Canada.

Geography. An island in the Atlantic about 300 miles (483 km) north of Venezuela, Barbados is only 21 miles long (34 km) and 14 miles across (23 km) at its widest point. It is circled by fine beaches and narrow coastal plains. The highest point is Mount Hillaby (1,105 ft; 337 m) in the north central area.

Government. The Barbados legislature dates from 1627. It is bicameral, with a Senate of 21 appointed members and an Assembly of 28 elected members. The major political parties are the Barbados Labour Party (19 seats in Assembly), led by Prime Minister Owen Arthur; Democratic Labour Party (8 seats), led by Erskine Sandiford; and the National Democratic Party (1 seat).

History. Barbados, with a population 90% black, was settled by the British in 1627. It became a crown colony in 1885. It was a member of the Federation of the West Indies from 1958 to 1962. Britain granted the colony independence on Nov. 30, 1966, and it became a parliamentary democracy.

Prime Minister Sandiford handily won a second five-year term as a result of parliamentary elections in January 1991.

With the support of several members of the governing party the House of Representatives passed a no-confidence motion, forcing the government to call new elections ahead of time. Elections in September 1994 led to a return to power of the Labour Party.

BELARUS

Republic of Belarus
President: Aleksandr Lukashenko (1994)
Prime Minister: Mikhail Chyhir (1994)
Area: 80,200 sq mi. (207,600 sq km)
Population (est. mid-1995): 10,300,000 (average annual rate of natural increase: −0.2%) (In 1989: Belarusian, 77.9%; Russian, 13.2%; Polish, 4.1%; Ukrainian, 2.9%; Jewish, 1.1%; birth rate: 11/1000; infant mortality rate: 13/1000; density per square mile: 128.4
Capital (1991): Mensk (Minsk), 1,658,000. Other large cities (est. 1991): Gomel, 503,300; Mogilyov, 363,000; Vitebsk, 361,500; Grodno, 284,800; Bobruysk, 223,000.
Monetary unit: Belarusian ruble; **Language:** Belarusian (white Russian); **Religion:** Orthodoxy is predominant; **Literacy rate:** 100%
Economic summary: Gross domestic product (U.N., World Bank 1993 est.): $61 billion; per capita $5,890; −9% real growth rate; inflation 30% per month; unemployment 1.4% (Dec. '93). Labor force (1990): 5.4 million. Industry accounts for about two-thirds of the country's income. Major industries include tractors, trucks, agricultural machinery, textiles, timber, chemical products including fertilizers, light manufacturing

including TV sets, refrigerators, and computers, and food processing. Belarus's land is not well suited for farming. One-quarter of the republic's work force is employed in agriculture. High-yield agricultural crops are potatoes and vegetables, flax, rye, oats, other grains, sugar beets, fruit, and considerable quantities of meat, milk, and eggs. Exports: $994,309,000 (f.o.b., 1994): to outside the successor states of the former USSR. Illicit drugs: is an illicit producer of opium and cannabis, mostly for domestic market; transshipment point for illicit drugs to Western Europe. Imports: $561,374,000 (c.i.f., 1994): from outside of the successor states of the former USSR.

Geography: Much of Belarus (formerly Byelorussia) is a hilly lowland with forests, swamps, and numerous rivers and lakes. There are wide rivers emptying into the Baltic and the Black Seas. Its forests cover over one-third of the land and its peat marshes are a valuable natural resource. The largest lake is Narach, 31 sq mi. (79.6 sq km). The republic borders Latvia and Lithuania on the north, Ukraine on the south, Russia on the east, and Poland on the west.

Government: A constitutional republic. The parliament (Supreme Soviet) has 260 deputies.

History: In the 5th century, Belarus (also known as White Russia) was colonized by east Slavic tribes and was dominated by Kiev from the 9th to 12th centuries. After the destruction of Kiev by the Mongols in the 13th century, the territory was conquered by the dukes of Lithuania. Belarus became part of the Grand Duchy of Lithuania which merged with Poland in 1569.

Following the partitions of Poland in 1772, 1793, and the final partition which divided Poland between Russia, Prussia, and Austria, Belarus became part of the Russian empire.

The peace Treaty of Riga in March 1921 ending the Polish-Soviet War ceded west Belarus to Poland. The eastern part of the country was joined to the U.S.S.R. in 1922. In 1939, the Soviet Union took back West Belarus under the secret protocol of the Nazi-Soviet Nonaggression Pact and incorporated it into the Byelorussian Soviet Socialist Republic.

Following the end of World War II, Belarus was given membership in the United Nations in 1945.

Belarus declared its sovereignty in July 1990 and its independence in August 1991.

The Belarus president, Nikolai Dementei, a communist hard-liner, was forced to resign under pressure following the August 1991 attempted coup and Stanislav S. Shushkevich, First Deputy Chairman of the Parliament, assumed leadership of the country.

Belarus became a co-founder of the Commonwealth of Independent States (CIS) on Dec. 8, 1991, and its capital Minsk became the seat of the new union's government. On Dec. 21, 1991, Belarus formally proclaimed its membership in the Commonwealth of Independent States along with ten other former Soviet republics.

In January 1994 the country's parliament ousted its reform-minded leader in protest against his support for market economics. In March parliament adopted a new constitution, creating a presidency, and reconstructed the 260-seat parliament. In the first-round, May 15 election Lukashenka received a plurality, and in the run-off June 23 balloting over 80% of the vote.

The prime ministers of Russia and Belarus signed a treaty in April to unify their monetary systems and lift customs barriers. The chairman of the Belarussian national bank opposed the monetary union leaving its implementation in doubt.

BELGIUM

Kingdom of Belgium
Sovereign: King Albert II (1993)
Prime Minister: Jean-Luc Dehaene (1992)
Area: 11,781 sq mi. (30,513 sq km)
Population (est. mid-1995): 10,200,000 (average annual rate of natural increase: 0.1%); birth rate: 12/1000; infant mortality rate: 7.6/1000; density per square mile: 865.8
Capital and largest city (1992): Brussels, 960,324; **other large cities (est. 1992):** Antwerp, 467,875; Ghent, 230,246; Charleroi, 206,928; Liege, 195,201; Bruges, 117,100; Namur, 104,372. **Monetary Unit:** Belgian franc; **Languages:** Flemish (Dutch), 56%; French, 32%; bilingual (Brussels), 11%; German, 1%.; **Religion:** Roman Catholic, 75%; **Literacy rate:** 99%
National name: Royaume de Belgique—Koningrijk van België
Economic summary: Gross domestic product (1993): $177.5 billion; per capita $20,597 (1994); real growth rate 0.8%; inflation rate 2.6% (1994); unemployment rate: 10% (1994). Arable land: 46%. Agricultural products: pork, beef, milk, fruits and vegetables, ornamental plants, meals, sugar beets, eggs, dairy products. Labor force (1988): 4,200,000; services, 69%; industry, 28%; agriculture, 3%. Major products: chemicals, mechanical, electrical and plastic equipment, textiles, nonferrous metals, iron and steel, glass. Exports: $117 billion (f.o.b., 1992): road vehicles and tractors, pearls, precious metals and stones, nuclear reactors, boilers and mechanical equipment, plastics, iron and steel, electrical machinery and equipment. Imports: $120 billion (c.i.f., 1992): road vehicles and tractors, pearls, precious metals and stones, nuclear reactors, boilers and mechanical equipment, mineral fuels and oils, plastics, iron and steel, electrical machinery and equipment. Major trading partners: European Union, Germany, Netherlands, France, U.K., U.S., Eastern Europe.

Geography. A neighbor of France, Germany, the Netherlands, and Luxembourg, Belgium has about 40 miles of seacoast on the North Sea at the Strait of Dover. In area, it is approximately the size of Maryland. The northern third of the country is a plain extending eastward from the seacoast. North of the Sambre and Meuse Rivers is a low plateau; to the south lies the heavily wooded Ardennes plateau, attaining an elevation of about 2,300 feet (700 m).
The Schelde River, which rises in France and flows through Belgium, emptying into the Schelde estuaries, enables Antwerp to be an ocean port.

Government. Belgium, a parliamentary democracy under a constitutional monarch, consists of nine provinces. Its bicameral legislature has a Senate, with its 184 members elected for four years—106 by general election, 50 by provincial councillors and 25 by the Senate itself. The 212-member Chamber of Representatives is directly elected for four years by proportional representation. There is universal suffrage, and those who do not vote are fined.
Belgium joined the North Atlantic Alliance in 1949 and is a member of the European Community. NATO and the European Community have their headquarters in Brussels.
The late sovereign, Baudouin I, was born Sept. 7, 1930, the son of King Leopold III and Queen Astrid. He became King on July 17, 1951, after the abdication of his father. He married Doña Fabiola de Mora y Aragón on Dec. 15, 1960. Since he had no children, his brother, Prince Albert, became king upon his death in 1993.

History. Belgium occupies part of the Roman province of Belgica, named after the Belgae, a people of ancient Gaul. The area was conquered by Julius Caesar in 57–50 B.C., then was overrun by the Franks in the 5th century. It was part of Charlemagne's empire in the 8th century, then in the next century was absorbed into Lotharingia and later into the Duchy of Lower Lorraine. In the 12th century it was partitioned into the Duchies of Brabant and Luxembourg, the Bishopric of Liège, and the domain of the Count of Hainaut, which included Flanders.
In the 16th century, Belgium, with most of the area of the Low Countries, passed to the Duchy of Burgundy and was the marriage portion of Archduke Maximilian of Hapsburg and the inheritance of his grandson, Charles V, who incorporated it into his empire. Then, in 1555, they were united with Spain.
By the treaty of Utrecht in 1713, the country's sovereignty passed to Austria. During the wars that followed the French Revolution, Belgium was occupied and later annexed to France. But with the downfall of Napoleon, the Congress of Vienna in 1815 gave the country to the Netherlands. The Belgians revolted in 1830 and declared their independence.
Germany's invasion of Belgium in 1914 set off World War I. The Treaty of Versailles (1919) gave the areas of Eupen, Malmédy, and Moresnet to Belgium. Leopold III succeeded Albert, King during World War I, in 1934. In World War II, Belgium was overwhelmed by Nazi Germany, and Leopold III was made prisoner. When he attempted to return in 1950, Socialists and Liberals revolted. He abdicated July 16, 1951, and his son, Baudouin, became King the next day.
Despite the increasingly strong divisions between the French- and Flemish-speaking communities, a Christian Democrat-Liberal coalition that took office in December 1981 came close to setting a record for longevity among the 32 governments that had ruled Belgium since World War II. In national elections of November 1991 the environmental and far-right parties made significant gains. Political instability in Zaire following riots there led to Belgian troops supervising an exodus of foreigners in September 1991.
In 1993 the constitution was changed, turning the country into a federal state. Compulsory military service was also eliminated.
National elections on May 21, 1995, gave the governing coalition a parliamentary majority, although the right-of-center Liberals made significant gains. Shortly thereafter the King asked Dehaene again to form a government.

BELIZE

Sovereign: Queen Elizabeth II (1952)
Governor-General: Corville Young (1993)
Prime Minister: Manuel Esquivel (1993)
Area: 8,867 sq mi. (22,965 sq km)
Population (est. mid-1995): 200,000 (average annual rate of natural increase: 3.3%); birth rate: 38/1000; infant mortality rate: 34/1000.; density per sq mi.: 22.5
Capital: Belmopan, 3,687; **Largest city (est. 1990):** Belize City, 43,621; **Monetary unit:** Belize dollar; **Languages:** English (official) and Spanish, Maya, Carib; **Religions:** Roman Catholic, 62%; Protestant, 30%;; **Literacy rate:** 91% (est.)

Member of Commonwealth of Nations
Economic summary: Gross domestic product (1993 est.): $550 million, per capita $2,700; real growth rate 5.3% (1992); inflation 5.5% (1991); unemployment 15% (1992 est.). Principal products: sugar cane, citrus concentrate, corn, molasses, rice, bananas, livestock. Labor force: 51,500; 10.3% in manufacturing. Major products: timber, processed foods, furniture, rum, soap. Natural resource: timber, fish. Exports: $116 million (f.o.b., 1992); sugar, molasses, clothing, lumber, citrus concentrates, fish. Imports: $273 million (c.i.f., 1992 est.): fuels, transportation equipment, foodstuffs, machinery, chemicals, pharmaceuticals, manufactured goods. Major trading partners: European Union, Mexico, CARICOM, U.S.

Geography. Belize (formerly British Honduras) is situated on the Caribbean Sea south of Mexico and east and north of Guatemala. In area, it is about the size of New Hampshire. Most of the country is heavily forested with various hardwoods. Mangrove swamps and cays along the coast give way to hills and mountains in the interior. The highest point is Victoria Peak, 3,681 feet (1,122 m).

Government. Formerly the colony of British Honduras, Belize became a fully independent commonwealth on Sept. 21, 1981, after having been self-governing since 1964. Executive power is nominally wielded by Queen Elizabeth II through an appointed Governor-General but effective power is held by the Prime Minister, who is responsible to a 29-member parliament elected by universal suffrage.

History. Once a part of the Mayan empire, the area was deserted until British timber cutters began exploiting valuable hardwoods in the 17th century. Efforts by Spain to dislodge British settlers, including a major naval attack in 1798, were defeated. The territory was formally named a British colony in 1862 but administered by the Governor of Jamaica until 1884.

Guatemala has long made claims to the territory. A tentative agreement was reached between Britain, Belize, and Guatemala in March 1981 that would offer access to the Caribbean through Belizean territory for Guatemala. The agreement broke down, however.

Guatemala recognized Belize's sovereignty in September 1991 and abandoned its territorial claim, although unease remains.

The general election of June 1993 saw a victory for the United Democratic Party, which won 16 of the 29 seats in the House of Representatives.

Local council elections in March 1994 provided victories to the UDP, putting the party in control of all seven councils, whereas previously it had but two.

BENIN

Republic of Benin
President: Nicephore Soglo (1991)
Area: 43,483 sq mi. (112,622 sq km)
Population (est. mid-1995): 5,400,000 (average annual rate of natural increase: 3.1%); birth rate: 49/1000; infant mortality rate: 86/1000; density per square mile: 124
Capital and largest city (est. 1985): Cotonou (official) 402,300; **Other large cities (est. 1985):** Porto-Novo (de facto capital), 163,260.. **Monetary unit:** Franc CFA; **Ethnic groups:** Fons and Adjas, Baribas, Yorubas, Mahis; **Languages:** French, African languages; **Religions:** indigenous, 70%; Christian, 15%; Islam, 15%; **National name:** Republique du Benin; **Literacy rate (1990 est.):** 23%
Economic summary: Gross domestic product (1993 est.): $6.2 billion; $1,200 per capita; real growth rate (1991): 3%; inflation rate 3.4% (1990). Arable land: 12%. Principal agricultural products: palm oils, peanuts, cotton, coffee, tobacco, corn, rice, livestock, fish. Labor force: 1,900,000; 60% in agriculture. Major industrial products: processed palm oil, palm kernel oil, textiles, beverages. Natural resources: limestone, some offshore oil, marble, timber. Exports: $328.8 million (f.o.b., 1991 est.): crude oil, cotton, palm products, cocoa. Imports: $482.3 million (f.o.b., 1991 est.): foodstuffs, beverages, tobacco, petroleum products, intermediate goods, capital goods, light consumer goods. Major trading partners: France and other Western European countries, Japan, U.S.

Geography. This West African nation on the Gulf of Guinea, between Togo on the west and Nigeria on the east, is about the size of Tennessee. It is bounded also by Burkina Faso and Niger on the north. The land consists of a narrow coastal strip that rises to a swampy, forested plateau and then to highlands in the north. A hot and humid climate blankets the entire country.

Government. The change in name from Dahomey to Benin was announced by President Mathieu Kerekou on November 30, 1975. Benin commemorates an African kingdom that flourished in the 17th century. Benin is a republic under a multiparty democratic rule with a unicameral legislature, the National Assembly. At the National Conference held at Cotonou, Feb. 19–28, 1990, Marxism-Leninism was abolished as the State philosophy, a multiparty system was established, and political detainees and prisoners were released.

History. One of the smallest and most densely populated states in Africa, Benin was annexed by the French in 1893. The area was incorporated into French West Africa in 1904. It became an autonomous republic within the French Community in 1958, and on Aug. 1, 1960, was granted its independence within the Community.

Gen. Christophe Soglo deposed the first president, Hubert Maga, in an army coup in 1963. He dismissed the civilian government in 1965, proclaiming himself chief of state. A group of young army officers seized power in December 1967, deposing Soglo. They promulgated a new Constitution in 1968.

In December 1969, Benin had its fifth coup of the decade, with the army again taking power. In May 1970, a three-man presidential commission was created to take over the government. The commission had a six-year term. In May 1972, yet another army coup ousted the triumvirate and installed Lt. Col. Mathieu Kerekou as President.

Student protests and widespread strikes in 1989 and 1990 moved Benin toward multiparty democracy. In March 1991 Prime Minister Soglo won the first free presidential election.

Nominally above partisan politics the president in mid-1993 said he would join the Renaissance Party.

In July 1994 the president decreed his own national budget over the objections of the Assembly. The Supreme Court declared the president's action to be unconstitutional, and the Assembly passed a new budget in late August. Major problems were left unfunded as a result.

BHUTAN

Kingdom of Bhutan
Ruler: King Jigme Singye Wangchuck (1972)
Area: 18,000 sq mi. (46,620 sq km)
Population (est. mid-1995): 800,000 (average annual rate of natural increase: 2.3%); birth rate: 39/1000; infant mortality rate: 138/1000; density per square mile: 44.4
Capital and largest city (est. 1987): Thimphu, 15,000; **Monetary unit:** Ngultrum; **Language:** Dzongkha (official); **Religions:** Buddhist, 75%; Hindu, 25%; **National name:** Druk-yul; **Literacy rate:** not available
Economic summary: Gross domestic product (1993 est.): $500 million; per capita $700; real growth rate 5%; inflation (Oct. '93) 11%. Arable land: 3%. Labor force in agriculture: 95%. Principal products: rice, barley, wheat, potatoes, fruit. Major industrial product: cement. Natural resources: timber, hydroelectric power. Exports: $66 million (f.o.b., FY93 est.): cardamom, gypsum, timber, handicrafts, cement, fruit, electricity (to India), precious stones, spices. Imports: $125 million (c.i.f., FY93 est.): fuels, machinery, vehicles, grain, fabrics. Major trading partner: India.

Geography. Mountainous Bhutan, half the size of Indiana, is situated on the southeast slope of the Himalayas, bordered on the north and east by Tibet and on the south and west and east by India. The landscape consists of a succession of lofty and rugged mountains running generally from north to south and separated by deep valleys. In the north, towering peaks reach a height of 24,000 feet (7,315 m).

Government. Bhutan is a constitutional monarchy. The King rules with a Council of Ministers and a Royal Advisory Council. There is a National Assembly (Parliament), which meets semiannually, but no political parties.

History. British troops invaded the country in 1865 and negotiated an agreement under which Britain undertook to pay an annual allowance to Bhutan on condition of good behavior. A treaty with India in 1949 increased this subsidy and placed Bhutan's foreign affairs under Indian control.

In the 1960s, Bhutan undertook modernization, abolishing slavery and the caste system, emancipating women and enacting land reform. In 1985, Bhutan made its first diplomatic links with non-Asian countries.

A pro-democracy campaign emerged in 1991 that the government claimed was composed largely of Nepalese immigrants. Some 70,000 Nepalese civil servants in 1992 fled the country as part of the pro-democracy campaign.

Nepalese activism and a refugee problem continue to plague the country. The International Red Cross investigated charges of human rights violations in 1993. In 1994 as many as 100,000 remained in refugee camps.

BOLIVIA

Republic of Bolivia
President: Gonzalo Sanchez de Lozada (1993)
Area: 424,162 sq mi. (1,098,581 sq km)
Population (est. mid-1995): 7,400,000 (average annual rate of natural increase: 2.03%); birth rate: 37/1000; infant mortality rate: 75/1000; density per sq mile: 17.5
Historic and Judicial capital (1992): Sucre, 130,952; **Administrative capital (1992):** La Paz, 711,036 **Largest cities (est. 1992):** Santa Cruz, 694,616; El Alto, 404,367; Cochabamba, 404,102; Oruro, 183,194. **Monetary unit:** Boliviano; **Languages:** Spanish, Quechua, Aymara; **Religion:** Roman Catholic, 85%; **National name:** República de Bolivia; **Literacy rate:** 78%
Economic summary: Gross national product (1994): $6.02 billion; per capita, $870; real growth rate, 4.3%; inflation rate 8.5%; unemployment rate (1993), 5.4%. Arable land: 3%. Principal agricultural products (1994): soybeans, timber, sugar, cotton, brazil nuts, coffee. Major industrial products: refined petroleum, processed foods, tires, textiles, clothing. Labor force: 2,508,000; agriculture, 33%; manufacturing, 9%; services, 22%; other, 36%. Natural resources: petroleum, natural gas, tin, lead, zinc, copper, tungsten, bismuth, antimony, gold, sulfur, silver, iron ore. Exports: $1.035 billion (f.o.b., 1994): metals, 44.9%; hydrocarbons, 10.6%; nontraditional, 44.5% (soybeans, timber, sugar, cotton). Imports: $1.207 billion (c.i.f., 1994): food, petroleum, consumer goods, capital goods. Major trading partners: U.S., Argentina, U.K., Peru, Chile, Brazil, Japan, Germany.

Geography. Landlocked Bolivia, equal in size to California and Texas combined, lies to the west of Brazil. Its other neighbors are Peru and Chile on the west and Argentina and Paraguay on the south.

The country is a low alluvial plain throughout 60% of its area toward the east, drained by the Amazon and Plata river systems. The western part, enclosed by two chains of the Andes, is a great plateau—the Altiplano, with an average altitude of 12,000 feet (3,658 m). More than 80% of the population lives on the plateau, which also contains La Paz. At an altitude of 11,910 feet (3,630 m), it is the highest administrative capital city in the world.

Lake Titicaca, half the size of Lake Ontario, is one of the highest large lakes in the world, at an altitude of 12,507 feet (3,812 m). Islands in the lake hold ruins of the ancient Incas.

Government. The Bolivian Constitution provides for a democratic, representative, unitary republic, with a government made up of three branches: legislative, executive, and judicial. Executive power is exercised by the president, elected by a direct vote for a five-year term. Legislative power is vested in the National Congress, consisting of the Chamber of Deputies and the Senate. Judicial power is in the hands of the Supreme Court of Justice, made up of twelve members.

History. Famous since Spanish colonial days for its mineral wealth, modern Bolivia was once a part of the ancient Incan Empire. After the Spaniards defeated the Incas in the 16th century, Bolivia's predominantly Indian population was reduced to slavery. The country won its independence in 1825 and was named after Simón Bolívar, the famed liberator.

Harassed by internal strife, Bolivia lost great slices of territory to three neighbor nations. Several thousand square miles and its outlet to the Pacific were taken by Chile after the War of the Pacific (1879–84). In 1903 a piece of Bolivia's Acre province, rich in rubber, was ceded to Brazil. And in 1938, after a war with Paraguay, Bolivia gave up claim to nearly 100,000 square miles of the Gran Chaco.

In 1965 a guerrilla movement mounted from Cuba and headed by Maj. Ernesto (Ché) Guevara began a revolutionary war. With the aid of U.S. military advisers, the Bolivian army, helped by the peasants, smashed the guerrilla movement, wounding and capturing Guevara on Oct. 8, 1967, and shooting him to death the next day.

Faltering steps toward restoration of civilian government were halted abruptly on July 17, 1980, when Gen. Luis Garcia Meza Tejada seized power. A series of military leaders followed before the military moved, in 1982, to return the government to civilian rule. Hernán Siles Zuazo was inaugurated President on Oct. 10, 1982.

Under Siles' left-of-center government, the country was regularly shut down by work stoppages, the bulk of Bolivia's natural resources—natural gas, gold, lithium, potassium and tungsten—were either sold on the black market or left in the ground, the country had the lowest per-capita income in South America, and inflation approached 3,000 percent. In 1985, the 73-year-old Siles decided he was unable to carry on and quit a year early.

As in 1985 the inconclusive presidential election of 1989 was decided in Congress, where the second place finisher Bánzer threw his support to Paz Zamora, who finished third, in exchange for naming a majority of the new cabinet.

The presidential elections of June 1993 gave the post to a millionaire mining entrepreneur who ran on a platform calling for free market policies and privatization. A presidential proposal to privatize six state companies was passed by Congress in March 1994 but aroused disruptive protests linked with wage demands in the first half of the year.

BOSNIA AND HERZEGOVINA

Republic of Bosnia and Herzegovina
President: Alija Izetbegovic (1990)
Prime Minister: Haris Siladzic (Bosnia)
Area: 19,741 sq mi. (51,129 sq km)
Population (est. mid-1995) 3,500,000 (official figures not available due to ethnic cleansing); (average annual rate of natural increase: 0.7%), Muslims 44%; Serbs, 31%; Croats, 17%; other, 8%. Birth rate: 14/1000; infant mortality rate: 15.3/1000; density per square mile: 177.3.
Capital and largest city (1994 est.): Sarajevo (Bosnia) 300,000 (unofficial); (1991 prewar est.): Banja Luka (Bosnia), 195,139.. Mostar is capital of Herzegovina;
Monetary unit: Dinar; **Language:** Bosnian, written in Latin and Cyrillic; **Religions:** Slavic Muslim, 40%; Orthodox, 31%; Catholic, 15%; Protestant, 4%
Economic summary: (Reliable economic statistics not available.) Gross domestic product (1991): $14 billion, real growth rate –37%; inflation 80%; unemployment (Feb. 92 est.): 28%. Labor force: 1,026,254 (1991 est.): 2% agriculture; 45% industry. Industries: steel production, mining (coal, iron ore, lead, zinc, manganese, and bauxite); vehicle assembly, textiles, tobacco products, wooden furniture, domestic appliances, oil refining. Agriculture: orchards, vineyards, livestock, some wheat and corn. Exports: $2,054 million. Imports: $1,891 million (1990). Major trading partners: principally the other former Yugoslav republics.

Geography: Bosnia and Herzegovina is a roughly triangular-shaped republic about one-half the size of the state of Kentucky. The Bosnian region in the north is mountainous and covered with thick forests. The Herzegovina region in the south is largely a rugged and flat farm land. The republic is bordered on the east by Serbia, the southeast by Montenegro, and in the north and west by the Republic of Croatia. It has a narrow coastline without natural harbors stretching 13 miles (20 km) along the Adriatic Sea.

The Sava and Drina Rivers form much of the country's northern and eastern boundaries with Croatia and Serbia, respectively. The Sava and its tributaries are the nation's chief rivers.

Government: Democratic republic with bicameral legislature. The parties of the three ethnic groups share power in the legislature.

History: Bosnia and Herzegovina were once part of the Roman provinces of Illyricum and Pannonia. Serbs first settled in the land during the 7th century A.D. and by the end of the 10th century, Bosnia became an independent state. Later Bosnia came under Hungarian rule in the middle of the 12th century.

Medieval Bosnia reached the height of its power and prestige during the 14th century when it controlled many of the surrounding territories including Herzegovina. During this period, religious strife arose among the Roman Catholic, Orthodox, and Muslim populations which weakened the country and in 1463, Ottoman Turks conquered the disunited nation.

At the Congress of Berlin in 1878 following the end of the Russo-Turkish War (1877–78), Austria was given a mandate to occupy and govern Bosnia and Herzegovina. Although the provinces were still officially part of the Ottoman Empire, they were annexed into the Austro-Hungarian empire on Oct. 7, 1908. As a result, relations with Serbia, which had claims on Bosnia and Herzegovina, became embittered. The hostile tension between the two countries climaxed in the assassination of Austrian archduke Francis Ferdinand at Sarajevo on June 28, 1914 by a Serbian nationalist. This event precipitated the start of World War I (1914–1918).

Bosnia and Herzegovina were annexed to Serbia as part of the newly formed Kingdom of Serbs, Croats, and Slovenes on Oct. 26, 1918. The name was later changed to Yugoslavia in 1929.

When Germany invaded Yugoslavia in 1941, Bosnia and Herzegovina were made part of a Croatian state that was controlled by a Fascist dictatorship. During the German and Italian occupation of their land Bosnian and Herzegovinan resistance fighters fought a fierce guerrilla warfare against the Fascist troops.

After the defeat of Germany in 1945, Bosnia and Herzegovina were reunited into a single state as one of the six republics of the newly reestablished Yugoslavia.

In December 1991, Bosnia and Herzegovina declared their independence from Yugoslavia and asked for recognition by the 12 member nations of the European Community (E.C.). The E.C. said that before it could recommend recognition, Bosnia and Herzegovina should hold a referendum on independence.

Most Bosnian voters chose independence during a referendum held in March 1992 and President Izetbegovic again declared the nation an independent state.

Attempting to carve out enclaves for themselves the Serbian minority, with the help of the largely Serbian Yugoslav army, took the offensive and laid siege, particularly on Sarajevo, resulting in countless deaths.

By the end of August, rebel Bosnian Serbs had conquered over 60% of Bosnia and Herzegovina.

The Serbs halted their siege of Sarajevo in February 1994 formally at the request of Russia. In March the government signed an agreement with Bosnian Croats linking their territories into a single federation.

A comprehensive ceasefire went into effect in December 1994 only to be punctuated with the fierce shelling of Sarajevo in the spring of 1995, perhaps as a response to a Bosnian army offensive to seize land in the hills overlooking the city in Serbian hands. In July Bosnian Serb forces overran Srebrenica in the heart of a U.N.-proclaimed safe area.

BOTSWANA

Republic of Botswana

President: Quett K.J. Masire (1980)
Area: 231,800 sq mi. (600,360 sq km)
Population (est. mid-1995): 1,500,000 (average annual rate of natural increase: 2.3%); birth rate: 31/1000; infant mortality rate: 39/1000; density per square mile: 6.4
Capital and largest city (est. 1991): Gaborone, 133,791;
Monetary unit: Pula; **Languages:** English, Setswana;
Religions: indigenous beliefs, 50%; Christian, 50%.
Member of Commonwealth of Nations; Literacy rate: 23%. **Literacy rate:** 23%
Economic summary: Gross domestic product (1993 est.): $6 billion, per capita $4,500; real growth rate 3%; inflation 14%; unemployment 25%. Arable land: 2%. Principal agricultural products: livestock, sorghum, corn, millet, cowpeas, beans. Labor force (1992): 428,000; 220,000 formal sector employees, most others involved in cattle raising and subsistence agriculture. 14,300 employed in South African mines. Major industrial products: diamonds, copper, nickel, salt, soda ash, potash, coal, frozen beef; tourism. Natural resources: diamonds, copper, nickel, salt, soda ash, potash, coal, natural gas. Exports: $1.7 billion (f.o.b., 1993): diamonds. 78%; copper and nickel, 6%; meat, 5%. Imports: $1.8 billion (c.i.f., 1992): foodstuffs, vehicles, textiles, petroleum products. Major trading partners: Switzerland, U.K., Southern African Customs Union (SACU), U.S.

Geography. Twice the size of Arizona, Botswana is in south central Africa, bounded by Namibia, Zambia, Zimbabwe, and South Africa. Most of the country is near-desert, with the Kalahari occupying the western part of the country. The eastern part is hilly, with salt lakes in the north.

Government. The Botswana Constitution provides, in addition to the unicameral National Assembly, for a House of Chiefs, which has a voice on bills affecting tribal affairs. There is universal suffrage.

History. Botswana is the land of the Batawana tribes, which, when threatened by the Boers in Transvaal, asked Britain in 1885 to establish a protectorate over the country, then known as Bechuanaland. In 1961, Britain granted a Constitution to the country. Self-government began in 1965, and on Sept. 30, 1966, the country became independent. Since 1975, it has been an associate member of the European Common Market.

Owing to a land scandal the vice president and the minister of agriculture were forced to resign in March 1992. The minister of finance was selected to be the new vice president.

October 1994 elections for the Assembly gave 26 of the 40 contested seats to the Botswana Democratic Party. The Botswana National Front, however, picked up 13 seats, 10 more than previously.

A scandal erupted when it was disclosed that several ministers had not repaid substantial loans from the National Development Bank.

BRAZIL

Federative Republic of Brazil

President: Fernando Enrique Cardoso (1994)
Area: 3,286,470 sq mi. (8,511,957 sq km)
Population (est. mid-1995): 157,800,000 (average annual rate of natural increase: 1.7%); birth rate: 25/1000; infant mortality rate: 58/1000; density per square mile: 48
Capital (est. 1985): Brasilia; **Largest cities (est. 1985):** São Paulo, 10,099,086; Rio de Janeiro, 5,615,149; Salvador, 1,811,367; Belo Horizonte, 2,122,073; Brasilia, 1,576,657; Recife, 1,289,627; Porto Alegre, 1,275,483;
Monetary unit: Novo cruzado; **Language:** Portuguese;
Religion: Roman Catholic, 90% (nominal); **National name:** República Federativa de Brasil; **Literacy rate:** 81%
Economic summary: Gross domestic product (1993 est.): $785 billion; per capita $5,000; 5% real growth rate; inflation 2,709%; unemployment 4.9%. Arable land: 7%. Principal products: world's largest producer of coffee. Sugar cane, oranges, cocoa, soybeans, tobacco, cattle. Labor force (1990 est.): 57,409,975; 27% in industry. Major industrial products: steel, chemicals, petrochemicals, machinery, motor vehicles, cement, lumber. Natural resources: iron ore, manganese, bauxite, nickel, other industrial metals, hydropower, timber. Exports: $38.8 billion (f.o.b., 1993): coffee, iron ore, soybeans, sugar, beef, transport equipment, footwear, orange juice. Imports: $25.7 billion (f.o.b., 1993): crude oil, capital goods, chemical products, foodstuffs, coal. Major trading partners: U.S., European Union, Japan, Latin America, Middle East.

Geography. Brazil covers nearly half of South America, extends 2,965 miles (4,772 km) north-south, 2,691 miles (4,331 km), east-west, and borders every nation on the continent except Chile and Ecuador.

More than a third of Brazil is drained by the Amazon and its more than 200 tributaries. The Amazon is navigable for ocean steamers to Iquitos, Peru, 2,300 miles (3,700 km) upstream. Southern Brazil is drained by the Plata system—the Paraguay, Uruguay, and Paraná Rivers. The most important stream entirely within Brazil is the São Francisco, navigable for 1,000 miles (1,903 km), but broken near its mouth by the 275-foot (84 m) Paulo Afonso Falls.

Government. A federal republic. The president and vice president are elected for a five-year term. They cannot be re-elected for a consecutive term. The National Congress maintains a bicameral structure—a Senate, whose members serve eight-year terms, and a Chamber of Deputies, elected for four-year terms. Brazil has had a democratically-elected president since March 1990.

History. Brazil is the only Latin American nation deriving its language and culture from Portugal. Adm. Pedro Alvares Cabral claimed the territory for the Portuguese in 1500. He brought to Portugal a cargo of wood, pau-brasil, from which the land received its name. Portugal began colonization in 1532 and made the area a royal colony in 1549.

During the Napoleonic wars, King João VI, then Prince Regent, fled the country in 1807 in advance of the French armies and in 1808 set up his court in Rio de Janeiro. João was drawn home in 1820 by a revolution, leaving his son as Regent. When Portugal sought to reduce Brazil again to colonial status, the prince declared Brazil's independence on Sept. 7, 1822, and became Pedro I, Emperor of Brazil.

Harassed by his parliament, Pedro I abdicated in 1831 in favor of his five-year-old son, who became Emperor in 1840 as Pedro II. The son was a popular monarch, but discontent built up and, in 1889, following a military revolt, he had to abdicate. Although a republic was proclaimed, Brazil was under two military dictatorships during the next four years. A revolt permitted a gradual return to stability under civilian Presidents.

The President during World War I, Wenceslau Braz, cooperated with the Allies and declared war on Germany.

In World War II, Brazil cooperated with the Western Allies, welcoming Allied air bases, patrolling the South Atlantic, and joining the invasion of Italy after declaring war on the Axis.

Gen. João Baptista de Oliveira Figueiredo, became President in 1979 and pledged a return to democracy in 1985.

The electoral college's choice of Tancredo Neves on Jan. 15, 1985, as the first civilian President since 1964 brought a nationwide wave of optimism, but the 75-year-old President-elect was hospitalized and underwent a series of intestinal operations. The civilian government was inaugurated on schedule on March 15, but only Neves' Vice Presidential running mate, José Sarney, was sworn in, and he was widely distrusted because he had previously been a member of the governing military regime's political party. When Neves died on April 21, Sarney became President.

Collor de Mello won the election of late 1989 and took office in March 1990 despite his lack of support from a major party. In the campaign he pledged to lower the chronic hyperinflation following the path of free-market economics. Yet an economic recession still saw the inflation rate running at about 400% during the president's first year in office.

On the basis of a corruption scandal Collor in 1992 faced impeachment by Congress. Just minutes after the trial began on December 29 the president resigned, and the vice president assumed the presidency.

A former finance minister, Fernando Cordoso won the presidency in the October 1994 election with 54% of the vote. However, his party and its coalition allies failed to win a majority in either of the congressional houses.

BRUNEI DARUSSALAM

State of Brunei Darussalam
Sultan: Haji Hassanal Bolkiah
Area: 2,226 sq mi. (5,765 sq km)
Population (est. mid-1995): 300,000 (annual rate of natural increase: 2.4%); birth rate: 27/1000; infant mortality rate: 7/1000; density per square mile: 134.7
Capital and largest city (est. 1991): Bandar Seri Begawan, 21,484; **Monetary unit:** Brunei dollar; **Ethnic groups:** 64% Malay, 20% Chinese, 16% other; **Languages:** Malay (official), Chinese, English; **Religions:** Islam (official religion), 63%; Christian, 8%; Buddhist, 14%; indigenous beliefs and other, 15%; **Literacy rate:** 85%
Economic summary: Gross domestic product (1992): $3.5 billion, per capita $17,000; real growth rate (1992) 1.8%; inflation (1993 est.) 2%; unemployment (1992 est.) 3.7%. Arable land: 1%; principle agricultural products: fruit, rice, pepper, buffaloes. Labor force (1992): 90,000; Commerce and services, 26.4; government and public authorities, 40%; construction, 33%. Major industrial products: crude petroleum, liquified natural gas. Natural resources: petroleum, natural gas, timber. Exports: $2.3 billion (f.o.b., 1992 est.): crude petroleum, liquified natural gas. Imports: $2 billion (c.i.f., 1992 est.): machinery, transport equipment, manufactured goods, foodstuffs, chemicals. Major trading partners: Japan, Thailand, U.S., U.K., Singapore, South Korea.

Geography. About the size of Delaware, Brunei is an independent sultanate on the northwest coast of the island of Borneo in the South China Sea, wedged between the Malaysian states of Sabah and Sarawak. Three quarters of the thinly populated country is covered with tropical rain forest; there are rich oil and gas deposits.

Government. Sultan Hassanal Bolkiah is ruler of the state, a former British protectorate which became fully sovereign and independent on New Year's Day, 1984, presiding over a Privy Council and Council of Ministers appointed by himself.

History. Brunei (pronounced broon-eye) was a powerful state from the 16th to the 19th century, ruling over the northern part of Borneo and adjacent island chains. But it fell into decay and lost Sarawak in 1841, becoming a British protectorate in 1888 and a British dependency in 1905.

The Sultan regained control over internal affairs in 1959, but Britain retained responsibility for the state's defense and foreign affairs until the end of 1983, when the sultanate became fully independent.

Sultain Bolkiah was crowned in 1968 at the age of 22, succeeding his father, Sir Omar Ali Saifuddin, who had abdicated. During his reign, exploitation of the rich Seria oilfield had made the sultanate wealthy.

Warning against opposition to his government, the Islamic religion and himself, the sultan in 1990 said that the laws of the sultanate would be restructured into conformity with Islamic law.

Along with three other Pacific-rim countries, Brunei created in March 1994 the East Asian Growth Area, creating a regional economic market committed to expanding trade within the area.

BULGARIA

Republic of Bulgaria
Prime Minister: Jan Videnov (1994)
President: Zhelyu Zhelev (1992)
Area: 42,823 sq mi. (110,912 sq km)
Population (est. mid-1995): 8,500,000 (average annual rate of natural increase: –0.3%); birth rate: 10/1000; infant mortality rate: 15.5/1000; density per square mile: 198.4
Capital and largest city (1992 est.): Sofia, 1,140,800; **Largest cities (est. 1992):** Plovdiv, 379,112; Varna, 316,231; Burgas, 211,580; Ruse, 190,230. **Monetary unit:** Lev; **Language:** Bulgarian; **Religions:** Eastern Orthodox, 90%; Muslim, Catholic, Protestant, Judaic, Armeno-Gerogorian; **National name:** Narodna Republika Bulgariya; **Literacy rate:** 95%
Economic summary: Gross domestic product (1994): approx. $12 billioon, per capita $1,400; real growth rate –4%; inflation 19% (Jan.–June 94); unemployment 16%. Arable land: 34%. Principal products: grains, tobacco, fruits, vegetables. Labor force: 4,300,000, 33% in industry; 33% in agriculture. Major products: processed agricultural products, machinery, electronics, chemicals. Natural resources: metals, minerals, timber. Exports: $4.15 billion (f.o.b., 1994): machinery and transport equipment, fuels, minerals, raw materials, agricultural products. Imports: $3.98 billion (f.o.b., 1994): machinery and transportation equipment, fuels, raw materials, metals, agricultural raw materials. Major trading partners: C.I.S., U.S., Eastern European countries, EEC.

Geography. Two mountain ranges and two great valleys mark the topography of Bulgaria, a country the size of Tennessee. Situated on the Black Sea in the eastern part of the Balkan peninsula, it shares borders with Serbia, Macedonia, Romania, Greece, and Turkey. The Balkan belt crosses the center of the country, almost due east-west, rising to a height of 6,888 feet (2,100 m). The Rhodope, Rila and Pirin mountains straightens out along the western and southern border. Between the two ranges, is the valley of the Maritsa, Bulgaria's principal river. Between the Balkan range and the Danube, which forms most of the northern boundary with Romania, is the Danubian tableland.

Southern Dobruja, a fertile region of 2,900 square miles (7,511 sq km), below the Danube delta, is an area of low hills, fens, and sandy steppes.

Government. An emerging democracy. The National Assembly, consisting of 240 members is the legislative body. Direct elections for president and vice president were held in January 1992.

History. The first Bulgarians, a tribe of wild horsemen akin to the Huns, crossed the Danube from the north in A.D. 679 and subjugated the Slavic population of Moesia. They adopted a Slav dialect and Slavic customs and twice conquered most of the Balkan peninsula between 893 and 1280. After the Serbs subjected their kingdom in 1330, the Bulgars gradually fell prey to the Turks, and from 1396 to 1878 Bulgaria was a Turkish province. In 1878, Russia forced Turkey to give the country its independence; but the European powers, fearing that Bulgaria might become a Russian dependency, intervened. By the Treaty of Berlin in 1878, Bulgaria became autonomous under Turkish sovereignty.

In 1887, Prince Ferdinand of Saxe-Coburg-Gotha was elected ruler of Bulgaria; on Oct. 5, 1908, he declared the country independent and took the title of Tsar.

Bulgaria joined Germany in World War I and lost. On Oct. 3, 1918, Tsar Ferdinand abdicated in favor of his son, Tsar Boris III. Boris assumed dictatorial powers in 1934–35. When Hitler awarded Bulgaria southern Dobruja, taken from Romania in 1940, Boris joined the Nazis in war the next year and occupied parts of Yugoslavia and Greece. Later the Germans tried to force Boris to send his troops against the Russians. Boris resisted and died under mysterious circumstances on Aug. 28, 1943. Simeon II, infant son of Boris, became nominal ruler under a regency. Russia declared war on Bulgaria on Sept. 5, 1944. An armistice was agreed to three days later, after Bulgaria had declared war on Germany. Russian troops streamed in the next day and under an informal armistice a coalition "Fatherland Front" cabinet was set up under Kimon Georgiev.

A Soviet-style people's Republic was established in 1947 and Bulgaria acquired the reputation of being the most slavishly loyal to Moscow of all the East European Communist countries.

Zhikov resigned in 1989 after 35 years in power. His successor, Peter Mladenov, purged the Politburo, ended the Communist monopoly on power and held free elections in May 1990 that led to a surprising victory for the Communists, renamed the Bulgarian Socialist Party. Mladenov was forced to resign in July 1990.

Parliamentary elections in October 1991 resulted in a victory for the opposition Union of Democratic Forces. In the presidential election of January 1992 UDF leader Zhelev won 53.5% of the vote. The principally Turkish party, the Movement for Rights and Freedoms, joined with the Socialists in 1992 to pass a no-confidence motion. Later in the year a non-Turk nominated by the MRF became prime minister.

December 1994 parliamentary elections gave an absolute majority in the Assembly to the Socialists. The economy, however, had deteriorated in recent years amid growing concern over the spread of organized crime. Bulgaria's international reputation has remained high in light of its stabilizing role in the Balkans.

BURKINA FASO

President: Blaise Compaore (1991)
Area: 105,870 sq mi. (274,200 sq km)
Population (est. mid-1995): 10,400,000 (average annual rate of natural increase: 2.8%); birth rate: 47/1000; infant mortality rate: 94/1000; density per sq mile: 98.2
Capital and largest city (est. 1994): Ouagadougou, 500,000; **Monetary unit:** Franc CFA; **Ethnic groups:** Mosse, Gourounsi, Lobi, Fulani, Gourmantche, Senofo, Boussance, Mande. **Languages:** French, Tribal languages; **Religions:** Muslim, 50%; Christian (mainly Roman Catholic), 10%: indigenous beliefs, 40%. **National name:** Burkina Faso; **Literacy rate:** 18%
Economic summary: Gross domestic product (1993 est.): $7 billion, per capita $700; real growth rate (1992) 0.7%; inflation (1992) –0.8%. Arable land: 10%. Labor force: 3,300,000; in agriculture, 82%. Principal products: millet, sorghum, corn, rice, livestock, peanuts, sugar cane, cotton. Major industrial products: processed agricultural products, light industrial items, brick, brewed products. Natural resources: manganese, limestone, marble, gold, uranium, bauxite, copper. Exports: $300 million (f.o.b., 1992): oilseeds, cotton, live animals, gold. Imports: $685 million (f.o.b., 1992): grain, dairy products, petroleum, machinery. Major trading partners: E.U., China, Côte d'Ivoire, Africa, Taiwan, U.S., Japan.

Geography. Slightly larger than Colorado, Burkina Faso, formerly known as Upper Volta, is a landlocked country in West Africa. Its neighbors are the Ivory Coast, Mali, Niger, Benin, Togo, and Ghana. The country consists of extensive plains, low hills, high savannas, and a desert area in the north.

Government. In June 1991 voters approved a draft constitution providing for three branches of government and presidential elections every seven years. Seventeen political parties are represented in the National Assembly.

History. The country, called Upper Volta by the French, consists chiefly of the lands of the Mossi Empire, where France established a protectorate over the Kingdom of Ouagadougou in 1897. Upper Volta became a separate colony in 1919, was partitioned among Niger, the Sudan, and the Ivory Coast in 1933 and was reconstituted in 1947. An autonomous republic within the French Community, it became independent on Aug. 5, 1960.

President Maurice Yameogo was deposed on Jan. 3, 1966, by a military coup led by Col. Sangoulé Lamizana, who dissolved the National Assembly and suspended the Constitution. Constitutional rule returned in 1978 with the election of an Assembly and a presidential vote in June in which Gen. Lamizana won by a narrow margin over three other candidates.

On Nov. 25, 1980, there was a bloodless coup which placed Gen. Lamizana under house arrest. Col. Sayé Zerbo took charge as the President of the Military Committee of Reform for National Progress. Maj. Jean-Baptiste Ouedraogo toppled Zerbo in a other coup on Nov. 7, 1982. Captain Thomas Sankara, in turn, deposed Ouedraogo a year later. His government changed the country's name on Aug. 3, 1984, to Burkina Faso (the "land of upright men") to sever ties with its colonial past. He was overthrown and killed by Blaise Compaore in 1987.

A devaluation of the local currency resulted in the resignation of the then prime minister in early 1994. The new government, however, was unable to meet trade union demands for a major wage hike. The National Assembly in July approved legislation furthering the privatization program begun in 1991.

BURMA

See Myanmar

BURUNDI

Republic of Burundi
President: Sylvestre Ntibantunganya (1994)
Prime Minister: Sylvie Kinigi (1993)
Area: 10,747 sq mi. (27,834 sq km)
Population (est. mid-1995): 6,400,000 (average annual rate of natural increase: 3.0%); birth rate: 46/1000; infant mortality rate: 102/1000; density per square mile: 595.5
Capital and largest city (est. 1990): Bujumbura, 235,440; **Monetary unit:** Burundi franc; **Languages:** Kirundi and French (official), Swahili; **Religions:** Roman Catholic, 62%; Protestant, 5%; indigenous, 32%; **National name:** Republika Y'Uburundi; **Literacy rate:** 50%
Economic summary: Gross domestic product (1993 est.): $4.4 billion, per capita $205; real growth rate –3.8% (!991); inflation 4.7% (1992 est.). Arable land: 43%; Principal agricultural products: coffee, tea, cotton, bananas, sorghum. Labor force: 1,900,000 (1983 est.); 93% in agriculture. Major industrial products: light consumer goods. Natural resources: nickel, uranium, rare earth oxide, peat, cobalt, copper, unexploited platinum, vanadium. Exports: $40.8 million (f.o.b., 1992 est/): coffee, tea, cotton, hides and skins. Imports: $188 million (c.i.f., 1992 est.): food, petroleum products, capital goods, consumer goods. Major trading partners: U.S., Western Europe, Asia.

Geography. Wedged among Tanzania, Zaire, and Rwanda in east central Africa, Burundi occupies a high plateau divided by several deep valleys. It is equal in size to Maryland.

Government. A republic. Legislative and executive power is vested in the president.

A new Constitution adopted by referendum on March 9, 1992, established a multi-party system.

History. Burundi was once part of German East Africa. An integrated society developed among the Watusi, a tall, warlike people and nomad cattle raisers, and the Bahutu, a Bantu people, who were subject farmers. Belgium won a League of Nations mandate in 1923, and subsequently Burundi, with Rwanda, was transferred to the status of a United Nations trust territory.

In 1962, Burundi gained independence and became a kingdom under Mwami Mwambutsa IV. His son deposed him in 1966 to rule as Ntaré V. He was overthrown by Premier Micombero.

One of Africa's worst tribal wars, which became genocide, occurred in Burundi in April 1972, following the return of Ntare V. He was given a safe-conduct promise in writing by President Micombero but was "judged and immediately executed" by the Burundi leader. His return was apparently attended by an invasion of exiles of Burundi's Hutu tribe. Whether Hutus living in Burundi joined the invasion is unclear, but after it failed, the victorious Tutsis

proceeded to massacre some 100,000 persons in six weeks, with possibly 100,000 more slain by summer.

On Nov. 1, 1976, Lt. Col. Jean-Baptiste Bagaye led a coup and assumed the presidency. He suspended the Constitution, and announced that a 30-member Supreme Revolutionary Council would be the governing body.

Bagaza was elected head of the only legal political party in 1979 and was overthrown as party chieftain in 1987.

The Burundi Democracy Front's candidate Melchior Ndadaye won the first democratic presidential elections held on June 2, 1993.

The presidents of Burundi and Rwanda were killed in a plane crash on April 6, 1994 after their plane had been hit by gunfire or a rocket. There had already been much strife in the year between government troops and gunmen from a rival tribe.

The possibility of ethnic clashes loomed ever present. In March 1995 thousands of residents fled the capital after shooting erupted between rival Hutu and Tutsi groups, later estimated to have resulted in 150 killings.

CAMBODIA

President: Prince Norodom Sihanouk (1991)
First Prime Minister: Norodom Ranariddh (1994)
Second Prime Minister: Hun Sen (1994)
Area: 69,884 sq mi. (181,035 sq km)
Population (est. mid-1995): 10,600,000 (average annual rate of natural increase: 2.8%); birth rate: 44/1000; infant mortality rate: 108/1000; density per square mile: 151.7
Capital and largest city (est. 1989 for metropolitan area): Phnom Penh, 800,000; **Monetary unit:** Riel; **Ethnic groups:** Khmer, 90%; Chinese, 5%; other minorities 5%; **Languages:** Khmer (official), French; **Religion:** Theravada Buddhist, 5% others; **Literacy rate:** 35%
Economic summary: Gross domestic product (1993 est.): $6 billion, per capita $600; real growth rate 7.5%; inflation 60%. Arable land: 16%. Principal agricultural products: rice, rubber, corn. Labor force: 2.5–3.0 million; 80% in agriculture. Major industrial products: fish, wood and wood products, milled rice, rubber, cement. Natural resources: timber, gemstones, iron ore, manganese, phosphate. Exports: $70 million (f.o.b., 1992 est.): natural rubber, rice, pepper, wood. Imports: $360 million (c.i.f., 1992 est.): foodstuffs, fuel, consumer goods. Major trading partners: Vietnam, Japan, India, Singapore, Malaysia, China, Thailand.

Geography. Situated on the Indochinese peninsula, Cambodia is bordered by Thailand and Laos on the north and Vietnam on the east and south. The Gulf of Siam is off the western coast. The country, the size of Missouri, consists chiefly of a large alluvial plain ringed by mountains and on the east by the Mekong River. The plain is centered on Lake Tonle Sap, which is a natural storage basin of the Mekong.

Government. Constitutional monarchy.

History. Cambodia came under Khmer rule about A.D. 600. Under the Khmers, magnificent temples were built at Angkor. The Khmer kingdom once ruled over most of Southeast Asia, but attacks by the Thai and the Vietnamese almost annihilated the empire until the French joined Cambodia, Laos, and Vietnam into French Indochina.

Under Norodom Sihanouk, enthroned in 1941, and particularly under Japanese occupation during World War II, nationalism revived. After the ouster of the Japanese, the Cambodians sought independence, but the French returned in 1946, granting the country a Constitution in 1947 and independence within the French Union in 1949. Sihanouk won full military control during the French--Indochinese War in 1953. He abdicated in 1955 in favor of his parents, remaining head of the government, and when his father died in 1960, becamechief of state without returning to the throne. In 1963, he sought a guarantee of Cambodia's neutrality from all parties to the Vietnam War.

On March 18, 1970, while Sihanouk was abroad trying to get North Vietnamese and the Vietcong out of border sanctuaries near Vietnam, anti-Vietnamese riots occurred, and Sihanouk was overthrown.

The Vietnam peace agreement of 1973 stipulated withdrawal of foreign forces from Cambodia, but fighting continued between Hanoi-backed insurgents and U.S.-supplied government troops.

Fighting climaxed in April 1975 when the Lon Nol regime was overthrown by Pot Pol, leader of the communist Khmer Rouge forces.

In the next two years, from 2 million to 4 million Cambodians are estimated to have died under the brutality of the Pol Pot regime. Border clashes with Vietnam developed into a Vietnamese invasion and Pot Pol was ousted by Vietnamese forces on Jan. 8, 1979 and a new government led by Heng Samrin was installed.

While Sihanouk remained in exile, about 9,000 noncommunist troops loyal to him and another 15,000 under Son Sann joined about 35,000 communist Pol Pot forces fighting the 170,000 Vietnamese troops supporting the Heng Samrin government.

The Vietnamese plan originally called for them to withdraw by early 1990 and negotiate a political settlement. The talks, however, stalled through 1990 on into 1991. In 1992 a UN agreement was signed in Paris under which Prince Sihanouk was to be the leader of a Supreme National Council that was to run the country until free elctions in 1993.

Free elections in May 1993 saw the defeat of the ruling party. In June the victors, the royalist opposition, completed a power sharing deal with the ruling party. In September the constitution was changed, restoring the monarchy. Later that month Sihanouk was formally installed.

Stepped-up attacks by the Khmer Rouge in western Cambodia sent 55,000 people fleeing their homes in May 1994. Despite the king's plea for a coalition government that would include the Khmer Rouge, legislation was passed in July outlawing the group. In response the Khmer Rouge proclaimed their own government led by the illusive Pol Pot.

CAMEROON

Republic of Cameroon
President: Paul Biya (1988)
Prime Minister: Simon Achidi Achu (1992)
Area: 183,569 sq mi. (475,442 sq km)
Population (est. mid-1995): 13,500,000 (average annual rate of natural increase: 2.9%); birth rate: 40/1000; infant mortality rate: 65/1000; density per sq mile: 73.5
Capital: Yaoundé; **Largest cities (est. 1991):** Douala, 908,000; Yaoundé, 730,000; **Monetary unit:** Franc CFA; **Languages:** French and English (both official); 24 major African language groups; **Religions:** 51% indigenous beliefs, 33% Christian, 16% Muslim; **National name:** République du Cameroun; **Literacy rate:** 56.2%

Economic summary: Gross domestic product (1993 est.): $19.1 billion, per capita $1,500; real growth rate n.a.; inflation, 3% (1990); unemployment, 25% (1990). Arable land: 13%. Agriculture: coffee, cocoa, timber, corn, peanuts, cotton, rubber, bananas, oilseed, grains, livestock, root starches. Labor force in agriculture: 74.4%. Industries: crude oil products, food processing, light consumer goods, textiles, sawmills. Natural resources: timber, some oil, bauxite, hydropower potential. Exports: $1.8 billion (f.o.b., 1991): cocoa, coffee, timber, petroleum, aluminum products. Imports: $1.2 billion (c.i.f., 1991): machines and electrical equipment, transport equipment, consumer goods. Major trading partners: France, U.S., Western European nations, African countries.

Geography. Cameroon is a West African nation on the Gulf of Guinea, bordered by Nigeria, Chad, the Central African Republic, the Congo, Equatorial Guinea, and Gabon. It is nearly twice the size of Oregon.

The interior consists of a high plateau, rising to 4,500 feet (1,372 m), with the land descending to a lower, densely wooded plateau and then to swamps and plains along the coast. Mount Cameroon (13,350 ft.; 4,069 m), near the coast, is the highest elevation in the country. The main rivers are the Benue, Nyong, and Sanaga.

Government. After a 1972 plebiscite, a unitary nation was formed out of East and West Cameroon to replace the former Federal Republic. At present the country is a multiparty democracy with a one house legislative body, the National Assembly, holding 180 seats.

History. The Republic of Cameroon is inhabited by Hamitic and Semitic peoples in the north, where Islam is the principal religion, and by Bantu peoples in the central and southern regions, where native animism prevails. The tribes were conquered by many invaders.

The land escaped colonial rule until 1884, when treaties with tribal chiefs brought the area under German domination. After World War I, the League of Nations gave the French a mandate over 80% of the area, and the British 20% adjacent to Nigeria. After World War II, when the country came under a U.N. trusteeship in 1946, self-government was granted, and the Cameroun People's Union emerged as the dominant party by campaigning for reunification of French and British Cameroon and for independence. Accused of being under Communist control, it waged a campaign of revolutionary terror from 1955 to 1958, when it was crushed. In British Cameroon, unification was pressed also by the leading party, the Kamerun National Democratic Party, led by John Foncha.

France set up Cameroon as an autonomous state in 1957, and the next year its legislative assembly voted for independence by 1960. In 1959 a fully autonomous government of Cameroon was formed under Ahmadou Ahidjo. Cameroon became an independent republic on Jan. 1, 1960.

Biya won the presidential election in October 1992 but by a narrow margin.

The government convened in mid-1993 a Grand National Debate on Constitutional Reform, which the main opposition party, the Social Democratic Front, declined to attend. Political reform was suspended by the president.

Acquiescing to a devaluation of the local currency, the government received assurances of financial aid from France. The government requested additional funds from international organizations in exchange for privatization of certain state-owned companies.

CANADA

Sovereign: Queen Elizabeth II (1952)
Governor General: Roméo LeBlanc (1995)
Prime Minister: Jean Chrétien (1993)
Area: 3,851,809 sq mi. (9,976,186 sq km)
Population (est. mid-1995): 29,600,000. Average annual rate of natural increase: 1.5% (1994); birth rate: 14/1000; infant mortality rate: 7.0/1000; density per square mile: 7.6
Capital: Ottawa, Ont.; **Largest cities (1991 census; metropolitan areas):** Toronto, 3,893,046; Montreal, 3,127,242; Vancouver: 1,602,502; Ottawa/Hull, 920,857; Edmonton, 839,924; Calgary, 754,033; Winnipeg, 652,354; Quebec, 645,550; Hamilton, 599,760; London, 381,522; St. Catherines-Niagara, 364,552; **Monetary Unit:** Canadian dollar; **Languages:** English, French; **Religions:** 46% Roman Catholic, 16% United Church, 10% Anglican; **Literacy rate:** 99%
Economic Summary: Gross domestic product (1994): $548.1 billion, per capita $17,115; real growth rate 4.5%; inflation 0.2%; unemployment (Dec. 94) 9.6%. Arable land: 7.47%. Principal products: wheat, barley, oats, livestock. Labor force (1994): 14,832,000; 75% in manufacturing. Major industrial products; transportation equipment, petroleum, chemicals, wood products. Exports: $147.9 billion (1994): newsprint, wood pulp, timber, crude petroleum, machinery, natural gas, aluminum, motor vehicles and parts, telecommunications equipment. Imports: $165.9 billion (1994): crude petroleum, chemicals, motor vehicles and parts, durable consumer goods, computers, telecommunications equipment and parts. Major trading partners: U.S., Japan, U.K., C.I.S. nations, Germany, Mexico, South Korea, Taiwan.

Geography. Covering most of the northern part of the North American continent and with an area larger than that of the United States, Canada has an extremely varied topography. In the east the mountainous maritime provinces have an irregular coastline on the Gulf of St. Lawrence and the Atlantic. The St. Lawrence plain, covering most of southern Quebec and Ontario, and the interior continental plain, covering southern Manitoba and Saskatchewan and most of Alberta, are the principal cultivable areas. They are separated by a forested plateau rising from lakes Superior and Huron.

Population by Provinces and Territories

Province	1993 (estimate)	1991 (Census)
Alberta	2,662,300	2,545,553
British Columbia	3,535,100	3,282,061
Manitoba	1,116,000	1,091,942
New Brunswick	750,900	723,900
Newfoundland	581,000	568,474
Nova Scotia	923,000	899,942
Ontario	10,746,000	10,084,885
Prince Edward Island	131,600	129,765
Quebec	7,208,800	6,895,963
Saskatchewan	1,003,100	988,928
Northwest Territories	62,900	57,649
Yukon Territory	32,000	27,797
Total	**28,752,700**	**27,296,859**

Source: Statistics Canada.

Westward toward the Pacific, most of British Columbia, Yukon, and part of western Alberta are covered by parallel mountain ranges including the Rockies. The Pacific border of the coast range is ragged with fiords and channels. The highest point in Canada is Mount Logan (19,850 ft; 6,050 m), which is in the Yukon.

Canada has an abundance of large and small lakes. In addition to the Great Lakes on the U.S. border, there are 9 others that are more than 100 miles long (161 km) and 35 that are more than 50 miles long (80 km). The two principal river systems are the Mackenzie and the St. Lawrence. The St. Lawrence, with its tributaries, is navigable for over 1,900 miles (3,058 km).

Government. Canada, a self-governing member of the Commonwealth of Nations, is a federation of 10 provinces (Alberta, British Columbia, Manitoba, New Brunswick, Newfoundland, Nova Scotia, Ontario, Prince Edward Island, Quebec, and Saskatchewan) and two territories (Northwest Territories and Yukon) whose powers were spelled out in the British North America Act of 1867. With the passing of the Constitution Act of 1981, the act and the Constitutional amending power were transferred from the British Parliament to Canada so that the Canadian Constitution is now entirely in the hands of the Canadians.

Actually the Governor General acts only with the advice of the Canadian Prime Minister and the Cabinet, who also sit in the federal Parliament. The Parliament has two houses: a Senate of 104 members appointed for life, and a House of Commons of 295 members apportioned according to provincial population. Elections are held at least every five years or whenever the party in power is voted down in the House of Commons or considers it expedient to appeal to the people. The Prime Minister is the leader of the majority party in the House of Commons—or, if no single party holds a majority, the leader of the party able to command the support of a majority of members of the House. Laws must be passed by both houses of Parliament and signed by the Governor General in the Queen's name.

The 10 provincial governments are nominally headed by Lieutenant Governors appointed by the federal government, but the executive power in each actually is vested in a Cabinet headed by a Premier, who is leader of the majority party. The provincial legislatures are composed of one-house assemblies whose members are elected for four-year terms. They are known as Legislative Assemblies, except in Newfoundland, where it is the House of Assembly, and in Quebec, where it is the National Assembly.

The judicial system consists of a Supreme Court in Ottawa (established in 1875), with appellate jurisdiction, and a Supreme Court in each province, as well as county courts with limited jurisdiction in most of the provinces. The Governor General in Council appoints these judges.

History. The Norse explorer Leif Ericson probably reached the shores of Canada (Labrador or Nova Scotia) in A.D. 1000, but the history of the white man in the country actually began in 1497, when John Cabot, an Italian in the service of Henry VII of England, reached Newfoundland or Nova Scotia. Canada was taken for France in 1534 by Jacques Cartier. The actual settlement of New France, as it was then called, began in 1604 at Port Royal in what is now Nova Scotia; in 1608, Quebec was founded. France's colonization efforts were not very successful, but French explorers by the end of the 17th century had pene-

Canadian Governors General and Prime Ministers Since 1867

Term of Office	Governor General	Term	Prime Minister	Party
1867–1868	Viscount Monck[1]	1867–1873	Sir John A. Macdonald	Conservative
1869–1872	Baron Lisgar	1873–1878	Alexander Mackenzie	Liberal
1872–1878	Earl of Dufferin	1878–1891	Sir John A. Macdonald	Conservative
1878–1883	Marquess of Lorne	1891–1892	Sir John J. C. Abbott	Conservative
1883–1888	Marquess of Lansdowne	1892–1894	Sir John S. D. Thompson	Conservative
1888–1893	Baron Stanley of Preston	1894–1896	Sir Mackenzie Bowell	Conservative
1893–1898	Earl of Aberdeen	1896	Sir Charles Tupper	Conservative
1898–1904	Earl of Minto	1896–1911	Sir Wilfrid Laurier	Liberal
1904–1911	Earl Grey	1911–1917	Sir Robert L. Borden	Conservative
1911–1916	Duke of Connaught	1917–1920	Sir Robert L. Borden	Unionist
1916–1921	Duke of Devonshire	1920–1921	Arthur Meighen	Unionist
1921–1926	Baron Byng of Vimy	1921–1926	W. L. Mackenzie King	Liberal
1926–1931	Viscount Willingdon	1926	Arthur Meighen	Conservative
1931–1935	Earl of Bessborough	1926–1930	W. L. Mackenzie King	Liberal
1935–1940	Baron Tweedsmuir	1930–1935	Richard B. Bennett	Conservative
1940–1946	Earl of Athlone	1935–1948	W. L. Mackenzie King	Liberal
1946–1952	Viscount Alexander	1948–1957	Louis S. St. Laurent	Liberal
1952–1959	Vincent Massey	1957–1963	John G. Diefenbaker	Conservative
1959–1967	George P. Vanier	1963–1968	Lester B. Pearson	Liberal
1967–1973	Roland Michener	1968–1979	Pierre Elliott Trudeau	Liberal
1974–1979	Jules Léger	1979–1980	Charles Joseph Clark	Conservative
1979–1984	Edward R. Schreyer	1980–1984	Pierre Elliott Trudeau	Liberal
1984–1990	Jeanne Sauvé	1984–1984	John Turner	Liberal
1990–	Raymond John Hnatyshyn	1984–1993	Brian Mulroney	Conservative
		1993–1993	Kim Campbell	Conservative
		1993–	Jean Chrétien	Liberal

1. Became Governor General of British North America in 1861.

trated beyond the Great Lakes to the western prairies and south along the Mississippi to the Gulf of Mexico. Meanwhile, the English Hudson's Bay Company had been established in 1670. Because of the valuable fisheries and fur trade, a conflict developed between the French and English; in 1713, Newfoundland, Hudson Bay, and Nova Scotia (Acadia) were lost to England.

During the Seven Years' War (1756–63), England extended its conquest, and the British Maj. Gen. James Wolfe won his famous victory over Gen. Louis Montcalm outside Quebec on Sept. 13, 1759. The Treaty of Paris in 1763 gave England control.

At that time the population of Canada was almost entirely French, but in the next few decades, thousands of British colonists emigrated to Canada from the British Isles and from the American colonies. In 1849, the right of Canada to self-government was recognized. By the British North America Act of 1867, the Dominion of Canada was created through the confederation of Upper and Lower Canada, Nova Scotia, and New Brunswick. Prince Edward Island joined the Dominion in 1873.

In 1869 Canada purchased from the Hudson's Bay Company the vast middle west (Rupert's Land) from which the provinces of Manitoba (1870), Alberta, and Saskatchewan (1905) were later formed. In 1871, British Columbia joined the Dominion. The country was linked from coast to coast in 1885 by the Canadian Pacific Railway.

During the formative years between 1866 and 1896, the Conservative Party, led by Sir John A. Macdonald, governed the country, except during the years 1873–78. In 1896, the Liberal Party took over and, under Sir Wilfrid Laurier, an eminent French Canadian, ruled until 1911.

By the Statute of Westminster in 1931 the British Dominions, including Canada, were formally declared to be partner nations with Britain, "equal in status, in no way subordinate to each other," and bound together only by allegiance to a common Crown.

Newfoundland became Canada's 10th province on March 31, 1949, following a plebiscite. Canada includes two territories—the Yukon Territory, the area north of British Columbia and east of Alaska, and the Northwest Territories, including all of Canada north of 60° north latitude except Yukon and the northernmost sections of Quebec and Newfoundland. This area includes all of the Arctic north of the mainland, Norway having recognized Canadian sovereignty over the Svendrup Islands in the Arctic in 1931.

The Liberal Party, led by William Lyon Mackenzie King, dominated Canadian politics from 1921 until 1957, when it was succeeded by the Progressive Conservatives. The Liberals, under the leadership of Lester B. Pearson, returned to power in 1963. Pearson remained Prime Minister until 1968, when he retired and was replaced by a former law professor, Pierre Elliott Trudeau. Trudeau maintained Canada's defensive alliance with the United States, but began moving toward a more independent policy in world affairs.

Trudeau's election was considered in part a response to the most serious problem confronting the country, the division between French- and English-speaking Canadians, which had led to a separatist movement in the predominantly French province of Quebec. In 1974, the provincial government voted to make French the official language of Quebec.

Despite Trudeau's removal of price and wage controls in 1978, continuing inflation and a high rate of unemployment caused him to delay elections until May 22, 1979. The delay gave Trudeau no advantage—the Progressive Conservatives under Charles Joseph Clark defeated the Liberals everywhere except in Quebec, New Brunswick, and Newfoundland.

His government collapsed after only six months when a motion to defeat the Tory budget carried by 139–133 on Dec. 13, 1979. On the same day, the Quebec law making French the exclusive official language of the province—an issue which had been expected to provide Clark's first major internal test—was voided by the Canadian Supreme Court.

In national elections Feb. 18, 1980, the resurgent Liberals under Trudeau scored an unexpectedly big victory.

Resolving a dispute that had occupied Trudeau since the beginning of his tenure, Queen Elizabeth II, in Ottawa on April 17, 1982, signed the Constitution Act, cutting the last legal tie between Canada and Britain.

The Constitution retains Queen Elizabeth as Queen of Canada and keeps Canada's membership in the Commonwealth.

In the national election on Sept. 4, 1984, the Progressive Conservative Party scored an overwhelming victory, fundamentally changing the country's political landscape. The Conservatives, led by Brian Mulroney, a 45-year-old corporate lawyer, won the highest political majority in Canadian history, Mulroney was sworn in as Canada's 18th Prime Minister on Sept. 17.

The dominant foreign issue was a free trade pact with the U.S., a treaty bitterly opposed by the Liberal and New Democratic parties. The conflict led to elections in Nov. 1988 that solidly re-elected Mulroney and gave him a mandate to proceed with the agreement.

The issue of separatist sentiments in French-speaking Quebec flared up again in 1990 with the failure of the Meech Lake accord. The accord was designed to ease the Quebecers' fear of losing their identity within the English-speaking majority by giving Quebec constitutional status as a "distinct society." In an attempt to keep Canada united, the three major political parties came to an agreement in February 1992 on constitutional reforms.

Voters in the Northwest Territories authorized the division of their region in two, creating a homeland for Eskimos.

Also in 1992 Canada announced its decision to withdraw its combat units from NATO command. The economy continued to be mired in a long recession many blamed on the free trade agreement.

A national referendum was held in October 1992 on the proposal to change the constitution to insure greater representation in parliament for the more populous regions and thereby the French-speaking Quebecers. The referendum, however was defeated.

Brian Mulroney's popularity continued to slump in 1992 and early 1993, leading to his decision to retire prior to the required November election. The governing Progressive Conservative Party chose Defense Minister Kim Campbell as its leader in June making her the first female prime minister in Canadian history.

The national election in October 1993 resulted in the reemergence of the Liberal Party, which won 177 seats in the House of Commons. The Progressive Conservatives captured but 2 seats, while the Bloc Québécois became the official opposition party.

Regarded as highly symbolic, Quebec separatists lost two parliamentary by-elections in February 1995, signaling trouble for the independence cause.

In April Canada reached an agreement with the European Union over fishing rights in the North Atlantic.

CAPE VERDE

Republic of Cape Verde
President: Antonio Mascarenhas Monteiro (1991)

Premier: Carlos Wahnon Veiga (1991)
Area: 1,557 sq mi. (4,033 sq km)
Population: (est. mid-1995): 400,000 (average annual rate of natural increase: 2.8%); birth rate: 36/1000; infant mortality rate: 50/1000; density per square mile: 256.9
Capital (1990): Praia 61,797; **Other large city (est. 1982):** Mindelo, 50,000; **Monetary unit:** Cape Verdean escudo; **Language:** Portuguese, Criuolo; **Religion:** Roman Catholic fused with indigenous beliefs; **National name:** República de Cabo Verde; **Literacy rate:** 66%
Economic summary: Gross domestic product (1991 est.): $415 million, per capita $1,070; real growth rate 3.3%; inflation 8.7%; unemployment (1988) 25%. Arable land: 9%. Labor force in agriculture: 57%. Principal agricultural products: bananas, corn, sugar cane, beans. Major industry: fishing, salt mining. Natural resources: salt, siliceous rock. Exports: $5.7 million (f.o.b., 1991 est.): fish, bananas, salt. Imports: $120 million (c.i.f., 1990 est.): petroleum, foodstuffs, consumer goods, industrial products. Major trading partners: Portugal, Angola, Algeria, Italy, Netherlands, Spain, France, U.S., Germany, Sweden.

Geography: Cape Verde, only slightly larger than Rhode Island, is an archipelago in the Atlantic 385 miles (620 km) west of Dakar, Senegal.

The islands are divided into two groups: Barlavento in the north, comprising Santo Antão (291 sq mi.; 754 sq km), Boa Vista (240 sq mi.; 622 sq km), São Nicolau (132 sq mi.; 342 sq km), São Vicente (88 sq mi.; 246 sq km), Sal (83 sq mi.; 298 sq km), and Santa Luzia (13 sq mi.; 34 sq km); and Sotavento in the south, consisting of São Tiago (383 sq mi.; 992 sq km), Fogo (184 sq mi.; 477 sq km), Maio (103 sq mi.; 267 sq km), and Brava (25 sq mi.; 65 sq km). The islands are mostly mountainous, with the land deeply scarred by erosion. There is an active volcano on Fogo.

Government. The islands became independent on July 5, 1975, under an agreement negotiated with Portugal in 1974. Elections of January 13, 1991 resulted in the ruling African Party for the Independence of Cape Verde losing its majority in the 79-seat parliament. The big winner was the Movement for Democracy, whose candidate, Antonio Monteiro, won the subsequent presidential election on February 17. These were the first free elections since independence in 1975.

History. Uninhabited upon their discovery in 1456, the Cape Verde islands became part of the Portuguese empire in 1495. A majority of their modern inhabitants are of mixed Portuguese and African ancestry.

The former opposition MPD that had won the parliamentary and the presidential elections early in 1991 also won 10 out of 14 councils in the country's first local elections.

The government in 1993 announced a four-year plan to privatize a number of industries and liberalize the economy.

CENTRAL AFRICAN REPUBLIC

Head of Government: Gen. André Kolingba (1986)
President: Ange-Félix Patassé (1993)
Prime Minister: Jean-Luc Mandaba (1993)
Area: 241,313 sq mi. (625,000 sq km)
Population (est. mid-1995): 3,200,000 (average annual rate of natural increase: 2.0%); birth rate: 42/1000; infant mortality rate: 136/1000; density per square mile: 13.2

Capital and largest city (1988): Bangui, 596,776; **Monetary unit:** Franc CFA; **Ethnic groups:** Baya, Banda, Sara, Mandjia, Mboum, M'Baka, 6,500 Europeans; **Languages:** French (official), Sangho, Arabic, Hansa, Swahili; **Religions:** 24% indigenous beliefs, 50% Protestant and Roman Catholic with animist influence, 15% Muslim, 11% other; **National name:** République Centrafricaine; **Literacy rate:** 33%

Economic summary: Gross domestic product (1993 est.): $2.5 billion, per capita $440 (1990 est.); real growth rate –3% (1990 est.); inflation –3.0% (1990 est.); unemployment (1988 est.): 30% in Bangui. Arable land: 3%. Principal products: cotton, coffee, peanuts, food crops, livestock. Labor force (1986 est.): 775,413; 85% in agriculture. Major industrial products: timber, textiles, soap, cigarettes, diamonds, processed food, brewed beverages. Natural resources: diamonds, uranium, timber. Exports: $123.5 million (f.o.b., 1992): diamonds, cotton, timber, coffee, tobacco. Imports: $165.1 million (f.o.b., 1992): machinery and electrical equipment, petroleum products, textiles, food, motor vehicles, chemicals, pharmaceuticals, consumer goods, industrial products. Major trading partners: France, Belgium, Italy, Japan, U.S., Western Europe, Algeria, Yugoslavia.

Geography. Situated about 500 miles north (805 km) of the equator, the Central African Republic is a landlocked nation bordered by Cameroon, Chad, the Sudan, Zaire, and the Congo. Twice the size of New Mexico, it is covered by tropical forests in the south and semidesert land in the east. The Ubangi and Shari are the largest of many rivers.

Government. The Central African Republic has been ruled since 1981 by General André Kolingba who came to power in a bloodless coup and was elected to a six-year term as President in 1986. A Constitution was adopted on November 21, 1987 establishing a unicameral National Assembly. The following year the Central African Democracy Party (R.D.C.) was formed as the only political party. Since April 1991 other political parties legally registered by the Ministry of the Interior are allowed to compete for legislative and presidential elections and presidential and legislative elections were held in September 1993.

History. As the colony of Ubangi-Shari, what is now the Central African Republic was united with Chad in 1905 and joined with Gabon and the Middle Congo in French Equatorial Africa in 1910. After World War II a rebellion in 1946 forced the French to grant self-government. In 1958 the territory voted to become an autonomous republic within the French Community, but on Aug. 13, 1960, President David Dacko proclaimed the republic's independence from France.

Dacko undertook to move the country into Peking's orbit, but was overthrown in a coup on Dec. 31, 1965, by the then Col. Jean-Bédel Bokassa, Army Chief of Staff.

On Dec. 4, 1976, the Central African Republic became the Central African Empire. Marshal Jean-Bédel Bokassa, who had ruled the republic since he took power in 1965, was declared Emperor Bokassa I. He was overthrown in a coup on Sept. 20, 1979. Former President David Dacko, returned to power and changed the country's name back to the Central African Republic. An army coup on Sept. 1, 1981, deposed President Dacko again.

Although President Kolingba in 1991, under pressure, announced a move toward multi-party democracy no specifics were given, leading to further civil unrest. A general strike called for in August resulted in the legalization of three opposition parties.

Elections in August 1993 saw the defeat of Kolingba. Former prime minister Patassé won the presidency in the second round. Kolingba attempted to thwart the process but protests and opposition from France obstructed his maneuvers.

Patassé struggled to improve his poor personal relations with France in 1994.

CHAD

Republic of Chad
President: Gen. Idriss Deby (1991)
Prime Minister: Mr. Koibla Djimasta (1995)
Area: 495,752 sq mi. (1,284,000 sq km)
Population (est. mid-1995): 6,400,000 (average annual rate of natural increase, 2.6%); birth rate: 44/1000; infant mortality rate: 122/1000; density per square mile: 12.9
Capital and largest city (est. 1992): N'Djamena, 687,800; **Monetary unit:** Franc CFA; **Ethnic groups:** Baguirmiens, Kanembous, Saras, Massas, Arabs, Toubous, others; **Languages:** French and Arabic (official), many tribal languages; **Religions:** Islam, 44%; Christian, 33%; traditional, 23%; **National name:** République du Tchad; **Literacy rate:** 17%
Economic summary: Gross domestic product (1993 est.): $2.7 billion, per capita $500; real growth rate 8.4%; inflation 2–3%. Arable land: 2%; principal agricultural products: cotton, cattle, sugar, subsistence crops. Labor force in agriculture: 85%. Major products: livestock and livestock products, beer, food processing, textiles, cigarettes. Natural resources: petroleum, unexploited uranium, kaolin. Exports: $193.9 million (f.o.b., 1991): cotton, livestock and animal products, fish, textiles. Imports: $294.1 million (f.o.b., 1991): machinery and transportation equipment, industrial goods, petroleum products, foodstuffs. Major trading partners: France, Nigeria, U.S., Cameroon.

Geography. A landlocked country in north central Africa, Chad is about 85% the size of Alaska. Its neighbors are Niger, Libya, the Sudan, the Central African Republic, Cameroon, and Nigeria. Lake Chad, from which the country gets its name, lies on the western border with Niger and Nigeria. In the north is a desert that runs into the Sahara.

Government. Hissen Habré was overthrown by Col. Idriss Deby in December 1990. A transitional government mandate expired April 1995.

History. Chad was absorbed into the colony of French Equatorial Africa, as part of Ubangi-Shari, in 1910. France began the country's development after 1920, when it became a separate colony. In 1946, French Equatorial Africa was admitted to the French Union. By referendum in 1958 the Chad territory became an autonomous republic within the French Union.

A movement led by the first Premier and President, François (later Ngarta) Tombalbaye, achieved complete independence on Aug. 11, 1960.

Tombalbaye was killed in the 1975 coup and was succeeded by Gen. Félix Malloum, who faced a Libyan-financed rebel movement throughout his tenure in office. A ceasefire backed by Libya, Niger, and the Sudan early in 1978 failed to end the fighting.

Nine rival groups meeting in Lagos, Nigeria, in March 1979 agreed to form a provisional government headed by Goukouni Oueddei, a former rebel leader. Fighting broke out again in Chad in March 1980, when Defense Minister Hissen Habré challenged Goukouni and seized the capital. By the year's end, Libyan troops supporting Goukouni recaptured N'djamena, and Libyan President Muammar el-Qaddafi, in January 1981, proposed a merger of Chad with Libya.

The Libyan proposal was rejected and Libyan troops withdrew from Chad but in 1983 poured back into the northern part of the country in support of Goukouni. France, in turn, sent troops into southern Chad in support of Habré.

Government troops then launched an offensive in early 1987 that drove the Libyans out of most of the country.

After the overthrow of Habré's government, Deby, a former defense minister, declared himself president, dissolved the legislature (elected the previous July), and suspended the constitution.

A national conference, convened in January 1993, was suspended after only 4 days. A coup attempt later that month was foiled. The reconvened conference in October elected Koumakoye prime minister.

Political violence erupted in 1994 leading to a peace agreement with the dissident factions in October.

CHILE

Republic of Chile
President: Eduardo Frei Ruiz-Tagle (1994)
Area: 292,132 sq mi. (756,622 sq km)
Population (est. mid-1995): 14,300,000 (average annual rate of natural increase: 1.7%); birth rate: 22/1000; infant mortality rate: 14.6/1000; density per square mile: 48.9
Capital and largest city (1992): Santiago (administrative), 4,385,481; **Other large cities (1992):** Valparaiso, 276,736; Concepción, 330,448; Viña del Mar, 302,765; Puente Alto, 254,534; Talcahuano, 246,566; Antofagasta, 226,749. **Monetary unit:** Peso; **Language:** Spanish; **Religion:** Roman Catholic, 89%; Protestant, 11%; small Jewish and Muslim populations.; **National name:** República de Chile; **Literacy rate:** 94%
Economic summary: Gross domestic product (1993 est.): $96 billion; $7,000 per capita est.; 5.8% real growth rate; inflation 12.3% est.; unemployment 5.1% est.. Arable land: 7%. Principal products: wheat, corn, sugar beets, vegetables, wine, livestock. Labor force: 4.728 million, 31.3% in industry. Major industrial products: processed fish, iron and steel, pulp, paper. Natural resources: copper, timber, iron ore, nitrates. Exports: $10 billion (f.o.b., 1992): copper, iron ore, paper and wood products, fruits. Imports: $9.2 billion (f.o.b., 1992): wheat, vehicles, petroleum, capital goods, spare parts, raw materials. Major trading partners: U.S., Japan, European Union, Brazil, Argentina.

Geography. Situated south of Peru and west of Bolivia and Argentina, Chile fills a narrow 1,800-mile (2,897 km) strip between the Andes and the Pacific. Its area is nearly twice that of Montana.

One third of Chile is covered by the towering ranges of the Andes. In the north is the mineral-rich Atacama Desert, between the coastal mountains and the Andes. In the center is a 700-mile-long (1,127 km) valley, thickly populated, between the Andes and the coastal plateau. In the south, the Andes border on the ocean.

At the southern tip of Chile's mainland is Punta Arenas, the southernmost city in the world, and beyond that lies the Strait of Magellan and Tierra del Fuego, an island divided between Chile and Argentina. The southernmost point of South America is Cape Horn, a 1,390-foot (424-m) rock on Horn Island in the Wollaston group, which belongs to Chile. Chile also claims sovereignty over 482,628 sq mi (1,250,000 sq km) of Antarctic territory.

The Juan Fernández Islands, in the South Pacific about 400 miles (644 km) west of the mainland, and Easter Island, about 2,000 miles (3,219 km) west, are Chilean possessions.

Government. The President serves a siz-year term (with the exception of the 1990–1994 term). There is a bicameral legislature, the National Congress.

History. Chile was originally under the control of the Incas in the north and the fierce Araucanian people in the south. In 1541, a Spaniard, Pedro de Valdivia, founded Santiago. Chile won its independence from Spain in 1818 under Bernardo O'Higgins and an Argentinian, José de San Martin. O'Higgins, dictator until 1823, laid the foundations of the modern state with a two-party system and a centralized government.

The dictator from 1830 to 1837, Diego Portales, fought a war with Peru in 1836–39 that expanded Chilean territory. The Conservatives were in power from 1831 to 1861. Then the Liberals, winning a share of power for the next 30 years, disestablished the church and limited presidential power. Chile fought the War of the Pacific with Peru and Bolivia from 1879 to 1883, winning Antofagasta, Bolivia's only outlet to the sea, and extensive areas from Peru. A revolt in 1890 led by Jorge Montt overthrew, in 1891, José Balmaceda and established a parliamentary dictatorship that existed until a new Constitution was adopted in 1925. Industrialization began before World War I and led to the formation of Marxist groups.

Juan Antonio Ríos, President during World War II, was originally pro-Nazi but in 1944 led his country into the war on the side of the U.S.

A small abortive army uprising in 1969 raised fear of military intervention to prevent a Marxist, Salvador Allende Gossens, from taking office after his election to the presidency on Sept. 4, 1970. Dr. Allende was the first President in a non-Communist country freely elected on a Marxist-Leninist program.

Allende quickly established relations with Cuba and the People's Republic of China and nationalized several American companies.

Allende's overthrow and death in an army assault on the presidential palace in September 1973 ended a 46-year era of constitutional government in Chile.

The takeover was led by a four-man junta headed by Army Chief of Staff Augusto Pinochet Ugarte, who assumed the office of President.

Committed to "exterminate Marxism," the junta embarked on a right-wing dictatorship. It suspended parliament, banned political activity, and broke relations with Cuba.

In 1977, Pinochet, in a speech marking his fourth year in power, promised elections by 1985 if conditions warranted. Earlier, he had abolished DINA, the secret police, and decreed an amnesty for political prisoners.

Pinochet was inaugurated on March 11, 1981, for an eight-year term as President, at the end of which, according to the Constitution adopted six months earlier, the junta would nominate a civilian as successor. He stepped down in January 1990 in favor of Patricio Aylwin who was elected Dec. 1989 as the head of a 17-party coalition.

The presidential election of December 1993 saw the reemergence of a member of the Frei family. Eduardo Frei, the candidate of a center-left coalition, won. His father had been president from 1964–70.

The president in 1994 proposed reforming the health care systems and providing additional funding for education, all to be paid through proceeds from the privatization of state-sector enterprises.

CHINA

People's Republic of China
President: Jiang Zemin (1993)
Premier: Li Peng (1987)
Area: 3,691,521 sq mi. (9,561,000 sq km)[1]
Population (est. mid-1995): 1,218,800,000 (average rate of natural increase: 1.1%); birth rate: 18/1000; infant mortality rate: 44/1000; density per square mile: 330.1 China has 56 ethnic groups. In 1991, the Han people accounted for 92% of the population.
Capital: Beijing; **Largest cities (est. 1991):** Shanghai, 7,500,000; Beijing (Peking) 5,700,000; Tianjin (Tientsin) 4,575,000; Canton, 2,914,000; Wuhan, 3,284,200; Shenyang (Mukden), 3,604,000; Nanjing (Nanking), 2,100,000; Chongqing (Chongking), 2,267,000; Harbin, 2,443,400; **Monetary unit:** Yuan; **Languages:** Chinese, Mandarin, also local dialects; **Religions:** Officially atheist but traditional religion contains elements of Confucianism, Taoism, Buddhism; **National name:** Zhonghua Renmin Gongheguo; **Literacy rate:** 73%
Economic summary: Gross domestic product (1993 U.N., World Bank est.); $2.61 trillion; $2,200 per capita; 13.4% real growth rate; inflation rate (Dec. 93–94): 17.6%; unemployment rate in urban areas: 2.3%. Arable land: 10%. Principal agricultural products: rice, wheat, grains, cotton. Labor force: 567,400,000; 60% in agriculture and forestry, 25% in industry and commerce. Major industrial products: iron and steel, textiles, armaments, petroleum. Natural resources: coal, natural gas, limestone, marble, metals, hydropower potential. Exports: $92 billion (f.o.b., 1993): textiles, garments, petroleum, minerals, footwear, toys. Imports: $104 billion (c.i.f., 1993): specialized industrial machinery, chemicals, manufactured goods, steel, textile yarn, fertilizer. Major trading partners: Japan, Hong Kong, U.S., Germany, Taiwan, and Macau, Russia.

1. Including Manchuria and Tibet.

Geography. China, which occupies the eastern part of Asia, is slightly larger in area than the U.S. Its coastline is roughly a semicircle. The greater part of the country is mountainous, and only in the lower reaches of the Yellow and Yangtze Rivers are there extensive low plains.

The principal mountain ranges are the Tien Shan, to the northwest; the Kunlun chain, running south of the Taklimakan and Gobi Deserts; and the Trans-Himalaya, connecting the Kunlun with the borders of China and Tibet. Manchuria is largely an undulating plain connected with the north China plain by a narrow lowland corridor. Inner Mongolia contains the relatively fertile southern and eastern portions of the Gobi. The large island of Hainan (13,200 sq mi.; 34,300 sq km) lies off the southern coast.

Hydrographically, China proper consists of three great river systems. The northern part of the country is drained by the Yellow River (Huang Ho), 2,109 miles long (5,464 km) and mostly unnavigable. The central part is drained by the Chang Jiang (Yangtze

Kiang), the third longest river in the world 2,432 miles (6,300 km). The Zhujiang (Si Kiang) in the south is 848 miles long (2,197 km) and navigable for a considerable distance. In addition, the Amur (1,144 sq mi.; 2,965 km) forms part of the northeastern boundary.

Government. With 2,978 deputies, elected for four-year terms by universal suffrage, the National People's Congress is the chief legislative organ. A State Council has the executive authority. The Congress elects the Premier and Deputy Premiers. All ministries are under the State Council, headed by the Premier.

The Communist Party controls the government.

History. By 2000 B.C. the Chinese were living in the Huang Ho basin, and they had achieved an advanced stage of civilization by 1200 B.C. The great philosophers Lao-tse, Confucius Mo Ti, and Mencius lived during the Chou dynasty (1122–249 B.C.). The warring feudal states were first united under Emperor Ch'in Shih Huang Ti, during whose reign (246–210 B.C.) work was begun on the Great Wall. Under the Han dynasty (206 B.C.–A.D. 220), China prospered and traded with the West.

In the T'ang dynasty (618–907), often called the golden age of Chinese history, painting, sculpture, and poetry flourished, and printing made its earliest known appearance.

The Mings, last of the native rulers (1368–1644), overthrew the Mongol, or Yuan, dynasty (1280–1368) established by Kublai Khan. The Mings in turn were overthrown in 1644 by invaders from the north, the Manchus.

China closely restricted foreign activities, and by the end of the 18th century only Canton and the Portuguese port of Macao were open to European merchants. Following the Anglo-Chinese War of 1839–42, however, several treaty ports were opened, and Hong Kong was ceded to Britain. Treaties signed after further hostilities (1856–60) weakened Chinese sovereignty and removed foreigners from Chinese jurisdiction. The disastrous Chinese-Japanese War of 1894–95 was followed by a scramble for Chinese concessions by European powers, leading to the Boxer Rebellion (1900), suppressed by an international force.

The death of the Empress Dowager Tzu Hsi in 1908 and the accession of the infant Emperor Hsüan T'ung (Pu-Yi) were followed by a nation-wide rebellion led by Dr. Sun Yat-sen, who became first President of the Provisional Chinese Republic in 1911. The Manchus abdicated on Feb. 12, 1912. Dr. Sun resigned in favor of Yuan Shih-k'ai, who suppressed the republicans but was forced by a serious rising in 1915–16 to abandon his intention of declaring himself Emperor. Yuan's death in June 1916 was followed by years of civil war between rival militarists and Dr. Sun's republicans.

Nationalist forces, led by Gen. Chiang Kai-shek and with the advice of Communist experts, soon occupied most of China, setting up a Kuomintang regime in 1928. Internal strife continued, however, and Chiang broke with the Communists.

An alleged explosion on the South Manchurian Railway on Sept. 18, 1931, brought invasion of Manchuria by Japanese forces, who installed the last Manchu Emperor, Henry Pu-Yi, as nominal ruler of the puppet state of "Manchukuo." Japanese efforts to take China's northern provinces in July 1937 were resisted by Chiang, who meanwhile had succeeded in uniting most of China behind him. Within two years, however, Japan seized most of the ports and railways. The Kuomintang government retreated first to Han-

Provinces and Regions of China

Name	Area (sq mi.)	Area (sq km)	Capital
Provinces			
Anhui (Anhwei)	54,015	139,900	Hefei (Hofei)
Fujian (Fukien)	47,529	123,100	Fuzhou (Fukien)
Gansu (Kansu)	137,104	355,100	Lanzhou (Lanchow)
Guangdong (Kwangtung)	76,100	197,100	Canton
Guizhou (Kweichow)	67,181	174,000	Guiyang (Kweiyang)
Hainan	13,200	34,300	Haikou
Hebei (Hopei)	81,479	211,030	Shijiazhuang (Shitikiachwang)
Heilongjiang (Heilungkiang)[1]	178,996	463,600	Harbin
Henan (Honan)	64,479	167,000	Zhengzhou (Chengchow)
Hubei (Hupeh)	72,394	187,500	Wuhan
Hunan	81,274	210,500	Changsha
Jiangsu (Kiangsu)	40,927	106,000	Nanjing (Nanking)
Jiangxi (Kiangsi)	63,629	164,800	Nanchang
Jilin (Kirin)[1]	72,201	187,000	Changchun
Liaoning[1]	53,301	138,050	Shenyang
Quinghai (Chinghai)	278,378	721,000	Xining (Sining)
Shaanxi (Shensi)	75,598	195,800	Xian (Sian)
Shandong (Shantung)	59,189	153,300	Jinan (Tsinan)
Shanxi (Shansi)	60,656	157,100	Taiyuan
Sichuan (Szechwan)	219,691	569,000	Chengdu (Chengtu)
Yunnan	168,417	436,200	Kunming
Zhejiang (Chekiang)	39,305	101,800	Hangzhou (Hangchow)
Autonomous Region			
Guangxi Zhuang (Kwangsi Chuang)	85,096	220,400	Nanning
Nei Monggol (Inner Mongolia)[1]	454,633	1,177,500	Hohhot (Huhehot)
Ningxia Hui	30,039	77,800	Yinchuan (Yinchwan)
Xinjiang Uygur (Sinkiang Uighur)[1]	635,829	1,646,800	Urumqi (Urumchi)
Xizang (Tibet)	471,660	1,221,600	Lhasa

1. Together constitute (with Taiwan) what has been traditionally known as Outer China, the remaining territory forming the historical China Proper. NOTE: Names are in Pinyin, with conventional spelling in parentheses.

kow and then to Chungking, while the Japanese set up a puppet government at Nanking headed by Wang Jingwei.

Japan's surrender in 1945 touched off civil war between Nationalist forces under Chiang and Communist forces led by Mao Zedong, the party chairman. Despite U.S. aid, the Chiang forces were overcome by the Maoists, backed by the Soviet bloc, and were expelled from the mainland. The Mao regime, established in Peking as the new capital, proclaimed the People's Republic of China on Oct. 1, 1949, with Zhou Enlai as Premier.

After the Korean War began in June 1950, China led the Communist bloc in supporting North Korea, and on Nov. 26, 1950, the Mao regime intervened openly.

In 1958, Mao undertook the "Great Leap Forward" campaign, which combined the establishment of rural communes with a crash program of village industrialization but it failed and was abandoned.

China exploded its first atomic (fission) bomb in 1964 and produced a fusion bomb in 1967.

Mao moved to Shanghai, and from that base he and his supporters waged what they called a Cultural Revolution. In the spring of 1966 the Mao group formed Red Guard units dominated by youths and students, closing the schools to free the students for agitation.

The Red Guards campaigned against "old ideas, old culture, old habits, and old customs." Often they were no more than uncontrolled mobs, and brutality was frequent. Early in 1967 efforts were made to restore control. The Red Guards were urged to return home. Schools started opening.

Persistent overtures by the Nixon Administration resulted in the dramatic announcement in July that Henry Kissinger, President Richard M. Nixon's national security adviser, had secretly visited Peking and reached agreement on a visit by the President to China.

The movement toward reconciliation, which signaled the end of the U.S. containment policy toward China, provided irresistible momentum for Chinese admission to the U.N. Despite U.S. opposition to expelling Taiwan (Nationalist China), the world body overwhelmingly ousted Chiang in seating Peking.

President Nixon went to Peking for a week early in 1972, meeting Mao as well as Zhou. The summit ended with a historic communiqué on February 28, in which both nations promised to work toward improved relations. Full diplomatic relations were barred by China as long as the U.S. continued to recognize Nationalist China.

On Jan. 8, 1976, Zhou died. His successor, Vice Premier Deng Xiaoping was supplanted within a month by Hua Guofeng, former Minister of Public Security. Hua became permanent Premier in April. In October he was named successor to Mao as Chairman of the Communist Party.

After Mao died on Sept. 10, a campaign against his widow, Jiang Qing, and three of her "radical" colleagues began. The "Gang of Four" was denounced for having undermined the party, the government, and the economy. They were tried and convicted in 1981.

At the Central Committee meeting of 1977, Deng was reinstated as Deputy Premier, Chief of Staff of the Army, and member of the Central Committee of the Politburo.

At the same time, Jiang Qing, Wang Hongwen, Zhang Chunqiao, and Yao Wenyuan—the notorious "Gang of Four"—were removed from all official posts and banished from the party.

In May 1978, expulsion of ethnic Chinese by Vietnam produced an open rupture. Peking sided with Cambodia in the border fighting that flared between Vietnam and Cambodia, charging Hanoi with aggression.

Peking and Washington announced that they would open full diplomatic relations on Jan. 1, 1979 and the Carter Administration abrogated the Taiwan defense treaty. Deputy Premier Deng sealed the agreement with a visit to the U.S. that coincided with the opening of embassies in both capitals on March 1.

On Deng's return from the U.S. Chinese troops invaded Vietnam to avenge alleged violations of Chinese territory. The action was seen as a reaction to Vietnam's invasion of Cambodia.

After the Central Committee meeting of June 27–29, 1981, Hu Yaobang, a Deng protégé, was elevated to the party chairmanship, replacing Hua Guofeng. Deng became chairman of the military commission of the central committee, giving him control over the army. The committee's 215 members concluded the session with a statement holding Mao Zedong responsible for the "grave blunder" of the Cultural Revolution.

Under Deng Xiaoping's leadership, meanwhile, China's Communist ideology was almost totally reinterpreted and sweeping economic changes were set in motion in the early 1980s. The Chinese scrapped the personality cult that idolized Mao Zedong, muted Mao's old call for class struggle and exportation of the Communist revolution, and imported Western technology and management techniques to replace the Marxist tenets that retarded modernization.

Also under Deng's leadership, the Chinese Communists worked out an arrangement with Britain for the future of Hong Kong after 1997. The flag of China will be raised but the territory will retain its present social, economic and legal system.

The removal of Hu Yaobang as party chairman in January 1987 was a sign of a hard-line resurgence. He was replaced by former Premier Zhao Ziyang. Conflict between hard-liners and moderates continued and reached a violent climax in 1989. Student demonstrations calling for accelerated liberalization were crushed by military force in June, resulting in several hundred deaths.

The rubber-stamp National People's Congress concluded its April 1992 session with a call to guard against "leftism," widely interpreted as a sign of consolidation and a call for accelerating the drive for economic reform. Nevertheless, several hard-liners remained in their conspicuous positions.

China settled its long-running feud with Vietnam and normalized its relations with Japan during 1991.

The annual session of the National People's Congress in March 1993 was widely seen as an effort by Deng Xiaoping, the paramount leader, to maintain China's moves toward a market economy while retaining political authoritarianism. Communist Party leader Jiang Zemin was elected president, while hard-liner Li Peng was reelected to another five-year term as prime minister despite, but perhaps because of, his politics.

The economy continued to grow rapidly in 1993. In November the Central Committee adopted a resolution envisaging the conversion of state-owned enterprises into joint-stock companies, the creation of a central bank and modern tax system.

A last-minute deal in February 1995 was reached between the U.S. and China protecting intellectual property rights to end China's reputedly widespread pirating of software, movies, and musical recordings.

COLOMBIA

Republic of Colombia
President: Ernesto Samper Pizano (1994)
Area: 439,735 sq mi. (1,138,910 sq km)
Population (est. mid-1995): 37,700,000 (average annual rate of natural increase, 1.8%); birth rate: 24/1000; infant mortality rate: 37/1000; density per square mile: 85.7
Capital: Bogotá; **Largest cities (1993 census):** Bogotá, 6,500,000; Medellín, 1,800,000; Cali, 1,800,000; Barranquilla, 1,400,000; Cartagena, 700,000; **Monetary unit:** Peso; **Language:** Spanish; **Religion:** 95% Roman Catholic; **National name:** República de Colombia; **Literacy rate:** 91.3
Economic summary: Gross domestic product (1994 est.): $59 billion, per capita $1,643; est. real growth rate 5.7%; inflation 22.6%; unemployment 7.4%. Arable land: 4%. Principal agricultural products: coffee, bananas, rice, corn, sugar cane, cotton, tobacco, oilseeds, fresh cut flowers. Labor force (1990): 12,000,000; 46% in services, 30% agriculture, 24% industry. Major industrial products: textiles, processed food, beverages, chemicals, cement. Natural resources: petroleum, natural gas, coal, iron ore, nickel, gold, copper, emeralds. Exports: $8.5 billion (f.o.b., 1994 est.): coffee, fuel oil, coal, bananas, fresh cut flowers, nickel, chemicals, emeralds. Imports: $10.9 billion (f.o.b., 1994 est.): machinery, paper products, aircraft, telecommunications equipment, vehicles, gasoline, wheat. Major trading partners: U.S., E.U., Japan, Venezuela, Brazil.

Geography. Colombia, in the northwestern part of South America, is the only country on that continent that borders on both the Atlantic and Pacific Oceans. It is nearly equal to the combined areas of California and Texas.

Through the western half of the country, three Andean ranges run north and south, merging into one at the Ecuadorean border. The eastern half is a low, jungle-covered plain, drained by spurs of the Amazon and Orinoco, inhabited mostly by isolated, tropical-forest Indian tribes. The fertile plateau and valley of the eastern range are the most densely populated parts of the country.

Government. Colombia's President, who appoints his own Cabinet, serves for a four-year term. The Senate, the upper house of Congress, has 102 members elected for four years by direct vote. The House of Representatives of 165 members is directly elected for four years. Mayors and state governors are also elected by direct vote for three-year terms.

History. Spaniards in 1510 founded Darien, the first permanent European settlement on the American mainland. In 1538 the Spaniards established the colony of New Granada, the area's name until 1861. After a 14-year struggle, in which Simón Bolívar's Venezuelan troops won the battle of Boyacá in Colombia on Aug. 7, 1819, independence was attained in 1824. Bolívar united Colombia, Venezuela, Panama, and Ecuador in the Republic of Greater Colombia (1819–30), but lost Venezuela and Ecuador to separatists. Bolívar's Vice President, Francisco de Paula Santander, founded the Liberal Party as the Federalists while Bolívar established the Conservatives as the Centralists.

Santander's presidency (1832–36) re-established order, but later periods of Liberal dominance (1849–57 and 1861–80), when the Liberals sought to disestablish the Roman Catholic Church, were marked by insurrection and even civil war. Rafael Nuñez, in a 15-year-presidency, restored the power of the central government and the church, which led in 1899 to a bloody civil war and the loss in 1903 of Panama over ratification of a lease to the U.S. of the Canal Zone. For 21 years, until 1930, the Conservatives held power as revolutionary pressures built up.

The Liberal administrations of Enrique Olaya Herrera and Alfonso López (1930–38) were marked by social reforms that failed to solve the country's problems, and in 1946, insurrection and banditry broke out, claiming hundreds of thousands of lives by 1958. Laureano Gómez (1950–53); the Army Chief of Staff, Gen. Gustavo Rojas Pinilla (1953–56), and a military junta (1956–57) sought to curb disorder by repression.

The Liberals won a solid majority in 1982, but a party split enabled Belisario Betancur Cuartas, the Conservative candidate, to win the presidency on May 31. After his inauguration, he ended the state of siege that had existed almost continuously for 34 years and renewed the general amnesty of 1981.

In an official war against drug trafficking Colombia became a public battleground with bombs, killings and kidnapping. In 1989 a leading presidential candidate, Luis Carlos Galán, was murdered. In an effort to quell the terror President Gaviria proposed lenient punishment in exchange for surrender by the leading drug dealers. In addition in 1991 the constitutional convention voted to ban extradition. In July 1992 Pablo Escobar of the Medellin drug cartel escaped from prison in an operation that left six dead.

A new constitution adopted in July 1991 provided for direct election of the state governors.

In the country's closest presidential contest in 24 years Mr. Samper, the candidate of the Liberal Party, won 50% of the vote in June 1994. Mr. Samper ran on a platform calling for the creation of new jobs and significantly higher social spending.

Following the capture of the head of the Cali drug cartel, the government in June 1995 announced plans to combat drug trafficking.

COMOROS

Federal Islamic Republic of the Comoros
President: Said Mohammed Djohar (1989)
Area: 690 sq mi. (1,787 sq km)
Population (est. mid-1995): 500,000 (average annual rate of natural increase: 3.6%); birth rate: 46/1000; infant mortality rate: 79/1000; density per square mile: 724.6
Capital and largest city (est. 1988): Moroni (on Grande Comoro), 22,000; **Monetary unit:** Franc CFA; **Languages:** Shaafi Islam (Swahili dialect), Malagasu, French, Arabic; **Religions:** Sunni Muslim, 86%; Roman Catholic, 14%.; **National name:** République Fédéral Islamique des Comores; **Literacy rate:** 48%
Economic summary: Gross domestic product (1993 est.): $360 million; $700 per capita; real growth rate 5% (!992); inflation 4% (1991); unemployment (1989): over 15.9%. Arable land: 35%. Labor force: 140,000 (1982); 80% in agriculture. Principal agricultural products: perfume essences, copra, coconuts, cloves, vanilla, cassava, bananas. Major industrial products: perfume distillations. Exports: $21 million (f.o.b., 1992 est.): perfume essences, vanilla, copra, cloves. Imports: $60 million (f.o.b., 1992 est.): foodstuffs, cement, petroleum products, consumer goods. Major trading partners: France, Germany, U.S., Africa, Pakistan, China.

Geography. The Comoros Islands—Grande Comoro, Anjouan, Mohéli, and Mayotte (which retains ties to France)—are an archipelago of volcanic origin in the Indian Ocean between Mozambique and Madagascar.

Government. Democratic elections were held in March 1990. The interim president Said Djohar won from among a field of eight candidates. The constitution dates from October 1, 1978, and the country is an Islamic republic with a 42-member unicameral legislature.

History. Under French rule since 1886, the Comoros declared themselves independent July 6, 1975. However, Mayotte, with a Christian majority, voted against joining the other, mainly Islamic, islands, in the move to independence and remains French.

A month after independence, Justice Minister Ali Soilih staged a coup with the help of mercenaries, overthrowing the new nation's first president, Ahmed Abdallah. He was overthrown on May 13, 1978.

Voters approved a new constitution in a referendum of June 1992.

In June 1993 the president dissolved the Federal Assembly, appointing an interim prime minister. Amid widespread irregularities the president's supporters won 50% of the seats in the Assembly.

In early 1994 the opposition rejected the validity of the elections and called for the president to resign. Quarreling between the then prime minister and the president of the Assembly led to the creation of a new government late in the year with a new prime minister.

CONGO

Republic of the Congo
President: Prof. Pascal Lissouba (1992)
Prime Minister: Jacques Joachin Yhombi-Opango (1993)
Area: 132,046 sq mi. (342,000 sq km)
Population (est. mid-1995): 2,500,000 (average annual rate of natural increase: 2.3%); birth rate: 40/1000; infant mortality rate: 109/1000. Density per sq mile: 18.9
Capital and largest city (est. 1992): Brazzaville, 937,580; **Other large city (est. 1992):** Pointe-Noire, 576,206.
Monetary unit: Franc CFA; **Ethnic groups:** About 15 Bantu groups, Europeans; **Languages:** French, Lingala, Kikongo, others; **Religions:** 50% Christian, 48% animist, 2% Muslim; **National name:** République Populaire du Congo; **Literacy rate:** 57%
Economic summary: Gross domestic product (1993 est.): $7 billion, per capita $2,900; real growth rate 0.6% (1991 est.); inflation −0.6%. (1991 est.) Arable land: 2%. Principal agricultural products: cassava, rice, corn, peanuts, coffee, cocoa. Labor force: 79,100; 75% in agriculture. Major industrial products: crude oil, cigarettes, cement, beverages, milled sugar. Natural resources: wood, potash, petroleum, natural gas. Exports: $1.1 billion (f.o.b., 1990): oil, lumber, coffee, cocoa, sugar, diamonds. Imports: $704 million (c.i.f., 1990): foodstuffs, consumer goods, intermediate manufactures, capital equipment. Major trading partners: France, U.S., Italy, other E.C. countries, Spain, Brazil, Germany, Japan.

Geography. The Congo is situated in west Central Africa astride the Equator. It borders on Gabon, Cameroon, the Central African Republic, Zaire, and the Angola exclave of Cabinda, with a short stretch of coast on the South Atlantic. Its area is nearly three times that of Pennsylvania.

Most of the inland is tropical rain forest, drained by tributaries of the Zaire (Congo) River, which flows south along the eastern border with Zaire to Stanley Pool. The narrow coastal plain rises to highlands separated from the inland plateaus by the 200-mile-wide Niari River Valley, which gives passage to the coast.

History. The inhabitants of the former French Congo, mainly Bantu peoples with Pygmies in the north, were subjects of several kingdoms in earlier times.

The Frenchman Pierre Savorgnan de Brazza signed a treaty with Makoko, ruler of the Bateke people, in 1880, which established French control. The area, with Gabon and Ubangi-Shari, was constituted the colony of French Equatorial Africa in 1910. It joined Chad in supporting the Free French cause in World War II. The Congo proclaimed its independence without leaving the French Community in 1960.

Maj. Marien Ngouabi, head of the National Council of the Revolution, took power as president on Jan. 1, 1969. He was sworn in for a second five-year term in 1975.

A four-man commando squad assassinated Ngouabi in Brazzaville on March 18, 1977.

Col. Joachim Yhombi-Opango, Army Chief of Staff, assumed the presidency on April 4. Yombhi-Opango resigned on Feb. 4, 1979, and was replaced by Col. Denis Sassou-Neguessou.

In July 1990 the leaders of the ruling party voted to end the one-party system. A national political conference, hailed as a model for sub-Saharan Africa, in 1991 renounced Marxism, and scheduled the country's first free elections for 1992. The national conference ending in June 1991 rewrote the constitution.

Political and ethnic tensions remained high in 1993 particularly after legislative elections in May and run-offs in June. Soon afterward a state of emergency was declared.

The opposition's rejection of the results developed into violence. An international arbitration committee in February 1994 invalidated the electoral results for nine seats. A new ceasefire agreement was reached in March and as the year went on there were further signs of political reconciliation.

trading partners: U.S., Central American countries, Germany, Japan, United Kingdom.

Geography. This Central American country lies between Nicaragua to the north and Panama to the south. Its area slightly exceeds that of Vermont and New Hampshire combined.

Most of Costa Rica is tableland, from 3,000 to 6,000 feet (914 to 1,829 m) above sea level. Cocos Island (10 sq mi.; 26 sq km), about 300 miles (483 km) off the Pacific Coast, is under Costa Rican sovereignty.

Government. Under the 1949 Constitution, the president and the one-house Legislative Assembly of 57 members are elected for terms of four years.

The army was abolished in 1949. There is a civil guard and a rural guard.

History. Costa Rica was inhabited by 25,000 Indians when Columbus discovered it and probably named it in 1502. Few of the Indians survived the Spanish conquest, which began in 1563. The region was administered as a Spanish province. Costa Rica achieved independence in 1821 but was absorbed for two years by Agustín de Iturbide in his Mexican Empire. It was established as a republic in 1848.

Except for the military dictatorship of Tomás Guardia from 1870 to 1882, Costa Rica has enjoyed one of the most democratic governments in Latin America.

Rodrigo Carazo Odio, leader of a four-party coalition called the Unity Party, won the presidency in February 1978. His tenure was marked by a disastrous decline in the economy.

On Feb. 2, 1986, Oscar Arias Sanchez won the national elections on a neutralist platform. Arias initiated a policy of preventing contra usage of Costa Rican territory. Rafael Calderón won the presidential election of February 4, 1990 with 51% of the vote.

The presidential election in February 1994 was won by Maria Figueres Olsen, although the tone of the campaign shocked many Costa Ricans. Mr. Figueres proposed more government intervention in the economy. Mr. Calderon was constitutionally prevented from running for a second term.

A free-trade agreement between the country and Mexico was implemented at the start of 1995.

COSTA RICA

Republic of Costa Rica
President: José Maria Figueres Olsen (1994)
Area: 19,652 sq mi. (50,898 sq km)
Population (est. mid-1995): 3,300,000 (average annual rate of natural increase: 2.2%); birth rate: 26/1000; infant mortality rate: 13.7/1000; density per square mile: 167.9
Capital and largest city (est. 1992): San José, 302,574; **Monetary unit:** Colón; **Language:** Spanish; **Religion:** 95% Roman Catholic; **National name:** República de Costa Rica; **Literacy rate (1984):** 93%
Economic summary: Gross domestic product (1993 est.): $19.3 billion; per capita $5,900; real growth rate 6.5%; inflation 9%; unemployment 4%. Arable land: 6%. Principal products: bananas, coffee, sugar cane, rice, corn, livestock. Labor force: 868,300; 35.1% in industry and commerce. Major products: processed foods, textiles and clothing, construction materials, fertilizer. Natural resource: hydropower potential. Exports: $1.9 billion (f.o.b., 1993): coffee, bananas, textiles, sugar. Imports: $2.9 billion (c.i.f., 1993): raw materials, consumer goods, capital equipment, petroleum. Major

CÔTE D'IVOIRE

Republic of Côte d'Ivoire
President: Henri Konan Bédié (1993)
Area: 124,502 sq mi. (322,462 sq km)
Population (est. mid-1995): 14,300,000 (average annual rate of natural increase: 3.5%); birth rate: 50/1000; infant mortality rate: 92/1000; density per square mile: 114.9
Capital (est. 1984): Yamoussoukro[1] (since March 1983), 120,000; **Largest city:** Abidjan, 1,900,000. **Monetary unit:** Franc CFA; **Ethnic groups:** 60 different groups: principals are Baoule, Bete, Senoufou, Malinke, Agni; **Languages:** French and African languages (Diaula esp.); **Religions:** 60% indigenous, 17% Christian, 23% Islam; **National name:** République de la Côte d'Ivoire; **Literacy rate:** 54%
Economic summary: Gross domestic product (1993 est.): $21 billion; per capita $1,500; real growth rate n.a.; inflation 1% (1991); unemployment (1985) 14%. Arable land: 9%; Labor force: 5,718,000; over 85% in agriculture. Principal products: coffee, cocoa, corn, beans, timber. Major industrial products: food, wood, refined oil, textiles, fertilizer. Natural resources: diamonds, iron ore, crude oil, manganese, cobalt, bauxite, cop-

per. Exports: $2.8 billion (f.o.b., 1990): cocoa, coffee, tropical woods, petroleum, cotton, bananas, pineapples, palm oil. Imports: $1.6 billion (f.o.b., 1990): food, capital goods, consumer goods, fuel. Major trading partners: France, other E.C. countries, Germany, Netherlands, Belgium, Spain, U.S., Nigeria, Japan.

1. Not recognized by U.S. which recognizes Abidjan.

Geography. Côte d'Ivoire (also known as the Ivory Coast), in western Africa on the Gulf of Guinea, is a little larger than New Mexico. Its neighbors are Liberia, Guinea, Mali, Burkina Faso, and Ghana.

The country consists of a coastal strip in the south, dense forests in the interior, and savannas in the north. Rainfall is heavy, especially along the coast.

Government. The government is headed by a President who is elected every five years by popular vote, together with a National Assembly of 175 members.

History. Côte d'Ivoire attracted both French and Portuguese merchants in the 15th century. French traders set up establishments early in the 19th century, and in 1842, the French obtained territorial concessions from local tribes, gradually extending their influence along the coast and inland. The area was organized as a territory in 1893, became an autonomous republic in the French Union after World War II, and achieved independence on Aug. 7, 1960.

The Côte d'Ivoire formed a customs union in 1959 with Dahomey (Benin), Niger, and Burkina Faso.

Roman Catholic Pres. Houphouët-Boigny ordered the building of the largest Christian church in the world, Notre Dame de la Pax, in the capital city, which he periodically paid for.

Falling cocoa and coffee prices made this nation the largest per capita debtor in Africa. Massive protests by students, farmers and professionals forced the president to legalize opposition parties and hold the first contested presidential election. In October 1990 Houphouët-Boigny won 81% of the vote and is currently serving his seventh consecutive five-year term. In the first multiparty legislative elections in November the president's Democratic Party won 163 of the 175 seats.

Negotiations with the IMF over aid were suspended in July 1992 when the government refused to consider reducing public expenditures.

The country's long-time president Houphouët-Boigny died in December 1993, but a smooth transition ensued to Bédié.

CROATIA

Republic of Croatia
President: Franjo Tudjman
Area: 21,829 sq mi. (56,537 sq km)
Population (est. mid-1995): 4,500,000 (average annual rate of natural increase: –0.1%), predominantly Croats, about 12% Serbs. Birth rate: 10/1000; infant mortality rate: 11.6/1000; density per square mile: 206.2
Capital (1991): Zagreb, 930,753. **Other large cities (1991):** Split, 189,444; Rijeka, 167,757; Osijek, 104,553. **Monetary unit:** Kuna (May 1994). **Languages:** Croatian; **Literacy rate:** est. 90%; **Religion:** predominantly Roman Catholic
Economic summary: Gross domestic product (1994): $14.5 billion; $3,020 per capita; real growth rate 0.8%; inflation: 3%; unemployment: 12.8%. Industries: chemicals, plastics, machine tools, fabricated metals, electronics, and rolled steel products, aluminum processing, wood products, building materials, petroleum and petroleum

refining, food processing, beverages, pharmaceuticals, shipbuilding. Agriculture: wheat, corn, oats, sugar beets, potatoes, livestock breeding and dairy farming, vineyards, fishing. Exports: $4.3 billion (1994). Imports: $5.2 billion (1994).

Geography: Croatia is about half the size of the state of Louisiana (or the size of West Virginia). It is bounded in the north by the Republic of Slovenia, in the northeast by Hungary, in the east and south by the Federal Republic of Yugoslavia (Serbia and Montenegro), in the south by the Republic of Bosnia and Herzegovina, and in the west by the Adriatic Sea. Part of Croatia is a barren, rocky region lying in the Dinaric Alps. The Zagorje region north of the capital, Zagreb, is a land of rolling hills, and the fertile agricultural region of the Pannonian Plain is bordered by the Drava, Danube, and Sava Rivers in the east. Over one-third of Croatia is forested.

Government: A parliamentary democracy with two legislative houses.

History: The original home of the Slavic Croats was in an area that was part of the Republic of Ukraine. Other tribes arrived in the region during the 6th century A.D., which was then part of the Roman province of Pannonia. The Croats converted to Christianity between the 7th and 9th centuries and adopted the Roman alphabet.

In 925 A.D. the Croats defeated Byzantine and Frankish invaders and established their own independent kingdom which reached its peak during the 11th century.

A civil war ensued in 1089 which later led to the country being conquered by the Hungarians in 1091. The signing of the *Pacta Conventa* by Croatian tribal chiefs and the Hungarian king in 1102 united the two nations politically under the Hungarian monarch.

When the Hungarians were defeated by the Turks in 1526, most of Croatia fell under Ottoman rule until the end of the 17th century. The rest of Croatia elected Ferdinand of Austria as their king and became associated with the Hapsburgs of Austria.

After the establishment of the Austro-Hungarian kingdom in 1867, Croatia and Slovenia became part of Hungary until the collapse of Austria-Hungary in 1918 following their defeat in World War I.

On Oct. 29, 1918, Croatia proclaimed its independence and joined in union with Montenegro, Serbia, and Slovenia to form the Kingdom of Serbs, Croats, and Slovenes. The name was changed to Yugoslavia in 1929.

When Germany invaded Yugoslavia in 1941, an independent Croatian state was created that was controlled by a Fascist dictatorship. After Germany was defeated in 1945, Croatia was made into a republic of the newly reestablished nation of Yugoslavia.

In May 1991, Croatian voters supported a referendum calling for their republic's independence and when the Croatian parliament passed a declaration of independence from Yugoslavia in June, a six-month civil war followed with the Serbian-dominated Yugoslavian army. The war claimed thousands of lives and wrought mass destruction on the land.

A UN cease-fire was arranged on Jan. 2, 1992. The Security Council in February approved sending a 14,000-member peacekeeping force to monitor the cease-fire and protect the minority Serbs in Croatia.

By the end of August, rebel Serbs in Croatia still controlled a third of that republic.

Elections in February 1992 for the 63-seat upper house of parliament produced a victory for the nationalist party of President Tudjman.

In a 1993 referendum the Serb-occupied portion of Croatia (Krajina) voters resoundingly voted for integration with Serbs in Bosnia and Serbia proper. Although the Zagreb government and representatives of Krajina signed a ceasefire in March 1994 further negotiations broke down shortly afterward over the political status of the latter region.

Tudjman agreed in March 1995 to allow the continued stationing of U.N. peacekeeping troops in Croatia.

CUBA

Republic of Cuba
President: Fidel Castro Ruz (1976)
Area: 44,218 sq mi. (114,524 sq km)
Population (est. mid-1995): 11,200,000 (average annual rate of natural increase: 0.7%); birth rate: 14/1000; infant mortality rate: 9.4/1000; density per square mile: 253.29
Capital and largest city (1990 est.): Havana, 2,100,000. **Other large cities (est. 1990):** Santiago de Cuba, 405,354; Camagüey, 283,000 Holguin, 228,052; Guantánamo, 200,400; Santa Clara, 194,354. **Monetary unit:** Peso; **Language:** Spanish; **Religion:** at least 85% nominally Roman Catholic before Castro assumed power; **National name:** República de Cuba; **Literacy rate:** 94%
Economic summary: Gross domestic product (1993 est.): $13.7 billion, per capita $1,250; real growth rate –10%. Arable land: 23%. Principal agricultural products: sugar, tobacco, coffee, rice, fruits, sugar and sugar by-products. Labor force (1988): 4,620,800; 30% in services and government, industry 22%, agriculture 20%. Major industrial products: processed sugar and tobacco, refined oil products, textiles, chemicals, paper and wood products, metals, consumer products. Natural resources: metals, primarily nickel, timber. Exports: $1.5 billion (f.o.b., 1993 est.): coffee, sugar (world's largest sugar exporter), nickel, shellfish, tobacco, medical products, citrus. Imports: $1.7 billion (c.i.f., 1993 est.): petroleum, food, machinery, chemicals. Trading partners: China, Canada, Japan, Italy, Argentina, Spain, Mexico, Russia, Ukraine.

Geography. The largest island of the West Indies group (equal in area to Pennsylvania), Cuba is also the westernmost—just west of Hispaniola (Haiti and the Dominican Republic), and 90 miles (145 km) south of Key West, Fla., at the entrance to the Gulf of Mexico.

The island is mountainous in the southeast and south central area (Sierra Maestra). Elsewhere it is flat or rolling.

Government. Since 1976, elections have been held every five years to elect the National Assembly, which in turn elects the 31-member Council of States, its President, First Vice-President, five Vice-Presidents, and Secretary. Fidel Castro is President of the Council of State and of the government and First Secretary of the Communist Party of Cuba, the only political party.

History. Arawak Indians inhabiting Cuba when Columbus discovered the island in 1492 died off from diseases brought by sailors and settlers. By 1511, Spaniards under Diego Velásquez were founding settlements that served as bases for Spanish exploration. Cuba soon after served as an assembly point for treasure looted by the conquistadores, attracting French and English pirates.

Black slaves and free laborers were imported to work sugar and tobacco plantations, and waves of chiefly Spanish immigrants maintained a European character in the island's culture. Early slave rebellions and conflicts between colonials and Spanish rulers laid the foundation for an independence movement that turned into open warfare from 1867 to 1878. The poet, José Marti, in 1895 led the struggle that finally ended Spanish rule, thanks largely to U.S. intervention in 1898 after the sinking of the battleship *Maine* in Havana harbor.

A treaty in 1899 made Cuba an independent republic under U.S. protection. The U.S. occupation, which ended in 1902, suppressed yellow fever and brought large American investment. From 1906 to 1909, Washington invoked the Platt Amendment to the treaty, which gave it the right to intervene in order to suppress any revolt. U.S. troops came back in 1912 and again in 1917 to restore order. The Platt Amendment was abrogated in 1934.

Fulgencio Batista, an army sergeant, led a revolt in 1933 that overthrew the regime of President Gerado Machado.

Batista's Cuba was a police state. Corrupt officials took payoffs from American gamblers who operated casinos, demanded bribes from Cubans for various public services and enriched themselves with raids on the public treasury. Dissenters were murdered and their bodies dumped in gutters.

Fidel Castro Ruz, a hulking, bearded attorney in his 30s, landed in Cuba on Christmas Day 1956 with a band of 12 fellow revolutionaries, evaded Batista's soldiers, and set up headquarters in the jungled hills of the Sierra Maestra range. By 1958 his force had grown to about 2,000 guerrillas, for the most part young and middle class. Castro's brother, Raul, and Ernesto (Ché) Guevara, an Argentine physician, were his top lieutenants. Businessmen and landowners who opposed the Batista regime gave financial support to the rebels. The United States, meanwhile, cut off arms shipments to Batista's army.

The beginning of the end for Batista came when the rebels routed 3,000 government troops and captured Santa Clara, capital of Las Villas province 150 miles from Havana, and a trainload of Batista reinforcements refused to get out of their railroad cars. On New Year's Day 1959, Batista flew to exile in the Dominican Republic and Castro took over the government. Crowds cheered the revolutionaries on their seven-day march to the capital.

The United States initially welcomed what looked like the prospect for a democratic Cuba, but a rude awakening came within a few months when Castro established military tribunals for political opponents, jailed hundreds, and began to veer leftward. Castro disavowed Cuba's 1952 military pact with the United States. He confiscated U.S. investments in banks and industries and seized large U.S. landholdings, turning them first into collective farms and then into Soviet-type state farms. The United States broke relations with Cuba on Jan. 3, 1961. Castro thereupon forged an alliance with the Soviet Union.

From the ranks of the Cuban exiles who had fled to the United States, the Central Intelligence Agency recruited and trained an expeditionary force, numbering less than 2,000 men, to invade Cuba, with the expectation that the invasion would spark an uprising of the Cuban populace against Castro. The invasion was planned under the Eisenhower administration and President John F. Kennedy gave the go-ahead for it in the first months of his administration, but rejected a

CIA proposal for U.S. planes to provide air support. The landing at the Bay of Pigs on April 17, 1961, was a fiasco. Not only did the invaders fail to receive any support from the populace, but Castro's tanks and artillery made short work of the small force.

A Soviet attempt to change the global power balance by installing in Cuba medium-range missiles—capable of striking targets in the United States with nuclear warheads—provoked a crisis between the superpowers in 1962 that had the potential of touching off World War III. After a visit to Moscow by Cuba's war minister, Raul Castro, work began secretly on the missile launching sites.

Denouncing the Soviets for "deliberate deception," President Kennedy on Oct. 22 announced that the U.S. navy would enforce a "quarantine" of shipping to Cuba and search Soviet bloc ships to prevent the missiles themselves from reaching the island. After six days of tough public statements on both sides and secret diplomacy, Soviet Premier Nikita Khrushchev on Oct. 28 ordered the missile sites dismantled, crated and shipped back to the Soviet Union, in return for a U.S. pledge not to attack Cuba. Limited diplomatic ties were re-established on Sept. 1, 1977.

Emigration increased dramatically after April 1, 1980, when Castro, irritated by the granting of asylum to would-be refugees by the Peruvian embassy in Havana, removed guards and allowed 10,000 Cubans to swarm into the embassy grounds.

As an airlift began taking the refugees to Costa Rica, Castro opened the port of Mariel to a "freedom flotilla" of ships and yachts from the United States, many of them owned or chartered by Cuban-Americans to bring out relatives. It wasn't until after they had reached the United States that it was discovered that the regime had opened prisons and mental hospitals to permit criminals, homosexuals and others unwanted in Cuba to join the refugees.

For most of President Ronald Reagan's first term, U.S.-Cuban relations were frozen. But late in 1984, an agreement was reached between the two countries. Cuba would take back more than 2,700 Cubans who had come to the United States in the Mariel exodus but were not eligible to stay in the country under U.S. immigration law because of criminal or psychiatric disqualification. Castro cancelled it when the U.S. began the Radio Marti broadcasts in May 1985 to bring a non-Communist view to the Cuban people.

In the face of sweeping changes in Eastern Europe and the Soviet Union itself, Cuba has reaffirmed its adherence to Marxism-Leninism.

With the collapse of Communism in Eastern Europe Cuba's foreign trade plummeted as did aid from Russia, producing the worst economic crisis in the island's history.

The government moved slightly toward a mixed economy in 1993 by permitting limited private enterprise in a number of trades and services and allowing Cubans to possess convertible currencies.

Emigration from Cuba continued to vex the governments of the U.S. and Cuba in 1994. Finally the U.S. agreed to admit at least 20,000 per year in exchange for Cuba's promise to prevent a further exodus by boat.

CYPRUS

Republic of Cyprus
President: Glafcos Clerides (1993)
Area: 3,572 sq mi (9,251 sq km)

Population (Dec. 31, 1993): 722,800; Greek Cypriots, 601,300; Turkish Cypriots, 93,000.; Maronites, Armenians, Latins, 7,000; (average annual rate of natural increase: 1.71%[1]); birth rate: 16.8/1000[1]; infant mortality rate: 9/1000[1]; density per square mile: 202.3

Capital and largest city (1993): Lefkosia (Nicosia) (in government controlled area), 186,400 (in government controlled area); **Monetary unit:** Cyprus pound; **Languages:** Greek, Turkish (official), English is widely spoken; **Religions (1993 est.):** Greek Orthodox, 78%; Sunni Moslem, 18%; Maronite Armenian, Apostolic, Latin, and other, 4%. **National name:** Kypriaki Dimokratia—Kibris Cumhuriyeti; **Member of Commonwealth of Nations; Literacy rate (1993):** 94%

Economic summary: Gross domestic product (1994[1]): $7.5 billion, per capita $11,500; real growth rate 5%; inflation rate 4.7%; unemployment rate: 2.7%. Arable land: 40%. Principal agricultural products: potatoes, vegetables, citrus, vine products, olives, barley. Labor force: 288,000; 87% in industry. Major industrial products: food, beverages, metal products, pharmaceuticals, clothing, footwear, furniture. Tourism contributed 10.2% to GDP in 1992 (est. 8.2% in 1993). Natural resources: copper, asbestos, gypsum, timber, marble, clay, umber, ochre. Exports: $1.0 billion (f.o.b., 1994): citrus, potatoes, grapes, wine, cement, clothing, footwear, chemical products, paper products. Imports: $3.2 billion (c.i.f., 1994): consumer goods, petroleum and lubricants, food and feed grains, machinery. Major trading partners: U.K., Greece, Lebanon, Germany, Saudi Arabia.

1. Government controlled area only.

Geography. The third largest island in the Mediterranean (one and one half times the size of Delaware), Cyprus lies off the southern coast of Turkey and the western shore of Syria. Most of the country consists of a wide plain lying between two mountain ranges that cross the island. The highest peak is Mount Olympus at 6,406 feet (1,953 m).

Government. The president is elected for a five-year term and exercises executive power through an appointed Council of Ministers.

Legislative power lies with the House of Representatives which comprises 80 members elected for five years. 56 members are Greek-Cypriot elected by the Greek-Cypriot community; 24 are Turkish-Cypriots elected by the Turkish-Cypriot community. Since the Turkish-Cypriot ministers and other officials withdrew from their posts in 1963, the 24 seats allotted to the Turkish Cypriots remain vacant. The Cypriot House assembly has been functioning only with its 56 Greek Cypriot members. Representatives from the Maronite, Armenian, and Latin minorities are also elected as observers. Mediation efforts by the U.N. seek to achieve reunification of the island under one federated system of government.

History. Cyprus was the site of early Phoenician and Greek colonies. For centuries its rule passed through many hands. It fell to the Turks in 1571, and a large Turkish colony settled on the island.

In World War I, on the outbreak of hostilities with Turkey, Britain annexed the island. It was declared a crown colony in 1925.

For centuries the Greek population, regarding Greece as its mother country, has sought self-determination and reunion with it *(enosis)*. The resulting quarrel with Turkey threatened NATO. Cyprus became an independent nation on Aug. 16, 1960, with Britain, Greece, and Turkey as guarantor powers.

Archbishop Makarios, president since 1959, was overthrown July 15, 1974, by a military coup led by the Cypriot National Guard. The new regime named Nikos Giorgiades Sampson as president and Bishop Gennadios as head of the Cypriot Church to replace Makarios.

Diplomacy failed to resolve the crisis. Turkey invaded Cyprus by sea and air July 20, 1974, asserting its right to protect the Turkish Cypriote minority.

Geneva talks involving Greece, Turkey, Britain, and the two Cypriote factions failed in mid-August, and the Turks subsequently gained control of 40% of the island. Greece made no armed response to the superior Turkish force, but bitterly suspended military participation in the NATO alliance.

The tension continued after Makarios returned to become President on Dec. 7, 1974. He offered self-government to the Turkish minority, but rejected any solution "involving transfer of populations and amounting to partition of Cyprus."

Turkish Cypriots proclaimed a separate state under Rauf Denktas in the northern part of the island in Nov. 1983, and proposed a "biregional federation."

Makarios died on Aug. 3, 1977, and Spyros Kyprianou was elected to serve the remainder of his term. Kyprianou was subsequently re-elected in 1978, 1983, and 1985. In 1988, George Vassiliou defeated Kyprianou.

Despite several attempts in 1991 by the UN to resolve the dispute little if any progress was made.

Then-President Vassiliou won a plurality in the presidential election of February 1993 but fell short of a majority. A 73-year-old conservative and critic of UN proposals to reunify Cyprus narrowly won the second round of elections to become president

Encouraging steps in contacts between the Greek and Turkish communities received a setback by mid-1994. The U.N. Secretary General blamed the Turks and proposed economic sanctions.

Northern Cyprus—In 1974, Turkey invaded Cyprus and has since occupied 37% of the island in the north. Some 180,000 Greek Cypriots (about 40% of the Greek Cypriot population) were forced by the Turkish troops to flee to the Government-controlled area in the south and are still prevented by the occupying forces from returning to their homes and properties.

On Nov. 15, 1993, Turkish Cypriot leader Rauf Denktash unilaterally declared the occupied area independent, naming it the "Turkish Republic of Northern Cyprus." The UN Security Council, in its resolution 541 of Nov. 18, 1983, declared this action legally invalid and called for withdrawal. No country except Turkey has recognized this illegal entity. The Government of the Republic of Cyprus is the only internationally recognized Government on the island.

Both sides have public called for the resolution of inter-communal differences and the creation of a new federal system of government. Diplomacy by the United Nations has failed to settle the dispute between the two de facto autonomous states.

NORTHERN CYPRUS

Turkish Republic of Northern Cyprus
President: Rauf Denktas (1990)

Area: 1,295 sq mi. (3,355 sq km)
Population (est. 1993): 175,433: Turkish Cypriots, 174,618; Greek Cypriots, 547; Maronites, 268; (average annual rate of natural increase: 1.14%); birth rate: 19/1,000; infant mortality rate: 12/1000; density per square km: 135.4
Capital and largest city (1993): Nicosia North (Lefkosa), 41,327; **Monetary unit:** Turkish lira; **Official language:** Turkish; **Religions:** Moslem, 99%; others, 1%; **National name:** Kuzey Kibris Türk Cumhuriyeti (Turkish Republic of Northern Cyprus); **Literacy rate (1993):** 99%
Economic summary: Gross national product (1993): $624.9 million; per capita $3,528.40. Average rate of growth (1975–1993): 5.8%. Arable land (1993): 56.7%. Principal agricultural products: citrus, potatoes, tobacco, vegetables. Labor force (1993): 75,378; 24% in agriculture; 10.8% in industry. Major industrial products: concentrated citrus, hides, leathers, P.V.C. covered electric cables, footwear, clothing, cosmetics. Natural resources: gypsum, pyrite mine. Exports: dairy products, citrus, live animals, potatoes, ready-made clothing, tobacco, carobs, hides and leathers. Imports: consumer goods, petroleum and lubricants, food, machinery and transport equipment, chemicals. Major trading partners: EU countries (mainly U.K. and Germany) and Turkey are the largest trading partners.

Geography. The Turkish Republic of Northern Cyprus covers the northern part of the island of Cyprus. North Cyprus consists of the coastal plains, the Besparmak (Five-Finger) Mountains (the highest peak is Mount Selvili at 3,360 feet), and the interior plains.

Government. The Constitution envisages a Parliamentary democracy. The legislative power is exercised by an Assembly composed of 50 deputies elected for five years. The President is Head of State and represents the unity of the state. He appoints the Prime Minister from among the deputies.

Denktas dissolved parliament in October 1993 with a call for new elections in December, whose results led to the formation of a coalition government.

The European Court of Justice in July 1994 ordered an embargo on exports, consisting chiefly of fruits and clothing. Although this led to some deprivations, financial assistance from Turkey helped ameliorate the situation.

CZECH REPUBLIC

President: Vaclav Havel (1993)
Premier: Vaclav Klaus (1992)
Area: 30,464 sq mi. (78,902 sq km)
Population (est. mid-1995): 10,400,000 (average annual rate of natural increase: 0.0%); birth rate: 12/1000; infant mortality rate: 8.5/1000; density per square mile: 341.39
Capital and largest city (1993): Prague, 1,200,000. Other large cities (1991): Brno, 387,986; Ostrava, 327,553; Plzen, 173,129; Olomouc, 105,690; **Monetary unit:** Koruna; **Language:** Czech; **Religions:** Roman Catholic major; other: Protestant, Orthodox; **Literacy rate:** 99%
Economic summary: Gross domestic product (1993 est.): $75 billion; Per capita $7,200; real growth rate, 0%; inflation 19%; unemployment, 3.3%. The Czech Republic has a developed but deteriorating industrialized economy—much of its plant equipment is among the oldest in Europe. Natural resources: hard coal, kaolin, clay, graphite. Industries: fuels, ferrous metallurgy, machinery and equipment, coal, motor vehicles, glass, armaments. Agriculture: diversified crops including grains, potatoes, sugar beets, hops, fruit, hogs, cattle

and poultry; exporter of forest products. Labor force (1990): 5.389 million; industry, 37.9%; agriculture, 8.1%; construction, 8.8%; communications and other, 45.2%. Exports: $12.6 billion (f.o.b., 1993 est.): manufactured goods, machinery and transport equipment, chemicals, fuels, minerals, and metals. Imports: $12.4 billion (f.o.b., 1993 est.): machinery and transport equipment, fuels and lubricants, manufactured goods, raw materials, chemicals, agricultural products. Major trading partners: C.I.S., Slovakia, Germany, Hungary, Poland, Austria, Switzerland.

1. 1991 data for the former united Czechoslovakia.

Geography. The Czech Republic lies in central Europe. It is bordered on the north by Poland, on the east by Slovakia, on the south by Austria, and on the west and northwest by Germany. The two principal regions are Bohemia and Moravia. The Bohemian landscape consists of rolling hills and plateaus surrounded by low mountains to the north, west, and south. Moravia is bordered on the north by mountains and generally has more hills than Bohemia. The Principal rivers are the Elbe and the Vltava which are vital to the nation's waterborne and agricultural commerce. The Czech Republic is about the size of the state of South Carolina.

Government. A parliamentary democracy headed by the president. The parliament consists of two chambers—the 200-member House, elected for four-year terms, and the 81-member Senate, elected for six-year terms. The president is elected for a five-year term by both chambers of parliament.

History. Probably about the 5th century A.D., Slavic tribes from the Vistula basin settled in the region of the traditional Czech lands of Bohemia, Moravia, and Silesia. The Czechs founded the kingdom of Bohemia, the Premyslide dynasty, which ruled Bohemia and Moravia from the 10th to the 16th century.

One of the Bohemian kings, Charles IV, Holy Roman Emperor, made Prague an imperial capital and a center of Latin scholarship. The Hussite movement founded by Jan Hus (1369?–1415) linked the Slavs to the Reformation and revived Czech nationalism, previously under German domination. A Hapsburg, Ferdinand I, ascended the throne in 1526. The Czechs rebelled in 1618. Defeated in 1620, they were ruled for the next 300 years as part of the Austrian Empire. Full independence from the Hapsburgs was not achieved until the end of World War I following the collapse of the Austrian-Hungarian Empire.

A union of the Czech lands and Slovakia was proclaimed in Prague on Nov. 14, 1918, and the Czech nation became one of the two component parts of the newly formed Czechoslovakian state.

In March 1939, German troops occupied Czechoslovakia and Czech Bohemia and Moravia became German protectorates for the duration of World War II. The former government returned in April 1945 when the war ended and the country's pre-1938 boundaries were restored.

When elections were held in 1946, the Communists became the dominant political party and gained control of the Czechoslovakian government in 1948. Thereafter, the former democracy was turned into a Soviet-style state.

Nearly 42 years of Communist rule ended when Vaclav Havel was elected president of Czechoslovakia in 1989. The return of democratic political reform saw a strong Slovak nationalist movement emerge by the end of 1991 which sought independence for Slo-

vakia as a sovereign nation and the breakup of the two Czechoslovakian republics.

When the general elections of June 1992 failed to resolve the continuing coexistence of the two republics within the Federation, Czech and Slovak political leaders agreed to separate their states into two fully independent nations. On Aug. 26, 1992 they announced their intentions to disolve the Czechoslovakian federation on Jan. 1, 1993.

Havel was elected for a 5-year term as president in January 1993 by the 200-member parliament.

While the country enjoyed low unemployment and inflation fundamental economic restructuring has not yet begun.

The increasing bickering during early 1995 among the junior partners of the ruling coalition and with the dominant member the Civic Democratic Party was widely interpreted as political posturing in anticiation of mid-1996 elections.

DENMARK

Kingdom of Denmark
Sovereign: Queen Margrethe II (1972)
Prime Minister: Steen Spore
Area: 16,631 sq mi. (43,075 sq km[1]
Population (est. mid-1995): 5,200,000 (average annual rate of natural increase: 0.1%; birth rate: 13/1000; infant mortality rate: 5.7/1000; density per square mile: 313
Capital and largest city (1992): Copenhagen, 1,339,395. **Other large cities (1992):** Aarhus, 204,139; Odense, 140,886; Alborg, 114,970. **Monetary unit:** Krone; **Language:** Danish, Faroese, Greenlandic (an Inuit dialect), small German-speaking minority; **Religion (1992):** 88% Evangelical Lutheran; **National name:** Kongeriget Danmark; **Literacy rate:** 99%
Economic summary: Gross domestic product (1993): $95.6 billion; $18,500 per capita; real growth rate, 0.5%; inflation rate 1.8% (est.); unemployment rate: 11.8% (est.). Arable land: 61%. Principal agricultural products: meat, dairy products, fish, grains. Labor force: 2,553,900: Private services, 37.1%; government services, 30.4%; manufacturing and mining, 20%. Major industrial products: processed foods, machinery and equipment, textiles. Natural resources: crude oil, natural gas, fish, salt, limestone. Exports: $36.7 billion (f.o.b., 1993): meat and dairy products, fish, industrial machinery, chemical products, transportation equipment. Imports: $29.7 billion (c.i.f., 1993 est.): machinery and equipment, transport equipment, petroleum, chemicals, grains and foodstuffs, textiles, paper. Major trading partners: Germany, Sweden, France, U.K., U.S., Norway, Japan.

1. Excluding Faeroe Islands and Greenland.

Geography. Smallest of the Scandinavian countries (half the size of Maine), Denmark occupies the Jutland peninsula, which extends north from Germany between the tips of Norway and Sweden. To the west is the North Sea and to the east the Baltic.

The country also consists of several Baltic islands; the two largest are Sjaelland, the site of Copenhagen, and Fyn. The narrow waters off the north coast are called the Skagerrak and those off the east, the Kattegat.

Government. Denmark has been a constitutional monarchy since 1849. Legislative power is held jointly by the Sovereign and parliament. The Constitution of 1953 provides for a unicameral parliament called the Folketing, consisting of 179 popularly elected members who serve for four years. The Cabinet is presided over by the Sovereign, who appoints the Prime Minister.

The Sovereign, Queen Margrethe II, was born April 16, 1940, and became Queen—the second in Denmark's history—Jan. 15, 1972, the day after her father, King Frederik IX, died at 72 in the 25th year of his reign. Margrethe was the eldest of his three daughters (by Princess Ingrid of Sweden). The nation's Constitution was amended in 1953 to permit her to succeed her father in the absence of a male heir to the throne. (Denmark was ruled six centuries ago by Margrethe I, but she was never crowned Queen since there was no female right of succession.)

History. Denmark emerged with establishment of the Norwegian dynasty of the Ynglinger in Jutland at the end of the 8th century. Danish mariners played a major role in the raids of the Vikings, or Norsemen, on Western Europe and particularly England. The country was Christianized by St. Ansgar and Harald Blaatand (Bluetooth)—the first Christian king—in the 10th century. Harald's son, Sweyn, conquered England in 1013. His son, Canute the Great, who reigned from 1014 to 1035, united Denmark, England, and Norway under his rule; the southern tip of Sweden was part of Denmark until the 17th century. On Canute's death, civil war tore the country until Waldemar I (1157–82) re-established Danish hegemony over the north.

In 1282, the nobles won the Great Charter, and Eric V was forced to share power with parliament and a Council of Nobles. Waldemar IV (1340–75) restored Danish power, checked only by the Hanseatic League of north German cities allied with ports from Holland to Poland. His daughter, Margrethe, in 1397 united under her rule Denmark, Norway, and Sweden. But Sweden later achieved autonomy and in 1523, under Gustavus I, independence.

Denmark supported Napoleon, for which it was punished at the Congress of Vienna in 1815 by the loss of Norway to Sweden. In 1864, Bismarck, together with the Austrians, made war on the little country as an initial step in the unification of Germany. Denmark was neutral in World War I.

In 1940, Denmark was invaded by the Nazis. King Christian X reluctantly cautioned his countrymen to accept the occupation, but there was widespread resistance against the Nazis. In 1944, Iceland declared its independence from Denmark, ending a union that had existed since 1380.

Liberated by British troops in May 1945, the country staged a fast recovery in both agriculture and manufacturing and was a leader in liberalizing trade. It joined the United Nations in 1945 and NATO in 1949.

Disputes over economic policy led to elections in 1981 that led to Poul Schlüter coming to power in early 1982. Further disputes over his pro-NATO posture led to elections in May, 1988 that marginally confirmed his position.

A second referendum on the Maastricht accord in May 1993 passed with 56.8 percent of the vote but confidence in European monetary and political unity was waning in other European/community countries.

The Social Democratic Party took over the reins of government at the head of a four-party slightly left leaning coalition in 1993.

Although the right-wing opposition scored gains in parliamentary elections in September 1994, Rasmussen managed to retain the premiership at the head of a three-party minority coalition.

Outlying Territories of Denmark

FAEROE ISLANDS

Status: Autonomous part of Denmark
Chief of State: Queen Margrethe II (1972)
High Commissioner: Bent Klinte
Prime Minister: Atli P. Dam (1991)
Lagmand (President): Jogran Sundstein (1989)
Area: 540 sq mi. (1,399 sq km)
Population (est. mid-1994): 48,427 (average annual growth rate: 0.83%); birth rate: 17.9/1000; infant mortality rate: 8.1/1000; density per square mile: 90
Capital and largest city (est. 1993): Thorshavn, 16,100; **Monetary unit:** Faeroese krone; **Literacy rate:** 99%
Economic summary: Gross domestic product (1989 est.): $662 million, per capita $14,000; real growth rate 2%; inflation (1988) 2%; unemployment (1991 est.) 5–6%. Arable land: 2%; principal agricultural products: sheep, vegetables. Labor force: 17,585, largely engaged in fishing manufacturing, transportation and commerce. Major industrial products: fish, ships, handicrafts. Exports: $386 million (f.o.b., 1990 est.): fish and fish products. Imports: $322 million (c.i.f., 1990 est.): machinery and transport equipment, foodstuffs, petroleum and petroleum products. Major trading partners: Denmark, U.S., U.K., Germany, Canada, France, Japan.

This group of 18 islands, lying in the North Atlantic about 200 miles (322 km) northwest of the Shetland Islands, joined Denmark in 1386 and has since been part of the Danish kingdom. The islands were occupied by British troops during World War II, after the German occupation of Denmark.

The Faeroes have home rule under a bill enacted in 1948; they also have two representatives in the Danish Folketing.

GREENLAND

Status: Autonomous part of Denmark
Chief of State: Queen Margrethe II (1972)
High Commissioner: Steen Spore
Premier: Lars Emil Johansen (1991)
Area: 840,000 sq mi. (incl. 708,069 sq mi. covered by ice-cap) (2,175,600 sq km)
Population (est. mid-1994): 57,040 (growth rate: 0.94%); birth rate: 18.6/1000; infant mortality rate: 26.7/1000; density per square mile: 15. Ethnic divisions: Greenlander (Inuit and Greenland-born Caucasians), 86%; Danish, 14%
Capital and largest city (1994 est.): Godthaab, 12,935; **Monetary unit:** Krone; **Literacy rate:** 99%
Economic summary: Gross national product (1988): $500 million, per capita $9,000; real growth rate 5%; inflation (1991) 1.6%; unemployment (1990 est.) 9%. Arable land: 0%; principal agricultural products: hay, sheep, garden produce. Labor force: 22,800, largely engaged in fishing, hunting, sheep breeding. Major industries: fish processing, lead and zinc processing, handicrafts. Natural resources: metals, cryolite, iron ore, coal, uranium, fish. Exports: $340.6 million (f.o.b., 1991): fish and fish products, metalic ores and concentrates. Imports: $403 million (c.i.f., 1991): petroleum and petroleum products, machinery and transport equipment, foodstuffs, manufactured goods. Major trading partners: Denmark, U.S., Germany, Sweden, Japan, Norway.

Greenland, the world's largest island, was colonized in 985–86 by Eric the Red. Danish sovereignty, which covered only the west coast, was extended over the whole island in 1917. In 1941 the U.S. signed an agreement with the Danish minister in Washington, placing it under U.S. protection during World War II but maintaining Danish sovereignty. A definitive agreement for the joint defense of Greenland within the framework of NATO was signed in 1951. A large U.S. air base at Thule in the far north was completed in 1953.

Under 1953 amendments to the Danish Constitution, Greenland became part of Denmark, with two representatives in the Danish Folketing. On May 1, 1979, Greenland gained home rule, with its own local parliament (Landsting), replacing the Greenland Provincial Council.

In February 1982, Greenlanders voted to withdraw from the European Community, which they had joined as part of Denmark in 1973. Danish Premier Anker Jørgensen said he would support the request, but with reluctance.

An election in early March 1991 gave the Siumut Party 11 of the 27 available seats. The early election was called after a scandal allegedly involving overspending by government officials on entertainment.

DJIBOUTI

Republic of Djibouti
President: Hassan Gouled Aptidon (1977)
Prime Minister: Barkat Gourad Hamadou (1978)
Area: 8,490 sq mi. (22,000 sq km)
Population (est. mid-1995): 600,000 (average annual rate of natural increase: 2.2%); birth rate: 38/1000; infant mortality rate: 115/1000; density per square mile: 71
Capital (1992 est.): Djibouti, 395,000; **Monetary unit:** Djibouti franc; **Languages:** Arabic, French, Afar, Somali; **Religions:** Muslim, 94%; Christian, 6%; **National name:** Jumhouriyya Djibouti; **Literacy rate:** 48%
Economic summary: Gross domestic product (1993 est.): $500 million, $1,200 per capita; real growth rate –1% (1992 est.); inflation 6% (1992); unemployment over 30% (1989). Arable land: 2%; principal agricultural products: goats, sheep, camels. Labor force: NA. Industries: small-scale enterprises such as dairy products and mineral- water bottling. Exports: $158 million (f.o.b., est. 1992): hides, skins, coffee (in transit from Ethiopia). Imports: $334 million (f.o.b., 1992 est.): petroleum, transport equipment, foodstuffs. Major trading partners: Middle East, Africa, Europe, Bahrain, Asia.

Geography. Djibouti lies in northeastern Africa on the Gulf of Aden at the southern entrance to the Red Sea. It borders on Ethiopia and Somalia. The country, the size of Massachusetts, is mainly a stony desert, with scattered plateaus and highlands.

Government. On May 8, 1977, the population of the French Territory of the Afars and Issas voted by more than 98% for independence. Voters also approved a 65-member interim Constituent Assembly. France transferred sovereignty to the new nation of Djibouti on June 27. Later in the year it became a member of the Organization of African Unity and the Arab League.

History. The territory that is now Djibouti was acquired by France between 1843 and 1886 by treaties with the Somali sultans. Small, arid, and sparsely populated, Djibouti is important chiefly because of the capital city's port, the terminal of the Djibouti-Addis Ababa railway that carries 60% of Ethiopia's foreign trade.

Originally known as French Somaliland, the colony voted in 1958 and 1967 to remain under French rule. It was renamed the Territory of the Afars and Issas in 1967 and took the name of its capital city on attaining independence.

The two principal opposition groups in exile banded to form a common front in early 1990.

A referendum in 1992 approved a new constitution permitting a multiparty system.

The President won the May 1993 election against four opponents in an election criticized for irregularities.

Feuding within the major rebel opposition led to the naming of a new leader in 1994. The group began negotiations with the government to end the civil war although suspicions persist among all parties.

DOMINICA

Commonwealth of Dominica
President: Crispin Sorhaindo (1993)
Prime Minister: Edison James (1995)
Area: 290 sq mi. (751 sq km)
Population: (est. mid-1995): 100,000 (average annual rate of natural increase: 1.3%); birth rate: 20/1000; infant mortality rate: 18.4/1000; density per square mile: 344.8
Capital and largest city (1991): Roseau, 15,853; **Monetary unit:** East Caribbean dollar; **Languages:** English and French patois; **Religions:** Roman Catholic, 77%; Protestant, 15%; **Member of Commonwealth of Nations; Literacy rate:** 94%
Economic summary: Gross domestic product (1992 est.): $185 million, per capita $2,100; real growth rate 2.6%; inflation 5.2%; unemployment 15%. Arable land: 9%. Principal products: bananas, citrus fruits, coconuts, plantains. Labor force: 30,600 (1989); 32% in industry and commerce. Major industries: agricultural processing; tourism. Exports: $54.6 million (1992): bananas, coconuts, soap, vegetables, grapefruit, oranges. Imports: 97.5 million (1992): manufactured goods, machinery and equipment, food, chemicals. Major trading partners: U.K., Caribbean countries, U.S., Italy, Canada.

Geography. Dominica is an island of the Lesser Antilles in the Caribbean south of Guadeloupe and north of Martinique.

Government. Dominica is a republic, with a president elected by the House of Assembly as head of state and a prime minister appointed by the president on the advice of the Assembly. The United Workers Party (11 of 21 seats in the Assembly) is led by Prime Minister Edison James. The Freedom Party holds five seats and the United Dominican Labor Party holds five seats.

History. Visited by Columbus in 1493, Dominica was claimed by Britain and France until 1815, when Britain asserted sovereignty. Dominica, along with other Windward Isles, became a self-governing member of the West Indies Associated States in free association with Britain in 1967.

Dissatisfaction over the slow pace of reconstruction after Hurricane David struck the island in September 1979 brought a landslide victory for the Freedom Party in July 1980. The vote gave the prime ministership to Mary Eugenia Charles, a strong advocate of free enterprise. The Freedom Party won again in 1985 elections, giving Miss Charles a second five-year term as prime minister. She and her party won a third term in elections on May 28, 1990, though with a greatly reduced mandate.

The government in 1993 pursued its policy of divesting itself of state enterprises.

A major demonstration by public transportation operators in April 1994 caused the government to declare a state of emergency and a curfew. The emergency was lifted a month later.

DOMINICAN REPUBLIC

President: Joaquin Balaguer (1986)
Vice President: Jacinto Peynado
Area: 18,704 sq mi. (48,442 sq km)
Population (est. mid-1995): 7,800,000 (average annual rate of natural increase: 2.1%); birth rate: 27/1000; infant mortality rate: 42/1000; density per square mile: 417
Capital: Santo Domingo; **Largest cities (1990):** Santo Domingo, 2,200,000; Santiago de los Caballeros, 500,000; **Monetary unit:** Peso; **Language:** Spanish, English widely spoken; **Religion:** 90% Roman Catholic; **National name:** República Dominicana; **Literacy rate:** 83%
Economic summary: Gross domestic product (est. 1993): $23 billion, $3,000 per capita, 3% real growth rate; inflation rate 8%; unemployment rate: 30%. Arable land: 23%. Principal agricultural products: sugar cane, coffee, cocoa, tobacco, beef, fruit and vegetables. Agriculture accounts for 15% of GDP and 49% of labor force. Labor force (1986): 2,300,000–2,600,000; 18% in industry. Major industries: tourism, sugar processing, ferronickel and gold mining, textiles, cement, tobacco. Natural resources: nickel, bauxite, gold, silver. Exports: $769 million (f.o.b., 1993): sugar, coffee, cocoa, gold, ferronickel. Imports: $2.2 billion (c.i.f., 1993 est.): foodstuffs, petroleum, cotton and fabrics, chemicals, and pharmaceuticals. Major trading partners: U.S., including Puerto Rico, E.U.

Geography. The Dominican Republic in the West Indies, occupies the eastern two thirds of the island of Hispaniola, which it shares with Haiti. Its area equals that of Vermont and New Hampshire combined.

Crossed from northwest to southeast by a mountain range with elevations exceeding 10,000 feet (3,048 m), the country has fertile, well-watered land in the north and east, where nearly two thirds of the population lives. The southwest part is arid and has poor soil, except around Santo Domingo.

Government. The president is elected by direct vote every four years. Legislative powers rest with a Senate and a Chamber of Deputies, both elected by direct vote, also for four years. All citizens must vote when they reach 18 years of age, or even earlier if they are married.

History. The Dominican Republic was discovered by Columbus in 1492. He named it La Española, and his son, Diego, was its first viceroy. The capital, Santo Domingo, founded in 1496, is the oldest European settlement in the Western Hemisphere. Spain ceded the colony to France in 1795, and Haitian blacks under Toussaint L'Ouverture conquered it in 1801.

In 1808 the people revolted and the next year captured Santo Domingo, setting up the first republic. Spain regained title to the colony in 1814. In 1821 the people overthrew Spanish rule, but in 1822 they were reconquered by the Haitians. They revolted again in 1844, threw out the Haitians, and established the Dominican Republic, headed by Pedro Santana. Uprisings and Haitian attacks led Santana to make the country a province of Spain from 1861 to 1865. The U.S. Senate refused to ratify a treaty of annexation. Disorder continued until the dictatorship of Ulíses Heureaux; in 1916, when disorder broke out again, the U.S. sent in a contingent of marines, who remained until 1934.

A sergeant in the Dominican army trained by the marines, Rafaél Leonides Trujillo Molina, overthrew Horacio Vásquez in 1930 and established a dictatorship that lasted until his assassination 31 years later.

Leftists rebelled April 24, 1965, and President Lyndon Johnson sent in marines and troops. After an OAS ceasefire request May 6, a compromise installed Hector Garcia-Godoy as provisional president. Joaquin Balaguer won in free elections in 1966 against Bosch, and a peacekeeping force of 9,000 U.S. troops and 2,000 from other countries withdrew. Balaguer restored political and economic stability.

In 1978, the army suspended the counting of ballots when Balaguer trailed in a fourth-term bid. After a warning from President Jimmy Carter, however, Balaguer accepted the victory of Antonio Guzmán of the opposition Dominican Revolutionary Party.

Salvador Jorge Blanco of the Dominican Revolutionary Party was elected President on May 16, 1982, defeating Balaguer and Bosch. Austerity measures imposed by the International Monetary Fund, including sharply higher prices for food and gasoline, provoked rioting in the spring of 1984 that left more than 50 dead.

Saying he feared they would provoke "some kind of revolution," Blanco dragged his feet about putting into effect further IMF demands for higher prices and taxes and devaluation of the peso, and came within weeks of defaulting on several big loans.

Balaguer was elected President in May 1986 and aimed economic policy at diversifying the economy.

In a bitter presidential contest Mr. Balaguer maintained a slim lead over his opponent in the May 1994 election before election officials stopped releasing tallies. The opposition charged widespread fraud. Eventually the crisis eased when a constitutional amendment gave the current president a two-year term with new elections scheduled for May 1996.

ECUADOR

Republic of Ecuador
President: Sixto Durán Ballén (1992)
Area: 106,822[1] sq mi. (276,670 sq km)
Population (est. mid-1995): 11,460,117 (average annual rate of natural increase: 2.19%); birth rate: 31/1000; infant mortality rate: 53/1000; density per square mile: 107
Capital: Quito; **Largest cities (1992):** Guayaquil, 1,475,118; Quito, 1,094,318; Cuenca, 195,738. **Monetary unit:** Sucre. **Languages:** Spanish (by 90% of population), Quéchua. **Religion:** Roman Catholic, 95%. **National name:** República del Ecuador. **Literacy rate:** 92%
Economic summary: Gross domestic product (1993, est.). $14.27 billion, per capita $1,407; real growth rate 3.9%; inflation 25.4%; unemployment 8%. Arable land: 6%; principal agricultural products: bananas, cocoa,

coffee, sugar cane, manioc, plantains, potatoes, rice. Labor force (1995 est.): 3,751,247; 21% in manufacturing; major industries: food processing, textiles, chemicals, fishing, timber, petroleum. Exports: $3.31 billion (f.o.b., 1994): petroleum, coffee, bananas, cocoa products, shrimp, fish products. Imports: $3.27 billion (f.o.b., 1994): transport equipment, vehicles, machinery, chemicals. Major trading partners: U.S., Latin America, EC, Caribbean, Japan.

1. Does not include area under dispute with Peru.

Geography. Ecuador, about equal in area to Nevada, is in the northwest part of South America fronting on the Pacific. To the north is Colombia and to the east and south is Peru. Two high and parallel ranges of the Andes, traversing the country from north to south, are topped by tall volcanic peaks. The highest is Chimborazo at 20,577 feet (6,272 m).

The Galápagos Islands (or Colón Archipelago) (3,029 sq mi.; 7,845 sq km), in the Pacific Ocean about 600 miles (966 km) west of the South American mainland, became part of Ecuador in 1832.

Government. A 1978 Constitution returned Ecuador to civilian government after eight years of military rule. The President is elected to a term of four years and a House of Representatives of 71 members is popularly elected for the same period.

History. The tribes in the northern highlands of Ecuador formed the Kingdom of Quito around A.D. 1000. It was absorbed, by conquest and marriage, into the Inca Empire. Pizarro conquered the land in 1532, and through the 17th century a thriving colony was built by exploitation of the Indians. The first revolt against Spain occurred in 1809. Ecuador then joined Venezuela, Colombia, and Panama in a confederacy known as Greater Colombia.

On the collapse of this union in 1830, Ecuador became independent. Subsequent history was one of revolts and dictatorships; it had 48 presidents during the first 131 years of the republic. Conservatives ruled until the Revolution of 1895 ushered in nearly a half century of Radical Liberal rule, during which the church was disestablished and freedom of worship, speech, and press was introduced.

In 1988, Rodrigo Borja was elected President. He was also able to form a coalition in the House, confirming a leftward shift in the government and promising smoother executive-legislative relations.

Blamed for econommic conditions the governing Social Democrats were defeated in elections of May 1992 by right-wing parties promising free-market reforms.

In the runoff presidential election of July 5, 1992 Sixto Duran Ballen captured 58% of the vote. A devaluation of the currency and the elimination of energy price subsidies led to a national strike in September.

Clashes flared in early 1995 with Peru over a disputed border. The arrival of international observers to monitor a ceasefire in February did not totally prevent an exchange of gunfire.

EGYPT

Arab Republic of Egypt
President: Hosni Mubarak (1981)
Premier: Dr. Atef Sedky (1986)
Area: 386,900 sq. mi. (1,002,000 sq km)
Population (est. mid-1995): 61,900,000 (average annual rate of natural increase: 2.3%); birth rate: 30/1000;

infant mortality rate: 62/1000; density per square mile: 159.9
Capital: Cairo; **Largest cities (est. 1990):** City of Cairo, 6,513,000; Greater Cairo, 12,560,000; Alexandria, 3,183,000; (est 1987): Giza, 1,670,800; Shubra el Khema, 533,300; El Mahalla el Kubra, 385,300; **Monetary unit:** Egyptian pound; **Language:** Arabic; **Religions:** Islam, 94%; Christian (mostly Coptic), 6%; **Literacy rate:** 50.2%

Economic summary: Gross domestic product (1994 est.): $42 billion; $800 per capita; 2.3% real growth rate; inflation rate 10%; unemployment rate: 13%. Arable land: 3%. Principal agricultural products: cotton, wheat, rice, corn, beans. Labor force: 15,000,000; 20% in privately owned services and manufacturing. Major industries: textiles, food processing, tourism, chemicals, petroleum, construction, cement, metals. Natural resources: crude oil, natural gas, iron ore, phosphates, manganese, limestone, gypsum, talc, asbestos, lead, zinc. Exports: $5.5 billion (f.o.b., 1994 est.): cotton, petroleum, yarn, textiles, metal products, chemicals. Imports: $12 billion (c.i.f., 1994 est.): foodstuffs, machinery, fertilizers, woods, durable consumer goods, capital goods. Major trading partners: U.S., Western Europe, Japan, Eastern Europe.

Geography. Egypt, at the northeast corner of Africa on the Mediterranean Sea, is bordered on the west by Libya, on the south by the Sudan, and on the east by the Red Sea and Israel. It is nearly one and one half times the size of Texas.

The historic Nile flows through the eastern third of the country. On either side of the Nile valley are desert plateaus, spotted with oases. In the north, toward the Mediterranean, plateaus are low, while south of Cairo they rise to a maximum of 1,015 feet (309 m) above sea level. At the head of the Red Sea is the Sinai Peninsula, between the Suez Canal and Israel.

Navigable throughout its course in Egypt, the Nile is used largely as a means of cheap transport for heavy goods. The irrigation of the land depends mainly on the Nile water. The Nile is one of the famous tourist spots in the country. The principal ports are Alexandria, Port Said and Damietta.

The Nile delta starts 100 miles (161 km) south of the Mediterranean and fans out to a sea front of 155 miles between the cities of Alexandria and Port Said. From Cairo north, the Nile branches into many streams, the principal ones being the Damietta and the Rosetta.

Except for a narrow belt along the Mediterranean, Egypt lies in an almost rainless area, in which high daytime temperatures fall quickly at night.

Government. Executive power is held by the President, who is elected every six years and can appoint one or more Vice Presidents.

The National Democratic Party, led by President Hosni Mubarak, is the dominant political party. Elections on Nov. 1990 confirmed its huge majority. There are also 14 opposition parties and some independents in the parliament—there are a total of 14 parties actively engaged in the political process.

History. Egyptian history dates back to about 4000 B.C., when the kingdoms of upper and lower Egypt, already highly civilized, were united. Egypt's "Golden Age" coincided with the 18th and 19th dynasties (16th to 13th centuries B.C.), during which the empire was established. Persia conquered Egypt in 525 B.C.; Alexander the Great subdued it in 332 B.C.; and then the dynasty of the Ptolemies ruled the land until 30 B.C., when Cleopatra, last of the line, committed suicide and Egypt became a Roman province. From 641 to 1517 the Arab caliphs ruled Egypt, and then the Turks took it for their Ottoman Empire.

Napoleon's armies occupied the country from 1798 to 1801. In 1805, Mohammed Ali, leader of a band of Albanian soldiers, became Pasha of Egypt. After completion of the Suez Canal in 1869, the French and British took increasing interest in Egypt.

British troops occupied Egypt in 1882, and British resident agents became its actual administrators, though it remained under nominal Turkish sovereignty. In 1914, this fiction was ended, and Egypt became a protectorate of Britain.

Egyptian nationalism forced Britain to declare Egypt an independent, sovereign state on Feb. 28, 1922, although the British reserved rights for the protection of the Suez Canal and the defense of Egypt. In 1936, by an Anglo-Egyptian treaty of alliance, all British troops and officials were to be withdrawn, except from the Suez Canal Zone. When World War II started, Egypt remained neutral. British imperial troops finally ended the Nazi threat to Suez in 1942 in the battle of El Alamein, west of Alexandria.

In 1951, Egypt abrogated the 1936 treaty and the 1899 Anglo-Egyptian condominium of the Sudan (*See* Sudan). Rioting and attacks on British troops in the Suez Canal Zone followed, reaching a climax in January 1952. The army, led by Gen. Mohammed Naguib, seized power on July 23, 1952. Three days later, King Farouk abdicated in favor of his infant son. The monarchy was abolished and a republic proclaimed on June 18, 1953, with Naguib holding the posts of Provisional President and Premier. He relinquished the latter in 1954 to Gamal Abdel Nasser, leader of the ruling military junta. Naguib was deposed seven months later and Nasser confirmed as President in a referendum on June 23, 1956.

Nasser's policies embroiled his country in continual conflict. In 1956, the U.S. and Britain withdrew their pledges of financial aid for the building of the Aswan High Dam. In reply, Nasser nationalized the Suez Canal and expelled British oil and embassy officials. Israel, barred from the Canal and exasperated by terrorist raids, invaded the Gaza Strip and the Sinai Peninsula. Britain and France, after demanding Egyptian evacuation of the Canal Zone, attacked Egypt on Oct. 31, 1956. Worldwide pressure forced Britain, France, and Israel to halt the hostilities. A U.N. emergency force occupied the Canal Zone, and all troops were evacuated in the spring of 1957.

On June 5, 1967, Israel invaded the Sinai Peninsula, the East Bank of the Jordan River, and the zone around the Gulf of Aqaba. A U.N. ceasefire on June 10 saved the Arabs from complete rout.

Nasser declared the 1967 cease-fire void along the Canal in April 1969 and began a war of attrition. The U.S. peace plan of June 19, 1971, resulted in Egypt's agreement to reinstate the cease-fire for at least three months, (from August) and to accept Israel's existence within "recognized and secure" frontiers that might emerge from U.N.-mediated talks. In return, Israel accepted the principle of withdrawing from occupied territories.

Then, on Sept. 28, 1970, Nasser died, at 52, of a heart attack. The new President was Anwar el-Sadat, an associate of Nasser and a former newspaper editor.

In July 1972, Sadat ordered the expulsion of Soviet "advisors and experts" from Egypt because the Russians had not provided the sophisticated weapons he felt were needed to retake territory lost to Israel in 1967.

The fourth Arab-Israeli war broke out Oct. 6, 1973, while Israelis were commemorating Yom Kippur, the Jewish high holy day. Egypt swept deep into the Sinai, while Syria strove to throw Israel off the Golan Heights.

A U.N.-sponsored truce was accepted on October 22. In January 1974, both sides agreed to a settlement negotiated by U.S. Secretary of State Henry A. Kissinger that gave Egypt a narrow strip along the entire Sinai bank of the Suez Canal. In June, President Nixon made the first visit by a U.S. President to Egypt and full diplomatic relations were established. The Suez Canal was cleared and reopened on June 5, 1975.

In the most audacious act of his career, Sadat flew to Jerusalem at the invitation of Prime Minister Menachem Begin and pleaded before Israel's Knesset on Nov. 20, 1977, for a permanent peace settlement. The Arab world reacted with fury—only Morocco, Tunisia, Sudan, and Oman approved.

Egypt and Israel signed a formal peace treaty on March 26, 1979. The pact ended 30 years of war and established diplomatic and commercial relations.

Egyptian and Israeli officials met in the Sinai desert on April 26, 1979, to implement the peace treaty calling for the phased withdrawal of occupation forces from the peninsula. By mid-1980, two thirds of the Sinai was transferred, but progress here was not matched—the negotiation of Arab autonomy in the Gaza Strip and the West Bank.

Sadat halted further talks in August 1980 because of continued Israeli settlement of the West Bank. On October 6 1981, Sadat was assassinated by extremist Muslim soldiers at a parade in Cairo. Vice President Hosni Mubarak, a former Air Force chief of staff, was confirmed by the parliament as president the next day.

Although feared unrest in Egypt did not occur in the wake of the assassination, and Israel completed the return of the Sinai to Egyptian control on April 25, 1982, Mubarak was unable to revive the autonomy talks. Israel's invasion of Lebanon in June imposed a new strain on him, and brought a marked cooling in Egyptian-Israeli relations, but not a disavowal of the peace treaty.

While President Mubarak's stand during the Persian Gulf war won wide praise in the West, domestically this position proved far less popular. Nevertheless Egypt emerged with new clout and respect in the international community as evidenced by the election of the Deputy Prime Minister as secretary-general of the U.N., which further contributed to the country's international prestige.

A presidential referendum in October 1993 supported Mubarak's bid for a third term although only a third of the population registered to vote.

The government concentrated much of its time and attention in recent years combatting Islamic extremists. In June 1995 the president escaped an assassination attempt by radicals during a vist to Ethiopia.

Suez Canal. The Suez Canal, in Egyptian territory between the Arabian Desert and the Sinai Peninsula, is an artificial waterway about 100 miles (161 km) long between Port Said on the Mediterranean and Suez on the Red Sea. Construction work, directed by the French engineer Ferdinand de Lesseps, was begun April 25, 1859, and the Canal was opened Nov. 17, 1869. The cost was 432,807,882 francs. The concession was held by an Egyptian joint stock company, *Compagnie Universelle du Canal Maritime de Suez,* in which the British government held 353,504 out of a total of 800,000 shares. The concession was to expire Nov. 17, 1968, but the company was nationalized July 26, 1956, by unilateral action of the Egyptian government.

The Canal was closed in June 1967 after the Arab-Israeli conflict. With the help of the U.S. Navy, work was begun on clearing the Canal in 1974, after the cease-fire ending the Arab-Israeli war. It was reopened to traffic June 5, 1975.

EL SALVADOR

Republic of El Salvador
President: Armando Calderón Sol (1994)
Area: 8,260 sq mi. (21,393 sq km)
Population (est. mid-1995): 5,900,000 (average annual rate of natural increase: 2.6%); birth rate: 32/1000; infant mortality rate: 41/1000; density per square mile: 714.2
Capital and largest city (1993 est.): San Salvador, 972,810; **Other large cities (est. 1993):** Santa Ana, 208,322; San Miguel, 161,156; Zacatecoluca, 81,035.
Monetary unit: Colón; **Language:** Spanish; **Religion:** Roman Catholic; **National name:** República de El Salvador; **Literacy rate:** 73%
Economic summary: Gross domestic product (1993 est..): $14.2 billion; $2,500 est. per capita; real growth rate 5%; inflation 12%; unemployment 6.7%. Arable land: 27%. Principal agricultural products: coffee, cotton, corn, sugar, rice, sorghum. Labor force: 1.7 million (1992 est.); 40% in agriculture. Major industrial products: processed foods, clothing and textiles, petroleum products. Natural resources: hydro- and geothermal power, crude oil. Exports: $730 million (f.o.b. 1993): coffee, cotton, sugar, shrimp. Imports: $1.9 billion (c.i.f., 1993): raw materials, consumer goods, capital goods. Major trading partners: U.S., Guatemala, Japan, Germany, Mexico, Venezuela, Costa Rica.

Geography. Situated on the Pacific coast of Central America, El Salvador has Guatemala to the west and Honduras to the north and east. It is the smallest of the Central American countries, its area equal to that of Massachusetts, and the only one without an Atlantic coastline.

Most of the country is a fertile volcanic plateau about 2,000 feet (607 m) high. There are some active volcanoes and many scenic crater lakes.

Government. The President is elected for a nonrenewable, five-year term, and legislative power is in a unicameral 84-member National Assembly elected by universal suffrage and proportional representation.

History. Pedro de Alvarado, a lieutenant of Cortés, conquered El Salvador in 1525. El Salvador, with the other countries of Central America, declared its independence from Spain on Sept. 15, 1821, and was part of a federation of Central American states until that union was dissolved in 1838. Its independent career for decades thereafter was marked by numerous revolutions and wars against other Central American republics.

On Oct. 15, 1979, a junta deposed the President, Gen. Carlos Humberto Romero, seeking to halt increasingly violent clashes between leftist and rightist forces.

On Dec. 4, 1980, three American nuns and an American lay worker were killed in an ambush near San Salvador, causing the Carter Administration to suspend all aid pending an investigation. The naming of José Napoleón Duarte, a moderate civilian, as head of the governing junta brought a resumption of U.S. aid.

In an election closely monitored by American and other foreign observers, Duarte was elected President in May 1984.

Duarte's Christian Democratic Party scored an unexpected electoral triumph in national legislative and municipal elections held in March 1985, a winning majority in the new National Assembly. The rightist parties that had been dominant in the previous Constituent Assembly demanded that the vote be nullified, but the army high command rejected their assertion that the voting had been fraudulent.

At the same time, U.S. officials said that while the rebels still were far from being defeated, there had been marked improvement in the effectiveness of government troops in the civil war against anti-government guerrillas that has been waged mainly in the countryside. Talks with the rebels broke down in September 1986. Duarte's inability to find solutions led to the rightwing ARENA party controlling half the seats in the National Assembly, in the elections of March 1988. The decisive victory of Alfredo Cristiani, the ARENA candidate for president, gives the right-wing party effective control of the country, given their political control of most of the municipalities.

On January 16, 1992 the government signed a peace treaty with the guerrilla forces formally ending a 12-year civil war that had claimed 75,000 lives.

The candidate of the right-wing Arena party, Calderón Sol won the presidential election of March 1994 on a pledge to continue the peace process. Although the left-wing alliance won 21 seats in the Assembly, its elected deputies almost immediately began feuding in the legislature.

EQUATORIAL GUINEA

Republic of Equatorial Guinea
President: Col. Teodoro Obiang Nguema Mbasogo (1979)
Prime Minister: Don Silvestre Siale Bileka (1992)
Area: 10,830 sq mi. (28,051 sq km)
Population (est. mid-1995): 400,000 (average annual rate of natural increase: 2.6%); birth rate: 40/1000; infant mortality rate: 99/1000; density per square mile: 36.9
Capital and largest city (1983): Malabo, 30,418; **Monetary unit:** CFA Franc; **Languages:** Spanish (official), pidgin English, Fang, Bubi, Creole; **Religions:** Roman Catholic, Protestant, traditional; **National name:** República de Guinea Ecuatorial; **Literacy rate:** 50%
Economic summary: Gross domestic product (1993 est.): $280 million; $700 per capita; n.a. real growth rate; inflation: 1.6% (1992 est.); unemployment: n.a. Arable land: 8%. Principal products: cocoa, wood, coffee, rice, yams. Natural resources: wood, crude oil. Exports: $52.8 million (f.o.b., 1992): cocoa, wood, coffee. Imports: $63.6 million (c.i.f., 1992): petroleum, foodstuffs, textiles, machinery. Major trading partners: Spain, France, Nigeria, Cameroon, U.S.

Geography. Equatorial Guinea, formerly Spanish Guinea, consists of Rio Muni (10,045 sq mi.; 26,117 sq km), on the western coast of Africa, and several islands in the Gulf of Guinea, the largest of which is Bioko (formerly Fernando Po) (785 sq mi.; 2,033 sq km). The other islands are Annobón, Corisco, Elobey Grande, and Elobey Chico. The total area is twice that of Connecticut.

Government. A president with an 80-member House of Representatives exercises power.

History. Fernando Po and Annobón came under Spanish control in 1778. From 1827 to 1844, with Spanish consent, Britain administered Fernando Po, but in the latter year Spain reclaimed the island. Río Muni was given to Spain in 1885 by the Treaty of Berlin.

Negotiations with Spain led to independence on Oct. 12, 1968.

In 1969, anti-Spanish incidents in Río Muni, including the tearing down of a Spanish flag by national troops, caused 5,000 Spanish residents to flee for their safety, and diplomatic relations between the two nations became strained. A month later, President

Masie Nguema Biyogo Negue Ndong charged that a coup had been attempted against him. He seized dictatorial powers and arrested 80 opposition politicians and even several of his Cabinet ministers and the secretary of the National Assembly.

A coup on Aug. 3, 1979, deposed Masie, and a junta led by Lieut. Col. Teodoro Obiang Nguema Mbasogo took over the government. Obiang expelled Soviet technicians and reinstated cooperation with Spain.

In January 1992 the president established a transitional government toward a supposedly multiparty system.

After delays the legislative elections of November 1993 resulted in an easy win for the governing party although turnout was low and opposition parties boycotted the process.

ERITREA

President: Isaias Afwerki (1993)
Area: 45,754 sq mi. (123,300 sq km)
Population (est. mid-1995): 3,500,000 (of which 0.75 million are refugees awaiting repatriation). Average annual rate of natural increase: 2.6%; birth rate: 42/1000; infant mortality rate: —/1000; density per square mile: 76.4.
Capital and largest city (1993): Asmara, 400,000. Other major cities: the ports of Massawa and Assab; **Monetary unit:** Birr. **Languages:** Afar, Bilen, Kunama, Nara, Arabic, Tobedawi, Saho, Tigre, Tigrinya. **Religions:** Islam and Eritrean Orthodox Christianity. **Literacy rate:** 20%.
Economic summary: Gross domestic product (1993 est.): $1.7 billion; $500 per capita. The economy and infrastructure were severely damaged by the long war for independence and natural disasters. Eritrea has inherited the entire coastline of Ethiopia and has long-term prospects for revenues from the development of offshore oil, offshore fishing, and tourism. Major manufacturing industries are textiles, leather, food products, beverages. Most Eritreans are employed in agriculture and important crops are cotton, wheat, and coffee. Major mineral resources are salt and copper. Major trading partners: Ethiopia, Saudi Arabia, Yemen, Italy, Germany, U.K.

Geography. Eritrea was formerly the northernmost province of Ethiopia and is about the size of Indiana. Much of the country is mountainous. Its narrow Red Sea coastal plain is one of the hottest and driest places in Africa. The cooler central highlands have fertile valleys that support agriculture. Eritrea is bordered by the Sudan on the north and west, the Red Sea on the north and east, and Ethiopia and Djibouti on the south.

Government. A transitional government committed to a democratic system.

History. Eritrea was part of the first Ethiopian kingdom of Askum until its decline in the 8th century A.D. It came under control of the Ottoman Empire in the 16th century, and later the Egyptians. The Italians captured the coastal areas in 1885, and the Treaty of Uccialli (May 2, 1889) gave Italy sovereignty over part of Eritrea. The Italians named their colony after the Roman name for the Red Sea—*Mare Erythraeum*—and ruled it up until World War II.

The British captured Eritrea in 1941 and later administered it as a U.N. Trust Territory until it became federated with Ethiopia on Sept. 15, 1952. It was made an Ethiopian province on Nov. 14, 1962.

A civil war broke out against the Ethiopian government led by rebel groups who opposed the union and

wanted independence for Eritrea. The bitter conflict raged on for 17 years against the hard-line communist regime of the Ethiopian dictator, Mengistu Haile Mariam until he was overthrown in May 1991.

The Eritrean People's Liberation Front (EPLF) took control of Eritrea and shared power in a multi-party government in Addis Ababa with the Ethiopian People's Revolutionary Democratic Front (EPRDF). They agreed to hold a referendum on Eritrean independence within two years and on April 23–25, 1993, Eritrean voters almost unanimously opted for an independent republic. Ethiopia recognized Eritrea's sovereignty on May 3, 1993, and sought a new era of cooperation between the two countries.

Soon relations with Sudan deteriorated as the government accused the latter of infiltrating Islamic radicals into the country. In December 1994 Eritrea broke off diplomatic relations.

ESTONIA

Republic of Estonia
President: Lennart Meri (1992)
Prime Minister: Tiit Vahi (1995)
Area: 18,370 sq mi. (47,549 sq km)
Population: (est. mid-1995): 1,500,000 (average annual rate of natural increase: –0.5%); (Estonians, 61.5%; Russians, 30.3%; Ukrainians, 3.1%; Byelorussians, 1.8%; Finns, 1.1%); birth rate: 9/1000; infant mortality rate: 16/1000; density per square mile: 81.6
Capital and largest city (1992 est.): Tallinn, 471,608. Other large city (1992 est.): Tartu, 113,400. **Monetary unit:** Kroon; **Languages:** Estonian (official), Latvian, Lithuanian, Russian, other. **Religions (1937):** Lutheran, 78%; Orthodox, 19%; **National name:** Eesti; **Literacy:** (n.a., there was a 100% literacy rate before the Soviet occupation). **Literacy rate:** 100%
Economic summary: Gross national product (1993, UN, World Bank est.): $8.8 billion; $5,480 per capita; real growth rate: –5%; Inflation: 2.6% avg. Unemployment (March 93): 3%. Labor force (1993): 681,000, manufacturing, 154,000; agriculture, 76,000; trade and catering, 59,000; construction, 36,000; finance and business services, 28,900. The Estonian government has pursued a program of market reforms and rough stabilization measures, which is rapidly transforming the economy. There is low inflation, living standards are rising, and the private sector is growing rapidly. Exports: $800 million (1993): animals, animal products, food, beverages, tobacco, textiles and textile products, machinery and electrical equipment, vehicles, base metals. Imports $944 million (1993): food, beverages, tobacco, mineral products, textiles, textile products, machinery, electrical equipment, vehicles. Major trading partners: Russia and other former Soviet republics, Finland, the West.

Geography. Estonia borders on the Baltic Sea in the west, the gulfs of Riga and Finland in the southwest and north, respectively, Latvia in the south, and Russia in the east. It is mainly a lowland country with numerous lakes. Lake Peipus is the largest and is important to the fishing and shipping industries.

Government. Parliamentary democracy.

History. Born out of World War I, this small Baltic state enjoyed a mere two short decades of independence before it was absorbed again by its powerful neighbor, Russia. In the 13th century, the Estonians had been conquered by the Teutonic Knights of Germany, who reduced them to serfdom. In 1526, the Swedes took over, and the power of the German (Balt) landowning class was curbed somewhat. But after 1721, when Russia succeeded Sweden as the ruling power, the Estonians were subjected to a double bondage—the Balts and the tsarist officials. The oppression lasted until the closing months of World War I, when Estonia finally achieved independence after a victorious War of Independence (1918–20).

Shortly after the start of World War II, the nation was occupied by Russian troops and was incorporated as the 16th republic of the U.S.S.R. in 1940. Germany occupied the nation from 1941 to 1944, when it was retaken by the Russians.

Soon after Lithuania's declaration of independence from the Soviet Union in March 1990, the Estonian congress renamed its country on May 8 and omitted the words "Soviet Socialist" and adopted the former (1918) Coat of Arms of the Republic of Estonia. Thereafter, the government cautiously promoted national autonomy.

After the attempted Soviet coup to remove President Gorbachev failed, Estonia formally declared its independence from the U.S.S.R. on August 20, 1991. Recognition by European and other countries followed. The Soviet Union recognized Estonia's independence on September 6 and it received UN membership on Sept. 17, 1991.

March 1995 elections gave 41 of the 101 seats in parliament to two left-leaning parties. The leader of the winning alliance, however, ran on a program embracing free-market reforms. A russophone coalition entered parliament with six seats.

ETHIOPIA

Transitional Government of Ethiopia
President: Meles Zenawi (1991)
Prime Minister: Tamirat Laynie (1991)
Area: 446,952 sq mi. (1,157,585 sq km)
Population (est. mid-1995): 56,000,000 (average annual rate of natural increase: 3.1%); birth rate: 46/1000; infant mortality rate: 120/1000; density per square mile: 125.2
Capital and largest city (1992): Addis Ababa, 3,000,000; **Monetary unit:** Birr; **Languages:** Amharic (official), English, Orominga, Tigrigna, over 70 languages spoken. **Religions:** Ethiopian Orthodox, 35–40%; Islam, 40–45%; animist, 15-20%; other, 5%; **Literacy rate:** 62%
Economic summary: Gross domestic product (1993 est.): $22.7 billion; $400 per capita; real growth rate 7.8%; inflation (1992 est.): 21%. Arable land: 12%. Principal agricultural products: coffee, barley, wheat, corn, sugar cane, cotton, oilseeds, livestock. Major industrial products: cement, textiles, processed foods, refined oil. Natural resources: potash, gold, platinum, copper. Exports: $189 million (f.o.b., FY91): coffee, leather products, gold, petroleum products. Imports: $472 million (c.i.f., FY91): machinery and equipment, industrial inputs, pharmaceuticals, chemicals. Major trading partners: Japan, U.S., Djibouti, Saudi Arabia, Germany, Italy, France.

Geography. Ethiopia is in east central Africa, bordered on the west by the Sudan, the east by Somalia and Djibouti, the south by Kenya, and northeast by Eritrea. It is nearly three times the size of California. Over its main plateau land, Ethiopia has several high mountains, the highest of which is Ras Dashan at 15,158 feet (4,620 m). The Blue Nile, or Abbai, rises in the northwest and flows in a great semicircle east, south, and northwest before entering the Sudan. Its chief reservoir, Lake Tana, lies in the northwestern part of the plateau.

Government. A constitution was written and submitted to a constituent assembly elected in June 1994. The new Parliament has 548 seats. Elections were held in May 1995, and the governing coalition the Ethiopian People's Revolutionary Democratic Party (EPRDF) won a new five-year term.

History. Black Africa's oldest state, Ethiopia can trace 2,000 years of recorded history. Its now deposed royal line claimed descent from King Menelik I, traditionally believed to have been the son of the Queen of Sheba and King Solomon. The present nation is a consolidation of smaller kingdoms that owed feudal allegiance to the Ethiopian Emperor.

Hamitic peoples migrated to Ethiopia from Asia Minor in prehistoric times. Semitic traders from Arabia penetrated the region in the 7th century B.C. Its Red Sea ports were important to the Roman and Byzantine Empires. Coptic Christianity came to the country in A.D. 341, and a variant of that communion became Ethiopia's state religion.

Ancient Ethiopia reached its peak in the 5th century, then was isolated by the rise of Islam and weakened by feudal wars. Modern Ethiopia emerged under Emperor Menelik II, who established its independence by routing an Italian invasion in 1896. He expanded Ethiopia by conquest.

Disorders that followed Menelik's death brought his daughter to the throne in 1917, with his cousin, Tafari Makonnen, as Regent, heir presumptive, and strongman. When the Empress died in 1930, Tafari was crowned Emperor Haile Selassie I.

As Regent, Haile Selassie outlawed slavery. As Emperor, he worked for centralization of his diffuse realm, in which 70 languages are spoken, and for moderate reform. In 1931, he granted a Constitution, revised in 1955, that created a parliament with an appointed Senate and an elected Chamber of Deputies, and a system of courts. But basic power remained with the Emperor.

Bent on colonial empire, fascist Italy invaded Ethiopia on Oct. 3, 1935, forcing Haile Selassie into exile in May 1936. Ethiopia was annexed to Eritrea, then an Italian colony, and Italian Somaliland to form Italian East Africa, losing its independence for the first time in recorded history. In 1941, British troops routed the Italians, and Haile Selassie returned to Addis Ababa.

In August 1974, the Armed Forces Committee nationalized Haile Selassie's palace and estates and directed him not to leave Addis Ababa. On Sept. 12, 1974, he was deposed after nearly 58 years as Regent and Emperor. The 82-year-old "Lion of Judah" was placed under guard. Parliament was dissolved, the Constitution suspended and Ethiopia was proclaimed a socialist state.

Lt. Col. Mengistu Haile Mariam was named head of state, Feb. 2, 1977, and when a communist regime was established on Sept. 10, 1984, Mengistu became party leader.

A cut-off of Soviet aid led to mass animosity, and a rebel offensive began in February 1991. Mengistu resigned and fled the country in May. A group called the Ethiopian People's Revolutionary Democratic Front seized the capital. Also in May a separatist guerrilla organization, the Eritrean People's Liberation Front, took control of the province of Eritrea.

The two groups agreed in early July that Eritrea would have an internationally supervised referendum on independence. This election took place in April 1993 with an almost unanimous support for Eritrean independence. Ethiopia accepted and recognized Eritrea as an independent state within a few days.

General elections in May 1995 gave the ruling coalition a landslide victory after a boycott by most opposition groups.

FIJI

Republic of Fiji
President: Ratu Sir Kamisese Mara (1994)
Prime Minister: Maj. Gen. Sitiveni Rabuka (1992)
Area: 7,078 sq mi. (18,333 sq km)
Population (est. mid-1995): 800,000 (average annual rate of natural increase: 2.0%); birth rate: 25/1000; infant mortality rate: 19/1000; density per square mile: 113
Capital (1986): Suva (on Viti Levu), 69,665; **Monetary unit:** Fiji dollar; **Languages:** Fijian, Hindustani, English (official); **Religions:** Christian, 52%; Hindu, 38%; Islam, 8%; other, 2%; **Literacy rate:** 86%
Economic summary: Gross domestic product (1993 est.): $3 billion; $4,000 per capita; real growth rate 1%; inflation rate 5.6%; unemployment rate (est. 1991): 5.9%. Arable land: 8%. Principal products: sugar, copra, rice, ginger. Labor force (1987): 235,000; 67% subsistence agriculture; 18% wage earners; salary earners, 15%. Major industrial products: refined sugar, gold, lumber. Natural resources: timber, fish, gold, copper. Exports: $417 million (f.o.b., 1992): sugar, copra, processed fish, lumber, gold, clothing. Imports: $517 million (c.i.f., 1992 est.): machinery and transport equipment, food, petroleum products, consumer goods, chemicals. Major trading partners: EU, Australia, Japan, U.S., New Zealand, Pacific islands.

Geography. Fiji consists of more than 330 islands in the southwestern Pacific Ocean about 1,960 miles (3,152 km) from Sydney, Australia. The two largest islands are Viti Levu (4,109 sq mi.; 10,642 sq km) and Vanua Levu (2,242 sq mi.; 5,807 sq km). The island of Rotuma (18 sq mi.; 47 sq km), about 400 miles (644 km) to the north, is a province of Fiji. Overall, Fiji is nearly as large as New Jersey.

The largest islands in the group are mountainous and volcanic, with the tallest peak being Mount Victoria (4,341 ft; 1,323 m) on Viti Levu. The islands in the south have dense forests on the windward side and grasslands on the leeward.

Government. Military coup leader Major General Sitiveni Rabuka formerly declared Fiji a republic on Oct. 6, 1987. The Sept. 23, 1988 constitution provided for a bicameral parliament consisting of a 342-member Senate and a 70-member House of Representatives.

The new constitution of July 1990 ensured ethnic Fijians a majority of seats in the parliament as well as the presidency, prime ministership and other central positions.

History. In 1874, an offer of cession by the Fijian chiefs was accepted, and Fiji was proclaimed a possession and dependency of the British Crown.

During World War II, the archipelago was an important air and naval station on the route from the U.S. and Hawaii to Australia and New Zealand.

Fiji became independent on Oct. 10, 1970. The next year it joined the five-island South Pacific Forum, which intends to become a permanent regional

group to promote collective diplomacy of the newly independent members.

In Oct., 1987, then Brig. Gen. Sitiveni Rabuka, the coup leader, declared Fiji a republic and removed it from the British Commonwealth.

In elections of May 1992 Rabuka, as leader of the Fijian Political Party, became prime minister.

Rabuka began his 2nd term in February 1994 after his party's victory in a general election that month. Rabuka's party won most of the seats allotted to ethnic Fijians.

FINLAND

Republic of Finland
President: Martti Ahtisaari (1994)
Premier: Paavo Lipponen (1995)
Area: 130,558 sq mi. (338,145 sq km)
Population (est. mid-1995): 5,100,000 (average annual rate of natural increase: 0.3%); birth rate: 13/1000; infant mortality rate: 4.4/1000; density per square mile: 39
Capital and largest city (1993 est.): Helsinki, 501,740; **Other large cities (est. 1993):** Tampere, 175,200; Turku, 160,320, Espoo, 178,900. **Monetary unit:** Markka; **Languages:** Finnish, Swedish; **Religions:** Evangelical Lutheran, 90%; Greek Orthodox, 1.2%; **National name:** Suomen Tasavalta—Republiken Finland; **Literacy rate:** 100%
Economic summary: Gross domestic product (1993): $81.1 billion; $16,100 per capita; 4% real growth rate (1994); inflation rate: 1.1% (1994); unemployment rate: 18.4% (1994). Arable land: 8.3%. Principal products: dairy and meat products, cereals, sugar beets, potatoes. Labor force: 2,470,000; 21% agriculture. Major products: metal manufactures, forestry and wood products, refined copper, ships, machinery, chemicals, clothing, footwear. Natural resource: timber. Exports: $23.4 billion (f.o.b., 1993): timber, paper and pulp, ships, machinery, clothing, footwear, chemicals. Imports: $18 billion (c.i.f., 1993 est.): petroleum and petroleum products, chemicals, transportation equipment, machinery, textile yarns, foodstuffs, fodder grain, iron and steel. Major trading partners: Germany, Sweden, U.K., U.S., France, Russia, Denmark, Norway, Netherlands.

Geography. Finland stretches 721 miles (1,160 km) south to north, Russia extends along the entire eastern frontier while Norway is on her northern border and Sweden lies on her western border. In area, Finland is three times the size of Ohio.

Off the southwest coast are the Aland Islands, controlling the entrance to the Gulf of Bothnia. Finland has more than 200,000 lakes.

The Swedish-populated Aland Islands (581 sq mi.; 1,505 sq km) have an autonomous status under a law passed in 1921.

Government. The president, chosen for six years by popular vote, appoints the Cabinet. The one-chamber Diet, the Eduskunta, consists of 200 members elected for four-year terms by proportional representation.

History. At the end of the 7th century, the Finns came to Finland from their Volga settlements, taking the country from the Lapps, who retreated northward. The Finns' repeated raids on the Scandinavian coast impelled Eric IX, the Swedish King, to conquer the country in 1157 and bring it into contact with Western Christendom. By 1809 the whole of Finland was conquered by Alexander I of Russia, who set up Finland as a Grand Duchy.

The first period of Russification (1809–1905) resulted in a lessening of the powers of the Finnish Diet. The Russian language was made official, and the Finnish military system was superseded by the Russian. The pace of Russification was intensified from 1908 to 1914. When Russian control was weakened as a consequence of the March Revolution of 1917, the Diet on July 20, 1917, proclaimed Finland's independence, which became complete on Dec. 6, 1917.

Finland rejected Soviet territorial demands, and the U.S.S.R. attacked on Nov. 30, 1939. The Finns made an amazing stand of three months and finally capitulated, ceding 16,000 square miles (41,440 sq km) to the U.S.S.R. Under German pressure, the Finns joined the Nazis against Russia in 1941, but were defeated again and ceded the Petsamo area to the U.S.S.R. In 1948, a 20-year treaty of friendship and mutual assistance was signed by the two nations and renewed for another 20 years in 1970.

Premier Mauno Koivisto, leader of the Social Democratic Party, was elected President on Jan. 26, 1982, winning decisively over a conservative rival with support from Finnish Communists.

Running on a platform calling to invigorate the economy Ahtisaari, a Social Democrat, won the country's first direct presidential election in a runoff of February 1994. Traditionally the president is concerned largely with foreign policy. Previously the president had been chosen by electors.

An advisory referendum held in October 1994 saw a clear majority support Finnish membership in the European Union.

FRANCE

French Republic
President: Jacques Chirac (1995)
Premier: Alaiy Juppé (1995)
Area: 212,918 sq mi. (547,026 sq km)
Population (est. mid-1995): 58,100,000 (average annual rate of natural increase: 0.3%); birth rate: 12/1000; infant mortality rate: 6.1/1000; density per square mile: 273
Capital: Paris; **Largest cities (1990):** Paris, 2,152,000 (10,650,600, Paris region); Marseilles, 801,000; Lyons, 415,000; Toulouse, 359,000; Nice, 342,000; Strasbourg, 252,000; Nantes, 245,000; Bordeaux, 201,000; **Monetary unit:** French Franc; **Language:** French, declining regional dialects; **Religion:** Roman Catholic, 81%; Protestant, 1.7%; Muslim, 5%; Jewish, 1.2%; **National name:** République Française; **Literacy rate:** 99%
Economic summary: Gross domestic product (1993): $1.05 trillion; $18,200 per capita; –0.7% real growth rate; inflation 2.1% (est.); unemployment (May '94) 12.2%. Arable land: 32%. Principal products: cereals, feed grains, livestock and dairy products, wine, fruits, vegetables, potatoes. Labor force (1987): 24,170,000: services 61.5%, industry 31.3%. Major products: chemicals, automobiles, processed foods, iron and steel, aircraft, textiles, clothing. Natural resources: coal, iron ore, bauxite, fish, forests. Exports: $270.5 billion (f.o.b., 1993): textiles and clothing, chemicals, machinery and transport equipment, agricultural products, foodstuffs. Imports: $250.2 billion (c.i.f., 1993): machinery, crude petroleum, chemicals, agricultural products, iron and steel products. Major trading partners: Germany, Italy, U.S., Belgium-Luxembourg, U.K., Netherlands, Spain, Japan.

Geography. France is about 80% the size of Texas. In the Alps near the Italian and Swiss borders is Europe's

highest point—Mont Blanc (15,781 ft; 4,810 m). The forest-covered Vosges Mountains are in the northeast, and the Pyrenees are along the Spanish border.

Except for extreme northern France, which is part of the Flanders plain, the country may be described as four river basins and a plateau. Three of the streams flow west—the Seine into the English Channel, the Loire into the Atlantic, and the Garonne into the Bay of Biscay. The Rhône flows south into the Mediterranean. For about 100 miles (161 km), the Rhine is France's eastern border.

West of the Rhône and northeast of the Garonne lies the central plateau, covering about 15% of France's area and rising to a maximum elevation of 6,188 feet (1,886 m). In the Mediterranean, about 115 miles (185 km) east-southeast of Nice, is Corsica (3,367 sq mi.; 8,721 sq km).

Government. The president is elected for seven years by universal suffrage. He appoints the premier, and the Cabinet is responsible to Parliament. The president has the right to dissolve the National Assembly or to ask Parliament for reconsideration of a law. The Parliament consists of two houses: the National Assembly and the Senate.

History. The history of France, as distinct from ancient Gaul, begins with the Treaty of Verdun (843), dividing the territories corresponding roughly to France, Germany, and Italy among the three grandsons of Charlemagne. Julius Caesar had conquered part of Gaul in 57–52 B.C., and it remained Roman until Franks invaded it in the 5th century.

Charles the Bald, inheritor of *Francia Occidentalis*, founded the Carolingian dynasty, which ruled over a kingdom increasingly feudalized. By 987, the crown passed to Hugh Capet, a princeling who controlled only the Ile-de-France, the region surrounding Paris. For 350 years, an unbroken Capetian line added to its domain and consolidated royal authority until the accession in 1328 of Philip VI, first of the Valois line. France was then the most powerful nation in Europe, with a population of 15 million.

The missing pieces in Philip's domain were the French provinces still held by the Plantagenet kings of England, who also claimed the French crown. Beginning in 1338, the Hundred Years' War eventually settled the contest. English longbows defeated French armored knights at Crécy (1346) and the English also won the second landmark battle at Agincourt (1415), but the final victory went to the French at Castillon (1453).

Absolute monarchy reached its apogee in the reign of Louis XIV (1643–1715), the Sun King, whose brilliant court was the center of the Western world.

Revolution plunged France into a blood bath beginning in 1789 and ending with a new authoritarianism under Napoleon Bonaparte, who had successfully defended the infant republic from foreign attack and then made himself First Consul in 1799 and Emperor in 1804.

The Congress of Vienna (1815) sought to restore the pre-Napoleonic order in the person of Louis XVIII, but industrialization and the middle class, both fostered under Napoleon, built pressure for change, and a revolution in 1848 drove Louis Philipe, last of the Bourbons, into exile.

A second republic elected as its president Prince Louis Napoleon, a nephew of Napoleon I, who declared the Second Empire in 1852 and took the throne as Napoleon III. His opposition to the rising power of Prussia ignited the Franco-Prussian War (1870–71), ending in his defeat and abdication.

Rulers of France

Name	Born	Ruled[1]
CAROLINGIAN DYNASTY		
Pepin the Short	c. 714	751–768
Charlemagne[2]	742	768–814
Louis I the Debonair[3]	778	814–840
Charles I the Bald[4]	823	840–877
Louis II the Stammerer	846	877–879
Louis III[5]	c. 863	879–882
Carloman[5]	?	879–884
Charles II the Fat[6]	839	884–887 [7]
Eudes (Odo), Count of Paris	?	888–898
Charles III the Simple[8]	879	893–923 [9]
Robert I[10]	c. 865	922–923
Rudolf (Raoul), Duke of Burgundy	?	923–936
Louis IV d'Outremer	c. 921	936–954
Lothair	941	954–986
Louis V the Sluggard	c. 967	986–987
CAPETIAN DYNASTY		
Hugh Capet	c. 940	987–996
Robert II the Pious[11]	c. 970	996–1031
Henry I	1008	1031–1060
Philip I	1052	1060–1108
Louis VI the Fat	1081	1108–1137
Louis VII the Young	c.1121	1137–1180
Philip II (Philip Augustus)	1165	1180–1223
Louis VIII the Lion	1187	1223–1226
Louis IX (St. Louis)	1214	1226–1270
Philip III the Bold	1245	1270–1285
Philip IV the Fair	1268	1285–1314
Louis X the Quarreler	1289	1314–1316
John I[12]	1316	1316
Philip V the Tall	1294	1316–1322
Charles IV the Fair	1294	1322–1328
HOUSE OF VALOIS		
Philip VI	1293	1328–1350
John II the Good	1319	1350–1364
Charles V the Wise	1337	1364–1380
Charles VI the Well–Beloved	1368	1380–1422
Charles VII	1403	1422–1461
Louis XI	1423	1461–1483
Charles VIII	1470	1483–1498
Louis XII the Father of the People	1462	1498–1515
Francis I	1494	1515–1547
Henry II	1519	1547–1559
Francis II	1544	1559–1560
Charles IX	1550	1560–1574
Henry III	1551	1574–1589
HOUSE OF BOURBON		
Henry IV of Navarre	1553	1589–1610
Louis XIII	1601	1610–1643
Louis XIV the Great	1638	1643–1715
Louis XV the Well–Beloved	1710	1715–1774
Louis XVI	1754	1774–1792 [13]
Louis XVII (Louis Charles de France)[14]	1785	1793–1795

Name	Born	Ruled[1]
FIRST REPUBLIC		
National Convention	—	1792–1795
Directory (Directoire)	—	1795–1799
CONSULATE		
Napoleon Bonaparte[15]	1769	1799–1804
FIRST EMPIRE		
Napoleon I	1769	1804–1815 [16]
RESTORATION OF HOUSE OF BOURBON		
Louis XVIII le Désiré	1755	1814–1824
Charles X	1757	1824–1830 [17]
BOURBON-ORLEANS LINE		
Louis Philippe ("Citizen King")	1773	1830–1848 [18]
SECOND REPUBLIC		
Louis Napoleon[19]	1808	1848–1852
SECOND EMPIRE		
Napoleon III (Louis Napoleon)	1808	1852–1870 [20]
THIRD REPUBLIC (PRESIDENTS)		
Louis Adolphe Thiers	1797	1871–1873
Marie E. P. M. de MacMahon	1808	1873–1879
François P. J. Grévy	1807	1879–1887
Sadi Carnot	1837	1887–1894
Jean Casimir–Périer	1847	1894–1895
François Félix Faure	1841	1895–1899
Émile Loubet	1838	1899–1906
Clement Armand Fallières	1841	1906–1913
Raymond Poincaré	1860	1913–1920
Paul E. L. Deschanel	1856	1920–1920
Alexandre Millerand	1859	1920–1924
Gaston Doumergue	1863	1924–1931
Paul Doumer	1857	1931–1932
Albert Lebrun	1871	1932–1940
VICHY GOVERNMENT (CHIEF OF STATE)		
Henri Philippe Pétain	1856	1940–1944
PROVISIONAL GOVERNMENT (PRESIDENTS)		
Charles de Gaulle	1890	1944–1946
Félix Gouin	1884	1946–1946
Georges Bidault	1899	1946–1947
FOURTH REPUBLIC (PRESIDENTS)		
Vincent Auriol	1884	1947–1954
René Coty	1882	1954–1959
FIFTH REPUBLIC (PRESIDENTS)		
Charles de Gaulle	1890	1959–1969
Georges Pompidou	1911	1969–1974
Valéry Giscard d'Estaing	1926	1974–1981
François Mitterrand	1916	1981–1995
Jacques Chirac		1995–

1. For Kings and Emperors through the Second Empire, year of end of rule is also that of death, unless otherwise indicated. 2. Crowned Emperor of the West in 800. His brother, Carloman, ruled as King of the Eastern Franks from 768 until his death in 771. 3. Holy Roman Emperor 814–840. 4. Holy Roman Emperor 875–877 as Charles II. 5. Ruled jointly 879–882. 6. Holy Roman Emperor 881–887 as Charles III. 7. Died 888. 8. King 893–898 in opposition to Eudes. 9. Died 929. 10. Not counted in regular line of Kings of France by some authorities. Elected by nobles but killed in Battle of Soissons. 11. Sometimes called Robert I. 12. Posthumous son of Louis X; lived for only five days. 13. Executed 1793. 14. Titular King only. He died in prison according to official reports, but many pretenders appeared during the Bourbon restoration. 15. As First Consul, Napoleon held the power of government. In 1804, he became Emperor. 16. Abdicated first time June 1814. Re-entered Paris March 1815, after escape from Elba; Louis XVIII fled to Ghent. Abdicated second time June 1815. He named as his successor his son, Napoleon II, who was not acceptable to the Allies. He died 1821. 17. Died 1836. 18. Died 1850. 19. President; became Emperor in 1852. 20. Died 1873.

A new France emerged from World War I as the continent's dominant power. But four years of hostile occupation had reduced northeast France to ruins. The postwar Third Republic was plagued by political instability and economic chaos.

From 1919, French foreign policy aimed at keeping Germany weak through a system of alliances, but it failed to halt the rise of Adolf Hitler and the Nazi war machine. On May 10, 1940, mechanized Nazi troops attacked, and, as they approached Paris, Italy joined with Germany. The Germans marched into an undefended Paris and Marshal Henri Philippe Pétain signed an armistice June 22. France was split into an occupied north and an unoccupied south, the latter becoming a totalitarian state with Pétain as its chief.

Allied armies liberated France in August 1944. The French Committee of National Liberation, formed in Algiers in 1943, established a provisional government in Paris headed by Gen. Charles de Gaulle. The Fourth Republic was born Dec. 24, 1946.

The Empire became the French Union; the National Assembly was strengthened and the presidency weakened; and France joined the North Atlantic Treaty Organization. A war against communist insurgents in Indochina was abandoned after the defeat at Dien Bien Phu. A new rebellion in Algeria threatened a military coup, and on June 1, 1958, the Assembly invited de Gaulle to return as premier with extraordinary powers. He drafted a new Constitution for a Fifth Republic, adopted Sept. 28, which strengthened the presidency and reduced legislative power. He was elected president Dec. 21.

De Gaulle took France out of the NATO military command in 1967 and expelled all foreign-controlled troops from the country. He later went on to attempt to achieve a long-cherished plan of regional reform. This, however, aroused wide opposition. He decided to stake his fate on a referendum. At the voting in April 1969, the electorate defeated the plan.

His successor Georges Pompidou continued the de Gaulle policies of seeking to expand France's influence in the Mideast and Africa.

Socialist François Mitterrand attained a stunning victory in the May 10, 1981, Presidential election over the Gaullist alliance that had held power since 1958.

The victors immediately moved to carry out campaign pledges to nationalize major industries, halt nuclear testing, suspend nuclear power plant construction, and impose new taxes on the rich. On Feb. 11, 1982, the nationalization bills became law.

The Socialists' policies during Mitterrand's first two years created a 12% inflation rate, a huge trade deficit, and devaluations of the franc. In early 1983, Mitterrand embarked on an austerity program to control inflation and reduce the trade deficit. He increased taxes and slashed government spending. A halt in economic growth, declining purchasing power for the average Frenchman, and an increase in unemployment to 10% followed. Mitterrand sank lower and lower in the opinion polls.

In March 1986, a center-right coalition led by Jacques Chirac won a slim majority in legislative elections. Chirac became Premier initiating a period of "co-habitation" between him and the Socialist President, Mitterrand.

Mitterrand's decisive reelection in May 1987, led to Chirac being replaced as Premier by Michel Rocard, a Socialist.

Relations, however, cooled with Rocard, and in May 1991 he was replaced with Edith Cresson, France's first female prime minister and like Mitterrand a Socialist.

The conservative coalition won a resounding victory in the March 1993 parliamentary elections.

Domestically the premier's center-right coalition did well in local elections in March 1994. In foreign policy France continued its active engagement in the Bosnian conflict and intervened in Rwanda to help halt the widespread slaughter there.

On his third try Chirac won the presidency in May 1995, gaining more than 52% of the vote. He campaigned vigorously on a platform to reduce unemployment, but moved quickly to cement ties with Germany.

Overseas Departments

Overseas Departments elect representatives to the National Assembly, and the same administrative organization as that of mainland France applies to them.

FRENCH GUIANA (including ININI)

Status: Overseas Department
Prefect: Jean-François Cordet
Area: 35,126 sq mi. (90,976 sq km)
Population (est. mid-1994): 139,929; growth rate: 4.27%; birth rate 25.8/1000; infant mortality rate 15.9/1000; density per square mile: 4
Capital (1990): Cayenne, 41,067; **Monetary unit:** Franc; **Language:** French; **Religion:** Roman Catholic; **Literacy rate:** 73%
Economic summary: Gross domestic product (1986): $421 million; $4,390 per capita; inflation (1987): 4.1%; unemployment (1990): 13%. Arable land: negligible; principal agricultural products: rice, cassava, bananas, sugar cane. Labor force: 23,265; 21.2% in industry. Major industrial products: timber, rum, rosewood essence, gold mining, processed shrimp. Natural resources: bauxite, timber, cinnabar, kaolin. Exports: $59 million (f.o.b., 1992): shrimp, timber, rum, rosewood essence. Imports: $1.5 billion (c.i.f., 1992): food, consumer and producer goods, petroleum. Major trading partners: U.S., France, Japan.

French Guiana, lying north of Brazil and east of Suriname on the northeast coast of South America, was first settled in 1604. Penal settlements, embracing the area around the mouth of the Maroni River and the Iles du Salut (including Devil's Island), were founded in 1852; they have since been abolished.

During World War II, French Guiana at first adhered to the Vichy government, but the Free French took over in 1943. French Guiana accepted in 1958 the new Constitution of the French Fifth Republic and remained an Overseas Department of the French Republic.

GUADELOUPE

Status: Overseas Department
Prefect: Franck Perriez
Area: 687 sq mi. (1,779 sq km)
Population (est. mid-1995): 400,000 (average annual growth rate: 1.2%); birth rate: 18/1000; infant mortality rate: 10.3/1000; density per square mile: 582
Capital (1990): Basse-Terre, 14,000; **Largest city (1987):** Pointe-à-Pitre, over 25,312; **Monetary unit:** Franc; **Language:** French, Creole patois; **Religions:** Roman Catholic; **Literacy rate:** over 70%

Economic summary: Gross domestic product (1991): $2.9 billion; $8,400 per capita; n.a. real growth rate; inflation (1990): 3.7%; unemployment (1990): 31.3%. Arable land: 18%; principal agricultural products: sugar cane, bananas, eggplant, flowers. Labor force: 120,000; 25.8% industry. Major industries: construction, public works, sugar, rum, tourism. Exports: $168 million (f.o.b., 1988): sugar, rum, bananas. Imports: $1.2 billion (c.i.f., 1988): foodstuffs, clothing, consumer goods, construction materials, petroleum products, vehicles. Major trading partners: France, Martinique, Italy, Germany, U.S.

Guadeloupe, in the West Indies about 300 miles (483 km) southeast of Puerto Rico, was discovered by Columbus in 1493. It consists of the twin islands of Basse-Terre and Grande-Terre and five dependencies—Marie-Galante, Les Saintes, La Désirade, St. Barthélemy, and the northern half of St. Martin. The volcano Soufrière (4,813 ft; 1,467 m), also called La Grande Soufrière, is the highest point on Guadeloupe. Violent activity in 1976 and 1977 caused thousands to flee their homes.

French colonization began in 1635. In 1958, Guadeloupe voted in favor of the new Constitution of the French Fifth Republic and remained an Overseas Department of the French Republic.

MARTINIQUE

Status: Overseas Department
Prefect: Michel Morin
Area: 431 sq mi. (1,116 sq km)
Population (est. mid-1995): 400,000 (average annual growth rate: 1.1%; birth rate: 17/1000; infant mortality rate: 8/1000; density per square mile: 928
Capital (1990): Fort-de-France, 101,540; Other cities: Le Lamentin, 26,683; Sainte-Marie, 18,533; **Monetary unit:** Franc; **Languages:** French, Creole patois; **Religion:** Roman Catholic; **Literacy rate:** over 70%
Economic summary: Gross domestic product (1991): $3.3 billion; $9,500 per capita; inflation (1990): 3.9%; unemployment (1990): 32.1%. Average annual growth rate n.a. Arable land: 10%; principal agricultural products: sugar cane, bananas, rum, pineapples. Labor force: 100,000; 31.7% in service industry. Major industries: sugar, rum, refined oil, cement, tourism. Natural resources: coastal scenery and beaches. Exports: $201.5 million (f.o.b., 1991): bananas, refined petroleum products, rum, sugar, pineapples. Imports: $1.5 billion (c.i.f., 1991): foodstuffs, clothing and other consumer goods, petroleum products, construction materials. Major trading partners: France, U.S., Guadeloupe, Germany, U.K., Italy, Japan.

Martinique, lying in the Lesser Antilles about 300 miles (483 km) northeast of Venezuela, was probably discovered by Columbus in 1502 and was taken for France in 1635. Following the Franco-German armistice of 1940, it had a semiautonomous status until 1943, when authority was relinquished to the Free French. The area, administered by a Prefect assisted by an elected council, is represented in the French Parliament. In 1958, Martinique voted in favor of the new Constitution of the French Fifth Republic and remained an Overseas Department of the French Republic.

RÉUNION

Status: Overseas Department
Prefect: Hubert Fournier

Area: 970 sq mi. (2,510 sq km)
Population (est. mid-1995): 700,000 (average annual growth rate, 1.8%); birth rate: 23/1000; infant mortality rate: 8/1000; density per square mile: 722
Capital (1990): Saint-Denis (metropolitan area), 142,000. Other cities: Saint-Paul, 58,494; Saint-Pierre, 50,419; Le Tampon, 41,305; Saint-Louis, 32,045; **Monetary unit:** Franc; **Languages:** French, Creole; **Religion:** Roman Catholic
Economic summary: Gross domestic product (1993 est.): $2.5 billion; $3,900 per capita; inflation (1988) 1.3%; unemployment (Feb. 91) 35%. Arable land: 20%; principal agricultural products: rum, vanilla, bananas, perfume plants. Major industrial products: rum, cigarettes, processed sugar. Exports: $166 million (f.o.b., 1988): sugar, perfume essences, rum, molasses. Imports: $1.7 billion (c.i.f., 1988): manufactured goods, foodstuffs, beverages, machinery and transportation equipment, petroleum products. Major trading partners: France, Mauritius, Bahrain, South Africa, Italy.

Discovered by Portuguese navigators in the 16th century, the island of Réunion, then uninhabited, was taken as a French possession in 1642. It is located about 450 miles (724 km) east of Madagascar, in the Indian Ocean. In 1958, Réunion approved the Constitution of the Fifth French Republic and remained an Overseas Department of the French Republic.

Overseas Territories

Overseas Territories are comparable to Departments, except that their administrative organization includes a locally-elected government.

ST. PIERRE AND MIQUELON

Status: Overseas Territory
Prefect: Yves Henri
Area: 93 sq mi. (242 sq km)
Population (est. mid-1994): 6,704; growth rate 0.78%; birth rate 13.23/1000; infant mortality rate 11.72/1000; density per square mile: 72.08
Capital (1990): Saint Pierre, 5,683
Economic summary: Gross domestic product (1992 est.): $65 million; $10,000 per capita; unemployment (1990) 9.6%. Major industries: fishing, canneries. Exports: $30 million (f.o.b., 1991 est.): fish, pelts. Imports: $82 million (c.i.f., 1991 est.): meat, clothing, fuel, electrical equipment, machinery, building materials. Major trading partners: Canada, France, U.S., U.K., the Netherlands.

The sole remnant of the French colonial empire in North America, these islands were first occupied by the French in 1604. Their only importance arises from proximity to the Grand Banks, located 10 miles south of Newfoundland, making them the center of the French Atlantic cod fisheries. On July 19, 1976, the islands became an Overseas Department of the French Republic.

FRENCH POLYNESIA

Status: Overseas Territory
President of the Territorial Government: Gaston Flosse (1991)
Area: 1,544 sq mi. (4,000 sq km)
Population (est. mid-1995): 200,000 (average annual growth rate: 2.1%); birth rate: 26/1000; infant mortality rate: 12/1000; density per square mile: 130

Capital (1988): Papeete (on Tahiti), 23,555; **Monetary unit:** Pacific financial community franc; **Language:** French; **Religions:** Protestant, 55%; Roman Catholic, 32%

Economic summary: Gross domestic product (1993 est.): $1.5 billion; $7,000 per capita; inflation (1991) –0.6%; unemployment (1990 est.) 10%. Principal agricultural product: copra. Major industries: tourism, maintenance of French nuclear test base. Exports: $88.9 million (f.o.b., 1989): coconut products, mother of pearl, vanilla. Imports: $765 million (c.i.f., 1989): fuels, foodstuffs, equipment. Major trading partners: France, U.S.

The term French Polynesia is applied to the scattered French possessions in the South Pacific—Mangareva (Gambier), Makatea, the Marquesas Islands, Rapa, Rurutu, Rimatara, the Society Islands, the Tuamotu Archipelago, Tubuai, Raivavae, and the island of Clipperton—which were organized into a single colony in 1903. There are 120 islands, of which 25 are uninhabited.

The President of the Territorial Government is assisted by a Council of Government and a popularly elected Territorial Assembly. The principal and most populous island—Tahiti, in the Society group—was claimed as French in 1768. In 1958, French Polynesia voted in favor of the new Constitution of the French Fifth Republic and remained an Overseas Territory of the French Republic. The natives are mostly Maoris.

The Pacific Nuclear Test Center on the atoll of Mururoa, 744 miles (1,200 km) from Tahiti, was completed in 1966.

MAYOTTE

Status: Territorial collectivity
Prefect: Jean-Jacques Debacq
Area: 146 sq mi. (378 sq km)
Population (est. mid-1994): 93,468; average annual rate of natural increase 3.8%; birth rate 48.8/1000; infant mortality rate 79.6/1000; density per square mile: 640
Capital (1985): Dzaoudzi (Mamoudzou), 7,325
Economic summary: Gross domestic product (1993 est.): $54 million; $600 per capita. Exports (1984): $4 million (f.o.b.). Imports $21.8 million (f.o.b., 1984). Principal products: vanilla, ylang-ylang, coffee, copra. Exports: Ylang-ylang, vanilla. Imports: building materials, transportation equipment, rice, clothing, flour. Major trading partners: France, Comoros, Reunion, Kenya, South Africa, Pakistan.

The most populous of the Comoro Islands in the Indian Ocean, with a Christian majority, Mayotte voted in 1974 and 1976 against joining the other, predominantly Moslem islands, in declaring themselves independent. It continues to retain its ties to France.

NEW CALEDONIA AND DEPENDENCIES

Status: Overseas Territory
High Commissioner: Alain Christnacht (1991)
Area: 7,374 sq mi. (19,103 sq km)[1]
Population (mid-1995): 200,000 (average annual growth rate: 2.0%); birth rate: 26/1000; infant mortality rate: 21/1000; density per square mile: 27
Capital (1989): Nouméa, 65,110; **Monetary unit:** Pacific financial community franc; **Languages:** French, Melanesian and Polynesian dialects; **Religion:** Roman Catholic, 60%; Protestant, 30%; **Literacy rate:** 91%

Economic summary: Gross domestic product (1991 est.): $1 billion; real growth rate (1988) 2.4%; per capita income $6,000; inflation (1989) 4.1%; unemployment (1989) 16%. Principal agricultural products: coffee, copra, beef, wheat, vegetables. Major industrial product: nickel. Natural resources: nickel, chromite, iron ore. Exports: $671 million (f.o.b., 1989): nickel, chrome. Imports: $764 million (c.i.f., 1989): mineral fuels, machinery, electrical equipment, foodstuffs. Major trading partners: France, Japan, U.S., Australia.

1. Including dependencies.

New Caledonia (6,466 sq mi.; 16,747 sq km), about 1,070 miles (1,722 km) northeast of Sydney, Australia, was discovered by Capt. James Cook in 1774 and annexed by France in 1853. The government also administers the Isle of Pines, the Loyalty Islands (Uvéa, Lifu, and Maré), the Belep Islands, the Huon Island group, and Chesterfield Islands.

The natives are Melanesians; about one third of the population is white and one fifth Indochinese and Javanese. The French National Assembly on July 31, 1984, voted a bill into law that granted internal autonomy to New Caledonia and opened the way to possible eventual independence. This touched off ethnic tensions and violence between the natives and the European settlers, with the natives demanding full independence and sovereignty while the settlers wanted to remain part of France. In June 1988, France resumed direct administration of the territory and promised a referendum on self-determination in 1998. This was agreed to by organizations representing the natives and the French settlers.

SOUTHERN AND ANTARCTIC LANDS

Status: Overseas Territory
Administrator: Philyje Legrix (1995)
Area: 3,004 sq mi. (7,781 sq km, excluding Adélie Land)
Capital: Port-au-Français

This territory is uninhabited except for the personnel of scientific bases. It consists of Adélie Land (166,752 sq mi.; 431,888 sq km) on the Antarctic mainland and the following islands in the southern Indian Ocean: the Kerguelen and Crozet archipelagos and the islands of Saint-Paul and New Amsterdam.

WALLIS AND FUTUNA ISLANDS

Status: Overseas Territory
Administrator: Jacques de Llenoff
Area: 106 sq mi. (274 sq km)
Population (est. mid-1994): 14,338; growth rate 1.13%; birth rate 25.7/1000; infant mortality rate 26.2/1000; density per square mile: 136
Capital (1983): Mata-Utu, 81. **Languages:** French, Wallisian. **Religion:** Roman Catholic. **Literacy rate:** 50%.
Economic summary: Gross domestic product (1991 est.): $25 million; $1,500 per capita. Exports: negligible. Imports (1984, c.i.f.): $13.3 million: foodstuffs, manufactured goods, transport equipment, fuel.

The two islands groups in the South Pacific between Fiji and Samoa were settled by French missionaries at the beginning of the 19th century. A protectorate was established in the 1880s. Following a referendum by the Polynesian inhabitants, the status was changed to that of an Overseas Territory in 1961.

GABON

Gabonese Republic
President: Omar Bongo (1967)
Premier: Paulin Obame–Nguema (1994)
Area: 103,346 sq mi. (267,667 sq km)
Population (est. mid-1995): 1,300,000 (average annual rate of natural increase: 2.2%); birth rate: 37/1000; infant mortality rate: 94/1000; density per square mile: 13
Capital and largest city (est. 1987): Libreville, 352,000;
Monetary unit: Franc CFA; **Ethnic groups:** Bateke, Obamba, Bakota, Shake, Pongwés, Adumas, Chiras, Punu, Lumbu, and Echiras Bapunu **Languages:** French (official) and Bantu dialects; **Religions:** Christian, 55–75%; Muslim, more than 1%; remainder animist;
National name: République Gabonaise; **Member of French Community; Literacy rate:** 95%
Economic summary: Gross domestic product (1993 est.): $5.4 billion; $4,800 per capita; real growth rate (1992 est.): 0.5%; inflation 0.7% (1991 est.). Arable land: more than 65%. Principal agricultural products: cocoa, coffee, wood, palm oil. Labor force: 120,000 salaried; 65% in agriculture. Major industrial products: petroleum, natural gas, processed wood, manganese, uranium. Natural resources: wood, petroleum, iron ore, manganese, uranium. Exports: $2.3 billion (f.o.b., 1992 est.): crude oil, manganese, wood, uranium. Imports: $702 million (c.i.f., 1992 est.): foodstuffs, chemical products, petroleum products, construction materials, manufactures, machinery. Major trading partners: France, U.S., Germany, Japan, African countries.

Geography. This West African land with the Atlantic as its western border is also bounded by Equatorial Guinea, Cameroon, and the Congo. Its area is slightly less than Colorado's.

From mangrove swamps on the coast, the land becomes divided plateaus in the north and east and mountains in the north. Most of the country is covered by a dense tropical forest.

Government. The president is elected for a five-year term. Legislative powers are exercised by a 120-seat National Assembly, which is elected for a five-year term. After his conversion to Islam in 1973, President Bongo changed his given name, Albert Bernard, to Omar. The Rassemblement Social Démocrate Gabonais is led by President Bongo. He was re-elected without opposition in 1973, 1980, and in 1993.

History. Little is known of Gabon's history, even in oral tradition, but Pygmies are believed to be the original inhabitants. Now there are many tribal groups in the country, the largest being the Fang people who constitute a third of the population.

Gabon was first visited by the Portuguese navigator Diego Cam in the 15th century. In 1839, the French founded their first settlement on the left bank of the Gabon Estuary and gradually occupied the hinterland during the second half of the 19th century. It was organized as a French territory in 1888 and became an autonomous republic within the French Union after World War II and an independent republic on Aug. 17, 1960.

Following strikes and riots the president called a national conference in March 1990. In May it adopted a transitional constitution legalizing political parties and calling for free elections.

In its first multiparty election in December 1993 the incumbent president received just over 51% of the vote while the opposition candidate refused to accept defeat charging fraud and tried to establish a rival government.

Rioting in the capital caused the issuance of a state of siege in February 1994. A university strike by students in May caused the government to close the institution for a period. Growing dissension within the army also led the president to call for a peace conference in September. As a result a coalition government was formed in November.

GAMBIA

Republic of the Gambia
Head of state: Capt. Yahya Ajj Jammeh
Area: 4,093 sq mi. (10,600 sq km)
Population (est. mid-1995): 1,100,000 (average annual rate of natural increase: 2.7%); birth rate: 48/1000; infant mortality rate: 90/1000; density per square mile: 269
Capital (1986): Banjul, 44,188. **Monetary unit:** Dalasi.
Languages: Native tongues, English (official). **Religions:** Islam, 90%; Christian, 9%; traditional, 1%. **Literacy rate:** 27%. **Member of Commonwealth of Nations**
Economic summary: Gross domestic product (1993 est.): $740 million; per capita $800; real growth rate 4.5% (FY92 est.); inflation (FY92 est.) 5%. Arable land: 16%. Principal products: peanuts, rice, palm kernels. Labor force: 400,000; 18.9% in industry, commerce and services. Major industrial products: processed peanuts, fish, and hides. Natural resources: fish. Exports: $164 million (f.o.b., FY92 est.): peanuts and peanut products, fish, cotton, lint, palm kernels. Imports: $214 million (f.o.b., FY92 est.): foodstuffs, fuel, machinery, transport equipment, manufactures, raw materials. Major trading partners: U.S., E.C., Asia.

Geography. Situated on the Atlantic coast in westernmost Africa and surrounded on three sides by Senegal, Gambia is twice the size of Delaware. The Gambia River flows for 200 miles (322 km) through Gambia on its way to the Atlantic. The country, the smallest on the continent, averages only 20 miles (32 km) in width.

Government. A military regime following a coup on July 22, 1994. The constitution was suspended and political parties were banned.

History. During the 17th century, Gambia was settled by various companies of English merchants. Slavery was the chief source of revenue until it was abolished in 1807. Gambia became a crown colony in 1843 and an independent nation within the Commonwealth of Nations on Feb. 18, 1965.

Full independence was approved in a 1970 referendum, and on April 24 of that year Gambia proclaimed itself a republic.

Elections of April 29, 1992 returned Jawara for a fifth term. His People's Progressive Party won 25 of the 36 seats in the House of Representatives.

A military coup in July 1994 deposed the president, suspended the constitution, and banned political parties.

An executrive committee was established to run the country on a daily basis with plans to merge the police and army.

GEORGIA

Republic of Georgia
Chairman of the Parliament: Eduard Shevardnadze (1994)
Prime Minister: Otar Patsatia (1993)
Area: 26,900 sq mi. (169,000 sq km)
Population (est. mid-1995): 5,400,000 (Georgians, 70%; largest minorities: Armenians, other: Russians and Azerbaijanis); average annual rate of natural increase: 0.2%; birth rate: 12/1000; infant mortality rate: 18/1000; density per square mile: 201
Capital and largest city (1991): Tbilisi, 1,279,000. Other cities (1989): Kutaisi, 235,000; Batumi, 136,000; and Sukhumi, 121,000; **Monetary unit:** coupon (temporary); **Language:** Georgian (official), 71%; Russian, 9%; Armenian, 7%; Azerbaijani, 6%; **Religion:** Georgian Orthodox, 65%; Russian Orthodox, 10%; Armenian Orthodox, 8%; Muslim, 11%
Economic summary: Gross domestic product (UN, World Bank 1993 est.): $7.8 billion, $1,390 per capita; −35% real growth rate; inflation (mid-93 est.) 40.5%; unemployment 5%. Labor force (1990): 2,763,000: industry and construction, 31%; agriculture and forestry, 25%. Industries: heavy industrial products include raw steel, rolled steel, cement, lumber, machine tools, foundry equipment, electric locomotives, tower cranes, welding equipment, meat packing, dairy and fishing, farm machinery. Agriculture: citrus fruits, grapes, sugar, vegetables, grains, cattle, sheep, goats, pigs, and poultry. Exports: $176 million (f.o.b., 1990): citrus fruits, tea, other agricultural products, diverse types of machinery, ferrous and non-ferrous metals, textiles. Imports: $1.5 billion (c.i.f., 1990): machinery and parts, fuel, transport equipment, textiles. Major trading partners: Russia, Turkey, Azerbaijan, Ukraine, Germany, U.S.

Geography. Georgia is a land of snow-capped mountains, turbulent rivers, dense forests, and fertile valleys. Mt. Kazbet, 16,541 ft (5,042 m) is the country's tallest peak. Georgia's principal rivers, Kura Mtkvari and the Rioni and their tributaries are harnessed to provide an abundance of hydroelectric power for the country. Georgia is bordered by the Black Sea in the west, by Turkey and Armenia in the south, by Azerbaijan in the east, and Russia in the north. The republic also includes the Abkhaz and Adzhar autonomous republics and the Yugo-Ossetian Autonomous Oblast.

Government. A republic. On March 10, 1992, a temporary legislative and executive body called the State Council was established which is headed by Eduard Shevardnadze. There is a 234-seat legislature.

History. Georgia became a kingdom about 4 B.C. and reached its greatest period of expansion in the 12th century when its territory included the whole of Transcaucasia. The country was the scene of a struggle between Persia and Turkey from the 16th century on, and in the 18th century became a vassal to Russia in exchange for protection from the Turks.

Georgia joined Azerbaijan and Armenia in 1917 to establish the anti-Bolshevik Transcaucasian Federation, and upon its dissolution, proclaimed its independence in 1918. In 1922, the Red Army invaded Georgia and replaced the republic with a Soviet government. In 1922, Georgia, Armenia, and Azerbaijan were annexed and formed into the Transcaucasian Soviet Socialist Republic affiliated with the U.S.S.R. In 1936, it became a separate Soviet republic.

Zviad Gamsakhurdia won the first directly elected Soviet presidency in 1990 with 86.5% of the vote, pledging to lead Georgia toward independence. Georgia proclaimed its independence on April 9, 1990.

Gamsakhurdia was later accused of dictatorial policies, the jailing of opposition leaders, human rights abuses, and clamping down on the media. A two week civil war centered in the capital of Tbilisi ensued and Gamsakhurdia was forced to flee to Azerbaijan and later to Armenia. A ruling military council was established by the opposition until a civilian authority can be restored.

During 1993 the government continued to fight separatists in Abkhazia.

In February 1994 Russia and Georgia signed a cooperation treaty that authorized Russia to keep three military bases in Georgia and allow Russians to train and equip the Georgian army. In March the country joined NATO's Partnership for Peace program.

The economy continued in free-fall, and the parliament failed to act on market reforms. In November, Abkhazia ratified a new constitution declaring it an independent republic.

GERMANY

Federal Republic of Germany
President: Roman Herzog (1994)
Chancellor: Helmut Kohl (1982)
Area: 137,838 sq mi. (357,000 sq km)
Population (est. mid-1995): 81,700,000 (average annual growth rate: −0.1%; birth rate: 10/1000; infant mortality rate: 5.8/1000; density per square mile: 593
Capital and largest city (1992): Berlin, 3,454,200; seat of parliament and government: Bonn[1], 294,300; **Largest cities (est. 1993):** Hamburg, 1,675,200; Munich, 1,241,300; Cologne, 958,600; Frankfurt/Main, 660,800; Essen, 627,800; Dortmund, 600,700; Stuttgart, 599,400; Dusseldorf, 577,400; Bremen, 553,200; Duisberg, 538,300; Leipzig, 496,600; Hannover, 520,900. **Monetary unit:** Deutsche Mark; **Language:** German; **Religions:** Protestant, 49%; Roman Catholic, 45%; **National name:** Bundesrepublik Deutschland; **Literacy rate:** 99%
Economic summary (1994): Gross domestic product: $1,476.1 trillion; **per capita:** $18,133; **Western Germany:** $1,323.4 trillion; per capita $20,089; **Eastern Germany:** $152.6 billion; per capita: $9,822 **real growth rate (1993):** 1.5%; West 0.9%; East 8.0%; **Inflation(1993):** West 4%; East n.a.; **Unemployment (1994):** West 8.2%, East 15.2%. Labor force: 36.75 million, 45% in industry, agriculture 6%. Exports: $392 billion (f.o.b., 1993): manufactures 86.6% (including machines and precision tools, chemicals, motor vehicles, iron and steel products), agricultural products 4.9%, raw materials 2.3%, fuels 1.3%. Imports: $374.6 billion (f.o.b., 1993): manufactures 68.5%, agricultural products 12%, fuels 9.7%, raw materials 1.3%. **Industries:** West: among the world's largest producers of iron, steel, coal, cement, chemicals, machinery, vehicles, machine tools, electronics, food and beverages. East: metal fabrication, chemicals, brown coal, shipbuilding, machine building, food and beverages, textiles, petroleum refining. **Agriculture:** West: fishing and forestry, diversified crop and livestock farming; principal crops include potatoes, wheat, rye, barley, sugar beets, fruit, cabbage, cattle, pigs, poultry. East: fishing and forestry, principal crops include wheat, rye, barley, potatoes, sugar beets, fruit, pork, beef, chicken, milk, hides and skins. Natural resources: iron ore, coal, potash, timber, lignite, uranium, copper, natural gas, salt, nickel. Major trading partners: France, Netherlands, Italy, Belgium-Luxembourg, U.S., U.K.

1. At present, seat of government will eventually move to the traditional capital of Berlin by the year 2000.

Rulers of Germany and Prussia

Name	Born	Ruled[1]	Name	Born	Ruled[1]
KINGS OF PRUSSIA			**GERMAN FEDERAL REPUBLIC (WEST) (CHANCELLORS)**		
Frederick I[2]	1657	1701–1713	Konrad Adenauer	1876	1949–1963
Frederick William I	1688	1713–1740	Ludwig Erhard	1897	1963–1966
Frederick II the Great	1712	1740–1786	Kurt Georg Kiesinger	1904	1966–1969
Frederick William II	1744	1786–1797	Willy Brandt	1913	1969–1974
Frederick William III	1770	1797–1840	Helmut Schmidt	1918	1974–1984
Frederick William IV	1795	1840–1861	Helmut Kohl	1930	1984–1990
William I	1797	1861–1871 [3]			
			GERMAN DEMOCRATIC REPUBLIC (EAST)		
EMPERORS OF GERMANY			Wilhelm Pieck[5]	1876	1949–1960
William I	1797	1871–1888	Walter Ulbricht[8]	1893	1960–1973
Frederick III	1831	1888–1888	Willi Stoph[9]	1914	1973–1976
William II	1859	1888–1918 [4]	Erich Honecker[9]	1912	1976–1989
			Egon Krenz[9]	1937	1989–1989
WEIMAR REPUBLIC			Manfred Gerlach[9]		1989–1990
Friedrich Ebert[5]	1871	1919–1925	Sabine Bergman–Pohl[9]		1990–1990
Paul von Hindenburg[5]	1847	1925–1934			
			GERMAN FEDERAL REPUBLIC CHANCELLORS		
THIRD REICH			Helmut Kohl	1930	1991–
Adolf Hitler[6, 7]	1889	1934–1945			
Karl Doenitz[6]	1891	1945–1945			

1. Year of end of rule is also that of death, unless otherwise indicated. 2. Was Elector of Brandenburg (1688–1701) as Frederick III. 3. Became Emperor of Germany in 1871. 4. Died 1941. 5. President. 6. Führer. 7. Named Chancellor by President Hindenburg in 1933. 8. Chairman of Council of State. Died 1973. 9. Chairman of Council of State.

Geography. The Federal Republic of Germany was occupied by the United States, Britain, and France after World War II, when the eastern half of prewar Germany was split roughly between a Soviet-occupied zone, which became the German Democratic Republic, and an area annexed by Poland. After being divided for more than four decades, the two Germanys were reunited on Oct. 3, 1990. The united Federal Republic is about the size of Montana.

Germany's neighbors are France, Belgium, Luxembourg, and the Netherlands on the west, Switzerland and Austria on the south, Czechoslovakia and Poland on the east, and Denmark on the north.

The northern plain, the central hill country, and the southern mountain district constitute the main physical divisions of West Germany, which is slightly smaller than Oregon. The Bavarian plateau in the southwest averages 1,600 feet (488 m) above sea level, but it reaches 9,721 feet (2,962 m) in the Zugspitze Mountains, the highest point in the country.

Important navigable rivers are the Danube, rising in the Black Forest and flowing east across Bavaria into Austria, and the Rhine, which rises in Switzerland and flows across the Netherlands in two channels to the North Sea and is navigable by ocean-going and coastal vessels as far as Cologne. The Elbe, which also empties into the North Sea, is navigable within Germany for smaller vessels. The Weser, flowing into the North Sea, and the Main and Mosel (Moselle), both tributaries of the Rhine, are also important. In addition, the Oder and Neisse Rivers form the border with Poland. The rivers Danube and Rhine in the Black Sea and the North Sea were connected in 1992 with the completion of the Rhine Main–Danube Canal.

Government. Under the Constitution of May 23, 1949, the Federal Republic was established as a parliamentary democracy. The Parliament consists of the Bundesrat, an upper chamber representing and appointed by the Länder, or states, and the Bundestag, a lower house elected for four years by universal suffrage. A federal assembly composed of Bundestag deputies and deputies from the state parliaments elects the President of the Republic for a five-year-term; the Bundestag alone chooses the Chancellor, or Prime Minister. Each of the 16 Länder have a legislature popularly elected for a four-year or five-year term.

The major political parties are the Christian Democratic Union-Christian Social Union (244 and Christian Socialist Union, 50 of 662 seats in the Bundestag), led by Chancellor Helmut Kohl; Social Democratic Party (252 seats); and the Free Democratic Party (47 seats), led by Otto Count Larbsdorff, the Alliance 90/Greens (49 seats) and Party of Democratic Socialism (30 seats). Kohl's government is a coalition with the Free Democrats.

History. Immediately before the Christian era, when the Roman Empire had pushed its frontier to the Rhine, what is now Germany was inhabited by several tribes believed to have migrated from Central Asia between the 6th and 4th centuries B.C. One of these tribes, the Franks, attained supremacy in western Europe under Charlemagne, who was crowned Holy Roman Emperor A.D. 800. By the Treaty of Verdun (843), Charlemagne's lands east of the Rhine were ceded to the German Prince Louis. Additional territory acquired by the Treaty of Mersen (870) gave Germany approximately the area it maintained throughout the Middle Ages. For several centuries after Otto the Great was crowned King in 936, the German rulers were also usually heads of the Holy Roman Empire.

Relations between state and church were changed by the Reformation, which began with Martin Luther's 95 theses, and came to a head in 1547, when Charles V scattered the forces of the Protestant League at Mühlberg. Freedom of worship was guaranteed by the Peace of Augsburg (1555), but a Counter Reformation took place later, and a dispute over the succession to the Bohemian throne brought on the Thirty Years' War (1618–48), which devastated Germany and left the empire divided into hundreds of small principalities virtually independent of the Emperor.

Meanwhile, Prussia was developing into a state of considerable strength. Frederick the Great (1740–86) reorganized the Prussian army and defeated Maria Theresa of Austria in a struggle over Silesia. After the defeat of Napoleon at Waterloo (1815), the struggle between Austria and Prussia for supremacy in Germany continued, reaching its climax in the defeat of Austria in the Seven Weeks' War (1866) and the formation of the Prussian-dominated North German Confederation (1867).

The architect of German unity was Otto von Bismarck, a conservative, monarchist, and militaristic Prussian Junker who had no use for "empty phrase-making and constitutions." From 1862 until his retirement in 1890 he dominated not only the German but also the entire European scene. He unified all Germany in a series of three wars against Denmark (1864), Austria (1866), and France (1870–71), which many historians believe were instigated and promoted by Bismarck in his zeal to build a nation through "blood and iron."

On Jan. 18, 1871, King Wilhelm I of Prussia was proclaimed German Emperor in the Hall of Mirrors at Versailles. The North German Confederation, created in 1867, was abolished, and the Second German Reich, consisting of the North and South German states, was born. With a powerful army, an efficient bureaucracy, and a loyal bourgeoisie, Chancellor Bismarck consolidated a powerful centralized state.

Wilhelm II dismissed Bismarck in 1890 and embarked upon a "New Course," stressing an intensified colonialism and a powerful navy. His chaotic foreign policy culminated in the diplomatic isolation of Germany and the disastrous defeat in World War I (1914–18).

The Second German Empire collapsed following the defeat of the German armies in 1918, the naval mutiny at Kiel, and the flight of the Kaiser to the Netherlands on November 10. The Social Democrats, led by Friedrich Ebert and Philipp Scheidemann, crushed the Communists and established a moderate republic with Ebert as President.

The Weimar Constitution of 1919 provided for a President to be elected for seven years by universal suffrage and a bicameral legislature, consisting of the Reichsrat, representing the states, and the Reichstag, representing the people. It contained a model Bill of Rights. It was weakened, however, by a provision that enabled the President to rule by decree.

President Ebert died Feb. 28, 1925, and on April 26, Field Marshal Paul von Hindenburg was elected president.

The mass of Germans regarded the Weimar Republic as a child of defeat, imposed upon a Germany whose legitimate aspirations to world leadership had been thwarted by a world conspiracy. Added to this were a crippling currency debacle, a tremendous burden of reparations, and acute economic distress.

Adolf Hitler, an Austrian war veteran and a fanatical nationalist, fanned discontent by promising a Greater Germany, abrogation of the Treaty of Versailles, restoration of Germany's lost colonies, and destruction of the Jews. When the Social Democrats and the Communists refused to combine against the Nazi threat, President Hindenburg made Hitler chancellor on Jan. 30, 1933.

With the death of Hindenburg on Aug. 2, 1934, Hitler repudiated the Treaty of Versailles and began full-scale rearmament. In 1935 he withdrew Germany from the League of Nations, and the next year he reoccupied the Rhineland and signed the anti-Comintern pact with Japan, at the same time strengthening relations with Italy. Austria was annexed in March 1938. By the Munich agreement in September 1938 he gained the Czech Sudetenland, and in violation of this agreement he completed the dismemberment of Czechoslovakia in March 1939. But his invasion of Poland on Sept. 1, 1939, precipitated World War II.

On May 8, 1945, Germany surrendered unconditionally to Allied and Soviet military commanders, and on June 5 the four-nation Allied Control Council became the *de facto* government of Germany.

(For details of World War II, *see* Headline History.)

At the Berlin (or Potsdam) Conference (July 17–Aug. 2, 1945) President Truman, Premier Stalin, and Prime Minister Clement Attlee of Britain set forth the guiding principles of the Allied Control Council. They were Germany's complete disarmament and demilitarization, destruction of its war potential, rigid control of industry, and decentralization of the political and economic structure. Pending final determination of territorial questions at a peace conference, the three victors agreed in principle to the ultimate transfer of the city of Königsberg (now Kaliningrad) and its adjacent area to the U.S.S.R. and to the administration by Poland of former German territories lying generally east of the Oder-Neisse Line.

For purposes of control Germany was divided in 1945 into four national occupation zones, each headed by a Military Governor.

The Western powers were unable to agree with the U.S.S.R. on any fundamental issue. Work of the Allied Control Council was hamstrung by repeated Soviet vetoes; and finally, on March 20, 1948, Russia walked out of the Council. Meanwhile, the U.S. and Britain had taken steps to merge their zones economically (Bizone); and on May 31, 1948, the U.S., Britain, France, and the Benelux countries agreed to set up a German state comprising the three Western Zones.

The U.S.S.R. reacted by clamping a blockade on all ground communications between the Western Zones and Berlin, an enclave in the Soviet Zone. The Western Allies countered by organizing a gigantic airlift to fly supplies into the beleaguered city, assigning 60,000 men to it. The U.S.S.R. was finally forced to lift the blockade on May 12, 1949.

The Federal Republic of Germany was proclaimed on May 23, 1949, with its capital at Bonn. In free elections, West German voters gave a majority in the Constituent Assembly to the Christian Democrats, with the Social Democrats largely making up the opposition. Konrad Adenauer became chancellor, and Theodor Heuss of the Free Democrats was elected first president.

When the Federal Republic of Germany was established in West Germany, the East German states adopted a more centralized constitution for the Democratic Republic of Germany, and it was put into effect on Oct. 7, 1949. The U.S.S.R. thereupon dissolved its occupation zone but Soviet troops remained. The Western Allies declared that the East German Republic was a Soviet creation undertaken without self-determination and refused to recognize it. It was recognized only within the Soviet bloc.

The area that was occupied by East Germany, as well as adjacent areas in Eastern Europe, consists of Mecklenburg, Brandenburg, Lusatia, Saxony, and Thuringia. Soviet armies conquered the five territories by 1945. In the division of 1945 they were allotted to the U.S.S.R. Soviet forces created a State controlled by the secret police with a single party, the Socialist Unity (Communist) Party. The Russians appropriated East German plants to restore their war-ravaged industry.

THE BERLIN WALL (1961–1990)

Major anti-Communist riots broke out in East Berlin in June 1953 and, on Aug. 13, 1961, the Soviet Sector was sealed off by a Communist-built wall, 26 1/2 miles (43 km) long, running through the city. It was built to stem the flood of refugees seeking freedom in the West, 200,000 having fled in 1961 before the wall was erected.

On Nov. 9, 1989, several weeks after the resignation of East Germany's long-time Communist leader, Erich Honecker, the wall's designer and chief defender, the East German government opened its borders to the West and allowed thousands of its citizens to pass freely through the Berlin Wall. They were cheered and greeted by thousands of West Berliners, and many of the jubilant newcomers celebrated their new freedom by climbing on top of the hated wall.

The following day, East German troops began dismantling parts of the wall. It was ironic that this wall was built to keep the citizens from leaving and, 28 years later, it was being dismantled for the same reason.

On Nov. 22, new passages were opened at the north and south of the Brandenburg Gate in an emotional ceremony attended by Chancellor Helmut Kohl of West Germany and Chancellor Hans Modrow of East Germany. The opening of the Brandenburg Gate climaxed the ending of the barriers that had divided the German people since the end of World War II. By the end of 1990, the entire wall had been removed.

By 1973, normal relations were established between East and West Germany and the two states entered the United Nations.

The 25-year diplomatic hiatus between East Germany and the U.S. ended Sept. 4, 1974, with the establishment of formal relations.

Agreements in Paris in 1954 giving the Federal Republic full independence and complete sovereignty came into force on May 5, 1955. Under it, West Germany and Italy became members of the Brussels treaty organization created in 1948 and renamed the Western European Union. West Germany also became a member of NATO. In 1955 the U.S.S.R. recognized the Federal Republic. The Saar territory, under an agreement between France and West Germany, held a plebiscite and despite economic links to France voted to rejoin West Germany. It became a state of West Germany on Jan. 1, 1957.

In 1963, Chancellor Adenauer concluded a treaty of mutual cooperation and friendship with France and then retired. He was succeeded by his chief inner-party critic, Ludwig Erhard, who was followed in 1966 by Kurt Georg Kiesinger. He, in turn, was succeeded in 1969 by Willy Brandt, former mayor of West Berlin.

The division between West Germany and East Germany was intensified when the Communists erected the Berlin Wall in 1961. In 1968, the East German Communist leader, Walter Ulbricht, imposed restrictions on West German movements into West Berlin. The Soviet-bloc invasion of Czechoslovakia in August 1968 added to the tension.

A treaty with the U.S.S.R. was signed in Moscow in August 1970 in which force was renounced and respect for the "territorial integrity" of present European states declared.

Three months later, West Germany signed a similar treaty with Poland, renouncing force and setting Poland's western border as the Oder-Neisse Line. It subsequently resumed formal relations with Czechoslovakia in a pact that "voided" the Munich treaty that gave Nazi Germany the Sudetenland.

Both German states were admitted to the United Nations in 1973.

Brandt, winner of a Nobel Peace Prize for his foreign policies, was forced to resign in 1974 when an East German spy was discovered to be one of his top staff members. Succeeding him was a moderate Social Democrat, Helmut Schmidt.

Helmut Schmidt, Brandt's successor as chancellor, staunchly backed U.S. military strategy in Europe nevertheless, staking his political fate on the strategy of placing U.S. nuclear missiles in Germany unless the Soviet Union reduced its arsenal of intermediate missiles.

The chancellor also strongly opposed nuclear freeze proposals and won 2–1 support for his stand at the convention of Social Democrats in April. The Free Democrats then deserted the Socialists after losing ground in local elections and joined with the Christian Democrats to unseat Schmidt and install Helmut Kohl as chancellor in 1982. An economic upswing in 1986 led to Kohl's re-election.

The fall of the Communist government in East Germany left only Soviet objections to German reunification to be dealt with. This was resolved in July 1990. Soviet objections to a reunified Germany belonging to NATO were dropped in return for German promises to reduce their military and engage in wide-ranging economic cooperation with the Soviet Union.

In ceremonies beginning on the evening of Tuesday, Oct. 2, 1990, and continuing throughout the next day, the German Democratic Republic acceded to the Federal Republic and Germany became a united and sovereign state for the first time since 1945. Some one million people gathered at midnight Oct. 2 at the Reichstag in Berlin. At midnight, a replica of the Liberty Bell, a gift from the United States, rang, and unity was officially proclaimed.

Following unification, the Federal Republic became the second largest country in Europe, after the Soviet Union. A reunited Berlin serves as the official capital, although the government will initially remain in Bonn.

During the national election campaign of late 1990 the central issue remained the cost of unification, including the modernization of the former East German economy. The ruling Christian Democrats promised no tax increases would be needed, while the opposition Social Democrats argued that this was mere wishful thinking.

In the December 2 election the Christian Democrats emerged as the strongest group, taking 43.8% of the vote. Analysts generally considered the vote to be an expression of thanks and support to the Chancellor for his forceful drive for political unity. The Party of Democratic Socialism, formerly the Communist Party, won 17 seats in Parliament.

The new Parliament convened in January 1991 reelecting Helmut Kohl chancellor. Nevertheless it soon became clear that previous official estimates of the cost and time required to absorb eastern Germany were considerably understated. The number of failed enterprises in the east continued to grow, and the exodus of personnel to western Germany ceased to abate.

On June 20, 1991 the German Parliament officially voted in favor of moving the seat of the federal government to Berlin, although given the huge expense of such a move it would be done slowly and require 12 years before Berlin would be a fully functional federal capital.

Germany ratified the Maastricht Treaty in October 1993, being the last of the 12 EC members to do so.

The Federal Constitutional Court in July 1994 ruled in favor of the use of German military forces outside the country if parliamentary approval is received first.

General elections in October 1994 gave the ruling coalition a majority in the Bundestag. In November Kohl received formal re-election in that body.

GHANA

Republic of Ghana
President: Jerry John Rawlings
Area: 92,100 sq mi. (238,537 sq km)
Population (est. mid-1995): 17,500,000 (average annual rate of natural increase: 3.0%); birth rate: 42/1000; infant mortality rate: 81/1000; density per square mile: 190
Capital: Accra; **Largest cities (est. 1988):** Accra, 949,100; Kumasi, 385,200 Tamale, 151,100; **Monetary unit:** Cedi; **Languages:** English (official), Native tongues (Brong Ahafo, Twi, Fanti, Ga, Ewe, Dagbani); **Religions:** indigenous belief, 38%; Islam, 30%; Christian, 24%; **Literacy rate:** 60%
Member of Commonwealth of Nations
Economic summary: Gross domestic product (1993 est.): $25 billion; per capita $1,500; real growth rate 3.9% (1992 est.); inflation 10% est.; (1992) unemployment (1991) 10%. Arable land: 5%. Principal products: cocoa, coconuts, coffee, cassava, yams, rice, rubber. Labor force (1983): 3,700,000; 18.7% in industry. Major products: mining products, cocoa products, aluminum. Natural resources: gold, industrial diamonds, bauxite, manganese, timber, fish. Exports: $1.1 billion (f.o.b., 1992): cocoa beans and products, gold, timber, tuna, bauxite, and aluminum. Imports: $1.4 billion (c.i.f., 1992 est.): petroleum, consumer goods, foods, intermediate goods, capital equipment. Major trading partners: U.K., U.S., Germany, France, Japan, South Korea.

Geography. A West African country bordering on the Gulf of Guinea, Ghana is bounded by Côte d'Ivoire to the west, Burkina Faso to the north, Togo to the east and the Atlantic Ocean to the south. It compares in size to Oregon.

The coastal belt, extending about 270 miles (435 km), is sandy, marshy, and generally exposed. Behind it is a gradually widening grass strip. The forested plateau region to the north is broken by ridges and hills. The largest river is the Volta.

Government. A republic. Presidential and Parliamentary elections were held Nov. 3, 1992 and ushered in the Fourth Republic on Jan. 7, 1993.

History. Created an independent country on March 6, 1957, Ghana is the former British colony of the Gold Coast. The area was first seen by Portuguese traders in 1470. They were followed by the English (1553), the Dutch (1595), and the Swedes (1640). British rule over the Gold Coast began in 1820, but it was not until after quelling the severe resistance of the Ashanti in 1901 that it was firmly established. British Togoland, formerly a colony of Germany, was incorporated into Ghana by referendum in 1956. As the result of a plebiscite, Ghana became a republic on July 1, 1960.

Premier Kwame Nkrumah attempted to take leadership of the Pan-African Movement, holding the All-African People's Congress in his capital, Accra, in 1958 and organizing the Union of African States with Guinea and Mali in 1961. But he oriented his country toward the Soviet Union and China and built an autocratic rule over all aspects of Ghanaian life.

In February 1966, while Nkrumah was visiting Peking and Hanoi, he was deposed by a military coup led by Gen. Emmanuel K. Kotoka.

A series of military coups followed and on June 4, 1979, Flight Lieutenant Jerry Rawlings overthrew Lt. Gen. Frederick Akuffo's military rule. Rawlings permitted the election of a civilian president to go ahead as scheduled the following month, and Hilla Limann, candidate of the People's National Party, took office. Charging the civilian government with corruption and repression, Rawlings staged another coup on Dec. 31, 1981. As chairman of the Provisional National Defense Council, Rawlings instituted an austerity program and reduced budget deficits.

In a referendum of May 1992 over 92% of the voters approved a new constitution, which provided for a multi-party system.

In the elections of late 1992 Rawlings won a majority of the votes for president. The governing National Democratic Congress held 189 of the 200 seats in parliament. The country's favorable standing with the World Bank enabled it to receive a $2.1 billion aid grant.

Despite consistent economic growth, almost daily demonstrations occurred largely in protest against the introduction of a 17.5% value-added tax in March 1995.

GREECE

Hellenic Republic
President: Costis Stephanopoulos (1995)
Premier: Andreas Papandreou (1993)
Area: 50,961 sq mi. (131,990 sq km)
Population (est. mid-1995): 10,500,000 (average annual rate of natural increase: 0.0%); birth rate: 10/1000; infant mortality rate: 8.3/1000; density per square mile: 206
Capital: Athens; **Largest cities (1991 est.):** Athens, 3,000,000; Salonika, 720,000; Piraeus, 170,000; Patras, 155,000; Heraklion, 117,000; Larissa, 113,500; **Monetary unit:** Drachma; **Language:** Greek; **Religion:** Greek Orthodox, 98%; Muslim, 1.3%; **National name:** Elliniki Dimokratia; **Literacy rate:** 93%
Economic summary: Gross domestic product (1993): $93.2 billion; $8,900 per capita; 1% real growth rate; inflation 14.4%; unemployment 9.5%. Arable land: 23%. Principal agricultural products: grains, fruits, vegetables, olives, olive oil, tobacco, cotton, livestock, dairy products. Labor force (1993): 4.083 million; 48% services, 24% agriculture, 28% industry. Major industrial products: textiles, chemicals, food processing. Natural resources: bauxite, lignite, magnesite, crude oil, marble. Exports: $6 billion (f.o.b., 1992): manufactured goods, food and live animals, fuels and lubricants, raw materials. Imports: $23.3 billion (c.i.f.,

1992): machinery and automotive equipment, petroleum, consumer goods, chemicals, foodstuffs. Major trading partners: Germany, Italy, France, U.S.A., U.K., Netherlands.

Geography. Greece, on the Mediterranean Sea, is the southernmost country on the Balkan Peninsula in southern Europe. It is bordered on the north by Albania, Yugoslavia, and Bulgaria; on the west by the Ionian Sea; and on the east by the Aegean Sea and Turkey. It is slightly smaller than Alabama.

North central Greece, Epirus, and western Macedonia all are mountainous. The main chain of the Pindus Mountains rises to 10,256 feet (3,126 m) in places, separating Epirus from the plains of Thessaly. Mt. Olympus, rising to 9,570 feet (2,909 m) in the north near the Aegean Sea, is the highest point in the country. Greek Thrace is mostly a lowland region separated from European Turkey by the lower Evros River.

Among the many islands are the Ionian group off the west coast; the Cyclades group to the southeast; other islands in the eastern Aegean, including the Dodecanese Islands, Euboea, Lesbos, Samos, and Chios; and Crete, the fourth largest Mediterranean island.

Government. A referendum in December 1974, five months after the collapse of a military dictatorship, ended the Greek monarchy and established a republic. Ceremonial executive power is held by the president; the Premier heads the government and is responsible to a 300-member unicameral Parliament.

History. Greece, with a recorded history going back to 766 B.C., reached the peak of its glory in the 5th century B.C., and by the middle of the 2nd century B.C., it had declined to the status of a Roman province. It remained within the Eastern Roman Empire until Constantinople fell to the Crusaders in 1204.

In 1453, the Turks took Constantinople, and by 1460 Greece was a Turkish province. The insurrection made famous by the poet Lord Byron broke out in 1821, and in 1827 Greece won independence with sovereignty guaranteed by Britain, France, and Russia.

The protecting powers chose Prince Otto of Bavaria as the first king of modern Greece in 1832 to reign over an area only slightly larger than the Peloponnese Peninsula. Chiefly under the next king, George I, chosen by the protecting powers in 1863, Greece acquired much of its present territory. During his 57-year reign, a period in which he encouraged parliamentary democracy, Thessaly, Epirus, Macedonia, Crete, and most of the Aegean islands were added from the disintegrating Turkish empire. An unsuccessful war against Turkey after World War I brought down the monarchy, to be replaced by a republic in 1923.

Two military dictatorships and a financial crisis brought George II back from exile, but only until 1941, when Italian and German invaders defeated tough Greek resistance. After British and Greek troops liberated the country in October 1944, Communist guerrillas staged a long campaign in which the government received U.S. aid under the Truman Doctrine, the predecessor of the Marshall Plan.

A military junta seized power in April 1967, sending young King Constantine II into exile December 14. Col. George Papadopoulos, as premier, converted the government to republican form in 1973 and as President ended martial law. He was moving to restore democracy when he was ousted in November of that year by his military colleagues. The regime of the "colonels," which had tortured its opponents and scoffed at human rights, resigned July 23, 1974, after having bungled an attempt to seize Cyprus.

Former Premier Karamanlis returned from exile to become premier of Greece's first civilian government since 1967.

On Jan. 1, 1981, Greece became the 10th member of the European Community.

Double-digit inflation and scandals in the Socialist government led to them losing their majority in the elections of June 1989. Elections in April 1990 finally gave the conservative New Democracy Party a one-seat majority in parliament. Soon afterwards Karamanlis, the founder of that party, was elected president by parliament.

An election in October 1993 saw the return to power of Mr. Papandreou, who two years earlier was acquitted of criminal charges.

In April 1994 the European Union started legal action against Greece for its refusal to remove a trade blockade against the Republic of Macedonia.

Parliament assented to the international Law of the Sea treaty in early-June 1995, immediately drawing protests from Turkey, fearing Greece would extend its territorial waters.

GRENADA

State of Grenada
Sovereign: Queen Elizabeth II
Governor General: Sir Reginald Palmer (1992)
Prime Minister: Hon. George T. Brizan (1995)
Area: 133 sq mi. (344 sq km)
Population (est. mid-1995): 100,000 (average annual growth rate, 2.4%); birth rate: 29/1000; infant mortality rate: 12/1000; density per square mile: 751.8
Capital and largest city (1991): St. George's, 4,439; **Monetary unit:** East Caribbean dollar; **Ethnic groups:** Blacks and Indians; **Language:** English; **Religions:** Roman Catholic, 64%; Anglican, 21%; **Literacy rate:** 98%; **Member of Commonwealth of Nations**
Economic summary: Gross domestic product (1992 est.): $250 million; $3,000 per capita; –0.4% real growth rate; inflation rate (1991 est.) 2.6%; est. unemployment rate 25%. Arable land: 15%. Principal products: spices, cocoa, bananas. Tourism is the leading foreign exchange earner followed by agricultural exports. Exports: $19.9 million (f.o.b., 1992 est.): nutmeg, cocoa beans, bananas, mace, textiles. Imports: $103.2 million (f.o.b., 1992 est.): foodstuffs, machinery, manufactured goods, petroleum, chemicals, fuel. Labor force: 36,000; 31% in services. Major trading partners: U.K., Trinidad and Tobago, U.S., Japan, Canada.

Geography. Grenada (the first "a" is pronounced as in "gray") is the most southerly of the Windward Islands, about 100 miles (161 km) from the South American coast. It is a volcanic island traversed by a mountain range, the highest peak of which is Mount St. Catherine (2,756 ft.; 840 m).

Government. A Governor-General represents the sovereign, Elizabeth II. The Prime Minister is the head of government, chosen by a 15-member House of Representatives elected by universal suffrage every five years.

History. Grenada was discovered by Columbus in 1498. After more than 200 years of British rule, most recently as part of the West Indies Associated States, it became independent Feb. 7, 1974, with Eric M. Gairy as Prime Minister.

Prime Minister Maurice Bishop, a protégé of Cuba's President Castro, was killed in a military coup on Oct. 19, 1983. At the request of five members of the Organization of Eastern Caribbean States, President Reagan ordered an invasion of Grenada on Oct. 25 involving over 1,900 U.S. troops and a small military force from Barbados, Dominica, Jamaica, St. Lucia, and St. Vincent. The troops met strong resistance from Cuban military personnel on the island.

A centrist coalition led by Herbert A. Blaize, a 66-year-old lawyer, won 14 of the 15 seats in Parliament in an election in December 1984, and Blaize became Prime Minister.

None of the four main parties won a clear victory in the election of March 1990. Negotiations led to the National Democratic Congress forming a government with the support of several members from other parties.

The income tax, which was abolished in 1986, was reinstated in 1994. In the interim the government found it was unable to obtain sufficient revenues to meet expenses.

GUATEMALA

Republic of Guatemala
President: Ramiro de Leon Carpio (1993)
Area: 42,042 sq mi. (108,889 sq km)
Population (est. mid-1995): 10,600,000 (average annual rate of natural increase: 3.1%); birth rate: 39/1000; infant mortality rate: 48/1000; density per sq mile: 252
Capital and largest city (est. 1993): Guatemala City, 2,000,000; **Monetary unit:** Quetzal; **Languages:** Spanish, Indian languages; **Religion:** Roman Catholic, Protestant, Mayan.; **National name:** República de Guatemala; **Literacy rate:** 55%
Economic summary: Gross domestic product (1993 est.): $31.3 billion; per capita $3,000; real growth rate 4%; inflation 11.6%; unemployment (1992 est.) 6.1%. Arable land: 12%. Principal products: corn, beans, coffee, cotton, cattle, sugar, bananas, fruits and vegetables. Labor force: 2,500,000; 14% in manufacturing. Principal products: sugar, textiles and clothing, furniture, chemicals, petroleum, metals, rubber. Natural resources: nickel, crude oil, rare woods, fish, chicle. Exports: $1.3 billion (f.o.b., 1993): coffee, sugar, bananas, beef. Imports: $2.6 billion (c.i.f., 1993): fuel and petroleum products, machinery, grain, fertilizers, motor vehicles. Major trading partners: U.S., Central-American nations, Caribbean, Mexico, Germany.

Geography. The northernmost of the Central American nations, Guatemala is the size of Tennessee. Its neighbors are Mexico on the north and west, and Belize, Honduras, and El Salvador on the east. The country consists of three main regions—the cool highlands with the heaviest population, the tropical area along the Pacific and Caribbean coasts, and the tropical jungle in the northern lowlands. The principal mountain range rises to the highest elevation in Central America and contains many volcanic peaks. Volcanic eruptions are frequent.

The Petén region in the north contains important resources and archaeological sites of the Mayan civilization.

Government. A republic with a unicameral legislative branch, the Congress of the Republic.

History. Once the site of the ancient Mayan civilization, Guatemala, conquered by Spain in 1524, set itself up as a republic in 1839. From 1898 to 1920, the dictator Manuel Estrada Cabrera ran the country, and from 1931 to 1944, Gen. Jorge Ubico Castaneda was the strongman.

Jacobo Arbenz Guzmán won the 1950 election. He expropriated the large estates, including plantations of the United Fruit Company. With covert U.S. backing, a revolt was led by Col. Carlos Castillo Armas, and Arbenz took refuge in Mexico. Castillo Armas became president but was assassinated in 1957. Gen. Miguel Ydigoras Fuentes was elected president in 1957.

A wave of terrorism, by left and right, began in 1967. Fear of anarchy led to the election in 1970 of Army Chief of Staff Carlos Araña Osorio. Araña, surprisingly, pledged social reforms when he took office. Another military candidate, Gen. Kjell Laugerud, won the presidency in 1974 amid renewed political violence.

The administration of Gen. Romeo Lucas Garcia, elected president in 1978, ended in a coup by a three-man military junta on March 23, 1982. Lucas Garcia was charged by Amnesty International with responsibility for at least 5,000 political murders in a reign of brutality and corruption that brought a cutoff of U.S. military aid in 1978. Hopes for improvement under the junta faded when Gen. José Efraín Ríos Montt took sole power in June.

President Oscar Mejía Victores, another general, seized power from Rios Montt in an August 1983 coup.

Jorge Serrano Elias presided over seven years of democratic rule until in May 1993 he moved to dissolve congress and the supreme court and suspend constitutional rights. Under strong foreign and domestic pressure the military deposed Serrano on June 1 and allowed the inauguration of de Leon Carpio, the former Attorney General of Human Rights and no particular friend of the military.

The basis for new negotiations to end a long-standing leftist rebellion was reached in January 1994. Yet rebel activity continued throughout the year with no end in sight.

August congressional elections gave a majority of seats to right-wing parties, but total voter turnout was very high, particularly in rural areas.

GUINEA

Republic of Guinea
President: Brig. Gen. Lansana Conté (1984)
Area: 94,925 sq mi. (245,857 sq km)
Population (est. mid-1995): 6,500,000 (average annual rate of natural increase: 2.4%); birth rate: 44/1000; infant mortality rate: 143/1000; density per square mile: 68.4
Capital and largest city (1983): Conakry, 705,280; **Monetary unit:** Guinean franc; **Languages:** French (official), native tongues (Malinké, Susu, Fulani); **Religions:** Islam, 85%; 7% indigenous, 8% Christian ; **National name:** République de Guinée; **Literacy rate:** 24% in French; 48% in local languages
Economic summary: Gross domestic product (1993 est.): $3.1 billion; per capita $500; real growth rate 3.2% (1992 est.); inflation 16.6%. (1992 est.). Arable land: 6%. Principal agricultural products: rice, cassava, millet, corn, coffee, bananas, pineapples. Labor force: 2,400,000 (1983); 11% in industry and commerce. Major industrial products: bauxite, alumina, light manufactured and processed goods, diamonds. Natural resources: bauxite, iron ore, diamonds, gold, water power. Exports: $622 million (f.o.b., 1992 est.): bauxite,

alumina, diamonds, pineapples, bananas, coffee. Imports: $768 million (c.i.f., 1992 est): petroleum, machinery, transport equipment, foodstuffs, textiles. Major trading partners: U.S., France, Brazil, Germany, Belgium, Ireland, Spain, Côte d'Ivoire, Hong Kong.

Geography. Guinea, in West Africa on the Atlantic, is also bordered by Guinea-Bissau, Senegal, Mali, the Ivory Coast, Liberia, and Sierra Leone. Slightly smaller than Oregon, the country consists of a coastal plain, a mountainous region, a savanna interior, and a forest area in the Guinea Highlands. The highest peak is Mount Nimba at 5,748 ft (1,752 m).

Government. Military government headed by President Lansana Conté, who promoted himself from colonel to brigadier general after a 1984 coup. In 1989, President Conté announced that Guinea would move to a multi-party democracy.

A new constitution approved in a nationwide referendum, December 1990, provided for the establishment of a directly elected multi-party parliament (five-year terms) and a popularly elected president for a maximum of two five-year terms, and a judiciary to be independent of either the presidency or the legislature. A transitional Committee for National Recovery (CTRN) replaced the military committee to guide implementation of the new constitution.

History. Previously part of French West Africa, Guinea achieved independence by rejecting the new French Constitution, and on Oct. 2, 1958, became an independent state with Sékou Touré as president. Touré led the country into being the first avowedly Marxist state in Africa. Diplomatic relations with France were suspended in 1965, with the Soviet Union replacing France as the country's chief source of economic and technical assistance.

Prosperity came in 1960 after the start of exploitation of bauxite deposits. Touré was re-elected to a seven-year term in 1974 and again in 1981.

After 26 years as President, Touré died in the United States in March 1984, following surgery. A week later, a military regime headed by Col. Lansana Conté took power with a promise not to shed any more blood after Touré's harsh rule. Conté became President and his co-conspirator in the coup, Col. Diara Traoré, became Prime Minister, but Conté later demoted Traoré to Education Minister. Traoré tried to seize power on July 4, 1985, while Conté was out of the country, but his attempted coup was crushed by troops loyal to Conté.

In 1991 voters approved a new constitution that would lead the country to democracy. Under mounting popular pressure Conté declared in April 1992 that constitutional rule would begin.

In December 1993 elections the president's Unity and Progress Party took almost 51% of the vote cast.

In a cabinet reshuffling in August 1994 the president dismissed all remaining opposition ministers.

GUINEA-BISSAU

Republic of Guinea-Bissau
President: João Bernardo Vieira (1980)
Area: 13,948 sq mi. (36,125 sq km)
Population (est. mid-1995): 1,100,000 (average annual rate of natural increase: 2.1%); birth rate: 43/1000; infant mortality rate: 140/1000; density per square mile: 78.8

Capital and largest city (est. 1988): Bissau, 125,000; **Monetary unit:** Guinea-Bissau peso; **Language:** Portugese Criolo, African languages; **Religions:** traditional, 65%; Islam, 30%; Christian, 5%; **National name:** República da Guiné-Bissau; **Literacy rate:** 36% (1991 est.)
Economic summary: Gross national product (1993 est.): $860 million; $800 per capita; real growth rate n.a.; inflation: 55% (1991 est.). Arable land: 9%. Principal products: palm kernels, cotton, cashew nuts, peanuts. Labor force: 403,000 (est.): Agriculture, 90%; industry, services, and commerce, 5%; government, 5%. Major industries: food processing, beer, soft drinks. Natural resources: unexploited deposits of bauxite, petroleum, phosphates; fish and timber. Exports: $20.4 million (f.o.b., 1991 est.): peanuts, cashews, fish, palm kernels. Imports: $63.5 million (f.o.b., 1991 est.): capital equipment, consumer goods, semiprocessed goods, foods, petroleum. Major trading partners: Portugal, Spain, and other European countries, Senegal, U.S., China, India, Nigeria.

Geography. A neighbor of Senegal and Guinea in West Africa, on the Atlantic coast, Guinea-Bissau is about half the size of South Carolina.

The country is a low-lying coastal region of swamps, rain forests, and mangrove-covered wetlands, with about 25 islands off the coast. The Bijagos archipelago extends 30 miles (48 km) out to sea. Internal communications depend mainly on deep estuaries and meandering rivers, since there are no railroads. Bissau, the capital, is the main port.

Government. After the overthrow of Louis Cabral in November 1980, the nine-member Council of the Revolution formed an interm government. At present the government consists of a president and a single 100-member legislative body.

History. Guinea-Bissau was discovered in 1446 by the Portuguese Nuno Tristao, and colonists in the Cape Verde Islands obtained trading rights in the territory. In 1879 the connection with the Cape Verde Islands was broken. Early in the 1900s the Portuguese managed to pacify some tribesmen, although resistance to colonial rule remained.

The African Party for the Independence of Guinea-Bissau and Cape Verde was founded in 1956 and several years later began guerrilla warfare that grew increasingly effective. By 1974 the rebels controlled most of the countryside, where they formed a government that was soon recognized by scores of countries. The military coup in Portugal in April 1974 brightened the prospects for freedom, and in August the Lisbon government signed an agreement granting independence to the province as of Sept. 10. The new republic took the name Guinea-Bissau.

In November 1980, Prémier João Bernardo Vieira headed a coup that deposed Luis Cabral, President since 1974. A Revolutionary Council assumed the powers of government, with Vieira as its head. An extraordinary congress of the ruling party in January 1991 approved a multi-party system. In June the constitution was amended to allow for opposition parties.

July 1994 multiparty presidential and legislative elections gave the president's party 64 seats in the Assembly although Vieira himself less than a majority. In the runoff election Vieira officially received 52% of the vote.

GUYANA

Cooperative Republic of Guyana
President: Dr. Cheddi Jagan (1992)
Area: 83,000 sq mi. (214,969 sq km)
Population (est. mid-1995): 800,000 (average annual rate of natural increase: 1.8%); birth rate: 25/1000; infant mortality rate: 48/1000; density per square mile: 9.6
Capital and largest city (est. 1990): Georgetown, 234,000; **Monetary unit:** Guyana dollar; **Languages:** English (official), Amerindian dialects; **Religions:** Hindu, 34%; Protestant, 18%; Islam, 9%; Roman Catholic, 18%; Anglican, 16%; **Member of Commonwealth of Nations; Literacy rate:** 95%
Economic summary: Gross national product (1993 est.): $1.4 billion; $1,900 per capita; real growth rate 8.3%; inflation: 13% (1994); unemployment (1994 est.): 8–10%. Arable land: 3%. Principal products: sugar, rice. Labor force (1985): 268,000; 44.5% industry and commerce. Major products: bauxite, alumina. Natural resources: bauxite, gold, diamonds, hardwood timber, shrimp. Exports: $400 million (f.o.b., 1993 est.): sugar, bauxite, rice, timber, shrimp, gold, molasses, rum. Imports: $520 million (c.i.f., 1993 est.): petroleum, food, machinery, manufactures. Major trading partners: U.K., U.S., Canada, Japan, Trinidad and Tobago, Germany.

Geography. Guyana is situated on the northern coast of South America east of Venezuela, west of Suriname, and north of Brazil. The country consists of a low coastal area and the Guiana Highlands in the south. There is an extensive north-south network of rivers. Guyana is the size of Idaho.

Government. Guyana, formerly British Guiana, proclaimed itself a republic on Feb. 23, 1970, ending its tie with Britain while remaining in the Commonwealth.

Guyana has a unicameral legislature, the National Assembly, with 53 members directly elected for five-year terms and 12 elected by local councils. A 13-member Cabinet is headed by the President.

History. British Guiana won internal self-government in 1952. The next year the People's Progressive Party, headed by Cheddi B. Jagan, an East Indian dentist, won the elections and Jagan became Prime Minister. British authorities deposed him for alleged Communist connections. A coalition ousted Jagan in 1964, installing a moderate Socialist, Forbes Burnham, a black, as Prime Minister. On May 26, 1966, the country became an independent member of the Commonwealth and resumed its traditional name, Guyana.

After ruling Guyana for 21 years, Burnham died on Aug. 6, 1985, in a Guyana hospital after a throat operation.

Jagan's People's Progressive Party won a majority in the general election of October 1992.

Local elections in 1994 gave a surprisingly strong showing for the governing alliance. The IMF also promised substantial financial aid.

HAITI

Republic of Haiti
President: Jean-Bertrand Aristide (in exile)
Prime Minister: Smarck Michel (1994)
Area: 10,714 sq mi. (27,750 sq km)
Population (est. mid-1995): 7,200,000 (average annual rate of natural increase: 2.3%); birth rate: 35/1000; infant mortality rate: 74/1000; density per square mile: 672
Capital and largest city (est. 1993): Port-au-Prince, 1.5 million
Monetary unit: Gourde
Languages: Creole, French
Religion: Roman Catholic, 80%; Protestant, 16%; Vaudou, 95%
National name: République d'Haïti
Literacy rate: 25%
Economic summary: Gross domestic product (1992 est.): $1.5 billion; $250 per capita; –4.0% real growth rate; inflation 20%; unemployment 25–50%. Arable land: 50%. Principal agricultural products: coffee, sugar cane, rice, corn, sorghum. Labor force: 2,300,000; 66% in agriculture. Major industrial products: refined sugar, textiles, flour, cement, light assembly products. Natural resource: bauxite. Exports: $135 million (f.o.b., 1992 est.): coffee, light industrial products, agricultural products. Imports: $423 million (f.o.b., 1992 est.): machines and manufactures, food and beverages, petroleum products, fats and oils, chemicals. IMajor trading partner: U.S., Italy, France, Japan.

Geography. Haiti, in the West Indies, occupies the western third of the island of Hispaniola, which it shares with the Dominican Republic. About the size of Maryland, Haiti is two thirds mountainous, with the rest of the country marked by great valleys, extensive plateaus, and small plains. The most densely populated region is the Cul-de-Sac plain near Port-au-Prince.

Government. A republic with a bicameral assembly consisting of an upper house or Senate and a lower house, the House of Deputies. The National Assembly consists of 27 senate seats and 83 deputies.

Democratically-elected Pres. Aristide was replaced by a de facto regime in October 1991 following a military coup on Sept. 30, 1991. He was reinstated in October 1993 by a U.S.-led multinational force appointed by U.N. Resolution 940. A U.S. peace mission in September 1994 reached a compromise with the military leaders, avoiding a U.S. invasion. Acting as peacekeepers U.S. troops landed in Haiti, allowing Aristide to return in mid-October.

History. Discovered by Columbus, who landed at Môle Saint Nicolas on Dec. 6, 1492, Haiti in 1697 became a French possession known as Saint Domingue. An insurrection among a slave population of 500,000 in 1791 ended with a declaration of independence by Pierre-Dominique Toussaint l'Ouverture in 1801. Napoleon Bonaparte suppressed the independence movement, but it eventually triumphed in 1804 under Jean-Jacques Dessalines, who gave the new nation the aboriginal name Haiti.

Its prosperity dissipated in internal strife as well as disputes with neighboring Santo Domingo during a succession of 19th-century dictatorships, a bankrupt Haiti accepted a U.S. customs receivership from 1905 to 1941. Direct U.S. rule from 1915 to 1934 brought a measure of stability and a population growth that made Haiti the most densely populated nation in the hemisphere.

In 1949, after four years of democratic rule by President Dumarsais Estimé, dictatorship returned under Gen. Paul Magloire, who was succeeded by François Duvalier in 1957.

Duvalier established a dictatorship based on secret police, known as the "Ton-ton Macoutes," who gunned down opponents of the regime. Duvalier's son, Jean-Claude, or "Baby Doc," succeeded his father in 1971 as ruler of the poorest nation in the Western Hemisphere. Duvalier fled the country in 1986 after strong unrest.

Following the election of December 6, 1990 which he won, Jean-Bertrand Aristide, a Roman Catholic priest, was sworn in as president on February 7, 1991—the country's first freely elected chief executive.

In September 1991 elements of the military seized the President and took control of the government. Although the OAS attempted to have Aristide reinstated the Army forced the Assembly officially to depose him. The OAS call for economic blockade led to a sharp downturn in an already poor economy.

The population largely ignored parliamentary elections the following January. In July Aristide and the army signed an accord to return the exiled president to power.

When the military leaders failed to resign the UN reimposed an embargo.

After Aristide's return to Haiti in October 1994 he moved quickly to replace the police force, downsize the military, and purge the officer corps. His cabinet choices were largely those with expertise in economic matters.

The first round of parliamentary elections was held in July 1995, but widespread irregularities forced the postponement of the second round.

HONDURAS

Republic of Honduras
President: Carlos Roberto Reina Idiáquez (1994)
Area: 43,872 sq mi. (112,492 sq km)
Population (est. mid-1995): 5,500,000 (average annual rate of natural increase: 2.8%); birth rate: 34/1000; infant mortality rate: 50/1000; density per sq mi.: 125.3
Capital and largest city (1995): Tegucigalpa, 1,500,000; **Monetary unit:** Lempira; **Languages:** Spanish (official), English widely spoken in business. **Religion:** Roman Catholic, 94%; Protestant minority; **National name:** República de Honduras; **Literacy rate:** 73%
Economic summary: Gross domestic product (1993 est.): $10 billion; $1,950 per capita; real growth rate 3.7%; inflation 13%; unemployment (1992) 10%. Arable land: 14%. Principal products: bananas, coffee, timber, beef, shrimp, citrus. Labor force (1985): 1,300,000; agriculture 62%; services 20%. Major industrial products: processed agricultural products, textiles and clothing, wood products. Natural resources: timber, gold, silver, copper, lead, zinc, iron ore, antimony. Exports: $850 million (f.o.b., 1993 est.): bananas, coffee, lumber, shrimp and lobster, minerals. Imports: $1.1 billion (c.i.f., 1993 est.): manufactured goods, machinery, transportation equipment, chemicals, petroleum. Major trading partners: U.S., Caribbean countries, Western Europe, Japan, Latin America.

Geography. Honduras, in the north central part of Central America, has a 400-mile (644-km) Caribbean coastline and a 40-mile (64-km) Pacific frontage. Its neighbors are Guatemala to the west, El Salvador to the south, and Nicaragua to the east. Honduras is slightly larger than Tennessee. Generally mountainous, the country is marked by fertile plateaus, river valleys, and narrow coastal plains.

Government. The President serves a four-year term. There is a 134-member National Congress.

History. Columbus discovered Honduras on his last voyage in 1502. Honduras, with four other countries of Central America, declared its independence from Spain in 1821 and was part of a federation of Central American states until 1838. In that year it seceded from the federation and became a completely independent country.

In July 1969, El Salvador invaded Honduras after Honduran landowners had deported several thousand Salvadorans. The fighting left 1,000 dead and tens of thousands homeless. By threatening economic sanctions and military intervention, the OAS induced El Salvador to withdraw.

Although parliamentary democracy returned with the election of Roberto Suazo Córdova as President in 1982 after a decade of military rule, Honduras faced severe economic problems and tensions along its border with Nicaragua. "Contra" rebels, waging a guerrilla war against the Sandinista regime in Nicaragua, used Honduras as a training and staging area. At the same time, the United States used Honduras as a site for military exercises and built bases to train both Honduran and Salvadoran troops.

In the first democratic transition of power since 1932 Rafael Callejas became president in January 1990. The immediate task was to deal with a deficit caused in part by reduced U.S. aid and the previous government's fiscal policies.

Running on a platform attacking governmental corruption and military influence the candidate of the Liberal Party, Carlos Reina, won the general election of November 1993 against the ruling National Party.

To improve the economic climate the president proposed to increase taxes and slash the budget by 10% while continuing social spending aimed at combating poverty.

HUNGARY

Republic of Hungary
President: Arpad Goncz (1990)
Premier: Gyula Horn (1994)
Area: 35,919 sq mi. (93,030 sq km)
Population (est. mid-1995): 10,200,000 (average annual rate of natural increase: –0.3%); birth rate: 12/1000; infant mortality rate: 11.6/1000; density per square mile: 283.9
Capital and largest city (1992 est.): Budapest, 2,016,000; **Other large cities (1992 est.):** Debrecen, 216,137; Miskolc, 192,355; Szeged, 177,680; Péces, 170,540; Gyór, 130,300; **Monetary unit:** Forint; **Language:** Magyar; **Religions:** Roman Catholic, 67.5%; Protestant, 25%; atheist and others, 7.5%; **National name:** Magyar Köztársaság; **Literacy rate:** 99%
Economic summary: Gross domestic product (1993 est.): $57 billion; $5,500 per capita; –1% real growth rate; inflation rate 23%; unemployment rate 13%. Arable land: 54%. Principal agricultural products: corn, wheat, potatoes, sugar beets, sun flowers, livestock, dairy products. Labor force (1991): 5,400,000; 43.2% in services, trade and government. Major industrial products: steel, chemicals, pharmaceuticals, textiles, transport equipment. Natural resources: bauxite, coal, natural gas. Exports: $10.9 billion (f.o.b., 1992 est.): raw materials, semi-finished goods, chemicals, machinery, light industry, food and agricultural, fuels and energy. Imports: $11.7 billion (f.o.b., 1992 est.): fuels and energy, raw materials, semi-finished goods, chemicals, machinery, light industry, food and agricultural. Major trading partners: C.I.S. countries, Eastern Europe.

Geography. This central European country the size of Indiana is bordered by Austria to the west, Slovakia to the north, Ukraine and Romania to the east, and Yugoslavia to the south.

Most of Hungary is a fertile, rolling plain lying east of the Danube River and drained by the Danube and Tisza rivers. In the extreme northwest is the Little Hungarian Plain. South of that area is Lake Balaton (250 sq mi.; 648 sq km).

Government. Hungary is a Republic with legislative power vested in the unicameral National Assembly, whose 386 members are elected directly for four-year terms. The National Assembly elects the President.

The major political parties are the Socialist Party, the Hungarian Democratic Forum, the Alliance of Free Democrats, the Independent Socialist Party and the Independent Smallholder's Party and the Young Democrats (FIDESZ).

History. About 2,000 years ago, Hungary was part of the Roman provinces of Pannonia and Dacia. In A.D. 896 it was invaded by the Magyars, who founded a kingdom. Christianity was accepted during the reign of Stephen I (St. Stephen) (997–1038).

The peak of Hungary's great period of medieval power came during the reign of Louis I the Great (1342–82), whose dominions touched the Baltic, Black, and Mediterranean seas.

War with the Turks broke out in 1389, and for more than 100 years the Turks advanced through the Balkans. When the Turks smashed a Hungarian army in 1526, western and northern Hungary accepted Hapsburg rule to escape Turkish occupation. Transylvania became independent under Hungarian princes. Intermittent war with the Turks was waged until a peace treaty was signed in 1699.

After the suppression of the 1848 revolt against Hapsburg rule, led by Louis Kossuth, the dual monarchy of Austria-Hungary was set up in 1867.

The dual monarchy was defeated with the other Central Powers in World War I. After a short-lived republic in 1918, the chaotic Communist rule of 1919 under Béla Kun ended with the Romanians occupying Budapest on Aug. 4, 1919. When the Romanians left, Adm. Nicholas Horthy entered the capital with a national army. The Treaty of Trianon of June 4, 1920, cost Hungary 68% of its land and 58% of its population. Meanwhile, the National Assembly had restored the legal continuity of the old monarchy; and, on March 1, 1920, Horthy was elected Regent.

Following the German invasion of Russia on June 22, 1941, Hungary joined the attack against the Soviet Union, but the war was not popular and Hungarian troops were almost entirely withdrawn from the eastern front by May 1943. German occupation troops set up a puppet government after Horthy's appeal for an armistice with advancing Soviet troops on Oct. 15, 1944, had resulted in his overthrow. The German regime soon fled the capital, however, and on December 23 a provisional government was formed in Soviet-occupied eastern Hungary. On Jan. 20, 1945, it signed an armistice in Moscow. Early the next year, the National Assembly approved a constitutional law abolishing the thousand-year-old monarchy and establishing a republic.

By the Treaty of Paris (1947), Hungary had to give up all territory it had acquired since 1937 and to pay $300 million reparations to the U.S.S.R., Czechoslovakia, and Yugoslavia. In 1948 the Communist Party, with the support of Soviet troops seized control. Hungary was proclaimed a People's Republic and one-party state in 1949. Industry was nationalized, the land collectivized into state farms, and the opposition terrorized by the secret police.

The terror, modeled after that of the U.S.S.R., reached its height with the trial of József Cardinal Mindszenty, Roman Catholic primate. He confessed to fantastic charges under duress of drugs or brainwashing and was sentenced to life imprisonment in 1949. Protests were voiced in all parts of the world.

On Oct. 23, 1956, anti-Communist revolution broke out in Budapest. To cope with it, the Communists set up a coalition government and called former Premier Imre Nagy back to head it. But he and most of his ministers were swept by the logic of events into the anti-Communist opposition, and he declared Hungary a neutral power, withdrawing from the Warsaw Treaty and appealing to the United Nations for help.

One of his ministers, János Kádár, established a counter-regime and asked the U.S.S.R. to send in military power. Soviet troops and tanks suppressed the revolution in bloody fighting after 190,000 people had fled the country and Mindszenty, freed from jail, had taken refuge in the U.S. Embassy.

Kádár was succeeded as Premier, but not party secretary, by Gyula Kallai in 1965. Continuing his program of national reconciliation, Kádár emptied prisons, reformed the secret police, and eased travel restrictions.

Following local and parliamentary elections in October 1990, József Antall's Hungarian Democratic Forum and its conservative coalition parties held 60% of the parliamentary seats. The last Soviet troops left Hungary in June 1991, thereby ending almost 47 years of military presence.

The transition to a market economy was proving difficult. Hungary strengthened its ties with Poland and Czechoslovakia but grew concerned about the fate of ethnic Hungarians in neighboring countries.

Hungary cautiously watched the birth of Slovakia and its treatment of a large ethnic Hungarian minority.

Hungary became the first country to accept formally a US-designed partnership plan with NATO in January 1994.

Parliamentary elections in May 1994 gave the Socialists, formerly the Communists, a 15-seat majority. A coalition government with the Free Democrats was formed in July. The expected economic reforms, however, were not immediately enacted as had been expected.

ICELAND

Republic of Iceland
President: Mrs. Vigdis Finnbogadottir (1980)
Prime Minister: David Oddsson (1991)
Area: 39,709 sq mi. (102,846 sq km)
Population (est. mid-1995): 300,000 (average annual rate of natural increase: 1.1%); birth rate: 17/1000; infant mortality rate: 4.8/1000; density per square mile: 7.56
Capital and largest city (est. 1993): Reykjavik, 101,855.
  Monetary unit: M.N. króna; **Language:** Icelandic; **Religion:** Evangelical Lutheran; **National name:** Lydveldid Island; **Literacy rate:** 100%
Economic summary: Gross domestic product (1993): $4.2 billion; $16,000 per capita; real growth rate 0.4%; inflation 4%; unemployment (est.) 4.5%. Arable land: NEGL%; principal agricultural products: livestock, potatoes and turnips. Labor force: 127,900; 60% in commerce, transportation and services. Major products: processed aluminum, fish. Natural resources: fish, diatomite, hydroelectric and geothermal power. Exports: $1.5 billion (f.o.b., 1992): fish, animal products, aluminum, diatomite, ferrosilicon. Imports: $1.5 billion (c.i.f., 1992): petroleum products, machinery and

Ct

transportation equipment, food, textiles. Major trading partners: European Communities (EC) countries, European Free Trade Association (EFTA) countries, U.S., Japan, and Denmark,.

1. Including some offshore islands.

Geography. Iceland, an island about the size of Kentucky, lies in the north Atlantic Ocean east of Greenland and just touches the Arctic Circle. It is one of the most volcanic regions in the world.

Small fresh-water lakes are to be found throughout the island, and there are many natural phenomena, including hot springs, geysers, sulfur beds, canyons, waterfalls, and swift rivers. More than 13% of the area is covered by snowfields and glaciers, and most of the people live in the 7% of the island comprising fertile coastlands.

Government. The president is elected for four years by popular vote. Executive power resides in the prime minister and his Cabinet. The Althing (Parliament) is composed of 63 members.

History. Iceland was first settled shortly before 900, mainly by Norse. A Constitution drawn up about 930 created a form of democracy and provided for an Althing, or General Assembly.

In 1262–64, Iceland came under Norwegian rule and passed to ultimate Danish control through the formation of the Union of Kalmar in 1483. In 1874, Icelanders obtained their own Constitution. In 1918, Denmark recognized Iceland as a separate state with unlimited sovereignty but still nominally under the Danish king.

On June 17, 1944, after a popular referendum, the Althing proclaimed Iceland an independent republic.

The British occupied Iceland in 1940, immediately after the German invasion of Denmark. In 1942, the U.S. took over the burden of protection. Iceland refused to abandon its neutrality in World War II and thus forfeited charter membership in the United Nations, but it cooperated with the Allies throughout the conflict. Iceland joined the North Atlantic Treaty Organization in 1949.

Iceland unilaterally extended its territorial waters from 12 to 50 nautical miles in 1972, precipitating a running dispute with Britain known as the "cod war."

Elections to the Althing in April 1991 gave the opposition Independence Party 26 of the 63 seats, up from 18. Prime Minister Hermannson resigned allowing David Oddsson of the Independence Party to enter into talks with the Social Democrats about a coalition government.

General election results in April 1995 gave the former coalition Independence Party and Social Democrats that would have been only a one-seat majority. A new coalition was formed between the Independence Party and the centrist Progressives, who also oppose Iceland seeking membership in the European Union.

INDIA

Republic of India
President: Dr. Shankar Dayal Sharma (1992)
Prime Minister: P.V. Narasimha Rao (1991)
Area: 1,229,737 sq mi. (3,185,019 sq km)
Population (est. mid-1995): 930,600,000 (average annual rate of natural increase: 1.9%); birth rate: 29/1000; infant mortality rate: 74/1000; density per square mile: 756.7

Capital (1991): New Delhi, 294,149; **Largest cities (1992):** Greater Bombay, 12,916,272; Calcutta, 10,916,272; Delhi, 8,375,188; Madras, 5,361,468; Ahmedabad, 4,775,670; Bangalore, 4,807,019; Kanpur, 2,284,000; **Monetary unit:** Rupee; **Principal languages:** Hindi (official), English (official), Bengali, Gujarati, Kashmiri, Malayalam, Marathi, Oriya, Punjabi, Tamil, Telugu, Urdu, Kannada, Assamese, Sanskrit, Sindhi (all recognized by the Constitution). Dialects, 1,652; **Religions:** Hindu, 82.6%; Islam, 11.3%; Christian, 2.4%; Sikh, 2%; Buddhists, 0.71%; Jains, 0.48%; **National name:** Bharat; **Literacy rate:** 52.11%; **Member of Commonwealth of Nations**
Economic summary: Gross domestic product (FY94 est.): $1.17 trillion; $1,300 per capita; real growth rate 3.8%; inflation 8%; unemployment n.a.. Arable land: 55%. Principal products: rice, wheat, oilseeds, cotton, tea, opium poppy (for pharmaceuticals). Labor force (1990): 314,751 million; 67% in agriculture. Major industrial products: jute, processed food, steel, machinery, transport machinery, cement. Natural resources: iron ore, coal, manganese, mica, bauxite, limestone, textiles. Exports: $21.4 billion (f.o.b., FY93 est.): gems and jewelry, clothing, engineering goods, leather manufacturers, cotton yarn and fabric. Imports: $22 billion (c.i.f., FY93 est.): crude oil and petroleum products, gems, fertilizer, chemicals, machinery. IMajor trading partners: U.S., C.I.S. nations, Germany, Italy, Belgium.

Geography. One third the area of the United States, the Republic of India occupies most of the subcontinent of India in south Asia. It borders on China in the northeast. Other neighbors are Pakistan on the west, Nepal and Bhutan on the north, and Burma and Bangladesh on the east.

The country contains a large part of the great Indo-Gangetic plain, which extends from the Bay of Bengal on the east to the Afghan frontier and the Arabian Sea on the west. This plain is the richest and most densely settled part of the subcontinent. Another distinct natural region is the Deccan, a plateau of 2,000 to 3,000 feet (610 to 914 m) in elevation, occupying the southern portion of the subcontinent.

Forming a part of the republic are several groups of islands—the Laccadives (14 islands) in the Arabian Sea and the Andamans (204 islands) and the Nicobars (19 islands) in the Bay of Bengal.

India's three great river systems, all rising in the Himalayas, have extensive deltas. The Ganges flows south and then east for 1,540 miles (2,478 km) across the northern plain to the Bay of Bengal; part of its delta, which begins 220 miles (354 km) from the sea, is within the republic. The Indus, starting in Tibet, flows northwest for several hundred miles in the Kashmir before turning southwest toward the Arabian Sea; it is important for irrigation in Pakistan. The Brahmaputra, also rising in Tibet, flows eastward, first through India and then south into Bangladesh and the Bay of Bengal.

Government. India is a federal republic. It is also a member of the Commonwealth of Nations, a status defined at the 1949 London Conference of Prime Ministers, by which India recognizes the Queen as head of the Commonwealth. Under the Constitution effective Jan. 26, 1950, India has a parliamentary type of government.

The constitutional head of the state is the President, who is elected every five years. He is advised by the Prime Minister and a Cabinet based on a majority of the bicameral Parliament, which consists of a Council of States (Rajya Sabha), representing the constituent units of the republic and a House of the People (Lok Sabha), elected every five years by universal suffrage.

History. The Aryans who invaded India between 2400 and 1500 B.C. from the northwest found a land already well civilized. Buddhism was founded in the 6th century B.C. and spread through northern India, most notably by one of the greatest ancient kings, Asoka (c. 269–232 B.C.), who also unified most of the Indian subcontinent.

In 1526, Moslem invaders founded the great Mogul empire, centered on Delhi, which lasted, at least in name, until 1857. Akbar the Great (1542–1605) strengthened and consolidated this empire. The long reign of his great-grandson, Aurangzeb (1658–1707), represents both the greatest extent of the Mogul empire and the beginning of its decay.

Vasco da Gama, the Portuguese explorer, visited India first in 1498, and for the next 100 years the Portuguese had a virtual monopoly on trade with the subcontinent. Meanwhile, the English founded the East India Company, which set up its first factory at Surat in 1612 and began expanding its influence, fighting the Indian rulers and the French, Dutch, and Portuguese traders simultaneously.

Bombay, taken from the Portuguese, became the seat of English rule in 1687. The defeat of French and Islamic armies by Lord Clive in the decade ending in 1760 laid the foundation of the British Empire in India. From then until 1858, when the administration of India was formally transferred to the British Crown following the Sepoy Mutiny of native troops in 1857, the East India Company suppressed native uprisings and extended British rule.

After World War I, in which the Indian states sent more than 6 million troops to fight beside the Allies, Indian nationalist unrest rose to new heights under the leadership of a little Hindu lawyer, Mohandas K. Gandhi, called Mahatma Gandhi. His tactics called for nonviolent revolts against British authority. He soon became the leading spirit of the All-India Congress Party, which was the spearhead of revolt. In 1919 the British gave added responsibility to Indian officials, and in 1935 India was given a federal form of government and a measure of self-rule.

In 1942, with the Japanese pressing hard on the eastern borders of India, the British War Cabinet tried and failed to reach a political settlement with nationalist leaders. The Congress Party took the position that the British must quit India. In 1942, fearing mass civil disobedience, the government of India carried out widespread arrests of Congress leaders, including Gandhi.

Gandhi was released in 1944 and negotiations for a settlement were resumed. Finally, in February 1947, the Labor government announced its determination to transfer power to "responsible Indian hands" by June 1948 even if a Constitution had not been worked out.

Lord Mountbatten as Viceroy, by June 1947, achieved agreement on the partitioning of India along religious lines and on the splitting of the provinces of Bengal and the Punjab, which the Moslems had claimed.

The Indian Independence Act, passed quickly by the British Parliament, received royal assent on July 18, 1947, and on August 15 the Indian Empire passed into history.

Jawaharlal Nehru, leader of the Congress Party, was made Prime Minister. Before an exchange of populations could be arranged, bloody riots occurred among the communal groups, and armed conflict broke out over rival claims to the princely state of Jammu and Kashmir. Peace was restored only with the greatest difficulty. In 1949 a Constitution, along the lines of the U.S. Constitution, was approved making India a sovereign republic. Under a federal structure the states were organized on linguistic lines.

The dominance of the Congress Party contributed to stability. In 1956 the republic absorbed the former French settlements. Five years later, it forcibly annexed the Portuguese enclaves of Goa, Damao, and Diu.

Nehru died in 1964. His successor, Lal Bahadur Shastri, died on Jan. 10, 1966. Nehru's daughter, Indira Gandhi, became Prime Minister, and she continued his policy of nonalignment.

In 1971 the Pakistani Army moved in to quash the independence movement in East Pakistan that was supported by clandestine aid from India, and some 10 million Bengali refugees poured across the border into India, creating social, economic, and health problems. After numerous border incidents, India invaded East Pakistan and in two weeks forced the surrender of the Pakistani army. East Pakistan was established as an independent state and renamed Bangladesh.

In the summer of 1975, the world's largest democracy veered suddenly toward authoritarianism when a judge in Allahabad, Mrs. Gandhi's home constituency, found her landslide victory in the 1971 elections invalid because civil servants had illegally aided her campaign. Amid demands for her resignation, Mrs. Gandhi decreed a state of emergency on June 26 and ordered mass arrests of her critics, including all opposition party leaders except the Communists.

In 1976, India and Pakistan formally renewed diplomatic relations.

Despite strong opposition to her repressive measures and particularly the resentment against compulsory birth control programs, Mrs. Gandhi in 1977 announced parliamentary elections for March. At the same time, she freed most political prisoners.

The landslide victory of Morarji R. Desai unseated Mrs. Gandhi.

Mrs. Gandhi staged a spectacular comeback in the elections of January 1980.

In 1984, Mrs. Gandhi ordered the Indian Army to root out a band of Sikh holy men and gunmen who were using the holiest shrine of the Sikh religion, the Golden Temple in Amritsar, as a base for terrorist raids in a violent campaign for greater political autonomy in the strategic Punjab border state. The perceived sacrilege to the Golden Temple kindled outrage among many of India's 14 million Sikhs and brought a spasm of mutinies and desertions by Sikh officers and soldiers in the army.

On Oct. 31, 1984, Mrs. Gandhi was assassinated by two men identified by police as Sikh members of her bodyguard. The ruling Congress I Party chose her older son, Rajiv Gandhi, to succeed her as Prime Minister.

One week after the resignation of Prime Minister Shekhar, India's president in March 1991 called for national elections. While at an election rally on May 22 former prime minister Rajiv Gandhi was assassinated. Final phases of the election were postponed a month. When they were resumed the Congress Party and its allies won 236 seats in the lower house, 20 short of a majority. P.V. Narasimha Rao was chosen to form a new government. In elections for 15 parliamentary seats in November 1991 Rao's government won more votes than expected, largely interpreted as a sign of willingness to move closer toward a free-market economy.

Owing to the possibility of renewed violence in the state of Jammu and Kashmir, the government decided in May 1995 to cancel planned elections there. The state has been ruled directly from New Delhi since January 1990, when the last elected government was dismissed.

Native States. Most of the 560-odd native states and subdivisions of pre-1947 India acceded to the new nation, and the central government pursued a vigorous policy of integration. This took three forms: merger into adjacent provinces, conversion into centrally administered areas, and grouping into unions of states. Finally, under a controversial reorganization plan effective Nov. 1, 1956, the unions of states were abolished and merged into adjacent states, and India became a union of 15 states and 8 centrally administered areas. A 16th state was added in 1962, and in 1966, the Punjab was partitioned into two states. Today India consists of 25 states and 7 Union Territories.

Resolution of the territorial dispute over Kashmir grew out of peace negotiations following the two-week India-Pakistan war of 1971. After sporadic skirmishing, an accord reached July 3, 1972, committed both powers to withdraw troops from a temporary cease-fire line after the border was fixed. Agreement on the border was reached Dec. 7, 1972.

In April 1975, the Indian Parliament voted to make the 300-year-old kingdom of Sikkim a full-fledged Indian state, and the annexation took effect May 16. Situated in the Himalayas, Sikkim was a virtual dependency of Tibet until the early 19th century. Under an 1890 treaty between China and Great Britain, it became a British protectorate, and was made an Indian protectorate after Britain quit the subcontinent.

INDONESIA

Republic of Indonesia
President: Soeharto (1993)[1]
Area: 735,268 sq mi. (1,904,344 sq km)[2]
Population (est. mid-1995): 198,400,000 (average annual rate of natural increase: 1.6%); birth rate: 24/1000; infant mortality rate: 64/1000; density per square mile: 269.8
Capital and largest city (1990):: Jakarta, 8,259,266.
  Other large cities (1990): Surabaya, 2,421,000; Medan, 1,685,972; Bandung, 2,026,893; Semarang, 1,005,316.
Monetary unit: Rupiah; **Languages:** Bahasa Indonesia (official), Dutch, English, and more than 583 languages, and dialects; **Religions:** Islam, 87%; Christian, 9%; Hindu, 2%; other, 2%; **National name:** Republik Indonesia; **Literacy rate:** 86.3%
Economic summary: Gross domestic product (1993 est.): $571 billion; $2,900 per capita; real growth rate 6.5%; inflation 10%; unemployment 3%. Arable land: 8%. Principal agricultural products: rice, cassava, peanuts, rubber, coffee. Labor force: 67,000,000; 10% in manufacturing. Major industrial products: petroleum, timber, textiles, cement, fertilizer, rubber. Natural resources: oil, timber, nickel, natural gas, tin, bauxite, copper. Exports: $38.2 billion (f.o.b, 1993 est.): petroleum and liquid natural gas, timber, rubber, coffee, textiles. Imports: $28.3 billion (f.o.b, 1993 est.): chemicals, machinery, manufactured goods. Illicit drugs: minor producer of cannabis for international trade. Government actively eradicating plantings. Major trading partners: Japan, U.S., Singapore, E.U.

1. Reelected President for the 6th five-year term in office.
2. Includes West Irian (former Netherlands New Guinea), renamed Irian Jaya in March 1973 (159,355 sq mi.; 421,981 sq km), and former Portuguese Timor (5,763 sq mi.; 14,874 sq km), annexed in 1976.

Geography. Indonesia is part of the Malay archipelago in Southeast Asia with an area nearly three times that of Texas. It consists of the islands of Sumatra, Java, Bali, Madura, Kalimantan (Indonesia's part of Borneo, except Malaysia's Sarawak and Brunei Darussalam in the north), the Sulawesi (Celebes), the Maluku Islands, Irian Jaya (eastern part of New Guinea), and about 30 smaller archipelagos, totaling 17,508 islands, of which about 6,000 are inhabited. Its neighbor to the north is Malaysia and to the east Papua New Guinea.

A backbone of mountain ranges extends throughout the main islands of the archipelago. Earthquakes are frequent, and there are many active volcanoes.

Government. The President is elected by the People's Consultative Assembly, whose 1,000 members include the functioning legislative arm, the 500-member House of Representatives. Meeting at least once every five years, the Assembly has broad policy functions. The House, 100 of whose members are appointed from the armed forces, meets at least once annually. General Soeharto was elected unopposed to a sixth five-year term in 1993.

History. Indonesia is inhabited by Malayan and Papuan peoples ranging from the more advanced Javanese and Balinese to the more primitive Dyaks of Borneo. Invasions from China and India contributed Chinese and Indian admixtures.

During the first few centuries of the Christian era, most of the islands came under the influence of Hindu priests and traders, who spread their culture and religion. Moslem invasions began in the 13th century, and most of the area was Moslem by the 15th. Portuguese traders arrived early in the 16th century but were ousted by the Dutch about 1595. After Napoleon subjugated the Netherlands homeland in 1811, the British seized the islands but returned them to the Dutch in 1816. In 1922 the islands were made an integral part of the Netherlands kingdom.

During World War II, Indonesia was under Japanese military occupation with nominal native self-government. When the Japanese surrendered to the Allies, President Sukarno and Mohammed Hatta, his Vice President, proclaimed Indonesian independence from the Dutch on Aug. 17, 1945. Allied troops—mostly British Indian troops—fought the nationalists until the arrival of Dutch troops. In November 1946, the Dutch and the Indonesians reached a draft agreement contemplating formation of a Netherlands-Indonesian Union, but differences in interpretation resulted in more fighting between Dutch and Indonesian forces.

On Nov. 2, 1949, Dutch and Indonesian leaders agreed upon the terms of union. The transfer of sovereignty took place at Amsterdam on Dec. 27, 1949. In February 1956 Indonesia abrogated the Union with the Netherlands and in August 1956 repudiated its debt to the Netherlands. In 1963, Netherlands New Guinea was transferred to Indonesia and renamed West Irian. In 1973 it became Irian Jaya.

Hatta and Sukarno, the co-fathers of Indonesian independence, split after it was achieved over Sukarno's concept of "guided democracy." Under Sukarno, the country's leading political figure for almost a half century, the Indonesian Communist Party gradually gained increasing influence.

After an attempted coup was put down by General Soeharto, the army chief of staff, and officers loyal to him, thousands of Communist suspects were sought out and killed all over the country. Soeharto took over the reins of government, gradually eased Sukarno out of office, and took full power in 1967.

Soeharto permitted national elections, which moved the nation back to representative government. He also ended hostilities with Malaysia. Under President Soeharto, Indonesia has been strongly anticommunist. It also has been politically stable and has made progress in economic development.

Indonesia invaded the former Portuguese half of the island of Timor in 1975, and annexed the territory in 1976. More than 100,000 Timorese, a sixth of the mostly Catholic population, were reported to have died from famine, disease, and fighting since the annexation.

Several new pro-democracy groups were formed in 1991 amid speculation over Soeharto's plans for a new five-year term. The government continued its reform program, cutting tariffs and barriers to foreign investment.

In March 1993 the 1,000 member People's Consultative Assembly, a body which meets every five years for the express purpose of choosing a president, reelected Soeharto, who ran unopposed.

In early 1995 the government began a crackdown on magazine and newspaper reporters who were critical of the government.

Negotiations with Portugal over East Timor proceeded extremely slowly.

IRAN

Islamic Republic of Iran

President: Hashemi Rafsanjani (1989)
Area: 636,293 sq mi. (1,648,000 sq km)
Population (est. mid-1995): 61,300,000 (average annual rate of natural increase: 2.9%); birth rate: 36/1000; infant mortality rate: 56/1000; density per square mile: 96.3
Capital: Teheran; **Largest cities (1991 est.):** Teheran, 6,450,500; Mashad, 1,500,000; Isfahan, 1,000,000; Tabriz, 1,090,000; **Monetary unit:** Rial; **Languages:** Farsi (Persian), Azari, Kurdish, Arabic; **Religions:** Shi'ite Moslem, 95%; Sunni Moslem, 4%; **Literacy rate:** 74% (1992)
Economic summary: Gross domestic product (1993 est.): $303 billion; $4,780 per capita; real growth rate 3%; inflation (Sept. 92–93) 30%; unemployment (1991 est.) 30%. Arable land: 8%. Principal agricultural products: wheat, barley, rice, sugar beets, cotton, dates, raisins, sheep, goats. Labor force: 15,400,000; 33% in agriculture. Major industrial products: crude and refined oil, textiles, petrochemicals, cement, processed foods, steel and copper fabrication. Natural resources: oil, gas, iron, copper. Exports: $15.5 billion (f.o.b., FY92 est.): petroleum, carpets, fruits, nuts, hides. Imports: $23.7 billion (c.i.f., FY92 est.): machinery, military supplies, foodstuffs, pharmaceuticals, metal works, technial services. Major trading partners: Japan, Germany, Netherlands, U.K., Italy, Spain, Turkey, France

Geography. Iran, a Middle Eastern country south of the Caspian Sea and north of the Persian Gulf, is three times the size of Arizona. It shares borders with Iraq, Turkey, Azerbaijan, Turkmenistan, Armenia, Afghanistan, and Pakistan.

In general, the country is a plateau averaging 4,000 feet (1,219 m) in elevation. There are also maritime lowlands along the Persian Gulf and the Caspian Sea. The Elburz Mountains in the north rise to 18,603 feet (5,670 m) at Mt. Damavend. From northwest to southeast, the country is crossed by a desert 800 miles (1,287 km) long.

Government. The Pahlavi monarchy regime was overthrown on Feb. 11, 1979. The Islamic Republic of Iran was established and endorsed by a universal referendum on March 30, the same year. A new Constitution was drafted by the Assembly of Experts and was approved in a national referendum in Dec. 1979.

The Constitution recognizes the executive, legislative, and judiciary, as independent branches. The President is elected by direct vote for a four years term. He runs the government and is accountable for the implementation of the Constitution before the Parliament (*Majles*), which consists of 270 representatives popularly elected for a period of four years.

In the course of the Islamic Revolution, Ayatollah Khomeini emerged as the leader of Iran. After Ayatollah Khomeini's demise, on July 3, 1989, the Assembly of Experts elected Ayatollah Ali Khameneie as his successor. The Assembly itself consists of experts elected directly by the nation.

History. Oil-rich Iran was called Persia before 1935. Its key location blocks the lower land gate to Asia and also stands in the way of traditional Russian ambitions for access to the Indian Ocean. After periods of Assyrian, Median, and Achaemenidian rule, Persia became a powerful empire under Cyrus the Great, reaching from the Indus to the Nile at its zenith in 525 B.C. It fell to Alexander in 331–30 B.C. and to the Seleucids in 312–02 B.C., and a native Persian regime arose about 130 B.C. Another Persian regime arose about A.D. 224, but it fell to the Arabs in 637. In the 12th century, the Mongols took their turn ruling Persia, and in the early part of the 18th century, the Turks occupied the country.

An Anglo-Russian convention of 1907 divided Persia into two spheres of influence. British attempts to impose a protectorate over the entire country were defeated in 1919. Two years later, Gen. Reza Pahlavi seized the government and was elected hereditary Shah in 1925. Subsequently he did much to modernize the country and abolished all foreign extraterritorial rights.

Increased pro-Axis activity led to Anglo-Russian occupation of Iran in 1941 and deposition of the Shah in favor of his son, Mohammed Reza Pahlavi.

Ali Razmara became premier in 1950 and pledged to restore efficient and honest government, but he was assassinated after less than nine months in office and Mohammed Mossadegh took over. Mossadegh was ousted in August 1953, by Fazollah Zahedi, whom the Shah had named premier.

Opposition to the Shah spread, despite the imposition of martial law in September 1978, and massive demonstrations demanded the return of the exiled Ayatollah Ruhollah Khomeini. Riots and strikes continued despite the appointment of an opposition leader, Shahpur Bakhtiar, as premier on Dec. 29. The Shah and his family left Iran on Jan. 16, 1979, for a "vacation," leaving power in the hands of a regency council.

Khomeini returned on Feb. 1 to a nation in turmoil as military units loyal to the Shah continued to support Bakhtiar and clashed with revolutionaries. Khomeini appointed Mehdi Bazargan as premier of the provisional government and in two days of fighting, revolutionaries forced the military to capitulate on Feb. 11.

The new government began a program of nationalization of insurance companies, banks, and industries both locally and foreign-owned. Oil production fell amid the political confusion.

Khomeini, ignoring opposition, proceeded with his plans for revitalizing Islamic traditions. He urged women to return to the veil or chador; banned alcohol and mixed bathing, and prohibited music from radio and television broadcasting, declaring it to be "no different from opium."

Revolutionary militants invaded the U.S. Embassy in Teheran on Nov. 4, 1979, seized staff members as hostages, and precipitated an international crisis.

Khomeini refused all appeals, even a unanimous vote by the U.N. Security Council demanding immediate release of the hostages.

Iranian hostility toward Washington was reinforced by the Carter administration's economic boycott and deportation order against Iranian students in the U.S., the break in diplomatic relations and ultimately an aborted U.S. raid in April aimed at rescuing the hostages.

As the first anniversary of the embassy seizure neared, Khomeini and his followers insisted on their original conditions: guarantee by the U.S. not to interfere in Iran's affairs, cancellation of U.S. damage claims against Iran, release of $8 billion in frozen Iranian assets, an apology, and the return of the assets held by the former imperial family.

These conditions were largely met and the 52 American hostages were released on Jan. 20, ending 444 days in captivity.

From the release of the hostages onward, President Bani-Sadr and the conservative clerics of the dominant Islamic Republican Party clashed with growing frequency. He was stripped of his command of the armed forces by Khomeini on June 6 and ousted as President on June 22. On July 24, Prime Minister Mohammed Ali Rajai was elected overwhelmingly to the Presidency.

Rajai and Prime Minister Mohammed Javad Bahonar were killed on Aug. 30 by a bomb in Bahonar's office. Hojatolislam Mohammed Ali Khamenei, a clergyman, leader of the Islamic Republican Party and spokesman for Khomeini, was elected President on Oct. 2, 1981.

The sporadic war with Iraq regained momentum in 1982, as Iran launched an offensive in March and regained much of the border area occupied by Iraq in late 1980.

Iran continued to be at war with Iraq well into 1988. Although Iraq expressed its willingness to cease fighting, Iran stated that it would not stop the war until Iraq agreed to make payment for war damages to Iran, and punish the Iraqi government leaders involved in the conflict.

On July 20, 1988, Khomeini, after a series of Iranian military reverses, agreed to cease-fire negotiations with Iraq. A cease-fire went into effect Aug. 20, 1988. Khomeini died in June 1989.

By early 1991 the Islamic Revolution appeared to have lost much of its militancy. Attempting to revive a stagnant economy President Rafsanjani took measures to decentralize the command system and introduce free-market mechanisms.

In 1995 Russia remained steadfast in the face of U.S. protests concerning the former's agreement with Iran to help build a nuclear power plant.

In February Iran called for the U.N. to end its sanctions against Iraq, accusing the U.S. of trying to divide the Arab world.

IRAQ

Republic of Iraq
President: Saddam Hussein (1979)
Area: 167,920 sq mi. (434,913 sq km)
Population (est. mid-1995): 20,600,000 (average annual rate of natural increase: 3.7%); birth rate: 43/1000; infant mortality rate: 62/1000; density per square mile: 122.6

Capital: Baghdad; **Largest cities (est. 1985):** Baghdad, 4,648,609; Basra, 616,700; Mosul, 570,926; **Monetary unit:** Iraqi dinar; **Languages:** Arabic (official) and Kurdish; **Religions:** Islam, 95%; Christian or other, 5%; **National name:** Jumhouriyat Al Iraq; **Literacy rate:** 55–65% (est.). **Literacy rate:** 60%

Economic summary: Gross domestic product (1993 est.): $38 billion, $2,000 per capita; n.a. real growth rate; inflation: 200% (est.). Arable land: 12%. Principal products: dates, livestock, wheat, barley, cotton, rice. Labor force: 4,400,000 (1989); services, 48%; agriculture, 30%; industry, 22%. Major products: petroleum, chemicals, textiles,, construction materials. Natural resources: oil, natural gas, phosphates, sulfur. Exports: $10.4 billion (f.o.b., 1990): petroleum and refined products, machinery, chemicals, dates. Imports: $6.6 billion (c.i.f., 1990): manufactured goods, food. Major trading partners: France, Italy, Japan, Germany, Brazil, U.K., U.S., Turkey, C.I.S. countries.

Geography. Iraq, a triangle of mountains, desert, and fertile river valley, is bounded on the east by Iran, on the north by Turkey, the west by Syria and Jordan, and the south by Saudi Arabia and Kuwait. It is twice the size of Idaho.

The country has arid desertland west of the Euphrates, a broad central valley between the Euphrates and Tigris, and mountains in the northeast. The fertile lower valley is formed by the delta of the two rivers, which join about 120 miles (193 km) from the head of the Persian Gulf. The gulf coastline is 26 miles (42 km) long. The only port for seagoing vessels is Basra, which is on the Shatt-al-Arab River near the head of the Persian Gulf.

Government. Since the coup d'etat of July 1968, Iraq has been governed by the Arab Ba'ath Socialist Party through a Council of Command of the Revolution headed by the President. There is also a Council of Ministers headed by the President and a National Council (Parliament).

History. From earliest times Iraq was known as Mesopotamia—the land between the rivers—for it embraces a large part of the alluvial plains of the Tigris and Euphrates.

An advanced civilization existed by 4000 B.C. Sometime after 2000 B.C. the land became the center of the ancient Babylonian and Assyrian empires. It was conquered by Cyrus the Great of Persia in 538 B.C., and by Alexander in 331 B.C. After an Arab conquest in A.D. 637–40, Baghdad became capital of the ruling caliphate. The country was cruelly pillaged by the Mongols in 1258, and during the 16th, 17th, and 18th centuries was the object of repeated Turkish-Persian competition.

Nominal Turkish suzerainty imposed in 1638 was replaced by direct Turkish rule in 1831. In World War I, an Anglo-Indian force occupied most of the country, and Britain was given a mandate over the area in 1920. The British recognized Iraq as a kingdom in 1922 and terminated the mandate in 1932 when Iraq was admitted to the League of Nations. In World War II, Iraq generally adhered to its 1930 treaty of alliance with Britain, but in 1941, British troops were compelled to put down a pro-Axis revolt led by Premier Rashid Ali.

Iraq became a charter member of the Arab League in 1945, and Iraqi troops took part in the Arab invasion of Palestine in 1948.

Faisal II, born on May 2, 1935, succeeded his father, Ghazi I, who was killed in an automobile accident on April 4, 1939. Faisal and his uncle, Crown Prince Abdul-Illah, were assassinated in July 1958 in a swift revolutionary coup that brought to power a military junta headed by Abdul Karem Kassim. Kassim, in turn, was overthrown and killed in a coup staged March 8, 1963, by the Ba'ath Socialist Party.

Abdel Salam Arif, a leader in the 1958 coup, staged another coup in November 1963, driving the Ba'ath members of the revolutionary council from power. He adopted a new constitution in 1964. In 1966, he, two Cabinet members, and other supporters died in a helicopter crash. His brother, Gen. Abdel Rahman Arif, assumed the presidency, crushed the opposition, and won an indefinite extension of his term in 1967. His regime was ousted in July 1968 by a junta led by Maj. Gen. Ahmed Hassan al-Bakr.

A long-standing dispute over control of the Shatt al-Arab waterway between Iraq and Iran broke into full-scale war on Sept. 20, 1980. Iraqi planes attacked Iranian airfields and the Abadan refinery, and Iraqi ground forces moved into Iran.

Despite the smaller size of its armed forces, Iraq took and held the initiative by seizing Abadan and Khurramshahr together with substantial Iranian territory by December and beating back Iranian counterattacks in January. Peace efforts by the Islamic nations, the nonaligned, and the United Nations failed as 1981 wore on and the war stagnated.

In 1982, the Iraqis fell back to their own country and dug themselves in behind sandbagged defensive fortifications. From the beginning of the war in September 1980 to September 1984, foreign military analysts estimated that more than 100,000 Iranians and perhaps 50,000 Iraqis had been killed.

The Iraqis clearly wanted to end the war, but the Iranians refused.

In February 1986, Iranian forces gained on two fronts; but Iraq retook most of the lost ground in 1988 and the war continued a stalemate. In August, Iraq and Iran agreed to hold direct talks after a ceasefire takes effect.

In July 1990, President Hussein claimed that Kuwait was flooding world markets with oil and forcing down prices. A mediation attempt by Arab leaders failed, and on Aug. 2, 1990, over this and territorial claims, Iraqi troops invaded Kuwait and set up a puppet government.

After the Gulf War, Saddam Hussein was still in power. The U.N. Security Council affirmed an embargo against military supplies to that country and a trade embargo was still in place.

The Iraqi parliament in November 1994 recognized Kuwait as an independent state and the legitimacy of the U.N. delineated a border between the state states. Despite this and other measures, U.N. sanctions remained in place.

IRELAND

President: Mary Robinson (1990)
Taoiseach (Prime Minister): John Bruton (1994)
Area: 27,136 sq mi. (70,282 sq km)
Population (est. mid-1995): 3,600,000 (average annual rate of natural increase: 0.5%); birth rate: 14/1000; infant mortality rate: 6.0/1000; density per square mile: 132.7
Capital: Dublin; **Largest cities (1991):** Dublin, 1,024,429; Cork, 282,790; Limerick, 109,816; **Monetary unit:** Irish pound (punt); **Languages:** Irish, English; **Religions:** Roman Catholic, 92%; others, 8%; **National name:** Ireland, or Eire in the Irish language; **Literacy rate:** 99%

Economic summary: Gross national product (1995 est.): $48.130 billion; $13,480 per capita; real growth rate 5%; inflation 2.5%; unemployment 14.8%. Arable land: 14%. Principal products: cattle and dairy products, pigs, poultry and eggs, sheep and wool, horses, barley, sugar beets. Labor force: 1,375,000; 27.9% in manufacturing and construction. Major products: processed foods, brews, textiles, clothing, chemicals, pharmaceuticals, machinery, transportation equipment, glass and crystal. Natural resources: zinc, lead, natural gas, crude oil, barite, copper, gypsum, limestone, dolomite, peat, silver. Exports: $35 billion (1995 est.): livestock, dairy products, machinery, chemicals, data processing equipment. Imports: $29 billion (1995 est.): food, animtal feed, chemicals, petroleum products, machinery, textile clothing. Major trading partners: U.K., Western European countries, U.S.

Geography. Ireland is situated in the Atlantic Ocean and separated from Britain by the Irish Sea. Half the size of Arkansas, it occupies the entire island except for the six counties which make up Northern Ireland.

Ireland resembles a basin—a central plain rimmed with mountains, except in the Dublin region. The mountains are low, with the highest peak, Carrantuohill in County Kerry, rising to 3,415 feet (1,041 m).

The principal river is the Shannon, which begins in the north central area, flows south and southwest for about 240 miles (386 km), and empties into the Atlantic.

Government. Ireland is a parliamentary democracy. The National Parliament (Oireachtas) consists of the president and two Houses, the House of Representatives (Dáil éireann) and the Senate (Seanad éireann), whose members serve for a maximum term of five years. The House of Representatives has 166 members elected by proportional representation; the Senate has 60 members of whom 11 are nominated by the prime minister, 6 by the universities and the remaining 43 from five vocational panels. The prime minister (Taoiseach), who is the head of government, is appointed by the president on the nomination of the House of Representatives, to which he is responsible.

History. In the Stone and Bronze Ages, Ireland was inhabited by Picts in the north and a people called the Erainn in the south, the same stock, apparently, as in all the isles before the Anglo-Saxon invasion of Britain. About the fourth century B.C., tall, red-haired Celts arrived from Gaul or Galicia. They subdued and assimilated the inhabitants and established a Gaelic civilization.

By the beginning of the Christian Era, Ireland was divided into five kingdoms—Ulster, Connacht, Leinster, Meath, and Munster. St. Patrick introduced Christianity in 432 and the country developed into a center of Gaelic and Latin learning. Irish monasteries, the equivalent of universities, attracted intellectuals as well as the pious and sent out missionaries to many parts of Europe and, some believe, to North America.

Norse depredations along the coasts, starting in 795, ended in 1014 with Norse defeat at the Battle of Clontarf by forces under Brian Boru. In the 12th century, the Pope gave all Ireland to the English Crown as a papal fief. In 1171, Henry II of England acknowledged "Lord of Ireland," but local sectional rule continued for centuries, and English control over the whole island was not reasonably absolute until the 17th century. By the Act of Union (1801), England and Ireland became the "United Kingdom of Great Britain and Ireland."

A steady decline in the Irish economy followed in the next decades. The population had reached 8.25 million when the great potato famine of 1846–48 took many lives and drove millions to emigrate to America. By 1921 it was down to 4.3 million.

In the meantime, anti-British agitation continued along with demands for Irish home rule. The advent of World War I delayed the institution of home rule and resulted in the Easter Rebellion in Dublin (April 24–29, 1916), in which Irish nationalists unsuccessfully attempted to throw off British rule. Guerrilla warfare against British forces followed proclamation of a republic by the rebels in 1919.

The Irish Free State was established as a dominion on Dec. 6, 1922, with the six northern counties as part of the United Kingdom. Ireland was neutral in World War II.

In 1948, Eamon de Valera, American-born leader of the Sinn Fein, who had won establishment of the Free State in 1921 in negotiations with Britain's David Lloyd George, was defeated by John A. Costello, who demanded final independence from Britain. The Republic of Ireland was proclaimed on April 18, 1949. It withdrew from the Commonwealth but in 1955 entered the United Nations.

Through the 1960s, two antagonistic currents dominated Irish politics. One sought to bind the wounds of the rebellion and civil war. The other was the effort of the outlawed extremist Irish Republican Army to bring Northern Ireland into the republic.

In the elections of June 11, 1981, Garret M. D. FitzGerald, leader of the Fine Gael, was elected Prime Minister. FitzGerald resigned Jan. 27, 1982, after his presentation of an austerity budget aroused the opposition of independents who had backed him previously. Former Prime Minister Haughey was sworn in on March 9 and presented a budget with nearly a $1 billion deficit.

Three candidates vied in the November 1990 presidential election. Although Brian Lenihan of Fianna Fail led in the first round, Mary Robinson, supported by the Labour Party and the Workers Party, won the second round with 52.8% of the vote, becoming the first non-Fianna Fail president since 1945.

Amid allegations of scandal Prime Minister Haughey resigned in early 1992. Reynolds was chosen by a majority of his Fianna Fail party to become the next prime minister.

The general election of November 1992 saw Reynolds's Fianna Fail receive a plurality.

Reynolds's government fell in January 1995 over a scandal involving the handling of the extradition of a priest convicted of child molestation in the North. Immediately plans for a referendum on divorce and for legalizing the distribution of information on abortion clinics abroad were postponed.

ISRAEL

State of Israel
President: Ezer Weizman (1993)
Prime Minister: Yitzhak Rabin (1992)
Area: 8,020 sq mi. (20,772 sq km)
Population (est. mid-1995): 5,500,000[1] (average annual rate of natural increase: 1.5%); birth rate: 21/1000; infant mortality rate: 7.0/1000; density per square mile: 685.7
Capital and largest city (1993 est.): Jerusalem[2], 550,500. **Other large cities (est. 1993):** Tel Aviv, 355,900; Haifa, 250,000; **Monetary unit:** Shekel; **Languages:** Hebrew,

Arabic, English; **Religions:** Judaism, 82%; Islam, 14%; Christian, 2%; others, 2%; **National name:** Medinat Yisra'el; **Literacy rate:** 92%
Economic summary: Gross domestic product (1993 est.): $65.7 billion; $13,350 per capita; real growth rate 3.5%; inflation 11.3%; unemployment 10.4%. Arable land: 17%. Principal agricultural products: citrus and other fruits, vegetables, beef, dairy and poultry products. Labor force: (1989): 1,348,000; 29.3% in public services. Major industrial products: processed foods, cut diamonds, clothing and textiles, chemicals, metal products, transport and electrical equipment, high-technology electronics. Natural resources: sulfur, copper, phosphates, potash, bromine. Exports: $14.1 billion (f.o.b., 1993 est.): polished diamonds, citrus and other fruits, clothing and textiles, processed foods, electronics, military hardware, fertilizer and chemical products. Imports: $20.3 billion (f.o.b., 1993 est.): rough diamonds, chemicals, oil, machinery, iron and steel, cereals, textiles, vehicles, ship, aircraft. Major trading partners: U.S., E.U., Switzerland, Japan, Hong Kong, Canada, South Africa.

1. Includes West Bank, Gaza Strip, East Jerusalem. 2. Not recognized by U.S. which recognizes Tel Aviv. 3. Includes East Jerusalem.

Geography. Israel, slightly smaller than Massachusetts, lies at the eastern end of the Mediterranean Sea. It is bordered by Egypt on the west, Syria and Jordan on the east, and Lebanon on the north. Northern Israel is largely a plateau traversed from north to south by mountains and broken by great depressions, also running from north to south.

The maritime plain of Israel is remarkably fertile. The southern Negev region, which comprises almost half the total area, is largely a wide desert steppe area. The National Water Project irrigation scheme is now transforming it into fertile land. The Jordan, the only important river, flows from the north through Lake Hule (Waters of Merom) and Lake Kinneret (Sea of Galilee or Sea of Tiberias), finally entering the Dead Sea, 1,290 feet (393 m) below sea level. This "sea," which is actually a salt lake (394 sq mi.; 1,020 sq km), has no outlet, its water balance being maintained by evaporation.

Government. Israel, which does not have a written constitution, has a republican form of government headed by a president elected for a five-year term by the Knesset. The president may serve no more than two terms. The Knesset has 120 members elected by universal suffrage under proportional representation for four years. The government is administered by the Cabinet, which is headed by the prime minister.

The Knesset decided in June 1950 that Israel would acquire a constitution gradually through the years by the enactment of fundamental laws. Israel grants automatic citizenship to every Jew who desires to settle within its borders, subject to control of the Knesset.

History. Palestine, cradle of two great religions and homeland of the modern state of Israel, was known to the ancient Hebrews as the "Land of Canaan." Palestine's name derives from the Philistines, a people who occupied the southern coastal part of the country in the 12th century B.C.

A Hebrew kingdom established in 1000 B.C. was later split into the kingdoms of Judah and Israel; they were subsequently invaded by Assyrians, Babylonians, Egyptians, Persians, Macedonians, Romans, and Byzantines. The Arabs took Palestine from the Byzantine Empire A.D. 634–40. With the exception of a Frankish Crusader kingdom from 1099 to 1187, Palestine remained under Moslem rule until the 20th century (Turkish rule from 1516), when British forces under Gen. Sir Edmund Allenby defeated the Turks and captured Jerusalem Dec. 9, 1917. The League of Nations granted Britain a mandate to govern Palestine, effective in 1923.

Jewish colonies—Jews from Russia established one as early as 1882—multiplied after Theodor Herzl's 1897 call for a Jewish state. The Zionist movement received official approval with the publication of a letter Nov. 2, 1917, from Arthur Balfour, British Foreign Secretary, to Lord Rothschild, a British Jewish leader. Balfour promised support for the establishment of a Jewish homeland in Palestine on the understanding that the civil and religious rights of non-Jewish Palestinians would be safeguarded.

A 1937 British proposal called for an Arab and a Jewish state separated by a mandated area incorporating Jerusalem and Nazareth. Arabs opposed this, demanding a single state with minority rights for Jews, and a 1939 British White Paper retreated, offering instead a single state with further Jewish immigration to be limited to 75,000. Although the White Paper satisfied neither side, further discussion ended on the outbreak of World War II, when the Jewish population stood at nearly 500,000, or 30% of the total. Illegal and legal immigration during the war brought the Jewish population to 678,000 in 1946, compared with 1,269,000 Arabs. Unable to reach a compromise, Britain turned the problem over to the United Nations in 1947, which on November 29 voted for partition—despite strong Arab opposition.

Britain did not help implement the U.N. decision and withdrew on expiration of its mandate May 14, 1948. Zionists had already seized control of areas designated as Jewish, and, on the day of British departure, the Jewish National Council proclaimed the State of Israel.

U.S. recognition came within hours. The next day, Jordanian and Egyptian forces invaded the new nation. At the cease-fire Jan. 7, 1949, Israel increased its original territory by 50%, taking western Galilee, a broad corridor through central Palestine to Jerusalem, and part of modern Jerusalem. (In April 1950, Jordan annexed areas of eastern and central Palestine that had been designated for an Arab state, together with the old city of Jerusalem).

Chaim Weizmann and David Ben-Gurion became Israel's first president and prime minister. The new government was admitted to the U.N. May 11, 1949.

The next clash with Arab neighbors came when Egypt nationalized the Suez Canal in 1956 and barred Israeli shipping. Coordinating with an Anglo-French force, Israeli troops seized the Gaza Strip and drove through the Sinai to the east bank of the Suez Canal, but withdrew under U.S. and U.N. pressure. In 1967, Israel threatened retaliation against Syrian border raids, and Syria asked Egyptian aid. Egypt demanded the removal of U.N. peace-keeping forces from Suez, staged a national mobilization, closed the Gulf of Aqaba, and moved troops into the Sinai. Starting with simultaneous air attacks against Syrian, Jordanian, and Egyptian air bases on June 5, Israel during a six-day war totally defeated its Arab enemies. Expanding its territory by 200%, Israel at the cease-fire held the Golan Heights, the West Bank of the Jordan River, the Old City, and all of the Sinai and the east bank of the Suez Canal.

Israel insisted that Jerusalem remain a unified city and that peace negotiations be conducted directly, something the Arab states had refused to do because it would constitute a recognition of their Jewish neighbor.

Egypt's President Gamal Abdel Nasser renounced the 1967 cease-fire in 1969 and began a "war of attri-

tion" against Israel, firing Soviet artillery at Israeli forces on the east bank of the canal. Nasser died of a heart attack on Sept. 28, 1970, and was succeeded by Anwar el-Sadat.

In the face of Israeli reluctance even to discuss the return of occupied territories, the fourth Mideast war erupted Oct. 6, 1973, with a surprise Egyptian and Syrian assault on the Jewish high holy day of Yom Kippur. Initial Arab gains were reversed when a cease-fire took effect two weeks later, but Israel suffered heavy losses in manpower.

U.S. Secretary of State Henry A. Kissinger arranged a disengagement of forces on both the Egyptian and Syrian fronts. Geneva talks, aimed at a lasting peace, foundered, however, when Israel balked at inclusion of the Palestine Liberation Organization.

A second-stage Sinai withdrawal signed by Israel and Egypt in September 1975 required Israel to give up the strategic Mitla and Gidi passes and to return the captured Abu Rudeis oil fields. Egypt guaranteed passage of Israeli cargoes through the reopened Suez Canal, and both sides renounced force in the settlement of disputes. Two hundred U.S. civilian technicians were stationed in a widened U.N. buffer zone to monitor and warn either side of truce violations.

A dramatic breakthrough in the tortuous history of Mideast peace efforts occurred Nov. 9, 1977, when Egypt's President Sadat declared his willingness to go anywhere to talk peace. Prime Minister Menachem Begin on Nov. 15 extended an invitation to the Egyptian leader to address the Knesset. Sadat's arrival in Israel four days later raised worldwide hopes. But optimism ebbed even before Begin was invited to Ismailia by Sadat, December 25–26.

An Israeli peace plan unveiled by Begin on his return, and approved by the Knesset, offered to end military administration in the West Bank and the Gaza Strip, with a degree of Arab self-rule but no relinquishment of sovereignty by Israel. Sadat severed talks on Jan. 18 and, despite U.S. condemnation, Begin approved new West Bank settlements by Israelis.

On March 14, 1979, after a visit by Carter, the Knesset approved a final peace treaty, and 12 days later Begin and Sadat signed the document, together with Carter, in a White House ceremony. Israel began its withdrawal from the Sinai on May 25 by handing over the coastal town of El Arish and the two countries opened their border on May 29.

One of the most difficult periods in Israel's history began with a confrontation with Syria over the placing by Syria of Soviet surface-to-air missiles in the Bekaa Valley of Lebanon in April 1981. President Reagan dispatched Philip C. Habib to prevent a clash. While Habib was seeking a settlement, Begin ordered a bombing raid against an Iraqi nuclear reactor on June 7, invoking the theory of preemptive self-defense because he said Iraq was planning to make nuclear weapons to attack Israel.

Although Israel withdrew its last settlers from the Sinai in April 1982 and agreed to a Sinai "peace patrol" composed of troops from four West European nations, the fragile peace engineered by Habib in Lebanon was shattered on June 9 by a massive Israeli assault on southern Lebanon. The attack was in retaliation for what Israel charged was a PLO attack that critically wounded the Israeli ambassador to London six days earlier.

Israeli armor swept through UNIFIL lines in southern Lebanon, destroyed PLO strongholds in Tyre and Sidon, and reached the suburbs of Beirut on June 10. As Israeli troops ringed Moslem East Beirut, where 5,000 PLO guerrillas were believed trapped, Habib sought to negotiate a safe exit for them.

A U.S.-mediated accord between Lebanon and Israel, signed on May 17, 1983, provided for Israeli withdrawal from Lebanon. Israeli withdrawal was conditioned on withdrawal of Syrian troops from the Bekaa Valley, however, and the Syrians refused to leave. Israel eventually withdrew its troops from the Beirut area, but kept them in southern Lebanon. Lebanon, under pressure from Syria, canceled the accord in March 1984.

Prime Minister Begin resigned on Sept. 15, 1983. On Oct. 10, Likud Party stalwart Yitzhak Shamir was elected Prime Minister.

After a close election, the two major parties worked out a carefully balanced power-sharing agreement and the Knesset, on Sept. 14, 1984 approved a national unity government including both the Labor Alignment and the Likud bloc.

In one hopeful development, the coalition government declared an economic emergency on July 1 and imposed sweeping austerity measures intended to break the country's 260% inflation. Key elements were an 18.8% devaluation of the shekel, price increases in such government-subsidized products as gasoline, dismissal of 9,000 government employees, government spending cuts and a wage and price freeze. By the end of Peres' term in October, 1986, the shekel had been revalued and stabilized and inflation was down to less than 20%.

In Dec. 1987, riots by Gazan Palestinians led to the current general uprising throughout the occupied territories which consists of low-level violence and civil disobedience. As a consequence, in 1988 the PLO formally declared an independent state. Also, in response to their ostensible recognition of Israel in that year, the U.S. established low-level diplomatic contacts with the PLO.

A deadlock in the elections of Dec. 1988 led to a continuation of the Likud-Labor national unity government. This collapsed in 1990, leading to Shamir forming a right-wing coalition that included the religious parties.

The relaxation of Soviet emigration rules resulted in a massive wave of Jews entering Israel. Citing for one the severe housing shortage, but probably owing as much to political considerations, Israel embarked on constructing new settlements in the West Bank.

Elections in late June 1992 scored a major victory for Rabin's Labor Party but without a parliamentary majority, forcing the new prime minister to search for coalition partners.

In highly secretive Norwegian-sponsored talks Israel and the PLO hammered out an agreement for limited Palestinian self-rule and measured Israeli withdrawal from the West Bank. The accord itself was signed in Cairo in May 1994.

Despite loud outcry the Israeli government in May 1995 decided to confiscate land in largely Palestinian areas of Jerusalem. In July the PLO and the government outlined an agreement calling for Israeli Army withdrawal and expanded Palestinian self-rule coupled with elections. Details, however, had yet to be completed.

ITALY

Italian Republic
President: Oscar Luigi Scalfaro (1992)
Prime Minister: Lamberto Dini (1995)
Area: 116,500 sq mi. (301,278 sq km)
Population (est. mid-1995): 57,700,000 (average annual rate of natural increase: –0.0%); birth rate: 9/1000; infant mortality rate: 7.4/1000; density per square mile: 495.2
Capital: Rome; **Largest cities (est. 1991):** Rome, 2,800,000; Milan, 1,432,200; Naples, 1,206,000; Turin, 992,000; Palermo, 734,250; Genoa, 710,000; Bologna, 411,800; Florence, 408,400; Catania, 364,200; Bari, 353,000; **Monetary unit:** Lira; **Language:** Italian; **Religion:** Roman Catholic, almost 100%; **National name:** Repubblica Italiana; **Literacy rate:** 97%
Economic summary: Gross domestic product (1993): $7.39 trillion, $13,000 per capita; –.7% real growth rate; inflation rate 4.2%; unemployment rate 11.3% (Jan. 94). Arable land: 32%. Principal agricultural products: grapes, olives, citrus fruits, vegetables, wheat, corn. Labor force (1993): 23,697,,000; 58.7% in services. Major industrial products: machinery, iron and steel, autos, textiles, shoes, chemicals. Natural resources: mercury, potash, sulfur, fish, gas, marble. Exports: $156.4 billion (f.o.b., 1993): textiles, wearing apparel, metals, transport equipment, chemicals. Imports: $138.65 billion (c.i.f., 1993): petroleum, industrial machinery, chemicals, food, metals. Major trading partners: United States, E.U., OPEC

Geography. Italy is a long peninsula shaped like a boot bounded on the west by the Tyrrhenian Sea and on the east by the Adriatic. Slightly larger than Arizona, it has for neighbors France, Switzerland, Austria, and Yugoslavia.

Approximately 600 of Italy's 708 miles (1,139 km) of length are in the long peninsula that projects into the Mediterranean from the fertile basin of the Po River. The Apennine Mountains, branching off from the Alps between Nice and Genoa, form the peninsula's backbone, and rise to a maximum height of 9,560 feet (2,912 m) at the Gran Sasso d'Italia (Corno). The Alps form Italy's northern boundary.

Several islands form part of Italy. Sicily (9,926 sq mi.; 25,708 sq km) lies off the toe of the boot, across the Strait of Messina, with a steep and rockbound northern coast and gentler slopes to the sea in the west and south. Mount Etna, an active volcano, rises to 10,741 feet (3,274 m), and most of Sicily is more than 500 feet (3,274 m) in elevation. Sixty-two miles (100 km) southwest of Sicily lies Pantelleria (45 sq mi.; 117 sq km), and south of that are Lampedusa and Linosa. Sardinia (9,301 sq mi.; 24,090 sq km), which is just south of Corsica and about 125 miles (200 km) west of the mainland, is mountainous, stony, and unproductive.

Italy has many northern lakes, lying below the snow-covered peaks of the Alps. The largest are Garda (143 sq mi.; 370 sq km), Maggiore (83 sq mi.; 215 sq km), and Como (55 sq mi.; 142 sq km).

The Po, the principal river, flows from the Alps on Italy's western border and crosses the Lombard plain to the Adriatic.

Government. The president is elected for a term of seven years by Parliament in joint session with regional representatives. The president nominates the premier and, upon the premier's recommendations, the members of the Cabinet. Parliament is composed of two houses: a Senate with 315 elective members and a Chamber of Deputies of 630 members elected by the people for a five-year term.

History. Until A.D. 476, when the German Odoacer became head of the Roman Empire in the west, the history of Italy was largely the history of Rome. From A.D. 800 on, the Holy Roman Emperors, Popes, Normans, and Saracens all vied for control over various segments of the Italian peninsula. Numerous city states, such as Venice and Genoa, and many small principalities flourished in the late Middle Ages.

In 1713, after the War of the Spanish Succession, Milan, Naples, and Sardinia were handed over to Austria, which lost some of its Italian territories in 1735. After 1800, Italy was unified by Napoleon, who crowned himself King of Italy in 1805; but with the Congress of Vienna in 1815, Austria once again became the dominant power in Italy.

Austrian armies crushed Italian uprisings in 1820–1821, and 1831. In the 1830s Giuseppe Mazzini, brilliant liberal nationalist, organized the Risorgimento (Resurrection), which laid the foundation for Italian unity.

Disappointed Italian patriots looked to the House of Savoy for leadership. Count Camille di Cavour (1810–61), Premier of Sardinia in 1852 and the architect of a united Italy, joined England and France in the Crimean War (1853–56), and in 1859, helped France in a war against Austria, thereby obtaining Lombardy. By plebiscite in 1860, Modena, Parma, Tuscany, and the Romagna voted to join Sardinia. In 1860, Giuseppe Garibaldi conquered Sicily and Naples and turned them over to Sardinia. Victor Emmanuel II, King of Sardinia, was proclaimed King of Italy in 1861.

Allied with Germany and Austria-Hungary in the Triple Alliance of 1882, Italy declared its neutrality upon the outbreak of World War I on the ground that Germany had embarked upon an offensive war. In 1915, Italy entered the war on the side of the Allies.

Benito (Il Duce) Mussolini, a former Socialist, organized discontented Italians in 1919 into the Fascist Party to "rescue Italy from Bolshevism." He led his Black Shirts in a march on Rome and, on Oct. 28, 1922, became premier. He transformed Italy into a dictatorship, embarking on an expansionist foreign policy with the invasion and annexation of Ethiopia in 1935 and allying himself with Adolf Hitler in the Rome-Berlin Axis in 1936. He was executed by Partisans on April 28, 1945 at Dongo on Lake Como.

Following the overthrow of Mussolini's dictatorship and the armistice with the Allies (Sept. 3, 1943), Italy joined the war against Germany as a co-belligerent. King Victor Emmanuel III abdicated May 9, 1946, and left the country after having installed his son as King Humbert II. A plebiscite rejected monarchy, however, and on June 13, King Humbert followed his father into exile.

The peace treaty of Sept. 15, 1947, required Italian renunciation of all claims in Ethiopia and Greece and the cession of the Dodecanese to Greece and of five small Alpine areas to France. Much of the Istrian Peninsula, including Fiume and Pola, went to Yugoslavia. ·

The Trieste area west of the new Yugoslav territory was made a free territory (until 1954, when the city and a 90-square-mile zone were transferred to Italy and the rest to Yugoslavia).

Scandal brought the long reign of the Christian Democrats to an end when Italy's 40th premier since World War II, Arnaldo Forlani, was forced to resign in the wake of disclosure that many high-ranking Christian Democrats and civil servants belonged to a secret Masonic lodge known as "P-2."

When the Socialists deserted the coalition, Forlani was forced to resign on May 26, 1981, leaving to Giovanni Spadolini of the small Republican Party the task of forming a new government.

In elections of April 1992 the Christian Democrats obtained less than one-third of the vote, its lowest ever but still making it the largest party. Andreotti routinely handed in his resignation but to compound matters President Cossiga also did so shortly afterwards.

During the early months of 1993 the nation was riveted by a political scandal of a seemingly ever-growing size involving the Mafia and many government leaders. In a referendum in mid-April voters approved changing the current proportional system of representation in the Senate for one utilizing majority voting.

As a result of March 1994 elections an alliance between the Forza Italia party and two other parties dislodged the Christian Democrats, who had dominated national politics since 1948.

In the face of a gradual erosion of support during the year, Berlusconi was forced to resign in December. The Dini government nominated in January 1995 was seen as a reprieve from the ongoing corruption inquiries.

Regional and local elections in April showed the country almost evenly split between right and left forces.

JAMAICA

Sovereign: Queen Elizabeth II
Governor-General: H.E. The Most Hon. Sir Howard F.H. Cooke (1991)
Prime Minister: The Rt. Hon. Percival J. Patterson (1992)
Area: 4,411 sq mi. (11,424 sq km)
Population (est. mid-1995): 2,400,000 (average annual rate of natural increase: 2.0%; birth rate: 25/1000; infant mortality rate: 13.2/1000; density per square mile: 544.1
Capital and largest city (est. 1991): Kingston, 104,000; **Monetary unit:** Jamaican dollar; **Language:** English, Jamaican Creole; **Religions:** Protestant, 55.9%; Roman Catholic, 5%; other, 39.1%; **Member of Commonwealth of Nations; Literacy rate:** 98%
Economic summary: Gross domestic product (1992 est.): $8 billion; $3,200 per capita; real growth rate 1.2%; inflation 15% (1995 est.); unemployment 15.4%. Arable land: 19%. Principal products: sugar cane, citrus fruits, bananas, coffee, potatoes, livestock. Labor force (1991): 1,072,500; services, 41%; agriculture, 22.5%; industry, 19%. Industries: Tourism, bauxite mining, textiles, processed foods, light manufactures. Natural resources: bauxite, gypsum. Exports: $1.1 billion (f.o.b., 1992): alumina, bauxite, sugar, bananas. Imports: $1.5 billion (f.o.b., 1992): fuels, machinery, consumer goods, construction goods, food. Major trading partners: U.S., U.K., Canada, Norway, Trinidad and Tobago, Venezuela, Japan.

Geography. Jamaica is an island in the West Indies, 90 miles (145 km) south of Cuba and 100 miles (161 km) west of Haiti. It is a little smaller than Connecticut.

The island is made up of a plateau and the Blue Mountains, a group of volcanic hills, in the east. Blue Mountain (7,402 ft.; 2,256 m) is the tallest peak.

Government. The legislature is a 60-member House of Representatives elected by universal suffrage and an appointed Senate of 21 members. The Prime Minister is appointed by the Governor-General and must, in the Governor-General's opinion, be the person best able to command the confidence of a majority of the members of the House of Representatives.

History. Jamaica was inhabited by Arawak Indians when Columbus visited it in 1494 and named it St. Iago. It remained under Spanish rule until 1655, then became a British possession. The island prospered from wealth brought by buccaneers to their base, Port Royal, the capital, until the city disappeared in the sea in 1692 after an earthquake. The Arawaks died off from disease and exploitation, and slaves, mostly black, were imported to work sugar plantations. Abolition of the slave trade (1807), emancipation of the slaves (1833), and a gradual drop in sugar prices led to depressed economic conditions that resulted in an uprising in 1865.

The following year Jamaica's status was changed to that of a colony, and conditions improved considerably. Introduction of banana cultivation made the island less dependent on the sugar crop for its well-being.

On May 5, 1953, Jamaica attained internal autonomy, and in 1958 it led in organizing the West Indies Federation. This effort at Caribbean unification failed. A nationalist labor leader, Sir Alexander Bustamente, led a campaign for withdrawal from the Federation. As the result of a popular referendum in 1961, Jamaica became independent on Aug. 6, 1962.

Michael Manley became Prime Minister in 1972 and initiated a socialist program.

The Labour Party defeated Manley's People's National Party in 1980 and its capitalist-oriented leader, Edward P.G. Seaga, became Prime Minister. He instituted measures to encourage private investment.

Like other Caribbean countries, Jamaica was hard-hit by the 1981–82 recession. By 1984, austerity measures that Seaga instituted in the hope of bringing the economy back into balance included elimination of government subsidies. Devaluation of the Jamaican dollar made Jamaican products more competitive on the world market and Jamaica achieved record growth in tourism and agriculture. Manufacturing also grew. But at the same time, the cost of many foods went up 50% to 75% and thousands of Jamaicans fell deeper into poverty.

The PNP decisively won local elections in mid-July, 1987, signaling a weakening in Seaga's position. In 1989, Manley swept back into power with a clear-cut victory. He indicated that he would pursue more centrist policies than he did in his previous administration.

Manley stepped down in 1992 for reasons of health, being replaced by P.J. Patterson.

Parliamentary elections in March 1993 were marred by violence in which 11 died. The PNP received 53 of the 60 seats in parliament.

The Labour Party refused to take part in elections until the polling system was reformed. In 1994 it refused to contest two parliamentary by-elections.

JAPAN

Emperor: Akihito (1989)
Prime Minister: Tomiichi Murayama (1994)
Area: 145,874 sq mi. (377,815 sq km)
Population (est. Oct. 1994): 125,030,000 (average annual rate of natural increase: 0.22%); birth rate: 9.6/1000; infant mortality rate: 4.4/1000; density per square mile: 857.1
Capital: Tokyo; **Largest cities (Jan. 1993):** Tokyo, 8,112,000; Yokohama, 3,276,000; Osaka 2,601,000; Nagoya, 2,162,000; Sapporo, 1,719,000; Kobe, 1,501,000; Kyoto, 1,456,000; Fukuoka, 1,263,000; Kawasaki, 1,196,000; Hiroshima, 1,099,000; **Monetary unit:** Yen;

Language: Japanese; **Religions:** Shintoist, 111.8 million; Buddhist, 93.1 million; Christian, 1.4 million; other, 11.4 million; **National name:** Nippon; **Literacy rate:** 99.9%
Economic summary: Gross national product (1994): $4,629.5 billion; $37,036 per capita; real growth rate 0.4%; inflation 0.7%; unemployment 2.9%. Arable land: 14%. Principal agricultural products: rice, vegetables, fruits, meat and dairy products. Labor force (1994): 66,450,000; 54% in trade and services. Major industrial products: machinery and equipment, metals and metal products, autos, consumer electronics, chemicals, electrical and electronic equipment. Natural resource: fish. Exports: $395.6 billion (1994 customs clearance): machinery and equipment, automobiles, metals and metal products, consumer electronics. Imports: $274.7 billion (1994 customs clearance): fossil fuels, metal ore, raw materials, foodstuffs. Major trading partners: U.S., Middle East, European Union, Southeast Asia

Geography. An archipelago extending in an arc more than 1,744 miles (2,790 km) from northeast to southwest in the Pacific, Japan is separated from the east coast of Asia by the Sea of Japan. It is approximately the size of Montana.

Japan's four main islands are Honshu, Hokkaido, Kyushu, and Shikoku. The Ryukyu chain to the southwest was U.S.-occupied and the Kuriles to the northeast are Russian-occupied. The surface of the main islands consists largely of mountains separated by narrow valleys. There are about 60 more or less active volcanoes, of which the best-known is Mount Aso. Mount Fuji, seen on postcards, is not active.

Government. Japan's Constitution, promulgated on Nov. 3, 1946, replaced the Meiji Constitution of 1889. The 1946 Constitution, sponsored by the U.S. during its occupation of Japan, brought fundamental changes to the Japanese political system, including the abandonment of the Emperor's divine rights. The Diet (Parliament) consists of a House of Representatives of 500 members, elected for four years, and a House of Councilors of 252 members, half of whom are elected every three years for four-year terms. Executive power is vested in the Cabinet, which is headed by a Prime Minister, nominated by the Diet from its members.

On Jan. 7, 1989, Emperor Hirohito, Japan's longest-reigning monarch died and was succeeded by his son, Akihito (born 1933). He was married in 1959 to Michiko Shoda (the first time a crown prince married a commoner).

History. A series of legends attributes creation of Japan to the sun goddess, from whom the later emperors were allegedly descended. The first of them was Jimmu Tenno, supposed to have ascended the throne in 660 B.C.

Recorded Japanese history begins with the first contact with China in the 5th century A.D. Japan was then divided into strong feudal states, all nominally under the Emperor, but with real power often held by a court minister or clan. In 1185, Yoritomo, chief of the Minamoto clan, was designated Shogun (Generalissimo) with the administration of the islands under his control. A dual government system—Shogun and Emperor—continued until 1867.

First contact with the West came about 1542, when a Portuguese ship off course arrived in Japanese waters. Portuguese traders, Jesuit missionaries, and Spanish, Dutch, and English traders followed. Suspicious of Christianity and of Portuguese support of a local Japanese revolt, the shoguns prohibited all trade with foreign countries; only a Dutch trading post at Nagasaki was permitted. Western attempts to renew trading relations failed until 1853, when Commodore Matthew Perry sailed an American fleet into Tokyo Bay.

Japan now quickly made the transition from a medieval to a modern power. Feudalism was abolished and industrialization was speeded. An imperial army was established with conscription. The shogun system was abolished in 1868 by Emperor Meiji, and parliamentary government was established in 1889. After a brief war with China in 1894–95, Japan acquired Formosa (Taiwan), the Pescadores Islands, and part of southern Manchuria. China also recognized the independence of Korea (Chosen), which Japan later annexed (1910).

In 1904–05, Japan defeated Russia in the Russo-Japanese War, gaining the territory of southern Sakhalin (Karafuto) and Russia's port and rail rights in Manchuria. In World War I Japan seized Germany's Pacific islands and leased areas in China. The Treaty of Versailles then awarded it a mandate over the islands.

At the Washington Conference of 1921–22, Japan agreed to respect Chinese national integrity. The series of Japanese aggressions that was to lead to the nation's downfall began in 1931 with the invasion of Manchuria. The following year, Japan set up this area as a puppet state, "Manchukuo," under Emperor Henry Pu-Yi, last of China's Manchu dynasty. On Nov. 25, 1936, Japan joined the Axis by signing the anti-Comintern pact. The invasion of China came the next year and the Pearl Harbor attack on the U.S. on Dec. 7, 1941.

(For details of World War II (1939–45), *see* Headline History.)

Japan surrendered formally on Sept. 2, 1945, aboard the battleship *Missouri* in Tokyo Bay after atomic bombs had hit Hiroshima and Nagasaki. Southern Sakhalin and the Kurile Islands reverted to the U.S.S.R., and Formosa (Taiwan) and Manchuria to China. The Pacific islands remained under U.S. occupation. General of the Army Douglas MacArthur was appointed Supreme Commander for the Allied Powers on Aug. 14, 1945.

A new Japanese Constitution went into effect in 1947. In 1949, many of the responsibilities of government were returned to the Japanese. Full sovereignty was granted to Japan by the Japanese Peace Treaty in 1951.

Following the visit of Prime Minister Eisaku Sato to Washington in 1969, the U.S. agreed to return Okinawa and other Ryukyu Islands to Japan in 1972, and both nations renewed the security treaty in 1970.

The general election of July 1989 for the upper house of parliament scored a loss for the ruling Liberal Democratic Party, the first in 35 years. The following month, however, the party's president, Toshiki Kaifu, was elected prime minister.

Kaifu pledged to provide $9 billion to the U.S. to help defray the expense of the latter's operations in the Persian Gulf. The government attempted to push legislation that would have permitted Japan to send a military contingent to the Gulf in noncombat roles. This was defeated amid public outcry against it.

During Soviet President Gorbachev's visit to Tokyo in April 1991 he and Prime Minister Kaifu attempted to resolve a territorial dispute arising out of the last days of World War II. No breakthrough resulted, and the issue still remained at an impasse.

Rebellious legislators in June 1993 joined with the opposition to force a vote of no confidence in the government. In its wake Prime Minister Miyazawa dissolved parliament. Many of the rebels quit the ruling Liberal Democrats to form three new parties.

The elections of July saw the largest loss for the Liberal Democrats since its creation. Yet it managed to retain 223 of the 511 seats, making it the largest single party.

An odd partnership was formed in June 1994 when the Liberal Democrats were instrumental in electing the Socialist Party head as prime minister. Fears were immediately raised that all progress toward deregulating the economy and reforming the political system would grind to a halt.

A devastating earthquake shook on October 4, 1994. Particularly hard hit was the city of Hokkaido.

In June 1995 the government passed a resolution expressing remorse for the pain Japan caused during World War II, but the statement was calculatingly ambiguous and unlikely to mollify foreign criticism.

JORDAN

The Hashemite Kingdom of Jordan
Ruler: King Hussein I (1952)
Prime Minister: Sharif Zeid Ben Shaker
Area: 34,573 sq mi (89,544 sq km) excludes West Bank
Population (est. mid-1995): 4,100,000 (average annual rate of natural increase: 3.3%); birth rate: 38/1000; infant mortality rate: 32/1000; density per square mile: 118.6
Capital: Amman; **Largest cities (est. 1990):** Amman, 1,300,000; Zarka, 420,900; Irbid, 280,000; Salt, 143,600; **Monetary unit:** Jordanian dinar; **Languages:** Arabic (official), English; **Religions:** Islam, 96%; Christian, 4%; **National name:** Al Mamlaka al Urduniya al Hashemiyah; **Literacy rate:** 82%
Economic summary: Gross domestic product (1993 est.): $11.5 billion; $3,000 per capita; 5% real growth rate; inflation: 5% (est.); unemployment: 20% (est.). Arable land: 4%. Principal products: wheat, fruits, vegetables, olive oil. Labor force (1992): 600,000: industry 11.4%; commerce, restaurants, and hotels 10.5%; constructin 10%; transport and communications 8.7%; agriculture 7.4%. Major products: phosphate, refined petroleum products, cement. Natural resources: phosphate, potash. Exports: $1.4 billion (f.o.b., 1993 est.): phosphates, fruits, and vegetables, shale oil, fertilizer, manufactures. Imports: $3.2 billion (c.i.f., 1993 est.): petroleum products, textiles, capital goods, motor vehicles, foodstuffs. Major trading partners: U.S., Japan, Saudi Arabia, Iraq, E.U., China, India, Iraq.

Geography. The Middle East kingdom of Jordan is bordered on the west by Israel and the Dead Sea, on the north by Syria, on the east by Iraq, and on the south Saudi Arabia. It is comparable in size to Indiana.

Arid hills and mountains make up most of the country. The southern section of the Jordan River flows through the country.

Government. Jordan is a constitutional monarchy with a bicameral parliament.

The upper house consists of 40 members appointed by the king and the lower house is composed of 80 members elected by popular vote. The Constitution guarantees freedom of religion, speech, press, association, and private property.

Political parties were legalized in 1991.

History. In biblical times, the country that is now Jordan contained the lands of Edom, Moab, Ammon, and Bashan. In A.D. 106 it became part of the Roman province of Arabia and in 633–36 was conquered by the Arabs.

Taken from the Turks by the British in World War I, Jordan (formerly known as Transjordan) was separated from the Palestine mandate in 1920, and in 1921, placed under the rule of Abdullah ibn Hussein.

In 1923, Britain recognized Jordan's independence, subject to the mandate. In 1946, grateful for Jordan's loyalty in World War II, Britain abolished the mandate. That part of Palestine occupied by Jordanian troops was formally incorporated by action of the Jordanian Parliament in 1950.

King Abdullah was assassinated in 1951. His son Talal was deposed as mentally ill the next year. Talal's son Hussein, born Nov. 14, 1935, succeeded him.

From the beginning of his reign, Hussein had to steer a careful course between his powerful neighbor to the west, Israel, and rising Arab nationalism, frequently a direct threat to this throne. Riots erupted when he joined the Central Treaty Organization (the Baghdad Pact) in 1955, and he incurred further unpopularity when Britain, France, and Israel attacked the Suez Canal in 1956, forcing him to place his army under nominal command of the United Arab Republic of Egypt and Syria.

The 1961 breakup of the UAR eased Arab national pressure on Hussein, who was the first to recognize Syria after it reclaimed its independence. Jordan was swept into the 1967 Arab-Israeli war, however, and lost the old city of Jerusalem and all of its territory west of the Jordan river, the West Bank. Embittered Palestinian guerrilla forces virtually took over sections of Jordan in the aftermath of defeat, and open warfare broke out between the Palestinians and government forces in 1970.

Despite intervention of Syrian tanks, Hussein's Bedouin army defeated the Palestinians, suffering heavy casualties. A U.S. military alert and Israeli armor massed on the Golan Heights contributed psychological weight, but the Jordanians alone drove out the Syrians and invited the departure of 12,000 Iraqi troops who had been in the country since the 1967 war. Ignoring protests from other Arab states, Hussein by mid-1971 crushed Palestinian strength in Jordan and shifted the problem to Lebanon, where many of the guerrillas had fled.

In October 1974, Hussein concurred in an Arab summit resolution calling for an independent Palestinian state and endorsing the Palestine Liberation Organization as the "sole legitimate representative of the Palestinian people." This apparent reversal of policy changed with the growing disillusion of Arab states with the P.L.O., however.

As Egypt and Israel neared final agreement on a peace treaty early in 1979, Hussein met with Yassir Arafat, the PLO leader, on March 17 and issued a joint statement of opposition. Although the U.S. pressed Jordan to break Arab ranks on the issue, Hussein elected to side with the great majority, cutting ties with Cairo and joining the boycott against Egypt.

In September 1980, Jordan declared itself with Iraq in its conflict with Iran and, despite threats from Syria, opened ports to war shipments for Iraq.

Jordan's stance during the Persian Gulf war strained relations with the U.S. and led to the termination of aid to the former. The signing of a national charter by King Hussein and leaders of the main political groups in June 1991 meant political parties were permitted in exchange for acceptance of the constitution and the monarchy.

Still smarting from its stance during the Gulf War unemployment soared. The King's decision to join the Middle East peace talks in mid-1991 helped his country's relations with the U.S.

In July 1994 King Hussein and the Israeli prime minister signed a declaration ending the state of belligerency between the two countries.

A peace between the two countries was signed on October 26, 1994, although a clause in it calling the King the "custodian" of Islamic holy shrines in Jerusalem angered the PLO.

KAZAKHSTAN

Republic of Kazakhstan
President: Nursultan A. Nazarbaev (1990)
Vice President: Erik M. Asanbaev
Prime Minister: Arkezhan Kazhgeldin (1994)
Area: 1,049,000 sq mi. (2,717,300 sq km)
Population (est. mid-1995): 16,900,000 (Kazaks, 38%; Russians, 36%; Germans, 5.5%; Ukranians, 5.3%; other minorities: Tatars, Izbeks, Belarus, and Koreans); average annual rate of natural increase: 0.9%; birth rate: 19/1000; infant mortality rate, 28/1000; density per square mile: 16.1
Capital and largest city (1991): Alma-Ata (Alamty), 1,156,200. Other large cities: Karaganda, 608,600; (1989): Shymkent, 393,000; Semipalatinsk (Semey), 334,000; Ust-Kamenogorsk, 324,000; Aktyubinsk (Aktobe), 253,000; Temiratau, 212,000; **Monetary unit:** Tenge; **Language:** Kazakh (Qazaq) official language, Russian; **Religion:** Muslim, 47%; Russian Orthodox; Lutheran. **Literacy rate:** 100%
Economic summary: Gross national product (UN, World Bank 1993 est.): $60.3 billion, $3,510 per capita; real growth rate –13%; inflation (per month) 28%; unemployment 0.6%. Labor force: 7,356,000 (1992); industry and construction 31%; agriculture and forestry 26%. Industries: extractive industries (oil, coal, iron ore, manganese, bauxite, gold, silver, phosphates, sulfur); iron and steel, nonferrous metals, tractors and other agricultural machinery, electric motors, construction materials. Agriculture: grains, spring wheat, meat, cotton, and wool. Exports: $1.3 billion (1993): to outside the former USSR: oil, ferrous and non-ferrous metals, chemicals, wool, grain, meat. Imports: $358.3 billion (1993): from outside the successor states of the former USSR: machinery and parts, industrial materials. Trading partners: Russia, Ukraine, Uzbekistan, and other former Soviet republics, China.

Geography: Kazakhstan lies in the north of the central Asian republics and is bounded by Russia in the north, China in the east, the Kyrgyzstan and Uzbekistan in the south, and the Caspian Sea and part of Turkmenistan in the west. It has almost 15,000 miles of coastline on the Caspian Sea. Kazakhstan is the second largest republic of the Commonwealth of Independent States in area and is slightly more than twice the size of Texas. The territory is mostly steppe land with hilly plains and plateaus.

Government: A constitutional republic.

History: The indigenous Kazakhs were a nomadic Turkic people who belonged to several divisions of Kazakh hordes. They grouped together in settlements and lived in dome-shaped tents made of felt called "yurts." Their tribes migrated seasonally to find pastures for their herds of sheep, horses, and goats. Although they had chiefs, the Kazakhs were rarely united as a single nation under one great leader. Their tribes fell under Mongol rule in the 13th century and they were dominated by Tartar Khanates until the area was conquered by Russia in the 18th century.

Kazakhstan became a constituent republic of the Soviet Union in 1936 and collective farming and modern industrial production methods were instituted.

The world's first fast-breeder nuclear reactor was built in the republic and the main space center for the Commonwealth of Independent States is located in Baikonur.

Kazakhstan sought greater political autonomy but delayed seeking independence from the former Soviet Union.

Kazakhstan proclaimed its membership in the Commonwealth of Independent States on Dec. 21, 1991, along with ten other former Soviet republics.

A draft constitution was adopted in June 1992 that guaranteed political pluralism.

In 1993 the country overwhelmingly approved the Nuclear Non-Proliferation Treaty. The U.S. in December signed an agreement to finance denuclearizaiton.

In a referendum held on April 29, 1995, the electorate voted in support of extending the president's term to December 2000.

KENYA

Republic of Kenya
President: Daniel arap Moi (1978)
Area: 224,960 sq mi. (582,646 sq km)
Population (est. mid-1995): 28,300,000 (average annual rate of natural increase: 3.3%); birth rate: 45/1000; infant mortality rate: 69/1000; density per square mile: 125.8
Capital: Nairobi; **Largest cities (est. 1990):** Nairobi, 1,200,000; Mombasa, 800,000; **Monetary unit:** Kenyan shilling; **Languages:** English (official), Swahili (national), and several other languages spoken by 40 ethnic groups; **Religions:** Protestant, 38%; Roman Catholic, 28%; traditional, 26%; Islam, 6%; **Literacy rate:** 69%; **Member of Commonwealth of Nations; National name:** Jamhuri ya Kenya
Economic summary: Gross domestic product (1993 est.): $33.2 billion; $1,200 per capita; real growth rate: 0.5%; inflation 55%; unemployment: 23.8% (urban est.). Arable land: 3%. Principal agricultural products: coffee, sisal, tea, pineapples, livestock. Labor force: 9.2 million: services, 54.8%; industry, 26.2%; agriculture, 19%. Major industrial products: textiles, processed foods, consumer goods, refined oil. Natural resources: gold, limestone, minerals, wildlife. Exports: $1.0 billion (f.o.b., 1992 est.): coffee, tea, refined petroleum. Imports: $1.6 billion (f.o.b., 1992 est.): machinery, transport equipment, crude oil, iron and steel products. Major trading partners: Western European countries, Far East, U.S., Africa, Middle East, Asia.

Geography. Kenya lies on the equator in east central Africa on the coast of the Indian Ocean. It is twice the size of Nevada. Kenya's neighbors are Tanzania, Uganda, the Sudan, Ethiopia, and Somalia.

In the north, the land is arid; the southwestern corner is in the fertile Lake Victoria Basin; and a length of the eastern depression of Great Rift Valley separates western highlands from those that rise from the lowland coastal strip. Large game reserves have been developed.

Government. Under its Constitution Kenya has a one-house National Assembly of 188 members, elected for five years by universal suffrage and 12 nominated and 2 ex-officio, for a total of 202. Since 1969, the president has been chosen by a general election.

History. Kenya, formerly a British colony and protectorate, was made a crown colony in 1920. The whites' domination of the rich plateau area, the White Highlands, long regarded by the Kikiyu people as their territory, was a factor leading to native terrorism, called the Mau Mau movement, in 1952. In 1954 the British began preparing the territory for African rule and independence. In 1961 Jomo Kenyatta was freed from banishment to become leader of the Kenya African National Union.

Internal self-government was granted in 1963; Kenya became independent on Dec. 12, 1963, with Kenyatta the first president.

Moi's tenure has been marked by a consolidation of power which has included the harassment of political opponents and the banning of secret ballots.

In reluctant elections of December 1992 Moi won re-election, although the opposition disputed the results.

The government reimposed price controls and broke with the IMF and World Bank in March 1993, threatening a break in Western aid. The opposition boycotted the opening of parliament in protest. The government assured foreign donors in July that it intended to service its huge debt despite its size.

President Moi in early 1995 moved against the opposition, ordering the arrest of anyone who insulted him. In June the renowned paleontologist Richard Leakey registered a new political party.

KIRIBATI

Republic of Kiribati
President: Teburoro Tito (1994)
Area: 280 sq mi. (726 sq km)
Population (est. mid-1994): 77,853 (average annual growth rate: 1.999%); birth rate: 31.6/1000; infant mortality rate: 98.4/1000; density per square mile: 278
Capital (1990): Tarawa, 25,154; **Monetary unit:** Australian dollar; **Language:** English; **Religions:** Roman Catholic, 52.6%; Protestant, 40.9%; **Member of Commonwealth of Nations; Literacy rate:** 90%
Economic summary: Gross domestic product (1990 est.): $36.8 million; $525 per capita; 1% real growth rate; inflation 4%. Arable land: NEGL%. Principal agricultural products: copra, vegetables. Exports: $5.8 million (f.o.b., 1990 est.): fish, copra. Imports: $26.7 million (c.i.f., 1990 est.): foodstuffs, fuel, transportation equipment. Major trading partners: New Zealand, Australia, Japan, American Samoa, U.K., U.S., Fiji.

Geography. Kiribati, formerly the Gilbert Islands, consists of three widely separated main groups of Southwest Pacific islands, the Gilberts on the equator, the Phoenix Islands to the east, and the Line Islands further east. Ocean Island, producer of phosphates until it was mined out in 1981, is also included in the two million square miles of ocean, which give Kiribati an important fishery resource.

Government. The president holds executive power. The legislature consists of a House Assembly with 39 members.

History. A British protectorate since 1892, the Gilbert and Ellice Islands became a colony in 1915–16. The two island groups were separated in 1975 and given internal self-government.

Tarawa and others of the Gilbert group were occupied by Japan during World War II. Tarawa was the site of one of the bloodiest battles in U.S. Marine Corps history when Marines landed in November 1943 to dislodge the Japanese defenders.

Princess Anne, representing Queen Elizabeth II, presented the independence documents to the new government on July 12, 1979.

President Tabai resigned in July 1991 after the maximum 12 years in office, being succeeded by his vice president.

The government continued its moves in 1993–94 to privatize the public sector with its plans to sell off several major enterprises.

A no-confidence vote in the Assembly in May 1994 led to general elections in July. A coalition of opposition parties won a majority.

KOREA, NORTH

Democratic People's Republic of Korea

Head of State: Kim Jong Il (1994)
Premier: Kang Song San (1992)
Area: 46,768 sq mi. (121,129 sq km)
Population (est. mid-1995): 23,500,000 (average annual rate of natural increase: 1.8%); birth rate: 23/1000; infant mortality rate: 26/1000; density per sq mi.: 502.4
Capital and largest city (est. 1987): Pyongyang, 2,355,000; **Monetary unit:** Won; **Language:** Korean; **Religions:** Buddhism and Confucianism, religious activities almost nonexistent; **National name:** Choson Minjujuui Inmin Konghwaguk; **Literacy rate:** 99%
Economic summary: Gross national product (1992 est.): $22 billion; $1,000 per capita; real growth rate –10 to 15%. Arable land: 18%. Principal agricultural products: corn, rice, vegetables. Labor force: 9,615,000; 64% nonagricultural. Major industrial products: machines, electric power, chemicals, textiles, processed food, metallurgical products. Natural resources: coal, iron ore, hydroelectric power. Exports: $1.3 billion (f.o.b., 1992 est.): minerals, metallurgical products, agricultural products, manufactures (including armaments). Imports: $1.9 billion (f.o.b., 1992 est.): machinery and equipment, petroleum, grain, coking coal. Major trading partners: C.I.S. countries, China, Japan, Hong Kong, Germany, Singapore.

Geography. Korea is a 600-mile (966 km) peninsula jutting from Manchuria and China (and a small portion of the U.S.S.R.) into the Sea of Japan and the Yellow Sea off eastern Asia. North Korea occupies an area slightly smaller than Pennsylvania north of the 38th parallel.

The country is almost completely covered by a series of north-south mountain ranges separated by narrow valleys. The Yalu River forms part of the northern border with Manchuria.

Government. The elected Supreme People's Assembly, as the chief organ of government, chooses a Presidium and a Cabinet. The Cabinet, which exercises executive authority, is subject to approval by the Assembly and the Presidium.

The Korean Workers (Communist) Party is the only political party.

History. According to myth, Korea was founded in 2333 B.C. by Tangun. In the 17th century, it became a vassal of China and was isolated from all but Chinese influence and contact until 1876, when Japan forced Korea to negotiate a commercial treaty, opening the land to the U. S. and Europe. Japan achieved control as the result of its war with China (1894–95) and with Russia (1904–05) and annexed Korea in 1910. Japan developed the country but never won over the Korean nationalists.

After the Japanese surrender in 1945, the country was divided into two occupation zones, the U.S.S.R. north of and the U.S. south of the 38th parallel. When the cold war developed between the U.S. and U.S.S.R., trade between the zones was cut off. In 1948, the division between the zones was made permanent with the establishment of separate regimes in the north and south. By mid-1949, the U.S. and U.S.S.R. withdrew all troops. The Democratic People's Republic of Korea (North Korea) was established on May 1, 1948. The Communist Party, headed by Kim Il Sung, was established in power.

On June 25, 1950, the North Korean army launched a surprise attack on South Korea. On June 26, the U.N. Security Council condemned the invasion as aggression and ordered withdrawal of the invading forces. On June 27, President Harry S. Truman ordered air and naval units into action to enforce the U.N. order. The British government did the same, and soon a multinational U.N. command was set up to aid the South Koreans. The North Korean invaders took Seoul and pushed the South Koreans into the southeast corner of their country.

Gen. Douglas MacArthur, U.N. commander, made an amphibious landing at Inchon on September 15 behind the North Korean lines, which resulted in the complete rout of the North Korean army. The U.N. forces drove north across the 38th parallel, approaching the Yalu River. Then Communist China entered the war, forcing the U.N. forces into headlong retreat. Seoul was lost again, then regained; ultimately the war stabilized near the 38th parallel but dragged on for two years while the belligerents negotiated. An armistice was agreed to on July 27, 1953.

Formerly strenuously opposed to separate membership for the two Koreas in the U.N., the North in May 1991 announced it would, albeit reluctantly, apply for such membership.

Tensions continued to build in early 1994 over international inspection of North Korea's nuclear sites.

Kim Il Sung's death on July 8, 1994, introduced a period of uncertainty. Negotiations over the country's suspected atomic weapons program proved lengthy and thorny, but an agreement was reached in June 1995 which included providing the North with a South Korean nuclear reactor.

KOREA, SOUTH

Republic of Korea

President: Kim Young Sam (1993)
Prime Minister: Lee Hong-Koo (1994)
Area: 38,031 sq mi. (99,392 sq km)
Population (est. mid-1995): 44,900,000 (average annual rate of natural increase: 1.0%); birth rate: 15/1000; infant mortality rate: 11/1000; density per square mile: 1,180.6.
Capital: Seoul; **Largest cities (est. 1990):** Seoul, 10,628,000; Pusan, 3,798,000; Taegu, 2,229,000; Inchon, 1,818,000; **Monetary unit:** Won; **Language:** Korean; **Religions (1989):** Buddhist, 46.9%; Confucianist, 2.8%; Catholic, 10.8%; Protestant, 37.7%; **National name:** Taehan Min'guk; **Literacy rate:** 96%
Economic summary: Gross national product (1994 est.): $29.6 billion; $8,483 per capita; 8.4% real growth rate; inflation 5.6%; unemployment 2.4%. Arable land: 21%. Principal agricultural products: rice, barley. Labor force: 19,864,000; 26% in mining and manufacturing. Major products: clothing and textiles, processed foods, automobiles, steel, electronics equipment. Natural resources: molybdenum, lead, tungsten, graphite, coal, hydropower. Exports: $80.9 billion (1993): foot-

wear, clothing, fish, textiles, automobiles, electric and electronics, ships, and steel. Imports: $79.090 billion (1993): transport equipment, organic chemicals, textiles, steel, oil, grains, chemicals, machinery, electronics. Major trading partners: U.S., Japan.

Geography. Slightly larger than Indiana, South Korea lies below the 38th parallel on the Korean peninsula. It is mountainous in the east; in the west and south are many harbors on the mainland and offshore islands.

Government. Constitutional amendments enacted in Sept. 1987 called for direct election of a President, who would be limited to a single five-year term, and increased the powers of the National Assembly *vis a vis* the President.

The National Assembly was expanded from 276 to 299 seats, filled by proportional representation.

History. South Korea came into being in the aftermath of World War II as the result of a 1945 agreement making the 38th parallel the boundary between a northern zone occupied by the U.S.S.R. and a southern zone occupied by U.S. forces. (For details, *see* North Korea.)

Elections were held in the U.S. zone in 1948 for a national assembly, which adopted a republican Constitution and elected Syngman Rhee president. The new republic was proclaimed on August 15 and was recognized as the legal government of Korea by the U.N. on Dec. 12, 1948.

On June 25, 1950, South Korea was attacked by North Korean Communist forces. U.S. armed intervention was ordered on June 27 by President Harry S. Truman, and on the same day the U.N. invoked military sanctions against North Korea. Gen. Douglas MacArthur was named commander of the U.N. forces. U.S. and South Korean troops fought a heroic holding action but, by the first week of August, they had been forced back to a 4,000-square-mile beachhead in southeast Korea.

There they stood off superior North Korean forces until September 15, when a major U.N. amphibious attack was launched far behind the Communist lines at Inchon, port of Seoul. By September 30, U.N. forces were in complete control of South Korea. They then invaded North Korea and were nearing the Manchurian and Siberian borders when several hundred thousand Chinese Communist troops entered the conflict in late October. U.N. forces were then forced to retreat below the 38th parallel.

On May 24, 1951, U.N. forces recrossed the parallel and had made important new inroads into North Korea when truce negotiations began on July 10. An armistice was finally signed at Panmunjom on July 27, 1953, leaving a devastated Korea in need of large-scale rehabilitation.

The U.S. and South Korea signed a mutual-defense treaty on Oct. 1, 1953.

Rhee, president since 1948, resigned in 1960 in the face of rising disorders. PoSun Yun was elected to succeed him, but political instability continued. In 1961, Gen. Park Chung Hee took power and subsequently built up the country. The U.S. stepped up military aid, building up South Korea's armed forces to 600,000 men. The South Koreans sent 50,000 troops to Vietnam, at U.S. expense.

Park's assassination on Oct. 26, 1979, by Kim Jae Kyu, head of the Korean Central Intelligence Agency, brought a liberalizing trend as Choi Kyu Hah, the new President, freed imprisoned dissidents. The release of opposition leader Kim Dae jung in February 1980 generated anti-government demonstrations that turned into riots by May. Choi resigned on Aug. 16.

Chun Doo Wha, head of a military Special Committee for National Security Measures, was the sole candidate as the electoral college confirmed him as President on Aug. 27.

Debate over the Presidential succession in 1988 was the main dispute in 1986–87 with Chun wanting election by the electoral college and the opposition demanding a direct popular vote, charging that Chun could manipulate the college. On April 13, 1987, Chun declared a close on the debate but when, in June, he appointed Roh Toe Woo, the DJP chairman as his successor, violent protests broke out. Roh, and later, Chun, agreed that direct elections should be held. A split in the opposition led to Roh's election on Dec. 16, 1987, with 36.6% of the vote.

Weeks of anti-government protests in May 1991 led to the resignation of then-Prime Minister Ro Ja Bong.

In early 1991 the Soviet Union announced it would not oppose South Korea's application for U.N. membership.

In his first year in office President Kim began a massive anticorruption campaign, purging thousands of military men with links to previous regimes, bureaucrats and businessmen.

As part of the GATT South Korea in December 1993 announced it would allow foreign rice imports, a move that led to a major Cabinet reshuffle.

Events in the North and their effect on the country dominated the political news in 1994. The crisis situation in the South in early year led to the resignation of the then prime minister. Abruptly, however, tensions eased with the first summit in June between the presidents of the two Koreas.

KUWAIT

State of Kuwait

Emir: Sheik Jaber al-Ahmad al-Sabah (1977)
Prime Minister: Sheik Sa'ad Abdullah al-Salim (1978)
Area: 6,880 sq mi. (17,820 sq km)
Population (est. mid-1995): 1,500,000 (average annual rate of natural increase: 2.2%); birth rate: 25/1000; infant mortality rate: 12/1000; density per square mile: 218
Capital (est. 1990): Kuwait, 151,060; **Largest city (est. 1985):** as-Salimiyah, 153,220; **Monetary unit:** Kuwaiti dinar; **Languages:** Arabic and English; **Religions:** Islam; **National name:** Dawlat al Kuwayt; **Literacy rate:** 74%

Economic summary: Gross domestic product (1993 est.): $25.7 billion; $15,100 per capita; real growth rate 15%; inflation 3%. Labor force: 566,000 (1986); 45% in services. Major products: crude and refined oil, petrochemicals, building materials, salt. Natural resources: petroleum, fish, shrimp. Exports: $10.5 billion (f.o.b., 1993 est.): oil 90%. Imports: $6 billion (f.o.b., 1993 est.): foodstuffs, automobiles, building materials, machinery, textiles. Major trading partners: U.S., Japan, Italy, U.K., Canada, France.

Geography. Kuwait is situated northeast of Saudi Arabia at the northern end of the Persian Gulf, south of Iraq. It is slightly larger than Hawaii. The low-lying land is mainly sandy and barren.

Government. Sheik Jaber al-Ahmad al-Sabah rules as Emir of Kuwait and appoints the Prime Minister, who appoints his Cabinet (Council of Ministers). National elections were held in 1992 and the National Assembly (legislative branch), dissolved in 1986 was reinstated. There are no political parties in Kuwait.

History. Kuwait obtained British protection in 1897 when the Sheik feared that the Turks would take over the area. In 1961, Britain ended the protectorate, giving Kuwait independence, but agreed to give military aid on request. Iraq immediately threatened to occupy the area and Sheik Sabah al-Salem al-Sabah called in British troops in 1961. Soon afterward the Arab League sent in troops, replacing the British. The prize was oil.

Oil was discovered in the 1930s. Kuwait proved to have 20% of the world's known oil resources. It has been a major producer since 1946, the world's second largest oil exporter. The Sheik, who gets half the profits, devotes most of them to the education, welfare, and modernization of his kingdom. In 1966, Sheik Sabah designated a relative, Jaber al-Ahmad al-Sabah, as his successor.

By 1968, the sheikdom had established a model welfare state, and it sought to establish dominance among the sheikdoms and emirates of the Persian Gulf.

In July 1990, Iraq President Hussein blamed Kuwait for falling oil prices. After a failed Arab mediation attempt to solve the dispute peacefully, Iraq invaded Kuwait on Aug. 2, 1990, and set up a pro-Iraqi provisional government.

A coalition of Arab and Western military forces drove Iraqi troops from Kuwait in February 1991. The Emir returned to his country from Saudi Arabia in mid-March. Martial law, in effect since the end of the Gulf war, ended in late June.

The U.S. sent 2,400 troops to the country in August 1992 as part of a training exercise but this was widely interpreted as a show of strength to Saddam Hussein.

The general election of October 1992 was widely interpreted as a success for supporters of a return to Islamic law. A political independent was named speaker of the parliament, and the opposition held 31 of the 50 seats.

In May 1993 Kuwait announced its plans to build a deep ditch along its entire land border with Iraq.

Iraqi "training" maneuvers near the Kuwaiti border in October 1994 renewed fears of aggression in the country. A Kuwaiti appeal brought the quick deployment of U.S. and British troops and equipment.

KYRGYZSTAN

The Kyrgyz Republic
President: Askar Akaev (1990)
Prime Minister: Apas Jumagulov
Area: 76,000 sq mi. (198,500 sq km)
Population (est. mid-1995): 4,400,000; (Kyrgyz, 52%; Russian, 22%); (average annual rate of natural increase: 1.8%); birth rate: 26/1000; infant mortality rate: 33/1000; density per square mile: 57.9
Capital and largest city (1994): Bishkek (Frunze), 631,000. Other (1994): Osh, 213,000; **Monetary unit:** The Som; **Language:** Kyrgyz (official), Russian is de facto second language of communication. **Religion:** Muslim, 70%; Russian Orthodox. **Literacy rate:** 100%
Economic summary: $810 per capita GNP 1992; −25% real growth rate (1992 est.); inflation (1st qtr. 1993) 29%; unemployment 0.1%. Important natural resources are rare earth metals and gold. Industrial production includes electrical engineering, hydroelectric power, agricultural machine building, washing machines, furniture, cement, paper, and brick. Agricultural products are food grains including wheat, cotton,

grapes, sugar beets, tobacco, and livestock raising, especially sheep. Labor force: 1,900,000 (1994): agriculture, 33%; industry, 28%. Exports: $76.6 million (c.i.f., 1994): wool, chemicals, cotton, ferrous and nonferrous metals, shoes, machinery, tobacco. Imports: $34.9 million (c.i.f., 1994): grain, lumber, industrial products, ferrous metals, fuel, machinery, textiles, footwear.. Trading partners: Russia, 70%; others Ukraine, Uzbekistan, Kazakhstan.

Geography: Kyrgyzstan (formerly Kirghizia) is a rugged country with the Tien Shan mountain range covering approximately 95 percent of the whole territory. The mountain tops are covered with perennial snow and glaciers. Kyrgyzstan borders Kazakhstan on the north and northwest, Uzbekistan in the southwest, Tajikistan in the south, and China in the southeast. The republic is the same size in area as the state of Nebraska.

Government: A constitutional republic.

History: The native Kyrgyz are a Turkic people who in ancient times first settled in the Tien Shan mountains. They were traditionally pastoral nomads. There was extensive Russian colonization in the 1900s and Russian settlers were given much of the best agricultural land. This led to an unsuccessful and disastrous revolt by the Kyrgyz people in 1916. Kyrgyzstan became part of the Soviet Federated Socialist Republic in 1924, and was made an autonomous republic in 1926. Kyrgyzstan became a constituent republic of the U.S.S.R. in 1936. The Soviets forced the Kyrgyz to abandon their nomadic culture and brought modern farming and industrial production techniques into their society. It has greatly changed their traditional way of life.

President Askar Akaev supported Soviet President Gorbachev's reform programs and promoted them in his country.

Kyrgyzstan proclaimed its independence from the Soviet Union on Aug. 31, 1991.

On Dec. 21, 1991, Kyrgyzstan the Commonwealth of Independent States.

The country joined the UN and the IMF in 1992 and adopted a shock-therapy economic program.

Voters formally and overwhelmingly endorsed market reforms in a referendum held in January 1994.

The introduction of its own monetary unit caused a predictable disruption in supplies from other republics. This, in turn, led to a production slowdown and a worsening of the living standards.

Political tensions rose between the president and the holdover Supreme Soviet during 1994.

LAOS

Lao People's Democratic Republic
President: Nouhak Phoumsavane (1992)
Premier: Khamtai Siphandon (1991)
Area: 91,429 sq mi. (236,800 sq km)
Population (est. mid-1995): 4,800,000 (average annual rate of natural increase: 2.8%); birth rate: 42/1000; infant mortality rate: 98/1000; density per square mile: 52.4
Capital and largest city (1990): Vientiane, 442,000; **Monetary unit:** Kip; **Languages:** Lao (official), French, English; **Religions:** Buddhist, 85%; animist and other, 15%; **Literacy rate:** 50%

Economic summary: Gross domestic product: (1993 est.): $4.1 billion; $900 per capita GNP 1992; 7% real growth rate (1993); inflation rate (1993): 7%; unemployment rate (1993): 3%. Arable land: 4%. Principal agricultural products: rice, corn, vegetables. Labor force: 1–1.5 million; 85–90% in agriculture. Major industrial products: tin, timber, electric power, gypsum. Natural resources: tin, timber, hydroelectric power. Exports: $158.6 million (1993 est.): electric power, forest products, tin concentrates, coffee, gypsum, cardamom, rattan, clothing and textiles. Imports: $320 million (1993 est.): rice, foodstuffs, petroleum products, machinery, transport equipment. Major trading partners: Thailand, Malaysia, Vietnam, C.I.S. countries, Japan, France, U.S., Hong Kong, Singapore.

Geography. A landlocked nation in Southeast Asia occupying the northwestern portion of the Indochinese peninsula, Laos is surrounded by China, Vietnam, Cambodia, Thailand, and Burma. It is twice the size of Pennsylvania.

Laos is a mountainous country, especially in the north, where peaks rise above 9,000 feet (2,800 m). Dense forests cover the northern and eastern areas. The Mekong River, which forms the boundary with Burma and Thailand, flows entirely through the country for 932 miles (1,500 km) of its course.

Government. Laos is a people's democratic republic with executive power in the hands of the premier. The monarchy was abolished Dec. 2, 1975, when the Pathet Lao ousted a coalition government and King Sisavang Vatthana abdicated. The King was appointed "Supreme Adviser" to the President, the former Prince Souphanouvong. Former Prince Souvanna Phouma, Premier since 1962, was made an "adviser" to the government. The Lao People's Revolutionary Party (Pathet Lao) is the only political party.

History. Laos became a French protectorate in 1893, and the territory was incorporated into the union of Indochina. A strong nationalist movement developed during World War II, but France reestablished control in 1946 and made the King of Luang Prabang constitutional monarch of all Laos. France granted semiautonomy in 1949 and then, spurred by the Viet Minh rebellion in Vietnam, full independence within the French Union in 1950. In 1951, Prince Souphanouvong organized the Pathet Lao, a Communist independence movement, in North Vietnam. The Viet Minh in 1953 established the Pathet Lao in power at Samneua. Viet Minh and Pathet Lao forces invaded central Laos, and civil war resulted.

By the Geneva agreements of 1954 and an armistice of 1955, two northern provinces were given the Pathet Lao, the royal regime the rest. Full sovereignty was given the kingdom by the Paris agreements of Dec. 29, 1954. In 1957, Prince Souvanna Phouma, the royal Premier, and the Pathet Lao leader, Prince Souphanouvong, the Premier's half-brother, agreed to reestablishment of a unified government, with Pathet Lao participation and integration of Pathet Lao forces into the royal army. The agreement broke down in 1959, and armed conflict broke out again.

In 1960, the struggle became three-way as Gen. Phoumi Nosavan, controlling the bulk of the royal army, set up in the south a pro-Western revolutionary government headed by Prince Boun Gum. General Phoumi took Vientiane in December, driving Souvanna Phouma into exile in Cambodia. The Soviet bloc supported Souvanna Phouma. In 1961, a cease-fire was arranged and the three princes agreed to a coalition government headed by Souvanna Phouma.

But North Vietnam, the U.S. (in the form of Central Intelligence Agency personnel), and China remained active in Laos after the settlement. North Vietnam used a supply line (Ho Chi Minh trail) running down the mountain valleys of eastern Laos into Cambodia and South Vietnam, particularly after the U.S.-South Vietnamese incursion into Cambodia in 1970 stopped supplies via Cambodian seaports.

An agreement, reached in 1973 revived coalition government. The Communist Pathet Lao seized complete power in 1975, installing Souphanouvong as president and Kaysone Phomvihane as premier. Since then other parties and political groups have been moribund and most of their leaders have fled the country.

The Supreme People's Assembly in August 1991 adopted a new constitution that dropped all references to socialism but retained the one-party state. In addition to implementing market-oriented policies, the country has passed laws governing property, inheritance and contracts. Laos agreed to trade with Moscow and Hanoi in hard currency.

While the Pathet Lao's political control in 1993 remained firm, they proceeded apace in the creation of a market economy.

The opening of the Thai–Laos Friendship Bridge, built with substantial Australian aid, across the Mekong River in April 1994 signaled both the importance of Thai–Laotian trade as well as burgeoning cross-cultural contacts.

Despite the rush to a free-market the Communists retained tight political control.

LATVIA

The Republic of Latvia
President: Guntis Ulmanis (1993)
Prime Minister: Maris Gailis (1994)
Area: 25,400 sq mi. (65,786 sq km)
Population (est. mid-1995): 2,500,000 (Latvian, 53%; Russian, 33%; Ukrainians, Byelorussians, other 14%); (average annual rate of natural increase: –0.5%); birth rate: 10/1000; infant mortality rate: 16/1000; density per square mile: 98.4
Capital and largest city (est. 1992): Riga, 897,078. **Other large cities (est. 1992):** Daugavpils, 127,280; Liepaja, 113,815; **Monetary unit:** Lats. **Language:** Latvian; **Religions:** Lutheran, Catholic, and Baptist; **National name:** Latvija. **Literacy rate:** 100%
Economic survey: Most industrialized of the Baltic states. Latvia is in the process of reforming a central planned economy into a market economy. Gross domestic product (UN, World Bank 1993 est.): $13.2 billion; per capita: $4,810; real growth rate: –5%; inflation rate: 2%, unemployment (Dec. 1993): 5.6%. Labor force: 1,407,000: industry and construction 41%, agriculture and forestry 16% (1990). Latvia's industries are highly diversified they produce buses, trains, street and railroad cars, synthetic fibres, agricultural machinery, fertilizers, pharmaceuticals, washing machines, radios, electronics, processed foods, and textiles. Agricultures is principally dairy farming and livestock raising. The government has fostered the development of the private sector and market mechanisms kept inflation low and created a dynamic private sector. Exports: $429 million from non-former Soviet Union countries (f.o.b., 1992). Imports: $9 billion (c.i.f., 1989): machinery, 35%; petroleum products, 13%; chemicals, 9%. Natural resources: Peat, sapropel, timber, limestone, dolomite, and clay. Major trading partners are

Russia, 50%; Ukraine, 15%; other former Soviet Republics, 30%; also Poland, Germany, Sweden, and Czech Republic. U.S.

Geography: Latvia borders Estonia on the north, Lithuania in the south, the Baltic Sea with the Gulf of Riga in the west, Russia in the east, and Belarus in the southeast. Latvia is largely a fertile lowland with numerous lakes and hills to the east.

Government: Latvia is a parliamentary democracy.

History: Descended from Aryan stock, the Latvians were early tribesmen who settled along the Baltic Sea and, lacking a central government, fell an easy prey to more powerful peoples. The German Teutonic knights first conquered them in the 13th century and ruled the area, consisting of Livonia and Courland, until 1562.

Poland conquered the territory in 1562 and ruled until 1795 in Courland; control of Livonia was disputed between Sweden and Poland from 1562 to 1629. Sweden controlled Livonia from 1629 to 1721. Russia took over Livonia in the latter year and Courland after the third partition of Poland in 1795.

From that time until 1918, the Latvians remained Russian subjects, although they preserved their language, customs, and folklore. The Russian Revolution of 1917 gave them their opportunity for freedom, and the Latvian republic was proclaimed on Nov. 18, 1918.

The republic lasted little more than 20 years. It was occupied by Russian troops in 1939 and incorporated into the Soviet Union in 1940. German armies occupied the nation from 1941 to 1943–44, when they were driven out by the Russians. Most countries, including the United States, refused to recognize the Soviet annexation of Latvia.

When the coup against Soviet President Mikhail Gorbachev failed, the Baltic nations saw a historic opportunity to free themselves from Soviet domination and, following the actions of Lithuania and Estonia, Latvia declared its independence on Aug. 21, 1991.

European and most other nations quickly recognized their independence, and on Sept. 2, 1991, President Bush announced full diplomatic recognition for Latvia, Estonia, and Lithuania. The Soviet Union recognized Latvia's independence on September 6, and UN membership followed on Sept. 17, 1991.

In addition to severe economic problems the issue of citizenship loomed explosive as almost half the population is non-Latvian.

In the first post-Soviet parliamentary elections in June 1993 an alliance of former Communists and emigres made a strong showing. The franchise, however, was by and large not extended to the non-ethnic-Latvian minority.

In the first post-Soviet parliamentary elections in June 1993 an alliance of former Communists and emigres made a strong showing. The franchise, however, was by and large not extended to the non-ethnic-Latvian minority.

One of the coalition parties withdrew its support over the issue of food-import duties in July 1994, forcing the formation of a new grouping.

Tight monetary policies by the central bank yielded the lowest rate of inflation in 1994 among the former Soviet republics.

In August Latvia celebrated the official withdrawal of Russian troops from the country, although Russia was allowed to retain control of its radar station in Skrunda until mid-1998.

The citizenship law was amended in August in accordance with the wishes of the Council of Europe.

LEBANON

Republic of Lebanon
President: Elias Hrawi (1989)
Premier: Rafik al-Hariri (1992)
Area: 4,015 sq mi. (10,400 sq km)
Population (est. mid-1995): 3,700,000 (average annual rate of natural increase: 2.0%); birth rate: 25/1000; infant mortality rate: 28/1000; density per square mile: 921.5
Capital: Beirut; **Largest cities (est. 1990):** Beirut, 1,100,000; Tripoli, 240,000; Sidon, 110,000; Tyre, 60,000; Zahleh, 55,000; **Monetary unit:** Lebanese pound; **Languages:** Arabic (official), French, English; **Religions:** Islam, 60%; Christian, 40% (17 recognized sects); Judaism Negl. % (1 sect); **National name:** Al-Joumhouriya al-Lubnaniya; **Literacy rate:** 80%
Economic summary: Gross domestic product (1993 est.): $6.1 billion; $1,720 per capita; real growth rate: 4.2% (1992); inflation: 35%; unemployment: 35%. Arable land: 21%; principal agricultural products: citrus fruits, vegetables, potatoes, tobacco, olives, shrimp. Labor force (1985): 650,000; 79% in industry, commerce and services. Major industrial products: processed foods, textiles, cement, chemicals, refined oil. Exports: $925 million (f.o.b., 1993 est.): fruits, vegetables, textiles, chemicals, semiprecious metals and jewelry, metals and metal products. Imports: $4.1 billion (c.i.f., 1993 est.): consumer goods, machinery and transport equipment, petroleum products. Major trading partners: U.S., Western European and Arab countries.

Geography. Lebanon lies at the eastern end of the Mediterranean Sea north of Israel and west of Syria. It is four fifths the size of Connecticut.

The Lebanon Mountains, which parallel the coast on the west, cover most of the country, while on the eastern border is the Anti-Lebanon range. Between the two lies the Bekaa Valley, the principal agricultural area.

Government. Lebanon is governed by a President, elected by Parliament for a six-year term, and a Cabinet of Ministers appointed by the President but responsible to Parliament.

The unicameral Parliament has 108 members elected for a four-year term by universal suffrage and chosen by proportional division of religious groups.

History. After World War I, France was given a League of Nations mandate over Lebanon and its neighbor Syria, which together had previously been a single political unit in the Ottoman Empire. France divided them in 1920 into separate colonial administrations, drawing a border that separated predominantly Moslem Syria from the kaleidoscope of religious communities in Lebanon in which Maronite Christians were then dominant. After 20 years of the French mandate regime, Lebanon's independence was proclaimed on Nov. 26, 1941, but full independence came in stages. Under an agreement between representatives of Lebanon and the French National Committee of Liberation, most of the powers exercised by France were transferred to the Lebanese government on Jan. 1, 1944. The evacuation of French troops was completed in 1946.

Civil war broke out in 1958, with Moslem factions led by Kamal Jumblat and Saeb Salam rising in insurrection against the Lebanese government headed by President Camille Chamoun, a Maronite Christian. At Chamoun's request, President Eisenhower on July 15 sent U.S. troops to reestablish the government's authority.

Clan warfare between various factions in Lebanon goes back centuries. The hodgepodge includes Maronite Christians, who since independence have dominated the government; Sunni Moslems, who have prospered in business and shared political power; the Druse, a secretive Islamic splinter group; and at the bottom of the heap until recently, Shiite Moslems.

A new—and bloodier—Lebanese civil war that broke out in 1975 resulted in the addition of still another ingredient in the brew—the Syrians. In the fighting between Lebanese factions, 40,000 Lebanese were estimated to have been killed and 100,000 wounded between March 1975 and November 1976. At that point, a Syrian-dominated Arab Deterrent Force intervened and brought large-scale fighting to a halt.

Palestinian guerrillas staging raids on Israel from Lebanese territory drew punitive Israeli raids on Lebanon, and two large-scale Israeli invasions. The Israelis withdrew in June after the U.N. Security Council created a 6,000-man peacekeeping force for the area, called UNIFIL. As they departed, the Israelis turned their strongpoints over to a Christian militia that they had organized, instead of to the U.N. force.

The second Israeli invasion came on June 6, 1982, and this time it was a total one. It was in response to an assassination attempt by Palestinian terrorists on the Israeli ambassador in London.

A U.S. special envoy, Philip C. Habib, negotiated the dispersal of most of the PLO to other Arab nations and Israel pulled back some of its forces. The violence seemed to have come to an end when, on Sept. 14, Bashir Gemayel, the 34-year-old President-elect, was killed by a bomb that destroyed the headquarters of his Christian Phalangist Party.

The day after Gemayel's assassination, Israeli troops moved into west Beirut in force. On Sept. 17 it was revealed that Christian militiamen had massacred hundreds of Palestinians in two refugee camps but Israel denied responsibility.

On Sept. 20, Amin Gemayel, older brother of Bashir Gemayel, was elected President by the parliament.

The massacre in the refugee camps prompted the return of a multinational peacekeeping force composed of U.S. Marines and British, French, and Italian soldiers. Their mandate was to support the central Lebanese government, but they soon found themselves drawn into the struggle for power between different Lebanese factions. During their stay in Lebanon, 260 U.S. Marines and about 60 French soldiers were killed, most of them in suicide bombings of the Marine and French Army compounds on Oct. 23, 1983. The multinational force left in the spring of 1984.

During 1984, Israeli troops remained in southern Lebanon and Syrian troops remained in the Bekaa Valley. By the third anniversary of the invasion, June 6, 1985, all Israeli troops had withdrawn except for several hundred "advisers" to a Christian militia trained and armed by the Israelis.

In July 1986, Syrian observers took position in Beirut to monitor a peacekeeping agreement. The agreement broke down and fighting between Shiite and Druze militia in West Beirut became so intense that Syrian troops moved in force in February 1987, suppressing militia resistance.

Amin Gemayel's Presidency expired on Sept. 23, 1988. The impossibility of setting up elections led Gemayel to designate a government under army chief Gen. Michael Aoun. Aoun's government was rejected by Prime Minister Selim al-Hoss who established a rival government in Muslim West Beirut.

In October 1989, Lebanese Christian and Moslem deputies approved a tentative peace accord and the new National Assembly selected a President.

In early 1991 the Lebanese government, backed by Syria, attempted to regain control over the south and disband all private militias, thereby ending the 16-year civil war.

In the general elections of August 1992 most Christians abstained from voting demanding that Syrian forces first leave the country. The new legislature consisted of mostly pro-Syrian members. The largest Christian party was further weakened when in January 1993 it appeared to split into two factions.

The prime minister's offer of resignation in early December 1994 was withdrawn four days later when Syria assured that it would not interfere with the planned reconstruction of the country.

In March 1995 Lebanon asked the U.N. to take measures to halt an Israeli naval blockade of its southern regions and stop artillery and air attacks.

LESOTHO

Kingdom of Lesotho
Sovereign: King Letsie III (1990)
Prime Minister: Dr. Ntsu Mokhehle
Area: 11,720 sq mi. (30,355 sq km)
Population (est. mid-1995): 2,100,000 (average annual rate of natural increase: 1.9%; birth rate: 31/1000; infant mortality rate: 79/1000; density per square mile: 179.1
Capital and largest city (1992): Maseru (1992), 170,000; **Monetary unit:** Loti; **Languages:** English and Sesotho (official); also Zulu and Xhosa; **Religions:** Christian, 80%; indigenous beliefs; Muslim; and Bahai; **Member of Commonwealth of Nations; Literacy rate:** 59% (1989)
Economic summary: Gross domestic product (1993 est.): $2.8 billion; $1,500 per capita; 2.4% real growth rate (FY93); inflation 17% (FY93); unemployment (adult males): 55% among adult males. Arable land: 10%. Principal products: corn, wheat, sorghum, barley. Labor force: 689,000; 86.2% in subsistence agriculture. Natural resources: diamonds. Exports: $109 million (f.o.b., 1992): wool, mohair, wheat, cattle, hides and skins, peas, beans, corn, baskets. Imports: $964 million (c.i.f., 1992): foodstuffs, building materials, clothing, vehicles, machinery, corn, medicines. Major trading partner: South Africa, E.U., North and South America, Asia.

Geography. Mountainous Lesotho, the size of Maryland, is surrounded by the Republic of South Africa in the east central part of that country except for short borders on the east and south with two discontinuous units of the Republic of Transkei. The Drakensberg Mountains in the east are Lesotho's principal chain. Elsewhere the region consists of rocky tableland.

Government. A constitutional monarchy. The executive power is with the prime minister and the cabinet (Council of Ministers).

History. Lesotho (formerly Basutoland) was constituted a native state under British protection by a treaty signed with the native chief Moshesh in 1843. It was annexed to Cape Colony in 1871, but in 1884 it was restored to direct control by the Crown.

The colony of Basutoland became the independent nation of Lesotho on Oct. 4, 1966.

In the 1970 elections, Ntsu Mokhehle, head of the Basutoland Congress Party, claimed a victory, but Jonathan declared a state of emergency, suspended the Constitution, and arrested Mokhehle.

The King returned after a compromise with Jonathan in which the new Constitution would name him head of state but forbid his participation in politics.

After the King refused to approve the replacements in February 1990 of individuals dismissed by Lekhanya, the latter stripped the King of his executive power. Then in early March Lekhanya sent the King into exile. In November the King was dethroned, and his son was sworn in as King Letsie III.

Lekhanya, the chairman of the Military Counccil, was himself forced to resign in April 1991. Col. Ramaema became the new chairman in May.

In August 1994 the king attempted to dissolve the government and the legislature. After violent demonstrations he also announced suspension of part of the constitution. The government, however, refused to step down. Mounting internal and international pressure led the king in September to restore the government officially.

LIBERIA

Republic of Liberia
Interim President: David Kpormakpor (March 1994)
Area: 43,000 sq mi. (111,370 sq km)
Population (est. mid-1995): 3,000,000 (average annual rate of natural increase: 3.3%); birth rate: 47/1000; infant mortality rate: 126/1000; density per square mile: 69.7
Capital and largest city (est. 1990): Monrovia, 660,000; **Monetary unit:** Liberian dollar; **Languages:** English (official) and tribal dialects; **Religions:** traditional, 70%; Christian, 10%; Islam, 20%; **Literacy rate:** 40%
Economic summary: Civil war since 1990 has destroyed much of Liberia's economy. Gross domestic product (1993 est.): $2.3 billion; $800 per capita; 1.5% real growth rate (1988); inflation (1989): 12%; unemployment (1988): 43% urban. Arable land: 1%. Principal agricultural products: rubber, rice, palm oil, cassava, coffee, cocoa. Labor force: 510,000; 70.5% in agriculture. Major industrial products: iron ore, diamonds, processed rubber, processed food, construction materials. Natural resources: iron ore, gold, timber, diamonds. Exports: $505 million (f.o.b., 1989 est.): iron ore, rubber, timber, coffee. Imports: $394 million (c.i.f., 1989 est.): machinery, petroleum products, transport equipment, foodstuffs. Major trading partners: U.S., E.U., Netherlands, Japan, China.

Geography. Lying on the Atlantic in the southern part of West Africa, Liberia is bordered by Sierra Leone, Guinea, and the Ivory Coast. It is comparable in size to Tennessee.

Most of the country is a plateau covered by dense tropical forests, which thrive under an annual rainfall of about 160 inches a year.

Government. A five-nation West African peacekeeping force installed an interim government in October 1990 and in November made Amos Sawyer interim president. The National Patriotic Front led by Charles Taylor controls most of the country.

History. Liberia was founded in 1822 as a result of the efforts of the American Colonization Society to settle freed American slaves in West Africa. In 1847, it became the Free and Independent Republic of Liberia.

The government of Africa's first republic was modeled after that of the United States, and Joseph J. Roberts of Virginia was elected the first president. He laid the foundations of a modern state and initiated efforts, never too successful but pursued for more than a century, to bring the aboriginal inhabitants of the territory to the level of the emigrants. The English-speaking descendants of U.S. blacks, known as Americo-Liberians, were the intellectual and ruling class. The indigenous inhabitants, divided, constitute 99% of the population.

After 1920, considerable progress was made toward opening up the interior, a process that was spurred in 1951 by the establishment of a 43-mile (69-km) railroad to the Bomi Hills from Monrovia.

In July 1971, while serving his sixth term as president, William V. S. Tubman died following surgery and was succeeded by his long-time associate, Vice President William R. Tolbert, Jr.

Tolbert was ousted in a military coup carried out April 12, 1980, by army enlisted men led by Master Sgt. Samuel K. Doe.

A rebellion led by Charles Taylor, a former Doe aide, started in December 1989 and, by mid-July 1990, had taken most of Liberia's key population and economic centers and surrounded the capital.

A West African peacekeeping force intervened in Liberia and effectively partitioned the country into two zones: One, containing the capital of Monrovia, led by President Sawyer, is backed by virtually all West African nations. The other, led by Mr. Taylor, constitutes about 95% of the territory. A national conference in March 1991 failed to reach an agreement but reelected Sawyer interim president.

Despite a 1991 peace factional fighting continued at times in the country's civil war. In July 1993 the disputants reached a peace agreement that included a cease-fire, the establishment of an interim government and democratic elections. The agreement fell apart, however, in November.

The various feuding parties met in May 1994 to form a government. Fighting, however, continued at various levels both then and in subsequent months. A cop attempt in September was quelled the following day. In late December another ceasefire was proclaimed. This, in turn, broke down in March 1995.

LIBYA

Socialist People's Libyan Arab Jamahiriya
Head of State: Col. Muammar el-Qaddafi (1969)
Secretary of the General People's Committee: Abdulmajid Almabruk Alqaod (1994)
Area: 679,536 sq mi. (1,759,998 sq km)
Population (est. mid-1995): 5,200,000 (average annual rate of natural increase: 3.4%); birth rate: 42/1000; infant mortality rate: 68/1000; density per sq mile: 7.65
Capital: Tripoli; **Largest cities (est. 1988):** Tripoli, 591,062; Benghazi, 446,250; **Monetary unit:** Libyan dinar; **Language:** Arabic, Italian and English widely understood in major cities; **Religion:** Islam; **National name:** Socialist People's Libyan Arab Jamahiriya; **Literacy rate:** 64%
Economic summary: Gross domestic product (1993 est.): $32 billion; $6,600 per capita; real growth rate 1%; inflation 6%; unemployment (1988 est.) 2%. Arable land: 1%. Principal products: wheat, barley, olives, dates, citrus fruits, peanuts. Labor force: 1,000,000 (includes about 280,000 resident foreigners); 31% industry, services 27%, government 24%, agriculture 18%. Major products: petroleum, processed foods, textiles, handicrafts, cement. Natural resources: petroleum, natural gas. Exports: $7.7 billion (f.o.b., 1993

est.): petroleum, peanuts, hides, natural gas. Imports: $8.26 billion (f.o.b., 1993 est.): machinery, foodstuffs, manufactured goods. Major trading partners: Italy, Germany, U.K., France, Spain, Japan, Turkey, former USSR, Korea, Belgium/Luxembourg.

Geography. Libya stretches along the northeastern coast of Africa between Tunisia and Algeria on the west and Egypt on the east; to the south are the Sudan, Chad, and Niger. It is one sixth larger than Alaska.

A greater part of the country lies within the Sahara. Along the Mediterranean coast and farther inland is arable plateau land.

Government. In a bloodless coup d'etat on Sept. 1, 1969, the military seized power in Libya. King Idris I, who had ruled since 1951, was deposed and the Libyan Arab Republic proclaimed. The official name was changed in 1977 to the Socialist People's Libyan Arab Jamahiriya—Jamahiriya (a state of the masses): in theory, governed by the populace through local councils; in fact, a military dictatorship. The Revolutionary Council that had governed since the coup was renamed the General Secretariat of the General People's Congress. The Arab Socialist Union Organization is the only political party.

History. Libya was a part of the Turkish dominions from the 16th century until 1911. Following the outbreak of hostilities between Italy and Turkey in that year, Italian troops occupied Tripoli; Italian sovereignty was recognized in 1912.

Libya was the scene of much desert fighting during World War II. After the fall of Tripoli on Jan. 23, 1943, it came under Allied administration. In 1949, the U.N. voted that Libya should become independent by 1952.

Discovery of oil in the Libyan Desert promised financial stability and funds for economic development.

On Aug. 19, 1981, two U.S. Navy F-14's shot down two Soviet-made SU-22's of the Libyan air force that had attacked them in air space above the Gulf of Sidra, claimed by Libya but held to be international by the U.S. In December, Washington asserted that Libyan "hit squads" had been dispatched to the U.S. and security was drastically tightened around President Reagan and other officials. When the Mobil Oil Company abandoned its operations in April 1982, only four U.S. firms were still in Libya, using Libyan or third-country personnel.

Qaddafi's troops also supported rebels in Chad but suffered major military reverses in 1987.

On March 24, 1986, U.S. and Libyan forces skirmished in the Gulf of Sidra, with two Libyan patrol boats being sunk.

A two-year-old U.S. covert policy to destabilize the Libyan government with U.S.-trained Libyan ex-P.O.W.s ended in failure in December 1990 when a Libyan-supplied guerrilla force assumed power in Chad, where the commandos were based, and asked the band to leave.

For its refusal to extradite two Libyans accused of involvement in an airline bombing back in 1988 the UN imposed sanctions in April 1992.

Relations with Chad improved as the two nations signed an agreement of mutual cooperation. The border dispute with Chad, however, was sent to the International Court at The Hague.

UN approved trade and air traffic embargoes on Libya, because of its refusal to surrender two suspects implicated in the Pan Am flight bombing, seriously affected the economy.

The U.S. attempted in March 1995 to get a total international embargo of Libyan oil.

LIECHTENSTEIN

Principality of Liechtenstein
Ruler: Prince Hans Adam (1989)
Prime Minister: Dr. Mario Frick (1994)
Area: 61 sq mi. (157 sq km)
Population (Dec. 1993): 30,310 (average annual growth rate: 1.4% [1983–1993]); birth rate: 13.7/1000; infant mortality rate: 0.03/1000 (1984–1993); density per square mile: 496.8
Capital and largest city (1993): Vaduz, 5,072; **Monetary unit:** Swiss franc; **Language:** German; **Religions:** Roman Catholic, 80.6%; Protestant, 7.3%; other 17.1%; **Literacy rate:** 100%
Economic summary: Gross domestic product (1990 est.): $630 million; $22,300 per capita; inflation (1994) 0.4%; unemployment 14.0% (1993). Arable land: 25%. Principal agricultural products: livestock, vegetables, corn, wheat, potatoes, grapes. Labor force (1993): 20,756 (12,569 are foreigners); industry, 48.1%; service, 50.2%. Major industrial products: electronics, metal products, textiles, ceramics, pharmaceuticals, food products, precision instruments. Natural resource: hydroelectric power. Exports: $2.6 billion (c.i.f., 1994): small specialty machinery, dental products, stamps, hardware, pottery. Imports: $n.a.: machinery, processed foods, metal goods, textiles, motor vehicles. Major trading partners: Switzerland and other Western European countries.

Geography. Tiny Liechtenstein, not quite as large as Washington, D.C., lies on the east bank of the Rhine River south of Lake Constance between Austria and Switzerland. It consists of low valley land and Alpine peaks. Falknis (8,401 ft; 2,561 m) and Naafkopf (8,432 ft; 2,570 m) are the tallest.

Government. The Constitution of 1921 provides for a legislature, the Landtag, of 25 members elected by direct suffrage.

History. Founded in 1719, Liechtenstein was a member of the German Confederation from 1815 to 1866, when it became an independent principality. It abolished its army in 1868 and has managed to stay neutral and undamaged in all European wars since then. In a referendum on July 1, 1984, male voters granted women the right to vote, a victory for Prince Hans Adam.

A June 1992 referendum to lower the voting age from 20 to 18 was rejected.

Parliamentary elections in October 1993 gave a plurality to the centrist Fatherland Union (VU) party.

A treaty negotiated between EFTA and the then-European Community was ratified in a December 1993 vote, but in Switzerland it was rejected. The treaty was under revision during 1994 so as to maintain the country's traditional link with Switzerland.

LITHUANIA

Republic of Lithuania
President: Algirdas Mykolas Brazauskas (1993)
Prime Minister: Adolfas Slezevicius (1993)
Area: 25,212 sq mi. (65,300 sq km)
Population (est. midd-1995): 3,700,000 (Lithuanian, 80.6%; Russian, 8.5%; Polish, 7%); (average annual rate of natural increase: 0.0%); birth rate: 13/1000; infant mortality rate: 16/1000; density per sq mi.: 146.7
Capital and largest city (1992): Vilnius, 590,100; **Monetary unit:** Litas; **Languages:** Lithuanian; **Religion (1939):** Catholic, 85%; **National name:** Lietuva; **Literacy:** very high

Economic survey: Gross national product (UN, World Bank 1993 est.): $12.4 billion; $3,240 per capita; real growth rate –10%; inflation 44.6% (1994). Labor force (June 1994): 1,690,000: private sector, 60.4%; public sector, 39.6%. Natural resources: peat, sand and gravel, quartz, gypsum, dolomite, clay, limestone, mineral water. Amber found on Baltic Sea coast. Industries: metal cutting, electric motors, TV sets, refrigerators and freezers, petroleum refining, shipbuilding, furniture, textiles, food processing, electronic components, computers. Agriculture (36% of labor force): Most developed are the livestock and dairy branches. Lithuania is a net exporter of meat, milk, and eggs. Exports (1994): mineral products, machinery, electrical equipment, TV and sound recording and reproduction equipment parts and associated equipment, chemicals. Imports (1994): mineral products, machinery, electrical equipment, metals, transport equipment. Major trading parters: CIS nations , E.U. including Germany, the Netherlands, and Italy.

Geography: Lithuania is situated on the eastern shore of the Baltic Sea and borders Latvia on the north, Belarus on the east and south, Poland and the Kaliningrad region of Russia on the southwest. It is a country of gently rolling hills, many forests, rivers and streams, and lakes. Its principal natural resource is agricultural land.

Government: Lithuania is a parliamentary democracy. The head of state is the directly-elected President. The president nominates the prime minister who is then approved by the parliament (Seimas).

History: Southernmost of the three Baltic states, Lithuania in the Middle Ages was a grand duchy joined to Poland through royal marriage. Poles and Lithuanians merged forces to defeat the Teutonic knights of Germany at Tannenberg in 1410 and extended their power far into Russian territory. In 1795, however, following the third partition of Poland, Lithuania fell into Russian hands and did not regain its independence until 1918, toward the end of the first World War.

The republic was occupied by the Soviet Union in June 1940 and annexed in August 1940. From June 1941 to 1944 it was occupied by German troops and then was retaken by Russia. Western countries, including the United States, never recognized the Russian annexation of Lithuania.

Nineteen eighty-eight saw a re-emergence of the Lithuanian independence movement. Elections were held on Feb. 24, 1990, and Vytautas Landsbergis, the non-communist head of the largest Lithuanian popular movement (Sajudis) was elected to parliament that day, and on March 11, 1990, the parliament elected him as its president. On the same day, the Supreme Council rejected Soviet rule and declared the restoration of Lithuania's independence, the first Baltic republic to take this action.

Confrontation with the Soviet Union ensued along with economic sanctions, but they were lifted after both sides agreed to a face-saving compromise.

After an abortive coup to depose Soviet President Mikhail Gorbachev, President Landsbergis called his country's independence a formality.

Lithuania's independence was quickly recognized by major European and other nations, and on Sept. 2, 1991, President Bush extended full diplomatic recognition for the Baltic republics. The Soviet Union finally recognized the independence of the Baltic states on September 6. UN admittance followed on Sept. 17, 1991.

Elections in February 1993 made Brazauskas, a former Communist Party leader, president.

An expected improved relationship with Russia did not occur. The latter's parliament refused to grant Lithuania most-favored-nation trade status until the two countries reached an agreement on military transit to and from Kaliningrad.

A law passed in January 1995 severely restricted the restitution of property nationalized after World War II from the Catholic Church.

LUXEMBOURG

Grand Duchy of Luxembourg
Ruler: Grand Duke Jean (1964)
Premier: Jean-Claude Jurcker (1994)
Area: 999 sq mi. (2,586 sq km)
Population (est. mid-1995: 400,000 (average annual rate of natural increase: 0.4%); birth rate: 13/1000; infant mortality rate: 6.0/1000; density per square mile: 400.4
Capital and largest city (1991: Luxembourg, 75,622;
   Monetary unit: Luxembourg franc; **Languages:** Luxermbourgish, French, German; **Religion:** Mainly Roman Catholic; **National name:** Grand-Duché de Luxembourg; **Literacy rate:** 100%
Economic summary: Gross domestic product (1994): $9 billion; $22,000 per capita; real growth rate 1% (1993); inflation: 3.6% (1992); unemployment: 5.1% (March 1994). Arable land: 24%. Principal agricultural products: livestock, dairy products, wine. Labor force (1994): 203,200; one-third are foreign workers. Services, 65%; industry, 31.6%; agriculture, 3.4%. Major industrial products: banking, steel, processed food, chemicals, metal products, tires, glass. Natural resource: Iron ore. Exports: $6.3 billion (f.o.b., 1992): steel, chemicals, rubber products, glass, aluminum. Imports: $7.8 billion (c.i.f., 1992): minerals, metals, foodstuffs, consumer goods. Major trading partners: European Common Market countries.

Geography. Luxembourg is a neighbor of Belgium on the west, Germany on the east, and France on the south. The Ardennes Mountains extend from Belgium into the northern section of Luxembourg.

Government. Luxembourg's unicameral legislature, the Chamber of Deputies, consists of 60 members elected for five years.

History. Sigefroi, Count of Ardennes, an offspring of Charlemagne, was Luxembourg's first sovereign ruler. In 1060, the country came under the rule of the House of Luxembourg. From the 15th to the 18th century, Spain, France, and Austria held it in turn. The Congress of Vienna in 1815 made it a Grand Duchy and gave it to William I, King of the Netherlands. In 1839 the Treaty of London ceded the western part of Luxembourg to Belgium.

The eastern part, continuing in personal union with the Netherlands and a member of the German Confederation, became autonomous in 1848 and a neutral territory by decision of the London Conference of 1867, governed by its Grand Duke. Germany occupied the duchy in World Wars I and II. Allied troops liberated the enclave in 1944.

In 1961, Prince Jean, son and heir of Grand Duchess Charlotte, was made head of state, acting for his mother. She abdicated in 1964, and Prince Jean became Grand Duke. Grand Duchess Charlotte died in 1985.

By a customs union between Belgium and Luxembourg, which came into force on May 1, 1922, to last for 50 years, customs frontiers between the two countries were abolished. On Jan. 1, 1948, a customs union with Belgium and the Netherlands (Benelux) came into existence. On Feb. 3, 1958, it became an economic union.

Luxembourg's parliament approved the "Maastricht Accord" in July 1992, with the proviso that the country negotiate an exemption to the clause granting foreigners the vote.

The country in 1993 tried to resist efforts from other EU members to introduce a withholding tax on savings and investments.

The governing coalition won the general election held in June 1994, thereby insuring the continuance of Santer's premiership.

MACEDONIA[1]

Republic of Macedonia
President: Kiro Gilgorov
Prime Minister: Branko Crvenkovski (1992)
Area: 9,928 sq mi. (25,713 sq km)
Population (est. mid-1995): 2,100,000; (1994): Macedonians, 65%; Albanians, 22%; Turkish, 4%; Serb, 2%; Gypsies, 3%. (Average annual rate of natural increase: 0.8%); birth rate: 16/1000; infant mortality rate: 24.4/1000; density per square mile: 211.5
Capital and largest city (1991 est.): Skopje, 448,229. Other large cities: Bitola, 84,002; Kumanovo, 69,231; Prelep, 70,152; Tetovo, 51,472; Titov Veles, 47,326; Ohrid, 42,903; Sitip, 42,826; **Monetary unit:** Dinar; **Languages:** Macedonian, 70%; Albanian, 21%; Turkish, 3%; other, 6%; **Religions (1994):** Eastern Orthodox, 67%; Muslim, 30%. **National name:** Republica Makedonija
Economic summary: Gross domestic product (1993 est.): $2.2 billion; $1,000 per capita; real growth rate, –14.7% (1992 est.); inflation: 13%; unemployment: 27%. Labor force: 507,324 (1990): manufacturing and mining, 40%; agriculture, 8%. Industries: low level technology (basic fuels) mining, basic textiles, wood products, and tobacco. Agriculture: rice, tobacco, wheat, corn, millet, cotton, citrus fruits, and vegetables. Exports (1993): $889 million: manufactured goods, 40%; machinery and transport equipment, 14%; misc. mfg. articles, 23%; raw materials, 7.6%; food (rice) and live animals, 5.7%; beverages and tobacco, 4.5%; chemicals, 4.7% (1990). Imports (1993): $963 million: fuel and lubricants, 19%; manufactured goods, 18%; machinery and transport euqipment, 15%; food and live animals, 14%; chemicals, 11.4%; raw materials, 10%. Major trading partners: Germany, Albania, Bulgaria, former Yugoslav republics, Greece

1. The U.N. recognized the Republic of Macedonia on April 8, 1993 under the temporary name the Former Yugoslav Republic of Macedonia. The U.S. recognized Macedonia as a state in February 1994.

Geography: Macedonia is a landlocked state in the heart of the Balkans and is slightly smaller than the state of Vermont. It is a mountainous country with small basins of agricultural land linked by rivers. It borders the Yugoslavian Republic of Serbia in the north, Bulgaria in the east, Greece in the south, and Albania in the west. The three major rivers are the Aliakmon, the Vardar, and the Strymon. The Vardar is the largest and most important river.

Government: A democratic republic with two legislative houses—the National Assembly consisting of 120 deputies, each elected for a four-year term. The assembly's president and vice presidents are elected from among its members.

History: The Republic of Macedonia occupies the western half of the ancient Kingdom of Macedonia. Historic Macedonia was defeated by Rome in 146 B.C. and became a Roman province in 148 B.C.

After the Roman Empire was divided in A.D. 395, Macedonia was intermittently ruled by the Byzantine Empire until Turkey took possession of the land in 1389. The Ottoman Turks dominated Macedonia for the next five centuries up until 1913.

During the 19th and 20th centuries, there was a constant struggle by the Balkan powers to possess Macedonia for its economic and strategic military corridors.

The Treaty of San Stefano in 1878 ending the Russo-Turkish War gave the largest part of Macedonia to Bulgaria. Bulgaria lost much of its Macedonian territory when it was defeated by the Greeks and Serbs in the Second Balkan War of 1913. Most of Macedonia went to Serbia and the remainder was divided among Greece and Bulgaria.

In 1914, Serbia, which included Macedonia, joined in union with Croatia, Slovenia, and Montenegro to form the Kingdom of Serbs, Croats, and Slovenes which was renamed Yugoslavia in 1929.

Bulgaria joined the Axis powers in World War II and occupied parts of Yugoslavia including Macedonia in 1941. During the occupation of their country, Macedonian resistance fighters fought a guerrilla warfare against the invading troops.

The Yugoslavian Republic was re-established after the defeat of Germany in 1945, and in 1946, the government removed Macedonia from Serbian control and made it an autonomous Yugoslavian republic. Later, when President Tito recognized the Macedonian people as a separate nation, the Macedonians strove to develop their own culture and language separate from Bulgaria and Serbia.

In January 1992, Macedonia declared its independence from Yugoslavia and asked for recognition from the European Community nations. While the E.C. approved the move in principle, it requested that the republic hold a referendum on independence.

In December 1993 six European nations recognized Macedonia. The following February the U.S. announced it had decided also to extend diplomatic recognition. Shortly thereafter Greece closed landlocked Macedonia's main trade route through the Greek port of Salonika.

The president won re-election in October 1994. As a result of that voting a coalition government was created from the Social Democratic Alliance, the Liberals, the Socialists, and a mainly ethnic-Albanian party.

MADAGASCAR

Republic of Madagascar
President and Head of State: Albert Zafy (1993)
Prime Minister: Francisque Ravony (1993)
Area: 226,660 sq mi. (587,050 sq km)
Population (est. mid-1995): 14,800,000 (average annual rate of natural increase: 3.2%); birth rate: 44/1000; infant mortality rate: 93/1000; density per square mile: 65.2
Capital and largest city (est. 1993): Antananarivo, 1,000,000; **Monetary unit:** Malagasy franc; **Languages:** Malagasy, French; **Ethnic groups:** Merina (or Hova), Betsimisaraka, Betsileo, Tsimihety, Antaisaka, Sakalava, Antandroy; **Religions:** traditional, 52%; Christian,

41%; Islam, 7%; **National name:** Repoblikan'i Madagasikara. **Literacy rate:** 80%
Economic summary: Gross domestic product (1993 est.): $10.4 billion; $800 per capita; 1% real growth rate (1992 est.); inflation 20%. (1992 est.) Arable land: 4%. Principal agricultural products: rice, livestock, coffee, vanilla, sugar, cloves, cardamom, beans, bananas. Labor force: 4,900,000; 90% in subsistence agriculture. Major industrial products: processed food, textiles, assembled automobiles, soap, cement. Natural resources: graphite, chromium, bauxite, semiprecious stones. Exports: $312 million (f.o.b., 1991 est.): coffee, cloves, vanilla, sugar, petroleum products. Imports: $350 million (f.o.b., 1992 est.): consumer goods, foodstuffs, crude petroleum. Major trading partners: France, U.S., Japan, Italy, Germany, U.K. and other E.U.

Geography. Madagascar lies in the Indian Ocean off the southeast coast of Africa opposite Mozambique. The world's fourth-largest island, it is twice the size of Arizona. The country's low-lying coastal area gives way to a central plateau. The once densely wooded interior has largely been cut down.

Government. A Republic. Under the new constitution of the Third Republic, August 19, 1992, Albert Zafy was elected President, February 1993 for a 5-year term. The Prime Minister, Francisque Ravony, was elected by the unicameral National Assembly, composed of 19 political parties, which voted in August 1993.

History. The present population is of black and Malay stock, with perhaps some Polynesian, called Malagasy. The French took over a protectorate in 1885, and then in 1894–95 ended the monarchy, exiling Queen Rànavàlona III to Algiers. A colonial administration was set up, to which the Comoro Islands were attached in 1908, and other territories later. In World War II, the British occupied Madagascar, which retained ties to Vichy France.

An autonomous republic within the French Community since 1958, Madagascar became an independent member of the Community in 1960. In May 1973, an army coup led by Maj. Gen. Gabriel Ramanantsoa ousted Philibert Tsiranana, president since 1959.

On June 15, 1975, Comdr. Didier Ratsiraka was named President. He announced that he would follow a socialist course and, after nationalizing banks and insurance companies, declared all mineral resources nationalized.

In July 1991 opposition leaders named an alternative government. After a 15-day strike the president offered a referendum on a multiparty constitution and named a new prime minister. An interim government was formed in May that included the opposition and would prepare constitutional changes.

Albert Zafy decidedly won the second round of the presidential election in February 1993. F. Ravony was elected prime minister in August and made his cabinet appointments shortly thereafter.

In line with demands from the IMF and the World Bank for a wage freeze and shrinking the size of the civil service, the government implemented a series of austerity measures.

MALAWI

Republic of Malawi
President: Bakili Muluzi (1994)
Area: 45,747 sq mi. (118,484 sq km)
Population (est. mid-1995): 9,700,000 (average annual rate of natural increase: 2.7%); birth rate: 47/1000;

infant mortality rate: 134/1000; density per square mile: 212
Capital (1993 est.): Lilongwe, 260,000; **Largest city (1993 est.):** Blantyre, 399,000; **Monetary unit:** Kwacha; **Languages:** English and Chichewa (National); **Religions:** Christian, 75%; Islam, 20%; **Member of Commonwealth of Nations; Literacy rate:** 41.2%
Economic summary: Gross domestic product (1993 est.): $6 billion; $600 per capita; growth rate –8% (1992 est.); inflation rate 21% (1992 est.). Arable land: 25%. Agriculture accounts for 40% of GDP and 90% of export revenues. Principal agricultural products: tobacco, tea, sugar, corn, cotton. Labor force: 428,000 wage earners; 43% in agriculture. Major industrial products: food, tobacco, cement, processed wood, consumer goods. Natural resources: limestone, uranium, coal, bauxite. Exports: $413 million (f.o.b., 1992): tobacco, sugar, tea, coffee, peanuts. Imports: $737 million (c.i.f., 1992): transport equipment, food, petroleum, consumer goods. Major trading partners: U.K., U.S., Japan, Germany, South Africa, Zambia, Zimbabwe.

Geography. Malawi is a landlocked country the size of Pennsylvania in southeastern Africa, surrounded by Mozambique, Zambia, and Tanzania. Lake Malawi, formerly Lake Nyasa, occupies most of the country's eastern border. The north-south Rift Valley is flanked by mountain ranges and high plateau areas.

Government. Under a Provisional Constitution which came into effect on May 17, 1994, the president is the Head of State and Government. There is a Vice President. The National Assembly (Parliament) is composed of 177 members. There are eight (8) registered parties and the ruling Party since May 17, 1994 is the United Democratic Front (UDF) of President Bakili Muluzi.

History. The first European to make extensive explorations in the area was David Livingstone in the 1850s and 1860s. In 1884, Cecil Rhodes's British South African Company received a charter to develop the country. The company came into conflict with the Arab slavers in 1887–89. After Britain annexed the Nyasaland territory in 1891, making it a protectorate in 1892, Sir Harry Johnstone, the first high commissioner, using Royal Navy gunboats, wiped out the slavers.

Nyasaland became the independent nation of Malawi on July 6, 1964. Two years later, it became a republic within the Commonwealth of Nations.

Dr. Hastings K. Banda, Malawi's first Prime Minister, became its first President. He pledged to follow a policy of "discretionary nonalignment." Banda alienated much of black Africa by maintaining good relations with South Africa.

The results of a referendum in June 1993 on Banda's one-party rule gave 63% in favor of a multiparty democracy.

Bakili Muluzi won the country's first free election in May 1994. He was sworn in a few days later and immediately released the remaining political prisoners. Muluzi restated his commitment to the alleviation of poverty.

MALAYSIA

Paramount Ruler: H.R.H. Tuanku Ja'afar Tuanku Abdul Rahman (1994)
Prime Minister: Dato' Seri Mahathir bin Mohamad (1981)

Area: 128,328 sq mi. (332,370 sq km)
Population (est. mid-1995): 19,900,000 (average annual rate of natural increase: 2.4%); birth rate: 29/1000; infant mortality rate: 12/1000; density per square mile: 155
Capital: Kuala Lumpur; **Largest cities (1991 est.):** Kuala Lumpur, 1,145,000; Georgetown (Pinang), 220,000; Ipoh, 382,600; **Monetary unit:** Ringgit; **Languages:** Malay (official), Chinese, Tamil, English; **Ethnic divisions:** 59% Malay and other indigenous; 32% Chinese; 9% Indian; **Religions:** Malays all Muslim, Chinese predominantly Buddhists, Indians predominantly Hindus; **Member of Commonwealth of Nations; Literacy rate:** 78%
Economic summary: Gross domestic product (1994 est.): $55.1 billion; $3,711 per capita; real growth rate 8% (1993 est.); inflation 3.5% (1995); unemployment 2.8% (1995). Arable land: 3%. Principal agricultural products: rice, rubber, palm products. Labor force (1994): 7,858,000. Major industrial products: processed rubber, timber, and palm oil, tin, petroleum, light manufactures, electronics equipment. Natural resources: tin, oil, copper, timber. Exports: $50.2 billion (f.o.b., 1994): natural rubber, palm oil, tin, timber, petroleum, electronics, textiles. Imports: $44.8 billion (f.o.b., 1994): food, crude oil, capital equipment, chemicals, consumer goods. Major trading partners: Japan, Singapore, U.S., Western European countries, Taiwan.

Geography. Malaysia is on the Malay Peninsula in southeast Asia. The nation also includes Sabah and Sarawak on the island of Borneo to the east. Its area slightly exceeds that of New Mexico.

Most of Malaysia is covered by forest, with a mountain range running the length of the peninsula. Extensive forests provide ebony, sandalwood, teak, and other woods.

Government. Malaysia is a sovereign constitutional monarchy practicing parliamentary democracy based on universal suffrage. Malaysia is a member of the Commonwealth of Nations. The Paramount Ruler is elected for a five-year term by the hereditary rulers of the states from among themselves. He is advised by the prime minister and his cabinet. There is a bicameral legislature. The Senate, whose role is comparable more to that of the British House of Lords than to the U.S. Senate, has 68 members, partly appointed by the Paramount Ruler to represent minority and special interests, and partly elected by the legislative assemblies of the various states.

The House of Representatives, is made up of 192 members, who are elected for five-year terms.

History. Malaysia came into existence on Sept. 16, 1963, as a federation of Malaya, Singapore, Sabah (North Borneo), and Sarawak. In 1965, Singapore withdrew from the federation. Since 1966, the 11 states of former Malaya have been known as West Malaysia, and Sabah and Sarawak have been known as East Malaysia.

The Union of Malaya was established April 1, 1946, being formed from the Federated Malay States of Negri Sembilan, Pahang, Perak, and Selangor; the Unfederated Malay States of Johore, Kedah, Kelantan, Perlis, and Trengganu; and two of the Straits Settlements—Malacca and Penang. The Malay states had been brought under British administration during the late 19th and early 20th centuries.

It became the Federation of Malaya on Feb. 1, 1948, and the Federation attained full independence within the Commonwealth of Nations in 1957.

Sabah, constituting the extreme northern portion of

the island of Borneo, was a British protectorate administered under charter by the British North Borneo Company from 1881 to 1946, when it assumed the status of a colony. It was occupied by Japanese troops from 1942 to 1945.

Sarawak extends along the northwestern coast of Borneo for about 500 miles (805 km). In 1841, part of the present territory was granted by the Sultan of Brunei to Sir James Brooke. Sarawak continued to be ruled by members of the Brooke family until the Japanese occupation.

From 1963, when Malaysia became independent, it was the target of guerrilla infiltration from Indonesia, but beat off invasion attempts. In 1966, when Sukarno fell and the Communist Party was liquidated in Indonesia, hostilities ended.

In the late 1960s, the country was torn by communal rioting directed against Chinese and Indians, who controlled a disproportionate share of the country's wealth. Beginning in 1968, the government moved to achieve greater economic balance through a rural development program.

Malaysia felt the impact of the "boat people" fleeing Vietnam early in 1978. Because the refugees were mostly ethnic Chinese, the government was apprehensive about any increase of a minority that previously had been the source of internal conflict in the country. In April 1988, it announced that starting in April 1989 it would accept no more refugees.

General elections were held in October 1990 producing another victory for Prime Minister Mahathir and his Barisan National coalition, which won 127 of the 180 parliamentary seats.

Constitutional amendments in 1993 removed legal immunity from the country's nine hereditary rulers in purely personal matters.

In 1994 the constitution was amended to state that the monarch had to obey the government's advice and that any bill not signed by him within 30 days became law automatically.

MALDIVES

Republic of Maldives
President: Maumoon Abdul Gayoom (1978)
Area: 115 sq mi. (298 sq km)
Population (1995 census): 244,000 (average annual rate of natural increase: 3.6%) (1994 est.)); birth rate: 43.5/1000 (1994 est.); infant mortality rate: 53.8/1000 (1994 est.); density per square mile: 2,121
Capital and largest city (1995 census): Malé, 62,973; **Monetary unit:** Maldivian rufiyaa; **Language:** Dhivehi; **Religion:** Islam (Sunni Muslim); **Literacy rate:** 98%
Economic summary: Gross domestic product (1993): $167.7 million; $703.4 per capita; real growth rate 6.2%; inflation (1992–93): 20.1%. Arable land: 10%. Principal agricultural products: maize, sorghum, finger millet, alocasia, cassava, sweet potato, onion, coconut. Labor force: 66,000; 80% in fishing. Major products: fish, processed coconuts, handicraft. Natural resource: fish. Tourism is also an important sector of the economy. Exports: $56.3 million (f.o.b., 1993 est.): fish, clothing. Imports: $173.6 million (c.i.f., 1993 est.): intermediate and capital goods, consumer goods, petroleum products. Major trading partners: Thailand, U.S., Singapore, U.K., Germany, India.

Geography. The Republic of Maldives is a group of atolls in the Indian Ocean about 417 miles (671 km) southwest of Sri Lanka. Its 1,190 coral islets stretch over an area of 35,200 square miles (90,000 sq km). With concerns over global warming and the shrinking of the polar ice caps, Maldives felt directly threatened as none of its islands rises more than six feet above sea level.

Government. The 15-member Cabinet is headed by the president. The Majlis (Parliament) is a unicameral legislature consisting of 48 members. Eight of these are appointed by the president. The others are elected for five-year terms, 2 from the capital island of Malé and 2 from each of the 19 administrative atolls. There are no political parties in the Maldives.

History. The Maldives (formerly called the Maldive Islands) are inhabited by an Islamic seafaring people. Originally the islands were under the suzerainty of Ceylon. They came under British protection in 1887 and were a dependency of the then colony of Ceylon until 1948. The independence agreement with Britain was signed July 26, 1965.

For centuries a sultanate, the islands adopted a republican form of government in 1952, but the sultanate was restored in 1954. In 1968, however, as the result of a referendum, a republic was again established in the islands.

Ibrahim Nasir, president since 1968, was removed from office by the Majlis in November 1978 and replaced by Maumoon Abdul Gayoom.

The president was elected to a fourth five-year term in October 1993. Economic growth continued. The national debt, however, was 75% of the GNP.

MALI

Republic of Mali
President of the Republic: Alpha Oumar Konaré (1992)
Area: 478,819 sq mi. (1,240,142 sq km)
Population (est. mid-1995): 9,400,000 (average annual rate of natural increase: 3.2%); birth rate: 51/1000; infant mortality rate: 104/1000; density per square mile: 19.6
Capital and largest city (1992 est.): Bamako, 746,000;
Monetary unit: Franc CFA; **Ethnic groups:** Bambara, Peul, Soninke, Malinke, Songhai, Dogon, Senoufo, Minianka, Berbers, and Moors; **Languages:** French (official), African languages; **Religions:** Islam, 90%; traditional, 9%; Christian, 1%; **National name:** République de Mali; **Literacy rate:** 32%
Economic summary: Gross domestic product (1993 est.): $5.8 billion; $650 per capita; real growth rate –6.1% (1992 est.); inflation 2% (1992 est.). Arable land: 2%; Principal agricultural products: millet, corn, rice, cotton, peanuts, livestock. Labor force: 2,666,000; 80% in agriculture. Major industrial products: consumer goods, phosphates, gold, fish. Natural resources: bauxite, iron ore, manganese, phosphate, salt, limestone, gold. Exports: $330 million (f.o.b., 1992 est.): cotton, livestock, gold. Imports: $682 million (f.o.b., 1992 est.): machinery and equipment, foodstuffs, construction materials, petroleum, textiles. Major trading partners: Western Europe.

Geography. Most of Mali, in West Africa, lies in the Sahara. A landlocked country four fifths the size of Alaska, it is bordered by Guinea, Senegal, Mauritania, Algeria, Niger, Burkina Faso, and the Ivory Coast.

The only fertile area is in the south, where the Niger and Senegal Rivers provide irrigation.

Government. The army overthrew the government on Nov. 19, 1968, and formed a provisional government. The Military Committee of National Liberation

consists of 14 members and forms the decision-making body.

Soldiers promising a multiparty democracy overthrew the dictatorship of General Traoré in March 1991.

The present government is a multiparty democracy with one parliamentary house of 129 seats, 13 of which are designated for Malians abroad.

History. Subjugated by France by the end of the 19th century, this area became a colony in 1904 (named French Sudan in 1920) and in 1946 became part of the French Union. On June 20, 1960, it became independent and, under the name of Sudanese Republic, was federated with the Republic of Senegal in the Mali Federation. However, Senegal seceded from the Federation on Aug. 20, 1960, and the Sudanese Republic then changed its name to the Republic of Mali on September 22.

In the 1960s, Mali concentrated on economic development, continuing to accept aid from both Soviet bloc and Western nations, as well as international agencies. In the late 1960s, it began retreating from close ties with China. But a purge of conservative opponents brought greater power to President Modibo Keita, and in 1968 the influence of the Chinese and their Malian sympathizers increased.

Mali, with Mauritania, the Ivory Coast, Senegal, Dahomey (Benin), Niger, and Burkina Faso signed a treaty establishing the Economic Community for West Africa.

Mali and Burkina Faso fought a brief border war from December 25 to 29, 1985.

The leader of the March 1991 coup, Lieut. Col. Amadou Toumani Touré, promised the army would return to the barracks. There were at least 59 casualties after the overnight coup, which France welcomed.

Multiparty elections in 1992 gave the Alliance for Democracy in Mali 76 of the 116 parliamentary seats, and the presidency went to that party's candidate Konaré with 70% of the vote.

Following large demonstrations and riots in early 1993 the prime minister resigned, being replaced by the then Minister of Defense Abdoulaye Sekou Sow.

Prime Minister Sow in turn resigned in February 1994 claiming political differences with the governing party. He was replaced with the foreign minister. The two chief opposition parties withdrew from the coalition government citing failure to be brought into the negotiations concerning the new cabinet.

MALTA

Malta
President: Dr. Ugo Mifsud Bonnici (1994)
Prime Minister: Dr. Edward Fenech Adami (1987)
Area: 122 sq mi. (316 sq km)
Population (est. mid-1995): 400,000 (average annual rate of natural increase: 0.7%); birth rate: 14/1000; infant mortality rate: 9.3/1000; density per square mile: 3,278.7
Capital (est. 1992): Valletta, 9,183; **Largest city (est. 1987):** Sliema; **Monetary unit:** Maltese lira; **Languages:** Maltese and English; **Religion:** Roman Catholic; **National name:** Malta; **Member of Commonwealth of Nations; Literacy rate:** 84%
Economic summary: Gross domestic product (1992 est.): $2.4 billion; $6,600 per capita; real growth rate 4.5%; inflation 1.64%; unemployment 4%. Arable land: 38%. Principal agricultural products: potatoes, wheat, barley, citrus, vegetables, hogs, poultry. Labor force: 125,674; 27% in manufacturing. Major manufacturing

products are high-tech semiconductors, electrical switchgear, gold and silver items, rubber products, and textiles. The same products are exported. Tourism is also important to the economy. Exports: $1.3 billion (f.o.b., 1992): clothing, textiles, footwear, ships. Imports: $1.93 million (f.o.b., 1992): food, petroleum, machinery, and semimanufactured goods. Major trading partners: Germany, Italy, UK, U.S.

Geography. The five Maltese islands—with a combined land area smaller than Philadelphia—are in the Mediterranean about 60 miles (97 km) south of the southeastern tip of Sicily.

Government. The government is headed by a Prime Minister, responsible to a 65-member House of Representatives elected by universal suffrage.

The major political parties are the Nationalists (34 of 65 seats in the House,) led by Prime Minister Dr. Dr. Edward Fenech-Adami; Malta Labor Party (31 seats), led by Dr. Alfred Sant.

History. The strategic importance of Malta was recognized by the Phoenicians, who occupied it, as did in their turn the Greeks, Carthaginians, and Romans. The apostle Paul was shipwrecked there in A.D. 58.

The Knights of St. John (Malta), who obtained the three habitable Maltese islands of Malta, Gozo, and Comino from Charles V in 1530, reached their highest fame when they withstood an attack by superior Turkish forces in 1565.

Napoleon seized Malta in 1798, but the French forces were ousted by British troops the next year, and British rule was confirmed by the Treaty of Paris in 1814.

Malta was heavily attacked by German and Italian aircraft during World War II, but was never invaded by the Axis.

Malta became an independent nation on Sept. 21, 1964, and a republic Dec. 13, 1974, but remained in the British Commonwealth. The Governor-General, Sir Anthony Mamo, was sworn in as first president and Dom Mintoff prime minister.

Fenech Adami won reelection in February 1992 when his party won an absolute majority of three seats in the parliament.

The European Council indicated in 1994 that Malta's application for membership in the European Union would be accepted in the next expansion phase.

MARSHALL ISLANDS

Republic of the Marshall Islands
President: Amata Kabua (1979)
Total land area: 70 sq mi (181.3 sq km), includes the atolls of Bikini, Eniwetok, and Kwajalein
Population (est. mid-1995): 100,000; growth rate 4.0%; birth rate 49/1000; infant mortality rate 63/1000; density per square mile: 1,428.5
Capital and largest city (1988): Majuro, 22,000; **Government:** Constitutional government in free association with the United States; **Ethnic divisions:** almost entirely Micronesian; **Religion:** predominantly Christian, mostly Protestant; **Literacy rate:** 93%; **Language:** Both Marshallese and English are official languages. Marshallese is a dialect of the Malayo-Polynesian family
Net migration rate (1992): 0 migrant/1000 population
Comparative land area: slightly larger than Washington, D.C.
Economic summary: Gross domestic product (1989 est.): $63 million; per capita, $1,500; real growth rate, n.a. Exports: $3.9 million (f.o.b., 1992 est.): coconut oil, fish,

live animals, trichus shells. Imports: $62.9 million (c.i.f., 1992 est.): foodstuffs, machinery and equipment, beverages and tobacco, fuels. Agriculture, marine resources, and tourism are the top development priorities for the Republic of the Marshall Islands (RMI). The government of the RMI is the largest employer with some 2,000 workers. Direct U.S. aid under the Compact of Free Association, the U.S. is to provide approximately $40 million annually in aid. Major trading partners: U.S., Japan, Australia.

The Government of the United States and the RMI signed a Compact of Free Association on October 15, 1986, which became effective as of October 21, 1986. The termination of the Trusteeship Agreement became effective on November 3, 1986. The Marshall Islands were admitted to the United Nations on Sept. 17, 1991.

The Marshall Islands, east of the Carolines, are divided into two chains: the western or Ralik group, including the atolls Jaluit, Kwajalein, Wotho, Bikini, and Eniwetok; and the eastern or Ratak group, including the atolls Mili, Majuro, Maloelap, Wotje, and Likiep. The islands are of the coral-reef type and rise only a few feet above sea level.

President Amata Kabua won reelection by the national legislature in January 1992.

The government again in 1994 considered allowing the dumping of nuclear waste on such islands as Bikini and Enewetak, which are already uninhabitable owing to nuclear tests decades ago.

MAURITANIA

Islamic Republic of Mauritania
Chief of State and Head of Government: Pres. Maaouye Ould Sidi Ahmed Taya (1984)
Area: 397,953 sq mi. (1,030,700 sq km)
Population (est. mid-1995): 2,300,000 (average annual rate of natural increase: 2.5%); birth rate: 40/1000; infant mortality rate: 101/1000; density per square mile: 5.7
Capital and largest city (est. 1992): Nouakchott, 480,000; **Monetary unit:** Ouguyia; **Ethnic groups:** Arabs, 80%; Africans, 20%. **Languages:** Arabic (official) and French; **Religion:** Islam; **National name:** République Islamique de Mauritanie; **Literacy rate:** 34%
Economic summary: Gross domestic product (1992 est.): $2.2 billion; $1,050 per capita; real growth rate 3.3% (1993 est.); inflation (1993 est.) 11.5%; unemployment (1991 est.) 20%. Arable land: 1%; Principal agricultural products: livestock, millet, maize, wheat, dates, rice. Labor force: 465,000 (1981 est.); 45,000 wage earners; 14% in industry and commerce. Major industrial products: iron ore, processed fish. Natural resources: copper, iron ore, gypsum, fish. Exports: $432 million (f.o.b., 1992 est.): iron ore, fish, gum arabic, gypsum. Imports: $413 million (c.i.f., 1992 est.): foodstuffs, petroleum, capital goods. Major trading partners: E.U., Japan, Côte d'Ivoire, Algeria, China, U.S.

Geography. Mauritania, three times the size of Arizona, is situated in northwest Africa with about 350 miles (592 km) of coastline on the Atlantic Ocean. It is bordered by Morocco on the north, Algeria and Mali on the east, and Senegal on the south.

The country is mostly desert, with the exception of the fertile Senegal River valley in the south and grazing land in the north.

Government. An Army coup on July 10, 1978, deposed Moktar Ould Daddah, who had been President since Mauritania's independence in 1960. President

Mohammed Khouna Ould Haldala, who seized power in the 1978 coup, was in turn deposed in a Dec. 12, 1984, coup by army chief of staff Maaouye Ould Sidi Ahmed Taya, who assumed the title of President.

In the January 1992 elections Pres. Taya won 62% of the electorate vote.

The constitution guarantees freedom of press, opinion, and assembly among others to all Mauritanian citizens. There are about 20 political parties. There is a bicameral legislature Senate (Majlis al-Shuyukh) and a National Assembly (Majlis al-Watani).

History. Mauritania was first explored by the Portuguese. The French organized the area as a territory in 1904.

Mauritania became an independent nation on Nov. 28, 1960, and was admitted to the United Nations in 1961 over the strenuous opposition of Morocco, which claimed the territory. With Moors, Arabs, Berbers, and blacks frequently in conflict, the government in the late 1960s sought to make Arab culture dominant to unify the land.

Mauritania acquired administrative control of the southern part of the former Spanish Sahara when the colonial administration withdrew in 1975, under an agreement with Morocco and Spain.

Increased military spending and rising casualties in Western Sahara helped bring down the civilian government of Ould Daddah in 1978. A succession of military rulers followed.

In 1989 Mauritania fought a border war with Senegal. Although the country voted in the U.N. to support the embargo against Iraq, the government actually leaned the other way.

The government in April 1991 announced a transition to a multiparty system. A constitutional reform embodying these changes won approcal in a referendum in July.

The opposition's call for a boycott of the March parliamentary elections reduced turnout to no more than 40%. Yet Taya's party won 67 of the 79 available seats.

Just days prior to the January 1994 local elections the army arrested a large number, charging them with printing counterfeit voter ID cards. Nevertheless, the governing party won in 172 of the 208 communes.

MAURITIUS

President: Cassam Uteem (1992)
Prime Minister: Aneerood Jugnauth (1982)
Area: 787 sq mi. (2,040 sq km)
Population (1994): 1,117,820 (average annual rate of natural increase: 1.1%); birth rate: 19.5/1000; infant mortality rate: 18/1000; density per square mile: 1,420.4
Capital and largest city (est. 1991): Port Louis, 142,087;
Monetary unit: Mauritian rupee; **Languages:** English (official), French, Creole, Hindi, Urdu, Hakka, Bojpoori; **Religions:** Hindu, 52%, Christian, 28.3%; Islam, 16.6%; other, 3.1%; **Member of Commonwealth of Nations;** Literacy rate: 82.8%
Economic summary: Gross domestic product (1993 est.): $8.6 billion; $7,800 per capita; real growth rate, 6.3% (1992 est.); inflation 4.6% (1992 est.); unemployment 2.4% (1991 est.). Arable land: 54%. Principal products: sugar cane, tea. Labor force: 335,000; 22% in manufacturing; 29% in government services; 27% in agriculture and fishing. Major products: processed sugar, wearing apparel, chemical products, textiles. Natural resources: fish. Exports: $1.32 billion (f.o.b., 1992 est.): sugar, light manufactures, textiles. Imports: $1.63 bil-

lion (f.o.b., 1992 est.): foodstuffs, manufactured goods. Major trading partners: E.U., S. Africa, U.S.

Geography. Mauritius is a mountainous island in the Indian Ocean east of Madagascar.

Government. Mauritius is a republic within the British Commonwealth. The unicameral Legislative Assembly has 70 members, 62 of whom are elected by direct suffrage. The remaining 8 are chosen from among the unsuccessful candidates.

History. After a brief Dutch settlement, French immigrants who came in 1715 gave the name of Isle de France to the island and established the first road and harbor infrastructure, as well as the sugar industry, under the leadership of Gov. Mahe de Labourdonnais. Negroes from Africa and Madagascar came as slaves to work in the cane fields. In 1810, the British captured the island and in 1814, by the Treaty of Paris, it was ceded to Great Britain along with its dependencies.

Indian immigration which followed the abolition of slavery in 1835 changed rapidly the fabric of Mauritian society, and the country flourished with the increased cultivation of sugar cane.

Mauritius became independent on March 12, 1968. The Labor Party government of Sir Seewoosagur Ramgoolam, who had ruled Mauritius since independence, was toppled in a 1982 election by the Movement Militant Mauricien, which had campaigned for recovery of Diego Garcia island, separated from Mauritius during the colonial period and leased by Britain to the United States for a naval base. But an Alliance Party coalition, including the Labor Party, regained power at the end of 1983 and brought back Ramgoolam as Prime Minister. He was succeeded by Aneerood Jugnauth of his party in 1982.

A transformation of the nation from a constitutional monarchy into a republic was attempted in mid-1990. Public dissent for the move, however, arose, and the required parliamentary vote was never taken.

The country formally broke ties with the British crown in March 1992 becoming a republic. The president was elected by the Legislative Assembly on June 30.

The government in 1993 offered interest-free loans to its citizens to invest on the local stock exchange. The loans could be repaid over a 10-month period. The finance minister took steps to enliven the stock exchange in early 1994. By midyear it was experiencing a boom, largely attributed to a larger than expected sugar crop.

MEXICO

United Mexican States
President: Ernesto Zedillo Ponce de Léon (1994)
Area: 761,600 sq mi. (1,972,547 sq km)
Population (est. mid-1995): 93,700,000 (average annual rate of natural increase: 2.2%); birth rate: 27/1000; infant mortality rate: 34/1000; density per square mile: 123
Capital: Federal District (Mexico City); **Largest cities (1989):** Federal District, 19,479,000; Guadalajara, 3,186,500; Monterey, 2,858,800; Puebla, 1,707,000; Leon, 1,006,700; **Monetary unit:** Peso; **Languages:** Spanish, Indian languages; **Religion:** nominally Roman Catholic, 97%; Protestant, 3%; **Official name:** Estados Unidos Mexicanos; **Literacy rate:** 88%

Economic summary: Gross domestic product (1993 est.): $740 billion; $8,200 per capita; real growth rate 0.4%; inflation 8%; unemployment (1992 est.) 10.7%. Arable land: 12%;principal products: corn, cotton, fruits, wheat, beans, coffee, tomatoes, rice. Labor force: 24,063,283 (1990); 27.9% in manufacturing; 22.6% in agriculture; 46.1% in services. Major products: processed foods, chemicals, basic metals and metal products, petroleum. Natural resources: petroleum, silver, copper, gold, lead, zinc, natural gas, timber. Exports: $50.5 billion (f.o.b., 1993 est.): motor vehicles, consumer electronics, cotton, shrimp, coffee, petroleum, petroleum products, engines. Imports: $65.5 billion (c.i.f., 1993 est.): grain, metal manufactures, agricultural machinery, electrical equipment, car parts for assembly, motor vehicle repair parts, aircraft and aircraft parts. Major trading partners: U.S., Japan, Western European countries.

Geography. The United States' neighbor to the south, Mexico is about one fifth its size. Baja California in the west, an 800-mile (1,287-km) peninsula, forms the Gulf of California. In the east are the Gulf of Mexico and the Bay of Campeche, which is formed by Mexico's other peninsula, the Yucatán.

The center of Mexico is a great, high plateau, open to the north, with mountain chains on east and west and with ocean-front lowlands lying outside of them.

Government. The President, who is popularly elected for six years and is ineligible to succeed himself, governs with a Cabinet of secretaries. Congress has two houses—a 500-member Chamber of Deputies, elected for three years, and a 64-member Senate, elected for six years half of which is renewed every three years. Popularly elected officials (President, members of Congress, mayors, etc.) cannot seek reelection.

Each of the 31 states has considerable autonomy, with a popularly elected governor, a legislature, and a local judiciary. The President of Mexico appoints the mayor of the Federal District.

History. At least two civilized races—the Mayas and later the Toltecs—preceded the wealthy Aztec empire, conquered in 1519–21 by the Spanish under Hernando Cortés. Spain ruled for the next 300 years until 1810 (the date was Sept. 16 and is now celebrated as Independence Day), when the Mexicans first revolted. They continued the struggle and finally won independence in 1821.

From 1821 to 1877, there were two emperors, several dictators, and enough presidents and provisional executives to make a new government on the average of every nine months. Mexico lost Texas (1836), and after defeat in the war with the U.S. (1846–48) it lost the area comprising the present states of California, Nevada, and Utah, most of Arizona and New Mexico, and parts of Wyoming and Colorado.

In 1855, the Indian patriot Benito Juárez began a series of liberal reforms, including the disestablishment of the Catholic Church, which had acquired vast property. A subsequent civil war was interrupted by the French invasion of Mexico (1861), the crowning of Maximilian of Austria as Emperor (1864), and then his overthrow and execution by forces under Juárez, who again became President in 1867.

The years after the fall of the dictator Porfirio Diaz (1877–80 and 1884–1911) were marked by bloody political-military strife and trouble with the U.S., culminating in the punitive expedition into northern Mexico (1916–17) in unsuccessful pursuit of the rev-

olutionary Pancho Villa. Since a brief period of civil war in 1920, Mexico has enjoyed a period of gradual agricultural, political, and social reforms. Relations with the U.S. were again disturbed in 1938 when all foreign oil wells were expropriated. Agreement on compensation was finally reached in 1941.

During 1983 and 1984, Mexico suffered its worst financial crisis in 50 years, leading to critically high unemployment and an inability to pay its foreign debt. The collapse of oil prices in 1986 cut into Mexico's export earnings and worsened the situation.

Although the ruling Institutional Revolutionary Party's candidate, Carlos Salinas de Gortari, won the presidential election of 1988, the opposition parties on the left and the right showed unprecedented strength.

In the economic sphere Mexico decided to apply for membership in the Organization for Economic Cooperation & Development and talks began on a comprehensive North American free-trade agreement. The national telephone company was privatized.

At the start of 1994 peasant rebels seized a colonial city and declared war on the state. Negotiations and a cease-fire began in mid-January. In March the leading presidential candidate was shot and killed in Tijuana. The campaign manager was then selected to be the party's presidential candidate. Zedillo won the election by more than 20% and the governing party retained its majority in both legislative houses.

In February 1995 agreement was reached with the U.S. to prevent the collapse of Mexico's private banks. The strict provisions, however, gave the U.S. virtual veto power over key elements in Mexico's economic policy.

MICRONESIA

Federated States of Micronesia

President: Bailey Olter (1991)

Total area: 271 sq mi (703 sq km). Land area, same (includes islands of Pohnpei, Truk, Yap, and Kosrae.

Population (est. mid-1995): 100,000 (average annual rate of natural increase: 3.0%); birth rate: 38/1000; infant mortality rate: 52/1000; density per square mile: 369

Capital: Palikir. **Ethnic divisions:** Nine ethnic Micronesian and Polynesian groups.; **Language:** English is the official and common language; major indigenous languages are Trukese, Pohnpeian, Yapese, and Kosrean.; **Literacy rate:** 90%

Government: A constitutional government in free association with the United States since November 1986.

Economic summary: Gross national product (1989 est.): $150 million, per capita, $1,500. Exports: $2.3 billion (f.o.b., 1988): copra. Imports: $67.7 million (c.i.f., 1988). Financial assistance from the U.S. is the primary source of revenue, with the U.S. pledged to spend $1 billion in the islands in the 1990s. Micronesia also earns about $4 million a year in fees from foreign fishing concerns. Economic activity consists primarily of subsistence farming and fishing. Unemployment rate: 80% **Aid:** Under the terms of the Compact of Free Association, the U.S. will provide $1.3 billion in grand aid during the period 1986–2001.

On April 2, 1947, the United Nations Security Council created the Trust Territory of the Pacific Islands under which the Northern Mariana, Caroline, and Marshall Islands were placed under the administration of the United States. These islands comprised what is now called the Federated States of Micronesia and only the Republic of Palau is still administered as a Trust Territory. Micronesia was admitted to the United Nations on September 17, 1991. In July 1993 the country became a member of the International Monetary Fund.

The Micronesian islands vary geologically from high mountainous islands to low, coral atolls; volcanic outcroppings on Pohnpei, Kosrae, and Truk. The climate is tropical with heavy, year-round rainfall. The islands are located 3,200 miles (5,150 km) west-southwest of Honolulu in the North Pacific Ocean, about three-quarters of the way between Hawaii and Indonesia.

In July 1993 the country became a member of the International Monetary Fund.

MOLDOVA

Republic of Moldova
President: Mircea Snegur (1990)
Prime Minister: Andrei Sangheli (1992)
Area: 13,000 sq mi. (33,700 sq km)
Population (est. mid-1995): 4,300,000 (Moldovans, 65.5%; Ukrainians, 13.9%; Russians, 13.0%; Gagauz, 3.5%; Bulgarians, 2.0%; Jews, 1.5%); (average annual rate of natural increase: 0.4%); birth rate: 15/1000; infant mortality rate: 22/1000, density per square mile: 330.7
Capital and largest city (1991): Chisinau, 676,700. Other large cities (est. 1991): Tiraspol, 186,000; Beltsy, 165,000; Bendery (Tighina), 141,500; **Monetary unit:** Moldovan lem; **Language:** Romanian official language since 1989
Economic summary: Gross domestic product (UN, World Bank 1993 est.): $16.3 billion, $3,650 per capita; real growth rate –4%; inflation: 30% (per mo.); unemployment: less than 1%. Agriculture and food processing are the main industries. Others include power engineering, textiles, metalworking, building materials, machine-building, TV sets, washing machines and other consumer goods, and manufacturing of electrical equipment. Agricultural products are wheat, corn, barley, sugar beets, fruits, and wine grapes, soybeans, tobacco, and animal husbandry. Eighty-five percent of all the land is cultivated. Exports: $108 million to outside former Soviet Union countries (Jan.–Sept. 1993): foodstuffs, wine, tobacco, textiles and footwear, machinery, chemicals (1991). Imports: $145 million from outside former Soviet Union countries (Jan.–Sept. 1993): oil, gas, coal, steel machinery, foodstuffs, automobiles, and other consumer durables. Major trading partners: Russia, Kazakhstan, Ukraine, Uzbekistan, Romania, Germany.

Geography: Moldova (formerly Moldavia) is a landlocked republic of hilly plains lying in the southwestern part of the former Soviet Union between the Prut and Dnestr (Dneister) Rivers. The Prut River separates it from Romania in the west and Ukraine borders it in the north, east, and south. The area is a very fertile region with rich black soil (chernozem) covering three-quarters of the territory.

Government: A democratic republic in transition with a parliament made up of 101 deputies. The working body of the parliament is the Presidium.

History: Most of Moldova was an independent principality in the 14th century. In the 16th century it came under Ottoman Turkish rule. Russia acquired Moldovan territory in 1791, and in 1812 (The Treaty of Bucharest) when Turkey gave up the province of Bessarabia[1] to Russia. Turkey held the rest of Moldova but it was passed to Romania in 1918. Russia did not recognize the cession of this territory.

In 1924, the U.S.S.R. established Moldova as an Autonomous Soviet Socialist Republic of the Ukraine. As a result of the Nazi-Soviet Nonaggression Pact of 1939, Romania was forced to cede all of Bessarabia to the Soviet Union in 1940 and the Moldovan A.S.S.R. was merged with the Romanian-speaking districts of Bessarabia to form the former Moldovan Soviet Socialist Republic.

During World War II, Romania joined Germany in the attack on the Soviet Union and reconquered Bessarabia. Soviet troops retook the territory in 1944 and reestablished the Moldovan S.S.R.

For many years, a controversy existed between Romania and the U.S.S.R. over Bessarabia. Following the aborted coup against Soviet President Mikhail Gorbachev, Moldova proclaimed its independence in September 1991.

Following the demise of the Soviet Union, Moldova joined the C.I.S. along with ten other former Soviet republics on Dec. 21, 1991.

Conflict between ethnic Romanians and Slavs in Trans-Dniester has erupted since independence. The prime minister and most of his Cabinet resigned in early June 1992 because of the continued strife. Russia and Moldova agreed in July 1992 to send a joint peace-keeping force to the region and outlined guarantees for its future.

The first parliamentary elections in February 1994 saw a victory for the former Communist establishment.

The implementation of a new constitution in October 1994 was seen as a setback for pro-Romanian forces. Also in that month an agreement was reached calling for the complete withdrawal of Russian troops within three years.

---

1. The area between the Prut and Dnestr Rivers.

MONACO

Principality of Monaco
Ruler: Prince Rainier III (1949)
Minister of State: Paul Dijoud (1994)
Area: 0.73 sq mi. (465 acres)
Population (est. mid-1994): 31,278 (average annual growth rate: 0.81%); birth rate 10.7/1000; infant mortality rate: 7.2/1000; density per square mile: 42,846.6
Capital and largest city (1990 est.): Monaco-Ville, 29,972; **Monetary unit:** French franc; **Languages:** French, Monégasque, Italian; **Religion:** Roman Catholic, 95%; **National name:** Principauté de Monaco; **Literacy rate:** 99%
Economic summary: Gross domestic product: (1991 est.): $475 million; $16,000 per capita; real growth rate, n.a. About 50% of Monaco's revenues come from value-added taxes on hotels, banks, and industrial sector. About 25% of revenues comes from tourism.

Geography. Monaco is a tiny, hilly wedge driven into the French Mediterranean coast nine miles east of Nice.

Government. Prince Albert of Monaco gave the principality a Constitution in 1911, creating a National Council of 18 members popularly elected for five years. The head of government is the Minister of State.

Prince Rainier III, born May 31, 1923, succeeded his grandfather, Louis II, on the latter's death, May 9, 1949. Rainier was married April 18, 1956, to Grace Kelly, U.S. actress. A daughter, Princess Caroline

Louise Margueritte, was born on Jan. 23, 1957 (married to Philippe Junot June 28, 1978 and divorced in 1980; married to Stefano Casiraghi Dec. 29, 1983, and gave birth to a son, Andrea Albert, June 9, 1984, a daughter, Charlotte, Aug. 3, 1986, a son, Pierre, Sept. 5, 1987. Stefano Casiraghi died Oct. 3, 1990); a son, Prince Albert Louis Pierre, on March 14, 1958; and Princess Stéphanie Marie Elisabeth, on Feb. 1, 1965. Princess Grace died Sept. 14, 1982, of injuries received the day before when the car she was driving went off the road near Monte Carlo. She was 52.

The special significance attached to the birth of descendants to Prince Rainier stems from a clause in the Treaty of July 17, 1919, between France and Monaco stipulating that in the event of vacancy of the Crown, the Monégasque territory would become an autonomous state under a French protectorate.

The National and Democratic Union (all 18 seats in National Council), led by Jean Louis Campola, is the only political party.

History. The Phoenicians, and after them the Greeks, had a temple on the Monacan headland honoring Hercules. From *Monoikos,* the Greek surname for this mythological strong man, the principality took its name. After being independent for 800 years, Monaco was annexed to France in 1793 and was placed under Sardinia's protection in 1815. In 1861, it went under French guardianship but continued to be independent.

By a treaty in 1918, France stipulated that the French government be given a veto over the succession to the throne.

Monaco is a little land of pleasure with a tourist business that runs as high as 1.5 million visitors a year. It had popular gaming tables as early as 1856. Five years later, a 50-year concession to operate the games was granted to François Blanc, of Bad Homburg. This concession passed into the hands of a private company in 1898.

Monaco's practice of providing a tax shelter for French businessmen resulted in a dispute between the countries. When Rainier refused to end the practice, France retaliated with a customs tax. In 1967, Rainier took control of the Société des Bains de Mer, operator of the famous Monte Carlo gambling casino, in a program to increase hotel and convention space.

With the recent tragedies in the royal family speculation has centered on Rainier's grooming of his son Prince Albert to assume the duties of chief of state.

The country was admitted to the UN in May 1993, making it the smallest country represented there.

MONGOLIA

Mongolia
President: Punsalmaagiin Ochirbat (1990)
Prime Minister: Puntsagiyn Jasray (1992)
Area: 604,250 sq mi. (1,565,000 sq km)
Population (est. mid-1995): 2,300,000 (average annual rate of natural increase: 1.4%); birth rate: 22/1000; infant mortality rate: 61/1000; density per square mile: 3.8
Capital and largest city (est. 1992): Ulan Bator, 600,900;
Monetary unit: Tugrik; **Language:** Mongolian, 90%; also Turkic, Russian, and Chinese; **Religion:** predominantly Tibetan Buddhist; Islam about 4%; **Literacy rate:** 90% (est.)
Economic summary: Gross national product (1993): $943 million; $400 per capita; real growth rate 2.1%. Arable land: 1%. Principal agricultural products: livestock, wheat, potatoes, forage, barley. Mongolia has the

highest number of livestock per person in the world. Major industrial products: coal, copper and molybdenum concentrate. Natural resources: coal, copper, molybdenum, iron, oil, lead, gold, and tungsten. Exports: $324.3 million (1994): copper, cashmere, livestock, animal products, wool, nonferrous metals. Imports: $221.7 million (1994): fuels, food products, industrial consumer goods, chemicals, building materials, machinery and equipment. Major trading partners: C.I.S. nations, China, Japan, Austria.

Geography. Mongolia lies in central Asia between Siberia on the north and China on the south. It is slightly larger than Alaska.

The productive regions of Mongolia—a tableland ranging from 3,000 to 5,000 feet (914 to 1,524 m) in elevation—are in the north, which is well drained by numerous rivers, including the Hovd, Onon, Selenga, and Tula.

Much of the Gobi Desert falls within Mongolia.

Government. In January 1992, the Great People's Hural (parliament) approved a new constitution which entered into force Feb. 12, 1992, and changed the name of the former communist state to Mongolia. Mongolia became an independent sovereign republic now in transition from communism. The highest organ of state power is the State Great Hural (SGH). The SGH has one chamber consisting of 76 members. Its chairman and vice-chairman are elected for a term of four years.

History. The State of Mongolia was formerly known as Outer Mongolia. It contains the original homeland of the historic Mongols, whose power reached its zenith during the 13th century under Kublai Khan. The area accepted Manchu rule in 1689, but after the Chinese Revolution of 1911 and the fall of the Manchus in 1912, the northern Mongol princes expelled the Chinese officials and declared independence under the Khutukhtu, or "Living Buddha."

In 1921, Soviet troops entered the country and facilitated the establishment of a republic by Mongolian revolutionaries in 1924 after the death of the last Living Buddha. China, meanwhile, continued to claim Outer Mongolia but was unable to back the claim with any strength. Under the 1945 Chinese-Russian Treaty, China agreed to give up Outer Mongolia, which, after a plebiscite, became a nominally independent country.

Allied with the U.S.S.R. in its dispute with China, Mongolia has mobilized troops along its borders since 1968 when the two powers became involved in border clashes on the Kazakh-Sinkiang frontier to the west and on the Amur and Ussuri Rivers. A 20-year treaty of friendship and cooperation, signed in 1966, entitled Mongolia to call upon the U.S.S.R. for military aid in the event of invasion.

Free elections were held in August 1990 that produced a multiparty government, though still largely Communist. As a result Mongolia has decided to move toward a market economy.

The former Communist Party won a landslide victory in parliamentary elections of June 1992, causing considerable consternation in the democratic forces.

As a result of a dispute between the president and the reformed communist party, the latter supported a hard-line candidate in the first presidential election of June 1993. The incumbent won as the nominee of the National Democrats and Social Democrats. Since that election political events have centered around the dispute between the president and the largely reform-Communist assembly.

Although inflation progressively slowed during 1993–94, industrial production remained depressed.

MOROCCO

Kingdom of Morocco
Ruler: King Hassan II (1961)
Prime Minister: Abd al-Latif Filali (1995)
Area: 172,413 sq mi. (446,550 sq km)
Population (est. mid-1995): 29,200,000 (average annual rate of natural increase: 2.2%); birth rate: 28/1000; infant mortality rate: 57/1000; density per square mile: 169.3
Capital: Rabat; **Largest cities:** Casablanca, 3,500,000; Rabat-Sale, 1,000,000; Fez, 600,000; Marrakesh, 500,000; Laayoune, 100,000; **Monetary unit:** Dirham; **Languages:** Arabic, French, Berber dialects, Spanish; **Religions:** Islam, 98.7%, Christian, 1.1%; Jewish, 0.2%; **National name:** al-Mamlaka al-Maghrebia; **Literacy rate:** 50%
Economic summary: Gross domestic product (1993 est.): $70.3 billion; $2,500 per capita; real growth rate 2%; inflation 4.5%; unemployment 16% (1992 est.). Arable land: 20%. Products: barley, wheat, citrus fruits, vegetables. Labor force (1985): 7,400,000: agriculture 50%; services 26%. Major products: textiles, processed food, phosphates, leather goods. Natural resources: phosphates, lead, manganese, fisheries. Exports: $5.7 billion (f.o.b., 1992): food and beverages, semiprocessed goods, consumer goods, phosphates. Imports: $8.4 billion (c.i.f., 1992): capital goods, fuels, foodstuffs, raw materials, consumer goods. Major trading partners: E.U., C.I.S. nations, Japan, U.S., India, Iraq.

Geography. Morocco, about one tenth larger than California, is just south of Spain across the Strait of Gibraltar and looks out on the Atlantic from the northwest shoulder of Africa. Algeria is to the east and Mauritania to the south.

On the Atlantic coast there is a fertile plain. The Mediterranean coast is mountainous. The Atlas Mountains, running northeastward from the south to the Algerian frontier, average 11,000 feet (3,353 m) in elevation.

Government. A constitutional monarchy. The King, after suspending the 1962 Constitution and dissolving Parliament in 1965, promulgated a new Constitution in 1972. He continued to rule by decree until June 3, 1977, when the first free elections since 1962 took place. The constitution was revised and approved by referendum in 1992. The National Assembly has 306 seats. Morocco has 14 political parties, 8 of whom are represented in the House of Representatives.

History. Morocco was once the home of the Berbers, who helped the Arabs invade Spain in A.D. 711 and then revolted against them and gradually won control of large areas of Spain for a time after 739.

The country was ruled successively by various native dynasties and maintained regular commercial relations with Europe, even during the 17th and 18th centuries when it was the headquarters of the famous Salé pirates. In the 19th century, there were frequent clashes with the French and Spanish. Finally, in 1904, France and Spain divided Morocco into zones of French and Spanish influence, and these were established as protectorates in 1912.

Meanwhile, Morocco had become the object of big-power rivalry, which almost led to a European war in 1905 when Germany attempted to gain a foothold in the rich mineral country. By terms of the Algeciras Conference (1906), Morocco was internationalized economically, and France's privileges were limited.

The Tangier Statute, concluded by Britain, France,

and Spain in 1923, created an international zone at the port of Tangier, permanently neutralized and demilitarized. In World War II, Spain occupied the zone, ostensibly to ensure order, but was forced to withdraw in 1945.

Sultan Mohammed V was deposed by the French in 1953 and replaced by his uncle, but nationalist agitation forced his return in 1955. On his death on Feb. 26, 1961, his son, Hassan, became King.

France and Spain recognized the independence and sovereignty of Morocco in 1956.

In 1975, tens of thousands of Moroccans crossed the border into Spanish Sahara to back their government's contention that the northern part of the territory was historically part of Morocco. At the same time, Mauritania occupied the southern half of the territory in defiance of Spanish threats to resist such a takeover. Abandoning its commitment to self-determination for the territory, Spain withdrew, and only Algeria protested.

When Mauritania signed a peace treaty with the Algerian-backed Polisario Front in August 1979, Morocco occupied and assumed administrative control of the southern part of the Western Sahara, in addition to the northern part it already occupied. Under pressure from other African leaders, Hassan agreed in mid-1981 to a cease-fire with a referendum under international supervision to decide the fate of the Sahara territory, but the referendum was never carried out.

King Hassan became the second Arab leader to meet with an Israeli leader when, on July 21, 1986, Israeli Prime Minister Shimon Peres came to Morocco. Libyan criticism of the meeting led to King Hassan's abrogation of the treaty with Libya.

Morocco became the first Arab state to condemn the 1990 Iraqi invasion of Kuwait and promised to send an 1,100-men contingent to Saudi Arabia. Public opinion, however, as evidenced by sanctioned marches in Rabat, mounted against Moroccan involvement and demanded withdrawal from the U.S.-led alliance.

The opposition was victorious in June 1993 parliamentary elections, although observers believed King Hassam's rule was secure owing to the need for a coalition and the limited powers of the Assembly.

Although tensions rose with Algeria, Morocco established low-level relations with Israel in September 1994.

In May 1995 the U.N. Security Council extended the mandate for U.N. forces in the Western Sahara by one month. In late June the Polisario rebels pulled out of a U.N.-sponsored voter registration program.

MOZAMBIQUE

Republic of Mozambique
President: Joaquim Chissano (1986)
Prime Minister: Dr. Pasejal Mocumbi (1994)
Area: 303,073 sq mi. (799,380 sq km)
Population (est. mid-1995): 17,400,000 (average annual rate of natural increase: 2.7%); birth rate: 45/1000; infant mortality rate: 148/1000; density per square mile: 57.4
Capital and largest city (1991 est.): Maputo, 931,591; **Monetary unit:** Metical; **Languages:** Portuguese (official), Bantu languages; **Religions:** traditional, 60%; Christian, 30%; Islam, 10%; **National name:** República de Moçambique; **Literacy rate:** 33%
Economic summary: Gross domestic product (1993 est.): $9.8 billion; $600 per capita; real growth rate 4.1%;

inflation 40%; unemployment (1989 est.) 50%. Arable land: 4%. Principal agricultural products: cotton, cashew nuts, sugar, tea, shrimp. Labor force: 90% in agriculture. Major industrial products: processed foods, petroleum products, beverages, textiles, tobacco. Natural resources: coal, titanium. Exports: $164.4 million (f.o.b., 1993 est.). Imports: $1.03 billion (c.i.f., 1993 est.) incl. aid: food, clothing, farm equipment, petroleum. Major trading partners: U.S., Western Europe, Japan, C.I.S. countries.

Geography. Mozambique stretches for 1,535 miles (2,470 km) along Africa's southeast coast. It is nearly twice the size of California. Tanzania is to the north; Malawi, Zambia, and Zimbabwe to the west; and South Africa and Swaziland to the south.

The country is generally a low-lying plateau broken up by 25 sizable rivers that flow into the Indian Ocean. The largest is the Zambezi, which provides access to central Africa. The principal ports are Maputo and Beira, which is the port for Zimbabwe.

Government. After having been under Portuguese colonial rule for 470 years, Mozambique became independent on June 25, 1975. The first President, Samora Moises Machel, headed the National Front for the Liberation of Mozambique (FRELIMO) in its 10-year guerrilla war for independence. He died in a plane crash on Oct. 19, 1986, and was succeeded by his Foreign Minister, Joaquim Chissano.

History. Mozambique was discovered by Vasco da Gama in 1498, although the Arabs had penetrated into the area as early as the 10th century. It was first colonized in 1505, and by 1510, the Portuguese had control of all the former Arab sultanates on the east African coast.

FRELIMO was organized in 1963. Guerrilla activity had become so extensive by 1973 that Portugal was forced to dispatch 40,000 troops to fight the rebels. A cease-fire was signed in September 1974, when Portugal agreed to grant Mozambique independence.

On Jan. 25, 1985, Mozambique's celebration of a decade of independence from Portugal was not a happy one. The government was locked in a five-year-old, stalemated, paralyzing war with anti-government guerrillas, known as the MNR, backed by the white minority government in South Africa.

President Chissano decided to abandon Marxism-Leninism in 1989. A new constitution was drafted calling for three branches of government and granting civil liberties.

A cease-fire agreement was signed in October 1992 between the government and the MNR to end 16 years of civil war.

In April 1994 the president announced that a multiparty general election would be held in late October. On the first day of balloting the opposition leader declared that he and his party would boycott the process, but he changed his mind the next day. Although he lost the presidency to the incumbent the main opposition party made a very respectable showing.

MYANMAR

Union of Myanmar
Head of State (Chairman): Senior Gen. Than Shwe (1992)
Area: 261,220 sq mi. (676,560 sq km)

Population (est. mid-1995): 44,800,000 (average annual rate of natural increase: 1.9%); birth rate: 28/1000; infant mortality rate: 48/1000; density per square mile: 171.5
Capital: Yangon; **Largest cities (est. 1983):** Yangon, 2,458,712; Mandalay, 532,895; **Monetary unit:** Kyat;
Language: Myanmar, minority languages; **Religions:** Buddhist, 89.5%; Christian, 4.9%; Muslim, 3.8%; Hindu, 0.05%; Animist, 1.3%. **National name:** Pyidaungsu Myanmar Naingngandau; **Literacy rate:** 81%
Economic summary: Gross domestic product (1993 est.): $41 billion; $950 per capita; real growth rate 5%; inflation 30%. Arable land: 15%. Principal products: oilseed, pulses, sugar cane, corn, rice. Labor force (FY89 est.): 16,036,000: 65.2% agriculture, 14.3% industry. Major products: textiles, footwear, processed agricultural products, wood and wood products, refined petroleum. Natural resources: timber, tin, antimony, zinc, copper, precious stones, crude oil and natural gas. Exports (FY93): $613.4 million: rice, teak, oilseeds, metals, rubber, gems. Imports (FY93): $1.02 billion: machinery, transportation equipment, chemicals, food products. Major trading partners: Japan, E.U., China, Singapore, Thailand, India, Hong Kong, Malaysia.

Geography. Myanmar occupies the northwest portion of the Indochinese peninsula. India lies to the northwest and China to the northeast. Bangladesh, Laos, and Thailand are also neighbors. The Bay of Bengal touches the southwestern coast.

Slightly smaller than Texas, the country is divided into three natural regions: the Arakan Yoma, a long, narrow mountain range forming the barrier between Myanmar and India; the Shan Plateau in the east, extending southward into Tenasserim; and the Central Basin, running down to the flat fertile delta of the Irrawaddy in the south. This delta contains a network of intercommunicating canals and nine principal river mouths.

Government. A military regime. On March 2, 1962, the government of U Nu was overthrown and replaced by a Revolutionary Council, which assumed all power in the state. Gen. U Ne Win, as chairman of the Revolutionary Council, became the chief executive. In 1972, Ne Win and his colleagues resigned their military titles. In 1974, Ne Win dissolved the Revolutionary Council and became President under the new Constitution. He voluntarily relinquished the presidency on Nov. 9, 1981. A military coup led by Gen. Saw Maung overthrew the civilian government in 1988.

In 1989, the military government changed the name of Burma to Myanmar.

On April 23, 1992, Senior Gen. Saw Maung handed over the power to Senior General Than Shwe, who continued to take the responsibility of the Chairman of the State Law and Order Restoration Council. The State Law and Order Restoration Council (SLORC) is a military government and is made up of the Chairman and 20 other members.

History. In 1612, the British East India Company sent agents to Burma, but the Burmese long resisted efforts of British traders, and Dutch and Portuguese as well, to establish posts on the Bay of Bengal. By the Anglo-Burmese War in 1824–26 and two following wars, the British East India Company expanded to the whole of Burma by 1886. Burma was annexed to India. It became a separate colony in 1937.

During World War II, Burma was a key battleground; the 800-mile Burma Road was the Allies' vital supply line to China. The Japanese invaded the country in December 1941, and by May 1942 had occupied most of it, cutting off the Burma Road. After one of the most difficult campaigns of the war, Allied forces liberated most of Burma prior to the Japanese surrender in August 1945.

Burma became independent on Jan. 4, 1948. In 1951 and 1952 the Socialists achieved power, and Burma became the first Asian country to introduce social legislation.

In 1968, after the government had made headway against the Communist and separatist rebels, the military regime adopted a policy of strict nonalignment and followed "the Burmese Way" to socialism. But the insurgents continued active.

In July 1988, Ne Win announced his resignation from the Burmese Socialist Program Party (BSPP), the only legal political party.

The civilian government was overthrown in Sept. 1988 by a military junta led by General Saw Maung, an associate of U Ne Win.

The new government held elections in May 1990 and the opposition National League for Democracy won in a landslide despite its leaders being in jail or under house arrest.

Under increasing international pressure and economic failure Saw Maung resigned in April 1992. In September martial law was lifted.

The ruling junta in July 1993 extended the house arrest of Nobel Peace Prize winner Aung San Suu Kyi. She was released on July 10, 1995 after being confined for almost six years.

A new constitution was drafted in 1994 that called for an elected executive branch.

NAMIBIA

President: Sam Nujoma (1990)
Status: Independent Country
Area: 318,261 sq mi. (824,296 sq km)
Population (est. mid-1995): 1,500,000 (average annual growth rate: 2.7%); birth rate: 37/1000; infant mortality rate: 57/1000; density per square mile: 4.71
Capital and largest city (est. 1991): Windhoek, 144,558; **Summer capital (est. 1980):** Swakopmund, 17,500;
Monetary unit: Namibian dollars. **Languages:** Afrikaans, German, English (official), several indigenous;
Religion: Predominantly Christian; **National name:** Republic of Namibia; **Literacy rate:** 58%
Economic summary: Gross domestic product (1993 est.): $3.85 billion; $2,500 per capita; real growth rate 3.5%; inflation 17.9% (1992, urban area); unemployment (1992) 30%. Arable land: 1%. Principal products: corn, millet, sorghum, livestock. Labor force: 500,000; 60% in agriculture, 19% in industry and commerce. Major products: canned meat, dairy products, tanned leather, textiles, clothing. Natural resources: diamonds, copper, lead, zinc, uranium, fish. Exports: $1.289 billion (f.o.b., 1992 est.): diamonds, copper, lead, zinc, beef cattle, karakul pelts, marble, semi-precious stones, uranium, beef, gold. Imports: $1.178 billion (f.o.b., 1992 est.): construction materials, fertilizer, grain, foodstuffs, petroleum products and fuel. Major trading partners: South Africa, France, Germany, Switzerland, U.S., Japan.

Geography. Namibia, bounded on the north by Angola and Zambia and on the east by Botswana and South Africa in the south. The Portuguese explorer Bartholomius Diaz was the first European to visit Namibia in the late 15th century. It is for the most part a portion of the high plateau of southern Africa with a general elevation of from 3,000 to 4,000 feet.

Government. Namibia became independent in 1990 after its new constitution was ratified. A multi-party democracy with an independent judiciary was established. There is a bicameral legislature consisting of a 26 seat National Council and a 72 seat National Assembly.

History. The territory became a German colony in 1884 but was taken by South African forces in 1915, becoming a South African mandate by the terms of the Treaty of Versailles in 1920.

South Africa's application for incorporation of the territory was rejected by the U.N. General Assembly in 1946 and South Africa was invited to prepare a trusteeship agreement instead. By a law passed in 1949, however, the territory was brought into much closer association with South Africa—including representation in its Parliament.

In 1969, South Africa extended its laws to the mandate over the objection of the U.N., particularly its black African members. When South Africa refused to withdraw them, the Security Council condemned it.

Under a 1974 Security Council resolution, South Africa was required to begin the transfer of power to the Namibians by May 30, 1975, or face U.N. action, but 10 days before the deadline Prime Minister Balthazar J. Vorster rejected U.N. supervision. He said, however, that his government was prepared to negotiate Namibian independence, but not with the South-West African People's Organization, the principal black separatist group. Meanwhile, the all-white legislature of South-West Africa eased several laws on apartheid in public places.

Despite international opposition, the Turnhalle Conference in Windhoek drafted a constitution to organize an interim government based on racial divisions, a proposal overwhelmingly endorsed by white voters in the territory in 1977. At the urging of ambassadors of the five Western members of the Security Council—the U.S., Britain, France, West Germany, and Canada—South Africa on June 11 announced rejection of the Turnhalle constitution and acceptance of the Western proposal to include the South-West Africa People's Organization (SWAPO) in negotiations.

Although negotiations continued between South Africa, the western powers, neighboring black African states, and internal political groups, there was still no agreement on a final independence plan. A new round of talks aimed at resolving the 18-year-old conflict ended in a stalemate on July 25, 1984.

As policemen wielding riot sticks charged demonstrators in a black, South-West Africa township, South Africa handed over limited powers to a new, multiracial administration in the former German colony on June 17, 1985. Installation of the new government ended South Africa's direct rule, but South Africa retained an effective veto over the new government's decisions along with responsibility for the territory's defense and foreign policy, and South Africa's efforts to quell the insurgents seeking independence continued.

An agreement between South Africa, Angola, and Cuba arranged for elections for a Constituent Assembly in Nov. 1989 to establish a new government. SWAPO won 57% of the vote, a majority but not enough to dictate a constitution unilaterally. In February 1990, SWAPO leader Sam Nujoma was elected President and took office when Namibia became independent on March 21, 1990.

SWAPO received a commanding vote in the December 1992 regional and local elections. The Namibian dollar was introduced in September 1993. Owing to the poor harvest of 1992 the country received World Food Program aid in 1993.

In December 1994 elections SWAPO obtained an overwhelming mandate winning not only the presidency again for the incumbent but also absolute control of the parliament.

NAURU

Republic of Nauru
President: Bernard Dowiyogo (1989)
Area: 8.2 sq mi. (21 sq km)
Population (est. mid-1994): 10,019; average annual growth rate: 1.33%; birth rate 18/1000; infant mortality rate 40.6/1000; density per square mile: 1,221.8
Capital (1983): Yaren, 559; **Monetary unit:** Australian dollar; **Languages:** Nauruan and English; **Religions:** Protestant, 58%; Roman Catholic, 24%; Confucian and Taoist, 8%; **Special relationship within the Commonwealth of Nations; Literacy rate:** 99%
Economic summary: Gross national product (1989): more than $90 million; $10,000 per capita. Major industrial products: phosphates. Natural resources: phosphates. Exports: $93 million (f.o.b., 1984): phosphates. Imports: $73 million (c.i.f., 1984): foodstuffs, fuel, machinery. Major trading partners: Australia, New Zealand, U.K., Japan.

Geography. Nauru (pronounced NAH oo roo) is an island in the Pacific just south of the equator, about 2,500 miles (4,023 km) southwest of Honolulu.

Government. Legislative power is invested in a popularly elected 18-member Parliament, which elects the President from among its members. Executive power rests with the President, who is assisted by a five-member Cabinet.

History. Nauru was annexed by Germany in 1888. It was placed under joint Australian, New Zealand, and British mandate after World War I, and in 1947 it became a U.N. trusteeship administered by the same three powers. On Jan. 31, 1968, Nauru became an independent republic.

In elections on December 9, 1989, Bernard Dowiyogo was elected and took office three days later.

In 1993 Australia offered an out of court settlement for damages Nauru presented to the International Court of Justice because of phosphate mining. Australia agreed to pay $2.5 million Australian dollars for 20 years, and New Zealand and the U.K. additionally agreed to pay a one-time settlement of $12 million each.

NEPAL

Kingdom of Nepal
Ruler: King Birendra Bir Bikram Shah Dev (1972)
Prime Minister: Man Mohan Adhikari (1994)
Area: 54,463 sq mi. (141,059 sq km)
Population (est. mid-1995): 22,600,000 (average annual rate of natural growth: 2.4%); birth rate: 38/1000; infant mortality rate: 102/1000; density per square mile: 414.9
Capital and largest city (1991): Kathmandu, 414,264; **Monetary unit:** Nepalese rupee; **Languages:** Nepali (official), Newari, Bhutia, Maithali; **Religions:** Hindu, 90%; Buddhist, 5%; Islam, 3%; **Literacy rate:** 36%
Economic summary: Gross domestic product (1993 est.): $20.5 billion; $1,000 per capita; real growth rate 2.9% (FY93); inflation (Sept. 93) 9%; unemployment (1987) 5%. Arable land: 17%. Labor force: 4,100,000. Principal products: rice, maize, wheat, millet, jute, sugar cane, oilseed, potatoes. Agriculture is the mainstay of the economy accounting for 60% of the GDP and 90% of the work force. Major products: sugar, textiles, jute, cigarettes, cement. Natural resources: water, timber, hydroelectric potential. Exports: $369 million (f.o.b., FY93 est.): clothing, carpets, leather goods, grain. Imports: $789 million (c.i.f., FY93 est.): petroleum products, fertilizer, machinery. Major trading partners: India, Japan, U.S., Europe.

Geography. A landlocked country the size of Arkansas, lying between India and the Tibetan Autonomous Region of China, Nepal contains Mount Everest (29,108 ft; 8,872 m), the tallest mountain in the world. Along its southern border, Nepal has a strip of level land that is partly forested, partly cultivated. North of that is the slope of the main section of the Himalayan range, including Everest and many other peaks higher than 20,000 feet (6,096 m).

Government. In November, 1990, King Birendra promulgated a new constitution and introduced a multiparty democracy in Nepal. In the general elections held in November 1994, the Nepal Communist Party (NML) emerged as the single largest party with 88 seats and formed a minority government headed by Prime Minister Man Mohan Adhikari on Nov. 30, 1994. Parliament consists of two houses: the higher with 60 members and a lower house with 205.

History. The Kingdom of Nepal was unified in 1768 by King Prithwi Narayan Shah. A commercial treaty was signed with Britain in 1792, and in 1816, after more than a year's hostilities, the Nepalese agreed to allow British residents to live in Katmandu, the capital. In 1923, Britain recognized the absolute independence of Nepal. Between 1846 and 1951, the country was ruled by the Rana family, which always held the office of prime minister. In 1951, however, the King took over all power and proclaimed a constitutional monarchy.

Mahendra Bir Bikram Shah became King in 1955. After Mahendra, who had ruled since 1955, died of a heart attack in 1972, Prince Birendra, at 26, succeeded to the throne.

In the first election in 22 years, on May 2, 1980, voters approved the continued autocratic rule by the King with the advice of a partyless Parliament. The King, however, permitted the election of a new legislature, in May 1986, to which the Prime Minister and Cabinet are responsible.

In 1990, pro-democracy movement forced King Birendra to lift the ban on political parties and appoint an opposition leader to head an interim government as Prime Minister.

The first free election in three decades provided a victory for the liberal Nepali Congress Party in 1991, although the Communists made a strong showing.

Parliamentary elections held in November 1994 placed the Communists in control of 88 seats in the House of Representatives. The Communist leader became prime minister later that month. In December he won a vote of confidence after the opposition decided not to risk another election.

THE NETHERLANDS

Kingdom of the Netherlands

Sovereign: Queen Beatrix (1980)
Premier: Win Kok (1994)
Area: 16,033 sq mi. (41,526 sq km)
Population (est. mid-1995): 15,500,000 (average annual rate of natural increase: 0.4%); birth rate: 13/1000; infant mortality rate: 5.9/1000; density per square mile: 966.7
Capital: Amsterdam; seat of government: The Hague; **Largest cities (est. 1993):** Amsterdam, 713,400; Rotterdam, 596,000; The Hague, 444,660; Utrecht, 234,170; Eindhoven, 195,267. **Monetary unit:** Guilder; **Language:** Dutch; **Religions:** Roman Catholic, 36%; Protestant, 27%; other, 4%; unaffiliated, 33%; **National name:** Koninkrijk der Nederlanden; **Literacy rate:** 99%
Economic summary: Gross domestic product (1993): $262.8 billion; $17,200 per capita; real growth rate –0.2%; inflation 3.5% (1992 est.); unemployment 9.1% (March 94). Arable land: 25%. Principal products: wheat, barley, sugar beets, potatoes, meat and dairy products. Labor force: 6,955,000; 50.1% in services, 28.2% in manufacturing and construction. Major products: metal fabrication, electrical machinery and equipment, chemicals, electronic equipment, petroleum, fishing. Exports: $139 billion (f.o.b., 1992): foodstuffs, natural gas, chemicals, metal products, textiles, tobacco, agricultural products. Imports: $130.3 billion (f.o.b., 1992): raw materials, consumer goods, transportation equipment, food products, crude petroleum. Major trading partners: Germany, Belgium–Luxembourg, France, U.K., U.S.

Geography. The Netherlands, on the coast of the North Sea, has Germany to the east and Belgium to the south. It is twice the size of New Jersey.

Part of the great plain of north and west Europe, the Netherlands has maximum dimensions of 190 by 160 miles (360 by 257 km) and is low and flat except in Limburg in the southeast, where some hills rise to 300 feet (92 m). About half the country's area is below sea level, making the famous Dutch dikes a requisite to the use of much land. Reclamation of land from the sea through dikes has continued through recent times.

All drainage reaches the North Sea, and the principal rivers—Rhine, Maas (Meuse), and Schelde—have their sources outside the country. The Rhine is the most heavily used waterway in Europe.

Government. The Netherlands and its former colony of the Netherlands Antilles form the Kingdom of the Netherlands.

The Netherlands is a constitutional monarchy with a bicameral Parliament. The Upper Chamber has 75 members elected for six years by representative bodies of the provinces, half of the members retiring every three years. The Lower Chamber has 150 members elected by universal suffrage for four years. The two Chambers have the right of investigation and interpellation; the Lower Chamber can initiate legislation and amend bills.

The Sovereign, Queen Beatrix Wilhelmina Armgard, born Jan. 31, 1938, was married on March 10, 1966, to Claus von Amsberg, a former West German diplomat. The marriage drew public criticism because of the bridegroom's service in the German army during World War II. In 1967, Beatrix gave birth to a son, Willem-Alexander Claus George Ferdinand, the first male heir to the throne since 1884. She also has two other sons, Johan Friso Bernhard Christian David, born in 1968, and Constantijn Christof Frederik Aschwin, born the next year.

History. Julius Caesar found the low-lying Netherlands inhabited by Germanic tribes—the Nervii, Frisii, and Batavi. The Batavi on the Roman frontier did not submit to Rome's rule until 13 B.C., and then only as allies.

A part of Charlemagne's empire in the 8th and 9th centuries A.D., the area later passed into the hands of Burgundy and the Austrian Hapsburgs, and finally in the 16th century came under Spanish rule.

When Philip II of Spain suppressed political liberties and the growing Protestant movement in the Netherlands, a revolt led by William of Orange broke out in 1568. Under the Union if Utrecht (1579), the seven northern provinces became the Republic of the United Netherlands.

The Dutch East India Company was established in 1602, and by the end of the 17th century Holland was one of the great sea and colonial powers of Europe.

The nation's independence was not completely established until after the Thirty Years' War (1618–48), after which the country's rise as a commercial and maritime power began. In 1814, all the provinces of Holland and Belgium were merged into one kingdom, but in 1830 the southern provinces broke away to form the Kingdom of Belgium. A liberal Constitution was adopted by the Netherlands in 1848.

In spite of its neutrality in World War II, the Netherlands was invaded by the Nazis in May 1940, and the East Indies were later taken by the Japanese. The nation was liberated in May 1945. In 1948, after a reign of 50 years, Queen Wilhelmina resigned and was succeeded by her daughter Juliana.

In 1949, after a four-year war, the Netherlands granted independence to the East Indies, which became the Republic of Indonesia. In 1963, it turned over the western half of New Guinea to the new nation, ending 300 years of Dutch presence in Asia. Attainment of independence by Suriname on Nov. 25, 1975, left the Dutch Antilles as the Netherlands' only overseas territory.

Prime Minister Van Agt lost his narrow majority in elections on May 26, 1981, in which the major issue was the deployment of U.S. cruise missiles on Dutch soil. Van Agt lost his centrist coalition in May 1982 in a dispute over economic policy, and was succeeded by Ruud Lubbers as Premier.

Lubbers formed his third government, a center-left coalition, in November 1989.

A general election in May 1994 resulted in the ruling coalition of the Christian Democratic and Labor Parties losing a third of its legislative seats. Nevertheless Labor became the largest party in parliament. The Christian Democratic Party leader attempted in vain to form a government. In August the Laborite leader succeeded in forming a cabinet without a single Christian Democratic member.

Netherlands Autonomous Countries

NETHERLANDS ANTILLES

Status: Part of the Kingdom of the Netherlands
Governor: Mr. J. M. Saleh (1990)
Premier: Mingull A. Pourier
Area: 313 sq mi. (800 sq km)
Population (est. mid-1994): 190,000 (average annual growth rate: 0.4%); birth rate: 19/1000; infant mortality rate: 6.3/1000; density per square mile: 607
Capital (est. 1985): Willemstad, 125,000; **Literacy rate:** 95%

Economic summary: Gross domestic product (1993 est.): $1.8 billion; $9,700 per capita; real growth rate 2%; inflation 2%; unemployment 16.4% (1991 est.). Arable land: 8%. Principal agricultural products: aloes, sorghum, peanuts. Labor force: 89,000; 28% industry and commerce (1983). Major industries: oil refining, tourism. Natural resource: phosphate. Export: $240 million (f.o.b., 1993): petroleum products. Imports: $1.2 billion (f.o.b. 1993): crude petroleum, food. Major trading partners: U.S., Venezuela, Netherlands, U.K., Guadeloupe.

Geography. The Netherlands Antilles comprise two groups of Caribbean islands 500 miles (805 km) apart: one, about 40 miles (64 km) off the Venezuelan coast, consists of Curaçao (173 sq mi.; 448 sq km), Bonaire (95 sq mi.; 246 sq km), the other, lying to the northeast, consists of three small islands with a total area of 34 square miles (88 sq km).

Government. There is a constitutional government formed by the Governor and Cabinet and an elected Legislative Council. The area has complete autonomy in domestic affairs.

ARUBA

Status: Part of the Kingdom of the Netherlands
Governor: F. B. Tromp
Prime Minister: Nelson Oduber
Area: 75 sq mi. (193 sq km)
Population: (est. mid-994): 65,545; growth rate 0.65%; birth rate: 14.9/1000; infant mortality rate 8..4/1000; density per square mile: 873.9
Capital and largest city: (1991 est.): Oranjestad, 20,050; **Literacy rate:** 95%
Economic summary: Gross domestic product (1993 est.): $1.2 billion; $17,400 per capita; real growth rate 5%; inflation 6.5%; unemployment 0.6% (1992). Little agriculture. Major industries: tourism, light manufacturing (tobacco, beverages, consumer goods. Exports: $1.3 billion (f.o.b., 1993): mostly petroleum products. Imports: $1.6 billion (f.o.b., 1993): food, consumer goods, manufacturers. Major trading partners: U.S., E.C.

Geography. Aruba, an island slightly larger than Washington D.C., lies 18 miles (28.9 km) off the coast of Venezuela in the southern Caribbean.

Government. The governmental structure comprises the Governor, appointed by the Queen for a term of six years; the Legislature consisting of 21 members elected by universal suffrage for terms not exceeding four years; and the Council of Ministers, presided over by the Prime Minister, which holds executive power.

NEW ZEALAND

Sovereign: Queen Elizabeth II
Governor-General: Dame Catherine Tizard (1990)
Prime Minister: Rt. Hon. James Brendan Bolger
Area: 103,884 sq mi. (270,534 sq km) (excluding dependencies)
Population (est. mid-1995): 3,500,000 (average annual growth rate: 0.9%); birth rate: 16/1000; infant mortality rate: 6.9/1000; density per square mile: 33.6

Capital: Wellington; **Largest cities (est. 1993):** Auckland, 910,200; Wellington, 326,900; Christchurch, 312,600.
Monetary unit: New Zealand dollar; **Languages:** English, Maori; **Religions:** Christian, 81%; none or unspecified, 18%; Hindu, Confucian, and other, 1%; **Member of Commonwealth of Nations; Literacy rate:** 99%
Economic summary: Gross domestic product (1993): $53 billion; $15,700 per capita; real growth rate 3%; inflation 2%; unemployment (Sept. 1993) 9.1%. Arable land: 2%. Principal products: wool, meat, dairy products, livestock. Labor force (June 1993): 1,640,000; services 67.4%; manufacturing 19.8%. Major products: processed foods, textiles, machinery, transport equipment, wood and paper products, financial services. Natural resources: forests, natural gas, iron ore, coal, gold. Exports: $10.3 billion (FY93): meat, dairy products, wool. Imports: $9.4 billion (FY93): consumer goods, petroleum, motor vehicles, industrial equipment. Major trading partners: Japan, Australia, E.U., U.S., China, South Korea, Taiwan.

Geography. New Zealand, about 1,250 miles (2,012 km) southeast of Australia, consists of two main islands and a number of smaller, outlying islands so scattered that they range from the tropical to the antarctic. The country is the size of Colorado.

New Zealand's two main components are North Island and South Island, separated by Cook Strait, which varies from 16 to 190 miles (26 to 396 km) in width. North Island (44,281 sq mi.; 115,777 sq km) is 515 miles (829 km) long and volcanic in its south-central part. This area contains many hot springs and beautiful geysers. South Island (58,093 sq mi.; 151,215 sq km) has the Southern Alps along its west coast, with Mount Cook (12,283.3 ft; 3,754 m) the highest point.

The largest of the outlying islands are the Auckland Islands (234 sq mi.; 606 sq km), Campbell Island (44 sq mi.; 114 sq km), the Antipodes Islands (24 sq mi.; 62 sq km), and the Kermadec Islands (13 sq mi.; 34 sq km).

Government. New Zealand was granted self government in 1852, a full parliamentary system and ministries in 1856, and dominion status in 1907. The Queen is represented by the Governor-General, and the Cabinet is responsible to a unicameral Parliament of 99 members who are elected by popular vote for three years.

New Zealand voted in a referendum (1993) for the mixed member system of proportional representation which will replace the present system in the 1996 general election.

History. New Zealand was discovered and named in 1642 by Abel Tasman, a Dutch navigator. Captain James Cook explored the islands in 1769. In 1840, Britain formally annexed them.

From the first, the country has been in the forefront in instituting social welfare legislation. It adopted old age pensions (1898); a national child welfare program (1907); social security for the aged, widows, and orphans, along with family benefit payments; minimum wages; a 40-hour week and unemployment and health insurance (1938); and socialized medicine (1941).

In the general elections of October 1990 the opposition National Party captured 49% of the vote, winning a 39-seat majority in Parliament.

The outcome of the November 1993 general election resulted in the governing National Party winning a bare majority of 50 seats to Labour's 45. Political maneuvering in 1994 kept the National Party with a majority despite anxious by-elections.

Cook Islands and Overseas Territories

The Cook Islands (93 sq mi.; 241 sq km) were placed under New Zealand administration in 1901. They achieved self-governing status in association with New Zealand in 1965. Population (July 1994 est.): 19,124; growth rate 1.15%; birth rate: 23.2/1000; density per square mile: 205.6. The seat of government is on Rarotonga Island.

Economic summary: Gross domestic product (1993 est.): $57 million; $3,000 per capita. Exports: $3.4 million (f.o.b., 1990): citrus juice, clothing, canned fruit, and pineapple juice. Imports: $50 million (c.i.f., 1990): foodstuffs, textiles, fuels, timber. Nearly all of the trade is with New Zealand, some with Japan, Australia, and U.S.

Niue (100 sq mi.; 259 sq km) was formerly administered as part of the Cook Islands. It was placed under separate New Zealand administration in 1901 and achieved self-governing status in association with New Zealand in 1974. The capital is Alofi. **Population (July 1994 est.):** 1,906; growth rate 3.66%. **Economic summary:** Gross national product (1989 est.): $2.1 million; per capita, $1,000. Exports: $175,274 (f.o.b., 1985): canned coconut cream, copra, honey, passion fruit products, pawpaw, root crops, limes, footballs, stamps, handicrafts. Imports: $3.8 million: food, live animals, manufactured goods, machinery, fuels, chemicals, lubricants, drugs. Major trading partners: New Zealand, 59%; Fiji, 20%; Japan, 13%.

The Ross Dependency (160,000 sq mi.; 414,400 sq km), an Antarctic region, was placed under New Zealand administration in 1923.

Tokelau (4 sq mi.; 10 sq km) was formerly administered as part of the Gilbert and Ellice Islands colony. It was placed under New Zealand administration in 1925. Its population is about 1,600.

NICARAGUA

Republic of Nicaragua
President: Violeta Barrios de Chamorro (1990)
Area: 50,180 sq mi. (130,000 sq km)
Population (est. mid-1995): 4,400,000 (average annual rate of natural increase: 2.7%); birth rate: 33/1000; infant mortality rate: 49/1000; density per sq mi.: 87.6
Capital and largest city (est. 1992): Managua, 974,000; **Monetary unit:** Cordoba; **Language:** Spanish; **Religion:** Roman Catholic, 95%; Protestant, 5%; **National name:** República de Nicaragua; **Literacy rate:** 57%
Economic summary: Gross domestic product (1993 est.): $6.4 billion; $1,600 per capita; real growth rate –0.5%; inflation 20%. Arable land: 9%. Principal products: cotton, coffee, sugar cane, rice, corn, beans, cattle. Labor force: 1,086,000; 13% in industry (1986). Major products: processed foods, chemicals, metal products, clothing and textiles, beverages, footwear. Natural resources: timber, fisheries, gold, silver, copper, tungsten, lead, zinc. Exports: $228 million (f.o.b., 1992): coffee, cotton, seafood, bananas, sugar, meat, chemicals. Imports: $907 million (c.i.f., 1992): machinery, chemicals, food, clothing, petroleum. Major trading partners: E.U., U.S., Japan, Costa Rica, El Salvador, Mexico, Venezuela, Guatemala.

Geography. Largest but most sparsely populated of the Central American nations, Nicaragua borders on Honduras to the north and Costa Rica to the south. It is slightly larger than New York State.

Nicaragua is mountainous in the west, with fertile valleys. A plateau slopes eastward toward the Caribbean.

Two big lakes—Nicaragua, about 100 miles long (161 km), and Managua, about 38 miles long (61 km)—are connected by the Tipitapa River. The Pacific coast is volcanic and very fertile. The Caribbean coast, swampy and indented, is aptly called the "Mosquito Coast."

Government. A republic. The president is chief of state and head of government. The National Assembly is the legislative branch.

History. Nicaragua, which established independence in 1838, was first visited by the Spaniards in 1522. The chief of the country's leading Indian tribe at that time was called Nicaragua, from whom the nation derived its name. A U.S. naval force intervened in 1909 after two American citizens had been executed, and a few U.S. Marines were kept in the country from 1912 to 1925. The Bryan-Chamorro Treaty of 1916 (terminated in 1970) gave the U.S. an option on a canal route through Nicaragua, and naval bases. Disorder after the 1924 elections brought in the marines again.

A guerrilla leader, Gen. César Augusto Sandino, began fighting the occupation force in 1927. He fought the U.S. troops until their withdrawal in 1933. Gen. Anastasio Somoza García emerged and ruled as dictator from 1936 until his assassination in 1956. He was succeeded by his son Luis, who alternated with trusted family friends in the presidency until his death in 1967. Another son, Maj. Gen. Anastasio Somoza Debayle, became President in 1967.

Sandinista guerrillas, leftists who took their name from Gen. Sandino, launched an offensive in May 1979. After seven weeks of fighting, Somoza fled the country on July 17, 1979. The Sandinistas assumed power on July 19, promising to maintain a mixed economy, a non-aligned foreign policy, and a pluralist political system.

On Jan. 23, 1981, the Reagan Administration suspended U.S. aid, charging that Nicaragua, with the aid of Cuba and the Soviet Union, was supplying arms to rebels in El Salvador. The Sandinistas denied the charges. Later that year, Nicaraguan guerrillas known as "contras," began a war to overthrow the Sandinistas.

The elections were finally held on Nov. 4, 1984, with Daniel Ortega Saavedra, the Sandinista junta coordinator, winning 63% of the votes cast for President. He began a six-year term on Jan. 10, 1985.

The war intensified in 1986–87, with the re-supplied contras establishing themselves inside the country. Negotiations sponsored by the Contadora (neutral Latin American) nations, but a peace plan sponsored by Arias, the Costa Rican president, led to a treaty signed by the Central American leaders in August 1987, that called for an end to outside aid to guerrillas and negotiations between hostile parties.

In 1989, an accord established a one-year advance in general elections to Feb. 1990.

Violetta Chamorro, owner of the opposition paper *La Prensa*, led a broad anti-Sandinista coalition to victory in the presidential and legislative elections, ending 11 years of Sandinista rule.

After a year in office Pres. Chamorro found herself besieged. Business groups were dissatisfied with the pace of reforms; Sandinistas with what they regarded as the dismantling of their earlier achievements and threatened to take up arms again. In Feb. 1991 the president brought the military under her direct command.

By early 1993 relations between the president and the coalition that backed her had soured over charges of corruption and the continuing influence of the Sandinistas in the government and the army.

In February 1995 the Sandinista military leader Humberto Ortego stepped down, marking the first peaceful transfer of that position in the country's history. Nevertheless, the President and the Assembly continued their bitter quarrel, this time over rival constitutions. Finally in June the President agreed to a new package that would bolster the legislative branch at the expense of the executive.

NIGER

Republic of Niger
President: Mahamane Ousmane (1993)
Prime Minister: Hama Amadou (1994)
Area: 489,206 sq mi. (1,267,044 sq km)
Population (est. mid-1995): 9,200,000 (average annual rate of natural increase: 3.4%); birth rate: 53/1000; infant mortality rate: 123/1000; density per square mile: 18.8
Capital and largest city (1988): Niamey, 398,265; **Other large cities:** Zinder, 120,900; Maradi, 112,970; **Monetary unit:** Franc CFA; **Ethnic groups:** Hausa, 54%; Djerma and Songhai, 24%; Peul, 11%; **Languages:** French (official); Hausa, Songhai; Arabic; **Religions:** Islam, 80%; Animist and Christian, 20%; **National name:** République du Niger; **Literacy rate:** 28%
Economic summary: Gross domestic product (1993 est.): $5.4 billion; $650 per capita; real growth rate 1.9% (1991 est.); inflation: 1.3% (1991 est.). Arable land: 3%. Principal products: peanuts, cotton, livestock, millet, sorghum, cassava, rice. Labor force: 2,500,000 (1982); 90% in agriculture. Major industrial products: uranium, cement, bricks, light industrial products. Natural resources: uranium, coal, iron ore, tin, phosphates. Exports: $294 million (f.o.b., 1991): uranium, cowpeas, livestock, hides, skins. Imports: $346 million (c.i.f., 1991): fuels, machinery, transport equipment, foodstuffs, consumer goods, pharmaceuticals, chemical products. Major trading partners: France, Nigeria, Algeria, U.S., Italy, Côte d'Ivoire, Germany.

Geography. Niger, in West Africa's Sahara region, is four-fifths the size of Alaska. It is surrounded by Mali, Algeria, Libya, Chad, Nigeria, Benin, and Burkina Faso.

The Niger River in the southwest flows through the country's only fertile area. Elsewhere the land is semiarid.

Government. Niger held its first democratic elections in April 1993 and formed a new coalition government on April 23, 1993. Eighty-three representatives from its different political parties formed a national assembly. The U.S. supports the new Nigerian government and its new democratic institutions.

History. Niger was incorporated into French West Africa in 1896. There were frequent rebellions, but when order was restored in 1922, the French made the area a colony. In 1958, the voters approved the French Constitution and voted to make the territory an autonomous republic within the French Community. The republic adopted a Constitution in 1959 and the next year withdrew from the Community, proclaiming its independence.

The 1974 army coup ousted President Hamani Dio-

ri, who had held office since 1960. An estimated 2 million people were starving in Niger, but 200,000 tons of imported food, half U.S.-supplied, substantially ended famine conditions by the year's end. The new President, Lt. Col. Seyni Kountché, Chief of Staff of the army, installed a 12-man military government. A predominantly civilian government was formed by Kountché in 1976.

The country's first multiparty election in February 1993 resulted in the need for a runoff for the presidency in March. Ousmane Mahamane, the candidate of the biggest opposition party, won.

A rebellion in the north that dominated most of 1994 subsided when an agreement was struck that granted the area a limited autonomy. One of the nine coalition parties in the parliamentary majority withdrew resulting in a vote of no confidence in October. The scheduled elections for December were postponed.

NIGERIA

Federal Republic of Nigeria
Head of State: Gen. Sani Abacha (1993)
Area: 356,700 sq mi. (923,853 sq km)
Population (est. mid-1995): 101,200,000; average annual rate of natural increase: 3.1%; birth rate: 43/1000; infant mortality rate: 72/1000; density per square mile: 283.7
Capital: Abuja, 298,300; **Largest cities (est. 1993):** Lagos, 1,408,000; Ibadan, 1,328,000; Ogbomosho, 677,200; Kano, 625,500. **Monetary unit:** Naira; **Languages:** English (official) Hausa, Yoruba, Ibo; **Religions:** Islam, 50%; Christian, 40%; indigenous, 10%; **Member of Commonwealth of Nations; Literacy rate:** 51%
Economic summary: Gross domestic product (1993 est.): $95.1 billion; $1,000 per capita; real growth rate 4.1% (1992); inflation 60% (1992 est.); unemployment 28%. (1992 est.) Arable land: 31%. Principal products: peanuts, rubber, cocoa, grains, fish, yams, cassava, livestock. Labor force (1985): 42,844,000, 54% in agriculture; 15% in government; 19% in industry, commerce and services. Major products: crude oil, natural gas, coal, tin, processed rubber, cotton, petroleum, hides, textiles, cement, chemicals. Natural resources: petroleum, tin, columbite, iron ore, coal, limestone, lead. Exports: $11.9 billion (f.o.b., 1992): oil, cocoa, palm products, rubber. Imports: $8.3 billion (c.i.f., 1992): consumer goods, capital equipment, raw materials, chemicals. Major trading partners: Western European countries, U.S., Japan

Geography. Nigeria, one-third larger than Texas and black Africa's most populous nation, is situated on the Gulf of Guinea in West Africa. Its neighbors are Benin, Niger, Cameroon, and Chad.

The lower course of the Niger River flows south through the western part of the country into the Gulf of Guinea. Swamps and mangrove forests border the southern coast; inland are hardwood forests.

Government. A military government since Dec. 31, 1983. The government annulled the results of the June 12, 1993 presidential election and suspended the return to civilian rule. Gen. Sani Abacha declared himself ruler in November 1993.

History. Between 1879 and 1914, private colonial developments by the British, with reorganizations of the Crown's interest in the region, resulted in the formation of Nigeria as it exists today. During World War I, native troops of the West African frontier force joined with French forces to defeat the German garrison in the Cameroons.

Nigeria became independent on Oct. 1, 1960.

Organized as a loose federation of self-governing states, the independent nation faced an overwhelming task of unifying a country with 250 ethnic and linguistic groups.

Rioting broke out again in 1966, the military commander was seized, and Col. Yakubu Gowon took power. Also in that year, the Moslem Hausas in the north massacred the predominantly Christian Ibos in the east, many of whom had been driven from the north. Thousands of Ibos took refuge in the Eastern Region. The military government there asked Ibos to return to the region and, in May 1967, the assembly voted to secede from the federation and set up the Republic of Biafra. Civil war broke out.

In January 1970, after 31 months of civil war, Biafra surrendered to the federal government.

Gowon's nine-year rule was ended in 1975 by a bloodless coup that made Army Brigadier Muritala Rufai Mohammed the new chief of state.

The return of civilian leadership was established with the election of Alhaji Shehu Shagari, as president in 1979.

A coup on December 31, 1983, restored military rule. The military regime headed by Maj. Gen. Mohammed Buhari was overthrown in a bloodless coup on Aug. 27, 1985, led by Maj. Gen. Ibrahim Babangida, who proclaimed himself president.

The presidential election of June 1993 was almost immediately voided by the government. Nevertheless, Babangida resigned as president in August. In November the military, headed by defense minister Sani Abacha, seized power again. A constitutional conference, called in 1994 after violent political protests against the military government, set January 1, 1995, as the deadline for a return to civilian rule. The government, however, did not step aside. In June 1995 a two-year ban on political parties was lifted, but Gen. Abacha said only that in October he would give a timetable for a return to civilian rule.

NORWAY

Kingdom of Norway
Sovereign: King Harald V (1991)
Prime Minister: Gro Harlem Brundtland (1991)
Area: 125,049 sq mi. (323,877 sq km)
Population (1993): 4,324,577 (average annual growth rate: 0.3%); birth rate: 13/1000 (1994 est.); infant mortality rate: 6.3/1000 (1994 est.); density per square mile: 34.5
Capital: Oslo; **Largest cities (est. 1993):** Oslo, 473,344; Bergen, 218,105; Trondheim, 140,718. **Monetary unit:** Krone; **Language:** Norwegian; **Religion:** Evangelical Lutheran (state), 94%; other Protestant and Roman Catholic, 4%; **National name:** Kongeriket Norge; **Literacy rate:** 100%
Economic summary: Gross domestic product (1993): $89.5 billion; $20,800 per capita; real growth rate 1.6%; inflation 2.3%; unemployment 5.5% (1993 est.). Labor force (Sept. 90): 2,167,000; services, 34.7%; commerce, 18%; mining and manufacturing, 16.6%:. Arable land: 3%. Principal products: dairy products, livestock, grain, potatoes, furs, wool. Major products: oil and gas, fish, pulp and paper, ships, aluminum, iron, steel, nickel, fertilizers, transportation equipment, hydroelectric power, petrochemicals. Natural resources: fish, timber, hydroelectric power, ores, oil, gas. Exports: $32.1 billion (f.o.b., 1993): oil, natural gas, fish products, ships, pulp and paper, aluminum. Imports:

$24.8 billion (c.i.f., 1993): machinery, fuels and lubricants, transportation equipment, chemicals foodstuffs, and clothing. Major trading partners: U.K., Sweden, Germany, U.S., Denmark, Netherlands, Japan.

Geography. Norway is situated in the western part of the Scandinavian peninsula. It extends about 1,100 miles (1,770 km) from the North Sea along the Norwegian Sea to more than 300 miles (483 km) above the Arctic Circle, the farthest north of any European country. It is slightly larger than New Mexico. Sweden borders on most of the eastern frontier, with Finland and the U.S.S.R. in the northeast.

Nearly 70% of Norway is uninhabitable and covered by mountains, glaciers, moors, and rivers. The hundreds of deep fiords that cut into the coastline give Norway an overall oceanfront of more than 12,000 miles (19,312 km). Nearly 50,000 islands off the coast form a breakwater and make a safe coastal shipping channel.

Government. Norway is a constitutional hereditary monarchy. Executive power is vested in the King together with a Cabinet, or Council of State, consisting of a Prime Minister and at least seven other members. The Storting, or Parliament, is composed of 165 members elected by the people under proportional representation. The Storting discusses and votes on political and financial questions, but divides itself into two sections (Lagting and Odelsting) to discuss and pass on legislative matters. The King cannot dissolve the Storting before the expiration of its term.

The sovereign is Harald V, born in 1937, son of Olav V and Princess Martha of Sweden. He succeeded to the throne upon the death of his father in January 1991. He married Sonja Haraldsen, a daughter of a merchant, in 1968.

History. Norwegians, like the Danes and Swedes, are of Teutonic origin. The Norsemen, also known as Vikings, ravaged the coasts of northwestern Europe from the 8th to the 11th century.

In 1815, Norway fell under the control of Sweden. The union of Norway, inhabited by fishermen, sailors, merchants, and peasants, and Sweden, an aristocratic country of large estates and tenant farmers, was not a happy one, but it lasted for nearly a century. In 1905, the Norwegian Parliament arranged a peaceful separation and invited a Danish prince to the Norwegian throne—King Haakon VII. A treaty with Sweden provided that all disputes be settled by arbitration and that no fortifications be erected on the common frontier.

When World War I broke out, Norway joined with Sweden and Denmark in a decision to remain neutral and to cooperate in the joint interest of the three countries. In World War II, Norway was invaded by the Germans on April 9, 1940. It resisted for two months before the Nazis took over complete control. King Haakon and his government fled to London, where they established a government-in-exile. Maj. Vidkun Quisling, whose name is now synonymous with traitor or fifth columnist, was the most notorious Norwegian collaborator with the Nazis. He was executed by the Norwegians on Oct. 24, 1945.

Despite severe losses in the war, Norway recovered quickly. The country led the world in social experimentation. It entered the North Atlantic Treaty Organization in 1949.

The Conservative government of Jan Syse resigned in October 1990 over the issue of Norway's future relationship to the E.C. A minority Labor government headed by Gro Brundtland was installed a few days later. Norway is a member of the European Free Trade Association.

In November 1992 the parliament voted to apply to join the European Community.

In an advisory referendum held in November 1994 voters rejected seeking membership for their nation in the European Union.

Dependencies of Norway

Svalbard (24,208 sq mi.; 62,700 sq km), in the Arctic Ocean about 360 miles north of Norway, consists of the Spitsbergen group and several smaller islands, including Bear Island, Hope Island, King Charles Land, and White Island (or Gillis Land). The capital is Longyearbyen. It came under Norwegian administration in 1925. Population (July 1994 est.): 3,018; growth rate –3.5%. **Economic summary (1993):** Coal mining is major economic activity. There is also some trapping of seal, polar bear, fox, and walrus.

Bouvet Island (23 sq mi.; 60 sq km), in the South Atlantic about 1,600 miles south-southwest of the Cape of Good Hope, came under Norwegian administration in 1928. It is uninhabited.

Jan Mayen Island (147 sq mi.; 380 sq km), in the Arctic Ocean between Norway and Greenland, came under Norwegian administration in 1929. There are no permanent inhabitants.

Peter I Island (96 sq mi.; 249 sq km), lying off Antarctica in the Bellinghausen Sea, came under Norwegian administration in 1931.

Queen Maud Land, a section of Antarctica, came under Norwegian administration in 1939.

OMAN

Sultanate of Oman
Sultan: Qabus Bin Said (1970)
Area: 82,030 sq mi. (212,458 sq km)[1]
Population (est. mid-1995): 2,200,000 (average annual rate of natural increase: 4.9%); birth rate: 53/1000; infant mortality rate: 24/1000; density per square mile: 24.3
Capital and largest city (est. 1991): Muscat, 350,000;
Monetary unit: Omani Rial; **Language:** Arabic (official); also English and Indian languages; **Religion:** Islam, 95%; **National name:** Saltonat Uman; **Literacy rate:** 65.8%
Economic summary: Gross domestic product (1993 est.): $16.4 billion; $10,000 per capita; real growth rate 6.1%; inflation 2%, unemployment n.a. Principal agricultural products: dates, fruit, cereal, livestock. Labor force: 430,000; 60% in agriculture. Major industries: petroleum drilling, fishing, construction. Natural resources: oil, marble, copper, limestone. Exports: $5 billion (f.o.b., 1993): oil, 87%; reexports: fish, processed copper, textiles. Imports: $3.7 billion (f.o.b., 1993): machinery and transport equipment, food, manufactured goods, livestock, lubricants. Major trading partners: U.K., U.S., Japan, UAE, South Korea, Singapore.

1. Excluding the Kuria Muria Islands.

Geography. Oman is a 1,000-mile-long (1,700-km)

coastal plain at the southeastern tip of the Arabian peninsula lying on the Arabian Sea and the Gulf of Oman. The interior is a plateau. The country is the size of Kansas.

Government. The Sultan of Oman (formerly called Muscat and Oman), an absolute monarch, is assisted by a council of ministers, seven specialized councils, a Majllis Ashura, and personal advisers.

There are no political parties.

History. Although Oman is an independent state under the rule of the Sultan, it has been under British protection since the early 19th century.

Muscat, the capital of the geographical area known as Oman, was occupied by the Portuguese from 1508 to 1648. Then it fell to Persian princes and later was regained by the Sultan.

In a palace coup on July 23, 1970, the Sultan, Sa'id bin Taimur, who had ruled since 1932, was overthrown by his son, who promised to establish a modern government and use new-found wealth to aid the people of this very isolated state.

A long border dispute with Yemen ended in late October 1992 when the Sultan signed an agreement with the Yemeni president.

The first border post was opened on June 1, 1993 and the governments announced their intention to establish a free-trade zone.

In the first round of voting for an expanded consultative assembly called by the Sultan in November 1994, four women were elected.

PAKISTAN

Islamic Republic of Pakistan
President: Farooq Ahmad Khan Leghari (1993)
Prime Minister: Benazir Bhutto (1993)
Area: 310,400 sq mi. (803,936 sq km)[1]
Population (est. mid-1995): 129,700,000 (average annual growth rate: 2.9%); birth rate: 39/1000; infant mortality rate: 91/1000; density per square mile: 417.8
Capital (1981 census): Islamabad, 201,000; **Largest cities (1981 census for metropolitan area):** Karachi, 5,208,100; Lahore, 2,952,700; Faisalabad, (Lyallpur) 1,920,000; Rawalpindi, 920,000; Hyderabad, 795,000;
Monetary unit: Pakistan rupee; **Principal languages:** Urdu (national), English (official), Punjabi, Sindhi, Pashtu, and Baluchi; **Religions:** Islam, 97%; Hindu, Christian, Buddhist, Parsi; **Literacy rate:** 35%
Economic summary: Gross national product (1993 est.): $239 billion; $1,900 per capita; real growth rate 3%; inflation (FY91) 12.7%; unemployment (FY91 est.) 10%. Arable land: 26%. Principal products: wheat, rice, cotton, sugarcane. Labor force (1987: 28,900,000; agriculture, 54%; services, 33%. Major products: cotton textiles, processed foods, petroleum products, construction materials. Natural resources: natural gas, limited petroleum, iron ore. Exports: $6.8 billion (FY92 f.o.b.): cotton, rice, textiles, clothing. Imports: $9.1 billion (f.o.b., FY92): edible oil, crude oil, machinery, chemicals, transport equipment. Major trading partners: U.S., E.U., Japan, Hong Kong.

1. Excluding Kashmir and Jammu.

Geography. Pakistan is situated in the western part of the Indian subcontinent, with Afghanistan and Iran on the west, India on the east, and the Arabian Sea on the south. The name "Pakistan" is derived from two Persian words "Pak" (meaning pure) and "stan" (meaning country).

Nearly twice the size of California, Pakistan consists of towering mountains, including the Hindu Kush in the west, a desert area in the east, the Punjab plains in the north, and an expanse of alluvial plains. The 1,000-mile-long (1,609 km) Indus River flows through the country from the Kashmir to the Arabian Sea.

Government. Pakistan is a federal republic with a bicameral legislature—a 217-member National Assembly and an 87-member Senate.

History. Pakistan was one of the two original successor states to British India. For almost 25 years following independence in 1947, it consisted of two separate regions East and West Pakistan, but now comprises only the western sector. It consists of Sind, Baluchistan, the former North-West Frontier Province, western Punjab, the princely state of Bahawalpur, and several other smaller native states.

The British became the dominant power in the region in 1757 following Lord Clive's military victory, but rebellious tribes kept the northwest in turmoil. In the northeast, the formation of the Moslem League in 1906 estranged the Moslems from the Hindus. In 1930, the league, led by Mohammed Ali Jinnah, demanded creation of a Moslem state wherever Moslems were in the majority. He supported Britain during the war. Afterward, the league received almost a unanimous Moslem vote in 1946 and Britain agreed to the formation of Pakistan as a separate dominion.

Pakistan was proclaimed a republic March 23, 1956. The election of 1970 set the stage for civil war when Sheik Muuibur told East Pakistanis to stop paying taxes to the central government. West Pakistan troops moved in and fighting began. The independent state of Bangladesh, or Bengali nation, was proclaimed March 26, 1971. The intervention of Indian troops protected the new state and brought President Yahya Kahn down. Bhutto took over and accepted Bangladesh as an independent entity.

Diplomatically, 1976 saw the resumption of formal relations between India and Pakistan.

Pakistan's first elections under civilian rule took place in March 1977 and provoked bitter opposition protest when Bhutto's party was declared to have won 155 of the 200 elected seats in the 216-member National Assembly. A rising tide of violent protest and political deadlock led to a military takeover on July 5. Gen. Mohammed Zia ul-Haq became Chief Martial Law Administrator.

Bhutto was tried and convicted for the 1974 murder of a political opponent, and despite worldwide protests was executed on April 4, 1979, touching off riots by his supporters. Zia declared himself President on Sept. 16, 1978, a month after Fazel Elahi Chaudhry left office upon the completion of his 5-year term.

A measure of representative government was restored with the election of a new National Assembly in February 1985, although leaders of opposition parties were banned from the elections.

On December 30, 1985, Zia ended martial law.

On August 19, 1988, President Zia was killed in a mid-air explosion of a Pakistani Air Force plane.

Elections at the end of 1988 brought longtime Zia opponent Benazir Bhutto, daughter of Zulfikar Bhutto, into office as Prime Minister.

In August 1990, Pakistan's President dismissed Prime Minister Bhutto on charges of corruption and incompetence and dissolved parliament. Sharif's coalition, the Islamic Democratic Alliance, won the elections of October 1990.

In April 1993 the president dismissed the prime minister on charges of corruption and dissolved the parliament. A month later, however, the country's supreme court overturned the order. The next day parliament gave the prime minister a vote of confidence. In July, however, the army demanded a resolution of the standoff.

October 1993 elections gave a plurality of parliamentary seats to Ms. Bhutto's Pakistan People's Party, ensuring her the prime ministry. A public feud with her mother, however, began in January 1994.

Continued support for Muslims during 1994 in the disputed Kashmir insured continued violence with civilians being the main victims.

REPUBLIC OF PALAU

President: Kuniwo Nakamura (1993)
Total area: 177 sq mi. (458 sq km)
Population (July 1994 est.): 16,366 (average rate of natural increase: 1.81%); birth rate: 22/1000; infant mortality rate: 25/1000; density per square mile: 92.4.
Capital: Koror. **Monetary unit:** U.S. dollar used. **Language:** Palauan is the official language, though English is commonplace. **Ethnic divisions:** Palauans are a composite of Polynesian, Malayan, and Melanesian races. **Religion:** Christian. About one-third islanders observe Modekngei religion, indigenous to Palau. **Literacy rate:** 92%.
Economic summary: Gross domestic product (1986): $31.6 million. Note: GDP numbers reflect U.S. spending. $2,260 per capita (1986); unemployment 20% (1986). Industries: Tourism, craft items (shell, wood, pearl), some commercial fishing, and agriculture (subsistence level production of coconut, copra, cassava, sweet potatoes. Exports: $500,000 (f.o.b., 1986) trochus (a shellfish), tuna, copra, handicrafts. Imports: $27.2 million (c.i.f., 1986). Major trading partners: U.S., Japan.

Geography. The Palau island chain consists of about 200 islands located in the North Pacific Ocean 528 mi. (650 km) southeast of the Philippines. The islands vary geologically from the high mountainous main island of Babelthuap to low, coral islands usually fringed by large barrier reefs.

Government. A republic with a bicameral parliament. There is a 14-member Senate and a 16-member House of Delegates. Palau became a sovereign nation in 1994.

History. Spain held the islands for 300 years before selling them to Germany in 1899. Japan occupied Palau during WWI and received a mandate over them from the League of Nations in 1920. It remained in Japanese control and served as an important naval base until the U.S. seized it during WWII. After the war it became a U.N. trusteeship (1947) and was administered by the U.S. until 1994.

PANAMA

Republic of Panama
President: Ernesto Perez Balladares (1994)
Area: 29,761 sq mi. (77,082 sq km)
Population (est. mid-1995): 2,600,000 (average annual rate of natural increase: 2.1%); birth rate: 29/1000; infant mortality rate: 28/1000; density per square mile: 87.3

Capital and largest city (1992 est.): Panama City, 625,000; **Monetary unit:** Balboa; **Language:** Spanish (official); many bilingual in English; **Religions:** Roman Catholic, over 93%; Protestant, 6%; **National name:** República de Panamá; **Literacy rate:** 88%

Economic summary: Gross domestic product (1993 est.): $11.6 billion; $4,500 per capita; real growth rate 5.9%; inflation 1%; unemployment 12.5%. Arable land: 6%. Principal agricultural products: bananas, corn, sugar, rice, coffee. Labor force: 921,000 (1992 est.): government and community services 31.8%, agriculture, hunting, fishing 26.8%, commerce, restaurants, hotels 16.4%. Major industrial products: refined petroleum, sugar, cement, paper products. Natural resources: copper, mahogany, shrimp. Exports: $545 million (f.o.b., 1993 est.): bananas, sugar, shrimp, coffee, clothing. Imports: $2.5 billion (f.o.b., 1993 est.): petroleum, manufactured goods, machinery and transportation equipment, food, chemicals. Major trading partners: U.S., Central America and the Caribbean, Western Europe, Mexico.

Geography. The southernmost of the Central American nations, Panama is south of Costa Rica and north of Colombia. The Panama Canal bisects the isthmus at its narrowest and lowest point, allowing passage from the Caribbean Sea to the Pacific Ocean.

Panama is slightly smaller than South Carolina. It is marked by a chain of mountains in the west, moderate hills in the interior, and a low range on the east coast. There are extensive forests in the fertile Caribbean area.

Government. Panama is a centralized republic. The executive power is vested in the president and two vice presidents who exercise power jointly with a cabinet of 12 ministers of state appointed by the president. Presidents and vice presidents are elected for five-year terms and may not succeed themselves. The legislative function is exercised through the National Assembly. The legislators are elected for five-year terms by direct vote and can be reelected.

History. Visited by Columbus in 1502 on his fourth voyage and explored by Balboa in 1513, Panama was the principal transshipment point for Spanish treasure and supplies to and from South and Central America in colonial days. In 1821, when Central America revolted against Spain, Panama joined Colombia, which already had declared its independence. For the next 82 years, Panama attempted unsuccessfully to break away from Colombia. After U.S. proposals for canal rights over the narrow isthmus had been rejected by Colombia, Panama proclaimed its independence with U.S. backing in 1903.

For canal rights in perpetuity, the U.S. paid Panama $10 million and agreed to pay $250,000 each year, increased to $430,000 after devaluation of the U.S. dollar in 1933 and was further increased under a revised treaty signed in 1955. In exchange, the U.S. got the Canal Zone—a 10-mile-wide strip across the isthmus—and a considerable degree of influence in Panama's affairs.

Panama and the U.S. agreed in 1974 to negotiate the eventual reversion of the canal to Panama, despite strongly expressed opposition in the U.S. Congress. The texts of two treaties—one governing the transfer of the canal and the other guaranteeing its neutrality after transfer—were negotiated by August 1977 and were signed by Pres. Omar Torrijos Herara and President Carter in Washington on September 7. A Panamanian referendum approved the treaties by more than two thirds on October 23, but further changes

were insisted upon by the U.S. Senate.

The principal change was a reservation specifying that despite the neutrality treaty's specification that only Panama shall maintain forces in its territory after transfer of the canal Dec. 31, 1999, the U.S. should have the right to use military force to keep the canal operating if it should become obstructed. The Senate approved the treaties in March-April 1978.

Nicolas Ardito Barletta, Panama's first directly elected President in 16 years, was inaugurated on Oct. 11, 1984, for a five-year term. He lacked the necessary support to solve the country's economic crisis and resigned September 28, 1985. He was replaced by Vice President Eric Arturo Delvalle.

In June 1986, reports surfaced that the behind-the-scenes strongman, Gen. Manuel Noriega, was involved in drug trafficking and the murder of an opposition leader. In 1987, Noriega was accused by his ex-Chief of Staff of assassinating Torrijos in 1981. He was indicted in the U.S. for drug trafficking but when Delvalle attempted to fire him, he forced the National Assembly to replace Delvalle with Manuel Solis Palma.

The crisis continued when Noriega called presidential elections for when the current term expired. Despite massive fraud by Noriega, the opposition seemed headed to a landslide. Noriega annulled the elections and suppressed protests by the opposition.

In December 1989, the Assembly named Noriega the "maximum leader" and declared the U.S. and Panama to be in a state of war. A further series of incidents led to a U.S. invasion overthrowing Noriega, who was brought to the U.S. to stand trial for drug trafficking. Guillermo Endara, who probably would have won the election suppressed by Noriega, was instated as President.

A military revolt in December 1990 was easily suppressed, although the leaders eluded capture.

In elections of May 1994 a left-of-center businessman won the country's first democratic presidential election since 1968. Although Mr. Balladares is an American-educated banker his victory was viewed as a defeat for the traditional elite.

Under the terms of agreement U.S. troops of the Southern Command began leaving the country in June.

Panama Canal. First conceived by the Spaniards in 1524, when King Charles V of Spain ordered a survey of a waterway across the Isthmus, a construction concession was granted by the Colombian government in 1878 to St. Lucien N. B. Wyse, representing a French company. Two years later, the French Canal Company, inspired by Ferdinand de Lesseps, began construction of what was to have been a sea-level canal. The effort ended in bankruptcy nine years later and the United States ultimately paid the French $40 million for their rights and assets.

The U.S. project, built on territory controlled by the United States, and calling for the creation of an interior lake connected to both oceans by locks, got under way in 1904. Completed in 1914, the Canal is 50.7 miles long and lifts ships 85 feet above sea level through a series of three locks on the Pacific and Atlantic sides. Enlarged in later years, each lock now measures 1,000 feet in length, 110 feet in width, and 40 feet in depth of water.

PAPUA NEW GUINEA

Sovereign: Queen Elizabeth II
Governor General: Wiwa Korowi
Prime Minister: Sir Julius Chan (1994)

Area: 178,704 sq mi. (462,840 sq km)
Population (est. mid-1995): 4,100,000 (average annual increase: 2.3%); birth rate: 33/1000; infant mortality rate: 63/1000; density per square mile: 22.9
Capital and largest city (est. 1990): Port Moresby, 193,242; **Monetary unit:** Kina; **Languages:** English, Melanesian pidgin, Hiri Motu, and 717 distinct native languages; **Religions:** over half Christian, remainder indigenous; **Member of Commonwealth of Nations; Literacy rate:** 52%
Economic summary: Gross domestic product (1993 est.): $8.2 billion; $2,000 per capita; 1.2% real growth rate; inflation (1992–93) 4.5%; unemployment n.a. Principal products: coffee, copra, palm oil, cocoa, tea, coconuts. Major industrial products: coconut oil, plywood, wood chips, gold, silver. Natural resources: copper, gold, silver, timber, natural gas. Exports: $1.14 billion (f.o.b., 1990): gold, copper, coffee, palm oil, copra, timber, lobster. Imports: $1.18 billion (c.i.f., 1990): food, machinery, transport equipment, fuels, chemicals, consumer goods. Major trading partners: Australia, U.K., Japan, Singapore, New Zealand, U.S., South Korea.

Geography. Papua New Guinea occupies the eastern half of the island of New Guinea, just north of Australia, and many outlying islands. The Indonesian province of Irian Jaya is to the west. To the north and east are the islands of Manus, New Britain, New Ireland, and Bougainville, all part of Papua New Guinea.

Papua New Guinea is about one-tenth larger than California. Its mountainous interior has only recently been explored. The high-plateau climate is temperate, in contrast to the tropical climate of the coastal plains. Two major rivers, the Sepik and the Fly, are navigable for shallow-draft vessels.

Government. Papua New Guinea attained independence Sept. 16, 1975, ending a United Nations trusteeship under the administration of Australia. Parliamentary democracy was established by a Constitution that invests power in a 109-member national legislature.

History. The eastern half of New Guinea was first visited by Spanish and Portuguese explorers in the 16th century, but a permanent European presence was not established until 1884, when Germany declared a protectorate over the northern coast and Britain took similar action in the south. Both nations formally annexed their protectorates and, in 1901, Britain transferred its rights to a newly independent Australia. Australian troops invaded German New Guinea in World War I and retained control under a League of Nations mandate that eventually became a United Nations trusteeship, incorporating a territorial government in the southern region, known as Papua.

Australia granted limited home rule in 1951. Autonomy in internal affairs came nine years later.

In February 1990 guerrillas of the Bougainville Revolutionary Army (BRA) attacked plantations, forcing the evacuation of numerous workers. In May the BRA declared Bougainville's independence, whereupon the government blockaded the island until January 1991, when a peace treaty was signed.

A general election of June 1992 saw the defeat of the incumbent prime minister. Wingti almost simultaneously resigned and was reelected in September 1993, thereby avoiding a vote of no-confidence.

Rebel guerrillas who had occupied the Bougainville copper mine withdrew to the surrounding hills in September 1994 allowing government forces to reclaim it.

PARAGUAY

Republic of Paraguay
President: Juan Carlos Wasmosy (1993)
Area: 157,047 sq mi. (406,752 sq km)
Population (est. mid-1995): 5,000,000 (average annual rate of natural increase: 2.8%); birth rate: 33/1000; infant mortality rate: 38/1000; density per square mile: 31.8
Capital and largest city (1992): Asunción, 502,426. **Other large cities (1992):** Ciudad del Este, 133,893; San Lorenzo, 133,311. **Monetary unit:** Guaraní; **Languages:** Spanish (official), Guaraní; **Religion:** Roman Catholic, 90%; **National name:** República del Paraguay; **Literacy rate:** 90%
Economic summary: Gross domestic product (1993 est.): $15.2 billion; $3,000 per capita; real growth rate 3.5%; inflation 20.4%; unemployment 11%. Arable land: 20%. Principal agricultural products: soybeans, cotton, timber, cassava, tobacco, corn, rice, sugar cane. Labor force (1993): 1,692,000; By occupation (1992 est.): 44% agriculture. Major industrial products: packed meats, crushed oilseeds, beverages, textiles, light consumer goods, cement. Natural resources: iron ore, timber, manganese, limestone, hydropower. Exports: $728 million (f.o.b., 1993 est.): cotton, soybeans, meat products, timber, coffee, tung oil, vegetable oils. Imports: $1.38 billion (c.i.f., 1993 est.): fuels and lubricants, beverages, tobacco, foodstuffs, capital goods, consumer goods, fuels and lubricants. Major trading partners: Argentina, Brazil, U.S., E.U., Japan.

Geography. California-size Paraguay is surrounded by Brazil, Bolivia, and Argentina in south central South America. Eastern Paraguay, between the Paraná and Paraguay Rivers, is upland country with the thickest population settled on the grassy slope that inclines toward the Paraguay River. The greater part of the Chaco region to the west is covered with marshes, lagoons, dense forests, and jungles.

Government. The President is elected by popular vote for five years. The legislature is bicameral, consisting of a Senate of 45 members and a Chamber of Representatives of 80 members. There is also a Council of State, whose members are nominated by the government.

History. In 1526 and again in 1529, Sebastian Cabot explored Paraguay when he sailed up the Paraná and Paraguay Rivers. From 1608 until their expulsion from the Spanish dominions in 1767, the Jesuits maintained an extensive establishment in the south and east of Paraguay. In 1811, Paraguay revolted against Spanish rule and became a nominal republic under two Consuls.

Actually, Paraguay was governed by three dictators during the first 60 years of independence. The third, Francisco López, waged war against Brazil and Argentina in 1865–70, a conflict in which the male population was almost wiped out. A new Constitution in 1870, designed to prevent dictatorships and internal strife, failed to do so, and not until 1912 did a period of comparative economic and political stability begin.

After World War II, politics became particularly unstable.

Stroessner ruled under a state of siege until 1965, when the dictatorship was relaxed and exiles returned. The Constitution was revised in 1967 to permit Stroessner to be re-elected.

The Stroessner regime was criticized by the U.S. State Department during the Carter administration as a violator of human rights, but unlike Argentina and

Uruguay, Paraguay did not suffer cuts in U.S. military aid.

Stroessner was overthrown by an army leader, Gen. Andres Rodriguez, in 1989. Rodriguez won in Paraguay's first multi-candidate elections in decades. He has promised to hand over power to an elected civilian successor in 1993.

The National Assembly in June 1991 approved a reform of the constitution.

The country's first ever democratic presidential election took place in May 1993. Wasmosy, a wealthy businessman and the candidate of the governing Colorado Party won a five-year term in an election that despite irregularities was regarded as reliable.

With the legislature in opposition hands, in May 1994 it passed a bill that made military service incompatible with political activity. The government immediately challenged the law's constitutionality.

PERU

Republic of Peru
President: Alberto Fujimori (1990)
Premier: Dr. Efrain Goldenberg Schreiber (1994)
Area: 496,222 sq mi. (1,285,216 sq km)
Population (est. mid-1995): 24,000,000 (average annual rate of natural increase: 2.1%); birth rate: 29/1000; infant mortality rate: 60/1000; density per sq mi.: 48.3
Capital: Lima; **Largest cities (est. 1990):** Lima, 5,826,000; Arequipa, 634,500; Callao, 589,000; Trujillo, 532,000; Chiclayo, 426,300; **Monetary unit:** Nuevo Sol (1991); **Languages:** Spanish, Quéchua, Aymara, and other native languages; **Religion:** Roman Catholic; **National name:** República del Perú; **Literacy rate:** 85%
Economic summary: Gross domestic product (1993 est.): $70 billion; $3,000 per capita; real growth rate 6%; inflation 39%; unemployment 15% (1992 est.). Arable land: 3%. Principal products: wheat, potatoes, beans, rice, sugar, cotton, coffee. Labor force: 8,000,000 (1992); by occupation (1988): government and other services, 44%; agriculture, 37%, industry, 19%. Major products: processed minerals, fish meal, refined petroleum, textiles. Natural resources: silver, gold, iron, copper, fish, petroleum, timber. Exports: $3.7 billion (f.o.b., 1993 est.): copper, fish products, cotton, sugar, coffee, lead, silver, zinc, oil. Imports: $4.5 billion (f.o.b., 1993 est.): machinery, foodstuffs, chemicals, pharmaceuticals, transport equipment. Major trading partners: U.S., Japan, Western European, and Latin American countries.

Geography. Peru, in western South America, extends for nearly 1,500 miles (2,414 km) along the Pacific Ocean. Colombia and Ecuador are to the north, Brazil and Bolivia to the east, and Chile to the south.

Five-sixths the size of Alaska, Peru is divided by the Andes Mountains into three sharply differentiated zones. To the west is the coastline, much of it arid, extending 50 to 100 miles (80 to 160 km) inland. The mountain area, with peaks over 20,000 feet (6,096 m), lofty plateaus, and deep valleys, lies centrally. Beyond the mountains to the east is the heavily forested slope leading to the Amazonian plains.

Government. A republic. The president, Alberto Fujimori was elected in 1990 by universal suffrage for a five-year term and holds executive power. He was reelected in April 1995 by an absolute majority for five more years. A new 120-member Congress was also elected by universal suffrage.

History. Peru was once part of the great Incan em-

pire and later the major vice-royalty of Spanish South America. It was conquered in 1531–33 by Francisco Pizarro. On July 28, 1821, Peru proclaimed its independence, but the Spanish were not finally defeated until 1824. For a hundred years thereafter, revolutions were frequent, and a new war was fought with Spain in 1864–66.

Peru emerged from 20 years of dictatorship in 1945 with the inauguration of President José Luis Bustamante y Rivero after the first free election in many decades. But he served for only three years and was succeeded in turn by Gen. Manual A. Odria, Manuel Prado y Ugarteche, and Fernando Belaúnde Terry. On Oct. 3, 1968, Belaúnde was overthrown by Gen. Juan Velasco Alvarado.

Velasco nationalized the nation's second biggest bank and turned two large newspapers over to Marxists in 1970, but he also allowed a new agreement with a copper-mining consortium of four American firms.

In 1975, Velasco was replaced in a bloodless coup by his Premier, Gen. Francisco Morales Bermudez, who promised to restore civilian government. In elections held on May 18, 1980, Belaunde Terry, the last previous civilian President and the candidate of the conservative parties that have traditionally ruled Peru, was elected President again.

But Peru's fragile democracy survived this period of stress and when he left office in 1985 Belaunde Terry was the first elected President to turn over power to a constitutionally elected successor since 1945.

In the June run-off to the April 1990 elections Alberto Fujimori won 56.5% of the vote. A newcomer to national politics, Fujimori is the son of Japanese immigrants.

Citing continuing terrorism, drug trafficking and corruption Fujimori in April 1992 dissolved Congress, suspended the constitution and imposed censorship.

A new constitution received approval in a referendum held in October 1993.

In January 1995 fighting flared once again along part of the disputed border with Ecuador, claiming nine lives. Peru declared a unilateral ceasefire in mid-February.

In the April elections, President Fujimori was reelected, and his party obtained a majority in the legislature.

THE PHILIPPINES

Republic of the Philippines
President: Fidel V. Ramos (1992)
Vice President: Joseph Estrada (1992)
Area: 115,830 sq mi. (300,000 sq km)
Population (est. mid-1995): 68,400,000 (average annual rate of natural increase: 2.1%); birth rate: 30/1000; infant mortality rate: 49/1000; density per square mile: 590.5
Capital: Manila; **Largest cities (1990):** Manila, 1,587,000[1]; Quezon City, 1,632,000; Cebu, 610,000; **Monetary unit:** Peso; **Languages:** Filipino (based on Tagalog), English; regional languages: Tagalog, Ilocano, Cebuano, others; **Religions:** Roman Catholic, 83%; Protestant, 9%; Islam, 5%; Buddhist and other, 3%; **National name:** Republika ng Pilipinas; **Literacy rate:** 93.5%
Economic summary: Gross domestic product (1993 est.): $171 billion; $2,500 per capita; real growth rate 1.4%; inflation 7.6%; unemployment 9.2%. Arable land: 9.8%. Principal products: rice, corn, coconuts, sugar cane,

bananas, pineapple. Labor force (1989): 24,120,000; agriculture, 46%; services, 18.5%; industry and commerce, 16%. Major products: textiles, pharmaceuticals, chemicals, food processing, electronics assembly. Natural resources: forests, crude oil, metallic and non-metallic minerals. Exports: $1.1 billion (f.o.b., 1993 est.): electrical equipment, coconut products, chemicals, logs and lumber, copper concentrates, nickel. Imports: $17.1 billion (f.o.b., 1993 est.): petroleum, industrial equipment, raw materials. Major trading partners: U.S., Japan, E.C., Taiwan, Saudi Arabia.

1. Metropolitan area population is 7,832,000.

Geography. The Philippine Islands are an archipelago of over 7,000 islands lying about 500 miles (805 km) off the southeast coast of Asia. The overall land area is comparable to that of Arizona. The northernmost island, Y'Ami, is 65 miles (105 km) from Taiwan, while the southernmost, Saluag, is 40 miles (64 km) east of Borneo.

Only about 7% of the islands are larger than one square mile, and only one third have names. The largest are Luzon in the north (40,420 sq mi.; 104,687 sq km), Mindanao in the south (36,537 sq mi.; 94,631 sq km), Samar (5,124 sq mi.; 13,271 sq km).

The islands are of volcanic origin, with the larger ones crossed by mountain ranges. The highest peak is Mount Apo (9,690 ft; 2,954 m) on Mindanao.

Government. On February 2, 1987, the Filipino people voted for a new Constitution that established a 24-seat Senate and a 250-seat House of Representatives and gave the President a six-year term. It limits the powers of the President, who can't be re-elected.

History. Fernando Magellan, the Portuguese navigator in the service of Spain, discovered the Philippines in 1521. Twenty-one years later, a Spanish exploration party named the group of islands in honor of Prince Philip, later Philip II of Spain. Spain retained possession of the islands for the next 350 years.

The Philippines were ceded to the U.S. in 1899 by the Treaty of Paris after the Spanish-American War. Meanwhile, the Filipinos, led by Emilio Aguinaldo, had declared their independence. They continued guerrilla warfare against U.S. troops until the capture of Aguinaldo in 1901. By 1902, peace was established except among the Moros.

The first U.S. civilian Governor-General was William Howard Taft (1901–04). The Jones Law (1916) provided for the establishment of a Philippine Legislature composed of an elective Senate and House of Representatives. The Tydings-McDuffie Act (1934) provided for a transitional period until 1946, at which time the Philippines would become completely independent.

Under a Constitution approved by the people of the Philippines in 1935, the Commonwealth of the Philippines came into being, with Manuel Quezon y Molina as President.

On Dec. 8, 1941, the Philippines were invaded by Japanese troops. Following the fall of Bataan and Corregidor, Quezon established a government-in-exile, which he headed until his death in 1944. He was succeeded by Vice President Sergio Osmeña.

U.S. forces led by Gen. Douglas MacArthur reinvaded the Philippines in October 1944 and, after the liberation of Manila in February 1945, Osmeña re-established the government.

The Philippines achieved full independence on July 4, 1946. Manual A. Roxas y Acuña was elected first president. Subsequent presidents have been Elpidio Quirino (1948–53), Ramón Magsaysay (1953–57). Carlos P. García (1957–61), Diosdado Macapagal (1961–65), Ferdinand E. Marcos (1965–86).

Marcos, who had freed the last of the national leaders still in detention, former Senator Benigno S. Aquino, Jr., in 1980 and permitted him to go to the United States, ended eight years of martial law on January 17, 1981.

Despite having been warned by First Lady Imelda Marcos that he risked being killed if he came back, opposition leader Aquino returned to the Philippines from self-exile on Aug. 21, 1983. He was shot to death as he was being escorted from his plane by military police at Manila International Airport. There was widespread suspicion that the Marcos government was involved in the murder.

In an attempt to re-secure American support, Marcos set Presidential elections for Feb. 7, 1986. With the support of the Catholic church, Corazon Aquino, widow of Benigno Aquino, declared her candidacy. Marcos was declared the winner, but the vote was widely considered to be rigged and anti-Marcos protests continued. The defection of Defense Minister Juan Enrile and Lt. Gen. Fidel Ramos signaled an end of military support for Marcos, who fled into exile in the U.S. on Feb. 25, 1986.

The Aquino government survived coup attempts by Marcos supporters and other right-wing elements including one, in November, by Enrile. Legislative elections on May 11, 1987, gave pro-Aquino candidates a large majority.

Negotiations on renewal of leases for U.S. military bases threatened to sour relations between the two countries. The volcanic eruptions from Mount Pinatubo, however, severely damaged Clark Air Base. In July 1991 the U.S. decided simply to abandon the base.

In elections of May 1992 Gen. Fidel Ramos, who had the support of outgoing Corazon Aquino, won the presidency in a seven-way race. The opposition gained control of the Congress.

The U.S. Navy turned over the Subic Bay naval base to the Philippines in September, ending a long U.S. military presence.

The government signs a cease-fire pact with Muslim separatists in late-January 1994, signaling a major step toward ending a long-standing war.

Elections for both houses of Congress in May 1995 gave a resounding victory to candidates backed by the president and were widely hailed as providing him with a fresh mandate to proceed with economic reforms.

POLAND

Republic of Poland
President: Lech Walesa (1990)
Prime Minister: Jozef Oleksy (1995)
Area: 120,727 sq mi. (312,683 sq km)
Population (est. mid-1995): 38,600,000 (average annual rate of natural increase: 0.2%; birth rate: 12/1000; infant mortality rate: 13.7/1000; density per square mile: 319.7
Capital: Warsaw; **Largest cities (est. 1991):** Warsaw, 1,655,000; Lodz, 846,500; Krakow, 750,600; Wroclaw, 643,000; Poznan, 590,000; Gdansk, 465,400; Szczecin, 413,600; **Monetary unit:** Zloty; **Language:** Polish; **Religions:** Roman Catholic, 95%; Russian Orthodox, Protestant, and other, 5%; **National name:** Rzeczpospolita Polska; **Literacy rate:** 98%
Economic summary: Gross domestic product (1994): $92 billion; $4,400 per capita; real growth rate 5%; inflation 29%; unemployment 16%. Arable land: 59%. Principal

products: rye, rapeseed, potatoes, hogs and other livestock. Labor force: 17,400,000 (1994): industry and construction 37%, agriculture and food products 23%. Major products: iron and steel, chemicals, textiles, processed foods, machine building. Natural resources: coal, sulfur, copper, natural gas. Exports: $172 billion (1994): coal, machinery and equipment, industrial products, chemicals, metals. Imports: $21.6 billion (1994): machinery and equipment, fuels, agricultural and food products, chemicals. Major trading partners: Germany, former USSR, Italy, U.K., The Netherlands, U.S.

Geography. Poland, a country the size of New Mexico in north central Europe, borders on Germany to the west, Czech and Slovak Republics to the south, and Ukraine, Balarus, Lithuania, and Russia to the east. In the north is the Baltic Sea.

Most of the country is a plain with no natural boundaries except the Carpathian Mountains in the south and the Oder and Neisse Rivers in the west. Other major rivers, which are important to commerce, are the Vistula, Warta, and Bug.

Government. Parliament adopted a new temporary constitution, Oct. 17, 1992, which describes Poland as the Republic of Poland. Work on a permanent constitution continues. The supreme organ of state authority is the Sejm (Parliament), which is composed of 460 members elected for four years and a 100-member Senate (Senat).

History. Little is known about Polish history before the 11th century, when King Boleslaus I (the Brave) ruled over Bohemia, Saxony, and Moravia. Meanwhile, the Teutonic knights of Prussia conquered part of Poland and barred the latter's access to the Baltic. The knights were defeated by Wladislaus II at Tannenberg in 1410 and became Polish vassals, and Poland regained a Baltic shoreline. Poland reached the peak of power between the 14th and 16th centuries, scoring military successes against the Russians and Turks. In 1683, John III (John Sobieski) turned back the Turkish tide at Vienna.

An elective monarchy failed to produce strong central authority, and Prussia and Austria were able to carry out a first partition of the country in 1772, a second in 1792, and a third in 1795. For more than a century thereafter, there was no Polish state, but the Poles never ceased their efforts to regain their independence.

Poland was formally reconstituted in November 1918, with Marshal Josef Pilsudski as Chief of State. In 1919, Ignace Paderewski, the famous pianist and patriot, became the first premier. In 1926, Pilsudski seized complete power in a coup and ruled dictatorially until his death on May 12, 1935, when he was succeeded by Marshal Edward Smigly-Rydz.

Despite a 10-year nonaggression pact signed in 1934, Hitler attacked Poland on Sept. 1, 1939. Russian troops invaded from the east on September 17, and on September 28 a German-Russian agreement divided Poland between Russia and Germany. Wladyslaw Raczkiewicz formed a government-in-exile in France, which moved to London after France's defeat in 1940.

All of Poland was occupied by Germany after the Nazi attack on the U.S.S.R. in June 1941.

The legal Polish government soon fell out with the Russians, and, in 1944, a Communist-dominated Polish Committee of National Liberation received Soviet recognition. Moving to Lublin after that city's liberation, it proclaimed itself the Provisional Government of Poland. Some former members of the Polish gov-

ernment in London joined with the Lublin government to form the Polish Government of National Unity, which Britain and the U.S. recognized.

On Aug. 2, 1945, in Berlin, President Harry S. Truman, Joseph Stalin, and Prime Minister Clement Attlee of Britain established a new *de facto* western frontier for Poland along the Oder and Neisse Rivers. (The border was finally agreed to by West Germany in a nonaggression pact signed Dec. 7, 1970.) On Aug. 16, 1945, the U.S.S.R. and Poland signed a treaty delimiting the Soviet-Polish frontier. Under these agreements, Poland was shifted westward. In the east it lost 69,860 square miles (180,934 sq km) with 10,772,000 inhabitants; in the west it gained (subject to final peace-conference approval) 38,986 square miles (100,973 sq km) with a prewar population of 8,621,000.

A New Constitution in 1952 made Poland a "people's democracy" of the Soviet type. In 1955, Poland became a member of the Warsaw Treaty Organization, and its foreign policy became identical with that of the U.S.S.R. The government undertook persecution of the Roman Catholic Church as a remaining source of opposition.

Wladyslaw Gomulka was elected leader of the United Workers (Communist) Party in 1956. He denounced the Stalinist terror, ousted many Stalinists, and improved relations with the church. Most collective farms were dissolved, and the press became freer.

A strike that began in shipyards and spread to other industries in August 1980 produced a stunning victory for workers when the economically hard-pressed government accepted for the first time in a Marxist state the right of workers to organize in independent unions.

Led by Solidarity, a free union founded by Lech Walesa, workers launched a drive for liberty and improved conditions. A national strike for a five-day week in January 1981 led to the dismissal of Premier Pinkowski and the naming of the fourth Premier in less than a year, Gen. Wojciech Jaruzelski.

Martial law was declared on Dec. 13, when Walesa and other Solidarity leaders were arrested. It was formally ended in 1984 but the government retained emergency powers.

Increasing opposition to the government because of the failing economy led to a new wave of strikes in 1988. Unable to totally quell the dissent, it relegalized Solidarity and allowed them to compete in elections.

Solidarity won a stunning victory, taking almost all the seats in the Senate and all of the 169 seats they were allowed to contest in the Sejm. This has given them substantial influence in the new government. Taduesz Mazowiecki was appointed prime minister.

The presidential election of 1990 was essentially a three-way race between Mazowiecki, Solidarity-leader Lech Walesa and an almost unknown businessman Stanislaw Tyminski. In the second round Walesa received 74% of the vote.

In 1991, the first fully free parliamentary election since WW II resulted in representation for 29 political parties.

In the second democratic parliamentary election of September 1993 voters returned power to ex-communists and their allies.

President Walesa in early 1995 demanded a change in the government run by Waldemar Pawlak, accusing it of slowing economic reform and of being indifferent to corruption within the Cabinet. The ruling coalition nominated Oleksy, a senior member of the Democratic Left Alliance, a direct descendent of the Communist Party.

PORTUGAL

Republic of Portugal
President: Mario Soares (1986)
Prime Minister: Anibal Cavaco Silva (1987)
Area: 35,550 sq mi. (92,075 sq km)
Population (est. mid-1995): 9,900,000 (average annual rate of natural increase: 0.1%); birth rate: 12/1000; infant mortality rate: 8.6/1000; density per square mile: 278.4
Capital and largest city (1991): Lisbon, 677,790. **Other large city (1991)):** Oporto, 350,000. **Monetary unit:** Escudo; **Language:** Portuguese; **Religion:** Roman Catholic 97%, 1% Protestant, 2% other; **National name:** República Portuguesa; **Literacy rate:** 85%
Economic summary: Gross domestic product (1993): $91.2 billion; $9,200 per capita; real growth rate –1%; inflation 6.8% (1995); unemployment 6.9% (1994). Arable land: 32%. Principal products: grains, potatoes, olives, wine grapes. Labor force (1988): 4,605,700; (1994): services 49%, industry 34%, agriculture 17%. Major products: textiles, footwear, wood pulp, paper, cork, metal products, refined oil, chemicals, canned fish, wine. Natural resources: fish, cork, tungsten, iron ore. Exports: $16 billion (f.o.b., 1994): cotton, textiles, cork and cork products, canned fish, wine, timber and timber products, resin, machinery, appliances. Imports: $24 billion (c.i.f., 1994): machinery and transport equipment, agricultural products, chemicals, petroleum, textiles. Major trading partners: Western European countries, U.S.

Geography. Portugal occupies the western part of the Iberian Peninsula, bordering on the Atlantic Ocean to the west and Spain to the north and east. It is slightly smaller than Indiana.

The country is crossed by many small rivers, and also by three large ones that rise in Spain, flow into the Atlantic, and divide the country into three geographic areas. The Minho River, part of the northern boundary, cuts through a mountainous area that extends south to the vicinity of the Douro River. South of the Douro, the mountains slope to the plains about the Tejo River. The remaining division is the southern one of Alentejo.

The Azores, stretching over 340 miles (547 km) in the Atlantic, consist of nine islands divided into three groups, with a total area of 902 square miles (2,335 sq km). The nearest continental land is Cape da Roca, Portugal, about 900 miles (1,448 km) to the east. The Azores are an important station on Atlantic air routes, and Britain and the U.S. established air bases there during World War II. Madeira, consisting of two inhabited islands, Madeira and Porto Santo, and two groups of uninhabited islands, lie in the Atlantic about 535 miles (861 km) southwest of Lisbon. The Madeiras are 307 square miles (796 sq km) in area.

Government. A republic. The president is elected for a five-year term. The unicameral legislature, the Assembly of the Republic, for four years.

History. Portugal was a part of Spain until it won its independence in the middle of the 12th century. King John I (1385–1433) unified his country at the expense of the Castilians and the Moors of Morocco. The expansion of Portugal was brilliantly coordinated by John's son, Prince Henry the Navigator. In 1488, Bartolomew Diaz reached the Cape of Good Hope, proving that the Far East was accessible by sea. In 1498, Vasco da Gama reached the west coast of India. By the middle of the 16th century, the Portuguese Empire was in West and East Africa, Brazil, Persia, Indochina, and Malaya.

In 1581, Philip II of Spain invaded Portugal and held it for 60 years, precipitating a catastrophic decline of Portuguese commerce. Courageous and shrewd explorers, the Portuguese proved to be inefficient and corrupt colonizers. By the time the Portuguese dynasty was restored in 1640, Dutch, English, and French competitors began to seize the lion's share of the world's colonies and commerce. Portugal retained Angola and Mozambique in Africa, and Brazil (until 1822).

The corrupt King Carlos, who ascended the throne in 1889, made Joao Franco the Premier with dictatorial power in 1906. In 1908, Carlos and his heir were shot dead on the streets of Lisbon. The new King, Manoel II, was driven from the throne in the Revolution of 1910 and Portugal became a French-style republic.

Traditionally friendly to Britain, Portugal fought in World War I on the Allied side in Africa as well as on the Western Front. Weak postwar governments and a revolution in 1926 brought Antonio Oliveira Salazar to power. He kept Portugal neutral in World War II but gave the Allies naval and air bases after 1943.

Portugal lost the tiny remnants of its Indian empire—Goa, Daman, and Diu—to Indian military occupation in 1961, the year an insurrection broke out in Angola. For the next 13 years, Salazar, who died in 1970, and his successor, Marcello Caetano, fought independence movements amid growing world criticism. Leftists in the armed forces, weary of a losing battle, launched a successful revolution on April 25, 1974.

In late 1985, a PSP-PSD split ended the Soares coalition government. Cavaco Silva, an advocate of free-market economics, was the Social Democratic candidate.

In July 1987, the governing Social Democratic Party was swept back into office with 50.22% of the popular vote, giving Portugal its first majority Government since democracy was restored in 1974.

Mario Soares easily won a second five-year term as president in January 1991 elections.

The general elections of October 1991 gave an absolute majority in the Assembly to the prime minister's Social Democratic Party.

Political maneuvering and the need to raise certain taxes dominated domestic news in 1994.

Portuguese Overseas Territory

After the April 1974 revolution, the military junta moved to grant independence to the territories, beginning with Portuguese Guinea in September 1974, which became the Republic of Guinea-Bissau.

Mozambique and Angola followed, leaving only Portuguese Timor and Macao of the former empire. Despite Lisbon's objections, Indonesia annexed Timor.

MACAO

Status: Territory
Governor: Vasco Rocha Vieira (1991)
Area: 6 sq mi. (15.5 sq km)
Population (est. mid-1995): 400,000 (average annual growth rate: 3.8%); birth rate: 16/1000; infant mortality rate: 9/1000; density per square mile: 66,666
Capital (1991): Macao, 326,460. **Monetary unit:** Patacá; **Languages:** Portuguese and Chinese are both official languages since December 31, 1991. Cantonese is most common, English is also spoken in business. **Religions:** Buddhist 17%, Roman Catholic 7%, Protestant 7%. **Literacy rate (1981):** almost 100% among Portuguese and Macanese, no data on Chinese

Economic summary: Gross domestic product (1993 est.): $5.83 billion; $14,970 per capita; real growth rate 5%; inflation 6.3%. Major industrial products: clothing, textiles, plastics, furniture. Exports: $1.8 billion (1992 est.): textiles, clothing, toys. Imports: $2 billion (1992 est.). raw materials, foodstuffs, capital goods. Major trading partners: Hong Kong, China, U.S., Germany, France, Japan.

Macao comprises the peninsula of Macao and the two small islands of Taipa and Colôane on the South China coast, about 35 miles (53 km) from Hong Kong. Established by the Portuguese in 1557, it is the oldest European outpost in the China trade, but Portugal's sovereign rights to the port were not recognized by China until 1887. The port has been eclipsed in importance by Hong Kong, but is still a busy distribution center and also has an important fishing industry. Portugal will return Macao to China in 1999.

QATAR

State of Qatar
Emir: Sheikh Khalifa bin Hamad al-Thani (1972)
Area: 4,000 sq mi. (11,437 sq km)
Population (est. mid-1995): 500,000 (average annual rate of natural increase: 1.8%); birth rate: 19/1000; infant mortality rate: 13/1000; density per square mile: 125
Capital (est. 1990): Doha, 300,000; **Monetary unit:** Qatari riyal; **Language:** Arabic; English is also widely spoken; **Religion:** Islam, 95%; **Literacy rate:** 76%
Economic summary: Gross domestic product (1993 est.): $8.8 billion; $17,500 per capita; –0.5% real growth rate; inflation: 3%. Labor force: 104,000. Major industrial product: oil. While Qatar depends on oil for much of its revenue, the government is increasing the development of its natural gas production. Qatar is one of the five leading gas producers in the world. Natural resources: oil, gas. Exports: $3.4 billion (f.o.b., 1993 est.): petroleum products 85%, steel, fertilizers. Imports: $1.8 billion (f.o.b., 1993 est.): machinery and equipment, consumer goods, food, chemicals. Major trading partners: France, U.K., U.S., Germany, Japan, Brazil, South Korea, UAE.

Geography. Qatar occupies a small peninsula that extends into the Persian Gulf from the east side of the Arabian Peninsula. Saudi Arabia is to the west and the United Arab Emirates to the south. The country is mainly barren.

Government. For a long time, Qatar was under Turkish protection, but in 1916, the Emir accepted British protection. After the discovery of oil in the 1940s and its exploitation in the 1950s and 1960s, political unrest spread to the sheikhdoms. Qatar declared its independence in 1971.

History. The Emir agreed to the deployment of Arab and Western forces in Qatar following the Iraqi invasion of Kuwait.

A border dispute with Saudi Arabia pushed Qatar somewhat closer to Iran. The dispute was settled in December 1992. A territorial dispute with Bahrain over the Hawar Islands remained unresolved, however.

In June Qatar signed a defense pact with the U.S., becoming the third Gulf state to do so.

In June 1995 Crown Prince Hamad bin Khalifa al-Thani asked his father the Emir to leave the country. The Emir's title was not stripped, and much of the power was already in the son's hands.

ROMANIA

Republic of Romania
President: Ion Iliescu (1990)
Prime Minister: Nicolae Vacaroiu (1992)
Area: 91,700 sq mi. (237,500 sq km)
Population (est. mid-1995): 22,700,000 Romanian, 89.4%; Hungarian, 7.1%; Gypsies, 1.8%. (average annual rate of natural increase: –0.1%); birth rate: 11/1000; infant mortality rate: 23.3/1000; density per square mile: 247.5
Capital: Bucharest; **Largest cities (1992):** Bucharest, 2,351,000; Constanta, 350,476; Iasi, 342,994; Timisoara, 334,278; Cluj-Napoca, 328,008; Galati, 325,788; Brasov, 323,835. **Monetary unit:** Leu; **Languages:** Romanian (official). **Religions:** Christian Orthodox, 86.8%; Roman Catholic, 5%; Protestant, 3.5%. **National name:** Romania. **Literacy rate:** 98%
Economic summary: Gross national product (1993 est.): $37.6 billion; $1,650 per capita; real growth rate 1.0%; inflation 12.1%; unemployment 10.2%. Arable land: 43%. Principal products: corn, wheat, livestock, sunflowers, potatoes. Labor force (1989): industry 31%, agriculture and forestry 33%, services 15%. Major products: timber, metal production and processing, chemicals, food processing, petroleum. Natural resources: oil, timber, natural gas, coal, iron ore. Exports: $4.5 billion (f.o.b., 1993 est.): machinery, metals, chemicals, timber, furniture, textiles, foodstuffs. Imports: $5.2 billion (f.o.b., 1993 est.): minerals, fuel, machinery, consumer goods. Major trading partners: Germany, Italy, Russia, France, U.K., U.S.

Geography. A country in southeastern Europe slightly smaller than Oregon, Romania is bordered on the west by Hungary and Yugoslavia, on the north and east by Moldova and Ukraine, on the east by the Black Sea, and on the south by Bulgaria.

The Carpathian Mountains divide Romania's upper half from north to south and connect near the center of the country with the Transylvanian Alps, running east and west.

North and west of these ranges lies the Transylvanian plateau, and to the south and east are the plains of Moldavia and Walachia. In its last 190 miles (306 km), the Danube River flows through Romania only. It enters the Black Sea in northern Dobruja, just south of the border with the Soviet Union.

Government. A multiparty republic with a bicameral Parliament consisting of an upper house or Senate and a lower house, the Chamber of Deputies.

History. Most of Romania was the Roman province of Dacia from about A.D. 100 to 271. From the 6th to the 12th century, wave after wave of barbarian conquerors overran the native Daco-Roman population. By the 16th century, the main Romanian principalities of Moldavia and Walachia had become satellites within the Ottoman Empire, although they retained much independence. After the Russo-Turkish War of 1828–29, they became Russian protectorates. The nation became a kingdom in 1881 after the Congress of Berlin.

King Ferdinand ascended the throne in 1914. At the start of World War I, Romania proclaimed its neutrality, but later joined the Allied side and in 1916 declared war on the Central Powers. The armistice of Nov. 11, 1918, gave Romania vast territories from Russia and the Austro-Hungarian Empire.

The gains of World War I, making Romania the largest Balkan state, included Bessarabia, Transylvania, and Bukovina. The Banat, a Hungarian area, was divided with Yugoslavia.

In 1925, Crown Prince Carol renounced his rights to the throne, and when King Ferdinand died in 1927, Carol's son, Michael (Mihai) became King under a regency. However, Carol returned from exile in 1930, was crowned King Carol II, and gradually became a powerful political force in the country. In 1938, he abolished the democratic Constitution of 1923.

In 1940, the country was reorganized along Fascist lines, and the Fascist Iron Guard became the nucleus of the new totalitarian party. On June 27, the Soviet Union occupied Bessarabia and northern Bukovina. By the Axis-dictated Vienna Award of 1940, two-fifths of Transylvania went to Hungary, after which Carol dissolved Parliament and granted the new premier, Ion Antonescu, full power. He abdicated and again went into exile.

Romania subsequently signed the Axis Pact on Nov. 23, 1940, and the following June joined in Germany's attack on the Soviet Union, reoccupying Bessarabia. Following the invasion of Romania by the Red Army in August 1944, King Michael led a coup that ousted the Antonescu government. An armistice with the Soviet Union was signed in Moscow on Sept. 12, 1944.

A Communist-dominated government bloc won elections in 1946, Michael abdicated on Dec. 30, 1947, and Romania became a "people's republic." In 1955, Romania joined the Warsaw Treaty Organization and the United Nations. Despite his liberal international record, at home Ceausescu harshly suppressed dissidents calling for freedom of expression in the wake of the Helsinki agreements.

An army-assisted rebellion in Dec. 1989 led to Ceausescu's overthrow. He was tried and executed. Elections in May 1990 led to the head of the interim government, Ion Iliescu, being elected President.

The government remains torn between introducing free-market reforms and its pledges to hold down unemployment and reduce shortages. While some, though few, measures have been implemented, price reforms in November 1990 led to strikes and demonstrations. The opposition remains weak and fragmented.

General elections in September 1992 saw the president returned for a second term and his party became the largest single party in parliament.

The IMF in 1994 provided $700 million over a 19-month period to support privatization. A privatization plan, however, was revised, and its implementation at least temporarily postponed, by the country's legislature. Exports rose during the year as did unemployment. The rate of inflation was significantly less than in the previous year.

RUSSIA

Russian Federation
President: Boris N. Yeltsin (1991)
Vice President: Aleksandr V. Rutskoi
Area: 6,592,800 sq mi. (17,075,400 sq km)
Population (est. mid-1995): 147,500,000 (Russian, 82%.
  Minorities: Tartars, Ukrainians, and Chuvashes); (average annual rate of natural increase: –0.6%); birth rate: 9/1000; infant mortality rate: 19/1000; density per square mile: 22.3
Capital and largest city (1992): Moscow, 8,747,000. ;
  Other large cities (1992): St. Petersburg, 4,437,000; Novosibirsk, 1,442,000; Samara, 1,239,000; Chelyabinsk, 1,143,000; Yekaterinburg, 1,371,000; Nizhny Novgorod, 1,441,000; Kazan, 1,104,000; Perm, 1,099,000; Ufa, 1,097,000; Omsk, 1,169,000. **Monetary unit:** Ruble;
  Religion: Mainly Eastern Orthodoxy; **Language:** Russian. **Literacy rate:** 100%

Economic summary: Russia is a highly industrialized-agrarian republic. Its vast mineral resources include oil and natural gas, coal, iron, zinc, lead, nickel, aluminum, molybdenum, gold, platinum, and other nonferrous metals. Russia has the world's largest oil and natural gas reserves. Three-quarters of the republic's mineral wealth is concentrated in Siberia and the Far East. Approximately ten million people are engaged in agriculture and they produce half of the region's grain, meat, milk, and other dairy products. The largest granaries are located in the North Caucasus and the Volga and Amur regions. Gross national product (UN, World Bank 1993 est.): $775.4 billion, $5,190 per capita; –12% real growth rate; inflation 21% (per mo.); unemployment: 1.4% (per mo., Jan. 94). Labor force (1993 est.): 75 million. Exports: $43 billion (f.o.b., 1993): petroleum and petroleum products, natural gas, wood and wood products, coal, nonferrous metals, chemicals, civilian and military manufacturers. Imports: $27 billion (f.o.b., 1993): machinery and equipment, chemicals, consumer goods, grain, meat, semifinished metal products. Foreign investment in Russia (1993 est.): $500 million. Major trading partners: Europe, N. America, Japan, Third World countries, Cuba.

Geography: The Russian Federation is the largest republic of the Commonwealth of Independent States. It is about one and four-fifths of the land area of the United States and occupies most of eastern Europe and north Asia. Russia stretches from the Baltic Sea in the west to the Pacific Ocean in the east and from the Arctic Ocean in the north to the Black Sea and the Caucasus, the Altai, and Sayan Mountains, and the Amur and Ussuri Rivers in the south. It is bordered by Norway and Finland in the northwest, Estonia, Latvia, Belarus and Ukraine in the west, Georgia and Azerbaijan in the southwest, and Kazakhstan, Mongolia, and China along the southern border. The federation comprises 21 republics.

Government: A constitutional republic. A new constitution adopted Dec. 12, 1993 gave the President considerable power to rule independently of the Parliament. The upper house or Federation Council has 176 elected members, two from each of Russia's 88 constituent regions. The State Duma or lower house has 450 elected members. The President and the parliament are elected for four-year terms. The president is limited to two terms. President Yeltsin will serve out the rest of his current five-year term until June 1996.

History. Tradition says the Viking Rurik came to Russia in A.D. 862 and founded the first Russian dynasty in Novgorod. The various tribes were united by the spread of Christianity in the 10th and 11th centuries; Vladimir "the Saint" was converted in 988. During the 11th century, the grand dukes of Kiev held such centralizing power as existed. In 1240, Kiev was destroyed by the Mongols, and the Russian territory was split into numerous smaller dukedoms, early dukes of Moscow extended their dominions through their office of tribute collector for the Mongols.

In the late 15th century, Duke Ivan III acquired Novgorod and Tver and threw off the Mongol yoke. Ivan IV, the Terrible (1533–84), first Muscovite Tsar, is considered to have founded the Russian state. He crushed the power of rival princes and boyars (great landowners), but Russia remained largely medieval until the reign of Peter the Great (1689–1725), grandson of the first Romanov Tsar, Michael (1613–45). Peter made extensive reforms aimed at westernization and, through his defeat of Charles XII of Sweden at the Battle of Poltava in 1709, he extended Russia's boundaries to the west.

Catherine the Great (1762–96) continued Peter's westernization program and also expanded Russian territory, acquiring the Crimea and part of Poland. During the reign of Alexander I (1801–25), Napoleon's attempt to subdue Russia was defeated (1812–13), and new territory was gained, including Finland (1809) and Bessarabia (1812). Alexander originated the Holy Alliance, which for a time crushed Europe's rising liberal movement.

Alexander II (1855–81) pushed Russia's borders to the Pacific and into central Asia. Serfdom was abolished in 1861, but heavy restrictions were imposed on the emancipated class. Revolutionary strikes following Russia's defeat in the war with Japan forced Nicholas II (1894–1917) to grant a representative national body (Duma), elected by narrowly limited suffrage. It met for the first time in 1906, little influencing Nicholas in his reactionary course.

World War I demonstrated tsarist corruption and inefficiency and only patriotism held the poorly equipped army together for a time. Disorders broke out in Petrograd (renamed Leningrad now St. Petersburg) in March 1917, and defection of the Petrograd garrison launched the revolution. Nicholas II was forced to abdicate on March 15, 1917, and he and his family were killed by revolutionists on July 16, 1918.

A provisional government under the successive premierships of Prince Lvov and a moderate, Alexander Kerensky, lost ground to the radical, or Bolshevik, wing of the Socialist Democratic Labor Party. On Nov. 7, 1917, the Bolshevik revolution, engineered by N. Lenin[1] and Leon Trotsky, overthrew the Kerensky government and authority was vested in a Council of People's Commissars, with Lenin as Premier.

The humiliating Treaty of Brest-Litovsk (March 3, 1918) concluded the war with Germany, but civil war and foreign intervention delayed Communist control of all Russia until 1920. A brief war with Poland in 1920 resulted in Russian defeat.

Emergence of the U.S.S.R.

The Union of Soviet Socialist Republics was established as a federation on Dec. 30, 1922.

The death of Lenin on Jan. 21, 1924, precipitated an intraparty struggle between Joseph Stalin, General Secretary of the party, and Trotsky, who favored swifter socialization at home and fomentation of revolution abroad. Trotsky was dismissed as Commissar of War in 1925 and banished from the Soviet Union in 1929. He was murdered in Mexico City on Aug. 21, 1940, by a political agent.

Stalin further consolidated his power by a series of purges in the late 1930s, liquidating prominent party leaders and military officers. Stalin assumed the premiership May 6, 1941.

Soviet foreign policy, at first friendly toward Germany and antagonistic toward Britain and France and then, after Hitler's rise to power in 1933, becoming anti-Fascist and pro-League of Nations, took an abrupt turn on Aug. 24, 1939, with the signing of a nonaggression pact with Nazi Germany. The next month, Moscow joined in the German attack on Poland, seizing territory later incorporated into the Ukrainian and Byelorussian S.S.R.'s. The war with Finland, 1939–40, added territory to the Karelian S.S.R. set up March 31, 1940; the annexation of Bessarabia and Bukovina from Romania became part of the new Moldavian S.S.R. on Aug. 2, 1940; and the annexation of the Baltic republics of Estonia, Latvia, and Lithuania in June 1940

created the 14th, 15th, and 16th Soviet Republics. The illegal annexation of the Baltic republics was never recognized by the U.S. for the 51 years leading up to Soviet recognition of Estonia, Latvia and Lithuania's independence on September 6, 1991.

The Soviet-German collaboration ended abruptly with a lightning attack by Hitler on June 22, 1941, which seized 500,000 square miles of Russian territory before Soviet defenses, aided by U.S. and British arms, could halt it. The Soviet resurgence at Stalingrad from November 1942 to February 1943 marked the turning point in a long battle, ending in the final offensive of January 1945.

Then, after denouncing a 1941 nonaggression pact with Japan in April 1945, when Allied forces were nearing victory in the Pacific, the Soviet Union declared war on Japan on Aug. 8, 1945, and quickly occupied Manchuria, Karafuto, and the Kurile islands.

The U.S.S.R. built a cordon of Communist states running from Poland in the north to Albania and Bulgaria in the south, including East Germany, Czechoslovakia, Hungary, and Romania, composed of the territories Soviet troops occupied at the war's end. With its Eastern front solidified, the Soviet Union launched a political offensive against the non-Communist West, moving first to block the Western access to Berlin. The Western powers countered with an airlift, completed unification of West Germany, and organized the defense of Western Europe in the North Atlantic Treaty Organization.

Stalin died on March 6, 1953, and was succeeded the next day by G. M. Malenkov as Premier.

The new power in the Kremlin was Nikita S. Khrushchev, First Secretary of the party.

Khrushchev formalized the Eastern European system into a Council for Mutual Economic Assistance (Comecon) and a Warsaw Pact Treaty Organization as a counterweight to NATO.

The Soviet Union exploded a hydrogen bomb in 1953, developed an intercontinental ballistic missile by 1957, sent the first satellite into space (Sputnik I) in 1957, and put Yuri Gagarin in the first orbital flight around the earth in 1961.

Khrushchev's downfall stemmed from his decision to place Soviet nuclear missiles in Cuba and then, when challenged by the U.S., backing down and removing the weapons. He was also blamed for the ideological break with China after 1963.

Khrushchev was forced into retirement on Oct. 15, 1964, and was replaced by Leonid I. Brezhnev as First Secretary of the Party and Aleksei N. Kosygin as Premier.

Carter and the ailing Brezhnev signed the SALT II treaty in Vienna on June 18, 1979, setting ceilings on each nation's arsenal of intercontinental ballistic missiles. Doubts about Senate ratification grew, and became a certainty on Dec. 27, when Soviet troops invaded Afghanistan.

Despite the tension between Moscow and Washington, Strategic Arms Reduction Talks (START) began in Geneva between U.S. and Soviet delegations in mid-1982. Negotiations on intermediate missile reduction also continued in Geneva.

On November 10, 1982, Soviet radio and television announced the death of Leonid Brezhnev. Yuri V. Andropov, who formerly headed the K.G.B., was chosen to succeed Brezhnev as General Secretary. By mid-June 1983, Andropov had assumed all of Brezhnev's three titles.

The Soviet Union broke off both the START talks and the parallel negotiations on European-based missiles in November 1983 in protest against the deployment of medium-range U.S. missiles in Western Europe.

---

1. N. Lenin was the pseudonym taken by Vladimir Ilich Ulyanov. It is sometimes given as Nikolai Lenin or V. Lenin.

Rulers of Russia Since 1533

Name	Born	Ruled[1]	Name	Born	Ruled[1]
Ivan IV the Terrible	1530	1533–1584	Alexander III	1845	1881–1894
Theodore I	1557	1584–1598	Nicholas II	1868	1894–1917 [7]
Boris Godunov	c.1551	1598–1605			
Theodore II	1589	1605–1605	**PROVISIONAL GOVERNMENT**		
Demetrius I[2]	?	1605–1606	**(PREMIERS)**		
Basil IV Shuiski	?	1606–1610 [3]	Prince Georgi Lvov	1861	1917–1917
"Time of Troubles"	—	1610–1613	Alexander Kerensky	1881	1917–1917
Michael Romanov	1596	1613–1645			
Alexis I	1629	1645–1676	**POLITICAL LEADERS OF U.S.S.R.**		
Theodore III	1656	1676–1682	N. Lenin	1870	1917–1924
Ivan V[4]	1666	1682–1689 [5]	Aleksei Rykov	1881	1924–1930
Peter I the Great[4]	1672	1682–1725	Vyacheslav Molotov	1890	1930–1941
Catherine I	c.1684	1725–1727	Joseph Stalin[8]	1879	1941–1953
Peter II	1715	1727–1730	Georgi M. Malenkov	1902	1953–1955
Anna	1693	1730–1740	Nikolai A. Bulganin	1895	1955–1958
Ivan VI	1740	1740–1741 [6]	Nikita S. Khrushchev	1894	1958–1964
Elizabeth	1709	1741–1762	Leonid I. Brezhnev	1906	1964–1982
Peter III	1728	1762–1762	Yuri V. Andropov	1914	1982–1984
Catherine II the Great	1729	1762–1796	Konstantin U. Chernenko	1912	1984–1985
Paul I	1754	1796–1801	Mikhail S. Gorbachev	1931	1985–1991
Alexander I	1777	1801–1825			
Nicholas I	1796	1825–1855	**PRESIDENT OF RUSSIA**		
Alexander II	1818	1855–1881	Boris Yeltsin	1931	1991–

1. For Tsars through Nicholas II, year of end of rule is also that of death, unless otherwise indicated. 2. Also known as Pseudo–Demetrius. 3. Died 1612. 4. Ruled jointly until 1689, when Ivan was deposed. 5. Died 1696. 6. Died 1764. 7. Killed 1918. 8. General Secretary of Communist Party, 1924–53.

After months of illness, Andropov died in February 1984. Konstantin U. Chernenko, a 72-year-old party stalwart who had been close to Brezhnev, succeeded him as General Secretary and, by mid-April, had also assumed the title of President. In the months following Chernenko's assumption of power, the Kremlin took on a hostile mood toward the West of a kind rarely seen since the height of the cold war 30 years before. Led by Moscow, all the Soviet bloc countries except Romania boycotted the 1984 Summer Olympic Games in Los Angeles—tit-for-tat for the U.S.-led boycott of the 1980 Moscow Games, in the view of most observers.

After 13 months in office, Chernenko died on March 10, 1985. He had been ill much of the time and left only a minor imprint on Soviet history.

Chosen to succeed him as Soviet leader was Mikhail S. Gorbachev, at 54 the youngest man to take charge of the Soviet Union since Stalin. Under Gorbachev, the Soviet Union began its long-awaited shift to a new generation of leadership. Unlike his immediate predecessors, Gorbachev did not also assume the title of President but wielded power from the post of party General Secretary. In a surprise move, Gorbachev elevated Andrei Gromyko, 75, for 28 years the Soviet Union's stony-faced Foreign Minister, to the largely ceremonial post of President. He installed a younger man with no experience in foreign affairs, Eduard Shevardnadze, 57, as Foreign Minister.

The Soviet Union took much criticism in early 1986 over the April 24 meltdown at the Chernobyl nuclear plant and its reluctance to give out any information on the accident.

In June 1987, Gorbachev obtained the support of the Central Committee for proposals that would loosen some government controls over the economy and in June 1988, an unusually open party conference approved several resolutions for changes in the structure of the Soviet system. These included a shift of some power from the Party to local soviets, a ten-year limit on the terms of elected government and party officials, and an alteration in the office of the

President to give it real power in domestic and foreign policy. Gorbachev was elected President in 1989. The elections to the Congress were the first competitive elections in the Soviet Union since 1917. Dissident candidates won a surprisingly large minority although pro-Government deputies maintained a strong lock on the Supreme Soviet.

The possible beginning of the fragmentation of the Communist party took place when Boris Yeltsin, leader of the Russian S.S.R. who urges faster reform, left the Communist party along with other radicals.

In March 1991 the Soviet people were asked to vote on a referendum on national unity engineered by President Gorbachev. The resultant victory for the federal government was tempered by the separate approval in Russia for the creation of a popularly-elected republic presidency. In addition, six republics boycotted the vote.

The bitter election contest for the Russian presidency principally between Yeltsin and a Communist loyalist resulted in a major victory for Yeltsin. He took the oath of office for the new position on July 10.

Reversing his relative hard-line position adopted in the autumn of 1990, Gorbachev together with leaders of nine Soviet republics signed an accord, called the Union Treaty, which was meant to preserve the unity of the nation. In exchange the federal government would have turned over control of industrial and natural resources to the individual republics.

An attempted coup d'état took place on August 19 orchestrated by a group of eight senior officials calling itself the State Committee on the State of Emergency. Boris Yeltsin, held up in the Russian Parliament building, defiantly called for a general strike. The next day huge crowds demonstrated in Leningrad, and Yeltsin supporters fortified barricades surrounding the Parliament building. On August 21 the coup committee disbanded, and at least some of its members attempted to flee Moscow. The Soviet Parliament formally reinstated Gorbachev as President. Two days later he resigned from his position as General Secretary of the Communist Party and recommended that its Central Committee be disbanded. On August 29 the Parliament approved the suspension of all Communist Party activities pending an investigation of its role in the failed coup.

At the time of the attempted coup, the republic's President Boris Yeltsin was the most popular political figure in the lands comprising the former Soviet Union. A leading reformer, he became the first directly elected leader in Russian history and received 60% of the vote for President of the Russian Republic.

During the attempted coup in August 1991 by hard-line Communists to dislodge Mikhail Gorbachev, Yeltsin risked his life and rallied the opposition against the coup leaders. His heroism won him worldwide acclaim when the coup failed and he gained new stature and influence.

Yeltsin championed the cause for national reconstruction and the adoption of a Union Treaty with the other republics to create a free-market economic association.

Dissolution of the U.S.S.R.

On Dec. 12, 1991, the Russian parliament ratified Yeltsin's plea to establish a new commonwealth of independent nations open to all former members of the Soviet Union. The new union was created with the governments of Ukraine and Belarus who along with Russia were the three original cofounders of the Soviet Union in 1922.

After the end of the Soviet Union, Russia and ten other Soviet republics joined in a Commonwealth of Independent States on Dec. 21, 1991.

At the start of 1992, Russia embarked on a series of dramatic economic reforms, including the freeing of prices on most goods, which led to an immediate downturn.

A national referendum on confidence in Yeltsin and his economic program took place in April 1993. To the surprise of many the president and his shock-therapy program won by a resounding margin. Yeltsin convened a constitutional conference in June which adopted a draft document in July. In September Yeltsin dissolved the legislative bodies left over from the Soviet era. The impasse between the executive and the legislature resulted in an armed conflict on October 3. Yeltsin prevailed largely through the support of the military and other forces.

The constitutional referendum on December 12 was a victory for Yeltsin, but the parliamentary election on the same day saw the rise of the extreme nationalist Vladimir Zhirinovsky, with western-oriented parties performing relatively poorly.

The southern republic of Chechnya's president accelerated his region's drive for independence in 1994. In December Russian troops closed the borders and sought to squelch the independence drive. The Russian military forces met firm and costly resistance that lasted well into 1995. Additionally in June of that year a Chechen commando unit raided a small Russian town, taking up to 2,000 hostages.

Also in June 1995 Russia agreed to participate actively in NATO's Partnership in Peace program but stated it would immediately suspend its participation should NATO expand eastward to Russia's borders.

RWANDA

Rwandese Republic
President: Pasteur Bizimungu (1994)

Prime Minister: Faustin Twagiramungu (1994)
Area: 10,169 sq mi. (26,338 sq km)
Population (est. mid-1995): 7,800,000 (average annual rate of natural increase: 2.3%); birth rate: 40/1000; infant mortality rate: 117/1000; density per square mile: 767
Capital and largest city (1991): Kigali, 232,733; **Monetary unit:** Rwanda franc; **Languages:** Kinyarwanda, French, Swahili, English. **Religions:** Roman Catholic, 56%; Protestant, 18%; Islam, 1%; Animist, 25%; **National name:** Republika y'u Rwanda; **Literacy rate:** 5%
Economic summary: Gross domestic product (1993 est.): $6.8 billion; $800 per capita; real growth rate 1.3% (1992 est.); inflation 9.5% (1992 est.); unemployment n.a. Arable land: 29%. Principal products: coffee, tea, bananas, yams, beans. Labor force 3,600,000; in agriculture, 93%; in industry: 2%. Major products: processed foods, light consumer goods, minerals. Natural resources: gold, cassiterite, wolfram. Exports: $66.6 million (f.o.b., 1992 est.): coffee, tea, tungsten, tin, pyrethrum. Imports: $259.5 million (f.o.b., 1992 est.): textiles, foodstuffs, machinery, and equipment, capital goods, steel. Major trading partners: Belgium, Germany, Kenya, Japan, France, U.S., Italy, U.K.

Geography. Rwanda, in east central Africa, is surrounded by Zaire, Uganda, Tanzania, and Burundi. It is slightly smaller than Maryland.

Steep mountains and deep valleys cover most of the country. Lake Kivu in the northwest, at an altitude of 4,829 feet (1,472 m) is the highest lake in Africa. Extending north of it are the Virunga Mountains, which include Volcan Karisimbi (14,187 ft; 4,324 m), Rwanda's highest point.

Government. A National Unity government was installed by the rebel Tutsu-dominated Rwandan Patriotic Front on July 19, 1994. The former government was a republic. Former President Gen. Juvénal Habyarimana was killed on April 6, 1994 in a mysterious plane crash over the capital Kigali. The new cabinet is composed of 22 members. Maj. Gen. Paul Kagame, the victorious Tutsi rebel leader, is both vice president and defense minister.

History. Rwanda, which was part of German East Africa, was first visited by European explorers in 1854. During World War I, it was occupied in 1916 by Belgian troops. After the war, it became a Belgian League of Nations mandate, along with Burundi, under the name of Ruanda-Urundi. The mandate was made a U.N. trust territory in 1946. Until the Belgian Congo achieved independence in 1960, Ruanda-Urundi was administered as part of that colony.

Ruanda became the independent nation of Rwanda on July 1, 1962.

In August 1992 a formal agreement was signed ending the civil war between the government and the Rwandan Patriotic Front.

After the downing of an aircraft in April 1994 carrying the presidents of Rwanda and Burundi, both of whom died in the crash, Tutsi rebels swept across the country in a 14-week civil war, routing the largely Hutu government. In the immediate aftermath an estimated 1.7 million Hutus fled across the border into neighboring Zaire, creating an international humanitarian problem.

Rwanda in June 1995 asked the U.N. Security Council to lift its arms embargo, imposed the previous year.

ST. KITTS AND NEVIS

Federation of St. Kitts and Nevis
Sovereign: Queen Elizabeth II
Governor General: Sir Clement Athelston Arrindell (1985)
Prime Minister: Dr. Denzil Douglas (1995)
Area: St. Kitts 65 sq mi. (169 sq km); Nevis 35 sq mi. (93 sq km)
Total population (est. mid-1995): 40,000 (average annual rate of natural increase: 1.4%); birth rate: 23/1000; infant mortality rate: 19/1000; density per square mile: 400
Capital: Basseterre (on St. Kitts), 19,000; **Largest town on Nevis:** Charlestown, 1,771; **Monetary unit:** East Caribbean dollar. **Literacy rate:** 98%.
Economic summary: Gross domestic product (1992): $163 million; per capita $4,000; real growth rate 4.1%; inflation 2.9%; unemployment (1990) 12.2%. Arable land: 22%. Principal agricultural products: sugar, rice, yams. Labor force: 20,000 (1981). Major industries: tourism, sugar processing, salt extraction. Exports: $32.4 million (f.o.b., 1992): sugar, manufactures, postage stamps. Imports: $100 million (f.o.b., 1992): foodstuffs, manufactured goods, machinery, fuels. Major trading partners: U.S., U.K., Japan, Trinidad and Tobago, Canada.

St. Christopher-Nevis, preferably St. Kitts and Nevis, was formerly part of the West Indies Associated States which were established in 1967 and consisted of Antigua and St. Kitts-Nevis-Anguilla of the Leeward Islands, and Dominica, Grenada, St. Lucia, and St. Vincent of the Windward Islands. Statehood for St. Vincent was held up until 1969 because of local political uncertainties. Anguilla's association with St. Christopher-Nevis ended in 1980.

St. Christopher-Nevis, now St. Kitts and Nevis, became independent on September 19, 1983.

The premier of Nevis in 1990 announced that he intended to seek an end to the federation with St. Kitts by the end of 1992, but a local election in June 1992 removed the threat of secession for now.

Parliamentary elections held on July 3, 1995, for the 11 seats resulted in a victory for the opposition Labour Party.

ST. LUCIA

Sovereign: Queen Elizabeth II
Governor-General: Sir Stanislaus A. James (1989)
Prime Minister: John Compton (1982)
Area: 238 sq mi. (616 sq km)
Population (est. mid-1994): 145,090 (average annual rate of natural increase: 0.52%); birth rate: 23.1/1000; infant mortality rate: 18.5/1000; density per square mile: 609.6
Capital and largest city (1992 est.): Castries, 13,600; **Monetary unit:** East Caribbean dollar; **Languages:** English and patois; **Religions:** Roman Catholic, 90%; Protestant, 7%; Anglican, 3%; **Member of Commonwealth of Nations;** **Literacy rate:** 90%
Economic summary: Gross domestic product (1993 est.): $433 million; $3,000 per capita; real growth rate 6.6% (1992 est.); inflation 5.1% (1992); unemployment (1988) 16%. Arable land: 8%. Principal products: bananas, coconuts, cocoa, citrus fruit. Major industrial products: clothing, assembled electronics, beverages. Exports: $122.8 million (f.o.b., 1992): bananas, cocoa, clothing, vegetables, fruits, coconut oil. Imports: $276 million (f.o.b., 1992): foodstuffs, machinery and equip-ment, fertilizers, petroleum products. Major trading partners: U.K., U.S., Caribbean countries, Japan, Canada.

Geography. One of the Windward Isles of the Eastern Caribbean, St. Lucia lies just south of Martinique. It is of volcanic origin. A chain of wooded mountains runs from north to south, and from them flow many streams into fertile valleys.

Government. A Governor-General represents the sovereign, Queen Elizabeth II. A Prime Minister is head of government, chosen by a 17-member House of Assembly elected by universal suffrage for a maximum term of five years.

History. Discovered by Spain in 1503 and ruled by Spain and then France, St. Lucia became a British territory in 1803. With other Windward Isles, St. Lucia was granted home rule in 1967 as one of the West Indies Associated States. On Feb. 22, 1979, St. Lucia achieved full independence in ceremonies boycotted by the opposition St. Lucia Labor Party, which had advocated a referendum before cutting ties with Britain.

Unrest and a strike by civil servants forced Prime Minister John Compton to hold elections in July, in which his United Workers Party lost its majority for the first time in 15 years.

A Labor Party government was ousted in turn by Compton and his followers, in elections in May 1982.

Formerly dependent on a single crop, bananas, St. Lucia has sought to lower its chronic unemployment and payments deficit.

Elections of April 1992 returned the prime minister and his party once again to office.

Banana farmers in 1994 protested against the low prices paid for their crop. In response the prime minister agreed to raise the price for certain grades of bananas.

ST. VINCENT AND THE GRENADINES

Sovereign: Queen Elizabeth II
Governor-General: David Jack (1989)
Prime Minister: James Mitchell (1984)
Area: 150 sq mi. (389 sq km)
Population (est. mid-1994): 115,437 (average annual rate of natural increase: 0.77%); birth rate: 20.2/1000; infant mortality rate: 17.2/1000; density per square mile: 769.5
Capital and largest city (1992 est.): Kingstown, 15,466. **Monetary unit:** East Caribbean dollar; **Language:** English, some French patois; **Religions:** Anglican, 47%; Methodist, 28%; Roman Catholic, 13%; **Member of Commonwealth of Nations;** Literacy rate: 96%
Economic summary: Gross domestic product (1992 est.): $215 million; $2,000 per capita; 6.5% real growth rate; inflation (1993 est.) 3.3%; unemployment: 35–40%. Arable land: 38%. Principal products: bananas, arrowroot, coconuts. Labor Force: 67,000 (1984 est.). Major industry: food processing. Exports: $77.5 million (f.o.b., 1992): bananas, arrowroot, eddos and dasheen (taro), tennis racquets. Imports: $118.6 million (f.o.b., 1992): foodstuffs, machinery and equipment, chemicals, fuels, minerals. Major trading partners: U.K., U.S., Caribbean nations.

Geography. St. Vincent, chief island of the chain, is 18 miles (29 km) long and 11 miles (18 km) wide. One of the Windward Islands in the Lesser Antilles, it is 100 miles (161 km) west of Barbados. The island is mountainous and well forested. The Grenadines, a chain of nearly 600 islets with a total area of only 17 square miles (27 sq km), extend for 60 miles (96 km) from northeast to southwest between St. Vincent and Grenada, southernmost of the Windwards.

St. Vincent is dominated by the volcano La Soufrière, part of a volcanic range running north and south, which rises to 4,048 feet (1,234 m). The volcano erupted over a 10-day period in April 1979, causing the evacuation of the northern two-thirds of the island. (There is also a volcano of the same name on Basse-Terre, Guadeloupe, which became violently active in 1976 and 1977.)

Government. A Governor-General represents the sovereign, Queen Elizabeth II. A Prime Minister, elected by a 15-member unicameral legislature, holds executive power.

History. Discovered by Columbus in 1498, and alternately claimed by Britain and France, St. Vincent became a British colony by the Treaty of Paris in 1783. The islands won home rule in 1969 as part of the West Indies Associated States and achieved full independence Oct. 26, 1979. Prime Minister Milton Cato's government quelled a brief rebellion Dec. 8, 1979, attributed to economic problems following the eruption of La Soufrière in April 1979. Unlike a 1902 eruption which killed 2,000, there was no loss of life but widespread losses to agriculture.

The House of Assembly in August 1993 approved a change in the criminal code that raised the minimum age for the death penalty from 16 to 18.

The election of February 1994 provided a victory for the prime minister and his party albeit with a reduced majority in parliament.

SAN MARINO

Most Serene Republic of San Marino
Co-Regents: Two selected every six months by Grand and General Council
Area: 23.6 sq mi. (62 sq km)
Population (est. mid-1995): 30,000 (average annual growth rate: 0.4%); birth rate: 10/1000; infant mortality rate: 9.3/1000; density per square mile: 1,271.2
Capital and largest city (est. 1992): San Marino, 2,397; **Monetary unit:** Italian lira; **Language:** Italian; **Religion:** Roman Catholic; **National name:** Repubblica di San Marino; **Literacy rate:** 96%
Economic summary: Gross domestic product (1992 est.): $370 million; $16,000 per capita; real growth rate, n.a.; inflation 6.2%; unemployment (1991) 3%. Arable land: 17%. Principal products: wheat and other grains, grapes, olives, cheese. Labor force: approx. 4,300. The tourist sector contributes over 50% of GDP. Key industries are wearing apparel, electronics and ceramics. Other industrial products: textiles, leather, cement, wine, olive oil. Exports: building stone, lime, chestnuts, wheat, hides, baked goods. Imports: manufactured consumer goods. Major trading partner: Italy.

Geography. One-tenth the size of New York City, San Marino is surrounded by Italy. It is situated in the Apennines, a little inland from the Adriatic Sea

near Rimini.

Government. The country is governed by two co-regents. Executive power is exercised by ten ministers. In 1959, the Grand Council granted women the vote. San Marino is a member of the Conference on Security and Cooperation in Europe.

History. According to tradition, San Marino was founded about A.D. 350 and had good luck for centuries in staying out of the many wars and feuds on the Italian peninsula. It is the oldest republic in the world.

A person born in San Marino remains a citizen and can vote no matter where he lives.

In September the country joined the IMF and the Social Democrats entered into a coalition with the Christian Democrats.

Spring 1993 elections for the Great and General Council gave a majority to the Christian Democrats and Socialists.

SÃO TOMÉ AND PRÍNCIPE

Democratic Republic of São Tomé and Príncipe
President: Miguel Trovoada (1991)
Prime Minister: Carlos da Graca (1994)
Area: 370 sq mi. (958 sq km)
Population (est. mid-1995): 100,000 (average annual growth rate: 2.6%); birth rate: 35/1000; infant mortality rate: 61.8/1000; density per square mile: 270.2
Capital and largest city (est. 1990): São Tomé, 43,420; **Monetary unit:** Dobra; **Language:** Portuguese; **Religions:** Roman Catholic, Evangelical Protestant, Seventh-Day Adventist; **Literacy rate:** 57% (est.)
Economic summary: Gross domestic product (1992 est.): $41.4 million; $315 per capita; 1.5% annual growth rate; inflation: 27%; unemployment: n.a. Arable land: 1%. Principal agricultural products: cocoa, copra, coconuts, palm oil, coffee, bananas. Labor force: 21,096 (1981): mostly in subsistence agriculture. Major industrial products: shirts, soap, beer, processed fish and shrimp. Exports: $5.4 million (f.o.b., 1992 est.): cocoa, coffee, copra, palm oil. Imports: $31.5 million (f.o.b., 1992 est.): textiles, machinery, electrical equipment, fuels, food products. Major trading partners: Netherlands, Portugal, Germany, China, Angola.

Geography. The tiny volcanic islands of São Tomé and Príncipe lie in the Gulf of Guinea about 150 miles (240 km) off West Africa. São Tomé (about 330 sq mi.; 859 sq km) is covered by a dense mountainous jungle, out of which have been carved large plantations. Príncipe (about 40 sq mi.; 142 sq km) consists of jagged mountains. Other islands in the republic are Pedras Tinhosas and Rolas.

Government. The Constitution grants supreme power to a 55-seat People's Assembly composed of members elected for four years. In 1990 a referendum approved a new constitution paving the way for a multi-party democracy.

History. São Tomé and Príncipe were discovered by Portuguese navigators in 1471 and settled by the end of the century. Intensive cultivation by slave labor made the islands a major producer of sugar during the 17th century but output declined until the introduction of coffee and cacao in the 19th century brought new prosperity. The island of São Tomé was the world's largest producer of cacao in 1908 and the crop is still the most important. An exile liberation movement was formed in 1953 after Portuguese land-owners quelled labor riots by killing several hundred African workers.

The Portuguese revolution of 1974 brought the end of the overseas empire and the new Lisbon government transferred power to the liberation movement on July 12, 1975.

A former prime minister and dissident Miguel Trovoada was elected president in March 1991 after the withdrawal of the two other candidates.

General elections, precipitated by tensions arising between the president and the ruling Party of Democratic Convergence, held in October 1994 gave 27 seats in the Assembly to a formerly Marxist party. As the single largest party the president appointed its leader prime minister.

SAUDI ARABIA

Kingdom of Saudi Arabia
King and Prime Minister: King Fahd bin 'Abdulaziz (1982)
Area: 865,000 sq mi. (2,250,070 sq km)
Population (est. mid-1995): 18,500,000 (average annual rate of natural increase: 3.2%); birth rate: 36/1000; infant mortality rate: 24/1000; density per square mile: 21.3
Capital: Riyadh; **Largest cities (1993):** Riyadh, 3,000,000; Jeddah, 2,500,000; Makkah (est. 1994) (Mecca,) 550,000. **Monetary unit:** Riyal; **Language:** Arabic, English widely spoken; **Religion:** Islam, 100%; **National name:** Al-Mamlaka al-'Arabiya as-Sa'udiya; **Literacy rate:** 65%
Economic summary: Gross domestic product (1993): $114 billion; $9,000 per capita; real growth rate (1992 est.) 3.6%; inflation 1%. Arable land: 5%. Principal agricultural products: dates, grains, livestock, wheat, fish, flowers. Labor force: 5,000,000; about 25% are foreign workers; in government, 34%; industry and oil, 28%. Major industrial products: petroleum, cement, plastic products, steel, packaged goods. Natural resources: oil, natural gas, iron ore. Exports: $42.3 billion (f.o.b., 1993 est.): petroleum and petroleum products. Imports: $26 billion (f.o.b., 1993 est.): manufactured goods, transport equipment, construction materials, processed food. Major trading partners: U.S., Germany, Great Britain and other Western European countries, South Korea, Taiwan, Japan.

Geography. Saudi Arabia occupies most of the Arabian Peninsula, with the Red Sea and the Gulf of Aqaba to the west, the Arabian Gulf to the east. Neighboring countries are Jordan, Iraq, Kuwait, Qatar, the United Arab Emirates, the Sultanate of Oman, Yemen, and Bahrain, connected to the Saudi mainland by a causeway.

A narrow coastal plain on the Red Sea rims a mountain range that spans the length of the western coastline. These mountains gradually rise in elevation from north to south. East of these mountains is a massive plateau which slopes gently downward toward the Arabian Gulf. Part of this plateau is covered by the world's largest continuous sand desert, the Rub Al-Khali, or Empty Quarter. Saudi Arabia's oil region lies primarily in the eastern province along the Arabian Gulf, but significant recent discoveries have also been made in the interior south of Riyadh.

Government. Saudi Arabia is a monarchy based on the Sharia (Islamic law), as revealed in the Koran (the

holy book) and the Hadith (teachings and sayings of the prophet Mohammed). A Council of Ministers was formed in 1953, which acts as a Cabinet under the leadership of the King. There are 21 Ministries.

Royal and ministerial decrees account for most of the promulgated legislation, treaties, and conventions. There are no political parties.

In March 1992 King Fahd announced new bylaws for the Consultative Council to propose and review laws. The Cabinet, composed of 21 members (four are members of the Saudi royal family) passes laws.

History. Mohammed united the Arabs in the 7th century, and his followers, led by the caliphs, founded a great empire, with its capital at Medina. Later, the caliphate capital was transferred to Damascus and then Baghdad, but Arabia retained its importance because of the holy cities of Mecca and Medina. In the 16th and 17th centuries, the Turks established at least nominal rule over much of Arabia, and in the middle of the 18th century, it was divided into separate principalities.

The Kingdom of Saudi Arabia is almost entirely the creation of King Ibn Saud (1882–1953). A descendant of earlier Wahabi rulers, he seized Riyadh, the capital of Nejd, in 1901 and set himself up as leader of the Arab nationalist movement. By 1906 he had established Wahabi dominance in Nejd. He conquered Hejaz in 1924–25, consolidating it and Nejd into a dual kingdom in 1926. In 1932, Hejaz and Nejd became a single kingdom, which was officially named Saudi Arabia. A year later the region of Asir was incorporated into the kingdom.

Oil was discovered in 1936, and commercial production began during World War II. Saudi Arabia was neutral until nearly the end of the war, but it was permitted to be a charter member of the United Nations. The country joined the Arab League in 1945 and took part in the 1948–49 war against Israel.

On Ibn Saud's death in 1953, his eldest son, Saud, began an 11-year reign marked by an increasing hostility toward the radical Arabism of Egypt's Gamal Abdel Nasser. In 1964, the ailing Saud was deposed and replaced by the Premier, Crown Prince Faisal, who gave vocal support but no military help to Egypt in the 1967 Mideast war.

Faisal's assassination by a deranged kinsman in 1975 shook the Middle East, but failed to alter his kingdom's course. His successor was his brother, Prince Khalid. Khalid gave influential support to Egypt during negotiations on Israeli withdrawal from the Sinai desert.

King Khalid died of a heart attack June 13, 1982, and was succeeded by his half-brother, Prince Fahd bin 'Abdulaziz, 60, who had exercised the real power throughout Khalid's reign. King Fahd, a pro-Western modernist, chose his 58-year-old half-brother, Abdullah, as Crown Prince.

Saudi Arabia and the smaller, oil-rich Arab states on the Persian Gulf, fearful that they might become Ayatollah Ruhollah Khomeini's next targets if Iran conquered Iraq, made large financial contributions to the Iraqi war effort. They began being dragged into the conflict themselves in the spring of 1984, when Iraq and Iran extended their ground war to attacks on Gulf shipping. First, Iraq attacked tankers loading at Iran's Kharg Island terminal with air-to-ground missiles, then Iran struck back at tankers calling at Saudi Arabia and other Arab countries.

At the same time, cheating by other members of the Organization of Petroleum Exporting Countries, competition from nonmember oil producers, and conservation efforts by consuming nations combined to drive down the world price of oil. Saudi Arabia has one-third of all known oil reserves, but falling demand and rising production outside OPEC combined to reduce its oil revenues from \$120 billion in 1980 to \$43 billion in 1984 to less the \$25 billion in 1985, threatening the country with domestic unrest and undermining its influence in the Gulf area.

In September 1993 the King confirmed organizing the country into 13 regions under governors. A consultative council, whose members were appointed by Faud, officially opened in December.

The first regular meeting of the council occurred in January 1994 and established various committees.

In May King Fahd promised a privatizing plan to sell certain state assets to the public.

SENEGAL

Republic of Senegal
President: Abdou Diouf (1981)
Area: 75,954 sq mi. (196,722 sq km)
Population (est. mid-1995): 8,300,000 (average annual rate of natural increase: 2.7%); birth rate: 43/1000; infant mortality rate: 68/1000; density per square mile: 109.2
Capital and largest city (1992 est.): Dakar, 1,729,823.
Monetary unit: Franc CFA; **Ethnic groups:** Wolofs, Sereres, Peuls, Tukulers, and others; **Languages:** French (official); Wolof, Serer, other ethnic dialects; **Religions:** Islam, 92%; indigenous, 6%; Christian, 2%; **National name:** République du Sénégal; **Literacy rate:** 38%
Economic summary: Gross domestic product (1993 est.): \$11.8 billion; \$1,400 per capita; real growth rate 1.2% (1991 est.); inflation (1991 est.) −1.8%; unemployment n.a. Arable land: 27%. Principal agricultural products: peanuts, millet, corn, rice, sorghum. Labor force: 2,509,000; 77% subsistence agriculture workers. Major industrial products: processed food, phosphates, refined petroleum, cement, and fish. Natural resources: fish, phosphate, iron ore. Exports: \$904 million (f.o.b., 1991 est.): peanuts, phosphate rock, canned fish, petroleum products. Imports: \$1.2 billion (c.i.f., 1991 est.): foodstuffs, consumer goods, machinery, transport equipment, petroleum. Major trading partners: U.S., Western European countries, African neighbors, Japan, China, India.

Geography. The capital of Senegal, Dakar, is the westernmost point in Africa. The country, slightly smaller than South Dakota, surrounds Gambia on three sides and is bordered on the north by Mauritania, on the east by Mali, and on the south by Guinea and Guinea-Bissau.

Senegal is mainly a low-lying country, with a semi-desert area in the north and northeast and forests in the southwest. The largest rivers include the Senegal in the north and the Casamance in the south tropical climate region.

Government. There is a National Assembly of 120 members, elected every five years. There is universal suffrage and a constitutional guarantee of equality before the law.

History. The Portuguese had some stations on the banks of the Senegal River in the 15th century, and the first French settlement was made at Saint-Louis about 1650. The British took parts of Senegal at various times, but the French gained possession in 1840 and organized the Sudan as a territory in 1904. In 1946, together with other parts of French West Africa, Senegal became part of the French Union. On

June 20, 1960, it became an independent republic federated with the Sudanese Republic in the Mali Federation, from which it withdrew two months later.

In 1973, Senegal joined with six other states to create the West African Economic Community.

In elections of February 21, 1993 President Diouf was reelected. In May legislative elections the president's Socialist Party captured 84 of the 120 seats.

A political demonstration in February 1994 organized by the opposition coalition resulted in the death of six policemen and injury to dozens more when more militant protesters attacked the security personnel.

SEYCHELLES

Republic of Seychelles
President: France-Albert René (1977)
Area: 175 sq mi. (453 sq km)
Population (est. mid-1995): 100,000 (average annual rate of natural increase: 1.5%); birth rate: 23/1000; infant mortality rate: 11.9/1000; density per square mile: 571.4
Capital: Victoria, 24,000; **Monetary unit:** Seychelles rupee; **Languages:** English and French (official); Creole; **Religions:** Roman Catholic, 90%; Anglican, 8%; **Member of Commonwealth of Nations; Literacy rate:** 58%
Economic summary: Gross domestic product (1992 est.): \$407 million; \$5,900 per capita; real growth rate 4%; inflation 3.3%; unemployment n.a.. Arable land: 4%. Principal agricultural products: vanilla, coconuts, cinnamon. Labor force: 27,700; 31% in industry and commerce. Major industrial products: processed coconut and vanilla, coir rope. Exports: \$47 million (f.o.b., 1992 est.): fish, canned tuna, copra, cinnamon bark. Imports: \$192 million (f.o.b., 1992 est.): food, tobacco, manufactured goods, machinery, petroleum products, transport equipment. Major trading partners: U.K., France, Japan, Pakistan, Reunion, South Africa.

Geography. Seychelles consists of an archipelago of about 100 islands in the Indian Ocean northeast of Madagascar. The principal islands are Mahé (55 sq mi.; 142 sq km), Praslin (15 sq mi.; 38 sq km), and La Digue (4 sq mi.; 10 sq km). The Aldabra, Farquhar, and Desroches groups are included in the territory of the republic.

Government. Seized from France by Britain in 1810, the Seychelles Islands remained a colony until June 29, 1976. The state is an independent republic within the Commonwealth.

On June 5, 1977, Prime Minister Albert René ousted the islands' first President, James Mancham, suspending the Constitution and the 25-member National Assembly. Mancham, whose "lavish spending" and flamboyance were cited by René in seizing power, charged that Soviet influence was at work. The new president denied this and, while more left than his predecessor, pledged to keep the Seychelles in the nonaligned group of countries.

An unsuccessful attempted coup against René attracted international attention when a group of 50 South African mercenaries posing as rugby players attacked the Victoria airport on Nov. 25, 1981.

An election was held in July 1992 for members of a commission to write a new constitution. 14 of the 23 seats went to the president's Seychelles People's Progressive Party. The draft constitution that emerged, however, was defeated in a referendum in November, failing to get the 60% of the vote needed for adoption.

The commission reconvened in January 1993 with the participation of the opposition Democratic Party. In May a draft constitution, institutionalizing a multiparty system and a 33-member National Assembly, was ready. In the June referendum more than 73% of the votes approved it. The presidential election in July under the new terms affirmed René's position and that of his party.

The country through its membership in the Indian Ocean Commission received substantial aid from the European Union in 1994. Tourism brought in income, and the overall economic picture remained bright.

SIERRA LEONE

Republic of Sierra Leone
President: Capt. Valentine Strasser (1992)
Area: 27,925 sq mi. (73,326 sq km)
Population (est. mid-1995): 4,500,000 (average annual rate of natural increase: 2.7%); birth rate: 46/1000; infant mortality rate: 143/1000; density per square mile: 161.1
Capital and largest city (1994 est.): Freetown, 1,300,000; **Monetary unit:** Leone; **Languages:** English (official), Mende, Temne, Krio; **Religions:** Islam, 40%; Christian, 35%; Indigenous, 20%. **Member of Commonwealth of Nations; Literacy rate:** 21%
Economic summary: Gross domestic product (FY 1993 est.): $4.5 billion; $1,000 per capita; real growth rate n.a.; inflation 35% (1992); unemployment n.a. Arable land: 25%; principal agricultural products: coffee, cocoa, palm kernels, rice. Labor force: 1,369,000 (est.); 65% in agriculture. Major industrial products: diamonds, bauxite, rutile, beverages, cigarettes, textiles, footwear. Natural resources: diamonds, bauxite, iron ore. Exports: $149 million (f.o.b., FY92): diamonds, rutile, bauxite, cocoa, coffee. Imports: $131 million (c.i.f., FY92): food, petroleum, products, capital goods. Major trading partners: U.K., U.S., Western European countries, Japan, China, Nigeria.

Geography. Sierra Leone, on the Atlantic Ocean in West Africa, is half the size of Illinois. Guinea, in the north and east, and Liberia, in the south, are its neighbors.

Mangrove swamps lie along the coast, with wooded hills and a plateau in the interior. The eastern region is mountainous.

Government. Sierra Leone became an independent nation on April 27, 1961, and declared itself a republic on April 19, 1971.

Sierra Leone became a one party state under the aegis of the All People's Congress Party in April 1978.

Sierra Leone has a military government which came into power in April 1992.

History. The coastal area of Sierra Leone was ceded to English settlers in 1788 as a home for blacks discharged from the British armed forces and also for runaway slaves who had found asylum in London. The British protectorate over the hinterland was proclaimed in 1896.

After elections in 1967, the British Governor-General replaced Sir Albert Margai, head of SLPP, which had held power since independence, with Dr. Stevens, head of APC, as prime minister. The Army took over the government; then another coup in April 1968 restored civilian rule and put the military leaders in jail.

A coup attempt early in 1971 by the army commander was apparently foiled by loyal army officers, but the

then Prime Minister Stevens called in troops of neighboring Guinea's army, under a 1970 mutual defense pact, to guard his residence. After perfunctorily blaming the U.S. for the coup attempt, Stevens switched Governors-General, changed the Constitution, and ended up with a republic, of which he was first president. Dr. Stevens' picked successor, Major-General Joseph Saidu Momoh was elected unopposed on Oct. 1, 1985.

Rebel soldiers in April 1992 toppled the government, voicing support for democracy. A few days later the ruling junta arrested their leader, placing in charge their second-in-command.

The government in December 1993 announced a timetable for a return to civilian rule and a multiparty democracy. Nevertheless, rebels continued to reject a government they considered corrupt. In January 1995 a rebel attack on a northern city sent many fleeing into Guinea. In mid-February government troops battled for six hours with rebels in the south.

SINGAPORE

Republic of Singapore
Prime Minister: Goh Chok Tong (1990)
Area: 246.7 sq mi. (639 sq km)
Population (est. mid-1995): 3,000,000 (average annual rate of natural increase: 1.2%); birth rate: 17/1000; infant mortality rate: 4.7/1000; density per square mile: 12,160.5
Capital (1992 est.): Singapore, 2,792,000. **Monetary unit:** Singapore dollar; **Languages:** Malay, Chinese (Mandarin), Tamil, English; **Religions:** Islam, Christian, Buddhist, Hindu, Taoist; **Member of Commonwealth of Nations; Literacy rate:** 91%
Economic summary: Gross domestic product (1993): $42.4 billion; $15,000 per capita; real growth rate 9.9%; inflation 2.4%; unemployment 1.9%. Arable land: 4%. Principal agricultural products: poultry, rubber, copra, vegetables, fruits. Labor force (June 1993): 1,635,700; manufacturing 429,500; commerce 363,600; community, social, and personal services 344,100; financial and business services 173,400. Major industries: petroleum refining, ship repair, electronics, financial and business services, biotechnology. Exports: $61.5 billion (f.o.b., 1992): petroleum products, rubber, manufactured goods, electrical and electronics, computers and computer peripherals. Imports: $66.4 billion (f.o.b., 1992): aircraft, petroleum, chemicals, foodstuffs. Major trading partners: U.S., E.U., Hong Kong, Japan.

Geography. The Republic of Singapore consists of the main island of Singapore, off the southern tip of the Malay Peninsula between the South China Sea and the Indian Ocean, and 58 nearby islands.

There are extensive mangrove swamps extending inland from the coast, which is broken by many inlets.

Government. There is a Cabinet, headed by the Prime Minister, and a Parliament of 81 members elected by universal suffrage.

History. Singapore, founded in 1819 by Sir Stamford Raffles, became a separate crown colony of Britain in 1946, when the former colony of the Straits Settlements was dissolved. The other two settlements—Penang and Malacca—were transferred to the Union of Malaya, and the small island of Labuan was transferred to North Borneo. The Cocos (or Keeling) Islands were transferred to Australia in 1955 and Christmas Island in 1958.

Singapore attained full internal self-government in 1959. On Sept. 16, 1963, it joined Malaya, Sabah (North Borneo), and Sarawak in the Federation of Malaysia. It withdrew from the Federation on Aug. 9, 1965, and proclaimed itself a republic the next month.

A law of January 1991 expanded the powers of the presidency. In August the ruling People's Action Party won 36 of the 40 contested parliamentary seats. The first direct presidential election took place in August 1993. Ong Teng Cheong faced what initially appeared to be only token opposition but which took 40% of the vote.

In April 1994 a 3% tax on goods and services was introduced.

The government announced in August 1994 that unwed mothers could no longer receive subsidized housing.

SLOVAKIA

Republic of Slovakia
President: Michal Kovac (1993)
Prime Minister: Vladimir Meciar (1994)
Area: 18,917 sq mi. (48,995 sq km)
Population (est. mid-1995): 5,400,000; 90% Slovaks, other: Hungarians, Czechs. (Average annual rate of natural increase: 0.4%); birth rate: 14/1000; infant mortality rate: 15.6/1000; density per square mile: 285.4
Capital and largest city (1993 est.): Bratislava, 446,600. Other large city (est. 1993): Kosice, 237,300. **Monetary unit:** Koruna. **Language:** Slovak (official), Hungarian. **Religions:** Protestant, Greek Catholic, Orthodox, Jewish. **Literacy rate:** 99%
Economic summary: Gross domestic product (1993 est.): $31 billion, $5,800 per capita; real growth rate: –5%; inflation: 23%; unemployment: 14.4%. Important industries are iron and nonferrous mining, metal processing, and shipbuilding. Other industries are construction materials, consumer appliances, and leather goods. Labor force: 2.484 million. Major agricultural products: grains, potatoes, sugar beets, fruit, vegetables, forestry. Livestock: pigs, cattle, poultry, sheep. Land use: 37% forest and woodland, 13% meadows and pastures, 1% permanent crops, 9% other. Exports: $5.13 billion (f.o.b., 1993 est.): machinery and transport equipment, chemicals, fuels, minerals, metals, agricultural products. Imports: $5.95 billion (f.o.b., 1993 est.): machinery, transport equipment, fuels and lubricants, manufactured goods, raw materials, chemicals, agricultural products. Major trading partners: Czech Republic, CIS republics, Germany, Poland, Austria, Hungary, Italy, France, U.K., U.S., Switzerland.

Geography. Slovakia is bordered by Poland in the north, Ukraine in the east, Hungary in the south, Austria in the southwest, and the Czech Republic in the west. The land has rugged mountains, rich in mineral resources, with vast forests and pastures. Southern Slovakia is a river island called "Zitny Ostrov," with fertile soil. Slovakia is about twice the size of the state of Maryland.

Government. A parliamentary democracy. The president is elected to a five-year term by the unicameral National Council (legislative branch). The 150 members of the National Council are elected for a four-year term.

History. Present day Slovakia was settled by Slavic Slovaks about the 5th century A.D. They were politically united in the Moravian empire in the 9th centu-

ry. In 907, the Germans and the Magyars conquered the Moravian state and the Slovaks fell under Hungarian control from the 10th century up until 1918.

When the Hapsburg state collapsed in 1918 following World War I, the Slovaks joined the Czech lands of Bohemia, Moravia, and part of Silesia to form the new joint state of Czechoslovakia.

In March 1939, Germany occupied Czechoslovakia, established a German "protectorate," and created a puppet state out of Slovakia with Monsignor Josef Tiso as premier. The country was liberated from the Germans by the Soviet army in the spring of 1945, and Slovakia was restored to its pre-war status and rejoined to a new Czechoslovakian state.

After the Communist party took power in February 1948, Slovakia was again subjected to a centralized Czech-dominated government and antagonism between the two republics developed. On January 1969, the nation became the Slovak Socialist Republic of Czechoslovakia.

Nearly 42 years of Communist rule for Slovakia ended when Vaclav Havel became president of Czechoslovakia in 1989 and democratic political reform began. However, with the demise of Communist power, a strong Slovak nationalist movement resurfaced and the rival relationship between the two states increased.

By the end of 1991, tensions heightened between Slovak and Czech political leaders following a debate over a Declaration of Slovak Sovereignty proclaimed by the Slovak parliament. Various attempts to resolve the issue by both parties failed. A crisis developed over whether the Czech and Slovak republics should continue to coexist within the federal structure or divide into two independent states.

The results of the general election in June 1992 failed to affirm the continuing coexistence of the Czech and Slovak Republics within a federal state and resulted in the Czech and Slovak political leaders agreeing to separate their nations into two fully independent republics. The Republic of Slovakia came into existence on January 1, 1993. The parliament in February elected Michael Kovac president.

Nationalistic prime minister Vladimir Meciar lost a vote of confidence in March 1994. A coalition of 5 parties chose the more moderate Moravcik to form a new government.

General elections later that year produced an unexpectedly strong showing for Meciar's party, thrusting him again into the premiership.

The signing of a bilateral treaty with Hungary in March 1995 failed to end concern for ethnic minorities owing to conflicting interpretations of the document.

SLOVENIA

Republic of Slovenia
President: Milan Kucan
Prime Minister: Janez Drnovsek
Area: 7,819 sq mi. (20,251 sq km)
Population (est. mid-1995): 2,000,000. Major ethnic groups: 87.6% Slovenes, 2.7% Croats, 2.4% Serbs, 1.4% Muslims; (average annual rate of natural increase: 0.1%); birth rate: 10/1000; infant mortality rate: 6.6/1000; density per square mile: 255.7
Capital and largest city (est. 1994): Ljubljana, 270,700 Other large city: Maribor, 103,500. **Monetary unit:** Slovenian Tolar; **Languages:** Slovenian; most can also speak Serbo-Croatian; **Religions:** predominantly Roman Catholic; **Literacy rate:** est. 96%

Economic summary: (1994) Gross domestic product: $13.8 billion; $6,900 per capita; real growth rate 5.5%; inflation 18.5%; unemployment (Feb. 1995): 14%. Principal products are corn, rye, oats, potatoes, fruit, livestock raising, and forestry. Mineral resources include coal, iron, and mercury. Major manufactured products are automobiles, iron and steel, cement, chemicals, textiles, furniture, shoes, electrical machinery, pharmaceuticals. Exports: $6.81 billion (f.o.b., 1994): machinery and transport equipment, 38%; other manufactured goods, 44%; chemicals, 9%; food and live animals, 4.6%; raw materials, 3%. Imports: $7.25 billion (c.i.f., 1994): machinery and transport equipment, 35%; other manufactured goods, 26.7%; chemicals, 14.5%; raw materials, 9.4%; fuels and lubricants, 7%. Trading partners: Germany, Italy, France, Croatia, Austria, Russia, Macedonia, U.S.

Geography: Slovenia occupies an area about the size of the state of Massachusetts. It borders Austria on the north, Hungary in the northeast, the Republic of Croatia in the south, and Italy and the Adriatic Sea in the west. It is largely a mountainous republic and almost half of the land is forested, with hilly plains spread across the central and eastern regions. Mount Triglav, the highest peak, rises to 9,393 ft (2,864 m).

Government: A parliamentary democracy with two legislative houses consisting of a 90-member National Assembly and 40-member State Council.

History: The Slovenes were a south-Slavic group that settled in the region during the 6th century A.D. During the 7th century, they established the Slavic state of Samu which owed its allegiance to the Avars, who dominated the Hungarian plain until Charlemagne defeated them in the late 8th century.

In the 11th century, Slovenia was a separate province of the Kingdom of Hungary. When the Hungarians were defeated by the Turks in 1526, Hungary accepted Austrian Hapsburg rule in order to escape Turkish domination. Thus, Slovenia and Croatia became part of the Austro-Hungarian kingdom when the dual-monarchy was established in 1857.

After 1848, nationalism was revived in Slovenia and following the defeat and collapse of Austria-Hungary in World War I, Slovenia declared its independence. It formally joined with Montenegro, Serbia, and Croatia on Dec. 4, 1918, to form the new nation called the Kingdom of the Serbs, Croats, and Slovenes. The name was later changed to Yugoslavia in 1929.

During World War II, Germany occupied Yugoslavia and Slovenia was divided among Germany, Italy, and Hungary. For the duration of the war many Slovenes fought a guerrilla warfare against the Nazis under the leadership of the Croatian-born communist re-sistance leader, Marshal Tito. After the final defeat of the Axis powers in 1945, Slovenia was again made into a republic of the newly established nation of Yugoslavia.

Slovenia declared its independence from Yugoslavia on June 25, 1991. The Serbian-dominated Yugoslavian army tried to keep Slovenia in line and some brief fighting took place, but the Yugoslavian army withdrew its forces and, unlike neighboring Croatia, Slovenia was able to maintain a peaceful status.

A coalition government of the Liberal Democrats and the Christian Democrats was formed in January 1993 in the wake of the December 1992 election.

The country's application for associate membership in the European Union received a setback when Italy demanded reparations for the property of its citizens who left or were expelled after 1945.

SOLOMON ISLANDS

Sovereign: Queen Elizabeth II
Governor-General: Sir Moses Pitakaka (1994)
Prime Minister: Hon. Solomon Mamaloni (1994)
Area: 11,500 sq mi. (29,785 sq km)
Population (est. mid-1995): 400,000 (average annual rate of natural increase: 3.7%); birth rate: 44/1000; infant mortality rate: 43/1000; density per square mile: 34.7
Capital and largest city (986): Honiara (on Guadalcanal), 30,499; **Monetary unit:** Solomon Islands dollar; **Languages:** English, Pidgin, 80 other languages and dialects; **Religions:** Anglican; Roman Catholic; South Seas Evangelical; Seventh-Day Adventist, United (Methodist) Church, other Protestant; **Member of British Commonwealth; Literacy rate:** 30%
Economic summary: Gross domestic product (1991 est.): $900 million; $2,500 per capita; real growth rate 1.8%; inflation 13%. Arable land: 1%. Principal agricultural products: coconuts, palm oil, rice, cocoa, yams, pigs. Labor force (1984): 23,448; agriculture, forestry, fishing 32.4%; services 25%. Major industrial products: processed fish, copra. Natural resources: fish, timber, gold, bauxite. Exports: $84 million (f.o.b., 1991): fish, timber, copra, palm oil. Imports: $110 million (c.i.f., 1991): machinery and transport equipment, foodstuffs, fuel. Major trading partners: Japan, EEC, Australia, U.K., Thailand, Singapore, Netherlands, Hong Kong, China.

Geography. Lying east of New Guinea, this island nation consists of the southern islands of the Solomon group: Guadalcanal, Malaita, Santa Isabel, San Cristóbal, Choiseul, New Georgia, Santa Cruz group, and numerous smaller islands.

Government. After 85 years of British rule, the Solomons achieved independence July 7, 1978. The Crown is represented by a Governor-General and legislative power is vested in a unicameral legislature of 47 members, led by the Prime Minister.

History. Discovered in 1567 by Alvaro de Mendana, the Solomons were not visited again for about 200 years. In 1886, Great Britain and Germany divided the islands between them. In 1914, Australian forces took over the German islands and the Solomons became an Australian mandate in 1920. In World War II, most of the islands were occupied by the Japanese. American forces landed on Guadalcanal on Aug. 7, 1942.

A border dispute with Papua New Guinea was the dominant political issue in 1992.

The general election in May 1993 resulted in a loss of a parliamentary majority for prime minister Mamaloni. The National Coalition Partners, an alliance of 7 groups, formed a new government.

The Hilly government lost its majority in parliament but continued in office. The governor-general in October 1994 swore in Mamaloni as interim prime minister, but the High Court ruled that parliament should decide on the premiership. In early November Mamaloni was again elected prime minister.

SOMALIA

Somali Democratic Republic
President: Vacant, no functioning government in place.
Prime Minister: Vacant.
Area: 246,199 sq mi. (637,655 sq km)
Population (est. mid-1995): 9,300,000 (average annual rate of natural increase: 3.2%); birth rate: 50/1000; infant mortality rate: 122/1000; density per sq mi.: 37.7
Capital and largest city (est. 1985): Mogadishu, 700,000; **Monetary unit:** Somali shilling; **Language:** Somali (official), Arabic, English, Italian; **Religion:** Islam (Sunni); **National name:** Al Jumhouriya As-Somalya al-Dimocradia; **Literacy rate:** 24%
Economic summary: Political turmoil in 1991–92 resulted in widespread famine and a substantial drop in economic output. Much of the economy has been devastated by the civil war. Agriculture is most important sector with livestock accounting for about 40% of GDP and about 65% of export earnings. Gross domestic product (1993 est.): $3.4 billion; $500 per capita; n.a. real growth rate. Arable land: 2%. Principal agricultural products: livestock, bananas, sorghum, cereals, sugar cane, maize. Labor force: 2,200,000; very few are skilled laborers. A few small industries: sugar refining, textiles, petroleum refining. Natural resources: uranium. Exports: $58 million (1990 est.) livestock, skins and hides, bananas. Imports: $249 million (1990 est.) textiles, foodstuffs, construction materials and equipment, petroleum products. Major trading partners: Saudi Arabia, Italy, U.S., U.K., Germany, Italy.

Geography. Somalia, situated in the Horn of Africa, lies along the Gulf of Aden and the Indian Ocean. It is bounded by Djibouti in the northwest, Ethiopia in the west, and Kenya in the southwest. In area it is slightly smaller than Texas.

Generally arid and barren, Somalia has two chief rivers, the Shebelle and the Juba.

Government. None. Last president was overthrown in January 1991 and Somalia was plunged into anarchy.

History. From the 7th to the 10th century, Arab and Persian trading posts were established along the coast of present-day Somalia. Nomadic tribes occupied the interior, occasionally pushing into Ethiopian territory. In the 16th century, Turkish rule extended to the northern coast and the Sultans of Zanzibar gained control in the south.

After British occupation of Aden in 1839, the Somali coast became its source of food. The French established a coaling station in 1862 at the site of Djibouti and the Italians planted a settlement in Eritrea. Egypt, which for a time claimed Turkish rights in the area, was succeeded by Britain. By 1920, a British protectorate and an Italian protectorate occupied what is now Somalia. The British ruled the entire area after 1941, with Italy returning in 1950 to serve as United Nations trustee for its former territory.

In mid-1960, Britain and Italy granted independence to their respective sectors, enabling the two to join as the Republic of Somalia on July 1. Somalia broke diplomatic relations with Britain in 1963 when the British granted the Somali-populated Northern Frontier District of Kenya to the Republic of Kenya.

On Oct. 15, 1969, President Abdi Rashid Ali Shermarke was assassinated and the army seized power, dissolving the legislature and arresting all government leaders. Maj. Gen. Mohamed Siad Barre, as President of a renamed Somali Democratic Republic, leaned heavily toward the U.S.S.R.

In 1977, Somalia openly backed rebels in the easternmost area of Ethiopia, the Ogaden desert, which had been seized by Ethiopia at the turn of the century. Somalia acknowledged defeat in an eight-month war against the Ethiopians, having lost much of its 32,000-man army and most of its tanks and planes. In 1988, guerrillas in the north went on the offensive and threatened the northern regional capital.

President Siad Barre fled the country in late January 1991. His departure left Somalia in the hands of a number of clan-based guerrilla groups, none of which trust each other.

U.S. troops were sent in to protect the delivery of food in December 1992. In May the U.N. took control of the relief efforts from the U.S.

Peace talks in Kenya appeared to be moving slowly but steadily toward an agreement on an interim government at least in principle when on March 23, 1994 they collapsed. Fears immediately arose that internecine fighting would resume.

The last of the U.S. troops left in late March, leaving 19,000 UN troops behind.

U.S. marines arrived again in February 1995 to evacuate the last 2,500 U.N. troops from the country. The last of the marines left on March 3.

SOUTH AFRICA

Republic of South Africa
President: Nelson Mandela (1994)
Deputy Presidents: Thabo Mbeki, F.W. deKlerk
Area: 471,440 sq mi. (1,221,030 sq km)
Population (est. mid-1995): 43,500,000 (average annual rate of natural increase: 2.3%); birth rate: 31/1000; infant mortality rate: 46/1000; density per sq mi.: 92.2
Administrative capital: Pretoria; **Legislative capital:** Capetown; **Judicial capital:** Bloemfontein. No decision has been made to relocate the seat of government. South Africa is demarcated into nine provinces, consisting of the Gauteng, Northern Transvaal, Eastern Transvaal, North West, KwaZulu/Natal, Eastern Cape, Western Cape, Northern Cape and Free State. Each province has its own capital. **Largest metropolitan areas (1994):** Capetown municipal area 1,319,590; Wanga Guguletu 303,808; Johannesburg 829,000; Randburg 150,000; Durban 844,000; Pinetown 100,000; Springs 300,000; Germiston 141,803. **Monetary unit:** Rand; **Languages:** English, Afrikaans, isiNdebele, Sesotho sa Leboa, Sesotho, siSwati, Xitsonga, Setswana, Tshivenda, isiXhosa and isiZulu are the official languages of the interim period. **Religions:** Christian; Hindu; Islam; **National name:** Republic of South Africa; **Literacy rate:** 76%
Economic summary: Gross domestic product (1994): $122 billion; $2,950 est. per capita; 2.3% real growth rate; inflation 9%; unemployment 44%. Arable land: 11.59%. Principal agricultural products: corn, wool, wheat, sugar cane, fruits, vegetables. Labor force (1994): 13,400,000; 34% in services, 30% agriculture, 29% industry and commerce. Major industrial products: gold, chromium, diamonds, assembled automobiles, machinery, textiles, iron and steel, chemicals, fertilizer. Natural resources: gold, diamonds, platinum, uranium, coal, iron ore, phosphates, manganese. Exports: $25.4 billion (1994): gold, diamonds, minerals and metals, food, chemicals. Imports: $24.4 billion (1994): motor vehicle parts, machinery, metals, chemicals, textiles, scientific instruments. Major trading partners: Germany, U.S., other E.U., Japan, U.K., Hong Kong, Italy.

Geography. South Africa, on the continent's southern tip, is washed by the Atlantic Ocean on the west and by the Indian Ocean on the south and east. Its neighbors are Namibia in the northwest, Zimbabwe and Botswana in the north, and Mozambique and Swaziland in the northeast. The kingdom of Lesotho forms an enclave within the southeastern part of South Africa. Bophuthatswana, Transkei, Ciskei, and Venda are independent states within South Africa, which occupies an area nearly three times that of California.

The country has a high interior plateau, or veld, nearly half of which averages 4,000 feet (1,219 m) in elevation.

There are no important mountain ranges, although the Great Escarpment, separating the veld from the coastal plain, rises to over 11,000 feet (3,350 m) in the Drakensberg Mountains in the east. The principal river is the Orange, rising in Lesotho and flowing westward for 1,300 miles (2,092 km) to the Atlantic.

The southernmost point of Africa is Cape Agulhas, located in Cape Province about 100 miles (161 km) southeast of the Cape of Good Hope.

Government. An Interim Constitution, adopted in January 1994, paved the way for the first all-inclusive democratic elections on April 26–29, 1994. Mr. Nelson R. Mandela was elected President. The interim period of power sharing will last until 1999 when the final government and constitution will be in place.

The constitution provides for a government of national unity, three tiers of government and a chapter for fundamental human rights. A schedule in the bill sets out binding and justiciable Constitutional principals to which a final constitution must adhere.

Parliament consists of a 400-member National Assembly, and a 90-person Senate. The National Assembly consists of 200 members elected from the national ballot and 200 members from the provincial ballot. Election to these bodies takes place on the basis of proportional representation.

Each of the nine provinces have their own constitution that is in accordance with the national constitution. A constitutional court has final jurisdiction on matters pertaining to the interpretation, protection, and enforcement of the constitution.

The interim constitution constituted that on April 27, 1994, the independence of Transkei, Bophuthatswana, Venda, and the Ciskei, along with the Self-Governing Territories, was repealed.

History. The Dutch East India Company landed the first settlers on the Cape of Good Hope in 1652, launching a colony that by the end of the 18th century numbered only about 15,000. Known as Boers or Afrikaners, speaking a Dutch dialect known as Afrikaans, the settlers as early as 1795 tried to establish an independent republic.

After occupying the Cape Colony in that year, Britain took permanent possession in 1814 at the end of the Napoleonic wars, bringing in 5,000 settlers. Anglicization of government and the freeing of slaves in 1833 drove about 12,000 Afrikaners to make the "great trek" north and east into African tribal territory, where they established the republics of the Transvaal and the Orange Free State.

The discovery of diamonds in 1867 and gold nine years later brought an influx of "outlanders" into the republics and spurred Cecil Rhodes to plot annexation. Rhodes's scheme of sparking an "outlander" rebellion to which an armed party under Leander Starr Jameson would ride to the rescue misfired in 1895, forcing Rhodes to resign as prime minister of the Cape colony. What British expansionists called the "inevitable" war with the Boers eventually broke out on Oct. 11, 1899.

The defeat of the Boers in 1902 led in 1910 to the Union of South Africa, composed of four provinces, the two former republics and the old Cape and Natal colonies. Louis Botha, a Boer, became the first Prime Minister.

Jan Christiaan Smuts brought the nation into World War II on the Allied side against Nationalist opposition, and South Africa became a charter member of the United Nations in 1945, but refused to sign the Universal Declaration of Human Rights. Apartheid—racial separation—dominated domestic politics as the Nationalists gained power and imposed greater restrictions on Bantus, Coloreds, and Asians.

Afrikaner hostility to Britain triumphed in 1961 with the declaration on May 31 of the Republic of South Africa and the severing of ties with the Commonwealth. Nationalist Prime Minister H. F. Verwoerd's government in 1963 asserted the power to restrict freedom of those who opposed rigid racial laws. Three years later, amid increasing racial tension and criticism from the outside world, Verwoerd was assassinated. His Nationalist successor, Balthazar J. Vorster, launched a campaign of conciliation toward conservative black African states, offering development loans and trade concessions.

Elections on May 7, 1987, increased the power of President Botha's Nationalist party while enabling the far-right Conservative Party to replace the liberal Progressives as the official opposition. The results of the whites-only vote indicated a strong conservative reaction against Botha's policy of limited reform.

A stroke led Botha to step down as leader of his party in 1989 in favor of Frederick de Klerk. De Klerk accelerated the pace of reform. He unbanned the African National Congress, the principal anti-apartheid organization, and released Nelson Mandela, the ANC deputy chief, after 27 1/2 years imprisonment. Negotiations between the government and the ANC commenced.

On June 5, 1991 the parliament scrapped the country's apartheid laws concerning property ownership. On June 17 the parliament did the same for the Population Registration Act of 1950, which classified all South Africans at birth by race.

In February 1993 the ANC approved a plan that would allow minority parties to participate in the government for five years after the end of white rule. Also in February the first nonwhites entered the cabinet in an apparent bid to broaden the base of the ruling National Party.

The 1994 election, as expected, resulted in a massive victory for Mandela and his ANC. The new president was sworn in on May 10, promising conciliation and a new era.

The new government included six ministers from the National Party and three from the Inkatha Freedom Party.

July 1994 saw a wave of industrial strikes in support of wage demands and against the slow pace of economic reform.

In its first major decision since its creation the country's Supreme Court abolished the death penalty in June 1995.

SPAIN

Kingdom of Spain
Ruler: King Juan Carlos I (1975)
Prime Minister: Felipe González Márquez (1982)

Area: 195,364.5 sq mi. (505,992 km²)[1]
Population (est. mid-1994): 39,300,000 (average annual growth rate: 0.1% (1995)); birth rate: 10/1000 (1995); infant mortality rate: 7.6/1000 (1995); density per square mile: 201 (1994)
Capital and largest city (1991): Madrid, 2,909,792. **Largest cities (1991):** Barcelona, 1,623,542; Valencia, 752,909; Seville, 659,126. **Monetary unit:** Peseta; **Languages:** Spanish, Basque, Catalan, Galician; **Religion:** Roman Catholic, 99%; **National name:** Reino de España; **Literacy rate:** 97%
Economic summary: Gross domestic product (1993): $498 billion; $12,700 per capita; real growth rate −1%; inflation 4.5%; unemployment (year-end 93) 22%. Arable land: 31%. Principal agricultural products: cereals, vegetables, citrus fruits, wine, olives and olive oil, livestock. Labor force (1988): 14,621,000: services 53%; 24% in industry. Major industrial products: processed foods, textiles, footwear, petro-chemicals, steel, automobiles, ships. Natural resources: coal, lignite, water power, uranium, mercury, pyrites, fluorospar, gypsum, iron ore, zinc, lead, tungsten, copper. Exports: $72.8 billion (f.o.b., 1993): cars and trucks, semifinished manufactured goods, foodstuffs, machinery and electrical equipment. Imports: $92.5 billion (c.i.f., 1993): machinery and transportation equipment, chemicals, petroleum, semifinished goods, consumer goods, machines and electrical equipment. Major trading partners: Germany, France, Italy, U.S., U.K.

1. Including the Balearic and Canary Islands.

Geography. Spain occupies 85% of the Iberian Peninsula in southwestern Europe, which it shares with Portugal; France is to the northeast, separated by the Pyrenees. The Bay of Biscay lies to the north, the Atlantic Ocean to the west, and the Mediterranean Sea to the south and east; Africa is less than 10 miles (16 km) south at the Strait of Gibraltar.

A broad central plateau slopes to the south and east, crossed by a series of mountain ranges and river valleys.

Principal rivers are the Ebro in the northeast, the Tajo in the central region, and the Guadalquivir in the south.

Off Spain's east coast in the Mediterranean are the Balearic Islands (1,936 sq mi.; 5,014 sq km), the largest of which is Majorca. Sixty miles (97 km) west of Africa are the Canary Islands (2,808 sq mi.; 7,273 sq km).

Government. A parliamentary monarchy.

The Cortes, or Parliament, consists of a Chamber of Deputies of 350 members and a Senate of 208, all elected by universal suffrage.

History. Spain, originally inhabited by Celts, Iberians, and Basques, became a part of the Roman Empire in 206 B.C., when it was conquered by Scipio Africanus. In A.D. 412, the barbarian Visigothic leader Ataulf crossed the Pyrenees and ruled Spain, first in the name of the Roman emperor and then independently. In 711, the Moslems under Tariq entered Spain from Africa and within a few years completed the subjugation of the country. In 732, the Franks, led by Charles Martel, defeated the Moslems near Poitiers, thus preventing the further expansion of Islam in southern Europe. Internal dissension of Spanish Islam invited a steady Christian conquest from the north.

Aragon and Castile were the most important Spanish states from the 12th to the 15th century, consolidated by the marriage of Ferdinand II and Isabella I in 1469. The last Moslem stronghold, Granada, was captured in 1492. Roman Catholicism was established as the official state religion and the Jews (1492) and the Moslems (1502) expelled.

In the era of exploration, discovery, and colonization, Spain amassed tremendous wealth and a vast colonial empire through the conquest of Peru by Pizarro (1532–33) and of Mexico by Cortés (1519–21). The Spanish Hapsburg monarchy became for a time the most powerful in the world.

In 1588, Philip II sent his Invincible Armada to invade England, but its destruction cost Spain its supremacy on the seas and paved the way for England's colonization of America. Spain then sank rapidly to the status of a second-rate power and never again played a major role in European politics. Its colonial empire in the Americas and the Philippines vanished in wars and revolutions during the 18th and 19th centuries.

In World War I, Spain maintained a position of neutrality. In 1923, Gen. Miguel Primo de Rivera became dictator. In 1930, King Alfonso XIII revoked the dictatorship, but a strong antimonarchist and republican movement led to his leaving Spain in 1931. The new Constitution declared Spain a workers' republic, broke up the large estates, separated church and state, and secularized the schools. The elections held in 1936 returned a strong Popular Front majority, with Manuel Azaña as President.

On July 18, 1936, a conservative army officer in Morocco, Francisco Franco Bahamonde, led a mutiny against the government. The civil war that followed lasted three years and cost the lives of nearly a million people. Franco was aided by Fascist Italy and Nazi Russia helped the Loyalist side. Several hundred leftist Americans served in the Abraham Lincoln Brigade on the side of the republic. The war ended when Franco took Madrid on March 28, 1939.

Franco became head of the state, national chief of the Falange Party (the governing party), and Premier and Caudillo (leader). In a referendum in 1947, the Spanish people approved a Franco-drafted succession law declaring Spain a monarchy again. Franco, however, continued as Chief of State.

In 1969, Franco and the Cortes designated Prince Juan Carlos Alfonso Victor María de Borbón (who married Princess Sophia of Greece on May 14, 1962) to become King of Spain when the provisional government headed by Franco came to an end.

Franco died of a heart attack on Nov. 20, 1975, after more than a year of ill health, and Juan Carlos was proclaimed King seven days later.

Under pressure from Catalonian and Basque nationalists, Premier Adolfo Suárez granted home rule to these regions in 1979.

With the overwhelming election of Prime Minister Felipe González Márquez and his Spanish Socialist Workers Party in the Oct. 20, 1982, parliamentary elections, the Franco past was finally buried. The thrust of González, a pragmatic moderate, was to modernize rather than radicalize Spain.

A treaty admitting Spain, along with Portugal, to the European Economic Community took effect on Jan. 1, 1986. Later that year, in June, Spain voted to remain in NATO, but outside of its military command.

General elections of June 1993 returned the Socialist Party to power through the assistance of Catalonia's main nationalist party, which increasingly pressed in 1994 for greater self-government for the region as the price for that support.

A fishing dispute with Canada in early 1995 threatened to disrupt diplomatic relations between the two countries.

In June the opposition called for early elections in light of the government's disclosure that its intelligence agency had eavesdropped on telephone conversations of a number of public figures.

SRI LANKA

Democratic Socialist Republic of Sri Lanka
President: Chandrika B. Kumaratunga (1994)
Prime Minister: Sirimao R.D. Bandaranayake
Area: 25,332 sq mi. (65,610 sq km)
Population (est. mid-1995): 18,200,000 (average annual rate of natural increase: 1.5%); birth rate: 21/1000; infant mortality rate: 19.4/1000; density per sq mi.: 718.4
Capital and largest city (1992 est.): Sri Jayewardenepura Kotte (Colombo), 1,994,000. **Other large cities (est. 1992):** Gampaha, 1,543,000; Kurunegala, 1,445,000; Kandy, 1,257,000. **Monetary unit:** Sri Lanka rupee; **Languages:** Sinhala, Tamil, English; **Religions:** Buddhist, 69%; Hindu, 15%; Islam, 8%; Christian, 8%; **Member of Commonwealth of Nations; Literacy rate:** 89%
Economic summary: Gross domestic product (1993 est.): $55.3 billion; $3,000 per capita; real growth rate 5%; inflation 11.6% (1992); unemployment (1991 est.) 15%. Arable land: 16%. Principal products: tea, coconuts, rubber, rice, spices. Labor force: 6,600,000; 13.3% in mining and manufacturing. Major products: processed rubber, tea, coconuts, textiles, cement, refined petroleum. Natural resources: limestone, graphite, gems. Exports: $2.3 billion (f.o.b., 1992): textiles, tea, rubber, petroleum products, gems and jewelry. Imports: $3 billion (c.i.f., 1992): petroleum, machinery, transport equipment, sugar. Major trading partners: U.S., U.K., Germany, Japan, Singapore, India, Iran, Taiwan, Belgium, Hong Kong, China.

Geography. An island in the Indian Ocean off the southeast tip of India, Sri Lanka is about half the size of Alabama. Most of the land is flat and rolling; mountains in the south central region rise to over 8,000 feet (2,438 m).

Government. Ceylon became an independent country in 1948 after British rule and reverted to the traditional name (resplendent island) on May 22, 1972. A new constitution adopted in 1978 set up the National State Assembly, a 225-member unicameral legislature that serves for six years unless dissolved earlier.

History. Following Portuguese and Dutch rule, Ceylon became an English crown colony in 1798. The British developed coffee, tea, and rubber plantations and granted six Constitutions between 1798 and 1924. The Constitution of 1931 gave a large measure of self-government.

Ceylon became a self-governing dominion of the Commonwealth of Nations in 1948.

Presidential elections were held in December 1982, and won by J.R. Jayewardene.

Tension between the Tamil minority and the Sinhalese majority continued to build and erupted in 1983 that has grown worse since. There are about 2.6 million Tamils in Sri Lanka, while the Sinhalese make up about three-quarters of the 17-million population. Tamil extremists are fighting for a separate nation.

The civil war continued during 1990 after a 13-month cease-fire collapsed. The president ruled month to month. The Tamil guerrillas announced a unilateral cease-fire to take effect on January 1, 1991, and the government, too, suspended operations. The cease-fire broke down ten days later. In the early months of 1991 the rebel forces suffered severe casualties.

India had sent soldiers in July 1987 to help enforce an accord granting the Tamil minority limited autonomy. The agreement failed, and Indian troops withdrew at the end of 1989.

President Premadasa was assassinated at a May Day political rally in 1993 when a Tamil rebel detonated explosives strapped to himself.

A general election in August 1994 gave a coalition of left-of-center opposition parties 105 seats in the parliament. A November presidential election was won by the coalition's head running on a peace platform and support for a free-market economy.

Tamil rebels, however, after the early April 1995 breakdown of a ceasefire, declared in January, shot down two airplanes carrying troops. More than 80 soldiers were killed.

SUDAN

Republic of the Sudan
Prime Minister: Brig. Omar Hassam Ahmed Bashir (1989)
Area: 967,491 sq mi. (2,505,802 sq km)
Population (est. mid-1995): 28,100,000 (average annual rate of natural increase: 3.0%); birth rate: 41/1000; infant mortality rate: 77/1000; density per sq mi.: 29
Capital: Khartoum; **Largest cities (est. 1988):** Khartoum, 817,000; Omdurman, 527,000; Port Sudan, 207,000;
Monetary unit: Sudanese pound; **Languages:** Arabic, English, tribal dialects; **Religions:** Islam, 70% (Sunni); indigenous, 20%; Christian, 5%; **National name:** Jamhuryat es-Sudan; **Literacy rate:** 27%
Economic summary: Gross domestic product (1993 est.): $21.5 billion; $750 per capita; real growth rate 7% (FY93 est.); inflation 105% (FY93 est.); unemployment 30% (FY93 est.). Arable land: 5%. Principal agricultural products: cotton, oil seeds, gum arabic, sorghum, wheat, millet, sheep. Labor force: 6,500,000; 80% in agriculture. Major industrial products: cement, textiles, pharmaceuticals, shoes, soap, refined petroleum, gold. Natural resources: crude oil, some iron ore, copper, chrome, industrial metals. Exports: $350 million (f.o.b., FY93 est.): cotton, peanuts, gum arabic, sesame. Imports: $1.1 billion (c.i.f., FY93 est.): petroleum products, machinery and equipment, medicines and chemicals. Major trading partners: Western Europe, Saudi Arabia, Eastern Europe, Japan.

Geography. The Sudan, in northeast Africa, is the largest country on the continent, measuring about one fourth the size of the United States. Its neighbors are Chad and the Central African Republic on the west, Egypt and Libya on the north, Ethiopia and Eritrea on the east, and Kenya, Uganda, and Zaire on the south. The Red Sea washes about 500 miles of the eastern coast.

The country extends from north to south about 1,200 miles (1,931 km) and west to east about 1,000 miles (1,609 km). The northern region is a continuation of the Libyan Desert. The southern region is fertile, abundantly watered, and, in places, heavily forested. It is traversed from north to south by the Nile, all of whose great tributaries are partly or entirely within its borders.

Government. On January 31, 1991, a criminal code became law that applied Islamic law in the predominantly Moslem north. The ruling military council passed a decree in 1993 dividing the country into 26 states each administered by a governor and a cabinet of ministers.

History. The early history of the Sudan (known as the Anglo-Egyptian Sudan between 1898 and 1955) is linked with that of Nubia, where a powerful local kingdom was formed in Roman times with its capital at Dongola. After conversion to Christianity in the

6th century, it joined with Ethiopia and resisted Mohammedanization until the 14th century. Thereafter the area was broken up into many small states until 1820–22, when it was conquered by Mohammed Ali, Pasha of Egypt. Egyptian forces were evacuated during the Mahdist revolt (1881–98), but the Sudan was reconquered by the Anglo-Egyptian expeditions of 1896–98, and in 1899 became an Anglo-Egyptian condominium, which was reaffirmed by the Anglo-Egyptian treaty of 1936.

Egypt and Britain agreed in 1953 to grant self-government to the Sudan under an appointed Governor-General. An all-Sudanese Parliament was elected in November-December 1953, and an all-Sudanese government was formed. In December 1955, the Parliament declared the independence of the Sudan, which, with the approval of Britain and Egypt, was proclaimed on Jan. 1, 1956.

In October 1969, Maj. Gen. Gaafar Mohamed Nimeiri, the president of the Council for the Revolution, took over as prime minister. He was elected the nation's first president in 1971.

In 1976, a third coup was attempted against Nimeiri. Nimeiri accused President Muammar el Qaddafi of Libya of having instigated the attempt and broke relations with Libya.

On April 6, 1985, while out of the country on visits to the United States and Egypt, Nimeiri lost power by a military coup headed by his Defense Minister, Gen. Abdel Rahman Siwar el-Dahab.

Among the problems that the new government faced were a debilitating civil war with rebels in the south of the country, other sectarian and tribal conflicts, and a famine.

During 1992 the government attempted to impose militant Islam throughout the nation as well as initiate capitalistic economic reforms, including the lifting of subsidies on basic commodities.

New fighting erupted in 1994 in the long civil war. In March peace talks began between two rebel delegations and the Khartoum government.

The Sudanese president in March 1995 declared a unilateral ceasefire for two months.

SURINAME

Republic of Suriname
President: Ronald Venetiaan (1991)
Vice President: Jules Adjodhia (1991)
Area: 63,251 sq mi. (163,820 sq km)
Population (est. mid-1995): 400,000 (average annual rate of natural increase: 2.0%; birth rate: 25/1000; infant mortality rate: 28/1000; density per square mile: 6.3
Capital and largest city (1986): Paramaribo, 77,558;
   Monetary unit: Suriname guilder; **Languages:** Dutch, Surinamese (lingua franca), English widely spoken;
   Religions: Protestant, 25.2%; Roman Catholic, 22.8%; Hindu, 27.4%; Islam, 19.6%; indigenous, about 5%;
   Literacy rate: 95%
Economic summary: Gross domestic product (1993 est.): $1.17 billion; $2,800 per capita; real growth rate –0.3%; inflation 109%; unemployment (1990) 16.5%. Arable land: NEGL %. Principal products: rice. Work force: 104,000. Major products: aluminum, alumina, processed foods, lumber. Natural resources: bauxite, iron ore, timber, fish, shrimp. Exports: $290 million (f.o.b, 1993 est.): bauxite, alumina, aluminum, rice, shrimp and fish, bananas. Imports: $250 million (f.o.b., 1993 est.): capital equipment, petroleum, cotton, foodstuffs, consumer goods.Major trading partners: U.S., Trini-

dad, Netherlands, Norway, Germany, Brazil, U.K., Japan, Netherlands Antilles.

Geography. Suriname lies on the northeast coast of South America, with Guyana to the west, French Guiana to the east, and Brazil to the south. It is about one-tenth larger than Michigan. The principal rivers are the Corantijn on the Guyana border, the Marowijne in the east, and the Suriname, on which the capital city of Paramaribo is situated. The Tumuc-Humac Mountains are on the border with Brazil.

Government. Suriname, formerly known as Dutch Guiana, became an independent republic on Nov. 25, 1975. The executive branch consists of the president and prime minister, Cabinet of Ministers, and Council of State. The legislative branch consists of a unicameral National Assembly with 51 members.

History. England established the first European settlement on the Suriname River in 1650 but transferred sovereignty to the Dutch in 1667 in the Treaty of Breda, by which the British acquired New York. Colonization was confined to a narrow coastal strip, and until the abolition of slavery in 1863, African slaves furnished the labor for the plantation economy. After 1870, laborers were imported from British India and the Dutch East Indies.

In 1948, the colony was integrated into the Kingdom of the Netherlands and two years later was granted full home rule in other than foreign affairs and defense. After race rioting over unemployment and inflation, the Netherlands offered complete independence in 1973.

During much of the 1980s Suriname has been under the control of Lieut. Col. Dési Bouterse, who in late December 1990 resigned as commander of the armed forces. The following night Pres. Shenkar was ousted in a bloodless coup. A few days later interim president Johan Krug acted to reinstate Bouterse.

A deadlocked parliament in 1991 gave way to an assembly, consisting of members of parliament and elected representatives of local councils, convened to select Venetiaan as president.

In 1992 a draft peace treaty was signed between the government and several guerrilla groups.

Rebel forces in March 1994 seized the highly important Afobaka Dam demanding among other things the government's resignation. Several days later the military regained the dam.

SWAZILAND

Kingdom of Swaziland
Ruler: King Mswati III (1986)
Prime Minister: Jameson Mbilini Dlamini (1993)
Area: 6,704 sq mi. (17,363 sq km)
Population (est. mid-1995): 1,000,000 (average annual rate of natural increase: 3.2%); birth rate: 43/1000; infant mortality rate: 90/1000; density per sq mi.: 149.1
Capital and largest city (1990 est.): Mbabane, 47,020;
   Monetary unit: Lilangeni; **Languages:** English and Swazi (official); **Religions:** Christian, 60%; indigenous, 40%; **Member of Commonwealth of Nations; Literacy rate:** 55%
Economic summary: Gross domestic product (1993 est.): $2.3 billion; $2,500 per capita; 1% real growth rate; inflation 11%; unemployment 15% (1992 est.) Arable land: 8%. The economy is based on subsistence agriculture, which occupies more than 60% of the population and contributes nearly 25% to GDP. Manufacturing, which includes a number of agroprocessing factories, accounts for another quarter of GDP. Principal

agricultural products: corn, livestock, sugar cane, citrus fruits, cotton, sorghum, peanuts. Labor force: 195,000; about 92,000 wage earners with 14% in manufacturing. Major industrial products: milled sugar, ginned cotton, processed meat and wood. Natural resources: asbestos, diamonds. Exports: $632 million (f.o.b., 1993 est.): sugar, wood pulp, asbestos, citrus fruits. Imports: $734 million (f.o.b., 1993 est.): motor vehicles, transport equipment, petroleum products, foodstuffs, chemicals. Major trading partners: South Africa, U.K., U.S.

Geography. Swaziland, 85% the size of New Jersey, is surrounded by South Africa and Mozambique. The country consists of a high veld in the west and a series of plateaus descending from 6,000 feet (1,829 m) to a low veld of 1,500 feet (457 m).

Government. In 1967, a new Constitution established King Sobhúza II as head of state and provided for an Assembly of 24 members elected by universal suffrage, together with a Senate of 12 members—half appointed by the Assembly and half by the King. In 1973, the King renounced the Constitution, suspended political parties, and took total power for himself. In 1977, he replaced the Parliament with an assembly of tribal leaders. The Parliament reconvened in 1979.

History. Bantu peoples migrated southwest to the area of Mozambique in the 16th century. A number of clans broke away from the main body in the 18th century and settled in Swaziland. In the 19th century they organized as a tribe, partly because they were in constant conflict with the Zulu. Their ruler, Mswazi, applied to the British in the 1840s for help against the Zulu. The British and the Transvaal governments guaranteed the independence of Swaziland in 1881.

South Africa held Swaziland as a protectorate from 1894 to 1899, but after the Boer War, in 1902, Swaziland was transferred to British administration. The Paramount Chief was recognized as the native authority in 1941.

In 1963, the territory was constituted a protectorate, and on Sept. 6, 1968, it became the independent nation of Swaziland.

The king in October 1992 dissolved parliament and announced plans for a new constitution allowing a multiparty democracy.

The first democratic elections took place in September 1993. The then-prime minister Obed Dlamini failed to win a seat in parliament.

A budget deficit in the 1993–94 fiscal year, the first in almost a decade, caused concern in the government.

SWEDEN

Kingdom of Sweden
Sovereign: King Carl XVI Gustaf (1973)
Prime Minister: Ingvar Carlsson (1994)
Area: 173,800 sq mi. (449,964 sq km)
Population (est. mid-1995): 8,900,000 (average annual rate of natural increase: 0.1%); birth rate: 13/1000; infant mortality rate: 4.8/1000; density per sq mi.: 51.2
Capital and largest city (1993 est.): Stockholm, 684,576.
Largest cities (est. 1993): Göteborg, 433,811; Malmö, 236,684. **Monetary unit:** Krona; **Language:** Swedish; **Religions:** Evangelical Lutheran, 93.5%; Roman Catholic, 1%; other, 5.5%; **National name:** Konungariket Sverige; **Literacy rate:** 99%
Economic summary: Gross domestic product (1993): $153.7 billion; $17,600 per capita; real growth rate –2.7%; inflation 4.4%; unemployment 8.2%. Arable

land: 7%. Principal agricultural products: dairy products, grains, sugar beets, potatoes. Labor force: 4,572,000 (1990); 37.4% in government services; 23.1% in mining, manufacturing, electricity, and water service; 22.2% in private services. Major products: iron and steel, precision equipment, wood pulp and paper products, automobiles. Natural resources: forests, iron ore, hydroelectric power, zinc, uranium. Exports: $49.7 billion (f.o.b., 1993 est.): machinery, motor vehicles, wood pulp, paper products, chemicals, petroleum and petroleum products, iron and steel products. Imports: $42.3 billion (c.i.f., 1993 est.): machinery, clothing, petroleum and petroleum products, foodstuffs, iron and steel, chemicals. Major trading partners: Norway, Germany, U.K., Denmark, U.S., France, Finland.

Geography. Sweden occupies the eastern part of the Scandinavian peninsula, with Norway to the west, Finland and the Gulf of Bothnia to the east, and Denmark and the Baltic Sea in the south. Sweden is the fourth largest country in Europe and is one-tenth larger than California.

The country slopes eastward and southward from the Kjölen Mountains along the Norwegian border, where the peak elevation is Kebnekaise at 6,965 feet (2,123 m) in Lapland. In the north are mountains and many lakes. To the south and east are central lowlands and south of them are fertile areas of forest, valley, and plain.

Along Sweden's rocky coast, chopped up by bays and inlets, are many islands, the largest of which are Gotland and Öland.

Government. Sweden is a constitutional monarchy. Under the 1975 Constitution, the Riksdag is the sole governing body. The prime minister is the political chief executive.

In 1967, agreement was reached on part of a new Constitution after 13 years of work. It provided for a single-house Riksdag of 350 members (later amended to 349 seats) to replace the 104-year old bicameral Riksdag. The members are popularly elected for three years. One hundred fifteen present members of the Riksdag are women.

The King, Carl XVI Gustaf, was born April 30, 1946, and succeeded to the throne Sept. 19, 1973, on the death at 90 of his grandfather, Gustaf VI Adolf. Carl Gustaf was married on June 19, 1976, to Silvia Sommerlath, a West German commoner. They have three children: Princess Victoria, born July 14, 1977; Prince Carl Philip, born May 13, 1979; and Princess Madeleine, born June 10, 1982. Under the new Act of Succession, effective Jan. 1, 1980, the first child of the reigning monarch, regardless of sex, is heir to the throne.

History. The earliest historical mention of Sweden is found in Tacitus' *Germania*, where reference is made to the powerful king and strong fleet of the Suiones. Toward the end of the 10th century, Olaf Sköttkonung established a Christian stronghold in Sweden. Around 1400, an attempt was made to unite the northern nations into one kingdom, but this led to bitter strife between the Danes and the Swedes.

In 1520, the Danish King, Christian II, conquered Sweden and in the "Stockholm Bloodbath" put leading Swedish personalities to death. Gustavus Vasa (1523–60) broke away from Denmark and fashioned the modern Swedish state.

Sweden played a leading role in the second phase (1630–35) of the Thirty Years' War (1618–48). By the Treaty of Westphalia (1648), Sweden obtained western Pomerania and some neighboring territory on the Baltic. In 1700, a coalition of Russia, Poland, and

Denmark united against Sweden and by the Peace of Nystad (1721) forced it to relinquish Livonia, Ingria, Estonia, and parts of Finland.

Sweden emerged from the Napoleonic Wars with the acquisition of Norway from Denmark and with a new royal dynasty stemming from Marshal Jean Bernadotte of France, who became King Charles XIV (1818–44). The artificial union between Sweden and Norway led to an uneasy relationship, and the union was finally dissolved in 1905.

Sweden maintained a position of neutrality in both World Wars.

An elaborate structure of welfare legislation, imitated by many larger nations, began with the establishment of old-age pensions in 1911. Economic prosperity based on its neutralist policy enabled Sweden, together with Norway, to pioneer in public health, housing, and job security programs.

Forty-four years of Socialist government were ended in 1976 with the election of a conservative coalition headed by Thorbjörn Fälldin, a 50-year-old sheep farmer.

Fälldin resigned on Oct. 5, 1978, when his conservative parties partners demanded less restrictions on nuclear power, and his successor, Ola Ullsten, resigned a year later after failing to achieve a consensus on the issue. Returned to office by his coalition partners, Fälldin said he would follow the course directed by a national referendum.

Olaf Palme and the Socialists were returned to power in the election of 1982.

In February 1986, Palme was killed by an unknown assailant.

Elections in September 1991 ousted the Social Democrats from power. The new coalition of four conservative parties pledged to cut taxes and cut back on the welfare state but not alter Sweden's traditional neutrality.

After coming to power the government has reduced unemployment benefits and injury compensations and raised the eligibility age for full pensions.

General elections in September 1994 saw the emergence again of the Social Democrats after three years of being in opposition. Short of a majority by 13 seats in parliament they decided to establish a minority government.

In a referendum held in November 1994 voters approved joining the European Union.

SWITZERLAND

Swiss Confederation
President: Villiger Kaspar (1995)
Vice President: Delamuraz Jean-Pascal (1995)
Area: 15,941 sq mi. (41,288 sq km)
Population (est. mid-1995): 7,000,000 (average annual rate of natural increase: 0.3%); birth rate: 12/1000; infant mortality rate: 5.6/1000; density per sq mi.: 439.1
Capital: Bern; **Largest cities (1992):** Zurich, 345,000; Basel, 174,000; Geneva, 170,000; Bern, 136,000; Lausanne, 125,000; **Monetary unit:** Swiss franc; **Languages:** German, 65%; French, 18%; Italian, 10%; Romansch, 1%; **Religions:** Roman Catholic, 49%; Protestant, 48%; **National name:** Schweiz/Suisse/Svizzera/Svizra; **Literacy rate:** 99%
Economic summary: Gross domestic product (1993): $149.1 billion; $21,300 per capita; real growth rate −0.6%; inflation 3.3%; unemployment 5.1% (est.). Arable land: 10%. Principal products: cheese and other dairy products, livestock. Labor force (1989): 3,310,000; 904,095 foreign workers, mostly Italian; 50% in industry and crafts. Major products: watches and clocks, precision instruments, machinery, chemicals, pharma-

ceuticals, textiles. Natural resources: water power, timber, salt. Exports: $63 billion (f.o.b., 1993): machinery and equipment, precision instruments, textiles, foodstuffs, metal products. Imports: $60.7 billion (c.i.f., 1993): transport equipment, foodstuffs, chemicals, textiles, construction material. Major trading partners: U.S., Japan, Western Europe.

Geography. Switzerland, in central Europe, is the land of the Alps. Its tallest peak is the Dufourspitze at 15,203 feet (4,634 m) on the Swiss side of the Italian border, one of 10 summits of the Monte Rose massif in the Apennines. The tallest peak in all of the Alps, Mont Blanc (15,771 ft; 4,807 m), is actually in France.

Most of Switzerland comprises a mountainous plateau bordered by the great bulk of the Alps on the south and by the Jura Mountains on the northwest. About one-fourth of the total area is covered by mountains and glaciers.

The country's largest lakes—Geneva, Constance (Bodensee), and Maggiore—straddle the French, German-Austrian, and Italian borders, respectively.

The Rhine, navigable from Basel to the North Sea, is the principal inland waterway. Other rivers are the Aare and the Rhône.

Switzerland, twice the size of New Jersey, is surrounded by France, West Germany, Austria, Liechtenstein, and Italy.

Government. The Swiss Confederation consists of 23 sovereign cantons, of which three are divided into six half-cantons. Federal authority is vested in a bicameral legislature. The Ständerat, or State Council, consists of 46 members, two from each canton. The lower house, the Nationalrat, or National Council, has 200 deputies, elected for four-year terms.

Executive authority rests with the Bundesrat, or Federal Council, consisting of seven members chosen by parliament. The parliament elects the President, who serves for one year and is succeeded by the Vice President. The federal government regulates foreign policy, railroads, postal service, and the national mint. Each canton reserves for itself important local powers.

History. Called Helvetia in ancient times, Switzerland in the Middle Ages was a league of cantons of the Holy Roman Empire. Fashioned around the nucleus of three German forest districts of Schwyz, Uri, and Unterwalden, the Swiss Confederation slowly added new cantons. In 1648 the Treaty of Westphalia gave Switzerland its independence from the Holy Roman Empire.

French revolutionary troops occupied the country in 1798 and named it the Helvetic Republic, but Napoleon in 1803 restored its federal government. By 1815, the French- and Italian-speaking peoples of Switzerland had been granted political equality.

In 1815, the Congress of Vienna guaranteed the neutrality and recognized the independence of Switzerland. In the revolutionary period of 1847, the Catholic cantons seceded and organized a separate union called the *Sonderbund*. In 1848 the new Swiss Constitution established a union modeled upon that of the U.S. The Federal Constitution of 1874 established a strong central government while maintaining large powers of control in each canton.

National unity and political conservatism grew as the country prospered from its neutrality. Its banking system became the world's leading repository for international accounts. Strict neutrality was its policy in World Wars I and II. Geneva was the seat of the League of Nations (later the European headquarters of the United Nations) and of a number of international organizations.

A referendum in December on merging the European Community with the 7 nation European Free Trade Association was narrowly defeated.

Another referendum in February 1994 resulted in an outright ban in 10 years on all heavy trucks passing through the country by road for other European countries. All such vehicles will have to be placed on railroad flatbeds. In addition, no new major highways can be built.

Voters in a national referendum in June 1994 rejected the creation of a volunteer military force for deployment as part of U.N. peacekeeping operations.

SYRIA

Syrian Arab Republic
President: Hafez al-Assad (1971)
Premier: Mahmoud al-Zubi (1987)
Area: 71,498 sq mi. (185,180 sq km)
Population (est. mid-1995): 14,700,000 (average annual rate of natural increase: 3.5%); birth rate: 41/1000; infant mortality rate: 39/1000; density per sq mi.: 205.6
Capital and largest city (1993 est.): Damascus, 1,500,000.
Largest cities (est. 1993): Aleppo, 1,490,000; Homs, 535,000; Hama, 230,000; Latakia, 290,000. **Monetary unit:** Syrian pound; **Language:** Arabic; **Religions:** Islam, 90%; Christian, 10%; **National name:** Al-Jamhouriya al Arabiya As-Souriya; **Literacy rate:** 64%
Economic summary: Gross domestic product (1993 est.): $81.7 billion; $5,700 per capita; real growth rate 7.6%; inflation 16.3%; unemployment: 7.5%. Arable land: 28%. Principal agricultural products: Cotton, wheat, barley, lentils, sheep, goats. Labor force: 2,951,000 (1989); miscellaneous and government services 36%, agriculture 32%, industry and construction 32%. Major industrial products: textiles, phosphate, petroleum, processed food. Natural resources: chrome, manganese, asphalt, iron ore, rock salt, phosphate, oil, gypsum. Exports: $3.4 billion (f.o.b., 1993 est.): petroleum, textiles, cotton, fruits and vegetables. Imports: $4.1 billion (c.i.f., 1993 est.): foodstuffs, metal products, machinery. Major trading partners: E.U. countries, U.S., Canada, Arab countries.

Geography. Slightly larger than North Dakota, Syria lies at the eastern end of the Mediterranean Sea. It is bordered by Lebanon and Israel on the west, Turkey on the north, Iraq on the east, and Jordan on the south.

Coastal Syria is a narrow plain, in back of which is a range of coastal mountains, and still farther inland a steppe area. In the east is the Syrian Desert, and in the south the Jebel Druze Range. The highest point in Syria is Mount Hermon (9,232 ft; 2,814 m) on the Lebanese border.

Government. A republic under a military regime since March 1963 with a unicameral legislature, the People's Council. The ruling party is the Arab Socialist Resurrectionist (Ba'th) Party.

History. Ancient Syria was conquered by Egypt about 1500 B.C., and after that by Hebrews, Assyrians, Chaldeans, Persians, and Greeks. From 64 B.C. until the Arab conquest in A.D. 636, it was part of the Roman Empire except during brief periods. The Arabs made it a trade center for their extensive empire, but it suffered severely from the Mongol invasion in 1260 and fell to the Ottoman Turks in 1516. Syria

remained a Turkish province until World War I.

A secret Anglo-French pact of 1916 put Syria in the French zone of influence. The League of Nations gave France a mandate over Syria after World War I, but the French were forced to put down several nationalist uprisings. In 1930, France recognized Syria as an independent republic, but still subject to the mandate. After nationalist demonstrations in 1939, the French High Commissioner suspended the Syrian Constitution. In 1941, British and Free French forces invaded Syria to eliminate Vichy control. During the rest of World War II, Syria was an Allied base.

Again in 1945, nationalist demonstrations broke into actual fighting, and British troops had to restore order. Syrian forces met a series of reverses while participating in the Arab invasion of Palestine in 1948. In 1958, Egypt and Syria formed the United Arab Republic, with Gamal Abdel Nasser of Egypt as President. However, Syria became independent again on Sept. 29, 1961, following a revolution.

In the war of 1967, Israel quickly vanquished the Syrian army. Before acceding to the U.N. cease-fire, the Israeli forces took over control of the fortified Golan Heights commanding the Sea of Galilee.

Syria joined Egypt in attacking Israel in October 1973 in the fourth Arab-Israeli war, but was pushed back from initial successes on the Golan Heights to end up losing more land. However, in the settlement worked out by U.S. Secretary of State Henry A. Kissinger in 1974, the Syrians recovered all the territory lost in 1973 and a token amount of territory, including the deserted town of Quneitra, lost in 1967.

Syrian troops, in Lebanon since 1976 as part of an Arab peacekeeping force whose other members subsequently departed, intervened increasingly during 1980 and 1981 on the side of Moslem Lebanese in their clashes with Christian militants supported by Israel. When Israeli jets shot down Syrian helicopters operating in Lebanon in April 1981, Syria moved Soviet-built surface-to-air (SAM 6) missiles into Lebanon's Bekaa Valley. Israel demanded that the missiles be removed because they violated a 1976 understanding between the governments. The demand, backed up by bombing raids, prompted the Reagan Administration to send veteran diplomat Philip C. Habib as a special envoy to avert a new conflict between the nations.

Habib's carefully engineered cease-fire was shattered by a new Israeli invasion in June 1982, when Israeli aircraft bombed Bekaa Valley missile sites.

Nevertheless, while the Israelis overran most of the rest of Lebanon, the Syrians retained their positions in the Bekaa Valley. As the various Lebanese factions fought each other, the Syrians became the dominant force in the country, both militarily and politically.

The first Arab country to condemn Iraq's invasion of Kuwait, Syria sent troops to help defend Saudi Arabia from possible Iraq attack. After the Gulf war hope for peace negotiations between Israel and Arab states, particularly Syria, rose then floundered.

In 1990 President Assad ruled out any possibility of legalizing opposition political parties. According to official sources, voters in December 1991 approved Assad staying on for a fourth term in office, giving him 99.98% of the vote.

With Israel's peace with Jordan, diplomatic eyes turned toward Syria in 1994. Nevertheless no major breakthroughts emerged. In November the European Union lifted an arms embargo, although this drew Israeli protests.

An August general election saw another victory for the ruling party and its allies, albeit with a relatively low voter turnout.

TAIWAN

Republic of China
President: Lee Teng-hui (1988)
Premier: Lien Chan (1993)
Area: 13,895 sq mi. (35,988 sq km)
Population (end 1994): 21,146,000 (average annual rate of natural increase: 0.96%); birth rate: 16/1000; infant mortality rate (est. mid-95): 5.6/1000; density per square mile: 1,521.8
Capital and largest city (1994): Taipei, 2,648,991; **Largest cities (1994):** Kaohsiung, 1,418,102; Tai Chung, 829,684; Tainan, 702,114; Keelung, 364,586; **Monetary unit:** New Taiwan dollar; **Languages:** Chinese (Mandarin). **Religions:** Buddhist, 4.86 million; Taoist, 3.3 million; Protestant, 422,000; Catholic, 304,000; **Literacy rate:** 93.4%
Economic summary: Gross national product (1994): $244.6 billion; per capita income $11,604; real growth rate 6.42%; inflation (1993) 3.4%; unemployment (1994): 1.56%. Arable land: 25%; principal products: rice, yams, sugar cane, bananas, pineapples, citrus fruits. Labor force (1993): 9,081,000; 39.1% in industry; 11.5% in agriculture; 49.4% in services. Major products: textiles, clothing, chemicals, processed foods, electronic equipment, cement, ships, plywood. Natural resources: coal, natural gas, limestone, marble. Exports: $85 billion (f.o.b., 1993 est.): textiles, electrical machinery, plywood. Imports: $77.1 billion (c.i.f., 1993 est.): machinery, basic metals, crude oil, chemicals. Major trading partners: U.S., Hong Kong, Japan, Germany.

Geography. The Republic of China today consists of the island of Taiwan, an island 100 miles (161 km) off the Asian mainland in the Pacific; two off-shore islands, Kinmen (Quemoy) and Matsu; and the nearby islets of the Pescadores chain. It is slightly larger than the combined areas of Massachusetts and Connecticut.

Taiwan is divided by a central mountain range that runs from north to south, rising sharply on the east coast and descending gradually to a broad western plain, where cultivation is concentrated.

Government. The President and the Vice President are elected by the National Assembly for a term of six years. There are five major governing bodies called Yuans: Executive, Legislative, Judicial, Control, and Examination. Taiwan's internal affairs are administered by the Taiwan Provincial Government under the supervision of the Provincial Assembly, which is popularly elected. In March 1996, the President and Vice President will be elected for the first time by popular vote for a proposed term of four years.

The majority and ruling party is the Kuomintang (KMT) (Nationalist Party) led by President Lee Teng-hui. The main opposition parties are the Democratic Progressive Party (DPP) and the New Party.

History. Taiwan was inhabited by aborigines of Malayan descent when Chinese from the areas now designated as Fukien and Kwangtung began settling it beginning in the 7th century, becoming the majority.

The Portuguese explored the area in 1590, naming it The Beautiful (Formosa). In 1624 the Dutch set up forts in the south, the Spanish in the North. The Dutch threw out the Spanish in 1641 and controlled the island until 1661, when the Chinese General Koxinga took it over, established an independent kingdom, and expelled the Dutch. The Manchus seized the island in 1683 and held it until 1895, when it passed to Japan after the first Sino-Japanese War. Japan developed and exploited it, and it was heavily bombed by American planes during World War II, after which it was restored to China.

After the defeat of its armies on the mainland, the Nationalist Government of Generalissimo Chiang Kai-shek retreated to Taiwan in December 1949. With only 15% of the population consisting of the 1949 immigrants, Chiang dominated the island, maintaining a 600,000-man army in the hope of eventually recovering the mainland. Japan renounced its claim to the island by the San Francisco Peace Treaty of 1951. By stationing a fleet in the Strait of Formosa the U.S. prevented a mainland invasion in 1953.

The "China seat" in the U.N., which the Nationalists held with U.S. help for over two decades was lost in October 1971, when the People's Republic of China was admitted and Taiwan ousted by the world body.

Chiang died at 87 of a heart attack on April 5, 1975. His son, Chiang Ching-kuo, continued as Premier and dominant power in the Taipei regime.

Martial law was lifted in 1987. In April 1991 President Lee Teng-Hui formally declared an end to emergency rule, yet without abandoning his government's claim to be the sole legitimate government of China.

In the first full election in many decades the governing Kuomintang in December 1991 won 71% of the vote, affirming the party's opposition to independence in principle from China.

In February 1993 the president, himself a native Taiwanese, nominated Lien Chan, another native to be prime minister marking a further generational shift away from mainland exiles. In April China and Taiwan concluded their first high level meeting by signing four agreements.

A group within the Kuomintang who feared the party was losing its commitment to a united China first formed a faction within the party and then quit, establishing itself as the Chinese New Party in August.

December 1994 regional and local elections gave a victory to the opposition Democratic Progressive Party's candidate in his bid for the mayoralty of Taipei, and the Nationalist Party candidate won in the second largest city.

TAJIKISTAN

Republic of Tajikistan
Chairman, Supreme Council: Imomali Rakhmonov (1993)
Prime Minister: Dzamshed Karimov
Area: 55,300 sq mi. (143,100 sq km)
Population (est. mid-1995): 5,800,000 (1989: Tajiks, 62.3%; Uzbeks, 23.5%; Russians, 7.6%; Tatars, 1.4%; Kyrgyz, 1.3%); (average annual rate of natural inmcrease: 2.4%); birth rate, 33/1000; infant motality rate: 47/1000; density per square mile: 104.8
Capital and largest city (1991): Dushanbe, 592,000; (1989): Khodzhent (Leninabad), 160,000; **Monetary unit:** Tajik ruble; **Religion:** Sunni Moslem, 80%; **Language:** Tajik
Economic summary: Gross national product (UN, Woirld Bank 1993 est.): $6.9 billion, per capita $1,180; real growth rate –21%; inflation (per mo. avg) 38%; unemployment 1.1% (registered unemployed). Arable land: 6%. Labor force: 1,950,000 (1992): agriculture and forestry 43%, government and services 24%, industry 14%, trade and communications 11%, construction (1990) 8%. Industries: Aluminum, zinc, lead, cement, vegetable oil, metal cutting machine tools, refrigerators and freezers. Agriculture: cotton, grain, fruits, and grapes. Exports: $263 million (1993) to outside the former USSR countries): aluminum, cotton, fruits, vegetable oil, textiles. Imports: $371 million from outside the former USSR countries (1993): chemicals, machinery and transport equipment, textiles, foodstuffs. Major trading partners: Russia, Kazakhstan, Ukraine, Uzbekistan, Turkmenistan.

Geography: Ninety-three percent of Tajikistan's territory is mountainous and the mountain glaciers are the source of its rivers. Tajikistan is an earthquake-prone area. The republic is bounded by China in the east, Afghanistan to the south, Uzbekistan and Kirghizia to the west and north. The central Asian republic also includes the Gorno-Badakh Shan Autonomous region. Tajikistan is slightly larger than the state of Illinois in area.

Government: A parliamentary democracy. The Assembly (parliament) is the Majlis.

History: The name Tadzhikstan (now Tajikistan) dates from the 1920s when the territory became an official Russian administrative area. The Tajiks had an ancient nomadic culture and were ruled at different times by Afghanistan and Persia.

Tajikistan declared its sovereignty in August 1990. In 1991, the republic's Communist leadership supported the attempted coup against Soviet President Mikhail Gorbachev. Shortly afterward pro-Communist president Makhkamov was forced to resign by mounting pressure from pro-democracy groups and the Tajikistan parliament restored an earlier ban on the Communist Party. The ban was rescinded in late September but again restored. The election of November 24 went to Nabiev, former head of the local Communist Party.

Tajikistan joined with ten other former Soviet republics in the Commonwealth of Independent States on Dec. 21, 1991. A parliamentary republic was proclaimed and presidential rule abolished on November 1992. Former Communists dominated the government.

The new government immediately set out to destroy the anti-Communist coalition, consisting principally of western-oriented intellectuals and Muslims. In 1993 the press was muzzled, and four opposition groups banned.

Armed oppositionist groups have since attacked government troops and at times seized roads. Peace talks in 1994 led nowhere.

A new constitution was approved in November, and the acting president won election, although opposition forces claimed fraud and other irregularities.

TANZANIA

United Republic of Tanzania
President: Ali Hassan Mwinyi (1985)
Prime Minister: Cleopa Msuya (1994)
Area: 364,879 sq mi. (945,037 sq km)[1]
Population (est. mid-1995): 28,500,000 (average annual rate of natural increase: 3.0%); birth rate: 45/1000; infant mortality rate: 92/1000; density per sq mi.: 78.1
Capital and largest city (1988): Dar es Salaam,[2] 1,360,850; **Monetary unit:** Tanzanian shilling; **Languages:** Swahili, English, local languages; **Religions:** Christian, 40%; Muslim, 33%. **Member of Commonwealth of Nations; Literacy rate:** 46%
Economic summary: Gross domestic product (1993 est.): $16.7 billion; $600 per capita; 3.2% real growth rate; inflation 21%. Arable land: 5%. Principal agricultural products: tobacco, corn, cassava, wheat, cotton, coffee, sisal, cashew nuts, pyrethrum, cloves. Labor force: 732,200; 90% in agriculture. Major industrial products: textiles, wood products, refined oil, processed agricultural products, diamonds, cement, fertilizer. Natural resources: hydroelectric potential, phosphates, iron and coal. Exports: $418 million (f.o.b., 1992 est.): coffee, cotton, sisal, cloves, cashew nuts, coffee, tobacco, tea. Imports: $1.51 billion (c.i.f., 1992 est.): manufactured goods, machinery and transport

equipment, crude oil, foodstuffs, cotton piece goods. Major trading partners: Germany, U.K., U.S., Japan, Italy, Denmark, Kenya, Netherlands, Hong Kong.

---

1. Including Zanzibar. 2. Some government offices have been transferred to Dodoma, which is planned as the new national capital by the end of the 1990s.

Geography. Tanzania is in East Africa on the Indian Ocean. To the north are Uganda and Kenya; to the west, Burundi, Rwanda, and Zaire; and to the south, Mozambique, Zambia, and Malawi. Its area is three times that of New Mexico.

Tanzania contains three of Africa's best-known lakes—Victoria in the north, Tanganyika in the west, and Nyasa in the south. Mount Kilimanjaro in the north, 19,340 feet (5,895 m), is the highest point on the continent.

Government. Under the republican form of government, Tanzania has a President elected by universal suffrage who appoints the Cabinet ministers. The 244-member National Assembly is composed of 119 elected members from the mainland, 50 elected from Zanzibar, 10 members appointed by the President (from both Tanganyika and Zanzibar), 5 national members (elected by the National Assembly after nomination by various national institutions), 20 members elected by Zanzibar's House of Representatives, 25 Regional Commissioners sitting as *ex officio* members, and 15 seats reserved for women (elected by the National Assembly).

The Tanganyika African National Union, the only authorized party on the mainland, and the Afro-Shirazi Party, the only party in Zanzibar and Pemba, merged in 1977 as the Revolutionary Party (Chama Cha Mapinduzi) and elected Julius K. Nyerere as its head. There are 13 registered political parties (including the CCM, the ruling party). Tanzania will hold general elections on Oct. 29, 1995 under a multi-party system.

History. Arab traders first began to colonize the area in A.D. 700. Portuguese explorers reached the coastal regions in 1500 and held some control until the 17th century, when the Sultan of Oman took power. With what are now Burundi and Rwanda, Tanganyika became the colony of German East Africa in 1885. After World War I, it was administered by Britain under a League of Nations mandate and later as a U.N. trust territory.

Although not mentioned in old histories until the 12th century, Zanzibar was believed always to have had connections with southern Arabia. The Portuguese made it one of their tributaries in 1503 and later established a trading post, but they were driven out by Arabs from Oman in 1698. Zanzibar was declared independent of Oman in 1861 and, in 1890, it became a British protectorate.

Tanganyika became independent on Dec. 9, 1961; Zanzibar, on Dec. 10, 1963. On April 26, 1964, the two nations merged into the United Republic of Tanganyika and Zanzibar. The name was changed to Tanzania six months later.

An invasion by Ugandan troops in November 1978 was followed by a counterattack in January 1979, in which 5,000 Tanzanian troops were joined by 3,000 Ugandan exiles opposed to President Idi Amin. Within a month, full-scale war developed.

Nyerere kept troops in Uganda in open support of former Ugandan President Milton Obote, despite protests from opposition groups, until the national elections in December 1980.

In November 1985, Nyerere stepped down as President. Ali Hassan Mwinyi, his Vice-President, succeeded him. Running unopposed Mwinyi was elected president in October. Shortly thereafter plans were announced to study the benefits of instituting a multi-party democracy.

In January 1993 Zanzibar joined the Organization of the Islamic Conference but held that this did not effect its union with Tanzania. Some legislators considered Zanzibar's action to be unconstitutional and demanded a separate government for the mainland. Zanzibar then promised to withdraw from the OIC.

The crisis in Rwanda in 1994 sent hundreds of thousands of refugees fleeing into Tanzania, taxing the already meager resources of the country. The government immediately appealed for international aid.

THAILAND

Kingdom of Thailand

Ruler: King Bhumibol Adulyadej (1946)
Prime Minister: Chuan Leekpai (1992)
Area: 198,455 sq mi. (514,000 sq km)
Population (est. mid-1995): 60,200,000 (average annual rate of natural increase: 1.4%); birth rate: 20/1000; infant mortality rate: 35/1000; density per square mile: 303.3
Capital and largest city (est. 1989): Bangkok, 5,876,000; **Monetary unit:** Baht; **Languages:** Thai (Siamese), Chinese, English; **Religions:** Buddhist, 94.4%; Islam, 4%; Hinduism, 1.1%; Christian, 0.5%; **National name:** Thailand; **Literacy rate:** 93%
Economic summary: Gross national product (1993 est.): $323 billion; $5,500 per capita; real growth rate 7.8%; inflation 4.1% (1992 est.); unemployment 3.1% (1992 est.). Arable land: 34%. Principal agricultural products: rice, rubber, corn, tapioca, sugar, coconuts. Labor force (1989 est.): 30,870,000; 62% in agriculture; 13% in commerce; 11% in services, including government. Major industries: Tourism largest source of foreign exchange; textiles and garments, agricultural processing, beverages, tobacco, cement, light manufacturing, electric appliances and components, integrated circuits, furniture, plastics, tungsten and tin. Natural resources: fish, natural gas, forests, fluorite, tin, tungsten. Exports: $32.9 billion (f.o.b., 1992): machinery and manufactures, 76.9%; agricultural products, 14.9%; fisheries products, 5.9%. Imports: $41.5 billion (c.i.f., 1992): capital goods, 41.4%; intermediate goods and raw materials, 32.8%; consumer goods, 10.4%; oil, 8.2%. Major trading partners: Japan, U.S., Singapore, Germany, Taiwan, Malaysia, Hong Kong, South Korea, U.K., France.

Geography. Thailand occupies the western half of the Indochinese peninsula and the northern two-thirds of the Malay peninsula in southeast Asia. Its neighbors are Myanmar on the north and west, Laos on the north and northeast, Cambodia on the east, and Malaysia on the south. Thailand is about the size of France.

Most of the population is supported in the fertile central alluvial plain, which is drained by the Chao Phraya River and its tributaries.

Government. A constitutional monarchy. The government is run by an elected civilian coalition of political parties. King Bhumibol Adulyadej, who was born Dec. 5, 1927, second son of Prince Mahidol of Songkhla, succeeded to the throne on June 9, 1946. He was married on April 28, 1950, to Queen Sirikit; their son, Vajiralongkorn, born July 28, 1952, is the Crown Prince.

History. The Thais first began moving down into their present homeland from the Asian continent in the 6th century A.D. and by the end of the 13th century ruled most of the western portion. During the next 400 years, the Thais fought sporadically with the

Cambodians and the Burmese. The British obtained recognition of paramount interest in Thailand in 1824, and in 1896 an Anglo-French accord guaranteed the independence of Thailand.

A coup in 1932 changed the absolute monarchy into a representative government with universal suffrage. After five hours of token resistance on Dec. 8, 1941, Thailand yielded to Japanese occupation and became one of the springboards in World War II for the Japanese campaign against Malaya.

After the fall of its pro-Japanese puppet government in July 1944, Thailand pursued a policy of passive resistance against the Japanese, and after the Japanese surrender, Thailand repudiated the declaration of war it had been forced to make against Britain and the U.S. in 1942.

Thailand's major problem in the late 1960s was suppressing guerrilla action by Communist invaders in the north.

Although Thailand had received $2 billion in U.S. economic and military aid since 1950 and had sent troops (paid by the U.S.) to Vietnam while permitting U.S. bomber bases on its territory, the collapse of South Vietnam and Cambodia in the spring of 1975 brought rapid changes in the country's diplomatic posture.

At the Thai government's insistence, the U.S. agreed to withdraw all 23,000 U.S. military personnel remaining in Thailand by March 1976. Diplomatic relations with China were established in 1975.

After three years of civilian government ended with a military coup on Oct. 6, 1976, Thailand reverted to military rule. Political parties, banned after the coup, gained limited freedom in 1980. The same year, the National Assembly elected Gen. Prem Tinsulanonda as prime minister. General elections on April 18, 1983, and July 27, 1986, resulted in Prem continuing as prime minister over a coalition government.

Refugees from Laos, Cambodia, and Vietnam flooded into Thailand in 1978 and 1979, and despite efforts by the United States and other Western countries to resettle them, a total of 130,000 Laotian and Vietnamese refugees were living in camps along the Cambodian border in mid-1980. A drive by Vietnamese occupation forces on western Cambodian areas loyal to the Pol Pot government, culminating in invasions of Thai territory in late June, drove an estimated 100,000 Cambodians across the line as refugees, adding to the 200,000 of their countrymen already in Thailand.

On April 3, 1981, a military coup against the Prem government failed. Another coup attempt on Sept. 9, 1985, was crushed by loyal troops after 10 hours of fighting in Bangkok. Four persons were killed and about 60 wounded.

In February 1991 a nonviolent military coup led by Gen. Suchinda Kraprayoon overthrew the democratic government charging corruption. The junta leaders declaring a state of emergency and martial law dismissed the houses of Parliament and abolished the Constitution.

Parliamentary elections in March 1992 gave more than half the seats at stake to pro-military parties. In April the top military commander was appointed prime minister. Violent street clashes ensued between pro-democracy civilians and the military leading to the King's rebuke of the government. Chuan Leekpai became prime minister in September.

A scandal over a land-reform program caused the fall of the government in May 1995. The prime minister dissolved parliament and set a date for new elections.

The results of the early July voting gave the largest number of seats in parliament to the Thai Nation Party, whose leader moved quickly to form a coalition government.

TOGO

Republic of Togo
President: Gen. Gnassingbé Eyadema (1967)
Prime Minister: Edem Kodjo (1994)
Area: 21,925 sq mi. (56,785 sq km)
Population (est. mid-1995): 4,400,000 (average annual rate of natural increase: 3.6%); birth rate: 47/1000; infant mortality rate: 86/1000; density per sq mi.: 200.6
Capital and largest city (1983): Lomé, 366,476; **Monetary unit:** Franc CFA; **Languages:** Ewé, Mina (south), Kabyé, Cotocoli (north), French (official), and many dialects; **Religions:** Indigenous beliefs, 70%; Christian, 20%; Islam, 10%; **National name:** République Togolaise; **Literacy rate:** 43%
Economic summary: Gross domestic product (1993 est.): $3.3 billion; $800 per capita; real growth rate 0%; inflation 0.5% (1991 est.); unemployment (1987 est.) 2%. Arable land: 25%. Principal agricultural products: yams, cotton, millet, sorghum, cocoa, coffee, rice. Labor force: 78% in agriculture. Major industrial products: phosphate, textiles, processed food. Natural resources: marble, phosphate, limestone. Exports: $558 million (f.o.b., 1991): phosphate, cocoa, coffee. cotton. Imports: $636 million (f.o.b., 1991): consumer goods, fuels, machinery, foodstuffs, chemical products. Major trading partners: E.U., Japan, U.S., Africa

Geography. Togo, twice the size of Maryland, is on the south coast of West Africa bordering on Ghana to the west, Burkina Faso to the north and Benin to the east.

The Gulf of Guinea coastline, only 32 miles long (51 km), is low and sandy. The only port is at Lomé. The Togo hills traverse the central section.

Government. The government of Nicolas Grunitzky was overthrown in a bloodless coup on Jan. 13, 1967, led by Lt. Col. Etienne Eyadema (now Gen. Gnassingbé Eyadema). A National Reconciliation Committee was set up to rule the country. In April, however, Eyadema dissolved the Committee and took over as President. In December 1979, a 67-member National Assembly was voted in by national referendum. The Assembly of the Togolese People is the only political party.

History. Freed slaves from Brazil were the first traders to settle in Togo. Established as a German colony (Togoland) in 1884, the area was split between the British and the French as League of Nations mandates after World War I and subsequently administered as U.N. trusteeships. The British portion voted for incorporation with Ghana.

Togo became independent on April 27, 1960.

Although political parties were legalized in 1991, violent protests continued. The president convened a national conference in July which declared itself sovereign.

The presidential election held in August 1993 gave Eyadema more than 96% of the vote, but only 36% of the electorate went to the polls. Many of the major opposition candidates withdrew prior to the election.

Elections to the National Assembly in February 1994 gave opposition parties a majority of seats. A coalition government was formed in June, although the president's party was allotted a disproportionately large number of ministries. As a result the principal opposition party boycotted the Assembly.

TONGA

Kingdom of Tonga
Sovereign: King Taufa'ahau Tupou IV (1965)
Prime Minister: Baron Vaea (1991)
Area: 290 sq mi. (751 sq km)
Population (est. mid-1994): 104,778 (average annual growth rate: 0.79%); birth rate: 24.7/1000; infant mortality rate: 20.7/1000; density per square mile: 361.3
Capital (1986): Nuku'alofa, 21,383; **Monetary unit:** Pa'anga; **Languages:** Tongan, English; **Religions:** Christian; Free Wesleyan Church claims over 30,000 adherents; **Member of Commonwealth of Nations; Literacy rate:** 57%
Economic summary: Gross domestic product (1993 est.): $200 million; $2,000 per capita; real growth rate 4%; inflation 9% (FY92). Arable land: 25%. Principal agricultural products: vanilla, coffee, ginger, black pepper, coconuts, bananas, copra. Labor force: 70% in agriculture. Natural resources: fish, copra. Exports: $18.8 million (f.o.b., FY92 est.): copra, coconut products, bananas, fruits, vegetables, fish, vanilla. Imports: $68.3 million (c.i.f., FY92 est.): foodstuffs, machinery and transport equipment, fuels, chemicals, building materials. Major trading partners: New Zealand, Australia, Fiji, U.S., Japan, E.U.

Geography. Situated east of the Fiji Islands in the South Pacific, Tonga (also called the Friendly Islands) consists of some 150 islands, of which 36 are inhabited.

Most of the islands contain active volcanic craters; others are coral atolls.

Government. Tonga is a constitutional monarchy. Executive authority is vested in the Sovereign, a Privy Council, and a Cabinet headed by the Prime Minister. Legislative authority is vested in the Legislative Assembly. Nine seats are reserved for commoners; the others filled by appointees of the king.

History. The present dynasty of Tonga was founded in 1831 by Taufa'ahau Tupou, who took the name George I. He consolidated the kingdom by conquest and in 1875 granted a Constitution.

In 1900, his great-grandson, George II, signed a treaty of friendship with Britain, and the country became a British protected state. The treaty was revised in 1959.

Tonga became independent on June 4, 1970.

Moves were made in 1992 to form a political party independent of the hereditary nobility that dominates the parliament.

A general election in February 1993 gave six of the nine contested parliamentary seats to pro-democracy candidates. The king, however, refused major changes in the system of government.

In September 1994 these six parliamentarians formed the Tonga Democratic Party.

TRINIDAD AND TOBAGO

Republic of Trinidad and Tobago
President: Noor Hassanali (1987)
Prime Minister: Patrick Manning (1991)
Area: 1,980 sq mi. (5,128 sq km)
Population (est. mid-1995): 1,300,000 (average annual rate of natural increase: 1.1%); birth rate: 17/1000; infant mortality rate: 10.5/1000; density per square mile: 656.5
Capital and largest city (1990): Port-of-Spain, 50,878; **Monetary unit:** Trinidad and Tobago dollar; **Languages:** English (official); Hindi, French, Spanish; **Religions:** Christian, 49%; Hindu, 25%. **Member of Commonwealth of Nations; Literacy rate:** 98%

Economic summary: Gross domestic product (1993 est.): $10.4 billion; $8,000 per capita; real growth rate −1%; inflation 9.5%; unemployment 18.5% (1991). Arable land: 14%. Principal products: sugar cane, cocoa, coffee, citrus. Labor force: 463,900; 14.8% in manufacturing, mining, and quarrying. Major industrial products: petroleum, processed food, cement; tourism. Natural resources: petroleum, natural gas, asphalt. Exports: $1.4 billion (f.o.b., 1993): including reexports—petroleum and petroleum products, steel products, fertilizer, sugar, cocoa, coffee, citrus fruits (1988). Imports: $900 million (f.o.b., 1993): raw materials, capital goods, consumer goods. Major trading partners: U.S., Caribbean, Latin America, Western Europe, UK, Canada.

Geography. Trinidad and Tobago lies in the Caribbean Sea off the northeast coast of Venezuela. The area of the two islands is slightly less than that of Delaware.

Trinidad, the larger, is mainly flat and rolling, with mountains in the north that reach a height of 3,085 feet (940 m) at Mount Aripo. Tobago is heavily forested with hardwood trees.

Government. A parliamentary democracy. The legislature consists of a 24-member Senate and a 36-member House of Representatives. The political parties are the Peoples National Movement led by Prime Minister Mr. Patrick Manning (21 seats in the House of Representatives); the United National Congress led by Mr. Basdeo Panday (19 seats); and the National Alliance for Reconstruction led by Mr. Selby Wilson (2 seats).

History. Trinidad was discovered by Columbus in 1498 and remained in Spanish possession, despite raids by other European nations, until it capitulated to the British in 1797 during a war between Britain and Spain.

Trinidad was ceded to Britain in 1802, and in 1899 it was united with Tobago as a colony. From 1958 to 1962, Trinidad and Tobago was a part of the West Indies Federation, and on Aug. 31, 1962, it became independent.

On Aug. 1, 1976, Trinidad and Tobago cut its ties wit Britain and became a republic, remaining within the Commonwealth and recognizing Queen Elizabeth II only as head of that organization.

The People's National Movement won a landslide victory in elections of December 1991, making Manning prime minister.

In March 1993 the government sold its controlling interest in two major industries.

Two of three parliamentary by-elections held in 1994 were won by opposition candidates.

TUNISIA

Republic of Tunisia
President: Mr. Zine El Abidine Ben Ali (1987)
Prime Minister: Hamed Karoui (1989)
Area: 63,379 sq mi. (164,152 sq km)
Population (est. mid-1995): 8,900,000 (average annual rate of natural increase: 1.9%); birth rate: 25/1000; infant mortality rate: 43/1000; density per sq mi.: 140.4
Capital and largest city (1991): Tunis, 834,629; **Monetary unit:** Tunisian dinar; **Languages:** Arabic, French; **Religion:** Islam (Sunni), 98%; Christian, 1%; Jewish, less than 1%; **National name:** Al-Joumhouria Attunisia; **Literacy rate:** 65%
Economic summary: Gross domestic product (1993 est.): $34.3 billion; $4,000 per capita; real growth rate 2.6%; inflation 4.5%; unemployment 16.2%. Arable land: 20%. Principal agricultural products: wheat, olives, oranges, grapes, dates. Labor force: 2,250,000. Manufacturing 19% of GDP, agriculture 18% of GDP, Tourism 6% of GDP. Major industrial products: textiles, and leather, chemical fertilizers, petroleum, phosphate, iron ore. Tourism is an important industry. Natural resources: oil, phosphates, iron ore, lead, zinc. Exports: $3.7 billion (f.o.b., 1992): textiles, crude oil, olive oil, phosphoric acid, chemical fertilizers, triple superphosphate, fish, dates. Imports: $6.1 billion (c.i.f., 1992): raw materials, consumer goods, machinery and equipment, foodstuffs. Major trading partners: France, Italy, Germany, U.S., Belgium and Luxembourg, Spain, the Netherlands.

Geography. Tunisia, at the northernmost bulge of Africa, thrusts out toward Sicily to mark the division between the eastern and western Mediterranean Sea. Twice the size of South Carolina, it is bordered on the west by Algeria and by Libya on the south.

Coastal plains on the east rise to a north-south escarpment which slopes gently to the west. Saharan in the south, Tunisia is more mountainous in the north, where the Atlas range continues from Algeria.

Government. Executive power is vested by the Constitution in the president, elected for five years and eligible for re-election to two additional terms. Legislative power is vested in a House of Deputies elected by universal suffrage.

In 1975, the National Assembly amended the Constitution to make Habib Bourguiba president for life. At 71, Bourguiba was re-elected to a fourth five-year term when he ran unopposed in 1974. He was deposed by Gen. Zine Ben Ali in 1987. Ben Ali was reelected in 1989, and again for another five-year term in 1994. Opposition parties entered Parliament for the first time (19 seats out of 163).

History. Tunisia was settled by the Phoenicians and Carthaginians in ancient times. Except for an interval of Vandal conquest in A.D. 439–533, it was part of the Roman Empire until the Arab conquest of 648–69. It was ruled by various Arab and Berber dynasties until the Turks took it in 1570–74. French troops occupied the country in 1881, and the Bey signed a treaty acknowledging a French protectorate.

Nationalist agitation forced France to grant internal autonomy to Tunisia in 1955 and to recognize Tunisian independence and sovereignty in 1956. The Constituent Assembly deposed the Bey on July 25, 1957, declared Tunisia a republic, and elected Habib Bourguiba as president.

Bourguiba maintained a pro-Western foreign policy that earned him enemies. Tunisia refused to break relations with the U.S. during the Israeli-Arab war in June 1967.

Tunisia ended its traditionally neutral role in the Arab world when it joined with the majority of Arab League members to condemn Egypt for concluding a peace treaty with Israel.

Developments in 1986–87 were characterized by a consolidation of power by the 84-year-old Bourguiba and his failure to arrange for a successor. This issue was settled when the then-Prime Minister, Gen. Ben Ali, deposed Bourguiba.

Concerned with Islamic fundamentalist plots against the state, the government stepped up efforts to eradicate the movement including censorship and frequent detention of suspects.

Elections in March 1994 gave a vast majority of seats to the ruling party. The president ran unopposed as no other candidate was able to qualify.

TURKEY

Republic of Turkey
President: Suleyman Demirel (1993)
Prime Minister: Tansu Ciller (1993)
Area: 300,947 sq mi. (incl. 9,121 in Europe) (779,452 sq km)
Population (est. mid-1995): 61,644,000 (population increase: 17.1/1000); birth rate: 22.4/1000; infant mortality rate: 44.4/1000; density per square mile: 204.8
Capital: Ankara; **Largest cities (1990 census):** Istanbul, 6,620,241; Ankara, 2,559,471; Izmir, 1,757,414; Adana, 916,150; Bursa, 834,576; Gaziantep, 603,434; **Monetary unit:** Turkish Lira; **Language:** Turkish; **Religion:** Islam (mostly Sunni), 98%; **National name:** Türkiye Cumhuriyeti; **Literacy rate:** 90.7%
Economic summary: Gross domestic product (1994): $132.2 billion; $2,181 per capita; real growth rate −5.4% (at 1987 prices); inflation: 106.3% (1987=100); unemployment: 8.3%. Arable land: 20%. Principal agricultural products: cotton, tobacco, cereals, sugar beets, fruits, olives. Labor force: 21,586,032; industry, 16.9%; agriculture, 47%; transportation, 4%. Major industrial products: textiles, coal, minerals, processed foods, steel, petroleum. Natural resources: coal, chromite, copper, borate, sulfur, petroleum. Exports: $18.1 billion (1994): agricultural products, textiles, leather, glass. Imports: $23.2 billion (1994): crude oil, machinery, motor vehicles, metals, mineral fuels, fertilizer, chemicals. Major trading partners: Germany, France, Italy, U.S., U.K., Iran, Japan, Russia.

Geography. Turkey is at the northeastern end of the Mediterranean Sea in southeast Europe and southwest Asia. To the north is the Black Sea and to the west the Aegean Sea. Its neighbors are Greece and Bulgaria to the west, Russia and Ukraine to the north (through the Black Sea), Georgia, Armenia, Azerbaijan, and Iran to the east, and Syria and Iraq to the south.

The Dardanelles, the Sea of Marmara, and the Bosporus divide the country.

Turkey in Europe comprises an area about equal to the state of Massachusetts. It is hilly country drained by the Maritsa River and its tributaries.

Turkey in Asia, or Anatolia, about the size of Texas, is roughly a rectangle in shape with its short sides on the east and west. Its center is a treeless plateau rimmed by mountains.

Government. The President is elected by the Grand National Assembly for a seven-year term and is not eligible for re-election.

The Prime Minister and her Council of Ministers hold the executive power although the President has the right to veto legislation.

History. The Ottoman Turks first appeared in the early 13th century in Anatolia, subjugating Turkish and Mongol bands pressing against the eastern borders of Byzantium. They gradually spread through the Near East and Balkans, capturing Constantinople in 1453 and storming the gates of Vienna two centuries later. At its height, the Ottoman Empire stretched from the Persian Gulf to western Algeria.

Defeat of the Turkish navy at Lepanto by the Holy League in 1571 and failure of the siege of Vienna in the 18th century, Russia was seeking to establish itself as the protector of Christians in Turkey's Balkan territories. Russian ambitions were checked by Britain and France in the Crimean War (1854–56), but the Russo-Turkish War (1877–78) gave Bulgaria virtual independence and Romania and Serbia liberation from their nominal allegiance to the Sultan.

Turkish weakness stimulated a revolt of young liberals known as the Young Turks in 1909. They forced Sultan Abdul Hamid to grant a constitution and install a liberal government. Reforms were no barrier to further defeats, however, in a war with Italy (1911–12) and the Balkan Wars (1912–13). Under the influence of German military advisors, Turkey signed a secret alliance with Germany on Aug. 2, 1914, that led to a declaration of war by the Allied powers and the ultimate humiliation of the occupation of Turkish territory by Greek and other Allied troops.

In 1919, the new Nationalist movement, headed by Mustafa Kemal, was organized to resist the Allied occupation and, in 1920, a National Assembly elected him President of both the Assembly and the government. Under his leadership, the Greeks were driven out of Smyrna, and other Allied forces were withdrawn.

The present Turkish boundaries (with the exception of Alexandretta, ceded to Turkey by France in 1939) were fixed by the Treaty of Lausanne (1923) and later negotiations. The caliphate and sultanate were separated, and the sultanate was abolished in 1922. On Oct. 29, 1923, Turkey formally became a republic, with Mustafa Kemal, who took the name Kemal Atatürk, as its first President. The caliphate was abolished in 1924, and Atatürk proceeded to carry out an extensive program of reform, modernization, and industrialization.

Gen. Ismet Inönü was elected to succeed Atatürk in 1938 and was re-elected in 1939, 1943, and 1946. Defeated in 1950, he was succeeded by Celâl Bayar. In 1939, a mutual assistance pact was concluded with Britain and France. Neutral during most of World War II Turkey, on Feb. 23, 1945, declared war on Germany and Japan, but took no active part in the conflict.

Turkey became a full member of NATO in 1952.

Turkey invaded Cyprus by sea and air July 20, 1974, following the failure of diplomatic efforts to resolve the crisis caused by the ouster of Archbishop Makarios. Talks in Geneva involving Greece, Turkey, Britain, and Greek Cypriot and Turkish Cypriot leaders broke down in mid-August. Turkey unilaterally announced a cease-fire August 16, after having gained control of 40% of the island. Turkish Cypriots established their own state in the north on Feb. 13, 1975.

In July 1975, after a 30-day warning, Turkey took over control of all the U.S. installations except the big joint defense base at Incirlik, which it reserved for "NATO tasks alone."

The establishment of military government in September 1980 stopped the slide toward anarchy and brought some improvement in the economy.

A Constituent Assembly, consisting of the six-member National Security Council and members appointed by them, drafted a new Constitution that was approved by an overwhelming (91.5%) majority of the voters in a Nov. 6, 1982, referendum. Prime Minister Turgut Özal's Motherland Party came to power in parliamentary elections held in late 1983. Özal was re-elected in November 1987.

In general elections in October 1991 Yilmaz's party was defeated. In November Demirel and his True Path Party formed a coalition government with the Social Democrats.

The sudden death of Turgut Ozal in April 1993 led to Demirel assuming the presidency in May. In June the True Path Party chose Tansu Ciller as its new leader leading to her appointment as Turkey's first female prime minister.

In March 1995 as many as 35,000 Turkish troops moved into northern Iraq seeking to root out Kurdish rebels, who have used Iraq as a base. That operation lasted six weeks but was followed by another incursion in July.

TURKMENISTAN

Republic of Turkmenistan
President: Saparmurad A. Niyazov (1990)
Prime Minister: Khan Akhmedov (1992)
Head of the Government: Saparmurad A. Niyazov
Area: 188,500 sq mi. (488,100 sq km)
Population (est. mid-1995): 4,500,000 (Turkmen, 72%; Russian, 10%; other minorities, Uzbeks, Kazakhs, Ukrainians); (average annual rate of natural increase: 2.5%); birth rate: 33/100; infant mortality rate: 44/100; density per square mile: 23.8
Capital and largest city (1991 est.): Ashkhabad, 412,200; **Largest cities (est. 1991):** Chardzhou, 166,400; Tashauz, 117,000. **Monetary unit:** Manat. **Languages:** Turkmen, 72%; Russian, 12%; Uzbek, 9%; **Religions:** Islam, 85%; Eastern Orthodox, 10%. **Literacy rate:** 100%.
Economic summary: Gross national product (UN, World Bank 1993 est.): $13 billion; $3,330 per capita; real growth rate 7.8%; inflation 45%; unemployment (1992 est.) 2.9%. Labor force: 1,573,000 (1992): agriculture and forestry, 44%; industry and construction, 20%. Industries: oil and gas, petrochemicals, fertilizers, food processing, textiles. Agriculture: cotton, fruits, vegetables. Exports: $1.2 billion to outside former USSR countries (1993): natural gas, oil, chemicals, cotton, textiles, carpets. Imports: $490 million from outside the former USSR countries (1993): machinery and parts, plastics and rubber, consumer durables, textiles, grain, foodstuffs. Major trading partners: Ukraine, Russia, Kazakhstan, Uzbekistan, Georgia, Azerbaijan, Eastern Europe, Turkey, Argentina.

Geography. Turkmenistan (formerly Turkmenia) lies between the Caspian Sea in the west and is bounded by Kazakhstan in the north, Uzbekistan in the east, and Iran and Afghanistan in the south. Eighty percent of the republic's territory is desert. The largest desert is the Kara-Kum (Black Sand) approximately 138,966 sq mi. (360,000 sq km) in area. A 684 mil (1,100 km) long canal runs across the Kara-Kum Desert and it supplies water from the Amu Darya River for irrigation and hydroelectric power.

Government. A republic. The constitution allows for a strong presidential rule. The president heads the Cabinet of Ministers, whose members he appoints with the consent of the Meglis (parliament) has the right to veto legislation. There are two parliaments, the unicameral People's Council (Halk Maslahaty) with over 100 members and the 50-member unicameral Assembly (Majlis).

History. Turkmenistan was once part of the ancient Persian empire. The Turkmen people were originally pastoral nomads and some of them continued their unsettled way of life up into the 20th century, living in transportable dome-shaped felt tents. The territory was ruled by the Seljuk Turks in the 11th century. The Mongols of Ghenghis Khan conquered the land in the 13th century and dominated the area for the next two centuries until they were deposed in the late 15th century by invading Uzbeks.

Prior to the 19th century, Turkmenia was divided into two lands, one belonging to the Khanate of Khiva and the other belonging to the Khanate of Bukhara. In 1868, the Khanate of Khiva was made part of the Russian empire and Turkmenia became known as the Transcaspia Region of Russian Turkistan. Turkmenistan was later formed out of the Turkistan Autonomous Soviet Socialist Republic, founded in 1922, and was made an independent Soviet Socialist Republic on May 13, 1925.

Turkmenistan declared its sovereignty in August 1990 and became a member of the Commonwealth of Independent States on Dec. 21, 1991 together with ten other former Soviet republics.

In the presidential election of June 1992 voters reelected Niyazov in a one-candidate race. A new constitution was adopted in May 1992 making it the first Central Asian state to do so.

The country left the ruble zone in November 1993, introducing its own currency emblazoned with the president's image.

A referendum held in January 1994 produced a resounding vote in favor of the ruling party's proposal to postpone presidential elections until 1997.

TUVALU

Sovereign: Queen Elizabeth II
Governor-General: Tulaga Manuella (1994)
Prime Minister: Kamuta Laatasi (1993)
Area: 10 sq mi. (26 sq km)
Population (est. mid-1994): 9,831; growth rate 1.66%; birth rate, 25.7/1000; infant mortality rate, 27.3/1000; density per square mile: 983.1
Capital and largest city (1985): Funafuti, 2,810; **Monetary unit:** Tvaluan dollar, Australian dollar. **Languages:** Tuvaluan, English; **Religion:** Church of Tuvalu (Congregationalist), 97%; **Member of the Commonwealth of Nations; Literacy rate:** less than 50%
Economic summary: Gross national product (1990): $6.4 million., per capita income: $700; 4% real growth rate (1993 est.); inflation 2.9% (1989). Principal agricultural products: copra and coconuts. Exports: $165,000 (f.o.b., 1989.): copra. Imports: $4.4 million (c.i.f., 1989) food, fuels, machinery, animals, manufactured goods. Major trading partners: Australia, Fiji, New Zealand

Geography. Formerly the Ellice Islands, Tuvalu consists of nine small islands scattered over 500,000 square miles of the western Pacific, just south of the equator.

Government. Official executive power is vested in a Governor-General, representing the Queen, who is appointed by her on the recommendation of the Tuvalu government. Actual executive power lies with a Prime Minister, who is responsible to a House of Assembly composed of eight elected members.

History. The Ellice Islands became a British protectorate in 1892 and were annexed by Britain in 1915–16 as part of the Gilbert and Ellice Islands Colony. The Ellice Islands were separated in 1975, given home rule, and renamed Tuvalu. Full independence was granted on Sept. 30, 1978.

Unable to select a prime minister after a mid-1993 election the governor-general dissolved parliament in September. A new election in November led ultimately to a new prime minister in December. In mid-1994 the prime minister removed the governor-general and replaced him with a former accountant.

UGANDA

Republic of Uganda
President: Yoweri Museveni (1986)
Prime Minister: Kintu Musoke
Area: 91,459 sq mi. (236,880 sq km)
Population (est. mid-1995): 21,300,000 (average annual rate of natural increase: 3.3%); birth rate: 52/1000; infant mortality rate: 115/1000; density per sq mi.: 232.8
Capital and largest city (est. 1991): Kampala, 773,463
Monetary unit: Ugandan shilling

Languages: English (official), Swahili, Luganda, Ateso, Luo
Religions: Christian, 66%; Islam, 16%
Member of Commonwealth of Nations
Literacy rate: 48%
Economic summary: Gross domestic product (1993 est.): $24.1 billion; $1,200 per capita; real growth rate 6%; inflation 41.5% (1992 est.). Arable land: 23%. Principal agricultural products: coffee, tea, cotton, sugar. Labor force: 4,500,000 (est.); 94% in subsistence activities. Major industrial products: refined sugar, beer, tobacco, cotton textiles, cement. Natural resources: copper, cobalt, limestone, salt. Exports: $150 million (f.o.b., 1992 est.): coffee 97%, cotton, tea. Imports: $513 million (c.i.f., 1992 est.): petroleum products, machinery, transport equipment, metals, food. Major trading partners: U.S., U.K., Kenya, Italy, France, Spain, South Africa.

Geography. Uganda, twice the size of Pennsylvania, is in east Africa. It is bordered on the west by Zaire, on the north by the Sudan, on the east by Kenya, and on the south by Tanzania and Rwanda.

The country, which lies across the Equator, is divided into three main areas—swampy lowlands, a fertile plateau with wooded hills, and a desert region. Lake Victoria forms part of the southern border.

Government. The country has been run by the National Resistance Movement (NRM) since January, 1986.

History. Uganda was first visited by European explorers as well as Arab traders in 1844. An Anglo-German agreement of 1890 declared it to be in the British sphere of influence in Africa, and the Imperial British East Africa Company was chartered to develop the area. The company did not prosper financially, and in 1894 a British protectorate was proclaimed.

Uganda became independent on Oct. 9, 1962.

Sir Edward Mutesa was elected the first President and Milton Obote the first Prime Minister of the newly independent country. With the help of a young army officer, Col. Idi Amin, Prime Minister Obote seized control of the government from President Mutesa four years later.

On Jan. 25, 1971, Col. Amin deposed President Obote. Obote went into exile in Tanzania. Amin expelled Asian residents and launched a reign of terror against Ugandan opponents, torturing and killing tens of thousands. In 1976, he had himself proclaimed President for Life. In 1977, Amnesty International estimated that 300,000 may have died under his rule, including church leaders and recalcitrant cabinet ministers.

After Amin held military exercises on the Tanzanian border, angering Tanzania's President Julius Nyerere, a combined force of Tanzanian troops and Ugandan exiles loyal to former President Obote invaded Uganda and chased Amin into exile.

After a series of interim administrations, President Obote led his People's Congress Party to victory in 1980 elections on charges that were rigged.

On July, 27, 1985, army troops staged a coup taking over the government. Obote fled into exile. The military regime installed Gen. Tito Okello as chief of state.

The National Resistance Army (NRA), an anti-Obote group led by Yoweri Musevni, kept fighting after being excluded from the new regime. They seized Kampala on January 29, 1986, and Musevni was declared President.

Voting for a constituent assembly to deliberate a draft constitution took place in March 1994. The draft, however, called for a suspension of party politics for at least five years.

Contending that Sudan supported a rebel force seeking the overthrow of the Ugandan government, the latter broke off diplomatic relations with the former.

UKRAINE

Ukraine
President: Leonid D. Kuchma (1994)
Prime Minister: Yevhen K. Marchuk (1995)
Area: 233,000 sq mi. (603,700 sq km)
Population (est. mid-1995): 52,000,000 (Ukrainians, 73%; Russians, 22%; Jews, Poles, Moldovians, Bulgarians); (average annual rate of natural increase: –0.4%): birth rate: 11/1000; infant mortality rate: 15/1000; density per square mile: 223.1
Capital: Kyiv (Kiev); **Largest cities:** Kyiv, 2,637,000; Kharkiv, 1,622,000; Donetske, 1,121,000; Odessa, 1,104,000; Lviv, 803,000; **Monetary unit:** Karbovanets. **Language:** Ukrainian; **Religion:** Orthodox, 76%; Ukrainian Catholic, 13.5%; Jewish, 2.3%; Baptist, Mennonite, Protestant, and Moslem, 8.2%; **Literacy rate (1992):** 99%
Economic summary: Gross domestic product (UN, World Bank 1993 est.): $205.4 billion; per capita: $3,960; real growth rate: –16%; inflation (per mo.): 45%; unemployment: 0.4% (officially registered). Labor force (1992: 23,985,000); industry and construction, 33%; agriculture and forestry, 21%; health, education, culture, 16%; trade and distribution, 7%; transport and communication, 7%. Mineral resources are iron ore, coal, manganese, natural gas, oil, salt, sulfur, graphite, titanium, magnesium, kaolin, nickel, mercury, and timber. Important agricultural crops are grain, vegetables, meat, and milk. Exports: $3 billion to countries outside of the former USSR (1993): coal, electric power, ferrous and nonferrous metals, chemicals, machinery and transportation equipment, grain and meat. Imports: $2.2 billion from countries outside of the former USSR (1993): machinery and parts, transportation equipment, chemicals, and textiles. Major trading partners: Russia, Belarus, and Kazakhstan, Germany, China, Austria.

Geography. Located in southeastern Europe, the country consists largely of fertile black soil steppes. Mountainous areas include the Carpathians in the southwest and the Crimean chain in the south. There are forest lakes in the north. It is bordered by Belarus on the north and the Russian Federation on the northeast and east, by Poland on the west, by Romania, and Moldova in the southwest, by Hungary, Slovakia, and Poland on the west, and the Baltic Sea and the Sea of Azov in the south.

Government. A constitutional republic. The unicameral parliament or Supreme Council has 450 members.

History. Ukraine was known as "Rus" (from which Russia is a derivative) up until the 16th century. In the 9th century, Kiev was the major political and cultural center in eastern Europe. Kievian Rus reached the height of its power in the 10th century and adopted Byzantine Christianity and the Cyrillic alphabet during that period.

The Mongol conquest in 1240 ended Kievian power. From the 13th to the 16th century, Kiev was under the influence of Poland and western Europe. In 1654, Ukraine asked the czar of Moscovy for protection against Poland and the Treaty of Pereyasav signed that year recognized the suzerainty of Moscow. The agreement was interpreted by Moscow as an invitation to take over Kiev and the Ukrainian state was eventually absorbed into the Russian empire.

After the Russian revolution, Ukraine declared its independence from Russia on Jan. 28, 1918 and several years of warfare ensued with several groups. The Red Army finally was victorious over Kiev and in

1920, Ukraine became a Soviet republic. In 1922, Ukraine became one of the founders of the United Soviet Socialist Republics.

Ukraine was one of the most devastated Soviet republics during World War II.

On April 15, 1986, the nation's nuclear power plant at Chernobyl was the site of the world's worst nuclear accident. On Oct. 29, 1991, the Ukrainian parliament voted to shut down the reactor within two years' time and asked for international assistance in dismantling it.

When president Leonid Kravchuk was elected by the Ukrainian parliament in 1990, he vowed to seek Ukrainian sovereignty. Ukraine declared its independence on Aug. 24, 1991.

New elections were held Dec. 1, 1991 and Mr. Kravchuk was elected president with 61.5% of the vote. Voters also overwhelmingly approved a referendum to establish full independence from the Soviet Union.

On December 8, 1991, Ukrainian, Russian, and Belarus leaders cofounded a new Commonwealth of Independent States with the new capital to be situated in Minsk, Belarus. The Commonwealth was formally established on Dec. 21, 1991 with ten other former Soviet republics.

After independence Ukraine sought to affirm and exercise its territorial claim on the Crimea, which was legally transferred from Russian jurisdiction in 1954. Tensions immediately arose with Russia over this as well as over control of the Black Sea Fleet.

The U.S. announced in January 1994 that an agreement had been reached with Russia and Ukraine for the destruction of Ukraine's entire nuclear arsenal. Later that month a candidate favoring the separation of Crimea from Ukraine and integration with Russia won that region's presidency. Parliamentary elections in April resulted in a deeply split legislature, divided principally between leftists in the east and nationalists in the west. A presidential election in July saw the surprise ascent of Leonid Kuchma to the presidency of Ukraine. His campaign called for closer ties to Moscow.

His promises notwithstanding, Kuchma in October 1994 began a program of economic liberalization and moved to re-establish central authority over Crimea. In March 1995 the region's separatist leader was removed and the Crimean constitution revoked. In June parliament approved legislation that expanded presidential powers.

UNITED ARAB EMIRATES

President: Sheik Zayed Bin Sultan Al-Nahayan (1971)
Prime Minister: Sheik Maktum ibn Rashid al-Maktum (1990)
Area: 32,000 sq mi. (82,880 sq km)
Population (est. mid-1995): 1,900,000 (average annual rate of natural increase: 1.9%); birth rate: 23/1000; infant mortality rate: 23/1000; density per square mile: 59.3
Capital and largest city (est. 1989): Abu Dhabi, 363,432
Monetary unit: Dirham
Language: Arabic; Farsi and English widely spoken
Religion: Islam (Sunni, 80%; Shiite, 16%); other, 4%
Literacy rate: 68%
Economic summary: Gross domestic product (1993 est.: $63.8 billion; $24,000 per capita; real growth rate 1%; inflation (1992 est.) 3.5%. Arable land: 0%, irrigated land, 19.3 sq mi. Principal agricultural products: vegetables, dates, poultry, fish. Labor force: 580,000 (1986 est.) 80% is foreign; 85% in industry and commerce. Major industrial products: light manufactures, petroleum, construction materials. Natural resource: oil.

Exports: $22.6 billion (f.o.b., 1993 est.): petroleum, dates, fish, natural gas. Imports: $18 billion (f.o.b, 1993 est.): consumer goods, food, capital goods. Major trading partners: Japan, Western Europe, U.S., Singapore, Korea, India, Iran.

Geography. The United Arab Emirates, in the eastern part of the Arabian Peninsula, extends along part of the Gulf of Oman and the southern coast of the Persian Gulf. The nation is the size of Maine. Its neighbors are Saudi Arabia in the west and south, Qatar in the north, and Oman in the east. Most of the land is barren and sandy.

Government. The United Arab Emirates was formed in 1971 by seven emirates known as the Trucial States—Abu Dhabi (the largest), Dubai, Sharjah, Ajman, Fujairah, Ras al Khaimah and Umm al-Qaiwain.

The loose federation allows joint policies in foreign relations, defense, and development, with each member state keeping its internal local system of government headed by its own ruler. A 40-member legislature consists of eight seats each for Abu Dhabi and Dubai, six seats each for Ras al Khaimah and Sharjah, and four each for the others. It is a member of the Arab League.

History. Originally the area was inhabited by a seafaring people who were converted to Islam in the seventh century. Later, a dissident sect, the Carmathians, established a powerful sheikdom, and its army conquered Mecca. After the sheikdom disintegrated, its people became pirates.

Threatening the sultanate of Muscat and Oman early in the 19th century, the pirates provoked the intervention of the British, who in 1820 enforced a partial truce and in 1853 a permanent truce. Thus what had been called the Pirate Coast was renamed the Trucial Coast.

A crisis with Iran over sovereignty of three islands near the Strait of Hormuz arose in 1992. Despite efforts to resolve the issue little progress was made. Throughout 1994 the UAE reiterated its wish to have the International Court of Justice settle the issue.

UNITED KINGDOM

United Kingdom of Great Britain and Northern Ireland
Sovereign: Queen Elizabeth II (1952)
Prime Minister: John Major (1990)
Area: 94,247 sq mi. (244,100 sq km)
Population (est. mid-1995): 58,600,000 (average annual rate of natural increase: 0.2%); birth rate: 13/1000; infant mortality rate: 6.6/1000; density per square mile: 621.7
Capital: London, England; **Largest cities (1991 mid-year est.):** London, 6,679,699 (metropolitan area); **(1992 mid-year est.):** Birmingham, 1,009,100; Leeds, 721,800; Glasgow, 681,470; Liverpool, 479,000; Bradford, 477,500; Edinburgh, 439,880; Manchester, 434,600; Bristol, 396,600. **Monetary unit:** Pound sterling (£); **Languages:** English, Welsh, Scots Gaelic; **Religions:** Church of England (established church); Church of Wales (disestablished); Church of Scotland (established church—Presbyterian); Church of Ireland (disestablished); Roman Catholic; Methodist; Congregational; Baptist; Jewish; **Literacy rate:** 99%
Economic summary: Gross domestic product (1993): $980.2 billion; $16,900 per capita; real growth rate 2.1%; inflation 2.6%; unemployment 10.3%. Arable land: 29%. Principal agricultural products: wheat, barley, potatoes,

sugar beets, livestock, dairy products. Labor force (June 1992): 28,048,000: services, 60.6%; mfg. and construction, 27.2%. Major industrial products: machinery and transport equipment, metals, processed food, paper, textiles, chemicals, clothing, aircraft, shipbuilding, electronics and communications. Natural resources: coal, oil, gas. Exports: $190.1 billion (f.o.b., 1993): machinery, transport equipment, chemicals, petroleum, manufactured goods, semifinished goods. Imports: $221.6 billion (c.i.f., 1993): foodstuffs, machinery, manufactured goods, semifinished goods, consumer goods. Major trading partners: Western European nations, U.S.

Area and Population of United Kingdom

Subdivision	Area sq mi.	Area sq km	Population 1992 (mid-year est.)
England and Wales	58,381	151,207	51,277,000
Scotland	30,414	78,772	5,111,000
Northern Ireland	5,452	14,121	1,610,000[1]
Total	**94,247**	**244,100**	**57,998,000**

1. Provisional.

Geography. The United Kingdom, consisting of England, Wales, Scotland, and Northern Ireland, is twice the size of New York State. England, in the southeast part of the British Isles, is separated from Scotland on the north by the granite Cheviot Hills; from them the Pennine chain of uplands extends south through the center of England, reaching its highest point in the Lake District in the northwest. To the west along the border of Wales—a land of steep hills and valleys—are the Cambrian Mountains, while the Cotswolds, a range of hills in Gloucestershire, extend into the surrounding shires.

The remainder of England is plain land, though not necessarily flat, with the rocky sand-topped moors in the southwest, the rolling downs in the south and southeast, and the reclaimed marshes of the low-lying fens in the east central districts.

Scotland is divided into three physical regions—the Highlands, the Central Lowlands, containing two-thirds of the population, and the Southern Uplands. The western Highland coast is intersected throughout by long, narrow sea-lochs, or fiords. Scotland also includes the Outer and Inner Hebrides and other islands off the west coast and the Orkney and Shetland Islands off the north coast.

Wales is generally hilly; the Snowdon range in the northern part culminates in Mount Snowdon (3,560 ft, 1,085 m), highest in both England and Wales.

Important rivers flowing into the North Sea are the Thames, Humber, Tees, and Tyne. In the west are the Severn and Wye, which empty into the Bristol Channel and are navigable, as are the Mersey and Ribble.

Government. The United Kingdom is a constitutional monarchy, with a Queen and a Parliament that has two houses: the House of Lords with about 830 hereditary peers, 26 spiritual peers, about 270 life peers and peeresses, and 9 law-lords, who are hereditary, or life, peers, and the House of Commons, which has 650 popularly elected members. Supreme legislative power is vested in Parliament, which sits for five years unless sooner dissolved.

The executive power of the Crown is exercised by the Cabinet, headed by the Prime Minister. The latter, normally the head of the party commanding a majority in the House of Commons, is appointed by the Sovereign, with whose consent he or she in turn appoints the rest of the Cabinet. All ministers must be members of one or the other house of Parliament; they are individually and collectively responsible to the Crown and Parliament. The Cabinet proposes bills and arranges the business of Parliament, but it depends entirely on the votes in the House of Commons. The Lords cannot hold up "money" bills, but they can delay other bills for a maximum of one year.

By the Act of Union (1707), the Scottish Parliament was assimilated with that of England, and Scotland is now represented in Commons by 71 members. The Secretary of State for Scotland, a member of the Cabinet, is responsible for the administration of Scottish affairs.

Ruler. Queen Elizabeth II, born April 21, 1926, elder daughter of King George VI and Queen Elizabeth, succeeded to the throne on the death of her father on Feb. 6, 1952; married Nov. 20, 1947, to Prince Philip, Duke of Edinburgh, born June 10, 1921; their children are Prince Charles[1] (heir presumptive), born Nov. 14, 1948; Princess Anne, born Aug. 15, 1950; Prince Andrew, born Feb. 19, 1960; and Prince Edward, born March 10, 1964. The Queen's sister is Princess Margaret, born Aug. 21, 1930. Prince William Arthur Philip Louis, son of the Prince and Princess of Wales and second in line to the throne, was born June 21, 1982. A second son, Prince Henry Charles Albert David, was born Sept. 15, 1984, and is third in line.

History. Roman invasions of the 1st century B.C. brought Britain into contact with the Continent. When the Roman legions withdrew in the 5th century A.D., Britain fell easy prey to the invading hordes of Angles, Saxons, and Jutes from Scandinavia and the Low Countries. Seven large kingdoms were established, and the original Britons were forced into Wales and Scotland. It was not until the 10th century that the country finally became united under the kings of Wessex. Following the death of Edward the Confessor (1066), a dispute about the succession arose, and William, Duke of Normandy, invaded England, defeating the Saxon King, Harold II, at the Battle of Hastings (1066). The Norman conquest introduced Norman law and feudalism.

The reign of Henry II (1154–89), first of the Plantagenets, saw an increasing centralization of royal power at the expense of the nobles, but in 1215 John (1199–1216) was forced to sign the Magna Carta, which awarded the people, especially the nobles, certain basic rights. Edward I (1272–1307) continued the conquest of Ireland, reduced Wales to subjection, and made some gains in Scotland. In 1314, however, English forces led by Edward II were ousted from Scotland after the Battle of Bannockburn. The late 13th and early 14th centuries saw the development of a separate House of Commons with tax-raising powers.

Edward III's claim to the throne of France led to the Hundred Years' War (1338–1453) and the loss of almost all the large English territory in France. In England, the great poverty and discontent caused by the war were intensified by the Black Death, a plague that reduced the population by about one-third. The Wars of the Roses (1455–85), a struggle for the throne between the House of York and the House of Lancaster, ended in the victory of Henry Tudor (Henry VII) at Bosworth Field (1485).

1. The title Prince of Wales, which is not inherited, was conferred on Prince Charles by his mother on July 26, 1958. The investiture ceremony took place on July 1, 1969. The previous Prince of Wales was Prince Edward Albert, who held the title from 1911 to 1936 before he became Edward VIII.

Rulers of England and Great Britain

Name	Born	Ruled[1]	Name	Born	Ruled[1]
SAXONS[2]			**HOUSE OF YORK**		
Egbert[3]	c.775	828–839	Edward IV	1442	1461–1483 [5]
Ethelwulf	?	839–858	Edward V	1470	1483–1483
Ethelbald	?	858–860	Richard III	1452	1483–1485
Ethelbert	?	860–866			
Ethelred I	?	866–871	**HOUSE OF TUDOR**		
Alfred the Great	849	871–899	Henry VII	1457	1485–1509
Edward the Elder	c.870	899–924	Henry VIII	1491	1509–1547
Athelstan	895	924–939	Edward VI	1537	1547–1553
Edmund I the Deed-doer	921	939–946	Jane (Lady Jane Grey)[6]	1537	1553–1553
Edred	c.925	946–955	Mary I ("Bloody Mary")	1516	1553–1558
Edwy the Fair	c.943	955–959	Elizabeth I	1533	1558–1603
Edgar the Peaceful	943	959–975			
Edward the Martyr	c.962	975–979	**HOUSE OF STUART**		
Ethelred II the Unready	968	979–1016	James I[7]	1566	1603–1625
Edmund II Ironside	c.993	1016–1016	Charles I	1600	1625–1649
DANES			**COMMONWEALTH**		
Canute	995	1016–1035	Council of State	—	1649–1653
Harold I Harefoot	c.1016	1035–1040	Oliver Cromwell[8]	1599	1653–1658
Hardecanute	c.1018	1040–1042	Richard Cromwell[8]	1626	1658–1659 [9]
SAXONS			**RESTORATION OF HOUSE OF**		
Edward the Confessor	c.1004	1042–1066	**STUART**		
Harold II	c.1020	1066–1066	Charles II	1630	1660–1685
			James II	1633	1685–1688 [10]
HOUSE OF NORMANDY			William III[11]	1650	1689–1702
William I the Conqueror	1027	1066–1087	Mary II[11]	1662	1689–1694
William II Rufus	c.1056	1087–1100	Anne	1665	1702–1714
Henry I Beauclerc	1068	1100–1135			
Stephen of Boulogne	c.1100	1135–1154	**HOUSE OF HANOVER**		
			George I	1660	1714–1727
HOUSE OF PLANTAGENET			George II	1683	1727–1760
Henry II	1133	1154–1189	George III	1738	1760–1820
Richard I Coeur de Lion	1157	1189–1199	George IV	1762	1820–1830
John Lackland	1167	1199–1216	William IV	1765	1830–1837
Henry III	1207	1216–1272	Victoria	1819	1837–1901
Edward I Longshanks	1239	1272–1307			
Edward II	1284	1307–1327	**HOUSE OF SAXE-COBURG**[12]		
Edward III	1312	1327–1377	Edward VII	1841	1901–1910
Richard II	1367	1377–1399 [4]			
			HOUSE OF WINDSOR[12]		
HOUSE OF LANCASTER			George V	1865	1910–1936
Henry IV Bolingbroke	1367	1399–1413	Edward VIII	1894	1936–1936 [13]
Henry V	1387	1413–1422	George VI	1895	1936–1952
Henry VI	1421	1422–1461 [5]	Elizabeth II	1926	1952–

1. Year of end of rule is also that of death, unless otherwise indicated. 2. Dates for Saxon kings are still subject of controversy. 3. Became King of West Saxons in 802; considered (from 828) first King of all England. 4. Died 1400. 5. Henry VI reigned again briefly 1470–71. 6. Nominal Queen for 9 days; not counted as Queen by some authorities. She was beheaded in 1554. 7. Ruled in Scotland as James VI (1567–1625). 8. Lord Protector. 9. Died 1712. 10. Died 1701. 11. Joint rulers (1689–1694). 12. Name changed from Saxe–Coburg to Windsor in 1917. 13. Was known after his abdication as the Duke of Windsor, died 1972.

During the reign of Henry VIII (1509–47), the Church in England asserted its independence from the Roman Catholic Church. Under Edward VI and Mary, the two extremes of religious fanaticism were reached, and it remained for Henry's daughter, Elizabeth I (1558–1603), to set up the Church of England on a moderate basis. In 1588, the Spanish Armada, a fleet sent out by Catholic King Philip II of Spain, was defeated by the English and destroyed during a storm. During Elizabeth's reign, England became a world power.

Elizabeth's heir was a Stuart—James VI of Scotland—who joined the two crowns as James I (1603–25). The Stuart kings incurred large debts and were forced either to depend on Parliament for taxes or to raise money by illegal means. In 1642, war

broke out between Charles I and a large segment of the Parliament; Charles was defeated and executed in 1649, and the monarchy was then abolished. After the death in 1658 of Oliver Cromwell, the Lord Protector, the Puritan Commonwealth fell to pieces and Charles II was placed on the throne in 1660. The struggle between the King and Parliament continued, but Charles II knew when to compromise. His brother, James II (1685–88), possessed none of his ability and was ousted by the Revolution of 1688, which confirmed the primacy of Parliament. James's daughter, Mary, and her husband, William of Orange, were now the rulers.

Queen Anne's reign (1702–14) was marked by the Duke of Marlborough's victories over France at Blen-

British Prime Ministers Since 1770

Name	Term	Name	Term
Lord North (Tory)	1770–1782	William E. Gladstone (Liberal)	1886–1886
Marquis of Rockingham (Whig)	1782–1782	Marquis of Salisbury (Conservative)	1886–1892
Earl of Shelburne (Whig)	1782–1783	William E. Gladstone (Liberal)	1892–1894
Duke of Portland (Coalition)	1783–1783	Earl of Rosebery (Liberal)	1894–1895
William Pitt, the Younger (Tory)	1783–1801	Marquis of Salisbury (Conservative)	1895–1902
Henry Addington (Tory)	1801–1804	Arthur James Balfour (Conservative)	1902–1905
William Pitt, the Younger (Tory)	1804–1806	Sir H. Campbell–Bannerman (Liberal)	1905–1908
Baron Grenville (Whig)	1806–1807	Herbert H. Asquith (Liberal)	1908–1915
Duke of Portland (Tory)	1807–1809	Herbert H. Asquith (Coalition)	1915–1916
Spencer Perceval (Tory)	1809–1812	David Lloyd George (Coalition)	1916–1922
Earl of Liverpool (Tory)	1812–1827	Andrew Bonar Law (Conservative)	1922–1923
George Canning (Tory)	1827–1827	Stanley Baldwin (Conservative)	1923–1924
Viscount Goderich (Tory)	1827–1828	James Ramsay MacDonald (Labor)	1924–1924
Duke of Wellington (Tory)	1828–1830	Stanley Baldwin (Conservative)	1924–1929
Earl Grey (Whig)	1830–1834	James Ramsay MacDonald (Labor)	1929–1931
Viscount Melbourne (Whig)	1834–1834	James Ramsay MacDonald (Coalition)	1931–1935
Sir Robert Peel (Tory)	1834–1835	Stanley Baldwin (Coalition)	1935–1937
Viscount Melbourne (Whig)	1835–1841	Neville Chamberlain (Coalition)	1937–1940
Sir Robert Peel (Tory)	1841–1846	Winston Churchill (Coalition)	1940–1945
Earl Russell (Whig)	1846–1852	Clement R. Attlee (Labor)	1945–1951
Earl of Derby (Tory)	1852–1852	Sir Winston Churchill (Conservative)	1951–1955
Earl of Aberdeen (Coalition)	1852–1855	Sir Anthony Eden (Conservative)	1955–1957
Viscount Palmerston (Liberal)	1855–1858	Harold Macmillan (Conservative)	1957–1963
Earl of Derby (Conservative)	1858–1859	Sir Alec Frederick Douglas–Home	
Viscount Palmerston (Liberal)	1859–1865	(Conservative)	1963–1964
Earl Russell (Liberal)	1865–1866	Harold Wilson (Labor)	1964–1970
Earl of Derby (Conservative)	1866–1868	Edward Heath (Conservative)	1970–1974
Benjamin Disraeli (Conservative)	1868–1868	Harold Wilson (Labor)	1974–1976
William E. Gladstone (Liberal)	1868–1874	James Callaghan (Labor)	1976–1979
Benjamin Disraeli (Conservative)	1874–1880	Margaret Thatcher (Conservative)	1979–1990
William E. Gladstone (Liberal)	1880–1885	John Major (Conservative)	1990–
Marquis of Salisbury (Conservative)	1885–1886		

heim, Oudenarde, and Malplaquet in the War of the Spanish Succession. England and Scotland meanwhile were joined by the Act of Union (1707). Upon the death of Anne, the distant claims of the elector of Hanover were recognized, and he became King of Great Britain and Ireland as George I.

The unwillingness of the Hanoverian kings to rule resulted in the formation by the royal ministers of a Cabinet, headed by a Prime Minister, which directed all public business. Abroad, the constant wars with France expanded the British Empire all over the globe, particularly in North America and India. This imperial growth was checked by the revolt of the American colonies (1775–81).

Struggles with France broke out again in 1793 and during the Napoleonic Wars, which ended at Waterloo in (1815).

The Victorian era, named after Queen Victoria (1837–1901), saw the growth of a democratic system of government that had begun with the Reform Bill of 1832. The two important wars in Victoria's reign were the Crimean War against Russia (1853–56) and the Boer War (1899–1902), the latter enormously extending Britain's influence in Africa.

Increasing uneasiness at home and abroad marked the reign of Edward VII (1901–10). Within four years after the accession of George V in 1910, Britain entered World War I when Germany invaded Belgium. The nation was led by coalition Cabinets, headed first by Herbert Asquith and then, starting in 1916, by the Welsh statesman David Lloyd George. Postwar labor unrest culminated in the general strike of 1926.

King Edward VIII succeeded to the throne on Jan. 20, 1936, at his father's death, but abdicated on Dec.

11, 1936 (in order to marry an American divorcee, Wallis Warfield Simpson) in favor of his brother, who became George VI.

The efforts of Prime Minister Neville Chamberlain to stem the rising threat of Nazism in Germany failed with the German invasion of Poland on Sept. 1, 1939, which was followed by Britain's entry into World War II on September 3. Allied reverses in the spring of 1940 led to Chamberlain's resignation and the formation of another coalition war Cabinet by the Conservative leader, Winston Churchill, who led Britain through most of World War II. Churchill resigned shortly after V-E Day, May 7, 1945, but then formed a "caretaker" government that remained in office until after the parliamentary elections in July, which the Labor Party won overwhelmingly. The government formed by Clement R. Attlee began a moderate socialist program.

For details of World War II (1939–45), *see* Headline History.

In 1951, Churchill again became Prime Minister at the head of a Conservative government. George VI died Feb. 6, 1952, and was succeeded by his daughter Elizabeth II.

Churchill stepped down in 1955 in favor of Sir Anthony Eden, who resigned on grounds of ill health in 1957, and was succeeded by Harold Macmillan and Sir Alec Douglas-Home. In 1964, Harold Wilson led the Labor Party to victory.

A lagging economy brought the Conservatives back to power in 1970. Prime Minister Edward Heath won Britain's admission to the European Community.

Margaret Thatcher became Britain's first woman Prime Minister as the Conservatives won 339 seats on May 3, 1979.

An Argentine invasion of the Falkland Islands on April 2, 1982, involved Britain in a war 8,000 miles from the home islands. Although Argentina had long claimed the Falklands, known as the Malvinas in Spanish, negotiations were in progress until a month before the invasion.

When more than 11,000 Argentine troops on the Falklands surrendered on June 14, 1982, Mrs. Thatcher declared her intention to garrison the islands indefinitely, together with a naval presence.

Although there were continuing economic problems and foreign policy disputes, an upswing in the economy in 1986–87 led Thatcher to call elections for June 11 in which she won a near-unprecedented third consecutive term.

Through much, if not all, of 1990 the Conservatives were losing the confidence of the electorate. The unpopularity of her poll tax together with an uncompromising position toward further European integration eroded support within her own party. When John Major won the Conservative Party leadership in November, Mrs. Thatcher resigned, paving the way for the Queen to ask Mr. Major to form a government.

In the middle of a long recession John Major called a national election for April 1992. Confounding many political observers the Conservatives won but by a far narrower margin than previously.

After months of political maneuvering the U.K. ratified the Maastricht treaty in August 1993.

In a bold gamble to shore up his support within the Conservative Party, Major resigned his leadership in late June 1995 and called for a party decision. Major won the position with a comfortable margin and immediately afterward reshuffled his Cabinet.

NORTHERN IRELAND

Status: Part of United Kingdom
Secretary of State: Sir Patrick Mayhew (1992)
Area: 5,452 sq mi. (14,121 sq km)
Population (est. mid-year 1992): 1,610,000 (provisional);
    Density per square mile: 295.3
Capital and largest city (June 30, 1992): Belfast, 287,500
Monetary unit: British pound sterling; **Languages:** English, Gaelic; **Religions:** Roman Catholic, Presbyterian, Church of Ireland, Methodist.

Geography. Northern Ireland comprises the counties of Antrim, Armagh, Down, Fermanagh, Londonderry, and Tyrone, which make up predominantly Protestant Ulster and form the northern part of the island of Ireland, westernmost of the British Isles. It is slightly larger than Connecticut.

Government. Northern Ireland is an integral part of the United Kingdom (it has 12 representatives in the British House of Commons), but under the terms of the government of Ireland Act in 1920, it had a semi-autonomous government. But in 1972, after three years of internal strife which resulted in over 400 dead and thousands injured, Britain suspended the Ulster parliament. The Ulster counties became governed directly from London after an attempt to return certain powers to an elected Assembly in Belfast.

The Northern Ireland Assembly was dissolved in 1975 and a Constitutional Convention was elected to write a Constitution acceptable to Protestants and Catholics. The convention failed to reach agreement and closed down the next year.

History. Ulster was part of Catholic Ireland until the reign of Elizabeth I (1558–1603) when, after crushing three Irish rebellions, the crown confiscated lands in Ireland and settled in Ulster the Scot Presbyterians who became rooted there. Another rebellion in 1641–51, crushed as brutally by Oliver Cromwell, resulted in the settlement of Anglican Englishmen in Ulster. Subsequent political policy favoring Protestants and disadvantaging Catholics encouraged further settlement in Northern Ireland.

But the North did not separate from the South until William Gladstone presented in 1886 his proposal for home rule in Ireland as a means of settling the Irish Question. The Protestants in the North, although they had grievances like the Catholics in the South, feared domination by the Catholic majority. Industry, moreover, was concentrated in the north and dependent on the British market.

When World War I began, civil war threatened between the regions. Northern Ireland, however, did not become a political entity until the six counties accepted the Home Rule Bill of 1920. This set up a semi-autonomous Parliament in Belfast and a Crown-appointed Governor advised by a Cabinet of the Prime Minister and eight ministers, as well as a 12-member representation in the House of Commons in London.

As the Republic of Ireland gained its sovereignty, relations improved between North and South, al-though the Irish Republican Army, outlawed in recent years, continued the struggle to end the partition of Ireland. In 1966–69, communal rioting and street fighting between Protestants and Catholics occurred in Londonderry, fomented by extremist nationalist Protestants, who feared the Catholics might attain a local majority, and by Catholics demonstrating for civil rights.

Rioting, terrorism, and sniping killed more than 2,200 people from 1969 through 1984 and the religious communities, Catholic and Protestant, became hostile armed camps. British troops were brought in to separate them but themselves became a target of Catholics.

In 1973, a new British charter created a 78-member Assembly elected by proportional representation that gave more weight to Catholic strength. It created a Province Executive with committee chairmen of the Assembly heading all government departments except law enforcement, which remained under London's control. Assembly elections in 1973 produced a majority for the new Constitution that included Catholic assemblymen.

Ulster's leaders agreed in 1973 to create an 11-member Executive Body with six seats assigned to Unionists (Protestants) and four to members of Catholic parties. Unionist leader Brian Faulkner headed the Executive. Also agreed to was a Council of Ireland, with 14 seats evenly divided between Dublin and Belfast, which could act only by unanimous vote.

Although the Council lacked real authority, its creation sparked a general strike by Protestant extremists in 1974. The two-week strike caused Faulkner's resignation from the Executive and resumption of direct rule from London.

In April 1974, London instituted a new program that responded to some Catholic grievances, but assigned more British troops to cut off movement of arms and munitions to Ulster's violence-racked cities.

Violence continued unabated, with new heights reached early in 1976 when the British government announced the end of special privileges for political prisoners in Northern Ireland. British Prime Minister James Callaghan visited Belfast in July and pledged that Ulster would remain part of the United Kingdom unless a clear majority wished to separate.

In October 1977, the 1976 Nobel Prize for Peace was awarded to Mairead Corrigan and Betty Williams for their campaign for peace in Northern Ireland. Intermittent violence continued, however, and on Aug.

27, 1979, an I.R.A. bomb killed Earl Mountbatten as he was sailing off southern Ireland.

New talks aimed at a restoration of home rule in Northern Ireland began and quickly ended in January 1980. In May, Mrs. Thatcher met with the new Prime Minister of the Irish Republic, Charles Haughey, but she insisted that the future of Ulster must be decided only by its people and the British Parliament.

On November 15, 1985, Mrs. Thatcher signed an agreement with Irish Prime Minister Garrett Fitzgerald giving Ireland a consultative role in the affairs of Northern Ireland. It was met with intense disapproval by the Ulster Unionists.

Two separate and secret dialogues were initiated in 1993 to bring peace.

The British and Irish governments in February 1995 announced an approved framework within which a settlement of the status of Northern Ireland could eventually be reached.

Dependencies of the United Kingdom

ANGUILLA

Status: Dependency
Governor: A.W. Shave (1992)
Area: 35 sq mi. (91 sq km)
Population (est. mid-1994): 7,052; average annual rate of natural increase: 0.67%; birth rate: 24.2/1000; infant mortality rate: 17.5/1000; density per sq mi.: 201.4
Capital (1992): The Valley, 1,400; **Monetary unit:** East Caribbean dollar; **Literacy:** 95%
Economy summary: Gross domestic product (1992 est.): $56.5 billion, $6,800 per capita; 7.5% real growth rate. Major industries: Tourism, boat building, salt, lobster fishing. Exports: $556,000 (f.o.b., 1992). Imports: $33.5 million (f.o.b., 1992)

Anguilla was originally part of the West Indies Associated States as a component of St. Kitts-Nevis-Anguilla.

In 1967, Anguilla declared its independence from the St. Kitts-Nevis-Anguilla federation. Britain however, did not recognize this action. In February 1969, Anguilla voted to cut all ties with Britain and become an independent republic. In March, Britain landed troops on the island and, on March 30, a truce was signed. In July 1971, Anguilla became a dependency of Britain and two months later Britain ordered the withdrawal of all its troops.

A new Constitution for Anguilla, effective in February 1976, provides for separate administration and a government of elected representatives. The Associated State of St. Kitts-Nevis-Anguilla ended Dec. 19, 1980.

BERMUDA

Status: Self-governing dependency
Governor: Lord Waddington (1992)
Premier: John Swan (1982)
Area: 20 sq mi. (52 sq km)
Population (est. mid-1994): 61,158; average annual rate of natural increase: 0.77%; birth rate: 15.1/1000; infant mortality rate: 13.1/1000; density per sq mi.: 3,057.9
Capital (1990): Hamilton, 2,000; **Monetary unit:** Bermuda dollar; **Literacy rate:** 98% domestic
Economic summary: Gross domestic product (1992): $1.63 billion; $27,100 per capita; −1.5% real growth rate (1991); unemployment: 6% (1991). Arable land: 0%. Principal agricultural products: bananas, vegetables, citrus fruits, dairy products. Labor force: 32,000; 47% clerical and in services. Major industrial prod-

ucts: structural concrete, paints, pharmaceuticals. Natural resource: limestone. Exports: $60 million (f.o.b., 1991) semi-tropical produce, light manufactures. Imports: $468 million (f.o.b., 1991) foodstuffs, fuel, machinery. Major trading partners: U.S., U.K., Canada, Venezuela, Japan.

Bermuda is an archipelago of about 360 small islands, 580 miles (934 km) east of North Carolina. The largest is (Great) Bermuda, or Long Island. Discovered by Juan de Bermúdez, a shipwrecked Spaniard, early in the 16th century, the islands were settled in 1612 by an offshoot of the Virginia Company and became a crown colony in 1684.

In 1940, sites on the islands were leased for 99 years to the U.S. for air and navy bases. Bermuda is also the headquarters of the West Indies and Atlantic squadron of the Royal Navy.

In 1968, Bermuda was granted a new Constitution, its first Prime Minister, and autonomy, except for foreign relations, defense, and internal security. The predominantly white United Bermuda Party has retained power in four elections against the opposition—the black-led Progressive Laborites—although Bermuda's population is 60% black.

The 1991 budget called for tax increases and control of the island's offshore banking sector was tightened.

BRITISH ANTARCTIC TERRITORY

Status: Dependency
Commissioner: Peter M. Newton (1992)
Area: 500,000 sq mi. (1,395,000 sq km)
Population (1992): no permanent residents

The British Antarctic Territory consists of the South Shetland Islands, South Orkney Islands, and nearby Graham Land on the Antarctic continent, largely uninhabited. They are dependencies of the British crown colony of the Falkland Islands but received a separate administration in 1962, being governed by a British-appointed High Commissioner who is Governor of the Falklands.

BRITISH INDIAN OCEAN TERRITORY

Status: Dependency
Commissioner: David Ross MacLennan (1994)
Administrative headquarters: Victoria, Seychelles
Area: 85 sq mi. (220 sq km)

This dependency, consisting of the Chagos Archipelago and other small island groups, was formed in 1965 by agreement with Mauritius and the Seychelles. There is no permanent civilian population in the territory.

BRITISH VIRGIN ISLANDS

Status: Dependency
Governor: Peter Alfred Penfold (1992)
Area: 59 sq mi. (153 sq km)
Population (est. mid-1994): 12,864; average annual rate of natural increase: 1.24%; birth rate: 20.3/1000; infant mortality rate: 19.5/1000; density per square mile: 218
Capital (1991 census): Road Town (on Tortola): 3,983; **Monetary unit:** U.S. dollar
Economic summary: Gross domestic product (1991): $133 million; $10,600 per capita; 2% real growth rate.

Some 36 islands in the Caribbean Sea northeast of Puerto Rico and west of the Leeward Islands, the British Virgin Islands are economically interdependent with the U.S. Virgin Islands to the south. They were formerly part of the administration of the Leeward Islands. They received a separate administration in 1956 as a crown colony. In 1967 a new Constitution was promulgated that provided for a ministerial system of government headed by the Governor. The principal islands are Tortola, Virgin Gorda, Anegada, and Jost Van Dyke.

CAYMAN ISLANDS

Status: Dependency
Governor: Michael E.J. Gore (1992)
Area: 100 sq mi. (259 sq km)
Population (est. mid-1994): 31,790; density per sq mi.: 317.9
Capital (est. 1992): George Town (on Grand Cayman), 15,000; **Monetary unit:** Cayman Islands dollar
Economic summary: Gross domestic product (1991 est.): $670 million, $23,000 per capita; inflation: 1.5% (1992 est.); unemployment: 7% (1992). Exports: $26 million (f.o.b., 1991, est.): turtle products, manufactured goods. Imports: $262.2 million (c.i.f., 1991 est.): foodstuffs, manufactured goods. Major trading partners: U.S., Trinidad and Tobago, U.K., Netherland Antilles, Japan.

This dependency consists of three islands—Grand Cayman (76 sq mi.; 197 sq km), Cayman Brac (22 sq mi.; 57 sq km), and Little Cayman (20 sq mi.; 52 sq km)—situated about 180 miles (290 km) northwest of Jamaica. They were dependencies of Jamaica until 1959, when they became a unit territory within the Federation of the West Indies. In 1962, upon the dissolution of the Federation, the Cayman Islands became a British dependency.

The islands' chief export is turtle products.

CHANNEL ISLANDS

Status: Crown dependencies
Lieutenant Governor of Jersey: Air Marshall Sir John Sutton (1990)
Lieutenant Governor of Guernsey: Vice Adm. Sir John Coward (1994)
Area: 120 sq mi. (311 sq km)
Populations (July 1992): Jersey, 85,026; Guernsey, 57,949
Capital of Jersey (1986): St. Helier, 27,083' **Capital of Guernsey (1986):** St. Peter Port, 16,085' **Monetary units:** Guernsey pound; Jersey pound

This group of islands, lying in the English Channel off the northwest coast of France, is the only portion of the Duchy of Normandy belonging to the English Crown, to which it has been attached since the conquest of 1066. It was the only British possession occupied by Germany during World War II.

For purposes of government, the islands are divided into the Bailiwick of Jersey (45 sq mi.; 117 sq km) and the Bailiwick of Guernsey (30 sq mi.; 78 sq km), including Alderney (3 sq mi.; 7.8 sq km); Sark (2 sq mi.; 5.2 sq km), Herm, Jethou, etc. The islands are administered according to their own laws and customs by local governments. Acts of Parliament in London are not binding on the islands unless they are specifically mentioned. The Queen is represented in each Bailiwick by a Lieutenant Governor.

FALKLAND ISLANDS AND DEPENDENCIES

Status: Dependency
Governor: David Evarard Tatham (1992)
Chief Executive: R. Sampson
Area: 4,700 sq mi. (12,173 sq km)
Population (est. mid-1994): 2,261; density per sq mi.: 2
Capital (1991): Stanley (on East Falkland), 1,643
Monetary unit: Falkland Island pound

This sparsely inhabited dependency consists of a group of islands in the South Atlantic, about 250 miles (402 km) east of the South American mainland. The largest islands are East Falkland and West Falkland. Dependencies are South Georgia Island (1,450 sq mi.; 3,756 sq km), the South Sandwich Islands, and other islets. Three former dependencies—Graham Land, the South Shetland Islands, and the South Orkney Islands—were established as a new British dependency, the British Antarctic Territory, in 1962.

The chief industry is sheep raising and, apart from the production of wool, hides and skins, and tallow, there are no known resources. The whaling industry is carried on from South Georgia Island.

The chief export is wool.

GIBRALTAR

Status: Self-governing dependency
Governor: Field Marshall Sir John Chapple
Chief Minister: J. Bossano
Area: 2.25 sq mi. (5.8 sq km)
Population (est. mid-1994): 31,684; average annual rate of natural increase: 0.58%; birth rate: 15.3/1000; infant mortality rate: 8.1/1000; density per sq mi.: 14,081.7.
Monetary unit: Gibraltar pound; **Literacy rate:** 99% (est.)
Economic summary: Gross national product (FY87 est.): $182 million; $4,600 per capita. Exports: $82 million (f.o.b., 1988): re-exports of tobacco, petroleum, wine. Imports: $258 million (c.i.f., 1988): manufactured goods, fuels, foodstuffs. Major trading partners: U.K., Morocco, Portugal, Netherlands, Spain, U.S.

Gibraltar, at the south end of the Iberian Peninsula, is a rocky promontory commanding the western entrance to the Mediterranean. Aside from its strategic importance, it is also a free port, naval base, and coaling station. It was captured by the Arabs crossing from Africa into Spain in A.D. 711. In the 15th century, it passed to the Moorish ruler of Granada and later became Spanish. It was captured by an Anglo-Dutch force in 1704 during the War of the Spanish Succession and passed to Great Britain by the Treaty of Utrecht in 1713. Most of the inhabitants of Gibraltar are of Spanish, Italian, and Maltese descent.

Spanish efforts to recover Gibraltar culminated in a referendum in 1967 in which the residents voted overwhelmingly to retain their link with Britain. Spain sealed Gibraltar's land border in 1969 and did not open communications until April 1980, after the two governments had agreed to solve their dispute in keeping with a United Nations resolution calling for restoration of the "Rock" to Spain.

The last British military battalion on the "Rock" was withdrawn in March 1991. Spain suggested a form of joint control, but the U.K. refused.

HONG KONG

Status: Dependency
Governor: Christopher Patten (1992)
Area: 416 sq mi. (1,077 sq km)

Population (est. mid-1995): 6,000,000 (average annual rate of natural increase: 0.7%); birth rate: 12/1000; infant mortality rate: 4.8/1000; density per square mile: 14,423
Capital (1993 est.): Victoria (Hong Kong Island), 5,932,000. **Monetary unit:** Hong Kong dollar; **Literacy rate:** 77%
Economic summary: Gross domestic product (1993 est.): $119 billion: $21,500 per capita; real growth rate 5.2%; inflation 9.5%; unemployment 2.3%. Arable land: 7%. Principal agricultural products: vegetables, rice, dairy products. Labor force (1990): 2,800,000: 28.5% manufacturing; 27.9%, wholesale, retail, hotels, restaurants. Major industrial products: textiles, clothing, toys, transistor radios, watches, electronic components. Exports: $145.1 billion (f.o.b., 1993 est.): clothing, textiles, toys, watches, electrical appliances, footwear. Imports: $149.6 billion (c.i.f., 1993 est.): raw materials, transport equipment, food. Major trading partners: U.S., U.K., Japan, Germany, China, Taiwan.

The crown colony of Hong Kong comprises the island of Hong Kong (32 sq mi.; 83 sq km), Stonecutters' Island, Kowloon Peninsula, and the New Territories on the adjoining mainland. The island of Hong Kong, located at the mouth of the Pearl River about 90 miles (145 km) southeast of Canton, was ceded to Britain in 1841.

Stonecutters' Island and Kowloon were annexed in 1860, and the New Territories, which are mainly agricultural lands, were leased from China in 1898 for 99 years. Hong Kong was attacked by Japanese troops Dec. 7, 1941, and surrendered the following Christmas. It remained under Japanese occupation until August 1945.

After two years of painstaking negotiation, authorities of Britain and the People's Republic of China agreed in 1984 that Hong Kong would return to Chinese sovereignty on June 30, 1997, when Britain's lease on the New Territories expires. They also agreed that the vibrant capitalist enclave on China's coast would retain its status as a free port and its social, economic, and legal system as a special administrative region of China. Current laws will remain basically unchanged.

Under a unique "One Country, Two Systems" arrangement, the Chinese government promised that Hong Kong's lifestyle would remain unchanged for 50 years, and that freedoms of speech, press, assembly, association, travel, right to strike, and religious belief would be guaranteed by law. However, the chief executive and some of the legislature will be appointed by Beijing.

Hong Kong will continue to have its own finances and issue its own travel documents, and Peking will not levy taxes.

Despite threats from China the legislature voted in June 1994 to transform that body into a much more democratic institution. Earlier in February they passed a bill to lower the voting age to 18 from 21 and introduced single-member districts.

ISLE OF MAN

Status: Self-Governing Crown Dependency
Lieutenant Governor: Air Marshall Sir Laurence Jones
Area: 221 sq mi. (572 sq km)
Population (1991 census): 69,788; growth rate 0.1%
Capital (1991): Douglas, 22,214; **Monetary unit:** Isle of Man pound

Situated in the Irish Sea, equidistant from Scotland, Ireland, and England, the Isle of Man is administered according to its own laws by a government composed of the Lieutenant Governor, a Legislative Council, and a House of Keys, one of the most ancient legislative assemblies in the world.

The chief exports are beef and lamb, fish, and livestock.

LEEWARD ISLANDS

See British Virgin Islands; Montserrat

MONTSERRAT

Status: Dependency
Governor: Frank Savage (1993)
Chief Minister: Reuben Meade (1991)
Area: 38 sq mi. (98 sq km)
Population (est. mid-1994): 12,701; average annual rate of natural increase: 0.33%; birth rate: 15.9/1000; infant mortality rate: 11.6/1000; density per square mile: 334.2
Capital (est. 1991): Plymouth, 2,500
Monetary unit: East Caribbean dollar
Econommic summary: Gross domestic product (1992 est.): $53.7 million, $4,300 per capita; inflation: 2.8%. Exports: $2.8 million (f.o.b., 1992): electric parts, plastic bags, apparel, hot peppers, live plants, cattle. Imports: $80.6 million (f.o.b., 1992): machinery and transportation equipment, foodstuffs, manufactured goods, fuels, lubricants and related materials.

The island of Montserrat is in the Lesser Antilles of the West Indies. Until 1956, it was a division of the Leeward Islands. It did not join the West Indies Associated States established in 1967.

The chief exports are cattle, potatoes, cotton, lint, recapped tires, mangoes, and tomatoes.

PITCAIRN ISLAND

Status: Dependency
Governor: Robert John Alston
Island Magistrate: J. Warren
Area: 1.75 sq mi. (4.5 sq km)
Population (mid-1994): 71; density per square mile: 40.5
Capital: Adamstown

Pitcairn Island, in the South Pacific about midway between Australia and South America, consists of the island of Pitcairn and the three uninhabited islands of Henderson, Duicie, and Oeno. The island of Pitcairn was settled in 1790 by British mutineers from the ship *Bounty,* commanded by Capt. William Bligh. It was annexed as a British colony in 1838. Overpopulation forced removal of the settlement to Norfolk Island in 1856, but about 40 persons soon returned.

The colony is governed by a 10-member Council presided over by the Island Magistrate, who is elected for a three-year term.

ST. HELENA

Status: Dependency
Governor: A.N. Hoole (1991)
Area: 120 sq mi. (310 sq km)
Population (est. mid-1994): 6,741; density per sq mi: 56.1
Capital (1987): Jamestown, 1,332
Monetary unit: Pound sterling

St. Helena is a volcanic island in the South Atlantic about 1,100 miles (1,770 km) from the west coast of Africa. It is famous as the place of exile of Napoleon (1815–21).

It was taken for England in 1659 by the East India Company and was brought under the direct government of the Crown in 1834.

St. Helena has two dependencies: Ascension (34 sq mi.; 88 sq km), an island about 700 miles (1,127 km) northwest of St. Helena; and Tristan da Cunha (40 sq mi.; 104 sq km), a group of six islands about 1,500 miles (2,414 km) south-southwest of St. Helena.

TURKS AND CAICOS ISLANDS

Status: Dependency
Governor: Martin Bourk (1993)
Area: 193 sq mi. (500 sq km)
Population (est. mid-1994): 13,552; average annual rate of natural increase: 2.69%; birth rate: 14.1/1000; infant mortality rate: 12.7/1000; density per square mile: 70.2
Capital (1990): Cockburn Town, 3,720
Monetary unit: U.S. dollar.
Economic summary: Gross domestic product (1992 est.): $80.8 million, $6,000 per capita. Exports: $6.8 million (f.o.b., 1992): lobster, dried and fresh conch, conch shells. Imports: $42.8 million (1992): food and beverages, tobacco, clothing, manufactures, construction materials. Major trading partners: U.S., U.K.

These two groups of islands are situated at the southeast end of the Bahamas. The principal islands in the Turks group are Grand Turk and Salt Cay; the principal ones in the Caicos group are South Caicos, East Caicos, Middle (or Grand) Caicos, North Caicos, Providenciales, and West Caicos.

The Turks and Caicos Islands were dependencies of Jamaica until 1959, when they became a unit territory within the Federation of the West Indies. In 1962, when Jamaica became independent, the Turks and Caicos became a British crown colony. The present Constitution has been in force since 1969.

Chief exports in 1974 were crayfish (73%) and conch (25%).

VIRGIN ISLANDS

See British Virgin Islands

UNITED STATES

The United States of America
President: William J. Clinton (1993)
Vice President: Albert A. Gore, Jr. (1993)
Land area: 3,536,341 sq mi. (9,159,123 sq km)
Population (est. Aug. 11, 1995): 263,081,710; **(1990 census):** 248,709,873 (% change 1980–1990: +9.80). White: 199,686,070 (80.3%); Black: 29,986,060 (12.1%); American Indian, Eskimo, or Aleut: 1,959,234 (0.8%); Asian or Pacific Islander: 7,273,662 (2.9%); Other Race: 9,804,847 (3.9%); Hispanic Origin[1]: 22,354,059 (9.0%); (average annual rate of natural increase: 0.7%); birth rate: 16/1000; infant mortality rate: 8.3/1000; density per square mile: 73.7
Capital (1990 census.): Washington, D.C., 606,900; **Largest cities (1990 census):** New York, 7,322,564; Los Angeles, 3,485,398; Chicago, 2,783,726; Houston, 1,630,553; Philadelphia, 1,585,577; San Diego, 1,110,549; Detroit, 1,027,974; Dallas, 1,006,877; Phoenix, 983,403; San Antonio, 935,933; **Monetary unit:** Dollar; **Languages:** predominantly English, sizable Spanish-speaking minority; **Religions:** Protestant, 61%; Roman Catholic, 25%; Jewish, 2%; other, 5%; none, 7%; **Literacy rate:** Age 15 and over having completed 5 or more years of schooling (1991) 97.9%

Economic summary: Gross domestic product (1994): $6,736.1 billion; per capita personal income (1994 est.): $21,809. Civilian labor force (April 1994): 130.7 million. Arable land: 20%. Principal products: corn, wheat, barley, oats, sugar, potatoes, soybeans, fruits, beef, veal, pork. Labor force: 125,557,000. Major industrial products: petroleum products, fertilizers, cement, pig iron and steel, plastics and resins, newsprint, motor vehicles, machinery, natural gas, electricity. Natural resources: coal, oil, copper, gold, silver, minerals, timber. Exports: machinery, chemicals, aircrafts, military equipment, cereals, motor vehicles, grains. Illicit drugs: illicit producer of cannabis for domestic consumption. Ongoing eradication program aimed at small plots and greenhouses unsuccessful. Imports: crude and partly refined petroleum, machinery, automobiles. Major trading partners: Canada, Japan, Western Europe.

1. Persons of Hispanic origin can be of any race.

Government. The president is elected for a four-year term and may be re-elected only once. In 1993, the bicameral Congress consisted of the 100-member Senate (46 Democrats, 54 Republicans), elected to a six-year term with one-third of the seats becoming vacant every two years, and the 435-member House of Representatives (201 Democrats, 233 Republicans, 1 Independent, as of July 25, 1994), elected every two years. The minimum voting age is 18.

URUGUAY

Oriental Republic of Uruguay
President: Julio Sanguinetti Cairolo
Area: 68,040 sq mi. (176,224 sq km)
Population (est. mid-1995): 3,200,000 (average annual rate of natural increase: 0.7%); birth rate: 17/1000; infant mortality rate: 18.6/1000; density per sq mi.: 47
Capital and largest city (est. 1992): Montevideo, 1,500,000; **Monetary unit:** Peso; **Language:** Spanish; **Religion:** Roman Catholic, 66%; Protestant, 2%; Jewish, 2%; **National name:** Republica Oriental del Uruguay; **Literacy rate:** 94%
Economic summary: Gross domestic product (1993 est.): $19 billion: $6,000 per capita; real growth rate 2%; inflation 50%; unemployment 8.8%. Arable land: 8%. Principal products: livestock, grains, Labor force (1991 est.): 1,355,000: government, 25%; manufacturing, 19%; commerce, 12%; agriculture, 11%. Major products: processed meats, wool and hides, textiles, shoes, handbags and leather wearing apparel, cement, refined petroleum. Natural resources: hydroelectric power potential. Exports: $1.6 billion (f.o.b., 1993 est.): meat, hides, wool, fish. Imports: $2 billion (f.o.b., 1993 est.): transportation equipment, chemicals, machinery, plastics, minerals. Major trading partners: U.S., Brazil, Argentina, Germany, China, Italy, Nigeria.

Geography. Uruguay, on the east coast of South America south of Brazil and east of Argentina, is comparable in size to the State of Oklahoma.

The country consists of a low, rolling plain in the south and a low plateau in the north. It has a 120-mile (193 km) Atlantic shore line, a 235-mile (378 km) frontage on the Rio de la Plata, and 270 miles (435 km) on the Uruguay River, its western boundary.

Government. A republic. Presidents serve a single five-year term. The bicameral Congress, the General Assembly, consists of the Chamber of Senators and the Chamber of Representatives.

History. Juan Díaz de Solis, a Spaniard, discovered Uruguay in 1516, but the Portuguese were first to settle it when they founded Colonia in 1680. After a long struggle, Spain wrested the country from Portugal in 1778. Uruguay revolted against Spain in 1811, only to be conquered in 1817 by the Portuguese from Brazil. Independence was reasserted with Argentine help in 1825, and the republic was set up in 1828.

Independence, however, did not restore order, and a revolt in 1836 touched off nearly 50 years of factional strife, with occasional armed intervention from Argentina and Brazil.

Uruguay, made prosperous by meat and wool exports, founded a welfare state early in the 20th century. A decline began in the 1950s as successive governments struggled to maintain a large bureaucracy and costly social benefits. Economic stagnation and political frustration followed.

A military coup ousted the civilian government in 1973. The military dictatorship that followed used fear and terror to demoralize the population, taking thousands of political prisoners, probably the highest proportion of citizens jailed for political reasons anywhere in the world.

After ruling for 12 years, the military regime permitted election of a civilian government in November 1984 and relinquished rule in March 1985.

Luis Lacalle became president in March 1990, becoming the first Blanco Party member to assume that office in 23 years.

The president's continuing attempts in 1993 at economic reform met much resistance from the opposition as well as from some within his own party, which itself lacks a majority in Congress.

Presidential and legislative elections in November 1994 resulted in a narrow victory for the Colorado Party and its presidential candidate Julio Sanguinetti Cairolo, who assumed office in March 1995.

UZBEKISTAN

Republic of Uzbekistan
President: Islam A. Karimov (1990)
Prime Minister: Abdulkhashim Mutalov
Area: 172,700 sq mi. (447,400 sq km)
Population (est. mid-1995): 22,700,000 (Uzbeks, 71%; Russians, 8%; other minorities: Tajiks, Kazakhs, and Tartars); (average annual rate of natural increase: 2.5%); birth rate: 31/1000; infant mortality rate: 37/1000; density per square mile: 131.4
Capital and largest city (1991): Tashkent, 2,113,300. Other: Samarkand, 370,500; **Language:** Uzbek, 85%; Russian, 5%; **Religion:** Muslim (mostly Sunnis) 75–80% **Literacy rate:** 100%
Economic summary: Gross domestic product (UN, World Bank 1993 est.): $53.7 billion, $2,430 per capita; –3.5% real growth rate; inflation: 18% (per mos.); unemployment: 0.2% (officially registered). Labor force (1990): 7,941,000: agriculture and forestry, 39%; industry and construction, 24%. Natural resources: natural gas, petroleum, coal, gold, uranium, silver, copper, lead and zinc, tungsten, molybdenum. Agriculture: major crop is cotton. Exports (1993): $706.5 million to outside the former USSR countries: cotton, gold, textiles, chemicals, mineral fertilizers, vegetable oil. Imports (1993): $947.3 million from outside the former USSR countries: machinery and parts, consumer durables, grain, and other food. Trading partners: Former Soviet republics, Czech Republic.

Geography. Uzbekistan is situated in the former Soviet Central Asia between the Amu Darya and Syr Darya Rivers, the Aral Sea, and the slopes of the Tien Shan Mountains. It is bounded by Kazakhstan in the north and northwest, Kyrgyzstan and Tajikistan in the east and southeast, and Turkmenistan in the southwest. The republic also includes the Kara-Kalpak Autonomous S.S.R. since 1936 with its capital, Nukus, 1987 population, 152,000. The land is made up of deserts, oases, and mountains with valleys. Two-thirds of the territory are occupied by deserts and semi-deserts. The country is about one-tenth larger in area than the state of California.

Government. A constitutional republic.

History. The Uzbekistan land was once part of the ancient Persian empire and was later conquered by Alexander the Great in 4 B.C. During the 8th century, the nomadic Turkic tribes living there were converted to Islam by invading Arab forces who dominated the area. The Mongols under Ghengis Khan took over the region from the Seljuk Turks in the 13th century and it later became part of Tamerlane the Great's empire and his successors until the 16th century.

The Uzbeks invaded the territory in the early 16th century and merged with the other inhabitants in the area. Their empire broke up into separate Uzbek principalities, the khanates of Khiva, Bukhara, and Kokand. These city-states resisted Russian expansion into the area, but were conquered by the Russian forces in the mid-19th century.

The territory was made into the Uzbek Republic in 1924 and became the independent Uzbekistan Soviet Socialist Republic in 1925.

Uzbekistan joined with ten other former Soviet republics on Dec. 21, 1991, in the Commonwealth of Independent States.

In February 1992, Karimov, a former Communist Party boss, affirmed his commitment to democracy and human rights. An election in December 1991 had given him 85% of the vote, but the main opposition parties were not allowed to field candidates.

Opposition forces in mid-1993 formed a coalition. However the government closed their headquarters and arrested the leaders. The criminal code was amended to impose stricter penalties for antigovernment activity.

The government implemented modest economic reforms in early 1994, authorizing the privatization of small shops and certain services. In mid-year a new currency, the sum, was introduced.

Parliamentary elections in December 1994 produced a huge victory for the ruling party and an allied party. Opposition groups were largely excluded.

VANUATU

Republic of Vanuatu
President: Jean-Marie Leye (1994)
Prime Minister: Maxime Carlot (1991)
Area: 5,700 sq mi. (14,763 sq km)
Population (est. mid-1995): 200,000 (average annual rate of natural increase: 2.9%); birth rate: 38/1000; infant mortality rate: 45/1000; density per square mile: 35
Capital (est. 1987): Port Vila, 15,100; **Monetary unit:** Vatu; **Religions:** Presbyterian, 36.7%; Roman Catholic, 15%; Anglican, 15%; other Christian, 10%; indigenous beliefs, 7.6%, other, 15.7%; **Literacy rate:** 53%
Economic Summary: Gross national product (1988 est.): $142 million, $1,050 per capita; real growth rate: 6% (1991); inflation (1992 est.) 2.3%. Arable land: 1%. Principal agricultural products: copra, cocoa, coffee. Agri-

culture accounts for 40% of GDP. Exports: $14.9 million (f.o.b., 1991): copra, cocoa, coffee, frozen fish, timber, beef Imports: $74 million (f.o.b., 1991): machines and vehicles, food, raw materials, fuel, chemicals. Major trading partners: France, New Zealand, Japan, Australia, Netherlands, Belgium, New Caledonia.

Geography. Formerly known as the New Hebrides, Vanuatu is an archipelago of some 80 islands lying between New Caledonia and Fiji in the South Pacific. Largest of the islands is Espiritu Santo (875 sq mi.; 2,266 sq km); others are Efate, Malekula, Malo, Pentecost, and Tanna. The population is largely Melanesian of mixed blood.

Government. The constitution by which Vanuatu achieved independence on July 30, 1980, vests executive authority in a President, elected by an electoral college for a five-year term. A unicameral legislature of 46 members exercises legislative power.

History. The islands were discovered by Pedro Fernandes de Queiros of Portugal in 1606 and were charted and named by the British navigator James Cook in 1774. Conflicting British and French interests were resolved by a joint naval commission that administered the islands from 1887. A condominium government was established in 1906.

The islands' plantation economy, based on imported Vietnamese labor, was prosperous until the 1920s, when markets for its products declined. The New Hebrides escaped Japanese occupation in World War II and the French population was among the first to support the Gaullist Free French movement.

A brief rebellion by French settlers and plantation workers on Espiritu Santo in May 1980 threatened the scheduled independence of the islands. Britain sent a company of Royal Marines and France a contingent of 50 policemen to quell the revolt, which the new government said was financed by the Phoenix Foundation, a right-wing U.S. group. With the British and French forces replaced by soldiers from Papua New Guinea, independence ceremonies took place on July 30. The next month it was reported that the revolt had been quelled.

Disaffection with Prime Minister Lini in August 1991 led to his dismissal as head of his party. Lini formed another to contest the November general elections. The Union of Moderate Parties won and formed an alliance with Lini's. Lini's party, however, withdrew from the coalition in August 1993. While the prime minister's party retained a parliamentary majority, its position became precarious.

The electoral college attempted twice in February 1994 to elect a president by the necessary two-thirds majority. The prime minister's choice was successful on the third attempt in March.

VATICAN CITY STATE

Ruler: Pope John Paul II (1978)
Area: 0.17 sq mi. (0.44 sq km)
Population (est. mid-1994): 821; population growth rate: 1.15%: density per square mile: 4,829.4
Monetary unit: Lira; **Languages:** Latin, Italian, and various other languages; **Religion:** Roman Catholic
Labor force: High dignataries, priests, nuns, guards, and 3,000 lay workers who live outside the Vatican
National name: Stato della Città del Vaticano

Geography. The Vatican City State is situated on the

Vatican hill, on the right bank of the Tiber River, within the commune of Rome.

Government. The Pope has full legal, executive, and judicial powers. Executive power over the area is in the hands of a Commission of Cardinals appointed by the Pope. The College of Cardinals is the Pope's chief advisory body, and upon his death the cardinals elect his successor for life. The cardinals themselves are created for life by the Pope.

In the Vatican the central administration of the Roman Catholic Church throughout the world (Holy See) is carried on by the Secretariat of State, nine Congregations, siz commissions, three tribunals, eleven councils, and five offices. In its diplomatic relations, the Holy See is represented by the Papal Secretary of State.

History. The Vatican City State, sovereign and independent, is the survivor of the papal states that in 1859 comprised an area of some 17,000 square miles (44,030 sq km). During the struggle for Italian unification, from 1860 to 1870, most of this area became part of Italy.

By an Italian law of May 13, 1871, the temporal power of the Pope was abrogated, and the territory of the Papacy was confined to the Vatican and Lateran palaces and the villa of Castel Gandolfo. The Popes consistently refused to recognize this arrangement and, by the Lateran Treaty of Feb. 11, 1929, between the Vatican and the Kingdom of Italy, the exclusive dominion and sovereign jurisdiction of the Holy See over the city of the Vatican was again recognized, thus restoring the Pope's temporal authority over the area.

The first session of Ecumenical Council Vatican II was opened by John XXIII on Oct. 11, 1962, to plan and set policies for the modernization of the Roman Catholic Church. Pope Paul VI continued the Council, opening the second session on Sept. 29, 1963.

On Aug. 26, 1978, Cardinal Albino Luciani was chosen by the College of Cardinals to succeed Paul VI, who had died of a heart attack on Aug. 6. The new Pope, who took the name John Paul I, was born on Oct. 17, 1912, at Forno di Canale in Italy.

(For a listing of all the Popes, *see* the Index.)

Only 34 days after his election, John Paul I died of a heart attack, ending the shortest reign in 373 years. On Oct. 16, Cardinal Karol Wojtyla, 58, was chosen Pope and took the name John Paul II.

On May 13, 1981, a Turkish terrorist shot the Pope in St. Peter's Square, the first assassination attempt against the Pontiff in modern times.

On June 3, 1985, the Vatican and Italy ratified a new church-state treaty, known as a concordat, replacing the Lateran Pact of 1929. The new accord affirmed the independence of Vatican City but ended a number of privileges the Catholic Church had in Italy, including its status as the state religion. The treaty ended Rome's status as a "sacred city."

Relations, diplomatic and ecclesiastical, with Eastern Europe have improved dramatically with the fall of communism. Relations with the Soviet Union, while improving, have not yet reached the ambassadorial level.

Diplomatic relations were established in 1992 with a host of new countries including Croatia, Slovenia, Armenia, Azerbaijan and Ukraine and reestablished with Mexico after 125 years.

Diplomatic ties were established in March 1994 with Jordan and full relations established with Israel in June. Six months earlier the two nations accorded each other mutual recognition.

The pontiff's fall in April 1994 made him curtail his busy schedule and postpone foreign trips. His only travel outside Italy in 1994 was to Croatia.

VENEZUELA

Republic of Venezuela
President: Rafael Caldera (1994)
Area: 352,143 sq mi. (912,050 sq km)
Population (est. mid-1995): 21,800,000 (average annual rate of natural increase: 2.6%); birth rate: 30/1000; infant mortality rate: 20.2/1000; density per sq mi.: 61.9
Capital: Caracas; **Largest cities (est. 1990):** Caracas, 1,290,087; Maracaibo, 1,206,726; Valencia, 616,000; Barquisimento, 723,587; **Monetary unit:** Bolivar; **Language:** Spanish, Indian dialects in interior; **Religion:** Roman Catholic; **National name:** Republica de Venezuela; **Literacy rate:** 85.6%
Economic summary: Gross domestic product (1993 est.): $161 billion, $8,000 per capita; real growth rate –1%; inflation 46%; unemployment 8.2%. Arable land: 3%. Principal agricultural products: rice, coffee, corn, cacao, sugar, bananas, dairy and meat products. Labor force: 5,800,000; 56% in services, 28% in industry. Principal industrial products: refined petroleum products, aluminum, iron and steel, cement, textiles, transport equipment. Natural resources: petroleum, natural gas, iron ore, hydroelectric power. Exports: $14.2 billion (f.o.b., 1993 est.): petroleum, iron ore, bauxite. Imports: $11 billion (f.o.b., 1993 est.): industrial machinery and equipment, manufactures, chemicals, foodstuffs. Major trading partners: U.S., Japan, Germany, Brazil, Italy.

Geography. Venezuela, a third larger than Texas, occupies most of the northern coast of South America on the Caribbean Sea. It is bordered by Colombia to the west, Guyana to the east, and Brazil to the south.

Mountain systems break Venezuela into four distinct areas: (1) the Maracaibo lowlands; (2) the mountainous region in the north and northwest; (3) the Orinoco basin, with the llanos (vast grass-covered plains) on its northern border and great forest areas in the south and southeast; and (4) the Guiana Highlands, south of the Orinoco, accounting for nearly half the national territory. About 80% of Venezuela is drained by the Orinoco and its tributaries.

Government. Venezuela is a federal republic consisting of 22 states, the Federal District, and 72 islands in the Caribbean. There is a bicameral Congress, the 50 members of the Senate and the 199 members of the Chamber of Deputies being elected by popular vote to five-year terms. The President is also elected for five years. He must be a Venezuelan by birth and over 30 years old. He is not eligible for re-election until 10 years after the end of his term.

History. Columbus discovered Venezuela on his third voyage in 1498. A subsequent Spanish explorer gave the country its name, meaning "Little Venice." There were no important settlements until Caracas was founded in 1567. Simón Bolívar, who led the liberation of much of the continent from Spain, was born in Caracas in 1783. With Bolívar taking part, Venezuela was one of the first South American colonies to revolt against Spain, in 1810, but it was not until 1821 that independence was won. Federated at first with Colombia and Ecuador, the country set up a republic in 1830 and then sank for many decades into a condition of revolt, dictatorship, and corruption.

From 1908 to 1935, Gen. Juan Vicente Gómez was an absolute dictator. A military junta ruled after his death in 1935. Dr. Rómulo Betancourt and the liberal Acción Democrática Party won a majority of seats in a constituent assembly to draft a new Constitution in 1946. A well-known writer, Rómulo Gallegos, candidate of Betancourt's party, easily won the presidential election of 1947. But, the army ousted Gallegos the next year and instituted a military junta.

The country overthrew the dictatorship in 1958 and thereafter enjoyed democratic government. Rafael Caldera Rodríguez, President from 1969 to 1974, legalized the Communist Party and established diplomatic relations with Moscow.

In 1974, President Carlos Andrés took office. In 1976, Venezuela nationalized 21 oil companies, mostly subsidiaries of U.S. firms, offering compensation of $1.28 billion. Oil income in that year was $9.9 billion, largely financing an ambitious social welfare program.

Despite difficulties at home, Pérez continued to play an active foreign role in extending economic aid to Latin neighbors, in backing the human-rights policy of President Carter, and in supporting Carter's return of the Panama Canal to Panama.

Opposition Christian Democrats capitalized on Pérez's domestic problems to elect Luis Herrera Campíns President in Venezuela's fifth consecutive free election, on Dec. 3, 1978.

When the Falklands war broke out, Venezuela became one of the most vigorous advocates of the Argentine cause and one of the sharpest critics of the U.S. decision to back Britain.

In the presidential election of December 1988 former president Carlos Andres Perez of the Democratic Action party easily won.

President Perez surrendered his powers in May 1993 in order to defend himself in impeachment proceedings arising out of corruption charges. Ramon Velasquez was elected by Congress to serve as acting president pending the outcome of the impeachment proceedings.

In the presidential election of December 1993 Mr. Velasquez came in fourth. After a partial recount Rafael Caldera, a former president, wsa declared the winner with 30 percent of the vote in January 1994.

In June 1994 approximately half of the country's banking sector collapsed, causing the government to suspend "temporarily" several constitutional guarantees.

Price increases of 20 percent were announced in February 1995, and the president's popularity has fallen. In March 150 leftists were arrested on the allegation that they were plotting an uprising.

VIETNAM

Socialist Republic of Vietnam
President: Le Duc Anh (1992)
Premier: Vo Van Kiet (1991)
Area: 127,246 sq mi. (329,566 sq km)
Population (est. mid-1995): 75,000,000 (average annual rate of natural increase: 2.3%); birth rate: 30/1000; infant mortality rate: 42/1000; Density per square mile: 589.4
Capital: Hanoi; **Largest cities (1992):** Ho Chi Minh City (Saigon),[1] 4,000,000; Hanoi, 2,000,000. Other large cities (1989): Haiphong, 456,049; Da Nang, 370,670; Nha Trang, 213,687; Qui Nho'n, 160,091; Hué 211,085; **Monetary unit:** Dong; **Languages:** Vietnamese (official), French, English, Khmer, Chinese; **Religions:** Buddhist, Roman Catholic, Islam, Taoist, Confucian, Animist; **National name:** Công Hòa Xa Hôi Chú Nghia Viêt Nam; **Literacy rate:** 88%
Economic summary: Gross national product (1993 est.): $72 billion; $1,000 per capita; 8.3% real growth rate (1994); inflation 5.2%; unemployment 25%. Arable land: 22%. Principal agricultural products: rice, rubber, fruits and vegetables, corn, sugar cane, fish. Labor force: 32,700,000; 65% in agriculture. Major industrial

products: processed foods, textiles, cement, chemical fertilizers, glass, tires. Natural resources: phosphates, forests, coal. Exports: $2.6 billion (f.o.b., 1993 est.): agricultural products, minerals, marine products, coffee, petroleum, rice. Imports: $3.1 billion (f.o.b., 1993 est.): petroleum, steel products, railroad equipment, chemicals, medicines, raw cotton, fertilizer, grain. Major trading partners: Singapore, Japan, Hong Kong, Thailand, Germany, Indonesia, South Korea, Taiwan.

1. Includes suburb of Cholon.

Geography. Vietnam occupies the eastern and southern part of the Indochinese peninsula in Southeast Asia, with the South China Sea along its entire coast. China is to the north and Laos and Cambodia to the west. Long and narrow on a north-south axis, Vietnam is about twice the size of Arizona.

The Mekong River delta lies in the south and the Red River delta in the north. Heavily forested mountain and plateau regions make up most of the country.

Government. On April 30, 1975, a joint National Assembly convened with 249 deputies representing the North and 243 representing the South. The Assembly set July 2, 1976, as the official reunification date. Hanoi became the capital.

A new constitution was adopted in April 1992 which called for the creation of a presidency and a prime ministry. The document affirmed the free-market economy and the role of the Communist Party is limited to that of guidance. Foreign assets are guaranteed against nationalization. The assembly has 395 members.

History. The Vietnamese are descendants of Mongoloid nomads from China and migrants from Indonesia. They recognized Chinese suzerainty until the 15th century, an era of nationalistic expansion, when Cambodians were pushed out of the southern area of what is now Vietnam.

A century later, the Portuguese were the first Europeans to enter the area. France established its influence early in the 19th century and within 80 years conquered the three regions into which the country was then divided—Cochin-China in the south, Annam in the center, and Tonkin in the north.

France first unified Vietnam in 1887, when a single governor-generalship was created, followed by the first physical links between north and south—a rail and road system. Even at the beginning of World War II, however, there were internal differences among the three regions.

Japan took over military bases in Vietnam in 1940 and a pro-Vichy French administration remained until 1945. A veteran Communist leader, Ho Chi Minh, organized an independence movement known as the Vietminh to exploit a confused situation. At the end of the war, Ho's followers seized Hanoi and declared a short-lived republic, which ended with the arrival of French forces in 1946.

Paris proposed a unified government within the French Union under the former Annamite emperor, Bao Dai. Cochin-China and Annam accepted the proposal, and Bao Dai was proclaimed emperor of all Vietnam in 1949. Ho and the Vietminh withheld support, and the revolution in China gave them the outside help needed for a war of resistance against French and Vietnamese troops armed largely by the U.S.

A bitter defeat at Dien Bien Phu in northwest Vietnam on May 5, 1954, broke the French military campaign and brought the division of Vietnam at the conference of Geneva that year.

In the new South, Ngo Dinh Diem, Premier under Bao Dai, deposed the monarch in 1955 and established a republic with himself as President. Diem used strong U.S. backing to create an authoritarian regime that suppressed all opposition but could not eradicate the Northern-supplied Communist Viet Cong.

Skirmishing grew into a full-scale war, with escalating U.S. involvement. A military coup, U.S.-inspired in the view of many, ousted Diem Nov. 1, 1963, and a kaleidoscope of military governments followed. The most savage fighting of the war occurred in early 1968, during the Tet holidays.

Although the Viet Cong failed to overthrow the Saigon government, U.S. public reaction to the apparently endless war forced a limitation of U.S. troops to 550,000 and a new emphasis on shifting the burden of further combat to the South Vietnamese. Ho Chi Minh's death on Sept. 3, 1969, brought a quadrumvirate to replace him but no fighting in Northern will to fight.

U.S. bombing and invasion of Cambodia in the summer of 1970—an effort to destroy Viet Cong bases in the neighboring state—marked the end of major U.S. participation in the fighting. Most American ground troops were withdrawn from combat by mid-1971 as heavy bombing of the Ho Chi Minh trail from North Vietnam appeared to cut the supply of men and matériel to the South.

Secret negotiations for peace by Secretary of State Henry A. Kissinger with North Vietnamese officials during 1972 after heavy bombing of Hanoi and Haiphong brought the two sides near agreement in October. When the Northerners demanded the removal of the South's President Nguyen Van Thieu as their price, President Nixon ordered the "Christmas bombing" of the North. The conference resumed and a peace settlement was signed in Paris on Jan. 27, 1973. It called for release of all U.S. prisoners, withdrawal of U.S. forces, limitation of both sides' forces inside South Vietnam, and a commitment to peaceful reunification.

An armored attack across the 17th parallel in January 1975 panicked the South Vietnamese army and brought the invasion within 40 miles of Saigon by April 9. Thieu resigned on April 21 and fled, to be replaced by Vice President Tran Van Huong, who quit a week later, turning over the office to Gen. Duong Van Minh. "Big Minh" surrendered Saigon on April 30, ending a war that took 1.3 million Vietnamese and 58,000 American lives, at the cost of $141 billion in U.S. aid.

On May 3, 1977, the U.S. and Vietnam opened negotiations in Paris to normalize relations. One of the first results was the withdrawal of U.S. opposition to Vietnamese membership in the United Nations, formalized in the Security Council on July 20. Two major issues remained to be settled, however: the return of the bodies of some 2,500 U.S. servicemen missing in the war and the claim by Hanoi that former President Nixon had promised reconstruction aid under the 1973 agreement. Negotiations failed to resolve these issues.

The new year also brought an intensification of border clashes between Vietnam and Cambodia and accusations by China that Chinese residents of Vietnam were being subjected to persecution. Peking cut off all aid and withdrew 800 technicians.

Hanoi was undoubtedly preoccupied with a continuing war in Cambodia, where 60,000 Vietnamese troops were aiding the Heng Samrin regime in suppressing the last forces of the pro-Chinese Pol Pot regime. In early 1979, Vietnam was conducting a two-front war, defending its northern border against a Chinese invasion and at the same time supporting its army in Cambodia.

Economic troubles continued, with the government seeking to reschedule its $1.4-billion foreign hard-currency debt, owed mainly to Japan and the International Monetary Fund. In late 1987, a shuffle of the Vietnamese Politburo brought in new leaders who are expected to slightly relax the government grip on the economy and crack down on corruption within the party.

In 1988, Vietnam also began limited troop withdrawals from Laos and Cambodia.

Vietnam supported the Cambodian peace agreement signed in October 1991.

General elections in July 1992 saw 601 candidates competing for the 395 seats in the assembly.

The economy grew remarkably during 1993. The currency stabilized and the rate of inflation fell to a relatively low level.

The U.S. trade embargo was lifted in February 1994 although the Party reiterated its opposition to political reform throughout the year despite its continued pursuit of major economic reforms.

Full diplomatic relations were announced between the U.S. and Vietnam in July 1995. The economy grew remarkably during 1993. The currency stabilized and the rate of inflation fell to a relatively low level. The country received large grants from a number of nations including Japan, France, and Britain.

(For a Vietnam War chronology, see Headline History.)

WESTERN SAMOA

Independent State of Western Samoa
Head of State: Malietoa Tanumafili II (1962)
Prime Minister: Tofilau Eti Alesana (1988)
Area: 1,093 sq mi. (2,831 sq km)
Population (est. mid-1995): 200,000 (average annual growth rate: 2.6%); birth rate: 34/1000; infant mortality rate: 21/1000; density per square mile: 182.9
Capital and largest city (1991): Apia, 32,859; **Monetary unit:** Tala; **Languages:** Samoan and English; **Religions:** Christian, 99.7%; **National name:** Western Samoa; **Member of Commonwealth of Nations; Literacy rate:** 97%
Economic summary: Gross domestic product (1992 est.): $400 million; $2,000 per capita; –4.3% real growth rate; inflation 7%. Arable land: 19%. Principal agricultural products: copra, coconuts, cocoa, bananas, taro, yams. Labor force (1987): 38,000; 22,000 employed in agriculture. Agriculture accounts for 50% of GDP. Major industrial products: timber, processed food, fish. Natural resource: timber. Exports: $5.7 million (f.o.b., 1992 est.): copra, cocoa, coconut oil and cream, timber. Imports: $11.5 million (c.i.f., 1992 est.): food, manufactured goods, machinery. Major trading partners: New Zealand, EC, Australia, U.S., Fiji, Japan

Geography. Western Samoa, the size of Rhode Island, is in the South Pacific Ocean about 2,200 miles (3,540 km) south of Hawaii midway to Sydney, Australia, and about 800 miles (1,287 km) northeast of Fiji. The larger islands in the Samoan chain are mountainous and of volcanic origin. There is little level land except in the coastal areas, where most cultivation takes place.

Government. Western Samoa has a 49-member Legislature, consisting mainly of the titleholders (chiefs) of family groups, with two non-title members. All members are elected by universal suffrage. When the present Head of State dies, successors will be elected by the Legislature for five-year terms.

History. The Samoan islands were discovered in the 18th century and visited by Dutch and French traders. Toward the end of the 19th century, conflicting interests of the U.S., Britain, and Germany resulted in a treaty signed in 1899. It recognized the paramount interests of the U.S. in those islands east of 171° west longitude (American Samoa) and Germany's interests in the other islands (Western Samoa).

New Zealand occupied Western Samoa in 1914, and was granted a League of Nations mandate. In 1947, the islands became a U.N. trust territory administered by New Zealand.

Western Samoa became independent on Jan. 1, 1962.

A referendum of 1990 gave most women the right to vote for the first time. The April 1991 election gave the ruling Human Rights Protection Party a narrow victory.

A value-added tax was introduced at the start of 1994 that produced widespread dissatisfaction and resistance. Government attempts to ameliorate the impact of the tax failed to soothe public opposition.

REPUBLIC OF YEMEN

President: Ali Abdullah Saleh
Prime Minister: Abd al-Aziz al-Ghani (1994)
Area: 203,850 sq mi. (527,970 sq km)
Population (1995): 15,800,000 (average annual rate of natural increase: 3.6%); birth rate: 50/1000; infant mortality rate: 109/1000; density per square mile: 77.5
Capital !995: Sanaá, 972,011; **Largest cities (1995):** Taiz, 2,205,947; Hodiedah, 1,749,944; Aden, 562,162. **Monetary unit:** Rial. **Language:** Arabic ; **Religion:** Islam (Sunni and Shiite) **Literacy rate:** 38%
Economic summary: Gross domestic product (1993 est.): $9 billion; $800 per capita; real growth rate 3.1%; inflation: 55%; unemployment: 30% (Dec. 92). Principal agricultural products: wheat, sorghum, cattle, sheep, cotton, fruits, coffee, dates. Principal industrial products: crude and refined oil, textiles, leather goods, handicrafts, fish. Exports: $695 million (f.o.b., 1993 est.): cotton, coffee, hides, vegetables, dried fish; Imports: $1.6 billion (f.o.b., 1993 est.): textiles, manufactured consumer goods, foodstuffs, sugar, grain, flour. Major trading partners: U.K., Japan, Saudi Arabia, Australia, U.S.

Geography. Formerly known as the states of Peoples Democratic Republic of Yemen and the Yemen Arab Republic, the Republic of Yemen occupies the southwestern tip of the Arabian Peninsula on the Red Sea opposite Ethiopia, and extends along the southern part of the Arabian Peninsula on the Gulf of Aden and the Indian Ocean. Saudi Arabia is to the north and Oman is to the east. The country is about the size of France.

It has a 700-mile (1,130-km) narrow coastal plain in the south that gives way to a mountainous region and then a plateau area. Some of the interior highlands in the west attain a height of 12,000 feet (3,660 m).

Government. Parliamentary. The Presidential Council was abolished by a new constitution approved in September 1994.

History. The history of Yemen dates back to the Minaean kingdom (1200–650 B.C.). It accepted Islam in A.D. 628, and in the 10th century came under the control of the Rassite dynasty of the Zaidi sect. The Turks occupied the area from 1538 to 1630 and from 1849 to 1918. The sovereign status of Yemen was confirmed by treaties signed with Saudi Arabia and Britain in 1934.

In 1962, a military revolt of elements favoring President Gamal Abdel Nasser of Egypt broke out. A ruling junta proclaimed a republic, and Yemen became an international battleground, with Egypt and the U.S.S.R. supporting the revolutionaries, and King Saud of Saudi Arabia and King Hussein of Jordan the royalists. The civil war continued until the war between the Arab states and Israel broke out in June 1967. Nasser had to pull out many of his troops and agree to a cease-fire and withdrawal of foreign forces. The war finally ended with the defeat of the royalists in mid-1969.

The People's Republic of Southern Yemen was established Nov. 30, 1967, when Britain granted independence to the Federation of South Arabia. This Federation consisted of the state (once the colony) of Aden and 16 of the 20 states of the Protectorate of South Arabia (once the Aden Protectorate). The four states of the Protectorate that did not join the Federation later became part of Southern Yemen.

The Republic of Yemen was established on May 23, 1990, when pro-western Yemen and Marxist Yemen Arab Republic merged after 300 years of separation to form the new nation. The union had been approved by both governments in November 1989.

The new president, Ali Abdullah Salen of Yemen, was elected by the parliaments of both countries. The parliaments also chose South Yemen's Ali Salem al-Baidh, secretary general of the ruling socialist party, to be the new vice-president.

In the Gulf War, Yemen favored Iraq. Consequently, many expatriates in Saudi Arabia were forced to return. A referendum in May 1992 on a constitution resulted in a landslide in favor of it.

Differences over power-sharing and the pace of integration between the north and south came to a head in 1994, resulting in a civil war. The north's superior forces quickly overwhelmed the south in May and early June despite the south's brief declaration of secession.

The victorious north presented a reconciliation plan providing for a general amnesty and pledges to protect political democracy. In September an Islamic fundamentalist party won six new seats in the cabinet.

YUGOSLAVIA

Federal Republic of Yugoslavia
President: Zoan Lilic (1993)
Prime Minister: Radoje Kontic (1993)
Area: 39,449 sq mi. (102,169 sq km)
Population (est. mid-1995): 10,800,000; (average annual rate of natural increase: 0.3%); birth rate: 13/1000; infant mortality rate: 18.4/1000; density per square mile: 273.7
Capital and largest city (1991): Belgrade, 1,168,454; **Largest cities (1991):** Novi Sad, 170,020; Nis 161,476; Pristina, 108,083, Subotica, 100,516. **Monetary unit:** Yugoslav new Dinar **Languages:** Serbo-Croatian 100%; **Religions:** Orthodox, 65%; Muslim, 19%; Christian religions, 5%; **National name:** Federativna Republika Jugoslavijā. **Literacy rate:** 90.5%
Economic summary: Gross domestic product (1993 est.): $10 billion; per capita $1,000; hyperinflation; unemployment: more than 60%. Labor force (1990): 2,640,909; industry and mining, 40%; agriculture, 5%. Industries: machine building (incl. aircraft, trucks, automobiles), nonferrous metallurgy, consumer goods, electronics, chemicals, petroleum products, pharmaceuticals. Exports: $4.4 billion (f.o.b., 1990): machinery and transportation equipment, manufactured goods and articles, chemicals, food, and live animals. Imports: $6.4 billion (c.i.f., 1990): machinery and transport equipment, fuels and lubricants, other manufac-

turers, chemicals, raw materials, food, and animals. Trading partners: C.I.S. countries, E.U., U.S., Eastern European countries.

Geography. Yugoslavia consists of the two states of Serbia and Montenegro. The nation is bordered by Hungary in the north, Romania and Bulgaria in the east, Macedonia in the south, Albania and the Adriatic Sea in the west, and the former Yugoslavian republics of Bosnia-Herzegovina and Croatia in the west. Yugoslavia is about the size of the state of Kentucky.

Yugoslavia is largely a mountainous country. The northeastern section of Serbia is part of the rich, fertile Danubian Plain drained by the Danube, Tisa, Sava, and Morava River systems. Montenegro is a jumbled mass of mountains, containing also some grassy slopes and fertile river valleys.

Government. Yugoslavia (Serbia and Montenegro) is a federal republic. The bicameral Federal Assembly consists of an upper house or Chamber of Republics and a lower house or Chamber of Deputies.

History. Yugoslavia was formed Dec. 4, 1918, from the patchwork of Balkan states and territories where World War I began with the assassination of Archduke Ferdinand of Austria at Sarajevo on June 28, 1914. The new Kingdom of Serbs, Croats, and Slovenes included the former kingdoms of Serbia and Montenegro; Bosnia-Herzegovina, previously administered jointly by Austria and Hungary; Croatia-Slavonia, a semi-autonomous region of Hungary; and Dalmatia, formerly administered by Austria. King Peter I of Serbia became the first monarch, his son acting as Regent until his accession as Alexander I on Aug. 16, 1921.

Croatian demands for a federal state forced Alexander to assume dictatorial powers in 1929 and to change the country's name to Yugoslavia. Serbian dominance continued despite his efforts, amid the resentment of other regions. A Macedonian associated with Croatian dissidents assassinated Alexander in Marseilles, France, on Oct. 9, 1934, and his cousin, Prince Paul, became Regent for the King's son, Prince Peter.

Paul's pro-Axis policy brought Yugoslavia to sign the Axis Pact on March 25, 1941, and opponents overthrew the government two days later. On April 6 the Nazis occupied the country, and the young King and his government fled. Two guerrilla armies —the Chetniks under Draza Mihajlovic supporting the monarchy and the Partisans under Tito (Josip Broz) leaning toward the U.S.S.R.—fought the Nazis for the duration of the war. In 1943, Tito established an Executive National Committee of Liberation to function as a provisional government.

Tito won the election held in the fall of 1945, as monarchists boycotted the vote. A new Assembly abolished the monarchy and proclaimed the Federal People's Republic of Yugoslavia, with Tito as Prime Minister. Ruthlessly eliminating opposition, the Tito government executed Mihajlovic in 1946.

Tito broke with the Soviet bloc in 1948 and Yugoslavia followed a middle road, combining orthodox Communist control of politics and general overall economic policy with a varying degree of freedom in the arts, travel, and individual enterprise. Tito became President in 1953 and President for life under a revised Constitution adopted in 1963.

After Tito's death on May 4, 1980, a rotating presidency designed to avoid internal dissension was put into effect immediately, and the feared clash of Yugoslavia's multiple nationalities and regions appeared to have been averted.

In May 1991 Croatian voters supported a referendum calling for their republic to become an independent nation. A similar referendum passed in December in Slovenia. In June the respective parliaments in both republics passed declarations of independence. Ethnic violence flared almost immediately. The largely Serbian-led Yugoslav military pounded break-away Bosnia and Herzegovina, leading the U.N. Security Council in May 1992 to impose economic sanctions on the Belgrade government.

Despite rampant inflation reaching approximately 3000% per month in December 1993 the Serbian government of Slobodan Milosevic maintained its effective control over the rump Yugoslavia. Final results of the late year parliamentary elections gave the Socialist Party the largest number of seats, just three short of a majority.

Despite continuing questions as to his sincerity, Milosevic trumpeted 1994 posed as a peacemaker in the Bosnian conflict. His appeal in July to the Bosnian Serbs to accept a plan was rejected. Serbia thereupon imposed an embargo on all supplies but medical and humanitarian goods to the Bosnian Serbs.

A new economic plan introduced at the start of 1994 moderated the country's hyperinflation.

ZAIRE

Republic of Zaire
President: Mobutu Sese Seko (1965)
Area: 905,365 sq mi. (2,344,885 sq km)
Population (est. mid-1995): 44,100,000 (average annual rate of natural increase: 3.2%); birth rate: 48/1000; infant mortality rate: 108/1000; density per sq mi.: 48.7
Capital: Kinshasa; **Largest cities (est. 1991):** Kinshasa, 3,804,000; Lubumbashi, 739,082; Mbuji-Mayi, 613,027; Kananga, 301,349; **Monetary unit:** Zaire; **Languages:** French (official), English, Bantu dialects, mainly Swahili, Lingala, Ishiluba, and Kikongo; **Religions:** Roman Catholic 50%, Protestant 20%, Kimbanguist 10%, Islam 10%; syncretic and traditional, 10%; **Ethnic groups:** Bantu, Sudanese, Nilotics, Pygmies, Hamites; **National name:** République du Zaïre; **Literacy rate:** 72%
Economic summary: Gross domestic product (1993 est.): $21 billion; $500 per capita; –6% real growth rate; unemployment: 30–40% per mo. (1992 est.). Arable land: 3%. Principal agricultural products: coffee, palm oil, rubber, quinine, cassava, bananas, plantains, vegetables, fruits. Labor force: 15,000,000; 13% in industry. Major industrial products: processed and unprocessed minerals, consumer goods. Natural resources: copper, cobalt, zinc, industrial diamonds, manganese, tin, gold, silver, bauxite, iron, coal, crude oil, hydroelectric potential. Exports: $1.5 billion (f.o.b., 1992 est.): copper, cobalt, diamonds, petroleum, coffee. Imports: $1.2 billion (f.o.b., 1992 est.): consumer goods, foodstuffs, mining and other machinery, transport equipment, and fuels. Major trading partners: Belgium, France, U.S., Germany, South Africa, Italy, Japan, UK.

Geography. Zaire is situated in west central Africa and is bordered by the Congo, the Central African Republic, the Sudan, Uganda, Rwanda, Burundi, Tanzania, Zambia, Angola, and the Atlantic Ocean. It is one quarter the size of the U.S.

The principal rivers are the Ubangi and Bomu in the north and the Zaire (Congo) in the west, which flows into the Atlantic. The entire length of Lake Tanganyika lies along the eastern border with Tanzania and Burundi.

Government. A republic with a multiparty unicameral legislature. The president and the legislature are elected by universal suffrage for five-year terms.

History. Formerly the Belgian Congo, this territory was inhabited by ancient Negrito peoples (Pygmies), who were pushed into the mountains by Bantu and Nilotic invaders. The American correspondent Henry M. Stanley navigated the Congo River in 1877 and opened the interior to exploration. Commissioned by King Leopold II of the Belgians, Stanley made treaties with native chiefs that enabled the King to obtain personal title to the territory at the Berlin Conference of 1885.

Criticism of forced labor under royal exploitation prompted Belgium to take over administration of the Congo, which remained a colony until agitation for independence forced Brussels to grant freedom on June 30, 1960. Moise Tshombe, Premier of the then Katanga Province seceded from the new republic on July 11, and another mining province, South Kasai, followed. Belgium sent paratroopers to quell the civil war, and with President Joseph Kasavubu and Premier Patrice Lumumba of the national government in conflict, the United Nations flew in a peacekeeping force.

Kasavubu staged an army coup in 1960 and handed Lumumba over to the Katangan forces. A U.N. investigating commission found that Lumumba had been killed by a Belgian mercenary in the presence of Tshombe. Dag Hammarskjold, U.N. Secretary-General, died in a plane crash en route to a peace conference with Tshombe on Sept. 17, 1961.

U.N. Secretary-General U Thant submitted a national reconciliation plan in 1962 that Tshombe rejected. Tshombe's troops fired on the U.N. force in December, and in the ensuing conflict Tshombe capitulated on Jan. 14, 1963. The peacekeeping force withdrew, and, in a complete about-face, Kasavubu named Tshombe Premier to fight a spreading rebellion. Tshombe used foreign mercenaries and, with the help of Belgian paratroops airlifted by U.S. planes, defeated the most serious opposition, a Communist-backed regime in the northeast.

Kasavubu abruptly dismissed Tshombe in 1965 and was himself ousted by Gen. Joseph-Desiré Mobutu, Army Chief of Staff. The new President nationalized the Union Minière, the Belgian copper mining enterprise that had been a dominant force in the Congo since colonial days. The plane carrying the exiled Tshombe was hijacked in 1967 and he was held prisoner in Algeria until his death from a heart attack was announced June 29, 1969.

Mobutu eliminated opposition to win election in 1970 to a term of seven years, which was renewed in a 1977 election. In 1975, he nationalized much of the economy, barred religious instruction in schools, and decreed the adoption of African names.

On March 8, 1977, invaders from Angola calling themselves the Congolese National Liberation Front pushed into Shaba and threatened the important mining center of Kolwezi. France and Belgium responded to Mobutu's pleas for help with weapons, but the U.S. gave only nonmilitary supplies.

In April, France flew 1,500 Moroccan troops to Shaba to defeat the invaders, who were, Mobutu charged, Soviet-inspired, and Cuban-led. U.S. intelligence sources, however, confirmed Soviet and Cuban denials of any participation and identified the rebels as former Katanga gendarmes who had fled to Angola after their 1963 defeat.

In April 1990 Mobutu announced he intended to introduce multiparty democracy, but that elections in January 1991 would reduce the number of political parties to two besides his own. Opposition leaders denounced the scheme as giving Mobutu's party an unfair advantage.

A national conference was scheduled for July 1991, but in June three opposition groups announced a boycott. The conference was postponed.

The conference finally convened in August, but, boycotted by the main opposition parties, it was adjourned without achieving anything. Mobutu offered the prime ministerial post to an opposition leader. The ensuing power struggle led to his dismissal in October.

In early 1993 Mobutu rejected Western demands that he yield power and announced plans to regroup his one-party parliament dismissing the main opposition leader Prime Minister Tshisekedi.

President Mobutu in January 1994 dissolved parliament and dismissed his prime minister, which led to a general strike in the capital. The strike was in response to a call from Mr. Tshisekedi, who never recognized his own dismissal the year before.

In early 1995 the world learned of an outbreak of an epidemic caused by the dreaded Ebola virus in Zaire. The World Health Organization moved quickly to impose sanitary control and curtail movement from the region concerned.

ZAMBIA

Republic of Zambia
President: Frederick T.J. Chiluba (1991)
Vice President: Levy Mwanawasa (1991)
Area: 290,586 sq mi. (752,618 sq km)
Population (est. mid-1995): 9,100,000 (average annual rate of natural increase: 3.1%); birth rate: 47/1000; infant mortality rate: 107/1000; density per sq mi.: 31.3
Capital: Lusaka; **Largest cities (1990):** Lusaka, 982,362; Kitwe, 338,207; Ndola, 376,311; Chingola, 167,954;
Monetary unit: Kwacha; **Languages:** English and local dialects; **Religions:** Christian, 50–75%; Islam and Hindu, 1%; remainder indigenous beliefs; **Member of Commonwealth of Nations; Literacy rate:** 75.7%
Economic summary: Gross domestic product (1993 est.): $7.3 billion; $800 per capita; real growth rate –2.8% (1992); inflation 191% (1992). Arable land: 7%. Principal agricultural products: corn, tobacco, rice, sugar cane. Labor force: 2,455,000; Agriculture 85%. Major industrial products: copper, textiles, chemicals, zinc, fertilizers. Natural resources: copper, zinc, lead, cobalt, coal. Exports: $1 billion (f.o.b., 1992 est.): copper, zinc, lead, cobalt, tobacco. Imports: $1.2 billion (c.i.f., 1992 est.): manufactured goods, machinery and transport equipment, foodstuffs, fuels. Major trading partners: Western Europe, Japan, South Africa, U.S., Saudi Arabia, India.

Geography. Zambia, a landlocked country in south central Africa, is about one-tenth larger than Texas. It is surrounded by Angola, Zaire, Tanzania, Malawi, Mozambique, Zimbabwe, Botswana, and Namibia (formerly South-West Africa). The country is mostly a plateau that rises to 8,000 feet (2,434 m) in the east.

Government. A multiparty system. Zambia (formerly Northern Rhodesia) is governed by a president, elected by universal suffrage, and a unicameral Legislative Assembly, consisting of 150 members elected by universal suffrage.

History. Empire builder Cecil Rhodes obtained mining concessions in 1889 from King Lewanika of the Barotse and sent settlers to the area soon thereafter. It was ruled by the British South Africa Company, which he established, until 1924, when the British

government took over the administration.

From 1953 to 1964, Northern Rhodesia was federated with Southern Rhodesia and Nyasaland in the Federation of Rhodesia and Nyasaland. On Oct. 24, 1964, Northern Rhodesia became the independent nation of Zambia.

Kenneth Kaunda, the first president, kept Zambia within the Commonwealth of Nations. The country's economy, dependent on copper exports, was threatened when Rhodesia declared its independence from British rule in 1965 and defied U.N. sanctions, which Zambia supported, an action that deprived Zambia of its trade route through Rhodesia. The U.S., Britain, and Canada organized an airlift in 1966 to ship gasoline into Zambia. In 1967, Britain agreed to finance new trade routes for Zambia.

Kaunda visited China in 1967, and China later agreed to finance a 1,000-mile railroad from the copper fields to Dar es Salaam in Tanzania. A pipeline was opened in 1968 from Ndola in Zambia's copper belt to the Indian Ocean at Dar es Salaam, ending the three-year oil drought.

In 1969, Kaunda announced the nationalization of the foreign copper-mining industry, with Zambia to take 51% (over $1 billion, estimated), and an agreement was reached with the companies on payment. He then announced a similar takeover of foreign oil producers.

With a soaring debt and inflation rate the government in 1990 turned to the International Monetary Fund and the World Bank, with whom an agreement was reached in exchange for economic reforms. Soaring prices in June 1990 led to riots in Lusaka, resulting in a number of killings. Mounting domestic pressure forced Kaunda to move Zambia toward multi-party democracy.

National elections on October 31, 1991 brought a stunning defeat to the long-serving President Kaunda and a repudiation of his long belief in a one-party state. The newly-elected chief executive, Chiluba, called for sweeping economic reforms including privatization and the establishing of a stock market.

The president declared a state of emergency in March 1993 after the uncovering of a plot to overthrow the government. The state of emergency was lifted in May. In November by-elections the president's party won only three of the eight contested seats.

The government in 1994 proposed making substantial cuts in the civil service and privatizing a large number of government-owned companies. In return international agencies promised more aid.

ZIMBABWE

Republic of Zimbabwe
Executive President: Robert Mugabe (1987)
Area: 150,698 sq mi. (390,308 sq km)
Population (est. mid-1995): 11,300,000 (average annual rate of natural increase: 2.7%); birth rate: 39/1000; infant mortality rate: 53/1000; density per square mile: 74.9
Capital: Harare; **Largest cities (est. 1987):** Harare, 863,000; Bulawayo, 495,317; Chitungwiza, 229,000.
Monetary unit: Zimbabwean dollar; **Languages:** English (official), Ndebele, Shona; **Religions:** Christian, 25%; Animist, 24%; Syncretic, 50%; **Literacy rate:** 74%
Economic summary: Gross domestic product (1993 est.): $15.9 billion; $1,400 per capita; real growth rate 2%; inflation 22% (Jan. 94 est.); unemployment: at least 35%. Arable land: 7%. Principal agricultural products: tobacco, corn, sugar, cotton, livestock. Labor force:

3,100,000; 74% in agriculture; 16%, transport and services. Major industrial products: steel, textiles, chemicals, vehicles, gold, copper. Natural resources: gold, copper, chrome, nickel, tin, asbestos. Exports: $1.5 billion (f.o.b., 1992 est.): gold, tobacco, asbestos, copper, meat, chrome, nickel, corn, sugar. Imports: $1.8 billion (c.i.f., 1992 est.): machinery, petroleum products, transport equipment. Major trading partners: South Africa, E.C., U.S.

Geography. Zimbabwe, a landlocked country in south central Africa, is slightly smaller than California. It is bordered by Botswana on the west, Zambia on the north, Mozambique on the east, and South Africa on the south.

A high veld up to 6,000 feet (1,829 m) crosses the country from northeast to southwest. This is flanked by a somewhat lower veld that contains ranching country. Tropical forests that yield hardwoods lie in the southeast.

In the north, on the border with Zambia, is the 175-mile-long (128-m) Kariba Lake, formed by the Kariba Dam across the Zambezi River. It is the site of one of the world's largest hydroelectric projects.

Government. A parliamentary democracy with a 150-seat unicameral legislature, the House of Assembly. The Executive President is chief of state and head of government. There are two co-vice presidents.

History. Zimbabwe was colonized by Cecil Rhodes's British South Africa Company at the end of the 19th century. In 1923, European settlers voted to become the self-governing British colony of Southern Rhodesia rather than merge with the Union of South Africa. After a brief federation with Northern Rhodesia and Nyasaland in the post-World War II period, Southern Rhodesia chose to remain a colony when its two partners voted for independence in 1963.

On Nov. 11, 1965, the white-minority government of Rhodesia unilaterally declared its independence from Britain.

In 1967, the U.N. imposed mandatory sanctions against Rhodesia. The country moved slowly toward meeting the demands of black Africans. The white-minority regime of Prime Minister Ian Smith withstood British pressure, economic sanctions, guerrilla attacks, and a right-wing assault.

On March 1, 1970, Rhodesia formally proclaimed itself a republic, and within the month nine nations, including the U.S., closed their consulates there.

Heightened guerrilla war and a withdrawal of South African military aid—particularly helicopters—marked the beginning of the collapse of Smith's 11 years of resistance in the spring of 1976. Under pressure from South Africa, Smith agreed with the U.S. that majority rule should come within two years.

In the fall, Smith met with black nationalist leaders in Geneva. The meeting broke up six weeks later when the Rhodesian Premier insisted that whites must retain control of the police and armed forces during the transition to majority rule. A British proposal called for Britons to take over these powers.

Divisions between Rhodesian blacks—Bishop Abel Muzorewa of the African National Congress and Ndabaningi Sithole as moderates versus Robert Mugabe and Joshua Nkomo of the Patriotic Front as advocates of guerrilla force—sharpened in 1977 and no agreement was reached. In July, with white residents leaving in increasing numbers and the economy showing the strain of war, Smith rejected outside mediation and called for general elections in order to work out an "internal solution" of the transfer of power.

On March 3, 1978, Smith, Muzorewa, Sithole, and Chief Jeremiah Chirau signed an agreement to transfer power to the black majority by Dec. 31, 1978. They constituted themselves an Executive Council, with chairmanship rotating but Smith retaining the title of Prime Minister. Blacks were named to each cabinet ministry, serving as co-ministers with the whites already holding these posts. African nations and the Patriotic Front leaders immediately denounced the action, but Western governments were more reserved, although none granted recognition to the new regime.

White voters ratified a new constitution on Jan. 30, 1979, enfranchising all blacks, establishing a black majority Senate and Assembly, and changing the country's name to Zimbabwe Rhodesia.

Muzorewa agreed to negotiate with Mugabe and Nkomo in British-sponsored talks beginning Sept. 9. By December, all parties accepted a new draft constitution, a cease-fire, and a period of British administration pending a general election.

In voting completed on Feb. 29, 1980, Mugabe's ZANU-Patriotic Front party won 57 of the 80 Assembly seats reserved for blacks. In an earlier vote on Feb. 14, the Rhodesian Front won all 20 seats reserved for whites in the Assembly.

On April 18, 1980, Britain formally recognized the independence of Zimbabwe.

In January 1981, Mugabe dismissed Nkomo as Home Minister and his onetime rival left the government in protest.

The 1985 harvest was good in Zimbabwe and the country could feed itself. But political turmoil and civil strife continued. In what Western analysts viewed as a free and fair election, President Mugabe's African National Union increased its sizeable majority in the House of Assembly but Mugabe was frustrated because it did not win the 70 seats he sought to cement one-party rule. After the election, Mugabe cracked down on Nkomo's ZAPU-Patriotic Front party.

In April 1990, Mugabe was re-elected and his ZANU(PF) party given virtual unanimity in the Assembly.

In December 1990 the parliament voted by 113 to 3 to amend the original 1980 constitution to allow the compulsory acquisition of white-owned farmland at government-set prices. Indeed, white farmers would have no judiciary recourse. Britain and the U.S. warned that forceful land acquisitions would deter foreign investments and further depress the country.

A split in the opposition Zimbabwe Unity Movement in June 1991 reduced pressure on the ruling ZANU(PF). At that time the latter deleted all references to Marxism-Leninism and scientific socialism from its constitution.

A long drought in southern Africa and government miscalculation on the expected maize harvest the previous year resulted in a shortage of that grain in 1992.

The Land Acquisition Act was amended in 1992 to permit compensation for compulsorily acquired land.

Parliamentary elections in April 1995 gave Mugabe's party a stunning victory with 63 of the 65 contested seats.

(For late reports, see Current Events of 1995)

UNITED NATIONS

The 185 Members of the United Nations

Country	Joined U.N.[1]	Country	Joined U.N.[1]	Country	Joined U.N.[1]
Afghanistan	1946	Germany	1973	Oman	1971
Albania	1955	Ghana	1957	Pakistan	1947
Algeria	1962	Greece	1945	Palau	1994
Andorra	1993	Grenada	1974	Panama	1945
Angola	1976	Guatemala	1945	Papua New Guinea	1975
Antigua and Barbuda	1981	Guinea	1958	Paraguay	1945
Argentina	1945	Guinea-Bissau	1974	Peru	1945
Armenia	1992	Guyana	1966	Philippines	1945
Australia	1945	Haiti	1945	Poland	1945
Austria	1955	Honduras	1945	Portugal	1955
Azerbaijan	1992	Hungary	1955	Qatar	1971
Bahamas	1973	Iceland	1946	Romania	1955
Bahrain	1971	India	1945	Russian Federation	1945
Bangladesh	1974	Indonesia	1950	Rwanda	1962
Barbados	1966	Iran	1945	St. Kitts and Nevis	1983
Belarus	1945	Iraq	1945	St. Lucia	1979
Belgium	1945	Ireland	1955	St. Vincent and the Grenadines	1980
Belize	1981	Israel	1949	San Marino	1992
Benin	1960	Italy	1955	São Tomé and Príncipe	1975
Bhutan	1971	Jamaica	1962	Saudi Arabia	1945
Bolivia	1945	Japan	1956	Senegal	1960
Bosnia and Hercegovina	1992	Jordan	1955	Seychelles	1976
Botswana	1966	Kazakhstan	1992	Sierra Leone	1961
Brazil	1945	Kenya	1963	Singapore	1965
Brunei Darussalam	1984	Korea, North	1991	Slovak Republic[3]	1993
Bulgaria	1955	Korea, South	1991	Slovenia	1992
Burkina Faso	1960	Kuwait	1963	Solomon Islands	1978
Burundi	1962	Kyrgyzstan	1992	Somalia	1960
Cambodia	1955	Laos	1955	South Africa	1945
Cameroon	1960	Latvia	1991	Spain	1955
Canada	1945	Lebanon	1945	Sri Lanka	1955
Cape Verde	1975	Lesotho	1966	Sudan	1956
Central African Republic	1960	Liberia	1945	Suriname	1975
Chad	1960	Libya	1955	Swaziland	1968
Chile	1945	Liechtenstein	1990	Sweden	1946
China[2]	1945	Lithuania	1991	Syria	1945
Colombia	1945	Luxembourg	1945	Tajikistan	1992
Comoros	1975	Madagascar	1960	Tanzania	1961
Congo	1960	Malawi	1964	Thailand	1946
Costa Rica	1945	Malaysia	1957	The former Yugoslav Republic of Macedonia[4]	1993
Côte d'Ivoire	1960	Maldives	1965	Togo	1960
Croatia	1992	Mali	1960	Trinidad and Tobago	1962
Cuba	1945	Malta	1964	Tunisia	1956
Cyprus	1960	Marshall Islands	1991	Turkey	1945
Czech Republic[3]	1993	Mauritania	1961	Turkmenistan	1992
Denmark	1945	Mauritius	1968	Uganda	1962
Djibouti	1977	Mexico	1945	Ukraine	1945
Dominica	1978	Micronesia	1991	United Arab Emirates	1971
Dominican Republic	1945	Moldova	1992	United Kingdom	1945
Ecuador	1945	Monaco	1993	United States	1945
Egypt	1945	Mongolia	1961	Uruguay	1945
El Salvador	1945	Morocco	1956	Uzbekistan	1992
Equatorial Guinea	1968	Mozambique	1975	Vanuatu	1981
Eritrea	1993	Myanmar	1948	Venezuela	1945
Estonia	1991	Namibia	1990	Vietnam	1977
Ethiopia	1945	Nepal	1955	Western Samoa	1976
Fiji	1970	Netherlands	1945	Yemen, Republic of	1947
Finland	1955	New Zealand	1945	Yugoslavia	1945
France	1945	Nicaragua	1945	Zaire	1960
Gabon	1960	Niger	1960	Zambia	1964
Gambia	1965	Nigeria	1960	Zimbabwe	1980
Georgia	1992	Norway	1945		

1. The U.N. officially came into existence on Oct. 24, 1945. 2. On Oct. 25, 1971, the U.N. voted membership to the People's Republic of China, which replaced the Republic of China (Taiwan) in the world body. 3. Czechoslovakia was an original member of the United Nations from Oct. 24, 1945. As of December 31, 1992 it ceased to exist and the Czech Republic and the Slovak Republic as successor States were admitted January 19, 1993. 4. The General Assembly on April 8, 1993 decided to admit the State provisionally being referred to as "The former Yugoslav Republic of Macedonia" pending settlement of the difference that has arisen over its name.

Member Countries' Assessments to U.N. Budget, 1995

Country	Total	Country	Total	Country	Total
Afghanistan	$109,278	Ghana	109,278	Pakistan	655,666
Albania	109,278	Greece	4,043,277	Palau[1]	—
Algeria	1,748,444	Grenada	109,278	Panama	109,278
Andorra	109,278	Guatemala	218,556	Papua New Guinea	109,278
Angola	109,278	Guinea	109,278	Paraguay	109,278
Antigua and Barbuda	109,278	Guinea-Bissau	109,278	Peru	655,666
Argentina	5,245,333	Guyana	109,278	Philippines	655,666
Armenia	874,222	Haiti	109,278	Poland	4,152,555
Australia	15,954,555	Honduras	109,278	Portugal	2,622,667
Austria	9,288,612	Hungary	1,639,166	Qatar	437,111
Azerbaijan	1,748,444	Iceland	327,833	Romania	1,639,166
Bahamas	218,556	India	3,387,611	Russian Federation	62,069,780
Bahrain	218,556	Indonesia	1,529,889	Rwanda	109,278
Bangladesh	109,278	Iran (Islamic Republic)	6,556,667	St. Kitts and Nevis	109,278
Barbados	109,278	Iraq	1,529,889	St. Lucia	109,278
Belarus	4,043,277	Ireland	2,185,555	St. Vincent & the Grenadines	109,278
Belgium	10,818,500	Israel	2,841,222	Samoa	109,278
Belize	109,278	Italy	52,344,057	San Marino	109,278
Benin	109,278	Jamaica	109,278	São Tomé and Príncipe	109,278
Bhutan	109,278	Japan	152,442,506	Saudi Arabia	8,742,223
Bolivia	109,278	Jordan	109,278	Senegal	109,278
Bosnia and Hercegovina	218,556	Kazakhstan	2,841,222	Seychelles	109,278
Botswana	109,278	Kenya	109,278	Sierra Leone	109,278
Brazil	17,703,001	Republic of Korea (north)	109,278	Singapore	1,529,889
Brunei Darussalam	218,556	Republic of Korea (south)	8,742,223	Slovakia	1,092,777
Bulgaria	1,092,777	Kuwait	2,185,555	Slovenia	764,945
Burkina Faso	109,278	Kyrgyzstan	437,111	Solomon Islands	109,278
Burundi	109,278	Lao People's Democratic	437,111	Somalia	109,278
Cambodia	109,278	Latvia	1,092,777	South Africa	3,715,445
Cameroon	109,278	Lebanon	109,278	Spain	24,478,223
Canada	33,548,279	Lesotho	109,278	Sri Lanka	109,278
Cape Verde	109,278	Liberia	109,278	Sudan	109,278
Central African Republic	109,278	Libyan Arab Jamahiriya	2,294,833	Suriname	109,278
Chad	109,278	Liechtenstein	109,278	Swaziland	109,278
Chile	874,222	Lithuania	1,202,055	Sweden	13,331,889
China	7,868,000	Luxembourg	764,945	Syrian Arab Republic	546,389
Colombia	1,202,055	Madagascar	109,278	Tajikistan	327,833
Comoros	109,278	Malawi	109,278	Tanzania	109,278
Congo	109,278	Malaysia	1,529,889	Thailand	1,420,611
Costa Rica	109,278	Maldives	109,278	The former Yugoslav	
Côte d'Ivoire	109,278	Mali	109,278	Republic of Macedonia	109,278
Croatia	1,092,777	Malta	109,278	Togo	109,278
Cuba	764,945	Marshall Islands	109,278	Trinidad and Tobago	437,111
Cyprus	327,833	Mauritania	109,278	Tunisia	327,833
Czech Republic	3,496,888	Mauritius	109,278	Turkey	3,733,092
Denmark	7,649,445	Mexico	8,523,666	Turkmenistan	437,111
Djibouti	109,278	Micronesia	109,278	Uganda	109,278
Dominica	109,278	Moldova	1,202,055	Ukraine	16,173,112
Dominican Republic	109,278	Monaco	109,278	United Arab Emirates	2,076,278
Ecuador	218,556	Mongolia	109,278	United Kingdom	57,589,390
Egypt	764,945	Morocco	327,833	United States	315,027,985
El Salvador	109,278	Mozambique	109,278	Uruguay	437,111
Equatorial Guinea	109,278	Myanmar	109,278	Uzbekistan	2,706,278
Eritrea	109,278	Namibia	109,278	Vanuatu	109,278
Estonia	546,389	Nepal	109,278	Venezuela	4,371,111
Ethiopia	109,278	Netherlands	17,265,889	Vietnam	109,278
Fiji	109,278	New Zealand	2,622,667	Yemen	109,278
Finland	6,665,944	Nicaragua	109,278	Yugoslavia	1,202,055
France	69,063,558	Niger	109,278	Zaire	109,278
Gabon	109,278	Nigeria	1,748,444	Zambia	109,278
Gambia	109,278	Norway	6,010,278	Zimbabwe	109,278
Georgia	1,748,444	Oman	437,111	**TOTAL**	**$1,134,628,998**
Germany	97,694,337				

1. Assessment rate of the Republic of Palau is to be determined.

Preamble of the United Nations Charter

The Charter of the United Nations was adopted at the San Francisco Conference of 1945. The complete text may be obtained by writing to the United Nations Sales Section, United Nations, New York, N.Y. 10017, and enclosing $1.

We the peoples of the United Nations determined to save succeeding generations from the scourge of war, which twice in our lifetime has brought untold sorrow to mankind, and

To reaffirm faith in fundamental human rights, in the dignity and worth of the human person, in the equal rights of men and women and of nations large and small, and

To establish conditions under which justice and respect for the obligations arising from treaties and other sources of international law can be maintained, and

To promote social progress and better standards of life in larger freedom, and for these ends

To practice tolerance and live together in peace with one another as good neighbors, and

To unite our strength to maintain international peace and security, and

To insure, by the acceptance of principles and the institution of methods, that armed force shall not be used, save in the common interest, and

To employ international machinery for the promotion of the economic and social advancement of all peoples, have resolved to combine our efforts to accomplish these aims.

Accordingly, our respective Governments, through representatives assembled in the city of San Francisco, who have exhibited their full powers found to be in good and due form, have agreed to the present Charter of the United Nations and do hereby establish an international organization to be known as the United Nations.

Principal Organs of the United Nations

Secretariat

This is the directorate on U.N. operations, apart from political decisions. All members contribute to its upkeep. Its headquarters staff of about 4,800 specialists is recruited from member nations on the basis of as wide a geographical distribution as possible. The staff works under the Secretary-General, whom it assists and advises.

Secretaries-General

Boutros Boutros-Ghali, Egypt, Jan. 1, 1992.

Javier Pérez de Cuéllar, Peru, Jan. 1, 1982, to Dec. 31, 1991.

Kurt Waldheim, Austria, Jan. 1, 1972, to Dec. 31, 1981.

U Thant, Burma (Myanmar), Nov. 3, 1961, to Dec. 31, 1971.

Dag Hammarskjöld, Sweden, April 11, 1953, to Sept. 17, 1961.

Trygve Lie, Norway, Feb. 1, 1946, to April 10, 1953.

General Assembly

The General Assembly is the world's forum for discussing matters affecting world peace and security, and for making recommendations concerning them. It has no power of its own to enforce decisions.

The Assembly is composed of the 51 original member nations and those admitted since, a total of 184. Each nation has one vote. On important questions including international peace and security, a two-thirds majority of those present and voting is required. Decisions on other questions are made by a simple majority.

The Assembly's agenda can be as broad as the Charter. It can make recommendations to member nations, the Security Council, or both. Emphasis is given on questions relating to international peace and security brought before it by any member, the Security Council, or nonmembers.

The Assembly also maintains a broad program of international cooperation in economic, social, cultural, educational, and health fields, and for assisting in human rights and freedoms.

Among other duties, the Assembly has functions relating to the trusteeship system, and considers and approves the U.N. Budget. Every member contributes to operating expenses according to its means.

Security Council

The Security Council is the primary instrument for establishing and maintaining international peace. Its main purpose is to prevent war by settling disputes between nations.

Under the Charter, the Council is permitted to dispatch a U.N. force to stop aggression. All member nations undertake to make available armed forces, assistance, and facilities to maintain international peace and security.

Any member may bring a dispute before the Security Council or the General Assembly. Any nonmember may do so if it accepts the charter obligations of pacific settlement.

The Security Council has 15 members. There are five permanent members: the United States, the Russian Federation, Britain, France, and China; and 10 temporary members elected by the General Assembly for two-year terms, from five different regions of the world.

Voting on procedural matters requires a nine-vote majority to carry. However, on questions of substance, the vote of each of the five permanent members is required.

Current temporary members are (term expires Dec. 31, 1995): Argentina, Czech Republic, Nigeria, Oman, and Rwanda; (term expires Dec. 31, 1996): Botswana, Germany, Honduras, Indonesia, and Italy.

Economic and Social Council

This council is composed of 54 members elected by the General Assembly to 3-year terms. It works closely with the General Assembly as a link with groups formed within the U.N. to help peoples in such fields as education, health, and human rights. It insures that there is no overlapping and sets up commissions to deal with economic conditions and collect facts and figures on conditions over the world. It issues studies and reports and may make recommendations to the Assembly and specialized agencies.

Functional Commissions

Population Commission; Commission for Social Development; Commission on Human Rights; Commission on the Status of Women, and Statistical Commission; Commission on Narcotic Drugs; Commission on Sustainable Development; Commission on Crime Prevention and Criminal Justice; Commission on Science and Technology for Development.

Regional Commissions

Economic Commission for Europe (ECE); Economic and Social Commission for Asia and the Pacific (ESCAP); Economic Commission for Latin America and the Caribbean (ECLAC); Economic Commission for Africa (ECA); Economic and Social Commission for Western Asia (ESCWA).

Trusteeship Council

The Trusteeship Council has five members: China, France, Russian Federation, United Kingdom, and the United States. With the independence of Palau, the last remaining United Nations trust territory, the Council formally suspended operation on November 1, 1994. By a resolution adopted on that day, the Council amended its rules of procedure to drop the obligation to meet annually and agreed to meet as occasion required—by its decision or the decision of its President, or at the request of a majority of its members or the General Assembly or the Security Council.

International Court of Justice

The International Court of Justice sits at The Hague, the Netherlands. Its 15-judge bench was established to hear disputes among states, which must agree to accept its verdicts. Its judges, charged with administering justice under international law, deal with cases ranging from disputes over territory to those concerning rights of passage.

Following are the members of the Court and the years in which their terms expire on Feb. 5:

President: Mohammed Bedjaoui, Algeria (1997 as president; 2000 term)
Vice President: Stephen M. Schwebel (1997)
Jens Evensen, Norway (1997)
Ni Zhengyu, China (1994)
Luigi Ferrari Bravo, Italy (1997)
Mohamed Shahabuddeen, Guyana (1997)
Stephen Schwebel, United States (1997)
Mohammed Bedjaoui, Algeria (2000)
Vladlen Vereshchetin, Russian Federation (1997)
Gilbert Guillaume, France (2000)
Andres Aguilar, Venezuela (2000)
Raymond Ranjeva, Madagascar (2000)
Christopher Gregory Weeramantry, Sri Lanka (2000)
Roslyn Higgins, United Kingdom (2000)
Carl-August Fleischauer, Germany (2003)
Géza Herczegh, Hungary (2003)
Abdul G. Koroma, Sierra Leone (2003)
Shigeru Oda, Japan (2003)
Jiuyong Shi, China (2003)

Agencies of the United Nations

INTL. ATOMIC ENERGY AGENCY (IAEA)

Established: Statute for IAEA, approved on Oct. 26, 1956, at a conference held at U.N. Headquarters, New York, came into force on July 29, 1957. The Agency is under the aegis of the U.N., but unlike the following, it is not a specialized agency.

Purpose: To promote the peaceful uses of atomic energy; to ensure that assistance provided by it or at its request or under its supervision or control is not used in such a way as to further any military purpose.

Headquarters: Vienna International Center, P.O. Box 100, Wargramer Strasse 5, A-1400 Vienna, Austria

FOOD AND AGRICULTURE ORGANIZATION OF THE UNITED NATIONS (FAO)

Established: October 16, 1945, when constitution became effective.

Purpose: To raise nutrition levels and living standards; to secure improvements in production and distribution of food and agricultural products.

Headquarters: Via delle Terme di Caracalla, 00100, Rome, Italy.

GENERAL AGREEMENT ON TARIFFS AND TRADE (GATT)

Established: Jan. 1, 1948.

Purpose: An International Trade Organization (ITO) was originally planned. Although this agency has not materialized, some of its objectives have been embodied in an international commercial treaty, the General Agreement on Tariffs and Trade. Its purpose is to sponsor trade negotiations.

Headquarters: Centre William Rappard, 154 Rue de Lausanne, CH-1211, Geneva 21, Switzerland.

INTERNATIONAL BANK FOR RECONSTRUCTION AND DEVELOPMENT (IBRD) (WORLD BANK)

Established: December 27, 1945, when Articles of Agreement drawn up at Bretton Woods Conference in July 1944 came into force. Began operations on June 25, 1946.

Purpose: To assist in reconstruction and development of economies of members by facilitating capital investment and by making loans to governments and furnishing technical advice.

Headquarters: 1818 H St., N.W., Washington, D.C. 20433.

INTL. CIVIL AVIATION ORGANIZATION (ICAO)

Established: April 4, 1947, after working as a provisional organization since June 1945.

Purpose: To study problems of international civil aviation; to establish international standards and regulations; to promote safety measures, uniform regulations for operation, simpler procedures at international borders, and the use of new technical methods and equipment. It has evolved standards for meteorological services, traffic control, communications, radio beacons and ranges, search and rescue organization, and other facilities. It has brought about much simplification of customs, immigration, and public health regulations as they apply to international air transport. It drafts international air law conventions, and is concerned with economic aspects of air travel.

Headquarters: 1000 Sherbrooke St. West, Montreal, Quebec, H3A 2R2, Canada.

INTL. DEVELOPMENT ASSOCIATION (IDA)

Established: Sept. 24, 1960. An affiliate of the World Bank, IDA has the same officers and staff as the Bank.

Purpose: To further economic development of its members by providing finance on terms which bear less heavily on balance of payments of members than those of conventional loans.

Headquarters: 1818 H St., N.W., Washington, D.C. 20433.

INTERNATIONAL FINANCE CORPORATION (IFC)

Established: Charter of IFC came into force on July 20, 1956. Although IFC is affiliated with the World Bank, it is a separate legal entity, and its funds are entirely separate from those of the Bank. However, membership in the Corporation is open only to Bank members.

Purpose: To further economic development by encouraging the growth of productive private enterprise in its member countries, particularly in the less developed areas; to invest in productive private enterprises in association with private investors, without government guarantee of repayment where sufficient private capital is not available on reasonable terms; to serve as a clearing house to bring together investment opportunities, private capital (both foreign and domestic), and experienced management.

Headquarters: 1818 H St., N.W., Washington, D.C. 20433.

INTERNATIONAL FUND FOR AGRICULTURAL DEVELOPMENT (IFAD)

Established: June 18, 1976. Began operations in December 1977.

Purpose: To mobilize additional funds for agricultural and rural development in developing countries through projects and programs directly benefiting the poorest rural populations.

Headquarters: 107 Via del Serafico, 00142, Rome, Italy.

INTERNATIONAL LABOR ORGANIZATION (ILO)

Established: April 11, 1919, when constitution was adopted as Part XIII of Treaty of Versailles. Became specialized agency of U.N. in 1946.

Purpose: To contribute to establishment of lasting peace by promoting social justice; to improve labor conditions and living standards through international action; to promote economic and social stability. The U.S. withdrew from the ILO in 1977 and resumed membership in 1980.

Headquarters: 4, Route des Morillons, CH-1211 Geneva 22, Switzerland.

INTERNATIONAL MARITIME ORGANIZATION (IMO)

Established: March 17, 1958.

Purpose: To give advisory and consultative help to promote international cooperation in maritime navigation and to encourage the highest standards of safety and navigation. Its aim is to bring about a uniform system of measuring ship tonnage; systems now vary widely in different parts of the world. Other activities include cooperation with other U.N. agencies on matters affecting the maritime field.

Headquarters: 4 Albert Embankment, London SE 1 7SR England.

INTERNATIONAL MONETARY FUND (IMF)

Established: Dec. 27, 1945, when Articles of Agreement drawn up at Bretton Woods Conference in July 1944 came into force. Fund began operations on March 1, 1947.

Purpose: To promote international monetary cooperation and expansion of international trade; to promote exchange stability; to assist in establishment of multilateral system of payments in respect of currency transactions between members.

Headquarters: 700 19th St., N.W., Washington, D.C. 20431.

INTERNATIONAL TELECOMMUNICATION UNION (ITU)

Established: 1865. Became specialized agency of U.N. in 1947.

Purpose: To extend technical assistance to help members keep up with present day telecommunication needs; to standardize communications equipment and procedures; to lower costs. It also works for orderly sharing of radio frequencies and makes studies and recommendations to benefit its members.

Headquarters: Place des Nations, 1211 Geneva 20, Switzerland.

UNITED NATIONS EDUCATIONAL, SCIENTIFIC, AND CULTURAL ORGANIZATION (UNESCO)

Established: Nov. 4, 1946, when twentieth signatory to constitution deposited instrument of acceptance with government of U.K.

Purpose: To promote collaboration among nations through education, science, and culture in order to further justice, rule of law, and human rights and freedoms without distinction of race, sex, language, or religion.

Headquarters: UNESCO House. 7, Place de Fontenoy, 75007 Paris, France.

UNITED NATIONS INDUSTRIAL DEVELOPMENT ORGANIZATION (UNIDO)

Established: Nov. 17, 1966. Became specialized agency of the U.N. in 1985.

Purpose: To promote and accelerate the industrialization of the developing countries.

Headquarters: UNIDO, Vienna International Centre, P.O. Box 300, A-1400 Vienna, Austria.

UNIVERSAL POSTAL UNION (UPU)

Established: Oct. 9, 1874. Became specialized agency of U.N. in 1947.

Purpose: To facilitate reciprocal exchange of correspondence by uniform procedures by all UPU members; to help governments modernize and speed up mailing procedures.

Headquarters: Weltpoststrasse 4, Berne, Switzerland.

WORLD HEALTH ORGANIZATION (WHO)

Established: April 7, 1948, when 26 members of the U.N. had accepted its constitution, adopted July 22, 1946, by the International Health Conference in New York City.

Purpose: To aid attainment by all people of highest possible level of health.

Headquarters: 20 Avenue Appia, 1211 Geneva 27, Switzerland.

WORLD INTELLECTUAL PROPERTY ORGANIZATION (WIPO)

Established: April 26, 1970, when its Convention came into force. Originated as International Bureau of Paris Union (1883) and Berne Union (1886), later succeeded by United International Bureau for the Protection of Intellectual Property (BIRPI). Became a specialized agency of the U.N. in December 1974.

Purpose: To promote legal protection of intellectual property, including artistic and scientific works, artistic performances, sound recordings, broadcasts, inventions, trademarks, industrial designs, and commercial names.

Headquarters: 34 Chemin des Colombettes, CH-1211 Geneva 20, Switzerland.

WORLD METEOROLOGICAL ORGANIZATION (WMO)

Established: March 23, 1950, succeeding the International Meteorological Organization, a non-governmental organization founded in 1878.

Purpose: To promote international exchange of weather reports and maximum standardization of observations; to help developing countries establish weather services for their own economic needs; to fill gaps in observation stations; to promote meteorological investigations affecting jet aircraft, satellites, energy resources, etc.

Headquarters: 41, Avenue Giuseppe-Motta, CH-1211 Geneva 2, Switzerland.

STRUCTURES

The Seven Wonders of the World

(Not all classical writers list the same items as the Seven Wonders, but most of them agree on the following.)

The Pyramids of Egypt. A group of three pyramids, *Khufu, Khafra,* and *Menkaura* at Giza, outside modern Cairo, is often called the first wonder of the world. The largest pyramid, built by Khufu (Cheops), a king of the fourth Dynasty, had an original estimated height of 482 ft (now approximately 450 ft). The base has sides 755 ft long. It contains 2,300,000 blocks; the average weight of each is 2.5 tons. Estimated date of construction is 2800 B.C. Of all the Seven Wonders, the pyramids alone survive.

Hanging Gardens of Babylon. Often listed as the second wonder, these gardens were supposedly built by Nebuchadnezzar about 600 B.C. to please his queen, Amuhia. They are also associated with the mythical Assyrian Queen, Semiramis. Archeologists surmise that the gardens were laid out atop a vaulted building, with provisions for raising water. The terraces were said to rise from 75 to 300 ft.

The Walls of Babylon, also built by Nebuchadnezzar, are sometimes referred to as the second (or seventh) wonder instead of the Hanging Gardens.

Statue of Zeus (Jupiter) at Olympia. The work of Phidias (5th century B.C.), this colossal figure in gold and ivory was reputedly 40 ft high. All trace of it is lost, except for reproductions on coins.

Temple of Artemis (Diana) at Ephesus. A beautiful structure, begun about 350 B.C. in honor of a non-Hellenic goddess who later became identified with the Greek goddess of the same name. The temple, with Ionic columns 60 ft high, was destroyed by invading Goths in A.D. 262.

Mausoleum at Halicarnassus. This famous monument was erected by Queen Artemisia in memory of her husband, King Mausolus of Caria in Asia Minor, who died in 353 B.C. Some remains of the structure are in the British Museum. This shrine is the source of the modern word "mausoleum."

Colossus at Rhodes. This bronze statue of Helios (Apollo), about 105 ft high, was the work of the sculptor Chares, who reputedly labored for 12 years before completing it in 280 B.C. It was destroyed during an earthquake in 224 B.C.

Pharos of Alexandria. The seventh wonder was the Pharos (lighthouse) of Alexandria, built by Sostratus of Cnidus during the 3rd century B.C. on the island of Pharos off the coast of Egypt. It was destroyed by an earthquake in the 13th century.

Famous Structures

Ancient

The *Great Sphinx of Egypt,* one of the wonders of ancient Egyptian architecture, adjoins the pyramids of Giza and has a length of 240 ft. It was built in the 4th dynasty.

Other Egyptian buildings of note include the *Temples of Karnak* and *Edfu* and the *Tombs at Beni Hassan.*

The *Parthenon of Greece,* built on the Acropolis in Athens, was the chief temple to the goddess Athena. It was believed to have been completed by 438 B.C. The present temple remained intact until the 5th century A.D. Today, though the Parthenon is in ruins, its majestic proportions are still discernible.

Other great structures of ancient Greece were the *Temples at Paestum* (about 540 and 420 B.C.); the *Temple of Poseidon* (about 460 B.C.); the *Temple of Apollo* at Corinth (about 540 B.C.); the *Temple of Apollo* at Bassae (about 450–420 B.C.); the famous *Erechtheum* atop the Acropolis (about 421–405 B.C.); the *Temple of Athena Niké* at Athens (about 426 B.C.); the *Olympieum* at Athens (174 B.C.–A.D. 131); the *Athenian Treasury* at Delphi (about 515 B.C.); the *Propylaea* of the Acropolis at Athens (437–432 B.C.); the *Theater of Dionysus* at Athens (about 350–325 B.C.); the *House of Cleopatra* at Delos (138 B.C.) and the *Theater* at Epidaurus (about 325 B.C.).

The *Colosseum (Flavian Amphitheater) of Rome,* the largest and most famous of the Roman amphitheaters, was opened for use A.D. 80. Elliptical in shape, it consisted of three stories and an upper gallery, rebuilt in stone in its present form in the third century A.D. Its seats rise in tiers, which in turn are buttressed by concrete vaults and stone piers. It could seat between 40,000 and 50,000 spectators. It was principally used for gladiatorial combat.

The *Pantheon* at Rome, begun by Agrippa in 27 B.C. as a temple, was rebuilt in its present circular form by Hadrian (A.D. 110–25). Literally the Pantheon was intended as a temple of "all the gods." It is remarkable for its perfect preservation today, and it has served continuously for 20 centuries as a place of worship.

Famous Roman arches include the *Arch of Constantine* (about A.D. 315) and the *Arch of Titus* (about A.D. 80).

Later European

St. Mark's Cathedral in Venice (1063–67), one of the great examples of Byzantine architecture, was begun in the 9th century. Partly destroyed by fire in 976, it was later rebuilt as a Byzantine edifice.

Other famous Byzantine examples of architecture are *St. Sophia* in Istanbul (A.D. 532–37); *San Vitale* in Ravenna (542); *St. Paul's Outside the Walls,* Rome (5th century); *Assumption Cathedral* in the Kremlin, Moscow (begun in 1475); and *St. Lorenzo Outside the Walls,* Rome, begun in 588.

The *Cathedral Group* at Pisa (1067–1173), one of the most celebrated groups of structures built in Romanesque-style, consists of the cathedral, the cathedral's baptistery, and the *Leaning Tower*. This trio forms a group by itself in the northwest corner of the city. The cathedral and baptistery are built in varicolored marble. The campanile *(Leaning Tower)* is 179 ft. high and leans more than 16 ft out of the perpendicular. There is little reason to believe that the architects intended to have the tower lean.

Other examples of Romanesque architecture include the *Vézelay Abbey* in France (1130); the *Church of Notre-Dame-du-Port* at Clermont-Ferrand in France (1100); the *Church of San Zeno* (begun in 1138) at Verona, and *Durham Cathedral* in England.

The *Alhambra* (1248–1354), located in Granada, Spain, is universally esteemed as one of the greatest masterpieces of Moslem architecture. Designed as a palace and fortress for the Moorish monarchs of Granada, it is surrounded by a heavily fortified wall more than a mile in perimeter. The location of the Alhambra in the Sierra Nevada provides a magnificent setting for this jewel of Moorish Spain.

The *Tower of London* is a group of buildings and towers covering 13 acres along the north bank of the Thames. The central *White Tower*, begun in 1078 during the reign of William the Conqueror, was originally a fortress and royal residence, but was later used as a prison. The *Bloody Tower* is associated with Anne Boleyn and other notables.

Westminster Abbey, in London, was begun in 1045 and completed in 1065. It was rebuilt and enlarged in 1245–50.

Notre-Dame de Paris (begun in 1163), one of the great examples of Gothic architecture, is a twin-towered church with a steeple over the crossing and immense flying buttresses supporting the masonry at the rear of the church.

Other famous Gothic structures are *Chartres Cathedral* (12th century); *Sainte Chapelle*, Paris (1246–48); *Laon Cathedral*, France (1160–1205); *Reims Cathedral* (about 1210–50; rebuilt after its almost complete destruction in World War I); *Rouen Cathedral* (13th–16th centuries); *Amiens Cathedral* (1218–69); *Beauvais Cathedral* (begun 1247); *Salisbury Cathedral* (1220–60); *York Minster* or the *Cathedral of St. Peter* (begun in the 7th century); *Milan Cathedral* (begun 1386); and *Cologne Cathedral* (13th–19th centuries); badly damaged in World War II.

The *Duomo* (cathedral) in Florence was founded in 1298, completed by Brunelleschi and consecrated in 1436. The oval-shaped dome dominates the entire structure.

The *Vatican* is a group of buildings in Rome comprising the official residence of the Pope. The *Basilica of St. Peter*, the largest church in the Christian world, was begun in 1450. The *Sistine Chapel*, begun in 1473, is noted for the art masterpieces of Michelangelo, Botticelli, and others. The *Basilica of the Savior* (known as *St. John Lateran*) is the first-ranking Catholic Church in the world, for it is the cathedral of the Pope.

Other examples of Renaissance architecture are the *Palazzo Riccardi*, the *Palazzo Pitti* and the *Palazzo Strozzi* in Florence; the *Farnese Palace* in Rome; *Palazzo Grimani* (completed about 1550) in Venice; the *Escorial* (1563–93) near Madrid; the *Town Hall* of Seville (1527–32); the *Louvre*, Paris; the *Château* at Blois, France; *St. Paul's Cathedral*, London (1675–1710; badly damaged in World War II); the *École Militaire*, Paris (1752); the *Pazzi Chapel*, Flor-

ence, designed by Brunelleschi (1429); the *Palace of Fontainebleau* and the *Château de Chambord* in France.

The *Palace of Versailles*, containing the famous Hall of Mirrors, was built during the reign of Louis XIV and served as the royal palace until 1793.

Outstanding European buildings of the 18th and 19th centuries are the *Superga* at Turin, the *Hôtel-Dieu* in Lyons, the *Belvedere Palace* at Vienna, the *Royal Palace* of Stockholm, the *Opera House* of Paris (1863–75); the *Bank of England*, the *British Museum*, the *University of London*, and the *Houses of Parliament*, all in London; the *Panthéon*, the *Church of the Madeleine*, the *Bourse*, and the *Palais de Justice* in Paris.

The *Eiffel Tower*, in Paris, was built for the Exposition of 1889 by Alexandre Eiffel. It is 984 ft high.[1]

1. 1,056 ft, including the television tower.

Asiatic and African

The *Taj Mahal* (1632–50), at Agra, India, built by Shah Jahan as a tomb for his wife, is considered by some as the most perfect example of the Mogul style and by others as the most beautiful building in the world. Four slim white minarets flank the building, which is topped by a white dome; the entire structure is of marble.

Other examples of Indian architecture are the temples at Benares and Tanjore.

Among famed Moslem edifices are the *Dome of the Rock* or *Mosque of Omar*, Jerusalem (A.D. 691); the *Citadel* (1166), and the *Tombs of the Mamelukes* (15th century), in Cairo; the *Tomb of Humayun* in Delhi; the *Blue Mosque* (1468) at Tabriz, and the *Tamerlane Mausoleum* at Samarkand.

Angkor Wat, outside the city of Angkor Thom, Cambodia, is one of the most beautiful examples of Cambodian or Khmer architecture. The sanctuary was built during the 12th century.

Great Wall of China (228 B.C.?), designed specifically as a defense against nomadic tribes, has large watch towers which could be called buildings. It was erected by Emperor Ch'in Shih Huang Ti and is 1,400 miles long. Built mainly of earth and stone, it varies in height between 18 and 30 ft.

Typical of Chinese architecture are the pagodas or temple towers. Among some of the better-known pagodas are the *Great Pagoda of the Wild Geese* at Sian (founded in 652); *Nan t'a* (11th century) at Fang Shan; the *Pagoda of Sung Yueh Ssu* (A.D. 523) at Sung Shan, Honan.

Other well-known Chinese buildings are the *Drum Tower* (1273), the *Three Great Halls* in the Purple Forbidden City (1627), *Buddha's Perfume Tower* (19th century), the *Porcelain Pagoda*, and the *Summer Palace*, all at Beijing.

United States

Rockefeller Center, in New York City, extends from 5th Ave. to the Avenue of the Americas between 48th and 52nd Sts. (and halfway to 7th Ave. between 47th and 51st Sts.). It occupies more than 22 acres and has 19 buildings.

The *Cathedral of St. John the Divine*, at 112th St. and Amsterdam Ave. in New York City, was begun in 1892 and is now in the final stages of completion. When completed, it will be the largest cathedral in the world: 601 ft long, 146 ft wide at the nave, 320 ft wide at the transept. The east end is designed in Romanesque-Byzantine style, and the nave and west end are Gothic.

St. Patrick's Cathedral, at Fifth Ave. and 50th St. in New York City, has a seating capacity of 2,500. The nave was opened in 1877, and the cathedral was dedicated in 1879.

Louisiana Superdome, in New Orleans, is the largest arena in the history of mankind. The main area can accommodate up to 95,000 people. It is the world's largest steel-constructed room. Unobstructed by posts, it covers 13 acres and reaches 27 stories at its peak.

World Trade Center, in New York City, was dedicated in 1973. Its twin towers are 110 stories high (1,350 ft), and the complex contains over 9 million sq ft of office space. A restaurant is on the 107th floor of the North Tower.

World's Highest Dams

Name	River, Country or State	Structural height		Gross reservoir capacity		Year completed
		feet	meters	thousands of acre feet	millions of cubic meters	
Rogun	Vakhsh, Tajikistan	1066	325	9,404	11,600	1985
Nurek	Vakhsh, Tajikistan	984	300	8,512	10,500	1980
Grande Dixence	Dixence, Switzerland	935	285	324	400	1962
Inguri	Inguri, Georgia	892	272	801	1,100	1984
Chicoasén	Grijalva, Mexico	869	265	1,346	1,660	1981
Vaiont	Vaiont, Italy	869	265	137	169	1961
Tehri	Bhagirathi, India	856	261	2,869	3,540	UC
Kinshau	Tons, India	830	253	1,946	2,400	1985
Guavio	Orinoco, Colombia	820	250	811	1,000	1989
Mica	Columbia, Canada	794	242	20,000	24,670	1972
Sayano-Shushensk	Yenisei, Russia	794	242	25,353	31,300	1980
Mihoesti	Aries, Romania	794	242	5	6	1983
Chivor	Batá, Colombia	778	237	661	815	1975
Mauvoisin	Drance de Bagnes, Switzerland	777	237	146	180	1957
Oroville	Feather, California	770	235	3,538	4,299	1968
Chirkey	Sulak, Ukraine	764	233	2,252	2,780	1977
Bhakra	Sutlej, India	741	226	8,002	9,870	1963
El Cajón	Humuya, Honduras	741	226	4,580	5,650	1984
Hoover	Colorado, Arizona/Nevada	726	221	28,500	35,154	1936
Contra	Verzasca, Switzerland	722	220	70	86	1965
Dabaklamm	Dorferbach, Austria	722	220	191	235	UC
Mratinje	Piva, Herzegovina	722	220	713	880	1973
Dworshak	N. Fk. Clearwater, Idaho	717	219	3,453	4,259	1974
Glen Canyon	Colorado, Arizona	710	216	27,000	33,304	1964
Toktogul	Naryn, Kyrgyzstan	705	215	15,800	19,500	1978
Daniel Johnson	Manicouagan, Canada	703	214	115,000	141,852	1968
San Roque	Agno, Philippines	689	210	803	990	UC
Luzzone	Brenno di Luzzone, Switzerland	682	208	71	87	1963
Keban	Firat, Turkey	679	207	25,110	31,000	1974
Dez	Dez, Abi, Iran	666	203	2,707	3,340	1963
Almendra	Tormes, Spain	662	202	2,148	2,649	1970
Kölnbrein	Malta, Austria	656	200	166	205	1977
Kärün	Karun, Iran	656	200	2,351	2,900	1976
Altinkaya	Kizil Irmak, Turkey	640	195	4,672	5,763	1986
New Bullards Bar	No. Yuba, California	637	194	960	1,184	1968
Lakhwar	Yamuna, India	630	192	470	580	1985
New Melones	Stanislaus, California	625	191	2,400	2,960	1979
Itaipu	Paraná, Brazil/Paraguay	623	190	23,510	29,000	1982
Kurobe 4	Kurobe, Japan	610	186	162	199	1964
Swift	Lewis, Washington	610	186	756	932	1958
Mossyrock	Cowlitz, Washington	607	185	1,300	1,603	1968
Oymopinar	Manavgat, Turkey	607	185	251	310	1983
Atatürk	Firat, Turkey	604	184	39,482	48,700	1990
Shasta	Sacramento, California	602	183	4,550	5,612	1945
Bennett WAC	Peace, Canada	600	183	57,006	70,309	1967
Karakaya	Firat, Turkey	591	180	7,767	9,580	1986
Tignes	Isère, France	591	180	186	230	1952
Amir Kabir (Karad)	Karadj, Iran	591	180	166	205	1962
Tachien	Tachia, Taiwan	591	180	188	232	1974
Dartmouth	Mitta-Mitta, Australia	591	180	3,243	4,000	1978
Özköy	Gediz, Turkey	591	180	762	940	1983
Emosson	Barberine, Switzerland	590	180	184	225	1974
Zillergründl	Ziller, Austria	590	180	73	90	1986
Los Leones	Los Leones, Chile	587	179	86	106	1986
New Don Pedro	Tuolumne, California	585	178	2,030	2,504	1971
Alpa-Gera	Cormor, Italy	584	178	53	65	1965

Name	River, Country or State	Structural height (feet)	Structural height (meters)	Gross reservoir capacity (thousands of acre feet)	Gross reservoir capacity (millions of cubic meters)	Year completed
Kopperston Tailings 3	Jones Branch, West Virginia	580	177	—	—	1963
Takase	Takase, Japan	577	176	62	76	1979
Nader Shah	Marun, Iran	574	175	1,313	1,620	1978
Hasan Ugurlu	Yesil Irmak, Turkey	574	175	874	1,078	1980
Pauti-Mazar	Mazar, Ecuador	540	165	405	500	1984
Hungry Horse	S.Fk., Flathead, Montana	564	172	3,470	4,280	1953
Longyangxia	Huanghe, China	564	172	20,025	24,700	1983
Cabora Bassa	Zambezi, Mozambique	561	171	51,075	63,000	1974
Maqarin	Yarmuk, Jordan	561	171	259	320	1987
Amaluza	Paute, Ecuador	558	170	81	100	1982
Idikki	Periyar, India	554	169	1,618	1,996	1974
Charvak	Chirchik, Uzbekistan	552	168	1,620	2,000	1970
Gura Apelor Retezat	Riul Mare, Romania	552	168	182	225	1980
Grand Coulee	Columbia, Washington	550	168	9,390	11,582	1942
Boruca	Terraba, Costa Rica	548	167	12,128	14,960	UC
Vidraru	Arges, Romania	545	166	380	465	1965
Kremasta (King Paul)	Achelöus, Greece	541	165	3,850	4,750	1965

NOTE: UC = under construction. *Source:* Department of the Interior, Bureau of Reclamation and *International Water Power and Dam Construction.*

World's Largest Dams

Dam	Location	Volume (thousands) Cubic meters	Volume (thousands) Cubic yards	Year completed
New Cornelia Tailings	Arizona	209,500	274,015	1973
Pati (Chapetón)	Argentina	200,000	261,590	UC
Tarbela	Pakistan	121,720	159,203	1976
Fort Peck	Montana	96,049	125,628	1940
Atatürk	Turkey	84,500	110,522	1990
Yacyretá-Apipe	Paraguay/Argentina	81,000	105,944	UC
Guri (Raul Leoni)	Venezuela	78,000	102,014	1986
Rogun	Tajikistan	75,500	98,750	1985
Oahe	South Dakota	70,339	92,000	1963
Mangla	Pakistan	65,651	85,872	1967
Gardiner	Canada	65,440	85,592	1968
Afsluitdijk	Netherlands	63,400	82,927	1932
Oroville	California	59,639	78,008	1968
San Luis	California	59,405	77,700	1967
Nurek	Tajikistan	58,000	75,861	1980
Garrison	North Dakota	50,843	66,500	1956
Cochiti	New Mexico	48,052	62,850	1975
Tabka (Thawra)	Syria	46,000	60,168	1976
Bennett W.A.C.	Canada	43,733	57,201	1967
Tucuruíi	Brazil	43,000	56,242	1984
Boruca	Costa Rica	43,000	56,242	UC
High Aswan (Sadd-el-Aali)	Egypt	43,000	56,242	1970
San Roque	Philippines	43,000	56,242	UC
Kiev	Russia	42,841	56,034	1964
Dantiwada Left Embankment	India	41,040	53,680	1965
Saratov	Russia	40,400	52,843	1967
Mission Tailings 2	Arizona	40,088	52,435	1973
Fort Randall	South Dakota	38,227	50,000	1953
Kanev	Ukraine.	37,860	49,520	1976
Mosul	Iraq	36,000	47,086	1982
Kakhovka	Ukraine	35,640	46,617	1955
Itumbiara	Brazil	35,600	46,563	1980
Lauwerszee	Netherlands	35,575	46,532	1969
Beas	India	35,418	46,325	1974
Oosterschelde	Netherlands	35,000	45,778	1986

NOTE: UC = under construction. *Source:* Department of the Interior, Bureau of Reclamation and *International Water Power and Dam Construction.*

World's Largest Hydroelectric Plants

Name of Dam	Location	Rated capacity (MW)		Year of initial operation
		Present	Ultimate	
Itaipu	Brazil/Paraguay	1,400	12,600	1984
Grand Coulee	Washington	6,480	10,080	1942
Guri (Raul Leoni)	Venezuela	2,800	10,060	1968
Tucuruí	Brazil	—	7,500	1985
Sayano-Shushensk	Former U.S.S.R.	—	6,400	1980
Krasnoyarsk	Russia	6,096	6,096	1968
Corpus-Posadas	Argentina/Paraguay	—	6,000	UC
LaGrande 2	Canada	5,328	5,328	1982
Churchill Falls	Canada	5,225	5,225	1971
Bratsk	Siberia	4,100	4,600	1964
Ust'—Ilimsk	Russia	3,675	4,500	1974
Cabora Bassa	Mozambique	2,075	4,150	1974
Yacyretá-Apipe	Argentina/Paraguay	—	4,050	UC
Rogun	Tajikistan	—	3,600	1985
Paulo Afonso	Brazil	3,409	3,409	1954
Salto Santiago	Brazil	1,332	3,333	1980
Pati (Chapetón)	Argentina	—	3,300	UC
Brumley Gap	Virginia	3,200	3,200	1973
Ilha Solteira	Brazil	3,200	3,200	1973
Inga I	Zaire	360	2,820	1974
Gezhouba	China	965	2,715	1981
John Day	Oregon/Washington	2,160	2,700	1969
Nurek	Tajikistan	900	2,700	1976
Revelstoke	Canada	900	2,700	1984
Sáo Simao	Brazil	2,680	2,680	1979
LaGrande 4	Canada	2,637	2,637	1984
Mica	Canada	1,736	2,610	1976
Volgograd—22nd Congress	Russia	2,560	2,560	1958
Fos do Areia	Brazil	2,511	2,511	1983
Itaparica	Brazil	—	2,500	1985
Bennett W.A.C.	Canada	2,116	2,416	1969
Chicoasén	Mexico	—	2,400	1980
Atatürk	Turkey	—	2,400	1990
LaGrande 3	Canada	2,310	2,310	1982
Volga—V.I. Lenin	Russia	2,300	2,300	1955
Iron Gates I	Romania/Yugoslavia	2,300	2,300	1970
Iron Gates II	Romania/Yugoslavia	270	2,160	1983
Bath County	Virginia	—	2,100	1985
High Aswan (Saad-el-Aali)	Egypt	2,100	2,100	1967
Tarbela	Pakistan	1,400	2,100	1977
Piedra del Aquila	Argentina	—	2,100	1993
Itumbiara	Brazil	2,080	2,080	1980
Chief Joseph	Washington	2,069	2,069	1956
McNary	Oregon	980	2,030	1954
Green River	North Carolina	—	2,000	1980
Tehri	India	—	2,000	UC
Cornwall	New York	—	2,000	1978
Ludington	Michigan	1,979	1,979	1973
Robert Moses—Niagara	New York	1,950	1,950	1961
Salto Grande	Argentina/Uruguay	—	1,890	1979

Note: MW = Megawatts, UC = under construction. *Source:* Department of the Interior, Bureau of Reclamation and *International Water Power and Dam Construction.*

Notable U.S. Skyscrapers

City	Building	Stories	Height ft	Height m	City	Building	Stories	Height ft	Height m
Chicago	Sears Tower	110	1,454	443	Atlanta	Nations Bank Plaza	55	1,025	312
New York	World Trade Center	110	1,377	419	Houston	Texas Commerce Tower	75	1,002	305
New York	Empire State	102	1,250	381	Houston	First Interstate Plaza	71	985	300
Chicago	AMOCO	80	1,136	346	Chicago	311 South Wacker Drive	65	969	295
Chicago	John Hancock Center	100	1,127	343	New York	American International	66	952	290
New York	Chrysler	77	1,046	319	Cleveland	Society Tower	57	948	289
Los Angeles	First Interstate World Center	73	1,017	310	Philadelphia	One Liberty Place	62	945	288

Seattle	Columbia Seafirst Center	76	943	287
New York	Citicorp Center	59	915	279
Atlanta	One Peachtree Center	60	902	275
New York	40 Wall Tower	71	900	274
Chicago	Two Prudential Center	64	900	274
Seattle	Two Union Square	56	886	270
Philadelphia	Mellon Bank Center	56	880	268
Charlotte	NationsBank Corporate Center	60	875	267
Chicago	Water Tower Place	74	859	262
Los Angeles	First Interstate Bank	62	858	261
San Francisco	Transamerica Pyramid	61	853	259
Chicago	First National Bank	60	851	259
New York	RCA	70	850	259
Seattle	Washington Mutual Tower	56	849	259
Philadelphia	Two Liberty Place	52	845	257
Pittsburgh	USX Tower	64	841	256
Atlanta	One Atlantic Center	50	825	251
New York	Chase Manhattan	60	813	248
New York	Met Life	59	808	246
New York	Woolworth	55	792	241
Boston	John Hancock Tower	60	790	241
San Francisco	Bank of America	52	779	237
Minneapolis	IDS Tower	57	775	236
New York	One Liberty Plaza	54	775	236
Chicago	Three First National Plaza	57	775	236
New York	One Penn Plaza	57	774	236
Minneapolis	Norwest Center	57	772	235
Minneapolis	First Bank Place	56	770	235
Miami	First Union Financial Center	55	765	233
Atlanta	Westin Peachtree Plaza	73	754	230
New York	Exxon	54	750	229
Boston	Prudential Tower	52	750	229
Dallas	First Interst. Bank Tower	60	744	227
Los Angeles	Security Pacific Plaza	55	743	226
Los Angeles	Wells Fargo Center	54	743	227
Atlanta	Georgia-Pacific Center	52	741	226
Atlanta	191 Peachtree Tower	50	740	225
New York	One Astor Plaza	54	730	222
Chicago	Olympia Centre	63	727	222
Houston	Chevron Tower	52	725	221
New York	Marine Midland	52	724	221
Los Angeles	Mitsui (North Tower) Fudosan Tower	52	716	218
Pittsburgh	One Mellon Bank Center	54	715	218
Houston	One Shell Plaza	50	714	218
Detroit	Detroit Westin Hotel	73	712	220
Indianapolis	Banc One Center Tower	51	711	216
Dallas	Renaissance Tower	56	710	216
Cleveland	Terminal Tower	52	708	216
New York	Union Carbide	52	707	215
New York	General Motors	50	705	215
Seattle	AT&T Gateway Tower	62	702	214
New York	Metropolitan Life	50	700	213
Philadelphia	Blue Cross Tower	50	700	213
Chicago	Leo Burnett Building	46	700	213

NOTE: Height does not include TV towers and antennas. *Source: Information Please* questionnaires.

Notable Tunnels

Name	Location	Length		Year completed
		mi.	km	
Railroad, excluding subways				
Seikan	Tsugara Strait, Japan	33.1	53.3	1983
Channel[1]	English Channel, England, France	31.0	49.9	1994
Simplon (I and II)	Alps, Switzerland-Italy	12.3	19.8	1906 & 1922
Apennine	Bologna-Florence, Italy	11.5	18.5	1934
St. Gotthard	Swiss Alps	9.3	14.9	1881
Lötschberg	Swiss Alps	9.1	14.6	1911
Mont Cénis	French Alps	8.5[2]	13.7	1871
New Cascade	Cascade Mountains, Washington	7.8	12.6	1929
Vosges	Vosges, France	7.0	11.3	1940
Flathead	Rocky Mountains, Montana	7.0	11.3	1970
Arlberg	Austrian Alps	6.3	10.1	1884
Moffat	Rocky Mountains, Colorado	6.2	9.9	1928
Shimuzu	Shimuzu, Japan	6.1	9.8	1931
Rimutaka	Wairarapa, New Zealand	5.5	8.9	1955
Vehicular				
St. Gotthard	Alps, Switzerland	10.2	16.4	1980
Mt. Blanc	Alps, France-Italy	7.5	12.1	1965
Mt. Ena	Japan Alps, Japan	5.3	8.5	1976[3]
Great St. Bernard	Alps, Switzerland-Italy	3.4	5.5	1964
Mount Royal	Montreal, Canada	3.2	5.1	1918
Lincoln	Hudson River, New York-New Jersey	1.6	2.6	1937
Queensway Road	Mersey River, Liverpool, England	2.2	3.5	1934
Brooklyn-Battery	East River, New York City	1.7	2.7	1950
Holland	Hudson River, New York-New Jersey	1.6	2.6	1927
Fort McHenry	Baltimore, Maryland	1.6	2.6	1985
Hampton Roads	Norfolk, Virginia	1.4	2.3	1957
Queens-Midtown	East River, New York City	1.3	2.1	1940
Liberty Tubes	Pittsburgh, Pennsylvania	1.2	1.9	1923
Baltimore Harbor	Baltimore, Maryland	1.2	1.9	1957
Allegheny Tunnels	Pennsylvania Turnpike	1.2	1.9	1940[4]

1. Twin-rail. One tunnel for passenger trains, the other for shuttle trains carrying vehicles plus a central service tunnel.
2. Lengthened to its present 8.5 miles in 1881. 3. Parallel tunnel begun in 1976. 4. Parallel tunnel built in 1965, twin tunnel in 1966. *Source:* American Society of Civil Engineers and International Bridge, Tunnel & Turnpike Association, Wittiker's.

Notable Modern Bridges

Name	Location	Length of main span		Year completed
		ft	m	
Suspension	**United States**			
Verrazano-Narrows	Lower New York Bay	4,260	1,298	1964
Golden Gate	San Francisco Bay	4,200	1,280	1937
Mackinac Straits	Michigan	3,800	1,158	1957
George Washington	Hudson River at New York City	3,500	1,067	1931
Tacoma Narrows II	Puget Sound at Tacoma, Wash.	2,800	853	1950
San Francisco-Oakland Bay[1]	San Francisco Bay	2,310	704	1936
Bronx-Whitestone	East River, New York City	2,300	701	1939
Delaware Memorial (twin)	Delaware River near Wilmington, Del.	2,150	655	1951, 1968
Seaway Skyway	St. Lawrence River at Ogdensburg, N.Y.	2,150	655	1960
Walt Whitman	Delaware River at Philadelphia	2,000	610	1957
Ambassador International	Detroit River at Detroit	1,850	564	1929
Throgs Neck	East River, New York City	1,800	549	1961
Benjamin Franklin	Delaware River at Philadelphia	1,750	533	1926
Bear Mountain	Hudson River at Peekskill, N.Y.	1,632	497	1924
Wm. Preston Lane, Jr., Memorial (twin)	Near Annapolis, Md.	1,600	488	1952, 1973
Williamsburg	East River, New York City	1,600	488	1903
Newport	Narragansett Bay at Newport, R.I.	1,600	488	1969
Chesapeake Bay	Sandy Point, Md.	1,600	488	1952
Brooklyn	East River, New York City	1,595	486	1883
	International			
Humber	Hull, Britain	4,626	1,410	1981
Minami Bisan–Seto	Japan	3,609	1,100	1988
Second Bosporus	Istanbul, Turkey	3,576	1,090	1988
First Bosporus	Istanbul	3,524	1,074	1973
Ponte 25 de Abril	Tagus River at Lisbon	3,323	1,013	1966
Forth Road	Queensferry, Scotland	3,300	1,006	1964
Kita Bisan–Seto	Japan	3,248	990	1988
Severn	Severn River at Beachley, England	3,240	988	1966
Shimotsui Straits	Japan	3,084	940	1988
Ohnaruto	Japan	2,874	876	1988
Cantilever	**United States**			
Commodore John Barry	Chester, Pa.	1,644	501	1974
Greater New Orleans[1]	Mississippi River, Louisiana	1,576	480	1958
Transbay Bridge	San Francisco Bay	1,400	427	1936
Baton Rouge	Mississippi River, Louisiana	1,235	376	1968
Tappan Zee	Hudson River at Tarrytown, N.Y.	1,212	369	1955
Longview	Columbia River at Longview, Wash.	1,200	366	1930
Patapsco River	Baltimore Outer Harbor Crossing	1,200	366	1976
Queensboro	East River, New York City	1,182	360	1909
	International			
Quebec Railway	St. Lawrence River at Quebec, Canada	1,800	549	1917
Forth Railway[1]	Queensferry, Scotland	1,710	521	1890
Minato Ohashi	Osaka, Japan	1,673	510	1974
Howrah	Hooghly River at Calcutta	1,500	457	1943
Steel Arch	**United States**			
New River Gorge	Fayetteville, W. Va.	1,700	518	1977
Bayonne	Kill Van Kull at Bayonne, N.J.	1,675	510	1931
Fremont	Portland, Ore.	1,255	383	1973
	International			
Sydney Harbor	Sydney, Australia	1,670	509	1932
Zdákov	Vltava River, Czech Republic	1,244	380	1967
Port Mann	Fraser River at Vancouver, British Columbia	1,200	366	1964
Thatcher Ferry	Panama Canal, Panama	1,128	344	1962
Laviolette	St. Lawrence River, Trois Rivieres, Quebec	1,100	335	1967
Runcorn-Widnes	Mersey River, England	1,082	330	1961
Birchenough	Sabi River at Fort Victoria, Zimbabwe	1,080	329	1935
Cable-Stayed	**United States**			
Dame Point	Jacksonville, Florida	1,300	396	1988
Houston Ship Channel	Baytown, Texas	1,250	381	1991
Hale Boggs Memorial	Luling, Louisiana	1,222	373	1983
Sunshine Skyway	Tampa, Florida	1,200	366	1987

Name	Location	Length of main span		Year completed
		ft	m	
Cable-Stayed	**International**			
Tatara	Ehime, Japan	2,920	890	UC
Ponte de Normandie	Le Havre, France	2,808	856	1994
Skarnsundet Bridge	near Trondheim, Norway	1,739	530	1991
Ikuchi	Honshu-Shikoku, Japan	1,608	490	1991
Alex Fraser	Vancouver, B.C., Canada	1,525	465	1986
Yokohama-ko-odan	Kanagawa, Japan	1,509	460	1989
Second Hooghly	Calcutta, India	1,500	457	1992
Second Severn Crossing	Severn River, England	1,496	456	1994
Dartford	Thames River, Dartford, England	1,476	450	1992
Dao Kanong	Chao Phraya River, Bangkok, Thailand	1,476	450	1987
Barrio de Luna	Cordillera, Spain	1,444	440	1983
Helgeland	Sandnessjoen, Nordland, Norway	1,394	425	1991
Continuous Truss	**United States**			
Mark Clark Expressway I-526	Cooper River, at Charleston, S.C.	1,600	487	1992
Astoria	Columbia River at Astoria, Oregon	1,232	376	1966
Croton Reservoir	Croton, N.Y.	1,052	321	1970
Ravenswood	Ohio River, Ravenswood, W. Va.	902	275	1981
Dubuque	Mississippi River at Dubuque, Iowa	845	258	1943
Braga Memorial	Taunton River at Somerset, Mass.	840	256	1966
	International			
Oshima	Oshima Island, Japan	1,066	325	1976
Tenmon	Kumamoto, Japan	984	300	1966
Kuronoseto	Nagashima-Kyushu, Japan	984	300	1974
Graf Spee	Germany	839	256	1936
Concrete Arch	**United States**			
Westinghouse	Pittsburgh, Pa.	460	140	1931
Jack's Run	Pittsburgh, Pa.	400	120	1930
Cappelen	Minneapolis, Minn.	400	120	1923
	International			
Gladesville	Parramatta River at Sydney, Australia	1,000	305	1964
Amizade	Paraná River at Foz do Iguassu, Brazil	951	290	1964
Arrábida	Porto, Portugal	886	270	1963
Sandö	Angerman River at Kramfors, Sweden	866	264	1943
Fiumarella	Catanzaro, Italy	758	231	1961
Zaporozhe	Old Dnepr River, Ukraine	748	228	1952
Segmental Concrete Box Girder	**United States**			
Jesse H. Jones Memorial	Houston Ship Channel, Texas	750	228	1982

1. Twin span. *Source: Encyclopaedia Britannica,* American Society of Civil Engineers, Bridge Division, Federal Highway Administration, and *Encyclopedia Americana.*

Famous Ship Canals

Name	Location	Length (miles)[1]	Width (feet)	Depth (feet)	Locks	Year opened
Albert	Belgium	80.0	53.0	16.5	6	1939
Amsterdam-Rhine	Netherlands	45.0	164.0	41.0	3	1952
Beaumont-Port Arthur	United States	40.0	200.0	34.0	—	1916
Chesapeake and Delaware	United States	19.0	250.0	27.0	—	1927
Houston	United States	50.0	[2]	40.0	—	1914
Kiel (Nord-Ostsee Kanal)	Germany	61.3	144.0	36.0	4	1895
Panama	Canal Zone	50.7	110.0	41.0	12	1914
St. Lawrence Seaway	U.S. and Canada	2,400.0[3]	([4])	—	—	1959
Montreal to Prescott	U.S. and Canada	11.5	80.0	30.0	7	1959
Welland	Canada	27.5	80.0	27.0	8	1931
Sault Ste. Marie	Canada	1.2	60.0	16.8	1	1895
Sault Ste. Marie	United States	1.6	80.0	25.0	4	1915
Suez	Egypt	100.6[5]	197.0	36.0	—	1869

1. Statute miles. 2. 300–400 feet. 3. From Montreal to Duluth. 4. 442–550 feet; there are 11.5 miles of locks, 80 feet wide and 30 feet deep. 5. From Port Said lighthouse to entrance channel in Suez roads. *Source:* American Society of Civil Engineers.

MEDIA

Leading Magazines: United States and Canada

Magazine	Circulation[1]	Magazine	Circulation[1]
American Health—Fitness of Body and Mind	827,643	Nation's Business	861,260
Architectural Digest	881,232	New Woman	1,301,859
Better Homes and Gardens	7,613,661	Newsweek	3,158,617
Bon Appetit	1,187,437	The New Yorker	830,307
Business Week (North America)	880,357	Organic Gardening	803,535
Car and Driver	1,125,119	Outdoor Life	1,503,257
Chatelaine	880,935	Parenting Magazine	856,019
Conde Nast Traveler	909,092	Parents Magazine	1,852,517
Consumers Digest	1,208,643	PC Magazine	1,051,381
Cooking Light	1,248,939	PC World	951,849
Cosmopolitan	2,527,928	PC/Computing	900,165
Country America	1,001,089	Penthouse	1,304,719
Country Home	1,018,362	People Weekly	3,424,858
Country Living	1,932,840	Playboy	3,401,264
Discover	1,008,916	Popular Mechanics	1,636,210
Disney Adventures	961,992	Popular Science	1,808,140
Ebony	1,937,095	Prevention	3,427,803
Elle	905,498	Reader's Digest	15,126,664
Entertainment Weekly	1,115,024	Reader's Digest (Canadian English Edition)	1,214,548
Esquire	756,030	Redbook	3,401,775
Essence	950,634	Rolling Stone	1,221,417
Family Circle	5,005,301	Sassy	800,592
The Family Handyman	1,041,098	Self	1,201,395
Field & Stream	2,004,087	Sesame Street Magazine	1,116,756
First for Women	1,236,019	Seventeen	1,978,155
Forbes	777,353	Shape	817,629
Fortune (North America)	750,971	Smithsonian	2,214,509
Glamour	2,181,316	Soap Opera Digest	1,422,958
Globe	1,021,929	Southern Living	2,472,649
Golf Digest	1,465,494	Sport	750,418
Golf Magazine	1,269,642	Sports Illustrated	3,252,641
Good Housekeeping	5,223,935	Star	2,752,280
Gourmet	912,342	Sunset, The Magazine of Western Living	1,498,417
Harper's Bazaar	752,711	'Teen	1,280,148
Health	916,952	Tennis	804,687
Home	1,005,751	Time	4,063,146
Home Mechanix	1,009,347	Traditional Home	771,552
Hot Rod	804,851	Travel & Leisure	927,790
House Beautiful	1,023,697	True Story	774,948
Jet	948,254	True Story Plus	1,143,479
Kiplinger's Personal Finance Magazine	1,095,652	TV Guide	14,037,062
Ladies Home Journal	5,048,081	TV Guide (Canada)	815,413
Life	1,596,862	U.S. News & World Report	2,240,710
Mademoiselle	1,304,059	US	1,177,395
McCall's	4,611,848	Vanity Fair	1,130,993
Men's Health	1,258,493	Victoria	907,034
Midwest Living	852,704	Vogue	1,181,313
Money	1,982,123	Weight Watchers Magazine	1,031,177
Motor Trend	951,650	Woman's Day	4,724,500
National Enquirer	3,066,032	Working Woman	783,006
National Geographic Magazine	9,203,079	YM	1,933,775

1. Average total paid circulation for the six-month period ending December 31, 1994. The table lists magazines with combined newsstand and subscription circulation of over 750,000. *Source:* Audit Bureau of Circulations. Publishers' Statements for six-month period ending December 31, 1994.

Major U.S. Daily Newspapers[1]

City and Newspaper	Net paid circulation			
	Morning[2]	All-Day[2]	Evening[2]	Sunday
Akron, Ohio: *Beacon Journal*	156,424		—	224,589
Albany, N.Y.: *Times-Union* (M & S)	100,585		—	162,588
Albuquerque, N.M.: *Journal* (M & S); *Tribune* (E)	116,653		32,014	168,166
Allentown, Pa.: *Call* (M & S)	135,601			188,521

City and Newspaper	Morning[2]	All-Day[2]	Evening[2]	Sunday
Anchorage, Alaska: *News*	71,667[3]		—	93,785
Ann Arbor, Mich.: *News*	—		58,584	75,627
Appleton, Wis.: *Post–Crescent*	—		60,540	76,143
Asbury Park, N.J.: *Press*	—		159,576	227,933
Asheville, N.C.: *Citizen–Times*	66,318		—	78,241
Atlanta: *Constitution* (M); *Journal* (E);				
Journal and Constitution (S)	300,890[4]		128,875[4]	713,835
Atlantic City, N.J.: *Press*	75,848		—	96,618
Augusta, Ga.: *Chronicle* (M & S)	76,442[5]		—	103,046
Austin, Tex.: *American-Statesman*	182,199		—	241,491
Bakersfield, Calif.: *Californian*	76,444		—	90,372
Baltimore: *Sun*	264,583[5]		86,360[5]	494,542
Bangor, Me.: *News*	69,215[5]		—	85,386[6]
Baton Rouge, La.: *Advocate* (M & S)	100,552[5]		—	137,293
Bergen County (Hackensack), N.J.: *Record*	161,991		—	217,932
Beaumont, Tex.: *Enterprise*	64,726		—	80,228
Binghamton, N.Y.: *Press & Sun-Bulletin* (M & S)	68,735		—	90,155
Birmingham, Ala.: *Post-Herald* (M); *News* (E & S)	61,611[5]		163,284[5]	207,474
Boise, Idaho: *Statesman*	66,376		—	88,406
Boston: *Globe*	500,587[5]		—	785,916
Herald	304,505[5]		—	223,447
Christian Science Monitor	90,095[5]		—	—
Buffalo, N.Y.: *News*	—	283,855[5]	—	365,049
Camden, N.J.: *Courier-Post*	89,690		—	99,736
Canton, Ohio: *Repository*	—		61,431	80,989
Cedar Rapids, Iowa: *Gazette Post*	70,747		—	86,203
Charleston, S.C.: *Post & Courier* (M);				
Post–Courier (S)	111,709		—	125,463
Charleston, W. Va.: *Gazette* (M); *Mail* (E);				
Gazette-Mail (S)	54,326		46,376	107,527
Charlotte, N.C.: *Observer*	237,435		—	305,286
Chattanooga, Tenn.: *Times* (M); *News-Free Press* (E & S)	41,531		42,003	115,682
Chicago: *Tribune*	691,283[5]		—	1,098,765
Sun-Times	500,969[5]		—	516,849
Cincinnati: *Enquirer* (M & S); *Post* (E)	203,104		84,172[5]	354,281
Cleveland: *Plain Dealer*	404,400		—	544,386
Colorado Springs, Colo.: *Gazette Telegraph*	103,742		—	123,597
Columbia, S.C.: *State*	131,411		—	168,218
Columbus, Ohio: *Dispatch*	261,002[5]		—	404,292
Corpus Christi, Tex.: *Caller-Times*	67,452		—	96,800
Dallas: *News*	515,571[4]		—	821,894
Wall Street Journal (Southwest edition)	171,689[5]		—	—
Davenport, Iowa: *Quad City Times*	53,236[5]		—	82,244
Dayton, Ohio: *News*	162,611		—	219,147
Daytona Beach, Fla.: *News-Journal*	104,606		—	124,776
Denver: *Post*	302,125		—	453,032
Rocky Mountain News	336,071		—	449,550
Des Moines, Iowa: *Register*	181,674		—	312,716
Detroit: *Free Press* (M); *News* (E);				
News & Free Press (S)	531,825[5]		354,403[5]	1,107,645
Duluth, Minn.: *News-Tribune*	54,284		—	81,524
Erie, Pa.: *News* (M); *Times* (E); *Times-News* (S)	32,755[5]		62,011[5]	101,769
El Paso, Tex.: *Times* (M & S); *Herald-Post* (E)	67,348[5]		24,081[5]	101,358
Eugene, Ore.: *Register-Guard*	75,770[5]		—	79,861
Evansville, Ind.: *Courier* (M); *Press* (E); *Courier & Press* (S)	62,227		25,739	116,328
Fayetteville, N.C.: *Observer-Times*	70,992[5]		—	84,384
Flint, Mich.: *Journal*	—		100,233	122,670
Fort Lauderdale, Fla.: *Sun-Sentinel*	284,215		—	390,205
Fort Myers, Fla.: *News-Press*	106,088		—	123,277
Fort Wayne, Ind.: *Journal-Gazette* (M & S); *News-Sentinel* (E)	62,428		52,806	137,321
Fort Worth: *Star-Telegram*	—		235,724[4]	350,596
Fresno, Calif.: *Bee*	154,997		—	191,036
Gary, Ind.: *Post-Tribune*	69,839		—	80,947
Grand Rapids, Mich.: *Press*	—		147,175	194,785
Green Bay, Wis.: *Press-Gazette*	—		60,262	87,625
Greensboro, N.C.: *News & Record*	95,679[5]		—	126,817
Greensburg, Pa.: *Tribune-Review*	72,143		—	127,163
Greenville, S.C.: *News* (M); *Piedmont* (E); *News & Piedmont* (S)	100,254[5]		15,376[5]	144,811
Harrisburg, Pa.: *Patriot* (M); *News* (E);				
Patriot-News (S)	65,505[5]		39,994[5]	178,450

City and newspaper	Net paid circulation			
	Morning[2]	All-Day[2]	Evening[2]	Sunday
Hartford, Conn.: *Courant*	229,092		—	317,953
Honolulu: *Advertiser* (M); *Star-Bulletin* (E); *Advertiser* (S)	107,799		79,519	196,003
Houston: *Chronicle*	413,717		—	608,467
Huntsville, Ala.: *News* (M); *Times* (E & S)	16,050[5]		58,568[5]	84,160
Indianapolis: *Star* (M & S); *News* (E)	226,562		83,208	399,583
Jackson, Miss.: *Clarion-Ledger*	112,185		—	131,009
Jacksonville, Fla.: *Times-Union*	200,501		—	257,818
Kalamazoo, Mich.: *Gazette*	—		63,899[5]	81,292
Kansas City, Mo.: *Star* (M & S)	288,295[5]		—	429,337
Knoxville, Tenn.: *News-Sentinel* (M & S)	119,787[4]		—	177,261
Lakeland, Fla.: *Ledger*	87,079		—	106,001
Lancaster, Pa.: *Intelligencer-Journal* (M); *New Era* (E); *News* (S)	44,493		50,705	106,594
Lansing, Mich.: *State-Journal*	72,002		—	95,269
Las Vegas, Nev.: *Review-Journal* (M); *Review–Journal–Sun* (E & S)	148,619[5]		38,904[5]	220,295
Levittown–Bristol–Langhorne, Pa.: *Bucks County Courier-Times* (M & S)	70,513[5]		—	77,224
Lexington, Ky.: *Herald-Leader*	117,652[4]		—	167,699
Lincoln, Neb.: *Star* (M); *Journal* (E); *Journal & Star* (S)	42,977[5]		38,303[5]	85,071
Little Rock, Ark.: *Democrat–Gazette*	178,619		—	296,974
Long Beach, Calif.: *Press-Telegram*	117,819[5]		—	137,006
Long Island (Melville), N.Y.: *Newsday*		669,739[5]	—	745,726
Los Angeles: *Times*	1,058,498[5]		—	1,457,583
Daily News	202,396[5]		—	218,165
Louisville, Ky.: *Courier-Journal*	244,379		—	331,268
Lubbock, Tex.: *Avalanche-Journal*	66,921		—	78,805
Macon, Ga.: *Telegraph*	77,665		—	105,920
Madison, Wis.: *State Journal* (M & S); *Capital Times* (E)	85,745[5]		22,048[5]	164,039
Melbourne, Fla.: *Today*	89,967		—	117,440
Memphis, Tenn.: *Commercial Appeal*	187,222[7]		—	280,317
Miami, Fla.: *Herald*	397,943		—	521,603
Middletown, N.Y.: *Times Herald-Record* (M); *Record* (S)	86,989		—	102,582
Milwaukee: *Sentinel* (M); *Journal* (E & S)	172,453[5]		208,844[5]	483,545
Minneapolis: *Star–Tribune*	404,757		—	695,548
Mobile, Ala.: *Register* (M); *Press* (E); *Press-Register* (S)	73,835[5]		34,904[5]	120,456
Modesto, Calif.: *Bee*	84,536		—	92,453
Montgomery, Ala. *Advertiser* (M); *Journal* (E); *Journal & Advertiser* (S)	63,577		—	77,935
Munster, Ind.: *Times*	72,228		—	78,491
Naperville, Ill.: *Wall Street Journal* (Midwest edition)	489,998[5]		—	—
Nashville, Tenn.: *Tennessean* (M & S); *Banner* (E)	148,247[5]		53,927[5]	285,436
New Haven, Conn.: *Register*	100,241		—	124,584
New Orleans: *Times-Picayune*		267,792[5]	—	321,347
New York: *News*	725,599[5]		—	974,034
Times	1,170,869[5]		—	1,770,504
Post	408,204[5]		—	331,243[8]
Wall Street Journal (Eastern edition)	775,153[5]		—	—
Newark, N.J.: *Star-Ledger*	450,316[5]		—	675,531
Newport News–Hampton, Va.: *Press*	103,966		—	126,547
Norfolk-Portsmouth-Virginia Beach-Chesapeake, Va.: *Virginian-Pilot* (M); *Ledger-Star* (E); *Virginian-Pilot/Ledger-Star* (S)	169,568[5]		35,740[5]	240,667
Oklahoma City: *Oklahoman* (M & S)	221,131[5]		—	318,439
Omaha, Neb.: *World-Herald*	—	238,462[5]	—	294,699
Orange County (Santa Ana), Calif.: *Register*	357,788		—	420,783
Orlando, Fla.: *Sentinel*	—	281,104	—	401,056
Palo Alto, Calif.: *Wall Street Journal* (Western edition)	386,367[5]		—	—
Pensacola, Fla.: *News-Journal*	62,375[5]		—	85,044
Peoria, Ill.: *Journal Star*	—	78,639[5]	—	107,201
Philadelphia: *Inquirer*	470,693[5]		—	919,389
News	200,035[5]		—	104,910[8]
Phoenix, Ariz.: *Republic* (M & S); *Gazette* (E)	399,702		75,872	611,704
Pittsburgh: *Post-Gazette, Sun-Telegraph* (M)	250,427[5]		—	455,716
Pontiac, Mich.: *Oakland Press*	71,077[5]		—	81,297

City and newspaper	Morning[2]	All-Day[2]	Evening[2]	Sunday
Portland, Me.: *Press-Herald*	74,789	—	—	—
Telegram	—		—	140,902
Portland, Or.: *Oregonian*	—	350,452[5]	—	446,296
Providence, R.I.: *Journal Bulletin;* Journal (S)	—	182,866[5]	—	264,321
Quincy, Mass.: *Patriot-Ledger*	—		87,838[5]	102,081[8]
Raleigh, N.C.: *News & Observer* (M & S)	151,840[5]		—	199,645
Reading, Pa.: *Times* (M); *Eagle* (E & S)	49,520[5]		23,804[5]	102,399
Reno, Nev.: *Gazette Journal*	68,976		—	86,976
Richmond, Va.: *Times-Dispatch* (M & S)	214,178		—	257,441
Riverside, Calif.: *Press-Enterprise* (M & S)	167,958		—	175,385
Roanoke, Va.: *Times & World-News*	113,054		—	125,569
Rochester, N.Y.: *Democrat & Chronicle* (M & S); *Times-Union* (E)	144,835[5]		57,777[5]	254,912
Rockford, Ill.: *Register Star*	77,237		—	89,309
Sacramento, Calif.: *Bee*	281,202		—	353,953
St. Louis: *Post-Dispatch*	332,713[5]		—	553,104
St. Paul: *Pioneer Press*	211,223[5]		—	276,540
St. Petersburg, Fla.: *Times*	372,451		—	470,924
Salt Lake City, Utah: *Tribune* (M & S);	125,915		—	159,251
Deseret News (E & S)			63,192	68,470
San Antonio: *Express News*	—	235,002[4]	—	401,895
San Bernardino, Calif.: *Sun*	83,433		—	97,835
San Diego, Calif.: *Union–Tribune*	382,800		—	457,835
Transcript	7,961		—	—
San Francisco: *Chronicle* (M); *Examiner* (E);				
Examiner & Chronicle (S)	499,526[5]		111,323[5]	660,149
San Jose, Calif.: *Mercury-News*	—	290,181[5]	—	354,542
Santa Rosa, Calif.: *Press Democrat*	95,394		—	103,391
Sarasota, Fla.: *Herald-Tribune* (M & S)	127,750		—	157,050
Savannah, Ga.: *News* (M & S); *Press* (E)	55,812[5]		14,335[5]	80,337
Scranton, Pa.: *Tribune* (M); *Times* (E & S)	31,305[5]		41,983[5]	83,231
Seattle: *Post-Intelligencer* (M); *Times* (E); combined (S)	204,905[5]		234,381[5]	507,171
Shreveport, La.: *Times* (M & S)	84,467		—	104,625
Sioux Falls, S.D.: *Argus Leader*	52,588		—	75,216
South Bend-Mishawaka, Ind.: *Tribune*	—		86,756	120,309
Spokane, Wash.: *Spokesman-Review* (M & S)	122,589[5]		—	152,339
Springfield, Ill.: *State Journal-Register*	66,656		—	76,009
Springfield, Mass.: *Union News; Republican* (S)	108,830		—	155,896
Springfield, Mo.: *News-Leader*	64,603		—	104,152
Staten Island, N.Y.: *Advance* (E&S)	—		75,906	93,537
Syracuse, N.Y.: *Post-Standard* (M); *Herald-Journal* (E);				
Herald-American (S)	86,152		77,241	194,799
Tacoma, Wash.: *News-Tribune*	129,589		—	150,212
Tallahassee, Fla.: *Democrat*	58,093		—	79,999
Tampa, Fla.: *Tribune* (M); *Tribune & Times* (S)	279,561		—	378,322
Toledo, Ohio: *Blade*	147,093		—	203,161
Trenton, N.J.: *Times* (M&S)	86,772		—	97,502
Trentonian (M & S)	73,352[5]		—	58,620
Tucson, Ariz.: *Star* (M & S); *Citizen* (E)	102,960		49,158	187,003
Tulsa, Okla.: *World* (M & S)	173,398		—	237,145
Walnut Creek, Calif.: *Contra Costa Times*	96,335		—	108,762
Washington, D.C.: *Post*	840,232[5]		—	1,153,822
Times	99,364[5]		—	66,326
USA Today	1,570,624[4]		—	1,979,092[10]
Waterbury, Conn.: *Republican–American* (M);				
Republican (S)	60,887		—	75,872
West Palm Beach, Fla.: *Post*	187,518		—	236,965
Wichita, Kan.: *Eagle*	111,317		—	189,643
Wilmington, Del.: *News Journal*	—	126,164	—	149,727
Winston-Salem, N.C.: *Journal*	90,420		—	102,698
Worcester, Mass.: *Telegram Gazette; Telegraph* (S)	111,470		—	141,896
York, Pa.: *Record* (M); *Dispatch* (E); *News* (S)	41,876[5]		40,273[5]	91,460
Youngstown, Ohio: *Vindicator*			86,117	128,016

1. Listing is of cities in which any one edition of a newspaper exceeds an average net paid circulation of 75,000; newspapers of smaller circulation in those cities are also included. 2. Unless otherwise indicated, figures are average Monday-through-Saturday circulation for six-month period ending March 31, 1995. 3. Average Monday through Thursday and Saturday. 4. Monday through Thursday. 5. Monday through Friday. 6. Week-end edition. 7. Monday, Tuesday and Thursday. 8. Saturday. 9. Tuesday through Saturday. 10. Friday morning. *Source:* Audit Bureau of Circulations.

English Language Daily and Sunday U.S. Newspapers

(number of newspapers as of Feb. 1, 1995; circulation as reported for Sept. 30, 1994)

State	Morning papers and circulation		Evening papers and circulation		Total M and E and circulation		Sunday papers and circulation	
Alabama	17	345,279	9	404,772	26	750,051	19	770,875
Alaska	5	101,310	2	10,122	7	111,432	4	129,843
Arizona	10	548,530	13	236,349	23	784,879	17	925,451
Arkansas	12	349,343	19	114,699	31	464,042	16	510,843
California[1]	66	5,189,250	37	997,510	101	6,186,760	65	6,530,267
Colorado	14	909,023	14	141,545	28	1,050,568	11	1,239,124
Connecticut[1]	13	666,404	9	155,389	19	821,790	12	844,838
Delaware[1]	3	87,713	1	62,871	3	150,584	2	182,720
District of Columbia	2	905,201	0	0	2	905,201	2	1,206,622
Florida[1]	33	2,920,911	8	198,738	40	3,119,649	35	3,997,910
Georgia	16	735,100	18	347,935	34	1,083,035	19	1,324,716
Hawaii	3	134,387	3	106,143	6	240,530	5	261,311
Idaho	7	141,446	5	78,719	12	220,165	8	237,058
Illinois[1]	18	1,866,072	51	658,723	68	2,524,795	28	2,696,205
Indiana	16	715,785	57	762,497	73	1,478,282	22	1,355,052
Iowa	13	451,552	25	241,835	38	693,387	10	712,964
Kansas	7	273,375	40	228,580	47	501,955	16	458,731
Kentucky	8	460,510	15	196,643	23	657,153	12	686,119
Louisiana[1]	12	503,398	14	247,256	25	750,654	20	861,846
Maine	5	235,810	2	25,388	7	261,198	2	191,795
Maryland	10	459,085	5	173,909	15	632,994	7	676,805
Massachusetts[2]	10	1,261,636	29	609,910	39	1,871,546	14	1,760,883
Michigan	10	724,786	41	1,359,293	51	2,084,079	27	2,376,106
Minnesota	14	803,606	11	139,107	25	942,713	14	1,189,155
Mississippi	6	218,465	16	187,913	22	406,378	15	388,425
Missouri	11	811,922	34	226,572	45	1,038,494	21	1,329,583
Montana	6	154,563	5	41,014	11	195,577	7	201,863
Nebraska[1]	5	212,905	14	258,251	18	471,155	7	444,063
Nevada	4	221,943	4	53,616	8	275,559	4	309,359
New Hampshire[1]	8	141,204	5	102,445	12	243,649	6	200,407
New Jersey	14	1,286,467	7	280,875	21	1,567,342	17	1,887,067
New Mexico	7	203,402	11	103,065	18	306,467	13	301,301
New York[1, 2]	27	5,528,255	46	1,230,685	70	6,758,940	43	5,583,199
North Carolina	18	1,002,872	31	400,596	49	1,403,468	37	1,520,487
North Dakota	7	170,685	3	13,709	10	184,394	7	187,654
Ohio	17	1,630,400	67	1,034,189	84	2,664,589	36	2,891,971
Oklahoma	10	472,090	35	217,665	45	689,755	40	862,099
Oregon[1]	5	319,155	15	365,431	19	684,586	10	701,119
Pennsylvania[1]	41	2,175,658	48	905,051	88	3,080,709	38	3,335,787
Rhode Island[1]	3	143,483	4	131,626	6	275,109	3	305,341
South Carolina	11	587,696	5	76,494	16	664,190	14	765,832
South Dakota	5	126,482	6	43,454	11	169,936	4	139,972
Tennessee[1]	11	637,999	17	282,320	27	920,319	16	1,113,766
Texas[1]	37	2,556,151	56	622,833	91	3,178,982	85	4,240,610
Utah	1	125,037	5	189,289	6	314,326	6	359,147
Vermont	4	96,195	4	33,336	8	129,531	3	105,660
Virginia[1, 2]	17	2,287,883	13	257,000	28	2,544,882	15	1,007,917
Washington	10	692,563	14	507,752	24	1,200,315	16	1,290,044
West Virginia	10	251,797	13	160,588	23	412,385	11	402,531
Wisconsin	10	465,867	26	680,944	36	1,146,811	21	1,224,020
Wyoming	6	70,927	3	19,219	9	90,146	4	68,336
Totals	**635**	**43,381,578**	**935**	**15,923,865**	**1,548**	**59,305,436**	**886**	**62,294,799**
Total, U.S., Sept. 30, 1993	623	43,093,866	954	16,717,737	1,556	59,811,584	884	62,565,574
Total U.S., Sept. 30, 1992	596	42,387,813	996	17,776,686	1,570	60,164,499	891	62,159,971
Total U.S., Sept. 30, 1991	571	41,469,756	1,042	19,217,369	1,586	60,687,125	875	62,067,820
Total U.S., Sept. 30, 1990	559	41,311,167	1,084	21,016,795	1,611	62,327,962	863	62,634,512
Total U.S., Sept. 30, 1989	530	40,759,016	1,125	21,890,202	1,626	62,649,218	847	62,008,154
Total U.S., Sept. 30, 1988	520	40,452,815	1,141	22,242,001	1,642	62,694,816	840	61,474,189
Total U.S., Sept. 30, 1987	511	39,123,807	1,166	23,702,466	1,645	62,826,273	820	60,111,863
Total U.S., Sept. 30, 1986	499	37,441,125	1,188	25,060,911	1,657	62,502,036	802	58,924,518
Total U.S., Sept. 30, 1985	482	36,361,561	1,220	26,404,671	1,676	62,766,232	798	58,825,978

1. "All-day" newspapers are listed in morning and evening columns but only once in the total, and their circulations are divided between morning and evening figures. Adjustments have been made in state and U.S. total figures. 2. Includes nationally circulated daily. Circulation counted only in the state indicated. *Source: Editor and Publisher International Yearbook, 1995.*

See the Entertainment and Culture section for additional Media information.

SPACE

DC–X Confirms Reusable Space Transportation

The McDonnell Douglas Delta Clipper Experimental (DC-X) is a one-third-size experimental vehicle that is being developed under contract for the Ballistic Missile Defense Organization's (BMDO) single-stage rocket technology (SSRT) program.

The *Clipper* differs radically from the space shuttle in that it is a reusable single-stage-to-orbit spacecraft. This means that it can take off and land with the same vehicle in a manner similar to aircraft, the take-offs and landings are performed vertically, it can be operated with or without a crew, and can remain in orbit for seven to fourteen days. Its advanced engineering design gives it the capability to abort a launch and return safely to base even if its engines fail. It is a totally new spacecraft design and it will greatly reduce the cost of going into space.

The DC–X made five successful vertical takeoffs and landing tests between August 1993 and June 1994 at the U.S. Army's White Sands Missile Range in New Mexico. During the fifth flight test on June 27, 1994, an external detonation of fuel cloud vapors caused by the ground support equipment damaged the spacecraft. Testing was resumed on May 16, 1995, and several more tests are planned for the remainder of 1995.

At the conclusion of the 1995 flight tests, McDonnell Douglas will integrate key advanced technology components into the experimental vehicle under a series of cooperative agreements awarded by NASA. Flight tests will continue in an upgraded vehicle called the DC–XA, scheduled for 1996.

The spacecraft is named "Delta" after the famous Thor/Delta launch vehicle and "Clipper" after the renowned Yankee Clipper ships that opened the sea trade routes more than two centuries ago. ☐

NASA's X–33

The X–33 experimental rocket project is a joint NASA/industry program to develop the technology required for a commercially operated fully reusable launch vehicle (RLV) capable of low-cost jetliner-like operations. NASA is studying competitive designs under agreements with three U.S. industry teams. The X–33 will be an unpiloted vehicle that will demonstrate the feasibility of building a single-stage rocket to replace the space shuttle early in the next century.

McDonnell Douglas, the leading U.S. defense contractor, and Boeing Company, the largest manufacturer of commercial jetliners in the world, are one of the industry teams entered in the intense competition to build the RLV and they are patterning their design after the successful DC–X rocket concept—a single-stage, vertical-lift, vertical landing spaceship.

Other companies selected by NASA to submit proposals for the X–33 design are Rockwell International and Lockheed. Lockheed has proposed a wingless, flat-bottomed rocket that would take off vertically and land horizontally, and Rockwell has proposed a winged ship that would also lift off vertically and land similar to the space shuttle.

NASA will choose an X–33 team in July 1996 to test the feasibility of replacing the shuttle with a new design and a joint government/industry decision is expected in 1999 as to whether to proceed with an operational reusable launch vehicle. A smaller two-stage reusable launch vehicle, the X–34, is scheduled to fly in late 1997. The X–34 will test the feasibility of launching small scientific and commercial satellites on a cost-saving reusable rocket. ☐

Space Station Alpha

Construction of a new space station nicknamed *Alpha* is scheduled to being in November 1997 with Russia as a partner. The former space station name *Freedom* was officially dropped by NASA.

The multinational space station design will utilize a modular build-up approach that will use existing flight-proven hardware as well as cost-effective designs from the former space station *Freedom* systems. The Johnson Space Center in Houston is the host center for *Alpha* and the Boeing Defense and Space Group is the prime contractor. Some of the components will come from parts originally intended for Russia's planned second generation *Mir-2* space station.

The crew-occupied modules will be rearranged to accommodate Russian hardware and the space station's orbit was also changed to accommodate Russian high-altitude launch sites.

The first phase of the joint program started on February 3, 1995, when the space shuttle *Discovery* made a close approach rendezvous with the *Mir*. On June 29, 1995, the shuttle *Atlantis* docked with the *Mir* for the first time. Additional docking missions are planned over a three-year period to test procedures and equipment for the new space station. The Space Shuttle will also assist with crew exchange, resupply, and payload activities for *Mir*.

During the second phase, Russia will launch a core module in May 1997, and nine American and Russian launches will bring additional hardware. Finally, the U.S. will develop a human-tended facility connected to the *Mir* module by December 1997.

During the third and last expansion phase, European and Japanese modules will be added along with supporting hardware. The space station will be completed and permanently manned with six crew members in June 2002.

The United States agreed to pay Russia $100 million each year through 1997 for access to *Mir*. It is believed that the Russian involvement will save the United States two to four billion dollars. ☐

Mars Pathfinder Mission

NASA's Mars Pathfinder Project will place a lander and a small six-wheeled robotic rover on the surface of Mars in July 1997. The spacecraft is being built at the Jet Propulsion Laboratory (JPL) in Pasadena, California.

The Pathfinder will be launched on a Delta–2 rocket in November 1996 and fly directly to Mars, enter its atmosphere, and land without first going into orbit around the planet. During its descent to the surface with the aid of parachutes, rockets, and airbags, the spacecraft will study the planet's atmospheric gases. After landing, the Pathfinder will deploy the rover to explore the ancient sediment-covered *Ares Vallis* floodplain.

The small rover weighs 22 lb (10 kg), is 10.9 inches (280 mm) high with a ground clearance of 5 inches (130 mm). It is 24.5 inches (630 mm) long and 18.7 inches (480 mm) wide. Three solar panels will provide the necessary power; however it will also have batteries. The rover will carry an X-ray spectrometer to determine soil composition.

The rover is technically named the Micro-rover Flight Experiment or MFEX. Although the information gained from the rover's technology experiments such as soil mechanics are of scientific interest, the rover's main science objectives are to deploy an alpha-proton-X-ray spectrometer (APXS) and take close-up images of Martian features. The APXS is provided by the Max Planck Institute of Mains, Germany, and the University of Chicago.

The APXS will be placed against a rock, collect a spectrum of the rock to determine its composition, and then transmit the spectrum to the lander for return to earth. A full APXS measurement of a rock requires ten hours. The microrover will also take black and white pictures of any rock on which the APXS is used.

The rover is controlled by an Earth-based operator, but because of the time delay between Earth and Mars (variously from six to 41 minutes), some autonomy is needed in the rover. The operator on Earth will view the work station with a stereo display of the lander's image of the terrain through three-dimensional glasses.   □

ULYSSES

Ulysses is an international project to study the poles of the Sun and interstellar space above and below the poles. The 814-lb (370-kg) spacecraft will be put into an orbit at right angles to the solar system's ecliptic plane. (The ecliptic is the plane in which the Earth and most of the planets orbit the Sun.) This special orbit will allow the spacecraft to examine for the first time the regions of the Sun's north and south poles. Besides examining the Sun's energy fields, instruments on *Ulysses* will study other phenomena from the Milky Way and beyond.

While scientists have studied the Sun for centuries, they know very little about matter reaching the solar system from other nearby stars. This is because particles reaching the Sun's magnetic field from beyond the solar system are greatly changed by the Sun's magnetic field and by collision with particles flowing outward from the Sun. No spacecraft has ever left the solar system to make actual measurements of the interstellar medium.

The *Ulysses* spacecraft was launched from the space shuttle *Discovery* on Oct. 6, 1990, reached the Sun's south pole in Septemebr 1994, and completed its pass in November. The spacecraft found that the Sun appears to have a south magnetic pole. A second encounter will take place when it passes over the Sun's north pole in October 1995. Afterwards, *Ulysses* will continue to orbit the Sun and will pass over the north and south poles again in 2000 and 2001.

On Feb. 8, 1992, *Ulysses* flew past Jupiter at 61,249 mph, using the planet's gravity as a slingshot to send it toward the Sun. During the flyby (Jan. 31–Feb. 16, 1992), the spacecraft studied unexplored portions of Jupiter's huge magnetic field.

THE CASSINI MISSION

The ringed planet Saturn, its major moon Titan, and a complex system of at least 18 other satellites[1] will be the destinations for NASA's and the European Space Agency's Cassini Mission. Cassini is named for the Italian-French astronomer, Gian Domenico Cassini (1625–1712), who discovered four of Saturn's major moons and a dark, narrow gap ("Cassini's Division") splitting the planet's rings.

The mission to Saturn is scheduled for launch on Oct. 6, 1997. Cassini is to arrive at Saturn in June 2004. The cost of the mission is approximately $1.9 billion.

Early during the spacecraft's four-year tour orbiting Saturn, it will launch a parachuted probe descending through Titan's dense atmosphere to the surface of the satellite which has unique organic-like chemistry that could provide clues to the origin of life on Earth.

In order to reach Saturn, Cassini will first execute flybys of the Earth and Jupiter to gain "gravity assist" boosts in velocity to send it on its way. The first flyby of Earth will take place 26 months after launch, followed by the Jupiter flyby some 19 months later. During the first leg of its trip, before its first Earth flyby, Cassini will navigate through part of the asteroid belt and could perform an encounter with the asteroid Maja. Maja is a carbonaceous, or "C" type asteroid about 50 miles (78 kilometers) in diameter. Two small asteroids are being considered as possible additional targets, but only one of them can be visited.

The spacecraft's final encounter before proceeding to Saturn will be with Jupiter, which it will pass at a distance of about 2.2 million miles (3.6 million kilometers). Its flight path will take it for 130 days down through a region that no spacecraft has explored more than briefly—the giant planet's magnetotail. Cassini will fly down the magnetotail[2] of Jupiter, performing studies complementing the Galileo mission to Jupiter.

Upon reaching Saturn, the spacecraft will begin the first of some three dozen highly elliptical orbits during the remainder of its mission. Eighty-five days later, it will release its probe to Titan. Eleven days later, the probe will enter Titan's dense atmosphere and descend to the surface by parachute.

The $260-million probe is called *Huygens* after the famous Dutch astronomer Christiaan Huygens (1629–1695) who was the first to correctly interpret the rings of Saturn. He was also the discoverer of Saturn's largest satellite, *Titan*.

Because of the dense atmosphere shrouding the moon Titan, little is known of its surface. Scientists hope to gain a better understanding of the abundances of elements and compounds in its atmosphere, winds, and temperatures, and its surface state and composition.

After relaying to Earth data from the Titan probe's experiments, Cassini will continue with orbits of Saturn and flybys of most of the planet's 16 or more moons. In addition to 36 close encounters with Titan, the spacecraft's orbits will allow it to study Saturn's polar regions after examining the planet's equatorial zone.   □

---

1. The International Astronomical Union has officially recognized 18 Saturnian moons. Photographs from *Voyager* flybys suggest that others may exist. 2. A tube of Jupiter's energy field, which trails away from the sun for several million miles.

GALILEO

Galileo is a project to orbit Jupiter and send an instrumented probe into the giant planet's atmosphere. The Galileo mission will allow scientists to study—at close range and for almost two years—the largest planet in the solar system, its satellites and massive energy field.

The Dawning of the Space Age

On Oct. 4, 1957, the Soviet Union put the world's first artificial satellite, *Sputnik I*, into Earth orbit and ushered in the modern space age. *Sputnik* ("traveling companion") was spherical in shape with four antennas about 8 to 9 feet in length, 23 inches in diameter, and weighed 183.4 pounds. It circled the globe every 96 minutes at a speed of 18,000 miles per hour for 92 days until Jan. 4, 1958, when it re-entered the atmosphere and burned up.

Sputnik I orbited the Earth between 156 miles at its perigee (low point) and 560 miles at its apogee (high point). Its two radio transmitters marked the first time in history that man-made radio signals were sent from space to the Earth.

A month later on Nov. 3, 1957, the Soviet Union launched *Sputnik II*, the world's first satellite put into orbit with an animal housed aboard, an 11 lb mongrel dog named *Laika* ("barker"). She died a week later after the oxygen supply ran out. The satellite carried more sophisticated instrumentation, weighed 1,120 lbs and circled the Earth every 103.7 minutes. Its orbit was approximately 145 miles at its perigee and 1,056 miles at its apogee. The satellite burned up after being in orbit for 162 days.

The spacecraft will study the chemical composition and physical state of Jupiter's atmosphere and the four moons, as well as the structure and dynamics of the Jovian magnetosphere.

The spacecraft was carried aloft by the space shuttle *Atlantis* and launched toward Jupiter on Oct. 18, 1989. After a six-year journey, it will reach the planet Dec. 7, 1995 and will release a probe into the planet's atmosphere.

On Oct. 29, 1991, Galileo took a historic photograph of asteroid 951 *Gaspera* from a distance of 10,000 miles (16,200 kilometers). It was the first close-up photo ever taken of an asteroid in space. Galileo encountered Asteroid 243 *Ida* on Aug. 28, 1993 and took first close up photos which revealed that *Ida* had a tiny moon.

Near-Earth Asteroid Rendezvous Mission (NEAR)

The NEAR spacecraft will be launched in February 1996; its main mission is to rendezvous with the near-Earth asteroid *Eros* in February 1999. The NEAR is the first of NASA's Discovery series of low-cost spacecraft, costing $122 million. The satellite will be placed in an orbit that will take it through the asteroid belt, back to Earth for a gravity assist, and then on to *Eros*.

Scientists would also like to have the NEAR pass within 750 miles (1,200 km) of the asteroid 253 Mathilde in June 1997.

Is There Ice on the Moon?

Unlike the rest of the Moon's surface, the temperature of its polar regions remains permanently about −390° to −315° F and some of its craters remain perpetually in the dark. Some scientists have speculated that ice may have accumulated in the dark craters over long eons of time.

The Lunar Prospector

NASA is planning on sending a small spacecraft to fly in a low-altitude orbit around the Moon. The mission, known as *Lunar Prospector*, is scheduled for launch in June 1997 and will last for at least one year. The $55-million *Prospector* will map the chemical composition of the lunar surface and the Moon's global magnetic and gravity fields at a level of detail greater than that achieved by previous missions. It will also detect traces of gases escaping from the lunar surface. The mission also should locate any significant quantities of frozen water in shadowed craters near the lunar poles. The presence of ice would be of great importance for any future human habitation on the Moon.

The *Lunar Prospector* will be built and launched on a Lockheed Launch Vehicle by Lockheed Missiles and Space Company of Sunnyvale, California.

The Mars Balloon

The original Mars program called for two launches, one in October 1994 for arrival in September 1995 and the other in 1996. During the first mission, the spacecraft will drop one or two balloons which will carry several scientific packages for analyzing Martian meteorological and surface conditions over a wide range of the planet.

The Mars mission program has encountered many delays, and one launch is scheduled for late 1996 and the other for late 1998. Russian financial problems have hampered the project. If additional delays occur, the next launch date will be in 2001.

The balloon segment of the mission is a joint undertaking by Russia, France, and the United States, which has greatly benefitted from the successful balloon deployed at Venus in 1985 under the Soviet VEGA program.

The balloon will carry both a suspended payload (gondola) and a distributed payload (SNAKE) which will come into contact with the planet's surface as the balloon descends during the Martian night. The SNAKE will carry its own instruments to investigate the Martian surface. The sun's light will heat the gases within the lightweight balloon during the daytime, causing the balloon to rise and drift with the winds above the planet's surface. At night, the gases will cool, causing the balloon to descend and rest on the Martian soil.

The French Space Agency, The Centre National d'Etudes Spatials (CENES) is building the balloon that will carry the SNAKE.

The total mass of the balloon system is targeted for 60 to 65 kilograms (130 to 134 pounds). The gondola will weigh about 15 kilograms (33 pounds).

Mars Global Surveyor

There has been a need to follow up in greater detail on what was learned from the Viking mission to Mars in 1976. The *Mars Global Surveyor* will be a polar-orbiting spacecraft at Mars designed to provide global maps of the planet's surface topography, distribution of minerals, and monitoring of the Martian weather.

The spacecraft will be launched with a Delta II expendable vehicle from Cape Canaveral, Florida, in November 1996, and will cruise 10 months to Mars, where it initially will be inserted into an elliptical capture orbit. During the following four months, thruster firings and aerobraking techniques will be used to reach the nearly circular mapping orbit over the Martian polar caps. Mapping operations are expected to begin in late January 1998.

The spacecraft will circle Mars once every two hours, maintaining a "sun synchronous" orbit that will put the sun at a standard angle above the horizon in each image and allow the mid-afternoon lighting to cast shadows in such a way that surface features will stand out.

The *Mars Global Surveyor* will carry a portion of the *Mars Observer* instrument payload and will use these instruments to acquire data of Mars for a full Martian year, the equivalent of about two Earth years. The spacecraft will then be used as a data relay station for signals from U.S. and international landers and low-altitude probes for an additional three years.

The *Mars Global Surveyor* is the first mission of a new decade-long program of robotic exploration of Mars, called the *Mars Surveyor Program.* This will be an aggressive series of orbiters and landers to be launched every 26 months, as Mars moves into alignment with Earth. International participation, collaboration, and coordination will enhance all missions of the program.

Landers in future years—1998, 2001, 2003, and 2005—will capitalize on the experience of the *Mars Pathfinder* lander mission to be launched in 1996. Small orbiters launched in the 1998 and 2003 opportunities will carry other instruments from the *Mars Observer* payload and will serve as data relay stations for international missions of the future. □

U.S. Unmanned Planetary and Lunar Programs

Lunar Orbiter. Series of spacecraft designed to orbit the Moon, taking pictures and obtaining data in support of the subsequent manned Apollo landings. The U.S. launched five *Lunar Orbiters* between Aug. 10, 1966 and Aug. 2, 1967.

Mariner. Designation for a series of spacecraft designed to fly past or orbit the planets, particularly Mercury, Venus, and Mars. *Mariners* provided the early information on Venus and Mars. *Mariner 9,* orbiting Mars in 1971, returned the most startling photographs of that planet and helped pave the way for a *Viking* landing in 1976. *Mariner 10* explored Venus and Mercury in 1973 and was the first probe to use a planet's gravity to whip it toward another.

Pioneer. Designation for the United States' first series of sophisticated interplanetary spacecraft. *Pioneers 10* and *11* reached Jupiter in 1973 and 1974 and continued on to explore Saturn and the other outer planets. *Pioneer 11,* renamed *Pioneer Saturn,* examined the Saturn system in September 1979. Significant discoveries were the finding of a small new moon and a narrow new ring. In 1986, *Pioneer 10* was the first man-made object to escape the solar system. *Pioneer Venus 1* and *2* reached Venus in 1978

First U.S. Satellite

The first successful U.S. satellite, *Explorer I,* was launched into Earth orbit by the Army on January 31, 1958, at Cape Canaveral, Florida, four months after Russia orbited *Sputnik.* The 18-pound satellite had a cylindrical shape and was 80 inches long and six inches in diameter.

Explorer I's small package of instruments produced the first major discovery of the Space Age—The Van Allen radiation belts surrounding the Earth. *Explorer I* burned up in the atmosphere on March 30, 1970.

---

and provided detailed information about that planet's surface and atmosphere.

Ranger. NASA's earliest Moon exploration program. Spacecraft were designed for a crash landing on the Moon, taking pictures and returning scientific data up to the moment of impact. Provided the first closeup views of the lunar surface. The *Rangers* provided more than 17,000 closeup pictures, giving us more information about the Moon in a few years than in all the time that had gone before.

Surveyor. Series of unmanned spacecraft designed to land gently on the Moon and provide information on the surface in preparation for the manned lunar landings. Their legs were instrumented to return data on the surface hardness of the Moon. *Surveyor* dispelled the fear that Apollo spacecraft might sink several feet or more into the lunar dust.

Viking. Designation for two spacecraft designed to conduct detailed scientific examination of the planet Mars, including a search for life. *Viking 1* landed on July 20, 1976; *Viking 2,* Sept. 3, 1976. More was learned about the Red Planet in a few short months than in all the time that had gone before. But the question of life on Mars remains unresolved.

Voyager. Designation for two spacecraft designed to explore Jupiter and the other outer planets. *Voyager 1* and *Voyager 2* passed Jupiter in 1979 and sent back startling color TV images of that planet and its moons. They took a total of about 33,000 pictures. *Voyager 1* passed Saturn November 1980. *Voyager 2* passed Saturn August 1981 and Uranus in January 1986.

It encountered Neptune on August 29, 1989 and made many startling discoveries. Found four rings around the planet, six new moons, a Giant Spot, and evidence of volcanic-like activity on its largest moon, Triton. The spacecraft sent back over 9,000 pictures of the planet and its system.

On February 13, 1990, at a distance of 3.7 billion miles, *Voyager 1* took its final pictures—the Sun and six of its planets as seen from deep space. NASA released the extraordinary images to the public on June 6, 1990. Only Mercury, Mars, and Pluto were not seen.

Notable Unmanned Lunar and Interplanetary Probes

Spacecraft	Launch date	Destination	Remarks
Pioneer 3 (U.S.)	Dec. 6, 1958	Moon	Max. alt.: 66,654 mi. Discovered outer Van Allen layer.
Luna 2 (U.S.S.R.)	Sept. 12, 1959	Moon	Impacted on Sept. 14. First space vehicle to reach moon.
Luna 3 (U.S.S.R.)	Oct. 4, 1959	Moon	Flew around Moon and transmitted first pictures of lunar far side, Oct. 7.
Mariner 2 (U.S.)	Aug. 27, 1962	Venus	Venus probe. Successful mid-course correction. Passed 21,648 mi. from Venus Dec. 14, 1962. Reported 800°F. surface temp. Contact lost Jan. 3, 1963 at 54 million mi.

Spacecraft	Launch date	Destination	Remarks
Mariner 4 (U.S.)	Nov. 28, 1964	Mars	Transmitted first close-up pictures on June 14, 1965, from altitude of 6,000 mi.
Ranger 7 (U.S.)	July 28, 1964	Moon	Impacted near Crater Guericke 68.5 h after launch. Sent 4,316 pictures during last 15 min of flight as close as 1,000 ft above lunar surface.
Luna 9 (U.S.S.R.)	Jan. 31, 1966	Moon	3,428 lb. Instrument capsule of 220 lb soft-landed Feb. 3, 1966. Sent back about 30 pictures.
Surveyor 1 (U.S.)	May 30, 1966	Moon	Landed June 2, 1966. Sent almost 10,400 pictures, a number after surviving the 14-day lunar night.
Lunar Orbiter 1 (U.S.)	Aug. 10, 1966	Moon	Orbited Moon Aug. 14. 21 pictures sent.
Surveyor 3 (U.S.)	April 17, 1967	Moon	Soft-landed 65 h after launch on Oceanus Procellarum. Scooped and tested lunar soil.
Venera 4 (U.S.S.R.)	June 12, 1967	Venus	Arrived Oct. 17. Instrument capsule sent temperature and chemical data.
Surveyor 5 (U.S.)	Sept. 8, 1967	Moon	Landed near lunar equator Sept. 10. Radiological analysis of lunar soil. Mechanical claw for digging soil.
Surveyor 7 (U.S.)	Jan. 6, 1968	Moon	Landed near Crater Tycho Jan. 10. Soil analysis. Sent 3,343 pictures.
Pioneer 9 (U.S.)	Nov. 8, 1968	Sun Orbit	Achieved orbit. Six experiments returned solar radiation data.
Venera 5 (U.S.S.R.)	Jan. 5, 1969	Venus	Landed May 16, 1969. Returned atmospheric data.
Mariner 6 (U.S.)	Feb. 24, 1969	Mars	Came within 2000 mi. of Mars July 31, 1969. Sent back data & TV pictures.
Luna 16 (U.S.S.R.)	Sept. 12, 1970	Moon	Soft-landed Sept. 20, scooped up rock, returned to Earth Sept. 24.
Luna 17 (U.S.S.R.)	Nov. 10, 1970	Moon	Soft-landed on Sea of Rains Nov. 17. Lunokhod 1, self-propelled vehicle, used for first time. Sent TV photos, made soil analysis, etc.
Mariner 9 (U.S.)	May 30, 1971	Mars	First craft to orbit Mars, Nov. 13. 7,300 pictures, 1st close-ups of Mars' moon. Transmission ended Oct. 27, 1972.
Luna 20 (U.S.S.R.)	Feb. 14, 1972	Moon	Soft-landed Feb. 21 in Sea of Fertility. Returned Feb. 25 with rock samples.
Pioneer 10 (U.S.)	March 3, 1972	Jupiter	620-million-mile flight path through asteroid belt passed Jupiter Dec. 3, 1973, to give man first closeup of planet. In 1986, it became first man-made object to escape solar system.
Luna 21 (U.S.S.R.)	Jan. 8, 1973	Moon	Soft-landed Jan. 16. Lunokhod 2 (moon-car) scooped up soil samples, returned them to Earth Jan. 27.
Mariner 10 (U.S.)	Nov. 3, 1973	Venus, Mercury	Passed Venus Feb. 5, 1974. Arrived Mercury March 29, 1974, for man's first closeup look at planet. First time gravity of one planet (Venus) used to whip spacecraft toward another (Mercury).
Viking 1 (U.S.)	Aug. 20, 1975	Mars	Carrying life-detection labs. Landed July 20, 1976, for detailed scientific research, including pictures. Designed to work for only 90 days, it operated for almost 6 1/2 years before it went silent in November 1982.
Viking 2 (U.S .)	Sept. 9, 1975	Mars	Like Viking 1. Landed Sept. 3, 1976. Functioned 3 1/2 years.
Luna 24 (U.S.S.R.)	Aug. 9, 1976	Moon	Soft-landed Aug. 18, 1976. Returned soil samples Aug. 22, 1976.
Voyager 1 (U.S.)[2]	Sept. 5, 1977	Jupiter, Saturn	Fly-by mission. Reached Jupiter in March 1979; passed Saturn Nov. 1980; passed Uranus 1986.
Voyager 2 (U.S.)[2]	Aug. 20, 1977	Jupiter, Saturn, Uranus	Launched before *Voyager 1*. Encountered Jupiter in July 1979; flew by Saturn Aug. 1981; passed Uranus January 1986; and passed Neptune in August 1989.
Pioneer Venus 1 (U.S.)	May 20, 1978	Venus	Arrived Dec. 4 and orbited Venus, photographing surface and atmosphere. Crashed into planet's surface mid-October 1992 after circling Venus for 14 years.
Pioneer Venus 2 (U.S.)	Aug. 8, 1978	Venus	Four-part multi-probe, landed Dec. 9.
Venera 13 (U.S.S.R.)	Oct. 30, 1981	Venus	Landed March 1, 1982. Took first X-ray fluorescence analysis of the planet's surface. Transmitted data 2 hours 7 minutes.
VEGA 1 (U.S.S.R.)	Deployed on Venus, June 10, 1985	Encounter with Halley's comet	In flyby over Venus while enroute to encounter with Halley's Comet, VEGA 1 and 2 dropped scientific capsules onto Venus to study atmosphere and surface material. Encountered Halley's Comet on March 6 and March 9, 1986. Took TV pictures and studied comet's dust particles.
VEGA 2 (U.S.S.R.)	Deployed on Venus, June 14, 1985		
Suisei (Japan)	Encountered Halley's Comet March 8, 1986	Halley's Comet	Spacecraft made fly-by of comet and studied atmosphere with ultraviolet camera. Observed rotation nucleus.
Sakigake (Japan)	Encountered Halley's Comet March 10, 1986	Halley's Comet	Spacecraft made fly-by to study solar wind and magnetic fields. Detected plasma waves.

Spacecraft	Launch date	Destination	Remarks
Giotto (ESA)	Encountered Halley's Comet March 13, 1986	Halley's Comet	European Space Agency spacecraft made closest approach to comet. Studied atmosphere and magnetic fields. Sent back best pictures of nucleus. Flew by comet Grigg-Skjellerup, July 10, 1992. Unable to send pictures.
Phobos Mission (U.S.S.R.)	July 7 and July 12, 1988	Mars and Phobos	Two spacecraft to probe Martian moon Phobos starting April 1989. Were to study orbit, soil chemistry, send TV pictures and data of planet. Contact was lost with Phobos 1 in August 1988 and later with Phobos 2 in March 1989 after it reached the Martian moon.
Magellan (U.S.)	May 4, 1989	Venus	Arrived at Venus on Aug. 10, 1990 and made a geologic map of planet with a powerful radar. Crashed into Venus Oct. 12, 1994.
Galileo (U.S.)	Oct. 18, 1989	Jupiter	To study Jupiter's atmosphere and its moons during 22-month mission. It will reach the planet in 1995.
Hubble Space Telescope (U.S., E.S.A.)[1]	April 25, 1990	Earth Orbit	Studies distant stars and galaxies and searches for evidence of planets in other solar systems. Crew of Endeavour STS-61 repaired telescope Dec. 2–13, 1993.
Ulysses (U.S., ESA)	Oct. 6, 1990	The Sun	To study the poles of the Sun and interstellar space above and below the poles. First solar encounter to be in 1994. Second encounter to be in 1995.
Gamma-Ray whole Observatory (U.S.)	April 7, 1991	Earth Orbit	To make first survey of gamma ray sources across the sky, studying explosive energic sources such as supernovae, quasars, neutron stars, pulsars, and black holes.
Mars Observer (U.S.)	Sept. 25, 1992	Mars	Spacecraft to arrive at Mars Aug. 1993 and orbit the planet for one full Martian year to study atmosphere and surface change during the planet's seasons. Mission failed after communications with *Observer* lost August 21, 1993.
Clementine (U.S.)	Jan. 25, 1994	Moon and asteroid Geographos 1620	Entered lunar orbit February 21 and took close-up photos of lunar surface for two months. Computer malfunction prevented planned rendezvous with *Geographos*.
Mars '96/'98 (Russia)	1996[1]	Mars	Two spacecraft to study Mars over an 18-month period. Will investigate Martian surface and deploy a balloon-borne package during second mission to study the planet's atmosphere.

1. European Space Agency (E.S.A.), responsible for furnishing the solar arrays, the Faint Object Camera, and participation in flight operations aspects of the mission. 2. The two *Voyager* spacecraft continue to explore and send data back to Earth.

U.S. Manned Space Flights

Mercury. *Project Mercury,* initiated in 1958 and completed in 1963, was the United States' first man-in-space program. It was designed to further knowledge about man's capabilities in space.

In April 1959, seven military jet test pilots were introduced to the public as America's first astronauts. They were: Lt. M. Scott Carpenter, USN; Capt. L. Gordon Cooper, Jr., USAF; Lt. Col. John H. Glenn, Jr., USMC; Cap. Virgil I. Grissom, USAF; Lt. Comdr. Walter M. Shirra, Jr., USN; Lt. Comdr. Alan B. Shepard, Jr., USN; and Capt. Donald K. Slayton, USAF. Six of the original seven would make a Mercury flight. Slayton was grounded for medical reasons, but remained a director of the astronaut office. He returned to flight status in 1975 as Docking Module Pilot on the Apollo-Soyuz flight.

Flight Summary

Each astronaut named his capsule and added the numeral 7 to denote the teamwork of the original astronauts.

May 5, 1961. Alan B. Shepard, Jr., makes a suborbital flight in *Freedom 7* and becomes the first American in space. Time: 15 minutes, 22 seconds.

July 21, 1961. Virgil I. Grissom makes the second successful suborbital flight in *Liberty Bell 7*, but spacecraft sank shortly after splashdown. Time: 15 minutes, 37 seconds. Grissom was later killed in *Apollo 1* fire, Jan. 27, 1967.

February 20, 1962. John H. Glenn, Jr., makes a three-orbit flight and becomes the first American in orbit. Time: 4 hours, 55 minutes.

May 24, 1962. M. Scott Carpenter duplicates Glenn's flight in *Aurora 7.* Time: 4 hours, 56 minutes.

October 3, 1962. Walter M. Schirra, Jr., makes a six-orbit engineering test flight in *Sigma 7.* Time: 9 hours, 13 minutes.

May 15–16, 1963. L. Gordon Cooper, Jr., performs the last *Mercury* mission and completes 22 orbits in *Faith 7* to evaluate effects of one day in space. Time: 34 hours, 19 minutes.

Gemini. *Gemini* was an extension of *Project Mercury,* to determine the effects of prolonged space flight on man—two weeks or longer—the time it takes to reach the Moon and return. "Walks in space" provided invaluable information for astronauts' later walks on the Moon. The *Gemini* spacecraft, twice as large as the *Mercury* capsule, accommodated two astronauts. Its crew named the project *Gemini* for the third constellation of the Zodiac and its twin stars, Castor and Pollux. The capsule differed from the *Mercury* spacecrafts in that it had hatches above the capsules so that the astronauts could leave the spacecraft and perform spacewalks or extra vehicular activities (EVAs).

There were ten manned flights in the *Gemini* program, starting with *Gemini 3* on March 23, 1965, and ending with the *Gemini 12* mission on Nov. 15, 1966. *Gemini 1* and *2* were unmanned test flights of the equipment.

When the *Gemini* program ended, U.S. astronauts had perfected rendezvous and docking maneuvers with other orbiting vehicles.

Apollo. *Apollo* was the designation for the United States' effort to land a man on the Moon and return him safely to Earth. The goal was successfully accomplished with *Apollo 11* on July 20, 1969, culminating eight years of rehearsal and centuries of dreaming. Astronauts Neil A. Armstrong and Col. Edwin E. Aldrin, Jr., scooped up and brought back the first lunar rocks ever seen on Earth—about 47 pounds.

Tragedy struck Jan. 27, 1967, on the launch pad during a preflight test of what would have become *Apollo 1*, the first manned mission. Astronauts Lt. Col. Virgil "Gus" Grissom, Lt. Col. Edward H. White, and Lt. Cdr. Roger Chafee lost their lives when a fire swept through the command module.

Six *Apollo* flights followed, ending with *Apollo 17* in December, 1972. The last three *Apollos* carried mechanized vehicles called lunar rovers for wide-ranging surface exploration of the Moon by astronauts. The rendezvous and docking of an *Apollo* spacecraft with a Russian *Soyuz* craft in Earth orbit on July 18, 1975, closed out the *Apollo* program.

During the Apollo project, the following 12 astronauts explored the lunar terrain:

Col. Edwin E. "Buzz" Aldrin, Jr., and Neil A. Armstrong, *Apollo 11;* Cdr. Alan L. Bean and Cdr. Charles Conrad, Jr., *Apollo 12;* Edgar D. Mitchell and Alan B. Shepard, *Apollo 14;* Lt. Col. James B. Irwin (1930–1991) and Col. David R. Scott, *Apollo 15;* Col. Charles M. Duke, Jr., and Capt. John W. Young, *Apollo 16;* and Capt. Eugene A. Cernan and Dr. Harrison H. Schmitt, *Apollo 17.*

Apollo was a three-part spacecraft: the command module (CM), the crew's quarters and flight control section; the service modules (SM) for the propulsion and spacecraft support systems (when together, the two modules were called CSM); and the lunar module (LM) to take two of the crew to the lunar surface, support them on the Moon, and return them to the CSM in orbit. The crews that made the lunar flights where both command modules and lunar modules were involved selected call names for the vehicles. The call names for the spacecraft in the six lunar landing missions with the command module and lunar module designations respectively were:

Apollo 11, Columbia and *Eagle; Apollo 12, Yankee Clipper* and *Intrepid;* (NOTE: The third lunar attempt, *Apollo 13,* April 11–17, 1970, 5 days, 22.9 hours, was aborted after the service module oxygen tank ruptured. The *Apollo 13* crew members were James A. Lovell, Jr., John L. Swigert, Jr., and Fred W. Haise, Jr. The mission was classified as a "Successful failure," because the crew was rescued. The call names for their spacecraft were *Odyssey* (CM) and *Aquarius* (LM).) *Apollo 14, Kitty Hawk* and *Antares; Apollo 15, Endeavor* and *Falcon; Apollo 16, Casper* and *Orion;* and *Apollo 17, America* and *Challenger.*

Skylab. America's first Earth-orbiting space station. *Project Skylab* was designed to demonstrate that men can work and live in space for prolonged periods without ill effects. Originally the spent third stage of a Saturn 5 moon rocket, *Skylab* measured 118 feet from stem to stern, and carried the most varied assortment of experimental equipment ever assembled in a single spacecraft. Three three-man crews visited the space stations, spending more than 740 hours observing the Sun and bringing home more than 175,000 solar pictures. These were the first recordings of solar activity above Earth's obscuring atmosphere. *Skylab* also evaluated systems designed to gather information on Earth's resources and environmental conditions. *Skylab*'s biomedical findings indicated that man adapts well to space for at least a period of three months, provided he has a proper diet and adequately programmed exercise, sleep, work, and recreation periods. *Skylab* orbited Earth at a distance of about 300 miles. Five years after the last *Skylab* mission, the 77-ton space station's orbit began to deteriorate faster than expected, owing to unexpectedly high sunspot activity. On July 11, 1979, the parts of *Skylab* that did not burn up in the atmosphere came crashing down on parts of Australia and the Indian Ocean. No one was hurt.

Space Shuttle. The NASA orbiter is 122.2 feet long and has a wingspan of 78.6 feet.

The *Space Shuttle Columbia* was successfully launched on April 12, 1981. It made five flights (the first four were test runs), the last completed on November 16, 1982. The second shuttle, *Challenger,* made its maiden flight on April 4, 1983. In April 1984, crew members of the *Challenger* captured, repaired, and returned the Solar Max satellite to orbit, making it the first time a disabled satellite had been repaired in space. The third shuttle, *Discovery,* made its first flight on August 30, 1984. The fourth space shuttle, *Atlantis,* made its maiden flight on Oct. 3, 1985.

A tragedy occurred on Jan. 28, 1986, when the shuttle *Challenger* exploded, killing the crew of seven 73 seconds after takeoff. It was the world's worst space flight disaster.

NASA has estimated that the risk of a catastrophic failure is about 1 in 78 for each shuttle flight. Eventually, another disaster could occur.

The first U.S. space mission since the *Challenger* disaster was launched 32 months later on Sept. 29, 1988, with the flight of *Discovery.* It had a crew of five and deployed a communications satellite.

The fifth and last orbiter, *Endeavour,* was built as a replacement for *Challenger.* It was named after the British explorer James Cook's first ship. *Endeavour* was launched on its maiden voyage on May 7, 1992 with a crew of seven astronauts. They made four spacewalks and retrieved a disabled Intelsat-6 communications satellite. During the mission, Dr. Kathryn Thornton became the second American woman to walk in space.

The shuttle *Endeavour* set a record 16 days, 15 hours in space, March 2–18, 1995.

The crew of the 50th mission aboard the *Endeavour,* launched Sept. 12, 1992, included the first black woman astronaut, Dr. Mae C. Jemison, and the first married couple to fly together in space, Air Force Lt. Col. Mark C. Lee and Dr. N. Jan Davis.

Lt. Col. Eileen M. Collins became the first woman to pilot a shuttle, *Discovery,* during the spacecraft's historic rendezvous with the Russian spacestation *Mir* on February 6, 1995. The shuttle *Atlantis* made the first linkup with the *Mir* on June 29, 1995.

Notable Manned Space Flights

Designation and country	Date	Astronauts	Flight time (h/min)	Remarks
Vostok 1 (U.S.S.R.)	April 12, 1961	Yuri A. Gagarin	1/48	First manned orbital flight
MR III (U.S.)	May 5, 1961	Alan B. Shepard, Jr.	0/15	Range 486 km (302 mi.), peak 187 km (116.5 mi); capsule recovered. First American in space.
Vostok 2 (U.S.S.R.)	Aug. 6–7, 1961	Gherman S. Titov	25/18	First long-duration flight
MA VI (U.S.)	Feb. 20, 1962	John H. Glenn, Jr.	4/55	First American in orbit
MA IX (U.S.)	May 15–16, 1963	L. Gordon Cooper, Jr.	34/20	Longest Mercury flight
Vostok 6 (U.S.S.R.)	June 16–19, 1963	Valentina V. Tereshkova	70/50	First orbital flight by female cosmonaut
Voskhod 1 (U.S.S.R.)	Oct. 12, 1964	Vladimir M. Komarov; Konstantin P. Feoktistov; Boris G. Yegorov	24/17	First 3-man orbital flight; also first flight without space suits
Voskhod 2 (U.S.S.R.)	March 18, 1965	Alexei A. Leonov; Pavel I. Belyayev	26/2	First "space walk" (by Leonov), 10 min
GT III (U.S.)	March 23, 1965	Virgil I. Grissom; John W. Young	4/53	First manned test of Gemini spacecraft
GT IV (U.S.)	June 3–7, 1965	James A. McDivitt; Edward H. White, 2d	97/48	First American "space walk" (by White), lasting slightly over 20 min
GT VIII (U.S.)	March 16–17, 1966	Neil A. Armstrong; David R. Scott	10/42	First docking between manned spacecraft and an unmanned space vehicle (an orbiting Agena rocket).
Apollo 7 (U.S.)	Oct. 11–22, 1968	Walter M. Schirra, Jr.; Donn F. Eisele; R. Walter Cunningham	260/9	First manned test of Apollo command module; first live TV transmissions from orbit
Soyuz 3 (U.S.S.R.)	Oct. 26–30, 1968	Georgi T. Bergeovoi	94/51	First manned rendezvous and possible docking by Soviet cosmonaut
Apollo 8 (U.S.)	Dec. 21–27, 1968	Frank Borman; James A. Lovell, Jr.; William A. Anders	147/00	First spacecraft in circumlunar orbit; TV transmissions from this orbit. The three astronauts were also the first men to view the Earth whole.
Apollo 9 (U.S.)	Mar. 3–13, 1969	James A. McDivitt; David R. Scott; Russell L. Schweikart	241/1	First manned flight of Lunar Module
Apollo 10 (U.S.)	May 18–26, 1969	Thomas P. Stafford; Eugene A. Cernan; John W. Young	192/3	First descent to within 9 miles of moon's surface by manned craft
Apollo 11 (U.S.)	July 16–24, 1969	Neil A. Armstrong; Edwin E. Aldrin, Jr.; Michael Collins	195/18	First manned landing and EVA on Moon; soil and rock samples collected; experiments left on lunar surface
Soyuz 6 (U.S.S.R.)	Oct. 11–16, 1969	Gorgiy Shonin; Valriy Kabasov	118/42	Three spacecraft and seven men put into earth orbit simultaneously for first time
Apollo 12 (U.S.)	Nov. 14–24, 1969	Charles Conrad, Jr.; Richard F. Gordon, Jr.; Alan Bean	244/36	Manned lunar landing mission; investigated Surveyor 3 spacecraft; collected lunar samples. EVA time: 15 h 30 min
Apollo 13 (U.S.)	April 11–17, 1970	James A. Lovell, Jr.; Fred W. Haise, Jr.; John L. Swigert, Jr.	142/54	Third manned lunar landing attempt; aborted due to pressure loss in liquid oxygen in service module and failure of fuel cells
Apollo 14 (U.S.)	Jan. 31–Feb. 9, 1971	Alan B. Shepard; Stuart A. Roosa; Edgar D. Mitchell	216/42	Third manned lunar landing: returned largest amount of lunar material
Soyuz 11 (U.S.S.R.)	June 6–30, 1971	Georgiy Tomofeyevich Dobrovolskiy; Vladislav Nikolayevich Volkov; Viktor Ivanovich Patsyev	569/40	Linked up with first space station, Salyut 1. Astronauts died just before re-entry due to loss of pressurization in spacecraft
Apollo 15 (U.S.)	July 26–Aug. 7, 1971	David R. Scott; James B. Irwin; Alfred M. Worden	295/12	Fourth manned lunar landing; first use of Lunar Rover propelled by Scott and Irving; first live pictures of LM lift-off from Moon; exploration time: 18 hours
Apollo 16 (U.S.)	April 16–27, 1972	John W. Young; Thomas K. Mattingly; Charles M. Duke, Jr.	265/51	Fifth manned lunar landing; second use of Lunar Rover Vehicle, propelled by Young and Duke Total exploration time on the Moon was 20 h 14 min, setting new record. Mattingly's in-flight "walk in space" was 1 h 23 min. Approximately 213 lb of lunar rock returned
Apollo 17 (U.S.)	Dec. 7–19, 1972	Eugene A. Cernan; Ronald E. Evans; Harrison H. Schmitt	301/51	Sixth and last manned lunar landing; third to carry lunar rover. Cernan and Schmitt, during three EVA's, completed total of 22 h 05 min 3 sec. USS Ticonderoga recovered crew and about 250 lbs of lunar samples
Skylab SL-2 (U.S.)	May 25–June 22, 1973	Charles Conrad, Jr.; Joseph P. Kerwin; Paul J. Weitz	672/50	First manned Skylab launch. Established Skylab Orbital Assembly and conducted scientific and medical experiments
Skylab SL-3 (U.S.)	July 28–Sept. 25, 1973	Alan L. Bean; Jack R. Lousma; Owen K. Garriott	1427/9	Second manned Skylab launch. New crew remained in space for 59 days, continuing scientific and medical experiments and earth observations from orbit

Designation and country	Date	Astronauts	Flight time (h/min)	Remarks
Skylab SL-4 (U.S.)	Nov. 16, 1973– Feb. 8, 1974	Gerald Carr; Edward Gibson; William Pogue	2017/16	Third manned Skylab launch; obtained medical data on crew for use in extending the duration of manned space flight; crews "walked in space" 4 times, totaling 44 h 40 min. Longest space mission yet—84 d 1 h 16 min. Splashdown in Pacific, Feb. 9, 1974
Apollo/Soyuz Test Project (U.S. and U.S.S.R.)	July 15–24, 1975 (U.S.)	U.S.: Brig. Gen. Thomas P. Stafford, Vance D. Brand, Donald K. Slayton	216/05	World's first international manned rendezvous and docking in space; aimed at developing a space rescue capability
	July 15–21, 1975 (U.S.S.R.)	U.S.S.R.: Col. A. A. Leonov, V. N. Kubasov	223/35	Apollo and Soyuz docked and crewmen exchanged visits on July 17, 1975. Mission duration for Soyuz: 142 h 31 min. For Apollo: 217 h, 28 min.
Columbia (U.S.)	April 12–14, 1981	Capt. Robert L. Crippen; John W. Young	54/20	Maiden voyage of *Space Shuttle*, the first spacecraft designed specifically for re-use up to 100 times
Salyut 7 (U .S.S.R.)	Feb. 8, 1984– Oct. 2, 1985	Leonid Kizim; Vladimir Solovyov; Oleg Atkov	237 days	Record Soviet team endurance flight in orbiting space station
Mir (U.S.S.R.)	Feb. 8, 1987– Dec. 29, 1987	Yuri V. Romanenko[1]	326.5 days	Record Soviet single endurance flight in orbiting space station.
Mir (U.S.S.R.)	Dec. 21, 1988– Dec. 21, , 1988	Col. Vladimir Titov and Musa Manarov[2]	366 days	Record Soviet team endurance flight in orbiting space station.
Endeavour (U.S.)	May 7–13, 1992	Richard J. Hieb; Maj. Thomas D. Akers; Comdr. Pierre J. Thugt	—	The three mission specialists remained free of the *Endeavour* for 8 hours and 20 minutes on May 13 during the repair of communications satellite, setting an absolute record for extravehicular duration in space. First capture of a satellite using hands only.
Endeavour (U.S.)	Dec. 2–13, 1993	Col. Richard O. Covey, Comdr. Kenneth D. Bowersox, Lt. Col. Tom Akers*, Dr. Jeffrey A. Hoffman**, Dr. Story Musgrave**, Claude Nicollier[3], Dr. Kathryn C. Thornton* (*two space walks, **three space walks)	10 days, 19 hr., 59 min.	Repaired Hubble Space Telescope. Replaced gyroscopes, solar arrays, camera, electronics and hardware. Installed COSTAR corrective optics to compensate for flaw in Hubble's primary mirror. Record five space walks in a single mission.
Discovery (U.S.)	Feb. 3–11, 1994	Col. Charles F. Bolden, Capt. Kenneth S. Reightier, Jr., Dr. N. Jan Davis, Dr. Frankling R. Chang-Diaz, Dr. Ronald M. Sega, Russian cosmonaut, Sergei K. Krikalev	8 days, 7 hr., 22 sec.	Test flight of Wake Shield Facility, an experimental, retrievable, free-flying satellite for use in developing exotic materials. Cargo bay carried a private, commercial pressurized-laboratory, Spacelab, for experimental use, leased by NASA. Crew member Sergei K. Krikalev, was first Russian cosmonaut to be launched in an American spacecraft.
Columbia (U.S.)	July 8–23, 1994	Col. Robert D. Cabana, Lieut. Col. James D. Halsell, Jr., Richard J. Hieb, Lieut. Col. Carl E. Walz, Dr. Leroy Chiao, Dr. Donald A. Thomas, and Dr. Chiaki Naito-Mukai, the first Japanese woman astronaut.	14 days, 17 hr., 55 min.	Old record for longest aerospace mission in duration and in orbit with more than two astronauts. Studied the effects of limited gravity of orbital flight on materials and living things including goldfish, killifish, jellyfish, sea urchins, and Japanese red-bellied newts.
Mir–17 (Russia)	Jan. 8, 1994– Mar. 22, 1995	Dr. Valery Polyakov	439[4] days	Record single endurance flight in orbiting space station. Returned to earth with crewmates cosmonaut Helena Kondakova and commander Alexander Viktorenko who spent 169 days each in the *Mir*.
Discovery (U.S.)	Feb. 3–11, 1995	Comdr. James D. Wetherbee, Lt. Col. Eileen M. Collins, Dr. Janice Voss, Dr. Bernard A. Harris, Jr.*, Dr. C. Michael Foale*, Russian cosmonaut Co. Vladimir G. Titov. *performed spacewalks.	8 days, 6 hr., 29 min.	First rendezvous of U.S. spacecraft with a Russian space station (*Mir*), Feb. 6. Lt. Col. Collins was first female shuttle pilot. Deployed and retrieved solar observatory satellite. Extra-vehicular activity to test new space suit modifications and practice space station assembly techniques. EVA time: 4 h, 35 min.
Endeavour (U.S.)	March 2–18, 1995	Comdr. Stephen Oswald, Lt. Col. William Gregory, Lt. Comdr. Wendy Lawrence, Dr. John Grunsfeld, Dr. Tamara Jernigan, Samuel Durrance, Ronald Parise	16 days, 15 hr., 8 min.	Longest aerospace mission in duration and in orbit with more than two astronauts. Performed astrophysics research with three ultraviolet telescopes. Studied ultraviolet light streaming from stars, galaxies, quasars, the Moon, and the Earth.

Designation and country	Date	Astronauts	Flight time (h/min)	Remarks
Soyuz TM–21 (Russia)	March 14–16, 1995	Russian cosmonauts: Lt. Col. Vladimir N. Dezhurov, Gennady M. Strekalov, and U.S. astronaut Dr. Norman E. Thagard	—	Dr. Thagard became the first American astronaut to fly aboard a Soyuz spacecraft with a Russian crew launched from Baikonur Space Center in Kazakhstan. He also became the first American to enter the *Mir* space station on March 16. Also see *Atlantis*, June 27–July 7, 1995.
Atlantis (U.S.)	June 27–July 7, 1995	Lt. Col. Charles J. Prescourt, Capt. Robert L. (Hoot) Gibson, Dr. Ellen S. Baker, Gregory J. Harbaugh, Dr. Bonnie Dunbar, Russian cosmonauts: *Mir–19* commander, Anatoly Y. Solovyev, Nikolai M. Budarin	10 days	Marked 100th human mission in U.S. space program and first shuttle linkup with the *Mir*: docked June 29, undocked July 4. Joined spacecraft held a record 10 people: 6 Americans and 4 Russians. Three *Mir* crew: cosmonauts: *Mir–18* commander, Lieut. Col. Vladimir N. Dezhurov, Gennady M. Strekalov, and U.S. astronaut Dr. Norman E. Thagard returned to earth aboard the *Atlantis*. Dr. Thagard set U.S. space record of 112 days in space aboard *Mir*. Cosmonauts Solovyez and Budarin remained aboard the *Mir*.

NOTE: The letters MR stand for Mercury (capsule) and Redstone (rocket); MA, for Mercury and Atlas (rocket); GT, for Gemini (capsule) and Titan-II (rocket). The first astronaut listed in the Gemini and Apollo flights is the command pilot. The Mercury capsules had names: MR-III was *Freedom 7*, MR-IV was *Liberty Bell 7*, MA-VI was *Friendship 7*, MA-VII was *Aurora 7*, MA-VIII was *Sigma 7*, and MA-IX was *Faith 7*. The figure 7 referred to the fact that the first group of U.S. astronauts numbered seven men. Only one Gemini capsule had a name: GT-III was called *Molly Brown* (after the Broadway musical *The Unsinkable Molly Brown*); thereafter the practice of naming the capsules was discontinued. 1. Returned to earth with two fellow cosmonauts, Aleksandr P. Aleksandrov and Anatoly Levchenko, who had spent a shorter stay aboard the *Mir*. 2. Also returned to earth with French astronaut Jean-Loup Chrétien who spent 3-1/2 weeks aboard the *Mir*. 3. European Space Agency Astronaut and operator of robot arm. 4. From launch to landing.

Soviet Manned Space Flight Programs

Vostok. The Soviets' first manned capsule, roughly spherical, used to place the first six cosmonauts in Earth orbit (1961–65).

Voskhod. Adaptation of the *Vostok* capsule to accommodate two and three cosmonauts. *Voskhod 1* orbited three persons, and *Voskhod 2* orbited two persons performing the world's first manned extra-vehicular activity.

Soyuz. Late-model manned spacecraft with provisions for three cosmonauts and a "working compartment" accessible through a hatch. Soyuz is the Russian word for "union." Since 1973, all *Soyuz* spacecraft have carried two cosmonauts. *Soyuz 19*, launched July 15, 1975, docked with the American *Apollo* spacecraft.

Salyut. Earth-orbiting space station intended for prolonged occupancy and re-visitation by cosmonauts. They are usually launched by Soviet Proton rockets. *Salyut 1* was launched April 19, 1971. *Salyut 2*, launched April 3, 1973, malfunctioned in orbit and was never occupied. *Salyut 3* was launched June 25, 1974. *Salyut 4* was launched Dec. 26, 1974. *Salyut 5* was launched June 22, 1976. *Salyut 6* was launched on Sept. 29, 1977. *Salyut 7* was launched on April 19, 1982. A record breaking Russian endurance flight was set (Feb. 8, 1984–Oct. 2, 1985) when Soviet astronauts spent 237 days in orbit aboard *Salyut 7*. *Salyut 7* re-entered the atmosphere and crashed into the Atlantic Ocean on Feb. 6, 1991.

Mir. The former Soviet Union's space station was launched into orbit on Feb. 20, 1986. Since that time, several space endurance records have been set in the *Mir*. On Dec. 29, 1987, Col. Yuri Romanenko set a single-mission record of 326.5 days in space. On Dec. 21, 1989, Col. Vladimir Titov and Musa Manarov returned to Earth after spending 366 days aboard the orbiting space station. On March 22, 1995, Russian cosmonaut Valeriy Polyakov set a new record for the longest human flight in space—439 days. U.S. astronaut Dr. Norman E. Thagard set a U.S. record of 112 days in space aboard the *Mir* on July 4, 1995.

The *Mir* will be abandoned when the international space station *Alpha* is constructed in 1997. However, the unpiloted *Mir* will be operated by remote control for a year or longer to test a solar power system to be used in *Alpha*.

The Russian Space Shuttle *Buran*

The successful test flight of the former Soviet Union's first reusable space shuttle *Buran* (Russian for "snowstorm") was made on Nov. 15, 1988. The unmanned flight circled the Earth for two orbits and lasted 3 hr 25 min.

The Russian and American space shuttles closely resemble each other in size and appearance and have similar delta wings and vertical tail structures. Some major differences between the two shuttles are that the Russian craft has no large rocket engines of its own. It uses the giant disposable *Energiya* rocket for most of its propulsion, and has only small rockets for maneuvering.

Unlike the American version, the *Buran* was designed for fully automatic flight, from takeoff to landing, a difficult engineering feat.

The crew cabin of *Buran* can accommodate two to four astronauts and has seats for six passengers or other crew members.

The Russian craft is 19 ft (5.6 m) in diameter compared with NASA's shuttle, 17 ft (5.2 m). The wingspan is 79.2 ft (24 m). NASA's orbiter is 78.6 ft (23.79 m). *Buran's* length is 119 ft (36 m), the U.S. shuttle is 122.2 ft long (37.24 m).

Additional flights in the *Buran* were never made.

ASTRONOMY

Astronomical Terms

Planet is the term used for a body in orbit around the Sun. Its origin is Greek; even in antiquity it was known that a number of "stars" did not stay in the same relative positions to the others. There were five such restless "stars" known—Mercury, Venus, Mars, Jupiter, and Saturn—and the Greeks referred to them as *planetes*, a word which means "wanderers." That the earth is one of the planets was realized later. The additional planets were discovered after the invention of the telescope.

In 1994, Dr. Alexander Wolszcan, an astronomer at Pennsylvania State University, presented convincing evidence of the first known planets to exist outside our solar system. They circle a pulsar or exploded star in the constellation *Virgo*. Two of the planets are two to three times the size of the Earth and a third is about the size of our Moon.

Satellite (or *moon*) is the term for a body in orbit around a planet. As long as our own Moon was the only moon known, there was no need for a general term for the moons of planets. But when Galileo Galilei discovered the four main moons of the planet Jupiter, Johannes Kepler (in a letter to Galileo) suggested "satellite" (from the Latin *satelles*, which means attendant) as a general term for such bodies. The word is used interchangeably with "moons": astronomers speak and write about the moons of Neptune, Saturn, etc. A satellite may be any size.

Orbit is the term for the path traveled by a body in space. It comes from the Latin *orbis*, which means circle, circuit, etc., and *orbita*, which means a rut or a wheel track. Theoretically, four mathematical figures are possible orbits: two are open (hyperbola and parabola) and two are closed (ellipse and circle), but in reality all closed orbits are ellipses. These ellipses can be nearly circular, as are the orbits of most planets, or very elongated, as are the orbits of most comets. In these orbits, the Sun is in one focal point of the ellipse, and the other focal point is empty. In the orbits of satellites, the planet stands in one focal point of the orbit. The *primary* of an orbit is the body in the focal point. For planets, the point of the orbit closest to the Sun is the *perihelion*, and the point farthest from the Sun is the *aphelion*. For orbits around the Earth, the corresponding terms are *perigee* and *apogee*; for orbits around other planets, corresponding terms are coined when necessary.

Two heavenly bodies are in *inferior* or *superior conjunction* when they have the same Right Ascension, or are in the same meridian; that is, when one is due north or south of the other. If the bodies appear near each other as seen from the Earth, they will rise and set at the same time. They are in *opposition* when they are opposite each other in the heavens: when one rises as the other is setting. *Greatest elongation* is the greatest apparent angular distance from the Sun, when a planet is most favorably suited for observation. Mercury can be seen with the naked eye only at about this time. An *occultation* of a planet or star is an eclipse of it by some other body, usually the Moon.

Stars are the basic units of population in the universe. Our Sun is the nearest star. Stars are very large (our Sun has a diameter of 865,400 miles—a compar-atively small star). Stars are composed of intensely hot gasses, deriving their energy from nuclear reactions going on in their interiors.

Galaxies are immense systems containing billions of stars. All that you can see in the sky (with a very few exceptions) belongs to our galaxy—a system of roughly 200 billion stars. The few exceptions are other galaxies. Our own galaxy, the rim of which we see as the "Milky Way," is about 100,000 light-years in diameter and about 10,000 light-years in thickness. Its shape is roughly that of a thick lens; more precisely it is a "spiral nebula," a term first used for other galaxies when they were discovered and before it was realized that these were separate and distant galaxies. The spiral galaxy nearest to ours is in the constellation Andromeda. It is somewhat larger than our own galaxy and is visible to the naked eye.

In 1994, English astronomers reported compelling evidence that a dwarf galaxy in the constellation *Sagittarius* lies 50,000 light-years from the Milky Way's center. Until then, the Large Magellanic Cloud, 169,000 light-years away from us, was considered the Milky Way's nearest neighbor.

Recent developments in radio astronomy have revealed additional celestial objects that are still incompletely understood.

Quasars ("quasi-stellar" objects), originally thought to be peculiar stars in our own galaxy, are now believed to be the most remote objects in the Universe. Spectral studies of quasars indicate that some are 9 billion light years away and moving away from us at the incredible rate of 150,000 miles per second. Quasars emit tremendous amounts of light and microwave radiation. Although they appear to be far smaller than ordinary galaxies, some quasars emit as much as 100 times more energy. Some astronomers believe that quasars are the cores of violently exploding galaxies.

Pulsars are believed to be rapidly spinning neutron stars, so crushed by their own gravity that a million tons of their matter would hardly fill a thimble. Pulsars are so named because they emit bursts of radio energy at regular intervals.

Pulsar *Geminga*, estimated to be within 300 light years from Earth, is the closest known pulsar to the solar system. In 1993, astronomers reported the discovery of a pulsar about 400 light years from Earth. Evidence of two Earth-sized planets circling a pulsar in *Virgo* was confirmed in 1994. A third is believed to be Moon-sized.

A *black hole* is the theoretical end-product of the total gravitational collapse of a massive star or group of stars. Crushed even smaller than an incredibly dense neutron star, such a body may become so dense that not even light can escape its gravitational field. It has been suggested that black holes may be detectable in proximity to normal stars when they draw matter away from their visible neighbors. Strong sources of X-rays in our galaxy and beyond may also indicate the presence of black holes. The first possible black hole to be studied is the invisible companion to a supergiant star in the constellation Cygnus.

In May 1994, astronomers using the Hubble Space Telescope found conclusive evidence of a massive black hole in the center of Galaxy M87 located 50 million light-years away in the constellation *Virgo*.

Origin of the Universe

Evidence tends to confirm that the universe began its existence about 15 billion years ago as a dense, hot globule of gas expanding rapidly outward. At that time, the universe contained nothing but hydrogen and a small amount of helium. There were no stars and no planets. The first stars probably began to condense out of the primordial hydrogen when the universe was about 100 million years old and continued to form as the universe aged. The Sun arose in this way 4.6 billion years ago. Many stars came into being before the Sun was formed; many others formed after the Sun appeared. This process continues, and through telescopes we can now see stars forming out of compressed pockets of hydrogen in outer space.

In 1992, instruments aboard the Cosmic Background Explorer (COBE) satellite, launched in 1989, showed that 99.97% of the radiant energy of the universe was released within the first year of the primeval explosion. This evidence seems to confirm the Big Bang theory which holds that the universe originated from a single violent explosion (a *big bang*) of a very small agglomeration of matter of extremely high density and temperatures. Astronomers also theorize that 99% of the matter in the universe is invisible or *dark matter* composed of some kind of matter that they cannot yet detect.

In March 1995, astronomers found supporting evidence for the Big Bang when they concluded data obtained from the space shuttle's *Astro 2* observatory showed that helium was widespread in the early universe. The theory holds that hydrogen and helium were the first elements created when the universe was formed.

Birth and Death of a Star

When a star begins to form as a dense cloud of gas, the individual hydrogen atoms fall toward the center of the cloud under the force of the star's gravity. As they fall, they pick up speed, and their energy increases. The increase in energy heats the gas. When this process has continued for some millions of years, the temperature reaches about 20 million degrees Fahrenheit. At this temperature, the hydrogen within the star ignites and burns in a continuing series of nuclear reactions in which all the elements in the universe are manufactured from hydrogen and helium. The onset of these reactions marks the birth of a star. When a star begins to exhaust its hydrogen supply, its life nears an end. The first sign of old age is a swelling and reddening of its outer regions. Such an aging, swollen star is called a red giant. The Sun, a middle-aged star, will probably swell to a red giant in 5 billion years, vaporizing the earth and any creatures that may be left on its surface. When all its fuel has been exhausted, a star cannot generate sufficient pressure at its center to balance the crushing force of gravity. The star collapses under the force of its own weight; if it is a small star, it collapses gently and remains collapsed. Such a collapsed star, at its life's end, is called a white dwarf. The Sun will probably end its life in this way. A different fate awaits a large star. Its final collapse generates a violent explosion, blowing the innards of the star out into space. There, the materials of the exploded star mix with the primeval hydrogen of the universe. Later in the history of the galaxy, other stars are formed out of this mixture. The Sun is one of these stars. It contains the debris of countless other stars that exploded before the Sun was born.

Supernovas

On Feb. 24, 1987, Canadian astronomer Ian Shelter at the Las Campas Observatory in Chile discovered a supernova—an exploding star—from a photograph taken on Feb. 23 of the Large Magellanic Cloud, a galaxy some 160,000 light years away from Earth. Astronomers believe that the dying star was Sanduleak –69°202, a 10-million-year-old blue supergiant.

Supernova 1987A was the closest and best studied supernova in almost 400 years. One was previously observed by Johannes Kepler in 1604, four years before the telescope was invented.

In April 1992, researchers observed the most distant supernova explosion, 5 billion light-years away from Earth.

Two mysterious giant rings around 1987A were discovered by the Hubble Space Telescope in 1994.

Formation of the Solar System

The sun's age was calculated in 1989 to be 4.49 billion years old, less than the 4.7 billion years previously believed. It was formed from a cloud of hydrogen mixed with small amounts of other substances that had been manufactured in the bodies of other stars before the Sun was born. This was the parent cloud of the solar system. The dense hot gas at the center of the cloud gave rise to the Sun; the outer regions of the cloud—cooler and less dense—gave birth to the planets.

Our solar system consists of one star (the Sun), nine planets and all their moons, several thousand minor planets called asteroids or planetoids, and an equally large number of comets.

The Sun

All the stars, including our Sun, are gigantic balls of superheated gas, kept hot by atomic reactions in their centers. In our Sun, this atomic reaction is hydrogen fusion: four hydrogen atoms are combined to form one helium atom. The temperature at the core of our Sun must be 20 million degrees centigrade, the surface temperature averages 6,000 degrees centigrade, or about 11,000 degrees Fahrenheit. The diameter of the sun is 865,400 miles, and its surface area is approximately 12,000 times that of the Earth. Compared with other stars, our Sun is just a bit below average in size and temperature, and is a yellow dwarf star. Its fuel supply (hydrogen) is estimated to last for another 5 billion years.

Our Sun is not motionless in space; in fact it has two proper motions. One is a seemingly straight-line motion in the direction of the constellation Hercules at the rate of about 12 miles per second. But since the Sun is a part of the Milky Way system and since the whole system rotates slowly around its own center, the Sun also moves at the rate of 175 miles per second as part of the rotating Milky Way system.

In addition to this motion, the Sun rotates on its axis. Observing the motion of sun spots (darkish areas which look like enormous whirling storms) and solar flares, which are usually associated with sun spots, has shown that the rotational period of our Sun is just short of 25 days. But this figure is valid for the Sun's equator only; the sections near the Sun's poles seem to have a rotational period of 34 days. Naturally, since the Sun generates its own heat and light, there is no temperature difference between poles and equator.

What we call the Sun's "surface" is technically known as the photosphere. Since the whole Sun is a ball of very hot gas, there is really no such thing as a

Astronomical Constants

Light–year (distance traveled by light in one year)	5,880,000,000,000 mi.
Parsec (parallax of one second, for stellar distances)	3.259 light-yrs.
Velocity of light	186,281.7 mi./sec.
Astronomical unit (A.U.), or mean distance earth-to-sun	ca. 93,000,000 mi.[1]
Mean distance, earth to moon	238,860 mi.
General precession	50".26
Obliquity of the ecliptic	$23° 27'8".26-0".4684(t-1900)^2$
Equatorial radius of the earth	3963.34 statute mi.
Polar radius of the earth	3949.99 statute mi.
Earth's mean radius	3958.89 statute mi.
Oblateness of the earth	1/297
Equatorial horizontal parallax of the moon	57' 2".70
Earth's mean velocity in orbit	18.5 mi./sec.
Sidereal year	365d.2564
Tropical year	365d.2422
Sidereal month	27d.3217
Synodic month	29d.5306
Mean sidereal day	23h56m4s.091 of mean solar time
Mean solar day	24h3m56s.555 of sidereal time

1. Actual mean distance derived from radar bounces: 92,935,700 mi. The value of 92,897,400 mi. (based on parallax of 8,.80) is used in calculations. 2. *t* refers to the year in question, for example, 1996.

surface; it is a question of visual impression. The next layer outside the photosphere is known as the chromosphere, which extends several thousand miles beyond the photosphere. It is in steady motion, and often enormous prominences can be seen to burst from it, extending as much as 100,000 miles into space. Outside the chromosphere is the corona. The corona consists of very tenuous gases (essentially hydrogen) and makes a magnificent sight when the Sun is eclipsed.

As the Sun ages, it gradually expands and heats. In 1994, American astrophysicists studying the eventual fate of the Sun estimated that its brilliancy will increase by 10% over the next 1.1 billion years or more and, in about 6.5 billion years hence, our aging star will have doubled its present luminosity. The extreme heat generated will cause a catastrophic greenhouse effect on Earth and our oceans will boil away, and life on Earth as we know it will end.

The Sun will eventually expand enormously to 166 times its present size and become over 2,000 times as bright. Eight billion years from now, the Sun's radius will engulf the planet Mercury and extend beyond the present orbit of Venus.

However, as the Sun expands, it will also lose considerable mass (as much as one-half) and weaken its gravitational pull on Venus and the other lifeless planets, causing them to orbit further away from the Sun and escape total destruction.

The Moon

Mercury and Venus do not have any moons. Therefore, the Earth is the planet nearest the Sun to be orbited by a moon.

The next planet farther out, Mars, has two very small moons. Jupiter has four major moons and twelve minor ones. Saturn, the ringed planet, has eighteen known moons (and possibly more), of which one (Titan) is larger than the planet Mercury. Uranus has fifteen moons, (four of them large) as well as rings, while Neptune has one large and seven small moons. Pluto has one moon, discovered in 1978. Some astronomers still consider Pluto to be a "runaway moon" of Neptune.

Our own Moon, with a diameter of 2,160 miles, is one of the larger moons in our solar system and is especially large when compared with the planet that it orbits. In fact, the common center of gravity of the Earth-Moon system is only about 1,000 miles below the Earth's surface. The closest our Moon can come to us (its perigee) is 221,463 miles; the farthest it can go away (its apogee) is 252,710 miles. The period of rotation of our Moon is equal to its period of revolution around the Earth. Hence from Earth we can see only one hemisphere of the Moon. Both periods are 27 days, 7 hours, 43 minutes and 11.47 seconds. But while the rotation of the Moon is constant, its velocity in its orbit is not, since it moves more slowly in apogee than in perigee. Consequently, some portions near the rim which are not normally visible will appear briefly. This phenomenon is called "libration," and by taking advantage of the librations, astronomers have succeeded in mapping approximately 59% of the lunar surface. The other 41% can never be seen from the earth but has been mapped by American and Russian Moon-orbiting spacecraft.

Though the Moon goes around the Earth in the time mentioned, the interval from new Moon to new Moon is 29 days, 12 hours, 44 minutes and 2.78 seconds. This delay of nearly two days is due to the fact that the Earth is moving around the Sun, so that the Moon needs two extra days to reach a spot in its orbit where no part is illuminated by the Sun, as seen from Earth.

If the plane of the Earth's orbit around the Sun (the ecliptic) and the plane of the Moon's orbit around the Earth were the same, the Moon would be eclipsed by the Earth every time it is full, and the Sun would be eclipsed by the Moon every time the Moon is "new" (it would be better to call it the "black Moon" when it is in this position). But because the two orbits do not coincide, the Moon's shadow normally misses the Earth and the Earth's shadow misses the Moon. The inclination of the two orbital planes to each other is 5 degrees. The tides are, of course, caused by the Moon with the help of the Sun, but in the open ocean they are surprisingly low, amounting to about one yard. The very high tides which can be observed near the shore in some places are due to funnelling effects of the shorelines. At new Moon and at full Moon the tides raised by the Moon are reinforced by the Sun; these are the "spring tides." If the Sun's tidal power acts at right angles to that of the Moon (quarter moons) we get the low "neap tides."

THE MILKY WAY GALAXY. Our sun is one of 200-billion stars banded together by gravity in an enormous spiral disk called the Milky Way Galaxy. The arrow indicates our position three-fifths of the way out from the center. It takes light 100,000 years to traverse our Galaxy, one of billions of galaxies in the universe. Copyright 1990 Hansen Planetarium, Salt Lake City, Utah. Reproduced with Permission.

OUR PLACE IN THE GALAXY

Data from the Defense Department's *Clementine* space probe has given support to the theory that the Moon was formed after a cosmic collision between the Earth and another celestial body. *Clementine* data show that the Moon is poor in iron while the Earth is relatively rich in iron under its crust. The data also show that the surface of the Moon was melted early in its history.

Our Planet Earth

The Earth, circling the Sun at an average distance of 93 million miles, is the fifth largest planet and the third from the Sun. It orbits the Sun at a speed of 67,000 miles per hour, making one revolution in 365 days, 5 hours, 48 minutes, and 45.51 seconds. The Earth completes one rotation on its axis every 23 hours, 56 minutes, and 4.09 seconds. Actually a bit pear-shaped rather than a true sphere, the Earth has a diameter of 7,927 miles at the Equator and a few miles less at the poles. It has an estimated mass of about 6.6 sextillion tons, with an average density of 5.52 grams per cubic centimeter. The Earth's surface area encompasses 196,949,970 square miles of which about three-fourths is water.

Origin of the Earth. The Earth, along with the other planets, is believed to have been born 4.5 billion years ago as a solidified cloud of dust and gases left over from the creation of the Sun. For perhaps 500 million years, the interior of the Earth stayed solid and relatively cool, perhaps 2000° F. The main ingredients, according to the best available evidence, were iron and silicates, with small amounts of other elements, some of them radioactive. As millions of years passed, energy released by radioactive decay—mostly of uranium, thorium, and potassium—gradually heated the Earth, melting some of its constituents. The iron melted before the silicates and, being heavi-

er, sank toward the center. This forced upward the silicates that it found there. After many years, the iron reached the center, almost 4,000 miles deep, and began to accumulate. No eyes were around at that time to view the turmoil which must have taken place on the face of the Earth—gigantic heaves and bubbling of the surface, exploding volcanoes, and flowing lava covering everything in sight. Finally, the iron in the center accumulated as the core. Around it, a thin but fairly stable crust of solid rock formed as the Earth cooled. Depressions in the crust were natural basins in which water, rising from the interior of the planet through volcanoes and fissures, collected to form the oceans. Slowly the Earth acquired its present appearance.

The Earth Today. As a result of radioactive heating over millions of years, the Earth's molten *core* is probably fairly hot today, around 11,000° F. By comparison, lead melts at around 800° F. Most of the Earth's 2,100-mile-thick core is liquid, but there is evidence that the center of the core is solid. The liquid outer portion, about 95% of the core, is constantly in motion, causing the Earth to have a magnetic field that makes compass needles point north and south. The details are not known, but the latest evidence suggests that planets which have a magnetic field probably have a solid core or a partially liquid one.

Outside the core is the Earth's *mantle*, 1,800 miles thick, and extending nearly to the surface. The mantle is composed of heavy silicate rock, similar to that brought up by volcanic eruptions. It is somewhere between liquid and solid, slightly yielding, and therefore contributing to an active, moving Earth. Most of the Earth's radioactive material is in the thin *crust* which covers the mantle, but some is in the mantle and continues to give off heat. The crust's thickness ranges from 5 to 25 miles.

The Brightest Stars

Star	Constellation	Mag.	Dist. (l.-y.)	Star	Constellation	Mag.	Dist. (l.-y.)
Sirius	Canis Major	−1.6	8	Antares	Scorpius	1.2	170
Canopus	Carina	−0.9	650	Fomalhaut	Piscis Austrinus	1.3	27
Alpha Centauri	Centaurus	+0.1	4	Deneb	Cygnus	1.3	465
Vega[1]	Lyra	0.1	23	Regulus	Leo	1.3	70
Capella	Auriga	0.2	42	Beta Crucis	Crux	1.5	465
Arcturus	Boötes	0.2	32	Eta Carinae	Carina	1–7	—
Rigel	Orion	0.3	545	Alpha-one Crucis	Crux	1.6	150
Procyon	Canis Minor	0.5	10	Castor	Gemini	1.6	44
Achernar	Eridanus	0.6	70	Gamma Crucis	Crux	1.6	—
Beta Centauri	Centaurus	0.9	130	Epsilon Canis Majoris	Canis Major	1.6	325
Altair	Aquila	0.9	18	Epsilon Ursae Majoris	Ursa Major	1.7	50
Betelgeuse	Orion	0.9	600	Bellatrix	Orion	1.7	215
Aldebaran	Taurus	1.1	54	Lambda Scorpii	Scorpius	1.7	205
Spica	Virgo	1.2	190	Epsilon Carinae	Carina	1.7	325
Pollux	Gemini	1.2	31	Mira	Cetus	2–10	250

1. In 1984, the discovery of a possible planetary system around Vega was reported.

Scientists recently discovered that the Earth's core is not a perfect sphere. X-ray like images of inside the Earth show that there are vast mountains six to seven miles high and deep valleys on the core. These features are in an upside down relationship to the Earth's surface.

Continental Drift. A great deal of recent evidence confirms the theory that the continents of the Earth, made mostly of relatively light granite, float in the slightly yielding mantle, like logs in a pond. For many years it had been noticed that if North and South America could be pushed toward western and southern Europe and western Africa, they would fit like pieces in a jigsaw puzzle. Today, there is little question—the continents have drifted widely and continue to do so.

In 10 million years, the world as we know it may be unrecognizable, with California drifting out to sea, Florida joining South America, and Africa moving farther away from Europe and Asia.

The Earth's Atmosphere. The thin blanket of atmosphere that envelops the Earth extends several hundred miles into space. From sea level—the very bottom of the ocean of air—to a height of about 60 miles, the air in the atmosphere is made up of the same gases in the same ratio: about 78% nitrogen, 21% oxygen, and the remaining 1% being a mixture of argon, carbon dioxide, and tiny amounts of neon, helium, krypton, xenon, and other gases. The atmosphere becomes less dense with increasing altitude: more than three-fourths of the Earth's huge envelope is concentrated in the first 5 to 10 miles above the surface. At sea level, a cubic foot of the atmosphere weighs about an ounce and a quarter. The entire atmosphere weighs 5,700,000,000,000,000 tons, and the force with which gravity holds it in place causes it to exert a pressure of nearly 15 pounds per square inch. Going out from the Earth's surface, the atmosphere is divided into five regions. The regions, and the heights to which they extend, are: *Troposphere*, 0 to 7 miles (at middle latitudes); *stratosphere*, 7 to 30 miles; *mesosphere*, 30 to 50 miles; *thermosphere*, 50 to 400 miles; and *exosphere*, above 400 miles. The boundaries between each of the regions are known respectively as the *tropopause, stratopause, meso-*

pause, and *thermopause.* Alternate terms often used for the layers above the troposphere are *ozonosphere* (for stratosphere) and *ionosphere* for the remaining upper layers.

The Seasons. Seasons are caused by the 23.4 degree tilt of the Earth's axis, which alternately turns the North and South Poles toward the Sun. Times when the Sun's apparent path crosses the Equator are known as *equinoxes.* Times when the Sun's apparent path is at the greatest distance from the Equator are known as *solstices.* The lengths of the days are most extreme at each solstice. If the Earth's axis were perpendicular to the plane of the Earth's orbit around the Sun, there would be no seasons, and the days always would be equal in length. Since the Earth's axis is at an angle, the Sun strikes the Earth directly at the Equator only twice a year: in March (vernal equinox) and September (autumnal equinox). In the Northern Hemisphere, spring begins at the vernal equinox, summer at the summer solstice, fall at the autumnal equinox, and winter at the winter solstice. The situation is reversed in the Southern Hemisphere.

Mercury

Mercury is the planet nearest the Sun. Appropriately named for the wing-footed Roman messenger of the gods, Mercury whizzes around the Sun at a speed of 30 miles per second completing one circuit in 88 days. The days and nights are long on Mercury. It takes 59 Earth days for Mercury to make a single rotation. It spins at a rate of about 10 kilometers (about 6 miles) per hour, measured at the equator, as compared to the Earth's spin of about 1,600 kilometers (about 1,000 miles) per hour at the equator.

The photographs *Mariner 10* (1974–75) radioed back to Earth revealed an ancient, heavily cratered surface on Mercury, closely resembling our own Moon. The pictures showed huge cliffs, or scarps, crisscrossing the planet. These apparently were created when Mercury's interior cooled and shrank, compressing the planet's crust. The cliffs are as high as two kilometers (1.2 miles) and as long as 1,500 kilometers (932 miles). Another unique feature is the Caloris Basin, a large impact crater about 1,300 kilometers (808 miles) in diameter.

(Continued on page 333)

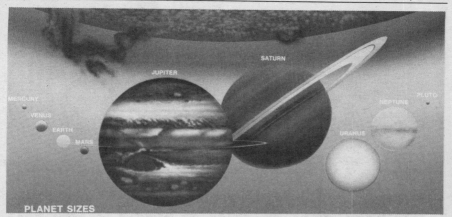

PLANET SIZES

PLANET SIZES. Shown from left to right: Mercury, Venus, Earth, Mars, Jupiter, Saturn, Uranus, Neptune, and Pluto.

Copyright 1990 Hansen Planetarium, Salt Lake City, Utah. Reproduced with Permission.

Basic Planetary Data

	Mercury	Venus	Earth	Mars	Jupiter
Mean distance from Sun (Millions of kilometers)	57.9	108.2	149.6	227.9	778.3
(Millions of miles)	36.0	67.24	92.9	141.71	483.88
Period of revolution	88 days	224.7 days	365.2 days	687 days	11.86 yrs
Rotation period	59 days	243 days retrograde	23 hr 56 min 4 sec	24 hr 37 min	9 hr 55 min 30 sec
Inclination of axis	Near 0°	3°	23°27′	25°12′	3°5′
Inclination of orbit to ecliptic	7°	3.4°	0°	1.9°	1.3°
Eccentricity of orbit	.206	.007	.017	.093	.048
Equatorial diameter (Kilometers)	4,880	12,100	12,756	6,794	142,800
(Miles)	3,032.4	7,519	7,926.2	4,194	88,736
Atmosphere (Main components)	Virtually none	Carbon dioxide	Nitrogen oxygen	Carbon dioxide	Hydrogen helium
Satellites	0	0	1	2	16
Rings	0	0	0	0	1

	Saturn	Uranus	Neptune	Pluto
Mean distance from Sun (Millions of kilometers)	1,427	2,870	4,497	5,900
(Millions of miles)	887.14	1,783.98	2,796.46	3,666
Period of revolution	29.46 yrs	84 yrs	165 yrs	248 yrs
Rotation period	10 hr 40 min 24 sec	16.8 hr(?) retrograde	16 hr 11 min(?)	6 days 9 hr 18 mins retrograde
Inclination of axis	26°44′	97°55′	28°48′	60° (?)
Inclination of orbit to ecliptic	2.5°	0.8°	1.8°	17.2°
Eccentricity of orbit	.056	.047	.009	.254
Equatorial diameter (Kilometers)	120,660	51,810	49,528	2,290 (?)
(Miles)	74,978	32,193	30,775	1,423 (?)
Atmosphere (Main components)	Hydrogen helium	Helium hydrogen methane	Hydrogen helium methane	None detected
Satellites	18+[1]	15	8	1
Rings	1,000 (?)	11	4	?

1. Two additional moons were found outside the outer F ring by the Hubble Space Telescope in 1995. They were temporarily named S3 and S4. *Source:* Basic NASA data and other sources.

THE SOLAR SYSTEM

THE SOLAR SYSTEM. Orbiting around the Sun are Mercury, Venus, Earth, Mars, Jupiter, Saturn, Uranus, Neptune, and Pluto. Our Solar System was born nearly five billion years ago out of a cloud of interstellar gas and dust. Gravity caused this nebula to contract and flatten into a spinning disk. Near the center, where the density was greatest, a body formed which was so massive that its internal pressures ignited and sustained a nuclear reaction, creating a star we call the Sun. Elsewhere in the cloud, smaller bodies coalesced and cooled—nine planets, perhaps fifty moons, millions of asteroids, and billions of comets. Within our Milky Way Galaxy, there may be billions of other solar systems. Copyright 1990 Hansen Planetarium, Salt Lake City, Utah. Reproduced with permission.

(Continued from page 330)

Mercury, like the Earth, appears to have a crust of light silicate rock. Scientists believe it has a heavy iron-rich core that makes up about half of its volume.

Instruments onboard *Mariner 10* discovered that the planet has a weak magnetic field and a trace of atmosphere—a trillionth the density of the Earth's and composed chiefly of argon, neon, and helium. The spacecraft reported temperatures ranging from 510° C (950° F) on Mercury's sunlit side to –210° C (–346° F) on the dark side. Mercury literally bakes in daylight and freezes at night.

Until the *Mariner 10* probe, little was known about the planet. Even the best telescopic views from Earth showed Mercury as an indistinct object lacking any surface detail. The planet is so close to the Sun that it is usually lost in the Sun's glare.

Radar images taken by astronomers at Jet Propulsion Laboratories and California Institute of Technology during the summer of 1991 suggest that the polar regions of Mercury may be covered with patches of water ice. Although this seems impossible due to the planet's sizzling heat, the polar regions receive very little sunlight and may get as cold as –235° F. The radar images showed bright patterns at the poles which are characteristic of ice reflecting the radar signals. Other explanations may be offered for this unexpected discovery.

• Mercury is a naked eye object at morning or evening twilight when it is at greatest elongation.

Venus

Although Venus is Earth's closest neighbor, very little is known about the planet because it is permanently covered with thick clouds. In 1962, Soviet and American space probes, coupled with Earth-based radar and infrared spectroscopy, began slowly unraveling some of the mystery surrounding Venus. Twenty-eight years later, the *Magellan* spacecraft sent by the United States arrived at Venus in August 1990 and began radar-mapping the planet's surface in greater detail.

According to the latest results, Venus' atmosphere exerts a pressure at the surface 94.5 times greater than Earth's. Walking on Venus would be as difficult as walking a half-mile beneath the ocean. Because of a thick blanket of carbon dioxide, a "greenhouse effect" exists on Venus. Venus intercepts twice as much of the Sun's light as does the Earth. The light enters freely through the carbon dioxide gas and is changed to heat radiation in molecular collisions. But carbon dioxide prevents the heat from escaping. Consequently, the temperature of the surface of Venus is over 800° F, hot enough to melt lead.

The atmospheric composition of Venus is about 96% carbon dioxide, 4% nitrogen, and minor amounts of water, oxygen, and sulfur compounds. There are at least four distinct cloud and haze layers that exist at different altitudes above the planet's surface. The haze layers contain small aerosol particles, possibly droplets of sulfuric acid. A concentration of sulfur dioxide above the cloud tops has been observed to be decreasing since 1978. The source of sulfur dioxide at this altitude is unknown; it may be injected by volcanic explosions or atmospheric overturning.

Measurements of the Venusian atmosphere and its cloud patterns reveal nearly constant high-speed zonal winds, about 100 meters per second (220 miles per hour) at the equator. The winds decrease toward the poles so that the atmosphere at cloud-top level rotates almost like a solid body. The wind speeds at the equator correspond to Venus' rotation period of four to five days at most latitudes. The circulation is always in the same direction—east to west—as Venus' slow retrograde motion. Earth's winds blow from west to east, the same direction as its rotation.

Venus is quite round, very different from the other planets and from the Moon. Venus has neither polar flattening nor an equatorial bulge. The diameter of Venus is 12,100 kilometers (7,519 miles). Venus has a retrograde axial rotation period of 243.1 Earth days. The surface atmospheric pressure is 1,396 pounds per square inch (95 Earth atmospheres). The planet's mean distance from the Sun is 108.2 million kilometers (67.2 million miles). The period of its revolution around the Sun is 224.7 days.

The highest point on Venus is the summit of Maxwell Montes, 10.8 kilometers (6.71 miles) above the mean level, more than a mile taller than Mount Everest. There is some evidence that this huge mountain is an active volcano. The lowest point is in the rift valley, Diana Chasma, 2.9 kilometers (1.8 miles) below the mean level. This point is about one-fifth the greatest depth on Earth in the Marianas Trench.

Venus has an extreme lowland basin, Atalanta Planitia, which is about the size of Earth's North Atlantic Ocean basin. The smooth surface of the Atalanta Planitia resembles the mare basins of the Moon.

There are only two highland or continental masses on Venus: Ishtar Terra and Aphrodite Terra. Ishtar Terra is 11 kilometers (6.8 miles) at its highest points (the highest peaks on Venus) and those of Aphrodite Terra rise to about 5 kilometers (3.10 miles) above the planet. Ishtar Terra is about the size of the continental United States and Aphrodite Terra is about the size of Africa.

The unmanned NASA spacecraft *Magellan* was launched on May 4, 1989, from the shuttle *Atlantis* and arrived at Venus Aug. 10, 1990, to map most of the planet. Despite some problems with its radio transmissions, the results of the radar mapping delighted scientists and provided them with the sharpest images ever taken of the planet's surface. Images taken from *Magellan* show ten times more detail than ever seen before.

The radar images provided scientists with compelling evidence that the planet has been dominated by volcanism on a global scale. The photos also showed that the planet's second highest mountain, Maat Mons, rising five miles (eight kilometers) above the Venusian plains, appears to be covered with fresh lava and is possibly an active volcano.

Magellan discovered the longest known channel in the solar system on Venus. It is 4,200 miles (6,800 kilometers) long and averages slightly over a mile (1.8 kilometers) wide. Its origin is puzzling to scientists because high temperature lava is unlikely to have caused such a long distance flow on the surface and there are no known substances that could remain liquid long enough under the planet's atmospheric pressure and temperature to have carved out this snake-like feature. The channel is slightly longer than the Nile River, the longest river on Earth. *Magellan* ended its radar and emissions mapping in September 1992 after covering 98% of the planet's surface. (Also see *Magellan* in the Space Section.)

• Venus is the brightest of all the planets and is often visible in the morning or evening, when it is frequently referred to as the Morning Star or Evening Star. At its brightest, it can sometimes be seen with the naked eye in full daylight, if one knows where to look.

(Continued on page 335)

LARGEST CHANNEL IN SOLAR SYSTEM. *Magellan* took the above image of the largest known channel on Venus. At 4,200 miles (6,800 kilometers) long and an average of 1.1 miles (1.8 kilometers) in width, it is longer than the Nile River, Earth's longest river, making it the longest known channel in the solar system. The channel was originally discovered by the Soviet *Venera 15* and *16* spacecraft orbiters. NASA.

Magellan radar image of Golubkina Crater on Venus. The impact crater is 20.4 miles (34 kilometers) in diameter. NASA.

Giant Olympus Mons, the tallest volcano on Mars, is also the highest mountain in the solar system. It is 540 kilometers (336 miles) across and rises 10 miles higher than Mount Everest. NASA photo.

Phobos, Mars' tiny inner moon, is covered with a large number of craters.

(Continued from page 333)

Mars

Mars, on the other side of the Earth from Venus, is Venus' direct opposite in terms of physical properties. Its atmosphere is cold, thin, and transparent, and readily permits observation of the planet's features. We know more about Mars than any other planet except Earth. Mars is a forbidding, rugged planet with huge volcanoes and deep chasms. The largest volcano, Olympus Mons (Olympic Mountain) rises 78,000 feet above the surface, higher than Mount Everest. The plains of Mars are pockmarked by the hits of thousands of meteors over the years.

Most of our information about Mars comes from the Mariner 9 spacecraft, which orbited the planet in 1971. Mariner 9, photographing 100% of the planet, uncovered spectacular geological formations, including a Martian Grand Canyon that dwarfs the one on Earth. Called Valles Marineris (Mariner Valley) it stretches more than 3,000 miles along the equatorial region of Mars and is over 4 kilometers (2.5 miles) deep in places and 80 to 100 kilometers (50 to 62 miles) wide. The spacecraft's cameras also recorded what appeared to be dried riverbeds, suggesting the onetime presence of water on the planet. The latter idea gives encouragement to scientists looking for life on Mars, for where there is water, there may be life. However, to date, no evidence of life has been found. Temperatures near the equator range from −17 degrees F. in the daytime to −130 degrees F. at night.

None of these probes have clearly shown whether Mars has its own magnetic field. Scientists hoped that the failed *Mars Observer,* launched Sept. 25, 1992, would provide a conclusive answer. (See *Mars Observer* in Space Section.)

Mars rotates upon its axis in nearly the same period as Earth—24 hours, 37 minutes—so that a Mars day is almost identical to an Earth day. Mars takes 687 days to make one trip around the Sun. Because of its eccentric orbit Mars' distance from the Sun can vary by about 36 million miles. Its distance from Earth can vary as much as 200 million miles. The atmosphere of Mars is much thinner than Earth's; atmospheric pressure is about 1% that of our planet. Its gravity is one-third of Earth's. Major constituents are carbon dioxide and nitrogen. Water vapor and oxygen are minor constituents. Mars' polar caps, composed mostly of frozen carbon dioxide (dry ice), recede and advance according to the Martian seasons.

Scientists have not yet determined if the Martian snow (as water ice or carbon dioxide particles) actually crystallizes on the polar caps or whether it falls from the clouds over them.

Mars has four seasons like Earth, but they are much longer. For example, in the northern hemisphere, the Martian spring is 198 days, and the winter season lasts 158 days.

Images taken by the Hubble space telescope in 1995 showed that the Martian climate has become cooler and drier since the *Viking* spacecraft visited the planet in the 1970s. NASA researchers believe that the planet's cooling may be due to diminished dust storms.

Mars was named for the Roman god of war, because when seen from Earth its distinct red color reminded the ancient people of blood. We know now that the reddish hue reflects the oxidized (rusted) iron in the surface material. The landing of two robot Viking spacecraft on the surface of Mars in 1976 provided more information about Mars in a few months than in all the time that has gone before.

The Martian Moons

Mars has two very small elliptical-shaped moons, Deimos and Phobos—the Greek names for the companions of the God Mars: Deimos (Terror) and Phobos (Fear). They were discovered in August 1877 by the American astronomer Asaph Hall (1829–1907) of the U.S. Naval Observatory in Washington, D.C.

The inner satellite Phobos is 27 kilometers (16.78 miles) long and it revolves around the planet in 7.6 hours. The outer moon, Deimos, is 15 kilometers (9.32 miles) long and it circles the planet in 30.35 hours. The short orbital period of Phobos means that the satellite travels around Mars twice in a Martian day. If an observer were suitably situated on the planet, he would see Phobos rise and set twice in a day.

Recent studies of Phobos indicate that its orbit is slowly decreasing downward and that in approximately 40 million years, it will crash into the planet's surface.

In 1988, the Soviet Union launched two spacecraft to study the geology, climate, and atmosphere of Mars, and explore its moon, Phobos. The attempt was unsuccessful as contact was lost with both spacecraft.

Russia plans to make unmanned studies of the Martian atmosphere and surface during 1996 and 1998. (*Also see* Space Section.)

Meteorites From Mars

Our knowledge of the origin and history of Mars has been greatly enhanced by recent research showing that a group of eight meteorites, labeled SNC[1] (named for towns where they were found: Shergotty, India, in 1865; Nakhla, Egypt, in 1911; and Chassigny, France, in 1815), are probably samples of Mars. This hypothesis is based largely on the composition of noble gases (particularly argon and xenon) trapped in the meteorites, and the Shergottites in particular, which resemble measurements of the Martian atmosphere made by the *Viking* spacecraft. Major element compositions of the SNCs are also similar to Martian soil analyses made by *Viking*.

These meteorites suggest that the Martian mantle is two to four times richer than Earth in moderately volatile elements such as potassium, rubidium, chlorine, bromine, sodium, zinc, and lead. In contrast, nitrogen, carbon dioxide, and the noble gases are more depleted than expected in the Martian atmosphere, suggesting an episode of severe atmospheric loss at some time in its history.

The relatively young isotopic ages of the SNC meteorites (1.3 billion years or less) suggest that Mars has been volcanically active during its recent past.

In 1991, a ninth meteorite, LEW 88516, was identified as having reached Earth from Mars some 180 million years ago. It was discovered in December 1988 near Lewis Cliff in Antarctica. The meteorite is very small with a dark pitted surface and weighs 13.2 grams (less than half an ounce).

A 4-pound, 7-ounce (1.9 kilograms) meteorite, ALH84001, found in the Allen Hills of Antarctica in 1984 was reclassified in 1993 as coming from the Red Planet, making it the tenth known to have originated from Mars. Its high carbonate content may have resulted when water rich in carbon dioxide crystallized within the meteorite, thus supporting the theory that Mars once had water.

A 40-pound meteorite that crashed to Earth in Nigeria in 1962 has been classified as coming from Mars. It was named Zagami for the region it was found in.

Scientists do not know how the meteorites were thrown off the Martian surface.

1. Pronounced "snick."

Jupiter's ring. A line has been drawn around a photograph of Jupiter to show the position of the extremely thin faint ring. NASA photo.

Jupiter

Jupiter is the largest planet in the solar system—a gaseous world as large as 1,300 Earths. Its equatorial diameter is 142,800 kilometers (88,736 miles), while from pole to pole, Jupiter measures only 133,500 kilometers (84,201 miles). For comparison, the diameter of the Earth is 12,756 kilometers (7,926.2 miles). The massive planet rotates at a dizzying speed—once every 9 hours and 55 minutes. It takes Jupiter almost 12 Earth years to complete a journey around the Sun.

The giant planet appears as a banded disk of turbulent clouds with all of its stripes running parallel to its bulging equator. Large dusky gray regions surround each pole. Darker Gray or brown stripes called belts intermingle with lighter, yellow-white stripes called zones. The belts are regions of descending air masses and the zones are rising cloudy air masses. The strongest winds—up to 400 kilometers (250 miles) per hour—are found at boundaries between the belts and zones.

This uniquely colorful atmosphere is mainly hydrogen and helium. It contains small amounts of methane, ammonia, ethane, acetylene, phosphene, germanium tetrahydride, and possibly hydrogen cyanide.

Cloud-type lightning bolts similar to those on Earth have been found in the Jovian atmosphere. At the polar regions, auroras have been observed. A very thin ring of material less than one kilometer (0.6 mile) in thickness and about 6,000 kilometers (4,000 miles) in radial extent has been observed circling the planet about 55,000 kilometers (35,000 miles) above the cloud tops.

The most prominent feature on Jupiter is its Great Red Spot, an oval larger than the planet Earth. It is a tremendous atmospheric storm that rotates counter-clockwise with one revolution every six days at the outer edge, while at the center almost no motion can be seen. The Spot is about 25,000 kilometers (16,000 miles) on its long axis, and would cover three Earths. The outer rim shows streamline shapes of 360-kilometer (225-mile) winds. Wind currents on the top flow east to west and currents on the top flow east to west and currents on the bottom flow west to east. The color of the Great Red Spot may indicate that it extends deep into the Jovian atmosphere.

The Spot was first seen more than three centuries ago. During the years, it has changed its color and size, and it escaped detection for nearly 50 years in the 1700s. *Voyager 1* and 2 found the Great Red Spot to be cooler at the top than the surrounding clouds, indicating that the Spot may tower above them.

Jupiter emits 67% more heat than it absorbs from the Sun. This heat is thought to be accumulated during the planet's formation several billion years ago.

Twenty-one fragments of Comet Shoemaker-Levy 9 bombarded the cloud-covered surface of Jupiter, July 16–22, 1994. It was the most violent event in the recorded history of our solar system. The cometary explosions caused towering plumes of debris and hot gas to rise from the darkened impact sites. It will take scientists many months and even years to analyze and interpret the results of the cosmic encounter.

Jovian Moons

The four great moons of Jupiter were discovered by Galileo Galilei (1564–1642) in January 1610, and are called the Galilean satellites after their discovery. Their names are Io, Europa, Ganymede, and Callisto. Like our Moon, the satellites always keep the same face turned toward the Earth. Jupiter has 16 known satellites.

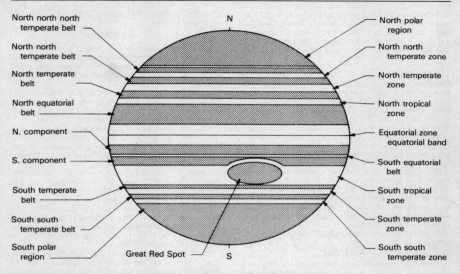

North north north
temperate belt

North north
temperate belt

North temperate
belt

North equatorial
belt

N. component

S. component

South temperate
belt

South south
temperate belt

South polar
region

N

Great Red Spot

S

North polar
region

North north
temperate zone

North temperate
zone

North tropical
zone

Equatorial zone
equatorial band

South equatorial
belt

South tropical
zone

South temperate
zone

South south
temperate zone

Schematic diagram of Jupiter's major features. NASA illustration.

Ganymede, Jupiter's largest satellite and also the largest known moon in the solar system. Its diverse surface indicates several periods of geologic activity.

A computer-generated image of Io, the most volcanically active planetary body known in the solar system. Io's volcanoes and lava lakes cover the landscape and continually reface it, so that many impact craters have disappeared. NASA photo.

Ganymede

Ganymede, 5,270 kilometers (3,275 miles) in diameter, is Jupiter's largest moon, and also it is the largest satellite in the solar system. Ganymede is about one and one-half times the size of our Moon. It is heavily cratered and probably has the greatest variety of geologic process recorded on its surface. Ganymede is half water and half rock, resulting in a density about two-thirds that of Europa, an ice-coated satellite. No atmosphere has been detected on it.

Europa

Europa, 3,130 kilometers (1,945 miles) in diameter, the brightest of Jupiter's Galilean satellites, may have

a surface of thin ice crust overlying water or softer ice, with large-scale fracture and ridge systems appearing in the crust. Europa has a density about three times that of water, suggesting that it is a mixture of silicate rock and some water. Very few impact craters are visible on the surface, implying a continual resurfacing process, perhaps by the production of fresh ice or snow along cracks and cold glacier-like flows.

Hubble space telescope observations of Europa in 1994 revealed that it has a tenuous oxygen-bearing atmosphere.

Callisto

Callisto, 4,840 kilometers (3,008 miles) in diameter, is the least active geologically of the Galilean satellites. Its icy, dirt-laden surface appears to be very ancient and heavily cratered. Callisto's density (less than twice that of water) is very close to that of Ganymede, yet there is little or no evidence of the crustal motion and internal activity that is visible on Ganymede.

Io

Io, 3,640 kilometers (2,262 miles) in diameter, is the most spectacular of the Galilean moons. Its brilliant colors of red, orange, and yellow set it apart from any other planet. Eight active volcanoes have been detected on Io, with some plumes extending up to 320 kilometers (200 miles) above the surface. The relative smoothness of Io's surface and its volcanic activity suggest that it has the youngest surface of Jupiter's moons. Its surface is composed of large amounts of sulfur and sulfur-dioxide frost, which account for the primarily yellow-orange surface color.

The volcanoes seem to eject a sufficient amount of sulfur dioxide to form a doughnut-shaped ring (torus) of ionized sulfur and oxygen atoms around Jupiter near Io's orbit. The Jovian magnetic field lines that go through the torus allow particles to precipitate into the polar regions of Jupiter, resulting in intense ultraviolet and visible auroras.

In 1995 astronomers observed two new volcanic eruptions on Io.

Amalthea

Amalthea, Jupiter's most innermost satellite, was discovered in 1892. It is so small—265 kilometers (165 miles) long and 150 kilometers (90 miles) wide—that it is extremely difficult to observe from Earth. Amalthea is an elongated, irregularly shaped satellite of reddish color. It orbits the planet every 12 hours and is in synchronous rotation, with its long axis always oriented toward Jupiter.

Jupiter's other moons are named Adrasta, Metis, Thebe, Leda, Himalia, Lysithea, Elara, Ananke, Carne, Pasiphae, and Sinope.

The Magnetosphere

Perhaps the largest structure in the solar system is the magnetosphere of Jupiter. This is the region of space which is filled with Jupiter's magnetic field and is bounded by the interaction of that magnetic field with the solar wind, which is the Sun's outward flow of charged particles. The plasma of electrically charged particles that exists in the magnetosphere is flattened into a large disk more than 4.8 million kilometers (3 million miles) in diameter, is coupled to the magnetic field, and rotates around Jupiter. The Galilean satellites are located in the inner regions of the magnetosphere and are subjected to intense radiation bombardment.

The intense radiation field that surrounds Jupiter is fatal to humans. If astronauts were one day able to approach the planet as close as the *Voyager 1* spacecraft did, they would receive a dose of 400,000 rads or roughly 1,000 times the lethal dose for humans.

In 1989, evidence from ground-based infrared spectra of Io indicated that the Jovian moon has hydrogen sulfide (H_2S) on its surface and in its atmosphere. It is the first time that the presence of H_2S has been detected outside the Earth.

• Even when nearest the Earth, Jupiter is still almost 400 million miles away. But because of its size, it may rival Venus in brilliance when near. Jupiter's four large moons may be seen through field glasses, moving rapidly around Jupiter and changing their position from night to night.

The United States launched its *Galileo* spacecraft toward Jupiter on Oct. 18, 1989. The unmanned spacecraft will reach Jupiter in 1995 and make a 22-month study of the planet. (Also see *Galileo* in the Space Section.)

Saturn

Saturn, the second largest planet in the solar system, is the least dense. Its mass is 95 times the mass of the Earth and its density is 0.70 gram per cubic centimeter, so that it would float in an ocean if there were one big enough to hold it.

Saturn radiates more energy than it receives from the Sun, about 80% more. However, the excess thermal energy cannot be primarily attributed to Saturn's primordial heat loss, as is speculated for Jupiter.

Saturn's diameter is 120,660 kilometers (74,978 miles) but 10% less at the poles, a consequence of its rapid rotation. Its axis of rotation is tilted by 27 degrees and the length of its day is 10 hours, 39 minutes, and 24 seconds.

Saturn is composed primarily of liquid metallic hydrogen (about 80%) and the second most common element is believed to be helium.

Saturn's atmospheric appearance is very similar to Jupiter's with dark and light cloud markings and swirls, eddies, and curling ribbons; the belts and zones are more numerous and a thick haze mutes the markings. The temperature ranges from 80° K to 90° K (176° F to −203° F).

Winds blow at extremely high speeds on Saturn. Near the equator, the *Voyagers* measured winds of about 500 meters per second (1,100 miles per hour). The winds blow primarily in an eastward direction.

Saturn's Rings

Saturn's spectacular ring system is unique in the solar system, with uncountable billions of tiny particles of water ice (with traces of other material) in orbit around the planet. The ring particles range in size from smaller than grains of sugar to as large as a house. The main rings stretch out from about 7,000 kilometers (4,350 miles) to above the atmosphere of the planet out to the F ring, a total span of 74,000 kilometers (45,984 miles). Saturn's rings can be likened to a phonograph, rings within rings numbering in the hundreds, and spokes in the B rings, and shepherding satellites controlling the F ring.

The main rings are called the A, B, and C rings moving from outside to inside. The gap between the A and B rings is called the Cassini Division and is named for the Italian-French astronomer, Gian Domenico Cassini, who discovered four of Saturn's major moons and the dark, narrow gap, "Cassini's Division," splitting the planet's rings.

Saturn's magnetic field has well-defined north and south magnetic poles, and is aligned with Saturn's axis of rotation to within one degree.

Saturn's Moons

Saturn has 18 recognized moons and two more were found outside Saturn's F ring by the Hubble Space Telescope in 1995. The five largest moons, Tethys, Dione, Rhea, Titan, and Iapetus, range from 1060 to 5150 kilometers (650 to 3,200 miles) in diameter. The planet's outstanding satellite is Titan, first discovered by the Dutch astronomer Christiaan Huygens in 1656.

Titan

Titan is remarkable because it is the only known moon in the solar system that has a substantial atmosphere—largely nitrogen with a minor amount of methane and a rich variety of other hydrocarbons. Its surface is completely hidden from view (except at infrared and radio wavelengths) by a dense, hazy atmosphere.

NASA illustration of the divisions in Saturn's ring system.

Photo of icy Mimas shows the largest meteorite crater which is about one-quarter the diameter of the entire moon. A huge mountain can be seen rising up almost 20,000 feet from the center of the crater. The crater's walls average 16,000 feet in height. NASA photo.

The diameter of Titan is 5,150 kilometers (3,200 miles) and it is the second largest satellite in the solar system after Jupiter's Ganymede. Titan is larger than the planet Mercury.

Titan's surface temperature is about −175° C (−280° F) and its surface pressure is about 50% greater than the surface pressure of the Earth. After the Voyager I flyby in 1980, scientists hypothesized that Titan may have an ocean of liquid hydrogen covering its surface. However, in 1990 it was shown that Titan's surface reflects and scatters radio waves, suggesting that the satellite has a solid surface with the possibility of small hydrocarbon lakes or ponds on the surface.

The data were obtained by using NASA's 70-meter antenna in California to transmit powerful radio waves to Titan, and the Very Large Array in New Mexico as the receiver of the reflected waves.

NASA plans to send a scientific probe to the surface of Titan in August 2002 as part of its Cassini Mission. The probe will be provided by the European Space Agency (ESA).

Other Notable Saturnian Moons

The other four largest moons of Saturn are: Tethys, Dione, Rhea, and Iapetus.

Tethys is 1,060 kilometers (650 miles) in diameter. Its surface is heavily cratered and it has a huge, globe-girdling canyon, Ithaca Chasma. Part of the canyon stretches over three-quarters of the satellite's surface. Ithaca Chasma is about 2,500 kilometers (1,550 miles) long. It has an average width of about 100 kilometers (62 miles) and a depth of 3 to 5 kilometers (1.8 to 3.1 miles).

Tethys also has a huge impact crater named Odysseus, 400 kilometers (244 miles) in diameter, or more than one-third its diameter.

Dione is slightly larger than Tethys, 1,120 kilometers (696 miles) and is more than half composed of water ice. It has bright, wispy markings resembling thin veils covering its features.

Rhea, the largest of the inner satellites, is 1,530 kilometers (951 miles) in diameter. It is composed mainly of water ice, causing its reflective surface to present an almost uniform white appearance.

Iapetus is the outermost of Saturn's icy satellites. Its appearance is unique because it has one dark and one bright hemisphere. The origin of the black coating of its dark face is unknown. Iapetus has a diameter of 1,460 kilometers (907 miles).

Other notable moons of Saturn are Mimas, Enceladus, Hyperion, and Phoebe.

Mimas is small, only 329 kilometers (244 miles) in diameter. It has a huge impact crater, Herschel, nearly one-third its diameter. The crater is about 130 kilometers (81 miles) wide and its icy peak rises almost 10 kilometers (6.2 miles) above the floor.

Mimas is believed to be composed mainly of water ice and to contain between 20 to 50% rock.

Enceladus is remarkable in that its surface shows signs of extensive and recent geological activity. There may be active water volcanism. The surface is extremely bright, reflecting more than 90% of incident sunlight. This suggests that its surface is composed of extremely pure ice without dust or rocks to contaminate it. Enceladus has a diameter of 500 kilometers (310 miles).

Hyperion orbits between Iapetus and Titan. It is irregular in shape, measuring about 400 by 250 by 200 kilometers (248 by 155 by 124 miles). It may be a remnant of a much larger object which was shattered by impact with another space body. It appears that Hyperion is composed primarily of water ice.

The Uranian moon Miranda is one of the strangest objects in the solar system. Photo shows some of its complex surface terrain. NASA photo.

Hyperion orbits Saturn in a random-like motion ("chaotic tumbling").

Phoebe is Saturn's outermost satellite. It travels in a retrograde orbit at a distance of over 10 million kilometers (6.2 million miles) away from the planet. It is the darkest moon of Saturn and is the planet's only known satellite that does not keep the same face always turned to Saturn. It has been speculated that it is an asteroid that was captured by the planet. Phoebe rotates in about nine hours and orbits Saturn in 406 days. It has a diameter of 200 kilometers (124 miles).

Pan was discovered in 1990 from *Voyager 2* photos taken in 1981. An official name, Pan, is to be approved by the International Astronomical Union. The satellite is estimated to be about 20 kilometers (12.43 miles) in diameter, which makes it the planet's smallest known moon. It orbits within the Encke Gap, a 325-kilometer (202 mile) division in Saturn's A ring. It was identified by Johann Franz Encke (1791–1865) in 1837.

The remaining eight moons range from 25 to 190 kilometers (15 to 120 miles) in diameter. They are all non-spherical in shape. Their names are Atlas, Prometheus, Pandora, Epimetheus, Janus, Telesto, Calypso, and Helene.

If NASA's planned Cassini Mission to Saturn in the later 1990s takes place, it will shed more light on the planet's mysteries. (*See* Cassini Mission in the Space Section.)

• Saturn is the last of the planets visible to the naked eye. Saturn is never an object of overwhelming brilliance, but it looks like a bright star. The rings can be seen with a small telescope.

Uranus

Uranus, the first planet discovered in modern times by Sir William Herschel in 1781, is the seventh planet from the Sun, twice as far out as Saturn. Its mean distance from the Sun is 2,869 million kilometers (1,783 million miles). Uranus's equatorial diameter is 51,810 kilometers (32,200 miles). The axis of Uranus is tilted at 97 degrees, so it goes around the Sun nearly lying on its side.

Due to Uranus' unusual inclination, the polar regions receive more sunlight during a Uranus year of 84 Earth years. Scientists had thought that the temperature of its poles would be warmer than that at its equator, but *Voyager 2* discovered that the equatorial temperatures were similar to the temperatures at the poles, –209° C (–344° F), implying that some redistribution of heat toward the equatorial region must occur within the atmosphere. The wind patterns are much like Saturn's, flowing parallel to the equator in the direction of the planet's rotation.

Ninety-eight percent of the upper atmosphere is composed of hydrogen and helium; the remaining two percent is methane. Scientists speculate that the bulk of the lower atmosphere is composed of water (perhaps as much as 50%), methane, and ammonia. Methane is responsible for Uranus' blue-green color because it selectively absorbs red sunlight and condenses to form clouds of ice crystals in the cooler, higher regions of Uranus' atmosphere.

It was also discovered that the planet's magnetic field was 60 degrees tilted from the planet's axis of rotation and offset from the planet's center by one-third of Uranus' radius. It may be generated at a depth where water is under sufficient pressure to be electrically conductive.

The Uranian Rings

Voyager 2 also expanded the body of information pertaining to the rings and moons of Uranus. *Voyager*'s cameras obtained the first images of nine previously known narrow rings and discovered at least two new rings, one narrow and one broadly diffused, bringing the total known rings to eleven. It was found that a highly structured distribution of fine dust exists throughout the ring system.

The outermost (epsilon) ring contains nothing smaller than fist-sized particles. It is flanked by two small moons discovered interior to the orbit of the Uranian moon Miranda. The moons exert a shepherding influence on the epsilon ring and on the outer edges of the gamma and delta rings.

All of the rings lie within one planetary radius[1] of Uranus' cloud tops. Most of Uranus' rings are narrow, ranging in width from 1 to 93 kilometers (0.6 to 58 miles) and are only a few kilometers thick. The Uranian rings are colorless and extremely dark. The dark material may be either irradiated methane ice or organic-rich minerals mixed with water-impregnated, silicon-based compounds. There is evidence that incomplete rings, or "ring arcs," exist at Uranus.

The Uranian Moons

There are 15 known moons of Uranus. In order of decreasing distance from the planet, the moons are Oberon, Titania, Umbriel, Ariel, Miranda, Puck, Belinda, Cressida, Portia, Rosalind, Desdemona, Juliet, Bianca, Ophelia, and Cordelia. Nine of the new moons range in size from 26 to 108 kilometers (16 to 67 miles) in diameter and, being closer to the planet, have faster periods of revolution (8 to 15 hours) than their more distant relatives.

---

1. The equatorial radius of Uranus is 25,560 kilometers (15,880 miles) at a pressure of 1 bar.

ABOVE LEFT: The rugged terrain of Triton, Neptune's largest moon. *Voyager 2* **photographed geyser-like eruptions of nitrogen gas on Triton. ABOVE RIGHT: High-altitude clouds in Neptune's atmosphere. BELOW RIGHT: The Great Dark Spot is the most prominent feature in the planet's atmosphere. It is a counter-clockwise storm about the size of the Earth.**

Oberon and Titania

The two largest moons, Oberon, 1,516 kilometers (942 miles) in diameter, and Titania (1,580 kilometers (982 miles) in diameter, are less than half the diameter of Earth's moon. Titania, the reddest of Uranus' moons, may have endured global tectonics as evidenced by complex valleys and fault lines etched into its surface. Smooth sections indicate that volcanic resurfacing has taken place.

Umbriel and Ariel

Umbriel and Ariel are roughly three-fourths the size of Oberon and Titania. Umbriel is the darkest of the large moons with huge craters peppering its surface. Umbriel has a paucity of what are known as bright ray craters, which are formed on an older darker surface when bright submerged ice is excavated and sprayed by meteoroid impacts.

In contrast, the surface of Ariel, the brightest of the Uranian moons, is relatively free of pockmarks due to volcanism which periodically erases the damage done by foreign projectiles. However, there are several extremely deep cuts on Ariel's surface.

Miranda

The smallest of Uranus' large moons, Miranda, 472 kilometers (293 miles) in diameter, has been described as "the most bizarre body in the solar system," with the most geologically complex surface. Miranda's remarkable terrain consists of rolling, heavily cratered plains (the oldest known in the Uranian system) adjoined by three huge, 200 to 300 kilometer (120 to 180 mile) oval-to-trapezoidal regions known as coronae, which are characterized by networks of concentric canyons.

Puck

Puck was the first new moon discovered by *Voyager,* and is 154 kilometers (96 miles) in diameter and makes a trip around Uranus every 18 hours. Puck is shaped somewhat like a potato with a huge impact crater marring roughly one-fourth of its surface.

• Uranus can—on rare occasions—become bright enough to be seen with the naked eye, if one knows exactly where to look; normally, a good set of field glasses or a small portable telescope is required.

Neptune

Little was known about Neptune until August 1989, when NASA's *Voyager 2* became the first spacecraft to observe the planet. Passing about 4,950 kilometers (3,000 miles) above Neptune's north pole, *Voyager 2* made its closest approach to any planet since leaving Earth twelve years prior. The spacecraft passed about 40,000 kilometers (25,000 miles) from Neptune's largest moon, Triton, the last solid body that *Voyager 2* will have studied.

Nearly 4.5 billion kilometers (3 billion miles) from the Sun, Neptune orbits the Sun once in 165 years, and therefore has made not quite a full circle around the Sun since it was discovered.[1]

With an equatorial diameter of 49,528 kilometers (30,775 miles), Neptune is the smallest of our solar system's four gas giants.[2] Even so, its volume could hold nearly 60 Earths. Neptune is also denser than the other gas giants—Jupiter, Saturn, and Uranus, about 64% heavier than if it were composed entirely of water.

Neptune has a blue color as a result of methane in its atmosphere. Methane preferentially absorbs the longer wavelengths of sunlight (those near the red end of the spectrum). What are left to be reflected are colors at the blue end of the spectrum.

The atmosphere of Neptune is mainly composed of hydrogen, with helium and traces of methane and ammonia.

Neptune is a dynamic planet even though it receives only three percent as much sunlight as Jupiter does. *Voyager 2* discovered several large, dark spots that were prominent features on the planet. The largest spot was about the size of the Earth and was designated the "Great Dark Spot" by its discoverers. It appeared to be an anticyclone similar to Jupiter's Great Red Spot. While Neptune's Great Dark Spot is comparable in size, relative to the planet, and at the same latitude (22° south latitude) as Jupiter's Great Red Spot, it was far more variable in size and shape than its Jovian counterpart. Bright, wispy "cirrus-type" clouds overlaid the Great Dark Spot at its southern and northeastern boundaries.

At about 42° south, a bright, irregularly shaped, eastward-moving cloud circles much faster than did the Great Dark Spot, "scooting" around Neptune in about 16 hours. This "scooter" may have been a cloud plume rising between cloud decks.

Another spot, designated D2," was located far to the south of the Great Dark Spot at 55° S latitude. It is almond-shaped, with a bright central core, and moves eastward around the planet in about 16 hours.

In 1995, images taken by the Hubble space telescope showed that the Great Dark Sport has vanished. The great storm center has either dissipated or is obscured by other atmospheric conditions.

The atmosphere above Neptune's clouds is hotter near the equator, cooler in the mid-latitudes, and warm again at the south pole. Temperatures in the stratosphere were measured to be 750 kelvins (900° F), while at the 100 millibar pressure level, they were measured to be 85° K (−360° F).

Long, bright clouds, reminiscent of cirrus clouds on Earth, were seen high in Neptune's atmosphere. They appear to form above most of the methane, and consequently are not blue.

At northern low latitudes (27° N), *Voyager* captured images of cloud streaks casting their shadows on cloud decks estimated to be about 50 to 100 kilometers (30 to 60 miles) below. The widths of these cloud streaks range from 50 to 200 kilometers (30 to 125 miles). Cloud streaks were also seen in the southern polar regions (71° S) where the cloud heights were about 50 kilometers (30 miles).

---

1. Astronomers have studied Neptune since Sept. 23, 1846, when Johann Gottfried Galle, of the Berlin Observatory, and Louis d'Arrest, an astronomy student, discovered the eighth planet on the basis of mathematical predictions by Urbain Jean Joseph Le Verrier. Similar predictions were made independently by John Couch Adams. Galileo Galilei had seen Neptune during several nights of observing Jupiter, in January 1613, but didn't realize he was seeing a new planet.
2. These four planets are about 4 to 12 times greater in diameter than Earth. They have no solid surfaces, but possess massive atmospheres that contain substantial amounts of hydrogen and helium with traces of other gases.

Most of the winds on Neptune blow in a westward direction, which is retrograde, or opposite to the rotation of the planet. Near the Great Dark Spot, there are retrograde winds blowing up to 1,500 miles an hour—the strongest winds measured on any planet.

The Magnetic Field

Neptune's magnetic field is tilted 47 degrees from the planet's rotation axis, and is offset at least 0.55 radii (about 13,500 kilometers or 8,500 miles) from the physical center. The dynamo electric currents produced within the planet, therefore, must be relatively closer to the surface than for Earth, Jupiter, or Saturn. Because of its unusual orientation, and the tilt of the planet's rotation axis, Neptune's magnetic field goes through dramatic changes as the planet rotates in the solar wind.

Voyager's planetary radio astronomy instrument measured the periodic radio waves generated by the magnetic field and determined that the rotation rate of the interior of Neptune is 16 hours 7 minutes.

Voyager also detected auroras, similar to the northern and southern lights on Earth, in Neptune's atmosphere. Unlike those on Earth, due to Neptune's complex magnetic field, the auroras are extremely complicated processes that occur over wide regions of the planet, not just near the planet's magnetic poles.

Neptune's Moons

Triton

The largest of Neptune's eight known satellites, Triton is different from all other icy moons that *Voyager* has studied. Triton circles Neptune in a tilted, circular, retrograde orbit, completing an orbit in 5.875 days at an average distance of 330,000 kilometers (205,000 miles) above the planet's cloud tops.

Triton shows evidence of a remarkable geologic history, and *Voyager 2* images show active geyser-like eruptions spewing invisible nitrogen gas and dark dust particles 2 to eight kilometers (1 to 5 miles) into space.

Triton is about three-quarters the size of Earth's moon and has a diameter of about 2,705 kilometers (1,680 miles), and a mean density of about 2.066 grams per cubic centimeter. (The density of water is 1.0 gram per cubic centimeter.) This means that Triton contains more rock in its interior than the icy satellites of Saturn and Uranus do.

The relatively high density and the retrograde orbit offer strong evidence that Triton did not originate near Neptune, but is a captured object.

An extremely thin atmosphere extends as much as 800 kilometers (500 miles) above the satellite's surface. Tiny nitrogen ice particles may form thin clouds a few kilometers above the surface. Triton is very bright, reflecting 60 to 95% of the sunlight that strikes it. (By comparison, Earth's moon reflects only 11 percent.)

The atmospheric pressure at Triton's surface is about 14 microbars, a mere 1/70,000th the surface pressure on Earth. Temperature at the surface is about 38 kelvins (−391° F), making it the coldest surface of any body yet visited in the solar system.

The Smaller Satellites

In addition to the previously known moons Triton and Nereid, *Voyager 2* found six more satellites, making the total eight.

Nereid

Nereid was discovered in 1948 through Earth-based telescopes. Little is known about Nereid, which is slightly smaller than Proteus, having a diameter of

340 kilometers (211 miles). The satellite's surface reflects about 14% of the sunlight that strikes it. Nereid's orbit is the most eccentric in the solar system, ranging from about 1,353,600 km (841,100 miles) to 9,623,700 (5,980,200 mi.).

Proteus

Like all six of Neptune's recently discovered small satellites, it is one of the darkest objects in the solar system—"as dark as soot" is a good description. It reflects only 6% of the sunlight that strikes it. Proteus is an ellipsoid about 258 kilometers (415 miles) in diameter, larger than Nereid. It circles Neptune at a distance of about 92,800 kilometers (57,700 miles) above the cloud tops, and completes one orbit in 26 hours 54 minutes. Scientists say that it is about as large as a satellite can be without being pulled into a spherical shape by its own gravity.

Larissa

This object is only about 48,800 kilometers (30,300 miles) from Neptune and circles the planet in 13 hours 18 minutes. Its diameter is 190 kilometers (120 miles).

Despina

The satellite is 27,700 kilometers (17,200 miles) from Neptune's clouds and makes one orbit every 8 hours. Its diameter is about 150 kilometers (90 miles).

Galatea

It lies 37,200 kilometers (23,100 miles) from Neptune. Its diameter is 180 kilometers (110 miles) and it completes an orbit in 10 hours 18 minutes.

Thalassa

The satellite appears to be about 80 kilometers (50 miles) in diameter. It orbits Neptune in 7 hours 30 minutes some 25,200 kilometers (15,700 miles) above the cloud tops.

Naiad

The last satellite discovered, it is about 60 kilometers (37 miles) in diameter and orbits Neptune about 23,200 kilometers (14,400 miles) above the clouds in 7 hours 6 minutes.

Proteus and its tiny companions are cratered and irregularly shaped—they are not round—and show no signs of any geologic modifications. All circle the planet in the same direction as Neptune rotates, and remain close to Neptune's equatorial plane.

Neptune's Rings

Voyager found four rings and evidence of ring *arcs* or incomplete rings. The "Main Ring" orbits Neptune at about 38,100 kilometers (23,700 miles) above the cloud tops. The "Inner Ring" is about 28,400 kilometers (17,700 miles) from Neptune's cloud tops. An "Inside Diffuse Ring"—a complete ring—is located about 17,100 kilometers (10,600 miles) from the planet's cloud tops. Some scientists suspect that this ring may extend all the way down to Neptune's cloud tops. An area called "the Plateau" is a broad, diffuse sheet of fine material just outside the so-called "Inner Ring." The fine material is approximately the size of smoke particles. All other rings contain a greater proportion of larger material.

Pluto

Pluto, the outermost and smallest planet in the solar system, is the only planet not visited by an exploring spacecraft. So little is known about it, that it is difficult to classify. Its distance is so great that the Hubble Space Telescope cannot reveal its surface features. Appropriately named for the Roman god of the underworld, it must be frozen, dark, and dead. Pluto's mean distance from the Sun is 5,900 million kilometers (3,666 million miles).

In 1978, light curve studies gave evidence of a moon revolving around Pluto with the same period as Pluto's rotation. Therefore, it stays over the same point on Pluto's surface. In addition, it keeps the same face toward the planet. The satellite was later named Charon and is estimated to be about 789 miles (1,270 kilometers) in diameter. Recent estimates indicate Pluto's diameter is about about 1,441.6 miles (2,220 kilometers), making the pair more like a double planet than any other in the solar system. Previously, the Earth-Moon system held this distinction. The density of Pluto is slightly greater than that of water.

There is evidence that Pluto has an atmosphere containing methane and polar ice caps that increase and decrease in size with the planet's seasons. It is not known to have water. The Hubble space telescope's faint object camera revealed light and dark regions on Pluto indicating an ice cap at the planet's north pole. It is not known if there is an ice cap at Pluto's south pole.

Pluto was predicted by calculation when Percival Lowell (1855–1916) noticed irregularities in the orbits of Uranus and Neptune. Clyde Tombaugh (1906–   ) discovered the planet in 1930, precisely where Lowell predicted it would be. The name Pluto was chosen because the first two letters represent the initials of Percival Lowell.

• Pluto has the most eccentric orbit in the solar system, bringing it at times closer to the Sun than Neptune. Pluto approached the perihelion of its orbit on Sept. 5, 1989, and for the rest of this century will be closer to the Sun than Neptune. Even then, it can be seen only with a large telescope.

The Asteroids

Between the orbits of Mars and Jupiter are an estimated 30,000 pieces of rocky debris, known collectively as the asteroids, or planetoids. The first and, incidentally, the largest (Ceres) was discovered during the New Year's night of 1801 by the Italian astronomer Father Piazzi (1746–1826), and its orbit was calculated by the German mathematician Karl Friedrich Gauss (1777–1855). Gauss invented a new method of calculating orbits on that occasion. A German amateur astronomer, the physician Olbers (1758–1840), discovered the second asteroid, Pallas. The number now known, catalogued, and named is over 6,000 and could reach 10,000 by the end of the 20th century. A few asteroids do not move in orbits beyond the orbit of Mars, but in orbits which cross the orbit of Mars. The first of them was named Eros because of this peculiar orbit. It had become the rule to bestow female names on the asteroids, but when it was found that Eros crossed the orbit of a major planet, it received a male name. Since then around two dozen orbit-crossers have been discovered, and they are often referred to as the "male asteroids." A few of them—Albert, Adonis, Apollo, Amor, and Icarus—cross the orbit of the Earth, and two of them may come closer than our Moon; but the crossing is like a bridge crossing a highway, not like two highways intersecting. Hence there is very little danger of collision from these bodies. They are all small, three to five miles in diameter, and therefore very difficult objects to identify, even when quite close. Some scientists believe the asteroids represent the remains of an exploded planet. Asteroid 1992 AD,

The First Ten Minor Planets (Asteroids)

Name	Year of discovery	Mean Distance from sun (millions of miles)	Orbital period (years)	Diameter (miles)	Magnitude
1. Ceres	1801	257.0	4.60	485	7.4
2. Pallas	1802	257.4	4.61	304	8.0
3. Juno	1804	247.8	4.36	118	8.7
4. Vesta	1807	219.3	3.63	243	6.5
5. Astraea	1845	239.3	4.14	50	9.9
6. Hebe	1847	225.2	3.78	121	8.5
7. Iris	1847	221.4	3.68	121	8.4
8. Flora	1847	204.4	3.27	56	8.9
9. Metis	1848	221.7	3.69	78	8.9
10. Hygeia	1849	222.6	5.59	40 (?)	9.5

discovered January 1992, is the outermost asteroid known. It takes 93 years to orbit the Sun. This minor planet's orbit crosses the paths of Saturn, Uranus, and Neptune.

On Oct. 29, 1991, the Galileo spacecraft took a historic photograph of asteroid 951 Gaspra from a distance of 10,000 miles (16,200 kilometers) away. It was the first close-up photo ever taken of an asteroid in space.

Gaspra was discovered to be an irregular, potato-shaped object about 12.5 mi (20 km) by 7.5 mi (12 km) by 7 mi (11 km) in size. Its surface is covered with a layer of loose rubble and its terrain is covered with several dozen small craters.

Scientists believe that Gaspra is a fragment of a larger body which was shattered from collisions with other asteroids.

The asteroid was named after a Black Sea retreat favored by Russian astronomer Grigoriy N. Neujmin who discovered it in 1916.

Closeup photos of Asteroid 243 Ida taken by the Galileo spacecraft on Aug. 28, 1993, revealed that Ida had a tiny egg-shaped moon measuring 0.9 miles by 0.7 miles (1.6 by 1.2 kilometers). The moon has been named Dactyl.

Comets

Comets, according to the noted astronomer, Fred L. Whipple (1906–   ), are enormous "snowballs" of frozen gases (mostly carbon dioxide, methane, and water vapor) and contain very little solid material. The whole behavior of comets can then be explained as the behavior of frozen gas being heated by the Sun. When the comet Kohoutek made its first appearance to man in 1973, its behavior seemed to confirm this theory and later, the international study by five spacecraft that encountered Comet Halley in March 1986 confirmed Whipple's idea of the make-up of comets.

Since comets appear in the sky without any warning, people in classical times and especially during the Middle Ages believed that they had a special meaning, which, of course, was bad. Since a natural catastrophe of some sort of a military conflict occurs every year, it was quite simple to blame the comet that happened to be visible. But even in the past, there were some people who used logical reasoning. When, in Roman times, a comet was blamed for the loss of a battle and hence was called a "bad omen," a Roman writer observed that the victors in the battle probably did not think so.

Up until the middle of the sixteenth century, comets were believed to be phenomena of the upper atmosphere; they were usually "explained" as "burning vapors" which had risen from "distant swamps." That nobody had ever actually seen burning vapors rise from a swamp did not matter.

But a large comet which appeared in 1577 was carefully observed by Tycho Brahe (1546–1601), a Danish astronomer who is often, and with the best of reasons, called "eccentric" but who insisted on precise measurements for everything. It was Tycho Brahe's accumulation of literally thousands of precise measurements which later enable his younger collaborator, Johannes Kepler (1571–1630), to discover the laws of planetary motion. Measuring the motion of the comet of 1577, Tycho Brahe could show that it had been far beyond the atmosphere, even though he could not give figures for the distance. Tycho Brahe's work proved that comets were astronomical and not meteorological phenomena.

In 1682, the second Astronomer Royal of Great Britain, Dr. Edmond Halley (1656–1742), checked the orbit of a bright comet that was in the sky then and compared it with earlier comet orbits which were known in part. Halley found that the comet of 1682 was the third to move through what appeared to be the same orbit. And the three appearances were roughly 76 years apart. Halley concluded that this was the same comet, moving around the Sun in a closed orbit, like the planets. He predicted that it would reappear in 1758 or 1759. Halley himself died in 1742, but a large comet appeared sixteen years after his death as predicted and was immediately referred to as "Halley's comet."

In the Spring of 1973, the discovery of comet Kohoutek, apparently headed for a close-Christmastime rendezvous with the Sun, created worldwide excitement. The comet was a visual disappointment, but turned out to be a treasure trove of information on these little-understood celestial objects. Given an unprecedented advance notice of nine months on the advent of the fiery object, scientists were able to study the comet in visible, ultraviolet and infrared light; with optical telescopes, radio telescopes, and radar. They observed it from the ground, from high-flying aircraft, with instruments aboard unmanned satellites, with sounding rockets, and telescopes and cameras on the Earth-orbiting Skylab space station.

Halley's Comet appeared again in 1986, sparking a worldwide interest to study it up close. Five satellites in all took readings from the comet at various distances. Two Soviet craft, *Vega 1* and *Vega 2*, went in close to provide detailed pictures of the comet, including the first of the comet's core. The European Space Agency's craft, *Giotto*, entered the comet itself, coming to within 450 miles of the comet's center and successfully passing through its tail. In addition, two Japanese craft, the *Suisei* and the *Sakigake*, passed at a longer distance in order to analyze the cloud and tail of the comet and the effect of solar radiation upon it. The United States declined to launch a similar mission, citing budgetary constraints imposed by the shuttle program. A space telescope was to study Halley's Comet but was destroyed in the *Challenger* disaster.

The information gained included measurements of the size of the nucleus, an idea of its configuration and the rate of its rotation. The gas and dust of the comet were analyzed as was the material of the tail. This information is considered important because comets are believed to be debris from the formation of the solar system and to have changed little since then.

Astronomers refer to comets as "periodic" or as "non-periodic" comets, but the latter term does not mean that these comets have no period; it merely means that their period is not known. The actual periods of comets run from 3.3 years (the shortest known) to many thousands of years. Their orbits are elliptical, like those of the planets, but they are very eccentric, long and narrow ellipses. Only comet Schwassmann-Wachmann has an orbit which has such a low eccentricity (for a cometary orbit) that it could be the orbit of a minor planet.

When a comet, coming from deep space, approaches the Sun, it is at first indistinguishable from a minor planet. Somewhere between the orbits of Mars and Jupiter its outline becomes fuzzy; it is said to develop a "coma" (the word used here is the Latin word *coma,* which means "hair," not the phonetically identical Greek word which means "deep sleep"). Then, near the orbit of Mars, the comet develops its tail, which at first trails behind. This grows steadily as the comet comes closer and closer to the Sun. As it rounds the Sun (as first noticed by Girolamo Fracastoro, 1483–1553) the tail always points away from the Sun so that the comet, when moving away from the Sun, points its tail ahead like the landing lights of an airplane.

The reason for this behavior is that the tail is pushed in these directions by the radiation pressure of the Sun. It sometimes happens that a comet loses its tail at perihelion; it then grows another one. Although the tail is clearly visible against the black of the sky, it is very tenuous. It has been said that if the tail of Halley's comet could be compressed to the density of iron, it would fit into a small suitcase.

Although very low in mass, comets are among the largest members of the solar system. The nucleus of a comet may be up to 10,000 miles in diameter; its coma between 10,000 and 50,000 miles in diameter; and its tail as long as 28 million miles.

Comet Shoemaker–Levy 9 broke up into 21 fragments in July 1992 and crashed into the surface of Jupiter July 16–22, 1994, in the worst violent event in the recorded history of the solar system.

Meteors and Meteorites

The term "meteor" for what is usually called a "shooting star" bears an unfortunate resemblance to the term "meteorology," the science of weather and weather forecasting. This resemblance is due to an ancient misunderstanding which wrongly considered meteors an atmospheric phenomenon. Actually, the streak of light in the sky that scientists call a meteor is essentially an astronomical phenomenon: the entry of a small piece of cosmic matter into our atmosphere.

The distinction between "meteors" and "fireballs" (formerly also called "bolides") is merely one of convenience; a fireball is an unusually bright meteor. Incidentally, it also means that a fireball is larger than a faint meteor.

Bodies which enter our atmosphere become visible when they are about 60 miles above the ground. The fact that they grow hot enough to emit light is not due to the "friction" of the atmosphere, as one can often read. The phenomenon responsible for the heating is one of compression. Unconfined air cannot move faster than the speed of sound. Since the entering meteorite moves with 30 to 60 times the speed of sound, the air simply cannot get out of the way. Therefore, it is compressed like the air in the cylinder of a Diesel engine and is heated by compression. This heat—or part of it—is transferred to the moving body. The details of this process are now fairly well understood as a result of re-entry tests with ballistic-missile nose cones.

The average weight of a body producing a faint "shooting star" is only a small fraction of an ounce. Even a bright fireball may not weigh more than 2 or 3 pounds. Naturally, the smaller bodies are worn to dust by the passage through the atmosphere; only rather large ones reach the ground. Those that are found are called meteorites. (The "meteor," to repeat, is the term for the light streak in the sky.) About 1,000 meteorites fall to the Earth each year.

The largest meteorite known is still imbedded in the ground near Grootfontein in SW Africa and is estimated to weight 70 tons. The second largest known is the 34-ton Anighito (on exhibit in the Hayden Planetarium, New York), which was found by Admiral Peary in 1892 at Cape York in Greenland. The largest meteorite found in the United States is the Willamette meteorite (found in Oregon, weight ca. 15 tons), but large portions of this meteorite weathered away before it was found. Its weight as it struck the ground may have been 20 tons.

All these are iron meteorites (an iron meteorite normally contains about 7% nickel), which form one class of meteorites. The other class consists of the stony meteorites, and between them there are the so-called "stony irons." The so-called "tektites" consist of glass similar to our volcanic glass obsidian, and because of the similarity, there is doubt in a number of cases whether the glass is of terrestrial or of extra-terrestrial origin.

Though no meteorite larger than the Grootfontein is actually known, we do know that the Earth has, on occasion, been struck by much larger bodies. Evidence for such hits are the meteorite craters, of which an especially good example is located near the Cañon Diablo in Arizona. Another meteor crater in the United States is a rather old crater near Odessa, Texas. A large number of others are known, especially in eastern Canada; and for many "probables," meteoric origin has now been proved.

The 13th known lunar meteorite was found in December 1993 by a team from the Antarctic Search for Meteorites project. It is approximately two inches long and weighs 0.75 of an ounce.

Some scientists theorize that the mass extermination of dinosaurs from the face of the Earth 65 million years ago was due to a large meteor that struck out planet at that time.

The meteor showers are caused by multitudes of very small bodies travelling in swarms. The Earth travels in its orbit through these swarms like a car driving through falling snow. The point from which the meteors seem to emanate is called the *radiant* and is named for the constellation in that area. The Perseid meteor shower in August is the most spectacular of the year, boasting at peak roughly 60 meteors per hour under good atmospheric conditions. The presence of a bright moon diminishes the number of visible meteors.

The 88 Recognized Constellations

In astronomical works, the Latin names of the constellations are used. The letter N or S following the Latin name indicates whether the constellation is located to the north or south of the Zodiac. The letter Z indicates that the constellation is within the Zodiac.

Latin name	Letter	English version	Latin name	Letter	English version	Latin name	Letter	English version
Andromeda	N	Andromeda	Delphinus	N	Dolphin	Pavo	S	Peacock
Antlia	S	Airpump	Dorado	S	Swordfish	Pegasus	N	Pegasus
Apus	S	Bird of Paradise			(Goldfish)	Perseus	N	Perseus
Aquarius	Z	Water Bearer	Draco	N	Dragon	Phoenix	S	Phoenix
Aquila	N	Eagle	Equuleus	N	Filly	Pictor	S	Painter (or his
Ara	S	Altar	Eridanus	S	Eridanus (river)			Easel)
Aries	Z	Ram	Fornax	S	Furnace	Pisces	Z	Fishes
Auriga	N	Charioteer	Gemini	Z	Twins	Piscis		
Boötes	N	Herdsmen	Grus	S	Crane	Austrinus	S	Southern Fish
Caelum	S	Sculptor's Tool	Hercules	N	Hercules	Puppis	S	Poop (of Argo)[1]
Camelopardalis	N	Giraffe	Horologium	S	Clock	Pyxis	S	Mariner's
Cancer	Z	Crab	Hydra	N	Sea Serpent			Compass
Canes Venatici	N	Hunting Dogs	Hydrus	S	Water Snake	Reticulum	S	Net
Canis Major	S	Great Dog	Indus	S	Indian	Sagitta	N	Arrow
Canis Minor	S	Little Dog	Lacerta	N	Lizard	Sagittarius	Z	Archer
Capricornus	Z	Goat (or Sea-	Leo	Z	Lion	Scorpius	Z	Scorpion
		Goat)	Leo Minor	N	Little Lion	Sculptor	S	Sculptor
Carina	S	Keel (of Argo)[1]	Lepus	S	Hare	Scutum	N	Shield
Cassiopeia	N	Cassiopeia	Libra	Z	Scales	Serpens	N	Serpent
Centaurus	S	Centaur	Lupus	S	Wolf	Sextans	N	Sextant
Cepheus	N	Cepheus	Lynx	N	Lynx	Taurus	Z	Bull
Cetus	S	Whale	Lyra	N	Lyre (Harp)	Telescopium	S	Telescope
Chameleon	S	Chameleon	Mensa	S	Table	Triangulum	N	Triangle
Circinus	S	Compasses			(mountain)	Triangulum	S	Southern
Columba	S	Dove	Microscopium	S	Microscope	Australe		Triangle
Coma Berenices	N	Berenice's Hair	Monoceros	S	Unicorn	Tucana	S	Toucan
Corona Australis	S	Southern Crown	Musca	S	Southern Fly	Ursa Major	N	Big Dipper
Corona Borealis	N	Northern Crown	Norma	S	Rule	Ursa Minor	N	Little Dipper
Corvus	S	Crow (Raven)			(straightedge)	Vela	S	Sail (of Argo)[1]
Crater	S	Cup	Octans	S	Octant	Virgo	Z	Virgin
Crux	S	Southern Cross	Ophiuchus	N	Serpent-Bearer	Volans	S	Flying Fish
Cygnus	N	Swan	Orion	S	Orion	Vulpecula	N	Fox

1. The original constellation Argo Navis (the Ship Argo) has been divided into Carina, Puppis, and Vela. Normally the brightest star in each constellation is designated by alpha, the first letter of the Greek alphabet, the second brightest by beta, the second letter of the Greek alphabet, and so forth. But the Greek letters run through Carina, Puppis, and Vela as if it were still one constellation.

The Constellations

Constellations are groupings of stars which form patterns that can be easily recognized and remembered, for example, Orion and the Big Dipper. The Big Dipper is actually an asterism, not a constellation, because it is only part of the constellation Ursa Major (the Big Bear). Actually, the stars of the majority of all constellations do not "belong together." Usually they are at greatly varying distances from the Earth and just happen to lie more or less in the same line of sight as seen from our solar system. But in a few cases the stars of a constellation are actually associated; most of the bright stars of the Big Dipper travel together and form what astronomers call an open cluster.

If you observe a planet, say Mars, for one complete revolution, you will see that it passes successively through twelve constellations. All planets (except Pluto at certain times) can be observed only in these twelve constellations, which form the so-called Zodiac, and the Sun also moves through the Zodiacal signs, though the Sun's apparent movement is actually caused by the movement of the Earth.

Although the constellations are due mainly to the optical accident of line of sight and have no real significance, astronomers have retained them as reference areas. It is much easier to speak of a star in

Orion than to give its geometrical position in the sky. During the Astronomical Congress of 1928, it was decided to recognize 88 constellations. A description of their agreed-upon boundaries was published at Cambridge, England, in 1930, under the title *Atlas Céleste*.

The Auroras

The "northern lights" (*Aurora borealis*) as well as the "southern lights" (*Aurora australis*) are upper-atmosphere phenomena of astronomical origin. The auroras center around the magnetic (not the geographical) poles of the Earth, which explains why, in the Western Hemisphere, they have been seen as far to the south as New Orleans and Florida while the equivalent latitude in the Eastern Hemisphere never sees an aurora. The northern magnetic pole happens to be in the Western Hemisphere.

The lower limit of an aurora is at about 50 miles. Upper limits have been estimated to be as high as 400 miles. Since about 1880, a connection between the auroras on Earth and the sun spots has been suspected and has gradually come to be accepted. It was said that the sun spots probably eject "particles" (later the word *electrons* was substituted) which on striking the Earth's atmosphere, cause the auroras.

But this explanation suffered from certain difficulties. Sometimes a very large sun spot group on the Sun, with individual spots bigger than the Earth itself, would not cause an aurora. Moreover, even if a sun spot caused an aurora, the time that passed between the appearance of the one and the occurrence of the other was highly unpredictable.

This problem of the time lag is, in all probability, solved by the discovery of the Van Allen layer by artificial satellite *Explorer I.* The Van Allen layer[1] is a double layer of charged sub-atomic particles around the Earth. The inner layer, with its center some 1,500 miles from the ground, reaches from about 40° N. to about 40° S. and does not touch the atmosphere. The outer layer, much larger and with its center several thousand miles from the ground, does touch the atmosphere in the vicinity of the magnetic poles.

It seems probable that the "leakage" of electrons from the outer Van Allen layer causes the auroras. A new burst of electrons from the Sun seems to be caught in the outer layer first. Under the assumption that all electrons are first caught in the outer layer, the time lag can be understood. There has to be an "overflow" from the outer layer to produce an aurora.

The Atmosphere

Astronomically speaking, the presence of our atmosphere is deplorable. Though reasonably transparent to visible light, the atmosphere may absorb as much as 60% of the visible and near-visible light. It is opaque to most other wave-lengths, except certain fairly short radio waves. In addition to absorbing much light, our atmosphere bends light rays entering at a slant (for a given observer) so that the true position of a star close to the horizon is not what it seems to be. One effect is that we see the Sun above the horizon before it actually is. And the unsteady movement of the atmosphere causes the "twinkling" of the stars, which may be romantic but is a nuisance when it comes to observing.

The composition of our atmosphere near the ground is 78% nitrogen and 21% oxygen, the remaining 1% consisting of other gases, most of it argon. The composition stays the same to an altitude of at least 70 miles (except that higher up two impurities, carbon dioxide and water vapor, are missing), but the pressure drops very fast. At 18,000 feet, half of the total mass of the atmosphere is below, and at 100,000 feet, 99% of the mass of the atmosphere is below. The upper limit of the atmosphere is usually given as 120 miles; no definitive figure is possible, since there is no boundary line between the incredibly attenuated gases 120 miles up and space.

Astronomical Telescopes

Optical telescopes used in astronomy are of two basic kinds: refracting and reflecting. In the *refractor telescope,* a lens is used to collect light from a distant object and bring it to a focus. A second lens, the eyepiece, then magnifies the image which may be examined visually or photographed directly. The *reflector telescope* uses a concave mirror instead of a lens, which reflects the light rays back toward the upper end of the telescope where they are magnified and observed or photographed. Most large optical telescopes now being built are reflectors.

1. Named after the American physicist, James Alfred Van Allen (1914–   ) who discovered the broad bands of intense radiation surrounding the Earth in 1958.

Radio telescopes are used to study radio waves coming from outside the Earth's atmosphere. The waves are gathered by an antenna or "dish," which is a parabolic reflecting surface made of metal or finely meshed wire. Radio signals have been received from the Sun, Moon, and planets, and from the center of our galaxy and other galaxies. Radio signals are the means by which the distant and mysterious quasars and pulsars were discovered.

Some Giant Telescopes

• The world's largest fixed-dish radio telescope (1963) is located near Arecibo, Puerto Rico. It is 1,000 ft (35 m) in diameter and spans some 25 acres.

• The Very Large Array (VLA) telescope (1980) near Socorro, N.M. is the world's most powerful radio telescope. It is Y-shaped and has 27 separate mobile antennas (each 82 ft in diameter) and is spread out over about a 25-mile area.

• The world's largest fully-steerable radio telescope (1972) located at Effelsberg, Germany, has a 100-meter (328 ft) antenna.

• The Very Long Baseline Array (VLBA) radio telescope was scheduled for operation in August 1993. The VLBA is a system linking ten widely scattered radio dishes—across the continental U.S., Hawaii, and the U.S. Virgin Islands—that will act as a single telescope. Each of the ten dish-shaped antenna is 82 feet (25.29 meters) in diameter. The VLBA is controlled by a "correlator" computer system located at Socorro, New Mexico.

The Very Long Baseline Array will study the most far out violent phenomena and exotic objects in the universe such as quasars, pulsars, and colliding galaxies with unprecedented accuracy. It should have a "seeing" ability that is 500 times better than the Hubble space telescope after it is repaired to operate in perfect condition.

• The Very Large Telescope of the European Southern Observatory (ESO) located at La Silla, Chile, will be the world's largest ground-based reflector when it is completed around the year 2000. It will consist of four 8-meter (26.24 ft) telescopes whose mirrors will combine their images to simulate a single 16 meter (52.49 ft) diameter telescope thereby giving it the power of a 630-inch primary mirror.

• The W.M. Keck Telescope (1991) at Mauna Kea, Hawaii, is the world's most powerful reflector telescope. It has a primary mirror composed of 36 hexagonal segments, each 1.8 meters in size. The Keck Telescope has a light gathering power four times greater than the 200-inch Hale.

• The 200-inch (5 meter) Hale telescope at Mount Palomar, Calif. (1948) is the second largest reflector in use.

• The 236-inch Special Astrophysical Observatory (1976) at Zelenchukskaya on the northern slopes of the Caucasus Mountains in the Russian Federation is the world's largest reflector telescope in use. However, problems with it make it less useful than the 200-inch Hale.

• The 40-inch (1.01 meter) telescope at Yerkes Observatory (1897) at Williams Bay, Wisc. is the world's largest refracting telescope.

• The Edwin P. Hubble Space Telescope was released by the space shuttle *Discovery* on April 25, 1990. It is able to peer far out in space and back in time, producing imagery of unprecedented clarity, of galaxies, star systems, and some of the universe's more intriguing objects: quasars, pulsars, and exploding galaxies. It can distinguish fine details—in planetary atmospheres or nearby star fields—with ten times the clarity of the best ground observatories. When pointed at Jupiter, for example, the telescope provides images comparable to those from Voyager flybys.

The $1.6-billion Space Telescope has a primary mirror 2.4 m (94 inches) in diameter. The mirror is almost half the diameter of the 5-m (200 inch) telescope at Mt. Palomar, the most powerful ground-based telescope in the western world.

After it was placed in orbit at 380 miles (611.5 km) altitude, the Hubble Telescope became the principal tool for exploring the universe through this decade and the next.

The Space telescope can view galaxies and quasars over distances up to 14 billion light years. Seeing that far will show us the universe as it was early in its lifetime and will reveal how matter has evolved over the eons. It will also teach us more about the large structure of the universe, providing clues as to whether the universe will continue to expand.

It was discovered in June 1990 that there was a spherical aberration in one of the telescope's mirrors. In 1991, two of the craft's six gyroscopes failed, and a third failed on Nov. 18, 1992, causing additional problems. NASA successfully repaired the Space Telescope during the Dec. 2–13, 1993, mission of the *Endeavour*.

Astronomers are now debating what instrument will be needed to replace the Hubble telescope when NASA deactivates it in 2005. NASA is planning a second mission to service the Hubble space telescope in February 1997.

The Gamma Ray Observatory

The Gamma Ray Observatory (GRO) launched from the space shuttle *Atlantis* April 7, 1991, is the second of the four "Great Observatories" NASA had planned for studying the Universe in this decade. The first of the "Great Observatories" was the Hubble Space Telescope, launched April 24, 1990. The others are the Advanced X-ray Astrophysics Facility (AXAF) expected to launch in 1997 but budget cuts delayed the project. It is now expected to lift off in 1998, and the Space Infrared Telescope Facility (SIRTF) which is being replaced and rescheduled for possible launching around the year 2000. The mission

will last two and one half years and it will study substellar objects in a wide range of infrared light.

Unlike visible radiation and radio waves, gamma rays cannot be focused with telescopes. Instead, gamma rays are detected when they interact with matter. Their passage through the detectors on the GRO convert the rays to flashes of visible light which are counted and measured. From those flashes, scientists can determine their energy level and source. Gamma rays cannot be detected on Earth because they do not penetrate the atmosphere.

The $617-million spacecraft was built by TRW and measures 70 feet (21 meters) between the tips of its solar arrays. The solar arrays provide 1800 watts of electrical power required for the operation of the observatory. The spacecraft was designed to have a minimum life of two years, but it is expected to operate for at least six years.

Gamma rays are the highest energy radiations in the electromagnetic spectrum, ranging from tens of thousands to tens of billions of electron volts (eV). An eV is a measure of the amount of energy impacted to an electron when subjected to an electrical potential of 1 volt. In contrast, visible light corresponds to only a few electron volts. These gamma rays provide a means of studying some of the primary forces of change in the astrophysical processes.

Gamma rays are thought to originate with the "Big Bang" and subsequent expansion of the universe we witness today. Through these gamma-ray observations, we may witness the birth of elements and deaths of stars, gain clues into the mysteries of quasars, pulsars, neutron stars, and get a glimpse into the spacetime precipice of a black hole. In all these cases, large amounts of energy are released and gamma rays produced.

Gamma rays are generated by **supernovas** and by their very dense remains, **neutron stars.** These stars spin very rapidly, some—perhaps all—emit radiation in pulses and are known as pulsars. Pulsars are thought to be remnants of supernova explosions. One of the fastest known **pulsars** makes 643 complete rotations in one second. How these stars convert their rotational energy to gamma rays is not known. Since the first pulsar was discovered in 1968, we now have located more than 500 of them.

How Bright Is Bright?

Source: U.S. Naval Observatory.

You will often hear astronomers refer to the brightness of an object in terms of an object's *apparent magnitude.* The term *apparent magnitude* relates to a star's apparent brightness, or, how bright the star looks to observers on the Earth. Apparent stellar brightness is a combination of two things: how bright the star actually is, and how far the star is from the Earth. A dim star close to the Earth could appear brighter than a bright star far away.

Back in the second century B.C., the Greek astronomer Hipparchus created the first known star catalog, listing star positions and brightnesses. This catalog contained about a thousand stars. In his catalog, he classified the stars by their magnitude. The brightest stars were called first magnitude, and the faintest were called sixth magnitude, with the rest being given intermediate magnitudes. This was a crude method of classification, for his observations were made with the unaided eye.

Today, magnitude classifications are made using highly precise instruments, but Hipparchus' general classification of magnitudes remains. The branch of

astronomy that deals with an object's brightness is called photometry.

In 1856, after more precise methods of photometry had been invented, British astronomer Norman Pogson proposed a quantitative scale of stellar magnitudes, which was adopted by the astronomical community.

Because of the nature of human perception, equal intervals of brightness are actually equal ratios of luminous flux. Pogson's proposal was that one increment in magnitude be the fifth root of 100. This means that each increment in magnitude corresponds to an increase in the amount of energy by 2.512, approximately. A fifth magnitude star is 2.512 times as bright as a sixth, and a fourth magnitude star is $2.512 \times 2.512 = 6.310$ times as a bright as a sixth, and so on.

The naked eye, under optimum conditions, can see down to around the sixth magnitude, that is, +6. Under the Pogson system, a few of the brighter stars now have negative magnitudes. For example, Sirius is −1.5. The lower the magnitude number, the brighter the object. The full Moon has a magnitude of about −12.5, and the Sun is a bright −26.5! ☐

Phenomena, 1996

Configurations of Sun, Moon, and Planets

NOTE: The hour listings are in Universal Time. For conversion to United States time zones, see conversion table on next page.

JANUARY
d	h	
1	01	Mercury 0°.9 S of Uranus
1	07	Mars 1°.6 S of Neptune
2	16	Mercury greatest elong. E (19°)
4	07	Earth at perihelion
5	12	Moon at apogee
5	21	FULL MOON
8	00	Mars 0°.6 S of Uranus
9	12	Mercury stationary
13	00	Mercury 3° N of Mars
13	21	LAST QUARTER
16	03	Neptune in conjunction with Sun
18	20	Jupiter 5° S of Moon
18	22	Mercury in inferior conjunction
19	23	Moon at perigee
20	13	NEW MOON
21	07	Uranus in conjunction with Sun
23	08	Venus 5° S of Moon
24	04	Saturn 5° S of Moon
26	05	Juno in conjunction with Sun
27	11	FIRST QUARTER
30	06	Mercury stationary

FEBRUARY
1	16	Moon at apogee
3	02	Venus 1°.3 N of Saturn
4	16	FULL MOON
11	14	Mercury 0°.07 N of Neptune
11	21	Mercury greatest elong. W (26°)
12	02	Passage of the Earth through the ring-plane of Saturn from N to S
12	09	LAST QUARTER
15	15	Jupiter 5° S of Moon
16	20	Neptune 5° S of Moon
16	22	Mercury 0°.2 N of Uranus
17	05	Uranus 6° S of Moon
17	06	Mercury 5° S of Moon
17	09	Moon at perigee
19	00	NEW MOON
20	19	Saturn 4° S of Moon
22	05	Venus 0°.06 N of Moon (Occn.)
26	06	FIRST QUARTER
29	07	Moon at apogee

MARCH
4	14	Mars in conjunction with Sun
5	09	FULL MOON
7	20	Pluto stationary
12	17	LAST QUARTER
13	00	Pallas stationary
14	06	Jupiter 5° S of Moon
15	05	Neptune 5° S of Moon
15	16	Uranus 6° S of Moon
16	06	Moon at perigee
17	19	Saturn in conjunction with Sun
19	11	NEW MOON
20	08	Equinox
22	20	Mars 1°.3 N of Saturn

23	00	Venus 5° N of Moon
23	11	Mercury 0°.3 N of Saturn
23	20	Mercury 0°.9 S of Mars
27	02	FIRST QUARTER
28	03	Moon at apogee
28	08	Mercury in superior conjunction
29	08	Vesta stationary

APRIL
1	01	Venus greatest elong. E (46°)
4	00	FULL MOON (Eclipse)
8	12	Ceres 1°.0 N of Moon (Occn.)
9	19	Ceres stationary
10	17	Jupiter 5° S of Moon
11	00	LAST QUARTER
11	03	Moon at perigee
11	12	Neptune 5° S of Moon
12	00	Uranus 6° S of Moon
15	22	Venus 10° N of Aldebaran
16	01	Saturn 4° S of Moon
17	23	NEW MOON (Eclipse)
18	21	Pallas at opposition
19	10	Mercury 5° N of Moon
21	14	Venus 9° N of Moon
23	08	Mercury greatest elong. E (20°)
24	22	Moon at apogee
25	21	FIRST QUARTER
29	09	Neptune stationary

MAY
3	12	FULL MOON
4	10	Mercury stationary
4	14	Venus greatest brilliancy
4	17	Jupiter stationary
5	15	Ceres 0°.3 N of Moon (Occn.)
6	22	Moon at perigee
8	00	Jupiter 5° S of Moon
8	17	Neptune 5° S of Moon
8	21	Vesta at opposition
9	00	Uranus stationary
9	06	Uranus 6° S of Moon
10	05	LAST QUARTER
13	13	Saturn 3° S of Moon
15	01	Mercury in inferior conjunction
16	03	Mars 1°.7 N of Moon
17	12	NEW MOON
20	01	Venus 8° N of Moon
20	07	Venus stationary
22	14	Pluto at opposition
22	16	Moon at apogee
25	14	FIRST QUARTER
27	07	Mercury stationary
30	00	Ceres at opposition
31	06	Mercury 4° S of Mars

JUNE
1	15	Ceres 9°.7 S of Moon (Occn.)
1	21	FULL MOON
3	16	Moon at perigee
4	06	Jupiter 5° S of Moon
5	00	Neptune 5° S of Moon
4	12	Uranus 6° S of Moon

8	11	LAST QUARTER
9	22	Saturn 3° S of Moon
10	09	Mercury greatest elong. W (24°)
10	16	Venus in inferior conjunction
14	00	Mercury 0°.4 N of Moon (Occn.)
14	01	Mars 4° N of Moon
14	13	Mercury 3° S of Mars
15	09	Pallas stationary
16	02	NEW MOON
19	06	Moon at apogee
21	02	Solstice
21	11	Mercury 4° N of Aldebaran
23	12	Mercury 1°.4 N of Venus
24	05	FIRST QUARTER
24	16	Vesta stationary
27	12	Mars 6° N of Aldebaran
30	04	Venus 4° S of Mars

JULY
1	04	FULL MOON
1	10	Jupiter 5° S of Moon
1	22	Moon at perigee
2	00	Venus stationary
2	08	Neptune 4° S of Moon
2	20	Uranus 5° S of Moon
4	12	Jupiter at opposition
5	18	Earth at aphelion
7	06	Saturn 3° S of Moon
7	19	LAST QUARTER
11	09	Mercury in superior conjunction
12	09	Venus 0°.4 S of Moon (Occn.)
12	23	Mars 5° N of Moon
15	16	NEW MOON
16	14	Moon at apogee
17	09	Venus greatest brilliancy
18	18	Neptune at opposition
20	00	Saturn stationary
20	18	Ceres stationary
23	18	FIRST QUARTER
25	07	Uranus at opposition
28	16	Jupiter 5° S of Moon
29	18	Neptune 4° S of Moon
30	04	Uranus 5° S of Moon
30	08	Moon at perigee
30	11	FULL MOON

AUGUST
1	10	Mercury 0°.5 N of Regulus
3	13	Saturn 3° S of Moon
4	03	Juno 0°.1 S of Moon (Occn.)
6	05	LAST QUARTER
8	07	Aldebaran 1°.0 S of Moon (Occn.)
10	04	Venus 1°.2 N of Moon
10	21	Mars 6° N of Moon
12	16	Moon at apogee
13	17	Pluto stationary
14	08	NEW MOON
16	18	Mercury 0°.3 N of Moon (Occn.)

Conversion of Universal Time (U. T.) to Civil Time

U.T.	E.D.T.[1]	E.S.T.[2]	C.S.T.[3]	M.S.T.[4]	P.S.T.[5]	U.T.	E.D.T.[1]	E.S.T.[2]	C.S.T.[3]	M.S.T.[4]	P.S.T.[5]
00	*8P	*7P	*6P	*5P	*4P	12	8A	7A	6A	5A	4A
01	*9P	*8P	*7P	*6P	*5P	13	9A	8A	7A	6A	5A
02	*10P	*9P	*8P	*7P	*6P	14	10A	9A	8A	7A	6A
03	*11P	*10P	*9P	*8P	*7P	15	11A	10A	9A	8A	7A
04	M	*11P	*10P	*9P	*8P	16	N	11A	10A	9A	8A
05	1A	M	*11P	*10P	*9P	17	1P	N	11A	10A	9A
06	2A	1A	M	*11P	*10P	18	2P	1P	N	11A	10A
07	3A	2A	1A	M	*11P	19	3P	2P	1P	N	11A
08	4A	3A	2A	1A	M	20	4P	3P	2P	1P	N
09	5A	4A	3A	2A	1A	21	5P	4P	3P	2P	1P
10	6A	5A	4A	3A	2A	22	6P	5P	4P	3P	2P
11	7A	6A	5A	4A	3A	23	7P	6P	5P	4P	3P

1. Eastern Daylight Time. 2. Eastern Standard Time, same as Central Daylight Time. 3. Central Standard Time, same as Mountain Daylight Time. 4. Mountain Standard Time, same as Pacific Daylight Time. 5. Pacific Standard Time. NOTES: *denotes previous day. N = noon. M = midnight.

20	04	Venus greatest elong. W (46°)
21	16	Mercury greatest elong. E (27°)
21	19	Vesta 0°.9 S of Moon (Occn.)
22	04	FIRST QUARTER
24	22	Jupiter 5° S of Moon
26	03	Neptune 5° S of Moon
26	13	Uranus 5° S of Moon
27	17	Moon at perigee
28	18	FULL MOON
30	21	Saturn 3° S of Moon
31	17	Mars 6° S of Pollux

SEPTEMBER

2	05	Venus 9° S of Pollux
2	11	Juno stationary
3	14	Jupiter stationary
3	20	Mercury stationary
4	14	Aldebaran 0°.9 S of Moon (Occn.)
4	15	Venus 3° S of Mars
4	19	LAST QUARTER
8	19	Mars 6° N of Moon
8	23	Venus 3° N of Moon
9	02	Moon at apogee
12	23	NEW MOON
17	13	Mercury in inferior conjunction
20	11	FIRST QUARTER
21	06	Jupiter 6° S of Moon
22	11	Neptune 5° S of Moon
22	18	Equinox
22	21	Uranus 6° S of Moon
24	22	Moon at perigee
25	22	Mercury stationary
26	19	Saturn at opposition
27	03	FULL MOON (Eclipse)
27	04	Saturn 3° S of Moon

OCTOBER

1	22	Aldebaran 0°.8 S of Moon (Occn.)
3	06	Mercury greatest elong. W (18°)
4	00	Venus 0°.2 S of Regulus
4	12	LAST QUARTER
5	00	Juno at opposition
6	12	Neptune stationary
6	18	Moon at apogee
7	15	Mars 6° N of Moon
9	04	Venus 4° N of Moon
10	03	Uranus stationary
12	14	NEW MOON (Eclipse)
18	16	Jupiter 6° S of Moon
19	17	Neptune 5° S of Moon
19	18	FIRST QUARTER
20	03	Uranus 6° S of Moon
22	09	Moon at perigee
24	10	Saturn 3° S of Moon
26	14	FULL MOON
29	04	Mars 1°.2 N of Regulus
29	08	Aldebaran 0°.9 S of Moon (Occn.)

NOVEMBER

2	00	Mercury in superior conjunction
3	08	LAST QUARTER
3	14	Moon at apogee
5	08	Mars 5° N of Moon
8	10	Venus 1°.4 N of Moon
11	04	NEW MOON
13	14	Juno stationary
15	05	Jupiter 5° S of Moon

15	23	Neptune 4° S of Moon
16	05	Moon at perigee
16	09	Uranus 5° S of Moon
16	18	Venus 4° N of Spica
18	01	FIRST QUARTER
20	15	Saturn 3° S of Moon
20	17	Mercury 3° N of Antares
25	00	Pluto in conjunction with Sun
25	04	FULL MOON
25	17	Aldebaran 0°.9 S of Moon (Occn.)

DECEMBER

1	11	Moon at apogee
3	05	LAST QUARTER
3	21	Mars 4° N of Moon
4	11	Saturn stationary
8	13	Venus 2° N of Moon
10	05	Pallas in conjunction with Sun
10	17	NEW MOON
12	05	Mercury 7° S of Moon
12	23	Jupiter 5° S of Moon
13	04	Moon at perigee
13	07	Neptune 4° S of Moon
13	18	Uranus 5° S of Moon
15	19	Mercury greatest elong. E (20°)
17	10	FIRST QUARTER
17	20	Saturn 3° S of Moon
21	14	Solstice
23	00	Aldebaran 0°.9 S of Moon (Occn.)
23	14	Mercury stationary
24	07	Venus 6° N of Antares
24	21	FULL MOON
29	05	Moon at apogee

When Is The Moon a "Blue Moon"?

Source: The U.S. Naval Observatory.

The second time the moon is full within a particular month, it is called a "blue moon." This condition occurs once every few years when the date of the first full moon is at or near the beginning of the month so that the following full moon comes before the end of the month. The expression "once in a blue moon," meaning "very seldom," stems from this phenomenon. Over the years a "blue moon" appears to have meant any rarely occurring kind of moon. A "blue moon" can also refer to a moon that appears to be blue in color, which is caused by unusual atmospheric conditions.

Full moons occur about every 29.53 days, or 12.3683 times a year. Therefore, months containing two full Moons occur on the average every 2.72 years. Approximately once every 19 years, one year will have two months with two full moons because February will have no full moon at all. February can never have two new or full moons because the shortest time between them is 29.27 days.

DECLINATIONS OF SUN AND PLANETS, 1996

Visibility of Planets, 1996

The planet diagram on page 353 shows, in graphical form for any date during the year, the local mean times of meridian passage of the Sun, of the five planets, Mercury, Venus, Mars, Jupiter, and Saturn, and of every 2^h of right ascension. Intermediate lines, corresponding to particular stars, may be drawn in by the user if desired. The diagram is intended to provide a general picture of the availability of planets and stars for observation during the year.

On each side of the line marking the time of meridian passage of the Sun, a band 45^m wide is shaded to indicate that planets and most stars crossing the meridian within 45^m of the Sun are generally too close to the Sun for observation.

For any date the diagram provides immediately the local mean time of meridian passage of the Sun, planets and stars, and thus the following information:
(a) whether a planet or star is too close to the Sun for observation;
(b) visibility of a planet or star in the morning or evening;
(c) location of a planet or star during twilight;
(d) proximity of planets to stars or other planets.
When the meridian passage of a body occurs at midnight, it is close to opposition to the Sun and is visible all night, and may be observed in both morning and evening twilights. As the time of meridian passage decreases, the body ceases to be observable in the morning, but its altitude above the eastern horizon during evening twilight gradually increases until it is on the meridian at evening twilight. From then onwards the body is observable above the western horizon, its altitude at evening twilight gradually decreasing, until it becomes too close to the Sun for observation. When it again becomes visible, it is seen in the morning twilight, low in the east. Its altitude at morning twilight gradually increases until meridian passage occurs at the time of morning twilight, then as the time of meridian passage decreases to 0^h, the body is observable in the west in the morning twilight with a gradually decreasing altitude, until it once again reaches opposition.

Notes on the visibility of the principal planets, except Pluto, are given on page 354. Further information on the visibility of planets may be obtained from the diagram above which shows, in graphical form for any date during the year, the declinations of the bodies plotted on the planet diagram on page 353.

Mercury can only be seen low in the east before sunrise, or low in the west after sunset (about the time of the beginning or end of civil twilight). It is visible in the mornings between the following approximate dates: January 25 to March 19, May 24 to July 4, and September 25 fo October 20. The planet is brighter at the end of each period, (the best conditions in northern latitudes occur from the beginning of October to mid-way through the second week of that month, and in southern latitudes during the last three weeks of February). It is visible in the evenings between the following approximate dates: January 1 to January 13, April 6 fo May 5, July 19 to September 11, and November 19 to December 27. The planet is brighter at the beginning of each period, (the best conditions in northern latitudes occur from mid-April to just a few days before the end of that month, and in southern latitudes from early August to early September)

Venus is a brilliant object in the evening sky from the beginning of the year until mid-way through the first week of June when it becomes too close to the Sun for observation. During the middle of June it reappears in the morning sky where it stays until the end of the year. Venus is in conjunction with Saturn on February 3, with Mercury on June 23 and with Mars on June 30 and September 4.

(Continued on page 352)

Visibility of Planets in Morning and Evening Twilight

Morning				Evening			
Venus	June 17	—	December 31	Venus	January 1	—	June 4
Mars	May 14	—	December 31	Jupiter	July 4	—	December 31
Jupiter	January 1	—	July 4	Saturn	January 1	—	February 29
Saturn	April 4	—	September 26		September 26	—	December 31

(Continued from page 351)

Mars is too close to the Sun for observation until the middle of May when it appears in the morning sky. Its westward elongation gradually increases moving from Aries at the beginning of May, into Taurus in early June (passing 6° N of *Aldebaran* on June 27) and into Gemini in the last week of July (passing 6° S of *Pollux* on August 31). It then continues through Cancer, Leo (passing 1°.2 N of *Regulus* on October 29) and into Virgo where after mid-December it can be seen for more than half the night. Mars is in conjunction with Mercury on May 31 and June 14, and with Venus on June 30 and September 4.

Jupiter rises just before sunrise in Sagittarius, in which constellation it remains throughout the year. Its westward elongation gradually increases and from the second week of April it can be seen for more than half the night. It is at opposition on July 4 when it is visible throughout the night. Its eastward elongation then decreases and from the beginning of October until the end of the year it can only be seen in the evening sky.

Saturn can be seen in the evening sky in Aquarius until the end of February when it becomes too close to the Sun for observation. It reappears in the morning sky during the first week of April in Pisces. Its westward elongation gradually increases passing into Cetus in early June and Pisces again from early September in which constellation it remains for the rest of the year. It is at opposition on September 26 when it it visible throughout the night. Its eastward elongation then gradually decreases until in the second half of December it can only be seen in the evening sky. Saturn is in conjunction with Venus on February 3.

Uranus is too close to the Sun for observation until mid-February when it appears in the morning sky in Capricornus, in which constellation it remains throughout the year. Its westward elongation gradually increases until on July 25 it is at opposition when it is visible throughout the night. Its eastward elongation gradually decreases and from mid-October until the end of the year it can only be seen in the evening sky.

Neptune is too close to the Sun for observation until the second week of February when it appears in the morning sky in Sagittarius, in which constellation it remains throughout the year. It is at opposition on July 18 when it can be seen throughout the night. Its eastward elongation gradually decreases and from mid-October until late December it can be seen in the evening sky, after which it again becomes too close to the Sun for observation.

Do not confuse (1) Venus with Saturn from the end of January to the end of the first week in February, with Mars from late June to early July and late August to mid-September and with Mercury in the fourth week of June; on all occasions Venus is the brighter object. (2) Mercury with Mars in the last week of May to the end of the third week of June; Mercury is the brighter object except for the last week in May. The reddish tint of Mars should assist in its identification. (3) Jupiter with Mercury around mid-December when Jupiter is the brighter object.

Eclipses of the Sun and Moon, 1996

NOTE: The day of an eclipse is given in Universal Time (U.T.) and may start a day earlier or later depending on your time zone. See Phenomena, 1996 table to find time of eclipse in your area.

April 3–4. Total eclipse of the Moon. The beginning of the umbral phase visible in extreme eastern North America, South America (except for the northwest and the west coast), southern and eastern Greenland, Europe, Africa, western and central Asia, the extreme western coast of Australia, parts of Antarctica, most of the North Atlantic Ocean, the South Atlantic Ocean, and the Indian Ocean; the end visible in eastern and central regions of the United States and Canada, most of Mexico, Central America, South America, Greenland, Europe, Africa, western Asia, parts of Antarctica, the eastern South Pacific Ocean, the Atlantic Ocean, and the western Indian Ocean.

April 17–18. Partial eclipse of the Sun. Visible in New Zealand, part of Antarctica, and the south Pacific Ocean.

September 27. Total eclipse of the Moon. The beginning of the umbral phase visible in eastern and central regions of the United States and Canada, most of Mexico, Central America, South America, Greenland, Europe, Africa, western Asia, parts of Antarctica, the eastern South Pacific Ocean, the Atlantic Ocean, and the western half of the Indian Ocean; the end visible in North America (except for extreme western Alaska), Hawaii, Central America, South America, the western half of Africa, Europe (except for the extreme east), Greenland, parts of Antarctica, the eastern Pacific Ocean, and the Atlantic Ocean.

October 12. Partial eclipse of the Sun. Visible in extreme northeast Canada, Greenland, Iceland, Europe, including the British Isles, and North Africa.

LOCAL MEAN TIME OF MERIDIAN PASSAGE

LOCAL MEAN TIME OF MERIDIAN PASSAGE

AVIATION

Famous Firsts in Aviation

Cayley's Helicopter

Sir George Cayley's Helicopter design

Sir George Cayley of England (1773-1857) designed the first practical helicopter in 1842-43. He designed and built the first successful man-carrying glider in 1853 and sent his coachman aloft in it on its first flight. He also formulated the basic principles of modern aerodynamics and is the father of British aeronautics.

1782 First balloon flight. Jacques and Joseph Montgolfier of Annonay, France, sent up a small smoke-filled balloon about mid-November.

1783 First hydrogen-filled balloon flight. Jacques A. C. Charles, Paris physicist, supervised construction by A. J. and M. N. Robert of a 13-ft diameter balloon that was filled with hydrogen. It got up to about 3,000 ft and traveled about 16 mi. in a 45-min flight (Aug. 27).

First human balloon flights. A Frenchman, Jean Pilâtre de Rozier made the first captive-balloon ascension (Oct. 15). With the Marquis d'Arlandes, Pilâtre de Rozier made the first free flight, reaching a peak altitude of about 500 ft, and traveling about 5 1/2 mi. in 20 min (Nov. 21).

1784 First powered balloon. Gen. Jean Baptiste Marie Meusnier developed the first propeller-driven and elliptically-shaped balloon—the crew cranking three propellers on a common shaft to give the craft a speed of about 3 mph.

First woman to fly. Mme. Thible, a French opera singer (June 4).

1793 First balloon flight in America. Jean Pierre Blanchard, a French pilot, made it from Philadelphia to near Woodbury, Gloucester County, N.J., in a little over 45 min (Jan. 9).

1794 First military use of the balloon. Jean Marie Coutelle, using a balloon built for the French Army, made two 4-hr observation ascents. The military purpose of the ascents seems to have been to damage the enemy's morale.

1797 First parachute jump. André-Jacques Garnerin dropped from about 6,500 ft over Monceau Park in Paris in a 23-ft diameter parachute made of white canvas with a basket attached (Oct. 22).

1843 First air transport company. In London, William S. Henson and John Stringfellow filed articles of incorporation for the Aerial Transit Company (March 24). It failed.

1852 First dirigible. Henri Giffard, a French engineer, flew in a controllable (more or less) steam-engine powered balloon, 144 ft long and 39 ft in diameter, inflated with 88,000 cu ft of coal gas. It reached 6.7 mph on a flight from Paris to Trappe (Sept. 24).

1860 First aerial photographers. Samuel Archer King and William Black made two photos of Boston, still in existence.

1872 First gas-engine powered dirigible. Paul Haenlein, a German engineer, flew in a semi-rigid-frame dirigible, powered by a 4-cylinder internal-combustion engine running on coal gas drawn from the supporting bag.

1873 First transatlantic attempt. *The New York Daily Graphic* sponsored the attempt with a 400,000 cu ft balloon carrying a lifeboat. A rip in the bag during inflation brought collapse of the balloon and the project.

1897 First successful metal dirigible. An all-metal dirigible, designed by David Schwarz, a Hungarian, took off from Berlin's Tempelhof Field and, powered by a 16-hp Daimler engine, got several miles before leaking gas caused it to crash (Nov. 13).

1900 First Zeppelin flight. Germany's Count Ferdinand von Zeppelin flew the first of his long series of rigid-frame airships. It attained a speed of 18 mi. per h and got 3 1/2 mi. before its steering gear failed (July 2).

1903 First successful heavier-than-air machine flight. Aviation was really born on the sand dunes at Kitty Hawk, N.C., when Orville Wright crawled to his prone position between the wings of the biplane he and his brother Wilbur had built, opened the throttle of their homemade 12-hp engine and took to the air. He covered 120 ft in 12 sec. Later that day, in one of four flights, Wilbur stayed up 59 sec and covered 852 ft (Dec. 17).

1904 First airplane maneuvers. Orville Wright made the first turn with an airplane (Sept. 15); 5 days later his brother Wilbur made the first complete circle.

Did the Wrights Fly First?

Supporters of Gustave A. Whitehead are seeking to prove that the German-born inventor flew a powered-batwing aircraft on Aug. 14, 1901, in Bridgeport, Conn., two years before the Wright Brothers made their first powered flight.

While photographs of Whitehead's plane exist, none of them show it flying, nor is there much useful evidence to prove or disprove this claim.

Although Whitehead supporters have built what they claim is a replica of his plane and have flown it on several short hops in 1986, it should be noted that blueprints of Whitehead's actual craft do not exist.

The current opinion of the Smithsonian is that none of Gustave Whitehead's planes actually flew and the controversy remains.

Dec. 17, 1903. Orville Wright at the controls, Wilbur runs alongside him. National Air and Space Museum, Smithsonian Institution. (SI Neg. No. A 26767B).

1905 **First airplane flight over half an hour.** Orville Wright kept his craft up 33 min 17 sec (Oct. 4).

1906 **First European airplane flight.** Alberto Santos-Dumont, a Brazilian, flew a heavier-than-air machine at Bagatelle Field, Paris (Sept. 13).

1908 **First airplane fatality.** Lt. Thomas E. Selfridge, U.S. Army Signal Corps, was in a group of officers evaluating the Wright plane at Fort Myer, Va. He was up about 75 ft with Orville Wright when the propeller hit a bracing wire and was broken, throwing the plane out of control, killing Selfridge and seriously injuring Wright (Sept. 17).

1909 **First cross-Channel flight.** Louis Blériot flew in a 25-hp Blériot VI monoplane from Les Baraques near Calais, France, and landed near Dover Castle, England, in a 26.61-mi. (38-km) 37-min flight across the English Channel (July 25).

First International Aviation Competition Meeting. American Glenn Curtis narrowly beats France's Louis Blériot in main event and wins the Gordon Bennett Cup. Meet held at Rheims, France (Aug. 22–28).

1910 **First licensed woman pilot.** Baroness Raymonde de la Roche of France, who learned to fly in 1909, received ticket No. 36 on March 8.

First flight from shipboard. Lt. Eugene Ely, USN, took a Curtiss plane off from the deck of cruiser *Birmingham* at Hampton Roads, Va., and flew to Norfolk (Nov. 14). The following January, he reversed the process, flying from Camp Selfridge to the deck of the armored cruiser *Pennsylvania* in San Francisco Bay (Jan. 18).

First aircraft to take off from water. Henri Fabrer in Gnome-powered floatplane, at Martigues, France (March 28).

1911 **First U.S. woman pilot.** Harriet Quimby, a magazine writer, got ticket No. 37, making her the second licensed female pilot in the world.

1912 **First woman's cross-Channel flight.** Harriet Quimby flew from Dover, England, across the English Channel, and landed at Hardelot, France (25 mi. south of Calais) in a Blériot monoplane loaned to her by Louis Blériot

Harriet Quimby was the leading woman aviator of her day. (Leslie's Weekly Illustrated Newspaper)

(April 16). She was later killed in a flying accident over Dorchester Bay during a Harvard-Boston aviation meet on July 1, 1912.

First parachute jump from a powered airplane. Albert Berry jumps in a test over Jefferson Barracks military post, St. Louis (March 1). Some sources credit Grant Morton as making first jump in 1911.

1913 **First multi-engined aircraft.** Built and flown by Igor Ivan Sikorsky while still in his native Russia.

1914 **First aerial combat.** In August, Allied and German pilots and observers started shooting at each other with pistols and rifles—with negligible results.

1915 **First air raids on England.** German Zeppelins started dropping bombs on four English communities (Jan. 19).

1918 **First U.S. air squadron.** The U.S. Army Air Corps made its first independent raids over enemy lines, in DH-4 planes (British-designed) powered with 400-hp American-designed Liberty engines (April 8).

First regular airmail service. Operated for the Post Office Department by the Army, the first regular service was inaugurated with one round trip a day (except Sunday) between Washington, D.C., and New York City (May 15).

1919 **First transatlantic flight.** The NC-4, one of four Curtiss flying boats commanded by Lt. Comdr. Albert C. Read, reached Lisbon, Portugal, (May

27) after hops from Trepassy Bay, Newfoundland, to Horta, Azores (May 16–17), to Ponta Delgada (May 20). The Liberty-powered craft was piloted by Walter Hinton.

First nonstop transatlantic flight. Capt. John Alcock and Lt. Arthur Whitten Brown, British World War I flyers, made the 1,900 mi. from St. John's, Newfoundland, to Clifden, Ireland, in 16 h 12 min in a Vickers-Vimy bomber with two 350-hp Rolls-Royce engines (June 15–16).

First lighter-than-air transatlantic flight. The British dirigible R-34, commanded by Maj. George H. Scott, left Firth of Forth, Scotland, (July 2) and touched down at Mineola, L.I., 108 h later. The eastbound trip was made in 75 h (completed July 13).

First scheduled London-Paris passenger service (using airplanes). Aircraft Travel and Transport inaugurated London-Paris service (Aug. 25). Later the company started the first trans-channel mail service on the same route (Nov. 10).

First free-fall parachute jump. Leslie Irvin jumps over McCook Field, Dayton, Ohio, to prove that you won't lose consciousness during a delayed free-fall using a manually-operated parachute (April 28).

1921 First U.S. black female pilot. Bessie Coleman received her license June 15. Was killed April 30, 1926, in flying accident.

First naval vessel sunk by aircraft. Two battleships being scrapped by treaty were sunk by bombs dropped from Army planes in demonstration put on by Brig. Gen. William S. Mitchell (July 21).

First helium balloon. The C-7, non-rigid Navy dirigible was first to use non-inflammable helium as lifting gas, making a flight from Hampton Roads, Va., to Washington, D.C. (Dec. 1).

1922 First member of Caterpillar Club. Lt. (later Maj. Gen.) Harold Harris bailed out of a crippled plane he was testing at McCook Field, Dayton, Ohio (Oct. 20), and became the first man to join the Caterpillar Club—those whose lives have been saved by parachute.

1923 First nonstop transcontinental flight. Lts. John A. Macready and Oakley Kelly flew a single-engine Fokker T-2 nonstop from New York to San Diego, a distance of just over 2,500 mi. in 26 h 50 min (May 2–3).

First autogyro flight. Juan de la Cierva, a brilliant Spanish mathematician, made the first successful flight in a rotary wing aircraft in Madrid (June 9).

1924 First round-the-world flight. Four Douglas Cruiser biplanes of the U.S. Army Air Corps took off from Seattle under command of Maj. Frederick Martin (April 6). 175 days later, two of the planes (Lt. Lowell Smith's and Lt. Erik Nelson's) landed in Seattle after a circuitous route—one source saying 26,345 mi., another saying 27,553 mi.

1926 First polar flight. Then-Lt. Cmdr. Richard E. Byrd, acting as navigator, and Floyd Bennett as pilot, flew a trimotor Fokker from Kings Bay, Spitsbergen, over the North Pole and back in 15 1/2 h (May 8–9).

1927 First solo, nonstop transatlantic flight. Charles Augustus Lindbergh lifted his Wright-powered Ryan monoplane, *Spirit of St. Louis,* from Roosevelt Field, L.I., to stay aloft 33 h 39 min and traveled 3,600 mi. to Le Bourget Field outside Paris (May 20–21). Although 91 persons in

Charles A. Lindbergh and *The Spirit of St. Louis.* National Air and Space Museum, Smithsonian Institution. (SI Neg. No. 87-8992).

13 separate flights crossed the Atlantic before him, he flew directly between two great world cities and did it alone.

First transatlantic passenger. Charles A. Levine was piloted by Clarence D. Chamberlin from Roosevelt Field, L.I., to Eisleben, Germany, in a Wright-powered Bellanca (June 4–5).

1928 First east-west transatlantic crossing. Baron Guenther von Huenefeld, piloted by German Capt. Hermann Koehl and Irish Capt. James Fitzmaurice, left Dublin for New York City (April 12) in a single-engine all-metal Junkers-monoplane. Some 37 h later, they crashed on Greely Island, Labrador. Rescued.

First U.S.-Australia flight. Sir Charles Kingsford-Smith and Capt. Charles T. P. Ulm, Australians, and two American navigators, Harry W. Lyon and James Warner, crossed the Pacific from Oakland to Brisbane. They went via Hawaii and the Fiji Islands in a trimotor Fokker (May 31–June 8).

First transarctic flight. Sir Hubert Wilkins, an Australian explorer and Carl Ben Eielson, who served as pilot, flew from Point Barrow, Alaska, to Spitsbergen (mid-April).

1929 First of the endurance records. With Air Corps Maj. Carl Spaatz in command and Capt. Ira Eaker as chief pilot, an Army Fokker, aided by refueling in the air, remained aloft 150 h 40 min at Los Angeles (Jan. 1–7).

First round-the-world airship flight. The LZ-127, known as the *Graf Zeppelin,* flew 21,300 miles in 20 days and 4 hours. Also set distance record (August).

First blind flight. James H. Doolittle proved the feasibility of instrument-guided flying when he took off and landed entirely on instruments (Sept. 24).

First rocket-engine flight. Fritz von Opel, a German auto maker, stayed aloft in his small rocket-powered craft for 75 sec, covering nearly 2 mi. (Sept. 30).

First South Pole flight. Comdr. Richard E. Byrd, with Bernt Balchen as pilot, Harold I. June, radio operator, and Capt. A. C. McKinley, photographer, flew a trimotor Fokker from the Bay of Whales, Little America, over the South Pole and back (Nov. 28–29).

1930 First Paris-New York nonstop flight. Dieudonné Coste and Maurice Bellonte, French pilots, flew a Hispano-powered Breguet biplane from Le Bourget Field to Valley Stream, L.I., in 37 h 18 min. (Sept. 2–3).

1931 First flight into the stratosphere. Auguste Piccard, a Swiss physicist, and Charles Knipfer ascended in a balloon from Augsburg, Germany, and reached a height of 51,793 ft in a 17-h flight that terminated on a glacier near Innsbruck, Austria (May 27).

First nonstop transpacific flight. Hugh Herndon and Clyde Pangborn took off from Sabishiro Beach, Japan, dropped their landing gear, and flew 4,860 mi. to near Wenatchee, Wash., in 41 h 13 min. (Oct. 4–5).

1932 First woman's transatlantic solo. Amelia Earhart, flying a Pratt & Whitney Wasp-powered Lockheed Vega, flew alone from Harbor Grace, Newfoundland, to Ireland in approximately 15 h (May 20–21).

First westbound transatlantic solo. James A. Mollison, a British pilot, took a de Havilland Puss Moth from Portmarnock, Ireland, to Pennfield, N.B. (Aug. 18).

First woman airline pilot. Ruth Rowland Nichols, first woman to hold three international records at the same time—speed, distance, altitude—was employed by N.Y.-New England Airways.

1933 First round-the-world solo. Wiley Post took a Lockheed Vega, *Winnie Mae,* 15,596 mi. around the world in 7 d 18 h 49 1/2 min (July 15–22).

1937 First successful helicopter. Hanna Reitsch, a German pilot, flew Dr. Heinrich Focke's FW-61 in free, fully controlled flight at Bremen (July 4).

1939 First turbojet flight. Just before their invasion of Poland, the Germans flew a Heinkel He-178 plane powered by a Heinkel S3B turbojet (Aug. 27).

1940 First wartime use of military gliders. German commandos make successful glider assault on Belgium's Fort Eben-Emael during WW II (May 10).

1941–1945 Most combat missions flown by a pilot in any war. Captain Hans-Ulrich Rudel of Germany flew 2,530 combat missions during WW II while flying a JU-87 Stuka dive bomber. He survived the war.

1942–1945 Top scoring fighter pilot of any war. German Luftwaffe ace Maj. Erich Hartmann scored 352 victories all while flying a Messerschmitt BF 109 during WW II. He was involved in 800 dogfights, and flew 1,425 missions. Maj. Hartmann survived the war.

1942 First and only enemy bombing of U.S. mainland. During World War II, a floatplane launched from a Japanese submarine off Cape Blanco, Oregon, dropped incendiary bombs on the Oregon forest in two attempts to start forest fires and terrorize American civilians, but the bombs did little damage (Sept. 9 and 29).

First American jet plane flight. Robert Stanley, chief pilot for Bell Aircraft Corp., flew the Bell XP-59 *Airacomet* at Muroc Army Base, Calif. (Oct. 1).

First woman fighter pilot to shoot down an enemy aircraft. Soviet Lieutenant, Lilya Litvyak, flying a Yak-1 fighter of the women's 586th Fighter Aviation Regiment, shoots down two German planes over Stalingrad on Sept. 13, 1942.

1944 The first production stage rocket-engine fighter plane, the German Messerschmitt Me 163B *Komet* (test flown 1941) becomes operational in June 1944. Some 350 of these delta-wing fighters were built before WW II in Europe ended.

Chuck Yeager alongside the Bell X-1 named *Glamorous Glennis* after his wife. National Air and Space Museum, Smithsonian Institution. (SI Neg. No. 86-4483).

1947 First piloted supersonic flight in an airplane. Capt. Charles E. Yeager, U.S. Air Force, flew the X-1 rocket-powered research plane built by Bell Aircraft Corp., faster than the speed of sound at Muroc Air Force Base, California (Oct. 14).

1949 First round-the-world nonstop flight. Capt. James Gallagher and USAF crew of 13 flew a Boeing B-50A Superfortress around the world nonstop from Ft. Worth, returning to same point: 23,452 mi. in 94 h 1 min, with 4 aerial refuelings enroute (Feb. 27–March 2).

1950 First nonstop transatlantic jet flight. Col. David C. Schilling (USAF) flew 3,300 mi. from England to Limestone, Maine, in 10 h 1 min (Sept. 22).

1951 First solo across North Pole. Charles F. Blair, Jr., flew a converted P-51 (May 29).

1952 First jetliner service. De Havilland Comet flight inaugurated by BOAC between London and Johannesburg, South Africa (May 2). Flight, including stops, took 23 h 38 min.

First transatlantic helicopter flight. Capt. Vincent H. McGovern and 1st Lt. Harold W. Moore piloted 2 Sikorsky H-19s from Westover, Mass., to Prestwick, Scotland (3,410 mi.). Trip was made in 5 steps, with flying time of 42 h 25 min (July 15–31).

First transatlantic round trip in same day. British Canberra twin-jet bomber flew from Aldergrove, Northern Ireland, to Gander, Newfoundland, and back in 7 h 59 min flying time (Aug. 26).

1955 First transcontinental round trip in same day. Lt. John M. Conroy piloted F-86 Sabrejet across U.S. (Los Angeles-New York) and back—5,085 mi.—in 11 h 33 min 27 sec (May 21).

1957 First round-the-world, nonstop jet plane flight. Maj. Gen. Archie J. Old, Jr., USAF, led a flight of 3 Boeing B-52 bombers, powered with 8 10,000-lb. thrust Pratt & Whitney Aircraft J57 engines around the world in 45 h 19 min; distance 24,325 mi.; average speed 525 mph. (Completed Jan. 18.)

1958 First transatlantic jet passenger service. BOAC, New York to London (Oct. 4). Pan American started daily service, N.Y. to Paris (Oct. 26).

First domestic jet passenger service. National Airlines inaugurated service between New York and Miami (Dec. 10).

1968 Prototype of world's first supersonic airliner, the Soviet-designed Tupolev Tu-144 made first flight, Dec. 31. It first achieved supersonic speed on June 5, 1969.

World's 25 Busiest Airports in 1994

	City/Code	Total passengers	% Chg	Cargo (metric tons)	% Chg	Aircraft movements	% Chg
1.	Chicago O'Hare (ORD)	66,468,269	2.1	1,255,844	9.5	883,062	2.8
2.	Atlanta Hartsfield (ATL)	54,093,051	13.3	805,599	10.5	715,920	6.4
3.	Dallas/Ft. Worth Airport (DFW)	52,601,125	5.9	798,781	10.1	840,406	4.6
4.	London Heathrow (LHR)	51,717,918	8.0	1,047,761	13.4	424,551	3.3
5.	Los Angeles Intl. (LAX)	51,050,275	6.7	1,545,025	16.5	689,888	1.1
6.	Tokyo Haneda (HND)	42,245,667	1.6	603,207	2.3	202,990	2.4
7.	Frankfurt/Main (FRA)	35,122,528	7.9	1,401,942	7.8	364,716	3.6
8.	San Francisco (SFO)	34,643,095	5.7	687,502	12.1	422,190	1.3
9.	Denver Stapleton (DEN)	33,133,428	1.6	381,157	4.4	530,839	−3.9
10.	Miami (MIA)	30,203,269	5.4	1,332,800	13.1	557,680	4.5
11.	Paris Charles De Gaulle (CDG)	29,630,222	13.5	882,486	17.6	324,944	4.8
12.	New York Kennedy (JFK)	28,806,638	7.5	1,449,723	4.9	343,252	2.8
13.	Newark, New Jersey (EWR)	28,020,482	8.6	861,681	22.8	436,686	−0.4
14.	Seoul (SEL)	27,333,241	19.6	1,029,166	17.4	183,292	10.2
15.	Las Vegas (LAS)	26,850,486	19.4	46,791	13.0	495,940	8.5
16.	Detroit (DTW)	26,800,951	10.9	328,518	22.1	485,306	4.9
17.	Paris Orly (ORY)	26,617,556	4.9	313,455	6.3	216,314	2.1
18.	Hong Kong (HKG)	25,948,789	3.3	1,320,206	13.1	161,893	4.8
19.	Phoenix Sky Harbour (PHX)	25,626,132	8.8	233,478	26.4	490,015	2.2
20.	Boston Logan (BOS)	25,195,005	4.8	417,600	10.0	470,318	−6.1
21.	Minneapolis/St. Paul (MSP)	24,471,944	4.6	377,533	17.7	454,723	3.3
22.	Tokyo Narita (NRT)	23,745,240	7.2	1,605,313	11.2	125,466	2.4
23.	Amsterdam Schiphol (AMS)	23,559,456	10.7	874,701	8.1	299,712	4.1
24.	St. Louis (STL)	23,362,671	17.3	127,628	16.0	479,943	5.9
25.	Honolulu, Hawaii (HNL)	22,995,976	4.2	429,352	10.9	359,569	0.3

Airports participating in the ACI Annual Traffic Statistics Collection. Total passengers: enplaned + deplaned passengers; passengers in transit counted once. Total cargo: freight and mail in metric tons. Total aircraft movements: landing and take off of an aircraft. *Source:* Airport Council International, Geneva, Switzerland.

1973 First female pilot of a U.S. major scheduled airline. Emily H. Warner became employed by Frontier Airlines on January 29 as second officer on a Boeing 737.

1976 First regularly-scheduled commercial supersonic transport (SST) flights begin. Air France and British Airways inaugurate service (January 21). Air France flies the Paris-Rio de Janeiro route; B.A., the London-Bahrain. Both airlines begin SST service to Washington, D.C. (May 24).

1977 First successful man-powered aircraft. Paul MacCready, an aeronautical engineer from Pasadena, Calif., was awarded the Kremer Prize for creating the world 's first successful man-powered aircraft. The *Gossamer Condor* was flown by Bryan Allen over the required 3-mile course on Aug. 23.

1978 First successful transatlantic balloon flight. Three Albuquerque, N.M., men, Ben Abruzzo, Larry Newman, and Maxie Anderson, completed the crossing (Aug. 16. Landed, Aug. 17) in their helium-filled balloon, *Double Eagle II.*

1979 First man-powered aircraft to fly across the English Channel. The Kremer Prize for the Channel crossing was won by Bryan Allen who flew the *Gossamer Albatross* from Folkestone, England to Cap Gris-Nez, France, in 2 h 55 min (June 12).

1980 First successful balloon flight over the North Pole. Sidney Conn and his wife Eleanor, in hot-air balloon *Joy of Sound* (April 11).

First nonstop transcontinental balloon flight, and also record for longest overland voyage in a balloon. Maxie Anderson and his son, Kris, completed four-day flight from Fort Baker, Calif., to successful landing outside Matane, Quebec, on May 12 in their helium-filled balloon, *Kitty Hawk.*

First long-distance solar-powered flight. Janice Brown, 98-lb former teacher, flew tiny experimental solar-powered aircraft, *Solar Challenger* six miles in 22-min near Marana, Ariz. (Dec. 3). The craft was powered by a 2.75-hp engine.

First solar-powered aircraft to fly across the English Channel. Stephen R. Ptacek flew the 210-lb *Solar Challenger* at the average speed of 30 mph from Cormeilles-en-Vexin near Paris to the Royal Manston Air Force Base on England's southeastern coast in 5 h 30 min (July 7).

1984 First solo transatlantic balloon flight. Joe W. Kittinger landed Sept. 18 near Savona, Italy, in his helium-filled balloon *Rosie O'Grady's Balloon of Peace* after a flight of 3,535 miles from Caribou, Me.

1986 First nonstop flight around the world without refueling. From Edwards AFB, Calif., Dick Rutan and Jeana Yeager flew in *Voyager* around the world (24,986.727 mi.), returning to Edwards in 216 h 3 min 44 s (Dec. 14–23).

1987 First transatlantic hot-air balloon flight. Richard Branson and Per Lindstrand flew 2,789.6 miles from Sugarloaf Mt., Maine, to Ireland in the hot-air balloon *Virgin Atlantic Flyer* (July 2–4).

1991 First transpacific hot-air balloon flight. Richard Branson and Per Lindstrand flew about 6,700 miles from Miyakonyo, Japan, to 150 miles west of Yellowknift, Northwest Territories, Canada (Jan. 15–17). Record pending verification.

1992 World's longest balloon flight. Americans Richard Abruzzo and Troy Bradley made a flight of 3,318.23 miles from Bangor, Maine to Sidi Amar El Kadmiri, Ben Slimane, Morocco in 144 hours and 16 minutes in Cameron R-77 (Sept. 16–22).

1993 First woman to co-pilot a commercial supersonic plane. Barbara Harmer, British Airways, flew as first officer on the Concorde from London to New York City (March 25).

1995 First solo transpacific balloon flight. Steve Fossett made a flight of more than 5,430 miles from Seoul, South Korea, to Leader, Saskatchewan, Canada, in a helium-filled balloon. Also set record for distance (Feb. 18–21, 1995). Record pending verification.

Active Pilot Certificates Held

Year	Total	Airline transport	Com-mercial	Private
1970	720,028	31,442	176,585	299,491
1980	814,667	63,652	182,097	343,276
1985	722,376	79,192	155,929	320,086
1990	702,659	107,732	149,666	299,111
1991	692,095	112,167	148,365	293,306
1992	682,959	115,855	146,385	288,078
1993	665,069	117,070	143,014	283,700
1994	654,088	117,434	138,728	284,236

NOTE: Includes other pilot categories—student 96,254, helicopter 8,719, glider 8,476, and recreational 241. Also nonpilot, i.e., mechanic, parachute rigger, etc. (total 574,358). Data as of Dec. 31, 1994. *Source:* Department of Transportation, Federal Aviation Administration.

World Class Helicopter Records

Selected records. *Source:* National Aeronautic Association.

Great Circle Distance Without Landing
International: 2,213.04 mi.; 3,561.55 km.
Robert G. Ferry (U.S.) in Hughes YOH-6A helicopter powered by Allison T-63-A-5 engine; from Culver City, Calif., to Ormond Beach, Fla., April 6–7, 1966.

Distance, Closed Circuit
International: 1,739.96 mi.; 2,800.20 km.
Jack Schweibold (U.S.) in Hughes YOH-6A helicopter powered by Allison T-62-A-5 engine; Edwards Air Force Base, Calif., March 26, 1966.

Altitude Without Payload
International: 40,820 ft; 12,442 m.
Jean Boulet (France) in Alouette SA 315-001 "Lama" powered by Artouste IIIB 735 KW engine; Istres, France, June 21, 1972.

Altitude in Horizontal Flight
International: 36,122 ft; 11,010 m.
CWO James K. Church, (U.S.) in Sikorsky CH-54B helicopter powered by 2 P&W JFTD-12 engines; Stratford, CT., Nov. 4, 1971.

Speed Around the World
35.40 mph; 56.97 kph.
H. Ross Perot, Jr., pilot; J.W. Coburn, co-pilot (U.S.) in Bell 206 L-II Long Ranger, powered by one Allison 250-C28B of 435 hp. Elapsed time: 29 days 3 h 8 min 13 sec, Sept. 10–30, 1982.

Speed Around the World, Eastbound
40.99 mph; 65.97 kph.
Joe Ronald Bower (U.S.) pilot, in Bell JetRanger III, powered by one Allison 250–C20J of 317 shp., covered 23,800 miles in 24 days, 4 hours, 36 minutes. June 28–July 22, 1994 (pending FAI approval).

Absolute World Records, Balloons

Selected records. *Source:* National Aeronautic Association.

Altitude (USA)
113,739.9 ft; 34,668 km.
Cmdr. M.D. Ross (USNR) and Lt. Cmdr. V.A. Prather, *Lee Lewis Memorial,* Gulf of Mexico, May 4, 1961.

Distance (USA)
5,208.67 mi; 8,382.54 km
Ben L. Abruzzo, pilot; Larry M. Newman, copilot; Rocky Aoki, pilot; Ron Clark, pilot. *Raven Exper-*

imental, Nagashima, Japan to Covello, Calif., Nov. 9–12, 1981.

Duration (USA)
144 hours, 16 minutes
Richard Abruzzo and Troy Bradley, *Cameron R–77,* Bangor, Maine, USA, to Ben Slimane, Morocco, Sept. 16–22, 1992.

World Class Records, Single-Seater Gliders

Selected records. *Source:* National Aeronautic Association.

Straight Distance (W. Germany)
907.70 mi; 1,460.80 km
Hans Werner Grosse, ASK 12, Luebeck to Biarritz, April 25, 1972.

Distance to a Goal and Return (USA)
1,023.25 mi; 1,646.68 km
Thomas L. Knauff, Nimbus III, Ridge Soaring Gliderport–Williamsport Airport, Pa., April 25, 1983.

Absolute Altitude (USA)
49,009 ft; 14,938 m
Robert Harris, Burkhart Grob, G–102, California City, Calif., February 17, 1986.

Speed Over a Commerical Air Route (U.S.)

Selected records. *Source:* National Aeronautic Association.

These records are for speed between two U.S. cities made by a commercial airliner on a regularly scheduled commercial route, and are timed from takeoff to landing.

West to East Transcontinental
680.90 mph
Capt. Wylie H. Drummond, American Airlines Boeing 707–123, powered by four P&W JT3D engines, from Los Angeles International to Idlewild International, 2,474 miles in 3 hr 38 min 00 sec. April 10, 1963.

East to West Transcontinental
575.52 mph
Capt. Gene Kruse, American Airlines, Boeing 707–720B, powered by four P&W JT3D engines, from Idlewild International to Los Angeles International, 2,474 miles in 4 hr 19 min 15 sec. Aug. 15, 1962.

Parachutes

Selected records. *Source:* National Aeronautic Association.

Largest Freefall Formations

General Category (International)
200 persons, Myrtle Beach, S.C., Oct. 23, 1992.

Feminine Category (International)
101 persons, Le Canet des Maures, France, Aug. 14, 1992.

Largest Canopy Formation

General Category (International)
46 persons, Davis, CA, October 12, 1994.

Feminine Category (International)
16 persons, Madera, Calif., Oct. 7, 1990.

Individual Altitude (Freefall Distance)

General Category
E. Andreev (U.S.S.R.), 80,360 ft, 24,500 m, Nov. 1, 1962.

Feminine Category
E. Fomitcheva (U.S.S.R.), 48,556 ft, 14,800 m, Oct. 26, 1977.

Absolute World Records

(Maximum Performance in Any Class)
Source: National Aeronautic Association

These official Absolute World Records are the supreme achievements of all the hundreds of records open to flying machines. They are the most outstanding of all the major types, and thus warrant the highest respect.

All types of airplanes are eligible for these few very special records. Airplanes may be powered by piston, turboprop, turbojet, rocket engines or a combination. They may be landplanes, seaplanes or amphibians; they may be lightplanes, business planes, military or commercial airplanes.

Over the years, many different categories of aircraft have held these records. In the past, the cost of developing high-performance aircraft has been so great that only airplanes created for military purposes have held these records. There have been two exceptions to this situation.

Most recently and most dramatically, the Rutan designed "Voyager" shattered the theory that only a complicated military behemoth could hold an Absolute World Record. The Voyager team and its nonstop, non-refueled flight around the world proved that the dreams of dedicated individuals, combined with creative engineering, new technology, and hard work, could conquer the world.

The other exception was the X-15 rocket-powered research airplane. Holder of one record, it was used for both civilian and military research during its highly productive lifetime.

Speed Around the World, Nonstop, Nonrefueled

Speed (mph)	Date	Type Plane	Pilots	Place
115.65	Dec. 14-23, 1986	*Voyager*	Dick Rutan & Jeana Yeager (U.S.)	Edwards AFB, Calif.—Edwards AFB, Calif.

Distance, Great Circle Without Landing, also Distance, Closed Circuit Without Landing

Distance (mi.)	Date	Pilots	Place
24,986.727	Dec. 14-23, 1986	Dick Rutan & Jeana Yeager (U.S.)	Edwards AFB, Calif.—Edwards AFB, Calif.

Speed Over a Straight Course

Speed (mph)	Date	Type Plane	Pilot	Place
2,193.16	July 28, 1976	Lockheed SR-71A	Capt. Eldon W. Joersz (USAF)	Beale AFB, Calif.

Speed Over A Closed Circuit

Speed (mph)	Date	Type Plane	Pilot	Place
2,092.294	July 27,1976	Lockheed SR-71A	Maj. Adolphus H. Bledsoe, Jr. (USAF)	Beale AFB, Calif.

Altitude

Height (ft)	Date	Type Plane	Pilot	Place
123,523.58	Aug. 31, 1977	MIG-25, E-266M	Alexander Fedotov (U.S.S.R.)	U.S.S.R.

Altitude in Horizontal Flight

Height (ft)	Date	Pilot	Place
85,068.997	July 28, 1976	Capt. Robert C. Helt (USAF)	Beale AFB, Calif.

Altitude, Aircraft Launched From A Carrier Airplane

Height (ft)	Date	Type Plane	Pilot	Place
314,750.00	July 17, 1962	N. American X-15-1	Maj. Robert White (USAF)	Edwards AFB, Calif.

The Speed of Sound

Source: Air & Space/Smithsonian.

The speed of sound varies with temperature. At sea level Mach 1 is around 742 mph. It decreases with altitude until it reaches about 661 mph at 36,000 feet, then remains at that speed in a band of steady temperature up to 60,000 feet. Because of the variation, it is possible for an airplane flying supersonic at high altitude to be slower than a subsonic flight at sea level. The transsonic band extends from around Mach .8—when the first supersonic shock waves form on the wing—to Mach 1.2, when the entire wing has gone supersonic.

The National Aviation Hall of Fame

Dedicated to honoring and preserving the history of outstanding air and space pioneers, the Aviation Hall of Fame was established in Dayton, Ohio on October 5, 1962, with five Daytonians as its founding fathers: James W. Jacobs, Gregory C. Karas, John A. Lombard, Larry E. O'Neil, and Gerald E. Weller. The first annual enshrinement ceremonies were held in December that same year. The United States Congress passed Public Law 88–372 in July 1964 granting the NAHF a national charter.

For additional information, contact the National Aviation Hall of Fame, Dayton Convention Center, Dayton, Ohio 45402, (513) 226-0800.

(With Year of Enshrinement)

Allen, William McPherson (1971)
Andrews, Frank M. (1986)
Armstrong, Neil Alden (1979)
Arnold, Henry Harley (1967)
Atwood, J. Leland (1984)
Balchen, Bernt (1973)
Baldwin, Thomas Scott (1964)
Beachey, Lincoln (1966)
Beech, Olive Ann (1981)
Beech, Walter Herschel (1977)
Bell, Alexander Graham (1965)
Bell, Lawrence Dale (1977)
Bellanca, Giuseppe Mario (1993)
Bendix, Vincent Hugo (1991)
Boeing, William Edward (1966)
Bong, Richard L. (1986)
Borman, Frank (1982)
Boyd, Albert (1984)
Bradley, Mark E. (1992)
Brown, George Scratchley (1985)
Byrd, Richard Evelyn (1968)
Cessna, Clyde Vernon (1978)
Chamberlin, Clarence Duncan (1976)
Chanute, Octave (1963)
Chennault, Claire Lee (1972)
Cochran, Jacqueline (1972)
Collins, Michael (1985)
Conrad, Charles, Jr. (1980)
Crawford, Frederick C. (1993)
Crossfield, A. Scott (1983)
Cunningham, Alfred Austell (1965)
Curtiss, Glenn Hammond (1964)
Davis, Jr. Benjamin O. (1994)
deSeversky, Alexander P. (1970)
Doolittle, James Harold (1967)
Douglas, Donald Wills (1969)
Draper, Charles Stark (1981)
Eaker, Ira Clarence (1970)
Eielson, Carl Benjamin (1985)
Ellyson, Theodore Gordon (1964)
Ely, Eugene Burton (1965)
Everest, Frank K. (1989)
Fairchild, Sherman Mills (1979)
Fleet, Rueben Hollis (1975)
Fokker, Anthony Herman Gerard (1980)
Ford, Henry (1984)
Foss, Joseph Jacob (1984)
Foulois, Benjamin Delahauf (1963)
Frye, William John (1992)
Gabreski, Francis Stanley (1978)
Gentile, Dominic S. (1995)
Gilruth, Robert R. (1994)
Glenn, John Herschel, Jr. (1976)

Goddard, George William (1976)
Goddard, Robert Hutchings (1966)
Godfrey, Arthur (1987)
Goldwater, Barry Morris (1982)
Grissom, Virgil I. (1987)
Gross, Robert Ellsworth (1970)
Grumman, Leroy Randle (1972)
Guggenheim, Harry Frank (1971)
Haughton, Daniel J. (1987)
Hegenberger, Albert Francis (1976)
Heinemann, Edward Henry (1981)
Hoover, Robert A. (1988)
Ingalls, David Sinton (1983)
James, Daniel, Jr. (1993)
Jeppesen, Elrey B. (1990)
Johnson, Clarence Leonard (1974)
Johnston, Alvin M. (1993)
Jones, Thomas V. (1992)
Kenney, George Churchill (1971)
Kettering, Charles Franklin (1979)
Kindelberger, James Howard (1972)
Knabenshue, A. Roy (1965)
Knight, William J. (1988)
Lahm, Frank Purdy (1963)
Langley, Samuel Pierpont (1963)
Lear, William Powerll, Sr. (1978)
LeMay, Curtis Emerson (1972)
LeVier, Anthony William (1978)
Lindbergh, Anne Morrow (1979)
Lindbergh, Charles Augustus (1967)
Link, Edwin Albert (1976)
Lockheed, Allan H. (1986)
Loening, Grover (1969)
Luke, Frank, Jr. (1975)
Macready, John Arthur (1968)
Macready, Paul B. (1991)
Martin, Glenn Luther (1966)
McDonnell, James Smith (1977)
Meyer, John C. (1988)
Mitchell, William (1966)
Mitscher, Marc A. (1988)
Montgomery, John Joseph (1964)
Moorer, Thomas H. (1987)
Moss, Sanford Alexander (1976)
Neumann, Gerhard (1986)
Nichols, Ruth Rowland (1992)
Norden, Carl L. (1994)
Northrop, John Knudsen (1974)
Pangborn, Clyde Edward (1995)
Patterson, William Allan (1976)

Piper, William Thomas, Sr. (1980)
Pitcairn, Harold Frederick (1995)
Post, Wiley Hardeman (1969)
Putnam, Amelia Earhart (1968)
Read, Albert Cushing (1965)
Reeve, Robert Campbell (1965)
Rentschler, Frederick Brant (1982)
Richardson, Holden Chester (1978)
Rickenbacker, Edward Vernon (1965)
Rodgers, Calbraith Perry (1964)
Rogers, Will (1977)
Rushworth, Robert A. (1990)
Rutan, Elbert L. (1995)
Ryan, T. Claude (1974)
Schirra, Walter M., Jr. (1986)
Schriever, Bernard Adolf (1980)
Selfridge, Thomas Etholen (1965)
Shepard, Alan Bartlett, Jr. (1977)
Sikorsky, Igor Ivan (1968)
Six, Robert Forman (1980)
Smith, C.R. (1974)
Spaatz, Carl Andrew (1967)
Sperry, Elmert Ambrose, Sr. (1973)
Sperry, Lawrence Burst, Sr. (1981)
Stanley, Robert M. (1990)
Stapp, John Paul (1985)
Stearman, Lloyd C. (1989)
Taylor, Charles Edward (1965)
Thomas, Lowell (1992)
Towers, John Henry (1966)
Trippe, Juan Terry (1970)
Turner, Roscoe (1975)
Twining, Nathan Farragut (1976)
Vandenberg, Hoyt S. (1991)
von Braun, Wernher (1982)
von Karman, Theodore (1983)
von Ohain, Hans P. (1990)
Vought, Chance M. (1989)
Wade, Leigh (1974)
Walden, Henry W. (1964)
Wells, Edward Curtis (1991)
Wilson, Thornton Arnold (1983)
Woolman, Collett Everman (1994)
Wright, Orville (1962)
Wright, Wilbur (1962)
Yeager, Charles Elwood (1973)
Young, John W. (1988)

TRAVEL

Ten Tips for Smooth Flying

By Elizabeth McGowan

**From making plane reservations to retrieving luggage,
you need a flight plan to avoid trouble.**

Just when you thought the skies were friendly again, along comes a dark cloud from the federal agency responsible for protecting air travelers' rights. The Department of Transportation reports that, after five years of decline, passenger complaints about everything from flight delays to lost luggage shot up last year, when almost 7,000 angry consumers reported the airlines to DOT, 16 percent more than in 1993. DOT promises a crackdown.

In the meantime, passengers are well advised to practice "defensive flying." While you can't control the weather or rude personnel, the following tactics will increase your odds for arriving at your destination with good temper and belongings intact.

1. Book your flight during non-peak hours. Runway backlog is worst on weekday mornings and early evenings, prime times for business travelers; Sunday nights, and the beginning and end of holiday weekends. Don't reserve the last flight of the day to your destination—if it's cancelled, you'll have no options for an alternative flight.

2. Fly nonstop rather than through or direct. "Through" or "direct" usually means that although you won't have to change planes, your flight will be making one or more stops en route to your destination, increasing potential for delays.

3. Allow a minimum of an hour between connecting flights. Although airlines typically suggest allowing 30 minutes between flights, don't believe it: an hour's window is the minimum you should request. If you are cutting it close, ask for an aisle seat near the front of the plane so you can disembark quickly. Reserve connecting flights on the same airline. If the first flight is delayed, the airline is more likely to hold up the second if the tardy passengers are on one of its own planes.

4. Pay for your ticket by credit card. This offers greater protection if an airline goes belly-up before your trip. Don't rely on the mail; pick up your ticket from a travel agency or airline office.

5. Arrive at the airport before check-in deadline. Airlines have a naughty habit of overselling seats to compensate for no-shows. When someone has to be bumped, latecomers are the likely candidates if there are no volunteers. If you are involuntarily bumped and the airline arranges substitute transportation that gets you to your final destination within one hour of your arrival time, don't expect compensation. If they switch you to a flight scheduled to land between one and two hours (four on international flights) after your original arrival time, you will be paid an amount equal to the fare of your overbooked flight, up to $200. If the alternate flight arrives more than two hours later (four for international flights) you'll get twice the fare, up to $400.

5. Pack only a carry-on bag if possible. If you're checking a bag, don't put anything in it that you can't live without—medicine, documents, your favorite sweater. And pack light. The airlines' liability limit is usually a maximum of $1,250 for lost luggage on domestic flights, $640 for international flights—not much considering the cost of a business suit these days.

7. Check your luggage tags. To prevent routing errors, remove old destination stubs from your bags. Make sure that the right airport code for your destination is on all your checked luggage.

8. Leave an address. Write your business address and phone number, and a destination phone number at which you can be reached on your luggage tag. Put the same information inside your suitcase.

9. File (and get a copy of) a claim for lost or damaged luggage before you leave the airport. Be sure to obtain the number to call to check on tracking progress. Play the role of squeaky wheel until you get your bag back or receive compensation. While carriers aren't required to pay you for necessities while your bag is missing, they often will when they are asked.

10. Know your rights. The brochure, "Fly Rights," is available for $1.75 (send check or money order payable to the Superintendent of Documents) from DOT's Consumer Information Center, Department 133–B, Pueblo, CO 81009. □

Elizabeth McGowan is a freelance writer based in New York City. This article was first published in *Car & Travel Monthly*, May 1995, the official publication of the Automobile Club of New York.

Emergency Help

The Citizens Emergency Center deals with emergencies involving Americans abroad—Americans who die, become destitute, get sick, disappear, have accidents, or get arrested.

In addition to individual emergencies, the Citizens Emergency Center is also the State Department's focal point for major disasters involving Americans abroad: plane crashes, hijackings, natural disasters, terrorist incidents, etc.

The Citizens Emergency Center's telephone number is: (202) 647-5225. The Center is open 8:15 a.m. to 10:00 p.m. Monday through Friday, and 9:00 a.m. to 3:00 p.m. Saturday. At other times, including holidays, a duty officer can be reached through the State Department's main number: (202) 647-4000.

Emergency assistance generally falls into four categories: deaths, arrests, financial/medical problems, and welfare/whereabouts queries. The Citizens Emergency Center, working through American embassies and consulates abroad, is a link between the citizen in distress and his or her family in the U.S. The Citizens Emergency Center is also responsible for the Department's consular information program consisting of Consular Information Sheets and Travel Warnings.

U.S. Passport and Customs Information

Source: Department of State, Bureau of Consular Affairs and Department of the Treasury, Customs Service.

Passports

With a few exceptions, a passport is required for all U.S. citizens to depart and enter the United States and to enter most foreign countries. A valid U.S. passport is the best documentation of U.S. citizenship available. Persons who travel to a country where a U.S. passport is not required should be in possession of documentary evidence of their U.S. citizenship and identity to facilitate reentry into the United States. Travelers should check passport and visa requirements with consular officials of the countries to be visited well in advance of their departure date.

Application for a passport may be made at a passport agency; to a clerk of any Federal court or State court of record; or a judge or clerk of any probate court accepting applications; or at a post office selected to accept passport applications. Passport agencies are located in Boston, Chicago, Honolulu, Houston, Los Angeles, Miami, New Orleans, New York, Philadelphia, San Francisco, Seattle, Stamford, Conn., and Washington, D.C.

All persons are required to obtain individual passports in their own names. Neither spouses nor children may be included in each others' passports. Applicants age 13 years and older must appear in person before the clerk or agent executing the application. For children under the age of 13, a parent or legal guardian may execute an application for them.

First time passport applicants must apply in person. Applicants must present evidence of citizenship (e.g., a certified copy of birth certificate), personal identification (e.g., a valid driver's license), two identical black and white or color photographs taken within six months (2 × 2 inches, with the image size measured from the bottom of the chin to the top of the head [including hair] not less than 1 inch nor more than 1 3/8 inches on a plain white or off–white background, vending machine photographs not acceptable), plus a completed passport application (DSP–11). If you were born abroad, you may also use as proof of citizenship: a Certificate of Naturalization, a Certificate of Citizenship, a Report of Birth Abroad of a Citizen of the United States of America or a Certification of Birth. A fee of $55 plus a $10 execution fee is charged for adults 18 years and older for a passport valid for ten years from the date of issue. The fee for minor children under 18 years of age is $30 for a five–year passport plus $10 for the execution of the application.

You may apply for a passport by mail if you have been the bearer of a passport issued within 12 years prior to the date of a new application, are able to submit your most recent U.S. passport with your new application, and your previous passport was not issued before your 18th birthday. If you are eligible to apply by mail, include your previous passport, a completed, signed, and dated DSP–82 "Application for Passport by Mail," new photographs, and the passport fee of $55. The $10 execution fee is not required when applying by mail. Mail the application and attachments in accordance with the instructions on the form.

Passports may be presented for amendment to show a married name or legal change of name or to correct descriptive data. Any alterations to the passport by the bearer other than in the spaces provided for change of address and next of kin data are forbidden.

If you **must** have your passport within 10 days, you will need to pay an additional $30 expedite fee and provide proof of the need for this service.

Loss, theft or destruction of a passport should be reported to Passport Services, 1111 19th Street, N.W., Washington, D.C. 20522-1705 immediately, or to the nearest passport agency. If you are overseas, report loss to the nearest U.S. Embassy or consulate and to local police authorities. Your passport is a valuable citizenship and identity document. It should be carefully safeguarded. Its loss could cause you unnecessary travel complications as well as significant expense. It is advisable to photocopy the data page of your passport and keep it in a place separate from your passport to facilitate the issuance of a replacement passport should one be necessary.

Portsmouth National Passport Center

The Department of State has the largest passport processing center in the United States at Portsmouth, New Hampshire. Known as the National Passport Center, the facility is capable of issuing 6,000 passports per day but can be expanded to issue 9,000 passports per day.

The Center is processing passport mail renewal applications from around the United States. Passport fees are deposited in Pittsburgh, with the applications subsequently express mailed to Portsmouth for processing. The other passport agencies will process first–time applications and any other requests for passport services presented in person.

To renew a passport by mail, applicants must:

1. Obtain an "Application for Passport by Mail" (Form DSP-82) from a passport acceptance facility (post office, court house or passport agency);

2. Complete and sign the application and attach the most recent passport issued not more than 12 years ago but after the applicant's 18th birthday, two identical 2″ × 2″ passport photographs, and a check or money order for $55.

3. Mail the above items to the National Passport Center, Post Office Box 371971, Pittsburgh, Pennsylvania 15250-7971.

Customs

United States residents must declare all articles acquired abroad and in their possession at the time of their return. In addition, articles acquired in the U.S. Virgin Islands, American Samoa, or Guam and not accompanying you must be declared at the time of your return. The wearing or use of an article acquired abroad does *not* exempt it from duty. Customs declaration forms are distributed on vessels and planes, and should be prepared in advance of arrival for presentation to the customs inspectors.

If you have not exceeded the duty–free exemption allowed, you may make an oral declaration to the customs inspector. However, the inspector can request a written declaration and may do so. A written declaration is necessary when (1) the total fair retail value of articles exceeds the personal exemption of $400; (2) over 1 liter of liquor, 200 cigarettes, or 100 cigars are included; (3) items are not intended for your personal or household use, or articles brought home for another person; (4) when a customs duty or internal revenue tax is collectible on any article in your possession; and (5) if your personal exemption was used in the last 30 days.

An exception to the above are regulations applicable to articles purchased in the U.S. Virgin Islands, American Samoa, or Guam where you may receive a customs exemption of $1,200. Not more than $400 of this exemption may be applied to merchandise obtained elsewhere than in these islands or $600 if acquired in a Caribbean Basin beneficiary country. Five liters of alcoholic beverages and 1000 cigarettes may be included provided not more than one liter and 200 cigarettes were acquired elsewhere than in these islands. Articles acquired in and sent from these islands to the United States may be claimed under your duty–free personal exemption if properly declared at the time of your return. For information on rules applying to beneficiary countries and a list of them check with your local Customs office or write for the pamphlet "GSP and the Traveler" from the U.S. Customs Services, P.O. Box 7407, Washington, D.C. 20044. Since rules change it is always wise to check with customs before leaving, to get information pertinent to the areas you will be visiting.

Articles accompanying you, in excess of your personal exemption, up to $1000 will be assessed at a flat rate of duty of 10% based on fair retail value in country of acquisition. (If articles were acquired in the insular possessions, the flat rate of duty is 5% and these goods may accompany you or be shipped home.) These articles must be for your personal use or for use as gifts and not for sale. This provision may be used every 30 days, excluding the day of your last arrival. Any items which have a "free" duty rate will be excluded before duty is calculated.

You may mail articles bought for your personal use back to the U.S. at a duty free rate of $200 per day (excluding restricted items such as liquor).

Other exemptions include in part: automobiles, boats, planes, or other vehicles taken abroad for non-commercial use. Foreign–made personal articles (e.g., watches, cameras, etc.) taken abroad should be registered with Customs before departure. Customs will register anything with a serial number or identifying marks. Sales receipt or insurance document are sufficient Customs identification. Registration of articles for which you have documented proof of purchase is redundant and is not necessary. Gifts of not more than $100 can be shipped back to the United States tax and duty free ($200 if mailed from the Virgin Islands, American Samoa, or Guam). Household effects and tools of trade which you take out of the United States are duty free at time of return.

Prohibited and restricted articles include in part: absinthe, narcotics and dangerous drugs, obscene articles and publications, seditious and treasonable materials, hazardous articles (e.g., fireworks, dangerous toys, toxic and poisonous substances, and switchblade knives), biological materials of public health or veterinary importance, fruit, vegetables and plants, meats, poultry and products thereof, birds, monkeys, and turtles. You can get additional information on this subject from the publication *Pets, Wildlife, U.S. Customs*. For a free copy write to the U.S. Customs Service, P.O. Box 7407, Washington, D.C. 20044.

If you understate the value of an article you declare, or if you otherwise misrepresent an article in your declaration, you may have to pay a penalty in addition to payment of duty. Under certain circumstances, the article could be seized and forfeited if the penalty is not paid.

If you fail to declare an article acquired abroad, not only is the article subject to seizure and forfeiture, but you will be liable for a personal penalty in an amount equal to the value of the article in the United States. In addition, you may also be liable to criminal prosecution.

If you carry more than $10,000 into or out of the United States in currency (either United States or foreign money), negotiable instruments in bearer form, or travelers checks, a report must be filed with United States Customs at the time you arrive or depart with such amounts.

For more information about Customs regulations for travelers, write the above address for a copy of "Know Before You Go."

Foreign Embassies in the United States

Source: U.S. Department of State.

Embassy of the Republic of Afghanistan, 2341 Wyoming Ave., N.W., Washington, D.C. 20008. Phone: (202) 234–3770, 3771.

Embassy of the Republic of Albania, 1511 K St., N.W., Suite 1010, Washington, D.C. 20005. Phone: (202) 223-4942, 8187.

Embassy of the Democratic & Popular Republic of Algeria, 2118 Kalorama Rd., N.W., Washington, D.C. 20008. Phone: (202) 265–2800.

Embassy of the Republic of Angola, 1819 L St., N.W., Suite 400, Washington, D.C. 20036. Phone: (202) 785-1156.

Embassy of Antigua & Barbuda, 3216 New Mexico Ave., N.W., Washington, D.C. 20016. Phone: (202) 362–5211, 5166, 5122.

Embassy of the Argentine Republic, 1600 New Hampshire Ave., N.W., Washington, D.C. 20009. Phone: (202) 939–6400 to 6403, inclusive.

Embassy of the Republic of Armenia, 1660 L St., N.W., Suite 210, Washington, D.C. 20036. Phone: (202) 628-5766.

Embassy of Australia, 1601 Massachusetts Ave., N.W., Washington, D.C. 20036. Phone: (202) 797–3000.

Embassy of Austria, 3524 International Court, N.W., Washington, D.C. 20008. Phone: (202) 895-6700.

Embassy of the Republic of Azerbaijan, 927 15th St., N.W., Suite 700, Washington, D.C. 20005. Phone: (202) 842-0001.

Embassy of The Commonwealth of The Bahamas, 2220 Massachusetts Ave., N.W., Washington, D.C. 20008. Phone: (202) 319-2660.

Embassy of the State of Bahrain, 3502 International Dr., N.W., Washington, D.C. 20008. Phone: (202) 342–0741, 0742.

Embassy of the People's Republic of Bangladesh, 2201 Wisconsin Ave., N.W., Washington, D.C. 20007. Phone: (202) 342–8372 to 8376.

Embassy of Barbados, 2144 Wyoming Ave., N.W., Washington, D.C. 20008. Phone: (202) 939–9200 to 9202.

Embassy of the Republic of Belarus, 1619 New Hampshire Ave., N.W., Washington, D.C. 20009. Phone: (202) 986-1640.

Embassy of Belgium, 3330 Garfield St., N.W., Washington, D.C. 20008. Phone: (202) 333–6900.

Embassy of Belize, 2535 Massachusetts Ave., N.W., Washington, D.C. 20008. Phone: (202) 332-9636.

Embassy of the Republic of Benin, 2737 Cathedral Ave., N.W., Washington, D.C. 20008. Phone: (202) 232–6656 to 6658.

Embassy of Bolivia, 3014 Massachusetts Ave., N.W., Washington, D.C. 20008. Phone: (202) 483–4410 to 4412.

Embassy of the Republic of Bosnia and Herzegovina, 1707 L St., N.W., Suite 760, Wshington, D.C. 20036. Phone: (202) 833-3612, 3613, and 3615.

Embassy of the Republic of Botswana, 3400 International Dr., N.W., Suite 7M, Washington, D.C. 20008. Phone: (202) 244–4990, 4991.

Brazilian Embassy, 3006 Massachusetts Ave., N.W., Washington, D.C. 20008. Phone: (202) 745–2700.

Embassy of the State of Brunei Darussalam, Watergate, 2600 Virginia Ave., N.W., Suite 300, Washington, D.C. 20037. Phone: (202) 342–0159.

Embassy of the Republic of Bulgaria, 1621 22nd St., N.W., Washington, D.C. Phone: (202) 387–7969.

Embassy of Burkina Faso, 2340 Massachusetts Ave., N.W., Washington, D.C. 20008. Phone: (202) 332–5577, 6895.

Embassy of the Republic of Burundi, 2233 Wisconsin Ave., N.W., Suite 212, Washington, D.C. 20007. Phone: (202) 342–2574.

Royal Embassy of Cambodia, 4500 16th St., N.W., Washington, D.C. 20011. Phone: (202) 726–7742.

Embassy of the Republic of Cameroon, 2349 Massachusetts Ave., N.W., Washington, D.C. 20008. Phone: (202) 265–8790 to 8794.

Embassy of Canada, 501 Pennsylvania Ave., N.W., Washington, D.C. 20001. Phone: (202) 682–1740.

Embassy of the Republic of Cape Verde, 3415 Massachusetts Ave., N.W., Washington, D.C. 20007. Phone: (202) 965–6820.

Embassy of Central African Republic, 1618 22nd St. N.W., Washington, D.C. 20008. Phone: (202) 483–7800, 7801.

Embassy of the Republic of Chad, 2002 R St., N.W., Washington, D.C. 20009. Phone: (202) 462–4009.

Embassy of Chile, 1732 Massachusetts Ave., N.W., Washington, D.C. 20036. Phone: (202) 785–1746.

Embassy of the People's Republic of China, 2300 Connecticut Ave., N.W., Washington, D.C. 20008. Phone: (202) 328–2500 to 2502.

Embassy of Colombia, 2118 Leroy Pl., N.W., Washington, D.C. 20008. Phone: (202) 387–8338.

Embassy of the Federal and Islamic Republic of Comoros, c/o Permanent Mission of the Federal and Islamic Republic of Comoros to the United Nations, 336 E. 45th St., 2nd floor, New York, N.Y. 10017. Phone: (212) 972–8010.

Embassy of the Republic of Congo, 4891 Colorado Ave., N.W., Washington, D.C. 20011. Phone: (202) 726–0825.

Embassy of Costa Rica, 2114 S St., N.W., Washington, D.C. 20008. Phone: (202) 234–2945.

Embassy of the Republic of Cote d'Ivoire, 2424 Massachusetts Ave., N.W., Washington, D.C. 20008. Phone: (202) 797–0300.

Embassy of the Republic of Croatia, 2343 Massachusetts Ave., N.W., Washington, D.C. 20008. Phone: (202) 588-5899.

Cuban Interests Section, 2630 and 2639 16th St., N.W., Washington, D.C. 20009. Phone: (202) 797–8518 to 8520, 8609, 8610.

Embassy of the Republic of Cyprus, 2211 R St. N.W., Washington, D.C. 20008. Phone: (202) 462–5772.

Embassy of the Czech Republic, 3900 Spring of Freedom St., N.W., Washington, D.C. 20008. Phone: (202) 363–6315, 6316.

Royal Danish Embassy, 3200 Whitehaven St., N.W., Washington, D.C. 20008. Phone: (202) 234–4300.

Embassy of the Republic of Djibouti, 1156 15th St., N.W., Suite 515, Washington, D.C. 20005. Phone: (202) 331-0270.

Embassy of the Commonwealth of Dominica, 3216 New Mexico Ave., N.W., Washington, D.C. 20016. Phone: (202) 364-6781.

Embassy of the Dominican Republic, 1715 22nd St., N.W., Washington, D.C. 20008. Phone: (202) 332–6280.

Embassy of Ecuador, 2535 15th St., N.W., Washington, D.C. 20009. Phone: (202) 234–7200.

Embassy of the Arab Republic of Egypt, 3521 International Court, N.W., Washington, D.C. 20008. Phone: (202) 895-5400.

Embassy of El Salvador, 2308 California St., N.W., Washington, D.C. 20008. Phone: (202) 265–9671, 9672.

Embassy of Equatorial Guinea, 57 Magnolia Ave., Mount Vernon, N.Y. 10553. Phone: (914) 738-9584 and 667-6913.

Embassy of the State of Eritrea, 910 17th St., N.W., Suite 400, Washington, D.C. 20006. Phone: (202) 429-1991.

Embassy of Estonia, 1030 15th St., N.W., Suite 1000, Washington, D.C. 20005. Phone: (202) 789-0320.

Embassy of Ethiopia, 2134 Kalorama Rd., N.W., Washington, D.C. 20008. Phone: (202) 234–2281, 2282.

Embassy of The Republic of Fiji, 2233 Wisconsin Ave., N.W., Suite 240, Washington, D.C. 20007. Phone: (202) 337–8320.

Embassy of Finland, 3301 Massachusetts Ave., N.W., Washington, D.C. 20008. Phone: (202) 298-5800.

Embassy of France, 4101 Reservoir Rd., N.W., Washington, D.C. 20007. Phone: (202) 944–6000.

Embassy of the Gabonese Republic, 2034 20th St., N.W., Suite 200, Washington, D.C. 20009. Phone: (202) 797–1000.

Embassy of The Gambia, 1155 15th St., N.W., Suite 1000, Washington, D.C. 20005. Phone: (202) 785-1399, 1379, 1425.

Embassy of the Republic of Georgia, 1511 K St., N.W., Suite 424, Washington, D.C. 20005. Phone: (202) 393-6060, 393-5959.

Embassy of the Federal Republic of Germany, 4645 Reservoir Rd., N.W., Washington, D.C. 20007. Phone: (202) 298–4000.

Embassy of Ghana, 3512 International Dr., N.W., Washington, D.C. 20008 (202) 686–4520.

Embassy of Greece, 2221 Massachusetts Ave., N.W., Washington, D.C. 20008. Phone (202) 939–5800.

Embassy of Grenada, 1701 New Hampshire Ave., N.W., Washington, D.C. 20009. Phone: (202) 265–2561.

Embassy of Guatemala, 2220 R St., N.W., Washington, D.C. 20008. Phone: (202) 745–4952 to 4954.

Embassy of the Republic of Guinea, 2112 Leroy Pl., N.W., Washington, D.C. 20008. Phone: (202) 483–9420.

Embassy of the Republic of Guinea–Bissau, 918 16th St., N.W., Mezzanine Suite, Washington, D.C. 20006. Phone: (202) 872-4222.

Embassy of Guyana, 2490 Tracy Pl., N.W. Washington, D.C. 20008. Phone: (202) 265–6900 to 6901.

Embassy of the Republic of Haiti, 2311 Massachusetts Ave., N.W., Washington, D.C. Phone: (202) 332–4090 to 4092.

Apostolic Nunciature of the Holy See, 3339 Massachusetts Ave., N.W., Washington, D.C. 20008. Phone: (202) 333–7121.

Embassy of Honduras, 3007 Tilden St., N.W., Washington, D .C. 20008. Phone: (202) 966–7702, 2604, 5008, 4596.

Embassy of the Republic of Hungary, 3910 Shoemaker St., N.W., Washington, D.C. 20008. Phone: (202) 362–6730.

Embassy of Iceland, 1156 15th St., N.W., Suite 1200, Washington, D.C. 20005. Phone: (202) 265–6653 to 6655.

Embassy of India, 2107 Massachusetts Ave., N.W., Washington, D.C. 20008. Phone: (202) 939–7000.

Embassy of the Republic of Indonesia, 2020 Massachusetts Ave., N.W., Washington, D.C. 20036. Phone: (202) 775–5200.

Iranian Interests Section, 2209 Wisconsin Ave., N.W., Washington, D.C. 20007. Phone: (202) 965-4990.

Iraqi Interests Section, 1801 P St., N.W., Washington, D.C. 20036. Phone: (202) 483–7500.

Embassy of Ireland, 2234 Massachusetts Ave., N.W., Washington, D.C. 20008. Phone: (202) 462–3939.

Embassy of Israel, 3514 International Dr., N.W., Washington, D.C. 20008. Phone: (202) 364–5500.

Embassy of Italy, 1601 Fuller St., N.W., Washington, D.C. 20009. Phone: (202) 328–5500.

Embassy of Jamaica, 1520 New Hampshire Ave., N.W. Washington, D.C. 20036. Phone: (202) 452–0660.

Embassy of Japan, 2520 Massachusetts Ave., N.W., Washington, D.C. 20008. Phone: (202) 939–6700.

Embassy of the Hashemite Kingdom of Jordan, 3504 International Dr., N.W., Washington, D.C. 20008. Phone: (202) 966–2664.

Embassy of the Republic of Kazakhstan, 3421 Massachusetts Ave., N.W., Wshington, D.C. 20008. Phone: (202) 333-4504–7.

Embassy of the Republic of Kenya, 2249 R St., N.W., Washington, D.C. 20008. Phone: (202) 387–6101.

Embassy of Korea, 2450 Massachusetts Ave., N.W., Washington, D.C. 20008. Phone: (202) 939–5600.

Embassy of the State of Kuwait, 2940 Tilden St., N.W., Washington, D.C. 20008. Phone: (202) 966–0702.

Embassy of the Republic of Kyrgystan, 1511 K St., N.W., Suite 705, Washington, D.C. 20005. Phone: (202) 347-3732, 3733, and 3718.

Embassy of the Lao People's Democratic Republic, 2222 S St., N.W., Washington, D.C. 20008. Phone: (202) 332–6416, 6417.

Embassy of Latvia, 4325 17th St., N.W., Washington, D.C. 20011. Phone: (202) 726–8213, 8214.

Embassy of Lebanon, 2560 28th St., N.W., Washington, D.C. 20008. Phone: (202) 939–6300.

Embassy of the Kingdom of Lesotho, 2511 Massachusetts Ave., N.W., Washington, D.C. 20008. Phone: (202) 797–5533 to 5536.

Embassy of the Republic of Liberia, 5201 16th St., N.W., Washington, D.C. 20011.

Embassy of the Republic of Lithuania, 2622 16th St., N.W., Washington, D.C. 20009. Phone: (202) 234–5860, 2639.

Embassy of Luxembourg, 2200 Massachusetts Ave., N.W., Washington, D.C. 20008. Phone: (202) 265–4171.

Embassy of the Democratic Republic of Madagascar, 2374 Massachusetts Ave., N. W., Washington, D.C. 20008. Phone: (202) 265–5525, 5526.

Malawi Embassy, 2408 Massachusetts Ave., N.W., Washington, D.C. 20008. Phone: (202) 797–1007.

Embassy of Malaysia, 2401 Massachusetts Ave., N.W., Washington, D.C. 20008. Phone: (202) 328–2700.

Embassy of the Republic of Mali, 2130 R St., N.W., Washington, D.C. 20008. Phone: (202) 332–2249; (202) 939–8950.

Embassy of Malta, 2017 Connecticut Ave., N.W., Washington, D.C. 20008. Phone: (202) 462–3611, 3612.

Embassy of the Republic of the Marshall Islands, 2433 Massachusetts Ave., N.W., Washington, D.C. 20008. Phone: (202) 234-5414.

Embassy of the Islamic Republic of Mauritania, 2129 Leroy Pl., N.W., Washington, D.C. 20008. Phone: (202) 232–5700.

Embassy of Mauritius, 4301 Connecticut Ave., N.W., Suite 441, Washington, D.C. 20008. Phone: (202) 244–1491, 1492.

Embassy of Mexico, 1911 Pennsylvania Ave., N.W., 20006, Washington, D.C. Phone: (202) 728–1600.

Embassy of the Federated States of Micronesia, 1725 N St., N.W., Washington, D.C. 20036. Phone: (202) 223-4383.

Embassy of the Republic of Moldova, 1511 K St., N.W., Suites 329, 333, Washington, D.C. 20005. Phone: (202) 783-3012.

Embassy of Mongolia, 2833 M St., N.W., Washington, D.C. 20007. Phone: (202) 333-7117.

Embassy of the Kingdom of Morocco, 1601 21st St., N.W., Washington, D.C. 20009. Phone: (202) 462–7979 to 7982, inclusive.

Embassy of the Republic of Mozambique, 1990 M St., N.W., Suite 570, Washington, D.C. 20036. Phone: (202) 293–7146.

Embassy of the Union of Myanmar, 2300 S St., N.W., Washington, D.C. 20008. Phone: (202) 332–9044, 9045.

Embassy of the Republic of Namibia, 1605 New Hampshire Ave., N.W., Washington, D.C. 20009. Phone: (202) 986-0540.

Royal Nepalese Embassy, 2131 Leroy Pl., N.W., Washington, D.C. 20008. Phone: (202) 667–4550.

Embassy of the Netherlands, 4200 Linnean Ave., N.W., Washington, D.C. 20008. Phone: (202) 244–5300; after 6 p.m. (202) 244–5304.

Embassy of New Zealand, 37 Observatory Circle, N.W., Washington, D.C. 20008. Phone: (202) 328–4800.

Embassy of Nicaragua, 1627 New Hampshire Ave., N.W., Washington, D.C. 20009. Phone: (202) 939–6570.

Embassy of the Republic of Niger, 2204 R St., N.W., Washington, D.C. 20008. Phone: (202) 483–4224 to 4227, inclusive.

Embassy of the Federal Republic of Nigeria, 1333 16th St., N.W., Washington, D.C. 20036. Phone: (202) 986-8400.

Royal Norwegian Embassy, 2720 34th St., N.W., Washington, D.C. 20008. Phone: (202) 333–6000.

Embassy of the Sultanate of Oman, 2535 Belmont Rd., N.W., Washington, D.C. 20008. Phone: (202) 387–1980 to 1982.

Embassy of Pakistan, 2315 Massachusetts Ave., N.W., Washington, D.C. 20008. Phone: (202) 939–6200.

Embassy of the Republic of Palau, 444 N. Capital St., N.W., Suite 619, Washington, D.C. 20001. Phone: (202) 624–7793.

Embassy of the Republic of Panama, 2862 McGill Terrace, N.W., Washington, D.C. 20008. Phone: (202) 483–1407.

Embassy of Papua New Guinea, 1615 New Hampshire Ave., N.W., 3rd floor, Washington, D.C. 20009. Phone: (202) 745-3680.

Embassy of Paraguay, 2400 Massachusetts Ave., N.W., Washington, D.C. 20008. Phone: (202) 483–6960 to 6962.

Embassy of Peru, 1700 Massachusetts Ave., N.W., Washington, D.C. 20036. Phone: (202) 833–9860 to 9869.

Embassy of the Philippines, 1600 Massachusetts Ave., N.W., Washington, D.C. 20036. Phone: (202) 467–9300..

Embassy of the Republic of Poland, 2640 16th St., N.W., Washington, D.C. 20009. Phone: (202) 234–3800 to 3802.

Embassy of Portugal, 2125 Kalorama Rd., N.W., Washington, D.C. 20008. Phone: (202) 328–8610.

Embassy of the State of Qatar, 600 New Hampshire Ave., N.W., Suite 1180, Washington, D.C. 20037. Phone: (202) 338–0111.

Embassy of Romania, 1607 23rd St., N.W., Washington, D.C. 20008. Phone: (202) 332-4846, 4848, 4851; after hours 332-4846.

Embassy of the Russian Federation, 2650 Wisconsin Ave., N.W. Washington, D.C. 20007. Phone: (202) 298-5700 to 5704 inclusive.

Embassy of the Republic of Rwanda, 1714 New Hampshire Ave., N.W., Washington, D.C. 20009. Phone: (202) 232–2882.

Embassy of Saint Kitts and Nevis, 3216 New Mexico Ave., N.W. Washington, D.C. 20016. Phone: (202) 686-2636..

Embassy of Saint Lucia, 3216 New Mexico Ave., N.W., Washington, D.C. 20016. Phone: (202) 364-6792 to 6795.

Embassy of Saint Vincent and the Grenadines, 1717 Massachusetts Ave., N.W., Suite 102, Washington, D.C. 20036. Phone: (202) 462-7806, 7846.

Embassy of Saudi Arabia, 601 New Hampshire Ave., N.W., Washington, D.C. 20037. Phone: (202) 342–3800.

Embassy of the Republic of Senegal, 2112 Wyoming Ave., N.W., Washington, D.C. 20008. Phone: (202) 234–0540, 0541.

Embassy of the Republic of Seychelles, c/o Permanent Mission of Seychelles to the United Nations, 820 Second Ave., Suite 900F, New York, N.Y. 10017. Phone: (212) 687–9766/9767.

Embassy of Sierra Leone, 1701 19th St., N.W., Washington, D.C. 20009. Phone: (202) 939–9261.

Embassy of the Republic of Singapore, 3501 International Pl., N.W., Washington, D.C. 20008. Phone: (202) 537–3100.

Embassy of the Slovak Republic, 2201 Wisconsin Ave., N.W., Suite 380, Washington, D.C. 20007. Phone: (202) 965–5166.

Embassy of the Republic of Slovenia, 1525 New Hampshire Ave., N.W., Washington, D.C. 20036. Phone: (202) 667–5363.

Embassy of South Africa, 3051 Massachusetts Ave., N.W., Washington, D.C. 20008. Phone: (202) 232–4400.

Embassy of Spain, 2375 Pennsylvania Ave. N.W., Washington, D.C. 20037. Phone: (202) 452–0100 and 728–2340.

Embassy of the Democratic Socialist Republic of Sri Lanka, 2148 Wyoming Ave., N.W., Washington, D.C. 20008. Phone: (202) 483–4025 to 4028.

Embassy of the Republic of the Sudan, 2210 Massachusetts Ave., N.W., Washington, D.C. 20008. Phone: (202) 338–8565 to 8570.

Embassy of the Republic of Suriname, 4301 Connecticut Ave., N.W., Suite 108, Washington, D.C. 20008. Phone: (202) 244–7488, 7490 to 7492.

Embassy of the Kingdom of Swaziland, 3400 International Drive, N.W., Washington, D.C. 20008. Phone: (202) 362–6683, 6685.

Embassy of Sweden, 1501 M St., N.W., Washington, D.C. 20005. Phone: (202) 467-2600.

Embassy of Switzerland, 2900 Cathedral Ave., N.W., Washington, D.C. 20008. Phone: (202) 745–7900.

Embassy of the Syrian Arab Republic, 2215 Wyoming Ave., N.W., Washington, D.C. 20008. Phone: (202) 232–6313.

Embassy of the United Republic of Tanzania, 2139 R St., N.W., Washington, D.C. 20008. Phone: (202) 939–6125.

Embassy of Thailand, 1024 Wisconsin Ave., N.W., Washington, D.C. 20007. Phone: (202) 944-3600.

Embassy of the Republic of Togo, 2208 Massachusetts Ave., N.W., Washington, D.C. 20008. Phone: (202) 234–4212.

Embassy of Trinidad and Tobago, 1708 Massachusetts Ave., N.W., Washington, D.C. 20036. Phone: (202) 467–6490.

Embassy of Tunisia, 1515 Massachusetts Ave., N.W., Washington, D.C. 20005. Phone: (202) 862–1850.

Embassy of the Republic of Turkey, 1714 Massachusetts Ave. N.W., Washington, D.C. 20036. Phone: (202) 659–8200.

Embassy of the Republic of Turkmenistan, 1511 K St., N.W., Suite 412, Washington, D.C. 20005. Phone: (202) 737-4800.

Embassy of the Republic of Uganda, 5911 16th St., N.W., Washington, D.C. 20011. Phone: (202) 726–7100 to 7102, 0416.

Embassy of Ukraine, 3350 M St., N.W., Washington, D.C. 20007. Phone: (202) 333-0606.

Embassy of the United Arab Emirates, 3000 K St., N.W., Suite 600, Washington, D.C. 20007. Phone: (202) 338–6500.

United Kingdom of Great Britain & Northern Ireland— British Embassy, 3100 Massachusetts Ave., N.W., Washington, D.C. 20008. Phone: (202) 462–1340.

Embassy of Uruguay, 1918 F St., N.W., Washington D.C. 20006. Phone: (202) 331–1313 to 1316, inclusive.

Embassy of the Republic of Uzbekistan, 1511 K St., N.W., Suites 619 and 623, Washington, D.C. 20005. Phone: (202) 638–4266, 4267.

Embassy of the Republic of Venezuela, 1099 30th St., N.W., Washington D.C. 20007. Phone: (202) 342-2214.

Embassy of Western Samoa, 820 Second Ave., Suite 800, New York, N.Y. 10017. Phone: (212) 599-6196, 6197.

Embassy of the Republic of Yemen, 2600 Virginia Ave., N.W. Suite 705, Washington, D.C. 20037. Phone: (202) 965–4760, 4761.

Embassy of the former Socialist Federal Republic of Yugoslavia, 2410 California St., N.W., Washington, D.C. 20008. Phone: (202) 462–6566.

Embassy of the Republic of Zaire, 1800 New Hampshire Ave., N.W., Washington, D.C. 20009. Phone: (202) 234–7690, 7691.

Embassy of the Republic of Zambia, 2419 Massachusetts Ave., N.W., Washington, D.C. 20008. Phone: (202) 265–9717 to 9719.

Embassy of the Republic of Zimbabwe, 1608 New Hampshire Ave., N.W., Washington, D.C. 20009. Phone: (202) 332-7100.

Diplomatic Personnel To and From the U.S.

Country	U.S. Representative to[1]	Rank	Representative from[2]	Rank
Afghanistan	—	—	Yar Mohammad Mohabbat	Cd'A.
Albania	Joseph E. Lake	Amb.	Lublin Dilja	Amb.
Algeria	Ronald E. Neumann	Amb.	Hadj Osmane Bencherif	Amb.
Angola	Edmund T. DeJarnette	Dir.	Jose Goncalves Martins Patricio	Amb.
Antigua and Barbuda	(Post closed)		Dr. Patrick Albert Lewis	Amb.
Argentina	James R. Cheek	Amb.	Raul Enrique Granillo Ocampo	Amb.
Armenia	Harry J. Gilmore	Amb.	Rouben Robert Shugarian	Amb.
Australia	Edward Perkins	Amb.	Dr. Donald Eric Russell	Amb.
Austria	Swanee G. Hunt	Amb.	Helmut Tuerk	Amb.
Azerbaijan	Richard D. Kauzlarich	Cd'A.	Hafiz Mir Jalal Pashayev	Amb.
Bahamas	Sidney Williams	Amb.	Timothy Baswell Donaldson	Amb.
Bahrain	David M. Ransom	Amb.	Muhammad Abdul Ghaffar Abdulla	Amb.
Bangladesh	David N. Merrill	Amb.	Humayun Kabir	Amb.
Barbados	Jeanette W. Hyde	Amb.	Courtney N.M. Blackman	Amb.
Belarus	Kenneth Spenser Yalowitz	Amb.	Serguei Nikolaevich Martynov	Amb.
Belgium	Alan J. Blinken	Amb.	Andre Adam	Amb.
Belize	George Charles Bruno	Amb.	Dean R. Lindo	Amb.

Country	U.S. Representative to[1]	Rank	Representative from[2]	Rank
Benin	Ruth A. Davis	Amb.	Lucien Edgar Tonoukouin	Amb.
Bermuda	Robert A. Farmer	Cons. Gen.	—	
Bolivia	Curt Warren Kamman	Amb.	Andres Petricevic R	Amb.
Bosnia-Herzegovina	Victor Jackovich	Amb.	Sven Alkalaj	Amb.
Botswana	Howard F. Jeter	Amb.	Botsweletse Kingsley Sebele	Amb.
Brazil	Melvyn Levitsky	Amb.	Paulo-Tarso Flecha de Lima	Amb.
Brunei	Theresa A. Tull	Amb.	Haji Jaya bin Abdul Latif	Amb.
Bulgaria	William D. Montgomery	Amb.	Snejana Damianova Botoucharova	Amb.
Burkina Faso	Donald J. McConnell	Amb.	Gaetan R. Ouedraogo	Amb.
Burundi	Robert C. Krueger	Amb.	Severin Ntahomvukiye	Amb.
Cambodia	Charles H. Twining	Dir.	Var Huoth	Amb.
Cameroon	Harriet W. Isom	Amb.	Jerome Mendouga	Amb.
Canada	James Johnston Blanchard	Amb.	Raymond A.J. Chretien	Amb.
Cape Verde	Joseph M. Segars	Amb.	Corentino Virgilio Santos	Amb.
Central African Republic	Robert E. Gribbin III	Amb.	Henry Koba	Amb.
Chad	Laurence E. Pope II	Amb.	Ahmat Mahamat-Saleh	Amb.
Chile	Curtis W. Kamman	Amb.	John Biehl	Amb.
China	J. Stapleton Roy	Amb.	Li Daoyu	Amb.
Colombia	Myles R.R. Frechette	Amb.	Carlos Lleras	Amb.
Comoros	(Post closed)		—	Amb.
Congo, Republic of	William C. Ramsay	Amb.	Pierre Damien Boussouko-Boumba	Amb.
Costa Rica	(Vacancy)		Sonia Picado	Min.
Côte d'Ivoire	Hume A. Horan	Amb.	Koffi Moise Koumoue	Amb.
Croatia	Peter W. Galbraith	Amb.	Peter A. Sarcevic	Amb.
Cyprus	Richard A. Boucher	Amb.	Andrew J. Jacovides	Amb.
Czech Republic	Adrian A. Basora	Amb.	Michael Zantovsky	Amb.
Denmark	Edward E. Elson	Amb.	Peter P. Dyvig	Amb.
Djibouti	Martin L. Cheshes	Amb.	Roble Olhaye	Amb.
Dominica	—	—	Edward I. Watty	Amb.
Dominican Republic	Donna Jean Hrinak	Amb.	Jose del Carmen Ariza	Amb.
Ecuador	Peter F. Romero	Amb.	Edgar Teran-Teran	Amb.
Egypt	Edward S. Walker, Jr.	Amb.	Ahmed Maher El Sayed	Amb.
El Salvador	Alan H. Flanigan	Amb.	Ana Cristina Sol	Amb.
Equatorial Guinea	John E. Bennett	Amb.	Theodoro Biyogo Nsue	1st Secy.
Eritrea	Robert G. Houdek	Amb.	Amdemicael Kahsai	Amb.
Estonia	(Vacancy)	Amb.	Toomas Hendrik Ilves	Amb.
Ethiopia	Irvin Hicks	Cd'A.	Berhane Gebre-Christos	Amb.
Fiji	(Vacancy)	Amb.	Pita Kewa Nacuva	Amb.
Finland	Derek N. Shearer	Amb.	Jukka Valtasaari	Amb.
France	Pamela C. Harriman	Amb.	Jacques Andreani	Amb.
Gabon	Joseph C. Wilson IV	Amb.	Paul Boundoukou-Latha	Amb.
Gambia	Andrew J. Winter	Amb.	Lamin A. Bojang	Attaché
Georgia	Kent N. Brown	Cd'A.	Tedo Djaparidze	Amb.
Germany	Charles E. Redman	Amb.	Juergen Chrobog	Amb.
Ghana	Kenneth L. Brown	Amb.	Ekwow Spio-Garbrah	Amb.
Greece	Thomas M.T. Niles	Amb.	Loucas Tsilas	Amb.
Grenada	(Vacancy)	Amb.	Denneth Modeste	Amb.
Guatemala	Marilyn McAfee	Amb.	Edmond Mulet	Amb.
Guinea	Joseph A. Saloom III	Amb.	Elhadj Boubacar Barry	Amb.
Guinea–Bissau	Roger A. McGuire	Amb.	Alfredo Lopes Cabral	Amb.
Guyana	George F. Jones	Amb.	Mohammed Ali Odeen Ishmael	Amb.
Haiti	William Lacy Swing	Amb.	Jean Casimir	Amb.
Holy See	Raymond L. Flynn	Amb.	Most Rev. Agostino Cacciavillan	Pro–Nuncio
Honduras	William T. Pryce	Amb.	Roberto Flores Bermudez	Amb.
Hong Kong	Richard W. Mueller	Cons. Gen.	—	—
Hungary	Donald M. Blinken	Amb.	Gyorgy Banlaki	Amb.
Iceland	Parker W. Borg	Amb.	Einar Benediktsson	Amb.
India	Frank G. Wisner	Amb.	Siddhartha S. Ray	Amb.
Indonesia	Robert L. Barry	Amb.	Arifin Mohamad Siregar	Amb.
Ireland	Jean Kennedy Smith	Amb.	Dermot A. Gallagher	Amb.
Israel	(Vacancy)	Amb.	Itamar Rabinovich	Amb.
Italy	Reginald Bartholomew	Amb.	Boris Biancheri	Amb.
Jamaica	(Vacancy)	Amb.	Richard Leighton Bernal	Amb.
Japan	Walter F. Mondale	Amb.	Takakazu Kuriyama	Amb.
Jordan	Wesley E. Egan, Jr.	Amb.	Fayez A. Tarawneh	Amb.
Kazakhstan	William H. Courtney	Amb.	Touleoutai S. Souleimenov	Amb.
Kenya	Aurelia Brazeal	Amb.	Benjamin Edgar Kipkorir	Amb.
Korea, South	James T. Laney	Amb.	Kun Woo Park	Amb.
Kuwait	Ryan C. Crocker	Amb.	Mohammed Sabah Al-Salim Al-Sabah	Amb.
Kyrgyzstan	Eileen A. Malloy	Amb.	Almas Chukin	Consl.
Laos	Victor L. Tomseth	Amb.	Hiem Phommachanh	Amb.

Country	U.S. Representative to[1]	Rank	Representative from[2]	Rank
Latvia	Ints M. Silins	Amb.	Ojars Eriks Kalnins	Amb.
Lebanon	Mark G. Hambley	Amb.	Riad Tabbarah	Amb.
Lesotho	(Vacancy)	Amb.	Eunice M. Bulane	Amb.
Liberia	William P. Twaddell	Cd'A.	Konah K. Blackett	Cd'A.
Lithuania	James W. Swihart, Jr.	Amb.	Alfonsas Eidintas	Amb.
Luxembourg	Clay Constantinou	Amb.	Alphonse Berns	Amb.
Macedonia (the former Yugoslav Republic of)	Victor R. Conras	P.O.	—	—
Madagascar	Dennis P. Barrett	Amb.	Pierrot J. Rajaonarivelo	Amb.
Malawi	Peter R. Chaveas	Amb.	W. Chokani	Amb.
Malaysia	John S. Wolf	Amb.	Dato Mohamed Abdul Majid	Amb.
Mali	William H. Dameron III	Amb.	Siragatou Ibrahim Cisse	Amb.
Malta	Joseph R. Paolino, Jr.	Amb.	Albert Borg Olivier De Puget	Amb.
Marshall Islands	David C. Fields	Amb.	Wilfred I. Kendall	Amb.
Mauritania	Dorothy Myers Sanpas	Amb.	Ismail Ould Iyahi	Amb.
Mauritius	Leslie M. Alexander	Amb.	Anund Priyay Neewoor	Amb.
Mexico	James R. Jones	Amb.	Jesus Silva Herzog	Amb.
Micronesia	March Fong Eu	Amb.	Jesse B. Marehalau	Amb
Moldova	Mary C. Pendleton	Amb.	Nicolae Tau	Amb.
Mongolia	Donald C. Johnson	Amb.	Luvsandorj Dawagiv	Amb.
Morocco	Marc C. Ginsberg	Amb.	Mohamed Benaissa	Amb.
Mozambique	Dennis Coleman Jett	Amb.	Hipolito Pereira Zozimo Patricio	Amb.
Myanmar (Burma)	(Vacancy)	Amb.	U Thaung	Amb.
Namibia	Marshall F. McCallie	Amb.	Tuliameni Kalomoh	Amb.
Nepal	Sandra L. Vogelgesang	Amb.	Basudev Prasad Dhungna	Amb.
Netherlands	K. Terry Dornbush	Amb.	Adriaan Pieter Roetert Jacobovits de Szeged	Amb.
New Zealand	Josiah Horton Beeman	Amb.	L. John Wood	Amb.
Nicaragua	John F. Maisto	Amb.	Roberto Genaro Mayorga-Cortes	Amb.
Niger	John S. Davison	Amb.	Adamou Seydou	Amb.
Nigeria	Walter C. Carrington	Amb.	Zubair Mahmud Kazaure	Amb.
Norway	Thomas A. Loftus	Amb.	Kjeld Vibe	Amb.
Oman	David J. Dunford	Amb.	Abdulla Moh'd Aqeel Al-Dhahab	Amb.
Pakistan	John C. Monjo	Amb.	Dr. Maleeha Lodhi	Amb.
Palau	Ihjod W. Moss	USLO	Isaac Ngewakl Soaladaob	Cd'A.
Panama	(Vacancy)	Amb.	Ricardo Alberto Arias	Amb.
Papua New Guinea	Richard W. Teare	Amb.	Kepas Isimel Watamgia	Amb.
Paraguay	(Vacancy)	Amb.	Jorge G. Prieto	Amb.
Peru	Alvin P. Adams, Jr.	Amb.	Ricardo V. Luna	Amb.
Philippines	John D. Negroponte	Amb.	Raul Ch. Rabe	Amb.
Poland	Nicholas Andrew Rey	Amb.	Jerzy Kozminski	Amb.
Portugal	Elizabeth Frawley Bagley	Amb.	Fernando Antonio Andresen Guimaraes	Amb.
Qatar	Kenton W. Keith	Amb.	Abdulrahman bin Saud Al-Thani	Amb.
Romania	Alfred H. Moses	Amb.	Mihail Horia Botez	Amb.
Russia	Thomas R. Pickering	Amb.	Yuli M. Vorontsov	Amb.
Rwanda	David P. Rawson	Amb.	Joseph W. Mutaboba	Consl.
Saint Kitts and Nevis	—	—	Erstein Mallet Edwards	Amb.
Saint Lucia	—	—	Dr. Joseph Edsel Edmunds	Amb.
Saint Vincent and the Grenadines	—	—	Kingsley C.A. Layne	Amb.
Saudi Arabia	Raymond E. Mabus, Jr.	Amb.	Prince Bandar Bin Sultan	Amb.
Senegal	Mark Johnson	Amb.	Mamadou Mansour Seck	Amb.
Serbia-Montenegro[3]	(Vacancy)	Amb.	Zoran Popovic	Consl.
Seychelles	Carl Burton Stokes	Amb.	Marc Michael Rogers Marengo	Amb.
Sierra Leone	Lauralee M. Peters	Amb.	Thomas Kahota Kargbo	Amb.
Singapore	Timothy A. Chorba	Amb.	S.R. Nathan	Amb.
Slovak Republic	Theodore E. Russell	Amb.	Branislav Lichardus	Amb.
Slovenia	E. Allan Wendt	Amb.	Dr. Ernest Petric	Amb.
Somalia	Richard W. Bogosian	Amb.	(Closed operations)	
South Africa	Princeton N. Lyman	Amb.	Franklin Sonn	Amb.
Spain	Richard N. Gardner	Amb.	Jaime de Ojeda	Amb.
Sri Lanka	Teresita C. Schaffer	Amb.	Janantha Cudah Bandara Dhanapala	Amb.
Sudan	Donald K. Petterson	Amb.	Ahmed Suliman	Amb.
Suriname	Roger R. Gamble	Amb.	Willem A. Udenhout	Amb.
Swaziland	John T. Sprott	Amb.	Mary M. Kanya	Amb.
Sweden	Thomas L. Siebert	Amb.	Carl Henrik Sihver Liljegren	Amb.
Switzerland	M. Larry Lawrence	Amb.	Carlo Jagmetti	Amb.
Syria	Christopher W.S. Ross	Amb.	Walid Al-Moualem	Amb.
Tajikistan	Stanley T. Escudero	Amb.	—	—
Tanzania	Steven A. Browning	Amb.	Mustafa Salim Nyang'anyi	Amb.
Thailand	David F. Lambertson	Amb.	Manaspas Xuto	Amb.

Country	U.S. Representative to[1]	Rank	Representative from[2]	Rank
Togo	Johnny Young	Amb.	Kossivi Osseyi	Amb.
Trinidad and Tobago	Sally G. Cowal	Amb.	Corinne Averille McKnight	Amb.
Tunisia	Mary Ann Casey	Amb.	Azouz Ennifar	Amb.
Turkey	Marc Grossman	Amb.	Nuzhet Kandemir	Amb.
Turkmenistan	Joseph S. Hulings III	Amb.	Halil Ugur	Amb.
Uganda	E. Michael Southwick	Amb.	Stephen Kapimpina Katenta–Apuli	Amb.
Ukraine	William Green Miller	Amb.	Yuriy Mikolayevych Shcherbak	Amb.
United Arab Emirates	William A. Rugh	Amb.	Mohammad bin Hussein Al-Shaali	Amb.
United Kingdom	William J. Crowe	Amb.	Sir Robin Renwick	Amb.
Uruguay	Thomas J. Dodd	Amb.	Alvaro Moerzinger	Amb.
Uzbekistan	Henry L. Clarke	Amb.	Fatikh Teshabaev	Amb.
Venezuela	Jeffery Davidow	Amb.	Pedro Luis Echeverria	Amb.
Western Samoa	Josiah Horton Beeman	Amb.	Tuiloma Neroni Slade	Amb.
Yemen	Arthur H. Hughes	Amb.	Mohsin A. Alaini	Amb.
Yugoslavia (former)			Zoran Popovic	Cd'A.
Zaire	(Vacancy)	Amb.	Tatanene Manata	Amb.
Zambia	Roland K. Kuchel	Amb.	Dunstan Weston Kamana	Amb.
Zimbabwe	E. Gibson Lanpher	Amb.	Amos Bernard Muvengwa Midzi	Amb.

1. As of Fall 1994. 2. As of May 1995. 3. Formerly Yugoslavia. NOTE: Amb.=Ambassador; Cd'A.=Charge d'Affaires; Secy.=Secretary; Cons. Gen.= Consul General. Consl.=Counselor; Min.=Minister; P.O.=Principal Officer; Dir.=Director; USLO=U.S. Liaison Office. *Source:* U.S. Department of State.

State and City Tourism Offices

The following is a selected list of state tourism offices. Where a toll–free 800 number is available, it is given. However, the numbers are subject to change.

ALABAMA
Bureau of Tourism & Travel
P.O. Box 4927
Montgomery, AL
36103-4927
334–242–4169 or
1–800–ALABAMA

ALASKA
Alaska Division of Tourism
P.O. Box 110801
Juneau, AK 99811-0801
907–465–2010

ARIZONA
Arizona Office of Tourism
1100 West Washington
Phoenix, AZ 85007
602 542–TOUR or
1–800–842–8257

ARKANSAS
Arkansas Department of
Parks and Tourism
1 Capitol Mall
Little Rock, AR 72201
501–682–7777 or
1–800–NATURAL
(to receive literature both
in and out of state)

CALIFORNIA
California Division
of Tourism
P.O. Box 1499
Sacramento, CA
95812–1499
1–800–862–2543 U.S. only

COLORADO
No longer has a tourism
board. Tourists need to contact individual cities.

CONNECTICUT
Tourism Promotion Service
CT Dept. of Economic
Development
865 Brook Street
Rocky Hill, CT 06067–3405
203–258–4355 or 800–CT
BOUND (nationwide)

DELAWARE
Delaware Tourism Office
Delaware Development
Office
99 Kings Highway
P.O. Box 1401
Dover, DE 19903
302–739–4271 or
1–800–441–8846
(both in and out of state)

DISTRICT OF COLUMBIA
Washington Convention
and Visitors Association
1212 New York Ave., NW
Suite 600
Washington, D.C.
20005–3992
202–789–7000

FLORIDA
Department of Commerce
Visitors Inquiry
126 Van Buren St.
Tallahassee, FL 32399–2000
904–487–1462

GEORGIA
Tourist Division
P.O. Box 1776
Atlanta, GA 30301-1776
404–656–3590
1-800-VISIT GA
(1-800-847-4842)

HAWAII
Hawaii Visitors Bureau
2270 Kalakaua Ave., Suite
801
Honolulu, HI 96815
808–923–1811

IDAHO
Department of Commerce
700 W. State St.
P.O. 83720
Boise, ID 83720-0093
208–334–2470 or
1–800–635–7820

ILLINOIS
Illinois Bureau of Tourism
100 W. Randolph,
Suite 3–400
Chicago, IL 60601
312–814–4732

INDIANA
Indiana Dept. of Commerce
Tourism & Film Develop-
ment Division
One North Capitol
Suite 700
Indianapolis, IN
46204–2288
317–232–8860 or
1–800–289–6646

IOWA
Iowa Department of
Economic Development
Division of Tourism
200 East Grand Avenue
Des Moines, IA 50309
515–242–4705
1-800-345-IOWA

Average Daily Temperatures (°F) in Tourist Cities

Location	January High	January Low	April High	April Low	July High	July Low	October High	October Low
U.S. CITIES (See Weather and Climate Section)								
CANADA								
Ottawa	21	3	51	31	81	58	54	37
Quebec	18	2	45	29	76	57	51	37
Toronto	30	16	50	34	79	59	56	40
Vancouver	41	32	58	40	74	54	57	44
MEXICO								
Acapulco	85	70	87	71	89	75	88	74
Mexico City	66	42	78	52	74	54	70	50
OVERSEAS								
Australia (Sydney)	78	65	71	58	60	46	71	56
Austria (Vienna)	34	26	57	41	75	59	55	44
Bahamas (Nassau)	77	65	81	69	88	75	85	73
Bermuda (Hamilton)	68	58	71	59	85	73	79	69
Brazil (Rio de Janeiro)	84	73	80	69	75	63	77	66
Denmark (Copenhagen)	36	29	50	37	72	55	53	42
Egypt (Cairo)	65	47	83	57	96	70	86	65
France (Paris)	42	32	60	41	76	55	59	44
Germany (Berlin)	35	26	55	38	74	55	55	41
Greece (Athens)	54	42	67	52	90	72	74	60
Hong Kong	64	56	75	67	87	78	81	73
India (Calcutta)	80	55	97	76	90	79	89	74
Italy (Rome)	54	39	68	46	88	64	73	53
Israel (Jerusalem)	55	41	73	50	87	63	81	59
Japan (Tokyo)	47	29	63	46	83	70	69	55
Nigeria (Lagos)	88	74	89	77	83	74	85	74
Netherlands (Amsterdam)	40	34	52	43	69	59	56	48
Puerto Rico (San Juan)	81	67	84	69	87	74	87	73
South Africa (Cape Town)	78	60	72	53	63	45	70	52
Spain (Madrid)	47	33	64	44	87	62	66	48
United Kingdom (London)	44	35	56	40	73	55	58	44
United Kingdom (Edinburgh)	43	35	50	39	65	52	53	44
Russia (Moscow)	21	9	47	31	76	55	46	34
Venezuela (Caracas)	75	56	81	60	78	61	79	61
Yugoslavia (Belgrade)	37	27	64	45	84	61	65	47

KANSAS
Kansas Department of
Commerce & Housing
Travel & Tourism
Development Division
700 SW Harrison St.,
Suite 1300
Topeka, KS 66603-3712
913-296-2009
1-800-2KANSAS

KENTUCKY
Department of Travel
Development
Dept. MR
P.O. Box 2011
Frankfort, KY 40602
1-800-225-TRIP Ext. 67
(From the United States
and Canada)

LOUISIANA
Office of Tourism
P.O. Box 94291 Dept. 5701
Baton Rouge, LA
70804-9291
504-342-8147 or
1-800-33GUMBO or
1-800-633-6970

MAINE
Maine Publicity Bureau
P.O. Box 2300
Hallowell, ME 04347-2300
207-623-0363

MARYLAND
Office of Tourism
Development
217 E. Redwood St.,
9th Floor
Baltimore, MD 21202
410-333-6611 Business
Office only
1-800-543-1036—
Maryland Travel Kit

MASSACHUSETTS
Office of Travel and
Tourism
100 Cambridge St., 13th
Floor
Boston, MA 02202
617-727-3201

MICHIGAN
Travel Bureau
Michigan Jobs
Commission
P.O. Box 3393
Livonia, MI 48151
1-800-5432-YES

MINNESOTA
Minnesota Office of
Tourism
100 Metro Square
121 Seventh Place E
St. Paul, MN 55101-2112
612-296-5029 or
1-800-657-3700

MISSISSIPPI
Department of Economic
and Community
Development
Tourism Development
P.O. Box 1705
Ocean Springs, MS
39566-1705
601-359-3297 or
1-800-927-6378

MISSOURI
Missouri Division of
Tourism
Truman State Office Bldg.
301 W. High St.
P.O. Box 1055
Jefferson City, MO 65102
314-751-4133
1-800-877-1234

MONTANA
Department of Commerce
Travel Montana
P.O. Box 200533
Helena, MT 59620-0533
406-444-2654 or
1-800-VISIT MT

NEBRASKA
Dept. of Economic
Development
Division of Travel and
Tourism
P.O. Box 98913
Lincoln, NE 68509
402-471-3796 or
1-800-228-4307
(In-state or out of state)

NEVADA
Commission on Tourism
Capitol Complex
Carson City, NV 89710
1-800-Nevada-8

NEW HAMPSHIRE
Office of Travel
and Tourism
P.O. Box 1856
Concord, NH 03302-1856
603-271-2666
or for recorded weekly
events, ski conditions,
foliage reports
1-800-258-3608

NEW JERSEY
Division of Travel and
Tourism
CN-826
Trenton, NJ 08625
1-800-JERSEY-7

NEW MEXICO
New Mexico Department
of Tourism
Room 751 Lamy Bldg.
491 Old Santa Fe Trail
Santa Fe, NM 87503
505-827-7400 or
1-800-545-2040 Ext. 751

NEW YORK
Division of Tourism
1 Commerce Plaza
Albany, NY 12245
Toll free from anywhere in
the U.S. and its territorial
possessions
1-800-225-5697. From
Canada, call (518) 474-4116

NORTH CAROLINA
Travel and Tourism Division
Department of Commerce
430 North Salisbury St.
Raleigh, NC 27611
919-733-4171 or
1-800-VISIT NC

NORTH DAKOTA
North Dakota Tourism
604 E. Boulevard
Bismarck, ND 58505
701-328-2525 or
1-800-435-5663

OHIO
Ohio Division of Travel and
Tourism
P.O. Box 1001
Columbus, OH 43266-1010
614-466-8844 (Business
Office)
1-800-BUCKEYE
(U.S. and Canada
Toll-Free Travel Hotline)

OKLAHOMA
Oklahoma Tourism and
Recreation Dept.
Literature Distribution
Center
P.O. Box 60789
Oklahoma City, OK
73146-9910
405-521-2409 (In
Oklahoma City area) or
nationwide at
1-800-652-6552

OREGON
Tourism Division
775 Summer St. NE
Salem, OR 97310
503-986-0000 (Business
Office)
1-800-547-7842 (Travel
Information)

PENNSYLVANIA
Office of Travel Marketing
Room 453 Forum Building
Harrisburg, PA 17120
717-787-5453 (Business
Office)
1-800-VISIT PA, ext. 257
(To order single free copy
of PA Travel Guide)

RHODE ISLAND
Rhode Island Tourism
Division
7 Jackson Walkway
Providence, RI 02903
401-277-2601 or
1-800-556-2484
U.S. and Canada

SOUTH CAROLINA
South Carolina Division of
Tourism
Box 71
Columbia, SC 29202
803-734-0122

SOUTH DAKOTA
Department of Tourism
711 E. Wells Ave.
Pierre, South Dakota 57501
605-773-3301 or
1-800-S-DAKOTA

TENNESSEE
Department of Tourist
Development
P.O. Box 23170
Nashville, TN 37202
615-741-2158
1-800-TENN-200

TEXAS
Travel Information Services
Texas Department of
Transportation
P.O. Box 5064
Austin, TX 78763-5064
1-800-452-9292

UTAH
Utah Travel Council
Council Hall, Capitol Hill
Salt Lake City, UT 84114
801-538-1030

VERMONT
Department of Travel
and Tourism
134 State St.
P.O. Box 1471
Montpelier, VT 05601-1471
1-800-VERMONT

VIRGINIA
Virginia Division
of Tourism
P.O. Box 798
Richmond, VA 23206-0798
804-786-4484
1-800-VISIT-VA

WASHINGTON
Washington State Dept. of
Community, Trade and
Economic Development
906 Columbia St. SW
P.O. Box 48300
Olympia, WA 98504-8300
360-753-2200

WASHINGTON, D.C.
See District of Columbia

WEST VIRGINIA
Division of Tourism
and Parks
2101 Washington St. E.
Charleston, WV 25305
304-558-2286 or
1-800-CALL-WVA

WISCONSIN
Travel Information
Division of Tourism
Box 7606
Madison, WI 53707
Toll free in WI and neigh-
bor states 1-800-372-2737
others: 608-266-2161
Nationally 1-800-432-TRIP

WYOMING
Wyoming Division of
Tourism
I-25 at College Drive
Cheyenne, WY 82002
307-777-7777 or
1-800-225-5996

Road Mileages Between U.S. Cities[1]

Cities	Birming–ham	Boston	Buffalo	Chicago	Cleveland	Dallas	Denver
Birmingham, Ala.	—	1,194	947	657	734	653	1,318
Boston, Mass.	1,194	—	457	983	639	1,815	1,991
Buffalo, N.Y.	947	457	—	536	192	1,387	1,561
Chicago, Ill.	657	983	536	—	344	931	1,050
Cleveland, Ohio	734	639	192	344	—	1,205	1,369
Dallas, Tex.	653	1,815	1,387	931	1,205	—	801
Denver, Colo	1,318	1,991	1,561	1,050	1,369	801	—
Detroit, Mich.	754	702	252	279	175	1,167	1,301
El Paso, Tex.	1,278	2,358	1,928	1,439	1,746	625	652
Houston, Tex.	692	1,886	1,532	1,092	1,358	242	1,032
Indianapolis, Ind.	492	940	510	189	318	877	1,051
Kansas City, Mo.	703	1,427	997	503	815	508	616
Los Angeles, Calif.	2,078	3,036	2,606	2,112	2,424	1,425	1,174
Louisville, Ky.	378	996	571	305	379	865	1,135
Memphis, Tenn.	249	1,345	965	546	773	470	1,069
Miami, Fla.	777	1,539	1,445	1,390	1,325	1,332	2,094
Minneapolis, Minn.	1,067	1,402	955	411	763	969	867
New Orleans, La.	347	1,541	1,294	947	1,102	504	1,305
New York, N.Y.	983	213	436	840	514	1,604	1,780
Omaha, Neb.	907	1,458	1,011	493	819	661	559
Philadelphia, Pa.	894	304	383	758	432	1,515	1,698
Phoenix, Ariz.	1,680	2,664	2,234	1,729	2,052	1,027	836
Pittsburgh, Pa.	792	597	219	457	131	1,237	1,411
St. Louis, Mo.	508	1,179	749	293	567	638	871
Salt Lake City, Utah	1,805	2,425	1,978	1,458	1,786	1,239	512
San Francisco, Calif.	2,385	3,179	2,732	2,212	2,540	1,765	1,266
Seattle, Wash.	2,612	3,043	2,596	2,052	2,404	2,122	1,373
Washington, D.C.	751	440	386	695	369	1,372	1,635

Cities	Detroit	El Paso	Houston	Indian–apolis	Kansas City	Los Angeles	Louisville
Birmingham, Ala.	754	1,278	692	492	703	2,078	378
Boston, Mass.	702	2,358	1,886	940	1,427	3,036	996
Buffalo, N.Y.	252	1,928	1,532	510	997	2,606	571
Chicago, Ill.	279	1,439	1,092	189	503	2,112	305
Cleveland, Ohio	175	1,746	1,358	318	815	2,424	379
Dallas, Tex.	1,167	625	242	877	508	1,425	865
Denver, Colo.	1,310	652	1,032	1,051	616	1,174	1,135
Detroit, Mich.	—	1,696	1,312	290	760	2,369	378
El Paso, Tex.	1,696	—	756	1,418	936	800	1,443
Houston, Tex.	1,312	756	—	1,022	750	1,556	981
Indianapolis, Ind.	290	1,418	1,022	—	487	2,096	114
Kansas City, Mo.	760	936	750	487	—	1,609	519
Los Angeles, Calif.	2,369	800	1,556	2,096	1,609	—	2,128
Louisville, Ky.	378	1,443	981	114	519	2,128	—
Memphis, Tenn.	756	1,095	586	466	454	1,847	396
Miami, Fla.	1,409	1,957	1,237	1,225	1,479	2,757	1,111
Minneapolis, Minn.	698	1,353	1,211	600	466	2,041	716
New Orleans, La.	1,101	1,121	365	839	839	1,921	725
New York, N.Y.	671	2,147	1,675	729	1,216	2,825	785
Omaha, Neb.	754	1,015	903	590	204	1,733	704
Philadelphia, Pa.	589	2,065	1,586	647	1,134	2,743	703
Phoenix, Ariz.	1,986	402	1,158	1,713	1,226	398	1,749
Pittsburgh, Pa.	288	1,778	1,395	360	847	2,456	416
St. Louis, Mo.	529	1,179	799	239	255	1,864	264
Salt Lake City, Utah	1,721	877	1,465	1,545	1,128	728	1,647
San Francisco, Calif.	2,475	1,202	1,958	2,299	1,882	403	2,401
Seattle, Wash.	2,339	1,760	2,348	2,241	1,909	1,150	2,355
Washington, D.C.	526	1,997	1,443	565	1,071	2,680	601

1. These figures represent estimates and are subject to change.

Road Mileages Between U.S. Cities

Cities	Memphis	Miami	Minne–apolis	New Orleans	New York	Omaha	Phila–delphia
Birmingham, Ala.	249	777	1,067	347	983	907	894
Boston, Mass.	1,345	1,539	1,402	1,541	213	1,458	304
Buffalo, N.Y.	965	1,445	955	1,294	436	1,011	383
Chicago, Ill.	546	1,390	411	947	840	493	758
Cleveland, Ohio	773	1,325	763	1,102	514	819	432
Dallas, Tex.	470	1,332	969	504	1,604	661	1,515
Denver, Colo.	1,069	2,094	867	1,305	1,780	559	1,698
Detroit, Mich.	756	1,409	698	1,101	671	754	589
El Paso, Tex.	1,095	1,957	1,353	1,121	2,147	1,015	2,065
Houston, Tex.	586	1,237	1,211	365	1,675	903	1,586
Indianapolis, Ind.	466	1,225	600	839	729	590	647
Kansas City, Mo.	454	1,479	466	839	1,216	204	1,134
Los Angeles, Calif.	1,847	2,757	2,041	1,921	2,825	1,733	2,743
Louisville, Ky.	396	1,111	716	725	785	704	703
Memphis, Tenn.	—	1,025	854	401	1,134	658	1,045
Miami, Fla.	1,025	—	1,801	892	1,328	1,683	1,239
Minneapolis, Minn.	854	1,801	—	1,255	1,259	373	1,177
New Orleans, La.	401	892	1,255	—	1,330	1,043	1,241
New York, N.Y.	1,134	1,328	1,259	1,330	—	1,315	93
Omaha, Neb.	658	1,683	373	1,043	1,315	—	1,233
Philadelphia, Pa.	1,045	1,239	1,177	1,241	93	1,233	—
Phoenix, Ariz.	1,464	2,359	1,644	1,523	2,442	1,305	2,360
Pittsburgh, Pa.	810	1,250	876	1,118	386	932	304
St. Louis, Mo.	295	1,241	559	696	968	459	886
Salt Lake City, Utah	1,556	2,571	1,243	1,743	2,282	967	2,200
San Francisco, Calif.	2,151	3,097	1,997	2,269	3,036	1,721	2,954
Seattle, Wash.	2,363	3,389	1,641	2,606	2,900	1,705	2,818
Washington, D.C.	902	1,101	1,114	1,098	229	1,170	140

Cities	Phoenix	Pitts–burgh	St. Louis	Salt Lake City	San Francisco	Seattle	Wash–ington
Birmingham, Ala.	1,680	792	508	1,805	2,385	2,612	751
Boston, Mass.	2,664	597	1,179	2,425	3,179	3,043	440
Buffalo, N.Y.	2,234	219	749	1,978	2,732	2,596	386
Chicago, Ill.	1,729	457	293	1,458	2,212	2,052	695
Cleveland, Ohio	2,052	131	567	1,786	2,540	2,404	369
Dallas, Tex.	1,027	1,237	638	1,239	1,765	2,122	1,372
Denver, Colo.	836	1,411	871	512	1,266	1,373	1,635
Detroit, Mich.	1,986	288	529	1,721	2,475	2,339	526
El Paso, Tex.	402	1,778	1,179	877	1,202	1,760	1,997
Houston, Tex.	1,158	1,395	799	1,465	1,958	2,348	1,443
Indianapolis, Ind.	1,713	360	239	1,545	2,299	2,241	565
Kansas City, Mo.	1,226	847	255	1,128	1,882	1,909	1,071
Los Angeles, Calif.	398	2,456	1,864	728	403	1,150	2,680
Louisville, Ky.	1,749	416	264	1,647	2,401	2,355	601
Memphis, Tenn.	1,464	810	295	1,556	2,151	2,363	902
Miami, Fla.	2,359	1,250	1,241	2,571	3,097	3,389	1,101
Minneapolis, Minn.	1,644	876	559	1,243	1,997	1,641	1,114
New Orleans, La.	1,523	1,118	696	1,743	2,269	2,626	1,098
New York, N.Y.	2,442	386	968	2,282	3,036	2,900	229
Omaha, Neb.	1,305	932	459	967	1,721	1,705	1,178
Philadelphia, Pa.	2,360	304	886	2,200	2,954	2,818	140
Phoenix, Ariz.	—	2,073	1,485	651	800	1,482	2,278
Pittsburgh, Pa.	2,073	—	599	1,899	2,653	2,517	241
St. Louis, Mo.	1,485	599	—	1,383	2,137	2,164	836
Salt Lake City, Utah	651	1,899	1,383	—	754	883	2,110
San Francisco, Calif.	800	2,653	2,137	754	—	817	2,864
Seattle, Wash.	1,482	2,517	2,164	883	817	—	2,755
Washington, D.C.	2,278	241	836	2,110	2,864	2,755	—

Air Distances Between U.S. Cities in Statute Miles

Cities	Birmingham	Boston	Buffalo	Chicago	Cleveland	Dallas	Denver
Birmingham, Ala.	—	1,052	776	578	618	581	1,095
Boston, Mass.	1,052	—	400	851	551	1,551	1,769
Buffalo, N. Y.	776	400	—	454	173	1,198	1,370
Chicago, Ill.	578	851	454	—	308	803	920
Cleveland, Ohio	618	551	173	308	—	1,025	1,227
Dallas, Tex.	581	1,551	1,198	803	1,025	—	663
Denver, Colo.	1,095	1,769	1,370	920	1,227	663	—
Detroit, Mich.	641	613	216	238	90	999	1,156
El Paso, Tex.	1,15 2	2,072	1,692	1,252	1,525	572	557
Houston, Tex.	567	1,605	1,286	940	1,114	225	879
Indianapolis, Ind.	433	807	435	165	263	763	1,000
Kansas City, Mo.	579	1,251	861	414	700	451	558
Los Angeles, Calif.	1,802	2,596	2,198	1,745	2,049	1,240	831
Louisville, Ky.	331	826	483	269	311	726	1,038
Memphis, Tenn.	217	1,137	803	482	630	420	879
Miami, Fla.	665	1,255	1,181	1,188	1,087	1,111	1,726
Minneapolis, Minn.	862	1,123	731	355	630	862	700
New Orleans, La.	312	1,359	1,086	833	924	443	1,082
New York, N. Y.	864	188	292	713	405	1,374	1,631
Omaha, Neb.	732	1,282	883	432	739	586	488
Philadelphia, Pa.	783	271	279	666	360	1,299	1,579
Phoenix, Ariz.	1,456	2,300	1,906	1,453	1,749	887	586
Pittsburgh, Pa.	608	483	178	410	115	1,070	1,320
St. Louis, Mo.	400	1,038	662	262	492	547	796
Salt Lake City, Utah	1,466	2,099	1,699	1,260	1,568	999	371
San Francisco, Calif.	2,013	2,699	2,300	1,858	2,166	1,483	949
Seattle, Wash.	2,082	2,493	2,117	1,737	2,026	1,681	1,021
Washington, D.C.	661	393	292	597	306	1,185	1,494

Cities	Detroit	El Paso	Houston	Indianapolis	Kansas City	Los Angeles	Louisville
Birmingham, Ala.	641	1,152	567	433	579	1,802	331
Boston, Mass.	613	2,072	1,605	807	1,251	2,596	826
Buffalo, N. Y.	216	1,692	1,286	435	861	2,198	483
Chicago, Ill.	238	1,252	940	165	414	1,745	269
Cleveland, Ohio	90	1,525	1,114	263	700	2,049	311
Dallas, Tex.	999	572	225	763	451	1,240	726
Denver, Colo.	1,156	557	879	1,000	558	831	1,038
Detr oit, Mich.	—	1,479	1,105	240	645	1,983	316
El Paso, Tex.	1,479	—	676	1,264	839	701	1,254
Houston, Tex.	1,105	676	—	865	644	1,374	803
Indianapolis, Ind.	240	1,264	865	—	453	1,809	107
Kansas City, Mo.	645	839	644	453	—	1,356	480
Los Angeles, Calif.	1,983	701	1,374	1,809	1,356	—	1,829
Louisville, Ky.	316	1,254	803	107	480	1,829	—
Memphis, Tenn.	623	976	484	384	369	1,603	320
Miami, Fla.	1,152	1,643	968	1,024	1,241	2,339	919
Minneapolis, Minn.	543	1,157	1,056	511	413	1,524	605
New Orleans, La.	939	983	318	712	680	1,673	623
New York, N. Y.	482	1,905	1,420	646	1,097	2,451	652
Omaha, Neb.	669	878	794	525	166	1,315	580
Philadelphia, Pa.	443	1,836	1,341	585	1,038	2,394	582
Phoenix, Ariz.	1,690	346	1,017	1,499	1,049	357	1,508
Pittsburgh, Pa.	205	1,590	1,137	330	781	2,136	344
St. Louis, Mo.	455	1,034	679	231	238	1,589	242
Salt Lake City, Utah	1,492	689	1,200	1,356	925	579	1,402
San Francisco, Calif.	2,091	995	1,645	1,949	1,506	347	1,986
Seattle, Wash.	1,938	1,376	1,891	1,872	1,506	959	1,943
Washington, D.C.	396	1,728	1,220	494	945	2,300	476

Source: National Geodetic Survey.

Air Distances Between U.S. Cities in Statute Miles

Cities	Memphis	Miami	Minne–apolis	New Orleans	New York	Omaha	Phila–delphiae
Birmingham, Ala.	217	665	862	312	864	732	783
Boston, Mass.	1,137	1,255	1,123	1,359	188	1,282	271
Buffalo, N. Y.	803	1,181	731	1,086	292	883	279
Chicago, Ill.	482	1,188	355	833	713	432	666
Cleveland, Ohio	630	1,087	630	924	405	739	360
Dallas, Tex.	420	1,111	862	443	1,374	586	1,299
Denver, Colo.	879	1,726	700	1,082	1,631	488	1,579
Detroit, Mich.	623	1,152	543	939	482	669	443
El Paso, Tex.	976	1,643	1,157	983	1,905	878	1,836
Houston, Tex.	484	968	1,056	318	1,420	794	1,341
Indianapolis, Ind.	384	1,024	511	712	646	525	585
Kansas City, Mo.	369	1,241	413	680	1,097	166	1,038
Los Angeles, Calif.	1,603	2,339	1,524	1,673	2,451	1,315	2,394
Louisville, Ky.	320	919	605	623	652	580	582
Memphis, Tenn.	—	872	699	358	957	529	881
Miami, Fla.	872	—	1,511	669	1,092	1,397	1,019
Minneapolis, Minn.	699	1,511	—	1,051	1,018	290	985
New Orleans, La.	358	669	1,051	—	1,171	847	1,089
New York, N. Y.	957	1,092	1,018	1,171	—	1,144	83
Omaha, Neb.	529	1,397	290	847	1,144	—	1,094
Philadelphia, Pa.	881	1,019	985	1,089	83	1,094	—
Phoenix, Ariz.	1,263	1,982	1,280	1,316	2,145	1,036	2,083
Pittsburgh, Pa.	660	1,010	743	919	317	836	259
St. Louis, Mo.	240	1,061	466	598	875	354	811
Salt Lake City, Utah	1,250	2,089	987	1,434	1,972	833	1,925
San Francisco, Calif.	1,802	2,594	1,584	1,926	2,571	1,429	2,523
Seattle, Wash.	1,867	2,734	1,395	2,101	2,408	1,369	2,380
Washington, D.C.	765	923	934	966	205	1,014	123

Cities	Phoenix	Pitts–burgh	St. Louis	Salt Lake City	San Francisco	Seattle	Wash–ington
Birmingham, Ala.	1,456	608	400	1,466	2,013	2,082	661
Boston, Mass.	2,300	483	1,038	2,099	2,699	2,493	393
Buffalo, N. Y.	1,906	17 8	662	1,699	2,300	2,117	292
Chicago, Ill.	1,453	410	262	1,260	1,858	1,737	597
Cleveland, Ohio	1,749	115	492	1,568	2,166	2,026	306
Dallas, Tex.	887	1,070	547	999	1,483	1,681	1,185
Denver, Colo.	586	1,320	796	371	949	1,021	1,494
Detroit, Mich.	1,690	205	455	1,492	2,091	1,938	396
El Paso, Tex.	346	1,590	1,034	689	995	1,376	1,728
Houston, Tex.	1,017	1,137	679	1,200	1,645	1,891	1,220
Indianapolis, Ind.	1,499	330	231	1,356	1,949	1,872	494
Kansas City, Mo.	1,049	781	238	925	1,506	1,506	945
Los Angeles, Calif.	357	2,136	1,589	579	347	959	2,300
Louisville, Ky.	1,508	344	242	1,402	1,986	1,943	476
Memphis, Tenn.	1,263	660	240	1,250	1,802	1,867	765
Miami, Fla.	1,982	1,010	1,061	2,089	2,594	2,734	923
Minneapolis, Minn.	1,280	743	466	987	1,584	1,395	934
New Orleans, La.	1,316	919	598	1,434	1,926	2,101	966
New York, N. Y.	2,145	317	875	1,972	2,571	2,408	205
Omaha, Neb.	1,036	836	354	833	1,429	1,369	1,014
Philadelphia, Pa.	2,083	259	811	1,925	2,523	2,380	123
Phoenix, Ariz.	—	1,828	1,272	504	653	1,114	1,983
Pittsburgh, Pa.	1,828	—	559	1,668	2,264	2,138	192
St. Louis, Mo.	1,272	559	—	1,162	1,744	1,724	712
Salt Lake City, Utah	504	1,668	1,162	—	600	701	1,848
San Francisco, Calif.	653	2,264	1,744	600	—	678	2,442
Seattle, Wash.	1,114	2,138	1,724	701	678	—	2,329
Washington, D.C.	1,983	192	712	1,848	2,442	2,329	—

Source: National Geodetic Survey.

Air Distances Between World Cities in Statute Miles

Cities	Berlin	Buenos Aires	Cairo	Calcutta	Cape Town	Caracas	Chicago
Berlin	—	7,402	1,795	4,368	5,981	5,247	4,405
Buenos Aires	7,402	—	7,345	10,265	4,269	3,168	5,598
Cairo	1,795	7,345	—	3,539	4,500	6,338	6,129
Calcutta	4,368	10,265	3,539	—	6,024	9,605	7,980
Cape Town, South Africa	5,981	4,269	4,500	6,024	—	6,365	8,494
Caracas, Venezuela	5,247	3,168	6,338	9,605	6,365	—	2,501
Chicago	4,405	5,598	6,129	7,980	8,494	2,501	—
Hong Kong	5,440	11,472	5,061	1,648	7,375	10,167	7,793
Honolulu, Hawaii	7,309	7,561	8,838	7,047	11,534	6,013	4,250
Istanbul	1,078	7,611	768	3,638	5,154	6,048	5,477
Lisbon	1,436	5,956	2,363	5,638	5,325	4,041	3,990
London	579	6,916	2,181	4,947	6,012	4,660	3,950
Los Angeles	5,724	6,170	7,520	8,090	9,992	3,632	1,745
Manila	6,132	11,051	5,704	2,203	7,486	10,620	8,143
Mexico City	6,047	4,592	7,688	9,492	8,517	2,232	1,691
Montreal	3,729	5,615	5,414	7,607	7,931	2,449	744
Moscow	1,004	8,376	1,803	3,321	6,300	6,173	4,974
New York	3,965	5,297	5,602	7,918	7,764	2,132	713
Paris	545	6,870	1,995	4,883	5,807	4,736	4,134
Rio de Janeiro	6,220	1,200	6,146	9,377	3,773	2,810	5,296
Rome	734	6,929	1,320	4,482	5,249	5,196	4,808
San Francisco	5,661	6,467	7,364	7,814	10,247	3,904	1,858
Shanghai, China	5,218	12,201	5,183	2,117	8,061	9,501	7,061
Stockholm	504	7,808	2,111	4,195	6,444	5,420	4,278
Sydney, Australia	10,006	7,330	8,952	5,685	6,843	9,513	9,272
Tokyo	5,540	11,408	5,935	3,194	9,156	8,799	6,299
Warsaw	320	7,662	1,630	4,048	5,958	5,517	4,667
Washington, D.C.	4,169	5,218	5,800	8,084	7,901	2,059	597

Cities	Hong Kong	Honolulu	Istanbul	Lisbon	London	Los Angeles	Manila
Berlin	5,440	7,309	1,078	1,436	579	5,724	6,132
Buenos Aires	11,472	7,561	7,611	5,956	6,916	6,170	11,051
Cairo	5,061	8,838	768	2,363	2,181	7,520	5,704
Calcutta	1,648	7,047	3,638	5,638	4,947	8,090	2,203
Cape Town, South Africa	7,375	11,534	5,154	5,325	6,012	9,992	7,486
Caracas, Venezuela	10,167	6,013	6,048	4,041	4,660	3,632	10,620
Chicago	7,793	4,250	5,477	3,990	3,950	1,745	8,143
Hong Kong	—	5,549	4,984	6,853	5,982	7,195	693
Honolulu, Hawaii	5,549	—	8,109	7,820	7,228	2,574	5,299
Istanbul	4,984	8,109	—	2,012	1,552	6,783	5,664
Lisbon	6,853	7,820	2,012	—	985	5,621	7,546
London	5,982	7,228	1,552	985	—	5,382	6,672
Los Angeles, Calif.	7,195	2,574	6,783	5,621	5,382	—	7,261
Manila	693	5,299	5,664	7,546	6,672	7,261	—
Mexico City	8,782	3,779	7,110	5,390	5,550	1,589	8,835
Montreal	7,729	4,910	4,789	3,246	3,282	2,427	8,186
Moscow	4,439	7,037	1,091	2,427	1,555	6,003	5,131
New York	8,054	4,964	4,975	3,364	3,458	2,451	8,498
Paris	5,985	7,438	1,400	904	213	5,588	6,677
Rio de Janeiro	11,021	8,285	6,389	4,796	5,766	6,331	11,259
Rome	5,768	8,022	843	1,161	887	6,732	6,457
San Francisco	6,897	2,393	6,703	5,666	5,357	347	6,967
Shanghai, China	764	4,941	4,962	6,654	5,715	6,438	1,150
Stockholm	5,113	6,862	1,348	1,856	890	5,454	5,797
Sydney, Australia	4,584	4,943	9,294	11,302	10,564	7,530	3,944
Tokyo	1,794	3,853	5,560	6,915	5,940	5,433	1,866
Warsaw	5,144	7,355	863	1,715	899	5,922	5,837
Washington, D.C.	8,147	4,519	5,215	3,562	3,663	2,300	8,562

Source: Encyclopaedia Britannica.

Air Distances Between World Cities in Statute Miles

Cities	Mexico City	Montreal	Moscow	New York	Paris	Rio de Janeiro	Rome
Berlin	6,047	3,729	1,004	3,965	545	6,220	734
Buenos Aires	4,592	5,615	8,376	5,297	6,870	1,200	6,929
Cairo	7,688	5,414	1,803	5,602	1,995	6,146	1,320
Calcutta	9,492	7,607	3,321	7,918	4,883	9,377	4,482
Cape Town, South Africa	8,517	7,931	6,300	7,764	5,807	3,773	5,249
Caracas, Venezuela	2,232	2,449	6,173	2,132	4,736	2,810	5,196
Chicago	1,691	744	4,974	713	4,134	5,296	4,808
Hong Kong	8,782	7,729	4,439	8,054	5,985	11,021	5,768
Honolulu	3,779	4,910	7,037	4,964	7,438	8,285	8,022
Istanbul	7,110	4,789	1,091	4,975	1,400	6,389	843
Lisbon	5,390	3,246	2,427	3,364	904	4,796	1,161
London	5,550	3,282	1,555	3,458	213	5,766	887
Los Angeles	1,589	2,427	6,003	2,451	5,588	6,331	6,732
Manila	8,835	8,186	5,131	8,498	6,677	11,259	6,457
Mexico City	—	2,318	6,663	2,094	5,716	4,771	6,366
Montreal	2,318	—	4,386	320	3,422	5,097	4,080
Moscow	6,663	4,386	—	4,665	1,544	7,175	1,474
New York	2,094	320	4,665	—	3,624	4,817	4,281
Paris	5,716	3,422	1,544	3,624	—	5,699	697
Rio de Janeiro	4,771	5,097	7,175	4,817	5,699	—	5,684
Rome	6,366	4,080	1,474	4,281	697	5,684	—
San Francisco	1,887	2,539	5,871	2,571	5,558	6,621	6,240
Shanghai, China	8,022	7,053	4,235	7,371	5,754	11,336	5,677
Stockholm	5,959	3,667	762	3,924	958	6,651	1,234
Sydney, Australia	8,052	9,954	9,012	9,933	10,544	8,306	10,136
Tokyo	7,021	6,383	4,647	6,740	6,034	11,533	6,135
Warsaw	6,365	4,009	715	4,344	849	6,467	817
Washington, D.C.	1,887	488	4,858	205	3,829	4,796	4,434

Cities	San Francisco	Shanghai	Stockholm	Sydney	Tokyo	Moscow	Washington
Berlin	5,661	5,218	504	10,006	5,540	320	4,169
Buenos Aires	6,467	12,201	7,808	7,330	11,408	7,662	5,218
Cairo	7,364	5,183	2,111	8,952	5,935	1,630	5,800
Calcutta	7,814	2,117	4,195	5,685	3,194	4,048	8,084
Cape Town, South Africa	10,247	8,061	6,444	6,843	9,156	5,958	7,901
Caracas, Venezuela	3,904	9,501	5,420	9,513	8,799	5,517	2,059
Chicago	1,858	7,061	4,278	9,272	6,299	4,667	597
Hong Kong	6,897	764	5,113	4,584	1,794	5,144	8,147
Honolulu	2,393	4,941	6,862	4,943	3,853	7,355	4,519
Istanbul	6,703	4,962	1,348	9,294	5,560	863	5,215
Lisbon	5,666	6,654	1,856	11,302	6,915	1,715	3,562
London	5,357	5,715	890	10,564	5,940	899	3,663
Los Angeles	347	6,438	5,454	7,530	5,433	5,922	2,300
Manila	6,967	1,150	5,797	3,944	1,866	5,837	8,562
Mexico City	1,887	8,022	5,959	8,052	7,021	6,365	1,887
Montreal	2,539	7,053	3,667	9,954	6,383	4,009	488
Moscow	5,871	4,235	762	9,012	4,647	715	4,858
New York	2,571	7,371	3,924	9,933	6,740	4,344	205
Paris	5,558	5,754	958	10,544	6,034	849	3,829
Rio de Janeiro	6,621	11,336	6,651	8,306	11,533	6,467	4,796
Rome	6,240	5,677	1,234	10,136	6,135	817	4,434
San Francisco	—	6,140	5,361	7,416	5,135	5,841	2,442
Shanghai, China	6,140	—	4,825	4,899	1,097	4,951	7,448
Stockholm	5,361	4,825	—	9,696	5,051	501	4,123
Sydney, Australia	7,416	4,899	9,696	—	4,866	9,696	9,758
Tokyo	5,135	1,097	5,051	4,866	—	5,249	6,772
Warsaw	5,841	4,951	501	9,696	5,249	—	4,457
Washington, D.C.	2,442	7,448	4,123	9,758	6,772	4,457	—

Source: Encyclopaedia Britannica.

MILITARY & VETERAN'S AFFAIRS

War Crimes Trials: Vengeance or Impartial Justice?

The Allies were confronted with legal and moral problems in bringing war criminals to justice.

Fifty years have passed since the Allies tried and convicted high-ranking German and Japanese defendants for war crimes committed by them during World War II. Historical precedent has given enemies the right to try citizens of other countries for suspected war crimes. The following scenario speculates on what might have happened to high-ranking American leaders if the United States had lost the war in 1945.

A Hypothetical Scenario

Shortly after midnight, October 16, 1945, President Harry S. Truman, escorted by a chaplain and two guards entered the Washington, D.C., prison gymnasium and mounted the thirteen steps to the gallows platform. The hangman adjusted the noose and placed a hood over his head. Minutes later, the trap door was sprung and the condemned President fell to his death.

The United States had lost the war and was occupied by Axis power troops. President Truman and other high American officials had been convicted of war crimes by a military tribunal of judges from the major Axis powers—Germany, Italy, and Japan. Next to be executed was U.S. Secretary of War Henry L. Stimson and General George C. Marshall, U.S. Army Chief of Staff. They were followed by Air Force general Curtis E. LeMay, who directed the firebombing of German and Japanese cities and the atomic attacks on Hiroshima and Nagasaki. General LeMay and other top U.S. military leaders had claimed that they were only following orders of their superiors, but this defense was not accepted. In fact, the tribunal had agreed prior to the trial to forbid this defense at all.[1]

Although this scenario never occurred, if the outcome of World War II were reversed, a defeated American leadership and their allies could have been put on trial by their victorious enemies for alleged war crimes, even if the accusations were not justified.

It is not unreasonable to think that our enemies might put some top American leaders on trial for acts committed by the military during the war.

For example, Japan conducted a war crimes trial against American servicemen only four months after Japan declared war on the United States. Eight American fliers were captured by Japanese troops following the first U.S. bombing attack on Tokyo's war industries, April 18, 1942. The airmen were falsely accused of war crimes and were tried by a vengeful Japanese military tribunal. All were sentenced to death; three fliers were executed and the rest had their sentences commuted to life imprisonment by Emperor Hirohito.[2]

Again, considering that Japan regards the atomic bombings of their cities in World War II to be unjustified atrocities—then and now—it is reasonable to assume that at the time the Japanese government would have sought punishment for the American leaders who authorized them.

Another possible example is the devastating attack on the German city of Dresden by American and British bombers on February 13–14, 1945, which was deliberately planned to wreak havoc on its civilian and refugee population. Eighty-five percent of the virtually undefended city was destroyed and an estimated 35,000 or more civilian and refugees from the Eastern front lost their lives in the controversial fire-bombings which historians are still debating today. Certainly Nazi Germany could have demanded punishment for those who planned the terror bombing attacks.

The victorious Allies of course did not attempt to bring charges against themselves for any possible war crimes committed by them. For example, take the crime of Katyn. In April 1943 during World War II, the Germans discovered mass graves in Katyn Forest of some 4,250 Polish officers who had been captured, bound, and executed by pistol shots in the back of the head during the Soviet invasion of Poland in 1939. The Soviet Union denied responsibility and blamed the Germans for the atrocities. Charges against Nazi leaders for the Katyn massacre were initially brought up at the Nuremberg Tribunal but were later quietly dropped. It wasn't until 1989 that the Soviets revealed that the Russian dictator Joseph Stalin had ordered the massacre.

The Nuremberg War Crimes Trials

Following the end of World War II, the Allies were confronted with legal and moral problems in bringing accused Nazi war criminals to justice because the defendants were being tried by a legal code that did not exist when their crimes were committed.

When the International Military Tribunal was held, many criticized it for retroactively criminalizing actions that had been legal and even required under orders at the time they occurred. It appeared to some that these were more like acts of vengeance than impartial justice. The trials were also criticized because the accusers were also the judges and the procedures used were unfamiliar to the defendants' German lawyers.

The International Military Tribunal was composed of one judge from each of the four major powers—the United States, Britain, France, and the Soviet Union—and 24 top Nazi leaders were tried for actions committed by them during the war. The trials were held from November 20, 1945, to October 1, 1946, in Nuremberg, West Germany.

The war crimes trials had been announced in the Moscow Declaration on November 1, 1943, when American, British, and Soviet foreign ministers met in the Soviet capital. It stated that German officers and Nazis responsible for war crimes would be tried and punished. Similarly, in respect to Japan, the Potsdam Declaration of July 26, 1945, stated that stern justice would be dealt to all war criminals including those who committed atrocities against prisoners of war.

There were three major categories of offenses: (1) Crimes against Peace—planning, preparing for, initiating, or waging a war of aggression or a war in violation of international treaties; (2) Conventional War Crimes—violations of the laws or customs of war: murder or ill treatment of civilians, hostages, and prisoners of war; the wanton destruction of cities, towns, and villages; and the plunder of public and private property; and (3) Crimes Against Humanity—murder, extermination, enslavement, deportation, and other inhumane acts against civilian populations, or persecution on religious, political, and racial grounds.

Twenty-four Nazi leaders were indicted and 22 were tried. One of them, S.S. leader Martin Bormann, was tried *in absentia*. Twelve were sentenced to hang, three were given life imprisonment, and four received lesser sentences. Three defendants were acquitted. Hermann Goering, who was second in position only to Adolf Hitler, was the principal defendant. He escaped hanging by committing suicide hours before he was scheduled to die.

Lesser officials, including officers and guards of the Dachau prison camp and German civilians who had murdered American airmen, were also tried.

Although the trials were criticized as not being impartial, the Chief Justice of the U.S. Supreme Court and the chief U.S. prosecutor at Nuremberg maintained that the Kellogg–Briand Pact of 1928 had outlawed aggressive warfare and held individuals responsible for their actions. The United Nations supported this argument and it set the precedent for future war crimes trials.

The Tokyo War Crimes Trials

The International Military Tribunal for the Far East began in Tokyo on May 3, 1946, and ended two years later with the judgments of the major Japanese war criminals on November 12, 1948. The tribunal held was similar to the one in Nuremberg. It consisted of one judge each from Australia, Canada, China, France, India, The Netherlands, New Zealand, The Philippines, The Soviet Union, the United Kingdom, and the United States.

Of twenty-five defendants who were sentenced, seven were hanged, sixteen received life imprisonment, and two were given lesser prison terms. The principal defendant was Gen. Hideki Tojo, the Japanese Prime Minister and Minister of War. Tojo had unsuccessfully tried to commit suicide and was the only enemy head of state to be executed by the Allies.

Not all war criminals were punished for their inhuman acts. Some Nazi scientists and S.S. members escaped prosecution in exchange for valuable information. What was not publicly known until recently was that Japan's notorious Unit 731, under the command of Gen. Shiro Ishii, conducted thousands of cold-blooded medical experiments on prisoners of war, including American POWs, and killed hundreds of thousands of Chinese villagers in germ warfare tests. The U.S. government exempted these experimenters from war-crimes prosecution in exchange for the knowledge they gained from their atrocities.

The first official war crimes indictment since World War II occurred on November 7, 1994, when the Yugoslav War Crimes Tribunal formed in 1993 by the United Nations at The Hague, Netherlands, indicted the former commander of a concentration camp run by the Bosnian Serbs and charged him with the murder and torture of Muslim prisoners.—*Ed.*

---

1. This is what the major Allied powers—the United States, Great Britain, the Soviet Union, and France—had agreed upon before the historic Nuremberg trials were held in 1945. They would not permit the accused to claim that they were acting under orders from their superiors.
2. A small force of 16 U.S. bombers led by Colonel James Doolittle made the first American bombing mission on Japan. They caused little damage to their war-industrial targets in Tokyo, Yokohama, Kobe, and Nagoya.

Bad weather forced most of the bomber crews to parachute or crash land in East China after completing their mission. Eight American fliers were captured by Japanese soldiers. They were tortured for three weeks and forced to sign false confessions that they had committed war crimes against civilians.

The retribution for Doolittle's raid didn't end here. Enraged Japanese military leaders also took their wrath out on the people of East China for aiding the downed fliers. Over fifty Japanese battalions fought their way 200 miles into China, destroying airfields and burning villages through which the airmen had passed. Japanese troops slaughtered the men, women, and children in these areas, killing an estimated quarter of a million Chinese civilians and soldiers.

Active Military Duty Personnel, 1940–1994[1]

Year	Total	Army[2]	Navy	Marine Corps	Air Force[2, 3]
1940	458,365	269,023	160,997	28,345	
1945	12,055,884	8,266,373	3,319,586	469,925	
1950	1,459,462	593,167	380,739	74,279	411,277
1955	2,935,107	1,109,296	660,695	205,170	959,946
1960	2,475,438	873,078	616,987	170,621	814,752
1965	2,653,926	969,066	669,985	190,213	824,662
1970	3,064,760	1,322,548	691,126	259,737	791,349
1975	2,128,120	784,333	535,085	195,951	612,751
1980	2,050,627	777,036	527,153	188,469	557,969
1985	2,151,032	780,787	570,705	198,025	601,515
1990	2,043,705	732,403	579,417	196,652	535,233
1991	1,985,555	710,821	570,262	194,040	510,432
1992	1,807,177	610,450	541,883	184,529	470,315
1993	1,705,103	572,423	509,950	178,379	444,351
1994	1,610,490	541,343	468,662	174,158	426,327

1. Military personnel on extended or continuous active duty. Excludes reserves on active duty for training. Prior year totals have been corrected. 2. Represents "Command Strength" prior to June 30, 1956. 3. Army Air Forces and its predecessors for period prior to September 18, 1947. *Source:* Department of Defense.

U.S. Military Pay Grades

Source: U.S. Department of Defense

Pay Grade	Army	Navy	Marines	Air Force
COMMISSIONED OFFICERS				
O–1	Second Lieutenant	Ensign	Second Lieutenant	Second Lieutenant
O–2	First Lieutenant	Lieutenant Junior Grade	First Lieutenant	First Lieutenant
O–3	Captain	Lieutenant	Captain	Captain
O–4	Major	Lieutenant Commander	Major	Major
O–5	Lieutenant Colonel	Commander	Lieutenant Colonel	Lieutenant Colonel
O–6	Colonel	Captain	Colonel	Colonel
O–7	Brigadier General	Commodore	Brigadier General	Brigadier General
O–8	Major General	Rear Admiral	Major General	Major General
O–9	Lieutenant General	Vice Admiral	Lieutenant General	Lieutenant General
O–10	General	Admiral	General	General
Special grades[1] (5 stars)	General of The Army	Fleet Admiral	(none)	General of The Air Force

WARRANT OFFICERS (ALL SERVICES)

W–1 Warrant Officer. Grades W–2 to W–5 Chief Warrant Officer

ENLISTED PERSONNEL				
E–1	Private	Seaman Recruit	Private	Airman Basic
E–2	Private	Seaman Apprentice	Private First Class	Airman
E–3	Private First Class	Seaman	Lance Corporal	Airman First Class
E–4	Corporal Specialist 4	Petty Officer, Third Class	Corporal	Sergeant Senior Airman
E–5	Sergeant Specialist 5	Petty Officer, Second Class	Sergeant	Staff Sergeant
E–6	Staff Sergeant Specialist 6	Petty Officer, First Class	Staff Sergeant	Technical Sergeant
E–7	Sergeant First Class Specialist 7	Chief Petty Officer	Gunnery Sergeant	Master Sergeant
E–8	First Sergeant Master Sergeant	Senior Chief Petty Officer	First Sergeant Master Sergeant	Senior Master Sergeant
E–9	Command Sergeant Major Sergeant Major	Master Chief Petty Officer	Sergeant Major Master Gunnery Sergeant	Chief Master Sergeant
Special grades[2]	Sergeant Major of the Army	Master Chief Petty Officer of the Navy	Sergeant Major of the Marine Corps	Chief Master Sergeant of the Air Force

1. There are no living 5-star commissioned officers. 2. Senior enlisted advisors. There is only one for each branch of service.

Monthly Basic Pay Rates by Grade Effective Jan. 1, 1995

Grade	Years of Service									
	< 2	2	4	6	10	14	16	18	20	26
COMMISSIONED OFFICERS										
O–10	6,978.30	7,223.70	7,223.70	7,223.70	7,501.20	7,916.70	8,482.80	8,482.80	9,016.80	9,016.80
O–9	6,184.50	6,346.50	6,481.80	6,481.80	6,646.50	6,923.10	7,501.20	7,501.20	7,916.70	8,482.80
O–8	5,601.60	5,769.60	5,906.40	5,906.40	6,346.50	6,846.50	6,923.10	7,223.70	7,501.20	7,686.00
O–7	4,654.50	4,971.00	4,971.00	5,193.90	5,494.80	5,769.60	6,346.50	6,783.00	6,783.00	6,783.00
O–6	3,449.70	3,790.20	4,038.60	4,038.60	4,038.60	4,176.00	4,836.30	5,082.90	5,193.90	5,959.50
O–5	2,759.10	3,239.70	3,463.80	3,463.80	3,588.50	4,012.80	4,313.10	4,580.00	4,698.50	4,862.70
O–4	2,325.60	2,832.00	3,021.00	3,077.10	3,432.00	3,790.20	3,956.70	4,065.60	4,065.60	4,065.60
O–3	2,161.20	2,416.50	2,858.10	2,994.90	3,270.30	3,516.30	3,516.30	3,516.30	3,516.30	3,516.30
O–2	1,884.50	2,058.00	2,558.00	2,608.80	2,608.80	2,608.80	2,608.80	2,608.80	2,608.80	2,608.80
O–1	1,636.20	1,703.10	2,058.00	2,058.00	2,058.00	2,058.00	2,058.00	2,058.00	2,058.00	2,058.00
WARRANT OFFICERS										
W–5	0.00	0.00	0.00	0.00	0.00	0.00	0.00	0.00	3,757.80	4,182.00
W–4	2,202.00	2,362.50	2,416.50	2,526.30	2,748.30	3,077.10	3,185.10	3,270.30	3,375.90	3,760.80
W–3	2,001.30	2,170.80	2,199.00	2,224.50	2,526.30	2,691.60	2,772.00	2,858.10	2,969.70	3,185.10
W–2	1,752.90	1,896.30	1,951.50	2,058.00	2,253.30	2,416.50	2,501.40	2,583.30	2,664.60	2,772.00
W–1	1,460.10	1,674.30	1,814.10	1,896.30	2,058.00	2,224.50	2,307.30	2,387.40	2,472.90	2,472.90

Grade	Years of Service									
	< 2	2	4	6	10	14	16	18	20	26
ENLISTED MEMBERS										
E–9	0.00	0.00	0.00	0.00	2,561.70	2,678.40	2,739.90	2,801.40	2,855.70	3,297.90
E–8	0.00	0.00	0.00	0.00	2,209.80	2,326.80	2,388.30	2,442.90	2,502.90	2,945.10
E–7	1,499.70	1,619.10	1,737.90	1,797.00	1,913.70	2,062.50	2,121.00	2,179.80	2,208.30	2,649.90
E–6	1,290.30	1,408.40	1,527.30	1,584.60	1,701.90	1,845.60	1,905.30	1,934.10	1,934.10	1,934.10
E–5	1,132.20	1,232.40	1,348.50	1,437.30	1,554.90	1,641.60	1,641.60	1,641.60	1,641.60	1,641.60
E–4	1,056.00	1,115.40	1,272.00	1,322.40	1,322.40	1,322.40	1,322.40	1,322.40	1,322.40	1,322.40
E–3	995.10	1,049.70	1,134.60	1,134.60	1,134.60	1,134.60	1,134.60	1,134.60	1,134.60	1,134.60
E–2	957.60	957.60	957.60	957.60	957.60	957.60	957.60	957.60	957.60	957.60
E–1	854.40	854.40	854.40	854.40	854.40	854.40	854.40	854.40	854.40	854.40

NOTE: E–1 with less than 4 months: $790.20. Basic allowance for quarters ranges from $183.90 per month for an enlisted E–1 with no dependents and less than 4 months service and up to $922.50 per month for an officer with dependents in grade O–10.

Service Academies

U.S. Military Academy

Source: U.S. Military Academy.

Established in 1802 by an act of Congress, the U.S. Military Academy is located on the west bank of the Hudson River some 50 miles north of New York City. To gain admission a candidate must first secure a nomination from an authorized source. These sources are:

Congressional Sources

Representatives
Senators
Other: Vice Presidential
District of Columbia
Puerto Rico
Am. Samoa, Guam, Virgin Is.

Military-Service-Connected Sources

Presidential—Sons or daughters of active duty or retired service members
Enlisted members of Army
Enlisted members of Army Reserve/
National Guard
Sons and daughters of deceased and disabled veterans
Honor military, naval schools and ROTC
Sons and daughters of persons awarded the Medal of Honor

Any number of applicants can meet the requirements for a *nomination* in these categories. *Appointments* (offers of admission), however, can only be made to a much smaller number, about 1,200 each year.

Candidates may be nominated for vacancies during the year preceding the day of admission, which occurs in late June or early July. The best time to apply is during the junior year in high school.

Candidates must be citizens of the U.S., be unmarried, be at least 17 but not yet 22 years old on July 1 of the year admitted, have a secondary-school education or its equivalent, and be able to meet the academic, medical, and physical aptitude requirements. Academic qualification is determined by an analysis of entire scholastic record, and performance on either the American College Testing (ACT) Assessment Program Test or the College Entrance Examination Board Scholastic Assessment Tests (SAT). Entrance requirements and procedures for appointment are described in the Admissions Bulletin and the Admissions Prospectus, available without charge from Admissions, U.S. Military Academy, West Point, N.Y.

10996-1797. Telephone: (914) 938-4041.

Cadets are members of the U.S. Army. As such they receive annual salaries from which they pay for their uniforms, textbooks, and incidental expenses. There is no tuition and room and board are provided. Upon successful completion of the four-year course, the graduate receives the degree of Bachelor of Science and is commissioned a second lieutenant in the U.S. Army with a requirement to serve as an officer for a minimum of six years.

U.S. Naval Academy

Source: U.S. Naval Academy.

The Naval School, established in 1845 at Fort Severn, Annapolis, Md., was renamed the U.S. Naval Academy in 1850. A four-year course was adopted a year later. The "Yard" as the campus is referred to, blends French Renaissance and modern architecture with many new academic, athletics, and laboratory facilities.

The Superintendent is a Navy admiral. A civilian academic dean heads the academic program. A captain heads the 4,000 members of the Brigade of Midshipmen and military, professional, and physical training. The faculty is half military and half civilian, with 650 members; 95% of the civilian faculty hold PhD's. The faculty-student ratio at 1:7 is one of the lowest in the nation and provides for classes that rarely exceed seventeen.

Eighteen majors are offered, including chemistry, math, computer science, economics, general engineering, history, English, ocean engineering, aerospace engineering, electrical engineering, oceanography, political science, mechanical engineering, marine engineering, physics, and naval architecture. Graduates are awarded the Bachelor of Science or Bachelor of Science in Engineering and are commissioned as officers in the U.S. Navy or Marine Corps.

To have basic eligibility for admission, candidates must be citizens of the U.S., of good moral character, at least 17 and not more than 22 years of age on July 1 of their entering year, unmarried, not pregnant, and without legal obligation for dependents.

The Admissions Board at the Naval Academy examines each candidate's school record, College Board or ACT scores, recommendations from school officials, extracurricular activities, and evidence from other sources concerning his or her character, leadership potential, academic preparation, and physical fitness. Qualification for admission is based on all of the above factors.

Tuition, board, lodging, and medical and dental care are provided. Midshipmen receive over $540 a month for books, uniforms, and personal needs.

For general information or answers to specific questions, write: Director of Candidate Guidance, U.S. Naval Academy, Annapolis, Md. 21402-5018, or call 1-800-638-9156.

U.S. Air Force Academy

Source: U.S. Air Force Academy.

The bill establishing the Air Force Academy was signed by President Eisenhower on April 1, 1954. The first class of 306 cadets was sworn in on July 11, 1955, at Lowry Air Force Base, Denver, the Academy's temporary location. The Cadet Wing moved into the Academy's permanent home north of Colorado Springs, Colorado, in 1958.

Cadets receive four years of academic, military, and physical education to prepare them for leadership as officers in the Air Force. The Academy is authorized a total of 4,000 cadets. Each new class averages 1,000. The candidates for the Academy must be at least 17 and not have passed their 22nd birthday on July 1 of the year for which they enter the Academy, must be a United States citizen, never married, and be able to meet the mental and physical requirements. International students authorized admission are exempt from the U.S. citizenship requirement. A candidate is required to take the following examinations and tests: (1) the Service Academies' Qualifying Medical Examination; (2) either the American College Testing (ACT) Assessment Program test or the College Entrance Examination Board Scholastic Aptitude Test (SAT); and (3) a Candidate Fitness Test.

Cadets receive their entire education at government expense and, in addition, are paid more than $540 per month base pay. From this sum, they pay for their uniforms, textbooks, tailoring, laundry, entertainment tickets, etc. Upon completion of the four-year program, leading to a Bachelor of Science degree, a cadet who meets the qualifications is commissioned a second lieutenant in the U.S. Air Force. For details on admissions, write: HQ USAFA/RRS, 2304 Cadet Drive, Suite 200, USAF Academy, CO 80840-5025.

U.S. Coast Guard Academy

Source: U.S. Coast Guard Academy.

The U.S. Coast Guard Academy, New London, Conn., was founded on July 31, 1876, to serve as the "School of Instruction" for the Revenue Cutter Service, predecessor to the Coast Guard.

The J.C. Dobbin, a converted schooner, housed the first Coast Guard Academy, and was succeeded in 1878 by the barque Chase, a ship built for cadet training. First winter quarters were in a sail loft at New Bedford, Mass. The school was moved in 1900 to Arundel Cove, Md., to provide a more technical education, and in 1910 was moved back to New England to Fort Trumbull, New London, Conn. In 1932 the Academy moved to its present location in New London.

The Academy today offers a four-year curriculum for the professional and academic training of cadets, which leads to a Bachelor of Science degree and a commission as ensign in the Coast Guard.

The U.S. Coast Guard Academy is the only one of the five federal service academies that offers appointments solely on the basis of an annual nationwide competition; there are no congressional nominations or geographical quotas involved. Competition is open to any young American who meets the basic eligibility requirements, which consist of satisfactory Scholastic Aptitude Test (SAT) or American College Testing Program examination (ACT) results, high school standing, and leadership potential. Either the SAT or the ACT must be completed prior to or during the December test administration of the year of application. All cadets must have reached their 17th but not their 22nd birthday by July 1 of the year of entrance to the Academy. All cadets must pass a rigid medical examination before being accepted.

Women were first admitted to the Coast Guard Academy in 1976 and first graduated in 1980. Cadets must be unmarried upon entry and must remain unmarried until after graduation. As ensigns, they must serve a five-year obligation following graduation. Cadets receive a stipend to cover incidentals and uniform expenses. Meals and quarters are provided.

A catalog can be obtained by writing to: Director of Admissions, U.S. Coast Guard Academy, 15 Mohegan Ave., New London, Conn. 06320-4195, or call (203) 444-8501 or (800) 424-8883.

U.S. Merchant Marine Academy

Source: U.S. Merchant Marine Academy.

The U.S. Merchant Marine Academy, situated at Kings Point, N.Y., on the north shore of Long Island, was dedicated Sept. 30, 1943. It is maintained by the Department of Transportation under direction of the Maritime Administration.

The Academy has a complement of approximately 950 men and women representing every state, D.C., the Canal Zone, Puerto Rico, Guam, American Samoa, and the Virgin Islands. It is also authorized to admit up to 12 candidates from the Western Hemisphere and 30 other foreign students at any one time.

Candidates are nominated by Senators and members of the House of Representatives. Nominations to the Academy are governed by a state and territory quota system based on population and the results of the College Entrance Examination Board tests.

A candidate must be a citizen not less than 17 and not yet 22 years of age by July 1 of the year in which admission is sought. Fifteen high school credits, including 3 units in mathematics (from algebra, geometry and/or trigonometry), 1 unit in science (physics or chemistry) and 3 in English are required.

The course is four years and includes one year of practical training aboard a merchant ship. Study includes marine engineering, navigation, satellite navigation and communications, electricity, ship construction, naval science and tactics, economics, business, languages, history, etc.

Upon completion of the course of study, a graduate receives a Bachelor of Science degree, a license as a merchant marine deck or engineering officer, and a commission as an Ensign in the Naval Reserve. ☐

Gays in the Military

Pentagon policy allows gay men and lesbians to serve in the armed forces as long as they do not engage in homosexual acts. They can privately acknowledge their homosexual feelings to another person provided they are not engaging in homosexual behavior. Under these somewhat ambiguous rules, holding hands, even off duty, could constitute evidence that such behavior was occurring. However, reading gay publications, displaying same-sex pictures, visiting a gay bar, and marching in a gay-rights parade are permissible.

Hostile treatment of or violence to gay or lesbian service personnel will not be tolerated. ☐

U.S. Casualties in Major Wars

War	Branch of service	Numbers engaged	Battle deaths	Other deaths	Total deaths	Wounds not mortal	Total casualties[1]
Revolutionary War	Army	n.a.	4,044	n.a.	n.a.	6,004	n.a.
1775 to 1783	Navy	n.a.	342	n.a.	n.a.	114	n.a.
	Marines	n.a.	49	n.a.	n.a.	70	n.a.
	Total	**n.a.**	**4,435**	**n.a.**	**n.a.**	**6,188**	**n.a.**
War of 1812	Army	n.a.	1,950	n.a.	n.a.	4,000	n.a.
1812 to 1815	Navy	n.a.	265	n.a.	n.a.	439	n.a.
	Marines	n.a.	45	n.a.	n.a.	66	n.a.
	Total	**286,730**	**2,260**	**n.a.**	**n.a.**	**4,505**	**n.a.**
Mexican War	Army	n.a.	1,721	11,550	13,271	4,102	17,373
1846 to 1848	Navy	n.a.	1	n.a.	n.a.	3	n.a.
	Marines	n.a.	11	n.a.	n.a.	47	n.a.
	Total	**78,718**	**1,733**	**n.a.**	**n.a.**	**4,152**	**n.a.**
Civil War[2]	Army	2,128,948	138,154	221,374	359,528	280,040	639,568
1861 to 1865	Navy	84,415	2,112	2,411	4,523	1,710	6,233
	Marines		148	312	460	131	591
	Total	**2,213,363**	**140,414**	**224,097**	**364,511**	**281,881**	**646,392**
Spanish-American War	Army	280,564	369	2,061	2,430	1,594	4,024
1898	Navy	22,875	10	0	10	47	57
	Marines	3,321	6	0	6	21	27
	Total	**306,760**	**385**	**2,061**	**2,446**	**1,662**	**4,108**
World War I	Army	4,057,101	50,510	55,868	106,378	193,663	300,041
1917 to 1918	Navy	599,051	431	6,856	7,287	819	8,106
	Marines	78,839	2,461	390	2,851	9,520	12,371
	Total	**4,734,991**	**53,402**	**63,114**	**116,516**	**204,002**	**320,518**
World War II	Army[3]	11,260,000	234,874	83,400	318,274	565,861	884,135
1941 to 1946	Navy	4,183,466	36,950	25,664	62,614	37,778	100,392
	Marines	669,100	19,733	4,778	24,511	67,207	91,718
	Total	**16,112,566**	**291,557**	**113,842**	**405,399**	**670,846**	**1,076,245**
Korean War	Army	2,834,000	27,704	9,429	37,133	77,596	114,729
1950 to 1953	Navy	1,177,000	458	4,043	4,501	1,576	6,077
	Marine	424,000	4,267	1,261	5,528	23,744	29,272
	Air Force	1,285,000	1,200	5,884	7,084	368	7,452
	Total	**5,720,000**	**33,629**	**20,617**	**54,246**	**103,284**	**157,530**
War in Southeast Asia[4]	Army	4,368,000	30,914	7,275	38,189	96,802	134,991
	Navy	1,842,000	1,631	928	2,559	4,178	6,737
	Marines	794,000	13,082	1,754	14,836	51,392	66,228
	Air Force	1,740,000	1,739	844	2,583	931	3,514
	Total	**8,744,000**	**47,366**	**10,801**	**58,167**	**153,303**	**211,470**

1. Excludes captured or interned and missing in action who were subsequently returned to military control. 2. Union forces only. Totals should probably be somewhat larger as data or disposition of prisoners are far from complete. Final Confederate deaths, based on incomplete returns, were 133,821, to which should be added 26,000–31,000 personnel who died in Union prisons. 178,975 blacks served in the Union Army. 2,894 were killed in battle or mortally wounded, 33,953 died from other causes including 29,658 deaths from disease. 3. Army data include Air Force. 4. Vietnam figures provided by the U.S. Center of Military History, Reference Division, Washington, D.C., February 1994. Navy figures exclude Coast Guard of which there were 5 battle deaths. NOTE: All data are subject to revision. For wars before World War I, information represents best data from available records. However, due to incomplete records and possible difference in usage of terminology, reporting systems, etc., figures should be considered estimates. n.a. = not available. *Source:* Department of Defense.

Female Military Personnel on Active Duty

Year	Army	Air Force	Navy	Marine Corps	Total
1970	16,724	13,654	8,683	2,418	41,479
1980	69,338	60,394	34,980	6,706	171,418
1985	79,247	70,061	52,603	9,695	211,606
1989	86,494	77,103	59,518	9,708	232,823
1990	83,621	74,134	59,907	9,356	227,018
1991	80,306	72,436	59,391	9,005	221,138
1992	73,430	68,789	59,305	8,524	210,048
1993	71,328	66,732	57,601	7,845	203,506
1994	69,878	66,314	55,825	7,671	199,688

Data as of September 30th.

The National Guard

Source: Departments of the Army and the Air Force, National Guard Bureau.

The National Guard is unique among the United States reserve military forces, filling both federal and state missions. In peacetime, the National Guard is commanded by the governors of the states and territories and may be called to state active duty by the governor in response to natural disasters, civil disturbances, or other state emergencies. During a war or national emergency, the National Guard may be called to active duty by the President or Congress, and serves as the primary source of augmentation for the active Army and active Air Force.

The men and women of the National Guard are described as citizen soldiers and airmen. They have full-time civilian careers, but, each month they meet with their unit for military training. National Guard members receive the same training, use the same equipment, and wear the same uniform as their active duty counterparts.

The foundation for the National Guard's dual state and federal mission can be traced to the earliest militias of the 13 original colonies. The oldest units were organized in the Massachusetts Bay Colony in 1636, and have been in continuous existence ever since. Framers of the U.S. Constitution provided for the continuation of the militia, a principle that has been further developed through subsequent legislation.

From its colonial beginnings, the militia system has evolved into today's Army National Guard and Air National Guard, our nation's community-based defense force of modern military units that serve their respective states and are part of the nation's overall military forces. In addition to countless call-ups for state duty, the National Guard has fought in every American war, from the Pequot War in 1637 to Operation DESERT STORM in which 75,000 members of the National Guard volunteered or were called to active duty.

As a reserve component of the U.S. military, the National Guard makes up a significant part of what is called the Total Force—active duty service members, the reserve components, and the civilians who are employed by the Department of Defense. The other federal reserve components include the Army Reserve, Naval Reserve, Marine Corps Reserve, Air Force Reserve, and Coast Guard Reserve. Members in all of these organizations are trained and equipped in units which are available for full-time duty in case of war or national emergency. However, the other federal reserve components of the military services, unlike the National Guard, are legally and operationally linked only to the active duty services, not the states. This distinction of having both federal and state missions makes the National Guard unique.

The Army National Guard is made up of more than 3,700 units located in 2,700 communities throughout the 50 states, Puerto Rico, Guam, the Virgin Islands, and the District of Columbia. The U.S. Army's largest reserve force, the Army National Guard provides roughly 55 percent of the Army's total combat capability, and approximately 35% of its combat support and 35% of its combat service support units. Units are provided modern military equipment including M-1 tanks, Bradley Fighting Vehicles, and Blackhawk helicopters.

The Air National Guard has 89 flying units and 1,500 support units at 200 locations. This represents approximately one-third of the U.S. Air Force's fighter and air transport assets. Air National Guard units fly F-16 fighters, KC-135 tankers, B–1B bombers, and C-130 transports, among other aircraft.

As part of the nation's total military force, Army and Air National Guard units are trained and equipped to mesh with active duty and other federal reserve component forces. Typically, members of the National Guard report for training duty one weekend per month, along with a minimum of 15 days of continuous unit training each year. Weekend training usually is performed at the unit's community armory or nearby military training facility. The annual training usually is performed at a large military training base or overseas location, frequently in cooperation with active duty and other reserve units. In recent years, Army National Guard units have trained in more than 30 nations, including locations in Central America, Europe, Asia, and Africa. Air National Guard units train with active Air Force and Air Force Reserve units on a regular basis at worldwide locations.

Approximately one-half of the National Guard's members join their units with no previous military experience. They complete basic military training and a technical school at an active duty training base and then return to their unit. The balance of the National Guard's membership consists of personnel who have had prior active duty in any U.S. military service.

National Guard members receive a full day's pay at their military rank for each unit training assembly they attend, for the 15 days of annual training, and for any military school or special assignment they may complete. All such training counts toward retirement. A member who has 20 or more years of qualifying military service begins to collect retired pay at age 60.

The National Guard offers its members a broad range of educational opportunities beyond the training and on-the-job experiences they receive for their military specialties. These benefits include participation in the Montgomery GI Bill and additional enlistment incentives for select military career fields. Members of the National Guard have access to active duty military shopping centers in addition to participation in many other active duty military benefit programs. Many states offer additional benefits and civilian educational incentives.

For 1995, the mission strength of the Army National Guard was 400,000, and the Air National Guard 112,400. The 1995 federal budget for the Army National Guard was $6.1 billion, the Air National Guard $4.3. States and territories provide additional funds to support state missions, recruiting and training administration, armory construction, and funding for state-salaried employees.

Additional information about the National Guard may be obtained from local units or from the National Guard Bureau, 2500 Army Pentagon, Washington, D.C. 20310-2500.

Veterans' Benefits

Veterans have been provided for by the individual states and the federal government since Colonial days. In 1944, Federal benefits for veterans were broadened in scope and value under the G.I. Bill. On March 15, 1989, the Veterans Administration, the federal agency that administers benefits for veterans, became the Department of Veterans Affairs.

The following benefits available to veterans generally require certain minimum periods of active duty during qualifying periods of service. Certain types of discharges are subject to special adjudication to determine eligibility.

For information or assistance in applying for veterans benefits, write, call, or visit a VA Regional Office. Consult your local telephone directory under United States Government, Department of Veterans Affairs (VA) for the address and telephone number. Toll-free telephone service is available in all 50 States: 1-800-827-1000.

Unemployment allowances. Veterans are provided job referral assistance through the Department of Labor and state employment agencies. Disabled veterans are provided a full range of assistance, including training, education, and placement by VA.

Loan Guaranty. VA will guarantee loans to buy or build a home; to purchase a manufactured home with or without a lot; and to refinance a home presently owned and occupied by the veteran. VA will guarantee the lender against loss up to 50% on loans of $45,000 or less, and between 40% and 50% of loans $22,500 to $144,000, and 25% on loans of more than $144,000. On manufactured home loans, the amount of the guarantee is 40% of the loan to a maximum of $20,000.

Disability compensation. Veterans with permanent service-connected disabilities are provided with from $89 to $1,823 per month, depending upon the extent of disability. For special conditions, an additional $5,212 a month may be paid, plus allowances for dependents when the disability is 30 percent or more.

Vocational Rehabilitation. VA provides professional counseling, training and other assistance to help compensably service-disabled veterans, rated 10 percent or more who have an employment handicap, to achieve maximum independence in daily living and, to the extent possible, to obtain and maintain suitable employment. Generally, a veteran may receive up to 48 months of this assistance within 12 years from the date he or she is notified of entitlement to VA compensation. All the expenses of a veteran's rehabilitation program are paid by VA. In addition, the veteran receives a subsistence allowance which varies based on the rate of training and number of dependents. For example, a single veteran training full time would receive $374.93 monthly.

Vocational Training for VA Pension Recipients. Veterans who are awarded pension before December 31, 1995, may participate in a program of vocational training essentially identical to that provided in VA's vocational rehabilitation program. Work income will affect the continuing receipt of pension.

Medical and dental care. Free medical care may be provided in VA and, in certain instances, in non-VA, or other federal hospitals to disabled and low-income veterans. This includes outpatient treatment at a VA field facility or, in some cases, by an approved private physician or dentist. Full domiciliary care also may be provided to veterans with low incomes. Nursing home care may be provided at certain VA medical facilities or in approved community nursing homes. Hospital and other medical care may also be provided for the spouse and child dependents of a veteran who is permanently and totally disabled due to a service-connected disability; or for survivors of a veteran who dies from a service-connected disability; or for survivors of a veteran who at the time of death had a total disability, permanent in nature, resulting from a service-connected disability. These latter benefits are usually provided in nonfederal facilities. Eligibility criteria for veterans' medical benefits vary. Veterans must agree to make a copayment for the care they receive from VA if their incomes exceed levels that vary with number of dependents and they do not have a service-connected disability or service in certain early war periods. Veterans and/or their dependents or survivors should always apply in advance. Contact the nearest VA medical facility for eligibility.

Readjustment Counseling. VA provides readjustment counseling to veterans of the Vietnam Era or the war or conflict zones of Lebanon, Grenada, Panama, or the Persian Gulf theaters in need of assistance in resolving post-war readjustment problems in the areas of family, education, and personal readjustment including post-traumatic stress disorder. Services are provided at community-based Vet Centers and at VA Medical Centers. Services include individual, family and group counseling, employment and educational counseling, and assistance in obtaining referrals to various governmental and nongovernmental agencies. Contact the nearest Vet Center or VA facility.

Dependents compensation. Payments are made to surviving dependents of veterans who died while on active duty or, after discharge, of a service-connected injury or disease. Beginning January 1, 1993, all surviving spouses of veterans who died on or after that date will receive $769 a month. In certain cases, parents and children may be eligible for additional payments.

Dependents' educational assistance. VA pays a maximum of $404 a month for up to 45 months of schooling to spouses and children of veterans who died of service-connected causes or who were permanently and totally disabled from service-connected causes or died while permanently and totally disabled or who are currently missing in action, captured in the line of duty, or forcibly detained or interned in line of duty by a foreign power for more than 90 days.

Montgomery GI Bill. This Act provides education benefits for individuals entering the military after June 30, 1985. Servicepersons entering active duty after that date will have their basic pay reduced by $100 a month for the first 12 months of their service, unless they specifically elect not to participate in the program.

Active duty for three years (two years, if the initial obligated period of active duty is less than three years), or two years active duty plus four years in the Selected Reserve or National Guard will entitle an individual to $404.88 a month basic benefits. Those who enlist for less than three years will receive $328.97 a month for 36 months. VA pays an additional amount, commonly called a "kicker," if directed by the Defense Department.

An educational entitlement program is also available for members of the Selected Reserve. Eligibility applies to individuals who, after June 30, 1985 enlist, re-enlist, or extend an enlistment for a six-year period. Benefits may be paid to eligible members of the Selected Reserve who complete their initial period of active duty training. Full-time payments are $192.32 a month for 36 months.

Pensions. Pension benefits ranging from $7,619 (pensions are similar to disability compensation, but of lesser amounts) a year may be payable to wartime veterans permanently and totally disabled from non-service-connected causes. These benefits are based on need. Surviving spouses and children of wartime veterans are eligible for Nonservice-Connected Death Pensions that range from $5,106 a year,

based on the veteran's honorable wartime service and their need.

Insurance. The VA life insurance programs have approximately 6.2 million policyholders with total coverage of about $512 billion. Detailed information on veterans insurance may be obtained by calling 1-800-669-8477.

Burial benefits. Burial is provided in any VA national cemetery with available grave space to any deceased veteran who was discharged under conditions other than dishonorable. Also eligible for burial in a national cemetery are the veteran's spouse, widow, widower, minor children, and under certain conditions, unmarried adult children. Arlington Cemetery is administered by the Army.

Headstone or marker. A government headstone or marker is furnished for any deceased veteran who was discharged under conditions other than dishonorable and is interred in a national, state veterans', military, or private cemetery. VA also will furnish markers to veterans' eligible dependents interred in a national, military, or state veterans' cemetery.

Highest Ranking Officers in the Armed Forces

ARMY

Generals: John M. Shalikashvili, Chairman of the Joint Chiefs of Staff; Dennis J. Reimer, Chief of Staff, U.S. Army; George A. Joulwan, Supreme Allied Commander, Europe; J.H. Binford Peay III, Commander in Chief, U.S. Central Command; Wayne A. Downing, Commander in Chief, U.S. Special Operations Command; Gary E. Luck, Commander in Chief, United Nations Command/U.S. Forces Korea/Combined Forces Command Korea; Leon E. Salomon, Commanding General, U.S. Army Materiel Command; Barry R. McCaffrey, Commander in Chief, U.S. Southern Command; John H. Tilelli, Jr., Vice Chief of Staff, U.S. Army; William W. Hartzog, Commanding General, U.S. Army Training and Doctrine Command; William W. Crouch, Commander in Chief, U.S. Army Europe and Seventh Army.

NAVY

Admirals: William A. Owens, Vice Chairman, Joint Chiefs of Staff; Jeremy H. Boorda, Chief of Naval Operations; Bruce Demars, Director, Naval Nuclear Propulsion; Charles R. Larson, Superintendent, U.S. Naval Academy; Henry G. Chiles, Jr., Commander in Chief, U.S. Strategic Command; Leighton W. Smith, Jr., Commander in Chief, U.S. Naval Forces Europe/ Allied Forces, Southern Europe; Richard C. Macke, Commander in Chief, U.S. Pacific Command; Ronald J. Zlatoper, Commander in Chief, U.S. Pacific Fleet; William J. Flanagan, Jr., Commander in Chief, U.S. Atlantic Fleet; Joseph W. Prueher, Vice Chief of Naval Operations.

AIR FORCE

Generals: Ronald R. Fogleman, Chief of Staff, U.S. Air Force; Ronald W. Yates, Commander, Air Force Materiel Command; John M. Low, Commander, Air Combat Command; Charles C. Boyd, Deputy Commander in Chief, U.S. European Command; Henry Viccellio, Jr., Commander, Air Education and Training Command; Robert L. Rutherford, Commander in Chief, U.S. Transportation Command and Commander, Air Mobility Command; Thomas S. Moorman, Jr., Vice Chief of Staff, U.S. Air Force; James L. Jamerson, Commander, Allied Air Forces Central Command, NATO/Commander, U.S. Air Forces in Europe/ Air Force Component Commander, U.S. European Command; Joseph W. Ashy, Commander in Chief, North American Aerospace Defense Command/Commander in Chief, U.S. Space Command/Commander, Air Force Space Command; John G. Lorber, Commander, Pacific Air Forces & Air Component Commander for U.S. Pacific Command; Billy J. Boles, Deputy Chief of Staff, Personnel.

MARINE CORPS

Generals: Charles C. Krulak, Commandant of the Marine Corps; Richard D. Hearney, Assistant Commandant of the Marine Corps and Chief of Staff; John J. Sheehan, Commander in Chief, U.S. Atlantic Command/Supreme Allied Commander, Atlantic.

Lieutenant Generals: Robert D. Johnston, Commander, U.S. Marine Forces Atlantic/Commanding General, Fleet Marine Force Atlantic/Commanding General, II Marine Expeditionary Force; George R. Christmas, Deputy Chief of Staff for Manpower and Reserve Affairs; Harold W. Blot, Deputy Chief of Staff for Aviation; James A. Brabham, Jr., Deputy Chief of Staff for Installations and Logistics; Charles E. Wilhelm, Commanding General, Marine Corps Combat Development Command; Arthur C. Blades, Deputy Chief of Staff for Plans, Policies and Operations; Anthony C. Zinni, Commanding General I. Marine Expeditionary Force; Richard I. Neal, Deputy Commander in Chief and Chief of Staff, U.S. Central Command.

Highest Ranking Officers in U.S. History

GENERAL AND COMMANDER-IN-CHIEF[1]

George Washington (1739–1799), b. Westmoreland County, Va., unanimously voted by Congress on June 15, 1775, to the rank of General and Commander-in-Chief (of the Continental Army).

GENERAL OF THE ARMIES[2]

John Joseph Pershing (1860–1948), b. Linn County, Mo., made permanent general of the armies, 1919.

GENERAL OF THE ARMY, GENERAL OF THE AIR FORCE (5-STARS)

George Catlett Marshall (1880–1959), b. Uniontown, Pa., promoted December 1944.

Douglas MacArthur (1880–1964), b. Little Rock, Ark., promoted December 1944.

Dwight David Eisenhower (1890–1969), b. Denison, Texas, promoted December 1944.

Henry Harley Arnold (1866–1950), b. Gladwyne, Pa. General Arnold had the unique distinction of being a five-star general twice—first conferred on him in 1944 as general of the army, and later in June 1949 as general of the air force. He is the only air force general to have held the five-star rank.

Omar Nelson Bradley (1893–1981), b. Clark, Mo., promoted September 1950.

FLEET ADMIRAL (5-STAR)

William Daniel Leahy (1875–1959), b. Hampton, Iowa, promoted December 1944.

Ernest Joseph King (1878–1956), b. Lorain, Ohio, promoted December 1944.

Chester William Nimitz (1885–1966), b. Fredericksburg, Texas, promoted December 1944.

William Frederick Halsey (1882–1959), b. Elizabeth, N.J., promoted December 1945.

---

1. On March 15, 1978, George Washington was promoted posthumously to the newly-created rank of General of the Armies of the United States. Congress authorized this title to make it clear that Washington is the Army's senior general. *Source:* Department of Defense. 2. General Pershing was given the option of 5 stars but he declined. *Source:* U.S. Army Historian, Research and Analysis Center.

Military Force Trends

	1989	1994	1995
Active Forces:			
Army Divisions	18	12	12
Navy Aircraft Carriers	16	12	11
Navy Air Wings	13	11	10
Navy Surface Combatants and Attack Submaries	287	196	198
Marine Divisions and Air Wings	3	3	3
Air Force Tactical Wings	25	13	13
Reserve Forces:			
Army Combat Brigades	56	48	46
Navy Air Wings	2	1	1
Navy Aircraft Carrier	—	—	1
Navy Ships	26	16	17
Marine Divisions	1	1	1
Marine Air Wings	1	1	1
Air Force Tactical Wings	12	9	8
Nuclear Deterrent:			
Intercontinental Ballistic Missiles	1,000	642	550
Ballistic Missile Submarines (Missiles)	34 (608)	15 (352)	15 (360)
Bombers	268	152	107
Mobility Forces:			
Strategic Airlift Aircraft	367	356	365
Sealift Ships[1]	163	174	178
Military Personnel (in thousands):			
Active Forces	2,130	1,611	1,526
Guard and Reserve Forces	1,171	1,025	979

1. Includes ships in the Ready Reserve Force funded by the Department of Transportation. *Source:* The Budget of the United States Government, Fiscal Year 1995.

Casualties in World War I

Country	Total mobilized forces	Killed or died[1]	Wounded	Prisoners or missing	Total Casualties
Austria-Hungary	7,800,000	1,200,000	3,620,000	2,200,000	7,020,000
Belgium	267,000	13,716	44,686	34,659	93,061
British Empire[2]	8,904,467	908,371	2,090,212	191,652	3,190,235
Bulgaria	1,200,000	87,500	152,390	27,029	266,919
France[2]	8,410,000	1,357,800	4,266,000	537,000	6,160,800
Germany	11,000,000	1,773,700	4,216,058	1,152,800	7,142,558
Greece	230,000	5,000	21,000	1,000	27,000
Italy	5,615,000	650,000	947,000	600,000	2,197,000
Japan	800,000	300	907	3	1,210
Montenegro	50,000	3,000	10,000	7,000	20,000
Portugal	100,000	7,222	13,751	12,318	33,291
Romania	750,000	335,706	120,000	80,000	535,706
Russia	12,000,000	1,700,000	4,950,000	2,500,000	9,150,000
Serbia	707,343	45,000	133,148	152,958	331,106
Turkey	2,850,000	325,000	400,000	250,000	975,000
United States	4,734,991	116,516	204,002	—	320,518

1. Includes deaths from all causes. 2. Official figures. NOTE: For additional U.S. figures, *see* the table on U.S. Casualties in Major Wars in this section.

Casualties in World War II

Country	Men in war	Battle deaths	Wounded
Australia	1,000,000	26,976	180,864
Austria	800,000	280,000	350,117
Belgium	625,000	8,460	55,513[1]
Brazil[2]	40,334	943	4,222
Bulgaria	339,760	6,671	21,878
Canada	1,086,343[7]	42,042[7]	53,145
China[3]	17,250,521	1,324,516	1,762,006
Czechoslovakia	—	6,683[4]	8,017
Denmark	—	4,339	—
Finland	500,000	79,047	50,000
France	—	201,568	400,000
Germany	20,000,000	3,250,000[4]	7,250,000
Greece	—	17,024	47,290
Hungary	—	147,435	89,313
India	2,393,891	32,121	64,354
Italy	3,100,000	149,496[4]	66,716
Japan	9,700,000	1,270,000	140,000
Netherlands	280,000	6,500	2,860
New Zealand	194,000	11,625[4]	17,000
Norway	75,000	2,000	—
Poland	—	664,000	530,000
Romania	650,000[5]	350,000[6]	—
South Africa	410,056	2,473	—
U.S.S.R.	—	6,115,000[4]	14,012,000
United Kingdom	5,896,000	357,116[4]	369,267
United States	16,112,566	291,557	670,846
Yugoslavia	3,741,000	305,000	425,000

1. Civilians only. 2. Army and Navy figures. 3. Figures cover period July 7, 1937–Sept. 2, 1945, and concern only Chinese regular troops. They do not include casualties suffered by guerrillas and local military corps. 4. Deaths from all causes. 5. Against Soviet Russia; 385,847 against Nazi Germany. 6. Against Soviet Russia; 169,822 against Nazi Germany. 7. National Defense Ctr., Canadian Forces Hq., Director of History. NOTE: The figures in this table are unofficial estimates obtained from various sources.

Merchant Marine Casualties in World War II

In 1988, the U.S. Government conferred official veterans status on those who served aboard oceangoing merchant ships in World War II. The officers and crews played a key role in transporting the troops and war material that enabled the United States and its allies to defeat the Axis powers.

During the war, merchant seamen died as a result of enemy attacks at a rate that proportionately exceeded all branches of the armed services, with the exception of the U.S. Marine Corps.

Enemy action sank more than 700 U.S.-flag merchant ships and claimed the lives of over 6,000 civilian seafarers. Untold thousands of additional seamen were wounded or injured during these attacks, and nearly 600 were made prisoners of war.

The Medal of Honor

Often called the Congressional Medal of Honor, it is the Nation's highest military award for "uncommon valor" by men and women in the armed forces. It is given for actions that are above and beyond the call of duty in combat against an armed enemy. The medal was first awarded by the Army on March 25, 1863. In April 1991, President Bush awarded posthumously the Medal of Honor to World War I veteran, Army Cpl. Freddie Stowers. He was the first black soldier to receive the nation's highest honor for valor in either World Wars.

The only conscientious objector to be awarded the medal was Pfc. Desmond Doss, a Seventh-Day Adventist who served as a medic in the Pacific Theater during WWII.

Recipients of the medal receive $400 per month for life, a right to burial at Arlington National Cemetery, admission for themselves or their children to a service academy (if they qualify and quotas permit), and free travel on government aircraft to almost anywhere in the world, on a space-available basis.

In 1989, medals were restored to William F. Cody (Buffalo Bill) and four other scouts who had them revoked in 1917 due to a new ruling.

President Clinton awarded the last medals to date. They were awarded posthumously on May 23, 1994, to two members of the ill-fated Delta Forces operation to capture warlord Gen. Aidid in Mogadishu on Oct. 3, 1993. The recipients were Master Sgt. Gary Gordon and Sgt. 1st Class Randall Shughart who were killed trying to protect and rescue wounded crew members under enemy fire.

Medal of Honor Recipients[1]

	Total	Army	Navy	Marines	Air Force	Coast Guard
Civil War	1,520	1,195	308	17	—	—
Indian Wars (1861-1898)	428	428	—	—	—	—
Korea (1871)	15	—	9	6	—	—
Spanish-American War	109	30	64	15	—	—
Philippines/Samoa	91	70	12	9	—	—
Boxer Rebellion	59	4	22	33	—	—
Veracruz (1914)	55	—	46	9	—	—
Haiti (1915)	6	—	—	6	—	—
Dominican Republic	3	—	—	3	—	—
Haiti (1919–1920)	2	—	—	2	—	—
Nicaragua (1927–1933)	2	—	—	2	—	—
Peacetime (1865–1870)	12	—	12	—	—	—
Peacetime (1871–1898)	103	—	101	2	—	—
Peacetime (1899–1911)	51	1	48	2	—	—
Peacetime (1915–1916)	8	—	8	—	—	—
Peacetime (1920-1940)	18	2	15	1	—	—
World War I	124	96	21	7	—	—
World War II	433	294	57	81	—	1
Korean War	131	78	7	42	4	—
Vietnam War	239	155	15	57	12	—
Somalia (1993)	2	2	—	—	—	—
Unknown Soldiers	9	—	—	—	—	—
Total	**3,420**	**2,355**	**745**	**294**	**16**	**1**

1. These totals reflect the total number of Medals of Honor awarded. Nineteen (19) men received a second award. The total number of Medal of Honor receipients is 3,401. *Source:* The Congressional Medal of Honor Society, Mt. Pleasant, S.C.

Estimated Educational Level of Active Duty Military Personnel, 1994

(Cumulative Percent—End of Fiscal Year)

Personnel/Educational Level	1994	Personnel/Educational Level	1994
Total Officers		**Warrant Officers**	
Graduated from college	94.0	Graduated from college	29.4
Completed 2 or more years college	97.6	Completed 2 or more years college	70.1
Completed some college	98.9	Completed some college	87.3
Graduated from high school	100.0	Graduated from high school	100.0
		Enlisted	
		Graduated from college	3.1
Commissioned Officers		Completed 2 or more years college	12.1
Graduated from college	97.7	Completed some college	22.5
Completed 2 or more years college	99.2	Graduated from high school	99.0
Completed some college	99.6	Completed some high school	100.0
Graduated from high school	100.0	Graduated from grade school	100.0

NOTE: The percentage distributions should be considered as approximate. *Source:* Department of Defense, Washington Headquarters Services, Directorate for Information Operations and Reports.

WEATHER & CLIMATE

Climate of 100 Selected U.S. Cities

| City | Average Monthly Temperature (°F)[1] | | | | Precipitation | | Snowfall | |
	Jan.	April	July	Oct	Average (in.)[1]	annual (days)[2]	Average annual (in.)[2]	Years[2]
Albany, N.Y.	21.1	46.6	71.4	50.5	35.74	134	65.5	38
Albuquerque, N.M.	34.8	55.1	78.8	57.4	8.12	59	10.6	45
Anchorage, Alaska	13.0	35.4	58.1	34.6	15.20	115	69.2	41[3]
Asheville, N.C.	36.8	55.7	73.2	56.0	47.71	124	17.5	20
Atlanta, Ga.	41.9	61.8	78.6	62.2	48.61	115	1.9	50
Atlantic City, N.J.	31.8	51.0	74.4	55.5	41.93	112	16.4	40[3]
Austin, Texas	49.1	68.7	84.7	69.8	31.50	83	0.9	43
Baltimore, Md.	32.7	54.0	76.8	56.9	41.84	113	21.8	34
Baton Rouge, La.	50.8	68.4	82.1	68.2	55.77	108	0.1	34[3]
Billings, Mont.	20.9	44.6	72.3	49.3	15.09	96	57.2	50
Birmingham, Ala.	42.9	62.8	80.1	62.6	54.52	117	1.3	41
Bismark, N.D.	6.7	42.5	70.4	46.1	15.36	96	40.3	45
Boise, Idaho	29.9	48.6	74.6	51.9	11.71	92	21.4	45
Boston, Mass.	29.6	48.7	73.5	54.8	43.81	127	41.8	49[3]
Bridgeport, Conn.	29.5	48.6	74.0	56.0	41.56	117	26.0	36
Buffalo, N.Y.	23.5	45.4	70.7	51.5	37.52	169	92.2	41
Burlington, Vt.	16.6	42.7	69.6	47.9	33.69	153	78.2	41
Caribou, Maine	10.7	37.3	65.1	43.1	36.59	160	113.3	45
Casper, Wyom.	22.2	42.1	70.9	47.1	11.43	95	80.5	34
Charleston, S.C.	47.9	64.3	80.5	65.8	51.59	113	0.6	42
Charleston, W.Va.	32.9	55.3	74.5	55.9	42.43	151	31.5	37
Charlotte, N.C.	40.5	60.3	78.5	60.7	43.16	111	6.1	45
Cheyenne, Wyom.	26.1	41.8	68.9	47.5	13.31	98	54.1	49
Chicago, Ill.	21.4	48.8	73.0	53.5	33.34	127	40.3	26
Cleveland, Ohio	25.5	48.1	71.6	53.2	35.40	156	53.6	43
Columbia, S.C.	44.7	63.8	81.0	63.4	49.12	109	1.9	37
Columbus, Ohio	27.1	51.4	73.8	53.9	36.97	137	28.3	37[3]
Concord, N.H.	19.9	44.1	69.5	48.3	36.53	125	64.5	43
Dallas–Ft. Worth, Texas	44.0	65.9	86.3	67.9	29.46	78	3.1	31
Denver, Colo.	29.5	47.4	73.4	51.9	15.31	88	59.8	50
Des Moines, Iowa	18.6	50.5	76.3	54.2	30.83	107	34.7	45
Detroit, Mich.	23.4	47.3	71.9	51.9	30.97	133	40.4	26
Dodge City, Kan.	29.5	54.3	80.0	57.7	20.66	78	19.5	42
Duluth, Minn.	6.3	38.3	65.4	44.2	29.68	135	77.4	41[3]
El Paso, Texas	44.2	63.6	82.5	63.6	7.82	47	5.2	45
Fairbanks, Alaska	−12.7	30.2	61.5	25.1	10.37	106	67.5	33
Fargo, N.D.	4.3	42.1	70.6	46.3	19.59	100	35.9	42
Grand Junction, Colo.	25.5	51.7	78.9	54.9	8.00	72	26.1	38
Grand Rapids, Mich.	22.0	46.3	71.4	50.9	34.35	143	72.4	21
Hartford, Conn.	25.2	48.8	73.4	52.4	44.39	127	50.0	30
Helena, Mont.	18.1	42.3	67.9	45.1	11.37	96	47.9	44
Honolulu, Hawaii	72.6	75.7	80.1	79.5	23.47	100	0.0	38[3]
Houston, Texas	51.4	68.7	83.1	69.7	44.76	105	0.4	50
Indianapolis, Ind.	26.0	52.4	75.1	54.8	39.12	125	23.1	53[3]
Jackson, Miss.	45.7	65.1	81.9	65.0	52.82	109	1.2	21
Jacksonville, Fla.	53.2	67.7	81.3	69.5	52.76	116	T	43
Juneau, Alaska	21.8	39.1	55.7	41.8	53.15	220	102.8	41
Kansas City, Mo.	28.4	56.9	80.9	59.6	29.27	98	20.0	43
Knoxville, Tenn .	38.2	59.6	77.6	59.5	47.29	127	12.3	42
Las Vegas, Nev.	44.5	63.5	90.2	67.5	4.19	26	1.4	36
Lexington, Ky.	31.5	55.1	75.9	56.8	45.68	131	16.3	40
Little Rock, Ark.	39.9	62.4	82.1	63.1	49.20	104	5.4	42
Long Beach, Calif.	55.2	60.9	72.8	67.5	11.54	32	T	41[3]
Los Angeles, Calif.	56.0	59.5	69.0	66.3	12.08	36	T	49
Louisville, Ky.	32.5	56.6	77.6	57.7	43.56	125	17.5	37
Madison, Wisc.	15.6	45.8	70.6	49.5	30.84	118	40.8	36
Memphis, Tenn.	39.6	62.6	82.1	62.9	51.57	107	5.5	34
Miami, Fla.	67.1	75.3	82.5	77.9	57.55	129	0.0	42
Milwaukee, Wisc.	18.7	44.6	70.5	50.9	30.94	125	47.0	44

City	Average Monthly Temperature (°F)[1]				Precipitation		Snowfall	
	Jan.	April	July	Oct	Average (in.)[1]	annual (days)[2]	Average annual (in.)[2]	Years[2]
Minneapolis–St. Paul, Minn.	11.2	46.0	73.1	49.6	26.36	115	48.9	46
Mobile, Ala.	50.8	68.0	82.2	68.5	64.64	123	0.3	43
Montgomery, Ala.	46.7	65.2	81.7	65.3	49.16	108	0.3	40
Mt. Washington, N.H.	5.1	22.4	48.7	30.5	89.92	209	246.8	52
Nashville, Tenn.	37.1	59.7	79.4	60.2	48.49	119	11.1	43
Newark, N.J.	31.2	52.1	76.8	57.2	42.34	122	28.2	43
New Orleans, La.	52.4	68.7	82.1	69.2	59.74	114	0.2	38[3]
New York, N.Y.	31.8	51.9	76.4	57.5	42.82	119	26.1	40[3]
Norfolk, Va.	39.9	58.2	78.4	61.3	45.22	115	7.9	36
Oklahoma City, Okla.	35.9	60.2	82.1	62.3	30.89	82	9.0	45
Olympia, Wash.	37.2	47.3	63.0	50.1	50.96	164	18.0	43
Omaha, Neb.	20.2	52.2	77.7	54.5	30.34	98	31.1	49[3]
Philadelphia, Pa.	31.2	52.9	76.5	56.5	41.42	117	21.9	42[3]
Phoenix, Ariz.	52.3	68.1	92.3	73.4	7.11	36	T	47[3]
Pittsburgh, Pa.	26.7	50.1	72.0	52.5	36.30	154	44.6	32
Portland, Maine	21.5	42.8	68.1	48.5	43.52	128	72.4	44
Portland, Ore.	38.9	50.4	67.7	54.3	37.39	154	6.8	44
Providence, R.I.	28.2	47.9	72.5	53.2	45.32	124	37.1	31
Raleigh, N.C.	39.6	59.4	77.7	59.7	41.76	112	7.7	40
Reno, Nev.	32.2	46.4	69.5	50.3	7.49	51	25.3	42
Richmond, Va.	36.6	57.9	77.8	58.6	44.07	113	14.6	47
Roswell, N.M.	41.4	61.9	81.4	61.7	9.70	52	11.4	37[3]
Sacramento, Calif.	45.3	58.2	75.6	63.9	17.10	58	0.1	36[3]
Salt Lake City, Utah	28.6	49.2	77.5	53.0	15.31	90	59.1	56
San Antonio, Texas	50.4	69.6	84.6	70.2	29.13	81	0.4	42
San Diego, Calif.	56.8	61.2	70.3	67.5	9.32	43	T	44
San Francisco, Calif.	48.5	54.8	62.2	60.6	19.71	63	T	57
Savannah, Ga.	49.1	66.0	81.2	66.9	49.70	111	0.3	34
Seattle–Tacoma, Wash.	39.1	48.7	64.8	52.4	38.60	158	12.8	40
Sioux Falls, S.D.	12.4	46.4	74.0	49.4	24.12	96	39.9	39
Spokane, Wash.	25.7	45.8	69.7	47.5	16.71	114	51.5	37
Springfield, Ill.	24.6	53.3	76.5	56.0	33.78	114	24.5	37
St. Louis, Mo.	28.8	56.1	78.9	57.9	33.91	111	19.8	48[3]
Tampa, Fla.	59.8	71.5	82.1	74.4	46.73	107	T	38
Toledo, Ohio	23.1	47.8	71.8	51.7	31.78	137	38.3	29
Tucson, Ariz.	51.1	64.9	86.2	70.4	11.14	52	1.2	44
Tulsa, Okla.	35.2	61.0	83.2	62.6	38.77	89	9.0	46
Vero Beach, Fla.	61.9	71.7	81.1	75.2	51.41	n.a.	n.a.	0
Washington, D.C.	35.2	56.7	78.9	59.3	39.00	112	17.0	41[3]
Wilmington, Del.	31.2	52.4	76.0	56.3	41.38	117	20.9	37
Wichita, Kan.	29.6	56.3	81.4	59.1	28.61	85	16.4	31

1. Based on 30 year period 1951–80. Data latest available. 2. Data through 1984 based on number of years as indicated in Years column. 3. For snowfall data where number of years differ from that for precipitation data. T = trace. n.a. = not available. *Source:* National Oceanic and Atmospheric Administration.

Wind Chill Factors

Wind speed (mph)	Thermometer reading (degrees Fahrenheit)																
	35	30	25	20	15	10	5	0	−5	−10	−15	−20	−25	−30	−35	−40	−45
5	33	27	21	19	12	7	0	−5	−10	−15	−21	−26	−31	−36	−42	−47	−52
10	22	16	10	3	−3	−9	−15	−22	−27	−34	−40	−46	−52	−58	−64	−71	−77
15	16	9	2	−5	−11	−18	−25	−31	−38	−45	−51	−58	−65	−72	−78	−85	−92
20	12	4	−3	−10	−17	−24	−31	−39	−46	−53	−60	−67	−74	−81	−88	−95	−103
25	8	1	−7	−15	−22	−29	−36	−44	−51	−59	−66	−74	−81	−88	−96	−103	−110
30	6	−2	−10	−18	−25	−33	−41	−49	−56	−64	−71	−79	−86	−93	−101	−109	−116
35	4	−4	−12	−20	−27	−35	−43	−52	−58	−67	−74	−82	−89	−97	−105	−113	−120
40	3	−5	−13	−21	−29	−37	−45	−53	−60	−69	−76	−84	−92	−100	−107	−115	−123
45	2	−6	−14	−22	−30	−38	−46	−54	−62	−70	−78	−85	−93	−102	−109	−117	−125

NOTES: This chart gives equivalent temperatures for combinations of wind speed and temperatures. For example, the combination of a temperature of 10° Fahrenheit and a wind blowing at 10 mph has a cooling power equal to −9° F. Wind speeds of higher than 45 mph have little additional cooling effect.

World and U.S. Extremes of Climate

Highest recorded temperature

	Place	Date	Degree Fahrenheit	Degree Centigrade
World (Africa)	El Azizia, Libya	Sept. 13, 1922	136	58
North America (U.S.)	Death Valley, Calif.	July 10, 1913	134	57
Asia	Tirat Tsvi, Israel	June 21, 1942	129	54
Australia	Cloncurry, Queensland	Jan. 16, 1889	128	53
Europe	Seville, Spain	Aug. 4, 1881	122	50
South America	Rivadavia, Argentina	Dec. 11, 1905	120	49
Canada	Midale and Yellow Grass, Saskatchewan	July 5, 1937	113	45
Persian Gulf (sea–surface)		August 5, 1924	96	36
South Pole		Dec. 27, 1978	7.5	−14
Antarctica	Vanda Station	Jan. 5, 1974	59	15

Lowest recorded temperature

	Place	Date	Degree Fahrenheit	Degree Centigrade
World (Antarctica)	Vostok	July 21, 1983	−129	−89
Asia	Verkhoyansk/Oimekon	Feb. 6, 1933	−90	−68
Greenland	Northice	Jan. 9, 1954	−87	−66
North America (excl. Greenland)	Snag, Yukon, Canada	Feb. 3, 1947	−81	−63
Alaska	Prospect Creek, Endicott Mts.	Jan. 23, 1971	−80	−62
U.S., excluding Alaska	Rogers Pass, Mont.	Jan. 20, 1954	−70	−56.5
Europe	Ust 'Shchugor, U.S.S.R.	n.a.	−67	−55
South America	Sarmiento, Argentina	Jan. 1, 1907	−27	−33
Africa	Ifrane, Morocco	Feb. 11, 1935	−11	−24
Australia	Charlotte Pass, N.S.W.	July 22, 1947	−8	−22
United States	Prospect Creek, Alaska	Jan. 23, 1971	−80	−62

Greatest rainfalls

	Place	Date	Inches	Centimeters
1 minute (World)	Unionville, Md.	July 4, 1956	1.23	3.1
20 minutes (World)	Curtea–de–Arges, Romania	July 7, 1889	8.1	20.5
42 minutes (World)	Holt, Mo.	June 22, 1947	12	30.5
12 hours (World)	Foc–Foc, La Réunion	Jan. 7–8, 1966	45	114
24 hours (World)	Foc–Foc, La Réeunion	Jan. 7–8, 1966	72	182.5
24 hours (N. Hemisphere)	Paishih, Taiwan	Sept. 10–11, 1963	49	125
24 hours (Australia)	Bellenden Ker, Queensland	Jan. 4, 1979	44	114
24 hours (U.S.)	Alvin, Texas	July 25–26, 1979	43	109
24 hours (Canada)	Ucluelet Brynnor Mines, British Columbia	Oct. 6, 1967	19	49
5 days (World)	Commerson, La Réunion	Jan. 23–28, 1980	156	395
1 month (World)	Cherrapunji, India	July 1861	366	930
12 months (World)	Cherrapunji, India	Aug. 1860–Aug. 1861	1,042	2,647
12 months (U.S.)	Kukui, Maui, Hawaii	Dec. 1981–Dec. 1982	739	1878

Greatest snowfalls

	Place	Date	Inches	Centimeters
1 month (U.S.)	Tamarack, Calif.	Jan. 1911	390	991
24 hours (N. America)	Silver Lake, Colo.	April 14–15, 1921	76	192.5
24 hours (Alaska)	Thompson Pass	Dec. 29, 1955	62	157.5
19 hours (France)	Bessans	April 5–6, 1969	68	173
1 storm (N. America)	Mt. Shasta Ski Bowl, Calif.	Feb. 13–19, 1959	189	480
1 storm (Alaska)	Thompson Pass	Dec. 26–31, 1955	175	445.5
1 season (N. America)	Paradise Ranger Sta., Wash.	1971–1972	1,122	2,850
1 season (Alaska)	Thompson Pass	1952–1953	974.5	2,475
1 season (Canada)	Revelstoke Mt. Copeland, British Columbia	1971–1972	964	2,446.5

Source: U.S. Army Corps of Engineers, Engineer Topographic Laboratories.

Tropical Storms and Hurricanes, 1886–1994

	Jan.–April	May	June	July	Aug.	Sept.	Oct.	Nov.	Dec.	Total
Number of tropical storms (incl. hurricanes)	4	14	57	69	223	313	189	44	6	919
Number of tropical storms that reached hurricane intensity	1	3	23	35	153	196	97	23	3	534

Other Recorded Extremes

Highest average annual mean temperature (World): Dallol, Ethiopia (Oct. 1960–Dec. 1966), 94° F (35° C). **(U.S.):** Key West, Fla. (30–year normal), 78.2° F (25.7° C).

Lowest average annual mean temperature (Antarctica): Plateau Station –70° F (–57° C). **(U.S.):** Barrow, Alaska (30–year normal), 9.3° F (–13° C).

Greatest average yearly rainfall (U.S.): Mt. Waialeale, Kauai, Hawaii (32–year avg), 460 in. (1,168 cm). **(India):** Cherrapunji (74–year avg), 450 in. (1,143 cm).

Minimum average yearly rainfall (Chile): Arica (59–year avg), 0.03 in. (0.08 cm) (no rainfall for 14 consecutive years). **(U.S.):** Death Valley, Calif. (42–year avg), 1.63 in. (4.14 cm). Bagdad, Calif., holds the U.S. record for the longest period with no measurable rain, 767 days, from Oct. 3, 1912 to Nov. 8, 1914).

Hottest summer avg in Western Hemisphere (U.S.): Death Valley, Calif., 98° F (36.7° C).

Longest hot spell (W. Australia): Marble Bar, 100° F (38° C) (or above) for 162 consecutive days, Oct. 30, 1923–Apr. 7, 1924.

Largest hailstone (U.S.): Coffeyville, KS, 17.5 in. (44.5 cm), Sept. 3, 1979.

Weather Glossary

blizzard: storm characterized by strong winds, low temperatures, and large amounts of snow.

cold wave warning: indicates that a change to abnormally cold weather is expected; greater than normal protective measures will be required.

cyclone: circulation of winds rotating counterclockwise in the northern hemisphere and clockwise in the southern hemisphere. Hurricanes and tornadoes are both examples of cyclones.

drifting snow: strong winds will blow loose or falling snow into significant drifts.

drizzle: uniform close precipitation of tiny drops with diameter of less than .02 inch.

flash flood: dangerous rapid rise of water levels in streams, rivers, or over land area.

freezing rain or drizzle: rain or drizzle that freezes on contact with the ground or other objects forming a coating of ice on exposed surfaces.

gale warning: winds in the 33–48 knot (38–55 mph) range forecast.

hail: small balls of ice falling separately or in lumps; usually associated with thunderstorms and temperatures that may be well above freezing.

heavy snow warnings: issued when 4 inches or more of snow are expected to fall in a 12–hour period or when 6 inches or more are anticipated in a 24–hour period.

hurricane: devastating cyclonic storm; winds over 74 mph near storm center; usually tropical in origin; called cyclone in Indian Ocean, typhoon in the Pacific.

hurricane warning: winds in excess of 64 knots (74 mph) in connection with hurricane.

rain: precipitation of liquid particles with diameters larger than .02 inch.

sleet: translucent or transparent ice pellets; frozen rain; generally a winter phenomenon.

small craft warning: indicates winds as high as 33 knots (38 mph) and sea conditions dangerous to small boats.

snow flurries: snow falling for a short time at intermittent periods; accumulations are usually small.

snow squall: brief, intense falls of snow, usually accompanied by gusty winds.

storm warnings: winds greater than 48 knots (55 mph) are forecast.

temperature–humidity index (THI): measure of personal discomfort based on the combined effects of temperature and humidity. Most people are uncomfortable when the THI is 75. A THI of 80 produces acute discomfort for almost everyone.

tidal waves: series of ocean waves caused by earthquakes; can reach speeds of 600 mph; they grow in height as they reach shore and can crest as high as 100 feet.

thunder: the sound produced by the rapid expansion of air heated by lightning.

tornado: dangerous whirlwind associated with the cumulonimbus clouds of severe thunderstorms; winds up to 300 mph.

tornado warning: tornado has actually been detected by radar or sighted in designated area.

tornado watch: potential exists in the watch area for storms that could contain tornadoes.

tsunami: *see* tidal waves.

wind–chill factor: combined effect of temperature and wind speed as compared to equivalent temperature in calm air .

The "Dog Days" of Summer

Source: Storm Phillips, STORMFAX, INC.

This expression describes a mid-Summer period of hot weather from July 3rd to August 11th. The exact dates are traced to the early Egyptians who recorded the appearance of *Sirius* (the bright Dog Star in the constellation *Canis Major*) rising with the Sun. They believed the star added heat to the Sun and caused exceptionally hot weather. The early-morning appearance of the star also coincided with the rising of the Nile River in Egypt, adding to ancient legends of its power.

The expression "dog days of summer" has lost its true meaning through the years, and now is often explained as **any** period of hot August weather that's "not fit for a dog" or a time when "dogs go mad in the heat."

Record Highest Temperatures by State

State	Temp. °F	Temp °C	Date	Station	Elevation, feet
Alabama	112	44	Sept. 5, 1925	Centerville	345
Alaska	100	38	June 27, 1915	Fort Yukon	est. 420
Arizona	127	53	July 7, 1905*	Parker	345
Arkansas	120	49	Aug. 10, 1936	Ozark	396
California	134	57	July 10, 1913	Greenland Ranch	−178
Colorado	118	48	July 11, 1888	Bennett	5,484
Connecticut	106	41	July 15, 1995	Danbury	457
Delaware	110	43	July 21, 1930	Millsboro	20
D.C.	106	41	July 20, 1930	Washington	410
Florida	109	43	June 29, 1931	Monticello	207
Georgia	113	45	May 27, 1978	Greenville	860
Hawaii	100	38	Apr. 27, 1931	Pahala	850
Idaho	118	48	July 28, 1934	Orofino	1,027
Illinois	117	47	July 14, 1954	E. St. Louis	410
Indiana	116	47	July 14, 1936	Collegeville	672
Iowa	118	48	July 20, 1934	Keokuk	614
Kansas	121	49	July 24, 1936*	Alton (near)	1,651
Kentucky	114	46	July 28, 1930	Greensburg	581
Louisiana	114	46	Aug. 10, 1936	Plain Dealing	268
Maine	105	41	July 10, 1911*	North Bridgton	450
Maryland	109	43	July 10, 1936*	Cumberland & Frederick	623;325
Massachusetts	107	42	Aug. 2, 1975	New Bedford & Chester	120;640
Michigan	112	44	July 13, 1936	Mio	963
Minnesota	114	46	July 6, 1936*	Moorhead	904
Mississippi	115	46	July 29, 1930	Holly Springs	600
Missouri	118	48	July 14, 1954*	Warsaw & Union	687;560
Montana	117	47	July 5, 1937	Medicine Lake	1,950
Nebraska	118	48	July 24, 1936*	Minden	2,169
Nevada	122	50	June 23, 1954*	Overton	1,240
New Hampshire	106	41	July 4, 1911	Nashua	125
New Jersey	110	43	July 10, 1936	Runyon	18
New Mexico	116	47	July 14, 1934*	Orogrande	4,171
New York	108	42	July 22, 1926	Troy	35
North Carolina	110	43	Aug. 21, 1983	Fayetteville	81
North Dakota	121	49	July 6, 1936	Steele	1,857
Ohio	113	45	July 21, 1934*	Gallipolis (near)	673
Oklahoma	120	49	July 26, 1943*	Tishomingo	670
Oregon	119	48	Aug. 10, 1898	Pendleton	1,074
Pennsylvania	111	44	July 10, 1936*	Phoenixville	100
Rhode Island	104	40	Aug. 2, 1975	Providence	51
South Carolina	111	44	June 28, 1954*	Camden	170
South Dakota	120	49	July 5, 1936	Gannvalley	1,750
Tennessee	113	45	Aug. 9, 1930*	Perryville	377
Texas	120	49	Aug. 12, 1936	Seymour	1,291
Utah	117	47	July 5, 1895	Saint George	2,880
Vermont	105	41	July 4, 1911	Vernon	310
Virginia	110	43	July 15, 1954	Balcony Falls	725
Washington	118	48	Aug. 5, 1961*	Ice Harbor Dam	475
West Virginia	112	44	July 10, 1936*	Martinsburg	435
Wisconsin	114	46	July 13, 1936	Wisconsin Dells	900
Wyoming	114	46	July 12, 1900	Basin	3,500

*Also on earlier dates at the same or other places. *Source:* National Climatic Data Center, Asheville, N.C., and Storm Phillips, STORMFAX, INC.

Record Lowest Temperatures by State

State	Temp. °F	Temp °C	Date	Station	Elevation, feet
Alabama	−27	−33	Jan. 30, 1966	New Market	760
Alaska	−80	−62	Jan. 23, 1971	Prospect Creek	1,100
Arizona	−40	−40	Jan. 7, 1971	Hawley Lake	8,180
Arkansas	−29	−34	Feb. 13, 1905	Pond	1,250
California	−45	−43	Jan. 20, 1937	Boca	5,532
Colorado	−60	−51	Jan. 1, 1979*	Maybell	5,920
Connecticut	−32	−36	Feb. 16, 1943	Falls Village	585
Delaware	−17	−27	Jan. 17, 1893	Millsboro	20
D.C.	−15	−26	Feb. 11, 1899	Washington	410
Florida	−2	−19	Feb. 13, 1899	Tallahassee	193
Georgia	−17	−27	Jan. 27, 1940	CCC Camp F−16	est. 1,000
Hawaii	14	−11	Jan. 2, 1961	Haleakala, Maui Is	9,750
Idaho	−60	−51	Jan. 18, 1943	Island Park Dam	6,285
Illinois	−35	−37	Jan. 22, 1930	Mount Carroll	817
Indiana	−36	−38	Jan. 19, 1994	New Whiteland	785
Iowa	−47	−44	Jan. 12, 1912	Washta	1,157
Kansas	−40	−40	Feb. 13, 1905	Lebanon	1,812
Kentucky	−34	−37	Jan. 28, 1963	Cynthiana	684
Louisiana	−16	−27	Feb. 13, 1899	Minden	194
Maine	−48	−44	Jan. 19, 1925	Van Buren	510
Maryland	−40	−40	Jan. 13, 1912	Oakland	2,461
Massachusetts	−34	−37	Jan. 18, 1957	Birch Hill Dam	840
Michigan	−51	−46	Feb. 9, 1934	Vanderbilt	785
Minnesota	−59	−51	Feb. 16, 1903*	Pokegama Dam	1,280
Mississippi	−19	−28	Jan. 30, 1966	Corinth	420
Missouri	−40	−40	Feb. 13, 1905	Warsaw	700
Montana	−70	−57	Jan. 20, 1954	Rogers Pass	5,470
Nebraska	−47	−44	Feb. 12, 1899	Camp Clarke	3,700
Nevada	−50	−46	Jan. 8, 1937	San Jacinto	5,200
New Hampshire	−46	−43	Jan. 28, 1925	Pittsburg	1,575
New Jersey	−34	−37	Jan. 5, 1904	River Vale	70
New Mexico	−50	−46	Feb. 1, 1951	Gavilan	7,350
New York	−52	−47	Feb. 18, 1979*	Old Forge	1,720
North Carolina	−29	−37	Jan. 30, 1966	Mt. Mitchell	6,525
North Dakota	−60	−51	Feb. 15, 1936	Parshall	1,929
Ohio	−39	−39	Feb. 10, 1899	Milligan	800
Oklahoma	−27	−33	Jan. 18, 1930	Watts	958
Oregon	−54	−48	Feb. 10, 1933*	Seneca	4,700
Pennsylvania	−42	−41	Jan. 5, 1904	Smethport	est. 1,500
Rhode Island	−23	−31	Jan. 11, 1942	Kingston	100
South Carolina	−20	−28	Jan. 18, 1977	Caesars Head	3,100
South Dakota	−58	−50	Feb. 17, 1936	McIntosh	2,277
Tennessee	−32	−36	Dec. 30, 1917	Mountain City	2,471
Texas	−23	−31	Feb. 8, 1933*	Seminole	3,275
Utah	−50	−51	Jan. 5, 1913*	Strawberry Tunnel	7,650
Vermont	−50	−46	Dec. 30, 1933	Bloomfield	915
Virginia	−29	−34	Feb. 10, 1899	Monterey	—
Washington	−48	−44	Dec. 30, 1968	Mazama & Winthrop	2,120;1,765
West Virginia	−37	−38	Dec. 30, 1917	Lewisburg	2,200
Wisconsin	−54	−48	Jan. 24, 1922	Danbury	908
Wyoming	−63	−53	Feb. 9, 1933	Moran	6,770

*Also on earlier dates at the same or other places. *Source:* National Climatic Data Center, Asheville, N.C., and Storm Phillips, STORMFAX, INC.

Record High and Low Temperature in U.S. for Each Month

Source: National Climatic Data Center, Asheville, N.C., and Storm Phillips, STORMFAX, Inc.
NOTE: for the conterminous states only.

January

The highest temperature ever recorded for the month of January occurred on January 17, 1936, again in 1954, in Laredo, Tex. (elevation 421 ft) where the temperature reached 98° F.

The lowest temperature ever recorded for the month of January occurred on January 20, 1954, in Rogers Pass, Mont. (elevation 5,470 ft) where the temperature fell to –70° F.

February

The highest temperature ever recorded for the month of February occurred on February 3, 1963, in Montezuma, Ariz. (elevation 735 ft) where the temperature reached 105° F.

The lowest temperature ever recorded for the month of February occurred on February 9, 1933, at the Riverside Ranger Station in Montana (elevation 6,700 ft) where the temperature fell to –66° F.

March

The highest temperature ever recorded for the month of March occurred on March 31, 1954, in Rio Grande City, Tex. (elevation 168 ft) where the temperature reached 108° F.

The lowest temperature ever recorded for the month of March occurred on March 17, 1906, in Snake River, Wyo. (elevation 6,862 ft) where the temperature dropped to –50° F.

April

The highest temperature ever recorded for the month of April occurred on April 25, 1898, at Volcano Springs, Calif. (elevation –220 ft) where the temperature reached 118° F.

The lowest temperature ever recorded for the month of April occurred on April 5, 1945, in Eagle Nest, N. Mex. (elevation 8,250 ft) where the temperature dropped to –36° F.

May

The highest temperature ever recorded for the month of May occurred on May 27, 1896, in Salton, Calif. (elevation –263 ft) where the temperature reached 124° F.

The lowest temperature ever recorded for the month of May occurred on May 7, 1964, in White Mountain 2, Calif. (elevation 12,470 ft) where the temperature dropped to –15° F.

June

The highest temperature ever recorded for the month of June occurred on June 23, 1902, at Volcano Springs, Calif. (elevation –220 ft) where the temperature reached 129° F.

The lowest temperature ever recorded for the month of June occurred on June 13, 1907, in Tamarack, Calif. (elevation 8,000 ft) where the temperature dropped to 2° F.

July

The highest temperature ever recorded for the month of July occurred on July 10, 1913, at Greenland Ranch, Calif. (elevation –178 ft) where the temperature reached 134° F.

The lowest temperature ever recorded for the month of July occurred on July 21, 1911, at Painter, Wyo. (elevation 6,800 ft) where the temperature fell to 10° F.

August

The highest temperature ever recorded for the month of August occurred on August 12, 1933, at Greenland Ranch, Calif. (elevation –178 ft) where the temperature reached 127° F.

The lowest temperature ever recorded for the month of August occurred on August 25, 1910, in Bowen, Mont. (elevation 6,080 ft) where the temperature fell to 5° F.

September

The highest temperature ever recorded for the month of September occurred on September 2, 1950, in Mecca, Calif. (elevation –175 ft) where the temperature reached 126° F.

The lowest temperature ever recorded for the month of September occurred on September 24, 1926, at Riverside Ranger Station, Mont. (elevation 6,700 ft) where the temperature fell to –9 F.

October

The highest temperature ever recorded for the month of October occurred on October 5, 1917, in Sentinel, Ariz. (elevation 685 ft) where the temperature reached 116° F.

The lowest temperature ever recorded for the month of October occurred on October 29, 1917, in Soda Butte, Wyo. (elevation 6,600 ft) where the temperature fell to –33° F.

November

The highest temperature ever recorded for the month of November occurred on November 12, 1906, in Craftonville, Calif. (elevation 1,759 ft) where the temperature reached 105° F.

The lowest temperature ever recorded for the month of November occurred on November 16, 1959, at Lincoln, Mont. (elevation 5,130 ft) where the temperature fell to –53° F.

December

The highest temperature ever recorded for the month of December occurred on December 8, 1938, in La Mesa, Calif. (elevation 539 ft) where the temperature reached 100° F.

The lowest temperature ever recorded for the month of December occurred on December 19, 1924, at Riverside Ranger Station, Mont. (elevation 6,700 ft) where the temperature fell to –59° F.

Temperature Extremes in The United States

Source: National Oceanic and Atmospheric Administration, Environmental Data and Information Service, and National Climatic Center

The Highest Temperature Extremes

Greenland Ranch, California, with 134° F on July 10, 1913, holds the record for the highest temperature ever officially observed in the United States. This station was located in barren Death Valley, 178 feet below sea level. Death Valley is about 140 miles long, four to six miles wide, and oriented north to south in southwestern California. Much of the valley is below sea level and is flanked by towering mountain ranges with Mt. Whitney, the highest landmark in the 48 conterminous states, rising to 14,495 feet above sea level, less than 100 miles to the west. Death Valley has the hottest summers in the Western Hemisphere, and is the only known place in the United States where nighttime temperatures sometimes remain above 100° F.

The highest annual normal (1941–70 mean) temperature in the United States, 78.2° F, and the highest summer (June–August) normal temperature, 92.8° F, are for Death Valley, California. The highest winter (December–February) normal temperature is 72.8° F for Honolulu, Hawaii.

Amazing temperature rises of 40° to 50° F in a few minutes occasionally may be brought about by chinook winds.[1]

Some Outstanding Temperature Rises

In 12 hours: 83° F, Granville, N.D., Feb. 21, 1918, from –33° F to 50° F from early morning to late afternoon.

In 15 minutes: 42° F, Fort Assiniboine, Mont., Jan. 19, 1892, from –5° F to 37° F.

In seven minutes: 34° F, Kipp, Mont., Dec. 1, 1896. The observer also reported that a total rise of 80° F occurred in a few hours and that 30 inches of snow disappeared in one–half day.

In two minutes: 49° F, Spearfish, S.D., Jan. 22, 1943 from –4° F at 7:30 a.m. to 45° F at 7:32 a.m.

The Lowest Temperature Extremes

The lowest temperature on record in the United States, –79.8° F, was observed at Prospect Creek Camp in the Endicott Mountains of northern Alaska (latitude 66° 48′N, longitude 150° 40′W) on Jan. 23, 1971. The lowest ever recorded in the conterminous 48 states, –69.7° F, occurred at Rogers Pass, in Lewis and Clark County, Mont., on Jan. 20, 1954. Rogers Pass is in mountainous and heavily forested terrain about one–half mile east of and 140 feet below the summit of the Continental Divide.

The lowest annual normal (1941–70 mean) temperature in the United States is 9.3° F for Barrow, Alaska, which lies on the Arctic coast. Barrow also has the coolest summers (June–August) with a normal temperature of 36.4° F. The lowest winter (December–February) normal temperature, is –15.7° F for Barter Island on the arctic coast of northeast Alaska.

In the 48 conterminous states, Mt. Washington, N.H. (elevation 6,262 feet) has the lowest annual normal temperature 26.9° F and the lowest normal summer temperature, 46.8° F. A few stations in the northeastern United States and in the upper Rocky Mountains have normal annual temperatures in the 30s; summer normal temperatures at these stations are in the low 50s. Winter normal temperatures are lowest in northeastern North Dakota, 5.6° F for Langdon Experiment Farm, and in northwestern Minnesota, 5.3° F for Hallock.

Some Outstanding Temperature Falls

In 24 hours: 100° F, Browing, Mont., Jan. 23–24, 1916, from 44° to –56° F.

In 12 hours: 84° F, Fairfield, Mont., Dec. 24, 1924, from 63° at noon to –21° F at midnight.

In 2 hours: 62° F, Rapid City, S.D., Jan. 12, 1911, from 49° F at 6:00 a.m. to –13° F at 8:00 a.m.

In 27 minutes: 58° F, Spearfish, S.D., Jan. 22, 1943, from 54° F at 9:00 a.m. to –4° F at 9:27 a.m.

In 15 minutes: 47° F, Rapid City, S.D., Jan. 10, 1911, from 55° F at 7:00 a.m. to 8° F. at 7:15 a.m.

1. A warm, dry wind that descends from the eastern slopes of the Rocky Mountains, causing a rapid rise in temperature.

Winter Indoor Comfort and Relative Humidity

Compared to summer when the moisture content of the air (relative humidity) is an important factor of body discomfort, air moisture has a lesser effect on the human body during outdoor winter activities. But it is a big factor for winter indoor comfort because it has a direct bearing on health and energy consumption.

The colder the outdoor temperature, the more heat must be added indoors for body comfort. However, the heat that is added will cause a drying effect and lower the indoor relative humidity, unless an indoor moisture source is present.

While a room temperature between 71° and 77° F may be comfortable for short periods of time under very dry conditions, prolonged exposure to dry air has varying effects on the human body and usually causes discomfort. The moisture content of the air is important, and by increasing the relative humidity to

above 50% within the above temperature range, 80% or more of all average dressed persons would feel comfortable.

Effects of Dry Air on the Body

Studies have shown that dry air has four main effects on the human body:

1. Breathing dry air is a potential health hazard which can cause such respiratory ailments as asthma, bronchitis, sinusitis, and nosebleeds, or general dehydration since body fluids are depleted during respiration.

2. Skin moisture evaporation can cause skin irritations and eye itching.

3. Irritative effects, such as static electricity which causes mild shocks when metal is touched, are common when the air moisture is low.

Average Indoor Relative Humidity, %, for January

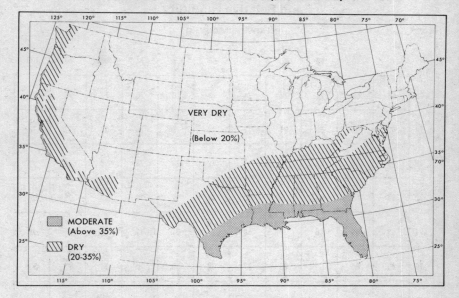

Source: National Oceanic and Atmospheric Administration, Environmental Data and Information Service, National Climatic Center.

4. The "apparent temperature" of the air is lower than what the thermometer indicates, and the body "feels" colder.

These problems can be reduced by simply increasing the indoor relative humidity. This can be done through use of humidifiers, vaporizers, steam ge nerators, sources such as large pans, or water containers made of porous ceramics. Even wet towels or water in a bathtub will be of some help. The lower the room temperature the easier the relative humidity can be brought to its desired level. A relative humidity indicator (hygrometer) may be of assistance in determining the humidity in the house.

Referring to item 4, a more detailed discussion is necessary. While the indoor temperature as read from a thermometer may be 75° F, the apparent temperature (what it feels like) may be warmer or colder depending on the moisture content of the air. Apparent temperature can vary as much as 8° F within a relative humidity range of 10 to 80 percent (these limits are generally possible in a closed room). Because of evaporation the human body cools when exposed to dry air, and the sense of coldness increases as the humidity decreases. With a room temperature of 70° F, for example, a person will feel colder in a dry room than in a moist room; this is especially noticeable when entering a dry room after bathing.

The table on the following page gives apparent temperatures for various combinations of room temperature and relative humidity. As an example of how to read the table, a room temperature of 70° F combined with a relative humidity of 10% feels like 64° F, but at 80% it feels like 71° F.

Although degrees of comfort vary with age, health, activity, clothing, and body characteristics, the table can be used as a general guideline when raising the apparent temperature and the level of comfort through an increase in room moisture, rather than by an addition of heat to the room. This method of changing the apparent temperature can give the direct benefit of reducing heating costs because comfort can be maintained with a lower thermostat setting if moisture is added. For example, an apparent comfortable temperature can be maintained with a thermostat setting of 75° F with 20% relative humidity or with a 70° F setting with 80 percent humidity. A relative humidity of 20 percent is common for homes without a humidifier during winter in the northern United States. ☐

Hurricane Advisories and Warnings

Source: Federal Emergency Management Agency and NOAA.

Thanks to modern detection and tracking devices, the National Weather Service can usually provide 12 to 24 hours of advance warning. Advisories are issued by the Weather Service if NOAA hurricanes approach land.

A "hurricane watch" is issued whenever a hurricane becomes a threat to coastal areas. Everyone in the area covered by the "watch" should listen for further advisories and be prepared to act promptly if a hurricane warning is issued.

A "hurricane warning" is issued when hurricane winds of 74 miles an hour or higher, or a combination of dangerously high water and very rough seas, are expected in a specific coastal area within 24 hours. Precautionary actions should begin immediately. ☐

Apparent Temperature for Values of Room Temperature and Relative Humidity

RELATIVE HUMIDITY (%)

ROOM TEMPERATURE (F)	0	10	20	30	40	50	60	70	80	90	100
75	68	69	71	72	74	75	76	76	77	78	79
74	66	68	69	71	72	73	74	75	76	77	78
73	65	67	68	70	71	72	73	74	75	76	77
72	64	65	67	68	70	71	72	73	74	75	76
71	63	64	66	67	68	70	71	72	73	74	75
70	63	64	65	66	67	68	69	70	71	72	73
69	62	63	64	65	66	67	68	69	70	71	72
68	61	62	63	64	65	66	67	68	69	70	71
67	60	61	62	63	64	65	66	67	68	68	69
66	59	60	61	62	63	64	65	66	67	67	68
65	59	60	61	61	62	63	64	65	65	66	67
64	58	59	60	60	61	62	63	64	64	65	66
63	57	58	59	59	60	61	62	62	63	64	64
62	56	57	58	58	59	60	61	61	62	63	63
61	56	57	57	58	59	59	60	60	61	61	62
60	55	56	56	57	58	58	59	59	60	60	61

Source: National Oceanic and Atmospheric Administration, Environmental Data and Information Service and National Climatic Center.

GREAT DISASTERS

The following lists are not all-inclusive due to space limitations. Only disasters involving great loss of life and/or property, historical interest, or unusual circumstances are listed. Data as of Aug. 1, 1995. For later disasters see *Current Events*.

WORST UNITED STATES DISASTERS

Aircraft
1979 May 25, Chicago: American Airlines DC-10 lost left engine upon take-off and crashed seconds later, killing all 272 persons aboard and three on the ground in worst U.S. air disaster.

Dam
1928 March 12, Santa Paula, Calif.: collapse of St. Francis Dam left 450 dead.

Drought
1930s Many states: longest drought of the 20th century. Peak periods were 1930, 1934, 1936, 1939, and 1940. During 1934, dry regions stretched solidly from New York and Pennsylvania across the Great Plains to the California coast. A great "dust bowl" covered some 50 million acres in the south central plains during the winter of 1935–1936.

Earthquake
1906 April 18, San Francisco: earthquake accompanied by fire razed more than 4 sq mi.; more than 500 dead or missing.

Epidemic
1918 Nationwide: Spanish influenza killed over 500,000 Americans.

Explosion
1947 April 16–18, Texas City, Texas: Most of the city destroyed by a fire and subsequent explosion on the French freighter *Grandcamp* carrying a cargo of ammonium nitrate. At least 516 were killed and over 3,000 injured.

Fire
1871 Oct. 8, Peshtigo, Wis.: over 1,200 lives lost and 2 billion trees burned in forest fire.

Flood
1889 May 31, Johnstown, Pa.: more than 2,200 died in flood.

Hurricane
1900 Aug. 27–Sept. 15, Galveston, Tex.: over 6,000 died from devastation due to both winds and tidal wave.

Marine
1865 April 27, Sultana: boiler explosion on Mississippi River steamboat near Memphis, 1,547 killed.

Mine
1907 Dec. 6, Monongha, W. Va.: coal mine explosion killed 361.

Oil Spill
1989 Mar. 24, Prince William Sound, Alaska: Tanker, *Exxon Valdez,* hit an undersea reef and released 10 million plus gallons of oil into the waters, causing the worst oil spill in U.S. history.

Railroad
1918 July 9, Nashville, Tenn.: 101 killed in a two-train collision near Nashville.

Submarine
1963 April 10, *Thresher:* atomic-powered submarine sank in North Atlantic: 129 dead.

Terrorist Attack
1995 April 19, Oklahoma City: Terrorist car bomb exploded outside Federal office building, collapsing wall and floors. 168 persons were killed, including 19 children and one person who died in rescue effort. Over 220 buildings sustained damage. Bombing motive believed to be in revenge for the deaths of Branch Davidians in the Waco, Texas, compound, April 19, 1993, resulting from a botched assault by government agents. It is worst terrorist bombing on U.S. soil. *See also,* Miscellaneous, 1993, April 19, Waco, Texas.

Tornado
1925 March 18, Great Tri-State Tornado: Missouri, Illinois, and Indiana; 695 deaths. Eight additional tornadoes in Kentucky, Tennessee, and Alabama raised day's toll to 792 dead.

Winter Storm
1888 March 11–14, East Coast: The Blizzard of 1888. 400 people died, as much as 5 feet of snow. Damage was estimated at $20 million.

Earthquakes and Volcanic Eruptions

A.D. 79 Aug. 24, Italy: eruption of Mt. Vesuvius buried cities of Pompeii and Herculaneum, killing thousands.

1556 Jan. 24, Shaanxi (Shensi) Province, China: most deadly earthquake in history; 830,000 killed.

1755 Nov. 1, Portugal: one of the most severe of recorded earthquakes leveled Lisbon and was felt as far away as southern France and North Africa; 10,000–20,000 killed in Lisbon.

1811 Dec. 16, Mississippi Valley near New Madrid, Missouri: The quake reversed the course of the Mississippi River. Fatalities unknown due to the sparse population in the area. Aftershocks and tremors continued into 1812. It has been estimated that three of the series of earthquakes had surface-wave magnitudes of 8.6, 8.4, and 8.8 on the Richter Scale. It is the largest series of earthquakes known to have occurred in North America.

1883 Aug. 26–28, Netherlands Indies: eruption of Krakatau; violent explosions destroyed two thirds of island. Sea waves occurred as far away as Cape Horn, and possibly England. Estimated 36,000 dead.

1886 Aug. 31, Charleston, S.C.: Sixty persons killed and damage to city extensive. The magnitude was 7.7 on the Richter Scale.

1902 May 8, Martinique, West Indies: Mt. Pelée erupted and wiped out city of St. Pierre; 40,000 dead.

1908 Dec. 28, Messina, Sicily: about 85,000 killed and city totally destroyed.

1915 Jan. 13, Avezzano, Italy: earthquake left 29,980 dead.

1920 Dec. 16, Gansu (Kansu) Province, China: earthquake killed 200,000.

1923 Sept. 1, Japan: earthquake destroyed third of Tokyo and most of Yokohama; more than 140,000 killed.

1933 March 10, Long Beach, Calif.: 117 left dead by earthquake.

1935 May 31, India: earthquake at Quetta killed an estimated 50,000.

1939 Jan. 24, Chile: earthquake razed 50,000 sq mi.; about 30,000 killed.
Dec. 27, Northern Turkey: severe quakes destroyed city of Erzingan; about 100,000 casualties.

1950 Aug. 15, India: earthquake affected 30,000 sq mi. in Assam; 20,000–30,000 believed killed.

1964 March 27, Alaska: strongest earthquake ever to strike North America hit 80 miles east of Anchorage; followed by seismic wave 50 feet high that traveled 8,445 miles at 450 miles per hour; 117 killed.

1970 May 31, Peru: earthquake left 50,000 dead, 17,000 missing.

1972 Dec. 22, Managua, Nicaragua: earthquake devastated city, leaving up to 6,000 dead.

1976 Feb. 4, Guatemala: earthquake left over 23,000 dead.
July 28, Tangshan, China: earthquake devastated 20-sq-mi. area of city leaving estimated 242,000 dead.
Aug. 17, Mindanao, Philippines: earthquake and tidal wave left up to 8,000 dead or missing.

1978 Sept. 16, Tabas, Iran: earthquake destroyed city in eastern Iran, leaving 25,000 dead.

1985 Sept. 19–20, Mexico: earthquake registering 8.1 on Richter scale struck central and southwestern regions, devastating part of Mexico City and three coastal states. An estimated 25,000 killed.
Nov. 14–16, Colombia: eruption of Nevada del Ruiz, 85 miles northwest of Bogotá, caused mud slides which buried most of the town of Armero and devastated Chinchiná. An estimated 25,000 were killed.

1988 Dec. 7, Armenia: an earthquake measuring 6.9 on the Richter scale killed nearly 25,000, injured 15,000, and left at least 400,000 homeless.

1989 Oct. 17, San Francisco Bay Area: an earthquake measuring 7.1 on the Richter Scale killed 67 and injured over 3,000. The quake damaged or destroyed over 100,000 buildings and caused billions of dollars of damage.

1990 June 21, Northwestern Iran: an earthquake measuring 7.7 on the Richter Scale destroyed cities, towns, and villages in Caspian Sea area. At least 50,000 dead, over 60,000 injured, and 400,000 homeless.

1994 Jan. 17, San Fernando Valley, Calif.: Earthquake measuring 6.6 on the Richter Scale killed 61 persons and injured over 8,000. Damage estimated at $13–20 billion.

1995 Jan. 17, Osaka, Kyoto, Kobe, Japan: 5,100 killed and 26,800 injured, estimated damage $100 billion. Epicenter 12 miles under Awaji Island in the Inland Sea. Magnitude: 7.2

Major U.S. Epidemics

1793 Philadelphia. More than 4,000 residents died from yellow fever.

1832 July–August, New York City. Over 3,000 people killed in a cholera epidemic. **October, New Orleans.** Cholera took the lives of 4,340 persons.

1848 New York City. More than 5,000 deaths caused by cholera.

1853 New Orleans. Yellow fever killed 7,790 residents.

1867 New Orleans. 3,093 persons perished from yellow fever.

1878 Southern States. Over 13,000 people died from yellow fever in lower Mississippi Valley.

1916 Nationwide. Over 7,000 deaths occurred and 27,363 cases were reported in polio (infantile paralysis) in America's worst polio epidemic.

1918 March–November, Nationwide. Outbreak of influenza killed over 500,000 people in the worst single U.S. epidemic.

1949 Nationwide. 2,720 deaths occurred from polio and 42,173 cases were reported.

1952 Nationwide. Polio killed 3,300; 57,628 cases reported; worst epidemic since 1916.

1981 To present. The Center for Disease Control projects that between 330,000 to 385,000 persons in the U.S. will have died of AIDS by 1995. The CDC estimates that approximately one in 250 Americans are infected with HIV.

Floods, Avalanches, and Tidal Waves

1228 Holland: 100,000 persons reputedly drowned by sea flood in Friesland.

1642 China: rebels destroyed Kaifeng seawall; 300,000 drowned.

1896 June 15, Sanriku, Japan: earthquake and tidal wave killed 27,000.

1953 Northwest Europe: storm followed by floods devastated North Sea coastal areas. Netherlands was hardest hit with 1,794 dead.

1959 Dec. 2, Frejus, France: flood caused by collapse of Malpasset Dam left 412 dead.

1960 Agadir, Morocco: 10, 000–12,000 dead as earthquake set off tidal wave and fire, destroying most of city.

1962 Jan. 10, Peru: avalanche down Huascaran, extinct Andean volcano, killed more than 3,000 persons.

1963 Oct. 9, Italy: landslide into the Vaiont Dam; flood killed about 2,000.

1966 Oct. 21, Aberfan, Wales: avalanche of coal, waste, mud, and rocks killed 144 persons, including 116 children in school.

1969 Jan. 18–26, Southern California: floods and mudslides from heavy rains caused widespread property damage; at least 100 dead. Another downpour (Feb. 23–26) caused further floods and mudslides; at least 18 dead.

1970 Nov. 13, East Pakistan: 200,000 killed by cyclone-driven tidal wave from Bay of Bengal. Over 100,000 missing.

1972 Feb. 26, Man, W. Va.: more than 118 died when slag-pile dam collapsed under pressure of torrential rains and flooded 17-mile valley.
June 9–10, Rapid City, S.D.: flash flood caused 237 deaths and $160 million in damage.
June 20, Eastern Seaboard: tropical storm Agnes, in 10-day rampage, caused widespread flash floods. Death toll was 129, 115,000 were left homeless, and damage estimated at $3.5 billion.
1976 Aug. 1, Loveland, Colo.: Flash flood along Route 34 in Big Thompson Canyon left 139 dead.
1988 August-September, Bangladesh: Heaviest monsoon in 70 years innundates three-fourths of country, killing more than 1,300 people and leaving 30 million homeless. Damage is estimated at over $1 billion.
1993 June–August, Ill., Iowa, Kan., Ky., Minn., Mo., Neb., N.D., S.D., Wis.: Two months of heavy rain caused Mississippi River and its tributaries to flood in ten states, causing almost 50 deaths and an estimated $12 billion in damage to property and agriculture in the Midwest. Almost 70,000 people left homeless.

Tropical Storms

Cyclones, typhoons, and hurricanes are the same kind of tropical storms but are called by different names in different areas of the world. For example: a typhoon is a severe tropical hurricane that occurs in the western Pacific and China Sea.

Cyclones

1864 Oct. 5, India: most of Calcutta denuded by cyclone; 70,000 killed.
1942 Oct. 16, India: cyclone devastated Bengal; about 40,000 lives lost.
1960 Oct. 10, East Pakistan: cyclone and tidal wave killed about 6,000.
1963 May 28–29, East Pakistan: cyclone killed about 22,000 along coast.
1965 May 11–12 and June 1–2, East Pakistan: cyclones killed about 47,000.
Dec. 15, Karachi, Pakistan: cyclone killed about 10,000.
1970 Nov. 12–13, East Pakistan: cyclone and tidal waves killed 200,000 and another 100,000 were reported missing.
1971 Sept. 29, Orissa State, India: cyclone and tidal wave off Bay of Bengal killed as many as 10,000.
1974 Dec. 25, Darwin, Australia: cyclone destroyed nearly the entire city, causing mass evacuation; 50 reported dead.
1977 Nov. 19, Andhra Pradesh, India: cyclone and tidal wave claimed lives of 20,000.
1991 April 30, southeastern Bangladesh: cyclone killed over 131,000 and left as many as 9 million homeless. Thousands of survivors died from hunger and water borne disease.

U.S. Hurricanes

(U.S. deaths only, except where noted)

1775 Sept. 2–Sept. 9, North Carolina to Nova Scotia: called the "Hurricane of Independence," it is believed that 4,170 in the U.S. and Canada died in the storm.
1856 Aug. 11, Last Island, La.: 400 died.

1893 Aug. 28, Savannah, Ga., Charleston, S.C., Sea Islands, S.C.: at least 1,000 died.
1900 Aug. 27–Sept. 15, Galveston, Tex. and Texas Gulf Coast: more than 6,000 died in hurricane and tidal wave.
1909 Sept. 10–21, Louisiana and Mississippi: 350 deaths.
1915 Aug. 5–23, East Texas and Louisiana: 275 killed.
1919 Sept. 2–15, Florida, Louisiana and Texas: 287 deaths, and 488 deaths at sea.
1926 Sept. 11–22, Florida and Alabama: 243 deaths.
1928 Sept. 6–20, Southern Florida: 1,836 died and 1,870 injured.
1935 Aug. 29–Sept. 10, Southern Florida: 408 killed.
1938 Sept. 10–22, Long Island and Southern New England: 600 deaths; 1,764 injured.
1944 Sept. 9–16, North Carolina to New England: 46 deaths, and 344 deaths at sea.
1947 Sept. 4–21, Florida and Mid-Gulf Coast: 51 killed.
1954 Aug. 25–31, North Carolina to New England: "Carol" killed 60 and injured 1,000 in Long Island–New England area.
Oct. 5–18, South Carolina to New York: "Hazel" killed 95 in U.S.; about 400-1000 in Haiti; 78 in Canada.
1955 Aug. 7–21, North Carolina to New England: "Diane" took 184 lives.
1957 June 25–28, Texas to Alabama: "Audrey" wiped out Cameron, La., causing 390 deaths.
1960 Aug. 29–Sept. 13, Florida to New England: "Donna" killed 50 in the United States. 115 deaths in Antilles—mostly from flash floods in Puerto Rico.
1961 Sept. 3–15, Texas coast: "Carla" devastated Texas gulf cities, taking 46 lives.
1965 Aug. 27–Sept. 12, Southern Florida and Louisiana: "Betsy" 75 people.
1969 Aug. 14–22, Mississippi, Louisiana, Alabama, Virginia, W. Virginia: 256 killed and 68 persons missing as a result of "Camille."
1972 June 14–23, Florida to New York: "Agnes" caused 117 deaths (50 in Pennsylvania.)
1979 Aug. 25–Sept. 7, Caribbean Islands to New England: "David" caused 5 U.S. deaths; 1,200 in the Dominican Republic.
1980 Aug. 3–10, Caribbean Islands to Texas Gulf: "Allen" killed 28 in the U.S.; over 200 killed in Caribbean.
1989 Sept. 10–22, Caribbean Sea and South and North Carolina: "Hugo" claimed 49 U.S. lives (71 killed overall) and $4.2 billion were paid in insurance claims.
1992 Aug. 22–26, South Florida, Louisiana, and Bahamas: Gulf Coast Hurricane "Andrew" with damage in South Florida alone estimated at $20.6 billion (est. $7.3 billion in private insurance claims) is most costly U.S. hurricane.

Other Hurricanes

1926 Oct. 20, Cuba: worst hurricane in 80 years, 650 reported dead.
1930 Sept. 3 Santo Domingo: hurricane killed about 2,000 and injured 6,000.
1934 Sept. 21, Japan: hurricane killed more than 4,000 on Honshu.
1955 Sept. 19, Mexico: Hurricane "Hilda" took 200 lives.
Sept. 22–28, Caribbean: Hurricane "Janet" killed 200 in Honduras and 300 in Mexico.
1961 Oct. 31, British Honduras: Hurricane "Hattie" devastated capital Belize, killed at least 400.

Nuclear Power Plant Accidents

1952 Dec. 12, Chalk River, near Ottawa, Canada: A partial meltdown of the reactor's uranium fuel core resulted after the accidental removal of four control rods. Although millions of gallons of radioactive water accumulated inside the reactor, there were no injuries.

1957 Oct. 7, Windscale Pile No. 1, north of Liverpool, England: Fire in a graphite-cooled reactor spewed radiation over the countryside, contaminating a 200 sq mi area.

South Ural Mountains: Explosion of radioactive wastes at Soviet nuclear weapons factory 12 miles from city of Kyshtym forces the evacuation of over 10,000 people from a contaminated area. No casualties were reported by Soviet officials.

1976 near Greifswald, East Germany. Radioactive core of reactor in the Lubmin nuclear power plant nearly melted down due to the failure of safety systems during a fire.

1979 March 28, Three Mile Island, near Harrisburg, Pa.: One of two reactors lost its coolant, which caused the radioactive fuel to overheat and caused a partial meltdown. Some radioactive material was released.

1986 April 26, Chernobyl, near Kiev, U.S.S.R.: Explosion and fire in the graphite core of one of four reactors released radioactive material which spread over part of the Soviet Union, Eastern Europe, Scandinavia, and later Western Europe. 31 claimed dead. Total casualties are unknown and estimates run into the thousands. Is the worst such accident to date.

1963 Oct. 2–7, Caribbean: Hurricane "Flora" killed up to 7,000 in Haiti and Cuba.
1966 Sept. 24–30, Caribbean area: Hurricane "Inez" killed 293.
1974 Sept. 20, Honduras: Hurricane "Fifi" struck northern section of country, leaving 8,000 dead, 100,000 homeless.
1988 Sept. 12–17, Caribbean Sea and Gulf of Mexico: Hurricane "Gilbert," worst Atlantic storm ever recorded, took at least 260 lives and caused some 39 tornadoes in Texas.

Tornadoes

1884 Feb. 19: tornadoes in Mississippi, Alabama, North and South Carolina, Tennessee, Kentucky and Indiana caused estimated 800 deaths.
1925 Mar. 18: tornadoes in Missouri, Illinois, Indiana, Kentucky, Tennessee, and Alabama killed 792.
1932 March 21: outbreak of tornadoes in Alabama, Mississippi, Georgia, and Tennessee killed 268.
1936 April 5–6: series of tornadoes in Arkansas, Alabama, Tennessee, Georgia, and South Carolina killed 498.
1952 March 21–22: tornadoes in Arkansas, Tennessee, Missouri, Mississippi, Alabama, and Kentucky caused 343 deaths.
1953 May 11: a single tornado struck Wako, Texas, killing 114.
June 8: another tornado killed 116 in Flint, Michigan.
1965 April 11: Tornadoes in Iowa, Illinois, Indiana, Ohio, Michigan, and Wisconsin caused 256 deaths.
1974 April 3–4: a series of tornadoes in East, South, and Midwest killed approximately 315.

Typhoons

1906 Sept. 18, Hong Kong: typhoon with tsunami killed an estimated 10,000 persons.
1949 Dec. 5, Off Korea: typhoon struck fishing fleet; several thousand men reported dead.
1959 Aug. 20, Fukien Province, China: Typhoon "Iris" killed 2,334.
Sept. 27, Honshu, Japan: Typhoon "Vera" killed an estimated 4,464.
1960 June 9, Fukien Province, China: Typhoon "Mary" caused at least 1,600 deaths.

1984 Sept. 2–3, Philippines: Typhoon "Ike" hit seven major islands leaving 1,300 dead.
1991 Nov. 5, Central Philippines: Flash floods triggered by tropical storm "Thelma" killed about 3,000 people. Leyte city of Ormoc was worst hit.

Fires and Explosions

1666 Sept. 2, England: "Great Fire of London" destroyed St. Paul's Church, etc. Damage £10 million.
1835 Dec. 16, New York City: 530 buildings destroyed by fire.
1871 Oct. 8, Chicago: the "Chicago Fire" burned 17,450 buildings, killed 250 persons; $196 million damage.
1872 Nov. 9, Boston: fire destroyed 800 buildings; $75-million damage.
1876 Dec. 5, New York City: fire in Brooklyn Theater killed more than 300.
1881 Dec. 8, Vienna: at least 620 died in fire at Ring Theatre.
1894 Sept. 1, Minnesota: forest fire over 480-square-mile area destroyed six towns and killed 480 people.
1900 May 1, Scofield, Utah: explosion of blasting powder in coal mine killed 200.
June 30, Hoboken, N.J.: piers of North German Lloyd Steamship line burned; 326 dead.
1903 Dec. 30, Chicago: Iroquois Theatre fire killed 602.
1906 March 10, France: explosion in coal mine in Courrières killed 1,060.
1907 Dec. 19, Jacobs Creek, Pa.: explosion in coal mine left 239 dead.
1909 Nov. 13, Cherry, Ill.: explosion in coal mine killed 259.
1911 March 25, New York City: fire in Triangle Shirtwaist Factory fatal to 145.
1913 Oct. 22, Dawson, N.M.: coal mine explosion left 263 dead.
1917 April 10, Eddystone, Pa.: explosion in munitions plant killed 133.
Dec. 6, Canada: 1,600 people died when French ammunition ship *Mont Blanc* collided with Belgium steamer in Halifax Harbor.
1930 April 21, Columbus, Ohio: fire in Ohio State Penitentiary killed 320 convicts.

1937 March 18, New London, Tex.: explosion destroyed schoolhouse; 294 killed.

1942 April 26, Manchuria: explosion in Honkeiko Colliery killed 1,549.

Nov. 28, Boston: Cocoanut Grove nightclub fire killed 491.

1944 July 6, Hartford, Conn.: fire and ensuing stampede in main tent of Ringling Brothers Circus killed 168, injured 487.

July 17, Port Chicago, Calif.: 322 killed as ammunition ships explode.

Oct. 20, Cleveland: liquid-gas tanks exploded, killing 130.

1946 Dec. 7, Atlanta: fire in Winecoff Hotel killed 119.

1948 Dec. 3, Shanghai: Chinese passenger ship *Kiangya*, carrying refugees fleeing Communist troops during civil war, struck an old mine, exploded, and sank off Shanghai. Over 3,000 people are believed killed.

1949 Sept. 2, China: fire on Chongqing (Chungking) waterfront killed 1,700.

1954 May 26, off Quonset Point, R.I.: explosion and fire aboard aircraft carrier *Bennington* killed 103 crewmen.

1956 Aug. 7, Colombia: about 1,100 reported killed when seven army ammunition trucks exploded at Cali.

Aug. 8, Belgium: 262 died in coal mine fire at Marcinelle.

1960 Jan. 21, Coalbrook, South Africa: coal mine explosion killed 437.

Nov. 13, Syria: 152 children killed in moviehouse fire.

1961 Dec. 17, Niteroi, Brazil: circus fire fatal to 323.

1962 Feb. 7, Saarland, West Germany: coal mine gas explosion killed 298.

1963 Nov. 9, Japan: explosion in coal mine at Omuta killed 447.

1965 May 28, India: coal mine fire in state of Bihar killed 375.

June 1, near Fukuoka, Japan: coal mine explosion killed 236.

1967 May 22, Brussels: fire in L'Innovation, major department store, left 322 dead.

July 29, off North Vietnam: fire on U.S. carrier *Forrestal* killed 134.

1969 Jan. 14, Pearl Harbor, Hawaii: nuclear aircraft carrier *Enterprise* ripped by explosions; 27 dead, 82 injured.

1970 Nov. 1, Saint-Laurent-du-Pont, France: fire in dance hall killed 146 young people.

1972 May 13, Osaka, Japan: 118 people died in fire in nightclub on top floor of Sennichi department store.

June 6, Wankie, Rhodesia: explosion in coal mine killed 427.

1973 Nov. 29, Kumamoto, Japan: fire in Taiyo department store killed 101.

1974 Feb. 1, Sao Paulo, Brazil: fire in upper stories of bank building killed 189 persons, many of whom leaped to death.

1975 Dec. 27, Dhanbad, India: explosion in coal mine followed by flooding from nearby reservoir left 372 dead.

1977 May 28, Southgate, Ky.: fire in Beverly Hills Supper Club; 167 dead.

1978 July 11, Tarragona, Spain: 140 killed at coastal campsite when tank truck carrying liquid gas overturned and exploded.

Aug. 20, Abadan, Iran: nearly 400 killed when arsonists set fire to crowded theater.

1982 Dec. 18–21, Caracas, Venezuela: power-plant fire leaves 128 dead.

1986 Dec. 31, San Juan, P. R.: arson fire in Dupont Plaza Hotel set by three hotel employees kills 96.

1989 June 3, Ural Mountains: Liquified petroleum gas leaking from a pipeline running alongside the Trans-Siberian railway near Uta, 720 miles east of Moscow, exploded and destroyed two passing passenger trains. About 500 travelers were killed and 723 injured of an estimated 1,200 passengers on both trains.

Oct. 23, Pasadena, Texas. A huge explosion followed by a series of others and a raging fire at a plastics manufacturing plant owned by Phillips Petroleum Co. killed 22 and injured more than 80 persons. A large leak of ethylene was presumed to be the cause.

1990 March 25, New York City. Arson fire in illegal *Happy Land Social Club*, Bronx, killed 87.

1991 Oct. 20–23, Oakland–Berkeley, Calif.: Brush fire in drought-stricken area destroyed over 3,000 homes and apartments. At least 24 persons died, damage estimated at $1.5 billion.

1993 May 10 near Bangkok, Thailand: Fire in doll factory killed at least 187 persons and injured 500 others. Is world's deadliest factory fire.

Shipwrecks

1833 May 11, *Lady of the Lake:* bound from England to Quebec, struck iceberg; 215 perished.

1853 Sept. 29 *Annie Jane:* emigrant vessel off coast of Scotland; 348 died.

1898 Nov. 26, *City of Portland:* Loss of 157 off Cape Cod.

1904 June 15, *General Slocum:* excursion steamer burned in East River, New York; 1,021 perished.

1912 March 5, *Principe de Asturias:* Spanish steamer struck rock off Sebastien Point; 500 drowned.

April 15, *Titanic:* sank after colliding with iceberg; 1,513 died.

1914 May 29, *Empress of Ireland:* sank after collision in St. Lawrence River; 1,024 perished.

1915 July 24, *Eastland:* Great Lakes excursion steamer overturned in Chicago River; 812 died.

1928 Nov. 12, *Vestris:* British steamer sank in gale off Virginia; 110 died.

1934 Sept. 8, *Morro Castle:* 134 killed in fire off Asbury Park, N.J.

1939 May 23, *Squalus:* submarine with 59 men sank off Hampton Beach, N.H.; 33 saved.

June 1, Submarine *Thetis:* sank in Liverpool Bay, England; 99 perished.

1942 Oct. 2, *Queen Mary:* rammed and sank a British cruiser; 338 aboard the cruiser died.

1945 April 9: U.S. ship, loaded with aerial bombs, exploded at Bari, Italy; at least 360 killed.

1947 November, Yingkow: Unidentified Chinese troopship evacuating Nationalist troops from Manchuria sank, killing an estimated 6,000 persons.

1949 Sept. 17, *Noronic:* Canadian Great Lakes cruise ship burned at Toronto dock; about 130 died.

1952 April 26, *Hobson:* minesweeper collided with aircraft carrier *Wasp* and sank during night maneuvers in mid-Atlantic; 176 persons lost.

1953 Jan. 9, *Chang Tyong-Ho:* South Korean ferry foundered off Pusan; 249 reported dead.

Jan. 31, *Princess Victoria:* British ferry sank in Irish Sea; 133 lost.

1956 **July 25, *Andrea Doria:*** Italian liner collided with Swedish liner *Stockholm* off Nantucket Island, Mass., sinking next day; 52, mostly passengers on Italian ship, dead or unaccounted for; over 1,600 rescued.

1962 **April 8, *Dara,*** British liner, exploded and sank in Persian Gulf; 236 persons dead. Caused by time bomb.

1963 **May 4:** U.A.R. ferry capsized and sank in upper Nile; over 200 died.

1968 **Late May, *Scorpion:*** nuclear submarine sank in Atlantic 400 miles S.W. of Azores; 99 dead. (Located Oct. 31.)

1970 **Dec. 15:** ferry in Korean Strait capsized; 261 lost.

1976 **Oct. 20, Luling, La.; *George Prince,*** Mississippi River ferry, rammed by Norwegian tanker *Frosta;* 77 dead.

1983 **May 25, *10th of Ramadan,*** Nile steamer, caught fire and sank in Lake Nasser, near Aswan, Egypt; 272 dead and 75 missing.

1987 **March 9, Belgium:** British ferry capsizes after leaving Belgian port of Zeebrugge with 500 aboard; 134 drowned. Water rushing through open bow is believed to be probable cause.

1987 **Dec. 20. Manila:** Over 1,500 people killed when passenger ferry *Dona Paz* collided with oil tanker *Victor* off Mindoro Is., 110 miles south of Manila.

1990 **April 7, Skagerrak Strait off Norway.** Suspected arson fire aboard Danish-owned North Sea ferry, *Scandinavian Star,* kills at least 110 passengers.

April 7, Myanmar (Burma). Double-decker ferry sinks in Gyaing River during a storm and 215 persons are believed drowned.

1991 **Dec. 14, off coast of Safaga, Egypt:** Ferry carrying 569 passengers sank in Red Sea after hitting a coral reef. Over 460 people believed drowned.

1993 **Feb. 17, off southern peninsula, Haiti:** Triple-deck ferry *Neptune* capsized during a squall. Over 1,000 passengers believed drowned. About 300 survived the sinking.

1994 **Sept. 28, off coast of southwest Finland:** Passenger ferry *Estonia* capsized and sank in a stormy Baltic Sea. Only about 140 of the estimated 1,040 passengers aboard survived.

Mysterious Disappearances

1872 The brigantine *Mary Celeste* set sail from New York harbor for Genoa, Italy, on November 5. A British brigantine, the *DeGratia,* discovered the ship derelict on December 5 and boarded her. Everyone aboard the *Mary Celeste* had vanished—her captain, his family, and its 14-man crew. The ship was in perfect order with ample supplies and there was no sign of violence or trouble. The fate of the crew remains unknown today.

1928 **Dec. 22:** The five-masted Danish steel barque *Köbenhavn,* a sail-training ship with a crew of 75 including 45 boy cadets, sailed from the River Plate for Melbourne, Australia, on December 14. The last radio contact with the ship was made on December 22 and all was well. The *Köbenhavn* and its crew disappeared without a trace and no one knows what happened to it.

Aircraft Accidents
(150 deaths or more, with exceptions)

1921 **Aug. 24, England:** *AR-2* British dirigible, broke in two on trial trip near Hull; 62 died.

1925 **Sept. 3, Caldwell, Ohio:** U.S. dirigible *Shenandoah* broke apart; 14 dead.

1930 **Oct. 5, Beauvais, France:** British dirigible R 101 crashed, killing 47.

1933 **April 4, New Jersey Coast:** U.S. dirigible *Akron* crashed; 73 died.

1937 **May 6, Lakehurst, N.J.:** German zeppelin *Hindenburg* destroyed by fire at tower mooring; 36 killed.

1945 **July 28, New York City:** U.S. Army bomber crashed into Empire State Building; 13 dead.

1960 **Dec. 16, New York City:** United and Trans World planes collided in fog, crashed in two boroughs, killing 134 in air and on ground.

1961 **Feb. 15, near Brussels:** 72 on board and farmer on ground killed in crash of Sabena plane; U.S. figure skating team wiped out.

1966 **Dec. 24, Binh Thai, South Vietnam:** crash of military-chartered plane into village killed 129.

1971 **July 30, Morioka, Japan:** Japanese Boeing 727 and F-86 fighter collided in mid-air; toll was 162.

1972 **Aug. 14, East Berlin, East Germany:** Soviet-built East German Ilyushin plane crashed, killing 156.
Dec. 3, Santa Cruz de Tenerife, Canary Islands: Spanish charter jet carrying West German tourists crashed on take-off; all 155 aboard killed.

1973 **Jan. 22, Kano, Nigeria:** 171 Nigerian Moslems returning from Mecca and five crewmen died in crash.

1973 **Feb. 21:** Civilian Libyan Arab Airlines Boeing 727 shot down by Israeli fighters over Sinai after it had strayed off course; 108 died, five survived. Officials claimed that the pilot had ignored fighters' warnings to land.

1974 **March 3, Paris:** Turkish DC-10 jumbo jet crashed in forest shortly after take-off; all 346 passengers and crew killed.
Dec. 4, Colombo, Sri Lanka: Dutch DC-8 carrying Moslems to Mecca crashed on landing approach, killing all 191 persons aboard.

1975 **April 4, near Saigon, Vietnam:** Air Force Galaxy C-5A crashed after take-off, killing 172, mostly Vietnamese children.
Aug. 3, Agadir, Morocco: Chartered Boeing 707, returning Moroccan workers home after vacation in France, plunged into mountainside; all 188 aboard killed.

1976 **Sept. 10, Zagreb, Yugoslavia:** midair collision between British Airways Trident and Yugoslav charter DC-9 fatal to all 176 persons aboard; worst mid-air collision on record.

1977 **March 27, Santa Cruz de Tenerife, Canary Islands:** Pan American and KLM Boeing 747s collided on runway. All 249 on KLM plane and 333 of 394 aboard Pan Am jet killed. Total of 582 is highest for any type of aviation disaster.

1978 **Jan. 1, Bombay:** Air India 747 with 213 aboard exploded and plunged into sea minutes after takeoff.
Sept. 25, San Diego, Calif.: Pacific Southwest plane collided in midair with Cessna. All 135 on airliner, 2 in Cessna, and 7 on ground killed for total of 144.
Nov. 15, Colombo, Sri Lanka: Chartered Icelandic Airlines DC-8, carrying 249 Moslem pilgrims from Mecca, crashed in thunderstorm during landing approach; 183 killed.

Space Accidents

1967 Jan. 27, Apollo 1: A fire aboard the space capsule on the ground at Cape Kennedy, Fla. killed astronauts Virgil I. Grissom, Edward H. White, and Roger Chaffee.
April 23–24, Soyuz 1: Vladimir M. Komarov was killed when his craft crashed after its parachute lines, released at 23,000 feet for re-entry, became snarled.
1971 June 6–30, Soyuz 11: Three cosmonauts, Georgi T. Dolrovolsky, Vladislav N. Volkov, and Viktor I. Patsayev, found dead in the craft after its automatic landing. Apparently the cause of death was loss of pressurization in the space craft during re-entry

into the earth's atmosphere.
1980 March 18, U.S.S.R. A Vostok rocket exploded on its launch pad while being refueled, killing 50 at the Plesetsk Space Center.
1986 Jan 28, Challenger Space Shuttle: Exploded 73 seconds after lift off, killing all seven crew members. They were: Christa McAuliffe, Francis R. Scobee, Michael J. Smith, Judith A. Resnick, Ronald E. McNair, Ellison S. Onizuka, and Gregory B. Jarvis. A booster leak ignited the fuel, causing the explosion.

1979 Nov. 26, Jidda, Saudi Arabia: Pakistan International Airlines 707 carrying pilgrims returning from Mecca crashed on take-off; all 156 aboard killed.
Nov. 28, Mt. Erebus, Antarctica: Air New Zealand DC-10 crashed on sightseeing flight; 257 killed.
1980 March 14, Warsaw: LOT Polish Airlines Ilyushin 62 crashed while attempting landing; 22 boxers and officials of a U.S. amateur boxing team killed along with 65 others.
Aug. 19, Riyadh, Saudi Arabia: all 301 aboard Saudi Arabian jet killed when burning plane made safe landing but passengers were unable to escape.
1981 Dec. 1, Ajaccio, Corsica: Yugoslav DC-9 Super 80 carrying tourists crashed into mountain on landing approach, killing all 178 aboard.
1983 Aug. 30, near island of Sakhalin off Siberia, South Korean civilian jetliner Boeing 747, flight KAL-007 shot down by Soviet fighter after it strayed off course into Soviet airspace. All 269 people aboard killed.

Secret Soviet documents released in October 1992, revealed that the plane was flying a straight course for two hours with its navigational lights on, it did not take evasive action, its crew members were unaware of its location, they never saw the Soviet fighter that shot them down and the Soviet fighter did not give a warning by firing tracer bullets as originally claimed. Recorded conversations indicated that the crew did not know what hit them.
Nov. 26, Madrid: A Columbian Avianca Boeing 747 crashed near Mejorada del Campó Airport killing 183 persons aboard. Eleven people survived the accident.
1985 June 23: Air-India Boeing 747 exploded over the Atlantic off the coast of Ireland, all 329 aboard killed.
Aug. 12, Japan Air Lines Boeing 747 crashed into a mountain, killing 520 of the 524 aboard.
Dec. 12, A chartered Arrow Air DC-8, bringing American soldiers home for Christmas, crashed on takeoff from Gander, Newfoundland. All 256 aboard died.
1987 May 9, Poland: Polish airliner, Ilyushin 62M on charter flight to New York, crashes after takeoff from Warsaw killing 183.

Aug. 16, Detroit: Northwest Airlines McDonnell Douglas MD-30 plunges to heavily traveled boulevard, killing 156. Girl 4, only survivor.
Nov. 26: South African Airways Boeing 747 goes down south of Mauritius in rough seas; 160 die.
Nov. 29: Korean Air Boeing 747 jetliner explodes from bomb planted by North Korean agents and crashes into sea off Burma, killing all 115 aboard.
1988 July 3, Persian Gulf: U.S. Navy cruiser *Vincennes* shot down Iran Air A300 Airbus, killing 290 persons, after mistaking it for an attacking jet fighter.
Aug. 28, Ramstein Air Force Base, West Germany: Three jets from Italian Air Force acr obatic team collided in mid-air during air show and crashed, killing 70 persons, including the pilots and spectators on the ground. It is worst air-show disaster in history.
Dec. 21, Lockerbie, Scotland: A New-York-bound Pan-Am Boeing 747 exploded in flight from a terrorist bomb and crashed into Scottish village, killing all 259 aboard and 11 persons on the ground. Passengers included 38 Syracuse University students and many U.S. military personnel.
1989 June 7, Paramaribo, Suriname: A Surinam Airways DC-8 carrying 174 passengers and nine crew members crashed into the jungle while making a third attempt to land in a thick fog, killing 168 aboard.
1991 July 11, Jedda, Saudi Arabia: Canadian-chartered DC-8 carrying pilgrims returning to Nigeria crashes after takeoff, killing 261 persons.
1994 April 14, northern Iraq: Two American F-15C fighter aircraft mistake two U.S. Army Blackhawk helicopters for Russian-made Iraqi MI-24 helicopters and shot them down over no-fly zone, killing all 26 on board them.
April 26, Nagoya, Japan: A China Airlines A-300 Airbus crash-landed and exploded on the tarmac. Only 7 of the 271 passengers aboard survived.
June 6, Xian, China: A Russian-built Tupolev-154 airliner of China Northwest Airlines crashed 10 minutes after takeoff, killing all 160 aboard.

Railroad Accidents

NOTE: Very few passengers were killed in a single U.S. train wreck up until 1853. These early trains ran slowly, made short trips, night travel was rare, and there were not many of them in operation.

1831 June 17: The boiler exploded on America's first passenger locomotive, *The Best Friend of Charleston,* killing the fireman. He was the first person in America to be killed in a railroad accident.

1833 Nov. 8, near Heightstown, N.J.: the world's first train wreck and the first passenger fatalities recorded. A 24-passenger Camden & Amboy train was derailed due to a broken axle, killing two passengers and injuring all others. Former president, John Quincy Adams and Cornelius Vanderbilt, who later made a fortune in railroads, were aboard the train.

1853 May 6, Norwalk, Conn: a New Haven Railroad train ran through an open drawbridge and plunged into the Norwalk River. Forty-six passengers were crushed to death or drowned. This was the first major drawbridge accident.

1856 July 17, Camp Hill, Pa.: two Northern Penn trains crashed head-on. Sixty-six church school children bound for a picnic died in the flaming wreckage.

1876 Dec. 29, Ashtabula, Ohio: a Lake Shore train fell into the Ashtabula River when a bridge it was crossing collapsed during a snowstorm. Ninety-two were killed.

1887 Aug. 10, near Chatsworth, Ill.: a burning railroad trestle collapsed while a Toledo, Peoria & Western train was crossing, killing 81 and injuring 372.

1904 Aug. 7, Eden, Colo.: Train derailed on bridge during flash flood; 96 killed.

1910 March 1, Wellington, Wash.: two trains swept into canyon by avalanche; 96 dead.

1915 May 22, Gretna, Scotland: two passenger trains and troop train collided; 227 killed.

1917 Dec. 12, Modane, France: nearly 550 killed in derailment of troop train near mouth of Mt. Cenis tunnel.

1918 Nov. 1, New York City: derailment of subway train in Malbone St. tunnel in Brooklyn left 92 dead.

1926 March 14, Virilla River Canyon, Costa Rica: An over-crowded train carrying pilgrims was derailed while crossing the Colima Bridge, killing over 300 people and injuring hundreds more.

1939 Dec. 22, near Magdeburg, Germany: more than 125 killed in collision; 99 killed in another wreck near Friedrichshafen.

1943 Dec. 16, near Rennert, N.C.: 72 killed in derailment and collision of two Atlantic Coast Line trains.

1944 March 2, near Salerno, Italy: 521 suffocated when Italian train stalled in tunnel.

1949 Oct. 22, near Nowy Dwor, Poland: more than 200 reported killed in derailment of Danzig-Warsaw express.

1950 Nov. 22, Richmond Hill, N.Y.: 79 died when one Long Island Rail Road commuter train crashed into rear of another.

1951 Feb. 6, Woodbridge, N.J.: 85 died when Pennsylvania Railroad commuter train plunged through temporary overpass.

1952 Oct. 8, Harrow-Wealdstone, England: two express trains crashed into commuter train; 112 dead.

1953 Dec. 24, near Sakvice, Czechoslovakia: two trains crashed; over 100 dead.

1957 Sept. 1, near Kendal, Jamaica: about 175 killed when train plunged into ravine.

Sept. 29, near Montgomery, West Pakistan: express train crashed into standing oil train; nearly 300 killed.

Dec. 4, St. John's, England: 92 killed, 187 injured as one commuter train crashed into another in fog.

1960 Nov. 14, Pardubice, Czechoslovakia: two trains collided; 110 dead, 106 injured.

1962 May 3, near Tokyo: 163 killed and 400 injured when train crashed into wreckage of collision between inbound freight train and outbound commuter train.

1963 Nov. 9, near Yokohama, Japan: two passenger trains crashed into derailed freight, killing 162.

1964 July 26, Custoias, Portugal: passenger train derailed; 94 dead.

1970 Feb. 4, near Buenos Aires: 236 killed when express train crashed into standing commuter train.

1972 July 21, Seville, Spain: head-on crash of two passenger trains killed 76.

Oct. 6, near Saltillo, Mexico: train carrying religious pilgrims derailed and caught fire, killing 204 and injuring over 1,000.

Oct. 30, Chicago: two Illinois Central commuter trains collided during morning rush hour; 45 dead and over 200 injured.

1974 Aug. 30, Zagreb, Yugoslavia: train entering station derailed, killing 153 and injuring over 60.

1981 June 6, Near Mansi, India: Driver of train carrying over 500 passengers, braked to avoid hitting cow, causing train to plunge off a bridge into Baghmati River; 268 passengers were reported killed, but at least 300 more were missing.

1982 July 11, Tepic, Mexico: Nogales-Guadalajara train plunges down mountain gorge killing 120.

1989 Jan. 15, Maizdi Khan, Bangladesh: A train carrying Muslim pilgrims crashed head-on with a mail train killing at least 110 persons and injuring as many as 1,000. Many people were riding on the roof of the trains and between the cars.

1989 Aug. 10, near Los Mochis, Mexico: A second-class passenger train traveling from Mazatlán to Mexicali, plunged off a bridge at Puente del Rio Bamoa into the river and killed an estimated 85 people and injured 107.

1990 Jan. 4, Sangi village, Sindh province, Pakistan: An overcrowded sixteen-car passenger train was switched to the wrong track and rammed into a standing freight train. At least 210 persons were killed and 700 were believed injured in what is said to be Pakistan's worst train disaster.

1993 Sept. 22, near Mobile, Ala.: Amtrak's Sunset Limited, enroute to Miami, jumps rails on weakened bridge that had been damaged by a barge, and plunges into Big Bayou Canot, killing 47 persons.

Oil Spills

1978 March 16, off Portsall, France: Wrecked supertanker *Amoco Cadiz* spilled 68 million gallons causing widespread environmental damage over 100 miles of coast of Brittany. Is world's largest tanker disaster.

1979 June 8, Gulf of Mexico: Exploratory oil well, Ixtoc 1, blew out, spilling an estimated 140 million gallons of crude into the open sea. Although it is the largest known oil spill, it had a low environmental impact.

1989 Dec. 19. Off Las Palmas, the Canary Islands. An explosion in Iranian supertanker, the *Kharg-5*, tore through its hull and caused 19 million gallons of crude oil to spill out into the Atlantic Ocean about 400 miles north of Las Palmas, forming a 100-square-mile oil slick.

1994 Aug. 12, near Ursinsk, Russia: Huge oil spill from ruptured pipeline. September 8: a dam built to contain oil bursts spilled oil into tributary of Kolva River. U.S. Energy Department estimates spill at 2 million barrels. Russian state-owned oil company claims spill was only 102,000 barrels.

Wartime Spills

1991 Jan. 25, Southern Kuwait: during the Persian Gulf War, Iraq deliberately released an estimated 460 million gallons of crude oil into the Persian Gulf from tankers at Mina al-Ahmadi and Sea Island Terminal 10 miles off Kuwait. Spill had little military significance. On Jan. 27, U.S. warplanes bombed pipe systems to stop the flow of oil.

Sports

1955 June 11, Le Mans, France: Racing car in Grand Prix hurtled into grandstand, killing 82 spectators.

1964 May 24, Lima, Peru: More than 300 soccer fans killed and over 500 injured during riot and panic following unpopular ruling by referee in Peru vs. Argentina soccer game. It is worst soccer disaster on record.

1971 Jan. 2, Glasgow, Scotland: Sixty-six persons killed in a crush at the Glasgow Rangers home stadium when fans trying to leave encountered fans trying to return to the stadium after hearing that a late goal had been scored.

1982 Oct. 20, Moscow: According to *Sovietsky Sport*, as many as 340 persons were killed at Lenin Stadium when exiting soccer fans collided with returning fans after final goal was scored. All the fans had been crowded into one section of stadium by police.

1985 May 11, Bradford, England: 56 persons burned to death and over 200 injured when fire engulfed the main grandstand at Bradford's soccer stadium.

May 29, Brussels, Belgium: Drunken group of British soccer fans supporting Liverpool club stormed stand filled with Italian supporters of Juventus team before European Champion's Cup final. While British fans attacked rival spectators at the Heysel Stadium, concrete retaining wall collapsed and 39 persons were crushed or trampled to death, 32 of them Italians. More than 400 persons were injured.

1988 March 12, Katmandu, Nepal: Some 80 soccer fans seeking cover during a violent hail storm at the national stadium were trampled to death in a stampede because the stadium doors were locked.

1989 April 15, Sheffield, England: Ninety-four people were killed and 170 injured at Hillsborough stadium when throngs of Liverpool soccer fans, many without tickets, collapsed a stadium barrier in a mad rush to see the game between Liverpool and Nottingham Forest. It was Britain's worst soccer disaster.

Terrorist Attacks in U.S.

1920 Sept. 16, New York City: TNT bomb planted in unattended horse-drawn wagon exploded on Wall Street opposite House of Morgan, killing 35 persons and injuring hundreds more. Bolshevist or anarchist terrorists believed responsible but crime never solved.

1975 Jan. 24, New York City: Bomb set off in historical Fraunces Tavern killed four and injured more than 50 persons. Puerto Rican nationalist group (FALN) claimed responsibility and police tied 13 other bombings to them.

Dec. 29, New York City: Bomb exploded in locker area of main terminal at La Guardia Airport, killing 11 persons and injuring 75 others. Puerto Rican nationalist group (FALN) was the prime suspect.

1993 Feb. 26, New York City: Bomb exploded in basement garage of World Trade Center; killed 6 persons and injured at least 1,040 others.

Miscellaneous

1958 January–October, Austria, France, Germany, Italy, and Switzerland: 283 people were killed in mountain climbing accidents in Alps Mountains.

1980 Jan. 20, Sincelejo, Colombia: Bleachers at a bullring collapsed, leaving 222 dead.

March 30, Stavanger, Norway: Floating hotel in North Sea collapsed, killing 123 oil workers.

1981 July 18, Kansas City, Mo.: suspended walkway in Hyatt Regency Hotel collapses; 113 dead, 186 injured.

1984 Dec. 3, Bhopal, India: Toxic gas, methyl isocyanate, seeped from Union Carbide insecticide plant, killing more than 2,000; injuring about 150,000.

1987 Sept. 18. Goiânia, Brazil: 244 people contaminated with cesium-137 removed from steel cyclinder taken from cancer-therapy machine in abandoned clinic and sold as scrap. Four people died in worst radiation disaster in Western Hemisphere.

1988 July 6, North Sea off Scotland: 166 workers killed in explosion and fire on Occidental Petroleum's Piper Alpha rig in North Sea off Scottish coast; 64 survivors rescued. It is the world's worst offshore oil disaster.

1990 July 2, Mecca, Saudi Arabia: a stampede in a 1,800 foot-long pedestrian tunnel leading from Mecca to a tent city for pilgrims, killed 1,426 pilgrims who were trampled to death.

1991 Nov. 29, near Coalinga, Calif.: A massive traffic accident occurred during a severe dust storm involving 104 vehicles in a pileup on Interstate 5; 17 persons killed.

1993 April 19, Waco, Texas: A 51-day stalemate between B.A.T.F. and F.B.I. agents seeking to investigate child abuse charges and members of the Christian Branch Davidian cult ended in a fiery tragedy after Federal agents botched their assault on the sect's compound. Earlier, on February 28, four Federal agents were shot to death in a failed attack on the heavily armed compound. About 80 Branch Davidians, including at least 17 children, died when the compound burned to the ground in a suspicious blaze. Child abuse charges weere never proven and jurors at criminal trial of surviving cult members were unable to determine who fired first shot on February 28. Surviving Davidians dispute the Government's version of how the cult members died.

1995 June 29, Seoul, Korea: Five-story wing of Sampoong Department Store collapsed, killing at least 206 people, injuring 910 others, with over 230 missing (as of mid-July).

Wartime Disasters

1915 May 6: Despite German warnings in newspapers, the Cunard Liner *Lusitania* sailed from New York for Liverpool, England, on May 1st and was sunk off the coast of Ireland by a German submarine. 1,198 passengers and crew, 128 of them Americans, died. Unknown to the passengers, the ship was carrying a cargo of small arms. The disaster contributed to the entry of the United States into World War I.

1916 Feb. 26: 3,100 people died when the French cruiser *Provence* was sunk by a German submarine in the Mediterranean.

1940 Sept. 13. The luxury liner *S.S. City of Benares* sailed from Liverpool with over 90 British children who were being evacuated to Canada to escape harm during World War II. About 600 miles out to sea, the ship was torpedoed by a German submarine during the night and only 13 of the children survived the disaster.[1]

1941 Dec. 7, Pearl Harbor, Hawaii: 1,177 crewmen were killed when U.S. Battleship *Arizona* was sunk during a surprise attack on the American naval base by Japanese warplanes. The devastating air strike, which damaged or destroyed the ships of the entire battleship force of the U.S. Pacific fleet, was the worst naval catastrophe in U.S. history.

1943 Nov. 26, Mediterranean Sea: 1,015 U.S. soldiers died when the British troopship *HMT Rohna*, was sunk by a German air-to-surface guided missile. It is the worst U.S. troopship disaster.

Dec., Bari Harbor, Italy: U.S. ship, damaged during German bombing attack, leaked mustard gas into harbor, killing 83 U.S. servicemen and nearly 1,000 civilians.

1944 Sept. 12, South China Sea: U.S. submarines torpedoed and sank two Japanese troop ships[2], the *Kachidoki Maru* and the *Rakuyo Maru*. Unknown to the submarines, the Japanese, in disregard for the rules of treatment of prisoners of war, had forced 2,000 British, Australian, and American POWs into the holds of the ships which were designed to hold only 300 troops. Later, when the subs discovered the tragedy, they sought to rescue as many survivors as possible. Japanese vessels picked up most of *Kachidoki Maru*'s prisoners but abandoned those

from the *Rakuyo Maru*, taking only the Japanese survivors. Of the 1,300 POWs aboard the *Rakuyo Maru*, 159 were rescued, but only seven lived.

Oct. 24, South China Sea: The *Arisan Maru*[2] carrying 1,800 American prisoners was torpedoed by a U.S. submarine and sunk. The Japanese destroyer escort rescued Japanese military and civilian personnel and left the POWs to their fate. It is estimated that only ten prisoners survived the disaster.

Dec. 17–18, Philippine Sea: A typhoon struck U.S. Third Fleet's Task Force 38, sank three destroyers, damaged seven other ships, destroyed 186 aircraft, and killed 800 officers and men.

1945 Jan. 30: 7,700 persons died in world's largest marine disaster when the Nazi passenger ship *Wilhelm Gustoff* car rying Germans fleeing Poland was torpedoed in the Baltic by a Soviet submarine.

May 3, *Cap Arcona*: Several days before World War II ended in Europe, the German passenger ship carrying about 6,000, of which an estimated 5,000 were concentration camp prisoners, was sunk by British aircraft. An estimated 5,000 persons were killed, most of them prisoners who were about to gain their freedom.

May 4, Gearhart Mountain, south-central Oregon: Six picnicking persons, including a mother and her unborn child, were the only persons ever killed by an exploding baloon-carried bomb launched from Japan. During war, Japan launched some six thousand FUGO ("windship weapons") balloons to drift across the Pacific to the U.S. and Canada, each carrying bombs and incendiaries for starting forest fires and creating death and havoc among the American people. Although over 200 of the deadly balloons floated to the U.S. before the war ended, the government kept it a secret from the American people.

July 29, near Leyte Gulf: The heavy cruiser *Indianapolis* was torpedoed and sunk by a Japanese submarine before the ship could send an SOS for help. Of the crew of 1,199 men, only 316 survived. Due to Navy blundering, the warship was not reported missing when it did not arrive at Leyte on July 31 as scheduled and therefore no search was made for its crew. The survivors were discovered by a Navy patrol plane 82 hours after the ship had gone down.

1991 February, Kuwait: during the Persian Gulf War, Iraqi troops systematically dynamited and set fire to 650 of Kuwait's 950 oil wells, causing the world's worst man-made environmental disaster. A total of 749 wells were damaged including those set ablaze. The last of the oil fires was extinguished on Nov. 6, 1991.

---

1. During the war (1939-1945), some 10,000 children were evacuated to stay with foster parents in the United States and Canada. The sinking of the *City of Benares* ended the British government's evacuation program.
2. The ships had no identification that they were transporting prisioners of war.

RELIGION

Major Religions of the World

Judaism

The determining factors of Judaism are: descendance from Israel, the *Torah,* and Tradition.

The name Israel (Jacob, a patriarch) also signifies his descendants as a people. During the 15th–13th centuries B.C., Israelite tribes, coming from South and East, gradually settled in Palestine, then inhabited by Canaanites. They were held together by Moses, who gave them religious unity in the worship of *Jahweh,* the God who had chosen Israel to be his people.

Under Judges, the 12 tribes at first formed an amphictyonic covenant. Saul established kingship (circa 1050 B.C.), and under David, his successor (1000–960 B.C.), the State of Israel comprised all of Palestine with Jerusalem as religio-political center. A golden era followed under Solomon (965–926 B.C.), who built *Jahweh* a temple.

After Solomon's death, the kingdom separated into Israel in the North and Judah in the South. A period of conflicts ensued, which ended with the conquest of Israel by Assyria in 722 B.C. The Babylonians defeated Judah in 586 B.C., destroying Jerusalem and its temple, and deporting many to Babylon.

The era of the kings is significant also in that the great prophets worked in that time, emphasizing faith in *Jahweh* as both God of Israel and God of the universe, and stressing social justice.

When the Persians permitted the Jews to return from exile (539 B.C.), temple and cult were restored in Jerusalem. The Persian rulers were succeeded by the Seleucides. The Maccabaean revolt against these Hellenistic kings gave independence to the Jews in 128 B.C., which lasted till the Romans occupied the country.

Important groups that exerted influence during these times were the Sadducees, priests in the temple in Jerusalem; the Pharisees, teachers of the Law in the synagogues; Essenes, a religious order (from whom Dead Sea Scrolls, discovered in 1947, came); Apocalyptists, who were expecting the heavenly Messiah; and Zealots, who were prepared to fight for national independence.

When the latter turned against Rome in A.D. 66, Roman armies under Titus suppressed the revolt, destroying Jerusalem and its temple in A.D. 70. The Jews were scattered in the *diaspora* (Dispersion), subject to oppressions until the Age of the Enlightenment (18th century) brought their emancipation, although persecutions did not end entirely.

Worldwide Adherents of All Religions, Mid–1994

Statistics of the world's religions are only very rough approximations. Aside from Christianity, few religions, if any, attempt to keep statistical records, and even Protestants and Catholics employ different methods of counting members. All persons of whatever age who have received baptism in the Catholic Church are counted as members, while in most Protestant Churches only those who "join" the church are numbered. The compiling of statistics is further complicated by the fact that in China one may be at the same time a Confucian, a Taoist, and a Buddhist. In Japan, one may be both a Buddhist and a Shintoist.

Religion	Africa	Asia	Europe[1]	Latin America	Northern America	Oceania	World
Christians	351,682,000	304,887,000	531,906,000	422,140,000	246,319,000	23,240,000	1,900,174,000
Roman Catholics	132,102,000	132,053,000	273,587,000	411,514,000	100,386,000	8,427,000	1,058,069,000
Protestants	93,865,000	87,051,000	85,344,000	17,513,000	99,652,000	7,718,000	391,143,000
Orthodox	30,685,000	3,904,000	130,998,000	1,789,000	6,217,000	591,000	174,184,000
Anglicans	28,873,000	755,000	33,626,000	1,322,000	7,593,000	5,872,000	78,038,000
Other Christians	66,158,000	81,125,000	8,352,000	10,004,000	33,445,000	623,000	199,707,000
Muslims	293,993,000	675,297,000	57,161,000	1,395,000	5,500,000	107,000	1,033,453,000
Hindus	1,608,000	759,059,000	727,000	912,000	1,315,000	379,000	764,000,000
Buddhists	23,000	336,755,000	680,000	559,000	578,000	26,000	338,621,000
Chinese folk religionists	14,000	149,037,000	62,000	76,000	126,000	21,000	149,336,000
New-Religionists	23,000	126,869,000	52,000	548,000	1,473,000	10,000	128,975,000
Tribal religionists	69,872,000	28,197,000	1,000	967,000	42,000	71,000	99,150,000
Sikhs	29,000	19,557,000	238,000	8,000	363,000	9,000	10,204,000
Jews	128,000	4,289,000	2,574,000	458,000	5,907,000	95,000	13,451,000
Shamanists	1,000	10,754,000	252,000	1,000	1,000	1,000	11,010,000
Confucians	1,000	6,300,000	4,000	2,000	26,000	1,000	6,334,000
Baha'is	1,631,000	2,817,000	100,000	827,000	379,000	81,000	5,835,000
Jains	57,000	3,906,000	15,000	4,000	4,000	1,000	3,987,000
Shintoists	0	3,383,000	1,000	1,000	1,000	1,000	3,387,000
Other religionists	472,000	12,912,000	1,842,000	3,686,000	1,503,000	4,000	20,419,000
Nonreligious	2,936,000	733,740,000	140,435,000	19,327,000	23,884,000	3,756,000	924,078,000
Atheists	344,000	167,739,000	65,769,000	3,329,000	1,367,000	563,000	239,111,000
Total Population	**722,814,000**	**3,345,498,000**	**801,819,000**	**474,240,000**	**288,788,000**	**28,366,000**	**5,661,525,000**

1. Includes the former U.S.S.R. Reprinted with permission from *1995 Britannica Book of the Year.* © 1995 Encyclopaedia Britannica, Inc.

The fall of the Jerusalem temple was an important event in the religious life of the Jews, which now developed around *Torah* (Law) and synagogue. Around A.D. 100 the Sacred Scriptures were codified. Synagogue worship became central, with readings from *Torah* and prophets. Most important prayers are the *Shema* (Hear) and the Prayer of the 18 Benedictions.

Religious life is guided by the commandments contained in the *Torah:* circumcision and *Sabbath,* as well as other ethical and ceremonial commandments.

The *Talmud,* based on the *Mishnah* and its interpretations, took shape over many centuries in the Babylonian and Palestinian Schools. It was a strong binding force of Judaism in the Dispersion.

In the 12th century, Maimonides formulated his "13 Articles of Faith," which carried great authority. Fundamental in this creed are: belief in God and his oneness *(Sherma),* belief in the changeless *Torah,* in the words of Moses and the prophets, belief in reward and punishment, the coming of the Messiah, and the resurrection of the dead.

Judaism is divided into theological schools, the main divisions of which are Orthodox, Conservative, and Reform.

Christianity

Christianity is founded upon Jesus Christ, to whose life the New Testament writings testify. Jesus, a Jew, was born in about 7 B.C. and assumed his public life, after his 30th year, in Galilee. The Gospels tell of many extraordinary deeds that accompanied his ministry. He proclaimed the Kingdom of God, a future reality that is at the same time already present. Nationalistic-Jewish expectations of the Messiah he rejected. Rather, he referred to himself as the "Son of Man," the Christ, who has power to forgive sins now and who shall also come as Judge at the end of time. Jesus set forth the religio-ethical demands for participation in the Kingdom of God as change of heart and love of God and neighbor.

At the Last Supper he signified his death as a sacrifice, which would inaugurate the New Covenant, by which many would be saved. Circa A.D. 30 he died on a cross in Jerusalem. The early Church carried on Jesus' proclamation, the apostle Paul emphasizing his death and resurrection.

The person of Jesus is fundamental to the Christian faith since it is believed that in his life, death, and resurrection, God's revelation became historically tangible. He is seen as the turning point in history, and man's relationship to God as determined by his attitude to Jesus.

Historically Christianity thus arose out of Judaism, claiming fulfillment of the promises of the Old Testament in Jesus. The early Church designated itself as "the true Israel," which expected the speedy return of Jesus. The mother church was at Jerusalem, but churches were soon founded in many other places. The apostle Paul was instrumental in founding and extending a Gentile Christianity that was free from Jewish legalism.

The new religion spread rapidly throughout the eastern and western parts of the Roman Empire. In coming to terms with other religious movements within the Empire, Christianity began to take definite shape as an organization in its doctrine, liturgy, and ministry circa A.D. 200. In the 4th century the Catholic Church had taken root in countries stretching from Spain in the West to Persia and India in the East. Christians had been repeatedly subject to persecution by the Roman state, but finally gained tolerance under Constantine the Great (A.D. 313). Since that time, the Church became favored under his successors and in 380 the Emperor Theodosius proclaimed Christianity the State religion. Paganism was suppressed and public life was gradually molded in accordance with Christian ethical demands.

It was in these years also that the Church was able to achieve a certain unity of doctrine. Due to differences of interpretation of basic doctrines concerning Christ, which threatened to divide the Catholic Church, a standard Christian Creed was formulated by bishops at successive Ecumenical Councils, the first of which was held in A.D. 325 (Nicaea). The chief doctrines formulated concerned the doctrine of the Trinity, i.e., that there is one God in three persons: Father, Son, and Holy Spirit (Constantinople, A.D. 381); and the nature of Christ as both divine and human (Chalcedon, A.D. 541).

Through differences and rivalry between East and West the unity of the Church was broken by schism in 1054. In 1517 a separation occurred in the Western Church with the Reformation. From the major Protestant denominations [Lutheran, Presbyterian, Anglican (Episcopalian)], many Free Churches separated themselves in an age of individualism.

In the 20th century, however, the direction is toward unity. The Ecumenical Movement led to the formation of the World Council of Churches in 1948 (Amsterdam), which has since been joined by many Protestant and Orthodox Churches.

Through its missionary activity Christianity has spread to most parts of the globe.

Eastern Orthodoxy

Eastern Orthodoxy comprises the faith and practice of Churches stemming from ancient Churches in the Eastern part of the Roman Empire. The term covers Orthodox Churches in communion with the See of Constantinople and Nestorian and Monophysite Churches.

The Orthodox, Catholic, Apostolic Church is the direct descendant of the Byzantine State Church and consists of a series of independent national churches that are united by Doctrine, Liturgy, and Hierarchical organization (deacons and priests, who may either be married or be monks before ordination, and bishops, who must be celibates). The heads of these Churches

U.S. Religious Bodies with Members Over 2,000,000

Religious body	Members
Roman Catholic Church	59,858,042
Southern Baptist Convention	15,398,642
United Methodist Church	8,646,595
National Baptist Convention, U.S.A.	8,200,000
Church of God in Christ	5,499,875
Evangelical Lutheran Church in America	5,212,785
Church of Jesus Christ of Latter-day Saints	4,520,000
Presbyterian Church (U.S.A.)	3,796,766
African Methodist Episcopal Church	3,500,000
National Baptist Convention of America (DAARB)	3,500,000
Lutheran Church–Missouri Synod	2,598,935
Episcopal Church	2,504,682
National Missionary Baptist Convention of America	2,500,000
Progressive National Baptist Convention	2,500,000
Assemblies of God	2,271,718

Source: Yearbook of American & Canadian Churches, 1995.

are patriarchs or metropolitans; the Patriarch of Constantinople is only "first among equals." Rivalry between the Pope of Rome and the Patriarch of Constantinople, aided by differences and misunderstandings that existed for centuries between the Eastern and Western parts of the Empire, led to a schism in 1054. Repeated attempts at reunion have failed in past centuries. The mutual excommunication pronounced in that year was lifted in 1965, however, and because of greater interaction in theology between Orthodox Churches and those in the West, a climate of better understanding has been created in the 20th century. First contacts were with Anglicans and Old Catholics. Orthodox Churches belong to the World Council of Churches.

The Eastern Orthodox Churches recognize only the canons of the seven Ecumenical Councils (325–787) as binding for faith and they reject doctrines that have been added in the West.

The central worship service is called the Liturgy, which is understood as representation of God's acts of salvation. Its center is the celebration of the Eucharist, or Lord's Supper.

In their worship icons (sacred pictures) are used that have a sacramental meaning as representation. The Mother of Christ, angels, and saints are highly venerated.

The number of sacraments in the Orthodox Church is the same as in the Western Catholic Church.

Orthodox Churches are found in the Balkans and the Soviet Union also, since the 20th century, in Western Europe and other parts of the world, particularly in America.

Eastern Rite Churches

These include the Uniate Churches that recognize the authority of the Pope but keep their own traditional liturgies and those Churches dating back to the 5th century that emancipated themselves from the Byzantine State Church: the Nestorian Church in the Near East and India and the Monophysite Churches (Coptic, Ethiopian, Syrian, Armenian, and the Mar Thoma Church in India).

Roman Catholicism

Roman Catholicism comprises the belief and practice of the Roman Catholic Church. The Church stands under the authority of the Bishop of Rome, the Pope, and is ruled by him and bishops who are held to be, through ordination, successors of Peter and the Apostles, respectively. Fundamental to the structure of the Church is the juridical aspect: doctrine and sacraments are bound to the power of jurisdiction and consecration of the hierarchy. The Pope, as the head of the hierarchy of archbishops, bishops, priests, and deacons, has full ecclesiastical power, granted him by Christ, through Peter. As successor to Peter, he is the Vicar of Christ. The powers that others in the hierarchy possess are delegated.

Roman Catholics believe their Church to be the one, holy, catholic, and apostolic Church, possessing all the properties of the one, true Church of Christ.

The faith of the Church is understood to be identical with that taught by Christ and his Apostles and contained in Bible and Tradition, i.e. the original deposit of faith, to which nothing new may be added. New definitions of doctrines, such as the Immaculate Conception of Mary (1854) and the bodily Assumption of Mary (1950), have been declared by Popes, however, in accordance with the principle of development (implicit-explicit doctrine).

At Vatican Council I (1870) the Pope was proclaimed "endowed with infallibility, *ex cathedra*, i.e.,

when exercising the office of Pastor and Teacher of all Christians."

The center of Roman Catholic worship is the celebration of the Mass, the Eucharist, which is the commemoration of Christ's sacrificial death and of his resurrection. Other sacraments are Baptism, Confirmation, Confession, Matrimony, Ordination, and Extreme Unction, seven in all. The Virgin Mary and saints, and their relics, are highly venerated and prayers are made to them to intercede with God, in whose presence they are believed to dwell.

The Roman Catholic Church is the largest Christian organization in the world, found in most countries. Since Vatican Council II (1962–65), and the effort to "update" the Church, many interesting changes and developments have been taking place.

Protestantism

Protestantism comprises the Christian churches that separated from Rome during the Reformation in the 16th century, initiated by an Augustinian monk, Martin Luther. "Protestant" was originally applied to followers of Luther, who protested at the Diet of Spires (1529) against the decree which prohibited all further ecclesiastical reforms. Subsequently, Protestantism came to mean rejection of attempts to tie God's revelation to earthly institutions, and a return to the Gospel and the Word of God as sole authority in matters of faith and practice. Central in the biblical message is the justification of the sinner by faith alone. The Church is understood as a fellowship and the priesthood of all believers stressed.

The Augsburg Confession (1530) was the principal statement of Lutheran faith and practice. It became a model for other Confessions of Faith, which in their turn had decisive influence on Church policy. Major Protestant denominations are the Lutheran, Reformed (Calvinist), Presbyterian, and Anglican (Episcopal). Smaller ones are the Mennonite, Schwenkfeldians, and Unitarians. In Great Britain and America there are the Congregationalists, Baptists, Quakers, Methodists, and other free church types of communities. (In regarding themselves as being faithful to original biblical Christianity, these Churches differ from such religious bodies as Unitarians, Mormons, Jehovah's Witnesses, and Christian Scientists, who either teach new doctrines or reject old ones.)

Since the latter part of the 19th century, national councils of churches have been established in many countries, e.g. the Federal Council of Churches of Christ in America in 1908. Denominations across countries joined in federations and world alliances, beginning with the Anglican Lambeth Conference in 1867.

Protestant missionary activity, particularly strong in the last century, resulted in the founding of many younger churches in Asia and Africa. The Ecumenical Movement, which originated with Protestant missions, aims at unity among Christians and churches.

Islam

Islam is the religion founded in Arabia by Mohammed between 610 and 632. There are an estimated 2.6 million Moslems in Northern America and 950 million Moslems worldwide.

Mohammed was born in A.D. 570 at Mecca and belonged to the Quraysh tribe, which was active in caravan trade. At the age of 25 he joined the caravan trade from Mecca to Syria in the employment of a rich widow, Khadiji, whom he married. Critical of the idolatry of the inhabitants of Mecca, he began to lead a contemplative life in the deserts. There he received a series of revelations. Encouraged by Khadiji, he gradually became convinced that he was given a God-appointed task to devote himself to the reform of religion and society. Idolatry was to be abandoned.

The *Hegira (Hijra)* (migration) of Mohammed from Mecca, where he was not honored, to Medina, where he was well received, occurred in 622 and marks the beginning of the Muslim era. In 630 he marched on Mecca and conquered it. He died at Medina in 632. His grave there has since been a place of pilgrimage.

Mohammed's followers, called Moslems, revered him as the prophet of *Allah* (God), beside whom there is no other God. Although he had no close knowledge of Judaism and Christianity, he considered himself succeeding and completing them as the seal of the Prophets. Sources of the Islamic faith are the *Qur'an*, regarded as the uncreated, eternal Word of God, and Tradition *(hadith)* regarding sayings and deeds of the prophet.

Islam means surrender to the will of *Allah*. He is the all-powerful, whose will is supreme and determines man's fate. Good deeds will be rewarded at the Last Judgment in paradise and evil deeds will be punished in hell.

The Five Pillars, primary duties, of Islam are: witness; confessing the oneness of God and of Mohammed, his prophet; prayer, to be performed five times a day; almsgiving to the poor and the mosque (house of worship); fasting during daylight hours in the month of Ramadan; and pilgrimage to Mecca at least once in the Moslem's lifetime.

Islam, upholding the law of brotherhood, succeeded in uniting an Arab world that had disintegrated into tribes and castes. Disagreements concerning the succession of the prophet caused a great division in Islam between *Sunnis* and *Shias*. Among these, other sects arose *(Wahhabi)*. Doctrinal issues also led to the rise of different schools of thought in theology. Nevertheless, since Arab armies turned against Syria and Palestine in 635, Islam has expanded successfully under Mohammed's successors. Its rapid conquests in Asia and Africa are unsurpassed in history. Turning against Europe, Moslems conquered Spain in 713. In 1453 Constantinople fell into their hands and in 1529 Moslem armies besieged Vienna. Since then, Islam has lost its foothold in Europe.

In modern times it has made great gains in Africa.

Hinduism

Hinduism is the major religion of India where there are over 550 million adherents. In contrast to other religions, it has no founder. Considered the oldest religion in the world, it dates back, perhaps, to prehistoric times.

Hinduism is hard to define, there being no common creed, no one doctrine to bind Hindus together. Intellectually there is complete freedom of belief, and one can be monotheist, polytheist, or atheist.

The most important sacred texts of the Hindu religion are written in Sanskrit and called the *Vedas* (*Veda*-knowledge). There are four Vedic books, of which the *Rig-Veda* is the oldest. It speaks of many gods and also deals with questions concerning the universe and creation. The dates of these works are unknown (1000 b.c.?).

The *Upanishads* (dated 1000–300 b.c.), commentaries on the Vedic texts, have philosophical speculations on the origin of the universe, the nature of deity, of *atman* (the human soul), and its relationship to *Brahman* (the universal soul).

Brahman is the principle and source of the universe who can be indicated only by negatives. As the

divine intelligence, he is the ground of the visible world, a presence that pervades all beings. Thus the many Hindu deities came to be understood as manifestations of the one *Brahman* from whom everything proceeds and to whom everything ultimately returns. The religio-social system of Hinduism is based on the concept of reincarnation and transmigration in which all living beings, from plants below to gods above, are caught in a cosmic system that is an everlasting cycle of becoming and perishing.

Life is determined by the law of *karma,* according to which rebirth is dependent on moral behavior in a previous phase of existence. In this view, life on earth is regarded as transient *(maya)* and a burden. The goal of existence is liberation from the cycle of rebirth and redeath and entrance into the indescribable state of what in Buddhism is called *nirvana* (extinction of passion).

Further important sacred writings are the Epics *(ithasas),* which contain legendary stories about gods and men. They are the *Mahabharata* (composed between 200 b.c. and a.d. 200) and the *Ramayana.* The former includes the poem *Bhagavad-Gita* (Song of the Lord).

The practice of Hinduism consists of rites and ceremonies centering on the main socio-religious occasions of birth, marriage, and death. There are many Hindu temples, which are dwelling places of the deities and to which people bring offerings. There are also places of pilgrimages, the chief one being Benares on the Ganges, most sacred among the rivers in India.

Orthodox Hindu society in India was divided into four major hereditary casts: 1) Brahmans (priestly and learned class); 2) Kshatriyas (military, professional, rulers and governing occupations); 3) Vaisyas (landowners, merchants, and business occupations); and 4) Sudras (artisans, laborers, and peasants). Below the Sudras was a fifth group, the untouchables (lowest menial occupations and no social standing). The Indian government banned discrimination against the untouchables in 1949.

In modern times work has been done to reform and revive Hinduism. One of the outstanding reformers was Ramakrishna (1836–86), who inspired many followers, one of whom founded the Ramakrishna mission. The mission is active both in India and in other countries and is known for its scholarly and humanitarian works.

Buddhism

Founded in the 6th century b.c. in northern India by Gautama Buddha, who was born in southern Nepal as son to a king. His birth is surrounded by many legends, but Western scholars agree that he lived from 563 to 483 b.c. Warned by a sage that his son would become an ascetic or a universal monarch, the king confined him to his home. He was able to escape and began the life of a homeless wanderer in search of peace, passing through many disappointments until he finally came to the Tree of Enlightenment, under which he lived in meditation till enlightenment came to him and he became a Buddha (enlightened one).

Now he understood the origin of suffering, summarized in the *Four Noble Truths,* which constitutes the foundation of Buddhism. The Four are the truth of suffering, which all living beings must endure; of the origin of suffering, which is craving and which leads to rebirth; that it can be destroyed; and of the way that leads to cessation of pain, i.e., the *Noble Eightfold Way,* which is the rule of practical Buddhism:

right views, right intention, right speech, right action, right livelihood, right effort, right concentration, and right ecstasy.

Nirvana is the goal of all existence, the state of complete redemption, into which the redeemed enters. Buddha's insight can free every man from the law of reincarnation through complete emptying of the self.

The nucleus of Buddha's church or association was originally formed by monks and lay-brothers, whose houses gradually became monasteries used as places for religious instruction. The worship service consisted of a sermon, expounding of Scripture, meditation, and confession. At a later stage pilgrimages to the holy places associated with the Buddha came into being, as well as veneration of relics.

In the 3rd century B.C., King Ashoka made Buddhism the State religion of India but, as centuries passed, it gradually fell into decay through splits, persecutions, and the hostile Brahmans. Buddhism spread to countries outside India, however.

At the beginning of the Christian era, there occurred a split that gave rise to two main types: *Hinayana* (Little Vehicle), or southern Buddhism, and *Mahayana* (Great Vehicle), or northern Buddhism. The former type, more individualistic, survived in Ceylon and southern Asia. *Hinayana* retained more closely the original teachings of the Buddha, which did not know of a personal god or soul. *Mahayana*, more social, polytheistic, and developing a pluralistic pompous cult, was strong in the Himalayas, Tibet, Mongolia, China, Korea, and Japan.

In the present century, Buddhism has found believers also in the West and there are an estimated 554,000 Buddhists in Northern America.

Confucianism

Confucius (K'ung Fu-tzu), born in the state of Lu (northern China), lived from 551 to 479 B.C. Tradition, exaggerating the importance of Confucius in life, has depicted him as a great statesman but, in fact, he seems to have been a private teacher. Anthologies of ancient Chinese classics, along with his own Analects (*Lun Yu*), became the basis of Confucianism. These Analects were transmitted as a collection of his sayings as recorded by his students, with whom he discussed ethical and social problems. They developed into men of high moral standing, who served the State as administrators.

In his teachings, Confucius emphasized the importance of an old Chinese concept *(li)*, which has the connotation of proper conduct. There is some disagreement as to the religious ideas of Confucius, but he held high the concepts handed down from centuries before him. Thus he believed in Heaven (*T'ien*) and sacrificed to his ancestors. Ancestor worship he indeed encouraged as an expression of filial piety, which he considered the loftiest of virtues.

Piety to Confucius was the foundation of the family as well as the State. The family is the nucleus of the State, and the "five relations," between king and subject, father and son, man and wife, older and younger brother, and friend and friend, are determined by the virtues of love of fellow men, righteousness, and respect.

An extension of ancestor worship may be seen in the worship of Confucius, which became official in the 2nd century B.C. when the emperor, in recognition of Confucius' teachings as supporting the imperial rule, offered sacrifices at his tomb.

Mencius (Meng Tse), who lived around 400 B.C., did much to propagate and elaborate Confucianism in its concern with ordering society. Thus, for two millennia, Confucius' doctrine of State, with its emphasis on ethics and social morality, rooted in ancient Chinese tradition and developed and continued by his disciples, has been standard in China and the Far East.

With the revolution of 1911 in China, however, students, burning Confucius in effigy, called for the removal of "the old curiosity shop."

Shintoism

Shinto, the Chinese term for the Japanese *Kami no Michi*, i.e., the Way of the Gods, comprises the religious ideas and cult indigenous to Japan. *Kami*, or gods, considered divine forces of nature that are worshipped, may reside in rivers, trees, rocks, mountains, certain animals, or, particularly, in the sun and moon. The worship of ancestors, heroes, and deceased emperors was incorporated later.

After Buddhism had come from Korea, Japan's native religion at first resisted it. Then there followed a period of compromise and amalgamation with Buddhist beliefs and ceremonies, resulting, since the 9th century A.D., in a syncretistic religion, a Twofold Shinto. Buddhist deities came to be regarded as manifestations of Japanese deities and Buddhist priests took over most of the Shinto shrines.

In modern times Shinto regained independence from Buddhism. Under the reign of the Emperor Meiji (1868–1912) it became the official State religion, in which loyalty to the emperor was emphasized. The line of succession of emperors is traced back to the first Emperor Jimmu (660 B.C.) and beyond him to the Sun-goddess *Amaterasuomikami*.

The centers of worship are the shrines and temples in which the deities are believed to dwell and believers approach them through *torii* (gateways). Most important among the shrines is the imperial shrine of the Sun-goddess at Ise, where state ceremonies were once held in June and December. The *Yasukuni* shrine of the war dead in Tokyo is also well known.

Acts of worship consist of prayers, clapping of hands, acts of purification, and offerings. On feast days processions and performances of music and dancing take place and priests read prayers before the gods in the shrines, asking for good harvest, the well-being of people and emperor, etc. In Japanese homes there is a god-shelf, a small wooden shrine that contains the tablets bearing the names of ancestors. Offerings are made and candles lit before it.

After World War II the Allied Command ordered the disestablishment of State Shinto. To be distinguished from State Shinto is Sect Shinto, consisting of 13 recognized sects. These have arisen in modern times. Most important among them is *Tenrikyo* in Tenri City (Nara), in which healing by faith plays a central role.

Taoism

Taoism, a religion of China, was, according to tradition, founded by Lao Tse, a Chinese philosopher, long considered one of the prominent religious leaders from the 6th century B.C.

Data about him are for the most part legendary, however, and the *Tao Te Ching* (the classic of the Way and of its Power), traditionally ascribed to him, is now believed by many scholars to have originated in the 3rd century B.C. The book is composed in short chapters, written in aphoristic rhymes. Central are the word *Tao*, which means way or path and, in a deeper sense, signifies the principle that underlies the reality of this world and manifests itself in nature and in the lives of men, and the word *Te* (power).

The virtuous man draws power from being absorbed in *Tao*, the ultimate reality within an ever-changing world. By non-action and keeping away from human striving it is possible for man to live in harmony with the principles that underlie and govern the universe. *Tao* cannot be comprehended by reason and knowledge, but only by inward quiet.

Besides the *Tao Te Ching*, dating from approximately the same period, there are two Taoist works, written by Chuang Tse and Lieh Tse.

Theoretical Taoism of this classical philosophical movement of the 4th and 3rd centuries B.C. in China differed from popular Taoism, into which it gradually degenerated. The standard of theoretical Taoism was maintained in the classics, of course, and among the upper classes it continued to be alive until modern times.

Religious Taoism is a form of religion dealing with deities and spirits, magic and soothsaying. In the 2nd century A.D. it was organized with temples, cult, priests, and monasteries and was able to hold its own in the competition with Buddhism that came up at the same time.

After the 7th century A.D., however, Taoist religion further declined. Split into numerous sects, which often operate like secret societies, it has become a syncretistic folk religion in which some of the old deities and saints live on.

Roman Catholic Pontiffs

St. Peter, of Bethsaida in Galilee, Prince of the Apostles, was the first Pope. He lived first in Antioch and then in Rome for 25 years. In AD 64 or 67, he was martyred. St. Linus became the second Pope.

Name	Birthplace	Reigned From	To	Name	Birthplace	Reigned From	To
St. Linus	Tuscia	67	76	St. Felix III (II)[2]	Rome	483	492
St. Anacletus (Cletus)	Rome	76	88	St. Gelasius I	Africa	492	496
				Anastasius II	Rome	496	498
St. Clement	Rome	88	97	St. Symmachus	Sardinia	498	514
St. Evaristus	Greece	97	105	St. Hormisdas	Frosinone	514	523
St. Alexander I	Rome	105	115	St. John I	Tuscany	523	526
St. Sixtus I	Rome	115	125	St. Felix IV (III)	Samnium	526	530
St. Telesphorus	Greece	125	136	Boniface II	Rome	530	532
St. Hyginus	Greece	136	140	John II	Rome	533	535
St. Pius I	Aquileia	140	155	St. Agapitus I	Rome	535	536
St. Anicetus	Syria	155	166	St. Silverius	Campania	536	537
St. Soter	Campania	166	175	Vigilius	Rome	537	555
St. Eleutherius	Epirus	175	189	Pelagius I	Rome	556	561
St. Victor I	Africa	189	199	John III	Rome	561	574
St. Zephyrinus	Rome	199	217	Benedict I	Rome	575	579
St. Callistus I	Rome	217	222	Pelagius II	Rome	579	590
St. Urban I	Rome	222	230	St. Gregory I (the Great)	Rome	590	604
St. Pontian	Rome	230	235				
St. Anterus	Greece	235	236	Sabinianus	Tuscany	604	606
St. Fabian	Rome	236	250	Boniface III	Rome	607	607
St. Cornelius	Rome	251	253	St. Boniface IV	Marsi	608	615
St. Lucius I	Rome	253	254	St. Deusdedit (Adeodatus I)	Rome	615	618
St. Stephen I	Rome	254	257				
St. Sixtus II	Greece	257	258	Boniface V	Naples	619	625
St. Dionysius	Unknown	259	268	Honorius I	Campania	625	638
St. Felix I	Rome	269	274	Severinus	Rome	640	640
St. Eutychian	Luni	275	283	John IV	Dalmatia	640	642
St. Caius	Dalmatia	283	296	Theodore I	Greece	642	649
St. Marcellinus	Rome	296	304	St. Martin I	Todi	649	655
St. Marcellus I	Rome	308	309	St. Eugene I[3]	Rome	654	657
St. Eusebius	Greece	309[1]	309[1]	St. Vitalian	Segni	657	672
St. Meltiades	Africa	311	314	Adeodatus II	Rome	672	676
St. Sylvester I	Rome	314	335	Donus	Rome	676	678
St. Marcus	Rome	336	336	St. Agatho	Sicily	678	681
St. Julius I	Rome	337	352	St. Leo II	Sicily	682	683
Liberius	Rome	352	366	St. Benedict II	Rome	684	685
St. Damasus I	Spain	366	384	John V	Syria	685	686
St. Siricius	Rome	384	399	Conon	Unknown	686	687
St. Anastasius I	Rome	399	401	St. Sergius I	Syria	687	701
St. Innocent I	Albano	401	417	John VI	Greece	701	705
St. Zozimus	Greece	417	418	John VII	Greece	705	707
St. Boniface I	Rome	418	422	Sisinnius	Syria	708	708
St. Celestine I	Campania	422	432	Constantine	Syria	708	715
St. Sixtus III	Rome	432	440	St. Gregory II	Rome	715	731
St. Leo I (the Great)	Tuscany	440	461	St. Gregory III	Syria	731	741
				St. Zachary	Greece	741	752
St. Hilary	Sardinia	461	468	Stephen II (III)[4]	Rome	752	757
St. Simplicius	Tivoli	468	483	St. Paul I	Rome	757	767

Name	Birthplace	Reigned From	To	Name	Birthplace	Reigned From	To
Stephen III (IV)	Sicily	768	772	Gelasius II	Gaeta	1118	1119
Adrian I	Rome	772	795	Callistus II	Burgundy	1119	1124
St. Leo III	Rome	795	816	Honorius II	Flagnano	1124	1130
Stephen IV (V)	Rome	816	817	Innocent II	Rome	1130	1143
St. Paschal I	Rome	817	824	Celestine II	Città di Castello	1143	1144
Eugene II	Rome	824	827				
Valentine	Rome	827	827	Lucius II	Bologna	1144	1145
Gregory IV	Rome	827	844	Bl. Eugene III	Pisa	1145	1153
Sergius II	Rome	844	847	Anastasius IV	Rome	1153	1154
St. Leo IV	Rome	847	855	Adrian IV	England	1154	1159
Benedict III	Rome	855	858	Alexander III	Siena	1159	1181
St. Nicholas I (the Great)	Rome	858	867	Lucius III	Lucca	1181	1185
				Urban III	Milan	1185	1187
Adrian II	Rome	867	872	Gregory VIII	Benevento	1187	1187
John VIII	Rome	872	882	Clement III	Rome	1187	1191
Marinus I	Gallese	882	884	Celestine III	Rome	1191	1198
St. Adrian III	Rome	884	885	Innocent III	Anagni	1198	1216
Stephen V (VI)	Rome	885	891	Honorius III	Rome	1216	1227
Formosus	Portus	891	896	Gregory IX	Anagni	1227	1241
Boniface VI	Rome	896	896	Celestine IV	Milan	1241	1241
Stephen VI (VII)	Rome	896	897	Innocent IV	Genoa	1243	1254
Romanus	Gallese	897	897	Alexander IV	Anagni	1254	1261
Theodore II	Rome	897	897	Urban IV	Troyes	1261	1264
John IX	Tivoli	898	900	Clement IV	France	1265	1268
Benedict IV	Rome	900	903	Bl. Gregory X	Piacenza	1271	1276
Leo V	Ardea	903	903	Bl. Innocent V	Savoy	1276	1276
Sergius III	Rome	904	911	Adrian V	Genoa	1276	1276
Anastasius III	Rome	911	913	John XXI[7]	Portugal	1276	1277
Landus	Sabina	913	914	Nicholas III	Rome	1277	1280
John X	Tossignano	914	928	Martin IV[8]	France	1281	1285
Leo VI	Rome	928	928	Honorius IV	Rome	1285	1287
Stephen VII (VIII)	Rome	928	931	Nicholas IV	Ascoli	1288	1292
John XI	Rome	931	935	St. Celestine V	Isernia	1294	1294
Leo VII	Rome	936	939	Boniface VIII	Anagni	1294	1303
Stephen VIII (IX)	Rome	939	942	Bl. Benedict XI	Treviso	1303	1304
Marinus II	Rome	942	946	Clement V	France	1305	1314
Agapitus II	Rome	946	955	John XXII	Cahors	1316	1334
John XII	Tusculum	955	964	Benedict XII	France	1334	1342
Leo VIII[5]	Rome	963	965	Clement VI	France	1342	1352
Benedict V[5]	Rome	964	966	Innocent VI	France	1352	1362
John XIII	Rome	965	972	Bl. Urban V	France	1362	1370
Benedict VI	Rome	973	974	Gregory XI	France	1370	1378
Benedict VII	Rome	974	983	Urban VI	Naples	1378	1389
John XIV	Pavia	983	984	Boniface IX	Naples	1389	1404
John XV	Rome	985	996	Innocent VII	Sul mona	1404	1406
Gregory V	Saxony	996	999	Gregory XII	Venice	1406	1415
Sylvester II	Auvergne	999	1003	Martin V	Rome	1417	1431
John XVII	Rome	1003	1003	Eugene IV	Venice	1431	1447
John XVIII	Rome	1004	1009	Nicholas V	Sarzana	1447	1455
Sergius IV	Rome	1009	1012	Callistus III	Jativa	1455	1458
Benedict VIII	Tusculum	1012	1024	Pius II	Siena	1458	1464
John XIX	Tusculum	1024	1032	Paul II	Venice	1464	1471
Benedict IX[6]	Tusculum	1032	1044	Sixtus IV	Savona	1471	1484
Sylvester III	Rome	1045	1045	Innocent VIII	Genoa	1484	1492
Benedict IX (2nd time)	—	1045	1045	Alexander VI	Jativa	1492	1503
				Pius III	Siena	1503	1503
Gregory VI	Rome	1045	1046	Julius II	Savona	1503	1513
Clement II	Saxony	1046	1047	Leo X	Florence	1513	1521
Benedict IX (3rd time)	—	1047	1048	Adrian VI	Utrecht	1522	1523
				Clement VII	Florence	1523	1534
Damasus II	Bavaria	1048	1048	Paul III	Rome	1534	1549
St. Leo IX	Alsace	1049	1054	Julius III	Rome	1550	1555
Victor II	Germany	1055	1057	Marcellus II	Montepulciano	1555	1555
Stephen IX (X)	Lorraine	1057	1058	Paul IV	Naples	1555	1559
Nicholas II	Burgundy	1059	1061	Pius IV	Milan	1559	1565
Alexander II	Milan	1061	1073	St. Pius V	Bosco	1566	1572
St. Gregory VII	Tuscany	1073	1085	Gregory XIII	Bologna	1572	1585
Bl. Victor III	Benevento	1086	1087	Sixtus V	Grottammare	1585	1590
Bl. Urban II	France	1088	1099	Urban VII	Rome	1590	1590
Paschal II	Ravenna	1099	1118	Gregory XIV	Cremona	1590	1591

Name	Birthplace	Reigned From	Reigned To		Name	Birthplace	Reigned From	Reigned To
Innocent IX	Bologna	1591	1591		Clement XIII	Venice	1758	1769
Clement VIII	Florence	1592	1605		Clement XIV	Rimini	1769	1774
Leo XI	Florence	1605	1605		Pius VI	Cesena	1775	1799
Paul V	Rome	1605	1621		Pius VII	Cesena	1800	1823
Gregory XV	Bologna	1621	1623		Leo XII	Genga	1823	1829
Urban VIII	Florence	1623	1644		Pius VIII	Cingoli	1829	1830
Innocent X	Rome	1644	1655		Gregory XVI	Belluno	1831	1846
Alexander VII	Siena	1655	1667		Pius IX	Senegallia	1846	1878
Clement IX	Pistoia	1667	1669		Leo XIII	Carpineto	1878	1903
Clement X	Rome	1670	1676		St. Pius X	Riese	1903	1914
Bl. Innocent XI	Como	1676	1689		Benedict XV	Genoa	1914	1922
Alexander VIII	Venice	1689	1691		Pius XI	Desio	1922	1939
Innocent XII	Spinazzola	1691	1700		Pius XII	Rome	1939	1958
Clement XI	Urbino	1700	1721		John XXIII	Sotto il Monte	1958	1963
Innocent XIII	Rome	1721	1724		Paul VI	Concesio	1963	1978
Benedict XIII	Gravina	1724	1730		John Paul I	Forno di Canale	1978	1978
Clement XII	Florence	1730	1740		John Paul II	Wadowice, Poland	1978	
Benedict XIV	Bologna	1740	1758					

1. Or 310. 2. He should be called Felix II, and his successors of the same name should be numbered accordingly. The discrepancy was caused by the erroneous insertion in some lists of the name of St. Felix of Rome, Martyr. 3. He was elected during the exile of St. Martin I, who endorsed him as Pope. 4. After St. Zachary died, a Roman priest named Stephen was elected but died before his consecration as Bishop of Rome. His name is not included in all lists for this reason. In view of this historical confusion, the *National Catholic Almanac* lists the true Stephen II as Stephen II (III), the true Stephen III as Stephen III (IV), etc. 5. Confusion exists concerning the legitimacy of claims. If the deposition of John was invalid, Leo was an antipope until after the end of Benedict's reign. If the deposition of John was valid, Leo was the legitimate Pope and Benedict an antipope. 6. If the triple removal of Benedict IX was not valid, Sylvester III, Gregory VI, and Clement II were antipopes. 7. Elimination was made of the name of John XX in an effort to rectify the numerical designation of Popes named John. The error dates back to the time of John XV. 8. The names of Marinus I and Marinus II were construed as Martin. In view of these two pontificates and the earlier reign of St. Martin I, this pontiff was called Martin IV. *Source: National Catholic Almanac, from Annuarto Pontificio.*

Both Students and Parents Approve of School Prayer

Source: The Princeton Religion Research Center.

Newt Gingrich captured headlines and sparked public debate when early after the Republicans captured the House and Senate he said one of his top priorities in the first 100 days of the new Congress was to pass a constitutional amendment to allow voluntary prayer in the schools. Although the proposed amendment was a key tenet among members of the Christian Right who helped elect the new Republican majority, both G.O.P. and Christian Right leaders quickly backed away from acting upon it immediately lest the ideological issues it raises would detract the new congress from its economic and social priorities the same way that the gays in the military issue derailed the Clinton administration's agenda in the first 100 days.

The irony of the postponement is that, unlike the issue of gays in the military on which the nation was sharply divided, most people in this country, young and old, favor voluntary prayer in the schools. In a Gallup Poll taken in late November 1994 about three adults in four said they favor an amendment to allow voluntary prayer in the public schools.

A New York Times/CBS News Poll in December 1994 found that 64 percent of adults felt that "organized prayer" should be permitted in the public schools, while 29 percent were opposed and 7 percent undecided.

Among teen-age public school students, six in 10 said in a Gallup Youth Survey taken before the 1994 elections that they favor prayer in their schools, while 37 percent opposed it. Approval is much higher among Protestant teens than among Catholics attending the public schools, and among recent church attenders. Little difference is found, however, among teens according to political preference.

Only 18 percent of adults polled in a September 1994 survey by the George H. Gallup International Institute believed that all children should be required to participate in public school prayer. Higher levels of approval were found among those who identify themselves with the Christian Right (28 percent) and among blacks (44 percent). Eight adults in 10 (81 percent) are opposed to any requirements that children be compelled to participate in school prayer. Critics are quick to point out that whether or not prayer is "voluntary," the normal reluctance of children to be non-conformists would make it difficult for them not to participate in organized activities such as school prayer. ☐

Reprinted with permission from *PRRC Emerging Trends*, March 1995, published by the Princeton Religion Research Center, Princeton, N.J. 08542. Copyright 1995.

PERSONAL FINANCE

The articles and opinions in this section are for general information only and are not intended to provide specific advice or recommendations for any individual.

Reverse Mortgages: A Good Idea?

Reverse mortgages allow homeowners over age 62 to tap their equity without having to move.

Owning a home free and clear has long been part of the American dream. Unfortunately for many retirees, that dream can be short-lived. Faced with inadequate pension and Social Security income, they may feel their only option is to sell the house and live off the proceeds, even if they would rather stay put.

Since 1989, more than 11,000 people have tried another option: the reverse mortgage. If you're planning for retirement or are already retired, it may be an option worth looking into.

A reverse mortgage allows homeowners age 62 and over to remain in their homes while using their built-up equity for any purpose—to make repairs, keep up with property taxes, or simply pay their bills. Some homeowners use a reverse mortgage to cover the high cost of home health care, others to forestall foreclosure (using the reverse mortgage to pay off the existing one), still others to help their children or grandchildren.

Reverse mortgages are now available in every state except Alaska, South Dakota, and Texas. However, willing lenders may still be scarce in some places.

The Basics

A reverse mortgage is a mortgage that pays the homeowner, instead of the other way around. When the homeowner dies or moves out, the loan is paid off through sale of the property. Any equity that is left over at that point belongs to the homeowner or the heirs.

Homeowners can choose how they wish to receive their money. Depending on the lender, borrowers can opt to receive monthly payments, a lump sum, a line of credit, or some combination. The line of credit is the most flexible choice, allowing homeowners to write checks on their equity whenever they need to, up to the limit of the loan. A few reverse-mortgage programs guarantee monthly payments for life, even after the borrower no longer lives in the home.

Turning Home Equity Into Debt

The bars show how debt grows over the life of a reverse mortgage. In this case, a 75-year old borrower receives a payment of $544 each month, on equity of $150,000. The home is assumed to appreciate at a moderate 3 percent a year, and interest remains stable at 8.8 percent throughout the loan period. Equity falls to zero by year 17, but the homeowner continues to collect $544 monthly until he or she moves out or dies.

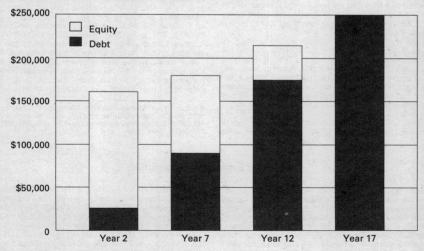

Source: National Center for Home Equity Conversion.

Maximum loan amounts are limited by the value of the home, the borrower's age and life expectancy, the loan's interest rate, and the lender's policies. No financial institution, for instance, will lend 100 percent of a home's market value; maximums are generally in the 50 to 75 percent range. In general, the older the homeowner and the more valuable the home, the more money will be available. For example, a 65-year-old homeowner, living in a home valued at $150,000 would qualify for a $30,000 lump sum (or credit line) when market interest rates are at 10 percent. A 90-year-old in the same circumstances could receive as much as $94,400.

Pluses, Minuses

All reverse mortgages must have "nonrecourse" clauses, meaning that the debt cannot exceed the value of the home. So the lender cannot pursue heirs or family members, or look to the borrower's income or other assets for repayment. In fact, the beauty of these loans is that borrowers can live in their homes as long as they like, even after they have completely exhausted their equity. (For their part, borrowers must maintain the value of the homes as much as possible with timely upkeep.)

A less attractive feature of today's reverse mortgages is their high up-front costs. Homeowners should realize that if they are forced to move soon after taking the mortgage (because of illness, for example), they will almost certainly end up with a great deal less equity to live on than if they had simply sold the house outright. That is particularly true for loans that are terminated in five years or less. Because of the high up-front costs on all reverse mortgages, the effective interest rates for loans of short duration can be staggering.

The up-front expenses can include origination fees, mortgage insurance (if any), closing costs, and servicing fees. Interest is most often adjustable annually or monthly and tied to a public index; most reverse mortgages have limits on how far the rate can rise or fall. The higher the rate, of course, the faster equity will be used up. Reverse mortgages that adjust monthly have no limit.

One lender requires "appreciation sharing," in which it lays claim to a portion of any increase in the home's value, over and above the debt, generally in exchange for a fixed interest rate. Another lender offers "percent of value pricing," collecting a fixed percentage of the home's value when the loan comes due; that can be an exceptionally expensive option for borrowers if the loan must be paid off after only a few years.

New Truth-in-Lending rules to go into effect in October [1995] require lenders to disclose all costs and fees. The total cost estimates must illustrate at least three loan periods (short-term, life expectancy, and long-term) and three likely appreciation rates (the predicted percentage increase in the home's value over the loan period). Armed with these estimates from several lenders, borrowers can more easily match programs to their needs and shop for the best mortgage value.

Choosing a Plan

The most widely available plan is the FHA's Government-insured Home Equity Conversion Mortgage (HECM) program. To qualify for a HECM loan, homeowners must be at least 62 and live in a single-family home or condominium as their principal residence. Under this program, the amount of equity homeowners may borrow against depends on where they live as well as on prevailing interest rates. In 1995, the maximum amount rages from $77,197 to $152,362.

For people who have more expensive homes or who need to borrow more, there are alternatives. Set to begin this fall, a new program from the Federal National Mortgage Association will grant reverse mortgages on up to $203,000 of home equity. Other, private lenders are planning to offer even higher limits.

A caution: Most of the "private" reverse mortgages are not insured. Only the strength of the company backs whatever promises it may make. So anyone looking to a reverse mortgage for future income, rather than a lump sum up front, would be much better off in a Federally insured program.

Counseling is required before homeowners can apply for a HECM loan. And it's a good idea regardless. Through counseling, homeowners can quickly discover whether a reverse mortgage is really the best answer to their cash-flow problems. For an approved counselor, contact any HECM lender.

A free Home Equity Conversion Information Kit, including an extensive state-by-state "Reverse Mortgage Lenders List" is a available from the American Association of Retired Persons. Address a postcard to: D15601, AARP Home Equity Information Center EE0756, 601 E St. NW, Washington, D.C. 20049. Another valuable resource on reverse mortgages is the book "Your New Retirement Nest Egg: A Consumer Guide to the New Reverse Mortgages," by Ken Scholen ($19.95 postpaid from National Center for Home Equity Conversion, 7373 147th St. W, Suite 115, Apple Valley, Minn. 55124). □

Source: "Your Money: Reverse Mortgages" Copyright 1995 by Consumers Union of U.S., Inc., Yonkers, N.Y. 10703-1057. Reprinted by permission from CONSUMER REPORTS, July 1995.

Housing Expense Guidelines

How much should families spend for housing? The banking and housing industries provide individuals and families with guidelines for determining how much they can afford for housing. Banks have traditionally suggested that homeowners borrow no more than 2-1/2 times the family income for a home mortgage. For example, a family with a total annual before-re-tax income of $50,000 should plan to allocate no more than $125,000 toward a home mortgage. Renters should typically plan to spend about one week's take-home pay each month for rent.

The National Association of Realtors publishes housing affordability indexes showing the median income American families need to qualify for a mortgage on a median-priced existing single-family home or a first-time buyer starter home.

The Federal National Mortgage Association (FNMA) states that monthly housing payments (principal and interest, taxes, insurance, and associated costs) for a conventional loan cannot exceed 28% of gross monthly family income, and total family debt cannot exceed 36% of that amount. □

It's In the Cards: Defending Yourself Against Bank Card Fraud

By Charlotte Rush, Vice President of Public Affairs,
MasterCard International Incorporated

Thirty years ago, the credit card was a new invention. Today nearly 80 percent of American families have at least one credit card account. Other payment options, like ATM cards, are commonplace and new payment products are being developed all the time. One key to using these financial tools successfully is knowing how to protect them.

Defending Yourself Against Credit Card Fraud

In 1994 alone, credit card scam artists bilked businesses and individuals out of more than $2 billion. The methods they used range from scavenging through garbage cans for receipt carbons and high-tech eavesdropping to counterfeit cards and telephone order scams. As clever as the payment service industry is in crime-proofing cards, enterprising con artists and thieves still find ways to cheat unsuspecting card holders.

Fortunately, by taking a few simple precautions, consumers can fight fraud and avoid unnecessary worry and expense.

• Keep your cards in a secure place and check them periodically to make sure none are missing.

• Keep card account numbers in a separate, confidential place.

• Sign new cards as soon as you receive them.

• Destroy carbon copies of receipts, copies of airline tickets, travel itineraries—anything that displays your credit card number—and discard them yourself.

• Know when new or reissued cards and billing statements should arrive. Contact your card issuer immediately if they don't.

• Memorize your personal identification number (PIN) for ATM transactions or keep it in a separate place from your card.

• Don't use an obvious PIN, such as your birth date, your telephone extension or consecutive numbers.

• When using your credit or cash card, be sure you take your receipt with you. Never throw it away at the site of the purchase or in a public trash container.

• When you receive your statement, review it carefully. Compare dates and amounts to verify expenditures. If you don't keep your monthly statements, destroy them carefully before discarding them.

Report Errors, Loss or Theft Immediately.

Contact your card issuer as soon as your discover that your card has been lost or stolen. There is no time limit for reporting unauthorized charges. If an unauthorized purchase is made and you report it immediately, your maximum liability is $50 per card. If your card is a MasterCard, most issuers will waive that liability.

Once you've reported by telephone that someone else has used your payment card number, send a letter to the issuer stating that an "unauthorized charge" was made. This language ensures that your issuer will treat the incident as fraud rather than a billing error. Furthermore, you are protected in a dispute with creditors by the federal Fair Credit Billing Act *only* if you report an error in writing.

• If a new or re-issued card does not arrive when expected, call your card issuer.

• Write your issuer if you discover errors in your statement.

• Pay at least the minimum on all undisputed charges. You need not pay for any charges under dispute until the issue is resolved.

Keep Your Personal Information Private

When making a purchase in person, as opposed to ordering over the phone, refuse merchant requests for personal information. Your address and telephone number are not required as a condition of purchase with a credit card.

Do not provide your account number over the phone unless you initiate the call. Your card number can be used to generate unauthorized purchases on your account. Telemarketers offering cheap vacations or merchandise awards and asking for your credit card number are among the most common telephone scams.

Do not allow a merchant to record your card number on a check, receipt or other document. Many states have laws prohibiting this practice.

If you receive a suspicious solicitation by phone or mail from someone who wants your credit card number (or if you have been a victim of fraud), you should immediately report it to the National Consumers League fraud hotline at 1–800–876–7060, 9:00 a.m. to 5:30 p.m., ET, Monday through Friday. This organization collects information on credit card scams and works with state and local law enforcement agencies to eliminate such operations. □

Choosing a Credit Card

Source: U.S. Office of Consumer Affairs.

Check the following terms before selecting a credit card.

• Annual Percentage Rate (APR)—the cost of credit as a yearly rate.

• Free or Grace Period—allows you to avoid any finance charge by paying your balance in full before the due date. If there is no free period, you will pay a finance charge from the date of the transaction, even if you pay your entire balance when you receive your bill.

• Fees and Charges—most issuers charge an annual fee; some might also charge a fee for a cash advance or if you fail to make a payment on time or go over your credit limit.

U.S. Currency to Get a Face-Lift

Source: Federal Deposit Insurance Corporation.

The U.S. Treasury Department is working on a re-design of our currency—the first major overhaul of paper money in sixty-five years. It won't change the value of our money and your old bills will still be good.

The first of the new notes will be that favorite of counterfeiters, the $100 bill. It will debut in 1996, and the other denominations will follow in descending value, every six months to a year or so.

The overhaul is needed because counterfeiters are using highly sophisticated photocopying equipment. To thwart the criminals, the Treasury is considering making the portraits larger and more detailed, so they become distorted if photocopied. Also a watermark—an image that is only visible when the note is held up to the light—of the person pictured on that note may be added. Other changes may include embedding in the paper bits of shiny paper that won't reproduce and creating a background that will become distorted if photocopied.

The new currency will maintain its current size and colors, with portraits of the same historical figures on the faces and the same buildings or monuments on the backs. Whatever the final design changes, the "new" bills will still have the traditional look of U.S. money.

Another feature that may be added is called color-shifting ink. This means that when the bill is viewed directly, the ink appears to be the traditional green, but when the bill is turned at an angle, it changes to gold. Also included will be hidden features that can be identified only by machines at banks and businesses, making it easier for the banking system to detect counterfeits.

Why Is Our Money Green?

No one is certain why U.S. paper money is green, but the generally accepted explanation goes like this: In 1929, the size of our currency was reduced to what it is today, and certain features of the bills, like portraits, emblems, and monuments, were standardized. At that time, green ink was plentiful and was known to stand up to a lot of handling. And, says the Bureau of Engraving and Printing, the color was thought to represent stability and strength.

Green ink also seemed best to meet certain requirements of the printing process used then for manufacturing the bills. And, as various changes were made to bills since then, the green tint was simply retained as the basic color.

Financial Tips for Senior Citizens

Source: Federal Deposit Insurance Corporation.

Guard Against Con Artists

Studies have shown that senior citizens are often targets for swindlers because they are easy to find at home, or at shopping malls, medical buildings and other public places; many seniors live alone and want to socialize, even with a stranger; declining physical and mental conditions make them less able to recognize and resist a con artist; and crooks know the elderly often have substantial sums in a bank.

Some danger signals include offers that sound too good to be true; the use of a company or association name that is close to, but not the same as, a reputable organization; unwillingness to send you written information about the firm; requests for money before a product or service is delivered; and pressure to accept an offer fast. While one of these conditions may not be enough to sound an alarm, two or three of them should tell you that something isn't right.

If you're suspicious about an unsolicited offer, don't send money and don't give out personal information like your credit card or Social Security number, at least until you've had a chance to check out the company with agencies like the Better Business Bureau (listed in your local phone book). If you think that you already have been victimized, immediately contact the Better Business Bureau, your state Attorney General (also in the phone book), or the National Fraud Information Center at 1–800–876–7060 (a nonprofit organization in Washington that forwards reports of fraud to law enforcement authorities).

Watch out for bad "great deals"—unsolicited phone calls about prizes or bargains for goods, services, or travel, but the real reason is to get your credit card

number, checking account information, or check.

Beware of the "Bogus Banker," a person who claims to work for your bank and asks you to "verify" account information, really just to get your credit card number or similar details. Another ruse is for a crook to impersonate an investigator who says that you can help catch a dishonest bank employee if you provide money from your account.

Protect Yourself Against Theft

It's a good idea to arrange for the direct deposit into your bank of Social Security checks and other regular income payments. This way, the check can't get lost or stolen on the street or from your mailbox.

Automatic teller machines (ATMs) are a great convenience, but use them safely. It's best to use an ATM during daylight hours, but if you *must* use one after dark, choose an ATM that is well-lit and free of bushes or other places where a thief can hide.

If you spot someone suspicious standing or parked near the ATM, or if a stranger tries to strike up a conversation, get away to another, safer ATM.

Don't needlessly expose your cash after you've made a withdrawal from a bank or ATM.. You can always count the money later in a safer place, even inside your parked car.

If your ATM card or credit card is lost or stolen, call your bank or credit card company immediately and even follow up with a letter. And always take your ATM and credit card receipt with you. Don't just leave the receive anywhere or toss it in the trash. The receipt contains important information about your account that can be valuable to a thief.

Know Your Rights When Borrowing Money

If you think that you've been denied a loan because of your age, or if the amount that you can borrow was dramatically reduced when you retired, you may have a legitimate complaint under the Equal Credit Opportunity Act (ECOA). This law doesn't give anyone the right to a loan, but it does prohibit a lender from discriminating against someone because of age, sex, race, or other factors.

Under the ECOA, for example, a lender cannot turn your loan application down or offer you less credit just because of your age, refuse to consider your Social Security income in judging your application for a loan, close your loan account, change the terms of the account, or require you to reapply just because you reached a certain age or retired.

If you have been denied credit, the lender must notify you in writing, explain the reasons why, and give you the name and address of the appropriate government agency to contact if you think you have been discriminated against.

Try working out problems with the lender first. But if that doesn't work, you may contact the government agency, which can decide to investigate. You're also entitled to bring a lawsuit for actual damages plus a penalty, and perhaps recover attorneys' fees and court costs.

Obtain a Credit Card

If you don't already have a major credit card, such as a Visa or MasterCard, consider getting one. According to the American Association of Retired Persons (AARP), a credit card offers the following advantages to senior citizens: It is safer to carry than cash; it can cover emergency expenses, such as medicine not covered by insurance; and repairs for a car or home appliance; and a credit card can be required if you need to rent a car.

For divorced or widowed women in particular, having your own credit card can give you a credit history that will help if you ever need a loan for a home, car, or other purpose. □

Red Flags of Fraud

Stay away from telemarketers who want to: have you send money by wire • automatically withdraw money from your checking account • offer you a free prize, but charge shipping and handling fees • ask for your credit card number, checking account number, social security number, or other personal information • get payment in advance especially for employment referrals, credit repair, or providing a loan or credit card. □

How to Measure the Shrinking Value of the Dollar

Source: Martin Lefkowitz, economist, U.S. Chamber of Commerce.

How to use this table. The value of a dollar is given for any year relative to the 1995 dollar. For example: What weekly salary would you need to earn in 1995 to equal the purchasing power of a weekly salary of $100 in 1960? Take the 1960 multiplier, 5.16, times $100 and you would need to earn $516 a week in 1995 to achieve the same salary.

Again, what income would you need in 1995 to equal the purchasing power of $1000 in 1985? The 1985 multiplier, 1.42, times $1000, equals $1,420 needed to stay even with inflation during those past ten years.

Year	Value of dollar in 1995 dollars	Year	Value of dollar in 1995 dollars	Year	Value of dollar in 1995 dollars
1930	9.14	1952	5.76	1974	3.10
1931	10.04	1953	5.72	1975	2.84
1932	11.17	1954	5.67	1976	2.68
1933	11.80	1955	5.70	1977	2.52
1934	11.40	1956	5.61	1978	2.34
1935	11.11	1957	5.43	1979	2.10
1936	11.00	1958	5.28	1980	1.85
1937	10.62	1959	5.25	1981	1.68
1938	10.82	1960	5.16	1982	1.58
1939	10.98	1961	5.11	1983	1.53
1940	10.89	1962	5.05	1984	1.47
1941	10.37	1963	4.99	1985	1.42
1942	9.36	1964	4.92	1986	1.39
1943	8.82	1965	4.85	1987	1.34
1944	8.67	1966	4.71	1988	1.29
1945	8.48	1967	4.57	1989	1.23
1946	7.83	1968	4.39	1990	1.17
1947	6.55	1969	4.16	1991	1.12
1948	6.33	1970	3.93	1992	1.09
1949	6.41	1971	3.77	1993	1.06
1950	6.33	1972	3.65	1994	1.03
1951	5.87	1973	3.44	1995	1.00

NOTE: These figures are based on projected consumer price increases of 3.0% in 1995.

Mortgage Highlights

Type	Description	Considerations
Fixed rate mortgage	Fixed interest rate, usually long–term; equal mnthly payments of principl and interest until debt is paid in full.	Offers stability and long–term tax advantages. Interest rates may be higher than other types of financing. New fixed rates are rarely assumable.
Fifteen–year mortgage	Fixed interest rate. Requires down payment or monthly payments higher than 30–year loan. Loan is fully repaid over 15–year term.	Frequently offered at slightly reduced interest rate. Offers faster accumulation of equity than traditional fixed rate mortgage but has higher monthly payments. Involves paying less interest but this may result in fewer tax deductions.
Adjustable rate mortgage	Interest rate changes over the life of the loan, resulting in possible changes in your monthly payments, loan term, and/or principal. Some plans have rate or interest caps.	Starting interest rate is slightly below market, but payments can increase sharply and frequently if index increases. Payment caps prevent wide fluctuations in payments but may cause negative amortization. Rate caps limit total amount debt can expand
Renegotiable rate mortgage (roll–over)	Interest rate and monthly payments are constant for several years; changes possible thereafter. Long–term mortgage.	Less frequent changes in interest rate offer some stability.
Balloon mortgage	Monthly payments based on fixed interest rate; usually short–term; payments may cover interest only with principal due in full at term end.	Offers low monthly payments but possibly no equity until loan is fully paid. When due, loan must be paid off or refinanced. Refinancing poses high risk if rates climb.
Graduated payment mortgage	Lower monthly payments rise gradually (usually over 5–10 years), then level off for duration of term. With adjustable interest rate, additional payment changes possible if index changes.	Easier to qualify for. Buyer's income must be able to keep pace with scheduled payment increases. With an adjustable rate, payment increases beyond the graduated payments can result in additional negative amortization..
Shared appreciation mortgage	Below–market interest rate and lower monthly payments, in exchange for a share of profits when property is sold or on a specified date. Many variations.	If home appreciates greatly, total cost of loan jumps. If home fails to appreciate, projected increase in value may still be due, requiring refinancing at possibly higher rates.
Assumable mortgage	Buyer takes over seller's original, below–market rate mortgage.	Lowers monthly payments. May be prohibited if "due on sale" clause is in original mortgage. Not permitted on most new fixed rate mortgages.
Seller take–back	Seller provides all or part of financing with a first or second mortgage.	May offer a below–market interest rate; may have a balloon payment requiring full payment in a few years or refinancing at market rates, which could sharply increase debt.
Wraparound	Seller keeps original low rate mortgage. Buyer makes payments to seller who forwards a portion to the lender holding original mortgage. Offers lower effective interest rate on total transaction.	Lender may call in old mortgage and require higher rate. If buyer defaults, seller must take legal action to collect debt.
Growing equity mortgage (rapid payoff mortgage)	Fixed interest rate but monthly payments may vary according to agreed–upon scchedule or index.	Permits rapid payoff of debt because payment increases reduce principal. Buyer's income must be able to keep up with payment increases.
Land contract	Seller retains original mortgage. No transfer of title until loan is fully paid. Equal monthly payments based on below–market interest rate with unpaid principal due at loan end.	May offer no equity until loan is fully paid. Buyer has few protections if conflict arises during loan.
Buy–down	Developer (or other party) provides an interest subsidy which lowers monthly payments during the first few years of the loan. Can have fixed or adjustable interest rate.	Offers a break from higher payments during early years. Enables buyer with lower income to qualify. With adjustable rate mortgage, payments may jump substantially at end of subsidy. Developer may increase selling price.
Rent with option	Renter pays "option fee" for right to purchase property at specified time and agreed–upon price. Rent may or may not be applied to sales price.	Enables renter to buy time to obtain down payment and decide whether to purchase. Locks in price during inflationary times. Failure to take option means loss of option fee and rental payments.
Reverse annuity mortgage (equity conversion)	Borrower owns mortgage–free property and needs income. Lender makes monthly payments to borrower, using property as collateral.	Can provide homeowners with needed cash. At end of term, borrower must have money available to avoid selling property or refinancing.

Source: The Mortgage Money Guide, Federal Trade Commission.

Two Different Worlds: Gender in the Workplace

The data for these findings are based upon the U.S. Census Bureau's 1982 Characteristics of Business Owners (CBO) survey. Every 5 years, the CBO survey gathers information on a sample of female and minority business owners and a comparable sample of nonminority male business owners. The businesses are sole proprietorships, partnerships, or sub-chapter S corporations.

Small Firms Employ Primarily One Gender

While previous studies have examined the distribution of men and women in large firms, this is the first research to examine their distribution in small firms and to link the characteristics of business owners to the gender composition (i.e., the proportional presence of males and females) of the workplace. A sizable segment—about 40 percent—of the nation's employees work in firms of under 100 workers.

Using the CBO data on small businesses, researchers found that nearly 60 percent of women worked in firms where 75–100 percent of their co-workers were women, and over 75 percent worked in firms where more than half the employees were women.

A full 56 percent of men worked in firms where more than 90 percent of all employees were men, and over 20 percent of men worked in an all male firm.

The Business Owner Makes a Difference

Two characteristics of the business owners—gender and education—show a systematic relationship to the gender composition of the firm's workers.

- Female small business owners hire more female employees than do male owners. While about 39 percent of employees hired by men are women, 52 percent of employees hired by women are women.
- The higher the educational attainment of the male small business owner, the larger the percentage of female employees he hires. The percent women rises from 31.8 in firms owned by men with 8 or fewer years of education to 49.7 in firms owned by men with 16 or more years of education.

One possible explanation for this finding is that men with more education are often doctors, dentists, or lawyers who are hiring support staff in female-dominated occupations (nurses, paralegals, receptionists). Men with less education may own firms characterized by occupations dominated by males, such as electrical appliance repairs or shoe repairs.

Preponderance of Men Means Higher Pay

Firms employing mostly men paid their workers more. For example,

- Firms with 76–90 percent male employees paid wages that, on average, were 40 percent higher than similar firms whose work force was entirely female.
- When firms with similar sales receipts were compared, firms with 76–90 percent males still paid, on average, wages that were 10 percent higher than comparable firms whose work force was almost entirely female.

The Gender Distribution in Small Firms

Percent in each category

□ All employees   ■ Male employees   ▨ Female employees

Category of firm according to its percentage of female employees

20.7 percent men worked in firms in which there were no female employees. 4.6 percent men worked in firms in which over 75 percent of the employees were female. 2.0 percent of women worked in firms in which there were 1–9% female employees. 59.1 percent of women worked in firms in which 75–100 percent of the employees were female.

Findings Have Implications for "Pay Equity" and "Comparable Worth"

These findings have distinct implications for "pay equity" and "comparable worth."

Although the Equal Pay Act of 1963 outlaws differential pay for men and women in the *same* occupation and in the *same* firm, this study shows that a large component of gender pay differences result from men and women working in *different* firms.

Moreover, the reasons for which men and women work in different firms (pastry shops vs. gun shops) may bear no relationship to discrimination, and thus, there may be no discriminatory component to this aspect of pay differentials between men and women.

Proposed "comparable worth" programs aim at equalizing compensation for equivalently valuable (i.e., "worthy") work across occupational categories—within a firm. However, when men and women work in different firms, then comparable worth policies will not resolve the matter of wage gaps across occupations.

Conventional Explanations Are Incomplete

The most popular explanation for the differences in pay between men and women—and for the preponderance of women in some workplaces and men in others—is that there is discrimination by employers against women in the labor market.

However,

• Some occupations and industries tend to have more of one gender in the first place, and thus, the owner and the employees may more likely be of the same gender. For example, auto repair shops tend to be male-dominated; hair-styling salons tend to be female-dominated.

("Occupation" is a way of classifying workers based on the tasks they perform. "Industry" is a way of classifying establishments based on what goods or services they produce.)

• Also, some industries, or segments within industries, that employ mostly women—such as health, educational, personal or social services—also tend to use more part-time workers.

Issues surrounding differential pay remain unresolved in the present study because of limited information—in the CBO survey—on the characteristics of the workers (education, occupation, employment history, and number of hours worked). Data on specific workers at specific firms would provide a far more complete picture of the worker in relationship to the workplace. □

Women's, Men's Earnings Compared by Occupation, 1991

Women's earnings exceed those of men in only two occupations, although they are close in several others. In these 16 occupations, women earned at least 89 percent as much as men did in 1991. The Women's Bureau of the U.S. Department of Labor, which published the table on which the chart is based, notes, "It is apparent from the table that the occupations in which women fare well when their earnings are compared with men's are not women's work or men's jobs; rather, they occur throughout the whole spectrum of jobs." Only occupations employing at least 50,000 women are compared.

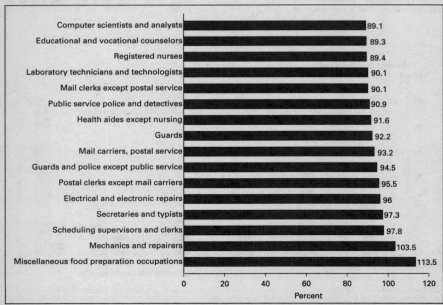

Occupation	Percent
Computer scientists and analysts	89.1
Educational and vocational counselors	89.3
Registered nurses	89.4
Laboratory technicians and technologists	90.1
Mail clerks except postal service	90.1
Public service police and detectives	90.9
Health aides except nursing	91.6
Guards	92.2
Mail carriers, postal service	93.2
Guards and police except public service	94.5
Postal clerks except mail carriers	95.5
Electrical and electronic repairs	96
Secretaries and typists	97.3
Scheduling supervisors and clerks	97.8
Mechanics and repairers	103.5
Miscellaneous food preparation occupations	113.5

Source: 1993 Handbook on Women Workers: Trends and Issues, Women's Bureau, U.S. Department of Labor, based on unpublished data from the Bureau of Labor Statistics.

The Fatherhood Movement

By Ken R. Canfield

One definition of a movement includes the following three parts: A movement has (1) a group of people who identify themselves as members of the movement, (2) literature that advances their cause, and (3) opposition from other forces.

Defined this way, the "fatherhood movement" is embryonic. By and large, public advocates of responsible fatherhood do not see themselves as a coherent group but as lone prophets shouting in a wilderness of neglect. And opposition to responsible fatherhood is difficult to find.

Still, there are some developments that have the feel of a movement:

The National Fatherhood Initiative has been formed to raise public awareness of the need for responsible fatherhood. The National Fatherhood Initiative is led by Don Eberly (president), who once served as a key aide to Jack Kemp; Wade Horn (director), commissioner of Children, Youth, and Families under President Bush; and David Blankenhorn (chairman), who was a civil-rights activist and community organizer before becoming involved in research on the need for fathers to be present and involved with their families. The group hosted a National Fatherhood Summit in October 1994 to educate civic leaders. After a tour this spring and summer [1995] featuring talks by David Blankenhorn, it will be aiming to spearhead an Ad Council campaign on the need for responsible fathers.

Another effort is that of Vice President Al Gore under the name "Father-to-Father." Through meetings of researchers and social-work practitioners (which have been deliberately low-key to ensure that this cause is not seen as partisan), the group is working to develop a private-sector mentoring program matching experienced fathers with newer dads. Gore personally signs on to Father-Net, a computer bulletin board sponsored by the Children, Youth, and Family Consortium of the University of Minnesota. Gore has brought together pioneers in the area of fathering such as Jim Levine and Ed Pitt of the Fatherhood Project and Ralph Smith of the Philadelphia Children's Network.

Levine's Fatherhood Project is sponsored by the Family and Work Institute in New York City. He champions "father-friendly" policies in the workplace and has developed practical materials on how to get men involved in early childhood development programs such as Head Start.

During his years as founder and president of the Philadelphia Children's Network, Ralph Smith promoted "father reengagement," refusing to accept the assumption of many social-welfare bureaucrats that fathers are unwilling or unable to support their children. Smith, now of the Annie E. Casey Foundation, recently helped found the National Center on Fathers and Families at the Graduate School of Education at the University of Pennsylvania. This center aims at closing the research gap in the social sciences on knowledge about fathers.

Meanwhile, a grass-roots group that makes no effort at changing public opinion, Promise Keepers, has motivated a stratum of men from the churches to take up the cause of fatherhood. The Christian group, headquartered in Denver, Colorado, is impressive through raw numbers: It attracted a total of more than 280,000 men for seven day-long events in stadiums across the nation last year [1994] and aims to conduct thirteen similar events this year.

While their speakers are a cross-section of evangelical Christians, the message is consistent: Men need to be servant-leaders of their families, get together with a few other men to encourage and support one another, and cross ethnic barriers to reach toward racial harmony. This group attracted some incidental opposition, as homosexual and feminist activists rallied outside one site last year, attacking and misinterpreting the group's motives.

Other developments, spontaneous and unconnected but portending bigger changes, include the following:

• Community colleges offering parent-education classes are starting to aim not just at mother-oriented preschool classes but at classes for fathers as well. Suzanne Spandau, an instructor at Pasadena City College in California, went so far as to offer a fathers-only class, "Being A Father and Loving It." Her class was well attended.

• Corporations are beginning to see resolving work-family tensions in a new light. IDS in Minneapolis recently hosted a fathering seminar taught by professional trainers that drew an overflow crowd, exceeding management's expectations. *Personnel Journal* reported in October 1994 that currently 60 percent of *Fortune* 500 companies offer parenting education programs. Those programs do not consistently take the fathers' needs and desires into account, but they may start to.

• A quasi-corporate municipal agency has gone one better than simply offering parenting education. The Los Angeles Department of Water and Power has an actual "Fathering Program" as part of its Work and Family Life Services office. The program coordinator arranges "Daddy-n-Me" recreation outings once a quarter for employees, lends beepers to dads with expectant wives, and sponsors noontime "information groups" for dads who get together monthly to talk and share ideas.

More Information

National Fatherhood Initiative:
800–790–DADS

FatherNet:
612–625–7251.
email address:
cyfcec@maroon.tc.umn.edu

The Fatherhood Project:
212–465–2044

National Center on Fathers and Families:
215–686–3910

Promise Keepers:
800–888–PK95

Los Angeles Department of Water and Power, Work and Family Life Services:
213–367–3546

National Institute for Responsible Fatherhood:
216–791–8336

Fathers' Education Network:
313–831–5838

MAD DADS:
402–451–3500

—K.R.C.

There may be a place for this kind of "affirmative action" for dads. Work and Family Life coordinator Ray Castro puts it this way, "Every time we hung out a sign 'Family Life Workshop' moms came, so the idea was to target men." No doubt part of the appeal of their offerings is that other men identify with Castro, who told me, "As a 22-year-old with all my degrees nobody had prepared me for the toughest job I would ever have: fatherhood."

• Programs to encourage unwed urban dads to form families are springing up as well. Charles Ballard's work in Cleveland, Ohio, has been so successful that he has been funded to replicate his program in five other cities. His program, the National Institute for Responsible Fatherhood, helps unwed young men acknowledge paternity, get regular jobs so they can support their kids, and develop stable relationships with their child's mother. Many formerly unwed couples have married as a result of participating in the program. Uncovering a man's paternal instinct is actually the first step in Ballard's program—and a much-neglected one.

• Fathers' Education Network in downtown Detroit, with Don Burwell, is taking fifty-two men through weekly gatherings aimed at instilling purpose in their lives and commitment to their children.

• MAD DADS in Omaha, Nebraska, was an "emergency response" when Eddie Staton and two other fathers founded it some five years ago. Dads were needed to take responsibility not just for their own children but for those wandering the streets at night. The group, which has thirty-two chapters nationally, has as its main focus patrolling the streets and talking with young people, especially those who are out after ten at night. The group confronts drug pushers with the consequences of their actions and brings together warring gangs simply to talk. MAD DADS is now taking the step of equipping both young and old fathers so that they may be more effective in rearing their children. □

This article appeared in the JUNE 1995 issue and is reprinted with permission from *The World & I*, a publication of *The Washington Times Corporation*, copyright © 1995.

Sexual Harassment

The term "sexual harassment" originated in the United States. It involves any unsolicited sexually motivated behavior whether physical or verbal that is perceived offensive by the victim. Federal courts first recognized sexual harassment as a prohibited form of sex discrimination in 1975.

In November 1993, the United States Supreme Court ruled unanimously that the Federal law against job discrimination as applied to sexual harassment was violated when the employee was in a work environment that "would be reasonably perceived, and is perceived, as hostile or abusive." The Court also rejected the requirement that plaintiffs show that sexual harassment made the workplace so hostile that it caused them "severe psychological injury." Justice Sandra Day O'Connor said that the Federal law's protection "comes into play before the harassing conduct leads to a nervous breakdown."

Unfortunately, the Court's broad interpretation did not define what is considered "reasonable," and that decision will be left to future jury trials to determine

the validity of each victim's "perceptions." Because there is a gray area in the definition of sexual harassment, male and female employees have to be concerned that their workplace behavior will not be misinterpreted as harassing and be careful not to send confused signals that may eventually put them at risk of being sued.

Although the vast majority of sexual harassment claims are brought by women, women can also harass men and male employees can complain that they weren't promoted or were fired because they refused the unwanted attentions of their female bosses. Nationwide, male charges of sexual harassment have doubled. Men have also filed complaints against male bosses.

In 1993, a 34-year-old Los Angeles man accused his female boss of sexually harassing him and he successfully sued her. A jury of ten women and two men awarded him over one million dollars in damages. This was the first time that a man won a sexual harassment case against a woman. □

Equal Rights Amendment

Next to abortion, the Equal Rights Amendment (ERA) was perhaps the most widely debated feminist issue of the 1970s. The ERA, which would provide for the legal equality of the sexes, was first proposed by the National Women's party in 1923. In its most recent form the amendment declared, "Equality of rights under the law shall not be denied or abridged by the United States or any State on account of sex." The amendment was approved by the requisite two-thirds vote of the House of Representatives in October 1971 and by the Senate in March 1972. Spurred by the revival of feminism in the late 1960s and 1970s, the ERA received much early support as thirty states ratified it within one year of its Senate approval. But it ultimately failed to achieve ratification by the required thirty-eight states, even though the deadline for ratification was extended to June 30, 1982. The defeat of the ERA was spearheaded by Phyllis Schlafly and her organization Stop ERA, which benefited from the conservative backlash

that gained momentum in the mid-1970s. Nonetheless, despite its defeat, public support for the amendment never fell below 54%, and as late as 1976 support for its passage was included in the platforms of both major political parties.

Opponents of the women's movement thought that the ERA would challenge traditional gender roles and ruin the stability of the family. They maintained that the ERA was unnecessary because women's rights were already protected. They also claimed that the ERA would lead to a draft of women into the military, abolish separate-sex public restrooms, and end alimony payments to divorced women.

In the view of ERA opponents, if men and women were equal in the eyes of the law, women would be as responsible as men for the support of the family. Therefore, a husband could not be held fully responsible for support of his wife and children.

The National Women's Hall of Fame

The National Women's Hall of Fame is the only national membership organization that honors and celebrates the achievements of American women. Founded in 1969 in Seneca Falls, New York, where in 1848 the first Women's Rights Convention was held, the Hall inducts distinguished women and offers programs and exhibits in Seneca Falls, the Finger Lakes area, Washington, D.C. and elsewhere.

Women are chosen for inclusion in the Hall of Fame on the basis of:

• The value of their contribution to society, to significant groups within society, or the progress and freedom of women.
• Their contributions to art, athletics, business, government, philanthropy, humanities, science, and education.
• The enduring value of their achievements.

For further information, contact The National Women's Hall of Fame, 76 Fall Street, Seneca Falls, N.Y. 13148. Phone: (315) 568–8060.

1995 Honorees

Virginia Apgar (1909–1974), Physician who invented lifesaving newborn health assessment test, the Apgar Scale.

Ann Bancroft (1955–), Polar explorer; first woman to reach the North and South Poles across the ice.

Amelia Bloomer (1818–1894), Suffragist and social reformer; founded and edited *The Lily*, the first newspaper devoted to reform and equality for women.

Mary Breckinridge (1881–1965), Nurse–midwife and founder of the Frontier Nursing Service, created to provide health care in rural areas.

Eileen Collins (1956–), First woman to pilot the space shuttle.

Elizabeth Hanford Dole (1936–), First woman Secretary of Transportation; Secretary of Labor; President of the American Red Cross.

Anne Dallas Dudley (1876–1955), Key leader in passage of the Nineteenth Amendment, giving women the right to vote; Tennessee suffrage and political leader.

Mary Baker Eddy (1821–1910), The first American woman to found a worldwide religion, the Church of Christ, Scientist (Christian Science).

Ella Fitzgerald (1917–), Singer.

Margaret Fuller (1810–1850), Author, feminist, Transcendentalist leader and teacher.

Matilda Joslyn Gage (1826–1898), Feminist, suffrage leader and author.

Lillian Moller Gilbreth (1878–1972), Industrial engineer and motion study expert whose ideas improved industry and the home.

Nannerl O. Keohane (1940–), Political scientist and educator; first woman President of Duke University; first woman to head a major women's college (Wellesley) and research university.

Maggie Kuhn (1905–1995), Founder of the Gray Panthers.

Sandra Day O'Connor (1930–), The first woman Justice of the U.S. Supreme Court.

Josephine St. Pierre Ruffin (1842–1924), Leader and organizer of Black women's organizations; Abolitionist and anti–lynching crusader.

Patricia Schroeder (1940–), Congresswoman who has pioneered passage of legislation helping women and families.

Hannah Greenebaum Solomon (1858–1942), Founder of the National Council of Jewish Women.

Past Honorees

Bella Abzug	Shirley Chisholm	Dorothy Height	Margaret Mead
Abigail Adams	Jacqueline Cochran	Grace Hopper	Maria Mitchell
Jane Addams	Ruth Colvin	Dolores Huerta	Constance Baker Motley
Ethel Percy Andrus	Jane Cunningham Croly	Helen Hunt	Lucretia Mott
Marian Anderson	Emily Dickinson	Zora Neale Hurston	Antonio Novello
Susan B. Anthony	Dorothea Dix	Anne Hutchinson	Annie Oakley
Ella Baker	Amelia Earhart	Mary Jacobi	Georgia O'Keeffe
Clara Barton	Catherine East	Frances Wisebart Jacobs	Rosa Parks
Mary McLeod Bethune	Marian Wright Edelman	Mae Jemison	Alice Paul
Antoinette Blackwell	Gertrude Belle Elion	Barbara Jordan	Frances Perkins
Elizabeth Blackwell	Alie Evans	Helen Keller	Esther Peterson
Emily Blackwell	Geraldine Ferraro	Billie Jean King	Jeannette Rankin
Margaret Bourke-White	Betty Friedan	Suzette La Flesche	Ellen Swallow Richards
Myra Bradwell	Charlotte Perkins Gilman	Belva Lockwood	Linda Richards
Gwendolyn Brooks	Ella Grasso	Juliette Gordon Low	Sally Ride
Pearl S. Buck	Martha Griffiths	Mary Lyon	Eleanor Roosevelt
Annie Jump Cannon	Fannie Lou Hamer	Mary Mahoney	Sister Elaine Roulet
Rachel Carson	Alice Hamilton	Wilma Mankiller	Wilma Rudolph
Mary Cassatt	Helen Hayes	Barbara McClintock	Florence Sabin
Willa Cather	Mary Harris "Mother	Louise McManus	Margaret Sanger
Carrie Chapman Catt	Jones"		

Katherine Siva Saubel	Elizabeth Cady Stanton	Harriet Tubman	Sarah Winnemucca
Betty Bone Schiess	Gloria Steinem	Lillian D. Wald	Fanny Wright
Mother Elizabeth Seton	Nettie Stevens	Madam C.J. Walker	Rosalyn Yalow
Florence Seibert	Lucy Stone	(Sarah Breedlove)	Gloria Yerkovich
Muriel Siebert	Harriet Beecher Stowe	Faye Wattleton	Mildred "Babe' Didrickson
Bessie Smith	Helen Brook Taussig	Ida B. Wells-Barnett	Zaharias
Margaret Chase Smith	Sojourner Truth	Oprah Winfrey	

Spouse Abuse: A Hidden Health Issue

Source: Health Words for Women, Summer 1995, a publication of Victory Memorial Hospital, Brooklyn, N.Y.

Many people think of domestic abuse as an interpersonal problem between partners. It's also a medical problem. The victims of domestic abuse account for 100,000 days of hospitalizations, almost 30,000 emergency department visits, and almost 40,000 physician visits each year. Battering is the single greatest cause of injury to women—more frequent, in fact, than car accidents, muggings and rapes combined.

But the physical injuries of any given incident of abuse aren't the only medical problems that victims experience. The stress of repeatedly suffering through the cycle of abuse—tension building (in which the batterer is moody and critical, acute explosion (in which the actual abuse occurs), and "honeymoon" (in which the batterer begs for forgiveness)—can cause additional medical problems. Those problems include headaches, low-back pain, chest pain, anxiety disorders, sleeplessness and eating disorders. The combination of physical and psychological symptoms that occur in women who suffer chronic abuse is known medically as the battered woman syndrome.

Doctors can help abused women by listening, by treating injuries and by referring women to appropriate support services—all with a guarantee of confidentiality. But doctors can't help if they don't know the true nature of the problem. In some cases, a physician may suspect abuse because of the nature of the injuries or the patient's history. Yet physicians can't always recognize the physical complains of battered women as abuse without help from the victims themselves.

To compound the problem, many women who are abused have difficulty admitting it because of the fear, guilt or shame they may feel, or because of a deep-seated denial that they are being abused.

Signs of Abuse

Keep in mind there are many forms of abuse directed toward women. Experts say that a woman's "Yes" answers to any of the following questions may suggest an abusive relationship:

1. Is she frightened at times by her partner's temper?
2. Is she afraid to disagree with him?
3. Is she constantly apologizing for her partner's behavior, especially when he has treated her badly?
4. Does she have to justify everything she does, every place she goes, or every person she sees to avoid her partner's anger?
5. Does her partner put her down, but then tell he that he loves her?
6. Has her partner ever hit, kicked, shoved or thrown things at her?
7. Does she not see friends or family because of her partner's jealousy?
8. Has her partner ever forced her to have sex?
9. Is she afraid to break up with her partner or leave him because he has threatened to hurt her, her children or himself?

Recognizing the Potential Batterer

Experts have found that male batterers tend to fit a profile. The characteristics listed below aren't definitive signs that a man is a batterer—only that he may have the potential to become one:

- The man reports having been physically or psychologically abused as a child.
- His mother was battered by his father.
- He plays with guns and uses them to protect himself against other people.
- He commits random acts of violence against objects and things.
- He drinks alcohol to excess.
- He becomes enraged when his partner doesn't listen to his advice.
- He appears to have a dual personality.
- There's a sense of "overdoing it" in his cruelty—or in his kindness.
- He has rigid ideas of what other people should or shouldn't doe that are determined by male or female sex-role stereotypes.

To receive the best care possible, a victim of abuse must be honest with her doctor about her home life. Admitting to abuse can be scary, to say the least, but it's the first step on the road to recovery.

A Closer Look at the Problem

- Between 2 and 6 million women experience at least one act of abuse each year. (The low number relates predominantly to physical acts. The higher number encompasses all acts of abuse.)
- In homes where spouse abuse occurs, children are abused at a rate 1,500 percent higher than the national average.
- More than a million adult American women have been victims of one or more forcible rapes by their husbands.
- In 1991, 28 percent of all female murder victims were slain by their husbands or boyfriends. That translates to four women a day killed by male partners.
- Family violence kills as many women every five years as the total number of Americans who died in the Vietnam war.

Research on Why Marriages Succeed or Fail

Successful marriages hinge on the ability of partners to handle conflict well.

By Randall Edwards

In the future, will engaged couples not only line up for blood tests and AIDS tests but also for marriage-endurance tests?

In the past year [1994], leading researchers in the field of family therapy have published the results of decades-long research into what makes some marriages last while others disintegrate. Some claim they are able to predict, with more than 90 percent accuracy, whether a marriage will succeed or fail, based on interviews with couples while they are still happily together.

Still, the researchers don't intend to use their findings to set up marital prognostication clinics. Instead, the information should be used to help all couples have happier marriages, said Howard J. Markman, PhD, a professor of psychology at the University of Denver.

Currently only about 50 percent of couples manage to avoid divorce. About 1.2 million couples divorce each year in the United States, affecting roughly 2 million children. Between 40 percent and 60 percent of new marriages will fail, depending upon which study is cited, or about 4.7 divorces for every 1,000 people in the country. That figure represents a decline since divorce hit its peak of 5.3 divorces per 1,000 people in the mid-1970s, and the rate generally is thought to be leveling off.

The new results challenge many of the popular assumptions about marriage. Among the beliefs debunked were:

• Incompatible couples cannot have successful marriages.

• Extramarital affairs are the result of problems in the marriage and will likely end the marriage.

• Volatile marriages are less likely to survive than more peaceful unions.

Love and commitment to the relationship are necessary for a good marriage, but they are not enough, said Markman.

"What are needed, on top of that, are skills in effective communication and how to handle conflict," Markman said. If divorce *is* unavoidable it doesn't have to be unbearable.

Markman and Clifford I. Notarius, PhD, a professor of psychology at Catholic University of America, studied 135 couples who were planning marriage when the study began 12 years ago. Their research is detailed in the 1993 book, *We Can Work It Out*. Seventy of the 103 couples who eventually married remain married, 18 divorced and three separated. They have identified a set of variables, which have predicted with 93 percent accuracy which couples would split. Most couples who divorce do so in the first 10 years of marriage.

"How you handle conflict is the single most important predictor of whether your marriage will survive," Markman said.

Markman's subjects have done better than the national average and he traces their success to the fact that about one-third of the couples participated in a divorce prevention and relationship-enhancing program that the two researchers devised.

Those who participated in the program, which emphasized conflict management and effective communication skills, showed lower rates of both divorce and domestic violence. The subjects participated in five two-and-a-half hour sessions over a five-week period, and were given extensive homework that required them to practice communication and problem-solving skills and discuss the expectations they had of their partners.

Markman found that certain behavior patterns usually signaled an impending collapse in a marriage:

• When either partner—although it is most often the male—withdraws from conflict.

• The tendency to escalate conflict in the face of disagreement and the inability to stop fights before they get ugly.

• The tendency to invalidate the relationship by hurling insults at each other.

"We tell couples that one 'zinger' counteracts 20 positive acts of kindness," he explained.

Squelching the Positive

A different formula is offered by John Gottman, PhD, professor of psychology at the University of Washington. Gottman, who has claimed a 94 percent accuracy rate in predicting divorces among the 2,000 couples he has studied over the past two decades, believes a successful marriage can be reduced to a simple mathematical equation: A couple must have at least five times as many positive as negative moments in their marriage.

In his recent book, *Why Marriages Succeed or Fail*, Gottman cites his research since 1980 to prove that marital satisfaction is linked to spouses' physiological responses to marital upsets. Gottman monitored changes in subjects' heart rates, sweat and adrenaline levels during laboratory conversations about issues that caused problems in the marriage. He discovered triggers as simple as a slight change in facial expression or tone of voice, a raised eyebrow or curl of the lip.

His data show that during emotional stress, the body's release of hormones such as adrenaline increases the heart rate and respiration, further heightening anxiety. Inner thoughts and the aroused nervous system "goad each other on," he said, making it difficult to break out of a pattern of escalating conflict.

The hormonal activity triggers a "fight or flight" stress reaction, with intense fear and anxiety. Gottman calls this phenomenon "flooding" and argues that partners in bad marriages often experience "chronic flooding," a conditioned response to certain situations that makes it impossible to work out problems.

"In short, you begin to react to your spouse like an animal conditioned to fear shock whenever it sees the color red," he wrote. "Show the red and the animal panics; let your spouse speak in a certain tone of voice or have a particular facial expression, and you react as though you have already been attacked."

Once flooding becomes chronic, the individual is unable to think positively about his or her spouse, and many partners even block out memories of good times in the relationship. Some cannot even remember the details of their first meetings or early dates.

Surviving Infidelity

Compatibility is not the issue, Gottman said. Couples need to identify the physical patterns that aggravate marital stress, break the cycles of negativity and learn to validate each other throughout the course of their marriages.

As for the old scapegoat, the extramarital affair, Shirley P. Glass, PhD, said her studies of more than 200 couples over the last 12 years indicate that two-thirds of marriages survive infidelity. She conducted the studies with Thomas Wright, PhD, director of clinical training at Catholic University.

"Some people say that an affair is always a symptom of a problem in a marriage, except in cases of sexual addiction. That's ridiculous," said Glass, a Baltimore therapist.

Attitudes that may be rooted in previous generations can lead men and women to look toward another partner, even when their own marriage is otherwise happy and fulfilling, she said.

Affairs involving the wife are more likely to lead to divorce, Glass said. First, women are more likely to be emotionally involved in sexual relationships than men, which leads to a detachment from their spouses that is hard to overcome. Second, "men are less patient in dealing with the aftermath" of an affair.

"But you never know," she added. "Sometimes when people are able to talk about their anger and their hurt, and the other partner really listens, that detachment and contempt can shift. It's hard to tell what's going to happen by the way they act toward each other when they first come in." □

The American Family Is in Transition

Since 1960, the American family has undergone many changes in the traditional family pattern of two biological or adoptive parents and a working breadwinner father and a full-time at-home mother. Among the forces of change were a massive influx of women into the workforce, an emphasis on self-gratification and self-fulfillment, and the destigmatization of divorce and cohabitation. The women's movement also contributed to the liberation of women from their former predetermined roles as homemakers and workers and subsequently family structures changed.

Since 1986, the United States has had the highest divorce rate in the world, and is now the world's leader in fatherless families.

Over the past three decades, the divorce rate doubled and gender roles changed with the growing number of working mothers (which may reach 70% by the year 2000), the burgeoning number of single-parent households[1] (30% of the nation's families in 1993), and the rise of couples living together and out of wedlock.

Not only are fewer people choosing to get married, but those that do are less likely to have children. Those who do have children have fewer of them. Only 10% of households in 1992 had five people or more compared to 21% in 1970.

According to a recent report, one out of two American children (33.4 million) lived in a situation other than the traditional "nuclear family" in 1991. These children lived in a home which included, for example, a single parent, a stepparent, grandparent, another relative, or a nonrelative.

Today, fathers are playing a larger role in taking care of their children. In 1991 (the latest data), 20% of preschoolers were cared for by their fathers while their mothers were at work, up from 15% in 1988. In addition, more of our preschoolers are enrolled in school. Nursery school enrollment has more than doubled from 1.3 million in 1973 to 3.0 million in 1993, due in part to the increasing educational levels and labor force participation of mothers.

These changes have resulted in new family groups such as dual-career couples, single parents, at-home fathers, gay and lesbian families, domestic partnerships, and even child-bearing families created by post-menopausal mothers.

Grandparents have also felt the impact of the new family structures. In 1993, there were 3.4 million grandchildren under 18 years old living in the home of their grandparent(s). This represented 5% of all children under 18, up from 3% in 1970.

Most of the increase in grandchildren living with grandparents has been among children with only a mother present in the household. Since 1970, the proportion of grandchildren with neither parent present has declined from 43 to 30% in 1993, while the proportion with mother only present has increased from 37 to 49 percent. Continued high levels of divorce and the rise in out-of-wedlock childbearing had a substantial role in this change.

In addition, people are living longer—persons 65 and older (33 million persons) are estimated at 13% of all Americans and that will probably increase to 18% (over 80 million) by 2020. Subsequently, more families will be challenged to care for older members who become more dependent on them.

Although the American family structure is in transition, recent statistics still give high marks to married couples. Studies presented at the Population Conference of America in April 1995 indicated that married life was more beneficial to the health, financial, and emotional well-being of couples than either cohabitation or single life.

In addition, it was reported that married people have frequent and more satisfying sex than do single persons or cohabiting couples. The research suggests that the lifelong commitment to marriage enhances all levels of support that the partners bring to the marriage relationship.

Researchers also found that those who live together before marriage have higher divorce rates than couples who didn't cohabit and they are generally less happy together than married couples are.

Two disturbing trends that have emerged in recent decades are the rise in family violence and the growing problem of child abuse and neglect. The disintegration of traditional family values has been blamed for many of today's societal problems and has become a controversial political issue. □

---

1. The proportion of single-parent families was only 13% in 1970. Nearly three-fourths of the single parents in 1993 either have never married or were divorced.

One-Parent Families Up Across the Nation

According to the latest (January 1995) census data on the nation's 46 metropolitan areas with one million or more people, New York led the list in 1990 with the highest percentage of single-parent families (36%), New Orleans, La., was second at 34%, followed by Miami–Hialeah, Fla. (31%), Detroit, Mich. (29%) and Sacramento, Calif., and Baltimore, Md., with 28% each.

At the lower end of the scale, the three large metropolitan areas with the lowest rates of single-parent families in 1990 were Nassau–Suffolk, N.Y. (14%), Middlesex, N.J. (15%), and Bergen–Passaic, N.J. (18%)—each bordered on New York, which had the highest rate.

The census report also showed that four in ten single-parent renters living in metro areas were either unemployed or not in the labor force. The rate for single-parent owners was less than half that, at 16 percent. □

Metro Areas With 25% or More Single-Parent Families, 1990

(Metro areas with 1 million or more persons)

	Number of family households with own children under 18	Percent of all family households with own children	Single-Parent Families		
			Number maintained by mothers	Number maintained by fathers	Mother-to-father ratio
New York, NY PMSA	925,042	35.9	286,976	44,839	6.4
New Orleans, LA MSA	160,702	33.6	46,801	7,134	6.6
Miami–Hialeah, FL PMSA	219,409	30.8	53,692	13,913	3.9
Detroit, MI PMSA	551,789	29.2	138,398	22,608	6.1
Sacramento, CA MSA	186,950	28.2	41,923	10,767	3.9
Baltimore, MD MSA	285,017	28.2	67,173	13,070	5.1
Milwaukee, WI PMSA	179,714	27.6	43,073	6,599	6.5
Cleveland, OH PMSA	217,724	27.4	51,270	8,489	6.0
Los Angeles–Long Beach, CA PMSA	1,015,965	27.2	208,090	68,140	3.1
Chicago, IL PMSA	709,586	27.2	162,982	30,131	5.4
Oakland, CA PMSA	251,284	26.7	53,609	13,447	4.0
Fort Lauderdale–Hollywood–Pompano Beach, FL PMSA	130,400	26.6	27.240	7,410	3.7
Tampa–St. Petersburg–Clearwater, FL MSA	215,622	26.5	46,280	10,821	4.3
San Antonio, TX MSA	173,352	25.6	37,408	6,997	5.3
Denver, CO PMSA	213,599	25.3	43,399	10,714	4.1
Rochester, NY MSA	125,191	25.2	26,415	5,163	5.1
St. Louis, MO–IL MSA	312,148	25.1	65,981	12,426	5.3
Cincinnati, OH–KY–IN PMSA	190,856	25.1	40,897	7,060	5.8
Phoenix, AZ MSA	259,911	25.1	50,044	15,255	3.3
Philadelphia, PA–NJ PMSA	560,904	25.0	116,248	23,977	4.8
San Diego, CA MSA	291,335	25.0	57,149	15,588	3.7

NOTE: Counts reflect 100-percent response rates and are not subject to sampling variability. Metro areas correspond to the definitions that were in place in 1990. MSA—Metropolitan Statistical Area. PMSA—Primary Metropolitan Statistical Area. *Source:* U.S. Bureau of the Census.

Unmarried-Couple Households, With Children: 1970 to 1993

(Numbers in thousands)

Year	Total married couples	Unmarried couples			Ratio of unmarried couples per 100 married couples
		Total	Without children under 15 years	With children under 15 years	
1993	54,199	3,510	2,274	1,236	6
1990	56,112	2,856	1,966	891	5
1985	51,114	1,983	1,380	603	4
1980	49,714	1,589	1,159	431	3
1970 Census	44,593	523	327	196	1

Source: "Current Population Reports, P20–478, Marital Status and Living Arrangements: March 1993." Source of 1970 data: "1970 Census of Population, PC(2)–4B, Persons by Family Characteristics," table 11.

Cohabitation

Source: Bureau of the Census.

In 1993, 3.5 million households consisted of unmarried adults living together compared with 2.9 million in 1990 and 523,000 in 1970. Today, there are six unmarried couples for every 100 married couples, compared with only one for every 100 in 1970. In 1993, there were 1.2 million children under age 15 living in unmarried households. ☐

Interracial Married Couples

According to the Census Bureau, a very small proportion of all married couples are interracial, and there has been very little increase in this percent over the past two decades. In 1991, there were 994,000 interracial married couples, representing only 1.9 percent of all married couples. A 1991 census report on Marital Status and Living Arrangements published in 1992 showed 231,000 Black married to White couples in 1991, 720,000 White married to "other" (other than White or Black), and 43,000 Black married to "other" couples. Between 1970 and 1991, the number of interracial married couples increased from 310,000 to 994,000. This increase is partially attributable to the difference between the sampling variability of the two census surveys [Current Population Survey (CPS) versus Decennial census]. ☐

Gay Marriages

In a case brought up by three homosexual couples, the Hawaiian State Supreme Court ruled three to one on May 5, 1993, that a ban on marriages between couples of the same sex may violate the State Constitution's prohibition against sex discrimination. However, the court did not overturn the ban. The Supreme Court sent the case back to the Trial Court to determine whether preserving the marriage ban was a "compelling state interest."

No state currently permits same sex couples to marry. If Hawaii eventually permitted same sex couples to marry, the union would have to be recognized nationwide because marriages in one state are legally recognized in all states. However, there may be legal problems with the states where sodomy is a criminal act.

In 1992, Denmark made homosexual marriages legal and survivors of same sex partnerships are granted the right to survivor benefits and the right to inherit the deceased partner's pension. However, they were not granted the right to adopt children. Sweden also permits gay marriages.

Domestic Partnerships

The newest category of family, called domestic partnerships, has been sanctioned by over 25 cities or counties in the United States to grant some of the rights of traditional married couples to unmarried heterosexual, homosexual, elderly, and disabled couples who share the traditional bond of a family.

In March 1993, New York City joined San Francisco, Seattle, Boston, Minneapolis, and other municipal governments in legally acknowledging domestic partnerships. To become recognized as domestic partners in New York, unmarried, unrelated couples over 18 years of age register at the City Clerk's office with two proofs of identification and place of residence and swear that they have a close committed personal relationship and have been living together on a continuing basis. They receive a notarized affidavit similar to a marriage license. To divorce from the partnership, couples simply have to advise the city that they no longer live together as couples.

The rights granted include the same unpaid leave that married city workers receive and the same standing as married couples in qualifying for apartments. The registered domestic partners of homosexuals and unmarried heterosexuals also receive the same health benefits that married city workers receive.

In June 1994, Vermont became the first state to extend health coverage to the unmarried heterosexual and homosexual partners of its state workers. ☐

Gay and Lesbian Parents

There is no accurate count of the number of gay and lesbian families. There may be millions of homosexual parents in this country. While the Census Bureau publishes official data about single parents and unmarried couples, it has never made a survey of gay and lesbian families or the number of homosexuals in the United States. The Census Bureau would need the approval of the U.S. Congress in order to request this information in the next census which will be taken in the year 2000. The need for these data would depend on our Government's policies at that time.

Gay parents have become more visible in recent years and more and more lesbians and gay men are considering parenthood. However, many of these couples fear public intolerance and retribution. In the past decade, scores of lesbian and gay parenting groups have arisen in many cities across the U.S. to offer information, support, and guidance. Many children of homosexual parents are children from a former marriage, others are either adopted, or conceived by artificial insemination. Gay parents love their children the same as straight parents do and the great majority of studies by social scientists show that children raised by same-sex parents are not in any way psychologically damaged in comparison with children of traditional opposite-sex couples. Unfortunately, the children of gay parents sometimes face hostility outside their homes from neighbors or schoolmates who can't accept their parents' homosexuality.

In a highly publicized case in September 1993, a 23-year-old mother, Sharon Bottoms, lost the custody of her 2-year-old son to her mother when a Virginia judge ruled that her lesbian relationship was immoral and made her an unfit mother. This case had contradictory moral standards because Ms. Bottoms testified that her mother's former live-in boyfriend of 17 years had sexually molested her at least twice a week for five years between the ages of 12 to 17 years old. Her mother denied knowing about her boyfriend's criminal actions.

In June 1994, the Virginia Court of Appeals overturned the lower court's decision and ruled that Ms. Bottoms' sexual conduct, although illegal in Virginia, does not create a presumption of unfitness and she regained custody of her son. However, in April 1995, the Virginia Supreme Court awarded the custody of her son to the boy's maternal grandmother. The court said "living daily under conditions stemming from active lesbianism practiced in the home may impose a burden upon a child by reason of the 'social condemnation' attached to such an arrangement."

As shown in this case, the laws regarding the rights of gay and lesbian parents are at best mixed. Some state courts approve gay adoption, others don't permit it. Courts in states such as New York, New Jersey, Vermont, Minnesota, and California have allowed homosexuals to adopt children. ☐

Divorce and Children: Guidelines for Parents

Source: American Academy of Pediatrics.

When parents divorce, it is often hard for their children to get used to a new way of life. There are many things parents going through a divorce can do to help their children. The American Academy of Pediatrics offers the following information and advice to parents who are thinking of divorce or are already divorced.

Preparing for a Divorce

Divorce can be seen as the loss of the family as a unit and, like a death, often includes feelings of sadness and loss by adults and children. How much stress occurs in children and how long it lasts will depend on many things, but largely on the kind of support children get from their parents. There are many ways parents can help prepare their children for the changes ahead.

Talk to your children about the separation or divorce.—Think about what your children can understand, and then be open and honest with them. It will help your children if they know what is going to happen, especially the changes that will directly affect them. Try to be sensitive to your children's needs and pace the changes so that not too many of them happen at one time. This will help your children feel more secure through this process.

Here are some questions you might expect from your children or that you can bring up yourself:
• Why are you getting divorced?
• Will you and daddy ever get back together again?
• Where am I going to live?
• Was the divorce my fault?
• Will I have to change schools?
• How often will I see daddy/mommy?
• Will I still be able to see my friends?
• Will I still be able to see my grandparents?
• Are we going to be poor?
• Can I still go to summer camp?
• Who will I spend holidays with?

Also, talk to your children about any changes in their roles within the family. If you are going back to work or changing work hours, talk to your children about how they might need to help more around the house, like setting the table or cleaning their rooms. However, do not use your children to replace your ex-spouse. Avoid statements such as, "You are the man in the family now," or "Now I have to depend on you." If these changes become too much for your children or for yourself to handle, talk to a counselor. He or she can help you understand your feelings and cope with these changes.

Be honest about the divorce with your children.—When going through a divorce, it might not be easy for you and your ex-partner to agree on every issue that affects your children. It's best for your children if you make as many decisions as you can before telling them about the separation. Talk with them about what is going on in terms that are honest and simple. Assure your children that, even though these changes will take getting used to, life can be happier under the new family arrangement.

Try your best to understand the feelings of your children.—Even though this may be a hard time for you, it is probably even harder for your children. Encourage them to talk about their feelings. Talking about feelings is good for everyone involved, and can reduce the stress you all feel.

Getting Through the Divorce Process

Once the divorce is under way, your children may need special attention and time with each parent. This is a hard time for everyone, but especially for children. Keep the following guidelines in mind:

Try not to let anger or legal battles cause you to overlook your child's needs.—Children shouldn't be exposed to arguments between divorced parents. Experts say this can be harmful to a child and can make it harder for them to adjust after a divorce. Both parents should step back and be willing to make compromises. If you are having trouble working out your differences, especially early in the process, see a mediator.

It is important to keep the lines of communication open with your ex-spouse and work together for the sake of your children. Remember, you both are responsible for raising your children. Sometimes parents choose to discuss parenting issues when they are bringing their child to or back from visiting the other parent. If such face-to-face talks result in arguments, talk about these issues over the phone or see a counselor to resolve on-going differences.

Try to work out an acceptable visitation/custody arrangement.—Today, parents are able to work out a wide variety of custody and visitation arrangements. **Physical custody** is based on where the children live. **Legal custody** is a parent's right to agree to key decisions such as a child's schooling and medical treatment. **Joint physical custody** allows children to live with both parents, usually by splitting their time between both homes. This can be done in a number of ways. In some cases, children may live halftime with each parent, or weekdays with one and weekends with another, or the school year with one and vacation with the other. Joint custody encourages both parents to be actively involved in the financial, emotional, and educational decisions of their children.

Respect the relationship between your children and their other parent.—Allow your children to spend time with their other parent without making them feel guilty or disloyal to you. Children often feel that if one parent left them, the other one may also. Reassure your children that you both still love them even though they may only be living with one parent at a time. It's important to let your children show their love to both parents. Unless your ex-spouse is unfit to parent, try not to let your differences keep your child away from him or her. Remember, one of the most important ways to help your children cope with a separation or divorce is to help them maintain a strong, loving relationship with *both* parents.

Keep your children's daily routines simple and predictable.—Children go through many changes during a separation or divorce. Try to keep as many of their regular routines as you can to help reduce their stress. Many divorced parents feel guilty that the divorce has upset their children and find it hard to discipline them when they need it. Even though a child's anger or difficult behavior may be a part of his or her attempts to cope with the divorce, children still need to have limits set. Be reliable and consistent. Even though you are not with your children all of the time, you are still their parent and they should know what you expect of them. As much as possible, parents living in separate households should try to set consistent rules with their children. This will help avoid any confusion about what is expected of them.   □

The Child Abuse and Neglect Epidemic

Source: The National Center on Child Abuse Prevention Research, a program of
The National Committee to Prevent Child Abuse.

Child abuse was formally recognized by the medical profession in 1961 as the "battered child syndrome." Since 1985, the number of reports of child abuse and neglect has risen by 50 percent. Many reasons have been cited as contributing to this increase. Among these reasons are (1) increased public awareness, (2) more families living at or near poverty level, (3) abuse of alcohol and other substances, and (4) fewer resources available to the increasing number of families needing child protective services.

In 1993, the National Committee to Prevent Child Abuse (NCPCA) determined that approximately 2.9 million children were identified and/or reported as victims of child abuse and neglect throughout the United States. About 45 out of every 1,000 children were reported as victims of maltreatment.

The reports of abuse have been separated into the following categories:

Neglect	1,404,830	47%
Physical abuse	896,700	30%
Sexual abuse	328,790	11%
*Other	269,010	9%
Emotional abuse	59,780	2%

*"Other" may indicate more than one form of abuse or abandonment.

The Four Types of Child Abuse

Physical Abuse: Is the nonaccidental physical injury of a child, including beatings, burns, bites, strangulation, immersion in scalding water, which result in bruises, welts, broken bones, scars, or serious injuries.
Sexual Abuse: Is the sexual contact between a child and adult or older child for the sexual gratification of the offender. It can include both physical and nonphysical contact and it is always forced.
Emotional Abuse: Is a pattern of behavior that attacks a child's emotional development and sense of self-worth.
Neglect: Is the withholding of or failure to provide a child with the basic necessities of life: food, clothing, shelter, medical care, attention to hygiene, or supervision needed for optimal physical growth and development.

Fatalities

In 1993, an estimated 1,299 child abuse and neglect related fatalities were confirmed by child protective service agencies in the United States. (The 1994 estimate was 1,271.) At least three children died each day as a result of maltreatment. The cause of death for 51% of the victims was abuse, 43% of deaths were the result of neglect, and 6% of the fatalities were caused by a combination of abuse and neglect.

Young children were most often victims of fatal injuries, with 86% of deaths occurring when children were under the age of five; 46% of these victims were under the age of one at the time of their death.

Sexual Abuse

Studies of the general population of adults show that anywhere from 6% to 63% of females were sexually abused as children. Females are more often the victims of sexual abuse than males. Generally, children are sexually abused by adults who are related to them or are known by them or their families. An estimated 77% of reported abusers are parents, 16% are other relatives, and 6% are non-related.

Abuse in Day Care and Foster Care

Reports of abuse in day care and foster care settings attract a great deal of attention from the media and the general public. However, it is important to remember that less than 1% of confirmed abuse cases occurred in these environments in 1993.

Factors Contributing to Abuse

Although child abuse occurs in all racial, ethnic, cultural, and socioeconomic groups, physical abuse and neglect are more likely among people in poverty. Reflecting the high rates of poverty among ethnic minorities, minority children enter the child protection system in disproportionately large numbers.

The link between substance abuse and child abuse has strengthened over the years. Parental abuse of alcohol and use of other drugs has been identified as a major factor contributing to child maltreatment and death. It is estimated that nearly 10 million children under age 18 are affected in some way by the substance abuse of their parents.

One well-known result of increased substance abuse by women is the growing number of infants born exposed to illegal substances taken by their mother during pregnancy. Estimates of this problem vary substantially from 100,000 to 350,000 infants nationwide.   □

SOCIAL SECURITY & AGING

Social Security

The original Social Security Act was passed in 1935 and amended in 1939, 1946, 1950, 1952, 1954, 1956, 1958, 1960, 1961, 1965, 1967, 1969, 1972, 1974, 1977, 1980-1984, 1986, and 1988-1989.

The act is administered by the Social Security Administration and the Health Care Financing Administration, and other agencies within the Department of Health and Human Services.

For purposes of clarity, the explanations given below will describe the provisions of the act as amended.

Old Age, Disability, and Survivors Insurance

Practically everyone who works fairly regularly is covered by social security. Most state and local government employees are covered under voluntary agreements between states and the Commissioner of Social Security. Those who are not members of their employer's retirement system are generally covered on a mandatory basis. Workers not covered include most federal civilian employees hired prior to January 1984, career railroad workers, and a few other exceptions.

Cash tips count for Social Security if they amount to $20 or more in a month from employment with a single employer.

To qualify for benefits or make payments possible for your survivors, you must be in work covered by the law for a certain number of "quarters of coverage." Before 1978, a quarter of coverage was earned if a worker was paid $50 or more wages in a 3-month calendar quarter. A self-employed person got 4 "quarters of coverage" for a year in which his net earnings were $400 or more.

In 1978, a worker, whether employed or self-employed, received one quarter of coverage for each $250 of covered annual earnings up to a maximum of four for a year. The quarter of coverage measure was increased to $260 in 1979 and $290 in 1980, $310 in 1981, $340 in 1982, $370 in 1983, $390 in 1984, $410 in 1985, $440 in 1986, $460 in 1987, $470 in 1988, $500 in 1989, $520 in 1990, $540 in 1991, $570 in 1992, $590 in 1993, $620 in 1994, $630 in 1995, and will increase automatically in future years to keep pace with increases in average wages. The number of quarters needed differs for different persons and depends on the date of your birth; in general, it is related to the number of years after 1950, or after the year you reach 21, if later, and up to the year you reach 62, become disabled, or die. One "quarter of coverage" is required for each such year in order for you or your family to get benefits. No one will need more than 40 quarters. Your local Social Security office can tell you how long you need to work.

Who Pays for the Insurance?

Both workers and their employers pay for the workers' insurance. Self-employed persons pay their own social security contributions annually along with their income tax. The rates include the cost of Medicare hospital insurance. The contribution and benefit base is $57,600 for 1993 for retirement, survivor and disability coverage, and $135,000 for 1993 for Medicare coverage, and will increase automatically in future years as earnings levels rise. The contribution rate schedules

Social Security Contribution and Rate Schedule
(percent of covered earnings)

Year	Retirement survivors, and disability insurance	Hospital insurance	Year
EMPLOYERS AND EMPLOYEES			
1978	4.95%	1.10%	6.05%
1979-80	5.08	1.05	6.13
1981	5.35	1.30	6.65
1982-83	5.40	1.30	6.70
1984	5.70	1.30	7.00
1985	5.70	1.35	7.05
1986-87	5.70	1.45	7.15
1988-89	6.06	1.45	7.51
1990 & later	6.20	1.45	7.65
SELF-EMPLOYED			
1978	7.00%	1.10%	8.10%
1979-80	7.05	1.05	8.10
1981	8.00	1.30	9.30
1982	8.05	1.30	9.35
1983	8.05	1.30	9.35
1984	11.40	2.60	*14.00
1985	11.40	2.70	*14.10
1986-87	11.40	2.90	*14.30
1988-89	12.12	2.90	*15.02
1990 & later	12.40	2.90	*15.30

*The law provides credit against self-employment tax liability in the following manner: 2.7% in 1984; 2.3% in 1985; 2.09% 1986-1989 and, beginning with the 1990 taxable year, the credit is replaced with two special provisions. First self-employed persons will be allowed a 7.65% deduction from net profit before computing their SECA tax and an income tax deduction equal to one-half of the SECA tax.

under present law are shown in a table in this section.

The separate payroll contribution to finance hospital insurance is placed in a separate trust fund in the U.S. Treasury. In addition, the medical insurance premiums, currently $46.10 a month in 1995, and the government's shares go into another separate trust fund.

How to Apply for Benefits

You apply for benefits by filing a claim either in person, by mail, or by telephone at any social security office. You can get the address of your nearest office either from the post office, from the phone book under the listing, United States Government—Social Security Administration, or by calling Social Security's toll-free number 1–800–772–1213. You will need certain kinds of proof, depending upon the type of benefit you are claiming. If it is a retirement benefit, you should provide your social security number and a birth certificate or religious record (preferably recorded before age 5). If you are unable to get these documents, other old documents showing your age or date of birth—such as census records, school records, early naturalization certificate, etc.—may be

Delayed Retirement Credit Rates

Age 62	Monthly percentage	Yearly percentage
Prior to 1979	1/12 of 1%	1%
1979-1986	1/4 of 1%	3%
1987-1988	7/24 of 1%	3.5%
1989-1990	1/3 of 1%	4%
1991-1992	3/8 of 1%	4.5%
1993-1994	5/12 of 1%	5%
1995-1996	11/24 of 1%	5.5%
1997-1998	1/2 of 1%	6%
1999-2000	13/24 of 1%	6.5%
2001-2002	7/12 of 1%	7%
2003-2004	5/8 of 1%	7.5%
2005 or later	2/3 of 1%	8%

acceptable. A widow, or widower, 60 or older who is claiming widow's benefits based on his/her spouse's earnings should have his/her own social security number, his/her spouse's social security number, proof of age and a copy of the marriage certificate. A child claiming child's benefits should provide a birth certificate, his/her own social security number, and the social security number of the parent on whose record benefits are being claimed. If formal proof is not available, the Social Security office will tell you what kinds of information will be acceptable. Do not delay applying even if you do not have the necessary information or proofs.

What Does Social Security Offer?

The Social Security contribution you pay gives you four different kinds of protection: (1) retirement benefits, (2) survivors' benefits, (3) disability benefits, and (4) Medicare hospital insurance benefits.

Retirement benefits. Currently, a worker becomes eligible for the full amount of his retirement benefits at age 65, if he has retired under the definition in the law. A worker may retire at 62 and get 80% of his full benefit. The closer he is to age 65 when he starts collecting his benefit, the larger is the fraction of his full benefit that he will get.

The amount of the retirement benefit you are entitled to at 65 is the key to all other benefits under the program. The retirement benefit is based on covered earnings, generally those after 1950. Your covered earnings will be updated (indexed) to the second year before you reach age 62, become disabled, or die, and will reflect the increases in average wages that have occurred since the earnings were paid.

Benefits to workers who attain age 62 after 1978 and their dependents are based, in part, on earnings that have been adjusted to take account of increases in average wages since they were earned. The adjusted earnings are averaged together and a formula is applied to the adjusted average to figure the benefit rate.

A worker who delays his retirement past age 65, or who does not receive a benefit for some months after age 65 because of high earnings will get a special credit that can mean a larger benefit. The credit adds to a worker's benefits 1% (3% for workers age 62 from 1979–1986) for each year (1/12 of 1% for each month) from age 65 to age 70 for which he did not get benefits. (*See* table.)

The law provides a special minimum benefit at retirement for people who worked under Social Security for many years. The provision will help people who had low incomes, but above a specific level, in

their working years. The amount of the special minimum depends on the number of years of coverage. For a worker retiring at 65 in Jan. 1995 with 30 or more years of coverage, the special minimum benefit would be $519.40. These benefits are reduced if a worker is under 65 and are increased automatically for increases in the cost of living.

If you retired at age 65 in Jan. 1995 with average earnings, you would get a benefit of $858.00.

If your spouse is also 65, then he or she will get a spouse's benefit that is equal to half your benefit. So if your benefit is $819.00, your spouse gets $409.00.

If your spouse is between ages 62 and 65, he or she can draw a reduced benefit; the amount depends on the number of months before 65 that he or she starts getting checks. If he or she draws his or her benefit when he or she is 62, he or she will get about 3/8 of your basic benefit, or $321.00. (He or she will get this amount for the rest of his or her life, unless you should die first; then he or she can start getting widow's or widower's benefits, described below.)

If the spouse is entitled to a worker's retirement benefit on his or her own earnings, he or she can draw whichever amount is larger. If the spouse is entitled to a retirement benefit which is less than the spouse's benefit, he or she will receive his or her own retirement benefit plus the difference between the retirement benefit and the spouse's benefit.

If you have children under 18 or a child under age 19 and in full-time attendance at an elementary or secondary school or a son or daughter who became totally disabled prior to reaching age 22, when you retire they will get a benefit equal to half your full retirement benefits (subject to maximum payments that can be made to a family). Children who can qualify for benefits include your biological or legally adopted child, or dependent stepchild or grandchild. If your spouse is caring for your child who is under 16 or who became disabled before 22 (and getting benefits too), he or she is eligible for benefits, even if he or she is under 62.

In general, the highest retirement check that can be paid to a worker who retired at 65 in Jan. 1995 is about $1199.00 a month. Maximum payment to the family of this retired worker is about $2,098.00 in Jan. 1995. When your children reach age 18, their benefits will stop except for children age 19 and under attending an elementary or secondary school full time and except for a benefit that is going to a son or daughter who became totally disabled before attaining age 22. Such a person can continue to get his benefits as long as his disability meets the definition in the law.

If you are divorced, you can get Social Security benefits (the same as a spouse or widow, or widower), based on your ex-spouse's earnings record if you were married at least 10 years and if your ex-spouse has retired, or become disabled. If a divorced spouse has been divorced for at least 2 years, the spouse may be eligible for benefits even if the worker is not receiving benefits. However, both the worker and spouse must be age 62 or over and the worker must be fully insured. The divorced spouse must be unmarried.

Survivor benefits. This feature of the social security program gives your family valuable life insurance protection—in some cases benefits to a family could amount to $100,000 or more over a period of years. The amount of protection is again geared to what the worker would be entitled to if he had been age 65 when he died. Your survivors could get:

1. A one-time cash payment. [NOTE: There is no restriction on the use of the lump-sum death payment.] This "lump-sum death payment" is $255.

2. A benefit for each child until he reaches 18, or 19 if the child is in full-time attendance at an elementary or secondary school or at any age if disabled before 22. "Child" includes biological or legally adopted child, or dependent stepchild or grandchild. Each eligible child receives 75% of the basic benefit (subject to reduction for the family maximum). (A disabled child can continue to collect benefits after age 22.) If certain conditions are met, dependent grandchildren of insured workers can receive survivor or dependent benefits.

3. A benefit for your widow(er) at any age, if she/he has your entitled children under 16 or disabled in care. "Your children" includes your biological or legally adopted children, dependent stepchildren or grandchildren. Her/his benefit is also 75% of the basic benefit. She/he can collect this as long as she/he has a child under 16 or disabled now "in care." Payments stop then (they will start again upon application when she/he is 60 at a slightly lower amount).

Total family survivor benefits are estimated to be as high as $2,534.00 a month if the worker dies in 1995.

4. Your spouse or divorced spouse can get a widow's, widower's, or surviving divorced spouse's benefit starting at age 60. This would come to 71 1/2% of the basic amount at age 60. A widow, or widower, who first becomes entitled at 65 or later may get 100% of his or her deceased spouse's basic amount (provided the deceased spouse did not draw reduced benefits). A widow(er) or surviving divorced spouse, including those who are disabled, must be unmarried. However, a marriage occurring after age 60, or after age 50 if disabled at the time of the remarriage, is disregarded.

5. Dependent parents can sometimes collect survivors' benefits. They are usually eligible if: (a) they were getting at least half their support from the deceased worker at (1) the time of the worker's death if the worker did not qualify for disability benefits before death, or (2) if the worker had been entitled to disability benefits which had not been terminated before death either at the beginning of the period of disability or at the time of death; (b) they have reached 62; and (c) they are not eligible for a greater retirement benefit based on their own earnings. A single surviving parent can then get 82 1/2% of the basic benefit. If two parents are eligible, each would get 75%.

Here is an example of survivors' benefits in one family situation: John Jones died at age 29 in June 1995 leaving a wife and two children aged one and three. He had average covered earnings under Social Security. Family survivors' benefits would include: (1) a lump-sum death payment of $255, and (2) a total monthly benefit of $1,529 for the family. When the children reach 18, their benefits stop unless they are attending an elementary or secondary school full time, in which case payments continue up to age 19. When the older child no longer collects benefits, the widow and younger child continue to get benefits until that child is 16. The child will still get a benefit until age 18 (or age 19, if he continues in elementary or secondary school full time), but Mrs. Jones' checks will stop. When Mrs. Jones becomes 60 (assuming she has not remarried), she will be able to get a reduced widow's benefit if she so chooses, or she can wait until age 65 to get a full benefit.

If in addition to your Social Security benefit as a wife, husband, divorced spouse, widow, widower, or surviving divorced spouse you receive a pension based on your work in employment not covered by Social Security, your benefit as a spouse or survivor will be reduced by 2/3rds of the amount of that pension. Under an exception in the law, your government pension will

Work Credit for Disabilty Benefits

Born after 1929, become disabled at age	Born before 1930, become disabled before 62 in	Years of work credit you need
42 or younger	1971	5
44	1973	5 1/2
46	1975	6
48	1977	6 1/2
50	1979	7
51	1980	7 1/4
52	1981	7 1/2
54	1983	8
56	1985	8 1/2
58	1987	9
60	1989	9 1/2
62 or older	1991 or later	10

NOTE: Five years of this credit must have been earned in the 10 years ending when you became disabled; years need not be continuous or in units of full years.

not affect your spouse's or survivor's benefit if you became eligible for that pension before December 1982 and if, at the time you apply or become entitled to your social security benefit as a spouse or survivor, you could have qualified for that benefit if the law in effect in January 1977 had remained in effect (e.g., at that time, men had to prove they were dependent upon their wives for 1/2 support to be eligible for benefits as a spouse or survivor.) There are also several other exceptions in the law. Your government pension, however, currently will not affect any Social Security benefit based on your own work covered by social security.

Disability Benefits. Disability benefits can be paid to several groups of people:

Disabled workers under 65 and their families.

Persons disabled before 22 who continue to be disabled. These benefits are payable as early as 18 when a parent (or stepparent or grandparent under certain circumstances) receives social security retirement or disability benefits or when an insured parent dies.

Disabled widows and widowers and (under certain conditions) disabled surviving divorced spouses of workers who were insured at death. These benefits are payable as early as 50.

A disabled person is eligible for Medicare after being entitled to disability payments for 24 months.

If you are a worker and become severely disabled, you will be eligible for monthly benefits if you have worked under Social Security long enough and recently enough. The amount of work you will need depends on your age when you become disabled:

Before 24: You need credit for 1 1/2 years of work in the 3-year period ending when your disability begins.

24 through 30: You need credit for having worked half the time during the period between 21 and the time you become disabled.

31 or older: All workers disabled at 31 or older—except the blind—need the amount of credit shown in the chart.

To be considered disabled under the social security law you must be: (1) unable to engage in any substantial activity because of any medically determinable physical or mental impairment which can be expected to result in death or has lasted for 12 continuous months, or (2) blind. A person whose vision is no better than 20/200 even with glasses, or who has a limited visual field of 20 degrees or less, is considered "blind" under the social security law.

If you meet these conditions, you may be able to get payments even if your recovery from the disability is expected.

The medical evidence from your physician or other sources will show the severity of your condition and the extent to which it prevents you from doing substantial gainful work. Your age, education, training, and work experience also may be considered in deciding whether you are able to work. If you can't do your regular work but can do other substantial gainful work, you will not be considered disabled.

While you are receiving benefits as a disabled worker, payments can also be made to certain members of your family. These family members include:

Your unmarried children under 18.

Your children [under 19] if they are unmarried and attending an elementary or secondary school full time.

Your unmarried children 18 or older who were disabled before reaching 22 and continue to be disabled.

Your spouse at any age if she/he has in-care a child who is under 16 or disabled and who is getting benefits based on your social security record.

Your spouse 62 or older even if there are no children entitled to benefits.

Children who can qualify for benefits include your biological or legally adopted child or dependent stepchild or grandchild.

Benefits begin after a waiting period of 5 full calendar months. No benefits can be paid for these first 5 months of disability; therefore, the first payment is for the 6th full month. If you are disabled more than 6 full months before you apply, back benefits may be payable, but not before the 6th full month of disability. It is important to apply soon after the disability starts because back payments are limited to the 12 months preceding the month you apply.

Certain disabled people under 65 are eligible for Medicare. They include disabled workers at any age, persons who became disabled before age 22, and disabled widows and widowers age 50 or over who have been entitled to disability checks for 2 years or more.

Medicare protection generally ends when monthly disability benefits end, and can continue an additional 3 years after benefits stop because an individual returns to gainful work. (Under certain circumstances, former disability beneficiaries may purchase continued Medicare coverage. *See* "Do You Qualify for Hospital Insurance?" in this section.)

If a person becomes entitled to disability benefits again, Medicare coverage starts at the same time if a worker becomes disabled again within 5 years after benefits end (or within 7 years for a disabled widow, widower, or person disabled before age 22).

Benefits to workers disabled after 1978 and their dependents are based, in part, on earnings that have been adjusted to take account of increases in average wages since they were earned. The adjusted earnings are averaged together and a formula is applied to the adjusted average to figure the benefit rate.

Monthly benefits in Jan. 1995 or later can be as high as $1,422.00 for a worker and as high as $2,488.00 for a worker with a family. Once a person starts receiving benefits, the amount will increase automatically in future years to keep pace with the rising cost of living.

If you receive benefits as a disabled worker, an adult disabled since childhood, or a disabled widow or widower, you are not subject to the general rule under which some benefits are withheld if you have substantial earnings. There are special rules, which include medical considerations, for determining how any work you do might affect your disability payments.

If one of your dependents who is under 65 and who is not disabled works and earns more than $8,040 in 1994, some of the dependent's benefits may be withheld. In general, $1 in benefits is withheld for each $2 over $8,040. Different rules apply to your dependents who are 65 or over. A person 65 or over can earn $11,160 in 1994 without having benefits withheld. For persons 65 or over, $1 in benefits is withheld for $3 in earnings over $11,160.

The amount a person can earn without having any benefits withheld will increase in future years as the level of average wages rises.

If you are receiving disability benefits, you are required by law to let the Social Security Administration know if your condition improves or if you return to work no matter how little you earn.

If at any time medical evidence shows that you no longer meet the requirements for entitlement to disability benefits, you will still receive benefits for a 3-month period of adjustment. Benefits will then be stopped.

Whether or not you report a return to work or that your condition has improved, Social Security will review your claim periodically to see if you continue to meet the requirements for benefits.

If you are a disabled worker or a person disabled in childhood and you return to work in spite of a severe condition, your benefits may continue to be paid during a trial work period of up to 9 months—not necessarily consecutive months. This will give you a chance to test your ability to work. If after 9 service months it is decided that you are able to do substantial gainful work, your benefits will be paid for an adjustment period of 3 additional months.

Thus, if you go to work in spite of your disability, you may continue to receive disability benefits for up to 12 months, even though the work is substantial gainful work. If it is decided that the work you are able to do is not substantial and gainful, you may continue to receive benefits. Of course, should you no longer meet the requirements for entitlement to disability, your benefits would be stopped after a 3-month adjustment period even though your trial work period might not be over.

Disabled widows and widowers also can have a trial work period. If your benefits are stopped because you return to work and you become unable to continue working within the next 33 months, your benefits can be restarted automatically. You do not have to file a new disability application.

You Can Earn Income Without Losing Benefits

If you are 70 or over you can earn any amount and still get all your benefits. If you are under 70, you can receive all benefits if your earnings do not exceed the annual exempt amount. The annual amount for 1995 is $11,280 for people 65 or over and $8,160 for people under 65.

If your earnings go over the annual amount, $1 in benefits is withheld for each $2 ($3 if age 65-69) of earnings above the limit.

The monthly measure used for 1977 and earlier years to determine whether benefits could be paid for any month during which they earned 1/12 or less of the annual exempt amount and did not perform substantial work in their business has been eliminated. A person can now use the monthly test only in the first year that he or she has a month in which earnings do not exceed 1/12 of the annual exempt amount or does not perform substantial services in self-employment. If such a month occurs in 1995, a benefit can be paid for any month in which you earn $940 or less (if 65 or older) or $680 or less (if under 65) and don't perform substantial services in self-employment even though your total yearly earnings exceed the annual amount.

The annual exempt amount will increase automatically as the level of average wages rises.

If a worker's earnings exceed the exempt amount, social security benefits to his dependents may be reduced. However, a dependent's benefits will not be reduced if another dependent has excess earnings.

Anyone earning over the annual exempt amount a year while receiving benefits (and under age 70) must report these earnings to the Social Security Administration. If you continue to work after you have applied for social security, your additional earnings may increase the amount of your monthly payment. This will be done automatically by the Social Security Administration. You need not ask for it.

Medicare

The Medicare program is administered by the Health Care Financing Administration.

Most people 65 and over and many under 65 who have been entitled to disability checks for at least 2 years have Medicare protection. So do insured people and their dependents who need a kidney transplant or dialysis treatment because of permanent kidney failure.

The hospital insurance part of Medicare helps pay the cost of inpatient hospital care and certain kinds of follow-up care. The medical insurance part helps pay for the cost of doctors' services, outpatient hospital services, and for certain other medical items and services.

A person who is eligible for monthly benefits at 65 gets hospital insurance automatically and does not have to pay a premium. He does pay a monthly premium for medical insurance.

Supplemental Security Income

The supplemental security income (SSI) program is a federally funded program administered by the Social Security Administration. Its basic purpose is to assure a minimum level of income to people who are elderly (65 or over), blind or disabled, and who have limited income and resources.

In 1995, the maximum Federal SSI payment was $458 a month for an individual and $687 a month for a couple. But in many States, SSI payments are much higher because the State adds to the Federal payment.

Countable resources must be valued at $2,000 or less for an individual or $3,000 or less for a couple. But not all the things people own count for SSI. For instance, the house a person lives in and the land around it, and usually, one car does not count.

Generally, depending on the State, people who get SSI can also get Medicaid to pay for their health care costs as well as food stamps and other social services. And in many States an application for SSI is an application for Medicaid, so people do not have to make separate applications. Certain people can also apply for food stamps at the same Social Security office where they apply for SSI.

Social Security representatives will need information about the income and resources and the citizenship or alien status of people applying for benefits. If the person is living with a spouse, or the application is for a disabled child living with parents, the same information is needed about the spouse/parents.

People who are age 65 or over will need proof of their age such as a birth certificate, or religious record. And if a person who is filing is disabled or blind, Social Security will need information about the impairment and its treatment history.

It helps if people have this information and evidence with them when they talk to their Social Security representative. But they do not need to have **any** of these things to **start** their application. All they need to do is to call Social Security to find out if they are eligible for SSI payments and the other benefits that come with it. Benefits are not retroactive, so delay can cost money.

The Social Security representative will explain just what information/evidence is needed for the SSI claim, and will provide help in getting it if help is needed. Most Social Security offices will make an appointment for an office visit or for a telephone interview if that is more convenient. Or people can just walk in, and wait until someone is free to help them.

Over 6 million people receive SSI benefits now. Many receive both SSI and Social Security. Do not wait. Call 1-800-772-1213, and find out more about SSI. Even the call is free!

How to Protect Your
Social Security Record

Always show your Social Security card when you start a new job. In that way you will be sure that your earnings will be credited to *your* Social Security record and not someone else's. If you lose your Social Security card, contact Social Security to find out how to apply for a new one. When a woman marries, she should apply for a new card showing her married name (and the same number).

Public Assistance

The Federal government makes grants to the states to help them provide financial assistance, medical care, and social services to certain persons in need, including children dependent because of the death, absence from home, incapacity, or (in some states) unemployment of a parent. In addition, some help is provided from only state and/or local funds to some other needy persons.

Federal sharing in state cash assistance expenditures made in accordance with the Social Security Act is based on formulas which are set forth in the Act. The Social Security Act gives the states the option of using one of two formulas, whichever is to its benefit. One formula limits the amount of assistance payment in which there is federal sharing. The other formula permits federal sharing without a limit on the amount of assistance payment. Administrative costs in all the programs are shared equally by the federal and state governments.

Within these and other general patterns set by the requirements of the Social Security Act and their administrative interpretations, each state initiates and administers its own public assistance programs, including the determination of who is eligible to receive assistance, and how much can be granted and under what conditions. Assistance is in the form of cash payments made to recipients, except that direct payments are used for medical care, and restricted payments may be used in cases of mismanagement. Other social services are provided, in some instances, to help assistance recipients increase their capacity for self-care and self-support or to strengthen family life.

In the medical assistance Medicaid program, federal funds pay 50% to 83% of the costs for medical care. If it is to a state's benefit, it may use the Medicaid formula for federal sharing for its money payment programs, ignoring the maximum on dollar amounts per recipient.

Medicare Program

The Medicare program is a federal health-insurance program for persons 65 and over, and certain disabled people under 65.

Enacted under the Social Security Amendments of 1965, Medicare's official name is Title XVIII of the Social Security Act. These amendments also carried Title XIX, providing federal assistance to state medical-aid programs, which has come to be known as Medicaid.

Medicare

It will be helpful to your understanding of the Medicare program if you keep the following points in mind:

- The federal health-insurance program does not of itself offer medical services. It helps pay hospital, doctor, and other medical bills. You choose your own doctor, who prescribes your treatment and place of treatment. But, you should always make sure that health care facilities or persons who provide you with treatment or services are participating in Medicare. Usually, Medicare cannot pay for care from non-participating health care organizations.
- There are two parts of the program: (1) The hospital insurance part for the payment of most of the cost of covered care provided by participating hospitals, skilled nursing facilities, home health agencies, and hospices. (2) The medical insurance part which helps pay doctors' bills and certain other expenses.
- Another important point to remember: While Medicare pays the major share of the costs of many illnesses requiring hospitalization, it does not offer adequate protection for long-term illness or mental illness and Medicare does not pay for custodial care.
- Therefore, it may be advisable not to cancel any private health insurance you now carry. You may wish to cancel a policy whose benefits are duplicated by the federal program, and consider a new policy that will provide for the payment of costs not covered by the federal program. Private insurance companies offer policies supplementing the protection offered by the federal program.
- If you want help in deciding whether to buy private supplemental insurance, ask at any social security office for the pamphlet, *Guide to Health Insurance for People with Medicare*. This free pamphlet describes the various types of supplemental insurance available.

Do You Qualify for Hospital Insurance?

If you're entitled to monthly social security or railroad retirement checks (as a worker, dependent, or survivor), you have hospital insurance protection automatically when you're 65. People 65 or older who are not entitled to monthly benefits must have worked long enough under Social Security or the railroad retirement system or in covered Federal, state, and local employment to get hospital insurance without paying a monthly premium. If they do not have enough work, they can get hospital insurance by paying a monthly premium. Disabled people under 65 will have hospital insurance automatically after they have been entitled to social security disability bene-

fits for 24 months. Effective July 1, 1990, former disability beneficiaries will be able to purchase hospital insurance if their premium-free coverage stops due to work activity. Federal, state, or local employees who are disabled before 65 may be eligible on the basis of their government employment. (Disabled people who get railroad annuities must meet special requirements.) People are eligible at any age if they need maintenance dialysis or a kidney transplant for permanent kidney failure and are getting monthly Social Security or railroad retirement benefits or have worked long enough.

To be sure your protection will start the month you reach 65, apply for Medicare insurance 3 months before reaching 65, even if you don't plan to retire.

Do You Qualify for Medicare Medical Insurance?

The medical insurance plan is a vital supplement to the hospital plan. It helps pay for doctors' and other medical services. Many people have not been able to obtain such insurance from private companies because they could not afford it or because of their medical histories.

Any person who can get premium-free hospital insurance benefits based on work as described above can enroll in the medical insurance plan and get medical insurance benefits. In addition, most United States residents age 65 or over can enroll in the medical insurance plan.

People who get social security benefits or retirement benefits under the railroad retirement system will be enrolled automatically for medical insurance—unless they say they don't want it—when they become entitled to hospital insurance. Automatic enrollment does not apply to people who plan to continue working past 65, who are disabled widows or widowers between 50 and 65 who aren't getting disability checks, who are 65 but have not worked long enough to be eligible for hospital insurance, who have permanent kidney failure, who are eligible for Medicare on the basis of government employment, or who live in Puerto Rico or foreign countries. These people have to apply for medical insurance if they want it. People who have medical insurance pay a monthly premium covering part of the cost of this protection. The other part is paid from general federal revenues. The basic premium for enrollees is $46.10 a month in 1995.

Is Other Insurance Necessary?

As already indicated, Medicare provides only partial reimbursement. Therefore, you should know how much medical cost you can bear and perhaps arrange for other insurance.

In 1995, for the first 60 days of inpatient hospital care in each benefit period, hospital insurance pays for all covered services except for the first $716. For the 61st through 90th day of a covered inpatient hospital stay, hospital insurance pays for all covered services except for $179 a day. People who need to be in a hospital for more than 90 days in a benefit period can use some or all of their 60 lifetime reserve days. Hospital insurance pays for all covered services except for $358 a day for each reserve day used. Hospital insurance pays the full cost of the first 20 days of an inpatient stay in a skilled nursing facility per benefit period.

Under medical insurance, the patient must meet an annual deductible. In 1995, the annual deductible is $100. After the patient has met the deductible, each year, medical insurance generally pays 80% of the approved amounts for any additional covered services the patient receives during the rest of the year.

How You Obtain Coverage

If you are receiving Social Security or railroad retirement monthly benefits, you will receive from the government information concerning Medicare about 3 months before you become eligible for hospital insurance.

All other eligible people have to file an application for Medicare. They should contact a social security office to apply for Medicare.

New Medicare Benefits

Breast Cancer Screening (Mammography): Medicare medical insurance now helps pay for X-ray screenings to detect breast cancer. Women 65 or older can use the benefit every other year. Younger disabled women covered by Medicare can use it more frequently. Medicare will pay 80 percent of up to $60.88 for each screening in 1995.

Physician Payment Reforms: In 1995, physicians who do not accept assignment may not charge you for office and hospital visits more than 115 percent of the Medicare-approved amount. Physicians who knowingly charge more than these amounts are subject to sanctions.

You no longer have to file claims to Medicare for covered medical insurance services. Doctors, suppliers, and other providers of services must submit the claims to Medicare within one year of providing the service to you or be subject to certain penalties. □

Receipt of Income

Source: Social Security Administration.

Sources of income, 1962 and 1992. Social Security benefits, which were the most common source of income in 1962, are now almost universal. The proportion of aged units with asset income, the next most common source, has grown from about one-half to two-thirds. Over the 30-year period, receipt of private pensions has more than tripled and receipt of government pensions has increased by two-thirds. A smaller proportion of couples and nonmarried persons aged 65 or older received earnings in 1992.

Benefits Affect Poverty

Source: Social Security Administration.

Benefits reduce poverty rates, 1992. Almost two-fifths of the aged were kept out of poverty in 1992 by their Social Security benefits, a proportion that varies little by marital status and race. Overall, 14% of the aged were poor; without Social Security, the total poverty rate would have been more than 52%. (Data are based on family income rather than aged unit income to conform with official measures of poverty.)

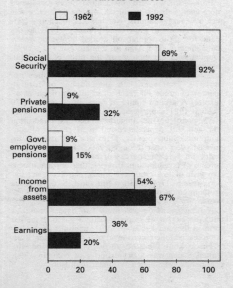

Percent of Aged Units Receiving Income From Various Sources

□ 1962   ■ 1992

Social Security: 69% / 92%
Private pensions: 9% / 32%
Govt. employee pensions: 9% / 15%
Income from assets: 54% / 67%
Earnings: 36% / 20%

Aged Units and Poverty Status

□ Poor even with Social Security   ■ Kept out of poverty with Social Security

Total beneficiaries: 14% / 38%
Married: 6% / 35%
Non-married: 21% / 40%
White: 12% / 39%
Black: 35% / 35%

ENERGY

Energy Overview

Source: Annual Energy Review, 1994.

Consumption

Energy consumption more than doubled during the 1949-through-1973 period, increasing from 30 quadrillion Btu in 1949 to 74 quadrillion Btu in 1973 and the U.S. economy grew at about the same rate. The domestic energy market was dominated by rapid growth in petroleum and natural gas consumption, which more than tripled during the period. After the 1973 oil price shock, energy consumption fluctuated, influenced by dramatic changes in oil prices, changes in the rate of growth of the domestic economy, and such factors as concerns about the effect of energy use on the environment. The post-1973 low point of energy consumption, 71 quadrillion Btu, occurred in 1983 during a period of very high oil prices. The highest level of energy consumption, 88 quadrillion Btu, occurred in 1994, when oil prices were low.

The composition of demand after 1973 reflected a shift away from petroleum and, to a lesser extent, natural gas towards electricity generated by other fuels. In 1973, petroleum and natural gas accounted for 77 percent of total energy consumption; by 1994, their share had declined to 63 percent.

Production

Historically, three fossil fuels have accounted for the bulk of domestic energy production, which by 1994 totaled 70 quadrillion Btu. Coal accounted for the largest share of domestic energy production in 1949–1951 and, after a long hiatus, again in 1982 and in 1984 through 1994. In the interim, first crude oil and then natural gas dominated domestic production. In 1994, coal production totaled 22 quadrillion Btu. Dry natural gas production totaled 19 quadrillion Btu and crude oil production totaled 14 quadrillion Btu. Natural gas plant liquids accounted for another 2.4 quadrillion Btu.

Indicators of Energy Intensity

The relationship between total energy consumption and real gross domestic product (GDP) is a traditional indicator of the energy intensity of the economy. In 1970, 23 thousand Btu of energy were consumed for each 1987 dollar of GDP. The energy intensity of the economy as a whole fell in 1985 to 17 thousand Btu per 1987 dollar, where it remained through 1994.

A second indicator of energy intensity is per capita consumption. Per capita consumption rose from 212 million Btu in 1960 to a peak of 285 million Btu in 1973. Thereafter, per capita consumption trended downward to as low as 226 million Btu in 1983. In the 1990s, low petroleum prices encouraged energy use, and end-use energy consumption rose to 260 million Btu per capita in 1994.

Net generation of electricity by electric utilities increased throughout the 1949-through-1994 period, registering only two year-to-year declines (during the 1982 recession and again in 1992). However, the rate of growth of electricity net generation slowed during the 46-year period. From 1949 through 1979, the annual growth rate averaged 7.1 percent, whereas from 1980 through 1994, the annual growth rate averaged 1.7 percent. After the mid-1970s, coal and nuclear fuels provided increasing shares of fuel input for electricity generation, displacing substantial quantities of both petroleum and natural gas.

Hydroelectric generation (conventional and pumped storage) accounted for over 1.4 quadrillion Btu of electricity in 1949 and from the 1970s through 1994 usually provided about 3 quadrillion Btu per year. However, in 1988, the second year of a drought, hydroelectric generation totaled only 2.3 quadrillion Btu and in 1992, a year of persistent drought in the West, it totaled 2.6 quadrillion Btu.

Other renewable energy sources also contributed to the domestic energy supply. Biofuels, a category which includes wood and waste, contributed 2.8 quadrillion Btu to the 1994 total. Geothermal, solar, and wind energy combined contributed 0.4 quadrillion Btu. Renewable energy production (including conventional hydroelectric power and excluding hydroelectric pumped storage) totaled 5.8 quadrillion Btu, 8.3 percent of U.S. total energy production.

Changing Patterns of Trade

From 1958 forward, the United States consumed more energy than it produced, and the difference was met by energy imports. Net imports of energy (primarily petroleum) grew rapidly through 1973, as demand for cheap foreign oil eroded quotas on petroleum imports. The Arab oil embargo of 1973–1974, coupled with the increase in the price of crude oil, interrupted growth in petroleum net imports; nevertheless they climbed to a peak of 18 quadrillion Btu in 1977. That year, U.S. dependence on foreign sources of crude oil reached an all-time high of 47 percent. A second round of price increases in 1979 through 1981 suppressed demand for foreign oil. In 1985, petroleum net imports totaled 9.0 quadrillion Btu, and U.S. dependence fell to 27 percent of consumption. Subsequently, petroleum net imports increased every year through 1989, when U.S. dependence on foreign sources of crude oil reached 42 percent of consumption. In 1994, the fourth consecutive year of low crude oil prices, petroleum net imports rose to 17 quadrillion Btu and U.S. dependence on them equaled 45 percent—the highest level in 17 years.

Natural gas trade was limited to border countries until the advent of shipping natural gas in liquefied form in the late 1960s. In 1994, natural gas net imports reached the record level of 2.4 quadrillion Btu.

Throughout the 1949-through-1994 period, the United States was a net exporter of coal. In 1994, coal net exports totaled 1.7 quadrillion Btu. ☐

Energy Production by Source, 1994

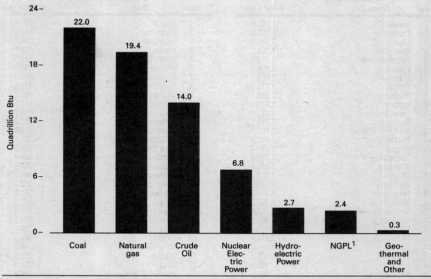

1. Natural gas plant liquids. *Source:* Energy Information Administration, *Annual Energy Review, 1994.*

Energy Consumption by Source, 1994

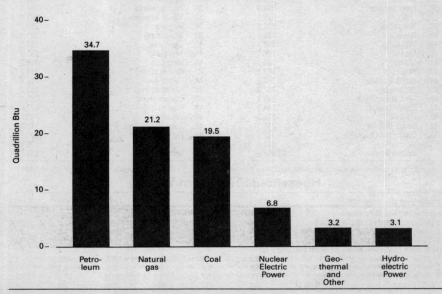

Source: Energy Information Administration, *Annual Energy Review, 1994.*

Energy Consumption and Consumption per Capita by State, 1993

	Consumption			Consumption per capita	
Rank	State	Trillion Btu	Rank	State	Million Btu
1.	Texas	10,081.1	1.	Alaska	1,001.6
2.	California	6,988.4	2.	Wyoming	864.6
3.	Ohio	3,790.6	3.	Louisiana	840.3
4.	New York	3,701.7	4.	Texas	559.4
5.	Pennsylvania	3,665.9	5.	North Dakota	519.5
6.	Louisiana	3,604.7	6.	West Virginia	454.1
7.	Illinois	3,582.1	7.	Indiana	440.6
8.	Florida	3,128.2	8.	Montana	425.6
9.	Michigan	2,898.7	9.	Oklahoma	419.1
10.	Indiana	2,513.8	10.	Kansas	417.1
11.	New Jersey	2,421.9	11.	Kentucky	415.7
12.	Georgia	2,236.7	12.	Alabama	399.3
13.	North Carolina	2,103.6	13.	Washington	369.6
14.	Washington	1,943.6	14.	Delaware	368.5
15.	Virginia	1,911.4	15.	New Mexico	368.2
16.	Tennessee	1,832.4	16.	Mississippi	364.8
17.	Alabama	1,669.4	17.	Idaho	362.9
18.	Missouri	1,597.4	18.	Tennessee	359.7
19.	Kentucky	1,577.0	19.	South Carolina	352.3
20.	Wisconsin	1,464.7	20.	Arkansas	351.7
21.	Minnesota	1,432.2	21.	Ohio	342.7
22.	Massachusetts	1,407.9	22.	Iowa	342.4
23.	Oklahoma	1,354.9	23.	Nebraska	330.2
24.	South Carolina	1,278.8	24.	Georgia	324.1
25.	Maryland	1,245.8	25.	Nevada	322.8
26.	Kansas	1,057.3	26.	Minnesota	316.6
27.	Colorado	1,023.1	27.	Oregon	315.3
28.	Iowa	965.8	28.	Utah	311.4
29.	Mississippi	963.1	29.	District of Columbia	308.3
30.	Arizona	958.0	30.	New Jersey	308.2
31.	Oregon	957.0	31.	Maine	306.7
32.	Arkansas	853.2	32.	Illinois	306.5
33.	West Virginia	825.5	33.	Michigan	306.4
34.	Connecticut	761.6	34.	South Dakota	305.8
35.	Alaska	599.0	35.	Missouri	305.1
36.	New Mexico	594.9	36.	Pennsylvania	304.7
37.	Utah	579.1	37.	North Carolina	302.6
38.	Nebraska	532.6	38.	Virginia	295.3
39.	Nevada	446.1	39.	Wisconsin	290.4
40.	Wyoming	406.4	40.	Colorado	287.1
41.	Idaho	399.2	41.	Maryland	251.3
42.	Maine	380.3	42.	Vermont	246.2
43.	Montana	357.9	43.	Rhode Island	244.9
44.	North Dakota	330.9	44.	Arizona	242.8
45.	Delaware	257.2	45.	Massachusetts	233.9
46.	New Hampshire	245.7	46.	Connecticut	232.3
47.	Rhode Island	244.9	47.	Florida	227.9
48.	Hawaii	229.3	48.	California	223.9
49.	South Dakota	219.0	49.	New Hampshire	218.6
50.	District of Columbia	178.5	50.	New York	203.9
51.	Vermont	141.8	51.	Hawaii	196.6
	United States	83,957.8		United States	325.7

Source: Energy Information Administration, _State Energy Data Report 1993, Consumption Eestimates_ (June 1995).

Households That Burn Wood

Household characteristic	1980	1982	1984	1987	1990	1993
Households That Burn Wood						
Numbers of households (millions)	21.6	21.4	22.9	22.5	22.9	20.4
Share of all U.S. households (percent)	26.4	25.6	26.6	24.8	24.3	21.1
Wood energy consumed (trillion Btu)	854	971	981	853	582	548
Households That Burn Wood as Main Heating Fuel						
Number of households (millions)	4.7	5.6	6.4	5.0	3.9	3.1
Share of all U.S. households (percent)	5.8	6.7	7.5	5.6	4.1	3.2
Number of cords burned (millions)	22.4	28.7	29.4	23.5	15.0	12.6
Wood energy consumed (trillion Btu)	448	574	589	470	300	252

Source: Energy Information Administration, Form EIA-457, "Residential Energy Consumption Survey."

steam spins generator that makes electricity

nuclear reactor
produces heat

condenser cools steam to water

water boiled to steam

uranium

reactor heat boils water

warm lake
water expelled

non-radioactive water

65°F   70°F   75°F   80°F

cool lake water drawn in

Simplified diagram of a nuclear reactor. Laurel Cook, Boston, MA.

Largest Nuclear Power Plants in the United States
(over a million kilowatts)

Plant	Operating utility	Capacity (kilowatts)	Year operative
South Texas 1, TX	Houston Lighting & Power	1,250,000	1988
South Texas 2	Houston Lighting	1,250,000	1989
Palo Verde 1, AZ	Arizona Public Service	1,221,000	1986
Palo Verde 2, AZ	Arizona Public Service	1,221,000	1986
Palo Verde 3, AZ	Arizona Public Service	1,221,000	1988
Perry 1, OH	Cleveland Electric Illumination	1,205,000	1987
Sequoyah 1, TN	Tennessee Valley Authority	1,148,000	1981
Sequoyah 2, TN	Tennessee Valley Authority	1,148,000	1982
Callaway, MO	Union Electric	1,145,000	1984
Grand Gulf 1, MS	System Energy Resources	1,142,000	1985
Millstone 3, CT	Northeast Nuclear Energy	1,142,000	1986
Catawba 1, SC	Duke Power Co.	1,129,000	1985
Catawba 2, SC	Duke Power Co.	1,129,000	1986
McGuire 1, NC	Duke Power Co.	1,129,000	1981
McGuire 2, NC	Duke Power Co.	1,129,000	1984
Wolf Creek 1, KS	Wolf Creek Nuclear Operating	1,128,000	1985
Braidwood 1, IL	Commonwealth Edison	1,120,000	1988
Braidwood 2, IL	Commonwealth Edison	1,120,000	1988
Salem 1, DE	Public Service Electric & Gas	1,106,000	1977
Salem 2, DE	Public Service Electric & Gas	1,106,000	1981
Byron 1, IL	Commonwealth Edison	1,105,000	1985
Byron 2, IL	Commonwealth Edison	1,105,000	1987
Vogtle 2	Georgia Power	1,083,000	1989
Trojan, OR	Portland General Electric	1,095,000	1976
Fermi 2, OH	Detroit Edison	1,093,000	1988
Diablo Canyon 2	Pacific Gas & Electric	1,087,000	1986
Nine Mile Point 2, NY	Niagara Mohawk Power	1,080,000	1988
San Onofre 3, CA	Southern California Edison	1,080,000	1984
Vogtle 1, GA	Georgia Power	1,079,000	1987
Waterford 3, LA	Louisiana Power & Light	1,075,000	1985
Diablo Canyon 1, CA	Pacific Gas & Electric	1,073,000	1985
San Onofre 2, CA	Southern California Edison	1,070,000	1983
Hope Creek 1, DE	Public Service Electric & Gas	1,067,000	1986
Browns Ferry 1, AL	Tennessee Valley Authority	1,065,000	1974
Browns Ferry 2, AL	Tennessee Valley Authority	1,065,000	1975
Browns Ferry 3, AL	Tennessee Valley Authority	1,065,000	1977
Limerick 2	Philadelphia Elec	1,065,000	1990
Cook 2, MI	Indiana & Michigan Power	1,060,000	1978
Limerick 1, PA	Philadelphia Electric	1,055,000	1986
Peach Bottom 2, PA	Philadelphia Electric	1,051,000	1974
Zion 1, IL	Commonwealth Edison	1,040,000	1973

Plant	Operating utility	Capacity (kilowatts)	Year operative
Zion 2, IL	Commonwealth Edison	1,040,000	1974
La Salle 1, IL	Commonwealth Edison	1,036,000	1984
La Salle 2, IL	Commonwealth Edison	1,036,000	1984
Peach Bottom 3, PA	Philadelphia Gas & Electric	1,035,000	1974
Susquehanna 1, PA	Pennsylvania Power & Light	1,032,000	1983
Susquehanna 2, PA	Pennsylvania Power & Light	1,032,000	1985
Comanche Peak 1, TX	Texas Utilities	1,159,000	1990
Seabrook 1, NH	Public Service of N.H.	1,150,000	1990
Comanche Peak 2, TX	Texas Utilities	1,150,000	1993

Source: Nuclear Regulatory Commission.

Production of Crude Petroleum by Countries

(in thousands of 42–gallon barrels)

Area and country	Est. 1995[1]	1994[1]	Est. percent change	Area and country	Est. 1995[1]	1994[1]	Est. percent change
Western Hemisphere	5,889,275	5,858,250	0.5	Iraq	219,000	182,500	20.0
Argentina	255,500	232,140	10.1	Kuwait	730,000	730,000	—
Bolivia	9,855	9,125	8.0	Oman	307,695	283,605	8.5
Brazil	254,770	242,360	5.1	Qatar	156,585	149,650	4.6
Canada	644,590	617,215	4.4	Saudi Arabia	2,937,155	2,920,000	0.6
Chile	4,015	5,110	−21.4	Syria	224,475	200,750	11.8
Colombia	189,435	169,360	11.9	United Arab Emirates	810,300	813,585	−0.4
Ecuador	149,650	131,035	14.2	Yemen	124,100	123,005	0.9
Mexico	972,360	992,070	−2.0	Asia Pacific	2,498,425	2,410,460	3.6
Peru	49,275	47,815	3.1	Australia	205,495	190,165	8.1
Trinidad	44,895	46,720	−3.9	Brunei	58,400	60,590	−3.6
United States	2,409,000	2,468,130	−2.4	China	1,078,940	1,076,750	0.2
Venezuela	892,425	884,760	0.9	India	250,755	202,940	23.6
Western Europe	2,141,455	2,001,295	7.0	Indonesia	482,165	480,340	0.4
Austria	8,395	8,760	−4.2	Japan	5,475	5,840	−6.3
Denmark	67,890	70,445	−3.6	Malaysia	248,200	237,250	4.6
France	18,615	21,170	−12.1	New Zealand	16,425	15,330	7.1
Germany	20,805	21,170	−11.4	Pakistan	21,170	21,170	—
Italy	31,025	31,390	−1.2	Papua New Guinea	36,865	43,435	−15.1
Netherlands	25,550	28,835	−11.4	Thailand	20,440	18,980	7.7
Norway	974,185	923,085	5.5	Vietnam	65,700	49,275	33.3
Spain	6,570	6,205	5.9	Africa	2,261,175	2,283,075	−1.0
Turkey	24,820	26,645	−6.8	Algeria	273,750	273,750	—
United Kingdom	960,315	859,940	11.7	Angola	211,700	193,450	9.4
Eastern Europe	2,648,075	2,771,445	−4.5	Cameroon	36,500	40,150	−9.1
Albania	4,380	4,380	—	Congo	60,590	67,525	−10.3
C.I.S.[2]	2,538,210	2,660,120	−4.6	Egypt	324,850	328,500	−1.1
Croatia	14,600	14,600	—	Gabon	124,100	111,325	11.5
Hungary	26,645	25,915	2.8	Libya	500,050	503,700	−0.7
Romania	49,640	50,005	−0.7	Nigeria	678,535	717,955	−5.5
Serbia	8,760	8,760	—	Tunisia	33,215	32,485	2.2
Middle East	6,857,620	6,747,025	1.6	Zaire	10,950	8,760	25.0
Bahrain	38,325	38,690	−0.9	**World Total**	**22,277,775**	**22,071,550**	**1.0**
Iran	1,309,985	1,305,240	0.4				

1. Based on Jan.–Feb. average. 2. Formerly the U.S.S.R. Totals may not add up due to rounding.

Energy Equivalents

(Source: Energy Information Administration.)

1 Btu of energy: one match tip, 250 calories (International Steam Table), or 0.25 kilocalories (food calories).

1,000 Btu of energy: two five–ounce glasses of table wine; 250 kilocalories (food calories), or 0.80 peanut butter and jelly sandwiches.

1 million Btu of energy: 90 pounds of coal, 120 pounds of oven dried hardwood, 8 gallons of motor gasoline, 10 therms of natural dry gas, 11 gallons of propane, 1.2 days of U.S. energy consumption per capita (1984), or two months dietary intake of a laborer.

1 barrel of crude oil: 14 days U.S. petroleum consumption per capita, 5.6 thousand cubic feet of dry natural gas, 0.26 short tons (520 pounds) of coal, or 1,700 kilowatts of electricity.

1 short ton of coal: 102 days of U.S. petroleum consumption per capita, 3.8 barrels of crude oil, 21 thousand cubic feet of dry natural gas, or 6,500 kilowatt-hours of electricity.

Petroleum Overview

Source: Annual Energy Review, 1994.

Fluctuations in Prices

In 1990, the Iraqi invasion of Kuwait drove up the real price of a barrel of crude oil to $19.61. In 1991, oil-producing nations' ability to replace Iraqi and Kuwaiti oil, coupled with an economic recession that restrained petroleum demand, caused the real price to decline to $16.21 per barrel. In 1992, despite political unrest in several oil-producing countries (most notably Russia) and the oil sales embargo on Iraq, as well as attempts by OPEC to bolster crude oil prices, the real price of crude oil declined to $15.24 per barrel. In 1993, due to restrained demand and increased production worldwide, the real price of crude oil fell to $13.29. In 1994, the real price of crude oil fell to $12.36, the lowest annual average in 21 years.

The end-use prices, excluding taxes, of almost all petroleum products also declined in 1994. The average price of all types of motor gasoline declined from 76 cents per gallon in 1993 to 74 cents per gallon in 1994. Distillate fuel oil and kerosene-type jet fuel average prices, excluding taxes, decreased. In contrast, the average price per gallon, excluding taxes, of residual fuel oil rose 4.5 percent to 35 cents in 1994.

Consumption of Petroleum Products

Consumption of motor gasoline, distillate fuel oil, jet fuel, and liquefied petroleum gases was higher in 1994 than in 1993. Consumption of motor gasoline, which consistently accounts for the largest share of all petroleum products supplied, rose 1.5 percent to 7.6 million barrels per day. Distillate fuel oil consumption rose 4.3 percent to 3.2 million barrels per day, consumption of jet fuel rose 4.1 percent to 1.5 million barrels per day, and consumption of liquefied petroleum gases rose 8.7 percent to 1.9 million barrels per day. By contrast, consumption of residual fuel oil fell 7.4 percent to 1.0 million barrels per day, the lowest level since at least 1949. Demand for residual fuel oil declined because its price was higher due to refiners' use of residual fuel oil to produce other petroleum products.

Production and Productivity

Of total U.S. production in 1994, 80 percent came from onshore wells and 20 percent from offshore. The 582 thousand producing wells attained an average productivity of 11 barrels per day per well, down 2.6 percent from the 1993 level and significantly below peak productivity of over 18 barrels attained in the early 1970s.

Imports and Exports

Despite import quotas, net imports of low-priced petroleum increased throughout most of the 1949-to-1973 period, and in 1973 totaled 6.0 million barrels per day. Thereafter, net imports fluctuated, peaking at 8.6 million barrels per day in 1977, then declining to 4.3 million barrels per day in 1985. In 1986, excess world production drove prices down, inhibiting domestic production and boosting demand. Those factors, as well as stockbuilding, resulted in an increase in net imports in 1986 to 5.4 million barrels per day. Subsequently, with prices significantly below peak levels, net imports rose to 7.2 million barrels per day in 1989 and 1990. In 1991, lower demand for petroleum due to the economic recession contributed to a decline in petroleum imports. In addition, in 1991, the United States exported a record level of petroleum products, and petroleum net imports declined to 6.6 million barrels per day. In 1992 through 1994, petroleum net imports rose; the 1994 level of 8.0 million barrels per day was the highest in 15 years.

U.S. dependence on petroleum net imports peaked at 47 percent of consumption in 1977, then fell in 1985 to 27 percent, the lowest level since 1971. In 1994, dependence on petroleum net imports reached a 17-year high of 45 percent. Saudi Arabia, Venezuela, Canada, Mexico, and Nigeria were the primary foreign suppliers of petroleum to the United States. □

Motor Vehicle Registrations and Motor Fuel Consumption

Year	Motor vehicle registrations (millions)					Motor fuel consumption[1] (thousand barrels per day)		
	Passenger Cars	Motorcycles	Buses	Trucks	Total	Gasoline[2]	Other Fuels[3]	Total[4]
1980	121.7	5.7	0.5	33.6	161.6	6,820	896	7,716
1985	132.1	5.4	[5]	39.6	177.1	7,020	1,158	8,178
1988	141.3	4.6	[5]	43.1	189.0	7,405	1,306	8,711
1989	143.1	4.4	[5]	44.2	191.7	7,437	1,385	8,822
1990	143.5	4.3	[5]	45.1	192.9	7,454	1,396	8,849
1991	143.0[R]	4.2	[5]	45.4[R]	192.5[R]	7,323[R]	1,349[R]	8,672[R]
1992	144.2	4.1	[5]	46.1	194.4	7,472	1,430	8,902
1993	146.3[R]	4.0	[5]	47.7[R]	198.0[R]	7,607[R]	1,534[R]	9,141[R]
1994E	147.2	3.9	[5]	48.3	199.4	7,333	1,630	9,362

1. Includes only motor fuel taxed at the prevailing tax rates in each State. Excludes motor fuel exempt from tax payment, subject to tax refund, or taxed at rates other than the prevailing tax rate. Experience has shown that the total motor fuel consumption quantity cited here equals more than 99.0% of gross reported motor fuel consumption. 2. Motor gasoline, aviation gasoline, and gasohol. 3. Distillate fuel oil (diesel oil), liquefied gases, and kerosene when they are used to operate vehicles on highways. Excludes jet fuel beginning in 1962. 4. Excludes losses allowed for evaporation, handling, etc. 5. Included in trucks. R = Revised data. E = Estimate. NOTE: Sum of components may not equal total due to independent rounding. *Sources:* 1976–86—Federal Highway Administration, *Highway Statistics Annual*, Tables MV-1, MF-21, and MF-25; 1987 forward—Federal Highway Administration, *Selected Highway Statistics and Charts 1994.*

Households With Selected Appliances, Selected Years, 1980–1993

Appliance	1980	1981	1982	1984	1987	1990	1993	Change 1980 to 1993
Electric Appliances								
Television set (color)	82	82	85	88	93	96	98	16
Television set (B/W)	51	48	47	43	36	31	20	−31
Clothes washer	75	74	72	74	76	76	77	2
Range (stove-top burner)	54	54	53	54	57	58	61	7
Oven, regular or microwave	59	58	59	63	79	88	91	32
Oven, microwave	14	17	21	34	61	79	84	70
Clothes dryer	47	45	45	46	51	53	57	10
Separate freezer	38	38	37	37	34	35	35	−3
Dishwasher	37	37	36	38	43	45	45	8
Dehumidifier	9	9	9	9	10	12	9	(s)
Waterbed heaters	n.a.	n.a.	n.a.	10	14	15	12	n.a.
Window or ceiling fan	n.a.	n.a.	28	35	46	51	60	n.a.
Whole house fan	n.a.	n.a.	8	8	9	10	4	n.a.
Evaporative cooler	4	4	4	4	3	4	3	−1
Personal computer	n.a.	n.a.	n.a.	n.a.	n.a.	16	23	n.a.
Pump for well water	n.a.	n.a.	n.a.	n.a.	n.a.	15	13	n.a.
Swimming-pool pump[1]	4	4	3	n.a.	n.a.	5	5	1
Gas Appliances[2]								
Range (stove-top or burner)	46	46	47	45	43	42	38	−8
Oven	42	40	42	42	41	41	36	−6
Clothes dryer	14	16	15	16	15	16	15	1
Outdoor gas grill	9	9	11	13	20	26	29	20
Outdoor gas light	2	2	2	1	1	1	1	−1
Swimming-pool heater[3]	n.a.	n.a.	n.a.	1	1	2	1	n.a.
Refrigerators[4]								
One	86	87	86	88	86	84	85	−1
Two or more	14	13	13	12	14	15	15	1
Air Conditioning (A/C)								
Central[5]	27	27	28	30	36	39	44	17
Individual room units[5]	30	31	30	30	30	29	25	−5
None	43	42	42	40	36	32	32	−11
Portable Kerosene Heaters	(s)	1	3	6	6	5	2	2

1. All reported swimming pools were assumed to have an electric pump for filtering and circulating the water, except in 1993 when a filtering system was made explicit. 2. Includes natural gas or liquefied petroleum gases. 3. In 1984 and 1987, also includes heaters for jacuzzis and hot tubs. 4. Fewer than 0.5 percent of the households do not have a refrigerator. 5. Households with both central and individual room units are counted only under "Central." n.a. = not available. (s) = Less than 0.5 percent. *Source:* Energy Information Administration (EIA), Form EIA–457, "Residential Energy Consumption Survey."

Renewable Energy Consumption

Source: Annual Energy Review, 1994.

In 1994, the United States consumed an estimated 6.3 quadrillion Btu of renewable energy. Conventional hydroelectric power and biofuels accounted for the largest shares (49 percent and 45 percent, respectively). Geothermal, solar, and wind energy accounted for the remainder. Over the 5-year period of 1990 through 1994 (the only years for which data are available) renewable energy consumption rose 4.6 percent. Among the five major renewable energy sources, biofuels showed the greatest nominal increase in consumption (171 trillion Btu), while wind energy showed the greatest percentage increase (52 percent).

Conventional Hydroelectric Power. Almost all of the 3.1 quadrillion Btu of conventional hydroelectric power generation in 1994 occurred at electric utilities. The industrial sector accounted for only 132 trillion Btu.

Biofuels. Biofuels are fuelwood, wood byproducts, waste wood, municipal solid waste, manufacturing process waste, and alcohol fuels. In 1994, biofuel consumption totaled an estimated 2.8 quadrillion Btu, most of which (2.2 quadrillion Btu) was wood energy. Some industries, such as the paper and lumber industries, have ready access to wood and wood byproducts, and those rely heavily on wood as an energy source. Consumption of municipal solid waste and

other wastes totaled 486 trillion Btu in 1994, and consumption of alcohol fuels (ethanol) totaled 96 trillion Btu.

Geothermal Energy. The third biggest source of renewable energy in 1994 was geothermal energy, which can be used directly, for purposes such as space heating, or converted to electricity. In 1960, The Geysers in California became the first U.S. power plant to generate electricity from geothermal steam. In 1994, geothermal energy consumption reached 265 trillion Btu, 145 trillion Btu at electric utilities and 120 trillion Btu by the industrial sector.

Solar Energy. Of the 71 trillion Btu of potential solar energy supplied in 1994, most (60 trillion Btu) was used in the residential and commercial sector. The industrial sector accounted for 11 trillion Btu and electric utilities accounted for less than 0.5 trillion Btu.

Because it is difficult to measure solar energy use directly, producer shipments of equipment are used as an indicator. Shipments of low temperature collectors, used primarily for heating swimming pools, totaled 6.0 million square feet in 1993. Shipments of medium-temperature collectors, used for pool heating and domestic hot water, peaked at 12 million square feet in 1983 and 1984 but, following the expiration of the

Federal energy tax credit in 1985, totaled only 0.9 million square feet in 1993. Shipments of high-temperature collectors, used for electricity generation, reached 5.2 million square feet in 1990 but fell to near zero in 1991 through 1993, when Luz International Ltd. ceased operating. Shipments of photovoltaic cells and modules, which have a wide variety of applications, rose to 21 thousand peak kilowatts in 1993.

Wind Energy. An estimated 35 trillion Btu of wind energy was consumed in 1993, almost all in the industrial sector. Very small amounts (less than 0.5 trillion Btu) were consumed at electric utilities. ☐

International Energy Production

World Leaders

Worldwide energy production of 349 quadrillion Btu in 1993 was 52 quadrillion Btu greater than in 1984. The relative contributions of the four leading energy producers changed markedly over the 10-year period.

In 1984, the United States was the leading producer of energy and U.S. production of 66 quadrillion Btu accounted for 22 percent of the world total. The former U.S.S.R., the second leading producer, accounted for 61 quadrillion Btu, a 21-percent share.

As of December 31, 1991, the U.S.S.R. ceased to exist as a political entity. Three of the U.S.S.R.'s constituent republics (Russia, Ukraine, and Kazakhstan) produced 50 quadrillion Btu of energy in 1993. That year the United States produced 68 quadrillion Btu.

China, the third largest energy producer in 1984, produced 22 quadrillion Btu of energy, much of which was coal. By 1993, Chinese production had reached 32 quadrillion Btu.

At 11 quadrillion Btu, Saudi Arabia was the fourth largest producer of energy in 1984. During the 1984-to-1993 period, Saudi Arabian production levels varied widely. But by 1993, Saudi Arabian production had risen to 20 quadrillion Btu.

Crude Oil Production in 1994

World production of crude oil totaled 61 million barrels per day in 1994, up 1.0 percent from the 1993 level. The most noticeable production increase occurred in the United Kingdom. The most noticeable production declines occurred in Russia, where production fell from 6.4 million barrels per day in 1993 to 5.8 million barrels per day in 1994, and in the United States, where production declined from 6.9 million barrels per day to 6.6 million barrels per day. In Saudi Arabia, the largest producer of crude oil in 1994, production declined slightly to 8.2 million barrels per day in 1994. Crude oil production by all members of the Organization of Petroleum Exporting Countries combined accounted for 43 percent of the world total in 1994.

Natural Gas Production in 1993

World production of dry natural gas totaled 76 trillion cubic feet and, on a Btu basis, equaled 22 percent of world energy production in 1993. Russia was the major producer of natural gas in 1993 and accounted for 22 trillion cubic feet, a 29-percent share of the world total. The United States was the second largest producer and accounted for 18 trillion cubic feet, a 24-percent share.

Coal Production in 1993

World production of coal totaled 4.9 billion short tons and, on a Btu basis, equaled 25 percent of world energy production in 1993. China, the leading producer, accounted for 1.3 billion short tons in 1993. Coal production in the United States, the second leading producer, totaled 945 million short tons. Russia, the world's third largest producer of coal in 1993, accounted for 336 million short tons, and Germany, the fourth largest, accounted for 315 million short tons.

Electricity

As of January 1, 1993, world electricity installed capacity at all sites (including nonutility power producers) totaled 2.8 billion kilowatts. Most of the capacity (64 percent) was fossil fuel-fired. Hydroelectric generating capacity accounted for 24 percent and nuclear electric generating capacity accounted for 12 percent. Renewable sources, such as biofuels and geothermal, solar, and wind energy, accounted for less than 1 percent of the world total.

World fossil fuel-fired net generation totaled 7.2 trillion kilowatthours in 1992. The United States, with 2.1 trillion kilowatthours, was by far the largest producer of fossil fuel-fired net generation. The former U.S.S.R. net generation totaled 1.1 trillion kilowatthours. World hydroelectric power net generation in 1993 totaled 2.3 trillion kilowatthours, up 3.8 percent from the 1992 level. Canada, the United States, Brazil, and Russia were the world leaders in hydroelectric power net generation and together accounted for 44 percent of the world total. In 1994, nuclear-based electricity gross generation totaled 2.2 trillion kilowatthours. The U.S. share of the world total was 30 percent. France accounted for 16 percent and Japan for 11 percent of the world total.

World Energy Reserves

As of January 1, 1994, world crude oil reserves were estimated to equal about 998 billion barrels.[1] Almost two-thirds of the reserves were located in the Middle East, especially in Saudi Arabia, where about 39 percent of the region's reserves were estimated to be. Iraq, the United Arab Emirates, Kuwait, and Iran each were estimated to have more crude oil reserves than entire regions in the rest of the world. The United States, at 23 billion barrels, ranked tenth in the world in amount of crude oil reserves.

The distribution of the world's 5.0 quadrillion cubic feet of natural gas reserves was different from the distribution of crude oil reserves. Former U.S.S.R. reserves of 2.0 quadrillion cubic feet made the Eastern Europe and U.S.S.R. regions first in the world in amount of natural gas reserves. The United States, at 162 trillion cubic feet, ranked sixth in the world in amount of natural gas reserves.

As of the end of 1990, recoverable reserves of coal were estimated to be 1.1 trillion short tons.[2] The three countries with the most plentiful coal reserves were estimated to be the U.S.S.R., with 266 billion short tons; the United States, with 265 billion short tons,[3] and China, with 126 billion short tons. ☐

---

1. *Oil and Gas Journal* data. 2. World Energy Council data, with the exception of U.S. data, which are estimated by the Energy Information Administration. Data for the U.S.S.R. and China are as of December 31, 1990, the most recent period for which they are available. 3. U.S. data are more current; they represent recoverable reserves as of December 31, 1991. *Source: Annual Energy Review, 1994.*

DRUG USE AND ABUSE

Commonly Abused Drugs

NARCOTICS

The term narcotic in its medical meaning refers to opium and opium derivatives or synthetic substitutes.[1]

Under medical supervision, narcotics are administered orally or by intramuscular injection. As drugs of abuse, however, they also are sniffed, smoked, or self-administered by the more direct routes of subcutaneous ("skin-popping") and intravenous ("mainlining") injection.

The relief of suffering, whether of physical or psychological origin, may result in a short-lived state of euphoria. The initial effects, however, are often unpleasant, leading many to conclude that those who persist in their illicit use may have latent personality disturbances.

To the extent that the response may be felt to be pleasurable, its intensity may be expected to increase with the amount of the dose administered. Repeated use, however, will result in increasing tolerance: the user must administer progressively larger doses to attain the desired effect, thereby reinforcing the compulsive behavior known as drug dependence.

Since addicts tend to become preoccupied with the daily ritual of obtaining and taking drugs, they often neglect themselves and may suffer from malnutrition, infections, and unattended diseases or injuries. Among the hazards of narcotic addiction are toxic reactions to contaminants, such as quindine, sugars, and talcum power, as well as unsterile needles and injection techniques, resulting in abscesses, blood poisoning, hepatitis, and AIDS.

NARCOTICS OF NATURAL ORIGIN

The poppy *Papaver somniferum* is the main source of the nonsynthetic narcotics. It was grown in the Mediterranean region as early as 300 B.C. and has since been cultivated in countries around the world, such as Hungary, Turkey, India, Burma, China, Lebanon, Pakistan, Afghanistan, Laos, and Mexico.

Opium

There were no legal restrictions on the importation or use of opium until the early 1900s. In those days, patent medicines often contained opium without any warning label. Today, there are state, federal, and international laws governing the production and distribution of narcotics substances, and there is little abuse of opium in the United States.

Although a small amount of opium is used to make antidiarrheal preparations, such as paregoric, virtually all the opium imported into this country is broken down into its alkaloid constituents, principally morphine and codeine.

Morphine

The principal constituent of opium, ranging in concentration from 4 to 21 percent, morphine is one of the most effective drugs known for the relief of pain.

1. Cocaine, ecgonine, and coca leaves, classified as narcotics under the Controlled Substances Act (CSA), are discussed in the text on stimulants.

It is marketed in the form of white crystals, hypodermic tablets, and injectable preparations. Its licit use is restricted primarily to hospitals. Morphine is odorless, tastes bitter, and darkens with age. It may be administered subcutaneously, intramuscularly, or intravenously, the latter method being the one most frequently resorted to by addicts.

Codeine

This alkaloid is found in raw opium in concentrations ranging from 0.7 to 2.5 percent. It was first isolated in 1832 as an impurity in a batch of morphine. Although it occurs naturally, most codeine is produced from morphine.

SEMI-SYNTHETIC NARCOTICS

Heroin

First synthesized from morphine in 1874, heroin was not extensively used in medicine until the beginning of this century. While it received widespread acceptance, the medical profession for years remained unaware of its potential for addiction. The first comprehensive control of heroin in the United States was established with the Harrison Narcotic Act of 1914.

Pure heroin is a white powder with a bitter taste. Illicit heroin may vary in both form and color. Most illicit heroin is a powder which may vary in color from white to dark brown because of impurities left from the manufacturing process or the presence of additives, such as food coloring, cocoa, or brown sugar.

Pure heroin is rarely sold on the street. A "bag"—slang for a single dosage unit of heroin—may weigh about 100 mg, usually containing about five percent heroin. To increase the bulk of the material sold to the addict, diluents are mixed with the heroin in ratios ranging from 9 to 1 to as much as 99 to 1. Sugars, starch, powdered milk, and quinine are among the diluents used.

Hydromorphone

Most commonly sold as Dilaudid, hydromorphone is the second oldest semi-synthetic narcotic analgesic. Marketed both in tablet and injectable form, it is shorter acting and more sedating than morphine, but its potency is from two to eight times as great. It is, therefore, a highly abusable drug, much sought after by narcotic addicts, who usually obtain it through fraudulent prescription or theft.

Oxycodone

Oxycodone is synthesized from thebaine. It is similar to codeine, but more potent and with a higher dependence potential. It is effective orally and is marketed in combination with aspirin as Percodan for the relief of pain. Addicts take Percodan orally or dissolve tablets in water, filter out the insoluble material, and "mainline" the active drug.

Teen Drug Use Continues to Climb

Source: The Monitoring the Future Study, the University of Michigan.

Researchers at the University of Michigan reported in their 20th annual survey of American high school seniors, and fourth national survey of eighth- and 10th-grade students, released December 1994, that illicit drug use among American secondary school students continued to rise in 1994.

The rise in illicit drug use, which began at least three years ago for eighth-graders and two years ago for the older students, has been particularly pronounced in the case of marijuana. Another number of illicitly-used drugs have been rising gradually as well. These include LSD, other hallucinogens taken as a class, inhalants, stimulants, barbiturates, and this year, cocaine and crack.

Teenagers on Drugs

	Percent			
	1992	1993	1994	1993–'94 change
Alcohol[1]				
8th grade	53.7	51.6	—	—
		45.4	46.8	+1.4
10th grade	70.2	69.3	—	—
		63.4	63.9	+0.5
12th grade	76.8	76.0	—	—
		72.7	73.0	+0.3
Marijuana/Hashish				
8th grade	7.2	9.2	13.0	+3.8
10th grade	15.2	19.2	25.2	+6.0
12th grade	21.9	26.0	30.7	+4.7
LSD				
8th grade	2.1	2.3	2.4	+0.1
10th grade	4.0	4.2	5.2	+1.0
12th grade	5.6	6.8	6.9	+0.1

	Percent			
	1992	1993	1994	1993–'94 change
Cocaine				
8th grade	1.5	1.7	2.1	+0.2
10th grade	1.9	2.1	2.8	+0.7
12th grade	3.1	3.3	3.6	+0.3
Crack				
8th grade	0.9	1.0	1.3	+0.3
10th grade	0.9	1.1	1.4	+0.3
12th grade	1.5	1.5	1.9	+0.4
Heroin				
8th grade	0.7	0.7	1.2	+0.5
10th grade	0.6	0.7	0.9	+0.2
12th grade	0.6	0.5	0.6	+0.1
Stimulants				
8th grade	6.5	7.2	7.9	+0.7
10th grade	8.2	9.6	10.2	+0.6
12th grade	7.1	8.4	9.4	+1.0

1. For 8th, 10th, and 12th graders: In 1993, the question text was changed slightly in one-half of the forms to indicate that a "drink" meant "more than a few sips." The data in the upper line for alcohol came from forms using the original wording, while the data in the lower line came from forms using the revised wording. In 1993, each line of data was based on one of two questionnaire forms for the 8th and 10th graders and three of six questionnaire forms for the 12th graders; N is one-half of N indicated for all groups. In 1994, data were based on all forms for all grades. *Source:* The Monitoring the Future Study, the University of Michigan.

SYNTHETIC NARCOTICS

In contrast to pharmaceutical products derived directly or indirectly from narcotics of natural origin, synthetic narcotics are produced entirely within the laboratory. A continuing search for a product that will retain the analgesic properties of morphine without the consequent dangers of tolerance and dependence has yet to yield a drug that is not susceptible to abuse. The two that are most widely available are meperidine and methadone.

Meperidine (Pethidine)

The first synthetic narcotic, meperidine, is chemically dissimilar to morphine but resembles it in its analgesic effect. It is probably the most widely used drug for the relief of moderate to severe pain. Available in pure form as well as in products containing other medicinal ingredients, it is administered either orally or by injection, the latter method being the most widely abused. Tolerance and dependence develop with chronic use, and large doses can result in convulsions or death.

Methadone

German scientists synthesized methadone during World War II because of a shortage of morphine. Although chemically unlike morphine or heroin, it produces many of the same effects. Introduced into the United States in 1947, it became widely used in the 1960s in the treatment of narcotic addicts. The effects of methadone differ from morphine-based drugs in that they have a longer duration of action, lasting up to 24 hours, thereby permitting administration only once a day in heroin detoxification and maintenance programs. Moreover, methadone is almost as effective when administered orally as it is by injection. But tolerance and dependence may develop, and withdrawal symptoms, though they develop more slowly and are less severe, are more prolonged. Ironically, methadone, designed to control narcotic addiction, has emerged in some metropolitan areas as a major cause of overdose deaths.

DEPRESSANTS

Depressants have a potential for abuse associated with both physical and psychological dependence. Taken as prescribed as a physician, depressants may be beneficial for the relief of anxiety, irritability, and tension, and for the symptomatic treatment of insomnia. In excessive amounts, however, they produce a state of intoxication that is remarkably similar to that of alcohol.

Tolerance to the intoxicating effects develops rapidly, leading to a progressive narrowing of the margin of safety between an intoxicating and lethal dose. The person who is unaware of the dangers of increasing dependence will often increase the daily dose up to 10 or 20 times the recommended therapeutic level. The source of supply may be no farther than the family medicine cabinet. Depressants are also frequently obtained by theft, illegal prescription, or purchase on the illicit market.

In the world of illicit drug use, depressants often are used as self-medication to soothe jangled nerves brought on by the use of stimulants, to quell the anxiety of "flashbacks" resulting from prior use of hallucinogens, or to ease withdrawal from heroin. The dangers, it should be stressed, are compounded when depressants are used in combination with alcohol or other drugs. Chronic intoxication, though it affects every age group, is not common in middle age. The problem often remains unrecognized until the user exhibits recurrent confusion or an obvious inability to function.

Barbiturates

Among the drugs most frequently prescribed to induce sedation and sleep by both physicians and veterinarians are the barbiturates. About 2,500 derivatives of barbituric acid have been synthesized, but of these only about 15 remain in medical use. Small therapeutic doses tend to calm nervous conditions, and larger dozes cause sleep 20 to 60 minutes after oral administration. As in the case of alcohol, some individuals may experience a sense of excitement before sedation takes effect. If dosage is increased, however, the effects of the barbiturates may progress through successive stages of sedation, sleep, and coma to death from respiratory arrest and cardiovascular complications.

STIMULANTS

The two most prevalent stimulants are nicotine in tobacco products and caffeine, the active ingredient of coffee, tea, and some bottled beverages that are sold in every supermarket. When used in moderation, these stimulants tend to relieve fatigue and increase alertness. They are an accepted part of our culture.

Users tend to rely on stimulants to feel stronger, more decisive, and self-possessed. Because of the cumulative effects of the drugs, chronic users often follow a pattern of taking "uppers" in the morning and "downers," such as alcohol or sleeping pills, at night. Such chemical manipulation interferes with normal body processes and can lead to mental and physical illness.

Cocaine

The most potent stimulant of natural origin, cocaine is extracted from the leaves of the coca plant (Erythroxylon coca), which has been grown in the Andean highlands of South America since prehistoric times. The leaves of the plant are chewed in the region for refreshment and relief from fatigue.

Pure cocaine, the principal psychoactive ingredient, was first isolated in the 1880s. It was used as an anesthetic in eye surgery for which no previously known drug had been suitable. It became particularly useful in surgery of the nose and throat because of its ability to anesthetize tissue while simultaneously constricting blood vessels and limiting bleeding. Many of its therapeutic applications are now obsolete because of the development of safer drugs as local anesthetics.

Illicit cocaine is usually distributed as a white crystalline powder, often diluted by a variety of other ingredients, the most common of which are sugars such as lactose, inositol, mannitol, and local anesthetics such as lidocaine. The frequent adulteration is to increase volume and thus to multiply profits.

The drug is most commonly administered by being "snorted" through the nasal passages. Symptoms of repeated use in this manner may resemble the congested nose of a common cold.

The intensity of the psychological effects of cocaine, as with many psychoactive drugs, depends on the rate of entry into the blood. Intravenous injection or smoking produces an almost immediate intense experience. Cocaine hydrochloride, the usual form in which cocaine is sold, while soluble in water and sometimes injected, is fairly insensitive to heat. Conversion of cocaine hydrochloride to cocaine base yields a substance that will become volatile when heated. "Crack," or cocaine base in the form of chips, chunks or "rocks," is usually vaporized in a pipe or smoked with plant material in a cigarette or a "joint." Inhalation of the cocaine fumes produces effects that are very fast in onset, very intense, and are quickly over. These intense effects are often followed within minutes by a dysphoric "crash," leading to frequently repeated doses and rapid addiction.

Excessive doses of cocaine may cause seizures and death from, for example, respiratory failure, stroke, cerebral hemorrhage, or heart failure. There is no specific treatment for cocaine overdose. Nor does tolerance develop to the toxic effects of cocaine. In fact, there are studies which indicate that repeated use lowers the dose at which toxicity occurs. There is no "safe" dose of cocaine.

Amphetamines

Amphetamine, dextroamphetamine, and methamphetamine are so similar in the effects they induce that they can be differentiated from one another only by laboratory analysis. Amphetamine was first used clinically in the mid-1930s to treat narcolepsy, a rare disorder resulting in an uncontrollable tendency to sleep. After the introduction of the amphetamines into medical practice, the number of conditions for which they were prescribed multiplied, as did the quantities made available.

For a time, they were sold without prescription in inhalers and other over-the-counter preparations. Abuse became popular. Many segments of the population, especially those concerned with extensive or irregular hours, were among those who used amphetamines orally in excessive amounts. "Speed freaks," who injected amphetamines, became known for their bizarre and often violent behavior. Over-the-counter availability (except inhalers) was terminated and amphetamines now are available only by prescription. Inhalers still are available over-the-counter.

Their illicit use closely parallels that of cocaine in the range of its short-term and long-term effects. Despite broad recognition of the risks, clandestine laboratories produce vast quantities of amphetamines, particularly methamphetamine, for distribution on the illicit market.

Methamphetamine Abusers

Abuse patterns suggest an estimated two- to four-year latency period from first use to full addiction. Most treatment clients interviewed initiated use by intranasal snorting, but then turned to intravenous (IV) administration. Compulsive abuse accelerates with IV use because of the drug's rapid onset of action in a pattern similar to crack cocaine abuse. Although crack is not injected, inhalation of its vapors provides a rapid pulmonary delivery of the drug in concentrated dose to the brain promoting an intensified onset of action. This method, like IV methamphetamine use, triggers an initial, short-term jolt which compels the user to repeat drug use again and again in a futile attempt to re-experience the drug's exhilarating effects.

CANNABIS

Cannabis sativa L., the hemp plant, grows wild throughout most of the tropic and temperate regions of the world. It is a single species. This plant has long been cultivated for the tough fiber of the stem, the seed used in feed mixtures, and the oil as an ingredient of paint, as well as for its biologically active substances, most highly concentrated in the leaves and resinous flowering tops.

The plant material has been used as a drug for centuries. In 1839, it entered the annals of western medicine with the publication of an article surveying its therapeutic potential, including possible uses as an analgesic and anticonvulsant agent. It was alleged to be effective in treating a wide range of physical and mental ailments during the remainder of the 19th century. With the introduction of many new synthetic drugs in the 20th century, interest in it as a medication waned.

The controls imposed with the passage of the Marijuana Tax Act of 1937 further curtailed its use in treatment, and by 1941 it had been deleted from the *U.S. Pharmacopoeia* and the *National Formulary,* the official compendia of drugs.

Cannabis products are usually smoked in the form of loosely rolled cigarettes ("joints"). They may be used alone or in combination with other substances. They may also be administered orally, but are reported to be about three times more potent when smoked. The effects are felt within minutes, reach their peak in 10 to 30 minutes, and may linger for 2 or 3 hours.

A condensed description of these effects is apt to be inadequate or even misleading. So much depends upon the experience and expectations of the individual as well as the activity of the drug itself. Low doses tend to induce restlessness and an increasing sense of well-being, followed by a dreamy state of relaxation, and frequently hunger, especially a craving for sweets. Changes of sensory perception—a more vivid sense of sight, smell, touch, taste, and hearing—may be accompanied by subtle alterations in thought formation and expression. Stronger doses intensify reactions. The individual may experience shifting sensory imagery, rapidly fluctuating emotions, a flight of fragmentary thoughts with disturbed associations, an altered sense of self-identity, impaired memory, and a dulling of attention despite an illusion of heightened insight. This state of intoxication may not be noticeable to an observer. High doses may result in image distortion, a loss of personal identity, and fantasies and hallucination. Very high doses may result in a toxic psychosis.

Marijuana

The term marijuana is used in this country to refer to the cannabis plant and to any part or extract of it that produces somatic or psychic changes in humans. A tobacco-like substance produced by drying the leaves and flowering tops of the plant, marijuana varies significantly in its potency, depending on the source and selectivity of plant materials used. Most wild U.S. cannabis is considered inferior because of a low concentration of THC[1], usually less than 0.5 percent. Jamaican, Colombian, and Mexican varieties range between 0.5 and 7 percent. The most selective produce is reputed to be sinsemilla (Spanish, *sin semilla:* without seed), prepared from the unpollinated female cannabis plant, samples of which have been found to contain up to 20 percent THC.

1. Delta-9-tetrahydro-cannabinol, believed to be responsible for most of its characteristic psychoactive effects.

HALLUCINOGENS

Hallucinogenic drugs, both natural and synthetic, are substances that distort the perception of objective reality. They induce a state of excitation of the central nervous system, manifested by alterations of mood, usually euphoric, but sometimes severely depressive. Under the influence of hallucinogens, the senses of direction, distance, and time becomes disoriented. A user may speak of "seeing" sounds and "hearing" colors. If taken in a large enough dose, the drug produces delusions and visual hallucinations. Occasionally, depersonalization and depression are so severe that suicide is possible, but the most common danger is impaired judgment, leading to rash decisions and accidents. Persons in hallucinogenic states should, therefore, be closely supervised and upset as little as possible to keep them from harming themselves and others. Acute anxiety, restlessness, and sleeplessness are common until the drug wears off.

Long after hallucinogens are eliminated from the body, users may experience flashbacks—fragmentary recurrences of psychedelic effects—such as the intensification of a perceived color, the apparent motion of a fixed object, or the mistaking of one object for another. Recurrent use produces tolerance, which tends to encourage resorting to greater amounts. Although no evidence of physical dependence is detectable when the drugs are withdrawn, recurrent use tends to produce psychic dependence, varying according to the drug, the dose, and the individual user. It should be stressed that the hallucinogens are unpredictable in their effects each time they are used.

Peyote and Mescaline

The primary active ingredient of the peyote cactus is the hallucinogen *mescaline.* It is derived from the fleshy parts or buttons of this plant, which has been employed by Indians in northern Mexico from the earliest recorded time as a part of traditional religious rites. Peyote, or mescal buttons, and mescaline should not be confused with mescal, the colorless Mexican liquor distilled from the leaves of maguey plants. Usually ground into a powder, peyote is taken orally. Mescaline can also be produced synthetically. A dose of 350 to 500 mg of mescaline produces illusions and hallucinations lasting from 5 to 12 hours.

LSD (LSD-25, lysergide)

LSD is an abbreviation of the German expression for lysergic acid diethylamide. It is produced from lysergic acid, a substance derived from the ergot fungus which grows on rye or from lysergic acid amide, a chemical found in morning glory seeds.

LSD was first synthesized in 1938. Its psychotomimetic effects were discovered in 1943 when a chemist accidentally took some LSD. As he began to experience the effects now known as a "trip," he was aware of vertigo and an intensification of light. Closing his eyes, he saw a stream of fantastic images of extraordinary vividness accompanied by a kaleidoscopic play of colors. This condition lasted for about two hours.

Because of the extremely high potency of LSD, its structural relationship to a chemical which is present in the brain, and its similarity in effects to certain aspects of psychosis, LSD was used as a tool of research to study the mechanism of mental illness.

LSD is usually sold in the form of tablets, thin squares of gelatin ("window panes"), or impregnated paper ("blotter acid"), The average effective oral dose is from 30 to 50 micrograms, but the amount per dosage unit varies greatly. The effects of higher doses persist for 10 to 12 hours. Tolerance develops rapidly.

Phencyclidine (PCP)

PCP is sold under at least 50 other names, including Angel Dust, Crystal, Supergrass, Killer Weed, Embalming Fluid, and Rocket Fuel, that reflect the range of its bizarre and volatile effects. It is also frequently misrepresented as mescaline, LSD, or THC. In its pure form, it is a white crystalline powder that readily dissolves in water. Most PCP now contains contaminants resulting from its makeshift manufacture, causing the color to range from tan to brown and the consistency from a powder to a gummy mass. Although sold in tablets and capsules, as well as in powder and liquid form, it is commonly applied to a leafy material, such as parsley, mint, oregano, or marijuana, and smoked.

The drug is as variable in its effects as it is in its appearance. A moderate amount often produces in the user a sense of detachment, distance, and estrangement from the surroundings. Numbness, slurred or blocked speech, and a loss of coordination may be accompanied by a sense of strength and invulnerability. A blank stare, rapid and involuntary eye movements, and an exaggerated gait are among the more common observable effects. Auditory hallucinations, image distortion as in a fun-house mirror, and severe mood disorders may also occur, producing in some acute anxiety and a feeling of impending doom, in others paranoia and violent hostility. PCP is unique among popular drugs of abuse in its power to produce psychoses indistinguishable from schizophrenia.

ALCOHOL

Source: U.S. Department of Education.

Alcohol is the number one drug problem among youth. The easy availability, widespread acceptability, and extensive promotion of alcoholic beverages within our society make alcohol the most widely used and abused drug.

Effects.—Alcohol consumption causes a number of marked changes in behavior. Even low doses significantly impair the judgment and coordination required to drive a car safely, increasing the likelihood that the driver will be involved in an accident. Low to moderate doses of alcohol also increase the incidence of a variety of aggressive acts, including spouse and child abuse. Moderate to high doses of alcohol cause marked impairments in higher mental functions, severely altering a person's ability to learn and remember information. Very high doses cause respiratory depression and death. If combined with other depressants of the central nervous system, much lower doses of alcohol will produce the effects just described.

Repeated use of alcohol can lead to dependence. Sudden cessation of alcohol intake is likely to produce withdrawal symptoms, including severe anxiety, tremors, hallucinations, and convulsions. Alcohol withdrawal can be life-threatening. Long-term consumption of large quantities of alcohol, particularly when combined with poor nutrition, can also lead to permanent damage to vital organs such as the brain and the liver.

Mothers who drink alcohol during pregnancy may give birth to infants with fetal alcohol syndrome. These infants have irreversible physical abnormalities and mental retardation. In addition, research indicates that children of alcoholic parents are at greater risk than other youngsters of becoming alcoholics.

TOBACCO

Source: U.S. Department of Education.

More than 25% of Americans smoke cigarettes regularly and the annual estimated number of cigarette-induced deaths is 50,000.

Effects.—The smoking of tobacco products is the chief avoidable cause of death in our society. Smokers are more likely than nonsmokers to contract heart disease. Lung, larynx, esophageal, bladder, pancreatic, and kidney cancers also strike smokers at increased rates. Some 30 percent of cancer deaths (130,000 per year) are linked to smoking. Chronic obstructive lung diseases such as emphysema and chronic bronchitis are 10 times more likely to occur among smokers than among nonsmokers.

Smoking during pregnancy also poses serious risks. Spontaneous abortion, preterm birth, low birth weights, and fetal and infant deaths are all more likely to occur when the pregnant woman/mother is a smoker.

Perhaps the most dangerous substance in tobacco smoke is nicotine. Although it is implicated in the onset of heart attacks and cancer, its most dangerous role is reinforcing and strengthening the desire to smoke. Because nicotine is highly addictive, addicts find it very difficult to stop smoking. Of 1,000 typical smokers, fewer than 20 percent succeed in stopping on the first try.

Although the harmful effects of smoking cannot be questioned, people who quit can make significant strides in repairing damage done by smoking. For pack-a-day smokers, the increased risk of heart attack dissipates after 10 years. The likelihood of contracting lung cancer as a result of smoking can also be greatly reduced by quitting.

Sources of Information

American Council for Drug Education.—This organization provides information on drug use, develops media campaigns, reviews scientific findings, publishes books and a newsletter, and offers films and curriculum materials for preteens. 204 Monroe St., Rockville, Md. 20850. Telephone (301) 294-0600.

U.S. Clearinghouse.—(A publication list is available on request, along with placement on a mailing list for new publications. Single copies are free.) National Clearinghouse for Alcohol and Drug Information (NCADI), P.O. Box 2345, Rockville, Md. 20852. Telephone (301) 468-2600

National Council on Alcoholism, Inc.—This national voluntary health agency provides information about alcoholism and alcohol problems through more than 300 local affiliates. 12 West 21st St., New York, N.Y. 10010. Telephone (212) 206-6770.

Narcotics Anonymous.—Similar to Alcoholics Anonymous, this program is a fellowship of men and women who meet to help one another with their drug dependency problems. World Service Office, P.O. Box 9999, Van Nuys, Calif. 91409. Telephone (818) 780-3951.

Families Anonymous.—This worldwide organization offers a 12-step, self-help program for families and friends of people with behavioral problems usually associated with drug abuse. The organization is similar in structure to Alcoholics Anonymous. P.O. Box 3475, Culver City, Calif. 90230. Telephone (310) 313-5800.

WORD TRENDS

A selection of new words recently introduced or that have taken on extended new meanings. *Source:* American Heritage Dictionary of the English Language, 3rd Edition, and The American Heritage College Dictionary, 3rd Edition.

ARC. A combination of symptoms, including fever, lymphadenopathy, blood abnormalities, and susceptibility to opportunistic infections. The complex was first considered to be a precursor to AIDS, but is now thought of as a milder form of the disease. [A(IDS) R(elated) C(omplex).]

Caregiver. 1. An individual, such as a physician, nurse, or social worker, who assists in the identification, prevention, or treatment of an illness or disability. 2. An individual, such as a parent, foster parent, or head of a household, who attends to the needs of a child or dependent adult.

Cash cow. A steady, dependable source of funds or income.

Chunnel. An underwater tunnel for the passage of motor vehicles, especially one under the English Channel.

Colorize. To impart color (to black-and-white film) by means of a computer-assisted process.

Cyberpunk. Fast-paced science fiction involving futuristic computer-based societies.

Date rape. Rape perpetrated by the victim's social escort.

Deconstruction. A philosophical movement and theory of literary criticism that questions traditional assumptions about certainty, identity, and truth, asserts that words can only refer to other words, and attempts to demonstrate how statements about any text subvert their own meanings.

Downlink. A transmission path for the communication of signals and data from a communications satellite or other space vehicle to the earth and back.

Eurocrat. An administrative official of the headquarters of the Common Market.

Four-by-four or **4 x 4.** A four-wheel-drive motor vehicle.

Fractal. A geometric pattern that is repeated at ever smaller scales to produce irregular shapes and surfaces that cannot be represented by classical geometry. Fractals are used especially in computer modeling of irregular patterns and structures in nature.

Fullerene. Any of various soccerball-shaped molecules that constitute the third form of carbon after graphite and diamond, including the extraordinarily stable fullerene C_{60}, the roundest molecule known.

Generation X. A group of people born between 1961 and 1972 typified by a college education, dissatisfaction with career opportunities, and pessimism.

Gonzo. 1. Using exaggerated, often highly subjective or self-indulgent style and tending toward bizarre or unconventional subjects, chiefly in journalism. 2. Bizarre; unconventional.

Greening. 1. Restoration of vitality or freshness; rejuvenation. 2. An adoption or alignment with the ideals or practices of the Green movement.

Greenmail. An antitakeover maneuver in which the target firm purchases the raider's stock at a price above that available to other stockholders.

HIV. A retrovirus that causes AIDS. HIV was formerly known as HTLV–III.

Home invasion. Burglary of a dwelling while the residents are at home.

Hypertext. A computer-based text retrieval system that enables the user to provide access to or gain information related to a particular text.

Jazz-rock. Music that blends jazz elements and the heavy repetitive rhythms of rock. Also called jazz-fusion.

Jersey barrier. A protective concrete barrier used as a highway divider and a means of preventing access to a prohibited area. [From the fact that they were first used on the New Jersey Turnpike.]

Junk bond. A corporate bond having a high yield and high risk.

Keypad. An input device, sometimes part of a standard typewriter keyboard, consisting of a separate grid of numerical and function keys arranged for efficient data entry.

Kickboxing. The martial art and sport of attack and defense, practiced in a boxing ring and combining many elements of karate and boxing.

Laffer curve. A curved graph that illustrates a relationship between tax rates and government revenues. As tax rates increase from zero, revenues increase until an optimum is reached. But if tax rates are further increased, they are supposed to discourage government spending and business investment, thereby reducing revenues.

Lake effect. The effect of any lake, especially the Great Lakes, in modifying the weather in nearby areas.

LAN. A system that links together electronic office equipment, such as computers, terminals, and word processors, and forms a network within an office or a building. [L(ocal) A(rea) N(etwork).]

Leveraged buyout (LBO). The use of a target company's asset value to finance the debt incurred in acquiring the company.

Liberation theology. A school of theology, especially prevalent in the Roman Catholic Church in Latin America, that finds in the Gospel a call to free people from political, social, and material oppression.

Liposuction. A usually cosmetic surgical procedure in which excess fatty tissue is removed from a specific area of the body, such as the thighs or abdomen, by means of suction.

Magical realism. A chiefly literary style or genre originating in Latin America that combines fantastic or dreamlike elements with reality.

Magnetic resonance imaging (MRI). The use of a nuclear magnetic resonance spectrometer to produce electronic images of specific atoms and molecular structures in solids, especially human cells, tissues, and organs.

Meta-analysis. The process or technique of synthesizing research results by using various statistical methods to retrieve, select, and combine results from previous separate but related studies.

Metafiction. Fiction that deals, often playfully and self-referentially, with the writing of fiction or its conventions.

MIDI. 1. A standard for representing sounds in a form that a computer can interpret. 2. Software that conforms to this standard, used for composing and editing electronic music. [M(usical) I(nstrument) D(igital) I(nterface).]

Minimalist. One who advocates a moderate or conservative approach, action, or policy, as in a political or governmental organization.

Music video. A filmed or videotaped rendition of a recorded song, often portraying musicians performing the song or including visual images interpreting the lyrics.

Narrowcast. To transmit, as by cable, programs confined to the interests of a specific group of viewers, subscribers, or listeners, such as physicians, businesspeople, or teenagers.

Novelize. 1. To write a novel based on. 2. To turn into fiction; fictionalize.

Off-road vehicle (ORV). A vehicle, such as a dune buggy, designed for use off paved or public roads or in rough terrain.

Ombudsperson. A person who investigates complaints, reports findings, and mediates fair settlements between aggrieved persons such as consumers or students and an institution, an organization, or a company.

Oncogene. A gene that causes the transformation of normal cells into cancerous tumor cells, especially a viral gene that transforms a host cell into a tumor cell.

Outplacement. The process of facilitating a terminated employee's search for a new job by provision of professional services, such as counseling, paid for by the employing company.

Outsource. To farm out (work, for example) to an outside provider or manufacturer in order to cut costs.

Passive smoking. The involuntary inhalation of tobacco smoke by a person, especially a nonsmoker, who occupies an area with smokers or a smoker.

Performance art. A form of theatrical art in which thematically related works in a variety of media are presented simultaneously or successively to an audience.

Photo opportunity. A brief period reserved for the press to photograph the participants in a newsworthy event.

Pixel. The smallest image-forming unit of a video display.

Politically correct. 1. Of, relating to, or supporting a program of broad social, political, and educational change, especially to redress historical injustices in matters such as race, class, gender, and sexual orientation. 2. Being or perceived as being overconcerned with this program, often to the exclusion of other matters.

Polymerase chain reaction. A laboratory technique in which trace amounts of DNA can be amplified into large quantities by repeatedly separating paired DNA strands and using each strand as a template for a new DNA segment.

Prequel. 1. A literary, cinematic, or dramatic work taking place in or concerned with a time before the action of a preexisting work. 2. A literary, cinematic, or dramatic work that precedes, introduces, or leads up to a later work.

Privatize. To change (an industry or a business, for example) from governmental or public ownership or control to private enterprise.

Quant. An expert in the use of mathematics and related subjects, particularly in investment management and stock trading.

Rear-end. To run into (another motor vehicle) from behind.

Serial killer. A person who attacks and slays more than three victims one by one during a relatively short period of time.

Sexually transmitted disease (STD). Any of various diseases, including chancroid, chlamydia, gonorrhea, and syphilis, that are usually contracted through sexual intercourse or other intimate sexual contact.

S/he. Used as a gender-neutral alternative to *he* or *she.*

Slam-dunk. 1. A very dramatic, highly forceful dunk shot. 2. A forceful, dramatic move.

Snowboard. A board resembling a small surfboard and equipped with bindings, used for descending snow-covered slopes on one's feet but without ski poles.

Sound bite. A very brief broadcast statement, as by a politician during a news report.

Spin control. Efforts made especially by politicians to ensure a favorable interpretation of their words and actions.

Spousal equivalent. One who cohabits and shares responsibility for common welfare with a nonrelative of the same sex in an exclusive relationship that one intends to maintain indefinitely.

Stress test. A graded test to measure an individual's heart rate and oxygen intake while undergoing strenuous physical exercise, as on a treadmill.

Supersaver. An airline ticket, purchased typically well ahead of the departure date, that affords the purchaser considerable savings over regular fare.

Talking head. 1. The image of a person, as on a television documentary or news show, who talks at length directly to the camera and usually appears on the screen with only the head and upper part of the body visible. 2. The person thus televised.

Traumatology. The branch of medicine that deals with the treatment of serious wounds, injuries, and disabilities.

Trilateral. Having or involving three sides, countries, or parties.

Underplot. A plot subordinate to the main plot of a literary work or film. Also called counterplot, subplot.

Urban wind. A strong wind generated near or around a group of high-rise buildings, creating areas of intense air turbulence especially at street level.

Venture capital. Money made available for investment in innovative enterprises or research, especially in high technology, in which both the risk of loss and the potential for profit may be considerable. Also called *risk capital.*

Video jockey (VJ). One who announces, plays, and provides commentary on videotaped programs, especially music videos, as on television or at a discotheque.

Voice mail. An interactive computerized system for answering and routing telephone calls, for recording, saving, and relaying messages, and sometimes for paging the user.

Waterbus. A large motorboat used for carrying passengers on rivers or canals.

Wellness. Good physical and mental health, especially when maintained by proper diet, exercise, and habits.

Wide-bodied. Being or relating to a jet aircraft having a wide fuselage with passenger seats divided by two lengthwise aisles.

Wind shear. A change in wind direction and speed between slightly different altitudes, especially a sudden downdraft.

Windsurfing. The sport of sailing while standing on a sailboard. Also called *boardsailing, windsailing.*

Xer. A member of Generation X.

Yellow rain. A powdery, poisonous, yellow substance reported as dropping from the air in southeast Asia and found to be the excrement of wild honeybees contaminated by a fungal toxin.

A Concise Guide to Style

From *Webster's II New Riverside University Dictionary.* © 1984 by Houghton Mifflin Company.

This section discusses and illustrates the basic conventions of American capitalization, punctuation, and italicization.

Capitalization

Capitalize the following: **1.** the first word of a sentence: Some spiders are poisonous; others are not. Are you my new neighbor?

2. the first word of a direct quotation, except when the quotation is split: Joyce asked, "Do you think that the lecture was interesting?" "No," I responded, "it was very boring." Tom Paine said, "The sublime and the ridiculous are often so nearly related that it is difficult to class them separately."

3. the first word of each line in a poem in traditional verse: Half a league, half a league,/Half a league onward,/All in the valley of Death/Rode the six hundred.—Alfred, Lord Tennyson

4. the names of people, of organizations and their members, of councils and congresses, and of historical periods and events: Marie Curie, Benevolent and Protective Order of Elks, an Elk, Protestant Episcopal Church, an Episcopalian, the Democratic Party, a Democrat, the Nuclear Regulatory Commission, the U.S. Senate, the Middle Ages, World War I, the Battle of Britain.

5. the names of places and geographic divisions, districts, regions, and locales: Richmond, Vermont, Argentina, Seventh Avenue, London Bridge, Arctic Circle, Eastern Hemisphere, Continental Divide, Middle East, Far North, Gulf States, East Coast, the North, the South Shore.

Do not capitalize words indicating compass points unless a specific region is referred to: Turn north onto Interstate 91.

6. the names of rivers, lakes, mountains, and oceans: Ohio River, Lake Como, Rocky Mountains, Atlantic Ocean.

7. the names of ships, aircraft, satellites, and space vehicles: U.S.S. *Arizona, Spirit of St. Louis,* the spy satellite Ferret-D, Voyager II, the space shuttle Challenger.

8. the names of nationalities, races, tribes, and languages: Spanish, Maori, Bantu, Russian.

9. words derived from proper names, except in their extended senses: the Byzantine Empire. *But:* byzantine office politics.

10. words indicating family relationships when used with a person's name as a title: Aunt Toni and Uncle Jack. *But:* my aunt and uncle, Toni and Jack Walker.

11. a title (i.e., civil, judicial, military, royal and noble, religious, and honorary) when preceding a name: Justice Marshall, General Jackson, Mayor Daley, Queen Victoria, Lord Mountbatten, Pope John Paul II, Professor Jacobson, Senator Byrd.

12. all references to the President and Vice President of the United States: The President has entered the hall. The Vice President presides over the Senate.

13. all key words in titles of literary, dramatic, artistic, and musical works: the novel *The Old Man and the Sea,* the short story "Notes from Underground," an article entitled "On Passive Verbs," James Dickey's poem "In the Tree House at Night," the play *Cat on a Hot Tin Roof,* Van Gogh's *Wheat Field and Cypress Trees,* Beethoven's *Emperor Concerto.*

14. *the* in the title of a newspaper if it is a part of the title: *The Wall Street Journal. But:* the New York *Daily News.*

15. the first word in the salutation and in the complimentary close of a letter: My dear Carol, Yours sincerely.

16. epithets and substitutes for the names of people and places: Old Hickory, Old Blood and Guts, The Oval Office, the Windy City.

17. words used in personifications: When is not Death at watch/Within those secret waters?/What wants he but to catch/Earth's heedless sons and daughters?—Edmund Blunden

18. the pronoun *I:* I told them that I had heard the news.

19. names for the Deity and sacred works: God, the Almighty, Jesus, Allah, the Supreme Being, the Bible, the Koran, the Talmud.

20. days of the week, months of the year, holidays, and holy days: Tuesday, May, Independence Day, Passover, Ramadan, Christmas.

21. the names of specific courts: The Supreme Court of the United States, the Massachusetts Appeals Court, the United States Court of Appeals for the First Circuit.

22. the names of treaties, accords, pacts, laws, and specific amendments: Panama Canal Treaty, Treaty of Paris, Geneva Accords, Warsaw Pact countries, Sherman Antitrust Law, Labor Management Relations Act, took the Fifth Amendment.

23. registered trademarks and service marks: Day-Glo, Comsat.

24. the names of geologic eras, periods, epochs, and strata and the names of prehistoric divisions: Paleozoic Era, Precambrian, Pleistocene, Age of Reptiles, Bronze Age, Stone Age.

25. the names of constellations, planets, and stars: Milky Way, Southern Crown, Saturn, Jupiter, Uranus, Polaris.

26. genus but not species names in binomial nomenclature: *Rana pipiens.*

27. New Latin names of classes, families, and all groups higher than genera in botanical and zoological nomenclature: Nematoda.

But do not capitalize derivatives from such names: nematodes.

28. many abbreviations and acronyms: Dec., Tues., Lt. Gen., M.F.A., UNESCO, MIRV.

Italicization

Use italics to:
1. indicate titles of books, plays, and epic poems:

War and Peace, The Importance of Being Earnest, Paradise Lost.

2. indicate titles of magazines and newspapers: *New York* magazine, *The Wall Street Journal*, the New York *Daily News.*

3. set off the titles of motion pictures and radio and television programs: *Star Wars, All Things Considered, Masterpiece Theater.*

4. indicate titles of major musical compositions: Handel's *Messiah,* Adam's *Giselle.*

5. set off the names of paintings and sculpture: *Mona Lisa, Pietà.*

6. indicate words, letters, or numbers that are referred to: The word *hiss* is onomatopoeic. *Can't* means *won't* in your lexicon. You form your *n*'s like *u*'s. A *6* looks like an inverted *9.*

7. indicate foreign words and phrases not yet assimilated into English: *C'est la vie* was the response to my complaint.

8. indicate the names of plaintiff and defendant in legal citations: *Roe* v. *Doe.*

9. emphasize a word or phrase: When you appear on the national news, you are *somebody.*

Use this device sparingly.

10. distinguish New Latin names of genera, species, subspecies, and varieties in botanical and zoological nomenclature: *Homo sapiens.*

11. set off the names of ships and aircraft but not space vehicles: U.S.S. *Arizona, Spirit of St. Louis,* Voyager II, the space shuttle Challenger, the spy satellite Ferret-D.

Punctuation

Apostrophe. 1. indicates the possessive case of singular and plural nouns, indefinite pronouns, and surnames combined with designations such as *Jr., Sr.,* and *II:* my sister's husband, my three sisters' husbands, anyone's guess, They answer each other's phones, John Smith, Jr.'s car.

2. indicates joint possession when used with the last of two or more nouns in a series: Doe and Roe's report.

3. indicates individual possession or authorship when used with each of two or more nouns in a series: Smith's, Roe's, and Doe's reports.

4. indicates the plurals of words, letters, and figures used as such: 60's and 70's; *x*'s, *y*'s, and *z*'s.

5. indicates omission of letters in contractions: aren't, that's, o'clock.

6. indicates omission of figures in dates: the class of '63.

Brackets.

1. enclose words or passages in quoted matter to indicate insertion of material written by someone other than the author: A tough but nervous, tenacious but restless race [the Yankees]; materially ambitious, yet prone to introspection. . . .—Samuel Eliot Morison

2. enclose material inserted within matter already in parentheses: (Vancouver [B.C.] January 1, 19—).

Colon.

1. introduces words, phrases, or clauses that explain, amplify, or summarize what has gone before: Suddenly I realized where we were: Rome.

"There are two cardinal sins from which all the others spring: impatience and laziness."—Franz Kafka

2. introduces a long quotation: In his original draft of the *Declaration of Independence,* Jefferson wrote: "We hold these truths to be sacred and undeniable; that all men are created equal and independent, that

from that equal creation they derive rights inherent and inalienable. . . ."

3. introduces a list: We need the following items: pens, paper, pencils, blotters, and erasers.

4. separates chapter and verse numbers in Biblical references: James 1:4.

5. separates city from publisher in footnotes and bibliographies: Chicago: Riverside Press, 1983.

6. separates hour and minute(s) in time designations: 9:30 a.m., a 9:30 meeting.

7. follows the salutation in a business letter: Gentlemen:

Comma. 1. separates the clauses of a compound sentence connected by a coordinating conjunction: A difference exists between the musical works of Handel and Haydn, and it is a difference worth noting.

The comma may be omitted in short compound sentences: I heard what you said and I am furious. I got out of the car and I walked and walked.

2. separates *and* or *or* from the final item in a series of three or more: Red, yellow, and blue may be mixed to produce all colors.

3. separates two or more adjectives modifying the same noun if *and* could be used between them without altering the meaning: a solid, heavy gait. *But:* a polished mahogany dresser.

4. sets off nonrestrictive clauses or phrases (i.e., those that if eliminated would not affect the meaning of the sentences): The burglar, who had entered through the patio, went straight to the silver chest.

The comma should not be used when a clause is restrictive (i.e., essential to the meaning of the sentence): The burglar who had entered through the patio went straight to the silver chest; the other burglar searched for the wall safe.

5. sets off words or phrases in apposition to a noun or noun phrase: Plato, the famous Greek philosopher, was a student of Socrates.

The comma should not be used if such words or phrases precede the noun: The Greek philosopher Plato was a student of Socrates.

6. sets off transitional words and short expressions that require a pause in reading or speaking: Unfortunately, my friend was not well traveled. Did you, after all, find what you were looking for? I live with my family, of course.

7. sets off words used to introduce a sentence: No, I haven't been to Paris. Well, what do you think we should do now?

8. sets off a subordinate clause or a long phrase that precedes a principal clause: By the time we found the restaurant, we were starved. Of all the illustrations in the book, the most striking are those of the tapestries.

9. sets off short quotations and sayings: The candidate said, "Actions speak louder than words." "Talking of axes," said the Duchess, "chop off her head"—Lewis Carroll

10. indicates omission of a word or words: To err is human; to forgive, divine.

11. sets off the year from the month in full dates: Nicholas II of Russia was shot on July 16, 1918.

But note that when only the month and the year are used, no comma appears: Nicholas II of Russia was shot in July 1918.

12. sets off city and state in geographic names: Atlanta, Georgia, is the transportation center of the South. 34 Beach Drive, Bedford, VA 24523.

13. separates series of four or more figures into thousands, millions, etc.: 67,000; 200,000.

14. sets off words used in direct address: "I tell you, folks, all politics is applesauce."—Will Rogers Thank you for your expert assistance, Dolores.

15. Separates a tag question from the rest of a sentence: You forgot your keys again, didn't you?

16. sets off sentence elements that could be misunderstood if the comma were not used: Some time after, the actual date for the project was set.

17. follows the salutation in a personal letter and the complimentary close in a business or personal letter: Dear Jessica, Sincerely yours.

18. sets off titles and degrees from surnames and from the rest of a sentence: Walter T. Prescott, Jr.; Gregory A. Rossi, S.J.; Susan P. Green, M.D., presented the case.

Dash.

1. indicates a sudden break or abrupt change in continuity: "If—if you'll just let me explain—" the student stammered. And the problem—if there really is one—can then be solved.

2. sets apart an explanatory, a defining, or an emphatic phrase: Foods rich in protein—meat, fish, and eggs—should be eaten on a daily basis.

More important than winning the election, is governing the nation. That is the test of a political party—the acid, final test.—Adlai E. Stevenson

3. sets apart parenthetical matter: Wolsey, for all his faults—and he had many—was a great statesman, a man of natural dignity with a generous temperament. . . .—Jasper Ridley

4. marks an unfinished sentence: "But if my bus is late—" he began.

5. sets off a summarizing phrase or clause: The vital measure of a newspaper is not its size but its spirit—that is its responsibility to report the news fully, accurately, and fairly.—Arthur H. Sulzberger

6. sets off the name of an author or source, as at the end of a quotation: A poet can survive everything but a misprint.—Oscar Wilde

Ellipses

1. indicate, by three spaced points, omission of words or sentences within quoted matter: Equipped by education to rule in the nineteenth century, . . . he lived and reigned in Russia in the twentieth century.—Robert K. Massie

2. indicate, by four spaced points, omission of words at the end of a sentence: The timidity of bureaucrats when it comes to dealing with . . . abuses is easy to explain. . . .—*New York*

3. indicate, when extended the length of a line, omission of one or more lines of poetry:

Roll on, thou deep and dark blue
    ocean—roll!

. . . .

Man marks the earth with ruin—his
    control
Stops with the shore.—Lord Byron

4. are sometimes used as a device, as for example, in advertising copy:

To help you Move and Grow
    with the Rigors of
Business in the 1980's . . .
    and Beyond.—*Journal of Business Strategy*

Exclamation Point.

1. terminates an emphatic or exclamatory sentence: Go home at once! You've got to be kidding!

2. terminates an emphatic interjection: Encore!

Hyphen. 1. indicates that part of a word of more than one syllable has been carried over from one line to the next:

During the revolution, the nation was
beset with problems—looting, fighting, and famine.

2. joins the elements of some compounds: great-grandparent, attorney-at-law, ne'er-do-well.

3. joins the elements of compound modifiers preceding nouns: high-school students, a fire-and-brimstone lecture, a two-hour meeting.

4. indicates that two or more compounds share a single base: four- and six-volume sets, eight- and nine-year olds.

5. separates the prefix and root in some combinations; check the Dictionary when in doubt about the spelling: anti-Nazi, re-elect, co-author, re-form/reform, re-cover/recover, re-creation/recreation.

6. substitutes for the word *to* between typewritten inclusive words or figures: pp. 145–155, the Boston-New York air shuttle.

7. punctuates written-out compound numbers from 21 through 99: forty-six years of age, a person who is forty-six, two hundred fifty-nine dollars.

Parentheses. 1. enclose material that is not essential to a sentence and that if not included would not alter its meaning: After a few minutes (some say less) the blaze was extinguished.

2. often enclose letters or figures to indicate subdivisions of a series: A movement in sonata form consists of the following elements; (1) the exposition, (2) the development, and (3) the recapitulation.

3. enclose figures following and confirming written-out numbers, especially in legal and business documents: The fee for my services will be two thousand dollars ($2,000.00).

4. enclose an abbreviation for a term following the written-out term, when used for the first time in a text: The patient is suffering from acquired immune deficiency syndrome (AIDS).

Period. 1. terminates a complete declarative or mild imperative sentence: There could be no turning back as war's dark shadow settled irrevocably across the continent of Europe.—W. Bruce Lincoln. Return all the books when you can. Would you kindly affix your signature here.

2. terminates sentence fragments: Gray clouds— and what looks like a veil of rain falling behind the East German headland. A pair of ducks. A tired or dying swan, head buried in its back feathers, sits on the sand a few feet from the water's edge.—Anthony Bailey

3. follows some abbreviations: Dec., Rev., St., Blvd., pp., Co.

Question Mark. 1. punctuates a direct question: Have you seen the new play yet? Who goes there? *But:* I wonder who said "Nothing is easy in war." I asked if they planned to leave.

2. indicates uncertainty: Ferdinand Magellan (1480?–1521), Plato (427?–347 B.C.).

Quotation Marks. 1. Double quotation marks enclose direct quotations: "What was Paris like in the Twenties?" our daughter asked. "Ladies and Gentlemen," the Chief Usher said, "the President of the United States." Robert Louis Stevenson said that "it is better to be a fool than to be dead." When advised not to become a lawyer because the profession was already overcrowded, Daniel Webster replied, "There is always room at the top."

2. Double quotation marks enclose words or phrases to clarify their meaning or use or to indicate that they are being used in a special way: This was the border of what we often call "the West" or "the Free World." "The Windy City" is a name for Chicago.

3. Double quotation marks set off the translation of a foreign word or phrase: *die Grenze,* "the border."

4. Double quotation marks set off the titles of series of books, of articles or chapters in publications, of essays, of short stories and poems, of individual radio and television programs, and of songs and short musical pieces: "The Horizon Concise History" series; an article entitled "On Reflexive Verbs in

English"; Chapter Nine, "The Prince and the Peasant"; Pushkin's "The Queen of Spades"; Tennyson's "Ode on the Death of the Duke of Wellington"; "The Bob Hope Special"; Schubert's "Death and the Maiden."

5. Single quotation marks enclose quotations within quotations: The blurb for the piece proclaimed, "Two years ago at Geneva, South Vietnam was virtually sold down the river to the Communists. Today the spunky little . . . country is back on its own feet, thanks to "a mandarin in a sharkskin suit who's upsetting the Red timetable.' "—Frances FitzGerald

Put commas and periods inside quotation marks; put semicolons and colons outside. Other punctuation, such as exclamation points and question marks, should be put inside the closing quotation marks only if part of the matter quoted.

Semicolon. 1. separates the clauses of a compound sentence having no coordinating conjunction: Do not let us speak of darker days; let us rather speak of sterner days.—Winston Churchill

2. separates the clauses of a compound sentence in which the clauses contain internal punctuation, even when the clauses are joined by conjunctions: Skis in hand, we trudged to the lodge, stowed our lunches, and donned our boots; and the rest of our party waited for us at the lifts.

3. separates elements of a series in which items already contain commas: Among those at the diplomatic reception were the Secretary of State; the daughter of the Ambassador to the Court of St. James's, formerly of London; and two United Nations delegates.

4. separates clauses of a compound sentence joined by a conjunctive adverb, such as *however, nonetheless,* or *hence:* We insisted upon a hearing; however, the Grievance Committee refused.

5. may be used instead of a comma to signal longer pauses for dramatic effect: But I want you to know that when I cross the river my last conscious thought will be of the Corps; and the Corps; and the Corps.—General Douglas MacArthur

Virgule. 1. separates successive divisions in an extended date: fiscal year 1983/84.

2. represents *per:* 35 km/hr, 1,800 ft/sec.

3. means *or* between the words *and* and *or:* Take water skis and/or fishing equipment when you visit the beach this summer.

4. separates two or more lines of poetry that are quoted and run in on successive lines of a text: The student actress had a memory lapse when she came to the lines "Double, double, toil and trouble/Fire burn and cauldron bubble/Eye of newt and toe of frog/Wool of bat and tongue of dog" and had to leave the stage in embarrassment.

Forms of Address[1]

Source: Webster's II New Riverside University Dictionary. Copyright © 1984 by Houghton Mifflin Company.

Academics

Dean, college or university. *Address:* **Dean** _____. *Salutation:* Dear Dean _____

President. *Address:* President _____ _____. *Salutation:* Dear President _____.

Professor, college or university. *Address:* Professor _____ _____. *Salutation:* Dear Professor _____.

Clerical and Religious Orders

Abbot. *Address:* The Right Reverend _____ _____ O.S.B. Abbot of _____. *Salutation:* Right Reverend Abbot or Dear Father Abbot.

Archbishop, Eastern Orthodox. *Address:* The Most Reverend Joseph, Archbishop of _____. *Salutation:* Your Eminence.

Archbishop, Roman Catholic. The Most Reverend _____ _____, Archbishop of _____. *Salutation:* Your Excellency.

Archdeacon, Episcopal. *Address:* The Venerable _____ _____, Archdeacon of _____. *Salutation:* Venerable Sir or Dear Archdeacon _____.

Bishop, Episcopal. *Address:* The Right Reverend _____ _____, Bishop of _____. *Salutation:* Right Reverend Sir or Dear Bishop _____.

Bishop, other Protestant. *Address:* The Reverend _____ _____. *Salutation:* Dear Bishop _____.

Bishop, Roman Catholic. *Address:* The Most Reverend _____ _____, Bishop of _____. *Salutation:* Your Excellency or Dear Bishop _____.

Brotherhood, Roman Catholic. *Address:* Brother _____ _____, C.F.C. *Salutation:* Dear Brother or Dear Brother Joseph.

Brotherhood, superior of. *Address:* Brother Joseph C.F.C. Superior. *Salutation:* Dear Brother Joseph.

Cardinal. *Address:* His Eminence Joseph Cardinal Stone. *Salutation:* Your Eminence.

Clergyman/woman, Protestant. *Address:* The Reverend _____ _____ or The Reverend _____ _____, D.D. *Salutation:* Dear Mr./Ms. _____ or Dear Dr. _____.

Dean of a cathedral, Episcopal. *Address:* The Very Reverend _____ _____, Dean of _____. *Salutation:* Dear Dean _____.

Monsignor. *Address:* The Right Reverend Monsignor _____ _____. *Salutation:* Dear Monsignor.

Patriarch, Greek Orthodox. *Address:* His All Holiness Patriarch Joseph. *Salutation:* Your All Holiness.

Patriarch, Russian Orthodox. *Address:* His Holiness the Patriarch of _____. *Salutation:* Your Holiness.

Pope. *Address:* His Holiness The Pope. *Salutation:* Your Holiness or Most Holy Father.

Priest, Roman Catholic. *Address:* The Reverend _____ _____, S.J. *Salutation:* Dear Reverend Father or Dear Father.

Rabbi, man or woman. *Address:* Rabbi _____ _____ or _____ _____ D.D.. *Salutation:* Dear Rabbi _____ or Dear Dr. _____.

Sisterhood, Roman Catholic. *Address:* Sister _____ _____, C.S.J. *Salutation:* Dear Sister or Dear Sister _____.

Sisterhood, superior of. *Address:* The Reverend Mother Superior, S.C. *Salutation:* Reverend Mother.

Diplomats

Ambassador, U.S. *Address:* The Honorable _____ _____ The Ambassador of the United States. *Salutation:* Sir/Madam or Dear Mr./Madam Ambassador.

Ambassador to the U.S. *Address:* His/Her Excellency _____ _____, The Ambassador of _____. *Salutation:* Excellency or Dear Mr./Madam Ambassador.

Chargé d'Affaires, U.S. *Address:* The Honorable _____ _____, United States Chargé d'Affaires. *Salutation:* Dear Mr./Ms. _____ .

Consul, U.S. *Address:* _____ _____, Esq., United States Consul. *Salutation:* Dear Mr./Ms. _____ .

Minister, U.S. or to U.S. *Address:* The Honorable _____ _____, The Minister of _____ . *Salutation:* Sir/Madam or Dear Mr./Madame Minister.

Secretary General, United Nations. *Address:* His/Her Excellency _____ _____, Secretary General of the United Nations. *Salutation:* Dear Mr./Madam/Madame Secretary General.

United Nations Representative (Foreign). *Address:* His/Her Excellency _____ _____ Representative of _____ to the United Nations. *Salutation:* Excellency or My dear Mr./Madame _____

United Nations Representative (U.S.) *Address:* The Honorable _____ _____, United States Representative to the United Nations. *Salutation:* Sir/Madam or Dear Mr./Ms. _____ .

Government Officials

Assemblyman. *Address:* The Honorable _____ _____. *Salutation:* Dear Mr./Ms. _____ .

Associate Justice, U.S. Supreme Court. *Address:* Mr./Madam Justice _____. *Salutation:* Dear Mr./Madam Justice or Sir/Madam.

Attorney General, U.S. *Address:* The Honorable _____ _____, Attorney General of the United States. *Salutation:* Dear Mr./Madam or Attorney General.

Cabinet member: *Address:* The Honorable _____ _____, Secretary of _____ . *Salutation:* Sir/Madam or Dear Mr./Madam Secretary.

Chief Justice, U.S. Supreme Court. *Address:* The Chief Justice of the United States. *Salutation:* Dear Mr. Chief Justice.

Commissioner (federal, state, local). *Address:* The Honorable _____ _____. *Salutation:* Dear Mr./Ms. _____ .

Governor. *Address:* The Honorable _____ _____, Governor of _____ . *Salutation:* Dear Governor _____

Judge, Federal: *Address:* The Honorable _____ _____, Judge of the United States District Court for the _____, District of _____ .

Salutation: Sir/Madam or Dear Judge _____ .

Judge, state or local. *Address:* The Honorable _____ _____, Judge of the Court of _____ . *Salutation:* Dear Judge _____ .

Lieutenant Governor. *Address:* The Honorable _____ _____, Lieutenant Governor of _____ . *Salutation:* Dear Mr./Ms. _____ .

Mayor. *Address:* The Honorable _____ _____, Mayor of _____ . *Salutation:* Dear Mayor _____ .

President, U.S. *Address:* The President. *Salutation:* Dear Mr. President.

President, U.S., former. *Address:* The Honorable _____ _____. *Salutation:* Dear Mr. _____ .

Representative, state. *Address:* The Honorable _____ _____. *Salutation:* Dear Mr./Ms. _____ .

Representative, U.S. *Address:* The Honorable _____ _____, United States House of Representatives. *Salutation:* Dear Mr./Ms. _____ .

Senator, state. *Address:* The Honorable _____ _____, The State Senate, State Capitol. *Salutation:* Dear Senator _____ .

Senator, U.S. *Address:* The Honorable _____ _____, United States Senate. *Salutation:* Dear Senator _____ .

Speaker, U.S. House of Representatives. *Address:* The Honorable _____ _____, Speaker of the House of Representatives. *Salutation:* Dear Mr./Madam Speaker.

Vice President, U.S. *Address:* The Vice President of the United States. *Salutation:* Sir or Dear Mr. Vice President.

Military and Naval Officers

Rank. *Address:* Full rank, USN (or USCG, USAF, USA, USMC). *Salutation:* Dear (full rank) _____ .

Professions

Attorney. *Address:* Mr./Ms. _____ _____, Attorney at law or _____ _____, Esq. *Salutation:* Dear Mr./Ms. _____ .

Dentist. *Address:* _____ _____, D.D.S. *Salutation:* Dear Dr. _____ .

Physician. *Address:* _____ _____, M.D. *Salutation:* Dear Dr. _____ .

Veterinarian. *Address:* _____ _____, D.V.M. *Salutation:* Dear Dr. _____ .

1. Forms of address do not always follow set guidelines; the type of salutation is often determined by the relationship between correspondents or by the purpose and content of the letter. However, a general style applies to most occasions. In highly formal salutations, when the addressee is a woman, "Madam" should be substituted for "Sir." When the salutation is informal, "Ms.," "Miss," or "Mrs." should be substituted for "Mr." If a woman addressee has previously indicated a preference for a particular form of address, that form should be used.

Selecting Child Care

Choosing child care is an important issue for parents. Here are some questions parents may want to ask when looking for child care:

1. What are the licensing laws for day care providers in your city, county, or state? Your local consumer protection office is a good place to check for this information.

2. Do caregivers have references? What about special training in child development and education? How many children does each adult look after?

3. Is the home or center clean? Is there enough space inside and outside for the children to play? Is the playground fenced?

4. If the center is large, do visitors and children sign in and out? What are the safety precautions in case of fire or other emergencies?

5. What about sick children? Do they stay home?

What if a child needs medical help?

6. How does the staff discipline children? How much of each day is filled with planned activities? Are activities geared to children's ages and development?

7. What are the fees for half-days, overtime, or sick children?

8. Are kids' pictures or projects hung up and changed often?

9. Do caregivers tell you what your child did that day? How he or she is doing overall?

After your child is in a program, you may wish to ask:

1. Does your child talk happily about the program?

2. Do you know new employees? Do they talk to your child?

WEIGHTS & MEASURES

Measures and Weights

Source: Department of Commerce, National Bureau of Standards.

The International System (Metric)

The International System of Units is a modernized version of the metric system, established by international agreement, that i.e. provides a logical and interconnected framework for all measurements in science, industry, and commerce. The system is built on a foundation of seven basic units, and all other units are derived from them. (Use of metric weights and measures was legalized in the United States in 1866, and our customary units of weights and measures are defined in terms of the meter and kilogram.)

Length. Meter. Up until 1893, the meter was defined as 1,650,764.73 wavelengths in vacuum of the orange-red line of the spectrum of krypton-86. Since then, it is equal to the distance traveled by light in a vacuum in 1/299,792,458 of a second.

Time. Second. The second is defined as the duration of 9,192,631,770 cycles of the radiation associated with a specified transition of the cesium 133 atom.

Mass. Kilogram. The standard for the kilogram is a cylinder of platinum-iridium alloy kept by the International Bureau of Weights and Measures at Paris. A duplicate at the National Bureau of Standards serves as the mass standard for the United States. The kilogram is the only base unit still defined by a physical object.

Temperature. Kelvin. The kelvin is defined as the fraction 1/273.16 of the thermodynamic temperature of the triple point of water; that is, the point at which water forms an interface of solid, liquid and vapor. This is defined as 0.01°C on the Centigrade or Celsius scale and 32.02°F on the Fahrenheit scale. The temperature 0°K is called "absolute zero."

Electric Current. Electric current. The ampere is defined as that current that, if maintained in each of two long parallel wires separated by one meter in free space, would produce a force between the two wires (due to their magnetic fields) of 2×10^{-7} newton for each meter of length. (A newton is the unit of force which when applied to one kilogram mass would experience an acceleration of one meter per second per second.)

Luminous Intensity. Candela. The candela is defined as the luminous intensity of 1/600,000 of a square meter of a cavity at the temperature of freezing platinum (2,042K).

Amount of Substance. Mole. The mole is the amount of substance of a system that contains as many elementary entities as there are atoms in 0.012 kilogram of carbon-12.

Tables of Metric Weights and Measures

LINEAR MEASURE

10 millimeters (mm) =	1 centimeter (cm)
10 centimeters =	1 decimeter (dm) = 100 millimeters
10 decimeters =	1 meter (m) = 1,000 millimeters
10 meters =	1 dekameter (dam)
10 dekameters =	1 hectometer (hm) = 100 meters
10 hectometers =	1 kilometer (km) = 1,000 meters

AREA MEASURE

100 square millimeters (mm^2) =	1 sq centimeter (cm^2)
10,000 square centimeters =	1 sq meter (m^2) = 1,000,000 sq millimeters
100 square meters =	1 are (a)
100 ares =	1 hectare (ha) = 10,000 sq meters
100 hectares =	1 sq kilometer (km^2) = 1,000,000 sq meters

VOLUME MEASURE

10 milliliters (ml) =	1 centiliter (cl)
10 centiliters =	1 deciliter (dl) = 100 milliliters

10 deciliters =	1 liter (l) = 1,000 milliliters
10 liters =	1 dekaliter (dal)
10 dekaliters =	1 hectoliter (hl) = 100 liters
10 hectoliters =	1 kiloliter (kl) = 1,000 liters

CUBIC MEASURE

1,000 cubic millimeters (mm^3) =	1 cu centimeter (cm^3)
1,000 cubic centimeters =	1 cu decimeter (dm^3) = 1,000,000 cu millimeters
1,000 cubic decimeters =	1 cu meter (m^3) = 1 stere = 1,000,000 cu centimeters = 1,000,000,000 cu millimeters

WEIGHT

10 milligrams (mg) =	1 centigram (cg)
10 centigrams =	1 decigram (dg) = 100 milligrams
10 decigrams =	1 gram (g) = 1,000 milligrams
10 grams =	1 dekagram (dag)
10 dekagrams =	1 hectogram (hg) = 100 grams
10 hectograms =	1 kilogram (kg) = 1,000 grams
1,000 kilograms =	1 metric ton (t)

Tables of Customary U.S. Weights and Measures

LINEAR MEASURE

12 inches (in.) =	1 foot (ft)
3 feet =	1 yard (yd)
5 1/2 yards =	1 rod (rd), pole, or perch (16 1/2 ft)
40 rods =	1 furlong (fur) = 220 yds = 660 ft
8 furlongs =	1 statute mile (mi.) = 1,760 yds = 5,280 ft
3 land miles =	1 league
5,280 feet =	1 statute or land mile
6,076.11549 feet =	1 international nautical mile

AREA MEASURE

144 square inches =	1 sq ft
9 square feet =	1 sq yd = 1,296 sq in.
30 1/4 square yards =	1 sq rd = 272 1/4 sq ft
160 square rods =	1 acre = 4,840 sq yds = 43,560 sq ft
640 acres =	1 sq mi.
1 mile square =	1 section (of land)
6 miles square =	1 township = 36 sections = 36 sq mi.

CUBIC MEASURE

1,728 cubic inches =	1 cu ft
27 cubic feet =	1 cu yd

LIQUID MEASURE

When necessary to distinguish the liquid pint or quart from the dry pint or quart, the word "liquid" or the abbreviation "liq" should be used in combination with the name or abbreviation of the liquid unit.

4 gills (gi) =	1 pint (pt) (= 28.875 cu in.)
2 pints =	1 quart (qt) (= 57.75 cu in.)
4 quarts =	1 gallon (gal) (= 231 cu in.) = 8 pts = 32 gills

APOTHECARIES' FLUID MEASURE

60 minims (min.) =	1 fluid dram (fl dr) (= 0.2256 cu in.)
8 fluid drams =	1 fluid ounce (fl oz) (= 1.8047 cu in.)
16 fluid ounces =	1 pt (= 28.875 cu in.) = 128 fl drs
2 pints =	1 qt (= 57.75 cu in.) = 32 fl oz = 256 fl drs
4 quarts =	1 gal (= 231 cu in.) = 128 fl oz = 1,024 fl drs

DRY MEASURE

When necessary to distinguish the dry pint or quart from the liquid pint or quart; the word "dry" should be used in combination with the name or abbreviation of the dry unit.

2 pints =	1 qt (=67.2006 cu in.)
8 quarts =	1 peck (pk) (=537.605 cu in.) = 16 pts
4 pecks =	1 bushel (bu) (= 2,150.42 cu in.) = 32 qts

AVOIRDUPOIS WEIGHT

When necessary to distinguish the avoirdupois dram from the apothecaries dram, or to distinguish the avoirdupois dram or ounce from the fluid dram or ounce, or to distinguish the avoirdupois ounce or pound from the troy or apothecaries, ounce or pound, the word "avoirdupois" or the abbreviation "avdp" should be used in combination with the name or abbreviation of the avoirdupois unit. (The "grain" is the same in avoirdupois, troy, and apothecaries weights.)

27 11/32 grains =	1 dram (dr)
16 drams =	1 oz = 437 1/2 grains
16 ounces =	1 lb = 256 drams = 7,000 grains
100 pounds =	1 hundredweight (cwt)[1]
20 hundredweights =	1 ton (tn) = 2,000 lbs[1]

In "gross" or "long" measure, the following values are recognized:

112 pounds =	1 gross or long cwt[1]
20 gross or long hundredweights =	1 gross or long ton = 2,240 lbs[1]

1. When the terms "hundredweight" and "ton" are used unmodified, they are commonly understood to mean the 100–pound hundredweight and the 2,000–pound ton, respectively; these units may be designated "net" or "short" when necessary to distinguish them from the corresponding units in gross or long measure.

UNITS OF CIRCULAR MEASURE

Second (") =	—
Minute (') =	60 seconds
Degree (°) =	60 minutes
Right angle =	90 degrees
Straight angle =	180 degrees
Circle =	360 degrees

TROY WEIGHT

24 grains =	1 pennyweight (dwt)
20 pennyweights =	1 ounce troy (oz t) = 480 grains
12 ounces troy =	1 pound troy (lb t) = 240 pennyweights = 5,760 grains

APOTHECARIES' WEIGHT

20 grains =	1 scruple (s ap)
3 scruples =	1 dram apothecaries' (dr ap) = 60 grains
8 drams apothecaries =	1 ounce apothecaries' (oz ap) = 24 scruples = 480 grains
12 ounces apothecaries =	1 pound apothecaries' (lb ap) = 96 drams apothecaries' = 288 scruples = 5,760 grains

GUNTER'S OR SURVEYOR'S CHAIN MEASURE

7.92 inches =	1 link (li)
100 links =	1 chain (ch) = 4 rods = 66 ft
80 chains =	1 statute mile = 320 rods = 5,280 ft

Metric and U.S. Equivalents

1 angstrom[1] (light wave measurement)	0.1 millimicron 0.000 1 micron 0.000 000 1 millimeter 0.000 000 004 inch	1 decimeter	3.937 inches
		1 dekameter	32.808 feet
1 cable's length	120 fathoms 720 feet 219.456 meters	1 fathom	6 feet 1.8288 meters
1 centimeter	0.3937 inch	1 foot	0.3048 meter
		1 furlong	10 chains (surveyor's) 660 feet 220 yards 1/8 statute mile 201.168 meters
1 chain (Gunter's or surveyor's)	66 feet 20.1168 meters		

1 inch	2.54 centimeters
1 kilometer	0.621 mile
1 league (land)	3 statute miles 4.828 kilometers
1 link (Gunter's or surveyor's)	7.92 inches 0.201 168 meter
1 meter	39.37 inches 1.094 yards
1 micron	0.001 millimeter 0.000 039 37 inch
1 mil	0.001 inch 0.025 4 millimeter
1 mile (statute or land)	5,280 feet 1.609 kilometers
1 mile (nautical international)	1.852 kilometers 1.151 statute miles 0.999 U.S. nautical miles
1 millimeter	0.03937 inch
1 millimicron (m+GRKm)	0.001 micron 0.000 000 039 37 inch
1 nanometer	0.001 micrometer or 0.000 000 039 37 inch
1 point (typography)	0.013 837 inch 1/72 inch (approximately) 0.351 millimeter
1 rod, pole, or perch	16 1/2 feet 5.0292 meters
1 yard	0.9144 meter

AREAS OR SURFACES

1 acre	43,560 square feet 4,840 square yards 0.405 hectare
1 are	119.599 square yards 0.025 acre
1 hectare	2.471 acres
1 square centimeter	0.155 square inch
1 square decimeter	15.5 square inches
1 square foot	929.030 square centimeters
1 square inch	6.4516 square centimeters
1 square kilometer	0.386 square mile 247.105 acres
1 square meter	1.196 square yards 10.764 square feet
1 square mile	258.999 hectares
1 square millimeter	0.002 square inch
1 square rod, square pole or square perch	25.293 square meters
1 square yard	0.836 square meters

CAPACITIES OR VOLUMES

1 barrel, liquid	31 to 42 gallons[2]
1 barrel, standard for fruits, vegetables, and other dry commodities except cranberries	7,056 cubic inches 105 dry quarts 3.281 bushels, struck measure
1 barrel, standard, cranberry	5.286 cubic inches 86 45/64 dry quarts 2.709 bushels, struck measure
1 bushel (U.S.) struck measure	2,150.42 cubic inches 35.238 liters
1 bushel, heaped (U.S.)	2,747.715 cubic inches 1.278 bushels, struck measure[3]
1 cord (firewood)	128 cubic feet
1 cubic centimeter	0.061 cubic inch
1 cubic decimeter	61.024 cubic inches
1 cubic foot	7.481 gallons 28.316 cubic decimeters
1 cubic inch	0.554 fluid ounce 4.433 fluid drams 16.387 cubic centimeters
1 cubic meter	1.308 cubic yards
1 cubic yard	0.765 cubic meter
1 cup, measuring	8 fluid ounces 1/2 liquid pint
1 dram, fluid or liquid (U.S.)	1/8 fluid ounce 0.226 cubic inch 3.697 milliliters 1.041 British fluid drachms
1 dekaliter	2.642 gallons 1.135 pecks
1 gallon (U.S.)	231 cubic inches 3.785 liters 0.833 British gallon 128 U.S. fluid ounces
1 gallon (British Imperial)	277.42 cubic inches 1.201 U.S. gallons 4.546 liters 160 British fluid ounces
1 gill	7.219 cubic inches 4 fluid ounces 0.118 liter
1 hectoliter	26.418 gallons 2.838 bushels
1 liter	1.057 liquid quarts 0.908 dry quart 61.024 cubic inches
1 milliliter	0.271 fluid dram 16.231 minims 0.061 cubic inch
1 ounce, fluid or liquid (U.S.)	1.805 cubic inch 29.574 milliliters 1.041 British fluid ounces

1 peck	8.810 liters	1 hundredweight, net or short	100 pounds 45.359 kilograms
1 pint, dry	33.600 cubic inches 0.551 liter	1 kilogram	2.205 pounds
1 pint, liquid	28.875 cubic inches 0.473 liter	1 microgram [μg (the Greek letter mu in combination with the letter g)]	0.000 001 gram
1 quart, dry (U.S.)	67.201 cubic inches 1.101 liters 0.969 British quart	1 milligram	0.015 grain
1 quart, liquid (U.S.)	57.75 cubic inches 0.946 liter 0.833 British quart	1 ounce, avoirdupois	437.5 grains 0.911 troy or apothecaries, ounce 28.350 grams
1 quart (British)	69.354 cubic inches 1.032 U.S. dry quarts 1.201 U.S. liquid quarts	1 ounce, troy or apothecaries	480 grains 1.097 avoirdupois ounces 31.103 grams
1 tablespoon, measuring	3 teaspoons 4 fluid drams 1/2 fluid ounce	1 pennyweight	1.555 grams
1 teaspoon, measuring	1/3 tablespoon 1 1/3 fluid drams	1 point	0.01 carat 2 milligrams
1 assay ton[4]	29.167 grams	1 pound, avoirdupois	7,000 grains 1.215 troy or apothecaries pounds 453.592 37 grams
1 carat	200 milligrams 3.086 grains	1 pound, troy or apothecaries	5,760 grains 0.823 avoirdupois pound 373.242 grams
1 dram, apothecaries'	60 grains 3.888 grams	1 ton, gross or long[5]	2,240 pounds 1.12 net tons 1.016 metric tons
1 dram, avoirdupois	27 11/32 (=27.344) grains 1.772 grams		
1 grain	64.798 91 milligrams	1 ton, metric	2,204.623 pounds 0 .984 gross ton 1.102 net tons
1 gram	15.432 grains 0.035 ounce, avoirdupois	1 ton, net or short	2,000 pounds 0.893 gross ton 0.907 metric ton
1 hundredweight, gross or long[5]	112 pounds 50.802 kilograms		

1. The angstrom is basically defined as 10^{-10} meter. 2. There is a variety of "barrels" established by law or usage. For example, federal taxes on fermented liquors are based on a barrel of 31 gallons; many state laws fix the "barrel for liquids" at 31 1/2 gallons; one state fixes a 36–gallon barrel for cistern measurement; federal law recognizes a 40–gallon barrel for "proof spirits"; by custom, 42 gallons comprise a barrel of crude oil or petroleum products for statistical purposes, and this equivalent is recognized "for liquids" by four states. 3. Frequently recognized as 1 1/4 bushels, struck measure. 4. Used in assaying. The assay ton bears the same relation to the milligram that a ton of 2,000 pounds avoirdupois bears to the ounce troy; hence the weight in milligrams of precious metal obtained from one assay ton of ore gives directly the number of troy ounces to the net ton. 5. The gross or long ton and hundredweight are used commercially in the United States to only a limited extent, usually in restricted industrial fields. These units are the same as the British "ton" and "hundredweight."

Miscellaneous Units of Measure

Acre: An area of 43,560 square feet. Originally, the area a yoke of oxen could plow in one day.

Agate: Originally a measurement of type size (5 1/2 points). Now equal to 1/14 inch. Used in printing for measuring column length.

Ampere: Unit of electric current. A potential difference of one volt across a resistance of one ohm produces a current of one ampere.

Astronomical Unit (A.U.): 93,000,000 miles, the average distance of the earth from the sun. Used for astronomy.

Bale: A large bundle of goods. In the U.S., the ap-

proximate weight of a bale of cotton is 500 pounds. The weight varies in other countries.

Board Foot (fbm): 144 cubic inches (12 in. × 12 in. × 1 in.). Used for lumber.

Bolt: 40 yards. Used for measuring cloth.

Btu: British thermal unit. Amount of heat needed to increase the temperature of one pound of water by one degree Fahrenheit (252 calories).

Carat (c): 200 milligrams or 3.086 grains troy. Originally the weight of a seed of the carob tree in the Mediterranean region. Used for weighing precious stones. *See also* Karat.

Chain (ch): A chain 66 feet or one–tenth of a furlong in length, divided into 100 parts called links. One mile is equal to 80 chains. Used in surveying and sometimes called Gunter's or surveyor's chain.

Cubit: 18 inches or 45.72 cm. Derived from distance between elbow and tip of middle finger.

Decibel: Unit of relative loudness. One decibel is the smallest amount of change detectable by the human ear.

Ell, English: 1 1/4 yards or 1/32 bolt. Used for measuring cloth.

Freight, Ton (also called Measurement Ton): 40 cubic feet of merchandise. Used for cargo freight.

Great Gross: 12 gross or 1728.

Gross: 12 dozen or 144.

Hand: 4 inches or 10.16 cm. Derived from the width of the hand. Used for measuring the height of horses at withers.

Hertz: Modern unit for measurement of electromagnetic wave frequencies (equivalent to "cycles per second").

Hogshead (hhd): 2 liquid barrels or 14,653 cubic inches.

Horsepower: The power needed to lift 33,000 pounds a distance of one foot in one minute (about 1 1/2 times the power an average horse can exert). Used for measuring power of steam engines, etc.

Karat (kt): A measure of the purity of gold, indicating how many parts out of 24 are pure. For example: 18 karat gold is 3/4 pure. Sometimes spelled *carat.*

Knot: Not a distance, but the rate of speed of one nautical mile per hour. Used for measuring speed of ships.

League: Rather indefinite and varying measure, but usually estimated at 3 miles in English-speaking countries.

Light-Year: 5,880,000,000,000 miles, the distance light travels in a vacuum in a year at the rate of 186,281.7 miles (299,792 kilometers) per second. (If an astronomical unit were represented by one inch, a light-year would be represented by about one mile.) Used for measurements in interstellar space.

Magnum: Two-quart bottle. Used for measuring wine, etc.

Ohm: Unit of electrical resistance. A circuit in which a potential difference of one volt produces a current of one ampere has a resistance of one ohm.

Parsec: Approximately 3.26 light-years of 19.2 million miles. Term is combination of first syllables of *par*allax and *sec*ond, and distance is that of imaginary star when lines drawn from it to both earth and sun form a maximum angle or parallax of one second (1/3600 degree). Used for measuring interstellar distances.

Pi (π): 3.14159265+. The ratio of the circumference of a circle to its diameter. For practical purposes, the value is used to four decimal places: 3.1416.

Pica: 1/6 inch or 12 points. Used in printing for measuring column width, etc.

Pipe: 2 hogsheads. Used for measuring wine and other liquids.

Point: .013837 (approximately 1/72) inch or 1/12 pica. Used in printing for measuring type size.

Quintal: 100,000 grams or 220.46 pounds avoirdupois.

Quire: Used for measuring paper. Sometimes 24 sheets but more often 25. There are 20 quires to a ream.

Ream: Used for measuring paper. Sometimes 480 sheets, but more often 500 sheets.

Roentgen: International Unit of radiation exposure produced by X-rays.

Score: 20 units.

Sound, Speed of: Usually placed at 1,088 ft per second at 32°F at sea level. It varies at other temperatures and in different media.

Span: 9 inches or 22.86 cm. Derived from the distance between the end of the thumb and the end of the little finger when both are outstretched.

Square: 100 square feet. Used in building.

Stone: Legally 14 pounds avoirdupois in Great Britain.

Therm: 100,000 Btu's.

Township: U.S. land measurement of almost 36 square miles. The south border is 6 miles long. The east and west borders, also 6 miles long, follow the meridians, making the north border slightly less than 6 miles long. Used in surveying.

Tun: 252 gallons, but often larger. Used for measuring wine and other liquids.

Watt: Unit of power. The power used by a current of one ampere across a potential difference of one volt equals one watt.

Kelvin Scale

Absolute zero, −273.16° on the Celsius (Centigrade) scale, is 0° Kelvin. Thus, degrees Kelvin are equivalent to degrees Celsuis plus 273.16. The freezing point of water, 0°C. and 32°F., is 273.16°K. The conversion formula is K° = C° + 273.16.

Conversion of Miles to Kilometers and Kilometers to Miles

Miles	Kilometers	Miles	Kilometers	Miles	Kilometers	Kilometers	Miles	Kilometers	Miles	Kilometers	Miles
1	1.6	8	12.8	60	96.5	1	0.6	8	4.9	60	37.2
2	3.2	9	14.4	70	112.6	2	1.2	9	5.5	70	43.4
3	4.8	10	16.0	80	128.7	3	1.8	10	6.2	80	49.7
4	6.4	20	32.1	90	144.8	4	2.4	20	12.4	90	55.9
5	8.0	30	48.2	100	160.9	5	3.1	30	18.6	100	62.1
6	9.6	40	64.3	1,000	1609	6	3.7	40	24.8	1,000	621
7	11.2	50	80.4			7	4.3	50	31.0		

Bolts and Screws: Conversion from Fractions of an Inch to Millimeters

Inch	mm	Inch	mm	Inch	mm	Inch	mm
1/64	0.40	17/64	6.75	33/64	13.10	49/64	19.45
1/32	0.79	9/32	7.14	17/32	13.50	25/32	19.84
3/64	1.19	19/64	7.54	35/64	13.90	51/64	20.24
1/16	1.59	5/16	7.94	9/16	14.29	13/16	20.64
5/64	1.98	21/64	8.33	37/64	14.69	53/64	21.03
3/32	2.38	11/32	8.73	19/32	15.08	27/32	21.43
7/64	2.78	23/64	9.13	39/64	15.48	55/64	21.83
1/8	3.18	3/8	9.53	5/8	15.88	7/8	22.23
9/64	3.57	25/64	9.92	41/64	16.27	57/64	22.62
5/32	3.97	13/32	10.32	21/32	16.67	29/32	23.02
11/64	4.37	27/64	10.72	43/64	17.06	59/64	23.42
3/16	4.76	7/16	11.11	11/64	17.46	15/16	23.81
13/64	5.16	29/64	11.51	45/64	17.86	61/64	24.21
7/32	5.56	15/32	11.91	23/32	18.26	31/32	24.61
15/64	5.95	31/64	12.30	47/64	18.65	63/64	25.00
1/4	6.35	1/2	12.70	3/4	19.05	1	25.40

U.S.—Metric Cooking Conversions

U.S. customary system				Metric			
Capacity		**Weight**		**Capacity**		**Weight**	
1/5 teaspoon	1 milliliter	1 fluid oz	30 milliliters	1 milliliter	1/5 teaspoon	1 gram	.035 ounce
1 teaspoon	5 ml		28 grams	5 ml	1 teaspoon	100 grams	3.5 ounces
1 tablespoon	15 ml	1 pound	454 grams	15 ml	1 tablespoon	500 grams	1.10 pounds
1/5 cup	50 ml			34 ml	1 fluid oz	1 kilogram	2.205
1 cup	240 ml						pounds
2 cups (1 pint)	470 ml			100 ml	3.4 fluid oz		35 oz
4 cups (1 quart)	.95 liter			240 ml	1 cup		
4 quarts (1 gal.)	3.8 liters			1 liter	34 fluid oz		
					4.2 cups		
					2.1 pints		
					1.06 quarts		
					0.26 gallon		

Cooking Measurement Equivalents

16 tablespoons =	1 cup		2 tablespoons =	1/8 cup
12 tablespoons =	3/4 cup		2 tablespoons + 2 teaspoons =	1/6 cup
10 tablespoons + 2 teaspoons =	2/3 cup		1 tablespoon =	1/16 cup
8 tablespoons =	1/2 cup		2 cups =	1 pint
6 tablespoons =	3/8 cup		2 pints =	1 quart
5 tablespoons + 1 teaspoon =	1/3 cup		3 teaspoons =	1 tablespoon
4 tablespoons =	1/4 cup		48 teaspoons =	1 cup

Prefixes and Multiples

Prefix	Suffix	Equivalent	Multiple/submultiple	Prefix	Suffix	Equivalent	Multiple/submultiple
atto	a	quintillionth part	10^{-18}	deci	d	tenth part	10^{-1}
femto	f	quadrillionth part	10^{-15}	deka	da	tenfold	10
pico	p	trillionth part	10^{-12}	hecto	h	hundredfold	10^2
nano	n	billionth part	10^{-9}	kilo	k	thousandfold	10^3
micro	μ	millionth part	10^{-6}	mega	M	millionfold	10^6
milli	m	thousandth part	10^{-3}	giga	G	billionfold	10^9
centi	c	hundredth part	10^{-2}	tera	T	trillionfold	10^{12}

Common Formulas

Circumference

Circle: $C = \pi d$, in which π is 3.1416 and d the diameter.

Area

Triangle: $A = \dfrac{ab}{2}$, in which a is the base and b the height.

Square: $A = a^2$, in which a is one of the sides.

Rectangle: $A = ab$, in which a is the base and b the height.

Trapezoid: $A = \dfrac{h(a + b)}{2}$, in which h is the height, a the longer parallel side, and b the shorter.

Regular pentagon: $A = 1.720a^2$, in which a is one of the sides.

Regular hexagon: $A = 2.598a^2$, in which a is one of the sides.

Regular octagon: $A = 4.828a^2$, in which a is one of the sides.

Circle: $A = \pi r^2$, in which π is 3.1416 and r the radius.

Volume

Cube: $V = a^3$, in which a is one of the edges.

Rectangular prism: $V = abc$, in which a is the length, b is the width, and c the depth.

Pyramid: $V = \dfrac{Ah}{3}$, in which A is the area of the base and h the height.

Cylinder: $V = \pi r^2 h$, in which π is 3.1416, r the radius of the base, and h the height.

Cone: $V = \dfrac{\pi r^2 h}{3}$, in which π is 3.1416, r the radius of the base, and h the height.

Sphere: $V = \dfrac{4 \pi r^3}{3}$, in which π is 3.1416 and r the radius.

Miscellaneous

Distance in feet traveled by falling body: $d = 16t^2$, in which t is the time in seconds.

Speed in sound in feet per second through any given temperature of air:
$$V = \frac{1087\sqrt{273 + t}}{16.52}$$
in which t is the temperature Centigrade.

Cost in cents of operration of electrical device: $C = \dfrac{Wtc}{1000}$, in which W is the number of watts, t the time in hours, and c the cost in cents per hilowatt-hour.

Conversion of matter into energy (Einstein's Theorem): $E = mc^2$, in which E is the energy in ergs, m the mass of the matter in grams, and c the speed of light in centimeters per second ($c^2 = 9 \times 10^{20}$).

Decimal Equivalents of Common Fractions

1/2	.5000	1/10	.1000	2/7	.2857	3/11	.2727	5/9	.5556	7/11	.6364
1/3	.3333	1/11	.0909	2/9	.2222	4/5	.8000	5/11	.4545	7/12	.5833
1/4	.2500	1/12	.0833	2/11	.1818	4/7	.5714	5/12	.4167	8/9	.8889
1/5	.2000	1/16	.0625	3/4	.7500	4/9	.4444	6/7	.8571	8/11	.7273
1/6	.1667	1/32	.0313	3/5	.6000	4/11	.3636	6/11	.5455	9/10	.9000
1/7	.1429	1/64	.0156	3/7	.4286	5/6	.8333	7/8	.8750	9/11	.8182
1/8	.1250	2/3	.6667	3/8	.3750	5/7	.7143	7/9	.7778	10/11	.9091
1/9	.1111	2/5	.4000	3/10	.3000	5/8	.6250	7/10	.7000	11/12	.9167

Conversion Factors

To change	To	Multi–ply by	To change	To	Multi–ply by
acres	hectares	.4047	liters	pints (dry)	1.8162
acres	square feet	43,560	liters	pints (liquid)	2.1134
acres	square miles	.001562	liters	quarts (dry)	.9081
atmospheres	cms. of mercury	76	liters	quarts (liquid)	1.0567
BTU	horsepower-hour	.0003931	meters	feet	3.2808
BTU	kilowatt-hour	.0002928	meters	miles	.0006214
BTU/hour	watts	.2931	meters	yards	1.0936
bushels	cubic inches	2150.4	metric tons	tons (long)	.9842
bushels (U.S.)	hectoliters	.3524	metric tons	tons (short)	1.1023
centimeters	inches	.3937	miles	kilometers	1.6093
centimeters	feet	.03281	miles	feet	5280
circumference	radians	6.283	miles (nautical)	miles (statute)	1.1516
cubic feet	cubic inches	.0283	miles (statute)	miles (nautical)	.8684
cubic meters	cubic feet	35.3145	miles/hour	feet/minute	88
cubic meters	cubic yards	1.3079	millimeters	inches	.0394
cubic yards	cubic meters	.7646	ounces avdp.	grams	28.3495
degrees	radians	.01745	ounces	pounds	.0625
dynes	grams	.00102	ounces (troy)	ounces (avdp)	1.09714
fathoms	feet	6.0	pecks	liters	8.8096
feet	meters	.3048	pints (dry)	liters	.5506
feet	miles (nautical)	.0001645	pints (liquid)	liters	.4732
feet	miles (statute)	.0001894	pounds ap or t	kilograms	.3782
feet/second	miles/hour	.6818	pounds avdp	kilograms	.4536
furlongs	feet	660.0	pounds	ounces	16
furlongs	miles	.125	quarts (dry)	liters	1.1012
gallons (U.S.)	liters	3.7853	quarts (liquid)	liters	.9463
grains	grams	.0648	radians	degrees	57.30
grams	grains	15.4324	rods	meters	5.029
grams	ounces avdp	.0353	rods	feet	16.5
grams	pounds	.002205	square feet	square meters	.0929
hectares	acres	2.4710	square kilometers	square miles	.3861
hectoliters	bushels (U.S.)	2.8378	square meters	square feet	10.7639
horsepower	watts	745.7	square meters	square yards	1.1960
hours	days	.04167	square miles	square kilometers	2.5900
inches	millimeters	25.4000	square yards	square meters	.8361
inches	centimeters	2.5400	tons (long)	metric tons	1.016
kilograms	pounds avdp or t	2.2046	tons (short)	metric tons	.9072
kilometers	miles	.6214	tons (long)	pounds	2240
kilowatts	horsepower	1.341	tons (short)	pounds	2000
knots	nautical miles/hour	1.0	watts	Btu/hour	3.4129
knots	statute miles/hour	1.151	watts	horsepower	.001341
liters	gallons (U.S.)	.2642	yards	meters	.9144
liters	pecks	.1135	yards	miles	.0005682

Fahrenheit and Celsius (Centigrade) Scales

Zero on the Fahrenheit scale represents the temperature produced by the mixing of equal weights of snow and common salt.

	F	C
Boiling point of water	212°	100°
Freezing point of water	32°	0°
Absolute zero	−459.6°	−273.1°

Absolute zero is theoretically the lowest possible temperature, the point at which all molecular motion would cease.

To convert Fahrenheit to Celsius (Centigrade), subtract 32 and multiply by 5/9.

To convert Celsius (Centigrade) to Fahrenheit, multiiply by 9/5 and add 32.

°Centigrade	°Fahrenheit	°Centigrade	°Fahrenheit
−273.1	−459.6	30	86
−250	−418	35	95
−200	−328	40	104
−150	−238	45	113
−100	−148	50	122
−50	−58	55	131
−40	−40	60	140
−30	−22	65	149
−20	−4	70	158
−10	14	75	167
0	32	80	176
5	41	85	185
10	50	90	194
15	59	95	203
20	68	100	212
25	77		

Roman Numerals

Roman numerals are expressed by letters of the alphabet and are rarely used today except for formality or variety.

There are three basic principles for reading Roman numerals:

1. A letter repeated once or twice repeats its value that many times (XXX = 30, CC = 200, etc.).

2. One or more letters placed after another letter of greater value increases the greater value by the amount of the smaller. (VI = 6, LXX = 70, MCC = 1200, etc.).

3. A letter placed before another letter of greater value decreases the greater value by the amount of the smaller. (IV = 4, XC = 90, CM = 900, etc.).

Letter	Value	Letter	Value	Letter	Value	Letter	Value	Letter	Value
I	1	VII	7	XXX	30	LXXX	80	V̄	5,000
II	2	VIII	8	XL	40	XC	90	X̄	10,000
III	3	IX	9	L	50	C	100	L̄	50,000
IV	4	X	10	LX	60	D	500	C̄	100,000
V	5	XX	20	LXX	70	M	1,000	D̄	500,000
VI	6							M̄	1,000,000

Mean and Median

The mean, also called the average, of a series of quantities is obtained by finding the sum of the quantities and dividing it by the number of quantities. In the series 1, 3, 5, 18, 19, 20, 25, the mean or average is 13—i.e., 91 divided by 7.

The median of a series is that point which so divides it that half the quantities are on one side, half on the other. In the above series, the median is 18.

The median often better expresses the commonrun, since it is not, as is the mean, affected by an excessively high or low figure. In the series 1, 3, 4, 7, 55, the median of 4 is a truer expression of the common-run than is the mean of 14.

Prime Numbers Between 1 and 1,000

2	3	5	7	11	13	17	19		23
29	31	37	41	43	47	53	59	61	67
71	73	79	83	89	97	101	103	107	109
113	127	131	137	139	149	151	157	163	167
173	179	181	191	193	197	199	211	223	227
229	233	239	241	251	257	263	269	271	277
281	283	293	307	311	313	317	331	337	347
349	353	359	367	373	379	383	389	397	401
409	419	421	431	433	439	443	449	457	461
463	467	479	487	491	499	503	509	521	523
541	547	557	563	569	571	577	587	593	599
601	607	613	619	631	641	643	647	653
659	661	673	677	683	691	701	709	719	727
733	739	743	751	757	761	769	773	787	797
809	811	821	823	827	829	839	853	857	859
863	877	881	883	887	907	911	919	929	937
941	947	953	967	971	977	983	991	997	(1009)

Definitions of Gold Terminology

The term "fineness" defines a gold content in parts per thousand. For example, a gold nugget containing 885 parts of pure gold, 100 parts of silver, and 15 parts of copper would be considered 885-fine.

The word "karat" indicates the proportion of solid gold in an alloy based on a total of 24 parts. Thus, 14-karat (14K) gold indicates a composition of 14 parts of gold and 10 parts of other metals.

The term "gold-filled" is used to describe articles of jewelry made of base metal which are covered on one or more surfaces with a layer of gold alloy. No article having a gold alloy portion of less than one twentieth by weight may be marked "gold-filled." Articles may be marked "rolled gold plate" provided the proportional fraction and fineness designations are also shown.

Electroplated jewelry items carrying at least 7 millionths of an inch of gold on significant surfaces may be labeled "electroplate." Plate thicknesses less than this may be marked "gold-flashed" or "gold-washed."

Portraits and Designs of U.S. Paper Currency[1]

Currency	Portrait	Design on back	Currency	Portrait	Design on back
$1	Washington	ONE between obverse and reverse of Great Seal of U.S.	$50	Grant	U.S. Capitol
$2[2]	Jefferson	Monticello	$100	Franklin	Independence Hall
$2[3]	Jefferson	"The Signing of the Declaration of Independence"	$500	McKinley	Ornate FIVE HUNDRED
			$1,000	Cleveland	Ornate ONE THOUSAND
$5	Lincoln	Lincoln Memorial	$5,000	Madison	Ornate FIVE THOUSAND
$10	Hamilton	U.S. Treasury Building	$10,000	Chase	Ornate TEN THOUSAND
$20	Jackson	White House	$100,000[4]	Wilson	Ornate ONE HUNDRED THOUSAND

1. Denominations of $500 and higher were discontinued in 1969. 2. Discontinued in 1966. 3. New issue, April 13, 1976.
4. For use only in transactions between Federal Reserve System and Treasury Department.

GEOGRAPHY

World Geography
Explorations
(All years are A.D. unless B.C. is specified.)

Country or place	Event	Explorer	Date
AFRICA			
Sierra Leone	Visited	Hanno, Carthaginian seaman	c. 520 B.C.
Zaire River (Congo)	Mouth visited[1]	Diogo Cão, Portuguese	c. 1484
Cape of Good Hope	Rounded	Bartolomeu Diaz, Portuguese	1488
Gambia River	Explored	Mungo Park, Scottish explorer	1795
Sahara	Crossed	Dixon Denham and Hugh Clapperton, English explorers	1822–23
Zambezi River	Visited[1]	David Livingstone, Scottish explorer	1851
Sudan	Explored	Heinrich Barth, German explorer	1852–55
Victoria Falls	Visited[1]	Livingstone	1855
Lake Tanganyika	Visited[1]	Richard Burton and John Speke, British explorers	1858
Zaire River (Congo)	Traced	Sir Henry M. Stanley, British explorer	1877
ASIA			
Punjab (India)	Visited	Alexander the Great	327 B.C.
China	Visited	Marco Polo, Italian traveler	c. 1272
Tibet	Visited	Odoric of Pordenone, Italian monk	c. 1325
Southern China	Explored	Niccolò dei Conti, Venetian traveler	c. 1440
India	Visited (Cape route)	Vasco da Gama, Portuguese navigator	1498
Japan	Visited	St. Francis Xavier of Spain	1549
Arabia	Explored	Carsten Niebuhr, German explorer	1762
China	Explored	Ferdinand Richthofen, German scientist	1868
Mongolia	Explored	Nikolai M. Przhevalsky, Russian explorer	1870–73
Central Asia	Explored	Sven Hedin, Swedish scientist	1890–1908
EUROPE			
Shetland Islands	Visited	Pytheas of Massilia (Marseille)	c. 325 B.C.
North Cape	Rounded	Ottar, Norwegian explorer	c. 870
Iceland	Colonized	Norwegian noblemen	c. 890–900
NORTH AMERICA			
Greenland	Colonized	Eric the Red, Norwegian	c. 985
Labrador; Nova Scotia(?)	Visited[1]	Leif Ericson, Norse explorer	1000
West Indies	Visited[1]	Christopher Columbus, Italian	1492
North America	Coast visited[1]	Giovanni Caboto (John Cabot), for British	1497
Pacific Ocean	Sighted[1]	Vasco Núñez de Balboa, Spanish explorer	1513
Florida	Explored	Ponce de León, Spanish explorer	1513
Mexico	Conquered	Hernando Cortés, Spanish adventurer	1519–21
St. Lawrence River	Visited[1]	Jacques Cartier, French navigator	1534
Southwest U. S.	Explored	Francisco Coronado, Spanish explorer	1540–42
Colorado River	Visited[1]	Hernando de Alarcón, Spanish explorer	1540
Mississippi River	Visited[1]	Hernando de Soto, Spanish explorer	1541
Frobisher Bay	Visited[1]	Martin Frobisher, English seaman	1576
Maine Coast	Explored	Samuel de Champlain, French explorer	1604

Country or place	Event	Explorer	Date
Jamestown, Va.	Settled	John Smith, English colonist	1607
Hudson River	Explored	Henry Hudson, English navigator	1609
Hudson Bay (Canada)	Visited[1]	Henry Hudson	1610
Baffin Bay	Visited[1]	William Baffin, English navigator	1616
Lake Michigan	Navigated	Jean Nicolet, French explorer	1634
Arkansas River	Visited[1]	Jacques Marquette and Louis Jolliet, French explorers	1673
Mississippi River	Explored	Sieur de La Salle, French explorer	1682
Bering Strait	Visited[1]	Vitus Bering, Danish explorer	1728
Alaska	Visited[1]	Vitus Bering	1741
Mackenzie River (Canada)	Visited[1]	Sir Alexander Mackenzie, Scottish–Canadian explorer	1789
Northwest U. S.	Explored	Meriwether Lewis and William Clark	1804–06
Northeast Passage (Arctic Ocean)	Navigated	Nils Nordenskjöld, Swedish explorer	1879
Greenland	Explored	Robert Peary, American explorer	1892
Northwest Passage	Navigated	Roald Amundsen, Norwegian explorer	1906
SOUTH AMERICA			
Continent	Visited	Columbus, Italian	1498
Brazil	Visited[1]	Pedro Alvarez Cabral, Portuguese	1500
Peru	Conquered	Francisco Pizarro, Spanish explorer	1532–33
Amazon River	Explored	Francisco Orellana, Spanish explorer	1541
Cape Horn	Visited[1]	Willem C. Schouten, Dutch navigator	1615
OCEANIA			
Papua New Guinea	Visited	Jorge de Menezes, Portuguese explorer	1526
Australia	Visited	Abel Janszoon Tasman, Dutch navigator	1642
Tasmania	Visited[1]		
Australia	Explored	John McDouall Stuart, English explorer	1828
Australia	Explored	Robert Burke and William Wills, Australian explorers	1861
New Zealand	Sighted (and named)	Abel Janszoon Tasman	1642
New Zealand	Visited	James Cook, English navigator	1769
ARCTIC, ANTARCTIC, AND MISCELLANEOUS			
Ocean exploration	Expedition	Magellan's ships circled globe	1519–22
Galápagos Islands	Visited	Diego de Rivadeneira, Spanish captain	1535
Spitsbergen	Visited	Willem Barents, Dutch navigator	1596
Antarctic Circle	Crossed	James Cook, English navigator	1773
Antarctica	Visited[1]	Nathaniel Palmer, U. S. whaler (archipelago) and Fabian Gottlieb von Bellingshausen, Russian admiral (mainland)	1820–21
Antarctica	Explored	Charles Wilkes, American explorer	1840
North Pole	Reached	Robert E. Peary, American explorer	1909
South Pole	Reached	Roald Amundsen, Norwegian explorer	1911

1. First European to reach the area.

The Continents

A continent is defined as a large unbroken land mass completely surrounded by water, although in some cases continents are (or were in part) connected by land bridges.

The hypothesis first suggested late in the 19th century was that the continents consist of lighter rocks that rest on heavier crustal material in about the same manner that icebergs float on water. That the rocks forming the continents are lighter than the material below them and under the ocean bottoms is now established. As a consequence of this fact, Alfred Wegener (for the first time in 1912) suggested that the continents are slowly moving, at a rate of about one yard per century, so that their relative positions are not rigidly fixed. Many geologists that were originally skeptical have come to accept this theory of Continental Drift.

When describing a continent, it is important to remember that there is a fundamental difference between a deep ocean, like the Atlantic, and shallow seas, like the Baltic and most of the North Sea, which are merely flooded portions of a continent. Another and entirely different point to remember is that political considerations have often overridden geographical facts when it came to naming continents.

Geographically speaking, Europe, including the British Isles, is a large western peninsula of the continent of Asia; and many geographers, when referring to Europe and Asia, speak of the Eurasian Continent. But traditionally, Europe is counted as a separate continent, with the Ural and the Caucasus mountains forming the line of demarcation between Europe and Asia.

To the south of Europe, Asia has an odd-shaped peninsula jutting westward, which has a large number of political subdivisions. The northern section is taken up by Turkey; to the south of Turkey there are Syria, Iraq, Israel, Jordan, Saudi Arabia, and a number of smaller Arab countries. All this is part of Asia. Traditionally, the island of Cyprus in the Mediterranean is also considered to be part of Asia, while the island of Crete is counted as European.

The large islands of Java, Borneo, and Sumatra and the smaller islands near them are counted as part of "tropical Asia," while New Guinea is counted as related to Australia. In the case of the Americas, the problem arises as to whether they should be considered one or two continents. There are good arguments on both sides, but since there is now a land bridge between North and South America (in the past it was often flooded) and since no part of the sea east of the land bridge is deep ocean, it is more logical to consider the Americas as one continent.

Politically, based mainly on history, the Americas are divided into North America (from the Arctic to the Mexican border), Central America (from Mexico to Panama, with the Caribbean islands), and South America. Greenland is considered a section of North America, while Iceland is traditionally counted as a European island because of its political ties with the Scandinavian countries.

The island groups in the Pacific are often called "Oceania," but this name does *not* imply that scientists consider them the remains of a continent.

The seven continents are North America, South America, Europe, Asia, Africa, Australia, and Antarctica.

Volcanoes of the World

About 500 volcanoes have had recorded eruptions within historical times. Almost two thirds of these are in the Northern Hemisphere. Most volcanoes occur at the boundaries of the earth's crustal plates, such as the famous "Ring of Fire" that surrounds the Pacific Ocean plate. Of the world's active volcanoes, about 60% are along the perimeter of the Pacific, about 17% on mid-oceanic islands, about 14% in an arc along the south of the Indonesian islands, and about 9% in the Mediterranean area, Africa, and Asia Minor. Many of the world's volcanoes are submarine and have unrecorded eruptions.

Pacific "Ring of Fire"

NORTHWEST
Japan: At least 33 active vents.

Aso (5,223 ft; 1,592 m), on Kyushu, has one of the largest craters in the world.

Asama (over 8,300 ft; 2,530 m), on Honshu, is continuously active; violent eruption in 1783.

Azuma (nearly 7,700 ft; 2,347 m), on Honshu, erupted in 1900.

Chokai (7,300 ft; 2,225 m), on Honshu, erupted in 1974 after having been quiescent since 1861.

Fujiyama (Fujisan) (12,385 ft; 3,775 m), on Honshu, southwest of Tokyo. Symmetrical in outline, snow-covered. Regarded as a sacred mountain.

On-take (3,668 ft; 1,118 m), on peninsula of Kyushu. Strong smoke emissions and explosions began November 1973 and continued through 1974.

Mt. Unzen (4,500 ft; 1,371 m), on Kyushu erupted on June 3, 1991. Last eruption was in 1792.

Russia: Kamchatka peninsula, 14–18 active volcanoes. Klyuchevskaya (Kluchev) (15,500 ft; 4,724 m) reported active in 1974.

Kurile Islands: At least 13 active volcanoes and several submarine outbreaks.

SOUTHWEST
New Zealand: Mount Tarawera (3,645 ft; 1,112 m), on North Island, had a severe eruption in 1886 that destroyed the famous Pink and White sinter terraces of Rotomahana, a hot lake.

Ngauruhoe (7,515 ft; 2,291 m), on North Island, emits steam and vapor constantly. Erupted 1974.

Papua New Guinea: Karkar Island (4,920 ft; 1,500 m). Mild eruptions 1974.

Philippine Islands: About 100 eruptive centers; Hibok Hibok, on Camiguin, erupted September 1950 and again in December 1951, when about 750 were reported killed or missing; eruptions continued during 1952–53.

Taal (4,752 ft; 1,448 m), on Luzon. Major eruption in 1965 killed 190; erupted again, 1968.

Mt. Pinatubo (4,795 ft; 1,462 m), on Luzon erupted on June 9, 1991. Last major eruption in 1380.

Volcano Islands: Mount Suribachi (546 ft; 166 m), on Iwo Jima. A sulfurous steaming volcano. Raising of U.S. flag over Mount Suribachi was one of the dramatic episodes of World War II.

NORTHEAST
Alaska: Mount Wrangell (14,163 ft; 4,317 m) and Mount Katmai (about 6,700 ft; 2,042 m). On June 6, 1912, a violent eruption (Nova Rupta) of Mount Katmai occurred, during which the "Valley of Ten Thousand Smokes" was formed.

Aleutian Islands: There are 32 active vents known and numerous inactive cones. Akutan Island (over 4,000 ft; 1,220 m) erupted in 1974, with ash and debris rising over 300 ft.

Great Sitkin (5,741 ft; 1,750 m). Explosive activity February–September 1974, accompanied by earthquake originating at volcano that registered 2.3 on Richter scale.

Augustine Island: Augustine volcano (4,000 ft; 1,220 m) erupted March 27, 1986. It last erupted in 1976.

California, Oregon, Washington: Lassen Peak (10,453 ft; 3,186 m) in California is one of two observed active volcanoes in the U.S. outside Alaska and Hawaii. The last period of activity was 1914–17. Mt. St. Helens (9,677 ft; 2,950 m) in the Cascade Range of southwest Washington became active on March 27, 1980, and erupted on May 18 after being inactive since 1857. From April 15 through May 1, 1986, weak activity began for the first time in two years. Other mountains of volcanic origin include Mount Shasta (California), Mount Hood (Oregon), Mount Mazama (Oregon)—the mountain containing Crater Lake, Mount Rainier (Washington), and Mount Baker (Washington), which has been steaming since

Continued on page 478

The Pacific Ocean "Ring of Fire"

Bezmianny

Vesuvius

Vulcano

Mt. Etna Stromboli

Mt. Fiji

Myōjin-shc

Barren Island

Mayon

Taal

Ulawun

Mt. Sinabung

Krakatau

●—Bouvet   ●—Heard

0°   60°   120°

Giant West Coast Quake Forecast

Segments of the Washington–Oregon coastline are rising faster than normal—in millimeters per year—providing additional strong evidence that the area is due for a massive earthquake. In 1994, a team of scientists from the University of Oregon and the University of Washington found that many areas of the Western coastline are rising almost ten times faster than expected each year.

This indicates that pressure is building underground, a sign of an imminent earthquake. According to Oregon State University geologist, Robert Yeats, there is little doubt among other geologists that the

Source: U.S. Department of the Interior, U.S. Geological Survey.

Northwest is due for a giant quake. The main question confronting scientists is whether the area known as the Cascadia subduction zone will buckle all at once or in smaller pieces.

The subduction zone is an area off the Northwestern coastline where two sections of the Earth's crust—the undersea Juan de Fuca plate and the North American plate—are pushing against each other. If the whole subduction zone goes at once, it may produce a massive quake stronger than the 1964 Alaska Good Friday earthquake, the strongest quake ever to strike North America. □

(Continued from p. 475)

October 1975, but gives no sign of an impending eruption.

SOUTHEAST

Chile and Argentina: About 25 active or potentially active.

Colombia: Huila (nearly 18,900 ft; 5,760 m), a vapor-emitting volcano, and Tolima (nearly 18,500 ft; 5,640 m). Eruption of Puracé (15,600 ft; 4,755 m) in 1949 killed 17 people. Nevado del Ruiz (16,200 ft; 4,938 m.), erupted Nov. 13, 1985, sending torrential floods of mud and water engulfing the town of Armero and killing more than 22,000 people.

Ecuador: Cayambe (nearly 19,000 ft; 5,791 m). Almost on the equator.

Cotopaxi (19,344 ft; 5,896 m). Perhaps highest active volcano in the world. Possesses a beautifully formed cone.

Reventador (11,434 ft; 3,485 m). Observed in active state in late 1973.

El Salvador: Izalco ("beacon of Central America") (7,830 ft; 2,387 m) first appeared in 1770 and is still growing (erupted in 1950, 1956; last erupted in October-November 1966). San Salvador (6,187 ft; 1,886 m) had a violent eruption in 1923. Conchagua (about 4100 ft; 1,250 m) erupted with considerable damage early in 1947.

Guatemala: Santa Maria Quezaltenango (12,361 ft; 3,768 m). Frequent activity between 1902–08 and 1922–28 after centuries of quiescence. Most dangerously active vent of Central America. Other volcanoes include Tajumulco (13,814 ft; 4,211 m) and Atitlán (11,633 ft; 3,546 m).

Mexico: Boquerón ("Big Mouth"), on San Benedicto, about 250 mi. south of Lower California. Newest volcano in Western Hemisphere, discovered September 1952.

Colima (about 14,000 ft; 4,270 m), in group that has had frequent eruptions.

Orizaba (Citlaltépetl) (18,701 ft; 5,700 m).

Parícutin (7,450 ft; 2,270 m). First appeared in February 1943. In less than a week, a cone over 140 ft high developed with a crater one quarter mile in circumference. Cone grew more than 1,500 ft (457 m) in 1943. Erupted 1952.

Popocatépetl (17,887 ft; 5,452 m). Large, deep, bell-shaped crater. Not entirely extinct; steam still escapes.

El Chinchonal (7,300 ft; 1,005.6 m) about 15 miles from Pichucalco. Long inactive, it erupted in March 1982.

Nicaragua: Volcanoes include Telica, Coseguina, and Momotombo. Between Momotombo on the west shore of Lake Managua and Coseguina overlooking the Gulf of Fonseca, there is a string of more than 20 cones, many still active. One of these, Cerro Negro, erupted in July 1947, with considerable damage and loss of life, and again in 1971.

Concepción (5,100 ft; 1,555 m). Ash eruptions 1973–74.

Mid-oceanic Islands

Canary Islands: Pico de Teide (12,192 ft; 3,716 m), on Tenerife.

Cape Verde Islands: Fogo (nearly 9,300 ft; 2,835 m). Severe eruption in 1857; quiescent until 1951.

Caribbean: La Soufrière (4,813 ft; 1,467 m), on Basse-Terre, Guadeloupe. Also called La Grande Soufrière. Violent activity in July-August 1976 caused evacuation of 73,000 people; renewed activity in April 1977 again caused thousands to flee their homes.

La Soufrière (4,048 ft; 1,234 m), on St. Vincent. Major eruption in 1902 killed over 1,000 people. Eruptions over 10-day period in April 1979 caused evacuation of northern two thirds of island.

Comoros: One volcano, Karthala (nearly 8,000 ft; 2,440 m), is visible for over 100 miles. Last erupted in 1904.

Hawaii: Mauna Loa ("Long Mountain") (13,680 ft; 4,170 m), on Hawaii, discharges from its high side vents more lava than any other volcano. Largest volcanic mountain in the world in cubic content. Area of crater is 3.7 sq mi. Violent eruption in June 1950, with lava pouring 25 miles into the ocean. Last major eruption in March 1984.

Mauna Kea (13,796 ft; 4,205 m), on Hawaii. Highest mountain in state.

Kilauea (4,090 ft; 1,247 m) is a vent in the side of Mauna Loa, but its eruptions are apparently independent. One of the most spectacular and active craters. Crater has an area of 4.14 sq mi. Earthquake in July 1975 caused major eruption. Eruptions began in September 1977 and reached a height of 980 ft (300 m). Activity ended Oct. 1. Became active again in January 1983, exploding in earnest in March 1983 forming the volcanic cone Pu'u O which has erupted periodically ever since. By May 1990, the lava flow had traveled 20 miles, obliterating the community of Kalapana on the southeast coast. By summer it had reached the Pacific Ocean.

Iceland: At least 25 volcanoes active in historical times. Very similar to Hawaiian volcanoes. Askja (over 4,700 ft; 1,433 m) is the largest. Hekla, one of the most active volcanoes in Iceland, erupted on Jan. 17, 1990 after 19 years of repose.

Lesser Antilles (West Indian Islands): Mount Pelée (over 4,500 ft; 1,370 m), northwestern Martinique. Eruption in 1902 destroyed town of St. Pierre and killed approximately 40,000 people.

Réunion Island (east of Madagascar): Piton de la Fournaise (Le Volcan) (8,610 ft; 2,624 m). Large lava flows. Last erupted in 1972.

Samoan archipelago: Savai'i Island had an eruption in 1905 that caused considerable damage. Niuafoo (Tin Can), in the Tonga Islands, has a crater that extends 6,000 feet below and 600 feet above water.

Indonesia

Sumatra: Ninety volcanoes have been discovered; 12 are now active. The most famous, Krakatau, is a small volcanic island in the Sunda Strait. Numerous volcanic discharges occurred in 1883. One extremely violent explosion caused the disappearance of the highest peak and the northern part of the island. Fine dust was carried around the world in the upper atmosphere. Over 36,000 persons lost their lives in resultant tidal waves that were felt as far away as Cape Horn. Active in 1972.

Mediterranean Area

Italy: Mount Etna (10,902 ft; 3,323 m), eastern Sicily. Two new craters formed in eruptions of February-March 1947. Worst eruption in 50 years occurred November 1950–January 1951. Erupted again in 1974, 1975, 1977, 1978, 1979, 1983, December 1991, and lava flows continued into April 1992.

Stromboli (about 3,000 ft; 914 m), Lipari Islands (north of Sicily). Called "Lighthouse of the Mediterranean." Reported active in 1971.

Mount Vesuvius (4,200 ft; 1,280 m), southeast of Naples. Only active volcano on European mainland. Pompeii buried by an eruption, A.D. 79.

Antarctica

The discovery of two small active volcanoes in 1982 brings to five the total number known on Antarctica. The new ones, 30 miles apart, are on the Weddell Sea side of the Antarctic Peninsula. The largest, Mount Erebus (13,000 ft; 3,962 m), rises from McMurdo Sound. Mount Melbourne (9,000 ft; 2,743 m) is in Victoria Land. The fifth, off the northern tip of the Antarctic Peninsula, is a crater known as Deception Island.

Principal Types of Volcanoes

(*Source:* U.S. Dept. of Interior, Geological Survey.)

Geologists generally group volcanoes into four main kinds—cinder cones, composite volcanoes, shield volcanoes, and lava domes.

Cinder Cones

Cinder cones are the simplest type of volcano. They are built from particles and blobs of congealed lava ejected from a single vent. As the gas-charged lava is blown violently into the air, it breaks into small fragments that solidify and fall as cinders around the vent to form a circular or oval cone. Most cinder cones have a bowl-shaped crater at the summit and rarely rise more than a thousand feet or so above their surroundings. Cinder cones are numerous in western North America as well as throughout other volcanic terrains of the world.

Composite Volcanoes

Some of the Earth's grandest mountains are composite volcanoes—sometimes called *stratovolcanoes.* They are typically steep-sided, symmetrical cones of large dimension built of alternating layers of lava flows, volcanic ash, cinders, blocks, and bombs and may rise as much as 8,000 feet above their bases. Some of the most conspicuous and beautiful mountains in the world are composite volcanoes, including Mount Fuji in Japan, Mount Cotopaxi in Ecuador, Mount Shasta in California, Mount Hood in Oregon, and Mount St. Helens and Mount Rainier in Washington.

Most composite volcanoes have a crater at the summit which contains a central vent or a clustered group of vents. Lavas either flow through breaks in the crater wall or issue from fissures on the flanks of the cone. Lava, solidified within the fissures, forms *dikes* that act as ribs which greatly strengthen the cone.

The essential feature of a composite volcano is a conduit system through which magma from a reservoir deep in the Earth's crust rises to the surface. The volcano is built up by the accumulation of material erupted through the conduit and increases in size as lava, cinders, ash, etc., are added to its slopes.

Shield Volcanoes

Shield volcanoes, the third type of volcano, are built almost entirely of fluid lava flows. Flow after flow pours out in all directions from a central summit vent, or group of vents, building a broad, gently sloping cone of flat, domical shape, with a profile much like that of a warrior's shield. They are built up slowly by the accretion of thousands of flows of highly fluid basaltic (from *basalt,* a hard, dense dark volcanic rock) lava that spread widely over great distances, and then cool as thin, gently dipping sheets. Lavas also commonly erupt from vents along fractures (rift zones) that develop on the flanks of the cone. Some of the largest volcanoes in the world are shield volcanoes. In northern California and Oregon, many shield volcanoes have diameters of 3 or 4 miles and heights of 1,500 to 2,000 feet. The Hawaiian Islands are composed of linear chains of these volcanoes, including Kilauea and Mauna Loa on the island of Hawaii.

In some shield-volcano eruptions, basaltic lava pours out quietly from long fissures instead of central vents and floods the surrounding countryside with lava flow upon lava flow, forming broad plateaus. Lava plateaus of this type can be seen in Iceland, southeastern Washington, eastern Oregon, and southern Idaho.

Lava Domes

Volcanic or lava domes are formed by relatively small, bulbous masses of lava too viscous to flow any great distance; consequently, on extrusion, the lava piles over and around its vent. A dome grows largely by expansion from within. As it grows its outer surface cools and hardens, then shatters, spilling loose fragments down its sides. Some domes form craggy knobs or spines over the volcanic vent, whereas others form short, steep-sided lava flows known as "coulees." Volcanic domes commonly occur within the craters or on the flanks of large composite volcanoes. The nearly circular Novarupta Dome that formed during the 1912 eruption of Katmai Volcano, Alaska, measures 800 feet across and 200 feet high. The internal structure of this dome—defined by layering of lava fanning upward and outward from the center—indicates that it grew largely by expansion from within. Mount Pelée in Martinique, West Indies, and Lassen Peak and Mono domes in California, are examples of lava domes.

Submarine Volcanoes

Submarine volcanoes and volcanic vents are common features on certain zones of the ocean floor. Some are active at the present time and, in shallow water, disclose their presence by blasting steam and rock-debris high above the surface of the sea. Many others lie at such great depths that the tremendous weight of the water above them results in high, confining pressure and prevents the formation and release of steam and gases. Even very large, deepwater eruptions may not disturb the ocean floor.

The famous black sand beaches of Hawaii were created virtually instantaneously by the violent interaction between hot lava and sea water.

Earth's Greatest Volcanic Field

The largest known concentration of active volcanoes on earth was discovered by scientists aboard the research vessel *Melville* during the period November 1992 to January 1993. The vast volcanic cluster is situated under the South Pacific Ocean, 600 miles northwest of Easter Island.

A total of 1,133 seamounts and volcanic cones were found in the area which is about the size of New York State. Some of them rise to a height of almost 7,000 feet and their peaks are 2,500 to 5,000 feet below the ocean's surface.

Plate-Tectonics Theory—The Lithosphere Plates of the Earth

Source: U.S. Department of the Interior, U.S. Geological Survey.

World Population, Land Areas, and Elevations

Area	Estimated population, mid-1995	Approximate land area sq mi.	Percent of total land area	Population density per sq mi.	Elevation, feet Highest	Lowest
WORLD 1,290	5,734,106,000	58,433,000	100.0	98.1 [1]	Mt. Everest, Asia, 29,028	Dead Sea, Asia, below sea level
ASIA, incl. Philippines, Indonesia, and European and Asiatic Turkey; excl. Asiatic former U.S.S.R	3,403,451,000	10,644,000	18.2	319.7	Mt. Everest, Tibet-Nepal, 29,028	Dead Sea, Israel-Jordan, 1,290 below sea level
AFRICA	721,472,000	11,707,000	20.0	61.2	Mt. Kilimanjaro, Tanzania, 19,340	Lake Assal, Djibouti, 571 below sea level
NORTH AMERICA, including Hawaii, Central America, and Caribbean region	454,187,000	9,360,000	16.0	48.5	Mt. McKinley, Alaska, 20,320	Death Valley, Calif., 282 below sea level
SOUTH AMERICA	319,553,000	6,883,000	11.8	46.2	Mt. Aconcagua, Arg.-Chile, 23,034	Valdes Peninsula, 131 below sea level
ANTARCTICA	—	6,000,000	10.3	—	Vinson Massif, Sentinel Range, 16,863	Sea level
EUROPE, incl. Iceland; excl. European former U.S.S.R. and European Turkey	509,254,000	1,905,000	3.3	267.3	Mont Blanc, France, 15,781	Sea level
OCEANIA, incl. Australia, New Zealand, Melanesia, Micronesia, and Polynesia [2]	28,680,000	3,284,000	5.6	8.7	Wilhelm, Papua New Guinea, 14,793	Lake Eyre, Australia, 38 below sea level
Former U.S.S.R., both European and Asiatic	297,508,000	8,647,000	14.8	34.4	Communism Peak, Pamir, 24,590	Caspian Sea, 96 below sea level

1. In computing density per square mile, the area of Antarctica is omitted. 2. Although Hawaii is geographically part of Oceania, its population is included in the population figure for North America. *Source:* U.S. Bureau of the Census, International Data Base, for population figures. NOTE: The land area of Asia including the Asiatic portion of the former U.S.S.R. is 17,240,000 sq miles.

Plate-Tectonics Theory

(*Source:* U.S. Dept. of the Interior, Geological Survey.)

According to the generally accepted "plate-tectonics" theory, scientists believe that the Earth's surface is broken into a number of shifting slabs or plates, which average about 50 miles in thickness. These plates move relative to one another above a hotter, deeper, more mobile zone at average rates as great as a few inches per year. Most of the world's active volcanoes are located along or near the boundaries between shifting plates and are called "plate-boundary" volcanoes. However, some active volcanoes are not associated with plate boundaries, and many of these so-called "intra-plate" volcanoes form roughly linear chains in the interior of some oceanic plates. The Hawaiian Islands provide perhaps the best example of an "intra-plate" volcanic chain, developed by the northwest-moving Pacific plate passing over an inferred "hot spot" that initiates the magma-generation and volcano-formation process. The peripheral areas of the Pacific Ocean Basin, containing the boundaries of several plates, are dotted by many active volcanoes that form the so-called "Ring of Fire." The "Ring" provides excellent examples of "plate-boundary" volcanoes, including Mount St. Helens.

The accompanying figure on page 464 shows the boundaries of lithosphere plates that are active at present. The double lines indicate zones of spreading from which plates are moving apart. The lines with barbs show zones of underthrusting (subduction), where one plate is sliding beneath another. The barbs on the lines indicate the overriding plate. The single line defines a strike-slip fault along which plates are sliding horizontally past one another. The stippled areas indicate a part of a continent, exclusive of that along a plate boundary, which is undergoing active extensional, compressional, or strike-slip faulting.

The Severity of an Earthquake

(*Source:* U.S. Dept. of the Interior, Geological Survey.)

The Richter Magnitude Scale

The Richter magnitude scale was developed in 1935 by Charles F. Richter of the California Institute of Technology as a mathematical device to compare the size of earthquakes. The magnitude of an earthquake is determined from the logarithm of the amplitude of waves recorded by seismographs. Adjustments are included in the magnitude formula to compensate for the variation in the distance between the various seismographs and the epicenter of the earthquakes. On the Richter Scale, magnitude is expressed in whole numbers and decimal fractions. For example, a magnitude of 5.3 might be computed for a moderate earthquake, and a strong earthquake might be rated as magnitude 6.3. Great earthquakes, such as the 1906 earthquake in San Francisco, have magnitudes of 8.0 or higher. Although the Richter Scale has no upper limit, the largest known shocks have had magnitudes in the 8.8 to 8.9 range.

The Richter Scale is not used to express damage. An earthquake in a densely populated area which results in many deaths and considerable damage may have the same magnitude as a shock in a remote area that does nothing more than frighten the wildlife. Large-magnitude earthquakes that occur beneath the oceans may not even be felt by humans.

The Richter scale has been largely abandoned by seismologists because it isn't very accurate for the biggest earthquakes, those in the range of 8 or 9. Because it is based on readings taken close to quakes, 100 miles or so, it is less precise in other parts of the world where the nearest seismograph may be many hundreds of miles away.

New ways have been developed to rate the magnitude of the quake in numbers similar to the familiar Richter scale. The U.S. Geological Survey's National Earthquake Information Center in Golden, Colorado, uses surface-wave magnitude which measures the seismic waves crackling around the Earth's surface. Other seismologists use a measure known as the moment magnitude which is based on the size of the fault on which an earthquake occurs and the amount the earth slips. So nowadays, when most seismologists announce a magnitude number, they no longer say "on the Richter scale."

The Modified Mercalli Intensity Scale

The effect of an earthquake on the Earth's surface is called the intensity. The intensity scale consists of a series of certain key responses such as people awakening, movement of furniture, damage to chimneys, and finally—total destruction. Although numerous *intensity scales* have been developed over the last several hundred years to evaluate the effects of earthquakes, the one currently used in the United States is the Modified Mercalli (MM) Intensity Scale. It was developed in 1931 by the American seismologists Harry Wood and Frank Neumann. This scale, composed of 12 increasing levels of intensity that range from imperceptible shaking to catastrophic destruction, is designated by Roman numerals. It does not have a mathematical basis; instead it is an arbitrary ranking based on observed effects.

The Modified Mercalli Intensity value assigned to a specific site after an earthquake has a more meaningful measure of severity to the nonscientist than the magnitude because intensity refers to the effects actually experienced at that place. After the occurrence of widely-felt earthquakes, the Geological Survey mails questionnaires to postmasters in the disturbed area requesting the information so that intensity values can be assigned. The results of this postal canvass and information furnished by other sources are used to assign an intensity value, and to compile isoseismal maps that show the extent of various levels of intensity within the felt area. The maximum observed intensity generally occurs near the epicenter.

The *lower* numbers of the intensity scale generally deal with the manner in which the earthquake is felt by people. The *higher* numbers of the scale are based on observed structural damage. Structural engineers usually contribute information for assigning intensity values of VIII or above.

The Mexico City earthquake on September 19, 1985, was assigned an intensity of IX on the Mercalli Scale.

The following is an abbreviated description of the 12 levels of Modified Mercalli intensity.

I. Not felt except by a very few under especially favorable conditions.

II. Felt only by a few persons at rest, especially on upper floors of buildings. Delicately suspended objects may swing.

III. Felt quite noticeably by persons indoors, especially on upper floors of buildings. Many people do not recognize it as an earthquake. Standing motor cars may rock slightly. Vibration similar to the passing of a truck. Duration estimated.

IV. Felt indoors by many, outdoors by few during the day. At night, some awakened. Dishes, windows, doors disturbed; walls make cracking sound. Sensation like heavy truck striking building. Standing motor cars rocked noticeably.

V. Felt by nearly everyone; many awakened. Some dishes, windows broken. Unstable objects overturned. Pendulum clocks may stop.

VI. Felt by all, many frightened. Some heavy furniture moved; a few instances of fallen plaster. Damage slight.

VII. Damage negligible in buildings of good design and construction; slight to moderate in well-built ordinary structures; considerable damage in poorly built or badly designed structures; some chimneys broken.

VIII. Damage slight in specially designed structures; considerable damage in ordinary substantial buildings with partial collapse. Damage great in poorly built structures. Fall of chimneys, factory stacks, columns, monuments, walls. Heavy furniture overturned.

IX. Damage considerable in specially designed structures; well-designed frame structures thrown out of plumb. Damage great in substantial buildings, with partial collapse. Buildings shifted off foundations.

X. Some well-built wooden structures destroyed; most masonry and frame structures destroyed with foundations. Rails bent.

XI. Few, if any (masonry) structures remain standing. Bridges destroyed. Rails bent greatly.

XII. Damage total. Lines of sight and level are distorted. Objects thrown into the air.

Latitude and Longitude of World Cities

(and time corresponding to 12:00 noon, eastern standard time)

City	Lat. °	Lat. '	Long. °	Long. '	Time
Aberdeen, Scotland	57	9 n	2	9 w	5:00 p.m.
Adelaide, Australia	34	55 s	138	36 e	2:30 a.m. [1]
Algiers	36	50 n	3	0 e	6:00 p.m.
Amsterdam	52	22 n	4	53 e	6:00 p.m.
Ankara, Turkey	39	55 n	32	55 e	7:00 p.m.
Asunción, Paraguay	25	15 s	57	40 w	1:00 p.m.
Athens	37	58 n	23	43 e	7:00 p.m.
Auckland, New Zealand	36	52 s	174	45 e	5:00 a.m. [1]
Bangkok, Thailand	13	45 n	100	30 e	midnight
Barcelona	41	23 n	2	9 e	6:00 p.m.
Beijing	39	55 n	116	25 e	1:00 a.m. [1]
Belém, Brazil	1	28 s	48	29 w	2:00 p.m.
Belfast, Northern Ireland	54	37 n	5	56 w	5:00 p.m.
Belgrade, Yugoslavia	44	52 n	20	32 e	6:00 p.m.
Berlin	52	30 n	13	25 e	6:00 p.m.
Birmingham, England	52	25 n	1	55 w	5:00 p.m.
Bogotá, Colombia	4	32 n	74	15 w	12:00 noon
Bombay	19	0 n	72	48 e	10:30 p.m.
Bordeaux, France	44	50 n	0	31 w	6:00 p.m.
Bremen, Germany	53	5 n	8	49 e	6:00 p.m.
Brisbane, Australia	27	29 s	153	8 e	3:00 a.m. [1]
Bristol, England	51	28 n	2	35 w	5:00 p.m.
Brussels	50	52 n	4	22 e	6:00 p.m.
Bucharest	44	25 n	26	7 e	7:00 p.m.
Budapest	47	30 n	19	5 e	6:00 p.m.
Buenos Aires	34	35 s	58	22 w	2:00 p.m.
Cairo	30	2 n	31	21 e	7:00 p.m.
Calcutta	22	34 n	88	24 e	10:30 p.m.
Canton, China	23	7 n	113	15 e	1:00 a.m. [1]
Cape Town, South Africa	33	55 s	18	22 e	7:00 p.m.
Caracas, Venezuela	10	28 n	67	2 w	1:00 p.m.
Cayenne, French Guiana	4	49 n	52	18 w	1:00 p.m.
Chihuahua, Mexico	28	37 n	106	5 w	11:00 a.m.
Chongqing, China	29	46 n	106	34 e	1:00 a.m. [1]
Copenhagen	55	40 n	12	34 e	6:00 p.m.
Córdoba, Argentina	31	28 s	64	10 w	2:00 p.m.
Dakar, Senegal	14	40 n	17	28 w	5:00 p.m.
Darwin, Australia	12	28 s	130	51 e	2:30 a.m. [1]
Djibouti	11	30 n	43	3 e	8:00 p.m.
Dublin	53	20 n	6	15 w	5:00 p.m.
Durban, South Africa	29	53 s	30	53 e	7:00 p.m.
Edinburgh, Scotland	55	55 n	3	10 w	5:00 p.m.
Frankfurt	50	7 n	8	41 e	6:00 p.m.
Georgetown, Guyana	6	45 n	58	15 w	1:15 p.m.
Glasgow, Scotland	55	50 n	4	15 w	5:00 p.m.
Guatemala City, Guatemala	14	37 n	90	31 w	11:00 a.m.
Guayaquil, Ecuador	2	10 s	79	56 w	12:00 noon
Hamburg	53	33 n	10	2 e	6:00 p.m.
Hammerfest, Norway	70	38 n	23	38 e	6:00 p.m.
Havana	23	8 n	82	23 w	12:00 noon
Helsinki, Finland	60	10 n	25	0 e	7:00 p.m.
Hobart, Tasmania	42	52 s	147	19 e	3:00 a.m. [1]
Iquique, Chile	20	10 s	70	7 w	1:00 p.m.
Irkutsk, Russia	52	30 n	104	20 e	1:00 a.m.
Jakarta, Indonesia	6	16 s	106	48 e	0:30 a.m. [1]
Johannesburg, South Africa	26	12 s	28	4 e	7:00 p.m.
Kingston, Jamaica	17	59 n	76	49 w	12:00 noon
Kinshasa, Zaire	4	18 s	15	17 e	6:00 p.m.
La Paz, Bolivia	16	27 s	68	22 w	1:00 p.m.
Leeds, England	53	45 n	1	30 w	5:00 p.m.
Lima, Peru	12	0 s	77	2 w	2:00 noon
Lisbon	38	44 n	9	9 w	5:00 p.m.
Liverpool, England	53	25 n	3	0 w	5:00 p.m.
London	51	32 n	0	5 w	5:00 p.m.
Lyons, France	45	45 n	4	50 e	6:00 p.m.
Madrid	40	26 n	3	42 w	6:00 p.m.
Manchester, England	53	30 n	2	15 w	5:00 p.m.
Manila	14	35 n	120	57 e	1:00 a.m. [1]
Marseilles, France	43	20 n	5	20 e	6:00 p.m.
Mazatlán, Mexico	23	12 n	106	25 w	10:00 a.m.
Mecca, Saudi Arabia	21	29 n	39	45 e	8:00 p.m.
Melbourne	37	47 s	144	58 e	3:00 a.m. [1]
Mexico City	19	26 n	99	7 w	11:00 a.m.
Milan, Italy	45	27 n	9	10 e	6:00 p.m.
Montevideo, Uruguay	34	53 s	56	10 w	2:00 p.m.
Moscow	55	45 n	37	36 e	8:00 p.m.
Munich, Germany	48	8 n	11	35 e	6:00 p.m.
Nagasaki, Japan	32	48 n	129	57 e	2:00 a.m. [1]
Nagoya, Japan	35	7 n	136	56 e	2:00 a.m. [1]
Nairobi, Kenya	1	25 s	36	55 e	8:00 p.m.
Nanjing (Nanking), China	32	3 n	118	53 e	1:00 a.m. [1]
Naples, Italy	40	50 n	14	15 e	6:00 p.m.
Newcastle-on-Tyne, England	54	58 n	1	37 w	5:00 p.m.
Odessa, Ukraine	46	27 n	30	48 e	8:00 p.m.
Osaka, Japan	34	32 n	135	30 e	2:00 a.m. [1]
Oslo	59	57 n	10	42 e	6:00 p.m.
Panama City, Panama	8	58 n	79	32 w	12:00 noon
Paramaribo, Surinam	5	45 n	55	15 w	1:30 p.m.
Paris	48	48 n	2	20 e	6:00 p.m.
Perth, Australia	31	57 s	115	52 e	1:00 a.m. [1]
Plymouth, England	50	25 n	4	5 w	5:00 p.m.
Port Moresby, Papua New Guinea	9	25 s	147	8 e	3:00 a.m. [1]
Prague	50	5 n	14	26 e	6:00 p.m.
Reykjavik, Iceland	64	4 n	21	58 w	4:00 p.m.
Rio de Janeiro	22	57 s	43	12 w	2:00 p.m.
Rome	41	54 n	12	27 e	6:00 p.m.
Salvador, Brazil	12	56 s	38	27 w	2:00 p.m.
Santiago, Chile	33	28 s	70	45 w	1:00 p.m.
St. Petersburg	59	56 n	30	18 e	8:00 p.m.
Sao Paulo, Brazil	23	31 s	46	31 w	2:00 p.m.
Shanghai, China	31	10 n	121	28 e	1:00 a.m. [1]
Singapore	1	14 n	103	55 e	0:30 a.m. [1]
Sofia, Bulgaria	42	40 n	23	20 e	7:00 p.m.
Stockholm	59	17 n	18	3 e	6:00 p.m.
Sydney, Australia	34	0 s	151	0 e	3:00 a.m. [1]
Tananarive, Madagascar	18	50 s	47	33 e	8:00 p.m.
Teheran, Iran	35	45 n	51	45 e	8:30 p.m.
Tokyo	35	40 n	139	45 e	2:00 a.m. [1]
Tripoli, Libya	32	57 n	13	12 e	7:00 p.m.
Venice	45	26 n	12	20 e	6:00 p.m.
Veracruz, Mexico	19	10 n	96	10 w	11:00 a.m.
Vienna	48	14 n	16	20 e	6:00 p.m.
Vladivostok, Russia	43	10 n	132	0 e	3:00 a.m. [1]
Warsaw	52	14 n	21	0 e	6:00 p.m.
Wellington, New Zealand	41	17 s	174	47 e	5:00 a.m. [1]
Yangon, Myanmar	16	50 n	96	0 e	11:30 p.m.
Zürich	47	21 n	8	31 e	6:00 p.m.

1. On the following day.

Highest Mountain Peaks of the World

(For U.S. peaks, see Index)

Mountain peak	Range	Location	Height	
			feet	meters
Everest	Himalayas	Nepal-Tibet	29,028[1]	8,848
Godwin Austen (K-2)	Karakoram	Kashmir	28,250[1]	8,611
Kanchenjunga	Himalayas	Nepal-Sikkim	28,208	8,598
Lhotse	Himalayas	Nepal-Tibet	27,890	8,501
Makalu	Himalayas	Tibet-Nepal	27,790	8,470
Dhaulagiri I	Himalayas	Nepal	26,810	8,172
Manaslu	Himalayas	Nepal	26,760	8,156
Cho Oyu	Himalayas	Nepal	26,750	8,153
Nanga Parbat	Himalayas	Kashmir	26,660	8,126
Annapurna I	Himalayas	Nepal	26,504	8,078
Gasherbrum I	Karakoram	Kashmir	26,470	8,068
Broad Peak	Karakoram	Kashmir	26,400	8,047
Gasherbrum II	Karakoram	Kashmir	26,360	8,033
Gosainthan	Himalayas	Tibet	26,291	8,013
Gasherbrum III	Karakoram	Kashmir	26,090	7,952
Annapurna II	Himalayas	Nepal	26,041	7,937
Gasherbrum IV	Karakoram	India	26,000	7,925
Kangbachen	Himalayas	Nepal	25,925	7,902
Gyachung Kang	Himalayas	Nepal	25,910	7,897
Himal Chuli	Himalayas	Nepal	25,895	7,893
Disteghil Sar	Karakoram	Kashmir	25,868	7,885
Nuptse	Himalayas	Nepal	25,850	7,829
Kunyang Kish	Karakoram	Kashmir	25,760	7,852
Dakum (Peak 29)	Himalayas	Nepal	25,760	7,852
Masherbrum	Karakoram	Kashmir	25,660	7,821
Nanda Devi	Himalayas	India	25,645	7,817
Chomolonzo	Himalayas	Nepal-Tibet	25,640	7,815
Rakaposhi	Karakoram	Kashmir	25,550	7,788
Batura	Karakoram	Kashmir	25,540	7,785
Kanjut Sar	Karakoram	Kashmir	25,460	7,760
Kamet	Himalayas	India-Tibet	25,447	7,756
Namche Barwa	Himalayas	Tibet	25,445	7,756
Dhaulagiri II	Himalayas	Nepal	25,427	7,750
Saltoro Kangri	Karakoram	India	25,400	7,742
Gurla Mandhata	Himalayas	Tibet	25,355	7,728
Ulugh Muztagh	Kunlun	Tibet	25,341	7,724
Trivor	Karakoram	Kashmir	25,330	7,721
Jannu	Himalayas	Nepal	25,294	7,710
Tirich Mir	Hindu Kush	Pakistan	25,230	7,690
Saser Kangri	Karakoram	India	25,170	7,672
Makalu II	Himalayas	Nepal	25,130	7,660
Chogolisa	Karakoram	India	25,110	7,654
Dhaulagiri IV	Himalayas	Nepal	25,064	7,639
Fang	Himalayas	Nepal	25,013	7,624
Kula Kangri	Himalayas	Bhutan	24,783	7,554
Changtse	Himalayas	Tibet	24,780	7,553
Muztagh Ata	Muztagh Ata	China	24,757	7,546
Skyang Kangri	Himalayas	Kashmir	24,750	7,544
Communism Peak	Pamir	Tajikstan	24,590	7,495
Victory Peak	Pamir	Tajikistan	24,406	7,439
Sia Kangri	Himalayas	Kashmir	24,340	7,419
Chamlang	Himalayas	Nepal	24,012	7,319
Alung Gangri	Himalayas	Tibet	23,999	7,315
Chomo Lhari	Himalayas	Tibet-Bhutan	23,996	7,314
Muztagh (K-5)	Kunlun	China	23,891	7,282
Amne Machin	Kunlun	China	23,490	7,160
Gaurisankar	Himalayas	Nepal-Tibet	23,440	7,145
Lenin Peak	Tien-Shan	Tajikistan/Kyrgyzstan	23,405	7,134
Korzhenevski Peak	Pamir	Tajikistan	23,310	7,105
Kangto	Himalayas	Tibet	23,260	7,090
Dunagiri	Himalayas	India	23,184	7,066
Pauhunri	Himalayas	India-Tibet	23,180	7,065
Aconcagua	Andes	Argentina-Chile	23,034	7,021
Revolution Peak	Pamir	Tajikistan	22,880	6,974
Kangchenjhan	Himalayas	India	22,700	6,919
Siniolchu	Himalayas	India	22,620	6,895

Mountain peak	Range	Location	Height feet	Height meters
Ojos des Salado	Andes	Argentina-Chile	22,588	6,885
Bonete	Andes	Argentina-Chile	22,546	6,872
Simvuo	Himalayas	India	22,346	6,811
Tup	Andes	Argentina	22,309	6,800
Kungpu	Himalayas	Bhutan	22,300	6,797
Falso-Azufre	Andes	Argentina-Chile	22,277	6,790
Moscow Peak	Pamir	Tajikistan	22,260	6,785
Veladero	Andes	Argentina	22,244	6,780
Pissis	Andes	Argentina	22,241	6,779
Mercedario	Andes	Argentina-Chile	22,211	6,770
Huascarán	Andes	Peru	22,198	6,766
Tocorpuri	Andes	Bolivia-Chile	22,162	6,755
Karl Marx Peak	Pamir	Tajikistan	22,067	6,726
Llullaillaco	Andes	Argentina-Chile	22,057	6,723
Libertador	Andes	Argentina	22,047	6,720
Kailas	Himalayas	Tibet	22,027	6,714
Lingtren	Himalayas	Nepal-Tibet	21,972	6,697
Incahuasi	Andes	Argentina-Chile	21,719	6,620
Carnicero	Andes	Peru	21,689	6,611
Kurumda	Pamir	Tajikistan	21,686	6,610
Garmo Peak	Pamir	Tajikistan	21,637	6,595
Sajama	Andes	Bolivia	21,555	6,570
Ancohuma	Andes	Bolivia	21,490	6,550
El Muerto	Andes	Argentina-Chile	21,456	6,540
Nacimiento	Andes	Argentina	21,302	6,493
Illimani	Andes	Bolivia	21,184	6,457
Antofalla	Andes	Argentina-Chile	21,129	6,440
Coropuña	Andes	Peru	21,079	6,425
Cuzco (Ausangate)	Andes	Peru	20,995	6,399
Toro	Andes	Argentina-Chile	20,932	6,380
Parinacota	Andes	Bolivia-Chile	20,768	6,330
Chimboraso	Andes	Ecuador	20,702	6,31
Salcantay	Andes	Peru	20,575	6,271
General Manuel Belgrano	Andes	Argentina	20,505	6,250
Chañi	Andes	Argentina	20,341	6,200
Caca Aca	Andes	Bolivia	20,328	6,196
McKinley	Alaska	Alaska	20,320	6,194
Vudor Peak	Pamir	Tajikistan	20,118	6,132
Condoriri	Andes	Bolivia	20,095	6,125
Solimana	Andes	Peru	20,069	6,117
Nevada	Andes	Argentina	20,023	6,103

1. India gives the height as 29,028 feet (8,848 meters), however, in 1987, an Italian expedition recalculated its height to be 29,108 feet and K-2 to be 29,064 feet.

Oceans and Seas

Name	Area sq mi.	Area sq km	Average depth feet	Average depth meters	Greatest known depth feet	Greatest known depth meters	Place greatest known depth
Pacific Ocean	64,000,000	165,760,000	13,215	4,028	36,198	11,033	Mariana Trench
Atlantic Ocean	31,815,000	82,400,000	12,880	3,926	30,246	9,219	Puerto Rico Trough
Indian Ocean	25,300,000	65,526,700	13,002	3,963	24,460	7,455	Sunda Trench
Arctic Ocean	5,440,200	14,090,000	3,953	1,205	18,456	5,625	77° 45′ N; 175° W
Mediterranean Sea[1]	1,145,100	2,965,800	4,688	1,429	15,197	4,632	Off Cape Matapan, Greece
Caribbean Sea	1,049,500	2,718,200	8,685	2,647	22,788	6,946	Off Cayman Islands
South China Sea	895,400	2,319,000	5,419	1,652	16,456	5,016	West of Luzon
Bering Sea	884,900	2,291,900	5,075	1,547	15,659	4,773	Off Buldir Island
Gulf of Mexico	615,000	1,592,800	4,874	1,486	12,425	3,787	Sigsbee Deep
Okhotsk Sea	613,800	1,589,700	2,749	838	12,001	3,658	146° 10′ E; 46° 50′ N
East China Sea	482,300	1,249,200	617	188	9,126	2,782	25° 16′ N; 125° E
Hudson Bay	475,800	1,232,300	420	128	600	183	Near entrance
Japan Sea	389,100	1,007,800	4,429	1,350	12,276	3,742	Central Basin
Andaman Sea	308,100	797,700	2,854	870	12,392	3,777	Off Car Nicobar Island
North Sea	222,100	575,200	308	94	2,165	660	Skagerrak
Red Sea	169,100	438,000	1,611	491	7,254	2,211	Off Port Sudan
Baltic Sea	163,000	422,200	180	55	1,380	421	Off Gotland

1. Includes Black Sea and Sea of Azov. NOTE: For Caspian Sea, *see* Large Lakes of World elsewhere in this section.

World's Greatest Man-Made Lakes[1]

Name of dam	Location	Millions of cubic meters	Thousands of acre-feet	Year completed
Owen Falls	Uganda	204,800	166,000	1954
Kariba	Zimbabwe	181,592	147,218	1959
Bratsk	Siberia	169,270	137,220	1964
High Aswan (Sadd-el-Aali)	Egypt	168,000	136,200	1970
Akosombo	Ghana	148,000	120,000	1965
Daniel Johnson	Canada	141,852	115,000	1968
Guri (Raul Leoni)	Venezuela	136,000	110,256	1986
Krasnoyarsk	Siberia	73,300	59,425	1967
Bennett W.A.C.	Canada	70,309	57,006	1967
Zeya	Russia	68,400	55,452	1978
Cabora Bassa	Mozambique	63,000	51,075	1974
LaGrande 2	Canada	61,720	50,037	1982
LaGrande 3	Canada	60,020	48,659	1982
Ust'-Ilimsk	Russia	59,300	48,075	1980
Volga-V.I. Lenin	Russia	58,000	47,020	1955
Caniapiscau	Canada	53,790	43,608	1981
Pati (Chapetón)	Argentina	53,700	43,535	UC
Upper Wainganga	India	50,700	41,103	1987
Sáo Felix	Brazil	50,600	41,022	1986
Bukhtarma	Former U.S.S.R.	49,740	40,325	1960
Atatürk (Karababa)	Turkey	48,700	39,482	1990
Cerros Colorados	Argentina	48,000	38,914	1973
Irkutsk	Russia	46,000	37,290	1956
Tucuruí	Brazil	36,375	29,489	1984
Vilyuy	Russia	35,900	29,104	1967
Sanmenxia	China	35,400	28,700	1960
Hoover	Nevada/Arizona	35,154	28,500	1936
Sobridinho	Brazil	34,200	27,726	1981
Glen Canyon	Arizona	33,304	27,000	1964
Jenpeg	Canada	31,790	25,772	1975

1. Formed by construction of dams. NOTE: UC = under construction. *Source:* Department of the Interior, Bureau of Reclamation and *International Water Power and Dam Construction.*

Large Lakes of the World
(Area more than 1,600 sq miles)

Name and location	Area		Length		Maximum depth	
	sq mi.	km	mi.	km	feet	meters
Caspian Sea, Azerbaijan-Russia-Kazakhstan-Turkmenistan-Iran[1]	152,239	394,299	745	1,199	3,104	946
Superior, U.S.-Canada	31,820	82,414	383	616	1,333	406
Victoria, Tanzania-Uganda	26,828	69,485	200	322	270	82
Aral, Kazakhstan-Uzbekistan	25,659	66,457	266	428	223	68
Huron, U.S.-Canada	23,010	59,596	247	397	750	229
Michigan, U.S.	22,400	58,016	321	517	923	281
Tanganyika, Tanzania-Zaire	12,700	32,893	420	676	4,708	1,435
Baikal, Russia	12,162	31,500	395	636	5,712	1,741
Great Bear, Canada	12,000	31,080	232	373	270	82
Nyasa, Malawi-Mozambique-Tanzania	11,600	30,044	360	579	2,316	706
Great Slave, Canada	11,170	28,930	298	480	2,015	614
Chad,[2] Chad-Niger-Nigeria	9,946	25,760	—	—	23	7
Erie, U.S.-Canada	9,930	25,719	241	388	210	64
Winnipeg, Canada	9,094	23,553	264	425	204	62
Ontario, U.S.-Canada	7,520	19,477	193	311	778	237
Balkhash, Kazakhstan	7,115	18,428	376	605	87	27
Ladoga, Russia	7,000	18,130	124	200	738	225
Onega, Russia	3,819	9,891	154	248	361	110
Titicaca, Bolivia-Peru	3,141	8,135	110	177	1,214	370
Nicaragua, Nicaragua	3,089	8,001	110	177	230	70
Athabaska, Canada	3,058	7,920	208	335	407	124
Rudolf, Kenya	2,473	6,405	154	248	—	—
Reindeer, Canada	2,444	6,330	152	245	—	—
Eyre, South Australia	2,400 [3]	6,216	130	209	varies	varies
Issyk-Kul, Kyrgyzstan	2,394	6,200	113	182	2,297	700
Urmia,[2] Iran	2,317	6,001	81	130	49	15
Torrens, South Australia	2,200	5,698	130	209	—	—

Name and location	Area		Length		Maximum depth	
	sq mi.	km	mi.	km	feet	meters
Vänern, Sweden	2,141	5,545	87	140	322	98
Winnipegosis, Canada	2,086	5,403	152	245	59	18
Mobutu Sese Seko, Uganda	2,046	5,299	100	161	180	55
Nettilling, Baffin Island, Canada	1,950	5,051	70	113	—	—
Nipigon, Canada	1,870	4,843	72	116	—	—
Manitoba, Canada	1,817	4,706	140	225	22	7
Great Salt, U.S.	1,800	4,662	75	121	15/25	5/8
Kioga, Uganda	1,700	4,403	50	80	about 30	9
Koko-Nor, China	1,630	4,222	66	106	—	—

1. The Caspian Sea is called "sea" because the Romans, finding it salty, named it *Mare Caspium*. Many geographers, however, consider it a lake because it is land-locked. 2. Figures represent high-water data. 3. Varies with the rainfall of the wet season. It has been reported to dry up almost completely on occasion.

Principal Rivers of the World

(For other U.S. rivers, see Index)

River	Source	Outflow	Approx. length	
			miles	km
Nile	Tributaries of Lake Victoria, Africa	Mediterranean Sea	4,180	6,690
Amazon	Glacier-fed lakes, Peru	Atlantic Ocean	3,912	6,296
Mississippi-Missouri-Red Rock	Source of Red Rock, Montana	Gulf of Mexico	3,710	5,970
Yangtze Kiang	Tibetan plateau, China	China Sea	3,602	5,797
Ob	Altai Mts., Russia	Gulf of Ob	3,459	5,567
Huang Ho (Yellow)	Eastern part of Kunlan Mts., west China	Gulf of Chihli	2,900	4,667
Yenisei	Tannu-Ola Mts., western Tuva, Russia	Arctic Ocean	2,800	4,506
Paraná	Confluence of Paranaiba and Grande rivers	Río de la Plata	2,795	4,498
Irtish	Altai Mts., Russia	Ob River	2,758	4,438
Zaire (Congo)	Confluence of Lualab and Luapula rivers, Zaire	Atlantic Ocean	2,716	4,371
Heilong (Amur)	Confluence of Shilka (Russia) and Argun (Manchuria) rivers	Tatar Strait	2,704	4,352
Lena	Baikal Mts., Russia	Arctic Ocean	2,652	4,268
Mackenzie	Head of Finlay River, British Columbia, Canada	Beaufort Sea (Arctic Ocean)	2,635	4,241
Niger	Guinea	Gulf of Guinea	2,600	4,184
Mekong	Tibetan highlands	South China Sea	2,500	4,023
Mississippi	Lake Itasca, Minnesota	Gulf of Mexico	2,348	3,779
Missouri	Confluence of Jefferson, Gallatin, and Madison rivers, Montana	Mississippi River	2,315	3,726
Volga	Valdai plateau, Russia	Caspian Sea	2,291	3,687
Madeira	Confluence of Beni and Maumoré rivers, Bolivia-Brazil boundary	Amazon River	2,012	3,238
Purus	Peruvian Andes	Amazon River	1,993	3,207
São Francisco	Southwest Minas Gerais, Brazil	Atlantic Ocean	1,987	3,198
Yukon	Junction of Lewes and Pelly rivers, Yukon Territory, Canada	Bering Sea	1,979	3,185
St. Lawrence	Lake Ontario	Gulf of St. Lawrence	1,900	3,058
Rio Grande	San Juan Mts., Colorado	Gulf of Mexico	1,885	3,034
Brahmaputra	Himalayas	Ganges River	1,800	2,897
Indus	Himalayas	Arabian Sea	1,800	2,897
Danube	Black Forest, Germany	Black Sea	1,766	2,842

River	Source	Outflow	Approx. length miles	Approx. length km
Euphrates	Confluence of Murat Nehri and Kara Su rivers, Turkey	Shatt-al-Arab	1,739	2,799
Darling	Central part of Eastern Highlands, Australia	Murray River	1,702	2,739
Zambezi	11°21′S, 24°22′E, Zambia	Mozambique Channel	1,700	2,736
Tocantins	Goiás, Brazil	Pará River	1,677	2,699
Murray	Australian Alps, New South Wales	Indian Ocean	1,609	2,589
Nelson	Head of Bow River, western Alberta, Canada	Hudson Bay	1,600	2,575
Paraguay	Mato Grosso, Brazil	Paraná River	1,584	2,549
Ural	Southern Ural Mts., Russia	Caspian Sea	1,574	2,533
Ganges	Himalayas	Bay of Bengal	1,557	2,506
Amu Darya (Oxus)	Nicholas Range, Pamir Mts., Turkmenistan	Aral Sea	1,500	2,414
Japurá	Andes, Colombia	Amazon River	1,500	2,414
Salween	Tibet, south of Kunlun Mts.	Gulf of Martaban	1,500	2,414
Arkansas	Central Colorado	Mississippi River	1,459	2,348
Colorado	Grand County, Colorado	Gulf of California	1,450	2,333
Dnieper	Valdai Hills, Russia	Black Sea	1,419	2,284
Ohio-Allegheny	Potter County, Pennsylvania	Mississippi River	1,306	2,102
Irrawaddy	Confluence of Nmai and Mali rivers, northeast Burma	Bay of Bengal	1,300	2,092
Orange	Lesotho	Atlantic Ocean	1,300	2,092
Orinoco	Serra Parima Mts., Venezuela	Atlantic Ocean	1,281	2,062
Pilcomayo	Andes Mts., Bolivia	Paraguay River	1,242	1,999
Xi Jiang (Si Kiang)	Eastern Yunnan Province, China	China Sea	1,236	1,989
Columbia	Columbia Lake, British Columbia, Canada	Pacific Ocean	1,232	1,983
Don	Tula, Russia	Sea of Azov	1,223	1,968
Sungari	China-North Korea boundary	Amur River	1,215	1,955
Saskatchewan	Canadian Rocky Mts.	Lake Winnipeg	1,205	1,939
Peace	Stikine Mts., British Columbia, Canada	Great Slave River	1,195	1,923
Tigris	Taurus Mts., Turkey	Shatt-al-Arab	1,180	1,899

Highest Waterfalls of the World

Waterfall	Location	River	Height feet	Height m
Angel	Venezuela	Tributary of Caroni	3,281	1,000
Tugela	Natal, South Africa	Tugela	3,000	914
Cuquenán	Venezuela	Cuquenán	2,000	610
Sutherland	South Island, N.Z.	Arthur	1,904	580
Takkakaw	British Columbia	Tributary of Yoho	1,650	503
Ribbon (Yosemite)	California	Creek flowing into Yosemite	1,612	491
Upper Yosemite	California	Yosemite Creek, tributary of Merced	1,430	436
Gavarnie	Southwest France	Gave de Pau	1,384	422
Vettisfoss	Norway	Mörkedola	1,200	366
Widows' Tears (Yosemite)	California	Tributary of Merced	1,170	357
Staubbach	Switzerland	Staubbach (Lauterbrunnen Valley)	984	300

Waterfall	Location	River	Height	
			feet	m
Middle Cascade (Yosemite)	California	Yosemite Creek, tributary of Merced	909	277
King Edward VIII	Guyana	Courantyne	850	259
Gersoppa	India	Sharavati	829	253
Kaieteur	Guyana	Potaro	822	251
Skykje	Norway	In Skykjedal (valley of Inner Hardinger Fjord)	820	250
Kalambo	Tanzania-Zambia	—	720	219
Fairy (Mount Rainier Park)	Washington	Stevens Creek	700	213
Trummelbach	Switzerland	Trummelbach (Lauterbrunnen Valley)	700	213
Aniene (Teverone)	Italy	Tiber	680	207
Cascata delle Marmore	Italy	Velino, tributary of Nera	650	198
Maradalsfos	Norway	Stream flowing into Ejkisdalsvand (lake)	643	196
Feather	California	Fall River	640	195
Maletsunyane	Lesotho	Maletsunyane	630	192
Bridalveil (Yosemite)	California	Yosemite Creek	620	189
Multnomah	Oregon	Multnomah Creek, tributary of Columbia	620	189
Vøringsfos	Norway	Bjoreia	597	182
Nevada (Yosemite)	California	Merced	594	181
Skjeggedal	Norway	Tysso	525	160
Marina	Guyana	Tributary of Kuribrong, tributary of Potaro	500	152
Tequendama	Colombia	Funza, tributary of Magdalena	425	130
King George's	Cape of Good Hope, South Africa	Orange	400	122
Illilouette (Yosemite)	California	Illilouette Creek, tributary of Merced	370	113
Victoria	Rhodesia-Zambia boundary	Zambezi	355	108
Handöl	Sweden	Handöl Creek	345	105
Lower Yosemite	California	Yosemite	320	98
Comet (Mount Rainier Park)	Washington	Van Trump Creek	320	98
Vernal (Yosemite)	California	Merced	317	97
Virginia	Northwest Territories, Canada	South Nahanni, tributary of Mackenzie	315	96
Lower Yellowstone	Wyoming	Yellowstone	310	94

NOTE: Niagara Falls (New York-Ontario), though of great volume, has parallel drops of only 158 and 167 feet.

Large Islands of the World

Island	Location and status	Area	
		sq mi.	sq km
Greenland	North Atlantic (Danish)	839,999	2,175,597
New Guinea	Southwest Pacific (Irian Jaya, Indonesian, west part; Papua New Guinea, east part)	316,615	820,033
Borneo	West mid-Pacific (Indonesian, south part, Brunei and Malaysian, north part)	286,914	743,107
Madagascar	Indian Ocean (Malagasy Republic)	226,657	587,042
Baffin	North Atlantic (Canadian)	183,810	476,068
Sumatra	Northeast Indian Ocean (Indonesian)	182,859	473,605
Honshu	Sea of Japan-Pacific (Japanese)	88,925	230,316
Great Britain	Off coast of NW Europe (England, Scotland, and Wales)	88,758	229,883
Ellesmere	Arctic Ocean (Canadian)	82,119	212,688
Victoria	Arctic Ocean (Canadian)	81,930	212,199
Celebes	West mid-Pacific (Indonesian)	72,986	189,034
South Island	South Pacific (New Zealand)	58,093	150,461
Java	Indian Ocean (Indonesian)	48,990	126,884
North Island	South Pacific (New Zealand)	44,281	114,688

Island	Location and status	Area sq mi.	Area sq km
Cuba	Caribbean Sea (republic)	44,218	114,525
Newfoundland	North Atlantic (Canadian)	42,734	110,681
Luzon	West mid-Pacific (Philippines)	40,420	104,688
Iceland	North Atlantic (republic)	39,768	102,999
Mindanao	West mid-Pacific (Philippines)	36,537	94,631
Ireland	West of Great Britain (republic, south part; United Kingdom, north part)	32,597	84,426
Hokkaido	Sea of Japan—Pacific (Japanese)	30,372	78,663
Hispaniola	Caribbean Sea (Dominican Republic, east part; Haiti, west part)	29,355	76,029
Tasmania	South of Australia (Australian)	26,215	67,897
Sri Lanka (Ceylon)	Indian Ocean (republic)	25,332	65,610
Sakhalin (Karafuto)	North of Japan (Russia)	24,560	63,610
Banks	Arctic Ocean (Canadian)	23,230	60,166
Devon	Arctic Ocean (Canadian)	20,861	54,030
Tierra del Fuego	Southern tip of South America (Argentinian, east part; Chilean, west part)	18,605	48,187
Kyushu	Sea of Japan—Pacific (Japanese)	16,223	42,018
Melville	Arctic Ocean (Canadian)	16,141	41,805
Axel Heiberg	Arctic Ocean (Canadian)	15,779	40,868
Southampton	Hudson Bay (Canadian)	15,700	40,663

Principal Deserts of the World

Desert	Location	Approximate size	Approx. elevation, ft
Atacama	North Chile	400 mi. long	7,000–13,500
Black Rock	Northwest Nevada	About 1,000 sq mi.	2,000–8,500
Colorado	Southeast California from San Gorgonio Pass to Gulf of California	200 mi. long and a maximum width of 50 mi.	Few feet above to 250 below sea level
Dasht-e-Kavir	Southeast of Caspian Sea, Iran	—	2,000
Dasht-e-Lut	Northeast of Kerman, Iran	—	1,000
Gobi (Shamo)	Covers most of Mongolia	500,000 sq mi.	3,000–5,000
Great Arabian	Most of Arabia	1,500 mi. long	—
An Nafud (Red Desert)	South of Jauf	400 mi. by avg of 140 mi.	3,000
Dahna	Northeast of Nejd	400 mi. by 30 mi.	—
Rub' al-Khali	South portion of Nejd	Over 200,000 sq. mi.	—
Syrian (Al-Hamad)	North of lat. 30°N	—	1,850
Great Australian	Western portion of Australia	About one half the continent	600–1,000
Great Salt Lake	West of Great Salt Lake to Nevada—Utah boundary	About 110 mi. by 50 mi.	4,500
Kalahari	South Africa—South-West Africa	About 120,000 sq mi.	Over 3,000
Kara Kum (Desert of Kiva)	Southwest Turkmenistan	115,000 sq mi.	—
Kyzyl Kum	Uzbekistan and Kazakhstan	Over 100,000 sq. mi.	160 near Lake Aral to 2,000 in southeast
Libyan	Libya, Egypt, Sudan	Over 500,000 sq mi.	—
Mojave	North of Colorado Desert and south of Death Valley, southeast California	15,000 sq mi.	2,000
Nubian	From Red Sea to great west bend of the Nile, Sudan	—	2,500
Painted Desert	Northeast Arizona	Over 7,000 sq mi.	High plateau, 5,000
Sahara	North Africa to about lat. 15°N and from Red Sea to Atlantic Ocean	3,200 mi. greatest length along lat. 20°N; area over 3,500,000 sq mi.	440 below sea level to 11,000 above; avg elevation, 1,400–1,600
Takla Makan	South central Sinkiang, China	Over 100,000 sq mi.	—
Thar (Indian)	Pakistan-India	Nearly 100,000 sq mi.	Over 1,000

Interesting Caves and Caverns of the World

Aggtelek. In village of same name, northern Hungary. Large stalactitic cavern about 5 miles long.

Altamira Cave. Near Santander, Spain. Contains animal paintings (Old Stone Age art) on roof and walls.

Antiparos. On island of same name in the Grecian Archipelago. Some stalactites are 20 ft long. Brilliant colors and fantastic shapes.

Blue Grotto. On island of Capri, Italy. Cavern hollowed out in limestone by constant wave action. Now half filled with water because of sinking coast. Name derived from unusual blue light permeating the cave. Source of light is a submerged opening, light passing through the water.

Carlsbad Caverns. Southeast New Mexico. Largest underground labyrinth yet discovered. Three levels: 754, 900, and 1,320 ft below the surface.

Fingal's Cave. On island of Staffa off coast of western Scotland. Penetrates about 200 ft inland. Contains basaltic columns almost 40 ft high.

Ice Cave. Near Dobsina, Czechoslovakia. Noted for its beautiful crystal effects.

Jenolan Caves. In Blue Mountain plateau, New South Wales, Australia. Beautiful stalactitic formations.

Kent's Cavern. Near Torquay, England. Source of much information on Paleolithic man.

Luray Cavern. Near Luray, Va. Has large stalactitic and stalagmitic columns of many colors.

Mammoth Cave. Limestone cavern in central Kentucky. Cave area is about 10 miles in diameter but has over 300 miles of irregular subterranean passageways at various levels. Temperature remains fairly constant at 54°F.

Peak Cavern or Devil's Hole. Derbyshire, England. About 2,250 ft into a mountain. Lowest part is about 600 ft below the surface.

Postojna (Postumia) Grotto. Near Postumia in Julian Alps, about 25 miles northeast of Trieste. Stalactitic cavern, largest in Europe. Piuca (Pivka) River flows through part of it. Caves have numerous beautiful stalactites.

Singing Cave. Iceland. A lava cave; name derived from echoes of people singing in it.

Wind Cave. In Black Hills of South Dakota. Limestone caverns with stalactites and stalagmites almost entirely missing. Variety of crystal formations called "boxwork."

Wyandotte Cave. In Crawford County, southern Indiana. A limestone cavern with five levels of passages; one of the largest in North America. "Monumental Mountain," approximately 135 ft high, is believed to be one of the world's largest underground "mountains."

U.S. Geography

Miscellaneous Data for the United States

Source: Department of the Interior, U.S. Geological Survey.

Highest point: Mount McKinley, Alaska	20,320 ft (6,198 m)
Lowest point: Death Valley, Calif.	282 ft (86 m) below sea level
Approximate mean elevation	2,500 ft (763 m)
Points farthest apart (50 states):	5,859 mi. (9,429 km)
Log Point, Elliot Key, Fla., and Kure Island, Hawaii	
Geographic center (50 states):	44° 58′ N. lat.103° 46′ W. long.
In Butte County, S.D. (west of Castle Rock)	
Geographic center (48 conterminous states):	39° 50′ N. lat.98° 35′ W. long.
In Smith County, Kan. (near Lebanon)	
Boundaries:	
Between Alaska and Canada	1,538 mi. (2,475 km)
Between the 48 conterminous states and Canada (incl. Great Lakes)	3,987 mi. (6,416 km)
Between the United States and Mexico	1,933 mi. (3,111 km)

Extreme Points of the United States (50 States)

Extreme point	Latitude	Longitude	Distance[1] mi.	km
Northernmost point: Point Barrow, Alaska	71°23′ N	156°29′ W	2,507	4,034
Easternmost point: West Quoddy Head, Me.	44°49′ N	66°57′ W	1,788	2,997
Southernmost point: Ka Lae (South Cape), Hawaii	18°55′ N	155°41′ W	3,463	5,573
Westernmost point: Cape Wrangell, Alaska (Attu Island)	52°55′ N	172°27′ E	3,625	5,833

1. From geographic center of United States (incl. Alaska and Hawaii), west of Castle Rock, S.D., 44°58′ N. lat., 103°46′ W long. If measured from the prime meridian in Greenwich, England, Cape Wrangell, Attu Island, Alaska would be the easternmost point.

Highest, Lowest, and Mean Elevations in the United States

State	Elevation ft[1]	Highest point	Elevation ft	Lowest point	Elevation ft
Alabama	500	Cheaha Mountain	2,405	Gulf of Mexico	Sea level
Alaska	1,900	Mount McKinley	20,320	Pacific Ocean	Sea level
Arizona	4,100	Humphreys Peak	12,633	Colorado River	70
Arkansas	650	Magazine Mountain	2,753	Ouachita River	55
California	2,900	Mount Whitney	14,494[2]	Death Valley	282[3]
Colorado	6,800	Mount Elbert	14,433	Arkansas River	3,350
Connecticut	500	Mount Frissell, on south slope	2,380	Long Island Sound	Sea level
Delaware	60	On Ebright Road	448	Atlantic Ocean	Sea level
D.C.	150	Tenleytown, at Reno Reservoir	410	Potomac River	1
Florida	100	Sec. 30, T6N, R20W[4]	345	Atlantic Ocean	Sea level
Georgia	600	Brasstown Bald	4,784	Atlantic Ocean	Sea level
Hawaii	3,030	Puu Wekiu, Mauna Kea	13,796	Pacific Ocean	Sea level
Idaho	5,000	Borah Peak	12,662	Snake River	710
Illinois	600	Charles Mound	1,235	Mississippi River	279[5]
Indiana	700	Franklin Township, Wayne County	1,257	Ohio River	320[5]
Iowa	1,100	Sec. 29, T100N, R41W[6]	1,670	Mississippi River	480
Kansas	2,000	Mount Sunflower	4,039[7]	Verdigris River	679
Kentucky	750	Black Mountain	4,139	Mississippi River	257[5]
Louisiana	100	Driskill Mountain	535	New Orleans	8[3]
Maine	600	Mount Katahdin	5,267	Atlantic Ocean	Sea level
Maryland	350	Backbone Mountain	3,360	Atlantic Ocean	Sea level
Massachusetts	500	Mount Greylock	3,487	Atlantic Ocean	Sea level
Michigan	900	Mount Arvon	1,979	Lake Erie	572[5]
Minnesota	1,200	Eagle Mountain	2,301	Lake Superior	600
Mississippi	300	Woodall Mountain	806	Gulf of Mexico	Sea level
Missouri	800	Taum Sauk Mountain	1,772	St. Francis River	230[5]
Montana	3,400	Granite Peak	12,799	Kootenai River	1,800
Nebraska	2,600	Johnson Township, Kimball County	5,424	Missouri River	840
Nevada	5,500	Boundary Peak	13,140	Colorado River	479
New Hampshire	1,000	Mount Washington	6,288	Atlantic Ocean	Sea level
New Jersey	250	High Point	1,803[7]	Atlantic Ocean	Sea level
New Mexico	5,700	Wheeler Peak	13,161	Red Bluff Reservoir	2,842
New York	1,000	Mount Marcy	5,344	Atlantic Ocean	Sea level
North Carolina	700	Mount Mitchell	6,684	Atlantic Ocean	Sea level
North Dakota	1,900	White Butte	3,506	Red River	750
Ohio	850	Campbell Hill	1,549	Ohio River	455[5]
Oklahoma	1,300	Black Mesa	4,973	Little River	289
Oregon	3,300	Mount Hood	11,239	Pacific Ocean	Sea level
Pennsylvania	1,100	Mount Davis	3,213	Delaware River	Sea level
Rhode Island	200	Jerimoth Hill	812	Atlantic Ocean	Sea level
South Carolina	350	Sassafras Mountain	3,560	Atlantic Ocean	Sea level
South Dakota	2,200	Harney Peak	7,242	Big Stone Lake	966
Tennessee	900	Clingmans Dome	6,643	Mississippi River	178[5]
Texas	1,700	Guadalupe Peak	8,749	Gulf of Mexico	Sea level
Utah	6,100	Kings Peak	13,528	Beaverdam Wash	2,000
Vermont	1,000	Mount Mansfield	4,393	Lake Champlain	95
Virginia	950	Mount Rogers	5,729	Atlantic Ocean	Sea level
Washington	1,700	Mount Rainier	14,410	Pacific Ocean	Sea level
West Virginia	1,500	Spruce Knob	4,861	Potomac River	240
Wisconsin	1,050	Timms Hill	1,951	Lake Michigan	579[5]
Wyoming	6,700	Gannett Peak	13,804	Belle Fourche River	3,099
United States	2,500	Mount McKinley (Alaska)	20,320	Death Valley (California)	282[3]

1. Approximate mean elevation. 2. National Geodetic Survey. 3. Below sea level. 4. Walton County. 5. Corps of Engineers 6. Osceola County. 7. State Surveys *Source:* Department of the Interior, U.S. Geological Survey.

The Continental Divide

The Continental Divide is a ridge of high ground which runs irregularly north and south through the Rocky Mountains and separates eastward-flowing from westward-flowing streams. The waters which flow eastward empty into the Atlantic Ocean, chiefly by way of the Gulf of Mexico; those which flow westward empty into the Pacific.

Mason and Dixon's Line

Mason and Dixon's Line (often called the Mason-Dixon Line) is the boundary between Pennsylvania and Maryland, running at a north latitude of 39°43′19.11″. The greater part of it was surveyed from 1763–67 by Charles Mason and Jeremiah Dixon, English astronomers who had been appointed to settle a dispute between the colonies. As the line was partly the boundary between the free and the slave states, it has come to signify the division between the North and the South.

Latitude and Longitude of U.S. and Canadian Cities

(and time corresponding to 12:00 noon, eastern standard time)

City	Lat. °	Lat. '	Long. °	Long. '	Time
Albany, N.Y.	42	40	73	45	12:00 noon
Albuquerque, N.M.	35	05	106	39	10:00 a.m.
Amarillo, Tex.	35	11	101	50	11:00 a.m.
Anchorage, Alaska	61	13	149	54	8:00 a.m.
Atlanta	33	45	84	23	12:00 noon
Austin, Tex.	30	16	97	44	11:00 a.m.
Baker, Ore.	44	47	117	50	9:00 a.m.
Baltimore	39	18	76	38	12:00 noon
Bangor, Me.	44	48	68	47	12:00 noon
Birmingham, Ala.	33	30	86	50	11:00 a.m.
Bismarck, N.D.	46	48	100	47	11:00 a.m.
Boise, Idaho	43	36	116	13	10:00 a.m.
Boston	42	21	71	5	12:00 noon
Buffalo, N.Y.	42	55	78	50	12:00 noon
Calgary, Alberta	51	1	114	1	10:00 a.m.
Carlsbad, N.M.	32	26	104	15	10:00 a.m.
Charleston, S.C.	32	47	79	56	12:00 noon
Charleston, W. Va.	38	21	81	38	12:00 noon
Charlotte, N.C.	35	14	80	50	12:00 noon
Cheyenne, Wyo.	41	9	104	52	10:00 a.m.
Chicago	41	50	87	37	11:00 a.m.
Cincinnati	39	8	84	30	12:00 noon
Cleveland	41	28	81	37	12:00 noon
Columbia, S.C.	34	0	81	2	12:00 noon
Columbus, Ohio	40	0	83	1	12:00 noon
Dallas	32	46	96	46	11:00 a.m.
Denver	39	45	105	0	10:00 a.m.
Des Moines, Iowa	41	35	93	37	11:00 a.m.
Detroit	42	20	83	3	12:00 noon
Dubuque, Iowa	42	31	90	40	11:00 a.m.
Duluth, Minn.	46	49	92	5	11:00 a.m.
Eastport, Me.	44	54	67	0	12:00 noon
El Centro, Calif.	32	38	115	33	9:00 a.m.
El Paso	31	46	106	29	10:00 a.m.
Eugene, Ore.	44	3	123	5	9:00 a.m.
Fargo, N.D.	46	52	96	48	11:00 a.m.
Flagstaff, Ariz.	35	13	111	41	10:00 a.m.
Fort Worth, Tex.	32	43	97	19	11:00 a.m.
Fresno, Calif.	36	44	119	48	9:00 a.m.
Grand Junction, Colo.	39	5	108	33	10:00 a.m.
Grand Rapids, Mich.	42	58	85	40	12:00 noon
Havre, Mont.	48	33	109	43	10:00 a.m.
Helena, Mont.	46	35	112	2	10:00 a.m.
Honolulu	21	18	157	50	7:00 a.m.
Hot Springs, Ark.	34	31	93	3	11:00 a.m.
Houston, Tex.	29	45	95	21	11:00 a.m.
Idaho Falls, Idaho	43	30	112	1	10:00 a.m.
Indianapolis	39	46	86	10	12:00 noon
Jackson, Miss.	32	20	90	12	11:00 a.m.
Jacksonville, Fla.	30	22	81	40	12:00 noon
Juneau, Alaska	58	18	134	24	8:00 a.m.
Kansas City, Mo.	39	6	94	35	11:00 a.m.
Key West, Fla.	24	33	81	48	12:00 noon
Kingston, Ont.	44	15	76	30	12:00 noon
Klamath Falls, Ore.	42	10	121	44	9:00 a.m.
Knoxville, Tenn.	35	57	83	56	12:00 noon
Las Vegas, Nev.	36	10	115	12	9:00 a.m.
Lewiston, Idaho	46	24	117	2	9:00 a.m.
Lincoln, Neb.	40	50	96	40	11:00 a.m.
London, Ont.	43	2	81	34	12:00 noon
Long Beach, Calif.	33	46	118	11	9:00 a.m.
Los Angeles	34	3	118	15	9:00 a.m.
Louisville, Ky.	38	15	85	46	12:00 noon
Manchester, N.H.	43	0	71	30	12:00 noon

City	Lat. °	Lat. '	Long. °	Long. '	Time
Memphis, Tenn	35	9	90	3	11:00 a.m.
Miami, Fla.	25	46	80	12	12:00 noon
Milwaukee	43	2	87	55	11:00 a.m.
Minneapolis	44	59	93	14	11:00 a.m.
Mobile, Ala.	30	42	88	3	11:00 a.m.
Montgomery, Ala.	32	21	86	18	11:00 a.m.
Montpelier, Vt.	44	15	72	32	12:00 noon
Montreal, Que.	45	30	73	35	12:00 noon
Moose Jaw, Sask.	50	37	105	31	10:00 a.m.
Nashville, Tenn.	36	10	86	47	11:00 a.m.
Nelson, B.C.	49	30	117	17	9:00 a.m.
Newark, N.J.	40	44	74	10	12:00 noon
New Haven, Conn.	41	19	72	55	12:00 noon
New Orleans	29	57	90	4	11:00 a.m.
New York	40	47	73	58	12:00 noon
Nome, Alaska	64	25	165	30	8:00 a.m.
Oakland, Calif.	37	48	122	16	9:00 a.m.
Oklahoma City	35	26	97	28	11:00 a.m.
Omaha, Neb.	41	15	95	56	11:00 a.m.
Ottawa, Ont.	45	24	75	43	12:00 noon
Philadelphia	39	57	75	10	12:00 noon
Phoenix, Ariz.	33	29	112	4	10:00 a.m.
Pierre, S.D.	44	22	100	21	11:00 a.m.
Pittsburgh	40	27	79	57	12:00 noon
Port Arthur, Ont.	48	30	89	17	12:00 noon
Portland, Me.	43	40	70	15	12:00 noon
Portland, Ore.	45	31	122	41	9:00 a.m.
Providence, R.I.	41	50	71	24	12:00 noon
Quebec, Que.	46	49	71	11	12:00 noon
Raleigh, N.C.	35	46	78	39	12:00 noon
Reno, Nev.	39	30	119	49	9:00 a.m.
Richfield, Utah	38	46	112	5	10:00 a.m.
Richmond, Va.	37	33	77	29	12:00 noon
Roanoke, Va.	37	17	79	57	12:00 noon
Sacramento, Calif.	38	35	121	30	9:00 a.m.
St. John, N.B.	45	18	66	10	1:00 p.m.
St. Louis	38	35	90	12	11:00 a.m.
Salt Lake City, Utah	40	46	111	54	10:00 a.m.
San Antonio	29	23	98	33	11:00 a.m.
San Diego, Calif.	32	42	117	10	9:00 a.m.
San Francisco	37	47	122	26	9:00 a.m.
San Jose, Calif.	37	20	121	53	9:00 a.m.
San Juan, P.R.	18	30	66	10	1:00 p.m.
Santa Fe, N.M.	35	41	105	57	10:00 a.m.
Savannah, Ga.	32	5	81	5	12:00 noon
Seattle	47	37	122	20	9:00 a.m.
Shreveport, La.	32	28	93	42	11:00 a.m.
Sioux Falls, S.D.	43	33	96	44	11:00 a.m.
Sitka, Alaska	57	10	135	15	9:00 a.m.
Spokane, Wash.	47	40	117	26	9:00 a.m.
Springfield, Ill.	39	48	89	38	11:00 a.m.
Springfield, Mass.	42	6	72	34	12:00 noon
Springfield, Mo.	37	13	93	17	11:00 a.m.
Syracuse, N.Y.	43	2	76	8	12:00 noon
Tampa, Fla.	27	57	82	27	12:00 noon
Toledo, Ohio	41	39	83	33	12:00 noon
Toronto, Ont.	43	40	79	24	12:00 noon
Tulsa, Okla.	36	09	95	59	11:00 a.m.
Victoria, B.C.	48	25	123	21	9:00 a.m.
Virginia Beach, Va.	36	51	75	58	12:00 noon
Washington, D.C.	38	53	77	02	12:00 noon
Wichita, Kan.	37	43	97	17	11:00 a.m.
Wilmington, N.C.	34	14	77	57	12:00 noon
Winnipeg, Man.	49	54	97	7	11:00 a.m.

Named Summits in the U.S. Over 14,000 Feet Above Sea Level

Name	State	Height	Name	State	Height	Name	State	Height
Mt. McKinley	Alaska	20,320	Castle Peak	Colo.	14,265	Mt. Eolus	Colo.	14,083
Mt. St. Elias	Alaska	18,008	Quandary Peak	Colo.	14,265	Windom Peak	Colo.	14,082
Mt. Foraker	Alaska	17,400	Mt. Evans	Colo.	14,264	Mt. Columbia	Colo.	14,073
Mt. Bona	Alaska	16,500	Longs Peak	Colo.	14,255	Mt. Augusta	Alaska	14,070
Mt. Blackburn	Alaska	16,390	Mt. Wilson	Colo.	14,246	Missouri Mtn.	Colo.	14,067
Mt. Sanford	Alaska	16,237	White Mtn.	Calif.	14,246	Humboldt Peak	Colo.	14,064
Mt. Vancouver	Alaska	15,979	North Palisade	Calif.	14,242	Mt. Bierstadt	Colo.	14,060
South Buttress	Alaska	15,885	Mt. Cameron	Colo.	14,238	Sunlight Peak	Colo.	14,059
Mt. Churchill	Alaska	15,638	Mt. Shavano	Colo.	14,229	Split Mtn.	Calif.	14,058
Mt. Fairweather	Alaska	15,300	Crestone Needle	Colo.	14,197	Handies Peak	Colo.	14,048
Mt. Hubbard	Alaska	14,950	Mt. Belford	Colo.	14,197	Culebra Peak	Colo.	14,047
Mt. Bear	Alaska	14,831	Mt. Princeton	Colo.	14,197	Mt. Lindsey	Colo.	14,042
East Buttress	Alaska	14,730	Mt. Yale	Colo.	14,196	Ellingwood Point	Colo.	14,042
Mt. Hunter	Alaska	14,573	Mt. Bross	Colo.	14,172	Little Bear Peak	Colo.	14,037
Browne Tower	Alaska	14,530	Kit Carson Mtn.	Colo.	14,165	Mt. Sherman	Colo.	14,036
Mt. Alverstone	Alaska	14,500	Mt. Wrangell	Alaska	14,163	Redcloud Peak	Colo.	14,034
Mt. Whitney	Calif.	14,494 [1]	Mt. Shasta	Calif.	14,162	Mt. Langley	Calif.	14,027
University Peak	Alaska	14,470	El Diente Peak	Colo.	14,159	Conundrum Peak	Colo.	14,022
Mt. Elbert	Colo.	14,433	Point Success	Wash.	14,158	Mt. Tyndall	Calif.	14,019
Mt. Massive	Colo.	14,421	Maroon Peak	Colo.	14,156	Pyramid Peak	Colo.	14,018
Mt. Harvard	Colo.	14,420	Tabeguache Mtn.	Colo.	14,155	Wilson Peak	Colo.	14,017
Mt. Rainier	Wash.	14,410	Mt. Oxford	Colo.	14,153	Wetterhorn Peak	Colo.	14,015
Mt. Williamson	Calif.	14,370	Mt. Sill	Calif.	14,153	North Maroon Peak	Colo.	14,014
La Plata Peak	Colo.	14,361	Mt. Sneffels	Colo.	14,150	San Luis Peak	Colo.	14,014
Blanca Peak	Colo.	14,345	Mt. Democrat	Colo.	14,148	Middle Palisade	Calif.	14,012
Uncompahgre Peak	Colo.	14,309	Capitol Peak	Colo.	14,130	Mt. Muir	Calif.	14,012
Crestone Peak	Colo.	14,294	Liberty Cap	Wash.	14,112	Mt. of the Holy Cross	Colo.	14,005
Mt. Lincoln	Colo.	14,286	Pikes Peak	Colo.	14,110	Huron Peak	Colo.	14,003
Grays Peak	Colo.	14,270	Snowmass Mtn.	Colo.	14,092	Thunderbolt Peak	Calif.	14,003
Mt. Antero	Colo.	14,269	Mt. Russell	Calif.	14,088	Sunshine Peak	Colo.	14,001
Torreys Peak	Colo.	14,267						

1. National Geodetic Survey. *Source:* Department of the Interior, U.S. Geological Survey.

Rivers of the United States

(350 or more miles long)

Alabama-Coosa (600 mi.; 966 km): From junction of Oostanula and Etowah R. in Georgia to Mobile R.

Altamaha-Ocmulgee (392 mi.; 631 km): From junction of Yellow R. and South R., Newton Co. in Georgia to Atlantic Ocean.

Apalachicola-Chattahoochee (524 mi.; 843 km): From Towns Co. in Georgia to Gulf of Mexico in Florida.

Arkansas (1,459 mi.; 2,348 km): From Lake Co. in Colorado to Mississippi R. in Arkansas.

Brazos (923 mi.; 1,490 km): From junction of Salt Fork and Double Mountain Fork in Texas to Gulf of Mexico.

Canadian (906 mi.; 1,458 km): From Las Animas Co. in Colorado to Arkansas R. in Oklahoma.

Cimarron (600 mi.; 966 km): From Colfax Co. in New Mexico to Arkansas R. in Oklahoma.

Colorado (1,450 mi.; 2,333 km): From Rocky Mountain National Park in Colorado to Gulf of California in Mexico.

Colorado (862 mi.; 1,387 km): From Dawson Co. in Texas to Matagorda Bay.

Columbia (1,243 mi.; 2,000 km): From Columbia Lake in British Columbia to Pacific Ocean (entering between Oregon and Washington).

Colville (350 mi.; 563 km): From Brooks Range in Alaska to Beaufort Sea.

Connecticut (407 mi.; 655 km): From Third Connecticut Lake in New Hampshire to Long Island Sound in Connecticut.

Cumberland (720 mi.; 1,159 km): From junction of Poor and Clover Forks in Harlan Co. in Kentucky to Ohio R.

Delaware (390 mi.; 628 km): From Schoharie Co. in New York to Liston Point, Delaware Bay.

Gila (649 mi.; 1,044 km): From Catron Co. in New Mexico to Colorado R. in Arizona.

Green (360 mi.; 579 km): From Lincoln Co. in Kentucky to Ohio R. in Kentucky.

Green (730 mi.; 1,175 km): From Sublette Co. in Wyoming to Colorado R. in Utah.

Illinois (420 mi.; 676 km): From St. Joseph Co. in Indiana to Mississippi R. at Grafton in Illinois.

James (sometimes called *Dakota*) (710 mi.; 1,143 km): From Wells Co. in North Dakota to Missouri R. in South Dakota.

Kanawha-New (352 mi.; 566 km): From junction of North and South Forks of New R. in North Carolina, through Virginia and West Virginia (New River becoming Kanawha River), to Ohio River.

Kansas (743 mi.; 1,196 km): From source of Arikaree R. in Elbert Co., Colorado, to Missouri R. at Kansas City, Kansas.

Koyukuk (470 mi.; 756 km): From Brooks Range in Alaska to Yukon R.

Kuskokwim (724 mi.; 1,165 km): From Alaska Range in Alaska to Kuskokwim Bay.

Licking (350 mi.; 563 km): From Magoffin Co. in Kentucky to Ohio R. at Cincinnati in Ohio.

Little Missouri (560 mi.; 901 km): From Crook Co. in Wyoming to Missouri R. in North Dakota.

Milk (625 mi.; 1,006 km): From junction of forks in Alberta Province to Missouri R.

Mississippi (2,340 mi.; 3,766 km): From Lake Itasca in Minnesota to mouth of Southwest Pass in La.

Coastline of the United States

State	Lengths, statute miles General coastline[1]	Lengths, statute miles Tidal shoreline[2]	State	Lengths, statute miles General coastline[1]	Lengths, statute miles Tidal shoreline[2]
Atlantic Coast:			**Gulf Coast:**		
Maine	228	3,478	Florida (Gulf)	770	5,095
New Hampshire	13	131	Alabama	53	607
Massachusetts	192	1,519	Mississippi	44	359
Rhode Island	40	384	Louisiana	397	7,721
Connecticut	—	618	Texas	367	3,359
New York	127	1,850	Total Gulf coast	1,631	17,141
New Jersey	130	1,792	**Pacific Coast:**		
Pennsylvania	—	89	California	840	3,427
Delaware	28	381	Oregon	296	1,410
Maryland	31	3,190	Washington	157	3,026
Virginia	112	3,315	Hawaii	750	1,052
North Carolina	301	3,375	Alaska (Pacific)	5,580	31,383
South Carolina	187	2,876	Total Pacific coast	7,623	40,298
Georgia	100	2,344	**Arctic Coast:**		
Florida (Atlantic)	580	3,331	Alaska (Arctic)	1,060	2,521
Total Atlantic coast	2,069	28,673	Total Arctic coast	1,060	2,521
			States Total	**12,383**	**88,633**

1. Figures are lengths of general outline of seacoast. Measurements made with unit measure of 30 minutes of latitude on charts as near scale of 1:1,200,000 as possible. Coastline of bays and sounds is included to point where they narrow to width of unit measure, and distance across at such point is included. 2. Figures obtained in 1939–40 with recording instrument on largest–scale maps and charts then available. Shoreline of outer coast, offshore islands, sounds, bays, rivers, and creeks is included to head of tidewater, or to point where tidal waters narrow to width of 100 feet. *Source:* Department of Commerce, National Oceanic and Atmospheric Administration, National Ocean Service.

Mississippi-Missouri-Red Rock (3,710 mi.; 5,970 km): From source of Red Rock R. in Montana to mouth of Southwest Pass in Louisiana.

Missouri (2,315 mi.; 3,726 km): From junction of Jefferson R., Gallatin R., and Madison R. in Montana to Mississippi R. near St. Louis.

Missouri-Red Rock (2,540 mi.; 4,090 km): From source of Red Rock R. in Montana to Mississippi R. near St. Louis.

Mobile-Alabama-Coosa (645 mi.; 1,040 km): From junction of Etowah R. and Oostanula R. in Georgia to Mobile Bay.

Neosho (460 mi.; 740 km): From Morris Co. in Kansas to Arkansas R. in Oklahoma.

Niobrara (431 mi.; 694 km): From Niobrara Co. in Wyoming to Missouri R. in Nebraska.

Noatak (350 mi.; 563 km): From Brooks Range in Alaska to Kotzebue Sound.

North Canadian (800 mi.; 1,290 km): From Union Co. in New Mexico to Canadian R. in Oklahoma.

North Platte (618 mi.; 995 km): From Jackson Co. in Colorado to junction with So. Platte R. in Nebraska to form Platte R.

Ohio (981 mi.; 1,579 km): From junction of Allegheny R. and Monongahela R. at Pittsburgh to Mississippi R. between Illinois and Kentucky.

Ohio-Allegheny (1,306 mi.; 2,102 km): From Potter Co. in Pennsylvania to Mississippi R. at Cairo in Illinois.

Osage (500 mi.; 805 km): From east-central Kansas to Missouri R. near Jefferson City in Missouri.

Ouachita (605 mi.; 974 km): From Polk Co. in Arkansas to Red R. in Louisiana.

Pearl (411 mi.; 661 km): From Neshoba County in Mississippi to Gulf of Mexico (Mississippi-Louisiana).

Pecos (926 mi.; 1,490 km): From Mora Co. in New Mexico to Rio Grande in Texas.

Pee Dee-Yadkin (435 mi.; 700 km): From Watauga Co. in North Carolina to Winyah Bay in South Carolina.

Pend Oreille-Clark Fork (531 mi.; 855 km): Near Butte in Montana to Columbia R. on Washington-Canada border.

Platte (990 mi.; 1,593 km) From source of Grizzly Creek in Jackson Co., Colorado, to Missouri R. south of Omaha, Nebraska.

Porcupine (569 mi.; 916 km): From Yukon Territory, Canada, to Yukon R. in Alaska.

Potomac (383 mi.; 616 km): From Garrett Co. in Md. to Chesapeake Bay at Point Lookout in Md.

Powder (375 mi.; 603 km): From junction of forks in Johnson Co. in Wyoming to Yellowstone R. in Montana.

Red (1,290 mi.; 2,080 km): From source of Tierra Blanca Creek in Curry County, New Mexico to Mississippi R. in Louisiana.

Red (also called *Red River of the North*) (545 mi.; 877 km): From junction of Otter Tail R. and Bois de Sioux R. in Minnesota to Lake Winnipeg in Manitoba.

Republican (445 mi.; 716 km): From junction of North Fork and Arikaree R. in Nebraska to junction with Smoky Hill R. in Kansas to form the Kansas R.

Rio Grande (1,900 mi.; 3,060 km): From San Juan Co. in Colorado to Gulf of Mexico.

Roanoke (380 mi.; 612 km): From junction of forks in Montgomery Co. in Virginia to Albemarle Sound in North Carolina.

Sabine (380 mi.; 612 km): From junction of forks in Hunt Co. in Texas to Sabine Lake between Texas and Louisiana.

Sacramento (377 mi.; 607 km): From Siskiyou Co. in California to Suisun Bay.

Saint Francis (425 mi.; 684 km): From Iron Co. in Missouri to Mississippi R. in Arkansas.

Salmon (420 mi.; 676 km): From Custer Co. in Idaho to Snake R.

San Joaquin (350 mi.; 563 km): From junction of forks in Madera Co. in California to Suisun Bay.

San Juan (360 mi.; 579 km): From Archuleta Co. in Colorado to Colorado R. in Utah.

Santee-Wateree-Catawba (538 mi.; 866 km): From McDowell Co. in North Carolina to Atlantic Ocean in South Carolina.

Smoky Hill (540 mi.; 869 km): From Cheyenne Co. in Colorado to junction with Republican R. in Kansas to form Kansas R.

Snake (1,038 mi.; 1,670 km): From Ocean Plateau in Wyoming to Columbia R. in Washington.
South Platte (424 mi.; 682 km): From Park Co. in Colorado to junction with North Platte R. in Nebraska to form Platte R.
Stikine (379 mi.; 610 km) From British Columbia in Canada to Stikine Strait near Wrangell, Alaska.
Susquehanna (444 mi.; 715 km): From Otsego Lake in New York to Chesapeake Bay in Maryland.
Tanana (659 mi.; 1,060 km): From Wrangell Mts. in Yukon Territory, Canada, to Yukon R. in Alaska.
Tennessee (652 mi.; 1,049 km): From junction of Holston R. and French Broad R. in Tennessee to Ohio R. in Kentucky.
Tennessee-French Broad (886 mi.; 1,417 km): From Transylvania Co. in North Carolina to Ohio R. at Paducah in Kentucky.

Tombigbee (525 mil; 845 km): From junction of forks in Itawamba Co. in Mississippi to Mobile R. in Alabama.
Trinity (360 mi.; 579 km): From junction of forks in Dallas Co. in Texas to Galveston Bay.
Wabash (512 mi.; 824 km): From Darke Co. in Ohio to Ohio R. between Illinois and Indiana.
Washita (500 mi.; 805 km): From Hemphill Co. in Texas to Red R. in Oklahoma.
White (722 mi.; 1,160 km): From Madison Co. in Arkansas to Mississippi R.
Wisconsin (430 mi.; 692 km): From Vilas Co. in Wisconsin to Mississippi R.
Yellowstone (692 mi.; 1,110 km): From Park Co. in Wyoming to Missouri R. in North Dakota.
Yukon (1,979 mi.; 3,185 km): From source of McNeil R. in Yukon Territory, Canada, to Bering Sea in Alaska.

Geysers in The United States

Geysers are natural hot springs that intermittently eject a column of water and steam into the air. They exist in many parts of the volcanic regions of the world such as Japan and South America but their greatest development is in Iceland, New Zealand, and Yellowstone National Park.

There are 120 named geysers in Yellowstone National Park, Wyoming, and perhaps half that numebr unnamed. Most of the geysers and the 4,000 or more hot springs are located in the western portion of the park. The most important are the following:

Norris Geyser Basin has 24 or more active geysers; the number varies. There are scores of steam vents and hot springs. *Valentine* is highest, erupting 50–75 ft at intervals varying from 18 hr to 3 days or more. *Minuté* erupts 15–20 ft high, several hours aprt. Others include *Steamboat, Fearless, Veteran, Vixen, Corporal, Whirligig, Little Whirligig,* and *Pinwheel.*

Lower Geyser Basin has at least 18 active geysers. *Fountain* throws water 50–75 ft in all directions at unpredictable intervals. *Clepsydra* erupts violently from four vents up to 30 ft. *Great Fountain* plays every 8 to 15 hr in spurts from 30 to 90 ft high.

Midway Geyser Basin has vast steaming terraces of red, orange, pink and other colors; there are pools and springs, including the beautiful *Grand Prismatic Spring. Excelsior* crater discharges boiling water into Firehole River at the rate of 6 cu ft per second.

Giant erupts up to 200 ft at intervals of 2 1/2 days to 3 mo; eruptions last about 1 1/2 hr. *Daisy* sends water up to 75 ft but is irregular and frequently inactive.

Old Faithful sends up a column varying from 116 to 175 ft at intervals of about 65 min, varying from 33 to 90 min. Eruptions last about 4 min, during which time about 12,000 gal are discharged.

Giantess seldom erupts, but during its active period sends up streams 150–200 ft.

Lion Group: *Lion* plays up to 60 ft every 2–4 days when active; *Little Cub* up to 10 ft every 1–2 hr. *Big Cub* and *Lioness* seldom erupt.

Mammoth Hot Springs: There are no geysers in this area. The formation is travertine. Sides of a hill are steps and terraces over which flow the steaming waters of hot springs laden with minerals. Each step is tinted by algae to many shades of orange, pink, yellow, brown, green, and blue. Terraces are white where no water flows.

One Lake or Two?

It is a widely accepted fact that Lake Superior, with an area of 31,820 square miles is the world's largest freshwater lake. However this fact is based on an historical inaccuracy in the naming of Lake Huron and Lake Michigan. What should have been considered one body of water, Lake Michigan-Huron with an area of 45,410 square miles, was mistakenly given two names, one for each lobe. The explorers in colonial times incorrectly believed each lobe to be a separate lake because of its great size.

Why should the two lakes be considered one? The Huron Lobe and the Michigan Lobe are at the same elevation and are connected by the 120-foot deep Mackinac Strait, also at the same elevation. Lakes are separated from each other by streams and rivers. The Strait of Mackinac is not a river. It is 3.6 to 5 miles wide, wider than most lakes are long. In essence, it is just a narrowing, not a separation of the two lobes of Lake Michigan-Huron.

The flow between the two lakes can reverse. Because of the large connecting channel, the two can equalize rapidly whenever a water level imbalance occurs. Gage records for the lakes clearly show them to have identical water level regimes and mean long-term behavior; that is, Lake Michigan and Lake Huron act as one lake for many purposes. Hydrologically they are considered one lake.

Historical names are not easily changed. The separate names for the lake are a part of history and are also legally institutionalized since Lake Michigan is treated as American and Lake Huron is bisected by the international boundary between the United States and Canada.

Of all the world's freshwater lakes, North America's Great Lakes are unique. Their five basins combine to form a single watershed with one common outlet to the ocean. The total volume of the lakes is about 5,475 cubic miles, more than 6,000 trillion gallons.

The Great Lakes are: Superior with an area of 31,820 square miles (82,414 km) shared by the United States and Canada; Huron with an area of 23,010 square miles (59,596 sq km) shared by the United States and Canada; Michigan with an area of 22,400 square miles (58,016 sq km) entirely in the United States; Erie with an area of 9,930 square miles (25,719 km) shared by the United States and Canada; and Ontario with an area of 7,520 square miles (19,477 km) shared by the United States and Canada.

The United States also has another large lake, Great Salt Lake in Utah with an area of 1,800 square miles (4,662 sq km). However it is not a freshwater lake.

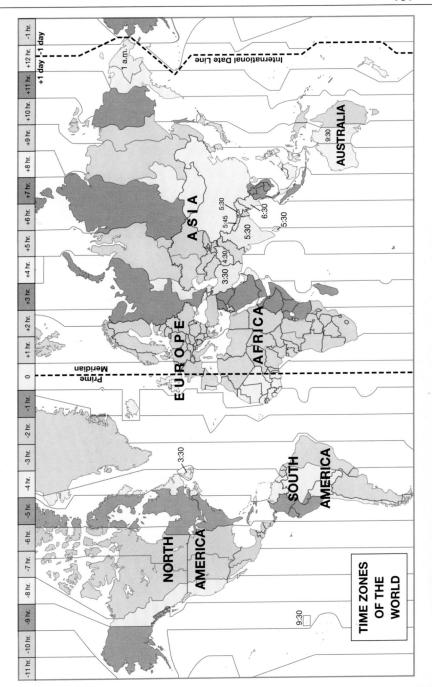

TIME ZONES
OF THE WORLD

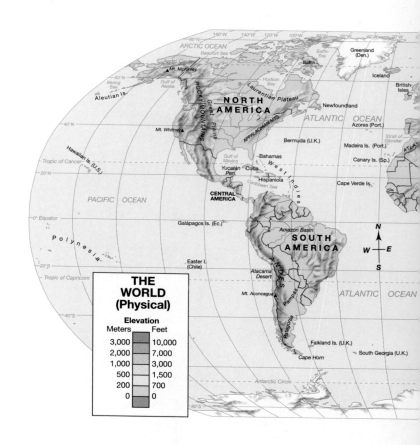

THE WORLD (Physical)

Elevation

Meters		Feet
3,000		10,000
2,000		7,000
1,000		3,000
500		1,500
200		700
0		0

ARCTIC OCEAN

Svalbard (Nor.) Novaya Zemlya

EUROPE

Siberia

ASIA

Sea of Okhotsk

Kamchatka Pen.

CARPATHIANS

CAUCASUS

Black Sea

Gobi Desert

Sea of Japan

Japan

Mt. Fuji

URAL MTS.

Balkan Pen.

Mt. Ararat

Mt. Damavand

Plateau of Tibet

PACIFIC OCEAN

Mediterranean Sea

HIMALAYAS

Mt. Everest

S a h a r a

Arabian Desert

Thar Desert

Taiwan

Arabian Sea

Deccan Plateau

Bay of Bengal

Hainan

D e s e r t

AFRICA

Sri Lanka

South China Sea

Philippine Is.

Micronesia

Maldives

Malay Pen.

Congo Basin

Mt. Kilimanjaro

Borneo

Java

Indonesia

New Guinea

Melanesia

Great Barrier Reef

Seychelles

Comoros

Great Rift Valley

Madagascar

Mauritius

INDIAN OCEAN

Sumatra

Great Sandy Desert

AUSTRALIA

Kalahari Desert

Nullarbor Plain

New Zealand

Cape of Good Hope

Tasmania

Kerguelen (Fr.)

0   1500   3000 Miles

0   1500   3000 Kilometers

Robinson Projection
1: 191,600,000

ANTARCTICA

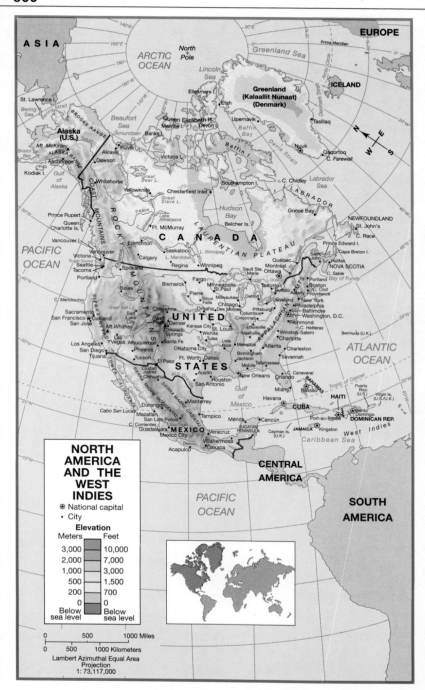

NORTH AMERICA AND THE WEST INDIES

⊗ National capital
• City

Elevation

Meters		Feet
3,000		10,000
2,000		7,000
1,000		3,000
500		1,500
200		700
0		0
Below sea level		Below sea level

```
0        500      1000 Miles
0    500      1000 Kilometers
```

Lambert Azimuthal Equal Area
Projection
1: 73,117,000

501

A D A

Minnesota
Duluth
Superior
St. Paul
Minneapolis
Green Bay
Eau Claire
Rochester
Wisconsin
Madison
Milwaukee
Kenosha
Lansing
Grand Rapids
Flint
Detroit
Sault Ste. Marie
Lake Superior
Michigan
Lake Huron
Lake Michigan
L. Ontario

Sioux City
Iowa
Cedar Rapids
Rockford
Chicago
Ann Arbor
Toledo
Gary
Fort Wayne
Ohio
L. Erie
Cleveland
Akron
Erie

Omaha
Des Moines
Illinois
Champaign
Springfield
Indianapolis
Indiana
Muncie
Springfield
Dayton
Cincinnati
Clarksburg
W. Va.
Wheeling
Pittsburgh

Topeka
Kansas City
Jefferson City
Missouri
Springfield
St. Louis
Louisville
Frankfort
Charleston
Lexington
Kentucky
Bowling Green
Knoxville
Nashville
Chattanooga
Tennessee

Tulsa
Arkansas
Fort Smith
Little Rock
Memphis
Birmingham
Alabama
Montgomery

Dallas
Shreveport
Mississippi
Jackson
Louisiana
Mobile
Pensacola
Baton Rouge
New Orleans
Port Arthur
Houston
Galveston

Rochester
Syracuse
Buffalo
New York
Albany
Pennsylvania
Reading
Harrisburg
Baltimore
Newark
Trenton
New Jersey
Philadelphia
Atlantic City
Delaware
Md.
Annapolis
Washington, D.C.
Dover
Virginia
Richmond
Lynchburg
Williamsburg
Norfolk
Virginia Beach
Chesapeake Bay
Winston-Salem
Durham
Raleigh
North Carolina
Charlotte
Wilmington
Columbia
South Carolina
Augusta
Charleston
Athens
Atlanta
Georgia
Macon
Savannah
Albany

Montpelier
Vt.
N.H.
Manchester
Concord
Portland
Portsmouth
Boston
Worcester
Mass.
Hartford
Conn.
Providence
R.I.
New Haven
New York
Long Island
Augusta
Mt. Washington
Maine
Gulf of Maine
L. Champlain

APPALACHIAN MTS.

ATLANTIC OCEAN

Cape Cod
Cape Hatteras

Jacksonville
St. Augustine
Daytona Beach
Tallahassee
Florida
Orlando
Cape Canaveral
Tampa
St. Petersburg
L. Okeechobee
Fort Lauderdale
Miami

Gulf of Mexico

Florida Keys
Straits of Florida
CUBA
BAHAMAS

N
W E
S

0   200   400 Miles
0   200   400 Kilometers
Albers Equal-Area Projection
1: 26,044,000

UNITED STATES
⊗ National capital
★ State capital
● City

Elevation
Meters		Feet
3,000		10,000
2,000		7,000
1,000		3,000
500		1,500
200		700
0		0

CENTRAL AMERICA

⊛ National capital
• City

Elevation

Meters	Feet
3,000	10,000
2,000	7,000
1,000	3,000
500	1,500
200	700
0	0

MEXICO

PACIFIC OCEAN

Gulf of Honduras

BELIZE
Belmopan ⊛

GUATEMALA
Cobán •
Quezaltenango ⊛
Guatemala City ⊛
San José •

EL SALVADOR
San Salvador ⊛
San Miguel •

HONDURAS
La Ceiba •
Tegucigalpa ⊛

Bay Is. (Hon.)

Is. Santanilla (Hon.)

C. Gracias a Dios

M O S Q U I T O   C O A S T

NICARAGUA
León •
Managua ⊛
Granada •
L. Managua
L. Nicaragua
Bluefields •

Providencia (Col.)

San Andrés (Col.)

Caribbean Sea

COSTA RICA
Puntarenas •
San José ⊛
Limón •
Golfito •
David •

PANAMA
Colón •
Panamá City ⊛
Panama Canal
Gulf of Panama

COLOMBIA

N
E
S
W

100 Miles
50
0

100 Kilometers
50
0

Chamberlin Trimetric Projection
1 : 12,500,000

80°W

85°W

90°W

15°N

10°N

SOUTH AMERICA

⊛ National capital
• City

Elevation

Meters		Feet
3,000		10,000
2,000		7,000
1,000		3,000
500		1,500
200		700
0		0

Lambert Azimuthal
Equal-Area Projection
1: 43,697,000

WESTERN EUROPE

⊛ National capital
• City

Elevation

Meters		Feet
3,000		10,000
2,000		7,000
1,000		3,000
500		1,500
200		700
0		0

0   200   400 Miles
0   200   400 Kilometers

Azimuthal Equal-Area Projection
1: 31,019,000

EASTERN EUROPE

⊛ National capital
• City

Elevation

Meters	Feet
3,000	10,000
2,000	7,000
1,000	3,000
500	1,500
200	700
0	0

Norwegian Sea
Barents Sea
Kolguyev I.
Cheshskaya Bay
C. Kanin
70°N
Murmansk
KOLA PENINSULA
Bay of Mezen
Arctic Circle
White Sea
Archangel
N. Dvina
Lake Onega
URAL MOUNTAINS
Perm
60°N
Lake Ladoga
RUSSIA
Izhevsk
Gulf of Finland
St. Petersburg
Tallinn
ESTONIA
Novgorod
Rybinsk Res.
Ufa
Tartu
Lake Peipus
Lake Il'men
Yaroslavl
Kazan
Tver
Nizhny Novgorod
Kuybyshev Res.
Riga
Liepaja
LATVIA
Moscow
Samara
Daugavpils
Smolensk
Ryazan
Ural
LITHUANIA
Vitsyebsk
Kaunas
Saratov
Kaliningrad
RUSSIA
Vilnius
Minsk
Mahilyow
Volgograd Res.
Gdansk
Hrodna
Babruysk
WESTERN EUROPE
Szczecin
POLAND
BELARUS
Homyel
Belgorod
Voronezh
Volgograd
Poznan
Warsaw
Lodz
Kiev
Kharkiv
Astrakhan
Wroclaw
Cracow
UKRAINE
Dnieper
Kremenchug Res.
Luhansk
Tsimlyansk Res.
CZECH REP.
Prague
Olomouc
Ostrava
Lviv
Don
Rostov-na-Donu
Caspian Sea
Plzen
Brno
SLOVAKIA
Vinnytsya
Dnipropetrovsk
Donetsk
Danube
Bratislava
Kosice
Miskolc
CARPATHIAN MTS.
Zaporizhya
Mariupol
L. Manych-Gudilo
HUNGARY
Gyor
Budapest
Debrecen
Cluj-Napoca
Balti
MOLDOVA
Kakhovka Res.
Sea of Azov
Krasnodar
Groznyy
Makhachkala
SLOVENIA
Maribor
Szeged
Timisoara
ROMANIA
Iasi
Tighina
Chisinau
Tiraspol
Odesa
CRIMEA
Simferopol
CAUCASUS MOUNTAINS
Ljubljana
Pecs
TRANSYLVANIAN ALPS
Galati
Sevastopol
Sukhumi
GEORGIA
Tbilisi
Sumqayit
Rijeka
Zagreb
Novi Sad
Bucharest
Constanta
Black Sea
Kutaisi
Ganca
Baku
CROATIA
Osijek
Belgrade
Ruse
Batumi
ARMENIA
AZERBAIJAN
Banja Luka
YUGOSLAVIA
Drava
Sava
BOSNIA & HERCEG.
Nis
BALKAN MTS.
Varna
Gyumri
AZER.
Split
Mostar
Sarajevo
Pristina
Sofia
BULGARIA
Burgas
Plovdiv
Yerevan
Dubrovnik
Podgorica
Skopje
MACEDONIA
TURKEY
Istanbul
Tirane
ALBANIA
Bosporus
Sea of Marmara
ASIA
Thessaloniki
Dardanelles
Adriatic Sea
Larissa
Mt. Olympus
Ionian Sea
GREECE
Aegean Sea
40°N
Patras
Athens
Corinth
Piraeus
C. Akritas
C. Matapan
Sea of Crete
Rhodes (Gr.)
Heraklion
Crete (Gr.)
Mediterranean Sea
30°N
AFRICA
0   200   400 Miles
0   200   400 Kilometers
Azimuthal Equal-Area Projection
1: 31,019,000
10°E 20°E 30°E 40°E 50°E 60°E 70°E

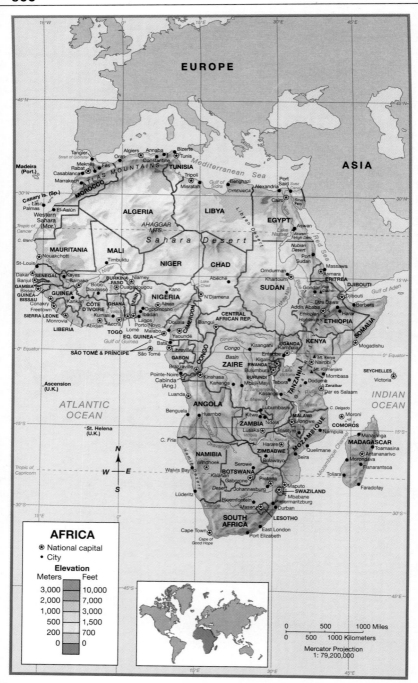

AFRICA

⊗ National capital
• City

Elevation

Meters	Feet
3,000	10,000
2,000	7,000
1,000	3,000
500	1,500
200	700
0	0

| 0 | 500 | 1000 Miles |
| 0 | 500 | 1000 Kilometers |

Mercator Projection
1: 79,200,000

NEAR AND
MIDDLE EAST

⊛ National capital
● City

Elevation
Meters | Feet
4,000 | 13,000
3,000 | 10,000
2,000 | 7,000
1,000 | 3,000
500 | 1,500
200 | 700
0 | 0

500 Miles

0   250   500 Kilometers

Albers Equal-Area Projection
1: 38,940,000

EUROPE

ASIA

AFRICA

Black Sea

Caspian Sea

Aral Sea

Mediterranean Sea

Red Sea

Arabian Sea

Persian Gulf

Gulf of Oman

Gulf of Aden

TURKEY
GEORGIA
ARMENIA
AZERBAIJAN
UZBEKISTAN
TURKMENISTAN
TAJIKISTAN
AFGHANISTAN
PAKISTAN
IRAN
IRAQ
SYRIA
LEBANON
ISRAEL
JORDAN
CYPRUS
EGYPT
SAUDI ARABIA
KUWAIT
BAHRAIN
QATAR
UNITED ARAB EMIRATES
OMAN
YEMEN

Qizilkum Desert
Garagum Desert
HINDU KUSH
CAUCASUS MTS.
PONTIC MTS.
TAURUS MTS.
ELBURZ MTS.
ZAGROS MTS.
KURDISTAN
MESOPOTAMIA
Syrian Desert
HEJAZ
ASIR
TUWAYQ MTS.
Rub 'al-Khali Desert
Arabian Desert
Libyan Desert

N
W   E
S

ASIA

⊕ National capital
• City
〰 Great Wall of China

Elevation

Meters	Feet
6,000	19,000
3,000	10,000
2,000	7,000
1,000	3,000
500	1,500
200	700
0	0

0   500   1000 Miles
0   500   1000 Kilometers

Lambert Azimuthal Equal-Area
Projection
1:61,016,000

OCEANIA

⊛ National capital
• City

Elevation

Meters	Feet
3,000	10,000
2,000	7,000
1,000	3,000
500	1,500
200	700
0	0

0   500   1,000 Miles
0   500 1,000 Kilometers

Mercator Projection
1: 58,400,000

THE YEAR IN PICTURES

SWEARING IN—Newt Gingrich takes the oath of office as House Speaker of the 104th Congress.

STATE OF THE UNION—President Clinton acknowledges the crowd during his address as Vice President Gore and House Speaker Gingrich look on.

513

EARTHQUAKE—Fire follows a powerful predawn earthquake in Kobe, Japan.

TUMBLING DOWN—The six-story Mitsubishi Bank in Kobe stands in ruins following the quake that claimed more than 2,000 lives.

AWASH—The church square in Givet, France, is a victim of record flood in the area when the Meuse River overflows its banks.

EVACUATION—Guerneville, California, residents line up to board a helicopter for evacuation from flooded area pounded by powerful Pacific storms.

THE TRIAL—O.J. Simpson sitting with his attorneys Johnnie Cochran, Jr., foreground, and Robert Shapiro, background.

WITNESS—Former Los Angeles police detective Mark Fuhrman invokes his Fifth Amendment rights during testimony at the Simpson trial.

FIGHTERS—Heavily armed Chechen volunteers make their way past a burning gas pipeline on the streets of Grozny, preparing to face Russian forces in the city.

BOMBED—Rescue personnel converge on the bomb-damaged Alfred Murrah Federal Building in Oklahoma City, following the worst act of terrorism in U.S. history.

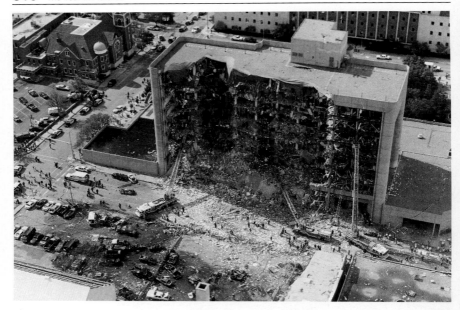

AFTERMATH—The north side of the federal building in Oklahoma City is missing in the wake of the car bomb explosion.

SUSPECT—Oklahoma City bombing suspect Timothy McVeigh is escorted from the Noble County courthouse in Perry, Okla.

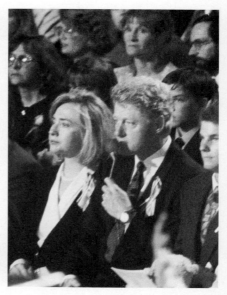

HEALING—President Clinton and the first lady join in the Time for Healing prayer service in Oklahoma City.

GASSED—A subway passenger is escorted by policemen at Tokyo's Akasaka Station as it was filled by toxic fumes. Eight people died and 4,700 injured in the rush hour terrorist attack.

REMEMBERING SELMA—Southern Christian Leadership Conference President Joseph Lowery, center, holds hands with former Alabama Governor George C. Wallace, at a rally marking the 30th anniversary of the Selma to Montgomery voting rights march.

U.N. AT FIFTY—United Nations Secretary–General Boutros Boutros-Ghali speaks at a forum in San Francisco in honor of the 50th anniversary of the founding of the U.N.

V–E DAY—President Clinton places a wreath at the Tomb of the Unknown Soldier in Arlington National Cemetery to mark the 50th anniversary of V–E Day.

CELEBRATION—Russian World War II veterans applaud during a veterans parade in Moscow's Red Square in celebration of the 50th anniversary of V–E Day.

KOREAN WAR MEMORIAL—South Korean President Kim Young-sam and President Clinton tour the Korean War Veterans Memorial in Washington prior to the dedication ceremony.

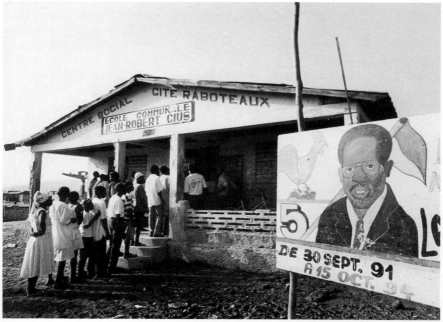

ELECTION DAY—Haitian voters line up to cast their ballots in the legislative and local elections at the polling station in Gonaives.

IWO JIMA REMEMBERED—President Clinton speaks at the Marine Corps War Memorial in Arlington, Va., paying tribute to a 50-year-old battle that turned the tide in the Pacific in World War II.

APOLOGY—Japanese Prime Minister Tomiichi Murayama expresses his feelings of deep remorse and apology as the country marks the 50th anniversary of the end of World War II.

GUILTY—Susan Smith is escorted from the Union County courthouse after a jury delivered a sentence of life in prison for the drowning of her two sons.

PASSING OF A LEGEND—New York Yankee slugger Mickey Mantle mirrors a painting of himself as a player in his restaurant in New York City. He died August 13, 1995, from liver cancer.

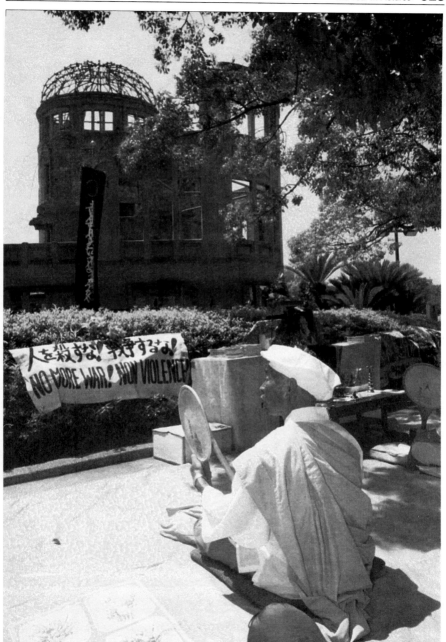

REMEMBERING THE BOMB—A Japanese Buddhist monk prays in front of Hiroshima's A–Bomb Dome at Peace Memorial Park marking the 50th anniversary of the dropping of the bomb.

BETTER LATE THAN NEVER—Seventy-seven years after his final season, Paul Robeson, the first black to win back-to-back All-American honors, was inducted into the College Hall of Fame.

COMEBACK—Monica Seles returns to competition after more than two years away from the court as a result of a stabbing mid-match in 1993. She celebrates after defeating Jana Novotna.

WRECK—Rescuers comb the wreckage of two passenger trains that collided near Firozabad, India, in which 300 people died and 500 were injured.

FIRST LADY—Hillary Rodham Clinton addresses a panel on women's health and security at the U.N. Women's Conference in Beijing, China.

FREE—Human rights activist Harry Wu holds up a yellow ribbon which he cut down from his hometown city hall in Milpitas, Calif., to celebrate.

TOGETHER IN SPACE—The combined crews of the space shuttle *Atlantis* and the Russian Space station *Mir* group together for a traditional in-flight portrait while docked for five days.

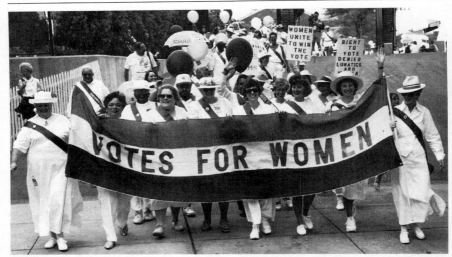

WOMEN'S SUFFRAGE—In celebration of the 75th anniversary of the passage of the constitutional amendment giving women the right to vote, people parade on the grounds of the Connecticut Tennis Center in New Haven.

BOMBED—Smoke rises from an ammunition dump in Bosnian Serb stronghold of Pale after NATO air strikes undertaken to eliminate threats to U.N. safe zones.

CROSSWORD PUZZLE GUIDE

First Aid to Crossword Puzzlers

We cannot begin to list all the odd words you will meet with in your daily and Sunday crossword puzzles, for such words run into many thousands. But we have tried to include those that turn up most frequently, as well as many others that should be of help to you when you are unable to go any further.

Also, we do not guarantee that the definitions in your puzzle will be exactly the same as ours, although we have checked every word with a standard dictionary and have followed its definition.

In nearly every case, we have used as the key word the principal noun of the definition, rather than any adjective, adjective phrase, or noun used as an adjective. And, to simplify your searching, we have grouped the words according to the number of spaces you have to fill.

For a list of Foreign Phrases, see Index. For Rulers of England and Great Britain, France, Germany and Prussia, and Russia, see Countries of the World.

Words of Two Letters

Ambary, DA
And (French, Latin), ET
Article (Arabic), AL
  (French), LA, LE, UN
  (Spanish), EL, LA, UN
At the (French), AU
  (Spanish), AL
Behold, LO
Bird: Hawaiian, OO
Birthplace: Abraham's, UR
Bone, OS
Buddha, FO
Butterfly: Peacock, IO
Champagne, AY
Chaos, NU
Chief: Burmese, BO
Coin: Roman, AS
  Siamese, AT
Concerning, RE
Dialect: Chinese, WU
Double (Egy. relig.), KA
Drama: Japanese, NO
Egg (comb. form), OO
Esker, OS
Eye (Scotch), EE
Factor: Amplification, MU
Fifty (Greek), NU
Fish: Carplike, ID
Force, OD
Forty (Greek), MU
From (French, Latin, Spanish), DE

(Latin prefix), AB
From the (French), DU
God: Babylonian, EA, ZU
  Egyptian sun, RA
  Hindu unknown, KA
  Semitic, EL
Goddess: Babylonian, AI
  Greek earth, GE
Gold (heraldry), OR
Gulf: Arctic, OB
Heart (Egy. relig.), AB
Indian: South American, GE
King: Of Bashan, OG
Language: Artificial, RO
  Assamese, AO
Lava: Hawaiian, AA
Letter: Greek, MU, NU, PI, XI
  Hebrew, HE, PE
Lily: Palm, TI
Measure: Annamese, LY
  Chinese, HO, HU, KO, LI, MU, PU, TO, TU
  Japanese, GO, JO, MO, RI, SE, TO
  Metric land, AR
  Netherlands, EL
  Portuguese, PE
  Siamese, WA
  Swedish, AM
  Type, EM, EN
Monk: Buddhist, BO
Month: Jewish, AB

Mouth, OS
Mulberry: Indian, AL
Native: Burmese, WA
Note: Of Scale, DO, FA, MI, LA, RE, TI
Of (French, Latin, Spanish), DE
Of the (French), DU
One (Scotch), AE
Pagoda: Chinese, TA
Plant: East Indian fiber, DA
Ridge: Sandy, AS, OS
River: Russian, OB
Sloth: Three-toed, AI
Soul (Egy. relig.), BA
Sound: Hindu mystic, OM
Suffix: Comparative, ER
The. See Article
To the: French, AU
  Spanish, AL
Tree: Buddhist sacred, BO
Tribe: Assamese, AO
Type: Jumbled, PI
Weight: Annamese, TA
  Chinese, LI
  Danish, ES
  Japanese, MO
  Roman, AS
Whirlwind: Faeroe Is., OE
Yes (German), JA
  (Italian, Spanish), SI
  (Russian), DA

Words of Three Letters

Adherent: IST
Again, BIS
Age, ERA
Antelope: African, GNU, KOB
Apricot: Japanese, UME
Article (German), DAS, DEM, DEN, DER, DES, DIE, EIN
  (French), LES, UNE
  (Spanish), LAS, LOS, UNA
Banana: Polynesian, FEI
Barge, HOY
Bass: African, IYO
Beak, NEB, NIB
Beard: Grain, AWN
Beetle: June, DOR
Being, ENS
Berry: Hawthorn, HAW
Beverage: Hawaiian, AVA
Bird: Australian, EMU
  Crowlike, JAY
  Extinct, MOA

Fabulous, ROC
Frigate, IWA
Parson, POE, TUE, TUI
Sea, AUK
Blackbird, ANI, ANO
Born, NEE
Bronze: Roman, AES
Bugle: Yellow, IVA
By way of, VIA
Canton: Swiss, URI
Cap: Turkish, FEZ
Catnip, NEP
Character: In "Faerie Queene," UNA
Coin: Afghan, PUL
  Albanian, LEK
  British Guiana, BIT
  Bulgarian, LEV, LEW
  French, ECU, SOU
  Indian, PIE
  Japanese, SEN, YEN
  Korean, WON

Lithuanian, LIT
Macao, Timor, AVO
Palestinian, MIL
Persian, PUL
Peruvian, SOL
Rumanian, BAN, LEU, LEY
Scandinavian, ORE
Siamese, ATT
  See also Money of account
Collection: Facts, ANA
Commune: Belgian, ANS, ATH
  Netherlands, EDE, EPE
Community: Russian, MIR
Constellation: Southern, ARA
Contraction: Poetic, EEN, EER, OER
Covering: Apex of roof, EPI
Crab: Fiddler, UCA
Crag: Rocky, TOR
Cry: Crow, rook, raven, CAW
Cup: Wine, AMA
Cymbal, Oriental, TAL, ZEL

Disease: Silkworm, UJI
Division: Danish territorial, AMT
  Geologic, EON
Doctrine, ISM
Dowry, DOT
Dry (French), SEC
Dynasty: Chinese, CHI, HAN, SUI,
  WEI, YIN
Eagle: Sea, ERN
Earth (comb. form), GEO
Egg: Louse, NIT
Eggs: Fish, ROE
Emmet, ANT
Enzyme, ASE
Equal (comb. form), ISO
Extension: building, ELL
Far (comb. form), TEL
Farewell, AVE
Fiber: Palm, TAL
Finial, EPI
Fish: Carplike, IDE
  Pikelike, GAR
Flatfish, DAB
Fleur-de-lis, LIS, LYS
Food: Hawaiian, POI
Formerly, NEE
Friend (French), AMI
Game: Card, LOO
Garment: Camel-hair, ABA
Gateway, DAR
Gazelle: Tibetan, GOA
Genus: Ducks, AIX
  Grasses, POA
  Grasses (maize), ZEA
  Herbs or shrubs, IVA
  Lizards, UTA
  Rodents (incl. house mice), MUS
  Ruminants (incl. cattle), BOS
  Swine, SUS
Gibbon: Malay, LAR
God: Assyrian, SIN
  Babylonian, ABU, ANU, BEL, HEA,
    SIN, UTU
  Irish sea, LER
  Phrygian, MEN
  Polynesian, ORO
Goddess: Babylonian, AYA
  Etruscan, UNI
  Hindu, SRI, UMA, VAC
  Teutonic, RAN
Governor: Algerian, DEY
  Turkish, BEY
Grampus, ORC
Grape, UVA
Grass: Meadow, POA
Gypsy, ROM
Hail, AVE
Hare: Female, DOE
Hawthorn, HAW
Hay: Spread for drying, TED
Herb: Japanese, UDO
  Perennial, PIA
  Used for blue dye, WAD
Herd: Whales, GAM, POD
Hero: Spanish, CID
High (music), ALT
Honey (pharm.), MEL
Humorist: American, ADE
I (Latin), EGO
I love (Latin), AMO
Indian: Algonquian, FOX, SAC, WEA
  Chimakuan, HOH
  Keresan, SIA
  Mayan, MAM
  Shoshonean, UTE
  Siouan, KAW, OTO
  South American, ITE, ONA, URO,
    URU, YAO
  Tierra del Fuego, ONA
  Wakashan, AHT
Ingot, PIG
Inlet: Narrow, RIA
Island: Cyclades, IOS
  Dodecanese, COS, KOS
  (French), ILE
  River, AIT

Jackdaw, DAW
John (Gaelic), IAN
Keelbill, ANI, ANO
Kiln, OST
King: British legendary LUD
Kobold, NIS
Lace: To make, TAT
Lamprey, EEL
Language: Artificial, IDO
  Bantu, ILA
  Siamese, LAO, TAI
Leaf: Palm, OLA, OLE
Leaving, ORT
Left: Cause to turn, HAW
Letter: Greek, CHI, ETA, PHI, PSI,
    RHO, TAU
  Hebrew, MEM, NUN, SIN, TAV, VAU
Lettuce, COS
Life (comb. form), BIO
Lily: Palm, TOI
Lizard, EFT
Louse: Young, NIT
Love (Anglo-Irish), GRA
Lute: Oriental, TAR
Macaw: Bralizian, ARA
Marble, TAW
Match: Shooting (French), TIR
Meadow, LEA
Measure: Abyssinian, TAT
  Algerian, PIK
  Annamese, GON, MAU, NGU,
    VUO, SAO, TAO, TAT
  Arabian, DEN, SAA
  Belgian, VAT
  Bulgarian, OKA, OKE
  Chinese, FEN, TOU, YIN
  Cloth, ELL
  Cyprus, OKA, OKE, PIK
  Czech, LAN, SAH
  Danish, FOD, MIL, POT
  Dominican Republic, ONA
  Dutch, old, AAM
  East Indian, KIT
  Egyptian, APT, HEN, PIK, ROB
  Electric, MHO, OHM
  Energy, ERG
  English, PIN
  Estonian, TUN
  French, POT
  German, AAM
  Greek, PIK
  Hebrew, CAB, HIN, KOR, LOG
  Hungarian, AKO
  Icelandic, FET
  Indian, GAZ, GUZ, JOW, KOS
  Japanese, BOO, CHO, KEN, RIN,
    SHO, SUN, TAN
  Malabar, ADY
  Metric land, ARE
  Netherlands, KAN, KOP, MUD,
    VAT, ZAK
  Norwegian, FOT, POT
  Persian, GAZ, GUZ, MOU, ZAR, ZER
  Polish, CAL
  Rangoon, DHA, LAN
  Roman, PES, URN
  Russian, FUT, LOF
  Scotch, COP
  Siamese, KEN, NIU, RAI, SAT,
    SEN, SOK, WAH, YOT
  Somaliland, TOP
  Spanish, PIE
  Straits Settlements, PAU, TUN
  Swedish, ALN, FOT, MIL, REF, TUM
  Swiss, POT
  Tunisian, SAA
  Turkish, OKA, OKE, PIK
  Wire, MIL
  Württemberg, IMI
  Yarn, LEA
  Yugoslavian, OKA, RIF
Milk, LAC
Milkfish, AWA
Moccasin, PAC
Money: Yap stone, FEI
Money of Account: Anglo-Saxon, ORA,

ORE
  French, SOU
  Indian, LAC
  Japanese, RIN
  Oman, GAJ
  Virgin Islands, BIT
  See also Coin
Monkey: Capuchin, SAI
Morsel, ORT
Mother: Peer Gynt's, ASE
Mountain: Asia Minor, IDA
Mulberry: Indian, AAL, ACH, AWL
Muttonbird: New Zealand, OII
Nahoor, SNA
Native: Mindanao, ATA
Neckpiece, BOA
Newt, EFT
No (Scotch), NAE
Note: Guido's highest, ELA
  Of scale, SOL
Nursemaid: Oriental, AMA, IYA
Ocher: Yellow, SIL
One (Scotch), YIN
Ornament: Pagoda, TEE
Oven: Polynesian, UMU
Ox: Tibetan, YAK
Pagoda: Chinese, TAA
Parrot: Hawk, HIA
  New Zealand, KEA
Part: Footlike, PES
Particle: Electrified, ION
Pasha, DEY
Pass: Mountain, COL
Paste: Rice, AME
Pea: Indian split, DAL
Peasant: Philippine, TAO
Penpoint, NEB, NIB
Piece out, EKE
Pigeon, NUN
Pine: Textile screw, ARA
Pistol (slang), GAT
Pit: Baking, IMU
Plant: Pepper, AVA
Play: By Capek, RUR
Poem: Old French, DIT
Porgy: Japanese, TAI
Priest: Biblical high, ELI
Prince Ethiopian, RAS
Pseudonym: Dickens', BOZ
Queen: Fairy, MAB
Quince: Bengal, BEL
Record: Ship's, LOG
Refuse: Flax (Scotch), PAB, POB
Resin, LAC
Resort, SPA
Revolver (slang), GAT
Right: Cause to turn, GEE
River: Scotch or English, DEE
  (Spanish), RIO
  Swiss, AAR
Room: Harem, ODA
Rootstock: Fern, ROI
Rose (Persian), GUL
Ruff: Female, REE
Rule: Indian, RAJ
Sailor, GOB, TAR
Saint: Female (abbr.), STE
  Mohammedan, PIR
Salt, SAL
Sash: Japanese, OBI
Scrap, ORT
Seed: Poppy, MAW
  Small, PIP
Self, EGO
Serpent: Vedic sky, AHI
Sesame, TIL
Sheep: Female, EWE
  Indian, SHA
  Male, RAM
Sheepfold (Scotch), REE
Shelter, LEE
Shield, ECU
Shooting match (French), TIR
Shrew: European, ERD
Shrub: Evergreen, YEW
Silkworm, ERI

Snake, ASP, BOA
Soak, RET
Son-in-law: Mohammed's, ALI
Sorrel: Wood, OCA
Spade: Long, narrow, LOY
Spirit: Malignant, KER
Spot: Playing-card, PIP
Spread for drying, TED
Spring: Mineral, SPA
Sprite: Water, NIX
Statesman: Japanese, ITO
Stern: Toward, AFT
Stomach: Bird's, MAW
Street (French), RUE
Summer (French), ETE
Sun, SOL
Swamp, BOG, FEN
Swan: Male, COB
Tea: Chinese, CHA
Temple: Shinto, SHA
The. *See* Article
Thing (law), RES
Title: Etruscan, LAR
  Monk's, FRA
  Portuguese, DOM
  Spanish, DON
  Turkish, AGA, BEY
Tool: Cutting, ADZ, AXE
  Mining, GAD
  Piercing, AWL
Tree: Candlenut, AMA
  Central American, EBO
  East Indian, SAJ, SAL

Evergreen, YEW
Hawaiian, KOA, KOU
Indian, BEL, DAR
Linden, LIN
New Zealand, AKE
Philippine, DAO, TUA, TUI
Rubber, ULE
South American, APA
Tribe: New Zealand, ATI
Turmeric, REA
Twice, BIS
Twin: Siamese, ENG
Uncle (dialect), EAM, EME
Veil: Chalice, AER, AIR
Vessel: Wine, AMA
Vestment: Ecclesiastical, ALB
Vetch: Bitter, ERS
Victorfish, AKU
Vine: New Zealand, AKA
  Philippine, IYO
Wallaba, APA
Wapiti, ELK
Water (French), EAU
Waterfall, LIN
Watering place: Prussian, EMS
Weave: Designating plain, UNI
Weight: Annamese, CAN
  Bulgarian, OKA, OKE
  Burmese, MOO, VIS
  Chinese, FEN, HAO, KIN, SSU,
    TAN, YIN
  Cyprus, OKA, OKE
  Danish, LOD, ORT, VOG

East Indian, TJI
Egyptian, KAT, OKA, OKE
English, for wool, TOD
German, LOT
Greek, MNA, OKA, OKE
Indian, SER
Japanese, FUN, KIN, RIN, SHI
Korean, KON
Malacca, KIP
Mongolian, LAN
Netherlands, ONS
Norwegian, LOD
Polish, LUT
Rangoon, PAI
Roman, BES
Russian, LOT
Siamese, BAT, HAP, PAI
Swedish, ASS, ORT
Turkish, OKA, OKE
Yugoslavian, OKA, OKE
Whales: Herd, GAM, POD
Wildebeest, GNU
Wing, ALA
Witticism, MOT
Wolframite, CAL
Worm: African, LOA
Wreath: Hawaiian, LEI
Yale, ELI
Yam: Hawaiian, HOI
Yes (French), OUI
Young: Bring forth, EAN
Z (letter), ZED

Words of Four Letters

Aborigine: Borneo, DYAK
Agave, ALOE
Animal: Footless, APOD
Ant: White, ANAI, ANAY
Antelope: African, ASSE, BISA,
  GUIB,KOBA, KUDU, ORYX, POKU,
  PUKU, TOPI, TORA
Apoplexy: Plant, ESCA
Apple, POME
Apricot, ANSU
Ardor, ELAN
Armadillo, APAR, PEBA, PEVA, TATU
Ascetic: Mohammedan, SUFI
Association: Chinese, TONG
Astronomer: Persian, OMAR
Avatar: Of Vishnu, RAMA
Axillary, ALAR
Band: Horizontal (heraldry), FESS
Barracuda, SPET
Bark: Mulberry, TAPA
Base: Column, DADO
Bearing (heraldry), ORLE
Beer: Russian, KVAS
Beige, ECRU
Being, ESSE
Beverage: Japanese rice, SAKE
Bird: Asian, MINA, MYNA
  Egyptian sacred, IBIS
  Extinct, DODO, MAMO
  Flightless, KIWI
  Gull-like, TERN
  Hawaiian, IIWI, MAMO
  Parson, KOKO
  Unfledged, EYAS
Birds: As class, AVES
Black, EBON
  (French), NOIR
Blackbird: European, MERL
Boat: Flat-bottomed, DORY
Bone: Forearm, ULNA
Bones, OSSA
Box, Japanese, INRO
Bravo (rare), EUGE
Buffalo: Indian wild, ARNA
Bull (Spanish), TORO
Burden, ONUS
Cabbage: Sliced, SLAW

Caliph: Mohammedan, OMAR
Canoe: Malay, PRAU, PROA
Cap: Military, KEPI
Cape, NESS
Capital: Ancient Irish, TARA
Case: Article, ETUI
Cat: Wild, BALU, EYRA
Chalcedony, SARD
Chamber: Indian ceremonial, KIVA
Channel: Brain, ITER
Cheese: Dutch, EDAM
Chest: Sepulchral stone, CIST
Chieftain: Arab, EMIR
Church: Part of, APSE, NAVE
  (Scotch), KIRK
Claim (law), LIEN
Cluster: Flower, CYME
Coin: Chinese, TAEL, YUAN
  German, MARK
  Indian, ANNA
  Iranian, RIAL
  Italian, LIRA
  Moroccan, OKIA
  Siamese, BAHT
  South American, PESO
  Spanish, DURO, PESO
  Turkish, PARA
Commune: Belgian, AATH
Composition: Musical, OPUS
Compound: Chemical, DIOL
Constellation: Southern, PAVO
Council: Russian, DUMA
Counsel, REDE
Covering: Seed, ARIL
Cross: Egyptian, ANKH
Cry: Bacchanalian, EVOE
Cup (Scotch), TASS
Cupbearer, SAKI
Dagger, DIRK
  Malay, KRIS
Dam: River, WEIR
Dash, ELAN
Date: Roman, IDES
Dawn: Pertaining to, EOAN
Dean: English, INGE
Decay: In fruit, BLET
Deer: Sambar, MAHA

Disease: Skin, ACNE
Disk: Solar, ATEN
Dog: Hunting, ALAN
Drink: Hindu intoxicating, SOMA
Duck, SMEE, SMEW, TEAL
Dynasty: Chinese, CHEN, CHIN,
  CHOU, CHOW, HSIA, MING, SUNG,
  TANG, TSIN
  Mongol, YUAN
Eagle: Biblical, GIER
  Sea, ERNE
Egyptian: Christian, COPT
Ear: Pertaining to, OTIC
Entrance: Mine, ADIT
Esau, EDOM
Escutcheon: Voided, ORLE
Eskers, OSAR
Evergreen: New Zealand, TAWA
Fairy: Persian, PERI
Family: Italian, ESTE
Far (comb. form), TELE
Farewell, VALE
Father (French), PERE
Fennel: Philippine, ANIS
Fever: Malarial, AGUE
Fiber: East Indian, JUTE
Firn, NEVE
Fish: Carplike, DACE
  Hawaiian, ULUA
  Herringlike, SHAD
  Mackerellike, CERO
  Marine, HAKE
  Sea, LING, MERO, OPAH
  Spiny-finned, GOBY
Food: Tropical, TARO
Foot: Metric, IAMB
Formerly, ERST
Founder: Of Carthage, DIDO
France: Southern, MIDI
Furze, ULEX
Gaelic, ERSE
Gaiter, SPAT
Game: Card, FARO, SKAT
Garlic: European wild, MOLY
Garment: Hindu, SARI
  Roman, TOGA
Gazelle, CORA

Gem, JADE, ONYX, OPAL, RUBY
Genus: Amphibians (incl. frogs), RANA
   Amphibians (incl. tree toads), HYLA
   Antelopes, ORYX
   Auks, ALCA, URIA
   Bees, APIS
   Birds (American ostriches), RHEA
   Birds (cranes), CRUS
   Birds (magpies), PICA
   Birds (peacocks), PAVO
   Cetaceans, INIA
   Ducks (incl. mallards), ANAS
   Fishes (burbots), LOTA
   Fishes (incl. bowfins), AMIA
   Geese (snow geese), CHEN
   Gulls, XEMA
   Herbs, ARUM, GEUM
   Insects (water scorpions), NEPA
   Lilies, ALOE
   Mammals (mankind), HOMO
   Orchids, DISA
   Owls, ASIO, BUBO, OTUS
   Palms, NIPA
   Sea birds, SULA
   Sheep, OVIS
   Shrubs, Eurasian, ULEX
   Shrubs (hollies), ILEX
   Shrubs (incl. Virginia Willow), ITEA
   Shrubs, tropical, EVEA
   Snakes (sand snakes), ERYX
   Swans, OLOR
   Trees, chocolate, COLA
   Trees (ebony family), MABA
   Trees (incl. maples), ACER
   Trees (olives), OLEA
   Trees, tropical, EVEA
   Turtles, EMYS
Goat: Wild, IBEX, KRAS, TAHR, TAIR, THAR
God: Assyrian, ASUR
   Babylonian, ADAD, ADDU, ENKI,
    ENZU, IRRA, NABU, NEBO, UTUG
   Celtic, LLEU, LLEW
   Hindu, AGNI, CIVA, DEVA, DEWA,
    KAMA, RAMA, SIVA, VAYU
   Phrygian, ATYS
   Semitic, BAAL
   Teutonic, HLER
Goddess: Babylonian, ERUA, GULA
   Hawaiian, PELE
   Hindu, DEVI, KALI, SHRI, VACH
Gooseberry: Hawaiian, POHA
Gourd, PEPO
Grafted (heraldry), ENTE
Grandfather (obsolete), AIEL
Grandparents: Pertaining to, AVAL
Grass: Hawaiian, HILO
Gray (French), GRIS
Green (heraldry), VERT
Groom: Indian, SYCE
Half (prefix), DEMI, HEMI, SEMI
Hamlet, DORP
Hammer-head: Part of, PEEN
Handle, ANSA
Harp: Japanese, KOTO
Hartebeest, ASSE, TORA
Hautboy, OBOE
Hawk: Taken from nest (falconry), EYAS
Hearing (law), OYER
Heater: For liquids, ETNA
Herb: Aromatic, ANET, DILL
   Fabulous, MOLY
   Perennial, GEUM, SEGO
   Pot, WORT
   Used for blue dye, WADE, WOAD
Hill: Flat-topped, MESA
   Sand, DENE, DUNE
Hoarfrost, RIME
Hog: Immature female, GILT
Holly, ILEX
House: Cow, BYRE
   (Spanish), CASA
Ice: Floating, FLOE
Image, ICON, IKON
Incarnation: Of Vishnu, RAMA

Indian: Algonquian, CREE, SAUK
   Central American, MAYA
   Iroquoian, ERIE
   Mexican, CORA
   Peruvian, CANA, INCA, MORO
   Shoshonean, HOPI
   Siouan, OTOE
   Southwestern, HOPI, PIMA,
YUMA, ZUNI
Insect: Immature, PUPA
Instrument: Stringed, LUTE, LYRE
Ireland, EIRE, ERIN
Jacket: English, ETON
Jail (British), GAOL
Jar, OLLA
Judge: Mohammedan, CADI
Juniper: European, CADE
Kiln, OAST, OVEN
King: British legendary, LUDD, NUDD
Kiss, BUSS
Knife: Philippine, BOLO
Koran: Section of, SURA
Laborer: Spanish American, PEON
Lake: Mountain, TARN
   (Scotch), LOCH
Lamp: Miner's, DAVY
Landing place: Indian, GHAT
Language: Buddhist, PALI
   Japanese, AINU
Latvian, LETT
Layer: Of iris, UVEA
Leaf: Palm, OLAY, OLLA
Legislature: Ukrainian, RADA
Lemur, LORI
Leopard, PARD
Let it stand, STET
Letter: Greek, BETA, IOTA, ZETA
   Hebrew, AYIN, BETH, CAPH, KOPH,
    RESH, SHIN, TETH, YODH
   Papal, BULL
Lily, ALOE
Literature: Hindu sacred, VEDA
Lizard, GILA
   Monitor, URAN
Loquat, BIWA
Magistrate: Genoese or Venetian, DOGE
Man (Latin), HOMO
Mark: Omission, DELE
   armoset: South American, MICO
Meadow: Fertile, VEGA
Measure: Electric, VOLT, WATT
   Force, DYNE
   Hebrew, OMER
   Printing, PICA
   Spanish or Portuguese, VARA
   Swiss land, IMMI
Medley, OLIO
Merganser, SMEW
Milk (French), LAIT
Molding, GULA
   Curved, OGEE
Mongoose: Crab-eating, URVA
Monk: Tibetan, LAMA
Monkey: African, MONA, WAAG
   Ceylonese, MAHA
   Cochin-China, DOUC
   South American, SAKI, TITI
Monkshood, ATIS
Month: Jewish, ADAR, ELUL, IYAR
Mother (French), MERE
Mountain: Thessaly, OSSA
Mouse: Meadow, VOLE
Mythology: Norse, EDDA
Nail (French), CLOU
Native: Philippine, MORO
Nest: Of pheasants, NIDE
Network, RETE
No (German), NEIN
Noble: Mohammedan, AMIR
Notice: Death, OBIT
Novel: By Zola, NANA
Nursemaid: Oriental AMAH, AYAH, EYAH
Nut: Philippine, PILI

Oak: Holm, ILEX
Oil (comb. form), OLEO
Ostrich: American, RHEA
Oven, KILN, OAST
Owl: Barn, LULU
Ox: Celebes wild, ANOE
   Extinct wild, URUS
Palm, ATAP, NIPA, SAGO
Parliament, DIET
Parrot: New Zealand, KAKA
Pass: Indian mountain, GHAT
Passage: Closing (music), CODA
Peach: Clingstone, PAVY
Peasant: Indian, RYOT
   Old English, CARL
Pepper: Australasian, KAVA
Perfume, ATAR
Persia, IRAN
Person: Extraordinary, ONER
Pickerel or pike, ESOX
Pitcher, EWER
Plant: Aromatic, NARD
   Century, ALOE
   Indigo, ANIL
   Pepper, KAVA
Platform: Raised, DAIS
Plum: Wild, SLOE
Pods: Vegetable, OKRA, OKRO
Poem: Epic, EPOS
Poet: Persian, OMAR
   Roman, OVID
Poison, BANE
   Arrow, INEE
Porkfish, SISI
Portico: Greek, STOA
Premium, AGIO
Priest: Mohammedan, IMAM
Prima donna, DIVA
Prong: Fork, TINE
Pseudonym: Lamb's, ELIA
Queen: Carthaginian, DIDO
   Hindu, RANI
Rabbit, CONY
Race: Of Japan, AINU
Rail: Ducklike, COOT
   North American, SORA
Redshank, CLEE
Refuse: After pressing, MARC
Regiment: Turkish, ALAI
Reliquary, ARCA
Resort: Italian, LIDO
Ridges: Sandy, ASAR, OSAR
River: German, ELBE, ODER
   Italian, ADDA
   Siberian, LENA
Road: Roman, ITER
Rockfish: California, RENA
Rodent: Mouselike, VOLE
   South American, PACA
Rootstock, TARO
Salamander, NEWT
Salmon: Silver, COHO
   Young, PARR
Same (Greek), HOMO
   (Latin), IDEM
Sauce: Fish, ALEC
School: English, ETON
Seaweed, AGAR, ALGA, KELP
Secular, LAIC
Sediment, SILT
Seed: Dill, ANET
   Of vetch, TARE
Serf, ILOT
Sesame, TEEL
Settlement: Eskimo, ETAH
Shark: Atlantic, GATA
   European, TOPE
Sheep: Wild, UDAD
Sheltered, ALEE
Shield, EGIS
Ship: Jason's, ARGO
   Left side of, PORT
   Two-masted, BRIG
Shrine: Buddhist, TOPE
Shrub: New Zealand, TUTU

Sign: Magic, RUNE
Silkworm, ERIA
Skin: Beaver, PLEW
Skink: Egyptian, ADDA
Slave, ESNE
Sloth: Two-toed, UNAU
Smooth, LENE
Snow: Glacial, NEVE
Soapstone, TALC
Society: African secret, EGBO, PORO
Son: Of Seth, ENOS
Song (German), LIED
  Unaccompanied, GLEE
Sound: Lung, RALE
Sour, ACID
Sow: Young, GILT
Spike: Brad-shaped, BROB
Spirit: Buddhist evil, MARA
Stake: Poker, ANTE
Star: Temporary, NOVA
Starch: East Indian, SAGO
Stone: Precious, OPAL
Strap: Bridle, REIN
Strewn (heraldry), SEME
Sweetsop, ATES, ATTA
Sword: Fencing, EPEE, FOIL
Tambourine: African, TAAR
Tapir: Brazilian, ANTA
Tax, CESS
Tea: South American, MATE
Therefore (Latin), ERGO
Thing: Extraordinary, ONER
Three (dice, cards, etc.), TREY
Thrush: Hawaiian, OMAO

Tide, NEAP
Tipster: Racing, TOUT
Tissue, TELA
Title: Etruscan, LARS
  Hindu, BABU
  Indian, RAJA
  Mohammedan, EMIR, IMAM
  Persian, BABA
  Spanish, DONA
  Turkish, AGHA, BABA
Toad: Largest-known, AGUA
  Tree, HYLA
Tool: Cutting, ADZE
Track: Deer, SLOT
Tract: Sandy, DENE
Tree: Apple, SORB
  Central American, EBOE
  East Indian, TEAK
  Eucalyptus, YATE
  Guiana and Trinidad, MORA
  Javanese, UPAS
  Linden, LIME, LINN, TEIL, TILL
  Sandarac, ARAR
  Sassafras, AGUE
  Tamarisk salt, ATLE
Tribe: Moro, SULU
Trout, CHAR
Urchin: Street, ARAB
Vessel: Arab, DHOW
Vestment: Ecclesiastical, COPE
Vetch, TARE
Vine: East Indian, SOMA
Violinist: Famous, AUER

Vortex, EDDY
Wampum, PEAG
Wapiti, STAG
Waste: Allowance for, TRET
Watchman: Indian, MINA
Water (Spanish), AGUA
Waterfall, LINN
Wavy (heraldry), ONDE, UNDE
Wax, CERE
  Chinese, PELA
Weed: Biblical, TARE
Weight: Ancient, MINA
  Danish (pl.), ESER
  East Asian, TAEL
  Greek, MINA
  Siamese, BAHT
Well done (rare), EUGE
Whale, CETE
  Killer, ORCA
  White, HUSE, HUSO
Whirlpool, EDDY
Wife: Of Geraint, ENID
Willow: Virginia, ITEA
Wine, PORT
Winged, ALAR
  (Heraldry), AILE
Wings, ALAE
Withered, SERE
Without (French), SANS
Wool: To comb, CARD
Work, OPUS
Wrong: Civil, TORT
Young: Bring forth, YEAN

Words of Five Letters

Abode of dead: Babylonian, ARALU
Aborigine: Borneo DAYAK
Aftersong, EPODE
Aloe, AGAVE
Animal: Footless, APODE
Ant, EMMET
Antelope: African, ADDAX, BEISA, CAAMA, ELAND,
  GUIBA, ORIBI, TIANG
  Goat, GORAL, SEROW
  Indian, SASIN
  Siberian, SAIGA
Arch: Pointed, OGIVE
Armadillo, APARA, POYOU, TATOU
Arrowroot, ARARU
Artery: Trunk, AORTA
Association: Russian, ARTEL
  Secret, CABAL
Author: English, READE
Automaton, GOLEM, ROBOT
Award: Motion-picture, OSCAR
Basket: Fishing, CREEL
Beer: Russian, KVASS
Bible: Mohammedan, KORAN
Bird: Asian, MINAH, MYNAH
  Indian, SHAMA
  Larklike, PIPIT
  Loonlike, GREBE
  Oscine, VIREO
  South American, AGAMI
  Swimming, GREBE
Black: (French), NOIRE
  (Heraldry), SABLE
Blackbird: European, MERLE, OUSEL, OUZEL
Block: Glacial, SERAC
Blue (heraldry), AZURE
Boat: Eskimo, BIDAR, UMIAK
Bobwhite, COLIN, QUAIL
Bone (comb. form), OSTEO
  Leg, TIBIA
  Thigh, FEMUR
Broom: Twig, BESOM
Brother (French), FRERE
  Moses, AARON
Canoe: Eskimo, BIDAR, KAYAK
Cape: Papal, FANON, ORALE
Caravansary, SERAI

Card: Old playing, TAROT
Caterpillar: New Zealand, AWETO
Catkin, AMENT
Cavity: Stone, GEODE
Cephalopod, SQUID
Cetacean, WHALE
Chariot, ESSED
Cheek: Pertaining to, MALAR
Chieftain: Arab, EMEER
Child (Scotch), BAIRN
Cigar, CLARO
Coating: Seed, TESTA
Cockatoo: Palm, ARARA
Coin: Costa Rican, COLON
  Danish, KRONE
  Ecuadorian, SUCRE
  English, GROAT, PENCE
  French, FRANC
  German, KRONE, TALER
  Hungarian, PENGO
  Icelandic, KRONA
  Indian, RUPEE
  Iraqi, DINAR
  Norwegian, KRONE
  Polish, ZLOTY
  Russian, COPEC, KOPEK, RUBLE
  Swedish, KRONA
  Turkish, ASPER
  Yugoslav, DINAR
Collar: Papal, FANON, ORALE
  Roman, RABAT
Commune: Italian, TREIA
Composition: Choral, MOTET
Compound: Chemical, ESTER
Conceal (law), ELOIN
Council: Ecclesiastical, SYNOD
Court: Anglo-Saxon, GEMOT
  Inner, PATIO
Crest: Mountain, ARETE
Crown: Papal, TIARA
Cuttlefish, SEPIA
Date: Roman, NONES
Decree: Mohammedan, IRADE
  Russian, UKASE
Deposit: Loam, LOESS
Desert: Gobi, SHAMO

Devilfish, MANTA
Disease: Cereals, ERGOT
Disk, PATEN
Dog: Wild, DHOLE, DINGO
Dormouse, LEROT
Drum, TABOR
Duck: Sea, EIDER
Dynasty: Chinese, CHING, LIANG, SHANG
Earthquake, SEISM
Eel, ELVER, MORAY
Ermine: European, STOAT
Ether: Crystalline, APIOL
Fabric: Velvetlike, PANNE
Fabulist, AESOP
Family: Italian, CENCI
Fiber: West Indian, SISAL
Fig: Smyrna, ELEME, ELEMI
Figure: Of speech, TROPE
Finch: European, SERIN
Fish: American small, KILLY
Flower: Garden, ASTER
Friend (Spanish), AMIGO
Fruit: Tropical, MANGO
Fungus: Rye, ERGOT
Furze, GORSE
Gateway, TORAN, TORII
Gem, AGATE, BERYL, PEARL, TOPAZ
Genus: Barnacles, LEPAS
   Bears, URSUS
   Birds (loons), GAVIA
   Birds (nuthatches), SITTA
   Cats, FELIS
   Dogs, CANIS
   Fishes (chiros), ELOPS
   Fishes (perch), PERCA
   Geese, ANSER
   Grasses, STIPA
   Grasses (incl. oats), AVENA
   Gulls, LARUS
   Hares, rabbits, LEPUS
   Hawks, BUTEO
   Herbs, old world, INULA
   Herbs, trailing or climbing, APIOS
   Herbs, tropical, TACCA, URENA
   Horses, EQUUS
   Insects (olive flies), DACUS
   Lice, plant, APHIS
   Lichens, USNEA
   Lizards, AGAMA
   Moles, TALPA
   Mollusks, OLIVA
   Monkeys, CEBUS
   Palms, ARECA
   Pigeons, GOURA
   Plants (amaryllis family), AGAVE
   Ruminants (goats), CAPRA
   Shrubs, Asiatic, SABIA
   Shrubs (heath), ERICA
   Shrubs (incl. raspberry), RUBUS
   Shrubs, tropical, IXORA, TREMA, URENA
   Ticks, ARGAS
   Trees (of elm family), TREMA, ULMUS
   Trees, tropical, IXORA, TREMA
Goat: Bezoar, PASAN
God: Assyrian, ASHIR, ASHUR, ASSUR
   Babylonian, DAGAN, SIRIS
   Gaelic, DAGDA
   Hindu, BHAGA, INDRA, SHIVA
   Japanese, EBISU
   Philistine, DAGON
   Phrygian, ATTIS
   Teutonic, AEGIR, GYMIR
   Welsh, DYLAN
Goddess: Babylonian, ISTAR, NANAI
   Hindu, DURGA, GAURI, SHREE
Group: Of six, HEXAD
Grove: Sacred to Diana, NEMUS
Growing out, ENATE
Guitar: Hindu, SITAR
Gull: PEWEE, PEWIT
Hartebeest, CAAMA
Headdress: Jewish or Persian, TIARA
   Liturgical, MITER, MITRE
Heath, ERICA
Herb: Grasslike marsh, SEDGE

Heron, EGRET
Hog: Young, SHOAT, SHOTE
Image, EIKON
Indian: Cariban, ARARA
   Iroquoian, HURON
   Mexican, AZTEC, OPATA, OTOMI
   Muskhogean, CREEK
   Siouan, OSAGE, TETON
   Spanish American, ARARA, CARIB
Inflorescence: Racemose, AMENT
Insect: Immature, LARVA
Intrigue, CABAL
Iris: Yellow, SEDGE
Juniper, GORSE, RETEM
Kidneys: Pertaining to, RENAL
King: British legendary, LLUDD
Kite: European, GLEDE
Kobold, NISSE
Land: Cultivated, ARADA, ARADO
Landholder (Scotch), LAIRD, THANE
Language: Dravidian, TAMIL
Lariat, LASSO, REATA
Laughing, RIANT
Lawgiver: Athenian, DRACO, SOLON
Leaf: Calyx, SEPAL
   Fern, FROND
Lemur, LORIS
Letter: English, AITCH
   Greek, ALPHA, DELTA, GAMMA, KAPPA, OMEGA,
      SIGMA, THETA
   Hebrew, ALEPH, CHETH, GIMEL, SADHE, ZAYIN
Lichen, USNEA
Lighthouse, PHARE
Lizard: Old World, AGAMA
Loincloth, DHOTI
Louse: Plant, APHID
Macaw: Brazilian, ARARA
Mahogany: Philippine, ALMON
Mammal: Badgerlike, RATEL
   Civetlike, GENET
   Giraffelike, OKAPI
   Raccoonlike, COATI
Man (French), HOMME
Marble, AGATE
Mark: Insertion, CARET
Market place: Greek, AGORA
Marsupial: Australian, KOALA
Measure: Electric, FARAD, HENRY
   Energy, JOULE
   Metric, LITER, STERE
   Printing, AGATE
   Russian, VERST
Mixture: Smelting, MATTE
Mohicans: Last of, UNCAS
Molding: Convex, OVOLO, TORUS
Mole, TALPA
Monkey: African, PATAS
   Capuchin, SAJOU
   Howling, ARABA
Monkshood, ATEES
Month: Jewish, NISAN, SIVAN, TEBET
Museum (French), MUSEE
Musketeer, ATHOS
Native: Aleutian, ALEUT
   New Zealand, MAORI
Neckpiece: Ecclesiastical, AMICE
Nerve (comb. form), NEURO
Nest: Eagle's or hawk's, AERIE
   Insect's, NIDUS
Net: Fishing, SEINE
Newsstand, KIOSK
Nitrogen, AZOTE
Noble: Mohammedan, AMEER
Nodule: Stone, GEODE
Nostrils, NARES
Notched irregularly, EROSE
Nymph: Mohammedan, HOURI
Official: Roman, EDILE
Oleoresin, ELEMI
Opening: Mouthlike, STOMA
Oration: Funeral, ELOGE
Ostiole, STOMA
Page: Left-hand, VERSO
   Right-hand, RECTO
Palm, ARECA, BETEL

Park: Colorado, ESTES
Perfume, ATTAR
Philosopher: Greek, PLATO
Pillar: Stone, STELA, STELE
Pinnacle: Glacial, SERAC
Plain, LLANO
Plant: Century, AGAVE
   Climbing, LIANA
   Dwarf, CUMIN
   East Asian perennial, RAMIE
   Medicinal, SENNA
   Mustard family, CRESS
Plate: Communion, PATEN
Poem: Lyric, EPODE
Point: Lowest, NADIR
Poplar, ABELE, ALAMO, ASPEN
Porridge: Spanish American, ATOLE
Post: Stair, NEWEL
Priest: Mohammedan, IMAUM
Protozoan, AMEBA
Queen: (French), REINE
   Hindu, RANEE
Rabbit, CONEY
Rail, CRAKE
Red (heraldry), GULES
Religion: Moslem, ISLAM
Resin, ELEMI
Revoke (law), ADEEM
Rich man, MIDAS, NABOB
Ridge: Sandy, ESKAR, ESKER
River: French, LOIRE, SEINE
Rockfish: California, REINA
Rootstock: Fragrant, ORRIS
Ruff: Female, REEVE
Sack: Pack, KYACK
Salt: Ethereal, ESTER
Saltpeter, NITER, NITRE
Salutation: Eastern, SALAM
Sandpiper: Old World, TEREK
Scented, OLENT
School: Fish, SHOAL
   French public, LYCEE
Scriptures: Mohammedan, KORAN
Seaweeds, ALGAE
Seed: Aromatic, ANISE
Seraglio, HAREM, SERAI
Serf, HELOT
Sheep: Wild, AUDAD
Sheeplike, OVINE
Shield, AEGIS
Shoe: Wooden, SABOT
Shoots: Pickled bamboo, ACHAR
Shot: Billiard, CAROM, MASSE
Shrine: Buddhist, STUPA
Shrub: Burning bush, WAHOO
   Ornamental evergreen, TOYON
   Used in tanning, SUMAC
Silk: Watered, MOIRE
Sister (French), SOEUR
   (Latin), SOROR
Six: Group of, HEXAD

Skeleton: Marine, CORAL
Slave, HELOT
Snake, ABOMA, ADDER, COBRA, RACER
Soldier: French, POILU
   Indian, SEPOY
Sour, ACERB
Spirit: Air, ARIEL
Staff: Shepherd's, CROOK
Starwort, ASTER
Steel (German), STAHL
Stockade: Russian, ETAPE
Stop (nautical), AVAST
Storehouse, ETAPE
Subway: Parisian, METRO
Tapestry, ARRAS
Tea: Paraguayan, YERBA
Temple: Hawaiian, HEIAU
Terminal: Positive, ANODE
Theater: Greek, ODEON, ODEUM
Then (French), ALORS
Thread: Surgical, SETON
Thrush: Wilson's, VEERY
Title: Hindu, BABOO
   Indian, RAJAH, SAHEB, SAHIB
   Mohammedan, EMEER, IMAUM
Tree: Buddhist sacred, PIPAL
   East Indian cotton, SIMAL
   Hickory, PECAN
   Light-wooded, BALSA
   Malayan, TERAP
   Mediterranean, CAROB
   Mexican, ABETO
   Mexican pine, OCOTE
   New Zealand, MAIRE
   Philippine, ALMON
   Rain, SAMAN
   South American, UMBRA
   Tamarack, LARCH
   Tamarisk salt, ATLEE
   West Indian, ACANA
Trout, CHARR
Troy, ILION, ILIUM
Twin: Siamese, CHANG
Vestment: Ecclesiastical, STOLE
Violin: Famous, AMATI, STRAD
Volcano: Mud, SALSE
Wampum, PEAGE
War cry: Greek, ALALA
Wavy (heraldry), UNDEE
Weight: Jewish, GERAH
Wen, TALPA
Wheat, SPELT
Wheel: Persian water, NORIA
Whitefish, CISCO
Willow, OSIER
Window: Bay, ORIEL
Wine, MEDOC, RHINE, TINTA, TOKAY
Winged, ALATE
Woman (French), FEMME
Year: Excess of solar over lunar, EPACT
Zoroastrian, PARSI

Words of Six or More Letters

Agave, MAGUEY
Alkaloid: Crystalline, ESERIN, ESERINE
Alligator, CAYMAN
Amphibole, EDENITE, URALITE
Ant: White, TERMITE
Antelope: African, DIKDIK, DUIKER, GEMSBOK, IMPALA, KOODOO
   European, CHAMOIS
   Indian, NILGAI, NILGAU, NILGHAI, NILGHAU
Ape: Asian or East Indian, GIBBON
Appendage: Leaf, STIPEL, STIPULE
Armadillo, PELUDO, TATOUAY
Arrowroot, ARARAO
Ascetic: Jewish, ESSENE
Ass: Asian wild, ONAGER
Avatar: Of Vishnu, KRISHNA
Babylonian, ELAMITE
Badge: Shoulder, EPAULET
Baldness, ALOPECIA

Barracuda, SENNET
Bark: Aromatic, SINTOC
Bearlike, URSINE
Beetle, ELATER
Bible: Zoroastrian, AVESTA
Bird: Sea, PETREL
   South American, SERIEMA
   Wading, AVOCET, AVOSET
Bone: Leg, FIBULA
Branched, RAMATE
Brother (Latin), FRATER
Bunting: European, ORTOLAN
Call: Trumpet, SENNET
Canoe: Eskimo, BAIDAR, OOMIAK
Caravansary, IMARET
Cat: Asian or African, CHEETAH
   Leopardlike, OCELOT
Cenobite: Jewish, ESSENE
Centerpiece: Table, EPERGNE

Cetacean, DOLPHIN, PORPOISE
Chariot, ESSEDA, ESSEDE
Chief: Seminole, OSCEOLA
Claim: Release as (law), REMISE
Clock: Water, CLEPSYDRA
Cloud, CUMULUS, NIMBUS
Coach: French hackney, FIACRE
Coin: Czech, KORUNA
  Ethiopian, TALARI
  Finnish, MARKKA
  German, THALER
  Greek, DRACHMA
  Haitian, GOURDE
  Honduran, LEMPIRA
  Hungarian, FORINT
  Indo-Chinese, PIASTER
  Netherlands, GUILDER
  Panamanian, BALBOA
  Paraguayan, GUARANI
  Portuguese, ESCUDO
  Russian, COPECK, KOPECK, ROUBLE
  Spanish, PESETA
  Venezuelan, BOLIVAR
Communion: Last holy, VIATICUM
Conceal (law), ELOIGN
Confection, PRALINE
Construction: Sentence, SYNTAX
Convexity: Shaft of column, ENTASIS
Court: Anglo-Saxon, GEMOTE
Cow: Sea, DUGONG, MANATEE
Cylindrical, TERETE
Dagger, STILETTO
  Malay, CREESE, KREESE
Date: Roman, CALENDS, KALENDS
Deer, CARIBOU, WAPITI
Disease: Plant, ERINOSE
Doorkeeper, OSTIARY
Dragonflies: Order of, ODANATA
Drink: Of gods, NECTAR
Drum: TABOUR
  Moorish, ATABAL, ATTABAL
Duck: Fish-eating, MERGANSER
  Sea, SCOTER
Dynasty: Chinese, MANCHU
Eel, CONGER
Edit, REDACT
Envelope: Flower, PERIANTH
Eskimo, AMERIND
Ether: Crystalline, APIOLE
Excuse (law), ESSOIN
Eyespots, OCELLI
Fabric, ESTAMENE, ESTAMIN, ETAMINE
Falcon: European, KESTREL
Figure: Used as column, CARYATID, TELAMON
Fine: For punishment, AMERCE
Fish: Asian fresh-water, GOURAMI
  Pikelike, BARRACUDA
Five: Group of, PENTAD
Fly: African, TSETSE
Foot: Metric, ANAPEST, IAMBUS
Foxlike, VULPINE
Frying pan, SPIDER
Fur, KARAKUL
Galley: Greek or Roman, BIREME, TRIREME
Game: Card, ECARTE
Garment: Greek, CHLAMYS
Gateway, GOPURA, TORANA
Genus: Birds (ravens, crows), CORVUS
  Eels, CONGER
  Fishes, ANABAS
  Foxes, VULPES
  Herbs, ANEMONE
  Insects, CICADA
  Lemurs, GALAGO
  Mints (incl. catnip), NEPETA
  Mollusks, ANOMIA, ASTARTE, TEREDO
  Mollusks (incl. oysters), OSTREA
  Monkeys (spider monkeys), ATELES
  Thrushes (incl. robins), TURDUS
  Trees (of elm family), CELTIS
  Trees (inc. dogwood), CORNUS
  Trees, tropical American, SAPOTA
  Wrens, NANNUS
Gibbon, SIAMANG, WOUWOU
Gland: Salivary, RACEMOSE

Goat: Bezoar, PASANG
Goatlike, CAPRINE
God: Assyrian, ASHSHUR, ASSHUR
  Babylonian, BABBAR, MARDUK, MERODACH,
    NANNAR, NERGAL, SHAMASH
  Hindu, BRAHMA, KRISHNA, VISHNU
  Tahitian, TAAROA
Goddess: Babylonian, ISHTAR
  Hindu, CHANDI, HAIMAVATI, LAKSHMI, PARVATI,
    SARASVATI, SARASWATI
Government, POLITY
Governor: Persian, SATRAP
Grandson (Scotch), NEPOTE
Group: Of five, PENTAD
  Of nine, ENNEAD
  Of seven, HEPTAD
Hare: in first year, LEVERET
Harpsichord, SPINET
Herb: Alpine, EDELWEISS
  Chinese, GINSENG
  South African, FREESIA
Hermit, EREMITE
Hero: Legendary, PALADIN
Heron, BITTERN
Horselike, EQUINE
Hound: Short-legged, BEAGLE
House (French), MAISON
Idiot, CRETIN
Implement: Stone, NEOLITH
Incarnation: Hindu, AVATAR
Indian, APACHE, COMANCHE, PAIUTE, SENECA
Inn: Turkish, IMARET
Insects: Order of, DIPTERA
Instrument: Japanese banjolike, SAMISEN
  Musical, CLAVIER, SPINET
Interstice, AREOLA
Ironwood, COLIMA
Juniper: Old Testament, RAETAM
Kettledrum, ATABAL
King: Fairy, OBERON
Kneecap, PATELLA
Knife, MACHETE
Langur: Sumatran, SIMPAI
Legislature: Spanish, CORTES
Lemur: African, GALAGO
  Madagascar, AYAYE
Letter: Greek, EPSILON, LAMBDA, OMICRON, UPSILON
  Hebrew, DALETH, LAMEDH, SAMEKH
Lighthouse, PHAROS
Lizard, IGUANA
Llama, ALPACA
Lockjaw, TETANUS
Locust, CICADA, CICALA
Macaw: Brazilian, MARACAN
Maid: Of Astolat, ELAINE
Mammal: Madagascar, TENDRAC, TENREC
Man (Spanish), HOMBRE
Marmoset: South American, TAMARIN
Marsupial, BANDICOOT, WOMBAT
Massacre, POGROM
Mayor: Spanish, ALCALDE
Measure: Electric, AMPERE, COULOMB, KILOWATT
Medicine: Quack, NOSTRUM
Member: Religious order, CENOBITE
Molasses, TREACLE
Monkey: African, GRIVET, NISNAS
  Asian, LANGUR
  Philippine, MACHIN
  South American, PINCHE, SAIMIRI, SAMIRI, SAPAJOU
Monster, CHIMERA, GORGON
  (Comb. form), TERATO
  Cretan, MINOTAUR
Month: Jewish, HESHVAN, KISLEV, SHEBAT, TAMMUZ,
    TISHRI, VEADAR
Mountain: Asia Minor, ARARAT
Mulct, AMERCE
Musketeer, ARAMIS, PORTHOS
Nearsighted, MYOPIC
Net, TRAMMEL
New York City, GOTHAM
Nine: Group of, ENNEAD
Nobleman: Spanish, GRANDEE
Official: Roman, AEDILE
Onyx: Mexican, TECALI
Order: Dragonflies, ODANATA

Insects, DIPTERA
Organ: Plant, PISTIL
Ornament: Shoulder, EPAULET
Overcoat: Military, CAPOTE
Ox: Wild, BANTENG
Oxidation: Bronze or copper, PATINA
Paralysis: Incomplete, PARESIS
Pear: Alligator, AVOCADO
Persimmon: Mexican, CHAPOTE
Pipe: Peace, CALUMET
Plaid (Scotch), TARTAN
Plain, PAMPAS, STEPPE, TUNDRA
Plant: Buttercup family, ANEMONE
   Century, MAGUEY
   On rocks, LICHEN
Plowing: Fit for, ARABLE
Poem: Heroic, EPOPEE
   Six-lined, SESTET
Point: Highest, ZENITH
Potion: Love, PHILTER, PHILTRE
Protozoan, AMOEBA
Punish, AMERCE
Purple (heraldry), PURPURE
Queen: Fairy, TITANIA
Race: Skiing, SLALOM
Rat, BANDICOOT, LEMMING
Retort, RIPOST, RIPOSTE
Ring: Harness, TERRET
   Little, ANNULET
Rodent: Jumping, JERBOA
   Spanish American, AGOUTI, AGOUTY
Sailor: East Indian, LASCAR
Salmon: Young, GRILSE
Salutation: Eastern, SALAAM
Sandpiper, PLOVER
Sandy, ARENOSE
Sapodilla, SAPOTA, SAPOTE
Saw: Surgical, TREPAN
Seven: Group of, HEPTAD
Sexes: Common to both, EPICENE
Shawl: Mexican, SERAPE
Sheathing: Flower, SPATHE
Sheep: Wild, AOUDAD, ARGALI
Shipworm, TEREDO
Shoes: Mercury's winged, TALARIA
Shortening: Syllable, SYSTOLE
Shrub, SPIRAEA

Sickle-shaped, FALCATE
Silver (heraldry), ARGENT
Snake, ANACONDA
Speech: Loss of, APHASIA
Spiral, HELICAL
Staff: Bishop's, CROSIER, CROZIER
Stalk: Plant, PETIOLE
State: Swiss, CANTON
Studio, ATELIER
Swan: Young, CYGNET
Swimming, NATANT
Sword-shaped, ENSATE
Terminal: Negative, CATHODE
Third (music), TIERCE
Thrust: Fencing, RIPOST, RIPOSTE
Tile: Pertaining to, TEGULAR
Tomb: Empty, CENOTAPH
Tooth (comb. form), ODONTO
Tower: Mohammedan, MINARET
Tree: African timber, BAOBAB
   Black gum, TUPELO
   East Indian, MARGOSA
   Locust, ACACIA
   Malayan, SINTOC
   Marmalade, SAPOTE
Urn: Tea, SAMOVAR
Vehicle, LANDAU, TROIKA
Verbose, PROLIX
Viceroy: Egyptian, KHEDIVE
Vulture: American, CONDOR
Warehouse (French), ENTREPOT
Whale: White, BELUGA
Whirlpool, VORTEX
Will: Addition to, CODICIL
   Having left, TESTATE
Wind, CHINOOK, MONSOON, SIMOOM, SIMOON, SI ROCCO
Window: In roof, DORMER
Wine, BARBERA, BURGUNDY, CABERNET, CHABLIS, CHIANTI, CLARET, MUSCATEL, RIESLING, SAUTERNE, SHERRY, ZINFANDEL
Wolfish, LUPINE
Woman: Boisterous, TERMAGANT
Woolly, LANATE
Workshop, ATELIER
Zoroastrian, PARSEE

Old-Testament Names

(We do not pretend that this list is all-inclusive. We include only those names which in our opinion one meets most often in crossword puzzles.)

Aaron: First high priest of Jews; son of Amram; brother of Miriam and Moses; father of Abihu, Eleazer, Ithamar, and Nadab.

Abel: Son of Adam; slain by Cain.

Abigail: Wife of Nabal; later, wife of David.

Abihu: Son of Aaron.

Abimelech: King of Gerar.

Abner: Commander of army of Saul and Ishbosheth; slain by Joab.

Abraham (or Abram): Patriarch; forefather of the Jews; son of Terah; husband of Sarah; father of Isaac and Ishmael.

Absalom: Son of David and Maacah; revolted against David; slain by Joab.

Achish: King of Gath; gave refuge to David.

Achsa (or Achsah): Daughter of Caleb; wife of Othniel.

Adah: Wife of Lamech.

Adam: First man; husband of Eve; father of Cain, Abel, and Seth.

Adonijah: Son of David and Haggith.

Agag: King of Amalek; spared by Saul; slain by Samuel.

Ahasuerus: King of Persia; husband of Vashti and, later, Esther; sometimes identified with Xerxes the Great.

Ahijah: Prophet; foretold accession of Jeroboam.

Ahinoam: Wife of David.

Amasa: Commander of army of David; slain by Joab.

Amnon: Son of David and Ahinoam; ravished Tamar; slain by Absalom.

Amram: Husband of Jochebed; father of Aaron, Miriam and Moses.

Asenath: Wife of Joseph.

Asher: Son of Jacob and Zilpah.

Balaam: Prophet; rebuked by his donkey for cursing God.

Barak: Jewish captain; associated with Deborah.

Baruch: Secretary to Jeremiah.

Bathsheba: Wife of Uriah; later, wife of David.

Belshazzar: Crown prince of Babylon.

Benaiah: Warrior of David; proclaimed Solomon King.

Ben-Hadad: Name of several kings of Damascus.

Benjamin: Son of Jacob and Rachel.

Bezaleel: Chief architect of tabernacle.

Bildad: Comforter of Job.

Bilhah: Servant of Rachel; mistress of Jacob.

Boaz: Husband of Ruth; father of Obed.

Cain: Son of Adam and Eve; slayer of Abel; father of Enoch.

Cainan: Son of Enos.

Caleb: Spy sent out by Moses to visit Canaan; father of Achsa.

Canaan: Son of Ham.

Chilion: Son of Elimelech; husband of Orpah.

Cush: Son of Ham; father of Nimrod.

Dan: Son of Jacob and Rachel.

Daniel: Prophet; saved from lions by God.

Deborah: Hebrew prophetess; helped Israelites conquer Canaanites.

Delilah: Mistress and betrayer of Samson.

Elam: Son of Shem.

Eleazar: Son of Aaron; succeeded him as high priest.

Eli: High priest and judge; teacher of Samuel; father of Hophni and Phinehas.

Eliakim: Chief minister of Hezekiah.

Eliezer: Servant of Abraham.

Elihu: Comforter of Job.

Elijah (or Elias): Prophet; went to heaven in chariot of fire.

Elimelech: Husband of Naomi; father of Chilion and Mahlon.

Eliphaz: Comforter of Job.

Elisha (or Eliseus): Prophet; successor of Elijah.

Elkanah: Husband of Hannah; father of Samuel.

Enoch: Son of Cain.

Enoch: Father of Methuselah.

Enos: Son of Seth; father of Cainan.

Ephraim: Son of Joseph.

Esau: Son of Isaac and Rebecca; sold his birthright to his brother Jacob.

Esther: Jewish wife of Ahasuerus; saved Jews from Haman's plotting.

Eve: First woman; created from rib of Adam.

Ezra (or Esdras): Hebrew scribe and priest.

Gad: Son of Jacob and Zilpah.

Gehazi: Servant of Elisha.

Gideon: Israelite hero; defeated Midianites.

Goliath: Philistine giant; slain by David.

Hagar: Handmaid of Sarah; concubine of Abraham; mother of Ishmael.

Haggith: Mother of Adonijah.

Ham: Son of Noah; father of Cush, Mizraim, Phut, and Canaan.

Haman: Chief minister of Ahasuerus; hanged on gallows prepared for Mordecai.

Hannah: Wife of Elkanah; mother of Samuel.

Hanun: King of Ammonites.

Haran: Brother of Abraham; father of Lot.

Hazael: King of Damascus.

Hephzi-Bah: Wife of Hezekiah; mother of Mannaseh.

Hiram: King of Tyre.

Holofernes: General of Nebuchadnezzar; slain by Judith.

Hophni: Son of Eli.

Isaac: Hebrew patriarch; son of Abraham and Sarah; half brother of Ishmael; husband of Rebecca; father of Esau and Jacob.

Ishmael: Son of Abraham and Hagar; half brother of Isaac.

Issachar: Son of Jacob and Leah.

Ithamar: Son of Aaron.

Jabal: Son of Lamech and Adah.

Jabin: King of Hazor.

Jacob: Hebrew patriarch, founder of Israel; son of Isaac and Rebecca; husband of Leah and Rachel; father of Asher, Benjamin, Dan, Gad, Issachar, Joseph, Judah, Levi, Naphtali, Reuben, Simeon, and Zebulun.

Jael: Slayer of Sisera.

Japheth: Son of Noah.

Jehoiada: High priest; husband of Jehoshabeath; revolted against Athaliah and made Joash King of Judah.

Jehoshabeath (or Jehosheba): Daughter of Jehoram of Judah; wife of Jehoiada.

Jephthah: Judge in Israel; sacrificed his only daughter because of vow.

Jesse: Son of Obed; father of David.

Jethro: Midianite priest; father of Zipporah.

Jezebel: Phoenician princess; wife of Ahab; mother of Ahaziah, Athaliah, and Jehoram.

Joab: Commander in chief under David; slayer of Abner, Absalom, and Amasa.

Job: Patriarch; underwent many afflictions; comforted by Bildad, Elihu, Eliphaz and Zophar.

Jochebed: Wife of Amram.

Jonah: Prophet; cast into sea and swallowed by great fish.

Jonathan: Son of Saul; friend of David.

Joseph: Son of Jacob and Rachel; sold into slavery by his brothers; husband of Asenath; father of Ephraim and Manassah.

Joshua: Successor of Moses; son of Nun.

Jubal: Son of Lamech and Adah.

Judah: Son of Jacob and Leah.

Judith: Slayer of Holofernes.

Kish: Father of Saul.

Laban: Father of Leah and Rachel.

Lamech: Son of Methuselah; father of Noah.

Lamech: Husband of Adah and Zillah; father of Jabal, Jubal, and Tubal-Cain.

Leah: Daughter of Laban; wife of Jacob.

Levi: Son of Jacob and Leah.

Lot: Son of Haran; escaped destruction of Sodom.

Maacah: Mother of Absalom and Tamar.

Mahlon: Son of Elimelech; first husband of Ruth.

Manasseh: Son of Joseph.

Melchizedek: King of Salem.

Methuselah: Patriarch; son of Enoch; father of Lamech.

Michal: Daughter of Saul; wife of David.

Miriam: Prophetess; daughter of Amram; sister of Aaron and Moses.

Mizraim: Son of Ham.

Mordecai: Uncle of Esther; with her aid, saved Jews from Haman's plotting.

Moses: Prophet and lawgiver; son of Amram; brother of Aaron and Miriam; husband of Zipporah.

Naaman: Syrian captain; cured of leprosy by Elisha.

Nabal: Husband of Abigail.

Naboth: Owner of vineyard; stoned to death because he would not sell it to Ahab.

Nadab: Son of Aaron.

Nahor: Father of Terah.

Naomi: Wife of Elimelech; mother-in-law of Ruth.

Naphtali: Son of Jacob and Bilhah.

Nathan: Prophet; reproved David for causing Uriah's death.

Nebuchadnezzar (or Nebuchadrezzar): King of Babylon; destroyer of Jerusalem.

Nehemiah: Jewish leader; empowered by Artaxerxes to rebuild Jerusalem.

Nimrod: Mighty hunter; son of Cush.

Noah: Patriarch; son of Lamech; escaped Deluge by building Ark; father of Ham, Japheth and Shem.

Nun (or Non): Father of Joshua.

Obed: Son of Boaz; father of Jesse.

Og: King of Bashan.

Orpah: Wife of Chilion.

Othniel: Kenezite; judge of Israel; husband of Achsa.

Phinehas: Son of Eleazer.

Phinehas: Son of Eli.

Phut (or Put): Son of Ham.

Potiphar: Egyptian official; bought Joseph.

Rachel: Wife of Jacob.

Rebecca (or Rebekah): Wife of Isaac.

Reuben: Son of Jacob and Leah.

Ruth: Wife of Mahlon, later of Boaz; daughter-in-law of Naomi.

Samson: Judge of Israel; famed for strength; betrayed by Delilah.

Samuel: Hebrew judge and prophet; son of Elkanah.

Sarah (or Sara, Sarai): Wife of Abraham.

Sennacherib: King of Assyria.

Seth: Son of Adam; father of Enos.

Shem: Son of Noah; father of Elam.

Simeon: Son of Jacob and Leah.

Sisera: Canaanite captain; slain by Jael.

Tamar: Daughter of David and Maachah; ravished by Amnon.

Terah: Son of Nahor; father of Abraham.

Tubal-Cain: Son of Lamech and Zillah.

Uriah: Husband of Bathsheba; sent to death in battle by David.

Vashti: Wife of Ahasuerus; set aside by him.

Zadok: High priest during David's reign.

Zebulun (or Zabulon): Son of Jacob and Leah.

Zillah: Wife of Lamech.

Zilpah: Servant of Leah; mistress of Jacob.

Zipporah: Daughter of Jethro; wife of Moses.

Zophar: Comforter of Job.

Kings of Judah and Israel

Kings Before Division of Kingdom

Saul: First King of Israel; son of Kish; father of Ish-Bosheth, Jonathan and Michal.

Ish-Bosheth (or Eshbaal): King of Israel; son of Saul.

David: King of Judah; later of Israel; son of Jesse; husband of Abigail, Ahinoam, Bathsheba, Michal, etc.; father of Absalom, Adonijah, Amnon, Solomon, Tamar, etc.

Solomon: King of Israel and Judah; son of David; father of Rehoboam.

Rehoboam:
Son of Solomon; during his reign the kingdom was divided into Judah and Israel.

Kings of Judah (Southern Kingdom)

Rehoboam: First King.

Abijah (or Abijam or Abia): Son of Rehoboam.

Asa: Probably son of Abijah.

Jehoshaphat: Son of Asa.

Jehoram (or Joram): Son of Jehoshaphat; husband of Athaliah.

Ahaziah: Son of Jehoram and Athaliah.

Athaliah: Daughter of King Ahab of Israel and Jezebel; wife of Jehoram.

Joash (or Jehoash): Son of Ahaziah.

Amaziah: Son of Joash.

Uzziah (or Azariah): Son of Amaziah.

Jotham: Regent, later King; son of Uzziah.

Ahaz: Son of Jotham.

Hezekiah: Son of Ahaz; husband of Hephzi-Bah.

Manasseh: Son of Hezekiah and Hephzi-Bah.

Amon: Son of Manasseh.

Josiah (or Josias): Son of Amon.

Jehoahaz (or Joahaz): Son of Josiah.

Jehoiakim: Son of Josiah.

Jehoiachin: Son of Jehoiakim.

Zedekiah: Son of Josiah; kingdom overthrown by Babylonians under Nebuchadnezzar.

Kings of Israel (Northern Kingdom)

Jeroboam I: Led secession of Israel.

Nadab: Son of Jeroboam I.

Baasha: Overthrew Nadab.

Elah: Son of Baasha.

Zimri: Overthrew Elah.

Omri: Overthrew Zimri.

Ahab: Son of Omri; husband of Jezebel.

Ahaziah: Son of Ahab.

Jehoram (or Joram): Son of Ahab.

Jehu: Overthrew Jehoram.

Jehoahaz (or Joahaz): Son of Jehu.

Jehoash (or Joash): Son of Jehoahaz.

Jeroboam II: Son of Jehoash.

Zechariah: Son of Jeroboam II.

Shallum: Overthrew Zechariah.

Menahem: Overthrew Shallum.

Pekahiah: Son of Menahem.

Pekah: Overthrew Pekahiah.

Hoshea: Overthrew Pekah; kingdom overthrown by Assyrians under Sargon II.

Prophets

Major.—Isaiah, Jeremiah, Ezekiel, Daniel.

Minor.—Hosea, Obadiah, Nahum, Haggai, Joel, Jonah, Habakkuk, Zechariah, Amos, Micah, Zephaniah, Malachi.

Greek and Roman Mythology

(Most of the Greek deities were adopted by the Romans, although in many cases there was a change of name. In the list below, information is given under the Greek name; the name in parentheses is the Latin equivalent. However, all Latin names are listed with cross references to the Greek ones. In addition, there are several deities which were exclusively Roman.)

Acheron: *See* Rivers.

Achilles: Greek warrior; slew Hector at Troy; slain by Paris, who wounded him in his vulnerable heel.

Actaeon: Hunter; surprised Artemis bathing; changed by her to stag and killed by his dogs.

Admetus: King of Thessaly; his wife, Alcestis, offered to die in his place.

Adonis: Beautiful youth loved by Aphrodite.

Aeacus: One of three judges of dead in Hades; son of Zeus.

Aeëtes: King of Colchis; father of Medea; keeper of Golden Fleece.

Aegeus: Father of Theseus; believing Theseus killed in Crete, he drowned himself, Aegean Sea named for him.

Aegisthus: Son of Thyestes; slew Atreus; with Clytemnestra, his paramour, slew Agamemnon; slain by Orestes.

Aegyptus: Brother of Danaus; his sons, except Lynceus, slain by Danaides.

Aeneas: Trojan; son of Anchises and Aphrodite; after fall of Troy, led his followers eventually to Italy; loved and deserted Dido.

Aeolus: *See* Winds.

Aesculapius: *See* Asclepius.

Aeson: King of Ioclus; father of Jason; overthrown by his brother Pelias; restored to youth by Medea.

Aether: Personification of sky.

Aethra: Mother of Theseus.

Agamemnon: King of Mycenae; son of Atreus; brother of Menelaus; leader of Greeks against Troy; slain on his return home by Clytemnestra and Aegisthus.

Agiaia: *See* Graces.

Ajax: Greek warrior; killed himself at Troy because Achilles' armor was awarded to Odysseus.

Alcestis: Wife of Admetus; offered to die in his place but saved from death by Hercules.

Alcmene: Wife of Amphitryon; mother by Zeus of Hercules.

Alcyone: *See* Pleiades.

Alecto: *See* Furies.

Alectryon: Youth changed by Ares into cock.

Althaea: Wife of Oeneus; mother of Meleager.

Amazons: Female warriors in Asia Minor; supported Troy against Greeks.

Amor: *See* Eros.

Amphion: Musician; husband of Niobe; charmed stones to build fortifications for Thebes.

Amphitrite: Sea goddess; wife of Poseidon.

Amphitryon: Husband of Alcmene.

Anchises: Father of Aeneas.

Ancile: Sacred shield that fell from heavens; palladium of Rome.

Andraemon: Husband of Dryope.

Andromache: Wife of Hector.

Andromeda: Daughter of Cepheus; chained to cliff for monster to devour; rescued by Perseus.

Anteia: Wife of Proetus; tried to induce Bellerophon to elope with her.

Anteros: God who avenged unrequited love.

Antigone: Daughter of Oedipus; accompanied him to Colonus; performed burial rite for Polynices and hanged herself.

Antinoüs: Leader of suitors of Penelope; slain by Odysseus.

Aphrodite (Venus): Goddess of love and beauty; daughter of Zeus; mother of Eros.

Apollo: God of beauty, poetry, music; later identified with Helios as Phoebus Apollo; son of Zeus and Leto.

Aquilo: *See* Winds.

Arachne: Maiden who challenged Athena to weaving contest; changed to spider.

Ares (Mars): God of war; son of Zeus and Hera.

Argo: Ship in which Jason and followers sailed to Colchis for Golden Fleece.

Argus: Monster with hundred eyes; slain by Hermes; his eyes placed by Hera into peacock's tail.

Ariadne: Daughter of Minos; aided Theseus in slaying Minotaur; deserted by him on island of Naxos and married to Dionysus.

Arion: Musician; thrown overboard by pirates but saved by dolphin.

Artemis (Diana): Goddess of moon; huntress; twin sister of Apollo.

Asclepius (Aesculapius): Mortal son of Apollo; slain by Zeus for raising dead; later deified as god of medicine. Also known as Asklepios.

Astarte: Phoenician goddess of love; variously identified with Aphrodite, Selene, and Artemis.

Astraea: Goddess of Justice; daughter of Zeus and Themis.

Atalanta: Princess who challenged her suitors to a foot race; Hippomenes won race and married her.

Athena (Minerva): Goddess of wisdom; known poetically as Pallas Athene; sprang fully armed from head of Zeus.

Atlas: Titan; held world on his shoulders as punishment for warring against Zeus; son of Iapetus.

Atreus: King of Mycenae; father of Menelaus and Agamemnon; brother of Thyestes, three of whose sons he slew and served to him at banquet; slain by Aegisthus.

Atropos: *See* Fates.

Aurora: *See* Eos.

Auster: *See* Winds.

Avernus: Infernal regions; name derived from small vaporous lake near Vesuvius which was fabled to kill birds and vegetation.

Bacchus: *See* Dionysus.

Bellerophon: Corinthian hero; killed Chimera with aid of Pegasus; tried to reach Olympus on Pegasus and was thrown to his death.

Bellona: Roman goddess of war.

Boreas: *See* Winds.

Briareus: Monster of hundred hands; son of Uranus and Gaea.

Briseis: Captive maiden given to Achilles; taken by Agamemnon in exchange for loss of Chryseis, which caused Achilles to cease fighting, until death of Patroclus.

Cadmus: Brother of Europa; planter of dragon seeds from which first Thebans sprang.

Calliope: *See* Muses.

Calypso: Sea nymph; kept Odysseus on her island Ogygia for seven years.

Cassandra: Daughter of Priam; prophetess who was never believed; slain with Agamemnon.

Castor: *See* Dioscuri.

Celaeno: *See* Pleiades.

Centaurs: Beings half man and half horse; lived in mountains of Thessaly.

Cephalus: Hunter; accidentally killed his wife Procris with his spear.

Cepheus: King of Ethiopia; father of Andromeda.

Cerberus: Three-headed dog guarding entrance to Hades.

Ceres: *See* Demeter.

Chaos: Formless void; personified as first of gods.

Charon: Boatman on Styx who carried souls of dead to Hades; son of Erebus.

Charybdis: Female monster; personification of whirlpool.

Chimera: Female monster with head of lion, body of goat, tail of serpent; killed by Bellerophon.

Chiron: Most famous of centaurs.

Chronos: Personification of time.

Chryseis: Captive maiden given to Agamemnon; his refusal to accept ransom from her father Chryses caused Apollo to send plague on Greeks besieging Troy.

Circe: Sorceress; daughter of Helios; changed Odysseus' men into swine.

Clio: *See* Muses.

Clotho: *See* Fates.

Clytemnestra: Wife of Agamemnon, whom she slew with aid of her paramour, Aegisthus; slain by her son Orestes.

Cocytus: *See* Rivers.

Creon: Father of Jocasta; forbade burial of Polynices; ordered burial alive of Antigone.

Creüsa: Princess of Corinth, for whom Jason deserted Medea; slain by Medea, who sent her poisoned robe; also known as Glaüke.

Creusa: Wife of Aeneas; died fleeing Troy.

Cronus (Saturn): Titan; god of harvests; son of Uranus and Gaea; dethroned by his son Zeus.

Cupid: *See* Eros.

Cybele: Anatolian nature goddess; adopted by Greeks and identified with Rhea.

Cyclopes: Race of one-eyed giants (singular: Cyclops).

Daedalus: Athenian artificer; father of Icarus; builder of Labyrinth in Crete; devised wings attached with wax for him and Icarus to escape Crete.

Danae: Princess of Argos; mother of Perseus by Zeus, who appeared to her in form of golden shower.

Danaïdes: Daughters of Danaüs; at his command, all except Hypermnestra slew their husbands, the sons of Aegyptus.

Danaüs: Brother of Aegyptus; father of Danaïdes; slain by Lynceus.

Daphne: Nymph; pursued by Apollo; changed to laurel tree.

Decuma: *See* Fates.

Deino: *See* Graeae.

Demeter (Ceres): Goddess of agriculture; mother of Persephone.

Diana: *See* Artemis.

Dido: Founder and queen of Carthage; stabbed herself when deserted by Aeneas.

Diomedes: Greek hero; with Odysseus, entered Troy and carried off Palladium, sacred statue of Athena.

Diomedes: Owner of man-eating horses, which Hercules, as ninth labor, carried off.

Dione: Titan goddess; mother by Zeus of Aphrodite.

Dionysus (Bacchus): God of wine; son of Zeus and Semele.

Dioscuri: Twins Castor and Pollux; sons of Leda by Zeus.

Dis: *See* Hades.

Dryads: Wood nymphs.

Dryope: Maiden changed to Hamadryad.

Echo: Nymph who fell hopelessly in love with Narcissus; faded away except for her voice.

Electra: Daughter of Agamemnon and Clytemnestra; sister of Orestes; urged Orestes to slay Clytemnestra and Aegisthus.

Electra: *See* Pleiades.

Elysium: Abode of blessed dead.

Endymion: Mortal loved by Selene.

Enyo: *See* Graeae.

Eos (Aurora): Goddess of dawn.

Epimetheus: Brother of Prometheus; husband of Pandora.

Erato: *See* Muses.

Erebus: Spirit of darkness; son of Chaos.

Erinyes: *See* Furies.

Eris: Goddess of discord.

Eros (Amor or Cupid): God of love; son of Aphrodite.

Eteocles: Son of Oedipus, whom he succeeded to rule alternately with Polynices; refused to give up throne at end of year; he and Polynices slew each other.

Eumenides: *See* Furies.

Euphrosyne: *See* Graces.

Europa: Mortal loved by Zeus, who, in form of white bull, carried her off to Crete.

Eurus: *See* Winds.

Euryale: *See* Gorgons.

Eurydice: Nymph; wife of Orpheus.

Eurystheus: King of Argos; imposed twelve labors on Hercules.

Euterpe: *See* Muses.

Fates: Goddesses of destiny; Clotho (Spinner of thread of life), Lachesis (Determiner of length), and Atropos (Cutter of thread); also called Moirae. Identified by Romans with their goddesses of fate; Nona, Decuma, and Morta; called Parcae.

Fauns: Roman deities of woods and groves.

Faunus: *See* Pan.

Favonius: *See* Winds.

Flora: Roman goddess of flowers.

Fortuna: Roman goddess of fortune.

Furies: Avenging spirits; Alecto, Megaera, and Tisiphone; known also as Erinyes or Eumenides.

Gaea: Goddess of earth; daughter of Chaos; mother of Titans; known also as Ge, Gea, Gaia, etc.

Galatea: Statue of maiden carved from ivory by Pygmalion; given life by Aphrodite.

Galatea: Sea nymph; loved by Polyphemus.

Ganymede: Beautiful boy; successor to Hebe as cupbearer of gods.

Glaucus: Mortal who became sea divinity by eating magic grass.

Glauke: *See* Creüsa.

Golden Fleece: Fleece from ram that flew Phrixos to Colchis; Aeëtes placed it under guard of dragon; carried off by Jason.

Gorgons: Female monsters; Euryale, Medusa, and Stheno; had snakes for hair; their glances turned mortals to stone. *See* Medusa.

Graces: Beautiful goddesses: Aglaia (Brilliance), Euphrosyne (Joy), and Thalia (Bloom); daughters of Zeus.

Graeae: Sentinels for Gorgons; Deino, Enyo, and Pephredo; had one eye among them, which passed from one to another.

Hades (Dis): Name sometimes given Pluto; also, abode of dead, ruled by Pluto.

Haemon: Son of Creon; promised husband of Antigone; killed himself in her tomb.

Hamadryads: Tree nymphs.

Harpies: Monsters with heads of women and bodies of birds.

Hebe (Juventas): Goddess of youth; cupbearer of gods before Ganymede; daughter of Zeus and Hera.

Hecate: Goddess of sorcery and witchcraft.

Hector: Son of Priam; slayer of Patroclus; slain by Achilles.

Hecuba: Wife of Priam.

Helen: Fairest woman in world; daughter of Zeus and Leda; wife of Menelaus; carried to Troy by Paris, causing Trojan War.

Heliades: Daughters of Helios; mourned for Phaëthon and were changed to poplar trees.

Helios (Sol): God of sun; later identified with Apollo.

Helle: Sister of Phrixos; fell from ram of Golden Fleece; water where she fell named Hellespont.

Hephaestus (Vulcan): God of fire; celestial blacksmith; son of Zeus and Hera; husband of Aphrodite.

Hera (Juno): Queen of heaven; wife of Zeus.

Hercules: Hero and strong man; son of Zeus and Alcmene; performed twelve labors or deeds to be free from bondage under Eurystheus; after death, his mortal share was destroyed, and he became immortal. Also known as Herakles or Heracles. Labors: (1) killing Nemean lion; (2) killing Lernaean Hydra; (3) capturing Erymanthian boar; (4) capturing Ceryneian hind; (5) killing man-eating Stymphalian birds; (6) procuring girdle of Hippolyte; (7) cleaning Augean stables; (8) capturing Cretan bull; (9) capturing man-eating horses of Diomedes; (10) capturing cattle of Geryon; (11) procuring golden apples of Hesperides; (12) bringing Cerberus up from Hades.

Hermes (Mercury): God of physicians and thieves; messenger of gods; son of Zeus and Maia.

Hero: Priestess of Aphrodite; Leander swam Hellespont nightly to see her; drowned herself at his death.

Hesperus: Evening star.

Hestia (Vesta): Goddess of hearth; sister of Zeus.

Hippolyte: Queen of Amazons; wife of Theseus.

Hippolytus: Son of Theseus and Hippolyte; falsely accused by Phaedra of trying to kidnap her; slain by Poseidon at request of Theseus.

Hippomenes: Husband of Atalanta, whom he beat in race by dropping golden apples, which she stopped to pick up.

Hyacinthus: Beautiful youth accidentally killed by Apollo, who caused flower to spring up from his blood.

Hydra: Nine-headed monster in marsh of Lerna; slain by Hercules.

Hygeia: Personification of health.

Hyman: God of marriage.

Hyperion: Titan; early sun god; father of Helios.

Hypermnestra: Daughter of Danaüs; refused to kill her husband Lynceus.

Hypnos (Somnus): God of sleep.

Iapetus: Titan; father of Atlas, Epimetheus, and Prometheus.

Icarus: Son of Daedalus; flew too near sun with wax-attached wings and fell into sea and was drowned.

Io: Mortal maiden loved by Zeus; changed by Hera into heifer.

Iobates: King of Lycia; sent Bellerophon to slay Chimera.

Iphigenia: Daughter of Agamemnon; offered as sacrifice to Artemis at Aulis; carried by Artemis to Tauris where she became priestess; escaped from there with Orestes.

Iris: Goddess of rainbow; messenger of Zeus and Hera.

Ismene: Daughter of Oedipus; sister of Antigone.

Ixion: King of Lapithae; for making love to Hera he was bound to endlessly revolving wheel in Tartarus.

Iulus: Son of Aeneas.

Janus: Roman god of gates and doors; represented with two opposite faces.

Jason: Son of Aeson; to gain throne of Ioclus from Pelias, went to Colchis and brought back Golden Fleece; married Medea; deserted her for Creüsa.

Jocasta: Wife of Laius; mother of Oedipus; unwittingly became wife of Oedipus; hanged herself when relationship was discovered.

Juno: *See* Hera.

Jupiter: *See* Zeus.

Juventas: *See* Hebe.

Lachesis: *See* Fates.

Laius: Father of Oedipus, by whom he was slain.

Laocoön: Priest of Apollo at Troy; warned against bringing wooden horse into Troy; destroyed with his two sons by serpents sent by Athena.

Lares: Roman ancestral spirits protecting descendants and homes.

Lavinia: Wife of Aeneas after defeat of Turnus.

Leander: Swam Hellespont nightly to see Hero; drowned in storm.

Leda: Mortal loved by Zeus in form of Swan; mother of Helen, Clytemnestra, Dioscuri.

Lethe: *See* Rivers.

Leto (Latona): Mother by Zeus of Artemis and Apollo.

Lucina: Roman goddess of childbirth; identified with Juno.

Lynceus: Son of Aegyptus; husband of Hypermnestra; slew Danaüs.

Maia: Daughter of Atlas; mother of Hermes.

Maia: *See* Pleiades.

Manes: Souls of dead Romans, particularly of ancestors.

Mars: *See* Ares.

Marsyas: Shepherd; challenged Apollo to music contest and lost; flayed alive by Apollo.

Medea: Sorceress; daughter of Aeëtes; helped Jason obtain Golden Fleece; when deserted by him for Creüsa, killed her children and Creüsa.

Medusa: Gorgon; slain by Perseus, who cut off her head.

Megaera: *See* Furies.

Meleager: Son of Althaea; his life would last as long as brand burning at his birth; Althaea quenched and saved it but destroyed it when Meleager slew his uncles.

Melpomene: *See* Muses.

Memnon: Ethiopian king; made immortal by Zeus; son of Tithonus and Eos.

Menelaus: King of Sparta; son of Atreus; brother of Agamemnon; husband of Helen.

Mercury: *See* Hermes.

Merope: *See* Pleiades.

Mezentius: Cruel Etruscan king; ally of Turnus against Aeneas; slain by Aeneas.

Midas: King of Phrygia; given gift of turning to gold all he touched.

Minerva: *See* Athena.

Minos: King of Crete; after death, one of three judges of dead in Hades; son of Zeus and Europa.

Minotaur: Monster, half man and half beast, kept in Labyrinth in Crete; slain by Theseus.

Mnemosyne: Goddess of memory; mother by Zeus of Muses.

Moirae: *See* Fates.

Momus: God of ridicule.

Morpheus: God of dreams.

Mors: *See* Thanatos.

Morta: *See* Fates.

Muses: Goddesses presiding over arts and sciences: Calliope (epic poetry), Clio (history), Erato (lyric and love poetry), Euterpe (music), Melpomene (tragedy), Polymnia or Polyhymnia (sacred poetry), Terpsichore (choral dance and song), Thalia (comedy and bucolic poetry), Urania (astronomy); daughters of Zeus and Mnemosyne.

Naiads: Nymphs of waters, streams, and fountains.

Napaeae: Wood nymphs.

Narcissus: Beautiful youth loved by Echo; in punishment for not returning her love, he was made to fall in love with his image reflected in pool; pined away and became flower.

Nemesis: Goddess of retribution.

Neoptolemus: Son of Achilles; slew Priam; also known as Pyrrhus.

Neptune: *See* Poseidon.

Nereids: Sea nymphs; attendants on Poseidon.

Nestor: King of Pylos; noted for wise counsel in expedition against Troy.

Nike: Goddess of victory.

Niobe: Daughter of Tantalus; wife of Amphion; her children slain by Apollo and Artemis; changed to stone but continued to weep her loss.

Nona: *See* Fates.

Notus: *See* Winds.

Nox: *See* Nyx.

Nymphs: Beautiful maidens; inferior deities of nature.

Nyx (Nox): Goddess of night.

Oceanids: Ocean nymphs; daughters of Oceanus.

Oceanus: Eldest of Titans; god of waters.

Odysseus (Ulysses): King of Ithaca; husband of Penelope; wandered ten years after fall of Troy before arriving home.

Oedipus: King of Thebes; son of Laius and Jocasta; unwittingly murdered Laius and married Jocasta; tore his eyes out when relationship was discovered.

Oenone: Nymph of Mount Ida; wife of Paris, who abandoned her; refused to cure him when he was poisoned by arrow of Philoctetes at Troy.

Ops: *See* Rhea.

Oreads: Mountain nymphs.

Orestes: Son of Agamemnon and Clytemnestra; brother of Electra; slew Clytemnestra and Aegisthus; pursued by Furies until his purification by Apollo.

Orion: Hunter; slain by Artemis and made heavenly constellation.

Orpheus: Famed musician; son of Apollo and Muse Calliope; husband of Eurydice.

Pales: Roman goddess of shepherds and herdsmen.

Palinurus: Aeneas' pilot; fell overboard in his sleep and was drowned.

Pan (Faunus): God of woods and fields; part goat; son of Hermes.

Pandora: Opener of box containing human ills; mortal wife of Epimetheus.

Parcae: *See* Fates.

Paris: Son of Priam; gave apple of discord to Aphrodite, for which she enabled him to carry off Helen; slew Achilles at Troy; slain by Philoctetes.

Patroclus: Great friend of Achilles; wore Achilles' armor and was slain by Hector.

Pegasus: Winged horse that sprang from Medusa's body at her death; ridden by Bellerophon when he slew Chimera.

Pelias: King of Ioclus; seized throne from his brother Aeson; sent Jason for Golden Fleece; slain unwittingly by his daughters at instigation of Medea.

Pelops: Son of Tantalus; his father cooked and served him to gods; restored to life; Peloponnesus named for him.

Penates: Roman household gods.

Penelope: Wife of Odysseus; waited faithfully for him for ten years while putting off numerous suitors.

Pephredo: *See* Graeae.

Periphetes: Giant; son of Hephaestus; slain by Theseus.

Persephone (Proserpine): Queen of infernal regions; daughter of Zeus and Demeter; wife of Pluto.

Perseus: Son of Zeus and Danaë; slew Medusa; rescued Andromeda from monster and married her.

Phaedra: Daughter of Minos; wife of Theseus; caused the death of her stepson, Hippolytus.

Phaethon: Son of Helios; drove his father's sun chariot and was struck down by Zeus before he set world on fire.

Philoctetes: Greek warrior who possessed Hercules' bow and arrows; slew Paris at Troy with poisoned arrow.

Phineus: Betrothed of Andromeda; tried to slay Perseus but turned to stone by Medusa's head.

Phlegethon: *See* Rivers.

Phosphor: Morning star.

Phrixos: Brother of Helle; carried by ram of Golden Fleece to Colchis.

Pirithous: Son of Ixion; friend of Theseus; tried to carry off Persephone from Hades; bound to enchanted rock by Pluto.

Pleiades: Alcyone, Celaeno, Electra, Maia, Merope, Sterope or Asterope, Taygeta; seven daughters of Atlas; transformed into heavenly constellation, of which six stars are visible (Merope is said to have hidden in shame for loving a mortal).

Pluto (Dis): God of Hades; brother of Zeus.

Plutus: God of wealth.

Pollux: *See* Dioscuri.

Polymnia: *See* Muses.

Polynices: Son of Oedipus; he and his brother Eteocles killed each other; burial rite, forbidden by Creon, performed by his sister Antigone.

Polyphemus: Cyclops; devoured six of Odysseus' men; blinded by Odysseus.

Polyxena: Daughter of Priam; betrothed to Achilles, whom Paris slew at their betrothal; sacrificed to shade of Achilles.

Pomona: Roman goddess of fruits.

Pontus: Sea god; son of Gaea.

Poseidon (Neptune): God of sea; brother of Zeus.

Priam: King of Troy; husband of Hecuba; ransomed Hector's body from Achilles; slain by Neoptolemus.

Priapus: God of regeneration.

Procris: Wife of Cephalus, who accidentally slew her.

Procrustes: Giant; stretched or cut off legs of victims to make them fit iron bed; slain by Theseus.

Proetus: Husband of Anteia; sent Bellerophon to lobates to be put to death.

Prometheus: Titan; stole fire from heaven for man. Zeus punished him by chaining him to rock in Caucasus where vultures devoured his liver daily.

Proteus: Sea god; assumed various shapes when called on to prophesy.

Psyche: Beloved of Eros; punished by jealous Aphrodite; made immortal and united with Eros.

Pygmalion: King of Cyprus; carved ivory statue of maiden which Aphrodite gave life as Galatea.

Pyramus: Babylonian youth; made love to Thisbe through hole in wall; thinking Thisbe slain by lion, killed himself.

Pyrrhus: *See* Neoptolemus.

Python: Serpent born from slime left by Deluge; slain by Apollo.

Quirinus: Roman war god.

Remus: Brother of Romulus; slain by him.

Rhadamanthus: One of three judges of dead in Hades; son of Zeus and Europa.

Rhea (Ops): Daughter of Uranus and Gaea; wife of Cronus; mother of Zeus; identified with Cybele.

Rivers of Underworld: Acheron (woe), Cocytus (wailing), Lethe (forgetfulness), Phlegethon (fire), Styx (across which souls of dead were ferried by Charon).

Romulus: Founder of Rome; he and Remus suckled in infancy by she-wolf; slew Remus; deified by Romans.

Sarpedon: King of Lycia; son of Zeus and Europa; slain by Patroclus at Troy.

Saturn: *See* Cronus.

Satyrs: Hoofed demigods of woods and fields; companions of Dionysus.

Sciron: Robber; forced strangers to wash his feet, then hurled them into sea where tortoise devoured them; slain by Theseus.

Scylla: Female monster inhabiting rock opposite Charybdis; menaced passing sailors.

Selene: Goddess of moon.

Semele: Daughter of Cadmus; mother by Zeus of Dionysus; demanded Zeus appear before her in all his splendor and was destroyed by his lightnings.

Sibyis: Various prophetesses; most famous, Cumaean sibyl, accompanied Aeneas into Hades.

Sileni: Minor woodland deities similar to satyrs (singular: silenus). Sometimes Silenus refers to eldest of satyrs, son of Hermes or of Pan.

Silvanus: Roman god of woods and fields.

Sinis: Giant; bent pines, by which he hurled victims against side of mountain; slain by Theseus.

Sirens: Minor deities who lured sailors to destruction with their singing.

Sisyphus: King of Corinth; condemned in Tartarus to roll huge stone to top of hill; it always rolled back down again.

Sol: *See* Helios.

Somnus: *See* Hypnos.

Sphinx: Monster of Thebes; killed those who could not answer her riddle; slain by Oedipus. Name also refers to other monsters having body of lion, wings, and head and bust of woman.

Sterope: *See* Pleiades.

Stheno: *See* Gorgons.

Styx: *See* Rivers.

Symplegades: Clashing rocks at entrance to Black Sea; Argo passed through, causing them to become forever fixed.

Syrinx: Nymph pursued by Pan; changed to reeds, from which he made his pipes.

Tantalus: Cruel king; father of Pelops and Niobe; condemned in Tartarus to stand chin-deep in lake surrounded by fruit branches; as he tried to eat or drink, water or fruit always receded.

Tartarus: Underworld below Hades; often refers to Hades.

Taygeta: *See* Pleiades.

Telemachus: Son of Odysseus; made unsuccessful journey to find his father.

Tellus: Roman goddess of earth.

Terminus: Roman god of boundaries and landmarks.

Terpsichore: *See* Muses.

Terra: Roman earth goddess.

Thalia: *See* Graces; Muses.

Thanatos (Mors): God of death.

Themis: Titan goddess of laws of physical phenomena; daughter of Uranus; mother of Prometheus.

Theseus: Son of Aegeus; slew Minotaur; married and deserted Ariadne; later married Phaedra.

Thisbe: Beloved of Pyramus; killed herself at his death.

Thyestes: Brother of Atreus; Atreus killed three of his sons and served them to him at banquet.

Tiresias: Blind soothsayer of Thebes.

Tisiphone: *See* Furies.

Titans: Early gods from which Olympian gods were derived; children of Uranus and Gaea.

Tithonus: Mortal loved by Eos; changed into grasshopper.

Triton: Demigod of sea; son of Poseidon.

Turnus: King of Rutuli in Italy; betrothed to Lavinia; slain by Aeneas.

Ulysses: *See* Odysseus.

Urania: *See* Muses.

Uranus: Personification of Heaven; husband of Gaea; father of Titans; dethroned by his son Cronus.

Venus: *See* Aphrodite.

Vertumnus: Roman god of fruits and vegetables; husband of Pomona.

Vesta: *See* Hestia.

Vulcan: *See* Hephaestus.

Winds: Aeolus (keeper of winds), Boreas (Aquilo) (north wind), Eurus (east wind), Notus (Auster) (south wind), Zephyrus (Favonius) (west wind).

Zephyrus: *See* Winds.

Zeus (Jupiter): Chief of Olympian gods; son of Cronus and Rhea; husband of Hera.

Norse Mythology

Aesir: Chief gods of Asgard.

Andvari: Dwarf; robbed of gold and magic ring by Loki.

Angerbotha (Angrbotha): Giantess; mother by Loki of Fenrir, Hel, and Midgard serpent.

Asgard (Asgarth): Abode of gods.

Ask (Aske, Askr): First man; created by Odin, Hoenir, and Lothur.

Asynjur: Goddesses of Asgard.

Atli: Second husband of Gudrun; invited Gunnar and Hogni to his court, where they were slain; slain by Gudrun.

Audhumia (Audhumbla): Cow that nourished Ymir, created by Buri by licking ice cliff.

Balder (Baldr, Baldur): God of light, spring, peace, joy; son of Odin; slain by Hoth at instigation of Loki.

Bifrost: Rainbow bridge connecting Midgard and Asgard.

Bragi (Brage): God of poetry; husband of Ithunn.

Branstock: Great oak in hall of Volsungs; into it, Odin thrust Gram, which only Sigmund could draw forth.

Brynhild: Valkyrie; wakened from magic sleep by Sigurd; married Gunnar; instigated death of Sigurd; killed herself and was burned on pyre beside Sigurd.

Bur (Bor): Son of Buri; father of Odin, Hoenir, and Lothur.

Buri (Bori): Progenitor of gods; father of Bur; created by Audhumla.

Embla: First woman; created by Odin, Hoenir, and Lothur.

Fafnir: Son of Rodmar, whom he slew for gold in Otter's skin; in form of dragon, guarded gold; slain by Sigurd.

Fenrir: Wolf; offspring of Loki; swallows Odin at Ragnarok and is slain by Vitharr.

Forseti: Son of Balder.

Frey (Freyr): God of fertility and crops; son of Njorth; originally one of Vanir.

Freya (Freyja): Goddess of love and beauty; sister of Frey; originally one of Vanir.

Frigg (Frigga): Goddess of sky; wife of Odin.

Garm: Watchdog of Hel; slays, and is slain by, Tyr at Ragnarok.

Gimle: Home of blessed after Ragnarok.

Giuki: King of Nibelungs; father of Gunnar, Hogni, Guttorm, and Gudrun.

Glathsehim (Gladsheim): Hall of gods in Asgard.

Gram (meaning "Angry"): Sigmund's sword; rewelded by Regin; used by Sigurd to slay Fafnir.

Greyfell: Sigmund's horse; descended from Sleipnir.

Grimhild: Mother of Gudrun; administered magic potion to Sigurd which made him forget Brynhild.

Gudrun: Daughter of Giuki; wife of Sigurd; later wife of Atli and Jonakr.

Gunnar: Son of Giuki; in his semblance Sigurd won Brynhild for him; slain at hall of Atli.

Guttorm: Son of Giuki; slew Sigurd at Brynhild's request.

Heimdall (Heimdallr): Guardian of Asgard.

Hel: Goddess of dead and queen of underworld; daughter of Loki.

Hiordis: Wife of Sigmund; mother of Sigurd.

Hoenir: One of creators of Ask and Embla; son of Bur.

Hogni: Son of Giuki; slain at hall of Atli.

Hoth (Hoder, Hodur): Blind god of night and darkness; slayer of Balder at instigation of Loki.

Ithunn (Ithun, Iduna): Keeper of golden apples of youth; wife of Bragi.

Jonakr: Third husband of Gudrun.

Jormunrek: Slayer of Swanhild; slain by sons of Gudrun.

Jotunnheim (Jotunheim): Abode of giants.

Lif and Lifthrasir: First man and woman after Ragnarok.

Loki: God of evil and mischief; instigator of Balder's death.

Lothur (Lodur): One of creators of Ask and Embla.

Midgard (Midgarth): Abode of mankind; the earth.

Midgard Serpent: Sea monster; offspring of Loki; slays, and is slain by, Thor at Ragnarok.

Mimir: Giant; guardian of well in Jotunnheim at root of Yggdrasill; knower of past and future.

Mjollnir: Magic hammer of Thor.

Nagifar: Ship to be used by giants in attacking Asgard at Ragnarok; built from nails of dead men.

Nanna: Wife of Balder.

Nibelungs: Dwellers in northern kingdom ruled by Giuki.

Niflheim (Nifelheim): Outer region of cold and darkness; abode of Hel.

Njorth: Father of Frey and Freya; originally one of Vanir.

Norns: Demigoddesses of fate: Urth (Urdur) (Past), Verthandi (Verdandi) (Present), Skuld (Future).

Odin (Othin): Head of Aesir; creator of world with Vili and Ve; equivalent to Woden (Wodan, Wotan) in Teutonic mythology.

Otter: Son of Rodmar; slain by Loki; his skin filled with gold hoard of Andvari to appease Rodmar.

Ragnarok: Final destruction of present world in battle between gods and giants; some minor gods will survive, and Lif and Lifthrasir will repeople world.

Regin: Blacksmith; son of Rodmar; foster-father of Sigurd.

Rerir: King of Huns; son of Sigi.

Rodmar: Father of Regin, Otter, and Fafnir; demanded Otter's skin be filled with gold; slain by Fafnir, who stole gold.

Sif: Wife of Thor.

Siggeir: King of Goths; husband of Signy; he and his sons slew Volsung and his sons, except Sigmund; slain by Sigmund and Sinflotli.

Sigi: King of Huns; son of Odin.

Sigmund: Son of Volsung; brother of Signy, who bore him Sinflotli; husband of Hiordis, who bore him Sigurd.

Signy: Daughter of Volsung; sister of Sigmund; wife of Siggeir; mother by Sigmund of Sinflotli.

Sigurd: Son of Sigmund and Hiordis; wakened Brynhild from magic sleep; married Gudrun; slain by Guttorm at instigation of Brynhild.

Sigyn: Wife of Loki.

Sinflotli: Son of Sigmund and Signy.

Skuld: *See* Norns.

Sleipnir (Sleipner): Eight-legged horse of Odin.

Surt (Surtr): Fire demon; slays Frey at Ragnarok.

Svartalfaheim: Abode of dwarfs.

Swanhild: Daughter of Sigurd and Gudrun; slain by Jormunrek.

Thor: God of thunder; oldest son of Odin; equivalent to Germanic deity Donar.

Tyr: God of war; son of Odin; equivalent to Tiu in Teutonic mythology.

Ull (Ullr): Son of Sif; stepson of Thor.

Urth: *See* Norns.

Valhalla (Valhall): Great hall in Asgard where Odin received souls of heroes killed in battle.

Vali: Odin's son: Ragnarok survivor.

Valkyries: Virgins, messengers of Odin, who selected heroes to die in battle and took them to Valhalla; generally considered as nine in number.

Vanir: Early race of gods; three survivors, Njorth, Frey, and Freya, are associated with Aesir.

Ve: Brother of Odin; one of creators of world.

Verthandi: *See* Norns.

Vili: Brother of Odin; one of creators of world.

Vingolf: Abode of goddesses in Asgard.

Vitharr (Vithar): Son of Odin; survivor of Ragnarok.

Volsung: Descendant of Odin, and father of Signy, Sigmund; his descendants were called Volsungs.

Yggdrasill: Giant ash tree springing from body of Ymir and supporting universe; its roots extended to Asgard, Jotunnheim, and Niffheim.

Ymir (Ymer): Primeval frost giant killed by Odin, Vili, and Ve; world created from his body; also, from his body sprang Yggdrasill.

Egyptian Mythology

Aaru: Abode of the blessed dead.

Amen (Amon, Ammdn): One of chief Theban deities; united with sun god under form of Amen-Ra.

Amenti: Region of dead where souls were judged by Osiris.

Anubis: Guide of souls to Amenti; son of Osiris; jackal-headed.

Apis: Sacred bull, an embodiment of Ptah; identified with Osiris as Osiris-Apis or Serapis.

Geb (Keb, Seb): Earth god; father of Osiris; represented with goose on head.

Hathor (Athor): Goddess of love and mirth; cow-headed.

Horus: God of day; son of Osiris and Isis; hawk-headed.

Isis: Goddess of motherhood and fertility; sister and wife of Osiris.

Khepera: God of morning sun.

Khnemu (Khnum, Chnuphis, Chnemu, Chnum): Ram-headed god.

Khonsu (Khensu, Khuns): Son of Amen and Mut.

Mentu (Ment): Solar deity, sometimes considered god of war; falcon-headed.

Min (Khem, Chem): Principle of physical life.

Mut (Maut): Wife of Amen.

Nephthys: Goddess of the dead; sister and wife of Set.

Nu: Chaos from which world was created, personified as a god.

Nut: Goddess of heavens; consort of Geb.

Osiris: God of underworld and judge of dead; son of Geb and Nut.

Ptah (Phtha): Chief deity of Memphis.

Ra: God of the Sun, the supreme god; son of Nut; Pharaohs claimed descent from him; represented as lion, cat, or falcon.

Serapis: God uniting attributes of Osiris and Apis.

Set (Seth): God of darkness or evil; brother and enemy of Osiris.

Shu: Solar deity; son of Ra and Hathor.

Tem (Atmu, Atum, Tum): Solar deity.

Thoth (Dhouti): God of wisdom and magic; scribe of gods; ibis-headed

Modern Wedding Anniversary Gift List

Anniversay	Gift	Anniversary	Gift	Anniversary	Gift
1st	Gold jewelry	10th	Diamond jewelry	19th	Aquamarine
2nd	Garnet	11th	Turquoise	20th	Emerald
3rd	Pearls	12th	Jade	25th	Silver jubilee
4th	Blue topaz	13th	Citrine	30th	Pearl jubilee
5th	Sapphire	14th	Opal	35th	Emerald
6th	Amethyst	15th	Ruby	40th	Ruby
7th	Onyx	16th	Peridot	45th	Sapphire
8th	Tourmaline	17th	Watches	50th	Golden jubilee
9th	Lapis	18th	Cat's—eye	60th	Diamond jubilee

Source: Jewelry Industry Council

Federal Funding of Selected Science and Technology Highlights

(Budget authority, dollar amounts in millions)

	1993 Actual	1995 Estimate[1]	1996 Proposed	Dollar change: 1995 to 1996	Percent change: 1995 to 1996
National Aeronautics and Space Administration:					
Reusable Launch Vehicle Technology Program	—	129	159	+30	−23%
International Space Station	2,262	2,113	2,115	+2	+*%
Aeronautics Initiative	129	347	434	+87	+25%
New Millennium Initiative	67	392	495	+103	+26%
Commerce–National Institute of Standards and Technology:					
Advanced Technology Program	68	431	491	+60	+14%
Manufacturing Extension Partnerships	18	91	147	+56	+62%
In-house R&D	193	259	300	+41	+16%
Defense-Advanced Research Project Agency:					
Technology Reinvestment Project	472	443	500	+57	+13%
Environmental Protection Agency:					
Environmental Technology Initiative	67	139	192	+53	+38%
National Institute of Health:					
Biomedical Research	10,326	11,321	11,789	+468	+4%
Department of Energy:					
Basic Research User Facilities	—	—	100	+100	n.a.
Fusion Energy Research	335	373	360	−12	−3%
Expanded Partnerships and Technology Transfer:[2]					
Funded Technology Transfer Investment	n.a.	1,611	1,768	+157	+10%
Number of CRADA Parterships	n.a.	6,093	6,816	+723	+12%
CRADA Value (Cash and non-cash contributions)	n.a.	5,104	5,806	+702	+14%
Academic R&D[2]	11,674	11,641	12,504	+863	+7%
Merit Reviewed Research[2]	n.a.	28,454	29,344	+890	+3%
National Science and Technology Council Initiatives:[2]					
Technology and Learning Challenge	n.a.	328	335	+8	+2%
Partnership for a New Generation of Vehicles	n.a.	246	333	+87	+35%
Construction & Building	n.a.	141	169	+28	+20%
Physical Infrastructure for Transportation	n.a.	247	321	+74	+30%
Environmental & Natural Resources	n.a.	5,339	5,536	+197	+4%
U.S. Global Change Research Program[3]	1,531	2,118	2,157	+39	+2%
Defense	6	6	6	*	+*%
Health and Human Services	1	31	32	+1	+5%
Energy	305	368	371	+3	+1%
National Aeronautics and Space Administration	917	1,338	1,341	+3	+*%
National Science Foundation	124	169	183	+14	+8%
Agriculture	46	61	67	+6	+9%
Commerce	66	78	97	+19	+24%
Interior	38	31	30	−1	−3%
Environmental Protection Agency	26	32	26	−6	−19%
Smithsonian	3	3	3	*	+*%
Tennessee Valley Authority	—	1	1	−*	−17%
High Performance Computing and Communications	762	1,080	1,142	+63	+6%
Defense	298	384	403	+19	+5%
Health and Human Services	47	68	78	+10	+15%
Energy	100	113	114	+1	+1%
National Aeronautics and Space Administration	82	131	131	−*	−*%
National Science Foundation	233	297	314	+17	+6%
Commerce	2	32	50	+18	+57%
Environmental Protection Agency	—	15	12	−3	−20%
Veterans Administration	—	24	24	+*	+*%
Education	—	16	17	+1	+6%

*Less than $500 thousand or 0.05 percent. 1. Includes proposed supplementals and rescissions. 2. These initiatives include double counting of other 1996 S&T initiatives, except for estimates from the Department of Energy. 3. U.S. Global Change Research Program is a subset of the Environment and Natural Resource initiative. n.a. = Not applicable. *Source: Budget of the United States Government, Fiscal Year 1996.*

Major Discoveries of Human Ancestors

Living and extinct human beings and their near human ancestors are called "Hominids," and belong to the family *Hominidae* of primates. They are not to be confused with "Hominoids" which belong to the family *Hominoidea* of primates that include apes and humans. Scientists theorize that the human and ape lines branched off from a common ancestor 8 to 6 million years ago.

Years	Species	Discovered	Remarks
c. 4.4 million	Ardipithecus ramidus	1994 in Ethiopia	Oldest known human ancestor. Had chimpanzee-like skull.
c. 4.2 million	Australopithecus anamensis	1995, two sites at Lake Turkana, Kanapoi, and Allia Bay, Kenya	Possible ancestor of A. afarensis (Lucy). Walked upright.
c. 3.2 million	Australopithecus afarensis	1974 at Hadar in the Afar triangle of eastern Ethiopia	Nicknamed "Lucy." Her skeleton was 3.5 feet (100 cm) tall. Had ape-like skull. Walked fully upright. Lived in family groups throughout eastern Africa.
c. 2.5 million	Australopithecus africanus	1924 at Taung, northern Cape Province, South Africa	Descendant of "Lucy." Lived in social groups.
c. 2 million	Australopithecus Robustus	1938 in Kromdraai, South Africa	Was related to africanus
c. 2 million	Homo habilus ("skillful man")	1960 in Olduvai Gorge, Tanzania	First brain expansion; is believed to have used stone tools.
c. 1.8 million	Homo erectus ("upright man")	1891 at Trinil, Java	Brain size twice that of Australopithecine species. Regarded as ancestor of Homo sapiens. Invented the hand ax. Could probably make fires. Was first to migrate out of Africa.
c. 100,000(?)	Homo sapien ("knowing or wise man"	1868, Cro-Magnon, France	Anatomically modern humans

Two Radically Different Types of Humans

The Neanderthals *(Homo sapiens neandertalensis),* c. 150,000–35,000 years ago, are the best known of all extinct human sub-species. They first appeared in Europe and their fossil remains, the first anatomically human forms to be discovered, were found in 1856 in the Neander Valley, Germany. They spread throughout Europe and Western Asia.

The Neanderthals' characteristics anatomical traits were prominent brow ridges, large front teeth, and chinless, heavy forward-jutting jaws. Their stature was shorter, more robust, and they were physically more powerful than contemporary *Homo sapiens sapiens.*

The Neanderthals were hunter-gatherers, could build crude artificial shelters of wood saplings and animal skins, fashion heavy clothing of skins laced with rawhide, make flaked stone tools, and were known to bury their dead. There is recent evidence that they coexisted with modern humans and no one knows why they suddenly vanished.

The Cro-Magnon *(Homo sapiens sapiens),* c. 100,000(?) years ago, completely resembled modern humans. Although usage of the term Cro-Magnon strictly applies only to those who lived in southwestern France, it has been used by many to generally describe *Homo sapiens sapiens* that lived everywhere else. Their skeletons were discovered in a rock shelter in the Cro-Magnon valley, Les Eyzies, southwestern France, in 1868. Early modern man was a hunter-gatherer, used more specialized stone tools and weapons than his human predecessors, baked pottery, and is well known for his rich artistic skills, i.e., beautiful cave paintings, jewelry, carvings, and clay figurines. He traveled throughout the habitable areas of the world and adapted to different terrain and climatic conditions.

There is evidence obtained through thermoluminescent (TL) dating and electron-spin resonance (ESR) dating at sites of modern hominids in Mount Carmel, Israel, that modern humans existed in Israel c. 100,000 years ago, long before the Neanderthal peoples arrived there. If these dates are correct, they imply that these two distinct human ancestors coexisted together for many thousands of years. ☐

Table of Geological Periods

It is now generally assumed that planets are formed by the accretion of gas and dust in a cosmic cloud, but there is no way of estimating the length of this process. Our earth acquired its present size, more or less, between 4,000 and 5,000 million years ago. Life on earth originated about 2,000 million years ago, but there are no good fossil remains from periods earlier than the Cambrian, which began about 550 million years ago. The largely unknown past before the Cambrian Period is referred to as the Pre-Cambrian and is subdivided into the Lower (or older) and Upper (or younger) Pre-Cambrian—also called the Archaeozoic and Proterozoic Eras.

The known geological history of the earth since the beginning of the Cambrian Period is subdivided into three "eras," each of which comprises a number of "periods." They, in turn, are subdivided into "subperiods." In a subperiod, a certain section may be especially well known because of rich fossil finds. Such a section is called a "formation," and it is usually identified by a place name.

Paleozoic Era

This era began 550 million years ago and lasted for 355 million years. The name was compounded from Greek *palaios* (old) and zoön *(animal).*

Period	Duration[1]	Subperiods	Events
Cambrian (from *Cambria,* Latin name for Wales)	70	Lower Cambrian Middle Cambrian Upper Cambrian	Invertebrate sea life of many types, proliferating during this and the following period
Ordovician (from Latin *Ordovices,* people of early Britain)	85	Lower Ordovician Upper Ordovician	
Silurian (from Latin *Silures,* people of eary Wales)	40	Lower Silurian Upper Silurian	First known fishes; gigantic sea scorpions
Devonian (from Devonshire in England)	50	Lower Devonian Upper Devonian	Proliferation of fishes and other forms of sea life, land still largely lifeless
Carboniferous (from Latin *carbo* = coal + *fero* = to bear)	85	Lower or Mississippian Upper or Pennsylvanian	Period of maximum coal formation in swampy forests; early insects and first known amphibians
Permian (from district of Perm in Russia)	25	Lower Permian Upper Permian	Early reptiles and mammals; earliest form of turtles

Mesozoic Era

This era began 195 million years ago and lasted for 135 million years. The name was compounded form Greek *mesos* (middle) and zoön (animal). Popular name: Age of Reptiles.

Period	Duration[1]	Subperiods	Events
Triassic (from *trias* = triad)	35	Lower or Buntsandstein (from German *bunt* = colorful + *Sandstein* = sandstone) Middle of Muschelkalk (from German *Muschel* = clam + *Kalk* = limestone) Upper or Keuper (old miner's term)	Early saurians
Jurrassic (from Jura Mountains)	35	Lower of Black Jurassic, or Lias (from French *liais* = hard stone) Middle or Brown Jurassic, or Dogger (old provincial English for ironstone) Upper or White Jurasic, or Malm (Middle English for sand)	Many sea-going reptiles; early large dinosaurs; somewhat later, flying reptile (pterosaurs), earliest known birds
Cretaceous (from Latin *creta* = chalk)	65	Lower Cretaceous Upper Cretaceous	Maximum development of dinosaurs; birds proliferating; opossum-like mammals

Cenozoic Era

This era began 60 million years ago and includes the geological present. The name was compounded from Greek *kainos* (new) and *zoön* (animal). Popular name: Age of Mammals.

Period	Duration[1]	Subperiods	Events
Tertiary (originally thought to be the third of only three periods)	c. 60	Palecene (from Greek *palaios* = old + *kainos* = new	First mammals other than marsupials
		Eocene (from Greek *eos* = dawn + *kainos* = new	Formation of amber; rich insect fauna; early bats
		Oligocene (from Greek *oligos* = few + *kainos* = new	Steady increase of large mammals
		Miocene (from Greek *meios* = less + *kainos* = new	
		Pliocene (from Greek *pleios* = more + *kainos* = new	Mammals closely resembling present types; protohumans
Pleistocene (from Greek *pleistos* = most + *kainos* = new) (popular name: Ice Age)	1	Four major glaciations, named Günz, Mindel, Riss, and Würm originally the name of rivers Last glaciation ended 10,000 to 15,000 years ago	Various forms of early man
Holocene (from Greek *holos* = entire + *kainos* = new)		The present	The last 3,000 years are called "history"

1. In millions of years.

Chemical Elements

Element	Symbol	Atomic no.	Atomic weight	Specific gravity	Melting point °C	Boiling point °C	Number of isotopes[1]	Discoverer	Year
Actinium	Ac	89	227[2]	10.07[2]	1050	3200±300	11	Debierne	1899
Aluminum	Al	13	26.9815	2.6989	660.37	2467	8	Wöhler	1827
Americum	Am	95	243[6]	13.67	994 ±4	2607	13[3]	Seaborg et al.	1944
Antimony	Sb	51	121.75	6.61	630.74	1750	29	Early historic times	
Argon	Ar	18	39.948	1.7837[4]	−189.2	−185.7	8	Rayleigh and Ramsay	1894
Arsenic (gray)	As	33	74.9216	5.73	817 (28 atm.)	613[5]	14	Albertus Magnus	1250?
Astatine	At	85	−210	—	302	337	21	Corson et al.	1940
Barium	Ba	56	137.34	3.5	725	1640	25	Davy	1808
Berkelium	Bk	97	247[6]	14.00[7]	—	—	8[3]	Seaborg et al.	1949
Berylium	Be	4	9.01218	1.848	1278 ±5	2970 (5 mm.)	6	Vauquelin	1798
Bismuth	Bi	83	208.9806	9.747	271.3	1560±5	19	Geoffroy	1753
Boron	B	5	10.81	2.37[8]	2300	2550[5]	6	Gay-Lussac and Thénard; Davy	1808
Bromine	Br	35	79.904	3.12[4]	−7.2	58.78	19	Balard	1826
Cadmium	Cd	48	112.40	8.65	320.9	765	22	Stromeyer	1817
Calcium	Ca	20	40.08	1.55	839 ±2	1484	14	Davy	1808
Californium	Cf	98	251[6]	—	—	—	12[3]	Seaborg et al.	1950
Carbon	C	6	12.011	1.8–3.5[9]	−3550	4827	7	Prehistoric	—
Cerium	Ce	58	140.12	6.771	798 ±3	3257	19	Berzelius and Hisinger; Klaproth	1803
Cesium	Cs	55	132.9055	1.873	28.40	678.4	22	Bunsen and Kirchoff	1860
Chlorine	Cl	17	35.453	1.56[4]	−100.98	−34.6	11	Scheele	1774
Chromium	Cr	24	51.996	7.18–7.20	1857 ±20	2672	9	Vauquelin	1797
Cobalt	Co	27	58.9332	8.9	1495	2870	14	Brandt	c.1735
Copper	Cu	29	63.546	8.96	1083.4±0.2	2567	11	Preshistoric	—
Curium	Cm	96	247[6]	13.51[2]	1340 ±40	—	13[3]	Seaborg et al.	1944
Dysprosium	Dy	66	162.50	8.540	1409	2335	21	Boisbaudran	1886
Einsteinium	Es	99	254[6]	—	—	—	12[3]	Ghiorso et al.	1952
Erbium	Er	68	167.26	9.045	1522	2510	16	Mosander	1843
Europium	Eu	63	151.96	5.283	822 ±5	1597	21	Demarcay	1896
Fermium	Fm	100	257[6]	—	—	—	10[3]	Ghiorso et al.	1953
Fluorine	F	9	18.9984	1.108[4]	−219.62	−188.14	6	Moissan	1886
Francium	Fr	87	223[6]	—	27[2]	677[2]	21	Perey	1938
Gadolinium	Gd	64	157.25	7.898	1311 ±1	3233	17	Marignac	1880
Gallium	Ga	31	69.72	5.904	29.78	2403	14	Boisbaudran	1875
Germanium	Ge	32	72.59	5.323	937.4	2830	17	Winkler	1886
Gold	Au	79	196.9665	19.32	1064.43	2807	21	Prehistoric	—
Hafnium	Hf	72	178.49	13.31	2227 ±20	4602	17	Coster and von Hevesy	1923
Hahnium	Ha	105	262	—	—	—	—	Ghiorso et al.	1970
Helium	He	2	4.00260	0.1785[4]	−272.2 (26 atm.)	−268.934	5	Janssen	1868
Holmium	Ho	67	164.9303	8.781	1470	2720	29	Delafontaine and Soret	1878
Hydrogen	H	1	1.0080	0.070[4]	−259.14	−252.87	3	Cavendish	1766
Indium	In	49	114.82	7.31	156.61	2080	34	Reich and Richter	1863
Iodine	I	53	126.9045	4.93	113.5	184.35	24	Cortois	1811
Iridium	Ir	77	192.22	22.42	2410	4130	25	Tennant	1803
Iron	Fe	26	55.847	7.894	1535	2750	10	Prehistoric	—
Krypton	Kr	36	83.80	3.733[4]	−156.6	−152.30±0.10	23	Ramsay and Travers	1898

Element	Symbol	Atomic no.	Atomic weight	Specific gravity	Melting point °C	Boiling point °C	Number of isotopes[1]	Discoverer	Year
Lanthanum	La	57	138.9055	6.166	920 ±5	3454	19	Mosander	1839
Lawrenceium	Lr	103	257[6]	—	—	—	20[3]	Ghiorso et al.	1961
Lead	Pb	82	207.2	11.35	327.502	1740	29	Prehistoric	—
Lithium	Li	3	6.941	0.534	180.54	1347	5	Arfvedson	1817
Lutetium	Lu	71	174.97	9.835	1656 ±5	3315	22	Urbain	1907
Magnesium	Mg	12	24.305	1.738	648.8±0.5	1090	8	Black	1755
Manganese	Mn	25	54.9380	7.21–7.44[10]	1244 ±3	1962	11	Gahn, Scheele, and Bergman	1774
Mendelevium	Md	101	256[6]	—	—	—	3[3]	Chiorso et al.	1955
Mercury	Hg	80	200.59	13.546	−38.87	356.58	26	Prehistoric	—
Molybdenum	Mo	42	95.94	10.22	2617	4612	20	Scheele	1778
Neodymium	Nd	60	144.24	6.80 & 7.004[10]	1010	3127	16	von Welsbach	1885
Neon	Ne	10	20.179	0.89990 (g/1 0°C/1 atm)	−248.67	−246.048	8	Ramsay and Travers	1898
Neptunium	Np	93	237.0482	20.25	640 ±1	3902	15[3]	McMillan and Abelson	1940
Nickel	Ni	28	58.71	8.902	1453	2732	11	Cronstedt	1751
Niobium (Columbium)	Nb	41	92.9064	8.57	2468 ±10	4742	24	Hatchett	1801
Nitrogen	N	7	14.0067	0.808[4]	−209.86	−195.8	8	Rutherford	1772
Nobelium	No	102	254[6]	—	—	—	7[3]	Ghiorso et al.	1957
Osmium	Os	76	190.2	22.57	3045 ±30	5027±100	19	Tennant	1803
Oxygen	O	8	15.9994	1.14[4]	−218.4	−182.962	8	Priestley	1774
Palladium	Pd	46	106.4	12.02	1552	3140	21	Wollaston	1803
Phosphorous	P	15	30.9738	1.82 (White)	44.1	280	7	Brand	1669
Platinum	Pt	78	195.09	21.45	1772	3827±100	32	Ulloa	1735
Plutonium	Pu	94	244[6]	19.84	641	3232	16[3]	Seaborg et al.	1940
Poionium	Po	84	210[6]	9.32	254	962	34	Curie	1898
Potassium	K	19	39.102	0.862	63.65	774	10	Davy	1807
Praseodymium	Pr	59	140.9077	6.772	931 ±4	3212	15	von Weisbach	1885
Promethium	Pm	61	145[6]	—	≈1080	2460?	14	Marinsky et al.	1945
Protactinium	Pa	91	231.0359	15.37[2]	<1600	—	14	Hahn and Meitner	1917
Radium	Ra	88	226.0254	5.0?	700	1140	15	P. and M. Curie	1898
Radon	Rn	86	222[6]	4.4[4]	−71	−61.8	20	Dorn	1900
Rhenium	Re	75	186.2	21.02	3180	5627[4]	21	Noddack, Berg, and Tacke	1925
Rhodium	Rh	45	102.9055	12.41	1966 ±3	3727±100	20	Wollaston	1803
Rubidium	Rb	37	85.4678	1.532	38.89	688	20	Bunsen and Kirchoff	1861
Rutherfordium	Rf	104	261	—	—	—	—	Ghiorso et al.	1969
Ruthenium	Ru	44	101.07	12.44	2310	3900	16	Klaus	1844
Samarium	Sm	62	150.4	7.536	1072 ±5	1778	17	Boisbaudran	1879
Scandium	Sc	21	44.9559	2.989	1539	2832	15	Nilson	1879
Seaborgium	Sg	106	263	—	—	—	—	Ghiorso et al.	1974
Selenium	Se	34	78.96	4.79 (gray)	217	684.9±1	20	Berzelius	1817
Silicon	Si	14	28.086	2.33	1410	2355	8	Berzelius	1824
Silver	Ag	47	107.868	10.5	961.93	2212	27	Prehistoric	—
Sodium	Na	11	22.9898	0.971	97.81±0.03	882.9	7	Davy	1807
Strontium	Sr	38	87.62	2.54	769	1384	18	Davy	1808
Sulfur	S	16	32.06	2.07[11]	112.8	444.674	10	Prehistoric	—
Tantalum	Ta	73	180.9479	16.654	2996	5425±100	19	Ekeberg	1801
Technetium	Tc	43	98.062	11.50[2]	2172	4877	23	Perrier and Segré	1937
Tellurium	Te	52	127.60	6.24	449.5±0.3	989.8±3.8	29	von Reichenstein	1782
Terbium	Tb	65	158.9254	8.234	1360 ±4	3041	24	Mosander	1843
Thallium	Tl	81	204.37	11.85	303.5	1457±10	28	Crookes	1861
Thorium	Th	90	232.0381	11.72	1750	4790	12	Berzelius	1828
Thulium	Tm	69	168.9342	9.314	1545 ±15	1727	18	Cleve	1879
Tin	Sn	50	118.69	7.31 (white)	231.9681	2270	28	Prehistoric	—
Titanium	Ti	22	47.90	4.55	1660 ±10	3287	9	Gregor	1791
Tungsten (Wolfram)	W	74	183.85	19.3	3410 ±20	5660	22	J. and F. d'Elhuyar	1783
Uranium	U	92	238.029	−18.95	1132.3±0.8	3818	15	Peligot	1841
Vanadium	V	23	50.9414	6.11	1890 ±10	3380	9	del Rio	1801
Xenon	Xe	54	131.30	3.52[4]	−111.9	−107.1±3	31	Ramsay and Travers	1898
Ytterbium	Yb	70	173.04	6.972	824 ±5	1193	16	Marignac	1878
Yttrium	Y	39	88.9059	4.457	1523 ±8	3337	21	Gadolin	1794
Zinc	Zn	30	65.38	7.133	419.58	907	15	Prehistoric	—
Zirconium	Zr	40	91.22	6.506[2]	1852 ±2	4377	20	Klaproth	1789

Elements No. 101–111—See NOTE at end of footnotes.

1. Isotopes are different forms of the same element having the same atomic number but different atomic weights. 2. Calculated figure. 3. Artificially produced. 4. Liquid 5. Sublimation point. 6. Mass number of the isotope of longest known life. 7. Estimated. 8. Amorphous. 9. Depending on whether amorphous, graphite or diamond. 10. Depending on allotropic form. 11. Rhombic. ≈ Is approximately. < Is less than. NOTE: In October 1994, the International Union of Pure and Applied Chemistry (IUPAC) recommended renaming the provisional names for elements 101 through 109. They rejected seaborgium for element 106 because of a newly adopted rule that no element may bear the name of a living person. If the IUPAC ratifies the proposed name changes in August 1995, the elements will have the following names: 104: dubnium, Db, named for the Joint Institute for Nuclear Research at Dubna, Russia; 105: joliotium, Jl, named for Frédéric Joliot-Curie, nuclear physics pioneer; 106: rutherfordium, Rf, named for Ernest Rutherford, atomic physics pioneer; 107: bohrium, Bh, named for Niels Bohr, a quantum mechanics founder; and 108: hahnium, Hn, named for Otto Hahn, a pioneer discoverer of nuclear fission. Unchanged, are elements 101: mendelevium, named for geneticist, Gregor Mendel; 102: nobelium, named for Alfred Nobel, founder of the Nobel Prizes; 103: lawrencium, named for the inventor of the cyclotron, Ernest O. Lawrence; and 109: meitnerium, named for Lise Meitner, a nuclear fission pioneer. **Elements 110 and 111.** In November 1994, German physicists at the Heavy Ion Research Center (GSI), Darmstadt, reported creating element 110, atomic mass 269. In December 1994, they announced they had produced element 111. Both unnamed new elements are extremely unstable.

INVENTIONS & DISCOVERIES

See also Famous Firsts in Aviation, Nobel Prize Awards

Abacus: *See* Calculating machine

Adding machine: *See* Calculating machine; Computer

Adrenaline: (isolation of) John Jacob Abel, U.S., 1897

Aerosol can: Erik Rotheim, Norway, 1926

Air brake: George Westinghouse, U.S., 1868

Air conditioning: Willis Carrier, U.S., 1911

Airplane: (first powered, sustained, controlled flight) Orville and Wilbur Wright, U.S., 1903. *See also* Jet propulsion

Airship: (non-rigid) Henri Giffard, France, 1852; (rigid) Ferdinand von Zeppelin, Germany, 1900

Aluminum manufacture: (by electrolytic action) Charles M. Hall, U.S., 1866

Anatomy, human: (*De fabrica corporis humani*, an illustrated systematic study of the human body) Andreas Vesalius, 1543; (comparative: parts of an organism are correlated to the functioning whole) Georges Cuvier, 1799–1805

Anesthetic: (first use of anesthetic—ether—on man) Crawford W. Long, U.S., 1842

Antibiotics: (first demonstration of antibiotic effect) Louis Pasteur, Jules-François Joubert, France, 1887; (discovery of penicillin, first modern antibiotic) Alexander Fleming, England, 1928; (penicillin's infection-fighting properties) Howard Florey, Ernst Chain, England, 1940

Antiseptic: (surgery) Joseph Lister, England, 1867

Antitoxin, diphtheria: Emil von Behring, Germany, 1890

Appliances, electric: (fan) Schuyler Wheeler, U.S., 1882; (flatiron) Henry W. Seely, U.S., 1882; (stove) Hadaway, U.S., 1896; (washing machine) Alva Fisher, U.S., 1906

Aqualung: Jacques-Yves Cousteau, Emile Gagnan, France, 1943

Aspirin: Dr. Felix Hoffman,, Germany, 1899

Astronomical calculator: The Antikythera device, first century B.C., Greece. Found off island of Antikythera in 1900

Atom: (nuclear model of) Ernest Rutherford, 1911

Atomic theory: (ancient) Leucippus, Democritus, Greece, c.500 B.C.; Lucretius, Rome, c.100 B.C.; (modern) John Dalton, England, 1808

Automobile: (first with internal combustion engine, 250 rpm) Karl Benz, Germany, 1885; (first with practical high-speed internal combustion engine, 900 rpm) Gottlieb Daimler, Germany, 1885; (first true automobile, not carriage with motor) René Panhard, Emile Lavassor, France, 1891; (carburetor, spray) Charles E. Duryea, U.S., 1892

Autopilot: (for aircraft) Elmer A. Sperry, U.S., c.1910, first successful test, 1912, in a Curtiss flying boat

Avogadro's law: (equal volumes of all gases at the same temperature and pressure contain equal number of molecules) Amedeo Avogadro, 1811

Bacteria: Anton van Leeuwenhoek, The Netherlands, 1683

Bakelite: *See* Plastics

Balloon, hot-air: Joseph and Jacques Montgolfier, France, 1783

Ball-point pen: *See* Pen

Barbed wire: (most popular) Joseph E. Glidden, U.S., 1873

Bar codes: (computer-scanned binary signal code) (retail trade use) Monarch Marking, U.S. 1970; (industrial use) Plessey Telecommunications, England, 1970

Barometer: Evangelista Torricelli, Italy, 1643

Bicycle: Karl D. von Sauerbronn, Germany, 1816; (first modern model) James Starley, England, 1884

Bifocal lens: *See* Lens, bifocal

Big Bang theory: (the universe originated with a huge explosion) Edwin Hubble, U.S., 1929; (confirmed) Arno Penzias, Robert Wilson, 1965

Blood, circulation of: William Harvey, England, 1628

Boyle's law: (relation between pressure and volume in gases) Robert Boyle, Ireland, 1662

Braille: Louis Braille, France, 1829

Bridges: (suspension, iron chains) James Finley, Pa., 1800; (wire suspension) Marc Seguin, Lyons, 1825; (truss) Ithiel Town, U.S., 1820

Bullet: (conical) Claude Minié, France, 1849

Calculating machine: (Abacus) China, c.190; (logarithms: made multiplying easier and thus calculators practical) John Napier, Scotland, 1614; (slide rule) William Oughtred, England, 1632; (digital calculator) Blaise Pascal, 1642; (multiplication machine) Gottfried Leibniz, Germany, 1671; (important 19th-century contributors to modern machine) Frank S. Baldwin, Jay R. Monroe, Dorr E. Felt, W. T. Ohdner, William Burroughs, all U.S.; ("analytical engine" design, included concepts of programming, taping) Charles Babbage, England, 1835. *See also* Computer

Calculus: Isaac Newton, England, 1669; (differential calculus) Gottfried Leibniz, Germany, 1684

Camera: (hand-held) George Eastman, U.S., 1888; (Polaroid Land) Edwin Land, U.S., 1948. *See also* Photography

"Canals" of Mars: Giovanni Schiaparelli, 1877

Carburetor: *See* Automobile

Carpet sweeper: Melville R. Bissell, U.S., 1876

Car radio: William Lear, Elmer Wavering, U.S., 1929, manufactured by Galvin Manufacturing Co., "Motorola"

Celanese: *See* Fibers, man-made

Celluloid: *See* Plastics

Cells: (word used to describe microscopic examination of cork) Robert Hooke, 1665; (theory: cells are common structural and functional unit of all living organisms) Theodor Schwann, Matthias Schleiden, 1838–39

Cement, Portland: Joseph Aspdin, England, 1724

Chewing gum: (spruce-based) John Curtis, U.S., 1848; (chicle-based) Thomas Adams, U.S., 1870

Cholera bacterium: Robert Koch, Germany, 1883

Circuit, integrated: (theoretical) G.W.A. Dummer, England, 1952; (phase-shift oscillator) Jack S. Kilby, Texas Instruments, U.S., 1959

Classification of plants: (first modern, based on comparative study of forms) Andrea Cesalpino, 1583; (classification of plants and animals by genera and species) Carolus Linnaeus, Sweden, 1737–53

The Double Helix—DNA

Clock, pendulum: Christian Huygens, The Netherlands, 1656

Coca-Cola: John Pemberton, U.S., 1886

Combustion: (nature of) Antoine Lavoisier, France, 1777

Compact disk: RCA, U.S., 1972

Computer: (differential analyzer, mechanically operated) Vannevar Bush, U.S., 1928; (Mark I, first information-processing digital computer) Howard Aiken, U.S., 1944; (ENIAC, Electronic Numerical Integrator and Calculator, first all-electronic) J. Presper Eckert, John W. Mauchly, U.S., 1946; (stored-program concept) John von Neumann, U.S., 1947

Concrete: (reinforced) Joseph Monier, 1877

Condensed milk: Gail Borden, U.S., 1853

Conditioned reflex: Ivan Pavlov, Russia, c.1910

Conservation of electric charge: (the total electric charge of the universe or any closed system is constant) Benjamin Franklin, U.S., 1751–54

Contagion theory: (infectious diseases caused by living agent transmitted from person to person) Girolamo Fracastoro, 1546

Continental drift theory: Antonio Snider-Pellegrini, 1858

Contraceptive, oral: Gregory Pincus, Min Chuch Chang, John Rock, Carl Djerassi, U.S., 1951

Converter, Bessemer: William Kelly, U.S., 1851

Cosmetics: Egypt, c.4000 B.C.

Cotton gin: Eli Whitney, U.S., 1793

Crossbow: China, c.300 B.C.

Cyclotron: Ernest O. Lawrence, U.S., 1931

Deuterium: (heavy hydrogen) Harold Urey, U.S., 1931

Disease: (chemicals in treatment of) crusaded by Philippus Paracelsus, 1527–1541; (germ theory) Louis Pasteur, 1862–77

DNA: (deoxyribonucleic acid) Friedrich Meischer, Germany, 1869; (determination of double-helical structure) F. H. Crick, England, James D. Watson, U.S., 1953

Dyes: (aniline, start of synthetic dye industry) William H. Perkin, 1856

Dynamite: Alfred Nobel, Sweden, 1867

Electric cooking utensil: (first) patented by St. George Lane-Fox, England, 1874

Electric generator (dynamo): (laboratory model) Michael Faraday, England, 1832; Joseph Henry, U.S., c.1832; (hand-driven model) Hippolyte Pixii, France, 1833; (alternating-current generator) Nikola Tesla, U.S., 1892

Electric lamp: (arc lamp) Sir Humphrey Davy, England, 1801; (fluorescent lamp) A.E. Becquerel, France, 1867; (incandescent lamp) Sir Joseph Swann, England, Thomas A. Edison, U.S., contemporaneously, 1870s; (carbon arc street lamp) Charles F. Brush, U.S., 1879; (first widely marketed incandescent lamp) Thomas A. Edison, U.S., 1879; (mercury vapor lamp) Peter Cooper Hewitt, U.S., 1903; (neon lamp) Georges Claude, France, 1911; (tungsten filament) Irving Langmuir, U.S., 1915

Electric motor: *See* Motor

Electrocardiography: demonstrated by Augustus Waller, 1887; (first practical device for recording activity of heart) Willem Einthoven, 1903, Dutch physiologist

Electromagnet: William Sturgeon, England, 1823

Electron: Sir Joseph J. Thompson, England, 1897

Elevator, passenger: (safety device permitting use by passengers) Elisha G. Otis, U.S., 1852; (elevator utilizing safety device) 1857

E = mc²: (equivalence of mass and energy) Albert Einstein, Switzerland, 1907

Engine, internal combustion: No single inventor. Fundamental theory established by Sadi Carnot, France, 1824; (two-stroke) Etienne Lenoir, France, 1860; (ideal operating cycle for four-stroke) Alphonse Beau de Roche, France, 1862; (operating four-stroke) Nikolaus Otto, Germany, 1876; (diesel) Rudolf Diesel, Germany, 1892; (rotary) Felix Wankel, Germany, 1956. *See also* Automobile

Engine, steam: *See* Steam engine

Evolution: (organic) Jean-Baptiste Lamarck, 1809; (by natural selection) Charles Darwin, England, 1859

Exclusion principle: (no two electrons in an atom can occupy the same energy level) Wolfgang Pauli, 1925

Expanding universe theory: (galaxies are receding from each other at speeds proportionate to their distance) George Lemaître, 1927

Falling bodies, law of: Galileo Galilei, Italy, 1590

Fermentation: (micro-organisms as cause of) Louis Pasteur, France, c.1860

Fiber optics: Narinder Kapany, England, 1955

Fibers, man-made: (nitrocellulose fibers treated to change flammable nitrocellulose to harmless cellulose, precursor of rayon) Sir Joseph Swann, England, 1883; (rayon) Count Hilaire de Chardonnet, France, 1889; (Celanese) Henry and Camille Dreyfuss, U.S., England, 1921; (research on polyesters and polyamides, basis for modern man-made fibers) U.S., England, Germany, 1930s; (nylon) Wallace H. Carothers, U.S., 1935

Fountain pen: *See* Pen

Frozen food: Clarence Birdseye, U.S. (1924)

Gene transfer: (human) Steven Rosenberg, R. Michael Blaese, W. French Anderson, U.S., 1989

Geometry, elements of: Euclid, Alexandria, Egypt, c.300 B.C.; (analytic) René Descartes, France; and Pierre de Fermat, Switzerland, 1637

Gravitation, law of: Sir Isaac Newton, England, c.1665 (published 1687)

Gunpowder: China, c.700

Gyrocompass: Elmer A. Sperry, U.S., 1905

Gyroscope: Léon Foucault, France, 1852

Halley's Comet: Edmund Halley, 1705

Heart, artificial: Dr. Robert Jarvik, U.S., 1982

Helicopter: (double rotor) Heinrich Focke, Germany, 1936; (single rotor) Igor Sikorsky, U.S., 1939

Helium first observed on sun: Sir Joseph Lockyer, England, 1868

Heredity, laws of: Gregor Mendel, Austria, 1865

Holograph: Dennis Gabor, England, 1947

Home videotape systems (VCR): (Betamax) Sony, Japan, 1975; (VHS) Matsushita, Japan, 1975

Ice age theory: Louis Agassiz, 1840

Induction, electric: Joseph Henry, U.S., 1828

Insulin: Sir Frederick G. Banting, J. J. R. MacLeod, Canada, 1922

Intelligence testing: Alfred Binet, Theodore Simon, France, 1905

Interferon: Alick Isaacs, Jean Lindemann, England, Switzerland, 1957

Isotopes: (concept of) Frederick Soddy, England, 1912; (stable isotopes) J. J. Thompson, England, 1913; (existence demonstrated by mass spectrography) Francis W. Ashton, 1919

Jet propulsion: (engine) Sir Frank Whittle, England, Hans von Ohain, Germany, 1936; (aircraft) *Heinkel He 178*, 1939

Kinetic theory of gases: (molecules of a gas are in a state of rapid motion) Daniel Bernoulli, 1738

Laser: (theoretical work on) Charles H. Townes, Arthur L. Schawlow, U.S., N. Basov, A. Prokhorov, U.S.S.R., 1958; (first working model) T. H. Maiman, U.S., 1960

Lawn mower: Edwin Budding, John Ferrabee, England, 1830 (31)

LCD (liquid crystal display): Hoffmann-La Roche, Switzerland, 1970

Lens, bifocal: Benjamin Franklin, U.S., c.1760

Leyden jar: (prototype electrical condenser) Canon E.G. von Kleist of Kamin, Pomerania, 1745; independently evolved by Cunaeus and P. van Musschenbroek, University of Leyden, Holland, 1746, from where name originated

Light, nature of: (wave theory) Christian Huygens, The Netherlands, 1678; (electromagnetic theory) James Clerk Maxwell, England, 1873

Light, speed of: (theory that light has finite velocity) Olaus Roemer, Denmark, 1675

Lightning rod: Benjamin Franklin, U.S., 1752

Linotype: *See* Printing

Lithography: *See* Printing

Locomotive: (steam powered) Richard Trevithick, England, 1804; (first practical, due to multiple-fire-tube boiler) George Stephenson, England, 1829; (largest steam-powered) Union Pacific's "Big Boy," U.S., 1941

Lock, cylinder: Linus Yale, U.S., 1851

Logarithms: *See* Calculating machine

Loom: (horizontal, two-beamed) Egypt, c.4400 B.C.; (Jacquard drawloom, pattern controlled by punch cards) Jacques de Vaucanson, France, 1745, Joseph-Marie Jacquard, 1801; (flying shuttle) John Kay, England, 1733; (power-driven loom) Edmund Cartwright, England, 1785

Machine gun: James Puckle, England, 1718; Richard J. Gatling, U.S., 1861

Magnet, Earth is: William Gilbert, 1600

Match: (phosphorus) François Derosne, France, 1816; (friction) Charles Sauria, France, 1831; (safety) J. E. Lundstrom, Sweden, 1855

Measles vaccine: John F. Enders, Thomas Peebles, U.S., 1953

Mendelian law: *See* Heredity

Metric system: revolutionary government of France, 1790–1801

Microphone: Charles Wheatstone, England, 1827

Microscope: (compound) Zacharias Janssen, The Netherlands, 1590; (electron) Vladimir Zworykin et al., U.S., Canada, Germany, 1932–1939

Microwave oven: Percy Spencer, U.S., 1947

Motion, laws of: Isaac Newton, England, 1687

Motion pictures: Thomas A. Edison, U.S., 1893

Motion pictures, sound: Product of various inventions. First picture with synchronized musical score: *Don Juan,* 1926; with spoken dialogue: *The Jazz Singer,* 1927; both Warner Bros.

Motor, electric: Michael Faraday, England, 1822; (alternating-current) Nikola Tesla, U.S., 1892

Motor, gasoline: *See* Engine, internal combustion

Motorcycle: (motor tricycle) Edward Butler, England, 1884; (gasoline-engine motorcycle) Gottlieb Daimler, Germany, 1885

National Science Foundation: established by U.S. Congress, 1950 based on report by Vannevar Bush, 1945

Neptune: (discovery of) Johann Galle, 1846

Neptunium: (first transuranic element, synthesis of) Edward M. McMillan, Philip H. Abelson, U.S., 1940

Neutron: James Chadwick, England, 1932

Neutron-induced radiation: Enrico Fermi et al., Italy, 1934

Nitroglycerin: Ascanio Sobrero, Italy, 1846

Bell demonstrating the long-distance capability of his invention at Salem, Mass., on March 15, 1877. A hook-up was made with Boston, 18 miles away, and an extended conversation took place between the two cities.

Nuclear fission: Otto Hahn, Fritz Strassmann, Germany, 1938

Nuclear reactor: Enrico Fermi, et al., 1942

Nylon: *See* Fibers, man-made

Ohm's law: (relationship between strength of electric current, electromotive force, and circuit resistance) Georg S. Ohm, Germany, 1827

Oil well: Edwin L. Drake, Titusville, Pa., 1859

Oxygen: (isolation of) Joseph Priestley, 1774; Carl Scheele, 1773

Ozone: Christian Schöonbein, Germany, 1839

Pacemaker: (internal) Clarence W. Lillehie, Earl Bakk, U.S., 1957

Paper: China, c.100 B.C.

Parachute: Louis S. Lenormand, France, 1783

Pen: (fountain) Lewis E. Waterman, U.S., 1884; (ball-point, for marking on rough surfaces) John H. Loud, U.S., 1888; (ball-point, for handwriting) Lazlo Biro, Argentina, 1944

Penicillin: *See* Antibiotics

Periodic law: (that properties of elements are functions of their atomic weights) Dmitri Mendeleev, Russia, 1869

Periodic table: (arrangement of chemical elements based on periodic law) Dmitri Mendeleev, Russia, 1869

Phonograph: Thomas A. Edison, U.S., 1877

Photography: (first paper negative, first photograph, on metal) Joseph Nicéphore Niepce, France, 1816–1827; (discovery of fixative powers of hyposulfite of soda) Sir John Herschel, England, 1819; (first direct positive image on silver plate, the daguerreotype) Louis Daguerre, based on work with Niepce, France, 1839; (first paper negative from which a number of positive prints could be made) William Talbot, England, 1841. Work of these four men, taken together, forms basis for all modern photography. (First color images) Alexandre Becquerel, Claude Niepce de Saint-Victor, France, 1848–60; (commercial color film with three emulsion layers, Kodachrome) U.S., 1935. *See also* Camera

Photovoltaic effect: (light falling on certain materials can produce electricity) Edmund Becquerel, France, 1839

Piano: (Hammerklavier) Bartolommeo Cristofori, Italy, 1709; (pianoforte with sustaining and damper pedals) John Broadwood, England, 1873

Planetary motion, laws of: Johannes Kepler, Germany, 1609, 1619

Plant respiration and photosynthesis: Jan Ingenhousz, 1779

Plastics: (first material, nitrocellulose softened by vegetable oil, camphor, precursor to Celluloid) Alexander Parkes, England, 1855; (Celluloid, involving recognition of vital effect of camphor) John W. Hyatt, U.S., 1869; (Bakelite, first completely synthetic plastic) Leo H. Baekeland, U.S., 1910; (theoretical background of macromolecules and process of polymerization on which modern plastics industry rests) Hermann Staudinger, Germany, 1922. *See also* Fibers, man-made

Plate tectonics: Alfred Wegener, Germany, 1912–15

Plow, forked: Mesopotamia, before 3000 B.C.

Plutonium, synthesis of: Glenn T. Seaborg, Edwin M. McMillan, Arthur C. Wahl, Joseph W. Kennedy, U.S., 1941

Polaroid Land camera: *See* Camera

Polio, vaccine against: (vaccine made from dead virus strains) Jonas E. Salk, U.S., 1954; (vaccine made from live virus strains) Albert Sabin, U.S., 1960

Positron: Carl D. Anderson, U.S., 1932

Pressure cooker: (early version) Denis Papin, France, 1679

Printing: (block) Japan, c.700; (movable type) Korea, c.1400; (movable type) Johann Gutenberg, Germany, c.1450 (lithography, offset) Aloys Senefelder, Germany, 1796; (rotary press) Richard Hoe, U.S., 1844; (linotype) Ottmar Mergenthaler, U.S., 1884

Probability theory: René Descartes, France; and Pierre de Fermat, Switzerland, 1654

Programming, information: *See* Calculating machine

Proton: Ernest Rutherford, England, 1919

Psychoanalysis: Sigmund Freud, Austria, c.1904

Pulsars: Jocelyn Bell Bunnell, England, 1968

Quantum theory: (general) Max Planck, Germany, 1900; (sub-atomic) Niels Bohr, Denmark, 1913; (quantum mechanics) Werner Heisenberg, Erwin Schrödinger, Germany, 1925

Quarks: Jerome Friedman, Henry Kendall, Richard Taylor, U.S. (1967)

Quasars: Marten Schmidt, U.S., 1963

Rabies immunization: Louis Pasteur, France, 1885

Radar: (limited to one-mile range) Christian Hulsmeyer, Germany, 1904; (pulse modulation, used for measuring height of ionosphere) Gregory Breit, Merle Tuve, U.S., 1925; (first practical radar—radio detection and ranging) Sir Robert Watson-Watt, England, 1934–35

Radio: (electromagnetism, theory of) James Clerk Maxwell, England, 1873; (spark coil, generator of electromagnetic waves) Henrich Hertz, Germany, 1886; (first practical system of wireless telegraphy) Guglielmo Marconi, Italy, 1895; (vacuum electron tube, basis for radio telephony) Sir John Fleming, England, 1904; (triode amplifying tube) Lee de Forest, U.S., 1906; (regenerative circuit, allowing long-distance sound reception) Edwin H. Armstrong, U.S., 1912; (frequency modulation—FM) Edwin H. Armstrong, U.S., 1933

Radioactivity: (X-rays) Wilhelm K. Roentgen, Germany, 1895; (radioactivity of uranium) Henri Becquerel, France, 1896; (radioactive elements, radium and polonium in uranium ore) Marie Sklodowska-Curie, Pierre Curie, France, 1898; (classification of alpha and beta particle radiation) Pierre Curie, France, 1900; (gamma radiation) Paul-Ulrich Villard, France, 1900; (carbon dating) Willard F. Libby et al., U.S., 1955

Radio signals, extraterrestrial: first known radio noise signals were received by U.S. engineer, Karl Jansky, originating from the Galactic Center, 1931.

Radio waves: (cosmic sources, led to radio astronomy) Karl Jansky, 1932

Rayon: *See* Fibers, man-made

Razor: (safety, successfully marketed) King Gillette, U.S., 1901; (electric) Jacob Schick, U.S., 1928(31)

Reaper: Cyrus McCormick, U.S., 1834

Refrigerator: Alexander Twining, U.S., James Harrison, Australia, 1850; (first with a compressor device) the Domelse, Chicago, U.S., 1913

Refrigerator ship: (first) the *Frigorifique*, 1877, cooling unit designed by Charles Teller, France

Relativity: (special and general theories of) Albert Einstein, Switzerland, Germany, U.S., 1905–53

Revolver: Samuel Colt, U.S., 1835

Richter scale: Charles F. Richter, U.S., 1935

Rifle: (muzzle-loaded) Italy, Germany, c1475; (breech-loaded) England, France, Germany, U.S., c.1866; (bolt-action) Paul von Mauser, Germany, 1889; (automatic) John Browning, U.S., 1918

Rocket: (liquid-fueled) Robert Goddard, U.S., 1926

Roller bearing: (wooden for cartwheel) Germany or France, c.100 B.C.

Rotation of earth: Jean Bernard Foucault, 1851

Royal Observatory, Greenwich: established by Charles II of England, John Flamsteed first Astronomer Royal

Rubber: (vulcanization process) Charles Goodyear, U.S., 1839

Saccharin: Constantine Fuhlberg, Ira Remsen, U.S., 1879

Safety match: *See* Match

Safety pin: Walter Hunt, U.S., 1849

Saturn, ring around: Christian Huygens, The Netherlands, 1659

"Scotch" tape: Richard Drew, U.S., 1929

Screw propeller: Sir Francis P. Smith, England, 1836; John Ericsson, England, worked independently of and simultaneously with Smith, 1837

Seismograph: (first accurate) John Milne, 1880

Sewing machine: Elias Howe, U.S., 1846; (continuous stitch) Isaac Singer, U.S., 1851

Solar energy: first realistic application of solar energy using parabolic solar reflector to drive caloric engine on steam boiler, Jon Ericsson, 1860s

Solar system, universe: (sun-centered universe) Nicolaus Copernicus, Warsaw, 1543; (establishment of planetary orbits as elliptical) Johannes Kepler, Germany, 1609; (infinity of universe) Giordano Bruno, Italian monk, 1584

Spectrum: (heterogeneity of light) Sir Isaac Newton, England, 1665–66

Spectrum analysis: Gustav Kirchoff, Robert Bunsen, 1859

Spermatozoa: Anton van Leeuwenhoek, The Netherlands, 1683

Spinning: (spinning wheel) India, introduced to Europe in Middle Ages; (Saxony wheel, continuous spinning of wool or cotton yarn) England, c.1500–1600; (spinning jenny) James Hargreaves, England, 1764; (spinning frame) Sir Richard Arkwright, England, 1769; (spinning mule, completed mechanization of spinning, permitting production of yarn to keep up with demands of modern looms) Samuel Crompton, England, 1779

Star catalog: (first modern) Tycho Brahe, 1572

Steam engine: (first commercial version based on principles of French physicist Denis Papin) Thomas Savery, England, 1639; (atmospheric steam engine) Thomas Newcomen, England, 1705; (steam engine for pumping water from collieries) Savery, Newcomen, 1725; (modern condensing, doubleacting) James Watt, England, 1782

Steam engine, railroad: *See* Locomotive

Steamship: Claude de Jouffroy d'Abbans, France, 1783; James Rumsey, U.S., 1787; John Fitch,

Johannes Gutenberg.

U.S., 1790. All preceded Robert Fulton, U.S., 1807, credited with launching first commercially successful steamship

Stethoscope: René Laënnec, 1819

Sulfa drugs: (parent compound, para-aminobenzenesulfanomide) Paul Gelmo, Austria, 1908; (antibacterial activity) Gerhard Domagk, Germany, 1935

Superconductivity: (theory) Bardeen, Cooper, Scheiffer, U.S., 1957

Symbolic logic: George Boule, 1854; (modern) Bertrand Russell, Alfred North Whitehead, 1910–13

Syphilis, test for: *See* Wassermann test

Tank, military: Sir Ernest Swinton, England, 1914

Tape recorder: (magnetic steel tape) Valdemar Poulsen, Denmark, 1899

Teflon: DuPont, U.S., 1943

Telegraph: Samuel F.B. Morse, U.S., 1837

Telephone: Alexander Graham Bell, U.S., 1876

Telescope: Hans Lippershey, The Netherlands, 1608; (astronomical) Galileo Galilei, Italy, 1609; (reflecting) Isaac Newton, England, 1668

Television: (mechanical disk-scanning method) successfully demonstrated by J.K. Baird, England, C.F. Jenkins, U.S., 1926; (electronic scanning method) Vladimir K. Zworykin, U.S., 1928; (color, all-electronic) Zworykin, 1926; (color, mechanical disk) Baird, 1928; (color, compatible with black and white) George Valensi, France, 1938; (color, sequential rotating filter) Peter Goldmark, U.S., first introduced, 1951; (color, compatible with black and white) commercially introduced in U.S., National Television Systems Committee, 1953

Thermodynamics: (first law: energy cannot be created or destroyed, only converted from one form to another) Julius von Mayer, Germany, 1842; James Joule, England, 1843; (second law: heat cannot of itself pass from a colder to a warmer body) Rudolph Clausius, Germany, 1850; (third law: the entropy of ordered solids reaches zero at the absolute zero of temperature) Walter Nernst, Germany, 1918

Thermometer: (open-column) Galileo Galilei, c.1593; (clinical) Santorio Santorio, Padua, c.1615; (mercury, also Fahrenheit scale) Gabriel D. Fahrenheit, Germany, 1714; (centigrade scale) Anders Celsius, Sweden, 1742; (absolute-temperature, or Kelvin, scale) William Thompson, Lord Kelvin, England, 1848

Tire, pneumatic: Robert W. Thompson, England, 1845; (bicycle tire) John B. Dunlop, Northern Ireland, 1888

Toilet, flush: Product of Minoan civilization, Crete, c.2000 B.C. Alleged invention by "Thomas Crapper" is untrue.

Tractor: Benjamin Holt, U.S., 1900

Transformer, electric: William Stanley, U.S., 1885

Transistor: John Bardeen, William Shockley, Walter Brattain, U.S., 1948

Tuberculosis bacterium: Robert Koch, Germany, 1882

Typewriter: Christopher Sholes, Carlos Glidden, U.S., 1867

Uncertainty principle: (that position and velocity of an object cannot both be measured exactly, at the same time) Werner Heisenberg, Germany, 1927

Uranus: (first planet discovered in recorded history) William Herschel, 1781

Vaccination: Edward Jenner, England, 1796

Vacuum cleaner: (manually operated) Ives W. McGaffey, 1869; (electric) Hubert C. Booth, England, 19091; (upright) J. Murray Spangler, U.S., 1907

Vacuum tube: *See* Radio

Van Allen (radiation) Belt: (around the earth) James Van Allen, U.S., 1958

Video disk: Philips Co., The Netherlands, 1972

Vitamins: (hypothesis of disease deficiency) Sir F. G. Hopkins, Casimir Funk, England, 1912; (vitamin A) Elmer V. McCollum, M. Davis, U.S., 1912–14; (vitamin B) Elmer V. McCollum, U.S., 1915–16; (thiamin, B_1) Casimir Funk, England, 1912; (riboflavin, B_2) D. T. Smith, E. G. Hendrick, U.S., 1926; (niacin) Conrad Elvehjem, U.S., 1937; (B_6) Paul Gyorgy, U.S., 1934; (vitamin C) C. A. Hoist, T. Froelich, Norway, 1912; (vitamin D) Elmer V. McCollum, U.S., 1922; (folic acid) Lucy Wills, England, 1933

Voltaic pile: (forerunner of modern battery, first source of continuous electric current) Alessandro Volta, 1800

Wallpaper: Europe, 16th and 17th century

Wassermann test: (for syphilis) August von Wassermann, Germany, 1906

Weaving, cloth: *See* Loom

Wheel: (cart, solid wood) Mesopotamia, c.3800–3600 B.C.

Windmill: Persia, c.600

X-ray: *See* Radioactivity

Xerography: Chester Carlson, U.S., 1938

Zero: India, c.600; (absolute zero temperature, cessation of all molecular energy) William Thompson, Lord Kelvin, England, 1848

Zipper, W.L. Judson, U.S., 1891

The National Inventors Hall of Fame

The Inventors Hall of Fame, located in Akron, Ohio, was established in 1973 by the National Council of Patent Law Associations, now the National Council of Intellectual Property Law Associations, and the Patent and Trademark Office of the U.S. Department of Commerce. The year of induction is in parentheses at the end of the entry.

Alexanderson, Ernst 1872–1975 (b. Sweden) HIGH FREQUENCY ALTERNATOR—Alexanderson built a high frequency machine that would operate at high speeds and produce a continuous wave transmission. His inventions included such fields as railway electrification, motors, telephone relays and radio and television. (1983)

Alford, Andrew 1904–1992 (b. Samara, Russia) LOCALIZER ANTENNA SYSTEM—Alford invented and developed antennas for radio navigation systems, including VOR and instrument landing systems, and the "Alford Loop" antenna. (1983)

Alvarez, Luis Walter 1911–1988 (b. San Francisco, Calif.) RADIO DISTANCE AND DIRECTION INDICATOR—Alvarez was awarded the Nobel Prize for Physics in 1968. He helped design a ground-controlled radar system for aircraft landings and with his son developed the meteorite theory of dinosaur extinction. (1978)

Armstrong, Edwin 1890–1954 (b. New York City) METHOD OF RECEIVING HIGH FREQUENCY OSCILLATIONS—Armstrong devised wide-band frequency modulation (FM radio) as a means of reducing background static. He also invented the regenerative circuit, the superheterodyne, and the super-regenerative circuit. (1980)

Baekeland, Leo Hendrik 1863–1944 (b. Ghent, Belgium) SYNTHETIC RESINS—Baekeland developed the thermosetting synthetic resin bakelite which helped found the modern plastics industry. He also invented Velox photographic paper. (1978)

Bardeen, John 1908–1991 (b. Madison, Wisconsin); **Shockley, William Bradford** 1910–1989 (b. London, England); **Brattain, Walter H.** 1902–1987 (b. Amoy, China) TRANSISTOR—Bardeen, Shockley and Brattain shared the 1956 Nobel Prize for Physics for the invention of the transistor. The transistor replaced the vacuum tube and paved the way for the integrated circuit. (1974)

Beckman, Arnold O. 1900– (b. Cullom, Ill.) APPARATUS FOR TESTING ACIDITY—Beckman founded Beckman Instruments, Inc. in 1935 with the development of a pH meter for measuring acidity and alkalinity. He also developed the helical potentiometer, a precision electronic component, and the quartz spectrophotometer, an instrument which pioneered automatic chemical analysis. (1987)

Bell, Alexander Graham 1847–1922 (b. Edinburgh, Scotland) TELEGRAPHY—In addition to the telephone, Bell held patents for the telegraph, photophone, phonograph, aerial vehicles, hydroairplanes, and a selenium cell. He was also noted for his medical research and work in teaching speech to the deaf. (1974)

Bennett, Willard Harrison 1903–1987 (b. Findlay, Ohio) RADIO FREQUENCY MASS SPECTROMETER—Bennett studies in gases ionized by high voltage electricity was used in controlled thermonuclear fusion research. His radio frequency mass spectrometer was the first launched into space to measure the masses of atoms. (1991)

Berliner, Emile 1851–1929 (b. Hanover, Germany) MICROPHONE AND GRAMOPHONE—The Berliner microphone enhanced Bell's telephone that had been limited to short transmissions. The gramophone introduced the flat disk which provided a method for inexpensive mass production. (1994)

Binnig, Gerd Karl 1947– (b. Frankfurt, Germany); **Rohrer, Heinrich** 1933– (b. Bucs, Switzerland) SCANNING TUNNELING MICROSCOPE—Binnig and Rohrer's microscope can trace details smaller than a single atom and has provided views of the atomic structure of atoms, the interaction of chemical catalysts, and views of microbe enviral interaction. (1994)

Bird, Forest M. 1921– (b. Stoughton, Mass.) MEDICAL RESPIRATORS—Bird developed the first highly reliable, low-cost mass-produced respirator in the world. His "Babybird" respirator reduced infant mortality from respiratory problems from 70% to 10% worldwide. (1995)

Black, Harold Stephen 1898–1983 (b. Leominster, Mass.) NEGATIVE FEEDBACK AMPLIFIER—Black's negative feedback concept involved feeding systems output back to the input as a method of system control thus helping to eliminate distortion in telecommunications and to extend the frequency range of the amplifier. (1981)

Blumberg, Baruch 1925– (b. New York City); **Millman, Irving** 1923– (b. New York City) TEST AND VACCINE FOR HEPATITIS B—The use of the test reduced the occurrence of hepatitis B after blood transfusions. The vaccine protects people exposed to the hepatitis B virus and has been administered to millions, particularly in Asia and Africa. With hepatitis B an unknown factor associated with the development of liver cancer, the vaccine was the first against a major form of cancer. (1993)

Brattain, Walter H. *See under* Bardeen, John.

Brown, Rachel Fuller *See under* Hazen, Elizabeth Lee.

Burbank, Luther 1849–1926 (b. Lancaster, Mass.) PEACH—Burbank developed more than 800 new strains and varieties of plants including varieties of potato, plums, prunes, berries, flowers and trees. (1986)

Burckhalter, Joseph H. 1912– (b. Columbia, S.C.); **Seiwald, Robert J.** 1925– (b. Fort Morgan, Colo.) DYES FOR DIAGNOSING INFECTIOUS DISEASES—Burckhalter and Seiwald synthesized fluorescein isothiocyanate (FITC), an antibody labeling agent. FITC has become widely used for rapid, accurate, and economic diagnosis of infectious diseases, including AIDS and syphilis. FITC and another agent are used together to quickly diagnose leukemia and lymphoma. (1995)

Burroughs, William Seward 1857–1898 (b. Rochester, N.Y.) CALCULATING MACHINE—In 1885 Burroughs submitted his first patent for his "calculating machine." This first model needed a special knack to use and Burroughs was dissatisfied with its durability. His 1892 patent not only improved the machine but added a printer. (1987)

Burton, William Meriam 1865–1954 (b. Cleveland, Ohio) MANUFACTURE OF GASOLINE—Burton developed the high heat and high pressure cracking process of fuel oil which more than doubled the potential yield of gasoline from crude oil. (1984)

Camras, Marvin 1916–1995 (b. Chicago, Ill.) METHOD AND MEANS OF MAGNETIC RECORDING—Camras's inventions are used in modern magnetic tape and wire recorders, including high frequency bias, improved recording heads, wire and tape material, magnetic sound for motion pictures, multi-track tape machines, stereophonic sound reproduction and video tape recording. (1985)

Carlson, Chester F. 1906–1968 (b. Seattle, Wash.) ELECTROPHOTOGRAPHY—Carlson invented xerographic dry-copy printing basing his process on electrostatics as opposed to chemical or photographic processes. (1981)

Carothers, Wallace Hume 1896–1937 (b. Burlington, Iowa) DIAMINE-DICARBOXYLIC ACID SALTS AND PROCESS OF PREPARING SAME AND SYNTHETIC FIBER—Carothers work involved the theory of linear polymerization which culminated in the production of the synthetic material nylon. Nylon was first commercially used in toothbrush bristles. Carothers's work also led others to develop the first successful synthetic rubber, neoprene. (1984)

Carrier, Willis Haviland 1876–1950 (b. Angola, N.Y.) APPARATUS FOR TREATING AIR—Carrier developed the first safe, low pressure centrifugal refrigeration machine using nontoxic, nonflammable refrigerant. By controlling humidity as well as temperature, he invented modern air conditioning. (1985)

Carver, George Washington 1864–1943 (b. Diamond Grove, Mo.) COSMETIC AND PROCESS OF PRODUCING SAME; PAINT AND STAIN AND PROCESS OF PRODUCING THE SAME—When Carver's method of crop rotation produced a surplus of peanuts, sweet potatoes and pecans he devised hundreds of uses for the extra crops, from cooking oil to highway paving material. He also synthesized organic dyes which proved superior to aniline dyes. (1990)

Colton, Frank B. 1923– (b. Poland) ORAL CONTRACEPTIVES—Colton has made many important contributions to medicinal organic chemistry, and particularly to steroid chemistry. His most important research resulted in the discovery of Enovid, the first oral contraceptive. (1988)

Conover, Lloyd H. 1923– (b. Orange, N.J.) TETRACYCLINE—Conover's invention of tetracycline in 1952 was the first creation of an antibiotic made by chemically modifying a naturally-produced drug. Tetracycline quickly became the most prescribed broad spectrum antibiotic in the U.S. 40 years later tetracycline is still being used to combat such serious infections as Rocky Mountain Spotted Fever and Lyme Disease. (1992)

Coolidge, William D. 1873–1974 (b. Hudson, Mass.) VACUUM TUBE—Coolidge invented ductile tungsten, the filament material still used in incandescent lamps. He also invented the "Coolidge tube", the model upon which all X-ray tubes for medical applications are patterned. (1975)

Cottrell, Frederick G. 1877–1948 (b. Oakland, Calif.) ELECTROSTATIC PRECIPITATOR—Cottrell's invention used high voltage electricity to remove from 90 to 98 percent of the ash, dust, and acid which industrial smokestacks spewed into the air. Besides eliminating this particulate pollution, this process also allowed some of the minerals and chemicals to be re-used. (1992)

Damadian, Raymond V. 1936– (b. Forest Hills, N.Y.) APPARATUS AND METHOD FOR DETECTING CANCER IN TISSUE—Damadian invented the magnetic resonance imaging (MRI) scanner that has revolutionized diagnostic medicine. The MRI yields radio signal outputs from the body's tissue that can be either transformed into images or analyzed to provide the chemical composition of the tissue. (1989)

Deere, John 1804–1886 (b. Rutland, Vt.) PLOW—Deere's plow had a cutting part made of steel and a moldboard made of polished wrought iron which proved more effective than implements then in use for cutting and turning prairie soils. (1989)

de Forest, Lee 1873–1961 (b. Council Bluffs, Iowa) AUDION AMPLIFIER—De Forest inserted a third electrode between the cathode and anode to make his audion tube. Radio signals are picked up by connecting an antenna to the tube's grid. (1977)

Diesel, Rudolf 1857–1913 (b. Paris, France) INTERNAL COMBUSTION ENGINE—Diesel is best known for his invention of the pressure-ignited heat engine that bears his name. The Diesel engine was able to supplant the large, expensive, and fuel-wasting steam engine. (1976)

Djerassi, Carl 1923– (b. Vienna, Austria) ORAL CONTRACEPTIVES—Along with developing the oral contraceptive Djerassi's research has included work with steroids, antibiotics, synthesis of antihistamines and anti-inflammatory agents. (1978)

Dow, Herbert Henry 1866–1930 (b. Belleville, Ontario) PROCESS OF EXTRACTING BROMINE—Dow invented an entirely new method of extracting bromine from underground brine. (1983)

Draper, Charles Stark 1901– (b. Windsor, Mo.) GYROSCOPIC APPARATUS—Draper developed a spinning gyroscope, stabilizing U.S. Navy antiaircraft gunsights which led to an inertial guidance system for launching long-range missiles at supersonic jet targets. His Instrumentation Lab at MIT contributed to Project Apollo and men on the moon. (1981)

Durant, Graham J. 1934– (b. Newport, England); **Emmett, John Colin** 1939– (b. Bradford, England); **Ganellin, C. Robin** 1934– (b. London, England) ANTIULCER COMPOUNDS AND COMPOSITIONS—Durant, Emmett and Ganellin discovered the drug cimetidine (trade name Tagamet) which inhibits the production of stomach acid. Cimetidine has the ability to heal stomach ulcers without surgery. (1990)

Eastman, George 1854–1932 (b. Waterville, N.Y.) METHOD AND APPARATUS FOR COATING PLATES FOR USE IN PHOTOGRAPHY—Before Eastman, photographers used glass plates with light-sensitive emulsions on them. Eastman put the emulsions first on paper, then on film rolls. He also developed a stronger motion picture film. (1977)

Edgerton, Harold E. 1903–1990 (b. Fremont, Neb.) STROBOSCOPE—Edgerton's research in the fields of stroboscopy and ultra-high speed photography led to the modern electronic speed flash. He was noted for his photographs revealing operations which move at speeds beyond the capacity of the human eye. (1986)

Edison, Thomas Alva 1847–1931 (b. Milan, Ohio) ELECTRIC LAMP—Edison held 1,093 patents, including those for the incandescent electric lamp, the phonograph, the carbon telephone transmitter, and the motion-picture projector. He also created the world's first industrial research laboratory. (1973)

Elion, Gertrude Belle 1918– (b. New York City) 6-MERCAPTOPURINE—Elion synthesized the leukemia-fighting drug 6-mercaptopurine. Her other developments were drugs used to block organ rejections in kidney transplant patients, for the treatment of gout and to battle herpes virus infections. (1991)

Emmett, John Colin *See under* Durant, Graham

Ericsson, John 1803–1889 (b. Vermland, Sweden) PROPELLER—Ericsson's propeller—still the main form of marine propulsion 150 years later—replaced the inefficient and vulnerable steam-driven oars and paddlewheels. He designed and built the Civil War ironclad *Monitor* which defeated the Confederate *Merrimac*. Ericsson also developed a caloric engine designed to use solar energy. (1993)

Farnsworth, Philo Taylor 1906–1971 (b. Beaver, Utah) TELEVISION SYSTEM—At the age of 20 Farnsworth produced the first all-electronic television image. In addition to his television system he invented the first cold cathode ray tubes and the first simple electronic microscope. He used radio waves to get direction (radar) and black light for seeing at night. (1984)

Fermi, Enrico 1901–1954 (b. Rome, Italy) NEUTRONIC REACTOR—Fermi was awarded the 1938 Nobel Prize for Physics for his work in the field of atomic fission. In 1942 he accomplished the controlled release of nuclear energy via the atomic pile. (1976)

Ford, Henry 1863–1947 (b. Wayne County, Mich.) TRANSMISSION MECHANISM—Ford holds numerous patents on automotive mechanisms and helped devise the factory assembly line method of mass production. (1982)

Forrester, Jay W. 1918– (b. Climax, Nebraska) MULTICOORDINATED DIGITAL INFORMATION STORAGE DEVICE—While working on the Whirlwind, the largest computer project in the late 1940s and early 1950s, Forrester devised the magnetic core memory storage which replaced the unreliable and short-lived electrostatic tubes which had previously been used. (1979)

Ganellin, C. Robin *See under* Durant, Graham

Ginsburg, Charles P. 1920–1992 VIDEOTAPE RECORDER—After World War II audio tape recorders were run at very high speeds to record the very high frequency television signals. Ginsburg developed a new machine that ran much slower for television recording. It was first used by CBS TV in 1956. (1990)

Goddard, Robert Hutchings 1882–1945 (b. Worcester, Mass.) CONTROL MECHANISM FOR ROCKET APPARATUS—Goddard launched the first liquid-fuel rocket in 1926. Other rocket design developments led to the bazooka and rocket-assisted takeoff of carrier planes. (1979)

Goodyear, Charles 1800–1860 (b. New Haven, Conn.) IMPROVEMENT IN INDIA-RUBBER FABRICS—Goodyear discovered the vulcanizing process when some rubber mixed with sulfur accidently dropped on a hot stove. Prior to this, rubber's applications were limited because of its adhesiveness and its inability to withstand temperature extremes. (1976)

Gould, Gordon 1920– (b. New York City) OPTICALLY-PUMPED LASER AMPLIFIERS, GAS-DISCHARGE-EXCITED LIGHT AMPLIFIERS—Gould's lasers are used in 80% of industrial, commercial, and medical applications. He also holds patents on laser uses and fiber optic communications. (1991)

Greatbatch, Wilson 1919– (b. Buffalo, N.Y.) MEDICAL CARDIAC PACEMAKER—Greatbatch's was trained as an electrical engineer but his research combined engineering with medical electronics, agricultural genetics, and the electrochemistry of pacemaker batteries. The first implantable pacemaker was a result of his pacemaker patent. (1986)

Greene, Leonard Michael 1918– (b. New York City) AIRPLANE STALL WARNING DEVICE—Greene developed his airplane stall warning device at a time when more than half of all aviation deaths were called by the stall/spin. He also developed a wind shear warning device for pilots. (1991)

Hall, Charles Martin 1863–1914 (b. Thompson, Ohio) MANUFACTURE OF ALUMINUM—Hall discovered the modern electrolytic method of producing aluminum cheaply which enabled the metal to be put into wide commercial use. (1976)

Hall, Robert N. 1919– (b. New Haven, Conn.) HIGH-VOLTAGE, HIGH-POWER SEMICONDUCTOR PIN RECTIFIER—Hall's invention boosted efficiency and reduced wasted power and destructive heat build-up in large-scale power transmission. (1994)

Hanford, William Edward 1908– (b. Bristol, Pa.); **Holmes, Donald Fletcher** 1910–1980 (b. Woodbury, N.J.) POLYURETHANE—The Hanford and Holmes process is the basis today for the manufacture of all polyurethane. Polyurethane is used as an upholstery material, heat insulating material, in artificial hearts, safety padding in automobiles and in carpeting. (1991)

Hazen, Elizabeth Lee 1885–1975 (b. rural Mississippi); **Brown, Rachel Fuller** 1898–1980 (b. Springfield, Mass.) NYSTATIN—Nystatin was the world's first non-toxic anti-fungal antibiotic. It cured fungal infections of the skin, mouth, throat and intestinal tract and could be combined with antibacterial drugs to balance their effects. (1994)

Hewlett, William R. 1913– (b. Ann Arbor, Mich.) VARIABLE FREQUENCY OSCILLATION GENERATOR—Also known as the "audio oscillator," this was the first practical method of generating high-quality audio frequencies needed in communications, geophysics, medicine, and defense work. Walt Disney Studios ordered eight audio oscillators to use in producing the soundtrack of the film, "Fantasia." (1992)

Higgonnet, Rene Alphonse *See under* Moyroud, Louis Marius.

Hillier, James 1915– (b. Ontario, Canada) ELECTRON LENS CORRECTION DEVICE—Hillier is noted for his contributions to the development of the electron microscope. The electron lens is used to focus a beam of electrons just as an optical lens focuses light rays. In 1937 he helped build a model that magnified 7000 times. (1980)

Hollerith, Herman 1860–1929 (b. Buffalo, N.Y.) ART OF COMPILING STATISTICS—Hollerith invented a punch card tabulation machine system that revolutionized statistical computation. His system enabled the 1890 census to save $5 million and more than two years time. (1990)

Holmes, Donald Fletcher *See under* Hanford, William

Houdry, Eugene 1892–1962 (b. Domont, France) LIQUID FUELS— Up until World War I enough gasoline was produced from crude oil by distillation. Cracking fuel oil, another product of distillation, was necessary to meet increased gasoline demands. Early processes used high heat and pressure but Houdry discovered that a catalyst enabled the process to be done at a lower temperature, more quickly, and more cheaply. He also invented the catalytic muffler which reduces the amount of carbon dioxide and unburned carbons released into the atmosphere. (1990)

Julian, Percy Lavon 1899–1975 (b. Montgomery, Ala.) PREPARATION OF CORTISONE—Julian's notable discoveries were the synthesis of cortisone, used in the treatment of arthritis; Aerofoam, used to suffocate gasoline and oil fires, and the synthesis of physostigmine, a treatment for glaucoma. Physostigmine is also being explored in the treatment of Alzheimer's Disease. (1990)

Keck, Donald *See under* Maurer, Robert.

Kettering, Charles Franklin 1876–1958 (b. Ohio) ENGINE STARTING DEVICES AND IGNITION SYSTEM—Kettering invented the first electrical ignition system and the self-starter for automobiles and the first practical engine-driven generator (the "Delco"). His other scientific work includes research in higher octane gasoline, high compression automobile engines, improved Diesel engine, and a nontoxic and nonflammable refrigerant. (1980)

Kilby, Jack S. 1923– (b. Jefferson City, Mo.) MINIATURIZED ELECTRONIC CIRCUITS—Kilby was responsible for the design and development of thick film integrated circuits, integrated circuit development and applications, and also invented the monolithic integrated circuit widely used in electronic systems. (1982)

Kolff, Willem J. 1911– (b. Netherlands) SOFT SHELL MUSHROOM SHAPED HEART—Kolff invented the artificial kidney dialysis machine and headed a team which invented and tested an artificial heart. (1985)

Kwolek, Stephanie Louise 1923– (b. New Kensington, KEVLAR (AROMATIC POLYAMIDES AND FIBERS)—Kwolek's processes have resulted in hundreds of new polymers used in producing mooring ropes, fiber-optic cables, aircraft parts, and canoes. The most famous product was Kevlar, five times stronger than the same weight in steel, used in light-weight bullet-resistant vests. (1995)

Land, Edwin 1909–1991 (b. Connecticut) PHOTOGRAPHIC PRODUCT COMPRISING A RUPTURABLE CONTAINING CARRYING A PHOTOGRAPHIC PROCESSING LIQUID—Land developed the first modern light polarizers and also optical devices. His most famous invention, the Polaroid camera, combined positive and negative film with developing chemicals. (1977)

Langmuir, Irving 1881–1957 (b. Brooklyn, N.Y.) INCANDESCENT ELECTRIC LAMP—Langmuir's major inventions were the high-vacuum electron tube and the gas-filled incandescent lamp. He also contributed to the fields of electronics, plasma physics, atomic, and molecular structure. (1989)

Lawrence, Ernest Orlando 1901–1958 (b. Canton, So. Dakota) METHOD AND APPARATUS FOR THE ACCELERATION OF IONS—Lawrence's cyclotron enabled him to study the structure of the atom, transmute certain elements, and produce artificial radioactivity. His research included the use of radiation in biology and medicine and he helped isolate uranium 235 which was used in the first atomic bomb. Lawrence received the 1939 Nobel Prize for Physics. (1982)

Lear, William 1902–1978 (b. Hannibal, Mo.) RADIO APPARATUS–AUTOMOBILE—Lear's design of a practical car radio launched the Motorola Company. He then turned to navigational aids for aircraft and formed Lear, Inc., LearAvia Corp., and then Learjet, a leading supplier of corporate jets. He also designed the eight-track tape player. (1993)

Ledley, Robert S. 1926– (b. New York City) DIAGNOSTIC X-RAY SYSTEMS—Ledley developed the ACTA diagnostic x-ray scanner, the first whole-body computerized tomography (CT) machine. He was the first to do medical imaging, three-dimensional reconstructions and to use CT in radiation therapy planning for cancer patients and the diagnosis of bone disease. (1990)

Maiman, Theodore Harold 1927– (b. Los Angeles, Calif.) RUBY LASER SYSTEMS—In 1960 Maiman built and patented the prototype of the ruby laser. The amplified light of the laser has many uses in industry, surgery, military range finders, as well as bar code scanners and compact disk players. (1984)

Marconi, Guglielmo 1874–1937 (b. Bologna, Italy) TRANSMITTING ELECTRICAL SIGNALS—Marconi's experiments led to practical wireless telegraphy and radio. In 1901 he successfully received signals transmitted from England to Newfoundland. He was awarded the 1909 Nobel Prize for Physics. (1975)

Maurer, Robert S. 1924– (b. St. Louis, Mo.); **Keck, Donald** 1941– (b. Lansing, Mich.); **Schultz, Peter** 1942– (b. Brooklyn, N.Y.) FUSED SILICA OPTICAL WAVEGUIDE—The inventors designed and produced the first optical fiber with light loss during transmission low enough for wide use in telecommunications. This paved the way for the commercialization of optical fiber and created a revolution in telecommunications. (1993)

McCormick, Cyrus 1809–1884 (b. Rockbridge County, Va.) REAPER—While others had also invented the mechanical grain reaper McCormick's constant improvements and astute business sense enabled him to turn his small family-run business into a worldwide corporation. (1976)

Mergenthaler, Ottmar 1854–1899 (b. Germany) MACHINE FOR PRODUCING PRINTING BARS—Mergenthaler's linotype composing machine allowed one operator to be machinist, typesetter, justifier, typefounder and type distributor by means of a board similar to a typewriter's keyboard. (1982)

Millman, Irving *See under* Blumberg, Baruch.

Morse, Samuel F.B. 1791–1872 (b. Charlestown, Mass.) TELEGRAPH SIGNALS—In 1844 Morse built the first telegraph line between Baltimore and Washington and relayed the first telegraphic message. He also devised the Morse code for his machine. (1975)

Moyer, Andrew J. 1899–1959 (b. Star City, Inc.) METHOD FOR PRODUCTION OF PENICILLIN—Moyer found that by culturing the *Penicillium* mold in a culture broth comprising corn steep liquor and lactose, penicillin yields could be increased many fold over the known methods. His discovery became the model for the development of all other antibiotic fermentations. (1987)

Moyroud, Louis Marius 1914– (b. Moirans, France); **Higonnet, Rene Alphonse** 1902–1983 (b. Valence, France) PHOTO COMPOSING MACHINE—Moyroud and Higgonet developed the first practical phototypesetting machine, the Lumitype—later known as the Photon—which was first demonstrated in 1946 and introduced in America in 1948. (1985)

Noyce, Robert N. 1927–1990 (b. Iowa) SEMICONDUCTOR DEVICE-AND-LEAD STRUCTURE—Noyce, as research director of Fairchild Semiconductor, was responsible for the initial development of silicon mesa and planar transistors, which led to a commercially applicable integrated circuit. He holds 16 patents for semiconductor devices, methods and structures. (1983)

Olsen, Kenneth H. 1926– (b. Stratford, Conn.) MAGNETIC CORE MEMORY—Olsen and his Digital Equipment Corporation developed the first successful minicomputer. Digital also developed the MicroVAX which placed a minicomputer structure on a single microchip. (1990)

Otis, Elisha Graves 1811–1861 (b. Halifax, Vt.) IMPROVEMENT IN HOISTING APPARATUS—Otis built the first modern passenger elevator which used his invention of a safety device which prevented the car from falling if the cables broke. (1988)

Otto, Nicolaus August 1832–1891 (b. Holzhausen, Germany) GAS MOTOR ENGINE—Otto introduced the four-stroke piston cycle on which most modern internal combustion engines are based. (1981)

Parker, Louis W. 1906–1993 (b. Budapest, Hungary) TELEVISION RECEIVER—Parker is best known for the "Intercarrier Sound System" used in all television receivers in the world. He also invented the first color television system using vertical color lines which made it possible to change from the original three color dot system to the simpler vertical color line system. (1988)

Parsons, John T. 1913– (b. Detroit, Mich.) NUMERICAL CONTROL OF MACHINE TOOLS—Parsons built a milling machine which was fed data to automatically activate servo-mechanisms to perform automatic contour cutting. First devevloped for making jet plane wings, the method is now widely used in the manufacture and assembly of many goods, from automobiles to computer chips. (1993)

Pasteur, Louis 1822–1895 (b. France) BREWING BEER AND ALE—Pasteur formulated the fundamental tenets of the germ theory of fermentation and of diseases which led to his pasteurization process of sterilization. He is also known for his pioneer work with vaccines, notably against anthrax and rabies. (1978)

Plank, Charles J. 1915–1989 (b. Calcutta, India); **Rosinski, Edward J.** 1921– (b. Gloucester County, N.J.) CATALYTIC CRACKING OF HYDROCARBONS WITH A CRYSTALLINE ZEOLITE CATALYST COMPOSITE—Plank and Rosinski developed the first commercially useful zeolite catalyst introduced in the petroleum industry for catalytic cracking. (1979)

Plunkett, Roy J. 1910–1994 (b. New Carlisle, Ohio) TETRAFLUOROETHYLENE POLYMERS—Plunkett discovered "Teflon" and also worked on the development of many other fluorochemical products and processes used in the refrigeration, aerosol, electronic and aerospace industries. (1985)

Rines, Robert H. 1922– (b. Boston, Mass.) HIGH RESOLUTION-IMAGE-SCANNING RADAR AND SONAR—Rines' radar and sonar inventions have been used by the military in the Persian Gulf War. In peacetime they have been used in locating the *Titanic* and *Bismarck* and also in a scientific sonar search for the Loch Ness Monster. (1994)

Rohrer, Heinrich *See under* Binnig, Gerd Karl.

Rosinski, Edward *See under* Plank, Charles J.

Rubin, Benjamin A. 1917– (b. New York City) BIFURCATED VACCINATION NEEDLE—Until 1967 smallpox killed at least 2 million people annually. In 1980 the World Health Organization declared that smallpox had been defeated. Rubin ground down the eyelet of a sewing machine needle to invent the bifurcated vaccination needle which could easily be used by natives under difficult conditions. (1992)

Sarett, Lewis Hastings 1917– (b. Champaign, Ill.) THE PROCESS OF TREATING PREGNENE COMPOUNDS—Sarett prepared the first synthetic cortisone. He and several collaborators developed synthesis from raw materials derived from coal, air, lime and water, leading to the first route which was independent of naturally occurring starting materials. (1980)

Schultz, Peter *See under* Maurer, Robert.

Seiwald, Robert J. *See under* Burckhalter, Joseph H.

Semon, Waldo L. 1898– (b. Demopolis, Ala.) PVC PLASTISOLS—Semon's work turned polyvinyl chloride (PVC), first considered worthless, into the world's second-best selling plastic. He also provided the technical leadership that led to the discovery of thermoplastic polyurethane, synthetic "natural" rubber, and the first oil-resistant synthetic rubber. (1995)

Sheehan, John C. 1915–1992 (b. Battle Creek, Mich.) SEMI-SYNTHETIC PENICILLIN—For almost 30 years after Sir Alexander Fleming's discovery of penicillin, the process for harvesting the drug took months to generate a small amount. Sheehan succeeded in a general total synthesis of the antibiotic. (1995)

Shockley, William Bradford *See under* Bardeen, John.

Sikorsky, Igor I. 1889–1972 (b. Kiev, Russia) HELICOPTER CONTROLS—Sikorsky's patents covered control and stability improvements. The single rotor helicopter developed by Sikorsky represented a major breakthrough in helicopter technology. (1987)

Sperry, Elmer Ambrose 1860–1930 (b. Cortland, N.Y.) GYROSCOPIC COMPASS—The gyroscope was the basis of Sperry's inventions of an autopilot and an airplane turn indicator that allowed flying without visual reference to the ground. His ideas are used today to stabilize space vehicles. (1991)

Stanley, Jr., William 1858–1916 (b. Brooklyn, N.Y.) INDUCTION COIL—Stanley designed a practical induction coil system that varied alternating current (AC) voltage. His coil became the prototype for all future transformers and made practical the transmitting of electricity for consumer uses such as lighting. (1995)

Steinmetz, Charles Proteus 1865–1923 (b. Breslau, Germany) SYSTEM OF ELECTRICAL DISTRIBUTION—Steinmetz developed theories for alternating current making possible the expansion of the electric power industry in the United States. (1977)

Stibitz, George R. 1904–1995 (b. York, Pa.) COMPLEX COMPUTER—Stibitz is internationally recognized as the father of the modern digital computer. In 1939 Stibitz helped design the Model I complex number calculator which could add two eight-digit decimal numbers in a tenth of a second. (1983)

Tabern, Donalee L. *See under* Volwiler, Ernest H.

Tesla, Nikola 1856–1943 (b. Smiljan Lika, Croatia) ELECTRO-MAGNETIC MOTOR—Tesla invented the induction motor which had a rotating magnetic field. The electro-magnetic motor was instrumental in converting electrical energy into mechanical energy, enabling electric motors to power machines. (1975)

Tishler, Max 1906–1989 (b. Boston, Mass.) SYNTHESIS OF RIBOFLAVIN AND SULFAQUINOXALINE—Tishler found a new process for the economical and large-scale synthesis of riboflavin (vitamin B_2). He also developed a production process for sulfaquinoxaline, the first effective antibiotic for the prevention and cure of the poultry disease coccidiosis. (1982)

Townes, Charles Hard 1915– (b. Greenville, South Carolina) MASERS—Townes constructed the maser (microwave amplification by stimulated emission of radiation) and also suggested the laser. Both are used in communications, medicine, industry, astronomy and navigation. (1976)

Volwiler, Ernest H. 1893–1992 (b. Hamilton, Ohio); **Tabern, Donalee L.** 1900–1974 (b. Bowling Green, Ohio) THIO-BARBITURIC ACID DERIVATIVES—Volwiler and Tabern came up with Pentothal when they were seeking an anesthetic which could be injected directly into the bloodstream. (1986)

Wang, An 1920–1990 (b. Shanghai, China) MAGNETIC PULSE CONTROLLING DEVICE—Wang's contributions to computer technology included the magnetic pulse controlling device, the principle upon which magnetic core memory is based. He is noted for his innovations in the office automation and information processing field. (1988)

Westinghouse, George 1846–1914 (b. Central Bridge, N.Y.) STEAM-POWER BRAKE DEVICES—Westinghouse invented a system of railroad brakes that would centralize control in the hands of the engineer. Westinghouse, Tesla and other inventors developed alternating current motors and apparatus for the transmission of high tension current leading to large scale municipal lighting. (1989)

Whitney, Eli 1765–1825 (b. Westboro, Mass.) COTTON GIN—Whitney invented the cotton gin, a machine that greatly increased the speed for separating the cotton from its pod and seeds and to clean it. Whitney also adopted the concept of interchangeable parts in manufacturing. (1974)

Williams, Robert R., Jr. 1886–1965 (b. Nellore, India) SYNTHESIS OF VITAMIN B_1—Williams isolated thiamine in crystalline form and synthesized vitamin B_1. He was instrumental in achieving enrichment of flour, cornmeal and other cereal grains, helping to eliminate pellagra and riboflavin deficiency among poor people. He also invented processes for making submarine insulation. (1991)

Wright, Orville 1871–1948 (b. Dayton, Ohio); **Wright, Wilbur** 1867–1912 (b. Millville, Ind.) FLYING MACHINE—The Wright brothers achieved the first powered, sustained and controlled flight of a heavier than air machine at Kitty Hawk, North Carolina in 1903. (1975)

Zworykin, Vladimir Kosma 1889–1982 (b. Murom, Russia) CATHODE RAY TUBE—Zworykin invented the iconoscope, a television transmitting tube and the kinetoscope, a cathode ray tube that projects pictures it receives onto a screen. He also invented an infrared image tube and helped develop an electron microscope. (1977) □

COMPUTER NOTES

How to Outwit a Cyber-Thief

By Farhan Memon, the New York Post

The first outbreak occurred in 1985 when the movie War Games showed two teen-agers and their home computer taking the world to the edge of nuclear annihilation.

Then there was a second epidemic in 1988 when Robert Tappan Morris inadvertently launched the Internet Worm, a computer virus that brought the world wide network to its knees.

Seven years later, the recent capture of Kevin Mitnick, the nation's most wanted cyber-thief, finds the United States once again in the grip of hacker hysteria.

The *Post* asked a group of computer security experts what you should know about hackers and how you can protect yourself against them both at home and at the office. Here's their advice:

1. Hackers don't normally attack home desktop computers, says Manny Kwahk, the founder of Interport, a Manhattan Internet service provider. "Hackers want a machine that they can give commands to and have it do something," he said. Your home PC "probably doesn't have information that would be of any interest to them."

2. You start exposing yourself to risk when you connect to a computer network. In the case of services like America Online and CompuServe it's your access to the service hackers would be interested in. They have the fun, you foot the bill.

3. The first and best line of defense to thwart a hacker is a good password says Erwin Mascardo, the computer security officer for Virginia-based AERA Inc. Don't make your password anything that identifies you personally, such as your name, log-in, E-mail address, etc.

4. A good password can be constructed by gluing together two easy-to-remember syllables (that don't form a word themselves) with a non-alpha character. A fairly good password can be constructed by taking a word that you SHOULDN'T use as a password and putting a non-alpha character somewhere in the middle. However, don't take a "bad" password and just stick a non-alpha character at the beginning or end.

5. It might seem clever to get around the "bad-password" rules by reversing or "rotating" the letters (taking some letters from the end and putting them at the beginning, or vice versa). It's not. Password-cracking programs check reversed and rotated forms as a matter of course.

6. Do not write down your password. Slips of paper can be lost or stolen. Don't tell anyone else your password, not even a trusted colleague.

7. If you believe that your password has been compromised, alert the system administrator. He or she should change your password. Do NOT log on yourself to change your password, because doing so may trigger a virus or other destructive program.

8. If you use more than one system, use a different password on each one.

9. Change your password periodically, but not so often that you have trouble remembering it. Once per month is good; more than once every two weeks is excessive.

10. There are smart cards available that generate a unique number every time you want to log in. Your computer will prompt you for the number to verify that you are a valid user and to ensure that the person logging-in is in physical possession of the device. The chances of someone knowing your password and having the smart card are remote.

11. There is only one aspect of physical security that the average user can control, and that is physical access to his or her terminal. If you leave your terminal unlocked when you step away from it, you have effectively given your password away.

12. Never insert a floppy disk or download a program from the Internet without running a virus check. Computer viruses can do serious damage to data. Also some viruses act as password sniffers, copying every keystroke you enter. The sniffer can give a hacker all he needs to break into your computer system.

13. E-mail sent through the Internet can be read by many people as it goes from sender to receiver. Jonathon Ezor, an attorney specializing in computer law, says he never E-mails confidential material to clients. If documents must be sent by E-mail, Ezor suggests encrypting the message.

14. Computer security consultant Ray Bengen says that companies who connect their network to the Internet must install a firewall, a machine that allows information from the corporate site to flow freely to the outside world, but examines and filters each incoming packet. This way it weeds out viruses and other non-acceptable entities.

15. Bengen also advises not to allow rogue modems into the office. These are modems that individuals hook up to their own desktop so they can work from home. But the same line that lets them access the system also provides a potential opening for hackers who use programs to sequentially dial hundreds of telephone numbers.

16. Don't add features to your machine that you don't need. For example the "finger" feature in UNIX allows users all over the Internet to ask about your log-in name. This helps when trying to find someone's E-mail address, but if not properly installed also allows hackers to gain access to the computer network. □

Access and Use of Computers in the United States

(Numbers in thousands)

Access, use and age	Number			Percent		
	1984	1989	1993	1984	1989	1993
Households with computer	6,980	13,683	22,605	8.2	15.0	22.8
ALL RACES						
3 to 17 years	51,482	52,667	55,827			
Access to a computer	7,697	12,082	17,829	15.3	24.2	31.9
Use home computer	5,679	8,547	12,527	74.2	71.1	74.7
Use computer at school	12,284	20,664	28,848	28.0	46.0	60.6
Use computer any place	15,542	24,216	32,659	30.2	46.0	58.5
18 years and over	169,786	180,123	187,405			
Access to a computer	14,999	29,615	47,988	9.1	17.3	25.6
Use home computer	7,757	16,758	30,165	53.3	58.4	65.6
Use computer at school	3,839	5,564	7,439	30.8	43.6	53.8
Use computer at work	24,172	40,245	51,106	24.6	36.8	45.8
Use computer any place	31,099	50,668	67,397	18.3	28.1	36.0
WHITE						
3 to 17 years	41,915	42,262	44,242			
Access to a computer	7,048	10,773	15,821	17.1	26.7	35.8
Use home computer	5,186	7,685	11,248	74.0	71.7	75.3
Use computer at school	10,827	17,463	23,799	30.3	48.2	62.7
Use computer any place	13,782	20,662	27,178	32.9	48.9	61.4
18 years and over	146,693	154,236	158,927			
Access to a computer	13,782	26,902	42,814	9.6	18.3	26.9
Use home computer	7,151	15,462	27,417	53.4	59.2	66.7
Use computer at school	3,269	4,709	5,980	31.0	43.6	53.1
Use computer at work	21,795	35,977	45,326	25.3	37.8	47.1
Use computer any place	27,940	45,264	59,532	19.0	29.4	37.5
BLACK						
3 to 17 years	7,721	8,212	8,836			
Access to a computer	461	806	1,152	6.1	10.6	13.0
Use home computer	350	518	721	75.9	65.0	67.3
Use computer at school	1,032	2,416	3,786	15.9	35.1	50.9
Use computer any place	1,254	2,622	4,031	16.2	31.9	45.6
18 years and over	18,403	20,007	21,361			
Access to a computer	780	1,573	2,949	4.4	8.4	13.8
Use home computer	406	733	1,582	54.0	50.6	56.8
Use computer at school	367	506	909	26.1	38.9	54.8
Use computer at work	1,724	2,990	4,072	18.3	27.6	36.1
Use computer any place	2,259	3,673	5,335	12.3	18.4	25.0
HISPANIC ORIGIN						
3 to 17 years	4,266	5,734	6,569			
Access to a computer	191	514	795	4.6	9.6	12.1
Use home computer	128	326	459	67.4	64.3	68.4
Use computer at school	634	1,724	2,829	18.2	37.5	52.7
Use computer any place	717	1,853	2,991	16.8	32.3	45.5
18 years and over	9,362	13,301	15,103			
Access to a computer	372	1,005	1,954	4.1	8.0	12.9
Use home computer	165	508	1,090	45.6	54.0	61.3
Use computer at school	177	323	534	28.0	37.7	50.0
Use computer at work	863	1,779	2,492	16.4	22.5	29.3
Use computer any place	1,091	2,246	3,322	11.7	16.9	22.0

NOTE: Percents based on the following: Use home computer based on persons with home computer. Use computer at school based on persons enrolled. Use computer at work based on persons with a job. Use computer any place (home, work, school combined) based on persons in age group. Persons of Hispanic origin may be of any race. *Source:* U.S. Bureau of the Census, "Computer Use in the United States: 1993." Data are from Current Population Survey (CPS), October 1993.

Countries With the Most Computers

(Year-End 1993)

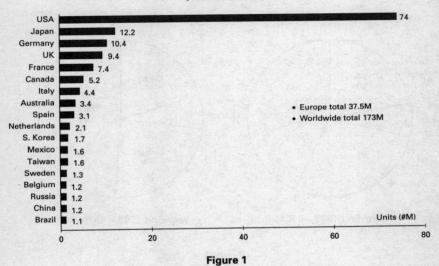

- Europe total 37.5M
- Worldwide total 173M

Figure 1

Computers per Capita

(Year-End 1993)

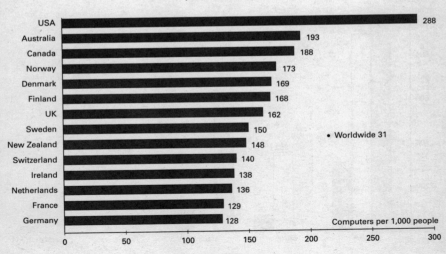

- Worldwide 31

Figure 2

Source: Karen Petska Juliussen and Egil Juliussen, *7th Annual Computer Industry Almanac,* Copyright © 1994 by Computer Industry Almanac, Inc., P.O. Box 9049, Incline Village, Nevada 89452.

U.S. vs Europe vs Japan

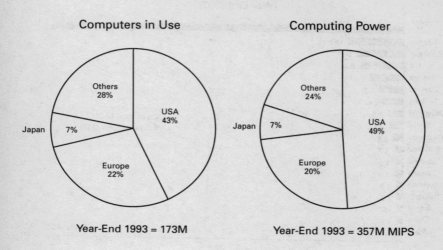

Computers in Use

Others 28%

USA 43%

Japan 7%

Europe 22%

Year-End 1993 = 173M

Computing Power

Others 24%

USA 49%

Japan 7%

Europe 20%

Year-End 1993 = 357M MIPS

Figure 3

Computers vs Phones vs TVs

In use per 1,000 people

Legend: Phones, TVs, Computers

	Phones	TVs	Computers
USA	965	900	288
Europe	446	363	76
Japan	650	635	98
Russia	150	350	8
Worldwide	156	182	31

Figure 4

Source: Karen Petska Juliussen and Egil Juliussen, *7th Annual Computer Industry Almanac,* Copyright © 1994 by Computer Industry Almanac, Inc., P.O. Box 9049, Incline Village, Nevada 89452.

Some Milestones in Modern Computing

1946—ENIAC (Electronic Numerical Integrator and Calculator), the first electronic digital computer, is designed by J.P. Eckert and J.W. Mauchly of the University of Pennsylvania to calculate ballistic trajectories. One trajectory took a human 3 days to calculate; ENIAC could do it in 20 seconds.

1947—John Bardeen and Walter Brattain invent the point-contact transistor to replace the bulky and fragile vacuum tube.

1949—EDSAC (Electronic Delay Storage Automatic Computer), the first electronic stored program computer, begins operating in England in June. BINAC (Binary Automatic Computer), America's version, tested in August. Claude Shannon of MIT builds the first chess-playing machine.

1951—The U.S. Census Bureau receives the first UNIVAC (Universal Automatic Computer). William Shockley invents the junction transistor. Whirlwind, the first real-time (instantaneous to human actions) computer is completed. It was built by MIT and designed by Jay W. Forestor and his team. Grace Hopper comes up with a compiler, a program that scans a programmer's instructions, produces an organized program, and carries it out.

1952—CBS-TV uses UNIVAC to successfully predict the presidential election result.

1953—Magnetic-core memory replaces electrostatic tubes on Whirlwind doubling speed, quadrupling input data rate, and slashing memory bank maintenance time from 4 hours a day to 2 hours a week.

1954—FORTRAN (Formula Translation). First major scientific programming language developed by John Backus and his team at IBM. It simplifies computer programming.

1955—Silicon Valley gets its start with William Shockley's Semiconductor Laboratory.

1957—Digital Equipment Company is founded by Kenneth H. Olsen.

1958—Jack Kilby of Texas Instruments creates an integrated circuit. ALGOL (Algorithmic Language). Developed as a result of international cooperation to obtain a standard algorithmic computer language. The first fully transistorized supercomputer, the CDC 1604, is built by Seymour Cray for Control Data Corporation.

1959—Robert Noyce invents the planar integrated circuit, opening the door for commercial development. COBOL (Common Business Oriented Language) was defined by the Conference on Data Systems Languages.

1961—MIT develops the first time-sharing computer.

1963—Minicomputer introduced by Digital Equipment Corp. Tandy Corporation purchases Radio Shack. The radio equipment company was named after the part of a ship's upper deck that housed the communications equipment. The first successful minicomputer, the PDP–8 (Programmed Data Processor model 8) is introduced by Digital Equipment Company.

1964—BASIC (Beginner's All-purpose Symbolic Instruction Code) developed by Thomas E. Kurtz and John G. Kemeny, Dartmouth College.

1965—MIT computer scientist, John McCarthy, coins the term "artificial intelligence."

1966—The first personal computer club, The Amateur Computer Society, is founded by Stephen B. Gray. The club's *ACS Newsletter* is possibly the first computer publication.

1968—Intel (Integrated Electronics) Corporation is founded by Gordon Moore and Robert Noyce.

1969—Gary Starkweather invents the laser printer while working for Xerox.

1970s—Researchers at the Xerox Palo Alto Research Center (PARC) developed the first workstations on a fully-distributed network called Alto. PARC also pioneered the use of windows, icons, and mouse pointing devices in workstations.

1971—Intel Corporation markets the first microprocessor, the 4004, developed by Marcian E. Hoff and his team.

1972—The first 8-bit microprocessor, the Intel 8008, is introduced.

1974—Intel introduces the first general-purpose microprocessor, the 8-bit 8080.

1975—*Byte*, the first computer magazine, begins publication. The term "personal computer" is coined by Ed Roberts and his company, MITS (Micro Instrumentation and Telemetry Systems). The MITS Altair 8800 (a computer kit) designed by Edward Roberts, William Yates, and Jim Bybee becomes the first personal computer on the market. William Gates and Paul Allen found Microsoft Corporation. Epson America, Inc. is formed by the Seiko.

1976—Apple Computer Corporation is founded by Stephen G. Wozniak and Steven P. Jobs.

1977—The Apple II, the first personal computer with color graphics capability, is introduced. Tandy Corp. introduces the Radio Shack TRS-80, Model 1 microcomputer. It sold for $599.

1978—Epson introduces the dot-matrix printer for personal computers. The 5.2-inch floppy diskette becomes the industry standard.

1980—The first spreadsheet for personal computers, VisCalc, was invented by Dan Bricklin and Bob Frankston for use on Apple II computer.

1981—IBM gets into personal computers with the IBM PC. Canon introduces Bubble Jet technology and announces a prototype Bubble Jet printer.

1982—Epson's HX-20 becomes the first laptop computer. *WordPerfect for DOS,* one of the all-time best-selling word processing programs, is introduced by WordPerfect Corporation. Compaq Computer Corporation is formed by Rod Canion and other Texas Instruments Inc. engineers. Compaq introduces the first clone of the IBM PC.

1983—Lotus 1–2–3 spreadsheet program is launched.

1984—The user-friendly Apple Macintosh makes its debut. The term "cyberspace" is coined by science fiction writer William Gibson in his first book, "Neuromancer." The 3.5-inch diskette debuts.

1985—Paul Brainerd, president and co-founder of Aldus Corporation, coins the term "desktop publishing" to describe his new Apple Macintosh computer-based program, *PageMaker.* It was the first program to easily integrate text and graphics, and thereby eliminated the need for paste-up. It incorporated the composition process in a what-you-see-is-what-you-get (WYSIWYG) environment. As a result, it opened a new field of careers in personal computing. The Apple LaserWriter laser printer opens up the desktop publishing area. AT&T Bell Labs produce the first fuzzy logic chips. The first *Windows* program, 1.0, is released by Microsoft Corporation.

1988—Notebook computers, smaller versions of laptops, become popular.

1989—First pen-based computer, the GRiDPAD, is announced by GRiD Systems Corporation.

1991—Clipboard computers appear. Clipboards replace the keyboard with a liquid crystal screen and electronic stylus.

1995—IBM acquires Lotus Development Corporation.

Computer Glossary

Alphanumeric: Letters and numbers.

ASCII: American Standard Code for Information Interchange, an encoding system for converting keyboard characters and instructions into the binary number code that the computer understands. (*See* Machine Language.)

Baud Rate: The speed of data transmission measured in bits per second.

Binary: A numbering system that uses only two digits, 0 and 1. Computers can *only* add and they can only add in 0's and 1's.

Bit: (Stands for binary digit). It is the smallest piece of computer information and is either the number 0 or 1. All information is given to the computer in the binary number system. With proper coding, the computer can "understand" any number, letter, punctuation mark, or symbol through an appropriate combination of the numbers 0 and 1.

Boot: To start up a program.

Bug: A malfunction due to an error in the program or a defect in the equipment.

Byte: Most computers use combinations of eight bits to represent one character of data. These eight-bit combinations are called bytes. Bytes can represent data or instructions. For example, the word "cat" has three characters, and it would be represented by three bytes.

CD-ROM: (Compact Disk Read-Only Memory.) A peripheral system that uses CD-ROM laser disks and a CD-ROM reader (similar to a CD music disk and player) connected to your computer. A single disk can hold an entire library of books such as encyclopedias, and other reference works and multi-media programs for quick, convenient viewing.

Chip: A tiny wafer of silicon containing miniature electric circuits which can store millions of bits of information.

CPU: Central Processing Unit. The "brains" or part of a computer where all the incoming information is controlled and executed by its electronic circuitry.

Cursor: A moving position-indicator displayed on the computer monitor that shows the computer operator where he is working.

Cyberspace: The continuum of computer networks and bulletin board systems in which on-line communication takes place.

Database: A program that enables you to create and update files of information in a well-organized manner.

Debug: Computer slang for finding and correcting in a computer program or equipment malfunction. (*See* Bug.)

Desktop Publishing: Use of a personal computer in combination with text, graphics, and page layout programs to produce publication quality documents.

Directory: A list of files stored in the computer.

Disk: On large computers, disks are hard and are about the same size as a phonograph record. PCs use smaller disks, 5 1/4 or 3 1/2 inches in diameter. Because they are made from a flexible mylar plastic, they are sometimes called *floppy disks*, or *diskettes*.

Disk Drive: The machine that a disk is inserted into so that information may be stored or retrieved from the disk.

Documentation: The instruction manual for a piece of hardware or software.

DOS: Disk Operating System. A program for controlling the storage of information on a disk commonly used in IBM computers and compatibles.

Dotted quad: An Internet address is a 32-bit number usually written as a set of 4 numbers separated by periods; for example: 120.210.49.30.

E-mail: Electronic Mail. It can refer to inter-office memos or letters sent by computer or messages sent by users to other computer users.

File: A set of data that is stored in the computer.

FTP (File Transfer Protocol): The format and rules for transferring files from a host to a remote computer.

Fonts: Sets of typefaces (or characters) that come in different styles and sizes.

Gigabyte (GB): One billion bytes.

Glitch: The cause of an unexpected malfunction.

Graphics: Pictorial matter such as charts, graphs, and diagrams that can be programmed into a computer's video display.

GUI: Graphical User Interface. A system that simplifies selecting computer commands by enabling the user to point to symbols or illustrations (called "icons") on the computer screen with a mouse.

Groupware: Software that allows networking groups to collaborate on documents.

Hacker: A person with technical expertise who enjoys tinkering with computer systems in order to produce additional features. Also one who intentionally accesses all or part of a computer or a computer system without authorization to do so. (A crime in some states.)

Hard Copy: A permanent record of what you have done on the computer in the form of a paper printout.

Hardware: The physical and mechanical components of a computer system. They include electronic circuitry, chips, screens, disk drives, keyboards, and printers.

Hexidecimal: A machine language written in a 16-base number system. In "Hex," the digits are 0 through 9, plus A, B, C, D, E, and F.

Home page: A site on the Web.

HTTP: Hypertext transfer protocol.

Hypermedia: Integrates audio, graphics, and/or video.

Hypertext: A system for retrieving and referencing related documents.

I/O: Input/output. Information into or out of a computer.

Icons: Symbols or illustrations appearing on the computer screen that indicate program files or other computer functions.

Input: Data that goes into a computer device.

Interface: A device that connects a computer with a peripheral so that they can communicate with each other.

Internet: The world's largest conglomeration of interconnecting communications networks accessed by millions of users. The Internet is a non-commercial, non-tangible entity. Its main focus is research and communications, but it offers a wide array of resources for business and home users.

Kilobyte (K or KB): Equal to 1,024 bytes. Computer memories are measured in terms of the number of bytes they can store. For example: a 64K memory means that the computer can handle 64×1024 or 65,536 bytes.

Language: A special set of symbols, characters, and numbers that you use to communicate with the computer.

Laptop and Notebook: Small, lightweight, portable battery-powered computers that can fit onto your lap. They have a thin, flat, liquid crystal display screen.

Liquid Crystal Display (LCD): The kind of display used to show numerals in digital watches and calculators.

Machine Language: The CPU or "brains" of the computer can only understand instructions written in binary form (bits of 0's and 1's). The commands the operator gives the computer are translated into data by the computer using the two-digit binary number system.

Megabyte (MB): Equal to 1,048,576 bytes, usually rounded off to one million bytes.

Memory: A computer device or series of devices that store information.

Menu: A list of options displayed on the computer terminal that you can choose from.

Merge: To combine two or more files into a single file arrangement.

Microcomputer: A personal computer containing a central processing unit (CPU) and one or more memory circuits.

Microprocessor: A complete central processing unit (CPU) contained on a single silicon chip.

Modem: A device that will connect two compatible computers together by a direct connection to the telephone line. Modems accomplish this by converting the computer's data into an audio signal.

Monitor: A video display terminal.

Mouse: A small hand-held device for controlling the cursor movement on the screen by moving the "mouse" back and forth on a desk.

Multimedia: Software application technology that combines text and graphics with sound and animation. A **multimedia PC** contains the hardware to support these capabilities.

Output: Data that come out of a computer device.

MS-DOS: An operating system developed by Microsoft Corporation.

Network: Computers that are connected to other computers.

OS/2: An operating system for IBM PCs and compatible computers.

PC: Personal computer.

Pen Computer: A type of laptop PC tat uses a stylus (pen) to write directly on the screen rather than using a keyboard.

Pentium chip: Intel's fifth generation of sophisticated high-speed microprocessors. Pentium means "the fifth element."

Peripherals: Extra equipment for the computer that will extend its usefulness and capability. Most peripherals either increase the computer's storage capacity or permit it to communicate with outside devices.

Power PC: A competitor to the Pentium chip. It is a new generation of powerful sophisticated microprocessors produced from an Apple–IBM–Motorola alliance.

Printer: A mechanical device for making a permanent printed record of your computer's output on paper. The three major types of printers are the **Dot Matrix:** In which individual letters are made up of a series of tiny ink dots. The dots are formed by punching a ribbon with the ends of tiny wires; **Ink**

Jet: Sprays tiny droplets of ink particles (which become electrically charged) onto paper and they are formed into characters by a varying electric field; and **Laser:** It uses the principle of dry process office copiers in which a modulated laser beam is used as the light source.

Program: A precise series of instructions written in a computer language that tells the computer what to do and how to do it. Programs are also called "software."

RAM: Random Access Memory. One of two basic types of memory. RAM is a memory that you can add to, retrieve from, or alter at will. RAM is also called Read/Write Memory. (*See* ROM.)

ROM: Read-Only Memory. One of the two basic types of memory. As its name implies, information in it cannot be altered by the computer operator. It can be transferred out, but not transferred in. ROM contains only permanent information put there by the manufacturer. (*See* RAM.)

Scanner: An electronic device that uses light-sensing equipment to scan paper images such as text, photos, and illustrations and translate the images into signals that the computer can understand and copy.

Server: A computer that shares its resources and information with other computers on a network.

Software: The various computer programs.

Spreadsheets: Software that allows one to calculate numbers in a format that is similar to pages in a conventional ledger.

Surfing: Exploring the Internet.

User Friendly: It means that the system and the instructions for it are supposed to be written in simple language and be easy to operate for people with a nontechnical background.

VGA: Video Graphics Array. A widely used monitor for personal computers.

Virtual Reality (VR): A technology that allows you to experience and interact with the image on the computer screen in a simulated three-dimensional environment. For example, you could design a room in a house on your computer and actually feel that you are walking around in it even though it was never built. (The holodeck in the science fiction TV series "Star Trek: The Next Generation" would be the ultimate virtual reality.) Current technology requires the user to wear a special helmet, viewing goggles, gloves, and other equipment that is wired to the computer.

Virus: An unauthorized piece of computer code attached to a computer program or portions of a computer system that secretly spreads from one computer to another by shared disks and over telephone lines.

Windows: A graphical user interface that enables users to select commands by pointing to illustrations or symbols displayed in a rectangular area on the computer screen with a mouse.

World Wide Web (WWW or The Web): A network of servers that utilize hypertext-linked databases and files. It was developed in 1989 by Tim Berners-Lee, a British computer specialist.

Word Processor: A computer system or program for setting, editing, revising, correcting, storing, and the printing of text.

Worm: An unauthorized independent program that penetrates computers and replicates itself, thereby affecting computers and computer networks. In 1988, Robert T. Morris, a Cornell University graduate student shut down a nationwide computer network with the best-known computer worm in history.

ENVIRONMENT

1995 Environmental Quality Review

Source: Copyright 1995 by the National Wildlife Federation.

Reprinted from the February-March 1995 issue of *National Wildlife Magazine.*

National Wildlife's annual Environmental Quality Review is a subjective analysis of the state of the nation's natural resources. The information included in each section is based on personal interviews, news reports, and the most current scientific studies.

Wildlife: New studies show the advantages of protecting biodiversity, but the U.S. Congress fails to take heed. After decades of decline the future of America's national symbol, the bald eagle, looks brighter. The U.S. Fish and Wildlife Service proposed that its status be downgraded from endangered to threatened everywhere in the lower 48 states except the Southwest. A month earlier, federal officials had removed the California gray whale from the endangered list. Conservationists viewed such recoveries as important milestones for the species and also for the Endangered Species Act. Its effectiveness was further documented by a Fish and Wildlife Service report which found nearly 40 percent of the animals and plants protected by the Act are stable or improving. Conservationists hoped such progress would help galvanize support for reauthorization by Congress of the Endangered Species Act, which was due in 1993, but was again postponed last year [1994]. On another front, the news regarding the nation's freshwater and saltwater fisheries was not encouraging. According to an Environmental Defense Fund report America's freshwater fish and shellfish are the nation's most endangered forms of wildlife.

Air: While states stall in complying with federal law one in four Americans continues to breathe unhealthful air. According to the Environmental Protection Agency (EPA) the number of U.S. citizens living in areas that do not meet the federal ozone standard declined by 37 percent to 54 million in 1992 (the most recent figures available) the lowest number in two decades of monitoring. Federal officials also reported that emissions of hydrocarbons—major components of smog—by new automobiles have been reduced by 90 percent since passage of the Clean Air Act in 1970. And EPA data on the release of airborne toxic chemicals by U.S. industry show a 9.4 percent improvement over 1991 and an overall reduction of 35 percent since 1988. Such reduction represents considerable improvement by any measure. But experts concede getting rid of air pollution—particularly ground-level ozone pollution—is a daunting task. In 1990 lawmakers set stiff new standards for reducing urban smog and other air pollution. Yet as last summer [1994] came to a close 10 states had not filed plans that were due in 1992 and some two dozen states that were required to file plans in 1993 had not yet responded.

Water: Despite grim news about pollution problems, U.S. lawmakers postpone strengthening the Clean Water Act. As Congress began considering reauthorization of the Clean Water Act early last year [1994], EPA officials reported 30 percent of rivers, 42 percent of lakes, and 32 percent of estuaries continue to be degraded, mainly by silt and nutrients from farm and urban runoff, combined sewer overflows, and municipal sewage. EPA also reported a 12 percent increase in the amount of toxic chemicals discharged into U.S. surface waters. Federal lawmakers also failed to reauthorize two other important measure that affect the quality of the nation's water: the Safe Drinking Water Act and the Superfund Law. On the positive side the U.S. Supreme Court ruled that under the Clean Water Act, states can protect not only the quality but also the quantity of water in streams and rivers.

Forests: While the old-growth dispute simmers in the Northwest, a plan to manage Northeast forests is unveiled. The Clinton administration took a long overdue step in 1994 in addressing the deadlock between the timber industry and conservationists over the future of remaining old-growth forests in the Pacific Northwest. A plan that the administration proposed in 1993 to end the conflict would permit logging of much of the old growth while preserving almost all of the habitat of the region's imperiled wildlife species. By June of 1994 the U.S. Forest Service began preparing timber sales that met the criteria of the plan. But by that time, the timber industry and environmentalists had filed lawsuits to challenge the plan. On the other side of the country, members of the Northern Forest Lands Council, an independent body created by Congress in 1990, sought to avoid the kinds of timber-related conflicts that plagued the Northwest. In another of the nation's major forest areas, the Southeast, EPA moved in 1994 to close a loophole in environmental law that has contributed to the destruction of millions of acres of wetlands by specifically banning clearing and draining wetlands for creating pine plantations.

Energy: As federal agencies strive to reduce energy consumption, low oil prices negate some conservation tactics. However, with the cost of converting sunlight to electricity dropping, electric utilities are increasingly plugging into solar power to avoid building new plants. Another boost for alternative energy sources came last year [1994] when the Clinton administration ordered federal agencies to reduce their energy consumption by 30 percent (of 1985 levels) in 10 years. An executive order mandated the use of high-efficiency fluorescent lights, better waste management practices, and renewable energy sources. Another government initiative involving the addition of oxygenates to gasoline—ethanol and methanol—resulted in competition of the nation's oil industry and the agribusiness establishment. Result, a federal appeals court temporarily blocked the EPA decision that at least 30 percent of the additives used be from ethanol while it considers oil industry legal challenges.

Soil: Last summer [1994] the U.S. Soil Conservation Service reported that American farmers were well on the way to reducing soil losses on at least 140 million acres of the country's most erodible farmland. A part of the success was due to the Conservation Reserve Program that has paid thousands of farmers to remove environmentally sensitive land from production and plant it with grass or trees to prevent erosion. Where it has worked effectively wildlife has benefited. Ironically, farmers in nine Midwest states along the Missouri and Mississippi Rivers struggled not with erosion but with sedimentation—millions of tons of sand and debris left on their cropland by the flood waters of 1993. In late 1993, the National Wildlife Federation and other groups persuaded lawmakers to make funds available for purchase of floodplain-damaged lands from farmers for restoration back to wetlands. Since then, nearly 100,000 acres have been offered to the program.

Quality of Life: Research uncovers potential new threats to human health from an ominous class of toxic pollutants. The pollutants in question often are found in traces so small that they are hard to measure and act so slowly that their full impact may not be known for generations. Instead of directly poisoning, these com-

pounds may imitate the natural hormones of living creatures well enough to take over and then sabotage the many functions the hormones control. The harm such compounds may do to human health is difficult for researchers to prove. What's more, every shred of evidence of a chemical's danger often is countered by massive campaigns of denial by industry. Although often confused by such claims and counterclaims, Americans held firm in 1994 to their concern about threats to their health. The Harvard Center for Risk Analysis reported that 66 percent of Americans interviewed agreed that "the government is not doing enough to protect people from environmental pollution" and 94 percent wanted to know the estimated costs and benefits of new clean-up regulations. ☐

Endangered Species

The number of threatened animal taxa identified by International Union for Conservation of Nature and Natural Resources (IUCN) is just under 6,000, comprised of 741 mammals, 971 birds, 316 reptiles, 169 amphibians, 977 fishes, and 2,574 invertebrates. However, except for birds, for which International Council for Bird Preservation (ICBP)/IUCN have now attempted a global review, these numbers represent only those taxa whose threatened status is known to IUCN; many, many more taxa, particularly invertebrates, are threatened, and becoming extinct every

year undescribed and unknown to the scientific and conservation communities. Thus the number of threatened taxa identified by IUCN represents only the visible fraction of a much greater problem.

The following list comprises some of the more familiar species that are endangered. Due to space limitations, it does not include all mammals, birds, reptiles, amphibians, and fish on the 1994 IUCN Red List nor does it include any clams, crustaceans, snails, insects, or plants.

Some Endangered and Threatened Species of the World[1]

Common Name	Scientific Name	Listed range
MAMMALS		
Bear, Baluchistan	Selenarctos thibetanus gedrosianus	Iran, Pakistan
Bear, Polar[2]	Ursus maritimus	Canada, Greenland, Norway, Svalbard and Jan Mayen Islands, Russia, U.S.
Cat, little spotted[3]	Felis tigrina	Argentina, Brazil, Colombia, Costa Rica, Ecuador, French Guiana, Guyana, Nicaragua? Paraguay? Peru? Suriname, Venezuela
Cheetah[2]	Acinonyx jubatus	Afghanistan (ex?), Algeria (?), Angola, Benin, Botswana, Burkina Faso, Cameroon, Chad, Ethiopia, Iran, Jordan (?), Kenya, Libya, Malawi, Mali, Mauritania, Morocco (ex?), Mozambique, Namibia, Niger, Nigeria, Pakistan (ex?), Saudi Arabia (ex?), Senegal, Somalia, South Africa, Sudan, Swaziland, Tanzania, Turkmenistan, Uganda, Western Sahara(?), Zaire, Zambia, Zimbabwe
Chimpanzee, West African	Pan troglodytes verus	Côte d'Ivoire, Ghana, Guinea, Guinea-Bissau (ex?), Liberia, Mali, Senegal, Sierra Leone, [Gambia]
Cougar, Florida	Felis concolor coryi	U.S.
Deer, Key	Odocoileus virginiaus clavium	U.S. Florida Keys
Deer, marsh[2]	Blastocerus dichotomus	Argentina, Bolivia, Brazil, Paraguay, Peru
Elephant, Indian	Elephas maximus	Bangladesh, Bhutan, Brunei, Cambodia, China, India, Indonesia, Kalimantan, Sumatra, Laos, Malaysia, Peninsular Malaysia, Sabah, Myanmar, Nepal, Sri Lanka, Thailand, Vietnam
Gazelle, Clark's (Dibatag)[2]	Ammodorcas clarkei	Ethiopia, Somalia
Gazelle, slender-horned	Gazella leptoceros	Algeria, Chad, Egypt, Libya, Mali, Mauritania?, Niger, Sudan, Tunisia, Western Sahara?
Gorilla, mountain	Gorilla gorilla beringei	Burundi (ex?), Rwanda, Uganda, Zaire, Virunga Volcano region
Ibex, Walia	Capra walie	Ethiopia
Leopard, snow	Panthera uncia	Afghanistan, Bhutan, China, India, Kazakhstan, Kyrgyzstan, Mongolia, Nepal, Pakistan, Russia, Tajikistan, Uzbekistan

Common Name	Scientific Name	Listed range
Lion, Asiatic	Panthera leo persica	India
Mandrill[2]	Mandrillus sphinx	Cameroon, Congo, Eq. Guinea, Gabon
Monkey, long-haired spider[2]	Ateles belzebuth	Brazil, Colombia, Ecuador, Peru, Venezuela
Prairie dog, Utah[2]	Cynomys parvidens	U.S.
Pronghorn, Sonoran	Antilocapra americana sonoriensis	Mexico, U.S.
Puma, Eastern	Felis concolor cougar	Canada, U.S.
Rat, Morro Bay kangaroo	Dipodomys heermanni morroensis	U.S.
Rhinoceros, great Indian	Rhinoceros unicornis	Bhutan, India, Nepal
Spanish Lynx	Lynx pardinus	Portugal, Spain
Sloth, maned	Bradypus torquatus	Brazil
Tiger	Panthera tigris	Afghanistan (ex?), Bangladesh, Bhutan, Cambodia, China, India, Indonesia, Java, Sumatra, Kazakhstan, North Korea (ex?), Kyrgyzstan, Laos, Malaysia, Peninsular Malaysia, Myanmar, Nepal, Russia, Tajikistan, Thailand, Turkmenistan, Uzbekistan, Vietnam
Wallaby, bridled nailtail	Onychogalea fraenata	Australia
Whale, humpback[2]	Megaptera novaeangliae	All oceans
Wolf, gray[2]	Canis lupus	Afghanistan, Albania, Armenia, Azerbaijan, Bangladesh (ex?), Belarus, Bhutan, Bulgaria, Canada, China, Czech Republic?, Estonia, Egypt, Finland, Greece, Greenland, India, Iran, Iraq, Israel, Italy, Jordan, Kazakhstan, Korea North, Korea South?, Kuwait, Kyrgyzstan, Latvia, Lebanon, Libya, Lithuania, Mexico, Moldova, Mongolia, Myanmar (ex?), Nepal, Norway, Oman, Pakistan, Poland, Portugal, Romania, Russia, Saudi Arabia, Slovakia, Slovenia, Spain, Sweden, Syria, Tajikistan, Turkey, Turkmenistan, Ukraine, U.S., Uzbekistan, Vietnam, Yemen, Yugoslavia
Wolf, red	Canis rufus	U.S.
Zebra, Cape Mountain	Equus zebra zebra	South Africa
BIRDS		
Albatross, short-tailed	Diomedea albatrus	Japan: Izu Islands * North Pacific inc. China, U.S.: Hawaiian Islands, Russia, Taiwan
Condor, California	Gymnogyps californianus	[Reintroduced to U.S.]
Crane, whooping	Grus americana	Canada* U.S.
Crow, Hawaiian	Corvus tropicus	Hawaiian Islands
Kestrel, Mauritius	Falco punctatus	Mauritius
Parrot, paradise	Psephotus pulcherrimus	Australia (ex?)
Stork, oriental	Ciconia boyciana	China, Russia * Japan, Korea North, Korea South
Woodpecker, ivory-billed[4]	Campephilus principalis	Cuba, U.S.
REPTILES		
Crocodile, American[2]	Crocodylus acutus	Belize?, Colombia, Costa Rica, Cuba, Dominican Republic, Ecuador, El Salvador, Guatemala, Haiti, Honduras, Jamaica, Mexico, Nicaragua, Panama, Peru, U.S.: Florida, Venezuela
Iguana, Anegada ground	Cyclura pinguis	British Virgin Is.: Anegada Island
Python, Indian[2]	Python molurus	Bangladesh, Cambodia, China, Hong Kong, India, Indonesia, Laos, Myanmar, Nepal, Pakistan, Sri Lanka, Thailand, Vietnam
Snake, Atlantic saltmarsh[5]	Nerodia fasciata taeniata	U.S.: Florida
AMPHIBIANS		
Frog, Israel painted[6]	Discoglossus nigriventer	Israel, Liberia?
Toad, Mount Nimba viviparous[2]	Nectophrynoides occidentalis	Guinea, Cote d'Ivoire
FISH		
Catfish, giant[2]	Pangasianodon gigas	Cambodia, China: Yunnan Province, Laos, Myanmar, Thailand, Vietnam
Trout, cutthroat[2]	Clarki ssp.	U.S.

1. Unless otherwise indicated the species is rated endangered. 2. Vulnerable. 3. Insufficiently known. 4. Extinct *[Former distribution]*. 5. Rare. 6. Extinct? *Within birds only an asterisk separates breeding range (left) from non-breeding range (right); vagrant records are excluded. NOTE: Square brackets indicate introduced populations. *Source: 1994 Red List of Threatened Animals,* published by the International Union for Conservation of Nature and Natural Resources and compiled by the World Conservation Monitoring Center. IUCN, Rue Mauverney 28, CH-1196 Gland, Switzerland.

Zoological Gardens

North America abounds in zoos from Canada to Mexico. The Metro Toronto Zoo, opened in 1974, is one of the largest in the world. Its six pavilions simulate the animals' natural habitats. So does the Calgary Zoo which also has a children's zoo. Mexico City's Chapultepec Park includes a large zoo featuring one of the few pairs of pandas outside of Red China, and a children's zoo.

The first zoological garden in the United States was established in Philadelphia in 1874. Since that time nearly every large city in the country has acquired a zoo. Among the largest are San Diego's on the West Coast; Chicago's Brookfield Zoo and those of St. Louis and Kansas City in the Middle West; New Orleans' Audubon Park and Zoological Garden in the South; and in the East the New York Zoological Society's park in the Bronx. The National Zoological Park in Washington, D.C., in a beautiful setting of hills, woods, and streams, was established in 1890 by an act of Congress. The major U.S. zoos now have created large naturalhabitat areas for their collections.

In Europe, zoological gardens have long been popular public institutions. The modern concept of zoo keeping may be dated from 1752 with the founding of the Imperial Menagerie at the Schönbrunn Palace in Vienna. It was opened to the public in 1765 and is still in operation. In 1793 the zoological collection of the Jardin des Plantes was established in Paris in the Bois de Boulogne. At Antwerp the Royal Zoological Society founded a large menagerie in 1843. Now its aviary is noted for the principle of lighted and darkened spaces for confining the birds. Germany's famous Tiergarten zoo, in Berlin, was founded in 1841 and officially opened in 1844.

In the British Isles, the Zoological Society of London established its collection in Regent's Park in 1828. It was also responsible for the establishment of the prototype of the openrange zoo, Whipsnade Park, in 1932. Edinburgh's zoo is famous for its collection of penguins, the largest colony in captivity.

U.S. Zoos and Aquariums

Source: The facilities listed are members of, and accredited by, the American Zoo and Aquarium Association (AZA) to ensure that they are maintaining professional standards. It also accredits facilities outside of the United States.

Abilene Zoological Gardens, Texas
Akron Zoological Park, Ohio
Alameda Park Zoo, Alamogordo, N.M.
Alexandria Zoological Park, La.
Aquarium for Wildlife Conservation, The, Brooklyn, N.Y.
Aquarium of the Americas, New Orleans, La.
Arizona-Sonora Desert Museum, Tucson
Audubon Park and Zoological Garden, New Orleans
John Ball Zoological Garden, Grand Rapids, Mich.
Baltimore Zoo, The, Md.
Beardsley Zoological Gardens, Bridgeport, Conn.
Belle Isle Zoo and Aquarium, Detroit
Bergen County Zoological Park, Paramus, N.J.
Binder Park Zoo, Battle Creek, Mich.
Birmingham Zoo, Ala.
Blank Park Zoo, Des Moines, Iowa
Bramble Park Zoo, Watertown, S.D.
Brandywine Zoo, Wilmington, Del.
Bronx Zoo/Wildlife Conservation Park, N.Y.
Brookfield Zoo, Ill.
Brookgreen Gardens, Murrells Inlet, S.C.
Buffalo Zoological Gardens, N.Y.
Burnet Park Zoo, Syracuse, N.Y.
Busch Gardens, Tampa, Fla.
Caldwell Zoo, Tyler, Texas
Cape May County Park Zoo, Cape May Court House, N.J.
Central Florida Zoological Park, Lake Monroe, Fla.
Central Park Wildlife Center, New York, N.Y.
Chaffee Zoological Gardens of Fresno, Calif.
Cheyenne Mountain Zoological Park, Colorado Springs
Cincinnati Zoo and Botanical Garden, Ohio
Cleveland Metroparks Zoo, Ohio
Columbus Zoological Gardens, Ohio
Dakota Zoo, Bismarck, N.D.
Dallas Aquarium, Texas
Dallas Zoo, Texas
Denver Zoological Gardens, Colo.
Detroit Zoological Park, Mich.
Dickerson Park Zoo, Springfield, Mo.

Discovery Island Zoological Park, Lake Buena Vista, Fla.
Dreher Park Zoo, West Palm Beach, Fla.
El Paso Zoo, Texas
Emporia Zoo, Kan.
Erie Zoo, Pa.
Folsom Children's Zoo & Botanical Garden, Lincoln, Neb.
Fort Wayne Children's Zoo, Ind.
Fort Worth Zoological Park, Texas
Fossil Rim Wildlife Center, Glen Rose, Texas
Franklin Park Zoo, Boston, Mass.
Glen Oak Zoo, Peoria, Ill.
Grassmere Wildlife Park, Nashville, Tenn.
Great Plains Zoo & Musem, Sioux Falls, S.D.
Greater Baton Rouge Zoo, La.
Greenville Zoo, S.C.
Happy Hollow Park and Zoo, San Jose, Calif.
Honolulu Zoo, Hawaii
Houston Zoological Gardens, Texas
Indianapolis Zoo, Ind.
International Crane Foundation, Baraboo, Wis.
Jackson Zoological Park, Miss.
Jacksonville Zoological Park, Fla.
Kansas City Zoological Gardens, Mo.
Knoxville Zoological Gardens, Tenn.
Lake Superior Zoological Gardens, Duluth, Minn.
Lincoln Park Zoological Gardens, Chicago
Little Rock Zoological Garden, Ark.
Living Desert, The, Palm Desert, Calif.
Living Seas, The, Lake Buena Vista, Fla.
Los Angeles Zoo, Calif.
Louisville Zoological Garden, Ky.
Lowry Park Zoological Garden, Tampa, Fla.
Marine World Africa USA, Vallejo, Calif.
Memphis Zoological Garden and Aquarium, Tenn.
Mesker Park Zoo, Evansville, Ind.
Metro Washington Park Zoo, Portland, Ore.
Miami Metrozoo, Fla.
Micke Grove Zoo, Lodi, Calif.
Miller Park Zoo, Bloomington, Ill.
Milwaukee County Zoological Gardens, Wis.

Minnesota Zoological Garden, Apple Valley, Minn.
Monterey Bay Aquarium, Calif.
Montgomery Zoo, Ala.
Mystic Marinelife Aquarium, Mystic, Conn.
National Aquarium in Baltimore, Md.
National Aviary in Pittsburgh, Pa.
National Zoological Park, Washington, D.C.
New England Aquarium, Boston
New Jersey State Aquarium at Camden
North Carolina Aquarium at Fort Fisher, Kure Beach
North Carolina Aquarium at Pine Knoll Shores, Atlantic Beach
North Carolina Aquarium on Roanoke Island, Manteo
North Carolina Zoological Park, Asheboro
Northwest Trek Wildlife Park, Eatonville, Wash.
Oakland Zoo, The Calif.
Oglebay's Good Children's Zoo, Wheeling, W.Va.
Oklahoma City Zoological Park, Okla.
Omaha's Henry Doorly Zoo, Neb.
Charles Paddock Zoo, Atascadero, Calif.
Parrot Jungle and Gardens, Miami, Fla.
Clyde Peeling's Reptiland Ltd., Allenwood, Pa.
Philadelphia Zoological Garden, Pa.
Phoenix Zoo, The Ariz.
Pittsburgh Zoo, Pa.
Point Defiance Zoo and Aquarium, Tacoma, Wash.
Gladys Porter Zoo, Brownsville, Texas
Potawatomi Zoo, South Bend, Ind.
Potter Park Zoological Gardens, Lansing, Mich.
Prospect Park Wildlife Center, Brooklyn, N.Y.
Pueblo Zoo, Colo.
Queens Wildlife Center, Flushing, N.Y.
Racine Zoological Gardens, Wis.
Reid Park Zoo, Tucson, Ariz.
Lee Richardson Zoo, Garden City, Kan.
Rio Grande Zoological Park, Albuquerque, N.M.
Riverbanks Zoological Park and Botanical Garden, Columbia, S.C.
Riverside Zoo, Scottsbluff, Neb.
Henson Robinson Zoo, Springfield, Ill.
Roosevelt Zoo, Minot, N.D.
Ross Park Zoo, Binghamton, N.Y.
Sacramento Zoo, Calif.

St. Augustine Alligator Farm, Fla.
St. Louis Zoological Park, Mo.
St. Paul's Como Zoo, Minn.
Salisbury Zoological Park, Md.
San Antonio Zoological Gardens and Aquarium, Texas
San Diego Wild Animal Park, Calif.
San Diego Zoo, Calif.
San Francisco Zoological Gardens, Calif.
Santa Ana Zoo, Calif.
Santa Barbara Zoological Gardens, Calif.
Sea Life Park Hawaii, Waimanalo
Sea World of California, San Diego
Sea World of Florida, Orlando
Sea World of Ohio, Aurora
Sea World of Texas, San Antonio
Seattle Aquarium, The Wash.
Sedgwick County Zoo, Wichita, Kan.
Seneca Park Zoo, Rochester, N.Y.
John G. Shedd Aquarium, Chicago
Staten Island Zoo, N.Y.
Steinhart Aquarium, San Francisco, Calif.
Sunset Zoological Park, Manhattan, Kan.
Tennessee Aquarium, Chattanooga, Tenn.
Texas State Aquarium, Corpus Christi
Texas Zoo, The Victoria, Texas
Toledo Zoological Gardens, Ohio
Topeka Zoological Park, Kan.
Tracy Aviary, Salt Lake City, Utah
Trevor Zoo, Millbrook, N.Y.
Ellen Trout Zoo, Lufkin, Texas
Tulsa Zoo and Living Museum, Okla.
Utah's Hogle Zoo, Salt Lake City
Utica Zoo, N.Y.
Henry Vilas Zoo, Madison, Wis.
Virginia Zoological Park, Norfolk, Va.
Waikiki Aquarium, Hawaii
Wildlife Safari, Winston, Ore.
Wildlife World Zoo, Litchfield Park, Ariz.
Roger Williams Park Zoo, Providence, R.I.
Woodland Park Zoological Gardens, Seattle
The ZOO, Gulf Breeze, Fla.
Zoo Atlanta, Ga.
ZOOAMERICA North American Wildlife Park, Hershey, Pa.

Speed of Animals

Most of the following measurements are for maximum speeds over approximate quarter–mile distances. Exceptions— which are included to give a wide range of animals—are the lion and elephant, whose speeds were clocked in the act of charging; the whippet, which was timed over a 200–yard course; the cheetah over a 100–yard distance; man for a 15–yard segment of a 100–yard run; and the black mamba, six–lined race runner, spider, giant tortoise, three–toed sloth, and garden snail, which were measured over various small distances.

Animal	Speed mph	Animal	Speed mph	Animal	Speed mph
Cheetah	70	Mongolian wild ass	40	Man	27.89
Pronghorn antelope	61	Greyhound	39.35	Elephant	25
Wildebeest	50	Whippet	35.5	Black mamba snake	20
Lion	50	Rabbit (domestic)	35	Six–lined race runner	18
Thomson's gazelle	50	Mule deer	35	Squirrel	12
Quarter horse	47.5	Jackal	35	Pig (domestic)	11
Elk	45	Reindeer	32	Chicken	9
Cape hunting dog	45	Giraffe	32	Spider (Tegenearia atrica)	1.17
Coyote	43	White–tailed deer	30	Giant Tortoise	0.17
Gray fox	42	Wart hog	30	Three–toed sloth	0.15
Hyena	40	Grizzly bear	30	Garden snail	0.03
Zebra	40	Cat (domestic)	30		

Source: Natural History Magazine, March 1974, copyright 1974. The American Museum of Natural History; and James G. Doherty, General Curator, The Wildlife Conservation Society.

Gestation, Incubation, and Longevity of Certain Animals

Animal	Gestation or incubation, in days & (average)	Longevity, in years (& record exceptions)	Animal	Gestation or incubation, in days & (average)	Longeveity, in years (& record exceptions)
Ass	365	18–20 (63)	Horse	329–345 (336)	20–25 (50+)
Bear	180–240[1]	15–30 (47)	Kangaroo	32–39[1]	4–6 (23)
Cat	52–69 (63)	10–12 (26+)	Lion	105–113 (108)	10 (29)
Chicken	22	7–8 (14)	Man	253–303	(2)
Cow	c. 280	9–12 (39)	Monkey	139–270[1]	12–15[1](29)
Deer	197–300[1]	10–15 (26)	Mouse	19–31[1]	1–3 (4)
Dog	53–71 (63)	10–12 (24)	Parakeet (Budgerigar)	17–20 (18)	8 (12+)
Duck	21–35[1](28)	10 (15)	Pig	101–130 (115)	10 (22)
Elephant	510–730 (624)[1]	30–40 (71)	Pigeon	11–19	10–12 (39)
Fox	51–63[1]	8–10 (14)	Rabbit	30–35 (31)	6–8 (15)
Goat	136–160 (151)	12 (17)	Rat	21	3 (5)
Groundhog	31–32	4–9	Sheep	144–152 (151)[1]	12 (16)
Guinea pig	58–75 (68)	3 (6)	Squirrel	44	8–9 (15)
Hamster, golden	15–17	2 (8)	Whale	365–547[1]	—
Hippopotamus	220–255 (240)	30 (49+)	Wolf	60–63	10–12 (16)

1. Depending on kind. 2. For life expectancy charts, *see* Index. *Source:* James G. Doherty, General Curator, The Wildlife Conservation Society.

Animal Group Terminology

Source: James G. Doherty, General Curator, The Wildlife Conservation Society and *Information Please* data.

ants: colony
bears: sleuth, sloth
bees: grist, hive, swarm
birds: flight, volery
cattle: drove
cats: clutter, clowder
chicks: brood, clutch
clams: bed
cranes: sedge, seige
crows: murder
doves: dule
ducks: brace, team
elephants: herd
elks: gang
finches: charm
fish: school, shoal, draught
foxes: leash, skulk
geese: flock, gaggle, skein
gnats: cloud, horde
goats: trip

gorillas: band
hares: down, husk
hawks: cast
hens: brood
hogs: drift
horses: pair, team
hounds: cry, mute, pack
kangaroos: troop
kittens: kindle, litter
larks: exaltation
lions: pride
locusts: plague
magpies: tidings
mules: span
nightingales: watch
oxen: yoke
oysters: bed
parrots: company
partridges: covey

peacocks: muster, ostentation
pheasants: nest, bouquet
pigs: litter
ponies: string
quail: bevy, covey
rabbits: nest
seals: pod
sheep: drove, flock
sparrows: host
storks: mustering
swans: bevy, wedge
swine: sounder
toads: knot
turkeys: rafter
turtles: bale
vipers: nest
whales: gam, pod
wolves: pack, route
woodcocks: fall

Animal Names: Male, Female, and Young

Animal	Male	Female	Young	Animal	Male	Female	Young	Animal	Male	Female	Young
Ass	Jack	Jenny	Foal	Duck	Drake	Duck	Duckling	Sheep	Ram	Ewe	Lamb
Bear	Boar	Sow	Cub	Elephant	Bull	Cow	Calf	Swan	Cob	Pen	Cygnet
Cat	Tom	Queen	Kitten	Fox	Dog	Vixen	Cub	Swine	Boar	Sow	Piglet
Cattle	Bull	Cow	Calf	Goose	Gander	Goose	Gosling	Tiger	Tiger	Tigress	Cub
Chicken	Rooster	Hen	Chick	Horse	Stallion	Mare	Foal	Whale	Bull	Cow	Calf
Deer	Buck	Doe	Fawn	Lion	Lion	Lioness	Cub	Wolf	Dog	Bitch	Pup
Dog	Dog	Bitch	Pup	Rabbit	Buck	Doe	Bunny				

Source: James G. Doherty, General Curator, The Wildlife Conservation Society.

The National Park System

Source: Department of the Interior, National Park Service.

The National Park System of the United States is administered by the National Park Service, a bureau of the Department of the Interior. Started with the establishment of Yellowstone National Park in 1872, the system includes not only the most extraordinary and spectacular scenic exhibits in the United States but also a large number of sites distinguished either for their historic or prehistoric importance or scientific interest, or for their superior recreational assets. The number and extent of the various types of areas that make up the system follow.

Type of area	Number	Total acreage[1]	Type of area	Number	Total acreage[1]
International Historic Site	1	35.39	National Parkways	4	170,546.79
National Battlefields	11	13,142.62	National Preserves	14	22,332,829.67
National Battlefield Parks	3	8,727.65	National Recreation Areas	18	3,699,550.55
National Battlefield Site	1	1.00	National Reserves	2	22,407.19
National Historic Sites	72	19,820.70	National Rivers	6	362,152.27
National Historical Parks	36	159,626.83	National Scenic Trails	3	176,351.97
National Lakeshores	4	228,745.27	National Seashores	10	592,531.64
National Memorials	26	7,951.16	National Wild and Scenic Rivers	9	212,682.12
National Military Parks	9	37,881.56	Parks (other)	11	46,809.00
National Monuments	76	4,787,743.69	**Total**	**367**	**80,663,217.42**
National Parks	51	47,783,680.35			

1. Acreages as of May 31, 1992.

National Parks

Name, location, and year authorized	Acreage	Outstanding characteristics
Acadia (Maine), 1919	41,951.06	Rugged seashore on Mt. Desert Island and adjacent mainland
Arches (Utah), 1971	73,373.98	Unusual stone arches, windows, pedestals caused by erosion
Badlands (S.D.), 1978	242,755.94	Arid land of fossils, prairie, bison, deer, bighorn, antelope
Big Bend (Tex.), 1935	801,163.02	Mountains and desert bordering the Rio Grande
Biscayne (Fla.), 1980	172,924.73	Aquatic, coral reef park south of Miami was a national monument, 1968–80
Bryce Canyon (Utah), 1924	35,835.08	Area of grotesque eroded rocks brilliantly colored
Canyonlands (Utah), 1964	337,570.43	Colorful wilderness with impressive red-rock canyons, spires, arches
Capitol Reef (Utah), 1971	241,904.26	Highly colored sedimentary rock formations in high, narrow gorges
Carlsbad Caverns (N.M.), 1930	46,766.45	The world's largest known caves
Channel Islands (Calif.) 1980	249,353.77	Area is rich in marine mammals, sea birds, endangered species and archeology
Crater Lake (Ore.), 1902	183,223.77	Deep blue lake in heart of inactive volcano
Denali (Alaska), 1917	4,741,910.00	Mt. McKinley National Park was renamed and enlarged by Act of Dec. 2, 1980. Contains Mt. McKinley, N. America's highest mountain (20,320 ft)
Dry Tortugas (Fla.), 1992	64,700.00	Formerly Ft. Jefferson National Monument. Located 70 miles off Key West. Features an underwater nature trail.
Everglades (Fla.), 1934	1,506,499.40	Subtropical area with abundant bird and animal life
Gates of the Arctic (Alaska), 1980	7,523,888.00	Diverse north central wilderness contains part of Brooks Range
Glacier Bay (Alaska), 1980	3,225,284.00	Park was a national monument (1925–1980) popular for wildlife, whale-watching, glacier-calving, and scenery
Glacier (Mont.), 1910	1,013,572.42	Rocky Mountain scenery with many glaciers and lakes
Grand Canyon (Ariz.), 1919	1,217,159.32	Mile-deep gorge, 4 to 18 miles wide, 217 miles long
Grand Teton (Wyo.), 1929	309,974.28	Picturesque range of high mountain peaks
Great Basin (Nev.), 1986	77,180.00	Exceptional scenic, biologic, and geologic attractions
Great Smoky Mts. (N.C.-Tenn), 1926	520,269.44	Highest mountain range east of Black Hills; luxuriant plant life
Guadalupe Mountains (Tex.), 1966	86,415.97	Contains highest point in Texas: Guadalupe Peak (8,751 ft)
Haleakala (Hawaii), 1960	28,099.00	World-famous 10,023-ft. Haleakala volcano (dormant)
Hawaii Volcanoes (Hawaii), 1916	229,177.03	Spectacular volcanic area; luxuriant vegetation at lower levels
Hot Springs (Ark.), 1921	5,839.24	47 mineral hot springs said to have therapeutic value
Isle Royale (Mich.), 1931	571,790.11	Largest wilderness island in Lake Superior; moose, wolves, lakes
Katmai (Alaska), 1980	3,586,000.00	Expansion may assure brown bear's preservation. Park was national monument 1918–80; is known for fishing, 1912 eruption, bears

Name, location, and year authorized	Acreage	Outstanding characteristics
Kenai Fjords (Alaska), 1980	689,541.00	Mountain goats, marine mammals, birdlife are features at this seacoast park near Seward
Kings Canyon (Calif.), 1940	461,901.20	Huge canyons; high mountains; giant sequoias
Kobuk Valley (Alaska), 1980	1,750,736.86	Native culture and anthropology center around the broad Kobuk River in northwest Alaska
Lake Clark (Alaska), 1980	2,636,839.00	Park provides scenic and wilderness recreation across Cook Inlet from Anchorage
Lassen Volcanic (Calif.), 1916	106,372.36	Exhibits of impressive volcanic phenomena
Mammoth Cave (Ky.), 1926	52,823.97	Vast limestone labyrinth with underground river
Mesa Verde (Colo.), 1906	52,121.93	Best-preserved prehistoric cliff dwellings in United States
Mount Rainier (Wash.), 1899	235,612.50	Single-peak glacial system; dense forests, flowered meadows
National Park of American Samoa	9,000.00	Samoa National Park, American Samoa: two rain forest preserves and a coral reef on the island of Ofu are home to unique tropical animals. The park also includes several thousand acres on the islands of Tutuila and Ta'u.
North Cascades (Wash.), 1968	504,780.94	Roadless Alpine landscape; jagged peaks; mountain lakes; glaciers
Olympic (Wash.), 1938	922,651.01	Finest Pacific Northwest rain forest; scenic mountain park
Petrified Forest (Ariz.), 1962	93,532.57	Extensive natural exhibit of petrified wood
Redwood (Calif.), 1968	110,232.40	Coastal redwood forests; contains world's tallest known tree (369.2 ft)
Rocky Mountain (Colo.), 1915	265,727.15	Section of the Rocky Mountains; 107 named peaks over 10,000 ft
Sequoia (Calif.), 1890	402,482.38	Giant sequoias; magnificent High Sierra scenery, including Mt. Whitney
Shenandoah (Va.), 1926	196,466.19	Tree-covered mountains; scenic Skyline Drive
Theodore Roosevelt (N.D.), 1978	70,446.59	Scenic valley of Little Missouri River; T.R. Ranch; Wildlife
Virgin Islands (U.S. V.I.), 1956	14,688.87	Beaches; lush hills; prehistoric Carib Indian relics
Voyageurs (Minn.), 1971	218,035.33	Wildlife, canoeing, fishing, and hiking
Wind Cave (S.D.), 1903	28,295.03	Limestone caverns in Black Hills; buffalo herd
Wrangell-St. Elias (Alaska), 1980	7,730,645.18	Largest Park System area has abundant wildlife, second highest peak in U.S. (Mt. St. Elias); adjoins Canadian park
Yellowstone (Wyo.-Mont.-Idaho), 1872	2,219,790.71	World's greatest geyser area; abundant falls, wildlife, and canyons
Yosemite (Calif.), 1890	761,236.20	Mountains; inspiring gorges and waterfalls; giant sequoias
Zion (Utah), 1919	146,597.64	Multicolored gorge in heart of southern Utah desert

NATIONAL HISTORICAL PARKS

Name and location	Total acreage
Appomattox Court House (Va.)	1,325.08
Boston (Mass.)	41.03
Chaco Culture (N.M.)	33,974.29
Chesapeake and Ohio Canal (Md.-W.Va.-D.C.).	19,236.60
Colonial (Va.)	9,327.37
Cumberland Gap (Ky.-Tenn.-Va.)	20,445.81
Dayton Aviation Heritage, (Oh.)	.00
George Rogers Clark (Ind.)	26.17
Harpers Ferry (W.Va.-Md.)	2,287.48
Hopewell Culture (Oh.)	1,032.20
Independence (Pa.)	44.85
Jean Lafitte (La.)	20,020.00
Kalaupapa (Hawaii)	10,778.88
Kaloko-Honokohau (Hawaii)	1,160.91
Keewenaw (Mich.)	.00
Klondike Goldrush (Alaska, Wash.)	13,191.35
Lowell (Mass.)	136.86
Lyndon B. Johnson (Tex.)	1,571.93
Marsh–Billings	643.10
Minute Man (Mass.)	789.53
Morristown (N.J.)	1,683.61
Natchez (Miss.)	108.29
Nez Perce (Idaho)	2,109.61
Pecos (N.M.)	6,570.54
Púuchonua o Honaunau (Hawaii)	181.80
Salt River Bay (U.S. V.I.)	912.00
San Antonio Missions (Tex.)	820.01

Name and location	Total acreage
San Franisco Maritime (Calif.)	50.00
San Juan Island (Wash.)	1,751.99
Saratoga (N.Y.)	3,392.82
Sitka (Alaska)	106.83
Tumacacori (Ariz.)	46.52
Valley Forge (Pa.)	3,468.06
War in the Pacific (Guam)	1,960.07
Women's Rights (N.Y.)	5.73
Yorktown National Cemetery	2.91
Zuni-Cibola (N.M.)	800.00

NATIONAL MONUMENTS

Agate Fossil Beds (Neb.)	3,055.22
Alibates Flint Quarries (Tex.)	1,370.97
Aniakchak (Alaska)	137,176.00
Aztec Ruins (N.M.)	319.47
Bandelier (N.M.)	32,737.20
Black Canyon (Colo.)	20,766.14
Booker T. Washington (Va.)	223.92
Buck Island Reef (U.S. V.I.)	880.00
Cabrillo (Calif.)	137.06
Canyon de Chelly (Ariz.)	83,840.00
Cape Krusenstern (Alaska)	659,807.00
Capulin Volcano (N.M.)	792.84
Casa Grande (Ariz.)	472.50
Castillo de San Marcos (Fla.)	20.51
Castle Clinton (N.Y.)	1.00
Cedar Breaks (Utah)	6,154.60
Chiricahua (Ariz.)	11,984.80

Name and location	Total acreage
Colorado (Colo.)	20,453.93
Congaree Swamp (S.C.)	22,200.00
Craters of the Moon (Idaho)	53,545.05
Custer Battlefield (Mont.)	765.34
Death Valley (Calif.-Nev.)	2,067,627.68
Devils Postpile (Calif.)	798.46
Devils Tower (Wyo.)	1,346.91
Dinosaur (Utah-Colo.)	210,844.02
Effigy Mounds (Iowa)	1,481.39
El Malpais (N.M.)	114,272.09
El Morro (N.M.)	1,278.72
Florissant Fossil Beds (Colo.)	5,998.09
Fort Frederica (Ga.)	216.35
Fort Jefferson (Fla.)	64,700.00
Fort Matanzas (Fla.)	227.76
Fort McHenry (Md.)	43.26
Fort Pulaski (Ga.)	5,623.10
Fort Stanwix (N.Y.)	15.52
Fort Sumter (S.C.)	194.60
Fort Union (N.M.)	720.60
Fossil Butte (Wyo.)	8,198.00
George Washington Birthplace (Va.)	550.23
George Washington Carver (Mo.)	210.00
Gila Cliff Dwellings (N.M.)	533.13
Grand Portage (Minn.)	709.97
Great Sand Dunes (Colo.)	38,662.18
Hagerman Fossil Beds (Idaho)	4,280.00
Hohokam Pima (Ariz.)	1,690.00
Homestead (Neb.)	195.11
Hovenweep (Utah-Colo.)	784.93
Jewel Cave (S.D.)	1,273.51
John Day Fossil Beds (Ore.)	14,014.10
Joshua Tree (Calif.)	559,954.50
Lava Beds (Calif.)	46,559.87
Little Big Horn Battlefield (N.M.)	765.34
Montezuma Castle (Ariz.)	857.69
Mound City Group (Ohio)	270.20
Muir Woods (Calif.)	553.55
Natural Bridges (Utah)	7,636.49
Navajo (Ariz.)	360.00
Ocmulgee (Ga.)	701.54
Oregon Caves (Ore.)	487.98
Organ Pipe Cactus (Ariz.)	330,688.86
Petroglyph (N.M.)	5,195.34
Pinnacles (Calif.)	16,265.44
Pipe Spring (Ariz.)	40.00
Pipestone (Minn.)	281.78
Poverty Point	910.85
Rainbow Bridge (Utah)	160.00
Russell Cave (Ala.)	310.45
Saguaro (Ariz.)	87,687.18
Salinas (N.M.)	1,100.64
Scotts Bluff (Neb.)	3,003.03
Statue of Liberty (N.Y.-N.J.)	58.38
Sunset Crater (Ariz.)	3,040.00
Timpanogos Cave (Utah)	250.00
Tonto (Ariz.)	1,120.00
Tuzigoot (Ariz.)	800.62
Walnut Canyon (Ariz.)	2,249.46
White Sands (N.M.)	143,732.92
Wupatki (Ariz.)	35,253.24
Yucca House (Colo.)	9.60

NATIONAL PRESERVES

Aniakchak (Alaska)	465,603.00
Bering Land Bridge (Alaska)	2,784,960.00
Big Cypress (Fla.)	716,000.00
Big Thicket (Tex.)	85,797.20
Denali (Alaska)	1,334,618.00
Ebey's Landing	17,400.00
Gates of the Arctic (Alaska)	948,629.00

Name and location	Total acreage
Glacier Bay (Alaska)	57,884.00
Katmai (Alaska)	374,000.00
Lake Clark (Alaska)	1,407,293.00
Little River Canyon	.00
Noatak (Alaska)	6,574,481.00
Timucuan Ecological and Historic Preserve (Fla.)	46,000.00
Wrangell-St. Elias (Alaska)	4,733,061.09
Yukon-Charley (Alaska)	2,523,509.00

NATIONAL RESERVE

City of Rocks (Idaho)	14.407.19

NATIONAL MILITARY PARKS

Chickamauga and Chattanooga (Ga.-Tenn.)	8,106.04
Fredericksburg and Spotsylvania (Va.)	7,780.73
Fredericksburg National Cemetery	12.00
Gettysburg Nat. Mil. Park (Pa.)	5,875.27
Gettysburg Nat. Cemetery (Pa.)	20.58
Guilford Courthouse (N.C.)	220.25
Horseshoe Bend (Ala.)	2,040.00
Kings Mountain (S.C.)	3,945.29
Pea Ridge (Ark.)	4,300.35
Shiloh Nat. Cemetery (Tenn.)	10.05
Shiloh Nat. Mil. Park (Tenn.)	3,962.82
Vicksburg Nat. Cemetery (Miss.)	116.28
Vicksburg Nat. Mil. Park (Miss.)	1,625.27

NATIONAL BATTLEFIELDS

Antietam (Md.)	3,244.37
Big Hole (Mont.)	655.61
Cowpens (S.C.)	841.56
Fort Donelson (Tenn.)	536.35
Fort Necessity (Pa.)	902.80
Monocacy (Md.)	1,647.01
Moores Creek (N.C.)	86.52
Petersburg (Va.)	2,735.38
Stones River (Tenn.)	719.81
Tupelo (Miss.)	1.00
Wilson's Creek (Mo.)	1,749.00

NATIONAL BATTLEFIELD PARKS

Kennesaw Mountain (Ga.)	2,884.52
Manassas (Va.)	5,071.62
Richmond (Va.)	771.51

NATIONAL BATTLEFIELD SITE

Brices Cross Roads (Miss.)	1.00

NATIONAL HISTORIC SITES

Abraham Lincoln Birthplace (Ky.)	116.50
Adams (Mass.)	9.82
Allegheny Portage Railroad (Pa.)	1,246.97
Andersonville (Ga.)	494.61
Andrew Johnson (Tenn.)	16.68
Bent's Old Fort (Colo.)	799.80
Boston African American (Mass.)	0.00
Carl Sandburg Home (N.C.)	263.52
Charles Pinckney (S.C.)	28.45
Christiansted (V.I.)	27.15
Clara Barton (Md.)	8.59
Edgar Allan Poe (Pa.)	0.52
Edison (N.J.)	21.25
Eisenhower (Pa.)	690.46
Eleanor Roosevelt (N.Y.)	180.50
Eugene O'Neill (Calif.)	13.19
Ford's Theatre (Lincoln Museum) (D.C.)	0.29
Fort Bowie (Ariz.)	1,000.00
Fort Davis (Tex.)	40.00
Fort Laramie (Wyo.)	832.85
Fort Larned (Kan.)	718.39

Name and location	Total acreage
Fort Point (Calif.)	29.00
Fort Raleigh (N.C.)	512.93
Fort Scott (Kan.)	16.69
Fort Smith (Ark.-Okla.)	75.00
Fort Union Trading Post (N.D.-Mont.)	442.45
Fort Vancouver (Wash.)	208.89
Frederick Douglass Home (D.C.)	8.53
Frederick Law Olmsted (Mass.)	1.75
Friendship Hill (Pa.)	674.56
Golden Spike (Utah)	2,735.28
Grant-Kohrs Ranch (Mont.)	1,498.38
Hampton (Md.)	62.04
Harry S Truman (Mo.)	1.41
Herbert Hoover (Iowa)	186.80
Home of F. D. Roosevelt (N.Y.)	290.34
Hopewell Furnace (Pa.)	848.06
Hubbell Trading Post (Ariz.)	160.09
James A. Garfield (Ohio)	7.82
Jimmy Carter (Ga.)	70.54
John F. Kennedy (Mass.)	0.09
John Muir (Calif.)	340.04
Knife River Indian Villages (N.D.)	1,758.35
Lincoln Home (Ill.)	12.24
Longfellow (Mass.)	1.98
M. McLeod Bethune Council House (N.H.)	.07
Maggie L. Walker (Va.)	1.29
Manzanar National Historic Site (Calif.)	500.00
Martin Luther King, Jr. (Ga.)	23.18
Martin Van Buren (N.Y.)	39.58
Mary McLeod Bethune Council House National Historic Site (D.C.)	—
Ninety Six (S.C.)	989.14
Palo Alto Battlefield (Tex.)	3,357.42
Pennsylvania Avenue (D.C.)	0.00
Puukohola Heiau (Hawaii)	80.47
Sagamore Hill (N.Y.)	83.02
Saint-Gaudens (N.H.)	148.23
Saint Paul's Church (N.Y.)	6.13
Salem Maritime (Mass.)	9.02
San Juan (P.R.)	75.13
Saugus Iron Works (Mass.)	8.51
Springfield Armory (Mass.)	54.93
Steamtown (Pa.)	62.48
Theodore Roosevelt Birthplace (N.Y.)	0.11
Theodore Roosevelt Inaugural (N.Y.)	1.03
Thomas Stone (Md.)	328.25
Tuskegee Institute (Ala.)	57.62
Ulysses S. Grant (Mo.)	9.60
Vanderbilt Mansion (N.Y.)	211.65
Weir Farm (Conn.)	58.77
Whitman Mission (Wash.)	98.15
William Howard Taft (Ohio)	3.07

NATIONAL MEMORIALS

Name and location	Total acreage
Arkansas Post (Ark.)	389.18
Arlington House, the Robert E. Lee Memorial (Va.)	27.91
Chamizal (Tex.)	54.90
Coronado (Ariz.)	4,750.22
De Sota (Fla.)	26.84
Federal Hall (N.Y.)	0.45
Fort Caroline (Fla.)	138.39
Fort Clatsop (Ore.)	125.20
General Grant (N.Y.)	0.76
Hamilton Grange (N.Y.)	0.11
Jefferson National Expansion Memorial (Mo.)	90.96
John F. Kennedy Center for Performing Arts (D.C.)	17.50
Johnstown Flood (Pa.)	164.12
Lincoln Boyhood (Ind.)	199.65
Lincoln Memorial (D.C.)	109.63

Name and location	Total acreage
Lyndon Baines Johnson Memorial Grove on the Potomac (D.C.)	17.00
Mount Rushmore (S.D.)	1,278.45
Perry's Victory and International Peace Memorial (Ohio)	25.38
Roger Williams (R.I.)	4.56
Thaddeus Kosciuszko (Pa.)	0.02
Theodore Roosevelt Island (D.C.)	88.50
Thomas Jefferson Memorial (D.C.)	18.36
USS Arizona Memorial (Hawaii)	0.00
Vietnam Veterans Memorial (D.C.)	2.00
Washington Monument (D.C.)	106.01
Wright Brothers (N.C.)	431.40

NATIONAL CEMETERIES[1]

	Total acreage
Antietam (Md.)	11.36
Battleground (D.C.)	1.03
Fort Donelson (Tenn.)	15.30
Poplar Grove (Va.)	8.72
Stones River (Tenn.)	719.81
Yorktown (Va.)	

1. The National Cemeteries are not independent areas of the National Park System; each is part of a military park, battlefield, etc., except Battleground. Their acreage is kept separately. Arlington National Cemetery is under the Department of the Army. *See* Index.

NATIONAL SEASHORES

Assateague Island (Md.-Va.)	39,636.75
Canaveral (Fla.)	57,661.69
Cape Cod (Mass.)	43,569.21
Cape Hatteras (N.C.)	30,319.43
Cape Lookout (N.C.)	28,243.36
Cumberland Island (Ga.)	36,415.09
Fire Island (N.Y.)	19,578.55
Gulf Islands (Fla.-Miss.)	135,624.51
Padre Island (Tex.)	130,434.27
Point Reyes (Calif.)	71,048.78

NATIONAL PARKWAYS

Blue Ridge (Va.-N.C.)	87,782.01
George Washington Memorial (Va.-Md.)	7,247.63
John D. Rockefeller, Jr., Memorial (Wyo.)	23,777.22
Natchez Trace (Miss.-Tenn.-Ala.)	51,739.93

NATIONAL LAKESHORES

Apostle Islands (Wis.)	69,371.89
Indiana Dunes (Ind.)	14,981.31
Pictured Rocks (Mich)	73,174.12
Sleeping Bear Dunes (Mich.)	71,189.15

NATIONAL WILD AND SCENIC RIVERS

Alagnak Wild River (Alaska)	24,038.00
Bluestone National Scenic River (W. Va.)	4,268.00
Delaware (N.Y.-N.J.-Pa.)	1,973.33
St. Croix (Minn.-Wis.)	92,735.85
Missouri National Recreational River (Neb., S.D.)	0.00
Obed Wild & Scenic River (Tenn.)	5,066.94
Rio Grande Wild & Scenic (Tex.)	9,600.00
Upper Delaware (N.Y., N.J.-Pa.)	75,000.00

NATIONAL RIVERS

Big South Fork National River & Recreation Area (Ky.-Tenn.)	125,000.00
Buffalo (Ark.)	94,218.55
Great Egg Harbor River (N.J.)	.00
Mississippi National River & Recreation Area (Minn.)	53,775.00
New River Gorge (W.Va.)	62,143.69
Niobrara/Missouri National Scenic Riverways (Neb.–S.D.)	.00

Name and location	Total acreage
Ozark (Mo.)	80,790.04

OTHER PARKS

Catoctin Mountain (Md.)	5,770.22
Constitution Gardens, (D.C.)	52.00
Fort Washington Park (Md.)	341.00
Greenbelt Park (Md.)	1,175.99
Piscataway (Md.)	4,262.52
Prince William Forest (Va.)	18,571.55
Rock Creek Park (D.C.)	1,754.37
Wolf Trap Farm Park for the Performing Arts (Va.)	130.28

NATIONAL RECREATION AREAS

Amistad (Tex.)	58,500.00
Bighorn Canyon (Wyo.-Mont.)	120,296.22
Chattahoochee River (Ga.)	9,259.91
Chickasaw (Okla.)	9,930.95
Coulee Dam (Wash.)	100,390.31
Curecanti (Colo.)	42,114.47
Cuyahoga Valley (Ohio)	32,524.76
Delaware Water Gap (Pa.-N.J.)	67,204.92
Gateway (N.Y.-N.J.)	26,310.93
Gauley River (W. Va.)	10,300.00
Glen Canyon (Ariz.-Utah)	1,236,880.00
Golden Gate (Calif.)	73,179.90
Lake Chelan (Wash.)	61,886.98
Lake Mead (Ariz.-Nev.)	1,495,665.52
Lake Meredith (Tex.)	44,977.63
Ross Lake (Wash.)	117,574.59
Santa Monica Mountains (Calif.)	150,050.00
Whiskeytown-Shasta-Trinity (Calif.)	42,503.46

NATIONAL SCENIC TRAIL

Appalachian (Maine, N.H., Vt., Mass., Conn., N.Y., N.J., Pa., Md., W.Va., Va., N.C., Tenn., Ga.)	165,504.63
Natchez Trace (Ga.-Ala.-Tenn.)	10,995.00
Potomac Heritage (D.C.-Md.-Va.-Pa.)	0.00

NATIONAL MALL

National Mall (D.C.)	146.35

INTERNATIONAL HISTORIC SITE

Saint Croix Island (Maine)	35.39

AFFILIATED AREAS

(National Historic Sites unless otherwise noted.)

American Memorial Park (N. Mariana Is.)	0.00
Benjamin Franklin (Pa.)[1]	0.00
Blackstone River Valley National Heritage Corridor (Mass., R.I.)	0.00
Chicago Portage (Ill.)	91.20
Chimney Rock (Neb.)	83.36
David Berger (Ohio)[1]	0.00
Delaware and Lehigh Navigation Canal National Heritage Corridor (Pa.)	0.00
Ebey's Landing (Wash.)	8,000.00
Father Marquette (Mich.)[1]	52.00
Gloria Dei Church (Pa.)	3.71
Green Springs Historic District (Va.)	5,490.59
Historic Camden (S.C.)	0.00
Ice Age Scenic Trail (Wis.)	0.00
Ice Age (Wis.)[2]	32,500.00
Iditarod National Historic Trail (Alaska)	0.00
Illinois and Michigan Canal National Heritage Corridor	0.00
International Peace Garden (N.D.)	2,330.30
Jamestown (Va.)	20.63
Lewis & Clark Natl. Historic Trail (Ill., Mo., Kan., Neb., Iowa, Idaho, S.D., N.D., Mont., Ore., Wash.)	39.11
M. McLeod Bethune Council House (D.C.)	0.00
McLaughlin House (Ore.)	0.63
Mormon Pioneer Natl. Historic Trail (Ill., Iowa, Neb., Wyo., Utah)	0.00
North Country Nat'l Scenic Trail (N.Y., Pa., Ohio, Mich., Wis., Minn., N.D.)	0.00
Oregon Natl. Historic Trail (Mo., Kan., Neb., Wyo., Idaho, Ore., Wash.)	0.00
Overmountain Victory Trail (Mo. to Ore.)	0.00
Pinelands Natl. Reserve (N.J.)	0.00
Red Hill Patrick Henry (Va.)[1]	0.00
Roosevelt-Campobello International Park (Canada)	2,721.50
Santa Fe National Historic Trail (Mo. to N.M.)	0.00
Sewell-Belmont House National Historic Site (D.C.)	0.35
Touro Synagogue (R.I.)	0.23
Trail of Tears National Historic Trail (N.C. to Okla.)	0.00

1. National Memorial. 2. National Scientific Reserve.

Water Supply of the World[1]

The Antarctic Icecap is the largest supply of fresh water, nearly 2 percent of the world's total of fresh and salt water. As can be seen from the table below, the amount of water in our atmosphere is over ten times as large as the water in all the rivers taken together. The fresh water actually available for human use in lakes and rivers and the accessible ground water amounts to only about one third of one percent of the world's total water supply.

	Surface area (square miles)	Volume (cubic miles)	Percentage of total
Salt Water			
The oceans	139,500,000	317,000,000	97.2
Inland seas and saline lakes	270,000	25,000	0.008
Fresh Water			
Freshwater lakes	330,000	30,000	0.009
All rivers (average level)	—	300	0.0001
Antarctic Icecap	6,000,000	6,300,000	1.9
Arctic Icecap and glaciers	900,000	680,000	0.21
Water in the atmosphere	197,000,000	3,100	0.001
Ground water within half a mile from surface	—	1,000,000	0.31
Deep-lying ground water	—	1,000,000	0.31
Total (rounded)	—	**326,000,000**	**100.00**

1. All figures are estimated. *Source:* Department of the Interior, Geological Survey.

Environmental Tips

Source: U.S. Office of Consumer Affairs, *Consumer's Resource Handbook.*

How to dispose of everyday trash or garbage (often called solid waste) is an issue of interest to many consumers, businesses, environmentalists and government officials. Here are some tips designed to help you understand the garbage, or solid waste, disposal issue. These tips also might help you evaluate the environmental claims some companies are making about their products and packages.

1. The Environmental Protection Agency (EPA) has outlined a three-part solid waste management plan. It includes source reduction or reducing the amount of waste created in the first place, recycling and composting, waste-to-energy incineration and landfilling.

2. The EPA also has issued its suggestions on how individual consumers can help solve the solid waste problem. They are **reduce** the amount of waste that you throw away, **reuse** products whenever possible, and **recycle** as many products and packages as you possibly can.

3. If you wish to use environmental claims to compare products, specific claims are usually more meaningful. Two examples of specific claims could be "50% less packaging than an earlier container" or "contains 25–30% recycled content." Claims about a product or package like "environmentally friendly" or "safe for the environment" can be misleading because they are so broad and vague. Environmental issues are very complex. If you have questions about a company's environmental claims, call or write the company.

4. The environmental benefits of a "degradable" product depend on how it is handled after disposal. A degradable product will break down if exposed to air, water, light and/or micro-organisms over time. Therefore, a degradable product might be appropriate for a composting system, if there is a composting system nearby that can safely and effectively compost the discarded product into a usable product. However, if the degradable product will end up in a landfill, and that is where more than 70% of waste ends up now, it might not degrade in any meaningful way because landfills are designed to keep out air, water and light. Additionally, if the product will be incinerated or recycled, the degradability of the product is not important. Check with your local solid waste management office to find out what waste disposal system is used in your community. If there is a composting facility in your area, be sure to ask what kinds of compostable materials it will accept. For example, some composting programs are limited to yard waste, leaves, etc.

5. It is technically possible to recycle many materials, for example, paper, metal, glass and plastic. The key question is whether these materials can be recycled in your community. Does your community ask you to separate one or more types of materials from the rest of your trash for curbside pick-up? Or, is there a drop-off recycling center that accepts that type of material? If a product labeled "recyclable" is not separated from the rest of your trash, it is not likely to be recycled. Check with your local solid waste management office to find out which products and packages are recyclable in your community.

6. Many products are being made from recycled materials. This helps "complete the loop" of recycling by using recycled materials to make new products. If you wish to buy a product made primarily from recycled material, check to see if the percentage of recycled material is listed on the product or package.

For additional information about environmental claims or the garbage disposal programs in your community, contact your state or local consumer protection office. This office will be able to refer you to the local solid waste management authority. ☐

Home Pesticide Survey

Source: U.S. Environmental Protection Agency, *Activities Update.*

EPA's National Home and Garden Pesticide Use Survey—a one-time measure of the non-agricultural use of pesticides in and around U.S. urban and rural homes—resulted in these findings:

About 75 percent of households that have no children under five years old had at least one pesticide stored within reach of children; about 47 percent of households with children under five had at least one pesticide within reach of children. (About 13 percent of children's poisoning incidents occur outside a child's own home.)

An estimated 85 percent of households had at least one pesticide stored in or around the home; about 76 percent of householder-respondents personally treated their homes for insects and related pests. About 15 percent of homes with lawns had pesticides applied by outsiders, usually a commercial lawn care company.

Sixty-seven percent of householders disposed of concentrated pesticides in regular trash, 16 percent in special collections and 17 percent gave them away, poured them down the sink or toilet or on the street, gutter, ground or into a sewer.

Thirty-six percent of users of pesticides from concentrates poured those mixtures down sinks or toilets, 29 percent disposed of them in regular trash and 35 percent burned, gave away, sprayed the mixtures elsewhere or poured them on the ground or into gutters or sewers. ☐

Waste Reducing Recipes

Source: "New York's Waste Reduction Handbook."

Here are substitutes for many household products that contain toxic chemicals. These common solutions, plus some elbow grease, are reliable and effective ways to get the job done while reducing excess packaging and toxic waste.

Clogs: Unclog drains by pouring boiling water with a few tablespoons of baking soda and a large splash of vinegar down drains. This treatment once-a-week prevents clogs too.

Ceramic tile cleaner: Mix one-quarter cup white vinegar with one gallon of water.

Furniture polish: Mix three parts olive oil with one part lemon juice or vinegar and apply with a clean, soft cloth.

Oven cleaner: Sprinkle water, then a layer of baking soda on oven surfaces. Rub gently with very fine steel wool for tough spots.

Toilet cleaner: Sprinkle some baking soda into the bowl, then drizzle with vinegar and scour with a toilet brush. ☐

CALENDAR & HOLIDAYS

1996

JANUARY

S	M	T	W	T	F	S
	1	2	3	4	5	6
7	8	9	10	11	12	13
14	15	16	17	18	19	20
21	22	23	24	25	26	27
28	29	30	31			

1 — New Year's Day
6 — Epiphany
15 — Martin Luther King Jr. Day Observed
21 — 1st Day of Ramadan

FEBRUARY

S	M	T	W	T	F	S
				1	2	3
4	5	6	7	8	9	10
11	12	13	14	15	16	17
18	19	20	21	22	23	24
25	26	27	28	29		

2 — Groundhog Day
12 — Lincoln's Birthday
14 — Valentine's Day
19 — Washington's Birthday Observed
21 — Ash Wednesday

MARCH

S	M	T	W	T	F	S
					1	2
3	4	5	6	7	8	9
10	11	12	13	14	15	16
17	18	19	20	21	22	23
24	25	26	27	28	29	30
31						

5 — Purim
17 — St. Patrick's Day
31 — Palm Sunday

APRIL

S	M	T	W	T	F	S
	1	2	3	4	5	6
7	8	9	10	11	12	13
14	15	16	17	18	19	20
21	22	23	24	25	26	27
28	29	30				

4 — 1st Day of Passover
5 — Good Friday
7 — Easter
7 — Daylight Savings Time begins

MAY

S	M	T	W	T	F	S
			1	2	3	4
5	6	7	8	9	10	11
12	13	14	15	16	17	18
19	20	21	22	23	24	25
26	27	28	29	30	31	

12 — Mother's Day
16 — Ascension Day
24 — 1st Day of Shavuot
26 — Pentecost
27 — Memorial Day Observed

JUNE

S	M	T	W	T	F	S
						1
2	3	4	5	6	7	8
9	10	11	12	13	14	15
16	17	18	19	20	21	22
23	24	25	26	27	28	29
30						

14 — Flag Day
16 — Father's Day

JULY

S	M	T	W	T	F	S
	1	2	3	4	5	6
7	8	9	10	11	12	13
14	15	16	17	18	19	20
21	22	23	24	25	26	27
28	29	30	31			

1 — Canada Day
4 — Independence Day

AUGUST

S	M	T	W	T	F	S
				1	2	3
4	5	6	7	8	9	10
11	12	13	14	15	16	17
18	19	20	21	22	23	24
25	26	27	28	29	30	31

SEPTEMBER

S	M	T	W	T	F	S
1	2	3	4	5	6	7
8	9	10	11	12	13	14
15	16	17	18	19	20	21
22	23	24	25	26	27	28
29	30					

2 — Labor day
14 — 1st Day of Rosh Hashana
23 — Yom Kippur

OCTOBER

S	M	T	W	T	F	S
		1	2	3	4	5
6	7	8	9	10	11	12
13	14	15	16	17	18	19
20	21	22	23	24	25	26
27	28	29	30	31		

14 — Columbus Day Observed
14 — Thanksgiving Day (Canada)
27 — Daylight Savings Time ends
31 — Halloween

NOVEMBER

S	M	T	W	T	F	S
					1	2
3	4	5	6	7	8	9
10	11	12	13	14	15	16
17	18	19	20	21	22	23
24	25	26	27	28	29	30

1 — All Saints Day
5 — Election Day
11 — Veterans Day
28 — Thanksgiving

DECEMBER

S	M	T	W	T	F	S
1	2	3	4	5	6	7
8	9	10	11	12	13	14
15	16	17	18	19	20	21
22	23	24	25	26	27	28
29	30	31				

1 — 1st Sunday of Advent
6 — 1st Day of Hanukkah
25 — Christmas

Seasons for the Northern Hemisphere, 1996

Eastern Standard Time

March 20, 3:03 a.m., sun enters sign of Aries; spring begins
June 20, 9:24 p.m., sun enters sign of Cancer; summer begins

Sept. 22, 1:00 p.m., sun enters sign of Libra; fall begins
Dec. 21, 9:06 a.m., sun enters sign of Capricorn; winter begins

1995

JANUARY
S	M	T	W	T	F	S
1	2	3	4	5	6	7
8	9	10	11	12	13	14
15	16	17	18	19	20	21
22	23	24	25	26	27	28
29	30	31				

FEBRUARY
S	M	T	W	T	F	S
			1	2	3	4
5	6	7	8	9	10	11
12	13	14	15	16	17	18
19	20	21	22	23	24	25
26	27	28				

MARCH
S	M	T	W	T	F	S
			1	2	3	4
5	6	7	8	9	10	11
12	13	14	15	16	17	18
19	20	21	22	23	24	25
26	27	28	29	30	31	

APRIL
S	M	T	W	T	F	S
						1
2	3	4	5	6	7	8
9	10	11	12	13	14	15
16	17	18	19	20	21	22
23	24	25	26	27	28	29
30						

MAY
S	M	T	W	T	F	S
	1	2	3	4	5	6
7	8	9	10	11	12	13
14	15	16	17	18	19	20
21	22	23	24	25	26	27
28	29	30	31			

JUNE
S	M	T	W	T	F	S
				1	2	3
4	5	6	7	8	9	10
11	12	13	14	15	16	17
18	19	20	21	22	23	24
25	26	27	28	29	30	

JULY
S	M	T	W	T	F	S
						1
2	3	4	5	6	7	8
9	10	11	12	13	14	15
16	17	18	19	20	21	22
23	24	25	26	27	28	29
30	31					

AUGUST
S	M	T	W	T	F	S
		1	2	3	4	5
6	7	8	9	10	11	12
13	14	15	16	17	18	19
20	21	22	23	24	25	26
27	28	29	30	31		

SEPTEMBER
S	M	T	W	T	F	S
					1	2
3	4	5	6	7	8	9
10	11	12	13	14	15	16
17	18	19	20	21	22	23
24	25	26	27	28	29	30

OCTOBER
S	M	T	W	T	F	S
1	2	3	4	5	6	7
8	9	10	11	12	13	14
15	16	17	18	19	20	21
22	23	24	25	26	27	28
29	30	31				

NOVEMBER
S	M	T	W	T	F	S
			1	2	3	4
5	6	7	8	9	10	11
12	13	14	15	16	17	18
19	20	21	22	23	24	25
26	27	28	29	30		

DECEMBER
S	M	T	W	T	F	S
					1	2
3	4	5	6	7	8	9
10	11	12	13	14	15	16
17	18	19	20	21	22	23
24	25	26	27	28	29	30
31						

1997

JANUARY
S	M	T	W	T	F	S
			1	2	3	4
5	6	7	8	9	10	11
12	13	14	15	16	17	18
19	20	21	22	23	24	25
26	27	28	29	30	31	

FEBRUARY
S	M	T	W	T	F	S
						1
2	3	4	5	6	7	8
9	10	11	12	13	14	15
16	17	18	19	20	21	22
23	24	25	26	27	28	

MARCH
S	M	T	W	T	F	S
						1
2	3	4	5	6	7	8
9	10	11	12	13	14	15
16	17	18	19	20	21	22
23	24	25	26	27	28	29
30	31					

APRIL
S	M	T	W	T	F	S
		1	2	3	4	5
6	7	8	9	10	11	12
13	14	15	16	17	18	19
20	21	22	23	24	25	26
27	28	29	30			

MAY
S	M	T	W	T	F	S
				1	2	3
4	5	6	7	8	9	10
11	12	13	14	15	16	17
18	19	20	21	22	23	24
25	26	27	28	29	30	31

JUNE
S	M	T	W	T	F	S
1	2	3	4	5	6	7
8	9	10	11	12	13	14
15	16	17	18	19	20	21
22	23	24	25	26	27	28
29	30					

JULY
S	M	T	W	T	F	S
		1	2	3	4	5
6	7	8	9	10	11	12
13	14	15	16	17	18	19
20	21	22	23	24	25	26
27	28	29	30	31		

AUGUST
S	M	T	W	T	F	S
					1	2
3	4	5	6	7	8	9
10	11	12	13	14	15	16
17	18	19	20	21	22	23
24	25	26	27	28	29	30
31						

SEPTEMBER
S	M	T	W	T	F	S
	1	2	3	4	5	6
7	8	9	10	11	12	13
14	15	16	17	18	19	20
21	22	23	24	25	26	27
28	29	30				

OCTOBER
S	M	T	W	T	F	S
			1	2	3	4
5	6	7	8	9	10	11
12	13	14	15	16	17	18
19	20	21	22	23	24	25
26	27	28	29	30	31	

NOVEMBER
S	M	T	W	T	F	S
						1
2	3	4	5	6	7	8
9	10	11	12	13	14	15
16	17	18	19	20	21	22
23	24	25	26	27	28	29
30						

DECEMBER
S	M	T	W	T	F	S
	1	2	3	4	5	6
7	8	9	10	11	12	13
14	15	16	17	18	19	20
21	22	23	24	25	26	27
28	29	30	31			

Hindu Festival Dates, 1996
Source: Jantri 500, by Pal Singh Purewal.

Jan. 14	Makara Sankranti	Aug. 28	Raksha Bandhan
Jan. 24	Vasanta Panchami	Sept. 4	Sri Krishna Jayanti
Feb. 17	Maha Shivaratri	Sept. 16	Sradhas begins
March 5	Holi (last day)	Sept. 27	Ganesh Chaturthi
March 20	Bikarami 2053 Samvat begins	Oct. 13	Asuj Navratras begins
March 20	Chetra Navratras begins	Oct. 21	Dassehra
March 28	Ram Navmi	Oct. 29	Karva Chauth Vrat (Fast)
April 13	Vaisakhi (solar new year)	Nov. 10	Diwali (Festival of Lights)

(For Sikh Festivals see page 589)

PERPETUAL CALENDAR

1800 ... 4	1844 ... 9	1888 ... 8	1932 . 13	1976 . 12	2020 . 11
1801 ... 5	1845 ... 4	1889 ... 3	1933 ... 1	1977 ... 7	2021 ... 6
1802 ... 6	1846 ... 5	1890 ... 4	1934 ... 2	1978 ... 1	2022 ... 7
1803 ... 7	1847 ... 6	1891 ... 5	1935 ... 3	1979 ... 2	2023 ... 1
1804 ... 4	1848 . 14	1892 . 13	1936 . 11	1980 . 10	2024 ... 9
1805 ... 3	1849 ... 2	1893 ... 1	1937 ... 6	1981 ... 5	2025 ... 4
1806 ... 4	1850 ... 3	1894 ... 2	1938 ... 7	1982 ... 6	2026 ... 5
1807 ... 5	1851 ... 4	1895 ... 3	1939 ... 1	1983 ... 7	2027 ... 6
1808 . 13	1852 . 12	1896 . 11	1940 ... 9	1984 ... 8	2028 . 14
1809 ... 1	1853 ... 7	1897 ... 6	1941 ... 4	1985 ... 3	2029 ... 2
1810 ... 2	1854 ... 1	1898 ... 7	1942 ... 5	1986 ... 4	2030 ... 3
1811 ... 3	1855 ... 2	1899 ... 1	1943 ... 6	1987 ... 5	2031 ... 4
1812 . 11	1856 . 10	1900 ... 2	1944 . 14	1988 . 13	2032 . 12
1813 ... 6	1857 ... 5	1901 ... 3	1945 ... 2	1989 ... 1	2033 ... 7
1814 ... 7	1858 ... 6	1902 ... 4	1946 ... 3	1990 ... 2	2034 ... 1
1815 ... 1	1859 ... 7	1903 ... 5	1947 ... 4	1991 ... 3	2035 ... 2
1816 ... 9	1860 ... 8	1904 . 13	1948 . 12	1992 . 11	2036 . 10
1817 ... 4	1861 ... 3	1905 ... 1	1949 ... 7	1993 ... 6	2037 ... 5
1818 ... 5	1862 ... 4	1906 ... 2	1950 ... 1	1994 ... 7	2038 ... 6
1819 ... 6	1863 ... 5	1907 ... 3	1951 ... 2	1995 ... 1	2039 ... 7
1820 . 14	1864 . 13	1908 . 11	1952 . 10	1996 ... 9	2040 ... 8
1821 ... 2	1865 ... 1	1909 ... 6	1953 ... 5	1997 ... 4	2041 ... 3
1822 ... 3	1866 ... 2	1910 ... 7	1954 ... 6	1998 ... 5	2042 ... 4
1823 ... 4	1867 ... 3	1911 ... 1	1955 ... 7	1999 ... 6	2043 ... 5
1824 . 12	1868 . 11	1912 ... 9	1956 ... 8	2000 . 14	2044 . 13
1825 ... 7	1869 ... 6	1913 ... 4	1957 ... 3	2001 ... 2	2045 ... 1
1826 ... 1	1870 ... 7	1914 ... 5	1958 ... 4	2002 ... 3	2046 ... 2
1827 ... 2	1871 ... 1	1915 ... 6	1959 ... 5	2003 ... 4	2047 ... 3
1828 . 10	1872 ... 9	1916 . 14	1960 . 13	2004 . 12	2048 . 11
1829 ... 5	1873 ... 4	1917 ... 2	1961 ... 1	2005 ... 7	2049 ... 6
1830 ... 6	1874 ... 5	1918 ... 3	1962 ... 2	2006 ... 1	2050 ... 7
1831 ... 7	1875 ... 6	1919 ... 4	1963 ... 3	2007 ... 2	2051 ... 1
1832 ... 8	1876 . 14	1920 . 12	1964 . 11	2008 . 10	2052 ... 9
1833 ... 3	1877 ... 2	1921 ... 7	1965 ... 6	2009 ... 5	2053 ... 4
1834 ... 4	1878 ... 3	1922 ... 1	1966 ... 7	2010 ... 6	2054 ... 5
1835 ... 5	1879 ... 4	1923 ... 2	1967 ... 1	2011 ... 7	2055 ... 6
1836 . 13	1880 . 12	1924 . 10	1968 ... 9	2012 ... 8	2056 . 14
1837 ... 1	1881 ... 7	1925 ... 5	1969 ... 4	2013 ... 3	2057 ... 2
1838 ... 2	1882 ... 1	1926 ... 6	1970 ... 5	2014 ... 4	2058 ... 3
1839 ... 3	1883 ... 2	1927 ... 7	1971 ... 6	2015 ... 5	2059 ... 4
1840 . 11	1884 . 10	1928 ... 8	1972 . 14	2016 . 13	2060 . 12
1841 ... 6	1885 ... 5	1929 ... 3	1973 ... 2	2017 ... 1	2061 ... 7
1842 ... 7	1886 ... 6	1930 ... 4	1974 ... 3	2018 ... 2	2062 ... 1
1843 ... 1	1887 ... 7	1931 ... 5	1975 ... 4	2019 ... 3	2063 ... 2

DIRECTIONS: The number given with each year in the key above is number of calendar to use for that year

Calendar 1

```
         JANUARY                FEBRUARY                 MARCH                  APRIL
 S  M  T  W  T  F  S     S  M  T  W  T  F  S     S  M  T  W  T  F  S     S  M  T  W  T  F  S
 1  2  3  4  5  6  7              1  2  3  4              1  2  3  4                       1
 8  9 10 11 12 13 14     5  6  7  8  9 10 11     5  6  7  8  9 10 11     2  3  4  5  6  7  8
15 16 17 18 19 20 21    12 13 14 15 16 17 18    12 13 14 15 16 17 18     9 10 11 12 13 14 15
22 23 24 25 26 27 28    19 20 21 22 23 24 25    19 20 21 22 23 24 25    16 17 18 19 20 21 22
29 30 31                26 27 28                26 27 28 29 30 31       23 24 25 26 27 28 29
                                                                        30

           MAY                     JUNE                   JULY                  AUGUST
 S  M  T  W  T  F  S     S  M  T  W  T  F  S     S  M  T  W  T  F  S     S  M  T  W  T  F  S
    1  2  3  4  5  6                 1  2  3                       1        1  2  3  4  5
 7  8  9 10 11 12 13     4  5  6  7  8  9 10     2  3  4  5  6  7  8     6  7  8  9 10 11 12
14 15 16 17 18 19 20    11 12 13 14 15 16 17     9 10 11 12 13 14 15    13 14 15 16 17 18 19
21 22 23 24 25 26 27    18 19 20 21 22 23 24    16 17 18 19 20 21 22    20 21 22 23 24 25 26
28 29 30 31             25 26 27 28 29 30       23 24 25 26 27 28 29    27 28 29 30 31
                                                30 31

        SEPTEMBER                OCTOBER                NOVEMBER                DECEMBER
 S  M  T  W  T  F  S     S  M  T  W  T  F  S     S  M  T  W  T  F  S     S  M  T  W  T  F  S
                1  2     1  2  3  4  5  6  7              1  2  3  4                    1  2
 3  4  5  6  7  8  9     8  9 10 11 12 13 14     5  6  7  8  9 10 11     3  4  5  6  7  8  9
10 11 12 13 14 15 16    15 16 17 18 19 20 21    12 13 14 15 16 17 18    10 11 12 13 14 15 16
17 18 19 20 21 22 23    22 23 24 25 26 27 28    19 20 21 22 23 24 25    17 18 19 20 21 22 23
24 25 26 27 28 29 30    29 30 31                26 27 28 29 30          24 25 26 27 28 29 30
                                                                        31
```

Calendar 2

```
         JANUARY                FEBRUARY                 MARCH                  APRIL
 S  M  T  W  T  F  S     S  M  T  W  T  F  S     S  M  T  W  T  F  S     S  M  T  W  T  F  S
    1  2  3  4  5  6              1  2  3                 1  2  3        1  2  3  4  5  6  7
 7  8  9 10 11 12 13     4  5  6  7  8  9 10     4  5  6  7  8  9 10     8  9 10 11 12 13 14
14 15 16 17 18 19 20    11 12 13 14 15 16 17    11 12 13 14 15 16 17    15 16 17 18 19 20 21
21 22 23 24 25 26 27    18 19 20 21 22 23 24    18 19 20 21 22 23 24    22 23 24 25 26 27 28
28 29 30 31             25 26 27 28             25 26 27 28 29 30 31    29 30

           MAY                     JUNE                   JULY                  AUGUST
 S  M  T  W  T  F  S     S  M  T  W  T  F  S     S  M  T  W  T  F  S     S  M  T  W  T  F  S
       1  2  3  4  5                    1  2     1  2  3  4  5  6  7              1  2  3  4
 6  7  8  9 10 11 12     3  4  5  6  7  8  9     8  9 10 11 12 13 14     5  6  7  8  9 10 11
13 14 15 16 17 18 19    10 11 12 13 14 15 16    15 16 17 18 19 20 21    12 13 14 15 16 17 18
20 21 22 23 24 25 26    17 18 19 20 21 22 23    22 23 24 25 26 27 28    19 20 21 22 23 24 25
27 28 29 30 31          24 25 26 27 28 29 30    29 30 31                26 27 28 29 30 31

        SEPTEMBER                OCTOBER                NOVEMBER                DECEMBER
 S  M  T  W  T  F  S     S  M  T  W  T  F  S     S  M  T  W  T  F  S     S  M  T  W  T  F  S
                   1        1  2  3  4  5  6                 1  2  3                       1
 2  3  4  5  6  7  8     7  8  9 10 11 12 13     4  5  6  7  8  9 10     2  3  4  5  6  7  8
 9 10 11 12 13 14 15    14 15 16 17 18 19 20    11 12 13 14 15 16 17     9 10 11 12 13 14 15
16 17 18 19 20 21 22    21 22 23 24 25 26 27    18 19 20 21 22 23 24    16 17 18 19 20 21 22
23 24 25 26 27 28 29    28 29 30 31             25 26 27 28 29 30       23 24 25 26 27 28 29
30                                                                      30 31
```

Calendar 3

```
         JANUARY                FEBRUARY                 MARCH                  APRIL
 S  M  T  W  T  F  S     S  M  T  W  T  F  S     S  M  T  W  T  F  S     S  M  T  W  T  F  S
       1  2  3  4  5                    1  2                    1  2        1  2  3  4  5  6
 6  7  8  9 10 11 12     3  4  5  6  7  8  9     3  4  5  6  7  8  9     7  8  9 10 11 12 13
13 14 15 16 17 18 19    10 11 12 13 14 15 16    10 11 12 13 14 15 16    14 15 16 17 18 19 20
20 21 22 23 24 25 26    17 18 19 20 21 22 23    17 18 19 20 21 22 23    21 22 23 24 25 26 27
27 28 29 30 31          24 25 26 27 28          24 25 26 27 28 29 30    28 29 30
                                                31

           MAY                     JUNE                   JULY                  AUGUST
 S  M  T  W  T  F  S     S  M  T  W  T  F  S     S  M  T  W  T  F  S     S  M  T  W  T  F  S
             1  2  3  4                    1        1  2  3  4  5  6              1  2  3
 5  6  7  8  9 10 11     2  3  4  5  6  7  8     7  8  9 10 11 12 13     4  5  6  7  8  9 10
12 13 14 15 16 17 18     9 10 11 12 13 14 15    14 15 16 17 18 19 20    11 12 13 14 15 16 17
19 20 21 22 23 24 25    16 17 18 19 20 21 22    21 22 23 24 25 26 27    18 19 20 21 22 23 24
26 27 28 29 30 31       23 24 25 26 27 28 29    28 29 30 31             25 26 27 28 29 30 31
                        30

        SEPTEMBER                OCTOBER                NOVEMBER                DECEMBER
 S  M  T  W  T  F  S     S  M  T  W  T  F  S     S  M  T  W  T  F  S     S  M  T  W  T  F  S
 1  2  3  4  5  6  7        1  2  3  4  5                    1  2     1  2  3  4  5  6  7
 8  9 10 11 12 13 14     6  7  8  9 10 11 12     3  4  5  6  7  8  9     8  9 10 11 12 13 14
15 16 17 18 19 20 21    13 14 15 16 17 18 19    10 11 12 13 14 15 16    15 16 17 18 19 20 21
22 23 24 25 26 27 28    20 21 22 23 24 25 26    17 18 19 20 21 22 23    22 23 24 25 26 27 28
29 30                   27 28 29 30 31          24 25 26 27 28 29 30    29 30 31
```

Calendar 4

```
         JANUARY                FEBRUARY                 MARCH                  APRIL
 S  M  T  W  T  F  S     S  M  T  W  T  F  S     S  M  T  W  T  F  S     S  M  T  W  T  F  S
          1  2  3  4                       1                       1        1  2  3  4  5
 5  6  7  8  9 10 11     2  3  4  5  6  7  8     2  3  4  5  6  7  8     6  7  8  9 10 11 12
12 13 14 15 16 17 18     9 10 11 12 13 14 15     9 10 11 12 13 14 15    13 14 15 16 17 18 19
19 20 21 22 23 24 25    16 17 18 19 20 21 22    16 17 18 19 20 21 22    20 21 22 23 24 25 26
26 27 28 29 30 31       23 24 25 26 27 28       23 24 25 26 27 28 29    27 28 29 30
                                                30 31

           MAY                     JUNE                   JULY                  AUGUST
 S  M  T  W  T  F  S     S  M  T  W  T  F  S     S  M  T  W  T  F  S     S  M  T  W  T  F  S
             1  2  3     1  2  3  4  5  6  7              1  2  3  4  5                1  2
 4  5  6  7  8  9 10     8  9 10 11 12 13 14     6  7  8  9 10 11 12     3  4  5  6  7  8  9
11 12 13 14 15 16 17    15 16 17 18 19 20 21    13 14 15 16 17 18 19    10 11 12 13 14 15 16
18 19 20 21 22 23 24    22 23 24 25 26 27 28    20 21 22 23 24 25 26    17 18 19 20 21 22 23
25 26 27 28 29 30 31    29 30                   27 28 29 30 31          24 25 26 27 28 29 30
                                                                        31

        SEPTEMBER                OCTOBER                NOVEMBER                DECEMBER
 S  M  T  W  T  F  S     S  M  T  W  T  F  S     S  M  T  W  T  F  S     S  M  T  W  T  F  S
    1  2  3  4  5  6              1  2  3  4                       1        1  2  3  4  5  6
 7  8  9 10 11 12 13     5  6  7  8  9 10 11     2  3  4  5  6  7  8     7  8  9 10 11 12 13
14 15 16 17 18 19 20    12 13 14 15 16 17 18     9 10 11 12 13 14 15    14 15 16 17 18 19 20
21 22 23 24 25 26 27    19 20 21 22 23 24 25    16 17 18 19 20 21 22    21 22 23 24 25 26 27
28 29 30                26 27 28 29 30 31       23 24 25 26 27 28 29    28 29 30 31
                                                30
```

Calendar 5

```
         JANUARY                FEBRUARY                 MARCH                  APRIL
 S  M  T  W  T  F  S     S  M  T  W  T  F  S     S  M  T  W  T  F  S     S  M  T  W  T  F  S
             1  2  3     1  2  3  4  5  6  7     1  2  3  4  5  6  7              1  2  3  4
 4  5  6  7  8  9 10     8  9 10 11 12 13 14     8  9 10 11 12 13 14     5  6  7  8  9 10 11
11 12 13 14 15 16 17    15 16 17 18 19 20 21    15 16 17 18 19 20 21    12 13 14 15 16 17 18
18 19 20 21 22 23 24    22 23 24 25 26 27 28    22 23 24 25 26 27 28    19 20 21 22 23 24 25
25 26 27 28 29 30 31                            29 30 31                26 27 28 29 30

           MAY                     JUNE                   JULY                  AUGUST
 S  M  T  W  T  F  S     S  M  T  W  T  F  S     S  M  T  W  T  F  S     S  M  T  W  T  F  S
                1  2        1  2  3  4  5  6              1  2  3  4                       1
 3  4  5  6  7  8  9     7  8  9 10 11 12 13     5  6  7  8  9 10 11     2  3  4  5  6  7  8
10 11 12 13 14 15 16    14 15 16 17 18 19 20    12 13 14 15 16 17 18     9 10 11 12 13 14 15
17 18 19 20 21 22 23    21 22 23 24 25 26 27    19 20 21 22 23 24 25    16 17 18 19 20 21 22
24 25 26 27 28 29 30    28 29 30                26 27 28 29 30 31       23 24 25 26 27 28 29
31                                                                      30 31

        SEPTEMBER                OCTOBER                NOVEMBER                DECEMBER
 S  M  T  W  T  F  S     S  M  T  W  T  F  S     S  M  T  W  T  F  S     S  M  T  W  T  F  S
       1  2  3  4  5                 1  2  3     1  2  3  4  5  6  7              1  2  3  4  5
 6  7  8  9 10 11 12     4  5  6  7  8  9 10     8  9 10 11 12 13 14     6  7  8  9 10 11 12
13 14 15 16 17 18 19    11 12 13 14 15 16 17    15 16 17 18 19 20 21    13 14 15 16 17 18 19
20 21 22 23 24 25 26    18 19 20 21 22 23 24    22 23 24 25 26 27 28    20 21 22 23 24 25 26
27 28 29 30             25 26 27 28 29 30 31    29 30                   27 28 29 30 31
```

Calendar 6

```
         JANUARY                FEBRUARY                 MARCH                  APRIL
 S  M  T  W  T  F  S     S  M  T  W  T  F  S     S  M  T  W  T  F  S     S  M  T  W  T  F  S
                1  2        1  2  3  4  5  6        1  2  3  4  5  6                 1  2  3
 3  4  5  6  7  8  9     7  8  9 10 11 12 13     7  8  9 10 11 12 13     4  5  6  7  8  9 10
10 11 12 13 14 15 16    14 15 16 17 18 19 20    14 15 16 17 18 19 20    11 12 13 14 15 16 17
17 18 19 20 21 22 23    21 22 23 24 25 26 27    21 22 23 24 25 26 27    18 19 20 21 22 23 24
24 25 26 27 28 29 30    28                      28 29 30 31             25 26 27 28 29 30
31

           MAY                     JUNE                   JULY                  AUGUST
 S  M  T  W  T  F  S     S  M  T  W  T  F  S     S  M  T  W  T  F  S     S  M  T  W  T  F  S
                   1           1  2  3  4  5                 1  2  3     1  2  3  4  5  6  7
 2  3  4  5  6  7  8     6  7  8  9 10 11 12     4  5  6  7  8  9 10     8  9 10 11 12 13 14
 9 10 11 12 13 14 15    13 14 15 16 17 18 19    11 12 13 14 15 16 17    15 16 17 18 19 20 21
16 17 18 19 20 21 22    20 21 22 23 24 25 26    18 19 20 21 22 23 24    22 23 24 25 26 27 28
23 24 25 26 27 28 29    27 28 29 30             25 26 27 28 29 30 31    29 30 31
30 31

        SEPTEMBER                OCTOBER                NOVEMBER                DECEMBER
 S  M  T  W  T  F  S     S  M  T  W  T  F  S     S  M  T  W  T  F  S     S  M  T  W  T  F  S
          1  2  3  4                    1  2        1  2  3  4  5  6              1  2  3  4
 5  6  7  8  9 10 11     3  4  5  6  7  8  9     7  8  9 10 11 12 13     5  6  7  8  9 10 11
12 13 14 15 16 17 18    10 11 12 13 14 15 16    14 15 16 17 18 19 20    12 13 14 15 16 17 18
19 20 21 22 23 24 25    17 18 19 20 21 22 23    21 22 23 24 25 26 27    19 20 21 22 23 24 25
26 27 28 29 30          24 25 26 27 28 29 30    28 29 30                26 27 28 29 30 31
                        31
```

7

```
JANUARY              FEBRUARY             MARCH                APRIL
S  M  T  W  T  F  S   S  M  T  W  T  F  S   S  M  T  W  T  F  S   S  M  T  W  T  F  S
                1                 1  2  3  4  5                 1  2  3  4  5                       1
 2  3  4  5  6  7  8   6  7  8  9 10 11 12   6  7  8  9 10 11 12   3  4  5  6  7  8  9
 9 10 11 12 13 14 15  13 14 15 16 17 18 19  13 14 15 16 17 18 19  10 11 12 13 14 15 16
16 17 18 19 20 21 22  20 21 22 23 24 25 26  20 21 22 23 24 25 26  17 18 19 20 21 22 23
23 24 25 26 27 28 29  27 28                 27 28 29 30 31        24 25 26 27 28 29 30
30 31

MAY                  JUNE                 JULY                 AUGUST
S  M  T  W  T  F  S   S  M  T  W  T  F  S   S  M  T  W  T  F  S   S  M  T  W  T  F  S
 1  2  3  4  5  6  7            1  2  3  4                 1  2            1  2  3  4  5  6
 8  9 10 11 12 13 14   5  6  7  8  9 10 11   3  4  5  6  7  8  9   7  8  9 10 11 12 13
15 16 17 18 19 20 21  12 13 14 15 16 17 18  10 11 12 13 14 15 16  14 15 16 17 18 19 20
22 23 24 25 26 27 28  19 20 21 22 23 24 25  17 18 19 20 21 22 23  21 22 23 24 25 26 27
29 30 31              26 27 28 29 30        24 25 26 27 28 29 30  28 29 30 31
                                            31

SEPTEMBER            OCTOBER              NOVEMBER             DECEMBER
S  M  T  W  T  F  S   S  M  T  W  T  F  S   S  M  T  W  T  F  S   S  M  T  W  T  F  S
             1  2  3                  1                 1  2  3  4  5                 1  2  3
 4  5  6  7  8  9 10   2  3  4  5  6  7  8   6  7  8  9 10 11 12   4  5  6  7  8  9 10
11 12 13 14 15 16 17   9 10 11 12 13 14 15  13 14 15 16 17 18 19  11 12 13 14 15 16 17
18 19 20 21 22 23 24  16 17 18 19 20 21 22  20 21 22 23 24 25 26  18 19 20 21 22 23 24
25 26 27 28 29 30     23 24 25 26 27 28 29  27 28 29 30           25 26 27 28 29 30 31
                      30 31
```

8

```
JANUARY              FEBRUARY             MARCH                APRIL
S  M  T  W  T  F  S   S  M  T  W  T  F  S   S  M  T  W  T  F  S   S  M  T  W  T  F  S
 1  2  3  4  5  6  7            1  2  3  4                1  2  3   1  2  3  4  5  6  7
 8  9 10 11 12 13 14   5  6  7  8  9 10 11   4  5  6  7  8  9 10   8  9 10 11 12 13 14
15 16 17 18 19 20 21  12 13 14 15 16 17 18  11 12 13 14 15 16 17  15 16 17 18 19 20 21
22 23 24 25 26 27 28  19 20 21 22 23 24 25  18 19 20 21 22 23 24  22 23 24 25 26 27 28
29 30 31              26 27 28 29           25 26 27 28 29 30 31  29 30

MAY                  JUNE                 JULY                 AUGUST
S  M  T  W  T  F  S   S  M  T  W  T  F  S   S  M  T  W  T  F  S   S  M  T  W  T  F  S
       1  2  3  4  5                  1  2   1  2  3  4  5  6  7            1  2  3  4
 6  7  8  9 10 11 12   3  4  5  6  7  8  9   8  9 10 11 12 13 14   5  6  7  8  9 10 11
13 14 15 16 17 18 19  10 11 12 13 14 15 16  15 16 17 18 19 20 21  12 13 14 15 16 17 18
20 21 22 23 24 25 26  17 18 19 20 21 22 23  22 23 24 25 26 27 28  19 20 21 22 23 24 25
27 28 29 30 31        24 25 26 27 28 29 30  29 30 31              26 27 28 29 30 31

SEPTEMBER            OCTOBER              NOVEMBER             DECEMBER
S  M  T  W  T  F  S   S  M  T  W  T  F  S   S  M  T  W  T  F  S   S  M  T  W  T  F  S
                1      1  2  3  4  5  6                1  2  3                    1
 2  3  4  5  6  7  8   7  8  9 10 11 12 13   4  5  6  7  8  9 10   2  3  4  5  6  7  8
 9 10 11 12 13 14 15  14 15 16 17 18 19 20  11 12 13 14 15 16 17   9 10 11 12 13 14 15
16 17 18 19 20 21 22  21 22 23 24 25 26 27  18 19 20 21 22 23 24  16 17 18 19 20 21 22
23 24 25 26 27 28 29  28 29 30 31           25 26 27 28 29 30     23 24 25 26 27 28 29
30                                                               30 31
```

9

```
JANUARY              FEBRUARY             MARCH                APRIL
S  M  T  W  T  F  S   S  M  T  W  T  F  S   S  M  T  W  T  F  S   S  M  T  W  T  F  S
    1  2  3  4  5  6               1  2  3                1  2               1  2  3  4  5  6
 7  8  9 10 11 12 13   4  5  6  7  8  9 10   3  4  5  6  7  8  9   7  8  9 10 11 12 13
14 15 16 17 18 19 20  11 12 13 14 15 16 17  10 11 12 13 14 15 16  14 15 16 17 18 19 20
21 22 23 24 25 26 27  18 19 20 21 22 23 24  17 18 19 20 21 22 23  21 22 23 24 25 26 27
28 29 30 31           25 26 27 28 29        24 25 26 27 28 29 30  28 29 30
                                            31

MAY                  JUNE                 JULY                 AUGUST
S  M  T  W  T  F  S   S  M  T  W  T  F  S   S  M  T  W  T  F  S   S  M  T  W  T  F  S
          1  2  3  4                     1      1  2  3  4  5  6               1  2  3
 5  6  7  8  9 10 11   2  3  4  5  6  7  8   7  8  9 10 11 12 13   4  5  6  7  8  9 10
12 13 14 15 16 17 18   9 10 11 12 13 14 15  14 15 16 17 18 19 20  11 12 13 14 15 16 17
19 20 21 22 23 24 25  16 17 18 19 20 21 22  21 22 23 24 25 26 27  18 19 20 21 22 23 24
26 27 28 29 30 31     23 24 25 26 27 28 29  28 29 30 31           25 26 27 28 29 30 31
                      30

SEPTEMBER            OCTOBER              NOVEMBER             DECEMBER
S  M  T  W  T  F  S   S  M  T  W  T  F  S   S  M  T  W  T  F  S   S  M  T  W  T  F  S
 1  2  3  4  5  6  7         1  2  3  4  5                  1  2   1  2  3  4  5  6  7
 8  9 10 11 12 13 14   6  7  8  9 10 11 12   3  4  5  6  7  8  9   8  9 10 11 12 13 14
15 16 17 18 19 20 21  13 14 15 16 17 18 19  10 11 12 13 14 15 16  15 16 17 18 19 20 21
22 23 24 25 26 27 28  20 21 22 23 24 25 26  17 18 19 20 21 22 23  22 23 24 25 26 27 28
29 30                 27 28 29 30 31        24 25 26 27 28 29 30  29 30 31
```

10

```
JANUARY              FEBRUARY             MARCH                APRIL
S  M  T  W  T  F  S   S  M  T  W  T  F  S   S  M  T  W  T  F  S   S  M  T  W  T  F  S
       1  2  3  4  5                  1  2                     1         1  2  3  4  5
 6  7  8  9 10 11 12   3  4  5  6  7  8  9   2  3  4  5  6  7  8   6  7  8  9 10 11 12
13 14 15 16 17 18 19  10 11 12 13 14 15 16   9 10 11 12 13 14 15  13 14 15 16 17 18 19
20 21 22 23 24 25 26  17 18 19 20 21 22 23  16 17 18 19 20 21 22  20 21 22 23 24 25 26
27 28 29 30 31        24 25 26 27 28 29     23 24 25 26 27 28 29  27 28 29 30
                                            30 31

MAY                  JUNE                 JULY                 AUGUST
S  M  T  W  T  F  S   S  M  T  W  T  F  S   S  M  T  W  T  F  S   S  M  T  W  T  F  S
             1  2  3   1  2  3  4  5  6  7         1  2  3  4  5                  1  2
 4  5  6  7  8  9 10   8  9 10 11 12 13 14   6  7  8  9 10 11 12   3  4  5  6  7  8  9
11 12 13 14 15 16 17  15 16 17 18 19 20 21  13 14 15 16 17 18 19  10 11 12 13 14 15 16
18 19 20 21 22 23 24  22 23 24 25 26 27 28  20 21 22 23 24 25 26  17 18 19 20 21 22 23
25 26 27 28 29 30 31  29 30                 27 28 29 30 31        24 25 26 27 28 29 30
                                                                 31

SEPTEMBER            OCTOBER              NOVEMBER             DECEMBER
S  M  T  W  T  F  S   S  M  T  W  T  F  S   S  M  T  W  T  F  S   S  M  T  W  T  F  S
    1  2  3  4  5  6            1  2  3  4                     1      1  2  3  4  5  6
 7  8  9 10 11 12 13   5  6  7  8  9 10 11   2  3  4  5  6  7  8   7  8  9 10 11 12 13
14 15 16 17 18 19 20  12 13 14 15 16 17 18   9 10 11 12 13 14 15  14 15 16 17 18 19 20
21 22 23 24 25 26 27  19 20 21 22 23 24 25  16 17 18 19 20 21 22  21 22 23 24 25 26 27
28 29 30              26 27 28 29 30 31     23 24 25 26 27 28 29  28 29 30 31
                                            30
```

11

```
JANUARY              FEBRUARY             MARCH                APRIL
S  M  T  W  T  F  S   S  M  T  W  T  F  S   S  M  T  W  T  F  S   S  M  T  W  T  F  S
          1  2  3  4                     1   1  2  3  4  5  6  7            1  2  3  4
 5  6  7  8  9 10 11   2  3  4  5  6  7  8   8  9 10 11 12 13 14   5  6  7  8  9 10 11
12 13 14 15 16 17 18   9 10 11 12 13 14 15  15 16 17 18 19 20 21  12 13 14 15 16 17 18
19 20 21 22 23 24 25  16 17 18 19 20 21 22  22 23 24 25 26 27 28  19 20 21 22 23 24 25
26 27 28 29 30 31     23 24 25 26 27 28 29  29 30 31              26 27 28 29 30

MAY                  JUNE                 JULY                 AUGUST
S  M  T  W  T  F  S   S  M  T  W  T  F  S   S  M  T  W  T  F  S   S  M  T  W  T  F  S
                1  2   1  2  3  4  5  6               1  2  3  4                     1
 3  4  5  6  7  8  9   7  8  9 10 11 12 13   5  6  7  8  9 10 11   2  3  4  5  6  7  8
10 11 12 13 14 15 16  14 15 16 17 18 19 20  12 13 14 15 16 17 18   9 10 11 12 13 14 15
17 18 19 20 21 22 23  21 22 23 24 25 26 27  19 20 21 22 23 24 25  16 17 18 19 20 21 22
24 25 26 27 28 29 30  28 29 30              26 27 28 29 30 31     23 24 25 26 27 28 29
31                                                               30 31

SEPTEMBER            OCTOBER              NOVEMBER             DECEMBER
S  M  T  W  T  F  S   S  M  T  W  T  F  S   S  M  T  W  T  F  S   S  M  T  W  T  F  S
       1  2  3  4  5               1  2  3   1  2  3  4  5  6  7         1  2  3  4  5
 6  7  8  9 10 11 12   4  5  6  7  8  9 10   8  9 10 11 12 13 14   6  7  8  9 10 11 12
13 14 15 16 17 18 19  11 12 13 14 15 16 17  15 16 17 18 19 20 21  13 14 15 16 17 18 19
20 21 22 23 24 25 26  18 19 20 21 22 23 24  22 23 24 25 26 27 28  20 21 22 23 24 25 26
27 28 29 30           25 26 27 28 29 30 31  29 30                 27 28 29 30 31
```

12

```
JANUARY              FEBRUARY             MARCH                APRIL
S  M  T  W  T  F  S   S  M  T  W  T  F  S   S  M  T  W  T  F  S   S  M  T  W  T  F  S
             1  2  3   1  2  3  4  5  6  7            1  2  3  4               1  2  3
 4  5  6  7  8  9 10   8  9 10 11 12 13 14   5  6  7  8  9 10 11   4  5  6  7  8  9 10
11 12 13 14 15 16 17  15 16 17 18 19 20 21  12 13 14 15 16 17 18  11 12 13 14 15 16 17
18 19 20 21 22 23 24  22 23 24 25 26 27 28  19 20 21 22 23 24 25  18 19 20 21 22 23 24
25 26 27 28 29 30 31  29                   26 27 28 29 30 31     25 26 27 28 29 30

MAY                  JUNE                 JULY                 AUGUST
S  M  T  W  T  F  S   S  M  T  W  T  F  S   S  M  T  W  T  F  S   S  M  T  W  T  F  S
                1            1  2  3  4               1  2  3   1  2  3  4  5  6  7
 2  3  4  5  6  7  8   6  7  8  9 10 11 12   4  5  6  7  8  9 10   8  9 10 11 12 13 14
 9 10 11 12 13 14 15  13 14 15 16 17 18 19  11 12 13 14 15 16 17  15 16 17 18 19 20 21
16 17 18 19 20 21 22  20 21 22 23 24 25 26  18 19 20 21 22 23 24  22 23 24 25 26 27 28
23 24 25 26 27 28 29  27 28 29 30          25 26 27 28 29 30 31  29 30 31
30 31

SEPTEMBER            OCTOBER              NOVEMBER             DECEMBER
S  M  T  W  T  F  S   S  M  T  W  T  F  S   S  M  T  W  T  F  S   S  M  T  W  T  F  S
          1  2  3  4                  1  2   1  2  3  4  5  6            1  2  3  4
 5  6  7  8  9 10 11   3  4  5  6  7  8  9   7  8  9 10 11 12 13   5  6  7  8  9 10 11
12 13 14 15 16 17 18  10 11 12 13 14 15 16  14 15 16 17 18 19 20  12 13 14 15 16 17 18
19 20 21 22 23 24 25  17 18 19 20 21 22 23  21 22 23 24 25 26 27  19 20 21 22 23 24 25
26 27 28 29 30        24 25 26 27 28 29 30  28 29 30              26 27 28 29 30 31
                      31
```

13

```
JANUARY              FEBRUARY             MARCH                APRIL
S  M  T  W  T  F  S   S  M  T  W  T  F  S   S  M  T  W  T  F  S   S  M  T  W  T  F  S
                1  2      1  2  3  4  5  6         1  2  3  4  5                  1  2
 3  4  5  6  7  8  9   7  8  9 10 11 12 13   6  7  8  9 10 11 12   3  4  5  6  7  8  9
10 11 12 13 14 15 16  14 15 16 17 18 19 20  13 14 15 16 17 18 19  10 11 12 13 14 15 16
17 18 19 20 21 22 23  21 22 23 24 25 26 27  20 21 22 23 24 25 26  17 18 19 20 21 22 23
24 25 26 27 28 29 30  28 29                 27 28 29 30 31        24 25 26 27 28 29 30
31

MAY                  JUNE                 JULY                 AUGUST
S  M  T  W  T  F  S   S  M  T  W  T  F  S   S  M  T  W  T  F  S   S  M  T  W  T  F  S
 1  2  3  4  5  6  7            1  2  3  4                 1  2            1  2  3  4  5  6
 8  9 10 11 12 13 14   5  6  7  8  9 10 11   3  4  5  6  7  8  9   7  8  9 10 11 12 13
15 16 17 18 19 20 21  12 13 14 15 16 17 18  10 11 12 13 14 15 16  14 15 16 17 18 19 20
22 23 24 25 26 27 28  19 20 21 22 23 24 25  17 18 19 20 21 22 23  21 22 23 24 25 26 27
29 30 31              26 27 28 29 30        24 25 26 27 28 29 30  28 29 30 31
                                            31

SEPTEMBER            OCTOBER              NOVEMBER             DECEMBER
S  M  T  W  T  F  S   S  M  T  W  T  F  S   S  M  T  W  T  F  S   S  M  T  W  T  F  S
             1  2  3                  1                 1  2  3  4  5                 1  2  3
 4  5  6  7  8  9 10   2  3  4  5  6  7  8   6  7  8  9 10 11 12   4  5  6  7  8  9 10
11 12 13 14 15 16 17   9 10 11 12 13 14 15  13 14 15 16 17 18 19  11 12 13 14 15 16 17
18 19 20 21 22 23 24  16 17 18 19 20 21 22  20 21 22 23 24 25 26  18 19 20 21 22 23 24
25 26 27 28 29 30     23 24 25 26 27 28 29  27 28 29 30           25 26 27 28 29 30 31
                      30 31
```

14

```
JANUARY              FEBRUARY             MARCH                APRIL
S  M  T  W  T  F  S   S  M  T  W  T  F  S   S  M  T  W  T  F  S   S  M  T  W  T  F  S
                1         1  2  3  4  5            1  2  3  4                        1
 2  3  4  5  6  7  8   6  7  8  9 10 11 12   5  6  7  8  9 10 11   2  3  4  5  6  7  8
 9 10 11 12 13 14 15  13 14 15 16 17 18 19  12 13 14 15 16 17 18   9 10 11 12 13 14 15
16 17 18 19 20 21 22  20 21 22 23 24 25 26  19 20 21 22 23 24 25  16 17 18 19 20 21 22
23 24 25 26 27 28 29  27 28 29              26 27 28 29 30 31     23 24 25 26 27 28 29
30 31                                                            30

MAY                  JUNE                 JULY                 AUGUST
S  M  T  W  T  F  S   S  M  T  W  T  F  S   S  M  T  W  T  F  S   S  M  T  W  T  F  S
    1  2  3  4  5  6            1  2  3                  1            1  2  3  4  5
 7  8  9 10 11 12 13   4  5  6  7  8  9 10   2  3  4  5  6  7  8   6  7  8  9 10 11 12
14 15 16 17 18 19 20  11 12 13 14 15 16 17   9 10 11 12 13 14 15  13 14 15 16 17 18 19
21 22 23 24 25 26 27  18 19 20 21 22 23 24  16 17 18 19 20 21 22  20 21 22 23 24 25 26
28 29 30 31          25 26 27 28 29 30     23 24 25 26 27 28 29  27 28 29 30 31
                                            30 31

SEPTEMBER            OCTOBER              NOVEMBER             DECEMBER
S  M  T  W  T  F  S   S  M  T  W  T  F  S   S  M  T  W  T  F  S   S  M  T  W  T  F  S
                1  2   1  2  3  4  5  6  7            1  2  3  4                  1  2
 3  4  5  6  7  8  9   8  9 10 11 12 13 14   5  6  7  8  9 10 11   3  4  5  6  7  8  9
10 11 12 13 14 15 16  15 16 17 18 19 20 21  12 13 14 15 16 17 18  10 11 12 13 14 15 16
17 18 19 20 21 22 23  22 23 24 25 26 27 28  19 20 21 22 23 24 25  17 18 19 20 21 22 23
24 25 26 27 28 29 30  29 30 31              26 27 28 29 30        24 25 26 27 28 29 30
                                                                 31
```

The Calendar

History of the Calendar

The purpose of a calendar is to reckon time in advance, to show how many days have to elapse until a certain event takes place—the harvest, a religious festival, or whatever. The earliest calendars, naturally, were crude, and they must have been strongly influenced by the geographical location of the people who made them. In the Scandinavian countries, for example, where the seasons are pronounced, the concept of the year was determined by the seasons, specifically by the end of winter. The Norsemen, before becoming Christians, are said to have had a calendar consisting of ten months of 30 days each.

But in warmer countries, where the seasons are less pronounced, the Moon became the basic unit for time reckoning; an old Jewish book actually makes the statement that "the Moon was created for the counting of the days." All the oldest calendars of which we have reliable information were lunar calendars, based on the time interval from one new moon to the next—a so-called "lunation." But even in a warm climate there are annual events that pay no attention to the phases of the Moon. In some areas it was a rainy season; in Egypt it was the annual flooding of the Nile. It was, therefore, necessary to regulate daily life and religious festivals by lunations, but to take care of the annual event in some other manner.

The calendar of the Assyrians was based on the phases of the Moon. The month began with the first appearance of the lunar crescent, and since this can best be observed in the evening, the day began with sunset. They knew that a lunation was 29 1/2 days long, so their lunar year had a duration of 354 days, falling eleven days short of the solar year.[1] After three years such a lunar calendar would be off by 33 days, or more than one lunation. We know that the Assyrians added an extra month from time to time, but we do not know whether they had developed a special rule for doing so or whether the priests proclaimed the necessity for an extra month from observation. If they made every third year a year of 13 lunations, their three-year period would cover 1,091 1/2 days (using their value of 29 1/2 days for one lunation), or just about four days too short. In one century this mistake would add up to 133 days by their reckoning (in reality closer to 134 days), requiring four extra lunations per century.

We now know that an eight-year period, consisting of five years with 12 months and three years with 13 months would lead to a difference of only 20 days per century, but we do not know whether such a calendar was actually used.

The best approximation that was possible in antiquity was a 19-year period, with seven of these 19 years having 13 months. This means that the period contained 235 months. This, still using the old value for a lunation, made a total of 6,932 1/2 days, while 19 solar years added up to 6,939.7 days, a difference of just one week per period and about five weeks per century. Even the 19-year period required constant adjustment, but it was the period that became the

basis of the religious calendar of the Jews. The Arabs used the same calendar at first, but Mohammed forbade shifting from 12 months to 13 months, so that the Islamic religious calendar, even today, has a lunar year of 354 days. As a result the Islamic religious festivals run through all the seasons of the year three times per century.

The Egyptians had a traditional calendar with 12 months of 30 days each. At one time they added five extra days at the end of every year. These turned into a five-day festival because it was thought to be unlucky to work during that time.

When Rome emerged as a world power, the difficulties of making a calendar were well known, but the Romans complicated their lives because of their superstition that even numbers were unlucky. Hence their months were 29 or 31 days long, with the exception of February, which had 28 days. However, four months of 31 days, seven months of 29 days, and one month of 28 days added up to only 355 days. Therefore, the Romans invented an extra month called Mercedonius of 22 or 23 days. It was added every second year.

Even with Mercedonius, the Roman calendar was so far off that Caesar, advised by the astronomer Sosigenes, ordered a sweeping reform in 45 B.C. One year, made 445 days long by imperial decree, brought the calendar back in step with the seasons. Then the solar year (with the value of 365 days and 6 hours) was made the basis of the calendar. The months were 30 or 31 days in length, and to take care of the six hours, every fourth year was made a 366-day year. Moreover, Caesar decreed, the year began with the first of January, not with the vernal equinox in late March.

This was the Julian calendar, named after Julius Caesar. It is still the calendar of the Eastern Orthodox churches.

However, the year is 11 1/2 minutes shorter than the figure written into Caesar's calendar by Sosigenes, and after a number of centuries, even 11 1/2 minutes add up. *See* table.

While Caesar could decree that the vernal equinox should not be used as the first day of the new year, the vernal equinox is still a fact of Nature that could not be disregarded. One of the first (as far as we know) to become alarmed about this was Roger Bacon. He sent a memorandum to Pope Clement IV, who apparently was not impressed. But Pope Sixtus IV (reigned 1471 to 1484) decided that another reform was needed and called the German astronomer Regiomontanus to Rome to advise him. Regiomontanus arrived in 1475, but one year later he died in an epidemic, one of the recurrent outbreaks of the plague. The Pope himself survived, but his reform plans died with Regiomontanus.

Less than a hundred years later, in 1545, the Council of Trent authorized the then Pope, Paul III, to reform the calendar once more. Most of the mathematical and astronomical work was done by Father Christopher Clavius, S.J. The immediate correction, advised by Father Clavius and ordered by Pope Gregory XIII, was that Thursday, Oct. 4, 1582, was to be the last day of the Julian calendar. The next day was Friday, with the date of October 15. For long-range accuracy, a formula suggested by the Vatican librarian Aloysius Giglio (latinized into Lilius) was adopted: every fourth year is a leap year *unless* it is a century year like 1700 or 1800. Century years can be

---

1. The correct figures are: lunation: 29 d, 12 h, 44 min, 2.8 sec (29.530585 d); solar year: 365 d, 5 h, 48 min, 46 sec (365.242216 d); 12 lunations: 354 d, 8 h, 48 min, 34 sec (354.3671 d).

Drift of the Vernal Equinox in the Julian Calendar

Date	Julian year	Date	Julian year	Date	Julian Year
March 21	325 A.D.	March 17	837 A.D.	March 13	1349 A.D.
March 20	453 A.D.	March 16	965 A.D.	March 12	1477 A.D.
March 19	581 A.D.	March 15	1093 A.D.	March 11	1605 A.D.
March 18	709 A.D.	March 14	1221 A.D.		

leap years *only* when they are divisible by 400 (e.g., 1600). This rule eliminates three leap years in four centuries, making the calendar sufficiently correct for all ordinary purposes.

Unfortunately, all the Protestant princes in 1582 chose to ignore the papal bull; they continued with the Julian calendar. It was not until 1698 that the German professor Erhard Weigel persuaded the Protestant rulers of Germany and of the Netherlands to change to the new calendar. In England the shift took place in 1752, and in Russia it needed the revolution to introduce the Gregorian calendar in 1918.

The average year of the Gregorian calendar, in spite of the leap year rule, is about 26 seconds longer than the earth's orbital period. But this discrepancy will need 3,323 years to build up to a single day.

Modern proposals for calendar reform do not aim at a "better" calendar, but at one that is more convenient to use, especially for commercial purposes. A 365-day year cannot be divided into equal halves or quarters; the number of days per month is haphazard; the months begin or end in the middle of a week; a holiday fixed by date (e.g., the Fourth of July) will wander through a week; a holiday fixed in another manner (e.g., Easter) can fall on thirty-five possible dates. The Gregorian calendar, admittedly, keeps the calendar dates in reasonable unison with astronomical events, but it still is full of minor annoyances. Moreover, you need a calendar every year to look up dates; an ideal calendar should be one that you can memorize for one year and that is valid for all other years, too.

In 1834 an Italian priest, Marco Mastrofini, suggested taking one day out of every year. It would be made a holiday and *not* be given the name of a weekday. That would make every year begin with January 1 as a Sunday. The leap-year day would be treated the same way, so that in leap years there would be two unnamed holidays at the end of the year.

About a decade later the philosopher Auguste Comte also suggested a 364-day calendar with an extra day, which he called Year Day.

Since then there have been other unsuccessful attempts at calendar reform.

Time and Calendar

The two natural cycles on which time measurements are based are the year and the day. The year is defined as the time required for the Earth to complete one revolution around the Sun, while the day is the time required for the Earth to complete one turn upon its axis. Unfortunately the Earth needs 365 days plus about six hours to go around the Sun once, so that the year does not consist of so and so many days; the fractional day has to be taken care of by an extra day every fourth year.

But because the Earth, while turning upon its axis, also moves around the Sun there are two kinds of days. A day may be defined as the interval between the highest point of the Sun in the sky on two succes-

sive days. This, averaged out over the year, produces the customary 24-hour day. But one might also define a day as the time interval between the moments when a certain point in the sky, say a conveniently located star, is directly overhead. This is called:

Sidereal time. Astronomers use a point which they call the "vernal equinox" for the actual determination. Such a sidereal day is somewhat shorter than the "solar day," namely by about 3 minutes and 56 seconds of so-called "mean solar time."

Apparent solar time is the time based directly on the Sun's position in the sky. In ordinary life the day runs from midnight to midnight. It begins when the Sun is invisible by being 12 hours from its zenith. Astronomers use the so-called "Julian Day," which runs from noon to noon; the concept was invented by the astronomer Joseph Scaliger, who named it after his father Julius. To avoid the problems caused by leap-year days and so forth, Scaliger picked a conveniently remote date in the past and just counting days without regard to weeks, months, and years. The Julian Day for 0^h Jan. 31, 1996 is 245 0082.5. The reason for having the Julian Day run from noon to noon is the practical one that astronomical observations usually extend across the midnight hour, which would require a change in date (or in the Julian Day number) if the astronomical day, like the civil day, ran from midnight to midnight.

Mean solar time, rather than apparent solar time, is what is actually used most of the time. The mean solar time is based on the position of a fictitious "mean sun." The reason why this fictitious sun has to be introduced is the following: the Earth turns on its axis regularly; it needs the same number of seconds regardless of the season. But the movement of the Earth around the Sun is not regular because the Earth's orbit is an ellipse. This has the result (as explained in the section The Seasons) that the Earth moves faster in January and slower in July. Though it is the Earth that changes velocity, it looks to us as if the Sun did. In January, when the Earth moves faster, the *apparent* movement of the Sun looks faster. The "mean sun" of time measurements, then, is a sun that moves regularly all year round; the real Sun will be either ahead of or behind the "mean sun." The difference between the real Sun and the fictitious mean sun is called the *equation of time.*

When the real Sun is west of the mean sun we have the "sun fast" condition, with the real Sun crossing the meridian ahead of the mean sun. The opposite is the "sun slow" situation when the real Sun crosses the meridian after the mean sun. Of course, what is observed is the real Sun. The equation of time is needed to establish mean solar time, kept by the reference clocks.

But if all clocks were actually set by mean solar time we would be plagued by a welter of time differences that would be "correct" but a major nuisance. A clock on Long Island, correctly showing mean solar time for its location (this would be *local civil time*), would be slightly ahead of a clock in Newark, N.J. The Newark clock would be slightly ahead of a

The Names of Days

Latin	Saxon	English	French	Italian	Spanish	German
Dies Solis	Sun's Day	Sunday	dimanche	domenica	domingo	Sonntag
Dies Lunae	Moon's Day	Monday	lundi	lunedì	lunes	Montag
Dies Martis	Tiw's Day	Tuesday	mardi	martedì	martes	Dienstag
Dies Mercurii	Woden's Day	Wednesday	mercredi	mercoledì	miércoles	Mittwoch
Dies Jovis	Thor's Day	Thursday	jeudi	giovedì	jueves	Donnerstag
Dies Veneris	Frigg's Day	Friday	vendredi	venerdì	viernes	Freitag
Dies Saturni	Seterne's Day	Saturday	samedi	sabato	sábado	Sonnabend

NOTE: The Romans gave one day of the week to each planet known, the Sun and Moon being considered planets in this connection. The Saxon names are a kind of translation of the Roman names: Tiw was substituted for Mars, Woden (Wotan) for Mercury, Thor for Jupiter (Jove), Frigg for Venus, and Seterne for Saturn. The English names are adapted Saxon. The Spanish, Italian, and French names, which are normally not capitalized, are derived from the Latin. The German names follow the Saxon pattern with two exceptions: Wednesday is Mittwoch (Middle of the Week), and Saturday is Sonnabend (Sunday's Eve).

clock in Trenton, N.J., which, in turn, would be ahead of a clock in Philadelphia. This condition prevailed until 1884, when a system of standard time was adopted by the International Meridian Conference. The earth's surface was divided into 24 zones. The standard time of each zone is the mean astronomical time of one of 24 meridians, 15 degrees apart, beginning at the Greenwich, England, meridian and extending east and west around the globe to the international dateline, (This system was actually put into use a year earlier by the railroad companies of the U.S. and Canada who, until then, had to contend with some 100 conflicting local sun times observed in terminals across the land.)

For practical purposes, this convention is sometimes altered. For example, Alaska, for a time, consisted of four of the eight U.S. time zones: the Pacific Standard Time zone (east of Juneau) and the 6th (Juneau), 7th (Anchorage), and 8th (Nome) zones, encompassing the 135°, 150°, and 165° meridians, respectively. In 1983, by Act of Congress, the entire state (except the westward-most Aleutians) was united into the 6th zone, Alaska Standard Time.

The eight U.S. Standard Time Zones are: Atlantic (includes Puerto Rico and the Virgin Islands), Eastern, Central, Mountain, Pacific, Alaska, Hawaii–Aleutian (includes all of Hawaii and those Aleutians west of the Fox Islands), and Samoa Standard Time.

The date line. While the time zones are based on the natural event of the Sun crossing the meridian, the date must be an arbitrary decision. The meridians are traditionally counted from the meridian of the observatory of Greenwich in England, which is called the zero meridian. The logical place for changing the date is 12 hours, or 180° from Greenwich. Fortunately, the 180th meridian runs mostly through the open

Pacific. The date line makes a zigzag in the north to incorporate the eastern tip of Siberia into the Siberian time system and then another one to incorporate a number of islands into the Hawaii-Aleutian time zone. In the south there is a similar zigzag for the purpose of tying a number of British-owned islands to the New Zealand time system. Otherwise the date line is the same as 180° from Greenwich. At points to the east of the date line the calendar is one day earlier than at points to the west of it. A traveller going eastward across the date line from one island to another would not have to re-set his watch because he would stay inside the time zone (provided he does so where the date line does *not* coincide with the 180° meridian), but it would be the same time of the previous day.

The Seasons

The seasons are caused by the tilt of the Earth's axis (23.4°) and not by the fact that the Earth's orbit around the Sun is an ellipse. The average distance of the Earth from the Sun is 93 million miles; the difference between aphelion (farthest away) and perihelion (closest to the Sun) is 3 million miles, so that perihelion is about 91.4 million miles from the Sun. The Earth goes through the perihelion point a few days after New Year, just when the northern hemisphere has winter. Aphelion is passed during the first days in July. This by itself shows that the distance from the Sun is not important within these limits. What is important is that when the Earth passes through perihelion, the northern end of the Earth's axis happens to tilt away from the Sun, so that the areas beyond the Tropic of Cancer receive only slanting rays from a Sun low in the sky.

The Names of the Months

January: named after Janus, protector of the gateway to heaven

February: named after Februalia, a time period when sacrifices were made to atone for sins

March: named after Mars, the god of war, presumably signifying that the campaigns interrupted by the winter could be resumed

April: from *aperire,* Latin for "to open" (buds)

May: named after Maia, the goddess of growth of plants

June: from *juvenis,* Latin for "youth"

July: named after Julius Caesar

August: named after Augustus, the first Roman Emperor

September: from *septem,* Latin for "seven"

October: from *octo,* Latin for "eight"

November: from *novem,* Latin for "nine"

December: from *decem,* Latin for "ten"

NOTE: The earliest Latin calendar was a 10-month one; thus September was the seventh month, October, the eighth, etc. July was originally called Quintilis, as the fifth month; August was originally called Sextilis, as the sixth month.

The tilt of the Earth's axis is responsible for four lines you find on every globe. When, say, the North Pole is tilted away from the Sun as much as possible, the farthest points in the North which can still be reached by the Sun's rays are 23 1/2° from the pole. This is the Arctic Circle. The Antarctic Circle is the corresponding limit 23.4° from the South Pole; the Sun's rays cannot reach beyond this point when we have mid-summer in the North.

When the Sun is vertically above the equator, the day is of equal length all over the Earth. This happens twice a year, and these are the "equinoxes" in March and in September. After having been over the equator in March, the Sun will seem to move northward. The northernmost point where the Sun can be straight overhead is 23.4° north of the equator. This is the Tropic of Cancer; the Sun can never be vertically overhead to the north of this line. Similarly the Sun cannot be vertically overhead to the south of a line 23.4° south of the equator—the Tropic of Capricorn.

This explains the climatic zones. In the belt (the Greek word *zone* means "belt") between the Tropic of Cancer and the Tropic of Capricorn, the Sun can be straight overhead; this is the tropical zone. The two zones where the Sun cannot be overhead but will be above the horizon every day of the year are the two temperate zones; the two areas where the Sun will not rise at all for varying lengths of time are the two polar areas, Arctic and Antarctic.

Holidays

Religious and Secular, 1996

Since 1971, by federal law, Washington's Birthday, Memorial Day, Columbus Day, and Veterans' Day have been celebrated on Mondays to create three-day weekends for federal employees. Many states now observe these holidays on the same Mondays. The dates given for the holidays listed below are the traditional ones.

New Year's Day, Monday, Jan. 1. A legal holiday in all states and the District of Columbia, New Year's Day has its origin in Roman Times, when sacrifices were offered to Janus, the two-faced Roman deity who looked back on the past and forward to the future.

Epiphany, Saturday, Jan. 6. Falls the twelfth day after Christmas and commemorates the manifestation of Jesus as the Son of God, as represented by the adoration of the Magi, the baptism of Jesus, and the miracle of the wine at the marriage feast at Cana. Epiphany originally marked the beginning of the carnival season preceding Lent, and the evening (sometimes the eve) is known as Twelfth Night.

Martin Luther King, Jr.'s Birthday, Monday, Jan. 15. Honors the late civil rights leader. Became a legal public holiday in 1986.

First Day of Ramadan. Sunday, Jan. 21. This day marks the beginning of a month-long fast which all Moslems must keep during the daylight hours. Only a few are exempt: the sick, those on a journey. It commemorates the first revelation of the Koran.

Ground-hog Day, Friday, Feb. 2. Legend has it that if the ground-hog sees his shadow, he'll return to his hole, and winter will last another six weeks.

Lincoln's Birthday, Monday, Feb. 12. A legal holiday in many states, this day was first formally observed in Washington, D.C., in 1866, when both houses of Congress gathered for a memorial address in tribute to the assassinated President.

St. Valentine's Day, Wednesday, Feb. 14. This day is the festival of two third-century martyrs, both named St. Valentine. It is not known why this day is associated with lovers. It may derive from an old pagan festival about this time of year, or it may have been inspired by the belief that birds mate on this day.

Washington's Birthday, Thursday, Feb. 22. The birthday of George Washington is celebrated as a legal holiday in every state of the Union, the District of Columbia, and all territories. The observance began in 1796.

Shrove Tuesday, Feb. 20. Falls the day before Ash Wednesday and marks the end of the carnival season, which once began on Epiphany but is now usually celebrated the last three days before Lent. In France, the day is known as Mardi Gras (Fat Tuesday), and Mardi Gras celebrations are also held in several American cities, particularly in New Orleans. The day is sometimes called Pancake Tuesday by the English because fats, which were prohibited during Lent, had to be used up.

Ash Wednesday, Feb. 21. The first day of the Lenten season, which lasts 40 days. Having its origin sometime before A.D. 1000, it is a day of public penance and is marked in the Roman Catholic Church by the burning of the palms blessed on the previous year's Palm Sunday. With his thumb, the priest then marks a cross upon the forehead of each worshipper. The Anglican Church and a few Protestant groups in the United States also observe the day, but generally without the use of ashes.

Purim (Feast of Lots), Tuesday, March 5. A day of joy and feasting celebrating deliverance of the Jews from a massacre planned by the Persian Minister Haman. The Jewish Queen Esther interceded with her husband, King Ahasuerus, to spare the life of her uncle, Mordecai, and Haman was hanged on the same gallows he had built for Mordecai. The holiday is marked by the reading of the Book of Esther (megillah), and by the exchange of gifts, donations to the poor, and the presentation of Purim plays.

St. Patrick's Day, Sunday, March 17. St. Patrick, patron saint of Ireland, has been honored in America since the first days of the nation. There are many dinners and meetings but perhaps the most notable part of the observance is the annual St. Patrick's Day parade on Fifth Avenue in New York City.

Palm Sunday, March 31. Is observed the Sunday before Easter to commemorate the entry of Jesus into Jerusalem. The procession and the ceremonies introducing the benediction of palms probably had their origin in Jerusalem.

Good Friday, April 5. This day commemorates the Crucifixion, which is retold during services from the Gospel according to St. John. A feature in Roman Catholic churches is the Liturgy of the Passion; there is no Consecration, the Host having been consecrated the previous day. The eating of hot cross buns on this day is said to have started in England.

First Day of Passover (Pesach), Thursday, April 4. The Feast of the Passover, also called the Feast of Unleavened Bread, commemorates the escape of the Jews from Egypt. As the Jews fled they ate unleavened bread, and from that time the Jews have allowed no leavening in the houses during Passover, bread being replaced by matzoh.

Easter Sunday, April 7. Observed in all Christian churches, Easter commemorates the Resurrection of Jesus. It is celebrated on the first Sunday after the full moon which occurs on or next after March 21 and is therefore celebrated between March 22 and April 25 inclusive. This date was fixed by the Council of Nicaea in A.D. 325. The Orthodox Church celebrates Easter on April 23, 1995.

Mother's Day, Sunday, May 12. Observed the second Sunday in May, as proposed by Anna Jarvis of Philadelphia in 1907.

Ascension Day, Thursday, May 16. Took place in the presence of His apostles 40 days after the Resurrection of Jesus. It is traditionally held to have occurred on Mount Olivet in Bethany.

First Day of Shavuot (Hebrew Pentecost), Friday, May 24. This festival, sometimes called the Feast of Weeks, or of Harvest, or of the First Fruits, falls 50 days after Passover and originally celebrated the end of the seven-week grain harvesting season. In later tradition, it also celebrated the giving of the Law to Moses on Mount Sinai.

Pentecost (Whitsunday), Sunday, May 26. This day commemorates the descent of the Holy Ghost upon the apostles 50 days after the Resurrection. The sermon by the Apostle Peter, which led to the baptism of 3,000 who professed belief, originated the ceremonies that have since been followed. "Whitsunday" is believed to have come from "white Sunday" when, among the English, white robes were worn by those baptized on the day.

Memorial Day, Thursday, May 30. Also known as Decoration Day, Memorial Day is a legal holiday in most of the states and in the territories, and is also observed by the armed forces. In 1868, Gen. John A. Logan (Retired), Commander in Chief of the Grand Army of the Republic, issued an order designating the day as one in which the graves of soldiers would be decorated. The holiday was originally devoted to honoring the memory of those who fell in the Civil War, but is now also dedicated to the memory of all war dead.

Flag Day, Friday, June 14. This day commemorates the adoption by the Continental Congress on June 14, 1777, of the Stars and Stripes as the U.S. flag. Although it is a legal holiday only in Pennsylvania, President Truman, on Aug. 3, 1949, signed a bill requesting the President to call for its observance each year by proclamation.

Father's Day, Sunday, June 16. Observed the third Sunday in June. First celebrated June 19, 1910.

Independence Day, Thursday, July 4. The day of the adoption of the Declaration of Independence in 1776, celebrated in all states and territories. The observance began the next year in Philadelphia.

Labor Day, Monday, Sept. 2. Observed the first Monday in September in all states and territories, Labor Day was first celebrated in New York in 1882 under the sponsorship of the Central Labor Union, following the suggestion of Peter J. McGuire, of the

Knights of Labor, that the day be set aside in honor of labor.

First Day of Rosh Hashana (Jewish New Year), Saturday, Sept. 14. This day marks the beginning of the Jewish year 5757 and opens the Ten Days of Penitence closing with Yom Kippur.

Yom Kippur (Day of Atonement), Monday, Sept. 23. This day marks the end of the Ten Days of Penitence that began with Rosh Hashana. It is described in *Leviticus* as a "Sabbath of rest," and synagogue services begin the preceding sundown, resume the following morning, and continue to sundown.

First Day of Sukkot (Feast of Tabernacles) Saturday, Sept. 28. This festival, also known as the Feast of the Ingathering, originally celebrated the fruit harvest, and the name comes from the booths or tabernacles in which the Jews lived during the harvest, although one tradition traces it to the shelters used by the Jews in their wandering through the wilderness. During the festival many Jews build small huts in their back yards or on the roofs of their houses.

Simhat Torah (Rejoicing of the Law), Sunday, Oct. 6. This joyous holiday falls on the eighth day of Sukkot. It marks the end of the year's reading of the Torah (Five Books of Moses) in the synagogue every Saturday and the beginning of the new cycle of reading.

Columbus Day, Saturday, Oct. 12. A legal holiday in many states, commemorating the discovery of America by Columbus in 1492. Quite likely the first celebration of Columbus Day was that organized in 1792 by the Society of St. Tammany, or Columbian Order, widely known as Tammany Hall.

United Nations Day, Thursday, Oct. 24. Marking the founding of the United Nations.

Halloween, Thursday, Oct. 31. Eve of All Saints' Day, formerly called All Hallows and Hallowmass. Halloween is traditionally associated in some countries with old customs such as bonfires, masquerading, and the telling of ghost stories. These are old Celtic practices marking the beginning of winter.

All Saints' Day, Friday, Nov. 1. A Roman Catholic and Anglican holiday celebrating all saints, known and unknown.

Election Day, (legal holiday in certain states), Tuesday, Nov. 5. Since 1845, by Act of Congress, the first Tuesday after the first Monday in November is the date for choosing Presidential electors. State elections are also generally held on this day.

Veterans Day, Monday, Nov. 11. Armistice Day was established in 1926 to commemorate the signing in 1918 of the Armistice ending World War I. On June 1, 1954, the name was changed to Veterans Day to honor all men and women who have served America in its armed forces.

Thanksgiving, Thursday, Nov. 28. Observed nationally on the fourth Thursday in November by Act of Congress (1941), the first such national proclamation having been issued by President Lincoln in 1863, on the urging of Mrs. Sarah J. Hale, editor of *Godey's Lady's Book.* Most Americans believe that the holiday dates back to the day of thanks ordered by Governor Bradford of Plymouth Colony in New England in 1621, but scholars point out that days of thanks stem from ancient times.

First Sunday of Advent, Dec. 1. Advent is the season in which the faithful must prepare themselves for the advent of the Saviour on Christmas. The four Sundays before Christmas are marked by special church services.

First Day of Hanukkah (Festival of Lights), Friday, Dec. 6. This festival was instituted by Judas Maccabaeus in 165 B.C. to celebrate the purification of the Temple of Jerusalem, which had been desecrated three years earlier by Antiochus Epiphanes, who set up a pagan altar and offered sacrifices to Zeus Olympius. In Jewish homes, a light is lighted on each night of the eight-day festival.

Christmas (Feast of the Nativity), Wednesday, Dec. 25. The most widely celebrated holiday of the Christian year, Christmas is observed as the anniversary of the birth of Jesus. Christmas customs are centuries old. The mistletoe, for example, comes from the Druids, who, in hanging the mistletoe, hoped for peace and good fortune. Use of such plants as holly comes from the ancient belief that such plants blossomed at Christmas. Comparatively recent is the Christmas tree, first set up in Germany in the 17th century, and the use of candles on trees developed from the belief that candles appeared by miracle on the trees at Christmas. Colonial Manhattan Islanders introduced the name Santa Claus, a corruption of the Dutch name for the 4th-century Asia Minor St. Nicholas.

Sikh Festival Dates, 1996
Source: Jantri 500, by Pal Singh Purewal.

Jan. 14	Maghi	Nov. 10	Diwali
March 6	Hola Mohalla	Nov. 12	Installation of Granth Sahib Ji as Guru
April 13	Vaisakhi (new year 298 KE)	Nov. 25	Birthday Guru Nanak Dev Ji
May 21	Martyrdom Guru Arjan Dev Ji	Dec. 15	Martyrdom Guru Teg Bahadur Ji
Sept. 13	First Parkash Granth Sahib Ji		

State Observances

January 6, Three Kings' Day: Puerto Rico.
January 8, Battle of New Orleans Day: Louisiana.
January 11, De Hostos' Birthday: Puerto Rico.
January 19, Robert E. Lee's Birthday: Arkansas, Florida, Kentucky, Louisiana, South Carolina, **(third Monday)** Alabama, Mississippi.
January 19, Confederate Heroes Day: Texas.
January (third Monday): Lee-Jackson-King Day: Virginia.
January 30, F.D. Roosevelt's Birthday: Kentucky.
February 15, Susan B. Anthony's Birthday: Florida, Minnesota.
March (first Tuesday), Town Meeting Day: Vermont.
March 2, Texas Independence Day: Texas.
March (first Monday), Casimir Pulaski's Birthday: Illinois.
March 17, Evacuation Day: Massachusetts (in Suffolk County).
March 20 (First Day of Spring), Youth Day: Oklahoma.
March 22, Abolition Day: Puerto Rico.
March 25, Maryland Day: Maryland.
March 26, Prince Jonah Kuhio Kalanianaole Day: Hawaii.
March (last Monday), Seward's Day: Alaska.
April 2, Pascua Florida Day: Florida
April 13, Thomas Jefferson's Birthday: Alabama, Oklahoma.
April 16, De Diego's Birthday: Puerto Rico.
April (third Monday), Patriots' Day: Maine, Massachusetts.
April 21, San Jacinto Day: Texas.
April 22, Arbor Day: Nebraska.
April 22, Oklahoma Day: Oklahoma.
April 26, Confederate Memorial Day: Florida, Georgia.
April (fourth Monday), Fast Day: New Hampshire.
April (last Monday), Confederate Memorial Day: Alabama, Mississippi.
May 1, Bird Day: Oklahoma.
May 8, Truman Day: Missouri.
May 11, Minnesota Day: Minnesota.

May 20, Mecklenburg Independence Day: North Carolina.
June (first Monday), Jefferson Davis's Birthday: Alabama, Mississippi.
June 3, Jefferson Davis's Birthday: Florida, South Carolina.
June 3, Confederate Memorial Day: Kentucky, Louisiana.
June 9, Senior Citizens Day: Oklahoma.
June 11, King Kamehameha I Day: Hawaii.
June 15, Separation Day: Delaware.
June 17, Bunker Hill Day: Massachusetts (in Suffolk County).
June 19, Emancipation Day: Texas.
June 20, West Virginia Day: West Virginia.
July 17, Muñoz Rivera's Birthday: Puerto Rico.
July 24, Pioneer Day: Utah.
July 25, Constitution Day: Puerto Rico.
July 27, Barbosa's Birthday: Puerto Rico.
August (first Sunday), American Family Day: Arizona.
August (first Monday), Colorado Day: Colorado.
August (second Monday), Victory Day: Rhode Island.
August 16, Bennington Battle Day: Vermont.
August (third Friday), Admission Day: Hawaii.
August 27, Lyndon B. Johnson's Birthday: Texas.
August 30, Huey P. Long Day: Louisiana.
September 9, Admission Day: California.
September 12, Defenders' Day: Maryland.
September 16, Cherokee Strip Day: Oklahoma.
September (first Saturday after full moon), Indian Day: Oklahoma.
October 10, Leif Erickson Day: Minnesota.
October 10, Oklahoma Historical Day: Oklahoma.
October 18, Alaska Day: Alaska.
October 31, Nevada Day: Nevada.
November 4, Will Rogers Day: Oklahoma.
November (week of the 16th), Oklahoma Heritage Week: Oklahoma.
November 19, Discovery Day: Puerto Rico.
December 7, Delaware Day: Delaware.

Movable Holidays, 1996–2000

CHRISTIAN AND SECULAR

Year	Ash Wednesday	Easter	Pentecost	Labor Day	Election Day	Thanksgiving	1st Sun. Advent
1996	Feb. 21	April 7	May 26	Sept.. 2	Nov. 5	Nov. 28	Dec. 1
1997	Feb. 12	March 30	May 18	Sept. 1	Nov. 4	Nov. 27	Nov. 30
1998	Feb. 25	April 12	May 31	Sept. 7	Nov. 3	Nov. 26	Dec. 6
1999	Feb. 17	April 4	May 23	Sept. 6	Nov. 2	Nov. 25	Nov. 28
2000	March 8	April 23	June 11	Sept. 4	Nov. 7	Nov. 23	Dec. 3

Shrove Tuesday: 1 day before Ash Wednesday
Palm Sunday: 7 days before Easter
Maundy Thursday: 3 days before Easter
Good Friday: 2 days before Easter

Holy Saturday: 1 day before Easter
Ascension Day: 10 days before Pentecost
Trinity Sunday: 7 days after Pentecost
Corpus Christi: 11 days after Pentecost

NOTE: Easter is celebrated on April 14, 1996, by the Orthodox Church.

JEWISH

Year	Purim[1]	1st day Passover[2]	1st day Shavuot[3]	1st day Rosh Hashana[4]	Yom Kippur[5]	1st day Sukkot[6]	Simhat Torah[7]	1st day Hanukkah[8]
1996	March 5	April 4	May 24	Sept. 14	Sept. 23	Sept. 28	Oct. 6	Dec. 6
1997	March 23	April 22	June 11	Oct. 2	Oct. 11	Oct. 16	Oct. 24	Dec. 24
1998	March 12	April 11	May 31	Sept. 21	Sept. 30	Oct. 5	Oct. 13	Dec. 14
1999	March 2	April 1	May 21	Sept. 11	Sept. 20	Sept. 25	Oct. 3	Dec. 4

1. Feast of Lots. 2. Feast of Unleavened Bread. 3. Hebrew Pentecost; or Feast of Weeks, or of Harvest, or of First Fruits. 4. Jewish New Year. 5. Day of Atonement. 6. Feast of Tabernacles, or of the Ingathering. 7. Rejoicing of the Law. 8. Festival of Lights.

Length of Jewish holidays (O=Orthodox, C=Conservative, R=Reform):

Passover: O & C, 8 days (holy days: first 2 and last 2); R, 7 days (holy days: first and last)
Shavuot: O & C, 2 days; R, 1 day
Rosh Hashana: O & C, 2 days; R, 1 day.
Yom Kippur: All groups, 1 day

Sukkot: All groups, 7 days (holy days: O & C, first 2; R, first only) O & C observe two additional days: Shemini Atseret (Eighth Day of the Feast) and Simhat Torah. R observes Shemini Atseret but not Simhat Torah
Hanukkah: All groups, 8 days

NOTE: All holidays begin at sundown on the evening before the date given.

Islamic 1996

Jan. 21 — First day of the month of Ramadan
Feb. 19 — 'Id al Fitr (Festival of end of Ramadan)
April 28 — 'Id al-Adha (Festival of Sacrifice at time of annual pilgrimage to Mecca)

June 14 — First day of month of Muharram (Beginning of liturgical year)
July 28 — Mawlid al-Nabi (Anniversary of Prophet Mohammad's birthday)

NOTE: All holidays begin at sundown on the evening before the date given.

Chinese Calendar

The Chinese lunar year is divided into 12 months of 29 or 30 days. The calendar is adjusted to the length of the solar year by the addition of extra months at regular intervals.

The years are arranged in major cycles of 60 years.

Each successive year is named after one of 12 animals. These 12-year cycles are continuously repeated. The Chinese New Year is celebrated at the second new moon after the winter solstice and falls between January 21 and February 19 on the Gregorian calendar.

Rat	Ox	Tiger	Cat (Rabbit)	Dragon	Snake	Horse	Sheep (Goat)	Monkey	Rooster	Dog	Pig
1900	1901	1902	1903	1904	1905	1906	1907	1908	1909	1910	1911
1912	1913	1914	1915	1916	1917	1918	1919	1920	1921	1922	1923
1924	1925	1926	1927	1928	1929	1930	1931	1932	1933	1934	1935
1936	1937	1938	1939	1940	1941	1942	1943	1944	1945	1946	1947
1948	1949	1950	1951	1952	1953	1954	1955	1956	1957	1958	1959
1960	1961	1962	1963	1964	1965	1966	1967	1968	1969	1970	1971
1972	1973	1974	1975	1976	1977	1978	1979	1980	1981	1982	1983
1984	1985	1986	1987	1988	1989	1990	1991	1992	1993	1994	1995
1996	1997	1998	1999	2000	2001	2002	2003	2004	2005	2006	2007

National Holidays Around the World, 1996

Afghanistan	Aug. 19	Ghana	March 6	Oman	Nov. 18		
Albania	Nov. 28	Greece	March 25	Pakistan	March 23		
Algeria	Nov. 1	Grenada	Feb. 7	Panama	Nov. 3		
Andorra	Sept. 8	Guatemala	Sept. 15	Papua New Guinea	Sept. 16		
Angola	Nov. 11	Guinea	Oct. 2	Paraguay	May 15		
Antigua and Barbuda	Nov. 1	Guinea-Bissau	Sept. 24	Peru	July 28		
Argentina	May 25	Guyana	Feb. 23	Philippines	June 12		
Armenia	Sept. 21	Haiti	Jan. 1	Poland	May 3		
Australia	Jan. 26	Honduras	Sept. 15	Portugal	June 10		
Austria	Oct. 26	Hungary	Aug. 20	Qatar	Sept. 3		
Azerbaijan	May 28	Iceland	June 17	Romania	Dec. 1		
Bahamas	July 10	India	Jan. 26	Rwanda	July 1		
Bahrain	Dec. 16	Indonesia	Aug. 17	St. Kitts and Nevis	Sept. 19		
Bangladesh	March 26	Iran	Feb. 11	St. Lucia	Feb. 22		
Barbados	Nov. 30	Iraq	July 17	St. Vincent and			
Belarus	July 27	Ireland	March 17	the Grenadines	Oct. 27		
Belgium	July 21	Israel	April 24[1]	Samoa	June 1		
Belize	Sept. 21	Italy	June 2	San Marino	Sept. 3		
Benin	Aug. 1	Jamaica	Aug. 5[2]	São Tomé and Príncipe	July 12		
Bhutan	Dec. 17	Japan	Dec. 23	Saudi Arabia	Sept. 23		
Bolivia	Aug. 6	Jordan	May 25	Senegal	April 4		
Botswana	Sept. 30	Kazakhstan	Oct. 25	Seychelles	June 18		
Brazil	Sept. 7	Kenya	Dec. 12	Sierra Leone	April 27		
Brunei	Feb. 23	North Korea	Sept. 9	Singapore	Aug. 9		
Bulgaria	March 3	South Korea	Aug. 15	Slovak Republic	Sept. 1		
Burkina Faso	Aug. 4	Kuwait	Feb. 25	Slovenia	June 25		
Burundi	July 1	Kyrgyzstan	Aug. 31	Solomon Islands	July 7		
Cambodia	Nov. 9	Laos	Dec. 2	Somalia	Oct. 21		
Cameroon	May 20	Latvia	Nov. 18	South Africa	May 31		
Canada	July 1	Lebanon	Nov. 22	Spain	Oct. 12		
Cape Verde	July 5	Lesotho	Oct. 4	Sri Lanka	Feb. 4		
Central African Republic	Dec. 1	Liberia	July 26	Sudan	Jan. 1		
Chad	Aug. 11	Libya	Sept. 1	Suriname	Nov. 25		
Chile	Sept. 18	Liechtenstein	Aug. 15	Swaziland	Sept. 6		
China	Oct. 1	Lithuania	Feb. 16	Sweden	June 6		
Colombia	July 20	Luxembourg	June 23	Switzerland	Aug. 1		
Comoros	July 6	Macedonia	Aug. 2	Syria	April 17		
Congo	Aug. 15	Madagascar	June 26	Tajikistan	Sept. 9		
Costa Rica	Sept. 15	Malawi	July 6	Tanzania	April 26		
Côte d'Ivoire	Dec. 7	Malaysia	Aug. 31	Thailand	Dec. 5		
Croatia	May 30	Maldives	July 26	Togo	Jan. 13		
Cuba	Jan. 1	Mali	Sept. 22	Tonga	June 4		
Cyprus	Oct. 1	Malta	Sept. 21	Trinidad and Tobago	Aug. 31		
Czech Republic	Oct. 28	Marshall Islands	May 1	Tunisia	March 20		
Denmark	April 16	Mauritania	Nov. 28	Turkey	Oct. 29		
Djibouti	June 27	Mauritius	March 12	Turkmenistan	Oct. 27		
Dominica	Nov. 3	Mexico	Sept. 16	Uganda	Oct. 9		
Dominican Republic	Feb. 27	Micronesia	Nov. 3	Ukraine	Aug. 24		
Ecuador	Aug. 10	Moldova	Aug. 27	United Arab Emirates	Dec. 2		
Egypt	July 23	Monaco	Nov. 19	United Kingdom	June 8[3]		
El Salvador	Sept. 15	Mongolia	July 11	United States	July 4		
Equatorial Guinea	Oct. 12	Morocco	March 3	Uruguay	Aug. 25		
Eritrea	May 24	Mozambique	June 25	Uzbekistan	Sept. 1		
Estonia	Feb. 24	Myanmar	Jan. 4	Vanuatu	July 30		
Ethiopia	Sept. 12	Namibia	March 21	Venezuela	July 5		
Fiji	Oct. 10	Nepal	Dec. 28	Viet Nam	Sept. 2		
Finland	Dec. 6	Netherlands	April 30	Western Samoa	June 1		
France	July 14	New Zealand	Feb. 6	Yemen, Republic of	May 22		
Gabon	Aug. 17	Nicaragua	Sept. 15	Yugoslavia	April 27		
Gambia	Feb. 18	Niger	Dec. 18	Zaire	June 30		
Georgia	May 26	Nigeria	Oct. 1	Zambia	Oct. 24		
Germany	Oct. 3	Norway	May 17	Zimbabwe	April 18		

1. Changes yearly according to Hebrew calendar. 2. Celebrated on first Monday in August. 3. Celebrated the second Saturday in June.

CONSUMER'S RESOURCE GUIDE

What You Should Know About Credit Card Blocking

Source: FDIC Consumer News, Spring 1995.

Credit card blocking is like having a slow leak in your spare tire: You are not aware of the problem until you need to do something about it.

Credit card blocking most often occurs when you rent a car or check into a hotel. It happens when you present your credit card and the clerk electronically asks the bank that issued the card to "block," or reserve, part of your line of credit to cover the expected cost before you go out and use it for your other vacation purchases. If it's a hotel, what's blocked—usually on arrival—could be the cost of your room for the length of your stay, plus incidental expenses you may incur, like meals and phone calls. In the case of cars, it could be the cost of the rental, plus gasoline. The Federal Trade Commission says the amounts that can be blocked "vary widely among merchants."

There is nothing sinister or illegal about it, as long as the amount blocked isn't out of line with what the customer is likely to pay at the end of the transaction. And most consumers are not aware that it happens at all, because the blocked amounts don't come close to their credit limits. But if you leave on vacation with your credit card near the limit, or if you are a business traveler who spends long periods on the road, you should be aware of credit blocking. This is because any additional transactions you attempt after you hit your credit limit would be rejected.

If the only block you want to be concerned with on your vacation is sun block, you might want to heed these tips from the FTC:

- Pay the bill using the same card you presented at the beginning of the transaction, so that the actual charge replaces the block in a day or two. If you use a different card to pay the bill, the block could remain on the original card for up to 15 days.
- When you check into the hotel or pick up the rental car, ask the clerk how much is being blocked, and how the amount was determined. This will allow you to factor the amount into your spending plans.
- If you use a different card or cash when it comes time to pay, ask the clerk to remove the block from the original card or call the issuer yourself.

Ruth Susswein, executive director of Bankcard Holders of America in Salem, Virginia, said some issuers will remove a block at the consumer's request, if they see the bill has been paid.

If you are trying to select from among potential credit cards, you might want to call the issuers to find out their policies on blocking, the FTC suggests.

Before you set off on your travels, you might want to call your credit card issuer and ask how long blocks are kept on credit lines. As important, Susswein said, ask how much of your credit line is available to you. ☐

Got a Yen . . . To Learn About Foreign Exchange?

Source: FDIC Consumer News, Spring 1995.

The value of the U.S. dollar has an impact on all our lives, not just those of us who travel abroad. So what does it mean when the dollar is "up" against the French franc or "down" against the Japanese yen? Is it better to have a "strong" or a "weak" dollar? Who determines the value of the dollar versus foreign currencies?

Economic conditions in the U.S. play a big role in why the dollar fluctuates in value. An example: Large trade deficits mean dollars are flooding the world markets, causing a greater supply than demand, which creates a weak dollar. And if foreign investors think U.S. interest rates are heading down, they'll put more money outside the U.S. looking for higher rates, which lessens the demand for dollars and weakens the dollar's value.

When the dollar is weak—or down—against a foreign currency, that means it takes more dollars to buy the same amount of foreign money, and items you buy while abroad will cost you more. When the dollar is strong—or up—against a foreign currency, that means it takes fewer dollars to buy the same amount of foreign money, and items you buy while abroad will cost you less (or as many like to look at it, you can buy more stuff).

Let's say you're planning a trip to England and you're told a cab ride from the airport to your hotel in London costs 25 British pounds. If it takes $1.50 to buy one British pound, that cab fare will cost the equivalent of about $37.50 ($1.50 × 25). If at the time of your trip the dollar has weakened, however, it might take $1.75 to equal one British pound. That same 25 pound cab ride would end up costing you about $6.25 more ($1.75 × 25 = $43.75). Likewise, if the dollar gets stronger, that cab ride might cost you only $1.25 per British pound, or $31.25 ($1.25 × 25 = $31.25).

This same principle applies to anything else you might buy—souvenirs, food and so on—while you're away.

Many people planning a trip try to predict what a foreign currency will be worth in the future. If they think the dollar will be strong they may hold off converting their dollars until right before they depart. Or if they think the dollar will be weaker, they may convert their dollars several weeks before they depart. It's a tough decision to make. It's like trying to predict what a stock will be worth on a certain day.

As a general rule, you shouldn't exchange all your money at one time because you could end up guessing wrong or converting too much money and losing again when you convert back to dollars or to another currency. Just because you got a good price exchanging dollars for pounds doesn't mean you'll get a good price exchanging pounds for French francs. ☐

Consumer Tips

Source: U.S. Office of Consumer Affairs.

Mail Fraud

More and more consumers are receiving misleading or downright fraudulent mail promotions. These promotions take several forms. Some examples are:
- sweepstakes that require you to pay an entry fee or order a product;
- notices of prizes that require you to call a 900 number or buy a product;
- mailings that look like they are from government agencies, but they are not;
- classified "employment" or "business opportunity" advertisements promising easy money for little work; and
- prize awards that ask for your credit card or bank account number.

Consumers should be particularly suspicious of one of the most prevalent forms of mail fraud, notices that you have received a prize, in some cases a very expensive prize like a car or vacation. Usually, you have to purchase a product, for example, a lifetime supply of cosmetics or large amounts of vitamins, to be eligible to receive the prize. In fact, few of the prizes are awarded, and of those received, most are worthless.

Contact your state or local consumer office or Better Business Bureau if you have any doubts about promotions you have received through the mail. Remember, if it sounds too good to be true, it almost certainly is. ☐

Warranties and Guarantees

An important feature to consider before buying a product or service is the warranty that comes with it. When reviewing warranties, use the guidelines below.
1. Do not wait until the product fails or needs repair to find out what is covered in the warranty.
2. If the product costs $15 or more, the law says that the seller must let you examine any warranty before you buy, if you ask to see it. So use your rights to compare the terms and conditions of warranties (or guarantees) on products or services before you buy. Look for the warranty that best meets your needs.
3. When purchasing a product or service, ask these questions:
- How long is the warranty, and when does it start and end?
- What is covered? Which parts? What kinds of problems?
- Will the warranty pay for 100% of repair costs, or will it pay for parts, but not the labor to do the repairs? Will it pay for testing the product before it is repaired? Will it pay for shipping and/or a loaner?
- What do you have to do and when? Are regular inspections or maintenance required? Do you have to ship the product out of state for repairs?
- Who offers the warranty, manufacturer or retailer? How reliable are they?
4. Keep sales receipts and warranties in a safe place.
5. Some states have additional warranty rights for consumers. Check with your state or local consumer protection office to find the laws in your state. ☐

Consumer Information Catalog

The *Consumer Information Catalog* lists approximately 200 free or low-cost Federal booklets with helpful information for consumers. Topics include careers and education, cars, child care, the environment, Federal benefits, financial planning, food and nutrition, health, housing, small business and more. This free *Catalog* is published quarterly by the Consumer Information Center of the U.S. General Services Administration. Single copies of the *Catalog* only may be ordered by sending your name and address to *Catalog,* Consumer Information Center, Pueblo, CO 81009 or by calling (719) 948-4000.

Non-profit groups that can distribute 25 copies or more each quarter can automatically receive copies by writing for a bulk mail card. ☐

Copyrights

Source: Library of Congress, Copyright Office.

On March 1, 1989, the United States joined the Berne Union by entering into an international treaty called the Berne Convention, whose full title is the Berne Convention for the Protection of Literary and Artistic Works. Also on that date, amendments to the U.S. copyright law that satisfy U.S. treaty obligations under the Convention took effect and some of them are listed herein. Contact the U.S. Copyright Office for details of Berne Convention obligations.

The U.S. Law continues to govern the protection and registration of works in the United States.

Beginning March 1, 1989, copyright in the works of U.S. authors is protected automatically in all member nations of the Berne Union and the works of foreign authors who are nationals of a Berne Union country, and works first published in a Berne Union country are automatically protected in the United States.

In order to fulfill its Berne Convention obligations, the United States made certain changes in its copyright law by passing the Berne Convention Implementation Act of 1988. These changes are not retroactive and are effective only on and after March 1, 1989.

The copyright law (Title 17 of the United States Code) was amended by the enactment of a statute for its general revision, Public Law 94–553 (90 Stat. 2541), which was signed by the President on October 19, 1976. The new law superseded the copyright act of 1909, as amended, which remained effective until the new enactment took effect on January 1, 1978.

Under the new law, all copyrightable works, whether published or unpublished, are subject to a single system of statutory protection which gives a copyright owner the exclusive right to reproduce the copyrighted work in copies or phonorecords and distribute them to the public by sale, rental, lease, or lending. Among the other rights given to the owner of a copyright are the exclusive rights to prepare derivative works based upon the copyrighted work, to perform the work publicly if it be literary, musical, dramatic, choreographic, a pantomime, motion picture, or other audiovisual work, and in the case of literary, musical, dramatic, and choreographic works, pantomimes, and pictorial, graphic, or sculptural works, including the individual images of a motion picture or other audiovisual work, to display the copyrighted work publicly. All of these rights are subject to certain exceptions, including the principle of "fair use" which the new statute specifically recognizes.

Special provisions are included which permit compulsory licensing for the recording of musical compositions, noncommercial transmissions by public broadcasters of published musical and graphic works, and the secondary transmission of copyrighted works on cable television systems; and voluntary licensing for performances of copyrighted music by jukeboxes.

Copyright protection under the new law extends to original works of authorship fixed in a tangible medium of expression, from which they can be perceived, reproduced, or otherwise communicated, either directly or with the aid of a machine or device. Works of authorship include books, periodicals and other literary works, musical compositions with accompanying lyrics, dramas and dramatico-musical compositions, pantomimes and choreographic works, motion pictures and other audiovisual works, sound recordings, and works of the visual arts.

As a mandatory condition of copyright protection under the law in effect before 1978, all published copies of a work were required to bear a copyright notice. The 1976 Act requires that all visually perceptible copies published in the United States or elsewhere bear a notice of copyright affixed in such manner and location as to give reasonable notice of the claim of copyright. (Abolished in or after March 1, 1989, according to the Berne agreement) The notice consists of the symbol © (the letter C in a circle), the word "Copyright," or the abbreviation "Copr.," and the year of first publication of the work, and the name of the owner of copyright in the work. EXAMPLE: © *1996 John Doe.*

The notice of copyright prescribed for sound recordings consists of the symbol ℗ (the letter P in a circle), the year of first publication of the sound recording, and the name of the owner of copyright in the sound recording, placed on the surface of the phonorecord, or on the phonorecord label or container, in such manner and location as to give reasonable notice of the claim of copyright. EXAMPLE: ℗ *1996 Doe Records, Inc.* Omission or errors in the notice will not immediately result in forfeiture of the copyright, and can be corrected within certain time limits. Innocent infringers misled by the omission or error may be shielded from liability.

In accordance with the Berne agreement, mandatory notice of copyright has been abolished for works published for the first time on or after March 1, 1989. Failure to place a notice of copyright on copies or phonorecords of such works can no longer result in the loss of copyright. Nevertheless, copyright owners must deposit in the Copyright Office two complete copies or phonorecords of the best edition of all works subject to copyright that are publicly distributed in the United States, whether or not the work contains a notice of copyright. In general, this deposit requirement may be satisfied by registration. For more information about mandatory deposit, request Circular 7d.

Voluntary use of notice is encouraged. Placing a notice of copyright on published works is still strongly recommended. One of the benefits is that an infringer will not be able to claim that he or she "innocently infringed" a work. (A successful innocent infringement claim may result in a reduction in damages for infringement that the copyright owner would otherwise receive.)

The notice requirement for works incorporating a predominant portion of U.S. government work has been eliminated as of March 1, 1989. For these works to receive the evidentiary benefit of voluntary notice, in addition to the notice, a statement is required on the copies identifying what is copyrighted.

A sample is: © 1994 Jane Brown. Copyright claimed in Chapters 7–10, exclusive of U.S. government maps.

Notice Unchanged for Works Published Before March 1, 1989

The Berne Convention Implementation Act is not retroactive. Thus, the notice requirements that were in place before March 1, 1989, govern all works first published during that period (regardless of national origin).

• Works first published between January 1, 1978, and February 28, 1989: If a work was first published without notice during this period, it is still necessary to register the work before or within five years after publication and add the notice to copies distributed in the United States after discovery of the omission.

• Works first published before January 1, 1978: If a work was first published without the required notice before 1978, copyright was lost immediately (with the possible exception of works seeking "ad interim" protection). Once copyright is lost, it can never be restored in the United States, except by special legislation.

Registration in the Copyright Office is not a condition of copyright protection but will be a prerequisite to bringing an action in a court of law for infringement. With certain exceptions, the remedies of statutory damages and attorney's fees will not be available for infringements occurring before registration. Most copies or phonorecords published in the United States with notice of copyright are required to be deposited for the collections of the Library of Congress, not as a condition of copyright protection, but under provisions of the law subjecting the copyright owner to certain penalties for failure to deposit after a demand by the Register of Copyrights. Registration is permissive, but may be made either at the time the depository requirements are satisfied or at any other time during the subsistence of the copyright.

For works protected under the 1909 Act, the new law retains the term of copyright of 28 years from first publication (or from registration in some cases), renewable by certain persons for a second period of protection, but it increases the length of the second period to 47 years.

Copyrights in their first term on January 1, 1978, *may* still be renewed to receive the maximum statutory term of 75 years (a first term of 28 years plus a renewal term of 47 years). Registering such renewal in the Copyright Office during the last (28th) year of the original copyright, or at any time during the renewed and extended term, accrues certain legal benefits:

• The renewal copyright will vest in the name of the renewal claimant on the effective date of the renewal registration;

• The renewal registration will constitute *prima facie* evidence as to the validity of the facts stated in the renewal certificate and the copyright in the renewed and extended term; and,

• The right to utilize the derivative work in the extended term may be affected.

However, recent legislation (Public Law 102-307, effective June 26, 1992) has made the renewal of works published or registered between January 1, 1964, and December 31, 1977, *automatic,* and the formality of registering such renewal in the Copyright Office *optional.*

Copyrights in their second term on January 1, 1978, are automatically extended up to a maximum of 75 years. Unpublished works that are already in existence on January 1, 1978, but are not protected by statutory copyright and have not yet gone into the public domain, will generally obtain automatic Federal copyright protection for the author's life, plus an additional 50 years after the author's death, but in any event, for a minimal term of 25 years (that is, until December 31, 2002), and if the work is published before that date, then for an additional term of 25 years, through the end of 2027.

For works created on or after January 1, 1978, the new law provides a term lasting for the author's life, plus an additional 50 years after the author's death. For works made for hire, and for anonymous and pseudonymous works (unless the author's identity is revealed in Copyright Office records), the new term will be 75 years from publication or 100 years from creation, whichever is shorter. The new law provides that all terms of copyright will run through the end of the calendar year in which they would otherwise expire. This will not only affect the duration of copyrights, but also the time-limits for renewal registrations.

Works already in the public domain cannot be protected under the new law. The 1976 Act provides no procedure for restoring protection to works in which copyright has been lost for any reason. In general, works published before January 1, 1921, are not under copyright protection in the United States, at least insofar as any version published before that date is concerned.

Recordation

Recordation as a Prerequisite to an Infringement Suit. The copyright owner no longer has to record a transfer before bringing a copyright lawsuit in that owner's name.

Benefits of recordation. The benefits of recordation in the Copyright Office are unchanged:

- Under certain conditions, recordation establishes priorities between conflicting transfers and nonexclusive licenses;
- Under certain conditions, recordation establishes priority between conflicting transfers; and,
- Recordation establishes a public record of the contents of the transfer or document.

Jukebox Licenses

Section 116 of the 1976 Copyright Act provides for a compulsory license to publicly perform nondra-matic musical works by means of coin-operated phonorecord players (jukeboxes). The Berne Convention Implementation Act amends the law to provide for negotiated licenses between the user (the jukebox operator) and the copyright owner. If necessary, the parties are encouraged to submit to arbitration to facilitate negotiated licenses. Such licenses take precedence over the compulsory license.

For detailed information about the amendments to U.S. copyright law under the Berne Convention agreement, request circulars 93, "Highlights of U.S. Adherence to the Berne Convention," and 93a, "The United States Joins The Berne Union" from the Copyright Office.

For publications, call the Forms and Publications Hotline, 202-707-9100, or write:

Copyright Office
Publications Section, LM-455
Library of Congress
Washington, D.C. 20559

To speak with an information specialist or to request further information, call 202-707-3000, or write:

Copyright Office
Information Section, LM-401
Library of Congress
Washington, D.C. 20559

Counterfeit Products

Source: U.S. Office of Consumer Affairs.

Counterfeit products include any product bearing an unauthorized representation of a manufacturer's trademark or trade name. Examples of products which have been counterfeited include prescription and over-the-counter drugs, clothing, credit cards, watches, pacemakers, and machine and automobile replacement parts. Because counterfeit products are often of sub-standard quality, there are potential safety risks which may cause personal injury as well as economic loss.

Avoiding counterfeit products takes practice. The following are usually associated with counterfeit products:

- incorrect, smeared or blurred product packaging
- incorrect spelling of brand name
- no warranty or guarantee available
- "unbelievably" low prices

Unemployment Insurance

Unemployment insurance is managed jointly by the states and the federal government. Most states began paying benefits in 1938 and 1939.

Under What Conditions Can the Worker Collect?

The laws vary from state to state. In general, a waiting period of one week is required in most states after a claim is filed before collecting unemployment insurance; the worker must be able to work, must not have quit without good cause or have been discharged for misconduct; he must not be involved in a labor dispute; above all, he must be ready and willing to work. He may be disqualified if he refuses, without good cause, to accept a job which is suitable for him in terms of his qualifications and experience, unless the wages, hours and working conditions offered are substantially less favorable than those prevailing for similar jobs in the community.

The unemployed worker must go to the local state employment security office and register for work. If that office has a suitable opening available, he must accept it or lose his unemployment payments, unless he has good cause for the refusal. If a worker moves out of his own state, he can still collect at his new residence; the state in which he is now located will act as agent for the other state, which will pay his benefits.

Benefits are paid only to unemployed workers who have had at least a certain amount of recent past employment or earnings in a job covered by the state law. The amount of employment or earnings, and the period used to measure them, vary from state to state, but the intent of the various laws is to limit benefits to workers whose recent records indicate that they are members of the labor force. The amount of benefits an unemployed worker may receive for any week is also determined by application to his past wages of a formula specified in the law. The general objective is to provide a weekly benefit which is about half the worker's customary weekly wages, up to a maximum set by the law (see table). In a majority of states, the total benefits a worker may receive in a 12-month period is limited to a fraction of his total wages in a prior 12-month period, as well as to a stated number of weeks. Thus, not all workers in a state are entitled to benefits for the number of weeks shown in the table.

Who Pays for the Insurance?

The total cost is borne by the employer in all but a few states. Each state has a sliding scale of rates. The standard rate is set at 6.2% of taxable payroll in most states. But employers with records of less unemployment (that is, with fewer unemployment benefits paid to their former workers) are rewarded with rates lower than the standard state rate.

During periods of high unemployment in a state, federal-state extended benefits are available to workers who have exhausted their regular benefits. An unemployed worker may receive benefits equal to the weekly benefit he received under the state program for one half the weeks of his basic entitlement to benefits up to a maximum (including regular benefits) of 39 weeks.

Federal Programs

Amendments to the Social Security Act provided unemployment insurance for Federal civilian employees (1954) and for ex-servicemen (1958). Benefits under these programs are paid by state employment security agencies as agents of the federal government under agreements with the Secretary of Labor. For federal civilian employees and ex-servicemembers, eligibility for benefits and the amount of benefits paid are determined according to the terms and conditions of the applicable state unemployment insurance law.

State Unemployment Compensation Maximums, 1995

State	Weekly benefit[1]	Maximum duration, weeks	State	Weekly benefit[1]	Maximum duration, weeks
Alabama	180	26	Nebraska	184	26
Alaska	212–284	26	Nevada	235	26
Arizona	185	26	New Hampshire	204	26
Arkansas	256	26	New Jersey	354	26
California	230	26	New Mexico	205	26
Colorado	267	26	New York	300	26
Connecticut	335–385	26	North Carolina	289	26
Delaware	265	26	North Dakota	237	26
D.C.	347	26	Ohio	245–328	26
Florida	250	26	Oklahoma	245	26
Georgia	195	26	Oregon	292	26
Hawaii	344	26	Pennsylvania	340–348	26
Idaho	240	26	Puerto Rico	133	26
Illinois	235–311	26	Rhode Island	317–396	26
Indiana	202	26	South Carolina	207	26
Iowa	216–265	26	South Dakota	174	26
Kansas	255	26	Tennessee	200	26
Kentucky	232	26	Texas	252	26
Louisiana	181	26	Utah	253	26
Maine	192–288	26	Vermont	210	26
Maryland	223	26	Virgin Islands	223	26
Massachusetts	336–504	30	Virginia	208	26
Michigan	293	26	Washington	343	30
Minnesota	304	26	West Virginia	282	26
Mississippi	165	26	Wisconsin	266	26
Missouri	175	26	Wyoming	229	26
Montana	223	26			

1. Maximum amounts. When two amounts are shown, higher includes dependents' allowances. *Source:* Department of Labor, Employment and Training Administration.

Trademarks

Source: Department of Commerce, Patent and Trademark Office.

A trademark may be defined as a word, letter, device, or symbol, as well as some combination of these, which is used in connection with merchandise and which points distinctly to the origin of the goods.

Certificates of registration of trademarks are issued under the seal of the Patent and Trademark Office and may be registered by the owner if he is engaged in interstate or foreign commerce which may lawfully be regulated by Congress since any Federal jurisdiction over trademarks arises under the commerce clause of the Constitution. Effective November 16, 1989, applications to register may also be based on a "bona fide intention to use the mark in commerce." Trademarks may be registered by foreign owners who comply with our law, as well as by citizens of foreign countries with which the U.S. has treaties relating to trademarks. American citizens may register trademarks in foreign countries by complying with the laws of those countries. The right to registration and protection of trademarks in many foreign countries is guaranteed by treaties.

General jurisdiction in trademark cases involving Federal Registrations is given to Federal courts. Adverse decisions of examiners on applications for registration are appealable to the Trademark Trial and Appeal Board, whose affirmances, and decisions in *inter partes* proceedings, are subject to court review. Before adopting a trademark, a person should make a search of prior marks to avoid infringing unwittingly upon them.

The duration of a trademark registration is 10 years, but it may be renewed indefinitely for 10-year periods, provided the trademark is still in use at the time of expiration.

The application fee is $245 per class.

Patents

Source: Department of Commerce, Patent and Trademark Office.

A patent, in the most general sense, is a document issued by a government, conferring some special right or privilege. The term is now restricted mainly to patents for inventions; occasionally, land patents.

The grant of a patent for an invention gives the inventor the privilege, for a limited period of time, of excluding others from making, using, or selling a certain article.

In the U.S., the law provides that a patent may be granted, for a term of 20* years, to any person who has invented or discovered any new and useful art, machine, manufacture, or composition of matter, as well as any new and useful improvements thereof. A patent may also be granted to a person who has invented or discovered and asexually reproduced a new and distinct variety of plant (other than a tuber-propagated one) or has invented a new, original and ornamental design for an article of manufacture for a term of 20 years and 14 years, respectively.

A patent is granted only upon a regularly filed application, complete in all respects; upon payment of the fees; and upon determination that the disclosure is complete and that the invention is new, useful, and, in view of the prior art, unobvious to one skilled in the art. The disclosure must be of such nature as to enable others to reproduce the invention.

A complete application, which must be addressed to the Commissioner of Patents and Trademarks, Washington, D.C. 20231, consists of a specification with one or more claims; oath or declaration; drawing (whenever the nature of the case admits of it); and a basic filing fee of $365.[1] The filing fee is not returned to the applicant if the patent is refused. If the patent is allowed, another fee of $605[1] is required before the patent is issued. The fee for design patent application is $150; the issue fee is $210[1]. The fee for a plant patent application is $245; the issue fee is $305. Maintenance fees are required on utility patents at stipulated intervals.

Applications are ordinarily considered in the order in which they are received. Patents are not granted for printed matter, for methods of doing business, or for devices for which claims contrary to natural laws are made. Applications for a perpetual-motion machine have been made from time to time, but until a working model is presented that actually fulfills the claim, no patent will be issued.

*As a result of the GATT Uruguay Round implementing legislation, the term of utility and plant patents is 20 years measured from the date of filing an application in the U.S. effective June 8, 1995.

1. Fees quoted are for small entities. Fees are double for corporations.

Beware of Illegal Patent Services

It is illegal under patent law (35 USC 33) for anyone to hold himself out as qualified to prepare and prosecute patent applications unless he is registered with the Patent Office. Also, Patent Office regulations forbid registered practitioners advertising for patent business. Some inventors, unaware of this, enter into binding contracts with persons and firms which advertise their assistance in making patent searches, preparing drawings, specifications, and patent applications, only to discover much later that their applications require the services of fully qualified agents or attorneys.

Birthstones

Month	Stone	Month	Stone
January	Garnet	July	Ruby or Star Ruby
February	Amethyst	August	Peridot or Sardonyx
March	Aquamarine or Bloodstone	September	Sapphire or Star Sapphire
April	Diamond	October	Opal or Tourmaline
May	Emerald	November	Topaz or Citrine
June	Pearl, Alexandrite or Moonstone	December	Turquoise, Lapis Lazuli, Blue Zircon or Blue Topaz

Source: Jewelry Industry Council.

How to Write a Complaint Letter

Source: United States Office of Consumer Affairs.

• Include your name, address, and home and work phone numbers.

• Type your letter if possible. If it is handwritten, make sure it is neat and easy to read.

• Make your letter brief and to the point. Include all important facts about your purchase, including the date and place where you made the purchase and any information you can give about the product or service such as serial or model numbers or specific type of service.

• State exactly what you want done about the problem and how long you are willing to wait to get it resolved. Be reasonable.

• Include all documents regarding your problem. Be sure to send COPIES, not originals.

• Avoid writing an angry, sarcastic, or threatening letter. The person reading your letter probably was not responsible for your problem, but may be very helpful in resolving it.

• Keep a copy of the letter for your records.

```
                    (Your Address)
                    (Your City, State, ZIP Code)
                    (Date)

(Name of Contact Person, if available)
(Title, if available)
(Company Name)
(Consumer Complaint Division, if you have no contact
person)
(Street Address)
(City, State, ZIP Code)

Dear (Contact Person):

Re: (account number, if applicable)

  On (date), I (bought, leased, rented, or had re-
paired) a (name of the product with serial or model
number or service performed) at (location, date and
other important details of the transaction).

Unfortunately, your product (or service) has not
performed well (or the service was inadequate) be-
cause (state the problem). I am disappointed because
(explain the problem: for example, the product does
not work properly, the service was not performed
correctly, I was billed the wrong amount, something
was not disclosed clearly or was misrepresented,
etc.)

To resolve the problem, I would appreciate your
(state the specific action you want—money back,
charge card credit, repair, exchange, etc.) Enclosed
are copies (do not send originals) of my records
(include receipts, guarantees, warranties, canceled
checks, contracts, model and serial numbers, and any
other documents).

I look forward to your reply and a resolution to
my problem, and will wait until (set a time limit)
before seeking help from a consumer protection
agency or the Better Business Bureau. Please contact
me at the above address or by phone at (home and/or
office numbers with area codes).

                    Sincerely,



                    (your name)

Enclosure(s)
cc: (reference to whom you are sending a copy of
this letter, if anyone)
```

WHERE TO FIND OUT MORE

Reference Books and Other Sources

This cannot be a record of all the thousands of available sources of information. Nevertheless, these selected references will enable the reader to locate additional facts about many subjects covered in the *Information Please Almanac*. The editors have chosen sources that they believe will be helpful to the general reader.

General References

Encyclopedias are a unique category, since they attempt to cover most subjects quite thoroughly. The most valuable multivolume encyclopedias are the **Encyclopaedia Britannica** and the **Encyclopedia Americana.** Useful one-volume encyclopedias are **The Columbia Encyclopedia 5th Edition** (Houghton Mifflin) and the **Random House Encyclopedia.**

Dictionaries and similar "word books" are also unique: **The American Heritage Dictionary, Second College Edition,** containing 200,000 definitions and specialized usage guidance; **The American Heritage Illustrated Encyclopedic Dictionary,** containing 180,000 entries, 275 boxed encyclopedic features, and 175 colored maps of the world; **Webster's Third New International Dictionary, Unabridged; Webster's II New Riverside University Dictionary,** containing 200,000 definitions plus hundreds of word history paragraphs; and the multivolume **Oxford English Dictionary,** providing definitions in historical order. **Roget's II The New Thesaurus,** containing thousands of synonyms grouped according to meaning, assists writers in choosing just the right word. The quick reference set—**The Word Book III** (over 40,000 words spelled and divided), **The Right Word III** (a concise thesaurus), and **The Written Word III** (a concise guide to writing, style, and usage)—are based on **The American Heritage Dictionary** and are intended for the busy reader needing information fast. Two excellent books of quotations are **Bartlett's Familiar Quotations** and **The Oxford Dictionary of Quotations.**

There are a number of useful atlases including **Times Atlas of the World, 9th Comprehensive Edition,** and the **Oxford Economic Atlas of the World.** Many contemporary road atlases of the United States and foreign countries are also available.

A source of information on virtually all subjects is the United States Government Printing Office (GPO). For information, write: Superintendent of Documents, Washington, D.C. 20402.

For help on any subject, consult: **Subject Guide to Books in Print, The New York Times Index,** and the **Reader's Guide to Periodical Literature** in your library.

Specific References

Address Book, The (Berkley)
AIDS Answer Book (ETR Assoc.)
America Votes (Congressional Quarterly, Inc.)
American Indian, Reference Encyclopedia of the (Todd Publications)
American Recipe Collection (Lifetime)
American Revolution, The (Houghton Mifflin)

Anatomy, Gray's (Churchill)
Antique Trader, Antiques and Collectibles Price Guide 1995: A Comprehensive Price Guide to the Entire Field of Antiques and Collectibles (Antique Trader)
Architectural & Building Technology, Dictionary of (Elsevier)
Art, History of (Abrams)
Art, Oxford Companion to (Oxford University Press)
Art, Who's Who in American (R.R. Bowker)
Art Directory, 1995–96, American (R.R. Bowker)
Associations, Encyclopedia of (Gale Research Co.)
Astronomy, Peterson First Guide (Houghton Mifflin)
Authors, 1000–1900, European (H.W. Wilson)
Authors, Twentieth Century (H.W. Wilson)
Automobile Facts and Figures (Kallman)
Automotive Yearbook (Wards Communication)
Ballet, Dictionary of Terms (Da Capo)
Banking and Finance, Encyclopedia of (Probus Publishing Co.)
Baseball Encyclopedia (Macmillan)
Biographical Dictionary, Cambridge (Cambridge University Press)
Biography Yearbook, Current (H.W. Wilson)
Birds, Field Guide to the, Peterson Field Guide Series (Houghton Mifflin)
Black Americans, Who's Who Among (Gale)
Book Review Digest, 1905–1994 (H.W. Wilson)
Business Almanac and Desk Reference, 1995 Information Please (Houghton Mifflin)
Catholic Encyclopedia, New (J. Heraty Assocs.)
Chemistry, Lange's Handbook of, 14th Edition (McGraw Hill)
Christian Church, Oxford Dictionary of the (Oxford University Press)
College Cost & Financial Aid Handbook, 1995 (The College Board)
Composers, Great 1300–1900 (H.W. Wilson)
Composers Since 1900 (H.W. Wilson)
Computer Science and Technology, Encyclopedia of (Dekker)
Computer Software (Harcourt Brace)
Computer Wisdom, The Little Book of (Houghton Mifflin)
Computer Words, Dictionary of (Houghton Mifflin)
Condo and Co-op Information Book, Complete (Houghton Mifflin)
Consumer Reports (Consumers Union)
Costume, The Dictionary of (Macmillan)
Cultural Literacy, The Dictionary of (Houghton Mifflin)
Drama As You'll Like It (DOK Publications)
Ecology (Dorling Kindersley)
Energy: Facts and Future (CRC Printing)
Environmental Politics and Policy, 2nd Edition (Congressional Quarterly)
Environmental Science, 4th Edition (Macmillan)
Europa World Year Book 1993 (Gale)
Fact Books, The Rand McNally (Macmillan)
Facts, Famous First (H.W. Wilson)
Facts on File (Facts on File, Inc.)

Film: A Reference Guide (Greenwood)
(Film) Leonard Maltin's Movie & Video Guide 1995, 25th Anniversary Edition (NAL–Dutton)
(Finance) Touche Ross Guide to Personal Financial Management (Prentice-Hall)
Football Made Easy (Jonathan David)
Games, Book of (Jazz Press)
Gardening, Wyman's Encyclopedia of: Updated Edition (Macmillan)
Gardening, Taylor's Pocket Guides (Houghton Mifflin)
Geography, Dictionary of (Penguin Books)
Government Manual, U.S. (U.S. Office of the Federal Register, Government Printing Office)
Health Care Choices for Today's Consumer: The Families USA Guide to Quality & Cost (Families USA Foundation)
History, Album of American (Macmillan)
History, Dictionary of American (Littlefield)
History, Documents of American (Prentice-Hall)
History, Encyclopedia of Latin-American (Greenwood)
History, Encyclopedia of World (Houghton Mifflin)
Hockey, the Illustrated History: An Official Publication of the National Hockey League (Doubleday)
Homosexuality: Lesbian and Gay Men in Society, History, and Literature (Hyer); **Understanding Homosexuality** (Crossroad Publishing Co., N.Y.)
How the World Works, A Guide to Science's Greatest Discoveries (Quill/William Morrow)
Islam, Dictionary of (Kazi Publications)
Jazz in the Seventies, Encyclopedia of (Da Capo)
Jewish Concepts, Encyclopedia of (Hebrew Publishers)
Legal Word Book, The (Houghton Mifflin)
Libraries, World Guide to (K. G. Saur)
Library Directory, 1994–95 American (R.R. Bowker)
Literary Market Place (R. R. Bowker)
Literature, Oxford Companion to American (Oxford University Press)
Literature, Oxford Companion to Classical (Oxford University Press)
Literature, Oxford Companion to English (Oxford University Press)
(Literature) Reader's Adviser: A Layman's Guide to Literature (R.R. Bowker)
Medical Encyclopedia, Home (Bern Porter)
Medical & Health Sciences Word Book (Houghton Mifflin)
Museums of the World (K.G. Saur)
Music and Musicians, Handbook of American (Da Capo)
Music, Concise Oxford Dictionary of (Oxford University Press)
Music, Harvard Dictionary of (Belknap Press)
Musical Terms, Dictionary of (Gordon Press)
Mystery Writers, Twentieth Century Crime and (St. Martin's Press)
Mythology (Little, Brown and Co.)
National Park Guide (Prentice-Hall)
New Nations: A Student Handbook (Shoe String)
Numismatist's Fireside Companion, Vol. 2 (Bowers & Merena)
Occupational Outlook Handbook (U.S. Bureau of Labor Statistics, Government Printing Office)
Operas, New Milton Cross Complete Stories of the Great (Doubleday)
Performing Arts Information (Kansas State University)
Physics (Wiley)
Pocket Data Book, U.S.A. (U.S. Department of Commerce, Bureau of the Census, Government Printing Office)

Poetry, Granger's Index to (Columbia University Press)
Politics, Almanac of American (National Journal)
Politics, Who's Who in American (R.R. Bowker)
Popular Music, American, Vol. 2 The Age of Rock (Bowling Green University)
Prescription & Non-Prescription Drugs, Complete Guide to, 1994 Edition (Putnam)
Private Schools of the United States Council for American Private Education Schools 1992 Edition (Market Data Res.)
Radon, A Citizen's Guide to (Government Printing Office)
Religions, The Facts on File Dictionary of (Facts on File)
Robert's Rules of Order Revised (Morrow & Co.)
Science, American Men and Women of (R.R. Bowker)
Science and Technology, Asimov's Biographical Encyclopedia of (Doubleday)
Scientific Encyclopedia, VanNostrand's (VanNostrand Reinhold)
Secretary's Handbook, The Professional (Houghton Mifflin)
Senior Citizens Information Resources, Encyclopedia of (Gale Research Co.)
Shakespeare, The Riverside (Houghton Mifflin)
Ships, Boats, & Vessels, Illustrated Encyclopedia of (Overlook Press)
Social Security Handbook (USGPO)
Sports Almanac, 1996 Information Please (Houghton Mifflin)
Stamp Collecting for Beginners (Wilshire)
Stars and Planets, Field Guide to the (Houghton Mifflin)
States, Book of the (Council of State Governments)
Statesman's Year-Book 1994–95 (St. Martin's)
Theater, Oxford Companion to the (Oxford University Press)
United Nations, Demographic Yearbook (Unipub)
United Nations, Statistical Yearbook of the (Unipub)
United States, Historical Statistics of the Colonial Times to 1970 (Revisionist Press)
United States, Statistical Abstract of the (U.S. Department of Commerce, Bureau of the Census, Government Printing Office)
Vitamin Book: A No-Nonsense Consumer Guide (Bantam)
Washington Information Directory 1993–94 (Congressional Quarterly, Inc.)
The Way Things Work (Houghton Mifflin)
Who's Who in America (Marquis)
Wines & Spirits, Alexis Lichine's New Encyclopedia of (Knopf)
Women, Notable American (Harvard University Press)
Writer's Market (Writers Digest)
Zip Code and Post Office Directory, National (U.S. Postal Service, Government Printing Office)

See the full range of publications of Dun & Bradstreet and Standard & Poor's for corporate financial and stockholder information.

For detailed information on American colleges and universities, see the many publications of the **American Council on Education.**

Also see many other specialized **Who's Who** volumes not listed here for biographies of famous people in many fields.

U.S. SOCIETIES & ASSOCIATIONS

Source: Information Please questionnaires to organizations. Names are listed alphabetically according to key word in title; figure in parentheses is year of founding; other figure is membership. An asterisk (*) before a name indicates that up-to-date information has not been provided.

The following is a partial list selected for general readership interest. A comprehensive listing of approximately 20,000 national and international organizations can be found in the **"Encyclopedia of Associations,"** 20th Ed., 1986, Vol. I, Parts 1-3 (Katherine Gruber, Editor; Iris Cloyd, Research Editor), published by Gale Research Company, Book Tower, Detroit, Mich. 48226, available in most public libraries.

AARP (American Association of Retired Persons) (1958): 601 E St. N.W., Washington, D.C. 20049. 32,000,000. Phone: (202) 434-2277.

Abortion Federation, National (1977): 1436 U St. N.W., Suite 103, Washington, D.C. 20009. Phone: (202) 667-5881 or (800) 772-9100.

Accountants, American Institute of Certified Public (1887): 1211 Avenue of the Americas, New York, N.Y. 10036-8775. 320,000. Phone: (212) 596-6200.

Acoustical Society of America (1929): 500 Sunnyside Blvd., Woodbury, N.Y. 11797. 7,000. Phone: (516) 576-2360.

ACSM: American Congress on Surveying and Mapping (1941): 5410 Grosvenor Lane, Bethesda, Md. 20814. 8,000. Phone: (301) 493-0200.

Actors' Equity Association (1913): 165 W. 46th St., New York, N.Y. 10036. Phone: (212) 869-8530.

Actuaries, Society of (1949): 475 N. Martingale Rd., Suite 800, Schaumburg, Ill. 60173-2226. 16,500. Phone: (708) 706-3500.

Adirondack Mountain Club (1922): RR 3, Box 3055, Luzerne Rd., Lake George, N.Y. 12845. 20,000+. Phone: (518) 668-4447.

Aeronautic Association, National (1905): 1815 N. Fort Myer Dr., Suite 700, Arlington, Va. 22209. 300,000. Phone: (703) 527-0226.

*****Aeronautics and Astronautics, American Institute of** (1930): 370 L'Enfant Promenade S.W., Washington, D.C. 20024-2518. 40,000+. Phone: (202) 646-7400.

Aerospace Industries Association of America Inc. (1919): 1250 Eye St. N.W., Washington, D.C. 20005. 50 companies. Phone: (202) 371-8400.

Aerospace Medical Association (1929): 320 S. Henry St., Alexandria, Va. 22314-3579. 4,000. Phone: (703) 739-2240.

African-American Institute, The (1953): 833 United Nations Plaza, New York, N.Y. 10017. Phone: (212) 949-5666.

Aging Association, American (1970): 2129 Providence Ave., Chester, Pa. 19013. 500. Phone: (610) 874-7550.

Agricultural History Society (1919): 1301 New York Ave. N.W., Washington, D.C. 20005-4788. 1,400. Phone: (202) 219–0786.

Agronomy, American Society of (1907): 677 S. Segoe Rd., Madison, Wis. 53711-1086. 13,000. Phone: (608) 273-8080.

Air & Waste Management Association (1907): One Gateway Center, 3rd Floor, Pittsburgh, Pa. 15222. Phone: (412) 232-3444.

Aircraft Association, Experimental (1953): 3000 Poberezny Rd., Oshkosh, Wis. 54903-3086. 130,000. Phone: (414) 426-4800.

Aircraft Owners and Pilots Association (1939): 421 Aviation Way, Frederick, Md. 21701-4798. 325,000. Phone: (301) 695-2000.

Air Force Association (1946): 1501 Lee Highway, Arlington, Va. 22209-1198. 173,000. Phone: (703) 247-5800.

Air Line Pilots Association (1931): 1625 Massachusetts Ave. N.W., Washington, D.C. 20036 and 535 Herndon Pkwy., Herndon, Va. 22070. 43,000. Phone: (703) 689-2270.

Air Transport Association of America (1936): 1301 Pennsylvania Ave. N.W., Washington, D.C. 20004-1707. 20 airlines. Phone: (202) 626-4000.

Al-Anon Family Group Headquarters, Inc. For families and friends of alcoholics. (1951): P.O. Box 862, Midtown Station, New York, N.Y. 10018-0862. 31,000 groups worldwide. Phone: (800) 356-9996.

Alateen. For children of alcoholics: P.O. Box 862, Midtown Station, New York, N.Y. 10018-0862. 4,100 groups worldwide. Phone: (800) 356–9996.

Alcoholics Anonymous (1935): General Service Office, A.A. World Services, Inc., 475 Riverside Dr., 11th Floor, New York, N.Y. 10115. 1,800,000. Phone: (212) 870-3400.

Alcoholism and Drug Dependence, National Council on (1944): 12 W. 21st St., New York, N.Y. 10010. 150 affiliates. Phone: (212) 206-6770.

Alcohol Problems, American Council on (1895): 3426 Bridgeland Dr., Bridgeton, Mo. 63044. 3,500. Phone: (314) 739-5944.

Alexander Graham Bell Association for the Deaf (1890): 3417 Volta Place N.W., Washington, D.C. 20007. 6,000. Phone: (202) 337-5220.

Allergy, Asthma, and Immunology, American Academy of (1943): 611 E. Wells St., Milwaukee, Wis. 53202. 5,000. Phone: (414) 272-6071.

Alzheimer's Disease and Related Disorders Association, Inc. (1980): 919 N. Michigan Ave., Suite 1000, Chicago, Ill. 60611-1676. More than 200 Chapters and Affiliates, over 2,000 Family Support Groups. Phone: (312) 335-8700; toll-free (800) 272-3900.

AMBUCS (1922): 3315 No. Main St., High Point, N.C. 27265. 7,000. Phone: (910) 869-2166.

American Alliance for Health, Physical Education, Recreation and Dance (1885): 1900 Association Dr., Reston, Va. 22091. 35,000. Phone: (703) 476-3400.

American Antiquarian Society (1812): 185 Salisbury St., Worcester, Mass. 01609. 600. Phone: (508) 755-5221.

American Automobile Association (1902): 1000 AAA Dr., Heathrow, Fla. 32746-5063. Phone: (407) 444-7000.

American Civil Liberties Union (1920): 132 W. 43rd St., New York, N.Y. 10036. 290,000. Phone: (212) 944-9800.

American Contract Bridge League (1927): 2990 Airways Blvd., Memphis, Tenn. 38116-3847. Phone: (901) 332-5586.

American Electroplaters and Surface Finishers Society (AESF) (1909): 12644 Research Pkwy.,

Orlando, Fla. 32826. 7,500. Phone: (407) 281-6441.

American Federation of Labor and Congress of Industrial Organizations (AFL-CIO) (1955): 815 16th St. N.W., Washington, D.C. 20006. 14,500,000. Phone: (202) 637-5000.

American Federation of Musicians of the United States and Canada (1896): 1501 Broadway, Suite 600 Paramount Bldg., New York, N.Y. 10036. Phone: (212) 869-1330.

American Field Service (1947): 220 E. 42nd St., 3rd Floor, New York, N.Y. 10017. 135,000. Phone: (212) 949-4242 or (800) AFS-INFO.

American Forest Foundation (1932): 1111 19th St. N.W., Suite 780, Washington, D.C. 20036. 100. Phone: (202) 463-2462.

American Forests (1875): 1516 P St. N.W., Washington, D.C. 20005. 115,000. Phone: (202) 667-3300.

American Foundrymen's Society, Inc. (1896): 505 State St., Des Plaines, Ill. 60016-8399. 14,000. Phone: (708) 824-0181.

American Friends Service Committee (1917): 1501 Cherry St., Philadelphia, Pa. 19102-1479. Phone: (215) 241-7000.

American Geographical Society, The (1851): 156 Fifth Ave., Suite 600, New York, N.Y. 10010-7002. 1,500. Phone: (212) 242-0214.

American Historical Association (1884): 400 A St. S.E., Washington, D.C. 20003. 19,000. Phone: (202) 544-2422.

American Hospital Association (1899): One North Franklin, Chicago, Ill. 60606. 5,000 institutions. Phone: (312) 422-3000.

American Indian Affairs, Association on (1923): 245 Fifth Ave., New York, N.Y. 10016-8728. 40,000. Phone: (212) 689-8720.

American Jail Association (1981): 2053 Day Rd., Suite 100, Hagerstown, Md. 21740-9795. 5,000. Phone: (301) 790-3930.

American Kennel Club (1884): 51 Madison Ave., New York, N.Y. 10010. 505 member clubs. Phone: (212) 696-8200.

American Legion, The (1919): P.O. Box 1055, Indianapolis, Ind. 46206. 3,100,000. Phone: (317) 630-1200.

American Legion Auxiliary (1919): 777 N. Meridian St., Indianapolis, Ind. 46204. 1,000,000. Phone: (317) 635-6291.

American Mensa, Ltd. (1960): 201 Main St., Suite 1101, Fort Worth, Texas 76102. 50,000. Phone: (817) 332-2600.

American Montessori Society (1960): 150 Fifth Ave., Suite 203, New York, N.Y. 10011. 12,000. Phone: (212) 924-3209.

American ORT (1922): 817 Broadway, 10th Floor, New York, N.Y. 10003. 200,000. Phone: (212) 677-4400.

American Philosophical Society (1743): 104 S. 5th St., Philadelphia, Pa. 19106-3387. 584 (resident), 126 (foreign). Phone: (215) 440-3400.

American Planning Association (1909): 1776 Massachusetts Ave. N.W., Washington, D.C. 20036 (headquarters). 30,000. Phone: (202) 872-0611. Administrative Offices: 122 S. Michigan Ave., Chicago, Ill. 60603. Phone: (312) 431-9100.

Americans for Democratic Action, Inc. (1947): 1625 K St. N.W., Suite 210, Washington, D.C. 20006. 70,000. Phone: (202) 785-5980.

American Society for Public Administration (ASPA) (1939): 1120 G St. N.W., Suite 700, Washington, D.C. 20005. 14,000. Phone: (202) 393-7878.

American Society of CLU & ChFC (1928): 270 S.

Bryn Mawr Ave., Bryn Mawr, Pa. 19010-2195. Phone: (610) 526-2500.

American Universities, Association of (1900): One Dupont Circle N.W., Suite 730, Washington, D.C. 20036. Phone: (202) 466-5030.

American Water Resources Association (1964): 950 Herndon Parkway, Ste. 300, Herndon, Va. 22070-5528. 4,000. Phone: (703) 904-1225.

America's Community Bankers (1992): 900 19th St. N.W., Suite 400, Washington, D.C. 20006. Phone: (202) 857-3100.

AMIDEAST (America-Mideast Educational and Training Services) (1951): 1730 M St. N.W., Suite 1100, Washington, D.C. 20036-4505. 168 institutional members. Phone: (202) 776-9600.

Amnesty International/USA (1961): 322 Eighth Ave., New York, N.Y. 10001-4808. 330,000. Phone: (212) 807-8400.

AMVETS (American Veterans of World War II, Korea, and Vietnam) (1944): 4647 Forbes Blvd., Lanham, Md. 20706-4380. 250,000. Phone: (301) 459-9600.

Animal Protection Institute (1968): 2831 Fruitridge Rd., P.O. Box 22505, Sacramento, Calif. 95822. Phone: (916) 731-5521.

Animals, The American Society for the Prevention of Cruelty to (ASPCA) (1866): 424 E. 92nd St., New York, N.Y. 10128. 400,000+. Phone: (212) 876-7700..

Animals, The Fund For, Inc. (1967): 200 W. 57th St., New York, N.Y. 10019. 175,000. Phone: (212) 246-2096.

Animal Welfare Institute (1951): P.O. Box 3650, Washington, D.C. 20007. 4,500. Phone: (202) 337-2332.

Anthropological Association, American (1902): 4350 N. Fairfax Dr., Suite 640, Arlington, Va. 22203. 11,500. Phone: (703) 528-1902.

Anti-Defamation League of B'nai B'rith (1913): 823 United Nations Plaza, New York, N.Y. 10017-3560. Phone: (212) 885-7700.

Anti-Vivisection Society, The American (1883): 801 Old York Rd., #204, Jenkintown, Pa. 19046-1685. 15,000. Phone: (215) 887-0816.

APMI International (1958): 105 College Rd. East, Princeton, N.J. 08540. 2,800. Phone: (609) 452-7700.

Appraisers, American Society of (1936): P.O. Box 17265, Washington, D.C. 20041. 6,500. Phone: (800) ASA-VALU or (703) 478-2228.

Arboriculture, International Society of (1924): P.O. Box GG, Savoy, Ill. 61874-9902. 8,000. Phone: (217) 355-9411.

Archaeological Institute of America (1879): 656 Beacon St., Boston, Mass. 02215-2010. 11,000. Phone: (617) 353-9361.

Architects, The American Institute of (1857): 1735 New York Ave. N.W., Washington, D.C. 20006-5292. 56,000. Phone: (202) 626-7300.

Architectural Historians, Society of (1940): 1365 N. Astor St., Chicago, Ill. 60610-2144. 4,000. Phone: (312) 753-1365.

Army, Association of the United States (1950): 2425 Wilson Blvd., Arlington, Va. 22210-3385. 117,000. Phone: (703) 841-4300.

***Arthritis Foundation** (1948): 1314 Spring St. N.W., Atlanta, Ga. 30309. 69 local chapters. Phone: (404) 872-7100 or (800) 283-7800.

Arts, National Endowment for the (1965): 1100 Pennsylvania Ave. N.W., Washington, D.C. 20506. Phone: (202) 682-5400.

Arts, The American Federation of (1909): 41 E. 65th St., New York, N.Y. 10021. 525+ institutional members (museums), 600+ individual members (patrons). Phone: (212) 988-7700.

Arts and Letters, American Academy of (1898): 633 W. 155th St., New York, N.Y. 10032. 250. Phone: (212) 368-5900.

ASAE—The Society for engineering in agricultural, food, and biological systems (1907): 2950 Niles Rd., St. Joseph, Mich. 49085. 12,000. Phone: (616) 429-0300.

ASM International® (1913): Materials Park, Ohio 44073-0002. 48,000. Phone: (216) 338-5151.

Association for Investment Management and Research (1990): 5 Boar's Head Lane, P.O. Box 3668, Charlottesville, Va. 22903. 26,000. Phone: (804) 980-3668.

Astronomical Society, American (1899): Dept. of Physics and Astronomy, Baton Rouge, La. 70803-4001. 6,300. Phone: (504) 388-1160.

Astronomical Society of the Pacific (1889): 390 Ashton Ave., San Francisco, Calif. 94112. 6,200. Phone: (415) 337-1100.

Atheists, American (1963): P.O. Box 140195, Austin, Tex. 78714-0195. 40,000 Families. Phone: (512) 458-1244.

Auctioneers Association, National (1949): 8880 Ballentine, Overland Park, Kan. 66214-1985. 5,900. Phone: (913) 541-8084.

Audubon Society, National (1905): 700 Broadway, New York, N.Y. 10003-9562. 600,000. Phone: (212) 979-3000.

Authors League of America (1912): 330 W. 42nd St., 29th Floor, New York, N.Y. 10036-6902. 14,000. Phone: (212) 564–8350.

Autism Society of America (1965): 7910 Woodmont Ave., Suite 650, Bethesda, Md. 20814. Phone: (301) 657-0881.

Automobile Club, National (1924): Bayside Plaza, 188 The Embarcadero, #300, San Francisco, Calif. 94105. 300,000. Phone: (415) 777-4000.

Automotive Hall of Fame (1939): P.O. Box 1727, Midland, Mich. 48641-1727. Phone: (517) 631-5760.

AZA (American Zoo and Aquarium Association) (1924): Exec. Office/Conservation Center, 7970-D Old Georgetown Rd., Bethesda, Md. 20814-2493. 6,000. Phone: (301) 907-7777.

Bar Association, American (1878): 750 N. Lake Shore Dr., Chicago, Ill. 60611-4497. 371,000. Phone: (312) 988-5000.

Barber Shop Quartet Singing in America, Society for the Preservation and Encouragement of (SPEBSQSA, Inc.) (1938): 6315 Third Ave., Kenosha, Wis., 53143-5199. 34,000. Phone: (414) 653-8440.

Better Business Bureaus, Council of (1970): 4200 Wilson Blvd., Suite 800, Arlington, Va. 22203-1804. Phone: (703) 276-0100.

Bible Society, American (1816): 1865 Broadway, New York, N.Y. 10023-9980. 300,000. Phone: (212) 408-1200.

Biblical Literature, Society of (1880): 1549 Clairmont Rd., Suite 204, Decatur, Ga. 30033-4635. 5,800 members, 1,200 subscribers. Phone: (404) 636-4744.

Bibliographical Society of America (1904): P.O. Box 397, Grand Central Station, New York, N.Y. 10163. 1,200. Phone: (212) 647-9171.

*Bide-A-Wee Home Association, Inc. (1903): 410 E. 38th St., New York, N.Y. 10016. Phone: Adoptions (pets) (212) 532-4455; Clinic and Hospital (212) 532-5884.

Big Brothers/Big Sisters of America (1977): 230 N. 13th St., Philadelphia, Pa. 19107. Phone: (215) 567-7000.

Biochemistry and Molecular Biology, American Society for (1906): 9650 Rockville Pike, Bethesda, Md. 20814. 9,000. Phone: (301) 530-7145.

Biological Sciences, American Institute of (1947): 730 11th St. N.W., Washington, D.C. 20001-4521. 14,000. Phone: (202) 628-1500.

Blind, American Council of the (1961): 1155 15th St. N.W., Suite 720, Washington, D.C. 20005. 40,000. Phone: (202) 467–5081.

Blind, National Federation of the (1940): 1800 Johnson St., Baltimore, Md. 21230. 50,000. Phone: (410) 659-9314.

Blindness, Research to Prevent (1960): 645 Madison Ave., New York, N.Y. 10022-1010. 1,250. Phone: (212) 752-4333.

*Blue Cross and Blue Shield Association (1948 and 1946): 676 N. St. Clair St., Chicago, Ill. 60611. 74 Plans. Phone: (312) 440-6000.

B'nai B'rith International (1843): 1640 Rhode Island Ave. N.W., Washington, D.C. 20036-3278. 500,000. Phone: (202) 857-6600.

Booksellers Association, American (1900): 828 So. Broadway, Tarrytown, N.Y. 10591. 8,400. Phone: (914) 591-2665, (800) 637-0037.

Botanical Gardens & Arboreta, American Association of (1940): 786 Church Rd., Wayne, Pa. 19087. 2,400. Phone: (610) 688-1120.

Boys & Girls Clubs of America (1906): 1230 W. Peachtree St. N.W., Atlanta, Ga. 30309. 2,210,281. Phone: (404) 815-5700.

Boy Scouts of America (1910): 1325 W. Walnut Hill Lane, P.O. Box 152079, Irving, Tex. 75015-2079. 4,882,700. Phone: (214) 580-2000.

Bridge, Tunnel, and Turnpike Association, International (1932): 2120 L St. N.W., Suite 305, Washington, D.C. 20037-1527. 250. Phone: (202) 659-4620.

Broadcasters, National Association of (1922): 1771 N St. N.W., Washington, D.C. 20036-2891. 6,500. Phone: (202) 429-5300.

Brookings Institution, The (1916): 1775 Massachusetts Ave. N.W., Washington, D.C. 20036-2188. Phone: (202) 797-6000.

*Brooks Bird Club, Inc., The (1932): 707 Warwood Ave., Wheeling, W. Va. 26003. 1,000. Phone: (614) 635-9246.

Business Education Association, National (1946): 1914 Association Dr., Reston, Va. 22091-1596. 14,000. Phone: (703) 860-8300.

Business Women's Association, American (1949): 9100 Ward Parkway, P.O. Box 8728, Kansas City, Mo. 64114-0728. 90,000. Phone: (816) 361-6621.

Camp Fire Boys and Girls (1910): 4601 Madison Ave., Kansas City, Mo. 64112-1278. 700,000. Phone: (816) 756-1950.

Camping Association, The American (1910): 5000 State Rd. 67 N., Martinsville, Ind. 46151-7902. 5,500. Phone: (317) 342-8456.

*Cancer Society, American (1913): 1599 Clifton Rd. N.E., Atlanta, Ga. 30329. 2,646,070 volunteers. Phone: (800) ACS-2345 or check local listings.

CARE, Inc. (1945): 151 Ellis St. NE, Atlanta, Ga. 30303. Programs in 61 developing countries. Phone: (404) 681-2552.

Carnegie Endowment for International Peᵃᶜᵉ (1910): 2400 N St. N.W., Washington, D̲.C̲. 20037. Phone: (202) 862-7900.

Catholic Charities USA (1910): 1731 King St., Alexandria, Va. 22314. 3,000 individuals, 1,200 agencies and institutions. Phone: (703) 549-1390.

Catholic Daughters of the Americas (1903): 10 W. 71st St., New York, N.Y. 10023. 130,000. Phone: (212) 877-3041.

Catholic Historical Society, American (1884): 263 S. Fourth St., Philadelphia, Pa. 19106. 950. Phone: (215) 925-5752.

Catholic War Veterans of the U.S.A. Inc. (1935): 441 N. Lee St., Alexandria, Va. 22314. 30,000. Phone: (703) 549-3622.

Ceramic Society, The American (1899): 735 Ceramic Place, Westerville, Ohio 43081-8720.

*Cerebral Palsy Associations, Inc., United (1949): 1522 K St. N.W., Suite 1112, Washington, D.C. 20005. 160 affiliates. Phone: (800) USA-5UCP/ TT (202) 842-1266.

Chamber of Commerce of the U.S. (1912): 1615 H St. N.W., Washington, D.C. 20062-2000. 220,000. Phone: (202) 659-6000.

Chemical Engineers, American Institute of (1908): 345 E. 47th St., New York, N.Y. 10017-2395. 59,000. Phone: (212) 705-7338.

Chemical Manufacturers Association, Inc. (1872): 2501 M St. N.W., Washington, D.C. 20037. 185 companies. Phone: (202) 887-1100.

Chemical Society, American (1876): 1155 16th St. N.W., Washington, D.C. 20036. 151,024. Phone: (202) 872-4600.

Chemists, The American Institute of (1923): 7315 Wisconsin Ave., Suite 502E, Bethesda, Md. 20814. 5,000. Phone: (301) 652-2447.

Chess Federation, United States (1939): 186 Rt. 9W, New Windsor, N.Y. 12553. 75,000. Phone: (914) 562-8350/(800) 388–KING.

Child Labor Committee, National (1904): 1501 Broadway, Rm. 1111, New York, N.Y. 10036. Phone: (212) 840-1801.

Children's Aid Society, The (1853): 105 E. 22nd St., New York, N.Y. 10010. Child welfare services, community centers, camps, health services, foster care/adoption, and community schools. Phone: (212) 949-4800.

Children's Book Council (1945): 568 Broadway, Suite 404, New York, N.Y. 10012. 77 imprints. Phone: (212) 966-1990.

Child Welfare League of America (1920): 440 First St. N.W., Suite 310, Washington, D.C. 20001-2085. Phone: (202) 638-2952.

Chiropractic Association, American (1963): 1701 Clarendon Blvd., Arlington, Va. 22209. 21,300. Phone: (703) 276-8800.

Churches of Christ in the USA, National Council of the (1950): 475 Riverside Drive, New York, N.Y. 10115. 32 Protestant and Orthodox communions. Phone: (212) 870-2227.

Cities, National League of (1924): 1301 Pennsylvania Ave. N.W., Washington, D.C. 20004. 17,000 cities and towns. Phone: (202) 626-3000.

Civil Air Patrol, National Headquarters (1941): 105 S. Hansell St., Bldg. 714, Maxwell AFB, Ala. 36116-6332. 52,048. Phone: (334) 953-4287.

Civil Engineers, American Society of (1852): 345 E. 47th St., New York, N.Y. 10017-2398. 115,000. Phone: (212) 705-7496.

Clinical Chemistry, Inc., American Association for (1948): 2101 L St. N.W., Suite 202, Washington, D.C. 20037. 11,000. Phone (202) 857-0717.

*Clinical Pathologists, American Society of (1922): 2100 W. Harrison St., Chicago, Ill. 60612-3798. 55,191. Phone: (312) 738-1336.

Collectors Association, American (1939): Box 39106, Minneapolis, Minn. 55439-0106. Over 3,600 debt collection agencies. Phone: (612) 926-6547.

College Board, The (1900): 45 Columbus Ave., New York, N.Y. 10023-6992. 2,900 institutions. Phone: (212) 713-8000.

Colleges and Employers, National Association of (formerly College Placement Council) (1956): 62 E. Highland Ave., Bethlehem, Pa. 18017. 3,100. Phone: (610) 868-1421.

Common Cause (1970): 2030 M St. N.W., Washington, D.C. 20036. 250,000. Phone: (202) 833-1200.

*Community Colleges, American Association of (1920): One Dupont Circle N.W., Suite 410, Washington, D.C. 20036-1176. 1,100 institutions. Phone: (202) 728-0200.

Community Cultural Center Association, American (1978): 19 Foothills Dr., Pompton Plains, N.J. 07444. Phone: (201) 835-2661.

*Composers, Authors, and Publishers, American Society of (ASCAP) (1914): One Lincoln Plaza, New York, N.Y. 10023. 55,000. Phone: (212) 621-6000.

Composers/USA, National Association of (1932): P.O. Box 49652, Barrington Station, Los Angeles, Calif. 90049. 550. Phone: (310) 541-8213.

Congress of Racial Equality (CORE) (1942): 30 Cooper Square, New York, N.Y. 10003. Phone: (212) 598-4000. Nationwide network of chapters.

Conscientious Objectors, Central Committee for (1948): 1515 Cherry St., Philadelphia, Pa. 19102. Phone: (215) 241-7196; 655 Sutter St., Suite 514, San Francisco, Calif. 94102. Phone: (415) 474-3002.

Conservation Engineers, Association of (1961): Alabama Dept. of Cons. & Natural Resources, Engineering Section, 64 N. Union St., Montgomery, Ala. 36130. Phone: (334) 242-3476.

Consulting Chemists & Chemical Engineers, Inc., Association of (1928): The Chemists Club, 40 W. 45th St., New York, N.Y. 10036. 130. Phone: (212) 983-3160.

Consumer Federation of America (1968): 1424 16th St. N.W., Suit 604, Washington, D.C. 20036. 240 member organizations. Phone: (202) 387-6121.

Consumer Interests, American Council on (1953): 240 Stanley Hall, Univ. of Missouri, Columbia, Mo. 65211. 1,500. Phone: (314) 882-3817.

Consumers League, National (1899): 1701 K St. N.W., Suite 1200, Washington, D.C. 20006. Phone: (202) 835-3323.

*Consumers Union (1936): 101 Truman Ave., Yonkers, N.Y. 10703-1057. 5,000,000 subscribers to *Consumer Reports*. Phone: (914) 378-2000.

Counselors, American College of (1984): 8038 Camellia Lane, Indianapolis, Ind. 46219. Phone: (317) 898-3211.

Country Music Association (1958): One Music Circle South, Nashville, Tenn. 37203. 7,000+. Phone: (615) 244-2840.

Credit Management, National Association of (1896): 8815 Centre Park Dr., Suite 200, Columbia, Md. 21045. Phone: (410) 740-5560.

Credit Union National Association (1934): P.O. Box 431, Madison, Wis. 53701. 51 state leagues representing 12,400 credit unions. Phone: (608) 231-4000.

Crime and Delinquency, National Council on (1907): 685 Market St., #620, San Francisco, Calif. 94105. Criminal justice research, nationwide membership. Phone: (415) 896-6223.

CSA/USA, Celiac Sprue Association/United States of America, Inc., P.O. Box 31700, Omaha, Neb. 68131-0700. 6 regions in U.S., 64 chapters, 20 active resource units. Phone: (402) 558-0600.

Dairy Council, National (1915): 10255 W. Higgins Rd., Suite 900, Rosemont, Ill. 60018-5616. Phone: (708) 803-2000.

Daughters of the American Revolution, National Society (1890): 1776 D St. N.W., Washington, D.C. 20006. 200,000. Phone: (202) 628-1776.

Daughters of the Confederacy, United (1894): 328 N. Boulevard, Richmond, Va. 23220-4057. 24,000. Phone: (804) 355-1636.

Deaf, National Association of the (1880): 814 Thayer Ave., Silver Spring, Md. 20910. Phone: (301) 587-1788; (301) 587-1789 TTY.

Defenders of Wildlife (1947): 1101 14th St. N.W., #1400, Washington, D.C. 20005. 105,000 members and supporters. Phone: (202) 682-9400.

Defense Preparedness Association, American (1919): Two Colonial Place, Suite 400, 2101 Wilson Blvd., Arlington, Va. 22201-3061. 27,000 individual, 675 corporate. Phone: (703) 522-1820.

Dental Association, American (1859): 211 E. Chicago Ave., Chicago, Ill. 60611. 140,000. Phone: (312) 440-2500.

Diabetes Association, American (1940): 1660 Duke St., Alexandria, Va. 22314. Phone: (703) 549-1500.

Dignity (1969): 1500 Massachusetts Ave. N.W., Suite 11, Washington, D.C. 20005. 5,000. Phone: (202) 861-0017 and (800) 877-8797.

Disabled American Veterans (1920): 807 Maine Ave. S.W., Washington, D.C. 20024. 1.4 million. Phone: (202) 554-3501.

Dowsers, Inc., The American Society of (1961): P.O. Box 24, Danville, Vt. 05828-0024. 5,000. Phone: (802) 684-3417.

Drug, Chemical & Allied Trades Association, Inc., The (1890): 2 Roosevelt Ave., Syosset, N.Y. 11791. 575. Phone (516) 496-3317.

Ducks Unlimited, Inc. (1937): One Waterfowl Way, Memphis, Tenn. 38120. 553,000. Phone: (901) 758-3825.

Earthwatch (1972): 680 Mt. Auburn St., Box 403N, Watertown, Mass. 02272. 75,000. Phone: (800) 776-0188.

Eastern Star, Order of, General Grand Chapter (1876): 1618 New Hampshire Ave. N.W., Washington, D.C. 20009. 1,207,301. Phone: (202) 667-4737.

Easter Seal Society, The National (1919): 230 W. Monroe, 18th Floor, Chicago, Ill. 60606-4802. 124 state and local affiliate societies. Phone: (312) 726-6200 and (312) 726-4258 TDD.

Economic Association, American (1885): 2014 Broadway, Suite 305, Nashville, Tenn. 37203-2418. 21,000. 6,000 inst. subscribers. Phone: (615) 322-2595.

Economic Development, Committee for (1942): 477 Madison Ave., New York, N.Y. 10022. 250 trustees. Phone: (212) 688-2063.

Edison Electric Institute (1933): 701 Pennsylvania Ave. N.W., Washington, D.C. 20004-2696.

Education, American Council on (1918): One Dupont Circle N.W., Washington, D.C. 20036. 1,600 institutions; over 200 organizations. Phone: (202) 939-9300.

Education, Council for Advancement and Support of (CASE) (1974): 11 Dupont Circle N.W., Suite 400, Washington, D.C. 20036-1261. 14,400. Phone: (202) 328-5900.

Educational Exchange, International, Council on (1947): 205 E. 42nd St., New York, N.Y. 10017. 265. Phone: (212) 661-1414.

*Educational Research Association, American (1916): 1230 17th St. N.W., Washington, D.C. 20036. 21,000. Phone: (202) 223-9485.

Education Association, National (1857): 1201 16th St. N.W., Washington, D.C. 20036-3290. 2.2 million. Phone: (202) 833-4000.

Electrochemical Society, The (1902): 10 S. Main St., Pennington, N.J. 08534-2896. 6,400. Phone: (609) 737-1902.

Electronic Industries Association (1924): 2500 Wilson Blvd., Arlington, Va. 22201. 1,000 member companies. Phone: (703) 907-7500.

Elks of the U.S.A., Benevolent and Protective Order of the (1868): 2750 N. Lakeview Ave., Chicago, Ill. 60614. 1,300,000. Phone: (312) 477-2750.

Energy Engineers, Association of (1977): 4025 Pleasantdale Rd., Suite 420, Atlanta, Ga. 30340. 8,500. Phone: (404) 447-5083.

Engineering Science & Mechanics, Dept. of, Virginia Polytechnic Institute & State Univ., Blacksburg, Va. 24061-0219. Phone: (703) 231-6651.

English-Speaking Union of the United States (1920): 16 E. 69th St., New York, N.Y. 10021. 18,000. Phone: (212) 879-6800.

Entomological Society of America (1889): 9301 Annapolis Rd., Lanham, Md. 20706-3115. 8,500. Phone: (301) 731-4535.

Esperanto League for North America, The (1952): P.O. Box 1129, El Cerrito, Calif. 94530. Over 1,000. Phone: (800) 828-5944.

Exceptional Children, The Council for (1922): 1920 Association Dr., Reston, Va. 22091. 54,000. Phone: (703) 620-3660.

Experimental Test Pilots, The Society of (1956): 44814 Elm St., Lancaster, Calif. 93534. 1,950. Phone: (805) 942-9574.

Exploration Geophysicists, Society of (1930): P.O. Box 702740, Tulsa, Okla. 74170-2740. 14,500. Phone: (918) 497-5500.

Family and Consumer Sciences, American Association of (1909): 1555 King St., Alexandria, Va. 22314. 20,000. Phone: (703) 706-4600.

Family Campers & RVers (1949): 4804 Transit Rd., Bldg. 2, Depew, N.Y. 14043-4906. 24,000 families. Phone: (716) 668-6242.

Family Physicians, American Academy of (1947): 8880 Ward Pkwy., Kansas City, Mo. 64114-2797. 80,000. Phone: (816) 333-9700.

Family Relations, National Council on (1938): 3989 Central Ave. N.E., #550, Minneapolis, Minn. 55421-3921. 3,800. Phone: (612) 781-9331.

Family Service America, Inc. (1911): 11700 W. Lake Park Dr., Park Place, Milwaukee, Wis. 53224. Approximately 300 member agencies. Phone: (414) 359-1040 or (800) 221-2681.

Farm Bureau Federation, American (1919): 225 Touhy Ave., Park Ridge, Ill. 60068. 4 million member families. Phone: (312) 399-5700.

Federal Bar Association (1920): 1815 H St. N.W., Suite 408, Washington, D.C. 20006-3697. 15,000. Phone: (202) 638-0252.

Federal Employees, National Federation of (1917): 1016 16th St. N.W., Washington, D.C. 20036. Rep. 150,000. Phone: (202) 862-4400.

Feline and Canine Friends, Inc. (1973): 505 N. Bush St., Anaheim, Calif. 92805. 1,000. Phone: (714) 635-7975.

Fellowship of Reconciliation (1915): Box 271, Nyack, N.Y. 10960. 20,000. Phone: (914) 358-4601.

Female Executives, National Association for (1972): 30 Irving Place, New York, N.Y. 10003. 250,000. Phone: (212) 477-2200.

FFA Organization, National (1928): 5632 Mt. Vernon Memorial Hwy., P.O. Box 15160, Alexandria, Va. 22309-0160. 401,574. Phone: (703) 360-3600.

Fire Protection Association, National (1896): One Batterymarch Park, P.O. Box 9101, Quincy, Mass. 02269-9101. 65,000. Phone: (617) 770-3000.

Flag Foundation, National (1968): Flag Plaza, Pittsburgh, Pa. 15219-3630. 3,000+. Phone: (412) 261-1776.

Fleet Reserve Association (1924): 125 N. West St., Alexandria, Va. 22314-2754. 167,000. Phone: (703) 683-1400.

Flight Test Engineers, Society of (1968): P.O. Box 4047, Lancaster, Calif. 93539-4047. 1,000. Phone: (805) 538-9715.

Foreign Policy Association (1918): 470 Park Ave. So., New York, N.Y. 10016. Phone: (212) 481-8100/(800) 628-5754.

*****Foreign Relations, Council on** (1921): 58 E. 68th St., New York, N.Y. 10021. 2,600. Phone: (212) 734-0400.

Foreign Study, American Institute for (1965): 102 Greenwich Ave., Greenwich, Conn. 06830. Phone: (203) 869-9090/(800) 727-AIFS.

Foreign Trade Council, Inc., National (1914): 1270 Avenue of the Americas, New York, N.Y. 10020-1702. Over 550 companies. Phone: (212) 399-7128. Also, 1625 K St. N.W., Washington, D.C. 20006. Phone: (202) 887-0278.

Forensic Sciences, American Academy of (1948): 410 N. 21st St., Suite 203/80904, P.O. Box 669, Colorado Springs, Colo. 80901-0669. 4,065. Phone: (719) 636-1100.

Foresters, Society of American (1900): 5400 Grosvenor Lane, Bethesda, Md. 20814-2198. 19,000. Phone: (301) 897-8720.

Fortean Organization, International (1965): P.O. Box 367, Arlington, Va. 22210-0367. 1,045.

4-H Program (early 1900s): Room 3441-S, U.S. Department of Agriculture, Washington, D.C. 20250. 5.6 million. Phone: (202) 720-2908.

Freedom of Information Center (1958): 20 Walter Williams Hall, Univ. of Missouri, Columbia, Mo. 65211. Phone: (314) 882-4856.

French-American Chamber of Commerce in the U.S. Inc. (1896): 509 Madison Ave., Suite 1900, New York, N.Y. 10022. 605. Membership Association. Phone: (212) 371-4466.

French Institute/Alliance Française (1911): 22 E. 60th St., New York, N.Y. 10022-1077. 9,000. Phone: (212) 355-6100.

Friendship and Good Will, International Society of (1978): 9538 Summerfield St., Spring Valley, San Diego County, Calif. 91977. 4,518 members in 189 countries. Phone: (619) 466-8882.

Friends of Animals Inc. (1957): 777 Post Rd., Suite 205, Darien, Conn. 06820. 120,000. Phone: (203) 656-1522.

Friends of the Earth (1969): 1025 Vermont Ave. N.W., Suite 300, Washington, D.C. 20005. 35,000. Phone: (202) 783-7400.

Future Homemakers of America, Inc. (1945): 1910 Association Dr., Reston, Va. 22091. 250,000. Phone: (703) 476-4900.

Gamblers Anonymous: Box 17173, Los Angeles, Calif. 90017. Phone: (213) 386-8789.

Gay and Lesbian Task Force, National (1973): 2320 17th St. N.W., Washington, D.C. 20009-2702. 35,000 members. Phone: (202) 332-6483.

Genealogical Society, National (1903): 4527 17th St. N., Arlington, Va. 22207-2399. 14,000. Phone: (703) 525-0050.

Genetic Association, American (1903): P.O. Box 39, Buckeystown, Md. 21717. 800. Phone: (301) 695-9292.

Geographers, Association of American (1904): 1710 16th St. N.W., Washington, D.C. 20009-3198. 6,300. Phone: (202) 234-1450.

Geographic Education, National Council for (1915): 16A Leonard Hall, Indiana University of Pennsylvania, Indiana, Pa. 15705. 3,700. Phone: (412) 357-6290.

Geographic Society, National (1888): 1145 17th St. N.W., Washington, D.C. 20036. 9,200,000. Phone: (202) 857-7000.

Geological Institute, American (1948): 4220 King St., Alexandria, Va. 22302-1507. 27 geoscience societies representing 80,000 geoscientists. Phone: (703) 379-2480.

Geological Society of America, Inc. (1888): 3300 Penrose Pl., P.O. Box 9140, Boulder, Colo. 80301. 15,200. Phone: (303) 447-2020.

Geriatrics Society, American (1942): 770 Lexington Ave., Suite 300, New York, N.Y. 10021. 6,500. Phone: (212) 308-1414.

German American National Congress, The (Deutsch-Amerikanischer National Congress—D.A.N.K.) (1958): 4740 N. Western Ave., Executive Office, Chicago, Ill. 60625-2097. 30,000, plus Associates. Phone: (312) 275-1100.

Gideons International, The (1889): 2900 Lebanon Rd., Nashville, Tenn. 37214-0800. 125,000. Phone: (615) 883-8533.

Gifted, The Association for the (1958): The Council for Exceptional Children, 1920 Association Dr., Reston, Va. 22091. 2,200. Phone: (703) 620-3660.

Girl Scouts of the U.S.A. (1912): 420 Fifth Ave., New York, N.Y. 10018. 3.5 million. Phone: (212) 852-8000.

Girls Incorporated (1945): 30 E. 33rd St., New York, N.Y. 10016. 350,000. Phone: (212) 689-3700.

Graphoanalysis Society, International (1929): 111 N. Canal St., Chicago, Ill. 60606. 10,000. Phone: (312) 930-9446.

Gray Panthers Project Fund (1970): 2025 Pennsylvania Ave. N.W., Suite 821, Washington, D.C. 20006. Over 50 chapters (networks). Phone: (202) 466-3132.

Greenpeace (1971): 1436 U St. N.W., Washington, D.C. 20009. 1,600,000. Phone: (202) 462-1177.

Group Psychotherapy Association, American (1942): 25 E. 21st St., 6th Floor, New York, N.Y. 10010. 4,400 Phone: (212) 477-2677.

Guide Dog Foundation for the Blind, Inc.® (1946): 371 E. Jericho Turnpike, Smithtown, N.Y. 11787-2976. 60,000. Phone: (516) 265-2121; outside N.Y. city call (800) 548-4337.

Hadassah, The Women's Zionist Organization of America (1912): 50 W. 58th St., New York, N.Y. 10019. 385,000. Phone: (212) 355-7900.

Handgun Control, Inc. (1974): 1225 Eye St. N.W., Washington, D.C. 20005. 400,000. Phone: (202) 898-0792.

Heart Association, American (1924): 7272 Greenville Ave., Dallas, Tex. 75231-4596. 4,200,000 volunteers. Phone: (214) 373-6300.

Heating, Refrigerating and Air-Conditioning Engineers, Inc., American Society of (1894): 1791 Tullie Circle N.E., Atlanta, Ga. 30329. 50,000. Phone: (404) 636-8400.

Helicopter Association International (1948): 1635 Prince St., Alexandria, Va. 22314. Phone: (703) 683-4646.

Hemispheric Affairs, Council on (1975): 724 9th St. N.W., Rm. 401, Washington, D.C. 20001. Phone: (202) 393-3322.

Historians, The Organization of American (1907): Indiana Univ., 112 N. Bryan St., Bloomington, Ind. 47408. 12,000. Phone: (812) 855-7311.

*Historic Preservation, National Trust for (1949): 1785 Massachusetts Ave. N.W., Washington, D.C. 20036. 250,000. Phone: (202) 673-4000.

Horse Council, Inc., American (1969): 1700 K St. N.W., #300, Washington, D.C. 20006. More than 190 organizations and 2,400 individuals. Phone: (202) 296-4031.

Horse Shows Association, Inc., American (1917): 220 E. 42nd St., New York, N.Y. 10017-5876. 65,000. Phone: (212) 972-2472.

Horticultural Association, National Junior (1935): 1424 N. 8th, Durant, Okla. 74701. Phone: (405) 924-0771.

Horticultural Society, American (1922): 7931 East Boulevard Dr., Alexandria, Va. 22308. 20,000. Phone: (703) 768-5700 or (800) 777-7931.

Hostelling International—American Youth Hostels (1934): 733 15th St. N.W., Suite 840, Washington, D.C. 20005. 124,000. Phone: (202) 783-6161; membership and reservations (800) 444-6111.

Housing Science, International Association for (1972): P.O. Box 340254, Coral Gables/Miami, Fla. 33114. 500 professionals. Phone: (305) 446-9462.

Humane Association, American (1877): 63 Inverness Drive East, Englewood, Colo. 80112-5117. Phone: (303) 792-9900.

Humane Association, The American—Children's Division (1877): 63 Inverness Dr. East, Englewood, Colo. 80112. Phone: (303) 792-9900.

Humane Society of the United States (1954): 2100 L St. N.W., Washington, D.C. 20037. 2,300,000. Phone: (202) 452-1100.

Humanities, National Endowment for the (1965): 1100 Pennsylvania Ave. N.W., Washington, D.C. 20506. Phone: (202) 606-8400.

Hydrogen Energy, International Association for (1975): P.O. Box 248266, Coral Gables, Fla. 33124. 2,500. Phone: (305) 284-4666.

Illustrators, Society of (1901): 128 E. 63rd St., New York, N.Y. 10021. 932. Phone: (212) 838-2560.

Industrial Engineers, Institute of (1948): 25 Technology Park/Atlanta, Norcross, Ga. 30092. 30,000. Phone: (404) 449-0461.

Interfraternity Conference, National (1909): 3901 W. 86th St., Suite 390, Indianapolis, Ind. 46268-1791. 62. Phone: (317) 872-1112.

International Credit Association (ICA) (1912): P.O. Box 419057, St. Louis, Mo. 63141-1757. 9,000 members, 110 local associations. Phone: (314) 991-3030.

*Investigative Pathology, American Society for (1976): 9650 Rockville Pike, Bethesda, Md. 20814-3993. 2,300. Phone: (301) 530-7130.

Iron and Steel Institute, American (1908): 1101 17th St. N.W., Washington, D.C. 20036-4700. 1,200. Phone: (202) 452-7100.

Izaak Walton League of America (1922): 707 Conservation Lane, Gaithersburg, Md. 20878-2983. 55,000. Phone: (301) 548-0150.

Jaycees, The United States (The U.S. Junior Chamber of Commerce) (1920): P.O. Box 7, Tulsa, Okla. 74102-0007. 155,000. Phone: (918) 584-2481.

Jewish Community Centers, World Confederation of (1946): 12 Hess St., Jerusalem, Israel 94185. Phone: (02) 251 265.

Jewish Community Centers Association of North America (1917): 15 E. 26th St., New York, N.Y. 10010-1579. 275 affiliated Jewish Community Centers, YM-YWHAs, and camps. Phone: (212) 532-4949.

*Jewish Congress, American (1918): 15 E. 84th St., New York, N.Y. 10028. 50,000. Phone: (212) 879-4500.

Jewish Historical Society, American (1892): 2 Thornton Rd., Waltham, Mass. 02154. 3,500. Phone: (617) 891-8110.

Jewish War Veterans of the U.S.A. (1896): 1811 R St. N.W., Washington, D.C. 20009-1659. Phone: (202) 265-6280.

Jewish Women, National Council of (1893): 53 W. 23rd St., New York, N.Y. 10010. 100,000. Phone: (212) 645-4048.

John Birch Society (1958): P.O. Box 8040, Appleton, Wis. 54913. Under 100,000. Phone: (414) 749-3780.

Journalists, Society of Professional, (1909): 16 S. Jackson, Greencastle, Ind. 46135-0077. 14,000. Phone: (317) 653-3333.

Journalists and Authors, American Society of (1948): 1501 Broadway, Suite 302, New York, N.Y. 10036. 800. Phone: (212) 997-0947.

Judaism, American Council for (1943): P.O. Box 9009, Alexandria, Va. 22304. 10,000. Phone: (703) 836-2546.

Junior Achievement Inc. (1919): One Education Way, Colorado Springs, Colo. 80906-4477. 2.3 million. Phone: (719) 540-8000.

*Junior Leagues International, Inc., Association of (1921): 660 First Ave., New York, N.Y. 10016-3241. 284 Leagues, 193,000 members. Phone: (212) 683-1515.

Junior Statesmen of America (1934): 60 E. Third Ave., Suite 320, San Mateo, Calif. 94401. 15,000. Phone: (415) 347-1600.

Kiwanis International (1915): 3636 Woodview Trace, Indianapolis, Ind. 46268-3196. 325,000. Phone: (317) 875-8755.

Knights of Columbus (1882): One Columbus Plaza, New Haven, Conn. 06510-3326. 1,551,919. Phone: (203) 772-2130.

Knights of Pythias, Supreme Lodge (1864): 2785 E. Desert Inn Rd. #150, Las Vegas, Nev. 89121. 75,000. Phone: (702) 735-3302.

Knights Templar, Grand Encampment of (1816): 5097 N. Elston, Suite 101, Chicago, Ill. 60630. 250,000. Phone: (312) 777-3300.

La Leche League International (1956): 1400 N. Meacham Rd., P.O. Box 4079, Schaumburg, Ill. 60168-4079. 50,000. Phone: (708) 519-7730.

Law, American Society of International (1906): 2223 Massachusetts Ave. N.W., Washington, D.C. 20008. 4,300. Phone: (202) 939-6000.

League of Women Voters of the U.S. (1920): 1730 M St. N.W., Washington, D.C. 20036. Phone: (202) 429-1965.

Legal Aid and Defender Association, National (1911): 1625 K St. N.W., Suite 800, Washington, D.C. 20006. 2,400. Phone: (202) 452-0620.

Legal Secretaries, National Association of (1950): 2250 E. 73rd St., Suite 550, Tulsa, Okla. 74136-6864. 14,000. Phone: (918) 493-3540.

Leukemia Society of America (1949): 600 Third Ave., 4th Floor, New York, N.Y. 10016. Phone: (212) 573-8484.

Library Association, American (1876): 50 E. Huron St., Chicago, Ill. 60611. 55,356. Phone: (312) 944-6780; (800) 545-2433.

Life Insurance, American Council of (1976): 1001 Pennsylvania Ave. N.W., Washington, D.C. 20004-2599. 606. Phone: (202) 624-2000.

Life Underwriters, National Association of (1890): 1922 F St. N.W., Washington, D.C. 20006-4387. Phone: (202) 331-6000.

Lions Clubs International (1917): 300 22nd St., Oak Brook, Ill. 60521-8842. 1,402,000. Phone: (708) 571-5466.

Lung Association, American (1904): 1740 Broadway, New York, N.Y. 10019-4374. 116 constituent and affiliate associations. Phone: (800) LUNG-USA/(800) 586-4872.

Magazine Editors, American Society of (1963): 919 Third Ave., 22nd Floor, New York, N.Y. 10022. 800. Phone: (212) 872-3700.

Magazine Publishers of America (1919): 919 Third Ave., New York, N.Y. 10022. 334 companies, 1,200+ publications. Phone: (212) 872-3700.

Management Accountants, Institute of (1919): 10 Paragon Dr., Montvale, N.J. 07645-1760. 84,000. Phone: (201) 573-9000.

Management Association, American (1923): 135 W. 50th St., New York, N.Y. 10020-1201. 70,000. Phone: (212) 586-8100.

Management Consultants, Institute of (1968): 521 Fifth Ave., 35th Floor, New York, N.Y. 10175-3598. 2,500 individuals. Phone: (212) 697-8262,.

Management Consulting Firms, Association of—ACME (1929): 521 Fifth Ave., 35th Floor, New York, N.Y. 10175-3598. 55 firms. Phone: (212) 697-9693.

Manufacturers, National Association of (1895): 1331 Pennsylvania Ave. N.W., Suite 1500-North, Washington, D.C. 20004-1790. 13,500. Phone: (202) 637-3065.

Manufacturers' Agents National Association (MANA) (1947): 23016 Mill Creek Rd., P.O. Box 3467, Laguna Hills, Calif. 92654-3467. 8,000. Phone: (714) 859-4040.

March of Dimes Birth Defects Foundation (1938): 1275 Mamaroneck Ave., White Plains, N.Y. 10605. 104 chapters. Phone: (914) 428-7100.

Marine Conservation, Center for (1972): 1725 De Sales St. N.W., Suite 500, Washington, D.C. 20036. 120,000. Phone: (202) 429-5609.

Marine Corps Association (1913): Bldg. #715, Marine Corps Base, Quantico, Va. 22134. 100,723. Phone: (703) 640-6161/(800) 336-0291.

Marine Corps League (1937): 8626 Lee Hwy., Suite 201, Fairfax, Va. 22031. Correspondence address: P.O. Box 3070, Merrifield, Va. 22116-3070. 42,000. Phone: (703) 207-9588 or (703) 207-9589.

Marine Technology Society (1963): 1828 L St. N.W., Suite 906, Washington, D.C. 20036-5104. 2,700. Phone: (202) 775-5966.

Masons, Ancient and Accepted Scottish Rite, Northern Masonic Jurisdiction, Supreme Council 33 (1813): 33 Marrett Rd., Lexington, Mass. 02173. 358,479. Phone: (617) 862-4410.

Masons, Ancient and Accepted Scottish Rite, Southern Jurisdiction, Supreme Council 33° (1801): 1733 16th St. N.W., Washington, D.C. 20009. 500,000. Phone: (202) 232-3579.

Masons, Royal Arch, General Grand Chapter International (1797): P.O. Box 489, 111 S. Fourth St., Danville, Ky. 40423-0489. 230,000. Phone: (606) 236-0757.

Massachusetts Audubon Society (1896): South Great Rd., Lincoln, Mass. 01773. 54,000 member households, 19 staffed wildlife sanctuaries. Phone: (617) 259-9500.

Mathematical Association of America (1915): 1529 18th St. N.W., Washington, D.C. 20036. 33,000. Phone: (202) 387-5200.

Mathematical Society, American (1888): P.O. Box 6248, Providence, R.I. 02940-6248. 29,018. Phone: (401) 455-4000.

Mathematical Statistics, Institute of (1935): 3401 Investment Blvd. #7, Hayward, Calif. 94545-3819. 4,000. Phone: (510) 783-8141.

Mayflower Descendants, General Society of (1897): 4 Winslow St., P.O. Box 3297, Plymouth, Mass. 02361. 25,000. Phone: (508) 746-3188.

*Mayors, U.S. Conference of (1932): 1620 Eye St. N.W., Washington, D.C. 20006. 9 standing committees. Phone: (202) 293-7330.

Mechanical Engineers, American Society of (1880): 345 E. 47th St., New York, N.Y. 10017. 125,000. Phone: (212) 705-7722.

Mechanics, American Academy of (1969): Dept. of Engineering Science & Mechanics, VPI & State University, Blacksburg, Va. 24061-0219. 1,600. Phone: (703) 231-6841.

Medical Association, American (1847): 515 N. State St., Chicago, Ill. 60610-4377. Phone: (312) 464-5000.

Medical Library Association (1898): Six N. Michigan Ave., Suite 300, Chicago, Ill. 60602. 5,000. Phone: (312) 419-9094.

Mental Health Association, National (1909): 1021 Prince St., Alexandria, Va., 22314-2971. 1,000,000. Phone: (703) 684-7722.

Meteorological Society, American (1919): 45 Beacon St., Boston, Mass. 02108-3693. 10,000. Phone: (617) 227-2425.

Military Chaplains Association of the U.S.A. (1925): P.O. Box 42660, Washington, D.C. 20015-0660. 1,500. Phone: (202) 574-2423.

Mining, Metallurgical, and Petroleum Engineers, The American Institute of (1871): 345 E. 47th St., New York, N.Y. 10017. 4 Member Societies: Society for Mining, Metallurgy and Exploration, The Minerals, Metals & Materials Society, Iron & Steel Society, Society of Petroleum Engineers. Phone: (212) 705-7695.

Mining and Metallurgical Society of America (1910): 9 Escalle Lane, Larkspur, Calif. 94939. 340. Phone: (415) 924-7441.

Model Aeronautics, Academy of (1936): 5151 East Memorial Dr., Muncie, Ind. 47302. 160,000. Phone: (317) 287-1256.

Modern Language Association of America (1883): 10 Astor Place, New York, N.Y. 10003. 32,000. Phone: (212) 475-9500.

Modern Woodmen of America (1883): 1701 1st Ave., Rock Island, Ill. 61201. 750,000. Phone: (309) 786-6481.

Moose International, Inc. (1888): Mooseheart, Ill. 60539. 1,750,000. Phone: (708) 859-2000.

Mothers Against Drunk Driving (MADD) (1980): 511 E. John Carpenter Freeway #700, Irving, Texas 75062-8187. 3.2 million. Phone: (214) 744-6233.

Motion Picture & Television Engineers, Society of (1916): 595 W. Hartsdale Ave., White Plains, N.Y. 10607. 9,500. Phone: (914) 761-1100.

Motion Picture Arts & Sciences, Academy of (1927): 8949 Wilshire Blvd., Beverly Hills, Calif. 90211-1972. Phone: (310) 247-3000.

Multiple Sclerosis Society, National (1946): 733 Third Ave., New York, N.Y. 10017-3288. 400,000. Phone: (212) 986-3240/(800) FIGHT-MS (344-4867).

Muscular Dystrophy Association (1950): 3300 East Sunrise Dr., Tucson, Ariz. 85718. 2,300,000 volunteers. Phone: (520) 529-2000.

Museum of Natural History, American (1869): Central Park West at 79th St., New York, N.Y. 10024-5192. 520,000. Phone: (212) 769-5100.

*Museums, American Association of (1906): 1225

Eye St. N.W., Suite 200, Washington, D.C. 20005. 12,400. Phone: (202) 289-1818.

*Music Publishers Association, Inc., National (1917): 205 E. 42nd St., New York, N.Y. 10017. Trade Organization/Harry Fox Agency-Licensing Organization. Phone: (212) 370-5330.

Muzzle Loading Rifle Association, National (1933): P.O. Box 67, Friendship, Ind. 47021. 25,000. Phone: (812) 667-5131.

NAFSA: Association of International Educators (1948): 1875 Connecticut Ave. N.W., Suite 1000, Washington, D.C. 20009-5728. 7,500. Phone: (202) 462-4811.

National Abortion and Reproductive Rights Action League (NARAL) (1969): 1156 15th St. N.W., Washington, D.C. 20005. 500,000. Phone: (202) 973-3000.

National Association for the Advancement of Colored People (1909): 4805 Mt. Hope Dr., Baltimore, Md. 21215-3297. 500,000+. Phone: (301) 358-8900.

National Audubon Society (1905): 700 Broadway, New York, N.Y. 10003-9501. 600,000. Phone: (212) 979-3000.

National Conference, The (founded as The Natl. Conf. of Christians & Jews) (1927): 71 Fifth Ave., New York, N.Y. 10003. 200,000. Phone: (212) 206-0006.

National Cooperative Business Association (formerly Cooperative League of the U.S.A.) (1916): 1401 New York Ave. N.W., Suite 1100, Washington, D.C. 20005. Phone: (202) 638-6222.

National Grange, The (1867): 1616 H St. N.W., Washington, D.C. 20006-4999. 300,000. Phone: (202) 628-3507.

National Press Club (1908): National Press Bldg., 529 14th St. N.W., Washington, D.C. 20015. 4,500. Phone: (202) 662-7500.

National PTA (National Congress of Parents and Teachers) (1897): 330 N. Wabash Ave., Chicago, Ill. 60611-3690. 7.0 million. Phone: (312) 670-6782.

National Rifle Association of America (1871): 11250 Waples Mill Rd., Fairfax, Va. 22030. 3,300,000. Phone: (703) 267-1000.

National Urban League, Inc. (1910): 500 E. 62nd St., New York, N.Y. 10021. 113 affiliates in 34 states and D.C. Phone: (212) 310-9000.

*Natural Science for Youth Foundation (1961): 130 Azalea Dr., Roswell, Ga. 30075. 350. Phone: (404) 594-9367.

Nature Conservancy, The (1951): 1815 N. Lynn St., Arlington, Va. 22209. 818,000. Phone: (703) 841-5300.

Naval Architects and Marine Engineers, The Society of (1893): 601 Pavonia Ave., Jersey City, N.J. 07306. 10,000. Phone: (201) 798-4800.

Naval Engineers, American Society of (1888): 1452 Duke St., Alexandria, Va. 22314. 6,800. Phone: (703) 836-6727.

Naval Institute, United States (1873): 118 Maryland Ave., Annapolis, Md. 21402-5035. 90,000. Phone: (410) 268-6110.

Navigation, The Institute of (1945): 1800 Diagonal Rd., Suite 480, Alexandria, Va. 22314. 3,800. Phone: (703) 683-7101.

Navy League of the United States (1902): 2300 Wilson Blvd., Arlington, Va. 22201-3308. 69,000; John R. Dalrymple, Rear Admiral, USN (Ret.), Executive Director.

Neurofibromatosis Foundation, Inc., The National (1978): 95 Pine St., 16th Floor, New York, N.Y. 10005. 27,000. Phone: (800) 323-7938; in

N.Y. State (212) 344NNFF.

Newspaper Association of America (1887): The Newspaper Center, 11600 Sunrise Valley Dr., Reston, Va. 22091-1412. 1,050. Phone: (703) 648-1000.

Newspaper Editors, American Society of (1922): P.O. Box 4090, Reston, Va. 22090-1700. 870. Phone: (703) 648-1144.

Ninety-Second Street Young Men's and Young Women's Hebrew Association (1874): 1395 Lexington Ave., New York, N.Y. 10128. Phone: (212) 996-1100.

Nondestructive Testing, Inc., The American Society for (1941): 1711 Arlingate Lane, P.O. Box 28518, Columbus, Ohio 43228-0518. 10,240. Phone: (800) 222-ASNT.

*North American Shortwave Assn. (1964): 45 Wildflower Rd., Levittown, Pa. 19057. 1,800. Phone: (215) 945-0543.

NOT SAFE (National Organization Taunting Safety and Fairness Everywhere) (1980): P.O. Box 5743, Montecito, Calif. 93150. 975. Phone: (805) 969-6217.

Nuclear Society, American (1954): 555 N. Kensington Ave., La Grange Park, Ill. 60526. 16,000. Phone: (708) 352-6611.

Numismatic Association, American (1891): 818 N. Cascade Ave., Colorado Springs, Colo. 80903-3279. 30,000. Phone: (719) 632-2646.

Nurses Association, American (1896): 600 Maryland Ave. S.W., Suite 100, Washington, D.C. 20024-2571. 209,000. Phone: (202) 651-7000.

Nutrition, American Institute of (1928): 9650 Rockville Pike, Bethesda, Md. 20814-3990. 3,600. Phone: (301) 530-7050.

Odd Fellows, Sovereign Grand Lodge, Independent Order of (1819): 422 Trade St., Winston-Salem, N.C. 27101-2830. 460,000. Phone: (910) 725-5955.

Olympic Committee, United States (1921): One Olympic Plaza, Colorado Springs, Colo. 80909-5760. Phone: (719) 632-5551.

Optical Society of America (1916): 2010 Massachusetts Ave. N.W., Washington, D.C. 20036. 12,000. Phone: (202) 223-8130.

Optimist International (1919): 4494 Lindell Blvd., St. Louis, Mo. 63108. 160,000. Phone: (314) 371-6000.

Optometric Association, American (1898): 243 N. Lindbergh Blvd., St. Louis, Mo. 63141. 31,000. Phone: (314) 991-4100.

*Organization of American States, General Secretariat (1890): 1889 F St. N.W., Washington, D.C. 20006. 35 member nations. Phone: (202) 458-3000.

Ornithologists' Union, American (1883): c/o National Museum of Natural History, NHB E607, MRC-116, Smithsonian Institution, Washington, D.C. 20560. 5,000. Phone: (202) 357-2051.

Overeaters Anonymous, Inc. (1960): P.O. Box 44020, Rio Rancho, N. Mex. 87174-4020. 150,000. Phone: (505) 891-2664.

Parents, Families and Friends of Lesbians and Gays (1981): 1101 14th St. N.W., Suite 1030, Washington, D.C. 20005. 42,000+ members. 365 chapters in 12 countries. Phone: (202) 638-4200.

Parents Without Partners (1957): 401 N. Michigan Ave., Chicago, Ill. 60611-4267. Phone: (312) 644-6610.

*Parks & Conservation Association, National (1919): 1776 Massachusetts Ave. N.W., Suite 200, Washington, D.C. 20036. 400,000. Phone: (202) 223-6722.

Pathology, American Society for Investigative (1976): 9650 Rockville Pike, Bethesda, Md. 20814-3993. 2,300. Phone: (301) 530-7130.

Peace Action (a merger of SANE and the Nuclear Weapons Freeze Campaign) (1957): 1819 H St. N.W., Suite 640, Washington, D.C. 20006-3603. 50,000. Phone: (202) 862-9740.

People for the American Way (1980): 2000 M St. N.W., Suite 400, Washington, D.C. 20036. 300,000. Phone: (202) 467-4999.

Petroleum Geologists, American Association of (1917): P.O. Box 979, Tulsa, Okla. 74101-0979. 31,846. Phone: (918) 584-2555.

Pharmaceutical Association, American (1852): 2215 Constitution Ave. N.W., Washington, D.C. 20037. 45,000. Phone: (202) 628-4410.

Philatelic Society, American (1886): P.O. Box 8000, State College, Pa. 16803. 57,000. Phone: (814) 237-3803.

Photogrammetry and Remote Sensing, American Society for (1934): 5410 Grosvenor Lane, Suite 210, Bethesda, Md. 20814-2160. Phone: (301) 493-0290.

Photographic Society of America (1934): 3000 United Founders Blvd., Suite 103, Oklahoma City, Okla. 73112. Phone: (405) 843-1437.

Photography, International Center of (1974): 1130 Fifth Ave., New York, N.Y. 10128. Midtown branch: 1133 Avenue of the Americas, New York, N.Y. 10036. Phone: (212) 860-1777.

Physical Society, The American (1899): One Physics Ellipse, College Park, Md. 20740-3844. 43,000. Phone: (301) 209-3200.

Physical Therapy Association, American (APTA) (1921): 1111 N. Fairfax St., Alexandria, Va. 22314. 67,000. Phone: (703) 684-2782.

Physics, American Institute of (1931): One Physics Ellipse, College Park, Md. 20740-3843. 125,000. Phone: (301) 209-3100.

Pilot International (1921): Pilot International Headquarters, 244 College St., P.O. Box 4844, Macon, Ga. 31213-0599. 18,000. Phone: (912) 743-7403.

Planetary Society, The (1979): 65 N. Catalina Ave., Pasadena, Calif. 91106. 120,000. Phone: (818) 793-5100.

***Plan International** (1937): Box 804, East Greenwich, R.I. 02818-1667. Phone: (401) 826-2500.

Planned Parenthood® Federation of America, Inc., (1916): 810 Seventh Ave., New York, N.Y. 10019. 160 affiliates. Phone: (212) 541-7800.

Plastics Engineers, Society of (1942): 14 Fairfield Dr., Brookfield, Conn. 06804-0403. 37,000. Phone: (203) 775-0471.

Police, American Federation of (1966): Records Center, 3801 Biscayne Blvd., Miami, Fla. 33137. 100,000. Phone: (305) 573-0070.

Police, International Association of Chiefs of (1893): 515 N. Washington St., Alexandria, Va. 22314-2357. 13,000. Phone: (703) 836-6767.

Police Hall of Fame, American (1960): 3801 Biscayne Blvd., Miami, Fla. 33137. 55,000. Phone: (305) 573-0070.

Political and Social Science, American Academy of (1889): 3937 Chestnut St., Philadelphia, Pa. 19104. Phone: (215) 386-4594.

Political Science, Academy of (1880): 475 Riverside Dr., Suite 1274, New York, N.Y. 10115-1274. 7,300. Phone: (212) 870-2500.

Prevent Blindness America (1908): 500 E. Remington Rd., Schaumburg, Ill. 60173-5611. 25 affiliates and divisions. Phone: (708) 843-2020/(800) 331-2020.

Professional Engineers, National Society of (1934): 1420 King St., Alexandria, Va. 22314. 75,000. Phone: (703) 684-2800.

Professional Photographers of America, Inc. (1880): 57 Forsyth St. N.W., Suite 1600, Atlanta, Ga. 30303. 14,000. Phone: (404) 522-8600.

Psychiatric Association, American (1844): 1400 K St. N.W., Washington, D.C. 20005. 39,677. Phone: (202) 682-6000.

Psychoanalytic Association, The American (1911): 309 E. 49th St., New York, N.Y. 10017. 3,030 psychoanalysts. Phone: (212) 752-0450.

Psychological Association, American (1892): 750 First St. N.E., Washington, D.C. 20002-4242. 132,000. Phone: (202) 336-5500; TDD: (202) 336-5662.

Public Health Association, American (1872): 1015 15th St. N.W., Washington, D.C. 20005. 50,000+. Phone: (202) 789-5600.

***Puppeteers of America** (1937): 5 Cricklewood Path, Pasadena, Calif. 91107-1002. Phone: (818) 797-5748.

Quality Control, The American Society for (1946): 611 E. Wisconsin Ave., P.O. Box 3005, Milwaukee, Wis. 53201-3005. 125,000+. Phone: (414) 272-8575.

***Railroads, Association of American** (1934): 50 F St. N.W., Washington, D.C. 20001-1564. Phone: (202) 639-2100.

Recording Arts & Sciences, Inc., National Academy of (1958): 3402 Pico Blvd., Santa Monica, Calif. 90405. 9,000. Phone: (310) 392-3777.

Red Cross, American (1881): 17th and D Sts. N.W., Washington, D.C. 20006. Approx. 2,000 chapters. Phone: (202) 737-8300.

Rehabilitation Association, National (1925): 633 S. Washington St., Alexandria, Va. 22314-4193. 18,000. Phone: (703) 836-0850.

Research and Enlightenment, Association for (Edgar Cayce Foundation) (1931): 67th St. & Atlantic Ave. (P.O. Box 595), Virginia Beach, Va. 23451. 55,000. Phone: (804) 428-3588.

Reserve Officers Association of the United States (1922): 1 Constitution Ave. N.E., Washington, D.C. 20002. 100,000. Phone: (202) 479-2200.

Retired Federal Employees, National Association: 1533 New Hampshire Ave. N.W., Washington, D.C. 20036-1279. 500,000. Phone: (202) 234-0832.

Reye's Syndrome Foundation, National (1974): 426 N. Lewis St., Bryan, Ohio 43506. Phone: (800) 233-7393.

RID-USA (Remove Intoxicated Drivers) (1978): Box 520, Schenectady, N.Y. 12301. Over 150/41 state chapters. Phone: (518) 372-0034/(518) 393-HELP.

Right to Life Committee, Inc., National (1973): 419 7th St. N.W., Suite 500, Washington, D.C. 20004. Phone: (202) 626-8800.

Rotary International (1905): One Rotary Center, 1560 Sherman Ave., Evanston, Ill. 60201. 1,196,100 in 150 countries and 34 geographical regions. Phone: (708) 866-3000.

SAE (Society of Automotive Engineers) (1905): 400 Commonweatlh Dr., Warrendale, Pa. 15096-0001. 64,000. Phone: (412) 776-4841.

Safety Council, National (1913): 1121 Spring Lake Dr., Itasca, Ill. 60143-3201. Phone: (708) 285-1121.

Salvation Army, The (1865): National Headquarters, 615 Slaters Lane, Alexandria, Va. 22313. 446,403. Phone: (703) 684-5500.

Save-the-Redwoods League (1918): 114 Sansome St., Suite 605, San Francisco, Calif. 94104. 45,000. Phone: (415) 362-2352.

Science, American Association for the Advancement of (1848): 1333 H St. N.W., Washington, D.C. 20005. 143,000. Phone: (202) 326-6400.

Science and Health, American Council on (1978): 1995 Broadway, 2nd Floor, New York, N.Y. 10023-5860. Phone: (212) 362-7044.

Science Fiction Society, World (1939): c/o Southern California Institute for Fan Interests, P.O. Box 8442, Van Nuys, Calif. 91409. 6,000. Phone: (818) 366-3827.

Science Writers, Inc., National Association of (1934): P.O. Box 294, Greenlawn, N.Y. 11740. 1,830. Phone: (516) 757-5664.

Scientists, Federation of American (FAS) (1945): 307 Massachusetts Ave. N.E., Washington, D.C. 20002. 4,000. Phone: (202) 546-3300.

SCRABBLE® Association, National (1972): P.O. Box 700, Front Street Garden, Greenport, N.Y. 11944. 15,000. Phone: (516) 477-0033.

Screen Actors Guild (1933): 5757 Wilshire Blvd., Los Angeles, Calif. 90036. 90,000. Phone: (213) 954-1600.

Sculpture Society, National (1893): 1177 Ave. of the Americas, New York, N.Y. 10036. 4,000. Phone: (212) 764-5645.

Seeing Eye Inc., The (1929): P.O. Box 375. Morristown, N.J. 07963-0375. Phone: (201) 539-4425.

Senior Citizens, National Alliance of (1974): 1700 18th St. N.W., Suite 401, Washington, D.C. 20009. 117,000. Phone: (202) 986-0117.

Separationists, Society of (1963): P.O. Box 140195, Austin, Tex. 78714-0195. Phone: (512) 458-1244.

Shriners of North America and Shriners Hospitals for Crippled Children, The (1872): Box 31356, Tampa, Fla. 33631-3356. 637,000. Phone: (813) 281-0300.

Sierra Club (1892): 730 Polk St., San Francisco, Calif. 94109. 550,000. Phone: (415) 776-2211.

SIETAR INTERNATIONAL (The International Society for Intercultural Education, Training and Research) (1974): 808 17th St. N.W., Suite 200, Washington, D.C. 20006-3910. 2,000+. Phone: (202) 466-7883.

Simon Wiesenthal Center (1978): 9760 W. Pico Blvd., Los Angeles, Calif. 90035-4792. 375,000 member families. Phone: (310) 553-9036.

Small Business United, National (1937): 1155 15th St. N.W., #710, Washington, D.C. 20005. 65,000. Phone: (202) 293-8830.

SMYAL, Sexual Minority Youth Assistance League (1984): 333 1/2 Pennsylvania Ave. SE, Washington, D.C. 20003-1148. 1,000 members. Phone: (202) 546-5940.

Social Work Education, Council on (1952): 1600 Duke St., Alexandria, Va. 22314-3421. Phone: (703) 683-8080.

Social Workers, National Association of (1955): 750 First St. N.E., Suite 700, Washington, D.C. 20002-4241. Phone: (202) 408-8600.

***Sociological Association, American** (1905): 1722 N St. N.W., Washington, D.C. 20036-2981. 13,000. Phone: (202) 833-3410.

Soil and Water Conservation Society (1945): 7515 N.E. Ankeny Rd., Ankeny, Iowa 50021-9764. 11,000. Phone: (515) 289-2331.

Songwriters Guild of America, The (1931): 1500 Harbor Blvd., Weehawken, N.J. 07087-6732. Phone: (201) 867-7603.

Sons of Italy in America, Order (1905): 219 E St. N.E., Washington, D.C. 20002. 475,000. Phone: (202) 547-2900.

Sons of the American Revolution, National Society of the (1889): 1000 S. 4th St., Louisville, Ky. 40203. 27,000. Phone: (502) 589-1776.

Soroptimist International of the Americas (1921): Two Penn Center Plaza, Suite 1000, Philadelphia, Pa. 19102-1883. 50,000. Phone: (215) 557-9300.

Southern Early Childhood Association (formerly SACUS) (1948): P.O. Box 56130, Little Rock, Ark. 72215-6130. 18,500. Phone: (501) 663-0353.

Space Education Association, U.S. (1973): Global Operations Center, 231 School Lane, P.O. Box 249, Rheems, Pa. 17570-0249. Voice/Fax: (717) 367-5196.

Space Society, National (1974): 922 Pennsylvania Ave. S.E., Washington, D.C. 20003. 30,000. Phone: (202) 543-1900.

Special Olympics International, Inc. (1968): 1325 G St. N.W., Suite 500, Washington, D.C., 20005-3104. 1,000,000. Phone: (202) 628-3630.

***Speech-Language-Hearing Association, American** (1925): 10801 Rockville Pike, Rockville, Md. 20852. 77,000. Phone: (301) 897-5700.

Sports Car Club of America Inc. (1944): 9033 E. Easter Place, Englewood, Colo. 80112-2105. 54,000. Phone: (303) 694-7222.

***State Garden Clubs, Inc., National Council of** (1929): 4401 Magnolia Ave., St. Louis, Mo. 63110. 280,992. Phone: (314) 776-7574.

State Governments, The Council of (1933): P.O. Box 11910, Lexington, Ky. 40578-1910. All state officials, all 50 states. Phone: (606) 244-8000.

Statistical Association, American (1839): 1429 Duke St., Alexandria, Va. 22314. 19,000.

Student Association, United States (1947): 815 15th St. N.W. #838, Washington, D.C. 20005. 350 schools (3.5 million students). Phone: (202) 347-8772.

Surgeons, American College of (1913): 55 E. Erie St., Chicago, Ill. 60611-2797. 52,000+. Phone: (312) 664-4050.

Symphony Orchestra League, American (1942): 1156 Fifteenth St. N.W., Suite 800, Washington, D.C. 20005-1704. 5,500. Phone: (202) 628-0099.

TASH: The Association for Persons with Severe Handicaps (1973): 29 W. Susquehanna Ave., Suite 210, Baltimore, Md. 21204. 8,500. Phone: (410) 828-TASH.

Tax Foundation, Inc. (1937): 1250 H St. N.W., Suite 750, Washington, D.C. 20005. Phone: (202) 783-2760.

Teachers, American Federation of (1916): 555 New Jersey Ave. N.W., Washington, D.C., 20001. 800,000+. Phone: (202) 879-4400.

Testing & Materials, American Society for (1898): 1916 Race St., Philadelphia, Pa. 19103-1187. 33,000. Phone: (215) 299-5400.

The Arc, a national organization on mental retardation (1950): 500 E. Border St., Suite 300, Arlington, Texas 76010. 140,000 members, 1,200 state and local chapters. Phone: (817) 261-6003.

Theatre Guild, Inc. (1919): 226 W. 47th St., New York, N.Y. 10036. 72,000. Phone: (212) 869-5470.

Theosophical Society in America, The (1875): P.O. Box 270, Wheaton, Ill. 60189-0270. 4,800. Phone: (708) 668-1571.

Tin Can Sailors, Inc. (1976): P.O. Box 100, Somerset, Mass. 02726-0100. 15,000+. Phone: (508) 677-0515.

612 U.S. Societies and Associations

Toastmasters International (1924): P.O. Box 9052, Mission Viejo, Calif. 92690-7052, and 23182 Arroyo Vista, Rancho Santa Margarita, Calif. 92688. 180,000. Phone: (714) 858-8255 and (714) 858-8255.

TOUGHLOVE International (1977): P.O. Box 1069, Doylestown, Pa. 18901. 750 registered groups. Phone: (215) 348-7090; (800) 333-1069.

TransAfrica Forum (1981): 1744 R St. N.W., Washington, D.C. 20009. Phone: (202) 797-2301.

Travel Agents, American Society of (ASTA) (1931): 1101 King St., Alexandria, Va. 22314. 25,000. Phone: (703) 739-2782.

Travelers Aid Services (1905/1982); 2 Lafayette St., New York, N.Y. 10007. Lucy N. Friedman, Executive Director. (Result of merger of Travelers Aid Society of New York and Victim Services Agency in 1982). Phone: (212) 577-7700. **Client Services:** Times Square Office, Port Authority Bus Terminal, No. Wing, 625 Eighth Ave., 2nd Fl., Manhattan (212) 944-0013; JFK Airport Office, International Arrivals Bldg. 50, Jamaica, Queens (718) 656-4870; 24-Hour Crime Victims Hotline (212) 577-7777; Immigration Hotline (718) 899-4000.

Tuberous Sclerosis Association, Inc., National (1975): 8000 Corporate Dr., Suite 120, Landover, Md. 20785. 5,000. Phone: (301) 459-9888 or (800) 225-6872.

UFOs, National Investigations Committee on (1967): 14617 Victory Blvd., Suite 4, Van Nuys, Calif. 91411. Phone & FAX: (818) 894-0914.

UNICEF, U.S. Committee for (1947): 333 E. 38th St., New York, N.Y. 10016. 20,000 volunteers. Phone: (212) 686-5522.

Union of Concerned Scientists (1969): 2 Brattle Square, Cambridge, Mass. 02238-9105. 80,000. Phone: (617) 547-5552.

United Jewish Appeal (1939): 99 Park Ave., New York, N.Y. 10016. Phone: (212) 818-9100.

United Negro College Fund Inc. (1944): 8260 Willow Oaks Corporate Dr., P.O. Box 10444, Fairfax, Va. 22031-4511. Phone: (703) 205-3400.

United Way of America (1918): 701 N. Fairfax St., Alexandria, Va. 22314-2045. 1,900 local United Ways. Phone: (703) 836-7100.

University Foundation, International (1973): 1301 S. Noland Rd., Independence, Mo. 64055. 67,000. Phone: (816) 461-3633.

University Women, American Association of (1881): 1111 16th St. N.W., Washington, D.C. 20036. 150,000. Phone: (202) 785-7700.

USO (United Service Organizations) (1941): World Headquarters, 601 Indiana Ave. N.W., Washington, D.C. 20004. Phone: (202) 783-8121.

*Variety Clubs International (1927): 1560 Broadway, Suite 1209, New York, N.Y. 10036. 15,000. Phone: (212) 704-9872.

Veterans Committee, American (AVC) (1944): 6309 Bannockburn Dr., Bethesda, Md. 20817. 15,000. Phone & FAX: (301) 320-6490.

Veterans of Foreign Wars of the U.S. (1899): 406 W. 34th St., Kansas City, Mo. 64111. VFW and Auxiliary, 2,850,000. Phone: (816) 756-3390.

Veterinary Medical Association, American (1863): 1931 N. Meacham Rd., Suite 100, Schaumburg, Ill. 60173-4360. 53,500. Phone: (708) 925-8070.

Visual Handicaps, Division on (1948): The Council for Exceptional Children, 1920 Association Dr., Reston, Va. 22091. 1,000. Phone: (703) 620-3660.

Volunteers of America (1896): 3939 N. Causeway Blvd., Metairie, La. 70002. Provides human services in more than 400 U.S. communities. Phone: 1-800-899-0089.

War Resisters League (1923): 339 Lafayette St., New York, N.Y. 10012. 12,000. Phone: (212) 228-0450.

Washington Legal Foundation (1976): 2009 Massachusetts Ave. N.W., Washington, D.C. 20036. 100,000. Phone: (202) 588-0302.

Water Quality Association (1974): 4151 Naperville Rd., Lisle, Ill. 60532. 2,500. Phone: (708) 505-0160.

Welding Society, American (1919): 550 N.W. LeJeune Rd., Miami, Fla. 33126. 45,000. Phone: (305) 443-9353; toll free (800) 443-9353.

Wildlife Federation, National (1936): 1400 16th St. N.W., Washington, D.C. 20036-2266. 4,000,000+. Phone: (202) 797-6800.

Wildlife Fund, World (1961): 1250 24th St. N.W., Washington, D.C. 20037-1175. 1.2 million. Phone: (202) 293-4800.

Woman's Christian Temperance Union, National (1874): 1730 Chicago Ave., Evanston, Ill. 60201. Under 20,000. Phone: (708) 864-1396.

Women, National Organization for (NOW) (1966): 1000 16th St. N.W., Suite 700, Washington, D.C. 20036-5705. 270,000. Phone: (202) 331-0066.

Women Police, The International Association of (1915): RR1, Box 149, Deer Isle, Me. 04627. 3,000. Phone: (207) 348-6976.

Women's American ORT (1927): 315 Park Ave. South, New York, N.Y. 10010. Chapters throughout the U.S. Phone: (212) 505-7700.

*Women's Clubs, General Federation of (1890): 1734 N St., N.W., Washington, D.C. 20036-2990. 350,000. Phone: (202) 347-3168.

Women's Educational and Industrial Union (1877): 356 Boylston St., Boston, Mass. 02116. 1,500. Phone: (617) 536-5651.

Women's International League for Peace and Freedom (1915): 1213 Race St., Philadelphia, Pa. 19107-1691. 10,000. Phone: (215) 563-7110.

World Future Society (1966): 7910 Woodmont Ave., Suite 450, Bethesda, Md. 20814. 30,000. Phone: (301) 656-8274.

World Health, American Association for (1953): 1129 20th St. N.W., Suite 400, Washington, D.C. 20036. Phone: (202) 466-5883.

World Peace, International Association of Educators for (1969): P.O. Box 3282, Mastin Lake Station, Huntsville, Ala. 35810-0282. 25,000. Phone: (205) 534-5501.

World Peace Foundation (1910): One Eliot Square, Cambridge, Mass. 02138. Phone: (617) 491-5085.

Worldwatch Institute (1974): 1776 Massachusetts Ave. N.W., Washington, D.C. 20036. Global environmental research organization. Phone: (202) 452-1999.

Writers Union, National (1983): 873 Broadway, Suite 203, New York, N.Y. 10003. 4,000. Phone: (212) 254-0279.

YMCA of the USA (1844): 101 N. Wacker Dr., Chicago, Ill. 60606. 12,800,000. Phone: (312) 977-0031.

Young Women's Christian Association of the U.S.A. (1858 in U.S.A., 1855 in England): 726 Broadway, New York, N.Y. 10003. 1,800,000. Phone: (212) 614-2700.

Zero Population Growth (1968): 1400 Sixteenth St. N.W., Suite 320, Washington, D.C. 20036. 55,000. Phone: (202) 332-2200.

Zionist Organization of America (1897): ZOA House, 4 E. 34th St., New York, N.Y. 10016. 110,000. Phone: (212) 481-1500.

*Zoologists, American Society of (1890): 401 N. Michigan Ave., Chicago, Ill. 60611. 2,800. Phone: (312) 527-6697.

THE DECLARATION OF INDEPENDENCE

In Congress, July 4, 1776

The unanimous Declaration of the thirteen united States of America.

When in the Course of human events it becomes necessary for one people to dissolve the political bands which have connected them with another, and to assume among the powers of the earth, the separate and equal station to which the Laws of Nature and of Nature's God entitle them, a decent respect to the opinions of mankind requires that they should declare the causes which impel them to the separation.

We hold these truths to be self-evident, that all men are created equal, that they are endowed by their Creator with certain unalienable Rights, that among these are Life, Liberty and the pursuit of Happiness.—That to secure these rights, Governments are instituted among Men, deriving their just powers from the consent of the governed,—That whenever any Form of Government becomes destructive of these ends, it is the Right of the People to alter or to abolish it, and to institute new Government, laying its foundation on such principles and organizing its powers in such form, as to them shall seem most likely to effect their Safety and Happiness. Prudence, indeed, will dictate that Governments long established should not be changed for light and transient causes; and accordingly all experience hath shewn that mankind are more disposed to suffer, while evils are sufferable, than to right themselves by abolishing the forms to which they are accustomed. But when a long train of abuses and usurpations, pursuing invariably the same Object evinces a design to reduce them under absolute Despotism, it is their right, it is their duty, to throw off such Government, and to provide new Guards for their future security.—Such has been the patient sufferance of these Colonies; and such is now the necessity which constrains them to alter their former Systems of Government. The history of the present King of Great Britain is a history of repeated injuries and usurpations, all having in direct object the establishment of an absolute Tyranny over these States. To prove this, let Facts be submitted to a candid world.

He has refused his Assent to Laws, the most wholesome and necessary for the public good.

He has forbidden his Governors to pass Laws of immediate and pressing importance, unless suspended in their operation till his Assent should be obtained; and when so suspended, he has utterly neglected to attend to them.

He has refused to pass other Laws for the accommodation of large districts of people, unless those people would relinquish the right of Representation in the Legislature, a right inestimable to them and formidable to tyrants only.

He has called together legislative bodies at places unusual, uncomfortable, and distant from the depository of their Public Records, for the sole purpose of fatiguing them into compliance with his measures.

He has dissolved Representative Houses repeatedly, for opposing with manly firmness his invasions on the rights of the people.

He has refused for a long time, after such dissolutions, to cause others to be elected; whereby the Legislative Powers, incapable of Annihilation, have returned to the People at large for their exercise; the State remaining in the mean time exposed to all the dangers of invasion from without, and convulsions within.

He has endeavoured to prevent the population of these States; for that purpose obstructing the Laws for Naturalization of Foreigners; refusing to pass others to encourage their migrations hither, and raising the conditions of new Appropriations of Lands.

He has obstructed the Administration of Justice, by refusing his Assent to Laws for establishing Judiciary Powers.

He has made Judges dependent on his Will alone, for the tenure of their offices, and the amount and payment of their salaries.

He has erected a multitude of New Offices, and sent hither swarms of Officers to harass our people, and eat out their substance.

He has kept among us, in times of peace, Standing Armies without the Consent of our legislatures.

He has affected to render the Military independent of and superior to the Civil Power.

He has combined with others to subject us to a jurisdiction foreign to our constitution, and unacknowledged by our laws; giving his Assent to their Acts of pretended Legislation:

For quartering large bodies of armed troops among us:

For protecting them, by a mock Trial, from punishment for any Murders which they should commit on the Inhabitants of these States:

For cutting off our Trade with all parts of the

NOTE: On April 12, 1776, the legislature of North Carolina authorized its delegates to the Continental Congress to join with others in a declaration of separation from Great Britain; the first colony to instruct its delegates to take the actual initiative was Virginia on May 15. On June 7, 1776, Richard Henry Lee of Virginia offered a resolution to the Congress to the effect "that these United Colonies are, and of right ought to be, free and independent States. . . ." A committee, consisting of Thomas Jefferson, John Adams, Benjamin Franklin, Robert R. Livingston, and Roger Sherman was organized to "prepare a declaration to the effect of the said first resolution." The Declaration of Independence was adopted on July 4, 1776.

Most delegates signed the Declaration August 2, but George Wythe (Va.) signed August 27; Richard Henry Lee (Va.), Elbridge Gerry (Mass.), and Oliver Wolcott (Conn.) in September; Matthew Thornton (N.H.), not a delegate until September, in November; and Thomas McKean (Del.), although present on July 4, not until 1781 by special permission, having served in the army in the interim.

world:

For imposing Taxes on us without our Consent:

For depriving us in many cases, of the benefits of Trial by Jury:

For transporting us beyond Seas to be tried for pretended offences:

For abolishing the free System of English Laws in a neighbouring Province, establishing therein an Arbitrary government, and enlarging its Boundaries so as to render it at once an example and fit instrument for introducing the same absolute rule into these Colonies:

For taking away our Charters, abolishing our most valuable Laws and altering fundamentally the Forms of our Governments:

For suspending our own Legislatures, and declaring themselves invested with power to legislate for us in all cases whatsoever.

He has abdicated Government here, by declaring us out of his Protection and waging War against us.

He has plundered our seas, ravaged our Coasts, burnt our towns, and destroyed the lives of our people.

He is at this time transporting large Armies of foreign Mercenaries to compleat the works of death, desolation, and tyranny, already begun with circumstances of Cruelty & Perfidy scarcely paralleled in the most barbarous ages, and totally unworthy the Head of a civilized nation.

He has constrained our fellow Citizens taken Captive on the high Seas to bear Arms against their Country, to become the executioners of their friends and Brethren, or to fall themselves by their Hands.

He has excited domestic insurrections amongst us, and has endeavoured to bring on the inhabitants of our frontiers, the merciless Indian Savages, whose known rule of warfare, is an undistinguished destruction of all ages, sexes and conditions.

In every stage of these Oppressions We have Petitioned for Redress in the most humble terms: Our repeated Petitions have been answered only by repeated injury. A Prince, whose character is thus marked by every act which may define a Tyrant, is unfit to be the ruler of a free people.

Nor have We been wanting in attentions to our Brittish brethren. We have warned them from time to time of attempts by their legislature to extend an unwarrantable jurisdiction over us. We have reminded them of the circumstances of our emigration and settlement here. We have appealed to their native justice and magnanimity, and we have conjured them by the ties of our common kindred to disavow these usurpations, which would inevitably interrupt our connections and correspondence. They too have been deaf to the voice of justice and of consanguinity. We must, therefore, acquiesce in the necessity, which denounces our Separation, and hold them, as we hold the rest of mankind, Enemies in War, in Peace Friends.

We, therefore, the Representatives of the United States of America, in General Congress, Assembled, appealing to the Supreme Judge of the world for the rectitude of our intentions, do, in the Name, and by Authority of the good People of these Colonies, solemnly publish and declare, That these United Colonies are, and of Right ought to be Free and Independent States; that they are Absolved from all Allegiance to the British Crown, and that all political connection between them and the State of Great Britain, is and ought to be totally dissolved; and that as Free and Independent States, they have full Power to levy War, conclude Peace, contract Alliances, establish Commerce, and to do all other Acts and Things which Independent States may of right do.—And for the support of this Declaration, with a firm reliance on the protection of Divine Providence, we mutually pledge to each other our Lives, our Fortunes and our sacred Honor.

—John Hancock

New Hampshire
Josiah Bartlett
Wm. Whipple
Matthew Thornton

Rhode Island
Step. Hopkins
William Ellery

Connecticut
Roger Sherman
Sam'el Huntington
Wm. Williams
Oliver Wolcott

New York
Wm. Floyd
Phil. Livingston
Frans. Lewis
Lewis Morris

New Jersey
Richd. Stockton
Jno. Witherspoon
Fras. Hopkinson
John Hart
Abra. Clark

Pennsylvania
Robt. Morris
Benjamin Rush
Benj. Franklin
John Morton
Geo. Clymer
Jas. Smith
Geo. Taylor
James Wilson
Geo. Ross

Massachusetts-Bay
Saml. Adams
John Adams
Robt. Treat Paine
Elbridge Gerry

Delaware
Caesar Rodney
Geo. Read
Tho. M'Kean

Maryland
Samuel Chase
Wm. Paca
Thos. Stone
Charles Carroll of Carrollton

Virginia
George Wythe
Richard Henry Lee
Th. Jefferson
Benj. Harrison
Ths. Nelson, Jr.
Francis Lightfoot Lee
Carter Braxton

North Carolina
Wm. Hooper
Joseph Hewes
John Penn

South Carolina
Edward Rutledge
Thos. Heyward, Junr.
Thomas Lynch, Junr.
Arthur Middleton

Georgia
Button Gwinnett
Lyman Hall
Geo. Walton

Constitution of the United States of America

(Historical text has been edited to conform to contemporary American usage.
The bracketed words are designations for your convenience; they are not part of the Constitution.)

The oldest federal constitution in existence was framed by a convention of delegates from twelve of the thirteen original states in Philadelphia in May, 1787, Rhode Island failing to send a delegate. George Washington presided over the session, which lasted until September 17, 1787. The draft (originally a preamble and seven Articles) was submitted to all thirteen states and was to become effective when ratified by nine states. It went into effect on the first Wednesday in March, 1789, having been ratified by New Hampshire, the ninth state to approve, on June 21, 1788. The states ratified the Constitution in the following order:

Delaware	December 7, 1787	South Carolina	May 23, 1788
Pennsylvania	December 12, 1787	New Hampshire	June 21, 1788
New Jersey	December 18, 1787	Virginia	June 25, 1788
Georgia	January 2, 1788	New York	July 26, 1788
Connecticut	January 9, 1788	North Carolina	November 21, 1789
Massachusetts	February 6, 1788	Rhode Island	May 29, 1790
Maryland	April 28, 1788		

[Preamble]

We the people of the United States, in order to form a more perfect Union, establish justice, insure domestic tranquility, provide for the common defence, promote the general welfare, and secure the blessings of liberty to ourselves and our posterity, do ordain and establish this Constitution for the United States of America.

Article I

Section 1

[Legislative powers vested in Congress.] All legislative powers herein granted shall be vested in a Congress of the United States, which shall consist of a Senate and House of Representatives.

Section 2

[Composition of the House of Representatives.—1.] The House of Representatives shall be composed of members chosen every second year by the people of the several States, and the electors in each State shall have the qualifications requisite for electors of the most numerous branch of the State Legislature.

[Qualifications of Representatives.—2.] No Person shall be a Representative who shall not have attained to the age of twenty-five years, and been seven years a citizen of the United States, and who shall not, when elected, be an inhabitant of that State in which he shall be chosen.

[Apportionment of Representatives and direct taxes—census.[1]—3.] (Representatives and direct taxes shall be apportioned among the several States which may be included within this Union, according to their respective numbers, which shall be determined by adding to the whole number of free persons, including those bound to service for a term of years, and excluding Indians not taxed, three fifths of all other persons.) The actual enumeration shall be made within three years after the first meeting of the Congress of the United States, and within every subsequent term of ten years, in such manner as they shall by law direct. The number of Representatives shall not exceed one for every thirty thousand, but each State shall have at least one Representative; and until such enumeration shall be made, the State of New Hampshire shall be entitled to choose three,

Massachusetts eight, Rhode-Island and Providence Plantations one, Connecticut five, New York six, New Jersey four, Pennsylvania eight, Delaware one, Maryland six, Virginia ten, North Carolina five, South Carolina five, and Georgia three.

[Filling of vacancies in representation.—4.] When vacancies happen in the representation from any State, the Executive Authority thereof shall issue writs of election to fill such vacancies.

[Selection of officers; power of impeachment.—5.] The House of Representatives shall choose their Speaker and other officers; and shall have the sole power of impeachment.

Section 3[2]

[The Senate.—1.] The Senate of the United States shall be composed of two Senators from each State, chosen by the Legislature thereof, for six years; and each Senator shall have one vote.

[Classification of Senators; filling of vacancies.—2.] Immediately after they shall be assembled in consequence of the first election, they shall be divided as equally as may be into three classes. The seats of the Senators of the first class shall be vacated at the expiration of the second year, of the second class at the expiration of the fourth year, and of the third class at the expiration of the sixth year, so that one-third may be chosen every second year; and if vacancies happen by resignation, or otherwise, during the recess of the Legislature of any State, the Executive thereof may make temporary appointments (until the next meeting of the Legislature, which shall then fill such vacancies).

[Qualification of Senators.—3.] No person shall be a Senator who shall not have attained to the age of thirty years, and been nine years a citizen of the United States, and who shall not, when elected, be an inhabitant of that State for which he shall be chosen.

[Vice President to be President of Senate.—4.] The Vice President of the United States shall be President of the Senate, but shall have no vote, unless they be equally divided.

[Selection of Senate officers; President pro tempore.—5.] The Senate shall choose their other officers, and also a President pro tempore, in the absence of the Vice President, or when he shall exercise the office of President of the United States.

[Senate to try impeachments.—6.] The Senate

shall have the sole power to try all impeachments. When sitting for that purpose, they shall be on oath or affirmation. When the President of the United States is tried, the Chief Justice shall preside: and no person shall be convicted without the concurrence of two thirds of the members present.

[Judgment in cases of Impeachment.—7.] Judgment in cases of impeachment shall not extend further than to removal from office, and disqualification to hold and enjoy any office of honor, trust, or profit under the United States: but the party convicted shall nevertheless be liable and subject to indictment, trial, judgment and punishment, according to Law.

Section 4

[Control of congressional elections.—1.] The times, places, and manner of holding elections for Senators and Representatives, shall be prescribed in each State by the Legislature thereof; but the Congress may at any time by law make or alter such regulations, except as to the places of choosing Senators.

[Time for assembling of Congress[3]—2.] The Congress shall assemble at least once in every year, and such meeting shall be on the first Monday in December, unless they shall by law appoint a different day.

Section 5

[Each house to be the judge of the election and qualifications of its members; regulations as to quorum.—1.] Each House shall be the judge of the elections, returns, and qualifications of its own members, and a majority of each shall constitute a quorum to do business; but a smaller number may adjourn from day to day, and may be authorized to compel the attendance of absent members, in such manner, and under such penalties as each House may provide.

[Each house to determine its own rules.—2.] Each House may determine the rules of its proceedings, punish its members for disorderly behavior, and, with the concurrence of two thirds, expel a member.

[Journals and yeas and nays.—3.] Each House shall keep a journal of its proceedings, and from time to time publish the same, excepting such parts as may in their judgment require secrecy; and the yeas and nays of the members of either House on any question shall, at the desire of one fifth of those present, be entered on the journal.

[Adjournment.—4.] Neither House, during the session of Congress, shall, without the consent of the other, adjourn for more than three days, nor to any other place than that in which the two Houses shall be sitting.

Section 6

[Compensation and privileges of members of Congress.—1.] The Senators and Representatives shall receive a compensation for their services, to be ascertained by law, and paid out of the Treasury of the United States. They shall in all cases, except treason, felony, and breach of the peace, be privileged from arrest during their attendance at the session of their respective Houses, and in going to and returning from the same; and for any speech or debate in either House, they shall not be questioned in any other place.

[Incompatible offices; exclusions.—2.] No Senator or Representative shall, during the time for which he was elected, be appointed to any civil office under the authority of the United States, which shall have been created, or the emoluments whereof shall have been increased during such time; and no person holding any office under the United States shall be a member of either House during his continuance in office.

Section 7

[Revenue bills to originate in House.—1.] All bills for raising revenue shall originate in the House of Representatives; but the Senate may propose or concur with amendments as on other bills.

[Manner of passing bills; veto power of President.—2.] Every bill which shall have passed the House of Representatives and the Senate, shall, before it becomes a law, be presented to the President of the United States; if he approve he shall sign it, but if not he shall return it, with his objections to that House in which it shall have originated, who shall enter the objections at large on their journal, and proceed to reconsider it. If after such reconsideration two thirds of that House shall agree to pass the bill, it shall be sent, together with the objections, to the other House, by which it shall likewise be reconsidered, and if approved by two thirds of that House, it shall become a law. But in all such cases the votes of both Houses shall be determined by yeas and nays, and the names of the persons voting for and against the bill shall be entered on the journal of each house, respectively. If any bill shall not be returned by the President within ten days (Sundays excepted) after it shall have been presented to him, the same shall be a law, in like manner as if he had signed it, unless the Congress by their adjournment prevent its return, in which case it shall not be a law.

[Concurrent orders or resolutions, to be passed by President.—3.] Every order, resolution, or vote to which the concurrence of the Senate and House of Representatives may be necessary (except on a question of adjournment) shall be presented to the President of the United States; and before the same shall take effect, shall be approved by him, or being disapproved by him, shall be repassed by two thirds of the Senate and House of Representatives, according to the rules and limitations prescribed in the case of a bill.

Section 8

[General powers of Congress.[4]]
[Taxes, duties, imposts, and excises.—1.] The Congress shall have power to lay and collect taxes, duties, imposts and excises, to pay the debts and provide for the common defense and general welfare of the United States; but all duties, imposts and excises shall be uniform throughout the United States;

[Borrowing of money.—2.] To borrow money on the credit of the United States;

[Regulation of commerce.—3.] To regulate commerce with foreign nations, and among the several States, and with the Indian tribes;

[Naturalization and bankruptcy.—4.] To establish a uniform rule of naturalization, and uniform laws on the subject of bankruptcies throughout the United States;

[Money, weights and measures.—5.] To coin money, regulate the value thereof, and of foreign coin, and fix the standard of weights and measures;

[Counterfeiting.—6.] To provide for the punishment of counterfeiting the securities and current coin of the United States;

[Post offices.—7.] To establish post offices and post roads;

[Patents and copyrights.—8.] To promote the

progress of science and useful arts, by securing for limited times to authors and inventors the exclusive right to their respective writings and discoveries;

[Inferior courts.—9.] To constitute tribunals inferior to the Supreme Court;

[Piracies and felonies.—10.] To define and punish piracies and felonies committed on the high seas, and offences against the law of nations;

[War; marque and reprisal.—11.] To declare war, grant letters of marque and reprisal, and make rules concerning captures on land and water;

[Armies.—12.] To raise and support armies, but no appropriation of money to that use shall be for a longer term than two years;

[Navy.—13.] To provide and maintain a navy;

[Land and naval forces.—14.] To make rules for the government and regulation of the land and naval forces;

[Calling out militia.—15.] To provide for calling forth the militia to execute the laws of the Union, suppress insurrections, and repel invasions;

[Organizing, arming, and disciplining militia.—16.] To provide for organizing, arming, and disciplining, the militia, and for governing such part of them as may be employed in the service of the United States, reserving to the States, respectively, the appointment of the officers, and the authority of training the militia according to the discipline prescribed by Congress;

[Exclusive legislation over District of Columbia.—17.] To exercise exclusive legislation in all cases whatsoever, over such district (not exceeding ten miles square) as may, by cession of particular States, and the acceptance of Congress, become the seat of the Government of the United States, and to exercise like authority over all places purchased by the consent of the Legislature of the State in which the same shall be, for the erection of forts, magazines, arsenals, dock-yards, and other needful buildings;—And

[To enact laws necessary to enforce Constitution.—18.] To make all laws which shall be necessary and proper for carrying into execution the foregoing powers, and all other powers vested by this Constitution in the Government of the United States, or in any department or officer thereof.

Section 9

[Migration or importation of certain persons not to be prohibited before 1808.—1.] The migration or importation of such persons as any of the States now existing shall think proper to admit, shall not be prohibited by the Congress prior to the year one thousand eight hundred and eight, but a tax or duty may be imposed on such importation, not exceeding ten dollars for each person.

[Writ of habeas corpus not to be suspended; exception.—2.] The privilege of the writ of habeas corpus shall not be suspended, unless when in cases of rebellion or invasion the public safety may require it.

[Bills of attainder and ex post facto laws prohibited.—3.] No bill of attainder or ex post facto law shall be passed.

[Capitation and other direct taxes.—4.] No capitation, or other direct, tax shall be laid, unless in proportion to the census or enumeration herein before directed to be taken.[5]

[Exports not to be taxed.—5.] No tax or duty shall be laid on articles exported from any State.

[No preference to be given to ports of any States; interstate shipping.—6.] No preference shall be given by any regulation of commerce or revenue

to the ports of one State over those of another: nor shall vessels bound to, or from, one State, be obliged to enter, clear, or pay duties in another.

[Money, how drawn from treasury; financial statements to be published.—7.] No money shall be drawn from the Treasury, but in consequence of appropriations made by law; and a regular statement and account of the receipts and expenditures of all public money shall be published from time to time.

[Titles of nobility not to be granted; acceptance by government officers of favors from foreign powers.—8.] No title of nobility shall be granted by the United States: and no person holding any office of profit or trust under them, shall, without the consent of the Congress, accept of any present, emolument, office, or title, of any kind whatever, from any king, prince, or foreign state.

Section 10

[Limitations of the powers of the several States.—1.] No State shall enter into any treaty, alliance, or confederation; grant letters of marque and reprisal; coin money; emit bills of credit; make any thing but gold and silver coin a tender in payment of debts; pass any bill of attainder, ex post facto law, or law impairing the obligation of contracts, or grant any title of nobility.

[State imposts and duties.—2.] No State shall, without the consent of the Congress, lay any imposts or duties on imports or exports, except what may be absolutely necessary for executing its inspection laws; and the net produce of all duties and imposts, laid by any State on imports or exports, shall be for the use of the Treasury of the United States; and all such laws shall be subject to the revision and control of the Congress.

[Further restrictions on powers of States.—3.] No State shall, without the consent of Congress, lay any duty of tonnage, keep troops, or ships of war in time of peace, enter into any agreement or compact with another state, or with a foreign power, or engage in war, unless actually invaded, or in such imminent danger as will not admit of delay.

Article II

Section 1

[The President; the executive power.—1.] The executive power shall be vested in a President of the United States of America. He shall hold his office during the term of four years, and, together with the Vice President, chosen for the same term, be elected, as follows

[Appointment and qualifications of presidential electors.—2.] Each State shall appoint, in such manner as the Legislature thereof may direct, a number of electors, equal to the whole number of Senators and Representatives to which the State may be entitled in the Congress: but no Senator or Representative, or person holding an office of trust or profit under the United States, shall be appointed an elector.

[Original method of electing the President and Vice President.[6]] (The electors shall meet in their respective States, and vote by ballot for two persons, of whom one at least shall not be an inhabitant of the same State with themselves. And they shall make a list of all the persons voted for, and of the number of votes for each; which list they shall sign and certify, and transmit sealed to the seat of the Government of the United States, directed to the President of the

Senate. The President of the Senate shall, in the presence of the Senate and House of Representatives, open all the certificates, and the votes shall then be counted. The person having the greatest number of votes shall be the President, if such number be a majority of the whole number of electors appointed; and if there be more than one who have such majority, and have an equal number of votes, then the House of Representatives shall immediately choose by ballot one of them for President; and if no person have a majority, then from the five highest on the list the said House shall in like manner choose the President. But in choosing the President, the votes shall be taken by States, the representation from each State having one vote; A quorum for this purpose shall consist of a member or members from two thirds of the States, and a majority of all the states shall be necessary to a choice. In every case, after the choice of the President, the person having the greatest number of votes of the electors shall be the Vice President. But if there should remain two or more who have equal votes, the Senate should choose from them by ballot the Vice President.)

[Congress may determine time of choosing electors and day for casting their votes.—3.] The Congress may determine the time of choosing the electors, and the day on which they shall give their votes; which day shall be the same throughout the United States.

[Qualifications for the office of President.[7]—4.] No person except a natural born citizen, or a citizen of the United States, at the time of the adoption of this Constitution, shall be eligible to the office of President; neither shall any person be eligible to that office who shall not have attained to the age of thirty-five years, and been fourteen years a resident within the United States.

[Filling vacancy in the office of President.[8]—5.] In case of the removal of the President from office, or of his death, resignation, or inability to discharge the powers and duties of the said office, the same shall devolve on the Vice President, and the Congress may by law provide for the case of removal, death, resignation or inability, both of the President and Vice President, declaring what officer shall then act as President, and such officer shall act accordingly, until the disability be removed, or a President shall be elected.

[Compensation of the President.—6.] The President shall, at stated times, receive for his services, a compensation, which shall neither be increased nor diminished during the period for which he shall have been elected, and he shall not receive within that period any other emolument from the United States, or any of them.

[Oath to be taken by the President.—7.] Before he enter on the execution of his office, he shall take the following oath or affirmation:—"I do solemnly swear (or affirm) that I will faithfully execute the office of President of the United States, and will to the best of my ability, preserve, protect, and defend the Constitution of the United States."

Section 2

[The President to be commander in chief of army and navy and head of executive departments; may grant reprieves and pardons.—1.] The President shall be Commander in Chief of the Army and Navy of the United States, and of the militia of the several States, when called into the actual service of the United States; he may require the opinion, in writing, of the principal officer in each of the executive departments, upon any subject relating to the duties of their respective offices, and he shall have power to grant reprieves and pardons for offences against the United States, except in cases of impeachment.

[President may, with concurrence of Senate, make treaties, appoint ambassadors, etc.; appointment of inferior officers, authority of Congress over.—2.] He shall have power, by and with the advice and consent of the Senate, to make treaties, provided two thirds of the Senators present concur; and he shall nominate, and by and with the advice and consent of the Senate, shall appoint ambassadors, other public ministers and consuls, judges of the Supreme Court, and all other officers of the United States, whose appointments are not herein otherwise provided for, and which shall be established by law: but the Congress may by law vest the appointment of such inferior officers, as they think proper, in the President alone, in the courts of law, or in the heads of departments.

[President may fill vacancies in office during recess of Senate.—3.] The President shall have power to fill up all vacancies that may happen during the recess of the Senate, by granting commissions which shall expire at the end of their session.

Section 3

[President to give advice to Congress; may convene or adjourn it on certain occasions; to receive ambassadors, etc.; have laws executed and commission all officers.] He shall from time to time give to the Congress information of the state of the Union, and recommend to their consideration such measures as he shall judge necessary and expedient; he may, on extraordinary occasions, convene both Houses, or either of them, and in case of disagreement between them, with respect to the time of adjournment, he may adjourn them to such time as he shall think proper; he shall receive ambassadors and other public ministers: he shall take care that the laws be faithfully executed, and shall commission all the officers of the United States.

Section 4

[All civil officers removable by impeachment.] The President, Vice President, and all civil officers of the United States shall be removed from office on impeachment for, and conviction of, treason, bribery, or other high crimes and misdemeanors.

Article III

Section 1

[Judicial powers; how vested; term of office and compensation of judges.] The judicial Power of the United States, shall be vested in one Supreme Court, and in such inferior courts as the Congress may from time to time ordain and establish. The judges, both of the supreme and inferior courts, shall hold their offices during good behavior, and shall, at stated times, receive for their services, a compensation, which shall not be diminished during their continuance in office.

Section 2

[Jurisdiction of Federal courts[9]—1.] The judicial power shall extend to all cases, in law and equity, arising under this Constitution, the laws of the United States, and treaties made, or which shall be made, under their authority; to all cases affecting ambassadors, other public ministers and consuls; to all cases of admiralty and maritime jurisdiction; to controversies to which the United States, shall be a party; to controversies between two or more States; between a State and citizens of another State; between citizens of different States; between citizens of the same State claiming lands under grants of different states, and between a State, or the citizens thereof, and foreign states, citizens, or subjects.

[Original and appellate jurisdiction of Supreme Court.—2.] In all cases affecting ambassadors, other public ministers and consuls, and those in which a State shall be party, the Supreme Court shall have original jurisdiction. In all the other cases before mentioned, the Supreme Court shall have appellate jurisdiction, both as to law and fact, with such exceptions, and under such regulations, as the Congress shall make.

[Trial of all crimes, except impeachment, to be by jury.—3.] The trial of all crimes, except in cases of impeachment, shall be by jury; and such trial shall be held in the State where the said crimes shall have been committed; but when not committed within any State, the trial shall be at such place or places as the Congress may by law have directed.

Section 3

[Treason defined; conviction of.—1.] Treason against the United States, shall consist only in levying war against them, or, in adhering to their enemies, giving them aid and comfort. No person shall be convicted of treason unless on the testimony of two witnesses to the same overt act, or on confession in open court.

[Congress to declare punishment for treason; proviso.—2.] The Congress shall have power to declare the punishment of treason, but no attainder of treason shall work corruption of blood, or forfeiture except during the life of the person attained.

Article IV

Section 1

[Each State to give full faith and credit to the public acts and records of other States.] Full faith and credit shall be given in each State to the public acts, records, and judicial proceedings of every other State. And the Congress may by general laws prescribe the manner in which such acts, records, and proceedings shall be proved, and the effect thereof.

Section 2

[Privileges of citizens.—1.] The citizens of each State shall be entitled to all privileges and immunities of citizens in the several States.

[Extradition between the several States.—2.] A person charged in any State with treason, felony, or other crime, who shall flee from justice, and be found in another State, shall on demand of the Executive authority of the State from which he fled, be delivered up, to be removed to the State having jurisdiction of the crime.

[Persons held to labor or service in one State, fleeing to another, to be returned.—3.] No person held to service or labor in one State, under the laws thereof, escaping into another, shall, in consequence of any law or regulation therein, be discharged from such service or labor, but shall be delivered up on claim of the party to whom such service or labor may be due.

Section 3

[New States.—1.] New States may be admitted by the Congress into this Union; but no new State shall be formed or erected within the jurisdiction of any other State; nor any State be formed by the junction of two or more States, or parts of States, without the consent of the Legislatures of the States concerned as well as of the Congress.

[Regulations concerning territory.—2.] The Congress shall have power to dispose of and make all needful rules and regulations respecting the territory or other property belonging to the United States; and nothing in this Constitution shall be so construed as to prejudice any claims of the United States, or of any particular State.

Section 4

[Republican form of government and protection guaranteed the several States.] The United States shall guarantee to every State in this Union a Republican form of government, and shall protect each of them against invasion; and on application of the Legislature, or of the Executive (when the Legislature cannot be convened) against domestic violence.

Article V

[Ways in which the Constitution can be amended.] The Congress, whenever two thirds of both Houses shall deem it necessary, shall propose amendments to this Constitution, or, on the application of the Legislatures of two thirds of the several States shall call a convention for proposing amendments, which, in either case, shall be valid to all intents and purposes, as part of this Constitution, when ratified by the Legislatures of three fourths of the several States, or by conventions in three fourths thereof, as the one or the other mode of ratification may be proposed by the Congress; provided that no amendment which may be made prior to the year one thousand eight hundred and eight shall in any manner affect the first and fourth clauses in the ninth Section of the first Article; and that no State, without its consent, shall be deprived of its equal suffrage in the Senate.

Article VI

[Debts contracted under the confederation secured.—1.] All debts contracted and engagements entered into, before the adoption of this Constitution, shall be as valid against the United States under this Constitution, as under the Confederation.

[Constitution, laws, and treaties of the United States to be supreme.—2.] This Constitution, and the laws of the United States which shall be made in pursuance thereof; and all treaties made, or which shall be made, under the authority of the United States, shall be the supreme law of the land; and the judges in every State shall be bound thereby, any thing in the Constitution or laws of any State to the

---

1. The clause included in parentheses is amended by the 14th Amendment, Section 2. 2. The first paragraph of this section and the part of the second paragraph included in parentheses are amended by the 17th Amendment. 3. Amended by the 20th Amendment, Section 2. 4. By the 16th Amendment, Congress is given the power to lay and collect taxes on income. 5. See the 16th Amendment. 6. This clause has been superseded by the 12th Amendment. 7. For qualifications of the Vice President, see 12th Amendment. 8. Amended by the 20th Amendment, Sections 3 and 4. 9. This section is abridged by the 11th Amendment. 10. See the 13th Amendment.

contrary notwithstanding.

[**Who shall take constitutional oath; no religious test as to official qualification.—3.**] The Senators and Representatives before mentioned, and the members of the several State Legislatures, and all executive and judicial officers, both of the United States and of the several States, shall be bound by oath or affirmation, to support this Constitution; but no religious test shall ever be required as a qualification to any office or public trust under the United States.

Article VII

[**Constitution to be considered adopted when ratified by nine States.**] The ratification of the conventions of nine States shall be sufficient for the establishment of this Constitution between the States so ratifying the same.

Done in convention by the unanimous consent of the States present the seventeenth day of September in the year of our Lord one thousand seven hundred and eighty seven and of the independence of the United States of America the Twelfth. In witness whereof we have hereunto subscribed our names.

GEORGE WASHINGTON
President and Deputy from Virginia

NEW HAMPSHIRE
John Langdon   Nicholas Gilman

MASSACHUSETTS
Nathaniel Gorham   Rufus King

CONNECTICUT
Wm. Saml. Johnson   Roger Sherman

NEW YORK
Alexander Hamilton

NEW JERSEY
Wil. Livingston   Wm. Paterson
David Brearley   Jona. Dayton

PENNSYLVANIA
B. Franklin   Thomas Mifflin
Robt. Morris   Geo. Clymer
Thos. FitzSimons   Jared Ingersoll
James Wilson   Gouv. Morris

DELAWARE
Geo. Read   Gunning Bedford Jun.
John Dickinson   Richard Bassett
Jaco. Broom

MARYLAND
James McHenry   Dan. of St. Thos. Jenifer
Danl. Carroll

VIRGINIA
John Blair   James Madison, Jr.

NORTH CAROLINA
Wm. Blount   Richd Dobbs Spaight
Hu. Williamson

SOUTH CAROLINA
J. Rutledge   Charles Cotesworth
Charles Pinckney   Pinckney
          Pierce Butler

GEORGIA
William Few   Abr. Baldwin
Attest: William Jackson, Secretary

Amendments to the Constitution of the United States

(Amendments I to X inclusive, popularly known as the Bill of Rights, were proposed and sent to the states by the first session of the First Congress. They were ratified Dec. 15, 1791.)

Article I

[**Freedom of religion, speech, of the press, and right of petition.**] Congress shall make no law respecting an establishment of religion, or prohibiting the free exercise thereof; or abridging the freedom of speech, or of the press; or the right of the people peaceably to assemble, and to petition the Government for a redress of grievances.

Article II

[**Right of people to bear arms not to be infringed.**] A well regulated militia, being necessary to the security of a free State, the right of the people to keep and bear arms, shall not be infringed.

Article III

[**Quartering of troops.**] No soldier shall, in time of peace be quartered in any house, without the consent of the owner, nor in time of war, but in a manner to be prescribed by law.

Article IV

[**Persons and houses to be secure from unreasonable searches and seizures.**] The right of the people to be secure in their persons, houses, papers, and effects, against unreasonable searches and seizures, shall not be violated, and no warrants shall issue, but upon probable cause, supported by oath or affirmation, and particularly describing the place to be searched, and the persons or things to be seized.

Article V

[**Trials for crimes; just compensation for private property taken for public use.**] No person shall be held to answer for a capital, or otherwise infamous crime, unless on a presentment or indictment of a Grand Jury, except in cases arising in the land or naval forces, or in the militia, when in actual service in time of war or public danger; nor shall any person be subject for the same offence to be twice put in jeopardy of life or limb; nor shall be compelled in any criminal case to be a witness against himself, nor be deprived of life, liberty, or property, without due process of law; nor shall private property be taken for public use, without just compensation.

Article VI

[**Civil rights in trials for crimes enumerated.**] In all criminal prosecutions, the accused shall enjoy the right to a speedy and public trial, by an impartial jury of the State and district wherein the crime shall have been committed, which district shall have been previously ascertained by law, and to be informed of the nature and cause of the accusation; to be confronted with the witnesses against him; to have compulsory process for obtaining witnesses in his favor, and to have the assistance of counsel for his defense.

Article VII

[**Civil rights in civil suits.**] In suits at common law, where the value in controversy shall exceed twenty dollars, the right of trial by jury shall be preserved, and no fact tried by a jury, shall be otherwise re-examined in any court of the United States, than according to the rules of the common law.

Article VIII

[**Excessive bail, fines, and punishments prohibited.**] Excessive bail shall not be required, nor excessive fines imposed, nor cruel and unusual punishments inflicted.

Article IX

[**Reserved rights of people.**] The enumeration in the Constitution, of certain rights, shall not be construed to deny or disparage others retained by the people.

Article X

[**Powers not delegated, reserved to states and people respectively.**] The powers not delegated to the United States by the Constitution, nor prohibited by it to the States, are reserved to the States, respectively, or to the people.

Article XI

(The proposed amendment was sent to the states Mar. 5, 1794, by the Third Congress. It was ratified Feb. 7, 1795.)

[**Judicial power of United States not to extend to suits against a State.**] The judicial power of the United States shall not be construed to extend to any suit in law or equity, commenced or prosecuted against one of the United States by citizens of another State, or by citizens or subjects of any foreign state.

Article XII

(The proposed amendment was sent to the states Dec. 12, 1803, by the Eighth Congress. It was ratified July 27, 1804.)

[**Present mode of electing President and Vice-President by electors.**[1]] The electors shall meet in their respective states, and vote by ballot for President and Vice President, one of whom, at least, shall not be an inhabitant of the same state with themselves; they shall name in their ballots the person voted for as President, and in distinct ballots the person voted for as Vice President, and they shall make distinct lists of all persons voted for as President, and of all persons voted for as Vice President, and of the number of votes for each, which lists they shall sign and certify, and transmit sealed to the seat of the government of the United States, directed to the President of the Senate; the President of the Senate shall, in the presence of the Senate and House of Representatives, open all the certificates and the votes shall then be counted; the person having the greatest number of votes for President, shall be the President, if such number be a majority of the whole number of electors appointed; and if no person have such majority, then from the persons having the highest numbers not exceeding three on the list of those voted for as President, the House of Representatives shall choose immediately, by ballot, the President. But in choosing the President, the votes shall be taken by states, the representation from each State having one vote; a quorum for this purpose shall consist of a member or members from two thirds of the states, and a majority of all the states shall be necessary to a choice. And if the House of Representatives shall not choose a President whenever the right of choice shall devolve upon them, before the fourth day of March next following, then the Vice President shall act as President, as in the case of the death or other constitutional disability of the President. The person having the greatest number of votes as Vice President, shall be the Vice President, if such number be a majority of the whole number of electors appointed, and if no person have a majority, then from the two highest numbers on the list, the Senate shall choose the Vice President; a quorum for the purpose shall consist of two thirds of the whole number of Senators, and a majority of the whole number shall be necessary to a choice. But no person constitutionally ineligible to the office of President shall be eligible to that of Vice President of the United States.

Article XIII

(The proposed amendment was sent to the states Feb. 1, 1865, by the Thirty-eighth Congress. It was ratified Dec. 6, 1865.)

Section 1

[**Slavery prohibited.**] Neither slavery nor involuntary servitude, except as a punishment for crime whereof the party shall have been duly convicted, shall exist within the United States, or any place subject to their jurisdiction.

Section 2

[**Congress given power to enforce this article.**] Congress shall have power to enforce this article by appropriate legislation.

Article XIV

(The proposed amendment was sent to the states June 16, 1866, by the Thirty-ninth Congress. It was ratified July 9, 1868.)

Section 1

[**Citizenship defined; privileges of citizens.**] All persons born or naturalized in the United States, and subject to the jurisdiction thereof, are citizens of the United States and of the State wherein they reside. No State shall make or enforce any law which shall abridge the privileges or immunities of citizens of the United States; nor shall any State deprive any person of life, liberty, or property, without due process of law; nor deny to any person within its jurisdiction the equal protection of the laws.

Section 2

[Apportionment of Representatives.] Representatives shall be apportioned among the several States according to their respective numbers, counting the whole number of persons in each State, excluding Indians not taxed. But when the right to vote at any election for the choice of electors for President and Vice President of the United States, Representatives in Congress, the executive and judicial officers of a State, or the members of the Legislature thereof, is denied to any of the male inhabitants of such State, being twenty-one years of age, and citizens of the United States, or in any way abridged, except for participation in rebellion, or other crime, the basis of representation therein shall be reduced in the proportion which the number of such male citizens shall bear to the whole number of male citizens twenty-one years of age in such State.

Section 3

[Disqualification for office; removal of disability.] No person shall be a Senator or Representative in Congress, or elector of President and Vice President, or hold any office, civil or military, under the United States, or under any State, who, having previously taken an oath, as a member of Congress, or as an officer of the United States, or as a member of any State Legislature, or as an executive or judicial officer of any State, to support the Constitution of the United States, shall have engaged in insurrection or rebellion against the same, or given aid or comfort to the enemies thereof. But Congress may, by a vote of two thirds of each House, remove such disability.

Section 4

[Public debt not to be questioned; payment of debts and claims incurred in aid of rebellion forbidden.] The validity of the public debt of the United States, authorized by law, including debts incurred for payment of pensions and bounties for services in suppressing insurrection or rebellion, shall not be questioned. But neither the United States nor any State shall assume or pay any debt or obligation incurred in aid of insurrection or rebellion against the United States, or any claim for the loss or emancipation of any slave; but all such debts, obligations, and claims shall be held illegal and void.

Section 5

[Congress given power to enforce this article.] The Congress shall have power to enforce, by appropriate legislation, the provisions of this article.

Article XV

(The proposed amendment was sent to the states Feb. 27, 1869, by the Fortieth Congress. It was ratified Feb. 3, 1870.)

Section 1

[Right of certain citizens to vote established.] The right of citizens of the United States to vote shall not be denied or abridged by the United States or by any State on account of race, color, or previous condition of servitude.

Section 2

[Congress given power to enforce this article.] The Congress shall have power to enforce this article by appropriate legislation.

Article XVI

(The proposed amendment was sent to the states July 12, 1909, by the Sixty-first Congress. It was ratified Feb. 3, 1913.)

[Taxes on income; Congress given power to lay and collect.] The Congress shall have power to lay and collect taxes on incomes, from whatever source derived, without apportionment among the several States, and without regard to any census or enumeration.

Article XVII

(The proposed amendment was sent to the states May 16, 1912, by the Sixty-second Congress. It was ratified April 8, 1913.)

[Election of United States Senators; filling of vacancies; qualifications of electors.] The Senate of the United States shall be composed of two Senators from each State, elected by the people thereof, for six years; and each Senator shall have one vote. The electors in each State shall have the qualifications requisite for electors of the most numerous branch of the State Legislatures.

When vacancies happen in the representation of any State in the Senate, the executive authority of such State shall issue writs of election to fill such vacancies: Provided, that the legislature of any State may empower the executive thereof to make temporary appointment until the people fill the vacancies by election as the legislature may direct.

This amendment shall not be so construed as to affect the election or term of any Senator chosen before it becomes valid as part of the Constitution.

Article XVIII[2]

(The proposed amendment was sent to the states Dec. 18, 1917, by the Sixty-fifth Congress. It was ratified by three quarters of the states by Jan. 16, 1919, and became effective Jan. 16, 1920.)

Section 1

[Manufacture, sale, or transportation of intoxicating liquors, for beverage purposes, prohibited.] After one year from the ratification of this article the manufacture, sale, or transportation of intoxicating liquors within, the importation thereof into, or the exportation thereof from the United States and all territory subject to the jurisdiction thereof for beverage purposes is hereby prohibited.

Section 2

[Congress and the several States given concurrent power to pass appropriate legislation to enforce this article.] The Congress and the several States shall have concurrent power to enforce this article by appropriate legislation.

Section 3

[Provisions of article to become operative, when adopted by three fourths of the States.] This article shall be inoperative unless it shall have been ratified as an amendment to the Constitution by the legislatures of the several States, as provided in the Constitution, within seven years from the date of the submission hereof to the States by Congress.

Article XIX

(The proposed amendment was sent to the states June 4, 1919, by the Sixty-sixth Congress. It was ratified Aug. 18, 1920.)

[The right of citizens to vote shall not be denied because of sex.] The right of citizens of the United States to vote shall not be denied or abridged by the United States or by any State on account of sex.

[Congress given power to enforce this article.] Congress shall have power to enforce this article by appropriate legislation.

Article XX

(The proposed amendment, sometimes called the "Lame Duck Amendment," was sent to the states Mar. 3, 1932, by the Seventy-second Congress. It was ratified Jan. 23, 1933; but, in accordance with Section 5, Sections 1 and 2 did not go into effect until Oct. 15, 1933.)

Section 1

[Terms of President, Vice President, Senators, and Representatives.] The terms of the President and Vice President shall end at noon on the twentieth day of January, and the terms of Senators and Representatives at noon on the third day of January, of the years in which such terms would have ended if this article had not been ratified; and the terms of their successors shall then begin.

Section 2

[Time of assembling Congress.] The Congress shall assemble at least once in every year, and such meeting shall begin at noon on the third day of January, unless they shall by law appoint a different day.

Section 3

[Filling vacancy in office of President.] If, at the time fixed for the beginning of the term of the President, the President-elect shall have died, the Vice President-elect shall become President. If a President shall not have been chosen before the time fixed for the beginning of his term, or if the President-elect shall have failed to qualify, then the Vice President shall have qualified; and the Congress may by law provide for the case wherein neither a President-elect nor a Vice President-elect shall have qualified, declaring who shall then act as President, or the manner in which one who is to act shall be selected, and such person shall act accordingly until a President or Vice President shall have qualified.

Section 4

[Power of Congress in Presidential succession.] The Congress may by law provide for the case of the death of any of the persons from whom the House of Representatives may choose a President whenever the right of choice shall have devolved upon them, and for the case of the death of any of the persons from whom the Senate may choose a Vice President whenever the right of choice shall have devolved upon them.

Section 5

[Time of taking effect.] Sections 1 and 2 shall take effect on the 15th day of October following the ratification of this article.

Section 6

[Ratification.] This article shall be inoperative unless it shall have been ratified as an amendment to the Constitution by the legislatures of three fourths of the several States within seven years from the date of its submission.

Article XXI

(The proposed amendment was sent to the states Feb. 20, 1933, by the Seventy-second Congress. It was ratified Dec. 5, 1933.)

Section 1

[Repeal of Prohibition Amendment.] The eighteenth article of amendment to the Constitution of the United States is hereby repealed.

Section 2

[Transportation of intoxicating liquors.] The transportation or importation into any State, territory, or possession of the United States for delivery or use therein of intoxicating liquors, in violation of the laws thereof, is hereby prohibited.

Section 3

[Ratification.] This article shall be inoperative unless it shall have been ratified as an amendment to the Constitution by convention in the several States, as provided in the Constitution, within seven years from the date of the submission thereof to the States by the Congress.

Article XXII

(The proposed amendment was sent to the states Mar. 21, 1947, by the Eightieth Congress. It was ratified Feb. 27, 1951.)

Section 1

[Limit to number of terms a President may serve.] No person shall be elected to the office of the President more than twice, and no person who has held the office of President, or acted as President, for more than two years of a term to which some other person was elected President shall be elected to the office of the President more than once. But this article shall not apply to any person holding the office of President when this article was proposed by the Congress, and shall not prevent any person who may be holding the office of President, or acting as President, during the term within which this article becomes operative from holding the office of President or acting as President during the remainder of such term.

Section 2

[Ratification.] This article shall be inoperative unless it shall have been ratified as an amendment to the Constitution by the legislatures of three fourths of the several States within seven years from the date of its submission to the States by the Congress.

Article XXIII

(The proposed amendment was sent to the states June 16, 1960, by the Eighty-sixth Congress. It was ratified March 29, 1961.)

Section 1

[Electors for the District of Columbia.] The District constituting the seat of Government of the United States shall appoint in such manner as the Congress may direct: A number of electors of President and Vice President equal to the whole number of Senators and Representatives in Congress to which the District would be entitled if it were a State, but in no event more than the least populous State; they shall be in addition to those appointed by the States, but they shall be considered, for the purposes of the election of President and Vice President, to be electors appointed by a State; and they shall meet in the District and perform such duties as provided by the twelfth article of amendment.

Section 2

[Congress given power to enforce this article.] The Congress shall have the power to enforce this article by appropriate legislation.

Article XXIV

(The proposed amendment was sent to the states Aug. 27, 1962, by the Eighty-seventh Congress. It was ratified Jan. 23, 1964.)

Section 1

[Payment of poll tax or other taxes not to be prerequisite for voting in federal elections.] The right of citizens of the United States to vote in any primary or other election for President or Vice President, for electors for President or Vice President, or for Senator or Representative in Congress, shall not be denied or abridged by the United States or any State by reasons of failure to pay any poll tax or other tax.

Section 2

[Congress given power to enforce this article.] The Congress shall have the power to enforce this article by appropriate legislation.

Article XXV

(The proposed amendment was sent to the states July 6, 1965, by the Eighty-ninth Congress. It was ratified Feb. 10, 1967.)

Section 1

[Succession of Vice President to Presidency.] In case of the removal of the President from office or of his death or resignation, the Vice President shall become President.

Section 2

[Vacancy in office of Vice President.] Whenever there is a vacancy in the office of the Vice President, the President shall nominate a Vice President who shall take office upon confirmation by a majority vote of both Houses of Congress.

Section 3

[Vice President as Acting President.] Whenever the President transmits to the President pro tempore of the Senate and the Speaker of the House of Representatives his written declaration that he is unable to discharge the powers and duties of his office, and until he transmits to them a written declaration to the contrary, such powers and duties shall be discharged by the Vice President as Acting President.

Section 4

[Vice President as Acting President.] Whenever the Vice President and a majority of either the princi-

pal officers of the executive departments or of such other body as Congress may by law provide, transmit to the President pro tempore of the Senate and the Speaker of the House of Representatives their written declaration that the President is unable to discharge the powers and duties of his office, the Vice President shall immediately assume the powers and duties of the office as Acting President.

Thereafter, when the President transmits to the President pro tempore of the Senate and the Speaker of the House of Representatives his written declaration that no inability exists, he shall resume the powers and duties of his office unless the Vice President and a majority of either the principal officers of the executive department or of such other body as Congress may by law provide, transmit within four days to the President pro tempore of the Senate and the Speaker of the House of Representatives their written declaration that the President is unable to discharge the powers and duties of his office. Thereupon Congress shall decide the issue, assembling within forty-eight hours for that purpose if not in session. If the Congress, within twenty-one days after receipt of the latter written declaration, or, if Congress is not in session, within twenty-one days after Congress is required to assemble, determines by two thirds vote of both Houses that the President is unable to discharge the powers and duties of his office, the Vice President shall continue to discharge the same as Acting President; otherwise, the President shall resume the powers and duties of his office.

Article XXVI

(The proposed amendment was sent to the states Mar. 23, 1971, by the Ninety-second Congress. It was ratified July 1, 1971.)

Section 1

[Voting for 18-year-olds.] The right of citizens of the United States, who are 18 years of age or older, to vote shall not be denied or abridged by the United States or by any state on account of age.

Section 2

[Congress given power to enforce this article.] The Congress shall have power to enforce this article by appropriate legislation.

Article XXVII

(Ratified May 7, 1992.)

[Congressional raises.] No law, varying the compensation for the services of the Senators and Representatives, shall take effect, until an election of Representatives shall have intervened.

1. Amended by the 20th Amendment, Sections 3 and 4. 2. Repealed by the 21st Amendment.

The White House

Source: Department of the Interior, U.S. National Park Service.

The White House, the official residence of the President, is at 1600 Pennsylvania Avenue in Washington, D.C. 20500. The site, covering about 18 acres, was selected by President Washington and Pierre Charles L'Enfant, and the architect was James Hoban. The design appears to have been influenced by Leinster House, Dublin, and James Gibb's *Book of Architecture.* The cornerstone was laid Oct. 13, 1792, and the first residents were President and Mrs. John Adams in November 1800. The building was fired by the British in 1814.

From December 1948 to March 1952, the interior of the White House was rebuilt, and the outer walls were strengthened.

The rooms for public functions are on the first floor; the second and third floors are used as the residence of the President and First Family. The most celebrated public room is the East Room, where formal receptions take place. Other public rooms are the Red Room, the Green Room, and the Blue Room. The State Dining Room is used for formal dinners. There are 132 rooms.

The Mayflower Compact

On Sept. 6, 1620, the *Mayflower,* a sailing vessel of about 180 tons, started her memorable voyage from Plymouth, England, with about 100[1] pilgrims aboard, bound for Virginia to establish a private permanent colony in North America. Arriving at what is now Provincetown, Mass., on Nov. 11 (Nov. 21, new style calendar), 41 of the passengers signed the famous "Mayflower Compact" as the boat lay at anchor in that Cape Cod harbor. A small detail of the pilgrims, led by William Bradford, assigned to select a place for permanent settlement landed at what is now Plymouth, Mass., on Dec. 21 (n.s.).

The text of the compact follows:

In the name of God, Amen. We, whose names are underwritten, the Loyal Subjects of our dread Sovereign Lord, King *James,* by the Grace of God, of *Great Britain, France and Ireland,* King, *Defender of the Faith, &*

Having undertaken for the Glory of God, and Advancement of the Christian Faith, and the Honour of our King and Country, a voyage to plant the first colony in the northern Parts of Virginia; do by these Presents, solemnly and mutually in the Presence of God and one of another, covenant and combine ourselves together into a civil Body Politick, for our better Ordering and Preservation, and Furtherance of the Ends aforesaid; And by Virtue hereof to enact, constitute, and frame, such just and equal Laws, Ordinances, Acts, Constitutions and Offices, from time to time, as shall be thought most meet and convenient for the General good of the Colony; unto which we promise all due Submission and Obedience.

In Witness whereof we have hereunto subscribed our names at *Cape Cod* the eleventh of *November,* in the Reign of our Sovereign Lord, King *James* of *England, France* and *Ireland,* the eighteenth, and of *Scotland* the fifty-fourth. *Anno Domini,* 1620

John Carver	William Mullins	John Billington	Peter Brown
Digery Priest	Thomas English	Thomas Tinker	John Turner
William Brewster	John Howland	Samuel Fuller	Edward Tilly
Edmund Margesson	Stephen Hopkins	Richard Clark	John Craxton
John Alden	Edward Winslow	John Allerton	Thomas Rogers
George Soule	Gilbert Winslow	Richard Warren	John Goodman
James Chilton	Miles Standish	Edward Liester	Edward Fuller
Francis Cooke	Richard Bitteridge	William Bradford	Richard Gardiner
Moses Fletcher	Francis Eaton	Thomas Williams	William White
John Ridgate	John Tilly	Isaac Allerton	Edward Doten
Christopher Martin			

1. Historians differ as to whether 100, 101, or 102 passengers were aboard.

The Monroe Doctrine

The Monroe Doctrine was announced in President James Monroe's message to Congress, during his second term on Dec. 2, 1823, in part as follows:

"In the discussions to which this interest has given rise, and in the arrangements by which they may terminate, the occasion has been deemed proper for asserting as a principle in which rights and interests of the United States are involved, that the American continents, by the free and independent condition which they have assumed and maintain, are henceforth not to be considered as subjects for future colonization by any European power. . . . We owe it, therefore, to candor and to the amicable relations existing between the United States and those powers to declare that we should consider any attempt on their part to extend their system to any portion of this hemisphere as dangerous to our peace and safety. With the existing colonies or dependencies of any European power we have not interfered and shall not interfere. But with the governments who have declared their independence and maintain it, and whose independence we have, on great consideration and on just principles, acknowledged, we could not view any interposition for the purpose of oppressing them or controlling in any other manner their destiny by any European power in any other light than as the manifestation of an unfriendly disposition toward the United States."

Order of Presidential Succession

1. The Vice President
2. Speaker of the House
3. President pro tempore of the Senate
4. Secretary of State
5. Secretary of the Treasury
6. Secretary of Defense
7. Attorney General
8. Secretary of the Interior
9. Secretary of Agriculture
10. Secretary of Commerce
11. Secretary of Labor
12. Secretary of Health and Human Services
13. Secretary of Housing and Urban Development
14. Secretary of Transportation
15. Secretary of Energy
16. Secretary of Education
17. Secretary of Veterans Affairs

NOTE: An official cannot succeed to the Presidency unless that person meets the Constitutional requirements.

The Star-Spangled Banner

Francis Scott Key, 1814

O say, can you see, by the dawn's early light,
What so proudly we hail'd at the twilight's last gleaming?
Whose broad stripes and bright stars, thro' the perilous fight,
O'er the ramparts we watch'd, were so gallantly streaming?
And the rockets' red glare, the bombs bursting in air,
Gave proof thro' the night that our flag was still there.
O say, does that star-spangled banner yet wave
O'er the land of the free and the home of the brave?

On the shore dimly seen thro' the mists of the deep,
Where the foe's haughty host in dread silence reposes,
What is that which the breeze, o'er the towering steep,
As it fitfully blows, half conceals, half discloses?
Now it catches the gleam of the morning's first beam,
In full glory reflected, now shines on the stream:
'T is the star-spangled banner: O, long may it wave
O'er the land of the free and the home of the brave!

And where is that band who so vauntingly swore
That the havoc of war and the battle's confusion,
A home and a country should leave us no more?
Their blood has wash'd out their foul footsteps' pollution.
No refuge could save the hireling and slave
From the terror of flight or the gloom of the grave:
And the star-spangled banner in triumph doth wave
O'er the land of the free and the home of the brave.

O thus be it ever when free-men shall stand
Between their lov'd home and the war's desolation;
Blest with vict'ry and peace, may the heav'n-rescued land
Praise the Pow'r that hath made and preserv'd us a nation!
Then conquer we must, when our cause it is just,
And this be our motto: "In God is our trust!"
And the star-spangled banner in triumph shall wave
O'er the land of the free and the home of the brave!

On Sept. 13, 1814, Francis Scott Key visited the British fleet in Chesapeake Bay to secure the release of Dr. William Beanes, who had been captured after the burning of Washington, D.C. The release was secured, but Key was detained on ship overnight during the shelling of Fort McHenry, one of the forts defending Baltimore. In the morning, he was so delighted to see the American flag still flying over the fort that he began a poem to commemorate the occasion. First published under the title "Defense of Fort M'Henry," and later as "The Star-Spangled Banner," the poem soon attained wide popularity as sung to the tune "To Anacreon in Heaven." The origin of this tune is obscure, but it may have been written by John Stafford Smith, a British composer born in 1750. "The Star-Spangled Banner" was officially made the National Anthem by Congress in 1931, although it had been already adopted as such by the Army and the Navy.

The Emancipation Proclamation

January 1, 1863

By the President of the United States of America:

A Proclamation.

Whereas on the 22d day of September, A.D. 1862, a proclamation was issued by the President of the United States, containing, among other things, the following, to wit:

"That on the 1st day of January, A.D. 1863, all persons held as slaves within any State or designated part of a State the people whereof shall then be in rebellion against the United States shall be then, thenceforward, and forever free; and the executive government of the United States, including the military and naval authority thereof, will recognize and maintain the freedom of such persons and will do not act or acts to repress such persons, or any of them, in any efforts they may make for their actual freedom.

"That the executive will on the 1st day of January aforesaid, by proclamation, designate the States and parts of States, if any, in which the people thereof, respectively, shall then be in rebellion against the United States; and the fact that any State or the people thereof shall on that day be in good faith represented in the Congress of the United States by members chosen thereto at elections wherein a majority of the qualified voters of such States shall have participated shall, in the absence of strong countervailing testimony, be deemed conclusive evidence that such State and the people thereof are not then in rebellion against the United States."

Now, therefore, I, Abraham Lincoln, President of

the United States, by virtue of the power in me vested as Commander-in-Chief of the Army and Navy of the United States in time of actual armed rebellion against the authority and government of the United States, and as a fit and necessary war measure for suppressing said rebellion, do, on this 1st day of January, A.D. 1863, and in accordance with my purpose so to do, publicly proclaimed for the full period of one hundred days from the first day above mentioned, order and designate as the States and parts of States wherein the people thereof, respectively, are this day in rebellion against the United States the following, to wit:

Arkansas, Texas, Louisiana (except the parishes of St. Bernard, Plaquemines, Jefferson, St. John, St. Charles, St. James, Ascension, Assumption, Terrebonne, Lafourche, St. Mary, St. Martin, and Orleans, including the city of New Orleans), Mississippi, Alabama, Florida, Georgia, South Carolina, North Carolina, and Virginia (except the forty-eight counties designated as West Virginia, and also the counties of Berkeley, Accomac, Northhampton, Elizabeth City, York, Princess Anne, and Norfolk, including the cities of Norfolk and Portsmouth), and which excepted parts are for the present left precisely as if this proclamation were not issued.

And by virtue of the power and for the purpose aforesaid, I do order and declare that all persons held as slaves within said designated States and parts of States are, and henceforward shall be, free; and that the Executive Government of the United States, including the military and naval authorities thereof, will recognize and maintain the freedom of said persons.

And I hereby enjoin upon the people so declared to be free to abstain from all violence, unless in necessary self-defense; and I recommend to them that, in all cases when allowed, they labor faithfully for reasonable wages.

And I further declare and make known that such persons of suitable condition will be received into the armed service of the United States to garrison forts, positions, stations, and other places, and to man vessels of all sorts in said service.

And upon this act, sincerely believed to be an act of justice, warranted by the Constitution upon military necessity, I invoke the considerate judgment of mankind and the gracious favor of Almighty God.

The Confederate States of America

State	Seceded from Union	Readmitted to Union[1]	State	Seceded from Union	Readmitted to Union[1]
1. South Carolina	Dec. 20, 1860	July 9, 1868	7. Texas	March 2, 1861	March 30, 1870
2. Mississippi	Jan. 9, 1861	Feb. 23, 1870	8. Virginia	April 17, 1861	Jan. 26, 1870
3. Florida	Jan. 10, 1861	June 25, 1868	9. Arkansas	May 6, 1861	June 22, 1868
4. Alabama	Jan. 11, 1861	July 13, 1868	10. North Carolina	May 20, 1861	July 4, 1868
5. Georgia	Jan. 19, 1861	July 15, 1870[2]	11. Tennessee	June 8, 1861	July 24, 1866
6. Louisiana	Jan. 26, 1861	July 9, 1868			

1. Date of readmission to representation in U.S. House of Representatives. 2. Second readmission date. First date was July 21, 1868, but the representatives were unseated March 5, 1869. NOTE: Four other slave states—Delaware, Kentucky, Maryland, and Missouri—remained in the Union.

Lincoln's Gettysburg Address

The Battle of Gettysburg, one of the most noted battles of the Civil War, was fought on July 1, 2, and 3, 1863. On Nov. 19, 1863, the field was dedicated as a national cemetery by President Lincoln in a two-minute speech that was to become immortal. At the time of its delivery the speech was relegated to the inside pages of the papers, while a two-hour address by Edward Everett, the leading orator of the time, caught the headlines.

The following is the text of the address revised by President Lincoln from his own notes:

Fourscore and seven years ago our fathers brought forth on this continent a new nation conceived in liberty and dedicated to the proposition that all men are created equal. Now we are engaged in a great civil war testing whether that nation, or any nation so conceived and so dedicated, can long endure. We are met on a great battlefield of that war. We have come to dedicate a portion of that field as a final resting-place for those who here gave their lives that that nation might live. It is altogether fitting and proper that we should do this. But, in a larger sense, we cannot dedicate, we cannot consecrate, we cannot hallow this ground. The brave men, living and dead, who struggled here have consecrated it far above our poor power to add or detract. The world will little note nor long remember what we say here, but it can never forget what they did here. It is for us the living rather to be dedicated here to the unfinished work which they who fought here have thus far so nobly advanced. It is rather for us to be here dedicated to the great task remaining before us—that from these honored dead we take increased devotion to that cause for which they gave the last full measure of devotion—that we here highly resolve that these dead shall not have died in vain, that this nation under God shall have a new birth of freedom, and that government of the people, by the people, for the people shall not perish from the earth.

Slavery in the United States

Source: The Reader's Companion to American History.

The Institution of Slavery

Slavery has been of signal importance in American history. During the antebellum period, it undergirded the nation's economy, increasingly dominated its politics, and finally led to civil war between North and South. After that war, the legacy of slavery continued to shape much of American history, from the struggle over Reconstruction in the 1860s and 1870s to the struggle over civil rights a century later.

Forced labor emerged in the American colonies, as it did elsewhere in the New World, to meet a pervasive labor shortage that resulted when settlers sought commercial exploitation of agricultural staples (primarily tobacco in the Upper South and rice in the Lower South) in areas of low population density. Although twenty Africans were sold to settlers in Virginia as early as 1619, throughout most of the seventeenth century white indentured servants were far more numerous in the English mainland colonies than African slaves. Only after 1680, when the flow of indentured migrants from Europe diminished, did European servitude increasingly give way to African slavery,. By the middle of the eighteenth century, slavery existed in all thirteen colonies and formed the heart of the agricultural labor system in the southern colonies.

In the years following the American Revolution, slavery, which had never been so prevalent or economically important in the North as in the South, became the South's "peculiar institution." Between 1774 and 1804 all the northern states undertook to abolish slavery. In some states emancipation was immediate, but more often—as in New York and New Jersey—it was gradual, freeing slaves born after passage of the state's emancipation act when they reached a given age (usually in their twenties). But despite widespread questioning of its morality and a proliferation of private manumissions in the Upper South during the revolutionary era, bondage actually expanded in the southern states. The spread of cotton production following the invention of the cotton gin in 1793 sharply increased the demand for slave labor and made possible the emergence of a vast new slave empire as southerners moved west. At the outbreak of the Revolution, the United States contained about half a million slaves, North and South; on the eve of the Civil War the country held almost 4 million slaves, confined entirely to the South.

Southern slavery was highly diverse. Slaveholdings varied according to size, location, and crops produced. Slavery in cities differed substantially from that in the countryside. Masters exhibited varying temperaments and used diverse methods to run their farms and plantations. Slaves served as skilled craftsmen, preachers, nurses, drivers, and mill workers, as well as field hands and house servants.

Despite these variations, southern slavery displayed some distinctive features. Unlike slavery in the rest of the New World, which depended on the continued importation of Africans, that in the southern United States was self-sustaining: during the half century after the end of legal importation in 1808, the slave population more than tripled. One consequence of this natural population growth was an equal ratio of males to females that—in contrast to the male preponderance in slave societies heavily dependent on imports from Africa—facilitated the formation of strong families. Another was the emergence of a slave population, that, despite its distinctive cultural norms, was increasingly American in birth and character. Slaves adopted the religion of their masters, for example, but adapted it to their own particular needs. In short, Africans became African-Americans.

Equally important was the moderate ratio of slaves to nonslaves, which set the South off both from societies in which slavery was legal but slaves were few and from Caribbean countries like Haiti and Jamaica, where slaves formed over 90 percent of the population, lived on immense estates with hundreds of other slaves, and rarely saw their owners. Throughout the antebellum period, slaves constituted about one-third of the southern population. Most lived on large farms and small plantations—three-quarters on holdings with fewer than fifty slaves—with resident masters who took an active role in directing them and were committed to slavery not just as an economic investment but as a way of life.

The slave-master relationship was intense and unstable. Slaves strove mightily to improve their conditions, sometimes by running away or striking back at hated individuals but more often by focusing on their families, friends, and churches. Although slaves were able to secure a measure of social autonomy in their quarters, that autonomy was severely limited by the masters' pervasive interference in their lives. Owners held Bible readings, nursed the sick, provided material conditions that were relatively high by international standards, and prided themselves on caring for their "people." But they (and their overseers) subjected the slaves to countless arbitrary regulations, resorted frequently to the lash, took sexual liberties with slave women, separated family members more often than they admitted, and strove to keep their human property in a state of complete dependence.

The unique sectional nature of antebellum slavery led to an increasingly bitter political struggle between North and South that culminated in civil war. A militant abolitionist movement, predicated on the sinfulness of slaveholding, emerged in the 1830s. Far more persuasive to most northerners was the "free-labor" argument that slavery was backward, inefficient, and socially degrading and must not be allowed to expand. Southern spokesmen responded with elaborate arguments in defense of slavery, including pseudoscientific demonstrations that blacks were unfit for freedom, reminders that the nation's economic well-being depended on slave labor, assertions that the Bible itself sanctioned the enslavement of the "sons of Ham," and claims that slavery produced a more humane and harmonious social order than the exploitative free-labor system of Great Britain and the North. From the late 1840s, the controversy over slavery increasingly dominated national politics. Finally, Abraham Lincoln's election to the presidency in 1860 on a free-labor Republican platform plunged the country into a secession crisis and civil war as southern politicians defended to the end their peculiar institution.

The chief casualty of the war to preserve slavery was slavery itself. Under the combined pressure of military necessity, growing northern antislavery sentiment, and the self-liberation of slaves who deserted in droves as federal troops neared, northern war aims, originally limited to preserving the Union, evolved to include the destruction of slavery. After Lincoln issued the Emancipation Proclamation that took effect on January 1, 1863, it became clear that northern victory would mean the end of slavery. The Thirteenth Amendment to the Constitution, ratified in 1865, provided legal confirmation. What should replace slavery, however, remained unanswered and would emerge as the primary issue of Reconstruction.

Slave Trade

The Atlantic slave trade began in the fifteenth century incidental to the Portuguese exploration of the African coast. Although trade in slaves dates back to ancient times, the Atlantic trade was marked by its westward direction, huge volume, long duration of the crossing, and racial character. Europe and the Iberian islands made the first imports; not until the second half of the sixteenth century did Latin America become the major market.

Dutch, French, and English colonization in America opened new markets for slave traders. The practice of importing labor from distant Africa sprang from the colonists' failure to develop a work force among Native Americans and white immigrants. Colonists, finding that Africans were cheap and relatively immune to tropical diseases, rationalized slavery on grounds that blacks were racially inferior.

Although the Dutch introduced the first Africans in North America in 1619, only about 20,500 had arrived by 1700. But the expansion of staple agriculture in the eighteenth century, especially tobacco, rice, and indigo, created a rising demand for slave labor: these crops required the performance of many manual tasks and a force that could be relied on to work through the long growing season.

Importation of Africans into the present United States occurred during a relatively short span of time. Only about one-third of the total arrived before 1760, more than one-half in the next half century, and a large influx—over one-sixth—in the decade before importation was abolished in 1808. Perhaps a thousand a year were brought in illegally over the next half century. Total imports, including those into Louisiana after 1761, amounted to some 600,000 persons—about 6 percent of the whole transatlantic traffic.

West Africa, stretching from the Senegal River through the Congo region, provided most of the slave trade's victims. Contrary to some historians, the West Indies did not ship many slaves to North America. A study of Virginia imports, 1727–1769, found that only about a tenth arrived from the West Indies, and another study, of South Carolina imports, 1735–1775, found that a seventh came from there. Most slaves entering the American mainland came directly from Africa, without the "seasoning" in the West Indies described by some writers.

The antebellum argument that New England slavers fastened the practice on the South is a myth. To the contrary, British ships from London, Bristol, and Liverpool introduced most of the slaves, with New England vessels contributing only in a small way to mainland trade.

The leading North American carrier was Newport, the fifth largest colonial port. Rhode Islanders, who were at a disadvantage competing with the more advanced economies of Europe in textiles, metalwares, and guns, had one product of superior quality—the rum they distilled. Often trading the liquor directly with Africans instead of Europeans, Rhode Islanders successfully plied the trade for a century, transporting over 106,000 Africans by 1808.

Rhode Island slavers supplied West Indian markets in far greater proportion than those on the mainland. Before the American Revolution Barbados was their most important destination, and after 1783 Cuba took half of their slave cargoes. The mainland market never averaged more than a third of the Rhode Island trade. New York, which sent out 151 voyages, and other ports, including Boston, Philadelphia, and Charleston, shared in transporting slaves. In general, southerners did not engage in the carrying business.

South Carolina and Virginia were the main markets, the first receiving about twenty thousand slaves between 1735 and 1775, and the second about the same number between 1699 and 1775. The trade virtually ceased during the American Revolution, but South Carolina afterward intermittently imported slaves in large numbers until 1808.

The Middle Passage, as the trip across the Atlantic was called, was undoubtedly horrible, with the frightened Africans mercilessly shackled, stowed, and sometimes cruelly handled and driven to suicide. Modern investigators, however, have lightened a little the grim picture painted by abolitionists by pointing out that traders had a financial stake in delivering slaves alive and healthy. It has been shown that white mortality on ocean voyages, especially in the tropics, was also heavy. Rhode Island averaged a 12 percent loss of slaves, higher than the English rate.

The slave trade came under attack in the egalitarian and anti-British atmosphere of the American Revolution. But in deference to certain objectors, drafters of the Declaration of Independence dropped a proposed condemnation of the practice in that document, and the Framers of the Constitution compromised on the issue. It was agreed that the trade could be abolished as early as 1808, an agreement that was fulfilled with a minimum of dissent. Efforts to end the subsequent illegal traffic were hampered for over half a century by southern objections as well as friction with the British, some of whom were crusading to suppress the traffic entirely. During the Civil War, with southerners out of Congress and an antislavery administration in power, the United States signed a treaty with Great Britain that led to ending the traffic.

The Constitution did not contemplate a ban on interstate slave trading, leaving the issue to the states. The federal government, however, prohibited trade in the District of Columbia and set regulations regarding the size of ships used in coastal trade. The exhaustion of soil in the older states, expansion of the cotton kingdom, and suppression of the foreign trade combined to encourage domestic trading. Many slaves migrated westward with their masters, and others were sold through a system that was well established by the early nineteenth century. The seaboard and border states exported an estimated twenty-five thousand slaves a year, with Virginia the largest resource.

Large-scale traders in the Upper South maintained agencies and representatives in the Lower South. Although water transport was used, slaves more commonly were marched overland, in coffles, to markets where they commanded prices that at least quadrupled between 1800 and 1860. At first only erratically regulated by the states and then unregulated altogether by 1850, the trade led to the breakup of families, which became the particular target of antislavery writers like Harriet Beecher Stowe. □

From THE READER'S COMPANION TO AMERICAN HISTORY, Eric Foner & John A. Garraty, Editors. Copyright © 1991 by Houghton Mifflin Company. Reprinted with permission.

The Early Congresses

At the urging of Massachusetts and Virginia, the First Continental Congress met in Philadelphia on Sept. 5, 1774, and was attended by representatives of all the colonies except Georgia. Patrick Henry of Virginia declared: "The distinctions between Pennsylvanians, New Yorkers and New Englanders are no more. I am not a Virginian but an American." This Congress, which adjourned Oct. 26, 1774, passed intercolonial resolutions calling for extensive boycott by the colonies against British trade.

The following year, most of the delegates from the colonies were chosen by popular election to attend the Second Continental Congress, which assembled in Philadelphia on May 10. As war had already begun between the colonies and England, the chief problems before the Congress were the procuring of military supplies, the establishment of an army and proper defenses, the issuing of continental bills of credit, etc. On June 15, 1775, George Washington was elected to command the Continental army. Congress adjourned Dec. 12, 1776.

Other Continental Congresses were held in Baltimore (1776–77), Philadelphia (1777), Lancaster, Pa. (1777), York, Pa. (1777–78), and Philadelphia (1778–81).

In 1781, the Articles of Confederation, although establishing a league of the thirteen states rather than a strong central government, provided for the continuance of Congress. Known thereafter as the Congress of the Confederation, it held sessions in Philadelphia (1781–83), Princeton, N.J. (1783), Annapolis, Md. (1783–84), and Trenton, N.J. (1784). Five sessions were held in New York City between the years 1785 and 1789.

The Congress of the United States, established by the ratification of the Constitution, held its first meeting on March 4, 1789, in New York City. Several sessions of Congress were held in Philadelphia, and the first meeting in Washington, D.C., was on Nov. 17, 1800.

Presidents of the Continental Congresses

Name	Elected	Brith and Death Dates	Name	Elected	Birth and Death Dates
Peyton Randolph, Va.	9/5/1774	c.1721–1775	John Hanson, Md.	11/5/1781	1715–1783
Henry Middleton, S.C.	10/22/1774	1717–1784	Elias Boudinot, N.J.	11/4/1782	1740–1821
Peyton Randolph, Va.	5/10/1775	c.1721–1775	Thomas Mifflin, Pa.	11/3/1783	1744–1800
John Hancock, Mass.	5/24/1775	1737–1793	Richard Henry Lee, Va.	11/30/1784	1732–1794
Henry Laurens, S.C.	11/1/1777	1724–1792	John Hancock, Mass.[1]	11/23/1785	1737–1793
John Jay, N.Y.	12/10/1778	1745–1829	Nathaniel Gorham, Mass.	6/6/1786	1738–1796
Samuel Huntington, Conn.	9/28/1779	1731–1796	Arthur St. Clair, Pa.	2/2/1787	1734–1818
Thomas McKean, Del.	7/10/1781	1734–1817	Cyrus Griffin, Va.	1/22/1788	1748–1810

1. Resigned May 29, 1786, never having served, because of continued illness.

The Great Seal of the U.S.

On July 4, 1776, the Continental Congress appointed a committee consisting of Benjamin Franklin, John Adams, and Thomas Jefferson "to bring in a device for a seal of the United States of America." After many delays, a verbal description of a design by William Barton was finally approved by Congress on June 20, 1782. The seal shows an American bald eagle with a ribbon in its mouth bearing the device *E pluribus unum* (One out of many). In its talons are the arrows of war and an olive branch of peace. On the reverse side it shows an unfinished pyramid with an eye (the eye of Providence) above it. Although this description was adopted in 1782, the first drawing was not made until four years later, and no die has ever been cut.

The American's Creed

William Tyler Page

"I believe in the United States of America as a government of the people, by the people, for the people; whose just powers are derived from the consent of the governed; a democracy in a republic; a sovereign Nation of many sovereign States; a perfect union, one and inseparable; established upon those principles of freedom, equality, justice, and humanity for which American patriots sacrificed their lives and fortunes.

"I therefore believe it is my duty to my country to love it, to support its Constitution, to obey its laws, to respect its flag, and to defend it against all enemies."

NOTE: William Tyler Page, Clerk of the U.S. House of Representatives, wrote "The American's Creed" in 1917. It was accepted by the House on behalf of the American people on April 3, 1918.

U.S. Capitol

When the French architect and engineer Maj. Pierre L'Enfant first began to lay out the plans for a new Federal city (now Washington, D.C.), he noted that Jenkins' Hill, overlooking the area, seemed to be "a pedestal waiting for a monument." It was here that the U.S. Capitol would be built. The basic structure as we know it today evolved over a period of more than 150 years. In 1792 a competition was held for the design of a capitol building. Dr. William Thornton, a physician and amateur architect, submitted the winning plan, a simple, low-lying structure of classical proportions with a shallow dome. Later, internal modifications were made by Benjamin Henry Latrobe. After the building was burned by the British in 1814, Latrobe and architect Charles Bulfinch were responsible for its reconstruction. Finally, under Thomas Walter, who was Architect of the Capitol from 1851 to 1865, the House and Senate wings and the imposing cast iron dome topped with the Statue of Freedom were added, and the Capitol assumed the form we see today. It was in the old Senate chamber that Daniel Webster cried out, "Liberty and Union, now and forever, one and inseparable!" In Statuary Hall, which used to be the old House chamber, a small disk on the floor marks the spot where John Quincy Adams was fatally stricken after more than 50 years of service to his country. A whisper from one side of this room can be heard across the vast space of the hall. Visitors can see the original Supreme Court chamber a floor below the Rotunda.

In addition to its historical association, the Capitol Building is also a vast artistic treasure house. The works of such famous artists as Gilbert Stuart, Rembrandt Peale, and John Trumbull are displayed on the walls. The Great Rotunda, with its 180-foot- (54.9-m-) high dome, is decorated with a massive fresco by Constantino Brumidi, which extends some 300 feet (90 m) in circumference. Throughout the building are many paintings of events in U.S. history and sculptures of outstanding Americans. The Capitol itself is situated on a 68-acre (27.5-ha) park designed by the 19th-century landscape architect Frederick Law Olmsted. There are free guided tours of the Capitol, which include admission to the House and Senate galleries. Those who wish to visit the visitors' gallery in either wing without taking the tour may obtain passes from their Senators or Congressmen. Visitors may ride on the monorail subway that joins the House and Senate wings of the Capitol with the Congressional office buildings.

Washington Monument

Construction of this magnificent Washington, D.C., monument, which draws some two million visitors a year, took nearly a century of planning, building, and controversy. Provision for a large equestrian statue of George Washington was made in the original city plan, but the project was soon dropped. After Washington's death it was taken up again, and a number of false starts and changes of design were made. Finally, in 1848, work was begun on the monument that stands today. The design, by architect Robert Mills, then featured an ornate base. In 1854, however, political squabbling and a lack of money brought construction to a halt. Work was resumed in 1880, and the monument was completed in 1884 and opened to the public in 1888. The tapered shaft, faced with white marble and rising from walls 15 feet thick (4.6 m) at the base was modeled after the obelisks of ancient Egypt. The monument, one of the tallest masonry constructions in the world, stands just over 555 feet (169 m). Memorial stones from the 50 States, foreign countries, and organizations line the interior walls. The top, reached only by elevator, commands a panoramic view of the city.

The Liberty Bell

The Liberty Bell was cast in England in 1752 for the Pennsylvania Statehouse (now named Independence Hall) in Philadelphia. It was recast in Philadelphia in 1753. It is inscribed with the words, "Proclaim liberty throughout all the land unto all the inhabitants thereof" (Lev. 25:10). The bell was rung on July 8, 1776, for the first public reading of the Declaration of Independence. Hidden in Allentown during the British occupation of Philadelphia, it was replaced in Independence Hall in 1778. The bell cracked on July 8, 1835, while tolling the death of Chief Justice John Marshall. In 1976 the Liberty Bell was moved to a special exhibition building near Independence Hall.

Arlington National Cemetery

Arlington National Cemetery occupies 612 acres in Virginia on the Potomac River, directly opposite Washington. This land was part of the estate of John Parke Custis, Martha Washington's son. His son, George Washington Parke Custis, built the mansion which later became the home of Robert E. Lee. In 1864, Arlington became a military cemetery. More than 230,000 servicemembers and their dependents are buried there. Expansion of the cemetery began in 1966, using a 180-acre tract of land directly east of the present site.

In 1921, an Unknown American Soldier of World War I was buried in the cemetery; the monument at the Tomb was opened to the public without ceremony in 1932. Two additional Unknowns, one from World War II and one from the Korean War, were buried May 30, 1958. The Unknown Serviceman of Vietnam was buried on May 28, 1984. The inscription carved on the Tomb of the Unknowns reads:

HERE RESTS IN
HONORED GLORY
AN AMERICAN
SOLDIER
KNOWN BUT TO GOD

History of the Flag

Source: Encyclopaedia Britannica.

The first official American flag, the Continental or Grand Union flag, was displayed on Prospect Hill, Jan. 1, 1776, in the American lines besieging Boston. It had 13 alternate red and white stripes, with the British Union Jack in the upper left corner.

On June 14, 1777, the Continental Congress adopted the design for a new flag, which actually was the Continental flag with the red cross of St. George and the white cross of St. Andrew replaced on the blue field by 13 stars, one for each state. No rule was made as to the arrangement of the stars, and while they were usually shown in a circle, there were various other designs. It is uncertain when the new flag was first flown, but its first official announcement is believed to have been on Sept. 3, 1777.

The first public assertion that Betsy Ross made the first Stars and Stripes appeared in a paper read before the Historical Society of Pennsylvania on March 14, 1870, by William J. Canby, a grandson. However, Mr. Canby on later investigation found no official documents of any action by Congress on the flag before June 14, 1777. Betsy Ross's own story, according to her daughter, was that Washington, Robert Morris, and George Ross, as representatives of Congress, visited her in Philadelphia in June 1776, showing her a rough draft of the flag and asking her if she could make one. However, the only actual record of the manufacture of flags by Betsy Ross is a voucher in Harrisburg, Pa., for 14 pounds and some shillings for flags for the Pennsylvania navy.

On Jan. 13, 1794, Congress voted to add two stars and two stripes to the flag in recognition of the admission of Vermont and Kentucky to the Union. By 1818, there were 20 states in the Union, and as it was obvious that the flag would soon become unwieldy, Congress voted April 18 to return to the original 13 stripes and to indicate the admission of a new state simply by the addition of a star the following July 4. The 49th star, for Alaska, was added July 4, 1959; and the 50th star, for Hawaii, was added July 4, 1960.

The first Confederate flag, adopted in 1861 by the Confederate convention in Montgomery, Ala., was called the Stars and Bars; but because of its similarity in colors to the American flag, there was much confusion in the Battle of Bull Run. To remedy this situation, Gen. G. T. Beauregard suggested a battle flag, which was used by the Southern armies throughout the war. The flag consisted of a red field on which was placed a blue cross of St. Andrew separated from the field by a white fillet and adorned with 13[1] white stars for the Confederate states. In May 1863, at Richmond, an official flag was adopted by the Confederate Congress. This flag was white and twice as long as wide; the union, two-thirds the width of the flag, contained the battle flag designed for Gen. Beauregard. A broad transverse stripe of red was added Feb. 4, 1865, so that the flag might not be mistaken for a signal of truce.

1. 11 states formally seceded, and unofficial groups in Kentucky and Missouri adopted ordinances of secession. On this basis, these two states were admitted to the Confederacy, although the official state governments remained in the Union.

The Pledge of Allegiance[1] to the Flag

"I pledge allegiance to the Flag of the United States of America, and to the Republic for which it stands, one Nation under God,[2] indivisible, with liberty and justice for all."

1. The original pledge was published in the Sept. 8, 1892, issue of *The Youth's Companion* in Boston. For years, the authorship was in dispute between James B. Upham and Francis Bellamy of the magazine's staff. In 1939, after a study of the controversy, the United States Flag Association decided that authorship be credited to Bellamy. 2. The phrase "under God" was added to the pledge on June 14, 1954.

The Statue of Liberty

The Statue of Liberty ("Liberty Enlightening the World") is a 225-ton, steel-reinforced copper female figure, 152 ft in height, facing the ocean from Liberty[1] Island in New York Harbor. The right hand holds aloft a torch, and the left hand carries a tablet upon which is inscribed: "July IV MDCCLXXVI."

The statue was designed by Frédéric Auguste Bartholdi of Alsace as a gift to the United States from the people of France to memorialize the alliance of the two countries in the American Revolution and their abiding friendship. The French people contributed the $250,000 cost.

The 150-foot pedestal was designed by Richard M. Hunt and built by Gen. Charles P. Stone, both Americans. It contains steel underpinnings designed by Alexander Eiffel of France to support the statue. The $270,000 cost was borne by popular subscription in this country. President Grover Cleveland accepted the statue for the United States on Oct. 28, 1886.

On Sept. 26, 1972, President Richard M. Nixon dedicated the American Museum of Immigration, housed in structural additions to the base of the stat-

1. Called Bedloe's Island prior to 1956.

ue. In 1984 scaffolding went up for a major restoration and the torch was extinguished on July 4. It was relit with much ceremony July 4, 1986 to mark its centennial.

On a tablet inside the pedestal is engraved the following sonnet, written by Emma Lazarus (1849–1887):

The New Colossus

Not like the brazen giant of Greek fame.
With conquering limbs astride from land to land;
Here at our sea-washed, sunset gates shall stand
A mighty woman with a torch, whose flame
Is the imprisoned lightning, and her name
Mother of Exiles. From her beacon-hand
Glows world-wide welcome; her mild eyes command
The air-bridged harbor that twin cities frame.
"Keep, ancient lands, your storied pomp!" cries she
With silent lips. "Give me your tired, your poor,
Your huddled masses yearning to breathe free,
The wretched refuse of your teeming shore.
Send these, the homeless, tempest-tost to me,
I lift my lamp beside the golden door!"

Presidents

Name and (party)[1]	Term	State of birth	Born	Died	Religion	Age at inaug.	Age at death
1. Washington (F)[2]	1789–1797	Va.	2/22/1732	12/14/1799	Episcopalian	57	67
2. J. Adams (F)	1797–1801	Mass.	10/30/1735	7/4/1826	Unitarian	61	90
3. Jefferson (DR)	1801–1809	Va.	4/13/1743	7/4/1826	Deist	57	83
4. Madison (DR)	1809–1817	Va.	3/16/1751	6/28/1836	Episcopalian	57	85
5. Monroe (DR)	1817–1825	Va.	4/28/1758	7/4/1831	Episcopalian	58	73
6. J. Q. Adams (DR)	1825–1829	Mass.	7/11/1767	2/23/1848	Unitarian	57	80
7. Jackson (D)	1829–1837	S.C.	3/15/1767	6/8/1845	Presbyterian	61	78
8. Van Buren (D)	1837–1841	N.Y.	12/5/1782	7/24/1862	Reformed Dutch	54	79
9. W. H. Harrison (W)[3]	1841	Va.	2/9/1773	4/4/1841	Episcopalian	68	68
10. Tyler (W)	1841–1845	Va.	3/29/1790	1/18/1862	Episcopalian	51	71
11. Polk (D)	1845–1849	N.C.	11/2/1795	6/15/1849	Methodist	49	53
12. Taylor (W)[3]	1849–1850	Va.	11/24/1784	7/9/1850	Episcopalian	64	65
13. Fillmore (W)	1850–1853	N.Y.	1/7/1800	3/8/1874	Unitarian	50	74
14. Pierce (D)	1853–1857	N.H.	11/23/1804	10/8/1869	Episcopalian	48	64
15. Buchanan (D)	1857–1861	Pa.	4/23/1791	6/1/1868	Presbyterian	65	77
16. Lincoln (R)[4]	1861–1865	Ky.	2/12/1809	4/15/1865	Liberal	52	56
17. A. Johnson (U)[5]	1865–1869	N.C.	12/29/1808	7/31/1875	(6)	56	66
18. Grant (R)	1869–1877	Ohio	4/27/1822	7/23/1885	Methodist	46	63
19. Hayes (R)	1877–1881	Ohio	10/4/1822	1/17/1893	Methodist	54	70
20. Garfield (R)[4]	1881	Ohio	11/19/1831	9/19/1881	Disciples of Christ	49	49
21. Arthur (R)	1881–1885	Vt.	10/5/1830	11/18/1886	Episcopalian	50	56
22. Cleveland (D)	1885–1889	N.J.	3/18/1837	6/24/1908	Presbyterian	47	71
23. B. Harrison (R)	1889–1893	Ohio	8/20/1833	3/13/1901	Presbyterian	55	67
24. Cleveland (D)[7]	1893–1897	—	—	—	—	55	—
25. McKinley (R)[4]	1897–1901	Ohio	1/29/1843	9/14/1901	Methodist	54	58
26. T. Roosevelt (R)	1901–1909	N.Y.	10/27/1858	1/6/1919	Reformed Dutch	42	60
27. Taft (R)	1909–1913	Ohio	9/15/1857	3/8/1930	Unitarian	51	72
28. Wilson (D)	1913–1921	Va.	12/28/1856	2/3/1924	Presbyterian	56	67
29. Harding (R)[3]	1921–1923	Ohio	11/2/1865	8/2/1923	Baptist	55	57
30. Coolidge (R)	1923–1929	Vt.	7/4/1872	1/5/1933	Congregationalist	51	60
31. Hoover (R)	1929–1933	Iowa	8/10/1874	10/20/1964	Quaker	54	90
32. F. D. Roosevelt (D)[3]	1933–1945	N.Y.	1/30/1882	4/12/1945	Episcopalian	51	63
33. Truman (D)	1945–1953	Mo.	5/8/1884	12/26/1972	Baptist	60	88
34. Eisenhower (R)	1953–1961	Tex.	10/14/1890	3/28/1969	Presbyterian	62	78
35. Kennedy (D)[4]	1961–1963	Mass.	5/29/1917	11/22/1963	Roman Catholic	43	46
36. L. B. Johnson (D)	1963–1969	Tex.	8/27/1908	1/22/1973	Disciples of Christ	55	64
37. Nixon (R)[8]	1969–1974	Calif.	1/9/1913	4/22/1994	Quaker	56	81
38. Ford (R)	1974–1977	Neb.	7/14/1913	—	Episcopalian	61	—
39. Carter (D)	1977–1981	Ga.	10/1/1924	—	Southern Baptist	52	—
40. Reagan (R)	1981–1989	Ill.	2/6/1911	—	Disciples of Christ	69	—
41. Bush (R)	1989–1993	Mass.	6/12/24	—	Episcopalian	64	—
42. Clinton (D)	1993–	Ark.	8/19/46	—	Baptist	46	—

1. F—Federalist; DR—Democratic-Republican; D—Democratic; W—Whig; R—Republican; U—Union. 2. No party for first election. The party system in the U.S. made its appearance during Washington's first term. 3. Died in office. 4. Assassinated in office. 5. The Republican National Convention of 1864 adopted the name Union Party. It renominated Lincoln for President; for Vice President it nominated Johnson, a War Democrat. Although frequently listed as a Republican Vice President and President, Johnson undoubtedly considered himself strictly a member of the Union Party. When that party broke apart after 1868, he returned to the Democratic Party. 6. Johnson was not a professed church member; however, he admired the Baptist principles of church government. 7. Second nonconsecutive term. 8. Resigned Aug. 9, 1974.

Vice Presidents

Name and (party)[1]	Term	State of birth	Birth and death dates	President served under
1. John Adams (F)[2]	1789–1797	Massachusetts	1735–1826	Washington
2. Thomas Jefferson (DR)	1797–1801	Virginia	1743–1826	J. Adams
3. Aaron Burr (DR)	1801–1805	New Jersey	1756–1836	Jefferson
4. George Clinton (DR)[3]	1805–1812	New York	1739–1812	Jefferson and Madison
5. Elbridge Gerry (DR)[3]	1813–1814	Massachusetts	1744–1814	Madison
6. Daniel D. Tompkins (DR)	1817–1825	New York	1774–1825	Monroe
7. John C. Calhoun[4]	1825–1832	South Carolina	1782–1850	J. Q. Adams and Jackson
8. Martin Van Buren (D)	1833–1837	New York	1782–1862	Jackson
9. Richard M. Johnson (D)	1837–1841	Kentucky	1780–1850	Van Buren
10. John Tyler (W)[5]	1841	Virginia	1790–1862	W. H. Harrison
11. George M. Dallas (D)	1845–1849	Pennsylvania	1792–1864	Polk
12. Millard Fillmore (W)[5]	1849–1850	New York	1800–1874	Taylor
13. William R. King (D)[3]	1853	North Carolina	1786–1853	Pierce
14. John C. Breckinridge (D)	1857–1861	Kentucky	1821–1875	Buchanan

Name and (party)[1]	Term	State of birth	Birth and death dates	President served under
15. Hannibal Hamlin (R)	1861–1865	Maine	1809–1891	Lincoln
16. Andrew Johnson (U)[5]	1865	North Carolina	1808–1875	Lincoln
17. Schuyler Colfax (R)	1869–1873	New York	1823–1885	Grant
18. Henry Wilson (R)[3]	1873–1875	New Hampshire	1812–1875	Grant
19. William A. Wheeler (R)	1877–1881	New York	1819–1887	Hayes
20. Chester A. Arthur (R)[5]	1881	Vermont	1830–1886	Garfield
21. Thomas A. Hendricks (D)[3]	1885	Ohio	1819–1885	Cleveland
22. Levi P. Morton (R)	1889–1893	Vermont	1824–1920	B. Harrison
23. Adlai E. Stevenson (D)	1893–1897	Kentucky	1835–1914	Cleveland
24. Garrett A. Hobart (R)[3]	1897–1899	New Jersey	1844–1899	McKinley
25. Theodore Roosevelt (R)[5]	1901	New York	1858–1919	McKinley
26. Charles W. Fairbanks (R)	1905–1909	Ohio	1852–1918	T. Roosevelt
27. James S. Sherman (R)[3]	1909–1912	New York	1855–1912	Taft
28. Thomas R. Marshall (D)	1913–1921	Indiana	1854–1925	Wilson
29. Calvin Coolidge (R)[5]	1921–1923	Vermont	1872–1933	Harding
30. Charles G. Dawes (R)	1925–1929	Ohio	1865–1951	Coolidge
31. Charles Curtis (R)	1929–1933	Kansas	1860–1936	Hoover
32. John N. Garner (D)	1933–1941	Texas	1868–1967	F. D. Roosevelt
33. Henry A. Wallace (D)	1941–1945	Iowa	1888–1965	F. D. Roosevelt
34. Harry S. Truman (D)[5]	1945	Missouri	1884–1972	F. D. Roosevelt
35. Alben W. Barkley (D)	1949–1953	Kentucky	1877–1956	Truman
36. Richard M. Nixon (R)	1953–1961	California	1913–1994	Eisenhower
37. Lyndon B. Johnson (D)[5]	1961–1963	Texas	1908–1973	Kennedy
38. Hubert H. Humphrey (D)	1965–1969	South Dakota	1911–1978	Johnson
39. Spiro T. Agnew (R)[6]	1969–1973	Maryland	1918–	Nixon
40. Gerald R. Ford (R)[7]	1973–1974	Nebraska	1913–	Nixon
41. Nelson A. Rockefeller (R)[8]	1974–1977	Maine	1908–1979	Ford
42. Walter F. Mondale (D)	1977–1981	Minnesota	1928–	Carter
43. George Bush (R)	1981–1989	Massachusetts	1924–	Reagan
44. J. Danforth Quayle (R)	1989–1993	Indiana	1947–	Bush
45. Albert A. Gore, Jr. (D)	1993–	Washington, D.C.	1948–	Clinton

1. F—Federalist; DR—Democratic-Republican; D—Democratic; W—Whig; R—Republican; U—Union. 2. No party for first election. The party system in the U.S. made its appearance during Washington's first term as President. 3. Died in office. 4. Democratic-Republican with J. Q. Adams; Democratic with Jackson. Calhoun resigned in 1832 to become a U.S. Senator. 5. Succeeded to presidency on death of President. 6. Resigned Oct. 10, 1973, after pleading no contest to Federal income tax evasion charges. 7. Nominated by Nixon on Oct. 12, 1973, under provisions of 25th Amendment. Confirmed by Congress on Dec. 6, 1973, and was sworn in same day. He became President Aug. 9, 1974, upon Nixon's resignation. 8. Nominated by Ford Aug. 20, 1974; confirmed by Congress on Dec. 19, 1974, and was sworn in same day.

Burial Places of the Presidents

President	Burial place	President	Burial place
Washington	Mt. Vernon, Va.	Hayes	Fremont, Ohio
J. Adams	Quincy, Mass.	Garfield	Cleveland, Ohio
Jefferson	Charlottesville, Va.	Arthur	Albany, N.Y.
Madison	Montpelier Station, Va.	Cleveland	Princeton, N.J.
Monroe	Richmond, Va.	B. Harrison	Indianapolis
J. Q. Adams	Quincy, Mass.	McKinley	Canton, Ohio
Jackson	The Hermitage, nr. Nashville, Tenn.	T. Roosevelt	Oyster Bay, N.Y.
		Taft	Arlington National Cemetery
Van Buren	Kinderhook, N.Y.	Wilson	Washington National Cathedral
W. H. Harrison	North Bend, Ohio	Harding	Marion, Ohio
Tyler	Richmond, Va.	Coolidge	Plymouth, Vt.
Polk	Nashville, Tenn.	Hoover	West Branch, Iowa
Taylor	Louisville, Ky.	F. D. Roosevelt	Hyde Park, N.Y.
Fillmore	Buffalo, N.Y.	Truman	Independence, Mo.
Pierce	Concord, N.H.	Eisenhower	Abilene, Kan.
Buchanan	Lancaster, Pa.	Kennedy	Arlington National Cemetery
Lincoln	Springfield, Ill.	L. B. Johnson	Stonewall, Tex.
A. Johnson	Greeneville, Tenn.	Nixon	Yorba Linda, Calif.
Grant	New York City		

"In God We Trust"

"In God We Trust" first appeared on U.S. coins after April 22, 1864, when Congress passed an act authorizing the coinage of a 2-cent piece bearing this motto. Thereafter, Congress extended its use to other coins. On July 30, 1956, it became the national motto.

Wives and Children of the Presidents

President	Wife's name	Year an place of wife's birth	Married	Wife died	Children of President[1]	
					Sons	Daughters
Washington	Martha Dandridge Custis	1732, Va.	1759	1802	—	—
John Adams	Abigail Smith	1744, Mass.	1764	1818	3	2
Jefferson	Martha Wayles Skelton	1748, Va.	1772	1782	1	5
Madison	Dorothy "Dolley" Payne Todd	1768, N.C.	1794	1849	—	—
Monroe	Elizabeth "Eliza" Kortright	1768, N.Y.	1786	1830	—	2
J. Q. Adams	Louisa Catherine Johnson	1775, England	1797	1852	3	1
Jackson	Mrs. Rachel Donelson Robards	1767, Va.	1791	1828	—	—
Van Buren	Hannah Hoes	1788, N.Y.	1807	1819	4	—
W. H. Harrison	Anna Symmes	1775, N.J.	1795	1864	6	4
Tyler	Letitia Christian	1790, Va.	1813	1842	3	4
	Julia Gardiner	1820, N.Y.	1844	1889	5	2
Polk	Sarah Childress	1803, Tenn.	1824	1891	—	—
Taylor	Margaret Smith	1788, Md.	1810	1852	1	5
Fillmore	Abigail Powers	1798, N.Y.	1826	1853	1	1
	Caroline Carmichael McIntosh	1813, N.J.	1858	1881	—	—
Pierce	Jane Means Appleton	1806, N.H.	1834	1863	3	—
Buchanan	(Unmarried)	—	—	—	—	—
Lincoln	Mary Todd	1818, Ky.	1842	1882	4	—
A. Johnson	Eliza McCardle	1810, Tenn.	1827	1876	3	2
Grant	Julia Dent	1826, Mo.	1848	1902	3	1
Hayes	Lucy Ware Webb	1831, Ohio	1852	1889	7	1
Garfield	Lucretia Rudolph	1832, Ohio	1858	1918	5	2
Arthur	Ellen Lewis Herndon	1837, Va.	1859	1880	2	1
Cleveland	Frances Folsom	1864, N.Y.	1886	1947	2	3
B. Harrison	Caroline Lavinia Scott	1832, Ohio	1853	1892	1	1
	Mary Scott Lord Dimmick	1858, Pa.	1896	1948	—	1
McKinley	Ida Saxton	1847, Ohio	1871	1907	—	2
T. Roosevelt	Alice Hathaway Lee	1861, Mass.	1880	1884	—	1
	Edith Kermit Carow	1861, Conn.	1886	1948	4	1
Taft	Helen Herron	1861, Ohio	1886	1943	2	1
Wilson	Ellen Louise Axson	1860, Ga.	1885	1914	—	3
	Edith Bolling Galt	1872, Va.	1915	1961	—	—
Harding	Florence Kling DeWolfe	1860, Ohio	1891	1924	—	—
Coolidge	Grace Anna Goodhue	1879, Vt.	1905	1957	2	—
Hoover	Lou Henry	1875, Iowa	1899	1944	2	—
F. D. Roosevelt	Anna Eleanor Roosevelt	1884, N.Y.	1905	1962	5	1
Truman	Bess Wallace	1885, Mo.	1919	1982	—	1
Eisenhower	Mamie Geneva Doud	1896, Iowa	1916	1979	2	—
Kennedy	Jacqueline Lee Bouvier	1929, N.Y.	1953	1994	2	1
L. B. Johnson	Claudia Alta "Lady Bird" Taylor	1912, Tex.	1934		—	2
Nixon	Thelma Catherine "Pat" Ryan	1912, Nev.	1940	1993	—	2
Ford	Elizabeth "Betty" Bloomer Warren	1918, Ill.	1948		3	1
Carter	Rosalynn Smith	1928, Ga.	1946		3	1
Reagan	Jane Wyman	1914, Mo.	1940[2]		1[3]	1
	Nancy Davis	1921 (?)[4], N.Y.	1952		1	1
Bush	Barbara Pierce	1925, N.Y.	1945		4	2
Clinton	Hillary Rodham	1946, Ill.	1975		—	1

1. Includes children who died in infancy. 2. Divorced in 1948. 3. Adopted. 4. Birthday officially given as 1923 but her high school and college records show 1921 for year of birth.

Elections

How a President Is Nominated and Elected

The National Conventions of both major parties are held during the summer of a presidential-election year. Earlier, each party selects delegates by primaries, conventions, committees, etc.

For their 1992 National Convention, the Republicans allow each state a base of 6 delegates at large; the District of Columbia, 14; Puerto Rico, 14; Guam and the Virgin Islands, 4 each. In addition, each state receives 3 district delegates for each representative it has in the House of Representatives, regardless of political affiliation. This did not apply to the District of Columbia, Puerto Rico, Guam and the Virgin Islands.

Each state is awarded additional delegates at large on the basis of having supported the Republican candidate for President in 1988 and electing Republican candidates for Senator, Governor, and U.S. Representative between 1988 and 1991 inclusive.

The number of delegates at the 1992 convention, to be held in Houston starting August 17, will be 2,206.[1]

Following is the apportionment of delegates:

Alabama	38	Florida	97	Kentucky	35	Montana	20	Ohio	83	Texas	121
Alaska	19	Georgia	52	Louisiana	38	Nebraska	24	Oklahoma	34	Utah	27
Arizona	37	Guam	4	Maine	22	Nevada	21	Oregon	23	Vermont	19
Arkansas	27	Hawaii	14	Maryland	42	N.H.	23	Pa.	90	V.I.	4
California	201	Idaho	22	Mass.	38	N. Jersey	60	P.R.	14	Virginia	54
Colorado	37	Illinois	85	Michigan	72	New Mexico	25	R.I.	15	Washington	35
Connecticut	35	Indiana	51	Minnesota	32	New York	100	S.C.	36	W. Va.	18
Delaware	19	Iowa	23	Mississippi	32	N.C.	57	S.D.	19	Wisconsin	35
D.C.	14	Kansas	30	Missouri	47	N.D.	17	Tennessee	45	Wyoming	20

1. Includes 4 delegates from American Samoa.

The Democrats base the number of delegates on a state's showing in the 1988 and 1990 elections. At the 1992 convention, to be held in New York starting July 13, there will be 4,313[1,2] delegates casting 4,282 votes. Following is the apportionment by states:

Alabama	62	Florida	160	Kentucky	62	Montana	22	Ohio	167	Texas	214
Alaska	18	Georgia	88	Louisiana	69	Nebraska	31	Oklahoma	52	Utah	28
Arizona	47	Guam	10[1]	Maine	30	Nevada	23	Oregon	53	Vermont	19
Arkansas	43	Hawaii	26	Maryland	80	N. H.	24	Pa.	188	V.I.	10[1]
California	382	Idaho	24	Mass.	107	New Jersey	117	P.R.	57	Virginia	92
Colorado	54	Illinois	183	Michigan	148	New Mexico	33	R.I.	28	Washington	80
Connecticut	61	Indiana	86	Minnesota	87	New York	268	S.C.	50	W. Va.	38
Delaware	19	Iowa	57	Mississippi	45	N.C.	93	S.D.	20	Wisconsin	91
D. C.	29	Kansas	42	Missouri	86	N.D.	20	Tennessee	77	Wyoming	19

1. Fractional votes. 2. Includes 22[1] delegates for Democrats Abroad and 10[1] for American Samoa. As of March 26, 1991.

The Conventions

At each convention, a temporary chairman is chosen. After a credentials committee seats the delegates, a permanent chairman is elected. The convention then votes on a platform, drawn up by the platform committee.

By the third or fourth day, presidential nominations begin. The chairman calls the roll of states alphabetically. A state may place a candidate in nomination or yield to another state.

Voting, again alphabetically by roll call of states, begins after all nominations have been made and seconded. A simple majority is required in each party, although this may require many ballots.

Finally, the vice-presidential candidate is selected. Although there is no law saying that the candidates *must* come from different states, it is, practically, necessary for this to be the case. Otherwise, according to the Constitution (*see* Amendment XII), electors from that state could vote for only one of the candidates and would have to cast their other vote for some person of another state. This could result in a presidential candidate's receiving a majority electoral vote and his running mate's failing to.

The Electoral College

The next step in the process is the nomination of electors in each state, according to its laws. These electors must not be Federal office holders. In the November election, the voters cast their votes for electors, not for President. In some states, the ballots include only the names of the presidential and vice-presidential candidates; in others, they include only names of the electors. Nowadays, it is rare for electors to be split between parties. The last such occurrence was in North Carolina in 1968[1]; the last before that, in Tennessee in 1948. On three occasions (1824, 1876, and 1888), the presidential candidate with the largest popular vote failed to obtain an electoral-vote majority.

Each state has as many electors as it has Senators and Representatives. For the 1992 election, the total electors were 538, based on 100 Senators, 435 Representatives, plus 3 electoral votes from the District of Columbia as a result of the 23rd Amendment to the Constitution.

On the first Monday after the second Wednesday in December, the electors cast their votes in their respective state capitols. Constitutionally they may vote for someone other than the party candidate but usually they do not since they are pledged to one party and its candidate on the ballot. Should the presidential or vice-presidential candidate die between the November election and the December meetings, the electors pledged to vote for him could vote for whomever they pleased. However, it seems certain that the national committee would attempt to get an agreement among the state party leaders for a replacement candidate.

The votes of the electors, certified by the states, are sent to Congress, where the president of the Senate opens the certificates and has them counted in the presence of both Houses on January 6. The new President is inaugurated at noon on January 20.

Should no candidate receive a majority of the electoral vote for President, the House of Representatives chooses a President from among the three highest candidates, voting, not as individuals, but as states, with a majority (now 26) needed to elect. Should no vice-presidential candidate obtain the majority, the Senate, voting as individuals, chooses from the highest two.

1. In 1956, 1 of Alabama's 11 electoral votes was cast for Walter B. Jones. In 1960, 6 of Alabama's 11 electoral votes and 1 of Oklahoma's 8 electoral votes were cast for Harry Flood Byrd. (Byrd also received all 8 of Mississippi's electoral votes.)

National Political Conventions Since 1856

Opening date	Party	Where held	Opening date	Party	Where held
June 17, 1856	Republican	Philadelphia	June 12, 1928	Republican	Kansas City
June 2, 1856	Democratic	Cincinnati	June 26, 1928	Democratic	Houston
May 16, 1860	Republican	Chicago	June 14, 1932	Republican	Chicago
April 23, 1860	Democratic	Charleston and Baltimore	June 27, 1932	Democratic	Chicago
			June 9, 1936	Republican	Cleveland
June 7, 1864	Republican[1]	Baltimore	June 23, 1936	Democratic	Philadelphia
Aug. 29, 1864	Democratic	Chicago	June 24, 1940	Republican	Philadelphia
May 20, 1868	Republican	Chicago	July 15, 1940	Democratic	Chicago
July 4, 1868	Democratic	New York City	June 26, 1944	Republican	Chicago
June 5, 1872	Republican	Philadelphia	July 19, 1944	Democratic	Chicago
June 9, 1872	Democratic	Baltimore	June 21, 1948	Republican	Philadelphia
June 14, 1876	Republican	Cincinnati	July 12, 1948	Democratic	Philadelphia
June 28, 1876	Democratic	St. Louis	July 17, 1948	(3)	Birmingham
June 2, 1880	Republican	Chicago	July 22, 1948	Progressive	Philadelphia
June 23, 1880	Democratic	Cincinnati	July 7, 1952	Republican	Chicago
June 3, 1884	Republican	Chicago	July 21, 1952	Democratic	Chicago
July 11, 1884	Democratic	Chicago	Aug. 20, 1956	Republican	San Francisco
June 19, 1888	Republican	Chicago	Aug. 13, 1956	Democratic	Chicago
June 6, 1888	Democratic	St. Louis	July 25, 1960	Republican	Chicago
June 7, 1892	Republican	Minneapolis	July 11, 1960	Democratic	Los Angeles
June 21, 1892	Democratic	Chicago	July 13, 1964	Republican	San Francisco
June 16, 1896	Republican	St. Louis	Aug. 24, 1964	Democratic	Atlantic City
July 7, 1896	Democratic	Chicago	Aug. 5, 1968	Republican	Miami Beach
June 19, 1900	Republican	Philadelphia	Aug. 26, 1968	Democratic	Chicago
July 4, 1900	Democratic	Kansas City	July 10, 1972	Democratic	Miami Beach
June 21, 1904	Republican	Chicago	Aug. 21, 1972	Republican	Miami Beach
July 6, 1904	Democratic	St. Louis	July 12, 1976	Democratic	New York City
June 16, 1908	Republican	Chicago	Aug. 16, 1976	Republican	Kansas City, Mo.
July 7, 1908	Democratic	Denver	Aug. 11, 1980	Democratic	New York City
June 18, 1912	Republican	Chicago	July 14, 1980	Republican	Detroit
June 25, 1912	Democratic	Baltimore	Aug. 20, 1984	Democratic	San Francisco
June 7, 1916	Republican	Chicago	Aug. 20, 1984	Republican	Dallas
June 14, 1916	Democratic	St. Louis	July 16, 1988	Democratic	Atlanta
June 8, 1920	Republican	Chicago	July 18, 1988	Democratic	Atlanta
June 28, 1920	Democratic	San Francisco	Aug. 15, 1988	Republican	New Orleans
June 10, 1924	Republican	Cleveland	July 13, 1992	Democratic	New York City
June 24, 1924[2]	Democratic	New York City	Aug. 17, 1992	Republican	Houston

1. The Convention adopted name Union party to attract War Democrats and others favoring prosecution of war. 2. In session until July 10, 1924. 3. States' Rights delegates from 13 Southern states.

National Committee Chairmen Since 1944

Chairman and (state)	Term	Chairman and (state)	Term
REPUBLICAN		Haley Barbour (Miss.)	1993–
Herbert Brownell, Jr. (N.Y.)	1944–46	**DEMOCRATIC**	
Carroll Reece (Tenn.)	1946–48	Robert E. Hannegan (Mo.)	1944–47
Hugh D. Scott, Jr. (Pa.)	1948–49	J. Howard McGrath (R.I.)	1947–49
Guy G. Gabrielson (N.J.)	1949–52	William M. Boyle, Jr. (Mo.)	1949–51
Arthur E. Summerfield (Mich.)	1952–53	Frank E. McKinney (Ind.)	1951–52
Wesley Roberts (Kan.)	1953–	Stephen A. Mitchell (Ill.)	1952–54
Leonard W. Hall (N.Y.)	1953–57	Paul M. Butler (Ind.)	1955–60
Meade Alcorn (Conn.)	1957–59	Henry M. Jackson (Wash.)	1960–61
Thruston B. Morton (Ky.)	1959–61	John M. Bailey (Conn.)	1961–68
William E. Miller (N.Y.)	1961–64	Lawrence F. O'Brien (Mass.)	1968–69
Dean Burch (Ariz.)	1964–65	Fred R. Harris (Okla.)	1969–70
Ray C. Bliss (Ohio)	1965–69	Lawrence F. O'Brien (Mass.)	1970–72
Rogers C. B. Morton (Md.)	1969–71	Jean Westwood (Utah)	1972
Robert Dole (Kan.)	1971–73	Robert S. Strauss (Tex.)	1972–77
George H. Bush (Tex.)	1973–74	Kenneth M. Curtis (Me.)	1977
Mary Louise Smith (Iowa)	1974–77	John C. White (Tex.)	1977–81
William E. Brock III (Tenn.)	1977–81	Charles T. Manatt (Calif.)	1981–85
Richard Richards (Utah)	1981–83	Paul G. Kirk, Jr. (Mass.)	1985–89
Frank J. Fahrenkopf, Jr. (Nevada)	1983–89	Ronald H. Brown (D.C.)	1989–93
Lee Atwater (S.C.)	1989–91	David Wilhelm (Ill.)	1993–94
Clayton K. Yeutter (Neb.)	1991–92	Christopher J. Dodd (Conn.)	1995–
Richard Bond (N.Y.)	1992–93		

Republican National Committee: 310 First St., S.E., Washington, D. C. 20003.
Democratic National Committee: 430 South Capitol St., S.E., Washington, D.C. 20003.

Presidential Elections, 1789 to 1992

For the original method of electing the President and the Vice President (elections of 1789, 1792, 1796, and 1800), see Article II, Section 1, of the Constitution. The election of 1804 was the first one in which the electors voted for President and Vice President on separate ballots. (See Amendment XII to the Constitution.)

Year	Presidential candidates	Party	Electoral vote	Year	Presidential candidates	Party	Electoral vote
1789[1]	George Washington	(no party)	69	1796	John Adams	Federalist	71
	John Adams	(no party)	34		Thomas Jefferson	Dem.-Rep.	68
	Scattering	(no party)	35		Thomas Pinckney	Federalist	59
	Votes not cast		8		Aaron Burr	Dem.-Rep.	30
					Scattering		48
1792	George Washington	Federalist	132				
	John Adams	Federalist	77	1800[2]	Thomas Jefferson	Dem.-Rep.	73
	George Clinton	Anti-Federalist	50		Aaron Burr	Dem.-Rep.	73
	Thomas Jefferson	Anti-Federalist	4		John Adams	Federalist	65
	Aaron Burr	Anti-Federalist	1		Charles C. Pinckney	Federalist	64
	Votes not cast		6		John Jay	Federalist	1

Year	Presidential candidates	Party	Electoral vote	Vice-presidential candidates	Party	Electoral vote
1804	Thomas Jefferson	Dem.-Rep.	162	George Clinton	Dem.-Rep.	162
	Charles C. Pinckney	Federalist	14	Rufus King	Federalist	14
1808	James Madison	Dem.-Rep.	122	George Clinton	Dem.-Rep.	113
	Charles C. Pinckney	Federalist	47	Rufus King	Federalist	47
	George Clinton	Dem.-Rep.	6	John Langdon	Ind. (no party)	9
	Votes not cast		1	James Madison	Dem.-Rep.	3
				James Monroe	Dem.-Rep.	3
				Votes not cast		1
1812	James Madison	Dem.-Rep.	128	Elbridge Gerry	Dem.-Rep.	131
	De Witt Clinton	Federalist	89	Jared Ingersoll	Federalist	86
	Votes not cast		1	Votes not cast		1
1816	James Monroe	Dem.-Rep.	183	Daniel D. Tompkins	Dem.-Rep.	183
	Rufus King	Federalist	34	John E. Howard	Federalist	22
	Votes not cast		4	James Ross	Ind. (no party)	5
				John Marshall	Federalist	4
				Robert G. Harper	Ind. (no party)	3
				Votes not cast		4
1820	James Monroe	Dem-Rep	231	Daniel D. Tompkins	Dem.-Rep.	218
	John Quincy Adams	Ind. (no party)	1	Richard Stockton	Ind. (no party)	8
	Votes not cast		3	Daniel Rodney	Ind. (no party)	4
				Richard Rush	Ind. (no party)	1
				Robert G. Harper	Ind. (no party)	1
				Votes not cast		3
1824[3]	John Quincy Adams	(no party)	84	John C. Calhoun	(no party)	182
	Andrew Jackson	(no party)	99	Nathan Sanford	(no party)	30
	William H. Crawford	(no party)	41	Nathaniel Macon	(no party)	24
	Henry Clay	(no party)	37	Andrew Jackson	(no party)	13
				Martin Van Buren	(no party)	9
				Henry Clay	(no party)	2
				Votes not cast		1
1828	Andrew Jackson	Democratic	178	John C. Calhoun	Democratic	171
	John Quincy Adams	Natl. Rep.	83	Richard Rush	Natl. Rep.	83
				William Smith	Democratic	7
1832	Andrew Jackson	Democratic	219	Martin Van Buren	Democratic	189
	Henry Clay	Natl. Rep.	49	John Sergeant	Natl. Rep.	49
	John Floyd	Ind. (no party)	11	Henry Lee	Ind. (no party)	11
	William Wirt	Antimasonic[4]	7	Amos Ellmaker	Antimasonic	7
	Votes not cast		2	William Wilkins	Ind. (no party)	30
				Votes not cast		2

Year	Presidential candidates	Party	Electoral vote	Vice-presidential candidates	Party	Electoral vote
1836	Martin Van Buren	Democratic	170	Richard M. Johnson[5]	Democratic	147
	William H. Harrison	Whig	73	Francis Granger	Whig	77
	Hugh L. White	Whig	26	John Tyler	Whig	47
	Daniel Webster	Whig	14	William Smith	Ind. (no party)	23
	W. P. Mangum	Ind. (no party)	11			
1840	William H. Harrison[6]	Whig	234	John Tyler	Whig	234
	Martin Van Buren	Democratic	60	Richard M. Johnson	Democratic	48
				L. W. Tazewell	Ind. (no party)	11
				James K. Polk	Democratic	1
1844	James K. Polk	Democratic	170	George M. Dallas	Democratic	170
	Henry Clay	Whig	105	Theo. Frelinghuysen	Whig	105
1848	Zachary Taylor[7]	Whig	163	Millard Fillmore	Whig	163
	Lewis Cass	Democratic	127	William O. Butler	Democratic	127
1852	Franklin Pierce	Democratic	254	William R. King	Democratic	254
	Winfield Scott	Whig	42	William A. Graham	Whig	42
1856	James Buchanan	Democratic	174	John C. Breckinridge	Democratic	174
	John C. Fremont	Republican	114	William L. Dayton	Republican	114
	Millard Fillmore	American[8]	8	A. J. Donelson	American[8]	8
1860	Abraham Lincoln	Republican	180	Hannibal Hamlin	Republican	180
	John C. Breckinridge	Democratic	72	Joseph Lane	Democratic	72
	John Bell	Const. Union	39	Edward Everett	Const. Union	39
	Stephen A. Douglas	Democratic	12	H. V. Johnson	Democratic	12
1864	Abraham Lincoln[9]	Union[10]	212	Andrew Johnson	Union[15]	212
	George B. McClellan	Democratic	21	G. H. Pendleton	Democratic	21
1868	Ulysses S. Grant	Republican	214	Schuyler Colfax	Republican	214
	Horatio Seymour	Democratic	80	Francis P. Blair, Jr.	Democratic	80
	Votes not counted[11]		23	Votes not counted[11]		23

Year	Presidential candidates	Party	Electoral vote	Popular vote	Vice-presidential candidates and party
1872	Ulysses S. Grant	Republican	286	3,597,132	Henry Wilson—R
	Horace Greeley	Dem., Liberal Rep.	[12]	2,834,125	B. Gratz Brown—D, LR—(47)
	Thomas A. Hendricks	Democratic	42		Scattering—(19)
	B. Gratz Brown	Dem., Liberal Rep.	18		Votes not counted—(14)
	Charles J. Jenkins	Democratic	2		
	David Davis	Democratic	1		
	Votes not counted		17		
1876[13]	Rutherford B. Hayes	Republican	185	4,033,768	William A. Wheeler—R
	Samuel J. Tilden	Democratic	184	4,285,992	Thomas A. Hendricks—D
	Peter Cooper	Greenback	0	81,737	Samuel F. Cary—G
1880	James A. Garfield[14]	Republican	214	4,449,053	Chester A. Arthur—R
	Winfield S. Hancock	Democratic	155	4,442,035	William H. English—D
	James B. Weaver	Greenback	0	308,578	B. J. Chambers—G
1884	Grover Cleveland	Democratic	219	4,911,017	Thomas A. Hendricks—D
	James G. Blaine	Republican	182	4,848,334	John A. Logan—R
	Benjamin F. Butler	Greenback	0	175,370	A. M. West—G
	John P. St. John	Prohibition	0	150,369	William Daniel—P
1888	Benjamin Harrison	Republican	233	5,440,216	Levi P. Morton—R
	Grover Cleveland	Democratic	168	5,538,233	A. G. Thurman—D
	Clinton B. Fisk	Prohibition	0	249,506	John A. Brooks—P
	Alson J. Streeter	Union Labor	0	146,935	Charles E. Cunningham—UL
1892	Grover Cleveland	Democratic	277	5,556,918	Adlai E. Stevenson—D
	Benjamin Harrison	Republican	145	5,176,108	Whitelaw Reid—R
	James B. Weaver	People's[15]	22	1,041,028	James G. Field—Peo
	John Bidwell	Prohibition	0	264,133	James B. Cranfill—P

Year	Presidential candidates	Party	Electoral vote	Popular vote	Vice-presidential candidates and party
1896	William McKinley	Republican	271	7,035,638	Garret A. Hobart—R
	William J. Bryan	Dem., People's[15]	176	6,467,946	Arthur Sewall—D—(149)
					Thomas E. Watson—Peo—(27)
	John M. Palmer	Natl. Dem.	0	133,148	Simon B. Buckner—ND
	Joshua Levering	Prohibition	0	132,007	Hale Johnson—P
1900	William McKinley[16]	Republican	292	7,219,530	Theodore Roosevelt—R
	William J. Bryan	Dem., People's[15]	155	6,358,071	Adlai E. Stevenson—D, Peo
	Eugene V. Debs	Social Democratic	0	94,768	Job Harriman—SD
1904	Theodore Roosevelt	Republican	336	7,628,834	Charles W. Fairbanks—R
	Alton B. Parker	Democratic	140	5,084,491	Henry G. Davis—D
	Eugene V. Debs	Socialist	0	402,400	Benjamin Hanford—S
1908	William H. Taft	Republican	321	7,679,006	James S. Sherman—R
	William J. Bryan	Democratic	162	6,409,106	John W. Kern—D
	Eugene V. Debs	Socialist	0	402,820	Benjamin Hanford—S
1912	Woodrow Wilson	Democratic	435	6,286,214	Thomas R. Marshall—D
	Theodore Roosevelt	Progressive	88	4,126,020	Hiram Johnson—Prog
	William H. Taft	Republican	8	3,483,922	Nicholas M. Butler—R[17]
	Eugene V. Debs	Socialist	0	897,011	Emil Seidel—S
1916	Woodrow Wilson	Democratic	277	9,129,606	Thomas R. Marshall—D
	Charles E. Hughes	Republican	254	8,538,221	Charles W. Fairbanks—R
	A. L. Benson	Socialist	0	585,113	G. R. Kirkpatrick—S
1920	Warren G. Harding[18]	Republican	404	16,152,200	Calvin Coolidge—R
	James M. Cox	Democratic	127	9,147,353	Franklin D. Roosevelt—D
	Eugene V. Debs	Socialist	0	917,799	Seymour Stedman—S
1924	Calvin Coolidge	Republican	382	15,725,016	Charles G. Dawes—R
	John W. Davis	Democratic	136	8,385,586	Charles W. Bryan—D
	Robert M. LaFollette	Progressive, Socialist	13	4,822,856	Burton K. Wheeler—Prog S
1928	Herbert Hoover	Republican	444	21,392,190	Charles Curtis—R
	Alfred E. Smith	Democratic	87	15,016,443	Joseph T. Robinson—D
	Norman Thomas	Socialist	0	267,420	James H. Maurer—S
1932	Franklin D. Roosevelt	Democratic	472	22,821,857	John N. Garner—D
	Herbert Hoover	Republican	59	15,761,841	Charles Curtis—R
	Norman Thomas	Socialist	0	884,781	James H. Maurer—S
1936	Franklin D. Roosevelt	Democratic	523	27,751,597	John N. Garner—D
	Alfred M. Landon	Republican	8	16,679,583	Frank Knox—R
	Norman Thomas	Socialist	0	187,720	George Nelson—S
1940	Franklin D. Roosevelt	Democratic	449	27,244,160	Henry A. Wallace—D
	Wendell L. Willkie	Republican	82	22,305,198	Charles L. McNary—R
	Norman Thomas	Socialist	0	99,557	Maynard C. Krueger—S
1944	Franklin D. Roosevelt[19]	Democratic	432	25,602,504	Harry S. Truman—D
	Thomas E. Dewey	Republican	99	22,006,285	John W. Bricker—R
	Norman Thomas	Socialist	0	80,518	Darlington Hoopes—S
1948	Harry S. Truman	Democratic	303	24,179,345	Alben W. Barkley—D
	Thomas E. Dewey	Republican	189	21,991,291	Earl Warren—R
	J. Strom Thurmond	States' Rights Dem.	39	1,176,125	Fielding L. Wright—SR
	Henry A. Wallace	Progressive	0	1,157,326	Glen Taylor—Prog
	Norman Thomas	Socialist	0	139,572	Tucker P. Smith—S
1952	Dwight D. Eisenhower	Republican	442	33,936,234	Richard M. Nixon—R
	Adlai E. Stevenson	Democratic	89	27,314,992	John J. Sparkman—D
1956	Dwight D. Eisenhower	Republican	457	35,590,472	Richard M. Nixon—R
	Adlai E. Stevenson	Democratic	73 [20]	26,022,752	Estes Kefauver—D
1960	John F. Kennedy[22]	Democratic	303	34,226,731	Lyndon B. Johnson—D
	Richard M. Nixon	Republican	219 [21]	34,108,157	Henry Cabot Lodge—R

Year	Presidential candidates	Party	Electoral vote	Popular vote	Vice-presidential candidates and party
1964	Lyndon B. Johnson	Democratic	486	43,129,484	Hubert H. Humphrey—D
	Barry M. Goldwater	Republican	52	27,178,188	William E. Miller—R
1968	Richard M. Nixon	Republican	301	31,785,480	Spiro T. Agnew—R
	Hubert H. Humphrey	Democratic	191	31,275,166	Edmund S. Muskie—D
	George C. Wallace	American Independent	46	9,906,473	Curtis F. LeMay—AI
1972	Richard M. Nixon[23]	Republican	520 [24]	47,169,911	Spiro T. Agnew—R
	George McGovern	Democratic	17	29,170,383	Sargent Shriver—D
	John G. Schmitz	American	0	1,099,482	Thomas J. Anderson—A
1976	Jimmy Carter	Democratic	297	40,830,763	Walter F. Mondale—D
	Gerald R. Ford	Republican	240 [25]	39,147,973	Robert J. Dole—R
	Eugene J. McCarthy	Independent	0	756,631	None
1980	Ronald Reagan	Republican	489	43,899,248	George Bush—R
	Jimmy Carter	Democratic	49	36,481,435	Walter F. Mondale—D
	John B. Anderson	Independent	0	5,719,437	Patrick J. Lucey—I
1984	Ronald Reagan	Republican	525	54,455,075	George Bush—R
	Walter F. Mondale	Democratic	13	37,577,185	Geraldine A. Ferraro—D
1988	George H. Bush	Republican	426	48,886,097	J. Danforth Quayle—R
	Michael S. Dukakis	Democratic	111 [26]	41,809,074	Lloyd Bentsen—D
1992	William J. Clinton	Democratic	370	44,909,889	Albert A. Gore, Jr.—D
	George H. Bush	Republican	168	39,104,545	J. Danforth Quayle—R
	H. Ross Perot	Independent	0	19,742,267	James B. Stockdale—I

1. Only 10 states participated in the election. The New York legislature chose no electors, and North Carolina and Rhode Island had not yet ratified the Constitution. 2. As Jefferson and Burr were tied, the House of Representatives chose the President. In a vote by states, 10 votes were cast for Jefferson, 4 for Burr; 2 votes were not cast. 3. As no candidate had an electoral-vote majority, the House of Representatives chose the President from the first three. In a vote by states, 13 votes were cast for Adams, 7 for Jackson, and 4 for Crawford. 4. The Antimasonic Party on Sept. 26, 1831, was the first party to hold a nominating convention to choose candidates for President and Vice-President. 5. As Johnson did not have an electoral-vote majority, the Senate chose him 33–14 over Granger, the others being legally out of the race. 6. Harrison died April 4, 1841, and Tyler succeeded him April 6. 7. Taylor died July 9, 1850, and Fillmore succeeded him July 10. 8. Also known as the Know-Nothing Party. 9. Lincoln died April 15, 1865, and Johnson succeeded him the same day. 10. Name adopted by the Republican National Convention of 1864. Johnson was a War Democrat. 11. 23 Southern electoral votes were excluded. 12. See Election of 1872 in *Unusual Voting Results* under Elections, Presidential, in Index. 13. See Election of 1876 in *Unusual Voting Results* under Elections, Presidential, in Index. 14. Garfield died Sept. 19, 1881, and Arthur succeeded him Sept. 20. 15. Members of People's Party were called Populists. 16. McKinley died Sept. 14, 1901, and Roosevelt succeeded him the same day. 17. James S. Sherman, Republican candidate for Vice President, died Oct. 30, 1912, and the Republican electoral votes were cast for Butler. 18. Harding died Aug. 2, 1923, and Coolidge succeeded him Aug. 3. 19. Roosevelt died April 12, 1945, and Truman succeeded him the same day. 20. One electoral vote from Alabama was cast for Walter B. Jones. 21. Sen. Harry F. Byrd received 15 electoral votes. 22. Kennedy died Nov. 22, 1963, and Johnson succeeded him the same day. 23. Nixon resigned Aug. 9, 1974, and Gerald R. Ford succeeded him the same day. 24. One electoral vote from Virginia was cast for John Hospers, Libertarian Party. 25. One electoral vote from Washington was cast for Ronald Reagan. 26. One electoral vote from West Virginia was cast for Lloyd Bentsen.

Gerrymander

Source: "The Reader's Companion to American History," Houghton Mifflin Company.

Gerrymander refers to the drawing of boundaries of legislative districts to benefit one party or group and handicap another. Although the practice dates back to the colonial period, its name is derived from Elbridge Gerry, a signer of the Declaration of Independence, a nonsigning delegate to the Federal Convention of 1787, and a leader of the Jeffersonian Republican party.

In 1812, while Gerry was governor of Massachusetts, the Republican-dominated legislature redrew district lines to weigh representation in favor of Republicans and against Federalists. The Federalists attacked the redistricting, specifically blaming Gerry although he had nothing to do with the project and, in private, opposed it. A Federalist newspaper published a political cartoon depicting the oddly shaped district covering Essex County as a salamander; the cartoonist dubbed his creation a "Gerry-mander." The word quickly passed into common parlance.

Since the 1950s, the federal courts have been increasingly willing to examine states' defining of representative districts to determine their adherence to the principle of "one man, one vote," as enunciated in *Baker* v. *Carr* (1962). Ironically, in light of the term's New England origins, most gerrymanders examined by the Supreme Court have come from southern states, where local legislatures sought to dilute the representation of urban residents and African-Americans.

Large Voter Turnout

Voter turnout for the presidential election of 1992 was the largest since 1972 with 61% of the voting-age population going to the polls. Furthermore, the 1992 turnout rate was four percentage points higher than in 1988 (57%).

Qualifications for Voting

The Supreme Court decision of March 21, 1972, declared lengthy requirements for voting in state and local elections unconstitutional and suggested that 30 days was an ample period. Most of the states have changed or eliminated their durational residency requirements to comply with the ruling, as shown.

NO DURATIONAL RESIDENCY REQUIREMENT

Alabama,[6] Arkansas, Connecticut,[13] Delaware,[12] District of Columbia,[16] Florida,[5] Georgia,[2] Hawaii,[2] Iowa,[6] Louisiana,[8] Maine,[22] Maryland, Massachusetts,[3] Missouri,[4] Nebraska,[9] New Hampshire,[17] New Mexico,[7] Oklahoma, South Carolina,[22] South Dakota,[10] Tennessee,[20] Texas,[2] Virginia, West Virginia,[2] Wyoming[2]

30-DAY RESIDENCY REQUIREMENT

Alaska,[18] Arizona,[11] Idaho,[23] Illinois, Indiana, Michigan, Mississippi,[21] Montana, Nevada, New Jersey, New York, North Carolina, North Dakota, Ohio, Pennsylvania[2] Rhode Island, Utah, Washington[2]

OTHER

California,[19] Colorado,[1] Minnesota,[15] and Oregon,[24] 20 days; Kentucky, 28 days; Kansas, 14 days; Vermont, 10–12 days;[14] Wisconsin, 10 days

1. 25 days immediately preceding the election. 2. 30-day registration requirement. 3. No residency required to register to vote. 4. Must be registered by the fourth Wednesday prior to election. 5. 29–day registration requirement before national election; 29-day registration requirement before first state primary, if change of party before second primary have to re-register. 6. 10-day registration requirement. In-person registration by 5 PM, eleven days before election date. 7. Must register 28 days before election. 8. Register 24 days prior to any election. 9. Registration requirement, 2nd Friday prior to elections. 10. 15-day registration requirement. 11. Residency in the state 29 days next preceding the election. 12. Must reside in Delaware and register by the last day that the books are open for registration. 13. Registration deadline 14th day before election; registration and party enrollment deadline by 12 noon the day before primary. 14. Administrative cut-off date for processing applications 2nd Saturday before the election by 12 noon. 15. Permits registration and voting on election day with approved ID. 16. Registration stops 30 days before any election. Voters must inform Board of Elections of change of address within 30 days of moving. 17. Registration requirement, 10 days prior to elections. Same day registration for Federal and State elections. 18. If otherwise qualified but has not been a resident of the election district for at least 30 days preceding the date of a presidential election, is entitled to register and vote for presidential and vice-presidential candidates. 19. Must be a registered voter 29 days before an election. 20. Must register at least 30 days before an election. 21. 30 days registration required, 60 days if registration is by mail. 22. Registration certificate not valid for 30 days but if you move within the state you can vote in old precinct during the 30 days. 23. May register 25 days prior to any election with County Clerk. If eligible to vote, an individual may register in person at the polling place on election day at the resident precinct and complete a registration card, make an oath and provide proof of residence. 24. By close of business day registering agencies (which varies) 21st day before the election. *Source: Information Please* questionnaires to the states.

Facts About Elections

Candidate with highest populate vote: Reagan (1984), 54,455,075.

Candidate with highest electoral vote: Reagan (1984), 525.

Candidate carrying most states: Nixon (1972) and Reagan (1984), 49.

Candidate running most times: Norman Thomas, 6 (1928, 1932, 1936, 1940, 1944, 1948).

Candidate elected, defeated, then reelected: Cleveland (1884, 1888, 1892).

Plurality and Majority

In order to win a plurality, a candidate must receive a greater number of votes than anyone running against him. If he receives 50 votes, for example, and two other candidates receive 49 and 2, he will have a plurality of one vote over his closest opponent.

However, a candidate does not have a majority unless he receives more than 50% of the total votes cast. In the example above, the candidate does not have a majority, because his 50 votes are less than 50% of the 101 votes cast.

Unusual Voting Results

Election of 1872

The presidential and vice-presidential candidates of the Liberal Republicans and the northern Democrats in 1872 were Horace Greeley and B. Gratz Brown. Greeley died Nov. 29, 1872, before his 66 electors voted. In the electoral balloting for President, 63 of Greeley's votes were scattered among four other men, including Brown.

Election of 1876

In the election of 1876 Samuel J. Tilden, the Democratic candidate, received a popular majority but lacked one undisputed electoral vote to carry a clear majority of the electoral college. The crux of the problem was in the 22 electoral votes which were in dispute because Florida, Louisiana, South Carolina, and Oregon each sent in two sets of election returns. In the three southern states, Republican election boards threw out enough Democratic votes to certify the Republican candidate, Hayes. In Oregon, the Democratic governor disqualified a Republican elector, replacing him with a Democrat. Since the Senate was Republican and the House of Representatives Democratic, it seemed useless to refer the disputed returns to the two houses for solution. Instead Congress appointed an Electoral Commission with five representatives each from the Senate, the House, and the Supreme Court. All but one Justice was named, giving the Commission seven Republican and seven Democratic members. The naming of the fifth Justice was left to the other four. He was a Republican who first favored Tilden but, under pressure from his party, switched to Hayes, ensuring his election by the Commission voting 8 to 7 on party lines.

Minority Presidents

Sixteen candidates have become President of the United States with a popular vote less than 50% of the total cast. It should be noted, however, that in elections before 1872, presidential electors were not chosen by popular vote in all states. Adams' election in 1824 was by the House of Representatives, which chose him over Jackson, who had a plurality of both electoral and popular votes, but not a majority in the electoral college.

Besides Jackson in 1824, only two other candidates receiving the largest popular vote have failed to gain a majority in the electoral college—Samuel J. Tilden (D) in 1876 and Grover Cleveland (D) in 1888. The "minority" Presidents follow:

Vote Received by Minority Presidents

Year	President	Electoral Percent	Popular vote Percent
1824	John Q. Adams	31.8	29.8
1844	James K. Polk (D)	61.8	49.3
1848	Zachary Taylor (W)	56.2	47.3
1856	James Buchanan (D)	58.7	45.3
1860	Abraham Lincoln (R)	59.4	39.9
1876	Rutherford B. Hayes (R)	50.1	47.9
1880	James A. Garfield (R)	57.9	48.3
1884	Grover Cleveland (D)	54.6	48.8
1888	Benjamin Harrison (R)	58.1	47.8
1892	Grover Cleveland (D)	62.4	46.0
1912	Woodrow Wilson (D)	81.9	41.8
1916	Woodrow Wilson (D)	52.1	49.3
1948	Harry S. Truman (D)	57.1	49.5
1960	John F. Kennedy (D)	56.4	49.7
1968	Richard M. Nixon (R)	56.1	43.4
1992	William J. Clinton (D)	68.8	43.0

Percent of Persons Voting in Presidential Elections 1964–1992

(Numbers in thousands. Civilian noninstitutional population.)

United States	1992	1988	1984	1980	1976	1972	1968	1964
Total voting age	185,684	178,098	169,963	157,085	146,548	136,203	116,535	110,604
Percent voted	61.3	57.4	59.9	59.2	59.2	63.0	67.8	69.3
White	63.6	59.1	61.4	60.9	60.9	64.5	69.1	70.7
Black	54.0	51.5	55.8	50.5	48.7	52.1	57.6	58.5[2]
Hispanic origin[1]	28.9	28.8	32.6	29.9	31.8	37.5	n.a.	n.a.
Male	60.2	56.4	59.0	59.1	59.6	64.1	69.8	71.9
Female	62.3	58.3	60.8	59.4	58.8	62.0	66.0	67.0
18 to 24 years	42.8	36.2	40.8	39.9	42.2	49.6	50.4[3]	50.9[3]
25 to 44 years	58.3	54.0	58.4	58.7	58.7	62.7	66.6	69.0
45 to 64 years	70.0	67.9	69.8	69.3	68.7	70.8	74.9	75.9
65 years and over	70.1	68.8	67.7	65.1	62.2	63.5	65.8	66.3

1. Persons of Hispanic origin may be of any race. 2. Black and other races in 1964. 3. Prior to 1972, includes persons 18 to 20 years old in Georgia and Kentucky, 19 and 20 in Alaska, and 20 years old in Hawaii. n.a. = not available. *Source:* Bureau of the Census, *Current Population Reports*, April 1993.

How a Bill Becomes a Law

When a Senator or a Representative introduces a bill, he sends it to the clerk of his house, who gives it a number and title. This is the *first reading,* and the bill is referred to the proper committee.

The committee may decide the bill is unwise or unnecessary and *table* it, thus killing it at once. Or it may decide the bill is worthwhile and hold hearings to listen to facts and opinions presented by experts and other interested persons. After members of the committee have debated the bill and perhaps offered amendments, a vote is taken; and if the vote is favorable, the bill is sent back to the floor of the house.

The clerk reads the bill sentence by sentence to the house, and this is known as the *second reading.* Members may then debate the bill and offer amendments. In the House of Representatives, the time for debate is limited by a *cloture rule,* but there is no such restriction in the Senate for cloture, where 60 votes are required. This makes possible a *filibuster,* in which one or more opponents hold the floor to defeat the bill.

The *third reading* is by title only, and the bill is put to a vote, which may be by voice or roll call, depending on the circumstances and parliamentary rules. Members who must be absent at the time but who wish to record their vote may be paired if each negative vote has a balancing affirmative one.

The bill then goes to the other house of Congress, where it may be defeated, or passed with or without amendments. If the bill is defeated, it dies. If it is passed with amendments, a joint Congressional committee must be appointed by both houses to iron out the differences.

After its final passage by both houses, the bill is sent to the President. If he approves, he signs it, and the bill becomes a law. However, if he disapproves, he *vetoes* the bill by refusing to sign it and sending it back to the house of origin with his reasons for the veto. The objections are read and debated, and a roll-call vote is taken. If the bill receives less than a two-thirds vote, it is defeated and goes no farther. But if it receives a two-thirds vote or greater, it is sent to the other house for a vote. If that house also passes it by a two-thirds vote, the President's veto is *overridden,* and the bill becomes a law.

Should the President desire neither to sign nor to veto the bill, he may retain it for ten days, Sundays excepted, after which time it automatically becomes a law without signature. However, if Congress has adjourned within those ten days, the bill is automatically killed, that process of indirect rejection being known as a *pocket veto.*

Government Officials
Cabinet Members With Dates of Appointment

Although the Constitution made no provision for a President's advisory group, the heads of the three executive departments (State, Treasury, and War) and the Attorney General were organized by Washington into such a group; and by about 1793, the name "Cabinet" was applied to it. With the exception of the Attorney General up to 1870 and the Postmaster General from 1829 to 1872, Cabinet members have been heads of executive departments.

A Cabinet member is appointed by the President, subject to the confirmation of the Senate; and as his term is not fixed, he may be replaced at any time by the President. At a change in Administration, it is customary for him to tender his resignation, but he remains in office until a successor is appointed.

The table of Cabinet members lists only those members who actually served after being duly commissioned.

The dates shown are those of appointment. "Cont." indicates that the term continued from the previous Administration for a substantial amount of time.

With the creation of the Department of Transportation in 1966, the Cabinet consisted of 12 members. This figure was reduced to 11 when the Post Office Department became an independent agency in 1970 but, with the establishment in 1977 of a Department of Energy, became 12 again. Creation of the Department of Education in 1980 raised the number to 13. Creation of the Department of Veterans' Affairs in 1989 raised the number to 14.

WASHINGTON

Secretary of State	Thomas Jefferson 1789
	Edmund Randolph 1794
	Timothy Pickering 1795
Secretary of the Treasury	Alexander Hamilton 1789
	Oliver Wolcott, Jr. 1795
Secretary of War	Henry Knox 1789
	Timothy Pickering 1795
	James McHenry 1796
Attorney General	Edmund Randolph 1789
	William Bradford 1794
	Charles Lee 1795

J. ADAMS

Secretary of State	Timothy Pickering (Cont.)
	John Marshall 1800
Secretary of the Treasury	Oliver Wolcott, Jr. (Cont.)
	Samuel Dexter 1801
Secretary of War	James McHenry (Cont.)
	Samuel Dexter 1800
Attorney General	Charles Lee (Cont.)
Secretary of the Navy	Benjamin Stoddert 1798

JEFFERSON

Secretary of State	James Madison 1801
Secretary of the Treasury	Samuel Dexter (Cont.)
	Albert Gallatin 1801
Secretary of War	Henry Dearborn 1801
Attorney General	Levi Lincoln 1801
	Robert Smith 1805
	John Breckinridge 1805
	Caesar A. Rodney 1807
Secretary of the Navy	Benjamin Stoddert (Cont.)
	Robert Smith 1801

MADISON

Secretary of State	Robert Smith 1809
	James Monroe 1811
Secretary of the Treasury	Albert Gallatin (Cont.)
	George W. Campbell 1814
	Alexander J. Dallas 1814
	William H. Crawford 1816
Secretary of War	William Eustis 1809
	John Armstrong 1813
	James Monroe 1814
	William H. Crawford 1815

Attorney General	Caesar A. Rodney (Cont.)
	William Pinckney 1811
	Richard Rush 1814
Secretary of the Navy	Paul Hamilton 1809
	William Jones 1813
	B. W. Crowninshield 1814

MONROE

Secretary of State	John Quincy Adams 1817
Secretary of the Treasury	William H. Crawford (Cont.)
Secretary of War	John C. Calhoun 1817
Attorney General	Richard Rush (Cont.)
	William Wirt 1817
Secretary of the Navy	B. W. Crowninshield (Cont.)
	Smith Thompson 1818
	Samuel L. Southard 1823

J. Q. ADAMS

Secretary of State	Henry Clay 1825
Secretary of the Treasury	Richard Rush 1825
Secretary of War	James Barbour 1825
	Peter B. Porter 1828
Attorney General	William Wirt (Cont.)
Secretary of the Navy	Samuel L. Southard (Cont.)

JACKSON

Secretary of State	Martin Van Buren 1829
	Edward Livingston 1831
	Louis McLane 1833
	John Forsyth 1834
Secretary of the Treasury	Samuel D. Ingham 1829
	Louis McLane 1831
	William J. Duane 1833
	Roger B. Taney[3] 1833
	Levi Woodbury 1834
Secretary of War	John H. Eaton 1829
	Lewis Cass 1831
Attorney General	John M. Berrien 1829
	Roger B. Taney 1831
	Benjamin F. Butler 1833
Postmaster General[1]	William T. Barry 1829
	Amos Kendall 1835
Secretary of the Navy	John Branch 1829
	Levi Woodbury 1831
	Mahlon Dickerson 1834

VAN BUREN

Secretary of State	John Forsyth (Cont.)
Secretary of the Treasury	Levi Woodbury (Cont.)
Secretary of War	Joel R. Poinsett 1837
Attorney General	Benjamin F. Butler (Cont.)
	Felix Grundy 1838
	Henry D. Gilpin 1840
Postmaster General	Amos Kendall (Cont.)
	John M. Niles 1840
Secretary of the Navy	Mahlon Dickerson (Cont.)
	James K. Paulding 1838

W. H. HARRISON

Secretary of State	Daniel Webster 1841
Secretary of the Treasury	Thomas Ewing 1841
Secretary of War	John Bell 1841
Attorney General	John J. Crittenden 1841
Postmaster General	Francis Granger 1841
Secretary of the Navy	George E. Badger 1841

TYLER

Secretary of State	Daniel Webster (Cont.)
	Abel P. Upshur 1843
	John C. Calhoun 1844
Secretary of the Treasury	Thomas Ewing (Cont.)
	Walter Forward 1841
	John C. Spencer[3] 1843
	George M. Bibb 1844
Secretary of War	John Bell (Cont.)
	John C. Spencer 1841
	James M. Porter[3] 1843
	William Wilkins 1844
Attorney General	John J. Crittenden (Cont.)
	Hugh S. Legaré 1841
	John Nelson 1843
Postmaster General	Francis Granger (Cont.)
	Charles A. Wickliffe 1841
Secretary of the Navy	George E. Badger (Cont.)
	Abel P. Upshur 1841
	David Henshaw[3] 1843
	Thomas W. Gilmer 1844
	John Y. Mason 1844

POLK

Secretary of State	James Buchanan 1845
Secretary of the Treasury	Robert J. Walker 1845
Secretary of War	William L. Marcy 1845
Attorney General	John Y. Mason 1845
	Nathan Clifford 1846
	Isaac Toucey 1848
Postmaster General	Cave Johnson 1845
Secretary of the Navy	George Bancroft 1845
	John Y. Mason 1846

TAYLOR

Secretary of State	John M. Clayton 1849
Secretary of the Treasury	William M. Meredith 1849
Secretary of War	George W. Crawford 1849
Attorney General	Reverdy Johnson 1849
Postmaster General	Jacob Collamer 1849
Secretary of the Navy	William B. Preston 1849
Secretary of the Interior	Thomas Ewing 1849

FILLMORE

Secretary of State	Daniel Webster 1850
	Edward Everett 1852
Secretary of the Treasury	Thomas Corwin 1850
Secretary of War	Charles M. Conrad 1850
Attorney General	John J. Crittenden 1850
Postmaster General	Nathan K. Hall 1850
	Samuel D. Hubbard 1852
Secretary of the Navy	William A. Graham 1850
	John P. Kennedy 1852
Secretary of the Interior	Thos. M. T. McKennan 1850
	Alex. H. H. Stuart 1850

PIERCE

Secretary of State	William L. Marcy 1853
Secretary of the Treasury	James Guthrie 1853
Secretary of War	Jefferson Davis 1853
Attorney General	Caleb Cushing 1853
Postmaster General	James Campbell 1853
Secretary of the Navy	James C. Dobbin 1853
Secretary of the Interior	Robert McClelland 1853

BUCHANAN

Secretary of State	Lewis Cass 1857
	Jeremiah S. Black 1860
Secretary of the Treasury	Howell Cobb 1857
	Philip F. Thomas 1860
	John A. Dix 1861
Secretary of War	John B. Floyd 1857
	Joseph Holt 1861
Attorney General	Jeremiah S. Black 1857
	Edwin M. Stanton 1860
Postmaster General	Aaron V. Brown 1857
	Joseph Holt 1859
	Horatio King 1861
Secretary of the Navy	Isaac Toucey 1857
Secretary of the Interior	Jacob Thompson 1857

LINCOLN

Secretary of State	William H. Seward 1861
Secretary of the Treasury	Salmon P. Chase 1861
	William P. Fessenden 1864
	Hugh McCulloch 1865
Secretary of War	Simon Cameron 1861
	Edwin M. Stanton 1862
Attorney General	Edward Bates 1861
	James Speed 1864
Postmaster General	Montgomery Blair 1861
	William Dennison 1864
Secretary of the Navy	Gideon Welles 1861
Secretary of the Interior	Caleb B. Smith 1861
	John P. Usher 1863

A. JOHNSON

Secretary of State	William H. Seward (Cont.)
Secretary of the Treasury	Hugh McCulloch (Cont.)
Secretary of War	Edwin M. Stanton (Cont.)
	John M. Schofield 1868
Attorney General	James Speed (Cont.)
	Henry Stanbery 1866
	William M. Evarts 1868
Postmaster General	William Dennison (Cont.)
	Alexander W. Randall 1866
Secretary of the Navy	Gideon Welles (Cont.)
Secretary of the Interior	John P. Usher (Cont.)
	James Harlan 1865
	Orville H. Browning 1866

GRANT

Secretary of State	Elihu B. Washburne 1869
	Hamilton Fish 1869
Secretary of the Treasury	George S. Boutwell 1869
	William A. Richardson 1873
	Benjamin H. Bristow 1874
	Lot M. Morrill 1876
Secretary of War	John A. Rawlins 1869
	William W. Belknap 1869
	Alphonso Taft 1876
	James D. Cameron 1876
Attorney General	Ebenezer R. Hoar 1869
	Amos T. Akerman 1870
	George H. Williams 1871
	Edwards Pierrepont 1875
	Alphonso Taft 1876
Postmaster General	John A. J. Creswell 1869
	Marshall Jewell 1874
	James N. Tyner 1876
Secretary of the Navy	Adolph E. Borie 1869
	George M. Robeson 1869
Secretary of the Interior	Jacob D. Cox 1869
	Columbus Delano 1870
	Zachariah Chandler 1875

HAYES

Secretary of State	William M. Evarts 1877
Secretary of the Treasury	John Sherman 1877
Secretary of War	George W. McCrary 1877
	Alexander Ramsey 1879

Attorney General	Charles Devens 1877
Postmaster General	David M. Key 1877
	Horace Maynard 1880
	Richard W. Thompson 1877
	Nathan Goff, Jr. 1881
Secretary of the Interior	Carl Schurz 1877

GARFIELD

Secretary of State	James G. Blaine 1881
Secretary of the Treasury	William Windom 1881
Secretary of War	Robert T. Lincoln 1881
Attorney General	Wayne MacVeagh 1881
Postmaster General	Thomas L. James 1881
Secretary of the Navy	William H. Hunt 1881
Secretary of the Interior	Samuel J. Kirkwood 1881

ARTHUR

Secretary of State	James G. Blaine (Cont.)
	F. T. Frelinghuysen 1881
Secretary of the Treasury	William Windom (Cont.)
	Charles J. Folger 1881
	Walter Q. Gresham 1884
	Hugh McCulloch 1884
Secretary of War	Robert T. Lincoln (Cont.)
Attorney General	Wayne MacVeagh (Cont.)
	Benjamin H. Brewster 1881
Postmaster General	Thomas L. James (Cont.)
	Timothy O. Howe 1881
	Walter Q. Gresham 1883
	Frank Hatton 1884
Secretary of the Navy	William H. Hunt (Cont.)
	William E. Chandler 1882
Secretary of the Interior	Samuel J. Kirkwood (Cont.)
	Henry M. Teller 1882

CLEVELAND

Secretary of State	Thomas F. Bayard 1885
Secretary of the Treasury	Daniel Manning 1885
	Charles S. Fairchild 1887
Secretary of War	William C. Endicott 1885
Attorney General	Augustus H. Garland 1885
Postmaster General	William F. Vilas 1885
	Don M. Dickinson 1888
Secretary of the Navy	William C. Whitney 1885
Secretary of the Interior	Lucius Q. C. Lamar 1885
	William F. Vilas 1888
Secretary of Agriculture	Norman J. Colman 1889

B. HARRISON

Secretary of State	James G. Blaine 1889
	John W. Foster 1892
Secretary of the Treasury	William Windom 1889
	Charles Foster 1891
Secretary of War	Redfield Proctor 1889
	Stephen B. Elkins 1891
Attorney General	William H. H. Miller 1889
Postmaster General	John Wanamaker 1889
Secretary of the Navy	Benjamin F. Tracy 1889
Secretary of the Interior	John W. Noble 1889
Secretary of Agriculture	Jeremiah M. Rusk 1889

CLEVELAND

Secretary of State	Walter Q. Gresham 1893
	Richard Olney 1895
Secretary of the Treasury	John G. Carlisle 1893
Secretary of War	Daniel S. Lamont 1893
Attorney General	Richard Olney 1893
	Judson Harmon 1895
Postmaster General	Wilson S. Bissell 1893
	William L. Wilson 1895
Secretary of the Navy	Hilary A. Herbert 1893
Secretary of the Interior	Hoke Smith 1893
	David R. Francis 1896
Secretary of Agriculture	Julius Sterling Morton 1893

MCKINLEY

Secretary of State	John Sherman 1897
	William R. Day 1898
	John Hay 1898
Secretary of the Treasury	Lyman J. Gage 1897
Secretary of War	Russell A. Alger 1897
	Elihu Root 1899
Attorney General	Joseph McKenna 1897

	John W. Griggs 1898
	Philander C. Knox 1901
Postmaster General	James A. Gary 1897
	Charles E. Smith 1898
Secretary of the Navy	John D. Long 1897
Secretary of the Interior	Cornelius N. Bliss 1897
	Ethan A. Hitchcock 1898
Secretary of Agriculture	James Wilson 1897

T. ROOSEVELT

Secretary of State	John Hay (Cont.)
	Elihu Root 1905
	Robert Bacon 1909
Secretary of the Treasury	Lyman J. Gage (Cont.)
	Leslie M. Shaw 1902
	George B. Cortelyou 1907
Secretary of War	Elihu Root (Cont.)
	William H. Taft 1904
	Luke E. Wright 1908
Attorney General	Philander C. Knox (Cont.)
	William H. Moody 1904
	Charles J. Bonaparte 1906
Postmaster General	Charles E. Smith (Cont.)
	Henry C. Payne 1902
	Robert J. Wynne 1904
	George B. Cortelyou 1905
	George von L. Meyer 1907
Secretary of the Navy	John D. Long (Cont.)
	William H. Moody 1902
	Paul Morton 1904
	Charles J. Bonaparte 1905
	Victor H. Metcalf 1906
	Truman H. Newberry 1908
Secretary of the Interior	Ethan A. Hitchcock (Cont.)
	James R. Garfield 1907
Secretary of Agriculture	James Wilson (Cont.)
Secretary of Commerce and Labor	George B. Cortelyou 1903
	Victor H. Metcalf 1904
	Oscar S. Straus 1906

TAFT

Secretary of State	Philander C. Knox 1909
Secretary of the Treasury	Franklin MacVeagh 1909
Secretary of War	Jacob M. Dickinson 1909
	Henry L. Stimson 1911
Attorney General	George W. Wickersham 1909
Postmaster General	Frank H. Hitchcock 1909
Secretary of the Navy	George von L. Meyer 1909
Secretary of the Interior	Richard A. Ballinger 1909
	Walter L. Fisher 1911
Secretary of Agriculture	James Wilson (Cont.)
Secretary of Commerce and Labor	Charles Nagel 1909

WILSON

Secretary of State	William J. Bryan 1913
	Robert Lansing 1915
	Bainbridge Colby 1920
Secretary of the Treasury	William G. McAdoo 1913
	Carter Glass 1918
	David F. Houston 1920
Secretary of War	Lindley M. Garrison 1913
	Newton D. Baker 1916
Attorney General	James C. McReynolds 1913
	Thomas W. Gregory 1914
	A. Mitchell Palmer 1919
Postmaster General	Albert S. Burleson 1913
Secretary of the Navy	Josephus Daniels 1913
Secretary of the Interior	Franklin K. Lane 1913
	John B. Payne 1920
Secretary of Agriculture	David F. Houston 1913
	Edwin T. Meredith 1920
Secretary of Commerce	William C. Redfield 1913
	Joshua W. Alexander 1919
Secretary of Labor	William B. Wilson 1913

HARDING

Secretary of State	Charles E. Hughes 1921
Secretary of the Treasury	Andrew W. Mellon 1921
Secretary of War	John W. Weeks 1921
Attorney General	Harry M. Daugherty 1921
Postmaster General	Will H. Hays 1921
	Hubert Work 1922

	Harry S. New 1923
Secretary of the Navy	Edwin Denby 1921
Secretary of the Interior	Albert B. Fall 1921
	Hubert Work 1923
Secretary of Agriculture	Henry C. Wallace 1921
Secretary of Commerce	Herbert Hoover 1921
Secretary of Labor	James J. Davis 1921

COOLIDGE

Secretary of State	Charles E. Hughes (Cont.)
	Frank B. Kellogg 1925
Secretary of the Treasury	Andrew W. Mellon (Cont.)
Secretary of War	John W. Weeks (Cont.)
	Dwight F. Davis 1925
Attorney General	Harry M. Daughtery (Cont.)
	Harlan F. Stone 1924
	John G. Sargent 1925
Postmaster General	
	Harry S. New (Cont.)
Secretary of the Navy	Edwin Denby (Cont.)
	Curtis D. Wilbur 1924
Secretary of the Interior	Hubert Work (Cont.)
	Roy O. West 1928
Secretary of Agriculture	Henry C. Wallace (Cont.)
	Howard M. Gore 1924
	William M. Jardine 1925
Secretary of Commerce	Herbert Hoover (Cont.)
	William F. Whiting 1928
Secretary of Labor	James J. Davis (Cont.)

HOOVER

Secretary of State	Frank B. Kellogg (Cont.)
	Henry L. Stimson 1929
Secretary of the Treasury	Andrew W. Mellon (Cont.)
	Ogden L. Mills 1932
Secretary of War	James W. Good 1929
	Patrick J. Hurley 1929
Attorney General	William D. Mitchell 1929
Postmaster General	Walter F. Brown 1929
Secretary of the Navy	Charles F. Adams 1929
Secretary of the Interior	Ray Lyman Wilbur 1929
Secretary of Agriculture	Arthur M. Hyde 1929
Secretary of Commerce	Robert P. Lamont 1929
	Roy D. Chapin 1932
Secretary of Labor	James J. Davis (Cont.)
	William N. Doak 1930

F. D. ROOSEVELT

Secretary of State	Cordell Hull 1933
	E. R. Stettinius, Jr. 1944
Secretary of the Treasury	William H. Woodin 1933
	Henry Morgenthau, Jr. 1934
Secretary of War	George H. Dern 1933
	Harry H. Woodring 1936
	Henry L. Stimson 1940
Attorney General	Homer S. Cummings 1933
	Frank Murphy 1939
	Robert H. Jackson 1940
	Francis Biddle 1941
Postmaster General	James A. Farley 1933
	Frank C. Walker 1940
Secretary of the Navy	Claude A. Swanson 1933
	Charles Edison 1940
	Frank Knox 1940
	James Forrestal 1944
Secretary of the Interior	Harold L. Ickes 1933
Secretary of Agriculture	Henry A. Wallace 1933
	Claude R. Wickard 1940
Secretary of Commerce	Daniel C. Roper 1933
	Harry L. Hopkins 1938
	Jesse H. Jones 1940
	Henry A. Wallace 1945
Secretary of Labor	Frances Perkins 1933

TRUMAN

Secretary of State	E. R. Stettinius, Jr. (Cont.)
	James F. Byrnes 1945
	George C. Marshall 1947
	Dean Acheson 1949
Secretary of the Treasury	Henry Morgenthau, Jr. (Cont.)
	Frederick M. Vinson 1945
	John W. Snyder 1946

Secretary of Defense	James Forrestal 1947
	Louis A. Johnson 1949
	George C. Marshall 1950
	Robert A. Lovett 1951
Attorney General	Francis Biddle (Cont.)
	Tom C. Clark 1945
	J. Howard McGrath 1949
	James P. McGranery 1952
Postmaster General	Frank C. Walker (Cont.)
	Robert E. Hannegan 1945
	Jesse M. Donaldson 1947
Secretary of the Interior	Harold L. Ickes (Cont.)
	Julius A. Krug 1946
	Oscar L. Chapman 1949
Secretary of Agriculture	Claude R. Wickard (Cont.)
	Clinton P. Anderson 1945
	Charles F. Brannan 1948
Secretary of Commerce	Henry A. Wallace (Cont.)
	W. Averell Harriman 1946
	Charles Sawyer 1948
Secretary of Labor	Frances Perkins (Cont.)
	Lewis B. Schwellenbach 1945
	Maurice J. Tobin 1948
Secretary of War [2]	Henry L. Stimson (Cont.)
	Robert P. Patterson 1945
	Kenneth C. Royall 1947
Secretary of the Navy [2]	James Forrestal (Cont.)

EISENHOWER

Secretary of State	John Foster Dulles 1953
	Christian A. Herter 1959
Secretary of the Treasury	George M. Humphrey 1953
	Robert B. Anderson 1957
Secretary of Defense	Charles E. Wilson 1953
	Neil H. McElroy 1957
	Thomas S. Gates, Jr. 1959
Attorney General	Herbert Brownell, Jr. 1953
	William P. Rogers 1958
Postmaster General	Arthur E. Summerfield 1953
Secretary of the Interior	Douglas McKay 1953
	Frederick A. Seaton 1956
Secretary of Agriculture	Ezra Taft Benson 1953
Secretary of Commerce	Sinclair Weeks 1953
	Lewis L. Strauss [3] 1958
	Frederick H. Mueller 1959
Secretary of Labor	Martin P. Durkin 1953
	James P. Mitchell 1953
Secretary of Health, Education, and Welfare	Oveta Culp Hobby 1953
	Marion B. Folsom 1955
	Arthur S. Flemming 1958

KENNEDY

Secretary of State	Dean Rusk 1961
Secretary of the Treasury	C. Douglas Dillon 1961
Secretary of Defense	Robert S. McNamara 1961
Attorney General	Robert F. Kennedy 1961
Postmaster General	J. Edward Day 1961
	John A. Gronouski 1963
Secretary of the Interior	Stewart L. Udall 1961
Secretary of Agriculture	Orville L. Freeman 1961
Secretary of Commerce	Luther H. Hodges 1961
Secretary of Labor	Arthur J. Goldberg 1961
	W. Willard Wirtz 1962
Secretary of Health, Education, and Welfare	Abraham A. Ribicoff 1961
	Anthony J. Celebrezze 1962

L. B. JOHNSON

Secretary of State	Dean Rusk (Cont.)
Secretary of the Treasury	C. Douglas Dillon (Cont.)
	Henry H. Fowler 1965
	Joseph W. Barr [4] 1968
Secretary of Defense	Robert S. McNamara (Cont.)
	Clark M. Clifford 1968
Attorney General	Robert F. Kennedy (Cont.)
	N. de B. Katzenbach 1965
	Ramsey Clark 1967
Postmaster General	John A. Gronouski (Cont.)
	Lawrence F. O'Brien 1965
	W. Marvin Watson 1968
Secretary of the Interior	Stewart L. Udall (Cont.)
Secretary of Agriculture	Orville L. Freeman (Cont.)

Secretary of Commerce	Luther H. Hodges (Cont.)
	John T. Connor 1964
	A. B. Trowbridge 1967
	C. R. Smith 1968
Secretary of Labor	W. Willard Wirtz (Cont.)
Secretary of Health, Education, and Welfare	Anthony J. Celebrezze (Cont.)
	John W. Gardner 1965
	Wilbur J. Cohen 1968
Secretary of Housing and Urban Development	Robert C. Weaver 1966
	Robert C. Wood[4] 1969
Secretary of Transportation	Alan S. Boyd 1966

NIXON

Secretary of State	William P. Rogers 1969
	Henry A. Kissinger 1973
Secretary of the Treasury	David M. Kennedy 1969
	John B. Connally 1971
	George P. Shultz 1972
	William E. Simon 1974
Secretary of Defense	Melvin R. Laird 1969
	Elliot L. Richardson 1973
	James R. Schlesinger 1973
Attorney General	John N. Mitchell 1969
	Richard G. Kleindienst 1972
	Elliot L. Richardson 1973
	William B. Saxbe 1974
Postmaster General[5]	William M. Blount 1969
Secretary of the Interior	Walter J. Hickel 1969
	Rogers C. B. Morton 1971
Secretary of Agriculture	Clifford M. Hardin 1969
	Earl L. Butz 1971
Secretary of Commerce	Maurice H. Stans 1969
	Peter G. Peterson 1972
	Frederick B. Dent 1973
Secretary of Labor	George P. Shultz 1969
	James D. Hodgson 1970
	Peter J. Brennan 1973
Secretary of Health, Education, and Welfare	Robert H. Finch 1969
	Elliot L. Richardson 1970
	Caspar W. Weinberger 1973
Secretary of Housing and Urban Development	George Romney 1969
	James T. Lynn 1973
Secretary of Transportation	John A. Volpe 1969
	Claude S. Brinegar 1973

FORD

Secretary of State	Henry A. Kissinger (Cont.)
Secretary of the Treasury	William E. Simon (Cont.)
Secretary of Defense	James R. Schlesinger (Cont.)
	Donald H. Rumsfeld 1975
Attorney General	William B. Saxbe (Cont.)
	Edward H. Levi 1975
Secretary of the Interior	Rogers C. B. Morton (Cont.)
	Stanley K. Hathaway 1975
	Thomas S. Kleppe 1975
Secretary of Agriculture	Earl L. Butz (Cont.)
	John Knebel 1976
Secretary of Commerce	Frederick B. Dent (Cont.)
	Rogers C. B. Morton 1975
	Elliot L. Richardson 1976
Secretary of Labor	Peter J. Brennan (Cont.)
	John T. Dunlop 1975
	William J. Usery, Jr. 1976
Secretary of Health, Education, and Welfare	Caspar W. Weinberger (Cont.)
	F. David Mathews 1975
Secretary of Housing and Urban Development	James T. Lynn (Cont.)
	Carla A. Hills 1975
Secretary of Transportation	Claude S. Brinegar (Cont.)
	William T. Coleman, Jr. 1975

CARTER

Secretary of State	Cyrus R. Vance 1977
	Edmund S. Muskie 1980
Secretary of the Treasury	W. Michael Blumenthal 1977
	G. William Miller 1979

Secretary of Defense	Harold Brown 1977
Attorney General	Griffin B. Bell 1977
	Benjamin R. Civiletti 1979
Secretary of the Interior	Cecil D. Andrus 1977
Secretary of Agriculture	Bob S. Bergland 1977
Secretary of Commerce	Juanita M. Kreps 1977
	Philip M. Klutznick 1979
Secretary of Labor	F. Ray Marshall 1977
Secretary of Health and Human Services[6]	Joseph A. Califano, Jr. 1977
	Patricia Roberts Harris 1979
Secretary of Housing and Urban Development	Patricia Roberts Harris 1977
	Moon Landrieu 1979
Secretary of Transportation	Brock Adams 1977
	Neil E. Goldschmidt 1979
Secretary of Energy	James R. Schlesinger 1977
	Charles W. Duncan, Jr. 1979
Secretary of Education	Shirley Mount Hufstedler 1979

REAGAN

Secretary of State	Alexander M. Haig, Jr. 1981
	George P. Shultz 1982
Secretary of the Treasury	Donald T. Regan 1981
	James A. Baker 3rd 1985
	Nicholas F. Brady 1988
Secretary of Defense	Caspar W. Weinberger 1981
	Frank C. Carlucci 1987
Attorney General	William French Smith 1981
	Edwin Meese 3rd 1985
	Richard L. Thornburgh 1988
Secretary of the Interior	James G. Watt 1981
	William P. Clark 1983
	Donald P. Hodel 1985
Secretary of Agriculture	John R. Block 1981
	Richard E. Lyng 1986
Secretary of Commerce	Malcolm Baldrige 1981
	C. William Verity, Jr. 1987
Secretary of Labor	Raymond J. Donovan 1981
	William E. Brock 1985
	Ann Dore McLaughlin 1987
Secretary of Health and Human Services	Richard S. Schweiker 1981
	Margaret M. Heckler 1983
	Otis R. Bowen 1985
Secretary of Housing and Urban Development	Samuel R. Pierce, Jr. 1981
Secretary of Transportation	Andrew L. Lewis, Jr. 1981
	Elizabeth H. Dole 1983
	James H. Burnley 4th 1987
Secretary of Energy	James B. Edwards 1981
	Donald P. Hodel 1983
	John S. Herrington 1985
Secretary of Education	T. H. Bell 1981
	William J. Bennett 1985
	Lauro F. Cavazos 1988

BUSH

Secretary of State	James A. Baker 3d 1989
	Lawrence S. Eagleburger 1992
Secretary of the Treasury	Nicholas F. Brady (Cont.)
Secretary of Defense	Richard Cheney 1989
Attorney General	Richard L. Thornburgh (Cont.)
	William P. Barr 1992
Secretary of the Interior	Manuel Lujan Jr. 1989
Secretary of Agriculture	Clayton K. Yeutter 1989
	Edward Madigan 1991
Secretary of Commerce	Robert A. Mosbacher Sr. 1989
	Barbara H. Franklin 1992
Secretary of Labor	Elizabeth H. Dole 1989
	Lynn Martin 1991
Secretary of Health and Human Services	Louis W. Sullivan 1989
Secretary of Housing and Urban Development	Jack F. Kemp 1989
Secretary of Transportation	Samuel K. Skinner 1989
	Andrew Card 1992
Secretary of Energy	James D. Watkins 1989
Secretary of Education	Lauro F. Cavazos (Cont.)
	Lamar Alexander 1991
Secretary of Veterans Affairs	Edward J. Derwinski 1989

CLINTON

Secretary of State	Warren M. Christopher 1993
Secretary of the Treasury	Lloyd Bentsen 1993
	Robert E. Rubin 1995
Secretary of Defense	Les Aspin 1993
	William J. Perry 1994
Attorney General	Janet Reno 1993
Secretary of the Interior	Bruce Babbitt 1993
Secretary of Agriculture	Mike Espy 1993
	Dan Glickman 1995
Secretary of Commerce	Ronald H. Brown 1993

Secretary of Labor	Robert B. Reich 1993
Secretary of Health and Human Services	Donna E. Shalala 1993
Secretary of Housing and Urban Development	Henry G. Cisneros 1993
Secretary of Transportation	Federico F. Pena 1993
Secretary of Energy	Hazel R. O'Leary 1993
Secretary of Education	Richard W. Riley 1993
Secretary of Veterans Affairs	Jesse Brown 1993

1. The Postmaster General did not become a Cabinet member until 1829. Earlier Postmasters General were: Samuel Osgood (1789), Timothy Pickering (1791), Joseph Habersham (1795), Gideon Granger (1801), Return J. Meigs, Jr. (1814), and John McLean (1823). 2. On July 26, 1947, the Departments of War and of the Navy were incorporated into the Department of Defense. 3. Not confirmed by the Senate. 4. Recess appointment. 5. The Postmaster General is no longer a Cabinet member. 6. Known as Department of Health, Education, and Welfare until May 1980.

The Beginning of the U.S. Supreme Court

In 1801, Chief Justice John Marshall and his colleagues had to meet in a tiny room in the basement of the Capitol because the planners of Washington, D.C., had forgotten to provide a space for the Supreme Court.

Although the Supreme Court is the most important judicial body in the world in terms of the role it plays within the political order, no one could have predicted this at the time the Constitution was written in 1787. The first chief justice, John Jay, resigned in 1795 to run for governor of New York. Nominated as his successor by President George Washington was John Rutledge, who had been named to the initial Court in 1789, but resigned in 1791, without ever sitting, to go to what was considered the more prestigious South Carolina Supreme Court. Because Rutledge failed to receive Senate confirmation, Oliver Ellsworth was nominated and confirmed in 1796 as chief justice, but he too resigned to accept a diplomatic post in France in 1800. Few decisions of this period were of great significance. The most important, a 1793 decision upholding federal jurisdiction in a suit brought by South Carolina land speculators against the state of Georgia, was met by a storm of protest that resulted in the quick proposal and ratification of the Eleventh Amendment effectively overruling the decision.

The rise in importance of the Supreme Court began with the appointment by President John Adams in 1801 of John Marshall, his secretary of state, to succeed Ellsworth. This appointment was widely interpreted as the symbol of the desire of the Federalists who had lost the recent election to retain control of the judicial branch after Thomas Jefferson and his supporters took over the presidency and Congress. This illustrates the extent to which the institutional mechanisms of checks and balances can help a repudiated political party. Given the lifetime tenure of justices, the Supreme Court is almost by definition a "conservative" force, even if what is being "conserved" is the liberal vision of an earlier party.

Not the least important of Marshall's contributions to the power of the Supreme Court was his establishment of the notion of a single "opinion of the Court" and his efforts, usually successful, to discourage the expression of any dissent from this opinion. Previously, the justices, like members of English courts, delivered separate opinions, with none being designated as the view of the institutional Court.

Marshall's opinion in *Marbury v. Madison* (1803) is famous for exemplifying the Court's power to invalidate even a congressional statute thought to violate the Constitution. Far more important, however, were a number of decisions upholding congressional power or limiting state power.

Most important was *McCulloch* v. *Maryland* (1819), which upheld the power of Congress to charter the (Second) Bank of the United States even though the Constitution contains no language specifically authorizing such an act. (This lack of authorization had led Representative James Madison, when the First Bank of the United States was chartered in 1791, to oppose the act as unconstitutional.) Moreover, the Court invalidated an attempt by Maryland to tax the Bank, viewing such a tax as an impermissible attack on the powers of the national government. What *McCulloch* illustrates is the crucial ability of the Supreme Court to legitimatize the decisions made by other branches of government by reassuring the public that they are, indeed, "constitutional."

Although "judicial review" is analyzed most often in terms of the ability of the Court to invalidate unconstitutional legislation, in fact the Court rarely finds legislation unconstitutional. Most often challenges, especially to federal legislation, fail, and the disputed legislation gains legitimacy from having survived judicial scrutiny.

Also more important than *Marbury*, practically speaking, was the 1810 decision in *Fletcher* v. *Peck*, in which for the first time the Court struck down state legislation as constitutionally invalid. Over the half century following *Marbury*, the combination of the Court's upholding federal legislation and invalidating state legislation deemed offensive to one or another constitutional principle (most often the contract clause or the commerce clause) served to bolster the power of the national government and to provide reins on state powers. □

Excerpted from THE READER'S COMPANION TO AMERICAN HISTORY, Copyright © 1991 by Houghton Mifflin Company. Reprinted with permission.

Figures and Legends in American Folklore

Appleseed, Johnny (John Chapman, 1774–1847): Massachusetts-born nurseryman; reputed to have spread seeds and seedlings from which rose orchards of the Midwest.

Billy the Kid (William H. Bonney, 1859–1881): New York-born desperado; killed his first man before he reached his teens; after short life of crime in Wild West, was gunned down by Sheriff Pat Garrett; symbol of lawless West.

Boone, Daniel (1734–1820): Frontiersman and Indian fighter, about whom legends of early America have been built; figured in Byron's *Don Juan*.

Brodie, Steve (1863–1901): Reputed to have dived off Brooklyn Bridge on July 23, 1886. (Whether he actually did so has never been proved.)

Buffalo Bill (William F. Cody, 1846–1917): Buffalo hunter and Indian scout; much of legend about him and Wild West stems from his own Wild West show, which he operated in late 19th century.

Bunyan, Paul: Mythical lumberjack; subject of tall tales throughout timber country (that he dug Grand Canyon, for example).

Crockett, David (1786–1836): Frontiersman and member of U.S. Congress, about whom legends have been built of heroic feats; died in defense of Alamo.

Fritchie (or Frietchie), Barbara: Symbol of patriotism; in ballad by John Greenleaf Whittier, 90-year-old Barbara Fritchie defiantly waves Stars and Stripes as "Stonewall" Jackson's Confederate troops march through Frederick, Md.

James, Jesse (1847–1882): Bank and train robber; folklore has given him quality of American Robin Hood.

Jones, Casey (John Luther Jones, 1863–1900): Example of heroic locomotive engineer given to feats of prowess; died in wreck with his hand on brake lever when his Illinois Central "Cannonball" express hit freight train at Vaughan, Miss.

Ross, Betsy (1752–1836): Member of Philadelphia flag-making family; reported to have designed and sewn first American flag. (Report is without confirmation.)

Uncle Sam: Personification of United States and its people; origin uncertain; may be based on inspector of government supplies in Revolutionary War and War of 1812.

Assassinations and Attempts in U. S. Since 1865

Cermak, Anton J. (Mayor of Chicago): Shot Feb. 15, 1933, in Miami by Giuseppe Zangara, who attempted to assassinate Franklin D. Roosevelt; Cermak died March 6.

Ford, Gerald R. (President of U.S.): Escaped assassination attempt Sept. 5, 1975, in Sacramento, Calif., by Lynette Alice (Squeaky) Fromm, who pointed but did not fire .45-caliber pistol. Escaped assassination attempt in San Francisco, Calif., Sept. 22, 1975, by Sara Jane Moore, who fired one shot from a .38-caliber pistol that was deflected.

Garfield, James A. (President of U.S.): Shot July 2, 1881, in Washington, D.C., by Charles J. Guiteau; died Sept. 19.

Jordan, Vernon E., Jr. (civil rights leader): Shot and critically wounded in assassination attempt May 29, 1980, in Fort Wayne, Ind.

Kennedy, John F. (President of U.S.): Shot Nov. 22, 1963, in Dallas, Tex., allegedly by Lee Harvey Oswald; died same day. Injured was Gov. John B. Connally of Texas. Oswald was shot and killed two days later by Jack Ruby.

Kennedy, Robert F. (U.S. Senator from New York): Shot June 5, 1968, in Los Angeles by Sirhan Bishara Sirhan; died June 6.

King, Martin Luther, Jr. (civil rights leader): Shot April 4, 1968, in Memphis by James Earl Ray; died same day.

Lincoln, Abraham (President of U.S.): Shot April 14, 1865, in Washington, D.C., by John Wilkes Booth; died April 15.

Long, Huey P. (U.S. Senator from Louisiana): Shot Sept. 8, 1935, in Baton Rouge by Dr. Carl A. Weiss; died Sept. 10.

McKinley, William (President of U.S.): Shot Sept. 6, 1901, in Buffalo by Leon Czolgosz; died Sept. 14.

Reagan, Ronald (President of U.S.): Shot in left lung in Washington by John W. Hinckley, Jr., on March 30, 1981; three others also wounded.

Roosevelt, Franklin D. (President-elect of U.S.): Escaped assassination unhurt Feb. 15, 1933, in Miami. *See* Cermak.

Roosevelt, Theodore (ex-President of U.S.): Escaped assassination (though shot) Oct. 14, 1912, in Milwaukee while campaigning for President.

Seward, William H. (Secretary of State): Escaped assassination (though injured) April 14, 1865, in Washington, D.C., by Lewis Powell (or Paine), accomplice of John Wilkes Booth.

Truman, Harry S. (President of U.S.): Escaped assassination unhurt Nov. 1, 1950, in Washington, D.C., as 2 Puerto Rican nationalists attempted to shoot their way into Blair House.

Wallace, George C. (Governor of Alabama): Shot and critically wounded in assassination attempt May 15, 1972, at Laurel, Md., by Arthur Herman Bremer. Wallace paralyzed from waist down.

Impeachments of Federal Officials

Source: Congressional Directory

The procedure for the impeachment of Federal officials is detailed in Article I, Section 3, of the Constitution. See Index

The Senate has sat as a court of impeachment in the following cases:

William Blount, Senator from Tennessee; charges dismissed for want of jurisdiction, January 14, 1799.
John Pickering, Judge of the U.S. District Court for New Hampshire; removed from office March 12, 1804.

Samuel Chase, Associate Justice of the Supreme Court; acquitted March 1, 1805.
James H. Peck, Judge of the U.S. District Court for Missouri; acquitted Jan. 31, 1831.
West H. Humphreys, Judge of the U.S. District Court for the middle, eastern, and western districts of Tennessee; removed from office June 26, 1862.
Andrew Johnson, President of the United States; acquitted May 26, 1868.
William W. Belknap, Secretary of War; acquitted Aug. 1, 1876.
Charles Swayne, Judge of the U.S. District Court for the northern district of Florida; acquitted Feb. 27, 1905.
Robert W. Archbald, Associate Judge, U.S. Commerce Court; removed Jan. 13, 1913.
George W. English, Judge of the U.S. District

Court for eastern district of Illinois; resigned Nov. 4, 1926; proceedings dismissed.
Harold Louderback, Judge of the U.S. District Court for the northern district of California; acquitted May 24, 1933.
Halsted L. Ritter, Judge of the U.S. District Court for the southern district of Florida; removed from office April 17, 1936.
Harry E. Claiborne, Judge of the U.S. District Court for the district of Nevada; removed from office October 9, 1986.
Alcee L. Hastings, Judge of the U.S. District Court for the southern district of Florida; removed from office October 20, 1989.
Walter L. Nixon, Jr., Judge of the U.S. District Court for Mississippi; removed from office November 3, 1989.

Members of the Supreme Court of the United States

Name; apptd. from	Service Term	Yrs	Birth Place	Date	Died	Religion
CHIEF JUSTICES						
John Jay, N.Y.	1789–1795	5	N.Y.	1745	1829	Episcopal
John Rutledge, S.C.	1795	0	S.C.	1739	1800	Church of England
Oliver Ellsworth, Conn.	1796–1800	4	Conn.	1745	1807	Congregational
John Marshall, Va.	1801–1835	34	Va.	1755	1835	Episcopal
Roger B. Taney, Md.	1836–1864	28	Md.	1777	1864	Roman Catholic
Salmon P. Chase, Ohio	1864–1873	8	N.H.	1808	1873	Episcopal
Morrison R. Waite, Ohio	1874–1888	14	Conn.	1816	1888	Episcopal
Melville W. Fuller, Ill.	1888–1910	21	Me.	1833	1910	Episcopal
Edward D. White, La.	1910–1921	10	La.	1845	1921	Roman Catholic
William H. Taft, Conn.	1921–1930	8	Ohio	1857	1930	Unitarian
Charles E. Hughes, N.Y.	1930–1941	11	N.Y.	1862	1948	Baptist
Harlan F. Stone, N.Y.	1941–1946	4	N.H.	1872	1946	Episcopal
Frederick M. Vinson, Ky.	1946–1953	7	Ky.	1890	1953	Methodist
Earl Warren, Calif.	1953–1969	15	Calif.	1891	1974	Protestant
Warren E. Burger, Va.	1969–1986	17	Minn.	1907	1995	Presbyterian
William H. Rehnquist, Ariz.	1986–		Wis.	1924	—	Lutheran
ASSOCIATE JUSTICES						
James Wilson, Pa.	1789–1798	8	Scotland	1742	1798	Episcopal
John Rutledge, S.C.	1790–1791	1	S.C.	1739	1800	Church of England
William Cushing, Mass.	1790–1810	20	Mass.	1732	1810	Unitarian
John Blair, Va.	1790–1796	5	Va.	1732	1800	Presbyterian
James Iredell, N.C.	1790–1799	9	England	1751	1799	Episcopal
Thomas Johnson, Md.	1792–1793	0	Md.	1732	1819	Episcopal
William Paterson, N.J.	1793–1806	13	Ireland	1745	1806	Protestant
Samuel Chase, Md.	1796–1811	15	Md.	1741	1811	Episcopal
Bushrod Washington, Va.	1799–1829	30	Va.	1762	1829	Episcopal
Alfred Moore, N.C.	1800–1804	3	N.C.	1755	1810	Episcopal
William Johnson, S.C.	1804–1834	30	S.C.	1771	1834	Presbyterian
Brockholst Livingston, N.Y.	1807–1823	16	N.Y.	1757	1823	Presbyterian
Thomas Todd, Ky.	1807–1826	18	Va.	1765	1826	Presbyterian
Gabriel Duval, Md.	1811–1835	23	Md.	1752	1844	French Protestant
Joseph Story, Mass.	1812–1845	33	Mass.	1779	1845	Unitarian
Smith Thompson, N.Y.	1823–1843	20	N.Y.	1768	1843	Presbyterian
Robert Trimble, Ky.	1826–1828	2	Va.	1777	1828	Protestant
John McLean, Ohio	1830–1861	31	N.J.	1785	1861	Methodist-Epis.
Henry Baldwin, Pa.	1830–1844	14	Conn.	1780	1844	Trinity Church
James M. Wayne, Ga.	1835–1867	32	Ga.	1790	1867	Protestant
Philip P. Barbour, Va.	1836–1841	4	Va.	1783	1841	Episcopal
John Catron, Tenn.	1837–1865	28	Pa.	1786	1865	Presbyterian
John McKinley, Ala.	1837–1852	14	Va.	1780	1852	Protestant
Peter V. Daniel, Va.	1841–1860	18	Va.	1784	1860	Episcopal
Samuel Nelson, N.Y.	1845–1872	27	N.Y.	1792	1873	Protestant
Levi Woodbury, N.H.	1845–1851	5	N.H.	1789	1851	Protestant
Robert C. Grier, Pa.	1846–1870	23	Pa.	1794	1870	Presbyterian
Benjamin R. Curtis, Mass.	1851–1857	5	Mass.	1809	1874	(2)
John A. Campbell, Ala.	1853–1861	8	Ga.	1811	1889	Episcopal

Name; apptd. from	Service Term	Yrs	Birth Place	Date	Died	Religion
Nathan Clifford, Maine	1858–1881	23	N.H.	1803	1881	(¹)
Noah H. Swayne, Ohio	1862–1881	18	Va.	1804	1884	Quaker
Samuel F. Miller, Iowa	1862–1890	28	Ky.	1816	1890	Unitarian
David Davis, Ill.	1862–1877	14	Md.	1815	1886	(⁴)
Stephen J. Field, Calif.	1863–1897	34	Conn.	1816	1899	Episcopal
William Strong, Pa.	1870–1880	10	Conn.	1808	1895	Presbyterian
Joseph P. Bradley, N.J.	1870–1892	21	N.Y.	1813	1892	Presbyterian
Ward Hunt, N.Y.	1872–1882	9	N.Y.	1810	1886	Episcopal
John M. Harlan, Ky.	1877–1911	33	Ky.	1833	1911	Presbyterian
William B. Woods, Ga.	1880–1887	6	Ohio	1824	1887	Protestant
Stanley Matthews, Ohio	1881–1889	7	Ohio	1824	1889	Presbyterian
Horace Gray, Mass.	1882–1902	20	Mass.	1828	1902	(³)
Samuel Blatchford, N.Y.	1882–1893	11	N.Y.	1820	1893	Presbyterian
Lucius Q. C. Lamar, Miss.	1888–1893	5	Ga.	1825	1893	Methodist
David J. Brewer, Kan.	1889–1910	20	Asia Minor	1837	1910	Protestant
Henry B. Brown, Mich.	1890–1906	15	Mass.	1836	1913	Protestant
George Shiras, Jr., Pa.	1892–1903	10	Pa.	1832	1924	Presbyterian
Howell E. Jackson, Tenn.	1893–1895	2	Tenn.	1832	1895	Baptist
Edward D. White, La.	1894–1910	16	La.	1845	1921	Roman Catholic
Rufus W. Peckham, N.Y.	1895–1909	13	N.Y.	1838	1909	Episcopal
Joseph McKenna, Calif.	1898–1925	26	Pa.	1843	1926	Roman Catholic
Oliver W. Holmes, Mass.	1902–1932	29	Mass.	1841	1935	Unitarian
William R. Day, Ohio	1903–1922	19	Ohio	1849	1923	Protestant
William H. Moody, Mass.	1906–1910	3	Mass.	1853	1917	Episcopal
Horace H. Lurton, Tenn.	1909–1914	4	Ky.	1844	1914	Episcopal
Charles E. Hughes, N.Y.	1910–1916	5	N.Y.	1862	1948	Baptist
Willis Van Devanter, Wyo.	1910–1937	26	Ind.	1859	1941	Episcopal
Joseph R. Lamar, Ga.	1910–1916	4	Ga.	1857	1916	Ch. of Disciples
Mahlon Pitney, N.J.	1912–1922	10	N.J.	1858	1924	Presbyterian
James C. McReynolds, Tenn.	1914–1941	26	Ky.	1862	1946	Disciples of Christ
Louis D. Brandeis, Mass.	1916–1939	22	Ky.	1856	1941	Jewish
John H. Clarke, Ohio	1916–1922	5	Ohio	1857	1945	Protestant
George Sutherland, Utah	1922–1938	15	England	1862	1942	Episcopal
Pierce Butler, Minn.	1923–1939	16	Minn.	1866	1939	Roman Catholic
Edward T. Sanford, Tenn.	1923–1930	7	Tenn.	1865	1930	Episcopal
Harlan F. Stone, N.Y.	1925–1941	16	N.H.	1872	1946	Episcopal
Owen J. Roberts, Pa.	1930–1945	15	Pa.	1875	1955	Episcopal
Benjamin N. Cardozo, N.Y.	1932–1938	6	N.Y.	1870	1938	Jewish
Hugo L. Black, Ala.	1937–1971	34	Ala.	1886	1971	Baptist
Stanley F. Reed, Ky.	1938–1957	19	Ky.	1884	1980	Protestant
Felix Frankfurter, Mass.	1939–1962	23	Austria	1882	1965	Jewish
William O. Douglas, Conn.	1939–1975	36	Minn.	1898	1980	Presbyterian
Frank Murphy, Mich.	1940–1949	9	Mich.	1890	1949	Roman Catholic
James F. Byrnes, S.C.	1941–1942	1	S.C.	1879	1972	Episcopal
Robert H. Jackson, Pa.	1941–1954	13	N.Y.	1892	1954	Episcopal
Wiley B. Rutledge, Iowa	1943–1949	6	Ky.	1894	1949	Unitarian
Harold H. Burton, Ohio	1945–1958	13	Mass.	1888	1964	Unitarian
Tom C. Clark, Tex.	1949–1967	17	Tex.	1899	1977	Presbyterian
Sherman Minton, Ind.	1949–1956	7	Ind.	1890	1965	Roman Catholic
John M. Harlan, N.Y.	1955–1971	16	Ill.	1899	1971	Presbyterian
William J. Brennan, Jr., N.J.	1956–1990	33	N.J.	1906	—	Roman Catholic
Charles E. Whittaker, Mo.	1957–1962	5	Kan.	1901	1973	Methodist
Potter Stewart, Ohio	1958–1981	23	Mich.	1915	1985	Episcopal
Byron R. White, Colo.	1962–1993	31	Colo.	1917	—	Episcopal
Arthur J. Goldberg, Ill.	1962–1965	2	Ill.	1908	1990	Jewish
Abe Fortas, Tenn.	1965–1969	3	Tenn.	1910	1982	Jewish
Thurgood Marshall, N.Y.	1967–1991	24	Md.	1908	1993	Episcopal
Harry A. Blackmun, Minn.	1970–1994	24	Ill.	1908	—	Methodist
Lewis F. Powell, Jr., Va.	1972–1987	15	Va.	1907	—	Presbyterian
William H. Rehnquist, Ariz.	1972–1986	14	Wis.	1924	—	Lutheran
John Paul Stevens, Ill.	1975–	—	Ill.	1920	—	Protestant
Sandra Day O'Connor, Ariz.	1981–	—	Tex.	1930	—	Episcopal
Antonin Scalia, D.C.	1986–	—	N.J.	1936	—	Roman Catholic
Anthony M. Kennedy, Calif.	1988–	—	Calif.	1936	—	Roman Catholic
David H. Souter, N.H.	1990–	—	Mass.	1939	—	Episcopal
Clarence Thomas, D.C.	1991–	—	Ga.	1948	—	Roman Catholic
Ruth Bader Ginsburg, D.C.	1993–	—	N.Y.	1933	—	Jewish
Stephen G. Breyer, Mass.	1994–	—	Calif.	1938	—	n.a.

1. Congregational; later Unitarian. 2. Unitarian; then Episcopal. 3. Unitarian or Congregational. 4. Not a member of any church. NOTE: n.a. = not available.

Executive Departments and Agencies

Source: United States Government Manual 1994–95.
Unless otherwise indicated, addresses shown are in Washington, D.C.

CENTRAL INTELLIGENCE AGENCY (CIA)
Washington, D.C. (20505).
 Established: 1947.
 Director: John M. Deutch.
COUNCIL OF ECONOMIC ADVISERS (CEA)
Room 314, Old Executive Office Bldg. (20500).
 Members: 3.
 Established: Feb. 20, 1946.
 Chairman: Laura D. Tyson.
COUNCIL ON ENVIRONMENTAL QUALITY
722 Jackson Pl., N.W. (20503).
 Members: 3.
 Established: 1969.
 Chairperson: Kathleen A. McGinty.
NATIONAL SECURITY COUNCIL (NSC)
Old Executive Office Bldg. (20506).
 Members: 4.
 Established: July 26, 1947.
 Chairman: The President.
 Other members: Vice President; Secretary of State; Secretary of Defense.
OFFICE OF ADMINISTRATION
Old Executive Office Bldg. (20500).
 Established: Dec. 12, 1977.
 Director: Patsy Thomasson.
OFFICE OF MANAGEMENT AND BUDGET
Old Executive Office Bldg. (20503).
 Established: July 1, 1970.
 Director: Alice M. Rivlin.
OFFICE OF SCIENCE AND TECHNOLOGY POLICY
Executive Office Building (20506).
 Established: May 11, 1976.
 Director: Dr. John H. Gibbons.
OFFICE OF THE UNITED STATES TRADE REPRESENTATIVE
600 17th St., N.W. (20506).
 Established: Jan. 15, 1963.
 Trade Representative: Michael Kantor.
OFFICE OF NATIONAL DRUG CONTROL POLICY
Suite 1011, 1825 Connecticut Ave., N.W. (20009).
 Established: March 13, 1989.
 Director: Dr. Lee Brown.

Executive Departments

DEPARTMENT OF STATE
2201 C St., N.W. (20520).
 Established: 1781 as Department of Foreign Affairs; reconstituted, 1789, following adoption of Constitution; name changed to Department of State Sept. 15, 1789.
 Secretary: Warren Christopher.
 Deputy Secretary: Strobe Talbott.
 Chief Delegate to U.N.: Madelaine Konibel Albright.
DEPARTMENT OF THE TREASURY
15th St. & Pennsylvania Ave., N.W. (20220).
 Established: Sept. 2, 1789.
 Secretary: Robert E. Rubin
 Deputy Secretary: Lawrence H. Summers[1].
 Treasurer of the U.S.: Mary Ellen Withrow.
 Comptroller of the Currency: Eugene Ludwig.
1. Nominated but not confirmed at press time.
DEPARTMENT OF DEFENSE
The Pentagon (20301).
 Established: July 26, 1947, as National Department Establishment; name changed to Department of Defense on Aug. 10, 1949. Subordinate to Secretary

of Defense are Secretaries of Army, Navy, Air Force.
 Secretary: William J. Perry.
 Deputy Secretary: John M. Deutch.
 Secretary of Army: Togo G. West, Jr.
 Secretary of Navy: John H. Dalton.
 Secretary of Air Force: Sheila E. Widnall
 Commandant of Marine Corps: Charles C. Krulak.
 Joint Chiefs of Staff: Gen. John M. Shalikashvili, Chairman; Adm. William A. Owens, Vice Chairman; Gen. Dennis J. Reimer, Army; Adm. Jeremy M. Boorda, Navy; Ronald R. Fogleman Air Force; Gen. Richard D. Hearney, Marine Corps.
DEPARTMENT OF JUSTICE
Constitution Ave. between 9th & 10th Sts., N.W. (20530).
 Established: Office of Attorney General was created Sept. 24, 1789. Although he was one of original Cabinet members, he was not executive department head until June 22, 1870, when Department of Justice was established.
 Attorney General: Janet Reno.
 Deputy Attorney General: Jamie S. Gorelick.
 Solicitor General: Drew Days 3rd
 Director of FBI: Louis Joseph Freeh.
DEPARTMENT OF THE INTERIOR
C St. between 18th & 19th Sts., N.W. (20240).
 Established: March 3, 1849.
 Secretary: Bruce Babbitt.
 Under Secretary: John Garamendi[1].
1. Nominated but not confirmed at press time.
DEPARTMENT OF AGRICULTURE
Independence Ave. between 12th & 14th Sts., S.W. (20250).
 Established: May 15, 1862. Administered by Commissioner of Agriculture until 1889, when it was made executive department.
 Secretary: Dan Glickman.
 Deputy Secretary: Richard Roninger.
DEPARTMENT OF COMMERCE
14th St. between Constitution Ave. & E St., N.W. (20230).
 Established: Department of Commerce and Labor was created Feb. 14, 1903. On March 4, 1913, all labor activities were transferred out of Department of Commerce and Labor and it was renamed Department of Commerce.
 Secretary: Ron Brown.
 Deputy Secretary: David L. Barram.
DEPARTMENT OF LABOR
200 Constitution Ave., N.W. (20210).
 Established: Bureau of Labor was created in 1884 under Department of the Interior; later became independent department without executive rank. Returned to bureau status in Department of Commerce and Labor, but on March 4, 1913, became independent executive department under its present name.
 Secretary: Robert Reich.
 Deputy Secretary: Thomas P. Glynn.
DEPARTMENT OF HEALTH AND HUMAN SERVICES[1]
200 Independence Ave., S.W. (20201).
 Established: April 11, 1953, replacing Federal Security Agency created in 1939.
 Secretary: Donna Shalala.
 Surgeon General: (Vacancy)
1. Originally Department of Health, Education and Welfare. Name changed in May 1980 when Department of Education was activated.

DEPARTMENT OF HOUSING AND URBAN DEVELOPMENT
451 7th St., S.W. (20410).
Established: 1965, replacing Housing and Home Finance Agency created in 1947.
Secretary: Henry Cisneros.
Under Secretary: Terry R. Duvernay.

DEPARTMENT OF TRANSPORTATION
400 7th St., S.W. (20590).
Established: Oct. 15, 1966, as result of Department of Transportation Act, which became effective April 1, 1967.
Secretary: Frederico Pena.
Deputy Secretary: Mort Downey.

DEPARTMENT OF ENERGY
1000 Independence Ave., S.W. (20585).
Established: Aug. 1977.
Secretary: Hazel R. O'Leary.
Deputy Secretary: William White.

DEPARTMENT OF EDUCATION
400 Maryland Avenue, S.W. (20202).
Established: Oct. 17, 1979.
Secretary: Richard Riley.
Under Secretary: Madeline Kunin.

DEPARTMENT OF VETERANS' AFFAIRS
810 Vermont Avenue, N.W. (20420).
Established: March 15, 1989, replacing Veterans Administration created in 1930.
Secretary: Jesse Brown.
Deputy Secretary: Hershel Gober.

Major Independent Agencies

CONSUMER PRODUCT SAFETY COMMISSION
4330 East West Towers, Bethesda, Md. (20814).
Members: 5.
Established: Oct. 27, 1972.
Chairperson: Ann Brown.

CORPORATION FOR NATIONAL SERVICE (Incorporating ACTION)
1100 Vermont Ave. N.W. (20525).
Established: April 9, 1994
CEO and President: Eli Segal.

ENVIRONMENTAL PROTECTION AGENCY (EPA)
401 M St., S.W. (20460).
Established: Dec. 2, 1970.
Administrator: Carol M. Browner.

EQUAL EMPLOYMENT OPPORTUNITY COMMISSION (EEOC)
1801 L St., N.W. (20507).
Members: 5.
Established: July 2, 1965.
Chairman: Gilbert Casellas.

FARM CREDIT ADMINISTRATION (FCA)
1501 Farm Credit Dr., McLean, Va. (22102).
Members: 13.
Established: July 17, 1916.
Chairman of Federal Farm Credit Board: Billy Ross Brown.

FEDERAL COMMUNICATIONS COMMISSION (FCC)
1919 M St., N.W. (20554).
Members: 7.
Established: 1934.
Chairman: Reed E. Hundt.

FEDERAL DEPOSIT INSURANCE CORPORATION (FDIC)
550 17th St., N.W. (20429).
Members: 3.
Established: June 16, 1933.

Chairman: Ricki Tigert Helfer.

FEDERAL ELECTION COMMISSION (FEC)
999 E St., N.W. (20463).
Members: 6.
Established: 1974.
Chairman: Danny L. McDonald.

FEDERAL MARITIME COMMISSION
800 North Capitol St., N.W. (20573–0001).
Members: 5.
Established: Aug. 12, 1961.
Chairman: William D. Hathaway.

FEDERAL MEDIATION AND CONCILIATION SERVICE (FMCS)
2100 K St., N.W. (20427).
Established: 1947.
Director: John Calhoun Wells.

FEDERAL RESERVE SYSTEM (FRS), BOARD OF GOVERNORS OF
20th St. & Constitution Ave., N.W. (20551).
Members: 7.
Established: Dec. 23, 1913.
Chairman: Alan Greenspan.

FEDERAL TRADE COMMISSION (FTC)
Pennsylvania Ave. at 6th St., N.W. (20580).
Members: 5.
Established: Sept. 26, 1914.
Chairperson: Robert Pitofsky.

GENERAL SERVICES ADMINISTRATION (GSA)
18th and F Sts., N.W. (20405).
Established: July 1, 1949.
Administrator: Roger W. Johnson.

INTERSTATE COMMERCE COMMISSION (ICC)
12th St. & Constitution Ave., N.W. (20423).
Members: 7.
Established: Feb. 4, 1887.
Chairperson: Linda Morgan.

NATIONAL AERONAUTICS AND SPACE ADMINISTRATION (NASA)
300 E St., S.W. (20546).
Established: 1958.
Administrator: Daniel S. Goldin.

NATIONAL FOUNDATION ON THE ARTS AND THE HUMANITIES
1100 Pennsylvania Ave., N.W., (20506).
Established: 1965.
Chairmen: National Endowment for the Arts, Chairperson, Jane Alexander; National Endowment for the Humanities, Chairman, Sheldon Hackney.

NATIONAL LABOR RELATIONS BOARD (NLRB)
1099 14th St. N.W. (20570).
Members: 5.
Established: July 5, 1935.
Chairman: William Gould IV.

NATIONAL MEDIATION BOARD
Suite 250 East, 1301 K St., N.W. (20572).
Members: 3.
Established: June 21, 1934.
Chairperson: Magdalena G. Jacobsen

NATIONAL SCIENCE FOUNDATION (NSF)
4201 Wilson Blvd., Arlington, Va. (22230)
Established: 1950.
Director: Dr. Neal F. Lane.

NATIONAL TRANSPORTATION SAFETY BOARD
490 L'Enfant Plaza, S.W. (20594).
Members: 5.
Established: April 1, 1975.
642Chairman: James Hall.

NUCLEAR REGULATORY COMMISSION (NRC)
Washington, D.C. (20555).
Members: 5.
Established: Jan. 19, 1975.
Chairperson: Shirley Jackson.

OFFICE OF PERSONNEL MANAGEMENT (OPM)
1900 E St., N.W. (20415).
Members: 3.
Established: Jan. 1, 1979.
Director: James B. King.

SECURITIES AND EXCHANGE COMMISSION (SEC)
450 5th St., N.W. (20549).
Members: 5.
Established: July 2, 1934.
Chairman: Arthur Levitt.

SELECTIVE SERVICE SYSTEM (SSS)
National Headquarters 1515 Wilson Blvd., Arlington, Va. 22209
Established: Sept. 16, 1940.
Director: Gil Coronado.

SMALL BUSINESS ADMINISTRATION (SBA)
409 3rd St., N.W. (20416).
Established: July 30, 1953.
Administrator: Philip Lader.

TENNESSEE VALLEY AUTHORITY (TVA)
400 West Summit Hill Drive, Knoxville, Tenn. (37902).
Washington office: One Massachusetts Ave., N.W. (20444–0001).
Members of Board of Directors: 3.
Established: May 18, 1933.
Directors: William Kennoy and Johnny H. Hayes.

U.S. AGENCY FOR INTERNATIONAL DEVELOPMENT
320 21st St., N.W. (20523).
Established: Oct. 1, 1979.
Administrator: J. Brian Atwood.

U.S. ARMS CONTROL AND DISARMAMENT AGENCY
320 21st St., N.W., (20451).
Established: Sept. 26, 1961.
Director: John Holum.

U.S. COMMISSION ON CIVIL RIGHTS
624 9th St., N.W. (20425).
Members: 8.
Established: 1957.
Chairperson: Mary Frances Berry.

U.S. INFORMATION AGENCY
301 Fourth St., S.W. (20547).
Established: Aug. 1, 1953. Reorganized April 1, 1978.
Director: Dr. Joseph Duffey.

U.S. INTERNATIONAL TRADE COMMISSION
500 E St., N.W. (20436).
Members: 6.
Established: Sept. 8, 1916.
Chairman: Peter S. Watson.

U.S. POSTAL SERVICE
475 L'Enfant Plaza West, S.W. (20260).
Postmaster General: Marvin T. Runyon.
Deputy Postmaster General: Michael S. Coughlin.
Established: In 1775 with the appointment of Benjamin Franklin as the first Postmaster General under the Continental Congress. In 1970 became independent agency headed by 11-member board of governors.

Other Independent Agencies

Administrative Conference of the United States—Suite 500, 2120 L St., N.W. (20037).
American Battle Monuments Commission—5127 Pulaski Bldg. 20 Massachusetts Ave., N.W. (20314).

Appalachian Regional Commission—1666 Connecticut Ave., N.W. (20235).
Board for International Broadcasting—Suite 400, 1201 Connecticut Ave., N.W. (20036).
Commission of Fine Arts—Pension Bldg. 441 F St., N.W. (20001).
Commodity Futures Trading Commission—2033 K St., N.W. (20581).
Export-Import Bank of the United States—811 Vermont Ave., N.W. (20571).
Federal Emergency Management Agency—500 C St., S.W. (20472).
Federal Housing Finance Board—1777 F St. N.W. (20006).
Federal Labor Relations Authority—607 14th St. N.W. (20424).
Inter-American Foundation—901 N. Stuart St., Arlington, Va. (22203).
Merit Systems Protection Board—1120 Vermont Ave., N.W. (20419).
National Commission on Libraries and Information Science—Suite 820, 1110 Vermont Ave., N.W. (20005).
National Credit Union Administration—1775 Duke St., Alexandria, Va. (22314–3428).
Occupational Safety and Health Review Commission—1120 20th St., N.W. (20036-3419).
Panama Canal Commission—Suite 1050, 1825 I St., N.W. (20006).
Peace Corps—1990 K St., N.W. (20526).
Pension Benefit Guaranty Corporation—1200 K St., N.W. (20006).
Postal Rate Commission—Suite 300, 1333 H St., N.W. (20268).
President's Committee on Employment of People With Disabilities—Suite 300, 1331 F St., N.W.
President's Council on Physical Fitness and Sports—701 Pennsylvania Ave., N.W., Suite 250 (20004).
Railroad Retirement Board (RRB)—844 Rush St., Chicago, Ill. (60611); Office of Legislative Affairs: Suite 500, 1310 G St., N.W. (20005-3004).
U.S. Parole Commission—5550 Friendship Blvd., Chevy Chase, Md. (20815).

Legislative Department

Architect of the Capitol—U.S. Capitol Building (20515).
General Accounting Office (GAO)—441 G St., N.W. (20548).
Government Printing Office (GPO)—North Capitol & H Sts., N.W. (20401).
Library of Congress—10 First St. S.E. (20540).
Office of Technology Assessment—600 Pennsylvania Ave., S.E. (20510).
United States Botanic Garden—Office of Director, 245 First St., S.W. (20024).

Quasi-Official Agencies

American National Red Cross—17th & D Sts., N.W. (20006).
Legal Services Corporation—750 First St., N.E. (20002-4250).
National Academy of Sciences, National Academy of Engineering, National Research Council, Institute of Medicine—2101 Constitution Ave., N.W. (20418).
National Railroad Passenger Corporation (Amtrak)—60 Massachusetts Ave., N.E. (20002).
Smithsonian Institution—1000 Jefferson Dr., S.W. (20560).

Biographies of the Presidents

GEORGE WASHINGTON was born on Feb. 22, 1732 (Feb. 11, 1731/2, old style) in Westmoreland County, Va. While in his teens, he trained as a surveyor, and at the age of 20 he was appointed adjutant in the Virginia militia. For the next three years, he fought in the wars against the French and Indians, serving as Gen. Edward Braddock's aide in the disastrous campaign against Fort Duquesne. In 1759, he resigned from the militia, married Martha Dandridge Custis, a widow, and settled down as a gentleman farmer at Mount Vernon, Va.

As a militiaman, Washington had been exposed to the arrogance of the British officers, and his experience as a planter with British commercial restrictions increased his anti-British sentiment. He opposed the Stamp Act of 1765 and after 1770 became increasingly prominent in organizing resistance. A delegate to the Continental Congress, Washington was selected as commander in chief of the Continental Army and took command at Cambridge, Mass., on July 3, 1775.

Inadequately supported and sometimes covertly sabotaged by the Congress, in charge of troops who were inexperienced, badly equipped, and impatient of discipline, Washington conducted the war on the policy of avoiding major engagements with the British and wearing them down by harrassing tactics. His able generalship, along with the French alliance and the growing weariness within Britain, brought the war to a conclusion with the surrender of Cornwallis at Yorktown, Va., on Oct. 19, 1781.

The chaotic years under the Articles of Confederation led Washington to return to public life in the hope of promoting the formation of a strong central government. He presided over the Constitutional Convention and yielded to the universal demand that he serve as first President. He was inaugurated on April 30, 1789, in New York, the first national capital. In office, he sought to unite the nation and establish the authority of the new government at home and abroad. Greatly distressed by the emergence of the Hamilton-Jefferson rivalry, Washington worked to maintain neutrality but actually sympathized more with Hamilton. Following his unanimous re-election in 1792, his second term was dominated by the Federalists. His Farewell Address on Sept. 17, 1796 (published but never delivered) rebuked party spirit and warned against "permanent alliances" with foreign powers.

He died at Mount Vernon on Dec. 14, 1799.

JOHN ADAMS was born on Oct. 30 (Oct. 19, old style), 1735, at Braintree (now Quincy), Mass. A Harvard graduate, he considered teaching and the ministry but finally turned to law and was admitted to the bar in 1758. Six years later, he married Abigail Smith. He opposed the Stamp Act, served as lawyer for patriots indicted by the British, and by the time of the Continental Congresses, was in the vanguard of the movement for independence. In 1778, he went to France as commissioner. Subsequently he helped negotiate the peace treaty with Britain, and in 1785 became envoy to London. Resigning in 1788, he was elected Vice President under Washington and was re-elected in 1792.

Though a Federalist, Adams did not get along with Hamilton, who sought to prevent his election to the presidency in 1796 and thereafter intrigued against his administration. In 1798, Adam's independent policy averted a war with France but completed the break with Hamilton and the right-wing Federalists; at the same time, the enactment of the Alien and Sedition Acts, directed against foreigners and against critics of the government, exasperated the Jeffersonian opposition. The split between Adams and Hamilton resulted in Jefferson's becoming the next President. Adams retired to his home in Quincy. He and Jefferson died on the same day, July 4, 1826, the 50th anniversary of the signing of the Declaration of Independence.

His *Defence of the Constitutions of Government of the United States* (1787) contains original and striking, if conservative, political ideas.

THOMAS JEFFERSON was born on April 13 (April 2, old style), 1743, at Shadwell in Goochland (now Albemarle) County, Va. A William and Mary graduate, he studied law, but from the start showed an interest in science and philosophy. His literary skill and political clarity brought him to the forefront of the revolutionary movement in Virginia. As delegate to the Continental Congress, he drafted the Declaration of Independence. In 1776, he entered the Virginia House of Delegates and initiated a comprehensive reform program for the abolition of feudal survivals in land tenure and the separation of church and state.

In 1779, he became governor, but constitutional limitations on his power, combined with his own lack of executive energy, caused an unsatisfactory administration, culminating in Jefferson's virtual abdication when the British invaded Virginia in 1781. He retired to his beautiful home at Monticello, Va., to his family. His wife, Martha Wayles Skelton, whom he married in 1772, died in 1782.

Jefferson's *Notes on Virginia* (1784–85) illustrate his many-faceted interests, his limitless intellectual curiosity, his deep faith in agrarian democracy. Sent to Congress in 1783, he helped lay down the decimal system and drafted basic reports on the organization of the western lands. In 1785 he was appointed minister to France, where the Anglo-Saxon liberalism he had drawn from John Locke, the British philosopher, was stimulated by contact with the thought that would soon ferment in the French Revolution. In 1789, Washington appointed him Secretary of State. While favoring the Constitution and a strengthened central government, Jefferson came to believe that Hamilton contemplated the establishment of a monarchy. Growing differences resulted in Jefferson's resignation on Dec. 31, 1793.

Elected vice president in 1796, Jefferson continued to serve as spiritual leader of the opposition to Federalism, particularly to the repressive Alien and Sedition Acts. He was elected President in 1801 by the House of Representatives as a result of Hamilton's decision to throw the Federalist votes to him rather than to Aaron Burr, who had tied him in electoral votes. He was the first President to be inaugurated in Washington, which he had helped to design.

The purchase of Louisiana from France in 1803, though in violation of Jefferson's earlier constitutional scruples, was the most notable act of his administration. Re-elected in 1804, with the Federalist Charles C. Pinckney opposing him, Jefferson tried desperately to keep the United States out of the Napoleonic Wars in Europe, employing to this end the unpopular embargo policy.

After his retirement to Monticello in 1809, he developed his interest in education, founding the University of Virginia and watching its development with never-flagging interest. He died at Monticello on July 4, 1826. Jefferson had an enormous variety of interests and skills, ranging from education and science to architecture and music.

JAMES MADISON was born in Port Conway, Va., on March 16, 1751 (March 5, 1750/1, old style). A Princeton graduate, he joined the struggle for independence on his return to Virginia in 1771. In the 1770s and 1780s he was active in state politics, where he championed the Jefferson reform program, and in the Continental Congress. Madison was influential in the Constitutional Convention as leader of the group favoring a strong central government and as recorder of the debates; and he subsequently wrote, in collaboration with Alexander Hamilton and John Jay, the *Federalist* papers to aid the campaign for the adoption of the Constitution.

Serving in the new Congress, Madison soon emerged as the leader in the House of the men who opposed Hamilton's financial program and his pro-British leanings in foreign policy. Retiring from Congress in 1797, he continued to be active in Virginia and drafted the Virginia Resolution protesting the Alien and Sedition Acts. His intimacy with Jefferson made him the natural choice for Secretary of State in 1801.

In 1809, Madison succeeded Jefferson as President, defeating Charles C. Pinckney. His attractive wife, Dolley Payne Todd, whom he married in 1794, brought a new social sparkle to the executive mansion. In the meantime, increasing tension with Britain culminated in the War of 1812—a war for which the United States was unprepared and for which Madison lacked the executive talent to clear out incompetence and mobilize the nation's energies. Madison was re-elected in 1812, running against the Federalist De Witt Clinton. In 1814, the British actually captured Washington and forced Madison to flee to Virginia.

Madison's domestic program capitulated to the Hamiltonian policies that he had resisted 20 years before and he now signed bills to establish a United States Bank and a higher tariff.

After his presidency, he remained in retirement in Virginia until his death on June 28, 1836.

JAMES MONROE was born on April 28, 1758, in Westmoreland County, Va. A William and Mary graduate, he served in the army during the first years of the Revolution and was wounded at Trenton. He then entered Virginia politics and later national politics under the sponsorship of Jefferson. In 1786, he married Elizabeth (Eliza) Kortright.

Fearing centralization, Monroe opposed the adoption of the Constitution and, as senator from Virginia, was highly critical of the Hamiltonian program. In 1794, he was appointed minister to France, where his ardent sympathies with the Revolution exceeded the wishes of the State Department. His troubled diplomatic career ended with his recall in 1796. From 1799 to 1802, he was governor of Virginia. In 1803, Jefferson sent him to France to help negotiate the Louisiana Purchase and for the next few years he was active in various negotiations on the Continent.

In 1808, Monroe flirted with the radical wing of the Republican Party, which opposed Madison's candicacy; but the presidential boom came to naught

and, after a brief term as governor of Virginia in 1811, Monroe accepted Madison's offer to become Secretary of State. During the War of 1812, he vainly sought a field command and instead served as Secretary of War from September 1814 to March 1815.

Elected President in 1816 over the Federalist Rufus King, and re-elected without opposition in 1820, Monroe, the last of the Virginia dynasty, pursued the course of systematic tranquilization that won for his administrations the name "the era of good feeling." He continued Madison's surrender to the Hamiltonian domestic program, signed the Missouri Compromise, acquired Florida, and with the able assistance of his Secretary of State, John Quincy Adams, promulgated the Monroe Doctrine in 1823, declaring against foreign colonization or intervention in the Americas. He died in New York City on July 4, 1831, the third president to die on the anniversary of Independence.

JOHN QUINCY ADAMS was born on July 11, 1767, at Braintree (now Quincy), Mass., the son of John Adams, the second President. He spent his early years in Europe with his father, graduated from Harvard, and entered law practice. His anti-Jeffersonian newspaper articles won him political attention. In 1794, he became minister to the Netherlands, the first of several diplomatic posts that occupied him until his return to Boston in 1801. In 1797, he married Louisa Catherine Johnson.

In 1803, Adams was elected to the Senate, nominally as a Federalist, but his repeated displays of independence on such issues as the Louisiana Purchase and the embargo caused his party to demand his resignation and ostracize him socially. In 1809, Madison rewarded him for his support of Jefferson by appointing him minister to St. Petersburg. He helped negotiate the Treaty of Ghent in 1814, and in 1815 became minister to London. In 1817 Monroe appointed him Secretary of State where he served with great distinction, gaining Florida from Spain without hostilities and playing an equal part with Monroe in formulating the Monroe Doctrine.

When no presidential candidate received a majority of electoral votes in 1824, Adams, with the support of Henry Clay, was elected by the House in 1825 over Andrew Jackson, who had the original plurality. Adams had ambitious plans of government activity to foster internal improvements and promote the arts and sciences, but congressional obstructionism, combined with his own unwillingness or inability to play the role of a politician, resulted in little being accomplished. After being defeated for re-election by Jackson in 1828, he successfully ran for the House of Representatives in 1830. There though nominally a Whig, he pursued as ever an independent course. He led the fight to force Congress to receive antislavery petitions and fathered the Smithsonian Institution.

Stricken on the floor of the House, he died on Feb. 23, 1848. His long and detailed *Diary* gives a unique picture of the personalities and politics of the times.

ANDREW JACKSON was born on March 15, 1767, in what is now generally agreed to be Waxhaw, S.C. After a turbulent boyhood as an orphan and a British prisoner, he moved west to Tennessee, where he soon qualified for law practice but found time for such frontier pleasures as horse racing, cockfighting, and dueling. His marriage to Rachel Donelson Robards in 1791 was complicated by subsequent legal uncertainties about the status of her divorce. During the 1790s, Jackson served in the Tennessee Constitutional Convention, the United States House of Representatives and Senate, and on the Tennessee Supreme Court.

After some years as a country gentleman, living at the Hermitage near Nashville, Jackson in 1812 was given command of Tennessee troops against the Creeks. He defeated the Indians at Horseshoe Bend in 1814; subsequently he became a major general and won the Battle of New Orleans over veteran British troops, though after the treaty of peace had been signed at Ghent. In 1818, Jackson invaded Florida, captured Pensacola, and hanged two Englishmen named Arbuthnot and Ambrister, creating an international incident. A presidential boom began for him in 1821, and to foster it, he returned to the Senate (1823–25). Though he won a plurality of electoral votes in 1824, he lost in the House when Clay threw his strength to Adams. Four years later, he easily defeated Adams.

As President, Jackson greatly expanded the power and prestige of the presidential office and carried through an unprecedented program of domestic reform, vetoing the bill to extend the United States Bank, moving toward a hard-money currency policy, and checking the program of federal internal improvements. He also vindicated federal authority against South Carolina with its doctrine of nullification and against France on the question of debts. The support given his policies by the workingmen of the East as well as by the farmers of the East, West, and South resulted in his triumphant re-election in 1832 over Clay.

After watching the inauguration of his handpicked successor, Martin Van Buren, Jackson retired to the Hermitage, where he maintained a lively interest in national affairs until his death on June 8, 1845.

MARTIN VAN BUREN was born on Dec. 5, 1782, at Kinderhook, N.Y. After graduating from the village school, he became a law clerk, entered practice in 1803, and soon became active in state politics as state senator and attorney general. In 1820, he was elected to the United States Senate. He threw the support of his efficient political organization, known as the Albany Regency, to William H. Crawford in 1824 and to Jackson in 1828. After leading the opposition to Adams's administration in the Senate, he served briefly as governor of New York (1828–29) and resigned to become Jackson's Secretary of State. He was soon on close personal terms with Jackson and played an important part in the Jacksonian program.

In 1832, Van Buren became vice president; in 1836, President. The Panic of 1837 overshadowed his term. He attributed it to the overexpansion of the credit and favored the establishment of an independent treasury as repository for the federal funds. In 1840, he established a 10-hour day on public works. Defeated by Harrison in 1840, he was the leading contender for the Democratic nomination in 1844 until he publicly opposed immediate annexation of Texas, and was subsequently beaten by the Southern delegations at the Baltimore convention. This incident increased his growing misgivings about the slave power.

After working behind the scenes among the anti-slavery Democrats, Van Buren joined in the movement that led to the Free-Soil Party and became its candidate for President in 1848. He subsequently returned to the Democratic Party while continuing to object to its pro-Southern policy. He died in Kinder-

hook on July 24, 1862. His *Autobiography* throws valuable sidelights on the political history of the times.

His wife, Hannah Hoes, whom he married in 1807, died in 1819.

WILLIAM HENRY HARRISON was born in Charles City County, Va., on Feb. 9, 1773. Joining the army in 1791, he was active in Indian fighting in the Northwest, became secretary of the Northwest Territory in 1798 and governor of Indiana in 1800. He married Anna Symmes in 1795. Growing discontent over white encroachments on Indian lands led to the formation of an Indian alliance under Tecumseh to resist further aggressions. In 1811, Harrison won a nominal victory over the Indians at Tippecanoe and in 1813 a more decisive one at the Battle of the Thames, where Tecumseh was killed.

After resigning from the army in 1814, Harrison had an obscure career in politics and diplomacy, ending up 20 years later as a county recorder in Ohio. Nominated for President in 1835 as a military hero whom the conservative politicians hoped to be able to control, he ran surprisingly well against Van Buren in 1836. Four years later, he defeated Van Buren but caught penumonia and died in Washington on April 4, 1841, a month after his inauguration. Harrison was the first president to die in office.

JOHN TYLER was born in Charles City County, Va., on March 29, 1790. A William and Mary graduate, he entered law practice and politics, serving in the House of Representatives (1817–21), as governor of Virginia (1825–27), and as senator (1827–36). A strict constructionist, he supported Crawford in 1824 and Jackson in 1828, but broke with Jackson over his United States Bank policy and became a member of the Southern state-rights group that co-operated with the Whigs. In 1836, he resigned from the Senate rather than follow instructions from the Virginia legislature to vote for a resolution expunging censure of Jackson from the Senate record.

Elected vice president on the Whig ticket in 1840, Tyler succeeded to the presidency on Harrison's death. His strict-constructionist views soon caused a split with the Henry Clay wing of the Whig party and a stalemate on domestic questions. Tyler's more considerable achievements were his support of the Webster-Ashburton Treaty with Britain and his success in bringing about the annexation of Texas.

After his presidency he lived in retirement in Virginia until the outbreak of the Civil War, when he emerged briefly as chairman of a peace convention and then as delegate to the provisional Congress of the Confederacy. He died on Jan. 18, 1862. He married Letitia Christian in 1813 and, two years after her death in 1842, Julia Gardiner.

JAMES KNOX POLK was born in Mecklenburg County, N.C., on Nov. 2, 1795. A graduate of the University of North Carolina, he moved west to Tennessee, was admitted to the bar, and soon became prominent in state politics. In 1825, he was elected to the House of Representatives, where he opposed Adams and, after 1829, became Jackson's floor leader in the fight against the Bank. In 1835, he became Speaker of the House. Four years later, he was elected governor of Tennessee, but was beaten in tries for re-election in 1841 and 1843.

The supporters of Van Buren for the Democratic

nomination in 1844 counted on Polk as his running mate; but, when Van Buren's stand on Texas alienated Southern support, the convention swung to Polk on the ninth ballot. He was elected over Henry Clay, the Whig candidate. Rapidly disillusioning those who thought that he would not run his own administration, Polk proceeded steadily and precisely to achieve four major objectives—the acquisition of California, the settlement of the Oregon question, the reduction of the tariff, and the establishment of the independent treasury. He also enlarged the Monroe Doctrine to exclude all non-American intervention in American affairs, whether forcible or not, and he forced Mexico into a war that he waged to a successful conclusion.

His wife, Sarah Childress, whom he married in 1824, was a woman of charm and ability. Polk died in Nashville, Tenn., on June 15, 1849.

ZACHARY TAYLOR was born at Montebello, Orange County, Va., on Nov. 24, 1784. Embarking on a military career in 1808, Taylor fought in the War of 1812, the Black Hawk War, and the Seminole War, meanwhile holding garrison jobs on the frontier or desk jobs in Washington. A brigadier general as a result of his victory over the Seminoles at Lake Okeechobee (1837), Taylor held a succession of Southwestern commands and in 1846 established a base on the Rio Grande, where his forces engaged in hostilities that precipitated the war with Mexico. He captured Monterrey in September 1846 and, disregarding Polk's orders to stay on the defensive, defeated Santa Anna at Buena Vista in February 1847, ending the war in the northern provinces.

Though Taylor had never cast a vote for president, his party affiliations were Whiggish and his availability was increased by his difficulties with Polk. He was elected president over the Democrat Lewis Cass. During the revival of the slavery controversy, which was to result in the Compromise of 1850, Taylor began to take an increasingly firm stand against appeasing the South; but he died in Washington on July 9, 1850, during the fight over the Compromise. He married Margaret Mackall Smith in 1810. His bluff and simple soldierly qualities won him the name Old Rough and Ready.

MILLARD FILLMORE was born at Locke, Cayuga County, N.Y., on Jan. 7, 1800. A lawyer, he entered politics with the Anti-Masonic Party under the sponsorship of Thurlow Weed, editor and party boss, and subsequently followed Weed into the Whig Party. He served in the House of Representatives (1833–35 and 1837–43) and played a leading role in writing the tariff of 1842. Defeated for governor of New York in 1844, he became State comptroller in 1848, was put on the Whig ticket with Taylor as a concession to the Clay wing of the party, and became president upon Taylor's death in 1850.

As president, Fillmore broke with Weed and William H. Seward and associated himself with the pro-Southern Whigs, supporting the Compromise of 1850. Defeated for the Whig nomination in 1852, he ran for president in 1856 as candidate of the American, or Know-Nothing Party, which sought to unite the country against foreigners in the alleged hope of diverting it from the explosive slavery issue. Fillmore opposed Lincoln during the Civil War. He died in Buffalo on March 8, 1874.

He was married in 1826 to Abigail Powers, who died in 1853, and in 1858 to Caroline Carmichael McIntosh.

FRANKLIN PIERCE was born at Hillsboro, N.H., on Nov. 23, 1804. A Bowdoin graduate, lawyer, and Jacksonian Democrat, he won rapid political advancement in the party, in part because of the prestige of his father, Gov. Benjamin Pierce. By 1831 he was Speaker of the New Hampshire House of Representatives; from 1833 to 1837, he served in the federal House and from 1837 to 1842 in the Senate. His wife, Jane Means Appleton, whom he married in 1834, disliked Washington and the somewhat dissipated life led by Pierce; in 1842 Pierce resigned from the Senate and began a successful law practice in Concord, N.H. During the Mexican War, he was a brigadier general.

Thereafter Pierce continued to oppose antislavery tendencies within the Democratic Party. As a result, he was the Southern choice to break the deadlock at the Democratic convention of 1852 and was nominated on the 49th ballot. In the election, Pierce overwhelmed Gen. Winfield Scott, the Whig candidate.

As president, Pierce followed a course of appeasing the South at home and of playing with schemes of territorial expansion abroad. The failure of his foreign and domestic policies prevented his renomination; and he died in Concord on Oct. 8, 1869, in relative obscurity.

JAMES BUCHANAN was born near Mercersburg, Pa., on April 23, 1791. A Dickinson graduate and a lawyer, he entered Pennsylvania politics as a Federalist. With the disappearance of the Federalist Party, he became a Jacksonian Democrat. He served with ability in the House (1821–31), as minister to St. Petersburg (1832–33), and in the Senate (1834–45), and in 1845 became Polk's Secretary of State. In 1853, Pierce appointed Buchanan minister to Britain, where he participated with other American diplomats in Europe in drafting the expansionist Ostend Manifesto.

He was elected president in 1856, defeating John C. Frémont, the Republican candidate, and former President Millard Fillmore of the American Party. The growing crisis over slavery presented Buchanan with problems he lacked the will to tackle. His appeasement of the South alienated the Stephen Douglas wing of the Democratic Party without reducing Southern militancy on slavery issues. While denying the right of secession, Buchanan also denied that the federal government could do anything about it. He supported the administration during the Civil War and died in Lancaster, Pa., on June 1, 1868.

The only president to remain a bachelor throughout his term, Buchanan used his charming niece, Harriet Lane, as White House hostess.

ABRAHAM LINCOLN was born in Hardin (now Larue) County, Ky., on Feb. 12, 1809. His family moved to Indiana and then to Illinois, and Lincoln gained what education he could along the way. While reading law, he worked in a store, managed a mill, surveyed, and split rails. In 1834, he went to the Illinois legislature as a Whig and became the party's floor leader. For the next 20 years he practiced law in Springfield, except for a single term (1847–49) in Congress, where he denounced the Mexican War. In 1855, he was a candidate for senator annd the next year he joined the new Republican Party.

A leading but unsuccessful candidate for the vice-presidential nomination with Frémont, Lincoln gained national attention in 1858 when, as Republican candidate for senator from Illinois, he engaged in a series of debates with Stephen A. Douglas, the Democratic candidate. He lost the election, but continued to prepare the way for the 1860 Republican convention and was rewarded with the presidential nomination on the third ballot. He won the election over three opponents.

From the start, Lincoln made clear that, unlike Buchanan, he believed the national government had the power to crush the rebellion. Not an abolitionist, he held the slavery issue subordinate to that of preserving the Union, but soon perceived that the war could not be brought to a successful conclusion without freeing the slaves. His administration was hampered by the incompetence of many Union generals, the inexperience of the troops, and the harassing political tactics both of the Republican Radicals, who favored a hard policy toward the South, and the Democratic Copperheads, who desired a negotiated peace. The Gettysburg Address of Nov. 19, 1863, marks the high point in the record of American eloquence. Lincoln's long search for a winning combination finally brought Generals Ulysses S. Grant and William T. Sherman on the top; and their series of victories in 1864 dispelled the mutterings from both Radicals and Peace Democrats that at one time seemed to threaten Lincoln's re-election. He was re-elected in 1864, defeating Gen. George B. McClellan, the Democratic candidate. His inaugural address urged leniency toward the South: "With malice toward none, with charity for all . . . let us strive on to finish the work we are in; to bind up the nation's wounds . . ." This policy aroused growing opposition on the part of the Republican Radicals, but before the matter could be put to the test, Lincoln was shot by the actor John Wilkes Booth at Ford's Theater, Washington, on April 14, 1865. He died the next morning.

Lincoln's marriage to Mary Todd in 1842 was often unhappy and turbulent, in part because of his wife's pronounced instability.

ANDREW JOHNSON was born at Raleigh, N.C., on Dec. 29, 1808. Self-educated, he became a tailor in Greeneville, Tenn., but soon went into politics, where he rose steadily. He served in the House of Representatives (1843–54), as governor of Tennessee (1853–57), and as a senator (1857–62). Politically he was a Jacksonian Democrat and his specialty was the fight for a more equitable land policy. Alone among the Southern Senators, he stood by the Union during the Civil War. In 1862, he became war governor of Tennessee and carried out a thankless and difficult job with great courage. Johnson became Lincoln's running mate in 1864 as a result of an attempt to give the ticket a nonpartisan and nonsectional character. Succeeding to the presidency on Lincoln's death, Johnson sought to carry out Lincoln's policy, but without his political skill. The result was a hopeless conflict with the Radical Republicans who dominated Congress, passed measures over Johnson's vetoes, and attempted to limit the power of the executive concerning appointments and removals. The conflict culminated with Johnson's impeachment for attempting to remove his disloyal Secretary of War in defiance of the Tenure of Office Act which required senatorial concurrence for such dismissals. The opposition failed by one vote to get the two thirds necessary for conviction.

After his presidency, Johnson maintained an interest in politics and in 1875 was again elected to the Senate. He died near Carter Station, Tenn., on July 31, 1875. He married Eliza McCardle in 1827.

ULYSSES SIMPSON GRANT was born (as Hiram Ulysses Grant) at Point Pleasant, Ohio, on April 27, 1822. He graduated from West Point in 1843 and served without particular distinction in the Mexican War. In 1848 he married Julia Dent. He resigned from the army in 1854, after warnings from his commanding officer about his drinking habits, and for the next six years held a wide variety of jobs in the Middle West. With the outbreak of the Civil War, he sought a command and soon, to his surprise, was made a brigadier general. His continuing successes in the western theaters, culminating in the capture of Vicksburg, Miss., in 1863, brought him national fame and soon the command of all the Union armies. Grant's dogged, implacable policy of concentrating on dividing and destroying the Confederate armies brought the war to an end in 1865. The next year, he was made full general.

In 1868, as Republican candidate for president, Grant was elected over the Democrat, Horatio Seymour. From the start, Grant showed his unfitness for the office. His Cabinet was weak, his domestic policy was confused, many of his intimate associates were corrupt. The notable achievement in foreign affairs was the settlement of controversies with Great Britain in the Treaty of London (1871), negotiated by his able Secretary of State, Hamilton Fish.

Running for re-election in 1872, he defeated Horace Greeley, the Democratic and Liberal Republican candidate. The Panic of 1873 graft scandals close to the presidency created difficulties for his second term.

After retiring from office, Grant toured Europe for two years and returned in time to accede to a third-term boom, but was beaten in the convention of 1880. Illness and bad business judgment darkened his last years, but he worked steadily at the *Personal Memoirs*, which were to be so successful when published after his death at Mount McGregor, near Saratoga, N.Y., on July 23, 1885.

RUTHERFORD BIRCHARD HAYES was born in Delaware, Ohio, on Oct. 4, 1822. A graduate of Kenyon College and the Harvard Law School, he practiced law in Lower Sandusky (now Fremont) and then in Cincinnati. In 1852 he married Lucy Webb. A Whig, he joined the Republican party in 1855. During the Civil War he rose to major general. He served in the House of Representatives from 1865 to 1867 and then confirmed a reputation for honesty and efficiency in two terms as Governor of Ohio (1868–72). His election to a third term in 1875 made him the logical candidate for those Republicans who wished to stop James G. Blaine in 1876, and he was nominated.

The result of the election was in doubt for some time and hinged upon disputed returns from South Carolina, Louisiana, Florida, and Oregon. Samuel J. Tilden, the Democrat, had the larger popular vote but was adjudged by the strictly partisan decisions of the Electoral Commission to have one fewer electoral vote, 185 to 184. The national acceptance of this result was due in part to the general understanding that Hayes would pursue a conciliatory policy toward the South. He withdrew the troops from the South, took a conservative position on financial and labor issues, and urged civil service reform.

Hayes served only one term by his own wish and

spent the rest of his life in various humanitarian endeavors. He died in Fremont on Jan. 17, 1893.

JAMES ABRAM GARFIELD, the last president to be born in a log cabin, was born in Cuyahoga County, Ohio, on Nov. 19, 1831. A Williams graduate, he taught school for a time and entered Republican politics in Ohio. In 1858, he married Lucretia Rudolph. During the Civil War, he had a promising career, rising to major general of volunteers; but he resigned in 1863, having been elected to the House of Representatives, where he served until 1880. His oratorical and parliamentary abilities soon made him the leading Republican in the House, though his record was marred by his unorthodox acceptance of a fee in the DeGolyer paving contract case and by suspicions of his complicity in the Crédit Mobilier scandal.

In 1880, Garfield was elected to the Senate, but instead became the presidential candidate on the 36th ballot as a result of a deadlock in the Republican convention. In the election, he defeated Gen. Winfield Scott Hancock, the Democratic candidate. Garfield's administration was barely under way when he was shot by Charles J. Guiteau, a disappointed office seeker, in Washington on July 2, 1881. He died in Elberton, N.J., on Sept. 19.

CHESTER ALAN ARTHUR was born at Fairfield, Vt., on Oct. 5, 1830. A graduate of Union College, he became a successful New York lawyer. In 1859, he married Ellen Herndon. During the Civil War, he held administrative jobs in the Republican state administration and in 1871 was appointed collector of the Port of New York by Grant. This post gave him control over considerable patronage. Though not personally corrupt, Arthur managed his power in the interests of the New York machine so openly that President Hayes in 1877 called for an investigation and the next year Arthur was suspended.

In 1880 Arthur was nominated for vice president in the hope of conciliating the followers of Grant and the powerful New York machine. As president upon Garfield's death, Arthur, stepping out of his familiar role as spoilsman, backed civil service reform, reorganized the Cabinet, and prosecuted political associates accused of post office graft. Losing machine support and failing to gain the reformers, he was not nominated for a full term in 1884. He died in New York City on Nov. 18, 1886.

STEPHEN GROVER CLEVELAND was born at Caldwell, N.J., on March 18, 1837. He was admitted to the bar in Buffalo, N.Y., in 1859 and lived there as a lawyer, with occasional incursions into Democratic politics, for more than 20 years. He did not participate in the Civil War. As mayor of Buffalo in 1881, he carried through a reform program so ably that the Democrats ran him successfully for governor in 1882. In 1884 he won the Democratic nomination for President. The campaign contrasted Cleveland's spotless public career with the uncertain record of James G. Blaine, the Republican candidate, and Cleveland received enough Mugwump (independent Republican) support to win.

As president, Cleveland pushed civil service reform, opposed the pension grab and attacked the high tariff rates. While in the White House, he married Frances Folsom in 1886. Renominated in 1888, Cleveland was defeated by Benjamin Harrison, polling more popular but fewer electoral votes. In 1892, he was elected over Harrison. When the Panic of 1893 burst upon the country, Cleveland's attempts to solve it by sound-money measures alienated the free-silver wing of the party, while his tariff policy alienated the protectionists. In 1894, he sent troops to break the Pullman strike. In foreign affairs, his firmness caused Great Britain to back down in the Venezuela border dispute.

In his last years Cleveland was an active and much-respected public figure. He died in Princeton, N.J., on June 24, 1908.

BENJAMIN HARRISON was born in North Bend, Ohio, on Aug. 20, 1833, the grandson of William Henry Harrison, the ninth president. A graduate of Miami University in Ohio, he took up the law in Indiana and became active in Republican politics. In 1853, he married Caroline Lavinia Scott. During the Civil War, he rose to brigadier general. A sound-money Republican, he was elected senator from Indiana in 1880. In 1888, he received the Republican nomination for President on the eighth ballot. Though behind on the popular vote, he won over Grover Cleveland in the electoral college by 233 to 168.

As President, Harrison failed to please either the bosses or the reform element in the party. In foreign affairs he backed Secretary of State Blaine, whose policy foreshadowed later American imperialism. Harrison was renominated in 1892 but lost to Cleveland. His wife died in the White House in 1892 and Harrison married her niece, Mary Scott (Lord) Dimmick, in 1896. After his presidency, he resumed law practice. He died in Indianapolis on March 13, 1901.

WILLIAM McKINLEY was born in Niles, Ohio, on Jan. 29, 1843. He taught school, then served in the Civil War, rising from the ranks to become a major. Subsequently he opened a law office in Canton, Ohio, and in 1871 married Ida Saxton. Elected to Congress in 1876, he served there until 1891, except for 1883–85. His faithful advocacy of business interests culminated in the passage of the highly protective McKinley Tariff of 1890. With the support of Mark Hanna, a shrewd Cleveland businessman interested in safeguarding tariff protection, McKinley became governor of Ohio in 1892 and Republican presidential candidate in 1896. The business community, alarmed by the progressivism of William Jennings Bryan, the Democratic candidate, spent considerable money to assure McKinley's victory.

The chief event of McKinley's administration was the war with Spain, which resulted in our acquisition of the Philippines and other islands. With imperialism an issue, McKinley defeated Bryan again in 1900. On Sept. 6, 1901, he was shot at Buffalo, N.Y., by Leon F. Czolgosz, an anarchist, and he died there eight days later.

THEODORE ROOSEVELT was born in New York City on Oct. 27, 1858. A Harvard graduate, he was early interested in ranching, in politics, and in writing picturesque historical narratives. He was a Republican member of the New York Assembly in 1882–84, an unsuccessful candidate for mayor of New York in 1886, a U.S. Civil Service Commissioner under Benjamin Harrison, Police Commissioner of New York City in 1895, and Assistant Secretary of the Navy under McKinley in 1897. He resigned in 1898 to help organize a volunteer regiment, the Rough Riders, and take a more direct part in the war with Spain. He was elected governor of New York in 1898 and vice president in 1900, in spite of lack of enthusiasm on the part of the bosses.

Assuming the presidency of the assassinated McKinley in 1901, Roosevelt embarked on a wide-ranging program of government reform and conservation of natural resources. He ordered antitrust suits against several large corporations, threatened to intervene in the anthracite coal strike of 1902, which prompted the operators to accept arbitration, and, in general, championed the rights of the "little man" and fought the "malefactors of great wealth." He was also responsible for such progressive legislation as the Elkins Act of 1901, which outlawed freight rebates by railroads; the bill establishing the Department of Commerce and Labor; the Hepburn Act, which gave the I.C.C. greater control over the railroads; the Meat Inspection Act; and the Pure Food and Drug Act.

In foreign affairs, Roosevelt pursued a strong policy, permitting the instigation of a revolt in Panama to dispose of Colombian objections to the Panama Canal and helping to maintain the balance of power in the East by bringing the Russo-Japanese War to an end, for which he won the Nobel Peace Prize, the first American to achieve a Nobel prize in any category. In 1904, he decisively defeated Alton B. Parker, his conservative Democratic opponent.

Roosevelt's increasing coldness toward his successor, William Howard Taft, led him to overlook his earlier disclaimer of third-term ambitions and to re-enter politics. Defeated by the machine in the Republican convention of 1912, he organized the Progressive Party (Bull Moose) and polled more votes than Taft, though the split brought about the election of Woodrow Wilson. From 1915 on, Roosevelt strongly favored intervention in the European war. He became deeply embittered at Wilson's refusal to allow him to raise a volunteer division. He died in Oyster Bay, N.Y., on Jan. 6, 1919. He was married twice: in 1880 to Alice Hathaway Lee, who died in 1884, and in 1886 to Edith Kermit Carow.

WILLIAM HOWARD TAFT was born in Cincinnati on Sept. 15, 1857. A Yale graduate, he entered Ohio Republican politics in the 1880s. In 1886 he married Helen Herron. From 1887 to 1890, he served on the Ohio Superior Court; 1890–92, as solicitor general of the United States; 1892–1900, on the federal circuit court. In 1900 McKinley appointed him president of the Philippine Commission and in 1901 governor general. Taft had great success in pacifying the Filipinos, solving the problem of the church lands, improving economic conditions, and establishing limited self-government. His period as Secretary of War (1904–08) further demonstrated his capacity as administrator and conciliator, and he was Roosevelt's hand-picked successor in 1908. In the election, he polled 321 electoral votes to 162 for William Jennings Bryan, who was running for the presidency for the third time.

Though he carried on many of Roosevelt's policies, Taft got into increasing trouble with the progressive wing of the party and displayed mounting irritability and indecision. After his defeat in 1912, he became professor of constitutional law at Yale. In 1921 he

was appointed Chief Justice of the United States. He died in Washington on March 8, 1930.

THOMAS WOODROW WILSON was born in Staunton, Va., on Dec. 28, 1856. A Princeton graduate, he turned from law practice to post-graduate work in political science at Johns Hopkins University, receiving his Ph.D. in 1886. He taught at Bryn Mawr, Wesleyan, and Princeton, and in 1902 was made president of Princeton. After an unsuccessful attempt to democratize the social life of the university, he welcomed an invitation in 1910 to be the Democratic gubernatorial candidate in New Jersey, and was elected. His success in fighting the machine and putting through a reform program attracted national attention.

In 1912, at the Democratic convention in Baltimore, Wilson won the nomination on the 46th ballot and went on to defeat Roosevelt and Taft in the election. Wilson proceeded under the standard of the New Freedom to enact a program of domestic reform, including the Federal Reserve Act, the Clayton Antitrust Act, the establishment of the Federal Trade Commission, and other measures designed to restore competition in the face of the great monopolies. In foreign affairs, while privately sympathetic with the Allies, he strove to maintain neutrality in the European war and warned both sides against encroachments on American interests.

Re-elected in 1916 as a peace candidate, he tried to mediate between the warring nations; but when the Germans resumed unrestricted submarine warfare in 1917, Wilson brought the United States into what he now believed was a war to make the world safe for democracy. He supplied the classic formulations of Allied war aims and the armistice of Nov. 11, 1918 was negotiated on the basis of Wilson's Fourteen Points. In 1919 he strove at Versailles to lay the foundations for enduring peace. He accepted the imperfections of the Versailles Treaty in the expectation that they could be remedied by action within the League of Nations. He probably could have secured ratification of the treaty by the Senate if he had adopted a more conciliatory attitude toward the mild reservationists; but his insistence on all or nothing eventually caused the diehard isolationists and diehard Wilsonites to unite in rejecting a compromise.

In September 1919 Wilson suffered a paralytic stroke that limited his activity. After leaving the presidency he lived on in retirement in Washington, dying on Feb. 3, 1924. He was married twice—in 1885 to Ellen Louise Axson, who died in 1914, and in 1915 to Edith Bolling Galt.

WARREN GAMALIEL HARDING was born in Morrow County, Ohio, on Nov. 2, 1865. After attending Ohio Central College, Harding became interested in journalism and in 1884 bought the *Marion* (Ohio) *Star.* In 1891 he married a wealthy widow, Florence Kling De Wolfe. As his paper prospered, he entered Republican politics, serving as state senator (1899–1903) and as lieutenant governor (1904–06). In 1910, he was defeated for governor, but in 1914 was elected to the Senate. His reputation as an orator made him the keynoter at the 1916 Republican convention.

When the 1920 convention was deadlocked between Leonard Wood and Frank O. Lowden, Harding became the dark-horse nominee on his solemn affirmation that there was no reason in his past that he should not be. Straddling the League question, Harding was easily elected over James M. Cox, his Democratic opponent. His Cabinet contained some able men, but also some manifestly unfit for public office. Harding's own intimates were mediocre when they were not corrupt. The impending disclosure of the Teapot Dome scandal in the Interior Department and illegal practices in the Justice Department and Veterans' Bureau, as well as political setbacks, profoundly worried him. On his return from Alaska in 1923, he died unexpectedly in San Francisco on Aug. 2.

JOHN CALVIN COOLIDGE was born in Plymouth, Vt., on July 4, 1872. An Amherst graduate, he went into law practice at Northampton, Mass., in 1897. He married Grace Anna Goodhue in 1905. He entered Republican state politics, becoming successively mayor of Northampton, state senator, lieutenant governor and, in 1919, governor. His use of the state militia to end the Boston police strike in 1919 won him a somewhat undeserved reputation for decisive action and brought him the Republican vice-presidential nomination in 1920. After Harding's death Coolidge handled the Washington scandals with care and finally managed to save the Republican Party from public blame for the widespread corruption.

In 1924, Coolidge was elected without difficulty, defeating the Democrat, John W. Davis, and Robert M. La Follette running on the Progressive ticket. His second term, like his first, was characterized by a general satisfaction with the existing economic order. He stated that he did not choose to run in 1928.

After his presidency, Coolidge lived quietly in Northampton, writing a unilluminating *Autobiography* and conducting a syndicated column. He died there on Jan. 5, 1933.

HERBERT CLARK HOOVER was born at West Branch, Iowa, on Aug. 10, 1874, the first president to be born west of the Mississippi. A Stanford graduate, he worked from 1895 to 1913 as a mining engineer and consultant throughout the world. In 1899, he married Lou Henry. During World War I, he served with distinction as chairman of the American Relief Committee in London, as chairman of the Commission for Relief in Belgium, and as U.S. Food Administrator. His political affiliations were still too indeterminate for him to be mentioned as a possibility for either the Republican or Democratic nomination in 1920, but after the election he served Harding and Coolidge as Secretary of Commerce.

In the election of 1928, Hoover overwhelmed Gov. Alfred E. Smith of New York, the Democratic candidate and the first Roman Catholic to run for the presidency. He soon faced the worst depression in the nation's history, but his attacks upon it were hampered by his devotion to the theory that the forces that brought the crisis would soon bring the revival and then by his belief that there were too many areas in which the federal government had no power to act. In a succession of vetoes, he struck down measures proposing a national employment system or national relief, he reduced income tax rates, and only at the end of his term did he yield to popular pressure and set up agencies such as the Reconstruction Finance Corporation to make emergency loans to assist business.

After his 1932 defeat, Hoover returned to private business. In 1946, President Truman charged him

with various world food missions; and from 1947 to 1949 and 1953 to 1955, he was head of the Commission on Organization of the Executive Branch of the Government. He died in New York City on Oct. 20, 1964.

FRANKLIN DELANO ROOSEVELT was born in Hyde Park, N.Y., on Jan. 30, 1882. A Harvard graduate, he attended Columbia Law School and was admitted to the New York bar. In 1910, he was elected to the New York State Senate as a Democrat. Reelected in 1912, he was appointed Assistant Secretary of the Navy by Woodrow Wilson the next year. In 1920, his radiant personality and his war service resulted in his nomination for vice president as James M. Cox's running mate. After his defeat, he returned to law practice in New York. In August 1921, Roosevelt was stricken with infantile paralysis while on vacation at Campobello, New Brunswick. After a long and gallant fight, he recovered partial use of his legs. In 1924 and 1928, he led the fight at the Democratic national conventions for the nomination of Gov. Alfred E. Smith of New York, and in 1928 Roosevelt was himself induced to run for governor of New York. He was elected, and was re-elected in 1930.

In 1932, Roosevelt received the Democratic nomination for president and immediately launched a campaign that brought new spirit to a weary and discouraged nation. He defeated Hoover by a wide margin. His first term was characterized by an unfolding of the New Deal program, with greater benefits for labor, the farmers, and the unemployed, and the progressive estrangement of most of the business community.

At an early stage, Roosevelt became aware of the menace to world peace posed by totalitarian fascism, and from 1937 on he tried to focus public attention on the trend of events in Europe and Asia. As a result, he was widely denounced as a warmonger. He was re-elected in 1936 over Gov. Alfred M. Landon of Kansas by the overwhelming electoral margin of 523 to 8, and the gathering international crisis prompted him to run for an unprecedented third term in 1940. He defeated Wendell L. Willkie.

Roosevelt's program to bring maximum aid to Britain and, after June 1941, to Russia was opposed, until the Japanese attack on Pearl Harbor restored national unity. During the war, Roosevelt shelved the New Deal in the interests of conciliating the business community, both in order to get full production during the war and to prepare the way for a united acceptance of the peace settlements after the war. A series of conferences with Winston Churchill and Joseph Stalin laid down the bases for the postwar world. In 1944 he was elected to a fourth term, running against Gov. Thomas E. Dewey of New York.

On April 12, 1945, Roosevelt died of a cerebral hemorrhage at Warm Springs, Ga., shortly after his return from the Yalta Conference. His wife, Anna Eleanor Roosevelt, whom he married in 1905, was a woman of great ability who made significant contributions to her husband's policies.

HARRY S. TRUMAN was born on a farm near Lamar, Mo., on May 8, 1884. During World War I, he served in France as a captain with the 129th Field Artillery. He married Bess Wallace in 1919. After engaging briefly and unsuccessfully in the haberdashery business in Kansas City, Mo., Truman entered local politics. Under the sponsorship of Thomas Pendergast, Democratic boss of Missouri, he held a number of local offices, preserving his personal honesty in the midst of a notoriously corrupt political machine. In 1934, he was elected to the Senate and was re-elected in 1940. During his first term he was a loyal but quiet supporter of the New Deal, but in his second term, an appointment as head of a Senate committee to investigate war production brought out his special qualities of honesty, common sense, and hard work, and he won widespread respect.

Elected vice president in 1944, Truman became president upon Roosevelt's sudden death in April 1945 and was immediately faced with the problems of winding down the war against the Axis and preparing the nation for postwar adjustment.

The years 1947–48 were distinguished by civil-rights proposals, the Truman Doctrine to contain the spread of Communism, and the Marshall Plan to aid in the economic reconstruction of war-ravaged nations. Truman's general record, highlighted by a vigorous Fair Deal campaign, brought about his unexpected election in 1948 over the heavily favored Thomas E. Dewey.

Truman's second term was primarily concerned with the Cold War with the Soviet Union, the implementing of the North Atlantic Pact, the United Nations police action in Korea, and the vast rearmament program with its accompanying problems of economic stabilization.

On March 29, 1952, Truman announced that he would not run again for the presidency. After leaving the White House, he returned to his home in Independence, Mo., to write his memoirs. He further busied himself with the Harry S. Truman Library there. He died in Kansas City, Mo., on Dec. 26, 1972.

DWIGHT DAVID EISENHOWER was born in Denison, Tex., on Oct. 14, 1890. His ancestors lived in Germany and emigrated to America, settling in Pennsylvania, early in the 18th century. His father, David, had a general store in Hope, Kan., which failed. After a brief time in Texas, the family moved to Abilene, Kan.

After graduating from Abilene High School in 1909, Eisenhower did odd jobs for almost two years. He won an appointment to the Naval Academy at Annapolis, but was too old for admittance. Then he received an appointment in 1910 to West Point, from which he graduated as a second lieutenant in 1915.

He did not see service in World War I, having been stationed at Fort Sam Houston, Tex. There he met Mamie Geneva Doud, whom he married in Denver on July 1, 1916, and by whom he had two sons: Doud Dwight (died in infancy) and John Sheldon Doud.

Eisenhower served in the Philippines from 1935 to 1939 with Gen. Douglas MacArthur. Afterward, Gen. George C. Marshall, the Army Chief of Staff, brought him into the War Department's General Staff and in 1942 placed him in command of the invasion of North Africa. In 1944, he was made Supreme Allied Commander for the invasion of Europe.

After the war, Eisenhower served as Army Chief of Staff from November 1945 until February 1948, when he was appointed president of Columbia University.

In December 1950, President Truman recalled Eisenhower to active duty to command the North Atlantic Treaty Organization forces in Europe. He held his post until the end of May 1952.

At the Republican convention of 1952 in Chicago, Eisenhower won the presidential nomination on the first ballot in a close race with Senator Robert A. Taft of Ohio. In the election, he defeated Gov. Adlai E. Stevenson of Illinois.

Through two terms, Eisenhower hewed to moderate domestic policies. He sought peace through Free World strength in an era of new nationalisms, nuclear missiles, and space exploration. He fostered alliances pledging the United States to resist Red aggression in Europe, Asia, and Latin America. The Eisenhower Doctrine of 1957 extended commitments to the Middle East.

At home, the popular president lacked Republican Congressional majorities after 1954, but he was re-elected in 1956 by 457 electoral votes to 73 for Stevenson.

While retaining most Fair Deal programs, he stressed "fiscal responsibility" in domestic affairs. A moderate in civil rights, he sent troops to Little Rock, Ark., to enforce court-ordered school integration.

With his wartime rank restored by Congress, Eisenhower returned to private life and the role of elder statesman, with his vigor hardly impaired by a heart attack, an ileitis operation, and a mild stroke suffered while in office. He died in Washington on March 28, 1969.

JOHN FITZGERALD KENNEDY was born in Brookline, Mass., on May 29, 1917. His father, Joseph P. Kennedy, was Ambassador to Great Britain from 1937 to 1940.

Kennedy was graduated from Harvard University in 1940 and joined the Navy the next year. He became skipper of a PT boat that was sunk in the Pacific by a Japanese destroyer. Although given up for lost, he swam to a safe island, towing an injured enlisted man.

After recovering from a war-aggravated spinal injury, Kennedy entered politics in 1946 and was elected to Congress. In 1952, he ran against Senator Henry Cabot Lodge, Jr., of Massachusetts, and won.

Kennedy was married on Sept. 12, 1953, to Jacqueline Lee Bouvier, by whom he had three children: Caroline, John Fitzgerald, Jr., and Patrick Bouvier (died in infancy).

In 1957 Kennedy won the Pulitzer Prize for a book he had written earlier, *Profiles in Courage*.

After strenuous primary battles, Kennedy won the Democratic presidential nomination on the first ballot at the 1960 Los Angeles convention. With a plurality of only 118,574 votes, he carried the election over Vice President Richard M. Nixon and became the first Roman Catholic president.

Kennedy brought to the White House the dynamic idea of a "New Frontier" approach in dealing with problems at home, abroad, and in the dimensions of space. Out of his leadership in his first few months in office came the 10-year Alliance for Progress to aid Latin America, the Peace Corps, and accelerated programs that brought the first Americans into orbit in the race in space.

Failure of the U.S.-supported Cuban invasion in April 1961 led to the entrenchment of the Communist-backed Castro regime, only 90 miles from United States soil. When it became known that Soviet offensive missiles were being installed in Cuba in 1962, Kennedy ordered a naval "quarantine" of the island and moved troops into position to eliminate this threat to U.S. security. The world seemed on the brink of a nuclear war until Soviet Premier Khrushchev ordered the removal of the missiles.

A sudden "thaw," or the appearance of one, in the cold war came with the agreement with the Soviet Union on a limited test-ban treaty signed in Moscow on Aug. 6, 1963.

In his domestic policies, Kennedy's proposals for medical care for the aged, expanded area redevelopment, and aid to education were defeated, but on minimum wage, trade legislation, and other measures he won important victories.

Widespread racial disorders and demonstrations led to Kennedy's proposing sweeping civil rights legislation. As his third year in office drew to a close, he also recommended an $11-billion tax cut to bolster the economy. Both measures were pending in Congress when Kennedy, looking forward to a second term, journeyed to Texas for a series of speeches.

While riding in a procession in Dallas on Nov. 22, 1963, he was shot to death by an assassin firing from an upper floor of a building. The alleged assassin, Lee Harvey Oswald, was killed two days later in the Dallas city jail by Jack Ruby, owner of a strip-tease place.

At 46 years of age, Kennedy became the fourth president to be assassinated and the eighth to die in office.

LYNDON BAINES JOHNSON was born in Stonewall, Tex., on Aug. 27, 1908. On both sides of his family he had a political heritage mingled with a Baptist background of preachers and teachers. Both his father and his paternal grandfather served in the Texas House of Representatives.

After his graduation from Southwest Texas State Teachers College, Johnson taught school for two years. He went to Washington in 1932 as secretary to Rep. Richard M. Kleberg. During this time, he married Claudia Alta Taylor, known as "Lady Bird." They had two children: Lynda Bird and Luci Baines.

In 1935, Johnson became Texas administrator for the National Youth Administration. Two years later, he was elected to Congress as an all-out supporter of Franklin D. Roosevelt, and served until 1949. He was the first member of Congress to enlist in the armed forces after the attack on Pearl Harbor. He served in the Navy in the Pacific and won a Silver Star.

Johnson was elected to the Senate in 1948 after he had captured the Democratic nomination by only 87 votes. He was 40 years old. He became the Senate Democratic leader in 1953. A heart attack in 1955 threatened to end his political career, but he recovered fully and resumed his duties.

At the height of his power as Senate leader, Johnson sought the Democratic nomination for president in 1960. When he lost to John F. Kennedy, he surprised even some of his closest associates by accepting second place on the ticket.

Johnson was riding in another car in the motorcade when Kennedy was assassinated in Dallas on Nov. 22, 1963. He took the oath of office in the presidential jet on the Dallas airfield.

With Johnson's insistent backing, Congress finally adopted a far-reaching civil-rights bill, a voting-rights bill, a Medicare program for the aged, and measures to improve education and conservation. Congress also began what Johnson described as "an all-out war" on poverty.

Amassing a record-breaking majority of nearly 16 million votes, Johnson was elected president in his own right in 1964, defeating Senator Barry Goldwater of Arizona.

The double tragedy of a war in Southeast Asia and urban riots at home marked Johnson's last two years in office. Faced with disunity in the nation and challenges within his own party, Johnson surprised the country on March 31, 1968, with the announcement that he would not be a candidate for re-election. He died of a heart attack suffered at his LBJ Ranch on Jan. 22, 1973.

RICHARD MILHOUS NIXON was born in Yorba Linda, Calif., on Jan. 9, 1913, to Midwestern-bred parents, Francis A. and Hannah Milhous Nixon, who raised their five sons as Quakers.

Nixon was a high school debater and was undergraduate president at Whittier College in California, where he was graduated in 1934. As a scholarship student at Duke University Law School in North Carolina, he graduated third in his class in 1937.

After five years as a lawyer, Nixon joined the Navy in August 1942. He was an air transport officer in the South Pacific and a legal officer stateside before his discharge in 1946 as a lieutenant commander.

Running for Congress in California as a Republican in 1946, Nixon defeated Rep. Jerry Voorhis. As a member of the House Un-American Activities Committee, he made a name as an investigator of Alger Hiss, a former high State Department official, who was later jailed for perjury. In 1950, Nixon defeated Rep. Helen Gahagan Douglas, a Democrat, for the Senate. He was criticized for portraying her as a Communist dupe.

Nixon's anti-Communism, his Western base, and his youth figured in his selection in 1952 to run for vice president on the ticket headed by Dwight D. Eisenhower. Demands for Nixon's withdrawal followed disclosure that California businessmen had paid some of his Senate office expenses. He televised rebuttal, known as "the Checkers speech" (named for a cocker spaniel given to the Nixons), brought him support from the public and from Eisenhower. The ticket won easily in 1952 and again in 1956.

Eisenhower gave Nixon substantive assignments, including missions to 56 countries. In Moscow in 1959, Nixon won acclaim for his defense of U.S. interests in an impromptu "kitchen debate" with Soviet Premier Nikita S. Khrushchev.

Nixon lost the 1960 race for the presidency to John F. Kennedy.

In 1962, Nixon failed in a bid for California's governorship and seemed to be finished as a national candidate. He became a Wall Street lawyer, but kept his old party ties and developed new ones through constant travels to speak for Republicans.

Nixon won the 1968 Republican presidential nomination after a shrewd primary campaign, then made Gov. Spiro T. Agnew of Maryland his surprise choice for vice president. In the election, they edged out the Democratic ticket headed by Vice President Hubert H. Humphrey by 510,314 votes out of 73,212,065 cast.

Committed to wind down the U.S. role in the Vietnamese War, Nixon pursued "Vietnamization"—training and equipping South Vietnamese to do their own fighting. American ground combat forces in Vietnam fell steadily from 540,000 when Nixon took office to none in 1973 when the military draft was ended. But there was heavy continuing use of U.S. air power.

Nixon improved relations with Moscow and re-opened the long-closed door to mainland China with a good-will trip there in February 1972. In May of that year, he visited Moscow and signed agreements on arms limitation and trade expansion and approved plans for a joint U.S.-Soviet space mission in 1975.

Inflation was a campaign issue for Nixon, but he failed to master it as president. On Aug. 15, 1971, with unemployment edging up, Nixon abruptly announced a new economic policy: a 90-day wage-price freeze, stimulative tax cuts, a temporary 10% tariff, and spending cuts. A second phase, imposing guide-lines on wage, price and rent boosts, was announced October 7.

The economy responded in time for the 1972 cam-paign, in which Nixon played up his foreign-policy achievements. Played down was the burglary on June 17, 1972, of Democratic national headquarters in the Watergate apartment complex in Washington. The Nixon-Agnew re-election campaign cost a record $60 million and swamped the Democratic ticket headed by Senator George McGovern of South Dakota with a plurality of 17,999,528 out of 77,718,554 votes. Only Massachusetts, with 14 electoral votes, and the Dis-trict of Columbia, with 3, went for McGovern.

In January 1973, hints of a cover-up emerged at the trial of six men found guilty of the Watergate bur-glary. With a Senate investigation under way, Nixon announced on April 30 the resignations of his top aides, H. R. Haldeman and John D. Ehrlichman, and the dismissal of White House counsel John Dean III. Dean was the star witness at televised Senate hear-ings that exposed both a White House cover-up of Watergate and massive illegalities in Republican fund-raising in 1972.

The hearings also disclosed that Nixon had routine-ly tape-recorded his office meetings and telephone conversations.

On Oct. 10, 1973, Agnew resigned as vice presi-dent, then pleaded no-contest to a negotiated federal charge of evading income taxes on alleged bribes. Two days later, Nixon nominated the House minority leader, Rep. Gerald R. Ford of Michigan, as the new vice president. Congress confirmed Ford on Dec. 6, 1973.

In June 1974, Nixon visited Israel and four Arab nations. Then he met in Moscow with Soviet leader Leonid I. Brezhnev and reached preliminary nuclear arms limitation agreements.

But, in the month after his return, Watergate ended the Nixon regime. On July 24 the Supreme Court or-dered Nixon to surrender subpoenaed tapes. On July 30, the Judiciary Committee referred three impeach-ment articles to the full membership. On August 5, Nixon bowed to the Supreme Court and released tapes showing he halted an FBI probe of the Water-gate burglary six days after it occurred. It was in ef-fect an admission of obstruction of justice, and im-peachment appeared inevitable.

Nixon resigned on Aug. 9, 1974, the first president ever to do so. A month later, President Ford issued an unconditional pardon for any offenses Nixon might have committed as president, thus forestalling possi-ble prosecution.

In 1940, Nixon married Thelma Catherine (Pat) Ryan. They had two daughters, Patricia (Tricia) Cox and Julie, who married Dwight David Eisenhower II, grandson of the former president.

He died on April 22, 1994, in New York City of a massive stroke.

GERALD RUDOLPH FORD was born in Omaha, Neb., on July 14, 1913, the only child of Leslie and Dorothy Gardner King. His parents were divorced in 1915. His mother moved to Grand Rapids, Mich., and married Gerald R. Ford. The boy was renamed for his stepfather.

Ford captained his high school football team in Grand Rapids, and a football scholarship took him to the University of Michigan, where he starred as varsi-ty center before his graduation in 1935. A job as as-sistant football coach at Yale gave him an opportunity to attend Yale Law School, from which he graduated in the top third of his class in 1941.

He returned to Grand Rapids to practice law, but entered the Navy in April 1942. He saw wartime service in the Pacific on the light aircraft carrier *Monterey* and was a lieutenant commander when he returned to Grand Rapids early in 1946 to resume law practice and dabble in politics.

Ford was elected to Congress in 1948 for the first of his 13 terms in the House. He was soon assigned to the influential Appropriations Committee and rose to become the ranking Republican on the subcommit-tee on Defense Department appropriations and an ex-pert in the field.

As a legislator, Ford described himself as "a mod-erate on domestic issues, a conservative in fiscal af-fairs, and a dyed-in-the-wool internationalist." He carried the ball for Pentagon appropriations, was a hawk on the war in Vietnam, and kept a low profile on civil-rights issues.

He was also dependable and hard-working and popular with his colleagues. In 1963, he was elected chairman of the House Republican Conference. He served in 1963–64 as a member of the Warren Com-mission that investigated the assassination of John F. Kennedy. A revolt by dissatisfied younger Republi-cans in 1965 made him minority leader.

Ford shelved his hopes for the Speakership on Oct. 12, 1973, when Nixon nominated him to fill the vice presidency left vacant by Agnew's resignation under fire. It was the first use of the procedures for filling vacancies in the vice presidency laid down in the 25th Amendment to the Constitution, which Ford had helped enact.

Congress confirmed Ford as vice president on Dec. 6, 1973. Once in office, he said he did not believe Nixon had been involved in the Watergate scandals, but criticized his stubborn court battle against releas-ing tape recordings of Watergate-related conversa-tions for use as evidence.

The scandals led to Nixon's unprecedented resigna-tion on Aug. 9, 1974, and Ford was sworn in imme-diately as the 38th president, the first to enter the White House without winning a national election.

Ford assured the nation when he took office that "our long national nightmare is over" and pledged "openness and candor" in all his actions. He won a warm response from the Democratic 93rd Congress when he said he wanted "a good marriage" rather than a honeymoon with his former colleagues. In De-cember 1974 Congressional majorities backed his choice of former New York Gov. Nelson A. Rocke-feller as his successor in the again-vacant vice pres-idency.

The cordiality was chilled by Ford's announce-ment on Sept. 8, 1974, that he had granted an uncon-ditional pardon to Nixon for any crimes he might have committed as president. Although no formal charges were pending, Ford said he feared "ugly pas-sions" would be aroused if Nixon were brought to trial. The pardon was widely criticized.

To fight inflation, the new president first proposed fiscal restraints and spending curbs and a 5% tax surcharge that got nowhere in the Senate and House. Congress again rebuffed Ford in the spring of 1975 when he appealed for emergency military aid to help the governments of South Vietnam and Cambodia resist massive Communist offensives.

In November 1974, Ford visited Japan, South Korea, and the Soviet Union, where he and Soviet leader Leonid I. Brezhnev conferred in Vladivostok and reached a tentative agreement to limit the number of strategic offensive nuclear weapons. It was Ford's first meeting as president with Brezhnev, who planned a return visit to Washington in the fall of 1975.

Politically, Ford's fortunes improved steadily in the first half of 1975. Badly divided Democrats in Congress were unable to muster votes to override his vetoes of spending bills that exceeded his budget. He faced some right-wing opposition in his own party, but moved to pre-empt it with an early announcement—on July 8, 1975—of his intention to be a candidate in 1976.

Early state primaries in 1976 suggested an easy victory for Ford despite Ronald Reagan's bitter attacks on administration foreign policy and defense programs. But later Reagan primary successes threatened the President's lead. At the Kansas City convention, Ford was nominated by the narrow margin of 1,187 to 1,070. But Reagan had moved the party to the right, and Ford himself was regarded as a caretaker president lacking in strength and vision. He was defeated in November by Jimmy Carter.

In 1948, Ford married Elizabeth Anne (Betty) Bloomer. They had four children, Michael Gerald, John Gardner, Steven Meigs, and Susan Elizabeth.

JAMES EARL CARTER, JR., was born in the tiny village of Plains, Ga., Oct. 1, 1924, and grew up on the family farm at nearby Archery. Both parents were fifth-generation Georgians. His father, James Earl Carter, was known as a segregationist, but treated his black and white workers equally. Carter's mother, Lillian Gordy, was a matriarchal presence in home and community and opposed the then-prevailing code of racial inequality. The future President was baptized in 1935 in the conservative Southern Baptist Church and spoke often of being a "born again" Christian, although committed to the separation of church and state.

Carter married Rosalynn Smith, a neighbor, in 1946. Their first child, John William, was born a year later in Portsmouth, Va. Their other children are James Earl III, born in Honolulu in 1950; Donnel Jeffrey, born in New London, Conn., in 1952, and Amy Lynn, born in Plains in 1967.

In 1946 Carter was graduated from the U.S. Naval Academy at Annapolis and served in the nuclear-submarine program under Adm. Hyman G. Rickover. In 1954, after his father's death, he resigned from the Navy to take over the family's flourishing warehouse and cotton gin, with several thousand acres for growing seed peanuts.

Carter was elected to the Georgia Senate in 1962. In 1966 he lost the race for Governor, but was elected in 1970. His term brought a state government reorganization, sharply reduced agencies, increased economy and efficiency, and new social programs, all with no general tax increase. In 1972 the peanut farmer-politician set his sights on the Presidency and in 1974 built a base for himself as he criss-crossed the country as chairman of the Democratic Campaign Committee, appealing for revival and reform. In 1975 his image as a typical Southern white was erased when he won support of most of the old Southern civil-rights coalition after endorsement by Rep. Andrew Young, black Democrat from Atlanta, who had been the closest aide to the Rev. Martin Luther King, Jr. At Carter's 1971 inauguration as Governor he had called for an end to all forms of racial discrimination.

In the 1976 spring primaries, he won 19 out of 31 with a broad appeal to conservatives and liberals, black and white, poor and well-to-do. Throughout his campaigning Carter set forth his policies in his soft Southern voice, and with his electric-blue stare faced down skeptics who joked about "Jimmy Who?" His toothy smile became his trademark. He was nominated on the first roll-call vote of the 1976 Bicentennial Democratic National Convention in New York, and defeated Gerald R. Ford in November. Likewise, in 1980 he was renominated on the first ballot after vanquishing Senator Edward M. Kennedy of Massachusetts in the primaries. At the convention he defeated the Kennedy forces in their attempt to block a party rule that bound a large majority of pledged delegates to vote for Carter. In the election campaign, Carter attacked his rivals, Ronald Reagan and John B. Anderson, independent, with the warning that a Reagan Republican victory would heighten the risk of war and impede civil rights and economic opportunity. In November Carter lost to Reagan, who won 489 Electoral College votes and 51% of the popular tally, to 49 electoral votes and 41% for Carter.

In his one term, Carter fought hard for his programs against resistance from an independent-minded Democratic Congress that frustrated many pet projects although it overrode only two vetoes. Many of his difficulties were traced to his aides' brusqueness in dealing with Capitol Hill and insensitivity to Congressional feelings and tradition. Observers generally viewed public dissatisfaction with the "stagflation" economy as a principal factor in his defeat. Others included his jittery performance in the debate Oct. 28 with Reagan and the final uncertainties in the negotiations for freeing the Iranians' hostages, along with earlier staff problems, friction with Congress, long gasoline lines, and the months-long Iranian crisis, including the abortive sally in April 1980 to free the hostages. The President, however, did deflect criticism resulting from the activities of his brother, Billy. Yet, assessments of his record noted many positive elements. There was, for one thing, peace throughout his term, with no American combat deaths and with a brake on the advocates of force. Regarded as perhaps his greatest personal achievements were the Camp David accords between Israel and Egypt and the resulting treaty—the first between Israel and an Arab neighbor. The treaty with China and the Panama Canal treaties were also major achievements. Carter worked for nuclear-arms control. His concern for international human rights was credited with saving lives and reducing torture, and he supported the British policy that ended internecine warfare in Rhodesia, now Zimbabwe. Domestically, his environmental record was a major accomplishment. His judicial appointments won acclaim; the Southerner who had forsworn racism made 265 choices for the Federal bench that included minority members and women. On energy, he ended by price decontrols the practice of holding U.S. petroleum prices far below world levels.

—Arthur P. Reed, Jr.

RONALD WILSON REAGAN rode to the Presidency in 1980 on a tide of resurgent right-wing sentiment among an electorate battered by winds of unwanted change, longing for a distant, simpler era.

He left office in January 1989 with two-thirds of the American people approving his performance during his two terms. It was the highest rating for any retiring President since World War II. In his farewell speech, Reagan exhorted the nation to cling to the revival of patriotism that he had fostered. And he spoke proudly of the economic recovery during his Administrations, although regretting the huge budget deficit, for which, in part, many blamed his policies.

Reagan had retained the public's affection as he applied his political magic to policy goals. His place in history will rest, perhaps, on the short- and intermediate-range missile treaty consummated on a cordial visit to the Soviet Union that he had once reviled as an "evil empire." Its provisions, including a ground-breaking agreement on verification inspection, were formulated in four days of summit talks in Moscow in May 1988 with the Soviet leader, Mikhail S. Gorbachev.

And Reagan can point to numerous domestic achievements: sharp cuts in income tax rates, sweeping tax reform; creating economic growth without inflation, reducing the unemployment rate, among others. He failed, however, to win the "Reagan Revolution" on such issues as abortion and school prayer, and he seemed aloof from "sleazy" conduct by some top officials.

In his final months Reagan campaigned aggressively to win election as President for his two-term Vice President, George Bush.

Reagan's popularity with the public dipped sharply in 1986 when the Iran-Contra scandal broke, shortly after the Democrats gained control of the Senate. Observers agreed that Reagan's presidency had been weakened, if temporarily, by the two unrelated events. Then the weeks-long Congressional hearings in the summer of 1987 heard an array of Administration officials, present and former, tell their tales of a White House riven by deceit and undercover maneuvering. Yet no breath of illegality touched the President's personal reputation; on Aug. 12, 1987, he told the nation that he had not known of questionable activities but agreed that he was "ultimately accountable."

Ronald Reagan, actor turned politician, New Dealer turned conservative, came to the films and politics from a thoroughly Middle-American background—middle class, Middle West and small town. He was born in Tampico, Ill., Feb. 6, 1911, the second son of John Edward Reagan and Nelle Wilson Reagan, and the family later moved to Dixon, Ill. The father, of Irish descent, was a shop clerk and merchant with Democratic sympathies. It was an impoverished family; young Ronald sold homemade popcorn at high school games and worked as a lifeguard to earn money for his college tuition. When the father got a New Deal WPA job, the future President became an ardent Roosevelt Democrat.

Reagan won a B.A. degree in 1932 from Eureka (Ill.) College, where a photographic memory aided in his studies and in debating and college theatricals. In a Depression year, he was making $100 a week as a sports announcer for radio station WHO in Des Moines, Iowa, from 1932 to 1937. His career as a film and TV actor stretched from 1937 to 1966, and his salary climbed to $3,500 a week. As a World War II captain in Army film studios, Reagan recoiled from what he saw as the laziness of Civil Service workers, and moved to the Right. As president of the Screen Actors Guild, he resisted what he considered a Communist plot to subvert the film industry. With advancing age, Reagan left leading-man roles and became a television spokesman for the General Electric Company at $150,000.

With oratorical skill his trademark, Reagan became an active Republican. At the behest of a small group of conservative Southern California businessmen, he ran for governor with a pledge to cut spending, and was elected by almost a million votes over the political veteran, Democratic Gov. Edmund G. Brown, father of the later governor.

In the 1980 election battle against Jimmy Carter, Reagan broadened his appeal by espousing moderate policies, gaining much of his support from disaffected Democrats and blue-collar workers. The incoming Administration immediately set out to "turn the government around" with a new economic program. Over strenuous Congressional opposition, Reagan triumphed on his "supply side" theory to stimulate production and control inflation through tax cuts and sharp reductions in government spending.

The President won high acclaim for his nomination of Sandra Day O'Connor as the first woman on the Supreme Court. His later nominations met increasing opposition but did much to tilt the Court's orientation to the Right.

In 1982, the President's popularity had slipped as the economy declined into the worst recession in 40 years, with persistent high unemployment and interest rates. Initial support for "supply side" economics faded but the President won crucial battles in Congress.

Internationally, Reagan confronted numerous critical problems in his first term. The successful invasion of Grenada accomplished much diplomatically. But the intervention in Lebanon and the withdrawal of Marines after a disastrous terrorist attack were regarded as military failures.

The popular President won reelection in the 1984 landslide, with the economy improving and inflation under control. Domestically, a tax reform bill that Reagan backed became law. But the constantly growing budget deficit remained a constant irritant, with the President and Congress persistently at odds over priorities in spending for defense and domestic programs. His foreign policy met stiffening opposition, with Congress increasingly reluctant to increase spending for the Nicarguan "Contras" and the Pentagon and to expand the development of the MX missile. But even severe critics praised Reagan's restrained but decisive handling of the crisis following the hijacking of an American plane in Beirut by Moslem extremists. The attack on Libya in April 1986 galvanized the nation, although it drew scathing disapproval from the NATO alliance.

Barely three months into his first term, Reagan was the target of an assassin's bullet; his courageous comeback won public admiration.

Reagan is devoted to his wife, Nancy, whom he married after his divorce from the screen actress Jane Wyman. The children of the first marriage are Maureen, his daughter by Miss Wyman, and Michael, an adopted son. In the present marriage the children are Patricia and Ron.

—Arthur P. Reed, Jr.

GEORGE H. BUSH became President on January 20, 1989, with his theme harmony and conciliation after the often-turbulent Reagan years. With his calm and unassuming manner, he emerged from his subordinate Vice-Presidential role with an air of quiet authority. His Inaugural address emphasized "A new breeze is blowing, and the old bipartisanship must be made new again."

In his first months, the President, the nation's 41st, established himself as his own man and all but erased memories of what many had regarded as his fiercely abrasive Presidential election campaign of 1988 and questionable tactics against his Democratic opponent. People liked his easy style and readiness to compromise even as he remained a staunch conservative, although that readiness had disconcerted some conservatives.

Bush's early Cabinet choices reflected a pragmatic desire for an efficient nonideological Government. And with his usual cautious instinct, in 1990 he nominated to the Supreme Court the scholarly David H. Souter, with broadly conservative views. Souter was confirmed without a bruising battle.

In his first year, Bush, a World War II hero, had won plaudits at home and abroad for his confident, competent conduct at the NATO 40th anniversary summit meeting in Brussels, the Paris economic conference, on his tour of Eastern Europe, and at the Malta conference with Gorbachev. Grave challenges in that year were the Lebanese hostage crisis and the ongoing war on the drug traffic.

Domestically, Bush had to cope with such issues as the *Exxon Valdez* oil spill in Alaska and the dispute over flag-burning restrictions, which was resolved, if only for a time, in mid-1990.

But in his second year, 1990, the President confronted a mounting array of problems, the most critical being on the domestic side. Chief among them were the staggering and mushrooming budget deficit and the savings and loan crisis. Other vexing issues were the question of cutting defense expenditures with consequent economic dislocation, the war on drugs and environmental matters.

At home, the President's popularity dipped sharply from its near-record public approval following the invasion of Panama in late 1989. This plunge followed Bush's recantation of his campaign "no new taxes" pledge as he sat down with Congressional leaders to tame the budge deficit and deal with a faltering economy.

In 1991, the 67-year-old President emerged as the leader of an international coalition of Western democracies, Japan, and even some Arab states that freed invaded Kuwait and vanquished, at least for a time, Iraq's President Saddam Hussein and his armies.

A nation grateful at feeling the end of the "Vietnam syndrome" gave the President an over-all rating of 89 percent in a Gallup poll in March after the end of the war. The approval rate fell as the year went on, but a solid majority continued to approve the President's performance, although with growing concern about the faltering economy and other domestic problems. And there were nagging doubts about the Persian Gulf war, its motives and conduct, and about the ensuing refugee crisis.

A major Bush accomplishment in 1991 was the Strategic Arms Reduction Treaty (Start), signed in July with Soviet President Mikhail S. Gorbachev at their fourth summit conference, marking the end of the long weapons buildup. Succeeding events in the Soviet Union and the apparent disintegration of the Communist empire could only enhance his status.

The year also saw the President undergoing treatment for Graves' disease, a thyroid disorder, from which he suffered serious side effects.

Bush, scion of an aristocratic New England family, came to the White House after a long career in public service, in which he held top positions in national and international organizations. As Vice President, he avoided the appearance of direct involvement in the Iran-Contra affair while not seeming to shy away from the President.

Earlier, in the 1960s, Bush won two contests for a Texas Republican seat in the House of Representatives, but lost two bids for a Senate seat and one for the Presidency. After his second race for the Senate, President Nixon appointed him U.S. delegate to the United Nations with the rank of Ambassador and he later became Republican National Chairman. He headed the United States liaison office in Beijing before becoming Director of Central Intelligence.

In 1980 Bush became Reagan's running mate despite earlier criticism of Reagan "voodoo economics" and by the 1984 election had won acclaim for devotion to Reagan's conservative agenda despite his own reputation as somewhat more liberally inclined. Nevertheless, die-hard right-wingers could find satisfaction in Bush's war record and his Government service, particularly with the C.I.A. Throughout he remained influential in White House decisions, particularly in foreign affairs.

In the 1988 campaign, Bush's choice of Senator Dan Quayle of Indiana for Vice President surprised his friends and provoked criticism and ridicule that continued even after the Administration was established in office. Nonetheless Bush strongly defended his choice.

In the 1992 Presidential election, Bush was defeated by Gov. Bill Clinton of Arkansas.

The future President joined the Navy after war broke out and at 18 became the Navy's youngest commissioned pilot, serving from 1942 to 1945. The man later derided by some as a "wimp" fought the Japanese on 58 missions and was shot down once. He won the Distinguished Flying Cross.

Throughout his whole career, Bush had the backing of an established family, headed by his father, the autocratic and wealthy Prescott Bush, who was elected to the Senate from Connecticut in 1952. And his family helped the young patrician became established in his early business ventures, a rich uncle raising most of the capital required for founding a new oil company in Texas.

George Herbert Walker Bush was born June 12, 1924, in Milton, Mass., to Prescott and Dorothy Bush. The family later moved to Connecticut. The youth studied at the elite Phillips Academy in Andover, Mass., before entering the Navy.

After the war, Bush earned an economics degree and a Phi Beta Kappa key in two and a half years at Yale University. While there he captained the baseball team and was initiated into "Skull and Bones," the prestigious Yale secret society.

In 1945 Bush married Barbara Pierce of Rye, N.Y., daughter of a magazine publisher. With his bride, Bush moved to Texas instead of entering his father's investment banking business. There he founded his oil company and in 1980 reported an estimated wealth of $1.4 million.

The Bushes have lived in 17 cities and more than a score of homes and have traveled in as many countries. In her husband's frequent absences during the early years, Mrs. Bush was often matriarch of a family of four boys and a girl. Bush is close to his immediate family and to 10 grandchildren, a sister, and three brothers.

After the Clinton inauguration in January, the Bushes flew to Houston, Texas, where they had rented a home. —*Arthur P. Reed, Jr.*

WILLIAM J. CLINTON became the 42nd U.S. President after a turbulent political campaign, only to face an array of daunting problems, with many setbacks and few victories. Almost immediately after his Inauguration in January 1993 he became embroiled with the military leadership over the politically sensitive issue of his campaign pledge to allow homosexuals to serve openly in the armed forces. He finally agreed to a compromise. And soon the new Administration was rocked by a "Nannygate" scandal, which caused his first two choices for Attorney General to fall victims to allegations concerning their employment of illegal aliens as household workers.

And early in his tenure, the new President encountered a major defeat when Congress rejected his program for economic stimulus. Later, he escaped a major disaster when the House and Senate passed his budget by the narrowest of margins. Even Democrats in Congress were restive at implementing Clinton's economic package. Politics was one factor. And conservatives, including Democrats, demanded more spending cuts, fewer taxes and caps on entitlement programs.

In his second year, Clinton faced persistent troubles on the domestic front, with acrimonious battles raging over health care, welfare reform, crime prevention, and White House personnel problems. Clinton could count a major victory in mid-term with the passage of the North American Free Trade Agreement. (NAFTA).

Among other Clinton initiatives approved by Congress were a deficit reduction bill, rules allowing abortion counseling in federally funded clinics, a waiting period for handgun purchases, and a national service program. On September 19, his Administration succeeded in getting Haiti's military rulers to step down by October 15, and restore Haiti's exiled president, Rev. Jean-Bertrand Aristide, to power.

And a major diplomatic success in the summer of 1994 was the Israeli-Jordan peace agreement, ending years of hostility, signed at the White House by Prime Minister Yitzhak Rabin and King Hussein as a beaming President watched.

The Arkansas Governor, elected on a platform stressing domestic economic issues, soon had to wrestle with the new, to him, field of international affairs. These grew more complicated and critical as his second year wore on. Such disparate places as Bosnia, Somalia, Rwanda, Cuba, and Haiti remained or became daily headaches.

Early in his presidency, Clinton succeeded, at least for a time, in shoring up Russia's President Yeltsin with promises of economic aid. But the agonizing situation in the former Yugoslavia immediately taxed the full powers of the new President and his advisers, particularly in view of the reluctance of the Western Allies to deal harshly with aggressors in Bosnia and Herzegovina.

In 1995, the President faced a hostile Congress, elected in the November 1994 Republican sweep. The year saw a tug-of-war between the White House and Capitol Hill over budget balancing and other key points of the Victorious G.O.P.'s "Contract With America." Foreign policy, particularly the U.S. stance toward the fighting in Bosnia and Herzegovina, was also a point of friction, with the President accused of vacillation and indecision and with Congress voting to lift unilaterally the embargo on arms for the Muslims. Welfare reform, a key point in the Clinton agenda, was held up in Congress, even though the President sought a compromise with Senate leaders.

Among other matters, the President offered his own plan for a balanced budget, calling for $1.1-trillion in spending cuts over 10 years. He established full diplomatic relations with Vietnam and met President Yeltsin in Moscow. And he sparked a crusade against teen-age smoking. On the negative side, Clinton's choice for Surgeon General was rejected in the Senate. And he and Hillary Rodham Clinton were still embroiled in the Whitewater affair, brushed by Congressional hearings on the Arkansas real estate deal before the 1992 Presidential election.

Clinton became the Democratic Presidential candidate after fighting back attacks on his personal life and public conduct to win a series of bruising primary contests. As a politician—and as a person—he displayed an empathy for the feelings of others and a genius for compromise that in his thinking and actions blended belief in programs for social welfare with fiscal responsibility and economic growth. These ideas had guided his role in the 1980s in striving to rebuild a Democratic Party that had lost key White House races.

The issue of "character" repeatedly haunted him as he sought the Presidency. He had to rebut allegations of adultery and in a television interview he and his wife reaffirmed their solid relationship.

Another target was Clinton's actions in the Vietnam War, which he actively opposed, and like many young men of his generation faced a series of unpalatable choices. In the event, he chose to sign a letter, much publicized in the primary campaign, signifying his intention of avoiding the draft by joining the Reserve Officers Training Corps. But he canceled his plans when draft calls were reduced.

After a series of primary victories, Clinton was nominated at the Democratic National Convention in New York. The platform reflected the nominee's own instinct for moderation in its appeal to middle-class values. Clinton's acceptance speech denounced years of Republican rule and President Bush's "failed economic policy." The speech reflected Clinton's record as Governor and earlier campaign positions. He had supported the death penalty and the use of force in the Persian Gulf.

He favored laws requiring minors seeking abortion to have the consent of parents or a judge. In the campaign he advocated a 10 percent middle-class tax cut and an $800-per-child tax credit. And he supported job training and health care for welfare recipients.

Clinton was born in Hope, Ark., on August 19, 1946, named William Jefferson Blythe 3rd for his father, who had been killed in an automobile accident before William's birth. His mother, Virginia Kelly, set an example of stamina by training to become a nurse anesthetist. The future Governor later changed his name to that of his stepfather, Roger Clinton, a car dealer. Meanwhile the family had moved to Hot Springs, Ark.

In high school young Clinton thought of becoming a doctor, but politics beckoned after a meeting with President John F. Kennedy in Washington on a Boys' Nation trip. He won a B.S. in international affairs at Georgetown University, where he spent his junior year working for Arkansas Senator J. William Fulbright, graduating in 1968. He was a Rhodes scholar at Oxford 1968–70. He then attended Yale Law School, where he met his future wife, Hillary Rodham, a Wellesley graduate. In 1974–76 he taught at the University of Arkansas and in 1976 was elected state Attorney General.

In 1979 he was elected Governor, at 32 the nation's youngest, but was defeated for re-election by voters irate at a rise in the state's automobile license fees.

In 1982 he was elected again. This time he reined in liberal tendencies to accommodate the conservative bent of the voters.

Hillary retained her maiden name until her husband's defeat for Governor, when it seemed politic to adopt his. The couple have one child, Chelsea, 15.

—*Arthur P. Reed, Jr.*

Milestones in the Gay Rights Movement

Source: Excerpted from *The Reader's Companion to American History.*
Copyright © 1991 by Houghton Mifflin Company.

Late in the [19th] century, as large cities allowed for greater anonymity, as wage labor apart from family became common, and as more women were drawn out of the home, evidence of a new pattern of homosexual expression surfaced. . . .

At first, these individuals developed ways of meeting one another and institutions to foster a sense of identity. . . . By 1915, one participant in this new gay world was referring to it as "a community distinctly organized." For the most part hidden from view because of social hostility, an urban gay subculture had come into existence by the 1920s and 1930s.

World War II served as a critical divide in the social history of homosexuality. Large numbers of the young left families, small towns, and closely knit ethnic neighborhoods to enter a sex-segregated military or to migrate to larger cities for wartime employment. . . .

After the war, many of them made choices designed to support their gay identities. Pat Bond, a woman from Iowa who first met other lesbians while in the military, decided to stay in San Francisco after her discharge. [Donald] Vining remained in New York City rather than return to his small hometown in New Jersey. They, along with countless others, sustained a vibrant gay subculture that revolved around bars and friendship networks. Many cities saw their first gay bars during the 1940s. . . .

This new visibility provoked latent cultural prejudices. . . . Firings from government jobs and purges from the military intensified in the 1950s. President Dwight D. Eisenhower issued an executive order in 1953 barring gay men and lesbians from all federal jobs. Many state and local governments and private corporations followed suit. The FBI began a surveillance program against homosexuals.

The lead taken by the federal government encouraged local police forces to harass gay citizens. Vice officers regularly raided gay bars, sometimes arresting dozens of men and women on a single night. . . . Under these conditions, some gays began to organize politically. In November 1950 in Los Angeles, a small group of men led by Harry Hay and Chuck Rowland met to form what would become the Mattachine Society. Mostly male in membership, it was joined in 1955 by a lesbian organization in San Francisco, the Daughters of Bilitis, founded by Del Martin and Phyllis Lyon. In the 1950s these organizations remained small, but they established chapters in several cities and published magazines that were a beacon of hope to the readers.

In the 1960s, influenced by the model of a militant black civil rights movement, the "homophile movement," as the participants dubbed it, became more visible. Activists, such as Franklin Kameny and Barbara Gittings, picketed government agencies in Washington to protest discriminatory employment policies. In San Francisco, Martin, Lyon, and others targeted police harassment. By 1969, perhaps fifty homophile organizations existed in the United States, with memberships of a few thousand.

Then, on Friday evening, June 27, 1969, the police in New York City raided a Greenwich Village gay bar, the Stonewall Inn. Contrary to expectations, the patrons fought back, provoking three nights of rioting in the area accompanied by the appearance of "gay power" slogans on the buildings. Almost overnight, a massive grassroots gay liberations movement was born. Owing much to the radical protest of blacks, women, and college students in the 1960s, gays challenged all forms of hostility and punishment meted out by society. Choosing to "come out of the closet" and publicly proclaim their identity, they ushered in a social change movement that has grown substantially. By 1973, there were almost eight hundred gay and lesbian organizations in the United States; by 1990, the number was several thousand. By 1970, 5,000 gay men and lesbians marched in New York City to commemorate the first anniversary of the Stonewall Riots; in October 1987, over 600,000 marched in Washington, to demand equality.

The changes were far-reaching. Over the next two decades, half the states decriminalized homosexual behavior, and police harassment was sharply contained. Many large cities included sexual orientation in their civil rights statutes, as did Wisconsin and Massachusetts, first among the states to do so. . . . [In 1975] the Civil Service Commission eliminated the ban on the employment of homosexuals in most federal jobs. Many of the nation's religious denominations engaged in spirited debates about the morality of homosexuality, and some, like Unitarianism and Reformed Judaism, opened their doors to gay and lesbian ministers and rabbis. The lesbian and gay world was no longer an underground subculture but, in larger cities especially, a well-organized community, with businesses, political clubs, social service agencies, community centers, and religious congregations bringing people together. In a number of places, openly gay candidates ran for elective office and won.

These changes spawned opposition. In 1977 the singer Anita Bryant led a campaign to repeal a gay rights ordinance in Dade County, Florida. Her success encouraged others, and by the early 1980s, a well-organized conservative force had materialized to target the gay rights movement. Politicians, such as Senator Jesse Helms of North Carolina, and fundamentalist ministers, such as Jerry Falwell of Lynchburg, Virginia, who formed Moral Majority, Inc., joined forces to slow the progress of the gay movement.

The onset of the AIDS epidemic in the 1980s, although it intensified the antigay rhetoric of the New Right, also stimulated further organizing within the gay community. AIDS made political mobilization a matter of life and death. With a large majority of the cases striking male homosexuals, the gay community in short order created a host of organizations, such as the Gay Men's Health Crisis in New York City, to provide services and assistance to those infected. Local and national gay civil rights groups also grew in size and number, as the community sought to increase funding for research and education and to win protection against discrimination. A personal and social tragedy of immense proportions, AIDS paradoxically strengthened the political arm of the gay movement. □

Firsts in America

This selection is based on our editorial judgment. Other sources may list different firsts.

Admiral in U.S. Navy: David Glasgow Farragut, 1866.

Air–mail route, first transcontinental: Between New York City and San Francisco, 1920.

Assembly, representative: House of Burgesses, founded in Virginia, 1619.

Bank established: Bank of North America, Philadelphia, 1781.

Birth in America to English parents: Virginia Dare, born Roanoke Island, N.C., 1587.

Black newspaper: *Freedom's Journal,* 1827, edited by John B. Russworm.

Black U.S. diplomat: Ebenezer D. Bassett, 1869, minister-resident to Haiti.

Black elected governor of a state: L. Douglas Wilder, Virginia, 1990.

Black elected to U.S. Senate: Hiram Revels, 1870, Mississippi.

Black elected to U.S. House of Representatives: Jefferson Long, Georgia, 1870.

Black associate justice of U.S. Supreme Court: Thurgood Marshall, Oct. 2, 1967.

Black U.S. cabinet minister: Robert C. Weaver, 1966, Secretary of the Department of Housing and Urban Development.

Botanic garden: Established by John Bartram in Philadelphia, 1728 and is still in existence in its original location.

Cartoon, colored: "The Yellow Kid," by Richard Outcault, in *New York World,* 1895.

College: Harvard, founded 1636.

College to confer degrees on women: Oberlin (Ohio) College, 1841.

College to establish coeducation: Oberlin (Ohio) College, 1833.

Electrocution of a criminal: William Kemmler in Auburn Prison, Auburn, N.Y., Aug. 6, 1890.

Five and Ten Cents Store: Founded by Frank Woolworth, Utica, N.Y., 1879 (moved to Lancaster, Pa., same year).

Fraternity, Greek-letter: Phi Beta Kappa; founded Dec. 5, 1776, at College of William and Mary.

Gay and lesbian civil rights advocacy organization: National Gay and Lesbian Task Force, founded in New York City, 1973.

Gay Power: Rioting following police raid on NYC gay bar mobilizes gay community and leads to birth of gay liberation movement, June 27, 1969.

Homosexual, acknowledged, elected to high local office: Harvey Milk, 1977, San Francisco Board of Supervisors.

Law to be declared unconstitutional by U.S. Supreme Court: Judiciary Act of 1789. Case: *Marbury* v. *Madison,* 1803.

Library, circulating: Philadelphia, 1731.

Newspaper, illustrated daily: *New York Daily Graphic,* 1873.

Newspaper published daily: *Pennsylvania Packet and General Advertiser,* Philadelphia, Sept., 1784.

Newspaper published over a continuous period: *The Boston News–Letter,* April, 1704.

Newsreel: Pathé Frères of Paris, in 1910, circulated a weekly issue of their *Pathé Journal.*

Oil well, commercial: Titusville, Pa., 1859.

Panel quiz show on radio: *Information Please,* May 17, 1938.

Postage stamps issued: 1847.

Public School: Boston Latin School, Boston, 1635.

Radio station licensed: KDKA, Pittsburgh, Pa., Oct. 27, 1920.

Railroad, transcontinental: Central Pacific and Union Pacific railroads, joined at Promontory, Utah, May 10, 1869.

Savings bank: The Provident Institute for Savings, Boston, 1816.

Science museum: Founded by Charleston (S.C.) Library Society, 1773.

Skyscraper: Home Insurance Co., Chicago, 1885 (10 floors, 2 added later).

Slaves brought into America: At Jamestown, Va., 1619, from a Dutch ship.

Sorority: Kappa Alpha Theta, at De Pauw University, 1870.

State to abolish capital punishment: Michigan, 1847.

State to enter Union after original 13: Vermont, 1791.

Steam–heated building: Eastern Hotel, Boston, 1845.

Steam railroad (carried passengers and freight): Baltimore & Ohio, 1830.

Strike on record by union: Journeymen Printers, New York City, 1776.

Subway: Opened in Boston, 1897.

"Tabloid" picture newspaper: *The Illustrated Daily News* (now *The Daily News*), New York City, 1919.

Vaudeville theater: Gaiety Museum, Boston, 1883.

Woman astronaut to ride in space: Dr. Sally K. Ride, 1983.

Woman astronaut to walk in space: Dr. Kathryn D. Sullivan, 1984.

Woman cabinet member: Frances Perkins, Secretary of Labor, 1933.

Woman candidate for President: Victoria Claflin Woodhull, nominated by National Woman's Suffrage Assn. on ticket of Nation Radical Reformers, 1872.

Woman candidate for Vice–President: Geraldine A. Ferraro, nominated on a major party ticket, Democratic Party, 1984.

Woman doctor of medicine: Elizabeth Blackwell; M.D. from Geneva Medical College of Western New York, 1849.

Woman elected governor of a state: Nellie Tayloe Ross, Wyoming, 1925.

Woman elected to U.S. Senate: Hattie Caraway, Arkansas; elected Nov., 1932.

Woman graduate of law school: Ada H. Kepley, Union College of Law, Chicago, 1870.

Woman member of U.S. House of Representatives: Jeannette Rankin; elected Nov., 1916.

Woman member of U.S. Senate: Rebecca Latimer Felton of Georgia; appointed Oct. 3, 1922.

Woman member of U.S. Supreme Court: Sandra Day O'Connor; appointed July 1981.

Woman suffrage granted: Wyoming Territory, 1869.

Written constitution: *Fundamental Orders of Connecticut,* 1639.

NATIVE AMERICANS

The 1990 census showed that nearly two million American Indians, Eskimos, and Aleuts lived in the United States. Of these, 437,079 American Indians, 182 Eskimos, and 97 Aleuts lived on reservations and trust lands.

Population

The 1890 census counted 248,000 American Indians throughout the country. In the first half of this century, their numbers increased slowly until 1950 when a rapid growth began reaching 1,878,285 in 1990. More than half of the American Indian population lived in just six states—Oklahoma, California, Arizona, New Mexico, Alaska, and Washington. Projections show that the American Indian population will reach 4.6 million by 2050.

In 1990, 39% of the American Indian, Eskimo, and Aleut population was under 20 years old compared with 29% of the rest of the Nation. About eight percent of all American Indians were 60 years old and over in 1990, about half the proportion (17%) for the total population.

Female Householder Families

Among the Nation's 442,000 American Indian families in 1990, only six in ten were married-couple families compared with about eight in ten of the Nation's 64.5 million families. Consistent with the national trend, the number of American Indian families maintained by a woman without a husband present increased during the last decade and reached 27% in 1990. This is considerably higher than the national figure of 17%.

The Sioux (36%) and the Chippewa (33.1%) had the largest proportions of families maintained by women without husbands.

Male Householder Families

The proportions of American Indian families maintained by men without wives for the ten largest tribes were: Navajo (10.3%), Sioux (9.8%), Pueblo (9.6%), Chippewa (8.5%), Apache (8.4%), Lumbee (7.6%), Iroquois (7.0%), Cherokee (6.1%), Choctaw (4.8%), and Creek (4.5%).

Educational Attainment

The educational attainment levels of American Indians, Eskimos, and Aleuts improved significantly during the 1980s. Sixty-six percent of American Indians 25 years old and over were high school graduates or higher in 1990 compared with only 56% in 1980. The total U.S. figure was 75%. About nine percent completed a bachelor's degree or higher compared with 20% for the total U.S. population.

The Creek (73.2%), Iroquois (71.9%), Pueblo (71.5%), Choctaw (70.3%), Chippewa (69.7%), Sioux (69.7%), and Cherokee (68.2%) all had about the same percentage of high school graduates, followed by the Apache (63.8%), Lumbee (51.6%), and Navajo (51.0%).

More than ten percent of the American Indian population had college degrees in four of the ten largest tribes—Choctaw (13.3%), Creek (12.7%), Iroquois (11.3%), and Cherokee (11.1%).

Labor Force

Sixty-two percent, including Eskimos and Aleuts, 16 years old and over were in the labor force in 1990, three percentage points below the 65% for the total population. Sixty-nine percent of American Indian males 16 years old and over were in the labor force compared with more than 74% for all U.S. males.

American Indian women have shared in the national trend of increased labor force participation by women. Their numbers in the work force grew from 48% in 1980 to 55% in 1990 compared with 57% for all women in 1990.

Occupations

The census reported that 729,000 American Indians, including Eskimos and Aleuts, were employed. They had fewer jobs in managerial and professional specialty occupations than that of the total population. This was also true for technical, sales, and administrative support jobs.

A larger proportion of American Indians than the overall population were employed in service occupations; farming, forestry, and fishing; precision production, craft, and repair occupations; or as operators, fabricators, and laborers.

Income

In 1990, the median family income in the U.S. was $35,225. The median family income of American Indians, Eskimos, and Aleuts was $21,750. Stated another way, for every $100 that U.S. families received, American Indian families received $62. The median income of American Indian married-couple families was $28,287, or 71% of the $39,584 median for all married-couple families.

Twenty-seven percent of all American Indian families were maintained by a female householder with no husband present. The median income for these families was $10,742, about 62% of the $17,414 median for all families maintained by women without husbands.

The tribe with the highest median family income in 1989 was the Iroquois ($27,025), and the Navajo had the lowest at $13,940, according to a November 1994 census report.

The report also showed that the Iroquois ($10,568) and the Cherokee ($10,469) tribes had the highest per capita incomes, and the Navajo ($4,788) had the lowest.

Poverty

Fifty-one percent of those residing on reservations and trust lands were living below the poverty level in 1989. The Hopi, Blackfeet, Zuni Pueblo, and Fort Apache Reservations had the lowest percentages of American Indians in poverty, about 50%.

Overall, about 603,000, or 31% were living below the poverty level compared to the national poverty rate of about 13% for the same period. Twenty-seven percent, or 125,000 American Indian families, were in poverty in 1989 compared with ten percent of all families.

Ten Largest American Indian Tribes: 1990
(Thousands)

Tribe	Value
Cherokee	369
Navajo	225
Chippewa	106
Sioux[1]	107
Choctaw	86.2
Pueblo	55.3
Apache	53
Iroquois[2]	53
Lumbee	51
Creek	46

1. Any entry with the spelling "Siouan" was miscoded to Sioux in North Carolina. 2. Reporting and/or processing problems have affected the data for this tribe. *Source:* U.S. Department of Commerce, Bureau of the Census.

Fifty percent of American Indian families maintained by females with no husband percent lived in poverty vs. 31% for all families maintained by women without husbands.

According to the 1990 census, the Navajo (48.8%) and the Sioux (44.4%) tribes had the highest proportions of people living in poverty, while the Iroquois had the lowest at 20.1 percent.

The tribes with the largest percentage of poor families were the Navajo (47.3%) and Lumbee (20.2%), and the Creek at 19.0 percent. The Iroquois had the lowest percent of poor families (17.3%).

Reservations and Trust Lands

Twenty-two percent, or 437,431, of all American Indians including Eskimos and Aleuts lived on reservations and trust lands in 1990. Reservations and trust lands are areas with boundaries established by treaty, statute, and/or executive or court order.

The per capita income in 1989 was about $4,478 for American Indians residing on all reservations and trust lands. On the ten largest reservations it ranged from $3,113 to $4,718. Blackfeet and Hopi had the highest per capita incomes, $4,718 and $4,566, respectively.

Ten percent of the total American Indian population lived in the Tribal Jurisdiction Statistical Areas in Oklahoma. Seven of the ten reservations and trust lands with the largest American Indian populations were entirely or partially located in Arizona.

School Enrollment

Overall, more than 31% of American Indians three years old and over living on reservations and trust lands were enrolled in elementary or high school. The enrollment rates for all American Indians three years old and over was 25%, higher than the U.S. population rate of 18%.

The proportion of adults 25 years old and older with high school diplomas or higher on the ten largest reservations and trust lands ranged from 37% to 66%. Overall, 54% of the adults were high school graduates or higher. Blackfeet and Hopi had the greatest proportions (66.3% and 62.6%) of high school graduates or higher.

ALASKA NATIVES
Population

The population rose by more than 50,000 persons (153%) between 1950 and 1990 and numbered 85,698 in 1990. The census reported that more than half of all Alaska Natives were Eskimos, about 36% were American Indians, and about 12% were Aleuts. The two main Eskimo groups, Inupiat and Yupik, are distinguished by their language and geography. The former live in the north and northwest parts of Alaska and speak Inupiaq, while the latter live in the south and southwest and speak Yupik.

The American Indian tribes are the Alaskan Athabaskan (11,696) in the central part of the State and the Tlingit (9,448), Tsimshian (1,653) and the Haida (1,083) in the southeast. The Aleuts (10,052) live mainly in the Aleutian Islands.

The median age of Alaska Natives was 24 years, compared with 29 years for the total State population and 33 years for the entire United States. About 44% were under 20 years old and seven percent were 60 years old and over.

Female Householder Families

Alaska Natives had proportionately fewer married-couple families and more families with a female householder and no husband present than the State as a whole. Only 58% of Alaska's 16,432 Native families consisted of a husband and wife compared with 80% of all families in Alaska. The Aleuts had the largest percentage of married-couple families among Alaska Natives.

The proportion of families with a female householder and no husband present was twice as high among Alaska Natives as Alaska's total population. Thirty-one percent of American Indian families, 28% of Eskimo families, and 26% of Aleut families were maintained by female householders with no husband present compared with 14% of all Alaska's families.

Education

Although Alaska Natives have made great strides in education during this century, they remain less likely to have high school diplomas and bachelor's degrees or higher than other Alaskans.

Sixty-three percent, 25 years old and over, had completed high school or higher compared with 87% statewide. Four percent were college graduates with a bachelor's degree or higher, while the statewide total was 23%.

Labor Force

Just 56% of the 54,614 Alaska Natives 16 years old and over were in the labor force compared with 75% of the State's total population. Fifty-one percent of all Alaska females 16 years old and over were in the labor force compared with 66% of all females in Alaska. Similarly, 61% of all Alaska Native males 16 years old and over were in the labor force in 1990 compared with 82% of all males in the State.

American Indians had the highest labor force participation rate of the three Alaska Native groups; this may be because they were more likely to live in urban areas where job opportunities were greater. Aleuts and Eskimos, who tend to live in rural areas, had lower rates.

Employment

Twenty percent of those 16 years old and over were in managerial and professional occupations compared with 30% of all workers in the State. However, Alaska Natives were as likely as the State's total population to work in technical, sales, and administrative jobs. About three of every ten workers in each population held such jobs. They were also more likely than the statewide population to be in service jobs and to be operators, fabricators, or laborers.

Income

Alaska, with a median family income of $46,581, had the highest income of any state in 1990. However, the median family income for Alaska natives was only $26,695. Aleut families earned an average of $36,472 followed by American Indians ($29,339) and Eskimos ($23,257). Among married-couple families, median income levels were $52,022 for the State and $37,406 for Alaska Natives.

Poverty

In 1989, 23% of Alaska Natives were poor compared with nine percent for the State as a whole. Twenty-eight percent of Eskimos lived in poverty compared with 20% of American Indians and 13% of Aleuts. Twenty-one percent of Native families and seven percent of families statewide lived below the poverty level. □

History: The Indigenous People of the Americas

Paleo-Indians

During the last Ice Age massive glaciers locked up so much water that the ocean level dropped. When that happened the Bering Strait between Asia and North America became dry land, a grassy "bridge" 1,000 miles wide between the two continents. The first humans in the Americas were probably hunters who wandered across the land bridge following herds of animals.

It is hard to say precisely when the first Indians arrived here from Asia. Some came as early as 20,000 or even 40,000 years ago. Most, however, moved into North America about 12,000 years ago.

At the height of the Ice Age the Paleo-Indians could go no farther than western Alaska, for walls of ice blocked their way. But about 12,000 years ago the climate began to warm up. As the glaciers started melting, great grassy corridors opened up between the mountains of ice. Bands of hunters migrated south through these corridors.

Hunter-Gatherers

As the climate warmed up, North America became drier. Within 2,000 years, the huge game animals became extinct. No one knows why for certain. Whatever happened, about 10,000 years ago the Paleo-Indians had to change their way of life to survive. Instead of depending on the meat of the giant mammoth, they learned to hunt smaller animals like deer. Their tools changed from huge throwing spears to small spears, and finally to the bow and arrow.

In adapting to a new environment, the Indians broadened their food-gathering patterns. Some came to depend on shellfish. Others became skilled at weaving nets to catch fish. People began to dig roots and gather berries, fruits, nuts, and grass seeds.

About 10,000 years ago agriculture began in the river valleys of the Near East with the domestication of both plants and animals. People of the Near East domesticated the wild grasses that became wheat and barley. By 5,000 years ago people had begun to cultivate rice in southern China. At about the same time, people in central Mexico began to sow the seeds of wild corn.

The cobs of this wild corn were tiny, about the size of a strawberry. Through selective breeding, the Indian farmers developed a corn cob like the one today. Although corn was first developed in central Mexico, its cultivation spread south to Peru and north to what is now the United States.

In time the Indians domesticated more than 100 plants. In Mexico people cultivated pumpkins, peppers, beans, and tomatoes. Indians in Peru domesticated gourds, lima beans, and potatoes. Other domestic plants once unique to the Western Hemisphere include pineapple, bananas, peanuts, tobacco, and cacao.

The Hohokam and Anasazi

Although scholars are still debating transoceanic diffusion, they do not question that Mesoamerican culture influenced Indian peoples to the north. The first influence was agriculture. The desert people of the Southwest began raising corn and squash 4,000 years ago. Later they learned to grow beans. Over time, they developed distinct farming cultures that depended on what the Indians called the Three Sisters—corn, squash, and beans.

The Hohokam people may have migrated from Mexico about 300 B.C. to settle in what is now central Arizona. To get water to their crops, they dug lengthy canals using only digging sticks as tools. The major canals in this system were more than 30 miles long.

The Hohokam culture broke up in the 1400s, perhaps because turbulent times in Mexico cut off trade and contact. The Hohokam people then became more like their neighbors. They survived through hunting, gathering, and a little farming.

During the same centuries the Anasazi people of the Colorado Plateau also developed a culture based on agriculture. Like the Hohokam, they built irrigation ditches to catch water, and they farmed on terraces to prevent erosion. To supplement their crops, they hunted game and gathered wild plants and nuts.

The Anasazi were also traders. Roads 30 feet wide radiated out from Pueblo Bonito in Chaco Canyon. A thousand years ago people traveled these roads carrying wood from the mountains, along with pottery, cloth, baskets, and turquoise. Pieces of the turquoise would end up in the markets of faraway Mexico.

By 1300, however, the Anasazi had abandoned their villages. No one knows exactly why. From the study of tree rings, scientists do know that a terrible, 25-year drought began in 1275. The drought might have been too much for these desert farmers to survive.

Whatever the cause, the Anasazi moved to other sites in the Southwest, including the Rio Grande Valley of New Mexico. Their descendants—the Pueblo Indians—live there still.

Woodland Cultures

To the east, meanwhile, complex cultures were emerging in the Eastern Woodlands—roughly the region between the Mississippi River and the Atlantic Coast. People there developed complex cultures based primarily on trade. As early as 3000 B.C. the Woodland Indians were engaged in long-distance trading of useful and decorative stones, copper tools, and carved beads. The later Crystal River culture along Florida's Gulf Coast, for example, carried on an extensive trade that reached south to the Olmecs of Mexico and north to the Great Lakes.

It is possible that the Crystal River culture was the first civilization north of Mexico to build pyramid mounds. Other Woodland cultures north of Florida also adopted this practice. Elaborate burial mounds became the most distinctive feature of the Hopewell culture, situated in the Ohio Valley. This culture, which emerged about 500 B.C., would last for about 1,200 years.

The Hopewell people began cultivating corn about A.D. 450. With the beginning of agriculture, some say, their trading activities declined and the communities became more isolated from each other. About 300 years later they took to the hills, where they built large defensive earthworks. Obviously there was unrest in the land, perhaps an invading people. These earthworks are the last evidence of the Hopewell culture.

The Mississippian Culture

About A.D. 900 another mound culture emerged in the Southeast and Mississippi Valley. This is known as the Mississippian culture and this culture had clear ties with Mexico.

Communities in the Mississippian culture clustered on the river flood plains where such locations were good for farming because floods constantly renewed the fertility of the soil. Their towns featured large flat-topped mounds on which were built temples, meeting houses, and residences of chiefs and priests. Common symbols in their art were the falcon and the jaguar, both of which had long been revered in Mesoamerica.

The crown jewel of the Mississippian culture was Cahokia, in western Illinois. In its heyday, Cahokia boasted 30,000 residents and more than 1,000 mounds. The tallest mound at Cahokia rises ten stories from a sixteen-acre base, rivaling Mexico's Pyramid of the Sun in size. By the time European explorers arrived in the region, the Mississippians had abandoned Cahokia. The Mississippian culture declined rapidly. Later Indians of the region could not say who had built the mounds. Yet there seems to be little doubt that the major tribes of the Southeast were descendants of the mound builders. These include the Cherokees, Catawbas, Creeks, Chickasaws, and Choctaws.

The first European explorers and settlers in the Americas left vivid accounts of the Indians they encountered, yet these accounts have tended to "freeze" Indians in time and place. This is because they assumed that the Indians had always lived in the same place and in the same way. But that is not true. Indian groups moved from one territory to another. As they did, they changed their way of life when it was necessary to do so.

The Cheyenne, for instance, are usually thought of as Plains Indians who hunted buffalo. Originally, however, they were farmers in southern Minnesota. Once they migrated to the Plains, the Cheyenne continued a life that included both farming and hunting-gathering. Then, when the Spanish brought horses to the Plains in the mid-1500s, the Cheyenne abandoned farming to rely on hunting.

The Indian societies in North America were a diverse lot. Some devoted themselves to warfare. Others were peaceful, fighting only if necessary. Some societies were egalitarian. Others were organized into social classes, often with slaves as the lowest class. Some societies emphasized the importance of individual feats of valor or of possessions to increase status. Others discouraged individualism and personal status-seeking.

Chiefs headed most Indian societies. The chief, either male or female depending on tradition, had only as much authority as the group was willing to give. Important decisions were made in consultation with other village leaders and sometimes a village chief might bow to the authority of the chief of a more powerful neighbor.

The Land

Concerned with survival rather than conservation, Indians did not always live in harmony with the earth. Many scientists, for example, think ancient big-game hunters may have hunted horses to extinction in the Western Hemisphere. They also think the Anasazi stripped large areas of forests and ruined the topsoil.

A major change in the use of the American land came with the rise of agriculture. In the Southwest the Indians adopted methods of irrigation. In the Eastern Woodlands the Indians practiced slash-and-burn farming. To prepare a field, they would kill the trees by cutting away strips of bark from around their trunks. Then they would burn the underbrush. The ashes helped fertilize the soil. Between the dead trees, the Indians used sticks to poke holes in the ground. In the holes they planted corn, beans, and squash, often mixing the seeds together. Whenever the soil became exhausted, usually after eight years, the Woodland Indians would move on to clear another plot and build another village. Meanwhile, forests would retake the old fields, thus renewing the land.

The Woodland Indians also used fire to reshape the forests and groups such as the Algonquin not only lived on the land; they managed it.

Their principal tool of management was fire. They regularly and systematically set fire in the woods to destroy the underbrush. These were low-heat fires that swept through an area quickly, not burning well-established trees. One effect of these fires was to make ashes that added nutrients to the soil. Another effect was that grass and berries were likely to establish themselves on the fire-cleared ground. The grass and berries in turn attracted animals such as deer, bears, and wild turkeys. By firing the woods, therefore, the Indians created an environment more supportive of wildlife.

The Woodland Indians were not alone in using fire to shape the environment. This technique was used throughout the continent. In California, for instance, the Indians set fire to the meadowlands each fall to ensure a good harvest of grass seed for the coming year.

The Clash of Cultures

The Europeans brought deadly new diseases that ravaged the Indians and their attitude toward land use, as well as their technology, destroyed the hunting-gathering environment on which the Indians depended.

The Indians had had no contact with diseases that were commonplace in the rest of the world. These included chicken pox, measles, smallpox, and flu. As a result, what was an ordinary case of flu to a European meant certain death for an Indian. With death rates as high as 90%, the social and economic foundations of whole tribes were wiped out. Millions died. The Indian population of North America dropped from about 10 or 12 million in 1500 to about half a million in 1900.

Differences over the meaning of land ownership became a principal source of conflict between the white and Indian cultures. To a white person, land ownership meant controlling what happened to the land. For the Indians, land ownership meant having access to the things on the land during different seasons of the year. No one could own the land itself, only have rights to its produce.

Disagreements between Indians and white settlers over the use of the land led to war and the settlers won because of their superior numbers and superior technology. □

LOCATIONS OF LARGEST AMERICAN INDIAN TRIBES
AND SELECTED RESERVATIONS

Population of Native Americans By State, 1990

States	American Indian	Eskimo	Aleut	States	American Indian	Eskimo	Aleut
Alabama	16,312	105	89	Montana	47,524	106	49
Alaska	31,245	44,401	10,052	Nebraska	12,344	38	28
Arizona	203,009	284	234	Nevada	19,377	156	104
Arkansas	12,641	80	52	New Hampshire	2,075	45	14
California	236,078	2,552	3,534	New Jersey	14,500	201	269
Colorado	27,271	297	208	New Mexico	134,097	162	96
Connecticut	6,472	83	99	New York	60,855	754	1,042
Delaware	1,982	19	18	North Carolina	79,825	152	178
D.C.	1,432	14	20	North Dakota	25,870	38	9
Florida	35,461	431	443	Ohio	19,859	230	269
Georgia	12,926	223	199	Oklahoma	252,089	202	129
Hawaii	4,738	155	206	Oregon	37,443	545	508
Idaho	13,594	132	54	Pennsylvania	14,210	264	259
Illinois	20,970	414	452	Rhode Island	3,987	42	42
Indiana	12,453	170	97	South Carolina	8,049	106	91
Iowa	7,217	67	65	South Dakota	50,501	62	12
Kansas	21,767	114	84	Tennessee	9,859	96	84
Kentucky	5,614	82	73	Texas	64,349	721	807
Louisiana	18,361	92	88	Utah	24,093	116	74
Maine	5,945	34	19	Vermont	1,650	32	14
Maryland	12,601	169	202	Virginia	14,893	200	189
Massachusetts	11,857	210	174	Washington	77,627	1,791	2,065
Michigan	55,131	253	282	West Virginia	2,385	36	37
Minnesota	49,392	235	282	Wisconsin	38,986	181	220
Mississippi	8,435	50	40	Wyoming	9,426	37	16
Missouri	19,508	173	154	**United States**	**1,878,285**	**57,152**	**23,797**

Source: U.S. Department of Commerce, Bureau of the Census.

Eskimos

The Eskimos are the most widely dispersed group in the world still leading a partly aboriginal way of life. They live in a region that spans more than 3,500 miles, including Greenland, the northern fringe of North America, and a sector of eastern Siberia.

Eskimos are racially distinct from American Indians, and are not, as previously believed, merely "Indians transformed." In fact, the Eskimos are most closely related to the Mongolian peoples of eastern Asia. Eskimos consider themselves to be "Inuit" (The People). The Eskimo-Aleut languages are unrelated to any American Indian language groups.

The Eskimo population was approximately 50,000 at the time of the first widespread contact with Europeans. An estimated 2,000 Siberian Eskimos lived near the Bering Strait, the Alaskan Eskimos numbered about 25,000, and the Central Eskimos (who inhabited what is now northern Canada) numbered about 10,000. The Labrador Eskimos totaled about 3,000, while the Greenland Eskimos totaled about 10,000.

The popular conception of the Eskimos—whale hunters dressed in heavy fur clothing and living in dome-shaped ice lodges—is derived from the Eskimos who live farthest north, on the Arctic islands of Canada and along northwestern Greenland. In reality, these northern Arctic dwellers formed a minority among Eskimos as a whole. No single environmental adaptation existed throughout the area of Eskimo occupancy. Eskimos along the Pacific coast probably obtained much of their food by fishing for salmon, while the Central Eskimos of Canada subsisted mainly on caribou. Eskimo groups lived in various types of shelters, including semi-subterranean sod houses and tents made of caribou skins.

At no time did the Eskimos possess a national or even well-defined tribal sense. The emphasis was on the local and familial group rather than on associations of land and territory.

The overall Eskimo population has remained fairly constant over the past several centuries, although not all groups have remained stable in number. According to the 1990 census, there are 57,152 Eskimos and 23,797 Aleuts living in the United States. □

Facts About American Indians Today

Source: U.S. Department of the Interior, Bureau of Indian Affairs.

Reservations. The number of Indian land areas in the U.S. administered as Federal Indian Reservations total 287. The largest is the Navajo Reservation of some 16 million acres of land in Arizona, New Mexico, and Utah. Many of the smaller reservations are less than 1,000 acres with the smallest less than 100 acres. On some reservations, a high percentage of the land is owned and occupied by non-Indians. Some 140 reservations have entirely tribally-owned land.

Indians do not have to live on reservations and are free to move about like all other Americans. Indians also have the right to buy and hold title to land purchased with their own funds. Over half of the total U.S. Indian and Alaska Native population now lives away from reservations. Many return home to participate in family and tribal life and sometimes to retire.

Indian Tribes. There are over 550 Federally recognized tribes in the United States, including about 226 village groups in Alaska. "Federally-recognized" means these tribes and groups have a special, legal relationship to the U.S. government and its agent, The Bureau of Indian Affairs (BIA).

A number of Indian tribes and groups in the U.S. do not have a federally-recognized status, although some are state-recognized. The Bureau of Indian Affairs has a special program to work with those seeking federal recognition status.

Who is an Indian? No single federal or tribal criterion establishes a person's identity as an Indian. Government agencies use differing criteria to determine who is an Indian eligible to participate in their programs. Tribes also have varying eligibility criteria for membership. To be eligible for Bureau of Indian Affairs services, an Indian must (1) be a member of a tribe recognized by the federal government and (2) must, for some purposes, be of one-fourth or more Indian ancestry. By legislative and administrative decision, the Aleuts, Eskimos, and Indians of Alaska are eligible for BIA services.

Tribal membership. A tribe sets up its own criteria, although the U.S. Congress can also establish tribal membership criteria. Becoming a member of a particular tribe requires meeting its membership rules, including adoption. Except for adoption, the amount of blood quantum needed varies, with some tribes requiring only a trace of Indian blood (of the tribe) while others require as much as one-half.

What is an Indian tribe? Originally, an Indian tribe was a body of people bound together by blood ties who were socially, politically, and religiously organized, who lived together in a defined territory, and who spoke a common language or dialect. The establishment of the reservation system created some new tribal groupings when two or three tribes were placed on one reservation, or when members of one tribe were spread over two or three reservations.

Taxes. Indians pay the same taxes as other citizens with the exceptions applying to those Indians living on federal reservations: (1) federal income taxes are not levied on income from trust lands held for them by the United States; (2) state income taxes are not paid on income earned on a federal reservation; (3) state sales taxes are not paid on transactions made on a federal reservation, and (4) local property taxes are not paid on reservation or trust land.

Citizenship. Indians are U.S. citizens and have the same right to vote as other Americans. They also have the right to hold federal, state, and local government offices. Ben Nighthorse Campbell, a member of the Northern Cheyenne Tribe of Montana, was elected to the U.S. House of Representatives in 1986 from the Third District of Colorado and was serving his third term in 1992. □

PEOPLE

Many public figures not listed here may be found elsewhere in the *Information Please Almanac*.

40	Governors	929	Sports Personalities
633	Presidents	651	Supreme Court Justices
635	Presidents' Wives	633	Vice Presidents
33	Senators		

A name in parentheses is the original name or form of name. Localities are places of birth. Country name in parenthesis is the present-day name. Dates of birth appear as month/day/year. **Boldface** years in parentheses are dates of (**birth-death**).

Information has been gathered from many sources, including the individuals themselves. However, the *Information Please Almanac* cannot guarantee the accuracy of every individual item.

A

Aalto, Alvar (architect); Kuortane, Finland **(1898-1976)**
Abbado, Claudio (orchestra conductor); Milan, Italy, 1933
Abbott, Bud (William) (comedian); Asbury Park, N.J. **(1898-1974)**
Abbott, George (stage producer); Forestville, N.Y. **(1887–1995)**
Abel, Walter (actor); St. Paul **(1898-1987)**
Abelard, Peter (theologian); nr. Nantes, France **(1079-1142)**
Abernathy, Ralph (civil rights leader); Linden, Ala., **(1926-1990)**
Acheson, Dean (statesman); Middletown, Conn. **(1893-1971)**
Acuff, Roy Claxton (musician); nr. Maynardsville, Tenm. **(1903-1992)**
Adams, Charles Francis (diplomat); Boston **(1807-1886)**
Adams, Don (actor); New York City, 4/19/1926
Adams, Edie (Edie Enke) (actress); Kingston, Pa., 4/16/1929
Adams, Franklin Pierce (columnist and author); Chicago **(1881-1960)**
Adams, Henry Brooks (historian); Boston **(1838-1918)**
Adams, Joey (comedian); New York City, 1/6/1911
Adams, Mason (actor); New York City, 2/26/19
Adams, Maude (Maude Kiskadden) (actress); Salt Lake City **(1872-1953)**
Adams, Samuel (American Revolutionary patriot); Boston **(1722-1803)**
Adamson, Joy (naturalist); Troppau, Silesia **(1910-1980)**
Addams, Charles (cartoonist); Westfield, N.J. **(1912-1988)**
Addams, Jane (social worker); Cedarville, Ill. **(1860-1935)**
Adderley, Julian "Cannonball" (jazz saxophonist); Tampa, Fla. **(1928-1975)**
Ade, George (humorist); Kentland, Ind. **(1866-1944)**
Adenauer, Konrad (statesman); Cologne, Germany **(1876-1967)**
Adler, Alfred (psychoanalyst); Vienna **(1870-1937)**
Adler, Larry (musician); Baltimore, 2/10/1914
Adler, Richard (songwriter); New York City, 8/3/1921
Adoree, Renée (Renée La Fonte) (actress); Lille, France **(1898-1933)**
Aeschylus (dramatist); Eleusis (Greece) **(525-456** B.C.)
Aesop (fabulist); birthplace unknown **(lived c. 600** B.C.)
Aherne, Brian (actor); King's Norton, England **(1902-1986)**
Aiello, Danny (actor); New York City, 6/20/33
Aiken, Conrad (poet); Savannah, Ga. **(1889-1973)**
Ailey, Alvin (choreographer); Rogers, Tex., **(1931-1989)**
Albanese, Licia (operatic soprano); Bari, Italy, 7/22/1913
Albee, Edward (playwright); Washington, D.C., 3/12/1928
Albers, Josef (painter); Bottrop, Germany **(1888-1976)**
Albert, Eddie (Edward Albert Heimberger) (actor); Rock Island, Ill., 4/22/1908
Albert, Edward (actor); Los Angeles, 2/20/51
Albertson, Jack (actor); Malden, Mass. **(1910?-1981)**
Albright, Lola (actress); Akron, Ohio, 7/20/1925
Alcott, Louisa May (novelist); Germantown, Pa. **(1832-1888)**
Alda, Alan (actor); New York City, 1/28/1936
Alda, Robert (Alphonso d'Abruzzo) (actor); New York City **(1914-1986)**
Alden, John (American Pilgrim); England **(1599?-1687)**
Alexander, Jane (Quigley) (actress); Boston, 10/28/39
Alexander the Great (monarch and conqueror); Pella, Macedonia (Greece) **(356-323** B.C.)
Alger, Horatio (author); Revere, Mass. **(1834-1899)**
Algren, Nelson (novelist); Detroit **(1909-1981)**
Allen, Debbie (dancer-choreographer, actress); Houston, Tex., 1/16/50
Allen, Ethan (American Revolutionary soldier); Litchfield, Conn. **(1738-1789)**
Allen, Fred (John Florence Sullivan) (comedian); Cambridge, Mass. **(1894-1956)**
Allen, Gracie (Grace Ethel Cecile Rosalie Allen) (comedienne); San Francisco **(1906-1964)**
Allen, Mel (Melvin Israel) (sportscaster); Birmingham, Ala., 2/14/1913
Allen, Peter (actor, songwriter); Tenterfield, Australia **(1944-1992)**
Allen, Steve (TV entertainer); New York City, 12/26/1921
Allen, Woody (Allen Stewart Konigsberg) (actor, writer, and director); Brooklyn, N.Y., 12/1/1935
Alley, Kirstie (actress); Wichita, Kan., 1/12/55
Allison, Fran (actress); LaPorte City, Iowa, **(1908?-1989)**
Allman, Gregg (singer); Nashville, Tenn., 12/8/1947
Allyson, June (Jan Allyson) (actress); New York City, 10/7/1923
Alonso, Alicia (ballerina); Havana, 12/21/1921(?)
Alpert, Herb (band leader); Los Angeles, 3/31/1935(?)
Alsop, Joseph W., Jr. (journalist); Avon, Conn., **(1910-1989)**
Alsop, Stewart (journalist); Avon, Conn. **(1914-1974)**
Altman, Robert (film director); Kansas City, Mo., 2/20/1925
Amati, Nicola (violin maker); Cremona, Italy **(1596-1684)**
Ambler, Eric (suspense writer); London, 6/28/1909
Ameche, Don (Dominic Amici) (actor); Kenosha, Wis. **(1908–1993)**
Ames, Leon (actor); Portland, Ind. **(1903–1993)**
Amis, Kingsley (novelist); London, 4/16/1922
Amory, Cleveland (writer and conservationist); Nahant, Mass., 9/2/1917
Amos (Freeman F. Gosden) (radio comedian); Richmond, Va. **(1899-1982)**
Amos, John (actor); Newark, N.J., 12/27/41
Amsterdam, Morey (actor); Chicago, 12/14/1914
Andersen, Hans Christian (author of fairy-tales); Odense, Denmark **(1805-1875)**
Anderson, Eddie. *See* Rochester
Anderson, Harry (actor); Newport, R.I., 10/14/52
Anderson, Ib (ballet dancer); Copenhagen, 12/14/1954
Anderson, Jack (journalist); Long Beach, Calif., 10/19/1922
Anderson, Dame Judith (actress); Adelaide, Australia **(1898-1992)**
Anderson, Lindsay (Gordon) (director); Bangalore, India **(1923–1994)**
Anderson, Loni (actress); St. Paul, Minn. 8/5/45
Anderson, Lynn (singer); Grand Forks, N.D., 9/26/1947
Anderson, Marian (contralto); Philadelphia **(1897-1993)**
Anderson, Maxwell (dramatist); Atlantic, Pa. **(1888-1959)**
Anderson, Richard Dean (actor); Minneapolis, Minn., 1/23/50
Anderson, Robert (playwright); New York City, 4/28/1917
Andersson, Bibi (actress); Stockholm, 11/11/1935
Andress, Ursula (actress); Switzerland, 3/19/1938
Andrews, Dana (actor); Collins, Miss. **(1909-1992)**
Andrews, Julie (Julia Wells) (actress and singer); Walton-on-Thames, England, 10/1/1935
Andrews, La Verne (singer); Minneapolis **(1916-1967)**
Andrews, Maxene (singer); Minneapolis, 1/3/1918
Andrews, Patti (singer); Minneapolis, 2/16/1920
Andy (Charles J. Correll) (radio comedian); Peoria, Ill. **(1890-1972)**
Angeles, Victoria de los (Victoria Gamez Cima) (operatic soprano); Barcelona, 11/1/1924
Anka, Paul (singer and composer); Ottawa, 7/30/1941
Ann-Margret (Ann-Margret Olsson) (actress); Valsjobyn, Sweden, 4/28/1941
Annabella (actress); Paris, 1912
Anouilh, Jean (playwright); Bordeaux, France **(1910-1987)**
Anthony, Susan Brownell (woman suffragist); Adams, Mass. **(1820-1906)**
Antonioni, Michelangelo (director); Ferrara, Italy, 9/2 9/1912
Antony, Mark (Marcus Antonius) (statesman); Rome **(83?-30** B.C.)
Anuszkiewicz, Richard (painter); Erie, Pa., 5/23/1930
Aquinas, St. Thomas (philosopher); nr. Aquino (Italy) **(1225?-1274)**
Arbuckle, Roscoe "Fatty" (actor and director); San Jose, Calif. **(1887-1933)**
Archimedes (physicist and mathematician); Syracuse, Sicily **(287?-212** B.C.)
Archipenko, Alexandre (sculptor); Kiev, Russia **(1887-1964)**
Arden, Elizabeth (Florence Nightingale Graham) (cosmetics executive); Woodbridge, Canada **(1891-1966)**

Arden, Eve (Eunice Quedens) (actress); Mill Valley, Calif. **(1907–1990)**
Arendt, Hannah (historian); Hannover, Germany **(1906-1975)**
Aristophanes (dramatist); Athens **(4487-380** B.C.)
Aristotle (philosopher); Stagirus, Macedonia **(384-322** B.C.)
Arkin, Alan (actor and director); New York City, 3/26/1934
Arledge, Roone (TV executive); Forest Hills, N.Y., 7/8/1931
Arlen, Harold (Hyman Arluck) (composer); Buffalo, N.Y. **(1905-1986)**
Arlen, Richard (actor); Charlottesville, Va. **(1900-1976)**
Arliss, George (actor); London **(1868-1946)**
Armstrong, Louis ("Satchmo") (musician); New Orleans **(1900-1971)**
Armstrong-Jones, Anthony. *See* Snowdon, Earl of
Arnaz, Desi (Desiderio) (actor and producer); Santiago, Cuba **(1917-1986)**
Arness, James (James Aurness) (TV actor); Minneapolis, 5/26/1923
Arno, Peter (cartoonist); New York City **(1904-1968)**
Arnold, Benedict (American Revolutionary War general, charged with treason); Norwich, Conn. **(1741-1801)**
Arnold, Eddy (singer); Henderson, Tenn., 5/15/1918
Arnold, Edward (actor); New York City **(1890-1956)**
Arnold, Matthew (poet and critic); Laleham, England **(1822-1888)**
Arp, Jean (sculptor and painter); Strasbourg (France) **(1887-1966)**
Arpino, Gerald (choreographer); Staten Island, N.Y., 1/14/28
Arquette, Cliff ("Charley Weaver") (actor); Toledo, Ohio **(1905-1974)**
Arquette, Rosanna (actress); New York City, 8/10/59
Arrau, Claudio (pianist); Chillán, Chile **(1903–1991)**
Arroyo, Martina (soprano); New York City, 2/2/1940
Arthur, Bea (Bernice Frankel) (actress); New York City, 5/13/1926(?)
Arthur, Jean (Gladys Greene) (actress); New York City **(1900–1991)**
Asch, Sholem (novelist); Kutno, Poland **(1880-1957)**
Ashcroft, Dame Peggy (actress); Croydon, England **(1907–1991)**
Ashkenazy, Vladimir (concert pianist); Gorki, U.S.S.R., 7/6/1937
Ashley, Elizabeth (actress); Ocala, Fla., 8/30/1939
Ashton, Sir Frederick William Mallandaine (choreographer); Guayaquil, Ecuador **(1904-1988)**
Asimov, Isaac (author); Petrovichi, Russia **(1920-1992)**
Asner, Edward (actor); Kansas City, Mo., 11/15/1929
Astaire, Fred (Frederick Austerlitz) (dancer and actor); Omaha, Neb. **(1899-1987)**
Astin, John (actor, director); Baltimore, Md., 3/30/30
Astor, John Jacob (financier); Waldorf (Germany) **(1763-1848)**
Astor, Mary (Lucile Langhanke) (actress); Quincy, Ill. **(1906-1987)**
Atkins, Chet (guitarist); nr. Luttrell, Tenn., 6/20/1924
Atkinson, Brooks (drama critic); Melrose, Mass. **(1894-1984)**
Attenborough, Richard (actor-director) Cambridge, England, 8/29/1923
Attila (King of Huns, called "Scourge of God") **(406?-453)**
Atwill, Lionel (actor); Croydon, England, **(1885-1946)**
Auberjonois, Rene (actor); New York City, 6/1/40
Auchincloss, Louis (author); Lawrence, N.Y., 9/27/1917
Auden, W(ystan) H(ugh) (poet); York, England **(1907-1973)**
Audubon, John James (naturalist and painter); Haiti **(1785-1851)**
Auer, Leopold (violinist and teacher); Veszprém, Hungary **(1845-1930)**
Auer, Mischa (actor); St. Petersburg, Russia **(1905-1967)**
Augustine, Saint (Aurelius Augustinus) (theologian); Tagaste, Numidia (Algeria) **(354-430)**
Augustus (Gaius Octavius) (Roman emperor); Rome **(63** B.C.-A.D. **14)**
Aumont, Jean-Pierre (actor); Paris, 1/5/1913
Austen, Jane (novelist); Steventon, England **(1775-1817)**
Autry, Gene (singer and actor); Tioga, Tex., 9/29/1907
Avalon, Frankie (singer); Philadelphia, 9/18/1940
Avedon, Richard (photographer); New York City, 5/15/1923
Avery, Milton (painter); Alt mar, N.Y. **(1893-1965)**
Ax, Emanuel (pianist); Lvov, U.S.S.R., 6/8/1949
Axelrod, George (playwright); New York City, 6/9/1922
Ayckbourn, Alan (playwright); London, 4/12/1939
Ayckroyd, Dan (actor); Ottawa, Ont., Canada, 7/1/1952
Ayres, Agnes (actress); Carbondale, Ill. **(1896-1940)**
Ayres, Lew (actor); Minneapolis, 12/28/1908
Aznavour, Charles (singer, composer); Paris, France, 5/22/24

B

Bacall, Lauren (Betty Joan Perske) (actress); New York City, 9/16/1924
Bach, Johann Sebastian (composer); Eisenach, Germany **(1685-1750)**
Bach, Karl Phillipp Emanuel (composer); Weimar, Germany **(1714-1788)**
Bacharach, Burt (songwriter); Kansas City, Mo., 5/12/1929
Backus, Jim (actor); Cleveland **(1913-1989)**
Bacon, Francis (painter); Dublin **(1910-1992)**
Bacon, Francis (philosopher and essayist); London **(1561-1626)**

Bacon, Roger (philosopher and scientist); Ilchester, England **(1214?-1294)**
Baez, Joan (folk singer); Staten Island, N.Y., 1/9/1941
Bagnold, Enid (novelist); Rochester, England **(1889-1981)**
Bailey, F. Lee (lawyer); Waltham, Mass., 6/10/1933
Bailey, Pearl (singer); Newport News, Va. **(1918-1990)**
Bain, Conrad (actor); Lethbridge, Alberta, Canada, 2/4/23
Bainter, Fay (actress); Los Angeles **(1891-1968)**
Baio, Scott (actor); Brooklyn, N.Y., 9/22/61
Baird, Bil (William B.) (puppeteer); Grand Island, Neb. **(1904-1987)**
Baker, Anita (singer); Toledo, Ohio, 1958
Baker, Carroll (actress); Johnstown, Pa., 5/28/1931
Baker, Josephine (singer and dancer); St. Louis **(1906-1975)**
Baker, Russell (columnist); Loudoun County, Va., 8/14/1925
Balanchine, George (choreographer); St. Petersburg, Russia **(1904-1983)**
Balboa, Vasco Nuñez de (explorer); Jerez de los Caballeros (Spain) **(1475-1517)**
Baldwin, Faith (novelist); New Rochelle, N.Y. **(1893-1978)**
Baldwin, James (novelist); New York City **(1924-1987)**
Balenciaga, Cristóbal (fashion designer); Guetaria, Spain **(1895–?72)**
Ball, Lucille (Désirée) (actress and producer); Celoron (nr. Jamestown), N.Y. **(1911-1989)**
Ballard, Kaye (Catherine Gloria Balotta) (actress); Cleveland, 11/20/1926
Balmain, Pierre (fashion designer); St.-Jean-de-Maurienne, France **(1914-1982)**
Balsam, Martin (actor); New York City, 11/4/1919
Balzac, Honoré de (novelist); Tours, France **(1799-1850)**
Bancroft, Anne (Annemarie Italiano) (actress); New York City, 9/17/1931
Bancroft, George (actor); Philadelphia **(1882-1956)**
Bankhead, Tallulah (actress); Huntsville, Ala. **(1903-1968)**
Banting, Fredrick Grant (physiologist); Alliston, Ont., Canada **(1891-1941)**
Bara, Theda (Theodosia Goodman) (actress); Cincinnati **(1890-1955)**
Barber, Red (Walter Lanier) (sportscaster); Columbus, Miss. **(1908-1992)**
Barber, Samuel (composer); West Chester, Pa. **(1910-1981)**
Bardot, Brigitte (actress); Paris, 1935
Barenboim, Daniel (concert pianist and conductor); Buenos Aires, 11/15/1942
Bari, Lynn (actress); Roanoke, Va., 12/18/13 (?)
Barker, Bob (host); Darrington, Wash., 12/12/23
Barnard, Christiaan N. (heart surgeon); Beauford West, South Africa, 1923
Barnes, Priscilla (actress); Fort Dix, N.J., 12/7/55
Barnum, Phineas Taylor (showman); Bethel, Conn. **(1810-1891)**
Barrie, Sir James Matthew (author); Kirriemuir, Scotland **(1860-1937)**
Barrie, Wendy (actress); Hong Kong **(1913-1978)**
Barry, Gene (Eugene Klass) (actor); New York City, 6/14/1921
Barry, John (naval officer); County Wexford, Ireland **(1745-1803)**
Barrymore, Diana (actress); New York City **(1921-1960)**
Barrymore, Ethel (Ethel Blythe) (actress); Philadelphia **(1879-1959)**
Barrymore, Georgiana Drew (actress); Philadelphia **(1856-1893)**
Barrymore, John (John Blythe) (actor); Philadelphia **(1882-1942)**
Barrymore, Lionel (Lionel Blythe) (actor); Philadelphia **(1878-1954)**
Barrymore, Maurice (Herbert Blythe) (actor and playwright); Agra, India **(1847-1905)**
Barthelme, Donald (novelist); Philadelphia **(1931 -1989)**
Barthelmess, Richard (actor); New York City **(1897-1963)**
Bartholomew, Freddie (actor); London **(1924-1992)**
Bartók, Béla (composer); Nagyszentmiklos (Hungary, now Romania) **(1881-1945)**
Barton, Clara (founder of American Red Cross); Oxford, Mass. **(1821-1912)**
Baruch, Bernard Mannes (statesman); Camden, S.C. **(1870-1965)**
Baryshnikov, Mikhail Nikolayevich (ballet dancer and artistic director); Riga, Latvia, 1/27/1948
Basehart, Richard (actor); Zanesville, Ohio **(1914-1984)**
Basie, Count (William) (band leader); Red Bank, N.J. **(1904-1984)**
Basinger, Kim (actress); Athens, Ga., 12/8/53
Bassey, Shirley (singer); Cardiff, Wales, 1/8/1937
Batchelor, Clarence Daniel (political cartoonist); Osage City, Kan. **(1888-1977)**
Bateman, Jason (actor); Rye, N.Y. 1/14/69
Bateman, Justine (actress); Rye, N.Y., 2/19/66
Bates, Alan (actor); Allestree, England, 2/17/1934
Bates, Kathy (Kathleen Doyle Bates) (actress); Memphis, Tenn., 6/28/1948
Battle, Kathleen (soprano); Portsmouth, Ohio, 8/13/48
Baudelaire, Charles Pierre (poet); Paris **(1821-1867)**
Baxter, Anne (actress); Michigan City, Ind. **(1923-1985)**
Baxter, Warner (actor); Columbus, Ohio **(1891-1951)**

Baxter, Meredith (actress); Los Angeles, 6/21/47
Bean, Orson (Dallas Frederick Burrows) (actor); Burlington, Vt., 7/22/1928
Beardsley, Aubrey Vincent (illustrator); Brighton, England **(1872-1898)**
Beaton, Cecil (photographer and designer); London **(1904-1980)**
Beatty, Clyde (animal trainer); Chillicothe, Ohio **(1903-1965)**
Beatty, Warren (actor and producer); Richmond, Va., 3/30/1937
Beaumont, Francis (dramatist); Grace-Dieu, England **(1584-1616)**
Beavers, Louise (actress); Cincinnati, Ohio **(1902-1962)**
Becket, Thomas à (Archbishop of Canterbury); London **(1118?-1170)**
Beckett, Samuel (playwright); Dublin **(1906-1989)**
Beckmann, Max (painter); Leipzig, Germany **(1884-1950)**
Bede, Saint ("The Venerable Bede") (scholar); Monkwearmouth, England **(673-735)**
Beecham, Sir Thomas (conductor); St. Helens, England **(1879-1961)**
Beecher, Henry Ward (clergyman); Litchf eld, Conn. **(1813-1887)**
Beerbohm, Sir Max (author); London **(1872-1956)**
Beery, Noah (actor); Kansas City, Mo. **(1884-1946)**
Beery, Noah, Jr. (actor); New York City **(1913-1994)**
Beery, Wallace (actor); Kansas City, Mo. **(1886-1949)**
Beethoven, Ludwig von (composer); Bonn (Germany) **(1770-1827)**
Begley, Ed (actor); Hartford, Conn. **(1901-1970)**
Belafonte, Harry (singer and actor); New York City, 3/1/1927
Belafonte-Harper, Shari (actress); New York City, 9/22/54
Belasco, David (dramatist and producer); San Francisco **(1854-1931)**
Bel Geddes, Barbara (actress); New York City, 10/31/22
Bell, Alexander Graham (inventor); Edinburgh, Scotland **(1847-1922)**
Bellamy, Edward (author); Chicopee Falls, Mass. **(1850-1898)**
Bellamy, Ralph (actor); Chicago **(1904-1991)**
Bellini, Giovanni (painter); Venice **(c.1430-1516)**
Bellow, Saul (novelist); Lachine, Quebec, Canada, 6/10/1915
Bellows, George Wesley (painter and lithographer); Columbus, Ohio **(1882-1925)**
Belmondo, Jean-Paul (actor); Neuilly-sur-Seine, France, 4/9/1933
Belushi, Jim (actor); Chicago, 6/15/54
Belushi, John (comedian, actor); Chicago **(1949-1982)**
Benchley, Peter Bradford (novelist); New York City, 5/8/1940
Benchley, Robert Charles (humorist); Worcester, Mass. **(1889-1945)**
Bendix, William (actor); New York City **(1906-1964)**
Benedict, Dirk (actor); Helena, Mont., 3/1/44
Benes, Eduard (statesman); Kozlany (Czechoslovakia) **(1884-1948)**
Benét, Stephen Vincent (poet and story writer); Bethlehem, Pa. **(1898-1943)**
Benét, William Rose (poet and novelist); Ft. Hamilton, Brooklyn, N.Y. **(1886-1950)**
Ben-Gurion, David (David Green) (statesman); Plónsk (Poland) **(1886-1973)**
Benjamin, Richard (actor); New York City, 5/22/1938
Bennett, Constance (actress); New York City **(1905-1965)**
Bennett, Enoch Arnold (novelist and dramatist); Hanley, England **(1867-1931)**
Bennett, James Gordon (editor); Keith, Scotland **(1795-1872)**
Bennett, Joan (actress); Palisades, N.J. **(1910-1990)**
Bennett, Robert Russell (composer); Kansas City, Mo. **(1894-1981)**
Bennett, Tony (Anthony Benedetto) (singer); Astoria, Queens, N.Y., 8/3/1926
Benny, Jack (Benjamin Kubelsky) (comedian); Chicago **(1894-1974)**
Benson, Robby (actor); Dallas, Tex., 1/21/56
Bentham, Jeremy Heinrich (economist); London **(1748-1832)**
Benton, Thomas Hart (painter); Neosho, Mo. **(1889-1975)**
Berg, Alban (composer); Vienna **(1885-1935)**
Berg, Gertrude (writer and actress); New York City **(1899-1966)**
Bergen, Candice (actress); Beverly Hills, Calif., 5/9/1946
Bergen, Edgar (ventriloquist); Chicago, **(1903-1978)**
Bergen, Polly (actress and singer); Knoxville, Tenn., 7/14/1930
Bergerac, Cyrano de (poet); Paris **(1619-1655)**
Bergman, Ingmar (film director); Uppsala, Sweden, 7/14/1918
Bergman, Ingrid (actress); Stockholm **(1918-1982)**
Bergson, Henri (philosopher); Paris **(1859-1941)**
Berkeley, Busby (choreographer, director); Los Angeles **(1885-1976)**
Berle, Milton (Milton Berlinger) (comedian); New York City, 7/12/1908
Berlin, Irving (Israel Baline) (songwriter); Temum, Russia **(1888-1989)**
Berlioz, Louis Hector (composer); La Côte-Saint-André, France **(1803-1869)**
Berman, Lazar (concert pianist); Leningrad, 1930.
Berman, Shelley (Sheldon) (comedian); Chicago, 2/3/1926
Bernardi, Herschel (actor); New York City **(1922-1986)**
Bernhardt, Sarah (Rosine Bernard) (actress); Paris **(1844-1923)**
Bernini, Gian Lorenzo (sculptor and painter); Naples (Italy) **(1598-1680)**
Bernoulli, Jacques (scientist); Basel, Switzerland **(1654-1705)**
Bernsen, Corbin (actor); North Hollywood, Calif., 7/7/?

Bertinelli, Valerie (actress); Wilmington, Del., 4/23/60
Bernstein, Leonard (conductor); Lawrence, Mass. **(1918-1990)**
Berry, Chuck (Charles Edward Berry) (singer and guitarist); San Jose, Calif., 1/15/1926
Berry, Ken (actor); Moline, Ill., 11/3/30
Betjeman, Sir John (Poet Laureate); London **(1906-1984)**
Bettelheim, Bruno (psychoanalyst); Vienna **(1903-1990)**
Bickford, Charles (actor); Cambridge, Mass. **(1889-1967)**
Bierce, Ambrose Gwinnett (journalist); Meigs County, Ohio **(1842-1914?)**
Bikel, Theodore (actor and folk singer); Vienna, 5 /2/1924
Bing, Sir Rudolf (opera manager); Vienna, 1/9/1902
Bingham, George Caleb (painter); Augusta Co., Va. **(1811-1879)**
Bishop, Joey (Joseph Gottlieb) (comedian); New York City, 2/3/1919
Bismarck-Schönhausen, Prince Otto Eduard Leopold von (statesman); Schönhausen, Germany **(1815-1898)**
Bisset, Jacqueline (actress); Weybridge, England, 9/13/1944
Bixby, Bill (actor); San Francisco **(1934-1993)**
Bizet, Georges (Alexandre César Léopold Bizet) (composer); Paris **(1838-1875)**
Bjoerling, Jussi (tenor); Stora Tuna, Sweden **(1911-1960)**
Black, Karen (actress); Park Ridge, Ill., 7/1/1942
Black, Shirley Temple (former actress); Santa Monica, Calif., 4/23/1928
Blackmer, Sidney (actor); Salisbury, N.C. **(1898-1973)**
Blackstone, Sir William (jurist); London **(1723-1780)**
Blaine, Vivian (actress and singer); Newark, N.J., 11/21/1924
Blair, Janet (actress); Altoona, Pa., 4/23/1921
Blake, Amanda (Beverly Louise Neill) (actress); Buffalo, N.Y. **(1929-1989)**
Blake, Eubie (James Hubert) (pianist); Baltimore **(1883-1983)**
Blake, Robert (Michael Gubitosi) (actor); Nutley, N.J., 9/18/1933
Blake, William (poet and artist); London **(1757-1827)**
Blanc, Mel(vin Jerome) (actor and voice specialist); San Francisco **(1908-1989)**
Blass, Bill (fashion designer); Fort Wayne, Ind., 6/22/1922
Bloch, Ernest (composer); Geneva **(1880-1959)**
Blondell, Joan (actress); New York City **(1909-1979)**
Bloom, Claire (actress); London, 2/15/1931
Bloomgarden, Kermit (producer); Brooklyn, N.Y. **(1904-1976)**
Blore, Eric (actor); London **(1887-1959)**
Blue, Monte (actor); Indianapolis **(1890-1963)**
Blyth, Ann (actress); New York City, 8/16/1928
Boccaccio, Giovanni (author); Paris **(1313-1375)**
Boccherini, Luigi (Rodolfo) (composer); Lucca, Italy **(1743-1805)**
Boccioni, Umberto (painter and sculptor); Reggio di Calabria, Italy **(1882-1916)**
Bock, Jerry (composer); New Haven, Conn., 11/23/1928
Bogarde, Dirk (Derek Van den Bogaerde) (film actor and director); London, 3/28/1921
Bogart, Humphrey DeForest (actor); New York City **(1899-1957)**
Bogdanovich, Peter (producer and director); Kingston, N.Y., 7/30/1939
Bohlen, Charles E. (diplomat); Clayton, N.Y. **(1904-1974)**
Bohr, Niels (atomic physicist); Copenhagen **(1885-1962)**
Boland, Mary (actress); Philadelphia, Pa. **(1880-1965)**
Boles, John (actor); Greenville, Tex. **(1895-1969)**
Bolger, Ray (dancer and actor); Dorchester, Mass **(1904-1987)**
Bolivar, Simón (South American liberator); Caracas, Venezuela **(1783-1830)**
Bologna, Giovanni da (sculptor); Douai (France) **(1529-1608)**
Bombeck, Erma (author, columnist); Dayton, Ohio 2/21/1927
Bonaparte, Napoleon (Emperor of the French); Ajaccio, Corsica (France) **(1769-1821)**
Bond, Julian (Georgia legislator); Nashville, Tenn., 1/14/1940
Bondi, Beulah (actress); Chicago **(1883-1981)**
Bonet, Lisa (actress); San Francisco, 11/16/67
Bonnard, Pierre (painter); Fontenayaux-Roses, France **(1867-1947)**
Bon Jovi, Jon (musician, songwriter); Sayreville, N.J., 3/2/62
Bono, Sonny (Salvatore) (singer, politician); Detroit, 2/16/1935
Boone, Daniel (frontiersman); nr. Reading, Pa. **(1734-1820)**
Boone, Pat (Charles) (singer); Jacksonville, Fla., 6/1/1934
Boone, Richard (actor); Los Angeles **(1917-1981)**
Booth, Edwin Thomas (actor); Bel Air, Md. **(1833-1893)**
Booth, Evangeline Cory (religious leader); London **(1865-1950)**
Booth, John Wilkes (actor; assassin of Lincoln); Harford County, Md. **(1838-1865)**
Booth, Shirley (Thelma Booth Ford) (actress); New York City **(1898(?)-1992)**
Bordoni, Irene (actress); Ajaccio (France) **(1895-1953)**
Borge, Victor (pianist and comedian); Copenhagen, 1/3/1909
Borgia, Cesare (nobleman and soldier); Rome **(1475?-1507)**
Borgia, Lucrezia (Duchess of Ferrara); Rome **(1480-1519)**
Borgnine, Ernest (actor); Hamden, Conn., 1/24/1917
Borromini, Francesco (architect); Bissone (Italy) **(1599-1667)**

Bosch, Hieronymus (Hieronymus van Aeken) (painter); Hertogen-bosch (Netherlands) **(c.1450-1516)**

Bosley, Tom (actor); Chicago, 10/1/1927

Bostwick, Barry (actor); San Mateo, Calif., 2/24/45

Boswell I, Connee (singer); New Orleans **(1907-1976)**

Boswell, James (diarist and biographer); Edinburgh, Scotland **(1740-1795)**

Botticelli, Sandro (Alessandro di Mariano dei Filipepi) (painter); Florence (Italy) **(1444?-1510)**

Bottoms, Joseph (actor); Santa Barbara, Calif., 4/16/33

Bottoms, Timothy (actor); Santa Barbara, Calif., 8/30/50

Boulez, Pierre (conductor); Montbrison, France, 3/26/1925

Bourke-White, Margaret (photographer); New York City **(1906-1971)**

Bow, Clara (actress); Brooklyn, N.Y. **(1905-1965)**

Bowen, Catherine Drinker (biographer); Haverford, Pa. **(1897-1973)**

Bowes, Edward (radio show director); San Francisco **(1874-1946)**

Bowie, David (David Robert Jones) (actor and musician); London, 1/8/1947(?)

Bowie, James (soldier); Burke County, Ga. **(1799-1836)**

Bowles, Chester (diplomat); Springfield, Mass. **(1901-1986)**

Boxleitner, Bruce (actor); Elgin, Ill., 5/12/50

Boyce, William (composer); London? **(1710-1779)**

Boyd, Bill (William) ("Hopalong Cassidy") (actor); Cambridge, Ohio **(1898-1972)**

Boyd, Stephen (Stephen Millar) (actor); Belfast, Northern Ireland **(1928-1977)**

Boyer, Charles (actor); Figeac, France **(1899-1978)**

Boy George (George Alan O'Dowd) (singer); London, 1961

Boyle, Peter (actor); Philadelphia, 10/18/33

Boyle, Robert (scientist); Lismore Castle, Munster, Ireland **(1627-1691)**

Bracken, Eddie (actor); Astoria, Queens, N.Y., 2/7/1920

Bradbury, Ray Douglas (science-fiction writer); Waukegan, Ill., 8/22/1920

Bradlee, Benjamin C. (editor); Boston, 8/26/1921

Bradley, Ed (broadcast journalist); Philadelphia, Pa., 6/22/1941

Bradley, Omar N. (5-star general); Clark, Mo. **(1893-1981)**

Brady, Alice (actress); New York City **(1892-1939)**

Brady, Scott (actor); Brooklyn, N.Y. **(1924-1985)**

Brahe, Tycho (astronomer); Knudstrup, Denmark **(1546-1601)**

Brahms, Johannes (composer); Hamburg **(1833-1897)**

Braille, Louis (teacher of blind); Coupvray, France **(1809-1862)**

Brailowsky, Alexander (pianist); Kiev, Russia **(1896-1976)**

Bramante, Donato D'Agnolo (architect); Monte Asdrualdo (now Fermignano, Italy) **(1444-1514)**

Brancusi, Constantin (sculptor); Pestisansi, Romania **(1876-1957)**

Brando, Marlon (actor); Omaha, Neb., 4/3/1924

Brandt, Willy (Herbert Frahm) (ex-Chancellor); Lübeck, Germany **(1913-1992)**

Braque, Georges (painter); Argenteuil, France **(1882-1963)**

Brazzi, Rossano (actor); Bologna, Italy **(1916–1994)**

Brecht, Bertolt (dramatist and poet); Augsburg, Bavaria **(1898-1956)**

Brel, Jacques (singer and composer); Brussels, **(1929-1978)**

Brennan, Walter (actor); Lynn, Mass. **(1894-1974)**

Brent, George (actor); Dublin **(1904-1979)**

Breslin, Jimmy (journalist: Jamaica, Queens, N.Y., 10/17/1930

Breuer, Marcel (architect and designer); Pécs, Hungary **(1902-1981)**

Brewer, Teresa (singer); Toledo, Ohio, 5/7/1931

Brewster, Kingman, Jr. (ex-president of Yale); Longmeadow, Mass. **(1919-1988)**

Brezhnev, Leonid I. (Communist Party Secretary); Dneprodzerzhinsk, Ukraine **(1906-1982)**

Brice, Fanny (Fannie Borach) (comedienne); New York City **(1892-1951)**

Bridges, Beau (actor); Los Angeles, 12/9/1941

Bridges, Jeff (actor); Los Angeles, 12/4/49

Bridges, Lloyd (actor); San Leandro, Calif. 1/15/1913

Brinkley, David (TV newscaster); Wilmington, N.C., 7/10/1920

Britt, May (Maybritt Wilkins) (actress); Sweden, 3/22/1936

Britten, Benjamin (composer); Lowestoft, England **(1913-1976)**

Britton, Barbara (actress); Long Beach, Calif. **(1920-1980)**

Broderick, Helen (actress); Philadelphia, Pa. **(1891-1959)**

Brolin, James (actor); Los Angeles, 7/18/40

Bromfield, Louis (novelist); Mansfield, Ohio **(1896-1956)**

Bronson, Charles (Charles Buchinsky) (actor); Ehrenfield, Pa., 11/3/1922(?)

Brontë, Charlotte (novelist); Thornton, England **(1816-1855)**

Brontë, Emily Jane (novelist); Thornton, England **(1818-1848)**

Bronzino, Agnolo (painter); Monticelli (Italy) **(1503-1572)**

Brook, Peter (director); London, 3/21/1925

Brooke, Rupert (poet); Rugby, England **(1887-1915)**

Brooks, Geraldine (Geraldine Stroock) (actress); New York City **(1925-1977)**

Brooks, Gwendolyn (poet); Topeka, Kan., 6/7/1917

Brooks, Mel (Melvin K aminsky) (writer and film director); Brooklyn,

N.Y., 1926(?)

Brosnan, Pierce (actor); County Meath, Ireland, 5/16/52

Brothers, Joyce (Bauer) (psychologist, author, radio-TV personality); New York City, 1927(?)

Broun, Matthew Heywood Campbell (journalist); Brooklyn, N.Y. **(1888-1939)**

Brown, Helen Gurley (author); Green Forest, Ark., 2/18/1922

Brown, James (singer); Augusta, Ga., 5/3/1934

Brown, Joe E. (comedian); Holgate, Ohio **(1892-1973)**

Brown, John (abolitionist); Torrington, Conn. **(1800-1859)**

Brown, John Mason (critic); Louisville, Ky. **(1900-1969)**

Brown, Les (band leader); Reinerton, Pa., 1912

Brown, Pamela (actress); London **(1918-1975)**

Brown, Vanessa (Smylla Brind) (actress); Vienna, 3/24/1928

Browne, Jackson (singer and guitarist); Heidelberg, Germany, 10/9/1948

Browning, Elizabeth Barrett (poet); Durham, England **(1806-1861)**

Browning, Robert (poet); London **(1812-1889)**

Brubeck, Dave (musician); Concord, Calif., 12/6/1920

Bruce, Lenny (comedian); Long Island, N.Y. **(1926-1966)**

Bruce, Nigel (actor); Ensenada, Mexico **(1895-1953)**

Bruce, Virginia (actress); Minneapolis, Minn. **(1910-1982)**

Brueghel, Pieter (painter); nr. Breda, Flanders (Netherlands) **(1520?-1569)**

Bruhn, Erik (Belton Evers) (ballet dancer); Copenhagen **(1928-1986)**

Brunelleschi, Filippo (architect); Florence (Italy) **(1377-1446)**

Bruno, Giordano (philosopher); Nola, Italy **(1548-1600)**

Brutus, Marcus Junius (Roman politician); **(85?-42 B.C.)**

Bryan, William Jennings (orator and politician); Salem, Ill. **(1860-1925)**

Bryant, Anita (singer); Barnsdall, Okla., 3/25/1940

Bryant, William Cullen (poet and editor); Cummington, Mass. **(1794-1878)**

Brynner, Yul (Taidje Khan) (actor); Sakhalin Island, Russia **(1920-1985)**

Brzezinski, Zbigniew (ex-presidential adviser); Warsaw, 3/28/1928

Buber, Martin (philosopher and theologian); Vienna **(1878-1965)**

Buchanan, Jack (actor); Glasgow, Scotland **(1891-1957)**

Buchanan, Edgar (actor); Humansville, Mo., **(1903-1979)**

Buchholz, Horst (actor); Berlin, 12/4/1933

Buchwald, Art (Arthur) (columnist); Mount Vernon, N.Y., 10/20/1925

Buck, Pearl S(ydenstricker) (author); Hillsboro, W. Va. **(1892-1973)**

Buckley, William F., Jr. (journalist); New York City, 11/24/1925

Buddha. *See* Gautama Buddha

Buffalo Bill (William Frederick Cody) (scout); Scott County, Iowa **(1846-1917)**

Bujold, Genevieve (actress); Montreal, 7/1/1942

Bujones, Fernando (ballet dancer); Miami, Fla., 3/9/1955

Bullins, Ed (playwright); Philadelphia, 7/2/1935

Bullock, Jm J. (actor); Casper Wyom., 2/9/?

Bumbry, Grace (mezzo-soprano); St. Louis, 1/4/1937

Bunche, Ralph J. (statesman); Detroit **(1904-1971)**

Bundy, McGeorge (educator); Boston, 3/30/1919

Bundy, William Putnam (editor); Washington, D.C., 9/24/1917

Buñuel, Luis (film director); Calanda, Spain, **(1900-1983)**

Bunyan, John (preacher and author); Elstow, England **(1628-1688)**

Burbank, Luther (horticulturist); Lancaster, Mass. **(1849-1926)**

Burke, Adm. Arleigh A. (ex-Chief of Naval Operations); Boulder, Colo., 10/19/1901

Burke, Billie (comedienne); Washington, D.C. **(1885-1970)**

Burke, Delta (actress); Orlando, Fla., 7/30/56

Burke, Edmund (statesman); Dublin **(1729-1797)**

Burne-Jones, Edward Coley (painter); Birmingham, England **(1833-1898)**

Burnett, Carol (comedienne); San Antonio, 4/26/1933

Burnette, Smiley (Lester Alvin) (actor); Summum, Ill. **(1911-1967)**

Burney, Fanny (Frances) (writer); King's Lynn, England **(1752-1840)**

Burns, George (Nathan Birnbaum) (comedian); New York City, 1/20/1896

Burns, Robert (poet); Alloway, Scotland **(1759-1796)**

Burr, Aaron (political leader); Newark, N.J. **(1756-1836)**

Burr, Raymond (William Stacey Burr) (actor); New Westminster, British Columbia, Canada **(1917–1993)**

Burroughs, Edgar Rice (novelist); Chicago **(1875-1950)**

Burrows, Abe (playwright and director); New York City **(1910-1985)**

Burstyn, Ellen (Edna Rae Gillooly) (actress); Detroit, 12/7/1932

Burton, LaVar (actor); Landsthul, Germany, 2/16/57

Burton, Richard (Richard Jenkins) (actor); Pontrhydfen, Wales **(1925-1984)**

Bushman, Francis X. (actor); Baltimore **(1883-1966)**

Butkus, Dick (actor); Chicago, 12/9/42

Butler, Samuel (author); Langar, England **(1835-1902)**

Butterworth, Charles (actor); South Bend, Ind. **(1896-1946)**

Buttons, Red (Aaron Chwatt) (actor); New York City, 2/5/1919

Buzzi, Ruth (comedienne); Wequetequock, Conn., 7/24/1936

Byington, Spring (actress); Colorado Springs, Colo. **(1893-1971)**

Byrd, Richard Evelyn (polar explorer); Winchester, Va. **(1888-1957)**
Byron, George Gordon (6th Baron Byron) (poet); London **(1788-1824)**

C

Caan, James (actor); The Bronx, N.Y., 3/26/1939
Caballé, Montserrat (soprano); Barcelona, Spain, 4/12/33
Cabot, Bruce (actor); Carlsbad, N.M. **(1904-1972)**
Cabot, John (Giovanni Caboto) (navigator); Genoa (?) **(1450-1498)**
Cabot, Sebastian (navigator); Venice **(1476?-1557)**
Cadmus, Paul (painter and etcher); New York City, 12/17/1904
Caesar, Gaius Julius (statesman); Rome **(100?-44 B.C.)**
Caesar, Sid (comedian); Yonkers, N.Y., 9/8/1922
Cage, Nicholas (Nicolas Coppola) (actor); Long Beach, Calif., 1/7/1964
Cagney, James (actor); New York City **(1899-1986)**
Cahn, Sammy (songwriter); New York City **(1913-1993)**
Caine, Michael (Maurice J. Micklewhite) (actor); London, 3/14/1933
Calder, Alexander (sculptor); Lawnton, Pa. **(1898-1976)**
Calderón del al Barca, Pedro (dramatist); Madrid **(1600-1681)**
Caldwell, Erskine (novelist); White Oak, Ga **(1903-1987)**
Caldwell, Sarah (opera director and conductor); Maryville, Mo., 1928
Caldwell, Taylor (novelist); Manchester, England **(1900-1985)**
Caldwell, Zoe (actress); Hawthorn, Australia, 9/14/1933
Calhern, Louis (Carl Henry Vogt) (actor); Brooklyn, N.Y. **(1895-1956)**
Calhoun, John Caldwell (statesman); nr. Calhoun Mills, S.C. **(1782-1850)**
Calisher, Hortense (novelist); New York City, 12/20/1911
Callas, Maria (Maria Calogeropoulos) (dramatic soprano); New York City **(1923-1977)**
Calloway, Cab (Cabell) (band leader); Rochester, N.Y. **(1907-1994)**
Calvet, Corinne (actress); Paris, 4/30/1926
Calvin, John (Jean Chauvin) (religious reformer); Noyon, Picardy **(1509-1564)**
Cambridge, Godfrey (comedian); New York City **(1933-1976)**
Cameron, Rod (Rod Cox) (actor); Calgary, Alberta, Canada **(1912-1983)**
Campbell, Glen (singer); nr. Delight, Ark., 4/22/1938
Campbell, Mrs. Patrick (Beatrice Stella Tanner) (actress); London **(1865-1940)**
Camus, Albert (author); Mondovi, Algeria **(1913-1960)**
Canaletto, (Giovanni Antonio Canale); (painter) Venice **(1697-1768)**
Candy, John (actor, comedian); Toronto, Ont., Canada **(1950-1994)**
Caniff, Milton (cartoonist); Hillsboro, Ohio **(1907-1988)**
Cannon, Dyan (actress); Tacoma, Wash., 1/4/1937
Canova, Judy (comedienne); Jacksonville, Fla. **(1916-1983)**
Cantinflas (Mario Moreno) (comedian); Mexico City **(1911-1993)**
Cantor, Eddie (Edward Iskowitz) (actor); New York City **(1892-1964)**
Capote, Truman (novelist); New Orleans **(1924-1984)**
Capp, Al (Alfred Gerald Caplin) (cartoonist); New Haven, Conn. **(1909-1979)**
Capra, Frank (film producer, director); Palermo, Italy **(1897-1991)**
Caravaggio, Michelangelo Merisi da (painter); Caravaggio (Italy) **(1573-1610)**
Cardin, Pierre (fashion designer); nr. Venice, 7/7/1922
Cardinale, Claudia (actress); Tunis, Tunisia, 1939
Carey, Harry (actor); New York City **(1878-1947)**
Carey, Macdonald (actor); Sioux City, Iowa **(1913-1994)**
Carlin, George (comedian); Bronx, N.Y., 5/12/1937
Carlisle, Kitty (singer and actress); New Orleans, 9/3/1915
Carlson, Richard (actor); Albert Lea, Minn. **(1912-1977)**
Carlyle, Thomas (essayist and historian); Ecclefechan, Scotland **(1795-1881)**
Carmichael, Hoagy (Hoagland Howard) (songwriter); Bloomington, Ind. **(1899-1981)**
Carne, Judy (Joyce Botterill) (singer); Northampton, England, 1939
Carnegie, Andrew (industrialist); Dunfermline, Scotland **(1835-1919)**
Carney, Art (actor); Mt. Vernon, N.Y., 11/4/1918
Carnovsky, Morris (actor); St. Louis **(1897-1992)**
Caron, Leslie (actress); Paris, 7/1/1931
Carr, Vikki (singer); El Paso, 7/19/1942
Carracci, Annibale (painter); Bologna (Italy) **(1560-1609)**
Carracci, Lodovico (painter); Bologna (Italy) **(1555-1619)**
Carradine, David (actor); Holly wood, Calif., 12/8/1936
Carradine, John (actor); New York City **(1906-1988)**
Carradine, Keith (actor); San Mateo, Calif., 8/8/49
Carreras, José (tenor); Barcelona, Spain, 12/5/1946
Carrillo, Leo (actor); Los Angeles **(1881-1961)**
Carroll, Diahann (Carol Diahann Johnson) (singer and actress); Bronx, N.Y., 7/17/1935
Carroll, Leo G. (actor); Weedon, England **(1892-1972)**
Carroll, Lewis (Charles Lutwidge Dodgson) (author and mathematician); Daresbury, England **(1832-1898)**
Carroll, Madeleine (actress); West Bromwich, England **(1906-1987)**

Carroll, Nancy (actress); New York City **(1904-1965)**
Carroll, Pat (comedienne); Shreveport, La., 5/5/1927
Carson, Jack (actor); Carmen, Man., Canada **(1910-1963)**
Carson, Johnny (TV entertainer); Corning, Iowa, 10/23/1925
Carson, Kit (Christopher) (scout); Madison County, Ky. **(1809-1868)**
Carson, Rachel (biologist and author); Springdale, Pa. **(1907-1964)**
Carter, Dixie (actress); McLemoresville, Tenn., 5/25/39
Carter, Jack (comedian); New York City, 1923
Carter, Lynda (actress); Phoenix, Ariz., 7/24/51
Cartier, Jacques (explorer); Saint-Malo, Brittany (France) **(1491-1557)**
Cartier-Brisson, Henri (photographer); Chanteloup, France, 8/22/1908
Cartland, Barbara (author); England, 7/9/1901
Caruso, Enrico (Errico) (tenor); Naples, Italy **(1873-1921)**
Carver, George Washington (botanist); Missouri **(1864-1943)**
Cary, Arthur Joyce Lunel (novelist); Londonderry, Ireland **(1888-1957)**
Casals, Pablo (cellist); Vendrell, Spain **(1876-1973)**
Casanova de Seingalt, Giovanni Jacopo (adventurer); Venice **(1725-1798)**
Cash, Johnny (singer); nr. Kingsland, Ark., 2/26/1932
Cass, Peggy (comedienne); Boston, 5/21/1924
Cassatt, Mary (painter); Allegheny, Pa. **(1844-1926)**
Cassavetes, John (actor and director); New York City **(1929-1989)**
Cassidy, David (singer); New York City, 4/12/1950
Cassidy, Jack (actor); Richmond Hill, Queens, N.Y. **(1927-1976)**
Cassidy, Shaun (actor); Los Angeles, 9/27/58
Cassini, Oleg (Oleg Lolewski-Cassini) (fashion designer); Paris, 4/11/1913
Castagno, Andrea del (painter); San Martino a Corella (Italy) **(c.1421-1457)**
Castellano, Richard (actor); New York City **(1934-1988)**
Castle, Irene (Irene Foote) (actress and dancer); New Rochelle, N.Y. **(1893-1969)**
Castle, Vernon Blythe (dancer and aviator); Norwich, England **(1887-1918)**
Castro Ruz, Fidel (Premier); Mayari, Oriente, Cuba, 8/13/1926
Cather, Willa Sibert (novelist); Winchester, Va. **(1876-1947)**
Cato, Marcus Porcius (called Cato the Elder) (statesman); Tusculum (Italy) **(234-149 B.C.)**
Catt, Carrie Chapman Lane (woman suffragist); Ripon, Wis. **(1859-1947)**
Catton, Bruce (historian); Petoskey, Mich. **(1899-1978)**
Cauldfield, Joan (actress); East Orange, N.J. **(1927-1991)**
Cavallaro, Carmen (band leader); New York City **(1913-1989)**
Cavett, Dick (Richard) (TV entertainer); Gibbon, Neb., 11/19/1936
Cellini, Benvenuto (goldsmith and sculptor); Florence (Italy) **(1500-1571)**
Cervantes Saavedra, Miguel de (novelist); Alcalá de Henares, Spain **(1547-1616)**
Cézanne, Paul (painter); Aix-en-Provence, France **(1839-1906)**
Chagall, Marc (painter); Vitebsk, Russia, **(1887-1985)**
Chaliapin, Feodor Ivanovitch (operatic basso); Kazan, Russia **(1873-1938)**
Chamberlain, Arthur Neville (statesman); Edgbaston, England **(1869-1940)**
Chamberlain, Richard (actor); Los Angeles, 3/31/1935(?)
Champion, Gower (choreographer); Geneva, Ill. **(1921-1980)**
Champion, Marge (dancer and actress); Los Angeles, 9/2/1923
Champlain, Samuel de (explorer); nr. Rochefort, France **(1567?-1635)**
Chancellor, John (TV commentator); Chicago, 7/14/1927
Chandler, Jeff (actor); Brooklyn, N.Y. **(1918-1961)**
Chandler, Raymond (writer); Chicago **(1883-1959)**
Chanel, "Coco" (Gabriel Bonheur) (fashion designer); Issoire, France **(1883-1971)**
Chaney, Lon (actor); Colorado Springs, Colo. **(1883-1930)**
Channing, Carol (actress); Seattle, 1/31/1923
Channing, Stockard (actress); New York City, 2/13/44
Chaplin, Geraldine (actress); Santa Monica, Calif., 7/31/1944
Chaplin, Sir Charles (actor); London **(1889-1977)**
Charisse, Cyd (Tula Finklea) (dancer and actress); Amarillo, Tex., 3/8/1923
Charlemagne (Holy Roman Emperor); birthplace unknown **(742-814)**
Charles, Ray (Ray Charles Robinson) (pianist, singer, and songwriter); Albany Ga., 9/23/1930
Charo (Maria Rosario Pilar Martinez) (actress); Murcia, Spain 1/15/51
Chase, Charlie (actor, director); Baltimore, Md. **(1893-1940)**
Chase, Chevy (Cornelius Crane Chase) (comedian); New York City, 10/8/1943
Chase, Ilka (author and actress); New York City **(1905-1978)**
Chase, Lucia (founder Ballet Theatre [now American Ballet Theatre]); Waterbury, Conn. **(1907-1986)**
Chatterton, Ruth (actress); New York City **(1893-1961)**

Chaucer, Geoffrey (poet); London **(1340?-1400)**

Chávez, Carlos (composer); nr. Mexico City **(1899-1978)**

Chavez, Cesar (labor leader); nr. Yuma, Ariz. **(1927-1993)**

Chayefsky, Paddy (Sidney) (playwright); New York City, **(1923-1981)**

Checker, Chubby (Ernest Evans) (performer); Philadelphia, 10/3/1941

Cheever, John (novelist); Quincy, Mass. **(1912-1982)**

Chekhov, Anton Pavlovich (dramatist and short-story writer); Taganrog, Russia **(1860-1904)**

Cher (Cherilyn LaPiere) (actress, singer); El Centro, Calif., 5/20/1946

Cherubini, Luigi (composer); Florence **(1760-1842)**

Chesterton, Gilbert Keith (author); Kensington, England **(1874-1936)**

Chevalier, Maurice (entertainer); Paris **(1888-1972)**

Chiang Kai-shek (Chief of State); Feng-hwa, China **(1887-1975)**

Child, Julia (food expert); Pasadena, Calif., 8/15/1912

Chippendale, Thomas (cabinet-maker); Otley, England **(1718?-1779)**

Chirico, Giorgio de (painter); Vólos, Greece, **(1888-1978)**

Chopin, Frédéric François (composer); nr. Warsaw **(1810-1849)**

Chou En-lai. *See* Zhou Enlai

Christie, Agatha (mystery writer); Torquay, England **(1890-1976)**

Christie, Julie (actress); Chukua, India, 4/14/1941

Christy, June (singer); Springfield, Ill. **(1925–1990)**

Chung, Connie (broadcast journalist); Washington, D.C., 8/20/1946

Churchill, Sir Winston Leonard Spencer (statesman); Blenheim Palace, Oxfordshire, England **(1874-1965)**

Cicero, Marcus Tullius (orator and statesman); Arpinum (Italy) **(106-43 B.C.)**

Cid, El (Rodrigo (or Ruy) DíezdeBivar)(Spanish nationl hero); nr. Burgos, Spain **(1040?-1099)**

Cilento, Diane (actress); Queensland, Australia, 10/5/1933

Cimabue, Giovanni (painter); Florence (Italy) **(c.1240-c.1302)**

Cimino, Michael (film director); New York City, 1943(?)

Clair, René (René Chomette) (film director); Paris **(1898-1981)**

Claire, Ina (Ina Fagan) (actress); Washington, D.C. **(1895-1985)**

Clapton, Eric (singer and guitarist); Ripley, England, 3/30/1945

Clark, Bobby (comedian, actor); Springfield, Ohio **(1888-1960)**

Clark, Dane (Barney Zanville) (actor); New York City, 2/18/1915

Clark, Dick (TV personality); Mt. Vernon, N.Y., 11/30/1929

Clark, Mark W. (general); Madison Barracks, N.Y. **(1896-1984)**

Clark, Petula (singer); Epsom, England, 11/15/1934

Clark, Roy (country music artist); Meherrin, Va., 4/15/1933

Clark, William (explorer); Caroline County, Va. **(1770-1838)**

Clarke, Arthur C. (science fiction writer); Minehead, England, 12/16/1917

Clary, Robert (actor); Paris, France, 3/1/26

Claude Lorrain (Claude Gellée) (painter); Champagne, France **(1600-1682)**

Clausewitz, Karl von (military strategist); Burg (East Germany) **(1780-1831)**

Clay, Henry (statesman); Hanover County, Va. **(1777-1852)**

Clay, Lucius D. (banker, ex-general); Marietta, Ga. **(1897-1978)**

Clayburgh, Jill (actress); New York City, 4/30/1944

Cleese, John (writer, actor); Weston-super-Mare, England, 10/27/39

Clemenceau, Georges (statesman); Mouilleron-en-Pareds, Vondée, France **(1841-1929)**

Clemens, Samuel L. *See* Mark Twain

Cleopatra (Queen of Egypt); Alexandria, Egypt **(69-30 B.C.)**

Cliburn, Van (Harvey Lavan Cliburn, Jr.) (concert pianist); Shreveport, La., 7/12/1934

Clift, Montgomery (actor); Omaha, Neb. **(1920-1966)**

Clooney, Rosemary (singer); Maysville, Ky., 5/23/1928

Close, Glenn (actress); Greenwich, Conn., 3/19/1947

Clurman, Harold (stage producer); New York City **(1901-1980)**

Cobb, Irvin Shrewsbury (humorist); Paducah, Ky. **(1876-1944)**

Cobb, Lee J. (Leo Jacob) (actor); New York City **(1911-1976)**

Coburn, Charles Douville (actor); Savannah, Ga. **(1877-1961)**

Coburn, James (actor); Laurel, Neb., 8/31/1928

Coca, Imogene (comedienne); Philadelphia, 11/18/1908

Cocker, Joe (John Robert Cocker) (singer); Sheffield, England, 5/20/1944

Coco, James (actor); New York City **(1929-1987)**

Cocteau, Jean (author); Maison-Lafitte, France **(1891-1963)**

Cody, W. F. *See* Buffalo Bill

Cohan, George Michael (actor and dramatist); Providence, R.I. **(1878-1942)**

Cohn, Mindy (actress); Los Angeles, 5/20/66

Colbert, Claudette (Lily Chauchoin) (actress); Paris, 9/13/1903

Cole, Nat "King" (singer); Montgomery, Ala. **(1919-1965)**

Cole, Natalie (singer); Los Angeles, 2/6/1950

Cole, Thomas (painter); Lancashire, England **(1801-1848)**

Coleman, Dabney (actor); Corpus Christi, Tex., 1/2/32

Coleman, Gary (actor); Zion, Ill., 2/8/68

Coleridge, Samuel Taylor (poet); Ottery St. Mary, England **(1772-1834)**

Colette (Sidonie-Gabrielle Colette) (novelist); St.-Sauveur, France **(c.1873-1954)**

Collier, Constance (actress); Windsor, England **(1878-1955)**

Collingwood, Charles (TV commentator); Three Rivers, Mich. **(1917-1985)**

Collins, Dorothy (Marjorie Chandler) (singer); Windsor, Ontario, Canada **(1926–1994)**

Collins, Joan (actress); London 5/23/1933

Collins, Judy (singer); Seattle, 5/1/1939

Colman, Ronald (actor); Richmond, England **(1891-1958)**

Colonna, Jerry (comedian); Boston **(1905-1986)**

Columbo, Russ (singer, bandleader); San Francisco **(1908-1934)**

Columbus, Christopher (Cristoforo Colombo) (discoverer of America); Genoa (Italy) **(1451-1506)**

Comden, Betty (writer); New York City, 5/3/1919

Comenius, Johann Amos (educational reformer) Nivnice, Moravia (Czechoslovakia) **(1592-1670)**

Commager, Henry Steele (historian); Pittsburgh, 10/25/1902

Como, Perry (Pierino) (singer); Canonsburg, Pa., 5/18/1912

Compton, Karl Taylor (phy sicist); Wooster, Ohio **(1887-1954)**

Comte, Auguste (philosopher); Montpellier, France **(1798-1857)**

Conant, James B. (educator and statesman); Dorchester, Mass. **(1893-1978)**

Condon, Eddie (jazz musician); Goodland, Ind. **(1905-1973)**

Confucius (K'ung Fu-tzu) (philosopher); Shantung province, China **(c.551-479 B.C.)**

Congreve, William (dramatist); nr. Leeds, England **(1670-1729)**

Connelly, Marc (playwright); McKeesport, Pa. **(1890-1980)**

Connery, Sean (actor); Edinburgh, Scotland, 8/25/1930

Conniff, Ray (band leader); Attleboro, Mass., 11/6/1916

Connolly, Walter (actor); Cincinnati, Ohio **(1887-1940)**

Connors, Chuck (actor); Brooklyn, N.Y. **(1921-1992)**

Connors, Mike (Krekor Ohanian) (actor); Fresno, Calif., 8/15/1925

Conrad, Joseph (Teodor Jozef Konrad Korzeniowski) (novelist); Berdichev, Ukraine **(1857-1924)**

Conrad, Robert (Conrad Robert Falk) (actor); Chicago, 3/1/1935

Conrad, William (actor); Louisville, Ky. **(1920–1994)**

Conried, Hans (Frank Foster) (actor); Baltimore **(1915-1982)**

Constable, John (painter); East Bergholt, Suffolk, England **(1776-1837)**

Constantine II (ex-king); Athens, 6/2/1940

Constantine, Michael (actor); Reading, Pa., 5/22/27

Conte, Richard (actor); New York City **(1916-1975)**

Conti, Tom (actor); Paisley, Scotland, 11/22/1941

Converse, Frank (actor); St. Louis, 1938

Convy, Bert (actor, host); St. Louis, Mo. **(1933–1991)**

Conway, Tim (comedian); Chagrin Falls, Ohio, 12/15/1933

Coogan, Jackie (actor); Los Angeles **(1914-1984)**

Cook, Peter (actor, writer); Torquay, England **(1937–1995)**

Cooke, Alistair (Alfred Alistair); (TV narrator and journalist); Manchester, England, 11/20/1908

Cooley, Denton A(rthur) (heart surgeon); Houston, Tex., 8/22/1920

Coolidge, Rita (singer); Nashville, Tenn., 1944

Cooper, Alice (Vincent Furnier) (rock musician); Detroit, 2/4/1948

Cooper, Gary (Frank James Cooper) (actor); Helena, Mont. **(1901-1961)**

Cooper, Dame Gladys (actress); Lewisham, England **(1898-1971)**

Cooper, Jackie (actor and director); Los Angeles, 9/15/1922

Cooper, James Fenimore (novelist); Burlington, N.J. **(1789-1 851)**

Cooper, Jeanne (actress); Taft, Calif., 10/25(?)

Cooper, Peter (industrialist and philanthropist); New York City **(1791-1883)**

Copernicus, Nicolaus (Mikolaj Kopernik) (astronomer); Thorn, Poland **(1473-1543)**

Copland, Aaron (composer); Brooklyn, N.Y. **(1900–1990)**

Copley, John Singleton (painter); Boston, Mass. **(1738-1815)**

Copperfield, David (illusionist); Matuchen, N.J., 9/16/1956

Coppola, Francis Ford (film director); Detroit, 4/7/1939

Corelli, Arcangelo (composer); Fusignano, Italy **(1653-1713)**

Corelli, Franco (operatic tenor); Ancona, Italy, 4/8/1923

Corneille, Pierre (dramatist); Rouen, France **(1606-1684)**

Cornell, Katharine (actress); Berlin **(1893-1974)**

Coret, Jean Baptiste Camille (painter); Paris **(1796-1875)**

Correggio, Antonio Allegri da (painter); Correggio (Italy) **(1494-1534)**

Corsaro, Frank (opera director); New York harbor, 12/22/1924

Cortés (or Cortez), Hernando (explorer); Medellin, Spain **(1485-1547)**

Cosby, Bill (actor); Philadelphia, 7/12/1937

Cosell, Howard (Howard Cohen) (sportscaster); Winston-Salem, N.C. **(1918–1995)**

Costa-Gavras, Henri (Kostantinos Gavras) (film director); Athens, 1933

Costello, Dolores (actress); Pittsburgh, Pa. **(1905-1979)**

Costello, Elvis (Declan Patrick McManus) (singer, musician, songwriter); London, 1954

Costello, Lou (comedian); Paterson, N.J. **(1908-1959)**

Costello, Maurice (actor); Pittsburgh **(1877-1950)**

Costner, Kevin (actor); Los Angeles, 1/18/1955

Cotten, Joseph (actor); Petersburg, Va. **(1905–1994)**
Couperin, François (composer); Paris **(1668-1733)**
Courbet, Gustave (painter); Ornans, France **(1819-1877)**
Courreges, André (fashion designer); Pau, France, 3/9/1923
Courtenay, Tom (actor); Hull, England, 2/25/1937
Cousins, Norman (publisher); Union Hill, N.J. **(1915–1990)**
Cousteau, Jacques-Yves (marine explorer); St. André-de-Cubzac, France, 6/11/1910
Coward, Sir Noel (playwright and actor); Teddington, England **(1899-1973)**
Cowl, Jane (actress); Boston **(1887-1950)**
Cowles, Gardner, Jr. (newspaper publisher); Algona, Iowa **(1903-1985)**
Cowper, William (poet); Great Berkhamstead, England **(1731-1800)**
Cox, Wally (actor); Detroit, Mich. **(1924-1973)**
Cozzens, James Gould (novelist); Chicago **(1903-1978)**
Crabbe, Buster (Clarence) (actor); Oakland, Calif. **(1908-1983)**
Crain, Jeanne (actress); Barstow, Calif., 5/25/1925
Cranach, Lucas, the elder (painter); Kronach (Germany) **(1472-1553)**
Crane, Hart (poet); Garrettsville, Ohio **(1899-1932)**
Crane, Stephen (novelist and poet); Newark, N.J. **(1871-1900)**
Cranmer, Thomas (churchman); Aslacton, England **(1489-1556)**
Crawford, Broderick (actor); Philadelphia **(1911-1986)**
Crawford, Cheryl (stage producer); Akron, Ohio **(1902-1986)**
Crawford, Joan (Lucille LeSueur) (actress and business executive); San Antonio **(1908-1977)**
Cregar, Laird (actor); Philadelphia, Pa. **(1916-1944)**
Crenna, Richard (actor); Los Angeles, 11/30/1927
Crespin, Régine (operatic soprano); Marseilles, France, 2/23/1929
Crichton, (John) Michael (novelist); Chicago, 10/23/1942
Crisp, Donald (actor); London **(1880-1974)**
Croce, Benedetto (philosopher); Peseasseroli, Aquila, Italy **(1866-1952)**
Croce, Jim (singer); Philadelphia **(1942-1973)**
Crockett, Davy (David) (frontiersman); Greene County, Tenn. **(1786-1836)**
Cromwell, Oliver (statesman); Huntingdon, England **(1599-1658)**
Cronin, A. J. (Archibald J. Cronin) (novelist); Cardross, Scotland **(1896-1981)**
Cronkite, Walter (TV newscaster); St. Joseph, Mo., 11/4/1916
Cronyn, Hume (actor); London, Ontario, Canada, 7/18/1911
Crosby, Bing (Harry Lillis) (singer, actor); Tacoma, Wash. **(1904-1977)**
Crosby, Bob (musician); Spokane, Wash. **(1913-1993)**
Crosby, Cathy Lee (actress); Los Angeles, 12/2/48
Crosby, Norm (comedian); Boston, 9/15/27
Cross, Ben (Bernard) (actor); Paddington, England, 12/16/1947
Cross, Milton (opera commentator); New York City **(1897-1975)**
Crouse, Russel (playwright); Findlay, Ohio **(1893-1966)**
Cruise, Tom (actor); Syracuse, N.Y., 7/3/1962
Crystal, Billy (comedian, actor); Long Beach, L.I., N.Y., 3/14/47
Cugat, Xavier (band leader); Barcelona, Spain **(1900-1990)**
Cukor, George (film director); New York City **(1899-1983)**
Cullen , Bill (William Lawrence Cullen) (radio and TV entertainer); Pittsburgh **(1920-1990)**
Culp, Robert (actor); Berkeley, Calif., 8/16/1930
Cummings, E. E. (Edward Estlin Cummings) (poet); Cambridge, Mass. **(1894-1962)**
Cummings, Robert (actor); Joplin, Mo. **(1908–1990)**
Curie, Marie (Marja Sklodowska) (physical chemist); Warsaw **(1867-1934)**
Curie, Pierre (physicist); Paris **(1859-1906)**
Curtin, Jane (actress); Cambridge, Mass., 9/6/47
Curtin, Phyllis (soprano); Clarksburg, W.Va., 12/3/1927
Curtis, Jamie Lee (actress); Los Angeles, 11/22/58
Curtis, Tony (Bernard Schwartz) (actor); Bronx, N.Y., 6/3/1925
Curzon, Clifford (concert pianist); London **(1907-1982)**
Custer, George Armstrong (army officer); New Rumley, Ohio **(1839-1876)**

D

da Gama, Vasco (explorer); Sines, Portugal **(1460-1524)**
Daguerre, Louis (photographic pioneer); nr. Paris **(1787-1851)**
Dahl, Arlene (actress); Minneapolis, 8/11/1928
Dailey, Dan (actor and dancer); New York City **(1917-1978)**
Dale, Jim (actor, singer, songwriter); Rothwell, England, 8/15/35
Daley, Richard J. (Mayor of Chicago); Chicago **(1902-1976)**
Dali, Salvador (painter); Figueras, Spain **(1904-1989)**
Dalton, Abby (actress); Las Vegas, Nev., 8/15/32
Dalton, John (chemist); nr. Cockermouth, England **(1766-1844)**
Daly, James (actor); Wisconsin Rapids, Wis. **(1918-1978)**
Daly, John (radio and TV news analyst); Johannesburg, South Africa **(1914–1991)**

Daly, Tyne (actress); Madison, Wis. 2/21/1946
d'Amboise, Jacques (ballet dancer); Dedham, Mass., 7/28/1934
Damone, Vic (Vito Farinola) (singer); Brooklyn, N.Y., 6/12/1928
Damrosch, Walter Johannes (orchestra conductor); Breslau (Poland) **(1862-1950)**
Dana, Charles Anderson (editor); Hinsdale, N.H. **(1819-1897)**
Dandridge, Dorothy (actress); Cleveland **(1923-1965)**
Dangerfield, Rodney (comedian); Babylon, L.I., N.Y., 1921
Daniels, Bebe (Virginia Daniels) (actress); Dallas **(1901-1971)**
Daniels, William (actor); Brooklyn, N.Y., 3/31/27
Danilova, Alexandra (ballerina); Peterhof, Russia, 1/20/1904
Dannay, Frederic (novelist, pseudonym Ellery Queen); Brooklyn, N.Y. **(1905-1982)**
Danner, Blythe (actress); Philadelphia, 1944(?)
D'Annunzio, Gabriele (soldier and author); Francaville at Mare, Pescara, Italy **(1863-1938)**
Danson, Ted (actor); San Diego, Calif., 12/29/47
Dante (or Durante) Alighieri (poet); Florence (Italy) **(1265-1321)**
Danton, Georges Jacques (French Revolutionary leader); Arcis-sur-Aube, France **(1759-1794)**
Danza, Tony (actor); Brooklyn, N.Y., 4/21/51
Darnell, Linda (actress); Dallas **(1921-1965)**
Darren, James (actor); Philadelphia, 6/8/1936
Darrieux, Danielle (actress); Bordeaux, France, 5/1/1917
Darrow, Clarence Seward (lawyer); Kinsman, Ohio **(1857-1938)**
Darwell, Jane (actress); Palmyra, Mo. **(1879-1967)**
Darwin, Charles Robert (naturalist); Shrewsbury, England **(1809-1882)**
daSilva, Howard (actor); Cleveland **(1909-1986)**
Dassin, Jules (film director); Middletown, Conn., 12/18/1911
Daumier, Honoré (caricaturist); Marseilles, France **(1808-1879)**
Dauphin, Claude (actor); Corbeil, France **(1903-1978)**
Davenport, Harry (actor); New York City **(1866-1949)**
David, Jacques-Louis (painter); Paris **(1748-1825)**
David (King of Israel and Judah) **(died c. 973 B.C.)**
Davidson, John (singer and actor); Pittsburgh, 12/13/1941
Davies, Marion (Marion Douras) (actress); New York City **(1898?-1961)**
da Vinci, Leonardo (painter and scientist); Vinci, Tuscany (Italy) **(1452-1519)**
Davis, Ann B. (actress); Schenectady, N.Y., 5/5/26
Davis, Bette (actress); Lowell, Mass. **(1908-1989)**
Davis, Elmer Holmes (radio commentator); Aurora, Ind. **(1890-1958)**
Davis, Jefferson (President of the Confederacy); Christian (now Todd) County, Ky. **(1808-1889)**
Davis, Joan (actress); St. Paul, Minn. **(1907-1961)**
Davis, Mac (singer); Lubbock, Tex., 1/21/1942
Davis, Miles (jazz trumpeter); Alton, Ill. **(1926-1991)**
Davis, Ossie (actor and writer); Cogdell, Ga., 12/18/1917
Davis, Sammy, Jr. (actor and singer); New York City **(1925-1990)**
Davis, Skeeter (Mary Francis Penick) (singer); Dry Ridge, Ky., 12/30/1931
Davis, Stuart (painter); Philadelphia **(1894-1964)**
Dawber, Pam (actress); Farmington Hills, Mich., 10/18/51
Dawson, Richard (actor, host); Gosport, Hampshire, England, 11/20/32
Day, Dennis (singer); New York City **(1917-1988)**
Day, Doris (Doris von Kappelhoff) (singer and actress); Cincinnati, 4/3/1924
Day, Laraine (La Raine Johnson) (actress); Roosevelt, Utah, 10/13/1920
Dayan, Moshe (ex-Defense Minister of Israel); Dagania, Palestine **(1915-1981)**
Dean, James (actor); Marion, Ind. **(1931-1955)**
Dean, Jimmy (singer); Seth Ward, nr. Plainview, Tex., 8/10/1928
De Bakey, Michael E. (heart surgeon); Lake Charles, La., 9/7/1908
de Beauvoir, Simone (novelist and philosopher); Paris **(1908-1986)**
Debs, Eugene Victor (Socialist leader); Terre Haute, Ind. **(1855-1926)**
Debussy, Claude Achille (composer); St. Germain-en-Laye, France **(1862-1918)**
DeCamp, Rosemary (actress); Prescott, Ariz., 11/14/14(?)
De Carlo, Yvonne (Peggy Yvonne Middleton) (actress); Vancouver, B.C., Canada, 9/1/1924
de Chirico, Giorgio (painter); Volos, Greece, **(1888-1978)**
Dee, Francis (actress); Los Angeles, 11/26/07
Dee, Ruby (actress); Cleveland, Ohio, 10/27/23(?)
Dee, Sandra (Alexandra Zuck) (actress); Bayonne, N.J., 4/23/1942
Defoe, Daniel (novelist); London **(1659?-1731)**
Defore, Don (actor); Cedar Rapids, Iowa **(1917–1993)**
Degas, Hilaire Germain Edgar (painter); Paris **(1834-1917)**
de Gaulle, Charles André Joseph Marie (soldier and statesman); Lille, France **(1890-1970)**
DeHaven, Gloria (actress); Los Angeles, 7/23/1925
de Havilland, Olivia (actress); Tokyo, 7/1/1916
Dekker, Albert (actor); Brooklyn, N.Y. **(1904-1968)**

de Kooning, Willem (painter); Rotterdam, 4/24/1904
Delacroix, Eugène (painter); Charenton-St. Maurice, France (1798-1863)
de la Renta, Oscar (fashion designer); Santo Domingo, Dominican Republic, 7/22/1932
Delaunay, Robert (painter); Paris (1885-1941)
De Laurentiis, Dino (film producer); Torre Annunziata, Bay of Naples, Italy, 8/8/1919
della Robbia, Andrea (sculptor) Florence (1435-1525)
della Robbia, Luca (sculptor); Florence (1400-1482)
Delon, Alain (actor); Sceaux, France, 11/8/1935
Del Rio, Dolores (Dolores Ansunsolo) (actress); Durango, Mexico (1905-1983)
DeLuise, Dom (comedian); Brooklyn, N.Y., 8/1/1933
Demarest, William (actor); St. Paul (1892-1983)
de Mille, Agnes (choreographer); New York City (1905–1993)
De Mille, Cecil Blount (film director); Ashfield, Mass. (1881-1959)
Demosthenes (orator); Athens (3857-322 B.C.)
Deneuve, Catherine (actress); Paris, 10/22/1943
De Niro, Robert (actor); New York City, 8/17/1943
Dennehy, Brian (actor); Brigeport, Conn., 7/9/40
Denning, Richard (actor); Poughkeepsie, N.Y., 3/27/14
Dennis, Sandy (actress); Hastings, Neb. (1937-1992)
Denny, Reginald (actor); Richmond, England (1891-1967)
Denver, John (Henry John Deutschendorf, Jr.) (singer); Roswell, N.M., 12/31/1943
De Palma, Brian (film director); Newark, N.J., 9/11/1940
Derain, André (painter); Chatou, Seine-et-Oise, France (1880-1954)
Derek, John (actor; director); Los Angeles, 8/12/26
Dern, Bruce (actor); Chicago, 6/4/1936
Descartes, René (philosopher and mathematician); La Haye, France (1596-1650)
De Seversky, Alexander P. (aviator); Tiflis, Russia (1894-1974)
De Sica, Vittorio (film director); Sora, Italy (1901-1974)
Desmond, Johnny (composer); Detroit (1921-1985)
Desmond, William (actor); Dublin (1878-1949)
De Soto, Hernando (explorer); Barcarrota, Spain (1500?-1542)
De Valera, Eamon (ex-President of Ireland); New York City (1882-1975)
Devane, William (actor); Albany, N.Y., 9/5/39
Devine, Andy (actor); Flagstaff, Ariz. (1905-1977)
DeVito, Danny (Daniel Michael); (actor, director); Neptune, N.J., 11/17/1944
De Vries, Peter (novelist); Chicago (1910–1993)
de Waart, Edo (conductor); Amsterdam, the Netherlands, 6/1/41
Dewey, George (admiral); Montpelier, Vt. (1837-1917)
Dewey, John (philosopher and educator); Burlington, Vt. (1859-1952)
Dewey, Thomas E. (politician); Owosso, Mich. (1902-1971)
Dewhurst, Colleen (actress); Montreal (1924–1991)
De Wilde, Brandon (actor); Brookly, N.Y. (1942-1972)
DeWitt, Joyce (actress); Wheeling W.Va., 4/23/49
De Wolfe, Billy (actor); Wollaston, Mass. (1907-1974)
Dey, Susan (actress); Pekin, Ill., 12/10/52
Diamond, Neil (singer); Brooklyn, N.Y., 1/24/1941
Diana (Diana Frances Spencer) (Princess of Wales); Sandringham, England, 7/1/61
Dichter, Misha (pianist); Shanghai, 9/27/1945
Dickens, Charles John Huffam (novelist); Portsea, England (1812-1870)
Dickey, James (poet); Atlanta, 2/2/1923
Dickinson, Angie (Angeline Brown) (actress); Kulm, N.D., 9/30/1932
Dickinson, Emily Elizabeth (poet); Amherst, Mass. (1830-1886)
Diddley, Bo (Elias McDaniel) (guitarist); McComb, Miss., 12/30/1928
Diderot, Denis (encyclopedist); Langres, France (1713-1784)
Dietrich, Marlene (Maria Magdalena von Losch) (actress); Berlin (1901-1992)
Diggs, Dudley (actor); Dublin (1879-1947)
Diller, Phyllis (Phyllis Driver) (comedienne); Lima, Ohio, 7/17/1917
Dillman, Bradford (actor); San Francisco, 4/14/1930
Dine, Jim (painter); Cincinnati, 6/16/1935
Diogenes (philosopher); Sinope (Turkey) (412?-323 B.C.)
Dion (Dion DiMucci) (singer); Bronx, N.Y., 7/18/1939
Dior, Christian (fashion designer); Granville, France (1905-1957)
Disney, Walt(er) Elias (film animator and producer); Chicago (1901-1966)
Disraeli, Benjamin (Earl of Beaconsfield) (statesman); London (1804-1881)
Dix, Dorothea (civil rights reformer); Hampden, Me. (1802-1887)
Dix, Richard (Ernest Carlton Brimmer) (actor); St. Paul (1894-1949)
Dixon, Jeane (Jeane Pinckert) (seer); Medford, Wis., 1918
Dobbs, Mattiwilda (soprano); Atlanta, Ga., 7/11/1925
Doctorow, E(dgar) L(aurence) (novelist); New York City, 1/6/1931
Dodgson, C. L. See Carroll, Lewis.
Dolin, Anton (dancer); Slinfold, England (1904-1983)
Domingo, Placido (tenor); Madrid, 1/21/1941

Domino, Fats (Antoine) (musician); New Orleans, 2/26/1928
Donahue, Phil (television personality); Cleveland, 12/21/1935
Donahue, Troy (actor); New York City, 1/27/36(?)
Donaldson, Sam (broadcast journalist); El Paso, Texas, 3/11/1934
Donat, Robert (actor); Withington, England (1905-1958)
Donatello (Donato Niccolò di Betto Bardi) (sculptor); Florence (c.1386-1466)
Donlevy, Brian (actor); Portadown, Ireland (1899-1972)
Donovan (Donovan Leitch) (singer and songwriter); Glasgow, Scotland, 2/10/1946
Donne, John (poet); London (1573-1631)
Doolittle, James H. (ex-Air Force general); Alameda, Calif. (1896–1993)
Dorati, Antal (orchestra conductor); Budapest (1906-1988)
Dorsey, Jimmy (band leader); Shenandoah, Pa. (1904-1957)
Dorsey, Tommy (band leader); Mahanoy Plane, Pa. (1905-1956)
Dos Passos, John (novelist); Chicago (1896-1970)
Dostoevski, Fyodor Mikhailovich (novelist); Moscow (1821-1881)
Dotrice, Roy (actor); Guernsey, Channel Islands, England, 5/26/23
Douglas, Helen Gahagan (ex-Representative); Boonton, N.J. (1900-1980)
Douglas, Kirk (Issur Danielovitch) (actor); Amsterdam, N.Y., 12/9/1916
Douglas, Melvyn (Melvyn Hesselberg) (actor); Macon, Ga., (1901-1981)
Douglas, Michael (actor; movie producer); New Brunswick, N.J., 9/25/1944
Douglas, Mike (Michael D. Dowd, Jr.) (TV personality); Chicago, 8/11/1925
Douglas, Paul (actor); Philadelphia (1907-1959)
Douglas, Stephen Arnold (politician); Brandon, Vt. (1813-1861)
Dowling, Eddie (Edward Goucher) (actor and stage producer); Woonsocket, R.I. (1894-1976)
Down, Lesley-Anne (actress); London, England, 3/17/54
Downs, Hugh (TV entertainer); Akron, Ohio, 2/14/1921
Doyle, Sir Arthur Conan (novelist and spiritualist); Edinburgh, Scotland (1859-1930)
Doyle, David (actor); Omaha, Neb., 12/1/25
Drake, Alfred (singer and actor); New York City (1914-1992)
Drake, Sir Francis (navigator); Tavistock, England (1545-1596)
Dreiser, Theodore (writer); Terre Haute, Ind. (1871-1945)
Dressler, Marie (Leila Koeber) (actress); Cobourg, Ontario, Canada (1869-1934)
Dreyfus, Alfred (French army officer); Mulhouse (France) (1859-1935)
Dreyfuss, Richard (actor); Brooklyn, N.Y., 10/29/1947
Drury, Allen (novelist); Houston, 9/2/1918
Dryden, John (poet); Northamptonshire, England (1631-1700)
Dryer, Fred (actor); Hawthorne, Calif., 7/6/46
Dru, Joan (actress); Logan, W. Va., 1/31/23
Dubček, Alexander (ex-President of Czechoslovakia); Uhroved (Czechoslovakia) (1921-1992)
Dubinsky, David (David Dobnievski) (labor leader); Brest-Litovsk (U.S.S.R.) (1892-1982)
Duchamp, Marcel (painter); Blainville, France (1887-1968)
Duchin, Eddy (pianist, bandleader); Cambridge, Mass. (1909-1951)
Duchin, Peter (pianist and band leader); New York City, 7/28/1937
Dufay, Guillaume (composer); Cambrai, France (c. 1400-1474)
Duff, Howard (actor); Bremerton, Wash. (1917-1990)
Duffy, Julia (actress); Minneapolis, Minn., 6/27/50
Dufy, Raoul (painter); Le Havre, France (1877-1953)
Dukakis, Olympia (actress); Lowell, Mass., 6/20/1931
Duke, James B. (industrialist); nr. Durham, N.C. (1856-1925)
Duke, Patty (Anna Marie Duke) (actress); New York City, 12/14/1946
Dullea, Keir (actor); Cleveland, 5/30/1936(?)
Dulles, Allen Welsh (ex-Director of CIA); Watertown, N.Y. (1893-1969)
Dulles, John Foster (statesman); Washington, D.C. (1888-1959)
Dumas, Alexandre (called Dumas fils) (novelist); Paris (1824-1895)
Dumas, Alexandre (called Dumas père) (novelist); Villers-Cotterets, France (1802-1870)
du Maurier, Daphne (novelist); London (1907-1989)
du Maurier, George Louis Palmella Busson (novelist); Paris (1834-1896)
Dumont, Margaret (actress); (1889-1965)
Dunaway, Faye (actress); Bascom, Fla., 1/14/1941
Duncan, Isadora (dancer); San Francisco (1878-1927)
Duncan, Sandy (actress); Henderson, Tex., 2/20/1946
Dunham, Katherine (dancer, choreographer); Chicago, 1914
Dunn, James (actor); Santa Monica, Calif. (1905-1967)
Dunne, Irene (actress); Louisville, Ky. (1901?-1990)
Dunnock, Mildred (actress); Baltimore (1901–1991)
Duns Scotus, John (theologian); Duns, Scotland (1265-1303)
Du Pont, Pierre S. (economist); Paris (1739-1817)
Durante, Jimmy (comedian); New York City (1893-1980)
Durbin, Deanna (Edna Mae) (actress); Winnipeg, Canada, 12/4/1922

Dürer, Albrecht (painter and engraver); Nürnberg (Germany) **(1471–1528)**
Durning, Charles (actor); Highland Falls, N.Y., 2/28/1923
Durrell, Lawrence George (novelist); Julundur, India **(1912–1990)**
Duryea, Dan (actor); White Plains, N.Y. **(1907–1968)**
Duse, Eleonora (actress); Chioggia, Italy **(1859–1924)**
Dussault, Nancy (actress); Pensacola, Fla., 6/30/1936
Duvall, Robert (actor); San Diego, Calif., 1931
Duvall, Shelley (actress); Houston, Tex., 1950
Dvořák, Antonin (composer); Nelahozeves (Czechoslovakia) **(1841–1904)**
Dylan, Bob (Robert Zimmerman) (folk singer and composer); Duluth, Minn., 5/24/1941
Dysart, Richard (actor); Brighton, Mass., 3/30/?

E

Eagels, Joanne (actress); Kansas City, Mo. **(1894–1929)**
Eakins, Thomas (painter and sculptor); Philadelphia **(1844–1916)**
Earhart, Amelia (aviator); Atchison, Kan. **(1898–1937)**
Eastman, George (inventor); Waterville, N.Y. **(1854–1932)**
Eastwood, Clint (actor); San Francisco, 5/31/1930
Ebert, Roger (film critic); Urbana, Ill., 6/18/42
Ebsen, Buddy (Christian Ebsen, Jr.) (actor); Belleville, Ill., 4/2/1908
Eckstine, Billy (singer); Pittsburgh **(1914–1993)**
Eddy, Mary Baker (founder of Christian Science Church); Bow, N.H. **(1821–1910)**
Eddy, Nelson (baritone and actor); Providence, R.I. **(1901–1967)**
Eden, Sir Anthony (Earl of Avon) (ex-Prime Minister); Durham, England **(1897–1977)**
Eden, Barbara (actress); Tucson, Ariz., 8/23/34
Edison, Thomas Alva (inventor); Milan, Ohio **(1847–1931)**
Edwards, Anthony (actor); Santa Barbara, Calif., 7/19/?
Edwards, Blake (film writer-producer); Tulsa, Okla. 7/26/1922
Edwards, Jonathan (theologian); East Windsor, Conn. **(1703–1758)**
Edwards, Ralph (TV and radio producer); Merino, Colo., 1913
Edwards, Vincent (actor); Brooklyn, N.Y., 7/7/1928
Egan, Richard (actor); San Francisco **(1923–1987)**
Eggar, Samantha (actress); London, 5/3/1939
Eglevsky, André (ballet dancer); Moscow **(1917–1977)**
Ehrlich, Paul (bacteriologist); Strzelin (Poland) **(1854–1915)**
Eikenberry, Jill (actress); New Haven, Conn., 1/21/47
Einstein, Albert (physicist); Ulm, Germany **(1879–1955)**
Eisenhower, Milton S. (educator); Abilene, Kan. **(1899–1985)**
Eisenstaedt, Alfred (photographer and photojournalist); Dirschau (Prussia, now Tczew, Poland) **(1898–1995)**
Ekberg, Anita (actress); Malmö, Sweden, 9/29/1931
Ekland, Britt (Britt-Marie) (actress); Stockholm, Sweden, 1942
Eldridge, Florence (Florence McKechnie) (actress); Brooklyn, N.Y. **(1901–1988)**
Elgar, Sir Edward (composer); Worcester, England **(1857–1934)**
Elgart, Larry (band leader); New London, Conn., 3/20/1922
El Greco (Domenicos Theotocopoulos) (painter); Candia, Crete (Greece) **(c.1541–1614)**
Eliot, George (Mary Ann Evans) (novelist); Chilvers Coton, England **(1819–1880)**
Eliot, Thomas Stearns (poet); St. Louis **(1888–1965)**
Ellington, Duke (Edward Kennedy) (jazz musician); Washington, D.C. **(1899–1974)**
Elliot, "Mama" Cass (Ellen Naomi Cohen) (singer); Baltimore **(1941–1974)**
Elliott, Denholm (actor); London **(1922–1992)**
Elliott, Sam (actor); California, 8/9/44
Elman, Mischa (violinist); Stalnoye, Ukraine **(1891–1967)**
Emerson, Ralph Waldo (philosopher and poet); Boston **(1803–1882)**
Enesco, Georges (composer); Dorohoi, Romania **(1881–1955)**
Engels, Friedrich (Socialist writer); Barmen (Germany) **(1820–1895)**
Englund, Robert (actor); Glendale, Calif., 6/6/49
Entremont, Philippe (concert pianist); Rheims, France, 6/7/1934
Epicurus (philosopher); Samos (Greece) **(341–270** B.C.)
Epstein, Sir Jacob (sculptor); New York City **(1880–1959)**
Erasmus, Desiderius (Gerhard Gerhards) (scholar); Rotterdam **(1466?–1536)**
Erickson, Leif (actor); Alameda, Calif. **(1911–1986)**
Ericson, Leif (navigator); **(c. 10th century** A.D.)
Erikson, Erik H. (psychoanalyst); Frankfurt, Germany **(1902–1994)**
Ernst, Max (painter); Brühl, Germany **(1891–1976)**
Erté (Romain de Tirtoff) (artist, designer); St. Petersburg, Russia **(1892–1990)**
Estrada, Erik (actor); New York City, 3/16/1949
Euclid (mathematician); Megara (Greece) **(c. 300** B.C.)
Euler, Leonhard (mathematician); Basel, Switzerland **(1707–1783)**
Euripides (dramatist); Salamis (Greece) **(c.484–407** B.C.)
Evans, Dale (Frances Butts) (actress and singer); Uvalde, Tex., 10/31/1912
Evans, Dame Edith (actress); London **(1888–1976)**
Evans, Linda (actress), Hartford, Conn., 11/18/1942
Evans, Maurice (actor); Dorchester, England **(1901–1989)**
Everett, Chad (actor); (Raymon Lee Cramton) South Bend, Ind., 6/11/1936
Evers, Charles (civil rights leader); Decatur, Miss., 9/14/1923(?)
Evers, Medgar (civil rights leader); Decatur, Miss. **(1925–1963)**
Evigan, Greg (actor); South Amboy, N.J., 10/14/1953
Ewell, Tom (Yewell Tompkins) (actor); Owensboro, Ky. **(1909–1994)**

F

Fabares, Shelley (actress); Santa Monica, Calif., 1/19/1944
Fabian (Fabian Anthony Forte) (singer); Philadelphia, 2/6/1943
Fabray, Nanette (Nanette Fabarés) (actress); San Diego, Calif., 10/27/1922
Fadiman, Clifton (literary critic); Brooklyn, N.Y., 5/15/1904
Fahrenheit, Gabriel (German physicist); Danzig (Poland), **(1686–1736)**
Fairbanks, Douglas (Douglas Ulman) (actor); Denver **(1883–1939)**
Fairbanks, Douglas, Jr. (actor); New York City, 12/9/1909
Fairchild, Morgan (actress); Dallas, Tex., 2/3/1950
Faith, Percy (conductor); Toronto **(1908–1976)**
Falk, Peter (actor); New York City, 9/16/1927
Falla, Manuel de (composer); Cadiz, Spain **(1876–1946)**
Faraday, Michael (physicist); Newington, England **(1791–1867)**
Farber, Barry (radio-TV broadcaster); Baltimore, Md., 1930
Farentino, James (actor); Brooklyn, N.Y., 2/24/1938
Farmer, Frances (actress); Seattle, Wash. **(1913–1970)**
Farmer, James (civil rights leader); Marshall, Tex., 1/12/1920
Farnum, William (actor); Boston **(1876–1953)**
Farr, Jamie (actor); Toledo, Ohio, 7/1/1934
Farrar, Geraldine (soprano, actress); Melrose, Mass. **(1882–1967)**
Farrell, Charles (actor); Onset Bay, Mass. **(1901–1990)**
Farrell, Eileen (operatic soprano); Willimantic, Conn., 2/13/1920
Farrell, Glenda (actress); Enid, Okla. **(1904–1971)**
Farrell, James T. (novelist); Chicago **(1904–1979)**
Farrell, Mike (actor); St. Paul, Minn., 2/6/1939
Farrell, Suzanne (Roberta Sue Ficker) (ballerina); Cincinnati, 8/16/1945
Farrow, Mia (actress); Los Angeles, 2/9/1946
Fasanella, Ralph (painter); New York City, 9/2/1914
Fassbinder, Rainer Werner (film and stage director); Bad Wörishofen, West Germany **(1946–1982)**
Fast, Howard (novelist); New York City, 11/11/1914
Faulkner, William (novelist); New Albany, Miss. **(1897–1962)**
Fauré, Gabriel Urbain (composer); Pamiers, France **(1845–1924)**
Fawcett, Farrah (actress); Corpus Christi, Tex., 2/2/1947(?)
Faye, Alice (Ann Leppert) (actress); New York City, 5/5/1912
Feiffer, Jules (cartoonist); New York City, 1/26/1929
Feininger, Lyonel (painter); New York City **(1871–1956)**
Feldman, Marty (actor, screenwriter, director); London **(1938–1982)**
Feldon, Barbara (actress); Pittsburgh, 3/12/1941
Feliciano, José (singer); Larez, Puerto Rico, 9/10/1945
Felker, Clay S. (editor and publisher); St. Louis, 10/2/1925(?)
Fell, Norman (actor); Philadelphia, 3/24/1923
Fellini, Federico (film director); Rimini, Italy **(1920–1993)**
Fender, Freddie (Baldemar Huerta) (singer); San Benito, Tex., 1937
Ferber, Edna (novelist); Kalamazoo, Mich. **(1885–1968)**
Ferguson, Maynard (jazz trumpeter); Verdun, Quebec, Canada, 5/4/1928
Fermi, Enrico (atomic physicist); Rome **(1901–1954)**
Fernandel (Fernand Joseph Desire Contandin) (actor); Marseilles, France **(1903–1971)**
Ferrer, José (actor and director); Santurce, Puerto Rico **(1912–1992)**
Ferrer, Mel (actor); Elberon, N.J., 8/25/1917
Ferrigno, Lou (actor); Brooklyn, N.Y., 11/9/1952
Fetchit, Stepin (Lincoln Theodore Perry) (comedian); Key West, Fla. **(1902–1985)**
Fiedler, Arthur (conductor); Boston **(1894–1979)**
Field, Betty (actress); Boston **(1918–1973)**
Field, Eugene (poet); St. Louis **(1850–1895)**
Field, Marshall (merchant); nr. Conway, Mass. **(1834–1906)**
Field, Sally (actress); Pasadena, Calif., 11/6/1946
Fielding, Henry (novelist); nr. Glastonbury, England **(1707–1754)**
Fields, Gracie (comedienne); Rochdale, England **(1898–1979)**
Fields, Totie (comedienne); Hartford, Conn. **(1931–1978)**
Fields, W. C. (William Claude Dukenfield) (comedian); Philadelphia **(1880–1946)**
Fierstein, Harvey (Forbes) (playwright and actor); Brooklyn, 6/6/1954
Filene, Edward A. (merchant); **(1860–1937)**
Finch, Peter (actor); Kensington, England **(1916–1977)**
Finney, Albert (actor); Salford, England, 5/9/1936
Firkusny, Rudolf (pianist); Napajedia (Czechoslovakia) **(1912–1994)**

Fischer-Dieskau, Dietrich (baritone); Berlin, 5/28/1925
Fisher, Carrie (actress); Los Angeles, 10/21/1956
Fisher, Eddie (Edwin) (singer); Philadelphia, 8/10/1928
Fitzgerald, Barry (William Joseph Shields) (actor); Dublin **(1888-1961)**
Fitzgerald, Edward (radio broadcaster); Troy, N.Y. **(1898(?)-1982)**
Fitzgerald, Ella (singer); Newport News, Va., 4/25/1918
Fitzgerald, F. Scott (Francis Scott Key) (novelist); St. Paul, Minn. **(1896-1940)**
Fitzgerald, Geraldine (actress); Dublin, 11/24/1914
Fitzgerald, Pegeen (radio broadcaster); Norcatur, Kan. **(1910-1989)**
Flack, Roberta (singer); Black Mountain, N.C., 2/10/1940
Flagstad, Kirsten (Wagnerian soprano); Hamar, Norway **(1895-1962)**
Flatt, Lester Raymond (bluegrass musician); Overton County, Tenn. **(1914-1979)**
Flaubert, Gustave (novelist); Rouen, France **(1821-1880)**
Fleming, Sir Alexander (bacteriologist); Lochfield, Scotland **(1881-1955)**
Fleming, Rhonda (Marilyn Louis) (actress); Los Angeles, 8/10/1923
Fletcher, John (dramatist); Rye? England **(1579-1625)**
Flynn, Errol (actor); Hobart, Tasmania **(1909-1959)**
Foch, Nina (actress); Leyden, Netherlands, 4/20/1924
Fodor, Eugene (violinist); Turkey Creek, Colo., 3/5/1950
Fokine, Michel (dancer, choreographer); St. Petersburg, Russia **(1880-1942)**
Fonda, Henry (actor); Grand Island, Neb. **(1905-1982)**
Fonda, Jane (actress); New York City, 12/21/1937
Fonda, Peter (actor); New York City, 2/23/1939
Fontaine, Frank (singer and comedian); Cambridge, Mass. **(1920-1979)**
Fontaine, Joan (Joan de Havilland) (actress); Tokyo, 10/22/1917
Fontanne, Lynn (actress); London **(1887-1983)**
Fonteyn, Dame Margot (Margaret Hookham) (ballerina); Reigate, England **(1919–1991)**
Forbes, Malcolm S(tevenson) (publisher and sportsman); Brooklyn, N.Y. **(1919-1990)**
Ford, Glenn (Gwyllyn Ford) (actor); Quebec, 5/1/1916
Ford, Harrison (actor); Chicago, 7/13/1942
Ford, Henry (industrialist); Greenfield, Mich. **(1863-1947)**
Ford, John (film director); Cape Elizabeth, Me. **(1895-1973)**
Ford, Paul (actor); Baltimore **(1901-1976)**
Ford, Tennessee Ernie (Ernie Jennings Ford) (singer); Bristol, Tenn. **(1919-1991)**
Forrester, Maureen (contralto); Montreal, 7/25/1930
Forsythe, John (actor); Penn's Grove, N.J., 1/29/1918
Fosdick, Harry Emerson (clergyman); Buffalo, N.Y. **(1878-1968)**
Fosse, Bob (Robert Louis) (choreographer and director); Chicago **(1927-1987)**
Foster, Jodie (actress); Bronx, N.Y., 1963
Foster, Preston (actor); Ocean City, N.J. **(1900-1970)**
Foster, Stephen Collins (composer); nr. Pittsburgh **(1826-1864)**
Fox, Michael J. (actor); Edmonton, Alta., Canada, 6/9/1961
Foxx, Redd (John Elroy Sanford) (actor and comedian); St. Louis **(1922-1991)**
Foy, Eddie, Jr. (dancer and actor); New Rochelle, N.Y. **(1905-1983)**
Fra Angelico (Giovanni da Fiesole) (painter); Vicchio in the Mugello, Tuscany (Italy) **(c.1387-1455)**
Fracci, Carla (ballerina); Milan, Italy, 8/20/1936
Fragonard, Jean Honoré (painter); Grasse, France **(1732-1806)**
Frampton, Peter (rock musician); Beckenham, England, 4/20/1950
France, Anatole (Jacques Anatole François Thibault) (author); Paris **(1844-1924)**
Francescatti, Zino (violinist); Marseilles, France **(1902–1991)**
Franciosa, Anthony (Anthony Papaleo) (actor); New York City, 10/25/1928
Francis, Anne (actress); Ossining, N.Y., 7/16/1930
Francis, Arlene (Arlene Francis Kazanjian) (actress); Boston, 10/20/1908
Francis, Connie (Concetta Franconero) (singer); Newark, N.J., 12/12/1938
Francis, Genie (actress); Englewood, N.J., 5/26/1962
Francis, Kay (Katherine Edwina Gibbs) (actress); Oklahoma City **(1903-1968)**
Francis of Assisi, Saint (Giovanni Francesco Barnardone) (founder of Franciscans); Assisi, Italy **(1182-1226)**
Franck, César Auguste (composer); Liège (Belgium) **(1822-1890)**
Franco Bahamonde, Francisco (Chief of State); El Ferrol, Spain **(1892-1975)**
Franklin, Aretha (singer); Memphis, Tenn., 3/25/1942
Franklin, Benjamin (statesman and scientist); Boston **(1706-1790)**
Franklin, Bonnie (actress); Santa Monica, Calif., 1/6/1944
Frann, Mary (actress); St. Louis, Mo., 2/27/1943
Frazer, Sir James George (anthropologist); Glasgow, Scotland **(1854-1941)**
Freeman, Morgan (actor); Memphis, Tenn., 6/1/1937
Freud, Sigmund (psychoanalyst); Moravia (Czechoslovakia) **(1856-1939)**
Friedan, Betty (Betty Naomi Goldstein) (feminist); Peoria, Ill., 2/4/1921
Fromm, Erich (psychoanalyst); Frankfurt-am-Main, Germany **(1900-1980)**
Frost, David (TV entertainer); Tenterden, England, 4/7/1939
Frost, Robert Lee (poet); San Francisco **(1874-1963)**
Fry, Christopher (playwright); Bristol, England, 12/18/1907
Frye, David (impressionist); Brooklyn, N.Y., 1934
Fugard, Athol (playwright); Middleburg, South Africa, 6/11/1932
Fuller, R(ichard) Buckminster (Jr.) (architect and educator); Milton, Mass. **(1895-1983)**
Fulton, Robert (inventor); Lancaster County, Pa. **(1765-1815)**
Funicello, Annette (actress); Utica, N..Y., 10/22/1942
Funt, Allen (TV producer); Brooklyn, N.Y., 9/16/1914
Furness, Betty (Elizabeth) (ex-actress and consumer advocate); New York City **(1916–1994)**

G

Gabel, Martin (actor and producer); Philadelphia **(1912-1986)**
Gabin, Jean (actor); Paris **(1904-1976)**
Gable, (William) Clark (actor); Cadiz, Ohio **(1901-1960)**
Gabo, Naum (sculptor); Briansk, Russia **(1890-1977)**
Gabor, Eva (actress); Budapest **(1926?–1995)**
Gabor, Zsa Zsa (Sari) (actress); Budapest, 2/6/1919(?)
Gabrieli, Giovanni (composer); Venice **(c.1557-1612)**
Gainsborough, Thomas (painter); Sudbury, Suffolk, England **(1727-1788)**
Galbraith, John Kenneth (economist); Iona Station, Ontario, Canada, 10/15/1908
Galilei, Galileo (astronomer and physicist); Pisa (Italy) **(1564-1642)**
Gallico, Paul (novelist); New York City **(1897-1976)**
Gallup, George H. (poll taker); Jefferson, Iowa **(1901-1984)**
Galsworthy, John (novelist and dramatist); Coombe, England **(1867-1933)**
Galway, James (flutist); Belfast, Northern Ireland, 12/8/1939
Gambling, John A. (radio broadcaster); New York City, 1930
Gandhi, Indira (Indira Nehru) (Prime Minister); Allahabad, India **(1917-1984)**
Gandhi, Mohandas Karamchand (called Mahatma Gandhi) (Hindu leader); Porbandar, India **(1869-1948)**
Gannett, Frank E. (editor and publisher); **(1876-1957)**
Garagiola, Joe (Joseph Henry) (sportscaster); St. Louis, 2/12/1926
Garbo, Greta (Greta Gustafsson) (actress); Stockholm **(1905-1990)**
Garcia Lorca, Frederico (author); Fuente Vaqueros, Spain **(1898-1936)**
Garden, Mary (soprano); Aberdeen, Scotland **(1874-1967)**
Gardenia, Vincent (actor); Naples, Italy **(1922-1992)**
Gardner, Ava (actress); Smithfield, N.C. **(1922-1990)**
Gardner, Erle Stanley (novelist); Malden, Mass. **(1889-1970)**
Garfield, John (Jules Garfinkle) (actor); New York City **(1913-1952)**
Garfunkel, Art (Arthur) (singer); Newark, N.J., 11/5/1941
Gargan, William (actor); Brooklyn, N.Y., **(1905-1979)**
Garibaldi, Giuseppe (Italian nationalist leader); Nice, France **(1807-1882)**
Garland, Judy (Frances Gumm) (actress and singer); Grand Rapids, Minn. **(1922-1969)**
Garner, Erroll (jazz pianist); Pittsburgh **(1921-1977)**
Garner, James (James Bumgarner) (actor); Norman, Okla., 4/7/1928
Garner, Peggy Ann (actress); Canton, Ohio **(1932-1984)**
Garr, Teri (actress); Lakewood, Ohio, 12/11/1949
Garrett, Betty (actress); St. Joseph, Mo., 5/23/1919
Garrick, David (actor); Hereford, England **(1717-1779)**
Garrison, William Lloyd (abolitionist); Newburyport, Mass. **(1805-1879)**
Garroway, Dave (TV host); Schenectady, N.Y. **(1913-1982)**
Garson, Greer (actress); County Down, Northern Ireland, 9/29/1912(?)
Gary, John (singer); Watertown, N.Y., 11/29/1932
Gassman, Vittorio (film actor and director); Genoa, Italy, 9/1/1922
Gaudí, Antonio (architect); Reus, Spain **(1852-1926)**
Gauguin, Eugène Henri Paul (painter); Paris **(1848-1903)**
Gautama Buddha (Prince Siddhartha) (philosopher); Kapilavastu (India) **(563?-?483 B.C.)**
Gavin, John (actor, diplomat); Los Angeles, 4/8/1935
Gayle, Crystal (Brenda Gayle Webb) (singer); Paintsville, Ky., 1/9/1951
Gaynor, Janet (actress); Philadelphia **(1906-1984)**
Gaynor, Mitzi (Francesca Mitzi Marlene de Czanyi von Gerber) (actress); Chicago, 9/4/1931
Gazzara, Ben (Biago Anthony Gazzara) (actor); New York City, 8/28/1930
Gedda, Nicolai (tenor); Stockholm, Sweden, 7/11/1925
Geddes, Barbara Bel (actress); New York City, 10/31/1922
Genet, Jean (playwright); Paris **(1910-1986)**

Genghis Khan (Temujin) (conqueror); nr. Lake Baikal, Russia **(1162-1227)**
Genn, Leo (actor); London **(1905-1978)**
Gentry, Bobbie (Roberta Streeter) (singer); Chickasaw Co., Miss., 7/27/1944
George, David Lloyd (statesman); Manchester, England **(1863-1945)**
Gere, Richard (actor); Philadelphia, 1950
Gericault, Jean Louis (painter); Rouen, France **(1791-1824)**
Geronimo (Goyathlay) (Apache chieftain); Arizona **(1829-1909)**
Gershwin, George (composer); Brooklyn, N.Y. **(1898-1937)**
Gershwin, Ira (lyricist); New York City, **(1896-1983)**
Getty, J. Paul (oil executive); Minneapolis **(1892-1976)**
Getz, Stan (saxophonist); Philadelphia **(1927–1991)**
Ghiberti, Lorenzo (goldsmith and sculptor); Florence **(1378-1455)**
Ghostley, Alice (actress); Eve, Mo., 8/14/1926
Giacometti, Alberto (sculptor); Switzerland **(1901-1966)**
Giannini, Giancarlo (actor); La Spezia, Italy, 8/1/1942
Gibbon, Edward (historian); Putney, England **(1737-1794)**
Gibson, Charles Dana (illustrator); Roxbury, Mass. **(1867-1944)**
Gibson, Henry (actor, comedian); Germantown, Pa., 9/21/35
Gibson, Hoot (Edward) (actor); Tememah, Neb. **(1892-1962)**
Gibson, Mel (actor); Peekskill, N.Y., 1/3/1956
Gide, André (author); Paris **(1869-1951)**
Gielgud, Sir John (actor); London, 4/14/1904
Gilbert, John (movie actor); Logan, Utah **(1897-1936)**
Gilbert, Melissa (actress); Los Angeles, 5/8/1964
Gilbert, Sir William Schwenck (librettist); London **(1836-1911)**
Gilels, Emil (concert pianist); Odessa, Ukraine **(1916-1985)**
Gillespie, Dizzy (John Birks Gillespie) (jazz trumpeter); Cheraw, S.C. **(1917-1993)**
Gillette, William (actor); Hartford, Conn. **(1855-1932)**
Gimbel, Bernard F. (merchant); Vincennes, Ind. **(1885-1966)**
Gingold, Hermione (actress and comedienne); London **(1897-1987)**
Ginsberg, Allen (poet); Newark, N.J., 6/3/1926
Giordano, Luca (painter); Naples, Italy **(1632-1705)**
Giorgione (painter); Castelfranco, (Italy) **(c.1477-1510)**
Giotto di Bondone (painter); Vespignamo (Italy) **(c.1266-1337)**
Giovanni, Nikki (poet); Knoxville, Tenn., 6/7/1943
Giroud, Françoise (French government official); Geneva, 9/21/1916
Gish, Dorothy (actress); Massillon, Ohio **(1898-1968)**
Gish, Lillian (Lillian de Guiche) (actress); Springfield, Ohio **(1893-1993)**
Givenchy, Hubert (fashion designer); Beauvais, France, 2/21/1927
Gladstone, William Ewart (statesman); Liverpool, England **(1809-1898)**
Glaser, Paul Michael (actor, director); Cambridge, Mass., 3/25/1943
Glass, Philip (composer); Baltimore, 1/31/1937
Gleason, Jackie (comedian); Brooklyn, N.Y. **(1916-1987)**
Gleason, James (actor); New York City **(1886-1959)**
Gless, Sharon (actress); Los Angeles, 5/31/1943
Gluck, Christoph Willibald (composer); Erasbach (Germany) **(1714-1787)**
Gobel, George (comedian); Chicago **(1920–1991)**
Godard, Jean Luc (film director); Paris, 12/3/1930
Goddard, Robert Hutchings (father of modern rocketry); Worcester, Mass. **(1882-1945)**
Goddard, Paulette (Marion Levy) (actress); Great Neck, N.Y. **(1911?-1990)**
Godfrey, Arthur (entertainer); New York City **(1903-1983)**
Goebbels, Joseph Paul (Nazi leader); Rheydt, Germany **(1897-1945)**
Goering, Hermann (Nazi leader); Rosenheim, Germany **(1893-1946)**
Goethals, George Washington (engineer); Brooklyn, N.Y. **(1858-1928)**
Goethe, Johann Wolfgang von (poet, playwright, and novelist); Frankfurt-am-Main, Germany **(1749-1832)**
Gogol, Nikolai Vasilievich (novelist); nr. Mirgorod, Ukraine **(1809-1852)**
Goldberg, Rube (cartoonist); San Francisco **(1883-1970)**
Goldberg, Whoopi (actress); New York City, 1949 (?)
Goldblum, Jeff (actor); Pittsburgh, Pa., 10/22/52
Golden, Harry (Harry Goldhurst) (auth or); New York City **(1902-1981)**
Goldsmith, Oliver (dramatist and poet); County Longford, Ireland **(1728-1774)**
Goldwyn, Samuel (Samuel Goldfish) (film producer); Warsaw **(1882-1974)**
Golenpaul, Dan (creator of Information Please radio show and editor of almanac of same name); New York City **(1900-1974)**
Gompers, Samuel (labor leader); London **(1850-1924)**
Goodall, Jane (Baroness van Lawick-Goodall) (ethologist); London, 4/3/1934
Goodman, Benny (clarinetist); Chicago **(1909-1986)**
Goodyear, Charles (inventor); New Haven, Conn. **(1800-1860)**
Gorbachev, Mikhail Sergeyevich (Soviet leader); Privolnoye, U.S.S.R., 3/2/1931
Gordimer, Nadine (novelist and short-story writer); Springs, South Africa, 12/20/1923

Gordon, Max (stage producer); New York City **(1892-1978)**
Gordon, Ruth (actress); Wollaston, Mass. **(1896-1985)**
Gordy, Berry, Jr. (record company executive); Detroit, 11/28/1929
Gore, Lesley (singer); Tenafly, N.J., 1946
Goren, Charles H. (bridge expert); Philadelphia **(1901–1991)**
Gorki, Maxim (Alexei Maximovich Peshkov) (author); Nizhni Novgorod, Russia **(1868-1936)**
Gorky, Arshile (painter); Armenia **(1904-1948)**
Gormé, Eydie (singer); Bronx, N.Y., 8/16/1932
Gorshin, Frank (actor); Pittsburgh, 4/5/1934
Gosden, Freeman F. *See* Amos
Gossett, Louis, Jr. (actor); Brooklyn, N.Y., 5/27/1936
Gottschalk, Louis Moreau (pianist, composer); New Orleans, La. **(1829-1869)**
Gould, Chester (cartoonist); Pawnee, Okla. **(1900-1985)**
Gould, Elliott (Elliott Goldstein) (actor); Brooklyn, N.Y., 8/29/1938
Gould, Glenn (concert pianist); Toronto, **(1932-1982)**
Gould, Morton (composer); Richmond Hill, Queens, N.Y., 12/10/1913
Goulet, Robert (singer); Lawrence, Mass., 11/26/1933
Gounod, Charles François (composer); Paris **(1818-1893)**
Goya y Lucientes, Francisco José de (painter); Fuendetodos, Spain **(1746-1828)**
Grable, Betty (actress); St. Louis **(1916-1973)**
Grace, Princess of Monaco (Grace Kelly) (ex-actress); Philadelphia **(1929-1982)**
Graham, Bill (Wolfgang Grajonca) (rock impresario); Berlin, 1931
Graham, Billy (William F.) (ev angelist); Charlotte, N.C., 11/7/1918
Graham, Katharine Meyer (newspaper publisher); New York City, 6/16/1917
Graham, Martha (choreographer); Pittsburgh **(1894–1991)**
Graham, Virgina (actress,host); Chicago, 7/4/1913
Grahame, Gloria (Gloria Hallwood) (actress); Los Angeles **(1929-1981)**
Grainger, Percy Aldridge (pianist and composer); Melbourne, Australia **(1882-1961)**
Gramm, Donald (Grambach) (bass-baritone); Milwaukee **(1927-1983)**
Granger, Farley (actor); San Jose, Calif., 7/1/1925
Granger, Stewart (James Stewart) (actor); London **(1913-1993)**
Grant, Cary (Alexander Archibald Leach) (actor); Bristol, England **(1904-1986)**
Grant, Kathryn (actress); Houston, Tex. 1933
Grant, Lee (Lyova Haskell Rosenthal) (actress); New York City, 10/31/1930
Granville, Bonita (actress); New York City **(1923-1988)**
Grass, Günter (novelist); Danzig (Poland), 10/16/1927
Grauer, Ben (radio and TV announcer); New York City **(1908-1977)**
Graves, Peter (Peter Arness) (actor); Minneapolis, 3/18/1926
Graves, Robert (writer); London **(1895-1985)**
Gray, Barry (Bernard Yaroslaw) (radio interviewer); Atlantic City, N.J., 7/2/1916
Gray, Dolores (singer and actress); Chicago, 6/7/1930
Gray, Linda (actress); Santa Monica, Calif., 9/12/1940
Gray, Thomas (poet); London **(1716-1771)**
Grayson, Kathryn (Zelma Hednick) (singer and actress); Winston-Salem, N.C., 2/9/1923
Greco, Buddy (singer); Philadelphia, 8/14/1926
Greco, José (dancer); Montorio nei Frentani, Itály, 12/23/1918
Greeley, Horace (journalist and politician); Amherst, N.H. **(1811-1872)**
Green, Adolph (actor and lyricist); New York City, 12/2/1915
Green, Al (singer); Forrest City, Ark., 4/13/1946
Greene, Graham (novelist); Berkhamsted, England **(1904–1991)**
Greene, Lorne (actor); Ottawa **(1915-1987)**
Greene, Martyn (actor); London **(1899-1975)**
Greene, Michele (actress); Las Vegas, Nev., 2/3/?
Greene, Shecky (comedian, actor); Chicago, 4/8/1925
Greenstreet, Sydney (actor); Sandwich, England **(1879-1954)**
Greenwood, Charlotte (actress); Philadelphia, Pa. **(1893-1978)**
Greenwood, Joan (actress and director); London **(19 21-1987)**
Greer, Germaine (feminist); Melbourne, 1/29/1939
Gregory, Cynthia (ballerina); Los Angeles, 7/8/1946
Gregory, Dick (comedian); St. Louis, 1932
Greuze, Jean-Baptiste (painter); Tournus, France **(1725-1805)**
Grey, Joel (Joel Katz) (actor); Cleveland, 4/11/1932
Grey, Zane (author); Zanesville, Ohio **(1875-1939)**
Grieg, Edvard Hagerup (composer); Bergen, Norway **(1843-1907)**
Griffin, Merv (TV entertainer); San Mateo, Calif., 7/6/1925
Griffith, Andy (actor); Mount Airy, N.C., 6/1/1926
Griffith, David Lewelyn Wark (film producer); La Grange, Ky. **(1875-1948)**
Griffith, Melanie (actress); New York City, 8/9/1957
Grigorovich, Yuri (choreographer); Leningrad, 1/1/1927
Grimes, Tammy (actress); Lynn, Mass., 1/30/1934
Grimm, Jacob (author of fairy tales); Hanau (Germany) **(1785-1863)**
Grimm, Wilhelm (author of fairy tales); Hanau (Germany) **(1786-1859)**

Gris, Juan (José Victoriano González) (painter); Madrid **(1887-1927)**
Grizzard, George (actor); Roanoke Rapids, N.C., 4/1/1928
Grodin, Charles (actor); Pittsburgh, Pa., 4/21/1935
Groh, David (actor); Brooklyn, N.Y., 5/21/1939
Gromyko, Andrei A. (diplomat); Starye Gromyki, Russia **(1909-1989)**
Gropius, Walter (architect); Berlin **(1883-1969)**
Gropper, William (painter, illustrator); New York City **(1897-1977)**
Gross, Michael (actor); Chicago, 6/21/1947
Grosz, George (painter); Germany **(1893-1959)**
Guardino, Harry (actor); New York City **(1925–1995)**
Guggenheim, Meyer (capitalist); Langnau, Switzerland **(1828-1905)**
Guillaume, Robert (actor); St. Louis, Mo. 11/30/1927
Guinness, Sir Alec (actor); London, 4/2/1914
Guitry, Sacha (Alexandre) (actor and film director); St. Petersburg, Russia **(1885-1957)**
Gumbel, Bryant Charles (TV newscaster); New Orleans, 9/29/1948
Gunther, John (author); Chicago **(1901-1970)**
Guténberg, Johannes (printer); Mainz (Germany) **(1400?-?1468)**
Guthrie, Arlo (singer); New York City, 7/10/1947
Guthrie, Woody (folk singer and composer); Okemah, Okla. **(1912-1967)**
Gwenn, Edmund (actor); London **(1875-1959)**
Gwynne, Fred (actor); New York City **(1926-1993)**

H

Hackett, Bobby (trumpeter); Providence, R.I. **(1915-1976)**
Hackett, Buddy (Leonard Hacker) (comedian and actor); Brooklyn, N.Y., 8/31/1924
Hackman, Gene (actor); San Bernardino, Calif., 1/30/1931
Hagen, Uta (actress); Göttingen, Germany, 6/12/1919
Haggard, Merle (songwriter); Bakersfield, Calif., 4/6/1937
Hagman, Larry (actor); Weatherford, Tex., 1931
Haig, Alexander Meigs, Jr. (ex-Secretary of State and ex-general); Bala-Cynwyd, Pa., 12/2/1924
Haile Selassie (Ras Tafari Makonnen) (ex-Emperor); Ethiopia **(1892-1975)**
Hailey, Arthur (novelist); Luton, England, 4/5/1920
Halberstam, David (journalist); New York City, 4/10/1934
Hale, Alan (actor, director); Washington, D.C. **(1892-1950)**
Hale, Barbara (actress); DeKalb, Ill., 4/18/1921
Hale, Edward Everett (clergyman and author); Boston **(1822-1909)**
Hale, Nathan (American Revolutionary officer); Coventry, Conn. **(1755-1776)**
Halevi, Judah (Jewish poet); Toledo, Spain **(1085-1140)**
Haley, Alex (writer); Ithaca, N.Y. **(1921-1992)**
Haley, Jack (actor); Boston **(1899-1979)**
Hall, Arsenio (comedian and talk show host); Cleveland, Ohio, 2/12/?
Hall, Donald (Andrew, Jr.) (poet) New Haven, Conn., 9/20/1928
Hall, Huntz (actor); New York City, 1920
Hall, Monty (TV personality); Winnipeg, Canada, 1923
Halley, Edmund (astronomer); London **(1656-1742)**
Hals, Frans (painter); Antwerp (Netherlands) **(1580?-1666)**
Halsey, William Frederick, Jr. (naval officer); Elizabeth, N.J. **(1882-1959)**
Hamel, Veronica (actress); Philadelphia, Pa., 11/20/1943
Hamill, Pete (journalist); Brooklyn, N.Y., 6/24/1935
Hamilton, Alexander (statesman); Nevis, British West Indies **(1757?-1804)**
Hamilton, George (actor); Memphis, Tenn., 8/12/1939
Hamilton, Margaret (actress); Cleveland **(1902-1985)**
Hamlin, Harry (actor); Pasadena, Calif., 10/30/1951
Hamlisch, Marvin (composer and pianist); New York City, 6/2/1944
Hammarskjöld, Dag (U.N. Secretary-General); Jönköping, Sweden **(1905-1961)**
Hammerstein, Oscar, II (librettist and stage producer); New York City **(1895-1960)**
Hampden, Walter (Walter Hampden Dougherty) (actor); Brooklyn, N.Y. **(1879-1955)**
Hampshire, Susan (actress); London, 5/12/1938
Hampton, Lionel (vibraharpist and band leader); Birmingham, Ala., 4/12/1913
Hamsun, Knut (Knut Pedersen) (novelist); Lom, Norway **(1859-1952)**
Hancock, John (statesman); Braintree, Mass. **(1737-1793)**
Hand, Learned (jurist); Albany, N.Y. **(1872-1961)**
Handel, George Frederick (Georg Friedrich Händel) (composer); Halle (East Germany) **(1685-1759)**
Handy, William Christopher (blues composer); Florence, Ala. **(1873-1958)**
Hanks, Tom (actor); Concord, Calif., 7/9/1956
Hannah, Daryl (actress); Chicago, 1961
Hannibal (Carthaginian general); North Africa **(247-182** B.C.)
Hanson, Howard (conductor); Wahoo, Neb., **(1896-1981)**
Harburg, E. Y. "Yip" (songwriter); New York City **(1896-1981)**
Harding, Ann (actress); San Antonio, Tex. **(1902-1981)**

Hardwicke, Sir Cedric (actor); Stourbridge, England **(1893-1964)**
Hardy, Oliver (comedian); Atlanta **(1892-1957)**
Hardy, Thomas (novelist); Dorsetshire, England **(1840-1928)**
Harkness, Edward S. (capitalist); Cleveland **(1874-1940)**
Harlow, Jean (Harlean Carpentier) (actress); Kansas City, Mo. **(1911-1937)**
Harnick, Sheldon (lyricist); Chicago, 4/30/1924
Harper, Valerie (actress); Suffern, N.Y., 8/22/1940(?)
Harrell, Lynn (cellist); New York City, 1/30/1944
Harriman, W. (William) Averell (ex-Governor of New York); New York City **(1891-1986)**
Harrington, Pat., Jr. (actor, comedian); New York City, 8/13/1929
Harris, Barbara (actress); Evanston, Ill., 1935
Harris, Emmylou (singer); Birmingham, Ala., 1949
Harris, Julie (actress); Grosse Pointe Park, Mich., 12/2/1925
Harris, Phil (actor and band leader); Linton, Ind. **(1906–1995)**
Harris, Richard (actor); Limerick, Ireland, 10/1/1933
Harris, Rosemary (actress); Ashby, England, 9/19/1930
Harris, Roy (composer); Lincoln County, Okla. **(1898-1979)**
Harrison, George (singer and songwriter); Liverpool, England, 2/25/1943
Harrison, Gregory (actor); Avalon, Catalina Island, Calif., 5/31/1950
Harrison, Sir Rex (Reginald Carey) (actor); Huyton, England **(1908-1990)**
Hart, Lorenz (lyricist); New York **(1895-1943)**
Hart, Mary (host); Sioux Falls, S.D., c.1950
Hart, Moss (playwright); New York City **(1904-1961)**
Hart, William S. (actor); Newburgh, N.Y. **(1862-1946)**
Harte, Bret (Francis Brett Harte) (author); Albany, N.Y. **(1836-1902)**
Hartford, Huntington (George Huntington Hartford II) (A.&P. heir); New York City, 4/18/1911
Hartford, John (singer and banjoist); New York City, 12/30/1937
Hartley, Mariette (actress); New York City, 6/21/1940
Hartman, David Downs (TV newscaster); Pawtucket, R.I., 5/19/1935
Hartman, Elizabeth (actress); Youngstown, Ohio **(1941-1987)**
Hartman, Lisa (actress); Houston, Tex., 6/1/1956
Harvey, Laurence (Larushka Skikne) (actor); Joniskis, Lithuania **(1928-1973)**
Harvey, William (physician); Folkestone, England **(1578-1657)**
Hasselhoff, David (actor); Baltimore, Md., 7/17/1952
Hasso, Signe (actress); Stockholm, 8/15/1915
Havoc, June (June Hovick) (actress); Seattle, 1916
Haver, June (actress); Rock Island, Ill., 6/10/1926
Hawkins, Jack (actor); London **(1910-1973)**
Hawn, Goldie (actress); Washington, D.C., 11/21/1945
Haworth, Jill (actress); Sussex, England, 1945
Hawthorne, Nathaniel (novelist); Salem, Mass. **(1804-1864)**
Hay, John Milton (statesman); Salem, Ind. **(1838-1905)**
Hayakawa, Sessue (actor); Honshu, Japan **(1890-1973)**
Hayden, Melissa (ballerina); Toronto, 4/25/1923
Hayden, Sterling (Sterling Relyea Walter) (actor and writer); Montclair, N.J. **(1916-1986)**
Haydn, Franz Joseph (composer); Rohrau (Austria) **(1732-1809)**
Hayes, Helen (Helen Hayes Brown) (actress); Washington, D.C. **(1900-1993)**
Hayes, Isaac (composer); Covington, Tenn., 8/20/1942
Hayes, Peter Lind (comedian, singer); San Francisco, 6/25/1915
Haymes, Dick (singer, actor); Buenos Aires **(1916-1980)**
Hayward, Leland (producer); Nebraska City, Neb. **(1902-1971)**
Hayward, Louis (actor); Johannesburg, South Africa **(1909-1985)**
Hayward, Susan (Edythe Marrener) (actress); Brooklyn, N.Y. **(1919?-1975)**
Hayworth, Rita (Margarita Cansino) (actress); New York City **(1918-1987)**
Head, Edith (costume designer); Los Angeles **(1907-1981)**
Hearst, William Randolph (publisher); San Francisco **(1863-1951)**
Hearst, William Randolph, Jr. (publisher); New York City **(1908-1993)**
Heatherton, Joey (actress); Rockville Centre, N.Y., 9/14/1944
Hecht, Ben (author); New York City **(1894-1964)**
Heckart, Eileen (actress); Columbus, Ohio, 3/29/1919
Heflin, Van (Emmet Evan Heflin) (actor); Walters, Okla. **(1910-1971)**
Hefner, Hugh (publisher); Chicago, 4/9/1926
Hegel, Georg Wilhelm Friedrich (philosopher); Stuttgart (Germany) **(1770-1831)**
Heifetz, Jascha (concert violinist); Vilna, Russia **(1901-1987)**
Heine, Heinrich (Harry) (poet); Düsseldorf (Germany) **(1797-1856)**
Heinemann, Gustav (ex-President of Germany); Schweim, Germany **(1899-1976)**
Heisenberg, Werner Karl (physicist); Würzburg, Germany **(1901-1976)**
Held, Anna (comedienne); Paris, France **(1873(?)-1918)**
Heller, Joseph (novelist); Brooklyn, N.Y., 5/1/1923
Hellman, Lillian (playwright); New Orleans **(1905-1984)**
Helmond, Katherine (actress); Galveston, Tex., 7/5/1934(?)
Hemingway, Ernest Miller (novelist); Oak Park, Ill. **(1899-1961)**
Hemingway, Margaux (actress); Portland, Ore., Feb. 1955

Hemmings, David (actor); Guilford, England, 11/2/1941
Henderson, Florence (actress); Dale, Ind., 2/14/1934
Henderson, Skitch (Lyle Russell Cedric) (conductor and pianist); Birmingham, England(?), 1/27/1918
Hendrix, Jimi (James Marshall Hendrix) (guitarist); Seattle **(1942-1970)**
Henley, Beth (playwright-actress); Jackson, Miss., 5/8/1952
Henner, Marilu (actress); Chicago, 4/6/1952
Henning, Doug (magician and actor); Winnipeg, Canada, 1947(?)
Henreid, Paul (actor); Trieste **(1908-1992)**
Henri, Robert (painter); Cincinnati **(1865-1926)**
Henry, O. (William Sydney Porter) (story writer); Greensboro, N.C. **(1862-1910)**
Henry, Patrick (statesman); Hanover County, Va. **(1736-1799)**
Henson, Jim (puppeteer); Greenville, Miss. **(1936-1990)**
Hepburn, Audrey (actress); Brussels, Belgium **(1929-1993)**
Hepburn, Katharine (actress); Hartford, Conn., 5/12/1907
Hepplewhite, George (furniture designer); England **(?-1786)**
Hepworth, Barbara (sculptor); Wakefield, England **(1903-1975)**
Herachel, William (Frederich Wilhelm) (astronomer); Hanover, Germany **(1738-1822)**
Herbert, George (poet); Montgomery Castle, Wales **(1593-1633)**
Herbert, Victor (composer); Dublin **(1859-1924)**
Herblock (Herbert L. Block) (political cartoonist); Chicago, 10/13/1909
Herman, Pee-wee (Paul Reubens) (comedian); Peekskill, N.Y., 1952
Herman, Woody (Woodrow Charles) (band leader); Milwaukee **(1913-1987)**
Herod (Herodes) (called Herod the Great) (King of Judea) **(73?-4 B.C.)**
Herodotus (historian); Halicarnassus, Asia Minor (Turkey) **(c. 484-425 B.C.)**
Herrick, Robert (poet); London? **(1591-1674)**
Hershey, Barbara (actress); Hollywood, Calif., 2/5/1948(?)
Hershfield, Harry (humorist and raconteur); Cedar Rapids, Iowa **(1885-1974)**
Hersholt, Jean (actor); Copenhagen **(1886-1956)**
Hesburgh, Theodore M. (educator); Syracuse, N.Y., 5/2/1917
Hesseman, Howard (actor); Salem, Ore., 2/27/1940
Heston, Charlton (actor); Evanston, Ill., 10/4/1924
Heyerdahl, Thor (ethnologist and explorer); Larvik, Norway, 10/6/1914
Hildegarde (Hildegarde Loretta Sell) (singer); Adell, Wis., 2/1/1906
Hill, Arthur (actor); Melfort, Canada, 8/1/1922
Hill, Benny (comedian); Southampton, England **(1925–1992)**
Hillary, Sir Edmund (mountain climber); New Zealand, 7/20/1919
Hiller, Wendy (actress); Bramhall, England, 8/15/1912
Hillerman, John (actor); Denison, Tex., 12/20(?)/1932
Hilliard, Harriet. *See* Nelson, Harriet
Hindemith, Paul (composer); Hanau, Germany **(1895-1963)**
Hines, Earl "Fatha" (jazz pianist); Duquesne, Pa. **(1905-1983)**
Hines, Gregory (dancer, actor); New York City, 2/14/1946
Hines, Jerome (Jerome Heinz) (basso); Los Angeles, 11/8/1921
Hingle, Pat (actor); Denver, 7/19/1924
Hippocrates (physician); Cos, Greece **(c. 460-c. 377 B.C.)**
Hirohito (Emperor); Tokyo, **(1901-1989)**
Hiroshige, Ando (pain ter); Edo? (Tokyo) **(1797-1858)**
Hirsch, Judd (actor); New York City, 3/15/1935
Hirschfeld, Al (Albert) (cartoonist); St. Louis, 6/21/1903
Hirschhorn, Joseph Herman (financier, speculator, and art collector); Mitau, Latvia **(1899-1981)**
Hirt, Al (trumpeter); New Orleans, 11/7/1922
Hitchcock, Alfred J. (film director); London **(1899-1980)**
Hitler, Adolf (German dictator); Braunau, Austria **(1889-1945)**
Hitzig, William Maxwell (physician); Austria, 12/15/1904
Hobbes, Thomas (philosopher); Westport, England **(1588-1679)**
Hobson, Laura Z. (Laura K. Zametkin) (novelist); New York City **(1900-1986)**
Hockney, David (artist); Bradford, England, 7/9/1937
Hodges, Eddie (actor); Hattiesburg, Miss., 3/5/1947
Hoffa, James R(iddle) (labor leader); Brazil, Ind. **(1913-75?)**; presumed murdered.
Hoffman, Dustin (film actor and director); Los Angeles, 8/8/1937
Hofmann, Hans (painter); Germany **(1880-1966)**
Hogan, Paul (actor); Lightning Ridge, NSW, Australia, 1941 (?)
Hogarth, William (painter and engraver); London **(1697-1764)**
Hokusai, Katauhika (artist); Yedo, Japan **(1760-1849)**
Holbein, Hans (the Elder) (painter); Augsburg (Germany) **(1465?-1524)**
Holbein, Hans (the Younger) (painter); Augsburg (Germany) **(1497?-1543)**
Holbrook, Hal (actor); Cleveland, 2/17/1925
Holden, William (William Franklin Beedle, Jr.) (actor); O'Fallon, Ill. **(1918-1981)**
Holder, Geoffrey (dancer); Port-of-Spain, Trinidad, 8/1/1930
Holiday, Billie (Eleanora Fagan) (jazz-blues singer); Baltimore **(1915-1959)**

Holliday, Judy (Judith Tuvim) (comedienne); New York City **(1922-1965)**
Holliday, Polly (actress); Jasper, Ala., 7/2/1937
Holliman, Earl (actor); Delhi, La., 9/11/1928
Holloway, Stanley (actor); London **(1890-1982)**
Holloway, Sterling (actor); Cedartown, Ga. **(1905-1992)**
Holm, Celeste (actress); New York City, 4/29/1919
Holmes, Oliver Wendell (jurist); Boston **(1841-1935)**
Holt, Jack (actor); Winchester, Va. **(1888-1951)**
Holt, Tim (actor); Beverly Hills, Calif. **(1918-1973)**
Holtz, Lou (comedian); San Francisco **(1898-1980)**
Home, Lord (Alexander Frederick Douglas-Home) (diplomat); London, 7/2/1903
Homeier, Skip (George Vincent Homeier) (actor); Chicago, 10/5/1930
Homer, Winslow (painter); Boston, Mass. **(1836-1910)**
Homer (Greek poet) **(c.850 B.C.?)**
Homolka, Oscar (actor); Vienna **(1898-1978)**
Honegger, Arthur (composer); Le Havre, France **(1892-1955)**
Hook, Sidney (philosopher); New York City **(1902-1989)**
Hoover, J. Edgar (FBI director); Washington, D.C. **(1895-1972)**
Hope, Bob (Leslie Townes Hope) (comedian); London, 5/29/1903
Hopkins, Sir Anthony (actor); Port Talbot, Wales, 12/31/1937
Hopkins, Gerald Manley (poet); Stratford, England **(1844-1899)**
Hopkins, Johns (financier); Anne Arundel County, Md. **(1795-1873)**
Hopkins, Miriam (actress); Bainbridge, Ga. **(1902-1972)**
Hopper, Dennis (actor); Dodge City, Kan., 5/17/1936
Hopper, Edward (painter); Nyack, N.Y. **(1882-1967)**
Horace (Quintus Horatius Flaccus) (poet); Venosa (Italy) **(65-8 B.C.)**
Horne, Lena (singer); Brooklyn, N.Y., 6/30/1917
Horne, Marilyn (mezzo-soprano); Bradford, Pa., 1/16/1934
Horowitz, Vladimir (pianist); Kiev, Russia **(1903-1989)**
Horsley, Lee (actor); Muleshoe, Tex., 5/15/1955
Horton, Edward Everett (comedian); Brooklyn, N.Y. **(1887-1970)**
Hoskins, Bob (actor); Bury St. Edminds, England, 10/26/1942
Houdini, Harry (Ehrich Weiss) (magician); Appleton, Wis. **(1874-1926)**
Houseman, John (Jacques Haussmann) (producer, director, and actor); Bucharest **(1902-1988)**
Housman, A(lfred) E(dward) (poet); Fockburg, England **(1859-1936)**
Houston, Samuel (political leader); Rockbridge County, Va. **(1793-1863)**
Houston, Whitney (singer); Newark, N.J., 8/9/1963
Howard, Ken (actor); El Centro, Calif., 3/28/1944
Howard, Leslie (Leslie Stainer) (actor); London **(1893-1943)**
Howard, Ron (actor, producer, director); Duncan, Okla., 3/1/1954
Howard, Trevor (actor); Kent, England **(1916-1988)**
Howe, Elias (inventor); Spencer, Mass. **(1819-1867)**
Howe, Irving (literary critic); New York City **(1920-1993)**
Howe, Julia Ward (poet and reformer); New York City **(1819-1910)**
Howes, Sally Ann (actress); London, 7/20/1934
Hudson, Henry (English navigator) **(?-1611)**
Hudson, Rock (born Roy Scherer, Jr.; took Roy Fitzgerald as legal name) (actor); Winnetka, Ill. **(1925-1985)**
Hughes, Barnard (actor); Bedford Hills, N.Y., 7/16/15
Hughes, Charles Evans (jurist); Glens Falls, N.Y. **(1862-1948)**
Hughes, Howard (industrialist and film producer); Houston **(1905-1976)**
Hughes, Langston (poet); Joplin, Mo. **(1902-1967)**
Hugo, Victor Marie (author); Besançon, France **(1802-1885)**
Hulce, Tom (actor); Detroit, Mich., 12/6/1953
Hull, Henry (actor); Louisville, Ky. **(1890-1977)**
Hume, David (philosopher); Edinburgh, Scotland **(1711-1776)**
Humperdinck, Engelbert (Arnold Dorsey) (singer); Madras, India, 5/2/1936
Humperdinck, Engelbert (composer); Siegburg (Germany) **(1854-1921)**
Hunt, Marsha (actress); Chicago, 10/17/1917
Hunter, Kim (Janet Cole) (actress); Detroit, 11/12/1922
Hunter, Tab (Arthur Andrew Gelien) (actor); New York City, 7/11/1931
Huntley, Chet (TV newscaster); Cardwell, Mont. **(1911-1974)**
Hurok, Sol (Solomon) (impresario); Pogar, Russia **(1884-1974)**
Hurst, Fannie (novelist); Hamilton, Ohio **(1889-1968)**
Hurt, John (actor); Shirebrook, England, 1/22/1940
Hurt, William (actor); Washington, D.C., 3/20/1950
Hus, Jan (Bohemian religious reformer); Husinetz, nr. Budweis (Czechoslovakia) **(c.1369-1415)**
Husing, Ted (sportscaster); New York City **(1901-1962)**
Hussein I (King); Jordan, 11/14/1935
Hussey, Ruth (Ruth Carol O'Rourke) (actress); Providence, R.I., 10/30/1914
Huston, Anjelica (actress); Los Angeles, 7/8/1951
Huston, John (film director and writer); Nevada, Mo. **(1906-1987)**
Huston, Walter (Walter Houghston) (actor); Toronto **(1884-1950)**
Hutchins, Robert M. (educator); Brooklyn, N.Y. **(1899-1977)**

Hutton, Barbara (Woolworth heiress); New York City **(1912-1979)**
Hutton, Betty (Betty Thornburg) (actress); Battle Creek, Mich., 2/26/1921
Hutton, Lauren (actress, model); Charleston, S.C., 11/17/1943
Hutton, Timothy (actor); Los Angeles, 8/16/1960
Huxley, Aldous (author); Godalming, England **(1894-1963)**
Huxley, Sir Julian S. (biologist and author); London **(1887-1975)**
Huxley, Thomas Henry (biologist); Ealing, England **(1825-1895)**

I

Ian, Janis (singer); New York City, 5/7/1951
Ibsen, Henrik (dramatist); Skien, Norway **(1828-1906)**
Inge, William (playwright); Independence, Kan. **(1913-1973)**
Ingres, Jean Auguste Dominique (painter); Montauban, France **(1780-1867)**
Inness, George (painter); nr. Newburgh, N.Y. **(1825-1894)**
Ionesco, Eugene (playwright); Slatina, Romania **(1912–1994)**
Ireland, Jill (actress); London, **(1936-1990)**
Ireland, John (actor); Vancouver, B.C., Canada **(1914-1992)**
Irons, Jeremy (actor); Cowes, Isle of Wight, England, 9/19/1948
Irving, Amy (actress); Palo Alto, Calif., 9/10/1953
Irving, John (Winslow) (writer); Exeter, N.H., 3/2/1942
Irving, Washington (author); New York City **(1783-1859)**
Isherwood, Christopher (novelist and playwright); nr. Dilsey and High Lane, England **(1904-1986)**
Iturbi, José (concert pianist); Valencia, Spain **(1895-1980)**
Ives, Burl (Icle Ivanhoe) (singer); Hunt, Ill. **(1909–1995)**
Ives, Charles E(dward) (composer); Danbury, Conn. **(1874-1954)**

J

Jackson, Anne (actress); Millvale, Pa., 9/3/1926
Jackson, Glenda (actress); Hoylake, England, 1937(?)
Jackson, Gordon (actor); Glasgow, Scotland, **(1923-1990)**
Jackson, Janet (singer); Gary, Ind., 5/16/1966
Jackson, Rev. Jesse (civil rights leader); Greenville, S.C., 10/8/1941
Jackson, Kate (actress); Birmingham, Ala., 10/29/1949
Jackson, Mahalia (gospel singer); New Orleans **(1911-1972)**
Jackson, Michael (singer); Gary, Ind., 8/29/1958
Jackson, Thomas Jonathan ("Stonewall") (general); Clarksburg, Va. (now W. Va.) **(1824-1863)**
Jacobi, Derek (actor); Leytonstone, England, 10/22/1938
Jacobi, Lou (actor); Toronto, 12/26/1913
Jacobs, Jane (urbanologist); Scranton, Pa., 5/1/1916
Jaffe, Sam (actor); New York City **(1891-1984)**
Jagger, Dean (actor); Lima, Ohio **(1903–1991)**
Jagger, Mick (Michael Phillip) (singer); Dartford, England, 7/26/1943
James, Harry (trumpeter); Albany, Ga. **(1916-1983)**
James, Henry (novelist); New York City **(1843-1916)**
James, Jesse Woodson (outlaw); Clay County, Mo. **(1847-1882)**
James, William (psychologist); New York City **(1842-1910)**
Jameson, (Margaret) Storm (novelist); Whitby, England **(1897-1986)**
Janis, Byron (pianist); McKeesport, Pa., 3/24/1928
Janis, Conrad (actor, musician); New York City, 2/11/1928
Jannings, Emil (actor); Brooklyn, N.Y. **(1886-1950)**
Janssen, David (David Meyer) (actor); Naponee, Neb. **(1930-1980)**
Jay, John (statesman and jurist); New York City **(1745-1829)**
Jeanmaire, Renée (dancer); Paris, 4/29/1924
Jenner, Edward (physician); Berkeley, England **(1749-1823)**
Jennings, Waylon (singer); Littlefield, Tex., 1937
Jessel, George (entertainer); New York City **(1898-1981)**
Jessup, Philip C. (diplomat); New York City **(1897-1986)**
Jillian, Ann (actress); Cambridge, Mass., 1/29/1951
Joan of Arc (Jeanne d'Arc) (saint and patriot); Domremy-la-Pucelle, France **(1412-1431)**
Joel, Billy (singer); New York City, 5/9/1949
Joffrey, Robert (Abdullah Jaffa Bey Khan) (choreographer); Seattle **(1930-1988)**
John, Elton (Reginald Kenneth Dwight) (singer and pianist); Pinner, England, 3/25/1947
Johns, Glynis (actress); Pretoria, South Africa, 10/5/1923
Johns, Jasper (painter and sculptor); Augusta, Ga., 5/15/1930
Johnson, Don (actor); Flatt Creek, Mo., 12/15/1949
Johnson, James Weldon (author and educator); Jacksonville, Fla. **(1871-1938)**
Johnson, Philip Cortalyou (architect); Cleveland, Ohio, 7/8/1906
Johnson, Samuel (lexicographer and author); Lichfield, England **(1709-1784)**
Johnson, Van (actor); Newport, R.I., 8/20/1916
Joliot-Curie, Frédéric (physicist); Paris **(1900-1958)**
Joliot-Curie, Irène (Irène Curie) (physicist); France **(1897-1956)**
Jolliet (or Joliet), Louis (explorer); Beaupré, Canada **(1645-1700)**

Jolson, Al (Asa Yoelson) (actor and singer); St. Petersburg, Russia **(1886-1950)**
Jones, Allan (singer, actor); Old Forge, Pa. **(1908-1992)**
Jones, Buck (Charles Frederick Gebhart) (actor); Vincennes, Ind. **(1889-1942)**
Jones, Carolyn (singer and actress); Amarillo, Tex., **(1933-1983)**
Jones, Dean (actor); Morgan County, Ala., 1/25/1935
Jones, George (singer); Saratoga, Tex., 9/12/1931
Jones, Inigo (architect); London **(1573-1652)**
Jones, James (novelist); Robinson, Ill. **(1921-1977)**
Jones, James Earl (actor); Arkabutla, Miss., 1/17/1931
Jones, Jennifer (Phyllis Isley) (actress); Tulsa, Okla., 3/2/1919
Jones, John Paul (John Paul) (naval officer); Scotland **(1747-1792)**
Jones, Quincy (composer); Chicago, 3/14/1933
Jones, Shirley (singer and actress); Smithtown, Pa., 3/31/1934
Jones, Spike (host, orchestra leader); Long Beach, Calif. **(1911-1965)**
Jones, Tom (Thomas Jones Woodward) (singer); Pontypridd, Wales, 6/7/1940
Jong, Erica (writer); New York City, 3/26/1942
Jonson, Ben (Benjamin) (poet and dramatist); Westminster, England **(1572-1637)**
Joplin, Janis (singer); Port Arthur, Tex. **(1943-1970)**
Joplin, Scott (ragtime pianist and composer); Texarkansas, Tex. **(1868-1917)**
Jordan, James Edward (radio actor-Fibber McGee); Peoria, Ill. **(1896-1988)**
Jordan, Marian (radio actress-Molly of Fibber McGee and Molly); Peoria, Ill. **(1898-1961)**
Jory, Victor (actor); Dawson City, Yukon, Canada **(1902-1982)**
Josquin des Prés (usually known as Josquin) (composer); Conde-sur-L'Escaut?, Hainaut (France or Belgium) (c.1445-1521)
Jourdan, Louis (Louis Gendre) (actor); Marseilles, France, 6/19/1920
Joyce, James (novelist); Dublin **(1882-1941)**
Juárez, Benito Pablo (statesman); Guelatao, Mexico **(1806-1872)**
Julia, Raul (Raúl Rafael Carlos Julia y Arcelay) (actor); San Juan, Puerto Rico **(1940–1994)**
Jung, Carl Gustav (psychoanalyst); Basel, Switzerland **(1875-1961)**
Jurado, Katy (actress); Guadalajara, Mexico, 1927

K

Kabalevsky, Dmitri (composer); St. Petersburg, Russia **(1904-1987)**
Kafka, Franz (author); Prague **(1883-1924)**
Kádár, János (Communist Party leader); Hungary **(1912-1989)**
Kahn, Gus (songwriter); Coblenz, Germany **(1886-1941)**
Kahn, Louis I. (architect); Oesel Island, Estonia **(1901-1974)**
Kahn, Madeline (actress); Boston, 9/29/1942
Kaminska, Ida (actress); Odessa, Russia **(1899-1980)**
Kandinsky, Wassily (painter); Moscow **(1866-1944)**
Kane, Helen (actress, singer); Bronx, N.Y. **(1903-1966)**
Kanin, Garson (playwright); Rochester, N.Y., 11/24/1912
Kant, Immanuel (philosopher); Königsberg (Kaliningrad, U.S.S.R.) **(1724-1804)**
Kantor, MacKinlay (novelist); Webster City, Iowa **(1904-1977)**
Kaplan, Gabe (Gabriel) (actor); Brooklyn, N.Y., 3/31/1945
Karloff, Boris (William Henry Pratt) (actor); London **(1887-1969)**
Kasem, Casey (disc jockey); Detroit, Mich., 4/27/1932
Katt, William (actor); Los Angeles, 2/16/1950
Kaufman, George S. (playwright); Pittsburgh **(1889-1961)**
Kavner, Julie (actress); Los Angeles, 9/7/1951
Kaye, Danny (David Daniel Kominski) (comedian); Brooklyn, N.Y. **(1913-1987)**
Kaye, Sammy (band leader); Cleveland **(1910-1987)**
Kazan, Elia (director); Constantinople, Turkey, 9/7/1909
Kazan, Lainie (Levine) (singer); New York City, 5/15/1940
Keach, Stacy (actor); Savannah, Ga., 6/2/1941
Kean, Edmund (actor); London **(1787-1833)**
Keaton, Buster (Joseph Frank Keaton) (comedian); Piqua, Kan. **(1896-1966)**
Keaton, Diane (actress); Los Angeles, 1/5/1946
Keaton, Michael (Michael Douglas); (actor); Robinson Township, Pa., 9/9/1951
Keats, John (poet); London **(1795-1821)**
Keel, Howard (singer and actor); Gillespie, Ill., 4/13/1919
Keeler, Ruby (Lehy Keeler) (actress and dancer); Halifax, Nova Scotia, Canada **(1910-1993)**
Kefauver, Estes (legislator); Madisonville, Tenn. **(1903-1963)**
Keith, Brian (actor); Bayonne, N.J., 11/14/1921
Keller, Helen Adams (author and educator); Tuscumbia, Ala. **(1880-1968)**
Kellerman, Sally (actress); Long Beach, Calif., 6/2/1938
Kelley, DeForest (actor); Atlanta, Ga., 1/20/1920
Kelly, Emmett (clown); Sedan, Kan., **(1898-1979)**
Kelly, Gene (dancer and actor); Pittsburgh, 8/23/1912

Kelly, Grace. *See* Grace, Princess of Monaco.
Kelly, Nancy (actress); Lowell, Mass. **(1921–1995)**
Kelly, Patsy (actress and comedienne); Brooklyn, N.Y. **(1910-1981)**
Kelly, Walt (cartoonist); Philadelphia **(1913-1973)**
Kemal Ataturk (Mustafa Kemal) (Turkish soldier and statesman); Salonika (Greece) **(1881-1938)**
Kemble, Fanny (F rances Anne) (actress); London **(1809-1893)**
Kempis, Thomas à (mystic); Kempis, Prussia (Germany) **(1380-1471)**
Kennan, George F. (diplomat); Milwaukee, 2/16/1904
Kennedy, Arthur (actor); Worcester, Mass. **(1914-1990)**
Kennedy, George (actor); New York City, 2/18/1925
Kennedy, Jacqueline. *See* Onassis, Jacqueline
Kennedy, Joseph P. (financier); Boston **(1888-1969)**
Kennedy, Robert Francis (legislator); Brookline, Mass. **(1925-1968)**
Kennedy, Rose Fitzgerald (President's mother); Boston **(1890–1995)**
Kent, Allegra (ballerina); Santa Monica, Calif., 8/11/1938
Kent, Rockwell (painter); Tarrytown Heights, N.Y. **(1882-1971)**
Kenton, Stan (Stanley Newcomb) (jazz musician); Wichita, Kan. **(1912-1979)**
Kepler, Johannes (astronomer); Weil (Germany) **(1571-1630)**
Kercheval, Ken (actor); Wolcottville, Ind., 7/15/1935
Kerensky, Alexander Fedorovich (statesman); Simbirks, Russia **(1881-1970)**
Kern, Jerome David (composer); New York City **(1885-1945)**
Kerns, Joanna (actress); San Francisco, 2/12/1953
Kerr, Deborah (actress); Helensburgh, Scotland, 9/30/1921
Kettering, Charles F. (engineer and inventor); nr. Loudonville, Ohio **(1876-1958)**
Key, Francis Scott (lawyer and author of national anthem); Frederick (now Carroll) County, Md. **(1779-1843)**
Keyes, Frances Parkinson (novelist); Charlottesville, Va. **(1885-1970)**
Keynes (1st Baron of Tilton) (John Maynard Keynes) (economist); Cambridge, England **(1883-1946)**
Khachaturian, Aram (composer); Tiflis, Russia **(1903-1978)**
Khrushchev, Nikita S. (Soviet leader); Kalinovka, nr. Kursk, Ukraine **(1894-1971)**
Kibbee, Guy (actor); El Paso **(1886-1956)**
Kidd, Michael (choreographer); Brooklyn, N.Y., 1917
Kidd, William (called Captain Kid) (pirate); Greenock, Scotland **(1645?-1701)**
Kidder, Margot (actress); Yellowknife, N.W.T., Canada, 10/17/1948
Kiepura, Jan (tenor); Sosnowiec, Poland **(1904(?)-1966)**
Kieran, John (writer); New York City **(1892-1981)**
Kierkegaard, Sören Aalys (philosopher); Copenhagen **(1813-1855)**
Kiesinger, Kurt Georg (diplomat); Ebingen, Germany **(1904-1988)**
Kiley, Richard (actor and singer); Chicago, 3/31/1922
Kilmer, Alfred Joyce (poet); New Brunswick, N.J. **(1886-1918)**
King, Alan (Irwin Alan Kniberg) (entertainer); Brooklyn, N.Y., 12/26/1927
King, B.B. (Riley King) (guitarist); Itta Bena, Miss., 9/16/1925
King, Carole (singer and songwriter); Brooklyn, N.Y., 2/9/1941
King, Coretta Scott (civil rights leader); Marion, Ala., 4/27/1927
King, Dennis (actor, singer); Coventry, England **(1897-1971)**
King, Martin Luther, Jr. (civil rights leader); Atlanta **(1929-1968)**
King, Pee Wee (Frank) (singer); Abrams, Wis., 2/18/1914
King, Stephen (writer); Portland, Maine, 9/21/1947
Kingsley, Ben (Krishna Bhanji) (actor); Snainton, England, 12/31/1943
Kingsley, Sidney (Sidney Kirschner) (playwright); New York City **(1906–1995)**
Kinski, Nastassja (Nastassja Nakszynski) (actress); West Berlin, 1/24/1961
Kipling, Rudyard (author); Bombay **(1865-1936)**
Kipnis, Alexander (basso); Ukraine, **(1891-1978)**
Kirby, George (comedian); Chicago, 1923(?)
Kirk, Grayson (educator); Jeffersonville, Ohio, 10/12/1903
Kirk, Lisa (actress and singer); Charleroi, Pa. **(1925–1990)**
Kirk, Phyllis (actress); Plainfield, N.J., 9/18/1930
Kirkland, Gelsey (ballerina); Bethlehem, Pa., 12/29/1952
Kirkpatrick, Jeane Jordan (educator-public affairs); Duncan, Okla., 11/19/1926
Kirkpatrick, Ralph (harpsichordist); Leominster, Mass. **(1911-1984)**
Kirkwood, James (actor); Grand Rapids, Mich. **(1883-1963)**
Kirsten, Dorothy (soprano); Montclair, N.J. **(1910-1992)**
Kissinger, Henry (Heinz Alfred Kissinger) (ex-Secretary of State); Furth, Germany, 5/27/1923
Kitt, Eartha (singer); North, S.C., 1/26/1928
Klee, Paul (painter); Münchenbuchsee, nr. Bern, Switzerland **(1879-1940)**
Klein, Calvin (fashion designer); Bronx, N.Y., 11/19/1942
Klein, Robert (comedian); New York City, 2/8/1942
Kline, Kevin (actor); St. Louis, Mo., 10/24/1947
Kleist, Henrich von (poet); Frankfurt an der Oder (East Germany) **(1777-1811)**
Klemperer, Otto (conductor); Breslau (Poland) **(1885-1973)**
Klemperer, Werner (actor); Cologne, Germany, 3/22/1920

Klugman, Jack (actor); Philadelphia, 4/27/1922
Knight, Gladys (singer); Atlanta, 5/28/1944
Knight, Ted (Tadeus Wladyslaw Konopka) (actor); Terryville, Conn., **(1923-1986)**
Knight, John S. (publisher); Bluefield, W. Va. **(1894-1981)**
Knopf, Alfred A. (publisher); New York City, **(1892-1984)**
Knotts, Don (actor); Morgantown, W.Va., 7/21/1924
Knox, John (religious reformer); Haddington, East Lothian, Scotland **(1505-1572)**
Koch, Robert (physician); Klausthal (Germany) **(1843-1910)**
Koestler, Arthur (novelist); Budapest **(1905-1983)**
Kokoschka, Oskar (painter); Póchlarn Austria **(1886-1980)**
Kooper, Al (singer and pianist); Brooklyn, N.Y., 2/5/1944
Kopell, Bernie (comedian); New York City, 6/21/1933
Koppel, Ted (broadcast journalist); Lancashire, England, 2/8/1940
Korman, Harvey (actor); Chicago, 2/15/1927
Kosciusko, Thaddeus (Tadeusz Andrzej Bonawentura Kosciuszko) (military officer); Grand Duchy of Lithuania **(1746-1817)**
Kossuth, Lajos (patriot); Monok, Hungary **(1802-1894)**
Kostelanetz, André (orchestra conductor); St. Petersburg, Russia **(1901-1980)**
Kosygin, Aleksei N. (Premier); St. Petersburg, Russia **(1904-1980)**
Koussevitzky, Serge (Sergei) Alexandrovitch (orchestra conductor); Vishni Volochek, Tver, Russia **(1874-1951)**
Kovacs, Ernie (comedian); Trenton, N.J. **(1919-1962)**
Kramer, Stanley E. (film producer and director); New York City, 9/29/1913
Kràus, Lili (pianist); Budapest **(1905-1986)**
Kreisler, Fritz (violinist and composer); Vienna **(1875-1962)**
Kresge, S. S. (merchant); Bald Mount, Pa. **(1867-1966)**
Krips, Josef (orchestra conductor); Vienna **(1902-1974)**
Kristofferson, Kris (singer); Brownsville, Tex., 6/22/1936
Kruger, Otto (actor); Toledo, Ohio **(1885-1974)**
Krupa, Gene (drummer); Chicago **(1909-1973)**
Krupp, Alfred (munitions magnate); Essen, Germany **(1812-1887)**
Kubelik, Rafael (conductor); Bychory (Czechoslovakia), 6/29/1914
Kublai Khan (Mongol conqueror) **(1216-1294)**
Kubrick, Stanley (producer and director); New York City, 7/26/1928
Kuralt, Charles (TV journalist); Wilmington, N.C., 9/10/1934
Kurosawa, Akira (film director); Tokyo, 3/23/1910
Kurtz, Efrem (conductor); St. Petersburg, Russia **(1900–1995)**
Kurtz, Swoosie (actress); Omaha, Neb., 9/6/1944

L

LaBelle, Patti (singer, actress); Philadelphia, Pa., 5/24/1944
Ladd, Alan (actor); Hot Springs, Ark. **(1913-1964)**
Ladd, Cheryl (Cheryl Stoppelmoor) (actress); Huron, S.D., 7/12/1951
Ladd, Diane (actress); Meridian, Miss., 11/29/1932
Lafayette, Marquis de (Marie Joseph Paul Yves Roch Gilbert du Motier) (military officer); Auvergne, France **(1757-1834)**
Lafitte, Jean (pirate); Bayonne? France **(1780-1826)**
La Follette, Robert Marin (politician); Primrose, Wis. **(1855-1925)**
La Guardia, Fiorello Henry (Mayor of New York); New York City **(1882-1947)**
Lahr, Bert (Irving Lahrheim) (comedian); New York City **(1895-1967)**
Laine, Cleo (Clementina Dinah Campbell) (singer, actress); Southall, England, 10/28/1927
Laine, Frankie (Frank Paul LoVecchio) (singer); Chicago, 3/30/1913
Laird, Melvin (ex-Secretary of Defense); Omaha, Neb., 9/1/1922
Lake, Veronica (actress); Brooklyn, N.Y. **(1919-1973)**
Lamarck, Chevalier de (Jean Baptiste Pierre Antoine de Monet) (naturalist); Bazantin, France **(1744-1829)**
Lamarr, Hedy (Hedwig Kiesler) (actress); Vienna, 1915
Lamas, Fernando (actor); Buenos Aires, **(1915-1982)**
Lamas, Lorenzo (actor); Los Angeles, 1/20/1958
Lamb, Charles (Elia) (essayist); London **(1775-1834)**
L'Amour, Louis (author); Jamestown, N.D. **(1908-1988)**
Lamour, Dorothy (Dorothy Kaumeyer) (actress); New Orleans, 10/10/1914
Lancaster, Burt (actor); New York City **(1913–1994)**
Lanchester, Elsa (Elsa Sullivan) (actress); London **(1902-1986)**
Landau, Martin (actor); Brooklyn, N.Y., 1934
Landers, Ann (columnist); Sioux City, Iowa, 7/4/1918
Landon, Michael (Eugene Maurice Orowitz) (actor); Forest Hills, Queens, N.Y. **(1936–1991)**
Lane, Abbe (singer); New York City, 1933
Lang, Fritz (film director); Vienna **(1890-1976)**
Lang, Paul Henry (music critic); Budapest **(1901-1991)**
Lange, Hope (actress); Redding Ridge, Conn., 11/28/1933
Lange, Jessica (actress); Cloquet, Minn., 4/20/1949
Langella, Frank (actor); Bayonne, N.J., 1/1/1940
Langford, Frances (singer); Lakeland, Fla., 4/4/1913
Langmuir, Irving (chemist); Brooklyn, N.Y. **(1881-1957)**

Langtry, Lillie (Emily Le Breton) (actress); Island of Jersey **(1852-1929)**
Lansbury, Angela (actress); London, 10/16/1925
Lansing, Robert (Robert Howell Brown) (actor); San Diego, Calif. **(1928–1994)**
Lanza, Mario (Alfred Arnold Cocozza) (singer and actor); Philadelphia **(1921-1959)**
Lao-Tzu (or Lao-Tse) (Li Erh) (philosopher); Honan Province, China (c. 604-531 B.C.)
Lardner, Ring (Ringgold Wilmar Lardner) (story writer); Niles, Mich. **(1885-1933)**
La Rochefoucauld, Francois duc de (author); Paris **(1613-1680)**
Larroquette, John (actor); New Orleans, 11/25/1947
La Salle, Sieur de (Robert Cavelier) (explorer); Rouen, France **(1643-1687)**
Lasser, Louise (actress); New York City, 1940(?)
Lauder, Sir Harry (Harry MacLennan) (singer); Portobello, Scotland **(1870-1950)**
Laughton, Charles (actor); Scarborough, England **(1899-1962)**
Lauper, Cyndi (singer); New York City, 6/20/1953
Laurel, Stan (Arthur Jefferson) (comedian); Ulverston, England **(1890-1965)**
Laurents, Arthur (playwright); New York City, 7/14/1918
Laurie, Piper (Rosetta Jacobs) (actress); Detroit, 1/22/1932
Lavin, Linda (actress); Portland, Me., 10/15/1937
Lavoisier, Antoine-Laurent (chemist); Paris **(1743-1794)**
Lawford, Peter (actor); London **(1923-1984)**
Lawrence, David Herbert (novelist); Nottingham, England **(1885-1930)**
Lawrence, Gertrude (Gertrud Klasen) (actress); London **(1900-1952)**
Lawrence, Marjorie (singer); Deans Marsh, Australia **(1908-1979)**
Lawrence, Steve (Sidney Leibowitz) (singer); Brooklyn, N.Y., 7/8/1935
Lawrence of Arabia (Thomas Edward Lawrence, later changed to Shaw) (author and soldier); Tremadoc, Wales **(1888-1935)**
Lawrence, Vicki (actress); Inglewood, Calif., 3/26/1949
Leach, Robin (host, producer); London, c.1941
Leachman, Cloris (actress); Des Moines, Iowa, 4/30/1926(?)
Lean, David (film director); Croydon, En gland **(1908–1991)**
Lear, Edward (nonsense poet); London **(1812-1888)**
Lear, Evelyn (Shulman) (soprano); Brooklyn, N.Y., 1/8/1929(?)
Lear, Norman (TV producer); New Haven, Conn., 7/27/1922
Learned, Michael (actress); Washington, D.C., 4/9/1939
le Carré, John (David John Moore Cornwell) (novelist); Poole, England, 10/19/1931
Le Corbusier (Charles Edouard Jeanneret) (architect); La Chaux-de-Fonds, Switzerland **(1887-1965)**
Lederer, Francis (actor); Prague, 11/6/1906
Lee, Christopher (actor); London, 5/27/1922
Lee, Gypsy Rose (Rose Louise Hovick) (entertainer); Seattle **(1914-1970)**
Lee, Manfred B. (novelist, pseudonym Ellery Queen); Brooklyn, N.Y. **(1905-1971)**
Lee, Michele (actress, singer); Los Angeles, 6/24/1942
Lee, Peggy (Norma Engstrom) (singer); Jamestown, N.D., 5/26/1920
Lee, Robert Edward (Confederate general); Stratford Estate, Va. **(1807-1870)**
Leeuwenhoek, Anton van (zoologist); Delft (Netherlands) **(1632-1723)**
Le Gallienne, Eva (actress); London **(1899–1991)**
Lehár Franz (composer); Komárom (Czechoslovakia) **(1870-1948)**
Lehman, Herbert H. (Governor and Senator); New York City **(1878-1963)**
Lehmann, Lotte (soprano); Perleberg (Germany) **(1888-1976)**
Lehrer, Jim (TV news co-anchor); Wichita, Kan., 5/19/1934
Leibniz, Gottfried W. von (scientist); Leipzig (East Germany) **(1646-1716)**
Leigh, Janet (Jeanetta Morrison) (actress); Merced, Calif., 7/6/1927
Leigh, Vivien (Vivien Mary Hartley) (actress); Darjeeling, India **(1913-1967)**
Leighton, Margaret (actress); nr. Birmingham, England **(1922-1976)**
Leinsdorf, Erich (conductor); Vienna **(1912–1993)**
Lemmon, Jack (actor); Boston, 2/8/1925
Lenin, Vladimir (Vladimir Ilich Ulyanov) (Soviet leader); Simbirsk, Russia **(1870-1924)**
Lennon, Dianne (singer); Los Angeles, 12/1/1939
Lennon, Janet (singer); Culver City, Calif., 11/15/1946
Lennon, John (singer and songwriter); Liverpool, England **(1940-1980)**
Lennon, Kathy (singer); Santa Monica, Calif., 8/22/1942
Lennon, Peggy (singer); Los Angeles, 4/8/1941
Leno, Jay (comedian, T.V. host); New Rochelle, N.Y., 4/28/1950
Lenya, Lotte (Karoline Blamauer) (singer and actress); Vienna, Austria **(1898-1981)**
Leonard, Sheldon (act or and director); New York City, 2/22/1907
Lerner, Alan Jay (lyricist); New York City **(1918-1986)**
Lerner, Max (columnist); Minsk, Russia **(1902-1992)**

Le Roy, Mervyn (film producer); San Francisco **(1900-1987)**
Leslie, Joan (actress); Detroit, 1/26/1925
Lessing, Doris (novelist); Kermanshah, Iran, 10/22/1919
Lester, Mark (actor); Richmond, England, 1958
Letterman, David (TV personality); Indianapolis, 1947
Levant, Oscar (pianist); Pittsburgh **(1906-1972)**
Levene, Sam (actor); New York City **(1905-1980)**
Levenson, Sam (humorist); New York City **(1911-1980)**
Levi, Carlo (novelist); Turin, Italy **(1902-1975)**
Levine, James (music director, Metropolitan Opera); Cincinnati, 6/23/1943
Levine, Joseph E. (film producer); Boston **(1905-1987)**
Lewis, Jerry (Joseph Levitch) (comedian and film director); Newark, N.J., 3/16/1926
Lewis, Jerry Lee (singer); Ferriday, La., 9/29/1935
Lewis, John Llewellyn (labor leader); Lucas, Iowa **(1880-1969)**
Lewis, Meriwether (explorer); Albemarle Co., Va. **(1774-1809)**
Lewis, Shari (Shari Hurwitz) (puppeteer); New York City, 1/17/1934
Lewis, Sinclair (novelist); Sauk Centre, Minn. **(1885-1951)**
Lewis, Ted (entertainer); Circleville, Ohio **(1891-1971)**
Ley, Willy (science writer); Berlin **(1906-1969)**
Liberace (Wladziu Liberace) (pianist); West Allis, Wis. **(1919-1987)**
Lichtenstein, Roy (painter); New York City, 10/27/1923
Lie, Trygve Halvdan (first U.N. Secretary-General); Oslo **(1896-1968)**
Light, Judith (actress); Trenton, N.J., 2/9/1949
Lightfoot, Gordon (singer and songwriter); Orillia, Ontario, Canada, 11/17/1938
Lillie, Beatrice (Lady Peel) (actress and comedienne); Toronto **(1898-1989)**
Lin Yutang (author); Changchow, China **(1895-1976)**
Lind, Jenny (Johanna Maria Lind) (soprano); Stockholm **(1820-1887)**
Lindbergh, Anne Morrow (author); Englewood, N.J., 6/22/1906
Lindbergh, Charles A. (aviator); Detroit **(1902-1974)**
Linden, Hal (Harold Lipshitz) (actor); New York City, 3/20/1931
Lindfors, Viveca (actress); Uppsala, Sweden, 12/29/1920
Lindsay, Howard (playwright); Waterford, N.Y. **(1889- 1968)**
Lindstrom, Pia (TV newscaster); Stockholm, 11/?/1938
Linkletter, Art (radio-TV personality); Moose Jaw, Saskatchewan, Canada, 7/17/1912
Linnaeus, Carolus (Carl von Linné (botanist); Råshult, Sweden **(1707-1778)**
Lipchitz, Jacques (sculptor); Druskieniki, Latvia **(1891-1973)**
Lippi, Fra Filippo (painter); Florence **(1406-1469)**
Lippmann, Walter (columnist, author, and political analyst); New York City **(1889-1974)**
Lister, (1st Baron of Lyme Regis) (Joseph Lister) (surgeon); Upton, England **(1827-1912)**
Liszt, Franz (composer and pianist); Raiding (Hungary) **(1811-1886)**
Lithgow, John (actor); Rochester, N.Y., 6/6/1945
Little, Cleavon (actor and comedian); Chickasha, Okla. **(1939-1992)**
Little, Rich (impressionist); Ottawa, 11/26/1938
Livesey, Roger (actor); Barry, Wales **(1906-1976)**
Livingstone, David (missionary and explorer); Lanarkshire, Scotland **(1813-1873)**
Livingstone, Mary (Sadye Marks) (comedienne); Seattle **(1909-1983)**
Llewellyn, Richard (novelist); St. David's, Wales **(1906-1983)**
Lloyd, Harold (comedian); Burchard, Neb. **(1894-1971)**
Lloyd George, David (Earl of Dwyfor) (statesman); Manchester, England **(1863-1945)**
Lloyd Webber, Andrew (composer); London, England, 3/22/1948
Locke, John (philosopher); Somersetshire, England **(1632-1704)**
Lockhart, Gene (actor); London, Ontario, Canada **(1891-1957)**
Lockhart, June (actress); New York City, 6/25/1925
Lockwood, Margaret (actress); Karachi (Pakistan) **(1916-1990)**
Lodge, Henry Cabot (legislator); Boston **(1850-1924)**
Lodge, Henry Cabot, Jr. (diplomat); Nahant, Mass. **(1902-1985)**
Loesser, Frank (composer); New York City **(1910-1969)**
Loewe, Frederick (composer); Vienna **(1901-1988)**
Logan, Joshua (director and producer); Texarkana, Tex. **(1908-1988)**
Lollobrigida, Gina (actress); Subiaco, Italy, 1928
Lombard, Carole (Carol Jane Peters) (actress); Ft. Wayne, Ind. **(1908-1942)**
Lombardo, Guy (band leader); London, Ontario, Canada **(1902-1977)**
London, George (baritone); Montreal **(1920-1985)**
London, Jack (John Griffith London) (novelist); San Francisco **(1876-1916)**
London, Julie (Julie Peck) (singer and actress); Santa Rosa, Calif., 9/26/1926
Long, Huey Pierce (politician); Winnfield, La. **(1893-1935)**
Long, Shelley (actress); Fort Wayne, Ind., 8/23/1949
Longfellow, Henry Wadsworth (poet); Portland, Me. **(1807-1882)**
Longworth, Alice Roosevelt (social figure); New York City **(1884-1980)**
Loos, Anita (novelist); Sissons, Calif., **(1888-1981)**
Lopez, Trini (singer); Dallas, Tex., 5/15/1937

Lopez, Vincent (band leader); Brooklyn, N.Y. **(1895-1975)**
Lord, Jack (John Joseph Ryan) (actor); New York City, 12/30/1930
Loren, Sophia (Sofia Scicolone) (actress); Rome, 9/20/1934
Lorre, Peter (Laszlo Löewenstein) (actor); Rosenberg (Czechoslovakia) **(1904-1964)**
Loudon. Dorothy (actress, singer); Boston, 9/17/1933
Louise, Tina (actress); New York City, 2/11/1937
Lovecraft, Howard Phillips (author); Providence, R.I., **(1890-1937)**
Lowe, Edmund (actor); San Jose, Calif. **(1892-1971)**
Lowell, Amy (poet); Brookline, Mass. **(1874-1925)**
Lowell, James Russell (poet); Cambridge, Mass. **(1819-1891)**
Lowell, Robert (poet); Boston **(1917-1977)**
Loy, Myrna (Myrna Williams) (actress); nr. Helena, Mont. **(1905–1993)**
Loyola, St. Ignatius of (Iñigo de Oñez y Loyola) (founder of Jesuits); Gúipuzcoa Province, Spain **(1491-1556)**
Lubitsch, Ernst (film director); Berlin **(1892-1947)**
Lucas, George (film director); Modesto, Calif., 5/14/1944
Lucci, Susan (actress); Scarsdale, N.Y., 12/23/1948
Luce, Clare Boothe (playwright and former Ambassador); New York City **(1903-1987)**
Luce, Henry Robinson (editor and publisher); Tengchow, China **(1898-1967)**
Ludlum, Robert (author); New York City, 5/25/1927
Lugosi, Bela (Bela Lugosi Blasko) (actor); Logos, Hungary **(1888-1956)**
Lukas, Paul (actor); Budapest **(1895-1971)**
Lully, Jean Baptiste (French composer); Florence **(1639-1687)**
Lumet, Sidney (film and TV director); Philadelphia, 6/25/1924
Lunden, Joan (TV host); Fair Oaks, Calif., 9/19/1950
Lunt, Alfred (actor); Milwaukee **(1892-1977)**
Lupino, Ida (actress and director); London **(1918–1995)**
LuPone, Patti (actress; singer); Northport, N.Y., 4/21/1949
Luther, Martin (religious reformer); Eisleben (East Germany) **(1483-1546)**
Lynde, Paul (comedian); Mt. Vernon, Ohio **(1926-1982)**
Lynley, Carol (actress); New York City, 2/13/1942
Lynn, Jeffrey (actor); Auburn, Mass., 1909
Lynn, Loretta (singer); Butcher's Hollow, Ky., 4/14/1935

M

Ma, Yo-Yo (cellist); Paris, 10/7/1955
Maazel, Lorin (conductor); Neuilly, France, 3/5/1930
MacArthur, Charles (playwright); Scranton, Pa. **(1895-1956)**
MacArthur, Douglas (five-star general); Little Rock Barracks, Ark. **(1880-1964)**
MacArthur, James (actor); Los Angeles, 12/8/1937
Macaulay, Thomas Babington (author); Rothley Temple, England **(1800-1859)**
MacCorkindale, Simon (actor); Ely, England, 2/12/1953
MacDermot, Galt (composer); Montreal, 12/19/1928
MacDonald, James Ramsay (statesman); Lossiemouth, Scotland **(1866-1937)**
MacDonald, Jeanette (actress and soprano); Philadelphia **(1907-1965)**
Macdonald, Ross (Kenneth Millar) (mystery writer); Los Gatos, Calif. **(1915-1983)**
MacDowell, Edward Alexander (composer); New York City **(1861-1908)**
Macfadden, Bernarr (physical culturist); nr. Mill Spring, Mo. **(1868-1955)**
MacGraw, Ali (actress); New York City, 4/1/1939
Machaut, Guillaume de (composer); Marchault, France **(1300-1377)**
Machiavelli, Niccolò (political philosopher); Florence (Italy) **(1469-1527)**
Mack, Ted (TV personality); Greeley, Colo. **(1904-1976)**
MacKenzie, Gisele (Marie Marguerite Louise Gisele LaFleche) (singer and actress); Winnipeg, Manitoba, Canada, 1/10/1927
Mackie, Bob (designer); Monterey Park, Calif., 3/24/1940
MacLaine, Shirley (Shirley MacLean Beatty) (actress); Richmond, Va., 4/24/1934
MacLeish, Archibald (poet); Glencoe, Ill. **(1892-1982)**
Macmillan, Harold (ex-Prime Minister); London **(1894-1986)**
MacMurray, Fred (actor); Kankakee, Ill. **(1908-1991)**
MacNeil, Cornell (baritone); Minneapolis, 1925
MacNeil, Robert (TV news co-anchor); Montreal, Que., Canada, 1/19/1931
MacRae, Gordon (singer); East Orange, N.J. **(1921-1986)**
MacRae, Sheila (comedienne); London, 9/24/1924
Madison, Guy (Robert Moseley) (actor); Bakersfield, Calif., 1/19/1922
Madonna (Madonna Louise Ciccone) (singer); Bay City, Mich., 8/16/1958
Maeterlinck, Count Maurice (author); Ghent, Belgium **(1862-1949)**

Magellan, Ferdinand (Fernando de Magalhaes) (navigator); Sabrosa, Portugal **(1480?-1521)**
Magnani, Anna (actress); Rome **(1908-1973)**
Magritte, René (painter); Belgium **(1898-1967)**
Magsaysay, Ramón (statesman); Iba, Luzon, Philippines **(1907-1957)**
Mahan, Alfred Thayer (naval historian); West Point, N.Y. **(1840-1914)**
Mahler, Gustav (composer and conductor); Kalischt (Czechoslovakia) **(1860-1911)**
Mailer, Norman (novelist); Long Branch, N.J., 1/31/1923
Maillol, Aristide (sculptor); Banyuls-sur-Mer, Rousillion, France **(1861-1944)**
Maimonides, Moses (Jewish philosopher); Cordoba, Spain **(1135-1204)**
Main, Marjorie (Mary Tomlinson Krebs) (actress); Acton, Ind. **(1890-1975)**
Mainbocher (Main Rousseau Bocher) (fashion designer); Chicago **(1891-1976)**
Majors, Lee (actor); Wyandotte, Mich., 4/23/1940
Makarova, Natalia (ballerina); Leningrad, 11/21/1940
Makeba, Miriam (singer); Johannesburg, South Africa, 3/4/1932
Malamud, Bernard (novelist); Brooklyn, N.Y., **(1914-1986)**
Malden, Karl (Miaden Sekulovich) (actor); Chicago, 3/22/1913
Malkovich, John (actor); Christopher, Ill., 12/9/1953
Malle, Louis (director); Thumeries, France, 10/30/1932
Malone, Dorothy (actress); Chicago, 1/30/1925
Malraux, André (author); Paris **(1901-1976)**
Malthus, Thomas Robert (economist); nr. Dorking, England **(1766-1834)**
Mamet, David (playwright); Chicago, 11/30/1947
Manchester, Melissa (singer); Bronx, N.Y., 2/15/1951
Manchester, William (writer); Attleboro, Mass., 4/1/1922
Mancini, Henry (composer and conductor); Cleveland **(1924–1994)**
Mandela, Nelson (Rolihlahla) (South African political activist) Umtata, Transkei, 1918
Mandela, Winnie (Nomzamo) (South African political activist); Pondoland district of the Transkei, 1936(?)
Mandrell, Barbara (singer); Houston, 12/25/1948
Manet, Edouard (painter); Paris **(1832-1883)**
Mangano, Silvana (actress); Rome **(1930-1989)**
Mangione, Chuck (hornist, pianist, and composer); Rochester, N.Y., 11/29/1940
Manilow, Barry (singer); Brooklyn, N.Y., 6/17/1946
Mankiewicz, Frank F. (columnist); New York City, 5/16/1924
Mankiewicz, Joseph L. (film writer and director); Wilkes-Barre, Pa. **(1909-1993)**
Mann, Horace (educator); Franklin, Mass. **(1796-1859)**
Mann, Thomas (novelist); Lübeck, Germany **(1875-1955)**
Mannes, Marya (writer); New York City, 11/14/1904
Mansfield, Jayne (Jayne Palmer) (actress); Bryn Mawr, Pa. **(1932-1967)**
Mansfield, Katherine (story writer); Wellington, New Zealand **(1888-1923)**
Mantovani, Annunzio (conductor); Venice **(1905-1980)**
Mao Zedong (Tse-tung) (Chinese leader); Shao Shan, China **(1893-1976)**
Mapplethorpe, Robert (photographer); Floral Park, Queens, N.Y. **(1946-1989)**
Marat, Jean Paul (French revolutionist); Boudry, Neuchâtei, Switzerland **(1743-1793)**
Marceau, Marcel (mime); Strasbourg, France, 3/22/1923
March, Fredric (Frederick Bickel) (actor); Racine, Wis. **(1897-1975)**
Marchand, Nancy (actress); Buffalo, N.Y., 6/19/1928
Marconi, Guglielmo (inventor); Bologna, Italy **(1874-1937)**
Marcus Aurelius (Marcus Annius Verus) (Roman emperor); Rome **(121-180)**
Marcuse, Herbert (philosopher); Berlin, **(1898-1979)**
Margaret Rose (Princess); Glamis Castle, Angus, Scotland, 8/21/1930
Margrethe II (Queen); Copenhagen, 4/16/1940
Marie Antoinette (Josephe Jeanne Marie Antoinette) (Queen of France); Vienna **(1755-1793)**
Marisol (sculptor); Venezuela, 1930
Markham, Edwin (poet); Oregon City, Ore. **(1852-1940)**
Markova, Dame Alicia (Lilian Alice Marks) (ballerina); London 12/1/1910
Marley, Bob (reggae singer and songwriter); Kingston, Jamaica **(1945-1981)**
Marlowe, Christopher (dramatist); Canterbury, England **(1564-1593)**
Marlowe, Julia (Sarah Frances Frost) (actress); Cumberlandshire, England **(1866-1950)**
Marquand, J(ohn) P(hillips) (novelist); Wilmington, Del. **(1893-1960)**
Marquette, Jacques (missionary and explorer); Laon, France **(1637-1675)**
Marriner, Neville (conductor); Lincoln, England, 4/15/1924
Marsalis, Wynton (musician); New Orleans, La., 10/18/1961

Marsh, Jean (actress); Stoke Newington, England, 7/1/1934
Marshall, E.G. (actor); Owatonna, Minn., 6/18/1910
Marshall, George Catlett (general); Uniontown, Pa. **(1880-1959)**
Marshall, Herbert (actor); London **(1890-1968)**
Marshall, John (jurist); nr. Germantown, Va. **(1755-1835)**
Marshall, Penny (actress); New York City, 10/15/1942
Martin, Dean (Dino Crocetti) (singer and actor); Steubenville, Ohio, 6/17/1917
Martin, Mary (singer and actress); Weatherford, Tex. **(1913–1990)**
Martin, Steve (comedian); Waco, Tex., 1945(?)
Martin, Tony (Alvin Morris) (singer); San Francisco, 12/25/1913
Martinelli, Giovanni (tenor); Montagnana, Italy **(1885-1969)**
Martins, Peter (dancer-choreographer); Copenhagen, 10/27/1945
Marvell, Andrew (poet); Winestead, England **(1621-1678)**
Marvin, Lee (actor); New York City **(1924-1987)**
Marx, Chico (Leonard) (comedian); New York City **(1891-1961)**
Marx, Groucho (Julius) (comedian); New York City **(1890-1977)**
Marx, Harpo (Arthur) (comedian); New York City **(1893-1964)**
Marx, Karl (Socialist writer); Treves (Germany) **(1818-1883)**
Marx, Zeppo (Herbert) (comedian); New York City **(1901-1979)**
Mary Stuart (Queen of Scotland); Linlithgow, Scotland **(1542-1587)**
Masaryk, Jan Garrigue (statesman); Prague (Czechoslovakia) **(1886-1948)**
Masaryk, Thomas Garrigue (statesman); Hodonin (Czechoslovakia) **(1850-1937)**
Masefield, John (poet); Ledbury, England **(1878-1967)**
Masekela, Hugh (trumpeter); Wilbank, South Africa, 4/4/1939
Mason, Jackie (comedian); Sheboygan, Wis., 6/9/1930(?)
Mason, James (actor); Huddersfield, England **(1909-1984)**
Mason, Marsha (actress); St. Louis, Mo., 4/3/1942
Massenet, Jules Emile Frédéric (composer); Montaud, France **(1842-1912)**
Massey, Raymond (actor); Toronto **(1896-1983)**
Massine, Léonide (choreographer); Moscow **(1895-1979)**
Masters, Edgar Lee (poet); Garnett, Kan. **(1869-1950)**
Mastroianni, Marcello (actor); Fontana Liri, Italy, 9/28/1924
Mather, Cotton (clergyman); Boston **(1663-1728)**
Mathis, Johnny (singer); San Francisco, 9/30/1935
Matisse, Henri (painter); Le Cateau, France **(1869-1954)**
Matthau, Walter (Walter Matuschanskayasky) (actor); New York City, 10/1/1920
Mature, Victor (actor); Louisville, Ky., 1/19/1916
Maugham, W(illiam) Somerset (author); Paris **(1874-1965)**
Mauldin, Bill (political cartoonist); Mountain Park, N.M., 10/29/1921
Maupassant, Henri René Albert Guy de (story writer); Normandy, France **(1850-1893)**
Maurois, André (Emile Herzog) (author); Elbauf, France **(1885-1967)**
Maximilian (Ferdinand Maximilian Joseph) (Emperor of Mexico); Vienna **(1832-1867)**
Maxwell, James Clerk (physicist); Edinburgh, Scotland **(1831-1879)**
May, Elaine (Elaine Berlin) (entertainer-writer); Philadelphia, 4/21/1932
May, Rollo (psychologist); Ada, Ohio **(1909–1994)**
Mayall, John (singer and songwriter); Manchester, England, 11/29/1933
Mayer, Louis B. (motion picture executive); Minsk, Russia **(1885-1957)**
Mayo, Charles H. (surgeon); Rochester, Minn. **(1865-1939)**
Mayo, Charles W. (surgeon); Rochester, Minn. **(1898-1968)**
Mayo, Virginia (Jones) (actress); St. Louis, 1920
Mayo, William J. (surgeon); Le Sueur, Minn. **(1861-1939)**
Mayron, Melanie (actress); Philadelphia, 10/20/1952
Mazzini, Giuseppe (patriot); Genoa **(1805-1872)**
McBride, Mary Margaret (radio personality); Paris, Mo. **(1899-1976)**
McBride, Patricia (ballerina); Teaneck, N.J., 8/23/1942
McCallum, David (actor); Glasgow, Scotland, 9/19/1933
McCambridge, Mercedes (actress); Joliet, Ill., 3/17/1918
McCarthy, Eugene J. (ex-Senator); Watkins, Minn., 3/29/1916
McCarthy, Joseph Raymond (Senator); Grand Chute, Wis. **(1908-1957)**
McCarthy, Kevin (actor); Seattle, 2/15/1914
McCarthy, Mary (novelist); Seattle **(1912-1989)**
McCartney, Paul (singer and songwriter); Liverpool, England, 6/18/1942
McClanahan, Rue (actress); Healdton, Okla., 2/21/1935
McClellan, George Brinton (general); Philadelphia **(1826-1885)**
McClintock, Barbara (geneticist); Hartford, Conn. **(1902–1992)**
McCloy, John J. (lawyer and banker); Philadelphia **(1895-1989)**
McClure, Doug (actor); Glendale, Calif. **(1938–1995)**
McCormack, John (tenor); Athlone, Ireland **(1884-1945)**
McCormack, John W. (ex-Speaker of House); Boston **(1891-1980)**
McCormack, Patty (actress); New York City, 8/21/1945
McCormick, Cyrus Hall (inventor); Rockbridge County, Va. **(1809-1884)**
McCormick, Myron (actor); Albany, Ind. **(1907-1962)**
McCoy, Col. Tim (actor); Saginaw, Mich. **(1891-1978)**

McCracken, James (dramatic tenor); Gary, Ind. **(1926-1988)**
McCrea, Joel (actor); Los Angeles **(1905–1990)**
McCullers, Carson (novelist); Columbus, Ga. **(1917-1967)**
McDaniel, Hattie (actress); Wichita, Kan. **(1895-1952)**
McDowall, Roddy (actor); London, 9/17/1928
McDowell, Malcolm (actor); Leeds, England, 6/19/1943
McFarland, Spanky (George Emmett) (actor); Fort Worth, Tex. **(1928-1993)**
McGavin, Darren (actor); San Joaquin, Calif., 5/7/1922
McGinley, Phyllis (poet and writer); Ontario, Ore. **(1905–1978)**
McGoohan, Patrick (actor); Astoria, Queens, N.Y., 1928
McGovern, Maureen (singer); Youngstown, Ohio, 7/27/1949
McGuire, Dorothy (actress); Omaha, Neb. 6/14/1919
McKellen, Ian (actor); Burnley, England, 5/25/1939
McKenna, Siobhan (actress); Belfast, Northern Ireland **(1923-1986)**
McKuen, Rod (singer and composer); Oakland, Calif., 4/29/1933
McLaglen, Victor (actor); Tunbridge Wells, Kent, England **(1886-1959)**
McLaughlin, John (guitarist); Yorkshire, England, 1942
McLean, Don (singer and songwriter); New Rochelle, N.Y., 10/2/1945
McLuhan, Marshall (Herbert Marshall) (communications writer); Edmonton, Canada **(1911-1980)**
McMahon, Ed (TV personality); Detroit, 3/6/1923
McQueen, Butterfly (Thelma) (actress); Tampa, Fla., 1/8/1911
McQueen, Steve (Terence Stephen McQueen) (actor); Indianapolis **(1930-1980)**
McRaney, Gerald (actor); Collins, Miss., 8/19/1947
Mead, Margaret (anthropologist); Philadelphia, **(1901-1978)**
Meadows, Audrey (actress); Wu Chang, China, 1922(?)
Meadows, Jayne (actress); Wu Chang, China 9/27/1926
Meany, George (labor leader); New York City **(1894-1980)**
Meara, Anne (actress); New York City, 1929
Medici, Lorenzo de' (called Lorenzo the Magnificent) (Florentine ruler); Florence (Italy) **(1449-1492)**
Meek, Donald (actor); Glasgow, Scotland **(1880-1946)**
Meeker, Ralph (Ralph Rathgeber) (actor); Minneapolis, **(1920-1988)**
Mehta, Zubin (conductor); Bombay, 4/29/1936
Meir, Golda (Golda Myerson, nee Mabovitz) (ex-Premier of Israel); Kiev, Russia **(1898-1978)**
Melanie (Melanie Safka) (singer and songwriter); New York City, 2/3/1947
Melba, Dame Nellie (Helen Porter Mitchell) (soprano); nr. Melbourne **(1861-1931)**
Melchior, Lauritz (Lebrecht Hommel) (heroic tenor); Copenhagen **(1890-1973)**
Mellon, Andrew William (financier); Pittsburgh **(1855-1937)**
Melville, Herman (novelist); New York City **(1819-1891)**
Mencken, Henry Louis (writer); Baltimore **(1880-1956)**
Mendel, Gregor Johann (geneticist); Heinzendorf, Austrian Silesia **(1822-1884)**
Mendeleyev, Dmitri Ivanovich (chemist); Tobolsk, Russia **(1834-1907)**
Mendelssohn-Bartholdy, Jakob Ludwig Felix (composer); Hamburg **(1809-1847)**
Mendès-France, Pierre (ex-Premier); Paris **(1905-1982)**
Menjou, Adolphe (actor); Pittsburgh **(1890-1963)**
Mennin, Peter (Peter Mennini) (composer); Erie, Pa. **(1923-1983)**
Menninger, William C. (psychiatrist); Topeka, Kan. **(1899-1966)**
Menotti, Gian Carlo (composer); Cadegliano, Italy, 7/7/1911
Menuhin, Yehudi (violinist and conductor); New York City, 4/22/1916
Menzies, Robert Gordon (ex-Prime Minister); Jeparit, Australia **(1894-1978)**
Mercer, Johnny (songwriter); Savannah, Ga. **(1909-1976)**
Mercer, Mabel (singer); Burton-on-Trent, England **(1900-1984)**
Mercer, Marian (actress, singer); Akron, Ohio, 11/26/1935
Mercouri, Melina (actress); Athens **(1925–1994)**
Meredith, Burgess (actor); Cleveland, 11/16/1908
Merkel, Una (actress); Covington, Ky. **(1903-1986)**
Merman, Ethel (Ethel Zimmerman) (singer and actress); Astoria, Queens, N.Y. **(1909-1984)**
Merrick, David (David Margulois) (stage producer); St. Louis, 11/27/1912
Merrill, Dina (actress); New York City, 12/9/1925
Merrill, Gary (actor); Hartford, Conn. **(1915-1990)**
Merrill, Robert (baritone); Brooklyn, N.Y., 6/4/1919
Merton, Thomas (clergyman and writer); France **(1915-1968)**
Mesmer, Franz Anton (physician); Itzmang, nr. Constance (Germany) **(1733-1815)**
Mesta, Perle (social figure); Sturgis, Mich. **(1889-1975)**
Metternich, Prince Klemens Wenzel Nepomuk Lothar von (statesman); Coblenz (Germany) **(1773-1859)**
Michelangelo Buonarroti (painter, sculptor, and architect); Caprese (Italy) **(1475-1564)**
Michener, James A. (novelist); New York City, 2/3/1907
Mickiewicz, Adam (Polish poet); Zozie, Belorussia (U.S.S.R.) **(1798-1855)**

Midler, Bette (singer); Honolulu, 1945
Mielziner, Jo (stage designer); Paris **(1901-1976)**
Mies van der Rohe, Ludwig (architect and designer); Aachen, Germany **(1886-1969)**
Mikoyan, Anastas I. (diplomat); Sanain, Armenia, **(1895-1978)**
Miles, Sarah (actress); Essex, England, 12/31/1943
Miles, Sylvia (actress); New York City, 9/9/1932
Miles, Vera (Vera Ralston) (actress); nr. Boise City, Okla., 8/23/1930
Milhaud, Darius (composer); Aix-en-Provence, France **(1892-1974)**
Mill, John Stuart (philosopher); London, **(1806-1873)**
Milland, Ray (Reginald Truscott-Jones) (actor); Neath, Wales **(1907-1986)**
Millay, Edna St. Vincent (poet); Rockland, Me. **(1892-1950)**
Miller, Ann (Lucille Ann Collier) (dancer and actress); Cherino, Tex., 4/12/1923
Miller, Arthur (playwright); New York City, 10/17/1915
Miller, Glenn (band leader); Clarinda, Iowa **(1904-1944)**
Miller, Henry (novelist); New York City **(1891-1980)**
Miller, Jason (John Miller) (playwright); New York City, 1939(?)
Miller, Marilyn (dancer-singer, actress); Evansville, Ind. **(1898-1936)**
Miller, Mitch (Mitchell) (musician); Rochester, N.Y., 7/4/1911
Miller, Roger (singer); Fort Worth **(1936-1992)**
Millet, Jean François (painter); Gruchy, France **(1814-1875)**
Millett, Kate (feminist); St. Paul, 9/14/1934
Millikan, Robert A. (physicist); Morrison, Ill. **(1869-1953)**
Mills, Donna (actress); Chicago, 12/11/1941
Mills, Hayley (actress); London, 4/18/1946
Mills, John (actor); Felixstowe, England, 2/22/1908
Mills, Juliet (actress); London, 11/21/1941
Milne, A(lan) A(lexander) (author); London **(1882-1956)**
Milner, Martin (actor); Detroit, Mich., 12/28/1931
Milnes, Sherrill (baritone); Downers Grove, Ill., 1/10/1935
Milstein, Nathan (concert violinist); Odessa, Russia **(1904-1992)**
Milton, John (poet); London **(1608-1674)**
Mimieux, Yvette (actress); Hollywood, Calif., 1/8/1941
Mineo, Sal (actor); New York City **(1939-1976)**
Minnelli, Liza (singer and actress); Hollywood, Calif., 3/12/1946
Minnelli, Vincente (film director); Chicago **(1913-1986)**
Minuit, Peter (Governor of New Amsterdam); Wesel (Germany) **(1580-1638)**
Miranda, Carmen (Maria do Carmo da Cunha) (singer and dancer); Lisbon **(1913-1955)**
Miró Joan (painter); Barcelona **(1893-1983)**
Mitchell, Cameron (actor); Dallastown, Pa. **(1918–1994)**
Mitchell, Guy (actor); Detroit, 2/27/1927
Mitchell, John N. (former Attorney General); Detroit **(1913-1988)**
Mitchell, Joni (Roberta Joan Anderson) (singer and songwriter); Ft. Macleod, Canada, 11/7/1943
Mitchell, Margaret (novelist); Atlanta **(1900-1949)**
Mitchell, Thomas (actor); Elizabeth, N.J. **(1892-1962)**
Mitchum, Robert (actor); Bridgeport, Conn., 8/6/1917
Mitropoulos, Dimitri (orchestra conductor); Athens **(1896-1960)**
Mix, Tom (actor); Mix Run, Pa. **(1880-1940)**
Moffo, Anna (soprano); Wayne, Pa., 6/27/1934
Modigliani, Amedeo (painter); Leghorn, Italy **(1884-1920)**
Mohammed (prophet); Mecca (Saudi Arabia) **(570-632)**
Molière (Jean Baptiste Poquelin) (dramatist); Paris **(1622-1673)**
Moll, Richard (actor); Pasadena, Calif. 1/13/(?)
Molnar, Ferenc (dramatist); Budapest **(1878-1952)**
Molotov, Vyacheslav M. (V. M. Skryabin) (diplomat); Kukarka, Russia **(1890-1986)**
Mondrian, Piet (painter); Amersfoort, Netherlands **(1872-1944)**
Monet, Claude (painter); Paris **(1840-1926)**
Monk, Meredith (choreographer-composer-performing artist); Lima, Peru, 11/20/1942
Monk, Thelonious (pianist); Rocky Mount, N.C. **(1918-1982)**
Monroe, Marilyn (Norma Jean Mortenson or Baker) (actress); Los Angeles **(1926-1962)**
Monroe, Vaughn (Wilton) (band leader); Akron, Ohio **(1912-1973)**
Monsarrat, Nicholas (novelist); Liverpool, England **(1910-1979)**
Montaigne, Michel Eyquem de (essayist); nr. Bordeaux, France **(1533-1592)**
Montalban, Ricardo (actor); Mexico City, 11/25/1920
Montand, Yves (Yvo Montand Livi) (actor and singer); Monsummano, Italy **(1921-1991)**
Montesquieu, Charles-Louis de Secondat, baron de La Brède and de, (philosopher) nr. Borleaux, France **(1689-1755)**
Monteux, Pierre (conductor); Paris **(1875-1964)**
Monteverdi, Claudio (composer); Cremona? Italy **(1567-1643)**
Montez, Maria (actress); Dominican Republican **(1918-1951)**
Montezuma II (Aztec emperor); Mexico **(1480?-1520)**
Montgomery, Elizabeth (actress); Hollywood, Calif. **(1938–1995)**
Montgomery, George (George Montgomery Letz) (actor); Brady, Mont., 8/29/1916
Montgomery, Robert (Henry, Jr.) (actor); Beacon, N.Y. **(1904-1981)**

Montgomery of Alamein, 1st Viscount of Hindhead (Sir Bernard Law Montgomery) (military leader); London **(1887-1976)**
Montoya, Carlos (guitarist); Madrid **(1903-1993)**
Moore, Clement Clarke (author); New York City **(1779-1863)**
Moore, Dudley (actor-writer-musician); Dagenham, England, 4/19/1935
Moore, Garry (Thomas Garrison Morfit) (TV personality); Baltimore **(1915–1993)**
Moore, Grace (soprano); Jellico, Tenn. **(1901-1947)**
Moore, Henry (sculptor); Castleford, England **(1898-1986)**
Moore, Marianne (poet); Kirkwood, Mo. **(1887-1972)**
Moore, Mary Tyler (actress); Brooklyn, N.Y., 12/29/1937
Moore, Melba (Beatrice) (singer and actress); New York City, 10/27/1945
Moore, Roger (actor); London, 10/14/1927(?)
Moore, Thomas (poet); Dublin **(1779-1852)**
Moore, Victor (actor); Hammonton, N.J. **(1876-1962)**
Moorehead, Agnes (actress); Clinton, Mass. **(1906-1974)**
More, Henry (philosopher); Grantham, England **(1614-1687)**
More, Sir Thomas (statesman and author); London **(1478-1535)**
Moreau, Jeanne (actress); Paris, 1/23/1928
Moreno, Rita (Rosita Dolores Alverio) (actress); Humacao, Puerto Rico, 12/11/1931
Morgan, Dennis (actor); Prentice, Wis. **(1910–1994)**
Morgan, Frank (actor); New York City **(1890-1949)**
Morgan, Harry (actor); Detroit, 4/10/1915
Morgan, Helen (singer); Danville, Ohio **(1900?-1941)**
Morgan, Henry (comedian); New York City **(1915–1994)**
Morgan, Jane (Florence Currier) (singer); Boston, 1920
Morgan, John Pierpont (financier); Hartford, Conn. **(1837-1913)**
Morgan, Ralph (actor); New York City **(1882-1956)**
Moriarty, Michael (actor); Detroit, 4/5/1941
Morini, Erica (concert violinist); Vienna, 1/5/1910
Morison, Samuel Eliot (historian); Boston **(1887-1976)**
Morley, Christopher Darlington (novelist); Haverford, Pa. **(1890-1957)**
Morley, Robert (actor); Semley, England **(1908-1992)**
Morris, Chester (actor); New York City **(1901-1970)**
Morris, Wayne (actor); Los Angeles, Calif. **(1914-1959)**
Morrison, Jim (James Douglas Morrison) (singer and songwriter); Melbourne, Fla. **(1943-1971)**
Morse, Marston (mathematician); Waterville, Me. **(1892-1977)**
Morse, Robert (actor); Newton, Mass., 5/18/1931
Morse, Samuel Finley Breese (painter and inventor); Charlestown, Mass. **(1791-1872)**
Moses, Grandma (Mrs. Anna Mary Robertson Moses) (painter); Greenwich, N.Y. **(1860-1961)**
Moses, Robert (urban planner); New Haven, Conn., **(1888-1981)**
Mostel, Zero (Samuel Joel Mostel) (actor); Brooklyn, N.Y. **(1915-1977)**
Moussorgsky, Modest Petrovich (composer); Karev, Russia **(1839-1881)**
Mowbray, Alan (actor); London **(1896-1969)**
Moyers, Bill D. (Billy Don) (journalist); Hugo, Okla., 6/5/1934
Moynihan, Daniel Patrick (New York Senator); Tulsa, Okla., 3/16/1927
Mozart, Wolfgang Amadeus (Johannes Chrysostomus Wolfgangus Theophilus Mozart) (composer); Salzburg (Austria) **(1756-1791)**
Mudd, Roger (TV newscaster); Washington, D.C., 2/9/1928
Muggeridge, Malcolm (Thomas) (writer); Croydon, England **(1903–1990)**
Muhammad, Elijah (Elijah Poole) (religious leader); Sandersville, Ga. **(1897-1975)**
Mulgrew, Kate (actress); Dubuque, Iowa, 4/?/1929
Mulhare, Edward (actor); Ireland, 1923
Mumford, Lewis (cultural historian and city planner); Flushing, Queens, N.Y. **(1895-1990)**
Munch, Edvard (painter); Löt en, Norway **(1863-1944)**
Munchhausen, Karl Friedrick Hieronymus, baron von (anecdotist); Hanover, Germany **(1720-1797)**
Muni, Paul (Muni Weisenfreund) (actor); Lemburg (Ukraine) **(1895-1967)**
Munsel, Patrice (soprano); Spokane, Wash., 5/14/1925
Murdoch, Iris (novelist); Dublin, 7/15/1919
Murdoch, Rupert (publisher); Melbourne, 3/11/1931
Murillo, Bartolomé Esteban (painter); Seville, Spain **(1617-1682)**
Murphy, Audie (actor and war hero); Kingston, Tex. **(1924-1971)**
Murphy, Eddie (actor-comedian); Brooklyn, N.Y. 4/3/1961
Murphy, George (actor, dancer, and ex-Senator); New Haven, Conn. **(1902-1992)**
Murray, Arthur (dance teacher); New York City **(1895–1991)**
Murray, Bill (actor-comedian); Wilmette, Ill. 9/21/1950
Murray, Kathryn (dance teacher); Jersey City, N.J., 1906
Murray, Ken (Don Court) (producer); Nyack, N.Y. **(1903-1988)**
Murray, Mae (Marie Adrienne Koenig) (actress); Portsmouth, Va. **(1890-1965)**

Murrow, Edward R. (commentator and government official); Greensboro, N.C. **(1908-1965)**
Mussolini, Benito (Italian dictator); Dovia, Forli, Italy **(1883-1945)**
Muti, Riccardo (orchestra conductor); Naples, Italy, 7/28/1941
Mutter, Anne-Sophie (violinist); Rheinfelden, West Germany, 6/29/1963
Myerson, Bess (consumer advocate); Bronx, N.Y., 1924
Myrdal, Gunnar (sociologist and economist); Gustaf Parish, Sweden **(1898-1987)**

N

Nabokov, Vladimir (novelist); St. Petersburg, Russia **(1899-1977)**
Nabors, Jim (actor and singer); Sylacauga, Ala., 6/12/1932
Nader, Ralph (consumer advocate); Winsted, Conn., 2/27/1934
Nagel, Conrad (actor); Keokuk, Iowa **(1897-1970)**
Naish, J. Carrol (actor); New York City **(1900-1973)**
Naldi, Nita (Anita Donna Dooley) (actress); New York City **(1899-1961)**
Napoleon Bonaparte. *See* Bonaparte, Napoleon
Nash, Graham (singer); Blackpool, England, 1942
Nash, Ogden (poet); Rye, N.Y. **(1902-1971)**
Nasser, Gamal Abdel (statesman); Beni Mor, Egypt **(1918-1970)**
Nast, Thomas (cartoonist); Landau (Germany) **(1840-1902)**
Nation, Carry Amelia (temperance leader); Garrard County, Ky. **(1846-1911)**
Natwick, Mildred (actress); Baltimore **(1905–1994)**
Nazimova, Alla (actress); Yalta, Crimea, Russia **(1879-1945)**
Neagle, Anna (Marjorie Robertson) (actress); London **(1908-1986)**
Neal, Patricia (actress); Packard, Ky., 1/20/1926
Neff, Hildegarde (actress); Ulm, Germany, 12/28/1925
Negri, Pola (Apolina Mathias-Chalupec) (actress); Bromberg (Poland) **(1899-1987)**
Nehru, Jawaharlal (first Prime Minister of India); Allahabad, India **(1889-1964)**
Nelligan, Kate (actress); London, Ont., Canada, 3/16/1951
Nelson, Barry (Neilsen) (actor); San Francisco, 1920
Nelson, David (actor); New York City, 10/24/1936
Nelson, Harriet Hilliard (Peggy Lou Snyder) (actress); Des Moines, Iowa **(1909–1994)**
Nelson, Ozzie (Oswald) (actor); Jersey City, N.J. **(1907-1975)**
Nelson, Ricky (Eric) (singer and actor); Teaneck, N.J. **(1940-1985)**
Nelson, Viscount Horatio (naval officer); Burnham Thorpe, England **(1758-1805)**
Nelson, Willie (singer); Waco, Texas, 4/30/1933
Nenni, Pietro (Socialist leader); Faenza, Italy **(1891-1980)**
Nero (Nero Claudius Caesar Drusus Germanicus) (Roman emperor); Antium (Italy) **(37-68)**
Nero, Peter (pianist); New York City, 5/22/1934
Nesbitt, Cathleen (actress); Cheshire, England **(1889-1982)**
Nevelson, Louise (sculptor); Kiev, Russia **(1899-1988)**
Newhart, Bob (entertainer); Chicago, 9/5/1929
Newhouse, Samuel I. (publisher); New York City **(1895-1979)**
Newley, Anthony (actor and song writer); London, 9/24/1931
Newman, Edwin (news commentator); New York City, 1/25/1919
Newman, John Henry (prelate); London **(1801-1890)**
Newman, Paul (actor and director); Cleveland, 1/26/1925
Newman, Randy (singer); Los Angeles, 11/28/1943
Newton, Huey (black activist); New Orleans **(1942-1989)**
Newton, Sir Isaac (mathematician and scientist); nr. Grantham, England **(1642-1727)**
Newton, Wayne (singer); Norfolk, Va., 4/3/1942
Newton-John, Olivia (singer); Cambridge, England, 9/26/1948
Nichols, Mike (Michael Peschkowsky) (stage and film director); Berlin, 11/6/1931
Nicholson, Jack (actor); Neptune, N.J., 4/22/1937
Nietzsche, Friedrich Wilhelm (philosopher); nr. Lützen Saxon y (East Germany) **(1844-1900)**
Nightingale, Florence (nurse); Florence (Italy) **(1820-1910)**
Nijinsky, Vaslav (ballet dancer); Warsaw **(1890-1950)**
Nilsson, Birgit (soprano); West Karup, Sweden, 5/17/1923
Nilsson, Harry (singer and songwriter); Brooklyn, N.Y. **(1941–1994)**
Nimitz, Chester W. (naval officer); Fredericksburg, Tex. **(1885-1966)**
Nimoy, Leonard (actor); Boston, 3/26/1931
Nin, Anais (author and diarist); Neuilly, France **(1903-1977)**
Niven, David (actor); Kirriemuir, Scotland, **(1910-1983)**
Nizer, Louis (lawyer and author); London **(1902–1994)**
Nobel, Alfred Bernhard (industrialist); Stockholm **(1833-1896)**
Noguchi, Isamu (sculptor); Los Angeles **(1904-1988)**
Nolan, Lloyd (actor); San Francisco **(1902-1985)**
Nolte, Nick (actor); Omaha, Neb., 1942
Norell, Norman (Norman Levinson) (fashion designer); Noblesville, Ind. **(1900-1972)**
Norman, Jessye (soprano); Augusta, Ga., 9/15/1945

Norman, Marsha (Marsha Williams) (playwright); Louisville, Ky., 9/21/1947
Normand, Mabel (actress); Boston **(1894-1930)**
Norstad, Gen. Lauris (ex-commander of NATO forces); Minneapolis **(1907-1988)**
North, John Ringling (circus director); Baraboo, Wis. **(1903-1985)**
North, Sheree (actress); Los Angeles, 1/17/1933
Norton, Eleanor Holmes (New York City government official, lawyer); Washington, D.C., 6/13/1937
Nostradamus (Michel de Notredame) (astrologer); St. Rémy, France **(1503-1566)**
Novaes, Guiomar (pianist); São João de Boa Vista, Brazil **(1895-1979)**
Novak, Kim (Marilyn Novak) (actress); Chicago, 2/13/1933
Novarro, Ramon (Ramon Samaniegoes) (actor); Durango, Mexico **(1899-1968)**
Novello, Ivor (actor, playwright, composer); Cardiff, Wales **(1893-1951)**
Nugent, Elliott (actor and director); Dover, Ohio, **(1899-1980)**
Nureyev, Rudolf (ballet dancer); Siberia **(1938-1993)**
Nuyen, France (actress); Marseilles, France, 7/31/1939
Nyro, Laura (singer and songwriter); Bronx, N.Y., 1947

O

Oakie, Jack (actor); Sedalia, Mo. **(1903-1978)**
Oakley, Annie (Phoebe Anne Oakley Mozee) (markswoman); Darke County, Ohio **(1860-1926)**
Oates, Joyce Carol (novelist); Lockport, N.Y., 6/16/1938
Oberon, Merle (Estelle Merle O'Brien Thompson) (actress); Calcutta, India **(1911-1979)**
Oberth, Hermann (rocketry and space flight pioneer); Hermannstadt, Romania **(1894-1989)**
O'Brian, Hugh (Hugh J. Krampe) (actor); Rochester, N.Y., 4/19/1930
O'Brien, Edmond (actor); New York City **(1915-1985)**
O'Brien, Margaret (Angela Maxine O'Brien) (actress); San Diego, Calif., 1/15/1937
O'Brien, Pat (William Joseph O'Brien, Jr.) (actor); Milwaukee **(1899-1983)**
O'Casey, Sean (playwright); Dublin **(1881-1964)**
Ochs, Adolph Simon (publisher); Cincinnati **(1858-1935)**
O'Connor, Carroll (actor); New York City, 8/2/1924
O'Connor, Donald (actor); Chicago, 8/28/1925
Odets, Clifford (playwright); Philadelphia **(1906-1963)**
Odetta (Odetta Holmes) (folk singer and actress); Birmingham, Ala., 12/31/1930
Offenbach, Jacques (composer); Cologne, Germany **(1819-1880)**
O'Hara, John (novelist); Pottsville, Pa. **(1905-1970)**
O'Hara, Maureen (Maureen FitzSimons) (actress); Dublin, 8/17/1921
Ohlsson, Garrick (pianist); Bronxville, N.Y., 4/3/1948
Ohrbach, Jerry (actor-singer); Bronx, N.Y., 10/20/1935
Oistrakh, David (concert violinist); Odessa, Russia **(1908-1974)**
O'Keefe, Dennis (actor); Fort Madison, Iowa **(1908-1968)**
O'Keeffe, Georgia (painter); Sun Prairie, Wis. **(1887-1986)**
Oland, Warner (actor); Umea, Sweden **(1880-1938)**
Oldenburg, Claes (painter); Stockholm, Sweden, 1/28/1929
Oliphant, Patrick B. (editorial cartoonist); Adelaide, Australia, 7/24/1935
Oliver, Edna May (actress); Malden, Mass. **(1883-1942)**
Olivier, Lord (Laurence) (actor); Dorking, England **(1907-1989)**
Olmsted, Frederick Law (landscape architect); Hartford, Conn. **(1822-1903)**
Olsen, Ole (John Sigvard Olsen) (comedian); Peru, Ind. **(1892-1963)**
Omar Khayyam (poet and astronomer); Nishapur (Iran) **(died c. 1123)**
Onassis, Aristotle (shipping executive); Smyrna, Turkey **(1906-1975)**
Onassis, Christina (shipping executive); New York City **(1950-1988)**
Onassis, Jacqueline Kennedy (Jacqueline Bouvier) (President's widow); Southampton, N.Y. **(1929–1994)**
O'Neal, Ryan (Patrick) (actor); Los Angeles, 4/20/1941
O'Neal, Tatum (actress); Los Angeles, Calif., 11/5/1963
O'Neill, Eugene Gladstone (playwright); New York City **(1888-1953)**
O'Neill, Jennifer (actress); Rio de Janeiro, 2/20/1949
Oppenheimer, J. Robert (nuclear physicist); New York City **(1904-1967)**
Orff, Carl (composer); Munich, Germany **(1895-1982)**
Orlando, Tony (Michael Anthony Orlando Cassavitis) (singer); New York City, 4/3/1944
Ormandy, Eugene (conductor); Budapest **(1899-1985)**
Orozco, José Clemente (painter); Zapotlán, Jalisco, Mexico **(1883-1949)**
Orwell, George (Eric Arthur Blair) (British author); Motihari, India **(1903-1950)**
Osborn, Paul (playwright); Evansville, Ind. **(1901-1988)**
Osborne, John (playwright); London **(1929–1994)**

Osler, Sir William (physician); Bondhead, Ontario, Canada **(1849-1919)**
Osmond, Donny (singer); Ogden, Utah, 12/9/1957
Osmond, Marie (singer); Ogden, Utah, 1959
O'Sullivan, Maureen (actress); County Roscommon, Ireland, 5/17/1911
Otis, Elisha (inventor); Halifax, Vt. **(1811-1861)**
O'Toole, Peter (actor); Connemara, Ireland, 8/2/1933
Ouspenskaya, Maria (actress); Tula, Russia **(1876-1949)**
Ovid (Publius Ovidius Naso) (poet); Sulmona (Italy) **(43** B.C.**-?**A.D. **17)**
Owen, Reginald (actor); Wheathampstead, England **(1887-1972)**
Owens, Buck (Alvis Edgar Owens) (singer); Sherman, Tex., 8/12/1929
Ozawa, Seiji (orchestra conductor); Fentian (Shenyan), Manchura, 7/1/1935

P

Paar, Jack (TV personality); Canton, Ohio, 5/1/1918
Pacino, Al (Alfred) (actor); New York City, 4/25/1940
Packard, Vance (author); Granville Summit, Pa., 5/22/1914
Paderewski, Ignace Jan (pianist and statesman); Kurylowka, Russian Podolia **(1860-1941)**
Paganini, Nicolò (violinist); Genoa (Italy) **(1782-1840)**
Page, Geraldine (actress); Kirksville, Mo. **(1924-1987)**
Page, Patti (Clara Ann Fowler) (singer and entertainer); Claremore, Okla., 11/8/1927
Paige, Janis (actress); Tacoma, Wash., 9/16/1922
Paine, Thomas (political philosopher); Thetford, England **(1737-1809)**
Palance, Jack (Walter Palanuik) (actor); Lattimer, Pa., 2/18/1920
Palestrina, Giovanni Pierluigi da (composer); Palestrina, Italy **(1526-1594)**
Paley, William S. (broadcasting executive); Chicago **(1901–1990)**
Palladio, Andrea (architect); Padua or Vicenza (Italy) **(1508-1580)**
Pallette, Eugene (actor); Winfield, Kan. **(1889-1954)**
Palmer, Betsy (actress); East Chicago, Ind., 1929
Palmer, Lilli (Lilli Peiser) (actress); Posen (Germany) **(1914-1986)**
Palmerston, Henry John Templeton (3rd Viscount) (statesman); Broadlands, England **(1784-1865)**
Pangborn, Franklin (actor); Newark, N.J. **(1893-1958)**
Papanicolaou, George N. (physician); Coumi, Greece **(1883-1962)**
Papas, Irene (actress); Chiliomodion, Greece, 1929
Papp, Joseph (Joseph Papirofsky) (stage producer and director); Brooklyn, N.Y. **(1921-1991)**
Paracelsus, Philippus (Aureolus Theophrastus Bombastus von Hohenheim) (physican); Einsiedeln, Switzerland **(1493-1541)**
Park, Chung Hee (President of South Korea); Sangmo-ri, Korea **(1917-1979)**
Parker, Dorothy (Dorothy Rothschild) (author); West End, N.J. **(1893-1967)**
Parker, Eleanor (actress); Cedarville, Ohio, 6/26/1922
Parker, Fess (actor); Fort Worth, Tex., 1925
Parker, Jean (actress); Butte, Mont., 8/11/1912
Parker, Suzy (model and actress); San Antonio, 10/28/1933
Parkinson, C(yril) Northcote (historian); Durham, England **(1909-1993)**
Parks, Bert (Bert Jacobson) (entertainer); Atlanta **(1914-1992)**
Parks, Gordon (film director); Ft. Scott, Kan., 11/30/1912
Parnell, Charles Stewart (statesman); Avondale, Ireland **(1846-1891)**
Parnis, Mollie (Mollie Parnis Livingston) (fashion designer); New York City **(1905(?)-1992)**
Parsons, Estelle (actress); Marblehead, Mass., 11/20/1927
Parton, Dolly (singer); Locust Ridge, Tenn. 1/19/1946
Pascal, Blaise (philosopher); Clermont, France **(1623-1662)**
Pasternak, Boris Leonidovich (author); Moscow **(1890-1960)**
Pasternak, Joseph (film producer); Silagy-Somlyo, Romania **(1901–1991)**
Pasteur, Louis (chemist); Dôle, France **(1822-1895)**
Pastor, Tony (Antonio) (actor, theater manager); New York City **(1837-1908)**
Paton, Alan (author); Pietermaritzburg, South Africa **(1903-1988)**
Patti, Adelina (soprano); Madrid **(1843-1919)**
Patton, George Smith, Jr. (general); San Gabriel, Calif., **(1885-1945)**
Paul, Les (Lester William Polfus) (guitarist); Waukesha, Wis., 6/9/1915
Paul VI (Giovanni Battista Montini) (Pope); Concesio, nr. Brescia, Italy **(1897-1978)**
Pauley, Jane (TV newscaster); Indianapolis, 10/31/1950
Pauling, Linus Carl (chemist); Portland, Ore. **(1901–1994)**
Pavarotti, Luciano (tenor); Modena, Italy, 10/12/1935
Pavlov, Ivan Petrovich (physiologist); Ryazan district, Russia **(1849-1936)**
Pavlova, Anna (ballerina); St. Petersburg, Russia **(1885-1931)**
Paxinou, Katina (actress); Piraeus, Greece **(1900-1973)**
Payne, John (actor); Roanoke, Va. **(1912-1989)**
Peale, Norman Vincent (clergyman); Bowersville, Ohio **(1898–1993)**

Pearl, Minnie (Sarah Ophelia Colley Cannon) (comedienne and singer); Centerville, Tenn., 10/25/1912
Pears, Peter (tenor); Farnham, England **(1910-1986)**
Pearson, Drew (Andrew Russel Pearson) (columnist); Evanston, Ill. **(1897-1969)**
Pearson, Lester B. (statesman); Toronto **(1897-1972)**
Peary, Robert Edwin (explorer); Cresson, Pa. **(1856-1920)**
Peck, Gregory (actor); La Jolla, Calif., 4/5/1916
Peckinpah, Sam (film director); Fresno, Calif. **(1925-1984)**
Peerce, Jan (tenor); New York City **(1904-1984)**
Pegler, (James) Westbrook (columnist); Minneapolis **(1894-1969)**
Pei, I(eoh) M(ing) (architect); Canton, China, 4/26/1917
Penn, Arthur (stage and film director); Philadelphia, 9/27/1922
Penn, William (American colonist); London **(1644-1718)**
Penner, Joe (comedian); Hungary **(1904-1941)**
Penney, James C. (merchant); Hamilton, Mo. **(1875-1971)**
Peppard, George (actor); Detroit **(1929–1994)**
Pepys, Samuel (diarist); Bampton, England **(1633-1703)**
Perelman, S(idney) J(oseph) (writer); Brooklyn, N.Y. **(1904-1979)**
Pergolesi, Giovanni Battista (composer); Jesi, Italy **(1710-1736)**
Pericles (statesman); Athens **(died 429** B.C.**)**
Perkins, Osgood (actor); West Newton, Mass. **(1892-1937)**
Perkins, Anthony (actor); New York City **(1932–1992)**
Perlman, Itzhak (violinist); Tel Aviv, Israel, 8/31/1945
Perlman, Rhea (actress); Brooklyn, N.Y., 3/31/1948
Perón, Isabel (María Estela Martínez Cartas) (former chief of state); La Rioja, Argentina, 2/4/1931
Perón, Juan D. (statesman); nr. Lobos, Argentina **(1895-1974)**
Perón, Maria Eva Duarte de (political leader); Los Toldos, Argentina **(1919-1952)**
Perrine, Valerie (actress and dancer); Galveston, Tex., 9/3/1943
Pershing, John Joseph (general); Linn County, Mo. **(1860-1948)**
Pestalozzi, Johann (educator); Zurich, Switzerland **(1746-1827)**
Peters, Bernadette (Bernadette Lazzara) (actress); New York City, 2/28/1948
Peters, Brock (actor-singer); New York City, 7/2/1927
Peters, Jean (actress); Canton, Ohio, 10/15/1926
Peters, Roberta (Roberta Peterman) (soprano); New York City, 5/4/1930
Petit, Roland (choreographer and dancer); Villemombe, France, 1924
Petrarch (Francesco Petrarca) (poet); Arezzo (Italy) **(1304-1374)**
Pfeiffer, Michelle (actress); Santa Ana, Calif., 4/29/1958
Philip (Philip Mountbatten) (Duke of Edinburgh); Corfu, Greece, 6/10/1921
Piaf, Edith (Edith Gassion) (chanteuse); Paris **(1916-1963)**
Piatigorsky, Gregor (cellist); Ekaterinoslav, Russia **(1903-1976)**
Piazza, Ben (actor); Little Rock, Ark., 7/30/1934
Piazza, Marguerite (soprano); New Orleans, 5/6/1926
Picasso, Pablo (painter and sculptor); Málaga, Spain **(1881-1973)**
Pickford, Jack (Jack Smith) (actor); Toronto **(1896-1933)**
Pickford, Mary (Gladys Mary Smith) (actress); Toronto **(1893-1979)**
Picon, Molly (actress); New York City **(1898-1992)**
Pidgeon, Walter (actor); East St. John, New Brunswick, Canada **(1898-1984)**
Pinter, Harold (playwright); London, 10/10/1930
Pinza, Ezio (basso); Rome **(1892-1957)**
Pirandello, Luigi (dramatist and novelist); nr. Girgenti, Italy **(1867-1936)**
Piranesi, Giambattista (artist); Mestre, Italy **(1720-1778)**
Pissaro, Camille Jacob (painter); St. Thomas (U.S. Virgin Islands) **(1830-1903)**
Piston, Walter (composer); Rockland, Me. **(1894-1976)**
Pitman, Sir (Isaac) James (educator a nd publisher); Bath, England, 8/14/1901
Pitt, William ("Younger Pitt") (statesman); nr. Bromley, England **(1759-1806)**
Pitts, ZaSu (actress); Parsons, Kan. **(1898-1963)**
Pius XII (Eugenio Pacelli) (Pope); Rome **(1876-1958)**
Pizarro, Francisco (explorer); Trujillo, Spain **(1470?-1541)**
Planck, Max (physicist); Kiel, Germany **(1858-1947)**
Plato (Aristocies) (philosopher); Athens (?) **(427?-347** B.C.**)**
Pleasence, Donald (actor); Worksop, England **(1919–1995)**
Pleshette, Suzanne (actress); New York City, 1/31/1937
Plimpton, George (author); New York City, 3/18/1927
Plisetskaya, Maya (ballerina); Moscow, 11/20/1925
Plowright, Joan (actress); Brigg, England, 10/28/1929
Plummer, Christopher (actor); Toronto, 12/13/1929
Plutarch (biographer); Chaeronea (Greece) **(46?-?120)**
Pocahontas (Matoaka) (American Indian princess); Virginia (?) **(1595?-1617)**
Podhoretz, Norman (author); Brooklyn, N.Y., 1/16/1930
Poe, Edgar Allan (poet and story writer); Boston, Mass. **(1809-1849)**
Poitier, Sidney (film actor and director); Miami, Fla., 2/20/1927
Polanski, Roman (film director); Paris, 8/18/1933
Pollard, Michael J. (actor); Passaic, N.J., 5/30/1939

Pollock, Jackson (painter); Cody, Wyo. **(1912-1956)**
Polo, Marco (traveler); Venice **(1254?-?1324)**
Pompadour, Mme. de (Jeanne Antoinette Poisson) (courtesan); Versailles **(1721-1764)**
Pompey (Gnaeus Pompeius Magnus) (general); Rome (?) **(106-48 B.C.)**
Ponce de León, Juan (explorer); Servas, Spain **(1460?-1521)**
Pons, Lily (coloratura soprano); Cannes, France **(1904-1976)**
Ponselle, Rosa (soprano); Meriden, Conn. **(1897-1981)**
Ponti, Carlo (director); Milan, Italy, 12/11/1913
Pope, Alexander (poet); London **(1688-1744)**
Porter, Cole (songwriter); Peru, Ind. **(1891-1964)**
Porter, Katherine Anne (novelist); Indian Creek, Tex. **(1891-1980)**
Post, Wiley (aviator); Grand Plain, Tex. **(1900-1935)**
Poston, Tom (actor); Columbus, Ohio, 10/17/1927
Potëmkin, Grigori Aleksandrovich, Prince (statesman); Khizovo (Khizov, Belorussia, U.S.S.R.) **(1739-1791)**
Potok, Chaim (author); New York City, 2/17/1929
Poulenc, Francis (composer); Paris **(1899-1963)**
Pound, Ezra (poet); Hailey, Idaho **(1885-1972)**
Poussin, Nicolas (painter); Villers, France **(1594-1665)**
Powell, Adam Clayton, Jr. (Congressman); New Haven, Conn. **(1908-1972)**
Powell, Colin L. (retired general); New York City, 4/5/1937
Powell, Dick (actor); Mt. View, Ark. **(1904-1963)**
Powell, Eleanor (actress and tap dancer); Springfield, Mass. **(1912-1982)**
Powell, Jane (Suzanne Burce) (actress and singer); Portland, Ore., 4/1/1929
Powell, William (actor); Pittsburgh, **(1892-1984)**
Power, Tyrone (actor); Cincinnati, Ohio **(1914-1958)**
Powers, Stephanie (Taffy Paul) (actress); Hollywood, Calif., 11/2/1942
Praxiteles (sculptor); Athens **(c.370-c.330 B.C.)**
Preminger, Otto (film director and producer); Vienna **(1906-1986)**
Prentiss, Paula (Paula Ragusa) (actress); San Antonio, 1939
Presley, Elvis (singer and actor); Tupelo, Miss. **(1935-1977)**
Presley, Priscilla (actress); Brooklyn, N.Y., 5/24/1945
Preston, Robert (Robert Preston Meservey) (actor); Newton Highlands, Mass **(1918-1987)**
Previn, André (conductor); Berlin, 4/6/1929
Previn, Dory (singer); Rahway, N.J., 10/22/1929(?)
Price, Leontyne (Mary) (soprano); Laurel, Miss., 2/10/1927
Price, Ray (country music artist); Perryville, Tex., 1/12/1926
Price, Vincent (actor); St. Louis **(1911-1993)**
Pride, Charley (singer); Sledge, Miss., 3/18/1938(?)
Priestley, J. B. (John B.) (author); Bradford, England **(1894-1984)**
Priestley, Joseph (chemist); nr. Leeds, England **(1733-1804)**
Primrose, William (violist); Glasgow, Scotland **(1904-1982)**
Prince (Prince Roger Nelson) (singer); Minneapolis, 6/7/58
Prince, Harold (stage producer); New York City, 1/30/1928
Principal, Victoria (actress); Fukuoka, Japan, 1/3/1945(?)
Prinze, Freddie (actor); New York City **(1954-1977)**
Pritchett, V(ictor) S(awdon) (literary critic); Ipswich, England, 12/16/1900
Procter, William (scientist); Cincinnati **(1872-1951)**
Prokofiev, Sergei Sergeevich (composer); St. Petersburg, Russia **(1891-1953)**
Proust, Marcel (novelist); Paris **(1871-1922)**
Provine, Dorothy (actress); Deadwood, S. Dak., 1/20/1937
Prowse, Juliet (actress); Bombay, 9/25/1936
Pryor, Richard (comedian); Peoria, Ill., 12/1/1940
Ptolemy (Claudius Ptolemaeus) (astronomer and geographer); Ptolemais Hermii (Egypt) **(2nd century A.D.)**
Pucci, Emilio (Marchese di Barsento) (fashion designer); Naples, Italy **(1914-1992)**
Puccini, Giacomo (composer); Lucca, Italy **(1858-1924)**
Puente, Tito (band leader); New York City, 4/20/1923
Pulaski, Casimir (military officer); Podolia, Poland **(1748-1779)**
Pulitzer, Joseph (publisher); Makó (Hungary) **(1847-1911)**
Pullman, George (inventor); Brockton, N.Y. **(1831-1897)**
Purcell, Henry (composer); London **(1658-1695)**
Pusey, Nathan M. (educator); Council Bluffs, Iowa, 4/4/1907
Pushkin, Alexander Sergeevich (poet and dramatist); Moscow **(1799-1837)**
Puzo, Mario (novelist); New York City, 10/15/1921
Pyle, Ernest Taylor (journalist); Dana, Ind. **(1900-1945)**
Pythagoras (mathematician and philosopher); Samos (Greece) **(6th century B.C.)**

Q

Quaid, Randy, (actor); Houston, Texas, 10/1/1950
Quayle, Anthony (actor); Ainsdale, England **(1913-1989)**

Queen, Ellery: pen name of the late Frederic Dannay and the late Manfred B. Lee
Queler, Eve (conductor); New York City, 1/1/1936
Quennell, Sir Peter Courtney (biographer); Bromley, England **(1905-1993)**
Quinn, Anthony (actor); Chihuahua, Mexico, 4/21/1916

R

Rabe, David (playwright); Dubuque, Iowa, 3/10/1940
Rabelais, François (satirist); nr. Chinon, France **(1494?-1553)**
Rabi, I(sidor) I(saac) (physicist); Rymanow (Poland) **(1898-1988)**
Rachmaninoff, Sergei Wassilievitch (pianist and composer); Oneg Estate, Novgorod, Russia **(1873-1943)**
Racine, Jean Baptiste (dramatist); La Ferté-Milon, France **(1639-1699)**
Radner, Gilda (comedienne); Detroit **(1946-1989)**
Raft, George (actor); New York City **(1895-1980)**
Rainer, Luise (actress); Vienna, 1912
Raines, Ella (actress); Snoqualmie Falls, Wash. **(1921-1988)**
Rainier III (Prince); Monaco, 5/31/1923
Rains, Claude (actor); London **(1889-1967)**
Raitt, Bonnie (singer); Burbank, Calif., 11/8/1949
Raitt, John (actor,singer); Santa Ana, Calif., 1/29(?)/17
Raleigh, Sir Walter (courtier and navigator); London **(1552?-1618)**
Rambeau, Marjorie (actress); San Francisco **(1889-1970)**
Rameau, Jean-Philippe (composer); Dijon? France **(1683-1764)**
Rampal, Jean-Pierre (Louis) (flutist); Marseilles, France, 7/1/22
Randall, Tony (Leonard Rosenberg) (actor); Tulsa, Okla., 2/26/1920
Randolph, A(sa) Philip (labor leader); Crescent City, Fla. **(1889-1979)**
Raphael (Raffaello Santi) (painter and architect); Urbino (Italy) **(1483-1520)**
Rasputin, Grigori Efimovich (monk); Tobolsk Province, Russia **(1871?-1916)**
Rathbone, Basil (actor); Johannesburg, South Africa **(1892-1967)**
Rather, Dan (TV newscaster); Wharton, Tex., 10/31/1931
Ratoff, Gregory (film director); St. Petersburg, Russia **(1897-1960)**
Rattigan, Terence (playwright); London **(1911-1977)**
Rauschenberg, Robert (painter); Port Arthur, Tex., 10/22/1925
Ravel, Maurice Joseph (composer); Ciboure, France **(1875-1937)**
Ray, Aldo (DaRe) (actor); Pen Argyl, Pa. **(1926-1991)**
Ray, Gene Anthony (actor, dancer); Harlem, N.Y., 5/24/1963
Ray, Man (painter); Philadelphia **(1890-1976)**
Ray, Satyajit (film director); Calcutta **(1921-1992)**
Rayburn, Gene (TV personality); Christopher, Ill., 12/22/1917
Raye, Martha (Margie Yvonne Reed) (comedienne and actress); Butte, Mont. **(1916-1994)**
Raymond, Gene (actor); New York City, 8/13/1908
Reasoner, Harry (TV commentator); Dakota City, Iowa **(1923-1991)**
Redding, Otis (singer); Dawson, Ga. **(1941-1967)**
Reddy, Helen (singer); Melbourne, 10/25/1941
Redford, Robert (Charles Robert Redford, Jr.) (actor); Santa Monica, Calif., 8/18/1937
Redgrave, Lynn (actress); London, 3/8/1943
Redgrave, Sir Michael (actor); Bristol, England **(1908-1985)**
Redgrave, Vanessa (actress); London, 1/30/1937
Reed, Donna (actress); Denison, Iowa **(1921-1986)**
Reed, Rex (critic); Ft. Worth, 10/2/1940
Reed, Walter (army surgeon); Belroi, Va. **(1851-1902)**
Reese, Della (Deloreese Patricia Early) (singer); Detroit, 7/6/1932
Reeve, Christopher (actor); New York City, 9/25/1952
Reeves, Jim (singer); Panola County, Tex. **(1923-1964)**
Reich, Steve (composer); New York City, 10/3/1936
Reid, Wallace (actor); St. Louis **(1891-1923)**
Reiner, Carl (actor); New York City, 3/20/1922
Reiner, Fritz (conductor); Budapest **(1888-1963)**
Reiner, Robert (actor); Bronx, N.Y., 1945
Reinhardt, Max (Max Goldmann) (theater producer); nr. Vienna **(1873-1943)**
Remarque, Erich Maria (novelist); Osnabrük, Germany **(1898-1970)**
Rembrandt (Rembrandt Harmensz van Rijn) (painter); Leyden (Netherlands) **(1605-1669)**
Remick, Lee (Ann) (actress); Boston **(1935-1991)**
Rennert, Günther (opera director and producer); Essen, Germany, 4/1/1911
Rennie, Michael (actor); Bradford, England **(1909-1971)**
Renoir, Jean (film director and writer); Paris, **(1894-1979)**
Renoir, Pierre Auguste (painter); Limoges, France **(1841-1919)**
Resnais, Alain (film director); Vannes, France, 6/3/1922
Resnik, Regina (mezzo-soprano); New York City, 8/30/1922
Respighi, Ottorino (composer); Bologna, Italy **(1879-1936)**
Reston, James (journalist); Clydebank, Scotland, 11/3/1909
Reuther, Walter (labor leader); Wheeling, W. Va. **(1907-1970)**

Revere, Paul (silversmith and hero of famous ride); Boston **(1735-1818)**
Revson, Charles (business executive); Boston **(1906-1975)**
Reynolds, Burt (actor); Lansing, Mich., 2/11/1936
Renolds, Debbie (Marie Frances Reynolds) (actress); El Paso, 4/1/1932
Reynolds, Sir Joshua (painter); nr. Plymouth, England **(1723-1792)**
Reynolds, Marjorie (Goodspeed) (actress); Buhl, Idaho, 8/12/1921
Rhodes, Cecil John (South African statesman); Bishop Stortford, England **(1853-1902)**
Rice, Elmer (playwright); New York City **(1892-1967)**
Rice, Grantland (sports writer); Murfreesboro, Tenn. **(1880-1954)**
Rich, Buddy (Bernard) (drummer); Brooklyn, N.Y. **(1917-1987)**
Rich, Charlie (singer); Colt, Ark. **(1932–1995)**
Richardson, Elliot L. (ex-Cabinet member); Boston, 7/20/1920
Richardson, Sir Ralph (actor); Cheltenham, England **(1902-1983)**
Richardson, Tony (director); Shipley, England **(1928-1991)**
Richelieu, Duc de (Armand Jean du Plessis) (cardinal); Paris **(1585-1642)**
Richie, Lionel (singer-songwriter); Tuskegee, Ala., 1949 (?)
Richter, Charles Francis (seismologist); Hamilton, Canada **(1900-1985)**
Richter, Sviatosiav (pianist); Zhitomir, Ukraine, 3/20/1914
Rickenbacker, Edward V. (aviator); Columbus, Ohio **(1890-1973)**
Rickles, Don (comedian); New York City, 5/8/1926
Rickover, Vice Admiral Hyman G. (atomic energy expert); Russia **(1900-1986)**
Riddle, Nelson (composer); Hackensack, N.J. **(1921-1985)**
Ride, Sally K(risten) (astronaut, astrophysicist); Encino, Calif., 5/26/1951
Ridgway, General Matthew B. (ex-Army Chief of Staff); Ft. Monroe, Va. **(1895-1993)**
Rigg, Diana (actress); Doncaster, England, 7/20/1938
Riley, James Whitcomb (poet); Greenfield, Ind. **(1849-1916)**
Rimsky-Korsakov, Nikolai Andreevich (composer); Tikhvin, Russia **(1844-1908)**
Rinehart, Mary (née Roberts) (novelist); Pittsburgh **(1876-1958)**
Ritchard, Cyril (actor and director); Sydney, Australia **(1898-1977)**
Ritter, John (Jonathan) (actor); Burbank, Calif., 9/17/1948
Ritter, Tex (Woodward Maurice Ritter) (singer); Panola County, Tex., **(1905-1973)**
Ritter, Thelma (actress); Brooklyn, N.Y. **(1905-1969)**
Rivera, Chita (Dolores Conchita Figuero del Rivero) (dancer-actress-singer); Washington, D.C. 1/23/1933
Rivera, Diego (painter); Guanajuato, Mexico **(1886-1957)**
Rivera, Geraldo (Miguel) (TV newscaster); New York City, 7/3/1943
Rivers, Joan (comedienne); Brooklyn, N.Y., 6/8/1933
Rivers, Larry (Yitzroch Loiza Grossberg) (painter); New York City, 8/17/1923
Roach, Hal (film producer); Elmira, N.Y. **(1892–1992)**
Robards, Jason, Jr. (actor); Chicago, 7/26/1922
Robards, Jason, Sr. (actor); Hillsdale, Mich. **(1892-1963)**
Robbins, Harold (Harold Rubin) (novelist); New York City, 5/21/1916
Robbins, Jerome (Jerome Rabinowitz) (choreographer); New York City, 10/11/1918
Robbins, Marty (singer); Glendale, Ariz., **(1925-1982)**
Roberts, Eric (actor); Bilox, Miss., 4/18/1956
Roberts, Julia (actress); Smyrna, Ga., 10/28/1967
Roberts, (Granville) Oral (evangelist and publisher); nr. Ada, Okla., 1/24/1918
Robertson, Cliff (actor); La Jolla, Cal if., 9/9/1925
Robertson, Dale (Dayle) (actor); Oklahoma City, 7/14/1923
Robeson, Paul (singer and actor); Princeton, N.J., **(1898-1976)**
Robespierre, Maximilien François Marie Isidore de (French Revolutionist); Arras, France **(1758-1794)**
Robinson, Bill "Bojangles" (Luther) (dancer); Richmond, Va. **(1878-1949)**
Robinson, Edward G. (Emanuel Goldenberg) (actor); Bucharest **(1893-1973)**
Robinson, Edwin Arlington (poet); Head Tide, Me. **(1869-1935)**
Robson, Dame Flora (actress); South Shields, England **(1902-1984)**
Robson, May (actress); Melbourne, Australia **(1858-1942)**
Rochester (Eddie Anderson) (actor); Oakland, Calif. **(1905-1977)**
Rockefeller, David (banker); New York City, 6/12/1915
Rockefeller, John Davison (capitalist); Richford, N.Y. **(1839-1937)**
Rockefeller, John Davison, Jr. (industrialist); Cleveland **(1874-1960)**
Rockefeller, John D., 3rd (philanthropist); New York City **(1906-1978)**
Rockefeller, Laurance S. (conservationist); New York City, 5/26/1910
Rockwell, Norman (painter and illustrator); New York City **(1894-1978)**
Rodgers, Jimmie (singer); Meridian, Miss. **(1897-1933)**
Rodgers, Richard (composer); New York City **(1902-1979)**
Rodin, François Auguste René (sculptor); Paris **(1840-1917)**
Rodzinski, Artur (conductor); Spalato, Dalmatia **(1894-1958)**
Roentgen, Wilhelm Konrad (physicist); Lennep, Prussia **(1845-1923)**

Rogers, Buddy (Charles) (actor); Olathe, Kan., 8/13/1904
Rogers, Fred (Television producer, host); Latrobe, Pa., 3/20/1928
Rogers, Ginger (Virginia McMath) (dancer and actress); Independence, Mo. **(1911–1995)**
Rogers, Kenny (singer); Houston, 1939(?)
Rogers, Roy (Leonard Slye) (actor); Cincinnati, 11/5/1912
Rogers, Wayne (actor); Birmingham, Ala. 4/7/1933
Rogers, Will (William Penn Adair Rogers) (humorist); Oologah, Okla. **(1879-1935)**
Rogers, William P. (ex-Secretary of State); Norfolk, N.Y., 6/23/1913
Roland, Gilbert (actor); Juarez, Mexico **(1905–1994)**
Rolland, Romain (author); Clamecy, France **(1866-1944)**
Rollins, Sonny (saxophonist); New York City, 9/7/1930
Romberg, Sigmund (comp oser); Szeged (Hungary) **(1887-1951)**
Rome, Harold (composer); Hartford, Conn. **(1908–1993)**
Romero, Cesar (actor); New York City **(1907–1994)**
Romney, George W. (automobile executive, governor); Chihuahua, Mexico **(1907–1995)**
Romulo, Carlos P. (diplomat and educator); Manila **(1899-1985)**
Ronsard, Pierre de (poet); La Possonnière nr. Couture (Couture-sur-Loir, France) **(1524-1585)**
Ronstadt, Linda (singer); Tucson, Ariz., 7/30/1946
Rooney, Andy (TV personality); Albany, N.Y., 1/14/1919
Rooney, Mickey (Joe Yule, Jr.) (actor); Brooklyn, N.Y., 9/23/1920
Roosevelt, Anna Eleanor (reformer and humanitarian); New York City **(1884-1962)**
Rorem, Ned (composer); Richmond, Ind., 10/23/1923
Rose, Billy (showman); New York City **(1899-1966)**
Rose, Leonard (concert cellist); Washington, D.C. **(1918-1984)**
Roseanne (Barr) (actress); Salt Lake City, 11/3/1952
Ross, Betsy (Betsey Griscom) (flagmaker); Philadelphia **(1752-1836)**
Ross, Diana (singer); Detroit, 3/26/1944
Ross, Katharine (actress); Hollywood, Calif., 1/29/1943
Rossellini, Isabella (model, actress); Rome, Italy, 6/18/1952
Rossellini, Roberto (film director); Rome **(1906-1977)**
Rossetti, Dante Gabriel (painter and poet); London **(1828-1882)**
Rossini, Gioacchino Antonio (composer); Pesaro (Italy) **(1792-1868)**
Rostand, Edmond (dramatist); Marseilles, France **(1868-1918)**
Rostow, Walt Whitman (economist); New York City, 10/7/1916
Rostropovich, Mstislav (cellist and conductor); Baku, U.S.S.R., 3/27/1927
Roth, Lillian (singer); Boston **(1910-1980)**
Roth, Philip (novelist); Newark, N.J., 3/19/1933
Rothko, Mark (Marcus Rothkovich) (painter); Russia **(1903-1970)**
Rouault, Georges (painter); Paris **(1871-1958)**
Roundtree, Richard (actor); New Rochelle, N.Y., 9/7/1942
Rousseau, Henri (painter); Laval, France **(1844-1910)**
Rousseau, Jean Jacques (philosopher); Geneva **(1712-1778)**
Rovere, Richard H. (journalist); Jersey City, N.J., 5/5/1915
Rowan, Dan (comedian); Beggs, Okla. **(1922-1987)**
Rowlands, Gena (actress); Cambria, Wis., 6/19/1936(?)
Rubens, Sir Peter Paul (painter); Siegen (Germany) **(1577-1640)**
Rubinstein, Arthur (concert pianist); Lódz (Poland) **(1887-1982)**
Rubinstein, Helena (cosmetics executive); Krakow (Poland) **(1882?-1965)**
Rubinstein, John (actor, composer); Los Angeles, 12/8/1946
Rudel, Julius (conductor); Vienna, 3/6/1921
Ruffo, Titta (baritone); Italy **(1878-1953)**
Ruggles, Charles (actor); Los Angeles **(1892-1970)**
Rule, Janice (actress); Norwood, Ohio, 8/15/1931
Runcie, Robert (Alexander Kennedy) (Archbishop of Canterbury); Liverpool, England, 10/2/1921
Runyon, (Alfred) Damon (journalist); Manhattan, Kan. **(1884-1945)**
Rusk, Dean (ex-Sec. of State); Cherokee County, Ga **(1909–1994)**
Ruskin, John (art critic); London **(1819-1900)**
Russell, Lord Bertrand (Arthur William) (mathematician and philosopher); Trelleck, Wales **(1872-1970)**
Russell, Jane (actress); Bemidji, Minn., 6/21/1921
Russell, Ken (film director); Southhampton, England, 4/3/1927
Russell, Leon (pianist and singer); Lawton, Okla., 4/2/1941
Russell, Lillian (Helen Louise Leonard) (soprano); Clinton, Iowa **(1861-1922)**
Russell, Mark (satirist); Buffalo, N.Y., 8/23/1932
Russell, Nipsy (comedian); Atlanta, 1924(?)
Russell, Rosalind (actress); Waterbury, Conn. **(1912-1976)**
Rustin, Bayard (civil rights leader); West Chester, Pa. **(1910-1987)**
Rutherford, Dame Margaret (actress); London **(1892-1972)**
Ryan, Robert (actor); Chicago **(1909-1973)**
Rydell, Bobby (singer); Philadelphia, 1942
Rysanek, Leonie (dramatic soprano); Vienna, 11/14/1928

S

Saarinen, Eero (architect); Finland **(1910-1961)**

Sabin, Albert B. (polio researcher); Bialystok (Poland) **(1906-1993)**
Sabu (Dastagir) (actor); Karapur, India **(1924-1963)**
Sadat, Anwar el- (President); Egypt **(1918-1981)**
Sade, Marquis de (Donatien Alphonse Francois, Comte de Sade) (libertine and writer); Paris **(1740-1814)**
Safer, Morley (TV newscaster); Toronto, 11/8/1931
Sagan, Carl (Edward) (astronomer, astrophysicist); New York City, 11/9/1934
Sagan, Françoise (novelist); Cajarc, France, 6/21/1935
Sahl, Mort (Morton Lyon Sahl) (comedian); Montreal, 5/11/1927
Saint, Eva Marie (actress); Newark, N.J., 7/4/1924
Saint-Gaudens, Augustus (sculptor); Dublin **(1848-1907)**
St. Denis, Ruth (dancer,choreographer); Newark, N.J. **(1878-1968)**
St. James, Susan (Susan Miller) (actress); Los Angeles, 8/14/1946
St. John, Jill (actress); Los Angeles, 8/19/1940
St. Johns, Adela Rogers (journalist and author); Los Angeles **(1894-1988)**
Saint-Laurent, Yves (Henri Donat Mathieu) (fashion designer); Oran, Algeria, 8/1/1936
Saint-Saens, Charles Camille (composer); Paris **(1835-1921)**
Sainte-Marie, Buffy (Beverly) (folk singer); Craven, Saskatchewan, Canada, 2/20/1942(?)
Sales, Soupy (Milton Hines); Franklinton, N.C., 1/6/1926
Salinger, J(erome) D(avid) (novelist); New York City, 1/1/1919
Salisbury, Harrison E. (journalist); Minneapolis **(1908-1993)**
Salk, Jonas (polio researcher); New York City **(1914–1995)**
Salk, Lee (psychologist); New York City **(1926–1992)**
Salomon, Haym (American Revolution financier); Leszno, Poland **(1740-1785)**
Sand, George (Amandine Lucille Aurore Dudevant, née Dupin) (novelist); Paris **(1804-1876)**
Sandburg, Carl (poet and biographer); Galesburg, Ill. **(1878-1967)**
Sanders, George (actor); St. Petersburg, Russia **(1906-1972)**
Sands, Tommy (singer); Chicago, 8/27/1937
Sanger, Margaret (birth control leader); Corning, N.Y. **(1883-1966)**
Santayana, George (philosopher); Madrid **(1863-1952)**
Sappho (poet); Lesbos (Greece) (lived c. 600 B.C.)
Sargent, John Singer (painter); Florence, Italy **(1856-1925)**
Sarnoff, David (radio executive); Minsk, Russia **(1891-1971)**
Saroyan, William (novelist); Fresno, Calif. **(1908-1981)**
Sarrazin, Michael (actor); Quebec, 5/22/1940
Sarto, Andrea del (Andrea Domenico d'Agnolo di Francesco) (painter); Florence (Italy) **(1486-1531)**
Sartre, Jean-Paul (existentialist writer); Paris **(1905-1980)**
Sassoon, Vidal (hair stylist); London, 1/(?)/1928
Saul (King of Israel) **(11th century** B.C.)
Savalas, Telly (Aristoteles) (actor); Garden City, N.Y. **(1924–1994)**
Savonarola, Girolamo (religious reformer); Ferrara, Italy **(1452-1498)**
Sawyer, Diane (broadcast journalist); Glasgow, Ky., 12/22/1945
Sayão, Bidú (soprano); Rio de Janeiro, 5/11/1902
Scaasi, Arnold (Arnold Isaacs) (fashion designer); Montreal
Scarlatti, Alessandro (composer); Palermo, Italy **(1659-1725)**
Scarlatti, Domenico (composer); Naples, Italy **(1685-1757)**
Scavullo, Francesco (photographer); Staten Island, N.Y. 1/16/1929
Schary, Dore (producer and writer); Newark, N.J. **(1905-1980)**
Schell, Maria (actress); Vienna, 1/15/1926
Schell, Maximilian (actor); Vienna, 12/8/1930
Schiaparelli, Elsa (fashion designer); Rome **(1890?-1973)**
Schiff, Dorothy (newspaper publisher); New York City **(1903-1989)**
Schildkraut, Joseph (actor); Vienna **(1896-1964)**
Schiller, Johann Christoph Friedrich von (dramatist and poet); Marbach (Germany) **(1759-1805)**
Schipa, Tito (tenor); Lecce, Italy **(1890-1965)**
Schippers, Thomas (conductor); Kalamazoo, Mich. **(1930-1977)**
Schlegel, Friedrich von (philosopher); Hanover? Germany **(1772-1829)**
Schlesinger, Arthur M., Jr. (historian); Columbus, Ohio, 10/15/1917
Schnabel, Artur (pianist,composer); Lipnik, Austria **(1882-1951)**
Schneider, Romy (Rose-Marie Albach) (actress); Vienna **(1938-1982)**
Schoenberg, Arnold (composer); Vienna **(1874-1951)**
Schopenhauer, Arthur (philosopher); Danzig (Poland) **(1788-1860)**
Schubert, Franz Peter (composer); Vienna **(1797-1828)**
Schulberg, Budd (novelist); New York City, 3/27/1914
Schulz, Charles M. (cartoonist); Minneapolis, 11/26/1922
Schuman, Robert (statesman); Luxembourg **(1886-1963)**
Schuman, William (composer); New York City **(1910-1992)**
Schumann, Robert Alexander (composer); Zwickau (East Germany) **(1810-1856)**
Schumann-Heink, Ernestine (contralto); near Prague **(1861-1936)**
Schwartz, Arthur (song writer); Brooklyn, N.Y. **(1900-1984)**
Schwarzenegger, Arnold (bodybuilder, actor); Graz, Austria, 7/30/1947
Schwarzkopf, Elisabeth (soprano); Jarotschin, Poznán (Poland), 12/9/1915
Schwarzkopf, H. Norman (retired general); Trenton, N.J., 8/22/1934

Schweitzer, Albert (humanitarian); Kaysersburg, Upper Alsace **(1875-1965)**
Scofield, Paul (actor); Hurstpierpoint, England, 1/21/1922
Scorsese, Martin (film director); Flushing, N.Y., 11/17/1942
Scott, George C. (actor); Wise, Va., 10/18/1927
Scott, Hazel (singer, pianist); Port of Spain, Trinidad **(1920-1981)**
Scott, Lizabeth (Emma Matso) (actress); Scranton, Pa., 1923
Scott, Martha (actress); Jamesport, Mo., 9/22/1914
Scott, Randolph (Randolph Crane) (actor); Orange County, Va **(1898-1987)**
Scott, Robert Falcon (explorer); Devonport, England **(1868-1912)**
Scott, Sir Walter (novelist); Edinburgh, Scotland **(1771-1832)**
Scott, Zachary (actor); Austin, Tex. **(1914-1965)**
Scotto, Renata (operatic soprano); Savona, Italy, 2/?/1936?
Scruggs, Earl Eugene (bluegrass musician); Cleveland County, N.C., 1/6/1924
Sebastian, John (composer); New York City, 3/17/1944
Seberg, Jean (actress); Marshalltown, Iowa **(1938-1979)**
Sedaka, Neil (singer); Brooklyn, N.Y., 3/13/1939
Seeger, Pete (folk singer); New York City, 5/3/1919
Segal, Erich (novelist); Brooklyn, N.Y., 6/16/1937
Segal, George (actor); New York City, 2/13/1936
Segovia, Andrés (guitarist); Linares, Spain **(1893-1987)**
Seinfeld, Jerry (comedian); Brooklyn, N.Y., 4/29/1954
Selleck, Tom (actor); Detroit, 1/29/1945
Sellars, Peter (theater director); Pittsburgh, Pa., 1958 (?)
Sellers, Peter (actor); Southsea, England **(1925-1980)**
Selznick, David O. (film producer); Pittsburgh **(1902-1965)**
Sendak, Maurice (Bernard) (children's book author and illustrator); Brooklyn, N.Y., 6/10/1928
Sennett, Mack (Michael Sinnott) (film producer); Richmond, Quebec, Canada **(1880-1960)**
Serkin, Peter (pianist); New York City, 7/24/1947
Serkin, Rudolf (pianist); Eger (Hungary) **(1903–1991)**
Serling, Rod (story writer); Syracuse, N.Y. **(1924-1975)**
Sessions, Roger (composer); Brooklyn, N.Y. **(1896-1985)**
Seurat, Georges (painter); Paris **(1859-1891)**
Seuss, Dr. (Theodor Seuss Geisel) (author and illustrator); Springfield, Mass. **(1904-1991)**
Sevareid, Eric (TV commentator); Velva, N.D. **(1912-1992)**
Severinsen, Doc (Carl) (band leader); Arlington, Ore., 7/7/1927
Sexton, Anne (poet); Newton, Mass. **(1928-1974)**
Seymour, Jane (actress); Wimbledon, England, 2/15/1951
Shaffer, Peter (playwright); Liverpool, England, 5/15/1926
Shahn, Ben(jamin) (painter); Kaunas, Lithuania **(1898-1969)**
Shakespeare, William (dramatist); Stratford on Avon, England **(1564-1616)**
Shandling, Garry (comedian); Chicago, Ill., 1950
Shankar, Ravi (sitar player); Benares, India, 4/7/1920
Sharif, Omar (Michael Shalhoub) (actor); Alexandria, Egypt, 4/10/1932
Shatner, William (actor); Montreal, 3/22/1931
Shaw, Artie (Arthur Arshawsky) (band leader); New York City, 5/23/1910
Shaw, George Bernard (dramatist); Dublin, **(1856-1950)**
Shaw, Irwin (novelist); Brooklyn, N.Y., **(1913-1984)**
Shaw, Robert (actor); Lancashire, England **(1927-1978)**
Shaw, Robert (chorale conductor); Red Bluff, Calif., 4/30/1916
Shawn, Ted (Edwin Myers Shawn) (dancer,choreographer); Kansas City, Mo. **(1891-1972)**
Shearer, Moira (ballerina); Dunfermline, Scotland, 1/17/1926
Shearer, Norma (actress); Montreal, **(1902?-1983)**
Shearing, George (pianist); London, 8/13/1920
Sheen, Fulton J. (Peter Sheen) (Roman Catholic bishop); El Paso, Ill. **(1895-1979)**
Sheen, Martin (Ramon Estevez) (actor); Dayton, Ohio, 8/3/1940
Shelley, Percy Bysshe (poet); nr. Horsham, England **(1792-1822)**
Shepard, Sam (playwright); Ft. Sheridan, Ill. 11/5/1943
Shepherd, Cybill (actress); Memphis, Tenn., 2/18/1950
Sheraton, Thomas (furniture designer); Stockton-on-Tees, England **(1751-1806)**
Sheridan, Ann (actress); Denton, Tex. **(1915-1967)**
Sheridan, Philip (army officer); Albany, N.Y. **(1831-1888)**
Sheridan, Richard Brinsley (dramatist); Dublin **(1751-1816)**
Sherman, William Tecumseh (army officer); Lancaster, Ohio **(1820-1891)**
Sherwood, Robert Emmet (playwright); New Rochelle, N.Y. **(1896-1955)**
Shevardnadze, Eduard Amvrosiyevich (State Council Chairman, Georgia); Mamati, Georgia, U.S.S.R. 1/25/1928
Shields, Brooke (actress); New York City, 5/31/1965
Shire, Talia (Coppola) (actress) Lake Success, N.Y. 4/25/1946(?)
Shirer, William L. (journalist and historian); Chicago **(1904–1993)**
Shirley, Anne (actress); New York City **(1918-1993)**
Sholokhov, Mikhail (novelist); Veshenskaya, Russia **(1905-1984)**

Shore, Dinah (Frances Rose Shore) (singer); Winchester, Tenn. **(1917–1994)**

Short, Bobby (Robert Waltrip Short) (singer and pianist); Danville, Ill., 9/15/1924

Shostakovich, Dmitri (composer); St. Petersburg, Russia **(1906-1975)**

Shriner, Herb (humorist,host); Toledo, Ohio **(1918-1970)**

Shriver, Maria (TV co-host); Chicago, 11/6/1955

Shriver, Sargent (Robert Sargent Shriver, Jr.) (business executive); Westminster, Md., 11/9/1915

Shulman, Max (novelist); St. Paul **(1919-1988)**

Sibelius, Jean (Johann Julius Christian Sibelius) (composer); Tavastehus (Finland) **(1865-1957)**

Siddons, Sarah (Sarah Kemble) (actress); Wales **(1755-1831)**

Sidney, Sylvia (actress); New York City, 8/8/1910

Siepi, Cesare (basso); Milan, Italy, 2/10/1923

Signoret, Simone (Simone Kaminker) (actress); Wiesbaden, Germany **(1921-1985)**

Sikorsky, Igor I. (inventor); Kiev, Russia **(1889-1972)**

Sills, Beverly (Belle Silverman) (soprano, opera director); Brooklyn, N.Y., 5/25/1929

Sills, Milton (actor); Chicago **(1882-1930)**

Silone, Ignazio (Secondo Tranquilli) (novelist); Pescina del Marsi, Italy **(1900-1978)**

Silverman, Fred (broadcasting executive); New York City, 9/13/1937

Silver, Ron (actor); New York City, 7/2/1946

Silvers, Phil (Philip Silversmith) (comedian); Brooklyn, N.Y. **(1912-1985)**

Sim, Alastair (actor); Edinburgh, Scotland **(1900-1976)**

Simenon, Georges (Georges Sim) (mystery writer); Liège, Belgium **(1903-1989)**

Simmons, Jean (actress); Crouch Hill, London, 1/31/1929

Simon, Carly (singer and songwriter); New York City, 6/25/1945

Simon, Neil (playwright); Bronx, N.Y., 7/4/1927

Simon, Norton (business executive); Portland, Ore. **(1907-1993)**

Simon, Paul (singer and songwriter); Newark, N.J., 11/5/1942

Simone, Nina (Eunice Kathleen Waymoa) (singer and pianist); Tryon, N.C., 2/21/1933

Sinatra, Frank (Francis Albert) (singer and actor); Hoboken, N.J., 12/12/1915

Sinclair, Upton Beall (novelist); Baltimore **(1878-1968)**

Singer, Isaac Bashevis (novelist); Radzymin (Poland) **(1904–1991)**

Siqueiros, David (painter); Chihuahua, Mexico **(1896-1974)**

Sisley, Alfred (painter); Paris **(1839-1899)**

Sitting Bull (Prairie Sioux Indian Chief); on Grand River, S.D. **(c. 1835-1890)**

Skelton, Red (Richard) (comedian); Vincennes, Ind., 7/18/1913

Skinner, B(urrhus) F(rederic) (psychologist); Susquehanna, Pa. **(1904-1990)**

Skinner, Cornelia Otis (writer and actress); Chicago, **(1901-1979)**

Skinner, Otis (actor); Cambridge, Mass. **(1858-1942)**

Slatkin, Leonard (conductor); Los Angeles, 9/1/1944

Slezak, Walter (actor); Vienna **(1902-1983)**

Sloan, Alfred P., Jr. (industrialist); New Haven, Conn. **(1875-1965)**

Sloan, John (painter); Lock Haven, Pa. **(1871-1951)**

Smetana, Bedrich (composer); Litomysl (Czechoslovakia) **(1824-1884)**

Smith, Adam (economist); Kirkaldy, Scotland **(1723-1790)**

Smith, Alexis (actress); Penticon, Canada **(1921-1993)**

Smith, Alfred Emanuel (politician); New York City **(1873-1944)**

Smith, Sir C. Aubrey (actor); London **(1863-1948)**

Smith, David (sculptor); Decatur, Ind. **(1906-1965)**

Smith, H. Allen (humorist); McLeansboro, Ill. **(1907-1976)**

Smith, Harry (TV co-anchor); Hammond, Ind., 8/21/1951

Smith, Howard K. (TV commentator); Ferriday, La., 5/12/1914

Smith, Jaclyn (actress); Houston, 10/26/1947

Smith, John (American colonist); Willoughby, Lincolnshire, England **(1580-1631)**

Smith, Joseph (religious leader); Sharon, Vt. **(1805-1844)**

Smith, Kate (Kathryn) (singer); Greenville, Va. **(1909-1986)**

Smith, Dame Maggie (actress); Ilford, England, 12/28/1934

Smith, Red (Walter) (sports columnist); Green Bay, Wis. **(1905-1982)**

Smits, Jimmy (actor); New York City, 7/9/1958

Smollet, Tobias (novelist); Dalquhurn, Scotland **(1721-1771)**

Smothers, Dick (Richard) (comedian); Governors Island, New York City, 11/20/1939

Smothers, Tom (Thomas) (comedian); Governors Island, New York City, 2/2/1937

Snow, Lord (Charles Percy) (author); Leicester, England **(1905-1980)**

Snowdon, Earl of (Anthony Armstrong-Jones) (photographer); London, 3/7/1930

Snyder, Tom (TV personality); Milwaukee, 5/12/1936

Socrates (philosopher); Athens **(469-399** B.C.)

Solomon (King of Israel); Jerusalem (?) **(died c. 933** B.C.)

Solon (lawgiver); Salamis (Greece) **(638?-559** B.C.)

Solti, Sir Georg (conductor); Budapest, 10/21/1912

Solzhenitsyn, Aleksandr (novelist); Kislovodsk, Russia, 12/11/1918

Somers, Suzanne (Suzanne Mahoney) (actress); San Bruno, Calif., 10/16/1946

Somes, Michael (ballet dancer); Horsley, England **(1917–1994)**

Sommer, Elke (Elke Schletz) (actress); Berlin, 11/5/1942

Sondheim, Stephen (composer); New York City, 3/22/1930

Sontag, Susan (author and film director); New York City, 1/28/1933

Sophocles (dramatist); nr. Athens **(496?-406** B.C.)

Sothern, Ann (Harriette Lake) (actress); Valley City, N.D., 1/22/1909

Soul, David (David Solberg) (actor); Chicago, 8/28/(?)

Sousa, John Philip (composer); Washington, D.C. **(1854-1932)**

Soyer, Raphael (painter); Borisoglebsk, Russia **(1899-1987)**

Spaak, Paul-Henri (statesman); Brussels **(1899-1972)**

Spacek, Sissy (Mary Elizabeth) (actress); Quitman, Tex., 12/25/1949

Spark, Muriel (novelist); Edinburgh, Scotland, 2/1/1918

Sparks, Ned (actor); Ontario **(1883-1957)**

Spector, Phil (rock producer); Bronx, N.Y., 12/25/1940

Spencer, Herbert (philosopher); Derby, England **(1820-1903)**

Spender, Stephen (poet); nr. London **(1909–1995)**

Spengler, Oswald (philosopher); Blankenburg, (East Germany) **(1880-1936)**

Spenser, Edmund (poet); London **(1552?-1599)**

Spewack, Bella (playwright); Hungary **(1899-1990)**

Spiegel, Sam (producer); Jaroslaw (Poland) **(1901-1985)**

Spielberg, Steven (film director); Cincinnati, 12/18/1947

Spillane, Mickey (Frank Spillane) (mystery writer); Brooklyn, N.Y., 3/9/1918

Spinoza, Baruch (philosopher); Amsterdam (Netherlands) **(1632-1677)**

Spitalny, Phil (orchestra leader); **(1890-1970)**

Spivak, Lawrence (TV producer); Brooklyn, N.Y. **(1900–1994)**

Spock, Benjamin (pediatrician); New Haven, Conn., 5/2/1903

Springsteen, Bruce (singer and songwriter); Freehold, N.J., 9/23/1949

Sproul, Robert G. (educator); San Francisco **(1891-1975)**

Stack, Robert (actor); Los Angeles, 1/13/1919

Stafford, Jo (singer); Coalinga, Calif., 1918

Stalin, Joseph Vissarionovich (Iosif V. Dzhugashvili) (Soviet leader); nr. Tiflis, Russia **(1879-1953)**

Stallone, Sylvester (actor and writer); New York City, 7/6/1946

Stamp, Terrence (actor); London, 1938

Stander, Lionel (actor); New York City **(1908–1994)**

Standing, Sir Guy (actor); London **(1873-1937)**

Stang, Arnold (comedian); Chelsea, Mass., 1925

Stanislavski (Konstantin Sergeevich Alekseev) (stage producer); Moscow **(1863-1938)**

Stanley, Sir Henry Morton (John Rowlands) (explorer); Denbigh, Wales **(1841-1904)**

Stanley, Kim (Patricia Reid) (actress); Tularosa, N.M., 2/11/1925

Stans, Maurice H. (ex-Secretary of Commerce); Shakope, Minn., 3/22/1908

Stanton, Frank (broadcasting executive); Muskegon, Mich., 3/20/1908

Stanwyck, Barbara (Ruby Stevens) (actress); Brooklyn, N.Y. **(1907-1990)**

Stapleton, Jean (Jeanne Murray) (actress); New York City, 1/19/1923

Stapleton, Maureen (actress); Troy, N.Y., 6/21/1925

Starker, János (cellist); Budapest, 7/5/1926

Starr, Kay (Starks) (singer); Dougherty, Okla., 7/21/1922

Starr, Ringo (Richard Starkey) (singer and songwriter); Liverpool, England, 7/7/1940

Stassen, Harold E. (ex-government official); West St. Paul, Minn., 4/13/1907

Steber, Eleanor (soprano); Wheeling, W. Va., 7/17/1916

Steegmuller, Francis (biographer); New Haven, Conn. **(1906–1994)**

Steele, Tommy (singer); London, 12/17/1936

Stegner, Wallace (Earle) (novelist and critic); Lake Mills, Iowa **(1909-1993)**

Steichen, Edward Jean (photographer, artist); Luxembourg **(1879-1973)**

Steiger, Rod (Rodney) (actor); Westhampton, N.Y., 4/14/1925

Stein, Gertrude (author); Allegheny, Pa. **(1874-1946)**

Steinbeck, John Ernst (novelist); Salinas, Calif. **(1902-1968)**

Steinberg, David (comedian); Winnipeg, Manitoba, Canada, 8/19/1942

Steinberg, William (conductor); Cologne, Germany **(1899-1978)**

Steinem, Gloria (feminist); Toledo, Ohio, 3/25/1934

Steinmetz, Charles (electrical engineer); Breslau (Poland) **(1865-1923)**

Stendhal (Marie Henri Beyle) (novelist); Grenoble, France **(1783-1842)**

Sterling, Jan (actress); New York City, 4/3/1923

Stern, Isaac (concert violinist); Kreminlecz, Russia, 7/21/1920

Sterne, Laurence (novelist); Clonmel, Ireland (**1713-1768)**

Theodorakis, Mikis (composer); Chios, Greece, 7/29/1925
Thicke, Alan (actor); Kirland Lake, Ont., Canada, 3/1/1947
Thieu, Nguyen Van (ex-President of South Vietnam); Trithuy (Vietnam) 4/5/1923
Thomas, Danny (Amos Jacobs) (entertainer and TV producer); Deerfield, Mich. **(1912–1991)**
Thomas, Dylan Marials (poet); Carmarthenshire, Wales **(1914–1953)**
Thomas, Lowell (explorer, commentator); Woodington, Ohio **(1892-1981)**
Thomas, Marlo (actress); Detroit, 11/21/1943
Thomas, Michael Tilson (conductor); Hollywood, Calif., 12/21/1944
Thomas, Norman Mattoon (Socialist leader); Marion, Ohio **(1884-1968)**
Thomas, Philip Michael (actor); Columbus, Ohio, 5/26/1949
Thomas, Richard (actor); New York City, 6/13/1951
Thompson, Dorothy (writer); Lancaster, N.Y. **(1894-1961)**
Thompson, Hunter (Stockton) (writer); Louisville, Ky. 7/18/1939
Thompson, Sada (actress); Des Moines, Iowa, 9/27/1929
Thomson, Virgil (Garnett) (composer); Kansas City, Mo. **(1896-1989)**
Thoreau, Henry David (naturalist and author); Concord, Mass. **(1817-1862)**
Thorndike, Dame Sybil (actress); Gainsborough, England **(1882-1976)**
Thurber, James Grover (author and cartoonist); Columbus, Ohio **(1894-1961)**
Tibbett, Lawrence (baritone); Bakersfield, Calif. **(1896-1960)**
Tiegs, Cheryl (model,actress); Minnesota, 9/25/1947
Tierney, Gene (actress); Brooklyn, N.Y. **(1920-1991)**
Tiffin, Pamela (actress); Oklahoma City, 10/13/1942
Tillstrom, Burr (puppeteer); Chicago **(1917-1985)**
Tintoretto, Il (Jacopo Robusti) (painter); Venice **(1518-1594)**
Tiny Tim (Herbert Khaury) (entertainer); New York City, 1923(?)
Tiomkin, Dmitri (composer); St. Petersburg, Russia **(1894-1979)**
Titian (Tiziano Vecelli) (painter); Pieve di Cadore (Italy) **(1477-1576)**
Tito (Josip Broz or Brozovich) (President of Yugoslavia); Croatia (Yugoslavia) **(1892-1980)**
Tocqueville, Alexis de (writer); Verneuil, France **(1805-1859)**
Todd, Ann (actress); Hartford, England **(1909-1993)**
Todd, Michael (producer); Minneapolis, Minn. **(1907-1958)**
Todd, Richard (actor); Dublin, Ireland, 6/11/1919
Todd, Thelma (actress); Lawrence, Mass. **(1905-1935)**
Tolstoi, Count Leo (Lev) Nikolaevich (novelist); Tula Province, Russia **(1828-1910)**
Tomlin, Lily (comedienne); Detroit, 1939(?)
Tone, Franchot (actor); Niagara Falls, N.Y. **(1905-1968)**
Toomey, Regis (actor); Pittsburgh, Pa. **(1902-1991)**
Tormé, Mel (Melvin) (singer); Chicago, 9/13/1925
Torn, Rip (Elmore Torn, Jr.) (actor and director); Temple, Tex., 2/6/1931
Torquamada, Tomásde (Spanish Inquisitor); Vlladolid, Spain **(1420-1498)**
Toscanini, Arturo (orchestra conductor); Parma, Italy **(1867-1957)**
Toulouse-Lautrec (Henri Marie Raymond de Toulouse-Lautrec Monfa) (painter); Albi, France **(1864-1901)**
Toynbee, Arnold J. (historian); London **(1889-1975)**
Tracy, Lee (actor); Atlanta, Ga. **(1898-1968)**
Tracy, Spencer (actor); Milwaukee **(1900-1967)**
Traubel, Helen (Wagnerian soprano); St. Louis **(1903-1972)**
Travanti, Daniel J. (actor); Kenosha, Wis., 3/7/1940
Travolta, John (actor); Englewood, N.J., 2/18/1954
Treacher, Arthur (actor); Brighton, England **(1894-1975)**
Tree, Sir Herbert Beerbolm (actor-manager); London **(1853-1917)**
Trevor, Claire (actress); New York City, 1911
Trigère, (Pauline (fashion designer); Paris, 11/4/1912
Trilling, Lionel (author and educator); New York City **(1905-1975)**
Trotsky, Leon (Lev Davidovich Bronstein) (statesman); Elisavetgrad, Russia **(1879-1940)**
Troyanos, Tatiana (mezzo-soprano); New York City **(1938-1993)**
Trudeau, Garry (cartoonist); New York City, 1948
Trudeau, Pierre Elliott (former Prime Minister); Montreal, 10/18/1919
Truffaut, François (film director); Paris **(1932-1984)**
Trujillo y Molina, Rafael Leonidas (Dominican Republic dictator); San Cristóbal, Dominican Republic **(1891-1961)**
Truman, Margaret (author); Independence, Mo., 2/17/1924
Tryon, Thomas (actor and novelist); Hartford, Conn. **(1926–1991)**
Tsiolkovsky, Konstantin E. (father of cosmonautics); Izhevskoye, Russia **(1857-1935)**
Tuchman, Barbara (Wertheim) (historian, author); New York City **(1912-1989)**
Tucker, Forrest (actor); Plainfield, Ind. **(1919-1986)**
Tucker, Richard (tenor); New York City **(1914-1975)**
Tucker, Sophie (Sophie Abuza) (singer); Europe **(1884?-1966)**
Tudor, Antony (choreographer); London **(1909-1987)**
Tune, Tommy (dancer-choreographer); Wichita Falls, Tex., 2/28/1939
Turgeniev, Ivan Sergeevich (novelist); Orel, Russia **(1818-18 83)**
Turner, Ike (singer); Clarksdale, Miss., 11/?/1931

Turner, Janine (actress); Lincoln, Neb., 12/6/1962
Turner, Joseph M.W. (painter); London **(1775-1851)**
Turner, Kathleen (actress); Springfield, Mo., 1956 (?)
Turner, Lana (Julia Jean Mildred Frances Turner) (actress); Wallace, Idaho **(1920–1995)**
Turner, Nat (civil rights leader); Southampton County, Va. **(1800-1831)**
Turner, Tina (Annie Mae Bullock) (singer); Nut Bush, nr. Brownsville, Tenn., 11/26/1939
Turpin, Ben (comedian); New Orleans **(1874-1940)**
Tushingham, Rita (actress); Liverpool, England, 3/14/1942
Twain, Mark (Samuel Langhorne Clemens) (author); Florida, Mo. **(1835-1910)**
Tweed, William Marcy (politician); New York City **(1823-1878)**
Twiggy (Leslie Hornby) (model); London, 9/19/1949
Twining, Gen. Nathan F. (former Air Force Chief of Staff); Monroe, Wis. **(1897-1982)**
Twitty, Conway (Harold Lloyd Jenkins) (singer and guitarist); Friars Point, Miss. **(1933-1993)**
Tyson, Cicely (actress); New York City, 12/19/1939(?)

U

Udall, Stewart L. (ex-Secretary of the Interior); St. Johns, Ariz., 1/31/1920
Uggams, Leslie (singer and actress); New York City, 5/25/1943
Ulanova, Galina (ballerina); St. Petersburg, Russia, 1/10/1910
Ullman, Tracey (actress, singer); Slough, England, 12/30/1959
Ullmann, Liv (actress); Tokyo, 12/16/1939
Ulric, Lenore (actress); New Ulm, Minn. **(1894-1970)**
Untermeyer, Louis (anthologist and poet); New York City **(1885-1977)**
Updike, John (novelist); Shillington, Pa., 3/18/1932
Urey, Harold C. (physicist); Walkerton, Ind. **(1893-1981)**
Uris, Leon (novelist); Baltimore, 8/3/1924
Ustinov, Peter (actor and producer); London, 4/16/1921
Utrillo, Maurice (painter); Paris **(1883-1955)**

V

Vaccaro, Brenda (actress); Brooklyn, N.Y., 11/18/1939
Vadim, Roger (Roger Vadim Plemiannikov) (film director); Paris, 1/26/1928
Valentine, Karen (actress); Santa Rosa, Calif., 1947
Valentino, Rudolph (Rodolpho d'Antonguolla) (actor); Castellaneta, Italy **(1895-1926)**
Valentino (Valentino Garavani) (fashion designer); nr. Milan, Italy, 5/11/1932
Vallee, Rudy (Hubert Prior Rudy Vallée) (band leader and singer); Island Pond, Vt. **(1901-1986)**
Valli, Frankie (Frank Castellaccio) (singer); Newark, N.J., 5/3/1937
Van Allen, James Alfred (space physicist); Mt. Pleasant, Iowa, 9/7/1914
Van Buren, Abigail (Mrs. Morton Phillips) (columnist); Sioux City, Iowa, 7/4/1918
Vance, Vivian (actress); Cherryvale, Kan. **(1912-1979)**
Vanderbilt, Alfred G. (sportsman); London, 9/22/1912
Vanderbilt, Cornelius (financier); Port Richmond, N.Y. **(1794-1877)**
Vanderbilt, Gloria (fashion designer New York City, 2/20/1924
Van Doren, Carl (writer and educator); Hope, Ill. **(1885-1950)**
Van Doren, Mamie (actress); Rowena, S.D., 2/6/1933
Van Dyke, Dick (actor); West Plains, Mo., 12/13/1925
Vandyke (or Van Dyck), Sir Anthony (painter); Antwerp (Belgium) **(1599-1641)**
Van Eyck, Jan (painter); Maeseyck (Belgium) **(c.1390-1441)**
Van Fleet, Jo (actress); Oakland, Calif., 12/30/1919
van Gogh, Vincent (painter); Groot Zundert, Brabant **(1853-1890)**
van Hamel, Martine (ballerina); Brussels, 11/16/1945
Van Heusen, Jimmy (Edward Chester Babcock) (songwriter); Syracuse, N.Y. **(1913-1990)**
Van Patten, Dick (actor); Richmond Hill, N.Y., 12/9/1928
Van Peebles, Melvin (playwright); Chicago, 9/21/1932
Vaughan, Sarah (singer); Newark, N.J. **(1924-1990)**
Vaughan Williams, Ralph (composer); Down Ampney, England **(1872-1958)**
Vaughn, Robert (actor); New York City, 11/22/1932
Veidt, Conrad (actor); Potsdam, Germany **(1893-1943)**
Velázquez, Diego Rodriguez de Silva y (painter); Seville, Spain **(1599-1660)**
Velez, Lupe (Guadelupe Velez de Villalobos) (actress); San Luis Potosi, Mexico **(1908-1944)**
Venturi, Robert (Charles) (architect); Philadelphia, 6/25/1925
Verdi, Giuseppe (composer); Roncole (Italy) **(1813-1901)**
Verdon, Gwen (actress); Culver City, Calif., 1/13/1925
Vereen, Ben (actor and singer); Miami, Fla., 10/10/1946

Vermeer, Jan (or Jan van der Meer van Delft) (painter); Delft (Netherlands) **(1632-1675)**

Verne, Jules (author); Nantes, France **(1828-1905)**

Veronese, Paolo (Paolo Cagliari) (painter); Verona **(1528-1588)**

Verrazano, Giovanni da (navigator); Florence (Italy) **(1485?-1528)**

Verrett, Shirley (mezzo-soprano); New Orleans, 5/31/1933

Vesalius, Andreas (anatomist); Brussels, Belgium **(1515-1564)**

Vespucci, Amerigo (navigator); Florence (Italy) **(1454-1512)**

Vickers, Jon (tenor); Prince Albert, Sask, Canada, 10/29/1926

Vico, Giovanni Battista (philosopher); Naples, Italy **(1668-1744)**

Vidal, Gore (novelist); West Point, N.Y., 10/3/1925

Vidor, King (film director and producer); Galveston, Tex. **(1895-1982)**

Vigoda, Abe (actor); New York City, 2/24/1921

Villa, Pancho (Doroteo Arango) (revolutionary); Hacienda de Rio Grande, San Juan del Rio, Meixco **(1877-1923)**

Villella, Edward (ballet dancer); Bayside, Queens, N.Y., 10/1/1936

Villon, François (François de Montcorbier) (poet); Paris **(1431-1463)**

Vincent, Helen (actress); Beaumont, Tex., 9/17/1907

Vinton, Bobby (singer); Canonsburg, Pa., 4/16/1935(?)

Virgil (or Vergil) (Publius Vergilius Maro) (poet); nr. Mantua (Italy) **(70-19** B.C.**)**

Vishnevskaya, Galina (soprano); Leningrad, 10/25/1926

Vivaldi, Antonio (composer); Venice **(1678-1741)**

Vlaminck, Maurice de (painter); Paris **(1876-1958)**

Voight, Jon (actor); Yonkers, N.Y., 12/29/1938

Volta, Alessandro (scientist); Como, Italy **(1745-1827)**

Voltaire (François Marie Arouet) (author); Paris **(1694-1778)**

von Aroldingen, Karin (Karin Awny Hannelore Reinbold von Aroedingen and Eltzinger) (ballet dancer); Greiz (East Germany) 7/9/1941

von Braun, Wernher (rocket scientist); Wirsitz, Germany **(1912-1977)**

von Furstenberg, Betsy (Elizabeth Caroline Maria Agatha Felicitas Therese von Furstenberg-Hedringen) (actress); Nelheim-Heusen, Germany, 8/16/1935

von Fürstenberg, Diane (Diane Simone Michelle Halfin) (fashion designer); Brussels, 12/31/1946

von Hindenburg, Paul (statesman); Posen (Poland) **(1847-1934)**

von Karajan, Herbert (conductor); Salzburg (Austria) **(1908-1989)**

Vonnegut, Kurt, Jr. (novelist); Indianapolis, 11/11/1922

Von Stade, Frederica (mezzo-soprano); Somerville, N.J., 1945

Von Stroheim, Erich Oswald Hans Carl Maria von Nordenwall (film actor and director); Vienna **(1885-1957)**

Von Zell, Harry (announcer); Indianapolis, Ind. **(1906-1981)**

Vreeland, Diana (Diana Da Iziel) (fashion journalist and museum consultant); Paris **(1903?-1989)**

W

Wagner, Lindsay (actress); Los Angeles, 6/22/1949

Wagner, Robert (actor); Detroit, 2/10/1930

Wagner, Robert F. (ex-Mayor of New York City); New York City **(1910-1991)**

Wagner, Wilhelm Richard (composer); Leipzig (East Germany) **(1813-1883)**

Waldheim, Kurt (ex-U.N. Secretary-General); St. Andrae-Wörden, Austria, 12/21/1918

Walker, Nancy (Ann Myrtle Swoyer); (actress and comedienne); Philadelphia **(1922-1992)**

Walker, Robert (actor); Salt Lake City, Utah **(1918-1951)**

Wallace, DeWitt (publisher); St. Paul **(1889-1981)**

Wallace, George C. (ex-govenor); Clio, Ala. 8/25/1919

Wallace, Irving (novelist); Chicago **(1916-1990)**

Wallace, Mike (Myron Wallace) (TV interviewer and commentator); Brookline, Mass., 5/9/1918

Wallach, Eli (actor); Brooklyn, N.Y., 12/7/1915

Wallenstein, Alfred (conductor); Chicago **(1898-1983)**

Waller, Thomas "Fats" (pianist); New York City **(1904-1943)**

Wallis, Hal (film producer); Chicago **(1899-1986)**

Waltari, Mika (novelist); Helsinki, Finland, **(1903-1979)**

Walter, Bruno (Bruno Walter Schlesinger) (orchestra conductor); Berlin **(1876-1962)**

Walters, Barbara (TV commentator); Boston, 9/25/1931

Walton, Izaak (author); Stafford, England **(1593-1683)**

Wambaugh, Joseph (author and screenwriter); East Pittsburgh, Pa., 1/22/1937

Wanamaker, John (merchant); Philadelphia **(1838-1922)**

Wanamaker, Sam (actor,director); Chicago **(1919-1993)**

Ward, Barbara (economist); York, England **(1914-1981)**

Warhol, Andy (artist and producer); Pennsylvania **(1928(?)-1987)**

Waring, Fred (band leader); Tyrone, Pa. **(1900-1984)**

Warner, H. B. (Henry Bryan Warner Lickford) (actor); London **(1876-1958)**

Warren, Lesley Ann (actress); New York City, 8/16/1946

Warren, Robert Penn (novelist); Guthrie, Ky. **(1905-1989)**

Warrick, Ruth (actress) St. Joseph, Mo., 6/29/1915

Warwick, Dionne (singer); East Orange, N.J., 1941

Washington, Booker Taliaferro (educator); Franklin County, Va. **(1856-1915)**

Waters, Ethel (actr ess and singer); Chester, Pa. **(1896-1977)**

Waters, Muddy (McKinley Morganfield) (singer and guitarist); Rolling Fork, Miss. **(1915-1983)**

Waterson, Sam (actor); Cambridge, Mass., 11/15/1940

Watson, Thomas John (industrialist); Campbell, N.Y. **(1874-1956)**

Watt, James (inventor); Greenock, Scotland **(1736-1819)**

Watteau, Jean-Antoine (painter); Valanciennes, France **(1684-1721)**

Wattleton, Faye (family planning advocate); St. Louis, Mo., 7/8/1943

Watts, André (concert pianist); Nuremberg, Germany, 6/20/1946

Waugh, Alec (Alexander Raban Waugh) (novelist); London **(1898-1981)**

Waugh, Evelyn (satirist); London **(1903-1966)**

Wayne, Anthony (military officer); Waynesboro (family farm), nr. Paoli, Pa. **(1745-1796)**

Wayne, David (David McMeekan); (actor); Traverse City, Mich. **(1914-1995)**

Wayne, John (Marion Michael Morrison) (actor); Winterset, Iowa **(1907-1979)**

Weaver, Dennis (actor); Joplin, Mo., 6/4/1925

Weaver, Fritz (actor); Pittsburgh, Pa., 1/19/1926

Weaver, Sigourney (actress); New York City, 10/8/1949

Webb, Clifton (Webb Parmelee Hollenbeck) (actor); Indianapolis **(1893-1966)**

Webb, Jack (film actor and producer); Santa Monica, Calif. **(1920-1982)**

Weber, Karl Maria Friedrich Ernst von (composer); nr. Lübeck (Germany) **(1786-1826)**

Webster, Daniel (statesman); Salisbury, N.H. **(1782-1852)**

Webster, Margaret (producer, director, actress); New York City **(1905-1973)**

Webster, Noah (lexicographer); West Hartford, Conn. **(1758-1843)**

Weill, Kurt (composer); Dessau, (East Germany) **(1900-1950)**

Weir, Peter (film director); Sydney, Australia, 8/21/1944

Weizmann, Chaim (statesman); Grodno Province, Russia **(1874-1952)**

Welch, Raquel (Raquel Tejada) (actress); Chicago, 9/5/1940

Weld, Tuesday (Susan) (actress); New York City, 8/27/1943

Welk, Lawrence (band leader); Strasburg, N.D. **(1903-1992)**

Welles, Orson (actor and producer); Kenosha, Wis. **(1915-1985)**

Wellington, Duke of (Arthur Wellesley) (statesman); Ireland **(1769-1852)**

Wells, H(erbert) G(eorge) (author); Bromley, England **(1866-1946)**

Welty, Eudora (novelist); Jackson, Miss., 4/13/1909

Werfel, Franz (novelist); Prague **(1890-1945)**

Werner, Oskar (Josef Schliessmayer) (film actor and director); Vienna **(1922-1984)**

Wertmuller, Lina (film director); Rome, 1926(?)

Wesley, John (religious leader); Epworth Rectory, Lincolnshire, England **(1703-1791)**

West, Dame Rebecca (Cicily Fairfield); (novelist); County Kerry, Ireland **(1892-1983)**

West, Jessamyn (novelist); nr. North Vernon, Ind. **(1902-1984)**

West, Mae (actress); Brooklyn, N.Y. **(1893-1980)**

West, Nathanael (Nathan Weinstein) (novelist); New York City **(1902-1940)**

Westheimer, Ruth (Karola Ruth Siegel) (psychologist, author, broadcaster); Frankfurt, Germany, 1928

Westinghouse, George (inventor); Central Bridge, N.Y. **(1846-1914)**

Westmoreland, William Childs (ex-Army Chief of Staff); Saxon, S.C., 3/26/1914

Wharton, Edith Newbold (née Jones) (novelist); New York City **(1862-1937)**

Wheeler, Bert (Albert Jerome Wheeler) (comedian); Paterson, N.J. **(1895-1968)**

Whistler, James Abbott McNeill (painter and etcher); Lowell, Mass. **(1834-1903)**

White, Betty (actress); Oak Park, Ill., 1/17/1924(?)

White, E(lwyn) B(rooks) (author); Mt. Vernon, N.Y. **(1899-1985)**

White, Pearl (actress); Green Ridge, Mo. **(1889-1938)**

White, Stanford (architect); New York City **(1853-1906)**

White, Theodore H. (historian); Boston **(1915-1986)**

White, Vanna (TV personality); Conway, S.C., 2/18/1957

White, William Allen (journalist); Emporia, Kan. **(1868-1944)**

Whitehead, Alfred North (mathematician and philosopher); Isle of Thanet, England **(1861-1947)**

Whiteman, Paul (band leader); Denver **(1891-1967)**

Whiting, Margaret (singer, actress); Detroit, Mich., 7/22/1924

Whitman, Walt (Walter) (poet); West Hills, N.Y. **(1819-1892)**

Whitmore, James (actor); White Plains, N.Y., 10/1/1921

Whitney, Cornelius Vanderbilt (sportsman); New York City **(1899-1992)**
Whitney, Eli (inventor); Westboro, Mass. **(1765-1825)**
Whitney, John Hay (publisher); Ellsworth, Me. **(1904-1982)**
Whittier, John Greenleaf (poet); Haverhill, Mass. **(1807-1892)**
Whitty, Dame May (actr ess); Liverpool, England **(1865-1948)**
Widmark, Richard (actor); Sunrise, Minn., 12/26/1914
Wiesel, Elie (Eliezer) (author); Signet, Romania, 9/30/1928
Wilde, Cornel (film actor and producer); New York City **(1915-1989)**
Wilde, Oscar Fingal O'Flahertie Wills (author); Dublin **(1854-1900)**
Wilder, Billy (film producer and director); Vienna, 6/22/1906
Wilder, Gene (Jerome Silberman) (actor); Milwaukee, 6/11/1935(?)
Wilder, Thornton (author); Madison, Wis. **(1897-1975)**
Wilding, Michael (actor); Westcliff, England **(1912-1979)**
Wilkins, Roy (civil rights leader); St. Louis **(1901-1981)**
Williams, Andy (singer); Wall Lake, Iowa, 12/3/1930
Williams, Billy Dee (actor); New York City, 4/6/1937
Williams, Cindy (actress); Van Nuys, Calif., 8/22/(?)
Williams, Edward Bennett (lawyer); Hartford, Conn. **(1920-1988)**
Williams, Emlyn (actor and playwright); Mostyn, Wales **(1905-1987)**
Williams, Esther (actress); Los Angeles, 8/8/1923
Williams, Gluyas (cartoonist); San Francisco **(1888-1982)**
Williams, Hank, Sr. (Hiram King Williams) (singer); Georgiana, Ala. **(1923-1953)**
Williams, Joe (singer); Cordele, Ga., 12/12/1918
Williams, Paul (singer, composer, actor); Omaha, Neb., 9/19/1940
Williams, Robin (comedian); Chicago, 7/?/1952
Williams, Roger (clergyman); London **(1603?-1683)**
Williams, Tennessee (Thomas L. Williams) (playwright); Columbus, Miss. **(1911-1983)**
Williams, William Carlos (physician and poet); Rutherford, N.J. **(1883-1963)**
Williamson, Nicol (actor); Hamilton, Scotland, 9/14/38
Willkie, Wendell Lewis (lawyer); Elwood, Ind. **(1892-1944)**
Willis, Bruce (actor); Germany, 3/19/1955
Willson, Meredith (composer); Mason City, Iowa **(1902-1984)**
Wilson, August (poet, writer, playwright); Pittsburgh, Pa., 1945
Wilson, Don (radio and TV announcer); Lincoln, Neb. **(1900-1982)**
Wilson, Dooley (actor, musician); Tyler, Tex. **(1894-1953)**
Wilson, Edmund (literary critic and author); Red Bank, N.J. **(1895-1972)**
Wilson, Flip (Clerow) (comedian); Jersey City, N.J., 12/8/1933
Wilson, Harold (ex-Prime Minister); Huddersfield, England **(1916–1995)**
Wilson, Marie (actress); Anaheim, Calif. **(1916-1972)**
Wilson, Nancy (singer); Chillicothe, Ohio, 2/20/1937
Wilson, Sloan (novelist); Norwalk, Conn., 5/8/1920
Winchell, Walter (columnist); New York City **(1897-1972)**
Windsor, Duchess of (Bessie Wallis Warfield); Blue Ridge Summit, Pa. **(1896-1986)**
Windsor, Duke of (formerly King Edward VIII of England); Richmond Park, England **(1894-1972)**
Winfrey, Oprah (talk show hostess, actress); Kosciusko, Miss., 1/29/1954
Winger, Debra (actress); Cleveland, Ohio, 1955
Winkler, Henry (actor); New York City, 10/30/1945
Winninger, Charles (actor); Athen, Wis. **(1884-1969)**
Winningham, Mare (actress); Phoenix, Ariz., 5/16/1959
Winter, Johnny (guitarist); Leland, Miss., 2/23/1944
Winters, Jonathan (comedian); Dayton, Ohio, 11/11/1925
Winters, Shelley (Shirley Schrift) (actress); East St. Louis, Ill., 8/18/1922
Winthrop, John (first Governor, Massachusetts Bay Colony); Suffolk, England **(1588-1649)**
Wise, Stephen Samuel (rabbi); Budapest **(1874-1949)**
Withers, Jane (actress); Atlanta, 1927
Wittgenstein, Ludwig (Josef Johann) (philosopher); Vienna **(1889-1951)**
Wodehouse, P(elham) G(renville) (novelist); Guildford, England **(1881-1975)**
Wolfe, Thomas Clayton (novelist); Asheville, N.C. **(1900-1938)**
Wolfe, Tom (journalist); Richmond, Va., 3/2/1931
Wolsey, Thomas (prelate and statesman); Ipswich, England **(1475?-1530)**
Wonder, Stevie (Steveland Judkins, later Steveland Morris) (singer and songwriter); Saginaw, Mich., 5/13/1950
Wong, Anna May (Lu Tsong Wong) (actress); Los Angeles **(1907-1961)**
Wood, Grant (painter); Anamosa, Iowa **(1892-1942)**
Wood, Natalie (Natasha Gurdin) (film actress); San Francisco **(1938-1981)**
Wood, Peggy (Margaret) (actress); Brooklyn, N.Y. **(1892-1978)**
Woodhouse, Barbara (Blackburn) (dog trainer, author, TV personality): Rathfarnham, Ireland **(1910-1988)**
Woodward, Edward (actor); Croydon, England, 6/1/1930

Woodward, Joanne (film actress); Thomasville, Ga., 2/27/1930
Woolf, Adeline Virginia (née Stephens) (novelist); London **(1882-1941)**
Woollcott, Alexander (author-critic); Phalanx, N.J. **(1887-1943)**
Woolley, Monty (Edgar Montillion Woolley) (actor); New York City **(1888-1963)**
Woolworth, Frank (merchant); Rodman, N.Y. **(1852-1919)**
Wopat, Tom (actor); Lodi, Wis., 9/9/1950
Wordsworth, William (poet); Cockermouth, England **(1770-1850)**
Wouk, Herman (novelist); New York City, 5/27/1915
Wray, Fay (actress); Alberta, Canada, 1907
Wren, Sir Christopher (architect); East Knoyle, England **(1632-1723)**
Wright, Frank Lloyd (architect); Richland Center, Wis. **(1869-1959)**
Wright, Martha (singer); Seattle, Wash., 3/23/1926
Wright, Orville (inventor); Dayton, Ohio **(1871-1948)**
Wright, Richard (novelist); nr. Natchez, Miss. **(1908-1960)**
Wright, Teresa (actress); New York City, 10/27/1918
Wright, Wilbur (inventor); Millville, Ind. **(1867-1912)**
Wyatt, Jane (film actress); Campgaw, N.J., 8/12/1912
Wycliffe, John (church reformer); Hipswell, England **(1320-1384)**
Wyeth, Andrew (painter); Chadds Ford, Pa., 7/12/1917
Wyler, William (film director); Mulhouse (France), **(1902-1981)**
Wyman, Jane (Sarah Jane Fulks) (actress); St. Joseph, Mo., 1/4/1914
Wynette, Tammy (Wynette Pugh) (singer); Tupelo, Miss. 5/5/1942
Wynn, Ed (Isaiah Edwin Leopold) (comedian); Philadelphia **(1886-1966)**
Wynn, Keenan (actor); New York City **(1916-1986)**
Wynter, Dana (actress); London, 6/8/1930

X

Xavier, St. Francis (Jesuit missionary); Pamplona, Navarre (Spain) **(1506-1552)**
Xenophon (soldier, historian and essayist): Athens, Greece **(434(?)-355(?)** B.C.**)**
Xerxes, the Great (king): Persian Empire **(519(?)-465** B.C.**)**

Y

Yeats, William Butler (poet); nr. Dublin **(1865-1939)**
Yevtushenko, Yevgeny (poet); Zima, U.S.S.R., 7/18/1933
York, Alvin Cullun (Sergeant York, World War I hero): Tennessee **(1887-1964)**
York, Michael (actor); Fulmer, England, 3/27/1942
York, Susannah (Fletcher) (actress); London, 1/9/1942
Yorty, Samuel W. (ex-Mayor of Los Angeles); Lincoln, Neb., 10/1/1909
Yothers, Tina (actress); Whittier, Calif., 5/5/1973
Young, Alan (actor); North Shield, England, 11/19/1919
Young, Brigham (religious leader); Whitingham, Vt. **(1801-1877)**
Young, Gig (Byron Barr) (actor); St. Cloud, Minn. **(1917-1978)**
Young, Loretta (Gretchen Young) (actress); Salt Lake City, Utah, 1/6/1913
Young, Neil (singer and songwriter); Toronto, 11/12/1945
Young, Robert (actor); Chicago, 2/22/1907
Young, Roland (actor); London **(1887-1953)**
Youngman, Henny (comedian); Whitechapel, London, England, 3/16/1906

Z

Zanuck, Darryl F. (film producer); Wahoo, Neb. **(1902-1979)**
Zappa, Frank (Francis Vincent Zappa, Jr.) (singer and songwriter); Baltimore **(1940–1993)**
Zeffirelli, Franco (director); Florence, Italy, 2/12/1923
Zenger, John Peter (printer and journalist); Germany, **(1697-1746)**
Zhou Enlai (Premier); Hualyin, China **(1898-1976)**
Ziegfeld, Florenz (theatrical producer); Chicago **(1869-1932)**
Zimbalist, Efrem (concert violinist); Rostov-on-Don, Russia **(1889-1985)**
Zimbalist, Efrem, Jr. (actor); New York City, 11/30/1923
Zimbalist, Stephanie (actress); New York City, 10/8/56
Zola, Emile (novelist); Paris **(1840-1902)**
Zoroaster (religious leader); Persian Empire **(c. 6th century** B.C.**)**
Zukerman, Pinchas (violinist); Tel Aviv, Israel, 7/16/1948
Zukor, Adolph (film executive); Risce, Hungary **(1873-1976)**
Zweig, Stefan (author); Vienna **(1881-1942)**
Zwingli, Huldrych (humanist); Wildaus, Switzerland **(1484-1531)**

AWARDS

Nobel Prizes

The Nobel prizes are awarded under the will of Alfred Bernhard Nobel, Swedish chemist and engineer, who died in 1896. The interest of the fund is divided annually among the persons who have made the most outstanding contributions in the fields of physics, chemistry, and physiology or medicine, who have produced the most distinguished literary work of an idealist tendency, and who have contributed most toward world peace.

In 1968, a Nobel Prize of economic sciences was established by Riksbank, the Swedish bank, in celebration of its 300th anniversary. The prize was awarded for the first time in 1969.

The prizes for physics and chemistry are awarded by the Swedish Academy of Science in Stockholm, the one for physiology or medicine by the Caroline Medical Institute in Stockholm, that for literature by the academy in Stockholm, and that for peace by a committee of five elected by the Norwegian Storting. The distribution of prizes was begun on December 10, 1901, the anniversary of Nobel's death. The amount of each prize varies with the income from the fund and currently is about $190,000. No Nobel prizes were awarded for 1940, 1941, and 1942; prizes for Literature were not awarded for 1914, 1918, and 1943.

PEACE

1901 Henri Dunant (Switzerland); Frederick Passy (France)
1902 Elie Ducommun and Albert Gobat (Switzerland)
1903 Sir William R. Cremer (England)
1904 Institut de Droit International (Belgium)
1905 Bertha von Suttner (Austria)
1906 Theodore Roosevelt (U.S.)
1907 Ernesto T. Moneta (Italy) and Louis Renault (France)
1908 Klas P. Arnoldson (Sweden) and Frederik Bajer (Denmark)
1909 Auguste M. F. Beernaert (Belgium) and Baron Paul H.B.B. d'Estournelles de Constant de Rebecque (France)
1910 Bureau International Permanent de la Paix (Switzerland)
1911 Tobias M. C. Asser (Holland) and Alfred H. Fried (Austria)
1912 Elihu Root (U.S.)
1913 Henri La Fontaine (Belgium)
1915 No award
1916 No award
1917 International Red Cross
1919 Woodrow Wilson (U.S.)
1920 Léon Bourgeois (France)
1921 Karl H. Branting (Sweden) and Christian L. Lange (Norway)
1922 Fridtjof Nansen (Norway)
1923 No award
1924 No award
1925 Sir Austen Chamberlain (England) and Charles G. Dawes (U.S.)
1926 Aristide Briand (France) and Gustav Stresemann (Germany)
1927 Ferdinand Buisson (France) and Ludwig Quidde (Germany)
1928 No award
1929 Frank B. Kellogg (U.S.)
1930 Lars O. J. Söderblom (Sweden)
1931 Jane Addams and Nicholas M. Butler (U.S.)
1932 No award
1933 Sir Norman Angell (England)
1934 Arthur Henderson (England)
1935 Karl von Ossietzky (Germany)
1936 Carlos de S. Lamas (Argentina)
1937 Lord Cecil of Chelwood (England)
1938 Office International Nansen pour les Réfugiés (Switzerland)
1939 No award
1944 International Red Cross
1945 Cordell Hull (U.S.)
1946 Emily G. Balch and John R. Mott (U.S.)
1947 American Friends Service Committee (U.S.) and British Society of Friends' Service Council (England)
1948 No award
1949 Lord John Boyd Orr (Scotland)

1950 Ralph J. Bunche (U.S.)
1951 Léon Jouhaux (France)
1952 Albert Schweitzer (French Equatorial Africa)
1953 George C. Marshall (U.S.)
1954 Office of U.N. High Commissioner for Refugees
1955 No award
1956 No award
1957 Lester B. Pearson (Canada)
1958 Rev. Dominique Georges Henri Pire (Belgium)
1959 Philip John Noel-Baker (England)
1960 Albert John Luthuli (South Africa)
1961 Dag Hammarskjöld (Sweden)
1962 Linus Pauling (U.S.)
1963 Intl. Comm. of Red Cross; League of Red Cross Societies (both Geneva)
1964 Rev. Dr. Martin Luther King, Jr. (U.S.)
1965 UNICEF (United Nations Children's Fund)
1966 No award
1967 No award
1968 René Cassin (France)
1969 International Labour Organization
1970 Norman E. Borlaug (U.S.)
1971 Willy Brandt (West Germany)
1972 No award
1973 Henry A. Kissinger (U.S.); Le Duc Tho (North Vietnam)[1]
1974 Eisaku Sato (Japan); Sean MacBride (Ireland)
1975 Andrei D. Sakharov (U.S.S.R.)
1976 Mairead Corrigan and Betty Williams (both Northern Ireland)
1977 Amnesty International
1978 Menachem Begin (Israel) and Anwar el-Sadat (Egypt)
1979 Mother Teresa of Calcutta (India)
1980 Adolfo Pérez Esquivel (Argentina)
1981 Office of the United Nations High Commissioner for Refugees
1982 Alva Myrdal (Sweden) and Alfonso García Robles (Mexico)
1983 Lech Walesa (Poland)
1984 Bishop Desmond Tutu (South Africa)
1985 International Physicians for the Prevention of Nuclear War
1986 Elie Wiesel (U.S.)
1987 Oscar Arias Sánchez (Costa Rica)
1988 U.N. Peacekeeping Forces
1989 Dalai Lama (Tibet)
1990 Mikhail S. Gorbachev (U.S.S.R.)
1991 Daw Aung San Suu Kyi (Myanmar)
1992 Rigoberta Menchú (Guatemala)
1993 F.W. de Klerk and Nelson Mandela (both South Africa)
1994 Yasir Arafat (Palestine) and Yitzhak Rabin (Israel)

1. Le Duc Tho refused prize, charging that peace had not yet been really established in South Vietnam.

LITERATURE

1901 René F. A. Sully Prudhomme (France)
1902 Theodor Mommsen (Germany)
1903 Björnstjerne Björnson (Norway)
1904 Frédéric Mistral (France) and José Echegaray (Spain)
1905 Henryk Sienkiewicz (Poland)
1906 Giosuè Carducci (Italy)
1907 Rudyard Kipling (England)
1908 Rudolf Eucken (Germany)
1909 Selma Lagerlöf (Sweden)
1910 Paul von Heyse (Germany)
1911 Maurice Maeterlinck (Belgium)
1912 Gerhart Hauptmann (Germany)
1913 Rabindranath Tagore (India)
1915 Romain Rolland (France)
1916 Verner von Heidenstam (Sweden)
1917 Karl Gjellerup (Denmark) and Henrik Pontoppidan (Denmark)
1919 Carl Spitteler (Switzerland)
1920 Knut Hamsun (Norway)
1921 Anatole France (France)
1922 Jacinto Benavente (Spain)
1923 William B. Yeats (Ireland)
1924 Wladyslaw Reymont (Poland)
1925 George Bernard Shaw (Ireland)
1926 Grazia Deledda (Italy)
1927 Henri Bergson (France)
1928 Sigrid Undset (Norway)
1929 Thomas Mann (Germany)
1930 Sinclair Lewis (U.S.)
1931 Erik A. Karlfeldt (Sweden)
1932 John Galsworthy (England)
1933 Ivan G. Bunin (Russia)
1934 Luigi Pirandello (Italy)
1935 No award
1936 Eugene O'Neill (U.S.)
1937 Roger Martin du Gard (France)
1938 Pearl S. Buck (U.S.)
1939 Frans Eemil Sillanpää (Finland)
1944 Johannes V. Jensen (Denmark)
1945 Gabriela Mistral (Chile)
1946 Hermann Hesse (Switzerland)
1947 André Gide (France)
1948 Thomas Stearns Eliot (England)
1949 William Faulkner (U.S.)
1950 Bertrand Russell (England)
1951 Pär Lagerkvist (Sweden)
1952 François Mauriac (France)
1953 Sir Winston Churchill (England)
1954 Ernest Hemingway (U.S.)
1955 Halldór Kiljan Laxness (Iceland)
1956 Juan Ramón Jiménez (Spain)
1957 Albert Camus (France)
1958 Boris Pasternak (U.S.S.R.) (declined)
1959 Salvatore Quasimodo (Italy)
1960 St-John Perse (Alexis St.-Léger Léger) (France)
1961 Ivo Andric (Yugoslavia)
1962 John Steinbeck (U.S.)
1963 Giorgios Seferis (Seferiades) (Greece)
1964 Jean-Paul Sartre (France) (declined)
1965 Mikhail Sholokhov (U.S.S.R.)
1966 Shmuel Yosef Agnon (Israel) and Nelly Sachs (Sweden)
1967 Miguel Angel Asturias (Guatemala)
1968 Yasunari Kawabata (Japan)
1969 Samuel Beckett (Ireland)
1970 Aleksandr Solzhenitsyn (U.S.S.R.)
1971 Pablo Neruda (Chile)
1972 Heinrich Böll (Germany)
1973 Patrick White (Australia)
1974 Eyvind Johnson and Harry Martinson (both Sweden)
1975 Eugenio Montale (Italy)

1976 Saul Bellow (U.S.)
1977 Vicente Aleixandre (Spain)
1978 Isaac Bashevis Singer (U.S.)
1979 Odysseus Elytis (Greece)
1980 Czeslaw Milosz (U.S.)
1981 Elias Canetti (Bulgaria)
1982 Gabriel García Márquez (Colombia)
1983 William Golding (England)
1984 Jaroslav Seifert (Czechoslovakia)
1985 Claude Simon (France)
1986 Wole Soyinka (Nigeria)
1987 Joseph Brodsky (U.S.)
1988 Naguib Mahfouz (Egypt)
1989 Camilo José Cela (Spain)
1990 Octavio Paz (Mexico)
1991 Nadine Gordimer (South Africa)
1992 Derek Walcott (Trinidad)
1993 Toni Morrison (U.S.)
1994 Kenzaburo Oe (Japan)

PHYSICS

1901 Wilhelm K. Roentgen (Germany), for discovery of Roentgen rays
1902 Hendrik A. Lorentz and Pieter Zeeman (Netherlands), for work on influence of magnetism upon radiation
1903 A. Henri Becquerel (France), for work on spontaneous radioactivity; and Pierre and Marie Curie (France), for study of radiation
1904 John Strutt (Lord Rayleigh) (England), for discovery of argon in investigating gas density
1905 Philipp Lenard (Germany), for work with cathode rays
1906 Sir Joseph Thomson (England), for investigations on passage of electricity through gases
1907 Albert A. Michelson (U.S.), for spectroscopic and metrologic investigations
1908 Gabriel Lippmann (France), for method of reproducing colors by photography
1909 Guglielmo Marconi (Italy) and Ferdinand Braun (Germany), for development of wireless
1910 Johannes D. van der Waals (Netherlands), for work with the equation of state for gases and liquids
1911 Wilhelm Wien (Germany), for his laws governing the radiation of heat
1912 Gustaf Dalén (Sweden), for discovery of automatic regulators used in lighting lighthouses and light buoys
1913 Heike Kamerlingh-Onnes (Netherlands), for work leading to production of liquid helium
1914 Max von Laue (Germany), for discovery of diffraction of Roentgen rays passing through crystals
1915 Sir William Bragg and William L. Bragg (England), for analysis of crystal structure by X rays
1916 No award
1917 Charles G. Barkla (England), for discovery of Roentgen radiation of the elements
1918 Max Planck (Germany), discoveries in connection with quantum theory
1919 Johannes Stark (Germany), discovery of Doppler effect in Canal rays and decomposition of spectrum lines by electric fields
1920 Charles E. Guillaume (Switzerland), for discoveries of anomalies in nickel steel alloys
1921 Albert Einstein (Germany), for discovery of the law of the photoelectric effect
1922 Niels Bohr (Denmark), for investigation of structure of atoms and radiations emanating from them
1923 Robert A. Millikan (U.S.), for work on elementary charge of electricity and photoelectric phenomena
1924 Karl M. G. Siegbahn (Sweden), for investigations in X-ray spectroscopy

1925 James Franck and Gustav Hertz (Germany), for discovery of laws governing impact of electrons upon atoms

1926 Jean B. Perrin (France), for work on discontinuous structure of matter and discovery of the equilibrium of sedimentation

1927 Arthur H. Compton (U.S.), for discovery of Compton phenomenon; and Charles T. R. Wilson (England), for method of perceiving paths taken by electrically charged particles

1928 In 1929, the 1928 prize was awarded to Sir Owen Richardson (England), for work on the phenomenon of thermionics and discovery of the Richardson Law

1929 Prince Louis Victor de Broglie (France), for discovery of the wave character of electrons

1930 Sir Chandrasekhara Raman (India), for work on diffusion of light and discovery of the Raman effect

1931 No award

1932 In 1933, the prize for 1932 was awarded to Werner Heisenberg (Germany), for creation of the quantum mechanics

1933 Erwin Schrödinger (Austria) and Paul A. M. Dirac (England), for discovery of new fertile forms of the atomic theory

1934 No award

1935 James Chadwick (England), for discovery of the neutron

1936 Victor F. Hess (Austria), for discovery of cosmic radiation; and Carl D. Anderson (U.S.), for discovery of the positron

1937 Clinton J. Davisson (U.S.) and George P. Thomson (England), for discovery of diffraction of electrons by crystals

1938 Enrico Fermi (Italy), for identification of new radioactivity elements and discovery of nuclear reactions effected by slow neutrons

1939 Ernest Orlando Lawrence (U.S.), for development of the cyclotron

1943 Otto Stern (U.S.), for detection of magnetic momentum of protons

1944 Isidor Isaac Rabi (U.S.), for work on magnetic movements of atomic particles

1945 Wolfgang Pauli (Austria), for work on atomic fissions

1946 Percy Williams Bridgman (U.S.), for studies and inventions in high-pressure physics

1947 Sir Edward Appleton (England), for discovery of layer which reflects radio short waves in the ionosphere

1948 Patrick M. S. Blackett (England), for improvement on Wilson chamber and discoveries in cosmic radiation

1949 Hideki Yukawa (Japan), for mathematical prediction, in 1935, of the meson

1950 Cecil Frank Powell (England), for method of photographic study of atom nucleus, and for discoveries about mesons

1951 Sir John Douglas Cockcroft (England) and Ernest T. S. Walton (Ireland), for work in 1932 on transmutation of atomic nuclei

1952 Edward Mills Purcell and Felix Bloch (U.S.), for work in measurement of magnetic fields in atomic nuclei

1953 Fritz Zernike (Netherlands), for development of "phase contrast" microscope

1954 Max Born (England), for work in quantum mechanics; and Walther Bothe (Germany), for work in cosmic radiation

1955 Polykarp Kusch and Willis E. Lamb, Jr. (U.S.), for atomic measurements

1956 William Shockley, Walter H. Brattain, and John Bardeen (U.S.), for developing electronic transistor

1957 Tsung Dao Lee and Chen Ning Yang (China), for disproving principle of conservation of parity

1958 Pavel A. Cherenkov, Ilya M. Frank, and Igor E. Tamm (U.S.S.R.), for work resulting in development of cosmic-ray counter

1959 Emilio Segre and Owen Chamberlain (U.S.), for demonstrating the existence of the anti-proton

1960 Donald A. Glaser (U.S.), for invention of "bubble chamber" to study subatomic particles

1961 Robert Hofstadter (U.S.), for determination of shape and size of atomic nucleus; Rudolf Mössbauer (Germany), for method of producing and measuring recoil-free gamma rays

1962 Lev D. Landau (U.S.S.R.), for his theories about condensed matter

1963 Eugene Paul Wigner, Maria Goeppert Mayer (both U.S.), and J. Hans D. Jensen (Germany), for research on structure of atom and its nucleus

1964 Charles Hard Townes (U.S.), Nikolai G. Basov, and Aleksandr M. Prochorov (both U.S.S.R.), for developing maser and laser principle of producing high-intensity radiation

1965 Richard P. Feynman, Julian S. Schwinger (both U.S.), and Shinichiro Tomonaga (Japan), for research in quantum electrodynamics

1966 Alfred Kastler (France), for work on energy levels inside atom

1967 Hans A. Bethe (U.S.), for work on energy production of stars

1968 Luis Walter Alvarez (U.S.), for study of subatomic particles

1969 Murray Gell-Mann (U.S.), for study of subatomic particles

1970 Hannes Alfvén (Sweden), for theories in plasma physics; and Louis Néel (France), for discoveries in antiferromagnetism and ferrimagnetism

1971 Dennis Gabor (England), for invention of holographic method of three-dimensional imagery

1972 John Bardeen, Leon N. Cooper, and John Robert Schrieffer (all U.S.), for theory of superconductivity, where electrical resistance in certain metals vanishes above absolute zero temperature

1973 Ivar Giaever (U.S.), Leo Esaki (Japan), and Brian D. Josephson (U.K.), for theories that have advanced and expanded the field of miniature electronics

1974 Antony Hewish (England), for discovery of pulsars; Martin Ryle (England), for using radiotelescopes to probe outer space with high degree of precision

1975 James Rainwater (U.S.) and Ben Mottelson and Aage N. Bohr (both Denmark), for showing that the atomic nucleus is asymmetrical

1976 Burton Richter and Samuel C. C. Ting (both U.S.), for discovery of subatomic particles known as J and psi

1977 Philip W. Anderson and John H. Van Vleck (both U.S.), and Nevill F. Mott (U.K.), for work underlying computer memories and electronic devices

1978 Arno A. Penzias and Robert W. Wilson (both U.S.), for work in cosmic microwave radiation; Piotr L. Kapitsa (U.S.S.R.), for basic inventions and discoveries in low-temperature physics

1979 Steven Weinberg and Sheldon L. Glashow (both U.S.) and Abdus Salam (Pakistan), for de-veloping theory that electromagnetism and the "weak" force, which causes radioactive decay in some atomic nuclei, are facets of the same phenomenon

1980 James W. Cronin and Val L. Fitch (both U.S.), for work concerning the assymetry of subatomic particles

1981 Nicolaas Bloembergen and Arthur L. Schawlow (both U.S.) and Kai M. Siegbahn (Sweden), for developing technologies with lasers and other devices to probe the secrets of complex forms of matter

1982 Kenneth G. Wilson (U.S.), for analysis of changes in matter under pressure and temperature

1983 Subrahmanyam Chandrasekhar and William A. Fowler (both U.S.) for complementary research on processes involved in the evolution of stars

1984 Carlo Rubbia (Italy) and Simon van der Meer (Netherlands), for their role in discovering three subatomic particles, a step toward developing a single theory to account for all natural forces

1985 Klaus von Klitzing (Germany), for developing an exact way of measuring electrical conductivity

1986 Ernst Ruska, Gerd Binnig (both Germany) and Heinrich Rohrer (Switzerland) for work on microscopes

1987 K. Alex Müller (Switzerland) and J. Georg Bednorz (Germany) for their discovery of high-temperature superconductors.

1988 Leon M. Lederman, Melvin Schwartz, and Jack Steinberger (all U.S.) for research that improved the understanding of elementary particles and forces.

1989 Norman F. Ramsey (U.S.), for work leading to development of the atomic clock, and Hans G. Dehmelt (U.S.) and Wolfgang Paul (Germany) for developing methods to isolate atoms and subatomic particles.

1990 Richard E. Taylor (Canada) and Jerome I. Friedman and Henry W. Kendall (both U.S.), for their "breakthrough in our understanding of matter" which confirmed the reality of quarks.

1991 Pierre-Gilles de Gennes (France) for his discoveries about the ordering of molecules in substances ranging from "super" glue to an exotic form of liquid helium.

1992 George Charpak (France), for his inventions of particle detectors.

1993 Joseph H. Taylor and Russell A. Hulse (U.S.) for their discovery of a binary pulsar.

1994 Clifford G. Shull (U.S.) and Bertram N. Brockhouse (Canada), for adapting beams of neutrons as probes to explore the atomic structure of matter.

CHEMISTRY

1901 Jacobus H. van't Hoff (Netherlands), for laws of chemical dynamics and osmotic pressure in solutions

1902 Emil Fischer (Germany), for experiments in sugar and purin groups of substances

1903 Svante A. Arrhenius (Sweden), for his electrolytic theory of dissociation

1904 Sir William Ramsay (England), for discovery and determination of place of inert gaseous elements in air

1905 Adolf von Baeyer (Germany), for work on organic dyes and hydroaromatic combinations

1906 Henri Moissan (France), for isolation of fluorine, and introduction of electric furnace

1907 Eduard Buchner (Germany), discovery of cell-less fermentation and investigations in biological chemistry

1908 Sir Ernest Rutherford (England), for investigations into disintegration of elements

1909 Wilhelm Ostwald (Germany), for work on catalysis and investigations into chemical equilibrium and reaction rates

1910 Otto Wallach (Germany), for work in the field of alicyclic compounds

1911 Marie Curie (France), for discovery of elements radium and polonium

1912 Victor Grignard (France), for reagent discovered by him; and Paul Sabatier (France), for methods of hydrogenating organic compounds

1913 Alfred Werner (Switzerland), for linking up atoms within the molecule

1914 Theodore W. Richards (U.S.), for determining atomic weight of many chemical elements

1915 Richard Willstätter (Germany), for research into coloring matter of plants, especially chlorophyll

1916 No award

1917 No award

1918 Fritz Haber (Germany), for synthetic production of ammonia

1919 No award

1920 Walther Nernst (Germany), for work in thermochemistry

1921 Frederick Soddy (England), for investigations into origin and nature of isotopes

1922 Francis W. Aston (England), for discovery of isotopes in nonradioactive elements and for discovery of the whole number rule

1923 Fritz Pregl (Austria), for method of microanalysis of organic substances discovered by him

1924 No award

1925 In 1926, the 1925 prize was awarded to Richard Zsigmondy (Germany), for work on the heterogeneous nature of colloid solutions

1926 Theodor Svedberg (Sweden), for work on disperse systems

1927 In 1928, the 1927 prize was awarded to Heinrich Wieland (Germany), for investigations of bile acids and kindred substances

1928 Adolf Windaus (Germany), for investigations on constitution of the sterols and their connection with vitamins

1929 Sir Arthur Harden (England) and Hans K. A. S. von Euler-Chelpin (Sweden), for research of fermentation of sugars

1930 Hans Fischer (Germany), for work on coloring matter of blood and leaves and for his synthesis of hemin

1931 Karl Bosch and Friedrich Bergius (Germany), for invention and development of chemical high-pressure methods

1932 Irving Langmuir (U.S.), for work in realm of surface chemistry

1933 No award

1934 Harold C. Urey (U.S.), for discovery of heavy hydrogen

1935 Frédéric and Irène Joliot-Curie (France), for synthesis of new radioactive elements

1936 Peter J. W. Debye (Netherlands), for investigations on dipole moments and diffraction of X rays and electrons in gases

1937 Walter N. Haworth (England), for research on carbohydrates and Vitamin C; and Paul Karrer (Switzerland), for work on carotenoids, flavins, and Vitamins A and B

1938 Richard Kuhn (Germany), for carotinoid study and vitamin research (declined)

1939 Adolf Butenandt (Germany), for work on sexual hormones (declined the prize); and Leopold Ruzicka (Switzerland), for work with polymethylenes

1943 Georg Hevesy De Heves (Hungary), for work on use of isotopes as indicators

1944 Otto Hahn (Germany), for work on atomic fission

1945 Artturi Illmari Virtanen (Finland), for research in the field of conservation of fodder

1946 James B. Sumner (U.S.), for crystallizing enzymes; John H. Northrop and Wendell M. Stanley (U.S.), for preparing enzymes and virus proteins in pure form

1947 Sir Robert Robinson (England), for research in plant substances

1948 Arne Tiselius (Sweden), for biochemical discoveries and isolation of mouse paralysis virus

1949 William Francis Giauque (U.S.), for research in thermodynamics, especially effects of low temperature

1950 Otto Diels and Kurt Alder (Germany), for discovery of diene synthesis enabling scientists to study structure of organic matter

1951 Glenn T. Seaborg and Edwin H. McMillan (U.S.), for discovery of plutonium

1952 Archer John Porter Martin and Richard Laurence Millington Synge (England), for development of partition chromatography

1953 Hermann Staudinger (Germany), for research in giant molecules

1954 Linus C. Pauling (U.S.), for study of forces holding together protein and other molecules

1955 Vincent du Vigneaud (U.S.), for work on pituitary hormones

1956 Sir Cyril Hinshelwood (England) and Nikolai N. Semenov (U.S.S.R.), for parallel research on chemical reaction kinetics

1957 Sir Alexander Todd (England), for research with chemical compounds that are factors in heredity

1958 Frederick Sanger (England), for determining molecular structure of insulin

1959 Jaroslav Heyrovsky (Czechoslovakia), for development of polarography, an electrochemical method of analysis

1960 Willard F. Libby (U.S.), for "atomic time clock" to measure age of objects by measuring their radioactivity

1961 Melvin Calvin (U.S.), for establishing chemical steps during photosynthesis

1962 Max F. Perutz and John C. Kendrew (England), for mapping protein molecules with X-rays

1963 Carl Ziegler (Germany) and Giulio Natta (Italy), for work in uniting simple hydrocarbons into large molecule substances

1964 Dorothy Mary Crowfoot Hodgkin (England), for determining structure of compounds needed in combating pernicious anemia

1965 Robert B. Woodward (U.S.), for work in synthesizing complicated organic compounds

1966 Robert Sanderson Mulliken (U.S.), for research on bond holding atoms together in molecule

1967 Manfred Eigen (Germany), Ronald G. W. Norrish, and George Porter (both Eng land), for work in high-speed chemical reactions

1968 Lars Onsager (U.S.), for development of system of equations in thermodynamics

1969 Derek H. R. Barton (England) and Odd Hassel (Norway), for study of organic molecules

1970 Luis F. Leloir (Argentina), for discovery of sugar nucleotides and their role in biosynthesis of carbohydrates

1971 Gerhard Herzberg (Canada), for contributions to knowledge of electronic structure and geometry of molecules, particularly free radicals

1972 Christian Boehmer Anfinsen, Stanford Moore, and William Howard Stein (all U.S.), for pioneering studies in enzymes

1973 Ernst Otto Fischer (W. Germany) and Geoffrey Wilkinson (U.K.), for work that could solve problem of automobile exhaust pollution

1974 Paul J. Flory (U.S.), for developing analytic methods to study properties and molecular structure of long-chain molecules

1975 John W. Cornforth (Australia) and Vladimir Prelog (Switzerland), for research on structure of biological molecules such as antibiotics and cholesterol

1976 William N. Lipscomb, Jr. (U.S.), for work on the structure and bonding mechanisms of boranes

1977 Ilya Prigogine (Belgium), for contributions to nonequilibrium thermodynamics, particularly the theory of dissipative structures

1978 Peter Mitchell (U.K.), for contributions to the understanding of biological energy transfer

1979 Herbert C. Brown (U.S.) and Georg Wittig (West Germany), for developing a group of substances that facilitate very difficult chemical reactions

1980 Paul Berg and Walter Gilbert (both U.S.) and Frederick Sanger (England), for developing methods to map the structure and function of DNA, the substance that controls the activity of the cell

1981 Roald Hoffmann (U.S.) and Kenichi Fukui (Japan), for applying quantum-mechanics theories to predict the course of chemical reactions

1982 Aaron Klug (U.K.), for research in the detailed structures of viruses and components of life

1983 Henry Taube (U.S.), for research on how electrons transfer between molecules in chemical reactions

1984 R. Bruce Merrifield (U.S.) for research that revolutionized the study of proteins

1985 Herbert A. Hauptman and Jerome Karle (both U.S.) for their outstanding achievements in the development of direct methods for the determination of crystal structures

1986 Dudley R. Herschback, Yuan T. Lee (both U.S.), and John C. Polanyi (Canada) for their work on "reaction dynamics"

1987 Donald J. Cram and Charles J. Pedersen (both U.S.) and Jean-Marie Lehn (France), for wide-ranging research that has included the creation of artificial molecules that can mimic vital chemical reactions of the processes of life.

1988 Johann Deisenhofer, Robert Huber, and Hartmut Michel (all West Germany) for unraveling the structure of proteins that play a crucial role in photosynthesis.

1989 Thomas R. Cech and Sidney Altman (both U.S.) for their discovery, independently, that RNA could actively aid chemical reactions in the cells.

1990 Elias James Corey (U.S.) for developing new ways to synthesize complex molecules ordinarily found in nature.

1991 Richard R. Ernst (Switzerland) for refinements he developed in nuclear magnetic resonance spectroscopy.

1992 Rudolph A. Marcus (U.S.), for his mathematical analysis of how the overall energy in a system of interacting molecules changes and induces an electron to jump from one molecule to another.

1993 Kary B. Mullis (U.S.) and Michael Smith (Canada) for their contributions to the science of genetics.

1994 George A. Olah (U.S.), University of Southern California in Los Angeles, for research that opened new ways to break apart and rebuild compounds of carbon and hydrogen.

PHYSIOLOGY OR MEDICINE

1901 Emil A. von Behring (Germany), for work on serum therapy against diptheria

1902 Sir Ronald Ross (England), for work on malaria

1903 Niels R. Finsen (Denmark), for his treatment of lupus vulgaris with concentrated light rays

1904 Ivan P. Pavlov (U.S.S.R.), for work on the physiology of digestion

1905 Robert Koch (Germany), for work on tuberculosis

1906 Camillo Golgi (Italy) and Santiago Ramón y Cajal (Spain), for work on structure of the nervous system

1907 Charles L. A. Laveran (France), for work with protozoa in the generation of disease

1908 Paul Ehrlich (Germany), and Elie Metchnikoff (U.S.S.R.), for work on immunity

1909 Theodor Kocher (Switzerland), for work on the thyroid gland

1910 Albrecht Kossel (Germany), for achievements in the chemistry of the cell

1911 Allvar Gullstrand (Sweden), for work on the dioptrics of the eye

1912 Alexis Carrel (France), for work on vascular ligature and grafting of blood vessels and organs

1913 Charles Richet (France), for work on anaphylaxy

1914 Robert Bárány (Austria), for work on physiology and pathology of the vestibular system

1915-1918 No award

1919 Jules Bordet (Belgium), for discoveries in connection with immunity

1920 August Krogh (Denmark), for discovery of regulation of capillaries' motor mechanism

1921 No award

1922 In 1923, the 1922 prize was shared by Archibald V. Hill (England), for discovery relating to heat-production in muscles; and Otto Meyerhof (Germany), for correlation between consumption of oxygen and production of lactic acid in muscles

1923 Sir Frederick Banting (Canada) and John J. R. Macleod (Scotland), for discovery of insulin

1924 Willem Einthoven (Netherlands), for discovery of the mechanism of the electrocardiogram

1925 No award

1926 Johannes Fibiger (Denmark), for discovery of the Spiroptera carcinoma

1927 Julius Wagner-Jauregg (Austria), for use of malaria inoculation in treatment of dementia paralytica

1928 Charles Nicolle (France), for work on typhus exanthematicus

1929 Christiaan Eijkman (Netherlands), for discovery of the antineuritic vitamins; and Sir Frederick Hopkins (England), for discovery of growth-promoting vitamins

1930 Karl Landsteiner (U.S.), for discovery of human blood groups

1931 Otto H. Warburg (Germany), for discovery of the character and mode of action of the respiratory ferment

1932 Sir Charles Sherrington (England) and Edgar D. Adrian (U.S.), for discoveries of the function of the neuron

1933 Thomas H. Morgan (U.S.), for discoveries on hereditary function of the chromosomes

1934 George H. Whipple, George R. Minot, and William P. Murphy (U.S.), for discovery of liver therapy against anemias

1935 Hans Spemann (Germany), for discovery of the organizer-effect in embryonic development

1936 Sir Henry Dale (England) and Otto Loewi (Germany), for discoveries on chemical transmission of nerve impulses

1937 Albert Szent-Györgyi von Nagyrapolt (Hungary), for discoveries on biological combustion

1938 Corneille Heymans (Belgium), for determining importance of sinus and aorta mechanisms in the regulation of respiration

1939 Gerhard Domagk (Germany), for antibacterial effect of prontocilate

1943 Henrik Dam (Denmark) and Edward A. Doisy (U.S.), for analysis of Vitamin K

1944 Joseph Erlanger and Herbert Spencer Gasser (U.S.), for work on functions of the nerve threads

1945 Sir Alexander Fleming, Ernst Boris Chain, and Sir Howard Florey (England), for discovery of penicillin

1946 Herman J. Muller (U.S.), for hereditary effects of X-rays on genes

1947 Carl F. and Gerty T. Cori (U.S.), for work on animal starch metabolism; Bernardo A. Houssay (Argentina), for study of pituitary

1948 Paul Mueller (Switzerland), for discovery of insect-killing properties of DDT

1949 Walter Rudolf Hess (Switzerland), for research on brain control of body; and Antonio Caetano de Abreu Freire Egas Moniz (Portugal), for development of brain operation

1950 Philip S. Hench, Edward C. Kendall (both U.S.), and Tadeus Reichstein (Switzerland), for discoveries about hormones of adrenal cortex

1951 Max Theiler (South Africa), for development of anti-yellow-fever vaccine

1952 Selman A. Waksman (U.S.), for co-discovery of streptomycin

1953 Fritz A. Lipmann (Germany-U.S.) and Hans Adolph Krebs (Germany-England), for studies of living cells

1954 John F. Enders, Thomas H. Weller, and Frederick C. Robbins (U.S.), for work with cultivation of polio virus

1955 Hugo Theorell (Sweden), for work on oxidation enzymes

1956 Dickinson W. Richards, Jr., André F. Cournand (both U.S.), and Werner Forssmann (Germany), for new techniques in treating heart disease

1957 Daniel Bovet (Italy), for development of drugs to relieve allergies and relax muscles during surgery

1958 Joshua Lederberg (U.S.), for work with genetic mechanisms; George W. Beadle and Edward L. Tatum (U.S.), for discovering how genes transmit hereditary characteristics

1959 Severo Ochoa and Arthur Kornberg (U.S.), for discoveries related to compounds within chromosomes, which play a vital role in heredity

1960 Sir Macfarlane Burnet (Australia) and Peter Brian Medawar (England), for discovery of acquired immunological tolerance

1961 Georg von Bekesy (U.S.), for discoveries about physical mechanisms of stimulation within cochlea

1962 James D. Watson (U.S.), Maurice H. F. Wilkins, and Francis H. C. Crick (England), for determining structure of deoxyribonucleic acid (DNA)

1963 Alan Lloyd Hodgkin, Andrew Fielding Huxley (both England), and Sir John Carew Eccles (Australia), for research on nerve cells

1964 Konrad E. Bloch (U.S.) and Feodor Lynen (Germany), for research on mechanism and regulation of cholesterol and fatty acid metabolism

1965 François Jacob, André Lwolff, and Jacques Monod (France), for study of regulatory activities in body cells

1966 Charles Brenton Huggins (U.S.), for studies in hormone treatment of cancer of prostate; Francis Peyton Rous (U.S.), for discovery of tumor-producing viruses

1967 Haldan K. Hartline, George Wald, and Ragnar Granit (U.S.), for work on human eye

1968 Robert W. Holley, Har Gobind Khorana, and Marshall W. Nirenberg (U.S.), for studies of genetic code

1969 Max Delbruck, Alfred D. Hershey, and Salvador E. Luria (U.S.), for study of mechanism of virus infection in living cells

1970 Julius Axelrod (U.S.), Ulf S. von Euler (Swed-en), and Sir Bernard Katz (England), for studies of how nerve impulses are transmitted within the body

1971 Earl W. Sutherland, Jr. (U.S.), for research on how hormones work

1972 Gerald M. Edelman (U.S.), and Rodney R. Porter (U.K.), for research on the chemical structure and nature of antibodies

1973 Karl von Frisch and Konrad Lorenz (Austria), and Nikolaas Tinbergen (Netherlands), for their studies of individual and social behavior patterns

1974 George E. Palade and Christian de Duve (both U.S.) and Albert Claude (Belgium), for contributions to understanding inner workings of living cells

1975 David Baltimore, Howard M. Temin, and Renato Dulbecco (all U.S.), for work in interaction between tumor viruses and genetic material of the cell

1976 Baruch S. Blumberg and D. Carleton Gajdusek (U.S.), for discoveries concerning new mechanisms for the origin and dissemination of infectious diseases

1977 Rosalyn S. Yalow, Roger C. L. Guillemin, and Andrew V. Schally (all U.S.), for research in role of hormones in chemistry of the body

1978 Daniel Nathans and Hamilton Smith (both U.S.) and Werner Arber (Switzerland), for discovery of restriction enzymes and their application to problems of molecular genetics

1979 Allan McLeod Cormack (U.S.) and Godfrey Newbold Hounsfield (England), for developing computed axial tomography (CAT scan) X-ray technique

1980 Baruj Benacerraf and George D. Snell (both U.S.) and Jean Dausset (France), for discoveries that explain how the structure of cells relates to organ transplants and diseases

1981 Roger W. Sperry and David H. Hubel (both U.S.) and Torsten N. Wiesel (Sweden), for studies vital to understanding the organization and functioning of the brain

1982 Sune Bergstrom and Bengt Samuelsson (Sweden) and John R. Vane (U.K.), for research in prostaglandins, a hormonelike substance involved in a wide range of illnesses

1983 Barbara McClintock (U.S.), for her discovery of mobile genes in the chromosomes of a plant that change the future generations of plants they produce

1984 Cesar Milstein (U.K./Argentina) Georges J.F. Kohler (West Germany), and Niels K. Jerne (U.K./Denmark) for their work in immunology

1985 Michael S. Brown and Joseph L. Goldstein (both U.S.) for their work which has drastically widened our understanding of the cholesterol metabolism and increased our possibilities to prevent and treat atherosclerosis and heart attacks

1986 Rita Levi-Montalcini (dual U.S./Italy) and Stanley Cohen (U.S.) for their contributions to the understanding of substances that influence cell growth

1987 Susumu Tonegawa (Japan), for his discoveries of how the body can suddenly marshal its immunological defenses against millions of different disease agents that it has never encountered before.

1988 Gertrude B. Elion, George H. Hitchings (both U.S.) and Sir James Black (U.K.) for their discoveries of important principles for drug treatment.

1989 J. Michael Bishop and Harold E. Varmus (both U.S.) for their unifying theory of cancer development.

1990 Joseph E. Murray and E. Donnall Thomas (both U.S.), for their pioneering work in transplants.

1991 Erwin Neher and Bert Sakmann (both Germany) for their research, particularly for the development of a technique called patch clamp.

1992 Edmond H. Fischer and Edwin G. Kerbs (U.S.), for their discovery of a regulatory mechanism affecting almost all cells.

1993 Phillip A. Sharp (U.S.) and Richard J. Roberts (U.K.), for their independent discovery in 1977 of "split genes."

1994 Alfred G. Gilman and Martin Rodbell (both U.S.), for discovery of G-proteins that help cells respond to outside signals.

ECONOMIC SCIENCE

1969 Ragnar Frisch (Norway) and Jan Tinbergen (Netherlands), for work in econometrics (application of mathematics and statistical methods to economic theories and problems)

1970 Paul A. Samuelson (U.S.), for efforts to raise the level of scientific analysis in economic theory

1971 Simon Kuznets (U.S.), for developing concept of using a country's gross national product to determine its economic growth

1972 Kenneth J. Arrow (U.S.) and Sir John R. Hicks (U.K.), for theories that help to assess business risk and government economic and welfare policies

1973 Wassily Leontief (U.S.), for devising the input–output technique to determine how different sectors of an economy interact

1974 Gunnar Myrdal (Sweden) and Friedrich A. von Hayek

(U.K.), for pioneering analysis of the interdependence of economic, social and institutional phenomena

1975 Leonid V. Kantorovich (U.S.S.R.) and Tjalling C. Koopmans (U.S.), for work on the theory of optimum allocation of resources

1976 Milton Friedman (U.S.), for work in consumption analysis and monetary history and theory, and for demonstration of complexity of stabilization policy

1977 Bertil Ohlin (Sweden) and James E. Meade (U.K.), for contributions to theory of international trade and international capital movements

1978 Herbert A. Simon (U.S.), for research into the decision-making process within economic organizations

1979 Sir Arthur Lewis (England) and Theodore Schultz (U.S.), for work on economic problems of developing nations

1980 Lawrence R. Klein (U.S.), for developing models for forecasting economic trends and shaping policies to deal with them

1981 James Tobin (U.S.), for analyses of financial markets and their influence on spending and saving by families and businesses

1982 George J. Stigler (U.S.), for work on government regulation in the economy and the functioning of industry

1983 Gerard Debreu (U.S.), in recognition of his work on the basic economic problem of how prices operate to balance what producers supply with what buyers want.

1984 Sir Richard Stone (U.K.), for his work to develop the systems widely used to measure the performance of national economics

1985 Franco Modigliani (U.S.) for his pioneering work in analyzing the behavior of household savers and the functioning of financial markets

1986 James M. Buchanan (U.S.) for his development of new methods for analyzing economic and political decision-making

1987 Robert M. Solow (U.S.), for seminal contributions to the theory of economic growth.

1988 Maurice Allais (France) for his pioneering development of theories to better understand market behavior and the efficient use of resources.

1989 Trygve Haavelmo (Norway) for his pioneering work in methods for testing economic theories.

1990 Harry M. Markowitz, William F. Sharpe, and Merton H. Miller (all U.S.), whose work provided new tools for weighing the risks and rewards of different investments and for valuing corporate stocks and bonds.

1991 Ronald Coase (U.S.) for his pioneering work in how property rights and the cost of doing business affect the economy.

1992 Gary S. Becker (U.S.), for "having extended the domain of economic theory to aspects of human behavior which had previously been dealth with—if at all—by other social science disciplines."

1993 Robert W. Fogel and Douglass C. North (U.S.), for their work in economic history.

1994 John F. Nash and John C. Harsanyi (both U.S.), and Reinhard Selten (Germany), for their pioneering work in game theory.

Motion Picture Academy Awards (Oscars)

1928

Picture: *Wings,* Paramount
Director: Frank Borzage, *Seventh Heaven;* Lewis Milestone, *Two Arabian Nights*
Actress: Janet Gaynor, *Seventh Heaven, Street Angel, Sunrise*

Actor: Emil Jannings, *The Way of All Flesh, The Last Command*

1929

Picture: *The Broadway Melody,* M–G–M
Director: Frank Lloyd, *The Divine Lady*
Actress: Mary Pickford, *Coquette*
Actor: Warner Baxter, *In Old Arizona*

1930

Picture: *All Quiet on the Western Front,* Universal
Director: Lewis Milestone, *All Quiet on the Western Front*
Actress: Norma Shearer, *The Divorcee*
Actor: George Arliss, *Disraeli*

1931

Picture: *Cimarron:* RKO Radio
Director: Norman Taurog, *Skippy*
Actress: Marie Dressler, *Min and Bill*
Actor: Lionel Barrymore, *A Free Soul*

1932

Picture: *Grand Hotel,* M–G–M
Director: Frank Borzage, *Bad Girl*
Actress: Helen Hayes, *The Sin of Madelon Claudet*
Actor: Fredric March, *Dr. Jekyll and Mr. Hyde,* and Wallace Beery, *The Champ*

1933

Picture: *Cavalcade,* Fox
Director: Frank Lloyd, *Cavalcade*
Actress: Katharine Hepburn, *Morning Glory*
Actor: Charles Laughton, *The Private Life of Henry VIII*

1934

Picture: *It Happened One Night,* Columbia
Director: Frank Capra, *It Happened One Night*
Actress: Claudette Colbert, *It Happened One Night*
Actor: Clark Gable, *It Happened One Night*

1935

Picture: *Mutiny on the Bounty,* MGM
Director: John Ford, *The Informer*
Actress: Bette Davis, *Dangerous*
Actor: Victor McLaglen, *The Informer*

1936

Picture: *The Great Ziegfeld,* M–G–M
Director: Frank Capra, *Mr. Deeds Goes to Town*
Actress: Luise Rainer, *The Great Ziegfeld*
Actor: Paul Muni, *The Story of Louis Pasteur*
Supporting Actress: Gale Sondergaard, *Anthony Adverse*
Supporting Actor: Walter Brennan, *Come and Get It*

1937

Picture: *The Life of Emile Zola,* Warner Bros.
Director: Leo McCarey, *The Awful Truth*
Actress: Luise Rainer, *The Good Earth*
Actor: Spencer Tracy, *Captains Courageous*
Supporting Actress: Alice Brady, *In Old Chicago*
Supporting Actor: Joseph Schildkraut, *The Life of Emile Zola*

1938

Picture: *You Can't Take It with You,* Columbia
Director: Frank Capra, *You Can't Take It with You*
Actress: Bette Davis, *Jezebel*
Actor: Spencer Tracy, *Boys Town*
Supporting Actress: Fay Bainter, *Jezebel*
Supporting Actor: Walter Brennan, *Kentucky*

1939

Picture: *Gone with the Wind,* SelznickM–G–M
Director: Victor Fleming, *Gone with the Wind*
Actress: Vivien Leigh, *Gone with the Wind*
Actor: Robert Donat, *Goodbye, Mr. Chips*
Supporting Actress: Hattie McDaniel, *Gone with the Wind*
Supporting Actor: Thomas Mitchell, *Stagecoach*

1940

Picture: *Rebecca,* Selznick–UA
Director: John Ford, *The Grapes of Wrath*
Actress: Ginger Rogers, *Kitty Foyle*
Actor: James Stewart, *The Philadelphia Story*
Supporting Actress: Jane Darwell, *The Grapes of Wrath*

Supporting Actor: Walter Brennan, *The Westerner*

1941

Picture: *How Green Was My Valley,* 20th CenturyFox
Director: John Ford, *How Green Was My Valley*
Actress: Joan Fontaine, *Suspicion*
Actor: Gary Cooper, *Sergeant York*
Supporting Actress: Mary Astor, *The Great Lie*
Supporting Actor: Donald Crisp, *How Green Was My Valley*

1942

Picture: *Mrs. Miniver,* M–G–M
Director: William Wyler, *Mrs. Miniver*
Actress: Greer Garson, *Mrs. Miniver*
Actor: James Cagney, *Yankee Doodle Dandy*
Supporting Actress: Teresa Wright, *Mrs. Miniver*
Supporting Actor: Van Heflin, *Johnny Eager*

1943

Picture: *Casablanca,* Warner Bros.
Director: Michael Curtiz, *Casablanca*
Actress: Jennifer Jones, *The Song of Bernadette*
Actor: Paul Lukas, *Watch on the Rhine*
Supporting Actress: Katina Paxinou, *For Whom the Bell Tolls*
Supporting Actor: Charles Coburn, *The More the Merrier*

1944

Picture: *Going My Way,* Paramount
Director: Leo McCarey, *Going My Way*
Actress: Ingrid Bergman, *Gaslight*
Actor: Bing Crosby, *Going My Way*
Supporting Actress: Ethel Barrymore, *None But the Lonely Heart*
Supporting Actor: Barry Fitzgerald, *Going My Way*

1945

Picture: *The Lost Weekend,* Paramount
Director: Billy Wilder, *The Lost Weekend*
Actress: Joan Crawford, *Mildred Pierce*
Actor: Ray Milland, *The Lost Weekend*
Supporting Actress: Anne Revere, *National Velvet*
Supporting Actor: James Dunn, *A Tree Grows in Brooklyn*

1946

Picture: *The Best Years of Our Lives,* Goldwyn–RKO Radio
Director: William Wyler, *The Best Years of Our Lives*
Actress: Olivia de Havilland, *To Each His Own*
Actor: Fredric March, *The Best Years of Our Lives*
Supporting Actress: Anne Baxter, *The Razor's Edge*
Supporting Actor: Harold Russell, *The Best Years of Our Lives*

1947

Picture: *Gentleman's Agreement,* 20th CenturyFox
Director: Elia Kazan, *Gentleman's Agreement*
Actress: Loretta Young, *The Farmer's Daughter*
Actor: Ronald Colman, *A Double Life*
Supporting Actress: Celeste Holm, *Gentleman's Agreement*
Supporting Actor: Edmund Gwenn, *Miracle on 34th Street*

1948

Picture: *Hamlet,* Rank–Two Cities–UI
Director: John Huston, *Treasure of Sierra Madre*
Actress: Jane Wyman, *Johnny Belinda*
Actor: Laurence Olivier, *Hamlet*
Supporting Actress: Claire Trevor, *Key Largo*
Supporting Actor: Walter Huston, *Treasure of Sierra Madre*

1949

Picture: *All the King's Men,* Rossen–Columbia
Director: Joseph L. Mankiewicz, *A Letter to Three Wives*
Actress: Olivia de Havilland, *The Heiress*

Actor: Broderick Crawford, *All the King's Men*
Supporting Actress: Mercedes McCambridge, *All the King's Men*
Supporting Actor: Dean Jagger, *Twelve O'Clock High*

1950

Picture: *All About Eve,* 20th Century–Fox
Director: Joseph L. Mankiewicz, *All About Eve*
Actress: Judy Holliday, *Born Yesterday*
Actor: José Ferrer, *Cyrano de Bergerac*
Supporting Actress: Josephine Hull, *Harvey*
Supporting Actor: George Sanders, *All About Eve*

1951

Picture: *An American in Paris,* M–G–M
Director: George Stevens, *A Place in the Sun*
Actress: Vivien Leigh, *A Streetcar Named Desire*
Actor: Humphrey Bogart, *The African Queen*
Supporting Actress: Kim Hunter, *A Streetcar Named Desire*
Supporting Actor: Karl Malden, *A Streetcar Named Desire*

1952

Picture: *The Greatest Show on Earth,* DeMille–Paramount
Director: John Ford, *The Quiet Man*
Actress: Shirley Booth, *Come Back, Little Sheba*
Actor: Gary Cooper, *High Noon*
Supporting Actress: Gloria Grahame, *The Bad and the Beautiful*
Supporting Actor: Anthony Quinn, *Viva Zapata!*

1953

Picture: *From Here to Eternity,* Columbia
Director: Fred Zinnemann, *From Here to Eternity*
Actress: Audrey Hepburn, *Roman Holiday*
Actor: William Holden, *Stalag 17*
Supporting Actress: Donna Reed, *From Here to Eternity*
Supporting Actor: Frank Sinatra, *From Here to Eternity*

1954

Picture: *On the Waterfront,* Horizon–American Corp., Columbia
Director: Elia Kazan, *On the Waterfront*
Actress: Grace Kelly, *The Country Girl*
Actor: Marlon Brando, *On the Waterfront*
Supporting Actress: Eva Marie Saint, *On the Waterfront*
Supporting Actor: Edmond O'Brien, *The Barefoot Contessa*

1955

Picture: *Marty,* Hecht and Lancaster, United Artists
Director: Delbert Mann, *Marty*
Actress: Anna Magnani, *The Rose Tattoo*
Actor: Ernest Borgnine, *Marty*
Supporting Actress: Jo Van Fleet, *East of Eden*
Supporting Actor: Jack Lemmon, *Mister Roberts*

1956

Picture: *Around the World in 80 Days,* Michael Todd Co., Inc.–U.A.
Director: George Stevens, *Giant*
Actress: Ingrid Bergman, *Anastasia*
Actor: Yul Brynner, *The King and I*
Supporting Actress: Dorothy Malone, *Written on the Wind*
Supporting Actor: Anthony Quinn, *Lust for Life*

1957

Picture: *The Bridge on the River Kwai,* Horizon Picture, Columbia
Director: David Lean, *The Bridge on the River Kwai*
Actress: Joanne Woodward, *The Three Faces of Eve*
Actor: Alec Guinness, *The Bridge on the River Kwai*
Supporting Actress: Miyoshi Umeki, *Sayonara*
Supporting Actor: Red Buttons, *Sayonara*

1958

Picture: *Gigi,* Arthur Freed Productions, Inc., M–G–M
Director: Vincente Minnelli, *Gigi*

Actress: Susan Hayward, *I Want to Live!*
Actor: David Niven, *Separate Tables*
Supporting Actress: Wendy Hiller, *Separate Tables*
Supporting Actor: Burl Ives, *The Big Country*

1959

Picture: *BenHur,* M–G–M
Director: William Wyler, *BenHur*
Actress: Simone Signoret, *Room at the Top*
Actor: Charlton Heston, *BenHur*
Supporting Actress: Shelley Winters, *The Diary of Anne Frank*
Supporting Actor: Hugh Griffith, *BenHur*

1960

Picture: *The Apartment,* Mirisch Co., Inc., United Artists
Director: Billy Wilder, *The Apartment*
Actress: Elizabeth Taylor, *Butterfield 8*
Actor: Burt Lancaster, *Elmer Gantry*
Supporting Actress: Shirley Jones, *Elmer Gantry*
Supporting Actor: Peter Ustinov, *Spartacus*

1961

Picture: *West Side Story,* Mirisch Pictures, Inc., and B and P Enterprises, Inc., United Artists
Director: Robert Wise and Jerome Robbins, *West Side Story*
Actress: Sophia Loren, *Two Women*
Actor: Maximillian Schell, *Judgment at Nuremberg*
Supporting Actress: Rita Moreno, *West Side Story*
Supporting Actor: George Chakiris, *West Side Story*

1962

Picture: *Lawrence of Arabia,* Horizon Pictures, Ltd.–Columbia
Director: David Lean, *Lawrence of Arabia*
Actress: Anne Bancroft, *The Miracle Worker*
Actor: Gregory Peck, *To Kill a Mockingbird*
Supporting Actress: Patty Duke, *The Miracle Worker*
Supporting Actor: Ed Begley, *Sweet Bird of Youth*

1963

Picture: *Tom Jones,* A Woodfall Production, UA–Lopert Pictures
Director: Tony Richardson, *Tom Jones*
Actress: Patricia Neal, *Hud*
Actor: Sidney Poitier, *Lilies of the Field*
Supporting Actress: Margaret Rutherford, *The V.I.P.s*
Supporting Actor: Melvyn Douglas, *Hud*

1964

Picture: *My Fair Lady,* Warner Bros.
Director: George Cukor, *My Fair Lady*
Actress: Julie Andrews, *Mary Poppins*
Actor: Rex Harrison, *My Fair Lady*
Supporting Actress: Lila Kedrova, *Zorba the Greek*
Supporting Actor: Peter Ustinov, *Topkapi*

1965

Picture: *The Sound of Music,* Argyle Enterprises Production, 20th CenturyFox
Director: Robert Wise, *The Sound of Music*
Actress: Julie Christie, *Darling*
Actor: Lee Marvin, *Cat Ballou*
Supporting Actress: Shelley Winters, *A Patch of Blue*
Supporting Actor: Martin Balsam, *A Thousand Clowns*

1966

Picture: *A Man for All Seasons,* Highland Films, Ltd., Production, Columbia
Director: Fred Zinnemann, *A Man for All Seasons*
Actress: Elizabeth Taylor, *Who's Afraid of Virginia Woolf?*
Actor: Paul Scofield, *A Man for All Seasons*
Supporting Actress: Sandy Dennis, *Who's Afraid of Virginia Woolf?*
Supporting Actor: Walter Matthau, *The Fortune Cookie*

1967

Picture: *In the Heat of the Night,* Mirisch Corp. Productions, United Artists
Director: Mike Nichols, *The Graduate*
Actress: Katharine Hepburn, *Guess Who's Coming to Dinner*
Actor: Rod Steiger, *In the Heat of the Night*
Supporting Actress: Estelle Parsons, *Bonnie and Clyde*
Supporting Actor: George Kennedy, *Cool Hand Luke*

1968

Picture: *Oliver!,* Columbia Pictures
Director: Sir Carol Reed, *Oliver!*
Actress: Katharine Hepburn, *The Lion in Winter* and Barbra Streisand, *Funny Girl*
Actor: Cliff Robertson, *Charly*
Supporting Actress: Ruth Gordon, *Rosemary's Baby*
Supporting Actor: Jack Albertson, *The Subject Was Roses*

1969

Picture: *Midnight Cowboy,* Jerome Hellman-John Schlesinger Production, United Artists
Director: John Schlesinger, *Midnight Cowboy*
Actress: Maggie Smith, *The Prime of Miss Jean Brodie*
Actor: John Wayne, *True Grit*
Supporting Actress: Goldie Hawn, *Cactus Flower*
Supporting Actor: Gig Young, *They Shoot Horses Don't They?*

1970

Picture: *Patton,* Frank McCarthy–Franklin J. Schaffner Production, 20th Century Fox
Director: Franklin J. Schaffner, *Patton*
Actress: Glenda Jackson, *Women in Love*
Actor: George C. Scott, *Patton*
Supporting Actress: Helen Hayes, *Airport*
Supporting Actor: John Mills, *Ryan's Daughter*

1971

Picture: *The French Connection,* D'Antoni Productions, 20th CenturyFox
Director: William Friedkin, *The French Connection*
Actress: Jane Fonda, *Klute*
Actor: Gene Hackman, *The French Connection*
Supporting Actress: Cloris Leachman, *The Last Picture Show*
Supporting Actor: Ben Johnson, *The Last Picture Show*

1972

Picture: *The Godfather,* Albert S. Ruddy Production, Paramount
Director: Bob Fosse, *Cabaret*
Actress: Liza Minnelli, *Cabaret*
Actor: Marlon Brando, *The Godfather*
Supporting Actress: Eileen Heckart, *Butterflies Are Free*
Supporting Actor: Joel Grey, *Cabaret*

1973

Picture: *The Sting,* Universal-Bill-Phillips-George Roy Hill Production, Universal
Director: George Roy Hill, *The Sting*
Actress: Glenda Jackson, *A Touch of Class*
Actor: Jack Lemmon, *Save the Tiger*
Supporting Actress: Tatum O'Neal, *Paper Moon*
Supporting Actor: John Houseman, *The Paper Chase*

1974

Picture: *The Godfather, Part II,* Coppola Co. Production, Paramount
Director: Francis Ford Coppola, *The Godfather, Part II*
Actress: Ellen Burstyn, *Alice Doesn't Live Here Anymore*
Actor: Art Carney, *Harry and Tonto*
Supporting Actress: Ingrid Bergman, *Murder on the Orient Express*
Suppo rting Actor: Robert De Niro, *The Godfather, Part II*

1975

Picture: *One Flew Over the Cuckoo's Nest,* Fantasy Films Production, United Artists
Director: Milos Forman, *One Flew Over the Cuckoo's Nest*
Actress: Louise Fletcher, *One Flew Over the Cuckoo's Nest*
Actor: Jack Nicholson, *One Flew Over the Cuckoo's Nest*
Supporting Actress: Lee Grant, *Shampoo*
Supporting Actor: George Burns, *The Sunshine Boys*

1976

Picture: *Rocky,* Robert Chartoff–Irwin Winkler Production, United Artists
Director: John G. Avildsen, *Rocky*
Actress: Faye Dunaway, *Network*
Actor: Peter Finch, *Network*
Supporting Actress: Beatrice Straight, *Network*
Supporting Actor: Jason Robards, *All the President's Men*

1977

Picture: *Annie Hall,* Jack Rollins–Charles H. Joffe Production, United Artists
Director: Woody Allen, *Annie Hall*
Actress: Diane Keaton, *Annie Hall*
Actor: Richard Dreyfuss, *The Goodbye Girl*
Supporting Actress: Vanessa Redgrave, *Julia*
Supporting Actor: Jason Robards, *Julia*

1978

Picture: *The Deer Hunter,* Michael Cimino Film Production, Universal
Director: Michael Cimino, *The Deer Hunter*
Actress: Jane Fonda, *Coming Home*
Actor: Jon Voight, *Coming Home*
Supporting Actress: Maggie Smith, *California Suite*
Supporting Actor: Christopher Walken, *The Deer Hunter*

1979

Picture: *Kramer vs. Kramer,* Stanley Jaffe Production, Columbia Pictures
Director: Robert Benton, *Kramer vs. Kramer*
Actress: Sally Field, *Norma Rae*
Actor: Dustin Hoffman, *Kramer vs. Kramer*
Supporting Actress: Meryl Streep, *Kramer vs. Kramer*
Supporting Actor: Melvyn Douglas, *Being There*

1980

Picture: *Ordinary People,* Wildwood Enterprises Production, Paramount
Director: Robert Redford, *Ordinary People*
Actress: Sissy Spacek, *Coal Miner's Daughter*
Actor: Robert De Niro, *Raging Bull*
Supporting Actress: Mary Steenburgen, *Melvin and Howard*
Supporting Actor: Timothy Hutton, *Ordinary People*

1981

Picture: *Chariots of Fire,* Enigma Productions, Ladd Company/Warner Bros.
Director: Warren Beatty, *Reds*
Actress: Katharine Hepburn, *On Golden Pond*
Actor: Henry Fonda, *On Golden Pond*
Supporting Actress: Maureen Stapleton, *Reds*
Supporting Actor: John Gielgud, *Arthur*

1982

Picture: *Gandhi,* Indo–British Films Production/Columbia
Director: Richard Attenborough, *Gandhi*
Actress: Meryl Streep, *Sophie's Choice*
Actor: Ben Kingsley, *Gandhi*
Supporting Actress: Jessica Lange, *Tootsie*
Supporting Actor: Louis Gossett, Jr., *An Officer and a Gentleman*

1983

Picture: *Terms of Endearment,* Paramount

Director: James L. Brooks, *Terms of Endearment*
Actress: Shirley MacLaine, *Terms of Endearment*
Actor: Robert Duvall, *Tender Mercies*
Supporting Actress: Linda Hunt, *The Year of Living Dangerously*
Supporting Actor: Jack Nicholson, *Terms of Endearment*

1984

Picture: *Amadeus,* Orion Pictures
Director: Milos Forman, *Amadeus*
Actress: Sally Field, *Places in the Heart*
Actor: F. Murray Abraham, *Amadeus*
Supporting Actress: Dame Peggy Ashcroft, *A Passage to India*
Supporting Actor: Haing S. Ngor, *The Killing Fields*

1985

Picture: *Out of Africa,* Universal
Director: Sydney Pollack, *Out of Africa*
Actress: Geraldine Page, *The Trip to Bountiful*
Actor: William Hurt, *Kiss of the Spider Woman*
Supporting Actress: Anjelica Huston, *Prizzi's Honor*
Supporting Actor: Don Ameche, *Cocoon*

1986

Picture: *Platoon,* Orion Pictures
Director: Oliver Stone, *Platoon*
Actress: Marlee Matlin, *Children of a Lesser God*
Actor: Paul Newman, *The Color of Money*
Supporting Actress: Dianne Wiest, *Hannah and Her Sisters*
Supporting Actor: Michael Caine, *Hannah and Her Sisters*

1987

Picture: *The Last Emperor,* Columbia Pictures
Director : Bernardo Bertolucci, *The Last Emperor*
Actress: Cher, *Moonstruck*
Actor: Michael Douglas, *Wall Street*
Supporting Actress: Olympia Dukakis, *Moonstruck*
Supporting Actor: Sean Connery, *The Untouchables*

1988

Picture: *Rain Man,* United Artists
Director: Barry Levinson, *Rain Man*
Actress: Jodie Foster, *The Accused*
Actor: Dustin Hoffman, *Rain Man*
Supporting Actress: Geena Davis, *The Accidental Tourist*

Supporting Actor: Kevin Kline: *A Fish Called Wanda*

1989

Picture: *Driving Miss Daisy,* Warner Brothers
Director: Oliver Stone, *Born on the Fourth of July*
Actress: Jessica Tandy, *Driving Miss Daisy*
Actor: Daniel Day-Lewis, *My Left Foot*
Supporting Actress: Brenda Fricker, *My Left Foot*
Supporting Actor: Denzel Washington, *Glory*

1990

Picture: *Dances With Wolves,* Orion
Director: Kevin Costner, *Dances With Wolves*
Actress: Kathy Bates, *Misery*
Actor: Jeremy Irons, *Reversal of Fortune*
Supporting Actress: Whoopi Goldberg, *Ghost*
Supporting Actor: Joe Pesci, *Goodfellas*

1991

Picture: *The Silence of the Lambs,* Orion
Director: Jonathan Demme, *The Silence of the Lambs*

Actress: Jodie Foster, *The Silence of the Lambs*
Actor: Anthony Hopkins, *The Silence of the Lambs*
Supporting Actress: Mercedes Ruehl, *The Fisher King*
Supporting Actor: Jack Palance, *City Slickers*

1992

Picture: *Unforgiven,* Warner Brothers
Director: Clint Eastwood, *Unforgiven*
Actress: Emma Thompson, *Howards End*
Actor: Al Pacino, *Scent of a Woman*
Supporting Actress: Marisa Tomei, *My Cousin Vinny*
Supporting Actor: Gene Hackman, *Unforgiven*

1993

Picture: *Schindler's List,* Universal
Director: Steven Spielberg, *Schindler's List*
Actress: Holly Hunter, *The Piano*
Actor: Tom Hanks, *Philadelphia*
Supporting Actress: Anna Paquin, *The Piano*
Supporting Actor: Tommy Lee Jones, *The Fugitive*

1994

Picture: *Forrest Gump,* Paramount
Director: Robert Zemeckis, *Forrest Gump*
Actress: Jessica Lange, *Blue Sky*
Actor: Tom Hanks, *Forrest Gump*
Supporting Actress: Dianne Wiest, *Bullets Over Broadway*
Supporting Actor: Martin Landau, *Ed Wood*

Other Academy Awards for 1994

Art Direction: Ken Adam and Carolyn Scott, *The Madness of King George*
Cinematography: John Toll, *Legends of the Fall*
Costume Design: Lizzy Gardiner and Tim Chappel, *The Adventures of Priscilla, Queen of the Desert*
Documentary (feature): *Maya Lin: A Strong Clear Vision;* **(short subject):** *A Time for Justiuce*
Editing: Arthur Schmidt, *Forrest Gump*
Foreign-language film: *Burnt by the Sun,* Russia
Makeup: Rick Baker, Ve Neill, and Yolanda Toussieng, *Ed Wood*
Music (original score): Hans Zimmer, *The Lion King;* **(song):** Elton John and Tim Rice, *Can You Feel the Love Tonight, The Lion King*
Screenplay, Original: Quentin Tarantino and Roger Avary, *Pulp Fiction*
Screenplay, Adapted: Eric Roth, *Forrest Gump*
Short subject (live action): *Franz Kafka's It's a Wonderful Life* and *Trevor;* **(animated):** *Bob's Birthday*
Sound: Gregg Landaker, Steve Maslow, Bob Beemer, and David R.B. MacMillan, *Speed*
Sound effects editing: Stephen Hunter Flick, *Speed*
Visual effects: Ken Ralson, George Murphy, Stephen Rosenbaum, and Allen Hall, *Forrest Gump*
Honorary Award: Michelangelo Antonioni for lifetime achievement
Irving G. Thalberg Memorial Award: Clinton Eastwood for a consistently high quality of motion picture production
Jean Hersholt Humanitarian Award: Quincy Jones
Technical Award of Merit: The Eastman Kodak Company for the development of the Eastman EXR Color Intermediate Film 5244
Technical Award of Merit: Petro and Paul Vlahos for the conception and development of the Ultimate Electric Blue Screen Composing Process.

1995 Bancroft Prizes in American History

The Refiner's Fire: The Making of Mormon Cosmology, 1644–1844, by John L. Brooke (Cambridge University Press)

Local People: The Struggle for Civil Rights in Mississippi, by John Dittmer (University of Illinois)

National Society of Film Critics Awards, 1994

Best Film: *Pulp Fiction*
Best Actress: Jennifer Jason Leigh, *Mrs. Parker and the Viscious Circle*
Best Actor: Paul Newman, *Nobody's Fool*
Best Supporting Actress: Dianne Wiest, *Bullets Over Broadway*
Best Supporting Actor: Martin Landau, *Ed Wood*
Best Director: Quentin Tarantino, *Pulp Fiction*

Best Screenwriter: Quentin Tarantino and Roger Avary, *Pulp Fiction*
Best Cinematography: Stefan Czapsky, *Ed Wood*
Best Documentary: *Hoop Dreams*
Best Foreign Film: *Red*, Kryzsztof Kieslowski
Experimental Work: *Satantango*, Bela Tarr and *The Pharoah's Belt*, Lewis Klahr

George Foster Peabody Awards for Broadcasting, 1994

Radio

National Public Radio: *Tobacco Stories.*
National Public Radio and the Smithsonian Institution: *Wade in the Water: African-American Sacred-Music Tradition.*
WRKS–FM, New York: *The Rise and Fall of Vee-Jay,* about one of America's most influential black-owned record companies.
WXXI–FM, Rochester, N.Y.: *Fascinatin' Rhythm,* a depiction of American culture through popular music.
WVXU–FM, Cincinnati: *D-Day and 50 Years.*

Television

PBS: Mini-series, *Armistead Maupin's "Tales of the City."*
NBC: Prime-time entertainment series *E.R., Frasier,* and *Mad About You.*
ABC: *Prime Time Live* report about errors at laboratories that test for cervical cancer and *20–20* story on a woman's fight to save victims of anorexia.
CBS and Arnold Shapiro Production: *Break the Silence: Kids Against Child Abuse.*
CBS News: *CBS Reports: D–Day.*
WGBH, Boston and Lennon Documentary Group: *The Battle of the Bulge* for *The American Experience.*
WGBH, Boston and David Grubin Productions: *F.D.R.* for *The American Experience.*
WGBH, Boston and Blackside and Roja: *Malcolm X: Make It Plain* for *The American Experience.*
J.E.G. Productions on HBO: *Barbra Streisand: The Concert.*
MTV Networks, New York: *MTV Unplugged.*
Nick News, a news magazine for children.
Lichtenstein Creative Media, New York: *Schizophrenia: Voices of an Illness.*
WTLV, Jacksonville, Fla.: *Buddy Check 12,* a public-service program.
Turner Original Productions–Varied Directions: *Moon Shoot.*
Discovery Communications, Bethesda, Md.: *Normandy: The Great Crusade.*
KGAN, Cedar Rapids, Iowa: *Sewer Solvent Scandal.*
WETA, Washington and Channel 4 London: *China: Beyond the Clouds,* a River Films Production for National Geographic Television.
National Geographic Television, Washington: *Reflections on Elephants.*
KSBW, Salinas, Calif.: *Just Because: Tales of Violence, Dreams of Peace,* a program on youth violence.
KGO, San Francisco: *Rwanda,* a report on the Rwandan civil war.
KSEE, Fresno, Calif.: *The Atomic Bombshell.*
National Film Board of Canada on TV Ontario: *Fat Chance.*
Case TV Production for Channel 4 London: *Fourways Farm,* a children's program dealing with issues of life and death.

Pulitzer Prize Awards

(For years not listed, no award was made.)
Source: Columbia University.

Pulitzer Prizes in Journalism

MERITORIOUS PUBLIC SERVICE

1918 *New York Times;* also special award to Minna Lewinson and Henry Beetle Hough
1919 *Milwaukee Journal*
1921 *Boston Post*
1922 *New York World*
1923 *Memphis Commercial Appeal*
1924 *New York World*
1926 *Columbus* (Ga.) *Enquirer Sun*
1927 *Canton* (Ohio) *Daily News*
1928 *Indianapolis Times*
1929 *New York Evening World*
1931 *Atlanta Constitution*
1932 *Indianapolis News*
1933 *New York World-Telegram*
1934 *Medford* (Ore.) *Mail Tribune*
1935 *Sacramento Bee*
1936 *Cedar Rapids* (Iowa) *Gazette*
1937 *St. Louis Post-Dispatch*
1938 *Bismarck* (N.D.) *Tribune*
1939 *Miami Daily News*
1940 *Waterbury* (Conn.) *Republican* and *American*
1941 *St. Louis Post-Dispatch*
1942 *Los Angeles Times*
1943 *Omaha World-Herald*
1944 *New York Times*
1945 *Detroit Free Press*
1946 *Scranton* (Pa.) *Times*
1947 *Baltimore Sun*
1948 *St. Louis Post-Dispatch*
1949 (Lincoln) *Nebraska State Journal*
1950 *Chicago Daily News;* and *St. Louis Post-Dispatch*
1951 *Miami Herald;* and *Brooklyn Eagle*
1952 *St. Louis Post-Dispatch*
1953 *Whiteville* (N.C.) *News Reporter;* and *Tabor City* (N.C.) *Tribune*
1954 *Newsday* (Garden City, L.I.)
1955 *Columbus* (Ga.) *Ledger* and *Sunday Ledger-Enquirer*
1956 *Watsonville* (Calif.) *Register-Pajaronian*
1957 *Chicago Daily News*
1958 (Little Rock) *Arkansas Gazette*
1959 *Utica* (N.Y.) *Observer Dispatch* and *Utica Daily Press*
1960 *Los Angeles Times*
1961 *Amarillo* (Tex.) *Globe-Times*
1962 *Panama City* (Fla.) *News-Herald*
1963 *Chicago Daily News*
1964 *St. Petersburg* (Fla.) *Times*
1965 *Hutchinson* (Kan.) *News*
1966 *Boston Globe*
1967 *Louisville Courier-Journal* and *Milwaukee Journal*

1968 *Riverside* (Calif.) *Press-Enterprise*
1969 *Los Angeles Times*
1970 *Newsday* (Garden City, L.I.)
1971 *Winston-Salem* (N.C.) *Journal and Sentinel*
1972 *New York Times*
1973 *Washington Post*
1974 *Newsday* (Garden City, L.I.)
1975 *Boston Globe*
1976 *Anchorage* (Alaska) *Daily News*
1977 *Lufkin* (Tex.) *News*
1978 *Philadelphia Inquirer*
1979 *Point Reyes* (Calif.) *Light*
1980 Gannett News Service
1981 *Charlotte* (N.C.) *Observer*
1982 *Detroit News*
1983 *Jackson* (Miss.) *Clarion-Ledger*
1984 *Los Angeles Times*
1985 *The Fort Worth Star-Telegram*
1986 *Denver Post*
1987 Andrew Schneider and Matthew Brelis, *Pittsburgh Press*
1988 *Charlotte* (N.C.) *Observer*
1989 *Anchorage Daily News*
1990 *Philadelphia Inquirer* and *Washington* (N.C.) *Daily News*
1991 *Des Moines Register,* reporting by Jane Schorer
1992 *Sacramento Bee* for "The Sierra in Peril" series by Tom Knudson
1993 *Miami Herald*
1994 *The Akron* (Ohio) *Beacon Journal*
1995 *The Virgin Islands Daily News*

EDITORIAL

1917 *New York Tribune*
1918 *Louisville Courier-Journal*
1920 Harvey E. Newbranch *(Omaha Evening World-Herald)*
1922 Frank M. O'Brien *(New York Herald)*
1923 William Allen White *(Emporia* [Kan.] *Gazette)*
1924 *Boston Herald* (Frank Buxton); special prize: Frank I. Cobb *(New York World)*
1925 *Charleston* (S.C.) *News and Courier*
1926 *New York Times* (Edward M. Kingsbury)
1927 *Boston Herald* (F. Lauriston Bullard)
1928 Grover Cleveland Hall *(Montgomery* [Ala.] *Advertiser)*
1929 Louis Isaac Jaffe *(Norfolk Virginian-Pilot)*
1931 Charles S. Ryckman *(Fremont* [Neb.] *Tribune)*
1933 *Kansas City* (Mo.) *Star*
1934 E. P. Chase *(Atlantic* [Iowa] *News Telegraph)*
1936 Felix Morley *(Washington Post);* George B. Parker (Scripps-Howard Newspapers)
1937 John W. Owens *(Baltimore Sun)*
1938 W. W. Waymack *(Des Moines Register and Tribune)*
1939 Ronald G. Callvert *(Portland Oregonian)*
1940 Bart Howard *(St. Louis Post-Dispatch)*
1941 Reuben Maury *(New York Daily News)*
1942 Geoffrey Parsons *(New York Herald Tribune)*
1943 Forrest W. Seymour *(Des Moines Register and Tribune)*
1944 *Kansas City* (Mo.) *Star* (Henry J. Haskell)
1945 George W. Potter *(Providence* [R.I.] *Journal-Bulletin)*
1946 Hodding Carter ([Greenville, Miss.] *Delta Democrat-Times)*
1947 William H. Grimes *(Wall Street Journal)*
1948 Virginius Dabney *(Richmond Times-Dispatch)*
1949 John H. Crider *(Boston Herald);* Herbert Elliston *(Washington Post)*
1950 Carl M. Saunders *(Jackson* [Mich.] *Citizen Patriot)*
1951 William H. Fitzpatrick *(New Orleans States)*
1952 Louis LaCoss *(St. Louis Globe-Democrat)*
1953 Vermont C. Royster *(Wall Street Journal)*
1954 *Boston Herald* (Don Murray)
1955 *Detroit Free Press* (Royce Howes)
1956 Lauren K. Soth *(Des Moines Register and Tribune)*
1957 Buford Boone *(Tuscaloosa* [Ala.] *News)*
1958 Harry S. Ashmore *(Arkansas Gazette)*

1959 Ralph McGill *(Atlanta Constitution)*
1960 Lenoir Chambers *(Virginian-Pilot)*
1961 William J. Dorvillier *(San Juan* [P.R.] *Star)*
1962 Thomas M. Storke *(Santa Barbara* [Calif.] *News-Press)*
1963 Ira B. Harkey, Jr. *(Pascagoula* [Miss.] *Chronicle)*
1964 Hazel Brannon Smith *(Lexington* [Miss.] *Advertiser)*
1965 John R. Harrison *(Gainesville* [Fla.] *Daily Sun)*
1966 Robert Lasch *(St. Louis Post-Dispatch)*
1967 Eugene Patterson *(Atlanta Constitution)*
1968 John S. Knight (Knight Newspapers)
1969 Paul Greenberg *(Pine Bluff* [Ark.] *Commercial)*
1970 Phillip L. Geyelin *(Washington Post)*
1971 Horance G. Davis, Jr. *(Gainesville* [Fla.] *Sun)*
1972 John Strohmeyer *(Bethlehem* [Pa.] *Globe Times)*
1973 Roger Bourne Linscott *(Berkshire Eagle* [Pittsfield, Mass.])
1974 F. Gilman Spencer *(Trenton* [N.J.] *Trentonian)*
1975 John Daniell Maurice *(Charleston* [W. Va.] *Daily Mail)*
1976 Philip P. Kerby *(Los Angeles Times)*
1977 Warren L. Lerude, Foster Church and Norman F. Cardoza *(Reno* [Nev.] *Gazette* and *Nevada State Journal)*
1978 Meg Greenfield *(Washington Post)*
1979 Edwin M. Yoder, Jr. *(Washington Star)*
1980 Robert L. Bartley *(Wall Street Journal)*
1981 Not awarded
1982 Jack Rosenthal *(New York Times)*
1983 *Miami Herald*
1984 Albert Scardino *(Georgia Gazette)*
1985 Richard Aregood *(Philadelphia Daily News)*
1986 Jack Fuller *(Chicago Tribune)*
1987 Jonathan Freedman *(San Diego Tribune)*
1988 Jane E. Healy *(Orlando Sentinel)*
1989 Lois Wille *(Chicago Tribune)*
1990 Thomas J. Hylton *(Pottstown* [Pa.] *Mercury)*
1991 Ron Casey, Harold Jackson, and Joey Kennedy *(Birmingham* [Ala.] *News)*
1992 Maria Henson *(Lexington* [Ky.] *Herald-Leader)*
1994 R. Bruce Dold *(Chicago Tribune)*
1995 Jeffrey Good *(St. Petersburg* (Fla.] *Times)*

CORRESPONDENCE

1929 Paul Scott Mowrer *(Chicago Daily News)*
1930 Leland Stowe *(New York Herald Tribune)*
1931 H. R. Knickerbocker *(Philadelphia Public Ledger* and *New York Evening Post)*
1932 Walter Duranty *(New York Times);* Charles G. Ross *(St. Louis Post-Dispatch)*
1933 Edgar Ansel Mowrer *(Chicago Daily News)*
1934 Frederick T. Birchall *(New York Times)*
1935 Arthur Krock *(New York Times)*
1936 Wilfred C. Barber *(Chicago Tribune)*
1937 Anne O'Hare McCormick *(New York Times)*
1938 Arthur Krock *(New York Times)*
1939 Louis P. Lochner (Associated Press)
1940 Otto D. Tolischus *(New York Times)*
1941 Group award[1]
1942 Carlos P. Romulo *(Philippines Herald)*
1943 Hanson W. Baldwin *(New York Times)*
1944 Ernie Pyle (Scripps-Howard Newspaper Alliance)
1945 Harold V. (Hal) Boyle (Associated Press)
1946 Arnaldo Cortesi *(New York Times)*
1947 Brooks Atkinson *(New York Times)*
1948 Discontinued

EDITORIAL CARTOONING

1922 Rollin Kirby *(New York World)*
1924 Jay Norwood Darling *(New York Tribune)*
1925 Rollin Kirby *(New York World)*
1926 D. R. Fitzpatrick *(St. Louis Post-Dispatch)*
1927 Nelson Harding *(Brooklyn Eagle)*

1. For the public services and the individual achievements of American news reporters in the war zones.

1928 Nelson Harding *(Brooklyn Eagle)*
1929 Rollin Kirby *(New York World)*
1930 Charles R. Macauley *(Brooklyn Eagle)*
1931 Edmund Duffy *(Baltimore Sun)*
1932 John T. McCutcheon *(Chicago Tribune)*
1933 H. M. Talburt *(Washington Daily News)*
1934 Edmund Duffy *(Baltimore Sun)*
1935 Ross A. Lewis *(Milwaukee Journal)*
1937 C. D. Batchelor *(New York Daily News)*
1938 Vaughn Shoemaker *(Chicago Daily News)*
1939 Charles G. Werner (*Daily Oklahoman*[Oklahoma City])
1940 Edmund Duffy *(Baltimore Sun)*
1941 Jacob Burck *(Chicago Times)*
1942 Herbert L. Block (NEA Service)
1943 Jay Norwood Darling *(New York Herald Tribune)*
1944 Clifford K. Berryman *(Washington Evening Star)*
1945 Bill Mauldin (United Features Syndicate)
1946 Bruce Alexander Russell *(Los Angeles Times)*
1947 Vaughn Shoemaker *(Chicago Daily News)*
1948 Reuben L. Goldberg *(New York Sun)*
1949 Lute Pease *(Newark Evening News)*
1950 James T. Berryman *(Washington Evening Star)*
1951 Reg (Reginald W.) Manning (*Arizona Republic* [Phoenix])
1952 Fred L. Packer *(New York Mirror)*
1953 Edward D. Kuekes *(Cleveland Plain Dealer)*
1954 Herbert L. Block *(Washington Post* and *Times-Herald)*
1955 Daniel R. Fitzpatrick *(St. Louis Post-Dispatch)*
1956 Robert York *(Louisville Times)*
1957 Tom Little *(Nashville Tennessean)*
1958 Bruce M. Shanks *(Buffalo Evening News)*
1959 Bill Mauldin *(St. Louis Post-Dispatch)*
1961 Carey Orr *(Chicago Tribune)*
1962 Edmund S. Valtman *(Hartford Times)*
1963 Frank Miller *(Des Moines Register)*
1964 Paul Conrad (formerly of *Denver Post,* later on *Los Angeles Times)*
1966 Don Wright *(Miami News)*
1967 Patrick B. Oliphant *(Denver Post)*
1968 Eugene Gray Payne *(Charlotte* [N.C.] *Observer)*
1969 John Fischetti *(Chicago Daily News)*
1970 Thomas F. Darcy *(Newsday* [Garden City, L.I.])
1971 Paul Conrad *(Los Angeles Times)*
1972 Jeffrey K. MacNelly *(Richmond* [Va.] *News Leader)*
1974 Paul Szep *(Boston Globe)*
1975 Garry Trudeau (Universal Press Syndicate)
1976 Tony Auth *(Philadelphia Inquirer)*
1977 Paul Szep *(Boston Globe)*
1978 Jeffrey K. MacNelly *(Richmond* [Va.] *News Leader)*
1979 Herbert L. Block *(Washington Post)*
1980 Don Wright *(Miami News)*
1981 Mike Peters *(Dayton* [Ohio] *Daily News)*
1982 Ben Sargent *(Austin* [Tex.] *American-Statesman)*
1983 Richard Locher *(Chicago Tribune)*
1984 Paul Conrad *(Los Angeles Times)*
1985 Jeff MacNelly *(Chicago Tribune)*
1986 Jules Feiffer *(Village Voice)*
1987 Berke Breathed *(Washington Post* Writers Group)
1988 Doug Marlette *(Atlanta Constitution* and *Charlotte* [N.C.] *Observer)*
1989 Jack Higgins *(Chicago Sun-Times)*
1990 Tom Toles *(Buffalo News)*
1991 Jim Borgman *(Cincinnati Inquirer)*
1992 Signe Wilkinson, *(Philadelphia Daily News)*
1993 Stephen R. Benson *(Arizona Republic)*
1994 Michael P. Ramirez *(The Commercial Appeal,* Memphis)
1995 Mike Luckovich *(The Atlanta Constitution)*

NEWS PHOTOGRAPHY

1942 Milton Brooks *(Detroit News)*
1943 Frank Noel (Associated Press)
1944 Frank Filan (Associated Press); Earle L. Bunker *(Omaha World-Herald)*
1945 Joe Rosenthal (Associated Press)
1947 Arnold Hardy
1948 Frank Cushing *(Boston Traveler)*
1949 Nat Fein *(New York Herald Tribune)*
1950 Bill Crouch *(Oakland Tribune)*
1951 Max Desfor (Associated Press)
1952 John Robinson and Don Ultang *(Des Moines Register & Tribune)*
1953 William M. Gallagher *(Flint* [Mich.] *Journal)*
1954 Mrs. Walter M. Schau
1955 John L. Gaunt, Jr. *(Los Angeles Times)*
1956 *New York Daily News*
1957 Harry A. Trask *(Boston Traveler)*
1958 William C. Beall *(Washington Daily News)*
1959 William Seaman *(Minneapolis Star)*
1960 Andrew Lopez (United Press International)
1961 Yasushi Nagao (Mainichi Newspapers, Tokyo)
1962 Paul Vathis (Harrisburg [Pa.] bureau of Associated Press)
1963 Hector Rondon (*La Republica,* Caracas, Venezuela)
1964 Robert H. Jackson *(Dallas Times Herald)*
1965 Horst Faas (Associated Press)
1966 Kyoichi Sawada (United Press International)
1967 Jack R. Thornell (Associated Press)
1968 News: Rocco Morabito *(Jacksonville* [Fla.] *Journal);* features: Toshio Sakai (United Press International)
1969 Spot news: Edward T. Adams (Associated Press); features: Moneta Sleet, Jr.
1970 Spot news: Steve Starr (Associated Press); features: Dallas Kinney *(Palm Beach Post)*
1971 Spot news: John Paul Filo (*Valley Daily News* and *Daily Dispatch*[Tarentum and New Kensington, Pa.]); features: Jack Dykinga *(Chicago Sun-Times)*
1972 Spot news: Horst Faas and Michel Laurent (Associated Press); features: Dave Kennerly (United Press International)
1973 Spot news: Huynh Cong Ut *(Associated Press);* features: Brian Lanker *(Topeka Capital-Journal)*
1974 Spot news: Anthony K. Roberts (Associated Press); features: Slava Veder (Associated Press)
1975 Spot news: Gerald H. Gay *(Seattle Times);* features: Matthew Lewis *(Washington Post)*
1976 Spot news: Stanley J. Forman *(Boston Herald-American);* features: photographic staff of *Louisville Courier-Journal* and *Times*
1977 Spot news: Neal Ulevich (Associated Press) and Stanley J. Forman *(Boston Herald-American);* features: Robin Hood *(Chattanooga News-Free Press)*
1978 Spot news: John Blair, freelance, Evansville, Ind.; features: J. Ross Baughman (Associated Press)
1979 Spot news: Thomas J. Kelly, 3rd *(Pottstown* [Pa.] *Mercury);* features: photographic staff of *Boston Herald-American*
1980 Features: Erwin H. Hagler *(Dallas Times Herald)*
1981 Spot news: Larry C. Price *(Fort Worth Star-Telegram);* features: Taro M. Yamasaki *(Detroit Free Press)*
1982 Spot news: Ron Edmonds (Associated Press); features: John H. White *(Chicago Sun-Times)*
1983 Spot news: Bill Foley (Associated Press); features: James B. Dickman *(Dallas Times Herald)*
1984 Spot news: Stan Grossfeld *(Boston Globe);* features: Anthony Suau *(Denver Post)*
1985 Spot news: photographic staff of *Register,* Santa Ana, Calif.; features: Stan Grossfeld *(Boston Globe)*
1986 Spot news: Michel duCille and Carol Guzy *(Miami Herald);* features: Tom Gralish *(Philadelphia Inquirer)*
1987 Spot news: Kim Komenich *(San Francisco Examiner);* features: David Peterson *(Des Moines Register)*
1988 Spot news: Scott Shaw *(Odessa* [Texas] *American);* features: Michel duCille *(Miami Herald)*
1989 Spot news: Ron Olshwanger *(St. Louis Post-Dispatch);* features: Manny Crisostomo *(Detroit Free Press)*

1990 Spot news: *Oakland Tribune;* features: David C. Turnley *(Detroit Free Press)*
1991 Spot news: Greg Marinovich (Associated Press); features: William Snyder *(Dallas Morning News)*
1992 Spot news: Associated Press staff; features: John Kaplan *(Herald* [Monterey, Calif.] and *Pittsburgh Post-Gazette)*
1993 Spot news: William Snyder and Ken Geiger *(Dallas Morning News)*; features: Associated Press
1994 Spot news: Paul Watson *(Toronto Star);* features: Kevin Carter, freelancer for *New York Times*
1995 Spot news: Carol Guzy *(Washington Post);* features: Associated Press Staff

NATIONAL TELEGRAPHIC REPORTING

1942 Louis Stark *(New York Times)*
1944 Dewey L. Fleming *(Baltimore Sun)*
1945 James Reston *(New York Times)*
1946 Edward A. Harris *(St. Louis Post-Dispatch)*
1947 Edward T. Folliard *(Washington Post)*

NATIONAL REPORTING

1948 Bert Andrews *(New York Herald Tribune);* Nat S. Finney *(Minneapolis Tribune)*
1949 C. P. Trussell *(New York Times)*
1950 Edwin O. Guthman *(Seattle Times)*
1952 Anthony Leviero *(New York Times)*
1953 Don Whitehead (Associated Press)
1954 Richard Wilson (Cowles Newspapers)
1955 Anthony Lewis *(Washington Daily News)*
1956 Charles L. Bartlett *(Chattanooga Times)*
1957 James Reston *(New York Times)*
1958 Relman Morin (Associated Press) and Clark Mollenhoff *(Des Moines Register & Tribune)*
1959 Howard Van Smith *(Miami News)*
1960 Vance Trimble (Scripps-Howard Newspaper Alliance)
1961 Edward R. Cony *(Wall Street Journal)*
1962 Nathan G. Caldwell and Gene S. Graham *(Nashville Tennessean)*
1963 Anthony Lewis *(New York Times)*
1964 Merriman Smith (United Press International)
1965 Louis M. Kohlmeier *(Wall Street Journal)*
1966 Haynes Johnson *(Washington Evening Star)*
1967 Stanley Penn and Monroe Karmin *(Wall Street Journal)*
1968 Howard James *(Christian Science Monitor);* Nathan K. (Nick) Kotz *(Des Moines Register* and *Minneapolis Tribune)*
1969 Robert Cahn *(Christian Science Monitor)*
1970 William J. Eaton *(Chicago Daily News)*
1971 Lucinda Franks and Thomas Powers (United Press International)
1972 Jack Anderson *(United Feature Syndicate)*
1973 Robert Boyd and Clark Hoyt *(Knight Newspapers)*
1974 Jack White *(Providence* [R.I.] *Journal-Bulletin);* and James R. Polk *(Washington Star-News)*
1975 Donald L. Barlett and James B. Steele *(Philadelphia Inquirer)*
1976 James Risser *(Des Moines Register)*
1977 Walter Mears (Associated Press)
1978 Gaylord D. Shaw *(Los Angeles Times)*
1979 James Risser *(Des Moines Register)*
1980 Bette Swenson Orsini and Charles Stafford *(St. Petersburg Times)*
1981 John M. Crewdson *(New York Times)*
1982 Rick Atkinson *(Kansas City* [Mo.] *Times)*
1983 *Boston Globe*
1984 John N. Wilford *(New York Times)*
1985 Thomas J. Knudson *(Des Moines Register)*
1986 Craig Flournoy and George Rodrigue *(Dallas Morning News)* and Arthur Howe *(Philadelphia Inquirer)*
1987 *Miami Herald,* staff; *New York Times,* staff
1988 Tim Weiner *(Philadelphia Inquirer)*
1989 Donald L. Barlett and James B. Steele *(Philadelphia Inquirer)*
1990 Ross Anderson, Bill Dietrich, Mary Ann Gwinn, and Eric Nalder *(Seattle Times)*
1991 Marjie Lundstrom and Rochelle Sharpe (Gannett News Service)
1992 Jeff Taylor and Mike McGraw *(Kansas City Star)*
1993 David Maranniss *(Washington Post)*
1994 Eileen Welsome *(Albuquerque* [N.M.] *Tribune)*
1995 Tony Horwitz *(Wall Street Journal)*

INTERNATIONAL TELEGRAPHIC REPORTING

1942 Laurence Edmund Allen (Associated Press)
1943 Ira Wolfert (North American Newspaper Alliance, Inc.)
1944 Daniel De Luce (Associated Press)
1945 Mark S. Watson *(Baltimore Sun)*
1946 Homer W. Bigart *(New York Herald Tribune)*
1947 Eddy Gilmore (Associated Press)

INTERNATIONAL REPORTING

1948 Paul W. Ward *(Baltimore Sun)*
1949 Price Day *(Baltimore Sun)*
1950 Edmund Stevens *(Christian Science Monitor)*
1951 Keyes Beech and Fred Sparks *(Chicago Daily News);* Homer Bigart and Marguerite Higgins *(New York Herald Tribune);* Relman Morin and Don Whitehead (Associated Press)
1952 John M. Hightower (Associated Press)
1953 Austin C. Wehrwein *(Milwaukee Journal)*
1954 Jim G. Lucas (Scripps-Howard Newspapers)
1955 Harrison E. Salisbury *(New York Times)*
1956 William Randolph Hearst, Jr. and Frank Conniff (Hearst Newspapers) and Kingsbury Smith (INS)
1957 Russell Jones (United Press)
1958 *New York Times*
1959 Joseph Martin and Philip Santora *(New York Daily News)*
1960 A. M. Rosenthal *(New York Times)*
1961 Lynn Heinzerling (Associated Press)
1962 Walter Lippmann (New York Herald Tribune Syndicate)
1963 Hal Hendrix *(Miami News)*
1964 Malcolm W. Browne (Associated Press) and David Halberstam *(New York Times)*
1965 J. A. Livingston *(Philadelphia Bulletin)*
1966 Peter Arnett (Associated Press)
1967 R. John Hughes *(Christian Science Monitor)*
1968 Alfred Friendly *(Washington Post)*
1969 William Tuohy *(Los Angeles Times)*
1970 Seymour M. Hersh (Dispatch News Service)
1971 Jimmie Lee Hoagland *(Washington Post)*
1972 Peter R. Kann *(Wall Street Journal)*
1973 Max Frankel *(New York Times)*
1974 Hedrick Smith *(New York Times)*
1975 William Mullen and Ovie Carter *(Chicago Tribune)*
1976 Sydney H. Schanberg *(New York Times)*
1978 Henry Kamm *(New York Times)*
1979 Richard Ben Cramer *(Philadelphia Inquirer)*
1980 Joel Brinkley and Jay Mather *(Louisville Courier-Journal)*
1981 Shirley Christian *(Miami Herald)*
1982 John Darnton *(New York Times)*
1983 Thomas L. Friedman *(New York Times)*
1984 Karen E. House *(Wall Street Journal)*
1985 Josh Friedman, Dennis Bell, and Ozier Muhammad *(Newsday)*
1986 Lewis M. Simons, Pete Carey, and Katherine Ellison *(San Jose Mercury News)*
1987 Michael Parks *(Los Angeles Times)*
1988 Thomas L. Friedman *(New York Times)*
1989 Bill Keller *(New York Times);* Glenn Frankel *(Washington Post)*
1990 Nicholas D. Kristof and Sheryl WuDunn *(New York Times)*

1991 Caryle Murphy *(Washington Post)* and Serge Schmemann *(New York Times)*
1992 Patrick J. Sloyan *(Newsday)*
1993 John F. Burns *(New York Times)* and Roy Gutman *(Newsday)*
1994 *Dallas Morning News,* team
1995 Mark Fritz (Associated Press)

REPORTING

1917 Herbert B. Swope *(New York World)*
1918 Harold A. Littledale *(New York Evening Post)*
1920 John J. Leary, Jr. *(New York World)*
1921 Louis Seibold *(New York World)*
1922 Kirke L. Simpson (Associated Press)
1923 Alva Johnston *(New York Times)*
1924 Magner White *(San Diego Sun)*
1925 James W. Mulroy and Alvin H. Goldstein *(Chicago Daily News)*
1926 William Burke Miller *(Louisville Courier-Journal)*
1927 John T. Rogers *(St. Louis Post-Dispatch)*
1929 Paul Y. Anderson *(St. Louis Post-Dispatch)*
1930 Russell D. Owen *(New York Times);* special award: W. O. Dapping *(Auburn* [N.Y.] *Citizen)*
1931 A. B. MacDonald *(Kansas City* [Mo.] *Star)*
1932 W. C. Richards, D. D. Martin, J. S. Pooler, F. D. Webb, J. N. W. Sloan (all of *Detroit Free Press)*
1933 Francis A. Jamieson (Associated Press)
1934 Royce Brier *(San Francisco Chronicle)*
1935 William H. Taylor *(New York Herald Tribune)*
1936 Lauren D. Lyman *(New York Times)*
1937 John J. O'Neill *(New York Herald Tribune);* William Leonard Laurence *(New York Times);* Howard W. Blakeslee (Associated Press); Gobind Behari Lal (Universal Service); David Dietz (Scripps-Howard Newspapers)
1938 Raymond Sprigle *(Pittsburg Post-Gazette)*
1939 Thomas L. Stokes *(New York World-Telegram)*
1940 S. Burton Heath *(New York World-Telegram)*
1941 Westbrook Pegler *(New York World-Telegram)*
1942 Stanton Delaplane *(San Francisco Chronicle)*
1943 George Weller *(Chicago Daily News)*
1944 Paul Schoenstein and associates *(New York Journal-American)*
1945 Jack S. McDowell *(San Francisco Call-Bulletin)*
1946 William Leonard Laurence *(New York Times)*
1947 Frederick Woltman *(New York World-Telegram)*
1948 George E. Goodwin *(Atlanta Journal)*
1949 Malcolm Johnson *(New York Sun)*
1950 Meyer Berger *(New York Times)*
1951 Edward S. Montgomery *(San Francisco Examiner)*
1952 George de Carvalho *(San Francisco Chronicle)*
1953 Editorial staff *(Providence Journal and Evening Bulletin);*[1] Edward J. Mowery *(New York World-Telegram and Sun)*[2]
1954 *Vicksburg* (Miss.) *Sunday Post-Herald;*[1] Alvin Scott McCoy *(Kansas City* [Mo.] *Star)*[2]
1955 Mrs. Caro Brown *(Alice* [Tex.] *Daily Echo);*[1] Roland Kenneth Towery *(Cuero* [Tex.] *Record)*[2]
1956 Lee Hills *(Detroit Free Press);*[1] Arthur Daley *(New York Times)*[2]
1957 *Salt Lake Tribune;*[1] Wallace Turner and William Lambert *(Portland Oregonian)*[2]
1958 *Fargo* [N.D.] *Forum;*[1] George Beveridge *(Washington* [D.C.] *Evening Star)*[2]
1959 Mary Lou Werner *(Washington* [D.C.] *Evening Star);*[1] John Harold Brislin *(Scranton* [Pa.] *Tribune & Scrantonian)*[2]
1960 Jack Nelson *(Atlanta Constitution);*[1] Miriam Ottenberg *(Washington Evening Star)*[2]
1961 Sanche de Gramont *(New York Herald Tribune);*[1] Edgar May *(Buffalo Evening News)*[2]
1962 Robert D. Mullins *(Deseret News,* Salt Lake City);[1] George Bliss *(Chicago Tribune)*[2]

1963 Sylvan Fox, Anthony Shannon, and William Longgood *(New York World-Telegram and Sun);*[1] Oscar Griffin, Jr. (former editor of *Pecos* [Tex.] *Independent and Enterprise,* now on staff of *Houston Chronicle)*[2]

1. Reporting under pressure of edition deadlines. 2. Reporting not under pressure of edition deadlines.

GENERAL LOCAL REPORTING

1964 Norman C. Miller *(Wall Street Journal)*
1965 Melvin H. Ruder *(Hungry Horse News,* Columbia Falls, Mont.)
1966 Staff of *Los Angeles Times*
1967 Robert V. Cox *(Chambersburg* [Pa.] *Public Opinion)*
1968 Staff of *Detroit Free Press*
1969 John Fetterman *(Louisville Times* and *Courier-Journal)*
1970 Thomas Fitzpatrick *(Chicago Sun-Times)*
1971 Staff of *Akron* (Ohio) *Beacon*
1972 Richard Cooper and John Machacek *(Rochester* [N.Y.] *Times-Union)*
1973 *Chicago Tribune*
1974 Arthur M. Petacque and Hugh F. Hough *(Chicago Sun-Times)*
1975 *Xenia* (Ohio) *Daily Gazette*
1976 Gene Miller *(Miami Herald)*
1977 Margo Huston *(Milwaukee Journal)*
1978 Richard Whitt *(Louisville Courier-Journal)*
1979 Staff of *San Diego* (Calif.) *Evening Tribune*
1980 Staff of *Philadelphia Inquirer*
1981 *Longview* (Wash.) *Daily News*
1982 *Kansas City* (Mo.) *Star* and *Kansas City* (Mo.) *Times*
1983 *Fort Wayne* (Ind.) *News-Sentinel*
1984 *Newsday*

GENERAL NEWS REPORTING

1985 Thomas Turcol *(Virginian-Pilot and Ledger-Star)*
1986 Edna Buchanan *(Miami Herald)*
1987 *Akron Beacon Journal,* staff
1988 *Alabama Journal* (Montgomery), staff, *Lawrence* (Mass.) *Eagle-Tribune,* staff
1989 *Louisville Courier-Journal* staff
1990 *San Jose* (Calif.) *Mercury News*

SPOT NEWS REPORTING

1991 *Miami Herald* staff
1992 *New York Newsday* staff
1993 *Los Angeles Times* staff
1994 *New York Times* staff
1995 *Los Angeles Times* staff

SPECIAL LOCAL REPORTING

1964 James V. Magee, Albert V. Gaudiosi, and Frederick A. Meyer *(Philadelphia Bulletin)*
1965 Gene Goltz *(Houston Post)*
1966 John A. Frasca *(Tampa Tribune)*
1967 Gene Miller *(Miami Herald)*
1968 J. Anthony Lukas *(New York Times)*
1969 Albert L. Delugach and Denny Walsh *(St. Louis Globe-Democrat)*
1970 Harold Eugene Martin *(Montgomery Advertiser)*
1971 William Hugh Jones *(Chicago Tribune)*
1972 Timothy Leland, Gerard N. O'Neill, Stephen A. Kurkjian, and Ann DeSantis *(Boston Globe)*
1973 Sun Newspapers of Omaha, Neb.
1974 William Sherman *(New York Daily News)*
1975 *Indianapolis Star*
1976 *Chicago Tribune*
1977 Acel Moore and Wendell Rawls, Jr. *(Philadelphia Inquirer)*
1978 Anthony R. Dolan *(Stamford* [Conn.] *Advocate)*
1979 Gilbert M. Gaul and Elliot G. Jaspin *(Pottsville* [Pa.] *Republican)*
1980 Nils J. Bruzelius, Alexander B. Hawes, Jr., Stephen A. Kurkjian, Robert M. Porterfield, and Joan Vennochi *(Boston Globe)*

1981 Clark Hallas and Robert B. Lowe (*Arizona Daily Star,* Tucson)
1982 Paul Henderson (*Seattle Times*)
1983 Loretta Tofani (*Washington Post*)
1984 Boston Globe

INVESTIGATIVE REPORTING

1985 Lucy Morgan and Jack Reed (*St. Petersburg* [Fla.] *Times*) and William K. Marimow (*Philadelphia Inquirer*)
1986 Jeffrey A. Marx and Michael M. York (*Lexington*[Ky.] *Herald Leader*)
1987 Daniel R. Biddle, H.G. Bissinger, and Fredric N. Tulsky (*Philadelphia Inquirer*)
1988 Dean Baquet, William C. Gaines, and Ann Marie Lipinski (*Chicago Tribune*)
1989 Bill Dedman (*Atlanta Journal and Constitution*)
1990 Lou Kilzer and Chris Ison (*Minneapolis-St. Paul Star Tribune*)
1991 Joseph T. Hallinan and Susan M. Headden (*Indianapolis Star*)
1992 Lorraine Adams and Dan Malone (*Dallas Morning News*)
1993 Jeff Brazil and Steve Berry (*Orlando* [Fla.] *Sentinel*)
1994 Providence (R.I.) *Journal-Bulletin* staff
1995 Stephanie Saul and Brian Donovan (*Newsday*)

FEATURE WRITING

1979 Jon D. Franklin (*Baltimore Evening Sun*)
1980 Madeleine Blais (*Miami Herald*)
1981 Teresa Carpenter (*Village Voice,* New York)
1982 Saul Pett (Associated Press)
1983 Nan Robertson (*New York Times*)
1984 Peter M. Rinearson (*Seattle Times*)
1985 Alice Steinbach (*Baltimore Sun*)
1986 John Camp (*St. Paul Pioneer Press and Dispatch*)
1987 Steve Twomey (*Philadelphia Inquirer*)
1988 Jacqui Banaszynski (*St. Paul Pioneer Press Dispatch*)
1989 David Zucchino (*Philadelphia Inquirer*)
1990 Dave Curtin (*Colorado Springs Gazette Telegraph*)
1991 Sheryl James, (*St. Petersburg* [Fla.] *Times*)
1992 Howell Raines (*New York Times*)
1993 George Lardner, Jr. (*Washington Post*)
1994 Isabel Wilkerson (*New York Times*)
1995 Ron Suskind (*Wall Street Journal*)

COMMENTARY

1970 Marquis W. Childs (*St. Louis Post-Dispatch*)
1971 William A. Caldwell (*Record* [Hackensack, N.J.])
1972 Mike Royko (*Chicago Daily News*)
1973 David S. Broder (*Washington Post*)
1974 Edwin A. Roberts, Jr. (*National Observer*)
1975 Mary McGrory (*Washington Star*)
1976 Walter W. (Red) Smith (*New York Times*)
1977 George F. Will (*Washington Post* Writers Group)
1978 William Safire (*New York Times*)
1979 Russell Baker (*New York Times*)
1980 Ellen H. Goodman (*Boston Globe*)
1981 Dave Anderson (*New York Times*)
1982 Art Buchwald (*Los Angeles Times* Syndicate)
1983 Claude Sitton (*Raleigh* [N.C.] *News & Observer*)
1984 Vermont Royster (*Wall Street Journal*)
1985 Murray Kempton (*Newsday*)
1986 Jimmy Breslin (*New York Daily News*)
1987 Charles Krauthammer (*Washington Post* Writers Group)
1988 Dave Barry (*Miami Herald*)
1989 Clarence Page (*Chicago Tribune*)
1990 Jim Murray (*Los Angeles Times*)
1991 Jim Hoagland (*Washington Post*)
1992 Anna Quindlen (*New York Times*)
1993 Liz Balmaseda (*Mami Herald*)
1994 William Raspberry (*Washington Post*)
1995 Jim Dwyer (*New York Newsday*)

CRITICISM

1970 Ada Louise Huxtable (*New York Times*)
1971 Harold C. Schonberg (*New York Times*)
1972 Frank Peters, Jr. (*St. Louis Post-Dispatch*)
1973 Ronald Powers (*Chicago Sun-Times*)
1974 Emily Genauer (Newsday Syndicate)
1975 Roger Ebert (*Chicago Sun-Times*)
1976 Alan M. Kriegsman (*Washington Post*)
1977 William McPherson (*Washington Post*)
1978 Walter Kerr (*New York Times*)
1979 Paul Gapp (*Chicago Tribune*)
1980 William A. Henry, 3rd (*Boston Globe*)
1981 Jonathan Yardley (*Washington Star*)
1982 Martin Bernheimer (*Los Angeles Times*)
1983 Manuela Hoelterhoff (*Wall Street Journal*)
1984 Paul Goldberger (*New York Times*)
1985 Howard Rosenberg (*Los Angeles Times*)
1986 Donal Henahan (*New York Times*)
1987 Richard Eder (*Los Angeles Times*)
1988 Tom Shales (*Washington Post*)
1989 Michael Skube (*News and Observer,* Raleigh, N.C.)
1990 Allan Temko (*San Francisco Chronicle*)
1991 David Shaw (*Los Angeles Times*)
1993 Michael Dirda (*Washington Post*)
1994 Lloyd Schwartz (*The Boston Phoenix*)
1995 Margo Jefferson (*New York Times*)

EXPLANATORY JOURNALISM

1985 Jon Franklin (*Baltimore Evening Sun*)
1986 New York Times
1987 Jeff Lyon and Peter Gorner (*Chicago Tribune*)
1988 Daniel Hertzberg and James B. Stewart (*Wall Street Journal*)
1989 David Hanners, William Snyder, and Karen Blessen (*Dallas Morning News*)
1990 David A. Vise and Coll (*Washington Post*)
1991 Susan C. Faludi (*Wall Street Journal*)
1992 Robert S. Capers and Eric Lipton (*Hartford Courant*)
1993 Mike Toner (*Atlanta Journal–Constitution*)
1994 Ronald Kotulak (*Chicago Tribune*)
1995 Leon Dash and Lucian Perkins (*Washington Post*)

SPECIALIZED REPORTING

1985 Randall Savage and Jackie Crosby (*Macon* [Ga.] *Telegraph and News*)
1986 Andrew Schneider and Mary Pat Flaherty (*Pittsburgh Press*)
1987 Alex S. Jones (*New York Times*)
1988 Walt Bogdanich (*Wall Street Journal*)
1989 Edward Humes (*Orange County Register*)
1990 Tamar Stieber (*Albuquerque* (N.M.) *Journal*)

BEAT REPORTING

1991 Natalie Angier (*New York Times*)
1992 Deborah Blum (*Sacramento Bee*)
1993 Paul Ingrassia and Joseph B. White, (*Wall Street Journal*)
1994 Eric Freedman and Jim Mitzelfeld (*Detroit News*)
1995 David M. Shribman (*Boston Globe*)

SPECIAL CITATIONS

1938 *Edmonton* (Alberta) *Journal,* special bronze plaque for editorial leadership in defense of freedom of press in Province of Alberta.
1941 *New York Times* for the public educational value of its foreign news report.
1944 Byron Price, Director of the Office of Censorship, for the creation and administration of the newspaper and radio codes. Mrs. William Allen White, for her husband's interest and services during the past seven years as a member of the Advisory Board of the Graduate School of Journalism, Columbia University. Richard Rodgers and Oscar Hammerstein II for their musical *Oklahoma!*

1945 The cartographers of the American press for their war maps.

1947 (Pulitzer centennial year.) Columbia University and the Graduate School of Journalism for their efforts to maintain and advance the high standards governing the Pulitzer Prize awards. The *St. Louis Post-Dispatch* for its unswerving adherence to the public and professional ideals of its founder and its leadership in American journalism.

1948 Dr. Frank D. Fackenthal for his interest and service.

1951 Cyrus L. Sulzberger *(New York Times)* for his exclusive interview with Archbishop Stepinac in a Yugoslav prison.

1952 *Kansas City Star* for coverage of 1951 floods; Max Kase *(New York Journal-American)* for exposures of bribery in college basketball.

1953 *New York Times* for its 17-year publication of "News of the Week in Review"; and Lester Markel, its founder.

1957 Kenneth Roberts for his historical novels.

1958 Walter Lippmann *(New York Herald Tribune)* for his "wisdom, perception and high sense of responsibility" in his commentary on national and international affairs.

1960 Garrett Mattingly, for *The Armada.*

1961 *American Heritage Picture History of the Civil War,* as distinguished example of American book publishing.

1964 Gannett Newspapers, Rochester, N.Y.

1973 James Thomas Flexner for his biography *George Washington.*

1974 Roger Sessions for his "life's work in music."

1976 John Hohenberg for "services for 22 years as administrator of the Pulitzer Prizes"; Scott Joplin for his contributions to American music.

1977 Alex Haley for his novel, *Roots.*

1978 E.B. White of *New Yorker* magazine and Richard L. Strout of *Christian Science Monitor.*

1982 Milton Babbitt, "for his life's work as a distinguished and seminal American composer."

1984 Theodor Seuss Geisel (Dr. Seuss) for "books full of playful rhymes, nonsense words and strange illustrations."

1985 William H. Schuman for "more than a half century of contribution to American music as a composer and educational leader."

1987 Joseph Pulitzer Jr., "for extraordinary services to American journalism and letters during his 31 years as chairman of the Pulitzer Prize Board and for his accomplishments as an editor and publisher."

Pulitzer Prizes in Letters

FICTION[1]

1918 *His Family.* Ernest Poole
1919 *The Magnificent Ambersons.* Booth Tarkington
1921 *The Age of Innocence.* Edith Wharton
1922 *Alice Adams.* Booth Tarkington
1923 *One of Ours.* Willa Cather
1924 *The Able McLaughlins.* Margaret Wilson
1925 *So Big.* Edna Ferber
1926 *Arrowsmith.* Sinclair Lewis
1927 *Early Autumn.* Louis Bromfield
1928 *The Bridge of San Luis Rey.* Thornton Wilder
1929 *Scarlet Sister Mary.* Julia Peterkin
1930 *Laughing Boy.* Oliver La Farge
1931 *Years of Grace.* Margaret Ayer Barnes
1932 *The Good Earth.* Pearl S. Buck
1933 *The Store.* T. S. Stribling
1934 *Lamb in His Bosom.* Caroline Miller
1935 *Now in November.* Josephine Winslow Johnson
1936 *Honey in the Horn.* Harold L. Davis
1937 *Gone With the Wind.* Margaret Mitchell
1938 *The Late George Apley.* John Phillips Marquand
1939 *The Yearling.* Marjorie Kinnan Rawlings
1940 *The Grapes of Wrath.* John Steinbeck
1942 *In This Our Life.* Ellen Glasgow
1943 *Dragon's Teeth.* Upton Sinclair
1944 *Journey in the Dark.* Martin Flavin
1945 *A Bell for Adano.* John Hersey
1947 *All the King's Men.* Robert Penn Warren
1948 *Tales of the South Pacific.* James A. Michener
1949 *Guard of Honor.* James Gould Cozzens
1950 *The Way West.* A. B. Guthrie, Jr.
1951 *The Town.* Conrad Richter
1952 *The Caine Mutiny.* Herman Wouk
1953 *The Old Man and the Sea.* Ernest Hemingway
1955 *A Fable.* William Faulkner
1956 *Andersonville.* MacKinlay Kantor
1958 *A Death in the Family.* James Agee
1959 *The Travels of Jaimie McPheeters.* Robert Lewis Taylor
1960 *Advise and Consent.* Allen Drury
1961 *To Kill a Mockingbird.* Harper Lee
1962 *The Edge of Sadness.* Edwin O'Connor
1963 *The Reivers.* William Faulkner
1965 *The Keepers of the House.* Shirley Ann Grau
1966 *Collected Stories of Katherine Anne Porter.* Katherine Anne Porter

1. Before 1948, award was for novels only.

1967 *The Fixer.* Bernard Malamud
1968 *The Confessions of Nat Turner.* William Styron
1969 *House Made of Dawn.* N. Scott Momaday
1970 *Collected Stories.* Jean Stafford
1972 *Angle of Repose.* Wallace Stegner
1973 *The Optimist's Daughter.* Eudora Welty
1975 *The Killer Angels.* Michael Shaara
1976 *Humboldt's Gift.* Saul Bellow
1978 *Elbow Room.* James Alan McPherson
1979 *The Stories of John Cheever.* John Cheever
1980 *The Executioner's Song.* Norman Mailer
1981 *A Confederacy of Dunces.* John Kennedy Toole
1982 *Rabbit Is Rich.* John Updike
1983 *The Color Purple.* Alice Walker
1984 *Ironweed.* William Kennedy
1985 *Foreign Affairs,* Alison Lurie
1986 *Lonesome Dove,* Larry McMurtry
1987 *A Summons to Memphis,* Peter Taylor
1988 *Beloved,* Toni Morrison
1989 *Breathing Lessons,* Anne Tyler
1990 *The Mambo Kings Play Songs of Love,* Oscar Hijeulos
1991 *Rabbit at Rest,* John Updike
1992 *A Thousand Acres,* Jane Smiley
1993 *A Good Scent From a Strange Mountain,* Robert Olen Butler
1994 *The Shipping News,* E. Annie Proulx
1995 *The Stone Diaries,* Carol Shields

DRAMA

1918 *Why Marry?* Jesse Lynch Williams
1920 *Beyond the Horizon.* Eugene O'Neill
1921 *Miss Lulu Bett.* Zona Gale
1922 *Anna Christie.* Eugene O'Neill
1923 *Icebound.* Owen Davis
1924 *Hell-Bent Fer Heaven.* Hatcher Hughes
1925 *They Knew What They Wanted.* Sidney Howard
1926 *Craig's Wife.* George Kelly
1927 *In Abraham's Bosom.* Paul Green
1928 *Strange Interlude.* Eugene O'Neill
1929 *Street Scene.* Elmer L. Rice
1930 *The Green Pastures.* Marc Connelly
1931 *Alison's House.* Susan Glaspell
1932 *Of Thee I Sing.* George S. Kaufman, Morrie Ryskind, and Ira Gershwin
1933 *Both Your Houses.* Maxwell Anderson
1934 *Men in White.* Sidney Kingsley
1935 *The Old Maid.* Zöe Akins
1936 *Idiot's Delight.* Robert E. Sherwood

1937 *You Can't Take It With You.* Moss Hart and George S. Kaufman
1938 *Our Town.* Thornton Wilder
1939 *Abe Lincoln in Illinois.* Robert E. Sherwood
1940 *The Time of Your Life.* William Saroyan
1941 *There Shall Be No Night.* Robert E. Sherwood
1943 *The Skin of Our Teeth.* Thornton Wilder
1945 *Harvey.* Mary Chase
1946 *State of the Union.* Russel Crouse and Howard Lindsay
1948 *A Streetcar Named Desire.* Tennessee Williams
1949 *Death of a Salesman.* Arthur Miller
1950 *South Pacific.* Richard Rodgers, Oscar Hammerstein II, and Joshua Logan
1952 *The Shrike.* Joseph Kramm
1953 *Picnic.* William Inge
1954 *The Teahouse of the August Moon.* John Patrick
1955 *Cat on a Hot Tin Roof.* Tennessee Williams
1956 *The Diary of Anne Frank.* Frances Goodrich and Albert Hackett
1957 *Long Day's Journey Into Night.* Eugene O'Neill
1958 *Look Homeward, Angel.* Ketti Frings
1959 *J.B.* Archibald MacLeish
1960 *Fiorello!* George Abbott, Jerome Weidman, Jerry Bock, and Sheldon Harnick
1961 *All the Way Home.* Tad Mosel
1962 *How to Succeed in Business Without Really Trying.* Frank Loesser and Abe Burrows
1965 *The Subject Was Roses.* Frank D. Gilroy
1967 *A Delicate Balance.* Edward Albee
1969 *The Great White Hope.* Howard Sackler
1970 *No Place to Be Somebody.* Charles Gordone
1971 *The Effect of Gamma Rays on Man-in-the-Moon Marigolds.* Paul Zindel
1973 *That Championship Season.* Jason Miller
1975 *Seascape.* Edward Albee
1976 *A Chorus Line.* Conceived by Michael Bennett
1977 *The Shadow Box.* Michael Cristofer
1978 *The Gin Game.* Donald L. Coburn
1979 *Buried Child.* Sam Shepard
1980 *Talley's Folly.* Lanford Wilson
1981 *Crimes of the Heart.* Beth Henley
1982 *A Soldier's Play.* Charles Fuller
1983 *'Night, Mother.* Marsha Norman
1984 *Glengarry Glen Ross.* David Mamet
1985 *Sunday in the Park with George.* Stephen Sondheim and James Lapine
1987 *Fences.* August Wilson
1988 *Driving Miss Daisy.* Alfred Uhry
1989 *The Heidi Chronicles,* Wendy Wasserstein
1990 *The Piano Lesson,* August Wilson
1991 *Lost in Yonkers,* Neil Simon
1992 *The Kentucky Cycle,* Robert Schenkkan
1993 *Angels in America: Millennium Approaches,* Tony Kushner
1994 *Three Tall Women,* Edward Albee
1995 *The Young Man from Atlanta,* Horton Foote

HISTORY OF UNITED STATES

1917 *With Americans of Past and Present Days.* J. J. Jusserand, Ambassador of France to United States
1918 *A History of the Civil War, 1861–1865.* James Ford Rhodes
1920 *The War With Mexico.* Justin H. Smith
1921 *The Victory at Sea.* William Sowden Sims in collaboration with Burton J. Hendrick
1922 *The Founding of New England.* James Truslow Adams
1923 *The Supreme Court in United States History.* Charles Warren
1924 *The American Revolution—A Constitutional Interpretation.* Charles Howard McIlwain
1925 *A History of the American Frontier.* Frederic L. Paxson

1926 *The History of the United States.* Edward Channing
1927 *Pinckney's Treaty.* Samuel Flagg Bemis
1928 *Main Currents in American Thought.* Vernon Louis Parrington
1929 *The Organization and Administration of the Union Army, 1861–1865.* Fred Albert Shannon
1930 *The War of Independence.* Claude H. Van Tyne
1931 *The Coming of the War: 1914.* Bernadotte E. Schmitt
1932 *My Experiences in the World War.* John J. Pershing
1933 *The Significance of Sections in American History.* Frederick J. Turner
1934 *The People's Choice.* Herbert Agar
1935 *The Colonial Period of American History.* Charles McLean Andrews
1936 *The Constitutional History of the United States.* Andrew C. McLaughlin
1937 *The Flowering of New England.* Van Wyck Brooks
1938 *The Road to Reunion, 1865–1900.* Paul Herman Buck
1939 *A History of American Magazines.* Frank Luther Mott
1940 *Abraham Lincoln: The War Years.* Carl Sandburg
1941 *The Atlantic Migration, 1607–1860.* Marcus Lee Hansen
1942 *Reveille in Washington.* Margaret Leech
1943 *Paul Revere and the World He Lived In.* Esther Forbes
1944 *The Growth of American Thought.* Merle Curti
1945 *Unfinished Business.* Stephen Bonsal
1946 *The Age of Jackson.* Arthur M. Schlesinger, Jr.
1947 *Scientists Against Time.* James Phinney Baxter, 3rd
1948 *Across the Wide Missouri.* Bernard DeVoto
1949 *The Disruption of American Democracy.* Roy Franklin Nichols
1950 *Art and Life in America.* Oliver W. Larkin
1951 *The Old Northwest, Pioneer Period 1815–1840.* R. Carlyle Buley
1952 *The Uprooted.* Oscar Handlin
1953 *The Era of Good Feelings.* George Dangerfield
1954 *A Stillness at Appomattox.* Bruce Catton
1955 *Great River: The Rio Grande in North American History.* Paul Horgan
1956 *The Age of Reform.* Richard Hofstadter
1957 *Russia Leaves the War: Soviet-American Relations, 1917–1920.* George F. Kennan
1958 *Banks and Politics in America: From the Revolution to the Civil War.* Bray Hammond
1959 *The Republican Era: 1869–1901.* Leonard D. White, assisted by Jean Schneider
1960 *In the Days of McKinley.* Margaret Leech
1961 *Between War and Peace: The Potsdam Conference.* Herbert Feis
1962 *The Triumphant Empire, Thunder-Clouds Gather in the West.* Lawrence H. Gipson
1963 *Washington, Village and Capital, 1800–1878.* Constance McLaughlin Green
1964 *Puritan Village: The Formation of a New England Town.* Sumner Chilton Powell
1965 *The Greenback Era.* Irwin Unger
1966 *Life of the Mind in America.* Perry Miller
1967 *Exploration and Empire: The Explorer and Scientist in the Winning of the American West.* William H. Goetzmann
1968 *The Ideological Origins of the American Revolution.* Bernard Bailyn
1969 *Origins of the Fifth Amendment.* Leonard W. Levy
1970 *Present at the Creation: My Years in the State Department.* Dean Acheson
1971 *Roosevelt: The Soldier of Freedom.* James McGregor Burns
1972 *Neither Black Nor White. Slavery and Race Relations in Brazil and the United States.* Carl N. Degler
1973 *People of Paradox: An Inquiry Concerning the Origin of American Civilization.* Michael Kammen
1974 *The Americans: The Democratic Experience, Vol. 3.* Daniel J. Boorstin
1975 *Jefferson and His Time.* Dumas Malone

1976 *Lamy of Santa Fe.* Paul Horgan
1977 *The Impending Crisis: 1841–1861.* David M. Potter (posth)
1978 *The Invisible Hand: The Managerial Revolution in American Business.* Alfred D. Chandler, Jr.
1979 *The Dred Scott Case: Its Significance in Law and Politics.* Don E. Fehrenbacher
1980 *Been in the Storm So Long.* Leon F. Litwack
1981 *American Education: The National Experience; 1783–1876.* Lawrence A. Cremin
1982 *Mary Chestnut's Civil War.* C. Vann Woodward, editor
1983 *The Transformation of Virginia, 1740–1790.* Rhys L. Isaac
1985 *The Prophets of Regulation.* Thomas K. McCraw
1986 *. . . the Heavens and the Earth: A Political History of the Space Age.* Walter A. McDougall
1987 *Voyagers to the West: A Passage in the Peopling of America on the Eve of the Revolution.* Bernard Bailyn
1988 *The Launching of Modern American Science 1846–1876.* Robert V. Bruce
1989 *Parting the Waters,* Taylor Branch; *Battle Cry of Freedom,* James M. McPherson
1990 *In Our Image: America's Empire in the Philippines,* Stanley Karnow
1991 *A Midwife's Tale: The Life of Martha Ballard, Based on Her Diary 1785–1812,* Laurel Thatcher Ulrich
1992 *The Fate of Liberty: Abraham Lincoln and Civil Liberties,* Mark E. Neely, Jr.
1993 *The Radicalism of the American Revolution,* Gordon S. Wood
1995 *No Ordinary Time: Franklin and Eleanor Roosevelt: The Home Front in World War II,* Doris Kearns Goodwin

BIOGRAPHY OR AUTOBIOGRAPHY

1917 *Julia Ward Howe.* Laura E. Richards and Maude Howe Elliott, assisted by Florence Howe Hall
1918 *Benjamin Franklin, Self-Revealed.* William Cabell Bruce
1919 *The Education of Henry Adams.* Henry Adams
1920 *The Life of John Marshall.* Albert J. Beveridge
1921 *The Americanization of Edward Bok.* Edward Bok
1922 *A Daughter of the Middle Border.* Hamlin Garland
1923 *The Life and Letters of Walter H. Page,* Burton J. Hendrick
1924 *From Immigrant to Inventor.* Michael Idvorsky Pupin
1925 *Barrett Wendell and His Letters.* M. A. DeWolfe Howe
1926 *The Life of Sir William Osler.* Harvey Cushing
1927 *Whitman.* Emory Holloway
1928 *The American Orchestra and Theodore Thomas.* Charles Edward Russell
1929 *The Training of an American. The Earlier Life and Letters of Walter H. Page.* Burton J. Hendrick
1930 *The Raven.* Marquis James
1931 *Charles W. Eliot.* Henry James
1932 *Theodore Roosevelt.* Henry F. Pringle
1933 *Grover Cleveland.* Allan Nevins
1934 *John Hay.* Tyler Dennett
1935 *R. E. Lee.* Douglas S. Freeman
1936 *The Thought and Character of William James.* Ralph Barton Perry
1937 *Hamilton Fish.* Allan Nevins
1938 *Pedlar's Progress.* Odell Shepard; *Andrew Jackson.* Marquis James
1939 *Benjamin Franklin.* Carl Van Doren
1940 *Woodrow Wilson. Life and Letters,* Vols. VII and VIII. Ray Stannard Baker
1941 *Jonathan Edwards.* Ola E. Winslow
1942 *Crusader in Crinoline.* Forrest Wilson
1943 *Admiral of the Ocean Sea.* Samuel Eliot Morison
1944 *The American Leonardo: The Life of Samuel F. B. Morse.* Carleton Mabee
1945 *George Bancroft: Brahmin Rebel.* Russel Blaine Nye
1946 *Son of the Wilderness.* Linnie Marsh Wolfe
1947 *The Autobiography of William Allen White*

1948 *Forgotten First Citizen: John Bigelow.* Margaret Clapp
1949 *Roosevelt and Hopkins.* Robert E. Sherwood
1950 *John Quincy Adams and the Foundations of American Foreign Policy.* Samuel Flagg Bemis
1951 *John C. Calhoun: American Portrait.* Margaret Louise Coit
1952 *Charles Evans Hughes.* Merlo J. Pusey
1953 *Edmund Pendleton, 1721–1803.* David J. Mays
1954 *The Spirit of St. Louis.* Charles A. Lindbergh
1955 *The Taft Story.* William S. White
1956 *Benjamin Henry Latrobe.* Talbot F. Hamlin
1957 *Profiles in Courage.* John F. Kennedy
1958 *George Washington.* Douglas Southall Freeman (Vols. 1–6) and John Alexander Carroll and Mary Wells Ashworth (Vol. 7)
1959 *Woodrow Wilson, American Prophet.* Arthur Walworth
1960 *John Paul Jones.* Samuel Eliot Morison
1961 *Charles Sumner and the Coming of the Civil War.* David Donald
1963 *Henry James: Vol. II, The Conquest of London, 1870–1881; Vol. III, The Middle Years, 1881–1895.* Leon Edel
1964 *John Keats.* Walter Jackson Bate
1965 *Henry Adams* (3 Vols.). Ernest Samuels
1966 *A Thousand Days.* Arthur M. Schlesinger, Jr.
1967 *Mr. Clemens and Mark Twain.* Justin Kaplan
1968 *Memoirs, 1925–1950.* George F. Kennan
1969 *The Man From New York.* B. L. Reid
1970 *Huey Long.* T. Harry Williams
1971 *Robert Frost: The Years of Triumph, 1915–1938.* Lawrence Thompson
1972 *Eleanor and Franklin: The Story of Their Relationship Based on Eleanor Roosevelt's Private Papers.* Joseph P. Lash
1973 *Luce and His Empire.* W. A. Swanberg
1974 *O'Neill, Son and Artist.* Louis Sheaffer
1975 *The Power Broker: Robert Moses and the Fall of New York.* Robert A. Caro
1976 *Edith Wharton: A Biography.* Richard W. B. Lewis
1977 *A Prince of Our Disorder.* John E. Mack
1978 *Samuel Johnson.* Walter Jackson Bate
1979 *Days of Sorrow and Pain: Leo Baeck and the Berlin Jews.* Leonard Baker
1980 *The Rise of Theodore Roosevelt.* Edmund Morris
1981 *Peter the Great.* Robert K. Massie
1982 *Grant: A Biography.* William S. McFeely
1983 *Growing Up.* Russell Baker
1984 *Booker T. Washington.* Louis R. Harlan
1985 *The Life and Times of Cotton Mather,* Kenneth Silverman
1986 *Louise Bogan: A Portrait,* Elizabeth Frank
1987 *Bearing the Cross: Martin Luther King Jr. and the Southern Christian Leadership Conference,* David J. Garrow
1988 *Look Homeward: A Life of Thomas Wolfe.* David Herbert Donald
1989 *Oscar Wilde.* Richard Ellmann
1990 *Machiavelli in Hell,* Sebastian de Grazia
1991 *Jackson Pollock: An American Saga,* Steven Naifeh and Gregory White Smith
1992 *Fortunate Son: The Healing of a Vietnam Vet,* Lewis B. Puller, Jr.
1993 *Truman,* David McCullough
1994 *W.E.B. Du Bois: Biography of a Race, 1868–1919,* David Levering Lewis
1995 *Harriet Beecher Stowe: A Life,* Joan D. Hedrick

POETRY[1]

1918 *Love Songs.* Sara Teasdale
1919 *Old Road to Paradise.* Margaret Widdemer; *Corn Huskers.* Carl Sandburg

1. This prize was established in 1922. The 1918 and 1919 awards were made from gifts provided by the Poetry Society.

1922 *Collected Poems.* Edwin Arlington Robinson
1923 *The Ballad of the Harp-Weaver; A Few Figs from Thistles; eight sonnets in American Poetry, 1922, A Miscellany.* Edna St. Vincent Millay
1924 *New Hampshire: A Poem With Notes and Grace Notes.* Robert Frost
1925 *The Man Who Died Twice.* Edwin Arlington Robinson
1926 *What's O'Clock.* Amy Lowell
1927 *Fiddler's Farewell.* Leonora Speyer
1928 *Tristram.* Edwin Arlington Robinson
1929 *John Brown's Body.* Stephen Vincent Benét
1930 *Selected Poems.* Conrad Aiken
1931 *Collected Poems.* Robert Frost
1932 *The Flowering Stone.* George Dillon
1933 *Conquistador.* Archibald MacLeish
1934 *Collected Verse.* Robert Hillyer
1935 *Bright Ambush.* Audrey Wurdemann
1936 *Strange Holiness.* Robert P. T. Coffin
1937 *A Further Range.* Robert Frost
1938 *Cold Morning Sky.* Marya Zaturenska
1939 *Selected Poems.* John Gould Fletcher
1940 *Collected Poems.* Mark Van Doren
1941 *Sunderland Capture.* Leonard Bacon
1942 *The Dust Which Is God.* William Rose Benét
1943 *A Witness Tree.* Robert Frost
1944 *Western Star.* Stephen Vincent Benét
1945 *V-Letter and Other Poems.* Karl Shapiro
1947 *Lord Weary's Castle.* Robert Lowell
1948 *The Age of Anxiety.* W. H. Auden
1949 *Terror and Decorum.* Peter Viereck
1950 *Annie Allen.* Gwendolyn Brooks
1951 *Complete Poems.* Carl Sandburg
1952 *Collected Poems.* Marianne Moore
1953 *Collected Poems, 1917–1952.* Archibald MacLeish
1954 *The Waking.* Theodore Roethke
1955 *Collected Poems.* Wallace Stevens
1956 *Poems—North & South.* Elizabeth Bishop
1957 *Things of This World.* Richard Wilbur
1958 *Promises: Poems, 1954–1956.* Robert Penn Warren
1959 *Selected Poems, 1928–1958.* Stanley Kunitz
1960 *Heart's Needle.* William Snodgrass
1961 *Times Three: Selected Verse From Three Decades.* Phyllis McGinley
1962 *Poems.* Alan Dugan
1963 *Pictures From Breughel.* William Carlos Williams
1964 *At the End of the Open Road.* Louis Simpson
1965 *77 Dream Songs.* John Berryman
1966 *Selected Poems.* Richard Eberhart
1967 *Live or Die.* Anne Sexton
1968 *The Hard Hours.* Anthony Hecht
1969 *Of Being Numerous.* George Oppen
1970 *Untitled Subjects.* Richard Howard
1971 *The Carrier of Ladders.* William S. Merwin
1972 *Collected Poems.* James Wright
1973 *Up Country.* Maxine Winokur Kumin
1974 *The Dolphin.* Robert Lowell
1975 *Turtle Island.* Gary Snyder
1976 *Self-Portrait in a Convex Mirror.* John Ashbery
1977 *Divine Comedies.* James Merrill
1978 *Collected Poems.* Howard Nemerov
1979 *Now and Then: Poems, 1976–1978.* Robert Penn Warren.
1980 *Selected Poems.* Donald Rodney Justice
1981 *The Morning of the Poem.* James Schuyler
1982 *The Collected Poems.* Sylvia Plath
1983 *Selected Poems.* Galway Kinnell
1984 *American Primitive.* Mary Oliver
1985 *Yin,* Carolyn Kizer
1986 *The Flying Change,* Henry Taylor
1987 *Thomas and Beulah,* Rita Dove
1988 *Partial Accounts: New and Selected Poems.* William Meredith
1989 *New and Collected Poems.* Richard Wilbur
1990 *The World Doesn't End,* Charles Simic

1991 *Near Changes,* Mona Van Duyn
1992 *Selected Poems,* James Tate
1993 *The Wild Iris,* Louise Gluck
1994 *Neon Vernacular,* Yusef Komunyakaa
1995 *Simple Truth,* Philip Levine

GENERAL NONFICTION

1962 *The Making of the President, 1960.* Theodore H. White
1963 *The Guns of August.* Barbara W. Tuchman
1964 *Anti-Intellectualism in American Life.* Richard Hofstadter
1965 *O Strange New World.* Howard Mumford Jones
1966 *Wandering Through Winter.* Edwin Way Teale
1967 *The Problem of Slavery in Western Culture.* David Brion Davis
1968 *Rousseau and Revolution.* Will and Ariel Durant
1969 *So Human an Animal.* Rene Jules Dubos; *The Armies of the Night.* Norman Mailer
1970 *Gandhi's Truth.* Erik H. Erikson
1971 *The Rising Sun.* John Toland
1972 *Stilwell and the American Experience in China, 1911–1945.* Barbara W. Tuchman
1973 *Fire in the Lake: The Vietnamese and the Americans in Vietnam.* Frances FitzGerald; and *Children of Crisis* (Vols. 1 and 2). Robert M. Coles
1974 *The Denial of Death.* Ernest Becker
1975 *Pilgrim at Tinker Creek.* Annie Dillard
1976 *Why Survive? Being Old in America.* Robert N. Butler
1977 *Beautiful Swimmers: Watermen, Crabs and the Chesapeake Bay.* William W. Warner
1978 *The Dragons of Eden.* Carl Sagan
1979 *On Human Nature.* Edward O. Wilson
1980 *Gödel, Escher, Bach: An Eternal Golden Braid.* Douglas R. Hofstadter
1981 *Fin-de-Siecle Vienna: Politics and Culture.* Carl E. Schorske
1982 *The Soul of a New Machine.* Tracy Kidder
1983 *Is There No Place on Earth for Me?* Susan Sheehan
1984 *Social Transformation of American Medicine.* Paul Starr
1985 *The Good War: An Oral History of World War II,* Studs Terkel
1986 *Move Your Shadow: South Africa, Black and White,* Joseph Lelyveld; *Common Ground: A Turbulent Decade in the Lives of Three American Families,* J. Anthony Lukas
1987 *Arab and Jew: Wounded Spirits in a Promised Land,* David K. Shipler
1988 *The Making of the Atomic Bomb.* Richard Rhodes
1989 *A Bright Shining Lie.* Neil Sheehan
1990 *And Their Children After Them,* Dale Maharidge and Michael Williamson
1991 *The Ants,* Bert Holldobler and Edward O. Wilson
1992 *The Prize: The Epic Quest for Oil, Money and Power,* Daniel Yergin
1993 *Lincoln at Gettysburg: The Words That Remade America,* Garry Wills
1994 *Lenin's Tomb: The Last Days of the Soviet Empire,* David Remick
1995 *The Beak of the Finch: A Story of Evolution in Our Time,* Jonathan Weiner

PULITZER PRIZES IN MUSIC

1943 *Secular Cantata No. 2, A Free Song.* William Schuman
1944 *Symphony No. 4* (Op. 34). Howard Hanson
1945 *Appalachian Spring.* Aaron Copland
1946 *The Canticle of the Sun.* Leo Sowerby
1947 *Symphony No. 3.* Charles Ives
1948 *Symphony No. 3.* Walter Piston
1949 *Louisiana Story* music. Virgil Thomson
1950 *The Consul.* Gian Carlo Menotti
1951 Music for opera *Giants in the Earth.* Douglas Stuart Moore
1952 *Symphony Concertante.* Gail Kubik

1954 *Concerto for Two Pianos and Orchestra.* Quincy Porter
1955 *The Saint of Bleecker Street.* Gian Carlo Menotti
1956 *Symphony No. 3.* Ernst Toch
1957 *Meditations on Ecclesiastes.* Norman Dello Joio
1958 *Vanessa.* Samuel Barber
1959 *Concerto for Piano and Orchestra.* John La Montaine
1960 *Second String Quartet.* Elliott Carter
1961 *Symphony No. 7.* Walter Piston
1962 *The Crucible.* Robert Ward
1963 *Piano Concerto No. 1.* Samuel Barber
1966 *Variations for Orchestra.* Leslie Bassett
1967 *Quartet No. 3.* Leon Kirchner
1968 *Echoes of Time and the River.* George Crumb
1969 *String Quartet No. 3.* Karel Husa
1970 *Time's Encomium.* Charles Wuorinen
1971 *Synchronisms No. 6 for Piano and Electronic Sound.* Mario Davidovsky
1972 *Windows.* Jacob Druckman
1973 *String Quartet No. 3.* Elliott Carter
1974 *Notturno.* Donald Martino
1975 *From the Diary of Virginia Woolf.* Dominick Argento
1976 *Air Music.* Ned Rorem
1977 *Visions of Terror and Wonder.* Richard Wernick
1978 *Déjà Vu for Percussion Quartet and Orchestra.* Michael Colgrass
1979 *Aftertones of Infinity.* Joseph Schwantner
1980 *In Memory of a Summer Day.* David Del Tredici
1981 Not awarded
1982 *Concerto for Orchestra.* Roger Sessions
1983 *Three Movements for Orchestra.* Ellen T. Zwilich
1984 *Canti del Sole.* Bernard Rands
1985 *Symphony RiverRun,* Stephen Albert
1986 *Wind Quintet IV,* George Perle
1987 *The Flight Into Egypt,* John Harbison
1988 *12 New Etudes for Piano.* William Bolcom
1989 *Whispers Out of Time,* Roger Reynolds
1990 *Duplicates: A Concerto for Two Pianos and Orchestra,* Mel Powell
1991 *Symphony,* Shulamit Ran
1992 *The Face of the Night, The Heart of the Dark,* Wayne Peterson
1993 *Trombone Concerto,* Christopher Rouse
1994 *Of Reminiscences and Reflections,* Gunther Schuller
1995 *Stringmusic,* Morton Gould

SPECIAL AWARD

1992 *Maus,* Art Spiegelman

Winners of Bollingen Prize in Poetry

($5,000[1] award is given biennially. It is administered by Yale University and the Bollingen Foundation.)

1949 Ezra Pound
1950 Wallace Stevens
1951 John Crowe Ransom
1952 Marianne Moore
1953 Archibald MacLeish and William Carlos Williams
1954 W. H. Auden
1955 Léonie Adams and Louise Bogan
1956 Conrad Aiken
1957 Allen Tate
1958 E.E. Cummings
1959 Theodore Roethke
1960 Delmore Schwartz
1961 Yvor Winters
1962 John Hall Wheelock and Richard Eberhart
1963 Robert Frost
1965 Horace Gregory
1967 Robert Penn Warren
1969 John Berryman and Karl Shapiro
1971 Richard Wilbur and Mona Van Duyn
1973 James Merrill
1975 Archie Randolph Ammons
1977 David Ignatow
1979 W. S. Merwin
1981 Howard Nemerov and May Swenson
1983 Anthony Hecht and John Hollander
1985 John Ashbery and Fred Chappell
1987 Stanley Kunitz
1989 Edgar Bowers
1991 Laura Riding Jackson and Donald Justin
1993 Mark Strand
1995 Kenneth Koch

1. Beginning 1989 award increased to $10,000. It now stands at $25,000.

New York Drama Critics' Circle Awards

1935–36
Winterset, Maxwell Anderson
1936–37
High Tor, Maxwell Anderson
1937–38
Of Mice and Men, John Steinbeck
Shadow and Substance, Paul Vincent Carroll[1]
1938–39
(No award) *The White Steed,* Paul Vincent Carroll[1]
1939–40
The Time of Your Life, William Saroyan
1940–41
Watch on the Rhine, Lillian Hellman
The Corn Is Green, Emlyn Williams[1]
1941–42
(No award) *Blithe Spirit,* Noel Coward[1]
1942–43
The Patriots, Sidney Kingsley
1943–44
(No award) *Jacobowsky and the Colonel.* Franz Werfel and S. N. Behrman[1]
1944–45
The Glass Menagerie, Tennessee Williams

1945–46
(No award) *Carousel,* Richard Rodgers and Oscar Hammerstein II[2]
1946–47
All My Sons, Arthur Miller
No Exit, Jean-Paul Sartre[1]
Brigadoon, Alan Jay Lerner and Frederick Loewe[2]
1947–48
A Streetcar Named Desire, Tennessee Williams
The Winslow Boy, Terence Rattigan[1]
1948–49
Death of a Salesman, Arthur Miller
The Madwoman of Chaillot, Jean Giraudoux and Maurice Valency[1]
South Pacific, Richard Rodgers, Oscar Hammerstein II, and Joshua Logan[2]
1949–50
The Member of the Wedding, Carson McCullers
The Cocktail Party, T. S. Eliot[1]
The Consul, Gian Carlo Menotti[2]
1950–51
Darkness at Noon, Sidney Kingsley[3]
The Lady's Not for Burning, Christopher Fry[1]

Guys and Dolls, Abe Burrows, Jo Swerling, and Frank Loesser[2]
1951–52
I Am a Camera, John Van Druten[4]
Venus Observed, Christopher Fry[1]
Pal Joey, Richard Rodgers, Lorenz Hart, and John O'Hara[2]
Don Juan in Hell, George B. Shaw[5]
1952–53
Picnic, William Inge *The Love of Four Colonels,* by Peter Ustinov[1]
Wonderful Town, Joseph Fields, Jerome Chodorov, Betty Comden, Adolph Green, and Leonard Bernstein[2]
1953–54
The Teahouse of the August Moon, John Patrick
Ondine, Jean Giraudoux[1]
The Golden Apple, John Latouche and Jerome Moross[2]
1954–55
Cat on a Hot Tin Roof, Tennessee Williams
Witness for the Prosecution, Agatha Christie[1]
The Saint of Bleecker Street, Gian Carlo Menotti[2]
1955–56
The Diary of Anne Frank, Frances Goodrich and Albert Hackett
Tiger at the Gates, Jean Giraudoux and Christopher Fry[1]
My Fair Lady, Frederick Loewe and Alan Jay Lerner[2]
1956–57
Long Day's Journey Into Night, Eugene O'Neill
Waltz of the Toreadors, Jean Anouilh[1]
The Most Happy Fella, Frank Loesser[2 6]
1957–58
Look Homeward, Angel, Ketti Frings[7]
Look Back in Anger, John Osborne[1]
The Music Man, Meredith Willson[2]
1958–59
A Raisin in the Sun, Lorraine Hansberry
The Visit, Friedrich Duerrenmatt-Maurice Valency[1]
La Plume de ma Tante, Robert Dhery and Gerard Calvi[2]
1959–60
Toys in the Attic, Lillian Hellman
Five Finger Exercise, Peter Shaffer[1]
Fiorello!, Jerome Weidman, George Abbott, Jerry Bock, and Sheldon Harnick[2]
1960–61
All the Way Home, Tad Mosel[3]
A Taste of Honey, Shelagh Delaney[1]
Carnival, Michael Stewart[2]
1961–62
The Night of the Iguana, Tennessee Williams
A Man for All Seasons, Robert Bolt[1]
How to Succeed in Business Without Really Trying, Abe Burrows, Jack Weinstock, Willie Gilbert, and Frank Loesser[2 9]
1962–63
Who's Afraid of Virginia Woolf?, Edward Albee
Beyond the Fringe, Alan Bennett, Peter Cook, Jonathan Miller, and Dudley Moore[10]
1963–64
Luther, John Osborne
Hello, Dolly!, Michael Stewart and Jerry Herman[2 11]
The Trojan Women, Euripides[10 12]
1964–65
The Subject Was Roses, Frank D. Gilroy
Fiddler on the Roof, Joseph Stein, Jerry Bock, and Sheldon Harnick[2 13]
1965–66
The Persecution and Assassination of Marat as Performed by the Inmates of the Asylum of Charenton Under the Direction of the Marquis de Sade, Peter Weiss
The Man of La Mancha, Dale Wasserman, Mitch Leigh, and Joe Darion

1966–67
The Homecoming, Harold Pinter
Cabaret, Joe Masteroff, John Kander, and Fred Ebb[2 14]
1967–68
Rosencrantz and Guildenstern Are Dead, Tom Stoppard
Your Own Thing, Donald Driver, Hal Hester, and Danny Apolinar[2]
1968–69
The Great White Hope, Howard Sackler
1776, Sherman Edwards and Peter Stone[2]
1969–70
Borstal Boy, Frank McMahon[15]
The Effect of Gamma Rays on Man-in-the-Moon Marigolds, Paul Zindel[16]
Company, George Furth and Stephen Sondheim[2]
1970–71
Home, David Storey
The House of Blue Leaves, John Guare[16]
Follies, James Goldman and Stephen Sondheim[2]
1971–72
That Championship Season, Jason Miller
Two Gentlemen of Verona, adapted by John Guare and Mel Shapiro[2]
The Screens, Jean Genet[1]
1972–73
The Changing Room, David Storey
The Hot l Baltimore, by Lanford Wilson[16]
A Little Night Music, Hugh Wheeler and Stephen Sondheim[2]
1973–74
The Contractors, David Storey
Short Eyes, Miguel Piñero[16]
Candide, Leonard Bernstein, Hugh Wheeler, and Richard Wilbur[2]
1974–75
Equus, Peter Shaffer
The Taking of Miss Janie, Ed Bullins[16]
A Chorus Line, James Kirkwood and Nicholas Dante[2]
1975–76
Travesties, Tom Stoppard
Streamers, David Rabe[16]
Pacific Overtures, Stephen Sondheim, John Weidman, and Hugh Wheeler[2]
1976–77
Otherwise Engaged, Simon Gray
American Buffalo, David Mamet[16]
Annie, Thomas Meehan, Charles Strouse, and Martin Charnin[2]
1977–78
Da, Hugh Leonard
Ain't Misbehavin', conceived by Richard Maltby, Jr.[2]
1978–79
The Elephant Man, Bernard Pomerance
Sweeney Todd, Hugh Wheeler and Stephen Sondheim[2]
1979–80
Talley's Folly, Lanford Wilson
Evita,[2] Andrew Lloyd Webber and Tim Rice
Betrayal, Harold Pinter[1]
1980–81
A Lesson From Aloes, Athol Fugard
Crimes of the Heart, Beth Henley[16]
1981–82
The Life and Adventures of Nicholas Nickleby, adapted by David Edgar
A Soldier's Play, Charles Fuller[16]
1982–83
Brighton Beach Memoirs, Neil Simon
Plenty, David Hare[1]
Little Shop of Horrors, Alan Menken and Howard Ashman[2 17]

1983–84
The Real Thing, Tom Stoppard
Glengarry Glen Ross, David Mamet[16]
Sunday in the Park with George, Stephen W Sondheim and James Lapine[2]
1984–85
Ma Rainey's Black Bottom, August Wilson
(No award for best musical or foreign play)
1985–86
Lie of the Mind, Sam Shepard
Benefactors, Michael Frayn[1]
The Search for Signs of Intelligent Life in the Universe, Lily Tomlin and Jane Wagner[10]
(No award for best musical)
1986–87
Fences, August Wilson
Les Liaisons Dangereuses, Christopher Hampton[1]
Les Miserables, Claude-Michel Schonberg and Alain Boublil[2]
1987–88
Joe Turner's Come and Gone, August Wilson
The Road to Mecca, Athol Fugard[1]
Into the Woods, Stephen Sondheim and James Lapine[2]
1988–89
The Heidi Chronicles, Wendy Wasserstein
Aristocrats, Brian Friel[1]
Largely New York, Bill Irwin[10]
(No award for best musical)
1989–90
The Piano Lesson, August Wilson
Privates on Parade, Peter Nichols[1]
City of Angels, Larry Gelbart, Cy Coleman, and David Zippel[2]
1990–91
Six Degrees of Separation, John Guare
Our Country's Good, Timberlake Wertenbaker[1]
The Will Rogers Follies, Cy Coleman, Peter Stone, Betty Comden, and Adolph Green[2]
Eileen Atkins, *A Room of One's Own*[10]
1991–92
Dancing at Lughnasa, Brian Friel
Two Trains Running, August Wilson[16]
(No award for best musical)
1992-93
Angels in America: Millennium Approaches, Tony Kushner
Someone Who'll Watch Over Me, Frank McGuinness[1]
Kiss of the Spider Woman, John Kander, Fred Ebb and Terrence McNally[2]
1993–94
Three Tall Women, Edward Albee
Twilight: Los Angeles, 1992, Anna Deavere Smith, writer/actress, a special award "for unique contribution to theatrical form."
(No award for best foreign play or best musical)
1994–95
Arcadia, Tom Stoppard
Love! Valour! Compassion! Terrence McNally
Signature Theater Company for outstanding achievement.
(No award for best musical or best foreign play)

1. Citation for best foreign play. 2. Citation for best musical. 3. Based on a novel by Arthur Koestler. 4. Based on Christopher Isherwood's *Berlin Stories.* 5. For "distinguished and original contribution to the theater." 6. Based on Sidney Howard's *They Knew What They Wanted.* 7. Based on a novel by Thomas Wolfe. 8. Based on James Agee's *A Death in the Family.* 9. Based on a book by Shepherd Mead. 10. Special citation. 11. Based on Thornton Wilder's *The Matchmaker.* 12. Translated by Edith Hamilton. 13. Based on Sholem Aleichem's Tevye stories, translated by Arnold Perl. 14. Based on John Van Druten's *I Am a Camera,* which won the award for the best play in 1951–52. 15. Based on Brendan Behan's autobiography. 16. Citation for best American play. 17. Based on a story by Roger Corman.

Antoinette Perry (Tony) Awards, 1995

Dramatic Play: *Love! Valour! Compassion!,* Terrence McNally
Musical: *Sunset Boulevard*
Actor (play): Ralph Fiennes, *Hamlet*
Actress (play): Cherry Jones, *The Heiress*
Actor, featured (play): John Glover, *Love! Valour! Compassion!*
Actress, featured (play): Frances Sternhagen, *The Heiress*
Actor (musical): Matthew Broderick, *How To Succeed in Business Without Really Trying*
Actress (musical): Glenn Close, *Sunset Boulevard*
Actor, featured (musical): George Hearn, *Sunset Boulevard*
Actress, featured (musical): Gretha Boston, *Show Boat*

Director (play): Gerald Gutierrez, *The Heiress*
Director (musical): Harold Prince, *Show Boat*
Best book of musical: *Sunset Boulevard*
Best original musical score: *Sunset Boulevard*
Scenic design: John Napier, *Sunset Boulevard*
Costume design: Florence Klotz, *Show Boat*
Lighting design: Andrew Bridge, *Sunset Boulevard*
Choreography: Susan Stroman, *Show Boat*
Play revival: *The Heiress*
Musical revival: *Show Boat*
Live Achievement: Carol Channing and Harvey Sabinson
Regional Theater: Goodspeed Opera House, East Haddam, Conn.
Outstanding Contribution: National Endowment for the Arts

1995 Obie Award Winners

Best New American Play: David Mamet, *The Cryptogram*
Performance: Randy Becker, Stephen Bogardus, John Glover, John Benjamin Hickey, Justin Kirk, Stephen Spinella, and Nathan Lane, all for *Love! Valour! Compassion!;* Vernel Bagneris and Morten Gunnar Larsen, *Jelly Roll*
Playwriting: Terrance McNally, *Love! Valour! Compassion!;* Tony Kushner, *Slavs!;* Susan Miller, *My Left Breast;* and David Hancock, *The Convention of Cartography*
Direction: Joe Mantello, *Love! Valour! Compassion!* and Susan Shulman, *Merrily We Roll Along*
Distinguished Performance: Eileen Atkins and Vanessa Redgrave, *Vita and Virginia* and Ron Liebman, *The Merchant of Venice*
Sustained Achievement: Set designer Ming Cho Lee

Poets Laureate of the United States

The post was established in 1985. Appointment is for a one-year term, but is renewable.

Robert Penn Warren	1986–1987	Joseph Brodsky	1991–1992
Richard Wilbur	1987–1988	Mona Van Duyn	1992–1993
Howard Nemerov	1988–1990	Rita Dove	1993–1995
Mark Strand	1990–1991	Robert Hass	1995–1996

Awards of the Society of Professional Journalists, 1994

(Sigma Delta Chi)

Deadline reporting: *Los Angeles Times*
Non-deadline reporting: *Syracuse Herald-Journal*
Investigative reporting: Russell Carollo and Cheryl Reed, *Dayton Daily News*
Feature writing: John Carlson, *The Des Moines Register*
Editorial writing: Tim Redmond, *San Francisco Bay Guardian*
Washington correspondence: John Hoeffel, *Winston–Salem* (N.C.) *Journal*
Foreign correspondence: John Balzar, *Los Angeles Times*
Public service in newspaper journalism: *The Lexington* (Ky.) *Herald–Leader* (greater than 100,000); *Virgin Islands Daily News* (less than 100,000)
Magazine reporting: Lisa DePaulo, *Philadelphia Magazine;* Mike Edwards, *National Geographic;* and Mary Kay Blakely, *Los Angeles Times*
Public service in magazine journalism: *U.S. News & World Report*
Photography: Ron Cortes, *Philadelphia Inquirer*
Editorial cartoons: Jim Borgman, *The Cincinnati Enquirer*

Informational graphics: *The Detroit News*
Radio spot news: Ross Simpson and Joe Walsh, Mutual/NBC
Radio editorial: Greg Shanley and Bob Wolf, KUNI, University of Northern Iowa
Radio investigative reporting: Mike Sugerman, KCBS, San Francisco
Public service in radio journalism: Stephen Smith and Bill Catlin, Minnesota Public Radio
Television spot-news: Renee Riddle and Bob Vermiglio, WISN, Milwaukee; Adrienne Arsenault, Margo Harper, and Deborah Goble, CBC, Vancouver, British Columbia
Television editorial: KGTV, San Diego, Calif.
Television investigative reporting: ABC World News and KSTP, St. Paul, Minn.
Television feature: ABC *Day One* and KARE, Minneapolis
Public service in television journalism: ABC News (top 40 markets); WXII, Winston–Salem, N.C. (other markets)
Research about journalism: John McManus, *Market-Driven Journalism: Let the Citizen Beware!*

1995 Christopher Awards

Adult Books

Conscience & Courage: Rescuers of Jews During the Holocaust, by Eva Fogelman (Anchor Books)
Harriet Beecher Stowe: A Life, by Joan D. Hedrick (Oxford University Press)
Let Someone Hold You: The Journey of a Hospice Priest, by Paul F. Morrissey (Crossroad)
Long Walk to Freedom: The Autobiography of Nelson Mandela, by Nelson Mandela (Little, Brown)
Not All of Us Are Saints: A Doctor's Journey with the Poor, by David Hilfiker, M.D. (Hill and Wang)

Young People's Books

I'll See You When the Moon Is Full, by Susi Gregg Fowler, pictures by Jim Fowler (Greenwillow Books)
Prize in the Snow, by Bill Easterling, illustration by Mary Beth Owens (Little, Brown)
The Ledgerbook of Thomas Blue Eagle, by Jewel H. Grutman and Gay Matthaei, illustration by Adam Cvijanovic (Thomasson–Grant)
Taking Hold: My Journey Into Blindness, by Sally Hobart Alexander (Macmillan)

Television Specials

Break the Silence: Kids Against Child Abuse (CBS)
CBS Schoolbreak Special: The Writing on the Wall (CBS)

Christy (CBS)
One More Mountain (ABC)
A Place for Annie (ABC)
The Vernon Johns Story (Independent Network)

Films

Forrest Gump (Paramount)
Little Women (Columbia Pictures)

Special Award

Pope John Paul II: As author of *Crossing the Threshold of Hope* (Knopf), the renowned spiritual leader of nearly one billion Catholics offers people of all faiths and those of no particular faith reflections on life, hope, and holiness.

James Keller Award

Mary Cunningham Agee: As founder and executive director of The Nurturing Network, a nationwide volunteer organization, she provides compassionate, positive, and practical support to women facing crisis pregnancies.

Life Achievement Award

Hugh Downs: As co-anchor of ABC News "20/20," he sets the standard for broadcasting excellence by communicating both ideas and ideals to the audience he has served so well throughout his unequaled media career.

National Book Critics Circle Awards, 1995

Fiction: *The Stone Diaries,* by Carol Shields (Viking)
General nonfiction: *The Rape of Europa: The Fate of Europe's Treasures in the Third Reich and the Second World War,* by Lynn H. Nicholas (Knopf)
Poetry: *Rider,* by Mark Rudman (Wesleyan University Press/University Press of New England)

Criticism: *The Culture of Bruising: Essays on Prizefighting, Literature and Modern American Culture,* by Gerald Early (Ecco Press)
Biography/Autobiography: *Shot in the Heart,* by Mikal Gilmore (Doubleday)

Poets Laureate of England

Edmund Spenser	1591–1599	Laurence Eusden	1718–1730	Alfred Lord Tennyson	1850–1892
Samuel Daniel	1599–1619	Colley Cibber	1730–1757	Alfred Austin	1896–1913
Ben Jonson	1619–1637	William Whitehead	1757–1785	Robert Bridges	1913–1930
William Davenant	1638–1668	Thomas Warton	1785–1790	John Masefield	1930–1967
John Dryden[1]	1670–1689	Henry James Pye	1790–1813	C. Day Lewis	1967–1972
Thomas Shadwell	1689–1692	Robert Southey	1813–1843	Sir John Betjeman	1972–1984
Nahum Tate	1692–1715	William Wordsworth	1843–1850	Ted Hughes	1984–
Nicholas Rowe	1715–1718				

1. First to bear the title officially. *Source: Encyclopaedia Britannica.*

Alfred I. du Pont-Columbia University Broadcast News Awards

(For work broadcast between July 1, 1993, and June 30, 1994)

Gold Baton Award: To ABC News for "the depth and range of its news coverage . . . in a single year." Five reports were cited: Haiti coverage by Linda Pattillo; a 10-part series on women's health issues, "American Agenda: Women's Health Week"; "Day One: Smokescreen," an investigation of the tobacco industry; "Turning Point: Inside the Struggle—The Amy Biel Story," about the young American Fulbright scholar who was murdered in South Africa; and "Peter Jennings Reporting: While America Watched—The Bosnia Tragedy."

Silver Baton Awards: Charles Kuralt, CBS newsman who retired in 1994, for his career; CBS "60 Minutes" for a report on the Soviet city of Semipalatin; CNN for the coverage of the Moscow uprising of October 1993; PBS "Frontline," one for "Innocence Lost: The Verdict," about child-abuse charges at a daycare center, and another for "Romeo and Juliet in Sarajevo," a story of two lovers killed in the violence there; Blackside, Inc., producer of the PBS documentary series "The Great Depression"; Filmmakers Alan and Susan Raymond and HBO for "I am a Promise: The Children of Stanton Elementary School," an inner city school in Philadelphia; National Public Radio won two batons for coverage of genocide in Rwanda and election in South Africa. Individual television station winners were WTVS Detroit and WCCO Minneapolis. Wisconsin Public Televisioon Madison was the remaining winner.

Enrico Fermi Award

Named in honor of Enrico Fermi, the atomic pioneer, the $100,000 award is given in recognition of "exceptional and altogether outstanding" scientific and technical achievement in atomic energy.

1954 Enrico Fermi	1972 Manson Benedict	1986 Ernest D. Courant and M.
1956 John von Neumann	1976 William L. Russell	Stanley Livingston
1957 Ernest O. Lawrence	1978 Harold M. Agnew and Wolfgang	1987 Luis W. Alvarez and Gerald F.
1958 Eugene P. Wigner	K.H. Panofsky	Tape
1959 Glenn T. Seaborg	1980 Alvin M. Weinberg and Rudolf	1988 Richard B. Setlow and Victor F.
1961 Hans A. Bethe	E. Peirls	Weisskopf
1962 Edward Teller	1981 W. Bennett Lewis	1989 Award not given
1963 J. Robert Oppenheimer	1982 Herbert Anderson and Seth	1990 George A. Cowan and Robley D.
1964 Hyman G. Rickover	Neddermeyer	Evans
1966 Otto Hahn, Lise Meitner, and	1983 Alexander Hollaender and	1991 Award not given
Fritz Strassman	John Lawrence	1992 Leon M. Lederman, Harold
1968 John A. Wheeler	1984 Robert R. Wilson and Georges	Brown, and John S. Foster, Jr.
1969 Walter H. Zinn	Vendryès	1993 Freeman J. Dyson and Liane B.
1970 Norris E. Bradbury	1985 Norman C. Rasmussen and	Russell
1971 Shields Warren and Stafford	Marshall N. Rosenblath	
L. Warren		

American Library Association Awards for Children's Books, 1995

(For books published in 1994)

John Newbery Medal for best book: *Walk Two Moons,* Sharon Creech (Harper–Collins)

Newbery Honor Books: *Catherine, Called Birdy,* Karen Cushman (Clarion Books); and *The Ear, the Eye and the Arm,* Nancy Farmer (Richard Jackson/Orchard Books)

Randolph Caldecott Medal for best picture book: *Smoky Night,* illustrated by David Diaz, written by Eve Bunting (Harcourt Brace & Company)

Caldecott Honor Books: *Swamp Angel,* illustrated by Paul Zelinsky, written by Anne Issacs (Dutton's Children's Books); *John Henry,* illustrated by Jerry Pinckney, written by Julius Lester (Dial Books); and *Time Flies,* illustrated and written by Eric Rohmann (Crown)

The Coretta Scott King Award: *Christmas in the Big House, Christmas in the Quarters,* Patricia C. and Frederick L. McKissack (Scholastic Inc.)

National Book Awards, 1994

Established by Association of American Publishers

(American Book Awards 1980–86. Reverted to original name in 1987.)

Fiction: *A Frolic of His Own,* by William Gaddis (Alfred A. Knopf)

Nonfiction: *How We Die: Reflections on Life's Final Chapter,* by Sherwin B. Nuland (Alfred A. Knopf)

Poetry: *Worshipful Company of Fletcher,* by James Tate (Ecco Press)

The National Book Foundation Medal for Distinguished Contribution to American Letters: Gwendolyn Brooks, poet.

Kingsley Tufts Poetry Prize

$50,000 award given to a poet for a book published in the previous year. Established 1992, it is administered by the Claremont (California) Graduate School.

1993 Susan Mitchell, *Rapture*
1994 Yusef Komunyakaa, *Neon Vernacular*

1995 Thomas Lux, *Split Horizon*

Recipients of Kennedy Center Honors

The Kennedy Center for the Performing Arts in Washington, D.C., created its Honors awards in 1978 to recognize the achievements of five distinguished contributors to the performing arts. Following are the recipients:

1978: Marian Anderson (contralto), Fred Astaire (dancer-actor), Richard Rodgers (Broadway composer), Arthur Rubinstein (pianist), George Balanchine (choreographer).

1979: Ella Fitzgerald (jazz singer), Henry Fonda (actor), Martha Graham (dancer-choreographer), Tennessee Williams (playwright), Aaron Copland (composer).

1980: James Cagney (actor), Leonard Bernstein (composer-conductor), Agnes de Mille (choreographer), Lynn Fontanne (actress), Leontyne Price (soprano).

1981: Count Basie (jazz composer-pianist), Cary Grant (actor), Helen Hayes (actress), Jerome Robbins (choreographer), Rudolf Serkin (pianist).

1982: George Abbott (Broadway producer), Lillian Gish (actress), Benny Goodman (jazz clarinetist), Gene Kelly (dancer-actor), Eugene Ormandy (conductor).

1983: Katherine Dunham (dancer-choreographer), Elia Kazan (director-author), James Stewart (actor), Virgil Thomson (music critic-composer), Frank Sinatra (singer).

1984: Lena Horne (singer), Danny Kaye (comedian-actor), Gian Carlo Menotti (composer), Arthur Miller (playwright), Isaac Stern (violinist).

1985: Merce Cunningham (dancer-choreographer), Irene Dunne (actress), Bob Hope (comedian), Alan Jay Lerner (lyricist-playwright), Frederick Loewe (composer), Beverly Sills (soprano and opera administrator).

1986: Lucille Ball (comedienne), Ray Charles (musician), Yehudi Menuhin (violinist), Antony Tudor (choreographer), Hume Cronyn and Jessica Tandy (husband-and-wife acting team).

1987: Perry Como (singer), Bette Davis (actress), Sammy Davis Jr. (entertainer), Nathan Milstein (violinist), Alwin Nikolais (choreographer).

1988: Alvin Ailey (choreographer), George Burns (comedian-actor), Myrna Loy (actress), Alexander Schneider (violinist), Roger L. Stevens (theatrical producer and the Kennedy Center's founding chairman).

1989: Harry Belafonte (singer-actor), Claudette Colbert (actress), Alexandra Danilova (ballerina-teacher), Mary Martin (actress), William Schuman (composer)

1990: Dizzy Gillespie (jazz trumpeter), Katharine Hepburn (actress), Risë Stevens (mezzo-soprano), Jule Styne (composer), Billy Wilder (director-author).

1991: Roy Acuff (country songwriter and singer), Betty Comden and Adloph Green (co-authors of books and lyrics of musicals), the brothers Fayard and Harold Nicholas (dancers), Gregory Peck (actor), Robert Shaw (choral director).

1992: Lionel Hampton (jazz musician), Paul Newman (actor), Joanne Woodward (actress), Ginger Rogers (dancer–actress), Mstislav Rostropovich (cellist–conductor), Paul Taylor (dancer–choreographer).

1993: Johnny Carson (talk show host), Arthur Mitchell (dancer and choreographer), Georg Solti (conductor), Stephen Sondheim (composer and lyricist), Marion Williams (gospel singer).

1994: Kirk Douglas (actor), Aretha Franklin (singer), Morton Gould (composer), Harold Prince (producer and director), Pete Seeger (folk singer and songwriter).

Presidential Medal of Freedom

The nation's highest civilian award, the Presidential Medal of Freedom, was established in 1963 by President John F. Kennedy to continue and expand Presidential recognition of meritorious service which, since 1945, had been granted as the Medal of Freedom. Kennedy selected the first recipients, but was assassinated before he could make the presentations. They were made by President Johnson. NOTE: An asterisk following a year denotes a posthumous award.

SELECTED BY PRESIDENT KENNEDY

Marian Anderson (contralto)	1963
Ralph J. Bunche (statesman)	1963
Ellsworth Bunker (diplomat)	1963
Pablo Casals (cellist)	1963
Genevieve Caulfield (educator)	1963
James B. Conant (educator)	1963
John F. Enders (bacteriologist)	1963
Felix Frankfurter (jurist)	1963
Karl Horton (youth authority)	1963
Robert J. Kiphuth (athletic director)	1963
Edwin H. Land (inventor)	1963
Herbert H. Lehman (statesman)	1963 *
Robert A. Lovett (statesman)	1963
J. Clifford MacDonald (educator)	1963 *
John J. McCloy (banker and statesman)	1963
George Meany (labor leader)	1963
Alexander Meiklejohn (philosopher)	1963
Ludwig Mies van der Rohe (architect)	1963
Jean Monnet (European statesman)	1963
Luis Muñoz-Marin (Governor of Puerto Rico)	1963
Clarence B. Randall (industrialist)	1963
Rudolf Serkin (pianist)	1963
Edward Steichen (photographer)	1963
George W. Taylor (educator)	1963
Alan T. Waterman (scientist)	1963
Mark S. Watson (journalist)	1963

Annie D. Wauneka (public health worker)	1963
E. B. White (author)	1963
Thornton N. Wilder (author)	1963
Edmund Wilson (author and critic)	1963
Andrew Wyeth (artist)	1963

AWARDED BY PRESIDENT CLINTON

Arthur Ashe, Jr. (athlete, tennis)	1993 *
Herbert Block (cartoonist)	1994
William J. Brennan, Jr. (public servant)	1993
Cesar Chavez (labor leader)	1994 *
Marjory Stoneman Douglas (conservationist)	1993
Arthur Flemming (government servant)	1994
J. William Fulbright (public servant()	1993
James Grant (Executive Director, UNICEF)	1994
Dorothy Height (civil rights leader)	1994
Barbara Jordan (public servant)	1994
Lane Kirkland (labor leader)	1994
Thurgood Marshall (public servant)	1993 *
Robert H. Michel (public servant)	1994
General Colin L. Powell[1] (soldier)	1993
Joseph L. Raugh, Jr. (civil rights and labor activist)	1993 *
Martha Raye (entertainer)	1993
R. Sargent Shriver (government servant)	1994
John Minor Wisdom (public servant)	1993

1. With Distinction.

Major Grammy Awards for Recording in 1994

Source: National Academy of Recording Arts and Sciences.

Record: "All I Wanna Do," Sheryl Crow
Album: "MTV Unplugged," Tony Bennett
Song: "Streets of Philadelphia," Bruce Springsteen
New Artist: Sheryl Crow
Pop Vocalists: (Female) Sheryl Crow, "All I Wanna Do"; (Male) Elton John, "Can You Feel the Love Tonight"
Pop Duo or Group: All 4 One, "I Swear"
Traditional Pop: "MTV Unplugged," Tony Bennett
Rock Vocalists: (Female) Melissa Etheridge, "Come to My Window"; (Male) Bruce Springsteen, "Streets of Philadelphia"
Rock Duo or Group: Aerosmith, "Crazy"
Rock Instrumental: "Marooned," Pink Floyd
Hard Rock: Soundgarden, "Black Hole Sun"
Metal: Soundgarden, "Spoonman"
Rhythm-and-Blues Vocalists: (Female) Toni Braxton, "Breathe Again"; (Male) Babyface, "When Can I See You"
Rhythm-and-Blues Duo or Group with Vocal: Boyz II Men, "I'll Make Love to You"
Rhythm-and-Blues Song: "I'll Make Love to You," Boyz II Men
Traditional Blues Album: "From the Cradle," Eric Clapton
Contemporary Blues Album: "Father Father," Pops Staples
Rap Solo: Queen Latifah, "U.N.I.T.Y."
Rap Duo or Group: Salt–N–Pepa, "None of Your Business"
Contemporary Jazz (Instrumental): Brecker Brothers, "Out of the Loop"
Jazz Vocalist: Etta James, "Mystery Lady (Songs of Billie Holiday)"
Jazz Instrumentalists: (Solo) Benny Carter, "Prelude to a Kiss"; (Individual or Group) Ron Carter, Herbie Hancock, Wallace Roney, Wayne Shorter, and Tony Williams, "A Tribute to Miles"
Large Jazz Ensemble: McCoy Tyner Big Band, "Journey"
Country Vocalists: (Female) Mary Chapin Carpenter, "Shut Up and Kiss Me"; (Male) Vince Gill, "When Love Finds You"
Country Duo or Group: Asleep at the Wheel with Lyle Lovett, "Blues for Dixie"
Country Instrumental: "Young Thing," Chet Atkins
Country Song: "I Swear," Gary Baker and Frank J. Myers
Rock Gospel Album: "Wake-Up Call," Petra
Pop-Contemporary Gospel: "Mercy," Andrae Crouch
Southern Gospel, Country Gospel or Bluegrass Gospel: "I Know Who Holds Tomorrow," Alison Krauss and the Cox Family
Traditional Soul Gospel: "Songs of the Church: Live in Memphis," Albertina Walker
Contemporary Soul Gospel: "Join the Band," Take 6
Gospel Choir or Chorus (choir director): (tie) "Through God's Eyes," the Rev. Milton Brunson and "Live in Atlanta at Morehouse College," Hezekiah Walker

Latin Pop: Luis Miguel, "Segundo Romance"
Tropical Latin: Cachao, "Master Sessions Volume 1"
Mexican-American: Vikki Carr, "Recuerdo a Javier Solis"
Traditional Folk: Bob Dylan, "World Gone Wrong"
Contemporary Folk: Johnny Cash, "American Recordings"
Polka Album: "Music and Friends," Walter Ostanek Band
Reggae Album: "Crucial! Roots Classic," Bunny Wailer
For Children: (Musical) "The Lion King," original motion picture soundtrack, various artists; (Spoken) "The Lion King Reading Along," Robert Guillaume, Ted Kryczko, and Randy Thornton
Comedy: Sam Kinison, "Live from Hell"
Spoken Word or Nonmusical: "Get in the Van: On the Road with Black Flag," Henry Rollins
Musical Show Album: "Passion"
Instrumental Composition: "African Skies," Michael Brecker
Instrumental Composition Written for a Motion Picture or Television: "Schindler's List," John Williams
Instrumental Arrangement: "Three Cowboy Songs," Dave Grusin
Music Video—Short Form: "Love Is Strong," Rolling Stones
Music Video—Long Form: "Zoo TV: Live from Sydney," U2
Historical Album: "The Complete Ella Fitzgerald Song Book on Verve," Michael Lang
Classical Album: "Bartok: Concerto for Orchestra; Four Orchestral Pieces (Op. 12)," Pieere Boulez, Chicago Symphony Orchestra
Classical Recording, Opera: "Floyd: Susannah," Kent Nagano, Orchestra and Chorus of the Lyons Opera
Classical Soloist With Orchestra: Yo–Yo Ma, cellist, "The New York Album (Works of Albert, Bartok, Bloch)"; **Without Orchestra:** Emanuel Ax, pianist, "Haydn: Piano Sonatas Nos. 32, 47, 53, 59"
Chamber Music: "Beethoven/Mozart: Quintets," Daniel Barenboim, Dale Clevenger, Larry Combs, Daniele Damiano, and Hansjorg Schellenberger
Classical Vocal Performance: Cecilia Bartoli, "The Impatient Lover" (Italian Songs by Beethoven, Schubert, Mozart, etc.)"
Classical Choral: "Berlioz: Messe Solennelle," John Eliot Gardiner, Orchestre Révolutionnaire et Romantique, the Monteverdi Choir and various artists
Contemporary Classical Composition: "Albert: Cello Concerto," Stephen Albert
Producer: Non-Classical: Don Was; **Classical:** Andrew Cornall
Engineers: Non-Classical: Ed Cherney, Paul Dieter and Rick Pekkonen, "I'm Alive"; **Classical:** William, Hoekstra, "Copland: Music for Films (The Red Pony, Our Town, etc.)"

TV Daytime Emmy Awards, 1995

Drama Series: *General Hospital* (ABC)
Actress: Erika Slezak, *One Life to Live* (ABC)
Actor: Justin Deas, *Guiding Light* (CBS)
Supporting Actress: Rena Sofer, *General Hospital* (ABC)
Supporting Actor: Jerry Ver Dorn, *Guiding Light* (CBS)
Younger Actress: Sara Michelle Gellar, *All My Children* (ABC)

Younger Actor: Jonathan Jackson, *General Hospital* (ABC)
Talk Show: *The Oprah Winfrey Show* (ABC)
Talk Show Host: Oprah Winfrey (ABC)
Children's Program: *Nick News* (Nickelodeon)
Animated Children's Program: *Where on Earth Is Carmen Sandiego?* (Fox)
Game Show: *Jeopardy* (Syndicated)

1995 MacArthur Foundation Awards

Allison Anders, independent film director and screenwriter, Los Angeles

Jed Z. Buchwald, professor of history of science at the Massachusetts Institute of Technology, Cambridge, Mass.

Octavia Butler, writer, Pasadena, California.

Sandra Cisneros, writer, San Antonio, Texas.

Sandy Close, Executive Editor, Pacific News Service, San Francisco

Frederick C. Cuny, Chairman, Intertect Relief and Reconstruction Corporation, Dallas

Sharon B. Emerson, Research professor, University of Utah, Salt Lake City

Richard Foreman, Artistic director, playwright, Ontological–Hysteric Theater, New York City

Alma Guillermoprieto, writer and journalist, New York City

Virginia Hamilton, writer, Yellow Springs, Ohio

Daniel Hopkins, consultant, Global 2000 program, Chicago

Susan Werner Kieffer, professor, department of geological sciences, University of British Columbia, Vancouver, B.C.

Elizabeth Le Compte, director, The Wooster Group, New York City

Patricia Nelson Limerick, professor of history, University of Colorado, Boulder

Michael Marletta, professor of medicinal and biological chemistry, University of Michigan, Ann Arbor

Pamela Anne Matson, professor of environmental science, University of California at Berkeley, Stanford, Calif.

Susan McClary, musicologist, professor, University of California at Los Angeles

Meredith Monk, composer, vocalist, filmmaker, theatrical director, choreographer, New York City

Rosalind Pollack Petchesky, professor of political science and women's studies, Hunter College, New York City

Joel Rogers, professor of law, political science, sociology, University of Wisconsin, Madison

Cindy Sherman, artist, New York City

Bryan Stevenson, Executive director, Alabama Capital Representation Resource Center, Montgomery

Nicholas Strausfeld, professor of neurobiology, of entomology, and of ecology and evolutionary biology, University of Arizona, Tucson

Richard White, professor of history, University of Washington, Seattle

Templeton Foundation Prize for Progress in Religion

The Templeton Prize, an award to encourage progress in religion, was established in 1972 by Sir John Templeton, a Tennessee-born financial analyst and Presbyterian layman, and first presented in 1973. Its value has increased over the years to nearly $1 million, depending on exchange rates.

Winners to date are:

1973 Mother Teresa of Calcutta, founder of the Missionaries of Charity

1974 Brother Roger, Founder and Prior of the Taize Community in France

1975 Dr. Sarvepalli Radhakrishnan, former President of India and Oxford Professor of Eastern Religions and Ethics

1976 H.E. Leon Joseph Cardinal Suenens, Archbishop of Malines-Brussels

1977 Chiara Lubich, Founder of the Focolare Movement, Italy

1978 Prof. Thomas F. Torrance, President of International Academy of Religion and Sciences, Scotland

1979 Nikkyo Niwano, Founder of Rissho Kosei Kai and World Conferences on Religion and Peace, Japan

1980 Prof. Ralph Wendell Burhoe, Founder and Editor of *Zygon*, Chicago

1981 Dame Cicely Saunders, Originator of Modern Hospice Movement, England

1982 The Rev'd Dr. Billy Graham, Founder, The Billy Graham Evangelistic Association

1983 Aleksandr Solzhenitsyn, U.S.A.

1984 The Rev'd Michael Bourdeaux, Founder of Keston College, England

1985 Sir Alister Hardy, Oxford, England

1986 Rev'd Dr. James McCord, Princeton, N.J.

1987 Rev'd Professor Stanley L. Jaki, Princeton, N.J.

1988 Dr. Inamullah Khan, Secretary-general of the World Moslem Congress

1989 The Very Reverend Lord MacLeod of the Iona Community, Scotland, and Professor Carl Friedrich von Weizsäcker of Starnberg, West Germany

1990 Baba Amte, India, and Professor Charles Birch, Sydney, Australia

1991 The Rt. Hon. Lord Jakobovits, Chief Rabbi of Great Britain and the Commonwealth

1992 Dr. Kyung-Chik Han, Founder of Seoul's Young Nak Presbyterian Church

1993 Charles W. Colson, Founder, Prison Fellowship, Virginia

1994 Michael Novak, Scholar at the American Enterprise Institute, Washington, D.C.

1995 Dr. Paul Davies, professor, Univbersity of Adelaide, Australia

1995 National Magazine Awards

Feature writing: *GQ* (Gentlemen's Quarterly) for "The Abortionist," by Tom Junod

Fiction: *Story* for short stories by three new writers

Reporting: *Atlantic Monthly* for two articles about American law enforcement involving marijuana

Essays and criticism: *Harper's Magazine* for three columns by its editor, Lewis H. Lapham

Public interest: *New Republic* for two articles by Elizabeth McCaughey about the Clinton health reform plan

Special-interest: *GQ* for three articles by Alan Richman, GQ's food writer

Personal service: *Smart Money* for three-part series about insurance

Single-topic issue: *Discover* for "The Science of Race"

Design: *Martha Stewart Living* for presenting a world where "calm and serenity reign"

Photography: *Rolling Stone*

General excellence: (for magazines with a circulation of more than one million): *Entertainment Weekly;* (for magazines with a circulation of 400,000 to one million): *The New Yorker;* (for magazines with a circulation of 100,000 to 400,000): *Men's Journal;* (for magazines with a circulation of under 100,000): *I.D. Magazine*

ENTERTAINMENT & CULTURE

U.S. Symphony Orchestras and Their Music Directors

(With expenses over $1,050,000)

Source: American Symphony Orchestra League.

Atlanta Symphony: Yoel Levi
Austin Symphony: Sung Kwak
Baltimore Symphony: David Zinman
Boston Symphony: Seiji Ozawa
Brooklyn Philharmonic: Robert Spano
Buffalo Philharmonic: Maximiano Valdes
Cedar Rapids Symphony: Christian Tiemeyer[1]
Charleston Symphony: David Stahl
Charlotte Symphony: Peter McCoppin
Chattanooga Symphony & Opera Assn.: Robert Bernhardt
Chicago Symphony: Daniel Barenboim
Cincinnati Symphony: Jesus Lopez-Cobos
Cleveland Orchestra: Christoph von Dohnanyi
Colorado Springs Symphony: Christopher P. Wilkins
Colorado Symphony (Denver): Martin Alsop[2]
Columbus Symphony: Alessandro Siciliani
Dallas Symphony: Andrew Litton
Dayton Philharmonic: Isaiah Jackson
Delaware Symphony: Stephen Gunzenhauser
Detroit Symphony: Neeme Jarvi
Florida Orchestra: Jahja Ling
Florida Philharmonic Orchestra: James Judd
Florida Symphonic Pops: Derek Stannard[3]
Fort Wayne Philharmonic: Edvard Tchivzhel
Fort Worth Symphony: John Giordano
Grand Rapids Symphony: Catherine Comet
Grant Park Symphony (Chicago): Hugh Wolff[2]
Hartford Symphony: Michael Lankester
Honolulu Symphony Society: Donald Johanos
Houston Symphony: Christopher Eschenbach
Hudson Valley Philharmonic (Poughkeepsie): Randall Craig Fleischer
Indianapolis Symphony: Raymond Leppard
Jacksonville Symphony: Roger Nierenberg
Kansas City Symphony: William McGlaughlin
Knoxville Symphony: Kirk Trevor
Long Beach Symphony: JoAnn Falletta
Long Island Philharmonic: Marin Alsop
Los Angeles Chamber Orchestra: Christof Perick
Los Angeles Philharmonic: Esa-Pekka Salonen
Louisville Orchestra: Joseph Silverstein[4]
Memphis Symphony: Alan Balter
Milwaukee Symphony: Zdenek Macal
Minnesota Orchestra: Eiji Oue[5]
Mississippi Symphony: Colman Pearce
Naples Philharmonic: Christopher Seaman

Nashville Symphony: Kenneth D. Schermerhorn
National Symphony (D.C.): Leonard Slatkin[5]
New Haven Symphony: Michael Palmer
New Jersey Symphony: Zdenek Macal[1]
New Mexico Symphony: David Lockington
New World Symphony (Fla.): Michael Tilson Thomas[1]
New York Chamber Symphony of the 92nd St. Y: Gerard Schwarz
New York Philharmonic: Kurt Masur
North Carolina Symphony: Gerhardt Zimmermann
Ohio Chamber Orchestra: David Lockington
Oklahoma City Philharmonic: Joel A. Levine
Omaha Symphony: Bruce B. Hangen[1]
Oregon Symphony: James DePreist
Pacific Symphony (Calif.): Carl St. Clair
Philadelphia Orchestra: Wolfgang Sawallisch
Phoenix Symphony: James Sedares
Pittsburgh Symphony: Lorin Maazel
Portland Symphony: Toshiyuki Shimada
Puerto Rico Symphony: Eugene Kohn[6]
Rhode Island Philharmonic: Zuohuang Chen
Richmond Symphony: George Manahan
Rochester Philharmonic: Peter Bay[7]
Sacramento Symphony: Geoffrey Simon
St. Louis Symphony: Hans Vonk[5]
St. Paul Chamber Orchestra: Hugh Wolff
San Antonio Symphony: Christopher Wilkins
San Diego Symphony: Yoav Talmi
San Francisco Symphony: Michael Tilson Thomas[5]
San Jose Symphony: Leonid Grin
Savannah Symphony: Philp B. Greenberg
Seattle Symphony: Gerard Schwarz
Shreveport Symphony: Peter Leonard
Spokane Symphony: Fabio Mechetti
Springfield Symphony (Mass.): Not designated
Syracuse Symphony: Fabio Mechetti
Toledo Symphony: Andrew Massey
Tucson Symphony: Robert E. Bernhardt
Tulsa Philharmonic: Bernard Rubenstein
Utah Symphony: Joseph Silverstein
Virginia Symphony: JoAnn Falletta
West Virginia Symphony: Thomas B. Conlin[1]
Wichita Symphony: Zuohuang Chen
Winston-Salem Symphony Assn.: Peter J. Perret

1. Artistic Director. 2. Principal conductor. 3. Conductor. 4. Artistic Advisor. 5. Music Director Designate. 6. Music conductor. 7. Music Advisor/Conductor.

Monet—Only in Chicago

From July 22 through November 26,1995, the Art Institute of Chicago presented the largest and most comprehensive exhibition of the work of Claude Monet ever. The exhibit included 159 works from 66 institutions and 37 private collections around the globe—15 countries in all.

Among the highlights were 31 water lily paintings including the rarely loaned triptych from the Museum of Modern Art in New York and the central panel from *Luncheon on the Grass* which had never been seen outside of Europe and will never again leave Paris. Also included were seven of the *Houses of Parliament* series Monet painted during his stay in London.

During the opening week, 48,580 persons viewed this once-in-a-lifetime exhibition.

Major Public Libraries

City (branches)	Volumes	Circulation	Budget (in millions)
Akron–Summit County, Ohio (17)	1,198,257	3,397,585	$15.5
Albuquerque, N.N. (15)	1,157,000	2,800,000	7.5
Annapolis, Md. (15)	1,241,549	5,122,106	11.2
Atlanta–Fulton County (31)	1,960,000	2,704,000	19.5
Austin, Tex. (17)	1,062,604	2,484,456	10.5
Baltimore (29)	2,231,799	1,460,241	19.8
Baton Rouge, La. (9)	1,015,165	2,517,159	10.2
Birmingham, Ala. (19)	906,590	1,701,817	10.0
Boston (25)	6,529,998	3,500,000	29.3
Buffalo–Erie County, N.Y. (53)	4,137,650[1]	8,523,174	22.8
*Charleston–Kanawna County, W.Va. (8)[2]	621,620	1,140,413	4.3
Charlotte, N.C. (22)	1,358,311	5,280,559	15.0
Chicago (81)	5,915,886	7,337,148	73.9
Cincinnati (41)	4,655,058	11,724,356	35.9
Cleveland (27)	3,000,000	5,210,449	37.7
Columbus Metropolitan, Ohio (21)	2,212,476	10,684,651	35.5
Dallas (19)	2,490,486	4,276,354	17.8
Dayton–Montgomery County, Ohio (20)	1,628,584	5,872,370	14.0
Denver (21)	3,832,699	5,668,758	19.0
Des Moines, Iowa (5)	548,495	1,406,799	4.8
Detroit (24)	2,718,961	1,585,372	25.5
D.C. (27)	2,155,761[3]	1,905,969	21.6
El Paso (10)	1,277,003[4]	1,731,820	6.6[5]
Erie, Pa. (6)	571,629	1,655,352	3.5
Evansville–Vanderburgh Ind. (7)	1,006,060	1,442,160	5.7
Fairfax County, Va. (23)	2,100,000	8,377,605	20.8
Fort Wayne–Allen County, Ind. (14)	2,477,541	3,785,817	14.6
Fort Worth (10)	1,964,507[6]	4,107,638[6]	6.0[6]
Grand Rapids, Mich. (5)	1,048,053	1,017,281	6.2[7]
Greenville City–County, S.C. (11)	810,542	1,777,809	6.6
Hawaii State Public Library System (49)[8]	3,094,457[3]	7,258,941	24.8
Houston (34)	4,113,095	6,482,882	24.4
Independence, Mo. (29)	2,341,680	6,125,000	18.0
Indianapolis–Marion County (21)	1,815,842	7,720,766	24.5
Jackson–Hinds County, Miss. (15)	548,415	817,789	2.9
Jacksonville, Fla. (18)	2,561,664	3,296,906	14.2
Kansas City, Mo. (9)	2,004,698	1,510,513	10.1
Knoxville, Tenn. (16)	665,212	1,884,239	5.2
Lincoln, Neb. (7)	647,521	1,796,793	4.3
Long Beach, Calif. (11)	1,112,102	2,749,095	11.4
Los Angeles County (87)	6,404,353[9]	11,500,000[7]	65.5[7]
Louisville, Ky. (15)	889,000[3]	2,336,182	9.8
Masicon, Wis. (8)	692,550	2,523,532	6.7
Memphis, Tenn. (21)	1,704,008	3,689,112	12.6
Miami–Dade County, Fla. (31)	3,795,890	9,089,185	34.4
Miilwaukee (12)	2,333,862	2,959,861	16.6
Minneapolis (14)	2,069,425	3,083,536	16.6
Nashville–Davidson County, Tenn. (18)	749,473[1]	2,140,043	10.6
*Newark, N.J. (11)	1,400,000	1,400,000	9.4
New Orleans (15)	928,639	1,130,289	5.6
New York City:			
*New York Public Library			
Branches (82)	5,910,000	10,712,622	96.0
Research	12,169,149	—	78.6
Brooklyn Public Library (60)	5,947,870	9,219,814	42.1
Queens Borough Public Library (62)	9,681,898	14,483,937[10]	51.0[10]
Norfolk, Va. (11)	938,436[11]	551,234	4.2
Oklahoma City–County (12)	878,688[6]	4,361,447[6]	10.1[6]
Omaha, Neb. (9)	664,421	2,086,226	8.3[12]
Philadelphia (52)	5,933,711	6,226,330	39.2
Phoenix, Ariz. (11)	1,754,000	6,267,218	15.5
Pittsburgh (20)	1,987,799	2,931,670	15.7
Portland–Multnomah County, Ore. (14)	1,360,601	7,718,120	20.9
Providence, R.I. (9)	934,471	643,734	4.3
Richmond, Va. (10)	814,723	842,297	3.7
Rochester, N.Y. (10)	2,000,000	1,498,143	10.0
Sacramento, Calif. (22)	1,659,985	3,454,842	13.4
St. Louis (15)	4,895,532[4]	2,054,592	16.5
St. Paul (12)	1,038,506[13]	2,561,497	7.8
St. Petersburg, Fla. (6)	440,000	1,000,000	3.1
Salt Lake County, Utah (15)	1,453,974	5,154,924	13.5
San Antonio (17)	1,822,743	3,206,795	12.7
San Diego, Calif. (3#)	2,452,366[1]	6,051,510	27.5[14]
San Francisco, Calif. (26)	2,161,733	3,392,372	31.1
San Jose, Calif. (18)	1,377,000	4,791,810	17.3
Seattle (22)	2,262,885[15]	4,727,384[16]	22.9[17]
Springfield, Mass. (8)	679,226	849,788	4.0
Tampa, Fla. (17)	1,961,722	3,007,915	14.6[18]
Tucson, Ariz. (19)	1,100,000	5,200,000	12.8
Tulsa City–County, Okla. (21)	999,872	3,659,189	10.2
Wichita, Kan. (12)	964,302[19]	1,667,155	4.8
Winston-Salem–Forsyth County, N.C. (9)	400,000	2,100,000	6.0
Worcester, Mass. (2)	537,146	544,400	3.0
Youngstown–Mahoning County, Ohio (22)	574,114[1]	1,591,205	9.0

1. Includes books and audio material. 2. Plus 1 affiliate. 3. Book collection only. 4. Includes books, periodicals, records, films, government documents (collection weeded). 5. Budget included both general and bonded funds. 6. FY 1993–94. 7. 1994–95. 8. State-wide system. 9. Includes books and audiovisual materials; excludes microforms. 10. Circulation 1994–95, budget 1993–94. 11. Volumes July 1, 1994. 12. Includes benefits, indirect costs, and county funding. 13. Includes books, audiovisual materials, government documents, musical scores, etc. 14. Includes capital improvements and grant-funded services. 15. As of 12/31/94, includes print and nonprint materials. 16. Jan. 1 through 12/31/94. 17. Jan. 1 through Dec. 31, 1995. 18. Plus $5,541,968 building fund. 19. Includes CDs, films, cassettes, pamphlets, periodicals, and microforms. *Did not reply to questionnaire with updated information.

Glossary of Art Movements

Abstract Expressionism. American art movement of the 1940s that emphasized form and color within a nonrepresentational framework. Jackson Pollock initiated the revolutionary technique of splattering the paint directly on canvas to achieve the subconscious interpretation of the artist's inner vision of reality.

Art Deco. A 1920s style characterized by setbacks, zigzag forms, and the use of chrome and plastic ornamentation. New York's Chrysler Building is an architectural example of the style.

Art Nouveau. An 1890s style in architecture, graphic arts, and interior decoration characterized by writhing forms, curving lines, and asymmetrical organization. Some critics regard the style as the first stage of modern architecture.

Ashcan School. A group of New York realist artists, formed in 1908, who abandoned decorous subject matter and portrayed the more common as well as the sordid aspects of city life.

Assemblage (Collage). Forms of modern sculpture and painting utilizing readymades, found objects, and pasted fragments to form an abstract composition. Louise Nevelson's boxlike enclosures, each with its own composition of assembled objects, illustrate the style in sculpture. Pablo Picasso developed the technique of cutting and pasting natural or manufactured materials to a painted or unpainted surface.

Barbizon School (Landscape Painting). A group of painters who, around the middle of the 19th century, reacted against classical landscape and advocated a direct study of nature. They were influenced by English and Dutch landscape masters. Theodore Rousseau, one of the principal figures of the group, led the fight for outdoor painting. In this respect, the school was a forerunner of Impressionism.

Baroque. European art and architecture of the 17th and 18th centuries. Giovanni Bernini, a major exponent of the style, believed in the union of the arts of architecture, painting, and sculpture to overwhelm the spectator with ornate and highly dramatized themes. Although the style originated in Rome as the instrument of the Church, it spread throughout Europe in such monumental creations as the Palace of Versailles.

Beaux Arts. Elaborate and formal architectural style characterized by symmetry and an abundance of sculptured ornamentation. New York's old Custom House at Bowling Green is an example of the style.

Black or Afro-American Art. The work of American artists of African descent produced in various styles characterized by a mood of protest and a search for identity and historical roots.

Classicism. A form of art derived from the study of Greek and Roman styles characterized by harmony, balance, and serenity. In contrast, the Romantic Movement gave free rein to the artist's imagination and to the love of the exotic.

Constructivism. A form of sculpture using wood, metal, glass, and modern industrial materials expressing the technological society. The mobiles of Alexander Calder are examples of the movement.

Cubism. Early 20th-century French movement marked by a revolutionary departure from representational art. Pablo Picasso and Georges Bracque penetrated the surface of objects, stressing basic abstract geometric forms that presented the object from many angles simultaneously.

Dada. A product of the turbulent and cynical post-World War I period, this anti-art movement extolled the irrational, the absurd, the nihilistic, and the nonsensical. The reproduction of Mona Lisa adorned with a mustache is a famous example. The movement is regarded as a precursor of Surrealism. Some critics regard HAPPENINGS as a recent development of Dada. This movement incorporates environment and spectators as active and important ingredients in the production of random events.

Expressionism. A 20th-century European art movement that stresses the expression of emotion and the inner vision of the artist rather than the exact representation of nature. Distorted lines and shapes and exaggerated colors are used for emotional impact.

Vincent Van Gogh is regarded as the precursor of this movement.

Fauvism. The name "wild beasts" was given to the group of early 20th-century French painters because their work was characterized by distortion and violent colors. Henri Matisse and Georges Roualt were leaders of this group.

Futurism. This early 20th-century movement originating in Italy glorified the machine age and attempted to represent machines and figures in motion. The aesthetics of Futurism affirmed the beauty of technological society.

Genre. This French word meaning "type" now refers to paintings that depict scenes of everyday life without any attempt at idealization. Genre paintings can be found in all ages, but the Dutch productions of peasant and tavern scenes are typical.

Impressionism. Late 19th-century French school dedicated to defining transitory visual impressions painted directly from nature, with light and color of primary importance. If the atmosphere changed, a totally different picture would emerge. It was not the object or event that counted but the visual impression as captured at a certain time of day under a certain light. Claude Monet and Camille Pissarro were leaders of the movement.

Mannerism. A mid-16th century movement, Italian in origin, although El Greco was a major practitioner of the style. The human figure, distorted and elongated, was the most frequent subject.

Neoclassicism. An 18th-century reaction to the excesses of Baroque and Rococo, this European art movement tried to recreate the art of Greece and Rome by imitating the ancient classics both in style and subject matter.

Neoimpressionism. A school of painting associated with George Seurat and his followers in late 19th-century France that sought to make Impressionism more precise and formal. They employed a technique of juxtaposing dots of primary colors to achieve brighter secondary colors, with the mixture left to the eye to complete (pointillism).

Op Art. The 1960s movement known as Optical Painting is characterized by geometrical forms that create an optical illusion in which the eye is required to blend the colors at a certain distance.

Pop Art. In this return to representational art, the artist returns to the world of tangible objects in a reaction against abstraction. Materials are drawn from the everyday world of popular culture—comic strips, canned goods, and science fiction.

Realism. A development in mid-19th-century France lead by Gustave Courbet. Its aim was to depict the customs, ideas, and appearances of the time using scenes from everyday life.

Rococo. A French style of interior decoration developed during the reign of Louis XV consisting mainly of asymmetrical arrangements of curves in paneling, porcelain, and gold and silver objects. The characteristics of ornate curves, prettiness, and gaiety can also be found in the painting and sculpture of the period.

Surrealism. A further development of Collage, Cubism, and Dada, this 20th-century movement stresses the weird, the fantastic, and the dreamworld of the subconscious.

Symbolism. As part of a general European movement in the latter part of the 19th century, it was closely allied with Symbolism in literature. It marked a turning away from painting by observation to transforming fact into a symbol of inner experience. Gauguin was an early practitioner.

Top 10 Videocassettes Sales, 1994

1. **Aladdin** (Walt Disney Home Video)
2. **Playboy Celebrity Centerfold: Dian Parkinson** (Uni Dist. Corp.)
3. **Yanni: Live at the Acropolis** (BMG Video)
4. **Free Willy** (Warner Home Video)
5. **Mrs. Doubtfire** (FoxVideo)
6. **The Fugitive** (Warner Home Video)
7. **The Return of Jafar** (Walt Disney Home Video)
8. **The Fox and the Hound** (Walt Disney Home Video)
9. **Ace Ventura: Pet Detective** (Warner Home Video)
10. **Beauty and the Beast** (Walt Disney Home Video)

Source: © 1995 BPI Communications Inc. Used with permission from *Billboard.*

Top 10 Music Videocassettes, 1994

1. **Live Shit: Binge & Purge,** Metallica (Elektra Entertainment)
2. **Our First Video,** Mary-Kate & Ashley Olsen (BMG Kidz)
3. **Live at the Acropolis,** Yanni (BMG Video)
4. **Comedy Video Classics,** Ray Stevens (Curb Video)
5. **Barbra–The Concert,** Barbra Streisand (SMV Enterprises)
6. **Live,** Ray Stevens (Curb Video)
7. **Livin', Lovin', & Rockin' that Jukebox,** Alan Jackson (6 West Home Video)
8. **The 3 Tenors in Concert 1994,** Carerras, Domingo, Pavarotti (A*Vison Entertainment)
9. **Dangerous: The Short Films,** Michael Jackson (SMV Enterprises)
10. **Mariah Carey,** Mariah Carey (SMV Enterprises)

Source: © 1995 BPI Communications Inc.. Used with permission from *Billboard.*

Top 10 Kid Videocassettes, 1994

1. **Aladdin** (Walt Disney Home Video)
2. **Beauty and the Beast** (Walt Disney Home Video)
3. **The Fox and the Hound** (Walt Disney Home Video)
4. **Pinocchio** (Walt Disney Home Video)
5. **The Return of Jafar** (Walt Disney Home Video)
6. **101 Dalmatians** (Walt Disney Home Video)
7. **There Goes a Bulldozer!** (A*Vison Entertainment)
8. **We're Back! A Dinosaur Story** (MCA/Universal Home Video)
9. **Batman: Mask of the Phantasm** (Warner Home Video)
10. **Thumbelina** (Warner Home Video)

Source: © 1995 BPI Communication Inc.. Used with permission from *Billboard.*

Top 10 Videocassettes Rentals, 1994

1. **Sleepless in Seattle** (Columbia TriStar Home Video)
2. **Philadelphia** (Columbia TriStar Home Video)
3. **In the Line of Fire** (Columbia TriStar Home Video)
4. **The Pelican Brief** (Warner Home Video)
5. **The Fugitive** (Warner Home Video)
6. **The Firm** (Paramount Home Video)
7. **Carlito's Way** (MCA/Universal Home Video)
8. **Sliver** (Paramount Home Video)
9. **Ace Ventura: Pet Detective** (Warner Home Video)
10. **Mrs. Doubtfire** (FoxVideo)

Source: © 1995 BPI Communications Inc. Used with permission from *Billboard.*

Top 10 Classical Crossover Albums, 1994

1. **The Piano,** Michael Nyman (Virgin)
2. **Schindler's List,** John Williams/Itzhak Perlman (MCA)
3. **Christmas in Vienna,** Domingo, Ross, Carreras (Sony Classical)
4. **Pavarotti & Friends,** Various Artists (London)
5. **Symphonic Music of Yes,** London Symphony Orchestry (RCA)
6. **Symphonic Rolling Stones,** London Symphony Orchestra (RCA)
7. **Yellow Shark,** Frank Zappa (Barking Pumpkin)
8. **The Star Wars Trilogy,** London Symphony (Williams) (Arista)
9. **The Wind Beneath My Wings,** James Galway (RCA)
10. **Unforgettable,** John Williams & The Boston Pops Orchestra (Sony Classical)

Source: © 1994 BPI Communications Inc. Used with permission from *Billboard*/SoundScan, Inc.

15 Top-Grossing Concerts
(Dec. 1993–Nov. 1994)

1. **Barbra Streisand,** $16,488,900, Madison Square Garden, New York, N.Y., June 20, 23, 26, 28, 30, July 10, 12.
2. **Billy Joel/Elton John,** $14,889,127, Giants Stadium, Rutherford, N.J., July 22, 24, 26, 28–29.
3. **Barbra Streisand,** $12,400,650, Arrowhead Pond, Anaheim, Calif., June 2, 4, July 18, 20, 22, 24.
4. **The Rolling Stones, Counting Crows,** $9,531,214, Giants Stadium, Rutherford, N.J., Aug. 12, 14–15, 17.
5. **The Rolling Stones, Seal,** $9,431,700, Oakland–Alameda County Stadium, Oakland, Calif., Oct. 26, 28–29, 31.
6. **Phil Collins,** $8,730,842, Niedersachsenstadion, Hanover, Germany, Sept. 3–4, 6–7.
7. **Barbra Streisand,** $7,780,700, Palace of Auburn Hills, Mich., May 15, 17, 19.
8. **Billy Joel/Elton John,** $7,315,495, Veterans Stadium, Philadelphia, Pa., July 8–9, 12.
9. **Paul McCartney,** $6,564,416, Hermanos Rodriguez Autodromo, Mexico City, Mexico, Nov. 25, 27.
10. **The Rolling Stones, Buddy Guy, Red Hot Chili Peppers,** $6,153,301, Rose Bowl, Pasadena, Calif., Oct. 19, 22.
11. **Luis Miguel,** $5,543,982, National Auditorium, Mexico City, Mexico, Aug. 4–28.
12. **Pink Floyd,** $5,301,117, Montreal (Que.) Olympic Stadium, May 22–24.
13. **Pink Floyd,** $5,249,778, Oakland–Alameda County Stadium, Oakland, Calif., April 20–22.
14. **Pink Floyd,,** $5,235,862, Hermanos Rodriguez Autodromo, Mexico City, Mexico, April 9–10.
15. **Eagles,** $5,129,091, Great Woods Center for the Performing Arts, Mansfield, Mass., Aug. 5–7, 9–10.

Source: © 1994, BPI Communications Inc. Used with permission from *Amusement Business.*

Top 10 Classical Albums, 1994

1. **Chant,** Benedictine Monks of Santo Domingo De Silo (Angel)
2. **The 3 Tenors in Concert 1994,** Jose Carreras, Placido Domingo, Luciano Pavarotti (Mehta) (Atlantic)
3. **In Concert,** Jose Carreras, Placido Domingo, Luciano Pavarotti (Mehta) (London)
4. **Gershwin Plays Gershwin,** George Gershwin/ Wodehouse (Nonesuch)
5. **Gorecki: Symphony No. 3,** Dawn Upshaw/ Zinman (Nonesuch)
6. **The Nutcracker,** NYC Ballet (Zinman) (Nonesuch)
7. **Ti Amo,** Luciano Pavarotti (London)
8. **Arvo Part: Te Deum,** Tallinn Chamber Orchestra (Kaljuste) (ECM)
9. **My Heart's Delight,** Luciano Pavarotti (London)
10. **If You Love Me,** Cecilia Bartoli (London)

Source: © 1994 BPI Communications Inc. Used with permission from *Billboard*/SoundScan, Inc.

Artists of the Year, 1994

Single of the Year: The Sign, Ace of Base
Album of the Year: The Sign, Ace of Base
Female Artist of the Year: Mariah Carey
Male Artist of the Year: Snoop Doggy Dogg
Group of the Year: Ace of Base
New Artist of the Year: Ace of Base
County Artist of the Year: Garth Brooks
Rhythm & Blues Artist of the Year: R. Kelly
Adult Contemporary Artist of the Year: Mariah Carey
Jazz Artist of the Year: Tony Bennett
Classical Artist of the Year: Benedictine Monks of Santo Domingo De Silos

Source: © 1994 BPI Communications Inc. Used with permission from *Billboard*/Broadcast Data Systems/SoundScan Inc.

Top 10 Country Single Recordings, 1994

1. **I Swear,** John Michael Montgomery (Atlantic)
2. **Wink,** Neal McCoy (Atlantic)
3. **Third Rock from the Sun,** Joe Diffie (Epic)
4. **Dreaming With My Eyes Open,** Clay Walker (Giant)
5. **Down on the Farm,** Tim McGraw (Curb)
6. **XXX's and OOO's (An American Girl),** Trisha Yearwood (MCA)
7. **Summertime Blues,** Alan Jackson (Arista)
8. **What the Cowgirls Do,** Vince Gill (MCA)
9. **Love a Little Stronger,** Diamond Rio (Arista)
10. **Foolish Pride,** Travis Tritt (Warner Bros.)

Source: © 1994 BPI Communications Inc. Used with permission from *Billboard*/Broadcast Data Systems/SoundScan, Inc.

Top 10 Pop Single Recordings, 1994

1. **The Sign,** Ace of Base (Arista)
2. **I Swear,** All-4-One (Blitzz)
3. **I'll Make Love to You,** Boyz II Men (Motown)
4. **The Power of Love,** Celine Dion (550 Music)
5. **Hero,** Mariah Carey (Columbia)
6. **Stay (I Missed You)** (from Reality Bites), Lisa Loeb & Nine Stories (RCA)
7. **Breathe Again,** Toni Braxton (LaFace)
8. **All for Love,** Bryan Adams, Rod Stewart, Sting (A&M)
9. **All That She Wants,** Ace of Base (Arista)
10. **Don't Turn Around,** Ace of Base (Arista)

Source: © 1994 BPI Communications Inc. Used with permission from *Billboard*/Broadcast Data Systems/SoundScan, Inc.

Top 10 Pop Albums, 1994

1. **The Sign,** Ace of Base (Arista)
2. **Music Box,** Mariah Carey (Columbia)
3. **Doggy Style,** Snoop Doggy Dogg (Death Row/ Interscope)
4. **The Lion King,** Soundtrack (Walt Disney)
5. **August & Everything After,** Counting Crows (DGC)
6. **VS.,** Pearl Jam (Epic)
7. **Toni Braxton,** Toni Braxton (LaFace)
8. **Janet,** Janet Jackson (Virgin)
9. **Bat Out of Hell II: Back Into Hell,** Meat Loaf (MCA)
10. **The One Thing,** Michael Bolton (Columbia)

Source: © 1994 BPI Communications Inc. Used with permission from *Billboard*/Broadcast Data Systems/SoundScan, Inc.

Manufacturers' Dollar[1] Shipments of Recordings
(in millions)

	1991	1992	1993	1994
Vinyl singles	63.9	66.4	51.2	47.2
LP's/EP's	29.4	13.5	10.6	17.8
CD's	4,337.7	5,326.5	6,511.4	8,464.5
Cassettes	3,019.6	3,116.3	2,915.8	2,976.4
Cassette singles	230.4	298.8	298.5	274.9
CD singles	35.1	45.1	45.8	56.1
Music videos	118.1	157.4	213.3	231.1

1. List price value. *Source:* Recording Industry Association of America, Inc.

Top 10 Rhythm & Blues Single Recordings, 1994

1. **Bump N' Grind,** R. Kelly (Jive)
2. **Back & Forth,** Aaliyah (Blackguard)
3. **I'll Make Love to You,** Boyz II Men (Motown)
4. **Can We Talk,** Tevin Campbell (Qwest)
5. **Cry for You,** Lodeci (Uptown)
6. **I Miss You,** Aaron Hall (Silas)
7. **Any Time, Any Place/And On and On,** Janet Jackson (Virgin)
8. **Never Keeping Secrets,** Babyface (Epic)
9. **Your Body's Callin',** R. Kelly (Jive)
10. **Send Me Swingin',** Mint Condition (Perspective)

Source: © 1994 BPI Communications Inc. Used with permission from *Billboard*/Broadcast Data Systems/SoundScan, Inc.

Top 15 Regularly Scheduled Network Programs, 1994–95[1]

Rank	Program name (network)	Total percent of TV households
1.	Seinfeld (NBC)	20.5
2.	E.R. (NBC)	20.0
3.	Home Improvement (ABC)	19.9
4.	Grace Under Fire (ABC)	18.8
5.	NFL Monday Night Football (ABC)	17.8
6.	60 Minutes (CBS)	17.1
7.	NYPD Blue (ABC)	16.5
8.	Friends (NBC)	16.1
9.	Roseanne (ABC)	15.6
9.	Murder, She Wrote (CBS)	15.6
11.	Mad About You (NBC)	15.2
12.	Madman of the People (NBC)	14.9
13.	Ellen (ABC)	14.7
14.	Hope & Gloria (NBC)	14.6
15.	Frasier (NBC)	14.3
Total U.S. TV households 95,400,000		

1. Sept. 19, 1994, through April 16, 1995. NOTE: Percentages are calculated from average audience viewings, 5 minutes or longer and 2 or more telecasts. *Source:* Nielsen Media Research. Copyright 1995, Nielsen Media Research.

Top 15 Syndicated TV Programs 1994–95 Season

Rank	Program	Rating (% U.S.)[1]
1.	Wheel of Fortune	13.8
2.	Jeopardy	11.4
3.	Oprah Winfrey Show	8.7
4.	Buena Vista I	8.1
4.	Star Trek	8.1
6.	Entertainment Tonight	7.9
7.	National Geographic on Assignment	7.6
8.	Star Trek: Deep Space Nine	7.5
9.	Magic II	7.3
10.	Roseanne	7.0
11.	Turner Pictures II	6.9
12.	Wheel of Fortune, Weekend	6.7
13.	Hard Copy	6.5
13.	Inside Edition	6.5
15.	Baywatch	6.4

1. Sept. 19, 1994, through April 16, 1995. *Source:* Nielsen Syndication Service National TV Ratings. Copyright 1995, Nielsen Media Research.

Top Sports Shows 1994–95[1]

Rank	Program name (network)	Rating (% of TV households)
1.	Super Bosl XXIX (ABC)	41.3
2.	Fox NFC Championship (Fox)	34.2
3.	Super Bowl XXIX Kickoff (ABC)	31.6
4.	AFC Championship Game (NBC)	28.3
5.	NFL Playoff Game (NBC)	25.1
6.	Super Bowl XXIX (Post Game) (ABC)	24.7
7.	AFC/NFC Playoff Game 2 (ABC)	24.1
8.	Fox NFC Playoff (Fox)	22.7
9.	AFC Wildcard Playoff (NBC)	22.0
10.	Fox NFC Wildcard Game (Fox)	21.0

1. Sept. 19, 1994, through April 16, 1995. *Source:* Nielsen Media Research. Copyright 1995, Nielsen Media Research.

Top Specials 1994–95[1]

Rank	Program name (network)	Rating (% of TV households)
1.	Academy Awards (ABC)	32.5
2.	Seinfeld Special (NBC)	22.6
3.	Mad About You Special (NBC)	21.6
4.	Seinfeld Special (NBC)	20.6
5.	Home Improvement Special (ABC)	18.5

1. Sept. 19, 1994, through April 16, 1995. *Source:* Nielsen Media Research. Copyright 1995, Nielsen Media Research.

Persons Viewing Prime Time[1]
(in millions)

	Total persons
Monday	98.2
Tuesday	94.6
Wednesday	91.7
Thursday	92.7
Friday	79.7
Saturday	78.2
Sunday	91.3
Total average	**89.5**

1. Average minute audiences May 1995. NOTE: Prime time is 8–11 p.m. (EST) except Sun. 7–11 pm. *Source:* Nielsen Media Research. Copyright 1995, Nielsen Media Research.

Top Rated Movies 1994–95[1]

Rank	Program name (network)	Rating (% of TV households)
1.	Scarlett—Part I (CBS)	21.4
2.	Rockford Files (CBS)	18.5
3.	Cagney & Lacey—Return (CBS)	18.4
4.	Someone She Knows (NBC)	18.3
5.	Scarlett—Part 3 (CBS)	17.8
5.	Presumed Innocent (CBS)	17.8
5.	Woman of Independent Means—Part 1 (NBC)	17.8
8.	Scarlett—Part 4 (CBS)	17.7
8.	A Friend To Die For (NBC)	17.7
10.	ER (NBC)	17.6

1. Sept. 19, 1994, through April 16, 1995. *Source:* Nielsen Media Research. Copyright 1995, Nielsen Media Research.

Average Hours of Household TV Usage

(In hours and minutes per day)

	Yearly average	February	July
1985–86	7 h 10 min	7 h 48 min	6 h 37 min
1986–87	7 h 05 min	7 h 35 min	6 h 32 min
1987–88	6 h 55 min	7 h 38 min	6 h 31 min
1988–89	7 h 02 min	7 h 32 min	6 h 27 min
1989–90	6 h 55 min	7 h 16 min	6 h 24 min
1990–91	6 h 56 min	7 h 30 min	6 h 26 min
1991–92	7 h 04 min	7 h 32 min	6 h 39 min
1992–93	7 h 17 min	7 h 41 min	6 h 47 min
1993–94	7 h 21 min	7 h 51 min	6 h 53 min

Source: Nielsen Media Research, copyright 1995, Nielsen Media Research.

Weekly TV Viewing by Age

(in hours and minutes)

	Time per week	
	Nov. 1994	Nov. 1993
Women 18–24 years old	26 h 23 min	25 h 42 min
Women 25–54	30 h 55 min	30 h 35 min
Women 55 and over	44 h 11 min	44 h 11 min
Men 18–24	22 h 41 min	22 h 31 min
Men 25–54	27 h 13 min	28 h 04 min
Men 55 and over	38 h 38 min	38 h 28 min
Female Teens	20 h 20 min	20 h 50 min
Male Teens	21 h 59 min	21 h 10 min
Children 6–11	21 h 30 min	19 h 59 min
Children 2–5	24 h 42 min	24 h 32 min

Source: Nielsen Media Research, copyright 1995, Nielsen Media Research.

Television Network Addresses

American Broadcasting Companies (ABC)
77 W. 66th Street
New York, N.Y. 10023
Cable News Network (CNN)
100 International Blvd., ICNN Center
Atlanta, Ga. 30348
Canadian Broadcasting Corporation (CBC)
1500 Bronson Avenue
Ottawa, Ontario, Canada K1G 3J5
Columbia Broadcasting System (CBS)
51 W. 52nd Street
New York, N.Y. 10019
Fox Television
10201 W. Pico Blvd.
Los Angeles, Calif. 90064
National Broadcasting Company (NBC)
30 Rockefeller Plaza
New York, N.Y. 10020
Public Broadcasting Service (PBS)
1320 Braddock Place
Alexandra, Va. 22314
Turner Network Television (TNT)
100 International Blvd., ICNN Center
Atlanta, Ga. 30348
Westinghouse Broadcasting Co.
888 7th Ave.
New York, N.Y. 10106

Television Set Ownership

(May 1995)

Homes with	Number	Percent
Color TV sets	94,446,000	99.0
B&W only	954,000	01.0
2 or more sets	62,964,000	66.0
One set	32,436,000	34.0
Cable	62,010,000	65.0
Total TV households	**95,400,000**	**98.0**

Source: Nielsen Media Research, copyright 1995, Nielsen Media Research.

Audience Composition by Selected Program Type[1]

(Average Minute Audience)

	General drama	Suspense and mystery drama	Situation comedy	Informational[2] 6-7 p.m.	Feature films	All regular network programs 7–11 p.m.
Women (18 and over)	7,610,000	10,220,000	8,882,000	6,910,000	8,810,000	8,270,000
Men (18 and over)	4,560,000	6,870,000	5,930,000	5,200,000	5,620,000	5,950,000
Teens (12–17)	1,010,000	760,000	1,610,000	320,000	1,220,000	1,180,000
Children (2–11)	1,180,000	990,000	2,620,000	540,000	1,820,000	1,640,000
Total persons (2+)	**14,360,000**	**18,840,000**	**18,990,000**	**12,980,000**	**17,480,000**	**17,040,000**

1. All figures are estimated for the period Nov. 1994. 2. Multiweekly viewing. *Source:* Nielsen Media Research, copyright 1995, Nielsen Media Research.

Hours of TV Usage Per Week by Household Income

	Under $30,000	$30,000+	$40,000+	$50,000+	$60,000+
Nov. 1992	53 h 35 min	52 h 05 min	50 h 24 min (includes $50,000+)		47 h 13 min
Nov. 1993	53 h 35 min	50 h 34 min	50 h 24 min (includes $50,000+)		47 h 13 min
Nov. 1994	53 h 46 min	52 h 05 min	50 h 04 min (includes $50,000+)		46 h 42 min

Source: Nielsen Media Research, copyright 1995, Nielsen Media Research.

Source of Household Viewing—Prime Time
Pay Cable, Basic Cable, and Non-Cable Households
(Mon.-Sun. 8–11 pm)

	Nov. 1994			Nov. 1993			Nov. 1992		
	Pay cable	Basic cable	Non-cable	Pay cable	Basic cable	Non-cable	Pay cable	Basic cable	Non-cable
% TV Usage	67.0	61.2	58.1	68.7	61.3	57.2	68.7	62.6	55.5
Pay Cable	9.3	—		9.2	—		10.0	—	
Cable-originated programming	22.1	20.5	—	21.0	20.2	—		20.5	20.3	—
Other-on-air stations	7.2	7.8	12.7	7.2	7.1	11.4	7.1	7.5	11.1
Network affiliated stations	41.6	40.7	50.6	44.4	40.7	50.3	43.8	42.7	48.2
Network share	(62)	(67)	(87)	(65)	(66)	(88)	(64)	(68)	(87)

Source: Nielsen Media Research, copyright 1995, Nielsen Media Research.

Major U.S. Fairs and Expositions

1853 Crystal Palace Exposition, New York City: modeled on similar fair held in London.

1876 Centennial Exposition, Philadelphia: celebrating 100th year of independence.

1893 World's Columbian Exposition, Chicago: commemorating 400th anniversary of Columbus' voyage to America.

1894 Midwinter International Exposition, San Francisco: promoting business revival after Depression of 1893.

1898 Trans-Mississippi and International Exposition, Omaha, Neb.: exhibiting products, resources, industries, and civilization of states and territories west of the Mississippi River.

1901 Pan-American Exposition, Buffalo, N.Y.: promoting social and commercial interest of Western Hemisphere nations.

1904 Louisiana Purchase Exposition, St. Louis: marking 100th anniversary of major land acquisition from France and opening up of the West.

1905 Lewis and Clark Centennial Exposition, Portland, Ore.: commemorating 100th anniversary of exploration of a land route to the Pacific.

1907 Jamestown Tercentennial Exposition, Hampton Roads, Va.: marking 300th anniversary of first permanent English settlement in America.

1909 Alaska-Yukon-Pacific Exposition, Seattle: celebrating growth of the Puget Sound area.

1915–16 Panama-Pacific International Exposition, San Francisco: celebrating opening of the Panama Canal.

1915–16 Panama-California Exposition, San Diego: promoting resources and opportunities for development and commerce of the Western states.

1926 Sesquicentennial Exposition, Philadelphia: marking 150th year of independence.

1933–34 Century of Progress International Exposition, Chicago: celebrating 100th anniversary of incorporation of Chicago as a city.

1935 California Pacific International Exposition, San Diego: marking 400 years of progress since the first Spaniard landed on the West Coast.

1939–40 New York World's Fair, New York City: "The World of Tomorrow," symbolized by Trylon and Perisphere. Officially commemorating 150th anniversary of inauguration of George Washington as President in New York.

1939–1940 Golden Gate International Exposition, Treasure Island, San Francisco: celebrating new Golden Gate Bridge and Oakland Bay Bridge.

1962 The Century 21 Exposition, Seattle: "Man in the Space Age," symbolized by 600-foot steel space needle.

1964–65 New York World's Fair, New York City: "Peace Through Understanding."

1974 Expo '74, Spokane: "Tomorrow's Fresh, New Environment."

1982 World's Fair, Knoxville, Tenn.: "Energy Turns the World," symbolized by the bronze-globed Sunsphere.

1984 Louisiana World Exposition, New Orleans: "The World of Rivers."

Longest Broadway Runs[1]

1.	A Chorus Line (M) (1975–90)	6,137
2.	Oh, Calcutta (M) (1976–89)	5,959
3.	Cats (M) (1982–)	5,357
4.	42nd Street (M) (1980–89)	3,486
5.	Les Miserables (M) (1987–)	3,445
6.	Grease (M) (1972–80)	3,388
7.	Fiddler on the Roof (M) (1964–72)	3,242
8.	Life with Father (1939–47)	3,224
9.	Tobacco Road (1933–41)	3,182
10.	Phantom of the Opera (1988–)	3,143
11.	Hello, Dolly! (M) (1964–71)	2,844
12.	My Fair Lady (M) (1956–62)	2,717
13.	Annie (M) (1977–83)	2,377
14.	Oklahoma (M) (1943–48)	2,377
15.	Man of La Mancha (M) (1965–71)	2,328
16.	Abie's Irish Rose (1922–27)	2,327
17.	Pippin (M) (1971–77)	1,994
18.	South Pacific (M) (1949–54)	1,925
19.	Magic Show (M) (1974–78)	1,920
20.	Miss Saigon (M)	1,797
21.	Deathtrap (1978–82)	1,792
22.	Gemini (1977–81)	1,788
23.	Harvey (1944–49)	1,775
24.	Dancin' (M) (1978–82)	1,774
25.	Cage aux Folles (M) (1983–87)	1,761

1. As of Aug. 6, 1995. M = musical. Years are those of opening and closing.

Motion Picture Revenues

(As of January 3, 1995)

All-Time Top Box Office Grosses[1]		Top Box Office Grosses 1994	
1. E.T. The Extra-Terrestrial (Universal, 1982)	$399,804,539	1. The Lion King (Buena Vista)	$300,352,905
2. Jurassic Park (Universal, 1993)	356,839,725	2. Forrest Gump (Paramount)	298,535,927
3. Star Wars (20th Century-Fox, 1977)	322,000,000	3. True Lies (20th Century-Fox)	146,273,950
4. The Lion King (Buena Vista, 1994)	300,352,905	4. The Santa Clause (Buena Vista)	137,826,098
5. Forrest Gump (Paramount, 1994)	298,535,927	5. The Flintstones (Universal)	130,512,915
6. Home Alone (20th Century-Fox, 1990)	285,016,000	6. Clear and Present Danger (Paramount)	121,758,219
7. Return of the Jedi (20th Century-Fox, 1983)	263,734,642	7. Speed (20th Century-Fox)	121,221,490
8. Jaws (Universal, 1975)	260,000,000	8. The Mask (New Line Cinema)	118,820,184
9. Batman (Warner Brothers, 1989)	251,188,924	9. Maverick (Warner Brothers)	101,619,662
10. Raiders of the Lost Ark (Paramount, 1981)	242,374,454	10. Interview With the Vampire (Warner Brothers)	100,689,360
11. Beverly Hills Cop (Paramount, 1984)	234,760,478	11. The Client (Warner Brothers)	92,112,663
12. The Empire Strikes Back (20th Century-Fox, 1980)	223,000,000	12. Ace Ventura: Pet Detective (Warner Brothers	72,208,397
13. Ghostbusters (Columbia, 1984)	220,855,498	13. Star Trek: Generations (Paramount)	71,293,610
14. Mrs. Doubtfire (20th Century-Fox, 1993)	219,194,773	14. Stargate (MGM)	68,644,252
15. Ghost (Paramount, 1990)	217,631,306	15. Dumb and Dumber (New Line Cinema)	66,469,339
16. Aladdin (Buena Vista, 1992)	217,042,825	16. Wolf (Columbia)	65,002,597
17. Back to the Future (Universal, 1985)	210,609,762	17. Pulp Fiction (Miramax)	63,617,560
18. Terminator 2 (TriStar, 1991)	204,446,562	18. The Specialist (Warner Brothers)	56,139,593
19. Indiana Jones and the Last Crusade (Paramount, 1989)	197,171,806	19. Four Weddings and a Funeral (Gramercy)	52,636,671
20. Gone With the Wind (MGM/United Artists/ (TEC, 1939)	193,597,756	20. The Little Rascals (Universal)	51,742,905
21. Snow White (RKO/Buena Vista, 1937)	184,925,486	21. Disclosure (Warner Brothers)	51,674,942
22. Dances With Wolves (Orion, 1990)	184,031,933	22. The Crow (Miramax/Dimension)	50,691,685
23. The Fugitive (Warner Brothers, 1993)	183,752,965	23. Angels in the Outfield (Buena Vista)	50,226,141
24. Indiana Jones and the Temple of Doom (Paramount, 1984)	179,870,271	24. Natural Born Killers (Warner Brothers)	50,215,945
25. Pretty Woman (Buena Vista, 1990)	178,406,268	25. When a Man Loves a Woman (Buena Vista)	50,000,813

1. Including reissues. *Source:* Exhibitor Relations Co. Inc.

Miss America Winners

1921	Margaret Gorman, Washington, D.C.	1964	Donna Axum, El Dorado, Ark.
1922-23	Mary Campbell, Columbus, Ohio	1965	Vonda Kay Van Dyke, Phoenix, Ariz.
1924	Ruth Malcolmson, Philadelphia, Pa.	1966	Deborah Irene Bryant, Overland Park, Kan.
1925	Fay Lamphier, Oakland, Calif.	1967	Jane Anne Jayroe, Laverne, Okla.
1926	Norma Smallwood, Tulsa, Okla.	1968	Debra Dene Barnes, Moran, Kan.
1927	Lois Delaner, Joliet, Ill.	1969	Judith Anne Ford, Belvidere, Ill.
1933	Marion Bergeron, West Haven, Conn.	1970	Pamela Anne Eldred, Birmingham, Mich.
1935	Henrietta Leaver, Pittsburgh, Pa.	1971	Phyllis Ann George, Denton, Texas
1936	Rose Coyle, Philadelphia, Pa.	1972	Laurie Lea Schaefer, Columbus, Ohio
1937	Bette Cooper, Bertrand Island, N.J.	1973	Terry Anne Meeuwsen, DePere, Wis.
1938	Marilyn Meseke, Marion, Ohio	1974	Rebecca Ann King, Denver, Colo.
1939	Patricia Donnelly, Detroit, Mich.	1975	Shirley Cothran, Fort Worth, Texas
1940	Frances Marie Burke, Philadelphia, Pa.	1976	Tawney Elaine Godin, Yonkers, N.Y.
1941	Rosemary LaPlanche, Los Angeles, Calif.	1977	Dorothy Kathleen Benham, Edina, Minn.
1942	JoCaroll Dennison, Tyler, Texas	1978	Susan Perkins, Columbus, Ohio
1943	Jean Bartel, Los Angeles, Calif.	1979	Kylene Baker, Galax, Va.
1944	Venus Ramey, Washington, D.C.	1980	Cheryl Prewitt, Ackerman, Miss.
1945	Bess Myerson, New York, N.Y.	1981	Susan Powell, Elk City, Okla.
1946	Marilyn Buferd, Los Angeles, Calif.	1982	Elizabeth Ward, Russellville, Ark.
1947	Barbara Walker, Memphis, Tenn.	1983	Debra Maffett, Anaheim, Calif.
1948	BeBe Shopp, Hopkins, Minn.	1984	Vanessa Williams, Milwood, N.Y.[1]
1949	Jacque Mercer, Litchfield, Ariz.		Suzette Charles, Mays Landing, N.J.
1951	Yolande Betbeze, Mobile, Ala.	1985	Sharlene Wells, Salt Lake City, Utah
1952	Coleen Kay Hutchins, Salt Lake City, Utah	1986	Susan Akin, Meridian, Miss.
1953	Neva Jane Langley, Macon, Ga.	1987	Kellye Cash, Memphis, Tenn.
1954	Evelyn Margaret Ay, Ephrata, Pa.	1988	Kaye Lani Rae Rafko, Toledo, Ohio
1955	Lee Meriwether, San Francisco, Calif.	1989	Gretchen Elizabeth Carlson, Anoka, Minn.
1956	Sharon Ritchie, Denver, Colo.	1990	Debbye Turner, Mexico, Mo.
1957	Marian McKnight, Manning, S.C.	1991	Marjorie Judith Vincent, Oak Park, Ill.
1958	Marilyn Van Derbur, Denver, Colo.	1992	Carolyn Suzanne Sapp, Honolulu, Hawaii
1959	Mary Ann Mobley, Brandon, Miss.	1993	Leanza Cornett, Jacksonville, Fla.
1960	Lynda Lee Mead, Natchez, Miss.	1994	Kimberly Clarice Aiken, Columbia, S.C.
1961	Nancy Fleming, Montague, Mich.	1995	Heather Whitestone, Birmingham, Ala.
1962	Maria Fletcher, Asheville, N.C.	1996	(*See* Current Events)
1963	Jacquelyn Mayer, Sandusky, Ohio		1. Resigned July 23, 1984.

U.S. Opera Companies

(Budgets $2,000,000 and over)

Arizona Opera Company (Tucson), Glynn Ross, Gen. Dir.

Baltimore Opera Company (Md.), Michael Harrison, Gen. Dir.

Boston Lyric Opera Company (Mass.), Janice Mancini Del Sesto, Gen. Dir.

Central City Opera House Association (Colo.), Daniel R. Rule, Gen. Mgr.

Cincinnati Opera Association (Ohio), James de Blasis, Art. Dir.

Civic Light Opera (Pittsburgh), Charles Gray, Exec. Dir. & Gen. Mgr.

Cleveland Opera (Ohio), David Bamberger, Gen. Dir.

Dallas Opera, The (Texas), Plato S. Karayanis, Gen. Dir.

Florentine Opera Company (Milwaukee), Dennis W. Hanthorne, Gen. Dir.

Florida Grand Opera (Miami), Robert M. Heuer, Gen. Mgr. & CEO.

Gimmerglass Opera (Cooperstown, N.Y.), Paul Kellogg, Gen. Dir.

Goodspeed Opera House (East Haddan, Conn.), Michael Price, Exec. Dir.

Hawaii Opera Theatre (Honolulu), J. Mario Ramos, Gen. Dir.

Houston Grand Opera Association (Texas), R. David Gockley, Gen. Dir.

Kentucky Opera (Louisville), Thomson Smillie, Gen. Dir.

Long Beach Civic Light Opera (Calif.), Barry Brown, Producer & CEO

Los Angeles Music Center Opera (Calif.), Peter Hemmings, Gen. Dir.

Lyric Opera of Chicago (Ill.), Ardis Krainik, Gen. Dir.

Lyric Opera of Kansas City (Mo.), Russell Patterson, Gen. & Art. Dir.

Metro Lyric Opera, (Allenhurst, N.J.), Era M. Tognoli, Gen. & Art. Dir.

Metropolitan Opera Association (N.Y.), James Levine, Art. Dir.

Michigan Opera Theatre (Detroit), David di Chiera, Gen. Dir.

Minnesota Opera, The (Minneapolis), Kevin Smith, President & Gen. Dir.

New York City Opera (N.Y.), Christopher Keene, Gen. Dir.

Ohio Light Opera (Wooster), James Stuart, Art. Dir.

Opera Colorado (Denver), Nathaniel Merrill, President & Gen. Dir.

Opera Company of Philadelphia (Pa.), Robert B. Driver, Gen. Dir.

Opera Pacific (Costa Mesa, Calif.), David Di Chiera, Gen. Dir.

Opera Theater Center (Aspen), Robert Hirth, President & CEO.

Opera Theatre of St. Louis (Mo.), Charles MacKay, Gen. Dir.

Palm Beach Opera Inc. (Fla.), Herbert P. Benn, Gen. Dir.

Pittsburgh Opera, Inc. (Pa.), Tito Capobianco, Gen. Dir.

Portland Opera Association (Ore.), Robert Bailey, Gen. Dir.

San Diego Civic Light Opera Association (Calif.), Leon Drew, Gen. Mgr.

San Diego Opera (Calif.), Ian D. Campbell, Gen. Dir.

San Jose Civic Light Opera (Calif.), Dianna Schuster, Art. Dir.

San Francisco Opera (Calif.), Lotfi Mansouri, Gen. Dir.

San Francisco Opera Center (Calif.), Christopher Hahn, Dir.

Santa Barbara Civic Light Opera (Calif.), Paul Jannacone, Exec. Prod.

Santa Fe Opera (N.M.), John Crosby, Gen. Dir.

Sarasota Opera Association (Fla.), Deane C. Allyn, Exec. Dir.

Seattle Opera Association (Wash.), Speight Jenkins, Gen. Dir.

Virginia Opera (Norfolk), Peter Mark, Gen. Dir.

Utah Opera Company (Salt Lake City), Anne Ewers, Gen. Dir.

Washington Opera, The (D.C.), Martin Feinstein, Gen. Dir.

U.S. Dance Companies

(Budget $2,500,000 and over)

(Figure in parentheses is year of founding)

Alvin Ailey American Dance Theatre (1958): Exec. Dir. Barbara B. Hauptman

American Ballet Theatre (1940): Art. Dir. Kevin McKenzie

Atlanta Ballet Company (1929): Art. Dir. John McCall

BalletMet, Inc. (1978): Art. Dir. David Nixon

Ballet West (1968[2]): Art. Dir. John Hart

Boston Ballet (1964): Art. Dir. Bruce Marks

Cincinnati/City Ballet (1955): Art. Dir. Peter Anastos

Cleveland/San Jose Ballet (1976[3]): Art. Dir. Dennis Nahat

Colorado Ballet (1961): Art. Dir. Martin Fredmann

Merce Cunningham Dance Company (1952): Dir. Merce Cunningham

Dance Theater of Harlem (1968): Art. Dir. Arthur Mitchell

Feld Ballet NY (1974): Dir. Eliot Feld

Martha Graham Dance Company (1927): Gen. Dir. Ron Protas

Houston Ballet (1968): Art. Dir. Ben Stevenson

Joffrey Ballet of Chicago[1] (1954): Art. Dir. Gerald Arpino

Miami City Ballet (1986): Art. Dir. Edward Villella

Milwaukee Ballet (1970): Art. Dir. Basil Thompson

New York City Ballet (1948): Peter Martin, Ballet Master in chief

Ocheami-Afrikan Dance Company (1978): Art. Dir. Kofe Anag

Pacific Northwest Ballet (1972): Art. Dirs. Kent Stowell and Francia Russell

Pennsylvania Ballet (1963): Gen. Mgr. Ellen C. Moran

Pittsburgh Ballet Theater (1970): Art. Dir. Patricia Wilde

San Francisco Ballet (1933): Art. Dir. Helgi Tomasson

Paul Taylor Dance Company (1954): Dir. Paul Taylor

Washington Ballet (1962): Art. Dir. Mary Day

1. Formerly Joffrey Ballet. Name changed in 1995. 2. Prior company founded 1963, name changed to Ballet West in 1968. 3. In 1986 joined in co-venture with San Jose Ballet.

Nureyev Memorabilia Sale Tops Expectations

Christie's, which estimated Nureyev's effects would bring between $3.3 and $4.8 million in its two-day auction, underestimated the power of his name. The sale raised more than $7.9 million.

PROFILE OF THE UNITED STATES

This Profile was created by the editors of *Information Please* from many data sources. Most figures are approximate. For additional details about the United States, please refer to the appropriate sections of the *Information Please Almanac*. NOTE: figures given are latest available at presstime.

GEOGRAPHY

Number of states: 50
Land area (1990): 3,536,341. Share of world land area (1990): 6.2%
Northernmost point: Point Barrow, Alaska
Easternmost point: West Quoddy Head, Maine
Southernmost point: Ka Lae (South Cape), Hawaii
Westernmost point: Pochnoi Point, Alaska[1]
Geographic center: in Butte County, S.D. (44″ 58′ N. lat., 103″ 46′ W. long.)

1. The extreme points are measured from the geographic center of the United States (incl. Alaska and Hawaii), west of Castle Rock, S.D. 44° 58′ N. lat., 103° 46′ W. long. If measured from the prime meridian in Greenwich, England Pochnoi Point, Alaska would be the easternmost point.

POPULATION

Total[1] (est. July 1, 1995): 262,777,000
Center of population (1990): 9.7 miles northwest of Steelville in Crawford County, Missouri.
Males (1990): 121,239,418
Females (1990): 127,470,455
White (July 1, 1995): 193,519,000
Black (July 1, 1995): 31,606,000
Hispanic origin (can be of any race) (July 1, 1995): 26,978,000
American Indian, Eskimo, Aleut (July 1, 1995): 1,931,000
Asian and Pacific Islanders (July 1, 1995): 8,743,000
Median age (1990): 32.9
Baby boomers (Nov. 1992): 77,000,000
Rural population (1990): 66,964,000
Metropolitan population (1990): 192,725,741
Families (March 1994): 68,490,000
Average family size (March 1994): 2.67
Home ownership (1990): 59,846,000
Married couples (March 1994): 54,251,000
Unmarried couples (1994): 3,661,000
Single parents (1990): female, 6,599,000; male, 1,153,000
Widows (1990): 11,477,000
Widowers (1990): 2,333,000

1. Resident population of the U.S. plus Armed Forces overseas.

VITAL STATISTICS

Births (1994 provisional): 3,979,000
Deaths (1994 provisional): 2,286,000
Marriages (1994 provisional): 2,362,000
Divorces (1994 provisional): 1,191,000
Infant Mortality Rate (1994 est.): 8.11/1,000
Legal abortions (1992): 1,528,930
Life Expectancy (1992): White men, 73.2; white women, 79.8; all other men, 67.7; all other women, 75.7

CIVILIAN LABOR FORCE

All (1994): 131,056,000 (93.9% employed)
Males (1994): 70,817,000 (93.8% employed)
Females (1994): 60,239,000 (94% employed)
Work at home (telecommuters, est. 1993): 7.6 million

Farms (June 1, 1994): 2,040,410; total acres (provisional 1993): 978,153,000. Farm population (1992): 4,665,000; percent of civilian population, 1.8%.

INCOME AND CREDIT

Gross Domestic Product (1994): 6,736,100,000,000
Federal budget (est. 1996): total receipts, $1,415.5 billion; total outlays, $1,612.1 billion; total deficit, $196.6 billion
Personal income per capita (1994 preliminary): $21,809
Median family income (1993): $36,950
Individual Shareholders (1990): 51,440,000
Number below poverty level (1993): white, 26,226,000; black, 10,877,000; Hispanic, 8,126,000

EDUCATION

Public elementary pupils, Grades 1–8 (Oct. 1994): 28,131,000
Public secondary pupils, Grades 9–12 (Oct. 1994): 13,539,000
Private elementary pupils, Grades 1–8 (Oct. 1994): 3,382,000
Private secondary pupils, Grades 9–12 (Oct. 1994): 1,077,000
College enrollment, public (Oct. 1994): 11,693,000
College enrollment, private (Oct. 1994): 3,327,000
College graduates (1993–94): 1,165,000
Money spent on public elementary and secondary education (1991–92): $234,485,729
Projected public school teachers (1994): 2,550,000; elementary, 1,536,000; secondary, 1,014,000; private elementary and secondary school teachers (1994): 370,000
Average salary for public school teachers (1993–94): $35,958

CONVENIENCES

Radio stations (standard and FM, est. 1994): 9,919
Television stations (est. 1994): 1,092
Registered automobiles (est. 1994): 147,171,000
Newspaper circulatioon (morning and evening, Sept. 30, 1994): 59,305,436
Cable TV subscribers (est. May 1995): 62,010,000
Total TV homes (est. May 1995): 95,400,000
TV Homes with VCRs (est. 1993): 80%
Households with computers (1994): 6,980,000

CRIME

Total arrests (est. 1993): 14,036,300; Males, 9,475,344; Under 18, 1,534,356; Females, 2,290,420; Under 18, 87,081
Child neglect and abuse cases (1992): 1,898,911
Prisoners under sentence of death (1992): 2,594
Law enforcement officers killed (1992): 128
Total murder victims (1993): 23,271
Households touched by crime (1992): 14,817,000
Violent crime (1993): 1,924,188
Theft (1993): 7,820,909

U.S. STATES

States and Territories

Sources for state populations, populations under 18, over 65, median age, largest cities and counties, and population by race are latest data provided by the U.S. Census Bureau. NOTE: Persons of Hispanic origin can be of any race. The population counts set forth herein by the Census Bureau are subject to possible correction for undercount or overcount. They include Armed Forces residing in each state. 1994 State populations are for July 1, 1994. Largest cities include incorporated places only, as defined by the U.S. Census Bureau. They do not include adjacent or suburban areas as do the Metropolitan Statistical Areas found in the "U.S. Statistics" section of this Almanac. For secession and readmission dates of the former Confederate states, see Index. For lists of Governors, Senators, and Representatives, see Index. For additional state information, see the sections on "Business and the Economy," "Elections," "Taxes," and "U.S. Statistics."

ALABAMA

Capital: Montgomery
Governor: Fob James, Jr., R (to Jan. 1999)
Lieut. Governor: Don Siegelman, D (to Jan. 1999)
Secy. of State: Jim Bennett, D (to Jan. 1999)
Treasurer: Lucy Baxley, D (to Jan. 1999)
Atty. General: Jeff Sessions, R (to Jan. 1999)
Auditor: Pat Duncan, R (to Jan. 1999)
Organized as territory: March 3, 1817
Entered Union & (rank): Dec. 14, 1819 (22)
Present constitution adopted: 1901
Motto: *Audemus jura nostra defendere* (We dare defend our rights)
STATE SYMBOLS: flower, Camellia (1959); **bird,** Yellowhammer (1927); **song,** "Alabama" (1931); **tree,** Southern pine (longleaf) (1949); **salt water fish,** Tarpon (1955); **fresh water fish,** Largemouth bass (1975); **horse,** Racking horse (1975); **mineral,** Hematite (1967); **rock,** Marble (1969); **game bird,** Wild turkey (1980); **dance,** Square dance (1981); **nut,** Pecan (1982); **fossil,** species *Basilosaurus Cetoides* (1984); **butterfly,** Eastern Tiger Swallowtail (1989); **insect,** Monarch butterfly (1989); **reptile,** Alabama red-bellied turtle (1990); **gemstone,** Star Blue Quartz (1990); **shell,** Scaphella junonia johnstoneae (1990).
Nickname: Yellowhammer State
Origin of name: May come from Choctaw meaning "thicket-clearers" or "vegetation-gatherers"
10 largest cities (1990 census): Birmingham, 265,968; Mobile, 196,278; Montgomery, 187,106; Huntsville, 159,789; Tuscaloosa, 77,759; Dothan, 53,589; Decatur, 48,761; Gadsden, 42,523; Hoover, 39,788; Florence, 36,426
Land area & (rank): 50,750 sq mi. (131,443 sq km) (28)
Geographic center: In Chilton Co., 12 mi. SW of Clanton
Number of counties: 67
Largest county: Baldwin (1,590 sq mi.)
Most populous county (1990 census): Jefferson, 651,525
State forests: 21 (48,000 ac.)
State parks: 22 (45,614 ac.)
1994 resident population est.: 4,219,000
1990 census population, sex, & (rank): 4,040,587 (22). **Male:** 1,936,162; **Female:** 2,104,425. **White:** 2,975,797 (73.6%); **Black:** 1,020,705 (25.3%); **American Indian, Eskimo, or Aleut:** 16,506 (0.4%); **Asian or Pacific Islander:** 21,797 (0.5%); **Other race:** 5,782 (0.1%); **Hispanic:** 24,629 (0.6%). **1990 percent population under 18:** 26.2; **65 and over:** 12.9; **median age:** 33.0.

Spanish explorers are believed to have arrived at Mobile Bay in 1519, and the territory was visited in 1540 by the explorer Hernando de Soto. The first permanent European settlement in Alabama was founded by the French at Fort Louis de la Mobile in 1702. The British gained control of the area in 1763 by the Treaty of Paris, but had to cede almost all the Alabama region to the U.S. after the American Revolution. The Confederacy was founded at Montgomery in February 1861 and, for a time, the city was the Confederate capital.

During the last part of the 19th century, the economy of the state slowly improved. At Tuskegee Institute, founded in 1881 by Booker T. Washington, Dr. George Washington Carver carried out his famous agricultural research.

In the 1950s and '60s, Alabama was the site of such landmark civil-rights actions as the bus boycott in Montgomery (1955–56) and the "Freedom March" from Selma to Montgomery (1965).

Today paper, chemicals, rubber and plastics, apparel and textiles, and primary metals comprise the leading industries of Alabama. Continuing as a major manufacturer of coal, iron, and steel, Birmingham is also noted for its world-renowned medical center, especially for heart surgery. The state ranks high in the production of poultry, soybeans, milk, vegetables, livestock, wheat, cattle, cotton, peanuts, fruits, hogs, and corn.

Points of interest include the Helen Keller birthplace "Ivy Green" at Tuscumbia, the Space and Rocket Center at Huntsville, the White House of the Confederacy, the restored state Capitol, the Civil Rights Memorial, and Shakespeare Festival Theater Complex in Montgomery, the Civil Rights Institute in Birmingham, the Russell Cave near Bridgeport, and Bellingrath Gardens at Theodore, the U.S.S. Alabama at Mobile, Mound State Monument near Tuscaloosa, and the Gulf Coast area.

Famous natives and residents: Hank Aaron, baseball player; Ralph Abernathy, civil rights activist; Tallulah Bankhead, actress; Hugo L. Black, jurist; George Washington Carver, educator, agricultural chemist; Nat "King" Cole, entertainer; Marva Collins, educator; Kenneth Gibson, first Black mayor of major eastern city (Newark); Lionel Hampton, jazz musician; W.C. Handy, composer; Kate Jackson, actress; Helen Keller, author and educator; Coretta Scott King, civil rights leader; Harper Lee, writer; Joe Louis, boxer; Willie Mays, baseball player; Jim Nabors, actor; Jesse Owens, athlete; Rosa Parks, civil rights activist; Wayne Rogers, actor; Tuscaloosa, Choctaw chief; George Wallace, ex-governor; William Weatherford (Red Eagle), Creek leader

ALASKA

Capital: Juneau
Governor: Tony Knowles, D (to Dec. 1998)
Lieut. Governor: Fran Ulmer, D (to Dec. 1998)
Commissioner of Administration: Mark Boyer
Atty. General: Bruce M. Botelho, D

Organized as territory: 1912
Entered Union & (rank): Jan. 3, 1959 (49)
Constitution ratified: April 24, 1956
Motto: North to the Future
STATE SYMBOLS: flower, Forget-me-not (1949); **tree,** Sitka spruce (1962); **bird,** Willow ptarmigan (1955); **fish,** King salmon (1962); **song,** "Alaska's Flag" (1955); **gem,** Jade (1968); **marine mammal,** Bowhead Whale (1983); **fossil,** Woolly Mammoth (1986); **mineral,** Gold (1968); **sport,** Dog Mushing (1972)
Nickname: The state is commonly called "The Last Frontier" or "Land of the Midnight Sun"
Origin of name: Corruption of Aleut word meaning "great land" or "that which the sea breaks against"
Largest cities: Anchorage, 248,296; Fairbanks, 33,281; Juneau, 29,078; Sitka, 9,052; Ketchikan, 8,846; Kodiak, 7,428; Kenai, 6,813
Land area & (rank): 570,374 sq mi. (1,477,267 sq km) (1)
Geographic center: 60 mi. NW of Mt. McKinley
Number of boroughs: 16
Largest borough (1994): Fairbanks North Star Borough, 82,428
State forests: None
State parks: 5; 59 waysides and areas (3.3 million ac.)
1994 resident population: 606,278
1990 resident census population, sex, & (rank): 550,043 (49). **Male:** 289,867; **Female:** 260,176. **White:** 415,492 (75.5%); **Black:** 22,451 (4.1%); **American Indian, Eskimo, or Aleut:** 85,698 (15.6%); **Asian or Pacific Islander:** 19,728 (3.6%); **Other race:** 6,675 (1.2%); **Hispanic:** 17,803 (3.2%). **1990 percent population under 18:** 31.3; **65 and over:** 4.1; **median age:** 29..4

Vitus Bering, a Dane working for the Russians, and Alexei Chirikov discovered the Alaskan mainland and the Aleutian Islands in 1741. The tremendous land mass of Alaska—equal to one fifth of the continental U.S.—was unexplored in 1867 when Secretary of State William Seward arranged for its purchase from the Russians for $7,200,000. The transfer of the territory took place on Oct. 18, 1867. Despite a price of about two cents an acre, the purchase was widely ridiculed as "Seward's Folly." The first official census (1880) reported a total of 33,426 Alaskans, all but 430 being of aboriginal stock. The Gold Rush of 1898 resulted in a mass influx of more than 30,000 people. Since then, Alaska has returned billions of dollars' worth of products to the U.S.

In 1968, a large oil and gas reservoir near Prudhoe Bay on the Arctic Coast was found. The Prudhoe Bay reservoir, with an estimated recoverable 10 billion barrels of oil and 27 trillion cubic feet of gas, is twice as large as any other oil field in North America. The Trans-Alaska pipeline was completed in 1977 at a cost of $7.7 billion. On June 20, oil started flowing through the 800-mile-long pipeline from Prudhoe Bay to the port of Valdez.

Other industries important to Alaska's economy are fisheries, wood and wood products, and furs, and tourism.

Denali National Park and Mendenhall Glacier in North Tongass National Forest are of interest, as is the large totem pole collection at Sitka National Historical Park. The Katmai National Park includes the "Valley of Ten Thousand Smokes," an area of active volcanoes.

Famous natives and residents: Clarence L. Andrews, author; Aleksandr Baranov, first governor of Russian America; Margaret Elizabeth Bell, author; Benny Benson, designed state flag at age 13; Vitus Bering, explorer; Charles E. Bunnell, educator; Susan Butcher, sled-dog racer; William A. Egan, first state governor; Carl Ben Eielson, pioneer pilot; Henry E. Gruennig, po-

litical leader; B. Frank Heintzleman, territorial governor; Walter J. Hickel, governor; Sheldon Jackson, educator and missionary; Joe Juneau, prospector; Austin Lathrop, industrialist; Sydney Lawrence, painter; Ray Mala, actor; Virgil F. Partch, cartoonist; Joe Redington, Sr., sled-dog musher and promoter; Peter Trinble Rowe, first Episcopal bishop; Ivan Popov-Veniaminov (St. Innocent), Russian Orthodox missionary; Ferdinand Wrangel, educator; Samuel Hall Young, founder of first American church

ARIZONA

Capital: Phoenix
Governor: Fife Symington, R (to Jan. 1999)
Secy. of State: Jane Dee Hull, R (to Jan. 1999)
Atty. General: Grant Woods, R (to Jan. 1999*)
State Treasurer: Tony West, R (to Jan. 1999)
Organized as territory: Feb. 24, 1863
Entered Union & (rank): Feb. 14, 1912 (48)
Present constitution adopted: 1911
Motto: *Ditat Deus* (God enriches)
STATE SYMBOLS: flower: Flower of saguaro cactus (1931); **bird:** Cactus wren (1931); **colors:** Blue and old gold (1915); **song:** "Arizona March Song" (1919); **tree:** Palo Verde (1954); **neckwear,** Bolo tie (1973); **fossil,** Petrified wood (1988); **gemstone,** Turquoise (1974); **animals, mammal,** Ringtail; **reptile,** Arizona ridgenose rattlesnake; **fish,** Arizona trout; **amphibian,** Arizona tree frog (1986)
Nickname: Grand Canyon State
Origin of name: From the Indian "Arizonac," meaning "little spring" or "young spring"
10 largest cities (1990 census): Phoenix, 983,403; Tucson, 405,390; Mesa, 288,091; Glendale, 148,134; Tempe, 141,865; Scottsdale, 130,069; Chandler, 90,533; Yuma, 54,923; Peoria, 50,618; Flagstaff, 45,857
Land area & (rank): 114,000 sq mi. (296,400 sq km) (6)
Geographic center: In Yavapai Co., 55 mi. ESE of Prescott
Number of counties: 15
Largest county (1990 census): Maricopa, 2,122,101
State forests: None
State parks: 28
1994 resident population est.: 4,071,650
1990 resident census population, sex, & (rank): 3,665,228 (24). **Male:** 1,810,691; **Female:** 1,854,537. **White:** 2,963,186 (80.8%); **Black:** 110,524 (3.0%); **American Indian, Eskimo, or Aleut:** 203,527 (5.6%); **Asian or Pacific Islander:** 55,206 (1.5%); **Other race:** 332,785 (9.1%); **Hispanic:** 688,338 (18.8%). **1990 percent population under 18:** 26.8; **65 and over:** 13.1; **median age:** 32.2

*Ran unopposed.

Marcos de Niza, a Spanish Franciscan friar, was the first European to explore Arizona. He entered the area in 1539 in search of the mythical Seven Cities of Gold. Although he was followed a year later by another gold seeker, Francisco Vásquez de Coronado, most of the early settlement was for missionary purposes. In 1775 the Spanish established Fort Tucson. In 1848, after the Mexican War, most of the Arizona territory became part of the U.S., and the southern portion of the territory was added by the Gadsden Purchase in 1853.

In 1973 one of the world's most massive dams, the New Cornelia Tailings, was completed near Ajo.

Arizona history is rich in legends of America's Old West. It was here that the great Indian chiefs Geronimo and Cochise led their people against the frontiersmen. Tombstone, Ariz., was the site of the West's most famous shoot-out—the gunfight at the O.K. Corral. Today, Arizona has the largest U.S. Indian population; more than 14 tribes are represented on 20 reservations.

Manufacturing has become Arizona's most important industry. Principal products include electrical, communications, and aeronautical items. The state produces over half the country's copper. Agriculture is also important to the state's economy.

State attractions include such famous scenery as the Grand Canyon, the Petrified Forest, and the Painted Desert. Hoover Dam, Lake Mead, Fort Apache, and the reconstructed London Bridge at Lake Havasu City are of particular interest.

Famous natives and residents: Apache Kid, Indian outlaw; Cesar Chavez, labor leader; Cochise, Apache chief; Joan Ganz Cooney, children's television executive; Lewis W. Douglas, public official; Max Ernst, painter; Geronimo (Goyathlay), Apache chief; Barry Goldwater, politician; Zane Grey, novelist; Carl Trumbull Hayden, politician; George Wylie Hunt, first state governor; Helen Hull Jacobs, tennis champion, writer; Ulysses S. Kay, composer; Eusebio Kino, missionary; Percival Lowell, astronomer; Frank Luke, Jr., WWI fighter ace; Charles Mingus, jazz musician, composer; Carlos Montezuma, doctor and Indian spokesman; William O'Neill, frontier sheriff; Alexander M. Patch, general; William H. Pickering, astronomer; Linda Ronstadt, singer; Clyde W. Tombaugh, astronomer; Stewart Udall, ex-Secretary of the Interior; Pauline Weaver, mountain man

Hernando de Soto, in 1541, was among the early European explorers to visit the territory. It was a Frenchman, Henri de Tonti, who in 1686 founded the first permanent white settlement—the Arkansas Post. In 1803 the area was acquired by the U.S. as part of the Louisiana Purchase.

Food products are the state's largest employing sector, with lumber and wood products a close second. Arkansas is also a leader in the production of cotton, rice, and soybeans. It also has the country's only active diamond mine; located near Murfreesboro, it is operated as a tourist attraction.

Hot Springs National Park, and Buffalo National River in the Ozarks are major state attractions.

Blanchard Springs Caverns, the Arkansas Territorial Restoration at Little Rock, and the Arkansas Folk Center in Mountain View are of interest.

Famous natives and residents: G.M. "Broncho Billy" Anderson, actor; Maya Angelou, author, poet; Katharine Susan Anthony, author; Helen Gurley Brown, author; Glen Campbell, singer; Hattie Caraway, first woman senator; Johnny Cash, singer; Eldridge Cleaver, Black activist; William Jefferson Clinton, 42nd President; Dizzy Dean, baseball player; Orval Faubus, governor; John Gould Fletcher, writer; James W. Fulbright, senator; John H. Johnson, publisher; Alan Ladd, actor; Douglas MacArthur, 5-star general; John Paul McConnell, U.S. Air Force officer; Ben Murphy, actor; Frank Pace, Jr., public official; Ben Piazza, actor; Albert Pike, pioneer teacher, lawyer; Dick Powell, actor; Opie P. Read, writer; Jenny D. Rice-Meyrowitz, painter; Brehon Burke Somervell, World Wars I and II U.S. Army officer; Mary Steenburgen, actress; Edward Durrell Stone, architect; Sam Walton, Wal-Mart founder; William C. Warfield, concert singer, actor

ARKANSAS

Capital: Little Rock
Governor: Jim Guy Tucker, D (to Jan. 1998)
Lieut. Governor: Mike Huckabee, R (to Jan. 1998)
Secy. of State: Sharon Priest, D (to Jan. 1998)
Atty. General: Winston Bryant, D (to Jan. 1998)
Auditor of State: Gus Wingfield, D (to Jan. 1998)
Treasurer of State: Jimmie Lou Fisher Lumpkin, D (to Jan. 1998)
Land Commissioner: Charles Daniels, D (to Jan. 1998)
Organized as territory: March 2, 1819
Entered Union & (rank): June 15, 1836 (25)
Present constitution adopted: 1874
Motto: *Regnat populus* (The people rule)
STATE SYMBOLS: flower, Apple Blossom (1901); **tree,** Pine (1939); **bird,** Mockingbird (1929); **insect,** Honeybee (1973); **song,** "Arkansas" (1963)
Nickname: Land of Opportunity
Origin of name: From the Quapaw Indians
10 largest cities (1990 census): Little Rock, 175,795; Fort Smith, 72,798; North Little Rock, 61,741; Pine Bluff, 57,140; Jonesboro, 46,535; Fayetteville, 42,099; Hot Springs, 32,462; Springdale, 29,941; Jacksonville, 29,101; West Memphis, 28,259
Land area & (rank): 52,075 sq mi. (134,875 sq km) (27)
Geographic center: In Pulaski Co., 12 mi. NW of Little Rock
Number of counties: 75
Largest county (1990 census): Pulaski, 349,660
State forests: None
State parks: 44
1994 resident population est.: 2,453,000
1990 resident population, sex, & rank: 2,350,725 (33). **Male:** 1,133,076; **Female:** 1,217,649. **White:** 1,944,744 (82.7%); **Black:** 373,912 (15.9%); **American Indian, Eskimo, or Aleut:** 12,773 (0.5%); **Asian or Pacific Islander:** 12,530 (0.5%); **Other race:** 6,766 (0.3%); **Hispanic:** 19,876 (0.8%). **1990 percent population under 18:** 26.4; **65 and over:** 14.9; **median age:** 33.8.

CALIFORNIA

Capital: Sacramento
Governor: Pete Wilson, R (to Jan. 1999)
Lieut. Governor: Gray Davis, D (to Jan. 1999)
Secy. of State: Bill Jones, R, (to Jan. 1999)
Controller: Cathleen Connell, D (to Jan. 1999)
Atty. General: Dan Lungren, R (to Jan. 1999)
Treasurer: Matt Fong, R (to Jan. 1999)
Supt. of Public Instruction: David Meaney
Entered Union & (rank): Sept. 9, 1850 (31)
Present constitution adopted: 1879
Motto: *Eureka* (I have found it)
STATE SYMBOLS: flower, Golden poppy (1903); **tree,** California redwoods (*Sequoia sempervirens* & *Sequoia gigantea*) (1937 % 1953); **bird,** California valley quail (1931); **animal,** California grizzly bear (1953); **fish,** California golden trout (1947); **colors,** Blue and gold (1951); **song,** "I Love You, California" (1951)
Nickname: Golden State
Origin of name: From a book, *Las Sergas de Esplandián,* by Garcia Ordóñez de Montalvo, c. 1500
10 largest cities (1990 census): Los Angeles, 3,485,398; San Diego, 1,110,549; San Jose, 782,248; San Francisco, 723,959; Long Beach, 429,433; Oakland, 372,242; Sacramento, 369,365; Fresno, 354,202; Santa Ana, 293,742; Anaheim, 266,406
Land area & (rank): 155,973 sq mi. (403,970 sq km) (3)
Geographic center: In Madera Co., 35 mi. NE of Madera
Number of counties: 58
Largest county (1990 census): Los Angeles, 8,863,164
State forests: 8 (70,283 ac.)
State parks and beaches: 180 (723,000 ac.)
1994 resident population est.: 31,431,000

1990 resident population, sex, & (rank): 29,760,021 (1). **Male:** 14,897,627; **Female:** 14,862,394. **White:** 20,524,327 (69.9%); **Black:** 2,208,801 (7.4%); **American Indian, Eskimo, or Aleut:** 242,164 (0.8%); **Asian or Pacific Islander,** 2,845,659 (9.6%); **Other race:** 3,939,070 (13.2%); **Hispanic,** 7,687,938 (25.8%). **1990 percent population under 18:** 26.0; **65 and over:** 10.5; **median age:** 31.5.

Although California was sighted by Spanish navigator Juan Rodríguez Cabrillo in 1542, its first Spanish mission (at San Diego) was not established until 1769. California became a U.S. Territory in 1847 when Mexico surrendered it to John C. Frémont. On Jan. 24, 1848, James W. Marshall discovered gold at Sutter's Mill, starting the California Gold Rush and bringing settlers to the state in large numbers.

In 1964, the U.S. Census Bureau estimated that California had become the most populous state, surpassing New York. California also leads the country in personal income and consumer expenditures.

Leading industries include manufacturing (transportation equipment, machinery, and electronic equipment), agriculture, biotechnology, and tourism. Principal natural resources include timber, petroleum, cement, and natural gas.

More immigrants settle in California than any other state—more than 30% of the nation's total in 1990. Asian-Pacific Islanders led the influx.

Death Valley, in the southeast, is 282 feet below sea level, the lowest point in the nation; and Mt. Whitney (14,491 ft) is the highest point in the contig-uous 48 states. Lassen Peak is one of two active U.S. volcanos outside of Alaska and Hawaii; its last eruptions were recorded in 1917. The General Sherman Tree in Sequoia National Park is estimated to be about 3,500 years old and a stand of bristlecone pine trees in the White Mountains may be over 4,000 years old.

Other points of interest include Yosemite National Park, Disneyland, Hollywood, the Golden Gate bridge, San Simeon State Park, and Point Reyes National Seashore.

Famous natives and residents: Gertrude Atherton, author; David Belasco, playwright and producer; Shirley Temple Black, actress, ambassador; Dave Brubeck, musician; Luther Burbank, horticulturalist; Julia Child, chef; Joe DiMaggio, baseball player; James H. Doolittle, Air Force general; Isadora Duncan, dancer; John Frémont, explorer; Robert Frost, poet; Henry George, economist; Richard "Pancho" Gonzales, tennis player; George E. Hale, astronomer; Bret Harte, writer; William Randolph Hearst, publisher; Sidney Howard, playwright; Collis Potter Huntington, financier; Helen Hunt Jackson, writer; Robinson Jeffers, poet; Anthony M. Kennedy, jurist; Jack London, author; James W. Marshall, first discovered gold; Aimee Semple McPherson, evangelist; Marilyn Monroe, actress; John Muir, naturalist; Richard M. Nixon, President; Isamu Noguchi, sculptor; Frank Norris, novelist; Kathleen Norris, novelist; George S. Patton, Jr, general; Robert Redford, actor; Sally K. Ride, astronaut; William Saroyan, author; Junípero Serra, missionary; Upton Sinclair, novelist; Leland Stanford, railroad magnate; Lincoln Steffens, journalist, author; John Steinbeck, author; Adlai Stevenson, statesman; Johann Sutter, pioneer; Michael Tilson Thomas, conductor; Earl Warren, jurist

COLORADO

Capital: Denver
Governor: Roy Romer, D (to Jan. 1999)
Lieut. Governor: Gail Schoettler, D (to Jan. 1999)

Secy. of State: Vikki Buckley, R (to Jan. 1999)
Treasurer: Bill Owens, R (to Jan. 1999)
Controller: Cliff Hall, R (appointed)
Atty. General: Gale Norton, R (to Jan. 1999)
Organized as territory: Feb. 28, 1861
Entered Union & (rank): Aug. 1, 1876 (38)
Present constitution adopted: 1876
Motto: *Nil sine Numine* (Nothing without Providence)
STATE SYMBOLS: flower, Rocky Mountain columbine (1899); **tree,** Colorado blue spruce (1939); **bird,** Lark bunting (1931); **animal,** Rocky Mountain bighorn sheep (1961); **gemstone,** Aquamarine (1971); **colors,** Blue and white (1911); **song,** "Where the Columbines Grow" (1915); **fossil,** Stegosaurus (1991)
Nickname: Centennial State
Origin of name: From the Spanish, "ruddy" or "red"
10 largest cities (1990 census): Denver, 467,610; Colorado Springs, 281,140; Aurora, 222,103; Lakewood, 126,481; Pueblo, 98,640; Arvada, 89,235; Fort Collins, 87,758; Boulder, 83,312; Westminster, 74,625; Greeley, 60,536
Land area & (rank): 103,730 sq mi. (268,660 sq km) (8)
Geographic center: In Park Co., 30 mi. NW of Pikes Peak
Number of counties: 63
Largest county (1990 census): Denver, 467,610
State forests: 1 (71,000 ac.)
State parks: 44
1994 resident population est.: 3,656,000
1990 resident census population, sex, & (rank): 3,294,394 (26). **Male:** 1,631,295; **Female:** 1,663,099. **White:** 2,095,474 (88.2%); **Black:** 133,146 (4.0%); **American Indian, Eskimo, or Aleut:** 27,776 (0.8%); **Asian or Pacific Islander,** 59,862 (1.8%); **Other race:** 168,136 (5.1%); **Hispanic,** 424,302 (12.9%). **1990 percent population under 18:** 26.1; **65 and over:** 10.0; **median age:** 32.5

First visited by Spanish explorers in the 1500s, the territory was claimed for Spain by Juan de Ulibarri in 1706. The U.S. obtained central Colorado as part of the Louisiana Purchase in 1803, the central portion in 1845 with the admission of Texas as a state, and the western part in 1848 as a result of the Mexican War.

Colorado has the highest mean elevation of any state, with more than 1,000 Rocky Mountain peaks over 10,000 feet high and 54 towering above 14,000 feet. Pikes Peak, the most famous of these mountains, was discovered by U.S. Army Lieut. Zebulon M. Pike in 1806.

Once primarily a mining and agricultural state, Colorado's economy is now driven by the service-producing industries, which provide jobs for approximately 82.4% of the state's non-farm work force. Tourism expenditures in the state total approximately 6 billion dollars annually. Tourist expenditures on the ski industry account for 1.8 billion dollars annually, approximately 1/3 of the total tourist expenditures. The main tourist attractions in the state include Rocky Mountain National Park, Curecanti National Recreation Area, Mesa Verde National Park, the Great Sand Dunes and Dinosaur National Monuments, Colorado National Monument, and the Black Canyon of the Gunnison National Monument.

The two primary facets of Colorado's manufacturing industry are food and kindred products, and printing and publishing.

The mining industry, which includes oil and gas, coal, and metal mining, was important to Colorado's economy, but it now employs only 1.2 percent of the state's workforce. Denver is home to companies that control half of the nation's gold production. The farm industry, which is primarily concentrated in livestock, is also an important element of the state's economy. The primary crops in Colorado are corn, hay, and wheat.

Famous natives and residents: William E. Barrett, writer; William Bent, fur trader and pioneer; Charles F. Brannan, lawyer and public official; M. Scott Carpenter, astronaut; Lon Chaney, actor; Mary Coyle Chase, playwright; Jack Dempsey, boxer; Ralph Edwards, entertainer; John Evans, physician, educator; Douglas Fairbanks, actor; John Thomas Fante, writer; Eugene Fodor, violinist; Gene Fowler, writer; Erick Hawkins, choreographer; Homer Lea, soldier, writer; Ted Mack, TV host; Jaye P. Morgan, singer; Peg Murray, actress; Ouray, Ute Indian chief; Anne Parrish, writer; Barbara Rush, actress; Horace A. Tabor, silver king, Lieut.-Governor; Lowell Thomas, commentator and author; Dalton Trumbo, screenwriter, novelist; Byron R. White, jurist; Paul Whiteman, conductor; Don Wilson, announcer

CONNECTICUT

Capital: Hartford
Governor: John G. Rowland, R (to Jan. 1999)
Lieut. Governor: M. Jodi Rell, R (to Jan. 1999)
Secy. of State: Miles S. Rapoport, D (to Jan. 1999)
Comptroller: Nancy Wyman, D (to Jan. 1999)
Treasurer: Christopher B. Burnham, R (to Jan. 1999)
Atty. General: Richard Blumenthal, D (to Jan. 1999)
Entered Union & (rank): Jan. 9, 1788 (5)
Present constitution adopted: Dec. 30, 1965
Motto: *Qui transtulit sustinet* (He who transplanted still sustains)
STATE SYMBOLS: flower, Mountain Laurel (1907); **tree,** White Oak (1947); **animal,** Sperm Whale (1975); **bird,** American Robin (1943); **hero,** Nathan Hale (1985); **insect,** Praying Mantis (1977); **mineral,** Garnet (1977); **song,** "Yankee Doodle" (1978); **ship,** USS Nautilus (SSN571) (1983); **shellfish,** Eastern Oyster (1989); **fossil,** Eubrontes Giganteus (1991)
Official designation: *Constitution State* (1959)
Nickname: Nutmeg State
Origin of name: From an Indian word (Quinnehtukqut) meaning "beside the long tidal river"
10 largest cities (1990 census): Bridgeport, 141,686; Hartford, 139,739; New Haven, 130,474; Waterbury, 108,961; Stamford, 108,056; Norwalk, 78,331; New Britain, 75,491; Danbury, 65,585; Bristol, 60,640; Meriden, 59,479
Land area & (rank): 4,845 sq mi. (12,550 sq km) (48)
Geographic center: In Hartford Co., at East Berlin
Number of counties: 8
Largest town (1990 census): West Hartford 60,110
State forests: 30 (143,699 ac.)
State parks: 92 (31,721 ac.)
1994 resident population est.: 3,275,000
1990 resident population, sex, & (rank): 3,287,116 (27). **Male:** 1,592,873; **Female:** 1,694,243. **White:** 2,859,353 (87.0%); **Black:** 274,269 (8.3%); **American Indian, Eskimo, or Aleut:** 6,654 (0.2%); **Asian or Pacific Islander:** 50,698 (1.5%); **Other race:** 96,142 (2.9%); **Hispanic:** 213,116 (6.5%). **1990 percent population under 18:** 22.8; **65 and over:** 13.6; **median age:** 34.4.

The Dutch navigator, Adriaen Block, was the first European of record to explore the area, sailing up the Connecticut River in 1614. In 1633, Dutch colonists built a fort and trading post near presentday Hartford, but soon lost control to English Puritans migrating south from the Massachusetts Bay Colony.

English settlements, established in the 1630s at Windsor, Wethersfield, and Hartford, united in 1639 to form the Connecticut Colony and adopted the *Fundamental Orders,* considered the world's first written constitution.

The colony's royal charter of 1662 was exception-

ally liberal. When Gov. Edmund Andros tried to seize it in 1687, it was hidden in the Hartford Oak, commemorated in Charter Oak Place.

Connecticut played a prominent role in the Revolutionary War, serving as the Continental Army's major supplier. Sometimes called the "Arsenal of the Nation," the state became one of the most industrialized in the nation.

Today, Connecticut factories produce weapons, sewing machines, jet engines, helicopters, motors, hardware and tools, cutlery, clocks, locks, ball bearings, silverware, and submarines. Hartford, which has the oldest U.S. newspaper still being published—the *Hartford Courant,* established 1764—is the insurance capital of the nation.

Poultry, fruit, and dairy products account for the largest portion of farm income, and Connecticut's shade-grown tobacco is acknowledged to be the state's most valuable crop per acre.

Connecticut is a popular resort area with its 250-mile Long Island Sound shoreline and many inland lakes. Among the major points of interest are Yale University's Gallery of Fine Arts and Peabody Museum. Other famous museums include the P.T. Barnum, Winchester Gun, and American Clock and Watch. The town of Mystic features a recreated 19th-century New England seaport and the Mystic Marinelife Aquarium.

Famous natives and residents: Dean Acheson, statesman; Ethan Allan, American Revolutionary soldier; Benedict Arnold, American Revolutionary general; Wadsworth Atheneum; P.T. Barnum, showman; Henry Ward Beecher, clergyman; John Brown, abolitionist; Oliver Ellsworth, jurist; Eileen Farrell, soprano; Charles Goodyear, inventor; Nathan Hale, American Revolutionary officer; Dorothy Hamill, ice skater; Katharine Hepburn, actress; Charles Ives, composer; Edwin H. Land, inventor; John Pierpont Morgan, financier; Frederick Law Olmsted, landscape planner; Rosa Ponselle, soprano; Adam Clayton Powell, Jr., congressman; Benjamin Spock, pediatrician; Harriet Beecher Stowe, author; Morris R. Waite, jurist; Noah Webster, lexicographer

DELAWARE

Capital: Dover
Governor: Thomas R. Carper, D (to Jan. 1997)
Lieut. Governor: Ruth Ann Minner, D (to Jan. 1997)
Secy. of State: William T. Quillen, D (Pleasure of Governor)
State Treasurer: Janet C. Rzewnicki, R (to Jan. 1996)
Atty. General: M. Jane Brady, R (to Jan. 1998)
Entered Union & (rank): Dec. 7, 1787 (1)
Present constitution adopted: 1897
Motto: Liberty and independence
STATE SYMBOLS: colors, Colonial blue and buff; **flower,** Peach blossom (1895); **tree,** American holly (1939); **bird,** Blue Hen chicken (1939); **insect,** Ladybug (1974); **fish,** Weakfish, *Cynoscion regalis* (1981); **song,** "Our Delaware"
Nicknames: Diamond State; First State; Small Wonder
Origin of name: From Delaware River and Bay; named in turn for Sir Thomas West, Lord De La Warr
10 largest cities (1990 census): Wilmington, 71,529; Dover, 27,630; Newark, 26,464; Milford, 6,040; Elsmere Town, 5,935; Seaford, 5,689; Smyrna Town, 5,213; New Castle, 4,837; Middletown Town, 3,834; Georgetown Town, 3,732
Land area & (rank): 1,982 sq mi. (5,153 sq km) (49)
Geographic center: In Kent Co., 11 mi. S of Dover

Number of counties: 3
Largest county (1990 census): New Castle, 441,946
State forests: 3 (6,149 ac.)
State parks: 12
1994 resident population est.: 706,000
1990 resident census population, sex, & (rank): 666,168 (46). **Male:** 322,968; **Female:** 343,200. **White:** 535,094 (80.3%); **Black:** 112,460 (16.9%); **American Indian, Eskimo, or Aleut:** 2,019 (0.3%); **Asian or Pacific Islander:** 9,057 (1.4%); **Other race:** 7,538 (1.1%); **Hispanic:** 15,820 (2.4%). **1990 percent population under 18:** 24.5; **65 and over:** 12.1; **median age:** 32.9.

Henry Hudson, sailing under the Dutch flag, is credited with Delaware's discovery in 1609. The following year, Capt. Samuel Argall of Virginia named Delaware for his colony's governor, Thomas West, Baron De La Warr. An attempted Dutch settlement failed in 1631. Swedish colonization began at Fort Christina (now Wilmington) in 1638, but New Sweden fell to Dutch forces led by New Netherlands' Gov. Peter Stuyvesant in 1655.

England took over the area in 1664 and it was transferred to William Penn as the southern Three Counties in 1682. Semiautonomous after 1704, Delaware fought as a separate state in the American Revolution and became the first state to ratify the constitution in 1787.

During the Civil War, although a slave state, Delaware did not secede from the Union.

In 1802, Éleuthère Irénée du Pont established a gunpowder mill near Wilmington that laid the foundation for Delaware's huge chemical industry. Delaware's manufactured products now also include vulcanized fiber, textiles, paper, medical supplies, metal products, machinery, machine tools, and automobiles.

Delaware also grows a great variety of fruits and vegetables and is a U.S. pioneer in the food-canning industry. Corn, soybeans, potatoes, and hay are important crops. Delaware's broiler chicken farms supply the big Eastern markets, fishing and dairy products are other important industries.

Points of interest include the Fort Christina Monument, Hagley Museum, Holy Trinity Church (erected in 1698, the oldest Protestant church in the United States still in use), and Winterthur Museum, in and near Wilmington; central New Castle, an almost unchanged late 18th-century capital; and the Delaware Museum of Natural History.

Popular recreation areas include Cape Henlopen, Delaware Seashore, Trapp Pond State Park, and Rehoboth Beach.

Famous natives and residents: Richard Allen, founder of African Methodist Episcopal Church; Valerie Bertinelli, actress; Robert Montgomery Bird, playwright and novelist; Henry S. Canby, editor and author; Annie Jump Cannon, astronomer; Elizabeth Margaret Chandler, author; Felix Darley, artist; John Dickinson, statesman; E.I. du Pont, industrialist; Oliver Evans, inventor; Thomas Garrett, abolitionist; Henry Heimlich, surgeon, inventor; Wilham Julius "Judy" Johnson, basketball player; J.P. Marquand, novelist; Howard Pyle, artist and author; George Read, jurist, signer of Declaration of Independence; Jay Saunders Redding, educator and author; Caesar Rodney, patriot, signer of Declaration of Independence; Frank Stephens, sculptor; Estelle Taylor, actress; George Alfred Townsend, journalist and author

DISTRICT OF COLUMBIA

See listing at end of *50 Largest Cities of the United States.*

FLORIDA

Capital: Tallahassee
Governor: Lawton Chiles, D (to Jan. 1999)
Lieut. Governor: Buddy McKay, D (to Jan. 1999)
Secy. of State: Sandra B. Mortham, R (to Jan. 1999)
Comptroller: Bob Milligan, R (to Jan. 1999)
Commissioner of Agriculture: Bob Crawford, D (to Jan. 1999)
Atty. General: Bob Butterworth, D (to Jan. 1999)
Organized as territory: March 20, 1822
Entered Union & (rank): March 3, 1845 (27)
Present constitution adopted: 1969
Motto: In God we trust (1868)
STATE SYMBOLS: flower, Orange blossom (1909); **bird,** Mockingbird (1927); **song,** "Suwannee River" (1935)
Nickname: Sunshine State (1970)
Origin of name: From the Spanish, meaning "feast of flowers" (Easter)
10 largest cities (1990 census): Jacksonville (CC[1]), 672,971; Miami, 358,548; Tampa, 280,015; St. Petersburg, 238,629; Hialeah, 188,004; Orlando, 164,693; Fort Lauderdale, 149,377; Tallahassee, 124,773; Hollywood, 121,697; Clearwater, 98,784
Land area & (rank): 53,997 sq mi. (139,852 sq km) (26)
Geographic center: In Hernando Co., 12 mi. NNW of Brooksville
Number of counties: 67
Largest county (1990 census): Dade, 1,937,094
State forests: 3 (306,881 ac.)
State parks: 105 (215,820 ac.)
1994 resident population est.: 13,953,000
1990 resident census population, sex, & (rank): 12,937,926 (4). **Male:** 6,261,719; **Female:** 6,676,207. **White:** 10,749,285 (83.1%); **Black:** 1,759,534 (13.6%); **American Indian, Eskimo, or Aleut:** 36,335 (0.3%); **Asian or Pacific Islander:** 154,302 (1.2%); **Other race:** 238,470 (1.8%); **Hispanic:** 1,574,143 (12.2%). **1990 percent population under 18:** 22.2; **65 and over:** 18.3; **median age:** 36.4.

1. Consolidated City (Coextensive with Duval County).

In 1513, Ponce De Leon, seeking the mythical "Fountain of Youth," discovered and named Florida, claiming it for Spain. Later, Florida would be held at different times by Spain and England until Spain finally sold it to the United States in 1819. (Incidentally, France established a colony named Fort Caroline in 1564 in the state that was to become Florida.)

Florida's early 19th-century history as a U.S. territory was marked by wars with the Seminole Indians that did not end until 1842, although a treaty was actually never signed.

One of the nation's fastest-growing states, Florida's population has gone from 2.8 million in 1950 to more than 12.9 million in 1990.

Florida's economy rests on a solid base of tourism (in 1992 the state entertained more than 40.5 million visitors from all over the world), manufacturing, agriculture, and international trade.

In recent years, oranges, grapefruit and tomatoes lead Florida's crop list, followed by vegetables, potatoes, melons, strawberries, sugar cane, dairy products, cattle and calves, and forest products.

Major tourist attractions are Miami Beach, Palm Beach, St. Augustine (founded in 1565, thus the oldest permanent city in the U.S.), Daytona Beach, and Fort Lauderdale on the East Coast. West Coast resorts include Sarasota, Tampa, Key West and St. Petersburg. The Orlando area, where Disney World is located on a 27,000-acre site, is Florida's most popular tourist destination.

Also drawing many visitors are the NASA Kennedy Space Center's Spaceport USA, located in the town of Kennedy Space Center, Everglades National Park, and the Epcot Center.

Famous natives and residents: Julian "Cannonball" Adderley, jazz saxophonist; Pat Boone, singer; Fernando Bujones, ballet dancer; Steve Carlton, baseball player; Fay Dunaway, actress; Stepin Fetchit (Lincoln Theodore Perry), comedian; Lue Gim Gong, horticulturist; Dwight Gooden, baseball player; James Weldon Johnson, author and educator; Frances Langford, singer; Butterfly McQueen, actress; Jim Morrison, singer; Osceola, Seminole Indian leader; Sidney Poitier, actor; A. Philip Randolph, labor leader; Marjorie Kinnan Rawlings, author; Charles and John Ringling, circus entrepreneurs; Joseph W. Stilwell, army general; Ben Vereen, actor

GEORGIA

Capital: Atlanta
Governor: Zell Miller, D (to Jan. 1995)
Lieut. Governor: Pierre Howard, D (to Jan. 1995)
Secy. of State: Max Cleland, D (to Jan. 1995)
Insurance Commissioner: Tim Ryles, D (to Jan. 1995)
Atty. General: Michael J. Bowers, R (to Jan. 1995)
Entered Union & (rank): Jan. 2, 1788 (4)
Present constitution adopted: 1977
Motto: Wisdom, justice, and moderation
STATE SYMBOLS: flower, Cherokee rose (1916); **tree,** Live oak (1937); **bird,** Brown thrasher (1935); **song,** "Georgia on My Mind" (1922)
Nicknames: Peach State, Empire State of the South
Origin of name: In honor of George II of England
10 largest cities (1990 census): Atlanta, 394,017; Columbus[1], 179,278; Savannah, 137,560; Macon, 106,612; Albany, 78,122; Roswell, 47,923; Athens, 45,734; Augusta, 44,639; Marietta, 44,129; Warner Robins, 43,726.
Land area & (rank): 57,919 sq mi. (150,010 sq km) (21)
Geographic center: In Twiggs Co., 18 mi. SE of Macon
Number of counties: 159
Largest county (1990 census): Fulton, 648,951
State forests: 25,258,000 ac. (67% of total state area)
State parks: 53 (42,600 ac.)
1994 resident population est.: 7,055,000
1990 resident census population, sex, & (rank): 6,478,216 (11). **Male:** 3,144,503; **Female:** 3,333,713. **White:** 4,600,148 (71.0%); **Black:** 1,746,565 (27.0%); **American Indian, Eskimo, or Aleut:** 13,348 (0.2%); **Asian or Pacific Islander:** 75,781 (1.2%); **Other race:** 42,374 (0.7%); **Hispanic:** 108,922 (1.7%). **1990 percent population under 18:** 26.7; **65 and over:** 10.1; **median age:** 31.6.

1. Consolidated City (Coextensive with Muscogee County).

Hernando de Soto, the Spanish explorer, first traveled parts of Georgia in 1540. British claims later conflicted with those of Spain. After obtaining a royal charter, Gen. James Oglethorpe established the first permanent settlement in Georgia in 1733 as a refuge for English debtors. In 1742, Oglethorpe defeated Spanish invaders in the Battle of Bloody Marsh.

A Confederate stronghold, Georgia was the scene of extensive military action during the Civil War. Union General William T. Sherman burned Atlanta and destroyed a 60-mile wide path to the coast where he captured Savannah in 1864.

The largest state east of the Mississippi, Georgia is typical of the changing South with an ever-increasing industrial development. Atlanta, largest city in the state, is the communications and transportation center for the Southeast and the area's chief distributor of goods.

Georgia leads the nation in the production of paper and board, tufted textile products, and processed chicken. Other major manufactured products are transportation equipment, food products, apparel, and chemicals.

Important agricultural products are corn, cotton, tobacco, soybeans, eggs, and peaches. Georgia produces twice as many peanuts as the next leading state. From its vast stands of pine come more than half the world's resins and turpentine and 74.4% of the U.S. supply. Georgia is also a leader in the production of marble, kaolin, barite, and bauxite.

Principal tourist attractions in Georgia include the Okefenokee National Wildlife Refuge, Andersonville Prison Park and National Cemetery, Chickamauga and Chattanooga National Military Park, the Little White House at Warm Springs where Pres. Franklin D. Roosevelt died in 1945, Sea Island, the enormous Confederate Memorial at Stone Mountain, Kennesaw Mountain National Battlefield Park, and Cumberland Island National Seashore.

Famous natives and residents: Conrad Aiken, poet; James Bowie, soldier; James Brown, singer; Jim Brown, actor and athlete; Erskine Caldwell, writer; James E. Carter, President; Ray Charles, singer; Lucius D. Clay, banker, ex-general; Ty Cobb, baseball player; Ossie Davis, actor & writer; James Dickey, poet; Mattiwilda Dobbs, soprano; Melvyn Douglas, actor; Rebecca Latimer Felton, first woman U.S. senator; Roosevelt Grier, entertainer and ex-athlete; Oliver Hardy, comedian; Joel Chandler Harris, journalist and author; Larry Holmes, boxer; Miriam Hopkins, actress; Harry James, trumpeter; Jasper Johns, painter and sculptor; Bobby Jones, golfer; Stacy Keach, actor; DeForest Kelley, actor; Martin Luther King, Jr., civil rights leader; Gladys Knight, singer; Joseph R. Lamar, jurist; Juliette Gordon Low, U.S. Girl Scouts founder; Carson McCullers, novelist; Johnny Mercer, songwriter; Margaret Mitchell, novelist; Elijah Muhammad, religious leader; Jessye Norman, soprano; Otis Redding, singer; Burt Reynolds, actor; Jackie Robinson, baseball player; Dean Rusk, ex-Secretary of State; Nipsey Russell, comedian; Alice Walker, author; Joanne Woodward, actress

HAWAII

Capital: Honolulu (on Oahu)
Governor: Benjamin Cayetano, D
Lieut. Governor: Mazie Hirono, D
Comptroller: Eugene Imai
Atty. General: Margery Bronster
Organized as territory: 1900
Entered Union & (rank): Aug. 21, 1959 (50)
Motto: *Ua Mau Ke Ea O Ka Aina I Ka Pono* (The life of the land is perpetuated in righteousness)
STATE SYMBOLS: flower, Hibiscus (yellow) 1988); **song,** "Hawaii Ponoi" (1967); **bird,** Nene (hawaiian goose) (1957); **tree,** Kukui (Candlenut) (1959)
Nickname: Aloha State (1959)
Origin of name: Uncertain. The islands may have been named by Hawaii Loa, their traditional discoverer. Or they may have been named after Hawaii or Hawaiki, the traditional home of the Polynesians.
10 largest cities[1] (1990 census): Honolulu, 377,059; Hilo, 37,808; Kailua, 36,818; Kaneohe, 35,448; Waipahu, 31,435; Pearl City, 30,993; Waimalu, 29,967; Mililani Town, 29,359; Schofield Barracks, 19,597; Wahiawa, 17,386
Land area & (rank): 6,423.4 sq mi. (16,636.5 sq km) (47)

Geographic center: Between islands of Hawaii and Maui

Number of counties: 4 plus one non-functioning county (Kalawao)

Largest county (1990 census): Honolulu, 836,231

State parks and historic sites: 70

1994 resident population est.: 1,178,564

1990 resident census population, sex, & (rank): 1,108,229 (40). **Male:** 563,891; **Female:** 544,338. **White:** 369,616 (33.4%); **Black:** 27,195 (2.5%); **American Indian, Eskimo, or Aleut:** 5,099 (0.5%); **Asian or Pacific Islander:** 685,236 (61.8%); **Other race:** 21,083 (1.9%); **Hispanic:** 81,390 (7.3%). **1990 percent population under 18:** 25.3; **65 and over:** 11.3; **median age:** 32.6

1. Census Designated Place. There are no political boundaries to Honolulu or any other place, but statistical boundaries are assigned under state law.

First settled by Polynesians sailing from other Pacific islands between 300 and 600 A.D., Hawaii was visited in 1778 by British Captain James Cook who called the group the Sandwich Islands.

Hawaii was a native kingdom throughout most of the 19th century when the expansion of the vital sugar industry (pineapple came after 1898) meant increasing U.S. business and political involvement. In 1893, Queen Liliuokalani was deposed and a year later the Republic of Hawaii was established with Sanford B. Dole as president. Then, following its annexation in 1898, Hawaii became a U.S. Territory in 1900.

The Japanese attack on the naval base at Pearl Harbor on Dec. 7, 1941, was directly responsible for U.S. entry into World War II.

Hawaii, 2,397 miles west-southwest of San Francisco, is a 1,523-mile chain of islets and eight main islands—Hawaii, Kahoolawe, Maui, Lanai, Molokai, Oahu, Kauai, and Niihau. The Northwestern Hawaiian Islands, other than Midway, are administratively part of Hawaii.

The temperature is mild and Hawaii's soil is fertile for tropical fruits and vegetables. Cane sugar and pineapple are the chief products. Hawaii also grows coffee, bananas and nuts. The tourist business is Hawaii's largest source of outside income.

Hawaii's highest peak is Mauna Kea (13,796 ft.). Mauna Loa (13,679 ft.) is the largest volcanic mountain in the world in cubic content.

Among the major points of interest are Hawaii Volcanoes National Park (Hawaii), Haleakala National Park (Maui), Puuhonua o Honaunau National Historical Park (Hawaii), Polynesian Cultural Center (Oahu), the U.S.S. *Arizona* Memorial at Pearl Harbor, and Iolani Palace (the only royal palace in the U.S.), Bishop Museum, and Waikiki Beach (all in Honolulu).

Famous natives and residents: George Ariyoshi, first Japanese-American elected governor; Hiram Bingham, missionary; Charles R. Bishop, banker and philanthropist; Tia Carrere, singer, actress; Samuel N. Castle, missionary, founder of Castle & Cooke Ltd. with Amos S. Cooke, missionary and educator; Father Damien, leper colony worker; Sanford B. Dole, territorial governor; Jean Erdman, dancer, choreographer; Hiram L. Fong, first Chinese-American senator; Don Ho, entertainer; Daniel K. Inouye, senator; Gerrit P. Judd, advisor of Hawaiian king; Keahumanu, female chief; Duke Paoa Kahanamoku, Olympic swimming champion; Kamehameha I, first Hawaiian king; Kamehameha V, last of the dynasty; George Parsons Lathrop, journalist and poet; Liliuokalani, queen, last Hawaiian monarch; Bette Midler, singer; Ellison Onizuka, astronaut; Kawaipuna Prejean, Hawaiian activist, proponent of Hawaiian sovereignty; Chad Rowan, Yokozuna sumo wrestler; Harold Sakata, actor; Carolyn Suzanne Sapp, 1991 Miss America; James Shigeta, actor; Claus Spreckels, developer of Hawaiian sugar industry; Don Stroud, actor

IDAHO

Capital: Boise

Governor: Philip E. Batt, R (to Jan. 1999)

Lieut. Governor: C. L. "Butch" Otter, R (to Jan. 1999)

Secy. of State: Pete T. Cenarrusa, R (to Jan. 1999)

State Auditor: J.D. Williams, D (to Jan. 1999)

Atty. General: Alan G. Lance, R (to Jan. 1999)

Treasurer: Lydia Justice Edwards, R (to Jan. 1999)

Organized as territory: March 3, 1863

Entered Union & (rank): July 3, 1890 (43)

Present constitution adopted: 1890

Motto: *Esto perpetua* (It is forever)

STATE SYMBOLS: flower, Syringa (1931); **tree,** White pine (1935); **bird,** Mountain bluebird (1931); **horse,** Appaloosa (1975); **gem,** Star garnet (1967); **song,** "Here We Have Idaho"; **folk dance,** Square Dance; **fish,** Cutthroat trout (1990); **fossil,** Hagerman horse fossil (1988)

Nicknames: Gem State; Spud State; Panhandle State

Origin of name: Unknown. It is an invented name and has no Indian translation meaning "Gem of the Mountains." Meaning of name, if any, is unknown.

10 largest cities (1992 est.): Boise, 135,506; Idaho Falls, 48,226; Pocatello, 47,914; Nampa, 31,416; Twin Falls, 29,684; Lewiston, 29,119; Coeur d'Alene, 26,611; Caldwell, 20,800; Moscow, 19,122; Rexburg, 14,497

Land area & (rank): 82,751 sq mi. (214,325 sq km) (11)

Geographic center: In Custer Co., at Custer, SW of Challis

Number of counties: 44, plus small part of Yellowstone National Park

Largest county (1994 est.): Ada, 243,337

State forests: 881,000 ac.

State parks: 22 (44,177 ac.)

1994 resident population est.: 1,133,034

1990 resident census population, sex, & (rank): 1,006,749 (42). **Male:** 500,956; **Female:** 505,793. **White:** 950,451 (94.4%); **Black:** 3,370 (0.3%); **American Indian, Eskimo, or Aleut:** 13,780 (1.4%); **Asian or Pacific Islander:** 9,365 (0.9%); **Other race:** 29,783 (3.0%); **Hispanic:** 52,927 (5.3%). **1990 percent population under 18:** 30.6; **65 and over:** 12.0; **median age:** 31.5.

After its acquisition by the U.S. as part of the Louisiana Purchase in 1803, the region was explored by Meriwether Lewis and William Clark in 1805–06. Northwest boundary disputes with Great Britain were settled by the Oregon Treaty in 1846 and the first permanent U.S. settlement in Idaho was established by the Mormons at Franklin in 1860.

After gold was discovered on Orofino Creek in 1860, prospectors swarmed into the territory, but left little more than a number of ghost towns.

In the 1870s, growing white occupation of Indian lands led to a series of battles between U.S. forces and the Nez Percé, Bannock, and Sheepeater tribes.

Mining, lumbering, and irrigation farming have been important for years. Idaho produces more than one fifth of all the silver mined in the U.S. It also ranks high among the states in antimony, lead, cobalt, garnet, phosphate rock, vanadium, zinc, mercury, and gold.

Idaho's most impressive growth began when World War II military needs made processing agricultural products a big industry, particularly the dehydrating and freezing of potatoes. The state produces about one fourth of the nation's potato crop, as well as wheat, apples, corn, barley, sugar beets, and hops.

With the growth of winter sports, tourism now outranks mining in dollar revenue. Idaho's many streams and lakes provide fishing, camping, and boating sites. The nation's largest elk herds draw hunters from all over the world and the famed Sun Valley resort attracts thousands of visitors to its swimming and skiing facilities.

Other points of interest are the Craters of the Moon National Monument; Nez Percé National Historic Park, which includes many sites visited by Lewis and Clark; and the State Historical Museum in Boise.

Famous natives and residents: Joe Albertson, grocery chain founder; Cecil Andrus, governor; T.H. Bell, educator; Ezra Taft Benson, Eisenhower's Secretary of Agriculture, pres. LDS church, marketing specialist; William E. Borah, senator; Gutzon Borglum, Mt. Rushmore sculptor; Carol R. Brink, author; Frank F. Church, senator; Fred Dubois, senator; Vardis Fisher, novelist; Lawrence H. Gipson, historian; Ernest Hemingway, author; Mariel Hemingway, actress; Chief Joseph, Nez Percé chief; Harmon Killebrew, baseball player; Jerry Kramer, football player, author; Ezra Pound, poet; Sacagawea, Shoshonean guide; J.R. Simplot, industrialist; Robert E. Smylie, political leader; Henry Spalding, missionary; Frank Steunenberg, governor; Picabo Street, skier; David Tompson, founded first trading post; Lana Turner, actress

ILLINOIS

Capital: Springfield
Governor: Jim Edgar, R (to Jan. 1999)
Lieut. Governor: Bob Kustra, R (to Jan. 1999)
Atty. General: Jim Ryan, R (to Jan. 1999)
Secy. of State: George H. Ryan, R (to Jan. 1999)
Comptroller: Loleta Didrickson, R (to Jan. 1999)
Treasurer: Judith Baar Topinka, R (to Jan. 1999)
Organized as territory: Feb. 3, 1809
Entered Union & (rank): Dec. 3, 1818 (21)
Present constitution adopted: 1970
Motto: State sovereignty, national union
STATE SYMBOLS: flower, Violet (1908); **tree,** White oak (1973); **bird,** Cardinal (1929); **animal,** White-tailed deer (1982); **fish,** Bluegill (1987); **insect,** Monarch butterfly (1975); **song,** "Illinois" (1925); **mineral,** Fluorite (1965)
Nickname: Prairie State
Origin of name: From an Indian word and French suffix meaning "tribe of superior men"
10 largest cities (1990 census): Chicago, 2,783,726; Rockford, 139,426; Peoria, 113,504; Springfield, 105,227; Aurora, 99,581; Naperville, 85,351; Decatur, 83,885; Elgin, 77,010; Joliet, 76,836; Arlington Heights Village, 75,460
Land area & (rank): 55,593 sq mi. (143,987 sq kkm) (24)
Geographic center: In Logan County 28 mi. NE of Springfield
Number of counties: 102
Largest county (1990 census): Cook, 5,105,067
Public use areas: 187 (275,000 ac.), incl. state parks, memorials, forests and conservation areas
1994 resident population est.: 11,752,000
1990 resident census population, sex, & (rank): 11,430,602 (6). **Male:** 5,552,233; **Female:** 5,878,369. **White:** 8,952,978 (78.3%); **Black:** 1,694,273 (14.8%); **American Indian, Eskimo, or Aleut:** 21,836 (0.2%); **Asian or Pacific Islander:** 285,311 (2.5%); **Other race:** 476,204 (4.2%); **Hispanic:** 904,446 (7.9%). **1990 percent population under 18:** 25.8; **65 and over:** 12.6; **median age:** 32.8.

French explorers Marquette and Joliet, in 1673, were the first Europeans of record to visit the region. In 1699 French settlers established the first permanent settlement at Cahokia, near present-day East St. Louis.

Great Britain obtained the region at the end of the French and Indian War in 1763. The area figured prominently in frontier struggles during the Revolutionary War and in Indian wars during the early 19th

century.

Significant episodes in the state's early history include the growing migration of Eastern settlers following the opening of the Erie Canal in 1825; the Black Hawk War, which virtually ended the Indian troubles in the area; and the rise of Abraham Lincoln from farm laborer to President-elect.

Today, Illinois stands high in manufacturing, coal mining, agriculture, and oil production. The sprawling Chicago district (including a slice of Indiana) is a great iron and steel producer, meat packer, grain exchange, and railroad center. Chicago is also famous as a Great Lakes port.

Illinois ranks third in the nation in export of agricultural products, first in corn and soybeans, and third hog production. An important dairying state, Illinois is also a leader in corn, oats, wheat, barley, rye, truck vegetables, and the nursery products.

The state manufactures a great variety of industrial and consumer products: railroad cars, clothing, furniture, tractors, liquor, watches, and farm implements are just some of the items made in its factories and plants.

Central Illinois is noted for shrines and memorials associated with the life of Abraham Lincoln. In Springfield are the Lincoln Home, the Lincoln Tomb, and the restored Old State Capitol. Other points of interest are the home of Mormon leader Joseph Smith in Nauvoo and, in Chicago: the Art Institute, Field Museum, Museum of Science and Industry, Shedd Aquarium, Adler Planetarium, Merchandise Mart, and Chicago Portage National Historic Site.

Famous natives and residents: Franklin Pierce Adams, author; Jane Addams, social worker; Mary Astor, actress; Jack Benny, comedian; Black Hawk, Sauk Indian chief; Harry A. Blackmun, jurist; Ray Bradbury, author; William Jennings Bryan, orator and politician; Edgar Rice Burroughs, novelist; Gower Champion, choreographer; John Chancellor, TV commentator; Raymond Chandler, writer; Jimmy Connors, tennis champion; James Gould Cozzens, novelist; Richard J. Daley, mayor of Chicago; Miles Davis, musician; Peter DeVries, novelist; Walt Disney, film animator and producer; John Dos Passos, author; James T. Farrell, novelist; Betty Friedan, feminist; Benny Goodman, musician; John Gunther, author; Ernest Hemingway, author; Charlton Heston, actor; Wild Bill Hickok, scout; William Holden, actor; Rock Hudson, actor; Burl Ives, singer; James Jones, novelist; John Jones, civil rights leader; Quincy Jones, composer; Keokuk (Watchful Fox), chief of the Sac and Fox Indians; Walter Kerr, drama critic; Archibalt MacLeish, poet; David Mamet, playwright; Robert A. Millikan, physicist; Sherrill Milnes, baritone; Bill Murray, actor; Bob Newhart, actor, comedian; William S. Paley, broadcasting executive; Drew Pearson, columnist; Richard Pryor, comedian, actor; Ronald Reagan, President; Carl Sandburg, poet; Sam Shepard, playwright; William L. Shirer, author and historian; John Paul Stevens, jurist; McLean Stevenson, actor; Preston Sturges, director; Gloria Swanson, actress; Carl Van Doren, writer and educator; Melvin Van Peebles, playwright; Irving Wallace, novelist; Alfred Wallenstein, conductor; Raquel Welch, actress; Florenz Ziegfield, theatrical producer

INDIANA

Capital: Indianapolis
Governor: Birch Evans Bayh III, D (to Jan. 1997)
Lieut. Governor: Frank O'Bannon, D (to Jan. 1997)
Secy. of State: Sue Anne Gilroy, R (to Feb. 1999)
Treasurer: Joyce Brinkman, R (to Feb. 1999)
Atty. General: Pamela Carter, D (to Jan. 1997)
Auditor: Morris Wooden, R (to Dec. 1998)
Organized as territory: May 7, 1800
Entered Union & (rank): Dec. 11, 1816 (19)

Present constitution adopted: 1851
Motto: The Crossroads of America
STATE SYMBOLS: flower: Peony (1957); **tree,** Tulip tree (1931); **bird,** Cardinal (1933); **song,** "On the Banks of the Wabash, Far Away" (1913)
Nickname: Hoosier State
Origin of name: Meaning "land of Indians"
10 largest cities (1990 census): Indianapolis, 731,327; Fort Wayne, 173,072; Evansville, 126,272; Gary, 116,646; South Bend, 105,511; Hammond, 84,236; Muncie, 71,035; Bloomington, 60,633; Anderson, 59,459; Terre Haute, 57,483
Land area & (rank): 35,870 sq mi. (92,904 sq km) (38)
Geographic center: In Boone Co., 14 mi. NNW of Indianapolis
Number of Counties: 92
Largest county (1990 census): Marion, 797,159
State parks: 20 (56,806 ac.)
State memorials: 16 (941.977 ac.)
1994 resident population est.: 5,752,000
1990 census population, sex, & (rank): 5,544,159 (14). **Male:** 2,688,281; **Female:** 2,855,878. **White:** 5,020,700 (90.6%); **Black:** 432,092 (7.8%); **American Indian, Eskimo, or Aleut:** 12,720 (0.2%); **Asian or Pacific Islander:** 37,617 (0.7%); **Other race:** 41,030 (0.7%); **Hispanic:** 98,788 (1.8%). **1990 percent population under 18:** 26.3; **65 and over:** 12.6; **median age:** 32.8.

First explored for France by La Salle in 1679–80, the region figured importantly in the Franco-British struggle for North America that culminated with British victory in 1763.

George Rogers Clark led American forces against the British in the area during the Revolutionary War and, prior to becoming a state, Indiana was the scene of frequent Indian uprisings until the victory of Gen. William Henry Harrison at Tippecanoe in 1811.

Indiana's 41-mile Lake Michigan waterfront—one of the world's great industrial centers—turns out iron, steel, and oil products. Products include automobile parts and accessories, mobile homes and recreational vehicles, truck and bus bodies, aircraft engines, farm machinery, and fabricated structural steel. Phonograph records, wood office furniture, and pharmaceuticals are also manufactured.

The state is a leader in agriculture with corn the principal crop. Hogs, soybeans, wheat, oats, rye, tomatoes, onions, and poultry also contribute heavily to Indiana's agricultural output. Much of the building limestone used in the U.S. is quarried in Indiana which is also a large producer of coal.

Wyandotte Cave, one of the largest in the U.S., is located in Crawford County in southern Indiana and West Baden and French Lick are well known for their mineral springs. Other attractions include Indiana Dunes National Lakeshore, Indianapolis Motor Speedway, Lincoln Boyhood National Memorial, and the George Rogers Clark National Historical Park.

Famous natives and residents: George Ade, humorist; Leon Ames, actor; Anne Baxter, actress; Albert J. Beveridge, political leader; Bill Blass, fashion designer; Frank Borman, astronaut; Hoagy Carmichael, songwriter; James Dean, actor; Eugene V. Debs, Socialist leader; Lloyd C. Douglas, author; Theodore Dreiser, writer; Bernard F. Gimbel, merchant; Virgil Grissom, astronaut; Phil Harris, actor and band leader; John Milton Hay, statesman; James R. Hoffa, labor leader; Michael Jackson, singer; Buck Jones, actor; Alfred C. Kinsey, zoologist; David Letterman, TV host, comedian; Eli Lilly, pharmaceuticals manufacturer; Carole Lombard, actress; Shelley Long, actress; Marjorie Main, actress; James McCracken, tenor; Joaquin Miller, poet; Paul Osborn, playwright; Cole Porter, songwriter; Gene Stratton Porter, naturalist and author; Ernest Taylor

Pyle, journalist; James Whitcomb Riley, poet; Knute Rockne, football coach; Ned Rorem, composer; Red Skelton, comedian; Rex Stout, mystery writer; Booth Tarkington, author; Twyla Tharp, dancer and choreographer; Forrest Tucker, actor; Harold C. Urey, physicist; Kurt Vonnegut, Jr., author; Jessamyn West, novelist; Wendell Willkie, lawyer; Wilbur Wright, inventor

IOWA

Capital: Des Moines
Governor: Terry E. Branstad, R (to Jan. 1999)
Lieut. Governor: Joy Corning, R (to Jan. 1999)
Secy. of State: Paul Pate, R (to Jan. 1999)
Treasurer: Michael L. Fitzgerald, D (to Jan. 1999)
Atty. General: Tom Miller, D (to Jan. 1999)
Organized as territory: June 12, 1838
Entered Union & (rank): Dec. 28, 1846 (29)
Present constitution adopted: 1857
Motto: Our liberties we prize and our rights we will maintain
STATE SYMBOLS: flower, Wild rose (1897); **bird,** Eastern goldfinch (1933); **colors,** Red, white, and blue (in state flag); **song,** "Song of Iowa"
Nickname: Hawkeye State
Origin of name: Probably from an Indian word meaning "I-o-w-a, this is the place," or "The Beautiful Land"
10 largest cities (1992 est.): Des Moines, 194,540; Cedar Rapids, 111,659; Davenport, 97,509; Sioux City, 81,907; Waterloo, 67,124; Iowa City, 59,313; Dubuque, 58,575; Council Bluffs, 54,884; Ames, 46,672; Cedar Falls, 35,094
Land area & (rank): 55,875 sq mi. (144,716 sq km) (23)
Geographic center: In Story Co., 5 mi. NE of Ames
Number of counties: 99
Largest county (1992 est.): Polk, 338,261
State forests: 5 (28,000 ac.)
State parks: 84 (49,237)
1994 resident population est.: 2,829,000
1990 resident census population, sex, & (rank): 2,776,755 (30). **Male:** 1,344,802; **Female:** 1,431,953. **White:** 2,683,090 (96.6%); **Black:** 48,090 (1.7%); **American Indian, Eskimo, or Aleut:** 7,349 (0.3%); **Asian or Pacific Islander:** 25,476 (0.9%); **Other race:** 12,750 (0.5%); **Hispanic:** 32,647 (1.2%). **1990 percent population under 18:** 25.9; **65 and over:** 15.3; **median age:** 34.0

The first Europeans to visit the area were the French explorers, Father Jacques Marquette and Louis Joliet in 1673. The U.S. obtained control of the area in 1803 as part of the Louisiana Purchase.

During the first half of the 19th century, there was heavy fighting between white settlers and Indians. Lands were taken from the Indians after the Black Hawk War in 1832 and again in 1836 and 1837.

When Iowa became a state in 1846, its capital was Iowa City; the more centrally located Des Moines became the new capital in 1857. At that time, the state's present boundaries were also drawn.

Although Iowa produces a tenth of the nation's food supply, the value of Iowa's manufactured products is twice that of its agriculture. Major industries are food and associated products, non-electrical machinery, electrical equipment, printing and publishing, and fabricated products.

Iowa stands in a class by itself as an agricultural state. Its farms sell over $10 billion worth of crops and livestock annually. Iowa leads the nation in all corn, soybeans, livestock, and hog marketings, with about 25% of the pork supply and 6% of the grain-fed cattle. Iowa's forests produce hardwood lumber, particularly walnut, and its mineral products include cement, limestone, sand, gravel, gypsum, and coal.

Tourist attractions include the Herbert Hoover birthplace and library near West Branch; the Amana Colonies; Fort Dodge Historical Museum, Fort, and Stockade; the Iowa State Fair at Des Moines in August; and the Effigy Mounds National Monument at Marquette, a prehistoric Indian burial site.

Famous natives and residents: Bix Beiderbecke, jazz musician; Norman Borlang, plant pathologist and geneticist, Nobel Peace Prize winner; William "Buffalo Bill" F. Cody, scout; Johnny Carson, TV entertainer; Gardner Cowles, Jr., publisher; Simon Estes, bass-baritone; William Frawley, actor; George H. Gallup, poll taker; Susan Glaspell, writer; Herbert Hoover, President; MacKinlay Kantor, novelist; Charles A. Kettering, inventor; Ann Landers, columnist; Cloris Leachman, actress; John L. Lewis, labor leader; Glenn L. Martin, aviator, manufacturer; Elsa Maxwell, writer; Frederick L. Maytag, inventor and manufacturer; Glenn Miller, bandleader; Harriet Nelson, actress; Nathan M. Pusey, educator; David Rabe, playwright; Harry Reasoner, TV commentator; Donna Reed, actress; Lillian Russell, soprano; Robert Schiller, evangelist; Wallace Stegner, novelist and critic; Billy Sunday, evangelist; James A. Van Allen, space physicist; Abigail Van Buren, columnist; Henry A. Wallace, statesman and vice president; John Wayne, actor; Andy Williams, singer; Meredith Willson, composer; Grant Wood, painter

KANSAS

Capital: Topeka
Governor: Bill Graves, R (to Jan. 1999)
Lieut. Governor: Sheila Frahm, R (to Jan. 1999)
Secy. of State: Ron Thornburgh, R (to Jan. 1999)
Treasurer: Sally Thompson, D (to Jan. 1999)
Atty. General: Carla Stovall, R (to Jan. 1999)
Commission of Insurance: Kathleen Sebelius, D (to Jan. 1999)
Organized as territory: May 30, 1854
Entered Union & (rank): Jan. 29, 1861 (34)
Present constitution adopted: 1859
Motto: *Ad astra per aspera* (To the stars through difficulties)
STATE SYMBOLS: flower, Sunflower (1903); **tree,** Cottonwood (1937); **bird,** Western meadowlark (1937); **animal,** Buffalo (1955); **song,** "Home on Range" (1947)
Nicknames: Sunflower State; Jayhawk State
Origin of name: From a Siouan word meaning "people of the south wind"
10 largest cities (1990 census): Wichita, 304,011; Kansas City, 149,767; Topeka, 119,883; Overland Park, 111,790; Lawrence, 65,608; Olathe, 63,352; Salina, 42,303; Hutchinson, 39,308; Leavenworth, 38,495; Shawnee, 37,993
Land area & (rank): 81,823 sq mi. (211,922 sq km) (13)
Geographic center: In Barton Co., 15 mi. NE of Great Bend
Number of counties: 105
Largest county (1990 census): Sedgwick, 403,662
State parks: 22 (14,394 ac.)
1994 resident population est.: 2,554,000
1990 resident census population, sex, & (rank): 2,477,574 (32). **Male:** 1,214,645; **Female:** 1,262,929. **White:** 2,231,986 (90.1%); **Black:** 143,076 (5.8%); **American Indian, Eskimo, or Aleut:** 21,965 (0.9%); **Asian or Pacific Islander:** 31,750 (1.3%); **Other race:** 48,797 (2.0%); **Hispanic:** 93,670 (3.8%). **1990 percent population under 18:** 26.7; **65 and over:** 13.8; **median age:** 32.9.

Spanish explorer Francisco de Coronado, in 1541, is considered the first European to have traveled this region. La Salle's extensive land claims for France (1682) included present-day Kansas. Ceded to Spain by France in 1763, the territory reverted back to France in 1800 and was sold to the U.S. as part of the Louisiana Purchase in 1803.

Lewis and Clark, Zebulon Pike, and Stephen H. Long explored the region between 1803 and 1819. The first permanent settlements in Kansas were outposts—Fort Leavenworth (1827), Fort Scott (1842), and Fort Riley (1853)—established to protect travelers along the Santa Fe and Oregon Trails.

Just before the Civil War, the conflict between the pro- and anti-slavery forces earned the region the grim title "Bleeding Kansas."

Today, wheat fields, oil well derricks, herds of cattle, and grain storage elevators are chief features of the Kansas landscape. A leading wheat-growing state, Kansas also raises corn, sorghums, oats, barley, soy beans, and potatoes. Kansas stands high in petroleum production and mines zinc, coal, salt, and lead. It is also the nation's leading producer of helium.

Wichita is one of the nation's leading aircraft manufacturing centers, ranking first in production of private aircraft. Kansas City is an important transportation, milling, and meat-packing center.

Points of interest include the Kansas Museum of History at Topeka, the Eisenhower boyhood home and the new Eisenhower Memorial Museum and Presidential Library at Abilene, John Brown's cabin at Osawatomie, recreated Front Street in Dodge City, Fort Larned (once the most important military post on the Santa Fe Trail), and Fort Leavenworth and Fort Riley.

Famous natives and residents: Roscoe "Fatty" Arbuckle, actor; Clarence D. Batchelor, political cartoonist; Gwendolyn Brooks, poet; Walter P. Chrysler, auto manufacturer; Clark M. Clifford, ex-Secretary of Defense; John Steuart Curry, painter; Amelia Earhart, aviator; Milton S. Eisenhower, educator; Gary Hart, politician; William Inge, playwright; Walter Johnson, baseball pitcher; Osa L. Johnson, documentary film producer; Buster Keaton, comedian; Emmett Kelly, clown; Stan Kenton, jazz musician; James Lehrer, broadcast journalist; Edgar Lee Masters, poet; Mary McCarthy, actress; Hattie McDaniel, actress; William C. Menninger, psychiatrist; Gordon Parks, film director; Zasu Pitts, actress; Samuel Ramey, opera singer; Charles Robinson, statesman and first governor; Charles (Buddy) Rogers, actor; Damon Runyon, journalist; Eugene W. Smith, photojournalist; Milburn Stone, actor; John Cameron Swayze, news commentator; William Allen White, journalist; Charles E. Whittaker, jurist; Jess Willard, boxer

KENTUCKY

Capital: Frankfort
Governor: Brereton C. Jones, D (to Dec. 1995)
Lieut. Governor: Paul E. Patton, D (to Dec. 1995)
Secy. of State: Bob Babbage, D (to Jan. 1996)
State Treasurer: Frances Jones Mills, D (to Jan. 1996)
State Auditor: Ben Chandler, D (to Jan. 1996)
Atty. General: Chris Gorman, D (to Jan. 1996)
Entered Union & (rank): June 1, 1792 (15)
Present constitution adopted: 1891
Motto: United we stand, divided we fall
STATE SYMBOLS: tree, Tulip poplar (1994); **flower,** Goldenrod; **bird,** Kentucky cardinal; **song,** "My Old Kentucky Home"
Nickname: Bluegrass State
Origin of name: From an Iroquoian word "Ken-tah-ten" meaning "land of tomorrow"

10 largest cities (1990 census): Louisville, 269,063; Lexington-Fayette, 225,366; Owensboro, 53,549; Covington, 43,264; Bowling Green, 40,641; Hopkinsville, 29,809; Paducah, 27,256; Frankfort, 25,968; Henderson, 25,945; Ashland, 23,622
Land area & (rank): 39,732 sq mi. (102,907 sq km) (36)
Geographic center: In Marion Co., 3 mi. NNW of Lebanon
Number of counties: 120
Largest county (1990 census): Jefferson, population 664,937
State forests: 9 (44,173 ac.)
State parks: 43 (40,574 ac.)
1994 resident population est.: 3,827,000
1990 resident census population, sex, & (rank): 3,685,296 (23). **Male:** 1,785,235; **Female:** 1,900,061. **White:** 3,391,832 (92.0%); **Black:** 262,907 (7.1%); **American Indian, Eskimo, or Aleut:** 5,769 (0.2%); **Asian or Pacific Islander:** 17,812 (0.5%); **Other race:** 6,976 (0.2%); **Hispanic:** 21,984 (0.6%). **1990 percent population below age 18:** 25.9; **65 and over:** 12.7; **median age:** 33.0.

Kentucky was the first region west of the Allegheny Mountains settled by American pioneers. James Harrod established the first permanent settlement at Harrodsburg in 1774; the following year Daniel Boone, who had explored the area in 1767, blazed the Wilderness Trail and founded Boonesboro.

Politically, the Kentucky region was originally part of Virginia, but early statehood was gained in 1792.

During the Civil War, as a slaveholding state with a considerable abolitionist population, Kentucky was caught in the middle of the conflict, supplying both Union and Confederate forces with thousands of troops.

In recent years, manufacturing has shown important gains particularly in automotive assembly and parts manufacturing. Kentucky also prides itself on producing some of the nation's best tobacco, horses, and whiskey. Corn, soybeans, wheat, fruit, hogs, cattle, and dairy farming are among the agricultural items produced.

Among the manufactured items produced in the state are motor vehicles, furniture, aluminum ware, brooms, apparel, lumber products, machinery, textiles, and iron and steel products. Kentucky also produces significant amounts of petroleum, natural gas, fluorspar, clay, and stone. However, coal accounts for 90% of the total mineral income.

Louisville, the largest city, famed for the Kentucky Derby at Churchill Downs, is also the location of a large state university, whiskey distilleries, and cigarette factories. The Bluegrass country around Lexington is the home of some of the world's finest race horses. Other attractions are Mammoth Cave, the George S. Patton, Jr., Military Museum at Fort Knox, and Old Fort Harrod State Park.

Famous natives and residents: John Adair, pioneer and political leader; Muhammad Ali, boxer; Alben W. Barkley, vice president; Louis D. Brandeis, jurist; John Mason Brown, critic; Kit Carson, scout; Champ Clark, politician; Rosemary Clooney, singer; Irvin S. Cobb, humorist; Jefferson Davis, President of Confederacy; Irene Dunne, actress; Crystal Gayle, singer; David W. Griffith, film producer; John M. Harlan, jurist; Elizabeth Hardwick, writer; Casey Jones, celebrated locomotive engineer; Abraham Lincoln, President; Loretta Lynn, singer; Carry Amelia Nation, temperance leader; Patricia Neal, actress; George Reeves, actor; Wiley B. Rutledge, jurist; Diane Sawyer, broadcast journalist; Phil Simms, football player; Adlai Stevenson, vice president; Allen Tate, poet and critic; Hunter Thompson, writer; Frederick M. Vinson, jurist; Robert Penn Warren, novelist

LOUISIANA

Capital: Baton Rouge
Governor: Edwin W. Edwards, D (to Jan. 1996)
Lieut. Governor: Melinda Schwegman, D (to Jan. 1996)
Secy. of State: W. Fox McKeithen, R (to Jan. 1996)
Treasurer: Mary L. Landieu, D (to Jan. 1996)
Atty. General: Richard P. Ieyoub, D (to Jan. 1996)
Organized as territory: March 26, 1804
Entered Union & (rank): April 30, 1812 (18)
Present constitution adopted: 1974
Motto: Union, justice, and confidence
STATE SYMBOLS: flower, Magnolia (1900); **tree,** Bald cypress (1963); **bird,** Pelican (1958); **songs,** "Give Me Louisiana" and "You Are My Sunshine"
Nicknames: Pelican State; Sportsman's Paradise; Creole State; Sugar State
Origin of name: In honor of Louis XIV of France
10 largest cities (1990 census): New Orleans, 496,938; Baton Rouge, 219,531; Shreveport, 198,525; Lafayette, 94,440; Kenner, 72,033; Lake Charles, 70,580; Monroe, 54,909; Bossier City, 52,721; Alexandria, 49,188; New Iberia, 31,828
Land area & (rank): 43,566 sq mi. (112,836 sq km) (33)
Geographic center: In Avoyelles Parish, 3 mi. SE of Marksville
Number of parishes (counties): 64
Largest parish (1990 census): Jefferson, 448,306
State forests: 1 (8,000 ac.)
State parks: 30 (13,932 ac.)
1994 resident population est.: 4,315,000
1990 resident census population, sex, & (rank): 4,219,973 (21). **Male:** 2,031,386; **Female:** 2,188,587. **White:** 2,839,138 (67.3%); **Black:** 1,299,281 (30.8%); **American Indian, Eskimo, or Aleut:** 18,541 (0.4%); **Asian or Pacific Islander:** 41,099 (1.0%); **Other race:** 21,914 (0.5%); **Hispanic:** 93,044 (2.2%). **1990 percent population under 18:** 29.1; **65 and over:** 11.1; **median age:** 31.0.

Louisiana has a rich, colorful historical background. Early Spanish explorers were Piñeda, 1519; Cabeza de Vaca, 1528; and de Soto in 1541. La Salle reached the mouth of the Mississippi and claimed all the land drained by it and its tributaries for Louis XIV of France in 1682.

Louisiana became a French crown colony in 1731, was ceded to Spain in 1763, returned to France in 1800, and sold by Napoleon to the U.S. as part of the Louisiana Purchase (with large territories to the north and northwest) in 1803.

In 1815, Gen. Andrew Jackson's troops defeated a larger British army in the Battle of New Orleans, neither side aware that the treaty ending the War of 1812 had been signed.

As to total value of its mineral output, Louisiana is a leader in natural gas, salt, petroleum, and sulfur production. Much of the oil and sulfur comes from offshore deposits. The state also produces large crops of sweet potatoes, rice, sugar cane, pecans, soybeans, corn, and cotton.

Leading manufactures include chemicals, processed food, petroleum and coal products, paper, lumber and wood products, transportation equipment, and apparel.

Louisiana marshes supply most of the nation's muskrat fur as well as that of opossum, raccoon, mink, and otter, and large numbers of game birds.

Major points of interest include New Orleans with its French Quarter and Superdome, plantation homes near Natchitoches and New Iberia, Cajun country in the Mississippi delta region, Chalmette National Historical Park, and the state capital at Baton Rouge.

Famous natives and residents: Louis Armstrong, musician; Geoffrey Beene, fashion designer; Truman Capote, writer; Kitty Carlisle, singer and actress; Van Cliburn, concert pianist; Michael De Bakey, heart surgeon; Fats Domino, musician; Louis Moreau Gottschalk, pianist, composer; Bryant Gumbel, TV newscaster; Lillian Hellman, playwright; Al Hirt, trumpeter; Mahalia Jackson, gospel singer; Jean Laffite, privateer; Dorothy Lamour, actress; John A. Lejeune, Marine Corps general; Elmore Leonard, author; Jerry Lee Lewis, singer; Huey P. Long, politician; Wynton Marsalis, musician; Jelly Roll Morton, jazz musician and composer; Huey Newton, black activist; Marguerite Piazza, soprano; Paul Prudhomme, chef; Howard K. Smith, TV commentator; Ben Turpin, comedian; Ray Walston, actor; Edward Douglas White, jurist

MAINE

Capital: Augusta
Governor: Angus S. King, Jr., I (to Jan. 1999)
Secy. of State: G. William Diamond, D (to Jan. 1999)
Controller: Carol Whitney, R (to Jan. 1999)
Atty. General: Andrew Ketterer, D (to Jan. 1999)
Entered Union & (rank): March 15, 1820 (23)
Present constitution adopted: 1820
Motto: *Dirigo* (I direct)
STATE SYMBOLS: flower, White pine cone and tassel (1895); **tree,** White pine tree (1945); **bird,** Chickadee (1927); **fish,** Landlocked salmon (1969); **mineral,** Tourmaline (1971); **song,** "State of Maine Song" (1937)
Nickname: Pine Tree State
Origin of name: First used to distinguish the mainland from the offshore islands. It has been considered a compliment to Henrietta Maria, Queen of Charles I of England. She was said to have owned the province of Mayne in France.
10 largest cities (1990 census): Portland, 64,358; Lewiston, 39,757; Bangor, 33,181; Auburn, 24,309; South Portland, 23,163; Augusta, 21,325; Biddeford, 20,710; Waterville, 17,173; Westbrook, 16,121; Saco, 15,181
Land area & (rank): 30,865 sq mi. (79,939 sq km) (39)
Geographic center: In Piscataquis Co., 18 mi. N of Dover–Foxcroft
Number of counties: 16
Largest town (1990 census): Brunswick, 20,906
State forests: 1 (21,000 ac.)
State parks: 26 (247,627 ac.)
State historic sites: 18 (403 ac.)
1994 resident population est.: 1,240,000
1990 resident census population, sex, & (rank): 1,227,928 (38). **Male:** 597,850; **Female:** 630,078. **White:** 1,208,360 (98.4%); **Black:** 5,138 (0.4%); **American Indian, Eskimo, or Aleut:** 5,998 (0.5%); **Asian or Pacific Islander:** 6,683; (0.5%); **Other race:** 1,749 (0.1%); **Hispanic:** 6,829 (0.6%).

John Cabot and his son, Sebastian, are believed to have visited the Maine coast in 1498. However, the first permanent English settlements were not established until more than a century later, in 1623.

The first naval action of the Revolutionary War occurred in 1775 when colonials captured the British sloop *Margaretta* off Machias on the Maine coast. In that same year, the British burned Falmouth (now Portland).

Long governed by Massachusetts, Maine became the 23rd state as part of the Missouri Compromise in 1820.

Maine produces 98% of the nation's low-bush blueberries. Farm income is also derived from apples, potatoes, dairy products, and vegetables, with poultry and eggs the largest items.

The state is one of the world's largest pulp-paper

producers. It ranks second in boot-and-shoe manufacturing. With almost 89% of its area forested, Maine turns out wood products from boats to toothpicks.

Maine leads the world in the production of the familiar flat tins of sardines, producing more than 75 million of them annually. Lobstermen normally catch 51% of the nation's true total of lobsters.

A scenic seacoast, beaches, lakes, mountains, and resorts make Maine a popular vacationland. There are more than 2,500 lakes and 5,000 streams, plus 26 state parks, to attract hunters, fishermen, skiers, and campers.

Major points of interest are: Bar Harbor, Allagash National Wilderness Waterway, the Wadsworth-Longfellow House in Portland, Roosevelt Campobello International Park, and the St. Croix Island National Monument.

Famous natives and residents: F. Lee Bailey, defense attorney; Charles F. Browne (Artemus Ward), humorist; Cyrus Curtis, publisher; Dorothea Dix, civil rights reformer; John Ford, film director; Melville Fuller, jurist; Marsden Hartley, painter; Henry Wadsworth Longfellow, poet; Sarah Orne Jewett, author; Stephen King, writer; Linda Lavin, actress; Edna St. Vincent Millay, poet; Marston Morse, mathematician; Frank Munsey, publisher; Walter Piston, composer; George Putnam, publisher; Kenneth Roberts, historical novelist; Edwin Arlington Robinson, poet; Margaret Chase Smith, politician; Samantha Smith, peacemaker, actress; John Hay Whitney, publisher

MARYLAND

Capital: Annapolis
Governor: Parris N. Glendening, D (to Jan. 1999)
Lieut. Gov.: Kathleen Kennedy Townsend, D (to Jan. 1999)
Secy. of State: John T. Willis, D (to Jan. 1999)
Comptroller of the Treasury: Louis L. Goldstein, D (to Jan. 1999)
Treasurer: Lucille Maurer, D (to Jan. 1999)
Atty. General: J. Joseph Curran, Jr., D (to Jan. 1999)
Entered Union & (rank): April 28, 1788 (7)
Present constitution adopted: 1867
Motto: *Fatti maschii, parole femine* (Manly deeds, womanly words)
STATE SYMBOLS: bird, Baltimore oriole (1947); **boat,** Skipjack (1985); **crustacean,** Maryland Blue Crab (1989); **dog,** Chesapeake Bay retriever (1964); **flower,** Black-eyed susan (1918); **tree,** White oak (1941); **fish,** Rockfish (1965); **folk dance,** Square dancing (1994); **fossil shell,** Ecphora gardnerae gardnerae (Wilson) (1994); **insect,** Baltimore checkerspot butterfly (1973); **song,** "Maryland! My Maryland!" (1939); **sport,** Jousting (1962)
Nicknames: Free State; Old Line State
Origin of name: In honor of Henrietta Maria (Queen of Charles I of England)
10 largest cities (1990 census): Baltimore, 736,014; Rockville, 44,835; Frederick, 40,148; Gaithersburg, 39,542; Bowie, 37,589; Hagerstown, 35,445; Annapolis, 33,187; Cumberland, 23,706; College Park, 21,927; Greenbelt, 21,096
Land area & (rank): 9,775 sq mi. (25,316 sq km) (42)
Geographic center: In Prince Georges Co., 4 1/2 mi. NW of Davidsonville
Number of counties: 23, and 1 independent city
Largest county (1990 census): Montgomery, 757,027
State forests: 13 (132,944 ac.)
State parks: 47 (87,670 ac.)
1994 resident population est.: 5,006,000
1990 resident census population, sex, & (rank): 4,781,468 (19). **Male:** 2,318,671; **Female:** 2,462,797. **White:** 3,393,964 (71.0%); **Black:** 1,189,899 (24.9%);

American Indian, Eskimo, or Aleut: 12,972 (0.3%); **Asian or Pacific Islander:** 139,719 (2.9%); **Other race:** 44,914 (0.9%); **Hispanic:** 125,102 (2.6%). **1990 percent population under 18:** 24.3; **65 and over:** 10.8; **median age:** 33.0

Maryland was inhabited by Indians as early as c. 10,000 B.C., and permanent Indian villages were established by c. 1,000 A.D.

In 1608, Capt. John Smith explored Chesapeake Bay. Charles I granted a royal charter for Maryland to Cecil Calvert, Lord Baltimore, in 1632, and English settlers, many of whom were Roman Catholic, landed on St. Clement's (now Blakistone) Island in 1634. Religious freedom, granted all Christians in the Toleration Act passed by the Maryland assembly in 1649, was ended by a Puritan revolt, 1654–58.

From 1763 to 1767, Charles Mason and Jeremiah Dixon surveyed Maryland's northern boundary line with Pennsylvania. In 1791, Maryland ceded land to form the District of Columbia.

In 1814, when the British unsuccessfully tried to capture Baltimore, the bombardment of Fort McHenry inspired Francis Scott Key to write *The Star Spangled Banner.*

The Baltimore clipper ship trade developed during the 19th century. During the Civil War, Maryland remained a Union state even while the battles of South Mountain (1862), Antietam (1862), and Monocacy (1864) were fought on her soil.

In 1904, the Great Fire of Baltimore occurred. In 1937, the City of Greenbelt, a New Deal model community, was chartered.

Maryland's Eastern Shore and Western Shore embrace the Chesapeake Bay, and the many estuaries and rivers create one of the longest waterfronts of any state. The Bay produces more seafood—oysters, crabs, clams, fin fish—than any comparable body of water. Important agricultural products, in order of cash value, are greenhouse and nursery products, chickens, dairy products, soy beans, corn, eggs, vegetables, melons and wheat. Maryland is a leader in vegetable canning. Stone, coal, sand, gravel, cement, and clay are the chief mineral products.

Manufacturing industries produce food and kindred products, instruments, chemicals, printing and publishing, transportation equipment, and primary metals. Baltimore, home of The Johns Hopkins University and Hospital, ranks as the nation's second port in foreign tonnage. Annapolis, site of the U.S. Naval Academy, has one of the earliest state houses (1772–79) still in regular use by a State government.

Among the popular attractions in Maryland are the Fort McHenry National Monument; Harpers Ferry and Chesapeake and Ohio Canal National Historic Parks; Antietam National Battlefield; National Aquarium, USS *Constellation,* and Maryland Science Center at Baltimore's Inner Harbor; Historic St. Mary's City; Jefferson Patterson Historical Park and Museum at St. Leonard; U.S. Naval Academy in Annapolis; Goddard Space Flight Center at Greenbelt; Assateague Island National Park Seashore; Ocean City beach resort; and Catoctin Mountain, Fort Frederick, and Piscataway parks.

Famous natives and residents: Benjamin Banneker, almanacker, mathetmatician-astronomer; John Barth, writer; Eubie Blake, musician; John Wilkes Booth, actor, Lincoln assassin; Francis X. Bushman, actor; James M. Cain, writer; Rachel Carson, writer; Samuel Chase, jurist; Frederick Douglass, abolitionist; John Hurst Fletcher, Methodist bishop and educator; Christopher Gist, frontiersman; Philip Glass, composer; Matthew Henson, reached North Pole with Peary; Billie Holiday, jazz-blues singer; Johns Hopkins, financier;

Reverdy Johnson, lawyer and statesman; Thomas Johnson, political leader; Francis Scott Key, laywer, author of National Anthem; Thurgood Marshall, jurist; H.L. Mencken, writer; Hezekiah Niles, journalist; Charles Wilson Peale, painter; Frank Perdue, farmer, businessman; James R. Randall, journalist, wrote state song; Babe Ruth, baseball player; Upton Sinclair, novelist; Roger B. Taney, jurist; George Alfred Townsend (Gath), journalist; Harriet Tubman, abolistionist; Leon Uris, novelist; Frank Zappa, singer

MASSACHUSETTS

Capital: Boston
Governor: William F. Weld, R (to Jan. 1999)
Lieut. Governor: A. Paul Cellucci, R (to Jan. 1999)
Secy. of the Commonwealth: William F. Galvin (to Jan. 1999)
Treasurer & Receiver-General: Joseph D. Malone, R (to Jan. 1999)
Auditor of the Commonwealth: A. Joseph DeNucci, D (to Jan. 1999)
Atty. General: L. Scott Harshbarger, D (to Jan. 1999)
Present constitution drafted: 1780 (oldest U.S. state constitution in effect today)
Entered Union & (rank): Feb. 6, 1788 (6)
Motto: *Ense petit placidam sub libertate quietem* (By the sword we seek peace, but peace only under liberty)
STATE SYMBOLS: flower, Mayflower (1918); **tree.** American elm (1941); **bird,** Chickadee (1941); **song,** "All Hail to Massachusetts" (1966); **beverage,** Cranberry juice (1970); **insect,** Ladybug (1974); **muffin,** corn muffin
Nicknames: Bay State; Old Colony State
Origin of name: From two Indian words meaning "Great mountain place"
10 largest cities (1990 census): Boston, 574,283; Worcester, 169,759; Springfield, 156,983; Lowell, 103,439; New Bedford, 99,922; Cambridge, 95,802; Brockton, 92,788; Fall River, 92,703; Quincy, 84,985; Newton, 82,585
Land area & (rank): 7,838 sq mi. (20,300 sq km) (45)
Geographic center: In Worcester Co., in S part of city of Worcester
Number of counties: 14
Largest county (1990 census): Middlesex, 1,398,468
State forests and parks: 129 (242,000 ac.)[1]
1994 resident population est.: 6,041,000
1990 resident census population, sex, & (rank): 6,016,425 (13). **Male:** 2,888,745; **Female:** 3,127,680. **White:** 5,405,374 (89.8%); **Black:** 300,130 (5.0%); **American Indian, Eskimo, or Aleut:** 12,241 (0.2%); **Asian or Pacific Islander:** 143,392 (2.4%); **Other race:** 155,288 (2.6%); **Hispanic:** 287,549 (4.8%). **1990 percent population under 18:** 22.5; **65 and over:** 13.6; **median age:** 33.6

1. The Metropolitan District Commission, an agency of the Commonwealth serving municipalities in the Boston area, has about 14,000 acres of parkways and reservations under its jurisdiction.

Massachusetts has played a significant role in American history since the Pilgrims, seeking religious freedom, founded Plymouth Colony in 1620.

As one of the most important of the 13 colonies, Massachusetts became a leader in resisting British oppression. In 1773, the Boston Tea Party protested unjust taxation. The Minute Men started the American Revolution by battling British troops at Lexington and Concord on April 19, 1775.

During the 19th century, Massachusetts was famous for the vigorous intellectual activity of famous writers and educators and for its expanding commercial fishing, shipping, and manufacturing interests.

Massachusetts pioneered in the manufacture of textiles and shoes. Today, these industries have been replaced in importance by activity in the electronics and communications equipment fields.

The state's cranberry crop is the nation's largest. Also important are dairy and poultry products, nursery and greenhouse produce, vegetables, and fruit.

Tourism has become an important factor in the economy of the state because of its numerous recreational areas and historical landmarks.

Cape Cod has summer theaters, water sports, and an artists' colony at Provincetown. Tanglewood, in the Berkshires, features the summer concerts of the Boston Symphony.

Among the many other points of interest are Old Sturbridge Village in Sturbridge in central Massachusetts, Minute Man National Historical Park between Lexington and Concord, and, in Boston: Old North Church, Old State House, Faneuil Hall, the USS *Constitution* and the John F. Kennedy Library and Museum.

Famous natives and residents: John Adams, President; John Quincy Adams, President; Samuel Adams, patriot; Horatio Alger, novelist; Susan B. Anthony, woman suffragist; Clara Barton, American Red Cross founder; Leonard Bernstein, conductor; George Bush, President; William Cullen Bryan, poet and editor; Luther Burbank, horticulturalist; John Cheever, novelist; John Singleton Copley, painter; E.E. Cummings, poet; Jacques d'Amboise, ballet dancer; Bette Davis, actress; Cecil B. De Mille, film director; Emily Dickinson, poet; Ralph Waldo Emerson, philosopher and poet; Geraldine Farrar, soprano, actress; Benjamin Franklin, statesman and scientist; Buckminster Fuller, architect and educator; Robert Goddard, father of modern rocketry; John Hancock, statesman; Nathaniel Hawthorne, novelist; Oliver Wendell Holmes, jurist; Winslow Homer, painter; Elias Howe, inventor; John F. Kennedy, President; Amy Lowell, poet; James Russell Lowell, poet; Robert Lowell, poet; Horace Mann, educator; Cotton Mather, clergyman; Samuel F.B. Morse, painter and inventor; Edgar Allan Poe, writer; Paul Revere, silversmith, hero of ride; Dr. Seuss (Theodore Geisel), author and illustrator; David Souter, jurist; Lucy Stone, woman suffragist; Louis Henry Sullivan, architect; Henry David Thoreau, author; Barbara Walters, TV commentator; James McNeill Whistler, painter; Eli Whitney, inventor; John Greenleaf Whittier, poet

MICHIGAN

Capital: Lansing
Governor: John M. Engler, R (to Jan. 1999)
Lieut. Governor: Connie Binsfeld, R (to Jan. 1999)
Secy. of State: Candice S. Miller, R (to Jan. 1999)
Atty. General: Frank J. Kelley, D (to Jan. 1999)
Organized as territory: Jan. 11, 1805
Entered Union & (rank): Jan. 26, 1837 (26)
Present constitution adopted: April 1, 1963, (effective Jan. 1, 1964)
Motto: *Si quaeris peninsulam amoenam circumspice* (If you seek a pleasant peninsula, look around you)
STATE SYMBOLS: flower, Apple blossom (1897); **bird,** Robin (1931); **fishes,** Trout (1965), Brook trout (1988); **gem,** Isle Royal Greenstone (Chlorastrolite) (1972); **stone,** Petoskey Stone (1965); **tree,** White pine (1955); **soil,** Kalkaska Soil series (1990); **flag,** "Blue charged with the arms of the state" (1911)
Nickname: Wolverine State
Origin of name: From Indian word "Michigana" meaning "great or large lake"
10 largest cities (1990 census): Detroit, 1,027,974; Grand Rapids, 189,126; Warren, 144,864; Flint, 140,761; Lansing, 127,321; Sterling Heights, 117,810; Ann Arbor, 109,592; Livonia, 100,850; Dearborn, 89,286; Westland, 84,724
Land area & (rank): 58,110 sq mi. (151,086 sq km) (22)
Geographic center: In Wexford Co., 5 mi. NNW of Cadillac
Number of counties: 83
Largest county (1990 census): Wayne, 2,111,687
State parks and recreation areas: 82 (250,000 ac.)
1994 resident population est.: 9,496,000
1990 resident census population, sex, & (rank): 9,295,297 (8). **Male:** 4,512,781; **Female:** 4,787,516. **White:** 7,756,086 (83.4%); **Black:** 1,291,706 (13.9%); **American Indian, Eskimo, or Aleut:** 55,638 (0.6%); **Asian or Pacific Islander:** 104,983 (1.1%); **Other race:** 86,884 (0.9%); **Hispanic:** 201,596 (2.2%). **1990 percent population under 18:** 26.5; **65 and over:** 11.9; **median age:** 32.6.

Indian tribes were living in the Michigan region when the first European, Etienne Brulé of France, arrived in 1618. Other French explorers, including Marquette, Joliet, and La Salle, followed, and the first permanent settlement was established in 1668 at Sault Ste. Marie. France was ousted from the territory by Great Britain in 1763, following the French and Indian War.

After the Revolutionary War, the U.S. acquired most of the region, which remained the scene of constant conflict between the British and U.S. forces and their respective Indian allies through the War of 1812.

Bordering on four of the five Great Lakes, Michigan is divided into Upper and Lower Peninsulas by the Straits of Mackinac, which link Lakes Michigan and Huron. The two parts of the state are connected by the Mackinac Bridge, one of the world's longest suspension bridges. To the north, connecting Lakes Superior and Huron are the busy Sault Ste. Marie Canals.

While Michigan ranks first among the states in production of motor vehicles and parts, it is also a leader in many other manufacturing and processing lines including prepared cereals, machine tools, airplane parts, refrigerators, hardware, steel springs, and furniture.

The state produces important amounts of iron, copper, iodine, gypsum, bromine, salt, lime, gravel, and cement. Michigan's farms grow apples, cherries, beans, pears, grapes, potatoes, and sugar beets. Michigan's forests contribute significantly to the state's economy. Forest-based industries (wood product industry, tourism, and recreation) support nearly 180,000 jobs and contribute over $18 billion to the state economy. With 10,083 inland lakes and 3,288 miles of Great Lakes' shoreline, Michigan is a prime area for both commercial and sport fishing.

Points of interest are the automobile plants in Dearborn, Detroit, Flint, Lansing, and Pontiac; Mackinac Island; Pictured Rocks and Sleeping Bear Dunes National Lakeshores, Greenfield Village in Dearborn; and the many summer resorts along both the inland and Great Lakes.

Famous natives and residents: Nelsen Algren, novelist; Ralph J. Bunche, statesman, Ellen Burstyn, actress; Bruce Catton, historian; Roger Chaffee, astronaut; Francis Ford Coppola, film director; Thomas E. Dewey, politician; Edna Ferber, novelist; Gerald R. Ford, U.S. President (1974–77); Henry Ford, industrialist; Ali Haji-Sheikh, football player; Julie Harris, actress; Earvin "Magic" Johnson, basketball player; Ring Lardner, story writer; Charles A. Lindbergh, aviator; Madonna, singer; Dick Martin, comedian; Terry McMillan, author; John N. Mitchell, former Attorney General; Gilda Radner, comedienne; Della Reese, singer; Jason Robards, Sr., actor; Diana Ross, singer; Thomas Schippers, conductor; Potter Stewart, jurist; Danny Thomas, entertainer; Margaret Whiting, singer; Stevie Wonder, singer

MINNESOTA

Capital: St. Paul
Governor: Arne Carlson, R (to Jan. 1999)
Lieut. Governor: Joanne Benson, R (to Jan. 1999)
Secy. of State: Joan Anderson Growe, D (to Jan. 1999)
State Auditor: Mark Dayton, D (to Jan. 1999)
Atty. General: Hubert H. Humphrey III, D (to Jan. 1999)
State Treasurer: Michael McGrath, D (to Jan. 1999)
Organized as territory: March 3, 1849
Entered Union & (rank): May 11, 1858 (32)
Present constitution adopted: 1858
Motto: L'Etoile du Nord (The North Star)
STATE SYMBOLS: flower, Showy lady slipper (1902); **tree,** Red (or Norway) pine (1953); **bird,** Common loon (also called Great Northern Diver) (1961); **song,** "Hail Minnesota" (1945); **fish,** Walleye (1965); **mushroom,** Morel (1984)
Nicknames: North Star State; Gopher State; Land of 10,000 Lakes
Origin of name: From a Dakota Indian word meaning "sky-tinted water"
10 largest cities (1991 est. population): Minneapolis, 368,993; St. Paul, 272,537; Bloomington, 86,453; Duluth, 85,382; Rochester, 72,480; Brooklyn Park, 57,359; Coon Rapids, 54,518; Plymouth, 52,492; Burnsville, 51,743; St. Cloud, 49,350
Land area & (rank): 79,617 sq mi. (206,207 sq km) (14)
Geographic center: In Crow Wing Co., 10 mi. SW of Brainerd
Number of counties: 87
Largest county (1991 est. population): Hennepin, 1,039,099
State forests: 56 (3,200,000+ ac.)
State parks: 66 (226,000 ac.)
1994 resident population est.: 4,567,000
1990 resident census population, sex, & (rank): 4,375,099 (20). **Male:** 2,145,183; **Female:** 2,229,916. **White:** 4,130,395 (94.4%); **Black:** 94,944 (2.2%); **American Indian, Eskimo, or Aleut:** 49,909 (1.1%); **Asian or Pacific Islander:** 77,886 (1.8%); **Other race:** 21,965 (0.5%); **Hispanic:** 53,884 (1.2%). **1990 percent population under 18:** 26.7; **65 and over:** 12.5; **median age:** 32.5.

Following the visits of several French explorers, fur traders, and missionaries, including Marquette and Joliet and La Salle, the region was claimed for Louis XIV by Daniel Greysolon, Sieur Duluth, in 1679.

The U.S. acquired eastern Minnesota from Great Britain after the Revolutionary War and 20 years later bought the western part from France in the Louisiana Purchase of 1803. Much of the region was explored by U.S. Army Lt. Zebulon M. Pike before cession of the northern strip of Minnesota bordering Canada by Britain in 1818.

The state is rich in natural resources. A few square miles of land in the north in the Mesabi, Cuyuna, and Vermillion ranges, produce more than 75% of the nation's iron ore. The state's farms rank high in yields of corn, wheat, rye, alfalfa, and sugar beets. Other leading farm products include butter, eggs, milk, potatoes, green peas, barley, soy beans, oats, and livestock.

Minnesota's factory production includes nonelectrical machinery, fabricated metals, flour-mill products, plastics, electronic computers, scientific instruments, and processed foods. It is also one of the nation's leaders in the printing and paper products industries.

Minneapolis is the trade center of the Northwest; and the headquarters of the world's largest super computer and grain distributor. St. Paul is the nation's biggest publisher of calendars and law books. These "twin cities" are the nation's third largest trucking

center. Duluth has the nation's largest inland harbor and now handles a significant amount of foreign trade. Rochester is the home of the Mayo Clinic, an internationally famous medical center.

Today, tourism is a major revenue producer in Minnesota, with arts, fishing, hunting, water sports, and winter sports bringing in millions of visitors each year.

Among the most popular attractions are the St. Paul Winter Carnival; the Tyrone Guthrie Theatre, the Institute of Arts, Walker Art Center, and Minnehaha Park, in Minneapolis; Boundary Waters Canoe Area; Voyageurs National Park; North Shore Drive; and the Minnesota Zoological Gardens and the state's more than 10,000 lakes.

Famous natives and residents: LaVerne, Maxene, and Patti Andrews, singers; Warren E. Burger, jurist; William E. Colby, ex-director of CIA; William Demarest, actor; William O. Douglas, jurist; Bob Dylan, singer and composer; F. Scott Fitzgerald, novelist; Judy Garland, singer and actress; J. Paul Getty, oil executive; Cass Gilbert, architect; Duane Hanson, sculptor; Hubert H. Humphrey, senator and vice president; Jessica Lange, actress; Sinclair Lewis, novelist; Cornell MacNeil, baritone; Roger Maris, baseball player; E.G. Marshall, actor; Charles H. Mayo, surgeon; William J. Mayo, surgeon; Eugene J. McCarthy, senator; Kate Millett, feminist; Gen. Lauris Norstad, ex-commander of NATO forces; Westbrook Pegler, columnist; John Sargent Pillsbury, flour milling; Marion Ross, actress; Jane Russell, actress; Harrison E. Salisbury, journalist; Charles M. Schulz, cartoonist; Max Shulman, novelist; Maurice H. Stans, ex-Secretary of Commerce; Harold E. Stassen, ex-government official; Michael Todd, producer; Frederick Weyerhaeuser, lumbering; Gig Young, actor

MISSISSIPPI

Capital: Jackson
Governor: Kirk Fordice, R (to Jan. 1996)
Lieut. Governor: Eddie Briggs, R (to Jan. 1996)
Secy. of State: Dick Molpus, D (to Jan. 1996)
Treasurer: Marshall Bennett, D (to Jan. 1996)
Atty. General: Mike Moore, D (to Jan. 1996)
Organized as Territory: April 7, 1798
Entered Union & (rank): Dec. 10, 1817 (20)
Present constitution adopted: 1890
Motto: *Virtute et armis* (By valor and arms)
STATE SYMBOLS: flower, Flower or bloom of the magnolia or evergreen magnolia (1952); **tree,** Magnolia (1938); **bird,** Mockingbird (1944); **song,** "Go, Mississippi" (1962); **stone,** Petrified wood (1976); **fish,** Largemouth or black bass (1974); **insect,** Honeybee (1980); **shell,** Oyster shell (1974); **water mammal,** Bottlenosed dolphin or porpoise (1974); **fossil,** Prehistoric whale (1981); **land mammal,** White-tailed deer (1974); **waterfowl,** Wood duck (1974); **beverage,** Milk (1984)
Nickname: Magnolia State
Origin of name: From an Indian word meaning "Father of Waters"
10 largest cities (1990 census): Jackson, 196,637; Biloxi, 46,319; Greenville, 45,226; Hattiesburg, 41,882; Meridian, 41,036; Gulfport, 40,775; Tupelo, 30,685; Pascagoula, 25,899; Columbus, 23,799; Clinton, 21,847
Land area & (rank): 46,914 sq mi. (121,506 sq km) (31)
Geographic center: In Leake Co., 9 mi. WNW of Carthage
Number of counties: 82
Largest county (1990 census): Hinds, 254,441
State forests: 1 (1,760 ac.)
State parks: 27 (16,763 ac.)
1994 resident population est.: 2,669,000

1990 resident census population, sex, & (rank):
2,573,216 (31). **Male:** 1,230,617; **Female:** 1,342,599.
White: 1,633,461 (63.5%); **Black:** 915,057 (35.6%);
American Indian, Eskimo, or Aleut: 8,525 (0.3%);
Asian or Pacific Islander: 13,016 (0.5%); **Other race:**
3,157 (0.1%); **Hispanic:** 15,931 (0.6%). **1990 percent
population under 18:** 29.0; **65 and over:** 12.5; **median
age:** 31.2.

First explored for Spain by Hernando de Soto who
discovered the Mississippi River in 1540, the region
was later claimed by France. In 1699, a French group
under Sieur d'Iberville established the first permanent
settlement near present-day Ocean Springs.

Great Britain took over the area in 1763 after the
French and Indian War, ceding it to the U.S. in 1783
after the Revolution. Spain did not relinquish its
claims until 1798, and in 1810 the U.S. annexed West
Florida from Spain, including what is now southern
Mississippi.

For a little more than one hundred years, from shortly after the state's founding through the Great Depression, cotton was the undisputed king of Mississippi's
largely agrarian economy. Over the last half-century,
however, Mississippi has progressively deepened its
commitment to diversification by balancing agricultural output with increased industrial activity.

Today, agriculture continues as a major segment of
the state's economy. While the most acreage is devoted to soybeans, cotton is the largest cash crop—
Mississippi remains third in the nation in cotton production. The state's farmlands yield important
harvests of corn, peanuts, pecans, rice, sugar cane,
sweet potatoes, soybeans and food grains as well as
poultry, eggs, meat animals, dairy products, feed
crops and horticultural crops. Mississippi remains the
world's leading producer of pond-raised catfish. The
total acres of catfish ponds nationwide is approximately 140,000 acres whereas Mississippi alone has
100,000 acres of the total nationwide figure.

The state abounds in historical landmarks and is
the home of the Vicksburg National Military Park.
Other National Park Service areas are Brices Cross
Roads National Battlefield Site, Tupelo National
Battlefield, and part of Natchez Trace National Park-
way. Pre-Civil War mansions are the special pride of
Natchez, Oxford, Columbus, Vicksburg, and Jackson.

Famous natives and residents: Red Barber, sportscaster; Jimmy Buffet, singer, songwriter; Craig Claiborne,
columnist and restaurant critic; Bo Diddley, guitarist;
Charles Evers, civil rights leader; Medgar Evers, civil
rights leader; William Faulkner, novelist; John Gri-
sham, novelist; Beth Henley, playwright and actress;
Jim Henson, puppeteer; James Earl Jones, actor; B.B.
King, guitarist; Mary Ann Mobley, actress; Willie Morris, writer; Elvis Presley, singer and actor; Leontyne
Price, soprano; Jerry Rice, football player; Jimmie
Rodgers, singer; Sela Ward, actress; Muddy Waters,
singer and guitarist; Eudora Welty, novelist; Tennessee
Williams, playwright; Oprah Winfrey, talk show host
and actress; Richard Wright, novelist; Tammy Wynette,
country music star; Zig Ziglar, speaker, author

MISSOURI

Capital: Jefferson City
Governor: Mel Carnahan, D (to Jan. 1997)
Lieut. Governor: Roger Wilson, D (to Jan. 1997)
Secy. of State: Rebecca McDowell "Bekki" Cook, D (to
Jan. 1997)
Auditor: Margaret Kelly, R (to Jan. 1999)
Treasurer: Bob Holden, D (to Jan. 1997)
Atty. General: Jeremiah W. "Jay" Nixon, D (to Jan. 1997)

Organized as territory: June 4, 1812
Entered Union & (rank): Aug. 10, 1821 (24)
Present constitution adopted: 1945
Motto: *Salus populi suprema lex esto* (The welfare of
the people shall be the supreme law)
STATE SYMBOLS: floral emblem, Hawthorn (1923); **bird,**
Bluebird (1927); **song,** "Missouri Waltz" (1949); **fossil,**
Crinoidea (1989); **musical instrument,** Fiddle (1987);
rock, Mozarkite (1967); **mineral,** Galena (1967); **insect,**
Honeybee (1985); **tree,** Flowering dogwood (1955); **tree
nut,** black walnut (1990); **Missouri Day,** third Wednes-
day in October (1915)
Nickname: Show-me State
Origin of name: Named after a tribe called Missouri
Indians. "Missouri" means "town of the large ca-
noes."
10 largest cities (1990 census): Kansas City, 435,146; St.
Louis, 396,685; Springfield, 140,494; Independence,
112,301; St. Joseph, 71,852; Columbia, 69,101; St.
Charles, 54,555; Florissant, 51,206; Lee's Summit,
46,418; St. Peter's, 45,779
Land area & (rank): 68,898 sq mi. (178,446 sq km) (18)
Geographic center: In Miller Co., 20 mi. SW of Jefferson
City
Number of counties: 114, plus 1 independent city
Largest county (1990 census): St. Louis, 993,529
Conservation areas[1]: 343 (602,272 ac.)
Conservation accesses: 218 (9,457 ac.)
State parks and historic sites: 79 (126,072 ac.)
1994 resident population est.: 5,278,000
1990 resident census population, sex, & (rank):
5,117,073 (15). **Male:** 2,464,315; **Female:** 2,652,758.
White: 4,486,228 (87.7%); **Black:** 548,208 (10.7%);
American Indian, Eskimo, or Aleut: 41,277 (0.8%);
Asian or Pacific Islander: 21,525 (0.4%); **Other race:**
21,525 (0.4%); **Hispanic:** 61,702 (1.2%). **1990 percent
population under 18:** 25.7; **65 and over:** 14.0; **median
age:** 33.5.

1. Includes wildlife areas, natural history areas, state forests, and tower sites.

De Soto visited the Missouri area in 1541. France's
claim to the entire region was based on La Salle's travels in 1682. French fur traders established Ste. Genevieve in 1735 and St. Louis was first settled in 1764.

The U.S. gained Missouri from France as part of
the Louisiana Purchase in 1803, and the territory was
admitted as a state following the Missouri Compromise of 1820. Throughout the pre-Civil War period
and during the war, Missourians were sharply divided
in their opinions about slavery and in their alle-
giances, supplying both Union and Confederate
forces with troops. However, the state itself remained
in the Union.

Historically, Missouri played a leading role as a
gateway to the West, St. Joseph being the eastern
starting point of the Pony Express, while the
much-traveled Santa Fe and Oregon Trails began in
Independence. Now a popular vacationland, Missouri
has 11 major lakes and numerous fishing streams,
springs, and caves. Bagnell Dam, across the Osage
River in the Ozarks, completed in 1931, created one
of the largest man-made lakes in the world, covering
65,000 acres of surface area.

Missouri's economy relies on a diversified industrial base. Service industries provide more income
and jobs than any other segment, and include a growing tourism and travel sector. Wholesale and retail
trade, manufacturing and agriculture also play significant roles in the state's economy. Missouri is a leading producer of transportation equipment (including
automobile manufacturing and auto parts), beer and
beverages, and defense and aerospace technology.

Food processing is the state's fastest-growing industry, well-suited to the state's blend of agricultural, natural, energy and transportation resources. Missouri mines also produce 90% of the nation's principal (non-recycled) lead supply.

Missouri's largest corporate employers include McDonnell-Douglas, Wal-Mart, Trans World Airlines and Southwestern Bell. The state's top agricultural products include: grain, sorghum, hay, corn, soybeans, wheat, oats, barley, tobacco and rice. A well-established grape and wine program brings together aspects of agriculture, manufacturing and tourism to support a vibrant vintner industry.

Tourism draws hundreds of thousands of visitors to a number of Missouri points of interest: the country-music shows of Branson; Bass Pro Shops national headquarters (Springfield); the Gateway Arch at the Jefferson National Expansion (St. Louis); Mark Twain's boyhood home and cave (Hanibal); the Harry S Truman home and library (Independence); the scenic beauty of the Ozark National Scenic Riverways; and the Pony Express and Jesse James museums (St. Joseph). The state's different lakes regions also attract fishermen and sun-seekers from throughout the Midwest.

Famous natives and residents: Robert Altman, film director; Burt Bacharach, songwriter; Josephine Baker, singer and dancer; Wallace Beery, actor; Robert Russell Bennett, composer; Yogi Berra, baseball player; Thomas Hart Benton, painter; Susan Elizabeth Blow, educator; Bill Bradley, basketball player and N.J. senator; Omar N. Bradley, 5-star general; Grace Bumbry, soprano; William Burroughs, writer; Sarah Caldwell, opera director and conductor; Martha Jane Canary (Calamity Jane), frontierswoman; George Washington Carver, scientist; Walter Cronkhite, TV newscaster; Robert Cummings, actor; Jane Darwell, actress; Walt Disney, artist; Jeanne Eagels, actress; T.S. Eliot, poet; Eugene Field, poet; Redd Foxx, actor and comedian; Betty Grable, actress; Dick Gregory, comic and activist; Jean Harlow, actress; George Hearn, actor; Al Hirschfeld, artist; Edwin Hubble, astronomer; Langston Hughes, poet; John Huston, film director; Jesse James, outlaw; Scott Joplin, composer; Bernarr MacFadden, physical culturist; Mary Margaret McBride, TV hostess; Marianne Moore, poet; Geraldine Page, actress; James C. Penney, merchant; Marlin Perkins, TV host, zoo director; John Joseph Pershing, general; Vincent Price, actor; Joseph Pulitzer, journalist; Doris Roberts, actress; Ginger Rogers, dancer and actress; Sacajawea, Indian guide for Lewis and Clark; Ted Shawn, dancer and choreographer; Casey Stengel, baseball; Gladys Swarthout, soprano; Sara Teasdale, poet; Virgil Thomson, composer; Harry S Truman, President; Mark Twain, author; Dick Van Dyke, actor; Ruth Warrick, actress; Dennis Weaver, actor; Pearl White, actress; Mary Wickes, actress; Laura Ingalls Wilder, author; Roy Wilkins, civil rights leader

MONTANA

Capital: Helena
Governor: Marc Racicot, R (to Jan. 1997)
Lieut. Governor: Dennis R. Rehberg, R (to Jan. 1997)
Secy. of State: Mike Cooney, D (to Jan. 1997)
Auditor: Mark O'Keefe, D (to Jan. 1997)
Atty. General: Joe Mazurek, D (to Jan. 1997)
Organized as territory: May 26, 1864
Entered Union & (rank): Nov. 8, 1889 (41)
Present constitution adopted: 1972
Motto: Oro y plata (Gold and silver)
STATE SYMBOLS: flower, Bitterroot (1895); **tree,** Ponderosa pine (1949); **stones,** Sapphire and agate (1969); **bird,** ·

Western meadowlark (1981); **song,** "Montana" (1945)
Nickname: Treasure State
Origin of name: Chosen from Latin dictionary by J. M. Ashley. It is a Latinized Spanish word meaning "mountainous."
10 largest cities (1990 census): Billings, 81,151; Great Falls, 55,097; Missoula, 42,918; Butte-Silver Bow[1], 33,941; Helena, 24,569; Bozeman, 22,660; Kalispell, 11,917; Anaconda-Deer Lodge County, 10,278; Havre, 10,201; Miles City, 8,461
Land area & (rank): 145,556 sq mi. (376,991 sq km) (4)
Geographic center: In Fergus Co., 12 mi. W of Lewistown
Number of counties: 56, plus small part of Yellowstone National Park
Largest county (1990 census): Yellowstone, 113,419
State forests: 7 (214,000 ac.)
State parks and recreation areas: 110 (18,273 ac.)
1994 resident population est.: 856,000
1990 resident census population, sex, & (rank): 799,065 (44). **Male:** 395,769; **Female:** 403,296. **White:** 741,111 (92.7%); **Black:** 2,381 (0.3%); **American Indian, Eskimo, or Aleut:** 47,679 (6.0%); **Asian or Pacific Islander:** 4,259 (0.5%); **Other race:** 3,635 (0.5%); **Hispanic:** 12,174 (1.5%). **1990 percent population under 18:** 27.8; **65 and over:** 13.3; **median age:** 33.8.

1. Consolidated City.

First explored for France by François and Louis-Joseph Verendrye in the early 1740s, much of the region was acquired by the U.S. from France as part of the Louisiana Purchase in 1803. Before western Montana was obtained from Great Britain in the Oregon Treaty of 1846, American trading posts and forts had been established in the territory.

The major Indian wars (1867–1877) included the famous 1876 Battle of the Little Big Horn, better known as "Custer's Last Stand," in which Cheyennes and Sioux killed George A. Custer and more than 200 of his men in southeastern Montana.

Much of Montana's early history was concerned with mining with copper, lead, zinc, silver, coal, and oil as principal products.

Butte is the center of the area that once supplied half of the U.S. copper.

Fields of grain cover much of Montana's plains; it ranks high among the states in wheat and barley, with rye, oats, flaxseed, sugar beets, and potatoes other important crops. Sheep and cattle raising make significant contributions to the economy.

Tourist attractions include hunting, fishing, skiing, and dude ranching. Glacier National Park, on the Continental Divide, is a scenic and vacation wonderland with 60 glaciers, 200 lakes, and many streams with good trout fishing.

Other major points of interest include the Custer Battlefield National Monument, Virginia City, Yellowstone National Park, Museum of the Plains Indians at Browning, and the Fort Union Trading Post and Grant-Kohr's Ranch National Historic Sites.

Famous natives and residents: Dorothy Baker, author; Dirk Benedict, actor; W.A. (Tony) Boyle, labor union official; Gary Cooper, actor; John Cowan, prospector and founder of Last Chance Gulch (now Helena); Alfred Bertram Guthrie, Pulitzer Prize-winning author; Chet Huntley, TV newscaster; Will James, writer and artist; Dorothy Johnson, author; Evel Knievel, daredevil motorcyclist; Myrna Loy, actress; David Lynch, filmmaker; Mike Mansfield, senator; George Montgomery, actor; Jeannette Rankin, first woman elected to Congress; Martha Raye, actress; Charles M. Russell, Old West painter; Michael Smuin, choreographer; Lester C. Thurow, economist, educator

NEBRASKA

Capital: Lincoln
Governor: Ben Nelson, D (to Jan. 1999)
Lieut. Governor: Kim Robak, D (to Jan. 1999)
Secy. of State: Scott Moore, R (to Jan. 1999)
Atty. General: Don Stenberg, R (to Jan. 1999)
Auditor: John Breslow, D (to Jan. 1999)
Treasurer: David Heineman, R (to Jan. 1999)
Organized as territory: May 30, 1854
Entered Union & (rank): March 1, 1867 (37)
Present constitution adopted: Oct. 12, 1875 (extensively amended 1919–20)
Motto: Equality before the law
STATE SYMBOLS: flower, Goldenrod (1895); **tree,** Cottonwood (1972); **bird,** Western meadowlark (1929); **insect,** Honeybee (1975); **gemstone,** Blue agate (1967); **rock,** Prairie agate (1967); **fossil;** Mammoth (1967); **song,** "Beautiful Nebraska" (1967); **soil,** Typic Arguistolls, Holdrege Series (1979); **mammal,** Whitetail deer (1981)
Nicknames: Cornhusker State (1945); Beef State; The Tree Planter State (1895)
Origin of name: From an Oto Indian word meaning "flat water"
10 largest cities (1990 census): Omaha, 335,795; Lincoln, 191,972; Grand Island, 39,386; Bellevue, 30,982; Kearney, 24,396; Fremont, 23,680; Hastings, 22,837; North Platte, 22,605; Norfolk, 21,476; Columbus, 19,480
Land area & (rank): 76,878 sq mi. (199,113 sq km) (15)
Geographic center: In Custer Co., 10 mi. NW of Broken Bow
Number of counties: 93
Largest county (1990 census): Douglas, 416,444
State forests: None
State parks: 86 areas, historical and recreational; 8 major areas
1994 resident population est.: 1,623,000
1990 resident census population, sex, & (rank): 1,578,385 (36). **Male:** 769,439; **Female:** 808,946. **White:** 1,480,558 (93.8%); **Black:** 57,404 (3.6%); **American Indian, Eskimo, or Aleut:** 12,410 (0.8%); **Asian or Pacific Islander:** 12,422 (0.8%); **Other race:** 15,591 (1.0%); **Hispanic:** 36,969 (2.3%). **1990 percent population under 18:** 27.2; **65 and over:** 14.1; **median age:** 33.0.

French fur traders first visited Nebraska in the early 1700s. Part of the Louisiana Purchase in 1803, Nebraska was explored by Lewis and Clark in 1804–06. Robert Stuart pioneered the Oregon Trail across Nebraska in 1812–13 and the first permanent settlement was established at Bellevue in 1823. Western Nebraska was acquired by treaty following the Mexican War in 1848. The Union Pacific began its transcontinental railroad at Omaha in 1865. In 1937, Nebraska became the only state in the Union to have a unicameral (one-house) legislature. Members are elected to it without party designation.

Nebraska is a leading grain-producer with bumper crops of rye, corn, and wheat. More varieties of grass, valuable for forage, grow in this state than in any other in the nation.

The state's sizable cattle and hog industries make Dakota City and Lexington among the nation's largest meat-packing centers.

Manufacturing has become diversified in Nebraska, strengthening the state's economic base. Firms making electronic components, auto accessories, pharmaceuticals, and mobile homes have joined such older industries as clothing, farm machinery, chemicals, and transportation equipment. Oil was discovered in 1939 and natural gas in 1949.

Among the principal attractions are Agate Fossil Beds, Homestead, and Scotts Bluff National Monuments; Chimney Rock National Historic Site; a recreated pioneer village at Minden; SAC Museum at Bellevue; the Stuhr Museum of the Prairie Pioneer with 57 original 19th-century buildings near Grand Island; the Sheldon Memorial Art Gallery at the University of Nebraska in Lincoln; and the Lied Center for the Performing Arts located on the University of Nebraska campus in Lincoln.

Famous natives and residents: Grace Abbott, social worker; Fred Astaire, dancer and actor; Max Baer, boxer; Bil Baird, puppeteer; George Beadle, geneticist; Marlon Brando, actor; Dick Cavett, TV entertainer; Richard B. Cheney, Secretary of Defense; Montgomery Clift, actor; James Coburn, actor; Sandy Dennis, actress; Mignon Eberhart, author; Ruth Etting, singer, actress; Henry Fonda, actor; Gerald Ford, President; Bob Gibson, baseball player; Hoot Gibson, actor; Howard Hanson, conductor; Leland Hayward, producer; Susette La Flesche, Omaha Indian artist; Francis La Flesche, ethnologist; Melvin Laird, politician, Secretary of Defense; Frank W. Leahy, football coach; Harold Lloyd, actor; David Janssen, actor; Irish McCalla, actress; Dorothy McGuire, actress; Julius Sterling Morton, politician, journalist, originated Arbor Day; Nick Nolte, actor; Inga Swenson, actress; Robert Taylor, actor; Paul Williams, singer, composer, actor; Julie Wilson, singer and actress; Daryl F. Zanuck, film producer

NEVADA

Capital: Carson City
Governor: Robert J. Miller, D (to Jan. 1999)
Lieut. Governor: Lonnie L. Hammargren, R (to Jan. 1999)
Secy. of State: Dean Heller, R (to Jan. 1999)
Treasurer: Bob Seale, R (to Jan. 1999)
Controller: Darrel R. Daines, R (to Jan. 1999)
Atty. General: Frankie Sue Del Papa, D (to Jan. 1999)
Organized as territory: March 2, 1861
Entered Union & (rank): Oct. 31, 1864 (36)
Present constitution adopted: 1864
Motto: All for Our Country
STATE SYMBOLS: flower, Sagebrush (1959); **trees,** Single-leaf pinon (1953) and Bristlecone pine (1987); **bird,** Mountain bluebird (1967); **animal,** Desert bighorn sheep (1973); **colors,** Silver and blue (1983); **song,** "Home Means Nevada" (1933); **rock,** Sandstone (1987); **precious gemstone,** Virgin Valley Black Fire Opal (1987); **semiprecious gemstone,** Nevada Turquoise (1987); **grass,** Indian Ricegrass (1977); **metal,** Silver (1977); **fossil,** Ichthyosaur (1977); **fish,** Lahontan Cutthroat Trout (1981); **reptile,** Desert tortoise (1989)
Nicknames: Sagebrush State; Silver State; Battle-born State
Origin of name: Spanish: "snowcapped"
10 largest cities (1990 census): Las Vegas, 258,295; Reno, 133,850; Henderson, 64,942; Sparks, 53,367; North Las Vegas, 47,707; Carson City, 40,443; Elko, 14,736; Boulder City, 12,567; Fallon, 6,438; Winnemucca, 6,134
Land area & (rank): 109,806 sq mi. (284,397 sq km) (7)
Geographic center: In Lander Co., 26 mi. SE of Austin
Number of counties: 16, plus 1 independent city
Largest county (1990 census): Clark, 741,459
State forests: None
State parks: 20 (150,000 ac., including leased lands)
1994 resident population est.: 1,457,000
1990 resident census population, sex, & (rank): 1,201,833 (39). **Male:** 611,880; **Female:** 589,953. **White:** 1,012,695 (84.3%); **Black:** 78,771 (6.6%); **American Indian, Eskimo, or Aleut:** 19,637 (1.6%); **Asian or Pacific Islander:** 38,127 (3.2%); **Other race:** 52,603 (4.4%); **Hispanic:** 124,419 (10.4%). **1990 percent population under 18:** 24.7; **65 and over:** 10.6; **median age:** 33.3.

Trappers and traders, including Jedediah Smith, and Peter Skene Ogden, entered the Nevada area in the 1820s. In 1843–45, John C. Fremont and Kit Carson explored the Great Basin and Sierra Nevada.

In 1848 following the Mexican War, the U.S. obtained the region and the first permanent settlement was a Mormon trading post near present-day Genoa.

The driest state in the nation with an average annual rainfall of only about 7 inches,[1] much of Nevada is uninhabited, sagebrush-covered desert.

Nevada was made famous by the discovery of the fabulous Comstock Lode in 1859 and its mines have produced large quantities of gold, silver, copper, lead, zinc, mercury, barite, and tungsten. Oil was discovered in 1954. Gold now far exceeds all other minerals in value of production.

In 1931, the state created two industries, divorce and gambling. For many years, Reno and Las Vegas were the "divorce capitals of the nation." More liberal divorce laws in many states have ended this distinction, but Nevada is the gambling and entertainment capital of the U.S. State gambling taxes account for 40.1% of general fund tax revenues. Although Nevada leads the nation in per capita gambling revenue, it ranks only fourth in total gambling revenue.

Near Las Vegas, on the Colorado River, stands Hoover Dam, which impounds the waters of Lake Mead, one of the world's largest artificial lakes.

The state's agricultural crop consists mainly of hay, alfalfa seed, barley, wheat, and potatoes.

Nevada manufactures gaming equipment; lawn and garden irrigation devices; titanium products; seismic and machinery monitoring devices; and specialty printing.

Major resort areas flourish in Lake Tahoe, Reno, and Las Vegas. Recreation areas include those at Pyramid Lake, Lake Tahoe, and Lake Mead and Lake Mohave, both in Lake Mead National Recreation Area. Among the other attractions are Hoover Dam, Virginia City, and Great Basin National Park (includes Lehman Caves).

Famous natives and residents: Eva Adams, director of U.S. Mint; Andre Agassi, tennis player; Raymond T. Baker, director of U.S. Mint; Helen Delich Bentley, government official, newspaperwoman; Robert Caples, painter; Walter Van Tilburg Clark, writer; Henry Comstock, prospector of "Comstock Lode" fame; Abby Dalton, actress; Michele Greene, actress; Sarah Winnemucca Hopkins, Paiute interpreter and peacemaker, author; Jack Kramer, tennis player; Paul Laxalt, politician; William Lear, aviation inventor; Robert C. Lynch, surgeon; John W. Mackay, benefactor, one of Big Four of Comstock Lode; Emma Nevada, opera singer; Thelma "Pat" Nixon, First Lady; James W. Nye, territory governor, U.S. senator; Lute Pease, cartoonist, Pulitzer Prize winner; Edna Purviance, actress; Patty Sheehan, golfer; Jack Wilson, Paiute Indian prophet; George Wingfield, mining millionaire

1. Wettest part of state receives about 40 inches of precipitation per year, while driest spot has less than four inches per year.

NEW HAMPSHIRE

Capital: Concord
Governor: Stephen E. Merrill, R (to Jan. 1997)
Treasurer: Georgie A. Thomas, R (to Dec. 1996)
Secy. of State: William M. Gardner, D (to Dec. 1996)
Commissioner: Patrick Duffy
Atty. General: Jeffrey R. Howard, R (to Mar. 1997)
Entered Union & (rank): June 21, 1788 (9)
Present constitution adopted: 1784

Motto: Live free or die
STATE SYMBOLS: flower, Purple lilac (1919); **tree,** White birch (1947); **bird,** Purple finch (1957); **songs,** "Old New Hampshire" (1949) and "New Hampshire, My New Hampshire" (1963)
Nickname: Granite State
Origin of name: From the English county of Hampshire
10 largest cities (1990 census): Manchester, 99,567; Nashua, 79,662; Concord, 36,006; Rochester, 26,630; Portsmouth, 25,925; Dover, 25,042; Keene, 22,430; Laconia, 15,743; Claremont, 13,902; Lebanon, 12,183
Land area & (rank): 8,969 sq mi. (23,231 sq km) (44)
Geographic center: In Belknap Co., 3 mi. E of Ashland
Number of counties: 10
Largest county (1990 census): Hillsborough, 336,073
State forests & parks: 175 (96,975 ac.)
1994 resident population est.: 1,137,000
1990 resident census population, sex, & (rank): 1,109,252 (41). **Male:** 543,544; **Female:** 565,708. **White:** 1,087,433 (98.0%); **Black:** 7,198 (0.6%); **American Indian, Eskimo, or Aleut:** 2,134 (0.2%); **Asian or Pacific Islander:** 9,343 (0.8%); **Other race:** 3,144 (0.3%); **Hispanic:** 11,333 (1.0%). **1990 percent population under 18:** 25.1; **65 and over:** 11.3; **median age:** 32.8.

Under an English land grant, Capt. John Smith sent settlers to establish a fishing colony at the mouth of the Piscataqua River, near present-day Rye and Dover, in 1623. Capt. John Mason, who participated in the founding of Portsmouth in 1630, gave New Hampshire its name.

After a 38-year period of union with Massachusetts, New Hampshire was made a separate royal colony in 1679. As leaders in the revolutionary cause, New Hampshire delegates received the honor of being the first to vote for the Declaration of Independence on July 4, 1776. New Hampshire is the only state that ever played host at the formal conclusion of a foreign war when, in 1905, Portsmouth was the scene of the treaty ending the Russo-Japanese War.

Abundant water power early turned New Hampshire into an industrial state and manufacturing is the principal source of income in the state. The most important industrial products are electrical and other machinery, textiles, pulp and paper products, and stone and clay products.

Dairy and poultry farming and growing fruit, truck vegetables, corn, potatoes, and hay are the major agricultural pursuits.

Tourism, because of New Hampshire's scenic and recreational resources, now brings over $3.5 billion into the state annually.

Vacation attractions include Lake Winnipesaukee, largest of 1,300 lakes and ponds; the 724,000-acre White Mountain National Forest; Daniel Webster's birthplace near Franklin; Strawbery Banke, restored building of the original settlement at Portsmouth; and the famous "Old Man of the Mountain" granite head profile, the state's official emblem, at Franconia.

Famous natives and residents: Sherman Adams, governor and presidential advisor; Salmon P. Chase, jurist; Charles Anderson Dana, editor; Mary Baker Eddy, founder of Christian Science Church; Dustin Farnum, actor; Thomas Green Fessenden, journalist and satirical poet; Daniel Chester French, sculptor; Horace Greeley, journalist and politician; Sarah J. Hale, editor; John Irving, writer; Benjamin F. Keith, theater entrepreneur; Jackson Hall Kelly, promoter of Oregon settlement; John Langdon, political leader; Sharon Christa McAuliffe, teacher and astronaut; Franklin Pierce, President; Augustus Saint-Gaudens, sculptor; Alan Shepard, astronaut; Harlan F. Stone, jurist; Daniel Webster, statesman; Henry Wilson, politician and U.S. vice president; Noah Worcester, clergyman and pacifist

NEW JERSEY

Capital: Trenton
Governor: Christine Todd Whitman, R (to Jan. 1998)
Secy. of State: Lonna R. Hooks, R (to Jan. 1998)
Treasurer: Bryan W. Clymer, R (to Jan. 1998)
Atty. General: Deborah T. Poritz, R (to Jan. 1998)
Entered Union & (rank): Dec. 18, 1787 (3)
Present constitution adopted: 1947
Motto: Liberty and prosperity
STATE SYMBOLS: flower, Purple violet (1913); **bird,** Eastern goldfinch (1935); **insect,** Honeybee (1974); **tree,** Red oak (1950); **animal,** Horse (1977); **colors,** Buff and blue (1965)
Nickname: Garden State
Origin of name: From the Channel Isle of Jersey
10 largest cities (1990 census)[1]: Newark, 275,221; Jersey City, 228,537; Paterson, 140,891; Elizabeth, 110,002; Edison[2], 88,680; Trenton, 88,675; Camden, 87,492; East Orange, 73,552; Clifton, 71,742; Cherry Hill[2], 69,319
Land area & (rank): 7,419 sq mi. (19,215 sq km) (46)
Geographic center: In Mercer Co., 5 mi. SE of Trenton
Number of counties: 21
Largest county (1990 census): Bergen, 825,380
State forests: 11
State parks: 35 (67,111 ac.)
1994 resident population est.: 7,904,000
1990 resident census population, sex, & (rank):
7,730,188 (9). **Male:** 3,735,685; **Female:** 3,994,503. **White:** 6,130,465 (79.3%); **Black:** 1,036,825 (13.4%); **American Indian, Eskimo, or Aleut:** 14,970 (0.2%); **Asian or Pacific Islander:** 272,521 (3.5%); **Other race:** 275,407 (3.6%); **Hispanic:** 739,861 (9.6%). **1990 percent population under 18:** 23.3; **65 and over:** 13.4; **median age:** 34.5.

1. These are the official 1990 census largest cities. However, the townships of Woodbridge, 93,086, and Hamilton, 86,553, are also legal municipalities or cities. 2. Census Designated Place.

New Jersey's early colonial history was involved with that of New York (New Netherlands), of which it was a part. One year after the Dutch surrender to England in 1664, New Jersey was organized as an English colony under Gov. Philip Carteret.

In the late 1600s the colony was divided between Carteret and William Penn; later it would be administered by the royal governor of New York. Finally, in 1738, New Jersey was separated from New York under its own royal governor, Lewis Morris.

Because of its key location between New York City and Philadelphia, New Jersey saw much fighting during the American Revolution.

Today, New Jersey, an area of wide industrial diversification, is known as the Crossroads of the East. Products from over 15,000 factories can be delivered overnight to almost 60 million people, representing 12 states and the District of Columbia. The greatest single industry is chemicals and New Jersey is one of the foremost research centers in the world. Many large oil refineries are located in northern New Jersey and other important manufactures are pharmaceuticals, instruments, machinery, electrical goods, and apparel.

Of the total land area, 37% is forested. Farmland is declining. In 1991 there were about 8,300 farms, with over 880,000 acres under harvest. The state ranks high in production of almost all garden vegetables. Tomatoes, asparagus, corn, and blueberries are important crops, and poultry farming and dairying make significant contributions to the state's economy.

Tourism is the second largest industry in New Jersey. The state has numerous resort areas on 127 miles of Atlantic coastline. In 1977, New Jersey voters approved legislation allowing legalized casino gambling in Atlantic City. Points of interest include the Delaware Water Gap, the Edison National Historic Site in West Orange, Princeton University, Liberty State Park, Jersey City, and the N.J. State Aquarium in Camden (opened 1992).

Famous natives and residents: Bud Abbott, comedian; Charles Addams, cartoonist; Edwin Aldrin, astronaut; Count Basie, band leader; Joan Bennett, actress; Jon Bon Jovi, musician; William J. Brennan, jurist; Aaron Burr, political leader; James Fenimore Cooper, novelist; Lou Costello, comedian; Stephen Crane, writer; Helen Gahagan Douglas, ex-Representative; Allen Ginsberg, poet; William Frederick Halsey, Jr., admiral; Alfred Joyce Kilmer, poet; Ernie Kovacs, comedian; Jerry Lewis, comedian, film director; Anne Morrow Lindbergh, author; Norman Mailer, novelist; Patricia McBride, ballerina; Richard Nixon, President; Dorothy Parker, author; Joe Piscopo, comedian, actor; Paul Robeson, singer and actor; Philip Roth, novelist; Ruth St. Denis, dancer and choreographer; Antonin Scalia, jurist; H. Norman Schwarzkopf, general; Frank Sinatra, singer and actor; Bruce Springsteen, musician; Alfred Stieglitz, photographer; Albert Payson Terhune, journalist and novelist; Sarah Vaughan, singer; William Carlos Williams, physician and poet; Edmund Wilson, literary crtic and author

NEW MEXICO

Capital: Santa Fe
Governor: Gary Johnson, R (to Jan. 1998)
Lieut. Governor: Walter Bradley, R (to Jan. 1998)
Secy. of State: Stephanie Gonzales, D (to Jan. 1998)
Atty. General: Tom Udall, D (to Jan. 1998)
State Auditor: Robert E. Vigil, D (to Jan. 1998)
State Treasurer: Michael A. Montoya, D (to Jan. 1998)
Commissioner of Public Lands: Ray Powell, D (to Jan. 1998)
Organized as territory: Sept. 9, 1850
Entered Union & (rank): Jan. 6, 1912 (47)
Present constitution adopted: 1911
Motto: Crescit eundo (It grows as it goes)
STATE SYMBOLS: flower, Yucca (1927); **tree,** Pinon (1949); **animal,** Black bear (1963); **bird,** Roadrunner (1949); **fish,** Cutthroat trout (1955); vegetables, Chili and frijol (1965); **gem,** Turquoise (1967); **colors,** Red and yellow of old Spain (1925); **song,** "O Fair New Mexico" (1917); **Spanish language song,** "Asi Es Nuevo Méjico" (1971); **poem,** A Nuevo México (1991); **grass,** Blue gramma; **fossil,** Coelophysis; **cookie,** Bizcochito (1989); **insect,** Tarantula hawk wasp (1989)
Nicknames: Land of Enchantment; Sunshine State
Origin of name: From the country of Mexico
10 largest cities (1990 census): Albuquerque, 384,736; Las Cruces, 62,126; Santa Fe, 55,859; Roswell, 44,654; Farmington, 33,997; Rio Rancho, 32,505; Clovis, 30,954; Hobbs, 29,115; Alamogordo, 27,596; Carlsbad, 24,952
Land area & (rank): 121,365 sq mi. (314,334 sq km) (5)
Geographic center: In Torrance Co., 12 mi. SSW of Willard
Number of counties: 33
Largest county (1990 census): Bernalillo, 480,577
State-owned forested land: 933,000 ac.
State parks: 29 (105,012 ac.)
1994 resident population est.: 1,654,000
1990 resident census population, sex, & (rank):
1,515,069 (37). **Male:** 745,253; **Female:** 769,816. **White:** 1,146,028 (75.6%); **Black:** 30,210 (2.0%); **American Indian, Eskimo, or Aleut:** 134,355 (8.9%); **Asian or Pacific Islander:** 14,124 (0.9%); **Other race:** 190,352 (12.6%); **Hispanic:** 579,224 (38.2%). **1990 percent population under 18:** 29.5; **65 and over:** 10.8; **median age:** 31.3.

Francisco Vásquez de Coronado, Spanish explorer searching for gold, traveled the region that became New Mexico in 1540–42. In 1598 the first Spanish settlement was established on the Rio Grande River by Juan de Onate and in 1610 Santa Fe was founded and made the capital of New Mexico.

The U.S. acquired most of New Mexico in 1848, as a result of the Mexican War, and the remainder in the 1853 Gadsden Purchase. Union troops captured the territory from the Confederates during the Civil War. With the surrender of Geronimo in 1886, the Apache Wars and most of the Indian troubles in the area were ended.

Since 1945, New Mexico has been a leader in energy research and development with extensive experiments conducted at Los Alamos Scientific Laboratory and Sandia Laboratories in the nuclear, solar, and geothermal areas.

Minerals are the state's richest natural resource and New Mexico is one of the U.S. leaders in output of uranium and potassium salts. Petroleum, natural gas, copper, gold, silver, zinc, lead, and molybdenum also contribute heavily to the state's income.

The principal manufacturing industries include food products, chemicals, transportation equipment, lumber, electrical machinery, and stone-clay-glass products. More than two thirds of New Mexico's farm income comes from livestock products, especially sheep. Cotton, pecans, and sorghum are the most important field crops. Corn, peanuts, beans, onions, chile, and lettuce are also grown.

Tourist attractions in New Mexico include the Carlsbad Caverns National Park, Inscription Rock at El Morro National Monument, the ruins at Fort Union, Billy the Kid mementos at Lincoln, the White Sands and Gila Cliff Dwellings National Monuments, and the Chaco Culture National Historical Park.

Famous natives and residents: Ernest L. Blumenshein, artist; William "Billy the Kid" Bonney, outlaw; Bruce Cabot, actor; Kit Carson, Army scout and trapper; Dennis Chavez, Congressman; John Chisum, cattle king; Mangus Coloradas, Apache leader; Edward Condon, physicist; John Denver, singer; Patrick Garrett, lawman; William Hanna, animator; Carl Hatch, senator; Conrad Hilton, hotel executive; Peter Hurd, artist; Preston Jones, playwright, actor; Ralph Kiner, baseball player, sportscaster; Nancy Lopez, golfer; Maria Martínez, San Ildefonso Pueblo potter; Bill Mauldin, political cartoonist; Popé, San Juan Pueblo medicine man, leader; Harrison Schmitt, astronaut; Kim Stanley, actress; Slim Summerville, actor; Al Unser, Bobby Unser, auto racers; Victorio, Apache chief; Kathy Whitworth, golfer

NEW YORK

Capital: Albany
Governor: George Pataki, R (to Jan. 1999)
Lieut. Governor: Elizabeth McCaughey, R (to Jan. 1999)
Secy. of State: Alexander Treadwell, R (to Jan. 1999)
Comptroller: Carl McCall, D (to Jan. 1999)
Atty. General: Dennis Vacco, R (to Jan. 1999)
Entered Union & (rank): July 26, 1788 (11)
Present constitution adopted: 1777 (last revised 1938)
Motto: *Excelsior* (Ever upward)
STATE SYMBOLS: animal, Beaver (1975); **fish,** Brook trout (1975); **gem,** Garnet (1969); **flower,** Rose (1955); **tree,** Sugar maple (1956); **bird,** Bluebird (1970); **insect,** Ladybug (1989); **song,** "I Love New York" (1980)
Nickname: Empire State
Origin of name: In honor of the English Duke of York
10 largest cities (1990 census): New York, 7,322,564;
Buffalo, 328,123; Rochester, 231,636; Yonkers, 188,082; Syracuse, 163,860; Albany, 101,082; Utica, 68,637; New Rochelle, 67,265; Mount Vernon, 67,153; Schenectady, 65,566
Land area & (rank): 47,224 sq mi. (122,310 sq km) (30)
Geographic center: In Madison Co., 12 mi. S of Oneida and 26 mi. SW of Utica
Number of counties: 62
Largest county (1990 census): Kings, 2,300,664
State forest preserves: Adirondacks, 2,500,000 ac., Catskills, 250,000 ac.
State parks: 150 (250,000 ac.)
1994 resident population est.: 18,169,000
1990 resident census population, sex, & (rank): 17,990,455 (2). **Male:** 8,625,673; **Female:** 9,364,782. **White:** 13,385,255 (74.4%); **Black:** 2,859,055 (15.9%); **American Indian, Eskimo, or Aleut:** 62,651 (0.3%); **Asian or Pacific Islander:** 693,760 (3.9%); **Other race:** 989,734 (5.5%); **Hispanic:** 2,214,026 (12.3%). **1990 percent population under 18:** 23.7; **65 and over:** 13.1; **median age:** 39.9,.

Giovanni da Verrazano, Italian-born navigator sailing for France, discovered New York Bay in 1524. Henry Hudson, an Englishman employed by the Dutch, reached the bay and sailed up the river now bearing his name in 1609, the same year that northern New York was explored and claimed for France by Samuel de Champlain.

In 1624 the first permanent Dutch settlement was established at Fort Orange (now Albany); one year later Peter Minuit is said to have purchased Manhattan Island from the Indians for trinkets worth about $24 and founded the Dutch colony of New Amsterdam (now New York City), which was surrendered to the English in 1664.

For a short time, New York City was the U.S. capital and George Washington was inaugurated there as first President on April 30, 1789.

New York's extremely rapid commercial growth may be partly attributed to Governor De Witt Clinton, who pushed through the construction of the Erie Canal (Buffalo to Albany), which was opened in 1825. Today, the 559-mile Governor Thomas E. Dewey Thruway connects New York City with Buffalo and with Connecticut, Massachusetts, and Pennsylvania express highways. Two toll-free superhighways, the Adirondack Northway (linking Albany with the Canadian border) and the North-South-Expressway (crossing central New York from the Pennsylvania border to the Thousand Islands) have been opened.

New York, with the great metropolis of New York City, is the spectacular nerve center of the nation. It is a leader in manufacturing, foreign trade, commercial and financial transactions, book and magazine publishing, and theatrical production.

New York City is not only a national but an international leader. A leading seaport, its John F. Kennedy International Airport is one of the busiest airports in the world. It is the largest manufacturing center in the country and its apparel industry is the city's largest manufacturing employer, with printing and publishing second.

Nearly all the rest of the state's manufacturing is done on Long Island, along the Hudson River north to Albany and through the Mohawk Valley, Central New York, and Southern Tier regions to Buffalo. The St. Lawrence seaway and power projects have opened the North Country to industrial expansion and have given the state a second seacoast.

The state ranks third in the nation in manufacturing with 1,057,100 employees in 1991. The principal industries are apparel, printing and publishing, leather products, instruments and electronic equipment.

The convention and tourist business is one of the state's most important sources of income.

New York farms are famous for raising cattle and calves, producing corn for grain, poultry, and the raising of vegetables and fruits. The state is a leading wine producer.

Among the major points of interest are Castle Clinton, Fort Stanwix, and Statue of Liberty National Monuments; Niagara Falls; U.S. Military Academy at West Point; National Historic Sites that include homes of Franklin D. Roosevelt at Hyde Park and Theodore Roosevelt in Oyster Bay and New York City; National Memorials, including Grant's Tomb and Federal Hall in New York City; Fort Ticonderoga; the Baseball Hall of Fame in Cooperstown; and the United Nations, skyscrapers, museums, theaters, and parks in New York City.

Famous natives and residents: Kareem Abdul-Jabbar, basketball player; Lucille Ball, actress; Humphrey Bogart, actor; James Cagney, actor; Maria Callas, soprano; Benjamin N. Cardozo, jurist; Paddy Chayefsky, playwright; Peter Cooper, industrialist and philanthropist; Aaron Copland, composer; Sammy Davis, Jr., actor and singer; Agnes de Mille, choreographer; Eamon De Valera, ex-President of Ireland; George Eastman, inventor; Millard Fillmore, President; Lou Gehrig, baseball plyer; George Gershwin, composer; Learned Hand, jurist; Edward Hopper, painter; Julia Ward Howe, poet and reformer; Charles Evans Hughes, jurist; Washington Irving, author; Henry James, novelist; John Jay, jurist; Michael Jordan, basketball; Jerome Kern, composer; Rockwell Kent, painter; Vince Lombardi, football coach; Chico, Groucho, Harpo, Zeppo Marx, comedians; Herman Melville, author; Ethel Merman, singer and actress; Ogden Nash, poet; Eugene O'Neill, playwright; Red Jacket, Seneca chief; John D. Rockefeller, industrialist; Norman Rockwell, painter and illustrator; Mickey Rooney, actor; Anna Eleanor Roosevelt, reformer and humanitarian; Franklin D. Roosevelt, President; Theodore Roosevelt, President; Jonas Salk, polio researcher; Margaret Sanger, birth control leader; Barbara Stanwyck, actress; Risë Stevens, mezzo-soprano; Richard Tucker, tenor; Martin Van Buren, President; Mae West, actress; Walt Whitman, poet; Edith Wharton, novelist

NORTH CAROLINA

Capital: Raleigh
Governor: James B. Hunt, Jr., D (to Jan. 1997)
Lieut. Governor: Dennis A. Wicker, D (to Jan. 1997)
Secy. of State: Rufus L. Edmisten, D (to Jan. 1997)
Treasurer: Harlan E. Boyles, D (to Jan. 1997)
Auditor: Ralph Campbell, D (to Jan. 1997)
Atty. General: Michael Easley, D (to Jan. 1997)
Entered Union & (rank): Nov. 21, 1789 (12)
Present constitution adopted: 1971
Motto: *Esse quam videri* (To be rather than to seem)
STATE SYMBOLS: flower, Dogwood (1941); **tree,** Pine (1963); **bird,** Cardinal (1943); **mammal,** Gray squirrel (1969); **insect,** Honeybee (1973); **reptile,** Eastern box turtle (1979); **gemstone,** Emerald (1973); **shell,** Scotch bonnet (1965); **historic boat,** Shad Boat (1987); **beverage,** Milk (1987); **rock,** Granite (1979); **dog,** Plott Hound (1989); **song,** "The Old North State" (1927); **colors,** Red and blue (1945)
Nickname: Tar Heel State
Origin of name: In honor of Charles I of England
10 largest cities (1990 census): Charlotte, 395,934; Raleigh, 207,951; Greensboro, 183,521; Winston-Salem, 143,485; Durham, 136,611; Fayetteville, 75,695; High Point, 69,496; Asheville, 61,607; Wilmington, 55,530; Gastonia, 54,732

Land area & (rank): 48,718 sq mi. (126,180 sq km) (29)
Geographic center: In Chatham Co., 10 mi. NW of Sanford
Number of counties: 100
Largest county (1990 census): Mecklenburg, 511,433
State forests: 1
State parks: 30 (125,000 ac.)
1994 resident population est.: 7,070,000
1990 resident census population, sex, & (rank): 6,628,637 (10). **Male:** 3,214,290; **Female:** 3,414,347. **White:** 5,008,491 (75.6%); **Black:** 1,456,323 (22.0%); **American Indian, Eskimo, or Aleut:** 80,155 (1.2%); **Asian or Pacific Islander:** 52,166 (0.8%); **Other race:** 31,502 (0.5%); **Hispanic:** 76,726 (1.2%). **1990 percent population under 18:** 24.2; **65 and over:** 12.1; **median age:** 33.1.

English colonists, sent by Sir Walter Raleigh, unsuccessfully attempted to settle Roanoke Island in 1585 and 1587. Virginia Dare, born there in 1587, was the first child of English parentage born in America.

In 1653 the first permanent settlements were established by English colonists from Virginia near the Roanoke and Chowan Rivers.

The region was established as an English proprietary colony in 1663–65 and its early history was the scene of Culpepper's Rebellion (1677), the Quaker-led Cary Rebellion of 1708, the Tuscarora Indian War in 1711–13, and many pirate raids.

During the American Revolution, there was relatively little fighting within the state, but many North Carolinians saw action elsewhere. Despite considerable pro-Union, anti-slavery sentiment, North Carolina joined the Confederacy.

North Carolina is the nation's largest furniture, tobacco, brick, and textile producer. It holds second place in the Southeast in population and first place in the value of its industrial and agricultural production. This production is highly diversified, with metal-working, chemicals, and paper constituting enormous industries. Tobacco, corn, cotton, hay, peanuts, and truck and vegetable crops are of major importance. It is the country's leading producer of mica and lithium.

Tourism is also important, with travelers and vacationers spending more than $1 billion annually in North Carolina. Sports include year-round golfing, skiing at mountain resorts, both fresh and salt water fishing, and hunting.

Among the major attractions are the Great Smoky Mountains, the Blue Ridge National Parkway, the Cape Hatteras and Cape Lookout National Seashores, the Wright Brothers National Memorial at Kitty Hawk, Guilford Courthouse and Moores Creek National Military Parks, Carl Sandburg's home near Hendersonville, and the Old Salem Restoration in Winston-Salem.

Famous natives and residents: David Brinkley, TV newscaster; Howard Cosell, sportscaster; Virginia Dare, first person born in America to English parents; James B. Duke, industrialist; Roberta Flack, singer; Ava Gardner, actress; Richard Gatling, inventor; Billy Graham, evangelist; Kathryn Grayson, singer and actress; Jesse Helms, politician; O. Henry, story writer; Barbara Howar, broadcaster, writer; Andrew Johnson, President; Michael Jordan, athlete; Charles Kuralt, TV journalist; Sugar Ray Leonard, boxer; Dolley Madison, First Lady; Ronni Milsap, country music singer; Theolonious Monk, pianist; Alfred Moore, jurist; Edward R. Murrow, commentator and government official; Walter Hines Page, journalist and ambassador; Floyd Patterson, boxer; Richard Petty, auto racer; James K. Polk, President; Soupy Sales, comedian; Earl Scruggs; bluegrass musician; Randy Travis, musician; John Scott Trotter, orchestra leader; Thomas Wolfe, novelist

NORTH DAKOTA

Capital: Bismarck
Governor: Edward T. Schafer, R (to Dec. 15, 1996)
Lieut. Governor: Rosemarie Myrdal, R (to Dec. 15, 1996)
Secy. of State: Alvin A. Jaeger, R (to Dec. 31, 1996)
Auditor: Robert W. Peterson, R (to Dec. 31, 1996)
State Treasurer: Kathi Gilmore, D (to Dec. 31, 1996)
Atty. General: Heidi Heitkamp, D (to Dec. 31, 1996)
Organized as territory: March 2, 1861
Entered Union & (rank): Nov. 2, 1889 (39)
Present constitution adopted: 1889
Motto: Liberty and union, now and forever: one and inseparable
STATE SYMBOLS: tree, American elm (1947); **bird,** Western meadowlark (1947); **song,** "North Dakota Hymn" (1947); **fish,** Northern Pike (1969); **grass,** Western wheatgrass (1977); **fossil,** Teredo petrified wood (1967); **beverage,** milk (1983); **state march,** Spirit of the Land (1975); **flower,** Wild prairie rose (1907); **state language,** English (1987); **honorary equine,** Nokota horse (1993); **state dance,** square dance (1995)
Nickname: Sioux State; Flickertail State, Peace Garden State
Origin of name: From the Sioux tribe, meaning "allies"
10 largest cities (1992 estimate): Fargo, 77,052; Grand Forks, 49,332; Bismarck, 51,319; Minot, 34,446; Dickinson, 16,264; Jamestown, 15,295; Mandan, 15,254; Williston, 13,033; West Fargo, 12,660; Wahpeton, 8,719
Land area & (rank): 68,994 sq mi. (178,695 sq km) (17)
Geographic center: In Sheridan Co., 5 mi. SW of McClusky
Number of counties: 53
Largest county (1990 census): Cass, 102,874
State forests: None
State parks: 14 (14,922.6 ac.)
1994 resident population est.: 638,000
1990 resident census population, sex, & (rank): 638,800 (47). **Male:** 318,201; **Female:** 320,599. **White:** 604,142 (94.6%); **Black:** 3,524 (0.6%); **American Indian, Eskimo, or Aleut:** 25,917 (4.1%); **Asian or Pacific Islander:** 3,462 (0.5%); **Other race:** 1,755 (0.3%); **Hispanic:** 4,665 (0.7%). **1990 percent population under 18:** 27.5; **65 and over:** 14.3; **median age:** 32.4.

North Dakota was explored in 1738–40 by French Canadians led by La Verendrye. In 1803, the U.S. acquired most of North Dakota from France in the Louisiana Purchase. Lewis and Clark explored the region in 1804–06 and the first settlements were made at Pembina in 1812 by Scottish and Irish families while this area was still in dispute between the U.S. and Great Britain.

In 1818, the U.S. obtained the northeastern part of North Dakota by treaty with Great Britain and took possession of Pembina in 1823.

North Dakota is the most rural of all the states, with farms covering more than 90% of the land. North Dakota ranks first in the Nation's production of spring and durum wheat, and the state's coal and oil reserves are plentiful.

Other agricultural products include barley, rye, sunflowers, dry edible beans, honey, oats, flaxseed, sugar beets, and hay; beef cattle, sheep, and hogs.

Recently, manufacturing industries have grown, especially food processing and farm equipment. The state also produces natural gas, lignite, salt, clay, sand, and gravel.

The Garrison Dam on the Missouri River provides extensive irrigation and produces 400,000 kilowatts of electricity for the Missouri Basin areas.

Known for its waterfowl, grouse, and deer hunting and bass, trout, and northern pike fishing, North Dakota has 20 state parks and recreation areas. Points of interest include the International Peace Garden near Dunseith, Fort Union Trading Post National Historic Site, the State Capitol at Bismarck, the Badlands, Theodore Roosevelt National Park, and Fort Lincoln, now a state park, from which Gen. George Custer set out on his last campaign in 1876.

Famous natives and residents: Lynn Anderson, singer; Maxwell Anderson, playwright; Dr. Robert H. Bahmer, U.S. archivist; Elizabeth Bodine, humanitarian; Dr. Anne Carlsen, educator; Ronald N. Davies, U.S. District judge; Angie Dickinson, actress; Ivan Dmitre, artist; Phyllis Frelich, actress; Bertin C. Gamble, founder of Gamble-Skogmo; William H. Gass, writer, philosopher; Rev. Richard C. Halverson, U.S. Senate chaplain; Phil D. Jackson, basketball player, coach; Dr. Leon O. Jacobson, researcher, educator; Harold K. Johnson, U.S. Army general; David C. Jones, U.S. Army general; Louis L'Amour, author; Peggy Lee, singer; William Lemke, U.S. Representative; Roger Maris, baseball player; Marquis de Mores, cattleman, established Medora; Gerald P. Nye, U.S. Senator; Casper Oimoen, skier; Arthur Peterson, radio and TV actor; Cliff (Fido) Purpur, hockey player, coach; James Rosenquist, paitner; Harold Schafer, founder of Gold Seal Co.; Eric Sevareid, TV commentator; Ann Sothern, actress; Dorothy Stickney, actress; Edward K. Thompson, Life magazine editor; Era Bell Thompson, Ebony magazine editor; Tommy Tucker, band leader; Lawrence Welk, band leader; Larry Woiwode, writer

OHIO

Capital: Columbus
Governor: George V. Voinovich, R (to Jan. 1999)
Lieut. Governor: Nancy Putnam–Hollister, R (to Jan. 1999)
Secy. of State: Bob Taft, R (to Jan. 1999)
Auditor: Jim Petro, R (to Jan. 1999)
Treasurer: J. Kenneth Blackwell, R (to Jan. 1999)
Atty. General: Betty D. Montgomery, R (to Jan. 1999)
Entered Union & (rank): March 1, 1803 (17)
Present constitution adopted: 1851
Motto: With God, all things are possible
STATE SYMBOLS: flower, Scarlet carnation (1904); **tree,** Buckeye (1953); **bird,** Cardinal (1933); **insect,** Ladybug (1975); **gemstone,** Flint (1965); **song,** "Beautiful Ohio" (1969); **drink,** Tomato juice (1965)
Nickname: Buckeye State
Origin of name: From an Iroquoian word meaning "great river"
10 largest cities (1992): Columbus, 642,987; Cleveland, 505,616; Cincinnati, 364,040; Toledo, 332,943; Akron, 223,019; Dayton, 182,044; Youngstown, 95,732; Parma, 87,876; Canton, 84,161; Lorain, 71,245
Land area & (rank): 40,953 sq mi. (106,067 sq km) (35)
Geographic center: In Delaware Co., 25 mi. NNE of Columbus
Number of counties: 88
Largest county (1990 census): Cuyahoga, 1,412,140
State forests: 19 (172,744 ac.)
State parks: 71 (198,027 ac.)
1994 resident population est.: 11,102,198
1990 resident census population, sex, & (rank): 10,847,115 (7). **Male:** 5,226,340; **Female:** 5,620,775. **White:** 9,521,756 (87.8%); **Black:** 1,154,826 (10.6%); **American Indian, Eskimo, or Aleut:** 20,358 (0.2%); **Asian or Pacific Islander:** 91,179 (0.8%); **Other race:** 58,996 (0.5%); **Hispanic:** 139,696 (1.3%). **1990 percent population under 18:** 25.8; **65 and over:** 13.0; **median age:** 33.3.

First explored for France by La Salle in 1669, the Ohio region became British property after the French and Indian War. Ohio was acquired by the U.S. after the Revolutionary War in 1783 and, in 1788, the first permanent settlement was established at Marietta, capital of the Northwest Territory.

The 1790s saw severe fighting with the Indians in Ohio; a major battle was won by Maj. Gen. Anthony Wayne at Fallen Timbers in 1794. In the War of 1812, Commodore Oliver H. Perry defeated the British in the Battle of Lake Erie on Sept. 10, 1813.

Ohio is one of the nation's industrial leaders, ranking third in the value of manufactured products. Important manufacturing centers are located in or near Ohio's major cities. Akron is known for rubber; Canton for roller bearings; Cincinnati for jet engines and machine tools; Cleveland for auto assembly and parts, refining, and steel; Dayton for office machines, refrigeration, and heating and auto equipment; Youngstown and Steubenville for steel; and Toledo for glass and auto parts.

The state's thousands of factories almost overshadow its importance in agriculture and mining. Its fertile soil produces soybeans, corn, oats, grapes, and clover. More than half of Ohio's farm receipts come from dairying and sheep and hog raising. Ohio is the top state in lime production and among the leaders in coal, clay, salt, sand, and gravel. Petroleum, gypsum, cement, and natural gas are also important.

Tourism is a valuable revenue producer, bringing in $8.5 billion in 1992, and ranking 10th among the 50 states. Attractions include the Indian burial grounds at Mound City Group National Monument, Perry's Victory International Peace Memorial, the Pro Football Hall of Fame at Canton, and the homes of Presidents Grant, Taft, Hayes, Harding, and Garfield.

Famous natives and residents: Neil Armstrong, astronaut; Kathleen Battle, soprano; George Bellows, painter and lithographer; Ambrose Bierce, journalist; Erma Bombeck, columnist; Bill Boyd (Hopalong Cassidy), actor; Milton Caniff, cartoonist; Hart Crane, poet; George Armstrong Custer, army officer; Dorothy Dandridge, actress; Doris Day, singer and actress; Clarence Darrow, lawyer; Ruby Dee, actress; Rita Dove, U.S. Poet Laureate; Hugh Downs, TV broadcaster; Thomas A. Edison, inventor; Clark Gable, actor; James A. Garfield, President; Lillian Gish, actress; John Glenn, astronaut and senator; Ulysses S. Grant, President; Warren G. Harding, President; Rutherford Hayes, President; Benjamin Harrison, President; William Dean Howells, novelist and critic; Zane Grey, author; Robert Henri, painter; Kenisaw Mountain Landis, first baseball commissioner; Dean Martin, singer and actor; William McKinley, President; Paul Newman, actor; Jack Nicklaus, golfer; Annie Oakley, markswoman; Norman Vincent Peale, clergyman; Tyrone Power, actor; Judith Resnik, astronaut; Eddie Rickenbacker, aviator; Arthur M. Schlesinger, Jr., historian; William Tecumseh Sherman, army general; Gloria Steinem, feminist; William H. Taft, President; Tecumseh, Shawnee Indian chief; Lowell Thomas, explorer and commentator; James Thurber, author and cartoonist; Orville Wright, inventor; Cy Young, baseball player

OKLAHOMA

Capital: Oklahoma City
Governor: Frank Keating, R (to Jan. 1999)
Lieut. Governor: Mary Fallin, R (to Jan. 1999)
Secy. of State: Tom Cole, R (to Jan. 1999)
Treasurer: Robert Butkin, D (to Jan. 1999)
Atty. General: Drew Edmondson, D (to Jan. 1999)
Organized as territory: May 2, 1890
Entered Union & (rank): Nov. 16, 1907 (46)
Present constitution adopted: 1907
Motto: *Labor omnia vincit* (Labor conquers all things)
STATE SYMBOLS: flower, Mistletoe (1893); **tree,** Redbud (1937); **bird,** Scissor-tailed flycatcher (1951); **animal,** Bison (1972); **reptile,** Mountain boomer lizard (1969); **stone,** Rose Rock (barite rose) (1968); **colors,** Green

and white (1915); **song,** "Oklahoma" (1953)
Nickname: Sooner State
Origin of name: From two Choctaw Indian words meaning "red people"
10 largest cities (1990 census): Oklahoma City, 444,719; Tulsa, 367,302; Lawton, 80,561; Norman, 80,071; Broken Arrow, 58,043; Edmond, 52,315; Midwest City, 52,267; Enid, 45,309; Moore, 40,318; Muskogee, 37,708
Land area & (rank): 68,679 sq mi. (177,877 sq km) (19)
Geographic center: In Oklahoma Co., 8 mi. N of Oklahoma City
Number of counties: 77
Largest county (1990 census): Oklahoma, 599,611
State forests: None
State parks: 36 (57,487 ac.)
1994 resident population est.: 3,258,000
1990 resident census population, sex, & (rank): 3,145,585 (28). **Male:** 1,530,819; **Female:** 1,614,766. **White:** 2,583,512 (82.1%); **Black:** 233,801 (7.4%); **American Indian, Eskimo, or Aleut:** 252,420 (8.0%); **Asian or Pacific Islander:** 33,563 (1.1%); **Other race:** 42,289 (1.3%); **Hispanic:** 86,160 (2.7%). **1990 percent population under 18:** 26.6; **65 and over:** 13.5; **median age:** 33.2.

Francisco Vásquez de Coronado first explored the region for Spain in 1541. The U.S. acquired most of Oklahoma in 1803 in the Louisiana Purchase from France; the Western Panhandle region became U.S. territory with the annexation of Texas in 1845.

Set aside as Indian Territory in 1834, the region was divided into Indian Territory and Oklahoma Territory on May 2, 1890. The two were combined to make a new state, Oklahoma, on Nov. 16, 1907.

On April 22, 1889, the first day homesteading was permitted, 50,000 people swarmed into the area. Those who tried to beat the noon starting gun were called "Sooners." Hence the state's nickname.

Oil made Oklahoma a rich state, but natural gas production has now surpassed it. Oil refining, meat packing, food processing, and machinery manufacturing (especially construction and oil equipment) are important industries.

Other minerals produced in Oklahoma include helium, gypsum, zinc, cement, coal, copper, and silver.

Oklahoma's rich plains produce bumper yields of wheat, as well as large crops of sorghum, hay, cotton, and peanuts. More than half of Oklahoma's annual farm receipts are contributed by livestock products, including cattle, dairy products, and broilers.

Tourist attractions include the National Cowboy Hall of Fame in Oklahoma City, the Will Rogers Memorial in Claremore, the Cherokee Cultural Center with a restored Cherokee village, the restored Fort Gibson Stockade near Muskogee, and the Lake Texoma recreation area, Pari-Mutuel horse racing at Remington Park in Oklahoma City, and Blue Ribbon Downs in Sallisaw.

Famous natives and residents: Johnny Bench, baseball player; John Berryman, poet; Iron Eyes Cody, Cherokee actor; L. Gordon Cooper, astronaut; Ralph Ellison, writer; James Garner, actor; Chester Gould, cartoonist; Woody Guthrie, singer and composer; Roy Harris, composer; Paul Harvey, broadcaster; Van Heflin, actor; Ron Howard, actor and director; Ben Johnson, actor; Jennifer Jones, actress; Jeane Kirkpatrick, educator and public affairs; Wilma P. Mankiller, Principal Chief of Cherokee Nation of Oklahoma; Mickey Mantle, baseball player; Bill Moyers, journalist; Daniel Patrick Moynihan, N.Y. Senator; Patti Page, singer; Mary Kay Place, actress and writer; Tony Randall, actor; Oral Roberts, evangelist; Dale Robertson, actor; Will Rogers, humorist; Dan Rowan, comedian; Maria Tallchief, ballerina; Jim Thorpe, athlete; Alfre Woodard, actress

OREGON

Capital: Salem
Governor: John A. Kitzhaber, D (to Jan. 1999)
Secy. of State: Phil Keisling, D (to Jan. 1999)
Treasurer: James A. Hill, D (to Jan. 1999)
Atty. General: Theodore R. Kulongoski, D (to Jan. 1999)
Organized as territory: Aug. 14, 1848
Entered Union & (rank): Feb. 14, 1859 (33)
Present constitution adopted: 1859
Motto: "Alis volat Propriis" ("She flies with her own wings") (1987)
STATE SYMBOLS: flower, Oregon grape (1899); **tree,** Douglas fir (1939); **animal,** Beaver (1969); **bird,** Western meadowlark (1927); **fish,** Chinook salmon (1961); **rock,** Thunderegg (1965); **colors,** Navy blue and gold (1959); **song,** "Oregon, My Oregon" (1927); **insect,** Swallowtail butterfly (1979); **dance,** Square dance (1977); **nut,** Hazelnut (1989); **gemstone,** Sunstone (1987)
Nickname: Beaver State
Poet Laureate: William E. Stafford (1974) [deceased]
Origin of name: Unknown. However, it is generally accepted that the name, first used by Jonathan Carver in 1778, was taken from the writings of Maj. Robert Rogers, an English army officer.
10 largest cities (1993 pop. est.): Portland, 471,328; Eugene, 119,235; Salem, 113,325; Gresham, 73,185; Beaverton, 60,000; Medford, 51,215; Springfield, 46,715; Corvallis, 46,260; Hillsboro, 42,280; Albany, 34,350
Land area & (rank): 96,003 sq mi. (248,647 sq km) (10)
Geographic center: In Crook Co., 25 mi. SSE of Prineville
Number of counties: 36
Largest county (1993 pop. est.): Multnomah, 615,000
State forests: 820,000 ac.
State parks: 240 (93,330 ac.)
1994 resident population est.: 3,086,000
1990 resident census population, sex, & (rank): 2,842,321 (29). **Male:** 1,397,073; **Female:** 1,445,248. **White:** 2,636,787 (92.8%); **Black:** 46,178 (1.6%); **American Indian, Eskimo, or Aleut:** 38,496 (1.4%); **Asian or Pacific Islander:** 69,269 (2.4%); **Other race:** 51,591 (1.8%); **Hispanic:** 112,707 (4.0%). **1990 percent population under 18:** 25.5; **65 and over:** 13.8; **median age:** 34.5.

Spanish and English sailors are believed to have sighted the Oregon coast in the 1500s and 1600s. Capt. James Cook, seeking the Northwest Passage, charted some of the coastline in 1778. In 1792, Capt. Robert Gray, in the *Columbia*, discovered the river named after his ship and claimed the area for the U.S.

In 1805 the Lewis and Clark expedition explored the area and John Jacob Astor's fur depot, Astoria, was founded in 1811. Disputes for control of Oregon between American settlers and the Hudson Bay Company were finally resolved in the 1846 Oregon Treaty in which Great Britain gave up claims to the region.

Oregon has a $3.3 billion lumber and wood products industry, and an $859 milliioon paper and allied manufacturing industry. Its salmon-fishing industry is one of the world's largest.

In agriculture, the state leads in growing peppermint, cover seed crops, blackberries, boysenberries, loganberries, black raspberries, and hazelnuts. It is second in raising hops, raspberries, sweet cherries, prunes, snap beans and onions. Oregon has the only nickel smelter in the United States.

With the low-cost electric power provided by Bonneville Dam, McNary Dam, and other dams in the Pacific Northwest, Oregon has developed steadily as a manufacturing state. Leading manufactures are lumber and plywood, metalwork, machinery, aluminum, chemicals, paper, food packing, and electronic equipment.

Crater Lake National Park, Mount Hood, and Bonneville Dam on the Columbia are major tourist attractions. Oregon Dunes National Recreation Area has been established near Florence. Other points of interest include the Oregon Caves National Monument, Cape Perpetua in Siuslaw National Forest, Columbia River Gorge between The Dalles and Troutdale, Hells Canyon, Newberry Volcanic National Monument, and John Day Fossil Beds National Monument.

Famous natives and residents: James Beard, food expert; Raymond Carver, writer, poet; Homer C. Davenport, political cartoonist; David Douglas, botanist; Abigail Scott Duniway, women's suffrage advocate; John E. Frohnmeyer, Chairman National Endowment of the Arts; Robert Gray, sea captain, discoverer of Columbia River; Matt Groening, cartoonist; Mark Hatfield, senator; Donald P. Hodel, Secretary of the Interior; Chief Joseph, Nez Percé chief; Dave Kingman, baseball player; Ursula LeGuin, writer; Edwin Markham, poet; Phyllis McGinley, author; Linus Pauling, chemist; Jane Powell, actress and singer; John Reed, poet and author; Harvey W. Scott, editor; Doc. Severinsen, band leader; Norton Simon, business executive; Paul M. Simon, Illinois senator; William E. Stafford, poet; Sally Struthers, actress

PENNSYLVANIA

Capital: Harrisburg
Governor: Tom Ridge, R (to Jan. 1999)
Lieut. Governor: Mark Schweiker, R (to Jan. 1999)
Secy. of the Commonwealth: Evette Kane, R (to Jan. 1999)
Auditor General: Barbara Hafer, R (to Jan. 1999)
Acting Atty. General: Walter W. Cowan, R
Entered Union & (rank): Dec. 12, 1787 (2)
Present constitution adopted: 1968
Motto: Virtue, liberty, and independence
STATE SYMBOLS: flower, Mountain laurel (1933); **tree,** Hemlock (1931); **bird,** Ruffed grouse (1931); **dog,** Great Dane (1965); **colors,** Blue and gold (1907); **song,** "Pennsylvania" (1990)
Nickname: Keystone State
Origin of name: In honor of Adm. Sir. William Penn, father of William Penn. It means "Penn's Woodland."
10 largest cities (1990 census): Philadelphia, 1,585,577; Pittsburgh, 369,879; Erie, 108,718; Allentown, 105,090; Scranton, 81,805; Reading, 78,380; Bethlehem, 71,428; Lancaster, 55,551; Harrisburg, 52,376; Altoona, 51,881
Land area & (rank): 44,820 sq mi. (116,083 sq km) (32)
Geographic center: In Centre Co., 2 1/2 mi. SW of Bellefonte
Number of counties: 67
Largest county (1990 census): Allegheny, 1,336,449
State forests: 1,991,526 ac.
State parks: 114 (277,164.18 ac.)
1994 resident population est.: 12,052,000
1990 resident census population, sex, & (rank): 11,881,643 (5). **Male:** 5,694,265; **Female:** 6,187,378. **White:** 10,520,201 (88.5%); **Black:** 1,089,795 (9.2%); **American Indian, Eskimo, or Aleut:** 14,733 (0.1%); **Asian or Pacific Islander:** 137,438 (1.2%); **Other race:** 119,476 (1.0%); **Hispanic:** 232,262 (2.0%). **1990 percent population under 18:** 23.5; **65 and over:** 15.4; **median age:** 35.

Rich in historic lore, Pennsylvania territory was disputed in the early 1600s among the Dutch, the Swedes, and the English. England acquired the region in 1664 with the capture of New York and in 1681 Pennsylvania was granted to William Penn, a Quaker, by King Charles II.

Philadelphia was the seat of the federal government almost continuously from 1776 to 1800; there the Declaration of Independence was signed in 1776 and the U.S. Constitution drawn up in 1787. Valley Forge, of Revolutionary War fame, and Gettysburg, the turning-point of the Civil War, are both in Pennsylvania. The Liberty Bell is located in a glass pavilion across from Independence Hall in Philadelphia.

With the decline of the coal, steel and railroad industries, Pennsylvania's industry has diversified, though the state still leads the country in the production of specialty steel. Pennsylvania is a leader in the production of chemicals, food, and electrical machinery and produces 10% of the nations's cement. Also important are brick and tiles, glass, limestone, and slate. Data processing is also increasingly important.

Pennsylvania's nine million agricultural acres (6 million acres for crops and pasture, 3 million acres in farm woodlands) produce a wide variety of crops and its 55,535 farms are the backbone of the state's economy. Leading products are milk, poultry and eggs, a variety of fruits, sweet corn, potatoes, mushrooms, cheese, beans, hay, maple syrup, and even Christmas trees.

Pennsylvania has the largest rural population in the nation. The state's farmers sell more than $3.3 billion in crops and livestock annually and agribusiness and food-related industries account for another $35 billion in economic activity annually.

Tourists now spend approximately $6 billion in Pennsylvania annually. Among the chief attractions: the Gettysburg National Military Park, Valley Forge National Historical Park, Independence National Historical Park in Philadelphia, the Pennsylvania Dutch region, the Eisenhower farm near Gettysburg, and the Delaware Water Gap National Recreation Area.

Famous natives and residents: Louisa May Alcott, novelist; Marian Anderson, contralto; Maxwell Anderson, dramatist; Samuel Barber, composer; John Barrymore, actor; Donald Barthelme, author; Stephen Vincent Benet, poet and story writer; Daniel Boone, frontiersman; Ed Bradley, TV anchorman; James Buchanan, President; Alexander Calder, sculptor; Rachel Carson, biologist and author; Mary Cassatt, painter; Henry Steele Commager, historian; Bill Cosby, actor; Stuart Davis, painter; Jimmy & Tommy Dorsey, band leaders; W.C. Fields, comedian; Stephen Foster, composer; Robert Fulton, inventor; Grace, Princess of Monaco; Martha Graham, choreographer; Alexander Haig, ex-Secretary of State; Marilyn Horne, mezzo-soprano; Lee Iacocca, auto executive; Reggie Jackson, baseball player; Gene Kelly, dancer and actor; Gelsey Kirkland, ballerina; S.S. Kresge, merchant; Mario Lanza, actor and singer; George C. Marshall, 5-star general; George McClellan, general; Margaret Mead, anthropologist; Andrew Mellon, financier; Tom Mix, actor; Arnold Palmer, golfer; Robert E. Peary, explorer; Man Ray, painter; Mary Roberts Rinehart, novelist; Betsy Ross, flagmaker; B.F. Skinner, psychologist; John Sloan, painter; Gertrude Stein, author; James Stewart, actor; John Updike, novelist; Honus Wagner, baseball player; Fred Waring, band leader; Ethel Waters, singer and actress; Anthony Wayne, military officer; August Wilson, poet, writer, and playwright; Duchess of Windsor (Wallis Warfield); Andrew Wyeth, painter

RHODE ISLAND

Capital: Providence
Governor: Lincoln Almond, R (to Jan. 1999)
Lieut. Governor: Robert A. Weygand, D (to Jan. 1999)
Secy. of State: Jim Langevin, D (to Jan. 1999)
Atty. General: Jeffery B. Pine, D (to Jan. 1999)
General Treasurer: Nancy J. Mayer, D (to Jan. 1999)
Entered Union & (rank): May 29, 1790 (13)
Present constitution adopted: 1843
Motto: Hope
STATE SYMBOLS: flower, Violet (unofficial) (1968); **tree,**

Red maple (official) (1964); **bird,** Rhode Island Red (official) (1954); **shell,** Quahog (official); **mineral,** Bowenite; **stone,** Cumberlandite; **colors,** Blue, white, and gold (in state flag); **song,** "Rhode Island" (1946)
Nickname: The Ocean State
Origin of name: From the Greek Island of Rhodes
10 largest cities (1990 census): Providence, 160,728; Warwick, 85,427; Cranston, 70,060; Pawtucket, 72,644; East Providence, 50,380; Woonsocket, 43,877; Newport, 28,227; Central Falls, 17,637
Land area & (rank): 1,045 sq mi. (2,706 sq km) (50)
Geographic center: In Kent Co., 1 mi. SSW of Crompton
Number of counties: 5
Largest town (1990 census): North Providence, 32,090
State forests: 11 (20,900 ac.)
State parks: 17 (8,200 ac.)
1994 resident population est.: 997,000
1990 resident census population, sex, & (rank): 1,003,464 (43). **Male:** 481,496; **Female:** 521,968. **White:** 917,375 (91.4%); **Black:** 38,861 (3.9%); **American Indian, Eskimo, or Aleut:** 4,071 (0.4%); **Asian or Pacific Islander:** 18,325 (1.8%); **Other race:** 24,832 (2.5%); **Hispanic:** 45,752 (4.6%). **1990 percent population under 18:** 22.5; **65 and over:** 15.0; **median age:** 34.

From its beginnings, Rhode Island has been distinguished by its support for freedom of conscience and action, started by Roger Williams, who was exiled by the Massachusetts Bay Colony Puritans in 1636, and was the founder of the present state capital, Providence. Williams was followed by other religious exiles who founded Pocasset, now Portsmouth, in 1638 and Newport in 1639.

Rhode Island's rebellious, authority-defying nature was further demonstrated by the burnings of the British revenue cutters *Liberty* and *Gaspee* prior to the Revolution, by its early declaration of independence from Great Britain in May 1776, its refusal to participate actively in the War of 1812, and by Dorr's Rebellion of 1842, which protested property requirements for voting.

Rhode Island, smallest of the fifty states, is densely populated and highly industrialized. It is a primary center for jewelry manufacturing in the United States. Electronics, metal, plastic products, and boat and ship construction are other important industries. Non-manufacturing employment includes research in health and medical areas, and the ocean environment. Providence is a wholesale distribution center for New England.

Two of New England's fishing ports are at Galilee and Newport. Rural areas of the state support small-scale farming including grapes for local wineries, turf grass and nursery stock.

Tourism is one of Rhode Island's largest industries, generating over a billion dollars a year in revenue.

Newport became famous as the summer capital of society in the mid-19th century. Touro Synagogue (1763) is the oldest in the U.S. Other points of interest include the Roger Williams National Memorial in Providence, Samuel Slater's Mill in Pawtucket, the General Nathanael Greene Homestead in Coventry and Block Island.

Famous natives and residents: Harry Anderson, actor; George M. Cohan, actor and dramatist; Eddie Dowling, actor and stage producer; Nelson Eddy, baritone and actor; Ann Smith Franklin, printer and almanac publisher; Charles Gorham, silversmith; Spalding Gray, writer, performance artist; Bobby Hackett, trumpeter; David Hartman, TV newscaster; Ruth Hussey, actress; Anne Hutchinson, religious leader; Thomas H. Ince, film producer; Wilbur John, Quaker leader; Van Johnson, actor; Clarence King, first director of the U.S. Geological Survey; Galway Kinnell, poet; Oliver LaFarge, writer; Irving R. Levine, news correspondent; H.P. Lovecraft, author;

Ida Lewis, lighthouse keeper; John McLaughlin, political commentator, broadcaster; Dana C. Munro, educator and historian; Matthew C. Perry, naval officer; Oliver Hazard Perry, naval officer; King Philip (Metacomet), Indian leader; Gilbert Stuart, painter; Sarah Helen (Power) Whitman, poet; Jemima Wilkinson, religious leader; Roger Williams, clergyman and founder of Rhode Island; Leonard Woodcock, labor union official

SOUTH CAROLINA

Capital: Columbia
Governor: David M. Beasley, R (to Jan. 1999)
Lieut. Governor: Robert L. Peeler, R (to Jan. 1999)
Secy. of State: Jim Miles, R (to Jan. 1999)
Comptroller General: Earle E. Morris, Jr., D (to Jan. 1999)
Atty. General: Charles M. Condon, R (to Jan. 1999)
Entered Union & (rank): May 23, 1788 (8).
Present constitution adopted: 1895
Mottoes: *Animis opibusque parati* (Prepared in mind and resources) and *Dum spiro spero* (While I breathe, I hope)
STATE SYMBOLS: flower, Carolina yellow jessamine (1924); **tree,** Palmetto tree (1939); **bird,** Carolina wren (1948); **song,** "Carolina" (1911)
Nickname: Palmetto State
Origin of name: In honor of Charles I of England
10 largest cities (1990 census): Columbia, 98,052; Charleston, 80,414; North Charleston, 70,218; Greenville, 58,282; Spartanburg, 43,467; Sumter, 41,943; Rock Hill, 41,643; Mount Pleasant Town, 30,108; Florence, 29,813; Anderson, 26,184
Land area & (rank): 30,111 sq mi. (77,988 sq km) (40)
Geographic center: In Richland Co., 13 mi. SE of Columbia
Number of counties: 46
Largest county (1990 census): Greenville, 320,167
State forests: 4 (124,052 ac.)
State parks: 50 (61,726 ac.)
1994 resident population est.: 3,664,000
1990 resident census population, sex, & (rank): 3,486,703 (25). **Male:** 1,688,510; **Female:** 1,798,193. **White:** 2,406,974 (69.0%); **Black:** 1,039,884 (29.8%); **American Indian, Eskimo, or Aleut:** 8,246 (0.2%); **Asian or Pacific Islander:** 22,382 (0.6%); **Other race:** 9,217 (0.3%); **Hispanic:** 30,551 (0.9%) **1990 percent population under 18:** 26.4; **65 and over:** 11.4; **median age:** 32.0

Following exploration of the coast in 1521 by De Gordillo, the Spanish tried unsuccessfully to establish a colony near present-day Georgetown in 1526 and the French also failed to colonize Parris Island near Fort Royal in 1562.

The first English settlement was made in 1670 at Albemarle Point on the Ashley River, but poor conditions drove the settlers to the site of Charleston (originally called Charles Town). South Carolina, officially separated from North Carolina in 1729, was the scene of extensive military action during the Revolution and again during the Civil War. The Civil War began in 1861 as South Carolina troops fired on federal Fort Sumter in Charleston Harbor and the state was the first to secede from the Union.

Once primarily agricultural, South Carolina has built so many large textile and other mills that today its factories produce eight times the output of its farms in cash value. Charleston makes asbestos, wood, pulp, and steel products; chemicals, machinery, and apparel are also important.

Farms have become fewer but larger in recent years. South Carolina grows more peaches than any other state

except California; it ranks fifth in overall tobacco production. Other farm products include cotton, peanuts, sweet potatoes, soybeans, corn, and oats. Poultry and dairy products are also important revenue producers.

Points of interest include Fort Sumter National Monument, Fort Moultrie, Fort Johnson, and aircraft carrier USS *Yorktown* in Charleston Harbor; the Middleton, Magnolia, and Cypress Gardens in Charleston; Cowpens National Battlefield; and the Hilton Head resorts.

Famous natives and residents: Bernard Baruch, statesman; Mary McLeod Bethune, educator; James F. Byrnes, senator, jurist, Secretary of State; John C. Calhoun, statesman; Mark Clark, general; Joe Frazier, prize fighter; Althea Gibson, tennis champion; Dizzy Gillespie, jazz trumpeter; DuBose Heyward, poet, playwright, novelist; Andrew Jackson, President; Jesse Jackson, civil rights leader; Eartha Kitt, singer; Francis Marion "Swamp Fox," Revolutionary general; Ronald McNair, astronaut; John Rutledge, jurist; Strom Thurmond, politician; Charles Townes, physicist; William Westmoreland, ex-Army Chief of Staff; Vanna White, television personality

SOUTH DAKOTA

Capital: Pierre
Governor: William J. Janklow, R (to Jan. 1999)
Lieut. Governor: Carole Hillard, R (to Jan. 1999)
Atty. General: Mark Barnett, R (to Jan. 1999)
Secy. of State: Joyce Hazeltine, R (to Jan. 1999)
State Auditor: Vern Larson, R (to Jan. 1999)
State Treasurer: Richard Butler, D (to Jan. 1999)
Organized as territory: March 2, 1861
Entered Union & (rank): Nov. 2, 1889 (40)
Present constitution adopted: 1889
Motto: Under God the people rule
STATE SYMBOLS: flower, American pasqueflower (1903); **grass,** Western wheat grass (1970); **soil,** Houdek (1990); **tree,** Black Hills spruce (1947); **bird,** Ring-necked pheasant (1943); **insect,** Honeybee (1978); **animal,** Coyote (1949); **mineral stone,** Rose quartz (1966); **gemstone,** Fairburn agate (1966); **colors,** Blue and gold (in state flag); **song,** "Hail! South Dakota" (1943); **fish,** Walleye (1982); **musical instrument,** Fiddle (1989); **soil,** Houdek soil (1990)
Nicknames: Mount Rushmore State; Coyote State
Origin of name: Same as for North Dakota
10 largest cities (1990 census): Sioux Falls, 100,814; Rapid City, 54,523; Aberdeen, 24,927; Watertown, 17,592; Brookings, 16,270; Mitchell, 13,798; Pierre, 12,906; Yankton, 12,703; Huron, 12,448; Vermillion, 10,034
Land area & (rank): 75,898 sq mi. (196,575 sq km) (16)
Geographic center: In Hughes Co., 8 mi. NE of Pierre
Number of counties: 67 (64 county governments)
Largest county (1990 census): Minnehaha, 123,809
State forests: None[1]
State parks: 13 plus 39 recreational areas (87,269 ac.)[2]
1994 resident population est.: 721,000
1990 resident census population, sex, & (rank): 696,004 (45). **Male:** 342,498; **Female:** 353,506. **White:** 637,515 (91.6%); **Black:** 3,258 (0.5%); **American Indian, Eskimo, or Aleut:** 50,575 (7.3%); **Asian or Pacific Islander:** 3,123 (0.4%); **Other race:** 1,533 (0.2%); **Hispanic:** 5,252 (0.8%). **1990 percent population under 18:** 28.5; **65 and over:** 14.7; **median age:** 32.5.

1. No designated state forests; about 13,000 ac. of state land is forestland. 2. Acreage includes 39 recreation areas and 80 roadside parks, in addition to 12 state parks.

Exploration of this area began in 1743 when Louis-Joseph and François Verendrye came from France in search of a route to the Pacific.

The U.S. acquired the region as part of the Louisiana Purchase in 1803 and it was explored by Lewis and Clark in 1804–06. Fort Pierre, the first permanent settlement, was established in 1817 and, in 1831, the first Missouri River steamboat reached the fort.

Settlement of South Dakota did not begin in earnest until the arrival of the railroad in 1873 and the discovery of gold in the Black Hills the following year.

Agriculture is the state's leading industry. South Dakota leads the nation in the production of oats and ranks second among the states in the production of rye, flaxseed, and sunflower seed.

South Dakota is the nation's second leading producer of gold and the Homestake Mine is the richest in the U.S. Other minerals produced include berylium, bentonite, granite, silver, petroleum, and uranium.

Processing of foods produced by farms and ranches is the largest South Dakota manufacturing industry, followed by lumber, wood products, and machinery, including farm equipment.

The Black Hills are the highest mountains east of the Rockies. Mt. Rushmore, in this group, is famous for the likenesses of Washington, Jefferson, Lincoln, and Theodore Roosevelt, which were carved in granite by Gutzon Borglum. A memorial to Crazy Horse is also being carved in granite near Custer.

Other tourist attractions include the Badlands; the World's Only Corn Palace in Mitchell; and the city of Deadwood where Wild Bill Hickok was killed in 1876 and where gambling was recently legalized to truly recapture the city's Old West flavor.

Famous natives and residents: Sparky Anderson, baseball manager; Gertrude Bonnin (Zitkala-Sa), Sioux writer and pan-Indian activist; Tom Brokaw, TV newscaster; Robert Casey, writer; Myron Floren, accordionist; Joseph J. Foss, WW II Marine fighter ace; Mary Hart, host; Crazy Horse, Oglala chief; Oscar Howe, Sioux artist; Hubert H. Humphrey, Vice President; Cheryl Ladd, actress; Ernest Orlando Lawrence, physicist; Russell Means, American Indian activist; George McGovern, politician; Arthur C. Mellette, first governor; Dorothy Provine, actress; Rain-in-the-Face, Hunkpapa Sioux chief; Red Cloud, chief of the Oglala Sioux; Ben Reifel, Brulé Sioux Congressman; Ole Edvart Rölvaag, writer; Sitting Bull, Chief of Hunkpappa Sioux; Norm Van Brocklin, football player; Mamie Van Doren, actress

TENNESSEE

Capital: Nashville
Governor: Don Sundquist, R (to Jan. 1999)
Lieut. Governor: John S. Wilder, D (to Jan. 1997)
Secy. of State: Riley C. Darnell, D (to Jan. 1997)
Atty. General: Charles W. Burson, D (to Aug. 1998)
State Treasurer: Steve Adams, D (to Jan. 1997)
Entered Union & (rank): June 1, 1796 (16)
Present constitution adopted: 1870; amended 1953, 1960, 1966, 1972, 1978
Motto: "Agriculture and Commerce" (1987)
Slogan: "Tennessee—America at its best!" (1965)
STATE SYMBOLS: flower, Iris (1933); **tree,** Tulip poplar (1947); **bird,** Mockingbird (1933); **horse,** Tennessee walking horse; **animal,** Raccoon (1971); **wild flower,** Passion flower (1973); **song,** "Tennessee Waltz" (1965)
Nickname: Volunteer State
Origin of name: Of Cherokee origin; the exact meaning is unknown
10 largest cities (1990 census): Memphis, 610,337; Nashville-Davidson (CC[1]), 510,784; Knoxville, 165,121; Chattanooga, 152,466; Clarksville, 75,494; Johnson City, 49,381; Jackson, 48,949; Murfreesboro, 44,922; Kingsport, 36,365; Germantown, 32,893
Land area & (rank): 41,220 sq mi. (106,759 sq km) (34)

Geographic center: In Rutherford Co., 5 mi. NE of Murfreesboro
Number of counties: 95
Largest county (1990 census): Shelby, 826,330
State forests: 13 (150,000 ac.)
State parks: 50 (133,000 ac.)
1994 resident population est.: 5,175,000
1990 resident census population, sex, & (rank): 4,877,185 (17). **Male:** 2,348,928; **Female:** 2,528,257. **White:** 4,048,068 (83.0%); **Black:** 778,035 (16.0%); **American Indian, Eskimo, or Aleut:** 10,039 (0.2%); **Asian or Pacific Islander:** 31,839 (0.7%); **Other race:** 9,204 (0.2%); **Hispanic:** 32,741 (0.7%). **1990 percent population under 18:** 24.9; **65 and over:** 12.7; **median age:** 33.6.

1. Consolidated City.

First visited by the Spanish explorer de Soto in 1540, the Tennessee area would later be claimed by both France and England as a result of the 1670s and 1680s explorations of Marquette and Joliet, La Salle, and the Englishmen James Needham and Gabriel Arthur.

Great Britain obtained the region following the French and Indian War in 1763 and it was rapidly occupied by settlers moving in from Virginia and the Carolinas.

During 1784–87, the settlers formed the "state" of Franklin, which was disbanded when the region was allowed to send representatives to the North Carolina legislature. In 1790 Congress organized the territory south of the Ohio River and Tennessee joined the Union in 1796.

Although Tennessee joined the Confederacy during the Civil War, there was much pro-Union sentiment in the state, which was the scene of extensive military action.

The state is now predominantly industrial; the majority of its population lives in urban areas. Among the most important products are chemicals, textiles, apparel, electrical machinery, furniture, and leather goods. Other lines include food processing, lumber, primary metals, and metal products. The state is known as the U.S. hardwood-flooring center and ranks first in the production of marble, zinc, pyrite, and ball clay.

Tennessee is one of the leading tobacco-producing states in the nation and its farming income is also derived from livestock and dairy products as well as corn, cotton, and soybeans.

With six other states, Tennessee shares the extensive federal reservoir developments on the Tennessee and Cumberland River systems. The Tennessee Valley Authority operates a number of dams and reservoirs in the state.

Among the major points of interest: the Andrew Johnson National Historic Site at Greenville, American Museum of Atomic Energy at Oak Ridge, Great Smoky Mountains National Park, The Hermitage (home of Andrew Jackson near Nashville), Rock City Gardens near Chattanooga, and three National Military Parks.

Famous natives and residents: James Agee, writer; Eddy Arnold, singer; Chet Atkins, guitarist; Julian Bond, Georgia legislator; Davy Crockett, frontiersman; David G. Farragut, first American admiral; Lester Flatt, bluegrass musician; Tennessee Ernie Ford, singer; Abe Fortas, jurist; Aretha Franklin, singer; Nikki Giovanni, poet; Al Gore, Jr., vice president; Red Grooms, artist; Isaac Hayes, composer; Benjamin L. Hooks, civil rights activist; Cordell Hull, US Sec. of State; Andrew Jackson, president; Andrew Johnson, president; Estes Kefauver, legislator; Anita Kerr, singer; Grace Moore, soprano; Dolly Parton, singer; Minnie Pearl, singer and comedienne; James K. Polk, president; Grantland Rice, sportswriter; Carl Rowan, journalist; Wilma Rudolph, sprinter; Sequoya, Cherokee scholar and educator; Cybil Shepherd, actress; Dinah Shore, actress, singer; Tina Turner, singer; Alvin York, World War I hero

TEXAS

Capital: Austin
Governor: George W. Bush, R (to Jan. 1999)
Lieut. Governor: Bob Bullock, D (to Jan. 1999)
Secy. of State: Tony Garza, R (Apptd. by Gov.)
Treasurer: Martha Whitehead, R (to Jan. 1999)
Comptroller: John Sharp, D (to Jan. 1999)
Atty. General: Dan Morales, D (to Jan. 1999)
Entered Union & (rank): Dec. 29, 1845 (28)
Present constitution adopted: 1876
Motto: Friendship
STATE SYMBOLS: flower, Bluebonnet (1901); **tree,** Pecan (1919); **bird,** Mockingbird (1927); **song,** "Texas, Our Texas" (1929); **fish,** Guadalupe bass (1989); **seashell,** Lightning whelk (1987); **dish,** Chili (1977); **folk dance,** Square dance (1991); **fruit,** Texas Red grapefruit (1993); **gem,** Texas blue topaz (1969); **gemstone cut,** Lone Star Cut (1977); **grass,** Sideoats grama (1971); **reptile,** Horned lizard (1993); **stone,** Petrified palmwood (1969)
Nickname: Lone Star State
Origin of name: From an Indian word meaning "friends"
10 largest cities (1990 census): Houston, 1,630,553, 1993: 1,630,864; Dallas, 1,006,877, 1993: 1,007,617; San Antonio, 935,933; El Paso, 515,342; Austin, 465,622; Fort Worth, 447,619; Arlington, 261,721; Corpus Christi, 257,453; Lubbock, 186,206; Garland, 180,650
Land area & (rank): 261,914 sq mi. (678,358 sq km) (2)
Geographic center: In McCulloch Co., 15 mi. NE of Brady
Number of counties: 254
Largest county (1995 est.): Harris, 3,043,400
State forests: 5 (7,609 ac.)
State parks: 218 (206 developed)
1995 resident population est.: 18,418,300
1990 resident census population, sex, & (rank): 16,986,510 (3). **Male:** 8,365,963; **Female:** 8,620,547. **White:** 12,774,762 (75.2%); **Black:** 2,021,632 (11.9%); **American Indian, Eskimo, or Aleut:** 65,877 (0.4%); **Asian or Pacific Islander:** 319,459 (1.9%); **Other race:** 1,804,780 (10.6%); **Hispanic:** 4,339,905 (25.5%). **1990 percent population under 18:** 28.5; **65 and over:** 10.1; **median age:** 30.8.

Spanish explorers, including Cabeza de Vaca and Coronado, were the first to visit the region in the 16th and 17th centuries, settling at Ysleta near El Paso in 1682. In 1685, La Salle established a short-lived French colony at Matagorda Bay.

Americans, led by Stephen F. Austin, began to settle along the Brazos River in 1821 when Texas was controlled by Mexico, recently independent from Spain. In 1836, following a brief war between the American settlers in Texas and the Mexican government, and famous for the battles of the Alamo and San Jacinto, the Independent Republic of Texas was proclaimed with Sam Houston as president.

After Texas became the 28th U.S. state in 1845, border disputes led to the Mexican War of 1846–48.

Today, Texas, second only to Alaska in land area, leads all other states in such categories as oil, cattle, sheep, and cotton. Possessing enormous natural resources, Texas is a major agricultural state and an industrial giant.

Sulfur, salt, helium, asphalt, graphite, bromine, natural gas, cement, and clays give Texas first place in mineral production. Chemicals, oil refining, food processing, machinery, and transportation equipment are among the major Texas manufacturing industries.

Texas ranches and farms produce beef cattle, poultry, rice, pecans, peanuts, sorghum, and an extensive variety of fruits and vegetables.

Millions of tourists spend well over $20.6 billion annually visiting more than 70 state parks, recreation areas, and points of interest such as the Gulf Coast resort area, the Lyndon B. Johnson Space Center in Houston, the Alamo in San Antonio, the state capital in Austin, and the Big Bend and Guadalupe Mountains National Parks.

Famous natives and residents: Alvin Ailey, choreographer; Mary Kay Ash, cosmetics entrepreneur; Steven Fuller Austin, founding father of Texas; Gene Autry, singer and actor; Carol Burnett, comedienne; Cyd Charisse, actress and dancer; Denton A. Cooley, heart surgeon; Joan Crawford, actress; Dwight David Eisenhower, President, general; A.J. Foyt, auto racer; Ben Hogan, golfer; Howard Hughes, industrialist and film producer; Jack Johnson, boxer; Lyndon B. Johnson, President; George Jones, singer; Scott Joplin, composer; Trini Lopez, singer; Mary Martin, singer and actress; Spanky McFarland, actor; Audie Murphy, actor and war hero; Chester Nimitz, admiral; Sandra Day O'Connor, jurist; Buck Owens, singer; Katherine Anne Porter, novelist; Wiley Post, aviator; Dan Rather, TV newscaster; Robert Rauschenberg, painter; Tex Ritter, singer; Rip Torn, actor and director; Tommy Tune, dancer and choreographer; Dooley Wilson, actor and musician; Babe Didrikson Zaharias, athlete, golfer

UTAH

Capital: Salt Lake City
Governor: Michael O. Leavitt, R (to Jan. 1997)
Lieut. Governor: Olene Walker, R (to Jan. 1997)
Atty. General: Jan Graham, D (to Jan. 1997)
Organized as territory: Sept. 9, 1850
Entered Union & (rank): Jan. 4, 1896 (45)
Present constitution adopted: 1896
Motto: Industry
STATE SYMBOLS: flower, Sego lily (1911); **tree,** Blue spruce (1933); **bird,** California gull (1955); **emblem,** Beehive (1959); **song,** "Utah, We Love Thee" (1953); **gem,** Topaz; **animal,** Rocky Mountain Elk (1971); **fish,** Rainbow trout (1971); **insect,** Honeybee (1983); **grass,** Indian rice grass (1990); **fossil,** Allosaurus (1988)
Nickname: Beehive State
Origin of name: From the Ute tribe, meaning "people of the mountains"
10 largest cities (1990 census): Salt Lake City, 159,936; West Valley City, 86,976; Provo, 86,835; Sandy, 75,058; Orem, 67,561; Ogden, 63,909; Taylorsville-Bennion, 52,351; West Jordan, 42,892; Layton, 41,784; Bountiful, 36,659
Land area & (rank): 82,168 sq mi. (212,816 sq km) (12)
Geographic center: In Sanpete Co., 3 mi. N. of Manti
Number of counties: 29
Largest county (1990 census): Salt Lake, 725,956
National parks: 5
National monuments: 6
State parks/forests: 44 (64,097 ac.)
1994 resident population est.: 1,908,000
1990 resident census population, sex, & (rank): 1,722,850 (35). **Male:** 855,759; **Female:** 867,091. **White:** 1,615,845 (93.8%); **Black:** 11,576 (0.7%); **American Indian, Eskimo, or Aleut:** 24,283 (1.4%); **Asian or Pacific Islander:** 33,371 (1.9%); **Other race:** 37,775 (2.2%); **Hispanic:** 84,597 (4.9%). **1990 percent population under 18:** 36.4; **65 and over:** 8.7; **median age:** 26.2.

The region was first explored for Spain by Franciscan friars, Escalante and Dominguez in 1776. In 1824 the famous American frontiersman Jim Bridger discovered the Great Salt Lake.

Fleeing the religious persecution encountered in eastern and middle-western states, the Mormons reached the Great Salt Lake in 1847 and began to build Salt Lake City. The U.S. acquired the Utah region in the treaty ending the Mexican War in 1848 and the first transcontinental railroad was completed with the driving of a golden spike at Promontory Summit in 1869.

Mormon difficulties with the federal government about polygamy did not end until the Mormon Church renounced the practice in 1890, six years before Utah became a state.

Rich in natural resources, Utah has long been a leading producer of copper, gold, silver, lead, zinc, and molybdenum. Oil has also become a major product. Utah, with Colorado and Wyoming, shares rich oil shale deposits. Utah also has large deposits of low sulphur coal.

Ranked eighth among the states in number of sheep in 1989, Utah also produces large crops of alfalfa, winter wheat, and beans. Utah's farmlands and crops require extensive irrigation.

Utah's traditional industries of agriculture and mining are being complemented by increased tourism business and growing aerospace, biomedical, and computer-related businesses. Utah is home to computer software giants Novell and WordPerfect.

Utah is a great vacationland with 11,000 miles of fishing streams and 147,000 acres of lakes and reservoirs. Among the many tourist attractions are Arches, Bryce Canyon, Canyonlands, Capitol Reef, and Zion National Parks; Dinosaur, Natural Bridges, and Rainbow Bridge National Monuments; the Mormon Tabernacle in Salt Lake City; and Monument Valley. Salt Lake City will be the site of the 2002 Winter Olympics.

Famous natives and residents: Maude Adams, actress; Roseanne Arnold, actress; Frank Borzage, film director and producer; John M. Browning, inventor; Butch Cassidy, outlaw; Laraine Day, actress; Bernard De Voto, writer; Avard Fairbanks, sculptor; Philo Farnsworth, television pioneer; Jake Garn, senator; John Gilbert, actor; J. Willard Marriott, restaurant and hotel chain founder; Peter Skene Ogden, fur trader, trapper; Merlin Olsen, football player; Donny Osmond, Marie Osmond, singers; Ivy Baker Priest, U.S. treasurer; Lee Greene Richards, painter; Leroy Robertson, composer; Brent Scowcroft, business executive, consultant; Reed Smoot, first Morman elected to U.S. Senate; Mack Swain, actor; Everett Thorpe, painter; Robert Walker, actor; James Woods, actor; Brigham Young, territory governor and religious leader; Loretta Young, actress

VERMONT

Capital: Montpelier
Governor: Howard B. Dean, D (to Jan. 1997)
Lieut. Governor: Barbara W. Snelling, R (to Jan. 1997)
Secy. of State: James F. Milne, R (to Jan. 1997)
Treasurer: James H. Douglas, R (to Jan. 1997)
Auditor of Accounts: Edward S. Flanagan D (to Jan. 1997)
Atty. General: Jeffrey L. Amestoy, R (to Jan. 1997)
Entered Union & (rank): March 4, 1791 (14)
Present constitution adopted: 1793
Motto: Vermont, Freedom, and Unity
STATE SYMBOLS: flower, Red clover (1894); **tree,** Sugar maple (1949); **bird,** Hermit thrush (1941); **animal,** Morgan horse (1961); **insect,** Honeybee (1978); **song,** "Hail, Vermont!" (1938)
Nickname: Green Mountain State
Origin of name: From the French "vert mont," meaning "green mountain"
10 largest cities (1990 census): Burlington, 39,127; Rutland, 18,230; South Burlington, 12,809; Barre, 9,482; Es-

sex Junction, 8,396; Montpelier, 8,247; St. Albans, 7,339; Winooski, 6,649; Newport, 4,434; Bellows Falls, 3,313
Land area & (rank): 9,249 sq mi. (23,956 sq km) (43)
Geographic center: In Washington Co., 3 mi. E of Roxbury
Number of counties: 14
Largest county (1990 census): Chittenden, 131,761
State forests: 34 (113,953 ac.)
State parks: 45 (31,325 ac.)
1994 resident population est.: 580,000
1990 resident census population, sex, & (rank): 562,758 (48). **Male:** 275,492; **Female:** 287,266. **White:** 555,088 (98.6%); **Black:** 1,951 (0.3%); **American Indian, Eskimo, or Aleut:** 1,696 (0.3%); **Asian or Pacific Islander:** 3,215 (0.6%); **Other race:** 808 (0.1%); **Hispanic:** 3,661 (0.7%). **1990 percent population under 18:** 25.4; **65 and over:** 11.8; **median age:** 33.0.

The Vermont region was explored and claimed for France by Samuel de Champlain in 1609 and the first French settlement was established at Fort Ste. Anne in 1666. The first English settlers moved into the area in 1724 and built Fort Drummer on the site of present-day Brattleboro. England gained control of the area in 1763 after the French and Indian War.

First organized to drive settlers from New York out of Vermont, the Green Mountain Boys, led by Ethan Allen, won fame by capturing Fort Ticonderoga from the British on May 10, 1775, in the early days of the Revolution.

In 1777 Vermont adopted its first constitution abolishing slavery and providing for universal male suffrage without property qualifications. In 1791 Vermont became the first state after the original 13 to join the Union.

Vermont leads the nation in the production of monument granite, marble, and maple syrup. It is also a leader in the production of talc.

In ratio to population, Vermont keeps more dairy cows than any other state. Vermont's soil is devoted to dairying, truck farming, and fruit growing because the rugged, rocky terrain discourages extensive farming.

Principal industrial products include electrical equipment, fabricated metal products, printing and publishing, and paper and allied products.

Tourism is a major industry in Vermont. Vermont's many famous ski areas include Stowe, Killington, Mt. Snow, Bromley, Jay Peak, and Sugarbush. Hunting and fishing also attract many visitors to Vermont each year. Among the many points of interest are the Green Mountain National Forest, Bennington Battle Monument, the Calvin Coolidge Homestead at Plymouth, and the Marble Exhibit in Proctor.

Famous natives and residents: Chester A. Arthur, President; Orson Bean, actor; Calvin Coolidge, President; George Dewey, admiral; John Dewey, philosopher and educator; Stephen A. Douglas, politician; James Fisk, financial speculator; Wilbur Fisk, clergyman and educator; Richard Morris Hunt, architect; William Morris Hunt, painter; Elisha Otis, inventor; Moses Pendleton, choreographer; Joseph Smith, religious leader; Ernest Thompson, actor, writer; Rudy Vallee, singer and band leader; Henry Wells, pioneer entrepreneur (Wells Fargo & Co.); Brigham Young, religious leader

VIRGINIA

Capital: Richmond
Governor: George Allen, R (to Jan. 1998)
Lieut. Governor: Donald S. Beyer, Jr., D (to Jan. 1998)
Secy. of the Commonwealth: Betsy David Beamer (apptd. by governor)

Comptroller: William E. Landsidle (apptd. by governor)
Atty. General: James S. Gilmore, III, R (to Jan. 1998)
Entered Union & (rank): June 25, 1788 (10)
Present constitution adopted: 1970
Motto: *Sic semper tyrannis* (Thus always to tyrants)
STATE SYMBOLS: flower, American dogwood (1918);
  bird, Cardinal (1950); **dog,** American foxhound (1966);
  shell, Oyster shell (1974); **song,** "Carry Me Back to
  Old Virginia" (1940)
Nicknames: The Old Dominion; Mother of Presidents
Origin of name: In honor of Elizabeth "Virgin Queen" of
  England
10 largest cities (1990 census): Virginia Beach, 393,069;
  Norfolk, 261,229; Richmond, 203,056; Newport News,
  170,045; Chesapeake, 151,976; Hampton, 133,793; Alex-
  andria, 111,183; Portsmouth, 103,907; Roanoke, 96,907;
  Lynchburg, 66,049
Land area & (rank): 39,598 sq mi. (102,558 sq km) (37)
Geographic center: In Buckingham Co., 5 mi. SW of
  Buckingham
Number of counties: 95, plus 41 independent cities
Largest county (1990 census): Fairfax, 818,384
State forests: 8 (49,566 ac.)
State parks and recreational parks: 27, plus 3 in proc-
  ess of acquisition and/or development (42,722 ac.)[1]
1994 resident population est.: 6,552,000
1990 resident census population, sex, & (rank):
  6,187,358 (12). **Male:** 3,033,974; **Female:** 3,153,384.
  White: 4,791,739 (77.4%); **Black:** 1,162,994 (18.8%);
  American Indian, Eskimo, or Aleut: 15,282 (0.2%);
  Asian or Pacific Islander: 159,053 (2.6%); **Other race:**
  58,290 (0.9%); **Hispanic:** 160,288 (2.6%). **1990 percent
  population under 18:** 24.3; **65 and over:** 10.7; **median
  age:** 32.6.

1. Does not include portion of Breaks Interstate Park
(Va.-Ky., 1,200 ac.) which lies in Virginia.

The history of America is closely tied to that of
Virginia, particularly in the Colonial period. Jamestown, founded in 1607, was the first permanent English settlement in North America and slavery was introduced there in 1619. The surrenders ending both
the American Revolution (Yorktown) and the Civil
War (Appomattox) occurred in Virginia. The state is
called the "Mother of Presidents" because eight chief
executives of the United States were born there.

Today, Virginia has a large number of diversified
manufacturing industries including transportation
equipment, textiles, food processing and printing. Other
important lines are electronic and other electric equipment, chemicals, apparel, lumber and wood products,
furniture, and industrial machinery and equipment.

Agriculture remains an important sector in the Virginia economy and the state ranks among the top 10
in the U.S. in tomatoes, tobacco, peanuts, summer
potatoes, turkeys, apples, broilers, and sweet potatoes. Other crops include corn, vegetables, and
barley. Famous for Smithfield hams, Virginia also has
a large dairy industry.

Coal mining accounts for roughly 75% of Virginia's mineral output, and lime, kyanite, and stone are
also mined.

Points of interest include Mt. Vernon and other places
associated with George Washington; Monticello, home
of Thomas Jefferson; Stratford, home of the Lees; Richmond, capital of the Confederacy and of Virginia; and
Williamsburg, the restored Colonial capital.

The Chesapeake Bay Bridge-Tunnel spans the
mouth of Chesapeake Bay, connecting Cape Charles
with Norfolk. Consisting of a series of low trestles,
two bridges and two mile-long tunnels, the complex
is 18 miles (29 km) long. It was opened in 1964.

Other attractions are the Shenandoah National

Park, Fredericksburg and Spotsylvania National Military Park, the Booker T. Washington birthplace near
Roanoke, Arlington House (the Robert E. Lee Memorial), the Skyline Drive, and the Blue Ridge National
Parkway.

Famous natives and residents: Richard Arlen, actor;
Arthur Ashe, tennis player; Pearl Bailey, singer; Russell
Baker, columnist; Warren Beatty, actor; George Bingham, painter; Richard E. Byrd, polar explorer; Willa
Cather, novelist; Roy Clark, country music artist; William Clark, explorer; Henry Clay, statesman; Joseph
Cotten, actor; Ella Fitzgerald, singer; William H. Harri-
son, President; Patrick Henry, statesman; Sam Hous-
ton, political leader; Thomas Jefferson, President;
Robert E. Lee, Confederate general; Meriwether Lewis,
explorer; Shirley MacLaine, actress; James Madison,
President; John Marshall, jurist; Cyrus McCormick, in-
ventor; James Monroe, President; Opechancanough,
Powhatan leader; John Payne, actor; Walter Reed,
army surgeon; Matthew Ridgway, ex-Army Chief of
Staff; Bill "Bojangles" Robinson, dancer; George C.
Scott, actor; Sam Snead, golfer; James "Jeb" Stuart,
Confederate army officer; Zachary Taylor, President;
Nat Turner, civil rights leader; John Tyler, President;
Booker T. Washington, educator; George Washington,
first President; Woodrow Wilson, President; Tom
Wolfe, journalist

WASHINGTON

Capital: Olympia
Governor: Mike Lowry, D (to 1997)
Lieut. Governor: Joel Pritchard, R (to 1997)
Secy. of State: Ralph Munro, R (to 1997)
State Treasurer: Daniel K. Grimm, D (to 1997)
Atty. General: Christine Gregoire, D (to 1997)
Organized as territory: March 2, 1853
Entered Union & (rank): Nov. 11, 1889 (42)
Present constitution adopted: 1889
Motto: *Al-Ki* (Indian word meaning "by and by")
STATE SYMBOLS: flower, Coast Rhododendron (1949);
  tree, Western hemlock (1947); **bird,** Willow goldfinch
  (1951); **fish,** Steelhead trout (1969); **gem,** Petrified
  wood (1975); **colors,** Green and gold (1925); **song,**
  "Washington, My Home" (1959); **folk song,** "Roll On
  Columbia, Roll On" (1987); **dance,** Square dance (1979)
Nicknames: Evergreen State; Chinook State
Origin of name: In honor of George Washington
10 largest cities (1990 census): Seattle, 516,259; Spokane, 177,196; Tacoma, 176,664; Bellevue, 86,874; Everett, 69,961; Yakima, 54,827; Bellingham, 42,155; Renton,
  41,688
Land area & (rank): 66,582 sq mi. (172,447 sq km) (20)
Geographic center: In Chelan Co., 10 mi. WSW of Wenatchee
Number of counties: 39
Largest county (1991 census): King, 1,542,300
State forest lands: 1,922,880 ac.
State parks: 215 (231,861 ac.)[1]
1994 resident population est.: 5,343,000
1990 resident census population, sex, & (rank):
  4,866,692 (18). **Male:** 2,413,747; **Female:** 2,452,945.
  White: 4,308,937 (88.5%); **Black:** 149,801 (3.1%); **American Indian, Eskimo, or Aleut:** 81,483 (1.7%); **Other
  race:** 115,513 (2.4%); **Hispanic:** 214,570 (4.4%). **1990
  percent population under 18:** 25.9; **65 and over:** 11.8;
  median age: 33.1.

1. Parks and undeveloped areas administered by State
Parks and Recreation Commission. Dept. of Wildlife administers wildlife and recreation areas totaling 428,989.5
acres.

As part of the vast Oregon Country, Washington
territory was visited by Spanish, American, and Brit-

ish explorers—Bruno Heceta for Spain in 1775, the American Capt. Robert Gray in 1792, and Capt. George Vancouver for Britain in 1792–94. Lewis and Clark explored the Columbia River region and coastal areas for the U.S. in 1805–06.

Rival American and British settlers and conflicting territorial claims threatened war in the early 1840s. However, in 1846 the Oregon Treaty set the boundary at the 49th parallel and war was averted.

Washington is a leading lumber producer. Its rugged surface is rich in stands of Douglas fir, hemlock, ponderosa and white pine, spruce, larch, and cedar. The state holds first place in apples, lentils, dry edible peas, hops, pears, red raspberries, spearmint oil, and sweet cherries, and ranks high in apricots, asparagus, grapes, peppermint oil, and potatoes. Livestock and livestock products make important contributions to total farm revenue and the commercial fishing catch of salmon, halibut, and bottomfish makes a significant contribution to the state's economy.

Manufacturing industries in Washington include aircraft and missiles, shipbuilding and other transportation equipment, lumber, food processing, metals and metal products, chemicals, and machinery.

The Columbia River contains one third of the potential water power in the U.S., harnessed by such dams as the Grand Coulee, one of the greatest power producers in the world. Washington has over 1,000 dams built for a variety of purposes including irrigation, power, flood control, and water storage. Its abundance of electrical power makes Washington one of the nation's major producers of refined aluminum.

Among the major points of interest: Mt. Rainier, Olympic, and North Cascades. In 1980, Mount St. Helens, a peak in the Cascade Range in Southwestern Washington erupted on May 18th. Also of interest are National Parks; Whitman Mission and Fort Vancouver National Historic Sites; and the Pacific Science Center and Space Needle in Seattle.

Famous natives and residents: Bob Barker, TV host; Dyan Cannon, actress; Carol Channing, actress; Judy Collins, singer; Bing Crosby, singer, actor; Bob Crosby, musician; Merce Cunningham, choreographer; Howard Duff, actor; Frances Farmer, actress; Jimi Hendrix, guitarist; Frank Herbert, writer; Robert Joffrey, choreographer; Gypsy Rose Lee, entertainer; Hank Ketcham, cartoonist; Mary McCarthy, novelist; Guthrie McClintic, theatrical producer and director; John McIntire, actor; Robert Motherwell, artist; Patrice Munsel, soprano; Ella Raines, actress; Jimmy Rogers, singer; Francis Scobee, astronaut; Seattle, Dwamish, Suquamish chief; Jeff Smith, TV cook; Smohalla, Indian prophet and chief; Adam West, actor; Martha Wright, singer; Audrey Wurdemann, poet

WEST VIRGINIA

Capital: Charleston
Governor: Gaston Caperton, D (to Jan. 1997)
Secy. of State: Ken Heckler, D (to Jan. 1997)
State Auditor: Glen Gainer (to Jan. 1997)
Atty. General: Darrell McGraw, D (to Jan. 1997)
Entered Union & (rank): June 20, 1863 (35)
Present constitution adopted: 1872
Motto: *Montani semper liberi* (Mountaineers are always free)
STATE SYMBOLS: flower, Rhododendron (1903); **tree,** Sugar maple (1949); **bird,** Cardinal (1949); **animal,** Black bear (1973); **colors,** Blue and gold (official) (1863); **songs,** "West Virginia, My Home Sweet Home," "The West Virginia Hills," and "This Is My West Virginia" (adopted by Legislature in 1947, 1961, and 1963 as official state songs)

Nickname: Mountain State
Origin of name: Same as for Virginia
10 largest cities (1990 census): Charleston, 57,287; Huntington, 54,844; Wheeling, 34,882; Parkersburg, 33,862; Morgantown, 25,879; Weirton, 22,124; Fairmont, 20,210; Beckley, 18,296; Clarksburg, 18,059; Martinsburg, 14,073
Land area & (rank): 24,087 sq mi. (62,384 sq km) (41)
Geographic center: In Braxton Co., 4 mi. E of Sutton
Number of counties: 55
Largest county (1990 census): Kanawha, 207,619
State forests: 9 (79,502 ac.)
State parks: 34 (74,508 ac.)
1994 resident population est.: 1,822,000
1990 resident census population, sex, & (rank): 1,793,477 (34). **Male:** 861,536; **Female:** 931,941. **White:** 1,725,523 (96.2%); **Black:** 56,295 (3.1%); **American Indian, Eskimo, or Aleut:** 2,458 (0.1%); **Asian or Pacific Islander:** 7,459 (0.4%); **Other race:** 1,742 (0.1%); **Hispanic:** 8,489 (0.5%). **1990 percent population under 18:** 24.7; **65 and over:** 15.0; **median age:** 35.4.

West Virginia's early history from 1609 until 1863 is largely shared with Virginia, of which it was a part until Virginia seceded from the Union in 1861. Then the delegates of 40 western counties formed their own government, which was granted statehood in 1863.

First permanent settlement dates from 1731 when Morgan Morgan founded Mill Creek. In 1742 coal was discovered on the Coal River, an event that would be of great significance in determining West Virginia's future.

The state usually ranks 3rd in total coal production with about 15% of the U.S. total. It also is a leader in steel, glass, aluminum, and chemical manufactures; natural gas, oil, quarry products, and hardwood lumber.

Major cash farm products are poultry and eggs, dairy products, apples, and feed crops. Nearly 80% of West Virginia is covered with forests.

Tourism is increasingly popular in mountainous West Virginia and visitors spent $2.475 billion in 1990. More than a million acres have been set aside in 34 state parks and recreation areas and in 9 state forests, and national forests.

Major points of interest include Harpers Ferry and New River Gorge National River, The Greenbrier and Berkeley Springs resorts, the scenic railroad at Cass, and the historic homes in the Eastern Panhandle.

Famous natives and residents: George Brett, baseball player; Pearl S. Buck, author; Phyllis Curtin, soprano; Martin R. Delany, first Black Army major; Billy Dixon, frontiersman and scout; Joanne Dru, actress; Thomas "Stonewall" Jackson, Confederate general; John S. Knight, publisher; Don Knotts, actor; Peter Marshall, TV host; Whitney D. Morrow, banker and diplomat; Mary Lou Retton, gymnast; Walter Reuther, labor leader; Eleanor Steber, soprano; Lewis L. Strauss, naval officer and scientist; Cyrus Vance, government official; William Lyne Wilson, legislator and university president; Chuck Yeager, test pilot and Air Force general

WISCONSIN

Capital: Madison
Governor: Tommy G. Thompson, R (to Jan. 1999)
Lieut. Governor: Scott McCallum, R (to Jan. 1999)
Secy. of State: Douglas J. La Follette, D (to Jan. 1999)
State Treasurer: Jack C. Voight, R (to Jan. 1999)
Atty. General: James E. Doyle, D (to Jan. 1999)
Superintendent of Public Instruction: John Benson Nonpartisan (to July 1997)
Organized as territory: July 4, 1836
Entered Union & (rank): May 29, 1848 (30)

Present constitution adopted: 1848
Motto: Forward
STATE SYMBOLS: flower, Wood violet (1949); **tree,** Sugar maple (1949); **grain,** corn (1990); **bird,** Robin (1949); **animal,** Badger; **"wild life" animal,** White-tailed deer (1957); **"domestic" animal,** Dairy cow (1971); **insect,** Honeybee (1977); **fish,** Musky (Muskellunge) (1955); **song,** "On Wisconsin"; **mineral,** Galena (1971); **rock,** Red Granite (1971); **symbol of peace:** Mourning Dove (1971); **soil,** Antigo Silt Loam (1983); **fossil,** Trilobite (1985); **dog,** American Water Spaniel (1986); **beverage,** Milk (1988); **grain,** Corn (1990); **dance,** Polka (1994)
Nickname: Badger State
Origin of name: French corruption of an Indian word whose meaning is disputed
10 largest cities (1990 census): Milwaukee, 628,088; Madison, 191,262; Green Bay, 96,466; Racine, 84,298; Kenosha, 80,352; Appleton, 65,695; West Allis, 63,221; Waukesha, 56,958; Eau Claire, 56,856; Oshkosh, 55,006
Land area & (rank): 54,314 sq mi. (140,673 sq km) (25)
Geographic center: In Wood Co., 9 mi. SE of Marshfield
Number of counties: 72
Largest county (1990 census): Milwaukee, 959,275
State forests: 9 (476,004 ac.)
State parks & scenic trails: 45 parks, 14 trails (66,185 ac.)
1994 resident population est.: 5,082,000
1990 resident census population, sex, & (rank): 4,891,769 (16). **Male:** 2,392,935; **Female:** 2,498,834. **White:** 4,512,523 (92.2%); **Black:** 244,539 (5.0%); **American Indian, Eskimo, or Aleut:** 39,387 (0.8%); **Asian or Pacific Islander:** 53,583 (1.1%); **Other race:** 41,737 (0.9%); **Hispanic:** 93,194 (1.9%). **1980 percent population under 18:** 26.4; **65 and over:** 13.3; **median age:** 32.9.

The Wisconsin region was first explored for France by Jean Nicolet, who landed at Green Bay in 1634. In 1660 a French trading post and Roman Catholic mission were established near present-day Ashland.

Great Britain obtained the region in settlement of the French and Indian War in 1763; the U.S. acquired it in 1783 after the Revolutionary War. However, Great Britain retained actual control until after the War of 1812. The region was successively governed as part of the territories of Indiana, Illinois, and Michigan between 1800 and 1836, when it became a separate territory.

Wisconsin is a leading state in milk and cheese production. In 1993 the state ranked first in the number of milk cows (1,500,000) and produced 15.2% of the nation's total output of milk. Other important farm products are peas, beans, corn, potatoes, oats, hay, and cranberries.

The chief industrial products of the state are automobiles, machinery, furniture, paper, beer, and processed foods. Wisconsin ranks second among the 47 paper-producing states.

Wisconsin pioneered in social legislation, providing pensions for the blind (1907), aid to dependent children (1913), and old-age assistance (1925). In labor legislation, the state was the first to enact an unemployment compensation law (1932) and the first in which a workman's compensation law actually took effect. Wisconsin had the first state-wide primary-election law and the first successful income-tax law. In April 1984, Wisconsin became the first state to adopt the Uniform Marital Property Act. The act took effect on January 1, 1986.

The state has over 14,000 lakes, of which Winnebago is the largest. Water sports, ice-boating, and fishing are popular, as are skiing and hunting. Public parks and forests take up one seventh of the land,

with 45 state parks, 9 state forests, 14 state trails, 3 recreational areas, and 2 national forests.

Among the many points of interest are the Apostle Islands National Lakeshore; Ice Age National Scientific Reserve; the Circus World Museum at Baraboo; the Wolf, St. Croix, and Lower St. Croix national scenic riverways; and the Wisconsin Dells.

Famous natives and residents: Don Ameche, actor; Ray Chapman Andrews, naturalist and explorer; Walter Annenberg, media tycoon and philanthropist; Carrie Catt, woman suffragist; John R. Commons, economist; Tyne Daly, actress; August Derleth, author; Jeanne Dixon, seer; Zona Gale, novelist; Eric Heiden, skater; Woody Herman, band leader; Hildegarde, singer; Harry Houdini, magician; Hans V. Kaltenborne, journalist; Pee Wee King, singer; George F. Kennan, diplomat; Robert La Follette, politician; William D. Leahy, Fleet Admiral; Liberace, pianist; Charles Litel, actor; Allen Ludden, TV host; Alfred Lunt, actor; Frederic March, actor; Jackie Mason, comedian; John Ringling North, circus director; Pat O'Brien, actor; Georgia O'Keeffe, painter; Charlotte Rae, actress; William H. Rehnquist, jurist; Gena Rowlands, actress; Tom Snyder, newscaster; Spencer Tracy, actor; Thorstein Veblen, economist; Orson Welles, actor and producer; Thornton Wilder, author; Charles Winninger, actor; Frank Lloyd Wright, architect.

WYOMING

Capital: Cheyenne
Governor: Jim Geringer, R (to Jan. 1999)
Secy. of State: Diana Ohman, R (to Jan. 1999)
Auditor: Dave Ferrari, R (to Jan. 1999)
Supt. of Public Instruction: Judy Catchpole, R (to Jan. 1999)
Treasurer: Stanford S. Smith, R (to Jan. 1999)
Atty. General: Bill Hill, R (apptd. by Governor)
Organized as territory: May 19, 1869
Entered Union & (rank): July 10, 1890 (44)
Present constitution adopted: 1890
Motto: Equal rights (1955)
STATE SYMBOLS: flower, Indian paintbrush (1917); **tree,** Cottonwood (1947); **bird,** Meadowlark (1927); **gemstone,** Jade (1967); **insignia,** Bucking horse (unofficial); **song,** "Wyoming" (1955)
Nickname: Equality State
Origin of name: From the Delaware Indian word, meaning "mountains and valleys alternating"; the same as the Wyoming Valley in Pennsylvania
10 largest cities (1990 census): Cheyenne, 50,008; Casper, 46,742; Laramie, 26,687; Rock Springs, 19,050; Gillette, 17,635; Sheridan, 13,900; Green River, 12,711; Evanston, 10,903; Rawlins, 9,380; Riverton, 9,202
Land area & (rank): 97,105 sq mi. (251,501 sq km) (9)
Geographic center: In Fremont Co., 58 mi. ENE of Lander
Number of counties: 23, plus Yellowstone National Park
Largest county (1990 census): Laramie, 73,142
State forests: None
State parks and historic sites: 23 (58,498 ac.)
1995 resident population est.: 474,970
1990 resident census population, sex, & (rank): 453,588 (50). **Male:** 227,007; **Female:** 226,581. **White:** 427,061 (94.2%); **Black:** 3,606 (0.8%); **American Indian, Eskimo, or Aleut:** 9,479 (2.1%); **Asian or Pacific Islander:** 2,806 (0.6%); **Other race:** 10,636 (2.3%); **Hispanic:** 25,751 (5.7%). **1990 percent population under 18:** 29.9; **65 and over:** 10.4; **median age:** 32.0.

The U.S. acquired the territory from France as part of the Louisiana Purchase in 1803. John Colter, a fur-trapper, is the first white man known to have entered present Wyoming. In 1807 he explored the Yellowstone area and brought back news of its geysers and hot springs.

Robert Stuart pioneered the Oregon Trail across Wyoming in 1812–13 and, in 1834, Fort Laramie, the first permanent trading post in Wyoming, was built. Western Wyoming was obtained by the U.S. in the 1846 Oregon Treaty with Great Britain and as a result of the treaty ending the Mexican War in 1848.

When the Wyoming Territory was organized in 1869 Wyoming women became the first in the nation to obtain the right to vote. In 1925 Mrs. Nellie Tayloe Ross was elected first woman governor in the United States.

Wyoming's towering mountains and vast plains provide spectacular scenery, grazing lands for sheep and cattle, and rich mineral deposits.

Mining, particularly oil and natural gas, is the most important industry. Wyoming has the world's largest sodium carbonate (natrona) deposits and has the nation's second largest uranium deposits.

Wyoming ranks second among the states in wool production. In January 1994, its sheep numbered 810,000, exceeded only by Texas and California; it also had 1,410,000 cattle. Principal crops include wheat, oats, sugar beets, corn, potatoes, barley, and alfalfa.

Second in mean elevation to Colorado, Wyoming has many attractions for the tourist trade, notably Yellowstone National Park. Cheyenne is famous for its annual "Frontier Days" celebration. Flaming Gorge, the Fort Laramie National Historic Site, and Devils Tower and Fossil Butte National Monuments are other National points of interest.

Famous natives and residents: James Bridger, trapper, guide, storyteller; Dick Cheney, ex-Secretary of Defense; Buffalo Bill Cody; John Colter, trader and first white man to enter Wyoming; June E. Downey, educator; Thomas Fitzpatrick, mountain man and guide; Curt Gowdy, sportscaster; Tom Horn, detective; Isabel Jewell, actress; Velma Linford, writer; Esther Morris, first woman judge; Ted Olson, writer; John "Portugee" Phillips, frontiersman; Jackson Pollock, painter; Nellie Tayloe Ross, first woman elected governor of a state; Alan K. Simpson, senator; Jedediah S. Smith, mountain man and first American to reach California from the East; Alan Swallow, publisher, author; Willis Van Devanter, Supreme Court justice; Francis E. Warren, first state governor; Chief Washakie, chief of the Shoshone; James G. Watt, ex-Secretary of the Interior

U.S. Territories and Outlying Areas

PUERTO RICO

(Commonwealth of Puerto Rico)
Governor: Pedro Rosselló, New Progressive Party (to 1997)
Capital: San Juan
Land area: 3,459 sq mi. (8,959 sq km)
Song: "La Borinqueña"
1990 census population: 3,522,037
Languages: Spanish and English
Literacy rate: 90%
Labor force (1994): 1,203,000; 24% services, 22% government, 20% commerce, 16% manufacturing, 5% construction, 5% communications and transportation, 3% agriculture, 5% other
Ethnic divisions: Almost entirely Hispanic.

10 largest municipalities (1990 census): San Juan, 437,745; Bayamón, 220,262; Ponce, 187,749; Carolina, 177,806; Caguas, 133,447; Mayagüez, 100,371; Arecibo, 93,385; Guaynabo, 92,886; Toa Baja, 89,454; Trujillo Alto, 61,120

Gross product (FY 1994): $26.6 billion; per capita, $7,294; real growth rate, 2.6%

Land use: 13% cropland, 41% meadows and pastures, 20% forest and woodland, 26% other.

Environment: Subtropical marine climate; high central mountain range circled by coastal plains; abundant agricultural production and foliage fostered by natural irrigation in all regions except relatively arid south coast.

The Commonwealth of Puerto Rico is located in the Caribbean Sea, about 1,000 miles east southeast of Miami, Florida. A possession of the United States, it consists of the island of Puerto Rico—smallest of the Greater Antilles, measuring about 100 miles from east to west and 35 miles across—plus the adjacent islets of Vieques, Culebra and Mona.

Discovered by Christopher Columbus in 1493, Puerto Rico subsequently became the only New World colony of Spain that never waged a war for independence. Despite this lack of animosity toward Madrid, however, Puerto Ricans warmly welcomed invading United States troops during the Spanish-American War of 1898. Since then, Puerto Rico has remained an unincorporated U.S. territory. Its people were granted

American citizenship in 1917; were permitted to elect their own governor, beginning in 1948; and now fully administer their internal affairs under a constitution approved by the U.S. Congress in 1952.

From 1940 to 1968, Puerto Rican politics was dominated by a party advocating voluntary association with the U.S. Since then, a party favoring U.S. statehood has won four of seven gubernatorial elections—including that of 1992.

Puerto Rican voters have twice had the opportunity to express themselves directly on political status alternatives. In 1967, the outcome was commonwealth 60%; statehood 39%; independence 1%. In 1993, commonwealth dropped to 48.6%; statehood rose to 46.3%; independence polled 4.4%; and 0.6% of the ballots were blank or spoiled.

Under the commonwealth formula, residents of Puerto Rico lack voting representation in Congress and the right to participate in Presidential elections. Also, funding caps limit their access to several key Federal programs. As U.S. citizens, Puerto Ricans are subject to military service and most Federal laws. Residents of the Commonwealth pay no Federal income tax on locally-generated earnings, but Puerto Rico government income tax rates are set at a level that closely parallels Federal-plus-state levies on the mainland.

Puerto Rico is a major hub of Caribbean commerce, finance, tourism, and communications. San Juan is one of the world's busiest cruise ship ports, and Puerto Rico hosts hundreds of modern manufacturing facilities. Its population's standard of living is among the highest in the hemisphere.

Famous natives and residents: Deborah Carthy-Deu, Miss Universe 1985; José Cabranes, U.S. appeals court judge; Pablo Casals, cellist; Roberto Clemente, baseball player; Angel Cordero, jockey; Justino Diaz, opera singer; Beatriz "Gigi" Fernández, U.S. Olympic tennis gold medalist; Luis Ferré, political leader, philanthropist; José Ferrer, actor; José Luis González, writer; Gabriel Guerra-Mondragón, U.S. Ambassador to Chile; Raúl Juliá, actor; Marisol Malaret, Miss Universe 1970; Jacobo Morales, filmmaker; Rita Moreno, actress; Luis Muñoz-Marín, political leader; Antonia Novello, U.S. Surgeon General; Miguel Piñero, dramatist; Chita Rivera, actress; Juan "Chi Chi" Rodríguez, golfer; José Serrano, (D–NY), member of Congress; Dayanara Torres, Miss Universe 1993; Juan Torruella, chief judge of U.S. First Circuit Court of Appeals.

GUAM

(Territory of Guam)
Governor: Carl T.C. Gutierrez
Capital: Agaña (1990) 1,139
Land area: 209 sq mi. (541 sq km)
1990 census population: 133,152
Population (est. 1995): 145,249; **Average annual rate of natural increase:** 2.53%; **birth rate:** 26.16/1000; **infant mortality rate:** 15.17/1000; **density per square mi.:** 698.2
1993 est. net migration: 3 migrants per 1,000 population
Ethnic divisions: Chamorro, 47%; Filipino, 25%; Caucasian, 10%; Chinese, Japanese, Korean, and other 18%
Language: English and Chamorro, most residents bilingual; Japanese also widely spoken
Literacy rate: 96%
Labor force (1994): 66,460; 30.6% government, 69.4% private
Gross national product (1994 est.): $3 billion, per capita $20,000; inflation, 11% (1993); unemployment, 7.3% (Dec. 1994) **Industries:** U.S. military, tourism, transshipment services, concrete products, printing and publishing, food processing, textiles.

Guam, the largest of the Mariana Islands, is independent of the trusteeship assigned to the U.S. in 1947. It was acquired by the U.S. from Spain in 1898 (occupied 1899) and was placed under the Navy Department.

In World War II, Guam was seized by the Japanese on Dec. 11, 1941; but on July 21, 1944, it was once more in U.S. hands.

On Aug. 1, 1950, President Truman signed a bill which granted U.S. citizenship to the people of Guam and established self-government. However, the people do not vote in national elections. In 1972 Guam elected its first delegate to the U.S. Congress. The Executive Branch of the Guam government is under the general supervision of the U.S. Secretary of the Interior. In November 1970, Guam elected its first Governor.

Currently, Guam is an unincorporated, organized territory of the United States. It is "unincorporated" because not all of the provisions of the U.S. constitution apply to the territory. It is an "organized" territory because the Congress provided the territory with an Organic Act in 1950 which organized the government much as a constitution would.

Guam's economy is based on two main sources of revenue: tourism and U.S. military spending (U.S. Naval and Air Force bases on Guam). Federal expenditures (FY93): $952 million; $472 million for wages and salaries and $166 million for purchases in the local economy.

The tourist industry has grown rapidly over the past 20 years. Visitors numbered about 1,078,720 in 1994. About 60% of the labor force works in the private sector and the rest for government.

U.S. VIRGIN ISLANDS

(Virgin Islands of the United States)
Governor: Alexander A. Farrelly
Capital: Charlotte Amalie (on St. Thomas), population 1990: 12,331
1990 population: 101,809 (St. Croix, 50,139; St. Thomas, 48,166; St. John, 3,504)
Population (est. July 1994): 97,564; average annual rate of natural increase: –0.52; birth rate: 19.4/1000; infant mortality rate: 12.5/1000; density per sq mi.: 739.1
Land area: 132 sq mi (342 sq km): St. Croix, 84 sq. mi. (218 sq km), St. Thomas, 32 sq mi (83 sq km), St. John, 20 sq mi. (52 sq km)
Ethnic divisions: West Indian, 74% (45% born in the

Virgin Islands and 29% born elsewhere in the West Indies), U.S. mainland, 13%; Puerto Rican, 5%; other, 8%; black, 80%, white, 15%, other, 5%; 14% of Hispanic origin.
Language: English (official), but Spanish and various dialects are widely spoken.
Literacy rate: 90%
Labor force (1992): 48,620
Gross domestic product (1989): $1.34 billion, per capita $11,052
Economic summary: Exports $2.8 billion (f.o.b. 1990), refined petroleum products. Imports $3.3 billion (c.i.f. 1990), crude oil, foodstuffs, consumer goods, building materials. Major trading partners: U.S., Puerto Rico.

The Virgin Islands, consisting of nine main islands and some 75 islets, were discovered by Columbus in 1493. Since 1666, England has held six of the main islands; the other three (St. Croix, St. Thomas, and St. John), as well as about 50 of the islets, were eventually acquired by Denmark, which named them the Danish West Indies. In 1917, these islands were purchased by the U.S. from Denmark for $25 million.

Congress granted U.S. citizenship to Virgin Islanders in 1927; and, in 1931, administration was transferred from the Navy to the Department of the Interior. Universal suffrage was given in 1936 to all persons who could read and write the English language. The Governor was elected by popular vote for the first time in 1970; previously he had been appointed by the President of the U.S. A unicameral 15-man legislature serves the Virgin Islands, and Congressional legislation gave the islands a non-voting Representative in Congress.

The "Constitution" of the Virgin Islands is the Revised Organic Act of 1954 in which the U.S. Congress defines the three branches of the territorial government, i.e., the Executive Branch, the Legislative Branch, and the Judicial Branch. Residents of the islands substantially enjoy the same rights as those enjoyed by mainlanders with one important exception: citizens of the U.S. who are residents may not vote in presidential elections.

Tourism is the primary economic activity, accounting for more than 70% of the GDP and 70% of employment. Tourist expenditures are estimated to be over $791.5 million annually. In 1992, 1,963,800 tourists arrived in the Virgin Islands; about two-thirds were day visitors on cruise ships. The manufacturing sector consists of textile, electronics, pharmaceutical, and watch assembly plants. The agricultural sector is small with most food imported. International business and financial services are a small but growing component of the economy. The world's largest petroleum refinery is at St. Croix.

AMERICAN SAMOA

(Territory of American Samoa)
Governor: A.P. Lutali
Lieut. Governor: Tauese Pita Sunia
Capital: Pago Pago, population 1990: 3,519
Population (est. July 1994): 55,223; average rate of natural increase: 3.86%; birth rate 36.6/1000; infant mortality rate: 18.7/1000; density per sq mi.: 717.1
Ethnic divisions: Samoan (Polynesian) 89%; Caucasian, 2%; Tongan 4%; other 6%
Language: Samoan (closely related to Hawaiian and other Polynesian languages) and English; most people are bilingual
Literacy rate: 99%

Labor force (1990): 13,250
Land area: 77 sq mi (199 sq km)
Gross domestic product (1991): $128 million; per capita, $2,600; real growth rate: n.a.; inflation: 7%
Aid (1991): $21.0 million in operational funds and $1,227,000 in construction for capital-improvement projects from the U.S. Department of Interior.

American Samoa, a group of five volcanic islands and two coral atolls located some 2,600 miles south of Hawaii in the South Pacific Ocean, is an unincorporated, unorganized territory of the U.S., administered by the Department of the Interior.

By the Treaty of Berlin, signed Dec. 2, 1899, and ratified Feb. 16, 1900, the U.S. was internationally acknowledged to have rights extending over all the islands of the Samoa group east of longitude 1715 west of Greenwich. On April 17, 1900, the chiefs of Tutuila and Anuu'u ceded those islands to the U.S. In 1904, the King and chiefs of Manu'a ceded the islands of Ofu, Olosega and Tau (composing the Manu'a group) to the U.S. Swains Island, some 214 miles north of Samoa, was included as part of the territory by Act of Congress March 4, 1925; and on Feb. 20, 1929, Congress formally accepted sovereignty over the entire group and placed the responsibility for administration in the hands of the President. From 1900 to 1951, by Presidential direction, the Department of the Navy governed the territory. On July 1, 1951, administration was transferred to the Department of the Interior. The first Constitution for the territory was signed on April 27, 1960, and was revised in 1967.

Congress has provided for a non-voting delegate to sit in the House of Representatives in 1981.

The people of American Samoa are U.S. nationals, not U.S. citizens. Like U.S. citizens, they owe allegiance to the United States.

Economic activity is strongly linked to the U.S., with which American Samoa does 80–90% of its foreign trade. Tuna fishing and tuna processing plants are the backbone of the private sector, with canned tuna the primary export. The tuna canneries and the government are by far the two largest employers. Other economic activities include a slowly developing tourist industry. Transfers from the U.S. government add substantially to American Samoa's economic well-being.

BAKER, HOWLAND, AND JARVIS ISLANDS

These Pacific islands were not to play a role in the extraterritorial plans of the U.S. until May 13, 1936. President F. D. Roosevelt, at that time, placed them under the control and jurisdiction of the Secretary of the Interior for administration purposes.

The three islands have a tropical climate with scant rainfall, constant wind, and a burning sun.

Baker Island is a saucer-shaped atoll with an area of approximately one square mile. It is about 1,650 miles from Hawaii.

Howland Island, 36 miles to the northwest, is approximately one and a half miles long and half a mile wide. It is a low-lying, nearly level, sandy, coral island surrounded by a narrow fringing reef.

Howland Island is related to the tragic disappearance of Amelia Earhart and Fred J. Noonan during the round-the-world flight in 1937. They left New Guinea on July 2, 1937, for Howland, but were never seen again.

Jarvis Island is several hundred miles to the east and is approximately one and three quarter miles long by one mile wide. It is a sandy coral island surrounded by a a narrow fringing reef.

Baker, Howland, and Jarvis have been uninhabited since 1942. In 1974, these islands became part of the National Wildlife Refuge System, administered by the U.S. Fish & Wildlife Service, Department of the Interior.

JOHNSTON ATOLL

Population (est. July 1994): 327
Land area: 1.08 sq. mi. (2.8 sq km); density per sq mi.: 302.7

Johnston is a coral atoll about 700 miles southwest of Hawaii. It consists of four small islands—Johnston Island, Sand Island, Hikina Island, and Akau Island—which lie on a reef about 9 miles long in a northeast-southwest direction.

The atoll was discovered by Capt. Charles James Johnston of *H.M.S. Cornwallis* in 1807. In 1858 it was claimed by Hawaii, and later became a U.S. possession.

Johnston Atoll is a Naval Defensive Sea Area and Airspace Reservation and is closed to the public. The airspace entry control has been suspended but is subject to immediate reinstatement without notice. The administration of Johnston Atoll is under the jurisdiction of the Defense Nuclear Agency, Commander, Johnston Atoll (FCDNA), APO San Francisco, CA 96305.

The Atoll is managed cooperatively by the Defense Nuclear Agency and the Fish and Wildlife Service of the U.S. Department of the Interior as part of the National Wildlife Refuge system.

KINGMAN REEF

Kingman Reef, located about 1,000 miles south of Hawaii, was discovered by Capt. E. Fanning in 1798, but named for Capt. W. E. Kingman, who rediscovered it in 1853. The reef, drying only on its northeast, east and southeast edges, is of atoll character. The reef is triangular in shape, with its apex northward; it is about 9.5 miles long, east and west, and 5 miles wide, north and south, within the 100-fathom curve. The island is uninhabited.

A United States possession, Kingman Reef is a Naval Defensive Sea Area and Airspace Reservation, and is closed to the public. The Airspace Entry Control has been suspended, but is subject to immediate reinstatement without notice. No vessel, except those authorized by the Secretary of the Navy, shall be navigated in the area within the 3-mile limit.

MIDWAY ISLANDS

Midway Islands, lying about 1,150 miles west-northwest of Hawaii, were discovered by Captain N. C. Brooks of the Hawaiian bark *Gambia* on July 5, 1859, in the name of the United States. The atoll was formally declared a U.S. possession in 1867, and in 1903 Theodore Roosevelt made it a naval reservation. The island was renamed "Midway" by the U.S. Navy in recognition of its geographic location on the route between California and Japan.

Midway Islands consist of a circular atoll, 6 miles in diameter, and enclosing two islands. Eastern Island, on its southeast side, is triangular in shape, and about 1.2 miles long. Sand Island, on its south side, is about 2.25 miles long in a northeast-southwest direction.

A National Wildlife Refuge was set up on Midway under an agreement with the Fish and Wildlife Service of the U.S. Dept. of the Interior.

The Midway Islands are within a Naval Defensive Sea Area. The Navy Department maintains an installation and has jurisdiction over the atoll. Permission to enter the Naval Defensive Sea Area must be obtained in advance from the Commander Third Fleet (N31), Pearl Harbor, HI 96860.

Midway has no indigenous population. It is currently populated with several U.S. military personnel.

WAKE ISLAND

Total area: 2.5 sq mi. (6.5 sq km)
Comparative size: about 11 times the size of The Mall in Washington, D.C.
Population (Jan. 1990): no indigenous inhabitants; temporary population consists of 11 U.S. Air Force personnel, 27 U.S. civilians, and 151 Thai contractors.
Economy: The economic activity is limited to providing services to U.S. military personnel and contractors on the island. All food and manufactured goods must be imported.

Wake Island, about halfway between Midway and Guam, is an atoll comprising the three islets of Wilkes, Peale, and Wake. They were discovered by the British in 1796 and annexed by the U.S. in 1899. The entire area comprises 3 square miles and has no native population. In 1938, Pan American Airways established a seaplane base and Wake Island has been used as a commercial base since then. On Dec. 8, 1941, it was attacked by the Japanese, who finally took possession on Dec. 23. It was surrendered by the Japanese on Sept. 4, 1945.

The President, acting pursuant to the Hawaii Omnibus Act, assigned responsibility for Wake to the Secretary of the Interior in 1962. The Department of Transportation exercised civil administration of Wake through an agreement with the Department of the Interior until June 1972, at which time the Department of the Air Force assumed responsibility for the Territory.

The Air Force had declared Wake Island excess to its operational requirements and the island will be returned to the Department of the Interior's jurisdiction on Oct. 1, 1994 if it is not utilized for other military activities.

CAROLINE ISLANDS

The Caroline Islands, east of the Philippines and south of the Marianas, include the Yap, Truk, and the Palau groups and the islands of Ponape and Kusqie, as well as many coral atolls.

The islands are composed chiefly of volcanic rock, and their peaks rise 2,000 to 3,000 feet above sea level. Chief exports of the islands are copra, fish products, and handicrafts.

Formerly members of the U.S. Trust Territory of the Pacific, all of the group but Palau joined the Federated States of Micronesia.

MARIANA ISLANDS

(The Commonwealth of The Northern Mariana Islands)
Governor: Lorenzo I. De Leon Guerrero (1989)
Total area: 184.17 sq mi. (477 sq km)
Population (est. July 1994): 49,799; growth rate: 3.04%; birth rate: 35/1000; infant mortality: 37.9/1000; density per sq mi.: 270.4. The population of the Commonwealth of the Northern Mariana Islands (CNMI) is concentrated on the three largest inhabited islands: Saipan, the government seat and commerce center; Rota; and Tinian. Of the CNMI's total population, approximately 22,063 are registered aliens, a 670% increase since 1980.
Language: English is the official language, but Chamorro and Carolinian are the spoken native tongues. Japanese is also spoken in many of the hotels and shops, reflecting a heavy tourism industry.
Literacy rate: 97%
Economy: The government of the CNMI benefits substantially from U.S. financial assistance. Gross national product (1992): $541 million; GNP reflects U.S. spending. Per capita: $11,500; exports: $263.4 million (f.o.b. 1991 est.): manufactured goods, garments, bread, pastries, concrete blocks, light iron work. Imports: $392.4 million (c.i.f. 1991 est.): food, construction equipment, materials.

The Mariana Islands, east of the Philippines and south of Japan, include the islands of Guam, Rota, Saipan, Tinian, Pagan, Guguan, Agrihan, and Aguijan. Guam, the largest, is independent of the trusteeship, having been acquired by the U.S. from Spain in 1898. (For more information, *see* the entry on Guam in this section.) The remaining islands, referred to as the Commonwealth of the Northern Mariana Islands (CNMI) became part of the United States pursuant to P.L. 94-241 as of November 3, 1986.

Tourism is the leading earning export employing about 50% of the work force. Seventy-five percent of the tourists are Japanese.

Agricultural products are coconuts, fruits, cattle, vegetables.

Minor Islands

NAVASSA ISLAND

Total area: 2 sq mi. (5.2 sq km)
Comparative size: About nine times the size of The Mall in Washington, D.C.

Navassa Island is strategically located in the Caribbean Sea, 99.4 miles (160 km) south of the U.S. Naval Base at Guantanamo, Cuba, between Cuba, Haiti, and Jamaica. It is an unincorporated territory of the United States, administered by the U.S. Coast Guard. The U.S. is responsible for its defense.

The island's terrain consists of a raised coral and limestone plateau, flat to undulating, and ringed by vertical cliffs, 30 to 50 feet (9 to 15 meters) high.

Navassa is uninhabited and transiet Haitian fishermen and others camp there.

PALMYRA ATOLL

Total area: 4.6 sq mi. (11.9 sq km)
Comparative size: About 20 times the size of The Mall in Washington, D.C.

Palmyra Atoll is an unincorporated territory of the U.S., privately owned, but administered by the Office of Territorial and International Affairs, U.S. Department of the Interior. The U.S. is responsible for its defense.

It is located in the North Pacific Ocean, 994 miles (1,600 kilometers) south–southwest of Honolulu, almost halfway between Hawaii and American Samoa. The Atoll consists of about 50 islets covered with dense vegetation, coconut trees, and balsa-like trees almost 100 feet (30 meters) high. Palmyra Atoll is uninhabited.

Tabulated Data on State Governments

	Governor		Legislature[1]					Highest Court[2]		
State	Term, years	Annual salary	Member-ship U[3]	L[4]	Term, yrs. U[3]	L[4]	Salaries of members[5]	Mem-bers	Term, years	Annual salary
Alabama	4 [10]	$81,151	35	105	4	4	$10 per diem[21]	9	6	$107,125 [6]
Alaska	4	81,648	20	40	4	2	24,012[25] per annum	5	([8])	99,996 [6]
Arizona	4	75,000	30	60	2	2	15,000 per annum	5	6	101,130 [6]
Arkansas	4	60,000	35	100	4	2	12,500 per annum	7	8	95,216 [6]
California	4	114,000	40	80	2	37	72,500 per annum	7	12	127,276 [6]
Colorado	4	70,000 [29]	35	65	4	2	17,500 per annum	7	10	88,000 [6]
Connecticut	4	78,000	36	151	2	2	16,760 per annum	7	8	106,553 [6]
Delaware	4 [9]	95,000	21	41	4	2	26,200[4] per annum	5	12	108,800
Florida	4 [10]	95,000	40	120	4	2	18,000 per annum	7	6	100,444
Georgia[10]	4	98,166	56	180	2	2	10,854. per annum	7	6	109,459
Hawaii	4	94,780	25	51	4	2	32,000 per year	5	10	93,780 [6]
Idaho	4	85,000	35	70	2	2	12,360[35] per annum[5]	5	6	79,183 [6]
Illinois	4	110,537	59	118	4-2	2	42,265 per annum	7	10	112,124
Indiana	4 [10]	77,200	50	100	4	2	11,600 per annum	5	([24])	81,000
Iowa	4	76,700	50	100	4	2	18,100 per annum	9	8	90,300 [6]
Kansas	4	76,091	40	125	4	2	119 per diem[22]	7	6	82,005 [6]
Kentucky	4 [7]	86,353	38	100	4	2	110 per diem[36]	7	8	83,752
Louisiana	4	95,000	39	105	4	4	16,800[5] per annum	7	10	85,000
Maine	4	70,000 [16]	35	151	2	2	25,000[37] per annum[16]	7	7	77,300
Maryland	4 [10]	120,000	47	141	4	4	29,700 per annum	7	10	91,700
Massachusetts	4	90,000	40	160	2	2	46,410 per annum	7	([13])	95,880 [6]
Michigan	4	112,025 [16]	38	110	4 [32]	2	47,723[38] per annum	7	8	111,941
Minnesota	4	109,053	67	134	4	2	27,979[5] per annum[16]	7	6	83,494
Mississippi	4	75,600	52	122	4	4	10,000 per session[5]	9	8	76,000 [6]
Missouri	4 [9]	94,563	34	163	4 [39]	2	24,313[5] per annum	7	12	95,897 [6]
Montana	4	53,006	50	100	4	2	55 per diem[16]	7	8	64,452
Nebraska	4 [10]	65,000	49 [11]	—	4 [10,11]	—	12,000 per biennium	7	6	88,157
Nevada	4	90,000	21	42	4	2	7,800[5] per biennium	5	6	85,000
New Hampshire	2	86,235	24	([12])	2	2	200 per biennium	5	([13])	98,611 [6]
New Jersey	4 [10]	130,000	40	80	4 [14]	2	35,000[30] per annum	7	7 [15]	112,000
New Mexico	4 [40]	90,000	42	70	4	2	75 per diem	5	8	77,250 [6]
New York	4	130,000	61	150	2	2	57,500 per annum	7	14	120,000 [6]
North Carolina	4 [41]	91,938 [16]	50	120	2	2	13,026 per annum[16]	7	8	89,532 [6]
North Dakota	4	69,650 [29]	49	98	4	2	90 per diem[16 23]	5	10	75,936 [6,29]
Ohio	4	115,752	33	99	4	2	42,427 per annum	7	6	101,150 [6]
Oklahoma	4 [10]	70,000	48	101	4	2	32,000 [16] per annum	([19])	6	87,700 [6]
Oregon	4 [10]	80,000	30	60	4	2	1,092[42] per month	7	6	83,700
Pennsylvania	4 [10]	105,000	50	203	4	2	47,000 per annum	7	10	105,000 [6]
Rhode Island	2	69,900	50	100	2	2	5[17] per diem[17]	5	([18])	104,403
South Carolina	4	103,998	46	124	4	2	10,400 per annum	5	10	92,986 [6]
South Dakota	4 [10]	79,875	35	70	2	2	8,000 per biennium	5	3 [26]	74,241 [6]
Tennessee	4	85,000	33	99	4	2	16,500[5] per annum	5	8	99,240
Texas	4	99,122	31	150	4	2	7,200[5] per annum	([20])	6	94,686 [6]
Utah	4	79,600	29	75	4	2	85 per diem[16]	5	([33])	94,800 [6]
Vermont	2	93,122	30	150	2	2	480 [16,28] per week[28]	5	6	80,031 [6]
Virginia	4 [7]	110,000	40	100	4	2	17,640[31] per annum	7	12	107,373 [6]
Washington	4 [43]	121,000	49	98	4 [44]	2	25,900 per annum	9	6	107,200
West Virginia	4 [10]	72,000	34	100	4	2	15,000 [16] per annum	5	12	72,000
Wisconsin	4	101,861	33	99	4	2	38,056 per annum	7	10	97,756
Wyoming	4	95,000	30	60	4	2	80 [16,27] per diem	5	8	85,000

1. Known as *General Assembly* in Ark., Colo., Conn., Del., Ga., Ill., Iowa, Ind., Ky., Md., Mo., N.C., Ohio, Pa., R.I., S.C., Tenn., Vt., Va.; *Legislative Assembly* in N.D., Ore.; *General Court* in Mass., N.H.; *Legislature* in other states. Meets biennially in Calif., Ky., Me., Mont., Nev., N.J., N.D., Ore., Pa., Texas. Wyoming Legislature has regular general session on odd numbered years and a budget session on even numbered years. Arkansas General Assembly meets every other year for 60 days in odd numbered years. Ohio General Assembly meets when deemed necessary. Legislative bodies meet annually in other states. 2. Known as *Court of Appeals* in Md., N.Y.; *Supreme Court of Virginia* in Va.; *Supreme Judicial Court* in Me., Mass.; *Supreme Court* in other states. 3. Upper house: *Senate* in all states. 4. Lower house: *Assembly* in Calif., Nev., N.Y., Wis.; *House of Delegates* in Md., Va., W.Va.; *General Assembly* in N.J.; *House of Representatives* in other states. 5. Base salary. Does not include additional payments for expenses, mileage, special sessions, etc., or additional per diem payments. 6. Chief Justice receives a higher salary. 7. Cannot succeed himself. 8. Appointed for 3 years; thereafter subject to approval or rejection on a nonpartisan ballot for 10-year term. 9. May serve only 2 terms, consecutive or otherwise. 10. May not serve 3rd consecutive term. 11. Unicameral legislature. 12. Constitutional number: 375-400. 13. Until 70 years old. 14. When term begins in Jan. of 2nd year following U.S. census, term shall be 2 years. 15. 2nd term receive tenure, mandatory retirement at 70. 16. Plus expense allowance. 17. For current legislators or $10,000 per year without a pension. Future legislators must take the $10,000. 18. Term of good behavior. 19. Nine members in Supreme Court, highest in civil cases; five in Court of Criminal Appeals. 20. Nine members in Supreme Court, highest in civil cases; nine in Court of Criminal Appeals. 21. Plus $50 per diem expenses up to $2,280 per month when

they are in session. 22. When in session, plus $600/mo. when not in session. 23. Plus $180 per month when not in session. 24. Appointed for 2 years; thereafter elected popularly for 10-year term. 25. Senate President and House Speaker receive an additional $500 per year. 26. Subsequent terms, 8 years. 27. $125 per annum. 28. To limit of $13,000 per biennium; $100 per diem for Special Session. 29. As of July 1, 1996, governor's salary jumps to $71,042 and the judges to $77,448. 30. Each legislator receives $70,000 annually for appointment of personal staff aides. 31. Senate $18,000. 32. Every 10 years (the year after census) term is only for 2 years. 33. Appointed by governor. Up for re-election at first general election that takes place at least 3 years after appointment. After that, face a retention election every 10 years. 34. Senator's salary higher. 35. $3,000 additional for speaker and president pro tem of the senate. 36. When in session, plus $950 a month when not in session. 37. For the 2-year term. 38. Expense accounts. 39. Legislators may serve only eight years in each house, 16 combined. 40. May serve two terms in office; after that ineligible to be governor until one term has expired. 41. May only serve two consecutive terms. 42. Plus $75 per day for expenses during session. 43. No person is eligible who would have served during eight of the previous 14 years. 44. Have term limitations. NOTE: Salaries are rounded to nearest dollar. Source: Information Please questionnaires to the states.

Land and Water Area of States, 1990

(in square miles)

State	Rank (total area)	Land[1] area	Water[2] area	Total area	State	Rank (total area)	Land[1] area	Water[2] area	Total area
Alabama	30	50,750.23	1,672.71	52,422.94	Montana	4	145,556.34	1,489.82	147,046.16
Alaska	1	570,373.55	86,050.59	656,424.14	Nebraska	16	76,877.73	480.67	77,358.40
Arizona	6	113,642.26	364.00	114,006.26	Nevada	7	109,805.89	761.02	110,566.91
Arkansas	29	52,075.29	1,107.07	53,182.36	New Hampshire	46	8,969.36	381.57	9,350.93
California	3	155,973.09	7,734.06	163,707.15	New Jersey	47	7,418.84	1,303.11	8,721.95
Colorado	8	103,729.54	370.78	104,100.32	New Mexico	5	121,364.54	233.69	123,598.23
Connecticut	48	4,845.39	698.26	5,543.65	New York	27	47,223.85	7,250.71	54,474.56
Delaware	49	1,954.62	534.76	2,489.38	North Carolina	28	48,718.08	5,103.27	53,821.35
Dist. of Columbia—		61.41	6.95	68.36	North Dakota	19	68,994.24	1,709.59	70,703.83
Florida	22	53,997.08	11,761.00	65,758.08	Ohio	34	40,952.59	3,874.94	44,827.53
Georgia	24	57,918.73	1,522.49	59,441.22	Oklahoma	20	68,678.57	1,224.33	69,902.90
Hawaii	43	6,423.34	4,508.24	10,931.58	Oregon	9	96,002.58	2,383.17	98,385.75
Idaho	14	82,750.93	822.84	83,573.77	Pennsylvania	33	44,819.61	1,238.63	46,058.24
Illinois	25	55,593.29	2,324.55	57,917.84	Rhode Island	50	1,044.98	500.12	1,545.10
Indiana	38	35,870.18	549.91	36,420.09	South Carolina	40	30,111.12	1,895.99	32,007.11
Iowa	26	55,874.90	400.64	56,275.54	South Dakota	17	75,897.74	1,223.72	77,121.46
Kansas	15	81,823.02	458.98	82,282.00	Tennessee	36	41,219.52	926.49	42,146.01
Kentucky	37	39,732.31	678.93	40,411.24	Texas	2	261,914.26	6,686.70	268,600.96
Louisiana	31	43,566.03	8,277.44	51,843.47	Utah	13	82,168.15	2,735.97	84,904.12
Maine	39	30,864.55	4,522.78	35,387.33	Vermont	45	9,249.33	365.67	9,615.00
Maryland	42	9,774.65	2,632.80	12,407.45	Virginia	35	39,597.79	3,171.09	42,768.88
Massachusetts	44	7,837.98	2,716.81	10,554.79	Washington	18	66,581.95	4,720.70	71,302.65
Michigan	11	56,809.18	40,001.04	96,810.22	West Virginia	41	24,086.55	144.89	24,231.44
Minnesota	12	79,616.66	7,326.05	86,942.71	Wisconsin	23	54,313.71	11,189.50	65,503.21
Mississippi	32	46,913.64	1,519.95	48,433.59	Wyoming	10	97,104.55	713.56	97,818.11
Missouri	21	68,898.01	810.80	69,708.81	**U.S. Total**		**3,536,341.73**	**251,083.35**	**3,787,425.08**

1. Dry land and land temporarily or partially covered by water, such as marshland, swamps, etc.; streams and canals under one-eighth statute mile wide; and lakes, reservoirs, and ponds under 40 acres. 2. Permanent inland water surface, such as lakes, reservoirs, and ponds having an area of 40 acres or more; streams, sloughs, estuaries, and canals one-eighth statute mile or more in width; deeply indented embayments and sounds, and other coastal waters behind or sheltered by headlands or islands separated by less than 1 nautical mile of water, and islands under 40 acres in area. Excludes areas of oceans, bays, sounds, etc. lying within U.S. jurisdiction but not defined as inland water. *Source:* Department of Commerce, Bureau of the Census.

Texas Now Second Largest

Source: Census and You, Bureau of the Census.

Texas passed New York to become the Nation's second largest state behind California, according to new 1994 population estimates from the Census Bureau. Texas expanded its population by 356,000 between 1993 and 1994 to reach 18.4 million. The last time Texas changed population rank was in 1973: it outgrew Pennsylvania and became third largest.

California was by far the most populous state, with an estimated 1994 population of 31.4 million. New York dropped to third at 18.2 million.

Eight of the ten fastest-growing states in the country were in the West. Nevada led all states, with a 5.4 percent gain from 1993 to 1994.

Two states—Rhode Island and Connecticut (each

−3,000) and the District of Columbia (−9,000) experienced population declines. In fact, Vermont passed the District of Columbia in population size and is our 49th largest state.

California (272,000), New York (101,000), and Texas (75,000) had the highest net international migration and the largest natural increases (births minus deaths)—California (358,000), Texas (188,000), and New York (114,000).

The Nation, as a whole, expanded its population from 257.8 million in 1993 to 260.3 million in 1994, an increase of 2.6 million or 1 percent. About 30 percent or 762,000 of the growth was attributed to international migration.

U.S. CITIES

50 Largest Cities of the United States

(According to the 1990 Census)

Data supplied by Bureau of the Census and by the cities in response to *Information Please* questionnaires. Ranking of 50 largest cities (April 1990 census data). Civilian labor force and unemployment figures (Annual averages, 1992); per capita personal income (1989); average daily temperature: *(County and City Data Book)*. NOTE: Persons of Hispanic origin may be of any race.

ALBUQUERQUE, N.M.

Mayor: Martin J. Chavez
1990 census population, sex & (rank): 384,736 (38); **% change,** 15.6; **Male,** 186,584; **Female,** 198,152; **White,** 301,010; **Black,** 11,484 (3.0%); **American Indian, Eskimo, or Aleut,** 11,708 (3.0%); **Asian or Pacific Islander,** 6,660 (1.7%); **Other race,** 53.874; **Hispanic origin,** 132,706 (34.5%). **1990 percent population under 18:** 25.0%; **65 and over:** 11.1%; **median age:** 32.5.
Land area: 137 sq mi. (356.2 sq km); **Alt.:** 4,958 ft.
Avg. daily temp: Jan., 34.8° F; July, 78.8° F
Churches: 211; **City-owned parks:** 169; **Radio stations:** 43 (AM, 19; FM, 24); **Television stations:** 11
CIVILIAN LABOR FORCE: 224,003; **Unemployed:** 10,305, **Percent:** 4.6; **Per capita personal income:** $15,806
Chamber of Commerce: Greater Albuquerque Chamber of Commerce, 401 2nd St., N.W., Albuquerque, N.M. 87102. Albuquerque Hispano Chamber of Commerce, 1520 Central Ave., S.E., Albuquerque, N.M. 87106

Albuquerque is the largest city in New Mexico and the seat of Bernalillo county. It is situated in west central New Mexico on the upper Rio Grande River. Early Spanish settlers arrived there in the mid-1600s. The old town was founded in 1706 by Don Francisco Cuervo y Valdés, the Governor of New Mexico, and named after the Duke of Alburquerque, the viceroy of New Spain. During the Civil War, Confederate forces briefly occupied the city in 1862. The new town section was founded in 1880. In 1883, Albuquerque became the county seat and was incorporated as a city in 1891.

The city is noted as a center for health and medical services in the region, and government agencies, nuclear research, banking, and tourism are important to the economy. There is a growing high-tech center in Albuquerque and Intel Corp.'s largest manufacturing facility is located there.

Famous natives: Erna Fergusson, author; Annabeth Gish, actress; Fred Haney, baseball player, executive; Ernie Pyle, WWII war correspondent; Slim Summerville, actor; Al and Bobby Unser, auto racers

ATLANTA, GA.

Mayor: Bill Campbell (to Jan. 1998)
1990 census population, sex, & (rank): 394,017 (36); **% change,** –7.3; **Male,** 187,877; **Female,** 206,140; **White,** 122,327; **Black,** 264,262 (67.1%); **American Indian, Eskimo, or Aleut,** 563 (0.1%); **Asian or Pacific Islander,** 3,498 (0.9%); **Other race,** 3,367; **Hispanic origin,** 7,525 (1.9%). **1990 percent population under 18:** 24.1; **65 and over:** 11.3; **median age:** 31.5.
City land area: 136 sq mi. (352.2 sq km); **Alt.:** Highest, 1,050 ft; lowest, 940
Avg. daily temp.: Jan., 41.9° F; July, 78.6° F
Churches (20-county area): 1,500; **City-owned parks:** 277 (3,178 ac.); **Radio stations (20-county area):** AM, 7; FM, 20; **Television stations (20-county area):** 7 commercial; 2 PBS

CIVILIAN LABOR FORCE: 1,846,646; **Unemployed:** 86,060, **Percent:** 4.7; **Per capita personal income:** $17,689
Chamber of Commerce: Atlanta Chamber of Commerce, 235 International Blvd., Atlanta, Ga. 30301-1740; Information is gathered on the 20-county MSA

Atlanta, the largest city and capital of Georgia, is the seat of Fulton county. It is situated in the northwest part of the state at the base of the Blue Ridge Mountains near the Chattahoochee River. The first European settler was Hardy Ivy who built a cabin there in 1833.

The town was founded as Terminus in 1837 as the end of the Georgia railroad line (Western and Atlantic Railroad) and became incorporated as Marthasville in 1843 in honor of ex-governor Lumpkin's daughter Martha. It was renamed Atlanta in 1845 and incorporated as a city in 1847. Its name was suggested by the railroad's chief engineer, J. Edgar Thomson, and was derived from its location at the end of the Georgia and Atlantic railroad line. The city later became the capital of Georgia in 1868.

During the Civil War, the city was burned and almost completely destroyed by General W.T. Sherman in November 1864. It was quickly rebuilt after the war and it grew rapidly due to the expansion of the railroads in the southwest. Atlanta's diverse economy is led by the service, communications, retail trade, manufacturing, and finance and insurance industries. The convention business is also important, and the 1996 Summer Olympic Games will be held there.

Famous natives: Hank Aaron, baseball player; Arrested Development, recording artists; Jimmy Carter, former President; Ray Charles, singer; James Dickey, poet; Mattivilda Dobbs, soprano; Walt Frazier, basketball player; Oliver Hardy, comedian; Evander Holyfield, boxer; Allan Jackson, singer; Bobby Jones, golfer; DeForest Kelley, actor; Martin Luther King, Jr., civil rights leader, Nobel Peace Prize winner; Gladys Knight, singer; Kriss Kross, recording artists; Margaret Mitchell, novelist; Bert Parks, entertainer; Eric Roberts, actor; Julia Roberts, actress; Ferroll Sams, author; Doug Stone, singer; Pamela Stone, comedienne; Gwen Torrence, Olympic athlete; Lee Tracy, actor; Travis Tritt, singer; Ted Turner, TBS, CNN founder; Jane Withers, actress; Joanne Woodward, actress; Andrew Young, civil rights activist

AUSTIN, TEX.

Mayor: Bruce Todd (to May 1997)
1990 census population, sex, & (rank): 465,622 (27); **% change,** 34.6; **Male,** 232,473; **Female,** 233,149; **White,** 328,542; **Black,** 57,868 (12.4%); **American Indian, Eskimo, or Aleut,** 1,756 (0.4%); **Asian or Pacific Islander,** 14,141 (3.0%); **Other race,** 63,315; **Hispanic origin,** 106,868 (23.0%). **1990 percent population under 18:** 23.1%; **65 and over:** 7.4%; **median age:** 28.9
Land area: 116 sq mi. (300 sq km); **Alt.:** From 425 ft. to over 1000 ft. elevation

Avg. daily temp.: Jan., 49.1° F; July, 84.7° F
Churches: 353 churches, representing 45 denominations;
City-owned parks and playgrounds: 169 (11,800 ac.);
Radio stations: AM, 6; FM, 12; **Television stations:** 3
commercial; 1 PBS; 1 independent
CIVILIAN LABOR FORCE: 285,190; **Unemployed:** 16,115,
Percent: 5.7; **Per capita personal income:** $16,113
Chamber of Commerce: Greater Austin Chamber of
Commerce, P.O. Box 1967, Austin, Tex. 78767

Austin, the capital and seat of Travis county, is the
fifth largest city in Texas. It is situated in the south
central part of the state on the Colorado River. The
site was called Waterloo in 1838 and in 1839 was
incorporated as a city and chosen to become the capital of the independent Republic of Texas. Waterloo
was renamed Austin in honor of Stephen F. Austin,
the founder of the Texas Republic. It became the permanent capital of the state of Texas in 1870.

Austin's growth was spurred by several developments after the Civil War—the railroads reached the
city in the 1870s; it was crossed by the important
Chisholm cattle trail, and it became the seat of the
state university in 1883.

Austin, the state capital, has a growing commercial
and diversified manufacturing sectors. Civilian government employment is 28% of the labor force and is
important to the economy. As home to the University
of Texas, Austin is a major research and development, and nationally-recognized high technology center. The city has a new convention center downtown.

Famous natives: Don Baylor, baseball player, manag-
er; Earl Campbell, football player; Liz Carpenter, au-
thor; Dabney Coleman, actor; Ben Crenshaw, golfer;
Michael Dell, founder Dell Computer Corp.; Tobe
Hooper, film director; Lady Bird Johnson, former First
Lady; Tom Kite, golfer; James Michener, author; Willie
Nelson, musician; Amado Pena, artist; Darrell Royal,
legendary UT football coach; Zachary Scott, actor;
Jerry Jeff Walker, musician; Dalhart Windberg, artist

BALTIMORE, MD.

Mayor: Kurt L. Schmoke (to Dec. 1995)
1990 census population, sex, & (rank): 736,014 (13); %
change, –6.4; **Male,** 343,513; **Female,** 392,501; **White:**
287,753; **Black:** 435,768 (59.2%); **American Indian,
Eskimo, or Aleut,** 2,555 (0.3%); **Asian or Pacific Islander:** 7,942 (1.1%); **Other race:** 1,996; **Hispanic origin:** 7,602 (1.0%). **1990 percent population under 18:**
24.4; **65 and over:** 13.7; **Median age:** 32.6.
Land area: 80.3 sq mi. (208 sq km); **Alt.:** Highest, 490 ft;
lowest, sea level
Avg. daily temp.: Jan., 35.5° F; July, 79.9° F
Churches: Roman Catholic, 72; Jewish, 50; Protestant
and others, 344; **City-owned parks:** 347 park areas
and tracts (6,314 ac.); **Radio stations:** AM, 10; FM, 11;
Television stations: 7 (including Home Shopping Network)
CIVILIAN LABOR FORCE: 333,043; **Unemployed:** 35,531,
Percent: 10.7; **Per capita personal income:** $20,267
Chamber of Commerce: Greater Baltimore Committee,
111 S. Calvert St., Ste. 1500, Baltimore, Md. 21202

Baltimore is the largest city in Maryland and is situated in the northern part of the state on the Pataps-
co River estuary, an arm of Chesapeake Bay. The city
is independent and is in no county.

The site was settled in the early 17th century and
founded as a town in 1729. The town was named after
Lord Baltimore, the founder of Maryland, and was incorporated as a city in 1797. It has an excellent harbor

and has been a principal port since the 18th century.
Baltimore was a pioneer ship-building center and the
Baltimore clipper was one of the best sailing ships of
its day and was used extensively in world trade. It ranks
today as the nation's second port in foreign tonnage.

Baltimore's economy is focused on manufacturing,
in steel, heavy and light industries, ship construction,
and scientific research and development.

Famous natives: Larry Adler, musician; John Astin, actor; Eubie Blake, pianist; Francis X. Bushman, actor;
Charlie Chase, actor; Hans Conried, actor; Mildred
Dunnock, actress; "Mama" Cass Elliot, singer; Barry
Farber, broadcaster; Paul Ford, actor; Philip Glass,
composer; Billy Holiday, singer; Barry Levinson, director; H.L. Mencken, writer; Babe Ruth, baseball player;
Upton Sinclair, novelist; Leon Uris, novelist; Frank Zappa, musician

BOSTON, MASS.

Mayor: Thomas Menino (to Dec. 1997)
1990 census population, sex, & (rank): 574,283 (20); %
change, 2.0; **Male,** 275,972; **Female,** 298,311; **White,**
360,875; **Black,** 146,945 (25.6%); **American Indian,
Eskimo, or Aleut,** 1,884 (0.3%); **Asian or Pacific Islander,** 30,388 (5.3%); **Other race,** 34,191; **Hispanic
origin,** 61,955 (10.8%). **1990 percent population under
18:** 19.1; **65 and over:** 11.5; **median age:** 30.3.
Land area: 47.2 sq mi. (122 sq km); **Alt.:** Highest, 330 ft;
lowest, sea level
Avg. daily temp.: Jan., 29.6° F; July, 73.5° F
Churches: Protestant, 187; Roman Catholic, 72; Jewish,
28; others, 100; **City-owned parks, playgrounds, etc.:**
2,276.36 ac.; **Radio stations:** AM, 9; FM, 12; **Television
stations:** 10
CIVILIAN LABOR FORCE: 294,320; **Unemployed:** 23,032,
Percent: 7.8; **Per capita personal income:** $23,746[1]
Chamber of Commerce: Boston Chamber of Commerce,
600 Atlantic Ave., Boston, Mass. 02210
1. Boston-Lawrence-Salem-Lowell-Brockton NECMA.

Boston is the capital and seat of Suffolk county
and the largest city in Massachusetts. It is located in
the eastern part of the state at the head of Boston
Bay. It was incorporated as a city in 1822. No city in
the U.S. is richer in historical associations than Boston, and no city has retained more of its original
buildings as memorials to America's past.

Puritans from England settled at Boston in 1630,
only ten years after the Pilgrims had landed at Plymouth in 1620. They named their new town Boston, after the former home of many of the Pilgrims in Lincolnshire, England. Fourteen years later, the pioneer
Bostonians set aside the first public park in the
U.S.—the Boston Common. The following year, 1635,
they opened the first free public school in America.
Today, Boston is home to 65 colleges and universities.

Boston is a major industrial, financial, and educational hub and has one of the finest ports in the
world. The Port of Boston ships more than $8 billion
worth of goods each year.

Although the city's banking and financial services,
insurance, and real estate sectors have declined in recent years other industries continue to grow, especially in the health care field. Boston has 25 medical research institutions, more than any other U.S. city, and
its health care industry is growing at a rate of about
3% a year. The city's unique cultural and historic heritage makes it a center of tourism and its hotel industry ranks first in the nation in occupancy. Boston's
other businesses are in high-technology, biotechnology, software, and electronics.

Famous natives: Samuel Adams, patriot; John Singleton Copley, painter; Ralph Waldo Emerson, philosopher and poet; Arthur Fiedler, conductor; Benjamin Franklin; Edward Everett Hale, clergyman, author; Oliver Wendell Holmes, jurist; Winslow Homer, painter; Joseph P. and Rose Fitzgerald Kennedy; Jack Lemmon, actor; Robert Lowell, poet; Edgar Allan Poe, writer; Paul Revere, patriot, silversmith; John L. Sullivan, boxer; Barbara Walters, TV journalist

BUFFALO, N.Y.

Mayor: Anthony M. Masiello (to Dec. 1998)
1990 census population, sex, & (rank): 328,123 (50); **% change,** –8.3; **Male,** 153,050; **Female,** 175,073; **White,** 212,449; **Black,** 100,733 (30.7%); **American Indian, Eskimo, or Aleut:** 2,547 (0.8%); **Asian or Pacific Islander,** 3,261 (1.0%); **Other race,** 9,287; **Hispanic origin,** 16,129 (4.9%). **1990 percent population under 18:** 24.2%; **65 and over:** 14.8%; **median age:** 32.0.
Land area: 40.6 sq. mi. (105.2 sq. km); **Alt.:** Highest 705 ft; lowest 571.84 ft
Avg. daily temp (1991).: Jan., 23.5° F; July, 70.7° F
Churches: 60 denominations, with over 1,100 churches; **County-owned parks:** 9 public parks (3,000 ac.); **Radio stations:** AM 22; FM 13; **Television stations:** 8 (plus reception from 3 Canadian stations)
CIVILIAN LABOR FORCE: 141,643; **Unemployed:** 13,420, **Percent:** 12.0; **Per capita personal income:** $19,467[1]
Chamber of Commerce: Greater Buffalo Partnership, 300 Main Place Tower, Buffalo, New York 14202.
1. MSA.

Buffalo is the second largest city in New York state and the seat of Erie county, situated in the western part of the state at the eastern end of Lake Erie and at the head of the Niagara River. It was named after Buffalo Creek which runs into Lake Erie. The origin of the city's name is in dispute and may have been a mispronunciation of "beau fleuve," French for "beautiful river."

The first ship to sail the Great Lakes—the *Griffon*—was built near the present site of Buffalo by La Salle in 1679. The town was laid out in 1803 at the site of the present-day city by Joseph Ellicot for the Holland Land Company and was known as New Amsterdam (but popularly called Buffalo). Buffalo was still a relatively small town in 1813 when the British captured it and set its homes and buildings afire. Two years later, the town was rebuilt, and it began to thrive with the coming of the Erie Canal (1825). Buffalo was incorporated as a village in 1816 and became the seat of Erie county in 1821. The city was incorporated in 1832.

Buffalo is a major Great Lakes port of entry, especially for grain distribution, and is an important milling (chiefly wheat) center. The city has one of the most diversified economies in the U.S. Major manufacturing products include automotive components, chemicals, fabricated metals, food processing, industrial machinery, medical instruments, and printing. In addition, Buffalo's economy is centered on trade, tourism, and finance.

Famous natives: Harold Arlen, composer; Michael Bennett, choreographer; Amanda Blake, actress; Don Criqui, television sportscaster; Diane English, television writer, producer; Tom Fontana, television writer; Harry Emerson Fosdick, clergyman; Wilson Greatbatch, pacemaker inventor; Orel Hershiser, baseball player; Christian Laettner, basketball player; Bob Lanier, basketball player; Nancy Marchand, actress; Cliff Robinson, basketball player; Susan Rothenberg, painter; Mark Russell, satirist; Warren Spahn, baseball player; Elizabeth Swados, composer, playwright

CHARLOTTE, N.C.

Mayor: Richard Vinroot (to Nov. 1995)
1990 census population, sex, & (rank): 395,934 (35); **% change,** 25.5; **Male,** 188,088; **Female,** 207,846; **White,** 259,760; **Black,** 125,827 (31.8%); **American Indian, Eskimo, or Aleut:** 1,425 (0.4%); **Asian or Pacific Islander:** 7,211 (1.8%); **Other race,** 1,711; **Hispanic origin,** 5,571 (1.4%). **1990 percent population under 18:** 24.2%; **65 and over:** 9.8%; **median age:** 32.1.
Land area: 209 sq mi. (541.3 sq km); **Alt.:** 765 ft
Avg. daily temp.: Jan., 40.5° F; July, 78.5° F
Churches: Protestant, over 400; Roman Catholic, 8; Jewish, 3; Greek Orthodox, 1; **City-owned parks and parkways:** 130; **Radio stations:** AM, 7; FM, 13; **Television stations:** 4 commercial; 2 PBS
CIVILIAN LABOR FORCE: 319,650; **Unemployed:** 11,610, **Percent:** 3.6; **Per capita personal income:** $19,884
Chamber of Commerce: Charlotte Chamber, P.O. Box 32785, Charlotte, N.C., 28232
1. Charlotte-Gastonia Rock Hill, N.C.–S.C. MSA.

Charlotte, North Carolina's largest city and seat of Mecklenburg county, is located in the southern part of the state near the South Carolina border. It was named for King George III of England's wife, Charlotte Sophia of Mecklenburg-Strelitz.

Settled about 1750, Charlotte was incorporated as a city in 1768 and made the county seat in 1774. Charlotte was a leading Confederate city during the Civil War and was the last meeting place of the full Confederate cabinet.

From 1800 to 1848, Charlotte was the center of U.S. gold production and a branch of the U.S. mint operated from there from 1837 to 1913.

The city has a highly diversified economy and is a foremost center for distribution, retailing, technology, and manufacturing. It is the third largest banking center in the U.S. It is the seat of the University of North Carolina at Charlotte.

Famous natives: Romare Bearden, artist; Richard G. Darman, government official; Billy Graham, evangelist; Charles Gwathmey, architect; Hamilton Jordan, government official; Donald Schollander, swimmer; Randolph Scott, actor

CHICAGO, ILL.

Mayor: Richard M. Daley (to April 1999)
1990 census population, sex, & (rank): 2,783,726 (3); **% change,** –7.4; **Male,** 1,334,705; **Female,** 1,449,021; **White,** 1,263,524; **Black,** 1,087,711 (39.1%); **American Indian, Eskimo, or Aleut:** 7,064 (0.3%); **Asian or Pacific Islander,** 104,118 (3.7%); **Other race,** 321,309; **Hispanic origin,** 545,852 (19.6%). **1990 percent population under 18:** 26.0%; **65 and over:** 11.9%; **median age:** 31.3.
Land area: 228.469 sq mi. (592 sq km); **Alt.:** Highest, 672 ft; lowest, 578.5
Avg. daily temp.: Jan., 21.4° F; July, 73.0° F
Churches: Protestant, 850; Roman Catholic, 252; Jewish, 51; **City-owned parks:** 552; **Radio stations:** AM, 15; FM, 24; **Television stations:** 14
CIVILIAN LABOR FORCE: 1,356,716; **Unemployed:** 124,195, **Percent:** 9.2; **Per capita personal income:** $20,349[1]
Chamber of Commerce: Chicagoland Chamber of Commerce, 200 N. LaSalle, Chicago, Ill. 60601
1. PMSA.

Chicago is the largest city in Illinois and the seat of Cook county. Built directly on a lake front, it stretches for 22 miles along the southwestern shore of Lake Michigan.

The first white men known to have visited Chicago were Joliet and Father Marquette in 1673. The first permanent white settler in the area was John Kinzie, sometimes called the father of Chicago, who took over a trading post in 1796 that had been established 1791 by Jean Baptiste Point Sable, a French-speaking black fur trapper. Fort Dearborn, a blockhouse and stockade, was built in 1804, but was evacuated in 1812, with more than half of its garrison massacred at what is now the foot of 18th Street. Not until 1830 was the town laid out. The name Chicago is thought to come from the Algonquian Indian word Chicagou meaning "strong" or "powerful." Some early Frenchmen believed that the name was derived from the Algonquian word for "onion place" because wild onions grew there.

Forty-one years later it was destroyed in the great Chicago fire of 1871. Chicago was incorporated as a village in 1833 and as a city in 1837.

Chicago is a major Great Lakes port and the commercial, financial, industrial, and cultural center of the Midwest. The manufacturing industries dominate the wholesale and retail trade, and trade in agricultural commodities is important to the economy. The Chicago Mercantile Exchange is the largest in the world.

Famous natives: Jack Benny, comedian; Edgar Rice Burroughs, author; Raymond Chandler, author; Hillary Rodham Clinton, lawyer, First Lady; Michael Crichton, author; Walt Disney, filmmaker; John Dos Passos, author; Bobby Fischer, chess player; Bob Fosse, choreographer, director; Benny Goodman, clarinetist; Dorothy Hamill, figure skater; Quincy Jones, composer; Gene Krupa, drummer; Dorothy Malone, actress; David Mamet, playwright; Bob Newhart, comedian; Kim Novak, actress; Donald O'Connor, actor; William L. Shirer, journalist, historian; Preston Sturges, film director; Gloria Swanson, actress; Melvin Van Peebles, playwright; Alfred Wallenstein, conductor; Robin Williams, comedian, actor; Robert Young, actor

CINCINNATI, OHIO

Mayor: Roxanne Qualls (to Nov. 1995)
City Manager: John F. Shirey
1990 census population, sex, & (rank): 364,040 (45); **% change,** −5.5; **Male,** 169,305; **Female,** 194,735; **White,** 220,285; **Black,** 138,1312 (37.9%); **American Indian, Eskimo, or Aleut,** 660 (0.2%); **Asian or Pacific Islander,** 4,030 (1.1%); **Other race,** 933; **Hispanic origin,** 2,386 (0.7%). **1990 percent population under 18:** 25.1%; **65 and over:** 13.9%; **median age:** 30.9.
Land area: 78.1 sq mi. (202 sq km); **Alt.:** Highest, 960 ft; lowest, 441
Avg. daily temp.: Jan., 30.3° F; July, 76.1° F
Churches: 850; **City-owned parks:** 96 (4,345 ac.); **Radio stations:** AM, 10; FM, 15 (Greater Cincinnati); **Television stations:** 8
CIVILIAN LABOR FORCE: 188,161; **Unemployed:** 14,318, **Percent:** 7.6; **Per capita personal income:** $17,624[1]
Chamber of Commerce: Cincinnati Chamber of Commerce, 441 Vine St. Suite 300, Cincinnati, Ohio 45202
1. PMSA.

Cincinnati is the third largest city in Ohio and the seat of Hamilton county. It is located on the Ohio River.

Cincinnati began as part of the Miami Purchase of 1788. The first settlement, Columbia, was begun by Benjamin Stites that same year. The town of Losantiville was founded in 1788 on a plateau above the Ohio River by Mathias Denman, Robert Patterson, and Israel Ludlow. Its strategic location in the Western Territory led to the building of Ft. Washington, the most ambitious military establishment in the territory. The community of Losantiville that grew up

around the fort was renamed Cincinnati in 1790 by Gen. Arthur St. Clair, Commander of Ft. Washington and first governor of the Northwest Territory, after the Revolutionary officers' Society of the Cincinnati, founded by George Washington. It was incorporated as a village in 1802 and chartered as a city in 1819.

The city began to flourish as a commercial hub with the arrival of the first steamboat in 1811, the completion of the Miami and Erie Canal in 1827, and the coming of the first railroad in 1843.

Cincinnati is a port of entry and more than 46 million tons pass through the Port of Cincinnati each year. The city has a diverse economy and is a major center for manufacturing, wholesaling, and retailing, as well as insurance and finance companies and health services. Prominent manufacturing groups include transportation equipment, which includes aircraft engines and auto parts, food and kindred products, metal working, general industrial machinery, chemicals, fabricated metal products, printing, and publishing.

Famous natives: Eddie Arcaro, jockey; Theda Bara, actress; Doris Day, actress; Jim Dine, painter; Suzanne Farrell, ballerina; Robert Henri, painter; James Levine, music director; Adolph Ochs, publisher; Tyrone Power, actor; William Procter, scientist; Roy Rogers, actor; Pete Rose, baseball player; Steven Spielberg, filmmaker; Roger Staubach, football player; Robert A. Taft, legislator; William Howard Taft, president

CLEVELAND, OHIO

Mayor: Michael R. White (to Dec. 1997)
1990 census population, sex, & (rank): 505,616 (24); **% change,** −11.9; **Male,** 237,211; **Female,** 268,405; **White,** 250,234; **Black,** 235,405 (46.6%); **American Indian, Eskimo, or Aleut,** 1,562 (0.3%); **Asian or Pacific Islander,** 5,115 (1.0%); **Other race,** 13,300; **Hispanic origin,** 23,197 (4.6%). **1990 percent population under 18:** 26.9; **65 and over:** 14.0; **median age:** 31.9.
Land area: 79 sq mi. (205 sq km); **Alt.:** Highest, 1048 ft.; lowest, 573
Avg. daily temp.: Jan., 25.5° F; July, 71.6° F
Churches: [1] Protestant, 980; Roman Catholic, 187; Jewish, 31; Eastern Orthodox, 22; **City-owned parks:** 41 (1,930 ac.); **Radio stations:** AM, 15; FM, 17; **Television stations:** 7
CIVILIAN LABOR FORCE: 219,836; **Unemployed:** 27,583, **Percent:** 12.5; **Per capita personal income:** $19,395[1]
Chamber of Commerce: Greater Cleveland Growth Association, 200 Tower City Center, Cleveland, Ohio 44113
1. PMSA.

Cleveland is the second largest city in Ohio and the seat of Cuyahoga county. It is located in the northeastern part of the state on Lake Erie. In the Colonial era, the Cleveland area was known as the Connecticut Western Reserve, part of a land grant made to Connecticut by King Charles II in 1662. The city was founded in 1796 by Gen. Moses Cleaveland, who was the head surveyor of the Connecticut Land Company. This company had bought three million acres in what is now northern Ohio. A permanent settlement was founded in 1799, named after the General, and the spelling was shortened to Cleveland. The city was incorporated in 1836.

Cleveland's industrial growth was stimulated by the opening of the Ohio and Erie Canals in 1832 and, later, the advent of the Civil War with the corresponding demand for machinery, railroad equipment, ships, and other items.

The Port of Cleveland is the largest overseas general cargo port on Lake Erie. Greater Cleveland has long been famous as a diversified durable goods manufacturing area. Following the national trend, Cleveland has been shifting to a more services-based economy. Greater Cleveland is a world corporate center for leading national and multinational companies, including transportation, insurance, retailing, utilities, and commercial banking and finance.

Famous natives: Jim Backus, actor; Dorothy Dandridge, actress; Ruby Dee, actress; Phil Donahue, talk show host; Joel Grey, actor; Arsenio Hall, talk show host; Margaret Hamilton, actress; Philip Johnson, architect; Henry Mancini, composer; Burgess Meredith, actor; Paul Newman, actor; Carl Stokes, judge; Andy Warhol, artist

COLUMBUS, OHIO

Mayor: Gregory S. Lashutka (to Jan. 1996)
1990 census population, sex, & (rank): 632,910 (16); **% change,** 12.0; **Male,** 305,574; **Female,** 327,336; **White,** 471,025; **Black,** 142,748 (22.6%); **American Indian, Eskimo, or Aleut,** 1,469 (0.2%); **Asian or Pacific Islander,** 14,993 (2.4%); **Other race,** 2,675; **Hispanic origin,** 6,741 (1.1%). **1990 percent population under 18:** 23.7; **65 and over:** 9.2; **median age:** 29.4.
Land area: 203.269 sq mi. (526.47 sq km); **Alt.:** Highest, 902 ft; lowest, 702
Avg. daily temp.: Jan.; 27.1° F; July, 73.8° F
Churches: Protestant, 436; Roman Catholic, 62; Jewish, 5; Other, 8; **City-owned parks:** 203 (12,891 ac.); **Radio stations:** AM, 10; FM, 16; **Television stations:** 9 commercial, 3 PBS
CIVILIAN LABOR FORCE: 366,600; **Unemployed:** 12,200, **Percent:** 3.3; **Per capita personal income:** $17,178
Chamber of Commerce: Columbus Area Chamber of Commerce, P.O. Box 1527, Columbus, Ohio 43216

Columbus, the largest city in Ohio, is the state capital and seat of Franklin county and is located in central Ohio on the Scioto River.

The first structures near downtown Columbus were earthen mounds constructed by Indian tribes known as the Mound Builders. The Indians lived alone in Central Ohio until the 1700s when the first explorers entered the Midwest. The first permanent settlement was founded by a surveyor from Kentucky, Lucas Sullivant, in 1797 and was named Franklinton. The site was laid out as the state capital in 1812 and named to honor Christopher Columbus and became the capital in 1816. Columbus was chartered as a city in 1834 and annexed Franklinton in 1870. The city's growth was stimulated by the development of transportation facilities—a feeder to the Ohio Canal completed in 1832, the National Road in 1833, and the arrival of the railroad in 1850.

Columbus is a port of entry and a major industrial, commercial, manufacturing, and cultural center. It is the seat of Ohio State University. The city has enjoyed steady growth over the years due largely in part to its economic diversity—there is no single activity that dominates the economy.

Famous natives: Warner Baxter, actor; George Bellows, painter; Michael Feinstein, singer, pianist; Eileen Heckart, actress; Jack Nicklaus, golfer; Tom Poston, actor; Eddie Rickenbacker, aviator; Arthur M. Schlesinger, historian; James Thurber, writer

DALLAS, TEX.

Mayor: Ron Kirk
City Manager: John Ware (apptd. Nov. 1993)

1990 census population, sex, & (rank): 1,006,877 (8); **% change,** 11.3; **Male,** 495,141; **Female,** 511,736; **White,** 556,760; **Black,** 296,994 (29.5%); **American Indian, Eskimo, or Aleut,** 4,792 (0.5%); **Asian or Pacific Islander,** 21,952 (2.2%); **Other race,** 126,379; **Hispanic origin,** 210,240 (20.9%). **1990 percent population under 18:** 25.0; **65 and over:** 9.7; **median age:** 30.6.
Land area: 378 sq mi. (979 sq km); **Alt.:** Highest, 750 ft; lowest, 375
Avg. daily temp.: Jan., 45.0° F; July, 86.3° F
Churches: 1,974 (in Dallas Co.); **City-owned parks:** 296 (47,025 ac.); **Radio stations:** AM, 19; FM, 30; **Television stations:** 10 commercial, 1 PBS
CIVILIAN LABOR FORCE: 570,661; **Unemployed:** 50,526, **Percent:** 8.9; **Per capita personal income:** $19,485[1]
Chamber of Commerce: Dallas Chamber of Commerce, 1201 Elm, Dallas, Tex. 75270
1. PMSA.

Dallas is the second largest city in Texas and is the seat of Dallas county. It is situated 185 miles northeast of Austin on the Trinity River near the junction of its three forks. It was first settled by Tennessee lawyer John Neely Bryan as a trading post on the Trinity River in 1841. Many historians believe that John Neely Bryan named the city after George Mifflin Dallas, Vice President under James K. Polk but there is no official agreement on this. It was incorporated as a town in 1856 and a city in 1871. The city developed as a cotton market in the 1870s and became the chief cotton producing region of Texas.

The economy is highly diversified and the city is the leading commercial, marketing, and industrial center of the southwest. The insurance business is important, and the service sector has experienced rapid growth. Dallas is also a popular tourist and convention city.

Famous natives: Tex Avery, animator, director; Robby Benson, actor; Ernie Banks, baseball player; Bebe Daniels, acteress; Linda Darnell, actress; Lee Elder, golfer; Morgan Fairchild, actress; Trini Lopez, singer; Aaron Spelling, producer; Stephen Stills, singer; Sharon Tate, actress; Lee Trevino, golfer

DENVER, COLO.

Mayor: Wellington Webb (to July 1997)
1990 census population, sex, & (rank): 467,610 (26); **% change,** −5.1; **Male,** 227,517; **Female,** 240,093; **White,** 337,198; **Black,** 60,046 (12.8%); **American Indian, Eskimo, or Aleut,** 5,381 (1.2%); **Asian or Pacific Islander,** 11,005 (2.4%); **Other race,** 53,980; **Hispanic origin,** 107,382 (23.0%); **1990 percent population under 18:** 22.0; **65 and over:** 13.9; **median age:** 33.9
Land area: 154.63 sq mi. (400.5 sq km); **Alt.:** Highest, 5,494 ft; lowest, 5,140
Avg. daily temp.: Jan., 29.5° F; July, 73.3° F
Churches:[1] Protestant, 859; Roman Catholic, 60; Jewish, 13; **City-owned parks:** 205 (4,166 ac.); **City-owned mountain parks:** 40 (13,600 ac.); **Radio stations:** AM, 23; FM, 20[1]; **Television stations:** 17[1]
CIVILIAN LABOR FORCE: 245,495[2]; **Unemployed:** 17,527[2]; **Percent:** 7.1[2]; **Per capita personal income:** $19,231[3]
Chamber of Commerce: Greater Denver Chamber of Commerce, 1445 Market Street, Denver, Colo. 80202
1. Metropolitan area. 2. Denver City/County. 3. PMSA.

Denver is the largest city and capital of Colorado and the seat of Denver county. It lies at the foot of the Rocky Mountains and is situated at the junction of the South Platte River and Cherry Creek. The city was born in 1858 when gold was discovered in the sands of Cherry Creek and it began as a tough village of cabins, shacks, and tents. It was incorporated as a city in 1861. In 1867, Denver became the territorial capital. The city is named for James W. Denver, governor of the Kansas Territory which included part of Colorado. The city prospered from the famous gold and silver mines of the 1870s and the 1880s.

Denver International Airport, the first major new airport to be opened in the U.S. in 21 years, opened to passenger traffic on Feb. 28, 1995, at a cost of $4.9 billion. At 53 square miles, it is the largest airport in North America.

Denver is an important cultural, industrial, transportation, tourist, and major marketing center. It is also a regional center for many federal government agencies and a leader in the development of western energy resources.

Denver's fastest growing industries include contract construction, real estate, retail trade, and federal government.

Famous natives: Tim Allen, comedian, actor; Ward Bond, actor; Douglas Fairbanks, Sr., actor; John Hart, newsman; Pat Hingle, actor; Ted Mack, TV host; Barbara Rush, actress; Alan K. Simpson, senator; Paul Whiteman, bandleader; Don Wilson, announcer

DETROIT, MICH.

Mayor: Dennis W. Archer
1990 census population, sex, & (rank): 1,027,974 (7); **% change,** –14.6; **Male,** 476,814; **Female,** 551,160; **White,** 222,316; **Black,** 777,916 (75.7%); **American Indian, Eskimo, or Aleut,** 3,655 (0.4%); **Asian or Pacific Islander,** 8,461 (0.8%); **Other race,** 15,626; **Hispanic origin,** 28,473 (2.8%). **1990 percent population under 18:** 29.4; **65 and over:** 12.2; **median age:** 30.8.
Land area: 143 sq mi. (370 sq km); **Alt.:** Highest, 685 ft; lowest, 574
Avg. daily temp.: Jan., 23.4° F; July, 71.9° F
Churches:[1] Protestant, 1,165; Roman Catholic, 89; Jewish, 2; **City-owned parks:** 56 parks (3,843 ac.); 393 sites (5,838 ac.); **Radio stations:** AM, 27; FM, 30 (includes 3 in Windsor, Ont.); **Television stations:** 8[2] (includes 1 in Windsor, Ont.)
CIVILIAN LABOR FORCE: 393,083; **Unemployed:** 64,712, **Percent:** 16.5; **Per capita personal income:** $19,660
Chamber of Commerce: Greater Detroit Chamber of Commerce, 622 W. Lafayette, Detroit, Mich. 48226
1. Six-county metropolitan area. 2. Within four counties of Metro Detroit.

Detroit, the largest city in Michigan, is situated in the southeastern part of the state on the Detroit River. It is the seat of Wayne county. Detroit was incorporated as a city in 1815 and reincorporated in 1824.

Detroit is the oldest city of any size west of the seaboard colonies, having been founded by Antoine de la Mothe Cadillac on July 24, 1701, more than a century before Chicago was founded. The French were the first settlers and they gave the city its name from their word meaning "straight." They referred to the 27-mile-long Detroit River which connects Lake Erie and Lake St. Clair. The river forms part of the international boundary, and marks the only point where Canada lies directly south of U.S. territory.

Because of its strategic location, Detroit was fought over by the French, the British, and the Indians. It was the headquarters for the British forces in the Northwest during the American Revolutionary War.

The first steam vessel, the *Walk-in-the-Water*, made its appearance on the Great Lakes in 1818, and Detroit was the western terminus for most of its voyages from Buffalo. Its link to all the important cities on the Great Lakes made it a major exporting port.

Detroit is one of the largest manufacturing cities in the U.S. and is the center of the automobile manufacturing industry, which has experienced a decline to foreign competition in the past decade. The health and medical care sector is important to the economy, and employment in the finance, insurance, and real estate industries has inched up in the Detroit metropolitan area since 1991.

Famous natives: Ralph Bunche, statesman; Francis Ford Coppola, director; Charles Lindbergh, aviator; Madonna, singer; John Mitchell; U.S. Attorney General; George Peppard, actor; Gilda Radner, comedian; Della Reese, singer; Sugar Ray Robinson, boxer; Diana Ross, singer; Tom Selleck, actor; Margaret Whiting, singer

EL PASO, TEX.

Mayor: Larry Francis
1990 census population, sex, & (rank): 515,342 (22); **% change,** 21.2; **Male,** 247,163; **Female,** 268,179; **White,** 396,122; **Black,** 17,708 (3.4%); **American Indian, Eskimo, or Aleut,** 2,239 (0.4%); **Asian or Pacific Islander,** 5,956 (1.2%); **Other race,** 93,317; **Hispanic origin,** 355,669 (69.0%). **1990 percent population under 18:** 31.9; **65 and over:** 8.7; **median age:** 28.7
1995 population (est.): 652,225
Land area: 247.4 sq mi. (641 sq km); **Alt.:** 4,000 ft
Avg. daily temp.: Jan., 44.2° F; July, 82.5° F
Churches: Protestant, 320; Roman Catholic, 39; Jewish, 3; others, 20; **City-owned parks:** 116[1] (1,180 ac.); **Radio Stations:** AM, 18; FM, 17; **Television stations:** 6
CIVILIAN LABOR FORCE: 234,891; **Unemployed:** 24,273, **Percent:** 10.3; **Per capita personal income:** $10,735
Chamber of Commerce: El Paso Chamber of Commerce, 10 Civic Center Plaza, El Paso, Tex. 79944
1. Includes 109 developed and 7 undeveloped parks.

El Paso, the fourth largest city in Texas and the seat of El Paso county, is located in the far western part of the state on the north bank of the Rio Grande River opposite the Mexican city of Ciudad Juárez on the south bank.

In 1581, Spanish explorers came through the Pass of the North to test the missionary and mining possibilities of New Mexico. The area had been inhabited for centuries by various Indian groups. On April 30, 1598, Juan de Onate took formal possession of the area for King Philip II of Spain and subsequently crossed the Rio Grande River near a site west of the present downtown El Paso which he called "El Paso del Rio del Norte," meaning the crossing of the river—the first use of the name "El Paso." In 1659, the mission of Nuestra Senora de Guadalupe was founded on a site that is present day downtown Ciudad Juárez; the mission is still in use today. In 1682, Spanish colonists from Mexico founded the settlement of Ysleta within the site of the present-day city. However, it wasn't until 1827 that the first permanent settlement at El Paso was established by Juan María Ponce de León. The city's real growth started with the arrival of the Southern Pacific Railroad in 1881. El Paso was incorporated as a city in 1873.

In 1888, Mexico changed the name of Paso del Norte to Ciudad Juárez in honor of Benito Juárez. Later in 1967, the United States agreed to cede a long disputed part of El Paso to Mexico due to changes in the course of the Rio Grande which forms the international boundary between the two countries. El Paso and its sister city of Ciudad Juárez across the U.S./Mexico border are inexorably joined by culture and economy. El Paso and Juárez make up the largest international metroplex in the world.

El Paso is an important port of entry to the U.S. from Mexico. The apparel industry plays a major role in the El Paso area. The high technology, medical device manufacturing, plastics, refining, automotive, food processing, and defense-related industries are important to the economy. El Paso's service sector has experienced the healthiest growth since 1983. El Paso is also a major tourist resort.

Famous natives: Manuel Acosta, artist; Don Bluth, animation director; Vicki Carr, singer; Sam Donaldson, newsman; Judith Ivey, actress; Guy Kibbee, actor; Sandra Day O'Connor, Supreme Court justice; Debbie Reynolds, actress; Irene Ryan, actress

FORT WORTH, TEX.

Mayor: Kay Granger (to May 1997)
City Manager: Bob Terrell
1990 census population, sex, & (rank): 447,619 (28); **% change,** 16.2; **Male,** 220,268; **Female:** 227,351; **White,** 285,549; **Black,** 98,532 (22.0%); **American Indian, Eskimo, or Aleut,** 1,914 (0.4%); **Asian or Pacific Islander,** 8,910 (2.0%); **Other race,** 52,714; **Hispanic origin,** 87,345 (19.5%). **1990 percent population under 18:** 26.6; **65 and over:** 11.2; **median age:** 30.3.
Land area: 295.301 sq mi. (765 sq km); **Alt.:** Highest, 780 ft; lowest, 520
Avg. daily temp.: Jan., 44.2° F; July, 82.5° F
Churches: 941, representing 72 denominations; **City-owned parks:** 171 (8,189 ac.; 3,500 ac. in Nature Center); **Radio stations:** AM, 5; FM, 20; **Television stations:** 15 (9 local)
CIVILIAN LABOR FORCE: 235,212; **Unemployed:** 21,653, **Percent:** 9.2; **Per capita personal income:** $17,259[1]
Chamber of Commerce: Fort Worth Chamber of Commerce, 777 Taylor Street, Suit 900, Fort Worth, Tex. 76102
1. Fort Worth–Arlington MSA.

Fort Worth, seat of Tarrant county, is situated in the north central part of Texas on the Trinity River.

The city was founded by Major Ripley Arnold in 1849 as a military outpost on the Trinity River to protect settlers moving westward from frequent Indian attacks. It was named after Gen. William J. Worth, the commander of the Texas army. Fort Worth was incorporated in 1873. Its growth was stimulated in the 1870s by the proximity to the Chisholm cattle trail. It prospered as a meat packing and shipping center when the Texas and Pacific Railway arrived in 1876, and later experienced a new boom when oil was discovered nearby in 1917. The establishment of military installations in the area during both world wars also spurred the economy.

Ft. Worth has traditionally been a diverse center of manufacturing and is not dependent on the oil or financial sectors. The city's industries range from clothing and food products to jet fighters, helicopters, computers, pharmaceuticals, and plastics. Ft. Worth is a national leader in aviation products, electronic equipment, and refrigeration equipment. It is home to a multitude of major corporate headquarters, office, and distribution centers.

Famous natives: Robert Bass, financier; Kate Capshaw, actress; Sandra Heynie, golfer; Patricia Highsmith, writer; Spanky McFarland, actor; R. Bruce Merrifield, Nobelist in chemistry; Roger Miller, singer; Fess Parker, actor; Rex Reed, critic; Johnny Rutherford, auto racer; Liz Smith, columnist

FRESNO, CALIF.

Mayor: Jim Patterson (to May 1997)
City Manager: Michael A. Bierman
1990 census population, sex, & (rank): 354,202 (47); **% change,** 62.9; **Male,** 172,241; **Female,** 181,961; **White,** 209,604; **Black,** 29,409 (8.3%); **American Indian, Eskimo, or Aleut,** 3,729 (1.1%); **Asian or Pacific Islander,** 44,358 (12.5%); **Other race,** 67,102; **Hispanic origin,** 105,787 (29.9%). **1990 percent population under 18:** 31.7; **65 and over:** 10.1; **median age:** 28.4.
Land area: 99.38 sq mi. (257.39 sq km); **Alt.:** 328 ft
Avg. daily temp.: Jan., 45.5° F; July, 81.0° F
Churches: 450 (approximate); **City-owned parks:** 38 (690 ac.); **Radio stations:** AM 11[1]; FM 13[1]; Bilingual 1; **Television stations:** 8[1]
CIVILIAN LABOR FORCE: 174,496; **Unemployed:** 22,708, **Percent:** 13.0; **Per capita personal income:** $15,927
Chamber of Commerce: Fresno County and City Chamber of Commerce, P.O. Box 1469, 2331 Fresno St., Fresno, CA 93716
1. Metropolitan area.

Fresno is located in central California, 184 miles southeast of San Francisco and 222 miles northwest of Los Angeles. It is the seat of Fresno county. Fresno was incorporated as a city in 1885.

Fresno began as a station for the Central Pacific Railroad in 1872 and was made the seat of Fresno county in 1874. The city's name is Spanish for the ash trees that the early explorers found in the area.

Fresno is the world capital of the agri-business with 250 different crops produced by 7,500 farmers on 1.9 million irrigated acres, worth $3 billion a year. Fresno county's top five leading crops are grapes, cotton, tomatoes, cattle and calves, and turkeys. The city is also a trade, financial, media, and commercial center. Its diverse industries include agricultural chemicals, farm equipment, canned fruit and vegetables, clothing, computer software, electric wire, pumps, glass, and plastic products.

Famous natives: Mike Connors, actor; Maynard Dixon, painter; Bruce Furniss, swimmer; Jon Hall, actor; Daryle Lamonica, football player; Sam Peckinpah, director; William Saroyan, novelist; Tom Seaver, baseball player

HONOLULU, HAWAII

Mayor: Jeremy Harris (to Jan. 1997)
1990 census population, sex, & (rank): 365,272 (44)[1]; **% change,** 0.1; **Male,** 180,357; **Female,** 184,915; **White,** 97,527; **Black,** 4,821 (1.3%); **American Indian, Eskimo, or Aleut,** 1,126 (0.3%); **Asian or Pacific Islander,** 257,552 (70.5%); **Other race,** 4,246; **Hispanic origin,** 16,704 (4.6%). **1990 percent population under 18:** 19.1; **65 and over:** 16.0; **median age:** 36.9.
Land area: 600 sq mi. (1,554 sq km)[2]; **Alt.:** Highest, 4,025 ft; lowest, sea level
Avg. daily temp.: Jan., 72.6° F; July, 81° F
Churches: Roman Catholic, 34; Buddhist, 35; Jewish, 2; Protestant and others, 329; **City-owned parks:** 6,053 ac.; **Radio stations:** AM, 8; FM, 4; **Television stations:** 10
CIVILIAN LABOR FORCE: 423,900[2]; **Unemployed:** 19,923[2], **Percent:** 4.7[2]; **Per capita personal income:** $23,864
Chamber of Commerce: Chamber of Commerce of Hawaii, 1132 Bishop St., Suite 200, Honolulu, Hawaii 96813
1. City only. 2. City and county. The census bureau does not include the entire city and county in its census of Honolulu. If it did, the 1990 census and rank would be 836,231 (12).

Honolulu is the capital (on Oahu) and largest city in Hawaii. It is also the seat of Honolulu county. The city and county of Honolulu include the entire island of Oahu, the major island of the state of Hawaii. It is situated in the central Pacific Ocean 2,397 miles westsouthwest of San Francisco. Honolulu's name means "sheltered harbor" and derives from the native words hono meaning "a bay" and lulu meaning "sheltered."

Honolulu's early history was one of turbulence and conflict. One of the last areas on the globe to be discovered and exploited (visited by British Captain James Cook 1778), Hawaii was subject to strong pressures from many powers, from American missionaries who arrived in 1820, and from the opportunism of whalers. These whalers were among those who built Honolulu originally, bringing trade, commerce, and prosperity that led to expansion into the sugar and pineapple industries.

As early as 1814, Russia tried to move in and Russian soldiers built a bastion at the harbor's edge. The British flag was raised in 1843 and French forces occupied Honolulu in 1849. Each time control was given back to the independent kingdom without bloodshed. In 1898, a group of Americans completed a project attempted at intervals during the previous 65 years—annexation to the United States. Honolulu was incorporated as a city in 1907.

Honolulu was bombed by Japan in a surprise attack on the unprepared U.S. naval base at Pearl Harbor on Dec. 7, 1941. This action forced the United States to enter World War II and "Remember Pearl Harbor," became a famous American wartime slogan.

Hawaiian statehood in 1959 and the arrival of fast jet air travel to the island brought boom times to Honolulu. Tourism is the city's principal industry, followed by federal defense expenditures and agricultural exports (chiefly sugar and pineapples).

Famous natives: Hiram Bingham, explorer; Jean Erdman, dancer, choreographer; Hiram Fong, senator; Daniel Inouye, senator; Duke Kahanamoku, surfer, Olympian swimmer; Bette Midler, actress; Kelly Preston, actress; Louise Morgan Sill, author; Don Stroud, actor; Merlin D. Tuttle, biologist, wildlife photographer

HOUSTON, TEX.

Mayor: Robert C. Lanier (to Dec. 1995)
1990 census population, sex, & (rank): 1,630,553 (4); **%
change,** 2.2; **Male,** 809,048; **Female,** 821,505; **White,**
859,069; **Black,** 457,990 (28.1%); **American Indian,
Eskimo, or Aleut,** 4,126 (0.3%); **Asian or Pacific Islander,** 67,113 (4.1%); **Other race,** 242,255; **Hispanic
origin,** 450,483 (27.6%). **1990 percent population under 18:** 26.7; **65 and over:** 8.3; **median age:** 30.4.
Land area: 594.03 sq mi. (1,521 sq km); **Alt.:** Highest, 120
ft; lowest, sea level
Avg. daily temp.: Jan., 51.4° F; July, 83.1° F
Churches: 1,750[2]; **City-owned parks:** 307 (32,598 ac.);
Radio stations: AM, 22; FM, 32[1]; **Television stations:**
13 commercial, 1 PBS
CIVILIAN LABOR FORCE: 979,931; **Unemployed:** 65,315,
Percent: 6.7; **Per capita personal income:** $17,598[3]
Chamber of Commerce: Greater Houston Partnership,
1200 Smith, Suite 700, Houston, Tex. 77002
1. Includes annexations since 1970. 2. Harris County. 3. PSMA

Houston, the largest city in Texas and seat of Harris county, is located in the southeastern part of the state near the Gulf of Mexico.

Sam Houston was the commander in chief of the Texas troops who fought a successful war of rebellion against the domination by Mexico, which had been in possession of Texas. On April 21, 1836, Houston's men won a decisive victory in which the Mexican dictator, Gen. Santa Anna, was taken prisoner, and signed the treaty which launched the Republic of Texas. In September, a constitution was ratified, and Houston was elected President. The Texas Republic was recognized by the U.S. and by the major European powers. The present city of Houston was incorporated in 1837 and named after Sam Houston, who was president of the republic. This was its first capital.

The port of Houston leads the U.S. in foreign tonnage handled. The city is a major business, financial, science, and technology center. Houston is outstanding in oil and natural gas production and is the energy capital of the world. It is the home of one of the largest medical facilities in the world—the Texas Medical Center—and the focus of the aerospace industry. The Lyndon B. Johnson Space Center is the nation's headquarters for manned spaceflight.

Famous natives: Debbie Allen, choreographer; Lance Alworth, football player; Denton Cooley, heart surgeon; Jim Demaret, golfer; Allen Drury, noveslit; Shelly Duvall, actress; A.J. Foyt, auto racer; Howard Hughes, industrialist; Barbara C. Jordan, educator, lawyer, politician; Barbara Mandrell, singer; Annette O'Toole, actress; Dennis and Randy Quaid, actors; Kenny Rogers, singer; Patrick Swayze, actor, dancer;

INDIANAPOLIS, IND.

Mayor: Stephen Goldsmith (to Dec. 31, 1995)
1990 census population, sex, & (rank)[2]: 741,952 (12); **%
change,** 4.3; **Male,** 352,309; **Female,** 389,643; **White,**
564,447; **Black,** 166,031 (22.4%); **American Indian,
Eskimo, or Aleut,** 1,580 (0.2%); **Asian or Pacific Islander,** 6,943 (0.9%); **Other race,** 2,951; **Hispanic origin,** 7,790 (1.0%). **1990 percent population under 18:**
25.6%; **65 and over:** 11.5; **median age:** 31.8.
Land area: 352 sq mi. (912 sq km); **Alt.:** Highest, 840 ft;
lowest, 700
Avg. daily temp.: Jan., 26.0 F; July, 75.1° F
Churches: 1,200[1]; **City-owned parks:** 130 (9,375 ac.); **Radio stations:** AM, 8[3]; FM, 17[3]; **Television stations:** 7[1]
CIVILIAN LABOR FORCE: 441,780[1], **Unemployed:** 20,820[1],
Percent: 4.7[1]; **Per capita personal income:** $19,522
Chamber of Commerce: Indianapolis Chamber of Com-
merce, 320 N Meridian St., Indianapolis, Ind. 46204
1. Marion County. 2. Consolidated city. 3. Metropolitan area.

Indianapolis, the largest city in Indiana and seat of Marion county, is located in the central part of the state on the West Fork of the White River. Its name derives from combining "Indiana" with "polis," the Greek word for city.

Indianapolis was settled in 1820 and, in 1825, its site was chosen as the state capital and it was incorporated as a city in 1832 and reincorporated in 1838. The city's growth began when the railroad reached it in 1847. Toward the end of the 19th century, the discovery of nearby natural gas and the start of the automobile industry hastened its industrial expansion. On Jan. 1, 1970, Indianapolis merged with the surrounding Marion county.

Indianapolis is an important center of a rich agricultural region and a major grain and livestock market. It is also a focal point of commerce, transportation, and manufacturing for the region. Some leading industries are electronics, pharmaceuticals, and food processing. The financial sector, and service and insurance industries are growing rapidly.

Indianapolis is the site of the world-famous 500-mile automobile race and the Indiana State Fair.

Famous natives: Monte Blue, actor; David Letterman, TV host; Steve McQueen, actor; Jane Pauley, TV newscaster; Booth Tarkington, author; Kurt Vonnegut, Jr., author; Harry Von Zell, announcer; Clifton Webb, actor

JACKSONVILLE, FLA.

Mayor: John Delaney (to June 30, 1999)
1990 census population, sex, & (rank)[1]: 681,126 (15); **% change,** 17.9; **Male,** 328,737; **Female,** 344,234; **White,** 489,604; **Black,** 163,902 (24.4%); **American Indian, Eskimo, or Aleut,** 1,904 (0.3%); **Asian or Pacific Islander,** 12,940 (1.9%); **Other race,** 4,621; **Hispanic origin,** 17,333 (2.6%). **1990 percent population under 18:** 25.9; **65 and over:** 10.7; **median age:** 31.5.
Land area: 759.6 sq mi. (1,967 sq km); **Alt.:** Highest, 71 ft; lowest, sea level
Avg. daily temp.: Jan., 53.2° F; July, 81.3° F
Churches: Protestant, 794; Roman Catholic, 21; Jewish, 5; others, 22; **City-owned parks and playgrounds:** 138 (1,522 ac.); **Radio stations:** AM, 14; FM, 16; **Television stations:** 6 commercial, 1 PBS, 1 religious
CIVILIAN LABOR FORCE: 328,211; **Unemployed:** 24,051, **Percent:** 7.3; **Per capita personal income:** $16,215
Chamber of Commerce: Jacksonville Area Chamber of Commerce, Jacksonville, Fla. 32202
1. Consolidated city.

Jacksonville, Florida's largest city, is located in Duval county in the northeast corner of Florida on the banks of the St. Johns River and adjacent to the Atlantic Ocean. It is the largest metropolitan area in northeast Florida and southeast Georgia.

Starting in the 16th century, French, Spanish, and English explorers and colonists were attracted to the region by the St. Johns River. The site was settled by Lewis Hogans in 1816. Jacksonville was laid out in 1822 and was named after Gen. Andrew Jackson, the first military governor of Florida. It was incorporated as a city in 1832.

During the Civil War, much of the city was destroyed by Union forces who occupied Jacksonville four times. The city was rebuilt and, following the development of its harbor and the railroads, fast became the transportation hub and leading industrial city in Florida by the 1880s. In 1968, Jacksonville annexed Duval county.

Jacksonville is the transportation hub and distribution focal point in the state. The strength of the city's economy lies in its broad diversification. The area's economic structure is composed of a balance between distribution, financial services, biomedical, consumer goods, information services, manufacturing, and other industries. Jacksonville has the largest deepwater port in the South Atlantic and is the leading port in the U.S. for automobile imports.

Famous natives: Mae Axton, songwriter; Pat Boone, singer; Judy Canova, comedian; Harold Carmichael, football player; Merion C. Cooper, producer, director; Billy Daniels, vocalist; Storm Davis, athlete; Bob Hayes, athlete; Wanda Hendrix, actress; James Weldon Johnson, author, educator; John Rosamond Johnson, musician, composer; Mark McCumber, pro golfer; Ray Mercer, boxer; Charles "Hoss" Singleton, songwriter; Bill Terry, Baseball Hall of Fame; Donnie Van Zant, rock musician; Ronnie Van Zant, rock musician; Leeroy Yarbrough, auto racer

KANSAS CITY, MO.

Mayor: Emanuel Cleaver II (to April 1999)
City Manager: Larry J. Brown (apptd. Nov. 1993)

1990 census population, sex, & (rank): 435,146 (31); **% change:** –2.9; **Male,** 206,965; **Female,** 228,181; **White,** 290,572; **Black,** 128,768 (29.6%); **American Indian, Eskimo, or Aleut,** 2,144 (0.5%); **Asian or Pacific Islander,** 5,239 (1.2%); **Other race,** 8,423; **Hispanic origin,** 17,017 (3.9%). **1990 percent population under 18:** 24.8; **65 and over:** 12.9; **median age:** 32.8.
Land area: 317 sq mi. (821 sq km); **Alt.:** Highest, 1,014 ft; lowest, 722
Avg. daily temp.: Jan., 28.4° F; July, 80.9 F
Churches: 1,100 churches of all denominations[1]; **City-owned parks and playgrounds:** 189 (10,647 ac.); **Radio stations:** AM, 14; FM, 19[1]; **Television stations:** 7[1]
CIVILIAN LABOR FORCE: 239,600; **Unemployed:** 15,400, **Percent:** 6.4; **Per capita personal income:** $17,899[2]
Chamber of Commerce: Chamber of Commerce of Greater Kansas City, 911 Main St., Kansas City, Mo. 64105
1. Metropolitan area. 2. Kansas City, Mo.–Kan. MSA.

Kansas City is the largest city in Missouri. It is located in the western part of the state, at the junction of the Missouri and Kansas Rivers. Kansas City is located in Jackson, Clay, Platte, and Cass counties.

In 1821, the year Missouri entered the Union, French trader François Chouteau came from St. Louis to establish a trading post on the site of the present city to take advantage of the growing fur trade with the Kansa, Osage, Wyandotte, and other tribes. In 1833, a settlement was laid out by John Calvin McCoy and developed, called the town of Westport Landing. The community became the Town of Kansas and was incorporated as a city in 1850 and renamed Kansas City in 1889. The city's name reflects its Native American heritage—its site was within the territory of the Kansa or Kaw Indians.

The city grew rapidly in the mid-1880s as the starting point for gold prospectors and settlers heading westward. The coming of the Missouri-Pacific railroad in 1865 and the spanning of the Missouri River by the Hannibal Bridge in 1869 also contributed to the city's growth, and it prospered as a center for the nation's cattle business.

The Kansas City metropolitan area once known primarily for agriculture and manufacturing, has expanded its economic base to include strong growth in areas of telecommunications, banking and finance, and the service industry. A transportation hub since the 1800s, the area enjoys a national and regional prominence as a distribution and manufacturing center. Kansas City ranks nationally as first in greeting card publishing, frozen food storage and distribution, and first in hard winter wheat marketing, second in wheat flour production, and third in auto and truck assembly. The area is one of ten federal regional centers and employs over 25,000 in local, state, and federal government. The city is also a regional center for health care, employing over 55,000 in this industry.

Famous natives: Robert Altman, director; Edward Asner, actor; Burt Bacharach, composer; Noah and Wallace Beery, actors; Robert Russell Bennett, composer; Jeanne Eagels, actress; Jean Harlow, actress; Ted Shawn, dancer, choreographer; Casey Stengel, baseball; Virgil Thompson, composer; Tom Watson, golfer

LONG BEACH, CALIF.

Mayor: Beverly O'Neill (to April 1998)
City Manager: James C. Hankla
1990 census population, sex, & (rank): 429,433 (32); **% change,** 18.8; **Male,** 216,685; **Female,** 212,748; **White,** 250,716; **Black,** 58,761 (13.7%); **American Indian, Eski-**

mo, or Aleut, 2,781 (0.6%); **Asian or Pacific Islander,**
58,266 (13.6%); **Other race,** 58,909; **Hispanic origin,**
101,419 (23.6%). **1990 percent population under 18:**
25.5; **65 and over:** 10.8; **median age:** 30.0.
Land area: 49.8 sq mi. (129 sq km); **Alt.:** Highest, 170 ft;
lowest, sea level
Avg. daily temp.: Jan., 55.2 F; July, 72.8° F
Churches: 236; **City-owned parks:** 48 (2,000 ac.); **Radio
stations:** AM, 2; FM, 2; **Television stations:** 8 (metro
area)
CIVILIAN LABOR FORCE: 201,900; **Unemployed:** 15,100,
Percent: 7.5; **Per capita personal income:** $19,906[1]
Chamber of Commerce: Long Beach Area Chamber of
Commerce, One World Trade Center, Suite 350, Long
Beach, CA 90831-0350
1. Los Angeles-Long Beach MSA.

Long Beach is the fifth largest city in California
and is situated on San Pedro Bay, south of Los Angeles, in Los Angeles county.
The town was laid out and settled in 1881 by developer W.E. Willmore who sold lots in the site as a
seaside resort community called Willmore City. It
was renamed Long Beach for its 8 1/2-mi. beach in
1884. The city was incorporated in 1888 and reincorporated in 1897.
Long Beach is a major industrial port. The services
and manufacturing industries together account for over
50% of the local economy. Retail trade and government are the next largest sectors, accounting for an additional 30% of employment. Tourism is also important to the economy. Minor industries include
transportation, communication and utilities, wholesale
trade, finance, insurance, and real estate. Long Beach's
economy has been adversely affected by cutbacks in
the defense and aircraft production industries.

Famous natives: Jack Anderson, journalist; Jennifer
Bartlett, artist; Barbara Britton, actress; Nicholas Cage,
actor; Spike Jones, orchestra leader; Sally Kellerman,
actress; Billie Jean King, tennis player; Martha Rae
Watson, track; Heather Watts, dancer

LOS ANGELES, CALIF.

Mayor: Richard Riordan (to June 1997)
1990 census population, sex, & (rank): 3,485,398 (2); **%
change,** 17.4; **Male,** 1,750,055; **Female,** 1,735,343;
White, 1,841,182; **Black,** 487,674 (14.0%); **American
Indian, Eskimo, or Aleut,** 16,379 (0.5%); **Asian or Pacific Islander,** 341,807 (9.8%); **Other race,** 798,356;
Hispanic origin, 1,391,411 (39.9%). **1990 percent population under 18:** 24.8; **65 and over:** 10.0; **median age:**
30.7.
Land area: 467.4 sq mi. (1,210.57 sq km); **Alt.:** Highest,
5,081 ft; lowest, sea level
Avg. daily temp.: Jan., 57.2° F; July, 74.1° F
Churches: 2,000 of all denominations; **City-owned parks:**
355 (15,357 ac.); **Radio stations:** AM, 35; FM, 53; **Television stations:** 19
CIVILIAN LABOR FORCE: 1,827,505; **Unemployed:**
198,626, **Percent:** 10.9; **Per capita personal income:**
$19,906[1]
Chamber of Commerce: Los Angeles Chamber of Commerce, 404 S Bixel St., Los Angeles, Calif. 90017
1. Los Angeles-Long Beach MSA.

Los Angeles is the largest city in California and
the second largest urban area in the nation. It is located in the southern part of the state on the Pacific
Ocean. It is the seat of Los Angeles county. Geographically, it extends more than 40 miles from the
mountains to the sea.

The Spanish explorer, Gaspar de Portolá visited the
site in 1769. On Sept. 4, 1781, the Mexican Provincial Governor, Filipe de Neve, founded "El Pueblo de
Nuestra Señora la Reina de Los Angeles"—meaning
"The Village of Our Lady, the Queen of the Angels."
The pueblo became the capital of the Mexican province, Alta California, and it was the last place to surrender to the U.S. at the time of the American occupation in 1847. By the Treaty of Guadalupe Hidalgo
in 1848, Mexico ceded California to the United States
and Los Angeles was incorporated as a city in 1850.
The city's phenomenal growth was brought about
primarily by its equable climate which attracted people and industry from all parts of the nation; the development of its citrus-fruit industry; the discovery of
oil in the area during the early 1890s; the development of its man-made harbor—its port is one of the
busiest in the U.S.; and the growth of the motion picture industry in the early 20th century. Today, Hollywood is a suburb of Los Angeles.
Los Angeles is a major hub of shipping, manufacturing, industry, and finance, and is world renowned
in the entertainment and communications fields. It is
a favorite vacation destination and attracts millions of
tourists to the area each year from all over the world.
Los Angeles county is the nation's largest manufacturing center, surpassing Chicago, New York, and
Detroit. The Ports of Los Angeles and Long Beach
are second only to New York as the largest customs
district in the United States.
Major employer in the Los Angeles Five-County
area is the business and management sector. Growth
in the key wholesale industries—apparel and textiles,
furniture, jewelry, and toys, and the boom in industrial trade have been forecast for the region in the
nineties. Other important sectors are health services
and international trade and investment. The aerospace
and technology industries have declined due to defense cutbacks but are still expected to be a viable
part of the region's economy.

Famous natives: Busby Berkeley, choreographer, director; Marge Champion, dancer, choreographer; Jackie Coogan, actor; Jackie Cooper, actor; Linda Fratianne, figure skater; Jodie Foster, actress, director;
John Gavin, actor, diplomat; Pancho Gonzalez, tennis
player; Cynthia Gregory, ballerina; Jerome Hines, basso; Dustin Hoffman, actor; Theodore Harold Maiman,
laser inventor; Marilyn Monroe, actress; Isamu Noguchi, sculptor; Leonard Slotkin, conductor; Duke Snider,
baseball player; Adlai E. Stevenson, statesman; Madeleine Stowe, actress; Darryl Strawberry, baseball player;

MEMPHIS, TENN.

Mayor: W.W. Herenton (to Dec. 1995)
1990 census population, sex, & (rank): 610,337 (18); **%
change,** −5.6; **Male,** 285,010; **Female,** 325,327; **White,**
268,600; **Black,** 334,737 (54.8%); **American Indian,
Eskimo, or Aleut,** 960 (0.2%); **Asian or Pacific Islander,** 4,805 (0.8%); **Other race,** 1,235; **Hispanic origin,**
4,455 (0.7%). **1990 percent population under 18:** 26.9;
65 and over: 12.2; **median age:** 31.5.
Land area: 277 sq mi. (702 sq km); **Alt.:** Highest, 417 ft
Avg. daily temp.: Jan., 39.6° G; July, 82.1° F
Churches: 2000+; **Parks and playgrounds:** 230 (13,291
ac.); **Radio stations:** AM, 14; FM, 15; **Television sta-
tions:** 6
CIVILIAN LABOR FORCE: 292,819; **Unemployed:** 25,640,
Percent: 8.8; **Per capita personal income:** $11,682
Chamber of Commerce: Memphis Area Chamber of
Commerce, P.O. Box 224, Memphis, Tenn. 38103

Memphis, the largest city in Tennessee and the seat of Shelby county, is located in the southwestern corner of the state, on the Mississippi River.

The first settlers of Memphis were the Chickasaw Indians, who had a village named Chisca there on the bluffs overlooking the Mississippi River. Hernando DeSoto, in 1541, is said to have had his first glimpse of the Mississippi from the site of Memphis; and in the next century, Joliet and Marquette stopped there to trade with the Indians. The French explorer Sieur de La Salle tried to claim the region for France in 1682 and built Fort Prudhomme there. The area was ceded to the United States by the Chickasaw Indians in 1818. Memphis was officially established in 1819 by three enterprising businessmen from Nashville, James Winchester, John Overton, and future-President Andrew Jackson. Jackson named it after the ancient Egyptian city because of its Nilelike site on the Mississippi River. Memphis was incorporated as a city in 1826 and became an important Mississippi River port.

During the Civil War, Memphis was a Confederate military center. In 1862, Federal forces won a gunboat battle on the river at Memphis and General Sherman was enabled to take the city.

Memphis's population was devastated by several yellow-fever epidemics during the 1870s and the city did not recover its prosperity until the end of the 19th century.

Memphis is one of the country's largest inland ports and is known as "America's Distribution Center" serving the northeast, southeast, and southwest regions of the country. Memphis is a leader in agribusiness, cultivating soybeans, rice, grain sorghum, winter wheat, corn, and livestock raising. The city is the world's largest trading center for spot cotton, handling over 40% of the nation's spot cotton crops annually. It is the largest hardwood lumber trading and processing center in the world and is estimated to be the nation's third largest total food processor.

Health care and related activities such as medical education and biomedical research is Memphis's largest industry bringing over $2.5 billion a year to the local economy. Also important are high tech communications.

Famous natives: Kathy Bates, actress; Dixie Carter, actress; Rosalind Cash, singer; Aretha Franklin, singer; Morgan Freeman, actor; Al Green, singer; George Hamilton, actor; Anfrenee "Penny" Hardaway, basketball; Isaac Hayes, singer; Hal Holbrook, actor; Benjamin Hooks, organization official; B.B. King, singer; Hal Needham, director; Charlie Rich, singer; Cybill Shepherd, actress; Robert Siodmak, director; Fred Smith, businessman; Rufus Thomas, singer; Kemmons Wilson, businessman

MIAMI, FLA.

Mayor: Stephen P. Clark (to Nov. 1997)
City manager: Cesar Odio (apptd. Dec. 1985)
1990 census population, sex, & (rank): 358,548 (46); **% change**, 3.4; **Male**, 173,223; **Female**, 185,325; **White**, 235,358; **Black**, 98,207 (27.4%); **American Indian, Eskimo, or Aleut**, 545 (0.2%); **Asian or Pacific Islander**, 2,272 (0.6%); **Other race**, 22,166; **Hispanic origin**, 223,964 (62.5%). **1990 percent population under 18:** 23.0; **65 and over**, 16.6; **median age**, 36.0.
Land area: 34.3 sq mi. (89 sq km); **Water area:** 19.5 sq mi.; **Alt.:** Average, 12 ft
Avg. daily temp.: Jan., 67.1° F; July, 82.4° F

Churches (Dade County): Protestant, 850; Roman Catholic, 61; Jewish, 64; **City-owned parks (Miami):** 109; **Radio stations (Dade County):** 29; **Television stations (Dade County):** 9 TV, 1 Cable
CIVILIAN LABOR FORCE: 181,684; **Unemployed:** 21,348, **Percent:** 11.8; **Per capita personal income:** $18,298
Chamber of Commerce: Greater Miami Chamber of Commerce, 1601 Biscayne Blvd., Miami, Fla. 33132

Miami, the second largest city in Florida and seat of Dade county, is located in the southeastern part of the state, on Biscayne Bay.

The area was once the home of the Tequesta Indians until they were nearly wiped out by European diseases and warfare brought on by two centuries of Spanish control of Florida. Miami was founded in 1870 near the site of Ft. Dallas built in 1835 during the Seminole Indian wars. The city's name is probably derived from "Mayaimi," the Indian word for "big water."

Miami is the only U.S. city to have been conceived by a woman. Julia Tuttle, a Clevelander, arrived there in 1891 and bought several hundred acres on the bank of the Miami River. She convinced New York financier Henry M. Flagler of the area's vast potential and persuaded him to extend his Florida East Coast Railroad to Miami in 1896, the year the city was incorporated. Flagler dredged Miami harbor, built the renowned Royal Palm Hotel which opened Jan. 1, 1897, and promoted the area as a winter playground. Tourists flocked there and, by 1910, the city was a thriving recreational area. Miami survived the collapse of a land speculation boom in the 1920s and severe hurricanes in 1926 and 1935 and continued to grow in the aftermath of these disasters.

Miami experienced one of its most monumental population boosts during the 1960s when about 260,000 Cuban refugees arrived on its shore seeking freedom. They made a great impact on Miami, now a bilingual metropolis, and spurred economic growth.

Miami is an international banking and finance center and the city has the greatest concentration of international and Edge Act banks[1] in North America which constitute a major employment base. Greater Miami[2] has a highly diversified economy with over 170 multinational Miami-based companies, a bevy of Fortune 500 companies, and a rapidly growing manufacturing and distribution center. Miami ranks number one in Florida for total manufacturing income, employment, and number of manufacturing establishments. Greater Miami is the nation's leader in biomedical technology and the health care sector is a major industry. It is also part of an area known as the Computer Coast of Florida, and its growing technologies include computers, electrical engineering, and plastics manufacturing.

Miami is one of the world's leading year-round resort centers with tourism contributing over 60% of the area's economy. The city is a major transportation hub and the port of Miami is the world's largest cruise port and a major seaport for cargo. The famous island resort of Miami Beach, incorporated in 1915, is part of Greater Miami and is connected to Miami by four causeways.

1. Edge Act banks may make only foreign loans and accept foreign deposits. 2. Greater Miami is made up of 27 municipalities of which the City of Miami is the largest.

Famous natives: Fernando Bujones, dancer; Steve Carlton, baseball player; Debbie Harry, singer; Dick Howser, baseball player and manager; Sidney Poitier, actor; Janet Reno, Attorney General of the U.S.; Ben Vereen, actor; Ellen Zwilich, composer

MILWAUKEE, WIS.

Mayor: John O. Norquist (to April 1996)
1990 census population, sex, & (rank): 628,088 (17); **% change,** –1.3; **Male,** 296,837; **Female,** 331,251; **White,** 398,033; **Black,** 191,255 (30.5%); **American Indian, Eskimo, or Aleut,** 5,858 (0.9%); **Asian or Pacific Islander,** 11,817 (1.9%); **Other race,** 21,125; **Hispanic origin,** 39,409 (6.3%). **1990 percent population under 18:** 27.4; **65 and over:** 12.4; **median age:** 30.3.
Land area: 95.8 sq mi. (248 sq km); **Alt.:** 580.60 ft
Avg. daily temp.: Jan., 18.7° F; July, 70.5° F
Churches: 411; **County-owned parks:** 14,758 ac.; **Radio stations:** AM, 15; FM, 8; **Television stations:** 10
CIVILIAN LABOR FORCE: 302,993; **Unemployed:** 17,468, **Percent:** 5.8; **Per capita personal income:** $18,842[1]
Chamber of Commerce: Metropolitan Milwaukee Association of Commerce, 828 N. Broadway, Milwaukee, Wis. 53202; Milwaukee Minority Chamber of Commerce, 2821 N. 4th St., Milwaukee, Wis. 53212; Hispanic Chamber of Commerce, 1125 W. National Ave., Milwaukee, Wis. 53204
1. PMSA.

Milwaukee, the largest city in Wisconsin and seat of Milwaukee county, is located in the southeastern part of the state on Lake Michigan.

French missionaries visited the site of Milwaukee in the seventeenth century, but it was not until 1795 that Jacques Vieau established a fur-trading post there. The first permanent white settler, Vieau's son-in-law, Solomon Juneau, an agent of the American Fur Company, made his home there in 1818. The settlement merged with several neighboring villages in 1838 to form Milwaukee, and the city was incorporated in 1846. Its name is derived from an Algonquian Indian word Milo-aki meaning "beautiful land." A large wave of German immigrants arrived after 1848 and contributed greatly to the city's political, economic, and cultural development.

Milwaukee is one of the great industrial centers in the country and one of the largest Great Lakes ports. Currently, port commerce runs over 2 million tons per year.

Its economy was forged by heavy industries but is now diversified. Manufacturing remains strong and Milwaukee manufacturers are national leaders in lithographic commercial printing and the production of medical diagnostic instruments, small gasoline engines, malt beverages, iron and steel forgings, mining and construction machinery, robotics, speed changers and drives, and electronic controls. Milwaukee's high-tech manufacturing community is the ninth-largest among the nation's 31 major metropolitan areas. Once known as a "beer town," less than one percent of Milwaukee's workforce is involved in beer production. However, beer still plays an important role and almost 11% of the nation's malt beverage is produced there.

Tourism is important to the economy and about 5 million people visit Milwaukee every year.

Famous natives: Donald Gramm, bass-baritone; Woody Herman, band leader; Al Jarreau, singer; George F. Kennan, diplomat; Alfred Lunt, actor; Pat O'Brien, actor; Tom Snyder, TV personality; Speech, member of rap group, "Arrested Development;" Spencer Tracy, actor; Gene Wilder, actor

MINNEAPOLIS, MINN.

Mayor: Sharon Sayles-Belton (to Jan. 1998)
1990 census population, sex, & (rank): 368,383 (42); **% change,** –0.7; **Male,** 178,671; **Female,** 189,712; **White,** 288,967; **Black,** 47,948 (13.0%); **American Indian, Eskimo, or Aleut,** 12,335 (3.3%); **Asian or Pacific Islander,** 15,723 (4.3%); **Other race,** 3,410; **Hispanic origin,** 7,900 (2.1%). **1990 percent population under 18:** 20.6; **65 and over:** 13.0; **median age:** 31.7
Land area: 58.7 sq mi. (143 sq km); **Alt.:** Highest, 945 ft; lowest, 695
Avg. daily temp.: Jan., 11.2° F; July, 73.1° F
Churches: 419; **City-owned parks:** 153; **Radio stations:** AM, 17; FM, 15 (metro area); **Television stations:** 6 (metro area)
CIVILIAN LABOR FORCE: 204,477; **Unemployed:** 9,905, **Percent:** 4.8; **Per capita personal income:** $20,227[1]
Chamber of Commerce: Greater Minneapolis Chamber of Commerce, Young Quinlan Building, 81 S. Ninth Street, Suite 200, Minneapolis, Minn. 55402-3223
1. Minneapolis-St. Paul Minn.–Wis. MSA.

Minneapolis, the largest city in Minnesota and seat of Hennepin county, is located in the southeast central part of the state on the Mississippi River. It is adjacent to its "twin city" of St. Paul. The Minneapolis-St. Paul Standard Metropolitan Statistical Area is the 15th largest in the United States.

In 1680, Father Louis Hennepin visited the future site of Minneapolis and gave the Falls of St. Anthony their name. Lieutenant Zebulon Pike made a treaty with the Sioux Indians in 1805–06 by which they ceded to the whites land including the Falls of St. Anthony and the site of Minneapolis. Fort Snelling was built in 1819–20 and, in 1823, the government built a lumber and flour mill. Flour milling became the major industry of early Minneapolis and made the city the milling capital of the world. The town of St. Anthony was established on the east bank of the Mississippi in 1848 and the town of Minneapolis grew up on the opposite bank of the river. The name Minneapolis is a combination of the Dakota Sioux word "minna" for water and the Greek word "polis" for city. Minneapolis was incorporated as a city in 1867 and, in 1872, the city of St. Anthony (chartered in 1860) was annexed to it. After the spread of the railroads in the 1870s, Minneapolis became the gateway to the Northern Great Plains.

Minneapolis is a center of industry and commerce serving a large agricultural region. During the 20th century, manufacturing, food processing, milling, computers, health services, and graphic arts developed as Minneapolis's major industries. Sixteen Fortune 500 industrial and 17 Fortune service companies are headquartered there. The city is the home of the world's largest cash grain market and is the headquarters of the Ninth Federal Reserve Bank.

Famous natives: La Verne, Maxene, Patti Andrews, singers; James Arness, actor; Lew Ayres, actor; Patty Berg, golfer; Virginia Bruce, actress; J. Paul Getty, oil executive; Peter Graves, actor; George Roy Hill, director; Cornell MacNeil, baritone; Ralph Meeker, actor; Gen. Lauris Norstad; Westbrook Pegler, columnist; Prince, singer; Harrison Salisbury, journalist; Charles Schulz, cartoonist; Anne Tyler, writer; Bud Wilkinson, football player; David Winfield, baseball player

NASHVILLE-DAVIDSON, TENN.

Mayor: Philip N. Bredesen
1900 census population, sex, & (rank)[1]: 510,784 (23); **% change,** 6.9; **Male,** 242,492; **Female,** 268,292; **White,** 381,740; **Black,** 119,273 (23.4%); **American Indian, Eskimo, or Aleut,** 1,162 (0.2%); **Asian or Pacific Islander,** 7,081 (1.4%); **Other race,** 1,528; **Hispanic origin,** 4,775 (0.9%). **1900 percent population under 18:** 22.8; **65 and over:** 11.6; **median age:** 32.6.

Land area: 533 sq mi. (1,380 sq km); **Altitude:** Highest, 1,100 ft; lowest, approx. 400 ft
Avg. daily temp.: Jan., 36.7° F; July, 76.6° F
Churches: Protestant, 781; Roman Catholic, 18; Jewish, 3; **City-owned parks:** 76 (6,650 ac.); **Radio stations:** AM, 11; FM, 8; **Television stations:** 7
CIVILIAN LABOR FORCE: 267,724; **Unemployed:** 12,893, **Percent:** 3.1; **Per capita personal income:** $22,273
Chamber of Commerce: Nashville Area Chamber of Commerce, 161 Fourth Ave. North, Nashville, Tenn. 37219
1. Consolidated city.

The consolidated city of Nashville–Davidson is the capital and second largest city in Tennessee and is located in the north central part of the state on the Cumberland River. It is the seat of Davidson county.

During the winter of 1779–80, James Robertson and John Donelson founded a settlement at Big Salt Lick by the Cumberland River at the present site of the city. They built forts on both sides of the river naming one of them Fort Nashborough in honor of Francis Nash, a Revolutionary War general. In 1784, the town was named Nashville and was incorporated as a city in 1806.

Nashville became the capital of Tennessee in 1843 and was the seat of Davidson county until 1963 when it merged with the county to become Nashville–Davidson.

Nashville's best known industries are recording, publishing, and the distribution of music, especially country music. The city is a port of entry and an important industrial and commercial center serving the Upper South. Its diverse economy includes chemicals, wearing apparel, publishing, insurance, and banking. Auto manufacturing and health care management are also important industries. Nashville is the home of several religious organizations and is a major tourist attraction and convention center.

Famous natives: Gregg Allman, singer; Rita Coolidge, singer; Al Gore, Vice President; Red Grooms, artist; Barbara Howar, hostess, writer; Minnie Pearl, comedienne; Annie Potts, actress; Paula Robeson, flutist; Dinah Shore, actress/singer

NEW ORLEANS, LA.

Mayor: Marc H. Morial
1990 census population, sex, & (rank): 496,938 (25); % **change,** –10.9; **Male,** 230,883; **Female,** 266,055; **White,** 173,554; **Black,** 307,728 (61.9%); **American Indian, Eskimo, or Aleut,** 759 (0.2%); **Asian or Pacific Islander,** 9,678 (1.9%); **Other race,** 5,219; **Hispanic origin,** 17,238 (3.5%). **1990 percent population under 18:** 27.5; **65 and over,** 13.0; **median age,** 31.6.
Land area: 199.4 sq mi. (516 sq km); **Alt.:** Highest, 15 ft; lowest, –4
Avg. daily temp.: Jan., 52.4° F; July, 77° F
Churches: 712; **City-owned parks:** 165 (299 ac.); **Radio stations:** AM, 12; FM, 14; **Television stations:** 7
CIVILIAN LABOR FORCE: 205,610[1]; **Unemployed:** 15,055[1], **Percent:** 7.3[1]; **Per capita personal income:** $14,745
Chamber of Commerce: The Chamber/New Orleans and the River Region, 301 Camp Street, New Orleans, La. 70130
1. New Orleans City/Orleans Parish.

New Orleans, the largest city in Louisiana and seat of Orleans Parish, is located in the southeastern part of the state, between the Mississippi River and Lake Ponchartrain.

One of the few cities of the nation that has been under three flags, New Orleans has belonged to Spain, France, and the U.S. The French founded it in 1718 and named it in honor of the Duke of Orleans. In 1762, France ceded the city and the territory to Spain. On 1800, the territory was returned to France, but government authorities did not take over until 1803, only 20 days before the region became part of the U.S. in the Louisiana Purchase.

As a memento of the old days, New Orleans has its famous French Quarter which has a fascination for tourists and gourmets. The most spectacular and gayest festival in the U.S. is held in New Orleans—The Mardi Gras—which involves a week of carnival before the beginning of Lent.

New Orleans is one of the world's greatest international ports, the second largest in the nation, and it is a major focus of the city's economy. New Orleans is home to the corporate offices of oil companies with major offshore operations in the Gulf of Mexico, as well as the distribution and service centers of offshore equipment suppliers and fabricators. Refining of petroleum and a broad range of petrochemicals is a leading manufacturing industry. The shipbuilding/repair and aerospace equipment sectors are the largest manufacturing industries in terms of jobs. The New Orleans region also functions as a mining, processing, and transportation center for other minerals, principally sulfur. The information services (telecommunications) industry is one of the fastest growing in the area. The largest service sector in terms of jobs is the health care industry and the region is a leading center of medical service and health care in the southern United States.

Tourism has grown rapidly in recent years and New Orleans hosts more than seven million visitors annually.

Famous natives: Louis Armstrong, musician; Truman Capote, author; Fats Domino, musician; Louis Gottschalk, pianist, composer; Bryant Gumbel, TV personality; Lillian Hellman, playwright, author; Al Hirt, musician; Mahalia Jackson, singer; Dorothy Lamour, actress; Wynton Marsalis, musician; Huey Newton, activist; Marguerite Piazza, soprano; Rusty Staub, baseball player; Ben Turpin, comedian; Shirley Verrett, mezzo-soprano; Carl Weathers, actor; Del Williams, football player

NEW YORK, N.Y.

Mayor: Rudolph W. Guiliani (to Dec. 1997)
Borough Presidents: Bronx, Fernando Ferrer; Brooklyn, Howard Golden; Manhattan, Ruth W. Messinger; Queens, Claire Shulman; Staten Island, Guy V. Molinari
1990 census population, sex, & (rank): 7,322,564 (1)[1]; % **change,** 3.5; **Male,** 3,437,687; **Female,** 3,884,877; **White,** 3,827,088; **Black,** 2,102,512 (28.7%); **American Indian, Eskimo, or Aleut,** 27,531 (0.4%); **Asian or Pacific Islander,** 512,719 (7.0%); **Other race,** 852,714; **Hispanic origin,** 1,783,511 (24.4%).[2] **1990 percent population under 18:** 23.0; **65 and over,** 13.0; **median age,** 33.7.
Land area: 321.8 sq mi. (826.68 sq km) (Queens, 112.1; Brooklyn, 81.8; Staten Island, 60.2; Bronx, 44.0 Manhattan, 23.7); **Alt.:** Highest, 410 ft; lowest, sea level
Avg. daily temp.: Jan., 31.8° F; July, 76.7° F
Churches: Protestant, 1,766; Jewish, 1,256; Roman Catholic, 437; Orthodox, 66; **City-owned parks:** 1,701 (26,295 ac.); **Radio stations:** AM, 13; FM, 18; **Television stations:** 6 commercial, 1 public
CIVILIAN LABOR FORCE: 3,311,000; **Unemployed:** 359,000, **Percent:** 10.8; **Per capita personal income:** $22,0645[1]
Chamber of Commerce: New York Chamber of Commerce and Industry, 65 Liberty St., New York, N.Y. 10005

1. PMSA. 2. Race breakdown figures according to N.Y.C. Dept. of City Planning: White, non-Hispanic, 3,163,125; Black, non-Hispanic, 1,847,049; American Indian, Eskimo and Aleut, non-Hispanic, 17,871; Asian and Pacific Islander, non-Hispanic, 489,157; Hispanic, 1,783,511.

New York City is the largest city in the United States. It is located in the southern part of New York State, at the mouth of the Hudson River (also known as North River as it passes Manhattan Island).

In 1609, Henry Hudson, who worked for the Dutch East India Company, sailed up the river that now bears his name and went as far as Albany. Five years later, a permanent settlement was established at what is now New York, but it was originally called New Amsterdam by the Dutch governors. One of them, Peter Minuit, was said to have bought Manhattan Island from the Indians for $24 worth of beads, buttons, and trinkets. In 1664, Great Britain's Duke of York sent a fleet which quietly seized the settlement from the Dutch, without bloodshed, and rechristened the colony in honor of the Duke.

Control of New York passed to the young U.S. at the end of the Revolutionary War, and George Washington was inaugurated President in New York's old City Hall. Congress met in New York from 1785 to 1790.

In 1898, when Greater New York was chartered, the city expanded to include the following five boroughs which are also counties in New York State: Manhattan (New York county); Brooklyn (Kings county); Bronx (Bronx county); Queens (Queens county); and Staten Island (Richmond county).

There is a growing effort among Staten Island residents to separate from Greater New York and become an independent city of Staten Island.

Today, the Big Apple is the most populous city in the United States, a major world capital, and the world leader in finance, the arts, and communications. The city is also the center of advertising, fashion, publishing, and radio broadcasting in the United States. New York has innumerable museums, art galleries, and educational institutions. The port of New York is one of the finest in the world. The city is the home of the United Nations and is headquarters for some of the world's largest corporations.

Famous natives: Kareem Abdul-Jabbar, basketball player; Woody Allen, actor, director; Robert Anderson, playwright; Martina Arroyo, soprano; Jean Arthur, actress; Lauren Bacall, actress; James Baldwin, novelist; Harry Belafonte, singer, actor; Humphrey Bogart, actor; James Cagney, actor; Maria Callas, soprano; Paddy Chayefsky, playwright; Aaron Copland, composer; Sammy Davis, Jr., singer, actor; Agnes de Mille, choreographer; Robert De Niro, actor; Eamon De Valera, President of Ireland; Gertrude Elion, Nobel Prize in medicine; Lou Gehrig, baseball player; George Gershwin, composer; Ira Gershwin, lyricist; Jackie Gleason, actor; Hank Greenberg, baseball player; Rita Hayworth, actress; Lena Horne, singer; Julia Ward Howe, poet, reformer; Washington Irving, author; Henry James, novelist; John Jay, statesman, jurist; Michael Jordan, basketball player; Jerome Kern, composer; Sandy Koufax, baseball player; Michael Landon, actor; Roy Lichtenstein, painter; Vince Lombardi, football player, coach; Chico, Groucho, Harpo, Zeppo Marx, comedians; Herman Melville, novelist; Yehudi Menuhin, violinist; Ethel Merman, singer, actress; James Michener, novelist; Arthur Miller, playwright; Eugene O'Neill, playwright; J. Robert Oppenheimer, nuclear physicist; Al Pacino, actor; Jan Peerce, tenor; Roberta Peters, soprano; Elmer Rice, playwright; Jerome Robbins, choreographer; Norman Rockwell, painter, illustrator; Eleanor Roosevelt, reformer, humanitarian; Theodore Roosevelt, President; Jonas Salk, polio researcher; Beverly Sills, soprano; Neil Simon, playwright; Risë Stevens, mezzo-soprano; Barbra Streisand, singer, actress; Ed Sullivan, TV personality; Fats Waller, pianist; Mae West, actress; Edith Wharton, novelist; Rosalyn Yalow, Nobel Prize in medicine

OAKLAND, CALIF.

Mayor: Elihu Mason Harris (to Jan. 1998)
City Manager: Craig Kocian (apptd. July 1994)
1990 census population, sex, & (rank): 372,242 (39); % change, 9.7; Male, 178,824; Female, 193,418; White, 120,849; Black, 163,335 (43.9%); American Indian, Eskimo, or Aleut, 2,371 (0.6%); Asian or Pacific Islander, 54,931 (14.8%); Other race, 30,756; Hispanic origin, 51,711 (13.9%). **1990 percent population under 18,** 24.9; **65 and over,** 12.0; **median age:** 32.7.
Land area: 53.9 sq mi. (140 sq km); **Alt.:** Highest, 1,700 ft; lowest, sea level
Avg. daily temp.: Jan., 49.0° F; July, 63.7° F
Churches: 374, representing over 78 denominations in the City; over 500 churches in Alameda County; **City-owned parks:** 2,196 ac.; **Radio stations:** AM, 1; **Television stations:** 1 commercial
CIVILIAN LABOR FORCE: 180,624; **Unemployed:** 18,148, **Percent:** 10.0; **Per capita personal income:** $22,249[1]
Chamber of Commerce: Oakland Chamber of Commerce, 475 Fourteenth St., Oakland, Calif. 94612-1903
1. PMSA.

Oakland is located in the west central part of California on the east side of San Francisco Bay. It is the seat of Alameda county.

Don Luis Peralta first settled the site of Oakland in 1820 when he established the Rancho San Antonio. The gold rush of 1849 attracted more people to the area and the city's population continued to grow after a ferry service to San Francisco was started in 1851. Oakland was incorporated as a town in 1852 and as a city in 1854. It was named after the numerous oak trees found in the area. Oakland became the western terminus of the Central Pacific Railroad in 1869 and the seat of Alameda county in 1873.

During the latter part of the 19th century and also in 1910, additional territory was annexed to Oakland and the city assumed its present size. In 1906, thousands of people fled to Oakland in the aftermath of the San Francisco earthquake and settled there permanently, furthering the city's growth. Oakland's economic development continued to rise with the opening of the San Francisco–Oakland Bay Bridge in 1936.

Oakland is a major center of culture and commerce. It is an important container shipping port and the terminus of three transcontinental railroads. Oakland's industries include shipbuilding, food processing, chemicals, pharmaceuticals, electrical and high technology manufacturing. Oakland is also a leading importer of foreign cars. The city is the headquarters of many national and international corporations.

Famous natives: Buster Crabbe, actor; Frederick Cottrell, inventor; Dennis Eckersley, athlete; Hammer, singer, dancer, songwriter; Rod McKuen, singer, composer; Russ Meyer, producer, director; (Eddie Anderson) Rochester, actor; George Stevens, director; Amy Tan, writer; Jo Van Fleet, actress

OKLAHOMA CITY, OKLA.

Mayor: Ron Norick (to April 1998)
City Manager: Don Bown
1990 census population, sex, & (rank): 444,719 (29); % change, 10.1; Male, 214,466; Female, 230,253; White, 332,539; Black, 71,064 (16.0%); American Indian, Eskimo, or Aleut, 18,794 (4.2%); Asian or Pacific Islander,

10,491 (2.4%); **Other race,** 11,831; **Hispanic origin,** 22,033 (5.0%). **1990 percent population under 18:** 26.0; **65 and over:** 11.9; **median age:** 32.4.
Land area: 608.2 sq mi. (1,575 sq km); **Alt.:** Highest, 1,320 ft; lowest, 1,140
Avg. daily temp.: Jan., 35.9° F; July, 82.1° F
Churches: Roman Catholic, 25; Jewish, 2; Protestant and others, 741; **City-owned parks:** 138 (3,944 ac.); **Television stations:** 8; **Radio stations:** AM, 10; FM, 14
CIVILIAN LABOR FORCE: 230,226; **Unemployed:** 13,059, **Percent:** 5.7; **Per capita personal income:** $17,645
Chamber of Commerce: Oklahoma City Chamber of Commerce, 123 Park Ave., Oklahoma City, Okla. 73102

Oklahoma City, the state capital and seat of Oklahoma county, is the largest city in Oklahoma. It is located in the central part of the state on the North Canadian River.

Oklahoma City sprang into being almost overnight. On April 22, 1889, the government threw open the territory for settlement, and there was a classic rush across the line to stake claims. Within a short time, a sprawling tent city sprang up near the Santa Fe railroad railroad tracks and Oklahoma City was a bustling town of 10,000. The city was incorporated in 1890 and replaced Guthrie as the state capital in 1910. Oil was discovered in the city in 1928 and petroleum production became a mainstay of the city's economy.

Oklahoma City is the wholesale and distributing center for the state, and the city's stockyards are the largest stocker and feeder cattle market in the world. Following the decline of the energy sector, Oklahoma City is fostering a private entrepreneurial environment and a more diversified economy. Within the service sector, health services are projected to grow, followed by retail trade and business services. Aerospace, distribution, and telecommunications have been targeted for business attraction. Nearby Tinker Air Force Base, one of the world's largest air depots, is a major city employer.

Famous natives: Johnny Bench, baseball; Lon Chaney, Jr., actor; Ralph Ellison, writer; Kay Francis, actress; Dale Robertson, actor; Ted Shackleford, actor; Pamela Tiffin, actress

OMAHA, NEB.

Mayor: Hal Daub (to June 1997)
1990 census population, sex, & (rank): 335,795 (48); % change, 7.0; **Male,** 160,392; **Female,** 175,403; **White,** 281,603; **Black,** 43,989 (13.1%); **American Indian, Eskimo, or Aleut,** 2,274 (0.7%); **Asian or Pacific Islander,** 3,412 (1.0%); **Other race,** 4,517; **Hispanic origin,** 10,288 (3.1%). **1990 percent population under 18:** 25.4; **65 and over:** 12.9; **median age:** 32.2.
Land area: 107 sq mi. (278.2 sq km); **Alt.:** Highest, 1,270 ft
Avg. daily temp.: Jan., 20.2° F; July, 77.7° F
Churches: Protestant, 246; Roman Catholic, 44; Jewish, 4; **City-owned parks:** 159 (over 7,000 ac.); **Radio stations:** AM, 7; FM, 13; **Television stations:** 4
CIVILIAN LABOR FORCE: 177,387; **Unemployed:** 8,298, **Percent:** 4.7; **Per capita personal income:** $13,957[1]
Chamber of Commerce: Omaha Chamber of Commerce, 1301 Harney St., Omaha, Neb. 68102
1. Omaha, Neb.–Iowa MSA.

Omaha, the largest city in Nebraska and the seat of Douglas county, is located in the eastern part of the state on the west bank of the Missouri River opposite Council Bluffs, Iowa.

The area was visited by the Lewis and Clark expedition in 1804, and the U.S. Army built Ft. Atkinson

nearby in 1819. Pierre Cabanne established a fur-trading post at the site in 1825. The first Mormon migrants wintered there in 1846–47 on their way to Utah. The city grew rapidly as the most northerly supply point for overland wagons to the Far West.

The city was officially founded in 1854 after the Nebraska Territory was opened for settlement. It was named for the Omaha Indians living nearby, whose tribal name means "those who go upstream or against the current." Omaha was incorporated as a city in 1857 and was the capital of the Nebraska Territory from 1855 to 1867. The city continued to thrive as a point of entry and a major transportation center when the Union Pacific trans-continental railroad arrived in 1869.

Omaha is a major market for food processing, telecommunications, and insurance. Other important industries include electrical equipment, finance, as well as printing and publishing.

Famous natives: Fred Astaire, dancer, actor; Max Baer, boxer; Ronald Boone, former NBA professional; Robert Boozer, former NBA professional; Marlon Brando, actor; Montgomery Clift, actor; David Doyle, actor; Gerald Ford, President; Bob Gibson, baseball; Swoosie Kurtz, actress; Melvin Laird, Secretary of Defense; Dorothy McGuire, actress; Nick Nolte, actor; Gale Sayers, football; Malcolm X, political activist; Paul Williams, singer, composer

PHILADELPHIA, PA.

Mayor: Edward G. Rendell (to first Monday, January 1996)
1990 census population, sex, & (rank): 1,585,577 (5); % change, –6.1; **Male,** 737,763; **Female,** 847,814; **White,** 848,586; **Black,** 631,936 (39.9%); **American Indian, Eskimo, or Aleut,** 3,454 (0.2%); **Asian or Pacific Islander,** 43,522 (2.7%); **Other race,** 58,079; **Hispanic origin,** 89,193 (5.6%). **1990 percent population under 18:** 23.9; **65 and over:** 15.2; **median age:** 33.2.
Land area: 136 sq mi. (352 sq km); **Alt.:** Highest, 440 ft; lowest, sea level
Avg. daily temp.: Jan., 31.2° F; July, 76.5° F
Churches: Roman Catholic, 133; Jewish, 55; Protestant and others, 830; **City-owned parks:** 630 (10,252 ac.); **Radio stations:** AM, 40[1]; FM, 43[1;] **Television stations:** 14[1]
CIVILIAN LABOR FORCE: 699,391[2]; **Unemployed:** 61,403[2], **Percent:** 8.8[2]; **Per capita personal income:** $19,750[1]
Chamber of Commerce: Philadelphia Chamber of Commerce, 1234 Market Street, Suite 1800, Philadelphia, Pa. 19107
1. PMSA. 2. Philadelphia City/County.

Philadelphia, the largest city in Pennsylvania and seat of Philadelphia county (coterminous), is located in the southeastern part of the state at the junction of the Schuylkill and Delaware Rivers.

Philadelphia, the "City of Brotherly Love," was settled in 1681 by Capt. William Markham, who, with a small band of colonists, was sent out by his cousin, William Penn. Penn arrived the following year.

In the period before the American Revolution, the city outstripped all others in the colonies in education, arts, science, industry, and commerce. In 1774–76, the First and Second Continental Congresses met in Philadelphia; and, from 1781–83, the city was the capital of the U.S. under the Articles of Confederation. In 1790, it became the nation's capital under the Constitution and remained so until the seat of the federal government moved to Washington in 1800.

Within a half-century of the founding of the nation at Independence Hall, Philadelphia had emerged as the "world's greatest workshop." The steam locomotives and hat factories of the 19th century have been replaced by diverse manufacturing specialties such as chemicals, including pharmaceuticals, medical devices, transportation equipment, and printing and publishing. In the services sector, Philadelphia is a major net "exporter" in subsectors such as health services, insurance carriers, legal services, and architecture and engineering services.

The city abounds in landmarks of early American history, including Independence Hall and the Liberty Bell.

Famous natives: Marian Anderson, contralto; John, Lionel, and Ethel Barrymore, actors; Wilt Chamberlain, basketball player; Bill Cosby, actor; Stuart Davis, painter; Thomas Eakins, painter, sculptor; W.C. Fields, comedian; Stan Getz, saxophonist; Grace (Kelly), Princess of Monaco; Walt Kelly, cartoonist; Jack Klugman, actor; Mario Lanza, singer, actor; George McClellan, general; Margaret Mead, anthropologist; Anna Quindlen, writer, Pulitzer Prize winner; Man Ray, painter; Betsy Ross, flagmaker; Jacqueline Susann, novelist; Robert Venturi, architect

PHOENIX, ARIZ.

Mayor: Skip Rimsza (to Oct. 1995)
City Manager: Frank Fairbanks (appt. May 1990)
Population (July 1995 est.): 1,071,045
1990 census population, sex, & (rank): 983,403 (9); **% change,** 24.5; **Male,** 487,589; **Female,** 495,814; **White,** 803,332; **Black,** 51,053 (5.2%); **American Indian, Eskimo, or Aleut,** 18,225 (1.9%); **Asian or Pacific Islander,** 16,303 (1.7%); **Other race,** 94,490; **Hispanic origin,** 197,103 (20.0%). **1990 percent population under 18:** 27.2; **65 and over,** 9.7; **median age,** 31.1.
Land area: 456.702 sq mi. (1,182.85 sq km); **Alt.:** Highest, 2,740 ft.; lowest, 1,017
Avg. daily temp.: Jan., 53.6° F; July, 93.5° F
City-owned parks: 200 (30,412 ac.); **Radio stations:** AM, 20; FM, 20; **Television stations:** 9 commercial; 1 PBS
CIVILIAN LABOR FORCE: 618,497; **Unemployed:** 25,593, **Percent:** 4.1; **Per capita personal income:** $18,042
Chamber of Commerce: Phoenix Chamber of Commerce, 201 N. Central, Phoenix, Ariz. 85073

Phoenix, the capital of Arizona and seat of Maricopa county, is the largest city in Arizona. It is located in the center of Arizona on the Salt River.

The prehistoric Hohokam Indians first settled the area about 300 B.C. and dug a system of extensive irrigation canals for farming. The Indian culture mysteriously broke up in the 1400s. The site was permanently resettled again by Jack Swilling and "Lord Darrell" Duppa about 1867. Because the city was founded on the ruins of the ancient civilization, it was named Phoenix after the legendary Phoenix bird that could regenerate itself. The irrigation canals were restored for farming, and ranching and prospecting began in the surrounding area. The city quickly grew as an important trading center.

Phoenix was incorporated as a city in 1881 and was made the territorial capital in 1889. It became the state capital when Arizona was admitted to the Union in 1912.

Phoenix is a center of agriculture and commerce. Major industries include government, agricultural products, aerospace technology, electronics, air-conditioning, leather goods, and Indian arts and crafts. The city of Phoenix is renowned as a leader in local government management and received the 1993 Bertelsmann Foundation award for the best managed city in the world.

Famous natives: Lynda Carter, actress; Joan Ganz Cooney, TV executive; Alice Cooper, musician; Arthur A. Fletcher, government official; Barry Goldwater, politician; Stevie Nicks, musician; Charles S. Robb, politician; Mare Winningham, actress

PITTSBURGH, PA.

Mayor: Tom Murphy (to Jan. 1998)
1990 census population, sex, & (rank): 369,879 (40); **% change,** −12.8; **Male,** 171,722; **Female,** 198,157; **White,** 266,791; **Black,** 95,362 (25.8%); **American Indian, Eskimo, or Aleut,** 671 (0.2%); **Other race,** 1,118; **Hispanic origin,** 3,468 (0.9%). **1990 percent population under 18:** 19.8; **65 and over,** 17.9; **median age:** 34.6.
Land area: 55.5 sq mi. (144 sq km); **Alt.:** Highest, 1,240 ft; lowest, 715
Avg. daily temp.: Jan., 26.7° F; July, 72.0° F
Churches: Protestant, 348; Roman Catholic, 86; Jewish, 28; Orthodox, 26; **City-owned parks and playgrounds:** 270 (2,572 ac.); **Radio stations:** AM, 12; FM, 20; **Television stations:** 8
CIVILIAN LABOR FORCE: 176,754; **Unemployed:** 11,613, **Percent:** 6.6; **Per capita personal income:** $17,763[1]
Chamber of Commerce: The Chamber of Commerce of Greater Pittsburgh, 3 Gateway Center, Pittsburgh, Pa. 15222
1. PMSA.

Pittsburgh, the second largest city in Pennsylvania and seat of Allegheny county, is located in the southwestern part of the state at the junction where the Allegheny and Monongahela Rivers join to form the Ohio River.

Some of the first inhabitants of the area were the Shawnee, Seneca, Delaware, and Iroquois Indians who had left the area by 1754. That year a detachment of troops from Virginia put a fort on the site of present Pittsburgh (Ft. Prince George) considering it a strategic spot. Following the original Virginia settlers, the French seized the spot and named it Ft. Duquesne; and, in 1758, the British took it away from the French. The British built a new fort and named it after the British Prime Minister, William Pitt. A town developed around the fort and was incorporated as the City of Pittsburgh in 1816.

By the late 1800s, Pittsburgh had become a world leader in iron and steelmaking, and it remained so for nearly a century. In the early 1980s, the country's domestic steel industry collapsed causing major upheavals in Pittsburgh's manufacturing sector.

The Pittsburgh region underwent a successful diversified economic transition, shifting from heavy industries to light manufacturing, advanced technologies such as industrial automation, advanced materials, software engineering and biomedical technology, medicine, education, finance, and corporate services. Pittsburgh is a national leader in health care services and is the world's leading center for organ transplantation. The city is a hub of international business and ranks fifth as a major corporate headquarters center.

Pittsburgh is also a major U.S. transportation center and is the nation's largest inland port in terms of tonnage.

Famous natives: Rachel Carson, ecologist; Henry Steele Commager, historian; Bill Cullen, radio and TV entertainer; John Davidson, singer, actor; Billy Eckstine, singer; Erroll Garner, jazz pianist; Scott Glenn, actor; Martha Graham, dancer, choreographer; George S. Kaufman, playwright; Michael Keaton, actor; Gene Kelly, actor, dancer; Oscar Levant, pianist; Andrew Mellon, financier; Adolphe Menjou, actor; William Powell, actor; Mary Roberts Rinehart, novelist; Peter Sellars, theater director; David O. Selznick, producer; Joseph Wambaugh, novelist; August Wilson, playwright

PORTLAND, ORE.

Mayor: Vera Katz (till Jan. 1997)
July 1, 1994 population est.: 495,482
1990 census population, sex, & (rank): 437,319 (30); % change, 18.8; **Male,** 211,914; **Female,** 225,405; **White,** 370,135; **Black,** 33,530 (7.7%); **American Indian, Eskimo, or Aleut,** 5,399 (1.2%); **Asian or Pacific Islander,** 23,185 (5.3%); **Other race,** 5,070; **Hispanic origin,** 13,874 (3.2%). **1990 percent population under 18:** 21.9; **65 and over,** 14.6; **median age:** 34.5.
Land area: 137.8 sq mi. (357 sq km.); **Alt.:** Highest, 1073 ft; lowest, sea level
Avg. daily temp.: Jan., 38.9° F; July, 67.7° F
Churches: Protestant, 450; Roman Catholic, 48; Jewish, 9; Buddhist, 6; other, 190; **City-owned parks:** 200 (over 9,400 ac.); **Radio stations:** AM: 14, FM: 14; **Television stations:** 5 commercial, 1 public
CIVILIAN LABOR FORCE: 248,724; **Unemployed:** 18,372, **Percent:** 7.4; **Per capita personal income:** $18,163[1]
Chamber of Commerce: Portland Chamber of Commerce, 221 NW 2nd Ave., Portland, Ore. 97209
1. PMSA.

Portland, the largest city in Oregon and seat of Multnomah county, is located in the northwestern part of the state on the Willamette River.

Lewis and Clark camped at the site of Portland in 1805 on their expedition across the continent. Portland was founded in 1845 and was almost called Boston after the city in Massachusetts. Its two founders, Amos Lovejoy from Massachusetts and Francis Pettygrove from Maine, flipped a coin to decide the name of the new town. Pettygrove won the toss and named the place Portland after his hometown in Maine. Portland was incorporated as a city in 1851.

Portland's growth was stimulated during the 1850s as a supply base for the California gold rush, the development of its salmon and lumber industries, and by the arrival of the railroad in 1883. The city continued to grow during 1879 to 1900 as a supply point for the Alaska gold rush and as the site of the Lewis and Clark Centennial Exposition in 1905.

The Port of Portland leads the west in grain exports and is among the top five auto import centers in the United States. The Port ranks third in overall volume behind Los Angeles and Long Beach.

Portland has a diverse economy with a broad base of manufacturing, distribution, wholesale and retail trade, regional government, and business services. Major manufacturing industries include machinery, electronics, metals, transportation equipment, and lumber and wood products. High technology is a thriving part of Portland's economy with over 500 high tech companies located in the metropolitan area. Tourism is also important to Portland's economy.

Famous natives: James Beard, food expert; Pietro Belluschi, architect; Richard Fosbury, high jumper; Matt Groening, cartoonist; Margaux Hemingway, actress; Phil Knight, founder of Nike; Terrance Knox, actor; Jeff Lorber, jazz musician; Linus Pauling, chemist; Jane Powell, singer, actress; Ahmad Rashad, football player, sportscaster; Susan Ruttan, actress; Pat Schroeder, congressperson; Doc Severinson, band leader; Norton Simon, business executive; Sally Ann Struthers, actress; Gus Van Sant, film director; Lindsay Wagner, actress; Mitch Williams, baseball pitcher

SACRAMENTO, CALIF.

Mayor: Joe Serna, Jr. (to Dec. 1996)
1994 population est.: 393,500; **1990 census population, sex, & (rank):** 369,365 (41); **% change,** 34.0; **Male,** 178,737; **Female,** 190,628; **White,** 221,963; **Black,** 56,521 (15.3%); **American Indian, Eskimo, or Aleut,** 4,561 (1.2%); **Asian or Pacific Islander,** 55,426 (15.0%); **Other race,** 30,894; **Hispanic origin,** 60,007 (16.2%). **1990 census population under 18:** 26.2; **65 and over,** 12.1; **median age:** 31.8.
Land area: 98 sq mi. (254 sq km);
Avg. daily temp.: Jan., 47.1° F; July, 76.6° F
City park & recreational facilities: 134+ (1,427+ ac.); **Television stations:** 7
CIVILIAN LABOR FORCE: 185,283 (1994); **Unemployed:** 16,418, **Percent:** 8.9; **Per capita personal income:** $14,087; **Chamber of Commerce:** Sacramento Chamber of Commerce, 917 7th St., Sacramento, Calif. 95814; West Sacramento Chamber of Commerce, 834-C Jefferson Blvd., Sacramento, Calif. 95691

Sacramento is the capital and seventh largest city in California and is the seat of Sacramento county. It is located in the north central part of the state at the confluence of the Sacramento and American Rivers.

In 1839, German-born Swiss citizen John Augustus Sutter obtained a grant from the Mexican governor to establish a colony for fellow Swiss emigrants on a large tract of land in the vicinity which he named New Helvetia (New Switzerland) and established Fort Sutter there as a trading post.

After gold was discovered on Sutter's property in 1848, the settlement rapidly expanded as the prominent supply point for gold prospectors coming from the East. Sacramento was laid out in 1848 and named after the principal river in California which ran beside it. The river's name in Spanish honors the Holy Sacrament. It became incorporated as a city in 1849 and was made the state capital in 1854. Sacramento was the terminus of the first railroad in 1856 and the western terminus of the Pony Express in 1860.

The city has always been a hub of river transportation and is a major deep-water port connected to the Pacific Ocean. Sacramento's economy is highly diversified and, along with state government and military installations, its industries include aerospace, high technology, furniture, chemicals, pharmaceuticals, meat packing, and food processing of crops from the Central Valley.

The defense sector of the economy declined and Mather Air Force Base and the Army Depot were closed in 1995.

Famous natives: Joan Didion, author; Mark Goodson, TV producer; Henry Hathaway, director; Anthony M. Kennedy, Supreme Court justice; Molly Ringwald, actress

ST. LOUIS, MO.

Mayor: Freeman Bosley, Jr. (to April 1997)
1990 census population, sex, & (rank): 396,685 (34); **% change,** -12.4; **Male,** 180,680; **Female,** 216,005; **White,** 202,085; **Black,** 188,408 (47.5%); **American Indian, Eskimo, or Aleut,** 950 (0.2%); **Asian or Pacific Islander,** 3,733 (0.9%); **Other race,** 1,509; **Hispanic origin,** 5,124 (1.3%). **1990 percent population under 18:** 25.2; **65 and over:** 16.6; **median age:** 32.8.
Land area: 61.4 sq mi. (159 sq km); **Alt.:** Highest, 616 ft; lowest, 413
Avg. daily temp.: Jan., 28.8° F; July, 78.9° F
Churches: 900[1]; **City-owned parks:** 89 (2,639 ac.); **Radio stations:** AM, 21; FM 27[1]; **Television stations:** 6 commercial; 1 PBS
CIVILIAN LABOR FORCE: 179,278; **Unemployed:** 14,379, **Percent:** 8.0; **Per capita personal income:** $18,957[2]

Chamber of Commerce: St. Louis Regional Commerce and Growth Association, 100 S. Fourth St., Ste. 500, St. Louis, Mo. 63102
1. Metropolitan area. 2. St. Louis, Mo.–Ill. MSA.

St. Louis, the second largest city in Missouri, is located in the east central part of the state on the Mississippi River. The city is independent and is in no county.

St. Louis was founded by the French in 1764 when Auguste Chouteau established a fur-trading post and Pierre Laclède Liguest, a New Orleans merchant, founded a town in February 1764 at the present site of the city and named it after King Louis XV of France and his patron saint, Louis IX of France. From 1770 to 1803, St. Louis was a Spanish possession and retroceded to France in 1803 in accordance with the Treaty of San Ildefonso (1800), only to be acquired by the U.S. as part of the Louisiana purchase that year.

The town was incorporated in 1809. From 1812 to 1821, St. Louis was the capital of the Missouri Territory and was incorporated as a city in 1822.

John Jacob Astor opened the Western branch of the American Fur Company in 1819 and the city prospered during the early part of the 19th century as a center for the transportation of the fur trade. St. Louis's commercial growth continued as a major transportation hub with the development of steamboat traffic and the later expansion of the railroads in the 1850s. The world-famous Louisiana Purchase Exposition was held here in 1904.

Manufacturing is important to the city's economy, and its highly developed industries include automobiles, aircraft and space technology, metal fabrication, beer, steelmaking, chemicals, food processing, and storage and distribution.

The giant stainless steel Gateway Arch, 630 feet high, standing on the banks of the Mississippi symbolizes St. Louis as the Gateway to the West.

Famous natives: Josephine Baker, singer; Yogi Berra, baseball player; Grace Bumbry, mezzo-soprano; Morris Carnovsky, actor; T.S. Eliot, poet; Eugene Field, poet; Redd Foxx, comedian; Joe Garagiola, baseball player; John Goodman, actor; Betty Grable, actress; Dick Gregory, comedian; Al Hirschfeld, cartoonist; Kevin Kline, actor; David Merrick, producer; Vincent Price, actor; Judy Rankin, golfer; Leon Spinks, boxer; Herbert Bayard Swope, journalist; Sara Teasdale, peot; Helen Traubel, soprano; Roy Wilkins, civil rights leader

San Antonio, the third largest city in Texas and seat of Bexar county, is located in the south central part of the state, on the San Antonio River.

The site of San Antonio was first visited in 1691 by a Franciscan friar on the feast day of St. Anthony and was named San Antonio de Padua in his honor. San Antonio was permanently settled on May 1, 1718, when the Spanish governor of Coahuila and Texas, Martin de Alarcón, founded the presidio (a fort) of San Antonio de Bejar (Bexar) and the mission of San Antonio de Valero (later called the Alamo[1]) on the site of a Coahuiltecan Indian village. San Antonio remained almost continuously under Spanish rule until 1812 when Mexico won its independence from Spain.

During the outbreak of the Texas revolution (1835) against the tyranny of Mexican dictator General Santa Anna, San Antonio was captured by a small band of rebels who occupied the fortified mission of the Alamo in December 1835. The historic battle of the Alamo was fought there (Feb. 24 to March 6, 1836) and its 183 besieged defenders were massacred by Santa Anna's troops. Their heroism aroused the anger and fighting spirit of Texans to shout their famous battle cry "Remember the Alamo!" and defeat the Mexicans six weeks later (April 21, 1836) at the battle of San Jacinto. Texas became an independent republic in 1836 and San Antonio was incorporated as a city on Jan. 5, 1837.

After the Civil War, San Antonio prospered as a major shipping point for cattle with the arrival of the railroad in 1877. The city has been an important military center since World War II and is the home to five of the largest military installations in the nation, including Fort Sam Houston constructed in 1876. San Antonio is a leading livestock center and one of the largest produce exchange markets. The city's industries are highly diversified and tourism is important to the economy.

1. Spanish for the cottonwood tree.

Famous natives: Carol Burnett, comedienne; Cody Carlson, football player; Henry G. Cisneros, Secretary HUD; Joan Crawford, actress; Cito Gaston, baseball manager; Ann Harding, actress; Jesse James Leija, boxer; Emilio Navaira, Tejano music singer; Oliver North, military officer, government official; Suzy Parker, model, actress; Paula Prentiss, actress; Kyle Rote, football player; David R. Scott, astronaut; John Silber, university president; Patsy Torres, Tejano music singer; Edward H. White, astronaut

SAN ANTONIO, TEX.

Mayor: William E. Thornton (to May 1997)
City Manager: Alexander E. Briseno (apptd. April 27, 1990)
1990 census population, sex, & (rank): 935,933 (10); **% change,** 19.1; **Male,** 450,695; **Female,** 485,238; **White,** 676,082; **Black,** 65,884 (7.0%); **American Indian, Eskimo, or Aleut,** 3,303 (0.4%); **Asian or Pacific Islander,** 10,703 (1.1%); **Other race,** 179,961; **Hispanic origin,** 520,282 (55.6%). **1990 percent population under 18:** 29.0; **65 and over:** 10.5; **median age:** 29.8.
Land area: 360 sq mi. (933.4 sq km); **Alt.:** 700 ft
Avg. daily temp.: Jan., 51.2° F; July, 86.1° F
City-owned parks: 6,717 ac.; **Radio stations:** AM, 20; FM, 22; **Television stations:** 9
CIVILIAN LABOR FORCE: 695,110; **Unemployed:** 32,177, **Percent:** 4.6; **Per capita personal income:** $15,300
Chamber of Commerce: Greater San Antonio Chamber of Commerce, P.O. Box 1628, 602 E Commerce, San Antonio, Tex. 78296

SAN DIEGO, CALIF.

Mayor: Susan Golding
City Manager: Jack McGrory (apptd. April 1991)
1990 census population, sex, & (rank): 1,110,549 (6); **% change,** 26.8; **Male,** 566,464; **Female,** 544,085; **White,** 745,406; **Black,** 104,261 (9.4%); **American Indian, Eskimo, or Aleut,** 6,800 (0.6%); **Asian or Pacific Islander,** 130,945 (11.8%); **Other race,** 123,137; **Hispanic origin,** 229,519 (20.7%). **1990 percent population under 18:** 23.1; **65 and over:** 10.2; **median age:** 30.5.
Land area: 330.7 sq miles (857 sq km); **Alt.:** Highest, 1,591 ft; lowest, sea level
Avg. daily temp.: Jan., 56.8° F; July, 70.3° F
Churches: Roman Catholic, 39; Jewish, 9; Protestant, 334; Eastern Orthodox, 8; other, 18; **City park and recreation facilities:** 164 (17,207 ac.); **Radio stations:** AM, 8; FM, 18; **Television stations:** 9

CIVILIAN LABOR FORCE: 548,687; **Unemployed:** 41,301,
  Percent: 7.5; **Per capita personal income:** $18,651
Chamber of Commerce: San Diego Chamber of Commerce, 402 West Broadway, Suite 1000, San Diego, Calif. 92101

San Diego is the second largest city in California. It is located in the southwestern part of the state, on San Diego Bay.

Portuguese navigator Juan Rodríguez Cabrillo discovered the bay in 1542 and claimed the area for Spain. The site was named San Miguel by Cabrillo. On Nov. 12, 1602, Don Sebastian de Viscaíno came ashore with his party on the day of St. Didacus (San Diego in Spanish) and celebrated a mass in the saint's honor. By coincidence, Viscaíno's flagship was named *San Diego*. He renamed the place San Diego after the 15th century saint.

In 1769, Franciscan Father Junípero Serra established the first California mission there—San Diego del Alcala. In 1822, Mexico won control of the town after it declared its independence from Spain. In 1846, during the Mexican War, San Diego was seized by the United States and incorporated into a city in 1850 after California joined the Union that same year.

Today, San Diego's excellent natural harbor is a busy commercial port and a hub of U.S. naval operations. However, the naval training center at San Diego is slated to be closed due to defense cutbacks. Other leading industries are electronics, aerospace and missiles, medical and scientific research, oceanography, and agriculture. Its magnificent climate and proximity to Mexico have made tourism a significant part of the city's economy.

Famous natives: Billy Casper, golfer; Florence Chadwick, swimmer; Dennis Conner, yacht racer; Ted Danson, actor; Robert Duvall, actor; Nanette Fabray, actress; Robert Lansing, actor; Margaret O'Brien, actress; Carol Vaness, soprano; Ted Williams, baseball player; Mickey Wright, golfer

SAN FRANCISCO, CALIF.

Mayor: Frank Jordan (to Jan. 1996)
1990 census population, sex, & (rank): 723,959 (14); **%
  change,** 6.6; **Male,** 362,497; **Female,** 361,462; **White,**
  387,783; **Black,** 79,039 (10.9%); **American Indian, Eskimo, or Aleut,** 3,456 (0.5%); **Asian or Pacific Islander,**
  210,876 (29.1%); **Other race,** 42,805; **Hispanic origin,**
  100,717 (13.9%). **1990 percent population under 18:**
  16.1; **65 and over:** 14.6; **median age:** 35.8.
Land area: 46.1 sq mi. (120 sq km); **Alt.:** Highest, 925 ft;
  lowest, sea level
Avg. daily temp.: Jan., 48.5° F; July, 62.2° F
Churches: 540 of all denominations; **City-owned parks
  and squares:** 225; **Radio stations:** 29; **Television stations:** 10
CIVILIAN LABOR FORCE: 396,584[1]; **Unemployed:** 27,795[1],
  Percent: 7.0[1]; **Per capita personal income:** $28,170[2]
Chamber of Commerce: Greater San Francisco Chamber of Commerce, 465 California St., San Francisco, Calif. 94104
1. San Francisco City/County. 2. PMSA.

San Francisco, the fourth largest city in California, is coextensive with San Francisco county. It is located in the northern part of the state between the Pacific Ocean and San Francisco Bay. A narrow arm of land embraces San Francisco Bay, the largest landlocked harbor in the world, and shelters it from the Pacific Ocean. On this arm of land is San Francisco, a city on hills, almost surrounded by water.

A Franciscan father who was sailing with Sebastián Rodríguez Cermeño named the bay San Francisco on Nov. 7, 1595. In 1776, the Spaniards established a presidio, or military post, and a Franciscan mission on the end of the beautiful peninsula. In the following year, a little town called Yerba Buena, Spanish for "Good Herb," because mint grew in abundance, was founded around the mission.

In 1846, during the Mexican War, Yerba Buena was taken over by the United States. It was renamed San Francisco in 1847 and became incorporated as a city in 1850.

When gold was discovered in California in 1848, the city's population jumped to 10,000, and it experienced turbulent years until order was established by Vigilance Committees, first in 1851, and again in 1856. Then followed a period of more orderly growth and the foundations of the great commerce and industry of today were laid.

In 1906, San Francisco experienced the nation's worst earthquake which, together with the fire that followed, practically destroyed the city. The city was quickly rebuilt and grew rapidly as a leading transportation, industrial, and cultural center. In the 19th century, the American explorer and soldier, John C. Frémont, known as The Pathfinder, named the entrance to the bay, the Golden Gate, and the famous bright orange Golden Gate Bridge was dedicated in May 1937.

San Francisco's outstanding port, together with the San Francisco Bay area, is the largest seaport on the Pacific Coast and trade with the Pacific Rim countries accounts for about two-thirds of general cargo through the Port of San Francisco.

San Francisco inspires entrepreneurs to start their own businesses, and small businesses have a very important place in the economy. More than90% of the city's 33,800 businesses have fewer than 15 employees. The high-tech industries of electronics and biotechnology are well represented throughout the Bay Area. With nearly 30% of the worldwide biotechnology labor force, the Bay Area has been appropriately called "Bionic Bay." Tourism is one of San Francisco's largest industries and the largest employer of city residents. Nearly 8.2 million persons visit San Francisco each year and spend an average of $10 million per day.

The military has played an important role in the San Francisco and the Bay Area's economy, but its impact will decline due to defense cutbacks.

San Francisco is also the banking and financial center of the West and is home to a Federal Reserve Bank and a United States Mint. More than 60 foreign banks maintain offices there.

Famous natives: Gracie Allen, comedienne; Luis Walter Alvarez, Nobel Prize in physics; David Belasco, dramatist, producer; Mel Blanc, actor, voice specialist; Rosemary Casals, tennis player; Isadora Duncan, dancer; Clint Eastwood, actor; Robert Frost, poet; Rube Goldberg, cartoonist; William Randolph Hearst, publisher; Bruce Lee, actor; Mervyn LeRoy, director; Jack London, novelist; Johnny Mathis, singer; Lloyd Nolan, actor; O.J. Simpson, football player; Robert G. Sproul, educator; Irving Stone, novelist; Natalie Wood, actress

SAN JOSE, CALIF.

Mayor: Susan Hammer (to Dec. 31, 1998)
City Manager: Regina V.K. Williams (apptd. Nov. 1994)
1995 population (est): 845,991
1990 census population, sex, & (rank): 782,248 (11); **%
  change,** 24.3; **Male,** 397,709; **Female,** 384,539; **White,**

491,280; **Black,** 36,790 (4.7%); **American Indian, Eskimo, or Aleut,** 5,416 (0.7%); **Asian or Pacific Islander,** 152,815 (19.5%); **Other race,** 95,947; **Hispanic origin,** 208,388 (26.6%). **1990 percent population under 18:** 26.7; **65 and over:** 7.2; **median age:** 30.4.
Land area: 180.8 sq mi. (468.27 sq km); **Alt.:** Highest, 4,372 ft.; lowest, sea level
Avg. daily temp.: Jan., 49.5° F; July, 68.8° F
Churches: 403; **City-owned parks and playgrounds:** 152 (3,136 ac.); **Radio stations:** 14; **Television stations:** 4
CIVILIAN LABOR FORCE: 420,686; **Unemployed:** 33,484, **Percent:** 8.0; **Per capita personal income:** $24,581[1]
Chamber of Commerce: San Jose Chamber of Commerce, One Paseo de San Antonio, San Jose, Calif. 95113
1. PMSA.

San Jose, the third largest city in California and seat of Santa Clara county, is located in the western part of the state in the Santa Clara Valley near South San Francisco Bay, 50 miles south of downtown San Francisco.

San Jose was founded on Nov. 29, 1777, by Spanish colonizers who named the settlement Pueblo de San José de Guadalupe in honor of Saint Joseph and after the Guadalupe River on which the pueblo (town) was situated. The town was the first city to be established in California.

After California became a U.S. territory in 1847, San Jose became the first state capital from December 1849 to 1852 and was incorporated as a city in 1850. The city developed commercially as a supply base for gold prospectors and, when the railroad connected it with San Francisco in 1864, it became the distribution point for agricultural products from the Santa Clara Valley.

Today, the city continues to be the distribution and food-processing center for the surrounding rich agricultural region producing seasonal fruits and grapes. More than 50 wineries grace the Valley.

Computers are big business here and San Jose is the capital of Silicon Valley (Santa Clara), the nation's center of high technology where more than 3,000 high tech companies are located. Silicon Valley is also one of the world's leading centers for medical treatment and research. Heart transplants, gene splicing, and transportable baby incubators were developed there.

San Jose has healthy retail, transportation, and tourism industries as well and is the primary center for real estate and industrial development in the area.

Famous natives: "Fatty" Arbuckle, actor; Chuck Berry, singer, guitarist; Cesar Chavez, labor leader; Peggy Fleming, figure skater; Farley Granger, actor; Edmund Lowe, actor; Jim Plunkett, football player

SEATTLE, WASH.

Mayor: Norman B. Rice (to Dec. 31, 1997)
1990 census population, sex, & (rank): 516,259 (21); **% change,** 4.5; **Male,** 252,042; **Female,** 264,217; **White,** 388,858 (75.3%); **Black,** 51,948 (10.1%); **American Indian, Eskimo, or Aleut,** 7,326 (1.4%); **Asian or Pacific Islander,** 60,819 (11.8%); **Other race,** 7,308 (1.4%); **Hispanic origin,** 18,349 (3.6%). **1990 percent population under 18:** 16.5; **65 and over:** 15.2; **median age:** 34.9.
Land area: 144.6 sq mi. (375 sq km); **Alt.:** Highest, 540 ft; lowest, sea level
Avg. daily temp.: Jan., 40.6° F; July, 65.3° F
Churches: Roman Catholic, 33; Jewish, 12; Protestant and others, 497; **City-owned parks, playgrounds, etc.):** 397 (6,000+ ac.); **Radio stations:** AM, 20; FM, 20; **Television stations:** 6 commercial; 1 educational

CIVILIAN LABOR FORCE: (3 counties) 1,068,000; **Unemployed:** 53,400, **Percent:** 5.0; **Per capita personal income:** (4 counties) $24,423
Chamber of Commerce: Greater Seattle Chamber of Commerce, 1301 5th Ave., Suite 2300, Seattle, Wash. 98101

Seattle is the largest city in Washington and the seat of King county. A city of steep hills, Seattle lies in western Washington between two bodies of water—Puget Sound on the west and Lake Washington on the east. Its fine land-locked harbor has made Seattle one of the major ports in the United States.

Seattle was first settled by five pioneer families from Illinois at Alki Point at the south end of Elliott Bay in 1851. They moved in 1852 to the eastern shore of the bay and laid out a town in 1853. It was named Seattle after a friendly Suquamish Indian Chief (Seattle is only an approximation of his name).

Seattle successfully withstood an Indian attack in 1856 and was incorporated as a city in 1869. A disastrous fire almost destroyed the entire business district in 1889. When the Great Northern Railway arrived in 1893, the city became a major rail terminus and it grew rapidly. It was a boom town during the Alaska gold rush of 1897 and continued to prosper as a major Pacific port of entry with the opening of the Panama Canal in 1914.

Seattle is the region's commercial and transportation hub and the center of manufacturing, trade, and finance. Its important diversified industries include aircraft, lumber and forest products, fishing, food processing, boat building, machinery, fabricated metals, chemicals, pharmaceuticals, and apparel.

Famous natives: Chester Carlson, Xerox inventor; Carol Channing, actress; Judy Collins, singer; Fred Couples, golfer; Gail Devers, athlete; Frances Farmer, actress; William Gates, Microsoft founder; June Havoc, actress; Jimi Hendrix, guitarist; Robert Joffrey, choreographer; Gypsy Rose Lee, entertainer; Mary Livingstone, comedienne; Kevin McCarthy, actor; Mary McCarthy, novelist; Jeff Smith, food expert; Martha Wright, singer

TOLEDO, OHIO

Mayor: Carlton Finkbeiner (to Jan. 1998)
1990 census population, sex, & (rank): 332,943 (49); **% change,** −6.1; **Male,** 157,941; **Female,** 175,002; **White,** 256,239; **Black,** 65,598 (19.7%); **Americn Indian, Eskimo, or Aleut,** 920 (0.3%); **Asian or Pacific Islander,** 3,487 (1.0%); **Other race,** 6,699; **Hispanic origin,** 13,207 (4.0%). **1990 percent population under 18:** 26.2; **65 and over:** 13.6; **median age:** 31.7.
Land area: 84.2 sq mi. (218 sq km); **Alt.:** 630 ft
Avg. daily temp.: Jan., 25.2° F; July, 74.6° F
Churches: Protestant, 301; Roman Catholic, 55; Jewish, 4; others, 98; **City-owned parks and playgrounds:** 134 (2,650.90 ac.); **Radio stations:** AM, 8; FM, 8; **Television stations:** 6
CIVILIAN LABOR FORCE: 156,800, **Unemployed:** 11,900, **Percent:** 7.6; **Per capita personal income:** $16,893
Chamber of Commerce: Toledo Area Chamber of Commerce, 300 Madison Ave., Ste. 200, Toledo, Ohio 43604

Toledo, the fourth largest city in Ohio and seat of Lucas county, is located in the northwestern part of the state on the Maumee River at Lake Erie.

The first European to visit the area was the French explorer Étienne Brulé in 1615. The first white settlement in the area was at Fort Industry built by Gen. "Mad Anthony" Wayne in 1794, after he defeated the Indians at the Battle of Fallen Timbers fought nearby. The village of Port Lawrence was established next to the fort in 1817 and the village of Vistula was established nearby in 1832. The two villages were united in 1833 and named Toledo after the city in Spain. They became incorporated as a city in 1837.

Both Michigan and Ohio claimed the Toledo area which at the time was part of Michigan Territory. The bloodless dispute (Toledo War of 1835) was settled by Congress which awarded the city to Ohio. In return, Michigan received the Upper Peninsula and admission to the Union.

The city developed as a transportation center with the arrival of the railroad in 1836 and the opening of canals in the 1840s. It continued to prosper with the development of the Ohio coalfields, the tapping of gas and oil deposits, and the establishment of the glassworks by Edward Libbey in 1888.

Toledo is a leading commercial and manufacturing center and a major Great Lakes port. Total annual tonnage through the Port of Toledo ranges from 10 to 15 million tons and includes three distinct types of cargo: coal and iron ore, grain, and a wide range of general cargoes.

Toledo is the home of numerous major corporate headquarters and has 13 financial institutions in the area. Major diversified manufacturing industries include Jeeps, glass and plastic containers, fiberglass, automotive components, petroleum refining, coal products, and natural gas distribution. Other important industries are printing and publishing, food products, furniture, and fabricated metal products.

Famous natives: Cliff Arquette, actor; Anita Baker, singer; Teresa Brewer, singer; Jamie Farr, actor; Otto Kruger, actor; Herb Shriner, humorist; Gloria Steinem, feminist

TUCSON, ARIZ.

Mayor: George Miller (to Dec. 1995)
1990 census population, sex, & (rank): 405,390 (33); **% change,** 22.6; **Male,** 197,319; **Female,** 208,071; **White,** 305,055; **Black,** 17,366 (4.3%); **American Indian, Eskimo, or Aleut,** 6,464 (1.6%); **Asian or Pacific Islander,** 8,901 (2.2%); **Other race,** 67,604; **Hispanic origin,** 118,595 (29.3%). **1990 percent population under 18:** 24.5; **65 and over:** 12.6; **median age:** 30.6.
Land area: 156.04 sq mi. (404 sq km); **Alt.:** 2,400 ft
Avg. daily temp.: Jan., 51.1° F; July, 86.2° F
Churches: Protestant, 340; Roman Catholic, 42; other, 150; **City-owned parks and parkways:** (25,349 ac.); **Radio stations:** AM, 16; FM, 11; **Television stations:** 3 commercial; 1 educational; 3 other
CIVILIAN LABOR FORCE: 293,300; **Unemployed:** 10,852, **Percent:** 3.7; **Per capita personal income:** $17,949
Chamber of Commerce: Tucson Metropolitan Chamber of Commerce, P.O. Box 991, Tucson, Ariz. 85702

Tucson is the second largest city in Arizona and the seat of Pima county. It is located in the southeastern part of the state on the Santa Cruz River.

The site was originally settled by the prehistoric Hohokam Indians (300 B.C.–1400s A.D.). The first Europeans to visit the area were Spanish missionaries in the 17th century. In 1700, the Jesuit missionary explorer Father Eusebio Francisco Kino close by the Papago Indian village of San Xavier del Bac close by the Papago Indian village of Stjukshon (later called Tucson). Stjukshon is an Indian word meaning "village of the dark spring at the foot of the mountain." The Papago Indians are descendants of the ancient Hohokam peoples.

In 1776, Spanish colonists from Mexico constructed a presidio (fort) at Tucson as protection against the hostile Apache Indians and also estab-

lished the mission of San Jose de Tucson nearby. Tucson remained a military outpost under Spanish rule and later Mexican control until the area was sold to the United States as part of the Gadsden Purchase in 1853. Tucson was the capital of the Arizona Territory from 1867 to 1877. It was incorporated as a city in 1877. The town grew rapidly when the Southern Pacific Railroad arrived in 1880 and silver and copper deposits were discovered nearby.

Tucson is a popular vacation and health resort due to its sunny, mild, and dry climate and unique desert location. Tourism is important to the city's economy. Major industries are aerospace and missile production, high technology, and electronics. Tucson is also the commercial center for the surrounding area's agriculture and mining industries.

Famous natives: Rose E. Bird, jurist; Dennis De Concini, senator; Barbara Eden, actress; Linda Ronstadt, singer

TULSA, OKLA.

Mayor: M. Susan Savage (to May 1998)
1990 census population, sex, & (rank): 367,302 (43); **% change,** 1.8; **Male,** 175,538; **Female,** 191,764; **White,** 291,444; **Black,** 49,825 (13.6%); **American Indian, Eskimo, or Aleut,** 17,091 (4.7%); **Asian or Pacific Islander,** 5,133 (1.4%); **Other race,** 3,809; **Hispanic origin,** 9,564 (2.6%). **1990 percent population under 18:** 24.4; **65 and over:** 12.7; **median age:** 33.1.
Land area: 192.24 sq mi. (499 sq km); **Alt.:** 674 ft
Avg. daily temp.: Jan., 35.2° F; July, 83.2° F
Churches: Protestant, 593; Roman Catholic, 32; Jewish, 2; others, 4; **City parks and playgrounds:** 121 (6,050 ac.); **Radio stations:** AM, 7; FM, 15; **Television stations:** 7 commercial; 1 PBS; 1 cable
CIVILIAN LABOR FORCE: 184,297; **Unemployed:** 10,935, **Percent:** 5.9; **Per capita personal income:** $16,016
Chamber of Commerce: Metropolitan Tulsa Chamber of Commerce, 616 S Boston, Tulsa, Okla. 74119

Tulsa, the second largest city in Oklahoma and seat of Tulsa county, is located in the northeastern part of the state on the Arkansas River.

Tulsa was settled in the 1830s by Creek Indians from Alabama who were forcibly sent to the area (then part of Indian Territory) under the Indian Removal Act of 1830. Creek medicine-men planted ashes from their old home at the new site and the Creeks named their new village "Tulsy" meaning old town in memory of their former home in Tallassee, Alabama. In time, the village became the town of Tulsa.

The coming of the first railroad in 1882 attracted white settlers to Tulsa and the town developed into a cattle shipping center. When enormous oil deposits were discovered at nearby Red Fork in 1901 and at Glenn Pool in 1905, the city experienced rapid growth as a center of a booming petroleum industry. Tulsa was incorporated as a city in 1898 and chartered in 1908.

Tulsa is the center of the state's petroleum industry and has a diversified economy. Important industries include aerospace, chemicals, computer parts, automobile glass, fabricated metals, and industrial machinery. The city became a major inland port when the Tulsa Port of Catoosa opened in 1971. It is the national headquarters of the U.S. Junior Chamber of Commerce (Jaycees).

Famous natives: Garth Brooks, singer; Blake Edwards, director; Paul Harvey, commentator; Jennifer Jones, actress; Henry R. Kravis, investment banker; Daniel Patrick Moynihan, senator; Tony Randall, actor; Alfre Woodard, actress; Judy Woodruff, journalist

VIRGINIA BEACH, VA.

Mayor: Meyera E. Obendorf (to June 30, 1996)
1994 population: 421,517
1990 census population, sex, & (rank): 393,069 (37); % change, 49.9; **Male,** 199,571; **Female,** 193,498; **White,** 316,408; **Black,** 54,671 (13.9%); **American Indian, Eskimo, or Aleut,** 1,384 (0.4%); **Asian or Pacific Islander,** 17,025 (4.3%); **Other race,** 3,581; **Hispanic origin,** 12,137 (3.1%); **1990 percent population under 18:** 28.0; **65 and over:** 5.9; **median age:** 28.9.
Land area: 258.7 sq mi. (670 sq km); **Alt.:** 12 ft
Avg. daily temp.: Jan., 39.9° F; July, 78.4° F
Churches: Protestant, 159; Catholic, 8; Jewish, 4;
City-owned parks: 182 (1,748 ac.); **Radio stations:** AM 18, FM 26; **Television stations:** 4 commercial, 1 PBS, 1 cable
CIVILIAN LABOR FORCE: 194,579; **Unemployed:** 11,541, **Percent:** 5.9; **Per capita personal income:** $15,721[1]
Chamber of Commerce: Hampton Roads Chamber of Commerce, 4512 Virginia Beach Blvd., Virginia Beach, Va., 23456
1. Norfolk-Virginia Beach-Newport News MSA.

Virginia Beach, the largest city in Virginia, is located in the southeasternmost portion of the state on the Atlantic coastline. It is independent and is not part of any county.

The first English settlers to set foot in America landed at Cape Henry at the tip of Virginia Beach on April 29, 1607. They were led by John Smith on his way to establishing Jamestown. The first permanent settlement within the city limits was made at Lynnhaven Bay in 1621. Cape Henry became an important port for British merchant ships calling on America, and it was here that the French Fleet led by Admiral Comte de Grasse blockaded the British Fleet during the American Revolution.

Virginia Beach gained its reputation as a famous vacation resort in the 19th century, following the building of a railroad connecting its oceanfront with Norfolk and the construction of its first hotel in 1883. Virginia Beach was incorporated as a town in 1906 and as a city in 1952. In 1963, Princess Anne County and Virginia Beach merged and gave the present city an area of 310 square miles of oceanfront.

Tourism is the mainstay of the economy and 2.5 million people visit Virginia Beach overnight each year. Four nearby military bases contribute to the city's employment and economy. There are 165 farms in the city and agribusiness is also an important industry. Diversified industries include computer software and engineering and technical services.

Famous natives and residents: V.C. Andrews, novelist; Raymond Brian Buckland, occult writer; Edgar Cayce, psychic; Ann Woodruff Compton, news correspondent; D.J. Dozier, football and baseball player; George Eastman, inventor; Scott McKenzie, singer; Juice Newton, singer; Kenneth S. Reightler, Jr., astronaut; Pat Robertson, evangelist; Grace Sherwood, accused witch; Henry Walke, naval officer in Mexican and Civil Wars; Pernell "Sweet Pea" Whitaker, boxer; Skip Wilkins, wheelchair athlete

WASHINGTON, D.C.

Created municipal corporation: Feb. 21, 1871
Mayor: Marion Barry (to Jan. 1999)
Motto: *Justitia omnibus* (Justice to all)
Flower: American beauty rose; **Tree:** Scarlet oak
1991 resident population est.: 598,000
1990 census population, sex, & (rank): 606,900 (19); % change, -4.9; **Male,** 282,970; **Female,** 323,930; **White,**
179,667; **Black,** 399,604 (65.8%); **American Indian, Eskimo, or Aleut,** 1,466 (0.2%); **Asian or Pacific Islander,** 11,214 (1.8%); **Other race,** 14,949; **Hispanic origin,** 32,710 (5.4%)
Land area: 68.25 sq mi. (177 sq km); **Alt.:** Highest, 420 ft; lowest, sea level
Avg. daily temp.: Jan., 35.2° F; July, 78.9° F
Churches: Protestant, 610; Roman Catholic, 132; Jewish, 9;
City parks: 753 (7,725 ac.); **Radio stations:** AM, 9; FM, 38; **Television stations:** 19
CIVILIAN LABOR FORCE: 276,000; **Unemployed:** 23,000, **Percent:** 8.4; **Per capita personal income:** $24,845[1]
Board of Trade: Greater Washington Board of Trade, 1129 20th Street, N.W., Washington, D.C. 20036
Chamber of Commerce: D.C. Chamber of Commerce, 1319 F St., NW, Washington, D.C. 20004
1. Washington, D.C.–Md.–Va. MSA.

The District of Columbia—identical with the City of Washington—is the capital of the United States and the first carefully planned capital in the world. It is located between Virginia and Maryland on the Potomac River. The district is named after Columbus.

D.C. history began in 1790 when Congress directed selection of a new capital site, 100 miles square, along the Potomac. When the site was determined, it included 30.75 square miles on the Virginia side of the river. In 1846, however, Congress returned that area to Virginia, leaving the 68.25 square miles ceded by Maryland in 1788. The seat of government was transferred from Philadelphia to Washington on Dec. 1, 1800, and President John Adams became the first resident in the White House.

The city was planned and partly laid out by Major Pierre Charles L'Enfant, a French engineer. This work was perfected and completed by Major Andrew Ellicott and Benjamin Banneker, a freeborn black man, who was an astronomer and mathematician. In 1814, during the War of 1812, a British force fired the capital including the White House.

Until Nov. 3, 1967, the District of Columbia was administered by three commissioners appointed by the President. On that day, a government consisting of a mayor-commissioner and a 9-member Council, all appointed by the President with the approval of the Senate, took office. On May 7, 1974, the citizens of the District of Columbia approved a Home Rule Charter, giving them an elected mayor and 13-member council—their first elected municipal government in more than a century. The District also has one non-voting member in the House of Representatives and an elected Board of Education.

On Aug. 22, 1978, Congress passed a proposed constitutional amendment to give Washington, D.C., voting representation in the Congress. The amendment had to be ratified by at least 28 state legislatures within seven years to become effective. As of 1985 it died.

A petition asking for the District's admission to the Union as the 51st State was filed in Congress on September 9, 1983. The District is continuing this drive for statehood.

The federal government and tourism are the mainstays of the city's economy, and many unions, business, professional and nonprofit organizations are headquartered there.

Famous natives: Edward Albee, playwright; Billie Burke, comedienne; Ina Claire, actress; John Foster Dulles, statesman; Duke Ellington, musician; Jane Greer, actress; Goldie Hawn, actress; Helen Hayes, actress; J. Edgar Hoover, F.B.I. director; William Hurt, actor; Noor al-Hussein, Queen of Jordan; Michael Learned, actress; Roger Mudd, newscaster; Eleanor Holmes Norton, government official; Chita Rivera, dancer, actress; Leonard Rose, cellist; John Philip Sousa, composer; Frances Sternhagen, actress

Top 50 Cities in the U.S. by Estimated 1992 Population and Rank

City and state	April 1, 1990 (census)	July 1, 1992 (estimate)	Change, 1990–92 Number	Change, 1990–92 Percent	City rank Population 1990	City rank Population 1992	Percent change 1990–92
New York, NY	7,322,564	7,311,966	−10,598	−0.1	1	1	156
Los Angeles, CA	3,485,398	3,489,779	4,381	0.1	2	2	150
Chicago, IL	2,783,726	2,768,483	−15,243	−0.5	3	3	163
Houston, TX	1,630,553	1,690,180	59,627	3.7	4	4	56
Philadelphia, PA	1,585,577	1,552,572	−33,005	−2.1	5	5	188
San Diego, CA	1,110,549	1,148,851	38,302	3.4	6	6	64
Dallas, TX	1,006,877	1,022,497	15,620	1.6	8	7	106
Phoenix, AZ	983,403	1,012,230	28,827	2.9	9	8	72
Detroit, MI	1,027,974	1,012,110	−15,864	−1.5	7	9	180
San Antonio, TX	935,933	966,437	30,504	3.3	10	10	67
San Jose, CA	782,248	801,331	19,083	2.4	11	11	82
Indianapolis (remainder), IN[1]	731,327	746,538	15,211	2.1	13	12	92
San Francisco, CA	723,959	728,921	4,962	0.7	14	13	127
Baltimore, MD	736,014	726,096	−9,918	−1.3	12	14	175
Jacksonville (remainder), FL[1]	635,230	661,177	25,947	4.1	15	15	51
Columbus, OH	632,910	642,987	10,077	1.6	16	16	105
Milwaukee, WI	628,088	617,043	−11,045	−1.8	17	17	184
Memphis, TN	610,337	610,275	−62	−	18	18	155
Washington, DC	606,900	585,221	−21,679	−3.6	19	19	196
Boston, MA	574,283	551,675	−22,608	−3.9	20	20	198
El Paso, TX	515,342	543,813	28,471	5.5	22	21	29
Seattle, WA	516,259	519,598	3,339	0.6	21	22	129
Cleveland, OH	505,616	502,539	−3,077	−0.6	23	23	165
Nashville–Davidson (remainder), TN[1]	488,374	495,012	6,638	1.4	25	24	108
Austin, TX	465,622	492,329	26,707	5.7	27	25	28
New Orleans, LA	496,938	489,595	−7,343	−1.5	24	26	179
Denver, CO	467,610	483,852	16,242	3.5	26	27	63
Fort Worth, TX	447,619	454,430	6,811	1.5	28	28	107
Oklahoma City, OK	444,719	453,995	9,276	2.1	29	29	91
Portland, OR	437,319	445,458	8,139	1.9	30	30	98
Long Beach, CA	429,433	438,771	9,338	2.2	32	31	90
Kansas City, MO	435,146	431,553	−3,593	−0.8	31	32	168
Virginia Beach, VA	393,069	417,061	23,992	6.1	37	33	23
Charlotte, NC	395,934	416,294	20,360	5.1	35	34	36
Tucson, AZ	405,390	415,079	9,689	2.4	33	35	84
Albuquerque, NM	384,736	398,492	13,756	3.6	38	36	59
Atlanta, GA	394,017	394,848	831	0.2	36	37	147
St. Louis, MO	396,685	383,733	−12,952	−3.3	34	38	193
Sacramento, CA	369,365	382,816	13,451	3.6	41	39	57
Fresno, CA	354,202	376,130	21,928	6.2	47	40	22
Tulsa, OK	367,302	375,307	8,005	2.2	43	41	89
Oakland, CA	372,242	373,219	977	0.3	39	42	146
Honolulu CDP, HI[2]	365,272	371,320	6,048	1.7	44	43	103
Miami, FL	358,548	367,016	8,468	2.4	46	44	85
Pittsburgh, PA	369,879	366,852	−3,027	−0.8	40	45	167
Cincinnati, OH	364,040	364,278	238	0.1	45	46	151
Minneapolis, MN	368,383	362,696	−5,687	−1.5	42	47	181
Omaha, NE	335,795	339,671	3,876	1.2	48	48	114
Toledo, OH	332,943	329,325	−3,618	−1.1	49	49	172
Buffalo, NY	328,123	323,284	−4,839	−1.5	50	50	178

1. The term "remainder" following a city name indicates that it is part of a consolidated city-county government and that the populations of other incorporated places in the county have been excluded from the population totals shown here. 2. Honolulu CDP (census designated place) is not incorporated as a city but is recognized for census purposes as a large urban place. Honolulu CDP is coextensive with Honolulu Judicial District within the City and County of Honolulu. NOTE: These estimates are consistent with the population as enumerated in the 1990 census, and have not been adjusted for census coverage errors. Source: U.S. Bureau of the Census.

195 Cities Have Populations Over 100,000

The 1990 census showed that 195 American cities had populations of 100,000 or more. Mesa, Arizona, was the greatest percentage gainer, growing by 89% from 152,404 in 1980 to 288,091 in 1990.

Five cities fell from the ranks of 100,000-plus cities since 1980: Columbia, South Carolina; Davenport, Iowa; Pueblo, Colorado; Roanoke, Virginia; and Youngstown, Ohio.

Tabulated Data on City Governments

City	Mayor		City manager's salary[2]	Council or Commission			
	Term, years	Salary[1]		Name	Members	Term, years	Salary[3]
Albuquerque, N.M.	4	$70,280	—	Council	9	4	$7,028
Atlanta	4	100,000	—	Council	19	4	22,000 [27]
Austin, Tex.	3	35,000	$125,000	Council	7 [2]	3	30,000
Baltimore	4	60,000	—	Council	19	4	29,000 [21]
Boston	4	110,000	—	Council	13	2	54,500
Buffalo, N.Y.	4	79,380	—	Council	13	2 [5]	41,895
Charlotte, N.C.	2	14,800	129,841	Council	11	2	8,000
Chicago	4	170,000	—	Council	50	4	75,000
Cincinnati	2	48,762	139,500	Council	9	2	45,262
Cleveland	4	93,600	—	Council	21	4	40,093
Columbus, Ohio	4	98,000	—	Council	7	4	25,000 [15]
Dallas	2	50 [6]	—	Council	15	2	50 [6]
Denver	4	97,812	—	Council	13	4	42,384 [28]
Detroit	4	117,000	—	Council	9 [7]	4	54,000 [29]
El Paso	2	25,000	—	Council	8 [7]	2	15,000
Fort Worth	2	75 [8]	109,000	Council	8	2	75 [8]
Fresno, Calif.	4	49,800	120,000	Council	7 [7]	4	28,800 [23]
Honolulu	4	100,000	95,000 [9]	Council	9	4	38,500
Houston	2	133,553	—	Council	14	2	36,614
Indianapolis	4	83,211	—	Council	29	4	14,705 [10]
Jacksonville, Fla.	4	100,613	105,000 [11]	Council	19	4	24,000
Kansas City, Mo.	4	58,200	117,000	Council	13 [7]	4	25,200
Long Beach, Calif.	4	84,545	155,786 [25]	Council	9	4	21,135
Los Angeles	4	127,491	169,880 [4]	Council	15	4	98,070
Memphis, Tenn.	4	100,000	84,736 [4]	Council	13	4	6,000
Miami, Fla.	4	5,000 [13]	116,887 [39]	Commission	5	4	5,000
Milwaukee	4	101,731	—	Council	17	4	45,146
Minneapolis	4	73,486	95,888 [40]	Council	13	4	54,578
Nashville, Tenn.	4	75,000	—	Council	41	4	7,500
New Orleans	4	90,000	57,900 [38]	Council	7	4	42,500
New York	4	130,000	112,000 [14]	Council	51	4	55,000 [26]
Oakland, Calif.	4	80,012	158,921	Council	9 [7]	4	35,300 [37]
Oklahoma City	4	2,000	100,000	Council	8	4	20 [17]
Omaha, Neb.	4	77,799	—	Council	7	4	22,384
Philadelphia	4	110,000	95,000 [18]	Council	17	4	65,000 [16]
Phoenix, Ariz.	4	37,500	138,000	Council	9 [7]	4	18,000
Pittsburgh	4	74,313	—	Council	9	4	42,372
Portland, Ore.	4	80,745	—	Council	4	4	68,016
Sacramento	4	2,175 [30]	115,772	Council	9 [12]	4	1,825 [31]
St. Louis	4	71,266	—	Board of Aldermen	29	4	18,500 [32]
San Antonio	2	3,000 [19]	115,000	Council	11 [7]	2	20 [20]
San Diego, Calif.	4	65,300	127,650	Council	8	4	49,000
San Francisco	4	138,669	137,521 [33]	Bd. of Supvrs.	11	4	23,924
San Jose, Calif.	4	82,500 [34]	145,000 [34]	Council	10	4	54,400 [34]
Seattle	4	109,555	—	Council	9	4	70,896
Toledo, Ohio	4	75,000	—	Council	12 [12]	4	18,500 [36]
Tucson, Ariz.	4	24,000	120,000	Council	7 [7]	4	12,000
Tulsa, Okla.	4	70,000	—	Council	9	2	12,000
Virginia Beach, Va.	4	20,000	108,000 [24]	Council	11	4	18,000
Washington, D.C.	4	90,705	115,700 [35]	Council	13	4	71,885 [22]

1. Annual salary unless otherwise indicated. 2. Annual salary. City Manager's term is indefinite and at will of Council (or Mayor). 3. Annual salary unless otherwise indicated. In some cities, President of Council receives a higher salary. 4. City Administrative Officer appointed by Mayor, approved by Council. 5. For 9 District Councilmen; 4 years for President and 3 Councilmen-at-Large. 6. Per Council meeting; not over $2,600 per year. 7. Including Mayor. 8. Per week and per Council meeting. 9. Managing Director appointed by Mayor; Council approval required. 10. $9,985 base plus $112 per council meeting (20 scheduled); $62 per committee meeting at a maximum of 40 meetings. President gets $1,982 extra, majority and minority leaders get $1,320 extra and the Committee Chairmen get $797 extra. 11. Chief Administrative Officer appointed by Mayor; not subject to Council confirmation. 12. Including the Council President. 13. Plus $2,500 expense account. 14. No City Manager; salary is for Deputy Mayors. 15. Per member. President earns $30,000. 16. Per member. President earns $80,000. 17. Per Council meeting; not to exceed 5 meetings a month. 18. Appointed by Mayor, with title of Managing Director. 19. Plus Council pay. 20. Per Council meeting; not over $1,040 per year. 21. Per member. President earns $53,000. 22. Council Chairman receives $81,885. 23. Mayor Pro Tempore, $31,200. 24. Plus $4,000 in travel expenses. 25. Plus $1,200 per month expense account. 26. Public Advocate receives $105,000. 27. Council President earns $25,000. 28. Council President receives $47,384. 29. Council President receives $56,700. 30. Per month includes $150 per month prorated for $1,800 a year entertainment expense, plus $60 per diem for lodging and meals when traveling outside the county. 31. Per month plus $60 per diem for lodging and meals when traveling outside the county. 32. For 12 Aldermen $18,500, 16 Aldermen $21,460. 33. Chief Administrative Officer. 34. Plus $4,200 annual vehicle expense allowance for Mayor/Council and $6,000 for City Manager. July 1, 1996, Mayor's salary increases to $85,000 and that of Council members to $56,000. 35. City Administrator. 36. Members of Council get $1,200 per year expense account. 37. Council also serves as the Redevelopment Agency for which there is additional compensation. 38. Minimum entrance base salary reported. 39. Approx. 40. City Coordinator. *Source: Information Please* questionnaires to the cities.

U.S. Telephone Area Codes and Time Zones

U.S. Cities Over 25,000 Population

Asterisk denotes more than one ZIP code for a city and refers to Postmaster. To find the ZIP code for a particular address, consult the ZIP code directory available in every post office. The ZIP codes printed herein were obtained either from the "National Five-Digit Zip Code & Post Office Directory," published by the U.S. Postal Service or from phone calls made to the postmaster in the areas where they were not listed in the Directory. We have tried to accurately list all the pertinent ZIP codes that were available. If there are any questions regarding the exact ZIP code for a particular street address, you should contact your local post office. NOTE: Census Designated Place (CDP)—A statistical area comprising a densely settled concentration of population that is not incorporated but which resembles an incorporated place in that local people can identify it with a name.

City and major zip code	1990 census	1990 rank
ALABAMA		
Anniston city (36201*)	26,623	1210
Auburn city (36830*)	33,830	904
Bessemer city (35020*)	33,497	921
Birmingham city (35203*)	265,968	60
Decatur city (35601*)	48,761	575
Dothan city (36302*)	53,589	496
Florence city (35630*)	36,426	828
Gadsden city (35902*)	42,523	685
Hoover city (35203*)	39,788	748
Huntsville city (35813*)	159,789	110
Mobile city (36601*)	196,278	79
Montgomery city (36119*)	187,106	86
Phenix City city (36867*)	25,312	1281
Prichard city (36610)	34,311	886
Tuscaloosa city (35401*)	77,759	287
ALASKA		
Anchorage city (99501*)	226,338	69
Fairbanks city (99701*)	30,843	1023
Juneau city (99801)	26,751	1204
ARIZONA		
Chandler city (85225*)	90,533	230
Flagstaff city (86004*)	45,857	627
Gilbert town (85234)	29,188	1090
Glendale city (85301*)	148,134	119
Mesa city (85201*)	288,091	53
Peoria city (85345*)	50,618	547
Phoenix city (85026*)	983,403	9
Prescott city (86301*)	26,455	1220
Scottsdale city (85251*)	130,069	141
Sierra Vista city (85635*)	32,983	938
Sun City CDP (85351*)	38,126	784
Tempe city (85282*)	141,865	124
Tucson city (85726*)	405,390	33
Yuma city (85364*)	54,923	471
ARKANSAS		
Conway city (72032)	26,481	1218
Fayetteville city (72701*)	42,099	694
Fort Smith city (72917*)	72,798	316
Hot Springs city (71901)	32,462	955
Jacksonville city (72076)	29,101	1096
Jonesboro city (72401)	46,535	613
Little Rock city (72231*)	175,795	96
North Little Rock city (72114*)	61,741	403
Pine Bluff city (71601*)	57,140	446
Springdale city (72764*)	29,941	1059
West Memphis city (72301*)	28,259	1132
CALIFORNIA		
Alameda city (94501)	76,459	292
Alhambra city (91715*)	82,106	271
Altadena CDP (91001*)	42,658	680
Anaheim city (92803*)	266,406	59
Antioch city (94509*)	62,195	395
Apple Valley town (92307*)	46,079	623
Arcadia city (91006*)	48,290	589
Arden-Arcade CDP (95825*)	92,040	228
Azusa city (91702)	41,333	710
Bakersfield city (93380*)	174,820	97
Baldwin Park city (91706)	69,330	343

City and major zip code	1990 census	1990 rank
Bell city (90201)	34,365	885
Bellflower city (90706*)	61,815	401
Bell Gardens city (90201)	42,355	687
Berkeley city (94704*)	102,724	194
Beverly Hills city (90210*)	31,971	974
Brea city (92622*)	32,873	945
Buena Park city (90622*)	68,784	347
Burbank city (91505*)	93,643	221
Burlingame city (94010*)	26,801	1201
Camarillo city (93010*)	52,303	519
Campbell city (95008*)	36,048	839
Carlsbad city (92008*)	63,126	391
Carmichael CDP (95608*)	48,702	579
Carson city (90745*)	83,995	266
Casa de Oro-Mount Helis CDP (91977*)	30,727	1030
Castro Valley CDP (94546)	48,619	582
Cathedral City city (92234*)	30,085	1053
Ceres city (95307)	26,314	1227
Cerritos city (90703)	53,240	503
Chico city (95926*)	40,079	742
Chino city (91710*)	59,682	423
Chino Hills CDP (91710)	27,608	1164
Chula Vista city (92010*)	135,163	133
Citrus Heights CDP (95621)	107,439	183
Claremont city (91711)	32,503	954
Clovis city (93612)	50,323	552
Colton city (92324)	40,213	735
Compton city (90221*)	90,454	231
Concord city (94520*)	111,348	167
Corona city (91720*)	76,095	294
Coronado city (92118*)	26,540	1215
Costa Mesa city (92628*)	96,357	212
Covina city (91722*)	43,207	669
Culver City city (90230*)	38,793	769
Cupertino city (95014*)	40,263	734
Cypress city (90630)	42,655	681
Daly City city (94015*)	92,311	227
Dana Point city (92629)	31,896	978
Danville city (94526*)	31,306	999
Davis city (95616*)	46,209	619
Diamond Bar city (91765)	53,672	494
Downey city (90241*)	91,444	229
East Los Angeles CDP (90055)	126,379	146
El Cajon city (92020*)	88,693	236
El Centro city (92244*)	31,384	997
El Monte city (91731*)	106,209	186
El Toro CDP (92630)	62,685	393
Encinitas city (92024*)	55,386	463
Escondido city (92025*)	108,635	180
Eureka city (95501*)	27,025	1193
Fairfield city (94533)	77,211	289
Fair Oaks CDP (95628)	26,867	1198
Florence-Graham CDP (90052*)	57,147	445
Fontana city (92335*)	87,535	241
Foster City city (94404)	28,176	1137
Fountain Valley city (92708*)	53,691	493
Fremont city (94537*)	173,339	98
Fresno city (93706*)	354,202	47
Fullerton city (92634*)	114,144	160
Folsom city (95630)	29,802	1066

City and major zip code	1990 census	1990 rank	City and major zip code	1990 census	1990 rank
Gardena city (90247*)	49,847	557	Pacifica city (94044)	37,670	802
Garden Grove city (92642*)	142,050	122	Palmdale city (93550*)	68,842	346
Gilroy city (95020*)	31,487	994	Palm Springs city (92263*)	40,181	736
Glendale city (92109*)	180,038	92	Palo Alto city (94303*)	55,900	458
Glendora city (91740)	47,828	593	Paradise town (95969*)	25,408	1276
Hacienda Heights CDP (91745)	52,354	515	Paramount city (90723)	47,669	595
Hanford city (93230*)	30,897	1020	Parkway-South Sacramento CDP (95823*)	31,903	977
Hawthorne city (90250*)	71,349	327	Pasadena city (91109*)	131,591	139
Hayward city (94544*)	111,498	166	Petaluma city (94952*)	43,184	671
Hemet city (92343*)	36,094	838	Pico Rivera city (90660)	59,177	429
Hesperia city (92345)	50,418	550	Pittsburg city (94565)	47,564	597
Highland city (92346)	34,439	881	Placentia city (92670)	41,259	711
Huntington Beach city (92647*)	181,519	90	Pleasant Hill city (94523)	31,585	992
Huntington Park city (90255)	56,065	456	Pleasanton city (94566*)	50,553	548
Imperial Beach city (92032)	26,512	1216	Pomona city (91768*)	131,723	138
Indio city (92201*)	36,793	821	Porterville city (93257*)	29,563	1073
Inglewood city (90311*)	109,602	173	Poway city (92064)	43,516	665
Irvine city (92713*)	110,330	171	Rancho Cordova CDP (95670*)	48,731	577
Laguna Hills CDP (92654*)	46,731	610	Rancho Cucamonga city (91739*)	101,409	196
Laguna Niguel city (92607)	44,400	650	Rancho Palos Verdes (90274)	41,659	706
La Habra city (90631*)	51,266	535	Redding city (96049*)	66,462	366
Lakeside CDP (92040)	39,412	754	Redlands city (92373*)	60,394	417
Lakewood city (90714*)	73,557	311	Redondo Beach city (92077*)	60,167	418
La Mesa city (92041*)	52,931	509	Redwood City city (94063*)	66,072	368
La Mirada city (90638*)	40,452	729	Rialto city (92376*)	72,388	319
Lancaster city (93534*)	97,291	209	Richmond city (94802*)	87,425	243
La Puente city (91744*)	36,955	816	Ridgecrest city (93555*)	27,725	1154
La Verne city (91750)	30,897	1020	Riverside city (92517*)	226,505	68
Lawndale city (90260)	27,331	1180	Rohnert Park city (94928*)	36,326	831
Livermore city (94550*)	56,741	451	Rosemead city (91770)	51,638	528
Lodi city (95240*)	51,874	526	Roseville city (95678*)	44,685	645
Lompoc city (93436*)	37,649	803	Rowland Heights CDP (91748)	42,647	682
Long Beach city (90809*)	429,433	32	Sacramento city (95813*)	369,365	41
Los Altos city (94022*)	26,303	1228	Salinas city (93907*)	108,777	177
Los Angeles city (90052*)	3,485,398	2	San Bernardino city (92403*)	164,164	106
Los Gatos town (95030*)	27,357	1176	San Bruno city (94066)	38,961	765
Lynwood city (90262)	61,945	397	San Buenaventura (Ventura) city (93001*)	92,575	226
Madera city (93638*)	29,281	1084	San Carlos city (94070)	26,167	1241
Manhattan Beach city (90266)	32,063	970	San Clemente city (92674*)	41,100	714
Manteca city (95336)	40,773	723	San Diego city (92199*)	1,110,549	6
Marina city (93933)	26,436	1222	San Dimas city (91773)	32,397	957
Martinez city (94553)	31,808	983	San Francisco city (94188*)	723,959	14
Maywood city (90270)	27,850	1151	San Gabriel city (91776*)	37,120	812
Menlo Park city (94025*)	28,040	1146	San Jose city (95101*)	782,248	11
Merced city (95340*)	56,216	454	San Juan Capistrano city (92690*)	26,183	1240
Milpitas city (95035*)	50,686	544	San Leandro city (94577*)	68,223	351
Mission Viejo city (92690*)	72,820	315	San Luis Obispo city (93401*)	41,958	698
Modesto city (95350*)	164,730	104	San Marcos city (92069)	38,974	764
Monrovia city (91016*)	35,761	844	San Mateo city (94402*)	85,486	254
Montclair city (91763)	28,434	1124	San Pablo city (94806)	25,158	1287
Montebello city (90640)	59,564	425	San Rafael city (94901*)	48,404	587
Monterey city (93940*)	31,954	975	San Ramon city (94583)	35,303	861
Monterey Park city (91754)	60,738	411	Santa Ana city (92799*)	293,742	52
Moorpark city (93021)	25,494	1273	Santa Barbara city (93102*)	85,571	252
Moreno Valley city (92388*)	118,779	155	Santa Clara city (95050*)	93,613	222
Mountain View city (94041*)	67,460	357	Santa Clarita city (91380*)	110,642	170
Napa city (94558*)	61,842	399	Santa Cruz city (95060*)	49,040	570
National City city (92050)	54,249	486	Santa Maria city (93454*)	61,284	408
Newark city (94560)	37,861	792	Santa Monica city (90406*)	86,905	246
Newport Beach city (92658*)	66,643	363	Santa Paula city (93060)	25,062	1294
North Highlands CDP (95660)	42,105	693	Santa Rosa city (95402*)	113,313	162
Norwalk city (90650*)	94,279	220	Santee city (92071*)	52,902	510
Novato city (94947*)	47,585	596	Saratoga city (95070*)	28,061	1145
Oakland city (94615*)	372,242	39	Seal Beach city (90740)	25,098	1289
Oceanside city (92054*)	128,398	143	Seaside city (93955)	38,901	768
Oildale CDP (93308*)	26,553	1214	Simi Valley city (93065*)	100,217	200
Ontario city (91761*)	133,179	136	South Gate city (90280)	86,284	250
Orange city (92613*)	110,658	169	South San Francisco city (94080*)	54,312	484
Orangevale CDP (95662)	26,266	1233	South Whittier CDP (90601*)	49,514	561
Oxnard city (93030*)	142,216	123	Spring Valley CDP (92078)	55,331	465

City and major zip code	1990 census	1990 rank
Stanton city (90680)	30,491	1042
Stockton city (95213*)	210,943	74
Sunnyvale city (94086*)	117,229	157
Temecula city (92390)	27,099	1189
Temple City city (91780)	31,100	1005
Thousand Oaks city (91359*)	104,352	190
Torrance city (90510*)	133,107	137
Tracy city (95376*)	33,558	918
Tulare city (93274*)	33,249	930
Turlock city (95380*)	42,198	689
Tustin city (92681*)	50,689	543
Union City city (94587)	53,762	491
Upland city (91786*)	63,374	388
Vacaville city (95687*)	71,479	325
Vallejo city (94590*)	109,199	175
Victorville city (92392*)	40,674	725
Visalia city (93277*)	75,636	300
Vista city (92083*)	71,872	321
Walnut city (91789*)	29,105	1095
Walnut Creek city (94596*)	60,569	414
Watsonville city (95076*)	31,099	1006
West Covina city (91790*)	96,086	214
West Hollywood city (90046)	36,118	837
Westminster city (92684*)	78,118	286
Westmont CDP (90250*)	31,044	1008
West Sacramento city (95691)	28,898	1101
Whittier city (90605*)	77,671	288
Willowbrook CDP (90223)	32,772	949
Woodland city (31365*)	39,802	747
Yorba Linda city (92686*)	52,422	513
Yuba City city (95991*)	27,437	1175
Yucaipa city (92399)	32,824	948
COLORADO		
Arvada city (80001*)	89,235	235
Aurora city (80010*)	222,103	72
Boulder city (80302*)	83,312	268
Colorado Springs city (80910*)	281,140	54
Denver city (80201*)	467,610	26
Englewood city (80110*)	29,387	1079
Fort Collins city (80521*)	87,758	240
Grand Junction city (81501*)	29,034	1099
Greeley city (80631*)	60,536	416
Lakewood city (80215*)	126,481	145
Littleton city (80120*)	33,685	912
Longmont city (80501*)	51,555	529
Loveland city (80538*)	37,352	809
Northglenn city (80233*)	27,195	1186
Pueblo city (81003*)	98,640	207
Southglenn CDP (80122*)	43,087	672
Thornton city (80229*)	55,031	468
Westminster city (80030)	74,625	309
Wheat Ridge city (80033*)	29,419	1078
CONNECTICUT		
Bridgeport city (06602*)	141,686	125
Bristol city (06010*)	60,640	412
Central Manchester CDP (06040*)	30,934	1018
Danbury city (06810*)	65,585	374
East Hartford CDP (06118*)	50,452	549
East Haven CDP (06512)	26,144	1242
Hartford city (06101*)	139,739	129
Meriden city (06450)	59,479	426
Middletown city (06457)	42,762	678
Milford city (remainder) (06460)	48,168	590
Naugatuck borough (06770)	30,625	1034
New Britain city (06050*)	75,491	302
New Haven city (06511*)	130,474	140
Newington CDP (06111*)	29,208	1086
New London city (06320)	28,540	1122
Norwalk city (06856*)	78,331	284
Norwich city (06360)	37,391	808
Shelton city (06484)	35,418	856
Stamford city (06910*)	108,056	181
Stratford CDP (06497)	49,389	565
Torrington city (06790)	33,687	911
Trumbull CDP (06611)	32,000	972
Waterbury city (06701*)	108,961	176
West Hartford CDP (06107*)	60,110	419
West Haven city (06516)	54,021	489
Wethersfield CDP (06109*)	25,651	1265
DELAWARE		
Dover city (19901*)	27,630	1160
Newark city (19711*)	25,098	1289
Wilmington city (19850*)	71,529	324
DISTRICT OF COLUMBIA		
Washington city (20066*)	606,900	19
FLORIDA		
Altamonte Springs city (32714*)	34,879	871
Boca Raton city (33431*)	61,492	405
Boynton Beach city (33436*)	46,194	620
Bradenton city (34206*)	43,779	658
Brandon CDP (33511*)	57,985	438
Cape Coral city (33990)	74,991	306
Carol City CDP (33055)	53,331	500
Clearwater city (34618*)	98,784	206
Coconut Creek city (33063)	27,485	1173
Coral Gables city (33114)	40,091	740
Coral Springs city (33075)	79,443	282
Davie town (33329)	47,217	601
Daytona Beach city (32114*)	61,921	398
Deerfield Beach city (33441*)	46,325	617
Delray Beach city (33444*)	47,181	603
Deltona CDP (32725*)	50,828	541
Dunedin city (34698*)	34,012	896
Ferry Pass CDP (32501*)	26,301	1230
Fort Lauderdale city (33310*)	149,377	118
Fort Myers city (33907*)	45,206	637
Fort Pierce city (34950*)	36,830	819
Gainesville city (32602*)	84,770	258
Golden Glades CDP (33054*)	25,474	1274
Hallandale city (33010*)	30,996	1010
Hialeah city (33010*)	188,004	85
Hollywood city (33022*)	121,697	152
Homestead city (33030*)	26,866	1199
Jacksonville city (32203*)	635,230	15
Kendale Lakes CDP (33152*)	48,524	584
Kendall CDP (33256)	87,271	244
Kissimmee city (34744*)	30,050	1054
Lakeland city (33805*)	70,576	334
Lakeside CDP	29,137	1092
Lake Worth city (33461*)	28,564	1121
Largo city (34640*)	65,674	372
Lauderdale Lakes city (33152*)	27,341	1178
Lauderhill city (33152*)	49,708	559
Margate city (33063)	42,985	673
Melbourne city (32901*)	59,646	424
Merritt Island CDP (32953*)	32,886	944
Miami city (33152*)	358,548	46
Miami Beach city (33119)	92,639	225
Miramar city (33023)	40,663	726
North Fort Myers CDP (33903)	30,027	1056
North Lauderdale city (33060*)	26,506	1217
North Miami city (33261)	49,998	556
North Miami Beach city (33160)	35,359	857
Oakland Park city (33334*)	26,326	1226
Ocala city (32678*)	42,045	695
Olympia Heights CDP (33265)	37,792	797

City and major zip code	1990 census	1990 rank
Orlando city (32862*)	164,693	105
Ormond Beach city (32176*)	29,721	1070
Palm Bay city (32901*)	62,632	394
Palm Harbor CDP (34683*)	50,256	553
Panama City city (32401*)	34,378	884
Pembroke Pines city (33084)	65,452	376
Pensacola city (32501*)	58,165	434
Pine Hills CDP (32862*)	35,322	858
Pinellas Park city (34665*)	43,426	667
Plantation city (33318)	66,692	361
Pompano Beach city (33060*)	72,411	318
Port Charlotte CDP (33949)	41,535	708
Port Orange city (32129)	35,317	859
Port St. Lucie city (34985)	55,866	459
Riviera Beach city (33419)	27,639	1158
St. Petersburg city (33730*)	238,629	65
Sanford city (32771*)	32,387	959
Sarasota city (34230*)	50,961	539
South Miami Heights CDP (33152*)	30,030	1055
Spring Hill CDP (34606*)	31,117	1004
Sunrise city (33322)	64,407	381
Tallahassee city (32301*)	124,773	149
Tamarac city (33320)	44,822	643
Tamiami CDP (33144)	33,845	901
Tampa city (33630*)	280,015	55
Titusville city (32780*)	39,394	756
Town 'n' Country CDP (33685)	60,946	409
Westchester CDP (33165)	29,883	1063
West Little River CDP (33152*)	33,575	916
West Palm Beach city (33406*)	67,643	354

GEORGIA

Albany city (31706*)	78,122	285
Athens city (30601*)	45,734	629
Atlanta city (30304*)	394,017	36
Augusta city (30901*)	44,639	648
Candler-McAfee CDP (30304*)	29,491	1075
Columbus city (remainder) (31908*)	178,681	93
Dunwoody CDP (30304*)	26,302	1229
East Point city (30304*)	34,402	883
La Grange city (30240*)	25,597	1268
Mableton CDP (30059)	25,725	1262
Macon city (31201*)	106,612	185
Marietta city (30060*)	44,129	653
Martinez CDP (30907)	33,731	908
North Atlanta CDP (30319)	27,812	1152
Rome city (30161*)	30,326	1045
Roswell city (30075*)	47,923	591
Sandy Springs CDP (30304*)	67,842	353
Savannah city (31402*)	137,560	131
Smyrna city (30080*)	30,981	1014
South Augusta CDP (30901*)	55,998	457
Tucker CDP (30084*)	25,781	1260
Valdosta city (31603*)	39,806	746
Warner Robins city (31088*)	43,726	661
West Augusta CDP (30901*)	27,637	1159

HAWAII

Hilo CDP (96720*)	37,808	796
Honolulu CDP (96820*)	365,272	44
Kailua CDP (96734)	36,818	820
Kaneohe CDP (96744)	35,448	854
Mililani Town CDP (96789)	29,359	1080
Pearl City CDP (96782)	30,993	1011
Waimalu CDP (96701)	29,967	1058
Waipahu CDP (96797)	31,435	996

IDAHO

Boise City city (83708*)	125,738	148
Idaho Falls city (83401*)	43,929	654
Lewiston city (83501)	28,082	1144

City and major zip code	1990 census	1990 rank
Nampa city (83651*)	28,365	1127
Pocatello city (83201*)	46,080	622
Twin Falls city (83301*)	27,591	1167

ILLINOIS

Addison village (60101)	32,058	971
Alton city (62002)	32,905	941
Arlington Heights village (60005*)	75,460	303
Aurora city (60505*)	99,581	203
Belleville city (62220*)	42,785	677
Berwyn city (60402)	45,426	633
Bloomington city (61701*)	51,972	524
Bolingbrook village (60440)	40,843	720
Buffalo Grove village (60089)	36,427	827
Burbank city (60459)	27,600	1165
Calumet City city (60409)	37,840	793
Carbondale city (62901*)	27,033	1192
Carol Stream village (60188)	31,716	987
Champaign city (61820*)	63,502	387
Chicago city (60607*)	2,783,726	3
Chicago Heights city (60411)	33,072	936
Cicero town (60650)	67,436	358
Danville city (61832*)	33,828	905
Decatur city (62523*)	83,885	267
De Kalb city (60115)	34,925	869
Des Plaines city (60018*)	53,223	504
Downers Grove village (60515*)	46,858	608
East St. Louis city (62201*)	40,944	718
Elgin city (60120*)	77,010	290
Elk Grove Village village (60007*)	33,429	924
Elmhurst city (60126)	42,029	696
Evanston city (60201*)	73,233	313
Freeport city (61032)	25,840	1258
Galesburg city (61401*)	33,530	919
Glendale Heights village (60139)	27,973	1147
Glenview village (60025)	37,093	813
Granite City city (62040)	32,862	946
Hanover Park village (60103)	32,895	942
Harvey city (60426)	29,771	1067
Highland Park city (60035)	30,575	1037
Hoffman Estates village (60195)	46,561	612
Joliet city (60436*)	76,836	291
Kankakee city (60901)	27,575	1168
Lansing village (60438)	28,086	1143
Lombard village (60148)	39,408	755
Maywood village (60153)	27,139	1187
Moline city (61265)	43,202	670
Mount Prospect village (60056)	53,170	505
Naperville city (60540*)	85,351	256
Niles village (60648)	28,284	1131
Normal town (61761)	40,023	744
Northbrook village (60062*)	32,308	963
North Chicago city (60064)	34,978	868
Oak Forest city (60452)	26,203	1238
Oak Lawn village (60455*)	56,182	455
Oak Park village (60301*)	53,648	495
Orland Park village (60462)	35,720	846
Palatine village (60067*)	39,253	760
Park Ridge city (60068)	36,175	835
Pekin city (61554*)	32,254	965
Peoria city (61601*)	113,504	161
Quincy city (62301*)	39,681	751
Rockford city (61125*)	139,426	130
Rock Island city (61201*)	40,552	728
Schaumburg village (60194*)	68,586	349
Skokie village (60077*)	59,432	428
Springfield city (62703*)	105,227	188
Streamwood village (60107)	30,987	1012
Tinley Park village (60477)	37,121	811
Urbana city (61801)	36,344	830
Waukegan city (60085*)	69,392	342

City and major zip code	1990 census	1990 rank
Wheaton city (60187*)	51,464	530
Wheeling village (60090)	29,911	1061
Wilmette village (60091)	26,690	1207
Woodridge village (60517)	26,256	1235
INDIANA		
Anderson city (46011*)	59,459	427
Bloomington city (47408*)	60,633	413
Carmel city (46032)	25,380	1279
Columbus city (47201*)	31,802	984
East Chicago city (46312)	33,892	899
Elkhart city (46515*)	43,627	663
Evansville city (47708*)	126,272	147
Fort Wayne city (46802*)	173,072	99
Gary city (46401*)	116,646	158
Greenwood city (46142*)	26,265	1234
Hammond city (46320*)	84,236	263
Indianapolis (46206*)	731,327	13
Kokomo city (46902*)	44,962	640
Lafayette city (47901*)	43,764	659
Lawrence city (46226)	26,763	1203
Marion city (46952*)	32,618	951
Merrillville town (46410)	27,257	1183
Michigan City city (46360)	33,822	907
Mishawaka city (46544*)	42,608	684
Muncie city (47302*)	71,035	330
New Albany city (47150*)	36,322	832
Portage city (46368)	29,060	1097
Richmond city (47374*)	38,705	772
South Bend city (46624*)	105,511	187
Terre Haute city (47808*)	57,483	442
West Lafayette city (47906*)	25,907	1252
IOWA		
Ames city (50010)	47,198	602
Bettendorf city (52722)	28,132	1141
Burlington city (52601)	27,208	1185
Cedar Falls city (50613)	34,298	887
Cedar Rapids city (52401*)	108,751	178
Clinton city (52732)	29,201	1089
Council Bluffs city (51501*)	54,315	483
Davenport city (52802*)	95,333	218
Des Moines city (50318*)	193,187	80
Dubuque city (52001*)	57,546	441
Fort Dodge city (50501)	25,894	1254
Iowa City city (52240*)	59,738	421
Marshalltown city (50158)	25,178	1286
Mason City city (50401)	29,040	1098
Sioux City city (51101*)	80,505	276
Waterloo city (50703*)	66,467	365
West Des Moines city (50265)	31,702	988
KANSAS		
Emporia city (66801)	25,512	1272
Hutchinson city (67501*)	39,308	759
Kansas City city (66106*)	149,767	116
Lawrence city (66044*)	65,608	373
Leavenworth city (66048)	38,495	775
Lenexa city (66215)	34,034	895
Manhattan city (66502)	37,712	800
Olathe city (66061*)	63,352	389
Overland Park city (66204)	111,790	165
Salina city (67401*)	42,303	688
Shawnee city (66203)	37,993	788
Topeka city (66603*)	119,883	153
Wichita city (67276*)	304,011	51
KENTUCKY		
Bowling Green city (42101*)	40,641	727
Covington city (41011*)	43,264	668
Frankfort city (40601*)	25,968	1249
Henderson city (42420)	25,945	1250

City and major zip code	1990 census	1990 rank
Hopkinsville city (42240*)	29,809	1065
Lexington-Fayette (40511*)	225,366	70
Louisville city (40231*)	269,063	58
Owensboro city (42301*)	53,549	497
Paducah city (42003*)	27,256	1184
Pleasure Ridge Park CDP (40268)	25,131	1288
LOUISIANA		
Alexandria city (71301*)	49,188	569
Baton Rouge city (70821*)	219,531	73
Bossier City city (71111*)	52,721	511
Chalmette CDP (70043*)	31,860	979
Houma city (70360*)	30,495	1041
Kenner city (70062*)	72,033	320
Lafayette city (70501*)	94,440	219
Lake Charles city (70601*)	70,580	333
Marerro CDP (70072*)	36,671	825
Metairie (70009*)	149,428	117
Monroe city (71203*)	54,909	472
New Iberia city (70560*)	31,828	981
New Orleans city (70113*)	496,938	24
Shreveport city (71102*)	198,525	77
MAINE		
Bangor city (04401*)	33,181	932
Lewiston city (04240*)	39,757	749
Portland city (04101*)	64,358	382
MARYLAND		
Annapolis city (21401*)	33,187	931
Aspen Hill CDP (20916)	45,494	632
Baltimore city (21233*)	736,014	12
Bel Air South CDP (21014*)	26,421	1223
Bethesda CDP (20814*)	62,936	392
Bowie city (20715*)	37,589	804
Carney CDP (21234)	25,578	1269
Catonsville CDP (21228)	35,233	863
Chillum CDP (20783)	31,309	998
Columbia CDP (21045*)	75,883	297
Dundalk CDP (21222*)	65,800	370
Ellicott City CDP (21043)	41,396	709
Essex CDP (21221)	40,872	719
Frederick city (21701*)	40,148	739
Gaithersburg city (20877*)	39,542	752
Germantown CDP (20874*)	41,145	713
Glen Burnie CDP (21061*)	37,305	810
Hagerstown city (21740*)	35,445	855
Lochearn CDP (21207)	25,240	1285
Montgomery Village CDP (20886)	32,315	961
North Bethesda CDP (20850)	29,656	1072
Oxon Hill-Glassmanor (20790*)	35,794	843
Parkville CDP (21234)	31,617	990
Potomac CDP (20859)	45,634	630
Randallstown CDP (21133)	26,277	1231
Rockville city (20850*)	44,835	642
St. Charles CDP (20601)	28,717	1111
Severna Park CDP (21146)	25,879	1255
Silver Spring CDP (20907*)	76,046	296
South Gate CDP (21061)	27,564	1169
Suitland-Silver Hill (20790*)	35,111	865
Towson CDP (21285)	49,445	563
Wheaton-Glenmont CDP (20915)	53,720	492
Woodlawn CDP (21207)	32,907	940
MASSACHUSETTS		
Arlington CDP (02174)	44,630	649
Attleboro city (02703)	38,383	777
Beverly city (01915)	38,195	779
Boston city (02205*)	574,283	20
Braintree CDP (02184)	33,836	903
Brockton city (02402*)	92,788	223

City and major zip code	1990 census	1990 rank
Brookline CDP (02147*)	54,718	479
Cambridge city (02139*)	95,802	215
Chelmsford CDP (01824)	32,388	958
Chelsea city (02150)	28,710	1113
Chicopee city (01020*)	56,632	452
Everett city (02149)	35,701	849
Fall River city (02720*)	92,703	224
Fitchburg city (01420)	41,194	712
Framingham CDP (01701)	64,994	379
Gloucester city (01930*)	28,716	1112
Haverhill city (01830*)	51,418	532
Holyoke city (01040*)	43,704	662
Lawrence city (01842*)	70,207	338
Leominster city (01453)	38,145	782
Lexington CDP (02173)	28,974	1100
Lowell city (01853*)	103,439	193
Lynn city (10901*)	81,245	273
Malden city (02148)	53,884	490
Marlborough city (01752)	31,813	982
Medford city (02155)	57,407	443
Melrose city (02176)	28,150	1139
Milton CDP (02186)	25,725	1262
Needham CDP (02194*)	27,557	1170
New Bedford city (02740*)	99,922	201
Newton city (02164*)	82,585	269
Northampton city (01060*)	29,289	1083
Norwood CDP (02062)	28,700	1115
Peabody city (01960*)	47,039	605
Pittsfield city (01201*)	48,622	581
Quincy city (02369*)	84,985	257
Randolph CDP (02368)	30,093	1052
Revere city (02151)	42,786	676
Salem city (01970*)	48,091	786
Saugus CDP (01906)	25,549	1271
Somerville city (02143*)	76,210	293
Springfield city (01101*)	156,983	112
Taunton city (02780)	49,832	558
Waltham city (02154)	57,878	439
Watertown CDP (02172)	33,284	929
Wellesley CDP (02181)	26,615	1211
Westfield city (01085*)	38,372	778
West Springfield CDP (01089*)	27,537	1172
Weymouth CDP (02188*)	54,063	487
Woburn city (01801)	35,943	841
Worcester city (01613*)	169,759	102

MICHIGAN

City and major zip code	1990 census	1990 rank
Allen Park city (48101)	31,092	1007
Ann Arbor city (48103*)	109,592	174
Battle Creek city (49016*)	53,540	498
Bay City city (48707*)	38,936	766
Bloomfield Township CDP (48302)	42,137	692
Burton city (48529*)	27,617	1162
Canton CDP (48185*)	57,047	447
Clinton city (48043)	85,866	251
Dearborn city (48120*)	89,286	234
Dearborn Heights city (48127*)	60,838	410
Detroit city (48283*)	1,027,974	7
East Detroit city (48021)	35,283	862
East Lansing city (48823*)	50,677	545
Farmington Hills city (48333*)	74,652	308
Ferndale city (48220)	25,084	1292
Flint city (48502*)	140,761	127
Garden City city (48135)	31,846	980
Grand Rapids city (49501*)	189,126	83
Holland city (49423*)	30,745	1028
Inkster city (48141)	30,772	1025
Jackson city (49201*)	37,446	806
Kalamazoo city (49001*)	80,277	279
Kentwood city (49518)	37,826	794
Lansing city (48924*)	127,321	144

City and major zip code	1990 census	1990 rank
Lincoln Park city (48146)	41,832	702
Livonia city (48150*)	100,850	198
Madison Heights city (48071)	32,196	967
Midland city (48640*)	38,053	787
Muskegon city (49440*)	40,283	733
Novi city (48376*)	32,998	937
Oak Park city (48237)	30,462	1043
Pontiac city (48343*)	71,166	329
Portage city (49081)	41,042	715
Port Huron city (48061*)	33,694	910
Redford CDP (48231*)	54,387	482
Rochester Hills city (48309)	61,766	402
Roseville city (48066)	51,412	533
Royal Oak city (48068*)	65,410	377
Saginaw city (48605*)	69,512	340
St. Clair Shores city (48080*)	68,107	352
Shelby CDP (48318*)	48,655	580
Southfield city (48037*)	75,728	298
Southgate city (48195)	30,771	1026
Sterling Heights city (48311*)	117,810	156
Taylor city (48180)	70,811	331
Troy city (48099*)	72,884	314
Warren city (48090*)	144,864	120
Waterford CDP (48329*)	66,692	361
West Bloomfield Township (48343*)	54,843	475
Westland city (48185)	84,724	259
Wyandotte city (48192)	30,938	1017
Wyoming city (49509)	63,891	384

MINNESOTA

City and major zip code	1990 census	1990 rank
Apple Valley city (55124)	34,598	876
Blaine city (55434)	38,975	763
Bloomington city (55431*)	86,335	249
Brooklyn Center city (55429*)	28,887	1102
Brooklyn Park city (55429*)	56,381	453
Burnsville city (55337)	51,288	534
Coon Rapids city (55433)	52,978	508
Duluth city (55806*)	85,493	253
Eagan city (55121)	47,409	599
Eden Prairie city (55344*)	39,311	758
Edina city (55424)	46,070	624
Fridley city (55432)	28,335	1128
Mankato city (56001*)	31,477	995
Maple Grove city (55369)	38,736	770
Maplewood city (55109)	30,954	1015
Minneapolis city (55401*)	368,383	42
Minnetonka city (55345)	48,370	588
Moorhead city (56560*)	32,295	964
Plymouth city (55441*)	50,889	540
Richfield city (55423)	35,710	847
Rochester city (55901*)	70,745	332
Roseville city (55113)	33,485	922
St. Cloud city (56301*)	48,812	574
St. Louis Park city (55426)	43,787	657
St. Paul city (55101*)	272,235	57
Winona city (55987)	25,399	1278

MISSISSIPPI

City and major zip code	1990 census	1990 rank
Biloxi city (39530*)	46,419	618
Greenville city (38701*)	45,226	635
Gulfport city (39503*)	40,775	722
Hattiesburg city (39402*)	41,882	700
Jackson city (39205*)	196,637	78
Meridian city (39301*)	41,036	716
Pascagoula city (39567*)	25,899	1253
Tupelo city (38801*)	30,685	1033

MISSOURI

City and major zip code	1990 census	1990 rank
Blue Springs city (64015*)	40,153	738
Cape Girardeau city (63701*)	34,438	882
Chesterfield city (63017*)	37,991	789

City and major zip code	1990 census	1990 rank
Columbia city (65201*)	69,101	345
Florissant city (63033*)	51,206	536
Gladstone city (64108*)	26,243	1236
Independence city (64050*)	112,301	164
Jefferson City city (65101*)	35,481	853
Joplin city (64801*)	40,961	717
Kansas City city (64108*)	435,146	31
Kirkwood city (63122)	27,291	1182
Lee's Summit city (64063*)	46,418	615
Maryland Heights city (64043)	25,407	1277
Mehlville CDP (63129)	27,557	1170
Oakville CDP (63129)	31,750	985
Raytown city (64108*)	30,601	1035
St. Charles city (63301*)	54,555	480
St. Joseph city (64501*)	71,852	322
St. Louis city (63155*)	396,685	34
St. Peters city (63376)	45,779	628
Springfield city (65801*)	140,494	128
University City city (63130)	40,087	741

MONTANA

Billlings city (59101*)	81,151	274
Butte-Silver Bow (remainder) (59701*)	33,336	928
Great Falls city (59401*)	55,097	466
Missoula city (59801*)	42,918	674

NEBRASKA

Bellevue city (68005)	30,982	1013
Grand Island city (68802*)	39,386	757
Lincoln city (68501*)	191,972	81
Omaha city (68108*)	335,795	48

NEVADA

Carson City (89701*)	40,443	730
Henderson city (89015*)	64,942	380
Las Vegas city (89199*)	258,295	63
North Las Vegas city (89030*)	47,707	594
Paradise CDP (89109*)	124,682	150
Reno city (89510*)	133,850	134
Sparks city (89431*)	53,367	499
Spring Valley CDP (89117*)	51,726	527
Sunrise Manor CDP (89110*)	95,362	217

NEW HAMPSHIRE

Concord city (03301*)	36,006	840
Dover city (03820)	25,042	1295
Manchester city (03103*)	99,567	204
Nashua city (03060*)	79,662	281
Portsmouth city (03801*)	25,925	1251
Rochester city (03867*)	26,630	1209

NEW JERSEY

Atlantic City city (08401*)	37,986	790
Bayonne city (07002)	61,444	406
Belleville CDP (07109)	34,213	890
Bloomfield CDP (07003)	45,061	638
Brick Township CDP (08723*)	66,473	364
Camden city (08101*)	87,492	242
Cherry Hill CDP (08034*)	69,319	344
Clifton city (07015*)	71,742	323
East Brunswick CDP (08816)	43,548	664
East Orange city (07019*)	73,552	312
Edison CDP (08818*)	88,680	237
Elizabeth city (07207*)	110,002	172
Ewing CDP (08650*)	34,185	892
Fair Lawn borough (07410)	30,548	1038
Fort Lee borough (07024)	31,997	973
Garfield city (07026)	26,727	1205
Hackensack city (07602*)	37,049	815
Hoboken city (07030)	33,397	926
Irvington CDP (07111)	59,774	420
Jersey City city (07303*)	228,537	67

City and major zip code	1990 census	1990 rank
Kearny town (07032)	34,874	872
Lakewood CDP (08701)	26,095	1243
Linden city (07036)	36,701	823
Livingston CDP (07039)	26,609	1212
Long Branch city (07740)	28,658	1117
Mercerville-Hamilton Square CDP (08619)	26,873	1197
Millville city (08332)	25,992	1248
Montclair CDP (07042*)	37,729	799
Newark city (07102*)	275,221	56
New Bunswick city (08901*)	41,711	704
North Bergen CDP (07047)	48,414	586
North Brunswick Township (08902)	31,287	1001
Nutley CDP (07110)	27,099	1189
Orange CDP (07051*)	29,925	1060
Paramus borough (07652*)	25,067	1293
Parsippany-Troy Hill (07054)	48,478	585
Passaic city (07055)	58,041	436
Paterson city (07510*)	140,891	126
Pennsauken CDP (08110)	34,733	874
Perth Amboy city (08861*)	41,967	697
Plainfield city (07061*)	46,567	611
Rahway city (07065)	25,325	1280
Sayreville borough (08872*)	34,986	867
Teaneck CDP (07666)	37,825	795
Trenton city (08650*)	88,675	238
Union CDP (07083)	50,024	554
Union City city (07087)	58,012	437
Vineland city (08360)	54,780	477
Wayne CDP (07470*)	47,025	606
Westfield town (07091*)	28,870	1103
West Milford CDP (07480)	25,430	1275
West New York town (07093)	38,125	785
West Orange CDP (07052)	39,103	762
Willingboro CDP (08046)	36,291	833

NEW MEXICO

Alamogordo city (88310*)	27,596	1166
Albuquerque city (87101*)	384,736	38
Clovis city (88101*)	30,954	1015
Farmington city (87401*)	33,997	897
Hobbs city (88240*)	29,115	1094
Las Cruces city (88001*)	62,126	396
Rio Rancho city (87124)	32,505	953
Roswell city (88201*)	44,654	647
Santa Fe city (87501*)	55,859	460
South Valley CDP (87101*)	35,701	849

NEW YORK

Albany city (12288*)	101,082	197
Auburn city (13021*)	31,258	1003
Binghamton city (13902*)	53,008	507
Brentwood CDP (11717)	45,218	636
Brighton CDP (14610)	34,455	880
Buffalo city (14240*)	328,123	50
Centereach CDP (11720)	26,720	1206
Central Islip CDP (11722)	26,028	1245
Cheektowaga CDP (14225)	84,387	261
Commack CDP (11725)	36,124	836
Coram CDP (11727)	30,111	1049
Deer Park CDP (11729)	28,840	1105
Dix Hills CDP (11746)	25,849	1257
East Meadow CDP (11554)	36,909	818
Elmira city (14901*)	33,724	909
Elmont CDP (11003)	28,612	1119
Franklin Square CDP (11010)	28,205	1136
Freeport village (11520)	39,894	745
Hempstead village (11551*)	49,453	562
Hicksville CDP (11805*)	40,174	737
Holbrook CDP (11741)	25,273	1284
Huntington Station CDP (11746)	28,247	1133
Irondequoit CDP (14617)	52,322	517

City and major zip code	1990 census	1990 rank
Ithaca city (14850*)	29,541	1074
Jamestown city (14701*)	34,681	875
Levittown CDP (11756)	53,286	502
Lindenhurst village (11757)	26,879	1196
Long Beach city (11561)	33,510	920
Mount Vernon city (10551*)	67,153	360
Newburgh city (12550*)	26,454	1221
New City CDP (10956)	33,673	913
New Rochelle city (10802*)	67,265	359
New York city (10199*)	7,322,564	1
Brooklyn (11256*)	2,300,664	
Bronx (10451*)	1,203,789	
Manhattan (10199*)	1,487,536	
Queens	1,951,598	
Staten Island (10314*)	378,977	
Niagara Falls city (14302*)	61,840	400
North Tonawanda city (14120)	34,989	866
Oceanside CDP (11572)	32,423	956
Plainview CDP (11803)	26,207	1237
Poughkeepsie city (12601*)	28,844	1104
Rochester city (14692*)	231,636	66
Rome city (13440)	44,350	652
Saratoga Springs city (12866)	25,001	1296
Schenectady city (12305*)	65,566	375
Smithtown CDP (11787)	25,638	1266
Syracuse city (13220*)	163,860	107
Tonawanda CDP (14150*)	65,284	378
Troy city (12180*)	54,269	485
Utica city (13504*)	68,637	348
Valley Stream village (11582*)	33,946	898
Watertown city (13601*)	29,429	1077
West Babylon CDP (11707)	42,410	686
West Islip CDP (11795)	28,419	1125
West Seneca CDP (14224)	47,866	592
White Plains city (10602*)	48,718	578
Yonkers city (10702*)	188,082	84
NORTH CAROLINA		
Asheville city (28810*)	61,607	404
Burlington city (27215*)	39,498	753
Camp Lejeune Central (28542)	36,716	822
Cary town (27511*)	43,858	656
Chapel Hill town (27514*)	38,719	771
Charlotte city (28228*)	395,934	35
Concord city (28025*)	27,347	1177
Durham city (27701*)	136,611	132
Fayetteville city (28302*)	75,695	299
Fort Bragg CDP (28307)	34,744	873
Gastonia city (28052*)	54,732	478
Goldsboro city (27530*)	40,709	724
Greensboro city (27420*)	183,521	88
Greenville city (27834*)	44,972	639
Hickory city (28603*)	28,301	1130
High Point city (27260*)	69,496	341
Jacksonville city (28540*)	30,013	1057
Kannapolis city (28081*)	29,696	1071
Kinston city (28501*)	25,295	1282
Raleigh city (27611*)	207,951	75
Rocky Mount city (27801*)	48,997	571
Wilmington city (28402*)	55,530	462
Wilson city (27893*)	36,930	817
Winston-Salem city (27102*)	143,485	121
NORTH DAKOTA		
Bismarck city (58501*)	49,256	568
Fargo city (58102*)	74,111	310
Grand Forks city (58201*)	49,425	564
Minot city (58701*)	34,544	878
OHIO		
Akron city (44309*)	223,019	71
Austintown CDP (44515)	32,371	960

City and major zip code	1990 census	1990 rank
Barberton city (44203)	27,623	1161
Beavercreek city (45430*)	33,626	914
Boardman CDP (44512*)	38,596	774
Bowling Green city (43402)	28,176	1137
Brunswick city (44212)	28,230	1134
Canton city (44711*)	84,161	264
Cincinnati city (45234*)	364,040	45
Cleveland city (44101*)	505,616	23
Cleveland Heights city (44118)	54,052	488
Columbus city (43216*)	632,910	16
Cuyahoga Falls city (44222*)	48,950	572
Dayton city (45401*)	182,044	89
East Cleveland city (44112)	33,096	935
Elyria city (44035*)	56,746	450
Euclid city (44117)	54,875	473
Fairborn city (45324)	31,300	1000
Fairfield city (45014)	39,729	750
Findlay city (45840*)	35,703	848
Gahanna city (43230)	27,791	1153
Garfield Heights city (44125)	31,739	986
Hamilton city (45011*)	61,368	407
Huber Heights city (45424)	38,696	773
Kent city (44240)	28,835	1106
Kettering city (45429)	60,569	414
Lakewood city (44107)	59,718	422
Lancaster city (43130)	34,507	879
Lima city (45802*)	45,549	631
Lorain city (44052*)	71,245	328
Mansfield city (44901*)	50,627	546
Maple Heights city (44137)	27,089	1191
Marion city (43302*)	34,075	894
Massillon city (44646*)	31,007	1009
Mentor city (44060*)	47,358	600
Middletown city (45042*)	46,022	625
Newark city (43055*)	44,389	651
North Olmsted city (44070)	34,204	891
Parma city (44129)	87,876	239
Reynoldsburg city (43068)	25,748	1261
Sandusky city (44870*)	29,764	1068
Shaker Heights city (44120)	30,831	1024
Springfield city (45501*)	70,487	335
Stow city (44224)	27,702	1155
Stongsville city (44136)	35,308	860
Toledo city (43601*)	332,943	49
Upper Arlington city (43221)	34,128	893
Warren city (44481*)	50,793	542
Westerville city (43081)	30,269	1046
Westlake city (44145)	27,018	1194
Youngstown city (44501*)	95,732	216
Zanesville city (43701*)	26,778	1202
OKLAHOMA		
Bartlesville city (74003*)	34,256	889
Broken Arrow city (74012*)	58,043	435
Edmond city (73034*)	52,315	518
Enid city (73701*)	45,309	634
Lawton city (73501*)	80,561	275
Midwest City city (73125*)	52,267	520
Moore city (73125*)	40,318	732
Muskogee city (74401*)	37,708	801
Norman city (73069*)	80,071	280
Oklahoma City city (73125*)	444,719	29
Ponca City city (74601*)	26,359	1225
Shawnee city (74801*)	26,017	1246
Stillwater city (74074*)	36,676	824
Tulsa city (74103*)	367,302	43
OREGON		
Albany city (97321)	29,462	1076
Aloha CDP (97006*)	34,284	888
Beaverton city (97005*)	53,310	501
Corvallis city (97333*)	44,757	644

City and major zip code	1990 census	1990 rank
Eugene city (97401*)	112,669	163
Gresham city (97030*)	68,235	350
Hillsboro city (97123*)	37,520	805
Lake Oswego city (97034*)	30,576	1036
Medford city (97501*)	46,951	607
Portland city (97208*)	437,319	30
Powellhurst-Centennial CDP (97208*)	28,756	1109
Salem city (97301*)	107,786	182
Springfield city (97477)	44,683	646
Tigard city (97208*)	29,344	1081
PENNSYLVANIA		
Allentown city (18101*)	105,090	189
Altoona city (16601*)	51,881	525
Bethel Park borough (15102)	33,823	906
Bethlehem city (18016*)	71,428	326
Chester city (19013*)	41,856	701
Drexel Hill CDP (19026)	29,744	1069
Easton city (18042*)	26,276	1232
Erie city (16515*)	108,718	179
Harrisburg city (17107*)	52,376	514
Johnstown city (15901*)	28,134	1140
Lancaster city (17604*)	55,551	461
Levittown CDP (19053*)	55,362	464
McCandless Township CDP (15237*)	28,781	1107
McKeesport city (15134*)	26,016	1247
Mount Lebanon CDP (15228)	33,362	927
Municipality of Monroeville borough (15146*)	29,169	1091
New Castle city (16108*)	28,334	1129
Norristown borough (19401*)	30,749	1027
Penn Hills CDP (15235)	51,430	531
Philadelphia city (19104*)	1,585,577	5
Pittsburgh city (15290*)	369,879	40
Plum borough (15239)	25,609	1267
Radnor Township CDP (19087)	28,705	1114
Reading city (19612*)	78,380	283
Ross Township CDP (15290*)	33,482	923
Scranton city (18505*)	81,805	272
Shaler Township CDP (15290*)	30,533	1040
State College borough (16801*)	38,923	767
Wilkes-Barre city (18701*)	47,523	598
Williamsport city (17701*)	31,933	976
York city (17405*)	42,192	690
RHODE ISLAND		
Cranston city (02920*)	76,060	295
East Providence city (02914)	50,380	551
Newport city (02840)	28,227	1135
Pawtucket city (02860*)	72,644	317
Providence city (02904*)	160,728	108
North Providence CDP (02908)	32,090	969
Warwick city (02886*)	85,427	255
West Warwick CDP (02886*)	29,268	1085
Woonsocket city (02895)	43,877	655
SOUTH CAROLINA		
Anderson city (29621*)	26,184	1239
Charleston city (29423*)	80,414	277
Columbia city (29292*)	98,052	208
Florence city (29501*)	29,813	1064
Greenville city (29602*)	58,282	433
Mount Pleasant town (29464*)	30,108	1050
North Charleston city (29406*)	70,218	337
Rock Hill city (29730*)	41,643	707
St. Andrews CDP (29407*)	25,692	1264
Spartanburg city (29301*)	43,467	666
Sumter city (29150*)	41,943	699
SOUTH DAKOTA		
Rapid City city (57701*)	54,523	481

City and major zip code	1990 census	1990 rank
Sioux Falls city (57101*)	100,814	199
TENNESSEE		
Bartlett town (38101*)	26,989	1195
Chattanooga city (37421*)	152,466	114
Clarksville city (37040*)	75,494	301
Cleveland city (37311*)	30,354	1044
Columbia city (38401*)	28,583	1120
Germantown city (38183)	32,893	943
Hendersonville city (37075*)	32,188	968
Jackson city (38301*)	48,949	573
Johnson City city (37601*)	49,381	566
Kingsport city (37660*)	36,365	829
Knoxville city (37950*)	165,121	103
Memphis city (38101*)	610,337	18
Murfreesboro city (37130*)	44,922	641
Nashville-Davidson city (37229*)	488,374	25
Oak Ridge city (37830*)	27,310	1181
TEXAS		
Abilene city (79604*)	106,654	184
Amarillo city (79120*)	157,615	111
Arlington city (76010*)	261,721	61
Austin city (78710*)	465,622	27
Baytown city (77520*)	63,850	385
Beaumont city (77707*)	114,323	159
Bedford city (76021*)	43,762	660
Brownsville city (78520*)	98,962	205
Bryan city (77801*)	55,002	470
Carrollton city (75006*)	82,169	270
Channelview CDP (77530)	25,564	1270
College Station city (77840*)	52,456	512
Conroe city (77301*)	27,610	1163
Corpus Christi (78469*)	257,453	64
Dallas city (75260*)	1,006,877	8
Deer Park city (77536)	27,652	1157
Del Rio city (78840*)	30,705	1032
Denton city (76201*)	66,270	367
DeSoto city (75115*)	30,544	1039
Duncanville city (75138*)	35,748	845
Edinburg city (78539*)	29,885	1062
El Paso city (79910*)	515,342	22
Euless city (76039*)	38,149	781
Fort Hood CDP (76541*)	35,580	851
Fort Worth city (76161*)	447,619	28
Galveston city (77550*)	59,070	430
Garland city (75040*)	180,650	91
Grand Prairie city (75051*)	99,616	202
Grapevine city (96051*)	29,202	1088
Haltom City city (76117)	32,856	947
Harlingen city (78550*)	48,735	576
Houston city (77201*)	1,630,553	4
Huntsville city (77340*)	27,925	1149
Hurst city (76053*)	33,574	917
Irving city (75015*)	155,037	113
Killeen city (76541*)	63,535	386
Kingsville city (78363*)	25,276	1283
Kingwood CDP (77338*)	37,397	807
La Porte city (77571*)	27,910	1150
Laredo city (78041*)	122,899	151
League City city (77573*)	30,159	1048
Lewisville city (75067*)	46,521	614
Longview city (75602*)	70,311	336
Lubbock city (79402*)	186,206	87
Lufkin city (75901*)	30,206	1047
McAllen city (78501*)	82,021	265
Mesquite city (75149*)	101,484	195
Midland city (79711*)	89,443	233
Mission city (78572)	28,653	1118
Missouri City city (77489*)	36,176	834
Nacogdoches city (75961*)	30,872	1022

City and major zip code	1990 census	1990 rank
New Braunfels city (78130*)	27,334	1179
North Richland Hills city (76182)	45,895	626
Odessa city (79761*)	89,699	232
Pasadena city (77501*)	119,363	154
Pharr city (78577)	32,921	939
Plano city (75075*)	128,713	142
Port Arthur city (77640*)	58,724	431
Richardson city (75080*)	74,840	307
Round Rock city (78681*)	30,923	1019
San Angelo city (76902*)	84,474	260
San Antonio city (78284*)	935,933	10
San Marcos city (78666*)	28,743	1110
Sherman city (75090*)	31,601	991
Spring CDP (77373*)	33,111	933
Temple city (76501*)	46,109	621
Texarkana city (75501*)	31,656	989
Texas City city (77590*)	40,822	721
The Woodlands CDP (77373*)	29,205	1087
Tyler city (75712*)	75,450	304
Victoria city (77901*)	55,076	467
Waco city (76702*)	103,590	192
Wichita Falls city (76307*)	96,259	213

UTAH

City and major zip code	1990 census	1990 rank
Bountiful city (84010*)	36,659	826
Cottonwood Heights CDP (84121)	28,766	1108
Kearns CDP (84118)	28,374	1126
Layton city (84041*)	41,784	703
Logan city (84321)	32,762	950
Millcreek CDP (84109)	32,230	966
Murray city (84199*)	31,282	1002
Ogden city (84401*)	63,909	383
Orem city (84057*)	67,561	355
Provo city (84601*)	86,835	248
St. George city (84770*)	28,502	1123
Salt Lake City city (84199*)	159,936	109
Sandy city (84070*)	75,058	305
Taylorsville-Bennion (84107*)	52,351	516
West Jordan city (84084*)	42,892	675
West Valley City city (84199*)	86,976	245

VERMONT

City and major zip code	1990 census	1990 rank
Burlington city (05401*)	39,127	761

VIRGINIA

City and major zip code	1990 census	1990 rank
Alexandria city (22313*)	111,183	168
Annandale CDP (22003)	50,975	538
Arlington CDP (22210*)	170,936	100
Blacksburg town (24060*)	34,590	877
Burke CDP (22015)	57,734	440
Centreville CDP (22020)	26,585	1213
Chantilly CDP (22030*)	29,337	1082
Charlottesville city (22906*)	40,341	731
Chesapeake city (23320*)	151,976	115
Dale City CDP (22191*)	47,170	604
Danville city (24541*)	53,056	506
Hampton city (23670*)	133,793	135
Harrisonburg city (22801)	30,707	1031
Jefferson CDP (22030*)	25,782	1259
Lynchburg city (24506*)	66,049	369
Manassas city (22110*)	27,957	1148
McLean CDP (22101*)	38,168	780
Mount Vernon CDP (22121)	27,485	1173
Newport News city (23607*)	170,045	101
Norfolk city (23501*)	261,229	62
Petersburg city (23804*)	38,386	776
Portsmouth city (23707*)	103,907	191
Reston CDP (22090)	48,556	583
Richmond city (23232*)	203,056	76
Roanoke city (24022*)	96,397	211
Suffolk city (23434*)	52,141	522

City and major zip code	1990 census	1990 rank
Tuckahoe CDP (23232*)	42,629	683
Virginia Beach city (23450*)	393,069	37
West Springfield CDP (22152)	28,126	1142
Woodbridge CDP (22191*)	26,401	1224

WASHINGTON

City and major zip code	1990 census	1990 rank
Auburn city (98002*)	33,102	934
Bellevue city (98009*)	86,874	247
Bellingham city (98225*)	52,179	521
Bremerton city (98310*)	38,142	783
Burien CDP (98166)	25,089	1291
Cascade-Fairwood CDP	30,107	1051
East Hill-Meridian CDP	42,696	679
Edmonds city (98020*)	30,744	1029
Everett city (98201*)	69,961	339
Inglewood-Finn Hill (98011*)	29,132	1093
Federal Way CDP (98063)	67,554	356
Kennewick city (99336*)	42,155	691
Kent city (98031*)	37,960	791
Kirkland city (98033*)	40,052	743
Lakewood CDP (98259)	58,412	432
Longview city (98632)	31,499	993
Lynnwood city (98036*)	28,695	1116
Olympia city (98501*)	33,840	902
Redmond city (98052*)	35,800	842
Renton city (98058*)	41,688	705
Richland city (99352)	32,315	961
Richmond Heights CDP (98177)	26,037	1244
Seattle city (98109*)	516,259	21
Spokane city (99210*)	177,196	94
Tacoma city (98413*)	176,664	95
University Place CDP	27,701	1156
Vancouver city (98661*)	46,380	616
Walla Walla city (99362)	26,748	1219
Yakima city (98903*)	54,827	476

WEST VIRGINIA

City and major zip code	1990 census	1990 rank
Charleston city (25301*)	57,287	444
Huntington city (25704*)	54,844	474
Morgantown city (26505*)	25,879	1255
Parkersburg city (26101*)	33,862	900
Wheeling city (26003)	34,882	870

WISCONSIN

City and major zip code	1990 census	1990 rank
Appleton city (54911*)	65,695	371
Beloit city (53511*)	35,573	852
Brookfield city (53045*)	35,184	864
Eau Claire city (54703*)	56,856	449
Fond du Lac city (54935*)	37,757	798
Green Bay city (54303*)	96,466	210
Greenfield city (53220)	33,403	925
Janesville city (53545*)	52,133	523
Kenosha city (53140*)	80,352	278
La Crosse city (54601*)	51,003	537
Madison city (53714*)	191,262	82
Manitowoc city (54220*)	32,520	952
Memomonee Falls village (53051*)	26,840	1200
Milwaukee city (53203*)	628,088	17
New Berlin city (53186*)	33,592	915
Oshkosh city (54901*)	55,006	469
Racine city (53403*)	84,298	262
Sheboygan city (53081*)	49,676	560
Superior city (54836)	27,134	1188
Waukesha city (53186*)	56,958	448
Wausau city (54401*)	37,060	814
Wauwatosa city (53213*)	49,366	567
West Allis city (53214)	63,221	390

WYOMING

City and major zip code	1990 census	1990 rank
Casper city (82601*)	46,742	609
Cheyenne city (82001*)	50,008	555
Laramie city (82070)	26,687	1208

U.S. STATISTICS

Demographic State of the Nation: 1995

Source: U.S. Bureau of the Census, Current Population Reports, Series P23, No. 188, December 1994.

Population Projections

The U.S. population would increase more than 50% from 258 million in 1993 to 392 million in 2050, under the Census Bureau's middle series population projection. The population would grow to 276 million in 2000, 300 million in 2010, 350 million in 2030, and 372 million in 2040. The average annual growth rate, however, would decrease by half from 1.10% from 1990 to 1995 to 0.54% from 2040 to 2050. The middle series assumes that in 2050 there would be 2.1 births per woman, an 82.6-year life expectancy, and net immigration of 880,000.

In 1993, there were 33 million persons 65 and over representing 13% of the population, and projections for 2050 indicate that there will be over 80 million people 65 and over who would represent 20% of the population. The 85 and over population is growing especially fast. It is projected to more than triple in size from 3 million (1%) in 1993 to 9 million (3%) in 2030 and to more than double in size from 2030 to 2050 (to 19 million people or 5% of the population).

Household Growth

There were an estimated 96 million households in 1993, 722,000 more than in 1992. The average annual rate of growth in the number of households has decreased over the past 20 years from 2.4% in the 1970s to 1.4% in the 1980s, to 1.1% from 1990 to 1993.

In 1993 there were 68 million family households: 78% (53 million) were married-couple families. 18% (12 million) were families maintained by a woman alone, and 4% (3 million) were maintained by a man alone. (A family has at least two members with at least one who is a relative of the householder.) There were 28 million nonfamily households, most of which contained only one person.

Single-Parent Families

The proportion of all parent-child family groups maintained by single parents rose dramatically from 13% in 1970 to 30% in 1993.[1] Nearly 75% of these "single" parents either had never married (36%) or were divorced (38%) in 1993. The absent parent was usually the father (86% of single-parent situations).

A majority of Black family groups with children were maintained by single parents in 1993 (63%), compared with 25% among Whites. This is much larger than in 1970, when the percentages were 36% and 10% respectively. More than 1 in 3 (35%) Hispanic family groups with children were maintained by single parents in 1993, compared with 26% in 1980 (comparable 1970 data are not available for Hispanics). (Persons of Hispanic origin may be of any race.)

Preschool Child Care

In fall 1991, there were 31 million children under 15 living with their employed mothers (55% of all children under 15). Of these 31 million children, 10 million were preschoolers under five. Among these preschoolers, 23% (2 million) were in an organized child care facility, such as a nursery school; 36% (4 million) were cared for in their own home; and 31% (3 million) were cared for in another home.

The proportion of children or preschool age cared for in a nonrelative's home declined from 24% in 1988 to 18% in 1991. In 1991, 20% of preschoolers were cared for by their fathers while their mothers were at work, up from 15% in 1988.

Poor families with only preschoolers paid less for child care than their non-poor counterparts: $52 compared with $70 per week. However, poor families with preschoolers spent a larger percentage of their family income on child care (20%) than similar non-poor families (8%).

Education

In October 1993, 65 million persons were enrolled in regular schools, compared with 59 million in 1983 and 60 million in 1973. There were seven million persons in nursery school and kindergarten, 31 million in elementary school, 14 million in high school, and 14 million in college. Nursery school enrollment has more than doubled from 1.3 million in 1973 to 3.0 million in 1993, due in part to the increasing educational levels and labor force participation rate of mothers.

High school graduation rates for persons 18 to 14 rose slightly from 81% in 1973 to 82% in 1993. The 1993 graduation figures were 83% for Whites, 75% for Blacks, and 61% for Hispanics. Of those recent graduates, 42% of Whites, 33% of Blacks, and 36% of Hispanics (not significantly different from Black) were enrolled in college.

The annual high school dropout rate[2] declined from 6.3% in 1973 to 4.2% in 1993. The 1993 rates were 4.1% for Whites, 5.4% for Blacks, and 6.4% for Hispanics (not significantly different from each other). The rate for men was 4.4%, not significantly different from the rate of 4.1% for women.

Public Assistance

In 1991, the average monthly number of persons participating in at least one major Federal public assistance program[3] was 30.9 million (12.4%), up from 28.5 million (11.5%) in 1990. Persons participating at least one month in 1991 numbered 38.0 million (15.5%), an increase of 2.3 million since 1990. Public assistance recipients for all 24 months of 1990 and

---

1. Parent-child family groups have at least one never-married own child under 18 living in them, and include family households, related subfamilies, and unrelated subfamilies.

2. The annual dropout rate is calculated as the proportion of persons 14 to 24 enrolled in grades 10–12 in Oct. 1992 who were no longer enrolled and had not graduated by Oct. 1993.

3. Major means-tested assistance programs include public housing assistance, AFDC, General Assistance, SSI, Medicaid, food stamps, and Federal or State rent assistance.

1991 numbered 18.1 million, representing 7.6% of the Nation's total population. More persons participated in the Medicaid program (19.1 million) and the Food Stamp program (17.1 million) in an average month in 1990 than any other program.

In an average month in 1990, 48.9% of program participants received at least half of their income (including the value of food stamps) from programs, and 29.6% received all of their income from programs. Median monthly family benefits from Aid to Families with Dependent Children (AFDC)/General Assistance, Supplemental Security Income (SSI), and food stamps were $420 in 1990 and 1991.

Among persons in families maintained by a woman alone, 37.2% were program participants in an average month in 1990, compared with 6.1% of persons in married-couple families. Female householder families also were more likely to have longer median spells of program participation than persons in married-couple families in 1990, 11.4 months compared with 7.3 months.

Health Insurance

An estimated 39.7 million people were without health insurance coverage during the entire 1993 calendar year, 1.1 million more than in 1992. Among poor persons, 11.5 million were uninsured in 1993, up about 500,000 from 1992. The proportions of all persons (15.3%) and poor persons (29.3%) lacking coverage were statistically unchanged from 1992 to 1993.

Among all persons in 1993, 70.2% were covered by a private insurance plan for some or all of the year (57.1% were covered through a plan offered by an employer or union). The rest of the insured were covered by Medicaid (12.2%), Medicare (12.7%), and military health care (3.7%). (Some persons carry coverage from more than one type of plan.)

Among all age groups, persons 18 to 24 were the most likely to be uninsured in 1993 (26.8%), while only 1.2% of persons 65 and over lacked any coverage. Among the poor, persons 18 to 64 had much higher noncoverage rates than persons under 18 or persons 65 and over.

In 1993, 51.9% of the 137.1 million workers had employer-provided health insurance policies in their own name. This proportion varied by size of employer. About 29.3% of workers employed by firms with less than 25 persons had policies in their own name, compared with 66.9% of workers employed by firms with 1,000 or more.

Median Household Income

Median household income[4] was $31,241 in 1993, down 1.0% in real terms from 1992 ($31,523). Although our most recent recessionary period ended in March 1991, household income has not recovered to the 1989 pre-recessionary level of $33,585 (in 1993 dollars). From 1989 to 1993, real median household income declined by 7.0%.

In central cities of metropolitan areas of one million or more persons, the real median income of households declined 3.2% from $27,498 in 1992 to $26,622 in 1993. Since 1989, the income of these households has declined by 12.0% in real terms. In

comparison, there was no change from 1992 to 1993 in the median income of households in the suburbs (outside central cities in these metropolitan areas) ($41,211) and households located outside all metropolitan areas ($25,309).

Real median household income by race and Hispanic origin showed no change from 1992 to 1993. However, household income for all of these groups declined from 1989 to 1993. Asian and Pacific Islanders had the highest median income in 1993 ($38,347), while Blacks had the lowest ($19,532). The median income of Hispanics was $22,886 in 1993, and for Whites it was $32,960.

From 1992 to 1993, real median earnings of year-round, full-time workers 15 and over declined by 2.2% for men, from $31,101 to $30,407, and 1.2% for women, from $22,015 to $21,747. (The difference between these declines is not statistically different.) The 1993 female-to-male earnings ratio for these workers was 0.72, comparable to the 1990 all-time high.

Poverty

There were 39.3 million persons below the official government poverty level of $14,763 for a family of four in 1993, up from 38.0 million in 1992 and 32.4 million in 1989. The 1993 poverty rate was 15.1%—not significantly different from the 1992 rate of 14.8 percent, but higher than the 1989 rate of 13.1%.

In 1993, about half of our Nation's poor were children under 18 or persons 65 and over, 40.1% and 9.6 percent, respectively. The poverty rate was 22.7% for all children under 18, 12.4% for persons 18 to 64, and 12.2% for the elderly. Over one-third (35.6%) of families maintained by a women alone were poor, compared with only 6.5% of married-couple families.

The poverty rates by race and Hispanic origin did not change from 1992 to 1993. Blacks had the highest rate in 1993 (33.1%), and Whites had the lowest rate (12.2%). The Hispanic poverty rate was 30.6%.

In nonmetropolitan areas, the 1993 poverty rate (17.2%) was higher than in metropolitan areas (14.6%). The poverty rate in central cities was the highest of the metro/nonmetro residence types (21.5%). The percentage of poor persons living in central cities was 42.8%, compared with 30.2% of all persons.

Low-Income Households

In 1991, 13 million households (14%) of the Nation's 93 million households were low income, that is, those with incomes below the poverty level.[5] An additional 5 million households (5%) were near low income, that is, those with incomes between 100 and 124% of the poverty line.

About 1% of all homeowners reported crowded living conditions (more than one person per room), compared with 4% each of low-income and near low-income owners. Among all renters, 5% lived in crowded homes, compared with 10% of low-income and 8% of near low-income renters.

A smaller proportion of all homeowners with mortgages (28%) spent at least 30% of their income on

---

4. All changes in income and earnings refer to comparisons after adjusting for inflation. The income data in this section are based on money income from regularly received sources before taxes and exclude capital gains and the value of noncash benefits.

5. The data on the numbers of poor and near-poor households in this section come from the American Housing Survey. They should not be compared to the data in the earlier sections on income and poverty which come from the Current Population Survey, the official source of annual poverty estimates in the United States.

housing costs than similar low-income (89%) and near low-income homeowners (72%). Low-income and near low-income householders owned homes with a median value of $47,000, compared with $80,000 for all owners.

Homeownership

There were 110 million housing units in the United States in 1993: 63 million were owner occupied, 35 million were renter occupied, and 12 million were vacant.

In 1993, 65% of U.S. households were owner occupied, the highest homeownership rate since 1985. The rate for married-couple families in 1993 was 79%, its highest level since 1988. The 1993 rates for families maintained by men alone and women alone were 55% and 45%., respectively. Among one-person households, the homeownership rate was 43% for men and 55% for women.

Among States, homeownership rates ranted from 53% in Hawaii to 74% in Delaware. The homeownership rate in the District of Columbia was 36%. □

Singles in the United States

The ratio of unmarried men per 100 unmarried women in U.S. Metro Areas, 1990

Highest Ratio Men to Women

Rank	Metro Area	Ratio
1	Jacksonville, NC MSA	223.64
2	Killeen–Temple, TX MSA	122.75
3	Fayetteville, NC MSA	117.66
4	Brazoria, TX PMSA	116.71
5	Lawton, OK MSA	115.63
6	State College, PA MSA	112.98
7	Clarksville–Hopkinsville, TN–KY MSA	112.71
8	Anchorage, AK MSA	112.45
9	Salinas–Seaside–Monterey, CA MSA	112.01
10	Bryan–College Station, TX MSA	111.40
11	Bremerton, WA MSA	108.30
12	San Diego, CA MSA	105.33
13	Honolulu, HI MSA	105.22
14	Las Vegas, NV MSA	104.65
15	Yuma, AZ MSA	104.64
16	Grand Forks, ND MSA	104.19
17	San Jose, CA PMSA	103.63
18	Reno, NV MSA	103.52
19	Lafayette–West Lafayette, IN MSA	102.01
20	Fort Walton Beach, FL MSA	101.70
21	Vallejo–Fairfield–Napa, CA PMSA	101.68
22	Lake County, IL PMSA	101.56
23	Champaign–Urbana–Rantoul, IL MSA	101.33
24	Jackson, MI MSA	101.24
25	Colorado Springs, CO MSA	99.42

Lowest Ratio Men to Women

Rank	Metro Area	Ratio
1	Sarasota, FL MSA	65.57
2	Bradenton, FL MSA	68.41
3	Altoona, PA MSA	69.42
4	Springfield, IL MSA	69.63
5	Jacksonville, TN, MSA	69.72
6	Gadsden, AL MSA	69.86
7	Wheeling, WV–OH MSA	70.48
8	Charleston, WV MSA	70.65
9	St. Joseph, MO MSA	70.93
10	Lynchburg, VA MSA	71.04
11	Roanoke, VA MSA	71.09
12	Asheville, NC MSA	71.14
13	Shreveport, LA MSA	71.54
14	Birmingham, AL MSA	71.63
15	Danville, VA MSA	71.72
16	Pittsburgh, PA PMSA	72.04
17	Monroe, LA MSA	72.06
18	Owensboro, KY MSA	72.14
19	Pittsburgh–Beaver Valley, PA CMSA	72.16
20	Florence, AL MSA	72.20
21	Sherman–Denison, TX MSA	72.27
22	Florence, SC MSA	72.32
23	Huntington–Ashland, WV–KY–OH MSA	72.67
24	Cumberland, MD–WV MSA	72.73
25	Steubenville–Weirton, OH–WV MSA	72.87

NOTE: Unmarried includes never-married, widowed, and divorced persons, 15 years or older. Metro Areas as defined June 30, 1990. The presence of a military base, college or university, etc. in a metropolitan area may have a significant impact on the size of the ratio. MSA—Metropolitan Statistical Area. CMSA—Consolidated Metropolitan Statistical Area. PMSA—Primary Metropolitan Statistical Area. *Source:* U.S. Bureau of the Census.

Persons Below Poverty Level
by Age, Region, Race, and Hispanic Origin, 1993

Age and region	Number below poverty level				Percent below poverty level			
	All races[2]	White	Black	Hispanic origin[1]	All races[2]	White	Black	Hispanic origin[1]
Under 18 years	15,727	9,752	5,125	3,873	22.7	17.8	46.1	40.9
18 to 21	2,799	1,801	834	592	20.2	16.3	39.9	31.7
22 to 44	12,275	8,360	3,143	2,614	12.9	10.6	26.0	25.5
45 to 54	2,522	1,776	586	446	8.5	7.0	19.2	20.2
55 to 59	1,057	742	254	154	9.9	8.0	23.6	20.6
60 to 64	1,129	857	233	151	11.3	9.7	24.4	24.4
65 and over	3,755	2,939	702	297	12.2	10.7	28.0	21.4
Northeast	6,839	4,817	1,744	1,527	13.1	11.0	31.2	37.3
Midwest	8,172	5,454	2,413	476	13.4	10.3	35.9	26.5
South	15,375	8,876	6,063	2,349	17.1	12.8	33.6	28.0
West	8,879	7,080	658	3,774	15.6	14.6	25.9	30.7
Total	**39,265**	**26,227**	**10,878**	**8,126**	**15.1**	**12.2**	**33.1**	**30.6**

1. Persons of Hispanic origin may be of any race. 2. Includes race not shown separately. *Source:* U.S. Bureau of the Census.

Population

Colonial Population Estimates (in round numbers)

Year	Population	Year	Population	Year	Population	Year	Population
1610	350	1660	75,100	1710	331,700	1760	1,593,600
1620	2,300	1670	111,900	1720	466,200	1770	2,148,100
1630	4,600	1680	151,500	1730	629,400	1780	2,780,400
1640	26,600	1690	210,400	1740	905,600		
1650	50,400	1700	250,900	1750	1,170,800		

National Censuses[1]

Year	Resident population[2]	Land area, sq mi.	Pop. per sq mi.	Year	Resident population[2]	Land area, sq mi.	Pop. per sq mi.
1790	3,929,214	864,746	4.5	1900	75,994,575	2,969,834	25.6
1800	5,308,483	864,746	6.1	1910	91,972,266	2,969,565	31.0
1810	7,239,881	1,681,828	4.3	1920	105,710,620	2,969,451	35.6
1820	9,638,453	1,749,462	5.5	1930	122,775,046	2,977,128	41.2
1830	12,866,020	1,749,462	7.4	1940	131,669,275	2,977,128	44.2
1840	17,069,453	1,749,462	9.8	1950	150,697,361	2,974,726	50.7
1850	23,191,876	2,940,042	7.9	1960	179,323,175	3,540,911	50.6
1860	31,443,321	2,969,640	10.6	1970	203,302,031	3,540,023	57.4
1870	39,818,449	2,969,640	13.4	1980	226,545,805	3,539,289	64.0
1880	50,155,783	2,969,640	16.9	1990	248,709,873	3,536,278	70.3
1890	62,947,714	2,969,640	21.2				

1. Beginning with 1960, figures include Alaska and Hawaii. 2. Excludes armed forces overseas. *Source:* Department of Commerce, Bureau of the Census.

Population Distribution by Age, Race, Nativity, and Sex

				Age				Race and Nativity				
									White[1]			
Year	Total	Under 5	5–19	20–44	45–64	65 and over	Total	Native born	Foreign born	Black	Other races[1]
PERCENT DISTRIBUTION											
1860[2]	100.0	15.4	35.8	35.7	10.4	2.7	85.6	72.6	13.0	14.1	0.3
1870[2]	100.0	14.3	35.4	35.4	11.9	3.0	87.1	72.9	14.2	12.7	0.2
1880[2]	100.0	13.8	34.3	35.9	12.6	3.4	86.5	73.4	13.1	13.1	0.3
1890[3]	100.0	12.2	33.9	36.9	13.1	3.9	87.5	73.0	14.5	11.9	0.3
1900	100.0	12.1	32.3	37.7	13.7	4.1	87.9	74.5	13.4	11.6	0.5
1910	100.0	11.6	30.4	39.0	14.6	4.3	88.9	74.4	14.5	10.7	0.4
1920	100.0	10.9	29.8	38.4	16.1	4.7	89.7	76.7	13.0	9.9	0.4
1930	100.0	9.3	29.5	38.3	17.4	5.4	89.8	78.4	11.4	9.7	0.5
1940	100.0	8.0	26.4	38.9	19.8	6.8	89.8	81.1	8.7	9.8	0.4
1950	100.0	10.7	23.2	37.6	20.3	8.1	89.5	82.8	6.7	10.0	0.5
1960	100.0	11.3	27.1	32.2	20.1	9.2	88.6	83.4	5.2	10.5	0.9
1970[2]	100.0	8.4	29.5	31.7	20.6	9.8	87.6	83.4	4.3	11.1	1.4
1980	100.0	7.2	24.8	37.1	19.6	11.3	83.1	n.a.	n.a.	11.7	5.2
1990	100.0	7.6	21.3	40.1	18.6	12.5	83.9	n.a.	n.a.	12.3	3.8
MALES PER 100 FEMALES											
1860[2]	104.7	102.4	101.2	107.9	111.5	98.3	105.3	103.7	115.1	99.6	260.8
1870[2]	102.2	102.9	101.2	99.2	114.5	100.5	102.8	100.6	115.3	96.2	400.7
1880[2]	103.6	103.0	101.3	104.0	110.2	101.4	104.0	102.1	115.9	97.8	362.2
1890[3]	105.0	103.6	101.4	107.3	108.3	104.2	105.4	102.9	118.7	99.5	165.2
1900	104.4	102.1	100.9	105.8	110.7	102.0	104.9	102.8	117.4	98.6	185.2
1910	106.0	102.5	101.3	108.1	114.4	101.1	106.6	102.7	129.2	98.9	185.6
1920	104.0	102.5	100.8	102.8	115.2	101.3	104.4	101.7	121.7	99.2	156.6
1930	102.5	103.0	101.4	100.5	109.1	100.5	102.9	101.1	115.8	97.0	150.6
1940	100.7	103.2	102.0	98.1	105.2	95.5	101.2	100.1	111.1	95.0	140.5

| | | | Age | | | | | Race and Nativity White[1] | | | |
Year	Total	Under 5	5–19	20–44	45–64	65 and over	Total	Native born	Foreign born	Black	Other races[1]
1950	98.6	103.9	102.5	96.2	100.1	89.6	99.0	98.8	102.0	93.7	129.7
1960	97.1	103.4	102.7	95.6	95.7	82.8	97.4	97.6	94.2	93.3	109.7
1970[2]	94.8	104.0	103.3	95.1	91.6	72.1	95.3	95.9	83.8	90.8	100.2
1980	94.5	104.7	104.0	98.1	90.7	67.6	94.8	n.a.	n.a.	89.6	100.3
1990	95.1	104.8	105.0	99.8	92.5	67.2	95.9	n.a.	n.a.	89.8	96.5

1. The 1980 and 1990 census data for white and other races categories are not directly comparable to those shown for the preceding years because of the changes in the way some persons reported their race, as well as changes in procedures relating to racial classification. 2. Excludes persons for whom age is not available. 3. Excludes persons enumerated in the Indian Territory and on Indian reservations. NOTES: Data exclude Armed Forces overseas. Beginning in 1960, includes Alaska and Hawaii. n.a. = not available. *Source:* Department of Commerce, Bureau of the Census.

Estimated 1992 Population of Metro Areas Over One Million

Metropolitan statistical area (MSA) Consolidated metropolitan statistical area (CMSA)	July 1, 1992
New York–Northern New Jersey–Long Island, NY–NJ–CT–PA CMSA	19,670,175
Los Angeles–Riverside–Orange County, CA CMSA	15,047,772
Chicago–Gary–Kenosha, IL–IN–WI CMSA	8,410,402
Washington–Baltimore, DC–MD–VA–WV CMSA	6,919,572
San Francisco–Oakland–San Jose, CA CMSA	6,409,891
Philadelphia–Wilmington–Atlantic City, PA–NJ–DE–MD CMSA	5,938,528
Boston–Worcester–Lawrence, MA–NH–ME–CT CMSA	5,438,815
Detroit–Ann Arbor–Flint, MI CMSA	5,245,906
Dallas–Fort Worth, TX CMSA	4,214,532
Houston–Galveston–Brazoria, TX CMSA	3,962,365
Miami–Fort Lauderdale, FL CMSA	3,309,246
Atlanta, GA MSA	3,142,857
Seattle–Tacoma–Bremerton, WA CMSA	3,131,392
Cleveland–Akron, OH CMSA	2,890,402
Minneapolis–St. Paul, MN–WI MSA	2,617,973
San Diego, CA MSA	2,601,055
St. Louis, MO–IL MSA	2,518,528
Pittsburgh, PA MSA	2,406,452
Phoenix–Mesa, AZ MSa	2,330,353
Tampa–St. Petersburg–Clearwater, FL MSA	2,107,271
Denver–Boulder–Greeley, CO CMSA	2,089,321
Portland–Salem, OR–WA CMSA	1,896,895
Cincinnati–Hamilton, OH–KY–IN CMSA	1,865,002
Milwaukee–Racine, WI CMSA	1,629,420
Kansas City, MO–KS MSA	1,616,930
Sacramento–Yolo, CA CMSA	1,563,374
Norfolk–Virginia Beach–Newport News, VA–NC MSA	1,496,672
Indianapolis, IN MSA	1,424,050
Columbus, OH MSA	1,394,067
San Antonio, TX MSA	1,378,619
Orlando, FL MSA	1,304,700
New Orleans, LA MSA	1,302,697
Charlotte–Gastonia–Rock Hill, NC–SC MSA	1,212,393
Buffalo–Niagara Falls, NY MSA	1,193,901
Hartford, CT MSA	1,155,725
Providence–Fall River–Warwick, RI–MA MSA	1,131,133
Salt Lake City–Ogden, UT MSA	1,128,121
Rochester, NY MSA	1,081,244
Greensboro–Winston-Salem–High Point, NC MSA	1,078,377
Memphis, TN–AR–MS MSA	1,033,813
Nashville, TN MSA	1,023,315

Source: U.S. Bureau of the Census. Areas defined by the Office of Management and Budget as of June 30, 1993. NOTE: These estimates are consistent with the population as enumerated in the 1990 census, and have not been adjusted for census coverage errors.

Homosexuality in the United States

There are no accurate data on the number of homosexuals in the United States. A 1991 national study published in 1993 by the Alan Guttmacher Institute showed that about 2% of American males surveyed had engaged in homosexual activity during the last ten years and that 1% considered themselves exclusively homosexual. These figures are similar to studies done by researchers at the University of Chicago and in Britain, France, and Denmark.

The survey was financed by a $1.8-billion grant from the National Institute of Child Health and Human Development and conducted by researchers from the Battelle Human Affairs Research Center. Gay activists do not accept these new figures and researchers do not know precisely how reliable the new data are. The margin of sampling error for the study was given less than one percentage point.

The Kinsey Report of over 40 years ago gave a figure of 10 percent for males who were predominantly homosexual for three years of their lives and 4 percent for those who were exclusively homosexual.

The United States population has increased by 93 million since the Kinsey sampling was taken and the four-decade-old data may not be representative today.□

The EXPANSION of the UNITED STATES

Population by State

State	1990	Percent change, 1980–90	Pop. per sq mi., 1990	Pop. rank, 1990	1980	1950	1900	1790
Alabama	4,040,587	+3.8	79.6	22	3,893,888	3,061,743	1,828,697	—
Alaska	550,403	+36.9	1.0	49	401,851	128,643	63,592	—
Arizona	3,665,228	+34.8	32.3	24	2,718,215	749,587	122,931	—
Arkansas	2,350,725	+2.8	45.1	33	2,286,435	1,909,511	1,311,564	—
California	29,760,021	+25.7	190.4	1	23,667,902	10,586,223	1,485,053	—
Colorado	3,294,394	+14.0	31.8	26	2,889,964	1,325,089	539,700	—
Connecticut	3,287,116	+5.8	674.7	27	3,107,576	2,007,280	908,420	237,946
Delaware	666,168	+12.1	344.8	46	594,338	318,085	184,735	59,096
D.C.	606,900	−4.9	—	—	638,333	802,178	278,718	—
Florida	12,937,926	+32.7	238.9	4	9,746,324	2,771,305	528,542	—
Georgia	6,478,216	+18.6	109.9	11	5,463,105	3,444,578	2,216,331	82,548
Hawaii	1,108,229	+14.9	172.5	41	964,691	499,794	154,001	—
Idaho	1,006,749	+6.7	12.2	42	943,935	588,637	161,772	—
Illinois	11,430,602	0.0	205.4	6	11,426,518	8,712,176	4,821,550	—
Indiana	5,544,159	+1.0	154.2	14	5,490,224	3,934,224	2,516,462	—
Iowa	2,776,755	−4.7	49.6	30	2,913,808	2,621,073	2,231,853	—
Kansas	2,477,574	+4.8	30.3	32	2,363,679	1,905,299	1,470,495	—
Kentucky	3,685,296	+0.7	92.9	23	3,660,777	2,944,806	2,147,174	73,677
Louisiana	4,219,973	+0.3	94.8	21	4,205,900	2,683,516	1,381,625	—
Maine	1,227,928	+9.2	39.6	38	1,124,660	913,774	694,466	96,540
Maryland	4,781,468	+13.4	486.0	19	4,216,975	2,343,001	1,188,044	319,728
Massachusetts	6,016,425	+4.9	768.9	13	5,737,037	4,690,514	2,805,346	378,787
Michigan	9,295,297	+0.4	163.2	8	9,262,078	6,371,766	2,420,982	—
Minnesota	4,375,099	+7.3	55.0	20	4,075,970	2,982,483	1,751,394	—
Mississippi	2,573,216	+2.1	54.5	31	2,520,638	2,178,914	1,551,270	—
Missouri	5,117,073	+4.1	74.2	15	4,916,686	3,954,653	3,106,665	—
Montana	799,065	+1.6	5.5	44	786,690	591,024	243,329	—
Nebraska	1,578,385	+0.5	20.6	36	1,569,825	1,325,510	1,066,300	—
Nevada	1,201,833	+50.1	10.9	39	800,493	160,083	42,335	—
New Hampshire	1,109,252	+20.5	123.3	40	920,610	533,242	411,588	141,885
New Jersey	7,730,188	+5.0	1,035.1	9	7,364,823	4,835,329	1,883,669	184,139
New Mexico	1,515,069	+16.3	12.5	37	1,302,894	681,187	195,310	—
New York	17,990,455	+2.5	379.7	2	17,558,072	14,830,192	7,268,894	340,120
North Carolina	6,628,637	+12.7	135.7	10	5,881,766	4,061,929	1,893,810	393,751
North Dakota	638,800	−2.1	9.0	47	652,717	619,636	319,146	—
Ohio	10,847,115	+0.5	264.5	7	10,797,630	7,946,627	4,157,545	—
Oklahoma	3,145,585	+4.0	45.8	28	3,025,290	2,233,351	790,391[1]	—
Oregon	2,842,321	+7.9	29.5	29	2,633,105	1,521,341	413,536	—
Pennsylvania	11,881,643	+0.1	264.7	5	11,863,895	10,498,012	6,302,115	434,373
Rhode Island	1,003,464	+5.9	951.1	43	947,154	791,896	428,556	68,825
South Carolina	3,486,703	+11.7	115.4	25	3,121,820	2,117,027	1,340,316	249,073
South Dakota	696,004	+0.8	9.1	45	690,768	652,740	401,570	—
Tennessee	4,877,185	+6.2	118.5	17	4,591,120	3,291,718	2,020,616	35,691
Texas	16,986,510	+19.4	64.8	3	14,229,191	7,711,194	3,048,710	—
Utah	1,722,850	+17.9	20.9	35	1,461,037	688,862	276,749	—
Vermont	562,758	+10.0	60.7	48	511,456	377,747	343,641	85,425
Virginia	6,187,358	+15.7	155.8	12	5,346,818	3,318,680	1,854,184	747,610[2]
Washington	4,866,692	+17.8	73.1	18	4,132,156	2,378,963	518,103	—
West Virginia	1,793,477	−8.0	73.8	34	1,949,644	2,005,552	958,800	—
Wisconsin	4,891,769	+4.0	89.9	16	4,705,767	3,434,575	2,069,042	—
Wyoming	453,588	−3.4	4.7	50	469,557	290,529	92,531	—
Total U.S.	**248,709,873**	**+9.8**	—	—	**226,545,805**	**151,325,798**	**76,212,168**	**3,929,214**

1. Includes population of Indian Territory: 1900, 392,960. 2. Until 1863, Virginia included what is now West Virginia.
Source: Department of Commerce, Bureau of the Census.

Americans Are on the Move

More than 42 million Americans moved in the one-year period between March 1992 and March 1993. This amounted to 16.8% of the population one year old and over. Most of these persons made local moves—26 million moved from one residence to another within the same county. Nearly eight million persons moved between counties in the same state and another nearly seven million changed states. During that same period, 1.3 million persons moved into the United States from abroad.

The highest mobility rates are found for young adults in their twenties. More than one-third of persons 20 to 24 years old (35.8%) moved between 1992 and 1993. This rate is twice that for all persons one year old and over. Persons 25 to 29 years old have nearly as high a rate of moving as persons in their early twenties; 30.9% moved in the previous year. □

Territorial Expansion

Accession	Date	Area[1]
United States	—	3,536,278
Territory in 1790	—	891,364
Louisiana Purchase	1803	831,321
Florida	1819	69,866
Texas	1845	384,958
Oregon	1846	283,439
Mexican Cession	1848	530,706
Gadsden Purchase	1853	29,640
Alaska	1867	591,004
Hawaii	1898	6,471
Other territory	—	4,664
Philippines	1898	115,600[2]
Puerto Rico	1899	3,426
Guam	1899	209
American Samoa	1900	77
Canal Zone[3]	1904	553
Virgin Islands of U.S.	1917	134
Trust Territory of Pacific Islands	1947	177[4]
All other	—	14
Total, 1990	—	**3,540,315**

1. Total land and water area in square miles. 2. Became independent in 1946. 3. Reverted to Panama. 4. Land area only; Palau only Trust Territory remaining. *Source:* Department of Commerce, Bureau of the Census.

Total Population

Area	1990	1980	1970
50 states of U.S.	248,709,873	226,545,805	203,302,031
48 conterminous	247,051,601	225,179,263	202,229,535
Alaska	550,043	401,851	302,583
Hawaii	1,108,229	964,691	769,913
American Samoa	46,773	32,297	27,159
Canal Zone	(1)	(1)	44,198
Corn Islands	—	—	(2)
Guam	133,152	105,979	84,996
Johnston Atoll	n.a.	327	1,007
Midway	(3)	453	2,220
Puerto Rico	3,522,037	3,196,520	2,712,033
Swan Islands	n.a.	n.a.	22
Trust Ter. of Pac. Is.	15,122[5]	132,929[4]	90,940
Virgin Is. of U.S.	101,809	96,569	62,468
Wake Island	(3)	302	1,647
Population abroad	922,819	995,546	1,737,836
Armed forces	910,611	515,408	1,057,776
Total	**253,451,585**	**231,106,727**	**208,066,557**

1. Reverted to Panama. 2. Returned to Nicaragua April 25, 1971. 3. No indigenous population. 4. Includes Northern Mariana Islands. 5. Palau only Trust Territory remaining. NOTE: n.a. = not available. *Source:* Department of Commerce, Bureau of the Census.

Resident Population, by Age Group, Race, and Hispanic Origin, 1995[1]

(in thousands)

Age	White	Black	Hispanic origin[2]	American Indian, Eskimo & Aleut	Asian & Pacific Islanders	All persons
Under 5	12,524	2,932	3,191	176	770	19,593
5–9	12,630	2,665	2,658	191	670	18,814
10–14	12,641	2,739	2,424	198	711	18,713
15–19	12,291	2,689	2,280	171	636	18,067
20–24	12,184	2,507	2,334	158	690	17,873
25–29	13,126	2,447	2,488	150	752	18,963
30–34	15,686	2,679	2,533	157	821	21,876
35–39	16,508	2,661	2,158	152	797	22,276
40–44	15,370	2,288	1,729	136	713	20,236
45–49	13,666	1,780	1,313	111	585	17,455
50–54	10,850	1,326	962	84	413	13,635
55–59	8,844	1,095	782	65	320	11,102
60–64	8,141	954	636	53	266	10,050
65–69	8,220	889	543	42	228	9,922
70–74	7,544	677	405	34	174	8,834
75–79	5,802	498	258	23	104	6,685
80–84	3,911	311	189	15	58	4,484
85–89	2,046	160	64	8	22	2,300
90–94	864	80	38	4	8	994
95–99	229	22	9	1	3	264
100 and over	42	7	2	1	1	53
All ages	193,519	31,606	26,978	1,931	8,743	262,777
16 and over	152,755	22,496	18,237	1,328	6,454	201,270
18 and over	147,835	21,422	17,332	1,258	5,199	193,046
65 and over	28,658	2,644	1,508	128	598	33,536

1. July 1, 1995. 2. Persons of Hispanic origin may be of any race. The information on the total and Hispanic population shown in this table was collected in the 50 states and the District of Columbia, and, therefore, does not include residents of Puerto Rico. *Source:* U.S. Bureau of the Census.

Gas or Electricity Heats Most New Homes

In 1950, many homes in the United States were heated with coal or coke; 40 years later, both had almost vanished as home-heating fuel, to be replaced by gas, electricity, and fuel oil/kerosene, according to a recent Census Bureau report.

The majority of our metropolitan homes in 1990 were heated by either utility or bottled gas (59%), electricity (26%), and fuel oil or kerosene (12%), with 3% using other or no fuel at all. The percentage of homes built between 1985 and March 1990 heated by electricity was nearly six times that of those built prior to 1940.

Immigrants to U.S. by Country of Origin

(Figures are totals, not annual averages, and were tabulated as follows: 1820–67, alien passengers arrived; 1868–91 and 1895–97, immigrant aliens arrived; 1892–94 and 1898 to present, immigrant aliens admitted. From 1989 totals include legalized immigrants. (Data before 1906 relate to country whence alien came; 1906–80, to country of last permanent residence; 1981 to present data based on country of birth.)

Countries	1994	1820–1994	1981–90	1971–80	1961–70	1951–60	1941–50	1820–1940
Europe: Albania[1]	1,489	6,803	479	329	98	59	85	2,040
Austria[2]	499	2,663,656	4,636	9,478	20,621	67,106	24,860	2,534,617
Belgium	516	211,674	5,706	5,329	9,192	18,575	12,189	158,205
Bulgaria[3]	981	74,166	2,342	1,188	619	104	375	65,856
Former Czechoslovakia[1]	874	154,285	11,500	6,023	3,273	918	8,347	120,013
Denmark	606	373,128	5,380	4,439	9,201	10,984	5,393	335,025
Estonia[1]	272	1,974	137	91	163	185	212	506
Finland[1]	471	39,237	3,265	2,868	4,192	4,925	2,503	19,593
France	2,715	789,675	23,124	25,069	45,237	51,121	38,809	594,998
Germany[2]	6,992	7,092,316	70,111	74,414	190,796	477,765	226,578	6,021,951
Great Britain	16,326	5,171,066	142,123	137,374	213,822	202,824	139,306	4,266,561
Greece	1,440	701,918	29,130	92,369	85,969	47,608	8,973	430,608
Hungary[2]	880	165,788	9,764	6,550	5,401	36,637	3,469	1,609,158
Ireland	17,256	4,773,845	32,823	11,490	32,966	48,362	14,789	4,580,557
Italy	2,305	5,348,481	32,894	129,368	214,111	185,491	57,661	4,719,223
Latvia[1]	762	4,916	359	207	510	352	361	1,192
Lithuania[1]	663	6,120	482	248	562	242	683	2,201
Luxembourg[1]	24	3,252	234	307	556	684	820	565
Netherlands	1,239	379,490	11,958	10,492	30,606	52,277	14,860	253,759
Norway[4]	459	755,674	3,901	3,941	15,484	22,935	10,100	697,095
Poland[5]	28,048	721,071	97,390	37,234	53,539	9,985	7,571	414,755
Portugal	2,169	512,372	40,020	101,710	76,065	19,588	7,423	256,044
Romania[6]	3,444	236,588	39,963	12,393	2,531	1,039	1,076	156,945
Spain	1,418	286,699	15,698	39,141	44,659	7,894	2,898	170,123
Sweden[4]	1,140	1,396,504	10,211	6,531	17,116	21,697	10,665	1,325,208
Switzerland	877	361,234	7,076	8,235	18,453	17,675	10,547	295,680
Former U.S.S.R.[7]	63,420	3,692,695	84,081	38,961	2,465	671	571	3,343,361
Former Yugoslavia[3]	3,405	148,222	19,182	30,540	20,381	8,225	1,576	56,787
Other Europe	226	61,837	2,661	4,049	4,904	9,799	3,447	36,060
Total Europe	160,916	37,644,936	705,630	800,368	1,123,492	1,325,727	621,147	32,468,776
Asia: China[8]	64,017	1,172,171	388,686	124,326	34,764	9,657	16,709	382,173
India	34,921	623,732	261,841	164,134	27,189	1,973	1,761	9,873
Israel	3,425	146,824	36,353	37,713	29,602	25,476	476	—
Japan[9]	6,093	487,485	43,248	49,775	39,988	46,250	1,555	277,591
Turkey	1,840	418,997	20,843	13,399	10,142	3,519	798	361,236
Other Asia	182,293	4,615,456	2,042,025	1,198,831	285,957	66,374	15,729	44,053
Total Asia[10]	292,589	7,464,575	2,066,455	1,588,178	427,642	153,249	37,028	1,074,926
America: Canada and Newfoundland[11]	16,068	4,319,784	119,204	169,939	413,310	377,952	171,718	3,005,728
Central America	39,908	1,077,114	458,753	134,640	101,330	44,751	21,665	49,154
Mexico[12]	11,398	5,172,888	1,653,250	640,294	453,937	299,811	60,589	778,255
South America	47,377	1,480,453	455,977	295,741	257,954	91,628	21,831	121,302
West Indies	104,686	3,159,127	892,392	741,126	470,213	123,091	49,725	446,971
Other America[12]	166	117,463	1,352	995	19,630	59,711	29,276	56
Total America	359,511	15,424,412	3,580,928	1,982,735	1,716,374	996,944	354,804	4,401,466
Africa	26,712	466,224	192,212	80,779	28,954	14,092	7,367	26,060
Australia and New Zealand	2,967	155,642	20,169	23,788	19,562	11,506	13,805	54,437
Pacific Islands[13]	1,625	60,817	21,041	17,454	5,560	1,470	746	11,089
Countries not specified[14]	4	272,247	196	12	93	12,491	142	253,689
Total all countries	804,416	61,503,866	7,338,062	4,493,314	3,321,677	2,515,479	1,035,039	38,290,443

1. Countries established since beginning of World War I are included with countries to which they belonged. 2. Data for Austria–Hungary not reported until 1861. Austria and Hungary recorded separately after 1905, Austria included with Germany 1938–45. 3. Bulgaria, Serbia, Montenegro first reported in 1899. Bulgaria reported separately since 1920. In 1920, separate enumeration for Kingdom of Serbs, Croats, Slovenes; since 1922, recorded as Yugoslavia. 4. Norway included with Sweden 1820–68. 5. Included with Austria–Hungary, Germany, and Russia 1899–1919. 6. No record of immigration until 1880. 7. From 1931–63, the U.S.S.R. was broken down into European U.S.S.R. and Asian U.S.S.R. Since 1964, total U.S.S.R. has been reported in Europe. 8. Beginning in 1957, China includes Taiwan. 9. No record of immigration until 1861. 10. From 1934, Asia included Philippines; before 1934, recorded in separate tables as insular travel. 11. Includes all British North American possessions, 1820–98. 12. No record of immigration, 1886–93. 13. Included with "Countries not specified" prior to 1925. 14. Includes 32,897 persons returning in 1906 to their homes in U.S. Source: Department of Justice, Immigration and Naturalization Service. NOTE: Data are latest available.

The Foreign Born Population in the United States: 1990 and 1980

25 Largest Places of Birth

1990 Rank	Place of Birth	Number	Percent	1980 Rank	Place of Birth	Number	Percent
	United States	**19,767,316**	**100.0**		**United States**	**14,079,906**	**100.0**
1	Mexico	4,298,014	21.7	1	Mexico	2,199,221	15.6
2	Philippines	912,674	4.6	2	Germany	849,384	6.0
3	Canada	744,830	3.8	3	Canada	842,859	6.0
4	Cuba	736,971	3.7	4	Italy	831,922	5.9
5	Germany	711,929	3.6	5	United Kingdom	669,149	4.8
6	United Kingdom	640,145	3.2	6	Cuba	607,814	4.3
7	Italy	580,592	2.9	7	Philippines	501,440	3.6
8	Korea	568,397	2.9	8	Poland	418,128	3.0
9	Vietnam	543,262	2.7	9	Soviet Union	406,022	2.9
10	China	529,837	2.7	10	Korea	289,885	2.1
11	El Salvador	465,433	2.4	11	China	286,120	2.0
12	India	450,406	2.3	12	Vietnam	231,120	1.6
13	Poland	388,328	2.0	13	Japan	221,794	1.6
14	Dominican Republic	347,858	1.8	14	Portugal	211,614	1.5
15	Jamaica	334,140	1.7	15	Greece	210,998	1.5
16	Soviet Union	333,725	1.7	16	India	206,087	1.5
17	Japan	290,128	1.5	17	Ireland	197,817	1.4
18	Colombia	286,124	1.4	18	Jamaica	196,811	1.4
19	Taiwan	244,102	1.2	19	Dominican Republic	169,147	1.2
20	Guatemala	225,739	1.1	20	Yugoslavia	152,967	1.1
21	Haiti	225,393	1.1	21	Austria	145,607	1.0
22	Iran	210,941	1.1	22	Hungary	144,368	1.0
23	Portugal	210,122	1.1	23	Colombia	143,508	1.0
24	Greece	177,398	0.9	24	Iran	121,505	0.9
25	Laos	171,577	0.9	25	France	120,215	0.9

Source: U.S. Bureau of the Census, 1993.

Ancestry of U.S. Population by Rank, 1990 Census

(Over one million)

1990 Rank	Ancestry group	Number	Percent	1990 Rank	Ancestry group	Number	Percent
	Total population	**248,709,873**	**100.0**	17	French Canadian	2,167,127	0.9
1	German	57,947,873	23.3	18	Welsh	2,033,893	0.8
2	Irish	38,735,539	15.6	19	Spanish	2,024,004	0.8
3	English	32,651,788	13.1	20	Puerto Rican	1,955,323	0.8
4	Afro American	23,777,098	9.6	21	Slovak	1,882,897	0.8
5	Italian	14,664,550	5.9	22	White	1,799,711	0.7
6	American	12,395,999	5.0	23	Danish	1,634,669	0.7
7	Mexican	11,586,983	4.7	24	Hungarian	1,582,302	0.6
8	French	10,320,935	4.1	25	Chinese	1,505,245	0.6
9	Polish	9,366,106	3.8	26	Filipino	1,450,512	0.6
10	American Indian	8,708,220	3.5	27	Czech	1,296,411	0.5
11	Dutch	6,227,089	2.5	28	Portuguese	1,153,351	0.5
12	Scotch-Irish	5,617,773	2.3	29	British	1,119,154	0.4
13	Scottish	5,393,581	2.2	30	Hispanic	1,113,259	0.4
14	Swedish	4,680,863	1.9	31	Greek	1,110,373	0.4
15	Norwegian	3,869,395	1.6	32	Swiss	1,045,495	0.4
16	Russian	2,952,987	1.2	33	Japanese	1,004,645	0.4

NOTE: Data are based on a sample and subject to sampling variability. Since persons who reported multiple ancestries were included in more than one group, the sum of the persons reporting the ancestry is greater than the total; for example, a person reporting "English-French" was tabulated in both the "English" and "French" categories. Ancestry groups with fewer than 2,000 persons were not included in this report. *Source:* U.S. Bureau of the Census, 1993.

A Quarter of Nation's Foreign Born Arrived Since 1985

Nearly one-fourth of the United States' nearly 20 million foreign-born residents entered the country between 1985 and 1990, according to tabulations from the 1990 census.

The listing shows that the number of foreign-born persons entering the United States has increased steadily since the early 1960s, from 1.5 million in 1960–64, to a peak of 5.6 million in 1985–90.

About 7.9 percent of the nation's population was foreign born in 1990, the highest proportion in the past four decades.

California was home to one-third of the nation's foreign-born population. Other states with large concentrations include New York, 14 percent; Florida and Texas, 8 percent each; and New Jersey and Illinois, 5 percent each.

The Foreign-Born Population: 1994

Nearly one in eleven Americans are foreign-born. Twenty percent came to the U.S in the last five years.

Source: Current Population Reports, P20–486, August 1995, Census Bureau.

In 1994, 8.7% of the United States population was foreign-born, nearly double the percent foreign-born in 1970 (4.8%). California is home to 7.7 million foreign-born persons—more than a third of all immigrants to the U.S. and nearly one-quarter of all California residents. New York ranks second with 2.9 million and Florida ranks third with 2.1 million foreign-born residents. Three other states have over one million foreign-born residents: Texas, Illinois, and New Jersey.

"Natives" are persons born in the United States, Puerto Rico, or an outlying area of the U.S., such as Guam or the U.S. Virgin Islands, and persons who were born in a foreign country but who had at least one parent who was a U.S. citizen. All other persons born outside the United States are "foreign-born."

Of the 22,568,000 foreign-born persons living in the United States in March 1994, 6.2 million came from Mexico. Mexico was by far the country of origin with the largest number of immigrants. The next largest group was from the Philippines—1,033,000.

Of the 4.5 million most recent immigrants, over a quarter (1.3 million) came from Mexico and an additional 243,000 came from Russia. Other countries with large numbers of recent immigrants include Vietnam, the Dominican Republic, the Philippines, India, and El Salvador.

During the 1980s, the largest numbers of immigrants came from Mexico (2,671,000) and the Philippines (424,000). China, Korea, the Dominican Republic, and Cuba also contributed large numbers. Prior to 1970, Mexico was still the most frequent country of origin (768,000), but the other top countries of origin were very different from today. They included Germany, Cuba, Italy, Canada, and England.

Note: The foreign-born population in this census report includes some undocumented immigrants, refugees, and temporary residents such as students and temporary workers, as well as the legally admitted immigrants included in data from the Immigration and Naturalization Service.

Citizenship

Foreign-born persons over the age of 18 can become "naturalized citizens" of the United States after they have lived here for a minimum number of five years and have passed a citizenship exam. Spouses of U.S. citizens (and certain others) can become naturalized after three years, and children who immigrate generally become citizens when their parents are naturalized. About 31% of foreign-born people in the United States are naturalized.

Race and Hispanic Origin

More than two-thirds of the foreign-born population are White, about one in five is Asian or Pacific Islander, and only 7.1% are Black. The remainder reported their race as either "American Indian, Eskimo, or Aleut" or "other race." Nearly half (44.5%) of all foreign-born persons are of Hispanic origin.

Nearly two-thirds of the Asian and Pacific Islanders in the United States are foreign-born and most of the immigrants (91.7%) entered this country since 1970. Although 38.5% of the persons of Hispanic origin in this country are foreign-born and have lived in the U.S. long enough to qualify for naturalization, only 18.3% are naturalized citizens.

Educational Attainment

Recent immigrants 25 years and over are more likely to have a college degree than either natives or earlier immigrants. While 11.5% of recent immigrants have a graduate or professional degree, only about 7.5% of natives and immigrants in earlier years have such degrees. Recent immigrants are also more likely to have a bachelor's degree (20.9%) than either natives (14.7%), or earlier immigrants (13.9%).

On the other hand, immigrants are also less likely to have graduated from high school than natives. Only 17.1% of natives over the age of 25 are not high school graduates while 36.0% of immigrants do not have high school degrees.

Labor Force Status

The foreign-born population has a higher unemployment rate than do natives (9.1% vs. 6.8%, respectively). However, the unemployment rate of naturalized citizens is no different statistically from that of natives. Foreign-born persons who are not citizens have the highest unemployment rate (10.7%).

Income in 1993

Foreign-born persons as a group had a lower median income in 1993 than natives ($12,179 vs. $15,876) but this difference seems to be related to length of residence. Those who immigrated during the 1970s have median incomes no different from that of natives. Recent immigrants have the lowest median income ($8,393) of all immigrants by period of entry into the United States.

Public Assistance

Recent immigrants are more likely to receive public assistance income than natives (5.7% vs. 2.9%). The rates drop significantly for immigrants who have been here for five or more years. Immigrants who arrived before 1970 are less likely to be receiving public assistance (1.4%) than natives.

Aid to Families with Dependent Children (AFDC) is the primary source of public assistance income.

Poverty Status.

The foreign-born are 1.6 times more likely to be in poverty than natives (22.9% vs. 14.4%). And recent immigrants are over twice as likely to be in poverty (37.1%). Only persons who immigrated prior to 1970 are less likely than natives to be in poverty (10.8%).

Spanish Leads Foreign Languages Spoken by U.S. Residents

According to the latest census studies released in April 1993, over 31.8 million people—14% of the nation's population five years or over—spoke a language other than English in 1990, compared with 23.1 million (or 11%) in 1980. After English, Spanish was the most common language spoken. About 4.5 million Americans spoke an Asian or Pacific Island language and nearly 332,000 spoke a Native North American language.

More than half of all non-English language speakers in 1990 lived in three states: California (8.6 million), New York (3.9 million), and Florida (4 million). New Mexico had the largest percentage of non-English language speakers at 36%, followed by California with 32 percent.

Spanish was the prevailing language in 39 states and the District of Columbia. The next most widely used language varied by region—Italian and German in the Northeast and Midwest, and French and Chinese in the South and West. French was most used in Louisiana, Maine, New Hampshire, and Vermont; and German in Montana, Minnesota, and North and South Dakota. In Rhode Island, Portuguese was first; in Alaska, it was Yupik; and in Hawaii, Japanese was the language of most non-English language speakers. ☐

Non-English Language Speaking Americans, 1990

Top languages spoken at home, ranked for persons five years old and over

Language	1990 Population 5 years and over	1980 Population 3 years and over	Percent change	Language	1990 Population 5 years and over	1980 Population 3 years and over	Percent change
United States	230,445,777	216,384,403	6.5	Navaho	148,530	123,169	20.6
Total	31,844,979	23,711,574	34.3	Hungarian	147,902	180,083	−17.9
Spanish	17,339,172	11,549,333	50.1	Hebrew	144,292	99,166	45.4
French	1,702,176	1,572,275	8.3	Dutch	142,684	146,429	−2.6
German	1,547,099	1,606,743	−3.7	Mon-Khmer[2]	127,441	16,417	676.3
Italian	1,308,648	1,633,279	−19.9	Gujarathi[3]	102,418	36,865	177.8
Chinese	1,249,213	631,737	97.7	Ukrainian	96,568	122,300	−21.0
Tagalog[1]	843,251	451,962	86.6	Czech	92,485	123,059	−24.8
Polish	723,483	826,150	−12.4	Pennsylvania Dutch	83,525	68,202	22.5
Korean	626,478	275,712	127.2	Miao[4]	81,877	16,189	405.8
Vietnamese	507,069	203,268	149.5	Norwegian	80,723	113,227	−28.7
Portuguese	429,860	361,101	19.0	Slovak	80,388	87,941	−8.6
Japanese	427,657	342,205	25.0	Swedish	77,511	100,886	−23.2
Greek	388,260	410,462	−5.4	Serbocroatian	70,964	83,216	−14.7
Arabic	355,150	225,597	57.4	Kru[5]	65,848	24,506	168.7
Hindi and related	331,484	129,968	155.1	Rumanian	65,265	32,502	100.8
Russian	241,798	174,623	38.5	Lithuanian	55,781	73,234	−23.8
Yiddish	213,064	320,380	−33.5	Finnish	54,350	69,386	−21.7
Thai	206,266	89,052	131.6	Panjabi	50,005	19,298	159.1
Persian	201,865	109,293	84.7	Formosan	46,044	13,661	237.0
French Creole	187,658	24,885	654.1	Croatian	45,206	42,479	6.4
Armenian	149,694	102,301	46.3	Turkish	41,876	27,459	52.5

NOTE: The data for 1980 in this table are for the population 3 years old and over; for 1990 they are for persons 5 years and over. *Source:* Census data published April 1993. 1. Filipino language of Manila and adjacent provinces. 2. Language spoken in southeast Asia, mostly in Cambodia. 3. Language of Gujarat region of western India. 4. Language of Hmong people of mountainous regions of southern China and adjacent areas of Vietnam, Laos, and Thailand. 5. Language spoken in Western Africa, chiefly in Liberia.

Hispanics Will Become Largest Minority in Future

Hispanics will become the nation's largest minority group by the year 2010 and outnumber blacks, according to the latest Census Bureau projections. By that time, the white non-Hispanic portion of the population will have declined sharply from 75% in 1990 to 68% in 2010 and finally, 53% in 2050. By the middle of the next century, the United States population will almost be evenly divided between non-Hispanic White and minorities. It is projected that the nation's population will have grown to 392 million by the year 2050.

After 1996, the Hispanic population is projected to add 870,000 people to the U.S. population each year. Nearly two-thirds of the growth will come from natural increase and about one-third from immigration.

Asian and Pacific Islanders will continue to be the fastest growing segment of the population at over four percent a year. At this rate, they will make up 10% of the population in 2050 (41 million people).

The African-American population is projected to grow from 31 million (12%) in 1990 to 62 million people (16%) by 2050. After 2012 more African-Americans will be added to the population each year than White non-Hispanics.

American Indians, Eskimos, and Aleuts may double their population size by the middle of the next century, growing from about 2.1 million in 1990 to 4.3 million in 2050. ☐

Immigrant and Nonimmigrant Aliens Admitted to U.S.

Period[1]	Immigrants	Non–immigrants[2]	Total	Period[1]	Immigrants	Non–immigrants[2]	Total
1901–10	8,795,386	1,007,909	9,803,295	1985	570,009	9,675,650	10,245,659
1911–20	5,735,811	1,376,271	7,112,082	1986	601,708	10,471,024	11,072,732
1921–30	4,107,209	1,774,896	5,882,090	1987	601,516	12,272,866	12,874,382
1931–40	528,431	1,574,071	2,102,502	1988	643,025	14,591,735	15,234,760
1941–50	1,035,039	2,461,359	3,496,398	1989	1,090,924[3]	16,144,576	17,235,500
1951–60	2,515,479	7,113,023	9,628,502	1990	1,536,483[3]	17,145,680	18,682,163
1961–70	3,321,677	24,107,224	27,428,901	1991	1,827,167[3]	18,962,520	20,789,687
1971–77	2,797,209	45,236,597	48,033,806	1992	973,977[3]	20,793,847	21,767,824
1984	543,903	9,426,759	9,970,662	1993	904,292[3]	21,446,993	22,351,285

1. Fiscal year ending June 30 prior to 1977. After 1977 for fiscal year ending Sept. 30. 2. Nonimmigrant aliens include visitors for business or pleasure, students, foreign government officials, and others temporarily in the U.S. 3. Includes immigrants and legalized immigrants. *Source:* Department of Justice, Immigration and Naturalization Service.

Persons Naturalized Since 1907

Period[1]	Civilian	Military	Total	Period[1]	Civilian	Military	Total
1907–30	2,713,389	300,506	3,013,895	1989	231,198	1,954	233,777[2]
1930–40	1,498,573	19,891	1,518,464	1990	246,845	1,630	270,101[3]
1941–50	1,837,229	149,799	1,987,028	1991	299,373	1,804	308,058[4]
1951–60	1,148,241	41,705	1,189,946	1992	222,519	5,702	240,252[4]
1961–70	1,084,195	36,068	1,120,263	1993	303,211	7,069	314,681[4]
1971–80	1,397,846	66,926	1,464,772	1907–93	12,660,095	657,787	13,317,882[5]

1. Fiscal year ending June 30. Starting 1977, fiscal year ending Sept. 30. 2. Including 625 unidentified. 3. Including 21,626 unidentified. 4. Includes 6,881 unidentified in 1991, 12,031 in 1992, and 4,401 in 1993. 5. Includes 53,742 unidentified. *Source:* Department of Justice, Immigration and Naturalization Service. NOTE: Data are latest available.

Marriage and Divorce

Marriages and Divorces

Year	Marriage Number	Marriage Rate[2]	Divorce[1] Number	Divorce[1] Rate[2]	Year	Marriage Number	Marriage Rate[2]	Divorce[1] Number	Divorce[1] Rate[2]
1900	709,000	9.3	55,751	.7	1971	2,190,481	10.6	773,000	3.7
1905	842,000	10.0	67,976	.8	1972	2,282,154	11.0	845,000	4.1
1910	948,166	10.3	83,045	.9	1973	2,284,108	10.9	915,000	4.4
1915	1,007,595	10.0	104,298	1.0	1974	2,229,667	10.5	977,000	4.6
1920	1,274,476	12.0	170,505	1.6	1975	2,152,662	10.1	1,036,000	4.9
1925	1,188,334	10.3	175,449	1.5	1976	2,154,807	10.0	1,083,000	5.0
1930	1,126,856	9.2	195,961	1.6	1977	2,178,367	10.1	1,091,000	5.0
1935	1,327,000	10.4	218,000	1.7	1978	2,282,272	10.5	1,130,000	5.2
1940	1,595,879	12.1	264,000	2.0	1979	2,341,799	10.6	1,181,000	5.4
1945	1,612,992	12.2	485,000	3.5	1980	2,406,708	10.6	1,182,000	5.2
1950	1,667,231	11.1	385,144	2.6	1981	2,438,000	10.6	1,219,000	5.3
1955	1,531,000	9.3	377,000	2.3	1982	2,495,000	10.8	1,180,000	5.1
1959	1,494,000	8.5	395,000	2.2	1983	2,444,000	10.5	1,179,000	5.0
1960	1,523,000	8.5	393,000	2.2	1984	2,487,000	10.5	1,155,000	4.9
1961	1,548,000	8.5	414,000	2.3	1985	2,425,000	10.2	1,187,000	5.0
1962	1,577,000	8.5	413,000	2.2	1986	2,400,000	10.0	1,159,000	4.8
1963	1,654,000	8.8	428,000	2.3	1987	2,421,000	9.9	1,157,000	4.8
1964	1,725,000	9.0	450,000	2.4	1988	2,389,000	9.7	1,183,000	4.8
1965	1,800,000	9.3	479,000	2.5	1989	2,404,000	9.7	1,163,000	4.7
1966	1,857,000	9.5	499,000	2.5	1990	2,448,000	9.8	1,175,000	4.7
1967	1,927,000	9.7	523,000	2.6	1991	2,371,000	9.4	1,187,000	4.7
1968	2,069,258	10.4	584,000	2.9	1992	2,362,000	9.3	1,215,000	4.8
1969	2,145,438	10.6	639,000	3.2	1993	2,334,000	9.0	1,187,000	4.6
1970	2,158,802	10.6	708,000	3.5	1994[3]	2,362,000	9.1	1,191,000	4.6

1. Includes annulments. 2. Per 1,000 population. Divorce rates for 1941–46 are based on population including armed forces overseas. Marriage rates are based on population excluding armed forces overseas. 3. Provisional. NOTE: Marriage and divorce figures for most years include some estimated data. Alaska is included beginning 1959, Hawaii beginning 1960. *Source:* Department of Health and Human Services, National Center for Health Statistics.

Percent of Population Never Married

Age group	All races			White			Black		
	1994	1980	1970	1994	1980	1970	1994	1980	1970
Males: 20 to 24	81.0	68.8	54.6	79.4	67.0	54.5	88.1	79.3	56.1
25 to 29	50.3	33.1	19.1	47.5	31.4	17.8	66.0	44.2	28.4
30 to 34	29.7	15.9	9.4	26.5	14.2	9.2	51.4	30.0	9.2
35 to 39	19.2	7.8	7.2	16.8	6.6	6.1	37.6	18.5	15.8
40 to 44	13.0	7.1	6.3	11.8	6.7	5.7	24.3	10.8	11.2
45 to 54	8.2	6.1	7.5	7.3	5.6	7.1	17.1	11.7	10.4
55 to 64	5.4	5.3	7.8	4.8	5.2	7.6	12.0	5.9	9.1
65 and over	4.7	4.9	7.5	4.6	4.8	7.4	5.6	5.5	5.7
Females: 20 to 24	66.0	50.2	35.8	63.0	47.2	34.6	80.9	68.5	43.5
25 to 29	35.3	20.9	10.5	30.5	18.3	9.2	60.7	37.2	18.8
30 to 34	19.9	9.5	6.2	16.2	8.1	5.5	42.7	19.0	10.8
35 to 39	12.8	6.2	5.4	9.9	5.2	4.6	31.1	12.2	12.1
40 to 44	9.2	4.8	4.9	7.3	4.3	4.8	21.7	9.0	6.9
45 to 54	5.9	4.7	4.9	4.9	4.4	4.9	18.8	7.7	4.4
55 to 64	4.1	4.5	6.8	3.6	4.4	7.0	8.2	5.7	4.7
65 and over	4.3	5.9	7.7	4.2	6.1	8.0	5.1	4.5	4.2

Source: U.S. Burea of the Census.

Persons Living Alone, by Sex and Age
(numbers in thousands)

Sex and Age[1]	1994		1993		1990		1980		1970	
	Number	Percent	Number	Percent	Number	Percent	Number	Percent	Number	Percent
BOTH SEXES										
15 to 24 years	1,126	4.8	1,186	5.0	1,210	5.3	1,726	9.4	556	5.1
25 to 44 years	7,235	30.6	7,021	29.7	7,110	30.9	4,729	25.8	1,604	14.8
45 to 64 years	5,967	25.3	6,081	25.7	5,502	23.9	4,514	24.7	3,622	33.4
65 years and over	9,285	39.3	9,355	39.6	9,176	39.9	7,328	40.1	5,071	46.7
Total, 15 years and over			23,642	100.0	22,999	100.0	18,296	100.0	10,851	100.0
MALE										
15 to 24 years	570	6.0	665	7.0	674	7.4	947	13.6	274	2.5
25 to 44 years	4,359	46.2	4,254	45.1	4,231	46.8	2,920	41.9	933	8.6
45 to 64 years	2,473	26.2	2,522	26.7	2,203	24.3	1,613	23.2	1,152	10.6
65 years and over	2,037	21.6	1,994	21.1	1,942	21.5	1,486	21.3	1,174	10.8
Total, 15 years and over			9,436	100.0	9,049	100.0	6,966	100.0	3,532	32.5
FEMALE										
15 to 24 years	557	3.9	521	3.7	536	3.8	779	6.9	282	2.6
25 to 44 years	2,872	20.3	2,764	19.5	2,881	20.7	1,809	16.0	671	6.2
45 to 64 years	3,493	24.6	3,559	25.1	3,300	23.7	2,901	25.6	2,470	22.8
65 years and over	7,248	51.1	7,361	51.8	7,233	51.8	5,842	51.6	3,897	35.9
Total, 15 years and over	14,171	100.0	14,206	100.0	13,950	100.0	11,330	100.0	7,319	67.5

1. Prior to 1980, data are for persons 14 years and older. NOTE: Details may not add because of rounding. *Source:* Department of Commerce, Bureau of the Census.

Characteristics of Unmarried–Couple Households, 1994
(number in thousands)

Characteristics	Number	Percent	Characteristics	Number	Percent
Unmarried–couple households	3,661	100.0	Presence of children:		
			No children under 15 years	2,391	65.3
Age of householders:			Some children under 15 years	1,270	34.7
Under 25 years	772	21.1			
25–44 years	2,169	59.2	Sex of householders:		
45–64 years	537	14.7	Male	2,057	56.2
65 years and over	183	5.0	Female	1,604	43.8

Source: U.S. Bureau of the Census.

Households, Families, and Married Couples

Date	Households		Families		Maried couples
	Number	Average population per household	Number	Average population per family	Number
June 1890	12,690,000	4.93	—	—	—
April 1930	29,905,000	4.11	—	—	25,174,000
April 1940	34,949,000	3.67	32,166,000	3.76	28,517,000
March 1950	43,554,000	3.37	39,303,000	3.54	36,091,000
April 1955	47,874,000	3.33	41,951,000	3.59	37,556,000
March 1960[1]	52,799,000	3.33	45,111,000	3.67	40,200,000
March 1965	57,436,000	3.29	47,956,000	3.70	42,478,000
March 1970	63,401,000	3.14	51,586,000	3.58	45,373,000
March 1975	71,120,000	2.94	55,712,000	3.42	47,547,000
March 1980	80,776,000	2.76	59,550,000	3.29	49,714,000
March 1985	86,789,000	2.69	62,706,000	3.23	51,114,000
March 1990	93,347,000	2.63	66,090,000	3.17	53,256,000
March 1994	97,107,000	2.67	68,490,000	3.20	54,251,000

1. First year in which figures for Alaska and Hawaii are included. *Source:* Department of Commerce, Bureau of the Census.

Families Maintained by Women, With No Husband Present
(numbers in thousands)

	1994		1990		1980		1970		1960	
	Number	Percent	Number	Percent	Number	Percent	Number	Percent	Number	Percent
Age of women:										
Under 35 years	4,232	34.1	3,699	34.0	3,015	34.6	1,364	24.4	796	17.7
35 to 44 years	3,370	27.2	2,929	26.9	1,916	22.0	1,074	19.2	940	20.9
45 to 64 years	3,216	25.9	2,790	25.6	2,514	28.9	2,021	36.1	1,731	38.5
65 years and over	1,587	12.8	1,471	13.5	1,260	14.5	1,131	20.2	1,027	22.9
Median age	40.2	—	40.7	—	41.7	—	48.5	—	50.1	—
Presence of children:										
No own children under 18 years	4,759	38.4	4,290	39.4	3,260	37.4	2,665	47.7	2,397	53.3
With own children under 18 years	7,647	61.6	6,599	60.6	5,445	62.6	2,926	52.3	2,097	46.7
Total own children under 18 years	13,397	—	11,378	—	10,204	—	6,694	—	4,674	—
Average per family	1.08	—	1.04	—	1.17	—	1.20	—	1.04	—
Average per family with children	1.75	—	1.72	—	1.87	—	2.29	—	2.24	—
Race:										
White	8,130	65.5	7,306	67.1	6,052	69.5	4,165	74.5	3,547	78.9
Black[1]	3,825	30.8	3,275	30.1	2,495	28.7	1,382	24.7	947	21.1
Other	451	3.6	309	2.8	158	1.8	44	0.8	n.a.	n.a.
Marital status:										
Married, husband absent	2,208	17.8	1,947	17.9	1,769	20.3	1,326	23.7	1,099	24.5
Widowed	2,421	19.5	2,536	23.3	2,570	29.5	2,396	42.9	2,325	51.7
Divorced	4,479	36.1	3,949	36.3	3,008	34.6	1,259	22.5	694	15.4
Never married	3,298	26.6	2,457	22.6	1,359	15.6	610	10.9	376	8.4
Total	12,406	100.0	10,890	100.0	8,705	100.0	5,591	100.0	4,494	100.0

1. Includes other races in 1960. NOTE: n.a. = not available. (—) as shown in this table, means "not applicable." *Source:* Department of Commerce, Bureau of the Census.

Median Age at First Marriage

Year	Males	Females	Year	Males	Females	Year	Males	Females	Year	Males	Females
1900	25.9	21.9	1930	24.3	21.3	1960	22.8	20.3	1990	26.1	23.9
1910	25.1	21.6	1940	24.3	21.5	1970	23.2	20.8	1993	26.5	24.5
1920	24.6	21.2	1950	22.8	20.3	1980	24.7	22.0	1994	26.7	24.5

Source: Department of Commerce, Bureau of the Census.

Characteristics of Mothers Who Receive AFDC Payments

Source: Bureau of the Census, Statistical Brief, March 1995.

In the summer of 1993, the Nation had 36 million mothers 15 to 44 years old; 3.8 million of them (10%) were receiving AFDC (Aid to Families with Dependent Children) payments to help with the rearing of 9.7 million children. An additional 0.5 million women over 45 years old and 0.3 million fathers living with their dependent children also received AFDC.

First designed primarily to aid widows with young children, AFDC has expanded over the years to serve children whose father or mother is absent, disabled, or unemployed. Rising rates of divorce and out-of-wedlock childbearing, along with an expansion of eligibility and higher participation rates among the eligible, swelled the population of AFDC recipients.

What is AFDC?

AFDC (Aid to Families with Dependent Children) is a program administered and funded by Federal and State governments to provide financial assistance to needy families. In an average State, more than half (55%) of the total costs of AFDC payments are funded by the Federal government. The States provide the balance of these payments, manage the program, and determine who receives benefits and how much they get.

In order to be eligible to receive AFDC payments, a family must have a dependent child who is:

Under age 18 and living with them. (An 18-year-old who is expected to complete secondary school or its equivalent before turning 19 may also be covered.)

Deprived of financial support from one of their parents due to the parent's death, continued absence, or incapacity. (This includes children in two-parent families where the principal family earner is unemployed.)

A resident of the State they live in.

A U.S. citizen or an alien who is permanently and lawfully residing in the United States.

Characteristics

AFDC mothers were nearly three times as likely as their non-AFDC counterparts to be under 25 years old (28 percent versus 10 percent). Twenty-five percent of mothers on AFDC had their first birth under age 18; the same was true for only 15% of non-AFDC mothers.

About one in four Black mothers of childbearing ages (1.5 million) were AFDC recipients, higher than the seven percent White mothers (2.1 million). Nearly one in five Hispanic mothers (784,000) aged 15 to 44 were on AFDC. By comparison, about one in ten (3.0 million) non-Hispanic mothers were AFDC recipients. About three in ten Hispanic mothers on AFDC were born outside the United States.

Length of Time on AFDC

Today, many believe AFDC fosters long-term dependency. Once a family begins to receive welfare, critics contend, parents may begin to rely on monthly cash payments instead of seeking work. While the charge is true of a small core of people that tend to stay on the rolls for a long time—about 9% stay continuously for at least eight years—most AFDC recipients receive assistance only temporarily.

Large numbers of recipients find jobs, and others marry and leave welfare. About 70% leave AFDC within two years, according to a recent study. But while they may want to remain independent, many families return to welfare. Some have trouble combining work and family responsibilities; others lack the social and work-related skills to keep a steady job.

About 9% (392,000) of the Nation's 4.2 million foreign-born mothers aged 15–44 were on AFDC, not statistically different from the 11% (3.4 million) U.S.-born mothers who were AFDC recipients. Incidentally, about three-quarters of all foreign-born mothers on AFDC were not citizens of the United States.

About 48% of the Nation's mothers receiving AFDC payments had never married and another 30% of the mothers were currently married. Most of these women (58%) or 648,000 were separated or had absent husbands. However, about half a million women in intact marriages need AFDC payments to help make ends meet.

Almost half of AFDC mothers do not have a high school diploma. An additional 38% had completed high school and another 19% had attended college for at least one year. About one in seven mothers were currently enrolled in school; these women, on average, had 2.1 children each and were 28 years old. Only 11% of these students were teenagers, suggesting that a large proportion of mothers on AFDC who are enrolled in school are trying to resume their education while raising a family under severe economic conditions.

Unlike mothers not getting AFDC payments, most AFDC mothers (87%) didn't have a job. Nearly three-quarters of mothers on AFDC lived in families with incomes of less than $1,000 a month. About four in every five AFDC mothers were below the poverty level.

Many mothers also participated in other programs designed to assist families needing economic support to provide basic nutrition for themselves and their children. About 5.3 million received food stamps; 2.4 million received support from the Women, Infants, and Children (WIC) program.   □

Selected Family Characteristics

Characteristics[1]	1993 Number (thous.)	Median income	Characteristics[1]	1993 Number (thous.)	Median income
ALL RACES			Wife not in paid labor force	18,913	$30,878
All families	68,506	$36,950	Male householder, no		
Location of residence			wife present	2,298	28,269
Inside metropolitan areas	52,770	39,759	Female householder, no		
1,000,000 or more	33,277	41,828	husband present	8,131	20,000
Inside central cities	11,682	31,018			
Outside central cities	21,595	48,266	Number of earners		
Under 1,000,000	19,494	36,329	No earners	8,622	17,656
Inside central cities	7,565	32,289	1 earner	15,556	28,574
Outside central cities	11,929	38,624	2 earners or more	33,703	51,129
Outside metropolitan areas	15,735	30,157	2 earners	26,336	48,332
			3 earners	5,486	58,651
Region			4 earners or more	1,882	73,269
Northeast	13,456	40,987	Size of family		
Midwest	16,210	37,942	2 persons	25,023	32,672
South	24,438	33,365	3 persons	13,180	41,494
West	14,402	38,881	4 persons	12,115	47,157
			5 persons	5,205	45,247
Type of family			6 persons	1,551	45,715
Married-couple family	53,181	43,005	7 persons or more	807	36,068
Wife in paid labor force	32,194	51,204			
Wife not in paid labor force	20,988	30,218	**BLACK**		
Male householder, no			All families	7,993	21,542
wife present	2,914	26,467	Location of residence		
Female householder, no			Inside metropolitan areas	6,840	22,811
husband present	12,411	17,443	1,000,000 or more	4,656	24,384
			Inside central cities	3,023	21,133
Number of earners			Outside central cities	1,633	32,707
No earners	10,546	15,515	Under 1,000,000	2,183	20,087
1 earner	19,301	26,193	Inside central cities	1,361	19,164
2 earners or more	38,659	50,308	Outside central cities	822	21,131
2 earners	30,137	47,424	Outside metropolitan areas	1,153	15,870
3 earners	6,367	57,745			
4 earners or more	2,155	72,673	Region		
Size of family			Northeast	1,298	25,002
2 persons	28,450	31,302	Midwest	1,643	20,794
3 persons	15,986	38,727	South	4,461	20,372
4 persons	14,479	45,161	West	591	26,182
5 persons	6,342	42,564			
6 persons	2,048	41,156	Type of family		
7 persons or more	1,201	33,158	Married-couple family	3,715	35,218
			Wife in paid labor force	2,417	44,805
WHITE			Wife not in paid labor force	1,298	22,207
All families	57,881	39,300	Male householder, no		
Location of residence			wife present	450	19,476
Inside metropolitan areas	43,645	42,313	Female householder, no		
1,000,000 or more	26,827	45,473	husband present	3,828	11,909
Inside central cities	7,843	35,634			
Outside central cities	18,983	49,729	Number of earners		
Under 1,000,000	16,818	38,603	No earners	1,574	6,858
Inside central cities	5,891	35,981	1 earner	2,999	16,571
Outside central cities	10,837	39,872	2 earners or more	3,420	41,172
Outside metropolitan areas	14,236	31,351	2 earners	2,620	37,124
			3 earners	651	49,489
Region			4 earners or more	149	59,678
Northeast	11,690	42,526	Size of family		
Midwest	14,258	40,158	2 persons	2,701	18,501
South	19,461	36,504	3 persons	2,187	21,679
West	12,472	39,614	4 persons	1,688	26,072
			5 persons	791	21,529
Type of family			6 persons	338	26,288
Married-couple family	47,452	43,575	7 persons or more	289	23,370
Wife in paid labor force	28,539	51,630			

Characteristics[1]	1993 Number (thous.)	1993 Median income	Characteristics[1]	1993 Number (thous.)	1993 Median income
HISPANIC ORIGIN OF HOUSEHOLDER[2]			Wife not in paid labor force	1,917	$20,721
All families	5,946	$23,654	Male householder, no		
Location of residence			wife present	410	21,717
Inside metropolitan areas	5,492	24,014	Female householder, no		
1,000,000 or more	4,198	24,228	husband present	1,498	12,047
Inside central cities	2,287	20,310			
Outside central cities	1,911	29,894	Number of earners		
Under 1,000,000	1,295	23,332	No earners	860	8,362
Inside central cities	750	22,412	1 earner	2,044	17,121
Outside central cities	545	24,106	2 earners or more	3,042	34,758
Outside metropolitan areas	453	21,027	2 earners	2,248	32,172
			3 earners	538	40,724
Region			4 earners or more	256	49,876
Northeast	1,001	19,580	Size of family		
Midwest	405	27,501	2 persons	1,567	20,275
South	1,915	23,651	3 persons	1,378	21,446
West	2,624	24,781	4 persons	1,351	25,694
			5 persons	903	28,775
Type of family			6 persons	397	26,894
Married-couple family	4,038	28,454	7 persons or more	350	29,355
Wife in paid labor force	2,121	35,973			

1. Family data as of March 1994. 2. Persons of Hispanic origin may be of any race. *Source:* Department of Commerce, Bureau of the Census Current Population Reports, Series P60-188, "Money Income of Households, Families, and Persons in the United States: 1993." NOTE: Data are the latest available.

Births

Live Births and Birth Rates

Year	Births[1]	Rate[2]	Year	Births[1]	Rate[2]	Year	Births[1]	Rate[2]
1910	2,777,000	30.1	1960[3]	4,257,850	23.7	1977	3,326,632	15.4
1915	2,965,000	29.5	1961[3]	4,268,326	23.3	1978	3,333,279	15.3
1920	2,950,000	27.7	1962[3]	4,167,362	22.4	1979	3,494,398	15.9
1925	2,909,000	25.1	1963[3]	4,098,020	21.7	1980	3,612,258	15.9
1930	2,618,000	21.3	1964[3]	4,027,490	21.0	1982	3,680,537	15.9
1935	2,377,000	18.7	1965[3]	3,760,358	19.4	1983	3,638,933	15.5
1940	2,559,000	19.4	1966[3]	3,606,274	18.4	1984	3,669,141	15.5
1945	2,858,000	20.4	1967[4]	3,520,959	17.8	1985	3,760,561	15.8
1950	3,632,000	24.1	1968[3]	3,501,564	17.5	1986	3,731,000	15.5
1952[3]	3,913,000	25.1	1969[3]	3,600,206	17.8	1987	3,829,000	15.7
1953[3]	3,965,000	25.1	1970[3]	3,731,386	18.4	1988	3,913,000	15.9
1954[3]	4,078,000	25.3	1971[3]	3,555,970	17.2	1989	4,021,000	16.2
1955	4,104,000	25.0	1972	3,258,411	15.6	1990	4,179,000	16.7
1956[3]	4,218,000	25.2	1973	3,136,965	14.9	1991	4,111,000	16.2
1957[3]	4,308,000	25.3	1974	3,159,958	14.9	1992	4,084,000	16.0
1958[3]	4,255,000	24.5	1975	3,144,198	14.8	1993	4,039,000	15.7
1959[3]	4,295,000	24.3	1976	3,167,788	14.8	1994[5]	3,979,000	15.3

1. Figures through 1959 include adjustment for underregistration; beginning 1960, figures represent number registered. For comparison, the 1959 registered count was 4,245,000. 2. Rates are per 1,000 population estimated as of July 1 for each year except 1940, 1950, 1960, 1970, and 1980, which are as of April 1, the census date; for 1942–46 based on population including armed forces overseas. 3. Based on 50% sample of births. 4. Based on a 20 to 50% sample of births. 5. Provisional. NOTE: Alaska is included beginning 1959; Hawaii beginning 1960. Since 1972, based on 100% of births in selected states and on 50% sample in all other states. *Sources:* Department of Health and Human Services, National Center for Health Statistics.

Day Care for Preschoolers

The choice of child care arrangements for pre-school-age children is one of the most important daily decisions parents make. In 1991, there were 9.9 million children under the age of five who were in need of care while their mothers were at work.

About two-thirds of preschool-age children were cared for in either their own home (36%) or another home (31%) for the majority of time their mothers were away at work. Most of the children were cared for by their fathers. In comparison, among those taken care of outside of the home, most were cared for by family day care providers—nonrelatives in the provider's home. Nearly one-quarter (23%) received care in an organized facility, such as a day care center.

Live Births by Age of Mother

Year[1] and race	Total	Under 15 yr	15–19 yr	20–24 yr	25–29 yr	30–34 yr	35–39 yr	40–44 yr	45 yr and over
					Age of Mother				
1940	2,558,647	3,865	332,667	799,537	693,268	431,468	222,015	68,269	7,558
1945	2,858,449	4,028	298,868	832,746	785,299	554,906	296,852	78,853	6,897
1950	3,631,512	5,413	432,911	1,155,167	1,041,360	610,816	302,780	77,743	5,322
1955	4,014,112	6,181	493,770	1,290,939	1,133,155	732,540	352,320	89,777	5,430
1960	4,257,850	6,780	586,966	1,426,912	1,092,816	687,722	359,908	91,564	5,182
1965	3,760,358	7,768	590,894	1,337,350	925,732	529,376	282,908	81,716	4,614
1970	3,731,386	11,752	644,708	1,418,874	994,904	427,806	180,244	49,952	3,146
1975	3,144,198	12,642	582,238	1,093,676	936,786	375,500	115,409	26,319	1,628
1980	3,612,258	10,169	552,161	1,226,200	1,108,291	550,354	140,793	23,090	1,200
1985	3,760,561	10,220	467,485	1,141,320	1,201,350	696,354	214,336	28,334	1,162
1990	4,158,212	11,657	521,826	1,093,730	1,277,108	886,063	317,583	48,607	1,638
1991	4,110,907	12,014	519,577	1,089,692	1,219,965	884,862	330,993	52,095	1,709
1992	4,065,014	12,220	505,415	1,070,490	1,179,264	895,271	344,644	55,702	2,008
White	3,201,678	5,367	342,739	814,422	964,586	745,510	282,617	44,866	1,571
Black	673,633	6,448	146,800	216,057	157,960	100,339	39,389	6,453	187
Other	189,703	405	15,876	40,011	56,718	49,422	22,638	4,383	250

1. Data for 1940–55 are adjusted for underregistration. Beginning 1960, registered births only are shown. Data for 1960–70 based on a 50% sample of births. For 1972–84, based on 100% of births in selected states and on 50% sample in all other states. Beginning 1960, including Alaska and Hawaii. For 1988 and prior years births were tabulated by race of child. Beginning 1989 births are tabulated by race of mother. NOTE: Data refer only to births occurring within the U.S. Figures are shown to the last digit as computed for convenience in summation. They are not assumed to be accurate to the last digit. Figures for age of mother not stated are distributed. Source: Department of Health and Human Services, National Center for Health Statistics.

Births to Unmarried Women
(in thousands, except as indicated)

Age and race	1992	1990	1985	1980	1975	1970	1965	1960	1950
By age of mother:									
Under 15 years	11.2	10.7	9.4	9.0	11.0	9.5	6.1	4.6	3.2
15–19 years	353.9	350.0	270.9	262.8	222.5	190.4	123.1	87.1	56.0
20–24 years	435.7	403.9	300.4	237.3	134.0	126.7	90.7	68.0	43.1
25–29 years	233.5	230.0	152.0	99.6	50.2	40.6	36.8	32.1	20.9
30–34 years	127.9	118.2	67.3	41.0	19.8	19.1	19.6	18.9	10.8
35–39 years	52.4	44.1	24.0	13.2	8.1	9.4	11.4	10.6	6.0
40 years and over	10.2	8.5	4.1	2.9	2.3	3.0	3.7	3.0	1.7
By race:[1]									
White	721.9	669.7	433.0	320.1	186.4	175.1	123.7	82.5	53.5
Black	458.9	495.7	395.2	345.7	261.6	223.6	167.5	141.8	88.1
Total of above births	1,224.8	1,165.4	828.2	665.8	447.9	398.7	291.2	224.3	141.6
Percent of all births[2]	30.1	28.0	22.0	18.4	14.2	10.7	7.7	5.3	3.9
Rate[3]	45.2	43.8	32.8	29.4	24.8	26.4	23.4	21.8	14.1

1. For 1988 and prior years births were tabulated by race of child. Beginning 1989, births are tabulated by race of mother. 2. Through 1955, based on data adjusted for underregistration; thereafter, registered births. 3. Rate per 1,000 unmarried (never married, widowed, and divorced) women, 15–44 years old. Source: Department of Health and Human Services, National Center for Health Statistics. NOTE: Data are latest available.

Who Gets Aid to Families With Dependent Children?

According to the most recent Census Bureau report, 29% of mothers 15 to 44 years old who received aid in 1993 had their first child before they turned 18 years old.

Almost 30% (1.1 million) were married mothers with an average of 2.8 children each. One-half million mothers were in intact marriages but most married mothers (648,000) had separated from their spouses or had husbands absent from the household. Another 23% were widowed or divorced.

Never-married mothers represented 48% of the mothers in the 15-to-44-year age group on AFDC. These 1.8 million never-married mothers supported about 4.2 million children, or an average of 2.4 children per mother.

Unlike mothers not receiving Aid to Families with Dependent Children payments, most mothers on AFDC (80%) were living in poverty. About 72% were living in households with monthly family incomes under $1,000. These low-income mothers supported an average of 2.7 children each.

Live Births and Birth Rates

State	1993[1] number	1993[1] rate	1992[2] number	1992[2] rate	State	1993[1] number	1993[1] rate	1992[2] number	1992[2] rate
Alabama	63,332	15.1	62,260	15.0	Montana	11,450	13.6	11,472	14.0
Alaska	10,555	17.6	11,726	20.0	Nebraska	22,847	14.2	23,397	14.6
Arizona	70,770	18.0	68,829	18.0	Nevada	21,129	15.2	22,374	16.7
Arkansas	34,248	14.1	34,820	14.5	New Hampshire	14,952	13.3	15,990	14.3
California	589,685	18.9	601,730	19.5	New Jersey	123,020	15.6	119,909	15.3
Colorado	54,817	15.4	54,535	15.7	New Mexico	27,658	17.1	27,922	17.7
Connecticut	45,821	14.0	47,573	14.5	New York	278,307	15.3	287,887	15.9
Delaware	10,555	15.1	10,656	15.4	North Carolina	100,597	14.5	103,967	15.2
D.C.	9,780	16.9	10,960	18.7	North Dakota	8,746	13.8	8,811	13.9
Florida	193,087	14.1	191,713	14.2	Ohio	156,748	14.1	162,247	14.7
Georgia	112,400	16.2	111,116	16.4	Oklahoma	46,711	14.5	47,557	14.8
Hawaii	19,589	16.7	19,864	17.2	Oregon	42,195	13.9	42,035	14.1
Idaho	17,162	15.6	17,362	16.3	Pennsylvania	159,189	13.2	164,625	13.7
Illinois	191,042	16.3	191,396	16.5	Rhode Island	14,275	14.3	14,500	14.5
Indiana	84,644	14.8	84,140	14.9	South Carolina	53,997	14.8	56,192	15.6
Iowa	37,044	13.2	38,469	13.7	South Dakota	10,830	15.1	11,018	15.6
Kansas	38,000	15.0	38,027	15.1	Tennessee	73,613	14.4	73,614	14.6
Kentucky	52,256	13.8	53,840	14.3	Texas	330,596	18.3	320,845	18.1
Louisiana	69,819	16.3	70,707	16.5	Utah	36,462	19.6	37,200	20.5
Maine	15,027	12.1	16,057	13.0	Vermont	7,286	12.6	7,737	13.5
Maryland	75,526	15.2	77,815	15.8	Virginia	95,161	14.7	97,198	15.2
Massachusetts	86,317	14.4	87,231	14.6	Washington	71,437	13.6	79,450	15.4
Michigan	143,576	15.1	144,089	15.3	West Virginia	22,044	12.1	22,170	12.3
Minnesota	63,761	14.1	65,607	14.7	Wisconsin	69,289	13.8	70,670	14.2
Mississippi	42,160	16.0	42,681	16.3	Wyoming	6,662	14.2	6,723	14.5
Missouri	77,424	14.8	76,301	14.7	**Total**	**4,013,638**	**15.4**	**4,065,014**	**15.9**

1. Provisional. 2. Revised. NOTE: Provisional data by place of residence. Rates are per 1,000 population. *Source:* Department of Health and Human Services, National Center for Health Statistics.

Live Births by Race or National Origin of Mother

Race	1992	1991	Race	1992	1991
White	3,201,678	3,241,273	Chinese	25,061	22,498
Black	673,633	682,602	Filipino	28,959	26,227
American Indian[1]	39,453	38,841	Other[2]	87,132	88,147
Japanese	9,098	8,500	Total[3]	4,065,014	4,110,907

1. Includes Eskimos and Aleuts. 2. Hawaiian and other Asian or Pacific Islander. 3. Includes births of other races not shown separately. Data are latest available. *Source:* Department of Health and Human Services, National Center for Health Statistics.

Live Births by Sex and Sex Ratio[1]

Year	Total[2] Male	Total[2] Female	Total[2] Males per 1,000 females	White[3] Male	White[3] Female	White[3] Males per 1,000 females	Black[3] Male	Black[3] Female	Black[3] Males per 1,000 females
1983[4]	1,865,553	1,773,380	1,052	1,492,385	1,411,865	1,057	297,011	289,016	1,028
1984[4]	1,879,490	1,789,651	1,050	1,500,326	1,423,176	1,054	300,951	291,794	1,031
1985	1,927,983	1,832,578	1,052	1,536,646	1,454,727	1,056	308,575	299,618	1,030
1986	1,924,868	1,831,679	1,051	1,523,914	1,446,525	1,053	315,788	305,433	1,034
1987	1,951,153	1,858,241	1,050	1,535,517	1,456,971	1,054	325,259	316,308	1,028
1988	2,002,424	1,907,086	1,050	1,562,675	1,483,487	1,053	341,441	330,535	1,033
1989	2,069,490	1,971,468	1,050	1,606,757	1,525,234	1,053	360,131	349,264	1,031
1990	2,129,495	2,028,717	1,050	1,654,928	1,570,415	1,054	367,455	357,121	1,029
1991	2,101,518	2,009,389	1,046	1,659,077	1,582,196	1,049	346,455	336,147	1,031
1992	2,082,097	1,982,917	1,050	1,641,811	1,559,867	1,053	342,726	330,907	1,036

1. Excludes births to nonresidents of U.S. 2. Includes races other than white and black. 3. Race of child through 1990. Race of mother from 1991. 4. Based on 100% of births for selected states and 50% sample in all others. *Source:* Department of Health and Human Services, National Center for Health Statistics. NOTE: Data are latest available.

Abortions and Abortion Rates

State	Number of Abortions			Abortion occurrence rate[1]			Change 1988–92
	1992	1991	1988	1992	1991	1988	
Alabama	17,450	17,400	18,220	18.2	18.2	18.7	-3
Alaska	2,370	2,400	2,390	16.5	16.9	18.2	-10
Arizona	20,600	19,690	23,070	24.1	23.2	28.8	-16
Arkansas	7,130	7,150	6,250	13.5	13.6	11.6	16
California	304,230	320,960	311,720	42.1	44.4	45.9	-8
Colorado	19,880	21,010	18,740	23.6	25.3	22.4	6
Connecticut	19,720	20,530	23,630	26.2	26.7	31.2	-16
Delaware	5,730	5,720	5,710	35.2	34.9	35.7	-1
District of Columbia	21,320	21,510	26,120	138.4	136.1	163.3	-15
Florida	84,680	84,570	82,850	30.0	29.9	31.5	-5
Georgia	39,680	39,720	36,720	24.0	24.2	23.5	2
Hawaii	12,190	12,130	11,170	46.0	45.9	43.0	7
Idaho	1,710	1,740	1,920	7.2	7.5	8.2	-12
Illinois	68,420	64,990	72,570	25.4	24.1	26.4	-4
Indiana	15,840	15,940	15,760	12.0	12.1	11.9	1
Iowa	6,970	7,200	9,420	11.4	11.7	14.6	-22
Kansas	12,570	12,770	11,440	22.4	22.9	20.1	11
Kentucky	10,000	8,270	11,520	11.4	9.5	13.0	-12
Louisiana	13,600	13,930	17,340	13.4	13.7	16.3	-18
Maine	4,200	4,210	4,620	14.7	14.7	16.2	-9
Maryland	31,260	33,000	32,670	26.4	27.5	28.6	-8
Massachusetts	40,660	44,150	43,720	28.4	30.2	30.2	-6
Michigan	55,580	55,800	63,410	25.2	25.1	28.5	-11
Minnesota	16,180	16,880	18,580	15.6	16.3	18.2	-14
Mississippi	7,550	8,160	5,120	12.4	13.5	8.4	48
Missouri	13,510	15,770	19,490	11.6	13.5	16.4	-29
Montana	3,330	3,680	3,050	18.2	20.6	16.5	11
Nebraska	5,580	6,230	6,490	15.7	17.5	17.7	-11
Nevada	13,300	14,450	10,190	44.2	49.0	40.3	10
New Hampshire	3,890	4,260	4,710	14.6	15.7	17.5	-17
New Jersey	55,320	55,800	63,900	31.0	30.9	35.1	-12
New Mexico	6,410	6,190	6,810	17.7	17.2	19.1	-7
New York	195,390	190,410	183,980	46.2	44.5	43.3	7
North Carolina	36,180	37,210	39,720	22.4	23.2	25.4	-12
North Dakota	1,490	1,600	2,230	10.7	11.4	14.9	-28
Ohio	49,520	52,030	53,400	19.5	20.4	21.0	-7
Oklahoma	8,940	9,130	12,120	12.5	12.8	16.2	-23
Oregon	16,060	16,580	15,960	23.9	24.9	23.9	0
Pennsylvania	49,740	51,780	51,830	18.6	19.2	18.9	-2
Rhode Island	6,990	7,500	7,190	30.0	31.5	30.6	-2
South Carolina	12,190	13,520	14,160	14.2	15.8	16.7	-15
South Dakota	1,040	980	900	6.8	6.4	5.7	19
Tennessee	19,060	19,840	22,090	16.2	16.9	18.9	-14
Texas	97,400	95,930	100,690	23.1	23.0	24.8	-7
Utah	3,940	4,250	5,030	9.3	10.4	12.8	-27
Vermont	2,900	3,110	3,580	21.2	22.7	25.8	-18
Virginia	35,020	35,170	35,420	22.7	22.8	23.7	-5
Washington	33,190	32,640	31,220	27.7	27.6	27.6	0
West Virginia	3,140	2,590	3,270	7.7	6.3	7.5	2
Wisconsin	15,450	15,510	18,040	13.6	13.6	16.0	-15
Wyoming	460	520	600	4.3	4.9	5.1	-16
Total	**1,528,930**	**1,556,510**	**1,590,750**	**25.9**	**26.3**	**27.3**	**-5**

1. Rate per 1,000 women aged 15–44. NOTE: Number of abortions are rounded to nearest 10. Source: Reproduced with the permission of The Alan Guttmacher Institute from Stanley K. Henshaw and Jennifer Van Vort, "Abortion Services in the United States, 1991 and 1992," Family Planning Perspectives, Volume 26, Number 3, May/June 1994.

Youth Suicides Are on Rise

Suicides by children 10 to 14 years of age have increased at rates twice as high as in 1980 according to an April 1995 report from the U.S. Centers for Disease Control and Prevention in Atlanta, Ga. It also noted that they are increasingly using guns to kill themselves. In 1992 firearms were the most common method of suicide for persons under 25, accounting for 64.9% of them. Among those in the 15 through 19 age group, firearm-related suicides accounted for 81% of the increase in the overall suicide rate from 1980 to 1992.

The increased use of guns in suicide attempts is seen as one factor in the rise of suicide rates. While the number of young people attempting suicide hasn't increased, they are using more lethal methods, making the attempts more successful.

The statistics for adolescents ages 10 to 14 show that the increased suicide rate for white boys was 86%, for white girls 233%, for black boys 300%, and for black girls 100% from 1980 to 1992.

Mortality
Death Rates for Selected Causes

Death rates per 100,000

Cause of death	1994[1]	1993	1990	1980	1950	1945–49	1920–24[4]	1900–04[4]
Typhoid fever	n.a.	n.a.	*	0.0	0.1	0.2	7.3	26.7
Communicable diseases of childhood	—	—	—	0.0	1.3	2.3	33.8	65.2
Measles	*	*	0.0	0.0	0.3	0.6	7.3	10.0
Scarlet fever	n.a.	n.a.	*	0.0	0.2	0.1	4.0	11.8
Whooping cough	*	*	*	0.0	0.7	1.0	8.9	10.7
Diphtheria	n.a.	n.a.	*	0.0	0.3	0.7	13.7	32.7
Pneumonia and influenza	31.4	30.9	32.8	23.3	31.3	41.3	140.3	184.3
Influenza	0.5	0.4	0.8	1.1	4.4	5.0	34.8	22.8
Pneumonia	30.9	30.5	31.1	22.0	26.9	37.2	105.5	161.5
Tuberculosis	0.6	0.6	0.7	0.8	22.5	33.3	96.7	184.7
Cancer	206.6	206.0	203.2	182.5	139.8	134.0	86.9	67.7
Diabetes mellitus	21.2	21.3	19.2	15.0	16.2	24.1	17.1	12.2
Major cardiovascular diseases	360.3	364.7	368.3	434.5	510.8	493.1	369.9	359.5
Diseases of the heart	280.3	285.8	289.5	335.2	356.8	325.1	169.8	153.0
Cerebrovascular diseases	59.1	58.0	57.9	74.6	104.0	93.8	93.5	106.3
Nephritis and nephrosis	9.5	9.6	8.3	7.6	16.4	48.4	81.5	84.3
Syphilis	*	*	0.0	0.1	5.0	8.4	17.6	12.9
Appendicitis	0.1	0.2	0.2	0.3	2.0	3.5	14.0	9.4
Accidents, all forms	33.9	33.7	37.0	46.0	60.6	67.6	70.8	79.2
Motor vehicle accidents	16.1	15.8	18.8	23.0	23.1	22.3	12.9	n.a.
Infant mortality[2]	n.a.	n.a.	9.2	12.5	29.2	33.3	76.7	n.a.
Neonatal mortality[2]	n.a.	n.a.	5.8	8.4	20.5	22.9	39.7	n.a.
Fetal mortality[3]	n.a.	n.a.	n.a.	9.2	19.2	21.6	n.a	n.a.
Maternal mortality[2]	0.1	0.1	8.2	0.1	0.8	1.4	6.9	n.a.
All causes	876.9	879.3	863.8	883.4	960.1	1,000.6	1,157.4	1,621.6

1. Provisional, based on a 10% sample of deaths. 2. Rates per 1,000 live births. 3. Ratio per 1,000 births. 4. Includes only deaths occurring within the registration areas. Beginning with 1933, area includes the entire United States; Alaska included beginning in 1959 and Hawaii in 1960. Rates per 100,000 population residing in areas, enumerated as of April 1 for 1940, 1950, and 1980 and estimated as of July 1 for all other years. Due to changes in statistical methods, death rates are not strictly comparable. Beginning in 1989 an asterisk is shown in place of a rate based on fewer than 20 deaths for final data and on 100 or fewer estimated deaths for provisional data. n.a. = not available. *Source:* Department of Health and Human Services, National Center for Health Statistics.

Accident Rates, 1993

Class of accident		One every	Class of accident		One every
All accidents	Deaths	6 minutes	Workers off-job	Deaths	16 minutes
	Injuries	2 seconds		Injuries	6 seconds
Motor-vehicle	Deaths	13 minutes	Home	Deaths	23 minutes
	Injuries	16 seconds		Injuries	5 seconds
Work	Deaths	58 minutes	Public non-motor-	Deaths	26 minutes
	Injuries	10 seconds	vehicle	Injuries	5 seconds

NOTE: Data are latest available. *Source:* National Safety Council.

Improper Driving as Factor in Accidents, 1993

Kind of improper driving	Fatal accidents			Injury accidents			All accidents		
	Total	Urban	Rural	Total	Urban	Rural	Total	Urban	Rural
Improper driving	57.7	54.7	59.4	72.7	74.3	69.6	68.6	69.8	66.1
Speed too fast or unsafe	16.5	14.4	17.7	13.5	11.8	17.6	12.2	11.1	15.4
Right of way	12.7	17.0	10.1	25.0	28.8	15.5	20.6	23.2	13.7
Failed to yield	*7.8*	*9.4*	*6.8*	*17.3*	*19.3*	*12.3*	*15.1*	*16.6*	*11.3*
Passed stop sign	*2.7*	*2.7*	*2.7*	*2.7*	*3.0*	*1.9*	*2.0*	*2.1*	*1.4*
Disregarded signal	*2.2*	*4.9*	*0.6*	*5.0*	*6.5*	*1.3*	*3.5*	*4.5*	*1.0*
Drove left of center	7.6	3.2	10.1	2.1	1.3	4.0	1.8	1.1	3.4
Improper overtaking	1.2	0.6	1.5	1.0	0.8	1.4	1.3	1.1	1.7
Made improper turn	2.9	2.7	3.0	3.4	3.3	3.7	4.5	4.6	4.2
Followed too closely	0.5	0.4	0.6	6.2	7.2	3.7	5.5	6.2	3.6
Other improper driving	16.3	16.4	16.4	21.5	21.1	23.7	22.7	22.5	24.1
No improper driving stated	42.3	45.3	40.6	27.3	25.7	30.4	31.4	30.2	33.9
Total	100.0%	100.0%	100.0%	100.0%	100.0%	100.0%	100.0%	100.0%	100.0%

Source: Motor-vehicle reports from 11 state traffic authorities to National Safety Council. NOTE: Figures are latest available.

Motor–Vehicle Deaths by Type of Accident

			Deaths from collisions with—					
Year	Pedes-trians	Other motor vehicles	Railroad trains	Pedalcycles[1]	Animal-drawn vehicle, animal, or streetcars	Fixed objects[1]	Deaths from non-collision accidents[1]	Total deaths[2]
1975	8,400	19,550	979	1,000	100	3,130	12,700	45,853
1980	9,700	23,000	739	1,200	100	3,700	14,700	53,172
1985	8,300	19,900	500	1,100	100	2,800	12,900	45,600
1990	7,400	19,400	600	1,000	100	12,900	4,900	46,300
1991	7,000	18,500	500	800	100	12,100	4,500	43,500
1992	6,500	17,400	500	700	100	10,900	4,200	40,300
1993	6,200	17,900	600	800	100	11,900	4,500	42,000

1. Estimates for 1990 and later are not comparable to earlier years. 2. Totals do not equal sums of various types because totals are estimated. NOTE: Figures are latest available. *Source:* National Safety Council.

Accidental Deaths by Principal Types

Year	Motor vehicle	Falls	Drown-ing[1]	Fire burns[2]	Ingestion of food or object	Fire-arms	Poison (solid, liquid)	Poison by gas
1986	47,900	11,000	5,600	4,800	3,600	1,800	4,000	900
1987	48,700	11,300	5,300	4,800	3,200	1,400	4,400	1,000
1988	49,000	12,000	5,000	5,000	3,600	1,400	5,300	1,000
1989	46,900	12,400	4,600	4,400	3,900	1,600	5,600	900
1990	46,300	12,400	5,200	4,300	3,200	1,400	5,700	800
1991	43,500	12,200	4,600	4,200	2,900	1,400	5,600	800
1992	40,300	12,400	4,300	4,000	2,700	1,400	5,200	700
1993	42,000	13,500	4,800	4,000	2,900	1,600	6,500	700

1. Includes drowning in water transport accidents. 2. Includes burns by fire and deaths resulting from conflagration regardless of nature of injury. NOTE: Figures are latest available. *Source:* National Safety Council.

Deaths and Death Rates

	Total deaths		Motor vehicle traffic deaths			Total deaths		Motor vehicle traffic deaths	
State	1993 number	1993 rate[1]	1993 number	1993 rate[2]	State	1993 number	1993 rate[1]	1993 number	1993 rate[2]
Alabama	41,540	9.9	1,016	2.2	Montana	7,502	8.9	194	2.2
Alaska	2,247	3.8	117	3.0	Nebraska	15,401	9.6	254	1.7
Arizona	32,090	8.2	803	2.2	Nevada	10,886	7.8	263	2.4
Arkansas	26,371	10.9	583	2.5	New Hampshire	8,919	7.9	122	1.2
California	217,559	7.0	3,903	1.5	New Jersey	72,776	9.2	787	1.3
Colorado	23,722	6.7	561	1.9	New Mexico	11,861	7.3	433	2.3
Connecticut	29,057	8.9	342	1.3	New York	170,203	9.4	1,756	1.6
Delaware	6,116	8.7	113	1.6	North Carolina	62,580	9.0	1,384	2.0
D.C.	6,713	11.6	n.a.	n.a.	North Dakota	5,925	9.3	89	1.4
Florida	146,309	10.7	2,693	2.3	Ohio	100,678	9.1	1,484	1.5
Georgia	55,851	8.1	1,406	1.8	Oklahoma	32,574	10.1	672	1.9
Hawaii	7,280	6.2	134	1.6	Oregon	27,275	9.0	522	1.8
Idaho	8,345	7.6	233	2.1	Pennsylvania	126,977	10.5	1,529	1.7
Illinois	107,563	9.2	1,392	1.6	Rhode Island	9,709	9.7	74	0.9
Indiana	52,210	9.1	891	1.5	South Carolina	31,404	8.6	845	2.4
Iowa	27,862	9.9	437	1.8	South Dakota	6,863	9.6	140	1.9
Kansas	23,337	9.2	428	1.7	Tennessee	49,628	9.7	1,175	2.3
Kentucky	36,921	9.7	876	2.2	Texas	135,603	7.5	3,037	1.8
Louisiana	40,117	9.3	881	2.5	Utah	10,193	5.5	303	1.8
Maine	11,479	9.3	186	1.5	Vermont	4,868	8.5	112	1.8
Maryland	43,087	8.7	672	1.6	Virginia	51,773	8.0	875	1.3
Massachusetts	56,460	9.4	474	1.0	Washington	41,986	8.0	662	1.3
Michigan	82,651	8.7	1,409	1.6	West Virginia	19,929	11.0	429	2.5
Minnesota	36,236	8.0	538	1.3	Wisconsin	44,033	8.7	703	1.4
Mississippi	26,575	10.1	813	3.0	Wyoming	3,544	7.5	120	1.9
Missouri	56,305	10.8	949	1.7	**Total**	**2,267,093**	**8.8**	**42,000**	**1.8**

1. Provisional rates per 1,000 population, by place of occurrence. 2. Per 100 million vehicle–miles. NOTE: n.a. = not available. *Sources:* Department of Health and Human Services, National Center for Health Statistics; National Safety Council.

Annual Death Rates

Year	Rate	Year	Rate	Year	Deaths	Rate
1900	17.2	1947	10.1	1971	1,927,542	9.3
1905	15.9	1948	9.9	1972	1,963,944	9.4
1910	14.7	1949	9.7	1973	1,973,003	9.3
1915	13.2	1950	9.6	1974	1,934,388	9.1
1920	13.0	1951	9.7	1975	1,892,879	8.8
1925	11.7	1952	9.6	1976	1,909,440	8.8
1930	11.3	1953	9.6	1977	1,899,597	8.6
1931	11.1	1954	9.2	1978	1,927,788	8.7
1932	10.9	1955	9.3	1979	1,913,841	8.5
1933	10.7	1956	9.4	1980	1,989,841	8.7
1934	11.1	1957	9.6	1982	1,974,797	8.5
1935	10.9	1958	9.5	1983	2,019,201	8.6
1936	11.6	1959	9.4	1984	2,039,369	8.6
1937	11.3	1960	9.5	1985	2,086,440	8.7
1938	10.6	1962	9.5	1986	2,099,000	8.7
1939	10.6	1963	9.6	1987	2,127,000	8.7
1940	10.8	1964	9.4	1988	2,171,000	8.8
1941	10.5	1965	9.4	1989	2,155,000	8.7
1942	10.3	1966	9.5	1990	2,162,000	8.6
1943	10.9	1967	9.4	1991	2,165,000	8.5
1944	10.6	1968	9.7	1992	2,177,000	8.5
1945	10.6	1969	9.5	1993	2,268,000	8.8
1946	10.0	1970[1]	9.5	1994	2,286,000[2]	8.8

1. First year for which deaths of nonresidents are excluded. 2. Provisional. NOTE: Includes only deaths occurring within the registration states. Beginning with 1933, area includes entire U.S.; with 1959 includes Alaska, and with 1960 includes Hawaii. Excludes fetal deaths. Rates per 1,000 population residing in area, as of April 1 for 1940, 1950, 1960, 1970, and 1980, and estimated as of July 1 for all other years. *Sources:* Department of Health and Human Services, National Center for Health Statistics.

Death Rates by Age, Race, and Sex

Age	1992	1991	1990	1980	1970[1]	1960	1992	1991	1990	1980	1970[1]	1960
	White males						White females					
Under 1 year	7.8	8.6	9.0	12.3	21.1	26.9	6.2	6.6	7.0	9.6	16.1	20.1
1–4	0.4	0.4	0.5	0.7	0.8	1.0	0.3	0.4	0.4	0.5	0.8	0.9
5–14	0.2	0.3	0.3	0.4	0.5	0.5	0.2	0.2	0.2	0.2	0.3	0.3
15–24	1.2	1.3	1.3	1.7	1.7	1.4	0.4	0.5	0.5	0.5	0.6	0.5
25–34	1.8	1.8	1.8	1.7	1.8	1.6	0.6	0.6	0.6	0.7	0.8	0.9
35–44	2.8	2.7	2.7	2.6	3.4	3.3	1.2	1.2	1.2	1.2	1.9	1.9
45–54	5.3	5.4	5.5	7.0	8.8	9.3	2.9	3.1	3.1	3.7	4.6	4.6
55–64	14.0	14.4	14.7	17.3	22.0	22.3	8.0	8.2	8.2	8.8	10.1	10.8
65–74	32.9	33.5	34.0	40.4	48.1	48.5	19.1	19.1	19.2	20.7	24.7	27.8
75–84	74.4	76.4	78.4	88.3	101.0	103.0	47.0	47.5	48.4	54.0	67.0	77.0
85 and over	179.6	180.2	183.0	191.0	185.5	217.5	140.2	141.9	144.0	149.8	159.8	194.8
	All other males						All other females					
Under 1 year	16.2	15.9	18.1	23.5	40.2	51.9	13.3	13.0	15.0	19.4	31.7	40.7
1–4	0.7	0.8	0.8	1.0	1.4	2.1	0.6	0.6	0.6	0.8	1.2	1.7
5–14	0.4	0.4	0.4	0.4	0.6	0.8	0.2	0.3	0.3	0.3	0.4	0.5
15–24	0.2	2.3	2.2	2.0	3.0	2.1	0.6	0.6	0.6	0.7	1.1	1.1
25–34	3.2	3.4	3.5	3.6	5.0	3.9	1.3	1.3	1.3	1.4	2.2	2.6
35–44	5.4	5.6	5.6	5.9	8.7	7.3	2.5	2.5	2.4	2.9	4.9	5.5
45–54	9.8	10.0	10.2	13.1	16.5	15.5	5.1	5.3	5.4	6.9	9.8	11.4
55–64	20.9	21.3	22.2	26.1	30.5	31.5	12.0	12.0	13.0	14.2	18.9	24.1
65–74	41.4	42.3	43.4	47.5	54.7	56.6	24.7	25.2	26.0	28.6	36.8	39.8
75–84	79.0	81.6	83.2	86.9	89.8	86.6	51.0	52.7	53.1	58.6	63.9	67.1
85 and over	157.2	158.0	160.8	157.7	114.1	152.4	126.3	127.2	129.0	119.2	102.9	128.7

1. Beginning 1970 excludes deaths of nonresidents of U.S. NOTE: Excludes fetal deaths. Rates are per 1,000 population in each group, enumerated as of April 1 for 1960, 1970, and 1980, and estimated as of July 1 for all other years. *Sources:* Department of Health and Human Services, National Center for Health Statistics.

Expectation of Life

Expectation of Life in the United States

Calendar period	Age								
	0	10	20	30	40	50	60	70	80
WHITE MALES									
1850[1]	38.3	48.0	40.1	34.0	27.9	21.6	15.6	10.2	5.9
1890[1]	42.50	48.45	40.66	34.05	27.37	20.72	14.73	9.35	5.40
1900–1902[2]	48.23	50.59	42.19	34.88	27.74	20.76	14.35	9.03	5.10
1909–1911[2]	50.23	51.32	42.71	34.87	27.43	20.39	13.98	8.83	5.09
1919–1921[3]	56.34	54.15	45.60	37.65	29.86	22.22	15.25	9.51	5.47
1929–1931	59.12	54.96	46.02	37.54	29.22	21.51	14.72	9.20	5.26
1939–1941	62.81	57.03	47.76	38.80	30.03	21.96	15.05	9.42	5.38
1949–1951	66.31	58.98	49.52	40.29	31.17	22.83	15.76	10.07	5.88
1959–1961[5]	67.55	59.78	50.25	40.98	31.73	23.22	16.01	10.29	5.89
1969–1971[6]	67.94	59.69	50.22	41.07	31.87	23.34	16.07	10.38	6.18
1979–1981	70.82	61.98	52.45	43.31	34.04	25.26	17.56	11.35	6.76
1990	72.7	63.5	54.0	44.7	35.6	26.7	18.7	12.1	7.1
1991	72.9	63.7	54.1	44.9	35.8	26.9	18.9	12.3	7.2
1992	73.2	64.0	54.3	45.1	36.0	27.1	19.1	12.4	7.2
WHITE FEMALES									
1850[1]	40.5	47.2	40.2	35.4	29.8	23.5	17.0	11.3	6.4
1890[1]	44.46	49.62	42.03	35.36	28.76	22.09	15.70	10.15	5.75
1900–1902[2]	51.08	52.15	43.77	36.42	29.17	21.89	15.23	9.59	5.50
1909–1911[2]	53.62	53.57	44.88	36.96	29.26	21.74	14.92	9.38	5.35
1919–1921[3]	58.53	55.17	46.46	38.72	30.94	23.12	15.93	9.94	5.70
1929–1931	62.67	57.65	48.52	39.99	31.52	23.41	16.05	9.98	5.63
1939–1941	67.29	60.85	51.38	42.21	33.25	24.72	17.00	10.50	5.88
1949–1951	72.03	64.26	54.56	45.00	35.64	26.76	18.64	11.68	6.59
1959–1961[5]	74.19	66.05	56.29	46.63	37.13	28.08	19.69	12.38	6.67
1969–1971[6]	75.49	66.97	57.24	47.60	38.12	29.11	20.79	13.37	7.59
1979–1981	78.22	69.21	59.44	49.76	40.16	30.96	22.45	14.89	8.65
1990	79.4	70.1	60.3	50.6	41.0	31.6	23.0	15.4	9.0
1991	79.6	70.2	60.4	50.7	41.1	31.8	23.1	15.5	9.1
1992	79.8	70.4	60.6	50.9	41.2	31.9	23.2	15.6	9.2
ALL OTHER MALES[4]									
1900–1902[2]	32.54	41.90	35.11	29.25	23.12	17.34	12.62	8.33	5.12
1909–1911[2]	34.05	40.65	33.46	27.33	21.57	16.21	11.67	8.00	5.53
1919–1921[3]	47.14	45.99	38.36	32.51	26.53	20.47	14.74	9.58	5.83
1929–1931	47.55	44.27	35.95	29.45	23.36	17.92	13.15	8.78	5.42
1939–1941	52.33	48.54	39.74	32.25	25.23	19.18	14.38	10.06	6.46
1949–1951	58.91	52.96	43.73	35.31	27.29	20.25	14.91	10.74	7.07
1959–1961[5]	61.48	55.19	45.78	37.05	28.72	21.28	15.29	10.81	6.87
1969–1971[6]	60.98	53.67	44.37	36.20	28.29	21.24	15.35	10.68	7.57
1979–1981	65.63	57.40	47.87	39.13	30.64	22.92	16.54	11.36	7.22
1990	67.0	58.5	49.0	40.3	31.9	23.9	17.0	11.4	7.0
1991	67.3	58.7	49.3	40.6	32.2	24.3	17.3	11.6	7.1
1992	67.7	59.0	49.6	40.9	32.4	24.5	17.5	11.7	7.2
ALL OTHER FEMALES[4]									
1900–1902[2]	35.04	43.02	36.89	30.70	24.37	18.67	13.60	9.62	6.48
1909–1911[2]	37.67	42.84	36.14	29.61	23.34	17.65	12.78	9.22	6.05
1919–1921[3]	46.92	44.54	37.15	31.48	25.60	19.76	14.69	10.25	6.58
1929–1931	49.51	45.33	37.22	30.67	24.30	18.60	14.22	10.38	6.90
1939–1941	55.51	50.83	42.14	34.52	27.31	21.04	16.14	11.81	8.00
1949–1951	62.70	56.17	46.77	38.02	29.82	22.67	16.95	12.29	8.15
1959–1961[5]	66.47	59.72	50.07	40.83	32.16	24.31	17.83	12.46	7.66
1969–1971[6]	69.05	61.49	51.85	42.61	33.87	25.97	19.02	13.30	9.01
1979–1981	74.00	65.64	55.88	46.39	37.16	28.59	20.49	14.44	9.17
1990	75.2	66.6	56.8	47.3	38.1	29.2	21.3	14.5	8.8
1991	75.5	66.8	57.0	47.5	38.3	29.4	21.5	14.6	8.8
1992	75.7	67.0	57.2	47.7	38.4	29.6	21.7	14.8	8.9

1. Massachusetts only; white and nonwhite combined, the latter being about 1% of the total. 2. Original Death Registration States. 3. Death Registration States of 1920. 4. Data for periods 1900–1902 to 1929–1931 relate to blacks only. 5. Alaska and Hawaii included beginning in 1959. 6. Deaths of nonresidents of the United States excluded starting in 1970.
Sources: Department of Health and Human Services, National Center for Health Statistics.

Expectation of Life and Mortality Probabilities, 1992

| | Expectation of life in years | | | | | Mortality probability per 1,000 | | | | |
| | Total persons | White | | All other | | Total persons | White | | All other | |
Age		Male	Female	Male	Female		Male	Female	Male	Female
0	75.8	73.2	79.8	67.7	75.7	8.5	7.6	6.1	5.7	3.0
1	75.4	72.8	79.3	67.7	75.7	0.6	0.6	0.4	0.9	0.7
2	74.5	71.8	78.3	66.8	74.8	0.4	0.4	0.3	0.7	0.6
3	73.5	70.9	77.3	65.9	73.8	0.3	0.3	0.2	0.5	0.5
4	72.5	69.9	76.3	64.9	72.9	0.2	0.2	0.2	0.4	0.4
5	71.6	68.9	75.4	63.9	71.9	0.2	0.2	0.1	0.4	0.3
6	70.6	67.9	74.4	62.9	70.9	0.2	0.2	0.1	0.3	0.2
7	69.6	66.9	73.4	62.0	69.9	0.2	0.2	0.1	0.3	0.2
8	68.6	65.9	72.4	61.0	68.9	0.1	0.2	0.1	0.3	0.1
9	67.6	65.0	71.4	60.0	68.0	0.1	0.1	0.1	0.2	0.1
10	66.6	64.0	70.4	59.0	67.0	0.1	0.1	0.1	0.1	0.1
11	65.6	63.0	69.4	58.0	66.0	0.1	0.1	0.1	0.1	0.1
12	64.6	62.0	68.4	57.0	65.0	0.1	0.2	0.1	0.2	0.2
13	63.7	61.0	67.4	56.1	64.0	0.3	0.3	0.2	0.5	0.2
14	62.7	60.0	66.5	55.1	63.0	0.4	0.5	0.2	0.8	0.2
15	61.7	59.1	65.5	54.1	62.0	0.6	0.7	0.3	1.2	0.3
16	60.7	58.1	64.5	53.2	61.1	0.7	0.9	0.4	1.6	0.4
17	59.8	57.2	63.5	52.3	60.1	0.8	1.1	0.4	1.9	0.4
18	58.8	56.2	62.5	51.4	59.1	0.9	1.2	0.4	2.1	0.5
19	57.9	55.3	61.6	50.5	58.1	0.9	1.2	0.4	2.3	0.5
20	56.9	54.3	60.6	49.6	57.2	1.0	1.2	0.4	2.4	0.6
21	56.0	53.4	59.6	48.7	56.2	1.0	1.3	0.4	2.5	0.6
22	55.1	52.5	58.7	47.9	55.3	1.0	1.3	0.4	2.7	0.7
23	54.1	51.6	57.7	47.0	54.3	1.0	1.3	0.4	2.7	0.8
24	53.2	50.6	56.7	46.1	53.3	1.1	1.4	0.4	2.8	0.8
25	52.2	49.7	55.7	45.2	52.4	1.1	1.4	0.4	2.8	0.9
26	51.3	48.8	54.8	44.4	51.4	1.1	1.4	0.5	2.8	1.0
27	50.4	47.8	53.8	43.5	50.5	1.1	1.5	0.5	2.9	1.0
28	49.4	46.9	52.8	42.6	49.5	1.2	1.5	0.5	3.0	1.1
29	48.5	46.0	51.8	41.8	48.6	1.3	1.6	0.5	3.1	1.2
30	47.5	45.1	50.9	40.9	47.7	1.3	1.7	0.6	3.3	1.3
31	46.6	44.1	49.9	40.0	46.7	1.4	1.8	0.6	3.5	1.4
32	45.7	43.2	48.9	39.2	45.8	1.5	1.9	0.6	3.6	1.5
33	44.7	42.3	48.0	38.3	44.9	1.6	2.0	0.7	3.8	1.6
34	43.8	41.4	47.0	37.4	43.9	1.7	2.1	0.7	4.1	1.7
35	42.9	40.5	46.0	36.6	43.0	1.8	2.2	0.8	4.3	1.9
36	42.0	39.6	45.1	35.8	42.1	1.9	2.3	0.9	4.5	2.0
37	41.0	38.7	44.1	34.9	41.2	2.0	2.4	0.9	4.8	2.1
38	40.1	37.8	43.2	34.1	40.3	2.1	2.5	1.0	5.1	2.3
39	39.2	36.9	42.2	33.3	39.3	2.2	2.6	1.1	5.3	2.4
40	38.3	36.0	41.2	32.4	38.4	2.3	2.8	1.1	5.6	2.6
41	37.4	35.1	40.3	31.6	37.5	2.4	2.9	1.2	5.9	2.7
42	36.5	34.2	39.3	30.8	36.6	2.6	3.1	1.3	6.2	2.9
43	35.6	33.3	38.4	30.0	35.8	2.7	3.2	1.5	6.6	3.1
44	34.7	32.4	37.5	29.2	34.9	2.9	3.4	1.6	7.0	3.3
45	33.8	31.5	36.5	28.4	34.0	3.1	3.7	1.8	7.4	3.5
46	32.9	30.6	35.6	27.6	33.1	3.3	3.9	2.0	7.8	3.8
47	32.0	29.7	34.7	26.8	32.2	3.6	4.2	2.2	8.3	4.1
48	31.1	28.8	33.7	26.0	31.4	3.9	4.6	2.4	8.8	4.4
49	30.2	28.0	32.8	25.3	30.5	4.2	5.0	2.7	9.3	4.8
50	29.3	27.1	31.9	24.5	29.6	4.6	5.4	3.0	9.8	5.2
51	28.5	26.3	31.0	23.7	28.8	5.1	5.9	3.3	10.4	5.6
52	27.6	25.4	30.1	23.0	28.0	5.6	6.5	3.7	11.2	6.2
53	26.8	24.6	29.2	22.2	27.1	6.1	7.1	4.1	12.2	6.8
54	25.9	23.7	28.3	21.5	26.3	6.7	7.9	4.5	13.4	7.5
55	25.1	22.9	27.5	20.8	25.5	7.4	8.7	5.0	14.7	8.3
56	24.3	22.1	26.6	20.1	24.7	8.1	9.5	5.5	16.0	9.1
57	23.5	21.3	25.7	19.4	23.9	8.9	10.5	6.0	17.4	9.9
58	22.7	20.6	24.9	18.8	23.2	9.7	11.6	6.6	18.7	10.7
59	21.9	19.8	24.1	18.1	22.4	10.7	12.8	7.3	20.0	11.4
60	21.1	19.1	23.2	17.5	21.7	11.7	14.2	8.1	21.4	12.2
61	20.4	18.3	22.4	16.8	20.9	12.7	15.6	8.9	22.9	13.0
62	19.7	17.6	21.6	16.2	20.2	13.9	17.1	9.7	24.4	14.0
63	18.9	16.9	20.8	15.6	19.5	15.1	18.7	10.6	26.2	15.1
64	18.2	16.2	20.0	15.0	18.8	16.4	20.5	11.5	28.0	16.4
65	17.5	15.5	19.3	14.4	18.1	17.8	22.4	12.5	29.9	17.7

		Expectation of life in years						Mortality probability per 1,000			
			White		All other				White		All other
Age	Total persons	Male	Female	Male	Female	Total persons	Male	Female	Male	Female	
66	16.8	14.9	18.5	13.9	17.4	19.3	24.4	13.6	31.9	19.1	
67	16.1	14.3	17.8	13.3	16.7	20.9	26.5	14.9	34.2	20.5	
68	15.5	13.6	17.0	12.8	16.1	22.6	28.8	16.3	36.8	22.1	
69	14.8	13.0	16.3	12.2	15.4	24.5	31.1	17.8	39.7	23.7	
70	14.2	12.4	15.6	11.7	14.8	26.5	33.6	19.5	42.9	25.6	
71	13.5	11.8	14.9	11.2	14.2	28.7	36.3	21.3	46.3	27.5	
72	12.9	11.3	14.2	10.8	13.6	31.0	39.3	23.3	49.5	29.4	
73	12.3	10.7	13.5	10.3	13.0	33.5	42.6	25.4	52.5	31.3	
74	11.7	10.2	12.9	9.8	12.4	36.2	46.4	27.7	55.2	33.1	
75	11.2	9.6	12.2	9.4	11.8	39.2	50.6	30.1	58.2	35.1	
76	10.6	9.1	11.6	8.9	11.2	42.5	55.0	32.9	61.4	37.4	
77	10.0	8.6	11.0	8.5	10.6	46.1	59.9	36.0	65.1	40.2	
78	9.5	8.1	10.4	8.1	10.0	50.0	65.1	39.6	69.6	43.5	
79	9.0	7.7	9.8	7.6	9.5	54.5	70.9	43.6	74.8	47.4	
80	8.5	7.2	9.2	7.2	8.9	59.5	77.2	48.2	81.0	52.1	
81	8.0	6.8	8.6	6.8	8.4	65.2	84.4	53.5	88.1	57.6	
82	7.5	6.4	8.1	6.4	7.9	71.7	92.5	59.5	96.1	64.0	
83	7.1	6.0	7.6	6.0	7.4	79.2	102.0	66.6	105.2	71.6	
84	6.6	5.6	7.1	5.7	6.9	88.1	113.3	75.0	115.2	80.6	
85	6.2	5.3	6.6	5.4	6.5	—	—	—	—	—	

Source: Department of Health and Human Services, National Center for Health Statistics.

Living Arrangements of the Elderly, 1992
(in thousands, noninstitutional population)

Living arrangement and age	All races			White			Black		
	Total	Men	Women	Total	Men	Women	Total	Men	Women
65 years and over	30,590	12,800	17,790	27,297	11,431	15,866	2,607	1,058	1,549
Living									
Alone	9,523	2,086	7,437	8,463	1,741	6,722	938	312	626
With spouse	16,537	9,448	7,089	15,220	8,664	6,556	956	572	384
With relatives	3,814	897	2,917	2,998	723	2,275	638	124	514
With nonrelatives	716	369	347	616	303	313	75	50	25
65 to 74 years	18,440	8,266	10,174	16,315	7,323	8,992	1,665	739	926
Living									
Alone	4,561	1,100	3,461	3,918	867	3,051	567	210	357
With spouse	11,606	6,372	5,234	10,626	5,808	4,818	722	425	297
With relatives	1,837	516	1,321	1,405	418	987	319	68	251
With nonrelatives	436	278	158	366	230	136	57	36	21
75 and over	12,149	4,533	7,616	10,983	4,108	6,875	941	318	623
Living									
Alone	4,962	986	3,976	4,546	875	3,671	371	102	269
With spouse	4,931	3,076	1,855	4,594	2,856	1,738	235	147	88
With relatives	1,976	380	1,596	1,594	305	1,289	310	54	256
With nonrelatives	280	91	189	249	72	177	25	15	10

Source: U.S. Bureau of the Census, Current Population Reports, Series P-20, No. 468, Marital Status and Living Arrangements: March 1992.

Elderly Homeownership on the Rise

The homeownership rate for householders aged 65 and over climbed from 70% in 1980 to 75% in 1990, while the rate for householdership in general declined slightly, according to a recent Census Bureau report.

The data indicate that all but three states recorded a gain in ownership among the elderly population.

There was no significant change in elderly homeownership rates between 1980 and 1990 for South Dakota, Nevada, and Alaska.

Elderly homeownership rates topped 80% in 11 states: Utah, Idaho, Oklahoma, West Virginia, Mississippi, Florida, South Carolina, New Mexico, Arizona, Wyoming, and Kansas. At the other end of the spectrum were New York and the District of Columbia where the rates were under 60.

For a majority of elderly homeowners, their most recent move was to either a new or a relatively new home. This was the case for slightly more than six out of 10 movers. For the purpose of this study a new or relatively new home means one built either during the decade or preceding the decade in which the householder moved.

LAW ENFORCEMENT & CRIME

Characteristics of Hate Crimes in 1993

Source: U.S. Department of Justice, *Uniform Crime Reports,* latest data.

Incidents

Bias-motivated crime is a phenomenon that touches all segments of society. It exacts an immeasurable toll on its victims who are targeted solely because of hatred toward their race, religion, ethnicity, or sexual orientation.

During 1993, a total of 7,587 bias-motivated criminal incidents were reported to the FBI by almost 7,000 law enforcement agencies in 46 states and the District of Columbia. Sixty-two percent of the incidents were motivated by racial bias; 17% by religious bias; 11% by sexual-orientation bias; and the remainder by ethnicity/national origin bias.

The 7,587 incidents involved 8,987 separate offenses, 9,372 victims, and 8,610 known offenders. Most of the incidents (84%) involved only one victim and a single offense type (98%).

Seven of every ten incidents involved crimes against persons; of these, eight of every ten were directed at individuals. Of the total incidents directed at individuals, 20% involved crimes against property, e.g., vandalism of an individual's car or home.

Offenses

Crimes against persons composed 70% of the 8,987 offenses reported. Intimidation was the single most frequently reported hate crime among all offenses measured, accounting for 34% of the total. Following were damage/destruction/vandalism of property, 26%; simple assault, 20%; and aggravated assault, 16 percent.

Sixteen persons were murdered in hate-motivated incidents. Racial bias motivated the highest number of murders in 1993: nine. Anti-white offenses alone accounted for six of the nine homicides in this category. Of the remaining murders, six were motivated

by sexual orientation, and one was motivated by bias against the victim's ethnic origin.

Victims

Eighty-five percent of the 9,372 reported hate crime victims were individuals, while the remaining 15% were businesses, religious organizations, or varied other targets. Of these victims, 67% were targets of crimes against persons. Six of every ten victims were attacked because of their race, with bias against blacks accounting for 38% of the total. Only crimes motivated by religious bias showed a higher percentage of crimes against property rather than persons. Sixty-seven percent of incidents involving victims targeted because of their religion were crimes against property.

Offenders

Law enforcement agencies reported 8,610 known offenders to be associated with the 7,587 incidents recorded in 1993. Fifty-one percent of the known offenders were white, and 34% were black. Characteristics of offenders for the remaining 39% of the incidents were unknown.

Considering the types of racial bias involved, nine of every ten white offenders were identified in connection with anti-black offenses. Similarly, nine out of every ten black offenders were associated with anti-white offenses.

Locations

Twenty-seven percent of hate crime incidents in 1993 occurred in residences. Following closely were highways, roads, alleys, or streets accounting for 23 percent. The remaining incidents were widely distributed among other locations. ▫

Summary of Hate Crime Statistics, 1993

	Number of incidents	Number of offenses	Number of victims	Number of known offenders
Total	**7,587**	**8,987**	**9,372**	**8,610**
BIAS MOTIVATION				
Race:	**4,732**	**5,786**	**6,011**	**6,258**
Anti-White	1,471	1,814	1,853	2,890
Anti-Black	2,815	3,410	3,559	2,845
Anti-American Indian/Alaskan Native	27	39	43	49
Anti-Multi-Racial Group	161	226	240	183
Ethnicity/National Origin:	**697**	**845**	**895**	**814**
Anti-Hispanic	472	596	643	653
Anti-Other Ethnicity/National Origin	225	249	252	161
Religion:	**1,298**	**1,358**	**1,423**	**461**
Anti-Jewish	1,143	1,197	1,252	371
Anti-Catholic	32	33	33	16
Anti-Protestant	30	30	38	13
Anti-Islamic	13	15	15	11
Anti-Other Religion	63	66	68	21
Anti-Multi-Religious Group	14	14	14	26
Anti-Atheism/Agnosticism/etc.	3	3	3	3

Sexual Orientation:	**860**	**998**	**1,043**	**1,077**
Anti-Male Homosexual	615	699	716	834
Anti-Female Homosexual	121	147	154	106
Anti-Homosexual	94	122	143	110
Anti-Heterosexual	28	28	28	26
Anti-Bisexual	2	2	2	1

Source: "Hate Crime Statistics 1993," *Uniform Crime Reports,* U.S. Department of Justice.

Justifiable Homicide

In 1993, the justifiable homicide total was 811, up 5 percent from the 1992 total of 769 and 28 percent higher than the 1989 total of 636. Of the justifiable homicides in 1993, 455 involved law enforcement officers and 356 were by private citizens.

Justifiable Homicide by Weapon, Law Enforcement,[1] 1989–1993

Year	Total	Total firearms	Handguns	Rifles	Shotguns	Firearms type not specified	Knives or other cutting instruments	Other dangerous weapons	Personal weapons
1989	363	360	299	15	42	4	—	2	1
1990	385	382	345	8	19	10	—	2	1
1991	367	361	319	10	25	7	1	3	2
1992	418	411	357	22	21	11	4	1	2
1993	455	451	391	22	26	12	—	2	2

1. The killing of a felon by a law enforcement officer in the line of duty.

Justifiable Homicide by Weapon, Private Citizen,[1] 1989–1993

Year	Total	Total firearms	Handguns	Rifles	Shotguns	Firearms type not specified	Knives or other cutting instruments	Other dangerous weapons	Personal weapons
1989	273	236	178	22	34	2	23	9	5
1990	328	276	210	20	39	7	39	9	4
1991	331	296	243	15	25	13	29	4	2
1992	351	311	264	20	24	3	31	5	4
1993	356	311	251	16	33	11	28	10	7

1. The killing of a felon, during the commission of a felony, by a private citizen. *Source: Crime in the Univted States 1993, Uniform Crime Reports,* Federal Bureau of Investigation.

Full–Time Law Enforcement Employees, 1993

City	Officers	Civilians	Total	1992 Total	City	Officers	Civilians	Total	1992 Total
Atlanta	1,626	478	2,104	1,996	Milwaukee	2,079	402	2,481	2,491
Baltimore	2,947	553	3,500	3,391	Minneapolis	876	162	1,038	957
Birmingham, Ala.	770	229	999	990	New York	29,327	10,115	39,442	37,922
Boston	1,944	660	2,604	2,586	Newark, N.J.	1,151	148	1,299	1,226
Buffalo, N.Y.	931	134	1,065	1,008	Norfolk, Va.	664	95	759	766
Chicago	12,093	2,103	14,196	14,446	Oakland, Calif.	719	370	1,089	1,133
Cincinnati	933	222	1,155	1,195	Oklahoma City	988	296	1,284	1,197
Cleveland	1,699	164	1,863	1,789	Philadelphia	6,225	744	6,969	7,101
Columbus, Ohio	1,543	357	1,900	1,775	Phoenix, Ariz.	1,978	680	2,658	2,606
Dallas	2,807	718	3,535	3,604	Pittsburgh	1,095	57	1,152	1,152
Denver	1,394	175	1,569	1,594	Portland, Ore.	881	252	1,133	1,072
Detroit	3,860	538	4,398	4,393	Rochester, N.Y.	670	140	810	800
El Paso	850	203	1,053	1,051	St. Louis	1,448	700	2,148	2,168
Fort Worth	1,074	316	1,390	1,376	St. Paul	521	154	675	686
Honolulu	1,921	449	2,370	2,374	San Antonio	1,662	361	2,023	1,926
Houston	4,734	1,966	6,700	6,021	San Diego, Calif.	1,861	752	2,613	2,741
Indianapolis	967	362	1,329	1,330	San Francisco	1,804	389	2,193	2,261
Jacksonvill, Fla.	1,253	947	2,200	2,180	San Jose, Calif.	1,203	421	1,624	1,581
Kansas City, Mo.	1,191	567	1,758	1,769	Seattle	1,245	504	1,749	1,803
Lincoln, Neb.	256	84	340	320	Shreveport, La.	452	132	584	551
Long Beach, Calif.	791	412	1,203	1,100	Tampa, Fla.	771	269	1,040	1,073
Los Angeles	7,637	2,462	10,099	10,392	Toledo, Ohio	654	55	709	677
Louisville, Ky.	627	216	843	801	Tucson, Ariz.	759	247	1,006	1,002
Memphis, Tenn.	1,437	373	1,810	1,710	Tulsa, Okla.	738	113	851	856
Miami, Fla.	1,062	433	1,495	1,318	Washington, D.C.	4,372	831	5,203	5,207

NOTE: As of Oct. 31, 1993. *Source:* Department of Justice, Federal Bureau of Investigation, *Uniform Crime Reports for the United States, 1993,* released 1994.

Estimated Arrests, 1993[1]

Murder and non–negligent manslaughter	23,400	Weapons—carrying, possession, etc.	262,300
Forcible rape	38,420	Prostitution and commercial vice	97,800
Robbery	173,620	Sex offenses, except forcible rape	
Aggravated assault	518,670	and prostitution	104,100
Burglary	402,700	Drug abuse violations	1,126,300
Larceny—theft	1,476,300	Gambling	17,300
Motor vehicle theft	195,900	Offenses against family and children	109,100
Arson	19,400	Driving under the influence	1,524,800
Total violent crime	754,110	Liquor laws	518,500
Total property crime	2,094,300	Drunkenness	726,600
Other assaults	1,144,900	Disorderly conduct	727,000
Forgery and counterfeiting	106,900	Vagrancy	28,200
Fraud	410,700	All other offenses, except traffic	3,518,700
Embezzlement	12,900	Curfew and loitering law violations	100,200
Stolen property—buying, receiving, possessing	158,100	Runaways	180,500
Vandalism	313,000	**Total**[2]	**14,036,300**

1. Arrest totals based on all reporting agencies and estimates for unreported areas. 2. Because of rounding, items may not add to totals. *Source:* Department of Justice, Federal Bureau of Investigation, *Uniform Crime Reports for the United States, 1993,* released 1994.

Reported Arrests by Sex and Age

	Male				Female			
	Total		Under 18		Total		Under 18	
Offense	1993	1992	1993	1992	1993	1992	1993	1992
Murder[1]	18,375	17,592	3,093	2,670	1,910	1,899	191	159
Forcible rape	32,107	32,965	5,212	5,258	416	420	91	111
Robbery	140,128	140,374	39,493	36,987	13,405	13,082	3,847	3,447
Aggravated assault	372,557	370,379	55,731	53,280	69,518	64,539	12,020	10,497
Burglary—breaking or entering	304,702	326,570	104,871	111,663	33,536	33,129	11,153	10,904
Larceny—theft	842,658	876,736	269,690	283,662	408,619	415,248	122,260	118,404
Motor vehicle theft	148,932	152,733	65,117	66,418	19,863	18,516	10,198	9,382
Arson	13,738	14,139	6,975	7,121	2,375	2,183	974	847
Violent crime[2]	563,167	561,310	103,529	98,195	85,249	79,940	16,149	14,214
Other assaults	792,848	755,933	115,714	108,649	172,470	156,584	40,554	35,148
Forgery and counterfeiting	58,425	57,849	4,243	4,575	31,062	30,800	2,263	2,449
Fraud	199,297	200,366	11,847	11,068	136,283	145,948	4,311	3,959
Embezzlement	6,493	7,147	366	372	4,423	4,560	250	299
Stolen property—buying, receiving, possessing	117,531	119,688	32,404	32,426	17,333	17,077	4,036	3,899
Vandalism	229,424	232,852	107,701	107,933	31,858	29,625	11,441	10,094
Weapons—carrying, possessing, etc.	206,990	188,797	48,159	42,960	17,405	15,319	4,193	3,296
Prostitution and commercialized vice	31,712	30,180	443	531	57,138	56,808	551	564
Sex offenses, except forcible rape and prostitution	80,211	84,540	14,969	15,429	7,501	7,020	1,424	1,203
Drug abuse violations	811,493	769,080	82,968	65,820	157,113	151,344	10,348	8,161
Gambling	13,186	12,942	1,115	1,012	2,150	2,087	52	76
Offenses against family and children	71,967	69,115	2,538	2,555	17,190	15,213	1,402	1,385
Driving under the influence	1,056,544	1,137,542	9,170	10,278	173,427	182,041	1,552	1,678
Liquor laws	338,276	357,669	65,586	69,546	80,806	85,316	26,115	27,897
Drunkenness	537,690	592,324	11,599	12,626	67,289	71,912	2,288	2,488
Disorderly conduct	481,553	480,677	93,472	85,598	125,919	124,690	27,740	24,086
Vagrancy	21,765	26,170	2,698	2,916	3,041	2,834	537	520
All other offenses, except traffic	2,410,082	2,448,952	2,158,448	233,874	525,408	505,488	69,002	61,201
Curfew and loitering law violations	61,343	54,622	61,343	54,622	24,011	19,997	24,011	19,997
Runaways	65,051	63,178	65,051	63,178	87,081	82,992	87,081	82,997
Total	**9,475,344**	**9,633,809**	**1,534,356**	**1,496,866**	**2,290,420**	**2,259,344**	**480,116**	**446,272**

1. Includes non–negligent manslaughter. 2. Violent crimes are offenses of murder, forcible rape, robbery, and aggravated assault. NOTE: 10,512 agencies reporting; 1993 estimated population 214,099,000. *Source:* Department of Justice, Federal Bureau of Investigation, *Uniform Crime Reports for the United States, 1993,* released Dec. 4, 1994.

Arrests by Race, 1993

Offense	White	Black	Other[1]	Total	Offense	White	Black	Other[1]	Total
Murder[2]	8,243	11,656	344	20,243	Sex offenses, except forcible rape and prostitution	67,435	18,304	1,842	87,581
Forcible rape	18,473	13,419	577	32,469					
Robbery	55,893	95,164	2,224	153,281					
Aggravated assault	257,628	175,827	8,000	441,455	Drug abuse violation	578,214	380,460	9,048	967,722
Burglary	226,857	104,473	6,480	337,810					
Larceny–theft	806,511	411,705	31,087	1,249,303	Gambling	7,382	7,178	760	15,320
Motor vehicle theft	96,328	67,938	4,325	168,591	Offenses against family and children	58,137	27,605	2,866	88,608
Arson	11,990	3,784	299	16,073					
Violent crimes[3]	340,237	296,066	11,145	647,448	Driving under the influence	1,069,632	130,026	27,631	1,227,289
Property crimes[4]	1,141,686	587,900	42,191	1,771,777					
Other assaults	606,211	336,360	20,856	963,427	Liquor laws	352,567	52,533	12,240	417,340
Forgery and counterfeiting	56,315	31,634	1,428	89,377	Drukenness	481,885	107,863	14,714	604,462
					Disorderly conduct	391,969	203,533	11,084	606,586
Fraud	208,601	122,614	3,836	335,051	Vagrancy	13,945	10,148	561	24,654
Embezzlement	7,357	3,380	177	10,914	All other offenses except traffic	1,833,220	1,039,100	55,342	2,927,662
Stolen property— buying, receiving, possessing	75,432	56,889	2,258	134,579					
Vandalism	194,940	59,820	5,964	260,724	Suspicion	5,690	6,304	131	12,125
Weapons— carrying, possession, etc.	124,135	96,189	3,616	223,940	Curfew and loitering law violations	67,091	15,382	2,683	85,156
					Runaways	118,125	25,973	7,119	151,217
Prostitution and commercial vice	55,081	31,913	1,798	88,792	**Total**	7,855,287	3,647,174	239,290	11,741,751

1. Includes American Indian, Alaskan Native, and Asian or Pacific Islander. 2. Includes non–negligent manslaughter. 3. Violent crimes are offenses of murder, forcible rape, robbery, and aggravated assault. 4. Property crimes are offenses of burglary, larceny-theft, motor vehicle theft. NOTE: Figures represent arrests reported by 10,509 agencies serving a total 1993 estimated population of 213,093,000. *Source:* Department of Justice, Federal Bureau of Investigation, *Uniform Crime Reports for the United States, 1993,* released Dec. 4, 1994.

Total Arrests, by Age Groups, 1993

Age	Arrests	Age	Arrests	Age	Arrests	Age	Arrests	Age	Arrests
Under 15	701,129	18	513,323	22	457,217	30–34	1,724,659	50–54	224,409
15	386,163	19	496,764	23	434,225	35–39	1,256,231	55 and	
16	454,004	20	471,617	24	404,678	40–44	759,580	over	282,222
17	473,176	21	457,570	25–29	1,856,055	45–49	412,742	**Total**	11,765,764

NOTE: Based on reports furnished to the FBI by 10,512 agencies covering a 1993 estimated population of 214,099,000. *Source:* Department of Justice, Federal Bureau of Investigation, *Uniform Crime Reports for the United States, 1993,* released Dec. 4, 1994.

Federal Prosecutions of Public Corruption: 1982 to 1991

(Prosecution of persons who have corrupted public office in violation of Federal Criminal Statutes. As of Dec. 31, 1991)

Prosecution status	1991	1990	1989	1988	1987	1986	1985	1984	1983	1982
Total:[1] Indicted	1,452	1,176	1,349	1,274	1,340	1,192	1,182	936	1,073	729
Convicted	1,194	1,084	1,444	1,067	1,075	1,027	997	934	972	671
Awaiting trial	346	300	375	288	368	246	256	269	222	186
Federal officials: Indicted	803	615	695	629	651	596	563	408	460[2]	158
Convicted	665	583	610	529	545	523	470	429	424[2]	147
Awaiting trial	149	103	126	86	118	83	90	77	58	38
State officials: Indicted	115	96	71	66	102	88	79	58	81	4
Convicted	77	79	54	69	76	71	66	52	65	43
Awaiting trial	42	28	18	14	26	24	20	21	26	18
Local officials: Indicted	242	257	269	276	246	232	248	203	270	257
Convicted	180	225	201	229	204	207	221	196	226	232
Awaiting trial	88	98	122	79	89	55	49	74	61	58

1. Includes individuals who are neither public officials nor employees, but who were involved with public officials or employees in violating the law, now shown separately. 2. Increases in the number indicted and convicted between 1982 and 1983 resulted from a greater focus on federal corruption nationwide and more consistent reporting of cases involving lower–level employees. NOTE: Figures are latest available. *Source:* U.S. Department of Justice, *Report to Congress on the Activities and Operations of the Public Integrity Section,* annual, from *Statistical Abstract of the United States 1994.*

Crime Rates for Selected Large Cities: 1992

(Offenses known to the police per 100,000 population.)

City ranked by population size, 1992[1]	Violent crime				Property crime		
	Murder	Forcible rape	Robbery	Aggravated assault	Burglary	Larceny-theft	Motor vehicle theft
New York, NY	27.1	38.2	1,237	861	1,403	3,202	1,722
Los Angeles, CA	30.3	51.8	1,093	1,285	1,598	3,426	1,880
Chicago, IL	33.1	([2])	1,357	1,450	1,731	4,225	1,588
Houston, TX	27.4	69.0	657	712	1,782	3,675	1,825
Philadelphia, PA	26.5	48.7	728	385	1,010	2,474	1,398
San Diego, CA	12.7	42.1	462	768	1,427	3,542	1,756
Dallas, TX	37.0	104.7	911	1,019	2,370	6,027	1,960
Phoenix, AZ	13.6	47.6	314	716	2,032	4,601	1,498
Detroit, MI	57.0	117.3	1,168	1,191	2,112	3,966	2,619
San Antonio, TX	22.5	63.3	358	289	2,258	6,714	1,513
San Jose, CA	5.3	55.2	152	457	835	2,934	468
Indianapolis, IN	17.8	109.5	437	816	1,640	3,185	1,055
San Francisco, CA	15.6	52.6	1,102	651	1,576	5,111	1,687
Baltimore, MD	44.3	99.1	1,623	1,119	2,157	5,389	1,496
Jacksonville, FL	18.5	107.4	544	1,069	2,456	4,991	1,324
Columbus, OH	17.6	106.4	558	412	2,336	4,543	1,083
Milwaukee, WI	22.7	81.3	674	207	1,360	4,111	2,215
Memphis, TN	28.0	109.4	849	566	2,589	3,605	2,101
Washington, DC	75.2	36.5	1,266	1,454	1,820	5,198	1,548
Boston, MA	12.7	93.7	832	1,099	1,522	4,294	1,992
El Paso, TX	8.2	50.8	301	728	1,429	5,513	1,014
Seattle, WA	11.0	64.8	473	796	1,697	7,547	1,413
Cleveland, OH	30.6	166.3	861	603	1,753	2,773	2,096
Nashville-Davidson, TN	17.5	96.7	518	996	1,989	5,071	998
Austin, TX	7.6	60.7	300	221	2,109	7,301	944
New Orleans, LA	55.2	56.8	1,058	812	2,172	4,028	1,807
Denver, CO	19.3	88.7	366	602	1,806	3,632	1,641
Fort Worth, TX	32.9	112.8	750	1,123	3,074	6,905	2,136
Oklahoma City, OK	13.4	104.0	404	878	2,476	5,991	1,310
Portland, OR	10.0	107.0	586	1,128	1,912	5,798	1,725
Long Beach, CA	23.3	48.9	804	678	1,696	3,264	1,419
Kansas City, MO	34.0	127.8	1,019	1,674	2,845	4,952	1,823
Virginia Beach, VA	5.7	37.8	151	91	916	3,729	286
Charlotte, NC	24.2	88.3	748	1,452	3,073	6,606	600
Tucson, AZ	9.9	91.1	229	691	1,608	6,755	1,029
Albuquerque, NM	10.5	73.2	364	1,089	2,168	5,040	724
Atlanta, GA	48.2	152.6	1,418	2,241	3,180	8,251	2,057
St. Louis, MO	57.4	86.7	1,226	1,920	3,056	6,359	2,094
Sacramento, CA	11.7	61.9	606	540	1,907	4,755	2,135
Fresno, CA	22.0	55.3	842	540	2,562	4,549	3,542
Tulsa, OK	8.8	98.1	358	870	2,147	3,449	1,277
Oakland, CA	42.7	108.3	1,194	1,281	2,297	5,520	2,012
Honolulu, HI	3.5	37.2	116	116	1,040	4,406	401
Miami, FL	34.2	72.8	1,890	1,734	3,232	8,195	2,330
Pittsburgh, PA	11.8	59.1	800	332	1,391	3,444	2,173
Cincinnati, OH	13.3	131.5	621	802	1,914	4,786	573
Minneapolis, MN	15.9	159.0	815	653	2,466	5,624	1,370
Toledo, OH	12.7	108.8	448	364	1,809	4,750	1,221
Buffalo, NY	23.0	104.7	907	892	2,484	3,960	1,660
Wichita, KS	9.4	82.3	432	365	2,102	5,217	916
Mesa, AZ	3.0	39.5	98	542	1,481	4,030	833
Colorado Springs, CO	5.7	76.3	151	287	1,278	4,657	364
Las Vegas, NV	14.6	57.9	532	284	1,524	3,850	1,091
Santa Ana, CA	19.0	23.6	652	366	1,244	3,234	1,379
Tampa, FL	16.8	103.8	1,027	2,231	3,427	6,482	2,514
Arlington, TX	5.9	53.7	267	430	1,577	5,073	1,083
Anaheim, CA	12.7	32.6	323	265	1,434	3,455	1,258
Louisville, KY	14.2	43.7	452	571	1,524	3,207	984
St. Paul, MN	11.8	85.0	300	543	1,672	4,209	856
Newark, NJ	31.3	112.8	1,942	1,415	2,205	3,899	5,019
Corpus Christi, TX	11.2	53.8	190	702	1,960	6,746	654
Birmingham, AL	48.8	132.9	681	1,393	2,734	5,591	1,370

1. Crime data are not available for Omaha, NE, in 1992. 2. The rate for forcible rape is not shown because the forcible rape figures were not in accordance with national Uniform Crime Reporting guidelines. *Source: Statistical Abstract of the United States, 1994.*

Child Abuse and Neglect Cases, 1992

State	Reports		Number of children substantiated[2]	State	Reports		Number of children substantiated[2]
	Number of reports[1]	Number of children			Number of reports[1]	Number of children	
Alabama	28,311	43,246	23,265	Montana	9,691	14,760	5,328
Alaska	9,892[3]	9,892	8,544	Nebraska	7,961	17,029	5,262
Arizona	29,339	51,216	30,556	Nevada	13,914	22,540	7,699
Arkansas	17,250	36,089	7,538	New Hampshire	6,755	10,943	917
California	326,120	463,090	73,675	New Jersey	50,443[3]	50,443	17,499
Colorado	34,409	55,740	9,237	New Mexico	26,969[3]	26,969	6,716
Connecticut	14,369	22,080	15,957	New York	137,779	228,457	92,238
Delaware	4,586	8,292	2,157	North Carolina	55,411	88,472	29,546
District of Columbia	5,596	12,093	3,718	North Dakota	4,515	7,565	3,669
Florida	116,403	180,285	88,563	Ohio	95,376	148,101	61,327
Georgia	51,225	46,192	46,192	Oklahoma	24,092[3]	24,092	8,063
Hawaii	5,310[3]	5,310	2,277	Oregon	25,622	41,506	8,705
Idaho	12,230	24,020	6,395	Pennsylvania	25,891[3]	25,891	8,419
Illinois	74,220	131,592	43,433	Rhode Island	8,395	12,886	4,931
Indiana	39,233	58,970	30,283	South Carolina	19,712	33,854	11,348
Iowa	19,432	28,094	7,834	South Dakota	10,486[3]	10,486	2,903
Kansas	22,079[3]	22,079	11,585	Tennessee	31,231[3]	31,231	11,469
Kentucky	35,997	56,438	24,437	Texas	110,937	174,255	62,342
Louisiana	26,087	47,893	16,050	Utah	15,910	27,047	10,875
Maine	4,286	10,177	4,927	Vermont	2,750	3,205	1,498
Maryland	30,062	48,699	n.a.	Virginia	35,880	55,680	14,472
Massachusetts	32,286	52,581	24,601	Washington	39,704	55,836	41,879
Michigan	51,601	117,316	26,931	West Virginia	12,932	20,949	n.a.
Minnesota	17,988	27,462	11,217	Wisconsin	47,622[3]	47,622	19,213
Mississippi	17,528	32,076	10,712	Wyoming	3,268	5,478	2,017
Missouri	49,286	79,493	24,339	**Total**	**1,898,911**	**2,855,691**	**991,758**

1. Except as noted, reports are on incident/family-based basis or based on the number of reported incidents regardless of the number of children involved. 2. Type of investigation disposition that determines that there is sufficient evidence under State law to conclude that maltreatment occurred or that the child is at risk of maltreatment. 3. Child-based report that enumerates each child who is a subject of the report. 4. 1990 data. n.a. = not available. NOTE: Based on reports that were referred for investigation by the child protective services agency in each state. The majority of states were unable to provide unduplicated counts except for Alaska, Hawaii, Michigan, Montana, Ohio, Oregon, South Carolina, Vermont, and Washington. *Source: Statistical Abstract of the United States, 1994.*

State Prison Populations, June 30, 1994

10 States with the largest total prison populations	Number of inmates	10 States with the highest incarceration rates, 1994*	Sentenced prisoners per 100,000 residents	10 States with highest annual growth, 6/30/93 to 6/30/94	Percent change	10 States with the largest number of female prisoners	Number of female prisoners
California	124,813	Texas	545	Connecticut	19.6%	California	7,934
Texas	100,136	Louisiana	514	Texas	18.4	Texas	7,760
New York	65,962	South Carolina	504	Tennessee	14.6	New York	3,607
Florida	56,052	Oklahoma	501	Montana	14.5	Florida	2,889
Ohio	41,156	Nevada	456	Virginia	13.6	Ohio	2,556
Michigan	40,220	Arizona	448	Georgia	12.2	Michigan	1,883
Illinois	35,614	Alabama	439	Mississippi	10.9	Georgia	1,862
Georgia	30,292	Michigan	423	Florida	10.8	Illinois	1,723
Pennsylvania	27,071	Georgia	417	Wyoming	10.8	Oklahoma	1,558
Virginia	24,822	Florida	404	Arizona	10.7	Virginia	1,399

NOTE: The District of Columbia as a wholly urban jurisdiction is excluded. *Prisoners with sentences greater than 1 year per 100,000 residents. *Source:* Bureau of Justice Statistics.

Prison Populations

The nation's prison population exceeded one million in 1994 for the first time in history. At the end of June 1994, 1,012,851 men and women were incarcerated in state and federal prisons. State prisons held 919,143 inmates and federal prisons held 93,708 inmates. California (124,813) and Texas (100,136) together accounted for more than one in five inmates in the country.

The prison population grew by almost 40,000 inmates during the first half of 1994, the equivalent of more than 1,500 a week—or three additional 500-bed prisons.

The states with the highest incarceration rates per 100,000 were Texas (545), Louisiana (514), South Carolina (504), and Oklahoma (501).

At the end of 1993, (the latest available data), there were 1,432 black inmates per 100,000 black U.S. residents and 203 white inmates per 100,000 white U.S. residents. On June 30, 1994, there were 61,872 women in state and federal prisons or 6.1% of all prisoners. The male incarceration rate for the same period was 719 per 100,000 male residents.

Family Violence, 1992

Source: "Criminal Victimization in the United States, 1992," A National Crime Victimization Survey Report, March 1994.

Family violence accounted for 7% of all violent crimes, including 9% of all completed crimes and 6% of all attempted crimes. Five percent of all robberies, and 8% of all assaults were committed by the victim's relatives.

Almost 86% of the violent crimes committed by relatives were assaults. Furthermore, simple assaults by family members accounted for 59% of the reported family violence, and aggravated assaults made up another 27% of these crimes.

The rate of violent crimes against women committed by relatives was 3.8 per 1,000, while the rate for men was 0.8 per 1,000. Men and women had comparable victimization rates when the offenders were well known but not related to the victims. Males, however, were significantly more likely than females to be victimized by a casual acquaintance.

Blacks were more likely than whites to be victims of violent crimes by persons who were well known but not related to them. There was not a significant difference between whites and blacks in the proportions of violent victimizations that were committed by relatives or casual acquaintances.

Marital status also affected the chances of an individual being victimized by a nonstranger. Widowed persons were excluded from the following analysis because the number of cases reported was too small to form reliable estimates. Among the other groups, married persons were the least likely to be victims of violence from well known offenders, and persons who had never married were the most likely. Persons who had never married were also most likely to be victimized by a casual acquaintance. Divorced or separated persons had the highest rate of violent crimes committed by relatives.

Fifty-three percent of the 489,460 violent crimes occurring between relatives involved the spouse or the ex-spouse of the victim. Family violence was more likely to involve the victim's spouse than ex-spouse, parents, or children. Violence between parents and children combined accounted for 14% of the crimes between relatives, while violence from other relatives accounted for nearly 33%. ☐

Murder Victims by Weapons Used

| Year | Murder victims, total | Guns | | Cutting or stabbing | Blunt object[1] | Strangulation, hands, fists, feet or pushing | Arson[3] | All other[2] |
		Total	Percent					
1965	8,773	5,015	57.2	2,021	505	894	226	112
1970	13,649	9,039	66.2	2,424	604	1,031	353	198
1975	18,642	12,061	64.7	3,245	1,001	1,646	193	496
1980	21,860	13,650	62.0	4,212	1,094	1,666	291	947
1985	17,545	10,296	58.7	3,694	972	1,491	243	849
1988	17,971	10,895	60.6	3,457	1,126	1,426	255	812
1989	18,954	11,832	62.4	3,458	1,128	1,416	234	886
1990	20,045	12,847	64.1	3,503	1,075	1,424	287	909
1991	21,505	14,265	66.3	3,405	1,082	1,519	194	1,040
1992	22,540	15,377	68.2	3,265	1,029	1,434	203	1,232
1993	23,271	16,189	69.6	2,957	1,024	1,493	217	1,391

1. Refers to club, hammer, etc. 2. Includes poison, explosives, unknown, drowning, asphyxiation, narcotics, other means, and weapons not stated. 3. Before 1973, includes drowning. Source: Department of Justice, Federal Bureau of Investigation, Uniform Crime Reports for the United States, 1993, released Dec. 4, 1994.

National Missing Children's Day

On May 25, 1979, Etan Patz vanished from the streets of New York City on his way to school. The massive search and media attention that were to follow helped to focus the Nation on the problem of child abduction and the lack of a national plan to address it.

In 1982, President Ronald Reagan signed into law the Missing Children Act, and in 1983, he proclaimed May 25 National Missing Children's Day.

Child victimization can often be prevented through education. The National Center for Missing and Exploited Children (NCMEC) believes that families should be careful, but they do not need to live in fear. Children can be taught what they need to know to keep themselves safe. For free information on child protection, write to NCMEC at 2101 Wilson Boulevard, Suite 550, Arlington, VA 22201, or call at 800–843–5678. ☐

Prison Offenders

According to a recent study by U.S. Department of Justice's Bureau of Justice Statistics, most Federal prisoners are drug offenders, but almost half of state prisoners are serving time for violent crimes.

About 58% of Federal prisoners are being held for drug law violations—more than 42% for drug trafficking, and about 15% for other types of drug crimes.

Among state inmates, approximately 21% are confined for drug offenses—about 13% for drug trafficking and 8% for other drug offenses. ☐

Law Enforcement Officers Killed or Assaulted: 1983 to 1992

(Covers officers killed feloniously and accidentally in line of duty; includes federal officers. 1988 excludes Florida and Kentucky.)

	1992	1991	1990	1989	1988	1987	1986	1985	1984	1983
Northeast	16	7	13	23	17	24	15	19	21	20
Midwest	15	20	20	22	18	31	19	23	22	26
South	68	29	68	68	77	51	62	64	69	64
West	23	7	23	23	39	40	29	29	32	34
Puerto Rico	6	7	8	8	1	1	6	10	3	6
Total killed	**128**	**70**	**132**	**146**	**155**	**147**	**131**	**148**	**147**	**152**
Assaults										
Population (1,000)[1]	217,997	191,397	199,065	189,641	186,418	190,025	196,030	198,935	195,794	198,341
Number of—										
Agencies	10,682	9,263	9,483	9,023	8,866	8,957	9,755	9,906	10,002	9,908
Police officers	460,430	405,069	412,314	380,232	369,743	378,977	380,249	389,808	372,268	377,620
Firearm	4,455	3,532	3,662	3,154	2,759	2,789	2,852	2,793	2,654	3,067
Knife or cutting instrument	2,095	1,493	1,641	1,379	1,367	1,561	1,614	1,715	1,662	1,829
Other dangerous weapon	8,604	7,014	7,390	5,778	5,573	5,685	5,721	5,263	5,148	5,527
Hands, fists, feet, etc.	66,098	50,813	59,101	51,861	49,053	53,807	54,072	51,953	50,689	51,901
Total assaulted	**81,252**	**62,852**	**71,794**	**62,172**	**58,752**	**63,842**	**64,259**	**61,724**	**60,153**	**62,324**

1. Represents the number of persons covered by agencies shown. NOTE: Data are latest available. *Source: Statistical Abstract of the United States, 1994.*

Crime Index by State, 1993

State	Crime index total	Rate per 100,000 inhabitants	Violent crime	Property crime	Murder and non-negligent manslaughter	State	Crime index total	Rate per 100,000 inhabitants	Violent crime	Property crime	Murder and non-negligent manslaughter
Ala.	204,274	4,878.8	32,676	171,598	484	Mont.	40,188	4,790.0	1,489	38,699	25
Alas.	33,352	5,567.9	4,557	28,795	54	Neb.	66,162	4,117.1	5,450	60,712	63
Ariz.	292,513	7,431.7	28,142	264,371	339	Nev.	85,842	6,180.1	12,157	73,685	144
Ark.	116,612	4,810.7	14,381	102,231	247	N.H.	32,681	2,905.0	1,550	31,131	23
Calif.	2,015,265	6,456.9	336,381	1,678,884	4,096	N.J.	378,257	4,800.8	49,390	328,867	418
Colo.	197,085	5,526.8	20,229	176,856	206	N.M.	101,260	6,266.1	15,024	86,236	130
Conn.	152,392	4,650.4	14,949	137,443	206	N.Y.	1,010,176	5,551.3	195,352	814,824	2,420
Del.	34,105	4,872.1	4,801	29,304	35	N.C.	392,555	5,652.3	47,178	345,377	785
D.C.	67,979	11,761.1	16,888	51,091	454	N.D.	17,909	2,820.3	522	17,387	11
Fla.	1,142,338	8,351.0	164,975	977,363	1,224	Ohio	497,465	4,485.3	55,915	441,550	667
Ga.	428,367	6,193.0	50,019	378,348	789	Okla.	171,058	5,294.3	20,512	150,546	273
Hi.	73,566	6,277.0	3,061	70,505	45	Ore.	174,812	5,765.6	15,254	159,558	140
Idaho	42,258	3,845.1	3,097	39,161	32	Pa.	394,136	3,271.4	50,295	343,841	823
Ill.	657,129	5,617.9	112,260	544,869	1,332	P.R.	121,029	n.a.	26,336	94,693	948
Ind.	255,090	4,465.1	27,941	227,149	430	R.I.	44,990	4,499.0	4,017	40,973	39
Iowa	108,239	3,846.4	9,159	99,080	66	S.C.	215,060	5,093.4	37,281	177,779	377
Kan.	125,924	4,975.3	12,564	113,360	161	S.D.	21,151	2,958.2	1,490	19,661	24
Ky.	123,509	3,259.7	17,530	105,979	249	Tenn.	267,164	5,239.5	39,047	228,117	521
La.	294,061	6,846.6	45,600	248,461	874	Tex.	1,161,031	6,439.1	137,419	1,023,612	2,147
Me.	39,077	3,153.9	1,558	37,519	20	Utah	97,415	5,237.4	5,599	91,816	58
Md.	303,187	6,106.5	49,540	253,647	632	Vt.	22,881	3,972.4	658	22,223	21
Mass.	294,224	4,893.9	48,393	245,831	233	Va.	267,135	4,115.5	24,160	242,975	539
Mich.	516,788	5,452.5	75,021	441,767	933	Wash.	312,793	5,952.3	27,040	285,753	271
Minn.	198,125	4,386.2	14,778	183,347	155	W. Va.	46,093	2,532.6	3,793	42,300	126
Miss.	116,775	4,418.3	11,447	105,308	357	Wis.	204,244	4,054.1	13,321	190,923	222
Mo.	266,694	5,095.4	38,963	227,731	590	Wyo.	19,566	4,163.0	1,345	18,221	16

Source: F.B.I. Uniform Crime Reports for the United States, 1993, published December 1994. NOTE: The Crime Index is composed of the violent and property crime categories. In 1993, 14% of the Index offenses reported to law enforcement agencies were violent crimes and 86% were property crimes. Violent crimes are murder, forcible rape, robbery, and aggravated assault. Property crimes are burglary, larceny–theft, and auto–theft. Data are not included for the property crime of arson. n.a. = not available.

Prisoners Under Sentence of Death[1]

Characteristic	1992	1991	1990	Characteristic	1992	1991	1990
White	1,519	1,450	1,368	Marital status:			
Black and other	1,075	1,016	978	Never married	1,141	1,071	998
Under 20 years	12	14	8	Married	665	663	632
20–24 years	189	179	168	Divorced or separated[2]	788	746	726
25–34 years	1,088	1,087	1,110	Time elapsed since sentencing:			
35–54 years	1,220	1,129	1,006	Less than 12 months	265	252	231
55 years and over	85	73	64	12–47 months	731	718	753
				48–71 months	450	441	438
Schooling completed:				72 months and over	1,148	1,071	934
7 years or less	182	173	178	Legal status at arrest:			
8 years	182	181	186	Not under sentence	1,493	1,415	1,345
9–11 years	841	810	775	On parole or probation[3]	704	615	578
12 years	840	783	729	In prison or escaped	101	102	128
More than 12 years	234	222	209	Unknown	296	321	305
Unknown	315	313	279	**Total**	**2,594**	**2,466**	**2,346**

1. For 1990 and 1991 revisions to the total number of prisoners were not carried to the characteristics except for race. 2. Includes widows, widowers, and unknown. 3. Includes persons on mandatory conditional release, work release, leave, AWOL, or bail covers 28 in 1990, and 29 in 1991 and 1992. NOTE: As of Dec. 31. Excludes prisoners under sentence of death confined in local correctional systems pending appeal or who had not been committed to prison. *Source:* U.S. Bureau of Justice Statistics, *Capital Punishment,* annual, from *Statistical Abstract of the United States, 1994.*

Methods of Execution[1]

State	Method	State	Method
Alabama	Electrocution	Nevada	Lethal injection
Alaska	No death penalty	New Hampshire	Lethal injection
Arizona	Lethal injection[9]	New Jersey	Lethal injection[4]
Arkansas	Lethal injection	New Mexico	Lethal injection
California	Lethal gas	New York	Lethal injection
Colorado	Lethal injection[6]	North Carolina	Lethal gas or injection
Connecticut	Lethal injection	North Dakota	No death penalty
Delaware	Lethal injection[2]	Ohio	Electrocution
D.C.	No death penalty	Oklahoma	Lethal injection
Florida	Electrocution	Oregon	Lethal injection[4]
Georgia	Electrocution	Pennsylvania	Lethal injection
Hawaii	No death penalty	Rhode Island	No death penalty
Idaho	Lethal injection[8]	South Carolina	Electrocution
Illinois	Lethal injection	South Dakota	Lethal injection
Indiana	Lethal injection	Tennessee	Electrocution
Iowa	No death penalty	Texas	Lethal injection
Kansas	Lethal injection	Utah	Firing squad or lethal injection
Kentucky	Electrocution	Vermont	No death penalty
Louisiana	Lethal injection	Virginia	Electrocution or lethal injection[10]
Maine	No death penalty	Washington[5]	Hanging or lethal injection
Maryland	Lethal injection	West Virginia	No death penalty
Massachusetts	No death penalty	Wisconsin	No death penalty
Michigan	No death penalty	Wyoming	Lethal injection
Minnesota	No death penalty	U.S. (Fed. Govt.)	([3])
Mississippi	Lethal injection[7]	American Samoa	No death penalty
Missouri	Lethal injection	Guam	No death penalty
Montana	Hanging, or lethal injection[5]	Puerto Rico	No death penalty
Nebraska	Electrocution	Virgin Islands	No death penalty

1. On July 1, 1976, by a 7–2 decision, the U.S. Supreme Court upheld the death penalty as not being "cruel or unusual." However, in another ruling the same day, the Court, by a 5–4 vote, stated that states may not impose "mandatory" capital punishment on every person convicted of murder. These decisions left uncertain the fate of condemned persons throughout the U.S. On Oct. 4, the Court refused to reconsider its July ruling, which allows some states to proceed with executions of condemned prisoners. The first execution in this country since 1967 was in Utah on Jan. 17, 1977. Gary Mark Gilmore was executed by shooting. 2. Prisoners originally sentenced to death prior to June 1986 may opt instead to hang. Those sentenced after June 1986 have no choice but lethal injection. 3. Is that of the state in which the inmate was sentenced. If that state makes no provision for the death penalty, the trial court designates another state. 4. Death penalty has been passed, but not been used. 5. Defendant may choose between hanging and a lethal injection. 6. Applies to offenses committed on or after July, 1 1988. Prior to that date the method of execution was lethal gas. 7. Prisoners sentenced prior to July 1, 1984, shall be executed by lethal gas. 8. If the director of the Idaho Department of Corrections finds it impractical to carry out a lethal injection, he may instead use a firing squad. 9. Defendant sentenced to death for an offense committed before Nov. 23, 1992, shall choose either lethal injection or lethal gas. 10. Beginning January 1995 inmates may choose lethal injection instead of electrocution. *Source: Information Please* questionnaires to the states.

Motor Vehicle Laws, 1994

State	Age for license Motor-cycle	Moped	Age for driver's license[1] Regular	Learner's	Restrictive	Driver's license duration	Fee	Annual safety inspection required
Alabama	14	14	16	15[5]	14[11]	4 yrs.	$20.00	no[15]
Alaska	16	14	16	14	14[6, 11]	5	15.00	no[15]
Arizona	16	16	18	15 7 mo.[5, 6]	16[6]	Until 60	10/25.00	no[16, 18]
Arkansas	16	10[10]	16	14–16[5]	14[6, 9]	4	14.00	yes
California	18[19]	16[19]	18	15[4, 7]	16[4]	4	12.00	no[18]
Colorado	16	16	21	15 9 mo.[6, 9]	15 1/4[6, 8, 9]	5	15.00	no[18]
Connecticut	16	16	16[4]	16[4]	16[4]	4	28.50/43.50	no
Delaware	18[19]	16	18	15 10 mo.[4]	16[4, 6]	5	12.50	yes
D.C.	16	16	18	(5, 7)	16[6]	4	20.00	yes[21]
Florida	15	15	16	15[5]	15[6]	4 or 6	20.00	no[18]
Georgia	16	15	16	15	16[6]	4	15.00	no[18]
Hawaii	15	15	18	15[5, 7]	15[6]	4[12]	6/12.00	yes
Idaho	16[19]	16[19]	17	16[4, 5, 7]	15[3, 4]	4	19.50	no
Illinois	18	16[19]	18	(5)	16[4, 6]	4 or 5	10.00	no[18]
Indiana	16	15	18	16[8, 9]	16 1 mo.[4, 6]	4[13]	6.00	no[18]
Iowa	16[19]	14	18	14	14[4, 6]	4[2]	8/16.00	no[15]
Kansas	14	14	16	(5)	14	4	8/14.00	no[15]
Kentucky	16	16	18	(5)	16[6]	4	10.00	no
Louisiana	15	15[27]	16[27]	16[6]	17[3]	4	18.00	yes[21]
Maine	16[4]	15[4]	17	15[4, 7]	16[4]	6	30.00	yes
Maryland	18[19]	16	18[28]	15 9 mo.[5, 9]	16[4, 6]	5	30.00	no[17, 20]
Massachusetts	17	16	17	(5)	16 1/3[4, 6]	5	33.75	yes[21]
Michigan	18[19]	15	18		16[4, 6]	2 or 4	6/12.00	no
Minnesota	18[22]	15	18	(5)	16[4]	4	18.50/37.50	no[15]
Mississippi	15	15	15	(5)		4	20.00	yes
Missouri	15.5[4]	16	16	15 1/2[23]	15 1/2[23]	3	7.50	yes[18]
Montana	15[4]	15[4]	18	(5)	15[4, 6]	4	16.00	no
Nebraska	16	16	16	15[7]	14	4	15.00	no
Nevada	16	15.5	18	15 1/2[5]		4	14/19.00	no[18]
New Hampshire	18[19]	16[4]	18		16[4]	4	32.00	yes[21]
New Jersey	17	15	17		16	4	16./17.50	yes
New Mexico	16	13	16	15[4]	14[9]	4	13.00	no[24]
New York	17	16	17[4]	16	16[6]	5	22.25	yes[17]
North Carolina	18	16	16	15[4, 6, 9]	16	5	10.00	yes
North Dakota	16	14	16	(5)	14[4, 6]	4	10.00	no[15]
Ohio	18	14	18	16[5, 6]	14[11]	4	10.75	no[15, 17]
Oklahoma	16	16	16	(8)	15 1/2[4]	4	18.00	yes
Oregon	16[19]	16	16	15[5]	14	4	26.25	no[15, 25]
Pennsylvania	16	16	16	16[6, 7]	16[6]	4	27.00	yes
Rhode Island	16	16	16	(5)	16[4]	5	30.00	yes
South Carolina	16	14	16	15[9]	15	5	10.00	yes
South Dakota	16	14	16	14[7]	14[3]	5	8.00	no
Tennessee	16	14	16	15[7]	15	4	19.50	no
Texas	18[19]	15	16[4]	15	15[4, 7]	4	16.00	yes[17]
Utah	16	16	16[4, 6]	16	15 9 mo.[8, 9]	5	15/20.00	yes[17]
Vermont	18	16	18	15[5, 9]	16[7]	2 or 4	12/20.00	yes
Virginia	18[19]	16	18	16[4, 6]	15 8 mo.[5, 6, 7]	5	12.00	yes[26]
Washington	18[19]	16	18	15[8]	16[4]	4	14.00	no[14]
West Virginia	18[19]	16	18	15[5]	15[6]	4	10.50	yes
Wisconsin	18[19]	16	18	15 1/2[5]	16[4, 6]	4	15.00	no
Wyoming	18	15[22]	16	15[6, 7]	15[6, 7]	4	20.00	no

1. Full driving privileges at age given in "Regular" column. A license restricted or qualified in some manner may be obtained at age given in "Restricted" column. 2. 2 years if under 18 or over 70. 3. Hours of operation restricted. 4. Must have completed approved driver education course. 5. Learner's permit required. 6. Guardian's or parental consent required. 7. Driver with learner's permit must be accompanied by locally licensed operator 18 years or older. 8. Must be enrolled in driver education course. 9. Driver with learner's permit must be accompanied by locally licensed operator 21 years or older. 10. Up to 50 cc. 11. Restricted to mopeds. 12. 2 years if 15–24 or over 65. 13. 3 years if over 75. 14. Individual inspection upon reasonable grounds. 15. State troopers are authorized to inspect at their discretion. 16. Arizona emission inspection fee $5.40. 17. Annual emissions test in some counties. 18. Annual emissions test in some counties. 19. 18; 16, if approved driver training course completed. 20. All used vehicles upon resale or transfer. 21. Required on out–of–state or salvaged vehicles. Emissions tested in some counties. 22. May obtain instruction permit with motorcycle endorsement. 23. Driver with learner's permit must be accompanied by a licensed parent or guardian. 24. Emission test every two years in Bernalillo County. 25. Biennial emission inspection in the Portland metro area and Rogue Valley. 26. Emission test required in some areas. 27. All first-time new licensees must complete state-approved pre-licensing course. 28. All new drivers must complete 3-hour alcohol-awareness program. NOTES: A driver's license is required in every state. All states have an *implied consent* Chemical Test Law for alcohol. *Source:* Reprinted with permission of the American Automobile Association, Heathrow, Fla.

EDUCATION

Parental Choice in Education: Home Schooling

The option of teaching children at home is appealing to more parents

One of the changing family roles in the United States is the growing phenomenon of home education. A Department of Education Survey taken 1990–1991 estimated that 250,000 to 300,000 children were taught at home. The Virginia-based Home School Defense Association (HSLDA) founded in March 1983 estimates that the current figure may be as high as one million or about one to two percent of the U.S. school population. It appears that the number of parent-taught children is growing at 15–20% annually, and that it will continue to grow as more families who are dissatisfied with public school education become aware of home schooling as an option.

Home schooling is legal in all 50 states, and each state sets its own laws governing home education. The requirements may be as simple as informing the school district of your intent to home school and having your child tested or as complex as fulfilling requirements to become a private school.

The Department of Defense recognizes home schooling as legal for U.S. military families at home and abroad and has instituted regulations regarding home education. This action is a boon to military home schoolers who are often reassigned and must relocate with their children to other geographic areas.

The Home School Family

Several studies have shown that a wide diversity of people teach their kids at home. Most parents are Christians who place a strong emphasis on orthodox and conservative biblical doctrine, and over 90% are white/Anglo in terms of racial/ethnic background.

According to the Home School Defense Association, both parents are actively involved with the mother/homemaker teaching most of the time. The learning program is flexible and highly individualized, involving both homemade and purchased curriculum materials. The children's formal instruction begins at 5.5 years of age and male and female students are equally represented. About 65% of the students are 5 to 11 years old. The children are "schooled" from three to four hours per day in a wide range of conventional subjects with an emphasis on math, reading, and science. They often spend additional time in individual learning endeavors.

Because the children have relatively little interaction with the public school system or its services, opponents of home education claim that this "social isolation" does not give these children a chance to learn social skills.

Two-parent families seem to be the norm for home school families and they typically have three children. Almost half of the parents have graduated from college and have two to three more years of formal education than adults in general nationwide. The family's median home income in 1990 was in the $30,000 to $40,000 category and was over $50,000 for 20% of the families.

Does Home Schooling Work?

Generally speaking, children who are taught by their parents have repeatedly scored above national averages on standardized achievement tests and have been accepted into hundreds of colleges and universities.

The question of "socialization" frequently comes up when home education is discussed. Do home schoolers need the experience of socializing with large groups of their peers in a conventional classroom in order to acquire necessary social skills? Several studies have shown that the home-educated appear to do as well in terms of participation in non-academic activities and measures of social and emotional adjustment.

In 1990, Dr. Brian Ray, president of the Salem, Oregon, National Home Education Research Institute, collected nationwide data on 1,516 home education families and about 4,600 children for the National Center for Home Education in Paeonian Springs, Virginia. The study found these home-educated children to average at or above the 80th percentile in all subject areas (the national average for conventionally schooled children is the 50th percentile).

The 2.2 million-plus member National Education Association (NEA) headquartered in Washington, D.C., disagrees with home educators on the issues of socialization, curriculums, and qualification requirements for parent-teachers.

The NEA believes that home schooling programs cannot provide the student with a comprehensive education experience.

The NEA believes that if parental preference home schooling study occurs, students enrolled must meet all state requirements and be taught by persons who are licensed by the appropriate state education licensure agency, and a curriculum approved by the state department of education should be used.

The Association further believes that such home schooling programs should be limited to children of the immediate family, with all expenses paid by the parents.—*Ed.*

Sources

The Home School Legal Defense Association, Post Office Box 159, Paeonian Springs, VA 22129. (703) 338-5600.

National Home Education Research Institute, Western Baptist College, 5000 Deer Park Drive, S.E., Salem, OR 97301.

The Teaching Home magazine, "Questions & Answers," Box 20219, Portland, OR 97220-0219.

The National Education Association, 1201 16th Street, N.W., Washington, D.C. 20036. (202) 833-4000.

School Enrollment, October 1994

(in thousands)

Age	White Enrolled	White Percent	Black Enrolled	Black Percent	Hispanic origin[1] Enrolled	Hispanic origin[1] Percent	Total Enrolled	Total Percent
3 and 4 years	3,059	47.0	697	51.9	376	30.8	3,917	47.3
5 and 6 years	6,052	96.6	1,296	97.2	1,065	96.1	7,752	96.7
7 to 9 years	9,057	99.2	1,832	99.7	1,483	99.2	11,487	99.3
10 to 13 years	12,095	99.3	2,398	99.6	2,025	99.4	15,281	99.4
14 and 15 years	5,909	98.7	1,220	99.2	904	96.1	7,519	98.8
16 and 17 years	5,421	94.3	1,151	95.4	784	88.3	6,895	94.4
18 and 19 years	3,386	60.9	549	54.0	475	51.4	4,180	60.2
20 and 21 years	2,532	46.2	371	34.9	252	24.9	3,133	44.9
22 to 24 years	2,149	23.5	356	22.6	240	15.1	2,724	24.1
25 to 29 years	1,625	10.4	264	10.5	197	8.1	2,070	10.8
30 to 34 years	1,197	6.6	203	7.2	146	5.7	1,468	6.7
Total	**52,482**	**52.6**	**10,337**	**56.4**	**7,947**	**49.0**	**66,427**	**53.3**

1. Persons of Hispanic origin may be of any race. NOTE: Figures include persons enrolled in nursery school, kindergarten, elementary school, high school, and college. *Source:* Department of Commerce, Bureau of the Census.

Persons Not Enrolled in School, October 1994

(in thousands)

Age	Population	Total not enrolled Number	Total not enrolled Percent	High school graduate Number	High school graduate Percent	Not high school graduate (dropouts)[1] Number	Not high school graduate (dropouts)[1] Percent
14 and 15 years	7,612	93	1.2	2	—	93	1.2
16 and 17 years	7,307	411	5.6	198	2.7	362	5.0
18 and 19 years	6,946	2,767	39.8	4,888	70.4	929	13.4
20 and 21 years	6,981	3,848	55.1	5,902	84.5	974	14.0
22 to 24 years	11,327	8,603	76.0	9,791	86.4	1,462	12.9

1. Persons who are not enrolled in school and who are not high school graduates are considered dropouts. *Source:* Department of Commerce, Bureau of the Census.

School Enrollment by Grade, Control, and Race

(in thousands)

Grade level and type of control	White Oct. 1994[3]	White Oct. 1990[3]	White Oct. 1980[4]	Black Oct. 1994[3]	Black Oct. 1990[3]	Black Oct. 1980[4]	All races[1] Oct. 1994[3]	All races[1] Oct. 1990[3]	All races[1] Oct. 1980[4]
Nursery school: Public	1,330	896	432	513	283	180	1,940	1,212	633
Private	2,046	1,961	1,205	208	148	115	2,320	2,188	1,354
Kindergarten: Public	2,505	2,609	2,172	603	574	440	3,278	3,322	2,690
Private	504	472	423	58	62	50	585	567	486
Grades 1–8: Public	21,902	20,997	19,743	4,709	4,431	4,058	28,131	26,615	24,398
Private	2,882	2,359	2,768	379	199	202	3,382	2,676	3,051
Grades 9–12: Public	10,515	9,429	12,056[2]	2,312	1,937	2,200[2]	13,539	11,911	14,556[2]
Private	916	810	—	120	65	—	1,077	906	—
College: Public	9,472	9,049	8,875[2]	1,439	1,120	1,007[2]	11,693	10,754	10,180[2]
Private	2,751	2,439	—	362	274	—	3,327	2,869	—
Total: Public	45,724	42,954	—	9,576	8,344	—	58,581	53,823	—
Private	9,099	8,041	—	1,127	748	—	10,691	9,204	—
Grand Total	**54,823**	**50,995**	**47,673**	**10,703**	**9,092**	**8,251**	**69,272**	**63,027**	**57.348**

1. Includes persons of Hispanic origin. 2. Total public and private. Breakdown not available. 3. Estimates controlled to 1980 census base. 4. Estimates controlled to 1970 census base. *Source:* Department of Commerce, Bureau of the Census.

State Compulsory School Attendance Laws, March 1994

State	Enactment[1]	Age limits	State	Enactment[1]	Age limits
Alabama	1915	7–16	Montana[7]	1883	7–16
Alaska[2]	1929	7–16	Nebraska	1887	7–16
Arizona[3]	1899	6–16	Nevada	1873	7–17
Arkansas	1909	5–17	New Hampshire	1871	6–16
California	1874	6–18	New Jersey	1875	6–16
Colorado	1889	7–16	New Mexico	1891	5–16
Connecticut	1872	7–16	New York[8]	1874	6–16
Delaware	1907	5–16	North Carolina	1907	7–16
D. C.	1864	7–17	North Dakota	1883	7–16
Florida	1915	6–16	Ohio	1877	6–18
Georgia	1916	7–16	Oklahoma	1907	5–18
Hawaii	1896	6–18	Oregon	1889	7–18
Idaho	1887	7–16	Pennsylvania	1895	8–17
Illinois	1883	7–16	Rhode Island	1883	6–16
Indiana[4]	1897	7–16	South Carolina[9]	1915	5–17
Iowa	1902	6–16	South Dakota[7]	1883	7–16
Kansas	1874	7–16	Tennessee	1905	7–17
Kentucky[5]	1896	6–16	Texas	1915	6–17
Louisiana	1910	7–17	Utah	1890	6–18
Maine	1875	7–17	Vermont	1867	7–16
Maryland	1902	5–16	Virginia	1908	5–18
Massachusetts	1852	6–16	Washington[10]	1871	8–18
Michigan	1871	6–16	West Virginia	1897	6–16
Minnesota[6]	1885	7–16	Wisconsin[11]	1879	6–18
Mississippi	1918	6–16	Wyoming	1876	7–16
Missouri	1905	7–16			

1. Date of enactment of first compulsory attendance law. 2. Ages 7 to 16 or high school graduation. 3. Ages 6 to 16 or tenth grade completion. 4. Students between 16 and 18 are required to submit to an exit interview and have written parental approval before leaving high school. 5. Must have parental signature for leaving school between ages of 16 and 18. 6. Will change to 7 to 18 in year 2000. 7. May leave after completion of eighth grade. 8. The ages are 6 to 17 for New York City and Buffalo. 9. Permits parental waiver of kindergarten at age 5. 10. Or can exit if age 15 and has completed grade 8, has a useful occupation, has met graduation requirements, or has certificate of education competency. 11. Ages 6 to 18 or high school graduation. *Source:* Department of Education, National Center for Educational Statistics, which prepared this table February 1993.

High School and College Graduates

School Year	High School			College[1]		
	Men	Women	Total	Men	Women	Total
1900	38,075	56,808	94,883	22,173	5,237	27,410
1910	63,676	92,753	156,429	28,762	8,437	37,199
1920	123,684	187,582	311,266	31,980	16,642	48,622
1929–30	300,376	366,528	666,904	73,615	48,869	122,484
1939–40	578,718	642,757	1,221,475	109,546	76,954	186,500
1949–50	570,700	629,000	1,199,700	328,841	103,217	432,058
1959–60	898,000	966,000	1,864,000	254,063	138,377	392,440
1969–70	1,433,000	1,463,000	2,896,000	484,174	343,060	827,234
1974–75	1,541,000	1,599,000	3,140,000	533,797	425,052	978,849
1977–78	1,535,000	1,599,000	3,134,000	487,000	434,000	921,000
1978–79	1,531,800	1,602,400	3,134,200	529,996	460,242	990,238
1979–80	1,500,000	1,558,000	3,058,000	526,327	473,221	999,548
1980–81	1,483,000	1,537,000	3,020,000	470,000	465,000	935,000
1981–82	1,474,000	1,527,000	3,001,000	473,000	480,000	953,000
1982–83	1,437,000	1,451,000	2,888,000	479,140	490,370	969,510
1983–84	n.a.	n.a.	2,767,000	482,319	491,990	974,309
1984–85	n.a.	n.a.	2,677,000	482,528	496,949	979,477
1985–86	n.a.	n.a.	2,643,000	485,923	501,900	987,823
1986–87	n.a.	n.a.	2,694,000	480,854	510,485	991,339
1987–88	n.a.	n.a.	2,773,000	477,203	517,626	994,829
1988–89	n.a.	n.a.	2,727,000	483,346	535,409	1,018,755
1989–90	n.a.	n.a.	2,588,000[2]	491,696	559,648	1,051,344
1990–91	n.a.	n.a.	2,503,000[2]	504,045	590,493	1,094,538
1991–92	n.a.	n.a.	2,471,000[2]	520,811[2]	615,742[2]	1,136,553[2]
1992–93[3]	n.a.	n.a.	2,512,000[2]	529,000[4]	616,000[4]	1,145,000[4]
1993–94[3]	n.a.	n.a.	2,513,000	537,000[4]	628,000[4]	1,165,000[4]

1. Bachelors's degrees. Includes first-professional degrees for years 1900–1960. 2. Revised from previously published data. 3. Public high school graduates based on state estimates. 4. Projected. n.a. = not available. NOTE: Includes graduates from public and private schools. Beginning in 1959–60, figures include Alaska and Hawaii. Because of rounding, details may not add to totals. Most recent data available. *Source:* Department of Education, Center for Education Statistics.

Federal Funds for Some Major Programs for Education, Fiscal Year 1996[1]

Program	Amount in thousands	Program	Amount in thousands
Elementary-secondary		**Vocational and adult education**	$1,669,000
Educationally disadvantaged	$7,441,000	**Education for the handicapped**	
School improvement programs	1,510,000	Special education	3,342,000
Bilingual education	300,000	Rehabilitation services and	
School assistance in federally		disability research	2,457,000
affected areas	619,000	All other	130,000
Higher education		**Indian education**	85,000
Student financial assistance	5,914,000	**Education research and improvement**	540,000
Higher education facliities loans	7,000	**Total**	**$24,061,000**
College housing loans	47,000		

1. Estimated outlay for fiscal year 1995. *Source: Budget of the United States Government,* Fiscal Year 1996.

Funding for Public Elementary and Secondary Education, 1985–86 to 1991–92

(In thousands except percent)

School year	Total	Federal	State	Local[1]	% Federal	& State	% Local[1]
1985–86	149,127,779	9,975,622	73,619,575	65,532,582	6.7	49.4	43.9
1986–87	158,523,693	10,146,013	78,830,437	69,547,243	6.4	49.7	43.9
1987–88	169,561,974	10,716,687	84,004,415	74,840,873	6.3	49.5	44.1
1988–89	191,210,310	11,872,419	91,158,363	88,179,529	6.2	47.4	46.1
1989–90	207,752,932	12,700,784	98,238,633	96,813,516	6.1	47.3	46.6
1990–91[2]	223,340,537	13,776,066	105,324,533	104,239,939	6.2	47.2	46.7
1991–92	234,485,729	15,493,330	108,792,779	110,199,621	6.6	46.4	47.0

1. Includes a relatively small amount from nongovernmental sources (gifts and tuition and transportation fees from patrons). 2. Revised from previously published figures. *Source:* U.S. Department of Education, National Center for Education Statistics, which prepared this table April 1994.

Major U.S. College and University Libraries—1993–94

(Top 50 based on number of volumes in library)

Institution	Volumes	Microforms[1]	Institution	Volumes	Microforms[1]
Harvard	12,877,360	7,244,390	Pennsylvania State	3,534,834	3,166,502
Yale	9,485,823	4,671,945	Rutgers	3,419,767	4,838,443
U of Illinois–Urbana	8,474,737	4,177,679	New York	3,335,176	3,417,044
U of California–Berkeley	8,078,685	5,379,562	U of Kansas	3,292,923	2,797,658
U of Texas	7,019,508	5,062,330	U of Southern California	3,232,617	4,090,605
U of Michigan	6,664,081	5,097,050	U of Georgia	3,215,717	5,204,977
Columbia	6,532,066	4,809,185	U of Pittsburgh	3,201,394	3,134,543
U of California–Los Angeles	6,460,391	5,612,521	U of Florida	3,092,189	5,586,785
Stanford	6,409,239	4,263,916	Johns Hopkins	3,061,736	2,562,936
U of Chicago	5,710,003	2,039,956	Washington U–St. Louis	3,045,378	2,576,767
Cornell	5,697,525	6,507,593	Arizona State	3,019,670	6,176,776
Indiana	5,554,529	3,442,457	SUNY–Buffalo	2,864,268	4,403,522
U of Wisconsin	5,535,592	4,139,554	Rochester	2,843,283	4,020,435
U of Washington	5,355,140	6,070,069	Wayne State	2,833,977	3,346,213
Princeton	5,186,097	3,436,709	U of Hawaii	2,786,852	5,488,805
U of Minnesota	5,101,275	4,910,404	Syracuse	2,780,040	3,273,792
Ohio State	4,786,385	3,822,981	Louisiana State	2,778,482	4,891,220
Duke	4,330,108	3,004,538	U of California–Davis	2,725,302	3,315,050
U of Pennsylvania	4,209,745	2,824,013	Brown	2,709,732	1,442,662
North Carolina	4,154,897	3,727,664	U of Missouri	2,683,566	5,334,134
U of Arizona	4,126,225	4,624,724	South Carolina	2,639,171	4,075,413
U of Virginia	4,059,252	4,224,549	U of Massachusetts	2,634,277	2,062,096
Michigan State	3,904,095	4,883,791	U of Colorado	2,575,290	5,319,494
Northwestern	3,709,164	2,898,653	U of Kentucky	2,556,807	5,239,342
Iowa	3,567,227	5,346,476	U of Oklahoma	2,484,094	3,394,894

1. Includes reels of microfilm and number of microcards, microprint sheets, and microfiches. *Source:* Association of Research Libraries.

College and University Endowments, 1993–94
(top 75 in millions of dollars)

Institution	Endowment (market value)	Voluntary support[1]	Expenditures[2]	Institution	Endowment (market value)	Voluntary support[1]	Expenditures[2]
Harvard U	$6,201.2	$289.1	$1,390.9	Boston C	449.7	20.5	216.7
Yale U	3,537.2	184.4	815.6	Smith C	442.1	28.0	92.3
Stanford U	3,212.5	226.1	907.4	Texas Christian U	439.9	16.6	86.4
Princeton U	3,146.6	85.6	359.4	Southern Methodist U	434.5	17.3	149.7
Columbia U	1,952.4	139.6	1,026.9	Loyola U of Chicago	422.7	16.4	261.1
Texas A&M U	1,793.1	91.7	747.0	Williams C	417.5	30.9	64.1
Massachusetts Inst. of Tech.	1,777.8	93.8	763.9	Carnegie–Mellon U	414.7	30.5	316.9
Washington U	1,715.5	62.3	730.6	Grinnell C	413.5	6.8	39.2
Northwestern U	1,619.6	96.8	633.6	Wake Forest U	412.3	32.9	339.3
U of Pennsylvania	1,464.5	259.6	887.1	U of North Carolina–Chapel Hill	407.8	82.7	655.0
Rice U	1,279.0	35.3	166.1	U of Delaware	407.5	20.2	297.3
Cornell U	1,249.0	175.7	972.7	U of Richmond	402.0	20.9	67.0
U of Chicago	1,180.0	86.2	573.7	Pomona C	388.5	16.2	50.1
Mayo Foundation	1,064.1	53.9	211.9	U of Wisconsin–Madison	379.0	147.3	1,048.4
U of Michigan	1,028.2	121.0	1,212.7	Indiana U	375.6	101.2	975.3
Dartmouth C	869.9	73.9	260.4	Lehigh U	354.7	25.5	160.9
U of Notre Dame	847.1	65.0	235.7	Berea C	352.7	11.7	30.1
Vanderbilt U	838.4	79.2	453.6	Boston U	346.9	33.2	669.5
U of Southern California	791.4	222.9	820.8	Trinity U	343.5	11.6	48.3
Johns Hopkins U	745.6	87.0	507.5	Georgetown U	342.4	36.7	392.8
U of California–Berkeley	734.2	99.2	789.0	George Washington U	333.8	23.8	346.5
U of Minnesota	733.9	116.4	1,186.2	U of Kansas	332.9	34.6	261.4
New York U	710.4	101.7	962.5	Amherst C	331.6	18.0	53.8
Duke U	699.0	148.3	600.2	Middlebury C	323.4	9.6	66.9
U of Texas–Austin	674.5	63.1	696.3	Wesleyan U	319.5	9.0	82.1
U of Rochester	656.4	40.1	481.3	Baylor U	318.4	28.8	125.0
U of Virginia	641.1	66.9	452.4	Vassar C	316.3	33.6	71.7
Brown U	622.4	50.6	248.7	Pennsylvania State U	312.3	82.5	1,016.2
California Inst. of Tech.	591.9	62.7	246.8	U of Illinois	308.3	124.2	1,307.9
U of Cincinnati	574.3	38.6	442.7	Washington and Lee U	308.3	22.6	42.3
Rockefeller U	571.2	31.8	96.3	U of Tennessee	304.0	50.0	725.3
Case Western Reserve U	557.1	77.0	312.9	U of Iowa	301.0	59.6	554.0
Purdue U	508.0	54.0	646.5	Lafayette C	288.6	10.7	50.7
Ohio State U	486.0	94.9	885.4	Oberlin C	280.9	10.7	69.7
Wellesley C	484.1	22.8	83.0	Georgia Inst. of Tech.	272.7	38.2	348.3
Macalester C	479.9	3.3	43.3	U of Nebraska	270.8	47.5	567.2
U of California–Los Angeles	464.9	90.9	1,097.6	Tulane U	268.1	41.3	293.8
Swarthmore C	458.1	16.2	57.6				

1. Gifts from alumni, other individuals, corporations, foundations, and other private organizations. 2. Figure represents about 80% of typical operating budget. Does not include auxiliary enterprises and capital outlays. NOTE: C = College; U = University. *Source:* Council for Aid to Education.

Institutions of Higher Education—Average Salaries and Fringe Benefits for Faculty Members, 1970–1993[1]
(in thousands of dollars)

Control and Acadmic Rank	1993	1992	1991	1990	1989	1988	1987	1985	1980	1975	1970
Average Salaries											
Public: All ranks	46.0	45.3	44.0	41.6	39.6	37.2	35.8	31.2	22.1	16.6	13.1
Professor	58.4	57.4	55.8	53.2	50.1	47.2	45.3	39.6	28.8	21.7	17.3
Associate professor	44.1	43.4	42.2	40.3	37.9	35.6	34.2	30.2	21.9	16.7	13.2
Assistant professor	37.0	36.3	35.2	33.5	31.7	29.6	28.5	25.0	18.0	13.7	10.9
Instructor	27.8	27.2	26.3	25.0	23.9	22.2	21.8	19.5	14.8	11.2	9.1
Private:[2] All ranks	51.6	50.0	47.0	45.1	42.4	39.7	37.8	33.0	22.1	16.6	13.1
Professor	68.7	66.1	61.6	59.6	55.9	52.2	50.3	44.1	30.1	22.4	17.8
Associate professor	46.9	45.6	43.2	41.2	38.8	36.6	34.9	30.9	21.0	16.0	12.6
Assistant professor	38.6	37.8	35.5	34.0	31.9	28.3	26.8	23.7	13.0	10.3	
Instructor	28.3	28.5	26.2	26.0	24.1	22.7	20.4	19.0	13.3	10.9	8.6
Average Fringe Benefits—All Ranks Combined											
Public	11.5	11.0	10.5	9.8	9.0	8.2	7.8	7.0	3.9	2.5	1.9
Private[2]	13.1	12.4	11.6	10.9	10.0	9.2	8.6	7.2	4.1	2.8	2.2

1. Figures are for 9 months teaching for full-time faculty members in four-year colleges and universities. 2. Excludes church-related colleges and universities. *Source:* Maryse Eymonerie Associates/American Association of University Professors. Washington, D.C. *AAUP Annual Report on the Economic Status of the Profession.* From *Statistical Abstract of the United States: 1994.* NOTE: Data are latest available.

Accredited U.S. Senior Colleges and Universities, 1995–96

Source: The Guidance Information System (trademark), a product of The Riverside Publishing Company, a Houghton Mifflin company.

Schools listed are four-year institutions that offer at least a Bachelor's degree and are fully accredited by one of the institutional and professional accrediting associations. Included are accredited colleges outside the U.S.

Tuition, room, and board listed are average annual figures (including fees) subject to fluctuation, usually covering two semesters, two out of three trimesters,

or three out of four quarters, depending on the school calendar.

For further information, write to the Registrar of the school concerned.

NOTE: n.a. = information not available. — = does not apply. Enrollment figures are approximate. (C) = Coeducational, (M) = primarily for men, (W) = primarily for women.

Abbreviations used for controls: **P** Private **Pub** Public

Institution and location	Enrollment	Control	Tuition ($)		Rm/Bd ($)
			Res.	Nonres.	
Abilene Christian University; Abilene, Tex. 79699	3,516 (C)	P	7,800	7,800	3,400
Academy of Art College; San Francisco, Calif. 94108–3893	2,156 (C)	P	9,200	9,200	4,900
Academy of the New Church College; Bryn Athyn, Pa. 19009	131 (C)	P	4,440	4,440	3,729
Adams State College; Alamosa, Colo. 81102	2,179 (C)	Pub	1,839	5,481	3,900
Adelphi University; Garden City, N.Y. 11530	3,835 (C)	P	12,730[1]	12,730[1]	6,880[1]
Adrian College; Adrian, Mich. 49221	1,059 (C)	P	11,640	11,640	3,690
Aeronautics, College of; Flushing, N.Y. 11371	1,070 (C)	P	8,800[1]	8,800[1]	n.a.[1]
Agnes Scott College; Decatur, Ga. 30030	568 (W)	P	13,935	13,935	5,800
Akron, University of; Akron, Ohio 44325-2001	22,755 (C)	Pub	3,192[1]	7,954[1]	3,844[1]
Alabama, University of; Tuscaloosa, Ala. 35487-0132	14,995 (C)	Pub	2,374	5,924	4,450[2]
Alabama, University of–Birmingham; Birmingham, Ala. 35294	11,658 (C)	Pub	4,348	8,696	3,454
Alabama, University of–Huntsville; Huntsville, Ala. 35899	5,512 (C)	Pub	2,480[1]	4,960[1]	3,500[1]
Alabama A&M University; Normal, Ala. 35762	3,914 (C)	Pub	1,700	3,400	2,550
Alabama State University; Montgomery, Ala. 36101-0271	5,117 (C)	Pub	1,650	3,250	3,100
Alaska, University of-Anchorage; Anchorage, Alas. 99508	19,624 (C)	Pub	1,886	5,342	2,650
Alaska, University of-Fairbanks; Fairbanks, Alas. 99701	7,393 (C)	Pub	2,490	7,114	3,690
Alaska Southeast, University of; Juneau, Alas. 99801	833 (C)	Pub	1,800	5,968	4,100
Alaska Bible College; Glennallen, Alas. 99588	43 (C)	P	3,300	3,300	3,400
Alaska Pacific University; Anchorage, Alas. 99508	307 (C)	P	7,560	7,560	4,120
Albany College of Pharmacy; Albany, N.Y. 12208	648 (C)	P	9,220[1]	9,220[1]	4,600[1]
Albany State College; Albany, Ga. 31705	2,936 (C)	Pub	1,899	5,109	2,910
Albertson College; Caldwell, Idaho 83605	604 (C)	P	14,100	14,100	3,075
Albertus Magnus College; New Haven, Conn. 06511	510 (C)	P	12,350	12,350	5,664
Albion College; Albion, Mich. 49224	1,641 (C)	P	15,334	15,334	4,850
Albright College; Reading, Pa. 19612-5234	1,277 (C)	P	16,375	16,375	4,820
Alcorn State University; Lorman, Miss. 39096	3,244 (C)	Pub	2,400	4,600	2,160
Alderson-Broaddus College; Philippi, W. Va. 26416	899 (C)	P	11,200	11,200	3,456
Alfred University; Alfred, N.Y. 14802	1,868 (C)	P	17,948	17,948	5,716
Alice Lloyd College; Pippa Passes, Ky. 41844	548 (C)	P	460	3,800	2,960
Allegheny College; Meadville, Pa. 16335	1,854 (C)	P	18,020	18,020	4,550
Allentown College of St. Francis de Sales; Center Valley, Pa. 18034-9568	1,007 (C)	P	10,340	10,340	5,050
Alma College; Alma, Mich. 48801-1599	1,404 (C)	P	13,332	13,332	4,762
Alvernia College; Reading, Pa. 19607–1799	1,249 (C)	P	9,500	9,500	4,400
Alverno College; Milwaukee, Wis. 53234-3922	2,457 (W)	P	8,928	8,928	3,770
Ambassador College; Big Sandy, Tex. 75755	1,111 (C)	P	3,650	3,650	3,000
Amber University; Garland, Tex. 75041	722 (C)	P	3,200	3,200	n.a.
American Baptist College; Nashville, Tenn. 37207	200 (C)	P	4,384	4,384	2,654
American College for the Applied Arts, The; Atlanta, Ga. 30326–1016	810 (C)	P	9,210	9,210	4,050
American College for the Applied Arts, The; Los Angeles, Calif. 90024	472 (C)	P	10,230	10,230	3,825
American College of Switzerland; Switzerland	70 (C)	P	23,372	23,372	7,954
American Conservatory of Music; Chicago, Ill. 60602–4792	n.a. (C)	P	11,200	11,200	n.a.
American International College; Springfield, Mass. 01109	1,010 (C)	P	9,630	9,630	4,775
American University; Washington, D.C. 20016	5,041 (C)	P	16,890	16,890	6,698
American University in Cairo; New York, N.Y. 10017	3,084 (C)	P	9,014	9,014	5,540
American University of Beirut; Beirut, Lebanon	4,371 (C)	P	4,860	4,860	2,860
American University of Paris; 75007 Paris, France	1,025 (C)	P	15,720[3]	15,720[3]	3,952[3]
American Universtity of Puerto Rico; Bayamon, P.R. 00621	4,208 (C)	P	2,500[1]	2,500[1]	n.a.[1]
Amherst College; Amherst, Mass. 01002	1,608 (C)	P	20,710	20,710	5,560
Anderson College; Anderson, SC 29621	932 (C)	P	8,821	8,821	4,145
Anderson University; Anderson, Ind. 46012	2,097 (C)	P	11,240	11,240	3,750
Andrews University; Berrien Springs, Mich. 49104	1,908 (C)	P	10,625	10,625	3,300
Angelo State University; San Angelo, Tex. 76909	5,567 (C)	Pub	1,754	5,984	4,048
Anna Maria College for Men and Women; Paxton, Mass. 01612	402 (C)	P	11,800	11,800	5,028

Institution and location	Enrollment	Control	Tuition ($) Res.	Tuition ($) Nonres.	Rm/Bd ($)
Antillian Adventist University; Mayaguez, P.R. 00709	854 (C)	P	2,850[1]	2,850[1]	3,150[1]
Antioch College; Yellow Springs, Ohio 45387	686 (C)	P	17,376	17,376	3,436
Antioch School for Adult & Experiential Learning; Yellow Springs, Ohio 45387	231 (C)	P	6,660	6,660	n.a.
Antioch Seattle; Seattle, Wash. 98121	176 (C)	P	11,620	11,620	n.a.
Antioch–Southern California at Los Angeles; Marina Del Rey, Calif. 90292	264 (C)	P	9,450	9,450	n.a.
Antioch–Southern California at Santa Barbara; Santa Barbara, Calif. 93101	107 (C)	P	8,550	8,550	n.a.
Appalachian Bible College; Bradley, W. Va. 25818	254 (C)	P	4,900	4,900	2,700
Appalachian State University; Boone, N.C. 28608	10,726 (C)	Pub	1,673	8,358	2,750
Aquinas College; Grand Rapids, Mich. 49506–1799	1,978 (C)	P	11,852	11,852	4,124
Arizona, University of; Tucson, Ariz. 85721	26,468 (C)	Pub	1,950	7,978	4,190
Arizona College of the Bible; Phoenix, Ariz. 85021	90 (C)	P	6,500	6,500	7,500
Arizona State University; Tempe, Ariz. 85287-0112	31,198 (C)	Pub	1,884	8,278	4,680
Arkansas, Univ. of; Fayetteville, Ark. 72701	11,597 (C)	Pub	2,130	5,322	3,687
Arkansas, Univ. of-Little Rock; Little Rock, Ark. 72204	9,403 (C)	Pub	2,136[1]	5,352[1]	3,940[1]
Arkansas, Univ. of-Monticello; Monticello, Ark. 71655	2,398 (C)	Pub	1,762	5,218	4,000
Arkansas, Univ. of-Pine Bluff; Pine Bluff, Ark. 71601–2799	3,709 (C)	Pub	1,818	3,822	2,464
Arkansas Baptist College; Little Rock, Ark. 72202	331 (C)	P	2,000	2,000	6,200
Arkansas College; Batesville, Ark. 72501	701 (C)	P	9,050	9,050	4,196
Arkansas State University; State University, Ark. 72467	8,657 (C)	Pub	1,950	3,600	2,580
Arkansas Tech. University; Russellville, Ark. 72801–2222	4,159 (C)	Pub	1,865	3,685	2,660
Arlington Baptist College; Arlington, Tex. 76012	179 (C)	P	1,795	1,795	3,100
Armstrong State College; Savannah, Ga. 31419	4,839 (C)	Pub	1,719	4,929	3,026
Armstrong University; Berkeley, Calif. 94704	60 (C)	P	6,060	6,060	n.a.
Art Academy of Cincinnati; Cincinnati, Ohio 45202	230 (C)	P	9,990	9,990	n.a.
Art Center College of Design; Pasadena, Calif. 91103	1,158 (C)	P	7,300	7,300	n.a.
Art Institute of Chicago, School of the; Chicago, Ill. 60603	1,422 (C)	P	15,300	15,300	4,880
Art Institute of Southern California; Laguna Beach, Calif. 92651	150 (C)	P	10,200	10,200	n.a.
Arts, The University of the; Philadelphia, Pa. 19102	1,306 (C)	P	13,670	13,670	3,860
Asbury College; Wilmore, Ky. 40390	1,159 (C)	P	9,051[1]	9,051[1]	2,842[1]
Ashland University; Ashland, Ohio 44805	2,692 (C)	P	12,494	12,494	4,832
Associated Arts, College of; St. Paul., Minn. 55102–2199	175 (C)	P	8,500	8,500	4,500
Assumption College; Worcester, Mass. 01615-0005	1,689 (C)	P	12,700	12,700	5,980
Athens State College; Athens, Ala. 35611	2,770 (C)	Pub	3,750	7,500	4,900
Atlanta Christian College; East Point, Ga. 30344	169 (C)	P	4,320	4,320	3,030
Atlanta College of Art; Atlanta, Ga. 30309	420 (C)	P	10,500	10,500	3,350
Atlantic, College of the; Bar Harbor, Maine 04609	246 (C)	P	15,150	15,150	4,800
Atlantic Union College; South Lancaster, Mass. 01561	938 (C)	P	11,150	11,150	3,600
Auburn University; Auburn University, Ala. 36849	18,680 (C)	Pub	2,100	6,300	4,680
Auburn University-Montgomery; Montgomery, Ala. 36117–3596	5,503 (C)	Pub	1,905	5,715	4,050
Audrey Cohen College; New York, N.Y. 10014	1,052 (C)	P	8,240	8,240	n.a.
Augsburg College; Minneapolis, Minn. 55454	1,512 (C)	P	12,602	12,602	4,591
Augusta College; Augusta, Ga. 30910	5,187 (C)	Pub	1,926	5,136	n.a.
Augustana College; Rock Island, Ill. 61201	2,054 (C)	P	13,968	13,968	4,257
Augustana College; Sioux Falls, S.D. 57197	1,890 (C)	P	11,780	11,780	3,370
Aurora University; Aurora, Ill. 60506	1,443 (C)	P	10,800	10,800	4,050
Austin College; Sherman, Tex. 75090	1,095 (C)	P	12,195	12,195	4,524
Austin Peay State University; Clarksville, Tenn. 37044	7,535 (C)	Pub	1,878[1]	5,812[1]	2,970[1]
Averett College; Danville, Va. 24541-3692	2,423 (C)	P	11,150	11,150	4,150
Avila College; Kansas City, Mo. 64145	1,168 (C)	P	9,600	9,600	3,950
Azusa Pacific University; Azusa, Calif. 91702-7000	1,975 (C)	P	12,416	12,416	4,460
Babson College; Wellesley, Mass. 02157	1,679 (C)	P	18,115	18,115	7,275
Baker College of Flint; Flint, Mich. 48507	4,179 (C)	P	6,000	6,000	1,650
Baker University; Baldwin City, Kan. 66006	860 (C)	P	9,600	9,600	4,300
Baldwin-Wallace College; Berea, Ohio 44017	4,087 (C)	P	12,270	12,270	4,635
Ball State University; Muncie, Ind. 47306	17,317 (C)	Pub	3,048	7,824	3,768
Baltimore, University of; Baltimore, Md. 21201	2,299 (C)	Pub	3,260	6,660	n.a.
Baltimore Hebrew University; Baltimore, Md. 21215	255 (C)	P	3,300	3,300	n.a.
Baptist Bible College; Springfield, Mo. 65803	793 (C)	P	2,466	2,466	2,812
Baptist Bible College of Pennsylvania; Clarks Summit, Pa. 18411	562 (C)	P	6,528	6,528	4,070
Barat College; Lake Forest, Ill. 60045	729 (C)	P	11,190	11,190	4,680
Barber-Scotia College; Concord, N.C. 28025	704 (C)	P	5,369	5,369	3,070
Barclay College; Haviland, Kan. 67059	106 (C)	P	4,265	4,265	2,700
Bard College; Annandale-on-Hudson, N.Y. 12504	1,070 (C)	P	20,677	20,677	6,382
Barnard College of Columbia University; New York, N.Y. 10027	2,190 (W)	P	19,452	19,452	8,172
Barry University; Miami Shores, Fla. 33161	4,410 (C)	P	11,990	11,990	5,980
Bartlesville Wesleyan College; Bartlesville, Okla. 74006	504 (C)	P	7,000	7,000	3,400
Barton College; Wilson, N.C. 27893	1,465 (C)	P	8,395	8,395	3,600
Bassist College; Portland, Ore. 97201	134 (C)	P	8,550	8,550	2,975
Bates College; Lewiston, Maine 04240	1,550 (C)	P	26,300	26,300	
Bay Path College; Longmeadow, Me. 01106	613 (W)	P	10,700	10,700	6,350
Baylor University; Waco, Tex. 76798-7008	10,421 (C)	P	8,990	8,990	4,139
Beaver College; Glenside, Pa. 19038	1,168 (C)	P	13,970	13,970	5,750

Institution and location	Enrollment	Control	Tuition ($) Res.	Tuition ($) Nonres.	Rm/Bd ($)
Behrend College. *See* Pennsylvania State–Erie					
Belhaven College; Jackson, Miss. 39202	1,109 (C)	P	1,890	1,890	
Bellarmine College; Louisville, Ky. 40205–0671	1,857 (C)	P	9,550	9,550	3,360
Bellevue University; Bellevue, Neb. 68005	1,973 (C)	P	4,000	4,000	n.a.
Bellin College of Nursing; Green Bay, Wis. 54305-3400	299 (C)	P	7,535	7,535	n.a.
Belmont Abbey College; Belmont, N.C. 28012	1,016 (C)	P	10,318	10,318	5,044
Belmont University; Nashville, Tenn. 37212	2,617 (C)	P	8,750	8,750	3,832
Beloit College; Beloit, Wis. 53511	1,246 (C)	P	17,544	17,544	3,846
Bemidji State University; Bemidji, Minn. 56601	4,813 (C)	Pub	3,311	5,936	2,798
Benedict College; Columbia, S.C. 29204	1,266 (C)	P	6,196	6,196	3,210
Benedictine College; Atchison, Kan. 66002	1,203 (C)	P	12,570	12,570	4,200
Bennett College; Greensboro, N.C. 27401	680 (W)	P	6,876	6,876	3,190
Bennington College; Bennington, Vt. 05201	573 (C)	P	21,700[1]	21,700[1]	4,100[1]
Bentley College; Waltham, Mass. 02254	3,389 (C)	P	14,770	14,770	6,200
Berea College; Berea, Ky. 40404	1,550 (C)	P	—	—	3,024
Berklee College of Music; Boston, Mass. 02215	2,686 (C)	P	12,390	12,390	7,190
Bernard M. Baruch Coll. *See* New York, City Univ. of					
Berry College; Mount Berry, Ga. 30149	1,714 (C)	P	9,216	9,216	3,662
Bethany Bible College; Scotts Valley, Calif. 95066–2898	589 (C)	P	7,300	7,300	3,644
Bethany College; Bethany, W. Va. 26032	743 (C)	P	15,750	15,750	5,390
Bethany College; Lindsborg, Kan. 67456	743 (C)	P	9,270	9,270	3,475
Bethel College; McKenzie, Tenn. 38201	463 (C)	P	7,500	7,500	2,050
Bethel College; Mishawaka, Ind. 46545	1,200 (C)	P	9,750	9,750	3,100
Bethel College; North Newton, Kan. 67117	644 (C)	P	9,270	9,270	3,800
Bethel College; St. Paul, Minn. 55112	1,832 (C)	P	12,260	12,260	4,460
Beth–El College of Nursing; Colorado Springs, Colo. 80917	364 (C)	Pub	4,230	4,230	n.a.
Bethune-Cookman College; Daytona Beach, Fla. 32015	2,345 (C)	P	6,458	6,458	3,522
Biola University; La Mirada, Calif. 90639	2,114 (C)	P	12,652	12,652	4,932
Birmingham-Southern College; Birmingham, Ala. 35254	1,669 (C)	P	11,660	11,660	4,350
Blackburn College; Carlinville, Ill. 62626	443 (C)	P	6,585	6,585	2,700
Black Hills State University; Spearfish, S.D. 57783	2,964 (C)	Pub	2,422	4,000	3,500
Bloomfield College; Bloomfield, N.J. 07003	2,174 (C)	P	8,850	8,850	4,500
Bloomsburg University of Pennsylvania; Bloomsburg, Pa. 17815	6,632 (C)	Pub	3,694[1]	8,452[1]	2,998[1]
Bluefield College; Bluefield, Va. 24605	707 (C)	P	7,770	7,770	4,430
Bluefield State College; Bluefield, W. Va. 24701	2,931 (C)	Pub	1,916	4,576	n.a.
Blue Mountain College; Blue Mountain, Miss. 38610	440 (W)	P	4,090	4,090	2,190
Bluffton College; Bluffton, Ohio 45817	849 (C)	P	10,620	10,620	4,377
Bob Jones University; Greenville, S.C. 29614	3,629 (C)	P	5,000	5,000	3,780
Boise State University; Boise, Idaho 83725	11,967 (C)	Pub	2,416	2,673	3,600
Boricua College; New York, N.Y. 10032	1,039 (C)	P	5,900	5,900	n.a.
Boston Architecture Center School of Architecture; Boston, Mass. 02115	613 (C)	P	4,620	4,620	n.a.
Boston College; Chestnut Hill, Mass. 02167	8,667 (C)	P	17,890	17,890	7,270
Boston Conservatory; Boston, Mass. 02215	309 (C)	P	13,400	13,400	6,280
Boston University; Boston, Mass. 02215	14,334 (C)	P	19,420	19,420	7,100
Bowdoin College; Brunswick, Me. 04011	1,489 (C)	P	20,230	20,230	5,945
Bowie State University; Bowie, Md. 20715	2,965 (C)	Pub	3,019	6,161	3,136
Bowling Green State University; Bowling Green, Ohio 43403	14,435 (C)	Pub	3,730	8,112	3,352
Bradford College; Bradford, Mass. 01835	600 (C)	P	15,380	15,380	6,490
Bradley University; Peoria, Ill. 61625	5,061 (C)	P	11,410	11,410	4,620
Brandeis University; Waltham, Mass. 02254	2,877 (C)	P	20,470	20,470	6,780
Brescia College; Owensboro, Ky. 42301	730 (C)	P	7,800	7,800	3,400
Brewton-Parker College; Mount Vernon, Ga. 30445	2,250 (C)	P	4,770	4,770	2,400
Briar Cliff College; Sioux City, Iowa 51104-2100	909 (C)	P	11,100	11,100	3,840
Bridgeport, University of; Bridgeport, Conn. 06601	731 (C)	P	13,700	13,700	7,150
Bridgewater College; Bridgewater, Va. 22812	1,007 (C)	P	11,925	11,925	4,975
Bridgewater State College; Bridgewater, Mass. 02325	6,862 (C)	Pub	3,422	7,596	4,041
Brigham Young University; Provo, Utah 84602	28,282 (C)	P	3,674	3,740	3,674
Brigham Young University-Hawaii; Laie, Oahu, Hawaii 96762	2,032 (C)	P	2,970	2,970	3,700
Brooklyn College. *See* New York, City University of					
Bristol University; Bristol, Tenn. 37625	532 (C)	P	5,400[3]	5,400[3]	3,800[3]
Brooks Institute of Photography; Santa Barbara, Calif. 93108	450 (C)	P	13,500	13,500	n.a.
Brown University; Providence, R.I. 02912	5,718 (C)	P	21,128	21,128	6,212
Bryan College; Dayton, Tenn. 37321	421 (C)	P	9,500	9,500	3,950
Bryant College; Smithfield, R.I. 02917	2,744 (C)	P	13,100	13,100	6,500
Bryn Mawr College; Bryn Mawr, Pa. 19010	1,169 (W)	P	19,250	19,250	7,085
Bucknell University; Lewisburg, Pa. 17837	3,298 (C)	P	19,470	19,470	4,925
Buena Vista University; Storm Lake, Iowa 50588	1,085 (C)	P	14,078	14,078	4,017
Burlington College; Burlington, Vt. 05401	184 (C)	P	6,276	6,276	n.a.
Butler University; Indianapolis, Ind. 46208	2,739 (C)	P	14,000	14,000	5,500
Cabrini College; Radnor, Pa. 19087–3699	829 (C)	P	11,100	11,100	6,500
Caldwell College; Caldwell, N.J. 07006	1,599 (C)	P	9,500	9,500	4,900
California, University of; Berkeley, Calif. 94720:					
UC-Berkeley; Berkeley, Calif. 94720	21,841 (C)	Pub	4,354	7,699	6,466
UC-Davis; Davis, Calif. 95616	17,273 (C)	Pub	4,332	12,031	5,822

Institution and location	Enrollment	Control	Tuition ($) Res.	Nonres.	Rm/Bd ($)
UC-Irvine; Irvine, Calif. 92717	13,597 (C)	Pub	4,324	12,023	5,824
UC-Los Angeles; Los Angeles, Calif. 90024	23,649 (C)	Pub	4,169	11,868	5,602
UC-Riverside; Riverside, Calif. 92521	7,217 (C)	Pub	3,750	11,451	5,430
UC-San Diego; La Jolla, Calif. 92093	14,320 (C)	Pub	4,200	11,698	6,500
UC-Santa Barbara; Santa Barbara, Calif. 93106	15,525 (C)	Pub	4,098	11,797	5,901
UC-Santa Cruz; Santa Cruz, Calif. 95064	9,099 (C)	Pub	4,384	12,083	6,081
California Baptist College; Riverside, Calif. 92504	808 (C)	P	8,800	8,800	4,464
California College of Arts and Crafts; Oakland, Calif. 94618	1,052 (C)	P	14,400	14,400	4,100
California Institute of Technology; Pasadena, Calif. 91125	912 (C)	P	17,370	17,370	5,283
California Institute of the Arts; Valencia, Calif. 91355	659 (C)	P	15,450	15,450	5,500
California Lutheran University; Thousand Oaks, Calif. 91360	1,834 (C)	P	13,680	13,680	5,450
California Maritime Academy; Vallejo, Calif. 94590	450 (C)	Pub	7.678[1]	13,768[1]	4,700[1]
California Polytechnic State University; San Luis Obispo, Calif. 93407	15,440 (C)	Pub	2,033	7,937	4,877
California State Polytechnic University-Pomona; Pomona, Calif. 91768	14,772 (C)	Pub	1,440[1]	7,872[1]	4,862[1]
California State University-Bakersfield; Bakersfield, Calif. 93311-1099	3,905 (C)	Pub	1,858[1]	9,238[1]	3,857[1]
California State University-Chico; Chico, Calif. 95929	12,385 (C)	Pub	2,006[1]	9,386[1]	4,632[1]
California St. Univ.-Dominguez Hills; Carson, Calif. 90747	6,929 (C)	Pub	1,796[1]	6,798[1]	4,844[1]
California State Univ.-Fresno; Fresno, Calif. 93740	15,279 (C)	Pub	1,802[1]	7,706[1]	4,184[1]
California State Univ.-Fullerton; Fullerton, Calif. 92634	18,346 (C)	Pub	1,622[1]	8,860[1]	5,176[1]
California State Univ.-Hayward; Hayward, Calif. 94542	9,888 (C)	Pub	1,776[1]	4,528[1]	4,345[1]
California State Univ.-Long Beach; Long Beach, Calif. 90840	21,424 (C)	Pub	1,551[1]	7,856[1]	5,330[1]
California State Univ.-Los Angeles; Los Angeles, Calif. 90032	13,882 (C)	Pub	1,710[1]	6,606[1]	2,805[1]
California State Univ.-Northridge; Northridge, Calif. 91330	21,681 (C)	Pub	1,916[1]	4,944[1]	3,540[1]
California State Univ.-Sacramento; Sacramento, Calif. 95819	18,401 (C)	Pub	1,860[1]	9,210[1]	4,623[1]
California State Univ.-San Bernardino; San Bernardino, Calif. 92407-2397	9,192 (C)	Pub	1,128[1]	8,508[1]	4,108[1]
California State Univ.-San Marcos; San Marcos, Calif. 92096	1,998 (C)	Pub	1,800	7,704	n.a.
California State Univ.-Stanislaus; Turlock, Calif. 95380	4,747 (C)	Pub	2,127	9,082	3,972
California Univ. of Pennsylvania; California, Pa. 15419-1394	5,475 (C)	Pub	7,632[1]	12,390[1]	3,730[1]
Calumet College of St. Joseph; Whiting, Ind. 46394	1,086 (C)	P	4,130	4,130	n.a.
Calvary Bible College; Kansas City, Mo. 64147	297 (C)	P	3,924	3,924	2,950
Calvin College; Grand Rapids, Mich. 49506	3,609 (C)	P	10,995	10,995	3,895
Cameron University; Lawton, Okla. 73505	5,988 (C)	Pub	1,297	2,430	2,947[4]
Campbellsville College; Campbellsville, Ky. 42718	1,260 (C)	P	6,420	6,420	3,210
Campbell University; Buies Creek, N.C. 27506	4,803 (C)	P	9,104	9,104	3,250
Canisius College; Buffalo, N.Y. 14208	3,048 (C)	P	11,976	11,976	5,500
Capital University; Columbus, Ohio 43209	1,669 (C)	P	13,700	13,700	4,000
Capitol College; Laurel, Md. 20708	679 (C)	P	8,781	8,781	4,412
Cardinal Stritch College; Milwaukee, Wis. 53217	3,017 (C)	P	8,320	8,320	3,725
Carleton College; Northfield, Minn. 55057	1,663 (C)	P	19,418[1]	19,418[1]	3,957[1]
Carlow College; Pittsburgh, Pa. 15213	2,029 (W)	P	10,588	10,588	4,512
Carnegie Mellon University; Pittsburgh, Pa. 15213	4,327 (C)	P	18,160	18,160	5,700
Carroll College; Helena, Mont. 59625	1,438 (C)	P	9,789	9,789	3,915
Carroll College; Waukesha, Wis. 53186	1,480 (C)	P	12,740	12,740	4,000
Carson-Newman College; Jefferson City, Tenn. 37760	2,150 (C)	P	9,000	9,000	3,320
Carthage College; Kenosha, Wis. 53140–1994	1,465 (C)	P	13,850	13,850	3,980
Case Western Reserve University; Cleveland, Ohio 44106	3,658 (C)	P	16,430	16,430	4,940
Castleton State College; Castleton, Vt. 05735	1,724 (C)	Pub	4,026	8,538	4,794
Catawba College; Salisbury, N.C. 28144	1,041 (C)	P	9,972	9,972	4,200
Catholic University of America; Washington, D.C. 20064	2,364 (C)	P	15,062	15,062	6,614
Cayey University College. See Puerto Rico, University of					
Cazenovia College; Cazenovia, N.Y. 13035	913 (C)	P	9,806	9,806	5,030
Cedar Crest College; Allentown, Pa. 18104-6196	1,342 (W)	P	14,770	14,770	5,365
Cedarville College; Cedarville, Ohio 45314	2,378 (C)	P	7,872	7,872	4,572
Centenary College; Hackettstown, N.J. 07840	343 (C)	P	11,100	11,100	5,500
Centenary College of Louisiana; Shreveport, La. 71104	796 (C)	P	9,322	9,322	3,690
Center for Creative Studies, College of Art and Design; Detroit, Mich. 48202	862 (C)	P	12,550	12,550	4,150
Central Arkansas, University of; Conway, Ark. 72032	8,525 (C)	Pub	2,000	3,586	2,600
Central Baptist College; Conway, Ark. 72032	273 (C)	P	3,792	3,792	2,880
Central Bible College; Springfield, Mo. 65803	991 (C)	P	4,200	4,200	2,930
Central Christian College of the Bible; Moberly, Mo. 65270	116 (C)	P	3,600	3,600	2,500
Central College; Pella, Iowa 50219	1,459 (C)	P	11,836	11,836	3,660
Central Connecticut State University; New Britain, Conn. 06050	6,088 (C)	Pub	3,684[1]	11,924[1]	4,614[1]
Central Florida, University of; Orlando, Fla. 32816	20,734 (C)	Pub	1,716[1]	6,618[1]	4,306[1]
Central Methodist College; Fayette, Mo. 65248	1,002 (C)	P	9,430	9,430	3,600
Central Michigan University; Mt. Pleasant, Mich. 48859	14,350 (C)	Pub	2,493	6,044	3,881
Central Missouri State University; Warrensburg, Mo. 64093	9,350 (C)	Pub	2,460	4,920	3,538
Central Oklahoma, University of; Edmond, Okla. 73034-0127	12,042 (C)	Pub	1,518[1]	3,580[1]	2,311[1]
Central State University; Wilberforce, Ohio 45384	3,263 (C)	Pub	2,895	6,432	4,575
Central Texas, University of; Killeen, Tex. 76540	527 (C)	P	5,432	5,432	4,698

Institution and location	Enrollment	Control	Tuition ($) Res.	Tuition ($) Nonres.	Rm/Bd ($)
Central Washington University; Ellensburg, Wash. 98926	7,694 (C)	Pub	2,256[1]	7,974[1]	3,778[1]
Central Wesleyan College; Central, S.C. 29630	1,349 (C)	P	8,882	8,882	3,234
Centre College; Danville, Ky. 40422–1394	955 (C)	P	13,100	13,100	4,350
Chadron State College; Chadron, Neb. 69337	2,371 (C)	Pub	1,459	2,419	2,814
Chaminade University of Honolulu; Honolulu, Hawaii 96816	800 (C)	P	10,600	10,600	3,225
Chapman University; Orange, Calif. 92666	2,141 (C)	P	17,687	17,687	6,744
Charleston, College of; Charleston, S.C. 29424	7,821 (C)	Pub	3,060	6,120	2,200
Charleston Southern University; Charleston, S.C. 29411	2,413 (C)	P	8,352	8,352	2,170
Charleston, University of; Charleston, W. Va. 25304	1,382 (C)	P	10,400	10,400	5,910
Charter Oak State College; Newington, Conn. 06111	1,216 (C)	Pub	585	765	n.a.
Chatham College; Pittsburgh, Pa. 15232	782 (W)	P	14,040	14,040	5,440
Chestnut Hill College; Philadelphia, Pa. 19118-2695	911 (W)	P	10,235	10,235	5,015
Cheyney University of Pennsylvania; Cheyney, Pa. 19319	1,084 (C)	Pub	3,591[1]	6,128[1]	3,900[1]
Chicago, University of—The College; Chicago, Ill. 60637	3,447 (C)	P	20,378	20,378	7,258
Chicago State University; Chicago, Ill. 60628	6,542 (C)	Pub	2,336	6,272	4,990
Christendom College; Front Royal, Va. 22630	173 (C)	P	9,254	9,254	3,600
Christian Brothers University; Memphis, Tenn. 38104	1,085 (C)	P	10,000	10,000	3,500
Christian Heritage College; El Cajon, Calif. 92019	310 (C)	P	9,240	9,240	4,120
Christian Life College; Stockton, Calif. 95210	173 (C)	P	2,475	2,475	2,500
Christopher Newport University; Newport News, Va. 23606-2998	4,788 (C)	Pub	3,350	7,946	4,750
Cincinnati, University of; Cincinnati, Ohio 45221	13,506 (C)	Pub	3,732[1]	9,405[1]	4,697[1]
Cincinnati Bible College; Cincinnati, Ohio 45204	609 (C)	P	4,770	4,770	3,450
Cincinnati College of Mortuary Science; Cincinnati, Ohio 45207	82 (C)	P	7,875	7,875	n.a.
Circleville Bible College; Circleville, Ohio 43113	186 (C)	P	4,028	4,028	3,628
Citadel-The Military College of South Carolina; Charleston, S.C. 29409	2,000 (M)	Pub	10,170[1]	14,164[1]	3,690[1]
City College (NYC). *See* New York, City University of					
City University; Bellevue, Wash. 98004	1,442 (C)	P	4,082	4,082	n.a.
Claflin College; Orangeburg, S.C. 29115	756 (C)	P	4,412[1]	4,412[1]	2,460[1]
Claremont Colleges:					
Claremont McKenna College; Claremont, Calif. 91711-6420	877 (C)	P	17,840	17,840	6,260
Harvey Mudd College; Claremont, Calif. 91711-5990	616 (C)	P	18,100	18,100	6,920
Pitzer College; Claremont, Calif. 91711	750 (C)	P	19,098[1]	19,098[1]	6,038[1]
Pomona College; Claremont, Calif. 91711	1,375 (C)	P	18,780	18,780	7,520
Scripps College; Claremont, Calif. 91711	630 (W)	P	18,180	18,180	7,450
Clarion University of Pennsylvania; Clarion, Pa. 16214	5,249 (C)	Pub	3,878	8,636	2,921
Clark Atlanta University; Atlanta, Ga. 30314	3,867 (C)	P	8,500	8,500	5,670
Clarke College; Dubuque, Iowa 52001	988 (C)	P	11,514	11,514	3,860
Clarkson College; Omaha, Neb. 68131–2739	450 (C)	P	6,000	6,000	3,450
Clarkson University; Potsdam, N.Y. 13676	2,077 (C)	P	16,770	16,770	5,830
Clark University; Worcester, Mass. 01610	2,100 (C)	P	18,700	18,700	4,250
Clayton State College; Morrow, Ga. 30260–1221	4,896 (C)	Pub	2,256	6,336	n.a.
Clearwater Christian College; Clearwater, Fla. 34619–9997	451 (C)	P	6,500	6,500	3,400
Cleary College; Ypsilanti, Mich. 48197	940 (C)	P	3,734	3,734	n.a.
Clemson University; Clemson, S.C. 29634	12,302 (C)	Pub	2,941[1]	8,021[1]	3,930[1]
Cleveland College of Jewish Studies; Beachwood, Ohio 44122	400 (C)	P	3,960	3,960	n.a.
Cleveland Institute of Art; Cleveland, Ohio 44106	520 (C)	P	11,900	11,900	4,510
Cleveland Institute of Music; Cleveland, Ohio 44106	201 (C)	P	15,726	15,726	4,855
Cleveland State University; Cleveland, Ohio 44115	11,966 (C)	Pub	3,231[1]	6,462[1]	4,161[1]
Clinch Valley College. *See* Virginia, University of					
Coastal Carolina University; Myrtle Beach, S.C. 29578	4,150 (C)	Pub	1,667	5,827	1,995
Coe College; Cedar Rapids, Iowa 52402	1,304 (C)	P	14,875	14,875	4,455
Cogswell College; Cupertino, Calif. 95014	350 (C)	P	6,960	6,960	n.a.
Cogswell College North; Kirkland, Wash. 98033	200 (C)	P	12,780	12,780	n.a.
Coker College; Hartsville, S.C. 29550	823 (C)	P	10,896	10,896	4,516
Colby College; Waterville, Me. 04901	1,650 (C)	P	20,990	20,990	5,650
Colby-Sawyer College; New London, N.H. 03257	675 (C)	P	14,720	14,720	5,640
Coleman College; La Mesa, Calif. 92041	650 (C)	P	6,000	6,000	n.a.
Colgate University; Hamilton, N.Y. 13346	2,740 (C)	P	20,500	20,500	5,765
College Misericordia; Dallas, Pa. 18612	1,614 (C)	P	12,200	12,200	6,000
College of West Virginia, The; Beckley, W. Va. 25802	1,736 (C)	P	3,240	3,240	3,500
Colorado, University of; Boulder, Colo. 80309:					
U. of Colorado-Boulder; Boulder, Colo. 80309	20,407 (C)	Pub	2,698[1]	12,780[1]	2,364[1]
U. of Colorado-Colorado Springs; Colorado Springs, Colo. 80933	4,127 (C)	Pub	2,375	8,375	4,800[5]
U. of Colorado-Denver; Denver, Colo. 80204	6,128 (C)	Pub	2,265[1]	9,759[1]	n.a.[1]
Colorado Christian University; Lakewood, Colo. 80226	980 (C)	P	7,080	7,080	3,910
Colorado College; Colorado Springs, Colo. 80903	1,903 (C)	P	18,084	18,084	4,562
Colorado School of Mines; Golden, Colo. 80401	2,207 (C)	Pub	4,392	13,134	4,440
Colorado State University; Fort Collins, Colo. 80523	17,800 (C)	Pub	2,708[1]	8,996[1]	4,534[1]
Colorado Technical College; Colorado Springs, Colo. 80907	1,026 (C)	P	4,980	4,980	n.a.
Columbia Christian College; Portland, Ore. 97216	250 (C)	P	6,725	6,725	3,300
Columbia College; Chicago, Ill. 60605	6,729 (C)	P	6,800[1]	6,800[1]	4,200[1]
Columbia College; Columbia, Mo. 65216	836 (C)	P	8,546	8,546	3,850
Columbia College; Columbia, S.C. 29203	1,180 (W)	P	10,995	10,995	4,160
Columbia College-Hollywood; Los Angeles, Calif. 90038	187 (C)	P	5,820	5,820	n.a.
Columbia International University; Columbia, S.C. 29230	473 (C)	P	6,950	6,950	3,828

Institution and location	Enrollment	Control	Tuition ($) Res.	Nonres.	Rm/Bd ($)
Columbia Union College; Takoma Park, Md. 20912	979 (C)	P	10,775	10,775	3,850
Columbia University-Columbia College; New York, N.Y. 10027	3,325 (C)	P	20,100	20,100	6,800
Columbia University School of General Studies; New York, N.Y. 10027	1,200 (C)	P	15,160	15,160	7,664
Columbus College; Columbus, Ga. 31993	4,832 (C)	Pub	1,653[1]	4,497[1]	3,375[1]
Columbus College of Art and Design; Columbus, Ohio 43215	1,695 (C)	P	10,300	10,300	5,700
Conception Seminary College; Conception, Mo. 64433	84 (M)	P	6,742	6,742	3,174
Concord College; Athens, W. Va. 24712	2,623 (C)	Pub	5,400[1]	5,400[1]	4,500[1]
Concordia College; Ann Arbor, Mich. 48105	523 (C)	P	10,440	10,440	4,650
Concordia College; Bronxville, N.Y. 10708	575 (C)	P	10,696	10,696	5,220
Concordia College; Irvine, Calif. 92715	885 (C)	P	12,500	12,500	4,990
Concordia College; Moorhead, Minn. 56562	2,970 (C)	P	10,720	10,720	3,280
Concordia College; Portland, Ore. 97211	1,017 (C)	P	10,500	10,500	3,500
Concordia College; St. Paul, Minn. 55104	1,258 (C)	P	10,815	10,815	3,930
Concordia College; Seward, Neb. 68434	919 (C)	P	9,480	9,480	3,470
Concordia Lutheran College; Austin, Tex. 78705	800 (C)	P	7,380	7,380	3,800
Concordia University; River Forest, Ill. 60305	1,316 (C)	P	9,888	9,888	4,443
Concordia University Wisconsin; Mequon, Wis. 53092	2,091 (C)	P	10,000	10,000	3,600
Connecticut, University of; Storrs, Conn. 06269	12,059 (C)	Pub	3,950	11,940	5,160
Connecticut College; New London, Conn. 06320	689 (C)	P	26,325	26,325	—
Conservatory of Music of Puerto Rico; Hato Rey, P.R. 00918	283 (C)	Pub	670[1]	670[1]	n.a.[1]
Converse College; Spartanburg, S.C. 29301	659 (W)	P	13,150	13,150	3,825
Cooper Union; New York, N.Y. 10003	983 (C)	P	400	400	6,500
Coppin State College; Baltimore, Md. 21216	2,638 (C)	Pub	2,749	5,963	4,640
Corcoran School of Art; Washington, D.C. 20006	268 (C)	P	11,550	11,550	7,150
Cornell College; Mt. Vernon, Iowa 52314	1,133 (C)	P	16,440	16,440	4,452
Cornell University; Ithaca, N.Y. 14853	13,228 (C)	P	20,066	20,066	6,762
Cornish College of the Arts; Seattle, Wash. 98102	603 (C)	P	10,400	10,400	5,000
Covenant College; Lookout Mountain, Ga. 30750	707 (C)	P	10,920	10,920	3,682
Creighton University; Omaha, Neb. 68178	3,296 (C)	P	11,652	11,652	4,548
Crichton College; Memphis, Tenn. 38175-7830	358 (C)	P	5,640	5,640	3,200
Crown College; St. Bonifacius, Minn. 55375-9001	620 (C)	P	7,950	7,950	3,920
Culver-Stockton College; Canton, Mo. 63435	1,057 (C)	P	8,400	8,400	3,800
Cumberland College; Williamsburg, Ky. 40769	1,319 (C)	P	7,098	7,098	3,526
Cumberland University of Tennessee; Lebanon, Tenn. 37087	980 (C)	P	7,150	7,150	3,220
Curry College; Milton, Mass. 02186	1,104 (C)	P	14,100	14,100	5,850
Curtis Institute of Music; Philadelphia, Pa. 19103	119 (C)	P	—	—	n.a.
C. W. Post. *See* Long Island Univ. Center					
Daemen College; Amherst, N.Y. 14226	1,855 (C)	P	9,720	9,720	4,900
Dakota State University; Madison, S.D. 57042	1,437 (C)	Pub	2,480	4,608	2,640
Dakota Wesleyan University; Mitchell, S.D. 57301	704 (C)	P	7,992	7,992	2,925
Dallas, University of; Irving, Tex. 75062	1,116 (C)	P	11,380	11,380	4,830
Dallas Baptist University; Dallas, Tex. 75211	2,989 (C)	P	7,110	7,110	3,413
Dallas Christian College; Dallas, Tex. 75234	99 (C)	P	3,400	3,400	2,700
Dana College; Blair, Neb. 68008-1099	650 (C)	P	10,180	10,180	3,520
Daniel Webster College; Nashua, N.H. 03063–1300	474 (C)	P	12,292[1]	12,292[1]	4,934[1]
Dartmouth College; Hanover, N.H. 03755	4,286 (C)	P	20,910	20,910	6,129
Davenport College; Grand Rapids, Mich. 49503	4,077 (C)	P	4,128	4,128	3,625
David Lipscomb University; Nashville, Tenn. 37204-3951	2,346 (C)	P	6,818	6,818	3,450
Davidson College; Davidson, N.C. 28036	1,614 (C)	P	18,626	18,626	5,364
Davis and Elkins College; Elkins, W. Va. 26241	877 (C)	P	10,330	10,330	4,670
Dayton, University of; Dayton, Ohio 45469	6,435 (C)	P	12,350	12,350	4,360
Defiance College, The; Defiance, Ohio 43512	965 (C)	P	12,950	12,950	3,800
Delaware, University of; Newark, Del. 19716	14,870 (C)	P	4,145[1]	10,675[1]	4,230[1]
Delaware State University*; Dover, Del. 19901	3,292 (C)	Pub	2,132[1]	5,364[1]	4,737[1]
Delaware Valley College of Science and Agriculture; Doylestown, Pa. 18901	1,350 (C)	P	13,208	13,208	5,290
Delta State University; Cleveland, Miss. 38732	3,332 (C)	Pub	2,294	4,888	4,474
Denison University; Granville, Ohio 43023	1,834 (C)	P	17,770	17,770	4,940
Denver, University of; Denver, Colo. 80208	3,242 (C)	P	15,948	15,948	5,172
The Women's College; Denver, Colo. 80220	420 (W)	P	7,830	7,830	n.a
DePaul University; Chicago, Ill. 60604	9,783 (C)	P	8,892	8,892	5,000
DePauw University; Greencastle, Ind. 46135	2,061 (C)	P	15,475	15,475	5,245
Deree College-Division of the American College of Greece; Athens, Greece GR-153 42	4,182 (C)	P	5,957[1]	5,957[1]	n.a.[1]
Design Institute of San Diego; San Diego, Calif. 92121	120 (C)	P	8,500	8,500	n.a.
Detroit College of Business; Dearborn, Mich. 48126	5,111 (C)	P	3,936	3,936	n.a.
Detroit Mercy, University of; Detroit, Mich. 48221	4,628 (C)	P	6,268	6,268	6,054
DeVry Institute of Technology; Chicago, Ill. 60618-5994	3,192 (C)	P	6,280	6,280	n.a.
DeVry Institute of Technology; Columbus, Ohio 43209-2764	2,752 (C)	P	6,280	6,280	n.a.
DeVry Institute of Technology; Decatur, Ga. 30030-2198	2,801 (C)	P	6,280	6,280	n.a.
DeVry Institute of Technology; Irving, Tex. 75038-4299	2,141 (C)	P	6,280	6,280	n.a.
DeVry Institute of Technology; Kansas City, Mo. 64131-3626	1,927 (C)	P	6,280	6,280	n.a.
DeVry Institute of Technology; Phoenix, Ariz. 85021-2995	3,016 (C)	P	6,280	6,280	n.a.
DeVry Institute of Technology University Center; Pomona, Calif. 91768	2,845 (C)	P	6,280	6,280	n.a.

Institution and location	Enrollment	Control	Tuition ($) Res.	Nonres.	Rm/Bd ($)
Dickinson College; Carlisle, Pa. 17013	2,916 (C)	P	19,750	19,750	5,270
Dickinson State University; Dickinson, N.D. 58601	1,591 (C)	Pub	1,890	4,732	2,250
Dillard University; New Orleans, La. 70122–3097	1,580 (C)	P	6,800[1]	6,800[1]	3,650[1]
District of Columbia, Univ. of the; Washington, D.C. 20008	10,599 (C)	Pub	1,118	4,142	1,046[6]
Divine Word College; Epworth, Iowa 52045	71 (M)	P	7,000	7,000	1,200
Doane College; Crete, Neb. 68333	885 (C)	P	10,410	10,410	3,165
Dominican College of Blauvelt; Orangeburg, N.Y. 10962	1,786 (C)	P	8,940	8,940	5,740
Dominican College of San Rafael; San Rafael, Calif. 94901-8008	936 (C)	P	13,890	13,890	6,410
Dominican School of Philosophy and Theology; Berkeley, Calif. 94709	8 (C)	P	6,360	6,360	n.a.
Dordt College; Sioux Center, Iowa 51250	1,156 (C)	P	10,300	10,300	2,770
Dowling College; Oakdale, N.Y. 11769	3,666 (C)	P	10,300	10,300	3,100
Drake University; Des Moines, Iowa 50311	3,918 (C)	P	14,100	14,100	4,950
Drew University-College of Liberal Arts; Madison, N.J. 07940	1,290 (C)	P	19,638	19,638	5,883
Drexel University; Philadelphia, Pa. 19104	7,269 (C)	P	13,305	13,305	4,851
Dr. Martin Luther College; New Ulm, Minn. 56073	570 (C)	P	4,035	4,035	2,010
Drury College; Springfield, Mo. 65802	1,110 (C)	P	9,391	9,391	3,696
Dubuque, University of; Dubuque, Iowa 52001	880 (C)	P	11,680	11,680	4,340
Duke University; Durham, N.C. 27706	6,057 (C)	P	19,995	19,995	6,320
Duquesne University; Pittsburgh, Pa. 15282	5,397 (C)	P	12,578	12,578	5,580
Dyke College; Cleveland, Ohio 44115	1,319 (C)	P	5,760	5,760	n.a.
D'Youville College; Buffalo, N.Y. 14201	1,337 (C)	P	9,330	9,330	4,630
Earlham College; Richmond, Ind. 47374	982 (C)	P	17,160	17,160	4,305
East Carolina University; Greenville, N.C. 27858	14,499 (C)	Pub	2,936[1]	9,002[1]	2,064[1]
East Central University; Ada, Okla. 74820-6899	4,473 (C)	Pub	1,528	3,591	2,068
Eastern College; St. Davids, Pa. 19087-3696	1,376 (C)	P	11,750	11,750	5,036
Eastern Connecticut State Univ.; Willimantic, Conn. 06226	2,695 (C)	Pub	3,202	8,294	5,248
Eastern Illinois University; Charleston, Ill. 61920	9,869 (C)	Pub	2,778	6,716	3,244
Eastern Kentucky University; Richmond, Ky. 40475	14,922 (C)	Pub	1,900	5,260	3,460
Eastern Mennonite College; Harrisonburg, Va. 22801	961 (C)	P	10,400	10,400	4,000
Eastern Michigan University; Ypsilanti, Mich. 48197	19,563 (C)	Pub	2,610[1]	6,750[1]	4,148[1]
Eastern Nazarene College; Quincy, Mass. 02170	664 (C)	P	10,160	10,160	3,600
Eastern New Mexico University; Portales, N.M. 88130	3,296 (C)	Pub	1,518[1]	5,586[1]	2,648[1]
Eastern Oregon State College; La Grande, Ore. 97850	1,931 (C)	Pub	2,766	2,766	3,636
Eastern Washington University; Cheney, Wash. 99004	7,041 (C)	Pub	7,572	15,524	5,560
Eastman School of Music; Rochester, N.Y. 14604	468 (C)	P	17,000	17,000	6,730
East Stroudsburg University of Pennsylvania; East Stroudsburg, Pa. 18301	4,558 (C)	Pub	7,465	12,439	3,448
East Tennessee State University; Johnson City, Tenn. 37614	9,923 (C)	Pub	1,658[1]	5,440[1]	3,018[1]
East Texas Baptist University; Marshall, Tex. 75670	1,204 (C)	P	6,260	6,260	3,000
East Texas State University; Commerce, Tex. 75429	5,485 (C)	Pub	1,424[1]	4,856[1]	3,384[1]
East-West University; Chicago, Ill. 60605	238 (C)	P	6,880	6,880	n.a.
Eckerd College; St. Petersburg, Fla. 33711	1,387 (C)	P	16,040	16,040	4,325
Edgewood College; Madison, Wis. 53711	1,690 (C)	P	9,500	9,500	3,500
Edinboro University of Pennsylvania; Edinboro, Pa. 16444	6,847 (C)	Pub	3,685[1]	8,443[1]	3,440[1]
Edward Waters College; Jacksonville, Fla. 32209	773 (C)	P	4,400	4,400	4,500
Electronic Data Processing College of Puerto Rico; Hato Rey, P.R. 00918	1,176 (C)	P	2,640[3]	2,640[3]	n.a.[3]
Elizabeth City State University; Elizabeth City, N.C. 27909	1,694 (C)	Pub	1,360	7,710	3,264
Elizabethtown College; Elizabethtown, Pa. 17022	1,553 (C)	P	15,490	15,490	4,550
Elmhurst College; Elmhurst, Ill. 60126-3296	1,604 (C)	P	10,264	10,264	4,390
Elmira College; Elmira, N.Y. 14901	1,121 (C)	P	16,700	16,700	5,380
Elms College; Chicopee, Mass. 01013-2839	550 (W)	P	12,470	12,470	5,000
Elon College; Elon College, N.C. 27244	3,316 (C)	P	9,750	9,750	4,008
Embry-Riddle Aeronautical Univ.-Daytona Beach Campus; Daytona Beach, Fla. 32114	3,984 (C)	P	8,500	8,500	3,462
Prescott Campus; Prescott, Ariz. 86301	1,378 (C)	P	8,500	8,500	3,900
Emerson College; Boston, Mass. 02116	2,087 (C)	P	15,936	15,936	7,850
Emmanuel College; Boston, Mass. 02115	1,393 (W)	P	12,775[1]	12,775[1]	6,030[1]
Emmanuel College; Franklin Springs, Ga. 30639	527 (C)	P	4,800	4,800	3,050
Emory and Henry College; Emory, Va. 24327	844 (C)	P	10,260	10,260	4,502
Emory University; Atlanta, Ga. 30322	5,100 (C)	P	19,000	19,000	6,220
Emporia State University; Emporia, Kan. 66801	4,476 (C)	Pub	1,758	5,776	3,220
Endicott College; Beverly, Mass. 01915	800 (W)	P	11,970	11,970	6,400
Erskine College; Due West, S.C. 29639	536 (C)	P	11,908	11,908	4,086
Esther Boyer College of Music; Philadelphia, Pa. 19122	350 (C)	Pub	5,389	5,389	5,282
ETI Technical College; Cleveland, Ohio 44114	361 (C)	P	6,192	6,192	3,850
Eugene Bible College; Eugene, Ore. 97405	212 (C)	P	4,767	4,767	2,904
Eureka College; Eureka, Ill. 61530	525 (C)	P	12,505	12,505	3,875
Evangel College; Springfield, Mo. 65802	1,420 (C)	P	7,300	7,300	3,170
Evansville, University of; Evansville, Ind. 47722	3,079 (C)	P	12,630	12,630	4,520
Evergreen State College; Olympia, Wash. 98505	3,250 (C)	Pub	2,256	7,974	4,000
Fairfield University; Fairfield, Conn. 06430	2,901 (C)	P	16,340	16,340	6,600
Fairhaven College-Western Washington University; Bellingham, Wash. 98225	400 (C)	Pub	2,406[1]	8,124[1]	4,144[1]

Institution and location	Enrollment	Control	Tuition ($) Res.	Tuition ($) Nonres.	Rm/Bd ($)
Fairleigh Dickinson Univ.-Madison; Madison, N.J. 07940	2,501 (C)	P	11,610	11,610	6,300
Fairleigh Dickinson Univ.-Rutherford; Rutherford, N.J. 07070	1,505 (C)	P	11,081[1]	11,081[1]	5,900[1]
Fairleigh Dickinson Univ.-Teaneck; Teaneck, N.J. 07666	4,557 (C)	P	12,254	12,254	5,550
Fairmont State College; Fairmont, W. Va. 26554	6,355 (C)	Pub	1,800[1]	4,238[1]	3,160[1]
Faith Baptist Bible College and Theological Seminary; Ankeny, Iowa 50021	222 (C)	P	5,800	5,800	3,160
Faulkner University; Montgomery, Ala. 36109–3398	2,363 (C)	P	6,240	6,240	3,400
Fayetteville State University; Fayetteville, N.C. 28301	3,251 (C)	Pub	1,400[1]	7,884[1]	2,550[1]
Felician College; Lodi, N.J. 07644	1,068 (C)	P	8,550	8,550	n.a.
Ferris State University; Big Rapids, Mich. 49307	9,991 (C)	Pub	3,412[1]	6,911[1]	2,086[1]
Ferrum College; Ferrum, Va. 24088	1,124 (C)	P	9,950	9,950	4,500
Findlay, University of; Findlay, Ohio 45840	3,190 (C)	P	12,500	12,500	5,210
Fisk University; Nashville, Tenn. 37208	900 (C)	P	6,990	6,990	3,948
Fitchburg State College; Fitchburg, Mass. 01420	4,500 (C)	Pub	3,234[1]	7,368[1]	4,030[1]
Five Towns College; Dix Hills, N.Y. 11746–6055	684 (C)	P	8,100	8,100	3,400
Flagler College; St. Augustine, Fla. 32085	1,282 (C)	P	5,350	5,350	3,320
Florida, University of; Gainesville, Fla. 32611	28,479 (C)	Pub	1,830	7,100	5,430
Florida A&M University; Tallahassee, Fla. 32307	9,879 (C)	Pub	1,796[1]	6,706[1]	2,822[1]
Florida Atlantic University; Boca Raton, Fla. 33431-0991	12,211 (C)	Pub	1,788	6,693	3,950
Florida Baptist Theological College; Graceville, Fla. 32440	491 (C)	P	2,634	2,634	3,000
Florida Christian College; Kissimmee, Fla. 34744	152 (C)	P	3,575[1]	3,575[1]	2,820[1]
Florida Institute of Technology; Melbourne, Fla. 32901–6988	1,881 (C)	P	14,111	14,111	4,264
Florida International University; Miami, Fla. 33199	18,636 (C)	Pub	1,448	5,360	3,647
Florida Memorial College; Miami, Fla. 33054	1,500 (C)	P	4,940	4,940	3,190
Florida Southern College; Lakeland, Fla. 33801	1,760 (C)	P	9,350	9,350	5,100
Florida State University; Tallahassee, Fla. 32306	22,202 (C)	Pub	1,935	7,210	4,980
Fontbonne College; St. Louis, Mo. 63105	1,532 (C)	P	9,040	9,040	4,460
Fordham University; Bronx, N.Y. 10458	6,393 (C)	P	14,900	14,900	7,473
Forsyth School for Dental Hygienists; Boston, Mass. 02115	108 (C)	P	11,860	11,860	8,010
Fort Hays State University; Hays, Kan. 67601	4,266 (C)	Pub	1,902	6,169	3,172
Fort Lauderdale College; Fort Lauderdale, Fla. 33304	503 (C)	P	5,520	5,520	6,280
Fort Lewis College; Durango, Colo. 81301	4,109 (C)	Pub	1,857[1]	7,153[1]	3,518[1]
Fort Valley State College; Fort Valley, Ga. 31030	2,549 (C)	Pub	1,920	5,130	2,805
Framingham State College; Framingham, Mass. 01701	3,106 (C)	Pub	3,228[1]	7,362[1]	3,794[1]
Franciscan University of Steubenville; Steubenville, Ohio 43952	1,533 (C)	P	10,230	10,230	4,500
Francis Marion University; Florence, S.C. 29501–0547	3,550 (C)	Pub	2,920	5,840	3,138
Franklin and Marshall College; Lancaster, Pa. 17604-3003	1,834 (C)	P	21,300	21,300	4,330
Franklin College; Franklin, Ind. 46131	909 (C)	P	10,950	10,950	4,210
Franklin College; Switzerland	200 (C)	P	19,540	19,540	6,800
Franklin Pierce College; Rindge, N.H. 03461	1,164 (C)	P	14,095	14,095	4,900
Franklin University; Columbus, Ohio 43215-5399	3,990 (C)	P	5,644	5,644	n.a.
Freed-Hardeman University; Henderson, Tenn. 38340	1,204 (C)	P	6,620	6,620	3,370
Free Will Baptist Bible College; Nashville, Tenn. 37205	334 (C)	P	3,492	3,492	3,188
Fresno Pacific College; Fresno, Calif. 93702	488 (C)	P	10,500	10,500	3,500
Friends University; Wichita, Kan. 67213	1,912 (C)	P	9,057	9,057	3,130
Friends World Program. See Long Island University					
Frostburg State University; Frostburg, Md. 21532	3,072 (C)	Pub	3,072	6,548	4,390
Furman University; Greenville, S.C. 29613–0645	7,448 (C)	P	14,432	14,432	4,168
Gallaudet University, Washington, D.C. 20002	1,602 (C)	P	4,700	4,700	5,400
Gannon University; Erie, Pa. 16541	3,095 (C)	P	11,780	11,780	4,520
Gannon University–Villa Marie Campus; Erie, Pa. 16505	2,632 (W)	P	10,350	10,350	4,560
Gardner-Webb College; Boiling Springs, N.C. 28017	1,460 (C)	P	8,590	8,590	4,360
General Motors Institute. See GMI Engineering and Management Institute					
Geneva College; Beaver Falls, Pa. 15010	1,334 (C)	P	10,000	10,000	4,400
George Fox College; Newberg, Ore. 97132	1,213 (C)	P	13,800	13,800	4,380
George Mason University; Fairfax, Va. 22030	13,331 (C)	Pub	4,212	11,604	5,050
Georgetown College; Georgetown, Ky. 40324	1,136 (C)	P	8,890	8,990	3,950
Georgetown University; Washington, D.C. 20057	6,229 (C)	P	19,230	19,230	7,100
George Washington University, The; Washington, D.C. 20052	5,900 (C)	P	19,032	19,032	6,590
Georgia, University of; Athens, Ga. 30602	22,832 (C)	Pub	2,542	6,829	3,820
Georgia Baptist College of Nursing; Atlanta, Ga. 30312-1239	392 (W)	P	4,737	4,737	1,065
Georgia College; Milledgeville, Ga. 31061	4,551 (C)	Pub	1,743[1]	4,587[1]	3,022[1]
Georgia Institute of Technology; Atlanta, Ga. 30332	9,240 (C)	Pub	2,345[1]	6,933[1]	5,141[1]
Georgian Court College; Lakewood, N.J. 08701	1,843 (W)	P	9,750	9,750	4,150
Georgia Southern University; Statesboro, Ga. 30458	12,245 (C)	Pub	1,800[1]	5,400[1]	2,721[1]
Georgia Southwestern College; Americus, Ga. 31709	2,563 (C)	Pub	1,926	3,210	3,486
Georgia State University; Atlanta, Ga. 30303	17,161 (C)	Pub	2,000	7,200	n.a.
Gettysburg College; Gettysburg, Pa. 17325–1484	2,100 (C)	P	20,800	20,800	4,522
Glenville State College; Glenville, W. Va. 26351	2,269 (C)	Pub	1,782[1]	4,080[1]	3,262[1]
GMI Engineering & Management Institute; Flint, Mich. 48504	2,367 (C)	P	12,480	12,480	3,502
Goddard College; Plainfield, Vt. 05667	104 (C)	P	10,056	15,056	4,936
God's Bible School and College; Cincinnati, Ohio 45210	169 (C)	P	3,560	3,560	2,550
Golden Gate University; San Francisco, Calif. 94105	2,027 (C)	P	6,360	6,360	n.a.
Goldey Beacom College; Wilmington, Del. 19808	1,757 (C)	P	6,450	6,450	4,585

Institution and location	Enrollment	Control	Tuition ($) Res.	Tuition ($) Nonres.	Rm/Bd ($)
Gonzaga University; Spokane, Wash. 99258	2,938 (C)	P	13,957	13,957	4,800
Gordon College; Wenham, Mass 01984	1,190 (C)	P	13,300[1]	13,300[1]	4,230[1]
Goshen College; Goshen, Ind. 46526	1,100 (C)	P	9,900	9,900	3,760
Goucher College; Baltimore, Md. 21204	909 (C)	P	16,530	16,530	6,360
Governors State University; University Park, Ill. 60466	2,764 (C)	Pub	3,147	9,051	n.a.
Grace Bible College; Grand Rapids, Mich. 49509	153 (C)	P	5,000	5,000	3,400
Grace College; Winona Lake, Ind. 46590	680 (C)	P	9,230	9,230	4,070
Grace University; Omaha, Neb. 68108	414 (C)	P	4,950	4,950	2,850
Graceland College; Lamoni, Iowa 50140	1,058 (C)	P	9,760	9,760	3,200
Grambling State University; Grambling, La. 71245	6,781 (C)	Pub	2,088[1]	4,038[1]	2,636[1]
Grand Canyon University; Phoenix, Ariz. 85017	1,641 (C)	P	8,250	8,250	3,260
Grand Rapids Baptist College; Grand Rapids, Mich. 49505	777 (C)	P	6,520	6,520	4,082
Grand Valley State University; Allendale, Mich. 49401-9401	10,527 (C)	Pub	2,940	6,620	4,180
Grand View College; Des Moines, Iowa 50316	1,477 (C)	P	10,470	10,470	3,500
Gratz College; Melrose Park , Pa. 19126	65 (C)	P	6,400	6,400	n.a.
Great Falls, College of; Great Falls, Mont. 59405	1,237 (C)	P	5,170	5,170	1,780
Great Lakes Christian College; Lansing, Mich. 48917	213 (C)	P	4,218	4,218	3,000
Green Mountain College; Poultney, Vt. 05764	494 (C)	P	13,180	13,180	2,920
Greensboro College; Greensboro, N.C. 27401	992 (C)	P	9,150	9,150	3,840
Greenville College; Greenville, Ill. 62246	781 (C)	P	10,950	10,950	4,750
Grinnell College; Grinnell, Iowa 50112	1,243 (C)	P	16,636	16,636	4,782
Grove City College; Grove City, Pa. 16127	2,280 (C)	P	6,174	6,174	3,474
Guam, University of; Mangilao, Guam 96913	2,626 (C)	Pub	1,500	2,528	2,905
Guilford College; Greensboro, N.C. 27410	1,187 (C)	P	14,390	14,390	5,270
Gustavus Adolphus College; St. Peter, Minn. 56082	2,334 (C)	P	14,760	14,760	3,750
Gwynedd-Mercy College; Gwynedd Valley, Pa. 19437	1,837 (C)	P	11,450	11,450	5,800
Hahnemann University School of Health Sciences and Humanities; Philadelphia, Pa. 19102	917 (C)	P	8,880	8,880	4,600
Hamilton College; Clinton, N.Y. 13323	1,710 (C)	P	20,700	20,700	5,050
Hamline University; St. Paul, Minn. 55104	1,491 (C)	P	13,808	13,808	4,342
Hampden-Sydney College; Hampden-Sydney, Va. 23943	970 (M)	P	14,322	14,322	5,011
Hampshire College; Amherst, Mass. 01002	1,173 (C)	P	20,665[1]	20,665[1]	5,465[1]
Hampton University; Hampton, Va. 23668	5,582 (C)	P	7,764[1]	7,764[1]	3,518[1]
Hannibal-LaGrange College; Hannibal, Mo. 63401	949 (C)	P	6,688	6,688	2,610
Hanover College; Hanover, Ind. 47243	1,055 (C)	P	9,135	9,135	3,710
Harding University; Searcy, Ark. 72143	3,817 (C)	P	6,400	6,400	3,900
Hardin-Simmons University; Abilene, Tex. 79698	1,802 (C)	P	5,760	5,760	3,200
Harrington Institute of Interior Design; Chicago, Ill. 60605	396 (C)	P	8,970[1]	8,970[1]	n.a.[1]
Harris Stowe State College; St. Louis, Mo. 63103	1,480 (C)	Pub	1,671	3,240	n.a.
Hartford, University of; West Hartford, Conn. 06117	5,182 (C)	P	15,610	15,610	6,265
Hartford College for Women; Hartford, Conn. 06105	214 (W)	P	12,850	12,850	6,340
Hartwick College; Oneonta, N.Y. 13820	1,465 (C)	P	17,665	17,665	5,310
Harvard and Radcliffe Colleges; Cambridge, Mass. 02138	6,643 (C)	P	20,865	20,865	6,710
Harvey Mudd College. *See* Claremont Colleges					
Hastings College; Hastings, Neb. 68901	1,055 (C)	P	9,754	9,754	3,472
Haverford College; Haverford, Pa. 19041-1392	1,109 (C)	P	20,075	20,075	6,550
Hawaii, Univ. of-Hilo; Hilo, Hawaii 96720-4091	2,670 (C)	Pub	504	4,914	4,914
Hawaii, University of-Manoa; Honolulu, Hawaii 96822	13,225 (C)	Pub	1,558	4,558	4,400
Hawaii, University of-West Oahu; Pearl City, Hawaii 96782	744 (C)	Pub	914	960	960[7]
Hawaii Pacific University; Honolulu, Hawaii 96813	6,140 (C)	P	6,700	6,700	7,000
Hawaii Pacific University–Hawaii Loa Campus; Kaneohe, Hawaii 96744	6,975 (C)	P	6,700	6,700	6,500
Health Sciences, University of-The Chicago Medical School; North Chicago, Ill. 60064	77 (C)	P	13,550[1]	13,550[1]	n.a.[1]
Hebrew Theological College; Skokie, Ill. 60077	218 (C)	P	6,370[1]	6,370[1]	4,625[1]
Heidelberg College; Tiffin, Ohio 44883	1,167 (C)	P	14,606	14,606	4,674
Hellenic College; Brookline, Mass. 02146	81 (C)	P	7,150[1]	7,150[1]	5,200[1]
Henderson State University; Arkadelphia, Ark. 71923	3,442 (C)	Pub	1,824	3,648	2,680
Hendrix College; Conway, Ark. 72023	954 (C)	P	9,453	9,453	3,500
Herbert H. Lehman College. *See* New York, City University of					
Heritage College; Toppenish, Wash. 98948	517 (C)	P	7,919	7,919	n.a.
High Point University; High Point, N.C. 27262-3598	2,326 (C)	P	9,050	9,050	4,470
Hillsdale College; Hillsdale, Mich. 49242	1,183 (C)	P	11,970	11,970	4,940
Hillsdale Free Will Baptist College; Moore, Okla. 73153	152 (C)	P	3,270	3,270	3,400
Hiram College; Hiram, Ohio 44234	847 (C)	P	15,000	15,000	4,722
Hobart and William Smith Colleges; Geneva, N.Y. 14456	1,808 (C)	P	20,393	20,393	6,075
Hofstra University; Hempstead, N.Y. 11550	7,662 (C)	P	11,710[1]	11,710[1]	5,920[1]
Hollins College; Roanoke, Va. 24020	882 (W)	P	14,234	14,234	5,745
Holy Apostles College and Seminary; Cromwell, Conn. 06416	70 (C)	P	4,290	4,290	6,150
Holy Cross, College of the; Worcester, Mass. 01610	2,742 (C)	P	18,355[1]	18,355[1]	6,300[1]
Holy Family College; Philadelphia, Pa. 19114	1,066 (C)	P	9,500	9,500	n.a.
Holy Names College; Oakland, Calif. 94619	603 (C)	P	12,000	12,000	4,080
Hong Kong Baptist College; Kowloon, Hong Kong	3,652 (C)	Pub	2,200[3]	2,200[3]	n.a.[3]
Hood College; Frederick, Md 21701	1,114 (W)	P	14,780	14,780	6,400
Hope College, Holland, Mich. 49423	2,825 (C)	P	13,234	13,234	4,516

Institution and location	Enrollment	Control	Tuition ($) Res.	Tuition ($) Nonres.	Rm/Bd ($)
Houghton College, Houghton, N.Y. 14744	1,357 (C)	P	10,890	10,890	3,720
Houston, Univ. of; Houston, Tex. 77294-2161	22,386 (C)	Pub	1,254	4,518	4,200
Houston, Univ.-of-Clear Lake; Houston, Tex. 77058	3,556 (C)	Pub	1,422	4,926	4,115
Houston, Univ.-of-Downtown; Houston, Tex .77002	8,056 (C)	Pub	1,440	4,880	n.a.
Houston, Univ.-of-Victoria; Victoria, Tex. 77901	638 (C)	Pub	1,488	4,992	n.a.
Houston Baptist University; Houston, Tex. 77074	1,700 (C)	P	6,954	6,954	3,440
Howard Payne University; Brownwood, Tex. 76801–2794	1,469 (C)	P	5,940	5,940	3,494
Howard University; Washington, D.C. 20059	7,996 (C)	P	9,105	9,105	2,835
Humboldt State University; Arcata, Calif. 95521	6,245 (C)	Pub	1,820[1]	9,200[1]	4,622[1]
Humphreys College; Stockton, Calif. 95207	792 (C)	P	5,460	5,460	3,345
Hunter College. See New York, City University of					
Huntingdon College; Montgomery, Ala. 36194	760 (C)	P	8,645	8,645	4,415
Huntington College; Huntington, Ind. 46750	531 (C)	P	10,450	10,450	4,470
Huron University; Huron, S.D. 57350	403 (C)	P	7,878	7,878	3,298
Husson College; Bangor, Me. 04401	1,832 (C)	P	8,140	8,140	4,300
Huston-Tillotson College; Austin, Tex. 78702	611 (C)	P	5,544	5,544	3,878
Idaho, University of; Moscow, Idaho 83843	8,046 (C)	Pub	1,620	7,000	3,680
Idaho State University; Pocatello, Idaho 83209	9,638 (C)	Pub	1,500[1]	6,000[1]	3,140[1]
Illinois, Univ. of, at Chicago; Chicago, Ill. 60680	16,206 (C)	Pub	3,974	8,894	5,188
Illinois, Univ. of, at Urbana-Champaign; Urbana, Ill. 61801	25,348 (C)	Pub	3,986	9,428	4,393
Illinois Benedictine College; Lisle, Ill. 60532	1,640 (C)	P	11,030	11,030	4,750
Illinois College; Jacksonville, Ill. 62650	986 (C)	P	8,600	8,600	4,000
Illinois Institute of Technology; Chicago, Ill. 60616	2,537 (C)	P	14,550	14,550	4,600
Illinois State University; Normal, Ill. 61761	16,516 (C)	Pub	3,544	8,926	3,627
Illinois Wesleyan University; Bloomington, Ill. 61702	1,809 (C)	P	15,510	15,510	4,290
Immaculata College; Immaculata, Pa. 19345	1,550 (W)	P	10,880	10,880	5,678
Incarnate Word College; San Antonio, Tex. 78209	2,282 (C)	P	9,655	9,655	4,337
Indiana Institute of Technology; Fort Wayne, Ind. 46803	477 (C)	P	8,960	8,960	3,970
Indianapolis, University of; Indianapolis, Ind. 46227	3,095 (C)	P	11,730	11,730	4,200
Indiana State University; Terre Haute, Ind. 47809	10,033 (C)	Pub	3,000	7,225	3,725
Indiana University of Pennsylvania; Indiana, Pa. 15705	12,825 (C)	Pub	3,431[1]	5,810[1]	—[1]
Indiana University-Bloomington; Bloomington, Ind. 47405	35,551 (C)	Pub	2,900[1]	9,766[1]	3,990[1]
Indiana University-East; Richmond, Ind. 47374	2,387 (C)	Pub	2,368[1]	6,139[1]	n.a.[1]
Indiana University-Kokomo; Kokomo, Ind. 46904–9003	3,442 (C)	Pub	2,000	5,200	n.a.
Indiana University-Northwest; Gary, Ind. 46408	5,029 (C)	Pub	1,895[1]	4,912[1]	n.a.[1]
Indiana University-Purdue University at Fort Wayne; Fort Wayne, Ind. 46805	11,513 (C)	Pub	3,156[1]	7,067[1]	n.a.[1]
Indiana University-Purdue University at Indianapolis; Indianapolis, Ind. 46202-5143	19,483 (C)	Pub	4,149[1]	12,735[1]	3,400[1]
Indiana University-South Bend; South Bend, Ind. 46634	6,125 (C)	Pub	2,027	5,540	n.a.
Indiana University-Southeast; New Albany, Ind. 47150	5,388 (C)	Pub	2,000	5,184	n.a.
Indiana Wesleyan University; Marion, Ind. 46953	1,656 (C)	P	9,725	9,725	3,820
Industrial Engineering College of Chicago; Chicago, Ill. 60607	240 (C)	P	4,800	4,800	n.a.
Insurance, College of; New York, N.Y. 10007	733 (C)	P	12,200	12,200	7,922
Inter-American University of Puerto Rico-Arecibo Campus; Arecibo, P.R. 00614	4,633 (C)	P	2,930[1]	2,930[1]	4,416[1]
International Institute of A.C.E.; Lewisville, Tex. 75067	75 (C)	P	2,000	2,000	2,800
International Training, School for; Brattleboro, Vt. 05301	55 (C)	P	11,500	11,500	4,593
Iona College; New Rochelle, N.Y. 10801	4,626 (C)	P	11,330	11,330	6,800
Iowa, University of; Iowa City, Iowa 52242	18,219 (C)	Pub	2,386	8,636	3,780
Iowa State University; Ames, Iowa 50011	20,132 (C)	Pub	2,386	8,004	3,382
Iowa Wesleyan College; Mount Pleasant, Iowa 52641	876 (C)	P	10,920	10,920	3,840
Ithaca College; Ithaca, N.Y. 14850	5,450 (C)	P	15,250	15,250	6,594
ITT Technical Institute; West Covina, Calif. 91790-2767	800 (C)	P	7,824	7,824	n.a.
Jackson State University; Jackson, Miss. 39217	6,346 (C)	Pub	2,430	4,664	3,816
Jacksonville State University; Jacksonville, Ala. 36265-9982	6,558 (C)	Pub	1,740[1]	2,610[1]	2,675[1]
Jacksonville University; Jacksonville, Fla. 32211	2,142 (C)	P	10,580	10,580	4,598
James Madison University; Harrisonburg, Va. 22807	10,152 (C)	Pub	4,014	8,294	4,680
Jamestown College; Jamestown, N.D. 58401	1,014 (C)	P	7,970	7,970	3,080
Jarvis Christian College; Hawkins, Tex. 75765	497 (C)	P	6,085	6,085	3,485
Jersey City State College; Jersey City, N.J. 07305	5,888 (C)	Pub	3,150	4,390	4,800
Jewish Theological Seminary of America; New York, N.Y. 10027	112 (C)	P	7,000	7,000	6,400
John Brown University; Siloam Springs, Ark. 72761	1,114 (C)	P	7,650	7,650	3,930
John Carroll University; University Heights, Ohio 44118	3,532 (C)	P	12,390	12,390	5,550
John F. Kennedy University; Orinda, Calif. 94563	377 (C)	P	6,336[1]	6,336[1]	n.a.[1]
John Jay Coll. of Criminal Justice. See New York, City Univ. of					
Johns Hopkins University; Baltimore, Md. 21218	3,297 (C)	P	19,750	19,750	6,500
School of Nursing; Baltimore, Md. 21205	214 (C)	P	20,480	20,480	n.a.
The Peabody Institute; Baltimore, Md. 21202–2397	269 (C)	P	18,320	18,320	7,910
Johnson and Wales University; Providence, R.I. 02903	7,365 (C)	P	10,900	10,900	5,100
Johnson Bible College; Knoxville, Tenn. 37998	403 (C)	P	4,475	4,475	3,125
Johnson C. Smith University; Charlotte, N.C. 28216	1,278 (C)	P	7,128	7,128	3,040
Johnson State College; Johnson, Vt. 05656	1,562 (C)	Pub	4,040	8,552	4,794
John Wesley College; High Point, N.C. 27265	77 (C)	P	4,534	4,534	3,000
Jones College—Jacksonville; Jacksonville, Fla. 32211	1,700 (C)	P	5,220	5,220	n.a.

Institution and location	Enrollment	Control	Tuition ($) Res.	Nonres.	Rm/Bd ($)
Jordan College; Cedar Springs, Mich. 49319	2,118 (C)	P	4,275	4,275	n.a.
Judson College; Elgin, Ill. 60123	605 (C)	P	5,644	5,644	4,690
Judson College; Marion, Ala. 36756	648 (W)	P	5,780	5,780	3,600
Juilliard School; New York, N.Y. 10023	505 (C)	P	13,600	13,600	6,300
Juniata College; Huntingdon, Pa. 16652	1,038 (C)	P	15,740	15,740	4,620
Kalamazoo College; Kalamazoo, Mich. 49006-3295	1,241 (C)	P	16,713	16,713	5,262
Kansas, University of; Lawrence, Kan. 66045	18,804 (C)	Pub	2,160	7,878	3,544
Kansas City Art Institute; Kansas City, Mo. 64111	559 (C)	P	14,785	14,785	4,340
Kansas City College and Bible School; Overland Park, Kan. 66204	41 (C)	P	4,560	4,560	2,780
Kansas Newman College; Wichita, Kan. 67213	1,954 (C)	P	8,100	8,100	5,116
Kansas State University; Manhattan, Kan. 66506	16,992 (C)	Pub	1,733	7,344	n.a.
Kansas Wesleyan University; Salina, Kan. 67401	738 (C)	P	9,220	9,220	3,600
Kean College of New Jersey; Union, N.J. 07083	10,907 (C)	Pub	2,810[1]	3,906[1]	4,142[1]
Keene State College; Keene, N.H. 03431	3,830 (C)	Pub	7,537[1]	12,757[1]	4,111[1]
Kendall College; Evanston, Ill. 60201	371 (C)	P	8,931	8,931	4,998
Kendall College of Art and Design; Grand Rapids, Mich. 49503	574 (C)	P	10,525	10,525	n.a.
Kennesaw College, Marietta, Ga. 30061	11,670 (C)	Pub	1,776	4,986	n.a.
Kent State University; Kent, Ohio 44242-0001	19,444 (C)	Pub	3,927[1]	7,854[1]	3,666[1]
Kentucky, University of; Lexington, Ky. 40506	17,658 (C)	Pub	2,260	6,780	3,078
Kentucky Christian College; Grayson, Ky. 41143	476 (C)	P	4,640	4,640	3,520
Kentucky State University; Frankfort, Ky. 40601	2,564 (C)	Pub	1,860	5,220	2,984
Kentucky Wesleyan College; Owensboro, Ky. 42301	767 (C)	P	8,950	8,950	4,300
Kenyon College; Gambier, Ohio 43022	1,510 (C)	P	20,794	20,794	3,866
Keuka College; Keuka Park, N.Y. 14478	808 (C)	P	10,200	10,200	4,780
King College; Bristol, Tenn. 37620	562 (C)	P	9,624	9,624	3,350
King's College; Wilkes-Barre, Pa 18711	2,176 (C)	P	12,260	12,260	5,500
King's College, The; Briarcliff Manor, N.Y. 10510	413 (C)	P	8,500[1]	8,500[1]	3,920[1]
Knox College; Galesburg, Ill. 61401	991 (C)	P	16,692	16,692	4,257
Knoxville College; Knoxville, Tenn. 37921	846 (C)	P	5,992	5,992	3,450
Kutztown University; Kutztown, Pa. 19530	6,960 (C)	Pub	3,698	8,552	3,000
Laboratory Institute of Merchandising; New York, N.Y. 10022	180 (C)	P	10,450	10,450	n.a.
Lafayette College; Easton, Pa. 18042	2,027 (C)	P	19,546	19,546	6,000
LaGrange College; LaGrange, Ga. 30240	999 (C)	P	8,200	8,200	5,912
Lake Erie College; Painesville, Ohio 44077	577 (C)	P	11,840	11,840	4,906
Lake Forest College; Lake Forest, Ill. 60045	964 (C)	P	18,036	18,036	4,204
Lakeland College; Sheboygan, Wis. 53082	3,303 (C)	P	10,270	10,270	4,020
Lake Superior State University; Sault Ste. Marie, Mich. 49783	3,157 (C)	Pub	3,426	6,612	4,332
Lakeview College of Nursing; Danville, Ill. 61832	116 (C)	P	6,000	6,000	n.a.
Lamar University; Beaumont, Tex. 77710	11,488 (C)	Pub	1,484	4,988	3,338
Lambuth College; Jackson, Tenn. 38301	1,464 (C)	P	5,600	5,600	3,570
Lancaster Bible College; Lancaster, Pa. 17601	572 (C)	P	7,770	7,770	3,500
Lander University; Greenwood S.C. 29649	2,378 (C)	Pub	3,390[1]	4,988[1]	3,170[1]
Lane College; Jackson, Tenn. 38301	744 (C)	P	5,196	5,196	3,202
Langston University; Langston, Okla. 73050	3,820 (C)	Pub	1,432	3,256	2,580
Laredo State University; Laredo, Tex. 78040-9960	794 (C)	Pub	1,030[1]	4,294[1]	3,380[1]
La Roche College; Pittsburgh, Pa. 15237	1,469 (C)	P	9,286	9,286	5,022
La Salle University; Philadelphia, Pa. 19141	2,506 (C)	P	13,160	13,160	6,200
Lasell College; Newton, Mass. 02166	620 (W)	P	12,700	12,700	6,300
LaSierra University; Riverside, Calif. 92515	1,330 (C)	P	12,750	12,750	3,885
La Verne, University of; La Verne, Calif 91750	1,489 (C)	P	14,220	14,220	4,500
Lawrence Technological University; Southfield, Mich. 48075	4,159 (C)	P	8,690	8,690	3,216
Lawrence University; Appleton, Wis. 54912	1,161 (C)	P	18,057	18,057	4,038
Lebanese American University; Beirut, Lebanon	2,634 (C)	P	10,500	10,500	4,500
Lebanon Valley College; Annville, Pa. 17003	1,545 (C)	P	14,785	14,785	4,755
Lee College; Cleveland, Tenn. 37311	2,197 (C)	P	4,992	4,992	3,420
Lee College at the University of Judaism; Los Angeles, Calif. 90077	93 (C)	P	12,040	12,040	6,300
Lehigh University; Bethlehem, Pa. 18015	4,406 (C)	P	19,650	19,650	5,810
Le Moyne College; Syracuse, N.Y. 13214-1399	2,386 (C)	P	11,700	11,700	5,040
Le Moyne-Owen College; Memphis, Tenn. 38126	1,082 (C)	P	6,400	6,400	3,916
Lenoir-Rhyne College; Hickory, N.C. 28603	1,422 (C)	P	10,900	10,900	4,060
Lesley College; Cambridge, Mass. 02138-2790	535 (W)	P	12,900	12,900	6,075
LeTourneau University; Longview, Tex. 75607	1,833 (C)	P	4,715	4,715	2,220
Lewis and Clark College; Portland, Ore. 97219	1,797 (C)	P	16,840	16,840	5,070
Lewis Clark State College; Lewiston, Idaho 83501	2,316 (C)	Pub	1,478	6,000	3,230
Lewis University; Romeoville, Ill. 60441	3,378 (C)	P	8,256	8,256	5,000
Liberty University; Lynchburg, Va. 24506	3,603 (C)	P	7,350	7,350	4,800
L.I.F.E. Bible College; San Dimas, Calif. 91773–3298	372 (C)	P	4,320	4,320	2,600
L.I.F.E. Bible College East; Christiansburg, V.A. 24073	105 (C)	P	2,750	2,750	2,300
Lifelong Learning, School for; Concord, N.H. 03301	3,144 (C)	Pub	3,144	3,480	n.a.
Limestone College, Gaffney, S.C. 29340	326 (C)	P	8,000	8,000	3,600
Lincoln Christian College; Lincoln, Ill. 62656	528 (C)	P	4,288	4,288	3,100
Lincoln Memorial University; Harrogate, Tenn. 37752	912 (C)	P	6,550	6,550	3,250
Lincoln University; San Francisco, Calif. 94118	185 (C)	P	10,510	10,.510	n.a.
Lincoln University; Jefferson City, Mo. 65101	3,149 (C)	Pub	2,216	4,232	2,728
Lincoln University; Lincoln University, Pa. 19352	1,279 (C)	Pub	4,431	6,618	3,750

Institution and location	Enrollment	Control	Tuition ($) Res.	Nonres.	Rm/Bd ($)
Lindenwood College; St. Charles, Mo. 63301–4949	2,143 (C)	P	14,700	14,700	4,800
Lindsey Wilson College; Columbia, Ky. 42728	1,327 (C)	P	7,128	7,128	3,820
Linfield College; McMinnville, Ore. 97128	1,528 (C)	P	14,270	14,270	4,721
Livingstone College; Salisbury, N.C. 28144	683 (C)	P	9,200	9,200	5,800
Lock Haven University of Pennsylvania; Lock Haven, Pa. 17745	3,878 (C)	Pub	7,378	12,136	—
Long Island University:					
Brooklyn Campus; Brooklyn, N.Y. 11201	6,279 (C)	P	10,483[1]	10,483[1]	4,620[1]
C.W. Post Campus; Greenvale, N.Y. 11548	4,460 (C)	P	12,855	12,855	5,880
Friends World Program–Southampton Campus;					
Southampton, N.Y. 11968	140 (C)	P	11,392	11,392	5,754
Southampton Campus; Southampton, N.Y. 11968	1,294 (C)	P	13,740	13,740	6,340
Longwood College; Farmville, Va. 23909	2,915 (C)	Pub	4,370	9,842	4,082
Loras College; Dubuque, Iowa 52001	1,807 (C)	P	11,826	11,826	4,370
Louisiana College; Pineville, La. 71359	983 (C)	P	5,810	5,810	2,940
Louisiana State Univ. and A&M Coll.; Baton Rouge, La. 70803	19,972 (C)	Pub	2,628[1]	5,928[1]	3,310[1]
Louisiana State University-Shreveport, Shreveport, La. 71115	4,017 (C)	Pub	1,930[1]	4,630[1]	n.a.[1]
Louisiana Tech University; Ruston, La. 71272	8,471 (C)	Pub	2,262	4,257	2,385
Louisville, University of; Louisville, Ky. 40292	15,469 (C)	Pub	2,470	6,990	3,800
Lourdes College; Sylvania, Ohio 43560	4,496 (C)	P	5,888	5,888	n.a.
Loyola College; Baltimore, Md. 21210	3,143 (C)	P	14,260	14,260	6,630
Loyola Marymount University; Los Angeles, Calif. 90045	3,956 (C)	P	14,640	14,640	6,000
Loyola University; New Orleans, La. 70118	3,602 (C)	P	12,031	12,031	5,660
Loyola University of Chicago; Chicago, Ill. 60611	5,236 (C)	P	13,000	13,000	5,910
Lubbock Christian University; Lubbock, Tex. 79407	1,147 (C)	P	7,742	7,742	3,080
Lutheran Bible Institute of Seattle; Issaquah, Wash. 98027	175 (C)	P	4,160	4,160	3,900
Luther College; Decorah, Iowa 52101	2,383 (C)	P	14,100	14,100	3,600
Lycoming College; Williamsport, Pa. 17701	1,523 (C)	P	14,700	14,700	4,400
Lynchburg College; Lynchburg, Va. 24501	1,646 (C)	P	14,080	14,080	4,400
Lyndon State College; Lyndonville, Vt. 05851	1,201 (C)	Pub	4,040	8,552	4,794
Lynn University; Boca Raton, Fla. 33431	1,200 (C)	P	15,250	15,250	6,950
Macalester College; St. Paul, Minn. 55105	1,712 (C)	P	16,686	16,686	4,975
MacMurray College; Jacksonville, Ill. 62650	615 (C)	P	10,190	10,190	3,900
Madonna University; Livonia, Mich. 48150	4,055 (C)	P	4,320	4,320	4,000
Maharishi International University; Fairfield, Iowa 52557-1155	459 (C)	P	13,976	13,976	3,600
Maine, Univ. of, at Augusta; Augusta, Maine 04330	5,320 (C)	Pub	2,940	6,600	n.a.
Maine, Univ. of, at Farmington; Farmington, Maine 04938	2,250 (C)	Pub	2,970[1]	7,020[1]	3,970[1]
Maine, Univ. of, at Fort Kent; Fort Kent, Maine 04743-1292	641 (C)	Pub	2,610[1]	6,360[1]	3,600[1]
Maine, Univ. of, at Machias; Machias, Maine 04654	948 (C)	Pub	2,875[1]	6,535[1]	3,680[1]
Maine, Univ. of, at Orono; Orono, Maine 04469	10,206 (C)	Pub	3,150	8,910	4,700
Maine, Univ. of, at Presque Isle; Presque Isle, Maine 04769	1,511 (C)	Pub	2,430	5,598	3,704
Maine College of Art; Portland, Maine 04101	281 (C)	P	12,300	12,300	5,494
Maine Maritime Academy—The Ocean College;					
Castine, Maine 04420	660 (C)	Pub	4,000	7,100	4,750
Malone College; Canton, Ohio 44709	1,820 (C)	P	10,345	10,345	4,020
Manchester College; North Manchester, Ind. 46962	1,001 (C)	P	11,470	11,470	4,030
Manhattan Christian College; Manhattan, Kan. 66502	251 (C)	P	4,730	4,730	2,946
Manhattan College; Riverdale, N.Y. 10471	2,300 (C)	P	13,000	13,000	7,000
Manhattan School of Music; New York, N.Y. 10027	414 (C)	P	14,730	14,730	9,000
Manhattanville College; Purchase, N.Y. 10577	980 (C)	P	15,900	15,900	7,370
Mankato State University; Mankato, Minn. 56001	11,048 (C)	Pub	2,582[1]	5,208[1]	2,768[1]
Mannes College of Music; New York, N.Y. 10024	96 (C)	P	13,850	13,850	7,900
Mansfield University of Pennsylvania; Mansfield, Pa. 16933	3,223 (C)	Pub	4,376	9,132	3,324
Marian College; Indianapolis, Ind. 46222	1,350 (C)	P	10,700	10,700	4,024
Marian College of Fond du Lac; Fond du Lac, Wis. 54935	1,856 (C)	P	10,120	10,120	3,700
Marietta College; Marietta, Ohio 45750	1,257 (C)	P	14,850	14,850	4,030
Marist College; Poughkeepsie, N.Y. 12601	3,557 (C)	P	11,700	11,700	6,230
Marlboro College; Marlboro, Vt. 05344	270 (C)	P	18,376	18,376	6,140
Marquette University; Milwaukee, Wis. 53233	7,691 (C)	P	12,370	12,370	5,100
Marshall University; Huntington, W. Va. 25755	10,341 (C)	Pub	3,826	5,696	3,920
Mars Hill College; Mars Hill, N.C. 28754	1,076 (C)	P	8,500	8,500	3,550
Martin University; Indianapolis, Ind. 46218	510 (C)	P	4,800	4,800	n.a.
Mary, University of; Bismarck, N.D. 58504	1,700 (C)	P	6,950	6,950	2,798
Mary Baldwin College; Staunton, Va. 24401	950 (W)	P	11,700	11,700	7,400
Marygrove College; Detroit, Mich. 48221	1,090 (C)	P	8,880[1]	8,880[1]	3,956[1]
Mary Hardin-Baylor, University of; Belton, Tex. 76513	2,244 (C)	P	5,850	5,850	3,890
Maryland, Univ. of-Baltimore County; Baltimore, Md. 21228	8,808 (C)	Pub	3,852	8,680	4,474
Maryland, Univ. of-College Park; College Park, Md. 20742	21,163 (C)	Pub	3,794	9,738	5,146
Maryland, Univ. of-Eastern Shore; Princess Anne, Md. 21853	2,266 (C)	Pub	2,855	7,536	4,030
Maryland, Univ. of, University College; College Park, Md. 20742	10,488 (C)	Pub	5,220	5,850	n.a.
Maryland Institute-College of Art; Baltimore, Md. 21217	814 (C)	P	14,950	14,950	5,050[1]
Marylhurst College; Marylhurst, Ore. 97036	1,048 (C)	P	9,087[1]	9,087[1]	n.a.[1]
Marymount College; Tarrytown, N.Y. 10591	1,031 (W)	P	12,500	12,500	6,750
Marymount Manhattan College; New York, N.Y. 10021	1,406 (C)	P	11,340	11,340	6,656
Marymount Univ.; Arlington, Va. 22207	2,066 (C)	P	11,900	11,900	5,470
Maryville College; Maryville, Tenn. 37801	843 (C)	P	12,096	12,096	4,378
Maryville University-St. Louis; St. Louis, Mo. 63141	2,859 (C)	P	9,800	9,800	4,750

Institution and location	Enrollment	Control	Tuition ($) Res.	Nonres.	Rm/Bd ($)
Mary Washington College; Fredericksburg, Va. 22401	3,637 (C)	Pub	3,300	8,190	5,024
Marywood College; Scranton, Pa. 18509	1,848 (C)	P	12,240	12,240	4,800
Massachusetts, Univ. of–Amherst; Amherst, Mass. 01003	17,504 (C)	Pub	5,574[1]	11,920[1]	4,162[1]
Massachusetts, Univ. of–Boston; Boston, Mass. 02125-3393	9,595 (C)	Pub	3,722[1]	11,657[1]	n.a.[1]
Massachusetts, Univ. of–Dartmouth; North Dartmouth, Mass. 02747	4,781 (C)	Pub	3,850[1]	9,627[1]	4,614[1]
Massachusetts, Univ. of–Lowell; Lowell, Mass. 01854	11,325 (C)	Pub	4,735	9,879	4,496
Massachusetts College of Art; Boston, Mass. 02115	1,261 (C)	Pub	4,822[1]	9,781[1]	5,800[1]
Massachusetts College of Pharmacy and Allied Health Sciences; Boston, Mass. 02115	765 (C)	P	11,875[1]	11,875[1]	6,720[1]
Massachusetts Institute of Technology; Cambridge, Mass. 02139	4,520 (C)	P	20,100[1]	20,100[1]	5,975[1]
Massachusetts Maritime Academy; Buzzards Bay, Mass. 02532	686 (C)	Pub	3,524[1]	8,483[1]	3,977[1]
Master's College, The; Newhall, Calif. 91322	819 (C)	P	9,992	9,992	4,314
Mayville State University; Mayville, N.D. 58257	716 (C)	Pub	1,920	4,726	2,572
McKendree College; Lebanon, Ill. 62258	1,632 (C)	P	8,640	8,640	3,865
McMurry College; Abilene, Tex. 79697	1,384 (C)	P	7,410	7,410	3,705
McNeese State University; Lake Charles, La. 70609	7,658 (C)	Pub	1,968[1]	4,516[1]	2,310[1]
McPherson College; McPherson, Kan. 67460	459 (C)	P	8,600	8,600	3,750
Medaille College; Buffalo, N.Y. 14214	1,144 (C)	P	9,360	9,360	4,400
Medcenter One College of Nursing; Bismarck, N.D. 58501	82 (C)	Pub	5,770[1]	5,770[1]	2,388[1]
Medical College of Georgia; Augusta, Ga. 30912	921 (C)	Pub	2,148[1]	5,946[1]	2,749[1]
Medical University of South Carolina; Charleston, S.C. 29425	995 (C)	Pub	3,060	6,120	3,460
Memphis College of Art; Memphis, Tenn. 38104	188 (C)	P	9,900	9,900	4,300
Memphis State University; Memphis, Tenn. 38152	15,767 (C)	Pub	2,130	6,264	3,140
Menlo College; Atherton, Calif. 94027-4185	560 (C)	P	16,975	16,975	6,200
Mercer University; Macon, Ga. 31207	2,224 (C)	P	12,987	12,987	4,365
Mercy College; Dobbs Ferry, N.Y. 10522	6,128 (C)	P	7,650	7,650	4,000
Mercyhurst College; Erie, Pa. 16546	2,259 (C)	P	11,010	11,010	4,251
Meredith College; Raleigh, N.C. 27607-5298	2,172 (W)	P	7,100	7,100	3,400
Merrimack College; North Andover, Mass. 01845	2,952 (C)	P	12,500[1]	12,500[1]	6,400[1]
Mesa State College; Grand Junction, Colo. 81502	4,638 (C)	Pub	1,872	5,642	4,100
Messiah College; Grantham, Pa. 17027	2,311 (C)	P	10,940	10,940	5,040
Methodist College; Fayetteville, N.C. 28311-1499	1,655 (C)	P	10,005	10,005	3,975
Metropolitan State College of Denver; Denver, Colo. 80204	17,461 (C)	Pub	1,729	6,198	n.a.
Metropolitan State University; St. Paul, Minn. 55101	5,444 (C)	Pub	9,011[1]	19,465[1]	n.a.[1]
Miami, University of; Coral Gables, Fla. 33124	8,046 (C)	P	17,700	17,700	6,852
Miami University; Oxford, Ohio 45056	16,104 (C)	Pub	4,612[1]	9,728[1]	3,960[1]
Michigan, Univ. of–Ann Arbor; Ann Arbor, Mich. 48109	23,088 (C)	Pub	5,550	16,776	4,898
Michigan, Univ. of–Dearborn; Dearborn, Mich. 48128	7,111 (C)	Pub	5,175	12,183	n.a.
Michigan, Univ. of–Flint; Flint, Mich. 48502	5,854 (C)	Pub	3,092	9,534	n.a.
Michigan Christian College; Rochester Hills, Mich. 48307	411 (C)	P	5,760	5,760	3,540
Michigan State University; East Lansing, Mich. 48824	31,056 (C)	Pub	4,443	11,028	3,764
Michigan Technological University; Houghton, Mich. 49931	5,473 (C)	Pub	3,636[1]	8,253[1]	3,978[1]
Mid-America Bible College; Oklahoma City, Okla. 73170	290 (C)	P	4,098	4,098	3,196
Mid-America Nazarene College; Olathe, Kan. 66062	1,270 (C)	P	7,878	7,878	3,928
Middlebury College; Middlebury, Vt. 05753–6002	1,950 (C)	P	27,020	27,020	—
Middle Tennessee State University; Murfreesboro, Tenn. 37132	12,744 (C)	Pub	1,792[1]	5,726[1]	2,840[1]
Midland Lutheran College; Fremont, Neb. 68025	1,019 (C)	P	10,990	10,990	3,060
Midway College; Midway, Ky. 40347	970 (W)	P	7,750	7,750	4,250
Midwestern State University; Wichita Falls, Tex. 76308	5,334 (C)	Pub	1,586[1]	5,876[1]	3,386[1]
Miles College; Birmingham, Ala. 35208	1,068 (C)	P	4,350	4,350	2,700
Millersville University of Pennsylvania; Millersville, Pa. 17551-0302	6,701 (C)	Pub	4,100	8,714	4,038
Milligan College; Milligan College, Tenn. 37682	786 (C)	P	8,800	8,800	3,500
Millikin University; Decatur, Ill. 62522	1,863 (C)	P	12,596	12,596	4,596
Millsaps College; Jackson, Miss. 39210	1,252 (C)	P	12,700	12,700	4,770
Mills College; Oakland, Calif. 94613	861 (W)	P	15,384	15,384	6,180
Milwaukee Institute of Art and Design; Milwaukee, Wis. 53202	511 (C)	P	12,600	12,600	5,500
Milwaukee School of Engineering; Milwaukee, Wis. 53202-0644	2,712 (C)	P	12,375	12,375	3,765
Minneapolis Coll. of Art and Design; Minneapolis, Minn. 55404	585 (C)	P	13,870	13,870	3,600
Minnesota, Univ. of–Duluth; Duluth, Minn. 55812	7,017 (C)	Pub	3,339[1]	9,284[1]	3,492[1]
Minnesota, Univ. of–Morris; Morris, Minn. 56267	2,000 (C)	Pub	4,020	11,214	3,359
Minnesota, Univ. of–Twin Cities; Minneapolis, Minn. 55455-0213	25,238 (C)	Pub	3,395[1]	9,190[1]	3,775[1]
Minnesota Bible College; Rochester, Minn. 55902	99 (C)	P	4,839	4,839	3,045
Minot State University; Minot, N.D. 58707	3,673 (C)	Pub	1,960	4,933	1,988
Mississippi, University of; University, Miss. 38677	7,850 (C)	Pub	2,456[1]	5,006[1]	2,900[1]
Mississippi, Univ. of, Medical Center; Jackson, Miss. 39216	472 (C)	Pub	7,955[1]	13,955[1]	n.a.[1]
Mississippi College; Clinton, Miss. 39058	2,418 (C)	P	4,975	4,975	3,040
Mississippi State University; Mississippi State, Miss. 39762	10,981 (C)	Pub	2,561	5,021	3,084
Mississippi University for Women; Columbus, Miss. 39701	2,773 (C)	Pub	2,244	6,630	2,367
Mississippi Valley State University; Itta Bena, Miss. 38941	2,169 (C)	Pub	2,287[1]	4,420[1]	2,425[1]
Missouri, Univ. of–Columbia; Columbia, Mo. 65211	16,439 (C)	Pub	3,538	9,720	3,619
Missouri, Univ. of–Kansas City; Kansas City, Mo. 64110	5,896 (C)	Pub	3,106	8,405	3,925
Missouri, Univ. of–Rolla; Rolla, Mo. 65401	4,487 (C)	Pub	3,954	10,136	3,735
Missouri, Univ. of–St. Louis; St. Louis, Mo. 63121	9,395 (C)	Pub	3,061	8,361	4,200
Missouri Baptist College; St. Louis, Mo. 63141	1,429 (C)	P	7,370	7,370	3,550
Missouri Southern State College; Joplin, Mo. 64801	5,334 (C)	Pub	1,596	3,192	2,924

Institution and location	Enrollment	Control	Tuition ($) Res.	Tuition ($) Nonres.	Rm/Bd ($)
Missouri Valley College; Marshall, Mo. 65340	1,206 (C)	P	9,500	9,500	5,000
Missouri Western State College; St. Joseph, Mo. 64507	5,124 (C)	Pub	2,126[1]	4,028[1]	2,444[1]
Mobile College; Mobile, Ala. 36613	1,986 (C)	P	9,990	9,990	3,680
Molloy College; Rockville Centre, N.Y. 11570	2,481 (C)	P	8,736	8,736	n.a.
Monmouth College; Monmouth, Ill. 61462	700 (C)	P	13,660	13,660	4,200
Monmouth University; West Long Branch, N.J. 07764	2,826 (C)	P	13,140	13,140	5,860
Montana, University of; Missoula, Mont. 59812	8,576 (C)	Pub	2,200	6,300	3,800
Montana State University–Billings; Billings, Mont. 59101	3,440 (C)	Pub	2,172	5,896	3,160
Montana State University; Bozeman, Mont. 59717	9,769 (C)	Pub	2,224	6,284	3,710
Montana Tech of the University of Montana; Butte, Mont. 59710	1,900 (C)	Pub	2,013[1]	6,073[1]	3,360[1]
Montclair State College; Upper Montclair, N.J. 07043-1624	10,349 (C)	Pub	2,390	3,374	5,060
Monterey Institute of Intl. Studies; Monterey, Calif. 93940	43 (C)	P	15,200	15,200	n.a.
Montevallo, University of; Montevallo, Ala. 35115	2,769 (C)	Pub	2,340[1]	4,680[1]	3,170[1]
Montreat-Anderson College; Montreat, N.C. 28757	317 (C)	P	8,690	8,690	3,540
Montserrat College of Art; Beverly, Mass. 01915	291 (C)	P	9,730	9,730	4,380
Moody Bible Institute; Chicago, Ill. 60610	1,422 (C)	P	—	—	6,000
Moore College of Art and Design; Philadelphia, Pa. 19103	440 (W)	P	14,400	14,400	5,143
Moorhead State University; Moorhead, Minn. 56560	8,214 (C)	Pub	2,299[3]	4,289[3]	2,644[3]
Moravian College; Bethlehem, Pa. 18018	1,211 (C)	P	15,880	15,880	4,950
Morehead State University; Morehead, Ky. 40351	7,049 (C)	Pub	2,000	5,200	2,950
Morehouse College; Atlanta, Ga. 30314	3,005 (M)	P	8,930	8,930	5,770
Morgan State University; Baltimore, Md. 21239	5,709 (C)	Pub	2,832	6,462	4,840
Morningside College; Sioux City, Iowa 51106	1,180 (C)	P	11,216	11,216	3,870
Morris Brown College; Atlanta, Ga. 30314	1,877 (C)	P	7,909[1]	7,909[1]	4,438[1]
Morris College; Sumter, S.C. 29150	889 (C)	P	4,867	4,867	2,601
Morrison College/Reno Business College; Reno, Nev. 89503	270 (C)	P	6,210	6,210	n.a.
Mount Aloysius College; Cresson, Pa. 16630	1,958 (C)	P	8,107[1]	8,107[1]	3,670[1]
Mount Holyoke College; South Hadley, Mass. 01075	1,925 (W)	P	20,150	20,150	5,950
Mount Ida College; Newton Centre, Mass. 02159	2,000 (C)	P	11,128	11,128	7,718
Mount Marty College; Yankton, S.D. 57078	1,050 (C)	P	8,196	8,196	3,320
Mount Mary College; Milwaukee, Wis. 53222	1,324 (W)	P	9,950	9,950	3,332
Mount Mercy College; Cedar Rapids, Iowa 52402	1,392 (C)	P	11,020	11,020	3,690
Mount Olive College; Mount Olive, N.C. 28365	874 (C)	P	7,895	7,895	2,950
Mount St. Joseph, College of; Mount St. Joseph, Ohio 45233-9314	2,333 (C)	P	10,600	10,600	4,750
Mount Saint Mary College; Newburgh, N.Y. 12550	1,589 (C)	P	8,830	8,830	5,000
Mount Saint Mary's College; Emmitsburg, Md. 21727	1,390 (C)	P	14,120	14,120	6,250
Mount St. Clare College; Clinton, Iowa 52732	411 (C)	P	10,380	10,380	3,800
Mount St. Mary's College; Los Angeles, Calif. 90049	1,156 (W)	P	13,347	13,347	6,842
Mount Saint Vincent, College of; New York, N.Y. 10471	1,100 (C)	P	12,580	12,580	5,944
Mount Senario College; Ladysmith, Wis. 54848	672 (C)	P	8,550	8,550	3,250
Mount Union College; Alliance, Ohio 44601	1,482 (C)	P	13,480	13,480	3,650
Mount Vernon College; Washington, D.C. 20007	245 (W)	P	14,350	14,350	7,200
Mount Vernon Nazarene College; Mount Vernon, Ohio 43050	1,061 (C)	P	8,740	8,740	3,576
Muhlenberg College; Allentown, Pa. 18104	1,636 (C)	P	17,550	17,550	4,728
Multnomah School of the Bible; Portland, Ore. 97220	479 (C)	P	6,700	6,700	3,260
Murray State University; Murray, Ky. 42071	6,686 (C)	Pub	1,960	5,320	3,100
Museum of Fine Arts, School of the–Affiliated with Tufts University; Boston, Mass. 02115	690 (C)	P	13,665	13,665	n.a.
Museum Art School, Portland. *See* Pacific Northwest College of Art					
Muskingum College; New Concord, Ohio 43762	1,113 (C)	P	14,240	14,240	4,090
NAES College; Chicago, Ill. 60659	80 (C)	P	4,410	4,410	n.a.
Naropa Institute; Boulder, Colo. 80302	140 (C)	P	7,080[1]	7,080[1]	n.a.[1]
Nathaniel Hawthorne College. *See* Hawthorne College					
National College; Rapid City, S.D. 57709	502 (C)	P	6,675	6,675	4,352
National College-Albuquerque; Albuquerque, N.M. 87110	122 (C)	P	5,680	5,680	n.a.
National College, Colorado Springs Branch; Colorado Springs, Colo. 80909	280 (C)	P	3,720	3,720	n.a.
National-Louis University; Evanston, Ill. 60201	2,934 (C)	P	8,280	8,280	4,821
National University; San Diego, Calif. 92108–4194	3,966 (C)	P	6,255	6,255	n.a.
Nazarene Bible College; Colorado Springs, Colo. 80935	1,400 (C)	P	4,000	4,000	n.a.
Nazareth College of Rochester; Rochester, N.Y. 14618	1,316 (C)	P	11,605	11,605	5,234
Nebraska, University of-Kearney; Kearney, Neb. 68849	7,120 (C)	Pub	1,557	2,721	2,610
Nebraska, University of-Lincoln; Lincoln, Neb. 68588-0415	19,746 (C)	Pub	2,004	4,476	3,350
Nebraska, University of–Medical Center; Omaha, Neb. 68198–4230	93 (C)	Pub	2,610[1]	6,990[1]	n.a.[1]
Nebraska, University of-Omaha; Omaha, Neb. 68182	15,570 (C)	Pub	1,966	5,161	n.a.
Nebraska Christian College; Norfolk, Neb. 68701	139 (C)	P	3,840	3,840	2,620
Nebraska Methodist College of Nursing and Allied Health; Omaha, Neb. 68114	467 (C)	P	5,808	5,808	2,960
Nebraska Wesleyan University; Lincoln, Neb. 68504	1,610 (C)	P	9,890	9,890	3,420
Neumann College; Aston, Pa. 19014	1,242 (C)	P	10,690	10,690	n.a.
Nevada, University of-Las Vegas; Las Vegas, Nev. 89154	15,707 (C)	Pub	1,780	7,700	5,492
Nevada, University of-Reno; Reno, Nev. 89557	12,137 (C)	Pub	1,740[1]	3,767[1]	4,285[1]
Newberry College; Newberry, S.C. 29108	620 (C)	P	10,950	10,950	2,600
New College of California; San Francisco, Calif. 94110	180 (C)	P	7,500	7,500	n.a.
New College of the University of South Florida; Sarasota, Fla. 34243-2197	541 (C)	Pub	2,030[1]	7,943[1]	3,717[1]

Institution and location	Enrollment	Control	Tuition ($) Res.	Tuition ($) Nonres.	Rm/Bd ($)
New England, University of; Biddeford, Me. 04005	801 (C)	P	11,450	11,450	5,070
New England College; Henniker, N.H. 03242	690 (C)	P	13,325[1]	13,325[1]	5,235[1]
New England College-Arundel Campus; England	119 (C)	P	14,226	14,226	5,620
New England Conservatory of Music; Boston, Mass. 02115	376 (C)	P	15,300[1]	15,300[1]	7,300[1]
New England Institute of Technology; Warwick, R.I. 02886	1,950 (C)	P	9,875	9,875	n.a.
New Hampshire, University of; Durham, N.H. 03824	10,415 (C)	Pub	4,649[1]	12,879[1]	4,038[1]
New Hampshire, Univ. at Manchester; Manchester, N.H. 03102	543 (C)	Pub	3,305[1]	9,695[1]	n.a.[1]
New Hampshire College; Manchester, N.H. 03104	1,048 (C)	P	11,142	11,142	4,884
New Haven, University of; West Haven, Conn. 06516	3,404 (C)	P	11,400	11,400	4,860
New Jersey Institute of Technology; Newark, N.J. 07102–9938	4,973 (C)	Pub	4,980[1]	9,324[1]	5,376[1]
New Mexico, University of; Albuquerque, N.M. 87131	18,998 (C)	Pub	1,997	7,542	4,176
New Mexico Highlands University; Las Vegas, N.M. 87701	2,053 (C)	Pub	1,500	5,700	2,598
New Mexico Inst. of Mining & Technology; Socorro, N.M. 87801	1,399 (C)	Pub	1,858[1]	5,932[1]	3,426[1]
New Mexico State University; Las Cruces, N.M. 88003-0001	13,097 (C)	Pub	2,088	6,798	3,210
New Orleans, University of; New Orleans, La. 70148	11,672 (C)	Pub	2,362	5,154	3,116
New Rochelle, College of-School of Arts & Sciences and School of Nursing; New Rochelle, N.Y. 10801	989 (W)	P	12,200	12,200	5,500
New Rochelle, College of-School of New Resources; New Rochelle, N.Y. 10805–2308	3,860 (C)	P	4,152	4,152	5,550
New School for Social Research Eugene Lang College; New York, N.Y. 10011	350 (C)	P	16,119	16,119	8,132
New York, City University of; New York, N.Y. 10021:					
Baruch College; New York, N.Y. 10010	12,730 (C)	Pub	2,490[1]	5,090[1]	n.a.[1]
Brooklyn College; Brooklyn, N.Y. 11210	11,326 (C)	Pub	2,450[1]	5,050[1]	n.a.[1]
City College; New York, N.Y. 10031	11,541 (C)	Pub	2,500[1]	4,850[1]	n.a.[1]
College of Staten Island; Staten Island, N.Y. 10301	10,972 (C)	Pub	2,490[1]	5,090[1]	n.a.[1]
Hunter College; New York, N.Y. 10021	14,934 (C)	Pub	2,557	5,157	3,440
John Jay College of Criminal Justice; New York, N.Y. 10019	7,918 (C)	Pub	2,500[1]	4,850[1]	5,050[1]
Lehman College; Bronx, N.Y. 10468	8,802 (C)	Pub	2,760	3,002	n.a.
Medgar Evers College; Brooklyn, N.Y. 11225–2201	2,823 (C)	Pub	2,352[1]	2,811[1]	n.a.[1]
New York City Technical College; Brooklyn, N.Y. 11201–2983	10,757 (C)	Pub	2,504[1]	5,104[1]	n.a.[1]
Queens College; Flushing, N.Y. 11367	14,478 (C)	Pub	2,540[1]	2,766[1]	n.a.[1]
York College; Jamaica, N.Y. 11451	6,869 (C)	Pub	2,493[1]	5,093[1]	n.a.[1]
New York, State University of; Albany, N.Y. 12246:					
SUNY-Albany; Albany, N.Y. 12222	11,787 (C)	Pub	3,350	7,250	4,898
SUNY-Binghamton; Binghamton, N.Y. 13901	9,314 (C)	Pub	3,350	7,250	4,410
SUNY-Buffalo; Buffalo, N.Y. 14214	16,411 (C)	Pub	3,350	7,250	4,635
SUNY-College at Brockport; Brockport, N.Y. 14420	7,229 (C)	Pub	3,350	7,250	4,440
SUNY-College at Buffalo; Buffalo, N.Y. 14222	10,204 (C)	Pub	3,350	7,250	4,460
SUNY-College at Cortland; Cortland, N.Y. 13045	5,600 (C)	Pub	3,350	7,250	4,540
SUNY-College at Fredonia; Fredonia, N.Y. 14063	4,536 (C)	Pub	3,350	7,250	4,350
SUNY-College at Geneseo; Geneseo, N.Y. 14454-1471	5,357 (C)	Pub	3,350	7,250	4,410
SUNY-College at New Paltz; New Paltz, N.Y. 12561–2499	4,874 (C)	Pub	3,350	7,250	4,520
SUNY-College at Old Westbury; Old Westbury, N.Y. 11568	4,111 (C)	Pub	3,350	7,250	4,808
SUNY-College at Oneonta; Oneonta, N.Y. 13820	5,400 (C)	Pub	3,350	7,250	4,606
SUNY-College at Oswego; Oswego, N.Y. 13126	7,611 (C)	Pub	3,350	7,250	4,640
SUNY-College at Plattsburgh; Plattsburgh, N.Y. 12901	5,275 (C)	Pub	3,350	7,250	4,220
SUNY-College at Potsdam; Potsdam, N.Y. 13676	3,946 (C)	Pub	3,350	7,250	4,450
SUNY-College of Agriculture and Life Sciences at Cornell University; Ithaca, N.Y. 14853	3,098 (C)	Pub	8,440	15,600	6,238
SUNY-College of Environmental Science and Forestry; Syracuse, N.Y. 13210	1,169 (C)	Pub	3,350	7,250	6,000
SUNY-College of Human Ecology at Cornell University; Ithaca, N.Y. 14853	1,330 (C)	Pub	8,556	16,526	6,550
SUNY-College of Technology-Farmingdale; Farmingdale, N.Y. 11735	6,717 (C)	Pub	3,124	6,550	2,745
SUNY-Empire State College; Saratoga Springs, N.Y. 12866	6,063 (C)	Pub	3,350	7,250	n.a.
SUNY-Fashion Institute of Technology; New York, N.Y. 10001-5992	4,253 (C)	Pub	3,495	6,910	4,754
SUNY-Health Science Center at Syracuse; Syracuse, N.Y. 13210	404 (C)	Pub	3,350	7,250	4,816
SUNY-Institute of Technology at Utica/Rome; Utica, N.Y. 13054-3050	2,271 (C)	Pub	3,350	7,250	4,650
SUNY-Maritime College; Throggs Neck, N.Y. 10465	655 (C)	Pub	3,350	7,250	4,600
SUNY-Purchase; Purchase, N.Y. 10577	3,909 (C)	Pub	3,350	7,250	4,730
SUNY-School of Industrial and Labor Relations at Cornell University; Ithaca, N.Y. 14853	628 (C)	Pub	8,440	15,600	6,238
SUNY-Stony Brook; Stony Brook, N.Y. 11794	10,759 (C)	Pub	3,350	7,250	4,768
New York, University of the State of, Regents College Degrees; Albany, N.Y. 12203	17,269 (C)	P	510[1]	510[1]	n.a.[1]
New York City Technical Coll. See New York, City Univ. of					
New York Institute of Technology; Old Westbury, N.Y. 11568	3,390 (C)	P	9,190	9,190	n.a.
New York Institute of Technology Central Islip Campus; Central Islip, N.Y. 11722	1,303 (C)	P	9,190[1]	9,190[1]	5,634[1]
New York Institute of Technology, Manhattan Capus; New York, N.Y. 10023	1,587 (C)	P	9,190[1]	9,190[1]	n.a.[1]
New York School of Interior Design; New York, N.Y. 10022	613 (C)	P	10,800	10,800	n.a.
New York University; New York, N.Y. 10011	15,335 (C)	P	19,948	19,948	7,552

Institution and location	Enrollment	Control	Tuition ($) Res.	Tuition ($) Nonres.	Rm/Bd ($)
Niagara University; Niagara University, N.Y. 14109	2,274 (C)	P	11,560	11,560	5,084
Nicholls State University; Thibodaux, La. 70310	6,775 (C)	Pub	1,986	4,578	2,700
Nichols College; Dudley, Mass. 01570	800 (C)	P	9,744[1]	9,744[1]	5,624[1]
Norfolk State University; Norfolk, Va. 23504	7,252 (C)	Pub	2,782[1]	6,276[1]	3,570[1]
North Adams State College; North Adams, Mass. 01247	1,600 (C)	Pub	3,555	7,689	4,400
North Alabama, University of; Florence, Ala. 35632	4,665 (C)	Pub	1,724[1]	2,990[1]	2,932[1]
North Carolina, Univ. of-Asheville; Asheville, N.C. 28804	3,155 (C)	Pub	1,588[1]	7,320[1]	3,500[1]
North Carolina, Univ. of-Chapel Hill; Chapel Hill, N.C. 27599-2200	15,895 (C)	Pub	1,569	9,095	4,200
North Carolina, Univ. of-Charlotte; Charlotte, N.C. 28223	12,972 (C)	Pub	1,457	7,941	3,620
North Carolina, Univ. of-Greensboro; Greensboro, N.C. 27412	9,337 (C)	Pub	1,800	9,500	3,800
North Carolina, Univ. of-Wilmington; Wilmington, N.C. 28403	7,486 (C)	Pub	1,528	8,012	4,000
North Carolina Agricultural and Technical State University; Greensboro, N.C. 27411	7,054 (C)	Pub	1,432[1]	7,914[1]	3,040[1]
North Carolina Central University; Durham, N.C. 27707	4,070 (C)	Pub	1,474	7,540	4,530[8]
North Carolina School of the Arts; Winston-Salem, N.C. 27127-2189	456 (C)	Pub	2,052[1]	9,459[1]	3,606[1]
North Carolina State University-Raleigh; Raleigh, N.C. 27695-7103	22,483 (C)	Pub	1,608[1]	9,134[1]	3,540[1]
North Carolina Wesleyan College; Rocky Mount, N.C. 27801	631 (C)	P	9,150	9,150	4,500
North Central Bible College; Minneapolis, Minn. 55404	1,055 (C)	P	5,950[1]	5,950[1]	3,390[1]
North Central College; Naperville, Ill. 60566-7063	2,446 (C)	P	12,513	12,513	4,692
North Dakota, University of; Grand Forks, N.D. 58202	9,550 (C)	Pub	2,428	5,952	2,816
North Dakota State University; Fargo, N.D. 58105	9,269 (C)	Pub	2,355[1]	5,879[1]	2,744[1]
Northeastern Illinois University, Chicago, Ill. 60625	7,403 (C)	Pub	3,206	9,210	n.a.
Northeastern State Univ.; Tahlequah, Okla. 74464	9,374 (C)	Pub	1,420[1]	3,460[1]	2,512[1]
Northeastern University; Boston, Mass. 02115	20,146 (C)	P	14,241	14,241	7,710
Northeast Louisiana University; Monroe, La. 71209	10,214 (C)	Pub	1,926[1]	4,086[1]	2,200[1]
Northeast Missouri State University; Kirksville, Mo. 63501	6,061 (C)	Pub	2,872	5,152	3,624
Northern Arizona University; Flagstaff, Ariz. 86011	14,018 (C)	Pub	1,950	7,176	3,206
Northern Colorado, University of; Greeley, Colo. 80639	8,751 (C)	Pub	2,317[1]	8,219[1]	4,128[1]
Northern Illinois University; De Kalb, Ill. 60115	16,423 (C)	Pub	3,730	7,460	3,316
Northern Iowa, University of; Cedar Falls, Iowa 50614	11,825 (C)	Pub	2,350	6,626	3,130
Northern Kentucky University; Highland Heights, Ky. 41099–7010	10,827 (C)	Pub	1,960	5,320	4,000
Northern Michigan University; Marquette, Mich. 49855	7,895 (C)	Pub	2,848	5,248	4,100
Northern Montana College; Havre, Mont. 59501	1,742 (C)	Pub	3,373	6,565	3,800
Northern State University; Aberdeen, S.D. 57401	2,895 (C)	Pub	2,368	4,629	2,250
North Florida, University of; Jacksonville, Fla. 32216	6,559 (C)	Pub	1,402	5,314	4,360
North Georgia College; Dahlonega, Georgia 30597	2,515 (C)	Pub	1,827	5,037	2,868
Northland College; Ashland, Wis. 54806	813 (C)	P	10,870	10,870	3,900
North Park College; Chicago, Illinois 60625	977 (C)	P	13,280	13,280	4,500
North Texas, University of; Denton, Tex. 76203	19,018 (C)	Pub	1,322	4,538	3,500
Northwest Christian College; Eugene, Ore. 97401	378 (C)	P	11,400	11,400	4,105
Northwest College; Kirkland, Wash. 98083-0579	839 (C)	P	7,800	7,800	3,660
Northwestern College; Orange City, Iowa 51041	1,038 (C)	P	10,400	10,400	3,175
Northwestern College; St. Paul, Minn. 55113	1,242 (C)	P	11,985	11,985	3,960
Northwestern Oklahoma State University; Alva, Okla. 73717	1,787 (C)	Pub	1,586[1]	3,786[1]	1,956[1]
Northwestern State Univ. of Louisiana; Natchitoches, La. 71497	7,906 (C)	Pub	2,067[1]	4,167[1]	2,352[1]
Northwestern University; Evanston, Ill. 60201-3060	7,615 (C)	P	17,184	17,184	5,781
Northwest Missouri State University; Maryville, Mo. 64468	5,168 (C)	Pub	2,280	3,975	3,290
Northwest Nazarene College; Nampa, Idaho 83686	1,095 (C)	P	11,145	11,145	3,145
Northwood Institute of Florida; West Palm Beach, Fla. 33409	524 (C)	P	9,948	9,948	5,883
Northwood University; Cedar Hill, Tex. 75104	765 (C)	P	10,128	10,128	4,634
Northwood Institute of Michigan; Midland, Mich. 48640	1,348 (C)	P	10,163	10,163	4,605
Norwich University; Northfield, Vt. 05663	1,660 (C)	P	14,346	14,346	5,310
Notre Dame, College of, Belmont, Calif. 94002–1997	937 (C)	P	13,500	13,500	6,100
Notre Dame, University of; Notre Dame, Ind. 46556	7,700 (C)	P	18,030	18,030	4,650
Notre Dame College; Manchester, N.H. 03104	815 (C)	P	10,927	10,927	5,050
Notre Dame College of Ohio; Cleveland, Ohio 44121	642 (W)	P	8,064[1]	8,064[1]	3,860[1]
Notre Dame of Maryland, College of; Baltimore, Md. 21210	645 (W)	P	11,740	11,740	5,845
Nova University; Ft. Lauderdale, Fla. 33314	3,509 (C)	P	9,150	9,150	4,890
Nyack College; Nyack, N.Y. 10960	577 (C)	P	9,450	9,450	4,380
Oakland City College; Oakland City, Ind. 47660	757 (C)	P	6,083	6,083	3,800
Oakland University; Rochester, Mich. 48063	10,553 (C)	Pub	3,110[1]	8,720[1]	2,015[1]
Oakwood College; Huntsville, Ala. 35896	1,344 (C)	P	7,064	7,064	3,680
Oberlin College; Oberlin, Ohio 44074	2,685 (C)	P	20,746	20,746	5,970
Oblate College; Washington, D.C. 20017	4 (C)	P	5,000	5,000	n.a.
Occidental College; Los Angeles, Calif. 90041–3393	1,677 (C)	P	16,894	16,894	5,440
Oglala Lakota College; Kyle, S.D. 57752	1,009 (C)	Pub	1,260	1,260	n.a.
Oglethorpe University; Atlanta, Ga. 30319	1,146 (C)	P	13,950	13,950	4,800
Ohio Dominican College; Columbus, Ohio 43219	1,713 (C)	P	8,100[1]	8,100[1]	4,270[1]
Ohio Northern University; Ada, Ohio 45810	2,500 (C)	P	16,950	16,950	4,290
Ohio State University–Columbus; Columbus, Ohio 43210	36,166 (C)	Pub	3,087[1]	9,315[1]	5,100[1]
Ohio State University-Lima; Lima, Ohio 45804	1,084 (C)	Pub	2,976[1]	9,204[1]	n.a.[1]
Ohio State University-Mansfield; Mansfield, Ohio 44906	1,327 (C)	Pub	2,976[1]	9,204[1]	n.a.[1]
Ohio State University-Marion; Marion, Ohio 43302	1,011 (C)	Pub	2,976[1]	9,204[1]	n.a.[1]
Ohio State University-Newark; Newark, Ohio 43055	1,626 (C)	Pub	2,976[1]	9,207[1]	4,150[1]
Ohio University; Athens, Ohio 45701	15,949 (C)	Pub	3,552[1]	7,629[1]	4,095[1]

Institution and location	Enrollment	Control	Tuition ($) Res.	Tuition ($) Nonres.	Rm/Bd ($)
Ohio University-Chillicothe; Chillicothe, Ohio 45601-0629	1,917 (C)	Pub	2,796[1]	6,831[1]	n.a.[1]
Ohio University-Lancaster; Lancaster, Ohio 43130	1,554 (C)	Pub	3,552[1]	7,629[1]	4,095[1]
Ohio University-Zanesville; Zanesville, Ohio 43701	1,111 (C)	Pub	2,796[1]	6,831[1]	n.a.[1]
Ohio Valley College; Parkersburg, W.Va. 26101	334 (C)	P	5,600	5,600	3,280
Ohio Wesleyan University; Delaware, Ohio 43015	1,732 (C)	P	17,569	17,569	5,876
Oklahoma, University of-Health Sciences Center; Oklahoma City, Okla. 73190	1,143 (C)	Pub	1,516	4,016	n.a.
Oklahoma, University of-Norman; Norman, Okla. 73019	15,088 (C)	Pub	1,450	4,043	3,808
Oklahoma Baptist University; Shawnee, Okla. 74801	2,412 (C)	P	6,525	6,525	3,210
Oklahoma Christian University of Science and Arts; Oklahoma City, Okla. 73136-1100	1,480 (C)	P	7,300	7,300	3,620
Oklahoma City University; Oklahoma City, Okla. 73106	2,234 (C)	P	7,350	7,350	3,830
Oklahoma Panhandle State University; Goodwell, Okla. 73939	1,262 (C)	Pub	1,519[1]	3,798[1]	1,800[1]
Oklahoma State University; Stillwater, Okla. 74078	14,281 (C)	Pub	1,306	5,182	3,804
Old Dominion University; Norfolk, Va. 23529-0050	11,624 (C)	Pub	4,104	9,192	4,676
Olivet College; Olivet, Mich. 49076	791 (C)	P	11,580	11,580	3,860
Olivet Nazarene University; Kankakee, Ill. 60901	1,532 (C)	P	9,300	9,300	4,260
O'More College of Design; Franklin, Tenn. 37604	147 (C)	P	7,300	7,300	n.a.
Oral Roberts University; Tulsa, Okla. 74171	2,811 (C)	P	8,538	8,538	4,150
Oregon, University of; Eugene, Ore. 97403	13,243 (C)	Pub	3,390	11,099	3,900
Oregon Health Sciences University; Portland, Ore. 97201	373 (C)	Pub	4,005	10,200	4,857
Oregon Institute of Technology; Klamath Falls, Ore. 97601	2,478 (C)	Pub	3,150	9,336	3,804
Oregon State University; Corvallis, Ore. 97331	11,258 (C)	Pub	3,312	10,113	4,000
Orlando College; Orlando, Fla. 32810	2,600 (C)	P	4,140	4,140	n.a.
Otis/Parsons School of Art and Design; Los Angeles, Calif. 90057	656 (C)	P	12,286[1]	12,286[1]	2,700[1]
Ottawa University; Ottawa, Kan. 66067	532 (C)	P	7,960	7,960	3,570
Ottawa University-Phoenix Center; Phoenix, Ariz. 85021	900 (C)	P	4,080	4,080	n.a.
Otterbein College; Westerville, Ohio 43081	2,488 (C)	P	13,611	13,611	4,569
Ouachita Baptist University; Arkadelphia, Ark. 71998-0001	1,440 (C)	P	7,070	7,070	2,900
Our Lady of Holy Cross College; New Orleans, La. 70131-7399	1,279 (C)	P	3,800	3,800	n.a.
Our Lady of the Lake-University of San Antonio; San Antonio, Tex. 78207–4689	2,295 (C)	P	9,000	9,000	4,200
Ozark Christian College; Joplin, Mo. 64801	574 (C)	P	3,515	3,515	2,980
Ozarks, College of the; Point Lookout, Mo. 65726	1,527 (C)	P	100	100	1,900
Ozarks, University of the; Clarksville, Ark. 72830	570 (C)	P	6,540	6,540	3,300
Pace University; New York, N.Y. 10038	5,614 (C)	P	11,400[1]	11,400[1]	5,000[1]
Pace University-College of White Plains; White Plains, N.Y. 10603	1,121 (C)	P	11,800	11,800	5,000
Pace University-Pleasantville-Briarcliff; Pleasantville, N.Y. 10570	3,651 (C)	P	11,100[1]	11,100[1]	4,940[1]
Pacific, University of the; Stockton, Calif. 95211	3,491 (C)	P	17,550	17,550	5,326
Pacific Christian College; Fullerton, Calif. 92631	500 (C)	P	8,515	8,515	4,000
Pacific Lutheran University; Tacoma, Wash. 98447	2,964 (C)	P	13,856	13,856	4,644
Pacific Northwest College of Art; Portland, Ore. 97205	269 (C)	P	9,104	9,104	n.a.
Pacific Oaks College; Pasadena, Calif. 91103	150 (C)	P	10,500	10,500	n.a.
Pacific States University; Los Angeles, Calif. 90006	300 (C)	P	7,200	7,200	n.a.
Pacific Union College; Angwin, Calif. 94508	1,578 (C)	P	11,925[1]	11,925[1]	3,825[1]
Pacific University; Forest Grove, Ore. 97116	943 (C)	P	14,435[1]	14,435[1]	3,994[1]
Paier College of Art, Inc.; Hamden, Conn. 06511	253 (C)	P	9,980	9,980	n.a.
Paine College; Augusta, Ga. 30910	686 (C)	P	5,920	5,920	2,967
Palm Beach Atlantic College; West Palm Beach, Fla. 33401	1,635 (C)	P	8,600	8,600	3,750
Park College; Parkville, Mo. 64152	490 (C)	P	3,990	3,990	4,100
Parks College of St. Louis University; Cahokia, Ill. 62206	1,070 (C)	P	9,560	9,560	4,400
Parsons School of Design; New York, N.Y. 10011	1,964 (C)	P	16,070	16,070	9,200
Patten College; Oakland, Calif. 94601	627 (C)	P	4,760[1]	4,760[1]	5,395[1]
Paul Quinn College; Waco, Tex. 75241	509 (C)	P	3,400	3,400	3,000
Pembroke State University; Pembroke, N.C. 28372	2,674 (C)	Pub	1,142[1]	6,874[1]	2,560[1]
Pennsylvania, University of; Philadelphia, Pa. 19104	9,949 (C)	P	19,898	19,898	7,500
Pennsylvania State Erie –The Behrend College; Erie, Pa. 16563	2,975 (C)	Pub	4,966[1]	10,654[1]	3,920[1]
Pennsylvania State Harrisburg–The Capital College; Middletown, Pa. 17057	2,314 (C)	Pub	4,966[1]	10,654[1]	3,920[1]
Pennsylvania State University Park; University Park, Pa. 16802	31,732 (C)	Pub	4,966[1]	10,654[1]	3,930[1]
Pepperdine University School of Business and Management; Culver City, Calif. 90230	451 (C)	P	18,000	18,000	n.a.
Pepperdine University-Seaver College; Malibu, Calif. 90263-4392	2,661 (C)	P	19,200	19,200	7,080
Peru State College; Peru, Neb. 68421	1,742 (C)	Pub	1,754[1]	2,954[1]	2,832[1]
Pfeiffer College; Misenheimer, N.C. 28109	653 (C)	P	8,990	8,990	3,950
Philadelphia College of Bible; Langhorne, Pa. 19047	699 (C)	P	7,800	7,800	4,460
Philadelphia College of Pharmacy and Science; Philadelphia, Pa. 19104	1,793 (C)	P	11,750	11,750	5,000
Philadelphia College of Textiles and Science; Philadelphia, Pa. 19144	1,624 (C)	P	12,240	12,240	5,676
Philander Smith College; Little Rock, Ark. 72202	915 (C)	P	3,048	3,048	2,540
Phillips University; Enid, Okla. 73701	808 (C)	P	6,600	6,600	3,904
Phoenix, University of; Phoenix, Ariz. 85040	20,000 (C)	P	5,850[1]	5,850[1]	n.a.[1]

Institution and location	Enrollment	Control	Tuition ($) Res.	Tuition ($) Nonres.	Rm/Bd ($)
Piedmont Bible College; Winston-Salem, N.C. 27101	300 (C)	P	4,600	4,600	2,950
Piedmont College; Demorest, Ga. 30535	640 (C)	P	6,360	6,360	3,850
Pikeville College; Pikeville, Ky. 41501	800 (C)	P	6,000	6,000	3,000
Pillsbury Baptist Bible College; Owatonna, Minn. 55060	338 (C)	P	5,490	5,490	2,800
Pine Manor College; Chestnut Hill, Mass. 02167	400 (W)	P	15,650	15,650	6,660
Pittsburgh, University of; Pittsburgh, Pa. 15260	16,721 (C)	Pub	5,416[1]	11,240[1]	4,560[1]
Pittsburgh, University of-Bradford; Bradford, Pa. 16701-2898	1,350 (C)	Pub	5,570[1]	11,290[1]	4,100[1]
Pittsburgh, University of-Greensburg; Greensburg, Pa. 15601	1,445 (C)	Pub	5,328[1]	11,152[1]	3,750[1]
Pittsburgh, University of-Johnstown; Johnstown, Pa. 15904	3,243 (C)	Pub	5,682[1]	10,786[1]	3,966[1]
Pittsburg State University; Pittsburg, Kan. 66762	5,129 (C)	Pub	1,806	5,788	3,126
Pitzer College. See Claremont Colleges.					
Plymouth State College; Plymouth, N.H. 03264	3,500 (C)	Pub	3,382	8,662	4,024
Point Loma Nazarene College; San Diego, Calif. 92106	2,051 (C)	P	11,120	11,122	4,480
Point Park College; Pittsburgh, Pa. 15222	2,317 (C)	P	10,522	10,522	5,072
Polytechnic University; Brooklyn, N.Y. 11201	1,568 (C)	P	17,335	17,335	6,100
Polytechnic University-Long Island Campus; Farmingdale, N.Y. 11735-3995	396 (C)	P	17,335	17,335	4,800
Pomona College. See Claremont Colleges.					
Pontifical Catholic University of Puerto Rico; Ponce, P.R. 00732	11,234 (C)	P	2,610[1]	2,610[1]	2,220[1]
Pontifical College Josephinum; Columbus, Ohio 43235-1498	53 (M)	P	5,896	5,896	4,044
Portland, University of; Portland, Ore. 97203	2,163 (C)	P	13,200	13,200	4,240
Portland State University; Portland, Ore. 97207–0751	10,283 (C)	Pub	4,746[1]	7,611[1]	4,950[1]
Potsdam Coll. of Arts & Science. See New York, State Univ. of					
Prairie View A&M University; Prairie View, Tex. 77446	5,660 (C)	Pub	1,744	6,124	3,620
Pratt Institute; Brooklyn, N.Y. 11205	1,979 (C)	P	15,194	15,194	6,326
Presbyterian College; Clinton, S.C. 29325	1,122 (C)	P	12,512	12,512	4,184
Prescott College; Prescott, Ariz. 86301	397 (C)	P	10,555	10,205	n.a.
Presentation College; Aberdeen, S.D. 57401	486 (C)	P	6,694	6,694	3,000
Princeton University; Princeton, N.J. 08544–0430	4,524 (C)	P	20,287[1]	20,287[1]	5,910[1]
Principia College; Elsah, Ill. 62028	543 (C)	P	13,047	13,047	5,424
Providence College; Providence, R.I. 02918	3,561 (C)	P	15,000	15,000	6,500
Puerto Rico, University of-Arecibo Campus; Arecibo, P.R. 00613	3,837 (C)	Pub	971	2,400	n.a.
Puerto Rico, University of-Cayey University College; Cayey, P.R. 00633	3,243 (C)	Pub	900[3]	2,400[3]	n.a.[3]
Puerto Rico, University of-Humacao University College; Humacao, P.R. 00661	3,884 (C)	Pub	1,242[3]	1,242[3]	3,150[3]
Puerto Rico, University of-Mayaguez Campus; Mayaguez, P.R. 00708	9,594 (C)	Pub	1,240[3]	1,240[3]	n.a.[3]
Puerto Rico, University of-Medical Science Campus; San Juan, P.R. 00936	996 (C)	Pub	1,080[3]	(9)	n.a.[3]
Puerto Rico, University of-Ponce Technological University College; Ponce, P.R. 00732	2,192 (C)	Pub	1,560[1]	1,560[1]	n.a.[1]
Puerto Rico, University of-Rio Piedras Campus; Rio Piedras, P.R. 00931	15,668 (C)	Pub	1,286[1]	(9)	2,100[1]
Puget Sound, University of; Tacoma, Wash. 98416	2,860 (C)	P	17,450	17,450	4,720
Puget Sound Christian College; Edmonds, Wash. 98020	92 (C)	P	5,280	5,280	3,420
Purdue University; West Lafayette, Ind. 47907	27,750 (C)	Pub	3,010	9,940	4,310
Purdue University-Calumet; Hammond, Ind. 46323	9,255 (C)	Pub	3,566[1]	8,978[1]	n.a.[1]
Purdue University-North Central; Westville, Ind. 46391	3,551 (C)	Pub	2,378[1]	3,608[1]	n.a.[1]
Queens College; Charlotte, N.C. 28274	1,213 (C)	P	11,520	11,520	5,170
Queens College (NYC). See New York, City University of					
Quincy University; Quincy, Ill. 62301	1,164 (C)	P	10,910	10,910	4,260
Quinnipiac College; Hamden, Conn. 06518	3,943 (C)	P	13,430	13,430	6,450[1]
Rabbinical College of America; Morristown, N.J. 07960	230 (M)	P	13,000[1]	13,000[1]	—[1]
Rabbinical Seminary of America; Forest Hills, N.Y. 11375	120 (M)	P	4,000	4,000	2,000
Radcliffe College. See Harvard and Radcliffe Colleges					
Radford University; Radford, Va. 24142	8,110 (C)	Pub	3,114	7,688	4,250
Ramapo College of New Jersey, Mahwah, N.J. 07403	4,674 (C)	Pub	3,352[1]	4,644[1]	5,552[1]
Randolph-Macon College; Ashland, Va. 23005	1,118 (C)	P	14,956	14,956	3,835
Randolph-Macon Woman's College; Lynchburg, Va. 24503	709 (W)	P	21,420	21,420	3,165
Ray College of Design; Chicago, Ill. 60654	610 (C)	P	8,880	8,880	n.a.
Redlands, University of; Redlands, Calif. 92373-0999	1,500 (C)	P	17,860	17,860	6,640
Reed College; Portland, Ore. 97202	1,230 (C)	P	20,760	20,760	5,750
Reformed Bible College; Grand Rapids, Mich. 49505-9749	196 (C)	P	6,530	6,530	3,350
Regis College; Weston, Mass. 02193	1,102 (W)	P	13,700	13,700	6,250
Regis University; Denver, Colo. 80221	1,170 (C)	P	13,400	13,400	5,600
Reinhardt College; Waleska, Ga. 30183	652 (C)	P	4,890	4,890	4,050
Rensselaer Polytechnic Institute; Troy, N.Y. 12180	4,398 (C)	P	18,565	18,565	6,155
Research College of Nursing; Kansas City, Mo. 64110-2508	302 (C)	P	10,200	10,200	4,320
Rhode Island, University of; Kingston, R.I. 02881	10,670 (C)	Pub	4,242[1]	4,242[1]	5,410[1]
Rhode Island, University of, College of Continuing Education; Providence, R.I. 02908-5090	4,400 (C)	Pub	3,204	10,692	n.a.
Rhode Island College; Providence, R.I. 02908	6,394 (C)	Pub	2,838[1]	7,162[1]	5,137[1]
Rhode Island School of Design; Providence, R.I. 02903	2,011 (C)	P	17,600	17,600	6,618
Rhodes College; Memphis, Tenn. 38112	1,469 (C)	P	15,920	15,920	4,912

Institution and location	Enrollment	Control	Tuition ($) Res.	Tuition ($) Nonres.	Rm/Bd ($)
Rice University; Houston, Tex. 77251	2,610 (C)	P	12,000	12,000	5,900
Richard Stocton College of New Jersey; the; Pomona, N.J. 08240	5,601 (C)	Pub	2,992[1]	3,744[1]	4,510[1]
Richmond, University of; Richmond, Va. 23173	2,857 (C)	P	15,500	15,500	3,435
Richmond College, The American International University in London; Richmond, Surrey, TW10 6JP England	915 (C)	P	12,413[1]	12,413[1]	6,279[1]
Rider College; Lawrenceville, N.J. 08648-3099	2,624 (C)	P	13,800	13,800	5,630
Ringling School of Art and Design; Sarasota, Fla. 34234	750 (C)	P	11,500	11,500	5,950
Rio Grande College of Sul Ross State University; Uvalde, Texas 78801	397 (C)	Pub	1,332	4,836	3,160
Rio Grande, University of; Rio Grande, Ohio 45674	2,024 (C)	P	2,976	2,976	4,221
Ripon College; Ripon, Wis. 54971	820 (C)	P	16,110	16,110	4,280
Rivier College; Nashua, N.H. 03060	995 (C)	P	11,010	11,010	5,250
Roanoke Bible College; Elizabeth City, N.C. 27909	141 (C)	P	2,960	2,960	2,750
Roanoke College; Salem, Va. 24153	1,694 (C)	P	14,100	14,100	4,640
Robert Morris College; Coraopolis, Pa. 15108	4,749 (C)	P	7,824	7,824	4,554
Roberts Wesleyan College; Rochester, N.Y. 14624	981 (C)	P	10,826	10,826	3,744
Rochester, University of; Rochester, N.Y. 14627	4,985 (C)	P	19,165	19,165	6,730
Rochester Institute of Technology; Rochester, N.Y. 14623	10,584 (C)	P	14,937	14,937	5,898
Rockford College; Rockford, Ill. 61108	1,251 (C)	P	13,500	13,500	4,400
Rockhurst College; Kansas City, Mo. 64110–2561	1,936 (C)	P	10,200	10,200	4,200
Rocky Mountain College; Billings, Mont. 59102	804 (C)	P	9,715	9,715	3,758
Roger Williams College; Bristol, R.I. 02809	2,111 (C)	P	15,900	15,900	6,660
Rollins College; Winter Park, Fla. 32789	1,422 (C)	P	17,995	17,995	5,555
Roosevelt University; Chicago, Ill. 60605	4,519 (C)	P	8,000	8,000	5,000
Rosary College; River Forest, Ill. 60305-1099	802 (C)	P	11,600	11,600	4,600
Rose-Hulman Institute of Technology; Terre Haute, Ind. 47803	1,320 (M)	P	14,400	14,400	4,400
Rosemont College; Rosemont, Pa. 19010	491 (W)	P	11,980	11,980	6,100
Rowan College of N.J.; Glassboro, N.J. 08028	6,380 (C)	Pub	3,096	5,109	4,900
Rush University Colleges of Nursing and Health Sciences; Chicago, Ill. 60612	276 (C)	P	13,148	13,148	4,800
Russell Sage College; Troy, N.Y. 12180	1,170 (W)	P	13,270	13,270	5,400
Rust College; Holly Springs, Miss. 38635	1,129 (C)	P	4,635	4,635	2,175
Rutgers, The State University of New Jersey–Camden College of Arts and Sciences; Camden, N.J. 08102	2,420 (C)	Pub	4,681	8,602	4,936
Rutgers, The State University of New Jersey–College of Engineering; New Brunswick, N.J. 08903	2,260 (C)	Pub	5,243	9,591	4,936
Rutgers, The State University of New Jersey–College of Nursing-Newark; Newark, N.J. 07102	372 (C)	Pub	4,627	8,548	4,936
Rutgers, The State University of New Jersey–College of Pharmacy; New Brunswick, N.J. 08903	889 (C)	Pub	5,243	9,591	4,936
Rutgers, The State Universit of New Jersey–Cook College; New Brunswick, N.J. 08903	3,010 (C)	Pub	5,231	9,579	4,936
Rutgers, The State University of New Jersey–Douglass College; New Brunswick, N.J. 08903	2,986 (W)	Pub	4,798	8,719	4,936
Rutgers, The State University of New Jersey–Livingston College; New Brunswick, N.J. 08903	3,273 (C)	Pub	4,862	4,862	4,936
Rutgers, The State University of New Jersey–Mason Gross School of the Arts; New Brunswick, N.J. 08903	418 (C)	Pub	4,827	8,748	4,936
Rutgers, The State University of New Jersey–Newark College of Arts and Sciences; Newark, N.J. 07102	3,724 (C)	Pub	4,644	4,644	4,936
Rutgers, The State University of New Jersey–Rutgers College; New Brunswick, N.J. 08903	8,908 (C)	Pub	4,836	8,757	4,936
Rutgers, The State University of New Jersey–University College– Camden; Camden, N.J. 08102	764 (C)	Pub	3,922	7,762	n.a.
Rutgers, The State University of New Jersey–University College– New Brunswick; New Brunswick, N.J. 08903	3,132 (C)	Pub	3,864	7,704	n.a.
Rutgers, The State University of New Jersey–University College– Newark; Newark, N.J. 07102	1,865 (C)	Pub	3,876	7,716	n.a.
Sacred Heart, Univ. of the; Santurce, P.R. 00924	4,753 (C)	P	3,190[1]	3,190[1]	3,000[1]
Sacred Heart Major Seminary; Detroit, Mich. 48206	220 (C)	P	4,820	4,820	4,160
Sacred Heart University; Fairfield, Conn. 06432	1,912 (C)	P	12,005	12,005	6,065
Saginaw Valley State University; University Center, Mich. 48710	5,680 (C)	Pub	2,317	4,731	3,990
Saint Ambrose University; Davenport, Iowa 52803	1,764 (C)	P	11,180	11,180	4,200
Saint Andrews Presbyterian College; Laurinburg, N.C. 28352	762 (C)	P	10,895	10,895	4,810
Saint Anselm College; Manchester, N.H. 03102	1,850 (C)	P	14,370	14,370	5,550
Saint Augustine's College; Raleigh, N.C. 27610–2298	1,737 (C)	P	5,872	5,872	3,708
St. Benedict, College of; St. Joseph, Minn. 56374-2099	1,787 (W)	P	13,089	13,089	4,370
St. Bonaventure University; St. Bonaventure, N.Y. 14778-2284	1,900 (C)	P	11,246[1]	11,246[1]	4,800[1]
St. Catherine, College of; St. Paul, Minn. 55105	2,638 (W)	P	9,835	9,835	4,592
St. Cloud State University; St. Cloud, Minn. 56301	13,260 (C)	Pub	2,539[1]	5,245[1]	2,769[1]
St. Edward's University; Austin, Tex. 78704	2,650 (C)	P	9,950	9,950	4,280
St. Elizabeth, College of; Convent Station, N.J. 07961	1,461 (W)	P	12,115	12,115	5,400
St. Francis, College of; Joliet, Ill. 60435	1,041 (C)	P	10,790	10,790	4,340
St. Francis College; Brooklyn Heights, N.Y. 11201	2,166 (C)	P	6,650[1]	6,650[1]	n.a.[1]
St. Francis College; Fort Wayne, Ind. 46808	787 (C)	P	9,550	9,550	3,950

Institution and location	Enrollment	Control	Tuition ($) Res.	Tuition ($) Nonres.	Rm/Bd ($)
St. Francis College; Loretto, Pa. 15940	1,136 (C)	P	9,660	9,660	5,350
St. Francis Medical Center College of Nursing; Peoria, Ill. 61603	163 (C)	P	7,593	7,593	1,380
St. Hyacinth College and Seminary; Granby, Mass. 01033	24 (M)	P	4,000	4,000	4,500
St. John Fisher College; Rochester, N.Y. 14618	1,522 (C)	P	11,540	11,540	5,580
St. John's College; Annapolis, Md. 21404	395 (C)	P	18,630	18,630	5,890
St. John's College; Santa Fe, N.M. 87501	391 (C)	P	18,180	18,180	5,995
St. John's College; Springfield, Ill. 62702	107 (C)	P	6,058	6,058	2,590
St. John's Seminary College; Camarillo, Calif. 93012	80 (M)	P	6,100	6,100	1,200
St. John's Seminary College of Liberal Arts; Brighton, Mass. 02135	42 (M)	P	5,200	5,200	2,600
St. John's University; Collegeville, Minn. 56321	1,812 (M)	P	13,094	13,094	4,736
St. John's University; Jamaica, N.Y. 11439	13,881 (C)	P	10,450	10,450	n.a.
St. John Vianney College Seminary; Miami, Fla. 33165	50 (M)	P	10,500	10,500	—
St. Joseph College; West Hartford, Conn. 06117	1,200 (W)	P	12,200	12,200	4,600
St. Joseph College of Nursing; Joliet, Ill. 60435	170 (C)	P	7,884	7,884	n.a.
St. Joseph in Vermont, College of; Rutland, Vt. 05701	378 (C)	P	9,070	9,070	5,100
Saint Joseph's College; Rensselaer, Ind. 47978	973 (C)	P	11,900	11,900	4,500
St. Joseph's College; Brooklyn, N.Y. 11205	1,343 (C)	P	7,817	7,817	n.a.
St. Joseph's College-Suffolk; Patchogue, N.Y. 11772	2,300 (C)	P	8,047	8,047	n.a.
Saint Joseph's College; Windham, Me. 04062-1198	820 (C)	P	10,630	10,630	5,380
St. Joseph Seminary College; St. Benedict, La. 70457	58 (M)	P	5,500[1]	5,500[1]	4,350[1]
Saint Joseph's University; Philadelphia, Pa. 19131	2,500 (C)	P	13,700	13,700	6,200
St. Lawrence University; Canton, N.Y. 13617	1,965 (C)	P	19,640	19,640	5,885
Saint Leo College; Saint Leo, Fla. 33574	819 (C)	P	10,190	10,190	5,240
St. Louis Christian College; Florissant, Mo. 63033	137 (C)	P	3,017	3,017	2,650
St. Louis College of Pharmacy; St. Louis, Mo. 63110	717 (C)	P	9,845[1]	9,845[1]	4,800[1]
St. Louis University; St. Louis, Mo. 63103	7,338 (C)	P	12,845	12,845	4,900
St. Martin's College; Lacey, Wash. 98503-1297	577 (C)	P	12,490	12,490	4,590
St. Mary, College of; Omaha, Neb. 68124	1,172 (W)	P	10,500	10,500	3,850
Saint Mary College; Leavenworth, Kan. 66048	839 (C)	P	8,736	8,736	4,120
St. Mary-of-the-Woods Coll.; St. Mary-of-the-Woods, Ind. 47876	1,215 (W)	P	11,370	11,370	4,410
St. Mary's College; Notre Dame, Ind. 46556	1,545 (W)	P	13,494	13,494	4,285
St. Mary's College; Orchard Lake, Mich. 48324	326 (C)	P	4,565	4,565	2,120
St. Mary's College of Minnesota; Winona, Minn. 55987	1,312 (C)	P	11,280	11,280	3,750
St. Mary's College of California; Moraga, Calif. 94575	2,580 (C)	P	14,250	14,250	6,608
St. Mary's College of Maryland; St. Mary's City, Md. 20686	1,510 (C)	Pub	5,435	8,735	4,970
St. Mary's University of San Antonio; San Antonio, Tex. 78228	2,595 (C)	P	9,688	9,688	3,698
Saint Meinrad College; St. Meinrad, Ind. 47577	125 (M)	P	6,725	6,725	4,226
Saint Michael's College; Colchester, Vt. 05439	1,704 (C)	P	13,810	13,810	6,010
St. Norbert College; De Pere, Wis. 54115	2,059 (C)	P	13,015	13,015	4,655
St. Olaf College; Northfield, Minn. 55057	3,015 (C)	P	14,430[1]	14,430[1]	3,750[1]
Saint Paul's College; Lawrenceville, Va. 23868	672 (C)	P	7,418	7,418	3,834
Saint Peter's College; Jersey City, N.J. 07306	3,145 (C)	P	11,035	11,035	5,620
St. Rose, College of; Albany, N.Y. 12203	1,698 (C)	P	10,735	10,735	5,646
St. Scholastica, College of; Duluth, Minn. 55811	1,588 (C)	P	12,534	12,534	3,807
St. Thomas, University of; Houston, Tex. 77006	1,403 (C)	P	7,540	7,540	4,050
St. Thomas, University of; St. Paul, Minn. 55105	4,196 (C)	P	13,106	13,106	4,374
St. Thomas Aquinas College; Sparkill, N.Y. 10968	2,100 (C)	P	9,300	9,300	6,050
Saint Thomas University; Miami, Fla. 33054	1,369 (C)	P	10,200	10,200	4,600
Saint Vincent College; Latrobe, Pa. 15650	1,237 (C)	P	11,625	11,625	4,200
St. Xavier University; Chicago, Ill. 60655	2,177 (C)	P	11,630	11,630	4,800
Salem College; Winston-Salem, N.C. 27108	760 (W)	P	11,260	11,260	6,640
Salem State College; Salem, Mass. 01970	5,468 (C)	Pub	3,208[1]	7,332[1]	3,672[1]
Salem-Teikyo University; Salem, W.Va. 26426	738 (C)	P	11,103	11,103	3,952
Salisbury State University; Salisbury, Md. 21801	5,398 (C)	Pub	3,364	6,478	4,940
Salve Regina University; Newport, R.I. 02840-4192	1,730 (C)	P	14,650	14,650	6,700
Samford University; Birmingham, Ala. 35229	3,231 (C)	P	8,648	8,648	3,844
Sam Houston State University; Huntsville, Tex. 77341	10,837 (C)	Pub	1,638	5,868	3,450
Samuel Merritt College; Oakland, Calif. 94609	323 (C)	P	13,330	13,330	3,150
San Diego, University of; San Diego, Calif. 92110	3,914 (C)	P	14,220	14,220	7,600
San Diego State University; San Diego, Calif. 92182	22,240 (C)	Pub	1,742[1]	9,122[1]	4,844[1]
Imperial Valley Campus; Calexico, Calif. 92231	253 (C)	Pub	1,558[1]	7,380[1]	n.a.[1]
San Francisco, University of; San Francisco, Calif. 94117	3,482 (C)	P	14,108	14,108	6,670
San Francisco Art Institute; San Francisco, Calif. 94133	513 (C)	P	15,486	15,486	n.a.
San Francisco Conservatory of Music; San Francisco, Calif. 94122	143 (C)	P	14,500	14,500	n.a.
San Francisco State Univ.; San Francisco, Calif. 94132	19,902 (C)	Pub	1,838[1]	9,218[1]	5,245[1]
Sangamon State University; Springfield, Ill. 62708	2,608 (C)	Pub	1,766	6,117	3,500
San Jose Christian College; San Jose, Calif. 95108	300 (C)	P	6,300	6,300	3,246
San Jose State University; San Jose, Calif. 95192-0009	21,655 (C)	Pub	1,970[1]	6,656[1]	5,100[1]
Santa Clara University; Santa Clara, Calif. 95053	4,079 (C)	P	14,604	14,604	6,500
Santa Fe, College of; Santa Fe, N.M. 87505	1,394 (C)	P	11,796	11,796	4,400
Sarah Lawrence College; Bronxville, N.Y. 10708	1,105 (C)	P	20,842	20,842	7,390
Savannah College of Art and Design; Savannah, Ga. 31401	2,090 (C)	P	10,800	10,800	3,600
Savannah State College; Savannah, Ga. 31404	3,187 (C)	Pub	1,965	5,175	4,665
Schiller International University; 6900 Heidelberg, Germany	1,280 (C)	P	11,440	11,440	5,950
Schreiner College; Kerrville, Tex. 78028	584 (C)	P	9,315	9,315	6,130

Institution and location	Enrollment	Control	Tuition ($) Res.	Tuition ($) Nonres.	Rm/Bd ($)
Science and Arts, University of, of Oklahoma; Chickasha, Okla. 73018	1,613 (C)	Pub	2,070[1]	3,375[1]	2,880[1]
Scranton, University of; Scranton, Pa. 18510-4699	4,304 (C)	P	12,559[1]	12,559[1]	5,786[1]
Scripps College. *See* Claremont Colleges					
Seattle Pacific University; Seattle, Wash. 98119	2,277 (C)	P	13,479	13,479	5,169
Seattle University; Seattle, Wash. 98122	3,193 (C)	P	13,635	13,635	5,091
Seaver College. *See* Pepperdine University					
Selma University; Selma, Ala. 36701	206 (C)	P	4,150	4,150	3,700
Seton Hall University; South Orange, N.J. 07079	5,179 (C)	P	12,250	12,250	6,710
Seton Hill College; Greensburg, Pa. 15601	923 (W)	P	11,775	11,775	4,435
Shawnee State University; Portsmouth, Ohio 45662	3,185 (C)	Pub	2,655	4,521	2,000
Shaw University; Raleigh, N.C. 27611	2,496 (C)	P	11,242	11,242	3,824
Sheldon Jackson College; Sitka, Alaska 99835	269 (C)	P	9,000	9,000	4,500
Shenandoah University; Winchester, Va. 22601-9986	1,201 (C)	P	11,470	11,470	4,800
Shepherd College; Shepherdstown, W. Va. 25443	3,648 (C)	Pub	2,064[1]	4,694[1]	3,800[1]
Shimer College; Waukegan, Ill. 60085-0500	120 (C)	P	12,600	12,600	4,100
Shippensburg University of Pennsylvania; Shippensburg, Pa. 17257	5,577 (C)	Pub	3,856[1]	7,844[1]	3,501[1]
Shorter College; Rome, Ga. 30165	899 (C)	P	7,610	7,610	3,925
Siena College; Loudonville, N.Y. 12211	3,492 (C)	P	11,340	11,340	5,270
Siena Heights College; Adrian, Mich. 49221	1,606 (C)	P	9,645	9,645	4,100
Sierra Nevada College; Incline Village, Nev. 89450	415 (C)	P	9,000	9,000	5,150
Silver Lake College; Manitowoc, Wis. 54220	829 (C)	P	8,950	8,950	3,700
Simmons Bible College; Louisville, Ky. 40210	109 (C)	P	930[1]	930[1]	n.a.[1]
Simmons College; Boston, Mass. 02115	1,360 (W)	P	17,496	17,496	7,228
Simon's Rock of Bard College; Great Barrington, Mass. 01230	318 (C)	P	19,770	19,770	5,860
Simpson College; Indianola, Iowa 50125	1,071 (C)	P	12,170	12,170	3,980
Simpson College; Redding, Calif. 96003	621 (C)	P	7,812	7,812	3,690
Sinte Gleska College; Rosebud, S.D. 57570	748 (C)	P	1,800	1,800	n.a.
Sioux Falls College; Sioux Falls, S.D. 57105	861 (C)	P	9,490	9,490	3,130
Skidmore College; Saratoga Springs, N.Y. 12866	2,128 (C)	P	19,945	19,945	5,890
Slippery Rock Univ. of Pennsylvania; Slippery Rock, Pa. 16057	7,162 (C)	Pub	4,025	9,075	3,374
Smith College; Northampton, Mass. 01063	2,631 (W)	P	19,650	19,650	6,670
Sojourner-Douglass College; Baltimore, Md. 21205	243 (C)	P	3,420	3,420	n.a.
Sonoma State University; Rohnert Park, Calif. 94928	5,536 (C)	Pub	1,035[1]	2,214[1]	5,753[1]
South, University of the; Sewanee, Tenn. 37375-1000	1,195 (C)	P	16,140	16,140	4,280
South Alabama, University of; Mobile, Ala. 36688	10,159 (C)	Pub	2,541	3,591	3,272
Southampton College. *See* Long Island Univ. Center					
South Carolina, University of; Columbia, S.C. 29208	16,028 (C)	Pub	3,278	8,282	3,589
South Carolina, Univ. of-Aiken; Aiken, S.C. 29801	3,235 (C)	Pub	2,500	6,250	3,175
South Carolina, Univ. of-Coastal Carolina; Myrtle Beach, S.C. 29578	4,023 (C)	Pub	3,082	7,180	3,890
South Carolina, Univ. of-Spartanburg; Spartanburg, S.C. 29303	3,270 (C)	Pub	2,500[1]	6,250[1]	3,062[1]
South Carolina State University; Orangeburg, S.C. 29117–0001	4,626 (C)	Pub	2,496	4,992	3,000
South Dakota, University of; Vermillion, S.D. 57069	5,952 (C)	Pub	2,191	2,191	2,757
South Dakota School of Mines and Technology; Rapid City, S.D. 57701	2,177 (C)	Pub	2,866	5,524	3,200
South Dakota State University; Brookings, S.D. 57007	9,140 (C)	Pub	2,705	5,537	2,330
Southeast Missouri State Univ.; Cape Girardeau, Mo. 63701	6,151 (C)	Pub	3,208	3,984	3,735
Southeastern Baptist College; Laurel, Miss. 39440	83 (C)	P	2,220	2,220	1,800
Southeastern Bible College; Birmingham, Ala. 35243	153 (C)	P	4,620	4,620	2,900
Southeastern College; Lakeland, Fla. 33801	1,137 (C)	P	3,552	3,552	3,234
Southeastern Louisiana University; Hammond, La. 70402	12,623 (C)	Pub	2,030	4,262	2,470
Southeastern Oklahoma State Univ.; Durant, Okla. 74701	3,650 (C)	Pub	1,543[1]	3,822[1]	2,619[1]
Southeastern University; Washington, D.C. 20024	220 (C)	P	6,910	6,910	n.a.
Southern Arkansas University; Magnolia, Ark. 71753	2,761 (C)	Pub	1,738	2,616	n.a.
Southern California, Univ. of; Los Angeles, Calif. 90089-0911	14,601 (C)	P	18,422	18,422	6,524
Southern California College; Costa Mesa, Calif. 92626	988 (C)	P	10,368	10,368	4,690
Southern California Institute of Architecture; Los Angeles, Calif. 90066	420 (C)	P	11,050[1]	11,050[1]	n.a.[1]
Southern College of Seventh-Day Adventists; Collegedale, Tenn. 37315	1,652 (C)	P	8,880	8,880	3,642
Southern College of Technology; Marietta, Ga. 30060	3,474 (C)	Pub	1,761	4,971	3,375
Southern Colorado, University of; Pueblo, Colo. 81001	4,508 (C)	Pub	2,066	7,866	4,100
Southern Connecticut State Univ.; New Haven, Conn. 06515	6,192 (C)	Pub	3,128	8,220	5,030
Southern Illinois Univ. at Carbondale; Carbondale, Ill. 62901	18,712 (C)	Pub	3,338	8,138	3,369
Southern Illinois Univ. at Edwardsville; Edwardsville, Ill. 62026	8,910 (C)	Pub	2,152	6,036	3,600
Southern Indiana, University of; Evansville, Ind. 47714	7,443 (C)	Pub	1,734	4,224	3,480
Southern Maine, University of; Gorham, Me. 04038	8,624 (C)	Pub	3,054[1]	8,334[1]	4,219[1]
Southern Methodist University; Dallas, Tex. 75275	5,247 (C)	P	15,228	15,228	5,206
Southern Mississippi, Univ. of; Hattiesburg, Miss. 39406	9,456 (C)	Pub	2,428	4,888	2,520
Southern Nazarene Univ.; Bethany, Okla. 73008	1,425 (C)	P	7,128	7,128	3,810
Southern Oregon State College; Ashland, Ore. 97520	4,519 (C)	Pub	3,780	10,432	4,000
Southern University at New Orleans; New Orleans, La. 70126	4,500 (C)	Pub	1,662	3,426	n.a.
Southern University-Baton Rouge; Baton Rouge, La. 70813	9,502 (C)	Pub	2,228[1]	4,550[1]	2,952[1]
Southern Utah State University; Cedar City, Utah 84720	4,592 (C)	Pub	1,776	5,628	2,895
Southern Vermont College; Bennington, Vt. 05201	743 (C)	P	9,810	9,810	4,650
South Florida, University of; Tampa, Fla. 33620	23,622 (C)	Pub	1,860	6,760	4,420

Institution and location	Enrollment	Control	Res.	Nonres.	Rm/Bd ($)
Southwest, College of the; Hobbs, N.M. 88240	365 (C)	P	4,100[1]	4,100[1]	2,483[1]
Southwest Baptist University; Bolivar, Mo. 65613	3,136 (C)	P	7,466	7,446	2,500
Southwestern Adventist College; Keene, Tex. 76059	971 (C)	P	7,728	7,728	3,812
Southwestern Assemblies of God College; Waxahachie, Tex. 75165	761 (C)	P	3,290[1]	3,290[1]	2,990[1]
Southwestern College; Winfield, Kan. 67156	738 (C)	P	7,850	7,850	3,692
Southwestern Conservative Baptist Bible College; Phoenix, Ariz. 85032	154 (C)	P	5,880	5,880	2,450
Southwestern Louisiana, University of; Lafayette, La. 70504	15,413 (C)	Pub	1,898	4,898	2,196
Southwestern Oklahoma State Univ.; Weatherford, Okla. 73096	5,453 (C)	Pub	1,461[1]	3,495[1]	2,016[1]
Southwestern University; Georgetown, Tex. 78626	1,238 (C)	P	12,700	12,700	4,868
Southwest Missouri State Univ.; Springfield, Mo. 65804	17,430 (C)	Pub	2,144	4,184	2,770
Southwest State University; Marshall, Minn. 56258	2,362 (C)	Pub	2,745	5,370	2,900
Southwest Texas State Univ.; San Marcos, Tex. 78666	17,928 (C)	Pub	1,806	5,280	3,676
Spalding University; Louisville, Ky. 40203	849 (C)	P	9,096	9,096	2,800
Spelman College; Atlanta, Ga. 30314	1,943 (W)	P	8,625	8,625	5,890
Spring Arbor College; Spring Arbor, Mich. 49283	850 (C)	P	10,000	10,000	3,850
Springfield College; Springfield, Mass. 01109	2,047 (C)	P	11,900	11,900	5,400
Spring Hill College; Mobile, Ala. 36608	1,117 (C)	P	12,489	12,489	4,788
Stanford University; Stanford, Calif. 94305	6,561 (C)	P	19,695	19,695	7,054
Staten Island, Coll. of (NYC). See New York, City Univ. of					
Stephen F. Austin State Univ. Nacogdoches, Tex. 75962	11,140 (C)	Pub	1,470	4,974	3,992
Stephens College; Columbia, Mo. 65215	1,045 (W)	P	14,400	14,400	5,370
Sterling College; Sterling, Kan. 67579	550 (C)	P	9,000	9,000	3,500
Stetson University; DeLand, Fla. 32720	2,045 (C)	P	13,110	13,110	5,390
Stevens Institute of Technology; Hoboken, N.J. 07030	1,280 (C)	P	17,500	17,500	3,016
Stillman College; Tuscaloosa, Ala. 35403	953 (C)	P	5,200	5,200	3,100
Stonehill College; North Easton, Mass. 02357	1,943 (C)	P	13,329	13,329	6,350
Strayer College Arlington Campus; Arlington, Va. 22204	5,784 (C)	P	6,075	6,075	n.a.
Suffolk University; Boston, Mass. 02108-2770	3,025 (C)	P	11,300	11,300	n.a.
Sul Ross State University; Alpine, Texas 79832	1,742 (C)	Pub	1,332	4,836	3,160
Sullivan College; Louisville, Ky. 40232	1,914 (C)	P	8,545	8,545	2,700
Susquehanna University; Selinsgrove, Pa. 17870–1001	1,608 (C)	P	17,080	17,080	4,900
Swarthmore College; Swarthmore, Pa. 19081	1,269 (C)	P	20,186	20,186	6,579
Sweet Briar College; Sweet Briar, Va. 24595	609 (W)	P	14,990	14,990	6,385
Syracuse University; Syracuse, N.Y. 13244	10,133 (C)	P	16,280	16,280	7,146
Tabor College; Hillsboro, Kan. 67063	433 (C)	P	9,000	9,000	3,600
Talladega College; Talladega, Ala. 35160	912 (C)	P	5,666	5,666	2,964
Tampa, University of; Tampa, Fla. 33606	1,976 (C)	P	13,620	13,620	5,780
Tampa College; Tampa, Fla. 33614	1,440 (C)	P	5,472	5,472	n.a.
Tarleton State University; Stephenville, Tex. 76402	5,600 (C)	Pub	1,494	4,998	3,172
Taylor University; Upland, Ind. 46989	1,817 (C)	P	11,914	11,914	4,150
Taylor University–Fort Wayne; Fort Wayne, Ind. 46807	423 (C)	P	9,700	9,700	3,840
Teikyo Marycrest University; Davenport, Iowa 52804	1,032 (C)	P	10,280	10,280	3,790
Teikyo Post College; Waterbury, Conn. 06723-2540	1,794 (C)	P	11,700	11,700	5,600
Teikyo Westmar University; Le Mars, Iowa 51031	761 (C)	P	10,100	10,100	4,100
Temple University; Philadelphia, Pa. 19122	19,529 (C)	Pub	5,464	10,246	5,426
Temple University-Ambler; Ambler, Pa. 19002	5,000 (C)	Pub	5,314	10,096	5,400
Tennessee, Univ. of-Chattanooga; Chattanooga, Tenn. 37403	7,001 (C)	Pub	1,850[1]	5,782[1]	3,798[1]
Tennessee, Univ. of-Knoxville; Knoxville, Tenn. 37996-0230	18,608 (C)	Pub	2,052[1]	5,986[1]	3,384[1]
Tennessee, Univ. of-Martin; Martin, Tenn. 38238	5,361 (C)	Pub	1,900[1]	5,832[1]	3,040[1]
Tennessee, Univ. of-Memphis, The Health Science Center; Memphis, Tenn. 38163	417 (C)	Pub	8,700	8,700	3,500
Tennessee State University; Nashville, Tenn. 37209	6,617 (C)	Pub	1,858	5,792	2,720
Tennessee Technological Univ.; Cookeville, Tenn. 38505	6,755 (C)	Pub	1,772[1]	5,706[1]	3,106[1]
Tennessee Temple University; Chattanooga, Tenn. 37404	653 (C)	P	5,240	5,240	3,990
Tennessee Wesleyan College; Athens, Tenn. 37303	632 (C)	P	6,200	6,200	3,700
Texas, University of-Arlington; Arlington, Tex. 76019	18,926 (C)	Pub	1,410	5,180	4,320
Texas, University of-Austin; Austin, Tex. 78712	34,746 (C)	Pub	1,815	6,105	3,528
Texas, University of-Dallas; Richardson, Tex. 75083-0688	4,727 (C)	Pub	1,678	6,058	4,953
Texas, University of-El Paso; El Paso, Tex. 79968	14,746 (C)	Pub	1,081	5,911	3,200
Texas, University of-Health Science Center-San Antonio; San Antonio, Tex. 78284	843 (C)	Pub	902[3]	4,982[3]	n.a.[3]
Texas, University of, Medical Branch-Galveston; Galveston, Tex. 77555-1305	972 (C)	Pub	1,550	6,626	1,756
Texas, University of–Pan American; Edinburg, Tex. 78539	12,733 (C)	Pub	1,230[1]	4,662[1]	2,050[1]
Texas, University of–Permian Basin; Odessa, Tex. 79762	2,219 (C)	Pub	1,390	4,894	3,580
Texas, University of-San Antonio; San Antonio, Tex. 78249-0616	14,663 (C)	Pub	1,562	4,946	6,840
Texas, University of, Southwestern Medical Center at Dallas; Dallas, Tex. 75235	379 (C)	Pub	859	5,083	n.a.
Texas, University of-Tyler; Tyler, Tex. 75701	2,590 (C)	Pub	1,222[1]	4,654[1]	3,850[1]
Texas A&I University-Kingsville; Kingsville, Tex. 78363	5,302 (C)	Pub	1,370	5,000	3,090
Texas A&M University; College Station, Tex. 77843	34,278 (C)	Pub	1,813	6,193	3,441
Texas A&M University–Corpus Christi; Corpus Christi, Tex. 78412	3,907 (C)	Pub	1,588	5,818	2,385
Texas A&M University-Galveston; Galveston, Tex. 77553	1,337 (C)	Pub	1,010[1]	5,360[1]	3,394[1]
Texas A&M University–Kingsville; Kingsville, Tex. 78363	5,302 (C)	Pub	1,370[1]	5,000[1]	3,090[1]
Texas Christian University; Fort Worth, Tex. 76129	5,566 (C)	P	10,040	10,040	3,400

Institution and location	Enrollment	Control	Tuition ($) Res.	Tuition ($) Nonres.	Rm/Bd ($)
Texas College; Tyler, Tex. 75702-2404	460 (C)	P	5,020	5,020	2,430
Texas Lutheran College; Seguin, Tex. 78155	1,091 (C)	P	8,026	8,026	3,806
Texas Southern University; Houston, Tex. 77004	6,113 (C)	Pub	1,130	4,562	3,320
Texas Tech University; Lubbock, Tex. 79409	19,652 (C)	Pub	1,867	6,247	3,853
Texas Wesleyan University; Fort Worth, Tex. 76105	1,493 (C)	P	6,900	6,900	3,550
Texas Woman's University; Denton, Tex. 76204	5,319 (W)	Pub	1,396	4,900	3,162
Thiel College; Greenville, Pa. 16125	892 (C)	P	12,000	12,000	5,025
Thomas Aquinas College; Santa Paula, Calif. 93060	221 (C)	P	13,700	13,700	5,500
Thomas College; Thomasville, Ga. 31792-7499	746 (C)	P	4,125	4,125	n.a.
Thomas College; Waterville, Me. 04901	450 (C)	P	9,720	9,720	4,825
Thomas Edison State College, Trenton, N.J. 08608-1176	8,619 (C)	Pub	458	811	n.a.
Thomas Jefferson University, College of Allied Health Sciences; Philadelphia, Pa. 19107	1,325 (C)	P	13,800[1]	13,800[1]	2,070[1]
Thomas More College; Crestview Hills, Ky. 41017	1,268 (C)	P	10,084	10,084	3,966
Tiffin University; Tiffin, Ohio 44883	1,023 (C)	P	8,200	8,200	4,000
Toccoa Falls College; Toccoa Falls, Ga. 30598	903 (C)	P	6,376	6,376	3,708
Toledo, University of; Toledo, Ohio 43606	21,162 (C)	Pub	3,396	8,145	3,717
Tougaloo College; Tougaloo, Miss. 39174	1,153 (C)	P	5,690	5,690	2,279
Touro College; New York, N.Y. 10001-4103	7,704 (C)	P	8,780	8,780	6,600
Towson State University; Towson, Md. 21204-7097	13,404 (C)	Pub	3,530	6,932	2,360
Transylvania University; Lexington, Ky. 40508-1797	974 (C)	P	8,200	8,200	3,040
Trenton State College; Trenton, N.J. 08650-4700	6,067 (C)	Pub	4,012[1]	6,287[1]	6,345[1]
Trevecca Nazarene College; Nashville, Tenn. 37210	973 (C)	P	7,856	7,856	3,410
Tri-State University; Angola, Ind. 46703	1,097 (C)	P	10,407	10,407	4,350
Trinity Bible College; Ellendale, N.D. 58436-7150	347 (C)	P	5,170	5,170	3,084
Trinity Christian College; Palos Heights, Ill. 60463	624 (C)	P	10,700	10,700	4,200
Trinity College; Burlington, Vt. 05401	1,046 (W)	P	11,830	11,830	5,703
Trinity College; Deerfield, Ill. 60015	1,006 (C)	P	11,140	11,140	4,420
Trinity College; Hartford, Conn. 06106	1,916 (C)	P	20,230	20,230	5,920
Trinity College; Washington, D.C. 20017	1,000 (W)	P	12,050	12,050	5,792
Trinity College of Fla.; New Port Richey, Fla. 34655	125 (C)	P	3,260	3,260	1,995
Trinity International University; Miami, Fla. 33101	405 (C)	P	7,340	7,340	n.a.
Trinity University; San Antonio, Tex. 78212	2,226 (C)	P	13,044	13,044	5,350
Troy State University; Troy, Ala. 36082	5,068 (C)	Pub	1,920[1]	3,330[1]	2,895[1]
Troy State University-Dothan; Dothan, Ala. 36303	1,707 (C)	Pub	1,920	3,456	n.a.
Troy State University-Montgomery; Montgomery, Ala. 36103-4419	2,718 (C)	Pub	1,845	2,016	n.a.
Tufts University; Medford, Mass. 02155	4,432 (C)	P	22,686	22,686	6,250
Tulane University; New Orleans, La. 70118	6,762 (C)	P	20,478	20,478	6,130
Tulsa, University of; Tulsa, Okla. 74104	3,369 (C)	P	12,300	12,300	4,074
Turabo University; Caguas, P.R. 00658	n.a.	n.a.	n.a.	n.a.	n.a.
Tusculum College; Greeneville, Tenn. 37743	930 (C)	P	8,700	8,700	3,500
Tuskegee University; Tuskegee, Ala. 36088	3,191 (C)	P	7,424	7,424	3,800
Union College; Barbourville, Ky. 40906	638 (C)	P	8,200	8,200	3,000
Union College; Lincoln, Neb. 68506	574 (C)	P	9,225	9,225	2,900
Union College; Schenectady, N.Y. 12308	2,025 (C)	P	19,972	19,972	6,234
Union Institute, The; Cincinnati, Ohio 45206-1947	482 (C)	P	7,776	7,776	n.a.
Union University; Jackson, Tenn. 38305	1,930 (C)	P	6,350	6,350	2,860
U.S. Air Force Academy; Colorado Springs, Colo. 80840	3,524 (C)	Pub	—	—	—
United States Coast Guard Academy; New London, Conn. 06320	906 (C)	Pub	—	—	—
United States International University; San Diego, Calif. 92131	355 (C)	P	11,070	11,070·	4,350
United States Merchant Marine Academy; Kings Point, N.Y. 11024	980 (C)	Pub	4,464[1]	4,464[1]	n.a.[1]
United States Military Academy; West Point, N.Y. 10996	4,054 (C)	Pub	—	—	—
U.S. Naval Academy; Annapolis, Md. 21402	4,100 (C)	Pub	—	—	—
Unity College; Unity, Me. 04988	487 (C)	P	9,430	9,930	4,895
Universidad de las Americas—Puebla; Puebla, Mexico 72820	5,481 (C)	P	3,400	3,400	3,000
Universidad Politecnica de Puerto Rico; Hato Rey, San Juan, P.R. 00918	4,322 (C)	P	3,310[1]	3,310[1]	n.a.[1]
Upper Iowa University; Fayette, Iowa 52142	2,641 (C)	P	8,840	8,840	3,360
Urbana Univ.; Urbana, Ohio 43078-2091	952 (C)	P	8,703	8,703	4,140
Ursinus College; Collegeville, Pa. 19426	1,113 (C)	P	15,835	15,835	5,330
Ursuline College; Pepper Pike, Ohio 44124	1,448 (C)	P	9,810	9,810	4,339
Utah, University of; Salt Lake City, Utah 84112	21,966 (C)	Pub	2,508	7,707	3,980
Utah State University; Logan, Utah 84322	16,032 (C)	Pub	1,992	6,042	3,165
Utica College of Syracuse University; Utica, N.Y. 13502	1,600 (C)	P	13,406	13,406	5,020
Valdosta State College; Valdosta, Ga. 31698	6,730 (C)	Pub	1,887	3,210	3,225
Valley City State University; Valley City, N.D. 58072	986 (C)	Pub	1,889[1]	4,695[1]	2,350[1]
Valley Forge Christian College; Phoenixville, Pa. 19460	517 (C)	P	5,032	5,032	3,140
Valparaiso University; Valparaiso, Ind. 46383	2,698 (C)	P	12,860	12,860	3,450
Vanderbilt University; Nashville, Tenn. 37203	5,652 (C)	P	21,065	21,065	6,656
Vandercook College of Music; Chicago, Ill. 60616	82 (C)	P	9,300	9,300	4,600
Vassar College; Poughkeepsie, N.Y. 12601	2,250 (C)	P	20,330	20,330	6,150
Vennard College; University Park, Iowa 52595	143 (C)	P	5,696	5,696	3,700
Vermont, University of; Burlington, Vt. 05401-3596	7,925 (C)	Pub	6,909	16,605	5,292
Villa Julie College; Stevenson, Md. 21153	1,858 (C)	P	8,200	8,200	4,600
Villanova University; Villanova, Pa. 19085	6,288 (C)	P	15,835	15,835	5,330
Virginia, University of; Charlottesville, Va. 22906	11,502 (C)	Pub	4,614	14,006	3,846[10]

Institution and location	Enrollment	Control	Tuition ($) Res.	Nonres.	Rm/Bd ($)
Virginia, University of—Clinch Valley College; Wise, Va. 24293	1,840 (C)	Pub	3,200	7,524	3,902
Virginia Commonwealth University; Richmond, Va. 23284-2526	12,604 (C)	Pub	4,030	11,633	4,306
Virginia Intermont College; Bristol, Va. 24201-4298	637 (C)	P	9,600	9,600	4,250
Virginia Military Institute; Lexington, Va. 24450	1,179 (M)	Pub	5,070[1]	11,110[1]	3,800[1]
Virginia Polytechnic Institute and State University; Blacksburg, Va. 24061–0202	19,229 (C)	Pub	4,087	10,739	3,120
Virginia State University; Petersburg, Va. 23806	4,260 (C)	Pub	3,356	7,365	4,845
Virginia Union University; Richmond, Va. 23220	1,209 (C)	P	8,219	8,219	3,638
Virginia Wesleyan College; Norfolk-Virginia Beach, Va. 23502	1,513 (C)	P	11,650	11,650	5,200
Virgin Islands, University of the; St. Thomas, V.I. 00802	2,668 (C)	Pub	1,650[1]	4,950[1]	4,850[1]
Visual Arts, School of; New York, N.Y. 10010	2,745 (C)	P	12,600	12,600	4,800
Viterbo College; La Crosse, Wis. 54601	1,548 (C)	P	9,850	9,850	3,750
Voorhees College; Denmark, S.C. 29042	723 (C)	P	8,900[1]	8,900[1]	5,084[1]
Wabash College; Crawfordsville, Ind. 47933	770 (M)	P	13,700	13,700	4,405
Wadhams Hall Seminary—College; Ogdensburg, N.Y. 13669-9308	31 (C)	P	4,120	4,120	4,115
Wagner College; Staten Island, N.Y. 10301	1,248 (C)	P	14,450	14,450	5,800
Wake Forest University; Winston-Salem, N.C. 27109	3,746 (C)	P	14,750	14,750	4,585
Walla Walla College; College Place, Wash. 99324	1,620 (C)	P	11,475	11,475	4,245
Walsh College of Accountancy and Business Administration; Troy, Mich. 48007	1,711 (C)	P	6,150	6,150	n.a.
Walsh University; North Canton, Ohio 44720	1,356 (C)	P	9,360	9,360	4,500
Warner Pacific College; Portland, Ore. 97215	692 (C)	P	8,940	8,940	4,340
Warner Southern College; Lake Wales, Fla. 33853	572 (C)	P	7,530	7,530	3,870
Warren Wilson College; Ashville, N.C. 28815	523 (C)	P	11,165	11,165	3,152
Wartburg College; Waverly, Iowa 50677	1,405 (C)	P	12,240	12,240	3,840
Warwick, University of; Coventry, CV4 7AL, England	6,706 (C)	Pub	4,748[1]	4,748[1]	3,806[1]
Washburn University; Topeka, Kan. 66621	5,661 (C)	Pub	2,264	4,616	3,800
Washington, University of; Seattle, Wash. 98195	24,592 (C)	Pub	2,807	8,199	4,218
Washington and Jefferson College; Washington, Pa. 15301	1,104 (C)	P	16,840	16,840	4,205
Washington and Lee University; Lexington, Va. 24450	1,617 (C)	P	14,655	14,655	4,935
Washington Bible College; Lanham, Md. 20706	352 (C)	P	4,608	4,608	3,390
Washington College; Chestertown, Md. 21620-9926	886 (C)	P	16,040	16,040	5,558
Washington State University; Pullman, Wash. 99164	16,123 (C)	Pub	2,909[1]	8,200[1]	4,050[1]
Washington University; St. Louis, Mo. 63130	4,962 (C)	P	19,100	19,100	5,961
Wayland Baptist University; Plainview, Tex. 79072	3,244 (C)	P	5,400	5,400	3,021
Waynesburg College; Waynesburg, Pa. 15370	1,281 (C)	P	9,370	9,370	3,892
Wayne State College; Wayne, Neb. 68787	3,273 (C)	Pub	1,632[1]	2,832[1]	2,660[1]
Wayne State University; Detroit, Mich. 48202	20,865 (C)	Pub	2,850	6,306	5,839
Webber College; Babson Park, Fla. 33827	370 (C)	P	6,540	6,540	3,000
Webb Institute of Naval Architecture; Glen Cove, N.Y. 11542	83 (C)	P	—	—	11,000
Weber State University; Ogden, Utah 84408	14,140 (C)	Pub	1,854	5,541	4,440
Webster University; St. Louis, Mo. 63119	3,709 (C)	P	9,700	9,700	4,384
Wellesley College; Wellesley, Mass. 02181	2,271 (W)	P	19,610	19,610	6,200
Wells College; Aurora, N.Y. 13026	400 (C)	P	16,800	16,800	5,800
Wentworth Institute of Technology; Boston, Mass. 02115	2,412 (C)	P	9,850	9,850	6,080
Wesleyan College; Macon, Ga. 31297	436 (W)	P	12,500	12,500	4,800
Wesleyan University; Middletown, Conn. 06457	2,724 (C)	P	20,820	20,820	5,810
Wesley College; Dover, Del. 19901	1,380 (C)	P	10,295	10,295	4,674
Wesley College; Florence, Miss. 39073–0070	65 (C)	P	2,000	2,000	2,250
West Alabama, The University of; Livingston, Ala. 35470	1,954 (C)	Pub	2,010	2,010	2,436
Westbrook College; Portland, Me. 04103	387 (C)	P	11,650	11,650	4,900
West Chester Univ. of Pennsylvania; West Chester, Pa. 19383	9,961 (C)	Pub	3,646[1]	8,404[1]	4,108[1]
West Coast University; Los Angeles, Calif. 90020-1765	500 (C)	P	10,200	10,200	n.a.
Western Baptist College; Salem, Ore. 97301	579 (C)	P	10,030	10,030	4,260
Western Carolina University; Cullowhee, N.C. 28723	5,948 (C)	Pub	1,695	8,503	2,516
Western Connecticut State University; Danbury, Conn. 06810	4,679 (C)	Pub	3,214	3,214	5,080
Western Illinois University; Macomb, Ill. 61455-1383	10,042 (C)	Pub	2,702	6,638	3,413
Western International University; Phoenix, Ariz. 85021	1,169 (C)	P	3,650	3,650	n.a.
Western Kentucky University; Bowling Green, Ky. 42101	12,709 (C)	Pub	1,901	5,261	3,450
Western Maryland College; Westminster, Md. 21157	1,251 (C)	P	15,300	15,300	5,365
Western Michigan University; Kalamazoo, Mich. 49008	19,499 (C)	Pub	2,549	5,825	4,100
Western Montana College; Dillon, Mont. 59725	1,120 (C)	Pub	1,934	5,658	3,372
Western New England College; Springfield, Mass. 01119	1,673 (C)	P	9,510	9,510	5,740
Western New Mexico University; Silver City, N.M. 88061	2,001 (C)	Pub	1,486	5,454	2,158
Western Oregon State College; Monmouth, Ore. 97361	3,975 (C)	Pub	2,820[1]	7,089[1]	3,631[1]
Western State College of Colorado; Gunnison, Colo. 81230	2,662 (C)	Pub	2,010	6,755	4,279
Western Washington University; Bellingham, Wash. 98225	9,732 (C)	Pub	2,406[1]	8,124[1]	4,144[1]
Westfield State College; Westfield, Mass. 01086	3,162 (C)	Pub	3,338	7,473	4,100
West Florida, University of; Pensacola, Fla. 32514	6,408 (C)	Pub	1,702[1]	6,605[1]	3,360[1]
West Georgia College; Carrollton, Ga. 30118	5,990 (C)	Pub	1,896	4,882	3,183
West Liberty State College; West Liberty, W. Va. 26074	2,381 (C)	Pub	1,900[1]	4,470[1]	2,890[1]
West Los Angeles, University of, School of Paralegal Studies; Los Angeles, Calif. 90066	235 (C)	P	5,160[1]	5,160[1]	n.a.[1]
Westminster College; Fulton, Mo. 65251	667 (C)	P	11,350	11,350	4,250
Westminster College; New Wilmington, Pa. 16172	1,543 (C)	P	12,810	12,810	3,980
Westminster Coll. of Salt Lake City; Salt Lake City, Utah 84105	947 (C)	P	9,600	9,600	4,190

Institution and location	Enrollment	Control	Tuition ($) Res.	Nonres.	Rm/Bd ($)
Westmont College; Santa Barbara, Calif. 93108	1,280 (C)	P	16,330	16,330	5,580
West Suburban College of Nursing; Oak Park, Ill. 60302	241 (C)	P	10,110	10,110	n.a.
West Texas State University; Canyon, Tex. 79016	4,813 (C)	Pub	1,586	5,966	2,716
West Virginia Institute of Technology; Montgomery, W. Va. 25136	3,027 (C)	Pub	2,270	4,940	3,940
West Virginia State College; Institute, W. Va. 25112	4,896 (C)	Pub	5,188	7,816	3,200
West Virginia University; Morgantown, W. Va. 26506-6009	15,383 (C)	Pub	2,128[1]	6,370[1]	4,310[1]
West Virginia University at Parkersburg; Parkersburg, W. Va. 26101-9577	3,979 (C)	Pub	1,164	1,824	n.a.
West Virginia Wesleyan College; Buckhannon, W. Va. 26201	1,620 (C)	P	14,750	14,750	3,850
Wheaton College; Norton, Mass. 02766	1,331 (C)	P	19,020	19,020	6,050
Wheaton College; Wheaton, Ill. 60187-5593	2,304 (C)	P	12,300	12,300	4,370
Wheeling Jesuit College; Wheeling, W. Va. 26003	1,296 (C)	P	12,000	12,000	4,670
Wheelock College; Boston, Mass. 02215	767 (C)	P	14,368	14,368	5,772
White Plains, Coll. of, of Pace Univ. *See* Pace Univ.					
Whitman College; Walla Walla, Wash. 99362	1,295 (C)	P	18,130	18,130	5,160
Whittier College; Whittier, Calif. 90608	1,321 (C)	P	17,187	17,187	5,813
Whitworth College; Spokane, Wash. 99251	1,577 (C)	P	13,620	13,620	4,900
Wichita State University; Wichita, Kan. 67208	14,558 (C)	Pub	4,642	16,197	3,465
Widener University; Chester, Pa. 19013	2,350 (C)	P	12,950	12,950	5,650
Wilberforce University; Wilberforce, Ohio 45384	880 (C)	P	7,010	7,010	3,720
Wiley College; Marshall, Tex. 75670	505 (C)	P	3,660	3,660	2,872
Wilkes University; Wilkes-Barre, Pa. 18766	2,408 (C)	P	12,478	12,478	5,410
Willamette University; Salem, Ore. 97301	1,701 (C)	P	16,490	16,490	4,800
William and Mary, College of; Williamsburg, Va. 23185	5,402 (C)	Pub	4,738	14,428	4,372
William Carey College; Hattiesburg, Miss. 39401	1,885 (C)	P	4,950[1]	4,950[1]	7,225[1]
William Jewell College; Liberty, Mo. 64068	1,360 (C)	P	10,580	10,580	2,970
William Paterson College; Wayne, N.J. 07470	8,044 (C)	Pub	3,000	3,952	4,500
William Penn College; Oskaloosa, Iowa 52577	693 (C)	P	10,940	10,940	3,490
Williams Baptist College; Walnut Ridge, Ark. 72476	607 (C)	P	4,550	4,550	2,522
Williams College; Williamstown, Mass. 01267	1,985 (C)	P	20,790	20,790	5,990
William Smith College. *See* Hobart and William Smith Colleges					
William Tyndale College; Farmington Hills, Mich. 48108	542 (C)	P	4,746	4,746	4,170
William Woods College; Fulton, Mo. 65251	823 (W)	P	11,300	11,300	4,700
Wilmington College; New Castle, Del. 19720	1,773 (C)	P	4,392	4,392	n.a.
Wilmington College of Ohio; Wilmington, Ohio 45177	1,000 (C)	P	11,050	11,050	4,200
Wilson College; Chambersburg, Pa. 17201-1285	861 (W)	P	11,999	11,999	5,338
Wingate College; Wingate, N.C. 28174	1,276 (C)	P	8,800	8,800	3,600
Winona State University; Winona, Minn. 55987	7,000 (C)	Pub	2,800	5,700	3,000
Winston-Salem State University; Winston-Salem, N.C. 27110	2,604 (C)	Pub	1,307	3,433	3,433
Winthrop University; Rock Hill, S.C. 29733	4,107 (C)	Pub	3,506[1]	4,896[1]	3,392[1]
Wisconsin, University of-Eau Claire; Eau Claire, Wis. 54701	9,801 (C)	Pub	2,208[1]	6,996[1]	2,705[1]
Wisconsin, University of-Green Bay; Green Bay, Wis. 54302	5,270 (C)	Pub	2,420	7,500	2,900
Wisconsin, University of-La Crosse; La Crosse, Wis. 54601	8,005 (C)	Pub	2,371	7,159	2,270
Wisconsin, University of-Madison; Madison, Wis. 53706	26,207 (C)	Pub	2,730	9,050	4,290
Wisconsin, University of-Milwaukee; Milwaukee, Wis. 53201	18,224 (C)	Pub	2,960	9,400	3,500
Wisconsin, University of-Oshkosh; Oshkosh, Wis. 54901	9,098 (C)	Pub	2,162[1]	7,950[1]	2,256[1]
Wisconsin, University of-Parkside; Kenosha, Wis. 53141–2000	4,828 (C)	Pub	2,420	7,495	3,600
Wisconsin, University of-Platteville; Platteville, Wis. 53818	4,381 (C)	Pub	2,485	7,560	3,600
Wisconsin, University of-River Falls; River Falls, Wis. 54022	5,400 (C)	Pub	2,304[1]	7,092[1]	2,500[1]
Wisconsin, University of-Stevens Point; Stevens Point, Wis. 54481	7,983 (C)	Pub	2,395	7,422	3,150
Wisconsin, University of-Stout; Menomonie, Wis. 54751	6,788 (C)	Pub	2,317[1]	7,105[1]	2,516[1]
Wisconsin, University of-Superior; Superior, Wis. 54880	2,402 (C)	Pub	2,182[1]	6,970[1]	2,780[1]
Wisconsin, University of-Whitewater; Whitewater, Wis. 53190	9,222 (C)	Pub	2,470	2,470	2,700
Wisconsin Lutheran College; Milwaukee, Wis. 53226	373 (C)	P	9,940	9,940	3,900
Wittenberg University; Springfield, Ohio 45501	2,279 (C)	P	17,696	17,696	4,536
Wofford College; Spartanburg, S.C. 29303-3663	1,127 (C)	P	13,795	13,795	4,185
Women's College of Brenau University, The; Gainesville, Ga. 30501	648 (W)	P	9,885	9,885	6,185
Woodbury University; Burbanks, Calif. 91510-7846	936 (C)	P	13,020	13,020	5,655
Wooster, College of; Wooster, Ohio 44691	1,785 (C)	P	17,600	17,600	4,640
Worcester Polytechnic Institute; Worcester, Mass. 01609	2,786 (C)	P	17,160	17,160	4,710
Worcester State College; Worcester, Mass. 01602–2597	3,600 (C)	Pub	2,653	6,187	3,800
Wright State University; Dayton, Ohio 45435	12,220 (C)	Pub	3,429	6,858	3,812
Xavier University; Cincinnati, Ohio 45207	3,996 (C)	P	12,270	12,270	5,050
Xavier University of Louisiana; New Orleans, La. 70125	2,916 (C)	P	7,300	7,300	4,300
Yale University; New Haven, Conn. 06520	5,166 (C)	P	21,000	21,000	6,630
Yeshiva University; New York, N.Y. 10033-3299	1,852 (C)	P	13,270	13,270	4,300
York College of Pennsylvania; York, Pa. 17405	3,149 (C)	P	5,250	5,250	3,810
Youngstown State Univ.; Youngstown, Ohio 44555	12,833 (C)	Pub	3,084	6,252	3,900

1. 1994–95. 2. Nonresident, $3,309. 3. 1993–94. 4. Nonresident, $2,430. 5. Nonresident, $5,500. 6. Nonresident, $3,854. 7. Nonresident, $3,280. 8. Nonresident, $11,113. 9. Varies. 10. Nonresident, $13,000.

Selected Degree Abbreviations

A.B. Bachelor of Arts
AeEng. Aeronautical Engineer
A.M.T. Master of Arts in Teaching
B.A. Bachelor of Arts
B.A.E. Bachelor of Arts in Education, or Bachelor of Art Education, Aeronautical Engineering, Agricultural Engineering, or Architectural Engineering
B.Ag. Bachelor of Agriculture
B.A.M. Bachelor of Applied Mathematics
B.Arch. Bachelor of Architecture
B.B.A. Bachelor of Business Administration
B.C.E. Bachelor of Civil Engineering
B.Ch.E. Bachelor of Chemical Engineering
B.C.L. Bachelor of Canon Law
B.D. Bachelor of Divinity
B.E. Bachelor of Education or Bachelor of Engineering
B.E.E. Bachelor of Electrical Engineering
B.F. Bachelor of Forestry
B.F.A. Bachelor of Fine Arts
B.J. Bachelor of Journalism
B.L.S. Bachelor of Liberal Studies or Bachelor of Library Science
B.Lit. Bachelor of Literature
B.M. Bachelor of Medicine or Bachelor of Music
B.M.S. Bachelor of Marine Science
B.N. Bachelor of Nursing
B.Pharm. Bachelor of Pharmacy
B.R.E. Bachelor of Religious Education
B.S. Bachelor of Science
B.S.Ed. Bachelor of Science in Education
C.E. Civil Engineer
Ch.E. Chemical Engineer
D.B.A. Doctor of Business Administration
D.C. Doctor of Chiropractic
D.D. Doctor of Divinity[1]
D.D.S. Doctor of Dental Surgery or Doctor of Dental Science
D.L.S. Doctor of Library Science
D.M.D. Doctor of Dental Medicine
D.O. Doctor of Osteopathy
D.M.S. Doctor of Medical Science
D.P.A. Doctor of Public Administration[2]
D.P.H. Doctor of Public Health
D.R.E. Doctor of Religious Education
D.S.W. Doctor of Social Welfare or Doctor of Social Work
D.Sc. Doctor of Science[3]
D.V.M. Doctor of Veterinary Medicine
Ed.D. Doctor of Education[2]
Ed.S. Education Specialist
E.E. Electrical Engineer

E.M. Engineer of Mines
E.Met. Engineer of Metallurgy
I.E. Industrial Engineer or Industrial Engineering
J.D. Doctor of Laws[2]
J.S.D. Doctor of Juristic Science
L.H.D. Doctor of Humane Letters[3]
Litt.B. Bachelor of Letters
Litt.M. Master of Letters[4]
LL.B. Bachelor of Laws
LL.D. Doctor of Laws[3]
LL.M. Master of Laws
M.A. Master of Arts
M.Aero.E. Master of Aeronautical Engineering
M.B.A. Master of Business Administration
M.C.E. Master of Christian Education or Master of Civil Engineering
M.C.S. Master of Computer Science
M.D. Doctor of Medicine
M.Div. Master of Divinity
M.E. Master of Engineering
M.Ed. Master of Education
M.Eng. Master of Engineering
M.F.A. Master of Fine Arts
M.H.A. Master of Hospital Administration
M.L.S. Master of Library Science
M.M. Master of Music
M.M.E. Master of Mechanical Engineering or Master of Music Education
M.Mus. Master of Music
M.N. Master of Nursing
M.R.E. Master of Religious Education
M.S. Master of Science
M.S.W. Master of Social Work
M.Th. Master of Theology
Nuc.E. Nuclear Engineer
O.D. Doctor of Optometry
Pharm.D. Doctor of Pharmacy[2]
Ph.B. Bachelor of Philosophy
Ph.D. Doctor of Philosophy
S.B. Bachelor of Science
Sc.D. Doctor of Science[3]
S.J.D. Doctor of Juridical Science or Doctor of the Science of Law
S.Sc.D. Doctor of Social Science
S.T.B. Bachelor of Sacred Theology
S.T.D. Doctor of Sacred Theology
S.T.M. Master of Sacred Theology
Th.B. Bachelor of Theology
Th.D. Doctor of Theology
Th.M. Master of Theology

1. Honorary. 2. Earned and honorary. 3. Usually honorary. 4. Sometimes honorary.

Academic Costume: Colors Associated With Fields

Field	Color	Field	Color
Agriculture	Maize	Medicine	Green
Arts, Letters, Humanities	White	Music	Pink
Commerce, Accountancy, Business	Drab	Nursing	Apricot
		Oratory (Speech)	Silver gray
Dentistry	Lilac	Pharmacy	Olive green
Economics	Copper	Philosophy	Dark blue
Education	Light blue	Physical Education	Sage green
Engineering	Orange	Public Admin. including Foreign Service	Peacock blue
Fine Arts, Architecture	Brown	Public Health	Salmon pink
Forestry	Russet	Science	Golden yellow
Journalism	Crimson	Social Work	Citron
Law	Purple	Theology	Scarlet
Library Science	Lemon	Veterinary Science	Gray

THE OLYMPIC GAMES

(W)—Site of Winter Games. (S)—Site of Summer Games

1896	Athens	1948	St. Moritz (W)	1976	Montreal (S)
1900	Paris	1948	London (S)	1980	Lake Placid (W)
1904	St. Louis	1952	Oslo (W)	1980	Moscow (S)
1906	Athens	1952	Helsinki (S)	1984	Sarajevo, Yugoslavia (W)
1908	London	1956	Cortina d'Ampezzo, Italy (W)	1984	Los Angeles (S)
1912	Stockholm	1956	Melbourne (S)	1988	Calgary, Alberta (W)
1920	Antwerp	1960	Squaw Valley, Calif. (W)	1988	Seoul, South Korea (S)
1924	Chamonix (W)	1960	Rome (S)	1992	Albertville, France (W)
1924	Paris (S)	1964	Innsbruck, Austria (W)	1992	Barcelona, Spain (S)
1928	St. Moritz (W)	1964	Tokyo (S)	1994	Lillehammer, Norway (W)
1928	Amsterdam (S)	1968	Grenoble, France (W)	1996	Atlanta, Ga. (S)
1932	Lake Placid (W)	1968	Mexico City (S)	1998	Nagano, Japan (W)
1932	Los Angeles (S)	1972	Sapporo, Japan (W)	2000	Sydney, Australia (S)
1936	Garnisch–Partenkirchen (W)	1972	Munich (S)	2002	Salt Lake City (W)
1936	Berlin (S)	1976	Innsbruck, Austria (W)		

The first Olympic Games of which there is record were held in 776 B.C., and consisted of one event, a great foot race of about 200 yards held on a plain by the River Alpheus (now the Ruphia) just outside the little town of Olympia in Greece. It was from that date the Greeks began to keep their calendar by "Olympiads," the four-year spans between the celebrations of the famous games.

The modern Olympic Games, which started in Athens in 1896, are the result of the devotion of a French educator, Baron Pierre de Coubertin, to the idea that, since young people and athletics have gone together through the ages, educaiton and athletics might go hand–in–hand toward a better international understanding.

The principal organization responsible for the staging of the Games is the International Olympic Committee (IOC). Other important roles are played by the National Olympic Committees in each participating country, international sports federations, and the organizing committee of the host city.

Beginning in 1994, the IOC decided to change the format of having both the Summer and Winter Games in the same year. Summer and Winter Olympics now alternate every two years. In 1994, the Winter Games were staged in Lillehammer, Norway, just two years after they'd been in Albertville, France. The Winter Games will next be held in Nagano, Japan, in 1998. The next Summer Olympics will be 1996 in Atlanta, Ga.

The headquarters of the 89–member International Olympic Committee are in Lausanne, Switzerland. The president of the IOC is Juan Antonio Samaranch of Spain.

The Olympic motto is "Citius, Altius, Fortius,"– "Faster, Higher, Stronger." The Olympic symbol is five interlocking circles colored blue, yellow, black, green, and red, on a white background, representing the five continents. At least one of those colors appears in the national flag of every country.

Norway Wins Medals Race, United States Best-Ever 13 Medals at 1994 Winter Olympics

The names Nancy Kerrigan and Tonya Harding dominated the 1994 Winter Olympics in Lillehammer, Norway. While Kerrigan won a silver medal and Harding none at all, the pre-Olympics attack on Kerrigan's knee, in which associates of Harding and even Harding herself were implicated, kept the spotlight on figure skating as soap opera rather than sport.

The on-ice big name for the United States, as it won a Winter Games record 13 medals, was Bonnie Blair of Milwaukee, Wis. Blair won gold in both the 500-meter and 1,000-meter speed skating races, giving her a career total of five gold medals. That's one more than any American woman had ever won, winter or summer. With one gold medal at Calgary in 1988, two at Albertville in 1992, and two at Lillehammer, Blair passed diver Pat McCormack, swimmer Janet Evans, and sprinter Evelyn Ashford.

Only speedskater Eric Heiden, the hero of the Lake Placid Winter Games in 1980, has won as many winter golds for the United States.

The United States ice hockey team's poor showing—1–1–3 in preliminary competition and an eighth place finish in the medal round—was the only mark on an otherwise stellar winter games for the Americans.

The U.S. won a surprising four medals in Alpine skiing, two by Tommy Moe of Palmer, Alaska, and one each by Diann Roffe-Steinrotter and Picabo Street.

The most emotional moment of the 1994 Winter Games for the American team came when Dan Jansen, in his final attempt, finally took the long-awaited gold medal in the 1,000-meter speedskating event. He not only won it, but did so in world record time.

Aside from Kerrigan's silver, the U.S. figure skating team came up empty.

Norway won the medals race with 26, two ahead of Germany with 24. Russia was third with 23, and Italy a surprising fourth with 20.

Calendar of 1996 Olympic Gold Medal Events

Atlanta, Georgia, July 19–August 4, 1996

Prepared by Robert A.T. Scalza

Friday, July 19, 1996
9:00 p.m.   Opening Ceremony

Saturday, July 20, 1996
9:00 a.m.   Shooting (M 10m Air Pistol)
3:00 p.m.   Judo (W & M Heavyweight)
3:00 p.m.   Fencing (M Individual Epee)
3:30 p.m.   Weightlifting (54 kg)
7:33 p.m.   Swimming (M 100 breast, 200 free; W 100 free, 400 im)

Sunday, July 21, 1996
9:00 a.m.   Shooting (M Trap; W 10m Air Pistol)
11:00 a.m.   Cycling (Women's Road Race)
3:00 p.m.   Judo (W & M Half-Heavyweights)
3:00 p.m.   Fencing (M Individual Sabre)
3:00 p.m.   Fencing (W Individual Epee)
3:30 p.m.   Greco–Roman Wrestling (48 kg, 57 kg, 68 kg, 82 kg, 100 kg)
3:30 p.m.   Weightligting (59 kg)
7:33 p.m.   Swimming (M 400 im, 200 free relay; W 200 free, 100 breast)

Monday, July 22, 1996
9:15 a.m.   Gymnastic (Men's Team Optional)
10:00 a.m.   Shooting (Men's 10m Air Rifle)
3:00 p.m.   Judo (W & M Middleweights)
3:00 p.m.   Fencing (W & M Individual Foil)
3:30 p.m.   Weightlifting (64 kg)
7:33 p.m.   Swimming (W 400 free, 100 back, 4 × 100 free relay)
7:33 p.m.   Swimming (M 100 free, 200 fly)

Tuesday, July 23, 1996
9:00 a.m.   Shooting (Men's 50m Free Pistol; Women's Double Trap)
3:00 p.m.   Fencing (Men's Team Epee)
3:00 p.m.   Judo (M & W Half-Middleweights)
3:00 p.m.   Gymnastics (Women's Team Optionals)
3:30 p.m.   Greco–Roman Wrestling (52 kg, 62 kg, 74 kg, 90 kg, 130 kg)
3:30 p.m.   Weightlifting (70 kg)
7:33 p.m.   Swimming (W 200 breast, 100 fly)
7:33 p.m.   Swimming (M 400 free, 100 back, 4 × 100 free relay)

Wednesday, July 24, 1996
8:30 a.m.   Shooting (W 3 × 20 rifle; M double trap)
10:00 a.m.   Cycling (M 1 km time trial)
3:00 p.m.   Judo (W & M Lightweight)
3:00 p.m.   Fencing (W & M Team Epee; M Team Sabre)
3:30 p.m.   Weightlifting (76 kg)
4:15 p.m.   Gymnastics (Men's Individual All-Around)
7:33 p.m.   Swimming (M 200 breast, 100 fly; W 200 im, 4 × 100 medley relay)

Thursday, July 25, 1996
8:30 a.m.   Shooting (M 50m Prone Rifle, 25m Rapid Fire Pistol)
9:00 a.m.   Cycling (W sprint octos final; M individual pursuit finals)
3:00 p.m.   Judo (M & W Half-Lightweight)
3:00 p.m.   Fencing (W & M Team Foil)
4:15 p.m.   Gymnastics (Women's Individual All-Around)
7:33 p.m.   Swimming (W 800 free, 200 back, 4 × 100 free)
7:33 p.m.   Swimming (M 500 free, 200 medley)

Friday, July 26, 1996
8:00 a.m.   Track (Men's 20 km walk)
8:30 a.m.   Shooting (W 25m Sport Pistol; M 10m Run Target)
8:30 a.m.   Cycling (M sprint octos final; W sprint 5–8 final)

3:00 p.m.   Judo (W & M Extra Lightweight)
3:30 p.m.   Weightlifting (83 kg)
5:30 p.m.   Men's Shot Put
7:33 p.m.   Swimming (W 200 fly, 50 free)
7:33 p.m.   Swimming (M 200 back, 1500 free, 4 × 100 medley)

Saturday, July 27, 1996
8:30 a.m.   Shooting (M 50m 3 × 40 Rifle; Skeet)
9:00 a.m.   Rowing (Men's & Women's Finals)
11:15 a.m.   Cycling (M sprint, team pursuit)
11:15 a.m.   Cycling (W sprint final; sprint final tie-break)
2:00 p.m.   Beach Volleyball (Women's Final)
3:30 p.m.   Weightlifting (91 kg)
5:30 p.m.   Track (M & W 100m; W Javelin)
10:00 p.m.   Diving (Women's Platform Final)

Sunday, July 28, 1996
7:30 a.m.   Track (Women's Marathon)
8:30 a.m.   Equestrian (Team Dressage Finals)
9:00 a.m.   Rowing (Men's & Women's Finals)
11:15 a.m.   Cycling (W & M points race final; W individual pursuit finals)
1:00 p.m.   Yachting (Star & Finn Finals)
1:30 p.m.   Beach Volleyball (Men's Final)
3:00 p.m.   Water Polo Finals
3:30 p.m.   Track (W triple jump, 5000m)
3:30 p.m.   Track & Field (M hammer throw, high jump)
3:30 p.m.   Weightlifting (99 kg)
9:30 p.m.   Gymnstics (W vault, uneven bars)
9:30 p.m.   Gymnstics (Men's Floor Exercise, Pommel Horse, Rings)

Monday, July 29, 1996
8:30 a.m.   Track (Women's 10 km walk)
1:00 p.m.   Yachting (M & W Mistral Finals)
1:00 p.m.   Table Tennis (Women's Doubles)
3:30 p.m.   Weightlifting (108 kg)
6:00 p.m.   Track (W discus, 800m)
6:00 p.m.   Track & Field (M 110m hurdles, triple jump, 10,000m)
7:30 p.m.   Gymnastics (W balance beam, floor exercise)
7:30 p.m.   Gymnastics (Men's Vault, Parallel Bars, High Bars)
10:00 p.m.   Diving (Men's Springboard Finals)

Tuesday, July 30, 1996
7:30 a.m.   Modern Pentathlon
10:00 a.m.   Mountain Bike Racing (W & M Cross Country)
1:00 p.m.   Yachting (M & W 470 finals; Laser, Europe, Tornado Finals)
1:00 p.m.   Table Tennis (Men's Doubles)
3:30 p.m.   Weightlifting (Over 109 kg)
4:00 p.m.   Gymnastics Exhibition
4:30 p.m.   Softball Final

Wednesday, July 31, 1996
8:30 a.m.   Cycling (Men's Road Race)
9:00 a.m.   Badminton (W & M Doubles Finals)
10:00 a.m.   Equestrian (Individual Dressage Finals)
1:00 p.m.   Yachting (Laser & Europe Finals)
2:00 p.m.   Archery (Women's Final)
3:30 p.m.   Freestyle Wrestling (48 kg, 57 kg, 68 kg, 82 kg, 100 kg)
4:30 p.m.   Table Tennis (Women's Singles)
5:15 p.m.   Track & Field (M 400m, 800m, discus; W 400m, 400m hurdles)
10:00 p.m.   Diving (Women's Springboard Finals)

(Continued on page 960)

Winter Games

FIGURE SKATING–MEN

1908	Ulrich Salchow, Sweden
1920	Gillis Grafstrom, Sweden
1924	Gillis Grafstrom, Sweden
1928	Gillis Grafstrom, Sweden
1932	Karl Schaefer, Austria
1936	Karl Schaefer, Austria
1948	Richard Button, United States
1952	Richard Button, United States
1956	Hayes Alan Jenkins, United States
1960	David Jenkins, United States
1964	Manfred Schnelldorfer, Germany
1968	Wolfgang Schwartz, Austria
1972	Ondrej Nepela, Czechoslovakia
1976	John Curry, Great Britain
1980	Robin Cousins, Great Britain
1984	Scott Hamilton, United States
1988	Brian Boitano, United States
1992	Viktor Petrenko, Unified Team*
1994	Alexei Urmanov, Russia

*Former Soviet Union team.

FIGURE SKATING–WOMEN

1908	Madge Syers, Britain
1920	Magda Julin–Maurey, Sweden
1924	Herma Szabo–Planck, Austria
1928	Sonja Henie, Norway
1932	Sonja Henie, Norway
1936	Sonja Henie, Norway
1948	Barbara Ann Scott, Canada
1952	Jeannette Altwegg, Great Britain
1956	Tenley Albright, United States
1960	Carol Heiss, United States
1964	Sjoukje Dijkstra, Netherlands
1968	Peggy Fleming, United States
1972	Beatrix Schuba, Austria
1976	Dorothy Hamill, United States
1980	Anett Poetzsch, East Germany
1984	Katarina Witt, East Germany
1988	Katarina Witt, East Germany
1992	Kristi Yamaguchi, United States
1994	Oksana Baiul, Ukraine

SPEED SKATING–MEN

(U.S. winners only)

500 Meters

1924	Charles Jewtraw	44.0
1932	John A. Shea	43.4
1952	Kenneth Henry	43.2
1964	Terrence McDermott	40.1
1980	Eric Heiden	38.03

1,000 Meters

1976	Peter Mueller	1:19.32
1980	Eric Heiden	1:15.18
1994	Dan Jansen	1:12.43[1]

1. World Record

1,500 Meters

1932	John A. Shea	2:57.5
1980	Eric Heiden	1:55.44

5,000 Meters

1932	Irving Jaffee	9:40.8
1980	Eric Heiden	7:02.29

10,000 Meters

1932	Irving Jaffee	19:13.6
1980	Eric Heiden	14:28.13

SPEED SKATING–WOMEN

500 Meters

1972	Anne Henning	43.33
1976	Sheila Young	42.76
1988	Bonnie Blair	39.10
1992	Bonnie Blair	40.33
1994	Bonnie Blair	39.25

1,000 Meters

1992	Bonnie Blair	1:21.90
1994	Bonnie Blair	1:18.74

1,500 Meters

1972	Dianne Holum	2:20.85

SKIING, ALPINE–MEN

Downhill

1948	Henri Oreiller, France	2m55.0s
1952	Zeno Colo, Italy	2m30.8s
1956	Anton Sailer, Austria	2m52.2s
1960	Jean Vuarnet, France	2m06.2s
1964	Egon Zimmermann, Austria	2m18.16s
1968	Jean–Claude Killy, France	1m59.85s
1972	Bernhard Russi, Switzerland	1m51.43s
1976	Franz Klammer, Austria	1m45.72s
1980	Leonhard Stock, Austria	1m45.50s
1984	Bill Johnson, United States	1m45.59s
1988	Pirmin Zurbriggen, Switzerland	1m59.63s
1992	Patrick Ortlieb, Austria	1m50.37s
1994	Tommy Moe, United States	1m45.75s

Slalom

1948	Edi Reinalter, Switzerland	2m10.3s
1952	Othmar Schneider, Austria	2m00.0s
1956	Anton Sailer, Austria	194.7 pts.
1960	Ernst Hinterseer, Austria	2m08.9s
1964	Josef Stiegler, Austria	2m10.13
1968	Jean–Claude Killy, France	1m39,73s
1972	Francisco Fernandez Ochoa, Spain	1m49.27s
1976	Piero Gros, Italy	2m03.29s
1980	Integmar Stenmark, Sweden	1m44.26s
1984	Phil Mahre, United States	1m39.41s
1988	Alberto Tomba, Italy	1m39.47s
1992	Finn Christian, Norway	1m44.39s
1994	Thomas Stangassinger, Austria	2m2.02s

Giant Slalom

1952	Stein Eriksen, Norway	2m25.0s
1956	Anton Sailer, Austria	3m00.1s
1960	Roger Staub, Switzerland	1m48.3s
1964	François Bonlieu, France	1m46.71s
1968	Jean–Claude Killy, France	3m29.28s
1972	Gustavo Thoeni, Italy	3m09.52s
1976	Heini Hemmi, Switzerland	3m26.97s
1980	Ingemar Stenmark, Sweden	2m40.74s
1984	Max Julen, Switzerland	1m20.54s
1988	Alberto Tomba, Italy	2m06.37s
1992	Alberto Tomba, Italy	2m06.98s
1994	Markus Wasmeier, Germany	2m52.46s

SKIING, ALPINE–WOMEN

Downhill

1948	Hedi Schlunegger, Switzerland	2m28.3s
1952	Trude Jochum–Beiser, Austria	1m47.1s
1956	Madeleine Berthod, Switzerland	1m40.1s
1960	Heidi Biebl, Germany	1m37.6s
1964	Christi Haas, Austria	1m55.39s
1968	Olga Pall, Austria	1m40.87s

1972	Marie–Therese Nadig, Switzerland	1m36.68s
1976	Rosi Mittermeier, West Germany	1m46.16s
1980	Annemarie Proell Moser, Austria	1m37.52s
1984	Michela Figini, Switzerland	1m13.36s
1988	Marina Kiehl, West Germany	1m25.86s
1992	Kerrin Lee-Gartner, Canada	1m52.55s
1994	Katja Seizinger, Germany	1m35.93s

Slalom

1948	Gretchen Fraser, United States	1m57.2s
1952	Andrea Mead Lawrence, United States	2m10.6s
1956	Renee Colliard, Switzerland	112.3 pts.
1960	Anne Heggtveigt, Canada	1m49.6s
1964	Christine Goitschel, France	1m29.86s
1968	Marielle Goitschel, France	1m25.86s
1972	Barbara Cochran, United States	1m31.24s
1976	Rosi Mittermeier, West Germany	1m30.54s
1980	Hanni Wenzel, Liechtenstein	1m25.09s
1984	Paoletta Magoni, Italy	1m36.47s
1988	Vreni Schneider, Switzerland	1m36.69s
1992	Petra Kronberger, Austria	1m32.68s
1994	Vreni Schneider, Switzerland	1m56.01s

Giant Slalom

1952	Andrea M. Lawrence, United States	2m06.8s
1956	Ossi Reichert, Germany	1m56.5s
1960	Yvonne Ruegg, Switzerland	1m39.9s
1964	Marielle Goitschel, France	1m52.24s
1968	Nancy Greene, Canada	1m51.97s
1972	Marie–Therese Nadig, Switzerland	1m29.90s
1976	Kathy Kreiner, Canada	1m29.13s
1980	Hanni Wenzel, Liechtenstein	2m41.66s
1984	Debbie Armstrong, United States	2m20.98s
1988	Vreni Schneider, Switzerland	2m06.49s
1992	Pernilla Wiberg, Sweden	2m12.74s
1994	Deborah Compagnoni, Italy	2m30.97s

1994 UNITED STATES MEDALISTS

Figure Skating
Women—SILVER—Nancy Kerrigan, Stoneham, Mass.

Alpine Skiing
Men's Downhill—GOLD—Tommy Moe, Palmer, Alaska.
Men's Super Giant Slalom—SILVER—Tommy Moe, Palmer, Alaska.
Women's Downhill—SILVER—Picabo Street, Sun Valley, Idaho.
Women's Super Giant Slalom—GOLD—Diann Roffe-Steinrotter, Potsdam, N.Y.

Freestyle Skiing
Women's Moguls—SILVER—Liz McIntyre, Winter Park, Colo.

Speedskating
Women's 500 meters—GOLD—Bonnie Blair, Milwaukee, Wis.
Women's 1,000 meters—GOLD—Bonnie Blair, Milwaukee, Wis.
Men's 1,000 meters—GOLD—Dan Jansen, Greenfield, Wis.

Short Track Speedskating
Women's 3,000 meter relay—BRONZE—United States (Karen Cashman, Quincy Mass.; Amy Peterson, Maplewood, Minn.; Cathy Turner, Hilton, N.Y.; Nicole Ziegelmayer, Milwaukee, Wis.)
Women's 500 meters—GOLD—Cathy Turner, Hilton, N.Y.—BRONZE—Amy Peterson, Maplewood, Minn.
Men's 5,000 meter relay—SILVER—United States (Randy Bartz, Milwaukee, Wis.; John Coyle, Milwaukee, Wis.; Eric Flaim, Hyde Park, Mass.; Andy Gabel, Northbrook, Ill.)

DISTRIBUTION OF MEDALS
1994 WINTER GAMES

(Lillehammer, Norway)

	Gold	Silver	Bronze	Total
Norway	10	11	5	26
Germany	9	7	8	24
Russia	11	8	4	23
Italy	7	5	8	20
United States	6	5	2	13
Canada	3	6	4	13
Austria	3	3	4	10
Switzerland	2	4	2	8
South Korea	4	1	1	6
Finland	0	1	5	6
Japan	1	2	2	5
France	0	1	4	5
Netherlands	0	1	3	4
Sweden	2	1	0	3
Kazakhstan	1	2	0	3
China	0	1	2	3
Slovenia	0	0	3	3
Ukraine	1	0	1	2
Belarus	0	2	0	2
Britain	0	0	2	2
Uzbekistan	1	0	0	1
Australia	0	0	1	1

ICE HOCKEY

1920	Canada	1964	U.S.S.R.
1924	Canada	1968	U.S.S.R.
1928	Canada	1972	U.S.S.R.
1932	Canada	1976	U.S.S.R.
1936	Great Britain	1980	United States
1948	Canada	1984	U.S.S.R.
1952	Canada	1988	U.S.S.R.
1956	U.S.S.R.	1992	Unified Team*
1960	United States	1994	Sweden

*Former Soviet Union team.

FINAL 1994 OLYMPIC HOCKEY
STANDINGS

Group A

	W	L	T	GF	GA
Finland	5	0	0	25	4
Germany	3	2	0	11	14
Czech Republic	3	2	0	16	11
Russia	3	2	0	20	14
Austria	1	4	0	13	28
Norway	0	5	0	5	19

Group B

	W	L	T	GF	GA
Slovakia	3	0	2	26	14
Canada	3	1	1	17	11
Sweden	3	1	1	23	13
United States	1	1	3	21	17
Italy	1	4	0	15	31
France	0	4	1	11	30

Championship
Sweden 3, Canada 2 (Shootout)

Bronze Medal
Finland 4, Russia 0

Fifth Place
Czech Republic 7, Slovakia 1

Seventh Place
Germany 4, United States 3

Other 1994 Winter Olympic Games Champions

Biathlon

Men's 10-kilometer—Sergei Tchepikov, Russia
Men's 20-kilometer—Sergei Tarasov, Russia
Men's 4 × 7.5 kilometer relay—Germany
Women's 7.5-kilometer—Myriam Bedard, Canada
Women's 15-kilometers—Myriam Bedard, Canada
Women's 4 × 7.5 kilometer relay—Russia

Bobsledding

2–man—Switzerland I
4–man—Germany II

Figure Skating

Men's singles—Alexei Urmanov, Russia
Women's singles—Oksana Baiul, Ukraine
Pairs—Ekaterina Gordeeva and Sergei Grinkov, Russia
Ice dancing—Oksana Gritschuk and Evgeni Platov, Russia

Speed Skating–Men

500m—Aleksandr Golubev, Russia
1,000m—Dan Jansen, United States
1,500m—Johann Olav Koss, Norway
5,000m—Johann Olav Koss, Norway
10,000m—Johann Olav Koss, Norway

Speed Skating–Women

500m—Bonnie Blair, United States
1,000m—Bonnie Blair, United States

1,500m—Emese Hunyady, Austria
3,000m—Svetlana Bazhanova, Russia
5,000m—Claudia Pechstein, Germany

Luge

Men's singles—Georg Hackl, Germany
Men's doubles—Kurt Brugger and Wilfried Huber, Italy
Women's singles—Gerda Weissensteiner, Italy

Skiing, Nordic–Men

Combined team—Japan
Combined—Fred Borre Lundberg, Norway
90-meter jump—Espen Bredesen, Norway
120-meter jump—Jens Weissflog, Germany
Team 120-meter jump—Germany
10-kilometer classical—Bjorn Dahlie, Norway
15-kilometer free pursuit—Bjorn Dahlie, Norway
30-kilometer freestyle—Thomas Alsgaard, Norway
50-kilometer classical—Vladimir Smirnov, Kazakhstan
4 × 10 kilometer relay—Italy

Skiing, Nordic–Women

5–kilometer classical—Lyubov Egorova, Russia
10-kilometer free pursuit—Lyubov Egorova, Russia
15-kilometer freestyle—Manuela Di Centa, Italy
30-kilometer classical—Manuela Di Centa, Italy
4 × 5 kilometer relay—Russia

1992 Summer Games

TRACK AND FIELD–MEN

100–Meter Dash

1896	Thomas Burke, United States	12s
1900	Francis W. Jarvis, United States	10.8s
1904	Archie Hahn, United States	11s
1906	Archie Hahn, United States	11.2s
1908	Reginald Walker, South Africa	10.8s
1912	Ralph Craig, United States	10.8s
1920	Charles Paddock, United States	10.8s
1924	Harold Abrahams, Great Britain	10.6s
1928	Percy Williams, Canada	10.8s
1932	Eddie Tolan, United States	10.3s
1936	Jesse Owens, United States	10.3s [1]
1948	Harrison Dillard, United States	10.3s
1952	Lindy Remigino, United States	10.4s
1956	Bobby Morrow, United States	10.5s
1960	Armin Hary, Germany	10.2s
1964	Robert Hayes, United States	10s
1968	James Hines, United States	9.9s
1972	Valery Borzow, U.S.S.R.	10.14s
1976	Hasely Crawford, Trinidad and Tobago	10.06s
1980	Allan Wells, Britain	10.25s
1984	Carl Lewis, United States	9.99s
1988	Carl Lewis, United States	9.92s [2]
1992	Linford Christie, Great Britain	09.96s

1. Wind assisted. 2. Lewis was awarded the gold medal when Ben Johnson of Canada, the original winner in 09.79s, was stripped of the medal after testing positive for steroid use.

200–Meter Dash

1900	John Tewksbury, United States	22.2s
1904	Archie Hahn, United States	21.6s
1908	Robert Kerr, Canada	22.6s

1912	Ralph Craig, United States	21.7s
1920	Allan Woodring, United States	22s
1924	Jackson Scholz, United States	21.6s
1928	Percy Williams, Canada	21.8s
1932	Eddie Tolan, United States	21.2s
1936	Jesse Owens, United States	20.7s
1948	Melvin E. Patton, United States	21.1s
1952	Andrew Stanfield, United States	20.7s
1956	Bobby Morrow, United States	20.6s
1960	Livio Berruti, Italy	20.5s
1964	Henry Carr, United States	20.3s
1968	Tommie Smith, United States	19.8s
1972	Vallery Borzov, U.S.S.R.	20s
1976	Don Quarrie, Jamaica	20.23s
1980	Pietro Mennea, Italy	20.19s
1984	Carl Lewis, United States	19.80s
1988	Joe DeLoach, United States	19.75s
1992	Mike Marsh, United States	20.01s

400–Meter Dash

1896	Thomas Burke, United States	54.2s
1900	Maxwell Long, United States	49.4s
1904	Harry Hillman, United States	49.2s
1906	Paul Pilgrim, United States	53.2s
1908	Wyndham Halswelle, Great Britain (walkover)	50s
1912	Charles Reidpath, United States	48.2s
1920	Bevil Rudd, South Africa	49.6s
1924	Eric Liddell, Great Britain	47.6s
1928	Ray Barbuti, United States	47.8s
1932	William Carr, United States	46.2s
1936	Archie Williams, United States	46.5s
1948	Arthur Wint, Jamaica, B.W.I.	46.2s
1952	George Rhoden, Jamaica, B.W.I.	45.9s
1956	Charles Jenkins, United States	46.7s
1960	Otis Davis, United States	44.9s

1964	Mike Larrabee, United States	45.1s
1968	Lee Evans, United States	43.8s
1972	Vincent Matthews, United States	44.66s
1976	Alberto Juantorena, Cuba	44.26s
1980	Viktor Markin, U.S.S.R.	44.60s
1984	Alonzo Babers, United States	44.27s
1988	Steve Lewis, United States	43.87s
1992	Quincy Watts, United States	43.50s

800–Meter Run

1896	Edwin Flack, Australia	2m11s
1900	Alfred Tysoe, Great Britain	2m1.4s
1904	James Lightbody, United States	1m56s
1906	Paul Pilgrim, United States	2m1.2s
1908	Mel Sheppard, United states	1m52.8s
1912	Ted Meredith, United States	1m51.9s
1920	Albert Hill, Great Britain	1m53.4s
1924	Douglas Lowe, Great Britain	1m52.4s
1928	Douglas Lowe, Great Britain	1m51.8s
1932	Thomas Hampson, Great Britain	1m49.8s
1936	John Woodruff, United States	1m52.9s
1948	Malvin Whitfield, United States	1m49.2s
1952	Malvin Whitfield, United States	1m49.2s
1956	Tom Courtney, United States	1m47.7s
1960	Peter Snell, New Zealand	1m46.3s
1964	Peter Snell, New Zealand	1m45.1s
1968	Ralph Doubell, Australia	1m44.3s
1972	David Wottle, United States	1m45.9s
1976	Alberto Juantorena, Cuba	1m43.5s
1980	Steve Ovett, Britain	1m45.4s
1984	Joaquin Cruz, Brazil	1m43.0s
1988	Paul Ereng, Kenya	1m43.45s
1992	WilliamTanui, Kenya	1m43.66s

1,500–Meter Run

1896	Edwin Flack, Australia	4m33.2s
1900	Charles Bennett, Great Britain	4m6s
1904	James Lightbody, United States	4m5.4s
1906	James Lightbody, United States	4m12s
1908	Mel Sheppard, United States	4m3.4s
1912	Arnold Jackson, Great Britain	3m56.8s
1920	Albert Hill, Great Britain	4m1.8s
1924	Paavo Nurmi, Finland	3m53.6s
1928	Harry Larva, Finland	3m53.2s
1932	Luigi Becali, Italy	3m51.2s
1936	Jack Lovelock, New Zealand	3m47.8s
1948	Henri Eriksson, Sweden	3m49.8s
1952	Joseph Barthel, Luxembourg	3m45.2s
1956	Ron Delany, Ireland	3m41.2s
1960	Herb Elliott, Australia	3m35.6s
1964	Peter Snell, New Zealand	3m38.1s
1968	Kipchoge Keino, Kenya	3m34.9s
1972	Pekka Vasala, Finland	3m36.3s
1976	John Walker, New Zealand	3m39.17s
1980	Sebastian Coe, Britain	3m38.4s
1984	Sebastian Coe, Britain	3m32.53s
1988	Peter Rono, Kenya	3m35.96s
1992	Fermin Cacho Ruiz, Spain	3m40.12s

5,000–Meter Run

1912	Hannes Kolehmainen, Finland	14m36.6s
1920	Joseph Guillemot, France	14m55.6s
1024	Paavo Nurmi, Finland	14m31.2s
1928	Willie Ritola, Finland	14m38s
1932	Lauri Lehtinen, Finland	14m30s
1936	Gunnar Hockert, Finland	14m22.2s
1948	Gaston Reiff, Belgium	14m17.6s
1952	Emil Zatopek, Czechoslovakia	14m6.6s
1956	Vladimir Kuts, U.S.S.R.	13m39.6s
1960	Murray Halberg, New Zealand	13m43.4s
1964	Bob Schul, United States	13m48.8s
1968	Mohamed Gammoudi, Tunisia	14m.05s
1972	Lasse Viren, Finland	13m26.4s

1976	Lasse Viren, Finland	13m24.76s
1980	Miruts Yifter, Ethiopia	13m21s
1984	Saud Aouita, Morocco	13m5.59s
1988	John Ngugi, Kenya	13m11.70s
1992	Dieter Baumann, Germany	13m12.52s

10,000–Meter Run

1912	Hannes Kolehmainen, Finland	31m20.8s
1920	Paavo Nurmi, Finland	31m45.8s
1924	Willie Ritola, Finland	30m23.2s
1928	Paavo Nurmi, Finland	30m18.8s
1932	Janusz Kusocinski, Poland	30m11.4s
1936	Ilmari Salminen, Finland	30m15.4s
1948	Emil Zatopek, Czechoslovakia	29m59.6s
1952	Emil Zatopek, Czechoslovakia	29ml7s
1956	Vladimir Kuts, U.S.S.R.	28m45.6s
1960	Peter Bolotnikov, U.S.S.R.	28m32.2s
1964	Billy Mills, United States	28m24.4s
1968	Nartali Temu, Kenya	29m27.4s
1972	Lasse Viren, Finland	27m38.4s
1976	Lasse Viren, Finland	27m40.38s
1980	Miruts Yifter, Ethiopia	27m42.7s
1984	Alberto Cova, Italy	27m47.5s
1988	Mly Brahim Boutaib, Morocco	27m21.46s
1992	Khalid Skah, Morocco	27m47.70s

Marathon

1896	Spiridon Loues, Greece	2h58m50s
1900	Michel Teato, France	2h59m45s
1904	Thomas Hicks, United States	3h28m53s
1906	William J. Sherring, Canada	2h51m23.65s
1908	John J. Hayes, United States	2h55m18.4s
1912	Kenneth McArthur, South Africa	2h36m54.8s
1920	Hannes Kolehmainen, Finland	2h32m35.8s
1924	Albin Stenroos, Finland	2h41m22.6s
1928	A.B. El Quafi, France	2h32m57s
1932	Juan Zabala, Argentina	2h31m36s
1936	Kitei Son, Japan	2h29m19.2s
1948	Delfo Cabrera, Argentina	2h34m51.6s
1952	Emil Zatopek, Czechoslovakia	2h23m3.2s
1956	Alain Mimoun, France	2h25m
1960	Abebe Bikila, Ethiopia	2h15m16.2s
1964	Abebe Bikila, Ethiopia	2h12m11.2s
1968	Mamo Wold, Ethiopia	2h20m26.4s
1972	Frank Shorter, United States	2h12m19.8s
1976	Walter Cierpinski, East Germany	2h09m55s
1980	Walter Cierpinski, East Germany	2h11m3s
1984	Carlos Lopes, Portugal	2h9m.55s
1988	Gelindo Bordin, Italy	2hr10m47s
1992	Hwang Young-Cho, South Korea	2h13m23s

110–Meter Hurdles

1896	Thomas Curtis, United States	17.6s
1900	Alvin Kraenzlein, United States	15.4s
1904	Frederick Schule, United States	16s
1906	R.G. Leavitt, United States	16.2s
1908	Forrest Smithson, United States	15s
1912	Frederick Kelly, United States	15.1s
1920	Earl Thomson, Canada	14.8s
1924	Daniel Kinsey, United States	15s
1928	Sydney Atkinson, South Africa	14.8s
1932	George Saling, United States	14.6s
1936	Forrest Towns, United States	14.2s
1948	William Porter, United States	13.9s
1952	Harrison Dillard, United States	13.7s
1956	Lee Calhoun, United States	13.5s
1960	Lee Calhoun, United States	13.8s
1964	Hayes Jones, United States	13.6s
1968	Willie Davenport, United States	13.3s
1972	Rodney Milburn, United States	13.24s
1976	Guy Drut, France	13.30s
1980	Thomas Munkett, East Germany	13.20s
1984	Roger Kingdom, United States	13.20s

| 1988 | Roger Kingdom, United States | 12.98s |
| 1992 | Mark McCoy, Canada | 13.12s |

200–Meter Hurdles

| 1900 | Alvin Kraenzlein, United States | 25.4s |
| 1904 | Harry Hillman, United States | 24.6s |

400–Meter Hurdles

1900	John Tewksbury, United States	57.6s
1904	Harry Hillman, United States	53s
1908	Charles Bacon, United States	55s
1920	Frank Loomis, United States	54s
1924	F. Morgan Taylor, United States	52.6s
1928	Lord David Burghley, Great Britain	53.4s
1932	Robert Tisdall, Ireland	51.8s [1]
1936	Glenn Hardin, United States	52.4s
1948	Roy Cochran, United States	51.1s
1952	Charles Moore, United States	50.8s
1956	Glenn Davis, United States	50.1s
1960	Glenn Davis, United States	49.3s
1964	Rex Cawley, United States	49.6s
1968	David Hemery, Great Britain	48.1s
1972	John Akii–Bua, Uganda	47.8s
1976	Edwin Moses, United States	47.64s
1980	Volker Beck, East Germany	48.70s
1984	Edwin Moses, United States	47.75s
1988	Andre Phillips, United States	47.19s
1992	Kevin Young, United States	46.78s

1. Record not allowed.

2,500–Meter Steeplechase

| 1900 | George Orton, United States | 7m34s |
| 1904 | James Lightbody, United States | 7m39.6s |

3,000–Meter Steeplechase

1920	Percy Hodge, Great Britain	10m0.4s
1924	Willie Ritola, Finland	9m33.6s
1928	Toivo Loukola, Finland	9m21.8s
1932	Volmari Iso–Hollo, Finland	10m33.4s [1]
1936	Volmari Iso–Hollo, Finland	9m3.8s
1948	Thure Sjoestrand, Sweden	9m4.6s
1952	Horace Ashenfelter, United States	8m45.4s
1956	Chris Brasher, Great Britain	8m41.2s
1960	Zdzislaw Krzyskowiak, Poland	8m34.2s
1964	Gaston Roelants, Belgium	8m30.8s
1968	Amos Biwott, Kenya	8m51s
1972	Kipchoge Keino, Kenya	8m23.6s
1976	Anders Gardervd, Sweden	8m08.02s
1980	Bronislaw Malinowski, Poland	8m9.7s
1984	Julius Korir, Kenya	8m11.80s
1988	Julius Karluki, Kenya	8m05.51s
1992	Matthew Birir, Kenya	8m08.84s

1. About 3,450 meters–extra lap by error.

10,000–Meter Walk

1912	George Goulding, Canada	46m28.4s
1920	Ugo Frigerio, Italy	48m6.2s
1924	Ugo Frigerio, Italy	47m49s
1948	John Mikaelsson, Sweden	45m13.2s
1952	John Mikaelsson, Sweden	45m2.8s

20,000–Meter Walk

1956	Leonid Spirin, U.S.S.R.	1h31m27.4s
1960	Vladimir Golubnichy, U.S.S.R.	1h34m7.2s
1964	Ken Mathews, Great Britain	1h29m34s
1968	Vladimir Golubnichy, U.S.S.R.	1h33m58.4s
1972	Peter Frenkel, East Germany	1h26m42.4s
1976	Daniel Bautista, Mexico	1h24m40.6s
1980	Maurizio Damiliano, Italy	1h23m35.5s
1984	Ernesto Conto, Mexico	1m23.13s
1988	Jozef Pribilinec, Czechoslovakia	1h19m57s

| 1992 | Daniel Plaza, Spain | 1h21m45s |

50,000–Meter Walk

1932	Thomas W. Green, Great Britain	4h50m10s
1936	Harold Whitlock, Great Britain	4h30m41.1s
1948	John Ljunggren, Sweden	4h41m52s
1952	Giuseppe Dordoni, Italy	4h28m7.8s
1956	Norman Read, New Zealand	4h30m42.8s
1960	Donald Thompson, Great Britain	4h25m30s
1964	Abdon Pamich, Italy	4h11m12.4s
1968	Christoph Hohne, East Germany	4h20m13.6s
1972	Bern Kannenberg, West Germany	3h56m11.6s
1980	Hartwig Guader, East Germany	3h49m24s
1984	Raul Gonzalez, Mexico	3hr37m26s
1988	Viacheslau Ivanenko, U.S.S.R.	3h438m29s
1992	Andrei Perlov, Unified Team	3h50m13s

400–Meter Relay (4x100)

1912	Great Britain	42.4s
1920	United States	42.2s
1924	United States	41s
1928	United States	41s
1932	United States	40s
1936	United States	39.8s
1948	United States	40.6s
1952	United States	40.1s
1956	United States	39.5s
1960	Germany	39.5s
1964	United States	39s
1968	United States	38.2s
1972	United States	38.19s
1976	United States	38.33s
1980	U.S.S.R.	38.26s
1984	United States	37.83s
1988	U.S.S.R.	38.19s
1992	United States	37.40s [1]

1. World record.

1,600–Meter Relay (4x400)

1912	United States	3m16.6s
1920	Great Britain	3m22.2s
1924	United States	3m16s
1928	United States	3m14.2s
1932	United States	3m8.2s
1936	Great Britain	3m9s
1948	United States	3m10.4s
1952	Jamaica, B.W.I.	3m3.9s
1956	United States	3m4.8s
1960	United States	3m2.2s
1964	United States	3m0.7s
1968	United States	2m56.1s
1972	Kenya	2m59.8s
1976	United States	2m58.65s
1980	U.S.S.R.	3m01.1s
1984	United States	2m57.91s
1988	United States	2m56.16s
1992	United States	2m55.74s [1]

1. World record.

Team Race

		Pts
1900	Great Britain (5,000 meters)	26
1904	United States (4 miles)	27
1908	Great Britain (3 miles)	6
1912	United States (3,000 meters)	9
1920	United States (3,000 meters)	10
1924	Finland (3,000 meters)	9

Standing High Jump

1900	Ray Ewry, United States	5 ft 5 in.
1904	Ray Ewry, United States	4 ft. 11 in.
1906	Ray Ewry, United States	5 ft 1 5/8 in.
1908	Ray Ewry, United States	5 ft 2 in.
1912	Platt Adams, United States	5 ft 4 1/8 in.

Running High Jump

1896	Ellery Clark, United States	5 ft 11 1/4 in.
1900	Irving Baxter, United States	6 ft 2 3/4 in.
1904	Samuel Jones, United States	5 ft 11 in.
1906	Con Leahy, Ireland	5 ft 9 7/8 in.
1908	Harry Porter, United States	6 ft 3 in.
1912	Alma Richards, United States	6 ft 4 in.
1920	Richmond Landon, United States	6 ft 4 1/4 in.
1924	Harold Osborn, United States	6 ft 5 15/16 in.
1928	Robert W. King, United States	6 ft 4 3/8 in.
1932	Duncan McNaughton, Canada	6 ft 5 5/8 in.
1936	Cornelius Johnson, United States	6 ft 7 15/16 in.
1948	John Winter, Australia	6 ft 6 in.
1952	Walter David, United States	6 ft 8 5/16 in.
1956	Charles Dumas, United States	6 ft 11 1/4 in.
1960	Robert Shavlakadze, U.S.S.R.	7 ft 1 in.
1964	Valeri Brumel, U.S.S.R.	7 ft 1 3/4 in.
1968	Dick Fosbury, United States	7 ft 4 1/4 in.
1972	Yuri Tarmak, U.S.S.R.	7 ft 3 3/4 in.
1976	Jacek Wszola, Poland	(2.25m) 7 ft 4 1/2 in.
1980	Gerd Wessig, East Germany	7 ft 8 3/4 in.
1984	Dietmar Mogenburg, West Germany	7 ft 8 1/2 in.
1988	Guennadi Avdeenko, U.S.S.R.	7 ft 9 1/2 in.
1992	Javier Sotomayar, Cuba	7ft 8 1/4 in.

Long Jump

1896	Ellery Clark, United States	20 ft 9 3/4 in.
1900	Alvin Kraenzlein, United States	23 ft 6 7/8 in.
1904	Myer Prinstein, United States	24 ft 1 in.
1906	Myer Prinstein, United States	23 ft 7 1/2 in.
1908	Frank Irons, United States	24 ft 6 1/2 in.
1912	Albert Gutterson, United States	24 ft 11 1/4 in.
1920	William Petterssen, Sweden	23 ft 5 1/2 in.
1924	DeHart Hubbard, United States	24 ft 5 1/8 in.
1928	Edward B. Hamm, United States	25 ft 4 3/4 in.
1932	Edward Gordon, United States	25 ft 3/4 in.
1936	Jesse Owens, United States	26 ft 5 5/16 in.
1948	Willie Steele, United States	25 ft 8 in.
1952	Jerome Biffle, United States	24 ft 10 in.
1956	Gregory Bell, United States	25 ft 8 1/4 in.
1960	Ralph Boston, United States	26 ft 7 3/4 in.
1964	Lynn Davies, Great Britain	26 ft 5 3/4 in.
1968	Bob Beamon, United States	29 ft 2 1/2 in.
1972	Randy Williams, United States	27 ft 1/2 in.
1976	Arnie Robinson, United States	(8.35m) 24 ft 7 3/4 in.
1980	Lutz Dombrowski, E. Germany	28 ft 1/4 in.
1984	Carl Lewis, United States	28 ft 1/4 in.
1988	Carl Lewis, United States	28 ft 7 1/4 in.
1992	Carl Lewis, United States	28 ft 5 1/2 in.

Triple Jump

1896	James B. Connolly, United States	45 ft
1900	Myer Prinstein, United States	47 ft 4 1/4 in.
1904	Myer Prinstein, United States	47 ft
1906	P.G. O'Connor, Ireland	46 ft 2 in.
1908	Timothy Ahearne, Great Britain	48 ft 11 1/4 in.
1912	Gustaf Lindblom, Sweden	48 ft 5 1/8 in.
1920	Vilho Tuulos, Finland	47 ft 6 7/8 in.
1924	Archie Winter, Australia	50 ft 11 1/8 in.
1928	Mikio Oda, Japan	49 ft 10 13/16 in.
1932	Chuhei Nambu, Japan	51 ft 7 in.
1936	Naoto Tajima, Japan	52 ft 5 7/8 in.
1948	Arne Ahman, Sweden	50 ft 6 1/4 in.
1952	Adhemar da Silva, Brazil	53 ft 2 1/2 in.
1956	Adhemar da Silva, Brazil	53 ft 7 1/2 in.
1960	Jozef Schmidt, Poland	55 ft 1 3/4 in.
1964	Jozef Schmidt, Poland	55 ft 3 1/4 in.
1968	Viktor Saneyev, U.S.S.R.	57 ft 3/4 in.
1972	Viktor Saneyev, U.S.S.R.	56 ft 11 in.
1976	Viktor Saneyev, U.S.S.R.	(17.29m) 56 ft 8 3/4 in.
1980	Jaak Uudmae, U.S.S.R.	56 ft 11 1/8 in.
1984	Al Joyner, United States	56 ft 7 1/2 in.
1988	Hristo Markov, Bulgaria	57 ft 9 1/4 in.

1992	Mike Conley, United States	59 ft 7 1/2 in.

Pole Vault

1896	William Hoyt, United States	10 ft 9 3/4 in.
1900	Irving Baxter, United States	10 ft 9 7/8 in.
1904	Charles Dvorak, United States	11 ft 6 in.
1906	Fernand Gouder, France	11 ft 6 in.
1908	Alfred Gilbert, United States, and Edward Cook, United States (tie)	12 ft 2 in.
1912	Harry Babcock, United States	12 ft 11 1/2 in.
1920	Frank Foss, United States	13 ft 5 9/16 in.
1924	Lee Barnes, United States	12 ft 11 1/2 in.
1928	Sabin W. Carr, United States	13 ft 9 3/8 in.
1932	William Miller, United States	14 ft 1 7/8 in.
1936	Earle Meadows, United States	14 ft 3 1/4 in.
1948	Guinn Smith, United States	14 ft 1 1/4 in.
1952	Robert Richards, United States	14 ft 11 1/8 in.
1956	Robert Richards, United States	14 ft 11 1/2 in.
1960	Don Bragg, United States	15 ft 5 1/8 in.
1964	Fred Hansen, United States	16 ft 8 3/4 in.
1968	Bob Seagren, United States	17 ft 8 1/2 in.
1972	Wolfgang Nordwig, East Germany	18 ft 1/2 in.
1976	Tadeusz Slusarski, Poland	(5.50m) 18 ft 1/2 in.
1980	Wladyslaw Kozakiewicz, Poland	18 ft 11 1/2 in.
1984	Pierre Quinon, France	18 ft 10 1/4 in.
1988	Sergei Bubka, U.S.S.R.	18 ft 4 1/4 in.
1992	Maxim Tarassov, Unified Team	19 ft 0 1/4 in.

16–lb Shot–Put

1896	Robert Garrett, United States	36 ft 9 3/4 in.
1900	Richard Sheldon, United States	46 ft 3 1/8 in.
1904	Ralph Rose, United States	48 ft 7 in.
1906	Martin Sheridan, United States	40 ft 4 4/5 in.
1908	Ralph Rose, United States	46 ft 7 1/2 in.
1912	Pat McDonald, United States	50 ft 4 in.
1920	Ville Porhola, Finland	48 ft 7 1/8 in.
1924	Clarence Houser, United States	49 ft 2 1/2 in.
1928	John Kuck, United States	52 ft 11 11/16 in.
1932	Leo Sexton, United States	52 ft 6 3/16 in.
1936	Hans Woellke, Germany	53 ft 1 3/4 in.
1948	Wilbur Thompson, United States	56 ft 2 in.
1952	Parry O'Brien, United States	57 ft 1 1/2 in.
1956	Parry O'Brien, United States	60 ft 11 in.
1960	Bill Nieder, United States	64 ft 6 3/4 in.
1964	Dallas Long, United States	66 ft 8 1/4 in.
1968	Randy Matson, United States	67 ft 4 3/4 in.
1972	Wladyslaw Komar, Poland	69 ft 6 in.
1976	Udo Beyer, East Germany	(21.05m) 69 ft 3/4 in.
1980	Vladmir Kiselyov, U.S.S.R.	70 ft 1/2 in.
1984	Alessandro Andrei, Italy	69 ft 9 in.
1988	Uhf Timmerman, East Germany	73 ft 8 3/4 in.
1992	Michael Stulze, United States	71 ft 2 1/2 in.

Discus Throw

1896	Robert Garrett, United States	95 ft 7 1/2 in.
1900	Rudolf Bauer, Hungary	118 ft 2 7/8 in.
1904	Martin Sheridan, United States	128 ft 10 1/2 in.
1906	Martin Sheridan, United States	136 ft 1/3 in.
1908	Martin Sheridan, United States	134 ft 2 in.
1912	Armas Taipale, Finland	145 ft 9/16 in.
1920	Elmer Niklander, Finland	146 ft 7 in.
1924	Clarence Houser, United States	151 ft 5 1/4 in.
1928	Clarence Houser, United States	155 ft 2 4/5 in.
1932	John Anderson, United States	162 ft 4 7/8 in.
1936	Ken Carpenter, United States	165 ft 7 3/8 in.
1948	Adolfo Consolini, Italy	173 ft 2 in.
1952	Simeon Iness, United States	180 ft 6 1/2 in.
1956	Al Oerter, United States	184 ft 10 1/2 in.
1960	Al Oerter, United States	194 ft 2 in.
1964	Al Oerter, United States	200 ft 1 1/2 in.
1968	Al Oerter, United States	212 ft 6 in.
1972	Ludvik Danek, Czechoslovakia	211 ft 3 in.

1976	Mac Wilkins, United States	(67.5m) 221 ft 5 in.
1980	Viktor Rashchupkin, U.S.S.R.	218 ft 8 in.
1984	Rolf Dannenberg, West Germany	218 ft 6 in.
1988	Jurgen Schult, East Germany	218 ft 9 1/4 in.
1992	Romas Ubartas, Lithuania	213 ft 7 3/4 in.

Javelin Throw

1906	Eric Lemming, Sweden	175 ft 6 in.
1908	Eric Lemming, Sweden	179 ft 10 1/2 in.
1912	Eric Lemming, Sweden	198 ft 11 1/4 in.
1920	Jonni Myyra, Finland	215 ft 9 3/4 in.
1924	Jonni Myyra, Finland	206 ft 6 3/4 in.
1928	Eric Lundquist, Sweden	218 ft 6 1/8 in.
1932	Matti Jarvinen, Finland	238 ft 7 in.
1936	Gerhard Stoeck, Germany	235 ft 8 5/16 in.
1948	Kaj Rautavaara, Finland	228 ft 10 1/2 in.
1952	Cy Young, United States	242 ft 3/4 in.
1956	Egil Danielsen, Norway	281 ft 2 1/4 in.
1960	Viktor Tsibuelnko, U.S.S.R.	277 ft 8 3/8 in.
1964	Pauli Nevala, Finland	271 ft 2 1/4 in.
1968	Janis Lusis, U.S.S.R.	295 ft 7 in.
1972	Klaus Wolfermann, West Germany	296 ft 10 in.
1976	Miklos Nemeth, Hungary	(94.58m) 310 ft 4 in.
1980	Dainis Kula, U.S.S.R.	299 ft 2 3/8 in.
1984	Arto Haerkoenen, Finland	284 ft 8 in.
1988	Tapio Korjus, Finland	276 ft 6 in.
1992	Jan Zelezny, Czechoslovakia	294 ft 2 in.

16–lb Hammer Throw

1900	John Flanagan, United States	167 ft 4 in.
1904	John Flanagan, United States	168 ft 1 in.
1908	John Flanagan, United States	170 ft 4 1/4 in.
1912	Matt McGrath, United States	179 ft 7 1/8 in.
1920	Pat Ryan, United States	173 ft 5 5/8 in.
1924	Fred Tootell, United States	174 ft 10 1/4 in.
1928	Patrick O'Callaghan, Ireland	168 ft 7 1/2 in.
1932	Patrick O'Callaghan, Ireland	176 ft 11 1/8 in.
1936	Karl Hein, Germany	185 ft 4 in.
1948	Imre Nemeth, Hungary	183 ft 11 1/2 in.
1952	Jozsef Csermak, Hungary	197 ft 11 9/16 in.
1956	Harold Connolly, United States	207 ft 2 3/4 in.
1960	Vasily Rudenkov, U.S.S.R.	220 ft 1 5/8 in.
1964	Romuald Klim, U.S.S.R.	228 ft 9 1/2 in.
1968	Gyula Zsivotzky, Hungary	240 ft 8 in.
1972	Anatoly Bondarchuk, U.S.S.R.	247 ft 8 1/2 in.
1976	Yuri Sedykh, U.S.S.R.	(77.52m) 254 ft 4 in.
1980	Yuri Sedykh, U.S.S.R.	(81.80m 268 ft 4 1/2 in.
1984	Juha Tiainen, Finland	256 ft 2 in.
1988	Sergei Litvinov, U.S.S.R.	278 ft 2 1/2 in.
1992	Andrey Abduvaliyev, Unified Team	270 ft 9 1/2 in.

Decathlon

1912	Jim Thorpe, United States	—
	Hugo Wieslander, Sweden	—
1920	Helge Lovland, Norway	6,804.35 pts.
1924	Harold Osborn, United States	7,710.775 pts.
1928	Paavo Yrjola, Finland	8,053.29 pts.
1932	James Bausch, United States	8,462.23 pts.
1936	Glenn Morris, United States	7,900 pts. [1]
1948	Robert B. Mathias, United States	7,139 pts.
1952	Robert B. Mathias, United States	7,887 pts.
1956	Milton Campbell, United States	7,937 pts.
1960	Rafer Johnson, United States	8,392 pts.
1964	Willi Holdorf, Germany	7,887 pts. [1]
1968	Bill Toomey, United States	8,193 pts.
1972	Nikolai Avilov, U.S.S.R.	8,454 pts.
1976	Bruce Jenner, United States	8,618 pts.
1980	Daley Thompson, Britain	8,495 pts.
1984	Daley Thompson, Britain	8,797 pts.
1988	Christian Schenk, East Germany	8,488 pts.
1992	Robert Zmelik, Czechoslovakia	8,611 pts.

1. Point system revised.

TRACK AND FIELD–WOMEN

100–Meter Dash

1928	Elizabeth Robinson, United States	12.2s
1932	Stella Walsh, Poland	11.9s
1936	Helen Stephens, United States	11.5s
1948	Fanny Blankers–Koen, Netherlands	11.9s
1952	Marjorie Jackson, Australia	11.5s
1956	Betty Cuthbert, Australia	11.5s
1960	Wilma Rudolph, United States	11s
1964	Wyomia Tyus, United States	11.4s
1968	Wyomia Tyus, United States	11s
1972	Renate Stecher, East Germany	11.07s
1976	Annegret Richter, West Germany	11.08s
1980	Lyudmila Kondratyeva, U.S.S.R.	11.06s
1984	Evelyn Ashford, United States	10.97s
1988	Florence Griffith–Joyner, United States	10.54s
1992	Gail Devers, United States	10.82s

200–Meter Dash

1948	Fanny Blankers–Koen, Netherlands	24.4s
1952	Marjorie Jackson, Australia	23.7s
1956	Betty Cuthbert, Australia	23.4s
1960	Wilma Rudolph, United States	24s
1964	Edith McGuire, United States	23s
1968	Irena Szewinska, Poland	22.5s
1972	Renate Stecher, East Germany	22.4s
1976	Baerbel Eckert, East Germany	22.37s
1980	Barbara Wockel, East Germany	22.03s
1984	Valerie Brisco–Hooks, United States	21.81s
1988	Florence Griffith–Joyner, United States	21.34s
1992	Gwen Torrence, United States	21.81s

400–Meter Dash

1964	Betty Cuthbert, Australia	52s
1968	Colette Besson, France	52s
1972	Monika Zehrt, East Germany	51.08s
1976	Irena Szewinska, Poland	49.29s
1980	Marita Koch, East Germany	48.88s
1984	Valerie Brisco–Hooks, United States	48.83s
1988	Olga Bryzguina, U.S.S.R.	48.65s
1992	Marie Jose-Perec, France	48.83s

800–Meter Run

1928	Lina Radke, Germany	2m16.8s
1960	Ljudmila Shevcova, U.S.S.R.	2m4.3s
1964	Ann Packer, Great Britain	2m1.1s
1968	Madeline Manning, United States	2m0.9s
1972	Hildegard Falck, West Germany	1m58.6s
1976	Tatiana Kazankina, U.S.S.R.	1m54.94s
1980	Nadezhda Olizarenko, U.S.S.R.	1m53.5s
1984	Doina Melinte, Romania	1m57.60s
1988	Sigrun Wodars, East Germany	1m56.10s
1992	Ellen Van Langen, Netherlands	1m55.54s

1,500–Meter Run

1972	Ludmila Bragina, U.S.S.R.	4m01.4s
1976	Tatiana Kazankina, U.S.S.R.	4m05.48s
1980	Tatiana Kazankina, U.S.S.R.	3m56.6s
1984	Gabriella Dorio, Italy	4m03.25s
1988	Paula Ivan, Romania	3m53.96s
1992	Hassiba Boulmerka, Algeria	3m55.30s

3,000–Meter Run

1984	Maricica Puica, Romania	8m35.96s
1988	Tatiana Samolenko, U.S.S.R.	8m26.53s
1992	Elena Romanova, Unified Team	8m46.04s

10,000-Meter Run

| 1992 | Derartu Tulu, Ethiopia | 31m6.02s |

80–Meter Hurdles

1932	Mildred Didrikson, United States	11.7s
1936	Trebisonda Valla, Italy	11.7s
1948	Fanny Blankers–Koen, Netherlands	11.2s
1952	Shirley S. de la Hunty, Australia	10.9s
1956	Shirley S. de la Hunty, Australia	10.7s
1960	Irina Press, U.S.S.R.	10.8s
1964	Karin Balzer, Germany	10.5s [1]
1968	Maureen Caird, Australia	10.3s

1. Wind assisted.

100–Meter Hurdles

1972	Annelie Ehrhardt, East Germany	12.59s
1976	Johanna Schaller, East Germany	12.77s
1980	Vera Komisova, U.S.S.R.	12.56s
1984	Benita Fitzgerald–Brown, United States	12.84s
1988	Jordanka Donkova, Bulgaria	12.38s
1992	Paraskevi Patoulidou, Greece	12.64s

400–Meter Hurdles

1984	Nawai El Moutawakel, Morocco	54.61s
1988	Debra Flintoff–King, Australia	53.17s
1992	Sally Gunnell, Great Britain	53.23s

400–Meter Relay

1928	Canada	48.4s
1932	United States	47s
1936	United States	46.9s
1948	Netherlands	47.5s
1952	United States	45.9s
1956	Australia	44.5s
1960	United States	44.5s
1964	Poland	43.6s
1968	United States	42.8s
1972	West Germany	42.81s
1976	East Germany	42.55s
1980	East Germany	41.60s
1984	United States	41.65s
1988	United States	41.98s
1992	United States	42.11s

1,600–Meter Relay

1972	East Germany	3m23s
1976	East Germany	3m19.23s
1980	U.S.S.R.	3m20.2s
1984	United States	3m18.29s
1988	U.S.S.R.	3m15.18s
1992	Unified Team	3m20.20s

10,000-Meter Walk

1992	Chen Yueling, China	44m32s

Marathon

1984	Joan Benoit, United States	2 hr 24 m 52s
1988	Rose Mota, Portugal	2 hr 25 m 40s
1992	Valentina Yegorova, Unified Team	2h32m41s

Running High Jump

1928	Ethel Catherwood, Canada	5 ft 3 in.
1932	Jean Shiley, United States	5 ft 5 1/4 in.
1936	Ibolya Csak, Hungary	5 ft 3 in.
1948	Alice Coachman, United States	5 ft 6 1/8 in.
1952	Ester Brand, South Africa	5 ft 5 3/4 in.
1956	Mildred McDaniel, United States	5 ft 9 1/4 in.
1960	Iolanda Balas, Romania	6 ft 3/4 in.
1964	Iolanda Balas, U.S.S.R.	6 ft 2 3/4 in.
1968	Miloslava Rezkova, Czechoslovakia	5 ft 11 3/4 in.
1972	Ulrike Meyfarth, West Germany	6 ft 3 5/8 in.
1976	Rosemarie Ackerman, E. Germany	(1.93m) 6 ft 4 in.
1980	Sara Simeoni, Italy	6 ft 5 1/2 in.
1984	Ulrike Meyfarth, West Germany	6 ft 7 1/2 in.
1988	Louise Ritter, United States	6 ft 8 in.
1992	Heike Henkel, Germany	6 ft 7 1/2 in.

Long Jump

1948	Olga Gyarmati, Hungary	18 ft 8 1/4 in.
1952	Yvette Williams, New Zealand	20 ft 5 3/4 in.
1956	Elzbieta Krzesinska, Poland	20 ft 9 3/4 in.
1960	Vera Krepkina, U.S.S.R.	20 ft 10 3/4 in.
1964	Mary Rand, Great Britain	22 ft 2 in.
1968	Viorica Ciscopoleanu, Romania	22 ft 4 1/2 in.
1972	Heidemarie Rosendahl, West Germany	22 ft 3 in.
1976	Angela Voigt, East Germany	(6.72m) 22 ft 1/2 in.
1980	Tatiana Kolpakova, U.S.S.R.	23 ft 2 in.
1984	Anisoara Stanciu, Romania	22 ft 10 in.
1988	Jackie Joyner–Kersee, United States	24 ft 3 1/2 in.
1992	Heike Drechsler, Germany	23 ft 5 1/4 in.

Shot–Put

1948	Micheline Ostermeyer, France	45 ft 1 1/2 in.
1952	Galina Zybina, U.S.S.R.	50 ft 1 1/2 in.
1956	Tamara Tishkyevich, U.S.S.R.	54 ft 5 in.
1960	Tamara Press, U.S.S.R.	56 ft 9 7/8 in.
1964	Tamara Press, U.S.S.R.	59 ft 6 in.
1968	Margitta Gummel, East Germany	64 ft 4 in.
1972	Nadezhda Chizhova, U.S.S.R.	69 ft
1976	Ivanka Christova, Bulgaria	(21.16m) 69 ft 5 in.
1980	Ilona Sluplanek, East Germany	73 ft 6 in.
1984	Claudia Losch, West Germany	67 ft 2 1/4 in.
1988	Natalya Lisovskaya, U.S.S.R.	72 ft 11 1/2 in.
1992	Svetlana Kriveleva, Unified Team	69 ft 1 1/4 in.

Discus Throw

1928	Helena Konopacka, Poland	129 ft 11 7/8 in.
1932	Lillian Copeland, United States	133 ft 2 in.
1936	Gisela Mauermayer, Germany	156 ft 3 3/16 in.
1948	Micheline Ostermeyer, France	137 ft 6 1/2 in.
1956	Olga Fikotova, Czechoslovakia	176 ft 1 1/2 in.
1960	Nina Ponomareva, U.S.S.R.	180 ft 8 1/4 in.
1964	Tamara Press, U.S.S.R.	187 ft 10 3/4 in.
1968	Lia Manoliu, Romania	191 ft 2 1/2 in.
1972	Faina Melnik, U.S.S.R.	218 ft 7 in.
1976	Evelin Schlaak, East Germany	(69.00m) 226 ft 4 in.
1980	Evelin Jahl, East Germany	229 ft 6 1/2 in.
1984	Ria Stalman, Netherlands	214 ft 5 in.
1988	Martina Hellmann, East Germany	237 ft 2 1/4 in.
1992	Maritza Marten, Cuba	229 ft 10 1/4 in.

Javelin Throw

1932	Mildred Didrikson, United States	143 ft 4 in.
1936	Tilly Fleischer, Germany	148 ft 2 3/4 in.
1948	Herma Bauma, Austria	149 ft 6 in.
1952	Dana Zatopek, Czechoslovakia	165 ft 7 in.
1956	Inessa Janzeme, U.S.S.R.	176 ft 8 in.
1960	Elvira Ozolina, U.S.S.R.	183 ft 8 in.
1964	Mihaela Penes, Romania	198 ft 7 1/2 in.
1968	Angela Nemeth, Hungary	198 ft 0 in.
1972	Ruth Fuchs, East Germany	209 ft 7 in.
1976	Ruth Fuchs, East Germany	(65.94m) 216 ft 4 in.
1980	Maria Colon, Cuba	224 ft 5 in.
1984	Tessa Sanderson, Britain	228 ft 2 in.
1988	Petra Felke, East Germany	245 ft
1992	Silke Renke, Germany	224 ft 2 1/2 in.

Pentathlon

1964	Irina Press, U.S.S.R.	5,246 pts.
1968	Ingrid Becker, West Germany	5,098 pts.
1972	Mary Peters, Britain	4,801 pts.
1976	Siegrun Siegl, East Germany	4,745 pts.
1980	Nadyeszhda Tkachenko, U.S.S.R.	5,083 pts.
1984	Daniele Masala, Italy	5,469 pts.
1988	Jackie Joyner–Kersee, United States	7,291 pts.

Heptathlon

1992	Jackie Joyner-Kersee, United States	7,044 pts.

SWIMMING–MEN

50 Meter Freestyle

1988	Matt Biondi, United States	22.14s
1992	Alexandre Popov, Unified Team	21.91s

100 Meter Freestyle

1896	Alfred Hajos, Hungary	1m22.2s
1904	Zoltan de Halmay, Hungary	1m2.8s [1]
1906	Charles Daniels, United States	1m13s
1908	Charles Daniels, United States	1m5.6s
1912	Duke P. Kahanamoku, United States	1m3.4s
1920	Duke P. Kahanamoku, United States	1m1.4s
1924	John Weissmuller, United States	59s
1928	John Weissmuller, United States	58.6s
1932	Yasuji Miyazaki, Japan	58.2s
1936	Ferenc Csik, Hungary	57.6s
1948	Walter Ris, United States	57.3s
1952	Clarke Scholes, United States	57.4s
1956	Jon Henricks, Australia	55.4s
1960	John Devitt, Australia	55.2s
1964	Don Schollander, United States	53.4s
1968	Michael Wenden, Australia	52.2s
1972	Mark Spitz, United States	51.22s
1976	Jim Montgomery, United States	49.99s
1980	Jorg Woithe, East Germany	50.40s
1984	Rowdy Gaines, United States	49.80s
1988	Matt Biondi, United States	48.63s
1992	Alexandre Popov, Unified Team	49.02s

1. 100 yards.

200–Meter Freestyle

1900	Frederick Lane, Australia	2m25.2s
1904	Charles Daniels, United States	2m44.2s [1]
1968	Michael Wenden, Australia	1m55.2s
1972	Mark Spitz, United States	1m52.78s
1976	Bruce Furniss, United States	1m50.29s
1980	Sergei Kopiliakov, U.S.S.R.	4m49.81s
1984	Michael Gross, West Germany	1m47.44s
1988	Duncan Armstrong, Australia	1m47.25s
1992	Evgueni Sadovyi, Unified Team	1m46.70s

1. 220 yards

400–Meter Freestyle

1896	Paul Neumann, Austria	8m12.6s [1]
1904	Charles Daniels, United States	6m16.2s [2]
1906	Otto Sheff, Austria	6m23.8s
1908	Henry Taylor, Great Britain	5m36.8s
1912	George Hodgson, Canada	5m24.4s
1920	Norman Ross, United States	5m26.8s
1926	John Weissmuller, United States	5m4.2s
1928	Albert Zorilla, Argentina	5m1.6s
1932	Clarence Crabbe, United States	4m48.4s
1936	Jack Medica, United States	4m44.5s
1948	William Smith, United States	4m41s
1952	Jean Boiteux, France	4m30.7s
1956	Murray Rose, Australia	4m27.3s
1960	Murray Rose, Australia	4m18.3s
1964	Don Schollander, United States	4m12.2s
1968	Mike Burton, United States	4m9s
1972	Bradford Cooper, Australia	4m00.27s [3]
1976	Brian Goodell, United States	3m51.93s
1980	Vladimir Salnikov, U.S.S.R.	3m51.31s
1984	George DiCarlo, United States	3m51.23s
1988	Uwe Dassier, East Germany	3m46.95s
1992	Evgueni Sadovyi, Unified Team	3m45.00s [4]

1. 500 meters. 2. 440 yards. 3. Rich DeMont, United States, won but was disqualified following day for medical reasons. 4. World record.

1,500 Meter Freestyle

1904	Emil Rausch, Germany	27m18.2s [1]
1906	Henry Taylor, Great Britain	28m28s [2]
1908	Henry Taylor, Great Britain	22m48.4s
1912	George Hodgson, Canada	22m
1920	Norman Ross, United States	22m23.2s
1924	Andrew Charlton, Australia	20m6.6s
1928	Arne Borg, Sweden	19m51.8s
1932	Kusuo Kitamura, Japan	19m12.4s
1936	Noboru Terada, Japan	19m13.7s
1948	James McLane, United States	19m18.5s
1952	Ford Konno, United States	18m30s
1956	Murray Rose, Australia	17m58.9s
1960	Jon Konrads, Australia	17m19.6s
1964	Robert Windle, Australia	17m1.7s
1968	Michael Burton, United States	16m38.9s
1972	Michael Burton, United States	15m52.58s
1976	Brian Goodell, United States	15m02.4s
1980	Vladimir Salnikov, U.S.S.R.	14m58.27s
1984	Michael O'Brien, United States	15m05.2s
1988	Vladimir Salnikov, U.S.S.R.	15m00.4s
1992	Kieren Perkins, Australia	14m43.48s

1. One mile. 2. 1,600 meters

100–Meter Backstroke

1904	Walter Brack, Germany	1m16.8s [1]
1908	Arno Bieberstein, Germany	1m24.6s
1912	Harry Hebner, United States	1m21.2s
1920	Warren Kealoha, United States	1m15.2s
1924	Warren Kealoha, United States	1m13.2s
1928	George Kojac, United States	1m8.2s
1932	Masaji Kiyokawa, Japan	1m8.6s
1936	Adolph Kiefer, United States	1m5.9s
1948	Allen Stack, United States	1m6.4s
1952	Yoshinobu Oyakawa, United States	1m5.4s
1956	David Thiele, Australia	1m2.2s
1960	David Thiele, Australia	1m1.9s
1968	Roland Matthes, East Germany	58.7s
1972	Roland Matthes, East Germany	56.58s
1976	John Naber, United States	55.49s
1980	Bengt Baron, Sweden	56.53s
1984	Rick Carey, United States	55.79s
1988	Daichi Suzuki, Japan	55.05s
1992	Mark Tewksbury, Canada	53.98s

1. 100 yards

200–Meter Backstroke

1900	Ernst Hoppenberg, Germany	2m47s
1964	Jed Graef, United States	2m10.3s
1968	Roland Matthes, East Germany	2m9.6s
1972	Roland Matthes, East Germany	2m2.82s
1976	John Naber, United States	1m59.19s
1980	Sandor Wladar, Hungary	2:01.93s
1984	Rick Carey, United States	2m00.23s
1988	Igor Polianski, U.S.S.R.	1m59.37s
1992	Martin Lopez Zubero, Spain	1m58.47s

100–Meter Breaststroke

1968	Donald McKenzie, United States	1m7.7s
1972	Nobutaka Taguchi, Japan	1m4.94s
1976	John Hencken, United States	1m03.11s
1980	Duncan Goodhew, Britain	1m03.34s
1984	Steve Lindquist, United States	1m01.65s
1988	Adrian Moorhouse, Great Britain	1m02.04s
1992	Nelson Diebel, United States	1m01.50s

200–Meter Breaststroke

1908	Frederick Holman, Great Britain	3m9.2s
1912	Walter Bathe, Germany	3m1.8s
1920	Haken Malmroth, Sweden	3m4.4s
1924	Robert Skelton, United States	2m56.6s
1928	Yoshiyuki Tsuruta, Japan	2m48.8s
1932	Yoshiyuki Tsuruta, Japan	2m45.4s
1936	Tetsuo Hamuro, Japan	2m41.5s
1948	Joseph Verdeur, United States	2m39.3s

1952	John Davies, Australia	2m34.4s
1956	Masaura Furukawa, Japan	2m34.7s
1960	Bill Muliken, United States	2m37.4s
1964	Ian O'Brien, Australia	2m27.8s
1968	Felipe Munoz, Mexico	2m28.7s
1972	John Hencken, United States	2m21.55s
1976	David Willkie, Britain	2m15.11s
1980	Robertas Zulpa, U.S.S.R.	2m15.85s
1984	Victor Davis, Canada	2m13.34s
1988	Jozef Szabo, Hungary	2m13.52s
1992	Mike Barrowman, United States	2m10.16s

100–Meter Butterfly

1968	Douglas Russell, United States	55.9s
1972	Mark Spitz, United States	54.27s
1976	Matt Vogel, United States	54.35s
1980	Par Arvidsson, Sweden	54.92s
1984	Michael Gross, West Germany	53.08s
1988	Anthony Nesty, Surinam	53.0s
1992	Pablo Morales, United States	53.32s

200–Meter Butterfly

1956	Bill Yorzyk, United States	2m19.3s
1960	Mike Troy, United States	2m12.8s
1964	Kevin Berry, Australia	2m6.6s
1968	Carl Robie, United States	2m8.7s
1972	Mark Spitz, United States	2m00.7s
1976	Mike Bruner, United States	1m59.23s
1980	Sergei Fesenko, U.S.S.R.	1m59.76s
1984	Jon Sieben, Australia	1m57.0s
1988	Michael Gross, East Germany	1m56.94s
1992	Mel Stewart, United States	1m56.26s

200–Meter Individual Medley

1968	Charles Hickcox, United States	2m12s
1972	Gunnar Larsson, Sweden	2m7.17s
1988	Tamas Darnyi, Hungary	2m0.17s
1992	Tamas Darnyi, Hungary	2m00.76s

400–Meter Individual Medley

1964	Dick Roth, United States	4m45.4s
1968	Charles Hickox, United States	4m48.4s
1972	Gunnar Larsson, Sweden	4m31.98s
1976	Rod Strachan, United States	4m23.68s
1980	Aleksandr Sidorenko, U.S.S.R.	4m22.8s
1984	Alex Baumann, Canada	4m17.41s
1988	Tamas Darnyi, Hungary	4m14.75s
1992	Tamas Darnyi, Hungary	4m14.23s

400–Meter Freestyle Relay

1964	United States	3m32.2s
1968	United States	3m31.7s
1972	United States	3m26.42s
1988	United States	3m16.52s
1992	United States	3m16.74s

800–Meter Freestyle Relay

1908	Great Britain	10m55.6s
1912	Australia	10m11.2s
1920	United States	10m4.4s
1924	United States	9m53.4s
1928	United States	9m36.2s
1932	Japan	8m58.4s
1936	Japan	8m51.5s
1948	United States	8m46.1s
1952	United States	8m31.1s
1956	Australia	8m23.6s
1960	United States	8m10.2s
1964	United States	7m52.1s
1968	United States	7m52.3s
1972	United States	7m35.78s
1976	United States	7m23.22s
1980	U.S.S.R.	7m23.50s

1984	United States	7m16.59s
1988	United States	7m12.51s
1992	Unified Team	7m11.95s

400–Meter Medley Relay

1960	United States	4m5.4s
1964	United States	3m58.4s
1968	United States	3m54.9s
1972	United States	3m48.16s
1976	United States	3m42.22s
1980	Australia	3m45.70s
1984	United States	3m39.30s
1988	United States	3m36.93s
1992	United States	3m36.93s[1]

1. World record.

Springboard Dive

		Points
1908	Albert Zuerner, Germany	85.5
1912	Paul Guenther, Germany	79.23
1920	Louis Kuehn, United States	675
1924	Albert White, United States	696.4
1928	Pete Desjardins, United States	185.04
1932	Michael Galitzen, United States	161.38
1936	Richard Degener, United States	163.57
1948	Bruce Harlan, United States	163.64
1952	David Browning, United States	205.59
1956	Robert Clotworthy, United States	159.56
1960	Gary Tobian, United States	170.00
1964	Ken Sitzberger, United States	159.90
1968	Bernard Wrightson, United States	170.15
1972	Vladimir Vasin, U.S.S.R.	594.09
1976	Phil Boggs, United States	619.05
1980	Alexsandr Portnov, U.S.S.R.	905.02
1984	Greg Louganis, United States	754.41
1988	Greg Louganis, United States	730.80
1992	Mark Lenzi, United States	676.53

Platform Dive

		Points
1904	G.E. Sheldon, United States	12.75
1906	Gottlob Walz, Germany	156
1908	Hialmar Johansson, Sweden	83.75
1912	Erik Adlerz, Sweden	73.94
1920	Clarence Pinkston, United States	100.67
1924	Albert White, United States	487.3
1928	Pete Desjardins, United States	98.74
1932	Harold Smith, United States	124.80
1936	Marshall Wayne, United States	113.58
1948	Samuel Lee, United States	130.05
1952	Samuel Lee, United States	156.28
1956	Joaquin Capilla, Mexico	152.44
1960	Bob Webster, United States	165.56
1964	Bob Webster, United States	148.58
1968	Klaus Dibiasi, Italy	164.18
1972	Klaus Dibiasi, Italy	504.12
1976	Klaus Dibiasi, Italy	600.51
1980	Falk Hoffman, E. Germany	835.65
1984	Greg Louganis, United States	710.91
1988	Greg Louganis, United States	638.61
1992	Sun Shuwei, China	677.31

SWIMMING–WOMEN

50–Meter Freestyle

1988	Kristin Otto, East Germany	25.49s
1992	Yang Wenyi, China	24.79s

100–Meter Freestyle

1912	Fanny Durack, Australia	1m22.2s
1920	Ethelda Bleibtrey, United States	1m13.6s
1924	Ethel Lackie, United States	1m12.4s
1928	Albina Osipowich, United States	1m11s
1932	Helene Madison, United States	1m6.8s

1936	Hendrika Mastenbroek, Netherlands	1m5.9s
1948	Greta Andersen, Denmark	1m6.3s
1952	Katalin Szoke, Hungary	1m6.8s
1956	Dawn Fraser, Australia	1m2s
1960	Dawn Fraser, Australia	1m1.2s
1964	Dawn Fraser, Australia	59.5s
1968	Marge Jan Henne, United States	1m
1972	Sandra Neilson, United States	58.59s
1976	Kornelia Ender, East Germany	55.65s
1980	Barbara Krause, East Germany	54.79s
1984	Carrie Steinseifer, United States	55.92s
1988	Kristin Otto, East Germany	54.93s
1992	Zhuang Yong, China	54.64s

200–Meter Freestyle

1968	Debbie Meyer, United States	2m10.5s
1972	Shane Gould, Australia	2m3.56s
1976	Kornelia Ender, East Germany	1m59.26s
1980	Barbara Krause, East Germany	1m58.33s
1984	Mary Wayle, United States	1m59.23s
1988	Heike Friedrich, East Germany	1m57.65s
1992	Nicole Haislett, United States	1m57.90s

400–Meter Freestyle

1920	Ethelda Bleibtrey, United States	4m34s [1]
1924	Martha Norelius, United States	6m2.2s
1928	Martha Norelius, United States	5m42.8s
1932	Helene Madison, United States	5m28.5s
1936	Hendrika Mastenbroek, Netherlands	5m26.4s
1948	Ann Curtis, United States	5m17.8s
1952	Valerie Gyenge, Hungary	5m12.1s
1956	Lorraine Crapp, Australia	4m54.6s
1960	Chris von Saltza, United States	4m50.6s
1964	Ginny Duenkel, United States	4m43.3s
1968	Debbie Meyer, United States	4m31.8s
1972	Shane Gould, Australia	4m19.04s
1976	Petra Thumer, East Germany	4m09.89s
1980	Ines Diers, East Germany	4m08.76s
1984	Tiffany Cohen, United States	4m07.10s
1988	Janet Evans, United States	4m03.85s
1992	Dagmar Hase, Germany	4m07.18s

1. 300 meters.

800–Meter Freestyle

1968	Debbie Meyer, United States	9m24s
1972	Keena Rothhammer, United States	8m53.68s
1976	Petra Thumer, East Germany	8m37.14s
1980	Michelle Ford, Australia	8m28.90s
1984	Tiffany Cohen, United States	8m24.95s
1988	Janet Evans, United States	8m20.20s
1992	Janet Evans, United States	8m25.52s

100–Meter Backstroke

1924	Sybil Bauer, United States	1m23.2s
1928	Marie Braun, Netherlands	1m22s
1932	Eleanor Holm, United States	1m19.4s
1936	Dina Senff, Netherlands	1m18.9s
1948	Karen Harup, Denmark	1m14.4s
1952	Joan Harrison, South Africa	1m14.3s
1956	Judy Grinham, Great Britain	1m12.9s
1960	Lynn Burke, United States	1m9.3s
1964	Cathy Ferguson, United States	1m7.7s
1968	Kaye Hall, United States	1m6.2s
1972	Melissa Belote, United States	1m5.78s
1976	Ulrike Richter, East Germany	1m01.83s
1980	Rica Reinisch, East Germany	1m00.86s
1984	Theresa Andrews, United States	1m02.55s
1988	Kristin Otto, East Germany	1m0.89s
1992	Kristina Egerszegi, Hungary	1m0.68s

200–Meter Backstroke

1968	Pokey Watson–United States	2m24.8s
1972	Melissa Belote, United States	2m19.19s

DISTRIBUTION OF MEDALS
1992 SUMMER GAMES

Country	Gold	Silver	Bronze	Total
Unified Team	45	38	29	112
United States	37	34	37	108
Germany	33	21	28	82
China	16	22	16	54
Cuba	14	6	11	31
Hungary	11	12	7	30
South Korea	12	5	12	29
France	8	5	16	29
Australia	7	9	11	27
Spain	13	7	2	22
Japan	3	8	11	22
Britain	5	3	12	20
Italy	6	5	8	19
Poland	3	6	10	19
Canada	6	5	7	18
Romania	4	6	8	18
Bulgaria	3	7	6	16
Netherlands	2	6	7	15
Sweden	1	7	4	12
New Zealand	1	4	5	10
North Korea	4	0	5	9
Kenya	2	4	2	8
Czechoslovakia	4	2	1	7
Norway	2	4	1	7
Turkey	2	2	2	6
Denmark	1	1	4	6
Indonesia	2	2	1	5
Finland	1	2	2	5
Jamaica	0	3	1	4
Nigeria	0	3	1	4
Brazil	2	1	0	3
Morocco	1	1	1	3
Ethiopia	1	0	2	3
Latvia	0	2	1	3
Belgium	0	1	2	3
Croatia	0	1	2	3
Iran	0	1	2	3
Yugoslavs	0	1	2	3
Greece	2	0	0	2
Ireland	1	1	0	2
Algeria	1	0	1	2
Estonia	1	0	1	2
Lithuania	1	0	1	2
Austria	0	2	0	2
Namibia	0	2	0	2
South Africa	0	2	0	2
Israel	0	1	1	2
Mongolia	0	0	2	2
Slovenia	0	0	2	2
Switzerland	1	0	0	1
Peru	0	1	0	1
Mexico	0	1	0	1
Taiwan	0	1	0	1
Argentina	0	0	1	1
Bahamas	0	0	1	1
Colombia	0	0	1	1
Ghana	0	0	1	1
Malaysia	0	0	1	1
Pakistan	0	0	1	1
Philippines	0	0	1	1
Puerto Rico	0	0	1	1
Qatar	0	0	1	1
Suriname	0	0	1	1
Thailand	0	0	1	1

1976	Ulrike Richter, East Germany	2m13.43s
1980	Rica Reinisch, East Germany	2m11.77s
1984	Jolanda DeRover, Netherlands	2m12.38s
1988	Krisztina Egerszegi, Hungary	2m09.29s
1992	Krisztina Egerszegi, Hungary	2m07.06s

100–Meter Breaststroke

1968	Djurdjica Bjedov, Yugoslavia	1m15.8s
1972	Catherine Carr, United States	1m13.58s
1976	Hannelore Anke, East Germany	1m11.16s
1980	Ute Geweniger, East Germany	1m10.22s
1984	Petra Van Staveren, Netherlands	1m09.88s
1988	Tainia Dangalakova, Bulgaria	1m07.95s
1992	Elena Roudkovskaia, Unified Team	1m08.00s

200–Meter Breaststroke

1924	Lucy Morton, Great Britain	3m33.2s
1928	Hilde Schrader, Germany	3m12.6s
1932	Clare Dennis, Australia	3m6.3s
1936	Hideko Maehata, Japan	3m3.6s
1948	Nel van Vliet, Netherlands	2m57.2s
1952	Eva Szekely, Hungary	2m51.7s
1956	Ursala Happe, Germany	2m53.1s
1960	Anita Lonsbrough, Great Britain	2m49.5s
1964	Galina Prozumenschikova, U.S.S.R.	2m46.4s
1968	Sharon Wichman, United States	2m44.4s
1972	Beverly Whitfield, Australia	2m41.71s
1976	Marina Koshevaia, U.S.S.R.	2m33.35s
1980	Lina Kachushite, U.S.S.R.	2m29.54s
1984	Anne Ottenbrite, Canada	2m30.38s
1988	Silke Hoerner, East Germany	2m26.71s
1992	Kyoko Iwasaki, Japan	2m26.65s

100–Meter Butterfly

1956	Shelley Mann, United States	1m11s
1960	Carolyn Schuler, United States	1m9.5s
1964	Sharon Stouder, United States	1m4.7s
1968	Lynn McClements, Australia	1m5.5s
1972	Mayumi Aoki, Japan	1m3.34s
1976	Kornelia Ender, East Germany	1m00.13s
1980	Caren Metschuck, East Germany	1m00.42s
1984	Mary Meagher, United States	59.26s
1988	Kristin Otto, East Germany	59s
1992	Qian Hong, China	58.62s

200–Meter Butterfly

1968	Ada Kok, Netherlands	2m24.7s
1972	Karen Moe, United States	2m15.57s
1976	Andrea Pollack, East Germany	2m11.41s
1980	Ines Geissler, East Germany	2m10.44s
1984	Mary Meagher, United States	2m06.90s
1988	Kathleen Nord, East Germany	2m9.51s
1992	Summer Sanders, United States	2m06.67s

200–Meter Individual Medley

1968	Claudia Kolb, United States	2m24.7s
1972	Shane Gould, Australia	2m23.07s
1984	Tracy Caulkins, United States	2m12.64s
1988	Daniela Hunger, East Germany	2m12.59s
1992	Lin Lee, China	2m11.55s[1]
1. World record.		

400–Meter Individual Medley

1964	Donna de Varona, United States	5m18.7s
1968	Claudia Kolk, United States	5m8.5s
1972	Gail Neall, Australia	5m2.97s
1976	Ulrike Tauber, East Germany	4m42.77s
1980	Petra Schneider, East Germany	4m36.29s
1984	Tracy Caulkins, United States	4m39.21s
1988	Janet Evans, United States	4m37.76s
1992	Krisztina Egerszegi, Hungary	4m36.54s

400–Meter Freestyle Relay

1912	Great Britain	5m52.8s
1920	United States	5m11.6s
1924	United States	4m58.8s
1928	United States	4m47.6s
1932	United States	4m38s
1936	Netherlands	4m36s
1948	United States	4m29.2s
1952	Hungary	4m24.4s
1956	Australia	4m17.1s
1960	United States	4m8.9s
1964	United States	4m3.8s
1968	United States	4m2.5s
1972	United States	3m55.19s
1976	United States	3m44.82s
1980	East Germany	3m42.71s
1984	United States	3m44.43s
1988	East Germany	3m40.63s
1992	United States	3m39.46s[1]
1. World record.		

400–Meter Medley Relay

1960	United States	4m41.1s
1964	United States	4m33.9s
1968	United States	4m28.3s
1972	United States	4m20.75s
1976	East Germany	4m07.95s
1980	East Germany	4m06.67s
1984	United States	4m08.34s
1988	East Germany	4m03.74s
1992	United States	4m02.54s[1]
1. World record.		

Springboard Dive

		Points
1920	Aileen Riggin, United States	539.90
1924	Elizabeth Becker, United States	474.5
1928	Helen Meany, United States	78.62
1932	Georgia Coleman, United States	87.52
1936	Marjorie Gestring, United States	89.27
1948	Victoria M. Draves, United States	108.74
1952	Patricia McCormick, United States	147.30
1956	Patricia McCormick, United States	142.36
1960	Ingrid Kramer, Germany	155.81
1964	Ingrid Kramer Engel, Germany	145.00
1968	Sue Gossick, United States	150.77
1972	Micki King, United States	450.03
1976	Jennifer Chandler, United States	506.19
1980	Irina Kalinina, U.S.S.R.	725.91
1984	Sylvie Bernier, Canada	530.70
1988	Gao Min, China	580.23
1992	Gao Min, China	572.40

Platform Dive

		Points
1912	Greta Johansson, Sweden	39.9
1920	Stefani Fryland, Denmark	34.60
1924	Caroline Smith, United States	166
1928	Elizabeth B. Pinkston, United States	31.60
1932	Dorothy Poynton, United States	40.26
1936	Dorothy Poynton Hill, United States	33.92
1948	Victoria M. Draves, United States	68.87
1952	Patricia McCormick, United States	79.37
1956	Patricia McCormick, United States	84.85
1960	Ingrid Kramer, Germany	91.28
1964	Lesley Bush, United States	99.80
1968	Milena Duchkova, Czechoslovakia	109.59
1972	Ulrika Knape, Sweden	390.00
1976	Elena Vaytsekhovskaia, U.S.S.R.	406.59
1980	Martina Jaschke, East Germany	596.25
1984	Zhou Jihong, China	435.51
1988	Xu Yanmei, China	445.20
1992	Fu Mingxia, China	461.43

BASKETBALL–MEN

1904	United States	1968	United States
1936	United States	1972	U.S.S.R.
1948	United States	1976	United States
1952	United States	1980	Yugoslavia
1956	United States	1984	United States
1960	United States	1988	U.S.S.R.
1964	United States	1992	United States

BASKETBALL–WOMEN

1976	U.S.S.R.	1988	United States
1980	U.S.S.R.	1992	Unified Team
1984	United States		

BOXING

(U.S. winners only)

(U.S. boycotted Olympics in 1980)

Flyweight–112 pounds (51 kilograms)

1904	George v. Finnegan	1952	Nate Brooks
1920	Frank De Genaro	1976	Leo Randolph
1924	Fidel La Barba	1984	Steve McCrory

Bantamweight–119 (54 kg)

1904	O.L. Kirk	1988	Kennedy McKinney

Featherweight–126 pounds (57 kg)

1904	O.L. Kirk	1984	Meldrick Taylor
1924	Jackie Fields		

Lightweight–132 pounds (60 kg)

1904	H.J. Spanger	1976	Howard Davis

1920	Samuel Mosberg	1984	Pernell Whitaker
1968	Ronnie Harris	1992	Oscar De La Hoya

Light Welterweight–140 pounds (63.5 kg)

1952	Charles Adkins	1976	Ray Leonard
1972	Ray Seales	1984	Jerry Page

Welterwight–148 pounds (67 kg)

1904	Al Young	1984	Mark Breland
1932	Edward Flynn		

Light Middleweight–157 pounds (71 kg)

1960	Wilbert McClure	1984	Frank Tate

Middleweight–165 pounds (75 kg)

1904	Charles Mayer	1960	Eddie Cook
1932	Carmen Barth	1976	Michael Spinks
1952	Floyd Patterson		

Light Heavyweight–179 pounds (81 kg)

1920	Edward Eagan	1960	Cassius Clay
1952	Norvel Lee	1976	Leon Spinks
1956	James Boyd	1988	Andrew Maynard

Heavyweight–201 pounds

1904	Sam Berger	1968	George Foreman
1952	Edward Sanders	1984	Henry Tilman
1956	Pete Rademacher	1988	Ray Mercer
1964	Joe Frazier		

Super Heavyweight (unlimited)

1984	Tyrell Biggs

Other 1992 Summer Olympic Games Champions

Archery
Men—Sebastien Flute, France
Men's Team—Spain
Women—Cho Youn-Jeong, South Korea
Women's Team—South Korea

Baseball
Men—Cuba

Canoe–Kayak—Men
Single Canoe Slalom—Lukas Pollert, Czechoslovakia
Double Canoe Slalom—United States (Scott Strausbaugh and Joe Jacobi)
Single Kayak Slalom—Pierpaolo Ferrazzi, Italy
Kayak 500m singles—Mikko Yrjoe Kolehmainen, Finland
Kayak 500m doubles—Germany (Kay Bluhm, Torsten Rene Gutsche)
Kayak 1,000m singles—Clint Robinson, Australia
Kayak 1,000m doubles—Germany (Kay Bluhm, Torsten Rene Gutsche)

Kayak 1,000m fours—Germany (Mario Von Appen, Oliver Kegel, Thomas Reineck, Andre Wohllebe)
Canoe 500m singles—Nikolai Boukhalov, Bulgaria
Canoe 500m doubles—Unified Team (Alexandre Masseikov, Dmitri Dovgalenok)
Canoe 1,000m singles—Nikolai Boukhalov, Bulgaria
Canoe 1,000m doubles—Germany (Ulrich Papke, Ingo Spelly)

Kayak—Women
Kayak slalom—Elisabeth Micheler, Germany
Kayak 500m singles—Birgit Schmidt, Germany
Kayak 500m doubles—Germany (Ramona Porturch, Anke Von Sek)
Kayak 500m fours—Hungary

Cycling—Men
4,000m individual pursuit—Chris Boardman, Great Britain
1,000m individual pursuit—Jens Fieldler, Germany

Individual points race—Giovanni Lombardi, Italy
Individual road race—Fabio Casartelli, Italy
1 km time trial—Jose Moreno, Spain
4,000m team pursuit—Germany
Team time trial—Germany

Cycling—Women
Individual road race—Kathryn Watt, Australia
1,000m individual sprint—Erika Salumae, Estonia
3,000m individual pursuit—Petra Rossner, Germany

Equestrian
Individual jumping—Ludger Beerbaum, Germany
Team jumping—Netherlands
Individual dressage—Nicole Uphoff, Germany
Team dressage—Germany
Individual three-day event—Matthew Ryan, Australia
Team three-day event—Australia

Fencing—Men
Individual foil—Philippe Omnes, France
Team foil—Germany
Individual sabre—Bence Szabo, Hungary
Team sabre—Unified Team
Individual épée—Eric Srecki, France
Team épée—Germany

Fencing—Women
Individual foil—Giovanna Trillini, Italy
Team foil—Italy

Field Hockey
Men—Germany
Women—Spain

Gymnastics—Men
All-around—Vitali Scherbo, Unified Team
Floor exercise—Li Xiaosqhuang, China
Horizontal bar—Trent Dimas, United States
Parallel bars—Vitali Scherbo, Unified Team
Pommel horse—Vitali Scherbo, Unified Team
Rings—Vitali Scherbo, Unified Team
Vault—Vitali Scherbo, Unified team
Team—Unified Team

Gymnastics—Women
All-around—Tatiana Gutsu, Unified Team
Balance beam—Tatiana Lisenko, Unified Team
Floor exercise—Lavania Milosovici, Romania
Uneven bars—Lu Li, China
Vault—Henrietta Onodi, Hungary and Lavinia Milosovici, Romania
Team—Unified Team

Judo—Men
132 lb—Nazim Gousseinov, Unified Team
143 lb—Rogerio Sampaio Cardoso, Brazil
157 lb—Toshihiko Koga, Japan
172 lb—Hidehiko Yoshida, Japan
198 lb—Waldemar Legien, Poland
209 lb—Antal Kovacs, Hungary
Over 209 lb—David Khakhaleichvili, Unified Team

Judo—Women
106 lb—Cecile Nowak, France
115 lb—Almudena Martinez, Spain
123 lb—Miriam Blasco Soto, Spain
134 lb—Catherine Fleury, France
146 lb—Odalis Reve, Cuba
159 lb—Kim Mi-Jung, South Korea
Over 159 lb—Zhuang Xiaoyan, China

Modern Pentathlon
Individual—Arkadiusz Skrzypaszek, Poland
Team—Poland

Rowing—Men
Singles—Thomas Lange, Germany
Doubles—Australia
Quadruples—Germany
Pairs—Great Britain
Pairs with coxswain—Great Britain
Fours—Australia
Fours with coxswain—Romania
Eights—Canada

Rowing—Women
Singles—Elisabeta Lipa, Romania
Doubles—Germany
Pairs—Canada
Fours with coxswain—Canada
Quadruple sculls—Germany
Eights—Canada

Shooting—Men
Skeet—Zhang Shan, China
Trap—Petr Hrdlicka, Czechoslovakia
Air pistol—Wang Yifu, China
Free pistol—Konstantine Loukqchik, Unified Team
Rapid-fire pistol—Ralf Schumann, Germany
Running game target—Michael Jakosits, Germany
Air rifle—Iouri Fedkine, Unified Team
Free rifle—Lee Eun Chui, South Korea
Three-position rifle—Gratchia Petikiane, Unified Team

Shooting—Women
Sport pistol—Marina Logvinenko, Unified Team
Air pistol—Marina Logvinenko, Unified Team
Air rifle—Yeo Kab Soon, South Korea
Three-position rifle—Launi Meili, United States

Synchronized Swimming
Solo—Kristin Babb-Sprague, United States
Duet—United States (Karen and Sarah Josephson)

Table Tennis
Men's singles—Jan Waldner, Sweden
Men's doubles—China (Lu Lin and Wang Tao)
Women's singles—Deng Yaping, China
Women's doubles—China (Deng Yaping and Qiao Hong)

Tennis
Men's singles—Marc Rosset, Switzerland
Men's doubles—Germany (Boris Becker and Michael Stich)
Women's singles—Jennifer Capriati, United States
Women's doubles—United States (Gigi Fernandez and Mary Jo Fernandez)

Weightlifting
115 lb—Ivan Ivanov, Bulgaria
123 lb—Chun Byung-Kwan, South Korea
132 lb—Naim Suleymanoglu, Turkey
148 lb—Israel Militossian, Unified Team
165 lb—Fedor Kassapu, Unified Team
181 lb—Pyrros Dimas, Greece
198 lb—Kakhi Kakhiachvili, Unified Team
220 lb—Victor Tregoubov, Unified Team
243 lb—Ronny Weller, Germany
Over 243 lb—Alexandre Fourlovitch, Unified Team

Wrestling—Freestyle
105.5 lb—Kim Il, North Korea
114.5 lb—Li Hak Son, South Korea
125.5 lb—Alejandro Puerto, Cuba
136.5 lb—John Smith, United States
149.5 lb—Arsen Fadzaev, Unified Team
163 lb—Park Jang Soon, South Korea
181 lb—Kevin Jackson, United States
198.5 lb—Makharbek Khadartsev, Unified Team
220 lb—Leri Khabelov, Unified Team
286 lb—Bruce Baumgartner, United States

Wrestling—Greco-Roman
105.5 lb—Oleg Koutherenko, Unified Team
114.5 lb—Joe Ronningen, Norway
125.5 lb—An Han-Bong, South Korea
136.5 lb—M. Akif Pirim, Turkey
149.5 lb—Attila Repka, Hungary
163 lb—Mnatsakan Iskandarian, Unified Team
181.5 lb—Peter Farkas, Hungary
198 lb—Malik Bullmann, Germany
220 lb—Hector Millian, Cuba
286 lb—Alexander Karelin, Unified Team

Yachting
Men's sailboard—Franck David, France
Women's sailboard—Barbara Kendall, New Zealand
Men's 470—Spain
Women's 470—Spain
Finn—Jose Van Der Ploeg, Spain
Europe—Linda Anderson, Norway
Flying Dutchman—Spain
Solins—Denmark
Star—United States (Mark Reynolds, Hal Haenel)
Tornado—France

Other Champions
Water polo—Italy
Volleyball, men—Brazil
Volleyball, women—Cuba
Soccer—Spain
Rhythmic gymnastics—Alexandra Timoshenka, Unified Team

FOOTBALL

The pastime of kicking around a ball goes back beyond the limits of recorded history. Ancient savage tribes played football of a primitive kind. There was a ball-kicking game played by Athenians, Spartans, and Corinthians 2500 years ago, which the Greeks called *Episkuros*. The Romans had a somewhat similar game called *Harpastum* and are supposed to have carried the game with them when they invaded the British Isles in the First Century, B.C.

Undoubtedly the game known in the United States as Football traces directly to the English game of Rugby, though the modifications have been many. Informal football was played on college lawns well over a century ago, and an annual Freshman-Sophomore series of "scrimmages" began at Yale in 1840. The first formal intercollegiate football game was the Princeton-Rutgers contest at New Brunswick, N.J. on Nov. 6, 1869, with Rutgers winning by 6 goals to 4.

In those days, games were played with 25, 20, 15, or 11 men on a side. In 1880, there was a convention at which Walter Camp of Yale persuaded the delegates to agree to a rule calling for 11 players on a side.

The first professional game was played in 1895 at Latrobe, Pa. The National Football League was founded in 1921. The All-American Conference went into action in 1946. At the end of the 1949 season the two circuits merged, retaining the name of the older league. In 1960, the American Football League began operations. In 1970, the leagues merged. The United States Football League played its first season in 1983, from March to July. It suspended spring operation after the 1985 season, and planned a 1986 move to fall, but suspended operations again.

In 1991, another effort at spring football was launched, but this time it had the backing of the National Football League. The World League of American Football debuted in March 1991 with 10 teams. Three of them were in Europe. The other seven were in North America, including the Montreal Machine in Canada. With television contracts signed with ABC and USA Cable Network, the league seemed to be on sound footing from the beginning. But after just two seasons, it was suspended. In the summer of 1994 the NFL announced the league would be back in 1995, but only with six teams in Europe.

College Football

NATIONAL COLLEGE FOOTBALL CHAMPIONS

The "National Collegiate A.A. Football Guide" recognizes as unofficial national champion the team selected each year by press association polls. If the Associated Press Poll (of writers) did not agree with the United Press International poll (of coaches) through 1991 or the USA Today–CNN poll from 1992, the guide lists both teams selected.

1937	Pittsburgh	1952	Mich. State	1963	Texas	1974	Oklahoma and
1938	Texas Christian	1953	Maryland	1964	Alabama		So. California
1939	Texas A & M	1954	Ohio State	1965	Alabama and	1975	Oklahoma
1940	Minnesota		and U.C.L.A.		Mich. State	1976	Pittsburgh
1941	Minnesota	1955	Oklahoma	1966	Notre Dame	1977	Notre Dame
1942	Ohio State	1956	Oklahoma	1967	So. California	1978	Alabama and
1943	Notre Dame	1957	Auburn and	1968	Ohio State		So. California
1944	Army		Ohio State	1969	Texas	1979	Alabama
1945	Army	1958	Louisiana	1970	Texas and	1980	Georgia
1946	Notre Dame		State		Nebraska	1981	Clemson
1947	Notre Dame	1959	Syracuse	1971	Nebraska	1982	Penn State
1948	Michigan	1960	Minnesota	1972	So. California	1983	Miami
1949	Notre Dame	1961	Alabama	1973	Notre Dame	1984	Brigham Young
1950	Oklahoma	1962	So. California		and U. of Ala.	1985	Oklahoma
1951	Tennessee						

1986	Penn State
1987	Miami
1988	Notre Dame
1989	Miami
1990	Colorado and
	Georgia Tech
1991	Miami and
	Washington
1992	Alabama
1993	Florida State
1994	Nebraska

RECORD OF ANNUAL MAJOR COLLEGE FOOTBALL BOWL GAMES

Rose Bowl

(At Pasadena, Calif.)

1902	Michigan 49, Stanford 0	1931	Alabama 24, Wash. State 0	1950	Ohio State 17, California 14
1916	Washington State 14, Brown 0	1932	So. California 21, Tulane 12	1951	Michigan 14, California 6
1917	Oregon 14, Pennsylvania 0	1933	So. California 35, Pittsburgh 0	1952	Illinois 40, Stanford 7
1918	Mare Island Marines 19, Camp Lewis 7	1934	Columbia 7, Stanford 0	1953	So. California 7, Wisconsin 0
		1935	Alabama 29, Stanford 13	1954	Michigan State 28, U.C.L.A. 20
1919	Great Lakes 17, Mare Island Marines 0	1936	Stanford 7, So. Methodist 0	1955	Ohio State 20, So. California 7
		1937	Pittsburgh 21, Washington 0	1956	Michigan State 17, U.C.L.A. 14
1920	Harvard 7, Oregon 6	1938	California 13, Alabama 0	1957	Iowa 35, Oregon State 19
1921	California 28, Ohio State 0	1939	So. California 7, Duke 3	1958	Ohio State 10, Oregon 7
1922	Washington and Jefferson 0, California 0	1940	So. California 14, Tennessee 0	1959	Iowa 38, California 12
		1941	Stanford 21, Nebraska 13	1960	Washington 44, Wisconsin 8
1923	So. California 14, Penn State 3	1942	Oregon State 20, Duke 16[1]	1961	Washington 17, Minnesota 7
1924	Navy 14, Washington 14	1943	Georgia 9, U.C.L.A. 0	1962	Minnesota 21, U.C.L.A. 3
1925	Notre Dame 27, Stanford 10	1944	So. California 29, Washington 0	1963	So. California 42, Wisconsin 37
1926	Alabama 20, Washington 19	1945	So. California 25, Tennessee 0	1964	Illinois 17, Washington 7
1927	Alabama 7, Stanford 7	1946	Alabama 34, So. California 14	1965	Michigan 34, Oregon State 7
1928	Stanford 7, Pittsburgh 6	1947	Illinois 45, U.C.L.A. 14	1966	U.C.L.A. 14, Michigan State 12
1929	Georgia Tech 8, California 7	1948	Michigan 49, So. California 0	1967	Purdue 14, So. California 13
1930	So. California 47, Pittsburgh 14	1949	Northwestern 20, California 14	1968	So. California 14, Indiana 3

1969 Ohio State 27, So. California 16
1970 So. California 10, Michigan 3
1971 Stanford 27, Ohio State 17
1972 Stanford 13, Michigan 12
1973 So. California 42, Ohio State 17
1974 Ohio State 42, So. California 21
1975 So. California 18, Ohio State 17
1976 U.C.L.A. 23, Ohio State 10
1977 So. California 14, Michigan 6
1978 Washington 27, Michigan 20
1979 So. California 17, Michigan 10
1980 So. California 17, Ohio State 16
1981 Michigan 23, Washington 6
1982 Washington 28, Iowa 8
1983 U.C.L.A. 24, Michigan 14
1984 U.C.L.A. 45, Illinois 9
1985 USC 20, Ohio St. 17
1986 U.C.L.A. 45, Iowa 28
1987 Arizona State 22, Michigan 15
1988 Michigan State 20, USC 17
1989 Michigan 22, So. California 14
1990 USC 17, Michigan 10
1991 Washington 46, Iowa 34
1992 Washington 34, Michigan 14
1993 Michigan 38, Washington 31
1994 Wisconsin 21, UCLA 16
1995 Penn State 38, Oregon 20
1. Played at Durham, N.C.

Orange Bowl
(At Miami)
1933 Miami (Fla.) 7, Manhattan 0
1934 Duquesne 33, Miami (Fla.) 7
1935 Bucknell 26, Miami (Fla.) 0
1936 Catholic 20, Mississippi 19
1937 Duquesne 13, Mississippi State 12
1938 Auburn 6, Michigan State 0
1939 Tennessee 17, Oklahoma 0
1940 Georgia Tech 21, Missouri 7
1941 Mississippi State 14, Georgetown 7
1942 Georgia 40, Texas Christian 26
1943 Alabama 37, Boston College 21
1944 Louisiana State 19, Texas A&M 14
1945 Tulsa 26, Georgia Tech 12
1946 Miami (Fla.) 13, Holy Cross 6
1947 Rice 8, Tennessee 0
1948 Georgia Tech 20, Kansas 14
1949 Texas 41, Georgia 28
1950 Santa Clara 21, Kentucky 13
1951 Clemson 15, Miami (Fla.) 14
1952 Georgia Tech 17, Baylor 14
1953 Alabama 61, Syracuse 6
1954 Oklahoma 7, Maryland 0
1955 Duke 34, Nebraska 7
1956 Oklahoma 20, Maryland 6
1957 Colorado 27, Clemson 21
1958 Oklahoma 48, Duke 21
1959 Oklahoma 21, Syracuse 6
1960 Georgia 14, Missouri 0
1961 Missouri 21, Navy 14
1962 Louisiana State 25, Colorado 7
1963 Alabama 17, Oklahoma 0
1964 Nebraska 13, Auburn 7
1965 Texas 21, Alabama 17
1966 Alabama 39, Nebraska 28
1967 Florida 27, Georgia Tech 12
1968 Oklahoma 26, Tennessee 24
1969 Penn State 15, Kansas 14
1970 Penn State 10, Missouri 3

1971 Nebraska 17, Louisiana State 12
1972 Nebraska 38, Alabama 6
1973 Nebraska 40, Notre Dame 6
1974 Penn State 16, Louisiana State 9
1975 Notre Dame 13, Alabama 11
1976 Oklahoma 14, Michigan 6
1977 Ohio State 27, Colorado 10
1978 Arkansas 31, Oklahoma 6
1979 Oklahoma 31, Nebraska 24
1980 Oklahoma 24, Florida State 7
1981 Oklahoma 18, Florida State 17
1982 Clemson 22, Nebraska 15
1983 Nebraska 21, Louisiana State 20
1984 Miami 31, Nebraska 30
1985 Washington 28, Oklahoma 17
1986 Oklahoma 25, Penn St. 10
1987 Oklahoma 42, Arkansas 8
1988 Miami 20, Oklahoma 14
1989 Miami 23, Nebraska 3
1990 Notre Dame 21, Colorado 6
1991 Colorado 10, Notre Dame 9
1992 Miami 22, Nebraska 0
1993 Florida State 27, Nebraska 14
1994 Florida State 18, Nebraska 16
1995 Nebraska 24, Miami 17

Sugar Bowl
(At New Orleans)
1935 Tulane 20, Temple 14
1936 Texas Christian 3, Louisiana State 2
1937 Santa Clara 21, Louisiana State 14
1938 Santa Clara 6, Louisiana State 0
1939 Texas Christian 15, Carnegie Tech 7
1940 Texas A & M 14, Tulane 13
1941 Boston College 19, Tennessee 13
1942 Fordham 2, Missouri 0
1943 Tennessee 14, Tulsa 7
1944 Georgia Tech 20, Tulsa 18
1945 Duke 29, Alabama 26
1946 Oklahoma A & M 33, St. Mary's (Calif.) 13
1947 Georgia 20, North Carolina 10
1948 Texas 27, Alabama 7
1949 Oklahoma 14, North Carolina 6
1950 Oklahoma 35, Louisiana State 0
1951 Kentucky 13, Oklahoma 7
1952 Maryland 28, Tennessee 13
1953 Georgia Tech 24, Mississippi 7
1954 Georgia Tech 42, West Virginia 19
1955 Navy 21, Mississippi 0
1956 Georgia Tech 7, Pittsburgh 0
1957 Baylor 13, Tennessee 7
1958 Mississippi 39, Texas 7
1959 Louisiana State 7, Clemson 0
1960 Mississippi 21, Louisiana State 0
1961 Mississippi 14, Rice 6
1962 Alabama 10, Arkansas 3
1963 Mississippi 17, Arkansas 13
1964 Alabama 12, Mississippi 7
1965 Louisiana State 13, Syracuse 10
1966 Missouri 20, Florida 18
1967 Alabama 34, Nebraska 7
1968 Louisiana State 20, Wyoming 13
1969 Arkansas 16, Georgia 2
1970 Mississippi 27, Arkansas 22
1971 Tennessee 34, Air Force Academy 13

1972 Oklahoma 40, Auburn 22
1973 Oklahoma 14, Penn State 0
1974 Notre Dame 24, Alabama 23
1975 Nebraska 13, Florida 10
1976 Alabama 13, Penn State 6
1977 Pittsburgh 27, Georgia 3
1978 Alabama 35, Ohio State 6
1979 Alabama 14, Penn State 7
1980 Alabama 24, Arkansas 9
1981 Georgia 17, Notre Dame 10
1982 Pittsburgh 24, Georgia 20
1983 Penn State 27, Georgia 23
1984 Auburn 9, Michigan 7
1985 Nebraska 28, LSU 10
1986 Tennessee 35, Miami, Fla. 7
1987 Nebraska 30, Louisiana State 15
1988 Syracuse 16, Auburn 16 (tie)
1989 Florida State 13, Auburn 7
1990 Miami 33, Alabama 25
1991 Tennessee 23, Virginia 22
1992 Notre Dame 39, Florida 28
1993 Alabama 34, Miami 13
1994 Florida 41, West Virginia 7
1995 Florida State 23, Florida 17

Cotton Bowl
(At Dallas)
1937 Texas Christian 16, Marquette 6
1938 Rice 28, Colorado 14
1939 St. Mary's (Calif.) 20, Texas Tech. 13
1940 Clemson 6, Boston College 3
1941 Texas A & M 13, Fordham 12
1942 Alabama 29, Texas A & M 21
1943 Texas 14, Georgia Tech 7
1944 Randolph Field 7, Texas 7
1945 Oklahoma A & M 34, Texas Christian 0
1946 Texas 40, Missouri 27
1947 Louisiana State 0, Arkansas 0
1948 So. Methodist 13, Penn State 13
1949 So. Methodist 21, Oregon 13
1950 Rice 27, North Carolina 13
1951 Tennessee 20, Texas 14
1952 Kentucky 20, Texas Christian 7
1953 Texas 16, Tennessee 0
1954 Rice 28, Alabama 6
1955 Georgia Tech 14, Arkansas 6
1956 Mississippi 14, Texas Christian 13
1957 Texas Christian 28, Syracuse 27
1958 Navy 20, Rice 7
1959 Air Force 0, Texas Christian 0
1960 Syracuse 23, Texas 14
1961 Duke 7, Arkansas 6
1962 Texas 12, Mississippi 7
1963 Louisiana State 13, Texas 0
1964 Texas 28, Navy 6
1965 Arkansas 10, Nebraska 7
1966 Louisiana State 14, Arkansas 7
1967 Georgia 24, So. Methodist 9
1968 Texas A & M 20, Alabama 16
1969 Texas 36, Tennessee 13
1970 Texas 21, Notre Dame 17
1971 Notre Dame 24, Texas 11
1972 Penn State 30, Texas 6
1973 Texas 17, Alabama 13
1974 Nebraska 19, Texas 3
1975 Penn State 41, Baylor 20
1976 Arkansas 31, Georgia 10
1977 Houston 30, Maryland 21
1978 Notre Dame 38, Texas 10

1979	Notre Dame 35, Houston 34	1955	Auburn 33, Baylor 13	1980	North Carolina 17, Michigan 15
1980	Houston 17, Nebraska 14	1956	Vanderbilt 25, Auburn 13	1981	Pittsburgh 37, South Carolina 9
1981	Alabama 30, Baylor 2	1957	Georgia Tech 21, Pittsburgh 14	1982	North Carolina 31, Arkansas 27
1982	Texas 14, Alabama 12	1958	Tennessee 3, Texas A & M 0	1983	Florida State 31, West Virginia
1983	South. Methodist 7, Pittsburgh 3	1959	Mississippi 7, Florida 3		12
1984	Georgia 10, Texas 9	1960	Arkansas 14, Georgia Tech 7	1984	Florida 14, Iowa 6
1985	Boston College 45, Houston 28	1961	Florida 13, Baylor 12	1985	Oklahoma St. 21, South Carolina
1986	Texas A & M 36, Auburn 16	1962	Penn State 30, Georgia Tech 15		14
1987	Ohio State 28, Texas A & M 12	1963	Florida 17, Penn State 7	1986	Florida State 34, Oklahoma St.
1988	Texas A & M 35, Notre Dame 10	1964	No. Carolina 35, Air Force 0		23
1989	UCLA 17, Arkansas 3	1965	Florida State 36, Oklahoma 19	1987	Clemson 27, Stanford 21
1990	Tennessee 31, Arkansas 27	1966	Georgia Tech 31, Texas Tech 21	1988	LSU 30, South Carolina 13
1991	Miami 46, Texas 3	1967	Tennessee 18, Syracuse 12	1989	Georgia 34, Michigan St. 27
1992	Florida State 10, Texas A&M 2	1968	Penn State 17, Florida State 17	1990	Clemson 27, West Virginia 7
1993	Notre Dame 28, Texas A&M 3	1969	Missouri 35, Alabama 10	1991	Michigan 35, Mississippi 3
1994	Notre Dame 24, Texas A&M 21	1970	Florida 14, Tennessee 13	1992	Oklahoma 38, Virginia 14
1995	Southern California 55, Texas	1971	Auburn 35, Mississippi 28	1993	Florida 27, No. Carolina St. 10
	Tech 14	1972	Georgia 7, North Carolina 3	1994	Alabama 24, No. Carolina 10
		1973	Auburn 24, Colorado 3	1995	Tennessee 45, Virginia Tech 23
		1974	Texas Tech 28, Tennessee 19		
		1975	Auburn 27, Texas 3		
Gator Bowl		1976	Maryland 13, Florida 0		
(At Jacksonville, Fla.)		1977	Notre Dame 20, Penn State 9		
1953	Florida 14, Tulsa 13	1978	Pittsburgh 34, Clemson 3		
1954	Texas Tech 35, Auburn 13	1979	Clemson 17, Ohio State 15		

RESULTS OF OTHER 1994 SEASON BOWL GAMES

Alamo (San Antonio, Texas, Dec. 31, 1994)—Washington State 10, Baylor 3

Aloha (Honolulu, Hawaii, Dec. 25, 1994)—Boston College 12, Kansas State 7

Carquest Classic (Miami, Fla., Jan. 2, 1995)—South Carolina 24, West Virginia 21

Citrus (Orlando, Fla., Jan. 2, ,1995)—Alabama 24, Ohio State 17

Copper (Tucson, Ariz., Dec. 29, 1994)—Brigham Young 31, Oklahoma 6

Fiesta (Tempe, Ariz., Jan. 2, 1995)—Colorado 41, Notre Dame 24

Freedom (Anaheim, Calif., Dec. 27, 1994)—Utah 16, Arizona 13

Hall of Fame (Tampa, Fla., Jan. 2, 1995)—Wisconsin 34,

Duke 20

Heritage (Atlanta, Ga., Dec. 30, 1994)—South Carolina State 31, Grambling 27

Holiday (San Diego, Calif., Dec. 30, 1994)—Michigan 24, Colorado State 14

Independence (Shreveport, La., Dec. 28, 1994)—Virginia 20, Texas Christian 10

Las Vegas (Las Vegas, Nev., Dec. 15, 1994)—Nevada-Las Vegas 52, Cent. Michigan 24

Liberty (Memphis, Tenn., Dec. 31, 1994)—Illinois 30, East Carolina 0

Peach (Atlanta, Ga., Jan. 1, 1995)—North Carolina State 28, Mississippi State 24

Sun (El Paso, Texas, Dec. 30, 1994)—Texas 35, North Carolina 31

HEISMAN MEMORIAL TROPHY WINNERS

The Heisman Memorial Trophy is presented annually by the Downtown Athletic club of New York City to the nation's outstanding college football player, as determined by a poll of sportswriters and sportscasters.

1935	Jay Berwanger, Chicago	1956	Paul Hornung, Notre Dame	1977	Earl Campbell, Texas
1936	Larry Kelley, Yale	1957	John Crow, Texas A & M	1978	Billy Sims, Oklahoma
1937	Clinton Frank, Yale	1958	Pete Dawkins, Army	1979	Charles White, Southern
1938	Davey O'Brien, Texas Christian	1959	Billy Cannon, Louisiana State		California
		1960	Joe Bellino, Navy	1980	George Rogers, South Carolina
1939	Nile Kinnick, Iowa	1961	Ernie Davis, Syracuse		ina
1940	Tom Harmon, Michigan	1962	Terry Baker, Oregon State	1981	Marcus Allen, Southern California
1941	Bruce Smith, Minnesota	1963	Roger Staubach, Navy		ifornia
1942	Frank Sinkwich, Georgia	1964	John Huarte, Notre Dame	1982	Hershel Walker, Georgia
1943	Angelo Bertelli, Notre Dame	1965	Mike Garrett, Southern California	1983	Mike Rozier, Nebraska
1944	Leslie Horvath, Ohio State		fornia	1984	Doug Flutie, Boston College
1945	Felix Blanchard, Army	1966	Steve Spurrier, Florida	1985	Bo Jackson, Auburn
1946	Glenn Davis, Army	1967	Gary Beban, U.C.L.A.	1986	Vinnie Testeverde, Miami
1947	Johnny Lujack, Notre Dame	1968	O.J. Simpson, Southern California	1987	Tim Brown, Notre Dame
1948	Doak Walker, So. Methodist		fornia	1988	Barry Sanders, Oklahoma State
1949	Leon Hart, Notre Dame	1969	Steve Owens, Oklahoma		State
1950	Vic Janowicz, Ohio State	1970	Jim Plunkett, Stanford	1989	Andre Ware, Houston
1951	Dick Kazmaier, Princeton	1971	Pat Sullivan, Auburn	1990	Ty Detmer, Brigham Young
1952	Billy Vessels, Oklahoma	1972	Johnny Rodgers, Nebraska	1991	Desmond Howard, Michigan
1953	Johnny Lattner, Notre Dame	1973	John Cappelletti, Penn State	1992	Gino Torretta, Miami
1954	Alan Ameche, Wisconsin	1974–75	Archie Griffin, Ohio State	1993	Charlie Ward, Florida State
1955	Howard Cassady, Ohio State	1976	Tony Dorsett, Pittsburgh	1994	Rashaan Salaam, Colorado

1994 N.C.A.A. CHAMPIONSHIP PLAYOFFS

DIVISION I-AA

Quarterfinals
(Dec. 3, 1994)

Youngstown St. 18, East. Kentucky 15
Montana 30, NcNeese State 28
Marshall 28, James Madison 21 (OT)
Boise State 17, Appalachian State 14

Semifinals
(Dec. 10, 1994)

Youngstown State 28, Montana 9
Boise State 28, Marshall 24

Championship
(Dec. 17, 1994 at Huntington, WV)

Youngstown State 28, Boise State 14

DIVISION II

Quarterfinals
(Nov. 26, 1994)

Indiana, Pa. 21, Ferris State, Mich. 17
Texas A&M–Kingsville 21, Portland
State, Ore. 16
North Dakota 14, North Dakota State 7
No. Alabama 27, Valdosta State, Ga. 24

Semifinals
(Dec. 3, 1994)

Texas A&M–Kingsville 46, Indiana 20
North Alabama 35, North Dakota 7

Championship
(Dec. 10, 1994 at Florence, Ala.)

No. Alabama 16, Tex. A&M–Kingsville 10

DIVISION III

Quarterfinals
(Nov. 26, 1994)

Albion, Mich. 34, Mount Union, Ohio 33
St. John's, Minn. 42, Wartburg, Iowa 14
Washington & Jefferson, Pa. 37, Wid-
ener, Pa. 21
Ithaca, N.Y. 22, Plymouth State, N.H. 7

Semifinals
(Dec. 3, 1994)

Washington & Jefferson 23, Ithaca 19
Albion 19, St. John's 16

Championship
(Dec. 10, 1994, at Salem, Va.)

Albion 38, Washington & Jefferson 15

1994 NATIONAL ASSOCIATION OF INTERCOLLEGIATE ATHLETICS CHAMPIONSHIPS

DIVISION I

Quarterfinals
(Nov. 26, 1994)

Arkansas–Pine Bluff 21, Central State, Ohio 14
Northeastern State, Okla. 14, Moorehead State, Minn. 7
Langston, Okla. 56, Arkansas Tech. 42
Western Montana 48, Glenville State, W. Va. 38

Semifinals
(Dec. 3, 1994)

Northeastern State, Okla. 3, Langston, Okla. 0
Arkansas–Pine Bluff 60, Western Montana 53 (OT)

Championship
(Dec. 10, 1994 at Pine Bluff, Ark.)

Northeastern State 13, Arkansas–Pine Bluff 12

DIVISION II

Quarterfinals
(Dec. 3, 1994)

Westminster, Pa. 42, Tiffin, Ohio 14
Lambuth, Tenn. 57, Hardin–Simmons, Texas 54
Northwestern Iowa 28, Minot State, S.D. 26
Pacific Lutheran, Wash. 25, Western Washington 20

Semifinals
(Dec. 10, 1994)

Westminster, Pa. 46, Lambuth, Tenn. 6
Pacific Lutheran, Wash. 28, Northwestern Iowa 7

Championship
(Dec. 17, 1994)

Westminster 27, Pacific Lutheran 7

COLLEGE FOOTBALL HALL OF FAME

(P.O. Box 11146, South Bend, Indiana) (Date given is player's last year of competition)

Players

Abell, Earl—Colgate, 1915
Agase, Alex—Purdue/Illinois, 1946
Agganis, Harry—Boston Univ., 1952
Albert, Frank—Stanford, 1941
Aldrich, Chas. (Ki)—T.C.U., 1938
Aldrich, Malcolm—Yale, 1921
Alexander, John—Syracuse, 1920
Alworth, Lance—Arkansas, 1961
Ameche, Alan (Horse)—Wisconsin, 1954
Amling, Warren—Ohio State, 1946
Anderson, Dick—Colorado, 1967
Anderson, Donny—Texas Tech, 1965
Andderson, H. (Hunk)—Notre Dame, 1921
Atkins, Doug—Tennessee, 1952
Babich, Bob—Miami–Ohio, 1968
Bacon, C. Everett—Wesleyan, 1912
Bagnell, Francis (Reds)—Penn, 1950
Baker, Hobart (Hobey)—Princeton, 1913
Baker, John—So. Calif., 1931
Baker, Terry—Oregon State, 1962
Ballin, Harold—Princeton, 1914
Banker, Bill—Tulane, 1929
Banonis, Vince—Detroit, 1941
Barnes, Stanley—S. California, 1921
Barrett, Charles—Cornell, 1915
Baston, Bert—Minnesota, 1916
Battles, Cliff—W. Va. Wesleyan, 1931
Baugh, Sammy—Texas Christian U., 1936
Baughan, Maxie—Georgia Tech, 1959
Bausch, James—Kansas, 1930
Beagle, Ron—Navy, 1955
Beban, Gary—UCLA, 1967
Bechtol, Hub—Texas Tech, 1946
Beckett, John—Oregon, 1916
Bednariok, Chuck—Pennsylvania 1948
Behm, Forrest—Nebraska, 1940
Bell, Bobby—Minnesota, 1962
Bellino, Joe—Navy, 1960

Below, Marty—Wisconsin, 1923
Benbrook, A.—Michigan, 1911
Bertelli, A.—Notre Dame, 1943
Berry, Charlie—Lafayette, 1924
Berwanger, John (Jay)—Chicago, 1935
Bettencourt, Larry—St. Mary's, 1927
Biletnikoff, Fred—Florida State, 1964
Blanchard, Felix (Doc)—Army, 1946
Bock, Ed—Iowa State, 1938
Bomar, Lynn—Vanderbilt, 1924
Bomeisler, Doug (Bo)—Yale, 1913
Booth, Albie–Yale, 1931
Borries, Fred—Navy, 1934
Bosely, Bruce—West Virginia, 1955
Bosseler, Don—Miami, Fla., 1956
Bottari, Vic—California, 1939
Boynton, Ben—Williams, 1920
Bozis, A.—Georgetown, 1941
Brewer, Charles—Harvard, 1895
Bright, John—Drake, 1951
Brodie, John—Stanford, 1956
Brooke, George—Pennsylvania, 1895
Brown, Bob—Nebraska, 1963
Brown, George—Navy, San Diego St., 1947
Brown, Gordon—Yale, 1900
Brown, Jim—Syracuse, 1956
Brown, John, Jr.—Navy, 1913
Brown, Johnny Mack—Alabama, 1925
Brown, Raymond (Tay)—So. Calif., 1932
Bunker, Paul—Army, 1902
Burford, Chris—Stanford, 1959
Burton, Ron—Northwestern, 1956
Butkus, Dick—Illinois, 1964
Butler, Robert—Wisconsin, 1912
Cafego, George—Tennessee, 1939
Cagle, Chris—SW La. / Army, 1929
Cain, John—Alabama, 1932
Cameron, Eddie—Wash. & Lee, 1924
Campbell, David C.—Harvard, 1901
Campbell, Earl—Texas, 1977

Cannon, Billy—L.S.U., 1959
Cannon, Jack—Notre Dame, 1929
Cappelletti, John—Penn State, 1973
Carideo, Frank—Notre Dame, 1930
Caroline, J.C.—Illinois, 1954
Carney, Charles—Illinois, 1921
Carpenter, Bill—Army, 1959
Carpenter, C. Hunter—VPI, 1905
Carroll, Charles—Washington, 1928
Casanova, Tommy—Louisiana State, 1971
Casey, Edward L.—Harvard, 1919
Cassady, Howard—Ohio State, 1955
Chamberlain, Guy—Nebraska, 1915
Chapman, Sam—Cal.–Berkeley, 1938
Chappuis, Bob—Michigan, 1947
Christman, Paul—Missouri, 1940
Clark, Earl (Dutch)—Colo. College, 1929
Cleary, Paul—USC, 1947
Clevenger, Zora—Indiana, 1903
Cloud, Jack—William & Mary, 1948
Cochran, Gary—Princeton, 1895
Cody, Josh—Vanderbilt, 1920
Coleman, Don—Mich. State, 1951
Conerly, Chuck—Mississippi, 1947
Connor, George—Notre Dame, 1947
Corbin, W.—Yale, 1888
Corbus, William—Stanford, 1933
Cowan, Hector—Princeton, 1889
Coy, Edward H. (Tad)—Yale, 1909
Crawford, Fred—Duke, 1933
Crow, John D.—Texas A&M, 1957
Crowley, James—Notre Dame, 1924
Csonka, Larry—Syracuse, 1967
Cutter, Slade—Navy, 1934
Czarobski, Ziggie—Notre Dame, 1947
Dale, Carroll—Virginia Tech, 1959
Dalrymple, Gerald—Tulane, 1931
Daniell, James—Ohio State, 1941
Dalton, John—Navy, 1912

Coaches

Bill Alexander
Dr. Ed Anderson
Ike Armstrong
Earl Banks
Harry Baujan
Matty Bell

Hugo Bezdek
Dana X. Bible
Bernie Bierman
Bob Blackman
Earl (Red) Blaik
Frank Broyles

Paul "Bear" Bryant
Charles W. Caldwell
Walter Camp
Len Casanova
Frank Cavanaugh
Richard Colman

Fritz Crisler
Duffy Daugherty
Bob Devaney
Dan Devine
Gil Dobie
Bobby Dodd

Michael Donohue
Vince Dooley
Gus Dorais
Bill Edwards
Charles (Rip) Engle
Don Faurot

Jake Gaither	L. (Biff) Jones	L.R. (Dutch) Meyer	Doyt LPerry	Amos A. Stagg
Sid Gillman	Thomas (Tad) Jones	Bernie Moore	James Phalea	Jock Sutherland
Ernest Godfrey	Ralph (Shug) Jordan	Scrappy Moore	Tommy Prothro	James Tatum
Ray Graves	Andy Kerr	Jack Mollenkopf	John Ralston	Frank W. Thomas
Andy Gustafson	Frank Kush	Ray Morrison	E.N. Robinson	Thad Vann
Jack Harding	Frank Leahy	George A. Munger	Knute Rockne	John H. Vaught
Edward K. Hall	George E. Little	Clarence Munn	E.L. (Dick) Romney	Wallace Wade
Richard Harlow	Lou Little	Frank Murray	William W. Roper	Lynn Waldorf
Jesse Harper	El (Slip) Madigan	William Murray	Darrell Royal	Glenn (Pop) Warner
Percy Haughton	Dave Maurer	Ed (Hooks) Mylin	George F. Sanford	E.E. (Tad) Wieman
Woody Hayes	Charley McClendon	Earle (Greasy) Neale	Bo Schembechler	John W. Wilce
John W. Heisman	Herbert McCracken	Jess Neely	Francis A. Schmidt	Bud Wilkinson
R.A. (Bob) Higgins	Daniel McGugin	David Nelson	Floyd (Ben) Schwartz-	Henry L. Williams
Orin E. Hollingberry	John McKay	Robert Neyland	walder	George W. Woodruff
Frank Howard	Allyn McKeen	Homer Norton	Clark Shaughnessy	Warren Woodson
William Ingram	DeOrmond (Tuss)	Frank (Buck) O'Neill	Buck Shaw	Fielding H. Yost
Morley Jennings	McLaughry	Bennie Owen	Andrew L. Smith	Robert Zuppke
Howard Jones	John Merritt	Ara Parseghian	Carl Snavely	

Professional Football

NATIONAL FOOTBALL LEAGUE FINAL STANDINGS 1994

AMERICAN FOOTBALL CONFERENCE

Eastern Division

	W	L	T	Pct	Pts	Op
Miami Dolphins[1]	10	6	0	.625	389	327
New England Patriots[2]	10	6	0	.625	351	312
Indianapolis Colts	8	8	0	.500	307	320
Buffalo Bills	7	9	0	.437	340	356
New York Jets	6	10	0	.375	264	320

Central Division

	W	L	T	Pct	Pts	Op
Pittsburgh Steelers[1]	12	4	0	.750	316	234
Cleveland Browns[2]	11	5	0	.687	340	204
Cincinnati Bengals	3	13	0	.187	276	406
Houston Oilers	2	14	0	.125	226	352

Western Division

	W	L	T	Pct	Pts	Op
San Diego Chargers[1]	11	5	0	.687	381	306
Kansas City Chiefs[2]	9	7	0	.563	319	298
L.A. Raiders	9	7	0	.563	303	327
Denver Broncos	7	9	0	.437	347	396
Seattle Seahawks	6	10	0	.375	287	323

1. Division champion. 2. Wild card qualifier for playoffs. Playoffs: Miami 27, Kansas City 17; Cleveland 20, New England 13; Pittsburgh 29, Cleveland 9; San Diego 22, Miami 21; San Diego 17, Pittsburgh 13.

NATIONAL FOOTBALL CONFERENCE

Eastern Division

	W	L	T	Pct	Pts	Op
Dallas Cowboys[1]	12	4	0	.750	414	248
New York Giants	9	7	0	.563	279	305
Arizona Cardinals	8	8	0	.500	235	267
Philadelphia Eagles	7	9	0	.437	308	308
Washington Redskins	3	13	0	.187	320	412

Central Division

	W	L	T	Pct	Pts	Op
Minnesota Vikings[1]	10	6	0	.625	356	314
Detroit Lions[2]	9	7	0	.563	357	342
Green Bay Packers[2]	9	7	0	.563	382	387
Chicago Bears[2]	9	7	0	.563	271	307
Tampa Bay Buccaneers	6	10	0	.375	251	351

Western Division

	W	L	T	Pct	Pts	Op
San Francisco 49ers[1]	13	3	0	.812	505	296
Atlanta Falcons	7	9	0	.437	317	385
New Orleans Saints	7	9	0	.437	348	407
L.A. Rams	4	12	0	.250	286	365

1. Division champion. 2. Wild card qualifier for playoffs. Playoffs: Green Bay 16, Detroit 12; Chicago 35, Minnesota 18; San Francisco 44, Chicago 15; Dallas 35, Green Bay 9; San Francisco 38, Dallas 28.

LEAGUE CHAMPIONSHIP—SUPER BOWL XXIX

(January 29, 1995, Joe Robbie Stadium, Miami, Fla. Attendance: 74,107, no shows: 0. Time: 3:36)

Scoring

	1st Q	2nd Q	3rd Q	4th Q	Final
San Diego (AFC)	7	3	8	8	26
San Francisco (NFC)	14	14	14	7	49

First Quarter: San Francisco—TD, Jerry Rice, 44-yd pass from Steve Young (Doug Brien kick) 1:24; San Francisco—TD, Ricky Watters 51-yd pass from Steve Young (Doug Brien kick) 4:55; San Diego—TD, Natrone Means 1-yd run (John Carney kick) 12:16.

Second Quarter: San Francisco—TD, William Floyd, 5-yd pass from Steve Young (Doug Brien kick) 1:58; San Francisco—TD, Ricky Watters 8-yd pass from Steve Young (Doug Brien kick) 10:16; San Diego—FG, John Carney, 31-yd, 13:16.

Third Quarter: San Francisco—TD, Ricky Watters, 9-yd run (Doug Brien kick) 5:25; San Francisco—TD, Jerry Rice, 15-yd pass from Steve Young (Doug Brien kick) 11:42; San Diego—TD, Andre Coleman, 98-yd kickoff return (Stan Humphries pass to Mark Seay for two-point conversion) 11.59.

Fourth Quarter: San Francisco—TD, Jerry Rice, 7-yd pass from Steve Young (Doug Brien kick) 1:11; San Diego—TD, Tony Martin, 30-yd pass from Stan Humphries (Stan Humphries pass to Alfred Pupunu for two-point conversion) 12:35.

Statistics of the Game

	San Diego	San Francisco
First downs	20	28
Total net yards	354	449
Net yards rushing	67	133
Net yards passing	287	316

Individual Statistics

Rushing: SAN DIEGO—Natrone Means 13–33, Ronnie Harmon 2–10, Shawn Jefferson 1–10, Gale Gilbert 1–8, Eric Bieniemy 1–3, Stan Humphries 1–3. SAN FRANCISCO—Steve Young 5–49, Ricky Watters 15–47, William Floyd 9–32, Jerry Rice 1–0, Dexter Carter 2–minus 5.

Passing: SAN DIEGO—Stan Humphries 24–49 for 275 yd, 2 interceptions, 1 touchdown; Gale Gilbert 3–6 for 30 yd, 1 interception, 0 touchdowns; SAN FRANCISCO—Steve Young 24–36 for 325 yd, 0 interceptions, 6 touchdowns; Bill Musgrave 1–1 for 6 yd, 0 interceptions, 0 touchdowns; Elvis Grbac 0–1 for 0 yards, 0 interceptions, 0 touchdowns.

Receiving: SAN DIEGO—Ronnie Harmon 8–68, Mark Seay 7–75, Mark Martin 2–59, Shawn Jefferson 2–15, Eric Bieniemy 1–33, Natrone Means 1–4, Duane Young 1–3; SAN FRANCISCO—Jerry Rice 10–149, John Taylor 4–43, William Floyd 4–26, Ricky Watters 3–61, Brent Jones 2–41, Ted Popson 1–6, Ed McCaffrey 1–5.

Officials: Referee—Jerry Markbreit. Umpire—Ron Botchan. Head linesman—Don Phares. Line judge—Ron Baynes. Back judge—Tim Millis. Side judge—Tom Fincken. Field judge—Jack Vaughan.

SUPER BOWLS I–XXIX

Game	Date	Winner	Loser	Site	Attendance
XXIX	Jan. 29, 1995	San Francisco (NFC) 49	San Diego (AFC) 26	Joe Robbie Stadium, Miami, Fla.	74,107
XXVIII	Jan. 30, 1994	Dallas (NFC) 30	Buffalo (AFC) 13	Georgia Dome, Atlanta, Ga.	72,817
XXVII	Jan. 31, 1993	Dallas (NFC) 52	Buffalo (AFC) 17	Rose Bowl, Pasadena, Calif.	98,374
XXVI	Jan. 26, 1992	Washington (NFC) 37	Buffalo (AFC) 24	Metrodome, Minneapolis, Minn.	63,130
XXV	Jan. 27, 1991	Giants (NFC) 20	Buffalo (AFC) 19	Tampa Stadium, Tampa, Fla.	73,813
XXIV	Jan. 28, 1990	San Francisco (NFC) 55	Denver (AFC) 10	Superdome, New Orleans	72,919
XXIII	Jan. 22, 1989	San Francisco (NFC) 20	Cincinnati (AFC) 16	Joe Robbie Stadium, Miami, Fla.	75,179
XXII	Jan. 31, 1988	Washington (NFC) 42	Denver (AFC) 10	Jack Murphy Stadium, San Diego, Calif.	73,302
XXI	Jan. 25, 1987	Giants (NFC) 39	Denver (AFC) 20	Rose Bowl, Pasadena, Calif.	101,063
XX	Jan. 26, 1986	Chicago (NFC) 46	New England (AFC) 10	Superdome, New Orleans	73,818
XIX	Jan. 20, 1985	San Francisco (NFC) 38	Miami (AFC) 16	Stanford Stadium, Palo Alto, Calif.	84,059
XVIII	Jan. 22, 1984	Los Angeles Raiders (AFC) 38	Washington (NFC) 9	Tampa Stadium, Tampa, Fla	72,920
XVII	Jan. 30, 1983	Washington (NFC) 27	Miami (AFC) 17	Rose Bowl, Pasadena, Calif.	103,667
XVI	Jan. 24, 1982	San Francisco (NFC) 26	Cincinnati (AFC) 21	Silverdome, Pontiac, Mich.	81,270
XV	Jan. 25, 1981	Oakland (AFC) 27	Philadelphia (NFC) 10	Superdome, New Orleans	75,500
XIV	Jan. 20, 1980	Pittsburgh (AFC) 31	Los Angeles (NFC) 19	Rose Bowl, Pasadena	103,985
XIII	Jan. 21, 1979	Pittsburgh (AFC) 35	Dallas (NFC) 31	Orange Bowl, Miami	79,484
XII	Jan. 15, 1978	Dallas (NFC) 27	Denver (AFC) 10	Superdome, New Orleans	75,583
XI	Jan. 9, 1977	Oakland (AFC) 32	Minnesota (NFC) 14	Rose Bowl, Pasadena	103,424
X	Jan. 18, 1976	Pittsburgh (AFC) 21	Dallas (NFC) 17	Orange Bowl, Miami	80,187
IX	Jan. 12, 1975	Pittsburgh (AFC) 16	Minnesota (NFC) 6	Tulane Stadium, New Orleans	80,997
VIII	Jan. 13, 1974	Miami (AFC) 24	Minnesota (NFC) 7	Rice Stadium, Houston	71,882
VII	Jan. 14, 1973	Miami (AFC) 14	Washington (NFC) 7	Memorial Coliseum, Los Angeles	90,182
VI	Jan. 16, 1972	Dallas (NFC) 24	Miami (AFC) 3	Tulane Stadium, New Orleans	81,591
V	Jan. 17, 1971	Baltimore (AFC) 16	Dallas (NFC) 13	Orange Bowl, Miami	79,204
IV	Jan. 11, 1970	Kansas City (AFL) 23	Minnesota (NFL) 7	Tulane Stadium, New Orleans	80,562
III	Jan. 12, 1969	New York (AFL) 16	Baltimore (NFL) 7	Orange Bowl, Miami	75,389
II	Jan. 14, 1968	Green Bay (NFL) 33	Oakland (AFL) 14	Orange Bowl, Miami	75,546
I	Jan. 15, 1967	Green Bay (NFL) 35	Kansas City (AFL) 10	Memorial Coliseum, Los Angeles	61,946

NOTE: Super Bowls I to IV were played before the American Football League and National Football League merged into the NFL, which was divided into two conferences, the NFC and AFC.

NATIONAL LEAGUE CHAMPIONS

Year	Champion (W–L–T)
1921	Chicago Bears (Staley's) (10–1–1)
1922	Canton Bulldogs (10–0–2)
1923	Canton Bulldogs (11–0–1)
1924	Cleveland Indians (7–1–1)
1925	Chicago Cardinals (11–2–1)
1926	Frankford Yellow Jackets!(14–1–1)
1927	New York Giants (11–1–1)
1928	Providence Steamrollers (8–1–2)
1929	Green Bay Packers (12–0–1)
1930	Green Bay Packers (10–3–1)
1931	Green Bay Packers (12–2–0)
1932	Chicago Bears (7–1–6)

Year	Eastern Conference winners (W–L–T)	Western Conference winners (W–L–T)	League champion playoff results
1933	New York Giants (11–3–0)	Chicago Bears (10–2–1)	Chicago Bears 23, New York 21
1934	New York Giants (8–5–0)	Chicago Bears (13–0–0)	New York 30, Chicago Bears 13
1935	New York Giants (9–3–0)	Detroit Lions (7–3–2)	Detroit 26, New York 7
1936	Boston Redskins (7–5–0)	Green Bay Packers (10–1–1)	Green Bay 21, Boston 6
1937	Washington Redskins (8–3–0)	Chicago Bears (9–1–1)	Washington 28, Chicago Bears 21
1938	New York Giants (8–2–1)	Green Bay Packers (8–3–0)	New York 23, Green Bay 17
1939	New York Giants (9–1–1)	Green Bay Packers (9–2–0)	Green Bay 27, New York 0
1940	Washington Redskins (9–2–0)	Chicago Bears (8–3–0)	Chicago Bears 73, Washington 0
1941	New York Giants (8–3–0)	Chicago Bears (10–1–1)[2]	Chicago Bears 37, New York 9
1942	Washington Redskins (10–1–1)	Chicago Bears (11–0–0)	Washington 14, Chicago Bears 6
1943	Washington Redskins (6–3–1)[2]	Chicago Bears (8–1–1)	Chicago Bears 41, Washington 21
1944	New York Giants (8–1–1)	Green Bay Packers (8–2–0)	Green Bay 14, New York 7
1945	Washington Redskins (8–2–0)	Cleveland Rams (9–1–0)	Cleveland 15, Washington 14
1946	New York Giants (7–3–1)	Chicago Bears (8–2–1)	Chicago Bears 24, New York 14
1947	Philadelphia Eagles (8–4–0)[2]	Chicago Cardinals (9–3–0)	Chicago Cardinals 28, Philadelphia 21
1948	Philadelphia Eagles (9–2–1)	Chicago Cardinals (11–1–0)	Philadelphia 7, Chicago Cardinals 0
1949	Philadelphia Eagles (11–1–0)	Los Angeles Rams (8–2–2)	Philadelphia 14, Los Angeles 0
1950[1]	Cleveland Browns (10–2–0)[2]	Los Angeles Rams (9–3–0)[2]	Cleveland 30, Los Angeles 28
1951[1]	Cleveland Browns (11–1–0)	Los Angeles Rams (8–4–0)	Los Angeles 24, Cleveland 17
1952[1]	Cleveland Browns (8–4–0)	Detroit Lions (9–3–0)[2]	Detroit 17, Cleveland 7
1953	Cleveland Browns (11–1–0)	Detroit Lions (10–2–0)	Detroit 17, Cleveland 16
1954	Cleveland Browns (9–3–0)	Detroit Lions (9–2–1)	Cleveland 56, Detroit 10
1955	Cleveland Browns (9–2–1)	Los Angeles Rams (8–3–1)	Cleveland 38, Los Angeles 14
1956	New York Giants (8–3–1)	Chicago Bears (9–2–1)	New York 47, Chicago Bears 7
1957	Cleveland Browns (9–2–1)	Detroit Lions (8–4–0)[2]	Detroit 59, Cleveland 14

1958	New York Giants (9–3–0)[2]	Baltimore Colts (9–3–0)	Baltimore 23, New York 17[3]
1959	New York Giants (10–2–0)	Baltimore Colts (9–3–0)	Baltimore 31, New York 16
1960	Philadelphia Eagles (10–2–0)	Green Bay Packers (8–4–0)	Philadelphia 17, Green Bay 13
1961	New York Giants (10–3–1)	Green Bay Packers (11–3–0)	Green Bay 37, New York 0
1962	New York Giants (12–2–0)	Green Bay Packers (13–1–0)	Green Bay 16, New York 7
1963	New York Giants (11–3–0)	Chicago Bears (11–1–2)	Chicago 14, New York 10
1964	Cleveland Browns (10–3–1)	Baltimore Colts (12–2–0)	Cleveland 27, Baltimore 0
1965	Cleveland Browns (11–3–0)	Green Bay Packers (11–3–1)[2]	Green Bay 23, Cleveland 12
1966	Dallas Cowboys (10–3–1)	Green Bay Packers (12–2–0)	Green Bay 34, Dallas 27
1967	Dallas Cowboys (9–5–0)[2]	Green Bay Packers (9–4–1)[2]	Green Bay 21, Dallas 17
1968	Cleveland Browns (10–4–0)[2]	Baltimore Colts (13–1–0)[2]	Baltimore 34, Cleveland 0
1969	Cleveland Browns (10–3–1)2	Minnesota Vikings (12–2–0)[2]	Minnesota 27, Cleveland 7

1. League was divided into American and National Conferences, 1950–52 and again in 1970, when leagues merged. 2. Won divisional playoff. 3. Won at 8:15 of sudden death overtime period.

NATIONAL CONFERENCE CHAMPIONS

Year	Eastern Division	Central Division	Western Division	Champion
1970	Dallas Cowboys (10–4–0)	Minnesota Vikings (12–2–0)	San Francisco 49ers (10–3–1)	Dallas
1971	Dallas Cowboys (11–3–0)	Minnesota Vikings (11–3–0)	San Francisco 49ers (9–5–0)	Dallas
1972	Washington Redskins (11–3–0)	Green Bay Packers (10–4–0)	San Francisco 49ers (8–5–1)	Washington
1973	Dallas Cowboys (10–4–0)	Minnesota Vikings (12–2–0)	Los Angeles Rams (12–2–0)	Minnesota
1974	St. Louis Cardinals (10–4–0)	Minnesota Vikings (10–4–0)	Los Angeles Rams (10–4–0)	Minnesota
1975	St. Louis Cardinals (11–3–0)	Minnesota Vikings (12–2–0)	Los Angeles Rams (10–4–0)	Dallas
1976	Dallas Cowboys (11–3–0)	Minnesota Vikings (11–2–1)	Los Angeles Rams (10–3–1)	Minnesota
1977	Dallas Cowboys (12–2–0)	Minnesota Vikings (9–5–0)	Los Angeles Rams (10–4–0)	Dallas
1978	Dallas Cowboys (12–4–0)	Minnesota Vikings (8–7–1)	Los Angeles Rams (12–4–0)	Dallas
1979	Dallas Cowboys (11–5–0)	Tampa Bay Buccaneers (10–6–0)	Los Angeles Rams (9–7–0)	Los Angeles
1980	Philadelphia Eagles (12–4–0)	Minnesota Vikings (9–7–0)	Atlanta Falcons (12–4–0)	Philadelphia
1981	Dallas Cowboys (12–4–0)	Tampa Bay Buccaneers (9–7–0)	San Francisco 49ers (13–3–0)	San Francisco
1982*	Washington Redskins won conference title and also had best regular–season record (8–1–0)			
1983	Washington Redskins (14–2–0)	Detroit Lions (8–8–0)	San Francisco 49ers (10–6–0)	Washington
1984	Washington Redskins (11–5–0)	Chicago Bears (10–6–0)	San Francisco 49ers (15–1–0)	San Francisco
1985	Dallas Cowboys (10–6–0)	Chicago Bears (15–1–0)	Los Angeles Rams (11–5–0)	Chicago
1986	New York Giants (14–2–0)	Chicago Bears (14–2–0)	San Francisco 49ers (10–5–1)	New York
1987	Washington Redskins (11–4–0)	Chicago Bears (11–4–0)	San Francisco 49ers (13–2–0)	Washington
1988	Philadelphia Eagles (10–6–0)	Chicago Bears (12–4–0)	San Francisco 49ers (10–6–0)	San Francisco
1989	New York Giants (12–4–0)	Minnesota Vikings (10–6–0)	San Francisco 49ers (14–2–0)	San Francisco
1990	New York Giants (13–3–0)	Chicago Bears (11–5–0)	San Francisco 49ers (14–2–0)	New York
1991	Washington (14–2–0)	Detroit Lions (12–4–0)	New Orleans Saints (11–5–0)	Washington
1992	Dallas (13–3–0)	Minnesota (11–5–0)	San Francisco (14–2–0)	Dallas
1993	Dallas (12–4–0)	Detroit (10–6–0)	San Francisco (10–6–0)	Dallas
1994	Dallas (12–4–0)	Minnesota (10–6–0)	San Francisco (13–3–0)	San Francisco

*Schedule reduced to 9 games from usual 16, with no standings kept in Eastern, Central, and Western Divisions, because of 57–day player strike.

AMERICAN LEAGUE CHAMPIONS

Year	Eastern Division (W–L–T)	Western Division (W–L–T)	League champion, playoff results
1960	Houston Oilers (10–4–0)	Los Angeles Chargers (10–4–0)	Houston 24, Los Angeles 16
1961	Houston Oilers (10–3–1)	San Diego Chargers (12–2–0)	Houston 10, San Diego 3
1962	Houston Oilers (11–3–0)	Dallas Texans (11–3–0)	Dallas 20, Houston 17[1]
1963	Boston Patriots (8–6–1)[2]	San Diego Chargers (11–3–0)	San Diego 51, Boston 10
1964	Buffalo Bills (12–2–0)	San Diego Chargers (8–5–1)	Buffalo 20, San Diego 7
1965	Buffalo Bills (10–3–1)	San Diego Chargers (9–2–3)	Buffalo 23, San Diego 0
1966	Buffalo Bills (9–4–1)	Kansas City Chiefs (11–2–1)	Kansas City 31, Buffalo 7
1967	Houston Oilers (9–4–1)	Oakland Raiders (13–1–0)	Oakland 40, Houston 7
1968	New York Jets (11–3–0)	Oakland Raiders (12–2–0)[2]	New York 27, Oakland 23
1969	New York Jets (10–4–0)	Oakland Raiders (12–1–1)	Kansas City 17, Oakland 7[3]

1. Won at 2:45 of second sudden death overtime period. 2. Won divisional playoff. 3. Kansas City defeated New York, 13–6, and Oakland defeated Houston, 56–7, in interdivisional playoffs.

AMERICAN CONFERENCE CHAMPIONS

Year	Eastern Division	Central Division	Western Division	Champion
1970	Baltimore Colts (11–2–1)	Cincinnati Bengals (8–6–0)	Oakland Raiders (8–4–2)	Baltimore
1971	Miami Dolphins (10–3–1)	Cleveland Browns (9–5–0)	Kansas City Chiefs (10–3–1)	Miami
1972	Miami Dolphins (14–0–0)	Pittsburgh Steelers (11–3–0)	Oakland Raiders (10–3–1)	Miami
1973	Miami Dolphins (12–2–0)	Cincinnati Bengals (10–4–0)	Oakland Raiders (9–4–1)	Miami
1974	Miami Dolphins (11–3–0)	Pittsburgh Steelers (10–3–1)	Oakland Raiders (12–2–0)	Pittsburgh
1975	Baltimore Colts (10–4–0)	Pittsburgh Steelers (12–2–0)	Oakland Raiders (12–2–0)	Pittsburgh
1976	Baltimore Colts (11–3–0)	Pittsburgh Steelers (10–4–0)	Oakland Raiders (13–1–0)	Oakland
1977	Baltimore Colts (10–4–0)	Pittsburgh Steelers (9–5–0)	Denver Broncos (12–2–0)	Denver
1978	New England Patriots (11–5–0)	Pittsburgh Steelers (14–2–0)	Denver Broncos (10–6–0)	Pittsburgh
1979	Miami Dolphins (10–6–0)	Pittsburgh Steelers (12–4–0)	San Diego Chargers (12–4–0)	Pittsburgh
1980	Buffalo Bills (11–5–0)	Cleveland Browns (11–5–0)	San Diego Chargers (11–5–0)	Oakland
1981	Miami Dolphins (11–4–1)	Cincinnati Bengals (12–4–0)	San Diego Chargers (10–6–0)	Cincinnati
1982*	Miami Dolphins won the conference title, but the Los Angeles Raiders had best regular–season record (8–1–0).			
1983	Miami (12–4–0)	Pittsburgh (10–6–0)	Los Angeles Raiders (12–4–0)	Los Angeles
1984	Miami (14–2–0)	Pittsburgh (9–7–0)	Denver (13–3–0)	Miami
1985	Miami (12–4–0)	Cleveland (8–8)	Los Angeles Raiders (12–4–0)	New England
1986	New England (11–5–0)	Cleveland (12–4–0)	Denver (11–5–0)	Denver
1987	Indianapolis Colts (9–6–0)	Cleveland Browns (10–5–0)	Denver Broncos (10–4–1)	Denver
1988	Buffalo Bills (12–4–0)	Cincinnati Bengals (12–4–0)	Seattle Seahawks (9–7–0)	Cincinnati
1989	Buffalo Bills (9–7–0)	Cleveland Browns (9–6–1)	Denver Broncos (11–5–0)	Denver
1990	Buffalo Bills (13–3–0)	Cincinnati Bengals (9–7–0)	Los Angeles Raiders (12–4–0)	Buffalo
1991	Buffalo Bills (13–3–0)	Houston Oilers (11–5–0)	Denver Broncos (12–4–0)	Buffalo
1992	Miami Dolphins (11–5–0)	Pittsburgh Steelers (11–5–0)	San Diego Chargers (11–5–0)	Buffalo
1993	Buffalo (12–4–0)	Houston (12–4–0)	Kansas City (11–5–0)	Buffalo
1994	Miami Dolphins (10–6–0)	Pittsburgh Steelers (12–4–0)	San Diego Chargers (11–5–0)	San Diego

*Schedule reduced to 9 games from usual 16, with no standings kept in Eastern, Central, and Western Divisions, because of 57–day player strike.

PRO FOOTBALL HALL OF FAME

(National Football Museum, Canton, Ohio)

Teams named are those with which player is best identified; figures in parentheses indicate number of playing seasons.

Adderley, Herb, defensive back, Packers, Cowboys (12)	1961–72
Alworth, Lance, wide receiver, Chargers, Cowboys (12)	1962–72
Atkins, Doug, defensive end, Browns, Bears, Saints (17)	1953–69
Badgro, Morris, and N.Y. Americans, Giants, Bklyn. Dodgers (8)	1927, 1930–36
Barney, Lem, defensive back, Lions (11)	1967–78
Battles, Cliff, back, Redskins (6)	1932–37
Baugh, Sammy, quarterback, Redskins (16)	1936–52
Bednarik, Chuck, center–lineback, Eagles (14)	1949–62
Bell, Bert, N.F.L. founder, Eagles and Steelers, N.F.L. Commissioner	1946–59
Bell, Bobby, linebacker, Chiefs (12)	1963–74
Berry, Raymond, end, Colts (13)	1955–67
Bidwell, Charles W., owner Chicago Cardinals	1933–47
Biletnikoff, Fred, wide receiver, Raiders (14)	1965–1978
Blanda, George, quarterback–kicker, Bears, Oilers, Raiders (27)	1949–75
Blount, Mel, cornerback, Pittsburgh Steelers (14)	1970–83
Bradshaw, Terry, quarterback, Pittsburgh Steelers (14)	1970–83
Brown, Jim, fullback, Browns (9)	1957–65
Brown, Paul E., coach, Browns (1946–62), Bengals (1968–75)	1946–75
Brown, Roosevelt, tackle, Giants (13)	1953–65
Brown, Willie, cornerback, Broncos, Raiders (16)	1963–78
Buchanan, Buck, tackle, Chiefs (11)	1963–73
Butkus, Dick, linebacker, Bears (9)	1965–73
Campbell, Earl, running back, Oilers, Saints (8)	1978–85
Canadeo, Tony, back, Packers (11)	1941–52
Carr, Joe, president N.F.L. (18)	1921–39
Chamberlin, Guy, end 4 teams (9)	1919–27
Christiansen, Jack, defensive back, Lions (8)	1951–58
Clark, Earl (Dutch), Qback, Spartans, Lions (7)	1931–38
Connor, George, tackle, linebacker, Bears (8)	1948–55
Conzelman, Jimmy, Qback 5 teams (10), owner	1921–48
Csonka, Larry, back, Dolphins, Giants (11)	1968–79
Davis, Al, owner, Raiders, coach, general manager	1963–present
Davis, Willie, defensive end, Packers (12)	1960–69
Dawson, Len, quarterback, Steelers, Browns, Texans, Chiefs (19)	1957–75
Ditka, Mike, tight end, Bears, Eagles, Cowboys (12)	1961–72
Donovan, Art, defensive tackle, Colts (12)	1950–61
Dorsett, Tony, running back, Cowboys, Broncos (12)	1977–88
Driscoll, John (Paddy), Qback, Cards, Bears (11)	1919–29
Dudley, Bill, back, Steelers, Lions, Redskins (9)	1942–53
Edwards, Albert Glen (Turk), tackle, Redskins (9)	1932–40
Ewbank, Weeb, coach Colts, Jets (20)	1954–73
Fears, Tom, end, Rams (9); coach, Saints	1948–56
Finks, Jim, administrator/general manager, Vikings, Bears, Saints	1964–93
Flaherty, Ray, end, Yankees, Giants (9); coach, Redskins, Yankees (14)	1928–49
Ford, Len, end, def. end, Browns, Packers (11)	1948–58
Fouts, Dan, quarterback, Chargers (15)	1973–87
Fortmann, Daniel J., guard, Bears (8)	1936–43
Gatski, Frank, offensive lineman, Browns (12)	1946–57
George, Bill, linebacker, Bears, Rams (15)	1952–66
Gifford, Frank, back, Giants (12)	1952–64
Gillman, Sid, coach, Rams, Chargers, Oilers (18)	1955–70, 73–74
Graham, Otto, quarterback, Browns (10)	1946–55
Grange, Harold (Red), back, Bears, Yankees (9)	1925–34
Grant, Bud, coach, Vikings (18)	1967–85
Greene, Joe, defensive tackle, Steelers (13)	1968–81
Gregg, Forrest, tackle, Packers (15)	1956–71
Griese, Bob, quarterback, Dolphins (14)	1967–80
Groza, Lou, place–kicker, tackle, Browns (21)	1946–67
Guyon, Joe, back, 6 teams (8)	1919–27
Halas, George, N.F.L. founder, owner and coach, Staleys and Bears, end (11)	1919–27
Ham, Jack, linebacker, Steelers (13)	1970–82
Hannah, John, guard, Patriots (13)	1973–85
Harris, Franco, running back, Steelers, Seahawks (13)	1972–84
Healey, Ed, Tackle, Bears (8)	1920–27
Hein, Mel, center, Giants (15)	1931–45
Hendricks, Ted, linebacker, Colts, Packers, Raiders (15)	1969–83
Henry, Wilbur (Pete), tackle, Bulldogs, Giants (8)	1920–28
Herber, Arnie, Qback, Packers, Giants (13)	1930–45
Hewitt, Bill, end, Bears, Eagles (9)	1932–43
Hinkle, Clarke, fullback, Packers (10)	1932–41
Hirsch, Elroy (Crazy Legs), back, end, Rams (12)	1946–57
Hornung, Paul, running back, Packers (9)	1957–62, 64–66
Houston, Ken, def. bck, Oilers, Redskins (14)	1967–80
Hubbard, R. (Cal), tackle, Giants, Packers (9)	1927–36
Huff, Sam, linebacker, Giants, Redskins (13)	1956–67, 1969
Hunt, Lamar, Founder A.F.L., owner Texans, Chiefs	1959–
Hutson, Don, end, Packers (11)	1935–45

All-Time Blockbuster NFL Trades

Twelve for one (Oct. 12, 1989)—The Dallas Cowboys trade RB Herschel Walker to Minnesota for five players (LB Jesse Solomon, LB David Howard, CB Issiac Holt, DE Alex Stewart and RB Darrin Nelson) and seven draft picks (1st in 1992 and six conditional picks over next three years).

Eleven for one (June 13, 1952)—The LA Rams trade 11 players (FB Dick Hoerner, DB Tom Keane, DB George Sims, C Joe Reid, HB Billy Baggett, T Jack Halliday, FB Dick McKissack, LB Vic Vasicek, Richard Wilkins, Aubrey Phillips and Dave Anderson) to the Dallas Texans for the draft rights to LB Les Richter.

Nine for one (Mar. 23, 1959)—The LA Rams trade seven players (DT Frank Fuller, DT Glenn Holtzman, DT Ken Panfil, G Art Hauser, LB John Tracey, FB Larry Hickman and Don Brown), a 2nd round draft pick in the 1960 Draft and a player to be named during training camp in 1959 for All-Pro HB Ollie Matson.

Eight for one (Oct. 31, 1987)—The LA Rams trade RB Eric Dickerson to the Indianapolis Colts for two players and six draft picks in a three-way deal involving the Buffalo Bills. The Colts send the draft rights to DE Cornelius Bennett to Buffalo for RB Greg Bell and three draft picks (1st in 1988 plus 1st and 2nd round picks in '89). The Colts then send Bell and the three Buffalo picks to the Rams along with RB Owen Gill and three more draft picks (the Colts 1st and 2nd in 1988 and 1st rounder in '89) for Dickerson.

N.F.L. INDIVIDUAL LIFETIME, SEASON, AND GAME RECORDS

(American Football League records were incorporated into N.F.L. records after merger of the leagues)
Players listed in boldface were active during the 1994 season. Players listed in capital letters are members of the Pro
Football Hall of Fame. The All-America Football Conference (AAFC) existed from 1946 to 1949. The 49ers, Browns,
and Colts merged with the NFL in 1949.

All–Time Leading Touchdown Scorers
(Through 1994)

Rank	Player	Yrs	Rush.	Rec.	Returns	TD
1.	**Jerry Rice**	10	8	131	0	139
2.	JIM BROWN	9	106	20	0	126
3.	WALTER PAYTON	13	110	15	0	125
4.	**Marcus Allen**	13	98	21	1	120
5.	JOHN RIGGINS	14	104	12	0	116
6.	Lenny Moore	12	63	48	2	113
7.	DON HUTSON	11	3	99	3	105
8.	STEVE LARGENT	14	1	100	0	101
9.	FRANCO HARRIS	13	91	9	0	100
10.	Eric Dickerson	11	90	6	0	96
11.	JIM TAYLOR	10	83	10	0	93
12.	TONY DORSETT	12	77	13	1	91
12.	BOBBY MITCHELL	11	18	65	8	91
14.	LEROY KELLY	10	74	13	3	90
14.	CHARLEY TAYLOR	13	11	79	0	90
16.	DON MAYNARD	15	0	88	0	88

All–Time Leading Receivers
(Through 1994)

Rank	Player	Yrs	No.	Yds.	Avg.	TD
1.	Art Monk	15	934	12,607	13.5	68
2.	Jerry Rice	10	820	13,275	16.2	131
3.	STEVE LARGENT	14	819	13,089	16.0	100
4.	James Lofton	16	764	14,004	18.3	75
5.	Charlie Joiner	18	750	12,146	16.2	65
6.	**Andre Reed**	10	676	9,536	14.1	66
7.	Henry Ellard	12	667	11,158	16.7	54
8.	**Gary Clark**	10	662	10,331	15.6	63
9.	Ozzie Newsome	13	662	7,890	12.1	47
10.	CHARLEY TAYLOR	13	649	9,110	14.0	79
11.	**Drew Hill**	14	634	9,831	15.5	60
12.	DON MAYNARD	15	633	11,834	18.7	88
13.	RAYMOND BERRY	13	631	9,275	14.7	68
14.	**Sterling Sharpe**	7	595	8,134	13.7	65
15.	Harold Carmichael	14	590	8,985	15.2	79

All–Time Leading Passers
(Minimum 1,500 attempts. Through 1994)

Rank	Player	Yrs	Att.	Comp.	Pct. Comp.	Yds	TD	Int.	Avg. Gain	Rating
1.	**Steve Young**	10	2,429	1,546	63.6	19,869	140	68	8.18	96.8
2.	Joe Montana	15	5,391	3,409	63.2	40,551	273	139	7.52	92.3
3.	Dan Marino	12	6,049	3,604	59.6	45,173	328	185	7.47	88.2
4.	Jim Kelly	9	3,942	2,397	60.8	29,527	201	143	7.49	85.8
5.	R. STAUBACH	11	2,958	1,685	57.0	22,700	153	109	7.67	83.4
6.	**Dave Krieg**	15	4,390	2,562	58.4	32,114	231	166	7.32	83.0
7.	Neil Lomax	8	3,153	1,817	57.6	22,771	136	90	7.22	82.7
8.	S. JURGENSEN	18	4,262	2,433	57.1	32,224	255	189	7.56	82.6
9.	LEN DAWSON	19	3,741	2,136	57.1	28,711	239	183	7.67	82.6
10.	Brett Favre	4	1,580	983	62.2	10,412	70	53	6.59	82.2
11.	Ken Anderson	16	4,475	2,654	59.3	32,838	197	160	7.34	81.9
12.	**Bernie Kosar**	10	3,225	1,896	58.8	22,394	120	82	6.94	81.8
13.	**Jeff Hostetler**	9	1,506	864	57.4	10,985	54	38	7.29	81.7
14.	Danny White	13	2,950	1,761	59.7	21,959	155	132	7.44	81.7
15.	B. Esiason	11	4,291	2,440	56.9	31,874	207	153	7.43	81.6

All–Time Leading Scorers
(Through 1994)

Rank	Player	Yrs	TD	FG	PAT	Pts
1.	GEORGE BLANDA	26	9	335	943	2,002
2.	JAN STENERUD	19	0	373	580	1,699
3.	**Nick Lowery**	16	0	349	512	1,559
4.	Pat Leahy	18	0	304	558	1,470
5.	Jim Turner	16	1	304	521	1,439
6.	Mark Moseley	16	0	300	482	1,382
7.	Jim Bakken	17	0	282	534	1,380
8.	Fred Cox	15	0	282	519	1,365
9.	**Eddie Murray**	17	0	298	465	1,359
10.	Lou Groza	17	1	234	641	1,349
11.	**Gary Anderson**	13	0	309	416	1,343
12.	**Matt Bahr**	16	0	277	495	1,326
13.	**Morten Andersen**	13	0	302	412	1,318
14.	Jim Breech	14	0	243	517	1,246
15.	Chris Bahr	14	0	241	490	1,213

All–Time Leading Rushers
(Through 1994)

Rank	Player	Yrs	Att.	Yds	Avg	TDs
1.	WALTER PAYTON	13	3,838	16,726	4.4	110
2.	Eric Dickerson	11	2,996	13,259	4.4	90
3.	TONY DORSETT	12	2,936	12,739	4.3	77
4.	JIM BROWN	9	2,359	12,312	5.2	106
5.	FRANCO HARRIS	13	2,949	12,120	4.1	91
6.	JOHN RIGGINS	14	2,916	11,352	3.9	104
7.	O.J. SIMPSON	11	2,404	11,236	4.7	61
8.	Ottis Anderson	14	2,562	10,273	4.0	81
9.	**Marcus Allen**	13	2,485	10,018	4.0	98
10.	EARL CAMPBELL	8	2,187	9,407	4.3	74
11.	**Thurman Thomas**	7	2,018	8,724	4.3	48
12.	**Barry Sanders**	6	1,763	8,672	4.9	62
13.	JIM TAYLOR	10	1,941	8,597	4.4	83
14.	Joe Perry	14	1,737	8,378	4.8	53
15.	Roger Craig	11	1,991	8,189	4.1	56

Scoring

Most points scored, lifetime—2,002, George Blanda, Chicago Bears, 1949–58; Baltimore, 1950; Houston, 1960–66; Oakland, 1967–75 (9tds, 943 pat, 335 fgs).

Most points, season—176, Paul Hornung, Green Bay, 1960 (15 td, 41 pat, 15 fg).

Most points, game—40, Ernie Nevers, Chicago Cardinals, 1929 (6 td, 4 pat).

Most points, per quarter—29, Don Hutson, Green Bay, 1945 (4 td, 5 pat).

Most touchdowns, lifetime—139, Jerry Rice, San Francisco, 1985–94.

Most touchdowns, season—24, John Riggins, Washington, 1983.

Most touchdowns, game—6, Ernie Nevers, Chicago Cardinals, 1929; William Jones, Cleveland, 1951; Gale Sayers, Chicago Bears, 1965.

Most points after touchdown, lifetime—959, George Blanda, Chicago Bears, 1949–58; Baltimore, 1950; Houston, 1960–66; Oakland, 1967–75.

Most points after touchdown, game—10, Charlie Gogolak, Washington, vs. N.Y. Giants, 1966

Most consecutive points after touchdown—234, Tommy Davis, San Francisco, 1959–65.

Most points after touchdown, no misses, season—56, Danny Villanueva, Dallas, 1966; Ray Wersching, San Francisco, 1984; Chip Lohmiller, Washington, 1991.

Most field goals, lifetime—373, Jan Stenerud, Kansas City Chiefs, 1967–79; Green Bay Packers, 1980–83; Minnesota Vikings, 1984–85.

Most field goals, season—35, Ali Haji-Sheikh, N.Y. Giants, 1983; Jeff Jaeger, L.A. Raiders, 1993.

Most field goals, game—7, Jim Bakken, St. Louis, 1967; and Rick Karlis, Minnesota, 1989.

Longest field goal—63 yards, Tom Dempsey, New Orleans, 1970.

Rushing

Most yards gained, lifetime—16,726, Walter Payton, Chicago Bears, 1975–1987.

Most yards gained, season—2,105, Eric Dickerson, Los Angeles, 1984.

Most yards gained, game—275, Walter Payton, Chicago, 1977.

Most touchdowns, lifetime—110, Walter Payton, Chicago, 1975–1987.

Most touchdowns, season—24, John Riggins, Washington, 1983.

Most touchdowns, game—6, Ernie Nevers, Chicago Cardinals, 1929; Dub Jones, Cleveland Browns, 1951; Gale Sayers, Chicago Bears, 1968.

Longest run from scrimmage—99 yards, Tony Dorsett, Dallas, Jan. 3, 1983.

Passing

Most touchdown passes, lifetime—342, Fran Tarkenton, Minnesota, 1961–66, 72–78; New York Giants, 1967–71.

Most touchdown passes, season—48, Dan Marino, Miami, 1984.

Most touchdown passes, game—7, Sid Luckman, Chicago Bears, 1943; Adrian Burk, Philadelphia, 1954; George Blanda, Houston, 1961; Y.A. Tittle, New York Giants, 1963; Joe Kapp, Minnesota, 1969.

Most consecutive games, touchdown passes—47, John Unitas, Baltimore, 1956–60.

Most consecutive passes attempted, none intercepted—308, Bernie Kosar, Cleveland, 1990–91.

Longest pass completion—99 yards, Frank Filchock (to Andy Farkas), Washington, 1939; George Izo (to Bob Mitchell), Washington, 1963; Karl Sweetan (to Pat Studstill), Detroit, 1966; Sonny Jurgensen (to Gerry Allen), Washington, 1968; Jim Plunkett (to Cliff Branch) L.A. Raiders, 1985; Ron Jaworksi (to Mike Quick), Philadelphia, 1985; Stan Humphries (to Tony Martin), San Diego, 1994.

Receiving

Most pass receptions, lifetime—934, Art Monk[1], Washington, 1980–93; N.Y. Jets, 1994.

Most pass receptions, season—122, Chris Carter, Minnesota, 1994.

Most pass receptions, game—18, Tom Fears, Los Angeles, 1950.

Most consecutive games, pass receptions—180, Art Monk, Washington, 1980–93; N.Y. Jets, 1994.

Most yards gained, pass receptions, lifetime—14,004, James Lofton, Green Bay, 1978–86; L.A. Raiders, 1987–88; Buffalo, 1989–92; L.A. Raiders, Philadelphia, 1993.

Most yards gained receptions, season—1,746, Charley Hennigan, Houston, 1961.

Most yards gained, game—336, Willie Anderson, Los Angeles Rams, Nov. 26, 1989 vs. New Orleans.

Most touchdown receptions, lifetime—131, Jerry Rice, San Francisco, 1985–94.

Most touchdown pass receptions, season—22, Jerry Rice, San Francisco 49ers, 1987.

Most touchdown pass receptions, game—5, Bob Shaw, Chicago Cards, 1950; Kellen Winslow, San Diego Chargers, 1981; Jerry Rice, San Francisco 49ers, 1990.

Most consecutive games, touchdown pass receptions—13, Jerry Rice, San Francisco 49ers, 1986–87.

Most pass interceptions, lifetime—81, Paul Krause, Washington, 1964–67; Minnesota, 1968–79.

Most pass interceptions, season—14, Richard (Night Train) Lane, Los Angeles, 1952.

Most pass interceptions, game—4, by 17 players.

Longest pass interception return—103 yards, Venice Glenn, San Diego, vs. Denver, Nov. 29, 1987.

1. Still active in the 1994 season.

Kicking

Longest punt—98 yrds, Steve O'Neal, New York Jets, 1969.

Highest average punting, lifetime—45.16 yards, Sammy Baugh, Washington, 1937–52.

Longest punt return—103 yards, Robert Bailey, L.A. Rams, 1994.

Longest kick-off return—106 yards, Roy Green, St. Louis, 1979; Al Carmichael, Green Bay, 1956; Noland Smith, Kansas City, 1967.

Most punts lifetime—1,154, Dave Jennings, N.Y. Giants 1974–84; N.Y. Jets, 1985–87.

Passing

Most passes completed, lifetime—3,686, Fran Tarkenton, Minnesota, 1961–66, 72–78; New York Giants, 1967–71.

Most passes completed, season—404, Warren Moon, 1991.

Most passes completed, game—45, Drew Bledsoe, New England, 1994.

Most consecutive passes completed—22, Joe Montana, San Francisco, 1987.

Most yards gained, lifetime—47,003, Fran Tarkenton, Minnesota, 1961–66, 72–78; New York Giants, 1967–71.

Most yards gained, season—5,084, Dan Marino, Miami, 1984.

Most yards gained, game—554, Norm Van Brocklin, Los Angeles, 1951.

NFL GOVERNMENT

Paul Tagliabue, Commissioner; Neil Austrian, President; Jay Moyer, Executive Vice President and League Counsel; Harold Henderson, Executive Vice President for Labor Relations/Chairman NFLMC; Joe Browne, Vice President of Communications & Development; Val Pinchbeck, Jr., Vice President of Broadcasting & Productions; Tom Sullivan, Vice President–Internal Audit; Jim Steeg, Executive Director for Special Events; Roger Goodell, Executive Director for Club Relations and International Development; Dennis Curran, General Counsel/Management Council; Pete Abitante, Director of Information; Greg Aiello, Director of Communications; Phil Ayoub, Comptroller; Nancy Behar, Assistant Director of Broadcasting and Productions; Joel Bussert, Director of Player Personnel; John Buzzeo, Director of Administration; David Cornwell, Director of Equal Employment and Assistant Counsel; Joe Ellis, Assistant Director of Club Administration; Bill Granholm, Director of Special Projects; Leslie Hammond, Director of Information, AFC; Charlie Jackson, Assistant Director of Security; John Jones, Director of Labor Operations; Dick Maxwell, Director of Broadcasting Services; Susan McCann Minogue, Assistant Director of Special Events; Jack Reader, Assistant Director of Officiating; Reggie Roberts, Director of Information, NFC; Peter Ruocco, Director of Planning for Player Employment; Jerry Seeman, Director of Officiating; Jan Van Duser, Director of Game Operations; Don Weiss, Director of Planning; Warren Welsh, Director of Security.

BASKETBALL

Basketball may be the one sport whose exact origin is definitely known. In the winter of 1891–92, Dr. James Naismith, an instructor in the Y.M.C.A. Training College (now Springfield College) at Springfield, Mass., deliberately invented the game of basketball in order to provide indoor exercise and competition for the students between the closing of the football season and the opening of the baseball season. He affixed peach baskets overhead on the walls at opposite ends of the gymnasium and organized teams to play his new game in which the purpose was to toss an association (soccer) ball into one basket and prevent the opponents from tossing the ball into the other

basket. The game is fundamentally the same today, though there have been improvements in equipment and some changes in rules.

Because Dr. Naismith had eighteen available players when he invented the game, the first rule was: "There shall be nine players on each side." Later the number of players became optional, depending upon the size of the available court, but the five-player standard was adopted when the game spread over the country. United States soldiers brought basketball to Europe in World War I, and it soon became a worldwide sport.

College Basketball

NATIONAL COLLEGIATE A.A. CHAMPIONS

1939	Oregon	1953	Indiana	1966	Texas Western	1984	Georgetown
1940	Indiana	1954	La Salle	1967–73	U.C.L.A.	1985	Villanova
1941	Wisconsin	1955	San Francisco	1974	No. Carolina State	1986	Louisville
1942	Stanford	1956	San Francisco	1975	U.C.L.A.	1987	Indiana
1943	Wyoming	1957	North Carolina	1976	Indiana	1988	Kansas
1944	Utah	1958	Kentucky	1977	Marquette	1989	Michigan
1945	Oklahoma A & M	1959	California	1978	Kentucky	1990	Nevada–Las Vegas
1946	Oklahoma A & M	1960	Ohio State	1979	Michigan State	1991	Duke
1947	Holy Cross	1961	Cincinnati	1980	Louisville	1992	Duke
1948	Kentucky	1962	Cincinnati	1981	Indiana	1993	North Carolina
1949	Kentucky	1963	Loyola (Chicago)	1982	North Carolina	1994	Arkansas
1950	C.C.N.Y.	1964	U.C.L.A.	1983	North Carolina	1995	U.C.L.A.
1951	Kentucky	1965	U.C.L.A.		State		
1952	Kansas						

NATIONAL INVITATION TOURNAMENT (NIT) CHAMPIONS

1939	Long Island U.	1954	Holy Cross	1968	Dayton	1982	Bradley
1940	Colorado	1955	Duquesne	1969	Temple	1983	Fresno State
1941	Long Island U.	1956	Louisville	1970	Marquette	1984	Michigan
1942	West Virginia	1957	Bradley	1971	North Carolina	1985	U.C.L.A.
1943–44	St. John's (N.Y.C.)	1958	Xavier (Cincinnati)	1972	Maryland	1986	Ohio State
1945	DePaul	1959	St. John's (N.Y.C.)	1973	Virginia Tech	1987	So. Mississippi
1946	Kentucky	1960	Bradley	1974	Purdue	1988	Connecticut
1947	Utah	1961	Providence	1975	Princeton	1989	St. John's (N.Y.C.)
1948	St. Louis	1962	Dayton	1976	Kentucky	1990	Vanderbilt
1949	San Francisco	1963	Providence	1977	St. Bonaventure	1991	Stanford
1950	C.C.N.Y.	1964	Bradley	1978	Texas	1992	Virginia
1951	Brigham Young	1965	St. John's (N.Y.C.)	1979	Indiana	1993	Minnesota
1952	La Salle	1966	Brigham Young	1980	Virginia	1994	Villanova
1953	Seton Hall	1967	So. Illinois	1981	Tulsa	1995	Virginia Tech

N.C.A.A. MAJOR COLLEGE INDIVIDUAL SCORING RECORDS

Single Season Averages

Player, Team	Year	G	FG	FT	Pts	Avg
Pete Maravich, Louisiana State	1969–70	31	522 [1]	337	1381 [1]	44.5 [1]
Pete Maravich, Louisiana State	1968–69	26	433	282	1148	44.2
Pete Maravich, Louisiana State	1967–68	26	432	274	1138	43.8
Frank Selvy, Furman	1953–54	29	427	355 [1]	1209	41.7
Johnny Neumann, Mississippi	1970–71	23	366	191	923	40.1
Freeman Williams, Portland State	1976–77	26	417	176	1010	38.8
Billy McGill, Utah	1961–62	26	394	221	1009	38.8
Calvin Murphy, Niagara	1967–68	24	337	242	916	38.2
Austin Carr, Notre Dame	1969–70	29	444	218	1106	38.1

1. Record.

N.C.A.A. CAREER SCORING TOTALS

Division I

Player, Team	Last year	G	FG	FT	Pts	Avg
Pete Maravich, Louisiana State	1970	83	1387 [1]	893 [1]	3667 [1]	44..2 [1]
Austin Carr, Notre Dame	1971	74	1017	526	2560	34.6
Oscar Robertson, Cincinnati	1960	88	1052	869	2973	33.8
Calvin Murphy, Niagara	1970	77	947	654	2548	33.1
Dwight Lamar [2]	1973	57	768	326	1862	32.7
Frank Selvy, Furman	1954	78	922	694	2538	32.5
Rick Mount, Purdue	1970	72	910	503	2323	32.3
Darrel Floyd, Furman	1956	71	868	545	2281	32.1
Nick Werkman, Seton Hall	1964	71	812	* 649	2273	32.0

1. Record. 2. Also played two seasons in college division.

Division II

Player, Team	Last year	G	FG	FT	Pts	Avg
Travis Grant, Kentucky State	1972	121	1760 [1]	525	4045 [1]	33.4 [1]
John Rinka, Kenyon	1970	99	1261	729	3251	32.8
Florindo Vieira, Quinnipiac	1957	69	761	741	2263	32.8
Willie Shaw, Lane	1964	76	960	459	2379	31.3
Mike Davis, Virginia Union	1969	89	1014	730	2758	31.0
Henry Logan, Western Carolina	1968	107	1263	764	3290	30.7
Willie Scott, Alabama State	1969	103	1277	601	3155	30.6
Gregg Northington, Alabama State	1972	75	894	403	2191	29.2
Bob Hopkins, Grambling	1956	126	1403	953	3759	29.8

1. Record.

TOP SINGLE–GAME SCORING MARKS

Player, Team (Opponent)	Yr	Pts	Player, Team (Opponent)	Yr	Pts
Selvy, Furman (Newberry)	1954	100 [1]	Maravich, LSU (Alabama)	1970	69
Arizin, Villanova (Phi. NAMC)	1949	85	Murphy, Niagara (Syracuse)	1969	68
Williams, Portland State (Rocky Mtn.)	1978	81	Floyd, Furman (Morehead)	1955	67
Mlkvy, Temple (Wilkes)	1951	73	Maravich, LSU (Tulane)	1969	66
Bradshaw, U.S. International (Loyola–CA)	1991	72	Handlan, W & L (Furman)	1951	66
Williams, Portland State (So. Oregon)	1977	71	Roberts, Oral Roberts (N.C. A&T)	1977	66

1. Record.

MEN'S N.C.A.A. BASKETBALL CHAMPIONSHIPS—1995

DIVISION I

First Round—East
Wake Forest 79, North Carolina A&T 47
St. Louis 64, Minnesota 61 (OT)
Alabama 91, Pennsylvania 85 (OT)
Oklahoma State 73, Drexel 49
Tulsa 68, Illinois 62
Old Dominion 89, Villanova 81 (3OT)
Stanford 70, North Carolina–Charlotte 68
Massachusetts 68, St. Peter's 51

First Round—Southeast
Kentucky 113, Mount St. Mary's 67
Tulane 76, Brigham Young 70
Arkansas State 81, Ball State 66
Manhattan 77, Oklahoma 67
Georgetown 68, Xavier 63
Weber State 79, Michigan State 72
Iowa State 64, Florida 61
North Carolina 80, Murray State 70

First Round—Midwest
Kansas 82, Colgate 68
Western Kentucky 82, Michigan 76 (OT)
Miami–Ohio 71, Arizona 62
Virginia 96, Nichols State 72
Memphis 75, Louisville 56
Purdue 49, Wisconsin–Green Bay 48
Syracuse 96, Southern Illinois 92
Arkansas 79, Texas Southern 78

First Round—West
UCLA 92, Florida International 56
Missouri 65, Indiana 60
Mississippi State 75, Santa Clara 67
Utah 76, Long Beach State 64
Texas 90, Oregon 73

Maryland 87, Gonzaga 63
Cincinnati 77, Temple 71
Connecticut 100, Tennessee–Chattanooga 71

Second Round—East
Wake Forest 64, St. Louis 59
Oklahoma State 66, Alabama 52
Tulsa 64, Old Dominion 52
Massachusetts 76, Stanford 51

Second Round—Southeast
Kentucky 82, Tulane 60
Arizona State 64, Manhattan 54
Georgetown 53, Weber State 51
North Carolina 73, Iowa State 51

Second Round—Midwest
Kansas 75, Western Kentucky 70
Virginia 60, Miami–Ohio 54 (OT)
Memphis 75, Purdue 73
Arkansas 96, Syracuse 94 (OT)

Second Round—West
UCLA 75, Missouri 74
Mississippi State 78, Utah 64
Maryland 82, Texas 68
Connecticut 76, Tulsa 51

Third Round—East
Oklahoma State 71, Wake Forest 66
Massachusetts 76, Tulsa 51

Third Round—Southeast
Kentucky 97, Arizona State 73
North Carolina 74, Georgetown 64

Third Round—Midwest
Virginia 67, Kansas 58
Arkansas 96, Memphis 91 (OT)

Third Round—West
UCLA 86, Mississippi State 67
Connecticut 99, Maryland 89

Regional Finals
East—Oklahoma State 68, Massachusetts 54
Southeast—North Carolina 74, Kentucky 61
Midwest—Arkansas 68, Virginia 61
West—UCLA 102, Connecticut 96

National Semifinals
(Sat., April 1, 1995, Seattle, Wash.)
UCLA 74, Oklahoma State 61
Arkansas 75, North Carolina 68

National Final
(Mon., April 3, 1995, Seattle, Wash.)
UCLA 89, Arkansas 78

DIVISION II

Semifinals
California Riverside 73, Indiana, Pa. 69
Southern Indiana 89, Norfolk (Va.) State 81

Championship
Southern Indiana 71, California–Riverside 63

DIVISION III

Semifinals
Wisconsin–Platteville 82, Trinity, Conn. 59
Manchester, Ind. 79, Rowan, N.J. 66

Championship
Wisconsin–Platteville 69, Manchester, Ind. 55

WOMEN'S N.C.A.A. BASKETBALL CHAMPIONSHIPS—1995

DIVISION I

First Round—East
Connecticut 105, Maine 75
Virginia Tech 62, St. Joseph's, Pa. 52
Duke 76, Oklahoma State 64
Alabama 82, Mount St. Mary's 55
Florida 89, Radford 49
Virginia 71, Dartmouth 68
Oklahoma 90, Loyola–Maryland 55
Louisiana Tech 90, Furman 52

First Round—Mideast
Tennessee 96, Florida A&M 59
Florida International 81, Old Dominion 76
Oregon State 88, Tennessee State 75 (OT)
Western Kentucky 77, Toledo 63
Arkansas 67, San Francisco 58
Washington 73, Ohio 56
Wisconsin 73, Kansas 72
Texas Tech 87, Tulane 72

First Round—Midwest
Colorado 83, Holy Cross 49
Southwest Missouri State 49, Utah 47
Drake 87, Mississippi 81 (OT)
George Washington 87, DePaul 79
Louisville 67, Oregon 65
Georgia 81, Indiana 64
North Carolina State 77, Marquette 62
Penn State 75, Jackson State 62

First Round—West
Vanderbilt 90, Northern Illinois 44
Memphis 74, Southern California 72
Montana 57, San Diego State 46
Purdue 74, Portland 59
Seton Hall 73, S.F. Austin 63

North Carolina 89, Western Illinois 48
SMU 96, Southern Mississippi 95 (OT)
Stanford 88, Cal–Irvine 55

Second Round—East
Connecticut 91, Virginia Tech 45
Alabama 121, Duke 120 (4OT)
Virginia 72, Florida 67
Louisiana Tech 48, Oklahoma 36

Second Round—Mideast
Tennessee 70, Florida International 44
Western Kentucky 85, Oregon State 78
Washington 54, Arkansas 50
Texas Tech 88, Wisconsin 65

Second Round—Midwest
Colorado 78, Southwest Missouri State 34
George Washington 96, Drake 93 (OT)
Georgia 81, Louisville 68
North Carolina State 76, Penn State 74

Second Round—West
Vanderbilt 95, Memphis 68
Purdue 62, Montana 51
North Carolina 59, Seton Hall 45
Stanford 95, SMU 73

Third Round—East
Connecticut 87, Alabama 56
Virginia 63, Louisiana Tech 62

Third Round—Mideast
Tennessee 87, Western Kentucky 65
Texas Tech 67, Washington 52

Third Round—Midwest
Colorado 77, George Washington 61
Georgia 98, North Carolina State 74

Third Round—West
Purdue 67, Vanderbilt 66
Stanford 81, North Carolina 71

Regional Finals
East—Connecticut 67, Virginia 63
Mideast—Tennessee 80, Texas Tech 59
Midwest—Georgia 82, Colorado 79
West—Stanford 69, Purdue 58

National Semifinals
(April 1, 1995, Minneapolis, Minn.)
Connecticut 87, Stanford 60
Tennessee 73, Georgia 51

National Championship
(April 2, 1995, Minneapolis, Minn.)
Connecticut 70, Tennessee 64

DIVISION II

Semifinals
Portland (Ore.) State 75, Stonehill, Mass. 59
North Dakota State 74, Missouri Western 67

Championship
North Dakota State 98, Portland (Ore.) State 85

DIVISION III

Semifinals
Wisconsin–Oshkosh 82, Salem State 69
Capital, Ohio 68, St. Thomas, Minn. 59

Championship
Capital, Ohio 59, Wisconsin–Oshkosh 55

LEADING N.C.A.A. SCORERS—1994–95

Division I

	TFG	3FG	FT	Pts	Avg
1. Kurt Thomas, Texas Christian	288	3	202	781	28.9
2. Frankie King, Western Caro.	249	52	193	743	26.5
3. Kenny Sykes, Grambling	245	82	112	684	26.3
4. Sherell Ford, Ill.–Chicago	265	47	130	707	26.2
5. Tim Roberts, Southern–B.R.	233	108	106	680	26.2
6. Kareem Townes, La Salle	242	103	112	699	25.9
7. Joe Griffin, LIU–Brooklyn	271	11	170	723	25.8
8. Shawn Respert, Michigan St.	229	119	139	716	25.6
9. Rob Feaster, Holy Cross	225	55	167	672	24.9
10. Shannon Smith, Wis.–Milwaukee	199	51	212	661	24.5
11. Mark Lueking, Army	204	98	176	682	24.4
12. Otis Jones, Air Force	213	71	173	670	23.9
13. Ryan Minor, Oklahoma	260	69	167	756	23.6
14. Alan Henderson, Indiana	284	2	159	729	23.5
15. Ronnie Henderson, LSU	219	68	124	630	23.3
16. Scott Drapeau, New Hampshire	241	21	145	648	23.1
17. Tucker Neale, Colgate	229	84	150	692	23.1
18. Gary Trent, Ohio	293	8	163	757	22.9
19. Joe Wilbert, Texas A&M	253	4	177	687	22.9
20. Damon Stoudamire, Arizona	222	112	128	684	22.8
21. Marcus Brown, Murray St.	219	44	189	671	22.4
22. Matt Alosa, New Hampshire	197	87	142	623	22.3
23. Danya Abrams, Boston Col.	215	0	190	620	22.1
24. Petey Sessoms, Old Dominion	213	89	215	730	22.1
25. Chris Carr, Southern Ill.	250	40	165	705	22.0

NATIONAL ASSOCIATION OF INTERCOLLEGIATE ATHLETICS—1995

MEN'S TOURNAMENT
DIVISION I

Quarterfinals
Birmingham Southern 109, Georgia Southwestern 76
Arkansas Tech 87, Montana State Northern 67
Pfeiffer, N.C. 92, Oklahoma City 78
Belmont, Tenn. 91, The Master's 72

Semifinals
Pfeiffer 68, Arkansas Tech 58
Birmingham Southern 90, Belmont 80

Championship
Birmingham Southern 92, Pfeiffer 76

WOMEN'S TOURNAMENT
DIVISION I

Quarterfinals
Lipscomb, Tenn. 91, Arkansas–Monticello 69
Southeastern Oklahoma 81, Auburn–Montgomery 76
Southern Nazarene, Okla. 76, Campbellsville 48
Southwestern Oklahoma 67, Simon Fraser 61

Semifinals
Southeastern Oklahoma 75, Lipscomb 74
Southern Nazarene 54, Southwestern Oklahoma 48

Championship
Southern Nazarene 78, Southeastern Oklahoma 77

NATIONAL INVITATION TOURNAMENT (N.I.T.)—1995

Semifinals

(March 27, 1995 at Madison Square Garden, N.Y., N.Y.)
Virginia Tech 71, Canisius 59
Marquette 87, Penn State 79

Championship

(March 29, 1995 at Madison Square Garden, N.Y., N.Y.)
Virginia Tech 65, Marquette 64

Consolation Game

Penn State 66, Canisius 62

FINAL 1994–95 N.C.A.A. REBOUNDING LEADERS

	Games	No.	Avg
1. Kurt Thomas, Texas Christian	27	393	14.6
2. Malik Rose, Drexel	30	404	13.5
3. Gary Trent, Ohio	33	423	12.8
4. Dan Callahan, Northeastern	29	364	12.6
5. Tim Duncan, Wake Forest	32	401	12.5
6. Adonal Foyle, Colgate	30	371	12.4
7. Tunji Awajobi, Boston U	31	378	12.2
8. Kareem Carpenter, Eastern Mich.	29	343	11.8
9. Marcus Mann, Mississippi Val.	27	317	11.7
10. Chris Ensminger, Valparaiso	28	315	11.3
11. Javan Rouzan, Stephen F. Austin	28	312	11.1
12. Harry Harrison, Idaho	26	283	10.9
13. Reggie Jackson, Nicholls St.	30	325	10.8
14. Rashard Griffith, Wisconsin	26	281	10.8
15. Larry Sykes, Xavier (Ohio)	27	291	10.8
16. Willie Fisher, Jacksonville	26	279	10.7
17. Carlin Warley, St. Joseph's (Pa.)	29	309	10.7
18. Joe Smith, Maryland	34	362	10.6
19. David Cully, William & Mary	28	287	10.6
20. Tim Moore, Houston	28	296	10.6

LACROSSE

NATIONAL INTERCOLLEGIATE CHAMPIONS

1946	Navy	1962–66	Navy	1983	Syracuse
1947–48	Johns Hopkins	1967	Johns Hopkins, Maryland, Navy	1984	Johns Hopkins
1949	Johns Hopkins, Navy	1968	Johns Hopkins	1985	Johns Hopkins
1950	Johns Hopkins	1969	Army, Johns Hopkins	1986	North Carolina
1951	Army, Princeton	1970	Johns Hopkins, Navy, Virginia	1987	Johns Hopkins
1952	Virginia, R.P.I.	1971[1]	Cornell	1988	Syracuse
1953	Princeton	1972	Virginia	1989	Syracuse
1954	Navy	1973	Maryland	1990	Syracuse
1955–56	Maryland	1974	Johns Hopkins	1991	North Carolina
1957	Johns Hopkins	1975	Maryland	1992	Princeton
1958	Army	1976–77	Cornell	1993	Syracuse
1959	Army, Johns Hopkins, Maryland	1978–80	Johns Hopkins	1994	Princeton
1960	Navy	1981	North Carolina	1995	Syracuse
1961	Army, Navy	1982	North Carolina		

1. First year of N.C.A.A. Championship Tournaments.

1995 N.C.A.A. LACROSSE

DIVISION I
Men's Championship
(May 29, 1995, at College Park, Md.)

Syracuse 13, Maryland 9

Women's Championship
(May 21, 1995, at Trenton, N.J.)

Maryland 13, Princeton 5

DIVISION III CHAMPIONSHIP
Men

Salisbury (Md.) 23, Nazareth (N.Y.) 13

Women

Trenton State (N.J.) 14, William Smith (N.Y.) 13

Professional Basketball

NATIONAL BASKETBALL ASSOCIATION CHAMPIONS

Source: National Basketball Association.

The National Basketball Association was originally the Basketball Association of America. It took its current name in 1949 when it merged with the National Basketball League.

Season	Eastern Conference (W–L)	Western Conference (W–L)	Playoff Champions[1]
1946–47	Washington Capitols (49–11)	Chicago Stags (39–22)	Philadelphia Warriors
1947–48	Philadelphia Warriors (27–21)	St. Louis Bombers (29–19)	Baltimore Bullets
1948–49	Washington Capitols (38–22)	Rochester Royals (45–15)	Minneapolis Lakers
1949–50	Syracuse Nationals (51–13)	Indianapolis Olympians (39–25)	Minneapolis Lakers
1950–51	Philadelphia Warriors (40–26)	Minneapolis Lakers (44–24)	Rochester Royals
1951–52	Syracuse Nationals (40–26)	Rochester Royals (41–25)	Minneapolis Lakers
1952–53	New York Knickerbockers (47–23)	Minneapolis Lakers (48–22)	Minneapolis Lakers
1953–54	New York Knickerbockers (44–28)	Minneapolis Lakers (46–26)	Minneapolis Lakers
1954–55	Syracuse Nationals (43–29)	Ft. Wayne Pistons (43–29)	Syracuse Nationals
1955–56	Philadelphia Warriors (45–27)	Ft. Wayne Pistons (37–35)	Philadelphia Warriors
1956–57	Boston Celtics (44–28)	St. Louis Hawks (38–34)	Boston Celtics
1957–58	Boston Celtics (48–23)	St. Louis Hawks (41–31)	St. Louis Hawks
1958–59	Boston Celtics (52–20)	St. Louis Hawks (49–23)	Boston Celtics
1959–60	Boston Celtics (59–16)	St. Louis Hawks (46–29)	Boston Celtics
1960–61	Boston Celtics (57–22)	St. Louis Hawks (51–28)	Boston Celtics
1961–62	Boston Celtics (60–20)	Los Angeles Lakers (54–26)	Boston Celtics
1962–63	Boston Celtics (58–22)	Los Angeles Lakers (53–27)	Boston Celtics
1963–64	Boston Celtics (59–21)	San Francisco Warriors (48–32)	Boston Celtics
1964–65	Boston Celtics (62–18)	Los Angeles Lakers (49–31)	Boston Celtics
1965–66	Philadelphia 76ers (55–25)	Los Angeles Lakers (45–35)	Boston Celtics
1966–67	Philadelphia 76ers (68–13)	San Francisco Warriors (44–37)	Philadelphia 76ers
1967–68	Philadelphia 76ers (62–20)	St. Louis Hawks (56–26)	Boston Celtics
1968–69	Baltimore Bullets (57–25)	Los Angeles Lakers (55–27)	Boston Celtics
1969–70	New York Knickerbockers (60–22)	Atlanta Hawks (48–34)	New York Knicks
1970–71	Baltimore Bullets (42–40)	Milwaukee Bucks (66–16)	Milwaukee Bucks
1971–72	New York Knickerbockers (48–34)	Los Angeles Lakers (69–13)	Los Angeles Lakers
1972–73	New York Knickerbockers (57–25)	Los Angeles Lakers (60–22)	New York Knicks
1973–74	Boston Celtics (56–26)	Milwaukee Bucks (59–23)	Boston Celtics
1974–75	Washington Bullets (60–22)	Golden State Warriors (48–34)	Golden State Warriors
1975–76	Boston Celtics (54–28)	Phoenix Suns (42–40)	Boston Celtics
1976–77	Philadelphia 76ers (50–32)	Portland Trail Blazers (49–33)	Portland Trail Blazers
1977–78	Washington Bullets (44–38)	Seattle Super Sonics (47–35)	Washington Bullets
1978–79	Washington Bullets (54–28)	Seattle Super Sonics (52–30)	Seattle Super Sonics
1979–80	Philadelphia 76ers (59–23)	Los Angeles Lakers (60–22)	Los Angeles Lakers
1980–81	Boston Celtics (62–20)	Houston Rockets (40–42)	Boston Celtics
1981–82	Philadelphia 76ers (58–24)	Los Angeles Lakers (57–25)	Los Angeles Lakers
1982–83	Philadelphia 76ers (65–17)	Los Angeles Lakers (58–24)	Philadelphia 76ers
1983–84	Boston Celtics (56–26)	Los Angeles Lakers (58–24)	Boston Celtics
1984–85	Boston Celtics (63–19)	Los Angeles Lakers (62–20)	Los Angeles Lakers
1985–86	Boston Celtics (67–15)	Houston Rockets (51–31)	Boston Celtics
1986–87	Boston Celtics (59–23)	Los Angeles Lakers (65–17)	Los Angeles Lakers
1987–88	Detroit Pistons (54–28)	Los Angeles Lakers (62–20)	Los Angeles Lakers
1988–89	Detroit Pistons (63–18)	Los Angeles Lakers (57–25)	Detroit Pistons
1989–90	Detroit Pistons (59–23)	Portland Trail Blazers (59–23)	Detroit Pistons
1990–91	Chicago Bulls (61–21)	Los Angeles Lakers (58–24)	Chicago Bulls
1991–92	Chicago Bulls (67–15)	Portland Trail Blazers (57–25)	Chicago Bulls
1992–93	Chicago Bulls (57–25)	Phoenix Suns (62–20)	Chicago Bulls
1993–94	New York Knicks (57–25)	Houston Rockets (58–24)	Houston Rockets
1994–95	Orlando Magic (57–25)	Houston Rockets (47–35)	Houston Rockets

1. Playoffs may involve teams other than conference winners.

INDIVIDUAL N.B.A. SCORING CHAMPIONS

Season	Player, Team	G	FG	FT	Pts	Avg
1953–54	Neil Johnston, Philadelphia Warriors	72	591	577	1759	24.4
1954–55	Neil Johnston, Philadelphia Warriors	72	521	589	1631	22.7
1955–56	Bob Pettit, St. Louis Hawks	72	646	557	1849	25.7
1956–57	Paul Arizin, Philadelphia Warriors	71	613	591	1817	25.6
1957–58	George Yardley, Detroit Pistons	72	673	655	2001	27.8
1958–59	Bob Pettit, St. Louis Hawks	72	719	667	2105	29.2
1959–60	Wilt Chamberlain, Philadelphia Warriors	72	1065	577	2707	37.6
1960–61	Wilt Chamberlain, Philadelphia Warriors	79	1251	531	3033	38.4
1961–62	Wilt Chamberlain, Philadelphia Warriors	80	1597	835	4029	50.4
1962–63	Wilt Chamberlain, San Francisco Warriors	80	1463	660	3586	44.8

Season	Player, Team	G	FG	FT	Pts	Avg
1963–64	Wilt Chamberlain, San Francisco Warriors	80	1204	540	2948	36.9
1964–65	Wilt Chamberlain, San Francisco Warriors–Phila. 76ers	73	1063	408	2534	34.7
1965–66	Wilt Chamberlain, Philadelphia 76ers	79	1074	501	2649	33.5
1966–67	Rick Barry, San Francisco Warriors	78	1011	753	2775	35.6
1967–68	Dave Bing, Detroit Pistons	79	835	472	2142	27.1
1968–69	Elvin Hayes, San Diego Rockets	82	930	467	2327	28.4
1969–70	Jerry West, Los Angeles Lakers	74	831	647	2309	31.2
1970–71	Lew Alcindor,[1] Milwaukee Bucks	82	1063	470	2596	31.7
1971–72	Kareem Abdul–Jabbar, Milwaukee Bucks	81	1159	504	2822	34.8
1972–73	Nate Archibald, Kansas City–Omaha Kings	80	1028	663	2719	34.0
1973–74	Bob McAdoo, Buffalo Braves	74	901	459	2261	30.8
1974–75	Bob McAdoo, Buffalo Braves	82	1095	641	2831	34.5
1975–76	Bob McAdoo, Buffalo Braves	78	934	559	2427	31.1
1976–77	Pete Maravich, New Orleans Jazz	73	886	501	2273	31.1
1977–78	George Gervin, San Antonio Spurs	82	864	504	2232	27.2
1978–79	George Gervin, San Antonio Spurs	80	947	471	2365	29.6
1979–80	George Gervin, San Antonio Spurs	78	1024	505	2585	33.1
1980–81	Adrian Dantley, Utah Jazz	80	909	632	2452	30.7
1981–82	George Gervin, San Antonio Spurs	79	993	555	2551	32.3
1982–83	Alex English, Denver Nuggets	82	959	406	2326	28.4
1983–84	Adrian Dantley, Utah Jazz	79	802	813	2418	30.6
1984–85	Bernard King, New York Knicks	55	691	426	1809	32.9
1985–86	Dominique Wilkins, Atlanta Hawks	78	888	527	2366	30.3
1986–87	Michael Jordan, Chicago Bulls[2]	82	1098	833	3041	37.1
1987–88	Michael Jordan, Chicago Bulls[3]	82	1069	723	2868	35.0
1988–89	Michael Jordan, Chicago Bulls[4]	81	966	674	2633	32.5
1989–90	Michael Jordan, Chicago Bulls[5]	82	1034	593	2753	33.6
1990–91	Michael Jordan, Chicago Bulls[6]	82	990	571	2580	31.5
1991–92	Michael Jordan, Chicago Bulls[7]	80	943	491	2404	30.1
1992–93	Michael Jordan, Chicago Bulls[8]	78	992	476	2541	32.6
1993–94	David Robinson, San Antonio Spurs[9]	80	840	693	2383	29.8
1994–95	Shaquille O'Neal, Orlando Magic[10]	79	930	455	2315	29.3

1. (Kareem Abdul–Jabbar). 2. Also had 12 3–point field goals. 3. Also had 7 3–point field goals. 4. Also had 27 3–point field goals. 5. Also had 92 3–point field goals. 6. Also had 29 3-point-field goals. 7. Also had 27 3-pt field goals in 1991–92. 8. Also had 81 3-pt field goals in 1992–93. 9. Also had 10 3-pt field goals in 1993–94. 10. O'Neal scored no 3-point field goals in 1994–95.

N.B.A. LIFETIME LEADERS

(Through 1994–95 season)

NBA and ABA records combined

Most Games Played

Kareem Abdul–Jabbar	1,560	Alex English	1,193
Robert Parish[1]	1,494	Tree Rollins[1]	1,156
Moses Malone[1]	1,329	James Edwards[1]	1,140
Elvin Hayes	1,303	Hal Greer	1,122
John Havlicek	1,270	Buck Williams[1]	1,122
Paul Silas	1,254		

Free Throw Percentage

(1,200 free throws made, minimum)

	FTA	FTM	Pct
Mark Price[1]	2,078	1,883	.906
Rick Barry	4,243	3,818	.900
Calvin Murphy	3,864	3,445	.892
Scott Skiles[1]	1,731	1,540	.890
Larry Bird	4,471	3,960	.886
Bill Sharman	3,559	3,143	.883
Reggie Miller[1]	3,624	3,186	.879
Ricky Pierce[1]	3,459	3,033	.877
Kiki Vandeweghe	3,997	3,484	.872
Jeff Malone[1]	3,351	2,918	.871

Blocked Shots

Kareem Abdul–Jabbar	3,189	Patrick Ewing[1]	2,143
Mark Eaton	3,064	Manute Bol[1]	2,086
Hakeem Olajuwon[1]	2,983	George T. Johnson	2,082
Tree Rollins[1]	2,542	Larry Nance	2,027
Robert Parish[1]	2,288	Elvin Hayes	1,771

1. Still active going into 1995–96 season.

Scoring Average

(400 games or 10,000 points minimum)

	G	Pts	Avg
Michael Jordan[1]	684	21,998	32.2
Wilt Chamberlain	1045	31,419	30.1
Elgin Baylor	846	23,149	27.4
Jerry West	932	25,192	27.0
Bob Pettit	792	20,880	26.4
George Gervin	791	20,708	26.2
Karl Malone[1]	816	21,237	26.0
Dominique Wilkins	984	25,389	25.8
David Robinson[1]	475	12,209	25.7
Oscar Robertson	1040	26,710	25.7

Steals

Maurice Cheeks	2,310
John Stockton[1]	2,225
Alvin Robertson	1,946
Isiah Thomas	1,861
Clyde Drexler[1]	1,857
Michael Jordan[1]	1,845
Magic Johnson	1,698
Lafayette Lever	1,666
Gus Williams	1,638
Derek Harper[1]	1,618

Rebounds

Wilt Chamberlain	23,924
Bill Russell	21,620
Kareem Abdul–Jabbar	17,440
Elvin Hayes	16,279
Moses Malone[1]	16,212
Nate Thurmond	14,464
Robert Parish[1]	14,323
Walt Bellamy	14,241
Wes Unseld	13,769
Jerry Lucas	12,942

Field Goal Percentage
(2,000 field goals made, minimum)

	FGA	FGM	Pct
Artis Gilmore	9,570	5,732	.599
Mark West[1]	3,958	2,330	.589
Shaquille O'Neal[1]	4,489	2,616	.583
Steve Johnson	4,965	2,841	.572
Darryl Dawkins	6,079	3,477	.572
James Donaldson[1]	5,442	3,105	.571
Jeff Ruland	3,734	2,105	.564
Kareem Abdul-Jabbar	28,307	15,837	.559
Otis Thorpe[1]	9,515	5,283	.555
Charles Barkley[1]	12,285	6,813	.555

1. Active going into 1995–96 season.

Assists

John Stockton[1]	10,394
Magic Johnson	9,921
Oscar Robertson	9,887
Isiah Thomas	9,061
Maurice Cheeks	7,392
Len Wilkens	7,211
Bob Cousy	6,955
Guy Rodgers	6,917
Nate Archibald	6,476
John Lucas	6,454

Points

Kareem Abdul-Jabbar	38,387
Wilt Chamberlain	31,419
Moses Malone[1]	27,409
Elvin Hayes	27,313
Oscar Robertson	26,710
John Havlicek	26,395
Alex English	25,613
Dominique Wilkins	25,389
Jerry West	25,192
Adrian Dantley	23,177

NATIONAL BASKETBALL ASSOCIATION
FINAL STANDINGS—1994–95

EASTERN CONFERENCE
Atlantic Division

	W	L	Pct	Games behind
x–Orlando Magic	57	25	.695	—
x–New York Knicks	55	27	.671	2
x–Boston Celtics	35	47	.427	22
Miami Heat	32	50	.390	25
New Jersey Nets	30	52	.366	27
Philadelphia 76ers	24	58	.293	33
Washington Bullets	21	61	.256	36

Central Division

	W	L	Pct	Games behind
x–Indiana Pacers	52	30	.634	—
x–Charlotte Hornets	50	32	.610	2
x–Chicago Bulls	47	35	.573	5
x–Cleveland Cavaliers	43	39	.524	9
x–Atlanta Hawks	42	40	.512	10
Milwaukee Bucks	34	48	.415	18
Detroit Pistons	28	54	.341	24

WESTERN CONFERENCE
Midwest Division

	W	L	Pct	Games behind
x–San Antonio Spurs	62	20	.756	—
x–Utah Jazz	60	22	.732	2
x–Houston Rockets	47	35	.573	15
x–Denver Nuggets	41	41	.500	21
Dallas Mavericks	36	46	.439	26
Minnesota Timberwolves	21	61	.256	41

Pacific Division

	W	L	Pct	Games behind
x–Phoenix Suns	59	23	.720	—
x–Seattle SuperSonics	57	25	.695	2
x–L.A. Lakers	48	34	.585	11
x–Portland Trail Blazers	44	38	.537	15
Sacramento Kings	39	43	.476	20
Golden St. Warriors	26	56	.317	33
L.A. Clippers	17	65	.207	42

x—Clinched playoff berth.

N.B.A. PLAYOFFS—1995

EASTERN CONFERENCE

First Round
(Best 3 out of 5)

Orlando defeated Boston, 3 games to 1
Indiana defeated Atlanta, 3 games to 0
New York defeated Cleveland, 3 games to 1
Chicago defeated Charlotte, 3 games to 1

Second Round

Indiana defeated New York, 4 games to 3
Orlando defeated Chicago, 4 games to 2

Conference Finals

Orlando defeated Indiana, 4 games to 3
    May 23—ORLANDO 105, Indiana 101
    May 25—ORLANDO 119, Indiana 114
    May 27—INDIANA 105, Orlando 100
    May 29—INDIANA 94, Orlando 93
    May 31—ORLANDO 108, Indiana 106
    June 2—INDIANA 123, Orlando 96
    June 4—ORLANDO 105, Indiana 81

NOTE: All caps denotes home team

WESTERN CONFERENCE

First Round
(Best 3 out of 5)

San Antonio defeated Denver, 3 games to 0
Phoenix defeated Portland, 3 games to 0
Houston defeated Utah, 3 games to 2
L.A. Lakers defeated Seattle, 3 games to 1

Second Round

San Antonio defeated L.A. Lakers, 4 games to 2
Houston defeated Phoenix, 4 games to 3

Conference Finals

Houston defeated San Antonio, 4 games to 2
    May 22—Houston 94, SAN ANTONIO 93
    May 24—Houston 106, SAN ANTONIO 96
    May 26—San Antonio 107, HOUSTON 102
    May 28—San Antonio 103, HOUSTON 81
    May 30—Houston 111, SAN ANTONIO 90
    June 1—HOUSTON 100, San Antonio 95

CHAMPIONSHIP

Houston defeated Orlando, 4 games to 0
    June 7—Houston 120, ORLANDO 118
    June 9—Houston 117, ORLANDO 106
    June 11—HOUSTON 106, Orlando 103
    June 14—HOUSTON 113, Orlando 101

N.B.A. INDIVIDUAL RECORDS
(Through 1994-95 season)

Most points, game—100, Wilt Chamberlain, Philadelphia vs. New York at Hershey, Pa. 1962
Most points, quarter—33, George Gervin, San Antonio, 1978
Most points, half—59, Wilt Chamberlain, Philadelphia, 1962
Most free throws, game—28, Wilt Chamberlain, Philadelphia vs. New York at Hershey, Pa. 1962; 28, Adrian Dantley, Utah vs. Houston, 1984
Most free throws, quarter—14, Rick Barry, San Francisco, 1966
Most free throws, half—19, Oscar Robertson, Cincinnati, 1964

Most field goals, game—36, Wilt Chamberlain, Philadelphia, 1962
Most consecutive field goals, game—18, Wilt Chamberlain, San Franciscco, 1963; Wilt Chamberlain, Philadelphia, 1967
Most assists, game—30, Scott Skiles, Orlando vs. Denver, 1990
Most rebounds, game—55, Wilt Chamberlain, Philadelphia vs. Boston, 1960
Most 3-pt. field goals, game—10, Brian Shaw, Miami vs. Milwaukee, 1993

N.B.A. MOST VALUABLE PLAYERS

1956	Bob Pettit	1973	Dave Cowens	1984	Larry Bird, Boston
1957	Bob Cousy	1974	Kareem Abdul-Jabbar, Milwaukee	1985	Larry Bird, Boston
1958	Bill Russell			1986	Larry Bird, Boston
1959	Bob Pettit	1975	Bob McAdoo, Buffalo	1987	Earvin Johnson, Los Angeles
1960	Wilt Chamberlain	1976-77	Kareem Abdul-Jabbar, Los Angeles	1988	Michael Jordan, Chicago
1961-63	Bill Russell			1989	Earvin Johnson, Los Angeles
1964	Oscar Robertson	1978	Bill Walton, Portland	1990	Earvin Johnson, Los Angeles
1965	Bill Russell	1979	Moses Malone, Houston	1991	Michael Jordan, Chicago
1966-68	Wilt Chamberlain	1980	Kareem Abdul-Jabbar, Los Angeles	1992	Michael Jordan, Chicago
1969	Wes Unseld			1993	Charles Barkley, Phoenix
1970	Willis Reed	1981	Julius Erving, Philadelphia	1994	Hakeem Olajuwon, Houston
1971-72	Lew Alcindor (Kareem Abdul-Jabbar)	1982	Moses Malone, Houston	1995	David Robinson, San Antonio
		1983	Moses Malone, Philadelphia		

N.B.A. TEAM RECORDS

Most points, game—186, Detroit vs. Denver, 3 overtimes, 1983
Most points, quarter—58, Buffalo vs. Boston, 1968
Most points, half—97, Atlanta vs. San Diego, 1970
Most points, overtime period—22, Detroit vs. Cleveland, 1973
Most field goals, game—74, Detroit, 1983
Most field goals, quarter—23, Boston, 1959; Buffalo, 1972
Most field goals, half—40, Boston, 1959; Syracuse, 1963; Atlanta, 1979
Most assists, game—53, Milwaukee, 1978
Most rebounds, game—109, Boston, 1960
Most points, both teams, game—370 (Detroit 186, Denver 184)

3 overtimes, Denver, December 13, 1983
Most points, both teams, quarter—96 (Boston 52, Minneapolis 44), 1959; (Detroit 53, Cincinnati 43), 1972
Most points, both teams, half—170 (Philadelphia 90, Cincinnati 80), Philadelphia, 1971
Longest winning streak—33, Los Angeles, 1971-72
Longest losing streak—20, Philadelphia, 1973
Longest winning streak at home—36, Philadelphia, 1966-67
Most games won, season—69, Los Angeles, 1971-72
Most games lost, season—73, Philadelphia, 1972-73
Highest average points per game—126.5, Denver, 1981-82

LEADING SCORERS—1994-1995

	GP	Pts	Avg
Shaquille O'Neal, Orlando	79	2315	29.3
Hakeem Olajuwon, Houston	72	2005	27.9
David Robinson, San Antonio	81	2238	27.6
Karl Malone, Utah	82	2187	26.7
Jim Jackson, Dallas	51	1309	25.7
Jamal Mashburn, Dallas	80	1926	24.1
Patrick Ewing, New York	79	1886	23.9
Charles Barkley, Phoenix	68	1561	23.0
Mitch Richmond, Sacramento	82	1867	22.8
Glen Rice, Miami	82	1831	22.3
Glenn Robinson, Milwaukee	80	1755	21.9
Clyde Drexler, Houston	76	1653	21.7
Cedric Ceballos, L.A. Lakers	58	1261	21.7
Scottie Pippen, Chicago	79	1692	21.4
Clifford Robinson, Portland	75	1601	21.4
Alonzo Mourning, Charlotte	77	1643	21.3
Anfernee Hardaway, Orlando	77	1613	21.0
Gary Payton, Seattle	82	1689	20.6
Latrell Sprewell, Golden St.	69	1420	20.6
Dana Barros, Philadelphia	82	1686	20.6
Derrick Coleman, New Jersey	56	1146	20.5
Isaiah Rider, Minnesota	75	1532	20.4

STEALS LEADERS—1994-1995

(minimum 100 steals)

	GP	Stl	Avg
Scottie Pippen, Chicago	79	232	2.9
Mookie Blaylock, Atlanta	80	200	2.5
Gary Payton, Seattle	82	204	2.5
John Stockton, Utah	82	194	2.4
Nate McMillian, Seattle	80	165	2.1
Eddie Jones, L.A. Lakers	64	131	2.1
Rod Strickland, Portland	64	123	1.9
Jason Kidd, Dallas	79	151	1.9
Elliott Perry, Phoenix	82	155	1.9
Hakeem Olajuwon, Houston	72	133	1.9
Dana Barros, Philadelphia	82	149	1.8
Clyde Drexler, Houston	76	136	1.8
Grant Hill, Detroit	70	124	1.8
Tom Gugliotta, Minnesota	77	132	1.7
Anfernee Hardaway, Orlando	77	130	1.7
David Robinson, San Antonio	81	133	1.6
Nick Anderson, Orlando	76	125	1.6
Kendall Gill, Seattle	73	120	1.6
Latrell Sprewell, Golden St.	69	112	1.6
Charles Barkley, Phoenix	68	110	1.6

ASSISTS LEADERS—1994–1995

	GP	No.	Avg
John Stockton, Utah	82	1011	12.3
Kenny Anderson, New Jersey	72	680	9.4
Tim Hardaway, Golden St.	62	578	9.3
Rod Strickland, Portland	64	562	8.8
Tyrone Bogues, Charlotte	78	675	8.7
Nick Van Exel, L.A. Lakers	80	660	8.3
Avery Johnson, San Antonio	82	670	8.2
Pooh Richardson, L.A. Clippers	80	632	7.9
Mookie Blaylock, Atlanta	80	616	7.7
Jason Kidd, Dallas	79	607	7.7
Dana Barros, Philadelphia	82	619	7.6
Mark Jackson, Indiana	82	616	7.5
Scott Skiles, Washington	62	452	7.3
Anfernee Hardaway, Orlando	77	551	7.2
Gary Payton, Seattle	82	583	7.1
Sherman Douglas, Boston	65	446	6.9
Eric Murdock, Milwaukee	75	482	6.4
Spud Webb, Sacramento	76	468	6.2
Bimbo Coles, Miami	68	416	6.1
Derek Harper, New York	80	458	5.7

BLOCKED–SHOTS LEADERS—1994–1995

	GP	No.	Avg
Dikembe Mutombo, Denver	82	321	3.9
Hakeem Olajuwon, Houston	72	242	3.4
Shawn Bradley, Philadelphia	82	274	3.3
David Robinson, San Antonio	81	262	3.2
Alonzo Mourning, Charlotte	77	225	2.9
Shaquille O'Neal, Orlando	79	192	2.4
Vlade Divac, L.A. Lakers	80	174	2.2
Patrick Ewing, New York	79	159	2.0
Charles Outlaw, L.A. Clippers	81	151	1.9
Oliver Miller, Detroit	64	116	1.8
Lorenzo Williams, Dallas	82	146	1.8
Elden Campbell, L.A. Lakers	73	130	1.8
Gheorghe Muresan, Washington	73	127	1.7
PJ Brown, New Jersey	80	135	1.7
Andrew Lang, Atlanta	82	138	1.7
Derrick Coleman, New Jersey	56	94	1.7
Dale Davis, Indiana	74	116	1.6
Mark West, Detroit	67	105	1.6
Chris Webber, Washington	54	85	1.6
Chris Dudley, Portland	82	126	1.5

FIELD GOAL PERCENTAGE LEADERS—1994–1995

	GP	FGM	FGA	Pct
Chris Gatling, Golden St.	58	324	512	.633
Shaquille O'Neal, Orlando	79	930	1594	.583
Horace Grant, Orlando	74	401	707	.567
Otis Thorpe, Portland	70	385	681	.565
Dale Davis, Indiana	74	324	576	.563
Gheorghe Muresan, Wash.	73	303	541	.560
Dikembe Mutombo, Denver	82	349	628	.556
Danny Manning, Phoenix	46	340	622	.547
Shawn Kemp, Seattle	82	545	1000	.545
Olden Polynice, Sacramento	81	376	691	.544
John Stockton, Utah	82	429	791	.542
Karl Malone, Utah	82	830	1548	.536
Eric Montross, Boston	78	307	575	.534
Marty Conlon, Milwaukee	82	344	647	.532
Antoine Carr, Utah	78	290	546	.531

FREE–THROW PERCENTAGE LEADERS—1994–1995

	GP	FTM	FTA	Pct
Spud Webb, Sacramento	76	226	242	.934
Mark Price, Cleveland	48	148	162	.914
Dana Barros, Philadelphia	82	347	386	.899
Reggie Miller, Indiana	81	383	427	.897
Tyrone Bogues, Charlotte	78	160	180	.889
Scott Skiles, Washington	62	179	202	.886
Mahmoud Abdul-Rauf, Denver	73	138	156	.885
BJ Armstrong, Chicago	82	206	233	.884
Jeff Hornacek, Utah	81	284	322	.882
Keith Jennings, Golden St.	80	134	153	.876
Hersey Hawkins, Charlotte	82	261	301	.867
Rex Chapman, Washington	46	137	159	.862
Allan Houston, Detroit	76	147	171	.860
Glen Rice, Miami	82	312	365	.855
Terrell Brandon, Cleveland	67	159	186	.855

REBOUND LEADERS—1994–1995

	GP	Reb	Avg
Dennis Rodman, San Antonio	49	833	16.8
Dikembe Mutombo, Denver	82	1029	12.6
Shaquille O'Neal, Orlando	79	901	11.4
Charles Barkley, Phoenix	68	756	11.1
Patrick Ewing, New York	79	867	11.0
Tyrone Hill, Cleveland	70	765	10.9
Kevin Willis, Miami	67	732	10.9
Shawn Kemp, Seattle	82	893	10.9
David Robinson, San Antonio	81	872	10.8
Hakeem Olajuwon, Houston	72	775	10.8
Karl Malone, Utah	82	870	10.6
Popeye Jones, Dallas	80	844	10.6
Derrick Coleman, New Jersey	56	591	10.6
Vlade Divac, L.A. Lakers	80	829	10.4
Vin Baker, Milwaukee	82	846	10.3
Alonzo Mourning, Charlotte	77	761	9.9
Horace Grant, Orlando	74	715	9.7
Loy Vaught, L.A. Clippers	80	772	9.7
Chris Webber, Washington	54	518	9.6
Dale Davis, Indiana	74	696	9.4

3–POINT FIELD GOAL LEADERS 1994–1995

	GP	3FG	3FA	Pct
Steve Kerr, Chicago	82	89	170	.524
Detlef Schrempf, Seattle	82	93	181	.514
Dana Barros, Philadelphia	82	197	426	.462
Hubert Davis, New York	82	131	288	.455
John Stockton, Utah	82	102	227	.449
Hersey Hawkins, Charlotte	82	131	298	.440
Wesley Person, Phoenix	78	116	266	.436
Kenny Smith, Houston	81	142	331	.429
Dell Curry, Charlotte	69	154	361	.427
BJ Armstrong, Chicago	82	108	253	.427
Dennis Scott, Orlando	62	150	352	.426
Allan Houston, Detroit	76	158	373	.424
Scott Skiles, Washington	62	96	228	.421
Reggie Miller, Indiana	81	195	470	.415
Nick Anderson, Orlando	76	179	431	.415

Sports Personalities

A name in parentheses is the original name or form of name. Localities are places of birth. Dates of birth appear as month/day/year. **Boldface** years in parentheses are dates of **(birth–death)**.
Information has been gathered from many sources, including the individuals themselves. However, the *Information Please Almanac* cannot guarantee the accuracy of every individual item.

Aaron, Hank (Henry) (baseball); Mobile, Ala., 2/5/1934
Abbott, Jim (baseball); Flint, Mich., 9/19/1967
Abdul–Jabbar, Kareem (Lewis Ferdinand Alcindor, Jr.) (basketball); New York City, 4/16/1947
Adderly, Herbert A. (football); Philadelphia, 6/8/1939
Affleck, Francis (auto racing) **(1951–1985)**
Aikman, Troy (football); Henryetta, Okla., 11/21/1966
Alcindor, Lew. *See* Abdul–Jabbar.
Ali, Muhammad (Cassius Clay) (boxing); Louisville, Ky., 1/18/1942
Allen, Dick (Richard Anthony) (baseball); Wampum, Pa., 3/8/1942
Allen, George (football) **(1918–1990)**
Allison, Bobby (Robert Arthur) (auto racing); Hueytown, Ala., 12/3/1937
Allison, Davey (auto racing); Hueytown, Ala. **(1961–1993)**
Alston, Walter (baseball); Venice, Ohio **(1911–1984)**
Alworth, Lance (football); Houston, 8/3/1940
Ameche, Alan (football); Houston, Tex., **(1933–1988)**
Anderson, Ken (football); Batavia, Ill., 2/15/1949
Anderson, Sparky (George) (baseball); Bridgewater, S.D., 2/22/1934
Andretti, Mario (auto racing); Montona, Trieste, Italy, 2/28/1940
Anthony, Earl (bowling); Kent, Wash., 4/27/1938
Appling, Luke (baseball); High Point, N.C **(1907–1990)**
Arcaro, Eddie (George Edward) (jockey); Cincinnati, 2/19/1916
Ashe, Arthur (tennis); Richmond, Va. **(1943–1993)**
Ashford, Evelyn (track & field); Shreveport, La., 4/15/1957
Austin, Tracy (tennis); Rolling Hills, Calif., 12/2/1962
Averill, Earl (baseball); Everett, Wash. **(1915–1983)**
Babashoff, Shirley (swimming); Whittier, Calif., 1/31/1957
Baer, Max (boxing); Omaha, Neb. **(1909–1959)**
Bagwell, Jeff (baseball); Boston, Mass., 5/17/1968
Banks, Ernie (baseball); Dallas, 1/31/1931
Bannister, Roger (runner); Harrow, England, 3/24/1929
Barkley, Charles (basketball); Leeds, Ala., 2/20/1963
Barry, Rick (Richard) (basketball); Elizabeth, N.J., 3/28/1944
Bauer, Hank (Henry) (baseball); East St. Louis, Ill., 7/31/1922
Baugh, Sammy (football); Temple, Tex., 3/17/1914
Bayi, Filbert (runner); Karratu, Tanganyika, 6/23/1953
Baylor, Elgin (basketball); Washington, D.C., 9/16/1934
Beamon, Bob (long jumper); New York City, 8/2/1946
Becker, Boris (tennis); Leiman, W. Germany, 11/22/1967
Bee, Clair (basketball); Cleveland, Ohio **(1896–1983)**
Beliveau, Jean (hockey); Three Rivers, Quebec, Canada, 8/31/1931
Bell, Rickey (football); Inglewood, Calif. **(1949–1984)**
Belle, Albert (baseball); Shreveport, La., 8/25/1966
Beman, Deane (golf); Washington, D.C., 4/22/1938
Bench, Johnny (Johnny Lee) (baseball); Oklahoma City, 12/7/1947
Berg, Patty (Patricia Jane) (golf); Minneapolis, 2/13/1918
Berra, Yogi (Lawrence) (baseball); St. Louis, 5/12/1925
Biletnikoff, Frederick (football); Erie, Pa., 2/23/1943
Bing, Dave (basketball); Washington, D.C., 11/24/1943
Bird, Larry (basketball); French Lick, Ind., 12/7/1956
Blaik, Earl H. (football); Detroit **(1897–1989)**
Blanda, George Frederick (football); Youngwood, Pa., 9/17/1927
Bledsoe, Drew (football); Walla Walla, Wash., 2/14/1972
Blue, Vida (baseball); Mansfield, La., 7/28/1949
Bodine, Brett (auto racing); Chemung, N.Y., 1/11/1959
Bodine, Geoff (auto racing); Chemung, N.Y., 4/18/1949
Bonds, Barry (baseball); Riverside, Calif., 7/24/1964
Borg, Björn (tennis); Stockholm, 6/6/1956
Boros, Julius (golf); Fairfield, Conn., 3/3/1920
Bossy, Mike (hockey); Montreal, 1/22/1957
Boston, Ralph (long jumper); Laurel, Miss., 5/9/1939
Bourque, Ray (hockey); Montreal, Que., 12/28/1960
Bradley, Bill (William Warren) (basketball); Crystal City, Mo., 7/28/1943
Bradshaw, Terry (football); Shreveport, La., 9/2/1948
Brathwaite, Chris (track); Eugene, Ore. **(1949–1984)**
Breedlove, Craig (Norman) (speed driving); Los Angeles, 3/23/1938
Brett, George (baseball); Glendale, W. Va., 5/15/1953
Brock, Louis Clark (baseball); El Dorado, Ark., 6/18/1939
Brown, Jimmy (football); St. Simon Island, Ga., 2/17/1936
Brumel, Valeri (high jumper); Tolbuzino, Siberia, 4/14/1942
Bryant, Paul "Bear" (football); Tuscaloosa, Ala., **(1913–1983)**
Bryant, Rosalyn Evette (track); Chicago, 1/7/1956
Burton, Michael (swimming); Des Moines, Iowa, 7/3/1947
Butkus, Dick (Richard Marvin) (football); Chicago, 12/9/1942

Campanella, Roy (baseball); Homestead, Pa. **(1921–1993)**
Campbell, Earl (football); Tyler, Tex., 3/29/1955
Canseco, Jose (baseball); Havana, Cuba, 7/2/1964
Caponi, Donna Maria (golf); Detroit, 1/29/1945
Cappelletti, Gino (football); Keewatin, Minn., 3/26/1934
Carew, Rod (Rodney Cline) (baseball); Gatun, Panama, 10/1/1945
Carlos, John (sprinter); New York City, 6/5/1945
Carlton, Steven Norman (baseball); Miami, Fla., 12/22/1944
Carner, Joanne Gunderson, Mrs. Don (golf); Kirkland, Wash., 3/4/1939
Casals, Rosemary (tennis); San Francisco, 9/16/1948
Casper, Billy (golf); San Diego, Calif., 6/24/1931
Caulkins, Tracy (swimming); Winona, Minn., 1/11/1963
Cauthen, Steve (jockey); Covington, Ky., 5/1/1960
Chamberlain, Wilt (Wilton) (basketball); Philadelphia, 8/21/1936
Chandler, A.B. (Happy) (baseball); Louisville, Ky. **(1899–1991)**
Chandler, Spud (baseball); Commerce, Ga., **(1907–1990)**
Chapot, Frank (equestrian); Camden, N.J., 2/24/1934
Chinaglia, Giorgio (soccer); Carrara, Italy, 1/24/1947
Clarke, Bobby (Robert Earle) (hockey); Flin Flon, Manitoba, Canada, 8/13/1949
Clay, Cassius. *See* Ali, Muhammad
Clemens, Roger (baseball); Dayton, Ohio, 8/4/1962
Clemente, Roberto Walker (baseball); Carolina, Puerto Rico **(1934–1972)**
Cobb, Ty (Tyrus Raymond) (baseball); Narrows, Ga., **(1886–1961)**
Cochran, Barbara Ann (skiing); Claremont, N.H., 1/14/1951
Cochran, Marilyn (skiing); Burlington, Vt., 2/7/1950
Cochran, Robert (skiing); Claremont, N.H., 12/11/1951
Coe, Sebastian Newblod (track); London, England, 9/29/1956
Colavito, Rocky (Rocco Domenico) (baseball); New York City, 8/10/1933
Coleman, Derrick (basketball); Mobile, Ala., 6/21/1967
Comaneci, Nadia (gymnast); Onesti, Romania, 11/12/1961
Conigliaro, Tony (baseball); Revere, Mass., **(1945–1990)**
Connors, Jimmy (James Scott) (tennis); East St. Louis, Ill., 9/2/1952
Cordero, Angel (jockey); Santurce, Puerto Rico, 5/8/1942
Cosell, Howard (broadcaster); Winston–Salem, N.C. **(1918–1995)**
Cournoyer, Yvan Serge (hockey); Drummondville, Quebec, Canada, 11/22/1943
Court, Margaret Smith (tennis); Albury, New South Wales, Australia, 7/16/1942
Cousy, Bob (basketball); New York City, 8/9/1928
Crabbe, Buster (swimming); Scottsdale, Ariz. **(1908–1983)**
Crenshaw, Ben (golf); Austin, Tex., 1/11/1952
Cronin, Joe (baseball executive); San Francisco, **(1906–1984)**
Cruyff, Johan (soccer); Amsterdam, Netherlands, 4/25/47
Csonka, Larry (Lawrence Richard) (football); Stow, Ohio, 12/25/1946
Dancer, Stanley (harness racing); New Egypt, N.J., 7/25/1927
Dantley, Adrian (basketball); Washington, D.C., 2/28/1956
Dark, Alvin (baseball); Comanche, Okla., 1/7/1922
Davenport, Willie (track); Troy, Ala., 6/6/1943
Dawson, Leonard Ray (football); Alliance, Ohio, 6/20/1935
Dean, Dizzy (Jay Hanna) (baseball); Lucas, Ark. **(1911–1974)**
DeBusschere, Dave (basketball); Detroit, 10/16/1940
Delvecchio, Alex Peter (hockey); Fort William, Ontario, Canada, 12/4/1931
Demaret, Jim (golf); Houston **(1910–1983)**
Dempsey, Jack (William H.) (boxing); Manassa, Colo. **(1895–1983)**
DeVicenzo, Roberto (golf); Buenos Aires, 4/14/1923
Dibbs, Edward George (tennis); Brooklyn, New York, 2/23/1951
Dietz, James W. (rowing); New York, N.Y., 1/12/1949
DiMaggio, Joe (baseball); Martinez, Calif., 11/25/1914
Dionne, Marcel (hockey); Drummondville, Quebec, Canada, 8/3/1951
Dominguín, Luis Miguel (matador); Madrid, 12/9/1926
Dorsett, Tony (football); Rochester, Pa., 4/7/1954
Dryden, Kenneth (hockey); Hamilton, Ontario, Canada, 8/4/1947
Drysdale, Don (baseball); Van Nuys, Calif. **(1936–1993)**
Duran, Roberto (boxing); Panama City, 6/16/1951
Durocher, Leo (baseball); West Springfield, Mass. **(1906–1991)**
Durr, Francois (tennis); Algiers, Algeria, 12/25/1942
El Cordobés, (Manuel Benitez Pérez) (matador); Palma del Rio, Córdoba, Spain, 5/4/1936(?)
Elder, Lee (golf); Dallas, 7/14/1934
Elway, John (football); Port Angeles, Wash., 6/28/1960

Emerson, Roy (tennis); Kingsway, Australia, 11/3/1936
Ender, Kornelia (swimming); Plauen, East Germany, 10/25/1958
Erving, "Dr. J" (Julius) (basketball); Roosevelt, N.Y., 2/22/1950
Esposito, Phil (Philip Anthony) (hockey); Sault Ste. Marie, Ontario, Canada, 2/20/1942
Evans, Lee (runner); Mandena, Calif., 2/25/1947
Everett, Chris (tennis); Fort Lauderdale, Fla., 12/21/1954
Ewbank, Weeb (football); Richmond, Ind., 5/6/1907
Ewing, Patrick (basketball); Kingston, Jamaica, 8/5/1962
Feller, Robert (Bobby) (baseball); Van Meter, Iowa, 11/3/1918
Feuerbach, Allan Dean (track); Preston, Iowa, 1/12/1948
Finley, Charles O. (sportsman); Ensley, Ala., 2/22/1918
Fischer, Bobby (chess); Chicago, 3/9/1943
Fitzsimmons, Bob (Robert Prometheus) (boxing); Cornwall, England **(1862–1917)**
Fleming, Peggy Gale (ice skating); San Jose, Calif., 7/27/1948
Ford, Whitey (Edward) (baseball); New York City, 10/21/1928
Foreman, George (boxing); Marshall, Tex., 1/10/1949
Fosbury, Richard (high jumper); Portland, Ore., 3/6/1947
Fox, Nellie (Jacob Nelson) (baseball); St. Thomas, Pa. **(1927–1975)**
Foxx, James Emory (baseball); Sudlersville, Md. **(1907–1967)**
Foyt, A. J. (auto racing); Houston, 1/16/1935
Fratianne, Linda (figure skating); Los Angeles, 8/2/1960
Frazier, Joe (boxing); Beauford, S.C., 1/17/1944
Frazier, Walt (basketball); Atlanta, 3/29/1945
Frick, Ford C. (baseball); Wawaka, Ind. **(1894–1978)**
Furillo, Carl (baseball); Stony Creek Mills, Pa. **(1922–1989)**
Furniss, Bruce (swimming); Fresno, Calif., 5/27/1957
Gable, Dan (wrestling); Waterloo, Iowa, 10/25/1945
Gabriel, Roman (football); Wilmington, N.C., 8/5/1940
Gallagher, Michael Donald (skiing); Yonkers, N.Y., 10/3/1941
Garms, Debs (baseball); Glen Rose, Tex. **(1908–1984)**
Garvey, Steve (baseball); Tampa, Fla., 12/22/1948
Gehrig, Lou (Henry Louis) (baseball); New York City **(1903–1941)**
Gehringer, Charlie (baseball); Fowlerville, Mich., 5/11/1903
Geoffrion, "Boom Boom" (Bernie) (hockey); Montreal, 2/14/1931
Gerulaitis, Vitas (tennis); Brooklyn, N.Y. **(1954–1994)**
Gervin, George (basketball); Long Beach, Calif., 4/27/52
Giacomin, Ed (hockey); Sudbury, Ontario, Canada, 6/6/1939
Giamatti, A. Bartlett (baseball); South Hadley, Mass. **(1938–1989)**
Gibson, Bob (baseball); Omaha, Neb., 11/9/1935
Gifford, Frank (football); Santa Monica, Calif., 8/16/1930
Gilbert, Rod (Rodrique) (hockey); Montreal, 7/1/1941
Giles, Warren (baseball executive); Tiskilwa, Ill. **(1896–1979)**
Gilmore, Artis (basketball); Chipley, Fla., 9/21/1949
Glance, Harvey (track); Phenix City, Ala., 3/28/1957
Gonzalez, Pancho (tennis); Los Angeles **(1928–1995)**
Goodell, Brian Stuart (swimming); Stockton, Calif., 4/2/1959
Gooden, Dwight (baseball); Tampa, Fla., 11/16/1964
Goodrich, Gail (basketball); Los Angeles, 4/23/1943
Goolagong, Cawley, Evonne (tennis); Griffith, Australia, 7/31/1951
Gossage, "Goose" (Rich) (baseball); Colorado Springs, Colo., 4/5/1951
Gottfried, Brian (tennis); Baltimore, Md., 1/27/1952
Graf, Steffi (tennis); Mannheim, W. Germany, 6/14/1969
Graham, David (golf); Windson, Australia, 5/23/1946
Graham, Otto Everett (football); Waukegan, Ill., 12/6/1921
Grange, Red (Harold) (football); Forksville, Pa. **(1904–1991)**
Green, Hubert (golf); Birmingham, Ala., 12/28/1946
Greene, Charles E. (sprinter); Pine Bluff, Ark., 3/21/1945
Greene, "Mean" (Joe); (football); Temple, Tex., 9/24/1946
Gretzky, Wayne (hockey); Brantford, Ont., 1/26/1961
Griese, Bob (Robert Allen) (football); Evansville, Ind., 2/3/1945
Griffey, Ken, Jr. (baseball); Donora, Pa., 11/21/1969
Groebli, "Mr. Frick" (Werner) (ice skating); Basil, Switzerland, 4/21/1915
Grove, Lefty (Robert Moses) (baseball); Lonaconing, Md., **(1900–1975)**
Groza, Lou (football); Martins Ferry Ohio, 1/25/1924
Guidry, Ronald Ames (baseball); Lafayette, La., 8/28/1950
Gunter, Nancy Richey (tennis); San Angelo, Tex., 8/23/1942
Halas, George (football); Chicago **(1895–1983)**
Hall, Gary (swimming); Fayetteville, N.C., 8/7/1951
Hamill, Dorothy (figure skating); Chicago, 1956(?)
Hamilton, Scott (figure skating); Bowling Green, Ohio, 8/28/1958
Hammond, Kathy (runner); Sacramento, Calif., 11/2/1951
Harris, Franco (football); Ft. Dix, N.J., 3/7/1950
Hartack, William, Jr. (jockey); Colver, Pa., 12/9/1932
Hasek, Dominik (hockey); Pardubice, Czechoslovakia, 1/29/1965
Haughton, William (harness racing); Gloversville, N.Y. **(1923–1986)**
Havlicek, John (basketball); Martins Ferry, Ohio, 4/8/1940
Hayes, Elvin (basketball); Rayville, La., 11/17/1945
Hayes, Woody (football); Upper Arlington, Ohio **(1913–1987)**
Haynie, Sandra (golf); Fort Worth, 6/4/1943
Heiden, Eric (speed skating); Madison, Wis., 6/14/1958

Hencken, John (swimming); Culver City, Calif., 5/29/1954
Henderson, Rickey (baseball); Chicago, 12/25/1958
Henie, Sonja (ice skater); Oslo **(1912–1969)**
Herman, Floyd Caves (Babe) (baseball); Buffalo, N.Y. **(1903–1987)**
Hernandez, Keith (baseball); San Francisco, 10/20/1953
Hershiser, Orel (baseball); Buffalo, N.Y., 9/16/1958
Hickcox, Charles (swimming); Phoenix, Ariz., 2/6/1947
Hines, James (sprinter); Dumas, Ark., 9/10/1946
Hodges, Gil (baseball); Princeton, Ind. **(1924–1972)**
Hogan, Ben (golf); Dublin, Tex., 8/13/1912
Holmes, Larry (boxing); Cuthert, Ga., 11/3/1949
Hornsby, Rogers (baseball); Winters, Tex. **(1896–1963)**
Hornung, Paul (football); Louisville, Ky., 12/23/1935
Houk, Ralph (baseball); Lawrence, Kan., 8/9/1919
Howard, Elston (baseball); St. Louis **(1929–1980)**
Howe, Gordon (hockey); Floral, Sask., Canada, 3/31/1928
Howell, Jim Lee (football); Lonoke, Ark. **(1914–1995)**
Howser, Dick (baseball); Miami, Fla. **(1937–1987)**
Hubbell, Carl (baseball); Carthage, Mo. **(1903–1988)**
Huff, Sam (Robert Lee) (football); Morgantown, W. Va., 10/4/1934
Hull, Bobby (hockey); Point Anne, Canada, 1/3/1939
Hunter, "Catfish" (Jim) (baseball); Hertford, N.C., 4/8/1946
Huntley, Joni (track); McMinnville, Ore., 8/4/1956
Hutson, Donald (football); Pine Bluff, Ark., 1/31/1913
Insko, Del (harness racing); Amboy, Minn., 7/10/1931
Irwin, Hale (golf); Joplin, Mo., 6/3/1945
Jackson, Reggie (baseball); Wyncote, Pa., 5/18/1946
Jagr, Jaromir (hockey); Kladno, Czechoslovakia, 2/15/1972
Jeffries, James J. (boxing); Carroll, Ohio **(1875–1953)**
Jenkins, Ferguson Arthur (baseball); Chatham, Ontario, Canada, 12/13/1943
Jenner, (W.) Bruce (track); Mt. Kisco, N.Y., 10/28/1949
Jezek, Linda (swimming); Palo Alto, Calif., 3/10/1960
Johnson, "Magic" (Earvin) (basketball); E. Lansing, Mich., 8/14/1959
Johnson, Anthony (rowing); Washington, D.C., 11/16/1940
Johnson, Jack (John Arthur) (boxing); Galveston, Tex. **(1876–1946)**
Johnson, Rafer (decathlon); Hillsboro, Tex., 8/18/1935
Johnson, Randy (baseball); Walnut Creek, Calif., 9/10/1963
Johnson, Wilham Julius (Judy) (baseball); Wilmington, Del. **(1899–1989)**
Jones, Deacon (David) (football); Eatonville, Fla., 12/9/1938
Jordan, Michael (basketball); Brooklyn, N.Y., 2/17/1963
Joyner, Florence Griffith (sprinter); Mojave Desert, Calif., 12/21/1959
Joyner-Kersee, Jackie (track); East St. Louis, Ill., 3/3/1962
Juantoreno, Alberto (track); Santiago, Cuba, 12/3/1951
Jurgensen, Sonny (football); Wilmington, N.C., 8/23/1934
Justice, Dave (baseball); Cincinnati, Ohio, 4/14/1966
Kaat, Jim (baseball); Zeeland, Mich., 11/7/1938
Kaline, Al (Albert) (baseball); Baltimore, 12/19/1934
Keino, Kipchoge (runner); Kapchemoiymo, Kenya 1/?/1940
Kelly, Leroy (football); Philadelphia, 5/20/1942
Kelly, Red (Leonard Patrick) (hockey); Simcoe, Ontario, Canada, 7/9/1927
Killebrew, Harmon (baseball); Payette, Idaho, 6/29/1936
Killy, Jean—Claude (skiing); Saint—Cloud, France, 8/30/1943
Kilmer, Bill (William Orland) (football); Topeka, Kan., 9/5/1939
King, Bille Jean (Bille Jean Moffitt) (tennis); Long Beach, Calif., 11/22/1943
Kinsella, John (swimming); Oak Park, Ill., 8/26/1952
Kluszeewski, Ted (baseball); Argo, Ill. **(1924–1988)**
Kodes, Jan (tennis); Prague, 3/1/1946
Kolb, Claudia (swimming); Hayward, Calif., 12/19/1949
Koosman, Jerry Martin (baseball); Appleton, Minn., 12/23/1942
Korbut, Olga (gymnast); Grodno, Byelorussia, U.S.S.R., 5/16/1955
Koufax, Sandy (Sanford) (baseball); Brooklyn, N.Y., 12/30/1935
Kramer, Jack (tennis); Las Vegas, Nev., 8/1/1921
Kramer, Jerry (football); Jordan, Mont., 1/23/1936
Kuenn, Harvey (baseball); West Allis, Wis. **(1930–1988)**
Kuhn, Bowie Kent (baseball); Takoma Park, Md., 10/28/1926
Kwalik, Ted (Thaddeus John) (football); McKees Rocks, Pa., 4/15/1947
Lafleur, Guy Damien (hockey); Thurson, Quebec, Canada, 8/20/1951
Laird, Ronald (walker); Louisville, Ky., 5/31/1935
Lamonica, Daryle (football); Fresno, Calif., 7/17/1941
Landis, Kenesaw Mountain (1st baseball commissioner); Millville, Ohio **(1866–1944)**
Landry, Tom (football); Mission, Tex., 9/11/1924
Landy, John (runner); Australia, 4/4/1930
Larrieu, Francie (track); Palo Alto, Calif., 11/28/1952
Lasorda, Tom (baseball); Norristown, Pa., 9/22/1927
Laver, Rod (tennis); Rockhampton, Australia, 8/9/1938
Layne, Bobby (football); Lubbock, Texas **(1927–1986)**

Leetch, Brian (hockey); Corpus Christi, Tex., 3/3/1968
Lemieux, Mario (hockey); Montreal, Quebec, Canada, 10/5/1965
Lendl, Ivan (tennis); Prague, 3/7/1960
Leonard, Benny (Benjamin Leiner) (boxing); New York City (1896–1947)
Leonard, Sugar Ray (boxing); Wilmington, N.C., 5/17/1956
Lewis, Carl (track); Willingboro, N.J., 7/1/1961
Lindros, Eric (hockey); London, Ont., 2/28/1973
Liquori, Marty (runner); Montclair, N.J., 9/11/1949
Little, Lou (football); Leominster, Mass., (1893–1979)
Littler, Gene (golf); La Jolla, Calif., 7/21/1930
Lombardi, Vince (football); Brooklyn, N.Y. (1913–1970)
Longden, Johnny (horse racing); Wakefield, England, 2/14/1907
Lopat, Eddie (baseball); New York, N.Y. (1918–1992)
Lopez, Al (baseball); Tampa, Fla., 8/20/1908
Lopez, Nancy (golf); Torrance, Calif., 1/6/1957
Louis, Joe (Joe Louis Barrow) (boxing); Lafayette, Ala. (1914–1981)
Lynn, Frederic Michael (baseball); Chicago, Ill., 2/3/1952
Lynn, Janet (figure skating); Rockford, Ill., 4/6/1953
Mack, Connie (Cornelius Alexander McGillicuddy) (baseball executive); East Brookfield, Mass. (1862–1956)
Mackey, John (football); New York City, 9/24/1941
Maddux, Greg (baseball); San Angelo, Texas, 4/15/1967
Mahovlich, Frank (Francis William) (hockey); Timmins, Ontario, Canada, 1/10/1938
Mahre, Phil (skiiing); White Pass, Wash., 5/10/1957
Malone, Karl (basketball); Summerfield, La., 7/24/1963
Malone, Moses (basketball); Petersburg, Va., 3/23/1955
Mandlikova, Hana (tennis); Prague, Czechoslovakia, 2/1962
Mann, Carol (golf); Buffalo, N.Y., 2/3/1941
Manning, Madeline (runner); Cleveland, 1/11/1948
Mantle, Mickey Charles (baseball); Spavinaw, Okla. (1931–1995)
Maravich, "Pistol Pete" (Peter) (basketball); Aliquippa, Pa. (1948–1988)
Marble, Alice (tennis); Palm Springs, Calif. (1913–1990)
Marciano, Rocky (boxing); Brockton, Mass. (1923–1969)
Marichal, Juan (baseball); Laguna Verde, Montecristi, Dominican Republic, 10/20/1937
Marino, Dan (football); Pittsburgh, Pa., 9/15/1961
Maris, Roger (baseball); Hibbing, Minn. (1934–1985)
Martin, Billy (Alfred Manuel) (baseball); Berkeley, Calif. (1928–1989)
Martin, Rick (Richard Lionel) (hockey); Verdun, Quebec, Canada, 7/26/1951
Mathews, Ed (Edwin) (baseball); Texarkana, Tex., 10/13/1931
Mattingly, Don (baseball); Evansville, Ind., 4/20/1961
Matson, Randy (shot putter); Kilgore, Tex., 3/5/1945
Mays, Willie (baseball); Westfield, Ala., 5/6/1931
McAdoo, Bob (basketball); Greensboro, N.C., 9/25/1951
McCarthy, Joe (Joseph Vincent) (baseball); Philadelphia (1887–1978)
McCovey, Willie Lee (baseball); Mobile, Ala., 1/10/1938
McDonald, Lanny (hockey); Hanna, Alberta, Canada, 2/16/1953
McDowell, Jack (baseball); Van Nuys, Calif., 1/16/1966
McEnroe, John Patrick, Jr. (tennis); Wiesbaden, Germany, 2/16/1959
McGraw, John Joseph (baseball); Truxton, N.Y. (1873–1934)
McGwire, Mark (baseball); Pomona, Calif., 10/1/1963
McLain, Dennis (baseball); Chicago, 3/24/1944
McMillan, Kathy Laverne (track); Raeford, N.C., 11/7/1957
Merrill, Janice (track); New London, Conn., 6/18/1962
Messier, Mark (hockey); Edmonton, Alberta, Canada, 1/18/1961
Meyer, Deborah (swimming); Haddonfield, N.J., 8/14/1952
Middlecoff, Cary (golf); Halls, Tenn., 1/6/1921
Mikita, Stan (hockey); Sokolce, Czechoslovakia, 5/20/1940
Milburn, Rodney, Jr. (hurdler); Opelousas, La., 5/18/1950
Miller, Johnny (golf); San Francisco, 4/29/1947
Montgomery, Jim (swimming); Madison, Wis., 1/24/1955
Moore, Archie (boxing); Benoit, Miss., 12/13/1916
Morgan, Joe Leonard (baseball); Bonham, Tex., 9/19/1943
Morrall, Earl (football); Muskegon, Mich., 5/17/1934
Morton, Craig L. (football); Flint, Mich., 2/5/1943
Mosconi, Willie (pocket billiards); Philadelphia, 6/27/1913
Moser, Annemarie. *See* Proell, Annemarie.
Moses, Edward Corley (track); Dayton, Ohio, 8/31/1958
Mungo, Van Lingo (baseball); Pageland, S.C. (1911–1985)
Munson, Thurman (baseball); Akron, Ohio (1947–1979)
Murphy, Calvin (basketball); Norwalk, Conn., 5/9/1948
Murray, Eddie (baseball); Los Angeles, Calif., 2/24/1956
Musial, Stan (baseball); Donora, Pa., 11/21/1920
Myers, Linda (archery); York, Pa., 6/19/1947
Naber, John (swimming); Evanston, Ill., 1/20/1956
Namath, Joe (Joseph William) (football); Beaver Falls, Pa., 5/31/1943
Nastase, Ilie (tennis); Bucharest, 7/19/1946

Navratilova, Martina (tennis); Prague, 10/18/1956
Nehemiah, Renaldo (track); Newark, N.J., 3/24/1959
Nelson, Cindy (skiing); Lutsen, Minn., 8/19/1955
Newcombe, John (tennis); Sydney, Australia, 5/23/1943
Niekro, Phil (baseball); Lansing, Ohio, 4/1/1939
Nicklaus, Jack (golf); Columbus, Ohio, 1/21/1940
Norman, Gregory (golf); Mount Isa, Australia, 2/10/1955
Oerter, Al (discus thrower); New York City, 9/19/1936
Olajuwon, Hakeem (basketball); Lagos, Nigeria, 1/21/1963
Oldfield, Barney (racing driver); Fulton County, Ohio (1878–1946)
Oliva, Tony (Pedro) (baseball); Pinar Del Rio, Cuba, 7/20/1940
Olsen, Merlin Jay (football); Logan, Utah, 9/15/1940
O'Malley, Walter (baseball executive); New York City (1903–1979)
O'Neal, Shaquille (basketball); Newark, N.J., 3/6/1972
Orantes, Manuel (tennis); Granada, Spain, 2/6/1949
Orr, Bobby (hockey); Parry Sound, Ontario, Canada, 3/20/1948
Ovett, Steve (track); Brighton, England, 10/9/1955
Owens, Jesse (track); Decatur, Ala. (1914–1980)
Paige, Satchell (Leroy) (baseball); Mobile, Ala. (1906–1982)
Palmer, Arnold (golf); Latrobe, Pa., 9/10/1929
Palmer, James Alvin (baseball); New York City, 10/15/1945
Parent, Bernard Marcel (hockey); Montreal, 4/3/1945
Park, Brad (Douglas Bradford) (hockey); Toronto, Ontario, Canada, 7/6/1948
Parseghian, Ara (football); Akron, Ohio, 5/21/1923
Pasarell, Charles (tennis); San Juan, Puerto Rico, 2/12/1944
Patterson, Floyd (boxing); Waco, N.C., 1/4/1935
Peete, Calvin (golf); Detroit, Mich., 7/18/1943
Pelé (Edson Arantes do Nascimento) (soccer); Tres Coracoes, Brazil, 10/23/1940
Perry, Gaylord (baseball); Williamston, N.C., 9/15/1938
Perry, Jim (baseball); Williamston, N.C., 10/30/1936
Petrovic, Drazen (basketball); Yugoslavia (1965–1993)
Pettit, Bob (basketball); Baton Rouge, La., 12/12/1932
Petty, Richard Lee (auto racing); Randleman, N.C., 7/2/1937
Pincay, Laffit, Jr. (jockey); Panama City, Panama, 12/29/1946
Plager, Barclay (ice hockey); Kirkland Lake, Ontario (1941–1988)
Plante, Jacques (hockey); Sahwinigan Falls, Quebec, Canada, 1/17/1929
Player, Gary (golf); Johannesburg, South Africa, 11/1/1935
Plunkett, Jim (football); San Jose, Calif., 12/5/1947
Potvin, Denis Charles (hockey); Hull, Quebec, Canada, 10/29/1953
Powell, Boog (John) (baseball); Lakeland, Fla., 8/17/1941
Powell, Mike (track); Philadelphia, 11/10/1963
Prefontaine, Steve Roland (runner); Coos Bay, Ore. (1951–1975)
Prince, Bob (baseball announcer); Pittsburgh (1917–1985)
Proell, Annemarie Moser (Alpine skier); Kleinarl, Austria, 3/27/1953
Ralston, Dennis (tennis); Bakersfield, Calif., 7/27/1942
Rankin, Judy Torluemke (golf); St. Louis, Mo., 2/18/1945
Raschi, Vic (baseball); West Springfield, Mass. (1919–1988)
Ratelle, Jean (Joseph Gilbert Yvon Jean) (hockey); St. Jean, Quebec, Canada, 10/29/1953
Rawls, Betsy (Elizabeth Earle) (golf); Spartanburg, S.C., 5/4/1928
Reed, Willis (basketball); Hico, La., 6/25/1942
Reese, Pee Wee (Harold) (baseball); Ekron, Ky., 7/23/1919
Resch, Glenn "Chico" (hockey); Moose Jaw, Saskatchewan, Canada, 7/10/1948
Rice, Jerry (football); Crawford, Miss., 10/13/1962
Richard, Maurice (hockey); Montreal, 8/14/1924
Riessen, Martin (tennis); Hinsdale, Ill., 12/4/1941
Rigney, William (baseball); Alameda, Calif., 1/29/1918
Ripken, Cal, Jr. (baseball); Havre de Grace, Md., 8/24/1960
Rizzuto, Phil (baseball); New York City, 9/25/1918
Roark, Helen Willis Moody (tennis); Centerville, Calif., 10/6/1906
Robertson, Oscar (basketball); Charlotte, Tenn., 11/24/1938
Robinson, Arnie (track); San Diego, Calif., 4/7/1948
Robinson, Brooks (baseball); Little Rock, Ark., 5/18/1937
Robinson, Dave (basketball); Key West, Fla., 8/6/1965
Robinson, Frank (baseball); Beaumont, Tex., 8/31/1935
Robinson, Jackie (baseball); Cairo, Ga. (1919–1972)
Robinson, Larry Clark (hockey); Marvelville, Ontario, Canada, 6/2/1951
Robinson, "Sugar" Ray (boxing); Detroit (1920–1989)
Rockne, Knute Kenneth (football); Voss, Norway (1888–1931)
Rockwell, Martha (skiing); Providence, R.I., 4/26/1944
Rono, Harry (track); Kiptaragon, Kenya, 2/12/1952
Rooney, Art (football); Pittsburgh, Pa. (1901–1988)
Rose, Pete (Peter Edward) (baseball); Cincinnati, 4/14/1942
Rosenbloom, Maxie (boxing); New York City (1904–1976)
Rosewall, Ken (tennis); Sydney, Australia, 11/2/1934
Rote, Kyle (football); San Antonio, 10/27/1928
Roush, Edd (baseball); Oakland City, Ind. (1893–1988)
Rozelle, Pete (Alvin Ray) (commissioner of National Football League); South Gate, Calif., 3/1/1926

Rudolph, Wilma Glodean (sprinter); St. Bethlehem, Tenn. **(1940–1994)**
Russell, Bill (basketball); Monroe, La., 2/12/1934
Ruth, Babe (George Herman Ruth) (baseball); Baltimore **(1895–1948)**
Rutherford, Johnny (auto racing); Fort Worth, 3/12/1938
Ryan, Nolan (Lynn Nolan, Jr.) (baseball); Refugio, Tex., 1/31/1947
Ryon, Luann (archery); Long Beach, Calif., 1/13/1953
Ryun, Jim (runner); Wichita, Kan., 4/29/1947
Salazar, Alberto (track); Havana, 8/7/1958
Samuels, Howard (horse racing soccer); New York City **(1920–1984)**
Sanders, Deion (baseball/football); Ft. Myers, Fla., 8/9/1967
Santana, Manuel (Manuel Santana Martinez) (tennis); Chamartin, Spain, 5/10/1938
Sayers, Gale (football); Wichita, Kan., 5/30/1943
Schmidt, Mike (baseball); Dayton, Ohio, 9/27/1949
Shoendienst, Al (Albert) (baseball); Germantown, Ill., 2/2/1923
Schollander, Donald (swimming); Charlotte, N.C., 4/30/1946
Seagren, Bob (Robert Lloyd) (pole vaulter); Pomona, Calif., 10/17/1946
Seau, Junior (football); Oceanside, Calif., 1/19/1969
Seaver, Tom (baseball); Fresno, Calif., 11/17/1944
Seidler, Maren (track); Brooklyn, N.Y., 6/11/1962
Selke, Frank (ice hockey); Canada **(1893–1985)**
Sewell, Joe (baseball); Titus, Ala., **(1898–1990)**
Shepherd, Lee (auto racing) **(1945–1985)**
Shero, Fred (hockey); Camden, N.J. **(1945–1990)**
Shoemaker, Willie (jockey); Fabens, Tex., 8/9/1931
Shore, Eddie (ice hockey); Saskatchewan, Canada **(1902–1985)**
Shorter, Frank (runner); Munich, Germany, 10/31/1947
Shriver, Pam (tennis); Baltimore, 7/4/1962
Shula, Don (Donald Francis) (football); Grand River, Ohio, 1/4/1930
Silvester, Jay (discus thrower); Tremonton, Utah, 2/27/1937
Simpson, O.J. (Orenthal James) (football); San Francisco, 7/9/1947
Sims, Billy (football); St. Louis, 9/18/1955
Smith, Bubba (Charles Aaron) (football); Orange, Tex., 2/28/1945
Smith, Emmitt (football); Escambia, Fla., 5/15/1969
Smith, Ozzie (baseball); Mobile, Ala., 12/26/1954
Smith, Ronnie Ray (sprinter); Los Angeles, 3/28/1949
Smith, Stanley Roger (tennis); Pasadena, Calif., 12/14/1946
Smith, Tommie (sprinter); Clarksville, Tex., 6/5/1944
Smoke, Marcia Jones (canoeing); Oklahoma City, 7/18/1941
Snead, Sam (golf); Hot Springs, Va., 5/27/1912
Sneva, Tom (auto racing); Spokane, Wash., 6/1/1948
Snider, Duke (Edwin) (baseball); Los Angeles, 9/19/1926
Solomon, Harold (tennis); Washington, D.C., 9/17/1952
Spahn, Warren (baseball); Buffalo, N.Y., 4/23/1921
Speaker, Tristram (baseball); Hubbard City, Tex. **(1888–1958)**
Spencer, Brian (ice hockey); Fort St. James, British Columbia **(1949–1988)**
Spinks, Leon (boxing); St. Louis, 7/11/1953
Spitz, Mark (swimming); Modesto, Calif., 2/10/1950
Stabler, Kenneth (football); Foley, Ala., 12/25/1945
Stagg, Amos Alonzo (football); West Orange, N.J. **(1862–1965)**
Stargell, Willie (Wilver Dornell) (baseball); Earlsboro, Okla., 3/6/1941
Starr, Bart (football); Montgomery, Ala., 1/9/1934
Staub, "Rusty" (Daniel) (baseball); New Orleans, 4/4/1944
Staubach, Roger (football); Cincinnati, 2/5/1942
Steinkraus, William C. (equestrian); Cleveland, 10/12/1925
Stenerud, Jan (football); Fetsund, Norway, 11/26/1942
Stengel, Casey (Charles Dillon) (baseball); Kansas City, Mo. **(1891–1975)**
Stenmark, Ingemar (Alpine skier); Tarnaby, Sweden, 3/18/1956
Stevens, Scott (hockey); Completon, New Brunswick, 5/4/1966
Stockton, Richard LaClede (tennis); New York City, 2/18/1951
Stones, Dwight Edwin (track); Los Angeles, 12/6/1953
Strawberry, Darryl (baseball); Los Angeles, 3/12/1962
Sullivan, John Lawrence (boxing); Boston **(1858–1918)**
Sutton, Don (Donald Howard) (baseball); Clio, Ala., 4/2/1945
Swann, Lynn (football); Alcoa, Tenn., 3/7/1952

Tanner, Leonard Roscoe III (tennis); Chattanooga, Tenn., 10/15/1951
Tarkenton, Fran (Francis) (football); Richmond, Va., 2/3/1940
Tebbetts, Birdie (George R.) (baseball); Nashua, N.H., 11/10/1914
Theismann, Joe (football); New Brunswick, N.J., 9/9/1946
Thomas, Frank (baseball); Columbus, Ga., 5/27/1968
Thomas, Isiah (basketball); Chicago, Ill., 4/30/1961
Thomas, Thurman (football); Houston, Texas, 5/16/1966
Thompson, David (basketball); Shelby, N.C., 7/13/1954
Thorpe, Jim (James Francis) (all–around athlete); nr. Prague, Okla. **(1888–1953)**
Tilden, William Tatem II (tennis); Philadelphia **(1893–1953)**
Tittle, Y. A. (Yelberton Abraham) (football); Marshall, Tex., 10/24/1926
Toomey, William (decathlon); Philadelphia, 1/10/1939
Trevino, Lee (golf); Dallas, 12/1/1939
Trottier, Bryan (hockey); Val Marie, Sask., Canada, 7/17/1956
Tunney, Gene (James J.) (boxing); New York City **(1898–1978)**
Tyus, Wyomia (runner); Griffin, Ga., 8/29/1945
Ueberroth, Peter (baseball); Evanston, Ill., 9/2/1937
Unitas, John (football); Pittsburgh, 5/7/1933
Unser, Al (auto racing); Albuquerque, N. Mex., 5/29/1939
Unser, Bobby (auto racing); Albuquerque, N. Mex., 2/20/1934
Valenzuela, Fernando (baseball); Sonora, Mexico, 11/1/1960
Valvano, Jim (basketball); New York, N.Y. **(1946–1993)**
Van Brocklin, Norm (football); Eagle Butte, S. Dak. **(1926–1983)**
Vilas, Guillermo (tennis); Mar del Plata, Argentina, 8/17/1952
Viola, Frank (baseball); Hempstead, N.Y., 4/19/1960
Viren, Lasse (track); Myrskyla, Finland, 7/12/1949
Wade, Virginia (tennis); Bournemouth, England, 7/10/1945
Wagner, Honus (John Peter Honus) (baseball); Carnegie, Pa. **(1867–1955)**
Waitz, Grete (Andersen) (running); Oslo, Norway, 10/1/1953
Walcott, Jersey Joe (Arnold Cream) (boxing); Merchantville, N.J. **(1914–1994)**
Wallace, Rusty (auto racing); St. Louis, Mo., 8/14/1956
Walsh, Adam (football) **(1902–1985)**
Walton, Bill (basketball); La Mesa, Calif., 11/5/1952
Waterfield, Bob (football); Burbank, Calif **(1921–1983)**
Watson, Martha Rae (track); Long Beach, Calif., 8/19/1946
Watson, Tom (golf); Kansas City, Mo., 9/4/1949
Weaver, Earl (baseball); St. Louis, 8/14/1930
Weiskopf, Tom (golf); Massillon, Ohio, 11/9/1942
Weiss, George (baseball executive); New Haven, Conn. **(1895–1972)**
Weissmuller, Johnny (swimmer and actor); Windber, Pa. **(1904–1984)**
West, Jerry (basketball); Cheylan, W. Va., 5/28/1938
White, Reggie (football); Chattanooga, Tenn., 12/19/1961
White, Willye B. (long jumper); Money, Miss., 1/1/1936
Whitworth, Kathy (golf); Monahans, Tex., 9/27/1939
Wilkens, Mac Maurice (track); Eugene, Ore., 11/15/1950
Wilkins, Lennie (basketball); 11/25/1937
Wilkinson, Bud (football); Minneapolis, 4/23/1916
Williams, Dick (baseball); St. Louis, 5/7/1929
Williams, Ted (baseball); San Diego, Calif., 8/30/1918
Wills, Maury (baseball); Washington, D.C., 10/2/1932
Winfield, Dave (baseball); St. Paul, Minn., 10/3/1951
Wohlhuter, Richard C. (runner); Geneva, Ill., 12/23/1945
Wood, "Smokey" (Joseph) (baseball); Kansas City, Mo. **(1890–1985)**
Woodhead, Cynthia (swimming); Riverside, Calif., 2/7/1964
Wottle, David James (runner); Canton, Ohio, 8/7/1950
Wright, Mickey (Mary Kathryn) (golf); San Diego, Calif., 2/14/1935
Yarborough, Cale (William Caleb) (auto racing); Timmonsville, S.C., 3/27/1939
Yarbrough, Leeroy (auto racing); Jacksonville, Fla. **(1938–1984)**
Yastrzemski, Carl (baseball); Southampton, N.Y., 8/22/1939
Young, Cy (Denton True) (baseball); Gilmore, Ohio **(1867–1955)**
Young, Shelia (speed skater, bicycle racer); Detroit, 10/14/1950
Young, Steve (football); Salt Lake City, Utah, 10/11/1961
Zaharias, Babe Didrikson (golf); Port Arthur, Tex. **(1913–1956)**

HOCKEY

Ice hockey, by birth and upbringing a Canadian game, is an offshoot of field hockey. Some historians say that the first ice hockey game was played in Montreal in December 1879 between two teams composed almost exclusively of McGill University students, but others assert that earlier hockey games took place in Kingston, Ontario, or Halifax, Nova Scotia. In the Montreal game of 1879, there were fifteen players on a side, who used an assortment of crude sticks to keep the puck in motion. Early rules allowed nine men on a side, but the number was reduced to seven in 1886 and later to six.

The first governing body of the sport was the Amateur Hockey Association of Canada, organized in 1887. In the winter of 1894–95, a group of college students from the United States visited Canada and saw hockey played. They became enthused over the game and introduced it as a winter sport when they returned home. The first professional league was the International Hockey League, which operated in northern Michigan in 1904–06.

Until 1910, professionals and amateurs were allowed to play together on "mixed teams," but this arrangement ended with the formation of the first "big league," the National Hockey Association, in eastern Canada in 1910. The Pacific Coast League was organized in 1911 for western Canadian hockey. The league included Seattle and later other American cities. The National Hockey League replaced the National Hockey Association in 1917. Boston, in 1924, was the first American city to join that circuit. The league expanded to include western cities in 1967. The Stanley Cup was competed for by "mixed teams" from 1894 to 1910, thereafter by professionals. It was awarded to the winner of the N.H.L. playoffs from 1926–67 and now to the league champion. The World Hockey Association was organized in October 1972 and was dissolved after the 1978–79 season when the N.H.L. absorbed four of the teams.

The National Hockey League Players Association staged a 10-day strike near the end of the 1991–92 season, the first strike in the league's 75-year history.

The agreement which settled the strike extended the regular season from 80 to 84 games beginning with the 1992–93 season, with owners and players sharing revenues from the final two games on a partnership basis.

The agreement also increased the players' playoff fund from $7.5 million to $9 million and the minimum salary to $100,000.

In addition, free agency for the players was made less restrictive and owners' contributions to the pension fund increased.

Shortly after the 1992 Stanley Cup playoffs concluded, John Ziegler, president of the NHL since 1977, resigned under pressure from the league's owners. Gil Stein was named as interim president and a search begun to name the league's first commissioner.

The search ended in 1993 when Gary Bettman was named to the position. Bettman served as an assistant to National Basketball Association Commissioner David Stern for 12 years.

The National Hockey League season, which usually begins in late October, didn't begin until Jan. 20, 1995, due to a labor dispute. Hockey owners, unable to reach an agreement with the National Hockey League Players Association, locked the players out, and the season, due to begin Oct. 24, was put on hold.

With cancellation of the entire season a possibility, the sides finally got together in January. The 103-day lockout ended with a new six-year contract which either side may reopen in 1998.

The key elements of the agreement included:

• Unrestricted free agency for players at age 32, dropping to age 31 after the first three years of the deal.

• A rookie salary cap of $850,000 in the first year of the deal, moving up to $1.075 million over the length of the agreement.

• 19-year-olds eligible for the draft and 18-year-olds able to opt in.

As a result of the lockout, the regular season was reduced to 48 games, with teams playing exclusively within their own conference.

STANLEY CUP WINNERS

Emblematic of World Professional Championship; N.H.L. Championship after 1967

1894	Montreal A.A.A.	1925	Victoria Cougars	1956–60	Montreal Canadiens
1895	Montreal Victorias	1926	Montreal Maroons	1961	Chicago Black Hawks
1896	Winnipeg Victorias	1927	Ottawa Senators	1962–64	Toronto Maple Leafs
1897–99	Montreal Victorias	1928	N.Y. Rangers	1965–66	Montreal Canadiens
1900	Montreal Shamrocks	1929	Boston Bruins	1967	Toronto Maple Leafs
1901	Winnipeg Victorias	1930–31	Montreal Candiens	1968–69	Montreal Canadiens
1902	Montreal A.A.A.	1932	Toronto Maple Leafs	1970	Boston Bruins
1903–05	Ottawa Silver Seven	1933	N.Y. Rangers	1971	Montreal Canadiens
1906	Montreal Wanderers	1934	Chicago Black Hawks	1972	Boston Bruins
1907	Kenora Thistles[1]	1935	Montreal Maroons	1973	Montreal Canadiens
1907	Mont. Wanderers[2]	1936–37	Detroit Red Wings	1974–75	Philadelphia Flyers
1908	Montreal Wanderers	1938	Chicago Black Hawks	1976–79	Montreal Canadiens
1909	Ottawa Senators	1939	Boston Bruins	1980–83	New York Islanders
1910	Montreal Wanderers	1940	N.Y. Rangers	1984	Edmonton Oilers
1911	Ottawa Senators	1941	Boston Bruins	1985	Edmonton Oilers
1912–13	Quebec Bulldogs	1942	Toronto Maple Leafs	1986	Montreal Canadiens
1914	Toronto	1943	Detroit Red Wings	1987	Edmonton Oilers
1915	Vancouver Millionaires	1944	Montreal Canadiens	1988	Edmonton Oilers
1916	Montreal Canadiens	1945	Toronto Maple Leafs	1989	Calgary Flames
1917	Seattle Metropolitans	1946	Montreal Canadiens	1990	Edmonton Oilers
1918	Toronto Arenas	1947–49	Toronto Maple Leafs	1991	Pittsburgh Penguins
1919	No champion	1950	Detroit Red Wings	1992	Pittsburgh Penguins
1920–21	Ottawa Senators	1951	Toronto Maple Leafs	1993	Montreal Canadiens
1922	Toronto St. Patricks	1952	Detroit Red Wings	1994	N.Y. Rangers
1923	Ottawa Senators	1953	Montreal Canadiens	1995	N.J. Devils
1924	Montreal Canadiens	1954–55	Detroit Red Wings	1. January. 2. March.	

NATIONAL HOCKEY LEAGUE YEARLY TROPHY WINNERS

The Hart Trophy—Most Valuable Player

1924	Frank Nighbor, Ottawa
1925	Billy Burch, Hamilton
1926	Nels Stewart, Montreal Maroons
1927	Herb Gardiner, Montreal Canadiens
1928	Howie Morenz, Montreal Canadiens
1929	Roy Worters, N.Y. Americans
1930	Nels Stewart, Montreal Maroons
1931–32	Howie Morenz, Montreal Canadiens
1933	Eddie Shore, Boston
1934	Aurel Joliat, Montreal Canadiens
1935–36	Eddie Shore, Boston
1937	Babe Siebert, Montreal Canadiens
1938	Eddie Shore, Boston
1939	Toe Blake, Montreal Canadiens
1940	Eddie Goodfellow, Detroit
1941	Bill Cowley, Boston
1942	Tom Anderson, N.Y. Americans
1943	Bill Cowley, Boston
1944	Babe Pratt, Toronto
1945	Elmer Lach, Montreal Canadiens
1946	Max Bentley, Chicago
1947	Maurice Richard, Montreal Canadiens
1948	Buddy O'Connor, N.Y. Rangers
1949	Sid Abel, Detroit
1950	Chuck Rayner, N.Y. Rangers
1951	Milt Schmidt, Boston
1952–53	Gordon Howe, Detroit
1954	Al Rollins, Chicago
1955	Ted Kennedy, Toronto
1956	Jean Belveau, Montreal Canadiens
1957–58	Gordon Howe, Detroit
1959	Andy Bathgate, N.Y. Rangers
1960	Gordon Howe, Detroit
1961	Bernie Geoffrion, Montreal Canadiens
1962	Jacques Plante, Montreal Canadiens
1963	Gordon Howe, Detroit
1964	Jean Beliveau, Montreal Canadiens
1965–66	Bobby Hull, Chicago
1967–68	Stan Mikita, Chicago
1969	Phil Esposito, Boston
1970–72	Bobby Orr, Boston
1973	Bobby Clarke, Philadelphia
1974	Phil Esposito, Boston
1975–76	Bobby Clarke, Philadelphia
1977–78	Guy Lafleur, Montreal
1979	Bryan Trottier, N.Y. Islanders
1980	Wayne Gretzky, Edmonton
1981	Wayne Gretzky, Edmonton
1982	Wayne Gretzky, Edmonton
1983	Wayne Gretzky, Edmonton
1984	Wayne Gretzky, Edmonton
1985	Wayne Gretzky, Edmonton
1986	Wayne Gretzky, Edmonton
1987	Wayne Gretzky, Edmonton
1988	Mario Lemieux, Pittsburgh
1989	Wayne Gretzky, Los Angeles
1990	Mark Messier, Edmonton
1991	Brett Hull, St. Louis
1992	Mark Messier, N.Y. Rangers
1993	Mario Lemieux, Pittsburgh
1994	Sergei Fedorov, Detroit
1995	Eric Lindros, Philadelphia

Vezina Trophy—Leading Goalkeeper

1956–60	Jacques Plante, Montreal
1961	Johnny Bower, Toronto
1962	Jacques Plante, Montreal
1963	Glenn Hall, Chicago
1964	Charlie Hodge, Montreal
1965	Terry Sawchuk—Johnny Bower, Toronto
1966	Lorne Worsley—Charlie Hodge, Montreal
1967	Glen Hall—Denis DeJordy, Chicago
1968	Lorne Worsley—Rogatien Vachon, Montreal
1969	Glen Hall—Jacques Plante, St. Louis
1970	Tony Esposito, Chicago
1971	Ed Giacomin—Gilles Villemure, New York
1972	Tony Esposito—Gary Smith, Chicago
1973	Ken Dryden, Montreal
1974	Bernie Parent, Philadelphia and Tony Esposito, Chicago
1975	Bernie Parent, Philadelphia
1976	Ken Dryden, Montreal
1977–79	Ken Dryden—Michel Larocque, Montreal
1980	Bob Sauve—Don Edwards, Buffalo
1981	Richard Sevigny, Denis Herron and Michel Larocque, Montreal
1982	Billy Smith, New York Islanders
1983	Pete Peeters, Boston
1984	Tom Barrasso, Buffalo
1985	Pelle Lindbergh, Philadelphia
1986	John Vanbiesbrouck, New York Rangers
1987	Ron Hextall, Philadelphia
1988	Grant Fuhr, Edmonton
1989	Patrick Roy, Montreal
1990	Patrick Roy, Montreal
1991	Ed Belfour, Chicago
1992	Patrick Roy, Montreal
1993	Ed Belfour, Chicago
1994	Dominik Hasek, Buffalo
1995	Dominik Hasek, Buffalo

James Norris Trophy—Defenseman

1954	Red Kelly, Detroit
1955–58	Doug Harvey, Montreal
1959	Tom Johnson, Montreal
1960–62	Doug Harvey, Montreal; New York (62)
1963–65	Pierre Pilote, Chicago
1966	Jacques Laperriere, Montreal
1967	Harry Howell, New York
1968–75	Bobby Orr, Boston
1976	Denis Potvin, N.Y. Islanders
1977	Larry Robinson, Montreal
1978–79	Denis Potvin, N.Y. Islanders
1980	Larry Robinson, Montreal
1981	Randy Carlyle, Pittsburgh
1982	Doug Wilson, Chicago
1983–84	Rod Langway, Washington
1985	Paul Coffey, Edmonton
1986	Paul Coffey, Edmonton
1987	Ray Bourque, Boston
1988	Ray Bourque, Boston
1989	Chris Chelios, Montreal
1990	Ray Bourque, Boston
1991	Ray Bourque, Boston
1992	Brian Leetch, N.Y. Rangers
1993	Chris Chelios, Chicago
1994	Ray Bourque, Boston
1995	Paul Coffey, Detroit

Lady Byng Trophy—Sportsmanship

1960	Don McKenney, Boston
1961	Red Kelly, Detroit
1962–63	Dave Keon, Toronto
1964	Ken Wharram, Chicago
1965	Bobby Hull, Chicago
1966	Alex Delvecchio, Detroit
1967–68	Stan Mikita, Chicago
1969	Alex Delvecchio, Detroit
1970	Phil Goyette, St. Louis
1971	John Bucyk, Boston
1972	Jean Ratelle, New York
1973	Gil Perrault, Buffalo
1974	John Bucyk, Boston
1975	Marcel Dionne, Detroit
1976	Jean Ratelle, N.Y. Rangers–Boston
1977	Marcel Dionne, Los Angeles
1978	Butch Goring, Los Angeles
1979	Bob MacMillan, Atlanta
1980	Wayne Gretzky, Edmonton
1981	Rick Kehoe, Pittsburgh
1982	Rick Middleton, Boston
1983–84	Mike Bossy, N.Y. Islanders
1985	Jari Kurri, Edmonton
1986	Mike Bossy, N.Y. Islanders
1987	Joe Mullen, Calgary
1988	Mats Naslund, Montreal
1989	Joe Mullen, Calgary
1990	Brett Hull, St. Louis
1991	Wayne Gretzky, Los Angeles
1992	Wayne Gretzky, Los Angeles
1993	Pierre Turgeon, N.Y. Islanders
1994	Wayne Gretzky, Los Angeles
1995	Ron Francis, Pittsburgh

Calder Trophy—Rookie

1962	Bobby Rousseau, Montreal
1963	Kent Douglas, Toronto
1964	Jacques Laperriere, Montreal
1965	Roger Crozier, Detroit
1966	Brit Selby, Toronto
1967	Bobby Orr, Boston
1968	Derek Sanderson, Boston
1969	Danny Grant, Minnesota
1970	Tony Esposito, Chicago
1971	Gilbert Perrault, Buffalo
1972	Ken Dryden, Montreal
1973	Steve Vickers, New York Rangers
1974	Denis Potvin, N.Y. Islanders
1975	Eric Vail, Atlanta
1976	Bryan Trottier, N.Y. Islanders

1977	Willi Plett, Atlanta	1993	Teemu Selanne, Winnipeg	1969	Phil Esposito, Boston
1978	Mike Bossy, N.Y. Islanders	1994	Martin Brodeur, New Jersey	1970	Bobby Orr, Boston
1979	Bobby Smith, Minnesota	1995	Peter Forsberg, Quebec	1971–74	Phil Esposito, Boston
1980	Ray Bourque, Boston			1975	Bobby Orr, Boston
1981	Peter Stastny, Quebec	**Art Ross Trophy—Leading scorer**		1976–78	Guy Lafleur, Montreal
1982	Dale Hawerchuk, Winnipeg	1955	Bernie Geoffrion, Montreal	1979	Bryan Trottier, N.Y. Islanders
1983	Steve Larmer, Chicago	1956	Jean Beliveau, Montreal	1980	Marcel Dionne, Los Angeles
1984	Tom Barrasso, Buffalo	1957	Gordie Howe, Detroit	1981–87	Wayne Gretzky, Edmonton
1985	Mario Lemieux, Pittsburgh	1958–59	Dickie Moore, Montreal	1988	Mario Lemieux, Pittsburgh
1986	Gary Suter, Calgary	1960	Bobby Hull, Chicago	1989	Mario Lemieux, Pittsburgh
1987	Luc Robitaille, Los Angeles	1961	Bernie Geoffrion, Montreal	1990	Wayne Gretzky, Los Angeles
1988	Joe Niewendyk, Calgary	1962	Bobby Hull, Chicago	1991	Wayne Gretzky, Los Angeles
1989	Brian Leetch, N.Y. Rangers	1963	Gordie Howe, Detroit	1992	Mario Lemieux, Pittsburgh
1990	Sergei Makarov, Calgary	1964–65	Stan Mikita, Chicago	1993	Mario Lemieux, Pittsburgh
1991	Ed Belfour, Chicago	1966	Bobby Hull, Chicago	1994	Wayne Gretzky, Los Angeles
1992	Pavel Bure, Vancouver	1967–68	Stan Mikita, Chicago	1995	Jaromir Jagr, Pittsburgh

N.H.L. CHAMPIONS

Wales Trophy		**Eastern Division**		1988	Boston	1976–77	Philadelphia
1939	Boston	1968–69	Montreal	1989	Montreal	1978–79	N.Y. Islanders
1940	Boston	1970	Chicago	1990	Boston	1980	Philadelphia
1941	Boston	1971	Boston	1991	Pittsburgh	1981	New York Islanders
1942	New York	1972	Boston	1992	Pittsburgh	1982	Edmonton
1943	Detroit	1973	Montreal	1993	Montreal	1983	Edmonton
1944–47	Montreal	1974	Boston	1994	N.Y. Rangers	1984	Edmonton
1948	Toronto			1995	Quebec	1985	Edmonton
1948–55	Detroit	**Eastern Conference**[1]				1986	Calgary
1956	Montreal	1975	Buffalo	**CAMPBELL BOWL**		1987	Edmonton
1957	Detroit	1976–79	Montreal	**Western Division**		1988	Edmonton
1958–62	Montreal	1980	Buffalo	1968	Philadelphia	1989	Calgary
1963	Toronto	1981	Montreal	1969	St. Louis	1990	Edmonton
1964	Montreal	1982	New York Islanders	1970	St. Louis	1991	Minnesota
1965	Detroit	1983	New York Islanders	1971–73	Chicago	1992	Chicago
1966	Montreal	1984	New York Islanders	1974	Philadelphia	1993	Los Angeles
1967	Chicago	1985	Philadelphia			1994	Detroit
		1986	Montreal	**Western Conference**[2]		1995	Detroit
		1987	Philadelphia	1975	Philadelphia		

1. Prior to 1994 was the Wales Conference. 2. Prior to 1994 was the Campbell Conference.

Stanley Cup Playoffs—1995

The labor dispute between players and owners limited the regular season to 48 games, but a full playoff schedule was played. The June 24 date of the last game of the Stanley Cup Final series was the latest date for a National Hockey League championship game in the history of the league.

The New Jersey Devils, without the benefit of home ice advantage in any of its playoff series, won the first Stanley Cup championship in their history.

The Devils beat the favored Detroit Red Wings in four straight games. This franchise, which began in Kansas City and played in Denver before settling in New Jersey for the 1982–83 season, was considering moving again even after winning the Stanley Cup.

For the second year of a new system, the playoffs pitted teams ranked instead of divisions. The league also saw its games televised nationally in the first year of a contract with the Fox television network and cable's ESPN.

FIRST ROUND
New York Rangers defeated the Quebec Nordiques, 4 games to 2

Philadelphia Flyers defeated the Buffalo Sabres, 4 games to 1

Pittsburgh Penguins defeated the Washington Capitals, 4 games to 3

New Jersey Devils defeated the Boston Bruins, 4 games to 1

Detroit Red Wings defeated the Dallas Stars, 4 games to 1

San Jose Sharks defeated the Calgary Flames, 4 games to 3

Vancouver Canucks defeated the St. Louis Blues, 4 games to 3

Chicago Black Hawks defeated the Toronto Maple Leafs, 4 games to 3

SECOND ROUND
Philadelphia Flyers defeated the New York Rangers, 4 games to 0

New Jersey Devils defeated the Pittsburgh Penguins, 4 games to 1

Detroit Red Wings defeated the San Jose Sharks, 4 games to 0

Chicago Black Hawks defeated the Vancouver Canucks, 4 games to 0

CONFERENCE FINALS
Eastern Conference
New Jersey Devils defeated Philadelphia Flyers, 4 games to 2
June 3—New Jersey 4, PHILADELPHIA 1
June 5—New Jersey 5, PHILADELPHIA 2
June 7—Philadelphia 3, NEW JERSEY 2 (OT)
June 10—Philadelphia 4, NEW JERSEY 2
June 11—New Jersey 3, PHILADELPHIA 2
June 13—NEW JERSEY 4, Philadelphia 2

Western Conference
Detroit Red Wings defeated Chicago Black Hawks, 4 games to 1
June 1—DETROIT 2, Chicago 1 (OT)
June 4—DETROIT 3, Chicago 2
June 6—Detroit 4, CHICAGO 3 (2OT)
June 8—CHICAGO 5, Detroit 2
June 11—DETROIT 2, Chicago 1 (2OT)

NOTE: Home teams are in capitals.

STANLEY CUP CHAMPIONSHIP FINALS

New Jersey Devils defeated Detroit Red Wings, 4 games to 0

June 17—New Jersey 2, DETROIT 1
June 20—New Jersey 4, DETROIT 2
June 22—NEW JERSEY 5, Detroit 2
June 24—NEW JERSEY 5, Detroit 2

OTHER N.H.L. AWARDS—1995

Frank Selke Trophy (top defensive forward)—Ron Francis, Pittsburgh
King Clancy Trophy (Humanitarian community involvement)—Joe Nieuwendyk, Calgary
Jack Adams Trophy (Coach of the Year)—Marc Crawford, Quebec
Bill Masterson Trophy (Sportsmanship)—Pat La Fontaine, Buffalo

NATIONAL HOCKEY LEAGUE
FINAL STANDINGS OF THE CLUBS—1994–95

EASTERN CONFERENCE
Northeast Division

	W	L	T	GF	GA	Pts
[1,2,3] Quebec Nordiques	30	13	5	185	134	65
[1] Pittsburgh Penquins	29	16	3	181	158	61
[1] Boston Bruins	27	18	3	150	127	57
[1] Buffalo Sabres	22	19	7	130	119	51
Hartford Whalers	19	24	5	127	141	43
Montreal Canadiens	18	23	7	125	148	43
Ottawa Senators	9	34	5	117	174	23

Atlantic Division

	W	L	T	GF	GA	Pts
[1,2] Philadelphia Flyers	28	16	4	150	132	60
[1] New Jersey Devils	22	18	8	136	121	52
[1] Washington Capitals	22	18	8	136	120	52
[1] New York Rangers	22	23	3	139	134	47
Florida Panthers	20	22	6	115	127	46
Tampa Bay Lightning	17	28	3	120	144	37
New York Islanders	15	28	5	126	158	35

WESTERN CONFERENCE
Central Division

	W	L	T	GF	GA	Pts
[1,2,3] Detroit Red Wings	33	11	4	180	117	70
[1] St. Louis Blues	28	15	5	178	135	61
[1] Chicago Black Hawks	24	19	5	156	115	53
[1] Toronto Maple Leafs	21	19	8	135	146	50
[1] Dallas Stars	17	23	8	136	135	42
Winnipeg Jets	16	25	7	157	177	39

Pacific Division

	W	L	T	GF	GA	Pts
[1,2] Calgary Flames	24	17	7	163	135	55
[1] Vancouver Canucks	18	18	12	153	148	48
San Jose Sharks	19	25	4	129	161	42
Los Angeles Kings	16	23	9	142	174	41
Edmonton Oilers	17	27	4	136	183	38
Anaheim Mighty Ducks	16	27	5	125	164	37

1. Clinched Playoff berth. 2. Clinched Division title. 3. Clinched Conference title.

N.H.L. LEADING GOALTENDERS—1994–95

	GPI	Min	GA	Avg
Dominik Hasek, Buffalo	41	2416	85	2.11
Rick Tabaracci, Wsh–Cgy	13	596	21	2.11
Jim Carey, Washington	28	1604	57	2.13
Chris Osgood, Detroit	19	1087	41	2.26
Ed Belfour, Chicago	42	2450	93	2.28

N.H.L. LEADING SCORERS—1994–95

	Team	GP	G	A	Pts
Jaromir Jagr	Pittsburgh	48	32	38	70
Eric Lindros	Philadelphia	46	29	41	70
Alexei Zhamnov	Winnipeg	48	30	35	65
Joe Sakic	Quebec	47	19	43	62
Ron Francis	Pittsburgh	44	11	48	59
Theoren Fleury	Calgary	47	29	29	58
Paul Coffey	Detroit	45	14	44	58
Mikael Renberg	Philadelphia	47	26	31	57
John Leclair	Mtl–Phi	46	26	28	54
Mark Messier	NY Rangers	46	14	39	53
Adam Oates	Boston	48	12	41	53
Bernie Nicholls	Chicago	48	22	29	51
Keith Tkachuk	Winnipeg	48	22	29	51
Brett Hull	St. Louis	48	29	21	50
Joe Nieuwendyk	Calgary	46	21	29	50
Sergei Fedorov	Detroit	42	20	30	50
Peter Forsberg	Quebec	47	15	35	50
Owen Nolan	Quebec	46	30	19	49
Teemu Selanne	Winnipeg	45	22	26	48
Mark Recchi	Phi–Mtl	49	16	32	48
Wayne Gretzky	Los Angeles	48	11	37	48

Team	GP	G	A	Pts
Pierre Turgeon	NYI–Mtl	49	24	23	47
Mats Sundin	Toronto	47	23	24	47
Alexander Mogilny	Buffalo	44	19	28	47

N.H.L. CAREER SCORING LEADERS
(Through 1994–95 season)

		Yrs	Games	G	A	Pts
1.	Wayne Gretzky[1]	16	1,173	814	1,692	2,506
2.	Gordie Howe	26	1,767	801	1,049	1,850
3.	Marcel Dionne	18	1,348	731	1,040	1,771
4.	Phil Esposito	18	1,282	717	873	1,590
5.	Stan Mikita	22	1,394	541	926	1,467
6.	Brian Trottier	18	1,279	524	901	1,425
7.	John Bucyk	23	1,540	556	813	1,369
7.	Mark Messier[1]	16	1,127	492	877	1,369
9.	Guy Lafleur	17	1,126	560	793	1,353
10.	Paul Coffey[1]	15	1,078	358	978	1,336
11.	Gilbert Perreault	17	1,191	512	814	1,326
12.	Dale Hawerchuk[1]	14	1,055	489	825	1,314
13.	Jari Kurri[1]	14	1,028	565	731	1,296
14.	Alex Delvecchio	24	1,549	456	825	1,281
15.	Ray Ratelle	21	1,281	491	776	1,267
16.	Denis Savard[1]	15	1,063	451	812	1,263
17.	Peter Stasny[1]	14	977	450	789	1,239
18.	Mario Lemieux[1]	16	1,146	323	907	1,230
19.	Norm Ullman	20	1,410	490	739	1,229
20.	Jean Beliveau	20	1,125	507	712	1,219
21.	Mario Lemieux[1]	11	599	494	717	1,211
22.	Bobby Clarke	15	1,144	358	852	1,210
23.	Mike Gartner[1]	16	1,208	629	562	1,191
24.	Bobby Hull	16	1,063	610	560	1,170
25.	Steve Yzerman[1]	12	862	481	679	1,160

1. Still active entering 1995–96 season.

BOWLING

The game of bowling in the United States is an indoor development of the more ancient outdoor game that survives as lawn bowling. The outdoor game is prehistoric in origin and probably goes back to Primitive Man and round stones that were rolled at some target. It is believed that a game something like nine-pins was popular among the Dutch, Swiss and Germans as long ago as A.D. 1200 at which time the game was played outdoors with an alley consisting of a single plank 12 to 18 inches wide along which was rolled a ball toward three rows of three pins each placed at the far end of the alley. When the first indoor alleys were built and how the game was modified from time to time are matters of dispute.

It is supposed that the early settlers of New Amsterdam (New York City) being Dutch, they brought their two bowling games with them. About a century ago the game of nine-pins was flourishing in the United States but so corrupted by gambling on matches that it was barred by law in New York and Connecticut. Since the law specifically barred "nine-pins," it was eventually evaded by adding another pin and thus legally making it a new game.

Various organizations were formed to make rules for bowling and supervise competition in the United States but none was successful until the American Bowling Congress, organized Sept. 9, 1895, became the ruling body.

AMERICAN BOWLING CONGRESS CHAMPIONS

Year	Singles	All–events	Year	Singles	All–events
1959	Ed Lubanski	Ed Lubanski	1979	Rick Peters	Bob Basacchi
1960	Paul Kulbaga	Vince Lucci	1980	Mike Eaton	Steve Fehr
1961	Lyle Spooner	Luke Karen	1981	Rob Vital	Rod Toft
1962	Andy Renaldo	Billy Young	1982	Bruce Bohm	Rich Wonders
1963	Fred Delello	Bus Owalt	1983	Rick Kendrick	Tony Cariello
1964	Jim Stefanich	Les Zikes, Jr.	1984	Bob Antczak and	
1965	Ken Roeth	Tom Hathaway		Neal Young (tie)	Bob Goike
1966	Don Chapman	John Wilcox	1985	Glen Harbison	Barry Asher
1967	Frank Perry	Gary Lewis	1986	Jess Mackey	Ed Marazka
1968	Wayne Kowalski	Vince Mazzanti	1987	Terry Taylor	Ryan Schafer
1969	Greg Campbell	Eddie Jackson	1988	Steve Hutkowski	Rick Steelsmith
1970	Jake Yoder	Mike Berlin	1989	Paul Tetreault	George Hall
1971	Al Cohn	Al Cohn	1990	Bob Hochrein	Mike Neumann
1972	Bill Pointer	Mac Lowry	1991	Ed Deines	Tom Howery
1973	Ed Thompson	Ron Woolet	1992	Bob Youker and	
1974	Gene Krause	Bob Hart		Gary Blatchford (tie)	Mike Tucker
1975	Jim Setser	Bobby Meadows	1993	Dan Bock	Jeff Nimke
1976	Mike Putzer	Jim Lindquist	1994	John Weltzien	Thomas Holt
1977	Frank Gadaleto	Bud Debenham	1995	Matt Surina	Jeff Kwiatkowski
1978	Rich Mersek	Chris Cobus			

PROFESSIONAL BOWLERS ASSOCIATION

National Championship Tournament

1960	Don Carter	1969	Mike McGrath	1978	Warren Nelson	1987	Randy Pedersen
1961	Dave Soutar	1970	Mike McGrath	1979	Mike Aulby	1988	Brian Voss
1962	Carmen Salvino	1971	Mike Lemongello	1980	Johnny Petraglia	1989	Pete Weber
1963	Billy Hardwick	1972	Johnny Guenther	1981	Earl Anthony	1990	Jim Pencak
1964	Bob Strampe	1973	Earl Anthony	1982	Earl Anthony	1991	Mike Miller
1965	Dave Davis	1974	Earl Anthony	1983	Earl Anthony	1992	Eric Forkel
1966	Wayne Zahn	1975	Earl Anthony	1984	Bob Chamberlain	1993	Ron Palombi
1967	Dave Davis	1976	Paul Colwell	1985	Mike Aulby	1994	David Traber
1968	Wayne Zahn	1977	Tommy Hudson	1986	Tom Crites	1995	Scott Alexander

BOWLING PROPRIETORS' ASSOCIATION OF AMERICA—MEN

United States Open[1]

1971	Mike Lemongello	1978	Nelson Burton, Jr.	1984	Mark Roth	1990	Ron Palumbi, Jr.
1972	Don Johnson	1979	Joe Berardi	1985	Marshall Holman	1991	Pete Weber
1973	Mike McGrath	1980	Steve Martin	1986	Steve Cook	1992	Robert Lawrence
1974	Larry Laub	1981	Marshall Holman	1987	Del Ballard	1993	Del Ballard, Jr.
1975	Steve Neff	1982	Dave Husted	1988	Pete Weber	1994	Justin Hromek
1976	Paul Moser	1983	Gary Dickinson	1989	Mike Aulby	1995	Dave Husted
1977	Johnny Petraglia						

1. Replaced All–Star tournament and is rolled as part of B.P.A. tour.

WOMEN'S INTERNATIONAL BOWLING CONGRESS CHAMPIONS

Year	Singles	All–events	Year	Singles	All–events
1959	Mae Bolt	Pat McBride	1980	Betty Morris	Cheryl Robinson
1960	Marge McDaniels	Judy Roberts	1981	Virginia Norton	Virginia Norton
1961	Elaine Newton	Evelyn Teal	1982	Gracie Freeman	Aleta Rzepecki
1962	Martha Hoffman	Flossie Argent	1983	Aleta Rzepecki	Virginia Norton
1963	Dot Wilkinson	Helen Shablis	1984	Freida Gates	Shinobu Saitoh
1964	Jean Havlish	Jean Havlish	1985	Polly Schwarzel	Aleta Sill
1965	Doris Rudell	Donna Zimmerman	1986	Dana Stewart	Robin Romeo
1966	Gloria Bouvia	Kate Helbig			Maria Lewis (tie)
1967	Gloria Paeth	Carol Miller	1987	Regi Junak	Leanne Barrette
1968	Norma Parks	Susie Reichley	1988	Michelle Meyer–Welty	Lisa Wagner
1969	Joan Bender	Helen Duval	1989	Lorraine Anderson	Nancy Fehn
1970	Dorothy Fothergill	Dorothy Fothergill	1990	Dana Miller–Mackie	
1971	Mary Scruggs	Lorrie Nichols		and Paula Carter	Carol Norman
1972	D. D. Jacobson	Mildred Martorella	1991	Debbie Kuhn	Debbie Kuhn
1973	Bobby Buffaloe	Toni Calvery	1992	Patty Ann	Mitsuko Tokimoto
1974	Shirley Garms	Judy C. Soutar	1993	Karen Collura and	Bertha Blackshur
1975	Barbara Leicht	Virginia Norton		Kari Murph (tie)	and Sharon Davis (tie)
1976	Bev Shonk	Betty Morris	1994	Vicki Fifield	Wendy Macpherson–
1977	Akiko Yamaga	Akiko Yamaga			Papanos
1978	Mae Bolt	Annese Kelly	1995	Beth Owen	Beth Owen
1979	Betty Morris	Betty Morris			

BOWLING PROPRIETORS' ASSOCIATION OF AMERICA—WOMEN[1]

United States Open

1971	Paula Carter	1977	Betty Morris	1983	Dana Miller	1989	Robin Romeo
1972	Lorrie Nichols	1978	Donna Adamek	1984	Karen Ellingsworth	1990	Dana Miller–Mackie
1973	Mildred Martorella	1979	Diana Silva	1985	Pat Mercatanti	1991	Anne Marie Duggan
1974	Pat Costello (Calif.)	1980	Pat Costello (Calif.)	1986	Wendy MacPherson	1992	Tish Johnson
1975	Paula Carter	1981	Donna Adamek	1987	Carol Nurman	1993	Dede Davidson
1976	Patty Costello (Pa.)	1982	Shinobu Saitoh	1988	Lisa Wagner	1994	Aleta Sill

1. The 1995 tournament was scheduled to be held after IPA went to press.

WIBC QUEENS TOURNAMENT CHAMPIONS

1961	Janet Harman	1970	Mildred Martorella	1979	Donna Adamek	1988	Wendy McPherson
1962	Dorothy Wilkinson	1971	Mildred Martorella	1980	Donna Adamek	1989	Carol Gianotti
1963	Irene Monterosso	1972	Dorothy Fothergill	1981	Katsuko Sugimoto	1990	Patty Ann
1964	D.D. Jacobson	1973	Dorothy Fothergill	1982	Katsuko Sugimoto	1991	Dede Davidson
1965	Betty Kuczynski	1974	Judy Soutar	1983	Aleta Rzepecki	1992	Cindy Coburn-Carroll
1966	Judy Lee	1975	Cindy Powell	1984	Kazue Inahashi	1993	Jan Schmidt
1967	Mildred Martorella	1976	Pamela Buckner	1985	Aleta Sill	1994	Anne Marie Duggan
1968	Phyllis Massey	1977	Dana Stewart	1986	Cora Fiebig	1995	Sandy Postma
1969	Ann Feigel	1978	Loa Boxberger	1987	Cathy Almeida		

PROFESSIONAL BOWLERS ASSOCIATION CHAMPIONSHIP—1995

(Toledo, Ohio, Feb. 19–25, 1995)

Winner—Scott Alexander, Seattle, Wash., defeated Wayne Webb, Canadaigua, N.Y., 246–210 in title match.
3. Mike Aulby, Indianapolis, Ind.
4. Don Genalo, Perrysburg, Ohio
5. Jason Couch, Claremont, Fla.

WOMEN'S INTERNATIONAL BOWLING CONGRESS TOURNAMENT—1995

(March 30–June 12, 1995, Tucson, Ariz.)

Singles—Beth Owen, Dallas, Tex.	749
Doubles—Carol Harsh and Debbie Villani, Las Vegas, Nev.	1,299
All Events—Beth Owen, Dallas, Tex.	1,983
Team—Contour Power Grips, West Bloomfield, Mich.	3,125

AMERICAN BOWLING CONGRESS TOURNAMENT—1995

(Feb. 4–July 1, Reno, Nev.)

Regular Division

Singles—Matt Surina, Mead, Wash.	826
Doubles—Michael Wambold and Scott Kruppenbacher, Rochester, N.Y.	1,486
All Events—Jeff Kwiatkowski, Maumee, Ohio	2,191
Team—Arden Lanes, Seattle, Wash.	3,387

Booster Division

Team—First Texas Bank, Killeen, Tex.	2,849

AMERICAN BOWLING CONGRESS MASTERS TOURNAMENT—1995

(May 2–6, 1995, Reno, Nev.)

Mike Aulby, Indianapolis, Ind. defeated Mark Williams, Beaumont, Tex., 200–187 in final match.

SKIING

HISTORY OF SKIING IN THE UNITED STATES

Skis were devised for utility, to aid those who had to travel over snow. The Norwegians, Swedes, Lapps, and other inhabitants of northern lands used skis for many centuries before skiing became a sport. Emigrants from these countries brought skis to the United States with them. The first skier of record in the United States was a mailman by the name of "Snowshoe" Thompson, born and raised in Telemarken, Norway, who came to the United States and, beginning in 1850, used skis through 20 successive winters in carrying mail from Northern California to Carson Valley, Idaho.

Ski clubs sprang up over 100 years ago where there were Norwegian and Swedish settlers in Wisconsin and Minnesota and ski contests were held in that territory in 1886. On Feb. 21, 1904, at Ishpenning, Mich., a small group of skiers organized the National Ski Association. In 1961 it was renamed the United States Ski Association.

ALPINE WORLD CUP OVERALL WINNERS

Year	Men	Women	Team
1967	Jean–Claude Killy, France	Nancy Greene, Canada	France
1968	Jean–Claude Killy, France	Nancy Greene, Canada	France
1969	Karl Schranz, Austria	Gertrude Gabl, Austria	Austria
1970	Karl Schranz, Austria	Michel Jacot, France	France
1971	Gustavo Thoeni, Italy	Annemarie Proell, Austria	France
1972	Gustavo Thoeni, Italy	Annemarie Proell, Austria	France
1973	Gustavo Thoeni, Italy	Annemarie Proell Moser, Austria	Austria
1974	Piero Gros, Italy	Annemarie Proell Moser, Austria	Austria
1975	Gustavo Thoeni, Italy	Annemarie Proell Moser, Austria	Austria
1976	Ingemar Stenmark, Sweden	Rosi Mittermaier, West Germany	Austria
1977	Ingemar Stenmark, Sweden	Lise–Marie Morerod, Switzerland	Austria
1978	Ingemar Stenmark, Sweden	Hanni Wenzel, Liechtenstein	Austria
1979	Peter Luescher, Switzerland	Annemarie Proell Moser, Austria	Austria
1980	Andreas Wenzel, Liechtenstein	Hanni Wenzel, Liechtenstein	Liechtenstein
1981	Phil Mahre, United States	Marie–Theres Nadig, Switzerland	Switzerland
1982	Phil Mahre, United States	Erika Hess, Switzerland	Austria
1983	Phil Mahre, United States	Tamara McKinney, United States	Switzerland
1984	Pirmin Zurbriggen, Switzerland	Erika Hess, Switzerland	Switzerland
1985	Marc Girardelli, Luxembourg	Michela Figini, Switzerland	Switzerland
1986	Marc Girardelli, Luxembourg	Maria Walliser, Switzerland	Switzerland
1987	Pirmin Zurbriggen, Switzerland	Maria Walliser, Switzerland	Switzerland
1988	Pirmin Zurbriggen, Switzerland	Michela Figini, Switzerland	Switzerland
1989	Marc Girardelli, Luxembourg	Vreni Schneider, Switzerland	Switzerland
1990	Pirmin Zurbriggen, Switzerland	Petra Kronberger, Austria	Austria
1991	Marc Girardelli, Luxembourg	Petra Kronberger, Austria	Austria
1992	Paul Accola, Switzerland	Petra Kronberger, Austria	Switzerland
1993	Marc Girardelli, Luxembourg	Anita Wachter, Austria	Austria
1994	Kjetil Andre Aamodt, Norway	Anita Wachter, Austria	Austria
1995	Alberto Tomba, Italy	Vreni Schneider, Switzerland	Austria

1995 UNITED STATES ALPINE CHAMPIONSHIPS

Men's Downhill
1. A.J. Kitt, U.S.A.
2. Craig Thrasher, U.S.A.
3. Kyle Rasmussen, U.S.A.
4. Jason Rosener, U.S.A.
5. Clic Bloomfield, U.S.A.

Men's Giant Slalom
1. Daron Rahives, U.S.A.
2. Paul Casey Puckett, U.S.A.
3. Casey Snyder, U.S.A.
4. Kyle Rasmussen, U.S.A.
5. Matthew Grosjean, U.S.A.

Women's Downhill
1. Megan Gerety, U.S.A.
2. Shana Sweitzer, U.S.A.
3. Hilary Lindh, U.S.A.
4. Kathleen Monahan, U.S.A.
5. Lisl Hager, U.S.A.

Women's Giant Slalom
1. Heidi Voelker, U.S.A.
2. Eva Twardokens, U.S.A.
3. Christi Hager, U.S.A.
4. Carrie Sheinberg, U.S.A.
5. Megan Gerety, U.S.A.

Men's Slalom
1. Matthew Grosjean, U.S.A.
2. Paul Casey Puckett, U.S.A.
3. Jeremy Nobis, U.S.A.
4. Michael Elvidge, Canada
5. Justin Yazmark, U.S.A.

Men's Combined
1. Paul Casey Puckett, U.S.A.
2. Matthew Grosjean, U.S.A.
3. Jeremy Nobis, U.S.A.
4. Jason Rosener, U.S.A.
5. Kyle Rasmussen, U.S.A.

Women's Slalom
1. Kristina Koznick, U.S.A.
2. Carrie Sheinberg, U.S.A.
3. Edith Rozsa, Canada
4. Heidi Voelker, U.S.A.
5. Kristi Terzian, U.S.A.

Women's Combined
1. Carrie Sheinberg, U.S.A.
2. Eva Twardokens, U.S.A.
3. Kathleen Monahan, U.S.A.
4. Heidi Voelker, U.S.A.
5. Lisl Hager, U.S.A.

1995 ALPINE WORLD CUP CHAMPIONS

Men	**Pts**
Overall—Alberto Tomba, Italy	1,150
Downhill—Luc Alphand, France	484
Slalom—Alberto Tomba, Itally	700
Giant Slalom—Alberto Tomba, Italy	450
Super G—Peter Runggaldier, Italy	332

Women |
--- | ---
Overall—Vreni Schneider, Switzerland | 1,248
Downhill—Picabo Street, United States | 709
Slalom—Vreni Schneider, Switzerland | 560
Giant Slalom—Vreni Schneider, Switzerland | 450
Super G—Katja Seizinger, Germany | 446

ALPINE WORLD CUP COMBINED—1995

Men |
--- | ---
1. Marc Giradelli, Luxembourg | 200
2. Harold Strand Nilsen, Norway | 140
3. Lasse Kjus, Norway | 125
4. Kjetil Andre Aamodt, Norway | 100
5. Espen Heilerud, Norway | 72

Women |
--- | ---
1. Pernilla Wiberg, Sweden | 100
2. Vreni Schneider, Switzerland | 80
3. Martina Ent, Germany | 60
4. Katja Seizinger, Germany | 50
5. Marianne Kjoerstad, Germany | 50

WORLD CUP NORDIC COMBINED—1995

1. Kenji Ogiwara, Japan	1,285
2. Bjarte Engen Vik, Norway	911
3. Knut Tore Apeland, Norway	898
4. Tsugiharu Ogiwara, Japan	825
5. Takanon Kono, Japan	710
Best American: 11. Todd Lodwick	464

1995 NATIONS CUP STANDINGS

Overall		**Men**	
1. Austria	6,862	1. Austria	5,884
2. Switzerland	6,015	2. Italy	3,756
3. Italy	5,962	3. Norway	3,139
4. Norway	4,382	4. Switzerland	2,158
5. Germany	3,894	5. France	1,976
6. France	3,885	6. United States	1,213
7. United States	3,314	**Women**	
8. Slovenia	2,887	1. Switzerland	3,857
9. Sweden	2,030	2. Germany	3,508
10. Luxembourg	744	3. Austria	2,978
		4. Italy	2,206
		5. United States	2,081

1995 WORLD CUP SKI JUMPING

1. Andi Goldberger, Austria	1,571
2. Roberto Cecon, Italy	935
3. Janne Ahonen, Finland	869
4. Kazuyoshi Funaki, Japan	843
5. Takanobu Okabe, Japan	821

1995 U.S. CROSS COUNTRY CHAMPIONSHIPS

Men
10-kilometer classic—Justin Wadsworth
30-kilomter classic—Justin Wadsworth
15-kilometer freestyle—Carl Swensen

Women
5-kilometer classic—Leslie Thompson
15-kilometer classic—Nina Kemppel
10-kilometer freestyle—Leslie Thompson

UNITED STATES SKI JUMPING CHAMPIONSHIPS—1995

1. Randy Weber	223.5
2. Tad Langlois	221.5
3. Matt Kuusinen	217.0
4. Brendan Doran	216.0
5. Taylor Hoffman	209.5

NORDIC WORLD CHAMPIONSHIPS—1995
WORLD CUP FINAL STANDINGS

Men	**Pts**	**Women**	
1. Bjorn Daehlie, Norway	930	1. Yelsna Vaelbe, Russia	1,060
2. Vladmir Smimov, Kazakhstan	866	2. Nina Gavnljuk, Russia	840
3. Silvio Faurier, Italy	591	3. Larissa Lazhutina, Russia	785
Best American: 62. Todd Boonstra	17	Best American: 46. Leslie Thompson	31

CURLING

UNITED STATES CHAMPIONSHIPS—1995

	Site	Winner's Home Club	Skip
Men's	Appleton, Wis.	Super, Wis.	Tim Somerville
Women's	Appleton, Wis.	Madison, Wis.	Lisa Schoeneberg
Junior Men's	Hibbing, Minn.	Centerville, Wis.	Mike Peplinski
Junior Women's	Hibbing, Minn.	Bemidji, Minn.	Risa O'Connell

WORLD CHAMPIONSHIPS—1995

	Site	Winner's Country	Skip
Men's	Manitoba, Canada	Canada	Kerry Burtnyk
Women's	Manitoba, Canada	Canada	Elisabet Johansson
Junior Men's	Perth, Scotland	Scotland	Tom Brewster
Junior Women's	Perth, Scotland	Canada	Kelly MacKenzie

SPEED SKATING

U.S. OUTDOOR CHAMPIONS (LONG TRACK)

Men

1959–60	Ken Bartholomew	1985	Andy Gabel	1970–71	Sheila Young
1961	Ed Rudolph	1986	Eric Klein	1972	Ruth Moore, Nancy Thorne
1962	Floyd Bedbury	1987	Dave Paulicic	1973	Nancy Class
1963	Tom Gray	1988	Patrick Wentland	1974	Kris Garbe
1964	Neil Blatchford	1989	Matt Trimble	1975	Nancy Swider
1965–66	Rich Wurster	1990	Andy Zak	1976	Connie Carpenter
1967	Mike Passarella	1991	Pat Seltsam	1977	Liz Crowe
1968–70	Peter Cefalu	1992	Dan Jansen	1978	Paula Class, Betsy Davis
1971	Jack Walters	1993	Brian Smith	1979	Gretchen Byrnes
1972	Barth Levy	1994	K.C. Boutiette	1980	Shari Miller
1973	Mike Woods	1995	David Tamburrino	1981–82	Lisa Merrifield
1974	Leigh Barczewski, Mike Passarella	**Women**		1983–84	Janet Hainstock
1975	Rich Wurster	1960	Mary Novak	1985	Betsy Davis
1976	John Wurster	1961	Jean Ashworth	1986	Deb Perkins
1977	Jim Chapin	1962	Jean Omelenchuk	1987	Laura Zuckerman
1978	Bill Heinkel	1963	Jean Ashworth	1988	Elise Brinich
1979	Erik Henriksen	1964	Diane White	1989	Liza Merrifield
1980	Greg Oly	1965	Jean Omelenchuk	1990	Jane Eickhoff
1981	Tom Grannes	1966	Diane White	1991	Liza Dennehy
1982	Greg Oly	1967	Jean Ashworth	1992	Hilary Mills
1983–84	Michael Ralston	1968	Helen Lutsch	1993	Chantal Bailey
		1969	Sally Blatchford	1994–95	Moira D'Andrea

WORLD SPEED SKATING RECORDS (LONG TRACK)

Men

Distance	Time	Skater	Place	Year
500m	0:35.76	Dan Jansen, United States	Calgary, Canada	1994
1000m	1:12.37	Yasunori Miyabe, Japan	Calgary, Canada	1994
1500m	1:51.29	Johann Olav Koss, Norway	Lillehammer, Norway	1994
3000m	3:56.16	Thomas Blos, Netherlands	Calgary, Canada	1992
5000m	6:34.96	Johann Olav Koss, Norway	Lillehammer, Norway	1994
10,000m	13:30.55	Johann Olav Koss, Norway	Lillehammer, Norway	1994

Women

Distance	Time	Skater	Place	Year
500m	0:38.69	Bonnie Blair, United States	Calgary, Canada	1995
1000m	1:17.65	Christa Rothenburger, Germany	Calgary, Canada	1988
1500m	1:59.30	Karin Kania, Germany	Medeo, U.S.S.R.	1986
3000m	4:09.32	Gunda Niemann, Germany	Calgary, Canada	1994
5000m	7:03.26	Gunda Niemann, Germany	Calgary, Canada	1994

U.S. LONG TRACK CHAMPIONSHIPS—1995

(Dec. 31, 1994–Jan. 1, 1995, Milwaukee, Wis.)

Men

	Points
500m—Casey FitzRandolph, Verona, Wis.	74.960
1000m—Brendan Eppert, St. Louis, Mo.	75.770

Overall standings:

1. Casey FitzRandolph, Verona, Wis.	150.930
2. Brendan Eppert, St. Louis, Mo.	151.630
3. David Cruikshank, Northbrook, Ill.	152.110

Women

500m—Bonnie Blair, Pewaukee, Wis.	80.280
1000m—Bonnie Blair, Pewaukee, Wis.	80.980

Overall standings:

1. Bonnie Blair, Pewaukee, Wis.	161.260
2. Christine Witty, West Allis, Wis.	163.630
3. Moira D'Andrea, Saratoga Springs, N.Y.	164.225

U.S. LONG TRACK ALL-AROUND CHAMPIONSHIPS—1995

(Jan. 7–8, 1995, Milwaukee, Wis.)

Men

	Points
500m—Cory Carpenter	38.410
1000m—K.C. Boutiette	38.940
5000m—David Tamburrino	42.093
10000m—K.C. Boutiette	43.990
Overall—David Tamburrino	164.046

Women

500m—Moira D'Andrea	41.440
1500m—Moira D'Andrea	42.453
3000m—Moira D'Andrea	45.273
5000m—Moira D'Andrea	46.997
Overall—Moira D'Andrea	176.163

U.S. SHORT TRACK CHAMPIONSHIPS—1995

(March 17–19, 1995, Muskegon, Mich.)

Men

Grand Master—Ed Lang
Master—Ken Mastrianna
Senior—Chad Powell
Intermediate—Tony Goskowicz
Junior—Chad Richards
Juvenile—Daniel Weinstein
Midget—J.P. Kepka
Men's relay—Northern New York

Women

Grand Master—Elaine Standler
Master—Carole Moore
Senior—Debra Cohen
Intermediate—Kelly Anderson
Junior—Julie Goskowicz
Juvenile—Sarah Elliott
Midget—Cherise Wilkins
Women's relay—Wisconsin

WORLD CHAMPIONSHIPS—1995
(Feb. 18–19, 1995, Milwaukee, Wis.)

Men	Points	Women	Points
500m—Kim Yoon-Man, Rep. of Korea	73,050	500m—Bonnie Blair, United States	78.670
1000m—Kim Yoon-Man, Rep. of Korea	72.975	1000m—Bonnie Blair, United States	79.475
Overall standings:		Overall standings:	
1. Kim Yoon-Man, Rep. of Korea	146.025	1. Bonnie Blair, United States	158.145
2. Hiroyasu Shimizu, Japan	146.975	2. Oksana Ravolova, Russia	160.820
3. Yasunori Miyabe, Japan	147.025	3. Franziska Schenk, Germany	160.830

FIGURE SKATING

WORLD CHAMPIONS

Men

1960	Alain Giletti, France	1985	Alexandr Fadeev, U.S.S.R.	1975	Dianne de Leeuw, Netherlands
1961	No competition	1986	Brian Boitano, United States	1976	Dorothy Hamill, United States
1962	Donald Jackson, Canada	1987	Brian Orser, Canada	1977	Linda Fratianne, United States
1963	Don McPherson, Canada	1988	Brian Boitano, United States	1978	Anett Poetzsch, East Germany
1964	Manfred Schnelldorfer, West Germany	1989–91	Kurt Browning, Canada	1979	Linda Fratianne, United States
		1992	Viktor Petrenko, Unified Team	1980	Anett Poetzsch, East Germany
1965	Alain Calmat, France	1993	Kurt Browning, Canada	1981	Denise Beillmann, Switzerland
1966–68	Emmerich Danzer, Austria	1994	Elvis Stoyko, Canada	1982	Elaine Zayak, United States
1969–70	Tim Wood, United States	1995	Elvis Stoyko, Canada	1983	Rosalynn Sumners, United States
1971–73	Ondrej Nepela, Czechoslovakia	**Women**			
1974	Jan Hoffman, East Germany	1956–60	Carol Heiss, United States	1984–85	Katarina Witt, East Germany
1975	Sergei Yolkov, U.S.S.R.	1961	No competition	1986	Debi Thomas, United States
1976	John Curry, Britain	1962–64	Sjoukje Dijkstra, Netherlands	1987–88	Katarina Witt, East Germany
1977	Vladimir Kovalev, U.S.S.R.	1965	Petra Burka, Canada	1989	Midori Ito, Japan
1978	Charles Tickner, United States	1966–68	Peggy Fleming, United States	1990	Jill Trenary, United States
1979	Vladimir Kovalev, U.S.S.R.	1969–70	Gabriele Seyfert, East Germany	1991–92	Kristi Yamaguchi, United States
1980	Jan Hoffman, East Germany	1971–72	Beatrix Schuba, Austria	1993	Oksana Baiul, Ukraine
1981–84	Scott Hamilton, United States	1973	Karen Magnusson, Canada	1994	Yuka Sato, Japan
		1974	Christine Errath, East Germany	1995	Chen Lu, China

U.S. CHAMPIONS

Men

1946–52	Richard Button	1981–84	Scott Hamilton	1964–68	Peggy Fleming
1953–56	Hayes Jenkins	1985–88	Brian Boitano	1969–73	Janet Lynn
1957–60	David Jenkins	1989	Christopher Bowman	1974–76	Dorothy Hamill
1961	Bradley Lord	1990–91	Todd Eldredge	1977–80	Linda Fratianne
1962	Monty Hoyt	1992	Christopher Bowman	1981	Elaine Zayak
1963	Tommy Liz	1993–94	Scott Davis	1982–84	Rosalynn Sumners
1964	Scott Allen	1995	Todd Eldredge	1985	Tiffany Chin
1965	Gary Visconti			1986	Debi Thomas
1966	Scott Allen	**Women**		1987	Jill Trenary
1967	Gary Visconti	1943–48	Gretchen Merrill	1988	Debi Thomas
1968–70	Tim Wood	1949–50	Yvonne Sherman	1989–90	Jill Trenary
1971	John M. Petkevich	1951	Sonya Klopfer	1991	Tonya Harding
1972	Ken Shelley	1952–56	Tenley Albright	1992	Kristi Yamaguchi
1973–75	Gordon McKellen	1957–60	Carol Heiss	1993	Nancy Kerrigan
1976	Terry Kubicka	1961	Laurence Owen	1994	Tonya Harding
1977–80	Charles Tickner	1962	Barbara Roles Pursley	1995	Nicole Bobek
		1963	Lorraine Hanlon		

1995 WORLD CHAMPIONSHIPS

(March 7–12, 1995, Birmingham, England)

Men's singles—Gold: Elvis Stoyko, Canada
  Silver: Todd Eldredge, United States
  Bronze: Philippe Candeloro, France
Women's singles—Gold: Chen Lu, China
  Silver: Surya Bonaly, France
  Bronze: Nicole Bobek, United States
Pairs—Gold: Radka Kovarikova and Rene Novotney, Czech Republic
  Silver: Yevgenia Shishkova and Vadim Naumov, Russia
  Bronze: Jenni Meno and Todd Sand, United States
Dance—Gold: Oksana Grischuk and Yevgeny Platov, Russia
  Silver: Susanna Rahkamo and Petri Kokko, Finland
  Bronze: Sophie Moniotte and Pascal Lavanchy, France

1995 UNITED STATES CHAMPIONSHIPS

Senior men—Todd Eldredge, South Chatham, Mass.

Senior women—Nicole Bobek, Chicago

Senior pairs—Jenni Meno, Westlake, Ohio, and Todd Sand, Thousand Oaks, Calif.

Senior dance—Renee Roca, Rochester, N.Y., and Gorsha Sur, Colorado Springs, Colo.

Junior men—Matt Kessinger, Indianapolis, Ind.

Junior women—Sydne Bogel, Anchorage, Alaska

Junior pairs—Danielle and Steve Hartsell, Westland, Mich.

Junior dance—Eve Chalom and Mathew Gates, Beverly Hills, Mich.

SWIMMING

WORLD RECORDS—MEN

(Through September 1, 1995)
Approved by the International Swimming Federation (F.I.N.A.)
(F.I.N.A. discontinued acceptance of records in yards in 1968)
Source: United States Swim Team

Distance	Record	Holder	Country	Date
Freestyle				
50 meters	0:21.81	Tom Jager	United States	March 24, 1990
100 meters	0:48.21	Alexander Popov	Russia	June 18, 1994
200 meters	1:46.69	Georgio Lamberti	Italy	Aug. 15, 1989
400 meters	3:43.80	Kieren Perkins	Australia	Sept. 9, 1994
800 meters	7:46.00	Kieren Perkins	Australia	Aug. 24, 1994
1,500 meters	14:41.66	Kieren Perkins	Australia	Aug. 24, 1994
Backstroke				
100 meters	53.86	Jeff Rouse	United States	July 31, 1992
200 meters	1:57.30	Martin Zubero	Spain	Aug. 13, 1991
Breaststroke				
100 meters	1:00.95	Karolyi Guttler	Hungary	Aug. 5, 1993
200 meters	2:10.16	Mike Barrowman	United States	July 29, 1992
Butterfly				
100 meters	0:52.84	Pablo Morales	United States	June 23, 1986
200 meters	1:55.22	Denis Pankratov	Russia	June 14, 1995
Individual Medley				
200 meters	1:58.16	Jani Sievinen	Finland	Sept. 11, 1994
400 meters	4:12.30	Tom Dolan	United States	Sept. 6, 1994
Freestyle Relay				
400 meters	3:15.11	United States	Pan Pacific Team	Aug. 12, 1995
800 meters	7:11.95	Unified Team	Former Soviet Union	July 27, 1992
Medley Relay				
400 meters	3:36.93	United States	National Team	Sept. 25, 1988

WORLD RECORDS—WOMEN

Distance	Record	Holder	Country	Date
Freestyle				
50 meters	0:24.51	Jingyi Le	China	Sept. 11, 1994
100 meters	0:54.01	Jingyi Le	China	Sept. 5, 1994
200 meters	1:56.78	Franziska van Almsick	Germany	Sept. 6, 1994
400 meters	4:03.85	Janet Evans	United States	Sept. 22, 1988
800 meters	8:16.22	Janet Evans	United States	Aug. 20, 1989
1,500 meters	15:52.10	Janet Evans	United States	March 26, 1988
Backstroke				
100 meters	1:00.16	Chijong He	China	Sept. 10, 1994
200 meters	2:06.62	Kristina Egerszegi	Hungary	Aug. 26, 1991
Breaststroke				
100 meters	1:07.69	Samantha Riley	Australia	Sept. 9, 1994
200 meters	2:24.76	Rebecca Brown	Australia	March 16, 1994
Butterfly				
100 meters	0:57.93	Mary T. Meagher	United States	Aug. 16, 1981
200 meters	2:05.96	Mary T. Meagher	United States	Aug. 13, 1981
Individual Medley				
200 meters	2:11.65	Lin Li	China	July 30, 1992
400 meters	4:36.10	Petra Schneider	East Germany	Aug. 1, 1982
Freestyle Relay				
400 meters	3:37.91	China	National Team	Sept. 7, 1994
800 meters	7:55.47	East Germany	National Team	Aug. 18, 1987
Medley Relay				
400 meters	4:01.67	China	National Team	Sept. 10, 1994

AMERICAN SWIMMING RECORDS
(As of September 1, 1995)

Distance	Holder	Record	Date
MEN			
Freestyle			
50 meters	Tom Jager	0:21.81	March 24, 1990
100 meters	Matt Biondi	0:48.42	August 10, 1988
200 meters	Matt Biondi	1:47.72	August 15, 1989
400 meters	Matt Cetlinski	3:48.06	August 11, 1988
800 meters	Sean Killion	7:52.45	July 27, 1987
1500 meters	George DiCarlo	15:01.51	June 30, 1984
Backstroke			
100 meters	Jeff Rouse	0:53.86	July 31, 1992
200 meters	Tripp Schwenk	1:58.33	Aug. 1, 1995
Breaststroke			
100 meters	Steve Lundquist	1:01.65	July 29, 1984
200 meters	Mike Barrowman	2:10.16	July 29, 1992
Butterfly			
100 meters	Pablo Morales	0:52.84	June 23, 1986
200 meters	Melvin Stewart	1:55.69	January 12, 1991
Individual Medley			
200 meters	David Wharton	2:00.11	August 20, 1989
400 meters	Tom Dolan	4:12.30	September 6, 1994
Freestyle Relay			
400 meters	US Pan Pacific Team	3:15.11	August 12, 1995
800 meters	US National Team	7:12.51	September 21, 1988
Medley Relay			
400 meters	US National Team	3:36.93	July 31, 1992
	US National Team	3:36.93	September 25, 1988

Distance	Holder	Record	Date
WOMEN			
Freestyle			
50 meters	Amy Van Dyken	0:25.03	August 13, 1995
100 meters	Jenny Thompson	0:54.48	March 1, 1992
200 meters	Nicole Haislett	1:57.55	March 27, 1992
400 meters	Janet Evans	4:03.85	September 22, 1988
800 meters	Janet Evans	8:16.22	August 20, 1989
1500 meters	Janet Evans	15:52.10	March 26, 1988
Backstroke			
100 meters	Lea Loveless	1:00.82	July 30, 1992
200 meters	Betsy Mitchell	2:08.60	June 27, 1986
Breaststroke			
100 meters	Anita Nall	1:08.17	July 29, 1992
200 meters	Anita Nall	2:25.35	March 3, 1992
Butterfly			
100 meters	Mary T. Meagher	0:57.93	August 16, 1981
200 meters	Mary T. Meagher	2:05.96	August 13, 1981
Individual Medley			
200 meters	Summer Sanders	2:11.91	July 30, 1992
400 meters	Summer Sanders	4:37.58	July 26, 1992
Freestyle Relay			
400 meters	US National Team	3:39.46	July 28, 1992
800 meters	US National Team	8:02.12	August 17, 1986
Medley Relay			
400 meters	US National Team	4:02.54	July 30, 1992

N.C.A.A. SWIMMING AND DIVING CHAMPIONSHIPS—1995

Men

(March 23–25, 1995, Indianapolis, Ind.)

50-yard freestyle—Gustavo Borges, Michigan	0:19.68
100-yard freestyle—Gustavo Borges, Michigan	0:42.85
200-yard freestyle—Gustavo Borges, Michigan	1:34.61
500-yard freestyle—Tom Dolan, Michigan	4:08.75
1,650-yard freestyle—Tom Dolan, Michigan	14:29.31
100-yard backstroke—Brian Retterer, Stanford	0:45.43
200-yard backstroke—Brian Retterer, Stanford	1:40.61
100-yard breaststroke—Kurt Grote, Stanford	0:53.21
200-yard breaststroke—Kurt Grote, Stanford	1:55.02
100-yard butterfly—Lars Frolander, SMU	0:46.26
200-yard butterfly—Ugur Taner, California	1:44.39
200-yard individual medley—Kurt Jachimowski, Auburn	1:45.11
400-yard individual medley—Tom Dolan, Michigan	3:38.18
200-yard medley relay—Stanford	1:26.08
400-yard medley relay—Stanford	3:07.28
200-yard freestyle relay—Stanford	1:16.98
400-yard freestyle relay—Stanford	2:52.57
800-yard freestyle relay—Michigan	6:21.65
1-meter dive—P.J. Bogart, Minnesota	593.60 pts
3-meter dive—Evan Stewart, Tennessee	655.40 pts
10-meter dive—Tyce Routson, Miami, Fla.	785.70 pts

Team standings: 1. Michigan, 561; 2. Stanford, 475; 3. Auburn, 393.

Division II champion—Oakland University
Division III champion—Kenyon College

Women

(March 16–18, 1995, University of Texas, Austin, Tex.)

50-yard freestyle—Ashley Tappin, Arizona	0:22.34
100-yard freestyle—Jenny Thompson, Stanford	0:48.38
200-yard freestyle—Ashley Tappin, Arizona	1:45.23
500-yard freestyle—Mimosa McNerney, Florida	4:41.86
1,650-yard freestyle—Mimosa McNerney, Florida	15:59.71
100-yard backstroke—Alecia Humphrey, Michigan	0:54.10
200-yard backstroke—Alecia Humphrey, Michigan	1:54.68
100-yard breaststroke—Beata Kaszuba, Arizona St.	0:59.71
200-yard breaststroke—Beata Kaszuba, Arizona St.	2:09.71
100-yard butterfly—Jenny Thompson, Stanford	0:52.77
200-yard butterfly—Berit Puggaard, SMU	1:57.86
200-yard individual medley—Jenny Thompson, Stanford	1:57.63
400-yard individual medley—Allison Wagner, Florida	4:09.04
200-yard freestyle relay—Georgia	1:30.84
400-yard freestyle relay—Stanford	3:17.17
800-yard freestyle relay—SMU	7:14.31
200-yard medley relay—Stanford	1:40.88
400-yard medley relay—Michigan	3:38.40
1-meter dive—Cheril Santini, SMU	454.00 pts
3-meter dive—Tracy Bonner, Tennessee	580.20 pts
10-meter dive—Eileen Richetelli, Stanford	630.10 pts

Team standings: 1. Stanford, 497.5; 2. Michigan 478.5; 3. Texas, 355.

Division II champion—U.S. Air Force Academy
Division III champion—Kenyon College

PHILLIPS 66 NATIONAL SWIMMING CHAMPIONSHIPS—1995

Women

50-meter freestyle—Amy Van Dyken, Unattached	0:25.13
100-meter freestyle—Angel Martino, Americus	0:55.91
200-meter freestyle—Cristinia Teuscher, Badger	2:00.78
400-meter freestyle—Brooke Bennett, BSTC Blue Wave	4:10.72
800-meter freestyle—Brooke Bennett, BSTC Blue Wave	8:31.84
1,500-meter freestyle—Brooke Bennett, BSTC Blue Wave	16:17.84
100-meter backstroke—Lea Loveless, Badger	1:02.44
200-meter backstroke—Beth Botsfoed, No. Baltimore	2:12.82
100-meter breaststroke—Amanda Beard, Irvine Novas	1:10.37
200-meter breaststroke—Annemieke McReynolds, Scenic City	2:28.92
100-meter butterfly—Jenny Thompson, Stanford	1:00.19
200-meter butterfly—Michelle Griglione, Curl–Burke	2:11.56
200-meter individual medley—Allison Wagner, Florida	2:15.99
400-meter individual medley—Kristine Quance, Trojan	4:45.97
400-meter freestyle relay—Hillenbrand	3:47.24
800-meter freestyle relay—Stanford	8:15.70
400-meter medley relay—Hillenbrand	4:11.01

Men

50-meter freestyle—Jon Olsen, Curl–Burke	0:22.42
100-meter freestyle—Jon Olsen, Curl–Burke	0:49.44
200-meter freestyle—Chad Carvin, Hillenbrand	1:48.43
400-meter freestyle—John Piersma, Club Wolverine	3:49.72
800-meter freestyle—Peter Wright, Jersey Wahoos	8:06.27
1,500-meter freestyle—Carlton Bruner, Club Wolverine	15:17.17
100-meter backstroke—Jeff Rouse, Phoenix	0:59.17
200-meter backstroke—Tripp Schwenk, Unattached	1:58.33
100-meter breaststroke—Kurt Grote, Stanford	1:01.91
200-meter breaststroke—Eric Wunderlich, Napa Valley	2:15.14
100-meter butterfly—Mark Henderson, Curl–Burke	0:53.59
200-meter butterfly—Ray Carey, Stanford	1:59.17
200-meter individual medley—Paul Nelsen, Ft. Lauderdale	2:02.11
400-meter individual medley—Eric Namesnik, Club Wolverine	4:15.57
400-meter freestyle relay—Curl–Burke	3:20.29
800-meter freesetyle relay—Curl–Burke	7:25.89
400-meter medley relay—Phoenix	3:41.56

U.S. DIVING CHAMPIONSHIPS—1995

INDOOR

(April 19–23, Midland, Texas)

Women's Events

1-meter—Carrie Zarse, unattached	264.48
3-meter—Melissa Moses, unattached	512.52
Platform—Patty Armstrong, Woodlands Diving Team	451.74

Men's Events

1-meter—David Pichler, Ft. Lauderdale Diving Team	390.42
3-meter—Mark Bradshaw, Ohio State Diving Team	646.50
Platform—David Pichler, Ft. Lauderdale Diving Team	593.13

OUTDOOR

(Aug. 9–13, Bartlesville, Okla.)

Women's Events

1-meter—Doris Glenn Easterly, Ft. Lauderdale Diving Team	242.79
3-meter—Eileen Richetelli, Stanford	494.43
Platform—Becky Ruchl, Stingrays	478.47

Men's Events

1-meter—David Pichler, Ft. Lauderdale Diving Team	377.97
3-meter—Kent Ferguson, Miami Diving	651.51
Platform—Patrick Jeffrey, Team Orlando	584.16

BOXING

Whether it be called pugilism, prize fighting or boxing, there is no tracing "the Sweet Science" to any definite source. Tales of rivals exchanging blows for fun, fame or money go back to earliest recorded history and classical legend. There was a mixture of boxing and wrestling called the "pancratium" in the ancient Olympic Games and in such contests the rivals belabored one another with hands fortified with heavy leather wrappings that were sometimes studded with metal. More than one Olympic competitor lost his life at this brutal exercise.

There was little law or order in pugilism until Jack Broughton, one of the early champions of England, drew up a set of rules for the game in 1743. Broughton, called "the father of English boxing," also is credited with having invented boxing gloves. However, these gloves—or "mufflers" as they were called—were used only in teaching "the manly art of self–defense" or in training bouts. All professional championship fights were contested with "bare knuckles" until 1892, when John L. Sullivan lost the heavyweight championship of the world to James J. Corbett in New Orleans in a bout in which both contestants wore regulation gloves.

The Broughton rules were superseded by the London Prize Ring Rules of 1838. The 8th Marquis of Queensberry, with the help of John G. Chambers, put forward the "Queensberry Rules" in 1866, a code that called for gloved contests. Amateurs took quickly to the Queensberry Rules, the professionals slowly.

HISTORY OF WORLD HEAVYWEIGHT CHAMPIONSHIP FIGHTS
(Bouts in which a new champion was crowned)

Date	Where held	Winner, weight, age	Loser, weight, age	Rounds	Referee
Sept. 7, 1892	New Orleans, La.	James J. Corbett, 178 (26)	John L. Sullivan, 212 (33)	21	Prof. John Duffy
March 17, 1897	Carson City, Nev.	Bob Fitzsimmons, 167 (34)	James J. Corbett, 183 (30)	KO 14	George Siler
June 9, 1899	Coney Island, N.Y.	James J. Jeffries, 206 (24)[1]	Bob Fitzsimmons, 167 (37)	KO 11	George Siler
Feb. 23, 1906	Los Angeles	Tommy Burns, 180 (24)[2]	Marvin Hart, 188 (29)	20	James J. Jeffries
Dec. 26, 1908	Sydney, N.S.W.	Jack Johnson, 196 (30)	Tommy Burns, 176 (27)	KO 14	Hugh McIntosh
April 5, 1915	Havana, Cuba	Jess Willard, 230 (33)	Jack Johnson, 205 1/2 (37)	KO 26	Jack Welch
July 4, 1919	Toledo, Ohio	Jack Dempsey, 187 (24)	Jess Willard, 245 (37)	KO 3	Ollie Pecord
Sept. 23, 1926	Philadelphia	Gene Tunney, 189 (28)[3]	Jack Dempsey, 190 (31)	10	Pop Reilly
June 12, 1930	New York	Max Schmeling, 188 (24)	Jack Sharkey, 197 (27)	WF 4	Jim Crowley
June 21, 1932	Long Island City	Jack Sharkey, 205 (29)	Max Schmeling, 188 (26)	15	Gunboat Smith
June 29, 1933	Long Island City	Primo Carnera, 260 1/2 (26)	Jack Sharkey, 201 (30)	KO 6	Arthur Donovan
June 14, 1934	Long Island City	Max Baer, 209 1/2 (25)	Primo Carnera, 263 1/4 (27)	KO 11	Arthur Donovan
June 13, 1935	Long Island City	Jim Braddock, 193 3/4 (29)	Max Baer, 209 1/2 (26)	15	Jack McAvoy
June 22, 1937	Chicago	Joe Louis, 197 1/4 (23)	Jim Braddock, 197 (31)	KO 8	Tommy Thomas
June 22, 1949	Chicago	Ezzard Charles, 181 3/4 (27)[4]	Joe Walcott, 195 1/2 (35)	15	Davey Miller
Sept. 27, 1950	New York	Ezzard Charles, 184 1/2 (29)[5]	Joe Louis, 218 (36)	15	Mark Conn
July 18, 1951	Pittsburgh	Joe Walcott, 194 (37)	Ezzard Charles, 182 (30)	KO 7	Buck McTiernan
Sept. 23, 1952	Philadelphia	Rocky Marciano, 184 (29)[6]	Joe Walcott, 196 (38)	KO 13	Charley Daggert
Nov. 30, 1956	Chicago	Floyd Patterson, 182 1/4 (21)	Archie Moore, 187 3/4 (42)	KO 5	Frank Sikora
June 26, 1959	New York	Ingemar Johansson, 196 (26)	Floyd Patterson, 182 (24)	KO 3	Ruby Goldstein
June 20, 1960	New York	Floyd Patterson, 190 (25)	Ingemar Johansson, 194 3/4 (27)	KO 5	Arthur Mercante
Sept. 25, 1962	Chicago	Sonny Liston, 214 (28)	Floyd Patterson, 189 (27)	KO 1	Frank Sikora
Feb. 25, 1964	Miami Beach, Fla.	Cassius Clay, 210 (22)[7]	Sonny Liston, 218 (30)	KO 7	Barney Felix
March 4, 1968	New York	Joe Frazier, 204 1/2 (24)[8]	Buster Mathis, 243 1/2 (23)	KO 11	Arthur Mercante
April 27, 1968	Oakland, Calif.	Jimmy Ellis, 197 (28)[9]	Jerry Quarry, 195 (22)	15	Elmer Costa
Feb. 16, 1970	New York	Joe Frazier, 205 (26)[10]	Jimmy Ellis, 201 (29)	KO 5	Tony Perez
Jan. 22, 1973	Kingston, Jamaica	George Foreman, 217 1/2 (24)	Joe Frazier, 214 (29)	KO 2	Arthur Mercante
Oct. 30, 1974	Kinshasa, Zaire	Muhammad Ali, 216 1/2 (32)	George Foreman, 220 (26)	KO 8	Zack Clayton
Feb. 15, 1978	Las Vegas, Nev.	Leon Spinks, 197 (25)	Muhammad Ali, 224 1/2 (36)	15	Howard Buck
June 9, 1978	Las Vegas, Nev.	Larry Holmes, 212 (28)[11]	Ken Norton, 220 (32)	15	Mills Lans
Sept. 15, 1978	New Orleans	Muhammad Ali, 221 (36)[12]	Leon Spinks, 201 (25)	15	Lucien Joubert
Oct. 20, 1979	Pretoria, S. Africa	John Tate, 240 (24)[13]	Gerrie Coetzee, 222 (24)	15	Carlos Berrocal
March 31, 1980	Knoxville, Tenn.	Mike Weaver, 207 1/2 (27)	John Tate, 232 (25)	KO 15	Ernesto Magana Ansorena
Dec. 10, 1982	Las Vegas, Nev.	Michael Dokes, 216 (24)	Mike Weaver, 209 1/2 (30)	KO 1	Joey Curtis
Sept. 23, 1983	Richfield, Ohio	Gerrie Coetzee, 215 (28)	Michael Dokes, 217 (25)	KO 10	Tony Perez
March 9, 1984	Las Vegas, Nev.	Tim Witherspoon, 220 1/2 (26)[14]	Greg Page, 239 1/2 (25)	12	Mills Lane
August 31, 1984	Las Vegas, Nev.	Pinklon Thomas, 216 (26)	Tim Witherspoon, 217 (26)	12	Richard Steele
Nov. 9, 1984	Las Vegas, Nev.	Larry Holmes, 221 1/2 (35)[15]	James Smith 227 (31)	KO 12	Dave Pearl
Dec. 1, 1984	Sun City, S. Africa	Greg Page, 236 (25)[16]	Gerry Coetzee, 217 (29)	KO 8	unavailable
April 29, 1985	Buffalo, N.Y.	Tony Tubbs, 229 (26)[16]	Greg Page, 239 1/2 (26)	15	unavailable
Sept. 21, 1985	Las Vegas, Nev.	Michael Spinks, 200 (29)	Larry Holmes, 221 (35)	15	Carlos Padilla
Jan. 17, 1986	Atlanta, Ga.	Tim Witherspoon, 227 (28)	Tony Tubbs, 229 (27)	15	unavailable
Nov. 23, 1986	Las Vegas, Nev.	Mike Tyson, 217 (20)[17]	Trevor Berbick, 220 (29)	KO 2	unavailable
Dec. 12, 1986	New York, N.Y.	James Smith, 230 (33)[16]	Tim Witherspoon, 218 (29)	KO 1	unavailable
March 7, 1987	Las Vegas, Nev.	Mike Tyson, 217 (20)[16]	James Smith, 230 (33)	12	unavailable
Feb. 10, 1990	Tokyo	James "Buster" Douglas,[18] 231 1/2 (29)	Mike Tyson (220) (23)	KO 10	Octavio Meyrom
Oct. 25, 1990	Las Vegas, Nev.	Evander Holyfield, 208 (28)	James "Buster" Douglas, 246 (30)	KO 3	Mills Lane
Nov. 13, 1992	Las Vegas, Nev.	Riddick Bowe,[19] 235 (25)	Evander Holyfield, 205 (30)	12	Joe Cortez

Date	Where held	Winner, weight, age	Loser, weight, age	Rounds	Referee
Nov. 6, 1993	Las Vegas, Nev.	Evander Holyfield, 217 (30)	Riddick Bowe, 246 (26)	12	Mills Lane
April 22, 1994	Las Vegas, Nev.	Michael Moorer, 214 (26)	Evander Holyfield[20] 214 (31)	12	unavailable
Sept. 24, 1994	London, England	Oliver McCall,[21] 228 (29)	Lennox Lewis, 238	2	Lupe Garcia
Nov. 5, 1994	Las Vegas, Nev.	George Foreman,[22] 250 (45)	Michael Moorer, 222 (26)	10	unavailable
April 8, 1995	Las Vegas, Nev.	Bruce Seldon,[23] 232 (28)	Tony Tucker, 238 (36)	7	unavailable

1. Jeffries retired as champion in March 1905. He named Marvin Hart and Jack Root as leading contenders and agreed to referee their fight in Reno, Nev., on July 3, 1905, with the stipulation that he would term the winner the champion. Hart, 190 (28), knocked out Root, 171 (29), in the 12th round. 2. Burns claimed the title after defeating Hart. 3. Tunney retired as champion after defeating Tom Heeney on July 26, 1928. 4. After Louis announced his retirement as champion on March 1, 1949, Charles won recognition from the National Boxing Association as champion by defeating Walcott. 5. Charles gained undisputed recognition as champion by defeating Louis, who came out of retirement. 6. Retired as Champion April 27, 1956. 7. The World Boxing Association later withdrew its recognition of Clay as champion and declared the winner of a bout between Ernie Terrell and Eddie Machen would gain its version of the title. Terrell, 199 (25), won a 15-round decision from Machen, 192 (32), in Chicago on March 5, 1965. Clay, 212 1/4 (25) and Terrell, 212 1/2 (27) met in Houston on Feb. 6, 1967, Clay winning a 15-round decision. 8. Winner recognized by New York, Massachusetts, Maine, Illinois, Texas and Pennsylvania to fill vacated title when Clay was stripped of championship for failing to accept U. S. Induction. 9. Bout was final of eight-man tournament to fill Clay's place and is recognized by World Boxing Association. 10. Bout settled controversy over title. 11. Holmes won World Boxing Council title after WBC had withdrawn recognition of Spinks, March 18, 1978, and awarded its title to Norton. WBC said Spinks had reneged on agreement to fight Norton 12. Ali regained World Boxing Association championship. 13. Tate won WBA title after Ali retired and left it vacant. 14. Tim Witherspoon and Greg Page fought for the WBC heavyweight title vacated by Larry Holmes, who could not come to agreement on a deal to fight Page, the No. 1 contender. Holmes declared he would fight under the banner of the International Boxing Federation. Several dates were set and postponed for fights between Holmes and Gerry Coetzee, the WBA champ, the latest being Nov. 16, 1984. 15. First fight under banner of International Boxing Federation. 16. New W.B.A. champion. 17. New W.B.C. champion. 18. New undisputed champion. 19. The W.B.C. stripped Bowe of its version of the title in December 1992 and named Lennox Lewis champion. 20. After the loss, Holyfield retired. 21. New WBC champion. Lennox Lewis had been named champion in 1992 and had won three title defenses before losing to McCall. 22. For combined WBA/IBF titles. Later WBA stripped Foreman of title for failing to fight no. 1 contender Tony Tucker. IBF also stripped Foreman on June 29, 1995. 23. New WBA champion.

OTHER WORLD BOXING TITLEHOLDERS

(Through June 25, 1995)

Light Heavyweight
1903 Jack Root, George Gardner
1903–05 Bob Fitzsimmons
1905–12 Philadelphia Jack O'Brien[1]
1912–16 Jack Dillon
1916–20 Battling Levinsky
1920–22 Georges Carpentier
1923 Battling Siki
1923–25 Mike McTigue
1925–26 Paul Berlenbach
1926–27 Jack Delaney[2]
1927 Mike McTigue
1927–29 Tommy Loughran
1930 Jimmy Slattery
1930–34 Maxie Rosenbloom
1934–35 Bob Olin
1935–39 John Henry Lewis
1939 Melio Bettina
1939–41 Billy Conn[2]
1941 Anton Christoforidis (NBA)
1941–48 Gus Lesnevich
1948–50 Freddie Mills
1950–52 Joey Maxim
1952–61 Archie Moore[3]
1961–63 Harold Johnson
1963–65 Willie Pastrano
1965–66 José Torres
1966–67 Dick Tiger
1968 Dick Tiger, Bob Foster
1969–70 Bob Foster
1971 Vicente Rondon (WBA), Bob!Foster (WBC)
1972–73 Bob Foster (WBA, WBC)
1974 John Conteh (WBA), Bob Foster (WBC)[1,4]
1975–76 Victor Galindez (WBA), John Conteh (WBC)
1977 Victor Galindez (WBA), John Conteh (WBC)[4] Miguel Cuello (WBC)

1978 Victor Galindez (WBA), Mike Rossman (WBA), Miguel Cuello (WBC), Mate Parlov (WBC), Marvin Johson (WBC)
1979 Mike Rossman (WBA), Victor Galindez (WBA), Marvin Johnson (WBC), Matthew (Franklin) Saad Muhammad (WBC)
1980 Matthew Saad Muhammad (WBC), Marvin Johnson (WBA), Eddie (Gregory), Mustafa Muhammad (WBA)
1981 Matthew Saad Muhammad (WBC), Eddie Mustafa Muhammad (WBA), Michael Spinks (WBA), Dwight Braxton (WBC)
1982 Dwight Braxton (WBC), Michael Spinks (WBA)
1983 Michael Spinks (undisputed)
1984 Michael Spinks (undisputed)
1985 Michael Spinks (undisputed)[5]
1986 Marvin Johnson (WBA), Dennis Andries (WBC)
1987 Thomas Hearns (WBC), Virgil Hill (WBA), Bobby Czyz (IBF)
1988 Charles Williams (IBF), Virgil Hill (WBA), Donny LaLonde (WBC), Sugar Ray Leonard (WBC)
1989 Dennis Andries (WBC), Virgil Hill (WBA), Charles Williams (IBF), Jeff Harding (WBC)

1990 Virgil Hill (WBA), Charles Williams (IBF), Jeff Harding (WBC), Dennis Andries (WBC)
1991 Virgil Hall (WBA), Thomas Hearns (WBA), Dennis Andries (WBC), Charles Williams (IBF)
1992 Charlie Williams (IBF), James Waring (IBF), Jeff Harding (WBC)
1993 Virgil Hill (WBA), Jeff Harding (WBC), Henry Maske (IBF)
1994 Virgil Hill (WBA), Mike McCallum (WBC), Henry Maske (IBF)
1995 Virgil Hill (WBA), Fabio Tiozzo (WBC), Henry Maske (IBF)

1. Retired. 2. Abandoned title. 3. NBA withdrew recognition in 1961, New York Commission in 1962; recognized thereafter only by California and Europe. 4. WBC withdrew recognition. 5. Spinks relinquished title in 1985 to fight for heavyweight title.

Middleweight
1867–72 Tom Chandler
1872–81 George Rooke
1881–82 Mike Donovan[1]
1884–91 Jack (Nonpareil) Dempsey
1891–97 Bob Fitzsimmons[2]
1908 Stanley Ketchel, Billy Papke
1908–10 Stanley Ketchel[3]
1913 Frank Klaus
1913–14 George Chip
1914–17 Al McCoy
1917–20 Mike O'Dowd
1920–23 Johnny Wilson
1923–26 Harry Greb

1926	Tiger Flowers
1926–31	Mickey Walker[2]
1931–41	Gorilla Jones, Ben Jeby, Marcel Thil, Lou Brouillard, Vince Dundee, Teddy Yarosz, Babe Risko, Freddy Steele, Al Hostak, Solly Kreiger, Fred Apostoli, Cerferino Garcia, Ken Overlin, Billy Soose, Tony Zale[4]
1941–47	Tony Zale
1947–48	Rocky Graziano
1948	Tony Zale
1948–49	Marcel Cerdan
1949–51	Jake LaMotta
1952	Ray Robinson, Randy Turpin
1951–52	Ray Robinson[1]
1953–55	Carl Olson
1955–57	Ray Robinson[5]
1957	Gene Fullmer, Ray Robinson
1957–58	Carmen Basilio
1958–60	Ray Robinson[6]
1960–61	Paul Pender[7]
1959–62	Gene Fullmer (NBA)
1961–62	Terry Downes[1]
1962	Paul Pender[1]
1962–63	Dick Tiger
1963–65	Joey Giardello
1965–66	Dick Tiger
1966	Emile Griffith
1967	Nino Benvenuti, Emile Griffith
1968	Emile Griffith, Nino Benvenuti
1969	Nino Benvenuti
1970	Nino Benvenuti, Carlos Monzon
1971–73	Carlos Monzon
1974–75	Carlos Monzon (WBA), Rodrigo Valdez (WBC)
1976	Carlos Monzon (WBA, WBC), Rodrigo Valdez (WBC)
1977	Carlos Monzon (WBA,WBC)[1], Rodrigo Valdez (WBA, WBC)
1978	Rodrigo Valdez, Hugo Corro
1979	Hugo Corro, Vito Antuofermo
1980	Vito Antuofermo, Alan Minter, Marvin Hagler
1981	Marvin Hagler
1982–86	Marvelous Marvin Hagler (undisputed)
1987	Marvin Hagler (undisputed) Sugar Ray Leonard (undisputed)
1988	Sumbu Kalambay (WBA), Thomas Hearns (WBC), Iran Barkley (WBC), Frank Tate (IBF), Michael Nunn (IBF), James Kinchen (NABF)
1989	Michael Nunn (IBF), Mike McCollum (WBA), Iran Barkley (WBC), Roberto Duran (WBC)
1990	Michael McCollum (WBA), Michael Nunn (IBF), Iran Barkley (WBC)

1991	Michael Nunn (IBF), James Toney (IBF), Michael McCallum (WBA)
1992	James Toney (IBF), Julian Jackson (WBC), Reggie Johnson (WBA)
1993	Reggie Johnson (WBA), Gerald McClellan (WBC), Roy Jones (IBF)
1994	Julian Jackson (WBA), Gerald McClellan (WBC), Roy Jones (IBF)
1995	Jorge Castro (WBA), Julian Jackson (WBC), Bernard Hopkins (IBF)

1. Retired. 2. Abandoned title. 3. Died. 4. National Boxing Association and New York Commission disagreed on champions. Those listed were accepted by one or the other until Zale gained world–wide recognition. 5. Ended retirement in 1954. 6. NBA withdrew recognition. 7. Recognized by New York, Massachusetts, and Europe.

Welterweight

1892–94	Mysterious Billy Smith
1894–96	Tommy Ryan
1896	Kid McCoy[2]
1896–	
1900	Mysterious Billy Smith
1900	Rube Ferns
1900–01	Matty Matthews
1901	Ruby Ferns
1901–04	Joe Walcott
1904	Dixie Kid[2]
1904–06	Joe Walcott
1906–07	Honey Mellody
1907	Mike (Twin) Sullivan[2]
1915–19	Ted Lewis
1919–22	Jack Britton
1922–26	Mickey Walker
1926–27	Pete Latzo
1927–29	Joe Dundee
1929–30	Jackie Fields
1930	Young Jack Thompson
1930–31	Tommy Freeman
1931	Young Jack Thompson
1931–32	Lou Brouillard
1932–33	Jackie Fields
1933	Young Corbett 3rd
1933–34	Jimmy McLarnin, Barney Ross
1934–35	Jimmy McLarnin
1935–38	Barney Ross
1938–40	Henry Armstrong
1940–41	Fritzie Zivic
1941–46	Freddie Cochrane
1946	Marty Servo[1]
1946–51	Ray Robinson[2]
1951	Johnny Bratton (NBA)
1951–54	Kid Gavilan
1954–55	Johnny Saxton
1955	Tony DeMarco
1955–56	Carmen Basilio
1956	Johnny Saxton
1956–57	Carmen Basilio[2]
1958	Virgil Akins
1959–60	Don Jordan
1960–61	Benny (Kid) Paret
1961	Emile Griffith
1961–62	Benny (Kid) Paret

1962–63	Emile Griffith, Luis Rodriguez
1963–66	Emile Griffith[2]
1966-69	Curtis Cokes
1969	Curtis Cokes, José Napoles
1970	José Napoles, Billy Backus
1971	Billy Backus, José Napoles
1972–74	José Napoles
1975	José Napoles (WBA, WBC),[3] Angel Espada (WBA), John Stracey (WBC)
1976	Angel Espada (WBA), José Cuevas (WBA), John Stracey (WBC), Carlos Palomino
1977–78	José Cuevas (WBA), Carlos Palomino (WBC)
1979	José Cuevas (WBA), Carlos Palomino (WBC), Wilfredo Benitez (WBC)
1980	José Cuevas (WBA), Ray Leonard (WBC), Roberto Duran (WBC), Thomas Hearns (WBA)
1981	Ray Leonard (WBC), Thomas Hearns (WBA), Ray Leonard (WBC,WBA)
1982	Ray Leonard
1983–85	Donald Curry (WBA)
1983–85	Milton McCrory (WBC)
1985–86	Donald Curry (undisputed)
1987	Mark Breland (WBA) Marlon Starling (WBA) Lloyd Honeychan (IBF)
1988	Marlon Starling (WBA), Tomas Molinares (WBA), Lloyd Honeyghan (WBC), Simon Brown (IBF)
1989	Mark Breland (WBA), Marlon Starling (WBC), Simon Brown (IBF)
1990	Mark Breland (WBA), Aaron Davis (WBA), Simon Brown (IBF), Marlon Starling (WBC), Maurice Blocker (WBC)
1991	Meldrick Taylor (WBA), Simon Brown (IBF, WBC)
1992	Meldrick Taylor (WBA), James "Buddy" McGirt (WBC), Maurice Blocker (IBF)
1993	Cristiano Espana (WBA), Pernell Whitaker (WBC), Felix Trinidad (IBF)
1994	Ike Quartey (WBA), Pernell Whitaker (WBC), Felix Trinidad (IBF)
1995	Ike Quartey (WBA), Pernell Whitaker (WBC), Felix Trinidad (IBF)

1. Retired. 2. Abandoned title. 3. WBA withdrew recognition.

Lightweight

1869–99	Kid Lavigne
1899–	
1902	Frank Erne
1902–08	Joe Gans
1908–10	Battling Nelson
1910–12	Ad Wolgast
1912–14	Willie Ritchie
1914–17	Freddy Welsh

1917–25 Benny Leonard[1]
1925 Jimmy Goodrich
1925–26 Rocky Kansas
1926–30 Sammy Mandell
1930 Al Singer
1930–33 Tony Canzoneri
1933–35 Barney Ross[2]
1935–36 Tony Canzoneri
1936–38 Lou Ambers
1938–39 Henry Armstrong
1939–40 Lou Ambers
1940–41 Lew Jenkins
1941–42 Sammy Angott[1]
1943–47 Beau Jack (N.Y.), Bob Montgomery (N.Y.), Sammy Angott (NBA), Juan Zurita (NBA), Ike Williams (NBA)
1947–51 Ike Williams
1951–52 James Carter
1952 Lauro Salas
1952–54 James Carter
1954 Paddy DeMarco
1954–55 James Carter
1955–56 Wallace Smith
1956–62 Joe Brown
1962–65 Carlos Ortiz
1965 Ismael Laguna
1965–68 Carlos Ortiz
1968 Teo Cruz
1969 Teo Cruz, Mando Ramos
1970 Mando Ramos, Ismael Laguna, Ken Buchanan
1971 Ken Buchanan (WBA), Mando Ramos (WBC), Pedro Carrasco (WBC)
1972 Ken Buchanan (WBA), Pedro Carrasco (WBC), Mando Ramos (WBC), Chango Carmona (WBC), Rodolfo Gonzalez (WBC)
1973 Roberto Duran (WBA), Rodolfo Gonzalez (WBC)
1974 Roberto Duran (WBA), Rodolfo Gonzalez (WBC), Guts Ishimatsu (WBC)
1975 Roberto Duran (WBA), Guts Ishimatsu (WBC)
1976 Roberto Duran (WBA), Guts Ishimatsu (WBC), Esteban!De Jesus (WBC)
1977 Roberto Duran (WBA), Esteban De Jesus (WBC)
1978 Roberto Duran (WBA, WBC)
1979 Roberto Duran[2], Jim Watt (WBC), Ernesto Espana (WBA)
1980 Ernesto Espana (WBA), Hilmer Kenty (WBA), Jim Watt (WBC)
1981 Hilmer Kenty (WBA), Sean O'Grady (WBA), James Watt (WBC), Alexis Arguello (WBC), Arturo Frias (WBA)
1982 Arturo Frias (WBA), Ray Mancini (WBA), Alexis Arguello (WBC)
1983 Edwin Rosario (WBC), Ray Mancini (WBA)
1984 Edwin Rosario (WBC), Livingstone Bramble (WBA)

1985 Jose Luis Ramirez (WBC), Hector Camacho (WBC), Livingstone Bramble (WBA)
1986 Hector Camacho (WBC) Livingstone Bramble (WBA), Jim Paul (IBF)
1987 Edwin Rosario (WBA) Jose Luis Ramirez (WBC), Greg Haugen (IBF)
1988 Jose Luis Ramirez (WBC), Julio Cesar Chavez (WBA), Greg Haugen (IBF), Julius Cesar Chavez (WBC & WBA title unified)
1989 Pernell Whitaker (IBF, WBC), Edwin Rosario (WBA)
1990 Pernell Whitaker (IBF, WBC) Juan Nazario (WBA)
1991 Pernell Whitaker (IBF, WBA, WBC)
1992 Pernell Whitaker (IBF, WBA, WBC)[3], Joey Gamache (WBA).
1993 Dingaan Thobela (WBA), Angel Gonzalez (WBC), Freddie Pendleton (IBF)
1994 Orzubek Nazarov (WBA), Angel Gonzalez (WBC), Rafael Ruelas (IBF)
1995 Orzubek Nazarov (WBA), Angel Gonzalez (WBC), Oscar de la Hoya (IBF)

1. Retired. 2. Abandoned title. 3. Moving up in weight class, so resigned titles.

Featherweight

1889 Dal Hawkins[1]
1890 Billy Murphy
1892–
1900 George Dixon
1900–01 Terry McGovern
1901 Young Corbett[1]
1901–12 Abe Attell
1912–23 Johnny Kilbane
1923 Eugene Criqui
1923–25 Johnny Dundee[1]
1925–27 Louis (Kid) Kaplan[1]
1927–28 Benny Bass
1928 Tony Canzoneri
1928–29 Andre Routis
1929–32 Battling Battalino[1]
1932 Tommy Paul (NBA), Kid Chocolate (N.Y.)
1933–36 Freddie Miller
1936–37 Petey Sarron
1937–38 Henry Armstrong[1]
1938–40 Joey Archibald
1940–41 Harry Jefra, Joey Archibald
1941–42 Chalky Wright
1942–48 Willie Pep
1948–49 Sandy Saddler[2]
1949–50 Willie Pep
1950–57 Sandy Saddler
1957–59 Kid Bassey
1959–63 Davey Moore
1963–64 Sugar Ramos
1964–67 Vicente Saldivar[2]
1968 Howard Winstone, José Legra[3], Paul Rojas (WBA), Sho Saijo (WBA)

1969 Sho Saijo (WBA), Johnny Famechon[3]
1970 Sho Saijo (WBA), Johnny Famechon,[3] Vicente Salvidar,[3] Kuniaki Shibata[3]
1971 Sho Saijo (WBA), Antonio Gomez (WBA), Kuniaki Shibata (WBC)
1972 Antonio Gomez (WBA), Ernesto Marcel (WBA), Kuniaki Shibata (WBC), Clemente Sanchez (WBC), José Legra (WBC)
1973 Ernesto Marcel (WBA), José Legra (WBC), Eder Jofre (WBC)
1974 Ernesto Marcel (WBA)[2], Ruben Olivares (WBA), Alexis Arguello (WBC), Eder Jofre (WBC), Bobby Chacon (WBC)
1975 Alexis Arguello (WBA), Bobby Chacon (WBC), Ruben Olivares (WBC), David Kotey (WBC)
1976 Alexis Arguello (WBA),[2] David Kotey (WBC), Danny Lopez (WBC)
1977 Rafael Ortega (WBA), Danny Lopez (WBC)
1978 Rafael Ortega (WBA), Cecilio Lastra (WBA), Eusebio Pedroza (WBA), Danny Lopez (WBC)
1979 Eusebio Pedroza (WBA), Danny Lopez (WBC)
1980 Eusebio Pedroza (WBA), Danny Lopez (WBC), Salvador Sanchez (WBC)
1981 Eusebio Pedroza (WBA), Salvador Sanchez (WBC)
1982 Eusebio Pedroza (WBA), Salvador Sanchez (WBC)[4]
1983 Juan Laporte (WBC), Eusebio Pedroza (WBA)
1984 Wilfred Gomez (WBC), Eusebio Pedroza (WBA)
1985 Eusebio Pedroza (WBA) Barry McGuigan (WBA) Azumah Nelson (WBC)
1986 Barry McGuigan (WBA) Stevie Cruz (WBA) Azumah Nelson (WBC)
1987 Azumah Nelson (WBC) Antonio Esparragoza (WBA)
1988 Calvin Grove (IBF), Jorge Paez (IBF), Antonio Esparragoza (WBA), Jeff Fenech (WBC)
1989 Jorge Paez (IBF), Antonio Esparragoza (WBA), Jeff Fenech (WBC)
1990 Marcos Villasana (WBC), Antonio Esparragoza (WBA), Jorge Paez (IBF)
1991 Park Young-Kyun (WBA), Troy Dorsey (IBF), Marcos Villagana (WBC)
1992 Paul Hodkinson (WBC), Manuel Medina (IBF), Yung Kyun Park (WBA)
1993 Yung-Kyun Park (WBA), Goyo Vargas (WBC), Tom Johnson (IBF)

| 1994 | Eloy Rojas (WBA), Kevin Kelley (WBC), Tom Johnson (IBF) |
| 1995 | Elroy Rojas (WBA), Alejandro Gonzalez (WBC), Tom Johnson (IBF) |

1. Abandoned title. 2. Retired. 3. Recognized in Europe, Mexico, and Orient. 4. Killed in auto accident.

Bantamweight

1890–92	George Dixon[1]
1894–99	Jimmy Barry[2]
1899–	
1900	Terry McGovern[1]
1901	Harry Harris[1]
1902–03	Harry Forbes
1903–04	Frankie Neil
1904	Joe Bowker[1]
1905–07	Jimmy Walsh[1]
1910–14	Johnny Coulon
1914–17	Kid Williams
1917–20	Pete Herman
1920	Joe Lynch
1920–21	Joe Lynch, Pete Herman, Johnny Buff
1922	Johnny Buff, Joe Lynch
1923	Joe Lynch
1924	Joe Lynch, Abe Goldstein
1924	Abe Goldstein, Eddie (Cannonball) Martin
1925	Eddie (Cannonball) Martin, Charlie (Phil) Rosenberg[3]
1927–28	Bud Taylor (NBA)[1]
1929–34	Al Brown
1935	Al Brown, Baltazar Sangchili
1936	Baltazar Sangchili, Tony Marino, Sixto Escobar
1937	Sixto Escobar, Harry Jeffra
1938	Harry Jeffra, Sixto Escobar
1939–40	Sixto Escobar[2]
1940–42	Lou Salica
1942–46	Manuel Ortiz
1947	Manuel Ortiz, Harold Dade
1948–50	Manuel Ortiz
1950–52	Vic Toweel
1952–54	Jimmy Carruthers[2]
1954–55	Robert Cohen
1956	Robert Cohen, Mario D'Agata, Raul Macias (NBA)
1957	Mario D'Agata, Alphonse Halimi
1958–59	Alphonse Halimi
1959–60	Jose Becerra[2]
1960–61	Alphonse Halimi[4]
1961–62	Johnny Caldwell[4]
1961–65	Eder Jofre
1965–68	Masahika (Fighting) Harada
1968	Masahika (Fighting) Harada, Lionel Rose
1969	Lionel Rose, Ruben Olivares
1970	Ruben Olivares, Chucho Castillo
1971	Chucho Castillo, Ruben Olivares
1972	Ruben Olivares, Rafael Herrera, Enrique Pinder
1973	Enrique Pinder (WBA), Romeo Anaya (WBA), Arnold Taylor (WBA), Rodolfo Martinez (WBC), Rafael Herrera

1974	Arnold Taylor (WBA), Soo Hwan Hong (WBA), Rafael Herrera (WBC), Rodolfo Martinez (WBC)
1975	Soo Hwan Hong (WBA), Alfonso Zamora (WBA), Rodolfo Martinez (WBC)
1976	Alfonso Zamora (WBA), Rodolfo Martinez (WBC), Carlos Zarate (WBC)
1977	Alfonso Zamora (WBA), Jorge Lujan (WBA), Carlos Zarate (WBC)
1978	Jorge Lujan (WBA), Carlos Zarate (WBC)
1979	Jorge Lujan (WBA), Carlos Zarate (WBC), Lupe Pintor (WBC)
1980	Jorge Lujan (WBA), Lupe Pintor (WBC), Julian Solis (WBA), Jeff Chandler (WBA)
1981	Lupe Pintor (WBC), Jeff Chandler (WBA)
1982	Lupe Pintor (WBC), Jeff Chandler (WBA)
1983	Jeff Chandler (WBA), Albert Dauila (WBC)
1984	Richie Sandqual (WBA), Albert Dauila (WBC)
1985	Richard Sandoval (WBA) Daniel Zaragoza (WBC) Miguel Lora (WBC)
1986	Richard Sandoval (WBA) Bernardo Pinango (WBA) Jeff Fenech (IBF)
1987	Bernardo Pinango (WBA) Takuya Muguruma (WBA) Miguel Lora (WBC)
1988	Wilfred Vasquez (WBA), Jibaro Perez (WBC), Moon Sung–gil (WBA) Orlando Canizales (IBF)
1989	Jibaro Perez (WBC), Moon Sung–gil (WBA), Orlando Canizales (IBF) Kaokor Galaxy (WBA), Luis Espinosa (WBA)
1990	Orlando Canizales (IBF), Jibaro Perez (WBC), Luis Espinosa (WBA)
1991	Greg Richardson (WBC), Orlando Canizales (IBF), Luis Espinosa (WBA)
1992	Joichiro Tatsuyoshi (WBC), Victor Manuel Rabanales (WBC), Eddie Cook (WBA), Orlando Gonzales (IBF)
1993	Jorge Julio (WBA), Byun-Jong-il (WBC), Orlando Canizales (IBF)
1994	John Michael Johnson (WBA), Yasuei Yakushiji (WBC), Orlando Canizales (IBF)
1995	Daorun Chuwatang (WBA), Yasuei Yakushiji (WBC), Mbulelo Botile (IBF)

1. Abandoned title. 2. Retired. 3. Deprived of title for failing to make weight. 4. Recognized in Europe.

Flyweight

1916–23	Jimmy Wilde
1923–25	Pancho Villa[1]
1925	Frankie Genaro
1925–27	Fidel La Barba[2]
1927–31	Corporal Izzy Schwartz, Frankie Genaro, Emile (Spider) Pladner, Midget Wolgast, Young Perez[3]
1932–35	Jackie Brown
1935–38	Bennie Lynch[4]
1939	Peter Kane[4]
1943–47	Jackie Paterson[1]
1947–50	Rinty Monaghan[2]
1950	Terry Allen
1950–52	Dado Marino
1952–54	Yoshio Shirai
1954–60	Pascual Perez
1960–62	Pone Kingpetch
1962–63	Masahika (Fighting) Harada
1963–64	Hiroyuki Ebihara
1964–65	Pone Kingpetch
1965–66	Salvatore Burrini
1966	Walter McGown, Chartchai Chionoi
1966–68	Charchai Chionoi
1969	Bernabe Villacampa, Efran Torres (WBA)
1970	Bernabe Villacampa, Chartchai Chionoi, Erbito Salavarria, Berkrerk Chartvanchai (WBA) Masao Ohba (WBA)
1971	Masao Ohba (WBA), Erbito Salavarria (WBC)
1972	Masao Ohba (WBA), Erbito Salavarria (WBC), Betulio Gonzalez (WBC), Venice Borkorsor (WBC)
1973	Masao Ohba (WBA), Chartchai Chionoi (WBA), Venice Borkorsor (WBC), Betulio Gonzalez (WBC)
1974	Chartchai Chionoi (WBA), Susumu Hanagata (WBA), Betulio Gonzalez (WBC), Shoji Oguma (WBC)
1975	Susumu Hanagata (WBA), Erbito Salavarria (WBA), Shoji Oguma (WBC), Miguel Canto (WBC)
1976	Erbito Salavarria (WBA), Alfonso Lopez (WBA), Guty Espadas (WBA), Miguel Canto (WBC)
1977	Guty Espadas (WBA), Miguel Canto (WBC)
1978	Guty Espadas (WBA), Betulio Gonzalez (WBA), Miguel Canto (WBC)
1979	Betulio Gonzalez (WBA), Miguel Canto (WBC), Park Chan–Hee (WBC)
1980	Luis Ibarra (WBA), Kim Tae Shik (WBA), Park Chan–Hee (WBC), Shoji Oguma (WBC)
1983	Frank Cedeno (WBC), Santos Lacia (WBA)
1984	Koji Kobayashy (WBA), Gabriel Bernal (WBC), Santos Laciar (WBA)

1985 Sot Chitlada (WBC) Santos Laciar (WBA)
1986 Hilario Zapata (WBA) Julio Cesar–Chevez (WBC)
1987 Shin Hi Sop (IBF) Chang Ho Choi (IBF) Sot Chitlada (WBC)
1988 Sot Chitlada (WBC), Kim Young Kang (WBC), Duke McKenzie (IBF), Fidel Bassa (WBA)
1989 Kim Young–gang (WBC), Sot Chitlada (WBC), Lee Yol–woo (WBA), Duke McKen-zie (IBF), Dave McAuley (IBF) Jesus Rojas (WBA)
1990 Sot Chitlada (WBC), Kim Bong–Jung (WBA), Lee Yul–woo (WBA), Dave McAuley (IBF), Leopard Tamakuma (WBA)
1991 Muangchai Kittasem (WBC), Kim-Young-Kang (WBC), Elvis Alvarez (WBA), Dave McAuley (IBF)
1992 Kim Young-Kang (WBA), Yuri Arbachakov (WBC), Rodolfo Blanco (IBF)
1993 David Griman (WBA), Yuri Arbachakov (WBC), P. Sitbangprachan (IBF)
1994 Saen Sor Ploenchit (WBA), Yuri Arbachakov (WBC), Humberto Gonzalez (IBF)
1995 Saen Sor Ploenchit (WBA), Yuri Arbachakov (WBC), Humberto Gonzalez (IBF)

1. Died. 2. Retired. 3. Claimants to NBA and New York Commission titles. 4. Abandoned title.

WEIGHTLIFTING

U.S. WEIGHTLIFTING FEDERATION

MEN'S NATIONAL CHAMPIONSHIPS
(April 28–30, 1995, Fresno, Calif.)

	Snatch	C&J[1]	Total[2]
54 kg—Chad Ikei	100.0	120.0	220.0
59 kg—Bryan Jacob	122.5	142.5	265.0
64 kg—Vernon Patao	125.0	145.0	270.0
70 kg—Michael Jacques	115.0	152.5	267.5
76 kg—David Santillo	137.5	170.0	307.5
83 kg—Dean Goad	140.0	182.5	322.5
91 kg—Tom Gough	152.5	197.5	350.0
99 kg—Pete Kelley	152.5	182.5	335.0
108 kg—Wes Barnett	162.5	207.5	370.0
Over 108 kg—Thomas McKinney	145.0	185.0	330.0

WOMEN'S NATIONAL CHAMPIONSHIPS
(April 28–30, 1995, Fresno, Calif.)

	Snatch	C&J[1]	Total[2]
46 kg—Sibby Flowers	65.0	80.0	145.0
50 kg—Kelly Rexroad	55.0	65.0	120.0
54 kg—Robin Byrd-Goad	80.0	90.0	170.0
59 kg—Lea Rentmeester	72.5	95.0	167.5
64 kg—Stephanie Bodie	75.0	90.0	165.0
70 kg—Diana Fuhrman	85.0	95.0	180.0
76 kg—Stacy Ketchum	82.5	112.5	195.0
83 kg—Decia Stenzel	95.0	107.5	202.5
Over 83 kg—Lisa Brien	87.5	110.0	197.5

1. Clean and jerk. 2. All results in kilograms.

WRESTLING

N.C.A.A. CHAMPIONSHIPS—1995

Division I

118 lb—Kelvin Jackson, Michigan State, d. Eric Ivins, Oklahoma, 6–3

126 lb—Jeff McGinness, Iowa, d. Sanshiro Abe, Penn State, 6–4

134 lb—T.J. Jaworsky, North Carolina, d. Babak Mohammadi, Oregon State, 13–6

142 lb—John Hughes, Penn State, d. Gerry Abas, Fresno State, 7–0

150 lb—Steve Marianetti, Illinois, d. Lincoln McIlravy, Iowa, 13–10

158 lb—Ernest Benior, Illinois, d. Dan Wimsberger, Michigan State, 6–5

167 lb—Markus Mollica, Arizona State, d. Mark Branch, Oklahoma State, 5–3

177 lb—Les Gutches, Oregon State, d. Quincey Clark, Oklahoma, 8–4

190 lb—J.J. McGrew, Oklahoma, d. Joel Sharratt, Iowa, 8–6

Heavyweight—Tolly Thompson, Nebraska, d. Justin Greenlee, Northern Iowa, 8–0

Team Standings
1. Iowa, 134; 2. Oregon State, 77.5; 3. Michigan State, 69.5; 4. Arizona State, 65.5; 5. Penn State, 60.5.

WORLD WRESTLING CHAMPIONSHIPS—1995
(Aug. 10–13, 1995, Atlanta, Ga.)

Freestyle
105.5 lb (48 kg)—Vugar Orudjev, Russia
114.5 lb (52 kg)—Valentin Jordanov, Bulgaria
125.5 lb (57 kg)—Terry Brands, United States
136.5 lb (62 kg)—Elbrus Tedeev, Ukraine
149.5 lb (68 kg)—Arayik Gevorkian, Armenia
163.0 lb (74 kg)—Buvaisa Saitev, Russia
180.5 lb (82 kg)—Kevin Jackson, United States
198.0 lb (90 kg)—Rasoul Khadem, Iran
220.0 lb (100 kg)—Kurt Angle, United States
286 lb (130 kg)—Bruce Baumgartner, United States
Team
1. United States, 71; 2. Iran, 59; 3. Russia, 58; 4. Turkey, 35; 5. Cuba, 34.

UNITED STATES OLYMPIC FESTIVAL
(June 22–30, 1995, Colorado Springs, Colo.)

Freestyle
105.5 lb—Dan Ramirez, Oceanside, Calif.
114.5 lb—Tim Dernlan, West Liberty, Ohio
125.5 lb—Eric Akin, Overland Park, Kan.
136.5 lb—Dunyasha Yetts, Steubenville, Ohio
149.5 lb—Steve Marianetti, Northbrook, Ill.
163.0 lb—Hardell Moore, Coweta, Okla.
180.5 lb—Jim McGovern, Coralville, Iowa
198.0 lb—Emilio Collions, Upper Nyack, N.Y.
220.0 lb—Seth Brady, Mount Prospect, Ill.
286.0 lb—Justin Greenlee, Waverly, Iowa

HORSE RACING

Ancient drawings on stone and bone prove that horse racing is at least 3000 years old, but Thoroughbred Racing is a modern development. Practically every thoroughbred in training today traces its registered ancestry back to one or more of three sires that arrived in England about 1728 from the Near East and became known, from the names of their owners, as the Byerly Turk, the Darley Arabian, and the Godolphin Arabian. The Jockey Club (English) was founded at Newmarket in 1750 or 1751 and became the custodian of the Stud Book as well as the court of last resort in deciding turf affairs.

Horse racing took place in this country before the Revolution, but the great lift to the breeding industry came with the importation in 1798, by Col. John Hoomes of Virginia, of Diomed, winner of the Epsom Derby of 1780. Diomed's lineal descendants included

such famous stars of the American turf as American Eclipse and Lexington. From 1800 to the time of the Civil War there were race courses and breeding establishments plentifully scattered through Virginia, North Carolina, South Carolina, Tennessee, Kentucky, and Louisiana.

The oldest stake event in North America is the Queen's Plate, a Canadian fixture that was first run in the Province of Quebec in 1836. The oldest stake event in the United States is The Travers, which was first run at Saratoga in 1864. The gambling that goes with horse racing and trickery by jockeys, trainers, owners, and track officials caused attacks on the sport by reformers and a demand among horse racing enthusiasts for an honest and effective control of some kind, but nothing of lasting value to racing came of this until the formation in 1894 of The Jockey Club.

"TRIPLE CROWN" WINNERS IN THE UNITED STATES[1]

(Kentucky Derby, Preakness and Belmont Stakes)

Year	Horse	Owner	Year	Horse	Owner
1919	Sir Barton	J. K. L. Ross	1946	Assault	Robert J. Kleberg
1930	Gallant Fox	William Woodward	1948	Citation	Warren Wright
1935	Omaha	William Woodward	1973	Secretariat	Meadow Stable
1937	War Admiral	Samuel D. Riddle	1977	Seattle Slew	Karen Taylor
1941	Whirlaway	Warren Wright	1978	Affirmed	Louis Wolfson
1943	Count Fleet	Mrs. John Hertz			

KENTUCKY DERBY

Churchill Downs; 3–year–olds; 1 1/4 miles.

Year	Winner	Jockey	Wt.	Win val.	Year	Winner	Jockey	Wt.	Win val.
1875	Aristides	O. Lewis	100	$2,850	1909	Wintergreen	V. Powers	117	$4,850
1876	Vagrant	R. Swim	97	2,950	1910	Donau	F. Herbert	117	4,850
1877	Baden Baden	W. Walker	100	3,300	1911	Meridian	G. Archibald	117	4,850
1878	Day Star	J. Carter	100	4,050	1912	Worth	C. H. Shilling	117	4,850
1879	Lord Murphy	C. Schauer	100	3,550	1913	Donerail	R. Goose	117	5,475
1880	Fonso	G. Lewis	105	3,800	1914	Old Rosebud	J. McCabe	114	9,125
1881	Hindoo	J. McLaughlin	105	4,410	1915	Regret	J. Notler	112	11,450
1882	Apollo	B. Hurd	102	4,560	1916	George Smith	J. Loftus	117	9,750
1883	Leonatus	W. Donohue	105	3,760	1917	Omar Khayyam	C. Borel	117	16,600
1884	Buchanan	I. Murphy	110	3,990	1918	Exterminator	W. Knapp	114	14,700
1885	Joe Cotton	E. Henderson	110	4,630	1919	Sir Barton	J. Loftus	1121/2	20,825
1886	Ben Ali	P. Duffy	118	4,890	1920	Paul Jones	T. Rice	126	30,375
1887	Montrose	I. Lewis	118	4,200	1921	Behave Yourself	C. Thompson	126	38,450
1888	Macbeth II	G. Covington	115	4,740	1922	Morvich	A. Johnson	126	46,775
1889	Spokane	T. Kiley	118	4,970	1923	Zev	E. Sande	126	53,600
1890	Riley	I. Murphy	118	5,460	1924	Black Gold	J. D. Mooney	126	52,775
1891	Kingman	I. Murphy	122	4,680	1925	Flying Ebony	E. Sande	126	52,950
1892	Azra	A. Clayton	122	4,230	1926	Bubbling Over	A. Johnson	126	50,075
1893	Lookout	E. Kunze	122	4,090	1927	Whiskery	L. McAtee	126	51,000
1894	Chant	F. Goodale	122	4,020	1928	Reigh Count	C. Lang	126	55,375
1895	Halma	J. Perkins	122	2,970	1929	Clyde Van Dusen	L. McAtee	126	53,950
1896	Ben Brush	W. Simms	117	4,850	1930	Gallant Fox	E. Sande	126	50,725
1897	Typhoon H	F. Garner	117	4,850	1931	Twenty Grand	C. Kurtsinger	126	48,725
1898	Plaudit	W. Simms	117	4,850	1932	Burgoo King	E. James	126	52,350
1899	Manuel	F. Taral	117	4,850	1933	Brokers Tip	D. Meade	126	48,925
1900	Lieut. Gibson	J. Boland	117	4,850	1934	Cavalcade	M. Garner	126	28,175
1901	His Eminence	J. Winkfield	117	4,850	1935	Omaha	W. Saunders	126	39,525
1902	Alan–a–Dale	J. Winkfield	117	4,850	1936	Bold Venture	I. Hanford	126	37,725
1903	Judge Himes	H. Booker	117	4,850	1937	War Admiral	C. Kurtsinger	126	52,050
1904	Elwood	F. Prior	117	4,850	1938	Lawrin	E. Arcaro	126	47,050
1905	Agile	J. Martin	122	4,850	1939	Johnstown	J. Stout	126	46,350
1906	Sir Huon	R. Troxler	117	4,850	1940	Gallahadion	C. Bierman	126	60,150
1907	Pink Star	A. Minder	117	4,850	1941	Whirlaway	E. Arcaro	126	61,275
1908	Stone Street	A. Pickens	117	4,850	1942	Shut Out	W. D. Wright	126	64,225

Year	Winner	Jockey	Wt.	Win val.	Year	Winner	Jockey	Wt.	Win val.
1943	Count Fleet	J. Longden	126	$60,725	1970	Dust Commander	M. Manganello	126	$127,800
1944	Pensive	C. McCreary	126	64,675	1971	Canonero II	G. Avila	126	145,500
1945	Hoop Jr.	E. Arcaro	126	64,850	1972	Riva Ridge	R. Turcotte	126	140,300
1946	Assault	W. Mehrtens	126	96,400	1973	Secretariat	R. Turcotte	126	155,050
1947	Jet Pilot	E. Guerin	126	92,160	1974	Cannonade	A. Cordero, Jr.	126	274,000
1948	Citation	E. Arcaro	126	83,400	1975	Foolish Pleasure	J. Vasquez	126	209,600
1949	Ponder	S. Brooks	126	91,600	1976	Bold Forbes	A. Cordero, Jr.	126	165,200
1950	Middleground	W. Boland	126	92,650	1977	Seattle Slew	J. Cruguet	126	214,700
1951	Count Turf	C. McCreary	126	98,050	1978	Affirmed	S. Cauthen	126	186,900
1952	Hill Gail	E. Arcaro	126	96,300	1979	Spectacular Bid	R. Franklin	126	228,650
1953	Dark Star	H. Moreno	126	90,050	1980	Genuine Risk	J. Vasquez	126	250,550
1954	Determine	R. York	126	102,050	1981	Pleasant Colony	J. Velasquez	126	317,200
1955	Swaps	W. Shoemaker	126	108,400	1982	Gato del Sol	E. Delahoussaye	126	417,600
1956	Needles	D. Erb	126	123,450	1983	Sunny's Halo	E. Delahoussaye	126	426,000
1957	Iron Liege	W. Hartack	126	107,950	1984	Swale	L. Pincay, Jr.	126	537,400
1958	Tim Tam	I. Valenzuela	126	116,400	1985	Spend a Buck	A. Cordero, Jr.	126	406,800
1959	Tomy Lee	W. Shoemaker	126	119,650	1986	Ferdinand	W. Shoemaker	126	609,400
1960	Venetian Way	W. Hartack	126	114,850	1987	Alysheba	C. McCarron	126	618,600
1961	Carry Back	J. Sellers	126	120,500	1988	Winning Colors	Gary Stevens	126	611,200
1962	Decidedly	W. Hartack	126	119,650	1989	Sunday Silence	Patrick Valen-zuela	126	574,200
1963	Chateauguay	B. Baeza	126	108,900					
1964	Northern Dancer	W. Hartack	126	114,300	1990	Unbridled	Craig Perret	126	581,000
1965	Lucky Debonair	W. Shoemaker	126	112,000	1991	Strike the Gold	Chris Antley	126	655,800
1966	Kauai King	D. Brumfield	126	120,500	1992	Lil E. Tee	P. Day	126	724,800
1967	Proud Clarion	R. Ussery	126	119,700	1993	Sea Hero	Jerry Bailey	126	735,900
1968	Forward Pass[1]	I. Valenzuela	126	122,600	1994	Go For Gin	Chris McCarron	126	628,800
1969	Majestic Prince	W. Hartack	126	113,200	1995	Thunder Gulch	Gary Stevens	126	707,400

1. Dancer's Image finished first but was disqualified after traces of drug were found in system.

PREAKNESS STAKES

Pimlico; 3–year–olds; 1 3/16 miles; first race 1873.

Year	Winner	Jockey	Wt.	Win val.	Year	Winner	Jockey	Wt.	Win val.
1919	Sir Barton	J. Loftus	126	$24,500	1963	Candy Spots	W. Shoemaker	126	$127,500
1930	Gallant Fox	E. Sande	126	51,925	1964	Northern Dancer	W. Hartack	126	124,200
1931	Mate	G. Ellis	126	48,225	1965	Tom Rolfe	R. Turcotte	126	128,100
1932	Burgoo King	E. James	126	50,375	1966	Kauai King	D. Brumfield	126	129,000
1933	Head Play	C. Kurtsinger	126	26,850	1967	Damascus	W. Shoemaker	126	141,500
1934	High Quest	R. Jones	126	25,175	1968	Forward Pass	I. Valenzuela	126	142,700
1935	Omaha	W. Saunders	126	25,325	1969	Majestic Prince	W. Hartack	126	129,500
1936	Bold Venture	G. Woolf	126	27,325	1970	Personality	E. Belmonte	126	151,300
1937	War Admiral	C. Kurtsinger	126	45,600	1971	Canonero II	G. Avila	126	137,400
1938	Dauber	M. Peters	126	51,875	1972	Bee Bee Bee	E. Nelson	126	135,300
1939	Challedon	G. Seabo	126	53,710	1973	Secretariat	R. Turcotte	126	129,900
1940	Bimelech	F.A. Smith	126	53,230	1974	Little Current	M. Rivera	126	156,000
1941	Whirlaway	E. Arcaro	126	49,365	1975	Master Derby	D. McHargue	126	158,100
1942	Alsab	B. James	126	58,175	1976	Elocutionist	J. Lively	126	129,700
1943	Count Fleet	J. Longden	126	43,190	1977	Seattle Slew	J. Cruguet	126	138,600
1944	Pensive	C. McCreary	126	60,075	1978	Affirmed	S. Cauthen	126	136,200
1945	Polynesian	W.D. Wright	126	66,170	1979	Spectacular Bid	R. Franklin	126	165,300
1946	Assault	W. Mehrtens	126	96,620	1980	Codex	A. Cordero	126	180,600
1947	Faultless	D. Dodson	126	98,005	1981	Pleasant Colony	J. Velasquez	126	270,800
1948	Citation	E. Arcaro	126	91,870	1982	Aloma's Ruler	J. Kaenel	126	209,900
1949	Capot	T. Atkinson	126	79,985	1983	Deputed Testimony	D. Miller	126	251,200
1950	Hill Prince	E. Arcaro	126	56,115					
1951	Bold	E. Arcaro	126	83,110	1984	Gate Dancer	A. Cordero	126	243,600
1952	Blue Man	C. McCreary	126	86,135	1985	Tank's Prospect	Pat Day	126	423,200
1953	Native Dancer	E. Guerin	126	65,200	1986	Snow Chief	A. Solis	126	411,900
1954	Hasty Road	J. Adams	126	91,600	1987	Alysheba	C. McCarron	126	421,100
1955	Nashua	E. Arcaro	126	67,550	1988	Risen Star	E. Delahoussaye	126	413,700
1956	Fabius	W. Hartack	126	84,250	1989	Sunday Silence	P. Valenzuela	126	438,230
1957	Bold Ruler	E. Arcaro	126	65,250	1990	Summer Squall	Pat Day	126	445,900
1958	Tim Tam	I. Valenzuela	126	97,900	1991	Hansel	Jerry Bailey	126	432,770
1959	Royal Orbit	W. Harmatz	126	136,200	1992	Pine Bluff	C. McCarron	126	484,120
1960	Bally Ache	R. Ussery	126	121,000	1993	Prairie Bayou	Mike Smith	126	471,835
1961	Carry Back	J. Sellers	126	126,200	1994	Tabasco Cat	Pat Day	126	447,720
1962	Greek Money	J. Rotz	126	135,800	1995	Timber Country	Pat Day	126	446,810

BELMONT STAKES

Belmont Park; 3–year–olds; 1 1/2 miles.

Run at Jerome Park 1867 to 1890; at Morris Park 1890–94; at Belmont Park 1905–62; at Aqueduct 1963–67. Distance 1 5/8 miles prior to 1874; reduced to 1 1/2 miles, 1874; reduced to 1 1/4 miles, 1890; reduced to 1 1/8 miles, 1893; increased to 1 1/4 miles, 1895; increased to 1 3/8 miles, 1896; reduced to 1 1/4 miles in 1904; increased to 1 1/2 miles, 1926.

Year	Winner	Jockey	Wt.	Win val.	Year	Winner	Jockey	Wt.	Win val.
1919	Sir Barton	J. Loftus	126	$11,950	1964	Quadrangle	M. Ycaza	126	$110,850
1930	Gallant Fox	E. Sande	126	66,040	1965	Hail to All	J. Sellers	126	104,150
1931	Twenty Grand	C. Kurtsinger	126	58,770	1966	Amberoid	W. Boland	126	117,700
1932	Faireno	T. Malley	126	55,120	1967	Damascus	W. Shoemaker	126	104,950
1933	Hurryoff	M. Garner	126	49,490	1968	Stage Door			
1934	Peace Chance	W.D. Wright	126	43,410		Johnny	H. Gustines	126	117,700
1935	Omaha	W. Saunders	126	35,480	1969	Arts and Letters	B. Baeza	126	104,050
1936	Granville	J. Stout	126	29,800	1970	High Echelon	J. Rotz	126	115,000
1937	War Admiral	C. Kurtsinger	126	38,020	1971	Pass Catcher	R. Blum	126	97,710
1938	Pasteurized	J. Stout	126	34,530	1972	Riva Ridge	R. Turcotte	126	93,540
1939	Johnstown	J. Stout	126	37,020	1973	Secretariat	R. Turcotte	126	90,120
1940	Bimelech	F.A. Smith	126	35,030	1974	Little Current	M. Rivera	126	101,970
1941	Whirlaway	E. Arcaro	126	39,770	1975	Avatar	W. Shoemaker	126	116,160
1942	Shut Out	E. Arcaro	126	44,520	1976	Bold Forbes	A. Cordero, Jr.	126	117,000
1943	Count Fleet	J. Longden	126	35,340	1977	Seattle Slew	J. Cruguet	126	109,080
1944	Bounding Home	G.L. Smith	126	55,000	1978	Affirmed	S. Cauthen	126	110,580
1945	Pavot	E. Arcaro	126	56,675	1979	Coastal	R. Hernandez	126	161,400
1946	Assault	W. Mehrtens	126	75,400	1980	Temperence Hill	E. Maple	126	176,220
1947	Phalanx	R. Donoso	126	78,900	1981	Summing	G. Martens	126	170,580
1948	Citation	E. Arcaro	126	77,700	1982	Conquistador			
1949	Capot	T. Atkinson	126	60,900		Cielo	L. Pincay, Jr.	126	159,720
1950	Middleground	W. Boland	126	61,350	1983	Caveat	L. Pincay, Jr.	126	215,100
1951	Counterpoint	D. Gorman	126	82,000	1984	Swale	L. Pincay, Jr.	126	310,020
1952	One Count	E. Arcaro	126	82,400	1985	Creme Fraiche	Eddie Maple	126	307,740
1953	Native Dancer	E. Guerin	126	82,500	1986	Danzig Connec-			
1954	High Gun	E. Guerin	126	89,000		tion	C. McCarron	126	338,640
1955	Nashua	E. Arcaro	126	83,700	1987	Bet Twice	C. Perret	126	329,160
1956	Needles	D. Erb	126	83,600	1988	Risen Star	E. Delahoussaye	126	303,720
1957	Gallant Man	W. Shoemaker	126	77,300	1989	Easy Goer	P. Day	126	413,520
1958	Cavan	P. Anderson	126	73,440	1990	Go And Go	Michael Kinane	126	411,600
1959	Sword Dancer	W. Shoemaker	126	93,525	1991	Hansel	Jerry Bailey	126	417,480
1960	Celtic Ash	W. Hartack	126	96,785	1992	A.P. Indy	E. Delahoussay	126	458,880
1961	Sherluck	B. Baeza	126	104,900	1993	Colonial Affair	Julie Krone	126	444,450
1962	Jaipur	W. Shoemaker	126	109,550	1994	Tabasco Cat	Pat Day	126	392,280
1963	Chateauguay	B. Baeza	126	101,700	1995	Thunder Gulch	Gary Stevens	126	415,440

TRIPLE CROWN RACES—1995

Kentucky Derby (Churchill Downs, Louisville, Ky., May 6, 1995). Gross purse: $957,400. Distance: 1 1/4 miles. Order of finish: 1. Thunder Gulch (Stevens), mutuel returns: $51.00, $24.20, $12.20. 2. Tejano Run (Bailey) $10.20, $6.80. 3. Timber Country (Day) $3.80. 4. Jumron (Almeida). 5. Mecke (Davis). 6. Eltish (Delahoussaye). 7. Knockadoon (McCarron). 8. Afternoon Deelites (Desormeaux). 9. Citadeed (Maple). 10. In Character (Antley). 11. Suave Prospect (Krone). 12. Talkin Man (Smith). 13. Dazzling Falls (Gomez). 14. Ski Captain (Mori). 15. Jambalaya Jazz (Perret). 16. Serena's Song (Nakatani). 17. Pyramid Peak (McCauley). 18. Lake George (Sellers). 19. Wild Syn (Romero) Winner's purse: $707,400. Margin of victory: 2 1/4 lengths. Time of race: 2:01 1/5.

Preakness Stakes (Pimlico, Md., May 20, 1995). Gross purse: $687,400. Distance: 1 3/16 miles. Order of finish: 1. Timber Country (Day), mutuel returns $5.80, $4.20, $2.80. 2. Oliver's Twist (Delgado) $16.80, $6.40. 3. Thunder Gulch (Stevens) $3.60. 4. Star Standard (McCarron). 5. Mecke (Davis). 6. Talkin Man (Smith). 7. Our Gatsby (Desormeaux). 8. Mystery Storm (Perret). 9. Tejano Run (Bailey). 10. Pana Brass (Maple). 11. Itron (Frazier). Winner's purse: $446,810. Margin of victory: 1 1/2 lengths. Time of race: 1:54 2/5.

Belmont Stakes (Elmont, N.Y., June 10, 1995). Gross purse: $692,400. Distance: 1 1/2 miles. Order of finish: 1. Thunder Gulch (Stevens), mutuel return: $5.00, $3.70, $2.90. 2. Star Standard (Krone) $5.80, $4.30. 3. Citadeed (Maple) $4.40. 4. Knockadoon (McCarron). 5. Pana Brass (Ramos). 6. Off n' Away (Smith). 7. Ave's Flag (Velazquez). 8. Composer (Bailey). 9. Colonial Secretary (Santos). 10. Is Sveikatas (Chavez). 11. Wild Syn (Romero). Winner's purse: $415,440. Margin of victory: 1/2 length. Time of race: 2:32.

ECLIPSE AWARDS—1994

(Presented January 12, 1995, and Jan. 27, 1995)

Horse of the Year	Holy Bull
4-year-old and up colt, horse, or gelding	The Wicked North
3-year-old horse or gelding	Holy Bull
3-year-old filly	Heavenly Prize
4-year-old and up filly or mare	Sky Beauty
Jockey	Mike Smith
Trainer	D. Wayne Lukas
Breeder	William T. Young
Owner	John Franks
Apprentice jockey	Dale Beckner
2-year-old colt	Timber Country
2-year-old filly	Flanders
Sprinter	Cherokee Run
Male turf horse	Paradise Creek
Female turf horse	Hatoof
Steeplechase	Warm Spell

(Based on vote by the Thoroughbred Racing Associations, the *Daily Racing Form*, and the National Turf Writers Association.)

TRACK AND FIELD

WORLD RECORDS—MEN
Source: USA Track & Field
(Through Aug. 17, 1995)

Recognized by the International Athletic Federation.
The I.A.A.F. decided late in 1976 not to recognize records in yards except for the one–mile run.
The I.A.A.F. also requires automatic timing for all records for races of 400 meters or less.

Event	Record	Holder	Home Country	Where Made	Date
Running					
100 m	0:09.85	Leroy Burrell	United States	Lausanne, Swtizerland	July 6, 1994
200 m	0:19.72	Pietro Mennea	Italy	Mexico City	Sept. 17, 1979
400 m	0:43.29	Butch Reynolds	United States	Indianapolis, Ind.	Aug. 17, 1988
800 m	1:41.80	Sebastian Coe	England	Florence, Italy	June 10, 1981
1,000 m	2:12.40	Sebastian Coe	England	Oslo, Norway	July 11, 1981
1,500 m	3:27.37	Noureddine Morceli	Algeria	Nice, France	July 12, 1995
1 mile	3:44.39	Noureddine Morceli	Algeria	Rieti, Italy	Sept. 5, 1993
2,000 m	4:47.88	Noureddine Morceli	Algeria	Paris	July 3, 1995
3,000 m	7:28.96	Moses Kiptanui	Kenya	Cologne	Aug. 16, 1992
3,000 m steeplechase	8:02.08	Moses Kiptanui	Kenya	Zurich	Aug. 19, 1992
5,000 m	12:44.39	Haile Gebrselassie	Ethiopia	Zurich, Switzerland	Aug. 16, 1995
10,000 m	26:43 53	Haile Gebrselassie	Ethiopia	Hengelo, Holland	June 5, 1995
25,000 m	1:13:55.80	Toshihiko Seko	Japan	Christchurch, N.Z.	March 22, 1981
30,000 m	1:29:18.80	Toshihiko Seko	Japan	Christchurch, N.Z.	March 22, 1981
20,000 m	56:55.60	Arturo Barrios	Mexico	La Fleche, France	March 30, 1991
1 hour	21,101 m	Arturo Barrios	Mexico	La Fleche, France	March 30, 1991
Marathon	2:06.50	Belayneh Densimo	Ethiopia	Rotterdam	April 17, 1988
Walking					
20,000 m	1:17:25.50	Bernardo Segura	Mexico	Fana, Norway	May 7, 1994
2 hours	17 mi. 1,092 yd	Ralph Kowalsky	East Germany	East Berlin	March 28, 1982
30,000 m	2:06:27.00	Maurizio Damilano	Italy	Milanese, Italy	May 5, 1985
50,000 m	3:41.28.2	Rene Piller	France	Fana, Norway	May 7, 1994
Hurdles					
110 m	0:12.91	Colin Jackson	Great Britain	Stuttgart, Germany	Aug. 20, 1993
400 m	0:46.78	Kevin Young	United States	Barcelona	Aug. 6, 1992
Relay Races					
400 m (4 × 100)	0:37.40	United States		Stuttgart, Germany	Aug. 21, 1993
800 m (4 × 200)	1:18.68	Santa Monica T.C.	United States	Walnut, Calif.	April 17, 1994
1,600 m (4 × 400)	2:54.29	United States		Stuttgart, Germany	Aug. 21, 1993
3,200 m (4 × 800)	7:03.89	National Team	Britain	London	Aug. 30, 1982
		(Peter Elliot, Garry Cook, Steve Cram, Sebastian Coe)			
Field Events					
High Jump	8 ft 1/2 in.	Javier Sotomayor	Cuba	Salamanca, Spain	July 27, 1993
Long jump	29 ft 4 3/4 in.	Ivan Pedroso	Cuba	Sestiere, Italy	July 29, 1995
Triple Jump	60 ft 1/4 in.	Jonathan Edwards	Great Britain	Gothenburg, Sweden	Aug. 7, 1995
Pole vault	20 ft 1 in.	Sergey Bubka	Unified Team	Padua	Aug. 30, 1992
Shot–put	75 ft 10 1/4 in.	Randy Barnes	United States	Los Angeles	May 20, 1990
Discus throw	243 ft 0 in.	Juergen Schult	East Germany	Neubrandenburg	June 6, 1986
Hammer throw	284 ft 7 in.	Yuriy Syedikh	U.S.S.R.	Stuttgart	Aug. 28, 1986
Javelin throw	313 ft 10 in.	Jon Zelezny	Czech Republic	Sheffield, Great Britain	Aug. 29, 1993
Decathlon	8,798 pts.	Jurgen Hingsen	W. Germany	Mannheim, W. Ger.	June 8–9, 1984

WORLD RECORDS—WOMEN
Source: USA Track & Field
(Through Aug. 17, 1995)

Event	Record	Holder	Home Country	Where Made	Date
Running					
100 m	0:10.49	Florence Griffith-Joyner	United States	Indianapolis, Ind.	July 16, 1988
200 m	0:21.56	Florence Griffith-Joyner	United States	Seoul, South Korea	Oct. 1, 1988
400 m	0:47.60	Martina Koch	East Germany	Canberra	Oct. 6, 1985
800 m	1:53.28	Jarmila Kratochvilova	Czechoslovakia	Munich, W. Ger.	July 26, 1983
1,500 m	3:50.46	Qu Yunxia	China	Beijing, China	Sept. 11, 1993
1 mile	4:15.61	Paula Ivan	Romania	Nice, Italy	July 10, 1989
3,000 m	8:06.11	Wang Junxia	China	Beijing, China	Sept. 13, 1993
5,000 m	14:36.45	Fernanda Ribeiro	Portugal	Hechtel, Belgium	July 22, 1995

10,000 m	29:31.78	Wang Junxia	China	Beijing, China	Sept. 8, 1993
Marathon	2:21:06.0	Ingrid Kristiansen	Norway	London	April 21, 1985

Walking

5,000 m	20:07.52	Beate Anders	East Germany	Rostock	June 23, 1990
10,000 m	41:37.90	Gao Hongmiao	China	Beijing, China	April 7, 1994

Hurdles

100–m hurdles	0:12.25	Ginka Zagorcheva	Bulgaria	Greece	August 8, 1987
400 m	0:52.61	Kim Batten	United States	Gothenburg, Sweden	Aug. 11, 1995

Relay Races

400 m (4 × 100)	0:41.53	East Germany	E. Germany	Berlin, E. Ger.	July 31, 1983
800 m (4 × 200)	1:28.15	East Germany	E. Germany	Jena, E. Ger.	Aug. 9, 1980
1,600 m (4 × 400)	3:15.18	Soviet Union	Soviet Union	Seoul, South Korea	Oct. 1, 1988
3,200 m (4 × 800)	7:52.3	U.S.S.R.	U.S.S.R.	Podolsk, U.S.S.R.	Aug. 16, 1976

Field Events

High jump	6 ft 10 1/4 in.	Stefka Kostadinova	Bulgaria	Rome	August 30, 1987
Long jump	24 ft 8 1/4 in.	Galina Chistyakova	Soviet Union	Leningrad	June 11, 1988
Triple jump	49 ft 6 1/4 in.	Ana Biryukova	Russia	Stuttgart, Germany	Aug. 21, 1993
Shot–put	74 ft 3 in.	Natalya Lisovskaya	U.S.S.R.	Moscow	June 7, 1987
Discus throw	252 ft 0 in.	Gabriele Reinsch	East Germany	Neubrandenburg, E. Ger.	July 9, 1988
Javelin throw	262 ft 5 in.	Petra Felke	East Germany	Potsdam	Sept. 9, 1988
Heptathlon	7,291 pts	Jackie Joyner–Kersee	United States	Seoul, South Korea	Sept. 24, 1988

AMERICAN RECORDS—MEN

Source: USA Track & Field
(Through Aug. 17, 1995)

Event	Record	Holder	Where Made	Date
Running				
100 m	0:09.85	Leroy Burrell	Lausanne, Switzerland	July 6, 1994
200 m	0:19.73	Mike Marsh	Barcelona	Aug. 5, 1992
400 m	0:43.29	Butch Reynolds	Indianapolis, Ind.	Aug. 17, 1988
800 m	1:42.60	Johnny Gray	Koblenz, W. Ger.	Aug. 29, 1985
1,000 m	2:13.9	Richard Wohlhuter	Oslo, Norway	July 30, 1974
1,500 m	3:29.77	Sydney Maree	Cologne, W. Ger.	Aug. 25, 1985
1 mile	3:47.69	Steve Scott	Oslo, Norway	July 7, 1982
2,000 m	4:54.71	Steve Scott	Ingelhem, W. Ger.	Aug. 31, 1982
3,000 m	7:35.84	Doug Padilla	Oslo, Norway	July 9, 1983
5,000 m	13:01.15	Sydney Maree	Oslo, Norway	July 27, 1985
10,000 m	27:20.56	Mark Nenow	Brussels	Sept. 5, 1986
20,000 m	58:15.0	Bill Rodgers	Boston, Mass.	Aug. 9, 1977
25,000 m	1:14:11.8	Bill Rodgers	Saratoga, Cal.	Feb. 21, 1979
30,000 m	1:31:49.0	Bill Rodgers	Saratoga, Cal.	Feb. 21, 1979
1 hour	12 mi., 1351 yds	Bill Rodgers	Boston, Mass.	Aug. 9, 1977
3,000–m steeplechase	8:09.17	Henry Marsh	Koblenz, W. Ger.	Aug. 29, 1985
Hurdles				
110 m	0:12.92	Roger Kingdom	Berlin	Aug. 16, 1989
400 m	0:46.78	Kevin Young	Barcelona	Aug. 6, 1992
Relay Races				
400 m (4 × 100)	0:37.40	USA National Team	Stuttgart, Germany	Aug. 21, 1993
800 m (4 × 200)	1:18.68	Santa Monica T.C.	Walnut, Calif.	April 17, 1994
1,600 m (4 × 400)	2:54.29	USA National Team	Stuttgart, Germany	Aug. 22, 1993
3,200 m (4 × 800)	7:06.50	Santa Monica T.C.	Walnut	Apr. 26, 1986
Field Events				
High jump	7 ft 10 1/2 in.	Charles Austin	Zurich	Aug. 7, 1991
Long jump	29 ft 4 1/2 in.	Mike Powell	Tokyo, Japan	Aug. 30, 1991
Triple jump	58 ft 11 1/2 in.	Willie Banks	Indianapolis, Ind.	June 16, 1985
Pole vault	19 ft 7 in.	Scott Huffman	Knoxville, Tenn.	June 18, 1994
Shot–put	75 ft 10 1/4 in.	Randy Barnes	Los Angeles	May 20, 1990
Discus throw	237 ft 4 in.	Ben Plucknett	Stockholm, Swe.	July 7, 1981
Javelin throw	281 ft 2 in.	Tom Pukstys	Kourtane, Finland	June 26, 1993
Hammer throw	270 ft 8 in.	Lance Deal	Knoxville, Tenn.	June 17, 1994
Decathlon	8,812 pts	Dan O'Brien	Tokyo, Japan	Aug. 29–30, 1991

AMERICAN RECORDS—WOMEN

Source: USA Track & Field (Through Aug. 17, 1995)

Event	Record	Holder	Where Made	Date
Running				
100 m	0:10.49	Florence Griffith–Joyner	Indianapolis, Ind.	July 16, 1988
200 m	0:21.56	Florence Griffith–Joyner	Seoul, South Korea	Oct. 1, 1988
400 m	0:48.83	Valerie Brisco–Hooks	Los Angeles, Cal.	Aug. 6, 1984
800 m	1:56.90	Mary Decker Slaney	Bern	Aug. 16, 1985
1,500 m	3:57.12	Mary Decker Slaney	Stockholm, Swe.	July 26, 1983
1000 m	2:34.8	Mary Decker Slaney	Eugene, Ore.	July 4, 1985
1 mile	4:16.71	Mary Decker Slaney	Zurich	Aug. 21, 1985
3,000 m	8:29.69	Mary Decker Slaney	Cologne	Aug. 25, 1985
5,000 m	14:56.07	Annette Peters	Berlin, Germany	Aug. 27, 1993
10,000 m	31:28.92	Francie L. Smith	Austin, Texas	April 4, 1991
Hurdles				
100 m hurdles	0:12.46	Gail Devers	Stuttgart, Germany	Aug. 20, 1993
400 m hurdles	0:52.61	Kim Batten	Gothenburg, Sweden	Aug. 11, 1995
Relay Races				
400 m (4 × 100)	0:41.49	U.S. National Team	Stuttgart, Germany	Aug. 22, 1993
800 m (4 × 200)	1:32.57	Louisiana State	Des Moines, Iowa	April 28, 1989
800 m (4 × 200)	1:32.57	Louisiana State	Philadelphia, Pa.	April 30, 1994
1,600 m (4 × 400)	3:15.51	U.S. Olympic Team	Seoul, South Korea	Oct. 1, 1988
Field Events				
High jump	6 ft 8 in.	Louise Ritter	Austin, Tex.	July 9, 1988
Long jump	24 ft. 7 in.	Jackie Joyner–Kersee	New York, N.Y.	May 22, 1994
Triple jump	46 ft. 9 in.	Sheila Hudson-Strudwick	Monte Carlo	July 25, 1995
Shot–put	66 ft. 2 1/2 in.	Ramon Pagel	San Diego, Calif.	June 25, 1988
Discus throw	216 ft 10 in.	Carol Cady	San Jose, Calif.	May 31, 1986
Javelin throw	227 ft 5 in.	Kate Schmidt	Furth, W. Ger.	Sept. 10, 1977
Heptathlon	7,291 pts	Jackie Joyner–Kersee	Seoul, South Korea	Sept. 23–24, 1988

HISTORY OF THE RECORD FOR THE MILE RUN

Source: USA Track & Field

Time	Athlete	Country	Year	Location
4:36.5	Richard Webster	England	1865	England
4:29.0	William Chinnery	England	1868	England
4:28.8	Walter Gibbs	England	1868	England
4:26.0	Walter Slade	England	1874	England
4:24.5	Walter Slade	England	1875	London
4:23.2	Walter George	England	1880	London
4:21.4	Walter George	England	1882	London
4:18.4	Walter George	England	1884	Birmingham, England
4:18.2	Fred Bacon	Scotland	1894	Edinburgh, Scotland
4:17.0	Fred Bacon	Scotland	1895	London
4:15.6	Thomas Conneff	United States	1895	Travers Island, N.Y.
4:15.4	John Paul Jones	United States	1911	Cambridge, Mass.
4:14.4	John Paul Jones	United States	1913	Cambridge, Mass.
4:12.6	Norman Taber	United States	1915	Cambridge, Mass.
4:10.4	Paavo Nurmi	Finland	1923	Stockholm
4:09.2	Jules Ladoumegue	France	1931	Paris
4:07.6	Jack Lovelock	New Zealand	1933	Princeton, N.J.
4:06.8	Glenn Cunningham	United States	1934	Princeton, N.J.
4:06.4	Sydney Wooderson	England	1937	London
4:06.2	Gundar Hägg	Sweden	1942	Goteborg, Sweden
4:06.2	Arne Andersson	Sweden	1942	Stockholm
4:04.6	Gunder Hägg	Sweden	1942	Stockholm
4:02.6	Arne Andersson	Sweden	1943	Goteborg, Sweden
4:01.6	Arne Andersson	Sweden	1944	Malmo, Sweden
4:01.4	Gunder Hägg	Sweden	1945	Malmo, Sweden
3:59.4	Roger Bannister	England	1954	Oxford, England
3:58.0	John Landy	Australia	1954	Turku, Finland
3:57.2	Derek Ibbotson	England	1957	London
3:54.5	Herb Elliott	Australia	1958	Dublin
3:54.4	Peter Snell	New Zealand	1962	Wanganui, N.Z.
3:54.1	Peter Snell	New Zealand	1964	Auckland, N.Z.
3:53.6	Michel Jazy	France	1965	Rennes, France
3:51.3	Jim Ryun	United States	1966	Berkeley, Calif.
3:51.1	Jim Ryun	United States	1967	Bakersfield, Calif.
3:51.0	Filbert Bayi	Tanzania	1975	Kingston, Jamaica
3:49.4	John Walker	New Zealand	1975	Goteborg, Sweden
3:49.0	Sebastian Coe	England	1979	Oslo

3:48.8	Steve Ovett	England	1980	Oslo
3:48.53	Sebastian Coe	England	1981	Zurich, Switzerland
3:48.40	Steve Ovett	England	1981	Koblenz, W. Ger.
3:47.33	Sebastian Coe	England	1981	Brussels
3:46.31	Steve Cram	England	1985	Oslo
3:44.39	Noureddine Morceli	Algeria	1993	Rieti, Italy

TOP TEN WORLD'S FASTEST OUTDOOR MILES

Source: USA Track & Field

Time	Athlete	Country	Date	Location
3:44.39	Noureddine Morceli	Algeria	Sept. 5, 1993	Rieti, Italy
3:46.31	Steve Cram	England	July 27, 1985	Oslo
3:47.33	Sebastian Coe	England	Aug. 28, 1981	Brussels
3:47.69	Steve Scott	United States	July 7, 1982	Oslo
3:47.79	Jose Gonzalez	Spain	July 27, 1985	Oslo
3:48.40	Steve Ovett	England	Aug. 26, 1981	Koblenz, W. Ger.
3:48.53	Sebastian Coe	England	Aug. 19, 1981	Zurich
3:48.53	Steve Scott	United States	June 26, 1982	Oslo
3:48.8	Steve Ovett	England	July 1, 1980	Oslo
3:48.83	Sydney Maree	United States	Sept. 9, 1981	Rieti, Italy

NOTE: Professional marks not included.

TOP TEN WORLD'S FASTEST INDOOR MILES

Source: USA Track & Field

Time	Athlete	Country	Date	Location
3:49.78	Eamonn Coghlan	Ireland	Feb. 27, 1983	East Rutherford, N.J.
3:50.6	Eamonn Coghlan	Ireland	Feb. 20, 1981	San Diego
3:50.7	Noureddine Morceli	Algeria	Feb. 20, 1993	Birmingham, England
3:50.94	Marcus O'Sullivan	Ireland	Feb. 13, 1988	East Rutherford, N.J.
3:51.2	Ray Flynn	Ireland	Feb. 27, 1983	East Rutherford, N.J.
3:51.66	Marcus O'Sullivan	Ireland	Feb. 10, 1989	East Rutherford, N.J.
3:51.8	Steve Scott[1]	United States	Feb. 20, 1981	San Diego
3:52.28	Steve Scott[2]	United States	Feb. 27, 1983	East Rutherford, N.J.
3:52.30	Frank O'Mara	Ireland	Feb. 1986	New York
3:52.37	Eamonn Coghlan	Ireland	Feb. 9, 1985	East Rutherford, N.J.

1. Finished second. 2. Finished third.

WORLD CHAMPIONSHIPS—1995

(Gothenburg, Sweden, Aug. 5–13, 1995)

Men's Events

100 m—Donovan Bailey, Canada	0:09.97
200 m—Michael Johnson, United States	0:19.79
400 m—Michael Johnson, United States	0:43.39
800 m—Wilson Kipketer, Denmark	1:45.08
1,500 m—Noureddine Morceli, Algeria	3:33.73
5,000 m—Ismael Kirui, Kenya	13:16.77
10,000 m—Hailie Gebrselassie, Ethiopia	27:12.95
Marathon—Martin Fiz, Spain	2:11:41
20-k walk—Michele Didoni, Italy	1:19:59
50-k walk—Valentin Kononen, Finland	3:43:42
4 x 100-m relay—Canada	0:38.31
4 x 400-m relay—United States	2:57.32
110-m hurdles—Allen Johnson, United States	0:13.00
400-m hurdles—Derrick Adkins, United States	0:47.98
3,000-m steeplechase—Moses Kiptaunui, Kenya	8:04.16
High jump—Troy Kemp, Bahamas	7 ft 9 1/4 in.
Pole vault—Sergei Bubka, Ukraine	19 ft 5 in
Long jump—Ivan Pedroso, Cuba	28 ft 6 1/2 in.
Triple jump—Jonathan Edwards, Great Britain	60 ft 1/4 in.
Shot-put—John Godina, United States	70 ft 5 1/4 in.
Discus—Lars Riedel, Germany	216 ft 3 in.
Hammer throw—Andrei Abdovaliyev, Tajikistan	267 ft 7 in.
Javelin throw—Jan Zelezny, Czech Republic	293 ft 11 in.
Decathlon—Dan O'Brien, United States	8,695 pts

Women's Events

100 m—Gwen Torrence, United States	0:10.85
200 m—Marlene Ottey, Jamaica	0:22.12
400 m—Marie-Jose Perec, France	0:49.28
800 m—Ana Fidelia Quirot, Cuba	1:56.11
1,500 m—Hassiba Boulmerka, Algeria	4:02.42
5,000 m—Sonia O'Sullivan, Ireland	14:46.47
10,000 m—Fernansa Ribeiro, Portugal	31:04.99
Marathon—Manuela Machado, Portugal	2:25:29
10-k walk—Irina Stankina, Russia	42:13
4 x 100-m relay—United States	0:42.12
4 x 400-m relay—United States	3:22.39
100-m hurdles—Gail Devers, United States	0:12.68
400-m hurdles—Kim Batten, United States	0:52.61
High jump—Stefka Kostadinova, Bulgaria	6 ft 7 in.
Long jump—Fiona May, Great Britain	22 ft 10 3/4 in.
Triple jump—Inessa Kravets, Ukraine	50 ft 10 1/4 in.
Shot-put—Astrid Kumbernuss, Germany	69 ft 7 1/2 in.
Discus throw—Ellina Zovereva, Bulgaria	225 ft 2 in.
Javelin throw—Natalya Shikolenko, Bulgaria	228 ft 8 in.
Heptathlon—Ghada Shouaa, Syria	6,651 pts

USA/MOBIL INDOOR TRACK AND FIELD CHAMPIONSHIP—1995

(March 3–4, 1995, Atlanta, Ga.)

Men's Events

60 m—Tim Harden	0:06.65
200 m—Tod Long	0:20.75
400 m—Michael Johnson	0:44.63
800 m—Joseph Tengelei	1:46.70
Mile—Niall Bruton	4:00.49
3,000 m—Bob Kennedy	7:48.39
5,000-m walk—Allen James	20:16.47
60-m hurdles—Allen Johnson	0:07.42
4 × 400-m relay—Louisiana State	3:07.37
4 × 800-m relay—Brooks Athletic Club	9:40.96
High jump—Tony Barton	7 ft 6 in.
Pole vault—Nick Hysong	19 ft 2 1/4 in.
Long jump—Joe Greene	26 ft 9 3/4 in.
Triple jump—Kenny Harrison	55 ft 9 in.
Shot-put—C.J. Hunter	69 ft 3/4 in.
35-pound weight throw—Lance Deal	84 ft 10 1/4 in.

Women's Events

60 m—Gwen Torrence	0:07.04
200 m—Carlette Guidry-White	0:22.73
400 m—Jearl Miles	0:50.99
800 m—Maria Mutola	1:58.41
Mile—Regina Jacobs	4:26.54
3,000 m—Lynn Jennings	8:57.62
3,000-m walk—Michelle Rohl	13:04.99
60-m hurdles—Lynda Tolbert–Goode	0:07.93
4 × 400-m relay—U. of Tennessee	3:38.64
4 × 800-m relay—Auburn University	11:19.45
High jump—Gwen Wentland	6 ft 5 in.
Pole vault—Melissa Price	11 ft 7 3/4 in.
Long jump—Jackie Joyner-Kersee	22 ft 3/4 in.
Triple jump—Shelia Hudson-Strudwick	46 ft 8 1/4 in.
Shot-put—Ramona Pagel	61 ft 3 1/2 in.
20-pound weight throw—Sonja Fitts	62 ft 7 1/4 in.

Team scoring—Men: 1. Nike International 25.33; 2. Reebok RC 13; 3. Team Adidas and New York Athletic Club (tie) 12. Women: 1. Reebok RC 23; 2. Nike Coast TC, Team Adidas and Honda TC (tie) 8.

Athletes of the Meet: Michael Johnson, Sheila Hudson-Strudwick.

USA/MOBIL OUTDOOR TRACK AND FIELD CHAMPIONSHIP—1995

(June 14–18, 1995, Sacramento, Calif.)

Men's Events

100 m—Mike Marsh	0:10.23
200 m—Michael Johnson	0:19.83
400 m—Michael Johnson	0:43.66
800 m—Brandon Rock	1:46.50
1,500 m—Paul McMullen	3:43.90
3,000-m steeplechase—Mark Croghan	8:17.54
5,000 m—Bob Kennedy	13:19.99
10,000 m—Todd Williams	28:01.84
110-m hurdles—Roger Kingdom	0:13.09
400-m hurdles—Derrick Adams	0:48.44
20-k walk—Allen James	1:24:46,00
High jump—Charles Austin	7 ft 6 1/2 in.
Pole vault—Scott Huffman	19 ft 1/4 in.
Long jump—Mike Powell	28 ft 3/4 in.
Triple jump—Mike Conley	56 ft 4 1/2 in.
Shot-put—Brent Noon	69 ft 2 in.
Discus—Mike Buncic	212 ft 8 in.
Hammer throw—Lance Deal	254 ft 10 in.
Javelin throw—Tom Pukstys	267 ft 4 in.
Decathlon—Dan O'Brien	8,682 pts

Women's Events

100 m—Gwen Torrence	0:11.04
200 m—Gwen Torrence	0:22.03
400 m—Jearl Miles	0:50.90
800 m—Meredith Rainey	2:00.07
1,500 m—Regina Jacobs	4:05.18
3,000-m steeplechase—Chris Morgan	10:51.92
5,000 m—Gina Procaccio	15:46.34
10,000 m—Lynn Jennings	31:77.19
100-m hurdles—Gail Devers	0:12.77
400-m hurdles—Kim Batten	0:54.74
10-k walk—Teresa Vaill	45:01.00
High jump—Amy Scuff	6 ft 4 3/4 in.
Pole vault—Melissa Price	12 ft 9 in.
Long jump—Jackie Joyner-Kersee	22 ft 7 in.
Triple jump—Sheila Hudson—Strudwick	48 ft 1 1/4 in.
Shot-put—Connie Price-Smith	62 ft 6 in.
Discus throw—Edie Boyer	205 ft 4 in.
Hammer throw—Dawn Ellerbe	181 ft 8 in.
Javelin throw—Donna Mayhew	191 ft 1 in.
Heptathlon—Jackie Joyner-Kersee	6,375 pts

BICYCLING

TOUR DE FRANCE—1995

(July 2–23, 1995)

Miguel Indurain captured a record fifth straight victory in the Tour de France, the premier event in cycling. Indurain, 31, finished 4:35 ahead of Alex Zulle of Switzerland.

Three other cyclists—Belgian Eddy Merckx and Frenchmen Jacques Anquetil and Bernard Hinault also won five Tours, but nobody had ever won five straight. Merckx and Anquetil each won four consecutive Tours.

The final order of finish:
1. Miguel Indurain, Spain—92 hours, 44 minutes, 59 seconds
2. Alex Zulle, Switzerland—4 minutes, 35 seconds behind
3. Bjarne Riis, Denmark—6:47 behind
4. Jalabert—8:24 behind
5. Ivan Gotti—Italy—11:33 behind
6. Melchor Mauri, Spain—15:20 behind
7. Fernado Escartin, Spain—15:49 behind
8. Tony Rominger, Switzerland—16:46 behind
9. Richard Virenque, France—17:31 behind
10. Herman Buenahora, Colombia—18:51 behind

AMATEUR BOXING

U.S. CHAMPIONSHIPS—1995

(April 3–8, 1995, Colorado Springs, Co.)

Light flyweight/106 pounds—Pedro Pena, Los Angeles, dec. Sean Johnson, Washington, D.C., 25–25 (tiebreaker)

Flyweight/112 pounds—Arnulfo Bravo, Virginia City, Nev., dec. Joey Garcia, Modesto, Calif., 3–0.

Bantamweight/119 pounds—Carlos Navarro, Los Angeles, dec. Jason Pines, New Bedford, Mass., 30–3.

Featherweight/125 pounds—Floyd Mayweather, Grand Rapids, Mich., won on medical walkover over James Baker, Washington, D.C.

Lightweight/132 pounds—Terrance Cauthen, Phildalphia, dec. Diego Corrales, Sacramento, Calif., 13–6.

Welterweight/147 pounds—Bobby Lewis, Cincinnati, Ohio, dec. Jorge Hawley, Pomona, Calif., 26–23.

Light middleweight/156 pounds—Jeffrey Clark, Army, Fort Bragg, N.C., won on disqualification over Rhoshii Wells, Riverdale, Ga., at 1:15 of 3rd round.

Middleweight/165 pounds—Shane Swartz, Fort Collins, Colo., dec. Eric Wright, Army, Fort Bragg, N.C., 28–15.

Light heavyweight/178 pounds—Antonio Tarver, Orlando, Fla., KO Anthony Stewart, Chicago, 1:43 of 3rd round.

Heavyweight/201 pounds—Lamon Brewster, Los Angeles, dec. Raynon Woods, Mesa, Ariz., 42–11.

Super heavyweight/More than 201 pounds—Lawrence Clay-Bey, Hartford, Conn., KO Marvin Artley, Madison, Wis., 1:47 of 2nd round.

(1996 Olympic Calendar,
continued from page 892)

Thursday, August 1, 1996

8:30 a.m.	Equestrian (Team Jumping Final)
9:00 a.m.	Badminton (W & M Singles' Finals; Mixed Doubles Finals)
1:00 p.m.	Yachting (Soling Match Race Finals)
2:00 p.m.	Track (W 100m hurdles, 200m)
2:00 p.m.	Track & Field (M long jump, 200m, 400m hurdles, decathlon)
2:00 p.m.	Archery (Men's Final)
4:30 p.m.	Table Tennis (Men's Singles)
5:30 p.m.	Field Hockey (Women's Final)
8:30 p.m.	Soccer (Women's Final)

Friday, August 2, 1996

7:30 a.m.	Track (Men's 50k walk)
8:00 a.m.	Track (Men's 1,500m wheelchair; Women's 800m wheelchair)
9:00 a.m.	Archery (W & M team 1/8 Finals)
10:00 a.m.	Tennis (Women's Singles, Men's Doubles)
1:30 p.m.	Archery (W & M Team Finals)
3:00 p.m.	Rhythmic Gymnastics (Group Finals)
3:30 p.m.	Freestyle Wrestling (52 kg, 62 kg, 74 kg, 90 kg, 120 kg)
3:30 p.m.	Soccer (Men's Final)
5:00 p.m.	Synchronized Swimming (Team Final)
5:00 p.m.	Field Hockey (Men's Final)
6:00 p.m.	Track (W shot put, long jump, 10,000m)
6:00 p.m.	Track & Field (M pole vault, 3,000m steeple-chase)

7:00 p.m.	Baseball Finals
10:00 p.m.	Diving (Men's Platform Finals)

Saturday, August 3, 1996

8:30 a.m.	Cycling (W & M Individual Time Trial)
9:00 a.m.	Equestrian (Individual Dressage Freestyle Finals)
9:00 a.m.	Canoe (C–1 M 1,000; C–2 M 1,000 Finals)
9:00 a.m.	Kayak (K–2 M 1,000, K–4 W 500, K–1 M 1,000, K–4 M 1,000)
10:00 a.m.	Tennis (Men's Singles; Women's Doubles)
1:30 p.m.	Boxing Finals
2:30 p.m.	Volleyball (Women's Final)
3:30 p.m.	Handball (Women's Final)
6:30 p.m.	Track (W high jump, 4 × 100m, 1,500m, 4 × 400m)
6:30 p.m.	Track & Field (M javelin, 4 × 100m, 1,500m, 5,000m, 4 × 400m)
8:00 p.m.	Basketball (Men's Finals)

Sunday, August 4, 1996

9:00 a.m.	Canoe (C–1 M 500; C–2 M 500)
9:00 a.m.	Kayak (K–2 M 500; K–1 W 500; K–1 M 500; K–2 W 500)
9:30 a.m.	Basketball (Women's Finals)
10:00 a.m.	Equestrian (Individual Jumping Final)
1:00 p.m.	Rhythmic Gymnastics (Individual Finals)
1:30 p.m.	Boxing Finals
2:30 p.m.	Volleyball (Men's Final)
3:00 p.m.	Handball (Men's Final)
6:30 p.m.	Track (Men's Marathon)
9:00 p.m.	Closing Ceremonies

GYMNASTICS

WORLD CHAMPIONSHIPS—1994[1]
(Brisbane, Australia, April 19–24, 1994)

Men	**Pts**
Floor exercise—1. Vitaly Scherbo, Belarus	9.725
2. Ioonnis Melissanidis, Germany and	9.687
Neil Thomas, Great Britain (tie)	9.687
Pommel horse—1. Marius Urzica, Romania	9.712
2. Eric Poujade, France	9.700
3. Li Donghua, Switzerland	9.662
Still Rings—1. Yui Chechi, Italy	9.787
2. Paul O'Neill, United States	9.725
3. Dan Burinca, Romania	9.700
Vault—1. Vitaly Scherbo, Belarus	9.674
2. Li Xiaoshuang, China	9.618
3. Yeo Hong-Chul, Korea	9.600
Parallel bars—1. Huang Liping, China	9.775
2. Rustam Charipov, Ukraine	9.612
3. Alexei Nemov, Russia	9.575
High bar—1. Vitaly Scherbo, Belarus	9.687
2. Zoltan Supola, Hungary	9.537
3. Ivan Ivankov, Belarus	9.500
All-Around—1. Ivan Ivankov, Belarus	57.012
2. Alexei Voropaev, Russia	56.924
3. Vitaly Scherbo, Belarus	56.350

Women	**Pts**
Vault—1. Gina Gogean, Romania	9.812
2. Svetlana Chorkina, Russia	9.800
3. Lavinia Milosovici, Romania	9.787
Bars—1. Luo Li, China	9.912
2. Svetlana Chorkina, Russia	9.875
3. Dina Kochetkova, Russia	9.850
Beam—1. Shannon Miller, United States	9.875
2. Lilia Podkopayeva, Ukraine	9.737
3. Oxana Fabrichnova, Russia	9.712
Floor—1. Dina Kochetkova, Russia	9.855
2. Lavinia Milosovici, Romania	9.837
3. Gina Gogean, Romania	9.762
All-Around—1. Shannon Miller, United States	39.274
2. Lavinia Milosovici, Romania	39.236
3. Dina Kochetkova, Russia	39.125

1. 1995 World Championships were scheduled for October 1995, after *Information Please Almanac* went to press.

UNITED STATES CHAMPIONSHIPS—1995
(Aug. 16–19, 1995, New Orleans, La.)

Men (Listed with club affiliation)	**Pts**
Floor exercise—1. Daniel Stover, Oklahoma	9.675
2. Blaine Wilson, Ohio State	9.500
3. Mike Racanelli, Bart Conner's	9.350
Pommel horse—1. Mark Sohn, unattached	9.812
2. Jason Bertram, California–Berkeley	9.650
3. Chris Waller, UCLA	9.562
Still rings—1. Paul O'Neill, USOTC	9.812
2. John Roethlisberger, Minnesota	9.575
3. Jarrod Hanks, Oklahoma	9.562
Vault—1. David. St. Pierre, Broadway	9.387
2. Brian Yee, Minnesota	9.187
3. John Macready, USOTC	9.175
Parallel bars—1. John Roethlisberger, Minnesota	9.450
2. Chris Waller, UCLA	9.425
3. Blaine Wilson, Ohio State	9.400
Horizontal bars—1. John Roethlisberger, Minnesota	9.837
2. John Macready, USOTC	9.612
3. Casey Bryan, Oklahoma	9.400
All-Around—1. John Roethlisberger, Minnesota	113.420
2. Mihai Bagiu, Gold Cup	110.560
3. Blaine Wilson, Ohio State	110.420

Women (Listed with club affiliation)	**Pts**
Vault—1. Shannon Miller, Dynamo	9.837
2. Heather Brink, Dynamo	9.781
3. Dominique Moceanu, Karolyi's	9.756
Bars—1. Dominique Dawes, Hill's Angels	9.912
2. Doni Thompson, Colorado Aerials	9.862
3. Kerri Strug, Colorado Aerials	9.812
Beam—1. Doni Thompson, Colorado Aerials	9.687
1. Monica Flammer, Cypress Academy (tie)	9.687
3. Dominique Dawes, Hill's Angels	9.600
Floor exercise—1. Dominique Dawes, Hill's Angels	9.900
2. Dominique Moceanu, Karolyi's	9.800
3. Shannon Miller, Dynamo	9.775
All-Around—1. Dominique Moceanu, Karolyi's	78.450
2. Shannon Miller, Dynamo's	78.250
3. Jaycie Phelps, Cincinnati	77.730

TENNIS

Lawn tennis is a comparatively modern modification of the ancient game of court tennis. Major Walter Clopton Wingfield thought that something like court tennis might be played outdoors on lawns, and in December, 1873, at Nantclwyd, Wales, he introduced his new game under the name of *Sphairistike* at a lawn party. The game was a success and spread rapidly, but the name was a total failure and almost immediately disappeared when all the players and spectators began to refer to the new game as "lawn tennis." In the early part of 1874, a young lady named Mary Ewing Outerbridge returned from Bermuda to New York, bringing with her the implements and necessary equipment of the new game, which she had obtained from a British Army supply store in Bermuda. Miss Outerbridge and friends played the first game of lawn tennis in the United States on the grounds of the Staten Island Cricket and Baseball Club in the spring of 1874.

For a few years, the new game went along in haphazard fashion until about 1880, when standard measurements for the court and standard equipment within definite limits became the rule. In 1881, the U.S. Lawn Tennis Association (whose name was changed in 1975 to U.S. Tennis Association) was formed and conducted the first national championship at Newport, R.I. The international matches for the Davis Cup began with a series between the British and United States players on the courts of the Longwood Cricket Club, Chestnut Hill, Mass., in 1900, with the home players winning.

Professional tennis, which got its start in 1926 when the French star Suzanne Lenglen was paid $50,000 for a tour, received full recognition in 1968. Staid old Wimbledon, the London home of what are considered the world championships, let the pros compete. This decision ended a long controversy over open tennis and changed the format of the competition. The United States championships were also opened to the pros and the site of the event, long held at Forest Hills, N.Y., was shifted to the National Tennis Center in Flushing Meadows, N.Y., in 1978. Pro tours for men and women became worldwide in play that continued throughout the year.

DAVIS CUP CHAMPIONSHIPS

No matches in 1901, 1910, 1915–18, and 1940–45.

1900	United States 3, British Isles 0	1934	Great Britain 4, United States 1	1968	United States 4, Australia 1
1902	United States 3, British Isles 2	1935	Great Britain 5, United States 0	1969	United States 5, Romania 0
1903	British Isles 4, United States 1	1936	Great Britain 3, Australia 2	1970	United States 5, West
1904	British Isles 5, Belgium 0	1937	United States 4, Great Britain 1		Germany 0
1905	British Isles 5, United States 0	1938	United States 3, Australia 2	1971	United States 3, Romania 2
1906	British Isles 5, United States 0	1939	Australia 3, United States 2	1972	United States 3, Romania 2
1907	Australasia 3, British Isles 2	1946	United States 5, Australia 0	1973	Australia 5, United States 0
1908	Australasia 3, United States 2	1947	United States 4, Australia 1	1974	South Africa (Default by India)
1909	Australasia 5, United States 0	1948	United States 5, Australia 0	1975	Sweden 3, Czechoslovakia 2
1911	Australasia 5, United States 0	1949	United States 4, Australia 1	1976	Italy 4, Chile 1
1912	British Isles 3, Australasia 2	1950	Australia 4, United States 1	1977	Australia 3, Italy 1
1913	United States 3, British Isles 2	1951	Australia 3, United States 2	1978	United States 4, Britain 1
1914	Australasia 3, United States 2	1952	Australia 4, United States 1	1979	United States 5, Italy 0
1919	Australasia 4, British Isles 1	1953	Australia 3, United States 2	1980	Czechoslovakia 3, Italy 2
1920	United States 5, Australasia 0	1954	United States 3, Australia 2	1981	United States 3, Argentina 1
1921	United States 5, Japan 0	1955	Australia 5, United States 0	1982	United States 3, France 0
1922	United States 4, Australasia 1	1956	Australia 5, United States 0	1983	Australia 3, Sweden 2
1923	United States 4, Australasia 1	1957	Australia 3, United States 2	1984	Sweden 4, United States 1
1924	United States 5, Australasia 0	1958	United States 3, Australia 2	1985	Sweden 3, West Germany 2
1925	United States 5, France 0	1959	Australia 3, United States 2	1986	Australia 3, Sweden 2
1926	United States 4, France 1	1960	Australia 4, Italy 1	1987	Sweden 5, Austria 0
1927	France 3, United States 2	1961	Australia 5, Italy 0	1988	West Germany 4, Sweden 1
1928	France 4, United States 1	1962	Australia 5, Mexico 0	1989	West Germany 3, Sweden 2
1929	France 3, United States 2	1963	United States 3, Australia 2	1990	United States 3, Australia 2
1930	France 4, United States 1	1964	Australia 3, United States 2	1991	France 3, United States 1
1931	France 3, Great Britain 2	1965	Australia 4, Spain 1	1992	United States 3, Switzerland 1
1932	France 3, United States 2	1966	Australia 4, India 1	1993	Germany 4, Australia 1
1933	Great Britain 3, France 2	1967	Australia 4, Spain 1	1994	Sweden 4, Russia 1

FEDERATION CUP CHAMPIONSHIPS

World team competition for women conducted by International Lawn Tennis Federation.

1963	United States 2, Australia 1	1971	Australia 3, Britain 0	1979	United States 3, Australia 0
1964	Australia 2, United States 1	1972	South Africa 2, Britain 1	1980	United States 3, Australia 0
1965	Australia 2, United States 1	1973	Australia 3, South Africa 0	1981	United States 3, Britain 0
1966	United States 3, West	1974	Australia 2, United States 1	1982	United States 3, West
	Germany 0	1975	Czechoslovakia 3, Australia 0		Germany 0
1967	United States 2, Britain 0	1976	United States 2, Australia 1	1983	Czechoslovakia 2, West
1968	Australia 3, Netherlands 0	1977	United States 2, Australia 1		Germany 1
1969	United States 2, Australia 1	1978	United States 2, Australia 1		
1970	Australia 3, West Germany 0				

1984	Czechoslovakia 2, Australia 1	1987	West Germany 2, United States 1	1990	United States 2, Soviet Union 1
1985	Czechoslovakia 2, United States 1	1988	Czechoslovakia 2, Soviet Union 1	1991	Spain 2, United States 1
1986	United States 3, Czechoslovakia 0	1989	United States 3, Spain 0	1992	Germany 2, Spain 1
				1993	Spain 3, Australia 0
				1994	Spain 3, United States 0

NOTE: 1995 Federation Cup championship scheduled Nov. 25–26, 1995, between United States and Spain, after *Information Please Almanac* went to press.

U.S. CHAMPIONS

Singles—Men

NATIONAL

1881–87	Richard D. Sears
1888–89	Henry Slocum, Jr.
1890–92	Oliver S. Campbell
1893–94	Robert D. Wrenn
1895	Fred H. Hovey
1896–97	Robert D. Wrenn
1898–	
1900	Malcolm Whitman
1901–02	William A. Larned
1903	Hugh L. Doherty
1904	Holcombe Ward
1905	Beals C. Wright
1906	William J. Clothier
1907–11	William A. Larned
1912–13	Maurice McLoughlin[1]
1914	R. N. Williams II
1915	William Johnston
1916	R. N. William II
1917–18	R. Lindley Murray[2]
1919	William Johnston
1920–25	Bill Tilden

1926–27	Jean Rene Lacoste
1928	Henri Cochet
1929	Bill Tilden
1930	John H. Doeg
1931–32	Ellsworth Vines
1933–34	Fred J. Perry
1935	Wilmer L. Allison
1936	Fred J. Perry
1937–38	Don Budge
1939	Robert L. Riggs
1940	Donald McNeill
1941	Robert L. Riggs
1942	Fred Schroeder
1943	Joseph Hunt
1944–45	Frank Parker
1946–47	Jack Kramer
1948–49	Richard Gonzales
1950	Arthur Larsen
1951–52	Frank Sedgman
1953	Tony Trabert
1954	Vic Seixas
1955	Tony Trabert

1956	Ken Rosewall
1957	Mal Anderson
1958	Ashley Cooper
1959–60	Neale Fraser
1961	Roy Emerson
1962	Rod Laver
1963	Rafael Osuna
1964	Roy Emerson
1965	Manuel Santana
1966	Fred Stolle
1967	John Newcombe
1968	Arthur Ashe
1969	Rod Laver

OPEN

1968	Arthur Ashe
1969	Rod Laver
1970	Ken Rosewall
1971	Stan Smith
1972	Ilie Nastase
1973	John Newcombe

1974	Jimmy Connors
1975	Manuel Orantes
1976	Jimmy Connors
1977	Guillermo Vilas
1978	Jimmy Connors
1979	John McEnroe
1980–81	John McEnroe
1982	Jimmy Connors
1983	Jimmy Connors
1984	John McEnroe
1985–87	Ivan Lendl
1988	Mats Wilander
1989	Boris Becker
1990	Pete Sampras
1991	Stefan Edberg
1992	Stefan Edberg
1993	Pete Sampras
1994	Andre Agassi
1995	Pete Sampras

Singles—Women

NATIONAL

1887	Ellen F. Hansel
1888–89	Bertha Townsend
1890	Ellen C. Roosevelt
1891–92	Mabel E. Cahill
1893	Aline M. Terry
1894	Helen R. Helwig
1895	Juliette P. Atkinson
1896	Elisabeth H. Moore
1897–98	Juliette P. Atkinson
1899	Marion Jones
1900	Myrtle McAteer
1901	Elisabeth H. Moore
1902	Marion Jones
1903	Elisabeth H. Moore
1904	May Sutton
1905	Elisabeth H. Moore
1906	Helen Homans
1907	Evelyn Sears

1908	Maud Bargar–Wallach
1909–11	Hazel V. Hotchkiss
1912–14	Mary K. Browne
1915–18	Molla Bjurstedt
1919	Hazel Hotchkiss Wightman
1920–22	Molla Bjurstedt Mallory
1923–25	Helen N. Wills
1926	Molla B. Mallory
1927–29	Helen N. Wills
1930	Betty Nuthall
1931	Helen Wills Moody
1932–35	Helen Jacobs
1936	Alice Marble
1937	Anita Lizana
1938–40	Alice Marble
1941	Sarah Palfrey Cooke
1942–44	Pauline Betz
1945	Sarah Cooke

1946	Pauline Betz
1947	Louise Brough
1948–50	Margaret Osborne duPont
1951–53	Maureen Connolly
1954–55	Doris Hart
1956	Shirley Fry
1957–58	Althea Gibson
1959	Maria Bueno
1960–61	Darlene Hard
1962	Margaret Smith
1963–64	Maria Bueno
1965	Margaret Smith
1966	Maria Bueno
1967	Billie Jean King
1968–69	Margaret Smith Court[3]

OPEN

1968	Virginia Wade
1969–70	Margaret Court
1971–72	Billie Jean King

1973	Margaret Court
1974	Billie Jean King
1975–78	Chris Evert
1979	Tracy Austin
1980	Chris Evert–Lloyd
1981	Tracy Austin
1982	Chris Evert–Lloyd
1983–84	Martina Navratilova
1985	Hana Mandlikova
1986–87	Martina Navratilova
1988	Steffi Graf
1989	Steffi Graf
1990	Grabriela Sabatini
1991	Monica Seles
1992	Monica Seles
1993	Steffi Graf
1994	Arantxa Sanchez Vicario
1995	Steffi Graf

Doubles—Men

NATIONAL

1920	Bill Johnston–C. J. Griffin	
1921–22	Bill Tilden–Vincent Richards	
1923	Bill Tilden–B. I. C. Norton	
1924	H. O. Kinsey––R. G. Kinsey	
1925–26	Vincent Richards––R. N. Williams II	
1927	Bill Tilden–Frank Hunter	
1928	G. M. Lott, Jr.–V. Hennessy	
1929–30	G. M. Lott, Jr.–J. H. Doeg	
1931	W. L. Allison–John Van Ryn	
1932	E. H. Vines, Jr.–Keith Gledh	
1933–34	G. M. Lott, Jr.–L. R. Stoefen	
1935	W. L. Allison–John Van Ryn	
1936	Don Budge–Gene Mako	
1937	G. von Cramm–H. Henkel	
1938	Don Budge–Gene Mako	
1939	A. K. Quist–J. E. Bromwich	
1940–41	Jack Kramer–F. R. Schroeder	

1942	Gardnar Mulloy–Bill Talbert	
1943	Jack Kramer––Frank Parker	
1944	Don McNeill––Bob Falkenburg	
1945	Gardnar Mulloy–Bill Talbert	
1946	Gardnar Mulloy–Bill Talbert	
1947	Jack Kramer–Fred Schroeder	
1948	Gardnar Mulloy–Bill Talbert	
1949	John Bromwich–William Sidwell	
1950	John Bromwich–Frank Sedgman	
1951	Frank Sedgman–Ken McGregor	
1952	Vic Seixas–Mervyn Rose	
1953	Mervyn Rose–Rex Hartwig	
1954	Vic Seixas–Tony Trabert	

1955	Kosei Kamo–Atsushi Miyagi	
1956	Lewis Hoad–Ken Rosewall	
1957	Ashley Cooper–Neale Fraser	
1958	Ham Richardson–Alex Olmedo	
1959–60	Neale Fraser–Roy Emerson	
1961	Chuck McKinley–Dennis Ralston	
1962	Rafael Osuna–Antonio Palafox	
1963–64	Chuck McKinley–Dennis Ralston	
1965–66	Fred Stolle–Roy Emerson	
1967	John Newcombe–Tony Roche	
1968	Stan Smith–Bob Lutz[3]	
1969	Richard Crealy–Allan Stone[3]	

OPEN

1968	Stan Smith–Bob Lutz	
1969	Fred Stolle–Ken Rosewall	
1970	Nikki Pilic–Fred Barthes	
1971	John Newcombe–Roger Taylor	
1972	Cliff Drysdale–Roger Taylor	
1973	John Newcombe–Owen Davidson	
1974	Bob Lutz–Stan Smith	
1975	Jimmy Connors–Ilie Nastase	
1976	Marty Riessen–Tom Okker	
1977	Frew McMillan–Bob Hewitt	
1978	Bob Lutz–Stan Smith	

1979	John McEnroe–Peter Fleming	
1980	Stan Smith–Bob Lutz	
1981	John McEnroe–Peter Fleming	
1982	Kevin Curren–Steve Denton	
1983	John McEnroe–Peter Fleming	
1984	John Fitzgerald–Tomas Smid	
1985	Ken Flach–Robert Seguso	
1986	Andres Gomez–Slobodan Zivojinovic	
1987	Stefan Edberg–Anders Jarryd	

1988	Sergio Casal–Emilio Sanchez	
1989	John McEnroe–Mark Woodforde	
1990	Pieter Aldrich–Danie Visser	
1991	John Fitzgerald–Anders Jarryd	
1992	Jim Grabb–Richey Reneberg	
1993	Ken Flach–Rick Leach	
1994	Jacco Hingh–Paul Haarhuis	
1995	Todd Woodbridge–Mark Woodforde	

1. Challenge round abandoned in 1912. 2. Patriotic Tournament in 1917. 3. With the inaugural of the Open Tournament in 1968, the United States Lawn Tennis Association held a national championship at Longwood, Chestnut Hill, Mass. which barred contract professionals in 1968 and 1969.

Doubles—Women

NATIONAL

1924	G. W. Wightman–Helen Wills	
1925	Mary K. Browne–Helen Wills	
1926	Elizabeth Ryan–Eleanor Goss	
1927	L. A. Godfree–Ermyntrude Harvey	
1928	Hazel Hotchkiss Wightman–Helen Wills	
1929	Phoebe Watson–L. R. C. Michell	
1930	Betty Nuthall–Sarah Palfrey	
1931	Betty Nuthall–E. B. Wittingstall	
1932	Helen Jacobs–Sarah Palfrey	
1933	Betty Nuthall–Freda James	
1934	Helen Jacobs–Sarah Palfrey	
1935	Helen Jacobs–Sarah Palfrey Fabyan	
1936	Marjorie G. Van Ryn–Carolin Babcock	
1937–40	Sarah Palfrey Fabyan–Alice Marble	
1941	Sarah Palfrey Cooke–Margaret Osborne	
1942–47	A. Louise Brough–Margaret Osborne	
1948–50	A. Louise Brough–Margaret	

	O. duPont	
1951–54	Doris Hart–Shirley Fry	
1955–57	A. Louise Brough–Margaret O. duPont	
1958–59	Darlene Hard–Jeanne Arth	
1960	Darlene Hard–Maria Bueno	
1961	Darlene Hard–Lesley Turner	
1962	Darlene Hard–Maria Bueno	
1963	Margaret Smith–Robyn Ebbern	
1964	Karen Hantze Susman–Billie Jean Moffitt	
1965	Nancy Richey–Carole Caldwell Graebner	
1966	Nancy Richey–Maria Bueno	
1967	Billie Jean King–Rosemary Casals	
1968	Margaret Court–Maria Bueno[3]	
1969	Margaret Court–Virginia Wade[3]	

OPEN

1968	Maria Bueno–Margaret Court	
1969	Darlene Hard–Francoise Durr	

1970	Margaret Court–Judy Dalton	
1971	Rosemary Casals–Judy Dalton	
1972	Francoise Durr–Betty Stove	
1973	Margaret Court–Virginia Wade	
1974	Billie Jean King–Rosemary Casals	
1975	Margaret Court–Virginia Wade	
1976	Linky Boshoff–Ilana Kloss	
1977	Martina Navratilova–Betty Stove	
1978	Billie Jean King–Martina Navratilova	
1979	Betty Stove–Wendy Turnbull	
1980	Billie Jean King–Martina Navratilova	
1981	Kathy Jordan–Anne Smith	
1982	Rosemary Casals–Wendy Turnbull	
1983–84	Martina Navratilova–Pam Shriver	
1985	Claudia Khode-Kilsch–Helena Sukova	

1986–87	Martina Navratilova–Pam Shriver	1991	Pam Shriver–Natalia Zvereva		Sanchez Vicario
1988	Gigi Fernandez–Robin White	1992	Gigi Fernandez–Natalia Zvereva	1995	Gigi Fernandez–Natasha Zvereva
1989	Hana Mandlikova–Martina Navratilova	1993	Arantxa Sanchez Vicario–Helena Sukova		
1990	Gigi Fernandez–Martina Navratilova	1994	Jana Novotna–Arantxa		

1. Challenge round abandoned in 1912. 2. Patriotic Tournament in 1917. 3. With the inaugural of the Open Tournament in 1968, the United States Lawn Tennis Association held a national championship at Longwood, Chestnut Hill, Mass. which barred contract professionals in 1968 and 1969.

BRITISH (WIMBLEDON) CHAMPIONS .

(Amateur from inception in 1877 through 1967)

Singles—Men

1908–09	Arthur Gore	1933	J. H. Crawford	1959	Alex Olmedo	1983–84	John McEnroe
1910–13	A. F. Wilding	1934–36	Fred Perry	1960	Neale Fraser	1985–86	Boris Becker
1914	N. E. Brookes	1937–38	Don Budge	1961–62	Rod Laver	1987	Pat Cash
1919	G. L. Patterson	1939	Robert L. Riggs	1963	Chuck McKinley	1988	Stefan Edberg
1920–21	Bill Tilden	1946	Yvon Petra	1964–65	Roy Emerson	1989	Boris Becker
1922	G. L. Patterson	1947	Jack Kramer	1966	Manuel Santana	1990	Stefan Edberg
1923	William Johnston	1948	R. Falkenburg	1967	John Newcombe	1991	Michael Stich
1924	Jean Borotra	1949	Fred Schroeder	1968–69	Rod Laver	1992	Andre Agassi
1925	Rene Lacoste	1950	Budge Patty	1970–71	John Newcombe	1993	Peter Sampras
1926	Jean Borotra	1951	Richard Savitt	1972	Stan Smith	1994	Pete Sampras
1927	Henri Cochet	1952	Frank Sedgman	1973	Jan Kodes	1995	Pete Sampras
1928	Rene Lacoste	1953	Vic Seixas	1974	Jimmy Connors		
1929	Jean Cochet	1954	Jaroslav Drobny	1975	Arthur Ashe		
1930	Bill Tilden	1955	Tony Trabert	1976–80	Bjorn Borg		
1931	S. B. Wood	1956–57	Lewis Hoad	1981	John McEnroe		
1932	Ellsworth Vines	1958	Ashley Cooper	1982	Jimmy Connors		

Singles—Women

1919–23	Lenglen	1946	Pauline M. Betz	1966–67	Billie Jean King	1981	Chris Evert–Lloyd
1924	Kathleen McKane	1947	Margaret Osborne	1968	Billie Jean King	1982–87	Martina Navratilova
1925	Lenglen	1948–50	A. Louise Brough	1969	Ann Jones	1988–89	Steffi Graf
1926	Godfree	1951	Doris Hart	1970	Margaret Court	1990	Martina Navratilova
1927–29	Helen Wills	1952–54	Maureen Connolly	1971	Evonne Goolagong	1991	Steffi Graf
1930	Helen Wills Moody	1955	A. Louise Brough	1972–73	Billie Jean King	1992	Steffi Graf
1931	Frl. C. Aussen	1956	Shirley Fry	1974	Chris Evert	1993	Steffi Graf
1932–33	Helen Wills Moody	1957–58	Althea Gibson	1975	Billie Jean King	1994	Conchita Martinez
1934	D. E. Round	1959–60	Maria Bueno	1976	Chris Evert	1995	Steffi Graf
1935	Helen Wills Moody	1961	Angela Mortimer	1977	Virginia Wade		
1936	Helen Jacobs	1962	Karen Susman	1978–79	Martina Navratilova		
1937	D. E. Round	1963	Margaret Smith	1980	Evonne Goolagong Cawley		
1938	Helen Wills Moody	1964	Maria Bueno				
1939	Alice Marble	1965	Margaret Smith				

Doubles—Men

1953	K. Rosewall–L. Hoad	1971	Rod Laver–Roy Emerson			Taroczy
1954	R. Hartwig–M. Rose	1972	Bob Hewitt–Frew McMillan	1986	Joakim Nystrom–Mats Wilander
1955	R. Hartwig–L. Hoad	1973	Jimmy Connors–Ilie Nastase		
1956	L. Hoad–K. Rosewall	1974	John Newcombe–Tony Roche	1987	Ken Flach–Robert Seguso
1957	Gardnar Mulloy–Budge Patty	1975	Vitas Gerulaitis–Sandy Mayer	1988	Ken Flach–Robert Seguso
1958	Sven Davidson–Ulf Schmidt	1976	Brian Gottfried–Raul Ramirez	1989	John Fitzgerald–Anders Jarryd
1959	Roy Emerson–Neale Fraser	1977	Ross Case–Geoff Masters	1990	Rick Leach–Jim Pugh
1960	Dennis Ralston–Rafael Osuna	1978	Fred McMillan–Bob Hewitt	1991	Anders Jarryd–John Fitzgerald
1961	Roy Emerson–Neale Fraser	1979	Peter Fleming–John McEnroe	1992	John McEnroe–Michael Stich
1962	Fred Stolle–Bob Hewitt	1980	Peter McNamara–Paul McNamee	1993	Todd Woodbridge–Mark Woodforde
1963	Rafael Osuna–Antonio Palafox				
1964	Fred Stolle–Bob Hewitt	1981	John McEnroe–Peter Fleming	1994	Todd Woodbridge–Mark Woodforde
1965	John Newcombe–Tony Roche	1982	Paul McNamee–Peter McNamara		
1966	John Newcombe–Ken Fletcher			1995	Todd Woodbridge–Mark Woodforde
1967	Bob Hewitt–Frew McMillan	1983–84	John McEnroe–Peter Fleming		
1968–70	John Newcombe–Tony Roche	1985	Heinz Gunthardt–Balazs		

Doubles—Women

1956	Althea Gibson–Angela Buxton		Moffitt	1965	Billie Jean Moffitt–Maria Bueno
1957	Althea Gibson–Darlene Hard	1962	Karen Hantze Susman–Billie Jean Moffitt		
1958	Althea Gibson–Maria Bueno			1966	Nancy Richey–Maria Bueno
1959	Darlene Hard–Jeanne Arth	1963	Darlene Hard–Maria Bueno	1967–68	Billie Jean King–Rosemary Casals
1960	Darlene Hard–Maria Bueno	1964	Margaret Smith–Les Turnerley		
1961	Karen Hantze–Billie Jean				

1969	Margaret Court–Judy Tegart	1977	Helen Cawley–JoAnne Russell	1987	Claudia Khode–Kilsch–Helena
1970–71	Billie Jean King–Rosemary	1978	Wendy Turnbull–Kerry Reid		Sukova
	Casals	1979	Billie Jean King–Martina	1988	Steffi Graf–Gabriela Sabatini
1972	Billie Jean King–Betty Stove		Navratilova	1989	Jana Novotna–Helena Sukova
1973	Billie Jean King–Rosemary	1980	Kathy Jordan–Anne Smith	1990	Jana Novotna–Helena Sukova
	Casals	1981	Martina Navratilova–Pam	1991	Pam Shriver–Natalia Zvereva
1974	Evonne Goolagong–Peggy		Shriver	1992	Gigi Fernandez–Natalia Zvereva
	Michel	1982–84	Pam Shriver–Martina	1993	Gigi Fernandez–Natalia Zvereva
1975	Ann Kiyomura–Kazuko		Navratilova	1994	Gigi Fernandez–Natalia Zvereva
	Sawamatsu	1985	Kathy Jordan–Elizabeth Smylie	1995	Jana Novotna–Arantxa
1976	Chris Evert–Martina	1986	Pam Shriver–Martina		Sanchez Vicario
	Navratilova		Navratilova		

UNITED STATES CHAMPIONS—1995

United States Open
(Flushing Meadow, N.Y., Aug. 28–Sept. 10, 1995)

Men's singles—Pete Sampras defeated Andre Agassi, 6–4, 6–3, 4–6, 7–5.

Women's singles—Steffi Graf defeated Monica Seles 7–6 (7–5), 0–6, 6–3.

Men's doubles—Mark Woodforde–Todd Woodbridge defeated Alex O'Brien–Sandon Stolle, 6–3, 6–3.

Women's doubles—Gigi Fernandez–Natash Zvereva, defeated Brenda Schultz McCarthy–Rennae Stubbs, 7–5, 6–3.

Mixed doubles—Meredith McGrath–Matt Lucena defeated Gig Fernandez–Cyril Suk, 6–4, 6–4.

OTHER 1995 CHAMPIONS

Wimbledon Open
(Wimbledon, England, June 26–July 9, 1995)

Men's singles—Pete Sampras defeated Boris Becker, 6–7 (5–7), 6–2, 6–4, 6–2.

Women's singles—Steffi Graf defeated Arantxa Sanchez Vicario, 4–6, 6–1, 7–5.

Men's doubles—Mark Woodforde–Todd Woodbridge defeated Rick Leach–Scott Mellvile, 7–5, 7–6 (10–8), 7–6 (7–5).

Women's doubles—Jana Novotna–Arantxa Sanchez Vicario defeated Gigi Fernandez–Natasha Zvereva, 5–7, 7–5, 6–4.

Mixed doubles—Jonathan Stark–Martina Navratilova defeated Cyril Suk–Gigi Fernandez, 6–4, 6–4.

French Open
(Paris, May 29–June 11, 1995)

Men's singles—Thomas Muster defeated Michael Chang, 7–5, 6–2, 6–4.

Women's singles—Steffi Graf defeated Arantxa Sanchez Vicario, 7–5, 4–6, 6–0.

Men's doubles—Jacco Eltingh–Paul Haarhuis defeated Nicklas Kulti–Magnus Larsson, 6–7 (3–7), 6–4, 6–1.

Women's doubles—Natasha Zvereva–Gigi Fernandez defeated Arantxa Sanchez Vicario–Jana Novotna, 6–7 (8–6), 6–4, 7–5.

Australian Open
(Jan. 16–29, 1995, Melbourne, Australia)

Men's singles—Andre Agassi defeated Pete Sampras, 4–6, 6–1, 7–6 (8–6), 6–4.

Women's singles—Mary Pierce defeated Arantxa Sanchez Vicario, 6–3, 6–2.

Men's doubles—Jared Palmer–Richey Reneberg defeated Mark Knowles–Daniel Nestor, 6–3, 3–6, 6–3, 6–2.

Women's doubles—Jana Novotna–Arantxa Sanchez Vicario defeated Gigi Fernandez–Natasha Zvereva, 6–3, 6–7 (3–7), 6–4.

Mixed doubles—Rick Leach–Natasha Zvereva defeated Cyril Zuk–Gigi Fernandez, 7–6 (7–4), 6–7 (3–7), 6–4.

DAVIS CUP RESULTS—1994

Finals
Sweden 4, Russia 1
(Dec. 2–4, 1994, Moscow, Russia)

Singles—Stefan Edberg, Sweden defeated Alexander Volkov, Russia, 6–4, 6–2, 6–7 (2–7), 0–6, 8–6; Magnus Larsson, Sweden defeated Yevgeny Kafeinkov, Russia, 6–0, 6–2, 3–6, 2–6, 6–3; Magnus Larsson, Sweden, defeated Alexander Volkov, Russia, 7–5, 6–4, 4–6, 6–4, 6–0; Yevgeny Kafeinkov, Russia, defeated Stefan Edberg, Sweden, 4–6, 6–4, 6–0.

Doubles—Jonas Bjorkman and Jan Apell, Sweden defeated Yevgeny Kafeinkov and Andrei Olhovskiy, 6–7 (4–7), 6–2, 6–3, 1–6, 8–6.

MEN'S MONEY WINNERS—1994

1.	Pete Sampras	$3,607,812
2.	Sergi Bruguera	3,031,874
3.	Stefan Edberg	2,489,161
4.	Goran Ivanisevic	2,060,278
5.	Michael Stich	2,033,623
6.	Boris Becker	2,029,756
7.	Andre Agassi	1,941,667
8.	Jim Courier	1,921,584
9.	Michael Chang	1,789,495
10.	Andrei Medvedev	1,211,134

WOMEN'S MONEY WINNERS—1994

1.	Arantxa Sanchez Vicario	$2,943,665
2.	Conchita Martinez	1,540,167
3.	Steffi Graf	1,487,980
4.	Jana Novotna	876,119
5.	Natasha Zvereva	874,592
6.	Gabriela Sabatini	874,470
7.	Martina Navratilova	851,082
8.	Mary Pierce	768,614
9.	Gigi Fernandez	742,650
10.	Lindsay Davenport	600,745

ROWING

Rowing goes back so far in history that there is no possibility of tracing it to any particular aboriginal source. The oldest rowing race still on the calendar is the "Doggett's Coat and Badge" contest among professional watermen of the Thames (England) that began in 1715. The first Oxford-Cambridge race was held at Henley in 1829. Competitive rowing in the United States began with matches between boats rowed by professional oarsmen of the New York waterfront. They were oarsmen who rowed the small boats that plied as ferries from Manhattan Island to Brooklyn and return, or who rowed salesmen down the harbor to meet ships arriving from Europe. Since the first salesman to meet an incoming ship had some advantage over his rivals, there was keen competition in the bidding for fast boats and the best oarsmen. This gave rise to match races.

Amateur boat clubs sprang up in the United States between 1820 and 1830 and seven students of Yale joined together to purchase a four-oared lap-streak gig in 1843. The first Harvard-Yale race was held Aug. 3, 1852, on Lake Winnepesaukee, N.H. The first time an American college crew went abroad was in 1869 when Harvard challenged Oxford and was defeated on the Thames. There were early college rowing races on Lake Quinsigamond, near Worcester, Mass., and on Saratoga Lake, N.Y., but the Intercollegiate Rowing Association in 1895 settled on the Hudson, at Poughkeepsie, as the setting for the annual "Poughkeepsie Regatta." In 1950 the I.R.A. shifted its classic to Marietta, Ohio, and in 1952 it was moved to Syracuse, N.Y. The National Association of Amateur Oarsmen, organized in 1872, has conducted annual championship regattas since that time.

INTERCOLLEGIATE ROWING ASSOCIATION REGATTA

(Varsity Eight-Oared Shells)

Rowed at 4 miles, Poughkeepsie, N.Y., 1895–97, 1899–1916, 1925–32, 1934–41. Rowed at 3 miles, Saratoga, N.Y., 1898; Poughkeepsie, 1921–24, 1947–49; Syracuse, N.Y., 1952–1963, 1965–67. Rowed at 2,000 meters, Syracuse, N.Y., 1964 and from 1968 on. Rowed at 2 miles, Ithaca, N.Y., 1920; Marietta, Ohio, 1950–51. Suspended 1917–19, 1933, 1942–46.

Year	Time	First	Second	Year	Time	First	Second
1895	21:25	Columbia	Cornell	1950	8:07.5	Washington	California
1896	19:59	Cornell	Harvard	1951	7:50.5	Wisconsin	Washington
1897	20:47 4/5	Cornell	Columbia	1952	15:08.1	Navy	Princeton
1898	15:51 1/2	Pennsylvania	Cornell	1953	15:29.6	Navy	Cornell
1899	20:04	Pennsylvania	Wisconsin	1954	16:04.4	Navy[1]	Cornell
1900	19:44 3/5	Pennsylvania	Wisconsin	1955	15:49.9	Cornell	Pennsylvania
1901	18:53 1/5	Cornell	Columbia	1956	16:22.4	Cornell	Navy
1902	19:03 3/5	Cornell	Wisconsin	1957	15:26.6	Cornell	Pennsylvania
1903	18:57	Cornell	Georgetown	1958	17:12.1	Cornell	Navy
1904	20:22 3/5	Syracuse	Cornell	1959	18:01.7	Wisconsin	Syracuse
1905	20:29	Cornell	Syracuse	1960	15:57	California	Navy
1906	19:36 4/5	Cornell	Pennsylvania	1961	16:49.2	California	Cornell
1907	20:02 2/5	Cornell	Columbia	1962	17:02.9	Cornell	Washington
1908	19:24 1/5	Syracuse	Columbia	1963	17:24	Cornell	Navy
1909	19:02	Cornell	Columbia	1964	6:31.1	California	Washington
1910	20:42 1/5	Cornell	Pennsylvania	1965	16:51.3	Navy	Cornell
1911	20:10 4/5	Cornell	Columbia	1966	16:03.4	Wisconsin	Navy
1912	19:31 2/5	Cornell	Wisconsin	1967	16:13.9	Pennsylvania	Wisconsin
1913	19:28 3/5	Syracuse	Cornell	1968	6:15.6	Pennsylvania	Washington
1914	19:37 4/5	Columbia	Pennsylvania	1969	6:30.4	Pennsylvania	Dartmouth
1915	19:36 3/5	Cornell	Stanford	1970	6:39.3	Washington	Wisconsin
1916	20:15 2/5	Syracuse	Cornell	1971	6:06	Cornell	Washington
1920	11:02 3/5	Syracuse	Cornell	1972	6:22.6	Pennsylvania	Brown
1921	14:07	Navy	California	1973	6:21	Wisconsin	Brown
1922	13:33 3/5	Navy	Washington	1974	6:33	Wisconsin	M.I.T.
1923	14:03 1/5	Washington	Navy	1975	6:08.2	Wisconsin	M.I.T.
1924	15:02	Washington	Wisconsin	1976	6:31	California	Princeton
1925	19:24 4/5	Navy	Washington	1977	6:32.4	Cornell	Pennsylvania
1926	19:28 3/5	Washington	Navy	1978	6:39.5	Syracuse	Brown
1927	20:57	Columbia	Washington	1979	6:26.4	Brown	Wisconsin
1928	18:35 4/5	California	Columbia	1980	6:46	Navy	Northeastern
1929	22:58	Columbia	Washington	1981	5:57.3	Cornell	Navy
1930	21:42	Cornell	Syracuse	1982	5:57.5	Cornell	Princeton
1931	18:54 1/5	Navy	Cornell	1983	6:14.4	Brown	Navy
1932	19:55	California	Cornell	1984	5:54.7	Navy	Pennsylvania
1934	19:44	California	Washington	1985	5:49.9	Princeton	Brown
1935	18:52	California	Cornell	1986	5:50.2	Brown	Pennsylvania
1936	19:09 3/5	Washington	California	1987	6:02.9	Brown	Wisconsin
1937	18:33 3/5	Washington	Navy	1988	6:14.0	Northeastern	Brown
1938	18:19	Navy	California	1989	5:56.0	Penn	Wisconsin
1939	18:12 3/5	California	Washington	1990	5:55.5	Wisconsin	Pennsylvania
1940	22:42	Washington	Cornell	1991	6:05.2	Northeastern	Pennsylvania
1941	18:53 3/10	Washington	California	1992	6:10.5	Dartmouth	Harvard
1947	13:59 1/5	Navy	Cornell	1993	5:59.1	Brown	Pennsylvania
1948	14:06 2/5	Washington	California	1994	5:54.4	Brown	Princeton
1949	14:42 3/5	California	Washington	1995	5:31.3[2]	Brown	Navy

1. Disqualified. 2. New course record.

JAMES E. SULLIVAN MEMORIAL AWARD WINNERS
(Amateur Athlete of Year Chosen in Amateur Athletic Union Poll)

1930	Robert Tyre Jones, Jr.	Golf	1963	John Pennel	Track and field
1931	Bernard E. Berlinger	Track and field	1964	Don Schollander	Swimming
1932	James A. Bausch	Track and field	1965	Bill Bradley	Basketball
1933	Glenn Cunningham	Track and field	1966	Jim Ryun	Track and field
1934	William R. Bonthron	Track and field	1967	Randy Matson	Track and field
1935	W. Lawson Little, Jr.	Golf	1968	Debbie Meyer	Swimming
1936	Glenn Morris	Track and field	1969	Bill Toomey	Decathlon
1937	J. Donald Budge	Tennis	1970	John Kinsella	Swimming
1938	Donald R. Lash	Track and field	1971	Mark Spitz	Swimming
1939	Joseph W. Burk	Rowing	1972	Frank Shorter	Marathon
1940	J. Gregory Rice	Track and field	1973	Bill Walton	Basketball
1941	Leslie MacMitchell	Track and field	1974	Rick Wohlhuter	Track
1942	Cornelius Warmerdam	Track and field	1975	Tim Shaw	Swimming
1943	Gilbert L. Dodds	Track and field	1976	Bruce Jenner	Track and field
1944	Ann Curtis	Swimming	1977	John Naber	Swimming
1945	Felix (Doc) Blanchard	Football	1978	Tracy Caulkins	Swimming
1946	Y. Arnold Tucker	Football	1979	Kurt Thomas	Gymnastics
1947	John B. Kelly, Jr.	Rowing	1980	Eric Heiden	Speed skating
1948	Robert B. Mathias	Track and field	1981	Carl Lewis	Track and field
1949	Richard T. Button	Figure skating	1982	Mary Decker Tabb	Track and field
1950	Fred Wilt	Track and field	1983	Edwin Moses	Track and field
1951	Robert E. Richards	Track and field	1984	Greg Louganis	Diving
1952	Horace Ashenfelter	Track and field	1985	Joan Benoit–Samuelson	Marathon
1953	Major Sammy Lee	Diving	1986	Jackie Joyner–Kersee	Heptathlon
1954	Malvin Whitfield	Track and field	1987	Jim Abbott	Baseball
1955	Harrison Dillard	Track and field	1988	Florence Griffith–Joyner	Track and field
1956	Patricia McCormick	Diving	1989	Janet Evans	Swimming
1957	Bobby Jo Morrow	Track and Field	1990	John Smith	Wrestling
1958	Glenn Davis	Track and field	1991	Mike Powell	Track and field
1959	Parry O'Brien	Track and field	1992	Bonnie Blair	Speed skating
1960	Rafer Johnson	Track and field	1993	Charles Ward	Football/basketball
1961	Wilma Rudolph Ward	Track and field	1994	Dan Jansen	Speed skating
1962	Jim Beatty	Track and field			

COLLEGE GOLF

N.C.A.A. DIVISION I CHAMPIONSHIP
(May 31–June 3, 1995, at Ohio State University, Columbus, Ohio)

Team scores (par 1152)

Oklahoma State	291–292–287–266—1,156
Stanford	289–292–286–289—1,156
Texas	289–296–282–290—1,157
Arizona State	288–300–289–287—1,164
Southern Cal	295–293–281–296—1,165
California	292–295–288–291—1,166
Florida State	289–293–292–294—1,168
North Carolina State	293–291–294–292—1,170
Ohio State	296–290–296–288—1,170
Arizona	294–290–291–296—1,171

Leading individual scorers

Chip Spratlin, Auburn	67–71–70–75—283
Ted Purdy, Arizona	74–70–70–70—284
Chris Tidland, Oklahoma State	69–69–72–74—284
Chris Wollmann, Ohio St.	70–73–71–71—285
Joey Snyder, Arizona St.	71–74–69–72—286
Tiger Woods, Stanford	73–72–70–71—286
Chad Wright, Southern Cal	71–73–67–75—286
Dennis Hillman, Tulsa	73–68–75–71—287
Scott Johnson, Arizona St.	72–72–74–69—287
Garrett Willis, E. Tenn. St.	72–70–76–69—287
Scott Rowe, Northwestern	71–70–75–72—288
Jeff Fahrenbruch, Texas	72–73–72–71—288

BADMINTON

WORLD BADMINTON CHAMPIONSHIPS—1995
(Lausanne, Switzerland, May 28, 1995)

Men

Singles—Heryanto Arbi, Indonesia, defeated Park Sung-woo, South Korea, 15–11, 15–8 in championship match

Doubles—Rexy Mainaky and Ricky Subagya, Indonesia, defeated Jon Holst–Christensen and Thomas Lund, Denmark, 15–5, 15–2 in championship march

Women

Singles—Ye Zhagying, China, defeated Han Jingna, China, 11–7, 11–0 in championship match

Doubles—Gil Young Ah and Jang Hye–ock, South Korea, defeated Fiharsih and Lili Tampi, Indonesia, 15–5, 15–2 in championship match

U.S. BADMINTON CHAMPIONSHIPS
(Georgia State Univ., Atlanta, Ga., Mar. 30–Apr. 2, 1995)

Men

Singles—Kevin Han, Palos Heights, Ill., defeated Tom Reidui, Tempe, Ariz., 15–6, 15–7 in championship match

Doubles—Tom Reidui, Tempe, Ariz. and Ben Lee, San Jose, Calif., defeated Andy Chong, Miami Lakes, Fla., and Kevin Han, Palos Heights, Ill., 15–7, 15–9 in championship match

Women

Singles—Andrea Andersson, Tempe, Ariz., defeated Kathy Zimmerman, Denver, Colo., 11–5, 11–9 in championship match

Doubles—Andrea Andersson, Tempe, Ariz., and Liz Aronsohn, Scottsdale, Ariz., defeated Kathy Zimmerman, Denver, Colo., and Ann French, LaJolla, Calif., 15–4, 15–4 in championship match

Mixed doubles—Andy Chong, Miami Lakes, Fla., and Linda French, Elmhurst, N.Y., defeated Trisha Gunadi, Alhambra, Calif., and Eileen Tang, Chino, Calif., 15–8, 15–2 in championship match

HARNESS RACING

Oliver Wendell Holmes, the famous Autocrat of the Breakfast Table, wrote that the running horse was a gambling toy but the trotting horse was useful and, furthermore, "horse–racing is not a republican institution; horse–trotting is." Oliver Wendell Holmes was a born–and–bred New Englander, and New England was the nursery of the harness racing sport in America. Pacers and trotters were matters of local pride and prejudice in Colonial New England, and, shortly after the Revolution, the Messenger and Justin Morgan strains produced many winners in harness racing "matches" along the turnpikes of New York, Connecticut, Rhode Island, Massachusetts, Vermont, and New Hampshire.

There was English thoroughbred blood in Messenger and Justin Morgan, and, many years later, it was blended in Rysdyk's Hambletonian, foaled in 1849. Hambletonian was not particularly fast under harness but his descendants have had almost a monopoly of prizes, titles, and records in the harness racing game. Hambletonian was purchased as a foal with its dam for a total of $124 by William Rysdyk of Goshen, N.Y., and made a modest fortune for the purchaser.

Trotters and pacers often were raced under saddle in the old days, and, in fact, the custom still survives in some places in Europe. Dexter, the great trotter that lowered the mile record from 2:19 3/4 to 2:17 1/4 in 1867, was said to handle just as well under saddle as when pulling a sulky. But as sulkies were lightened in weight and improved in design, trotting under saddle became less common and finally faded out in this country.

WORLD RECORDS

Established in a race or against time at one mile. *Source:* United States Trotting Association
(Through Sept. 1, 1995)

Trotting on Mile Track

	Record	Holder	Driver	Where Made	Year
All Age	1:52 1/5	Mack Lobell	John Campbell	Springfield, Ill.	1987
	1:52 4/5	Peace Corps	John Campbell	Du Quoin, Ill.	1989
	1:53	Express Ride	Berndt Lindstedt	Lexington, Ky.	1987
	* 1:55 1/4	Greyhound	Sep Palin	Lexington, Ky.	1938
2–year–old	* 1:55	Noxie Hanover	Jim Simpson	Lexington, Ky.	1988
	1:55 3/5	Mack Lobell	John Campbell	Lexington, Ky.	1986
	1:57 2/5	I'm Impeccable	Dave Rankin	Lexington, Ky.	1989
3–year–old	1:52 1/5	Mack Lobell	John Campbell	Springfield, Ill.	1987
	1:52 4/5	Peace Corps	John Campbell	Du Quoin, Ill.	1989
	1:53 2/5	Champion on Ice	Dave Magee	Springfield, Ill.	1994
4–year–old	1:52 4/5	Pine Chip	John Campbell	East Rutherford, N.J.	1994
	1:53	Express Ride	Berndt Lindstedt	Lexington, Ky.	1987
	1:54 1/5	Imperfection	D. Magee	Balmoral, Illinois	1993
5–year–old and older	1:54 1/5	Earl	Roger Hayotte	Toronto, Ontario	1994
	1:54 1/5	Napoletano	Stig Johansson	East Rutherford, N.J.	1989
	1:54 4/5	Kit Lobell	Berndt Lindstedt	East Rutherford, N.J.	1990
	1:55	Franconia	John Campbell	East Rutherford, N.J.	1987
	* 1:55 1/4	Greyhound	Sep Palin	Lexington, Ky.	1938

Trotting on Five-Eighths-Mile Track

	Record	Holder	Driver	Where Made	Year
All Age	1:54 1/5	Mack Lobell	John Campbell	Pompano Beach, Fla.	1987
2–year–old	1:57 3/5	Royal Troubador	Carl Allen	Pompano Beach, Fla.	1989
3–year–old	1:54 1/5	Mack Lobell	John Campbell	Pompano Beach, Fla.	1987
4–year–old	1:54 4/5	Mack Lobell	John Campbell	Solvalla, Sweden	1988
5–year–old and older	1:54 3/5	Mack Lobell	John Campbell	Pompano Beach, Fla.	1991

Trotting on Half-Mile Track

	Record	Holder	Driver	Where Made	Year
All Age	1:56	Mack Lobell	John Campbell	Saratoga Springs, N.Y.	1988
2–year–old	1:58 1/5	Royal Troubador	Carl Allen	Delaware, Ohio	1989
3–year–old	1:56 4/5	Editor In Chief	John Campbell	Delaware, Ohio	1988
4–year–old	1:56	Mack Lobell	John Campbell	Saratoga Springs, N.Y.	1988
5–year–old and older	1:57 3/5	Atkinson Ridge	H. Filion	Yonkers, N.Y.	1992
	1:57 3/5	Chief Litigator	J. Marsh, Jr.	Yonkers, N.Y.	1992

Pacing on a Mile Track

	Record	Holder	Driver	Where Made	Year
All Age	* 1:48 2/5	Matt's Scooter	Michel Lachance	Lexington, Ky.	1988
	1:49 2/5	Artsplace	C. Manzi	East Rutherford, N.J.	1992
	1:49 4/5	Dorunrun	J. Schwind	East Rutherford, N.J.	1992
2–year–old	1:51 4/5	America's Pasttime	W. Hennessey	East Rutherford, N.J.	1992
	1:52	L Dees Trish	Michel Lachance	Lexington, Ky.	1988
	1:52 1/5	Raque Bogart	Bill Fahy	Lexington, Ky.	1988
3–year–old	* 1:48 2/5	Matt's Scooter	Michel Lachance	Lexington, Ky.	1988
	1:50 4/5	Western Hanover	W. Fahy	East Rutherford, N.J.	1992
	* 1:51 2/5	Trini Hanover	Ron Waples	Springfield, Ill.	1987
	1:51 4/5	Indian Alert	Larry Noggle	Lexington, Ky.	1987
4–year–old	1:49 2/5	Artsplace	C. Manzi	East Rutherford, N.J.	1992
	* 1:49 2/5	Jaguar Spur	Dick Stillings	Lexington, Ky.	1988
	* 1:50 4/5	Fan Hanover	Glen Garnsey	Lexington, Ky.	1982
	1:51 1/5	Indian Alert	Jack Moiseyev	East Rutherford, N.J.	1988
5–year–old and older	1:49 4/5	Dorunrun	J. Schwind	East Rutherford, N.J.	1992

Pacing on Five-Eighths-Mile Track

All Age	1:50 4/5	In the Pocket	John Campbell	Meadow Lands, Pa.	1990
2–year–old	1:53 2/5	Kentucky Spur	Dick Stillings	Pompano Beach, Fla.	1988
3–year–old	1:50 4/5	In the Pocket	John Campbell	Meadow Lands, Pa.	1990
	1:51 1/5	Goalie Jeff	Michel Lachance	Montreal, Canada	1989
4–year–old	1:51	Falcon Seelster	Tom Harmer	Meadow Lands, Pa.	1986
	1:51	Matt's Scooter	Michel Lachance	Campbellville, Ont., Canada	1989
5–year–old and older	1:52 2/5	Ring of Light	James Morand	Laurel, Md.	1988

Pacing on a Half-Mile Track

All Age	1:50 4/5	Nihilator	Jim Morrill, Jr.	Yonkers, N.Y.	1993
2–year–old	1:54 1/5	Tooter Scooter	Bill Fahy	Louisville, Ky.	1990
	1:54 1/5	W.R.H.	John Campbell	Delaware, Ohio	1990
3–year–old	1:51	Falcon Seelster	Tom Harmer	Delaware, Ohio	1985
4–year–old	1:51 4/5	Arrive at Five	John Campbell	Northfield Park, Ohio	1994
5–year–old and older	1:54 1/5	Port Stanley	John Reese	Maywood, Ill.	1988

*Set in a time trial.

HARNESS RACING RECORDS FOR THE MILE

Trotters				**Pacers**			
Time	Trotter, age, driver		Year	Time	Pacer, age, driver		Year
2:00	Lou Dillon, 5, Millard Sanders		1903	2:00 1/2	John R. Gentry, 7, W.J. Andrews		1896
1:58 1/2	Lou Dillon, 5, Millard Sanders		1903	1:59 1/4	Star Pointer, 8, D. McClary		1897
1:58	Uhlan, 8, Charles Tanner		1912	1:59	Dan Patch, 7, M. E. McHenry		1903
1:58	Peter Manning, 5, T. W. Murphy		1921	1:56 1/4	Dan Patch, 7, M. E. McHenry		1903
1:57 3/4	Peter Manning, 5, T. W. Murphy		1921	1:56	Dan Patch, 8, H. C. Hersey		1904
1:57	Peter Manning, 6, T. W. Murphy		1922	1:55	Billy Direct, 4, Vic Fleming		1938
1:56 3/4	Peter Manning, 6, T. W. Murphy		1922	1:55	Adios Harry, 4, Luther Lyons		1955
1:56 3/4	Greyhound, 5, Sep Palin		1937	1:54 3/5	Adios Butler, 4, Paige West		1960
1:56	Greyhound, 5, Sep Palin		1937	1:54	Bret Hanover, 4, Frank Ervin		1966
1:55 1/4	Greyhound, 6, Sep Palin		1938	1:53 3/5	Bret Hanover, 4, Frank Ervin		1966
1:54 4/5	Nevele Pride, 4, Stanley Dancer		1969	1:52	Steady Star, 4, Joe O'Brien		1971
1:54 4/5	Lindy's Crown, 4, Howard Beissinger		1980	1:49 1/5	Niatross, 3, Clint Galbraith		1980
1:54	Arndon, 3, Del Miller		1982	1:48 2/5	Matt's Scooter, 3, Michel Lachance		1989
1:52 1/5	Mack Lobell, 3, John Campbell		1987	1:46 1/5	Cambest, 5, W. Hennessey		1993

HISTORY OF TRADITIONAL HARNESS RACING STAKES

The Hambletonian

Three–year–old trotters. One mile. Guy McKinney won first race at Syracuse in 1926; held at Goshen, N.Y., 1930–1942, 1944–1956; at Yonkers, N.Y., 1943; at Du Quoin, Ill., 1957–1980. Since 1981, the race has been held at The Meadowlands in East Rutherford, N.J.

Year	Winner	Driver	Best time	Total purse
1967	Speedy Streak	Del Cameron	2:00	$122,650
1968	Nevele Pride	Stanley Dancer	1:59 2/5	116,190
1969	Lindy's Pride	Howard Beissinger	1:57 3/5	124,910
1970	Timothy T.	John Simpson, Jr.	1:58 2/5[1]	143,630
1971	Speedy Crown	Howard Beissinger	1:57 3/5	129,770
1972	Super Bowl	Stanley Dancer	1:56 2/5	119,090
1973	Flirth	Ralph Baldwin	1:57 1/5	144,710
1974	Christopher T	Billy Haughton	1:58 3/5	160,150
1975	Bonefish	Stanley Dancer	1:59[2]	232,192
1976	Steve Lobell	Billy Haughton	1:56 3/5	263,524
1977	Green Speed	Billy Haughton	1:55 3/5	284,131
1978	Speedy Somolli	Howard Beissinger	1:55[3]	241,280
1979	Legend Hanover	George Sholty	1:56 1/5	300,000
1980	Burgomeister	Billy Haughton	1:56 3/5	293,570
1981	Shiaway St. Pat	Ray Remmen	2:01 1/5[4]	838,000
1982	Speed Bowl	Tommy Haughton	1:56 4/5	875,750
1983	Duenna	Stanley Dancer	1:57 2/5	1,000,000
1984	Historic Free	Ben Webster	1:56 2/5	1,219,000
1985	Prakas	Bill O'Donnell	1:54 3/5	1,272,000
1986	Nuclear Kosmos	Ulf Thoresen	1:56	1,172,082
1987	Mack Lobell	John Campbell	1:53 3/5	1,046,300
1988	Armbro Goal	John Campbell	1:54 3/5	1,156,800
1989	Park Avenue Joe	Ron Wayples	1:55 3/5	1,131,000
1990	Embassy Lobell	Michel Lachance	1:56 1/5	1,346,000
1991	Giant Victory	Jack Moiseyev	1:54 4/5	1,238,000
1992	Alf Palema	Mickey McNichol	1:56 3/5	1,288,000
1993	American Winner	Ron Pierce	1:53 1/5	1,200,000
1994	Victory Dream	Michel Lachance	1:53 4/5	1,200,000
1995	Tagliabue	John Campbell	1:54 3/5	1,200,000

1. By Formal Notice. 2. By Yankee Bambino. 3. By Speedy Somolli and Florida Pro. 4. By Super Juan.

Little Brown Jug

Three–year–old pacers. One Mile. Raced at Delaware County Fair Grounds, Delaware, Ohio.

Year	Winner	Driver	Best time	Total purse
1967	Best of All	Jim Hackett	1:59[1]	S84,778
1968	Rum Customer	Billy Haughton	1:59 3/5	104,226
1969	Laverne Hanover	Billy Haughton	2:00 2/5	109,731
1970	Most Happy Fella	Stanley Dancer	1:57 1/5	100,110
1971	Nansemond	Herve Filion	1:57 2/5	102,994
1972	Strike Out	Keith Waples	1:56 3/5	104,916
1973	Melvin's Woe	Joe O'Brien	1:57 3/5	120,000
1974	Ambro Omaha	Billy Haughton	1:57	132,630
1975	Seatrain	Ben Webster	1:57[2]	147,813
1976	Keystone Ore	Stanley Dancer	1:56 4/5[3]	153,799
1977	Governor Skipper	John Chapman	1:56 1/5	150,000
1978	Happy Escort	William Popfinger	1:55 2/5[4]	186,760
1979	Hot Hitter	Herve Filion	1:55 3/5	226,455
1980	Niatross	Clint Galbraith	1:54 4/5	207,361
1981	Fan Hanover	Glen Garnsey	1:56[5]	243,799
1982	Merger	John Campbell	1:56 3/5	328,900
1983	Ralph Hanover	Ron Waples	1:55 3/5	358,800
1984	Colt 46	Norman Boring	1:53 3/5	366,717
1985	Nihilator	Bill O'Donnell	1:52 1/5	350,730
1986	Barberry Spur	Bill O'Donnell	1:52 4/5	407,684
1987	Jaguar Spur	Richard Stillings	1:55 3/5	412,330
1988	B.J. Scoot	Michel Lachance	1:52 3/5	486,050
1989	Goalie Jeff	Michel Lachance	1:54 1/5	500,200
1990	Beach Towel	Ray Remmen	1:53 3/5	253,049
1991	Precious Bunny	Jack Moiseyev	1:54 1/5	575,150
1992	Fake Left	Ron Waples	1:54 2/5	556,210
1993	Life Sign	John Campbell	1:52	465,500
1994	Magical Mike	Michel LaChance	1:52 3/5	512,830
1995	Nick's Fantasy	John Campbell	1:51 2/5	543,670

1. By Nardin's Byrd. 2. By Albert's Star. 3. By Armbro Ranger. 4. By Falcon Almahurst. 5. By Seahawk Hanover.

HARNESS HORSE OF THE YEAR

Chosen in poll conducted by United States Trotting Association in conjunction with the U.S. Harness Writers Assn.

1959	Bye Bye Byrd, Pacer	1974	Delmonica Hanover, Trotter
1960–61	Adios Butler, Pacer	1975	Savoir, Trotter
1962	Su Mac Lad, Trotter	1976	Keystone Ore, Pacer
1963	Speedy Scot, Trotter	1977	Green Speed, Trotter
1964–66	Bret Hanover, Pacer	1978	Abercrombie, Pacer
1967–69	Nevele Pride, Trotter	1979–80	Niatross, Pacer
1970	Fresh Yankee, Trotter	1981	Fan Hanover, Pacer
1971–72	Albatross, Pacer	1982–83	Cam Fella, Pacer
1973	Sir Dalrae, Pacer	1984	Fancy Crown, Trotter

1985	Nihilator, Trotter
1986	Forrest Skipper
1987–88	Mack Lobell
1989	Matt's Scooter
1990	Beach Towel
1991	Precious Bunny
1992	Artsplace
1993	Staying Together
1994	Cam's Card Shark

RODEO

A rodeo was originally a contest held after a roundup where the cowboys competed among themselves in contests such as horse racing, steer riding, and calf roping. This display of cowboy skills originated in Mexico and the word "rodeo" comes from the Spanish word *rodear* which means a cattle roundup. The first real rodeo is commonly believed to have been held in Kansas in 1882 and was organized by Col. George Miller of the famous 101 Ranch. Others think that the first organized rodeo was held in Pecos, Texas, in 1883.

These cowboy displays of skill developed into the annual rodeo events held in the West today where millions of people watch professional rodeo performers compete. The Rodeo Cowboy Association was founded in 1936 to establish uniform regulations for the sport. There are five standard events in a modern rodeo. They are saddle bronc riding, bareback riding, bull riding, calf roping, and steer wrestling or "bulldogging."

PROFESSIONAL RODEO COWBOY ASSOCIATION, ALL AROUND COWBOY

1953	Bill Linderman	1962	Tom Nesmith	1975	Leo Camarillo and	1983	Roy Cooper
1954	Buck Rutherford	1963–65	Dean Oliver		Tom Ferguson	1984	Dee Pickett
1955	Casey Tibbs	1966–70	Larry Mahan	1976–79	Tom Ferguson	1985–87	Lewis Field
1956–59	Jim Shoulders	1971–72	Phil Lyne	1980	Paul Tierney	1988	Dave Appleton
1960	Harry Tompkins	1973	Larry Mahan	1981	Jimmie Cooper	1989–93	Ty Murray
1961	Benny Reynolds	1974	Tom Ferguson	1982	Chris Lybbert	1994	Ty Murray

NOTE: 1995 Championship scheduled after *Information Please Almanac* went to press.

GOLF

It may be that golf originated in Holland—historians believe it did—but certainly Scotland fostered the game and is famous for it. In fact, in 1457 the Scottish Parliament, disturbed because football and golf had lured young Scots from the more soldierly exercise of archery, passed an ordinance that "futeball and golf be utterly cryit doun and nocht usit." James I and Charles I of the royal line of Stuarts were golf enthusiasts, whereby the game came to be known as "the royal and ancient game of golf."

The golf balls used in the early games were leather-covered and stuffed with feathers. Clubs of all kinds were fashioned by hand to suit individual players. The great step in spreading the game came with the change from the feather ball to the guttapercha ball about 1850. In 1860, formal competition began with the establishment of an annual tournament for the British Open championship. There are records of "golf clubs" in the United States as far back as colonial days but no proof of actual play before John Reid and some friends laid out six holes on the Reid lawn in Yonkers, N.Y., in 1888 and played there with golf balls and clubs brought over from Scotland by Robert Lockhart. This group then formed the St. Andrews Golf Club of Yonkers, and golf was established in this country.

However, it remained a rather sedate and almost aristocratic pastime until a 20-year-old ex-caddy, Francis Ouimet of Boston, defeated two great British professionals, Harry Vardon and Ted Ray, in the United States Open championship at Brookline, Mass., in 1913. This feat put the game and Francis Ouimet on the front pages of the newspapers and stirred a wave of enthusiasm for the sport. The greatest feat so far in golf history is that of Robert Tyre Jones, Jr., of Atlanta, who won the British Open, the British Amateur, the U.S. Open, and the U.S. Amateur titles in one year, 1930.

THE MASTERS TOURNAMENT WINNERS

Augusta National Golf Club, Augusta, Ga.

Year	Winner	Score	Year	Winner	Score	Year	Winner	Score
1934	Horton Smith	284	1956	Jack Burke	289	1976	Ray Floyd	271
1935	Gene Sarazen[1]	282	1957	Doug Ford	283	1977	Tom Watson	276
1936	Horton Smith	285	1958	Arnold Palmer	284	1978	Gary Player	277
1937	Byron Nelson	283	1959	Art Wall, Jr.	284	1979	Fuzzy Zoeller[1]	280
1938	Henry Picard	285	1960	Arnold Palmer	282	1980	Severiano Ballesteros	275
1939	Ralph Guldahl	279	1961	Gary Player	280	1981	Tom Watson	280
1940	Jimmy Demaret	280	1962	Arnold Palmer[1]	280	1982	Craig Stadler[1]	284
1941	Craig Wood	280	1963	Jack Nicklaus	286	1983	Severiano Ballesteros	280
1942	Byron Nelson[1]	280	1964	Arnold Palmer	276	1984	Ben Crenshaw	277
1943–45	No Tournaments		1965	Jack Nicklaus	271	1985	Bernhard Langer	282
1946	Herman Keiser	282	1966	Jack Nicklaus[1]	288	1986	Jack Nicklaus	279
1947	Jimmy Demaret	281	1967	Gay Brewer, Jr.	280	1987	Larry Mize[1]	285
1948	Claude Harmon	279	1968	Bob Goalby	277	1988	Sandy Lyle	281
1949	Sam Snead	282	1969	George Archer	281	1989	Nick Faldo[1]	283
1950	Jimmy Demaret	283	1970	Billy Casper[1]	279	1990	Nick Faldo	278
1951	Ben Hogan	280	1971	Charles Coody	279	1991	Ian Woosnam	277
1952	Sam Snead	286	1972	Jack Nicklaus	286	1992	Fred Couples	275
1953	Ben Hogan	274	1973	Tommy Aaron	283	1993	Bernard Langer	277
1954	Sam Snead[1]	289	1974	Gary Player	278	1994	Jose Maria Olazabal	279
1955	Cary Middlecoff	279	1975	Jack Nicklaus	276	1995	Ben Crenshaw	274

1. Winner in playoff.

U.S. OPEN CHAMPIONS

Year	Winner	Score	Where played	Year	Winner	Score	Where played
1895	Horace Rawlins	173	Newport	1915	Jerome D. Travers[2]	297	Baltusrol
1896	James Foulis	152	Shinnecock Hills	1916	Charles Evans, Jr.[2]	286	Minikahda
1897	Joe Lloyd	162	Chicago	1917–18	No tournaments[4]		
1898[3]	Fred Herd	328	Myopia	1919	Walter Hagen[2]	301	Brae Burn
1899	Willie Smith	315	Baltimore	1920	Edward Ray	295	Inverness
1900	Harry Vardon	313	Chicago	1921	Jim Barnes	289	Columbia
1901	Willie Anderson[1]	331	Myopia	1922	Gene Sarazen	288	Skokie
1902	Laurie Auchterlonie	307	Garden City	1923	R. T. Jones, Jr.[1][2]	296	Inwood
1903	Willie Anderson[1]	307	Baltusrol	1924	Cyril Walker	297	Oakland Hills
1904	Willie Anderson	303	Glen View	1925	Willie Macfarlane[1]	291	Worcester
1905	Willie Anderson	314	Myopia	1926	R. T. Jones, Jr.[2]	293	Scioto
1906	Alex Smith	295	Onwentsia	1927	Tommy Armour[1]	301	Oakmont
1907	Alex Ross	302	Philadelphia	1928	Johnny Farrell[1]	294	Olympia Fields
1908	Fred McLeod[1]	322	Myopia	1929	R. T. Jones, Jr.[1][2]	294	Winged Foot
1909	George Sargent	290	Englewood	1930	R. T. Jones, Jr.[2]	287	Interlachen
1910	Alex Smith[1]	298	Philadelphia	1931	Billy Burke[1]	292	Inverness
1911	John McDermott[1]	307	Chicago	1932	Gene Sarazen	286	Fresh Meadow
1912	John McDermott	294	Buffalo	1933	John Goodman[2]	287	North Shore
1913	Francis Ouimet[1][2]	304	Brookline	1934	Olin Dutra	293	Merion
1914	Walter Hagen	290	Midlothian	1935	Sam Parks, Jr.	299	Oakmont

Year	Winner	Score	Where played	Year	Winner	Score	Where played
1936	Tony Manero	282	Baltusrol	1968	Lee Trevino	275	Oak Hill
1937	Ralph Guldahl	281	Oakland Hills	1969	Orville Moody	281	Champions G. C.
1938	Ralph Guldahl	284	Cherry Hills	1970	Tony Jacklin	281	Hazeltine
1939	Byron Nelson[1]	284	Philadelphia	1971	Lee Trevino[1]	280	Merion
1940	Lawson Little[1]	287	Canterbury	1972	Jack Nicklaus	290	Pebble Beach
1941	Craig Wood	284	Colonial	1973	Johnny Miller	279	Oakmont
1942–45	No tournaments[5]			1974	Hale Irwin	287	Winged Foot
1946	Lloyd Mangrum[1]	284	Canterbury	1975	Lou Graham[1]	287	Medinah
1947	Lew Worsham[1]	282	St. Louis	1976	Jerry Pate	277	Atlanta A.C.
1948	Ben Hogan	276	Riviera	1977	Hubert Green	278	Southern Hills
1949	Cary Middlecoff	286	Medinah	1978	Andy North	285	Cherry Hills
1950	Ben Hogan[1]	287	Merion	1979	Hale Irwin	284	Inverness
1951	Ben Hogan	287	Oakland Hills	1980	Jack Nicklaus	272	Baltusrol
1952	Julius Boros	281	Northwood	1981	David Graham	273	Merion
1953	Ben Hogan	283	Oakmont	1982	Tom Watson	282	Pebble Beach
1954	Ed Furgol	284	Baltusrol	1983	Larry Nelson	280	Oakmont
1955	Jack Fleck[1]	287	Olympic	1984	Fuzzy Zoeller[1]	276	Winged Foot
1956	Cary Middlecoff	281	Oak Hill	1985	Andy North	279	Oakland Hills
1957	Dick Mayer[1]	298	Inverness	1986	Ray Floyd	279	Shinnecock Hills
1958	Tommy Bolt	283	Southern Hills	1987	Scott Simpson	277	Olympic Golf Club
1959	Bill Casper, Jr.	282	Winged Foot	1988	Curtis Strange[1]	278	The Country Club
1960	Arnold Palmer	280	Cherry Hills	1989	Curtis Strange	278	Oak Hill Country Club
1961	Gene Littler	281	Oakland Hills	1990	Hale Irwin[1]	280	Medinah C.C.
1962	Jack Nicklaus[1]	283	Oakmont	1991	Payne Stewart[1]	282	Hazeltine
1963	Julius Boros[1]	293	Country Club	1992	Tom Kite	285	Pebble Beach
1964	Ken Venturi	278	Congressional	1993	Lee Janzen	272	Baltusrol
1965	Gary Player[1]	282	Bellerive	1994	Ernie Els	279	Oakmont
1966	Bill Casper[1]	278	Olympic	1995	Corey Pavin	280	Shinnecock Hills
1967	Jack Nicklaus	275	Baltusrol				

1. Winner in playoff. 2. Amateur. 3. In 1898, competition was extended to 72 holes. 4. In 1917, Jock Hutchison, with a 292, won an Open Patriotic Tournament for the benefit of the American Red Cross at Whitemarsh Valley Country Club. 5. In 1942, Ben Hogan, with a 271 won a Hale American National Open Tournament for the benefit of the Navy Relief Society and USO at Ridgemoor Country Club.

U.S. AMATEUR CHAMPIONS

1895	Charles B. Macdonald	1923	Max R. Marston	1952	Jack Westland	1975	Fred Ridley
1896–97	H. J. Whigham	1924–25	R. T. Jones, Jr.	1953	Gene Littler	1976	Bill Sander
1898	Findlay S. Douglas	1926	George Von Elm	1954	Arnold Palmer	1977	John Fought
1899	H. M. Harriman	1927–28	R. T. Jones, Jr.	1955–56	Harvie Ward	1978	John Cook
1900–01	Walter J. Travis	1929	H. R. Johnston	1957	Hillman Robbins	1979	Mark O'Meara
1902	Louis N. James	1930	R. T. Jones, Jr.	1958	Charles Coe	1980	Hal Sutton
1903	Walter J. Travis	1931	Francis Ouimet	1959	Jack Nicklaus	1981	Nathaniel Crosby
1904–05	H. Chandler Egan	1932	Ross Somerville	1960	Deane Beman	1982	Jay Sigel
1906	Eben M. Byers	1933	G. T. Dunlap, Jr.	1961	Jack Nicklaus	1983	Jay Sigel
1907–08	Jerome D. Travers	1934–35	Lawson Little	1962	Labron Harris, Jr.	1984	Scott Verplank
1909	Robert A. Gardner	1936	John W. Fischer	1963	Deane Beman	1985	Sam Randolph
1910	W. C. Fownes, Jr.	1937	John Goodman	1964	Bill Campbell	1986	Buddy Alexander
1911	Harold H. Hilton	1938	Willie Turnesa	1965[2]	Robert Murphy, Jr.	1987	Bill Mayfair
1912–13	Jerome D. Travers	1939	Marvin H. Ward	1966	Gary Cowan[1]	1988	Eric Meeks
1914	Francis Ouimet	1940	R. D. Chapman	1967	Bob Dickson	1989	Chris Patton
1915	Robert A. Gardner	1941	Marvin H. Ward	1968	Bruce Fleisher	1990	Phil Mickelson
1916	Charles Evans, Jr.	1946	Ted Bishop	1969	Steven Melnyk	1991	Mitch Voges
1919	S. D. Herron	1947	Robert Riegel	1970	Lanny Wadkins	1992	Justin Leonard
1920	Charles Evans, Jr.	1948	Willie Turnesa	1971	Gary Cowan	1993	John Harris
1921	Jesse P. Guilford	1949	Charles Coe	1972	Vinny Giles 3d	1994	Tiger Woods
1922	Jess W. Sweetser	1950	Sam Urzetta	1973[3]	Craig Stadler	1995	Tiger Woods
		1951	Billy Maxwell	1974	Jerry Pate		

1. Winner in playoff. 2. Tourney switched to medal play through 1972. 3. Return to match play.

U.S. P.G.A. CHAMPIONS

1916	Jim Barnes	1930	Tommy Armour	1938	Paul Runyan	1946	Ben Hogan
1919	Jim Barnes	1931	Tom Creavy	1939	Henry Picard	1947	Jim Ferrier
1920	Jock Hutchison	1932	Olin Dutra	1940	Byron Nelson	1948	Ben Hogan
1921	Walter Hagen	1933	Gene Sarazen	1941	Victor Ghezzi	1949	Sam Snead
1922–23	Gene Sarazen	1934	Paul Runyan	1942	Sam Snead	1950	Chandler Harper
1924–27	Walter Hagen	1935	Johnny Revolta	1944	Bob Hamilton	1951	Sam Snead
1928–29	Leo Diegel	1936–37	Denny Shute	1945	Byron Nelson	1952	Jim Turnesa

1953	Walter Burkemo	1964	Bobby Nichols	1975	Jack Nicklaus	1986	Bob Tway
1954	Chick Harbert	1965	Dave Marr	1976	Dave Stockton	1987	Larry Nelson
1955	Doug Ford	1966	Al Geiberger	1977	Lanny Wadkins[1]	1988	Jeff Sluman
1956	Jack Burke, Jr.	1967	Don January[1]	1978	John Mahaffey	1989	Payne Stewart
1957	Lionel Hebert	1968	Julius Boros	1979	David Graham[1]	1990	Mac Grady
1958[2]	Dow Finsterwald	1969	Ray Floyd	1980	Jack Nicklaus	1991	John Daly
1959	Bob Rosburg	1970	Dave Stockton	1981	Larry Nelson	1992	Nick Price
1960	Jay Hebert	1971	Jack Nicklaus	1982	Ray Floyd	1993	Paul Azinger[1]
1961	Jerry Barber[1]	1972	Gary Player	1983	Hal Sutton	1994	Nick Price
1962	Gary Player	1973	Jack Nicklaus	1984	Lee Trevino	1995	Steve Elkington
1963	Jack Nicklaus	1974	Lee Trevino	1985	Hubert Green		

1. Winner in playoff. 2. Switched to medal play.

U.S. WOMEN'S AMATEUR CHAMPIONS

1916	Alexa Stirling	1939–40	Betty Jameson	1961	Anne Quast Decker	1977	Beth Daniel
1919–20	Alexa Stirling	1941	Mrs. Frank Newell			1978	Cathy Sherk
1921	Marion Hollins	1946	Mildred Zaharias	1962	JoAnne Gunderson	1979	Carolyn Hill
1922	Glenna Collett	1947	Louise Suggs			1980	Juli Inkster
1923	Edith Cummings	1948	Grace Lenczyk	1963	Anne Quast Welts	1981	Juli Inkster
1924	Dorothy Campbell .Hurd	1949	Mrs. D. G. Porter	1964	Barbara McIntire	1982	Juli Inkster
1925	Glenna Collett	1950	Beverly Hanson	1965	Jean Ashley	1983	Joanne Pacillo
1926	Helen Stetson	1951	Dorothy Kirby	1966	JoAnne Gunderson	1984	Deb Richard
1927	Mrs. M. B. Horn	1952	Jacqueline Pung			1985	Michiko Hattori
1928–30	Glenna Collett	1953	Mary Lena Faulk	1967	Lou Dill	1986	Kay Cockerill
1931	Helen Hicks	1954	Barbara Romack	1968	JoAnne G. Carner	1987	Kay Cockerill
1932–34	Virginia Van Wie	1955	Patricia Lesser	1969	Catherine LaCoste	1988	Pearl Sinn
1935	Glenna Collett Vare	1956	Marlene Stewart	1970	Martha Wilkinson	1989	Vicki Goetze
1936	Pamela Barton	1957	JoAnne Gunderson	1971	Laura Baugh	1990	Pat Hurst
1937	Mrs. J. A. Page, Jr.	1958	Anne Quast	1972	Mary Ann Budke	1991	Amy Fruhwirth
1938	Patty Berg	1959	Barbara McIntire	1973	Carol Semple	1992	Vicki Goetze
		1960	JoAnne Gunderson	1974	Cynthia Hill	1993	Jill McGill
				1975	Beth Daniel	1994	Wendy Ward
				1976	Donna Horton	1995	Kelli Kuehne

U.S. WOMEN'S OPEN CHAMPIONS

Year	Winner	Score	Year	Winner	Score	Year	Winner	Score
1946	Patty Berg (match play)	—	1963	Mary Mills	289	1980	Amy Alcott	280
1947	Betty Jameson	295	1964	Mickey Wright[1]	290	1981	Pat Bradley	279
1948	Mildred D. Zaharias	300	1965	Carol Mann	290	1982	Janet Alex	283
1949	Louise Suggs	291	1966	Sandra Spuzich	297	1983	Jan Stephenson	290
1950	Mildred D. Zaharias	291	1967	Catherine LaCoste[2]	294	1984	Hollis Stacy	290
1951	Betsy Rawls	293	1968	Susie Berning	289	1985	Kathy Baker	280
1952	Louise Suggs	284	1969	Donna Caponi	294	1986	Jane Geddes[1]	287
1953	Betsy Rawls[1]	302	1970	Donna Caponi	287	1987	Laura Davies[1]	285
1954	Mildred D. Zaharias	291	1971	JoAnne Carner	288	1988	Liselotte Neumann	277
1955	Fay Crocker	299	1972	Susie Berning	299	1989	Betsy King	278
1956	Katherine Cornelius[1]	302	1973	Susie Berning	290	1990	Betsy King	284
1957	Betsy Rawls	299	1974	Sandra Haynie	295	1991	Meg Mallon	283
1958	Mickey Wright	290	1975	Sandra Palmer	295	1992	Patty Sheehan	280
1959	Mickey Wright	287	1976	JoAnne Carner[1]	292	1993	Lauri Merten	280
1960	Betsy Rawls	291	1977	Hollis Stacy	292	1994	Patty Sheehan	277
1961	Mickey Wright	293	1978	Hollis Stacy	289	1995	Annika Sorenstam	278
1962	Murle Lindstrom	301	1979	Jerilyn Britz	284			

. Winner in playoff. 2. Amateur.

BRITISH OPEN CHAMPIONS

(First tournament, held in 1860, was won by Willie Park, Sr.)

Year	Winner	Score	Year	Winner	Score	Year	Winner	Score
1920	George Duncan	303	1928	Walter Hagen	292	1936	A. H. Padgham	287
1921	Jock Hutchison[1]	296	1929	Walter Hagen	292	1937	Henry Cotton	290
1922	Walter Hagen	300	1930	R. T. Jones, Jr.	291	1938	R. A. Whitcombe	295
1923	A. G. Havers	295	1931	Tommy Armour	296	1939	R. Burton	290
1924	Walter Hagen	301	1932	Gene Sarazen	283	1940	Sam Snead	290
1925	Jim Barnes	300	1933	Denny Shute[1]	292	1947	Fred Daly	294
1926	R. T. Jones, Jr.	291	1934	Henry Cotton	283	1948	Henry Cotton	283
1927	R. T. Jones, Jr.	285	1935	A. Perry	283	1949	Bobby Locke[1]	283

. Winner in playoff.

Year	Winner	Score	Year	Winner	Score	Year	Winner	Score
1950	Bobby Locke	279	1966	Jack Nicklaus	282	1981	Bill Rogers	276
1951	Max Faulkner	285	1967	Roberto de Vicenzo	278	1982	Tom Watson	284
1952	Bobby Locke	287	1968	Gary Player	289	1983	Tom Watson	275
1953	Ben Hogan	282	1969	Tony Jacklin	280	1984	Severiano Ballesteros	276
1954	Peter Thomson	283	1970	Jack Nicklaus[1]	283	1985	Sandy Lyle	282
1955	Peter Thomson	281	1971	Lee Trevino	278	1986	Greg Norman	280
1956	Peter Thomson	286	1972	Lee Trevino	278	1987	Nick Faldo	279
1957	Bobby Locke	279	1973	Tom Weiskopf	276	1988	Seve Ballesteros	273
1958	Peter Thomson[1]	278	1974	Gary Player	282	1989	Mark Calcavecchia	275
1959	Gary Player	284	1975	Tom Watson[1]	279	1990	Nick Faldo	270
1960	Kel Nagle	278	1976	Johnny Miller	279	1991	Ian Baker-Finch	272
1961	Arnold Palmer	284	1977	Tom Watson	268	1992	Nick Faldo	272
1962	Arnold Palmer	276	1978	Jack Nicklaus	281	1993	Greg Norman	267
1963	Bob Charles[1]	277	1979	Severiano Ballesteros	283	1994	Nick Price	268
1964	Tony Lema	279	1980	Tom Watson	271	1995	John Daly	282
1965	Peter Thomson	285						

1. Winner in playoff.

OTHER 1995 PGA TOUR WINNERS

(Through Aug. 22, 1995)

The International—Lee Janzen (34 pts)	$270,000
Buick Open—Woody Austin (270)	216,000
Ideon Classic—Fred Funk (268)	180,000
Anheuser–Busch Classic—Ted Tryba (272)	198,000
Western Open—Billy Mayfair (279)	360,000
St. Jude Classic—J. Gallagher (267)	225,000
Greater Hartford Open—Greg Norman (267)	216,000
Kemper Open—Lee Janzen (272)	252,000
The Memorial—Greg Norman (269)	306,000
Colonial—Tom Lehman (271)	252,000
Buick Classic—Vijay Singh (278)	216,000
Byron Nelson Classic—Ernie Els (263)	234,000
BellSouth Classic—Mark Calcavecchia (271)	234,000
Greater Greensboro Open—J. Gallagher (274)	270,000
MCI Classic—Bob Tway (275)	234,000
The Players Championship—Lee Janzen (283)	540,000
Doral Open—Nick Faldo (273)	270,000
Los Angeles Open—Corey Pavin (268)	216,000
Bob Hope Classic—Kenny Perry (335)	216,000
Buick Invitational—Peter Jacobsen (269)	216,000
Pebble Beach Pro–Am—Peter Jacobsen (271)	252,000
Phoenix Open—Vijay Singh (269)	234,000
Northern Telecom Open—Phil Mickelson (269)	225,000
Hawaiian Open—John Morse (269)	216,000
Mercedes Championship—Steve Elkington (278)	180,000

OTHER 1995 LPGA TOUR WINNERS

British Open—Karrie Webb (278)	96,000
PING Welch's Championship—Beth Daniel (271)	67,500
McCall's Classic—Dottie Mochrie (204)	75,000
Friendly's Classic—Becky Iverson (276)	75,000
Big Apple Classic—Tracy Kerdyk (273)	105,000
Jamie Farr Toledo Classic—Kathryn Marshall (205)	75,000
ShopRite Classic—Betsy King (204)	97,500
Rochester International—Pat Sheehan (278)	82,500
Edina Realty Classic—Julie Larsen (205)	75,000
Oldsmobile Classic—Dale Eggeling (274)	90,000
Coming Classic—Alison Nicholas (275)	82,500
Star Bank Classic—Chris Johnson (210)	75,000
LPGA Championship—Kelly Robbins (274)	180,000
Sara Lee Classic—Michelle McGann (202)	78,750
Sprint Championship—Val Skinner (273)	180,000
Chick–Fil–A Championship—Laura Davies (201)	75,000
Pinewald Championship—Rosie Jones (211)	97,500
Nabisco Dinah Shore—Nanci Bowen (285)	127,500
Standard Register/PING—Laura Davies (280)	105,000
Hawaiian Open—Barb Thomas (204)	82,500
Healthsouth Inaugural—Pat Bradley (211)	67,500
Tournament of Champions—Dawn Coe–Jones (281)	115,000

FENCING

1995 WORLD CHAMPIONS

Individual

Men's sabre—Grigori Kirienko, Russia
Men's epee—Eric Srecki, France
Women's epee—Joanna Kakimiuk, Poland
Women's foil—Laura Badea, Romania
Men's foil—Dmitry Chevtchenko, Russia

Team

Women's foil—Italy
Men's sabre—Italy

Wonen's epee—Hungary
Men's foil—Cuba
Men's epee—Germany

1995 UNITED STATES CHAMPIONS

Women's foil—Ann Marsh, Royal Oak, Mich.
Women's epee—Teresa Orcutt, Fairfield, Calif.
Men's sabre—Peter Westbrook, New York City, N.Y.
Men's foil—Cliff Bayer, New York City, N.Y.
Men's epee—Robert Stull, Austin, Tex.

SOCCER

The early history of the sport is uncertain. A form of the game in which a leather ball was dribbled was played in China as early as the 4th century B.C. The Romans played a variation of soccer which eventually spread throughout Europe. British schools and universities played soccer (known as football) during the 1800s, however, each school used different sets of rules and the number of players varied. This difficulty was corrected on Oct. 26, 1863 when the Football Association (FA) was formed in London for the purpose of unifying the rules of the game.

The Federation of International Football Associations (FIFA) was created in 1913 as a world governing body to coordinate all of the national associations in the world. The FIFA held the first World Cup Championship tournament in 1930 in Montevideo, Uruguay. Today, soccer is the world's most popular sport.

WORLD CUP

1930	Uruguay	1950	Uruguay	1970	Brazil	1990	West Germany
1934	Italy	1954	West Germany	1974	West Germany	1994	Brazil
1938	Italy	1958	Brazil	1978	Argentina		
1942	No competition	1962	Brazil	1982	Italy		
1946	No competition	1966	England	1986	Argentina		

WORLD CUP—1994

QUARTERFINALS
Italy 2, Spain 1
Brazil 3, Netherlands 2

Bulgaria 2, Germany 1
Sweden 2, Romania 2 (Sweden won 5–4 in shootout)

SEMIFINALS
Italy 2, Bulgaria 1
Brazil 1, Sweden 0

CHAMPIONSHIP
Italy 0, Brazil 0 (Brazil won 3–2 in shootout)

FINAL GROUP STANDINGS

Group A

	W	L	T	GF	GA	Pts
x–Romania	2	1	0	5	5	6
x–Switzerland	1	1	1	5	4	4
x–United States	1	1	1	3	3	4
y–Colombia	1	2	0	4	5	3

Group B

	W	L	T	GF	GA	Pts
x–Brazil	2	0	1	6	1	7
x–Sweden	1	0	2	6	4	5
y–Russia	1	2	0	7	6	3
y–Cameroon	0	2	1	3	11	1

Group C

	W	L	T	GF	GA	Pts
x–Germany	2	0	1	5	3	7
x–Spain	1	0	2	6	4	5
y–South Korea	0	1	2	4	5	2
y–Bolivia	0	2	1	1	4	1

Group D

	W	L	T	GF	GA	Pts
x–Nigeria	2	1	0	6	2	6
x–Bulgaria	2	1	0	6	3	6
x–Argentina	2	1	0	6	3	6
y–Greece	0	3	0	0	10	0

Group E

	W	L	T	GF	GA	Pts
x–Mexico	1	1	1	3	3	4
x–Ireland	1	1	1	2	2	4
x–Italy	1	1	1	2	2	4
y–Norway	1	1	1	1	1	4

Group F

	W	L	T	GF	GA	Pts
x–Netherlands	2	1	0	4	3	6
x–Saudi Arabia	2	1	0	4	3	6
x–Belgium	2	1	0	2	1	6
y–Morocco	0	3	0	2	4	0

x–Advance to next round. y–Eliminated.

BRAZIL WINS RECORD FOURTH WORLD CUP ON SHOOTOUT

Brazil became the first country to win four World Cup championships and the first ever to win on a penalty kick shootout as the first World Cup tournament ever played in the United States ended on a high note.

The championship, Brazil's first since 1970, when it defeated Italy 4–1 at Mexico City, came as Brazil won the post-game penalty kick shootout, 3–2.

The game ended in a 0–0 tie.

The teams played 90 minutes of regulation and 30 minutes of overtime before the shootout.

Romario, Branco, and Dunga recorded the shootout scores for Brazil. Albergio Evani and Demetrio Albertini converted the penalty kicks for Italy.

With Italy trailing 3–2 and one opportunity left to keep the shootout going, Roberto Baggio's shot sailed over the crossbar, clinching the championship for Brazil.

Brazil had the best scoring opportunity of the game in the second overtime, when Romario found himself alone in front of the goal, having only to beat the Italian goalie Gianluca Pagliuca. But he shanked the ball and the ball rolled slowly wide of the net.

CUP A SUCCESS IN THE UNITED STATES ESCOBAR SHOOTING ADDS TRAGIC NOTE

Eventual champion Brazil ended the United States' dream of a miracle World Cup championship, beating Team USA 1–0 in the second round of the 1994 World Cup tournament.

But the loss couldn't change the fact that holding the tournament in the United States had turned out to be a huge success, despite a lot of international skepticism over the United States lukewarm fan reaction to soccer in general.

The games were well attended and there were none of the incidents of violence that have plagued previous tournaments.

The United States was involved in the lone tragedy of the 1994 World Cup, albeit indirectly. After a 2–1 first round victory over Colombia, Colombian soccer star Andres Escobar, who inadvertently deflected a cross pass into the Colombian goal to give the Americans the victory, was shot to death in his hometown of Medellin, Colombia, allegedly by gamblers who had bet heavily on the game.

As for the United States subsequent loss to Brazil, it came before a crowd of 84,147 at Stanford University Stadium.

In the tournament's first round, Team USA had beaten Colombia, tied Switzerland, and lost by one goal to Romania.

The United States was eliminated on July 4, 1994, exactly five years after the Federation Internationale de Football Association awarded the 1994 World Cup to the United States.

WORLD CUP
All-Time Top 10

	Tourneys	Total Games	Record (W–L–T)	Total Pts
1. Brazil	14	66	44–11–11	99
2. West Germany	12	68	39–14–15	93
3. Italy	12	54	31–11–12	74
4. Argentina	10	48	24–15–9	57
5. England	9	41	18–11–12	48
6. Uruguay	9	37	15–14–8	38
7. Soviet Union	7	31	15–10–6	36
8. France	9	34	15–14–5	35
9. Yugoslavia	8	33	14–12–7	35
10. Hungary	9	32	15–14–3	33
Spain	8	32	13–12–7	33

NATIONAL PROFESSIONAL SOCCER LEAGUE (NPSL) (Indoor)—1995
Standings—1995

AMERICAN DIVISION

	W	L	Pct	GB
y–Cleveland Crunch	30	10	.750	—
x–Harrisburg Heat	23	17	.575	7
x–Baltimore Spirit	23	17	.575	7
x–Buffalo Blizzard	20	20	.500	10
Dayton Dynamo	15	25	.375	15
Canton Invaders	6	34	.150	24

NATIONAL DIVISION

	W	L	Pct	GB
y–St. Louis Ambush	30	10	.750	—
x–Kansas City Attack	29	11	.725	1
x–Milwaukee Wave	23	17	.575	7
x–Detroit Rockets	18	22	.450	12
Wichita Wings	17	23	.425	13
Chicago Power	6	34	.150	24

y–Clinched division championsip. x–Clinched playoff berth.

CHAMPIONSHIP (BEST-OF-FIVE)
St. Louis vs. Harrisburg

(St. Louis wins championship, 4 games to 0)

April 20—St. Louis 19, Harrisburg 9
April 22—St. Louis 18, Harrisburg 8
April 23—St. Louis 12, Harrisburg 7
April 25—St. Louis 14, Harrisburg 11

TOURNAMENT TO EXPAND TO 32 TEAMS IN 1998

Soccer's world governing body, the Federation Internationale de Football Association, voted in 1994 to expand the World Cup from 24 to 32 teams, beginning with the 1998 tournament, to be held in France. The tournament's first round will expand to eight groups of four, with the two top teams in each group advancing to the second round. Previously, there were six groups with the two top teams and the four best third place teams advancing.

U.S. PRO LEAGUES OUTDOOR

National Professional Soccer League (1967)

Not sanctioned by FIFA, the international soccer federation. The NPSL recruited individual players to fill the rosters of its 10 teams. The leage lasted only one season with the Oakland Clippers beating the Baltimore Bays on the basis of goal differential.

United Soccer Association (1967)

Sanctioned by FIFA. Originally called the North American Soccer League, it became the USA to avoid being confused with the National Professional Soccer League. Instead of recruiting individual players, the USA imported 12 entire teams from Europe to represent its 12 franchises. It, too, only lasted a season. The league champion Los Angeles Wolves were actually Wolverhampton of England and the runner-up Washington Whips were Aberdeen of Scotland.

North American Soccer League (1968–1984)

The NPSL and USA merged to form the NASL in 1968 and the new league lasted until 1985. The NASL championship was known as the Soccer Bowl from 1975–84. One game decided the NASL title every year but five.

NORTH AMERICAN SOCCER LEAGUE CHAMPIONS

1968—Atlanta Chiefs	1973—Philadelphia Atoms	1978—New York Cosmos	1982—New York Cosmos
1969—Kansas City Stars	1974—Los Angeles Aztecs	1979—Vancouver Whitecaps	1983—Tulsa Roughnecks
1970—Rochester Lancers	1975—Tampa Bay Rowdies	1980—New York Cosmos	1984—Chicago Sting
1971—Dallas Tornado	1976—Toronto Metro–Croatia	1981—Chicago Sting	
1972—New York Cosmos	1977—New York Cosmos		

AUTO RACING

INDIANAPOLIS 500

Year	Winner	Car	Time	mph	Second place
1911	Ray Harroun	Marmon	6:42:08	74.59	Ralph Mulford
1912	Joe Dawson	National	6:21:06	78.72	Teddy Tetzloff
1913	Jules Goux	Peugeot	6:35:05	75.93	Spencer Wishart
1914	René Thomas	Delage	6:03:45	82.47	Arthur Duray
1915	Ralph DePalma	Mercedes	5:33:55.51	89.84	Dario Resta
1916[1]	Dario Resta	Peugeot	3:34:17	84.00	Wilbur D'Alene
1919	Howard Wilcox	Peugeot	5:40:42.87	88.05	Eddie Hearne
1920	Gaston Chevrolet	Monroe	5:38:32	88.62	René Thomas
1921	Tommy Milton	Frontenac	5:34:44.65	89.62	Roscoe Sarles
1922	Jimmy Murphy	Murphy Special	5:17:30.79	94.48	Harry Hartz
1923	Tommy Milton	H. C. S. Special	5:29:50.17	90.95	Harry Hartz
1924	L. L. Corum–Joe Boyer	Dusenberg Special	5:05:23.51	98.23	Earl Cooper
1925	Peter DePaolo	Dusenberg Special	4:56:39.45	101.13	Dave Lewis
1926[2]	Frank Lockhart	Miller Special	4:10:14.95	95.904	Harry Hartz
1927	George Souders	Dusenberg Special	5:07:33.08	97.54	Earl DeVore
1928	Louis Meyer	Miller Special	5:01:33.75	99.48	Lou Moore
1929	Ray Keech	Simplex Special	5:07:25.42	97.58	Louis Meyer
1930	Billy Arnold	Miller–Hartz Special	4:58:39.72	100.448	Shorty Cantlon
1931	Louis Schneider	Bowes Special	5:10:27.93	96.629	Fred Frame
1932	Fred Frame	Miller–Hartz Special	4:48:03.79	104.144	Howard Wilcox
1933	Louis Meyer	Tydol Special	4:48:00.75	104.162	Wilbur Shaw
1934	Bill Cummings	Boyle Products Special	4:46:05.20	104.863	Mauri Rose
1935	Kelly Petillo	Gilmore Special	4:42:22.71	106.240	Wilbur Shaw
1936	Louis Meyer	Ring Free Special	4:35:03.39	109.069	Ted Horn
1937	Wilbur Shaw	Shaw–Gilmore Special	4:24:07.80	113.580	Ralph Hepburn
1938	Floyd Roberts	Burd Piston Ring Special	4:15:58.40	117.200	Wilbur Shaw
1939	Wilbur Shaw	Boyle Special	4:20:47.39	115.035	Jimmy Snyder
1940	Wilbur Shaw	Boyle Special	4:22:31.17	114.277	Rex Mays
1941	Floyd Davis–Mauri Rose	Noc–Out Hose Clamp Special	4:20:36.24	115.117	Rex Mays
1946	George Robson	Thorne Engineering Special	4:21:26.71	114.820	Jimmy Jackson
1947	Mauri Rose	Blue Crown Special	4:17:52.17	116.338	Bill Holland
1948	Mauri Rose	Blue Crown Special	4:10:23.33	119.814	Bill Holland
1949	Bill Holland	Blue Crown Special	4:07:15.97	121.327	Johnny Parsons
1950[3]	Johnnie Parsons	Wynn's Friction Proof Special	2:46:55.97	124.002	Mike Nazaruk
1951	Lee Wallard	Belanger Special	3:57:38.05	126.244	Jim Rathmann
1952	Troy Ruttman	Agajanian Special	3:52:41.88	128.922	Art Cross
1953	Bill Vukovich	Fuel Injection Special	3:53:01.69	128.740	Jim Bryan
1954	Bill Vukovich	Fuel Injection Special	3:49:17.27	130.840	Jimmy Bryan
1955	Bob Sweikert	John Zink Special	3:53:59.13	128.209	Tony Bettenhausen
1956	Pat Flaherty	John Zink Special	3:53:28.84	128.490	Sam Hanks
1957	Sam Hanks	Belond Exhaust Special	3:41:14.25	135.601	Jim Rathmann
1958	Jimmy Bryan	Belond A–P Special	3:44:13.80	133.791	George Amick
1959	Rodger Ward	Leader Card 500 Roadster	3:40:49.20	135.857	Jim Rathmann
1960	Jim Rathmann	Ken–Paul Special	3:36:11.36	138.767	Rodger Ward
1961	A. J. Foyt	Bowes Special	3:35:37.49	139.130	Eddie Sachs
1962	Rodger Ward	Leader Card Special	3:33:50.33	140.293	Len Sutton
1963	Parnelli Jones	Agajanian Special	3:29:35.40	143.137	Jim Clark
1964	A. J. Foyt	Sheraton–Thompson Spl.	3:23:35.83	147.350	Rodger Ward
1965	Jim Clark	Lotus–Ford	3:19:05.34	150.686	Parnelli Jones
1966	Graham Hill	Red Ball Lola–Ford	3:27:52.53	144.317	Jim Clark
1967[4]	A. J. Foyt	Sheraton-Thompson Coyote–Ford	3:18:24.22	151.207	Al Unser
1968	Bobby Unser	Rislone Eagle–Offenhauser	3:16:13.76	152.882	Dan Gurney
1969	Mario Andretti	STP Hawk–Ford	3:11:14.71	156.867	Dan Gurney
1970	Al Unser	Johnny Lightning P. J. Colt–Ford	3:12:37.04	155.749	Mark Donohue
1971	Al Unser	Johnny Lightning P. J. Colt–Ford	3:10:11.56	157.735	Peter Revson
1972	Mark Donohue	Sunoco McLaren–Offenhauser	3:04:05.54	162.962	Al Unser
1973[5]	Gordon Johncock	STP Eagle–Offenhauser	2:05:26.59	159.036	Bill Vukovich, Jr.
1974	Johnny Rutherford	McLaren–Offenhauser	3:09:10.06	158.589	Bobby Unser
1975[6]	Bobby Unser	Jorgensen Eagle–Offenhauser	2:54:55.08	149.213	Johnny Rutherford
1976[7]	Johnny Rutherford	Hy-gain McLaren–Offenhauser	1:42:52.48	148.725	A. J. Foyt
1977	A. J. Foyt	Gilmore Coyote–Foyt	3:05:57.16	161.331	Tom Sneva
1978	Al Unser	1st Nat'l City Lola–Cosworth	3:05:54.99	161.363	Tom Sneva
1979	Rick Mears	Gould Penske–Cosworth	3:08:27.97	158.899	A. J. Foyt
1980	Johnny Rutherford	Pennzoil Chaparral–Cosworth	3:29:59.56	142.862	Tom Sneva
1981[8]	Bobby Unser	Norton Penske–Cosworth	3:35:41.78	139.029	Mario Andretti
1982	Gordon Johncock	STP Wildcat–Cosworth	3:05:09.14	162.029	Rick Mears
1983	Tom Sneva	Texaco Star March–Cosworth	3:05:03.06	162.117	Al Unser
1984	Rick Mears	Pennzoil March–Cosworth	3:03:21.00	162.962	Roberto Guerrero

Year	Winner	Car	Time	mph	Second place
1985	Danny Sullivan	Miller March–Cosworth	3:16:06.069	152.982	Mario Andretti
1986	Bobby Rahal	Budweiser March–Cosworth	2:55:43.48	170.722	Kevin Cogan
1987	Al Unser, Sr.	Cummins March–Cosworth	3:04:59.147	162.175	Roberto Guerrero
1988	Rick Mears	Pennzoil Penske P.C.17–Chevrolet	3:27:10.204	144.809	Emerson Fittipaldi
1989	Emerson Fittipaldi	Marlboro Penske-Cosworth	2:59:01.04	167.581	Al Unser, Jr.
1990	Arie Luyendyk	Domino's Pizza Lola–Cosworth	2:41:18.248	185.987	Bobby Rahal
1991	Rick Mears	Marlboro Penske–Cosworth	2:50:01.018	176.460	Michael Andretti
1992	Al Unser, Jr.	Valvoline–Chevrolet	3:43.05.148	134.477	Scott Goodyear
1993	Emerson Fittipaldi	Penske–Chevrolet	3:10:49.860	157.207	Arie Luyendyk
1994	Al Unser, Jr.	Penske–Mercedes	3:06:29.006	160.872	Jacques Villeneuve
1995	Jacques Villeneuve	Reynard–Ford	3:15:17.561	156.616	Christian Fittipaldi

1. 300 miles. 2. Race ended at 400 miles because of rain. 3. Race ended at 345 miles because of rain. 4. Race, postponed after 18 laps because of rain on May 30, was finished on May 31. 5. Race postponed May 28 and 29 was cut to 332.5 miles because of rain, May 30. 6. Race ended at 435 miles because of rain. 7. Race ended at 255 miles because of rain. 8. Andretti was awarded the victory the day after the race after Bobby Unser, whose car finished first, was penalized one lap and dropped from first place to second for passing other cars illegally under a yellow caution flag. Unser appealed the decision to the U.S. Auto Club and was upheld. A panel ruled the penalty was too severe and instead fined Unser $40,000, but restored the victory to him.

INDY CAR NATIONAL CHAMPIONS

1910	Ray Harroun	1928–29	Louis Meyer	1954	Jimmy Bryan	1977–78	Tom Sneva
1911	Ralph Mulford	1930	Billy Arnold	1955	Bob Sweikert	1979	Rick Mears (CART)
1912	Ralph DePalma	1931	Louis Schneider	1956–57	Jimmy Bryan		A.J. Foyt (USAC)[1]
1913	Earl Cooper	1932	Bob Carey	1958	Tony Bettenhausen	1980	Johnny Rutherford
1914	Ralph DePalma	1933	Louis Meyer	1959	Rodger Ward	1981–82	Rick Mears
1915	Earl Cooper	1934	Bill Cummings	1960–61	A. J. Foyt	1983	Al Unser
1916	Dario Resta	1935	Kelly Petillo	1962	Rodger Ward	1984	Mario Andretti
1917	Earl Cooper	1936	Mauri Rose	1963–64	A. J. Foyt	1985	Al Unser
1918	Ralph Mulford	1937	Wilbur Shaw	1965–66	Mario Andretti	1986–87	Bobby Rahal
1919	Howard Wilcox	1938	Floyd Roberts	1967	A. J. Foyt	1988	Danny Sullivan
1920	Gaston Chevrolet	1939	Wilbur Shaw	1968	Bobby Unser	1989	Emerson Fittipaldi
1921	Tommy Milton	1940–41	Rex Mays	1969	Mario Andretti	1990	Al Unser Jr.
1922	James Murphy	1946–48	Ted Horn	1970	Al Unser	1991	Michael Andretti
1923	Eddie Hearne	1949	Johnnie Parsons	1971–72	Joe Leonard	1992	Bobby Rahal
1924	James Murphy	1950	Henry Banks	1973	Roger McCluskey	1993	Nigel Mansell
1925	Peter DePaolo	1951	Tony Bettenhausen	1974	Bobby Unser	1994	Al Unser, Jr.
1926	Harry Hartz	1952	Chuck Stevenson	1975	A. J. Foyt	1995	Jacques Villeneuve
1927	Peter DePaolo	1953	Sam Hanks	1976	Gordon Johncock		

1. Two separate series were held in 1979. NOTE: There have been three sanctioning bodies for the series: the Automobile Association of America (1909–1955), the U.S. Auto Club (1956–1979), and the Championship Auto Racing Team (CART), 1979–present.

WORLD GRAND PRIX DRIVER CHAMPIONS

1950	Giuseppe Farina, Italy, Alfa Romeo	1974	Emerson Fittipaldi, Brazil, McLaren–Ford
1951	Juan Fangio, Argentina, Alfa Romeo	1975	Niki Lauda, Austria, Ferrari
1952	Alberto Ascari, Italy, Ferrari	1976	James Hunt, Britain, McLaren–Ford
1953	Alberto Ascari, Italy, Ferrari	1977	Niki Lauda, Austria, Ferrari
1954	Juan Fangio, Argentina, Maserati, Mercedes–Benz	1978	Mario Andretti, United States, Lotus
1955	Juan Fangio, Argentina, Mercedes–Benz	1979	Jody Scheckter, South Africa, Ferrari
1956	Juan Fangio, Argentina, Lancia–Ferrari	1980	Alan Jones, Australia, Williams–Ford
1957	Juan Fangio, Argentina, Maserati	1981	Nelson Piquet, Brazil, Brabham–Ford
1958	Mike Hawthorn, England, Ferrari	1982	Kiki Rosberg, Finland, Williams–Ford
1959	Jack Brabham, Australia, Cooper	1983	Nelson Piquet, Brazil. Brabham–BMW
1960	Jack Brabham, Australia, Cooper	1984	Nikki Lauda, Austria, McLaren–Porsche
1961	Phil Hill, United States, Ferrari	1985	Alain Prost, France, McLaren–Porsche
1962	Graham Hill, England, BRM	1986	Alain Prost, France, McLaren–Porsche
1963	Jim Clark, Scotland, Lotus–Ford	1987	Nelson Piquet, Brazil, Williams–Honda
1964	John Surtees, England, Ferrari	1988	Aryton Senna, Brazil, McLaren–Honda
1965	Jim Clark, Scotland, Lotus–Ford	1989	Alain Prost, France, McLaren–Honda
1966	Jack Brabham, Australia, Brabham–Repco	1990	Ayrton Senna, Brazil, McLaren–Honda
1967	Denis Hulme, New Zealand, Brabham–Repco	1991	Ayrton Senna, Brazil, McLaren–Honda
1968	Graham Hill, England, Lotus–Ford	1992	Nigel Mansell, Britain, Williams–Renault
1969	Jackie Stewart, Scotland, Matra–Ford	1993	Alain Prost
1970	Jochen Rindt, Austria, Lotus–Ford	1994	William Schumacher, Benetton
1971	Jackie Stewart, Scotland, Tyrrell–Ford	1995	Champion to be determined after *Information Please* went to press
1972	Emerson Fittipaldi, Brazil, Lotus–Ford		
1973	Jackie Stewart, Scotland, Tyrrell–Ford		

NATIONAL ASSOCIATION FOR STOCK CAR AUTO RACING
WINSTON CUP CHAMPIONS

1949	Red Byron	1961	Ned Jarrett	1974–75	Richard Petty	1986	Dale Earnhardt
1950	Bill Rexford	1962–63	Joe Weatherly	1976–78	Cale Yarborough	1987	Dale Earnhardt
1951	Herb Thomas	1964	Richard Petty	1979	Richard Petty	1988	Bill Elliott
1952	Tim Flock	1965	Ned Jarrett	1980	Dale Earnhardt	1989	Rusty Wallace
1953	Herb Thomas	1966	David Pearson	1981	Darrell Waltrip	1990	Dale Earnhardt
1954	Lee Petty	1967	Richard Petty	1982	Darrell Waltrip	1991	Dale Earnhardt
1955	Tim Flock	1968–69	David Pearson	1983	Bobby Allison	1992	Alan Kulwicki[1]
1956–57	Buck Baker	1970	Bobby Isaac	1984	Terry Labonte	1993	Dale Earnhardt
1958–59	Lee Petty	1971–72	Richard Petty	1985	Darrell Waltrip	1994	Dale Earnhardt
1960	Rex White	1973	Benny Parsons				

1. Kulwicki was killed in a plane crash in April 1993.

1994 NASCAR LEADING MONEY WINNERS

1.	Dale Earnhardt	$3,400,000
2.	Rusty Wallace	1,959,072
3.	Jeff Gordon	1,799,523
4.	Mark Martin	1,678,906
5.	Ernie Irvan	1,311,522
6.	Geoff Bodine	1,287,626
7.	Ken Schrader	1,211,062
8.	Terry Labonte	1,150,921
9.	Sterling Martin	1,140,683
10.	Morgan Shepherd	1,119,038

1994 WINSTON CUP POINT LEADERS

1.	Dale Earnhardt	4,694
2.	Mark Martin	4,250
3.	Rusty Wallace	4,207
4.	Ken Schrader	4,060
5.	Ricky Rudd	4,050
6.	Morgan Shepherd	4,029
7.	Terry Labonte	3,876
8.	Jeff Gordon	3,776
9.	Darrell Waltrip	3,688
10.	Bill Elliott	3,617

1994 INDY CAR POINTS LEADERS

1.	Al Unser, Junior	225
2.	Emerson Fittipaldi	178
3.	Paul Tracy	152
4.	Michael Andretti	118
5.	Robby Gordon	104
6.	Jacques Villeneuve	94
7.	Raul Boesel	90
8.	Nigel Mansell	88
9.	Teo Fabi	79
10.	Bobby Rahal	59

HANDBALL

U.S.H.A. NATIONAL FOUR–WALL CHAMPIONS

Singles

1960	Jimmy Jacobs
1961	John Sloan
1962–63	Oscar Obert
1964–65	Jimmy Jacobs
1966–67	Paul Haber
1968	Simon (Stuffy) Singer
1969–71	Paul Haber
1972	Fred Lewis
1973	Terry Muck
1974	Fred Lewis
1975	Jay Bilyeu
1976	Vern Roberts, Jr.
1977	Naty Alvarado
1978	Fred Lewis
1979	Naty Alvarado
1980	Naty Alvarado
1981	Fred Lewis
1982	Naty Alvarado
1983	Naty Alvarado
1984	Naty Alvarado
1985	Naty Alvarado
1986	Naty Alvarado
1987	Naty Alvarado
1988	Naty Alvarado[1]
1989	Ponch Monreal
1990	Naty Alvarado
1991	John Bike
1992	Octavio Silveyra
1993	David Chapman[2]
1994	Octavio Silveyra
1995	David Chapman

Doubles

1960	Jimmy Jacobs–Dick Weisman
1961	John Sloan–Vic Hershkowitz
1962–63	Jimmy Jacobs–Marty Decatur
1964	John Sloan–Phil Elbert
1965	Jimmy Jacobs–Marty Decatur
1966	Pete Tyson–Bob Lindsay
1967–68	Jimmy Jacobs–Marty Decatur
1969	Lou Kramberg–Lou Russo
1970	Karl and Ruby Obert
1971	Ray Neveau–Simie Fein
1972	Kent Fusselman–Al Drews
1973–74	Ray Neveau–Simie Fein
1975	Marty Decatur–Steve Lott
1976	Gary Rohrer–Dan O'Connor
1977	Skip McDowell–Matt Kelly
1978	Stuffy Singer–Marty Decatur
1979	Stuffy Singer–Marty Decatur
1980	Skip McDowell–Harry Robertson
1981	Tom Kopatich–Jack Roberts
1982	Naty Alvarado–Vern Roberts
1983	Naty Alvarado–Vern Roberts
1984	Naty Alvarado–Vern Roberts
1985	Naty Alvarado–Vern Roberts
1986–87	Jon Kemdler–Poncho Monreal
1988	Doug Glatt–Dennis Haynes
1989	Danny Bell—Charlie Kalil
1990	Doug Glatt–Rod Prince
1991	John Bike–Octavio Silveyra
1992	David Chapman–Naty Alvarado, Jr.
1993	David Chapman[2]–Naty Alvarado, Jr.
1994	John Bike–Octavio Silveyra
1995	David Chapman–Naty Alvarado, Jr.

1. 10th time—American record. 2. Chapman, at 17, is the youngest to win the singles and doubles championship in the same year.

BASEBALL

The popular tradition that baseball was invented by Abner Doubleday at Cooperstown, N.Y., in 1839 has been enshrined in the Hall of Fame and National Museum of Baseball erected in that town, but research has proved that a game called "Base Ball" was played in this country and England before 1839. The first team baseball as we know it was played at the Elysian Fields, Hoboken, N.J., on June 19, 1846, between the Knickerbockers and the New York Nine. The next fifty years saw a gradual growth of baseball and an improvement of equipment and playing skill.

Historians have it that the first pitcher to throw a curve was William A. (Candy) Cummings in 1867. The Cincinnati Red Stockings were the first all-professional team, and in 1869 they played 64 games without a loss. The standard ball of the same size and weight, still the rule, was adopted in 1872. The first catcher's mask was worn in 1875. The National League was organized in 1876. The first chest protector was worn in 1885. The three-strike rule was put on the books in 1887, and the four-ball ticket to first base was instituted in 1889. The pitching distance was lengthened to 60 feet 6 inches in 1893, and the rules have been modified only slightly since that time.

The American League, under the vigorous leadership of B. B. Johnson, became a major league in 1901. Judge Kenesaw Mountain Landis, by action of the two major leagues, became Commissioner of Baseball in 1921. Peter Ueberroth became baseball's fifth commissioner and took office Oct. 1, 1984.

Ueberroth did not seek a new term in 1989 and was succeeded by Bart Giamatti who died suddenly on Sept. 1, 1989. Francis T. Vincent, Jr., replaced him on Sept. 13, 1989.

Vincent, under pressure from owners to relinquish some of his powers, resigned in late 1992. Bud Selig, principal owner of the Milwaukee Brewers, headed a baseball executive committee that ruled baseball during the search for a new commissioner that extended late into 1993. The search was put on hold pending resolution of baseball's labor situation. No progress had been made through late 1995.

MAJOR LEAGUE ALL-STAR GAME

Year	Date	Winning league and manager	Runs	Losing league and manager	Runs	Winning pitcher	Losing pitcher	Site	Paid attendance
1933	July 6	A.L. (Mack)	4	N.L. (McGraw)	2	Gomez	Hallahan	Chicago A.L.	47,595
1934	July 10	A.L. (Cronin)	9	N.L. (Terry)	7	Harder	Mungo	New York N.L.	48,363
1935	July 8	A.L. (Cochrane)	4	N.L. (Frisch)	1	Gomez	Walker	Cleveland A.L.	69,831
1936	July 7	N.L. (Grimm)	4	A.L. (McCarthy)	3	J. Dean	Grove	Boston N.L.	25,556
1937	July 7	A.L. (McCarthy)	8	N.L. (Terry)	3	Gomez	J. Dean	Washington A.L.	31,391
1938	July 6	N.L. (Terry)	4	A.L. (McCarthy)	1	Vander Meer	Gomez	Cincinnati N.L.	27,067
1939	July 11	A.L. (McCarthy)	3	N.L. (Hartnett)	1	Bridges	Lee	New York A.L.	62,892
1940	July 9	N.L. (McKechnie)	4	A.L. (Cronin)	0	Derringer	Ruffing	St. Louis N.L.	32,373
1941	July 8	A.L. (Baker)	7	N.L. (McKechnie)	5	E. Smith	Passeau	Detroit A.L.	54,674
1942	July 6	A.L. (McCarthy)	3	N.L. (Durocher)	1	Chandler	Cooper	New York N.L.	34,178
1943	July 13[1]	A.L. (McCarthy)	5	N.L. (Southworth)	3	Leonard	Cooper	Philadelphia A.L.	31,938
1944	July 11[1]	N.L. (Southworth)	7	A.L. (McCarthy)	1	Raffensberger	Hughson	Pittsburgh N.L.	29,589
1946	July 9	A.L. (O'Neill)	12	N.L. (Grimm)	0	Feller	Passeau	Boston A.L.	34,906
1947	July 8	A.L. (Cronin)	2	N.L. (Dyer)	1	Shea	Sain	Chicago N.L.	41,123
1948	July 13	A.L. (Harris)	5	N.L. (Durocher)	2	Raschi	Schmitz	St. Louis A.L.	34,009
1949	July 12	A.L. (Boudreau)	11	N.L. (Southworth)	7	Trucks	Newcombe	Brooklyn N.L.	32,577
1950	July 11	N.L. (Shotton)	4	A.L. (Stengel)	3[3]	Blackwell	Gray	Chicago A.L.	46,127
1951	July 10	N.L. (Sawyer)	8	A.L. (Stengel)	3	Maglie	Lopat	Detroit A.L.	52,075
1952	July 8	N.L. (Durocher)	3	A.L. (Stengel)	2[4]	Rush	Lemon	Philadelphia N.L.	32,785
1953	July 14	N.L. (Dressen)	5	A.L. (Stengel)	1	Spahn	Reynolds	Cincinnati N.L.	30,846
1954	July 13	A.L. (Stengel)	11	N.L. (Alston)	9	Stone	Conley	Cleveland A.L.	68,751
1955	July 12	N.L. (Durocher)	6	A.L. (Lopez)	5[5]	Conley	Sullivan	Milwaukee N.L.	45,643
1956	July 10	N.L. (Alston)	7	A.L. (Stengel)	3	Friend	Pierce	Washington A.L.	28,843
1957	July 9	A.L. (Stengel)	6	N.L. (Alston)	5	Bunning	Simmons	St. Louis N.L.	30,693
1958	July 8	A.L. (Stengel)	4	N.L. (Haney)	3	Wynn	Friend	Baltimore A.L.	48,829
1959[2]	July 7	N.L. (Haney)	5	A.L. (Stengel)	4	Antonelli	Ford	Pittsburgh N.L.	35,277
	Aug. 3	A.L. (Stengel)	5	N.L. (Haney)	3	Walker	Drysdale	Los Angeles N.L.	55,105
1960[2]	July 11	N.L. (Alston)	5	A.L. (Lopez)	3	Friend	Monbouquette	Kansas City A.L.	30,619
	July 13	N.L. (Alston)	6	A.L. (Lopez)	0	Law	Ford	New York A.L.	38,362
1961[2]	July 11	N.L. (Murtaugh)	5	A.L. (Richards)	4[6]	Miller	Wilhelm	San Francisco N.L.	44,115
	July 31	A.L. (Murtaugh)	1	N.L. (Richards)	1[7]	—	—	Boston A.L.	31,851
1962[2]	July 10	N.L. (Hutchinson)	3	A.L. (Houk)	1	Marichal	Pascual	Washington A.L.	45,480
	July 30	A.L. (Houk)	9	N.L. (Hutchinson)	4	Herbert	Mahaffey	Chicago N.L.	38,359
1963	July 9	N.L. (Dark)	5	A.L. (Houk)	3	Jackson	Bunning	Cleveland A.L.	44,160
1964	July 7	N.L. (Alston)	7	A.L. (Lopez)	4	Marichal	Radatz	New York N.L.	50,850
1965	July 13	N.L. (March)	6	A.L. (Lopez)	5	Koufax	McDowell	Minnesota A.L.	46,706
1966	July 12	N.L. (Alston)	2	A.L. (Mele)	1[6]	Perry	Rickert	St. Louis N.L.	49,926
1967	July 11	N.L. (Alston)	2	A.L. (Bauer)	1[8]	Drysdale	Hunter	Anaheim A.L.	46,309
1968	July 9	N.L. (Schoendienst)	1	A.L. (Williams)	0	Drysdale	Tiant	Houston N.L.	48,321
1969	July 23	N.L. (Schoendienst)	9	A.L. (M. Smith)	3	Carlton	Stottlemyre	Washington A.L.	45,259
1970	July 14	N.L. (Hodges)	5	A.L. (Weaver)	4	Osteen	Wright	Cincinnati N.L.	51,838
1971	July 13	A.L. (Weaver)	6	N.L. (Anderson)	4	Blue	Ellis	Detroit A.L.	53,559

Year	Date	Winning league and manager	Runs	Losing league and manager	Runs	Winning pitcher	Losing pitcher	Site	Paid attendance
1972	July 25	N.L. (Murtaugh)	4	A.L. (Weaver)	3[6]	McGraw	McNally	Atlanta N.L.	53,107
1973	July 24[1]	N.L. (Anderson)	7	A.L. (Williams)	1	Wise	Blyleven	Kansas City A.L.	40,849
1974	July 23[1]	N.L. (Berra)	7	A.L. (Williams)	2	Brett	Tiant	Pittsburgh N.L.	50,706
1975	July 15[1]	N.L. (Alston)	6	A.L. (Dark)	3	Matlack	Hunter	Milwaukee A.L.	51,540
1976	July 13	N.L. (Anderson)	7	A.L. (D. Johnson)	1	R. Jones	Fidrych	Philadelphia N.L.	63,974
1977	July 19[1]	N.L. (Anderson)	7	A.L. (Martin)	5	Sutton	Palmer	New York A.L.	56,683
1978	July 11[1]	N.L. (Lasorda)	7	A.L. (Martin)	3	Sutter	Gossage	San Diego N.L.	51,549
1979	July 17[1]	N.L. (Lasorda)	7	A.L. (Lemon)	6	Sutter	Kern	Seattle A.L.	58,905
1980	July 8[1]	N.L. (Tanner)	4	A.L. (Weaver)	2	Reuss	John	Los Angeles N.L.	56,088
1981	Aug. 9[1]	N.L. (Green)	5	A.L. (Frey)	4	Blue	Fingers	Cleveland* A.L.	72,086
1982	July 13[1]	N.L. (Lasorda)	4	A.L. (Martin)	1	Rogers	Eckersley	Montreal N.L.	59,057
1983	July 6[1]	A.L. (Kuenn)	13	N.L. (Herzog)	3	Steib	Soto	Chicago A.L.	43,801
1984	July 11[1]	N.L. (Owens)	3	A.L. (Altobelli)	1	Leg	Steib	San Francisco, N.L.	57,756
1985	July 16[1]	N.L. (Williams)	6	A.L. (Anderson)	1	Hoyt	Morris	Minneapolis, A.L.	54,960
1986	July 15[1]	A.L. (Howser)	3	N.L. (Herzog)	2	Clemens	Gooden	Houston, N.L.	45,774
1987	July 14[1]	N.L. (Johnson)	2	A.L. (McNamara)	0	Smith	Howell	Oakland, A.L.	49,671
1988	July 12[1]	A.L. (Kelly)	2	N.L. (Herzog)	1	Viola	Gooden	Cincinnati, N.L.	55,837
1989	July 11[1]	A.L. (LaRussa)	5	N.L. (Lasorda)	3	Ryan	Smoltz	California, N.L.	64,036
1990	July 10[1]	A.L. (LaRussa)	2	N.L. (Craig)	0	Saberhagen	Brantley	Chicago, N.L.	39,071
1991	July 9[1]	A.L. (LaRussa)	4	N.L. (Piniella)	2	Key	Martinez	Toronto, A.L.	52,383
1992	July 14	A.L. (Kelly)	13	N.L. (Cox)	6	Brown	Glavine	San Diego, N.L.	59,372
1993	July 13	A.L. (Gaston)	9	N.L. (Cox)	3	McDowell	Burkett	Baltimore, A.L.	48,147
1994	July 12	N.L. (Fregosi)	8	A.L. (Gaston)	7	Jones	Bere	Pittsburgh, N.L.	59,568
1995	July 11	N.L. (Alou)	3	A.L. (Showalter)	2	Slocumb	Rogers	Texas, A.L.	50,920

1. Night game. 2. Two games. 3. Fourteen innings. 4. Five innings, rain. 5. Twelve innings. 6. Ten innings. 7. Called because of rain after nine innings. 8. Fifteen innings. NOTE: No game in 1945. *Game was originally scheduled for July 14, but was put off because of players' strike.

NATIONAL BASEBALL HALL OF FAME
Cooperstown, N.Y.

Fielders

Member	Active years
Aaron, Henry (Hank)	1954–1976
Anson, Adrian (Cap)	1876–1897
Aparicio, Luis	1956–1973
Appling, Lucius (Luke)	1930–1950
Ashburh, Richie	1948–1962
Averill, H. Earl	1929–1941
Baker, J. Frank (Home Run)	1908–1922
Bancroft, David	1915–1930
Banks, Ernest	1953–1971
Beckley, Jacob	1888–1907
Bell, James (Cool Papa)[1]	1920–1947
Bench, John	1967–1983
Berra, Lawrence (Yogi)	1946–1965
Bottomley, James	1922–1937
Boudreau, Louis	1938–1952
Bresnahan, Roger	1897–1915
Brock, Lou	1961–1980
Brouthers, Dennis	1879–1896
Burkett, Jesse	1890–1905
Campanella, Roy	1948–1957
Carew, Rod	1967–1985
Carey, Max	1910–1929
Chance, Frank	1898–1914
Charleston, Oscar[1]	1915–1954
Clarke, Fred	1894–1915
Clemente, Roberto	1955–1972
Cobb, Tyrus	1905–1928
Cochrane, Gordon (Mickey)	1925–1937
Collins, Edward	1906–1930
Collins, James	1895–1908
Comiskey, Charles	1882–1894
Combs, Earle	1924–1935
Connor, Roger	1880–1897
Crawford, Samuel	1899–1917
Cronin, Joseph	1926–1945
Cuyler, Hazen (Kiki)	1921–1938
Dandridge, Ray[1]	1933–1953
Delahanty, Edward	1888–1903
Dickey, William	1928–1946
Dihigo, Martin[1]	1923–1945
DiMaggio, Joseph	1936–1951
Doerr, Bobby	1937–1951
Duffy, Hugh	1888–1906
Ewing, William	1880–1897
Eyers, John	1902–1919
Ferrell, Rick	1929–1947
Flick, Elmer	1898–1910
Foxx, James	1925–1945
Frisch, Frank	1919–1937
Gehrig, H. Louis (Lou)	1923–1939
Gehringer, Charles	1924–1942
Gibson, Josh[1]	1929–1946
Goslin, Leon (Goose)	1921–1938
Greenberg, Henry (Hank)	1933–1947
Hafey, Charles (Chick)	1924–1937
Hamilton, William	1888–1901
Hartnett, Charles (Gabby)	1922–1941
Heilmann, Harry	1914–1932
Herman, William	1931–1947
Hooper, Harry	1909–1925
Hornsby, Rogers	1915–1937
Irvin, Monford (Monte)[1]	1939–1956
Jackson, Reggie	1967–1987
Jackson, Travis	1922–1936
Jennings, Hugh	1891–1918
Johnson, William (Judy)[1]	1921–1937
Kaline, Albert W.	1953–1974
Keeler, William (Wee Willie)	1892–1910
Kell, George	1943–1957
Kelley, Joseph	1891–1908
Kelly, George	1915–1932
Kelly, Michael (King)	1878–1893
Killebrew, Harmon	1954–1975
Kiner, Ralph	1946–1955
Klein, Charles H. (Chuck)	1928–1944
Lajoie, Napoleon	1896–1916
Lazzeri, Tony	1926–1939
Leonard, Walter (Buck)[1]	1933–1955
Lindstrom, Frederick	1924–1936
Lloyd, John Henry[1]	1905–1931
Lombardi, Ernie	1932–1947
Mantle, Mickey	1951–1968
Manush, Henry (Heinie)	1923–1939
Maranville, Walter (Rabbit)	1912–1935
Matthews, Edwin	1952–1968
Mays, Willie	1951–1973
McCarthy, Thomas	1884–1896
McGraw, John J.	1891–1906
McCovey, Willie	1959–1980
Medwick, Joseph (Ducky)	1932–1948
Mize, John (The Big Cat)	1936–1953
Morgan, Joe	1963–1984
Musial, Stanley	1941–1963
O'Rourke, James	1876–1894
Ott, Melvin	1926–1947
Reese, Harold (Pee Wee)	1940–1958
Rice, Edgar (Sam)	1915–1934
Rizzuto, Phil	1941–1956
Robinson, Brooks	1955–1977
Robinson, Frank	1956–1976
Robinson, Jack	1947–1956
Robinson, Wilbert	1886–1902
Roush, Edd	1913–1931
Ruth, Babe	1914–1935
Schalk, Raymond	1912–1929
Schoendienst, Red	1945–1963
Schmidt, Mike	1973–1989
Sewell, Joseph	1920–1933
Simmons, Al	1924–1944
Sisler, George	1915–1930
Slaughter, Enos	1938–1959
Snider, Edwin D. (Duke)	1947–1964
Speaker, Tristram	1907–1928
Stargell, Willie	1962–1982
Terry, William	1923–1936
Thompson, Samuel	1885–1906
Tinker, Joseph	1902–1916

Traynor, Harold (Pie)	1920–1937	Waner, Paul	1926–1945	Williams, Theodore	1939–1960
Vaughan, Arky	1932–1948	Ward, John (Monte)	1878–1894	Wilson, Lewis R. (Hack)	1923–1934
Wagner, John (Honus)	1897–1917	Wheat, Zachariah	1909–1927	Yastrzemski, Carl	1961–1983
Wallace, Roderick (Bobby)	1894–1918	Williams, Billy	1959–1976	Youngs, Ross (Pep)	1917–1926
Waner, Lloyd	1927–1945				

1. Negro League player selected by special committee.

Pitchers

Alexander, Grover	1911–1930	Grove, Robert (Lefty)	1925–1941	Palmer, Jim	1965–1984
Bender, Charles (Chief)	1903–1925	Haines, Jesse	1918–1937	Pennock, Herbert	1912–1934
Brown, Mordecai (3–Finger)	1903–1916	Hoyt, Waite	1918–1938	Perry, Gaylord	1962–1983
Carlton, Steve	1965–1988	Hubbell, Carl	1928–1943	Plank, Edward	1901–1917
Chesbro, John	1899–1909	Hunter, Jim (Catfish)	1965–1979	Radbourn, Charles (Hoss)	1880–1891
Clarkson, John	1882–1894	Jenkins, Ferguson	1965–1983	Rixey, Eppa	1912–1933
Coveleski, Stanley	1912–1928	Johnson, Walter	1907–1927	Roberts, Robert (Robin)	1948–1966
Day, Leon[1]	1935–1955	Joss, Adrian	1902–1910	Ruffing, Charles (Red)	1924–1947
Dean, Jerome (Dizzy)	1930–1947	Keefe, Timothy	1880–1893	Rusie, Amos	1889–1901
Drysdale, Don	1956–1969	Koufax, Sanford (Sandy)	1955–1966	Seaver, Tom	1967–1986
Faber, Urban (Red)	1914–1933	Lemon, Robert	1946–1958	Spahn, Warren	1942–1965
Feller, Robert	1936–1956	Lyons, Theodore	1923–1946	Vance, Arthur (Dazzy)	1915–1935
Fingers, Rollie	1968–1985	Marichal, Juan	1960–1975	Waddell, Rube	1897–1910
Ford, Edward (Whitey)	1950–1967	Marquard, Richard (Rube)	1908–1924	Walsh, Edward	1904–1917
Foster, Andrew (Rube)	1897–1926	Mathewson, Christopher	1900–1916	Welch, Michael (Mickey)	1880–1892
Galvin, James (Pud)	1876–1892	McGinnity, Joseph	1899–1908	Wilhelm, Hoyt	1952–1972
Gibson, Bob	1959–1975	Neuhouser, Hal	1939–1955	Willis, Vic	1898–1910
Gomez, Vernon (Lefty)	1930–1943	Nichols, Charles (Kid)	1890–1906	Wynn, Early	1939–1963
Griffith, Clark	1891–1914	Paige, Leroy (Satchel)[1]	1926–1965	Young, Denton (Cy)	1890–1911
Grimes, Burleigh	1916–1934				

1. Negro League player selected by special committee.

Officials and Others

Alston, Walter[1]	Cummings, William A.[5]	Hulbert, William[2]	McKechnie, William B.[1]
Barlick, Al[4]	Durocher, Leo[1]	Johnson, B. Bancroft[2]	Rickey, W. Branch[1, 2]
Barrow, Edward[1, 2]	Evans, William G.[4, 2]	Klem, William[4]	Spalding, Albert G.[4]
Bulkeley, Morgan G.[2]	Foster, Rube[2]	Landis, Kenesaw M.[6]	Stengel, Charles D.[7]
Cartwright, Alexander[2]	Frick, Ford C.[6, 2]	Lopez, Alfonso R.[7]	Veeck, Bill[2]
Chadwick, Henry[3]	Giles, Warren C.[2]	Mack, Connie[1, 2]	Weiss, George M.[2]
Chandler, A.B.[6]	Harridge, William[2]	MacPhail, Leland S.[2]	Wright, George[5]
Comiskey, Charles[1]	Harris, Stanley R.[7]	McCarthy, Joseph V.[1]	Wright, Harry[5, 1]
Conlan, John[2]	Hubbard, R. Calvin[4]	McGowan, Bill[4]	Yawkey, Thomas[2]
Connolly, Thomas[4]	Huggins, Miller J.[1]		

1. Manager. 2. Executive. 3. Writer–statistician. 4. Umpire. 5. Early player. 6. Commissioner. 7. Player–manager.

BASEBALL'S BACK IN 1995, BUT LABOR SETTLEMENT ELUSIVE

Major League Baseball's eighth work stoppage since 1972, which began when the Major League Players Association went on strike Aug. 12, 1994, ended on March 31, 1995, when the players returned to work after U.S. District Judge Sonia Sotomayor issued an injunction forcing owners to return to the terms of the expired agreement.

The season began on April 26, with each team scheduled to play 144 games instead of the usual 162.

While the games resumed, there was no progress in getting a new labor agreement, so the possibility of an additional work stoppage, either through another strike or a lockout by the owners, still existed throughout the 1995 season.

As a result of the 1994 strike, the playoffs and the World Series were cancelled by acting commissioner Bud Selig.

Though there were many issues to argue, the primary focus of both the players and ownership was a player salary cap. The owners insisted that many small-market teams would be unable to survive in the future if player salaries were not restricted.

The players argued that salaries should remain open in a free market, and refused to accept the cap proposal, which would lower the average salary.

The strike came in the midst of one of baseball's most exciting seasons in recent memory. Several records appeared within reach. By the strike date, Ken Griffey, Jr., of the Seattle Mariners had 40 home runs and Matt Williams of the San Francisco Giants 43—both in reach during a full season of the record of 61 set by Roger Maris in 1961.

San Diego Padres outfielder Tony Gwynn was making a bid to become the first hitter to bat .400 since Ted Williams hit .406 in 1941. He was batting .394 at the start of the strike.

LIFETIME BATTING, PITCHING, AND BASE–RUNNING RECORDS
(An asterisk indicates active player)

Source: The Complete Handbook of Baseball, published and copyrighted by New American Library, New York, N.Y. 10019. All records through 1994 unless noted.

(Records Through 1994)

Hits (3,000 or more)

Pete Rose	4,256
Ty Cobb	4,191
Henry Aaron	3,771
Stan Musial	3,630
Tris Speaker	3,535
Honus Wagner	3,430
Carl Yastrzemski	3,419
Eddie Collins	3,309
Willie Mays	3,283
Nap Lajoie	3,252
George Brett	3,154
Paul Waner	3,152
Robin Yount	3,142
Dave Winfield**	3,088
Cap Anson	3,081
Rod Carew	3,053
Lou Brock	3,023
Al Kaline	3,007
Roberto Clemente	3,000

Earned Run Average
(Minimum 1,500 innings pitched)

Ed Walsh	1.82
Addie Joss	1.88
Joe Wood	2.03
Three Finger Brown	2.06
Christy Mathewson	2.13
Rube Waddell	2.16
Walter Johnson	2.17
Orvie Overall	2.23
Ed Ruelbach	2.28
Jim Scott	2.32
Ed Plank	2.34
Ed Cicotte	2.37
Ed Killian	2.38
Doc White	2.38
Nap Rucker	2.42
Jeff Tesreau	2.43
Chief Bender	2.46
Sam Leaver	2.47

Runs Scored

Ty Cobb	2,245
Henry Aaron	2,174
Babe Ruth	2,174
Pete Rose	2,165
Willie Mays	2,062
Stan Musial	1,949
Lou Gehrig	1,888
Tris Speaker	1,881
Mel Ott	1,859
Frank Robinson	1,829
Eddie Collins	1,816
Carl Yastrzemski	1,816
Ted Williams	1,798
Charlie Gehringer	1,774
Jimmie Foxx	1,751
Honus Wagner	1,740
Willie Keeler	1,720
Cap Anson	1,712
Jesse Burkett	1,708
Billy Hamilton	1,690
Mickey Mantle	1,677
John McPhee	1,674
Dave Winfield**	1,658
Rickey Henderson**	1,652
Joe Morgan	1,650
George Van Haltren	1,650

Strikeouts, Pitching

Nolan Ryan	5,668
Steve Carlton	4,136
Bert Blyleven	3,701
Tom Seaver	3,640
Don Sutton	3,569
Gaylord Perry	3,534
Walter Johnson	3,509
Phil Niekro	3,342
Ferguson Jenkins	3,192
Bob Gibson	3,117
Jim Bunning	2,855
Mickey Lolich	2,832
Cy Young	2,819
Frank Tanana	2,657
Warren Spahn	2,583
Bob Feller	2,581
Jerry Koosman	2,556
Tim Keefe	2,538
Christy Mathewson	2,505

Home Runs (350 or More)

Henry Aaron	755
Babe Ruth	714
Willie Mays	660
Frank Robinson	586
Harmon Killebrew	573
Reggie Jackson	563
Mike Schmidt	548
Mickey Mantle	536
Jimmie Foxx	534
Ted Williams	521
Willie McCovey	521
Eddie Mathews	512
Ernie Banks	512
Mel Ott	511
Lou Gehrig	493
Stan Musial	475
Willie Stargell	475
Dave Winfield**	463
Eddie Murray**	458
Carl Yastrzemski	452
Dave Kingman	442
Andre Dawson**	428
Billy Williams	426
Darrell Evans	414
Duke Snider	406
Al Kaline	399
Dale Murphy	398
Johnny Bench	389
Frank Howard	382
Jim Rice	382
Orlando Cepeda	379
Norm Cash	377
Carlton Fisk	375
Rocky Colavito	374
Tony Perez	371
Gil Hodges	370
Ralph Kiner	369
Joe DiMaggio	361
Lee May	360
Johnny Mize	359
Yogi Berra	358
Dick Allen	351

Shutouts

Walter Johnson	110
Grover Alexander	90
Christy Mathewson	83
Cy Young	77
Ed Plank	64
Warren Spahn	63
Nolan Ryan	61
Bert Blyleven	60
Tom Seaver	60
Ed Walsh	58
Don Sutton	58
James Galvin	57
Bob Gibson	56
Steve Carlton	55
Bert Blyleven	55
Jim Palmer	53
Gaylord Perry	53
Juan Marichal	52

Strikeouts, Batting

Reggie Jackson	2,597
Willie Stargell	1,936
Mike Schmidt	1,883
Tony Perez	1,867
Dave Kingman	1,816
Bobby Bonds	1,757
Dale Murphy	1,733
Lou Brock	1,730
Mickey Mantle	1,710
Harmon Killebrew	1,699
Dwight Evans	1,697
Dave Winfield**	1,660
Lee May	1,570
Dick Allen	1,566
Willie McCovey	1,550
Dave Parker	1,537
Frank Robinson	1,532
Willie Mays	1,526

Bases on Balls

Babe Ruth	2,056
Ted Williams	2,019
Joe Morgan	1,865
Carl Yastrzemski	1,845
Mickey Mantle	1,734
Mel Ott	1,708
Eddie Yost	1,614
Darrell Evans	1,605
Stan Musial	1,599
Pete Rose	1,566
Harmon Killebrew	1,559
Lou Gehrig	1,508
Mike Schmidt	1,507
Eddie Collins	1,503
Rickey Henderson**	1,478
Willie Mays	1,463
Jimmie Foxx	1,452
Eddie Mathews	1,444
Frank Robinson	1,420
Henry Aaron	1,402

**Active coming into 1995 season

BASEBALL'S PERFECTLY PITCHED GAMES[1]
(no opposing runner reached base)

Lee Richmond—Worcester vs. Cleveland (NL) June 12, 1880 (1–0)

John M. Ward—Providence vs. Buffalo (NL) June 17, 1880 (5–0)

Cy Young—Boston vs. Philadelphia (AL) May 5, 1904 (3–0)

Addie Joss—Cleveland vs. Chicago (AL) Oct. 2, 1908 (1–0)

Ernest Shore[2]—Boston vs. Washington (AL) June 23, 1917 (4–0)

Charles Robertson—Chicago vs. Detroit (AL) April 30, 1922 (2–0)

Don Larsen[3]—New York (AL) vs. Brooklyn (NL) Oct. 8, 1956 (2–0)

Jim Bunning—Philadelphia vs. New York (NL) June 21, 1964 (6–0)

Sandy Koufax—Los Angeles vs. Chicago (NL) Sept. 9, 1965 (1–0)

Jim Hunter—Oakland vs. Minnesota (AL) May 8, 1968 (4–0)

Len Barker—Cleveland vs. Toronto (AL) May 15, 1981 (3–0)

Mike Witt—California vs. Texas (AL) Sept. 30, 1984 (1–0)

Tom Browning—Cincinnati vs. Los Angeles (NL) Sept. 16, 1988 (1–0)

Dennis Martinez—Montreal vs. Los Angeles (NL) July 28, 1991 (2–0)

Kenny Rogers—Texas vs. California (AL) July 28, 1994 (4–0)

1. Harvey Haddix, of Pittsburgh, pitched 12 perfect innings against Milwaukee (NL), May 26, 1959 but lost game in 13th on error and hit. 2. Shore, relief pitcher for Babe Ruth who walked first batter before being ejected by umpire, retired 26 batters who faced him and baserunner was out stealing. 3. World Series.

RECORD OF WORLD SERIES GAMES
(Through 1994)

Source: The Book of Baseball Records, published by Seymour Siwoff, New York City.

Figures in parentheses for winning pitchers (WP) and losing pitchers (LP) indicate the game number in the series.

1903—Boston A.L. 5 (Jimmy Collins); Pittsburgh N.L. 3 (Fred Clarke). WP—Bos.: Dinneen (2, 6, 8), Young (5, 7); Pitts.: Phillippe (1, 3, 4). LP—Bos.: Young (1), Hughes (3), Dinneen (4); Pitts.: Leever (2, 6), Kennedy (5), Phillippe (7, 8).

1904—No series.

1905—New York N.L. 4 (John J. McGraw); Philadelphia A.L. 1 (Connie Mack). WP—N.Y.: Mathewson (1, 3, 5); McGinnity (4); Phila.: Bender (2). LP—N.Y.: McGinnity (2); Phila.: Plank (1, 4), Coakley (3), Bender (5).

1906—Chicago A.L. 4 (Fielder Jones); Chicago N.L. 2 (Frank Chance). WP—Chi.: A.L.: Altrock (1), Walsh (3, 5), White (6); Chi.: N.L.: Reulbach (2), Brown (4). LP—Chi. A.L.: White (2), Altrock. (4); Chi.: N.L.: Brown (1, 6), Pfeister (3, 5).

1907—Chicago N.L. 4 (Frank Chance); Detroit A.L. 0 (Hugh Jennings). First game tied 3–3, 12 innings. WP—Pfeister (2), Reulbach (3), Overall (4), Brown (5). LP—Mullin (2, 5), Siever (3), Donovan (4).

1908—Chicago N.L. 4 (Frank Chance); Detroit A.L. 1 (Hugh Jennings). WP—Chi.: Brown (1, 4), Overall (2, 5); Det.: Mullin (3). LP—Chi.: Pfeister (3); Det.: Summers (1, 4), Donovan (2, 5).

1909—Pittsburgh N.L. 4 (Fred Clarke); Detroit A.L. 3 (Hugh Jennings). WP—Pitts.: Adams (1, 5, 7), Maddox (3); Det.: Donovan (2), Mullin (4, 6). LP—Pitts.: Camnitz (2), Leifield (4), Willis (6); Det.: Mullin (1), Summers (3, 5), Donovan (7).

1910—Philadelphia A.L. 4 (Connie Mack); Chicago N.L. 1 (Frank Chance). WP—Phila.: Bender (1), Coombs (2, 3, 5); Chi.: Brown (4). LP—Phila.: Bender (4); Chi.: Overall (1), Brown (2, 5), McIntyre (3).

1911—Philadelphia A.L. 4 (Connie Mack); New York N.L. 2 (John J. McGraw). WP—Phila.: Plank (2), Coombs (3), Bender (4, 6); N.Y.: Mathewson (1), Crandall (5). LP—Phila.: Bender (1), Plank (5); N.Y.: Marquard (3, 4), Ames (3).

1912—Boston A.L. 4 (J. Garland Stahl); New York N.L. 3 (John J. McGraw). Second game tied, 6–6, 11 innings. WP—Bos.: Wood (1, 4, 8), Bedient (5); N.Y.: Marquard (3, 6), Tesreau (7). LP—Bos.: O'Brien (3, 6), Wood (7); N.Y.: Tesreau (1, 4), Mathewson (5, 8).

1913—Philadelphia A.L. 4 (Connie Mack); New York N.L. 1 (John J. McGraw). WP—Phila.: Bender (1, 4), Bush (3), Plank (5); N.Y.: Mathewson (2); LP—Phila.: Plank (2); N.Y.: Marquard (1), Tesreau (3), Demaree (4), Mathewson (5).

1914—Boston N.L. 4 (George Stallings); Philadelphia A.L. 0 (Connie Mack). WP—Rudolph (1, 4), James (2, 3). LP—Bender (1), Plank (2), Bush (3), Shawkey (4).

1915—Boston A.L. 4 (Bill Carrigan); Philadelphia N.L. 1 (Pat Moran). WP—Bos.: Foster (2, 5), Leonard (3), Shore (4); Phila.: Alexander (1). LP—Bos.: Shore (1); Phila.: Mayer (2), Alexander (3), Chalmers (4), Rixey (5).

1916—Boston A.L. 4 (Bill Carrigan); Brooklyn N.L. 1 (Wilbert Robinson). WP—Bos.: Shore (1, 5), Ruth (2), Leonard (4), Bklyn.: Coombs (3). LP—Bos.: Mays (3); Bklyn.: Marquard (1, 4), Smith (2), Pfeffer (5).

1917—Chicago A.L. 4 (Clarence Rowland); New York N.L. 2 (John J. McGraw). WP—Chi.: Cicotte (1), Faber (2, 5, 6); N.Y.: Benton (3), Schupp (4). LP—Chi.: Cicotte (3), Faber (4); N.Y.: Sallee (1, 5), Anderson (2), Benton (6).

1918—Boston A.L. 4 (Ed Barrow); Chicago N.L. 2 (Fred Mitchell). WP—Bos.: Ruth (1, 4), Mays (3, 6); Chi.: Tyler (2), Vaughn (5). LP—Bos.: Bush (2), Jones (5); Chi.: Vaughn (1, 3), Douglas (4), Tyler (6).

1919—Cincinnati N.L. 5 (Pat Moran); Chicago A.L. 3 (William Gleason). WP—Cin.: Ruether (1), Sallee (2), Ring (4), Eller (5, 8); Chi.: Kerr (3, 6), Cicotte (1). LP—Cin.: Fisher (3), Ring (6), Sallee (7); Chi.: Cicotte (1, 4), Williams (2, 5, 8).

1920—Cleveland A.L. 5 (Tris Speaker); Brooklyn N.L. 2 (Wilbert Robinson). WP—Cleve.: Coveleski (1, 4, 7), Bagby (5), Mails (6); Bklyn.: Grimes (2), Smith (3). LP—Cleve.: Bagby (2), Caldwell (3). Bklyn.: Marquard (1), Cadore (4), Grimes (5, 7), Smith (6).

1921—New York N.L. 5 (John J. McGraw); New York A.L. 3 (Miller Huggins). WP—N.Y. N.L.: Barnes (3, 6), Douglas (4, 7), Nehf (8); N.Y. A.L.: Mays (1), Hoyt (2, 5). LP—N.Y. N.L.: Nehf (2, 5), Douglas (1). N.Y. A.L.: Quinn (3), Mays (4, 7), Shawkey (6), Hoyt (8).

1922—New York N.L. 4 (John J. McGraw); New York A.L. 0 (Miller Huggins). Second game tied 3–3, 10 innings. WP—Ryan (1), Scott (3), McQuillan (4), Nehf (5); LP—Bush (1, 5), Hoyt (3), Mays (4).

1923—New York A.L. 4 (Miller Huggins); New York N.L. 2 (John J. McGraw). WP—N.Y. A.L.: Pennock (2, 6), Shawkey (4), Bush (5); N.Y. N.L.: Ryan (1), Nehf (3). LP—N.Y. A.L.: Bush (1), Jones (3); N.Y. N.L.: McQuillan (2), Scott (4), Bentley (5), Nehf (6).

1924—Washington A.L. 4 (Bucky Harris); New York N.L. 3 (John J. McGraw). WP—Wash.: Zachary (2, 6), Mogridge (4), Johnson (7); N.Y.: Nehf (1), McQuillan (3), Bentley (5). LP—Wash.: Johnson (1, 5), Marberry (3); N.Y.: Bentley (2, 7), Barnes (4), Nehf (6).

1925—Pittsburgh N.L. 4 (Bill McKechnie); Washington A.L. 3 (Bucky Harris). WP—Pitts.: Aldridge (2, 5), Kremer (6, 7); Wash.: Johnson (1, 4), Ferguson (3). LP—Pitts.: Meadows (1), Kremer (3), Yde (4); Wash.: Coveleski (2, 5), Ferguson (6), Johnson (7).

1926—St. Louis N.L. 4 (Rogers Hornsby); New York A.L. 3 (Miller Huggins). WP—St. L.: Alexander (2, 6), Haines (3, 7); N.Y.: Pennock (1, 5), Hoyt (4). LP—St. L.: Sherdel (1, 5), Reinhart (4); N.Y.: Shocker (2), Ruether (3), Shawkey (6), Hoyt (7).

1927—New York A.L. 4 (Miller Huggins); Pittsburgh N.L. 0 (Donie Bush). WP—Hoyt (1), Pipgras (2), Pennock (3), Moore (4). LP—Kremer (1), Aldridge (2), Meadows (3), Miljus (4).

1928—New York A.L. 4 (Miller Huggins); St. Louis N.L. 0 (Bill McKechnie). WP—Hoyt (1, 4), Pipgras (2), Zachary (3). LP—Sherdel (1, 4), Alexander (2), Haines (3).

1929—Philadelphia A.L. 4 (Connie Mack); Chicago N.L. 1 (Joe McCarthy). WP—Phila.: Ehmke (1), Earnshaw (2), Rommel (4), Walberg (5); Chi.: Bush (3). LP—Phila.: Earnshaw (3) Chi.: Root (1), Malone (2, 5), Blake (4).

1930—Philadelphia A.L. 4 (Connie Mack); St. Louis N.L. 2 (Gabby Street). WP—Phila.: Grove (1, 5), Earnshaw (2, 6); St. L.: Hallahan (3), Haines (4). LP—Phila.: Walberg (3), Grove (4); St. L.: Grimes (1, 5), Rhem (2), Hallahan (6).

1931—St. Louis N.L. 4 (Gabby Street); Philadelphia A.L. 3 (Connie Mack). WP—St. L.: Hallahan (2, 5), Grimes (3, 7); Phila.: Grove (1, 6), Earnshaw (4). LP—St. L.: Derringer (1, 6), Johnson (4); Phila.: Earnshaw (2, 7), Grove (3), Hoyt (5).

1932—New York A.L. (Joe McCarthy); Chicago N.L. 0 (Charles Grimm). WP—Ruffing (1), Gomez (2), Pipgras (3), Moore (4). LP—Bush (1), Warneke (2), Root (3), May (4).

1933—New York N.L. 4 (Bill Terry); Washington A.L. 1 (Joe Cronin). WP—N.Y.: Hubbell (1, 4), Schumacher (2), Luque (5); Wash.: Whitehill (3). LP—N.Y.: Fitzsimmons (3); Wash.: Stewart (1), Crowder (2), Weaver (4), Russell (5).

1934—St. Louis N.L. 4 (Frank Frisch); Detroit A.L. 3 (Mickey Cochrane). WP—St. L.: J. Dean (1, 7), P. Dean (3, 6); Det.: Rowe (2), Auker (4), Bridges (5). LP—St. L.: W. Walker (2, 4), J. Dean (5); Det.: Crowder (1), Bridges (3), Rowe (6), Auker (7).

1935—Detroit A.L. 4 (Mickey Cochrane); Chicago N.L. 2 (Charles Grimm). WP—Det.: Bridges (2, 6), Rowe (3), Crowder (4); Chi.: Warneke (1, 5); LP—Det.: Rowe (1, 5), Chi.: Root (2), French (3, 6), Carleton (4).

1936—New York A.L. 4 (Joe McCarthy); New York N.L. 2 (Bill Terry). WP—N.Y. A.L.: Gomez (2, 6), Hadley (3), Pearson (4); N.Y. N.L.: Hubbell (1), Schumacher (5); LP—N.Y. A.L.: Ruffing (1), Malone (5); N.Y. N.L.: Schumacher (2), Fitzsimmons (3, 6), Hubbell (4).

1937—New York A.L. 4 (Joe McCarthy); New York N.L. 1 (Bill Terry). WP—N.Y. A.L.: Gomez (1, 5), Ruffing (2), Pearson (3); N.Y. N.L.: Hubbell (4). LP—N.Y. A.L.: Hadley (4); N.Y. N.L.: Hubbell (1), Melton (2, 5), Schumacher (3).

1938—New York A.L. 4 (Joe McCarthy); Chicago N.L. 0 (Gabby Hartnett). WP—Ruffing (1, 4), Gomez (2), Pearson (3) LP—Lee (1, 4), Dean (2), Bryant (3).

1939—New York A.L. 4 (Joe McCarthy); Cincinnati N.L. 0 (Bill McKechnie). WP—Ruffing (1), Pearson (2), Hadley (3), Murphy (4). LP—Derringer (1), Walters (2, 4), Thompson (3).

1940—Cincinnati N.L. 4 (Bill McKechnie); Detroit A.L. 3

(Del Baker). WP—Cin.: Walters (2, 6), Derringer (4, 7); Det.: Newsom (1, 5), Bridges (3). LP—Cin.: Derringer (1), Turner (3), Thompson (5); Det.: Rowe (2, 6), Trout (4), Newsom (7).

1941—New York A.L. 4 (Joe McCarthy); Brooklyn N.L. 1 (Leo Durocher). WP—N.Y.: Ruffing (1), Russo (3), Murphy (4), Bonham (5); Bklyn: Wyatt (2). LP—N.Y.: Chandler (2); Bklyn: Davis (1), Casey (3, 4), Wyatt (5).

1942—St. Louis N.L. 4 (Billy Southworth); New York A.L. 1 (Joe McCarthy). WP—St. L.: Beazley (2, 5), White (3), Lanier (4); N.Y.: Ruffing (1). LP—St. L.: Cooper (1); N.Y.: Bonham (2), Chandler (3), Donald (4), Ruffing (5).

1943—New York A.L. 4 (Joe McCarthy); St. Louis N.L. 1 (Billy Southworth). WP—N.Y.: Chandler (1, 5), Borowy (3), Russo (4); St. L.: Cooper (2). LP—N.Y.: Bonham (2); St. L.: Lanier (1), Brazle (3), Brecheen (4), Cooper (5).

1944—St. Louis N.L. 4 (Billy Southworth); St. Louis A.L. 2 (Luke Sewell). WP—St. L. N.L.: Donnelly (2), Brecheen (4), Cooper (5), Lanier (6); St. L. A.L.: Galehouse (1), Kramer (3). LP—St. L. N.L.: Cooper (1), Wilks (3); St. L. A.L.: Muncrief (2), Jakucki (4), Galehouse (5), Potter (6).

1945—Detroit A.L. 4 (Steve O'Neill); Chicago N.L. 3 (Charles Grimm). WP—Det.: Trucks (2), Trout (4), Newhouser (5, 7); Chi.: Borowy (1, 6), Passeau (3). LP—Det.: Newhouser (1), Overmire (3), Trout (6); Chi.: Wyse (2), Prim (4), Borowy (5, 7).

1946—St. Louis N.L. 4 (Eddie Dyer); Boston A.L. 3 (Joe Cronin). WP—St. L.: Brecheen (2, 6, 7), Munger (4); Bos.: Johnson (1), Ferriss (3), Dobson (5). LP—St. L.: Pollet (1), Dickson (3), Brazle (5); Bos.: Harris (2, 6), Hughson (4), Klinger (7).

1947—New York A.L. 4 (Bucky Harris); Brooklyn N.L. 3 (Burt Shotton). WP—N.Y.: Shea (1, 5), Reynolds (2), Page (7); Bklyn.: Casey (3, 4), Branca (6). LP—N.Y.: Newsom (3), Bevens (4), Page (6); Bklyn.: Branca (1), Lombardi (2), Barney (5), Gregg (7).

1948—Cleveland A.L. 4 (Lou Boudreau); Boston N.L. 2 (Billy Southworth). WP—Cleve.: Lemon (2, 6), Bearden (3), Gromek (4); Bos.: Sain (1), Spahn (5). LP—Cleve.: Feller (1, 5); Bos.: Spahn (2), Bickford (3), Sain (4), Voiselle (6).

1949—New York A.L. 4 (Casey Stengel); Brooklyn N.L. 1 (Burt Shotton). WP—N.Y.: Reynolds (1), Page (3), Lopat (4), Raschi (5); Bklyn.: Roe (2). LP—N.Y.: Raschi (2); Bklyn.: Newcombe (1, 4), Branca (3), Barney (5).

1950—New York A.L. 4 (Casey Stengel); Philadelphia N.L. 0 (Eddie Sawyer). WP—Raschi (1), Reynolds (2), Ferrick (3), Ford (4). LP—Konstanty (1), Roberts (2), Meyer (3), Miller (4).

1951—New York A.L. 4 (Casey Stengel); New York N.L. 2 (Leo Durocher). WP—N.Y. A.L.: Lopat (2, 5), Reynolds (4), Raschi (6); N.Y. N.L.: Koslo (1), Hearn (3). LP—N.Y. A.L.: Reynolds (1), Raschi (3); N.Y. N.L.: Jansen (2, 5), Maglie (4), Koslo (6).

1952—New York A.L. 4 (Casey Stengel); Brooklyn N.L. 3 (Chuck Dressen). WP—N.Y.: Raschi (2, 6), Reynolds (4, 7); Bklyn.: Black (1), Roe (3), Erskine (5). LP—N.Y.: Reynolds (1), Lopat (3), Sain (5); Bklyn.: Erskine (2), Black (4), Loes (6).

1953—New York A.L. 4 (Casey Stengel); Brooklyn N.L. 2 (Chuck Dressen). WP—N.Y.: Sain (1), Lopat (2), McDonald (5), Reynolds (6); Bklyn.: Erskine (3), Loes (4). LP—N.Y.: Raschi (3), Ford (4); Bklyn.: Labine (1, 6), Roe (2), Podres (5).

1954—New York N.L. 4 (Leo Durocher); Cleveland A.L. 0 (Al Lopez). WP—Grissom (1), Antonelli (2), Gomez (3), Liddle (4). LP—Lemon (1, 4), Wynn (2), Garcia (3).

1955—Brooklyn N.L. 4 (Walter Alston); New York A.L. 3 (Casey Stengel). WP—Bklyn.: Podres (3, 7), Labine (4), Craig (5); N.Y.: Ford (1, 6), Byrne (2). LP—Bklyn.: Newcombe (1), Loes (2), Spooner (6); N.Y.: Turley (3), Larsen (4), Grim (5), Byrne (7).

1956—New York A.L. 4 (Casey Stengel); Brooklyn N.L. 3 (Walter Alston). WP—N.Y.: Ford (3), Sturdivant (4), Larsen (5), Kucks (7); Bklyn.: Maglie (1), Bessent (2), Labine (6). LP—N.Y.: Ford (1), Morgan (2), Turley (6); Bklyn.: Craig (3), Erskine (4), Maglie (5), Newcombe (7).

1957—Milwaukee N.L. 4 (Fred Haney); New York A.L. 3 (Casey Stengel). WP—Mil.: Burdette (2, 5, 7), Spahn (4); N.Y.: Ford (1), Larsen (3), Turley (6). LP—Mil.: Spahn (1), Buhl (3), Johnson (6); N.Y.: Shantz (2), Grim (4), Ford (5), Larsen (7).

1958—New York A.L. 4 (Casey Stengel); Milwaukee N.L. 3 (Fred Haney). WP—N.Y.: Larsen (3), Turley (5, 7), Duren (6); Mil.: Spahn (1, 4), Burdette (2). LP—N.Y.: Duren (1), Turley (2), Ford (4); Mil.: Rush (3), Burdette (5, 7), Spahn (6).

1959—Los Angeles N.L. 4 (Walter Alston); Chicago A.L. 2 (Al Lopez). WP—L.A.: Podres (2), Drysdale (3), Sherry (4, 6); Chi.: Wynn (1), Shaw (5). LP—L.A.: Craig (1), Koufax (5); Chi.: Shaw (2), Donovan (3), Staley (4), Wynn (6).

1960—Pittsburgh N.L. 4 (Danny Murtaugh); New York A.L. 3 (Casey Stengel). WP—Pitts.: Law (1, 4), Haddix (5, 7); N.Y.: Turley (2), Ford (3, 6). LP—Pitts.: Friend (2, 6), Mizell (3); N.Y.: Ditmar (1, 5), Terry (4, 7).

1961—New York A.L. 4 (Ralph Houk); Cincinnati N.L. 1 (Fred Hutchinson). WP—N.Y.: Ford (1, 4), Arroyo (3), Daley (5); Cin.: Jay (2). LP—N.Y.: Terry (2); Cin.: O'Toole (1, 4), Purkey (3), Jay (5).

1962—New York A.L. 4 (Ralph Houk); San Francisco N.L. 3 (Al Dark). WP—N.Y.: Ford (1), Stafford (3), Terry (5, 7); S.F. Sanford (2), Larsen (4), Pierce (6). LP—N.Y.: Terry (2), Coates (4), Ford (6); S.F.: O'Dell (1), Pierce (3), Sanford (5, 7).

1963—Los Angeles N.L. 4 (Walter Alston); New York A.L. 0 (Ralph Houk). WP—Koufax (1, 4), Podres (2), Drysdale (3). LP—Ford (1, 4), Downing (2), Bouton (3).

1964—St. Louis N.L. 4 (Johnny Keane); New York A.L. 3 (Yogi Berra). WP—St. L.: Sadecki (1), Craig (4), Gibson (5, 7); N.Y.: Stottlemyre (2), Bouton (3, 6). LP—St. L.: Gibson (2), Schultz (3), Simmons (6); N.Y.: Ford (1), Downing (4), Mikkelsen (5), Stottlemyre (7).

1965—Los Angeles N.L. 4 (Walter Alston); Minnesota A.L. 3 (Sam Mele). WP—L.A.: Osteen (3), Drysdale (4), Koufax (5, 7); Minn.: Grant (1, 6), Kaat (2). LP—L.A.: Drysdale (1), Koufax (2), Osteen (6); Minn.: Pascual (3), Grant (4), Kaat (5, 7).

1966—Baltimore A.L. 4 (Hank Bauer); Los Angeles N.L. 0 (Walter Alston). WP—Drabowsky (1), Palmer (2), Bunker (3), McNally (4). LP—Drysdale (1, 4), Koufax (2), Osteen (3).

1967—St. Louis N.L. 4 (Red Schoendienst); Boston A.L. 3 (Dick Williams). WP—St. L.: Gibson (1, 4, 7), Briles (5); Bos.: Lonborg (2, 5), Wyatt (6). LP—St. L.: Hughes (2), Carlton (5), Lamabe (6); Bos.: Santiago (1, 4), Bell (3), Lonborg (7).

1968—Detroit A.L. 4 (Mayo Smith); St. Louis N.L. 3 (Red Schoendienst). WP—Det.: Lolich (2, 5, 7), McLain (6); St. L.: Gibson (1, 4), Washburn (3). LP—Det.: McLain (1, 4), Wilson (3); St. L.: Briles (2), Hoerner (5), Washburn (6), Gibson (7).

1969—New York N.L. 4 (Gil Hodges); Baltimore A.L. 1 (Earl Weaver). WP—N.Y.: Koosman (2, 5), Gentry (3), Seaver (4); Balt.: Cuellar (1). LP—N.Y.: Seaver (1); Balt.: McNally (2), Palmer (3), Hall (4), Watt (5).

1970—Baltimore A.L. 4 (Earl Weaver); Cincinnati N.L. 1 (Sparky Anderson) 1. WP—Balt.: Palmer (1), Phoebus (2), McNally (3), Cuellar (5); Cin.: Carroll (4). LP—Cin.: Nolan (1), Wilcox (2), Cloninger (3), Merritt (5); Balt.: Watt (4).

1971—Pittsburgh N.L. 4 (Danny Murtaugh); Baltimore A.L. 3 (Earl Weaver). WP—Pitts.: Blass (3, 7), Kison (4), Briles (5); Balt.: McNally (1, 6), Palmer (2). LP—Pitts.: Ellis (1), R. Johnson (2), Miller (6); Balt.: Cuellar (3, 7), Watt (4) McNally (5).

1972—Oakland A.L. 4 (Dick Williams); Cincinnati N.L. (Sparky Anderson) 3. WP—Oakland: Holtzman (2, 7), Hunter (2, 7), Fingers (4); Cincinnati: Billingham (3), Grimsley (5, 6). LP—Oakland: Odom (3), Fingers (5), Blue (6); Cincinnati: Nolan (1), Grimsley (2), Carroll (4), Borbon (7).

1973—Oakland A.L. 4 (Dick Williams); New York N.L. 3 (Yogi Berra). WP—Oakland: Holtzman (1, 7), Lindblad (3), Hunter (6). New York: McGraw (2), Matlack (4), Koosman (5). LP—Oakland: Fingers (2), Holtzman (4), Blue (5). New York: Matlack (1, 7) Parker (3), Seaver (6).

1974—Oakland A.L. 4 (Al Dark); Los Angeles N.L. 1 (Walter Alston). WP—Oakland: Fingers (1), Hunter (3), Holtzman (4), Odom (5). Los Angeles: Sutton (2). LP—Oakland: Blue (2), Los Angeles: Messersmith (1, 4), Downing (3), Marshall (5).

1975—Cincinnati N.L. 4 (Sparky Anderson); Boston A.L. 3 (Darrell Johnson). WP—Cincinnati: Eastwick (2, 3), Gullett (5), Carroll (7); Boston: Tiant (1, 4), Wise (6). LP—Cincinnati: Gullett (1), Norman (4), Darcy (6); Boston: Drago (2), Willoughby (3), Cleveland (5), Burton (7).

1976—Cincinnati N.L. 4 (Sparky Anderson); New York A.L. 0 (Billy Martin). WP—Gullett (1), Billingham (2), Zachry (3), Nolan (4). LP—Alexander (1), Hunter (2), Ellis (3), Figueroa (4).

1977—New York A.L. 4 (Billy Martin); Los Angeles N.L. 2

(Tom Lasorda). WP—New York: Lyle (1), Torrez (3, 6), Guidry (4); Los Angeles: Hooton (2), Sutton (5). LP—New York: Hunter (2), Gullett (5); Los Angeles: Rhoden (1), John (3), Rau (4), Hooton (6).

1978—New York A.L. 4 (Bob Lemon), Los Angeles N.L. 2 (Tom Lasorda); WP—New York: Guidry (3), Gossage (4); Beattie (5), Hunter (6); Los Angeles: John (1), Hooton (2). LP—New York: Figueroa (1), Hunter (2); Los Angeles: Sutton (3, 6), Welch (4), Hooton (5).

1979—Pittsburgh N.L. 4 (Chuck Tanner), Baltimore A.L. 3 (Earl Weaver); WP—Pittsburgh: D. Robinson (2), Blyleven (5), Candelaria (6), Jackson (7); Baltimore: Flanagan (1), McGregor (3), Stoddard (4). LP—Pittsburgh: Kison (1), Candelaria (3), Tekulve (4); Baltimore: Stanhouse (2), Flanagan (5), Palmer (6), McGregor (7).

1980—Philadelphia N.L. 4 (Dallas Green), Kansas City A.L. 2 (Jim Frey); WP—Philadelphia: Walk (1), Carlton (2), McGraw (5), Carlton (6); Kansas City: Quisenberry (3). LP—Philadelphia: McGraw (3), Christenson (4); Kansas City: Leonard (1), Quisenberry (2), Quisenberry (5), Gale (6).

1981—Los Angeles N.L. 4 (Tom Lasorda), New York A.L. 2 (Bob Lemon); WP—Los Angeles: Valenzuela (3), Howe (4), Reuss (5), Hooton (6); New York: Guidry (1), John (2). LP—Los Angeles: Reuss (1), Hooton (2); New York: Frazier (3), Frazier (4), Guidry (5), Frazier (6).

1982—St. Louis N.L. 4 (Whitey Herzog), Milwaukee A.L. 3 (Harvey Kuenn); WP—St. Louis: Sutter (2), Andujar (3), Stuper (6), Andujar (7). Milwaukee: Caldwell (1), Slaton (4), Caldwell (5). LP—St. Louis: Forsch (1), Bair (4), Forsch (5). Milwaukee: McClure (2), Vuckovich (3), Sutton (6), McClure (7).

1983—Baltimore A.L. 4 (Joe Altobelli), Philadelphia N.L. 1 (Paul Owens); WP—Baltimore: Boddicker (2), Palmer (3), Davis (4), McGregor (5). Philadelphia: Denny (1).

1984—Detroit A.L. 4 (Sparky Anderson), San Diego N.L. 1 (Dick Williams); WP—Det.: Morris (1,4), Wilcox (3), Lopez (5); San Diego: Hawkins (2). LP—Det.: Petry (2), San Diego: Thurmond (1), Lollar (4), Show (4), Hawkins (5).

1985—Kansas City A.L. 4 (Dick Howser), St. Louis N.L. 3 (Whitey Herzog); WP—KC: Saberhagen (3,7) Quisenberry (6), Jackson

(5). St. Louis: Tudor (1,4) Dayley (2). LP—KC: Jackson (1), Leibrandt (2), Black (4); St. Louis: Andujar (3), Forsch (5), Worrell (6), Tudor (7).

1986—New York N.L. 4 (Dave Johnson); Boston A.L. (John McNamara) 3 WP—N.Y.—Ojeda (3), Darling (4), Aguilera (6), McDowell (7), Bos: Hurst (1), (5), Crawford (3). LP—N.Y. Darling (1), Gooden (2, 5).

1987—Minnesota, A.L. 4 (Tom Kelly); St. Louis N.L. (Whitey Herzog) 3. WP—Minn. Viola (1, 7), Blyleven (2), Schatzeder (6), St. Louis: Tudor (3), Forsch (4), Cox (5). LP—Minn. Berenguer (3), Viola (4), Blyleven (5); St. Louis: Magrane (1), Cox (2, 7), Tudor (6).

1988—Los Angeles N.L. 4 (Tommy Lasorda); Oakland A.L. (Tony LaRussa) 1. WP—Los Angeles: Hershiser (2, 5), Pena (1), Belcher (4); Oakland: Honeycutt (3). LP—Los Angeles: Howell (3); Oakland: Davis (2), Eckersley (1), Stewart (4).

1989—Oakland, A.L. 4 (Tony LaRussa); San Francisco N.L. 0 (Roger Craig). WP—Oakland: Stewart (1, 4), Mike Moore (2, 4). LP—San Francisco: Scott Garrelts (1, 3), Don Robinson (4), Rick Reuschel (2).

1990—Cincinnati N.L. 4 (Lou Piniella); Oakland A.L. 0 (Tony LaRussa). WP—Cincinnati: Jose Rijo (1, 4), Rob Dibble (2), Tom Browning (3). LP—Oakland: Dave Stewart (1, 4), Dennis Eckersley (2), Mike Moore (3).

1991—Minnesota, A.L. 4 (Tom Kelly); Atlanta, N.L. 3 (Bobby Cox). WP—Minnesota: Morris (1,7), Tapani (2), Aguilera (6). Atlanta: Clancy (3), Stanton (4), Glavine (5). LP—Minnesota: Aguilera (3), Guthrie (4), Tapani (5). Atlanta: Leibrandt (1, 6), Glavine (2), Pena (7).

1992—Toronto, A.L. 4 (Cito Gaston), Atlanta, N.L. 2 (Bobby Cox); WP—Toronto: Ward (2, 3), Key (4, 6). Atlanta: Glavine (1), Smoltz (5). LP—Toronto: Morris (1, 5). Atlanta: Leibrandt (6), Reardon (2), Avery (3), Glavine (4).

1993—Toronto, A.L. 4 (Cito Gaston), Philadelphia, N.L. 2 (Jim Fregosi); WP—Toronto: Leiter (1), Hentgen (3), Castillo (4), Ward (6). Philadelphia: Mulholland (2), Schilling (5). LP—Toronto: Stewart (2), Guzman (5). Philadelphia: Schilling (1), Jackson (3), Williams (4,6).

1994—World Series cancelled due to players' strike.

Before the World Series

Source: Information Please Sports Almanac

The NL–American Assn. Series, 1882–90

When the National League met the American League for the first time in the 1903 World Series, it was not the N.L.'s first venture into post–season play.

From 1882–90, the N.L. pennant winner engaged in a championship series with the champion of the American Association. The Nationals won four of the eight series, lost once, and tied three times.

Year	Champion	Loser	Series	Year	Champion	Loser	Series
1882	Chicago (NL) &			1886	St. Louis (AA)	Chicago (NL)	4–2
	Cincinnati (AA)	—	1–1	1887	Detroit (NL)	St. Louis (AA)	10–5
1883	No series			1888	New York (NL)	St. Louis (AA)	6–4
1884	Providence (NL)	New York (AA)	3–0	1889	New York (NL)	Brooklyn (AA)	6–3
1885	Chicago (NL) &			1890	Brooklyn (NL) &		
	St. Louis (AA)	—	3–3–1		Louisville (AA)	—	3–3–1

Early NL and AL Pennant Winners

The National League had been around 27 years before the 1903 World Series. The AL, however, was only in its third season when the two leagues met. The following lists account for the pennant winners in those pre–World Series years and in 1904 when the NL champion New York Giants refused to play Boston.

NL Pennant Winners, 1876–1902, '04

Year	Winner	Manager	Year	Winner	Manager	Year	Winner	Manager
1876	Chicago	Al Spalding	1885	Chicago	Cap Anson	1895	Baltimore	Ned Hanlon
1877	Boston	Harry Wright	1886	Chicago	Cap Anson	1896	Baltimore	Ned Hanlon
1878	Boston	Harry Wright	1887	Detroit	Bill Watkins	1897	Boston	Frank Selee
1879	Providence	George Wright	1888	New York	Jim Mutrie	1898	Boston	Frank Selee
1880	Chicago	Cap Anson	1889	New York	Jim Mutrie	1899	Brooklyn	Ned Hanlon
1881	Chicago	Cap Anson	1890	Brooklyn	Bill McGunnigle	1900	Brooklyn	Ned Hanlon
1882	Chicago	Cap Anson	1891	Boston	Frank Selee	1901	Pittsburgh	Fred Clarke
1883	Boston	John Morrill	1892	Boston	Frank Selee	1902	Pittsburgh	Fred Clarke
1884	Providence	Frank Bancroft	1893	Boston	Frank Selee	1904	New York	John McGraw
			1894	Baltimore	Ned Hanlon			

AL Pennant Winners, 1901–02, '04

Year	Winner	Manager	Year	Winner	Manager	Year	Winner	Manager
1901	Chicago	Clark Griffith	1902	Philadelphia	Connie Mack	1904	Boston	Jimmy Collins

WORLD SERIES CLUB STANDING
(Through 1994)

	Series	Won	Lost	Pct.		Series	Won	Lost	Pct.
Toronto (A)	2	2	0	1.000	Detroit (A)	9	4	5	.444
Pittsburgh (N)	7	5	2	.714	New York (N–Giants)	14	5	9	.357
New York (A)	33	22	11	.667	Washington (A)	3	1	2	.333
Oakland (A)	6	4	2	.667	Philadelphia (N)	5	1	4	.200
Cleveland (A)	3	2	1	.667	Chicago (N)	10	2	8	.200
Minnesota (A)	3	2	1	.667	Brooklyn (N)	9	1	8	.111
New York (N–Mets)	3	2	1	.667	St. Louis (A)	1	0	1	.000
Philadelphia (A)	8	5	3	.625	San Francisco (N)	2	0	2	.000
St. Louis (N)	15	9	6	.600	Milwaukee (A)	1	0	1	.000
Boston (A)	9	5	4	.550	San Diego (N)	1	0	1	.000
Los Angeles (N)	9	5	4	.550	Atlanta (N)	2	0	2	.000
Cincinnati (N)	9	5	4	.550					
Milwaukee (N)	2	1	1	.500	**Recapitulation**				
Boston (N)	2	1	1	.500					
Chicago (A)	4	2	2	.500					Won
Baltimore (A)	6	3	3	.500	American League				52
Kansas City (A)	2	1	1	.500	National League				36

LIFETIME WORLD SERIES RECORDS
(Through 1994)

Most hits—71, Yogi Berra, New York A.L., 1947, 1949–53, 1955–58, 1960–63.

Most runs—42, Mickey Mantle, New York A.L., 1951–53, 1955–58, 1960–64.

Most runs batted in—40, Mickey Mantle, New York A.L., 1951–53, 1955–58, 1960–64.

Most home runs—18, Mickey Mantle, New York A.L., 1951–53, 1955–58, 1960–64.

Most bases on balls—43, Mickey Mantle, New York A.L., 1951–53, 1955–58, 1960–64.

Most strikeouts—54, Mickey Mantle, New York A.L., 1951–53, 1955–58, 1960–64.

Most stolen bases—14, Eddie Collins, Philadelphia A.L. 1910–11, 13–14; Chicago A.L., 1917, 1919. Lou Brock, St. Louis N.L., 1964, 67–68.

Most victories, pitcher—10, Whitey Ford, New York A.L., 1950, 1953, 1955–58, 1960–64.

Most times member of winning team—10, Yogi Berra, New York A.L., 1947, 1949–53, 1956, 1958, 1961–62.

Most victories, no defeats—6, Vernon Gomez, New York A.L., 1932, 1936(2), 1937(2), 1938.

Most shutouts—4, Christy Mathewson, New York N.L., 1905 (3), 1913.

Most innings pitched—146, Whitey Ford, New York A.L., 1950, 1953, 1955–58, 1960–64.

Most consecutive scoreless innings—33 2/3, Whitey Ford, New York A.L., 1960 (18), 1961 (14), 1962 (1 2/3).

Most strikeouts by pitcher—94, Whitey Ford, New York A.L., 1950, 1953, 1955–58, 1960–64.

SINGLE GAME AND SINGLE SERIES RECORDS
(Through 1994)

Most hits game—5, Paul Molitor, Milwaukee A.L., first game vs. St. Louis, N.L., 1982.

Most 4-hit games, series—2, Robin Yount, Milwaukee A.L., first and fifth games vs. St. Louis N.L., 1982.

Most hits inning—2, held by many players.

Most hits series—13 (7 games) Bobby Richardson, New York A.L., 1964; Lou Brock, St. Louis N.L., 1968; 12 (6 games) Billy Martin, New York A.L., 1953; 12 (8 games) Buck Herzog, New York N.L., 1912; Joe Jackson, Chicago A.L., 1919; 10 (4 games) Babe Ruth, New York A.L., 1928; 9 (5 games) held by 8 players.

Most home runs, series—5 (6 games) Reggie Jackson, New York A.L., 1977; 4 (7 games) Babe Ruth, New York A.L., 1926; Duke Snider, Brooklyn N.L., 1952, 1955; Hank Bauer, New York A.L., 1958; Gene Tenace, Oakland A.L., 1972; 4 (4 games) Lou Gehrig, New York A.L., 1928; 3 (6 games) Babe Ruth, New York A.L., 1923; Ted Kluszewski, Chicago A.L., 1959; 3 (5 games) Donn Clendenon, New York Mets N.L., 1969.

Most home runs, game—3, Babe Ruth, New York A.L., 1926 and 1928; Reggie Jackson, New York A.L., 1977.

Most strikeouts, series—12 (6 games) Willie Wilson, Kansas City A.L., 1980; 11 (7 games) Ed Mathews, Milwaukee N.L., 1958; Wayne Garrett, New York N.L., 1973: 10 (8 games) George Kelly, New York N.L., 1921; 9 (6 games) Jim Bottomley, St. Louis N.L., 1930; 9 (5 games) Carmelo Martinez, San

Diego, N.L., 1984; Duke Snider, Brooklyn N.L., 1949; 7 (4 games) Bob Muesel, New York A.L., 1927.

Most stolen bases, game—3, Honus Wagner, Pittsburgh N.L., 1909; Willie Davis, Los Angeles N.L., 1965; Lou Brock, St. Louis N.L., 1967 and 1968.

Most strikeouts by pitcher, game—17, Bob Gibson, St. Louis N.L. 1968.

Most strikeouts by pitcher in succession—6, Horace Eller, Cincinnati N.L., 1919; Moe Drabowsky, Baltimore N.L., 1966.

Most strikeouts by pitcher, series—35 (7 games) Bob Gibson, St. Louis N.L., 1968; 28 (8 games) Bill Dinneen, Boston A.L., 1903; 23 (4 games) Sandy Koufax, Los Angeles N.L., 1963; 20 (6 games) Chief Bender, Philadelphia A.L., 1911; 18 (5 games) Christy Mathewson, New York N.L., 1905.

Most bases on balls, series—11 (7 games) Babe Ruth, New York A.L., 1926; Gene Tenace, Oakland A.L., 1973; 9 (6 games) Willie Randolph, New York A.L., 1981; 7 (5 games) James Sheckard, Chicago N.L., 1910; Mickey Cochrane, Philadelphia A.L., 1929; Joe Gordon, New York A.L., 1941; 7 (4 games) Hank Thompson, New York N.L., 1954.

Most consecutive scoreless innings one series—27, Christy Mathewson, New York N.L., 1905.

AMERICAN LEAGUE HOME RUN CHAMPIONS

Year	Player, team	No.	Year	Player, team	No.	Year	Player, team	No.
1901	Nap Lajoie, Phila.	13	1935	Jimmy Foxx, Phila., and		1968	Frank Howard, Wash.	44
1902	Ralph Seybold, Phila.	16		Hank Greenberg, Det.	36	1969	Harmon Killebrew, Minn.	49
1903	Buck Freeman, Bost.	13	1936	Lou Gehrig, N.Y.	49	1970	Frank Howard, Wash.	44
1904	Harry Davis, Phila.	10	1937	Joe DiMaggio, N.Y.	46	1971	Bill Melton, Chicago	33
1905	Harry Davis, Phila.	8	1938	Hank Greenberg, Det.	58	1972	Dick Allen, Chicago	37
1906	Harry Davis, Phila.	12	1939	Jimmy Foxx, Bost.	35	1973	Reggie Jackson, Oak.	32
1907	Harry Davis, Phila.	8	1940	Hank Greenberg, Det.	41	1974	Dick Allen, Chicago	32
1908	Sam Crawford, Det.	7	1941	Ted Williams, Bost.	37	1975	Reggie Jackson, Oak., and	
1909	Ty Cobb, Det.	9	1942	Ted Williams, Bost.	36		George Scott, Mil.	36
1910	J. Garland Stahl, Bost.	10	1943	Rudy York, Det.	34	1976	Graig Nettles, N.Y.	32
1911	Franklin Baker, Phila.	9	1944	Nick Etten, N.Y.	22	1977	Jim Rice, Boston	39
1912	Franklin Baker, Phila.	10	1945	Vern Stephens, St. L.	24	1978	Jim Rice, Boston	46
1913	Franklin Baker, Phila.	12	1946	Hank Greenberg, Det.	44	1979	Gorman Thomas, Milwaukee	45
1914	Franklin Baker, Phila., and		1947	Ted Williams, Bost.	32	1980	Reggie Jackson, N.Y., and	
	Sam Crawford, Det.	8	1948	Joe DiMaggio, N.Y.	39		Ben Oglivie, Mil.	41
1915	Robert Roth, Chi.–Cleve.	7	1949	Ted Williams, Bost.	43	1981*	Tony Armas, Oak., Dwight	
1916	Wally Pipp, N.Y.	12	1950	Al Rosen, Cleve.	37		Evans, Bost., Bobby Grich,	
1917	Wally Pipp, N.Y.	9	1951	Gus Zernial, Chi.–Phila.	33		Calif., and Eddie	
1918	Babe Ruth, Bost., and		1952	Larry Doby, Cleve.	32		Murray, Balt. (tie)	22
	Clarence Walker, Phila.	11	1953	Al Rosen, Cleve.	43	1982	Gorman Thomas, Mil., and	
1919	Babe Ruth, Bost.	29	1954	Larry Doby, Cleve.	32		Reggie Jackson, Calif.	39
1920	Babe Ruth, N.Y.	54	1955	Mickey Mantle, N.Y.	37	1983	Jim Rice, Boston	39
1921	Babe Ruth, N.Y.	59	1956	Mickey Mantle, N.Y.	52	1984	Tony Armas, Boston	43
1922	Ken Williams, St. L.	39	1957	Roy Sievers, Wash.	42	1985	Darrell Evans, Detroit	40
1923	Babe Ruth, N.Y.	41	1958	Mickey Mantle, N.Y.	42	1986	Jesse Barfield, Toronto	40
1924	Babe Ruth, N.Y.	46	1959	Rocky Colavito, Cleve., and		1987	Mark McGwire, Oakland	49
1925	Bob Meusel, N.Y.	33		Harmon Killebrew, Wash.	42	1988	Jose Canseco, Oakland	42
1926	Babe Ruth, N.Y.	47	1960	Mickey Mantle, N.Y.	40	1989	Fred McGriff, Toronto	36
1927	Babe Ruth, N.Y.	60	1961	Roger Maris, N.Y.	61	1990	Cecil Fielder, Detroit	51
1928	Babe Ruth, N.Y.	54	1962	Harmon Killebrew, Minn.	48	1991	Jose Canseco, Oakland	
1929	Babe Ruth, N.Y.	46	1963	Harmon Killebrew, Minn.	45		Cecil Fielder, Detroit (tie)	44
1930	Babe Ruth, N.Y.	49	1964	Harmon Killebrew, Minn.	49	1992	Juan Gonzalez, Texas	43
1931	Lou Gehrig, N.Y., and		1965	Tony Conigliaro, Bost.	32	1993	Juan Gonzalez, Texas	46
	Babe Ruth, N.Y.	46	1966	Frank Robinson, Balt.	49	1994[1]	Ken Griffey, Jr., Seattle	40
1932	Jimmy Foxx, Phila.	58	1967	Carl Yastrzemski, Bost., and		1995	Albert Belle, Cleveland	50
933	Jimmy Foxx, Phila.	48		Harmon Killebrew, Minn.	44			
1934	Lou Gehrig, N.Y.	49						

AMERICAN LEAGUE BATTING CHAMPIONS

Year	Player, team	Avg	Year	Player, team	Avg	Year	Player, team	Avg
1901	Nap Lajoie, Phila.	.422	1927	Harry Heilmann, Det.	.398	1953	Mickey Vernon, Wash.	.337
1902	Ed Delahanty, Wash.	.376	1928	Goose Goslin, Wash.	.379	1954	Bobby Avila, Cleve.	.341
1903	Nap Lajoie, Cleve.	.355	1929	Lew Fonseca, Cleve.	.369	1955	Al Kaline, Det.	.340
1904	Nap Lajoie, Cleve.	.381	1930	Al Simmons, Phila.	.381	1956	Mickey Mantle, N.Y.	.353
1905	Elmer Flick, Cleve.	.306	1931	Al Simmons, Phila.	.390	1957	Ted Williams, Bost.	.388
1906	George Stone, St. L.	.358	1932	Dale Alexander, Det.–Bost.	.367	1958	Ted Williams, Bost.	.328
1907	Ty Cobb, Det.	.350	1933	Jimmy Foxx, Phila.	.356	1959	Harvey Kuenn, Det.	.353
1908	Ty Cobb, Det.	.324	1934	Lou Gehrig, N.Y.	.363	1960	Pete Runnels, Bost.	.320
1909	Ty Cobb, Det.	.377	1935	Buddy Myer, Wash.	.349	1961	Norman Cash, Det.	.361
1910	Ty Cobb, Det.	.385	1936	Luke Appling, Chi.	.388	1962	Pete Runnels, Bost.	.326
1911	Ty Cobb, Det.	.420	1937	Charley Gehringer, Det.	.371	1963	Carl Yastrzemski, Bost.	.321
1912	Ty Cobb, Det.	.410	1938	Jimmy Foxx, Bost.	.349	1964	Tony Oliva, Minn.	.323
1913	Ty Cobb, Det.	.390	1939	Joe DiMaggio, N.Y.	.381	1965	Tony Oliva, Minn.	.321
1914	Ty Cobb, Det.	.368	1940	Joe DiMaggio, N.Y.	.352	1966	Frank Robinson, Balt.	.316
1915	Ty Cobb, Det.	.369	1941	Ted Williams, Bost.	.406	1967	Carl Yastrzemski, Bost.	.326
1916	Tris Speaker, Cleve.	.386	1942	Ted Williams, Bost.	.356	1968	Carl Yastrzemski, Bost.	.301
1917	Ty Cobb, Det.	.383	1943	Luke Appling, Chi.	.328	1969	Rod Carew, Minn.	.332
1918	Ty Cobb, Det.	.382	1944	Lou Boudreau, Cleve.	.327	1970	Alex Johnson, Calif.	.329
1919	Ty Cobb, Det.	.384	1945	George Sternweiss, N.Y.	.309	1971	Tony Oliva, Minn.	.337
1920	George Sisler, St. L.	.407	1946	Mickey Vernon, Wash.	.353	1972	Rod Carew, Minn.	.318
1921	Harry Heilmann, Det.	.394	1947	Ted Williams, Bost.	.343	1973	Rod Carew, Minn.	.350
1922	George Sisler, St. L.	.420	1948	Ted Williams, Bost.	.369	1974	Rod Carew, Minn.	.364
1923	Harry Heilmann, Det.	.403	1949	George Kell, Det.	.343	1975	Rod Carew, Minn.	.359
1924	Babe Ruth, N.Y.	.378	1950	Billy Goodman, Bost.	.354	1976	George Brett, Kansas City	.333
1925	Harry Heilmann, Det.	.393	1951	Ferris Fain, Phila.	.344	1977	Rod Carew, Minn.	.388
1926	Heinie Manush, Det.	.378	1952	Ferris Fain, Phila.	.327			

*Split season because of player strike. 1. Season ended on August 12 because of a player's strike.

Year	Player, team	Avg	Year	Player, team	Avg	Year	Player, team	Avg
1978	Rod Carew, Minn.	.333	1984	Don Mattingly, New York	.343	1990	George Brett, Kansas City	.328
1979	Fred Lynn, Boston	.333	1985	Wade Boggs, Boston	.368	1991	Julio Franco, Texas	.341
1980	George Brett, Kansas City	.390	1986	Wade Boggs, Boston	.357	1992	Edgar Martinez, Seattle	.343
1981*	Carney Lansford, Bost.	.336	1987	Wade Boggs, Boston	.363	1993	John Olerud, Toronto	.363
1982	Willie Wilson, Kansas City	.332	1988	Wade Boggs, Boston	.366	1994[1]	Paul O'Neill, New York	.359
1983	Wade Boggs, Boston	.361	1989	Kirby Puckett, Minnesota	.339	1995	Edgar Martinez, Seattle	.356

NATIONAL LEAGUE HOME RUN CHAMPIONS

Year	Player, team	No.	Year	Player, team	No.	Year	Player, team	No.
1876	George Hall, Phila. Athletics	5	1916	Davis Robertson, N.Y., and Fred Williams, Chi.	12		Hank Sauer, Chi.	37
1877	George Shaffer, Louisville	3	1917	Davis Robertson, N.Y., and Cliff Cravath, Phila.	12	1953	Ed Mathews, Mil.	47
1878	Paul Hines, Providence	4	1918	Cliff Cravath, Phila.	8	1954	Ted Kluszewski, Cin.	49
1879	Charles Jones, Bost.	9	1919	Cliff Cravath, Phila.	12	1955	Willie Mays, N.Y.	51
1880	James O'Rourke, Bost., and Harry Stovey, Worcester	6	1920	Cy Williams, Phila.	15	1956	Duke Snider, Bklyn.	43
1881	Dan Brouthers, Buffalo	8	1921	George Kelly, N.Y.	23	1957	Henry Aaron, Mil.	44
1882	George Wood, Det.	7	1922	Rogers Hornsby, St. L.	42	1958	Ernie Banks, Chi.	47
1883	William Ewing, N.Y.	10	1923	Cy Williams, Phila.	41	1959	Ed Mathews, Mil.	46
1884	Ed Williamson, Chi.	27	1924	Jacques Fournier, Bklyn.	27	1960	Ernie Banks, Chi.	41
1885	Abner Dalrymple, Chi.	11	1925	Rogers Hornsby, St. L	39	1961	Orlando Cepeda, San Fran.	46
1886	Arthur Richardson, Det.	11	1926	Hack Wilson, Chi.	21	1962	Willie Mays, San Fran.	49
1887	Roger Connor, N.Y., and Wm. O'Brien, Wash.	17	1927	Hack Wilson, Chi., and Cy Williams, Phila.	30	1963	Henry Aaron, Mil., and Willie McCovey, San Fran.	44
1888	Roger Connor, N.Y.	14	1928	Hack Wilson, Chi., and Jim Bottomley, St. L.	31	1964	Willie Mays, San Fran.	47
1889	Sam Thompson, Phila.	20	1929	Chuck Klein, Phila.	43	1965	Willie Mays, San Fran.	52
1890	Tom Burns, Bkln, and Mike Tiernan, N.Y.	13	1930	Hack Wilson, Chi.	56	1966	Henry Aaron, Atlanta	44
1891	Harry Stovey, Bost., and Mike Tiernan, N.Y.	16	1931	Chuck Klein, Phila.	31	1967	Henry Aaron, Atlanta	39
1892	Jim Holliday, Cin.	13	1932	Chuck Klein, Phila., and Mel Ott, N.Y.	38	1968	Willie McCovey, San Fran.	36
1893	Ed Delahanty, Phila.	19	1933	Chuck Klein, Phila.	28	1969	Willie McCovey, San Fran.	45
1894	Hugh Duffy, Bost., and Robert Lowe, Bost.	18	1934	Mel Ott, N.Y., and Rip Collins, St. L.	35	1970	Johnny Bench, Cin.	45
1895	Bill Joyce, Wash.	17	1935	Wally Berger, Bost.	34	1971	Willie Stargell, Pitts.	48
1896	Ed Delahanty, Phila., and Sam Thompson, Phila.	13	1936	Mel Ott, N.Y.	33	1972	Johnny Bench, Cin.	40
1897	Nap Lajoie, Phila.	10	1937	Mel Ott, N.Y., and Joe Medwick, St. L.	31	1973	Willie Stargell, Pitts.	44
1898	James Colins, Bost.	14	1938	Mel Ott, N.Y.	36	1974	Mike Schmidt, Phila.	36
1899	John Freeman, Wash.	25	1939	John Mize, St. L.	28	1975	Mike Schmidt, Phila.	38
1900	Herman Long, Bost.	12	1940	John Mize, St. L.	43	1976	Mike Schmidt, Phila.	38
1901	Sam Crawford, Con.	16	1941	Dolph Camilli, Bklyn.	34	1977	George Foster, Cin.	52
1902	Tom Leach, Pitts.	6	1942	Mel Ott, N.Y.	30	1978	George Foster, Cin.	40
1903	James Sheckard, Bklyn.	9	1943	Bill Nicholson, Chi.	29	1979	Dave Kingman, Chicago	48
1904	Harry Lumley, Bklyn.	9	1944	Bill Nicholson, Chi.	33	1980	Mike Schmidt, Phila.	48
1905	Fred Odwell, Cin.	9	1945	Tommy Holmes, Bost.	28	1981*	Mike Schmidt, Phila.	31
1906	Tim Jordan, Bklyn	12	1946	Ralph Kiner, Pitts.	23	1982	Dave Kingman, N.Y.	37
1907	David Brain, Bost.	10	1947	Ralph Kiner, Pitts., and John Mize, N.Y.	51	1983	Mike Schmidt, Phila.	40
1908	Tim Jordan, Bklyn	12	1948	Ralph Kiner, Pitts., and John Mize, N.Y.	40	1984	Mike Schmidt, Phila. and Dale Murphy, Atlanta	36
1909	John Murray, N.Y.	7	1949	Ralph Kiner, Pitts.	54	1985	Dale Murphy, Atlanta	37
1910	Fred Beck, Bost., and Frank Schulte, Chi.	10	1950	Ralph Kiner, Pitts.	47	1986	Mike Schmidt, Phila.	37
1911	Frank Schulte, Chi.	21	1951	Ralph Kiner, Pitts.	42	1987	Andre Dawson, Chicago	49
1912	Henry Zimmerman, Chi.	14	1952	Ralph Kiner, Pitts., and		1988	Darryl Strawberry, N.Y.	39
1913	Cliff Cravath, Phila.	19				1989	Kevin Mitchell, San Francisco	47
1914	Cliff Cravath, Phila.	19				1990	Ryne Sandberg, Chicago	40
1915	Cliff Cravath, Phila.	24				1991	Howard Johnson, N.Y.	38
						1992	Fred McGriff, San Diego	35
						1993	Barry Bonds, San Francisco	46
						1994[1]	Matt Williams, San Francisco	43
						1995	Dante Bichette, Colorado	40

*Split season because of player strike. 1. Season ended on August 12 because of a player's strike.

NATIONAL LEAGUE BATTING CHAMPIONS

Year	Player, team	Avg	Year	Player, team	Avg	Year	Player, team	Avg
1876	Roscoe Barnes, Chicago	.404	1882	Dan Brouthers, Buffalo	.367	1888	Cap Anson, Chicago	.343
1877	Jim White, Boston	.385	1883	Dan Brouthers, Buffalo	.371	1889	Dan Brouthers, Boston	.373
1878	Abner Dalrymple, Mil.	.356	1884	James O'Rourke, Buffalo	.350	1890	John Glasscock, N. Y.	.336
1879	Cap Anson, Chicago	.407	1885	Roger Connor, N. Y.	.371	1891	William Hamilton, Phila.	.338
1880	George Gore, Chicago	.365	1886	King Kelly, Chicago	.388	1892	Dan Brouthers, Bklyn., and	
1881	Cap Anson, Chicago	.399	1887	Cap Anson, Chicago	.421		Clarence Childs, Cleve.	.335

Year	Player, team	Avg	Year	Player, team	Avg	Year	Player, team	Avg
1893	Hugh Duffy, Boston	.378	1928	Rogers Hornsby, Boston	.387	1962	Tommy Davis, L. A.	.346
1894	Hugh Duffy, Boston	.438	1929	Lefty O'Doul, Phila.	.398	1963	Tommy Davis, L. A.	.326
1895	Jesse Burkett, Cleveland	.423	1930	Bill Terry, N.Y.	.401	1964	Roberto Clemente, Pitts.	.339
1896	Jesse Burkett, Cleveland	.410	1931	Chick Hafey, St. Louis	.349	1965	Roberto Clemente, Pitts.	.329
1897	Willie Keeler, Baltimore	.432	1932	Lefty O'Doul, Brooklyn	.368	1966	Matty Alou, Pittsburgh	.342
1898	Willie Keeler, Baltimore	.379	1933	Chuck Klein, Phila.	.368	1967	Roberto Clemente, Pitts.	.357
1899	Ed Delahanty, Phila.	.408	1934	Paul Waner, Pittsburgh	.362	1968	Pete Rose, Cincinnati	.335
1900	Honus Wagner, Pittsburgh	.381	1935	Arky Vaughan, Pittsburgh	.385	1969	Pete Rose, Cincinnati	.348
1901	Jesse Burkett, St. Louis	.382	1936	Paul Waner, Pittsburgh	.373	1970	Rico Carty, Atlanta	.366
1902	Clarence Beaumont, Pitts.	.357	1937	Joe Medwick, St. Louis	.374	1971	Joe Torre, St. Louis	.363
1903	Honus Wagner, Pittsburgh	.355	1938	Ernie Lombardi, Cin.	.342	1972	Billy Williams, Chicago	.333
1904	Honus Wagner, Pittsburgh	.349	1939	John Mize, St. Louis	.349	1973	Pete Rose, Cincinnati	.338
1905	Cy Seymour, Cincinnati	.377	1940	Debs Garms, Pittsburgh	.355	1974	Ralph Garr, Atlanta	.353
1906	Honus Wagner, Pittsburgh	.339	1941	Pete Reiser, Brooklyn	.343	1975	Bill Madlock, Chicago	.354
1907	Honus Wagner, Pittsburgh	.350	1942	Ernie Lombardi, Boston	.330	1976	Bill Madlock, Chicago	.339
1908	Honus Wagner, Pittsburgh	.354	1943	Stan Musial, St. Louis	.357	1977	Dave Parker, Pittsburgh	.338
1909	Honus Wagner, Pittsburgh	.339	1944	Dixie Walker, Brooklyn	.357	1978	Dave Parker, Pittsburgh	.334
1910	Sherwood Magee, Phila.	.331	1945	Phil Cavarretta, Chicago	.355	1979	Keith Hernandez, St. Louis	.344
1911	Honus Wagner, Pittsburgh	.334	1946	Stan Musial, St. Louis	.365	1980	Bill Buckner, Chicago	.324
1912	Henry Zimmerman, Chicago	.372	1947	Harry Walker, St. L.–Phila.	.363	1981*	Bill Madlock, Pittsburgh	.341
1913	Jake Daubert, Brooklyn	.350	1948	Stan Musial, St. Louis	.376	1982	Al Oliver, Montreal	.331
1914	Jake Daubert, Brooklyn	.329	1949	Jackie Robinson, Brooklyn	.342	1983	Bill Madlock, Pittsburgh	.323
1915	Larry Doyle, New York	.320	1950	Stan Musial, St. Louis	.346	1984	Tony Gwynn, San Diego	.351
1916	Hal Chase, Cincinnati	.339	1951	Stan Musial, St. Louis	.355	1985	Willie McGee, St. Louis	.353
1917	Edd Roush, Cincinnati	.341	1952	Stan Musial, St. Louis	.336	1986	Tim Raines, Montreal	.334
1918	Zack Wheat, Brooklyn	.335	1953	Carl Furillo, Brooklyn	.344	1987	Tony Gwynn, San Diego	.370
1919	Edd Roush, Cincinnati	.321	1954	Willie Mays, N. Y.	.345	1988	Tony Gwynn, San Diego	.313
1920	Rogers Hornsby, St. Louis	.370	1955	Richie Ashburn, Phila.	.338	1989	Tony Gwynn, San Diego	.336
1921	Rogers Hornsby, St. Louis	.397	1956	Henry Aaron, Mil.	.328	1990	Willie McGee, St. Louis	.335
1922	Rogers Hornsby, St. Louis	.401	1957	Stan Musial, St. Louis	.351	1991	Terry Pendleton, Atlanta	.319
1923	Rogers Hornsby, St. Louis	.384	1958	Richie Ashburn, Phila.	.350	1992	Gary Sheffield, San Diego	.330
1924	Rogers Hornsby, St. Louis	.424	1959	Henry Aaron, Mil.	.355	1993	Andres Galarraga, Colorado	.370
1925	Rogers Hornsby, St. Louis	.403	1960	Dick Groat, Pittsburgh	.325	1994[1]	Tony Gwynn, San Diego	.394
1926	Gene Hargrave, Cincinnati	.353	1961	Roberto Clemente, Pitts.	.351	1995	Tony Gwynn, San Diego	.368
1927	Paul Waner, Pittsburgh	.380						

1. Season ended on August 12 because of a player's strike.

AMERICAN LEAGUE PENNANT WINNERS

Year	Club	Manager	Won	Lost	Pct	Year	Club	Manager	Won	Lost	Pct
1901	Chicago	Clark C. Griffith	83	53	.610	1933	Washington	Joseph E. Cronin	99	53	.651
1902	Philadelphia	Connie Mack	83	53	.610	1934	Detroit	Gordon Cochrane	101	53	.656
1903[1]	Boston	Jimmy Collins	91	47	.659	1935[1]	Detroit	Gordon Cochrane	93	58	.616
1904[2]	Boston	Jimmy Collins	95	59	.617	1936[1]	New York	Joseph V. McCarthy	102	51	.667
1905	Philadelphia	Connie Mack	92	56	.622	1937[1]	New York	Joseph V. McCarthy	102	52	.662
1906[1]	Chicago	Fielder A. Jones	93	58	.616	1938[1]	New York	Joseph V. McCarthy	99	53	.651
1907	Detroit	Hugh A. Jennings	92	58	.613	1939[1]	New York	Joseph V. McCarthy	106	45	.702
1908	Detroit	Hugh A. Jennings	90	63	.588	1940	Detroit	Delmar D. Baker	90	64	.584
1909	Detroit	Hugh A. Jennings	98	54	.645	1941[1]	New York	Joseph V. McCarthy	101	53	.656
1910[1]	Philadelphia	Connie Mack	102	48	.680	1942	New York	Joseph V. McCarthy	103	51	.669
1911[1]	Philadelphia	Connie Mack	101	50	.669	1943[1]	New York	Joseph V. McCarthy	98	56	.636
1912[1]	Boston	J. Garland Stahl	105	47	.691	1944	St. Louis	Luke Sewell	89	65	.578
1913[1]	Philadelphia	Connie Mack	96	57	.627	1945[1]	Detroit	Steve O'Neill	88	65	.575
1914	Philadelphia	Connie Mack	99	53	.651	1946	Boston	Joseph E. Cronin	104	50	.675
1915[1]	Boston	William F. Carrigan	101	50	.669	1947[1]	New York	Stanley R. Harris	97	57	.630
1916[1]	Boston	William F. Carrigan	91	63	.591	1948[1]	Cleveland	Lou Boudreau	97	58	.626
1917	Chicago	Clarence H. Rowland	100	54	.649	1949[1]	New York	Casey Stengel	97	57	.630
1918[1]	Boston	Ed Barrow	75	51	.595	1950[1]	New York	Casey Stengel	98	56	.636
1919	Chicago	William Gleason	88	52	.629	1951[1]	New York	Casey Stengel	98	56	.636
1920	Cleveland	Tris Speaker	98	56	.636	1952[1]	New York	Casey Stengel	95	59	.617
1921	New York	Miller J. Huggins	98	55	.641	1953[1]	New York	Casey Stengel	99	52	.656
1922	New York	Miller J. Huggins	94	60	.610	1954	Cleveland	Al Lopez	111	43	.721
1923[1]	New York	Miller J. Huggins	98	54	.645	1955	New York	Casey Stengel	96	58	.623
1924[1]	Washington	Stanley R. Harris	92	62	.597	1956[1]	New York	Casey Stengel	97	57	.630
1925	Washington	Stanley R. Harris	96	55	.636	1957	New York	Casey Stengel	98	56	.636
1926	New York	Miller J. Huggins	91	63	.591	1958[1]	New York	Casey Stengel	92	62	.597
1927[1]	New York	Miller J. Huggins	110	44	.714	1959	Chicago	Al Lopez	94	60	.610
1928[1]	New York	Miller J. Huggins	101	53	.656	1960	New York	Casey Stengel	97	57	.630
1929[1]	Philadelphia	Connie Mack	104	46	.693						
1930[1]	Philadelphia	Connie Mack	102	52	.662						
1931	Philadelphia	Connie Mack	107	45	.704						
1932[1]	New York	Joseph V. McCarthy	107	47	.695						

Year	Club	Manager	Won	Lost	Pct	Year	Club	Manager	Won	Lost	Pct
1961[1]	New York	Ralph Houk	109	53	.673	1979	Baltimore[8]	Earl Weaver	102	57	.642
1962[1]	New York	Ralph Houk	96	66	.593	1980	Kansas City[9]	Jim Frey	97	65	.599
1963	New York	Ralph Houk	104	57	.646	1981	New York[10]	Gene Michael–			
1964	New York	Yogi Berra	99	63	.611			Bob Lemon	59	48	.551 *
1965	Minnesota	Sam Mele	102	60	.630	1982	Milwaukee[11]	Harvey Kuenn	95	67	.586
1966[1]	Baltimore	Hank Bauer	97	53	.606	1983[1]	Baltimore[12]	Joe Altobelli	98	64	.605
1967	Boston	Dick Williams	92	70	.568	1984[1]	Detroit[13]	Sparky Anderson	104	58	.642
1968[1]	Detroit	Mayo Smith	103	59	.636	1985[1]	Kansas City[14]	Dick Howser	91	71	.562
1969	Baltimore[3]	Earl Weaver	109	53	.673	1986	Boston[11]	John McNamara	95	66	.590
1970[1]	Baltimore[3]	Earl Weaver	108	54	.667	1987	Minnesota[15]	Tom Kelly	85	77	.525
1971	Baltimore[4]	Earl Weaver	101	57	.639	1988	Oakland[16]	Tony LaRussa	104	58	.642
1972[1]	Oakland[5]	Dick Williams	93	62	.600	1989	Oakland[17]	Tony LaRussa	99	63	.611
1973[1]	Oakland[6]	Dick Williams	94	68	.580	1990	Oakland[18]	Tony LaRussa	103	59	.636
1974[1]	Oakland[6]	Alvin Dark	90	72	.556	1991	Minnesota[19]	Tom Kelly	95	67	.586
1975	Boston[4]	Darrell Johnson	95	65	.594	1992	Toronto[10]	Cito Gaston	96	66	.593
1976	New York[7]	Billy Martin	97	62	.610	1993	Toronto[12]	Cito Gaston	95	67	.586
1977[1]	New York[7]	Billy Martin	100	62	.617	1994	Strike ended season Aug. 11. No playoffs, no pennant				
1978[1]	New York[7]	Billy Martin and					winner.				
		Bob Lemon	100	63	.613	1995	Cleveland[20]	Mike Hargrove	100	44	.694

*Split season because of player strike. 1. World Series winner. 2. No World Series. 3. Defeated Minnesota, Western Division winner, in playoff. 4. Defeated Oakland, Western Division Leader, in playoff. 5. Defeated Detroit, Eastern Division winner, inplayoff. 6. Defeated Baltimore, Eastern Division winner, in playoff. 7. Defeated Kansas City, Western Division winner, in playoff. 8. Defeated California, Western Division winner, in playoff. 9. Defeated New York, Eastern Division winner, in playoff. 10. Defeated Oakland, Western Division winner, in playoff. 11. Defeated California, Western Division winner, in playoff. 12. Defeated Chicago, Western Division winner in playoff. 13. Defeated Kansas City, Western Division winner, in playoff. 14. Defeated Toronto, Eastern Division winner, in playoff. 15. Defeated Detroit, Eastern Division winner, in playoff. 16. Defeated Boston, Eastern division winner, in playoffs. 17. Defeated Toronto, Eastern Division winner, in playoffs. 18. Defeated Boston, Eastern Division winner, in playoffs. 19. Defeated Toronto, Eastern Division winner, in playoffs. 20. Defeated Seattle Mariners, Western Division winner in playoffs.

NATIONAL LEAGUE PENNANT WINNERS

Year	Club	Manager	Won	Lost	Pct	Year	Club	Manager	Won	Lost	Pct
1876	Chicago	Albert G. Spalding	52	14	.788	1917	New York	John J. McGraw	98	56	.636
1877	Boston	Harry Wright	31	17	.646	1918	Chicago	Fred L. Mitchell	84	45	.651
1878	Boston	Harry Wright	41	19	.683	1919	Cincinnati[1]	Patrick J. Moran	96	44	.686
1879	Providence	George Wright	55	23	.705	1920	Brooklyn	Wilbert Robinson	93	61	.604
1880	Chicago	Adrian C. Anson	67	17	.798	1921	New York[1]	John J. McGraw	94	59	.614
1881	Chicago	Adrian C. Anson	56	28	.667	1922	New York[1]	John J. McGraw	93	61	.604
1882	Chicago	Adrian C. Anson	55	29	.655	1923	New York	John J. McGraw	95	58	.621
1883	Boston	John F. Morrill	63	35	.643	1924	New York	John J. McGraw	93	60	.608
1884	Providence	Frank C. Bancroft	84	28	.750	1925	Pittsburgh[1]	Wm. B. McKechnie	95	58	.621
1885	Chicago	Adrian C. Anson	87	25	.777	1926	St. Louis[1]	Rogers Hornsby	89	65	.578
1886	Chicago	Adrian C. Anson	90	34	.726	1927	Pittsburgh	Donie Bush	94	60	.610
1887	Detroit	W. H. Watkins	79	45	.637	1928	St. Louis	Wm. B. McKechnie	95	59	.617
1888	New York	James J. Mutrie	84	47	.641	1929	Chicago	Joseph V. McCarthy	98	54	.645
1889	New York	James J. Mutrie	83	43	.659	1930	St. Louis	Gabby Street	92	62	.597
1890	Brooklyn	Wm. H. McGunnigle	86	43	.667	1931	St. Louis[1]	Gabby Street	101	53	.656
1891	Boston	Frank G. Selee	87	51	.630	1932	Chicago	Charles J. Grimm	90	64	.584
1892	Boston	Frank G. Selee	102	48	.680	1933	New York[1]	William H. Terry	91	61	.599
1893	Boston	Frank G. Selee	86	44	.662	1934	St. Louis[1]	Frank F. Frisch	95	58	.621
1894	Baltimore	Edward H. Hanlon	89	39	.695	1935	Chicago	Charles J. Grimm	100	54	.649
1895	Baltimore	Edward H. Hanlon	87	43	.669	1936	New York	William H. Terry	92	62	.597
1896	Baltimore	Edward H. Hanlon	90	39	.698	1937	New York	William H. Terry	95	57	.625
1897	Boston	Frank G. Selee	93	39	.705	1938	Chicago	Gabby Hartnett	89	63	.586
1898	Boston	Frank G. Selee	102	47	.685	1939	Cincinnati	Wm. B. McKechnie	97	57	.630
1899	Brooklyn	Edward H. Hanlon	88	42	.677	1940	Cincinnati[1]	Wm. B. McKechnie	100	53	.654
1900	Brooklyn	Edward H. Hanlon	82	54	.603	1941	Brooklyn	Leo E. Durocher	100	54	.649
1901	Pittsburgh	Fred C. Clarke	90	49	.647	1942	St. Louis[1]	Wm. H. Southworth	106	48	.688
1902	Pittsburgh	Fred C. Clarke	103	36	.741	1943	St. Louis	Wm. H. Southworth	105	49	.682
1903	Pittsburgh	Fred C. Clarke	91	49	.650	1944	St. Louis[1]	Wm. H. Southworth	105	49	.682
1904	New York[2]	John J. McGraw	106	47	.693	1945	Chicago	Charles J. Grimm	98	56	.636
1905	New York[1]	John J. McGraw	105	48	.686	1946	St. Louis[1]	Edwin H. Dyer	98	58	.628
1906	Chicago	Frank L. Chance	116	36	.763	1947	Brooklyn	Burton E. Shotton	94	60	.610
1907	Chicago[1]	Frank L. Chance	107	45	.704	1948	Boston	Wm. H. Southworth	91	62	.595
1908	Chicago[1]	Frank L. Chance	99	55	.643	1949	Brooklyn	Burton E. Shotton	97	57	.630
1909	Pittsburgh[1]	Fred C. Clarke	110	42	.724	1950	Philadelphia	Edwin M. Sawyer	91	63	.591
1910	Chicago	Frank L. Chance	104	50	.675	1951	New York	Leo E. Durocher	98	59	.624
1911	New York	John J. McGraw	99	54	.647	1952	Brooklyn	Charles W. Dressen	96	57	.630
1912	New York	John J. McGraw	103	48	.682	1953	Brooklyn	Charles W. Dressen	105	49	.682
1913	New York	John J. McGraw	101	51	.664	1954	New York[1]	Leo E. Durocher	97	57	.630
1914	Boston[1]	George T. Stallings	94	59	.614	1955	Brooklyn[1]	Walter Alston	98	55	.641
1915	Philadelphia	Patrick J. Moran	90	62	.592	1956	Brooklyn	Walter Alston	93	61	.604
1916	Brooklyn	Wilbert Robinson	94	60	.610	1957	Milwaukee1	Fred Haney	95	59	.617

Year	Club	Manager	Won	Lost	Pct	Year	Club	Manager	Won	Lost	Pct
1958	Milwaukee	Fred Haney	92	62	.597	1978	Los Angeles[7]	Tom Lasorda	95	67	.586
1959	Los Angeles[1]	Walter Alston	88	68	.564	1979[1]	Pittsburgh[6]	Chuck Tanner	98	64	.605
1960	Pittsburgh[1]	Danny Murtaugh	95	59	.617	1980[1]	Philadelphia[8]	Dallas Green	91	71	.562
1961	Cincinnati	Fred Hutchinson	93	61	.604	1981	Los Angeles[1 9]	Tom Lasorda	63	*47	.573
1962	San Francisco	Alvin Dark	103	62	.624	1982[1]	St. Louis[3]	Whitey Herzog	92	70	.568
1963	Los Angeles[1]	Walter Alston	99	63	.611	1983	Philadelphia[11]	Paul Owens	90	72	.556
1964	St. Louis[1]	Johnny Keane	93	69	.574	1984	San Diego[12]	Dick Williams	92	70	.568
1965	Los Angeles[1]	Walter Alston	97	65	.599	1985	St. Louis[11]	Whitey Herzog	101	61	.623
1966	Los Angeles	Walter Alston	95	67	.586	1986	New York[8]	Dave Johnson	108	54	.667
1967	St. Louis[1]	Red Schoendienst	101	60	.627	1987	St. Louis[5]	Whitey Herzog	95	67	.586
1968	St. Louis	Red Schoendienst	97	65	.599	1988	Los Angeles[10]	Tom Lasorda	94	67	.584
1969	New York[1 3]	Gil Hodges	100	62	.617	1989	San Francisco[12]	Roger Craig	92	70	.568
1970	Cincinnati[4]	Sparky Anderson	102	60	.630	1990	Cincinnati[4]	Lou Piniella	91	71	.562
1971	Pittsburgh[1 5]	Danny Murtaugh	97	65	.599	1991	Atlanta[4]	Bobby Cox	94	68	.580
1972	Cincinnati[4]	Sparky Anderson	95	59	.617	1992	Atlanta[4]	Bobby Cox	98	64	.605
1973	New York[6]	Yogi Berra	82	79	.509	1993	Philadelphia[3]	Jim Fregosi	97	65	.599
1974	Los Angeles[4]	Walter Alston	102	60	.630	1994	Strike ended season Aug. 11. No playoffs, no pennant winner.				
1975	Cincinnati[1 4]	Sparky Anderson	108	54	.667	1995	Atlanta[13]	Bobby Cox	90	54	.625
1976	Cincinnati[7 1]	Sparky Anderson	102	60	.630						
1977	Los Angeles[7]	Tom Lasorda	98	64	.605						

*Split season because of player strike. 1. World Series winner. 2. No World Series. 3. Defeated Atlanta, Western Division winner, in playoff. 4. Defeated Pittsburgh, Eastern Division winner, in playoff. 5. Defeated San Francisco, Western Division winner, in playoff. 6. Defeated Cincinnati, Western Division winner, in playoff. 7. Defeated Philadelphia, Eastern Division winner, in playoff. 8. Defeated Houston, Western Division winner, in playoff. 9. Defeated Montreal, Eastern Division winner, in playoff. 10. Defeated New York, Eastern Division winner, in playoff. 11. Defeated Los Angeles, Western Division in playoff. 12. Defeated Chicago, Eastern Division champion in playoff. 13. Defeated Cincinnati, Central Division winner in playoff.

MOST VALUABLE PLAYERS

(Baseball Writers Association selections)

American League

1931	Lefty Grove, Philadelphia
1932–33	Jimmy Foxx, Philadelphia
1934	Mickey Cochrane, Detroit
1935	Hank Greenberg, Detroit
1936	Lou Gehrig, New York
1937	Charlie Gehringer, Detroit
1938	Jimmy Foxx, Boston
1939	Joe DiMaggio, New York
1940	Hank Greenberg, Detroit
1941	Joe DiMaggio, New York
1942	Joe Gordon, New York
1943	Spurgeon Chandler, New York
1944–45	Hal Newhouser, Detroit
1946	Ted Williams, Boston
1947	Joe DiMaggio, New York
1948	Lou Boudreau, Cleveland
1949	Ted Williams, Boston
1950	Phil Rizzuto, New York
1951	Yogi Berra, New York
1952	Bobby Shantz, Philadelphia
1953	Al Rosen, Cleveland
1954–55	Yogi Berra, New York
1956–57	Mickey Mantle, New York
1958	Jackie Jensen, Boston
1959	Nellie Fox, Chicago
1960–61	Roger Maris, New York
1962	Mickey Mantle, New York
1963	Elston Howard, New York
1964	Brooks Robinson, Baltimore
1965	Zoilo Versalles, Minnesota
1966	Frank Robinson, Baltimore
1967	Carl Yastrzemski, Boston
1968	Dennis McLain, Detroit
1969	Harmon Killebrew, Minnesota
1970	John (Boog) Powell, Baltimore
1971	Vida Blue, Oakland
1972	Dick Allen, Chicago
1973	Reggie Jackson, Oakland
1974	Jeff Burroughs, Texas
1975	Fred Lynn, Boston
1976	Thurman Munson, New York
1977	Rod Carew, Minnesota
1978	Jim Rice, Boston
1979	Don Baylor, California
1980	George Brett, Kansas City
1981	Rollie Fingers, Milwaukee
1982	Robin Yount, Milwaukee
1983	Cal Ripken, Jr., Baltimore
1984	Willie Hernandez, Detroit
1985	Don Mattingly, New York
1986	Roger Clemens, Boston
1987	George Bell, Toronto
1988	Jose Canseco, Oakland
1989	Robin Yount, Milwaukee
1990	Rickey Henderson, Oakland
1991	Cal Ripken, Jr., Baltimore
1992	Dennis Eckersley, Oakland
1993	Frank Thomas, Chicago
1994	Frank Thomas, Chicago

National League

1931	Frank Frisch, St. Louis
1932	Chuck Klein, Philadelphia
1933	Carl Hubbell, New York
1934	Dizzy Dean, St. Louis
1935	Gabby Hartnett, Chicago
1936	Carl Hubbell, New York
1937	Joe Medwick, St. Louis
1938	Ernie Lombardi, Cincinnati
1939	Bucky Walters, Cincinnati
1940	Frank McCormick, Cincinnati
1941	Dolph Camilli, Brooklyn
1942	Mort Cooper, St. Louis
1943	Stan Musial, St. Louis
1944	Marty Marion, St. Louis
1945	Phil Cavarretta, Chicago
1946	Stan Musial, St. Louis
1947	Bob Elliott, Boston
1948	Stan Musial, St. Louis
1949	Jackie Robinson, Brooklyn
1950	Jim Konstanty, Philadelphia
1951	Roy Campanella, Brooklyn
1952	Hank Sauer, Chicago
1953	Roy Campanella, Brooklyn
1954	Willie Mays, New York
1955	Roy Campanella, Brooklyn
1956	Don Newcombe, Brooklyn
1957	Henry Aaron, Milwaukee
1958–59	Ernie Banks, Chicago
1960	Dick Groat, Pittsburgh
1961	Frank Robinson, Cincinnati
1962	Maury Wills, Los Angeles
1963	Sandy Koufax, Los Angeles
1964	Ken Boyer, St. Louis
1965	Willie Mays, San Francisco
1966	Roberto Clemente, Pittsburgh
1967	Orlando Cepeda, St. Louis
1968	Bob Gibson, St. Louis
1969	Willie McCovey, San Francisco
1970	Johnny Bench, Cincinnati
1971	Joe Torre, St. Louis
1972	Johnny Bench, Cincinnati
1973	Pete Rose, Cincinnati
1974	Steve Garvey, Los Angeles
1975–76	Joe Morgan, Cincinnati
1977	George Foster, Cincinnati
1978	Dave Parker, Pittsburgh
1979	Willie Stargell, Pittsburgh
1979	Keith Hernandez, St. Louis
1980	Mike Schmidt, Philadelphia
1981	Mike Schmidt, Philadelphia
1982	Dale Murphy, Atlanta
1983	Dale Murphy, Atlanta
1984	Ryne Sandberg, Chicago
1985	Willie McGee, St. Louis
1986	Mike Schmidt, Philadelphia
1987	Andre Dawson, Chicago
1988	Kirk Gibson, Los Angeles
1989	Kevin Mitchell, San Francisco
1990	Barry Bonds, Pittsburgh
1991	Terry Pendleton, Atlanta
1992	Barry Bonds, Pittsburgh
1993	Barry Bonds, Pittsburgh
1994	Jeff Baswell, Houston

MAJOR LEAGUE LIFETIME RECORDS
(Through 1994)

Leading Pitchers—Wins
* Indicates left-handed pitcher.

		Yrs	GS	W	L	Pct
1.	Cy Young	22	815	511	313	.620
2.	Walter Johnson	21	666	416	279	.599
3.	Christy Mathewson	17	551	373	188	.665
	Grover Alexander	20	598	373	208	.642
5.	Warren Spahn*	21	665	363	245	.597
6.	Kid Nichols	15	561	361	208	.634
	Pud Galvin	14	682	361	308	.540
8.	Tim Keefe	14	594	342	225	.603
9.	Steve Carlton*	24	709	329	244	.574
10.	Eddie Plank*	17	527	327	193	.629
11.	John Clarkson	12	518	326	177	.648
12.	Don Sutton	23	756	324	256	.559
13.	Nolan Ryan	27	773	324	292	.539
14.	Phil Niekro	24	716	318	274	.537
15.	Gaylord Perry	22	690	314	265	.542
16.	Old Hoss Radbourn	12	503	311	194	.616
	Tom Seaver	20	647	311	205	.603
18.	Mickey Welch	13	549	308	209	.596
19.	Lefty Grove*	17	456	300	141	.680
	Early Wynn	23	612	300	244	.551
21.	Tommy John*	26	700	288	231	.555
22.	Bert Blyleven	22	685	287	250	.534
23.	Robin Roberts	19	609	286	245	.539
24.	Tony Mullane	13	505	285	220	.564
25.	Ferguson Jenkins	19	594	284	226	.557

Pitchers Active in 1994 Season
(200 or more lifetime victories)

		Yrs	W	L	Pct
1.	Jack Morris	17	254	186	.577
2.	Frank Tanana*	21	240	236	.504
3.	Dennis Martinez	18	219	171	.562
4.	Charlie Hough	24	216	216	.500
5.	Bob Welch	16	211	146	.591

Leading Batters, by Average
* Indicates left-handed hitter.

		Years	AB	H	Avg
1.	Ty Cobb*	24	11,429	4191	.367
2.	Rogers Hornsby	23	8,137	2930	.358
3.	Joe Jackson*	13	4,981	1774	.356
4.	Ed Delahanty	16	7,502	2591	.345
5.	Ted Williams*	19	7,706	2654	.344
6.	Tris Speaker*	22	10,208	3515	.344
7.	Billy Hamilton*	14	6,284	2163	.344
8.	Willie Keeler*	19	8,585	2947	.343
9.	Dan Brouthers*	19	6,711	2296	.342
10.	Babe Ruth*	22	8,399	2873	.342
11.	Harry Heilmann	17	7,787	2660	.342
12.	Pete Browning	13	4,820	1646	.341
13.	Bill Terry*	14	6,428	2193	.341
14.	George Sisler*	15	8,267	2812	.340
15.	Lou Gehrig*	17	8,001	2721	.340
16.	Jesse Burkett*	16	8,413	2853	.339
17.	Nap Lajoie	21	9,592	3244	.338
18.	**Wade Boggs***	12	6,579	2392	.335
19.	Riggs Stephenson	14	4,508	1515	.336
20.	Al Simmons	20	8,761	2927	.334
21.	Paul Waner*	20	9,459	3152	.333
22.	Eddie Collins*	25	9,949	3311	.333
23.	**Tony Gwynn***	12	6,120	2204	.333
24.	Stan Musial*	22	10,972	3630	.331
25.	Sam Thompson*	14	6,005	1986	.331

NOTE: Players active in 1995 in boldfaces.

Players Active in 1994 Season
(1,500 or more lifetime hits)

		Years	H	Avg
1.	Wade Boggs*	12	2,392	.335
2.	Tony Gwynn*	12	2,204	.333
3.	Kirby Puckett	10	2,135	.318
4.	Don Mattingly*	12	2,021	.309
5.	Paul Molitor	16	2,647	.307

Realignment of Major Leagues

The move by the American and National leagues to three divisions in 1994 doubled the number of teams qualifying for the postseason from four to eight overall. All three divisional winners plus a wild-card team (the non-division winner with the best record) will reach the playoffs, which will expand to two rounds. The first round will be a Best-of-5 series, followed by a Best-of-7 championships series.

American League

West	Central	East
California	Chicago	Baltimore
Oakland	Cleveland	Boston
Seattle	Kansas City	Detroit
Texas	Milwaukee	New York
	Minnesota	Toronto

National League

West	Central	East
Colorado	Chicago	Atlanta
Los Angeles	Cincinnati	Florida
San Diego	Houston	Montreal
San Francisco	Pittsburgh	New York
	St. Louis	Philadelphia

CY YOUNG AWARD

1956	Don Newcombe, Brooklyn N.L.
1957	Warren Spahn, Milwaukee N.L.
1958	Bob Turley, New York A.L.
1959	Early Wynn, Chicago A.L.
1960	Vernon Law, Pittsburgh, N.L
1961	Whitey Ford, New York A.L.
1962	Don Drysdale, Los Angeles N.L.
1963	Sandy Koufax, Los Angeles N.L.
1964	Dean Chance, Los Angeles A.L.
1965	Sandy Koufax, Los Angeles N.L.
1966	Sandy Koufax, Los Angeles N.L.

1967	Jim Lonborg, Boston A.L.; Mike McCormick, San Francisco N.L.
1968	Dennis, McLain, Detroit A.L.; Bob Gibson, St. Louis N.L.
1969	Mike Cuellar, Baltimore, and Dennis McLain, Detroit, tied in A.L.; Tom Seaver, N.Y. N.L.
1970	Jim Perry, Minnesota A.L; Bob Gibson, St. Louis N.L.
1971	Vida Blue, Oakland A.L.; Ferguson Jenkins, Chicago N.L.
1972	Gaylord Perry, Cleveland A.L.; Steve Carlton, Phila. N.L.

1973	Jim Palmer, Baltimore A.L.; Tom Seaver, New York N.L.
1974	Catfish Hunter, Oakland A.L.; Mike Marshall, Los Angeles N.L.
1975	Jim Palmer, Baltimore A.L.; Tom Seaver, New York N.L.
1976	Jim Palmer, Baltimore A.L.; Randy Jones, San Diego N.L.
1977	Sparky Lyle, N.Y., A.L.; Steve Carlton, Philadelphia N.L.
1978	Ron Guidry, N.Y., A.L.; Gaylord Perry, San Diego N.L.

1979	Mike Flanagan, Baltimore, A.L.; Bruce Sutter, Chicago, N.L.	1984	Willie Hernandez, Detroit, A.L.; Rick Sutcliffe, Chica- go, N.L.	1990	Bob Welch, A.L.; Doug Drabek, N.L.
1980	Steve Stone, Baltimore, A.L.; Steve Carlton, Philadelphia, N.L.	1985	Bret Saberhagen, A.L.; Dwight Gooden, N.L.	1991	Roger Clemens, A.L.; Tom Glavine, N.L.
1981	Rollie Fingers, Milwaukee, A.L.; Fernando Valenzuela, Los Angeles, N.L.	1986	Roger Clemens, A.L.; Mike Scott, N.L.	1992	Dennis Eckersley, A.L.; Greg Maddux, N.L.
1982	Pete Vuckovich, Milwaukee, A.L.; Steve Carlton, Phila- delphia, N.L.	1987	Roger Clemens, A.L.; Steve Bedrosian, N.L.	1993	Jack McDowell, A.L.; Greg Maddux, N.L.
1983	LaMarr Hoyt, Chicago, A.L.; John Denny, Philadelphia, N.L.	1988	Frank Viola, A.L.; Orel Her- shiser, N.L.	1994	David Cone, A.L. Greg Maddux, N.L.
		1989	Bret Saberhagen, A.L.; Mark Davis, N.L.		

MAJOR LEAGUE INDIVIDUAL ALL–TIME RECORDS
(Through 1994)

Highest Batting Average—.442, James O'Neill, St. Louis, A.A., 1887; .438, Hugh Duffy, Boston, N.L., 1894 (Since 1900—.424, Rogers Hornsby, St. Louis, N.L., 1924; .422, Nap Lajoie, Phil., A.L., 1901)

Most Times at Bat—12,364, Henry Aaron, Milwaukee N.L., 1954–65; Atlanta N.L., 1966–74; Milwaukee A.L., 1975–76.

Most Years Batted .300 or Better—23, Ty Cobb, Detroit A.L., 1906–26, Philadelphia A.L., 1927–28.

Most hits—4,256, Pete Rose, Cincinnati 1963–79, Philadelphia 1980–83, Montreal 1984, Cincinnati 1984–86.

Most Hits, Season—257, George Sisler, St. Louis A.L., 1920.

Most Hits, Game (9 innings)—7, Wilbert Robinson, Baltimore N.L., 4 singles, 2 doubles, 1 triple, 1892. Rennie Stennett, Pittsburgh N.L., 4 singles, 2 doubles, 1 triple, 1975.

Most Hits, Game (extra innings)—9, John Burnett, Cleveland A.L., 18 innings, 7 singles, 2 doubles, 1932.

Most Hits in Succession—12, Mike Higgins, Boston A.L., in four games, 1938; Walt Dropo, Detroit A.L., in three games, 1952.

Most Consecutive Games Batted Safely—56, Joe DiMaggio, New York A.L., 1941.

Most Runs—2,244, Ty Cobb, Detroit A.L., 1905–26, Philadelphia A.L., 1927–28.

Most Runs, Season—196, William Hamilton, Philadelphia N.L., 1894. (Since 1900—177, Babe Ruth, New York A.L.)

Most Runs, Game—7, Guy Hecker, Louisville A.A., 1886. (Since 1900—6, by Mel Ott, New York N.L., 1934, 1944; Johnny Pesky, Boston A.L., 1946; Frank Torre, Milwaukee N.L., 1957.)

Most Runs Batted in—2,297, Henry Aaron, Milwaukee N.L., 1954–1965; Atlanta N.L., 1966–74; Milwaukee A.L., 1975–76.

Most Runs Batted in, Season—190, Hack Wilson, Chicago N.L., 1930.

Most Runs Batted In, Game—12, Jim Bottomley, St. Louis N.L., 1924, and Mark Whiten, St. Louis N.L., 1993.

Most Home Runs—755, Henry Aaron, Milwaukee N.L., 1954–1965; Atlanta N.L., 1966–74; Milwaukee A.L., 1975–76.

Most Home Runs, Season—61, Roger Maris, New York A.L., 1961 (162–game season); 60, Babe Ruth, New York A.L., 1927 (154–game season)

Most Home Runs with Bases Filled—23, Lou Gehrig, New York A.L., 1927–39.

Most 2–Base Hits—793, Tris Speaker, Boston A.L., 1907–15, Cleveland A.L., 1916–26, Washington A.L., 1927, Philadelphia A.L., 1928.

Most 2–Base Hits, Season—67, Earl Webb, Boston A.L., 1931.

Most 2–base Hits, Game—4, by many.

Most 3–Base Hits—312, Sam Crawford, Cincinnati N.L.,

1899–1902, Detroit A.L., 1903–17.

Most 3–Base Hits, Season—36, Owen Wilson, Pittsburgh N.L., 1912.

Most 3–Base Hits, Game—4, George Strief, Philadelphia A.A., 1885; William Joyce, New York N.L., 1897. (Since 1900—3, by many.)

Most Games Played—3,562, Pete Rose, Cincinnati N.L., Phila-delphia N.L., Montreal N.L., 1964–86

Most Consecutive Games Played—2,130, Lou Gehrig, New York A.L., 1925–39.

Most Bases on Balls—2,056, Babe Ruth, Boston A.L., 1914–19; New York A.L., 1920–34, Boston N.L., 1935.

Most Bases on Balls, Season—170, Babe Ruth, New York A.L., 1923.

Most bases on Balls, Game—6, Jimmy Foxx, Boston A.L., 1938.

Most Strikeouts, Season—189, Bobby Bonds, San Francisco N.L., 1970.

Most Strikeouts, Game (9 innings)—5, by many.

Most Strikeouts, Game (extra innings)—6, Carl Weilman, St. Louis A.L., 15 innings, 1913; Don Hoak, Chicago N.L., 17 in-nings, 1956; Fred Reichardt, California A.L., 17, innings, 1966; Billy Cowan, California A.L., 20, 1971; Cecil Cooper, Boston A.L., 15, 1974.

Most pinch—hits, lifetime—150, Manny Mota, S.F., 1962; Pitt., 1963–68; Montreal, 1969; L.A., 1969–80, N.L.

Most Pinch–hits, season—25, Jose Morales, Montreal N.L., 1976.

Most consecutive pinch–hits—9, Dave Philley, Phil., N.L., 1958 (8), 1959 (1).

Most pinch–hit home runs, lifetime—18, Gerald Lynch, Pitt.–Cin. N.L., 1957–66.

Most pinch–hit home runs, season—6, Johnny Frederick, Brooklyn, N.L., 1932.

Most stolen bases, lifetime (since 1900)—1,042, Rickey Hender-son,* 1979–84 Oakland, 1985–89 New York (A.L.), 1989–92 Oakland

Most stolen bases, season—156, Harry Stovey, Phil., A.A., 1888. Since 1900: 130, Rickey Henderson, Oak., A.L., 1982; 118, Lou Brock, St. Louis, N.L., 1974.

Most stolen bases, game—7, George Gore, Chicago N.L. 1881; William Hamilton, Philadelphia N.L. 1894. (Since 1900—6, Ed-die Collins, Philadelphia A.L., 1912.) and Otis Nixon*, Atlanta N.L., 1991.

Most time stealing home, lifetime—35, Ty Cobb, Detroit–Phil. A.L., 1905–28.

*Still active coming into 1995 season.

MAJOR LEAGUE ALL–TIME PITCHING RECORDS
(Through 1994)

Most Games Won—511, Cy Young, Cleveland N.L., 1890–98, St. Louis N.L., 1899–1900, Boston A.L., 1901–08, Cleveland A.L., 1909–11, Boston N.L., 1911.

Most Games Won, Season—60, Hoss Radbourne, Providence N.L., 1884. (Since 1900—41, Jack Chesbro, New York A.L., 1904.)

Most Consecutive Games Won—24, Carl Hubbell, New York N.L., 1936 (16) and 1937 (8).

Most Consecutive Games Won, Season—19, Tim Keefe, New York N.L., 1888; Rube Marquard, New York N.L., 1912.

Most Years Won 20 or More Games—16, Cy Young, Cleveland N.L., 1891–98, St. Louis N.L., 1899–1900, Boston A.L., 1901–04, 1907–08.

Most Shutouts—110, Walter Johnson, Wash. A.L., 1907–27.

Most Shutouts, Season—16, Grover Alexander, Philadelphia N.L., 1916.

Most Consecutive Shutouts—6, Don Drysdale, Los Angeles, N.L., 1968.

Most Consecutive Scoreless Innings—59, Orel Hershiser, Los Angeles Dodgers, 1988.

Most Strikeouts—5,714, Nolan Ryan, New York N.L., California A.L., Houston N.L., 1968–1988 Texas, 1989–93.

Most Strikeouts, Season—505, Matthew Kilroy, Baltimore A.A., 1886. (Since 1900—383, Nolan Ryan, California, A.L., 1973.)

Most Strikeouts, Game—21, Tom Cheney, Washington A.L., 1962, 16 innings. Nine innings: 20, Roger Clemens, Boston, A.L., 1986; 19, Charles McSweeney, Providence N.L., 1884; Hugh Dailey, Chicago U.A., 1884. (Since 1900—19, Steve Carlton, St. Louis N.L. vs. New York, Sept. 15, 1969; Tom Seaver, New York N.L. vs. San Diego, April 22, 1970; Nolan Ryan, California A.L. vs. Boston, Aug. 12, 1974; David Cone, New York N.L. vs. Philadelphia, Oct. 6, 1991.)

Most Consecutive Strikeouts—10, Tom Seaver, New York N.L. vs. San Diego, April 22, 1970.

Most Games, Season—106, Mike Marshall, Los Angeles, N.L., 1974.

Most Complete Games, Season—74, William White, Cincinnati N.L., 1879. (Since 1900—48, Jack Chesbro, New York A.L., 1904.)

ROOKIE OF THE YEAR
(Baseball Writers Association selections)

American League

1949	Roy Sievers, St. Louis	
1950	Walt Dropo, Boston	
1951	Gil McDougald, New York	
1952	Harry Byrd, Philadelphia	
1953	Harvey Kuenn, Detroit	
1954	Bob Grim, New York	
1955	Herb Score, Cleveland	
1956	Luis Aparicio, Chicago	
1957	Tony Kubek, New York	
1958	Albie Pearson, Washington	
1959	Bob Allison, Washington	
1960	Ron Hansen, Baltimore	
1961	Don Schwall, Boston	
1962	Tom Tresh, New York	
1963	Gary Peters, Chicago	
1964	Tony Oliva, Minnesota	
1965	Curt Blefary, Baltimore	
1966	Tommy Agee, Chicago	
1967	Rod Carew, Minnesota	
1968	Stan Bahnsen, New York	
1969	Lou Piniella, Kansas City	
1970	Thurman Munson, New York	
1971	Chris Chambliss, Cleveland	
1972	Carlton Fisk, Boston	
1973	Alonzo Bumbry, Baltimore	
1974	Mike Hargrove, Texas	
1975	Fred Lynn, Boston	
1976	Mark Fidrych, Detroit	
1977	Eddie Murray, Baltimore	
1978	Lou Whitaker, Detroit	
1979	Alfredo Griffin, Toronto	
1979	John Castino, Minnesota	

1980	Joe Charboneau, Cleveland	
1981	Dave Righetti, New York	
1982	Cal Ripken, Jr., Baltimore	
1983	Ron Kittle, Chicago	
1984	Alvin Davis, Seattle	
1985	Ozzie Guillen, Chicago	
1986	Jose Canseco, Oakland	
1987	Mark McGwire, Oakland	
1988	Walter Weiss, Oakland	
1989	Gregg Olson, Baltimore	
1990	Sandy Alomar Jr., Cleveland	
1991	Chuck Knoblauch, Minnesota	
1992	Pat Listach, Milwaukee	
1993	Tim Salmon, California	
1994	Bob Hamelin, Kansas City	

National League

1949	Don Newcombe, Brooklyn	
1950	Sam Jethroe, Boston	
1951	Willie Mays, New York	
1952	Joe Black, Brooklyn	
1953	Jim Gilliam, Brooklyn	
1954	Wally Moon, St. Louis	
1955	Bill Virdon, St. Louis	
1956	Frank Robinson, Cincinnati	
1957	Jack Sanford, Philadelphia	
1958	Orlando Cepeda, San Francisco	
1959	Willie McCovey, San Francisco	
1960	Frank Howard, Los Angeles	
1961	Billy Williams, Chicago	
1962	Ken Hubbs, Chicago	
1963	Pete Rose, Cincinnati	
1964	Richie Allen, Philadelphia	

1965	Jim Lefebvre, Los Angeles	
1966	Tommy Helms, Cincinnati	
1967	Tom Seaver, New York	
1968	Johnny Bench, Cincinnati	
1969	Ted Sizemore, Los Angeles	
1970	Carl Morton, Montreal	
1971	Earl Williams, Atlanta	
1972	Jon Matlack, New York	
1973	Gary Matthews, San Francisco	
1974	Bake McBride, St. Louis	
1975	John Montefusco, San Francisco	
1976	Pat Zachry, Cincinnati	
1976	Bruce Metzger, San Diego	
1977	Andre Dawson, Montreal	
1978	Bob Horner, Atlanta	
1979	Rick Sutcliffe, Los Angeles	
1980	Steve Howe, Los Angeles	
1981	Fernando Valenzuela, Los Angeles	
1982	Steve Sax, Los Angeles	
1983	Darryl Strawberry, New York	
1984	Dwight Gooden, New York	
1985	Vince Coleman, St. Louis	
1986	Todd Worrell, St. Louis	
1987	Benito Santiago, San Diego	
1988	Chris Sabo, Cincinnati	
1989	Jerome Walton, Chicago	
1990	Dave Justice, Atlanta	
1991	Jeff Baguell, Houston	
1992	Eric Karros, Los Angeles	
1993	Mike Piazza, Los Angeles	
1994	Raul Mondesi, Los Angeles	

MAJOR LEAGUE ATTENDANCE RECORDS
(Through 1994)

Single game—78,672, San Francisco at Los Angeles (N.L.), April 18, 1958. (At Memorial Coliseum.)

Doubleheader—84,587, New York at Cleveland (A.L.), Sept. 12, 1954.

Night—78,382, Chicago at Cleveland (A.L.), Aug. 20, 1948.

Season, home—4,483,350, Colorado (N.L.), 1993.

Season, league—36,912,502, National League, 1993.

Season, both leagues—70,257,938, 1993.

Season, road—2,461,240, New York (A.L.), 1980.

World Series, single game—92,706, Chicago (A.L.) at Los Angeles (N.L.), Oct. 6, 1959.

World Series, all games (6)—420,784, Chicago (A.L.) and Los Angeles (N.L.), 1959.

MOST HOME RUNS IN ONE SEASON
(45 or More)

HR	Player/Team	Year	HR	Player/Team	Year
61	Roger Maris, New York (AL)	1961	48	Harmon Killebrew, Minnesota (AL)	196
60	Babe Ruth, New York (AL)	1927	48	Willie Stargell, Pittsburgh (NL)	197
59	Babe Ruth, New York (AL)	1921	48	Dave Kingman, Chicago (NL)	197
58	Jimmy Foxx, Philadelphia (AL)	1932	48	Mike Schmidt, Philadelphia (NL)	198
58	Hank Greenberg, Detroit (AL)	1938	47	Babe Ruth, New York (AL)	192
56	Hack Wilson, Chicago (NL)	1930	47	Ralph Kiner, Pittsburgh (NL)	195
54	Babe Ruth, New York (AL)	1920	47	Ed Mathews, Milwaukee (NL)	195
54	Babe Ruth, New York (AL)	1928	47	Ernie Banks, Chicago (NL)	195
54	Ralph Kiner, Pittsburgh (NL)	1949	47	Willie Mays, San Francisco (NL)	196
54	Mickey Mantle, New York (AL)	1961	47	Henry Aaron, Atlanta (NL)	197
52	Mickey Mantle, New York (AL)	1956	47	Reggie Jackson, Oakland (AL)	196
52	Willie Mays, San Francisco (NL)	1965	47	George Bell, Toronto (AL)	198
52	George Foster, Cincinnati (NL)	1977	47	Kevin Mitchell, San Francisco (NL)	198
51	Ralph Kiner, Pittsburgh (NL)	1947	46	Babe Ruth, New York (AL)	192
51	John Mize, New York (NL)	1947	46	Babe Ruth, New York, (AL)	192
51	Willie Mays, New York (NL)	1955	46	Babe Ruth, New York (AL)	193
51	Cecil Fielder (AL)	1990	46	Lou Gehrig, New York (AL)	193
50	Jimmy Foxx, Boston (AL)	1938	46	Joe DiMaggio, New York (AL)	193
49	Babe Ruth, New York (AL)	1930	46	Ed Mathews, Milwaukee (NL)	195
49	Lou Gehrig, New York (AL)	1934	46	Orlando Cepeda, San Francisco (NL)	196
49	Lou Gehrig, New York (AL)	1936	46	Jim Rice, Boston (AL)	1978
49	Ted Kluszewski, Cincinnati (NL)	1954	46	Juan Gonzalez, Texas (AL)	1993
49	Willie Mays, San Francisco (NL)	1962	46	Barry Bonds, San Francisco (NL)	1993
49	Harmon Killebrew, Minnesota (AL)	1964	45	Harmon Killebrew, Minnesota (AL)	1963
49	Frank Robinson, Baltimore (AL)	1966	45	Willie McCovey, San Francisco (NL)	1969
49	Harmon Killebrew, Minnesota (AL)	1969	45	Johnny Bench, Cincinnati (NL)	1970
49	Mark McGwire, Oakland (AL)	1987	45	Gorman Thomas, Milwaukee (AL)	1979
49	Andre Dawson, Chicago (NL)	1987	45	Henry Aaron, Milwaukee (NL)	1962
48	Jimmy Foxx, Philadelphia (AL)	1933	45	Ken Griffey, Jr., Seattle (AL)	1993
48	Frank Howard, Washington (AL)	1969			

MAJOR LEAGUE BASEBALL—1995[1]

AMERICAN LEAGUE
(Final Standing—1995)

EASTERN DIVISION

Team	W	L	Pct	GB
Boston Red Sox[x]	86	58	.597	—
New York Yankees[y]	79	65	.549	7
Baltimore Orioles	71	73	.493	15
Detroit Tigers	60	84	.417	26
Toronto Blue Jays	56	88	.389	30

CENTRAL DIVISION

Team	W	L	Pct	GB
Cleveland Indians[x]	100	44	.694	—
Kansas City Royals	70	74	.486	30
Chicago White Sox	68	76	.472	32
Milwaukee Brewers	65	79	.451	35
Minnesota Twins	56	88	.389	44

WESTERN DIVISION

Team	W	L	Pct	GB
Seattle Mariners[x]	79	66	.545	—
California Angels	78	67	.538	1
Texas Rangers	74	70	.514	4 1/2
Oakland Athletics	67	77	.465	11 1/2

NATIONAL LEAGUE
(Final Standing—1995)

EASTERN DIVISION

Team	W	L	Pct	GB
Atlanta Braves[x]	90	54	.625	—
New York Mets	69	75	.479	21
Philadelphia Phillies	69	75	.479	21
Florida Marlins	67	76	.469	22 1/2
Montreal Expos	66	78	.458	24

CENTRAL DIVISION

Team	W	L	Pct	GB
Cincinnati Reds[x]	85	59	.590	—
Houston Astros	76	68	.528	9
Chicago Cubs	73	71	.507	12
St. Louis Cardinals	62	81	.434	22 1/2
Pittsburgh Pirates	58	86	.403	27

WESTERN DIVISION

Team	W	L	Pct	GB
Los Angeles Dodgers[x]	78	66	.542	—
Colorado Rockies[y]	77	67	.535	1
San Diego Padres	70	74	.486	8
San Francisco Giants[ʼ]	67	77	.465	11

1. Season reduced to 144 games instead of normal 162 due to players strike. x—Clinched division championship. y—Clinched wild card berth.

AMERICAN LEAGUE LEADERS—1995

Batting—Edgar Martinez, Seattle		.356
Runs—Albert Belle, Cleveland		121
Hits—Lance Johnson, Chicago		186
Runs batted in—Albert Belle, Cleveland		126
Triples—Kenny Lofton, Cleveland		13
Doubles—Albert Belle, Cleveland		52
Home runs—Albert Belle, Cleveland		50
Stolen bases—Kenny Lofton, Cleveland		54
Total bases—Albert Belle, Cleveland		377
Slugging percentage—Albert Belle, Cleveland		.690
On-base percentage—Edgar Martinez, Seattle		.479

NATIONAL LEAGUE LEADERS—1995

Batting—Tony Gwynn, San Diego		.368
Runs—Craig Biggio, Houston		123
Hits—Dante Bichette, Colorado		197
Runs batted in—Dante Bichette, Colorado		128
Triples—Brett Butler, N.Y./L.A.		9
Doubles—Mark Grace, Chicago		51
Home runs—Dante Bichette, Colorado		40
Stolen bases—Quilvio Veras, Florida		56
Total bases—Dante Bichette, Colorado		359
Slugging percentage—Dante Bichette, Colorado		.620
On-base percentage—Barry Bonds, San Francisco		.431

A.L. Pitching

Victories—Mike Mussina, Baltimore	19
Earned run average—Randy Johnson, Seattle	2.48
Strikeouts—Randy Johnson, Seattle	294
Shutouts—Mike Mussina, Baltimore	4
Complete games—Jack McDowell, New York	8
Saves—Jose Mesa, Cleveland	46
Innings pitched—David Cone, Toronto/N.Y.	229 1/3

N.L. Pitching

Victories—Greg Maddux, Atlanta	19
Earned run average—Greg Maddux, Atlanta	1.63
Strikeouts—Hideo Nomo, Los Angeles	236
Shutouts—Greg Maddux, Atlanta	3
Complete games—Greg Maddux, Atlanta	10
Saves—Randy Myers, Chicago	38
Innings pitched—Greg Maddux, Atlanta	209 2/3

•AMERICAN LEAGUE DIVISIONAL SERIES

Seattle Mariners defeated New York Yankees, 3 games to 2.
Oct. 3—NEW YORK 9, Seattle 6
Oct. 4—NEW YORK 7, Seattle 5 (15 innings)
Oct. 6—SEATTLE 7, New York 4
Oct. 7—SEATTLE 11, New York 8
Oct. 8—SEATTLE 6, New York 5 (11 innings)
Cleveland Indians defeated Boston Red Sox, 3 games to 0.
Oct. 3—CLEVELAND 5, Boston 4 (13 innings)
Oct. 4—CLEVELAND 4, Boston 0
Oct. 6—Cleveland 8, BOSTON 2

(HOME TEAM IN CAPS.)

NATIONAL LEAGUE DIVISIONAL SERIES

Cincinnati Reds defeated Los Angeles Dodgers, 3 games to 0.
Oct. 3—Cincinnati 7, LOS ANGELES 2
Oct. 4—Cincinnati 5, LOS ANGELES 4
Oct. 6—CINCINNATI 10, Los Angeles 1
Atlanta Braves defeated Colorado Rockies, 3 games to 1.
Oct. 3—Atlanta 5, COLORADO 4
Oct. 4—Atlanta 7, COLORADO 4
Oct. 6—Colorado 7, ATLANTA 5
Oct. 7—ATLANTA 10, Colorado 4

(HOME TEAM IN CAPS.)

NOTE: New York Yankees and Colorado Rockies advanced to new Divisional Series as wild card teams—second place team with the best record in the American and National Leagues, respectively. 1995 was the first year for the Divisional round.

AMERICAN LEAGUE AVERAGES—1995

Team Batting

	AB	R	H	HR	RBI	Avg
Cleveland	5028	840	1461	207	803	.290
Chicago	5060	755	1417	146	712	.280
Minnesota	5005	703	1398	120	662	.279
Boston	4997	791	1399	175	754	.279
California	5019	801	1390	180	761	.276
Seattle	4996	796	1377	182	767	.275
New York	4947	749	1365	122	709	.275
Texas	4913	691	1304	138	651	.265
Milwaukee	5000	740	1329	128	700	.265
Oakland	4915	730	1296	169	694	.263
Baltimore	4837	704	1207	173	688	.261
Kansas City	4903	629	1275	119	578	.260
Toronto	5036	642	1309	140	613	.259
Detroit	4865	654	1204	159	619	.247

Individual Batting

(Based on 300 plate appearances.)

Player/Team	AB	R	H	HR	RBI	Avg
EMartinez, Sea	511	121	182	29	113	.356
Knoblauch, Minn	538	107	179	11	63	.333
Salmon, Cal	537	111	177	34	105	.330
Boggs, NY	460	76	149	5	63	.324
Murray, Cle	436	68	141	21	82	.323
GAnderson, Cal	374	50	120	16	69	.321
Surhoff, Mil	415	72	133	13	73	.320
CDavis, Cal	424	81	135	29	86	.318
Belle, Cle	546	121	173	50	126	.317
Thome, Cle	452	92	142	25	73	.314
Baerga, Cle	557	87	175	15	90	.314
Puckett, Minn	538	83	169	23	99	.314
Seitzer, Mil	492	56	153	5	69	.311
Lofton, Cle	481	93	149	7	53	.310
RPalmeiro, Bal	554	89	172	39	104	.310
Joyner, KC	465	69	144	12	83	.310

Individual Pitching

(Based on 3 decisions)

Player/Club	IP	H	BB	SO	W	L	ERA
Tavares, Cle	85	76	21	68	10	2	2.44
RJohnson, Sea	214	189	86	294	18	2	2.48
Wakefield, Bos	195	163	68	119	16	8	2.95
DWells, Det	130	120	37	83	10	3	3.04
DeMartinez, Cle	187	174	46	99	12	5	3.08
Mussina, Bal	221	187	50	158	19	9	3.29
Rogers, Tex	208	192	76	140	17	7	3.37

Player/Club	IP	H	BB	SO	W	L	ERA
Cone, NY	229	185	88	191	18	8	3.57
KBrown, Bal	172	155	48	117	10	9	3.60
ALeiter, Tor	183	162	108	153	11	11	3.64
JAbbott, Cal	197	209	64	86	11	8	3.70
Gubicza, KC	213	222	62	81	12	14	3.75
AFernandez, Chi	203	200	85	159	12	8	3.80
Hershiser, Cle	167	151	51	111	16	6	3.87
Appier, KC	201	163	80	185	15	10	3.89
JMcDowell, NY	217	211	78	157	15	10	3.93

Team Pitching

	ERA	H	ER	BB	SO	ShO	Sv
Cleveland	3.83	1261	554	445	928	10	50
Baltimore	4.31	1165	607	523	930	10	29
Boston	4.39	1338	631	476	888	9	39
Kansas City	4.48	1323	642	503	763	10	37
Seattle	4.49	1343	644	591	1056	8	39
California	4.51	1310	645	486	901	9	42
New York	4.56	1286	651	535	908	5	35
Texas	4.65	1385	665	514	838	4	34
Milwaukee	4.82	1391	689	603	699	4	31
Chicago	4.85	1374	693	617	892	4	36
Toronto	4.88	1336	701	654	994	8	22
Oakland	4.93	1320	698	556	890	4	34
Detroit	5.49	1509	778	536	729	3	38
Minnesota	5.76	1450	815	533	790	2	27

NATIONAL LEAGUE AVERAGES—1995

Team Batting

	AB	R	H	HR	RBI	Avg
Colorado	4894	785	1406	200	749	.281
Houston	5087	747	1404	109	694	.276
San Diego	4950	668	1345	116	618	.271
Cincinnati	4903	747	1326	161	694	.270
New York	4958	657	1323	125	617	.266
Chicago	4983	693	1315	158	648	.264
Los Angeles	4942	634	1303	140	593	.263
Philadelphia	4950	615	1286	94	576	.261
Florida	4886	673	1278	144	636	.261
Pittsburgh	4937	629	1281	125	587	.259
Montreal	4905	621	1268	118	572	.258
San Francisco	4871	652	1256	152	610	.252
Atlanta	4814	645	1202	168	618	.249
St. Louis	4779	563	1182	107	533	.247

Individual Batting
(Based on 300 plate appearances.)

Player/Team	AB	R	H	HR	RBI	Avg
TGwynn, SD	535	82	197	9	90	.368
Piazza, LA	434	82	150	32	93	.346
Bichette, Col	579	102	197	40	128	.340
DBell, Hou	452	63	151	8	86	.334
Grace, Chi	552	97	180	16	92	.326
Larkin, Cin	496	98	158	15	66	.319
EYoung, Col	366	68	116	6	36	.317
Eisenreich, Phi	377	46	119	10	55	.316
Magadan, Hou	348	44	109	2	51	.313
Klesko, Atl	329	48	102	23	70	.310
Castilla, Col	527	82	163	32	90	.309
Segui, Mon	456	68	141	12	68	.309
Mabry, StL	388	35	119	5	41	.307
RSanders, Cin	484	91	148	28	99	.306
LWalker, Col	494	96	151	36	101	.306
Jefferies, Phi	480	89	147	11	56	.306

Individual Pitching
(Based on 10 decisions)

Player/Team	IP	H	BB	SO	W	L	ERA
GMaddux, Atl	208	147	23	181	19	2	1.63
Nomo, LA	191	124	78	236	13	6	2.54
BHenry, Mon	126	133	28	60	7	9	2.84
Ashby, SD	192	180	62	150	12	10	2.94
Valdes, LA	197	168	51	150	13	11	3.05
Glavine, Atl	198	182	66	127	16	7	3.08

Player/Team	IP	H	BB	SO	W	L	ERA
Hamilton, SD	204	189	56	123	6	9	3.08
Smoltz, Atl	192	166	72	193	12	7	3.18
FCastillo, Chi	188	179	52	135	11	10	3.21
Schourek, Cin	190	158	45	160	16	7	3.22
Navarro, Chi	200	194	56	128	14	6	3.28
Hampton, Hou	150	141	49	115	9	8	3.35
DeLucia, StL	82	63	38	76	8	7	3.39
Neagle, Pit	209	221	45	150	13	8	3.43
Rapp, Fla	167	158	76	102	14	7	3.44
Smiley, Cin	176	173	39	124	12	5	3.46
Reynolds, Hou	189	196	37	175	10	11	3.47
Candiotti, LA	190	187	58	141	7	14	3.50

Team Pitching

	ERA	H	ER	BB	SO	ShO	Sv
Atlanta	3.44	1184	494	436	1087	11	34
Los Angeles	3.85	1188	526	462	1060	11	36
New York	3.87	1296	556	401	901	9	36
Cincinnati	4.03	1270	578	424	903	10	38
Houston	4.06	1357	598	460	1056	8	32
St. Louis	4.08	1290	575	445	842	6	38
Montreal	4.10	1286	588	416	950	9	42
Chicago	4.12	1314	597	518	927	12	45
San Diego	4.13	1242	590	512	1047	10	35
Philadelphia	4.20	1241	603	538	980	8	41
Florida	4.26	1299	610	562	994	7	29
Pittsburgh	4.69	1407	666	477	871	7	29
San Francisco	4.86	1368	699	505	801	5	34
Colorado	4.95	1443	711	512	891	1	43

MAJOR LEAGUE BASEBALL—1995

AMERICAN LEAGUE CHAMPIONSHIP SERIES—1995
(Cleveland Indians win series, 4 games to 2)

1st Game, Seattle Wash., Oct. 10, 1995

Cleveland	001	000	100	—	2	10	1
Seattle	000	000	10x	—	3	7	0

Cleve: D. Martinez, Tavarez, Assenmacher, Plunk; Sea: Wolcott, Nelson, Charlton.
Winner: Wolcott. Loser: Martinez. Attendance: 57,065.

2nd Game, Seattle, Wash., Oct. 11, 1995

Cleveland	000	022	010	—	5	12	0
Seattle	000	001	001	—	2	6	1

Cleve: Hershiser, Mesa; Sea: Belcher, Ayala, Risley.
Winner: Hershiser. Loser: Belcher. Attendance: 58,144.

3rd Game, Cleveland, Ohio, Oct. 13, 1995

Seattle	001	000	000	03—	5	9	1
Cleveland	000	100	010	00—	2	4	2

Sea: Johnson, Charlton; Cleve: Nagy, Mesa, Tavarez, Assenmacher, Plunk.
Winner: Charlton. Loser: Tavarez. Attendance: 43,543.

4th Game, Cleveland, Ohio, Oct. 14, 1995

Seattle	000	000	000	—	0	6	1
Cleveland	312	001	00x	—	7	9	0

Sea: Benes, Wells, Ayala, Nelson, Risley; Cleve: Hill, Poole, Ogea, Embree.
Winner: Hill. Loser: Benes. Attendance: 43,686.

5th Game, Cleveland, Ohio, Oct. 15, 1995

Seattle	001	010	000	—	2	5	2
Cleveland	100	002	00x	—	3	10	4

Sea: Bosio, Nelson, Risley; Cleve: Hershiser, Tavarez, Assenmacher, Plunk, Mesa.
Winner: Hershiser. Loser: Bosio. Attendance: 43,607.

6th Game, Seattle, Wash., Oct. 17, 1995

Cleveland	000	010	030	—	4	8	0
Seattle	000	000	000	—	0	4	1

Cleve: Martinez, Tavarez, Mesa; Sea: Johnson, Charlton.
Winner: Martinez. Loser: Johnson. Attendance: 58,489.

NATIONAL LEAGUE CHAMPIONSHIP SERIES—1995
(Atlanta Braves win series, 4 games to 0)

1st Game, at Cincinnati, Ohio, Oct. 10, 1995

Atlanta	000	000	001	01—	2	7	0
Cincinnati	000	100	000	00—	1	8	0

Atl: Glavine, Pena, Wohlers, Clontz, Avery, McMichael; Cin: Schourek, Brantley, Jackson.
Winner: Wohlers. Loser: Jackson. Attendance: 40,382.

2nd Game, at Cincinnati, Ohio, Oct. 11, 1995

Atlanta	100	100	000	4—	6	11	1
Cincinnati	000	200	000	0—	2	9	1

Atl: Smoltz, Pena, McMichael, Wohlers; Cin: Smiley, Burba, Jackson, Brantly, Portugal.
Winner: McMichael. Loser: Portugal. Attendance: 44,624.

3rd Game, at Atlanta, Ga., Oct. 13, 1995

Cincinnati	000	000	011	—	2	8	0
Atlanta	000	003	20x	—	5	12	1

Cin: Wells, Hernandez, Carrasco; Atl: Maddux, Wohlers.
Winner: Maddux. Loser: Wells. Attendance: 51,424.

4th Game, at Atlanta, Ga., Oct. 14, 1995

Cincinnati	000	000	000	—	0	3	1
Atlanta	001	000	50x	—	6	12	1

Cin: Schourek, Jackson, Burba; Atl: Avery, McMichael, Pena, Wohlers.
Winner: Avery. Loser: Schourek. Attendance: 52,067.

WORLD SERIES—1995

1st Game—Atlanta, Oct. 21
Atlanta 3, Cleveland 2

CLEVELAND (A)	AB	R	H	RBI	ATLANTA (N)	AB	R	H	RBI
Lofton cf	4	2	1	0	Grissom cf	4	0	1	0
Vizquel ss	4	0	0	0	Lemke 2b	3	0	1	0
Baerga 2b	4	0	0	1	CpJones 3b	4	0	0	0
Belle lf	3	0	0	0	McGriff 1b	3	2	1	1
Murray 1b	3	0	0	0	Justice rf	1	1	0	0
Tavarez p	0	0	0	0	Klesko lf	2	0	0	0
Embree p	0	0	0	0	a–Devereaux	0	0	0	0
Thome 3b	3	0	1	0	ph–lf	0	0	0	0
MRamirez rf	3	0	0	0	O'Brien c	2	0	0	0
SAlomar c	3	0	0	0	b–Polonia ph	1	0	0	1
Hershiser p	2	0	0	0	JLopez c	0	0	0	0
Assenmacher p	0	0	0	0	Belliard ss	2	0	0	1
Sorrento 1b	1	0	0	0	GMaddux p	3	0	0	0
Totals	**30**	**2**	**2**	**1**	**Totals**	**25**	**3**	**3**	**3**

Cleveland	100	000	001	—	2	2	0
Atlanta	010	000	20x	—	3	3	2

a–walked for Klesko in the 7th. b–grounded into fielder's choice for O'Brien in the 7th. E—McGriff (1), Belliard (1). LOB—Cleveland 1, Atlanta 4. HR—McGriff (1) off Hershiser. RBI—Baerga (1), McGriff (1), Polonia (1), Belliard (1). SB—Lofton 2 (2). S—Belliard. Runners left in scoring position—Atlanta 1 (GMaddux). Runners moved up—Vizquel, Baerga, Lemke, Polonia. DP—Cleveland 1 (Vizquel and Baerga).

Cleveland	IP	H	R	ER	BB	SO	NP	ERA
Hershiser L, 0–1	6	3	3	3	3	7	101	4.50
Assenmacher	0	0	0	0	1	0	5	0.00
Tavarez	1 1/3	0	0	0	1	0	15	0.00
Embree	2/3	0	0	0	0	2	8	0.00
Atlanta								
GMaddux W, 1–0	9	2	2	0	0	4	95	0.00

Hershiser pitched to 2 batters in the 7th. Assenmacher pitched to 1 batter in the 7th. Inherited runners–scored—Tavarez 3–2, Embree 1–0, Assenmacher 2–0. Umpires—Home, Wendelstedt; First, McKean; Second, Froemming; Third, Hirshbeck; Left, Pulli; Right, Brinkman. T—2:37. A—51,876 (52,710).

2nd Game—Atlanta, Oct. 22
Atlanta 4, Cleveland 3

CLEVELAND (A)	AB	R	H	RBI	ATLANTA (N)	AB	R	H	RBI
Lofton cf	5	1	1	0	Grissom cf	3	1	1	0
Vizquel ss	4	0	1	0	Lemke 2b	3	1	1	0
Baerga 2b	4	0	0	0	CpJones 3b	3	0	2	1
Belle lf	3	1	1	0	McGriff 1b	4	0	0	0
Murray 1b	3	1	1	0	Justice rf	3	1	2	1
MRamirez rf	4	0	2	0	Wohlers p	0	0	0	0
Thome 3b	3	0	0	0	Klesko lf	3	0	0	0
Pena c	3	0	0	0	Devereaux lf–rf	1	0	0	0
c–Sorrento ph	1	0	0	0	JLopez c	3	1	1	2
SAlomar c	0	0	0	0	Belliard ss	4	0	0	0
DeMartinez p	2	0	0	0	Glavine p	1	0	0	0
Embree p	0	0	0	0	a–DwSmith ph	1	0	0	0
b–Kirby ph	1	0	0	0	McMichael p	0	0	0	0
Poole p	0	0	0	0	APena p	0	0	0	0
Tavarez p	0	0	0	0	Polonia lf	0	0	0	0
d–Amaro ph	1	0	0	0					
Totals	**34**	**3**	**6**	**2**	**Totals**	**29**	**4**	**8**	**4**

Cleveland	020	000	100	—	3	6	2
Atlanta	002	002	00x	—	4	8	2

a–singled for Glavine in the 6th. b–struck out for Embree in the 7th. c–flied out for Pena in the 8th. d–struck out for Tavarez in the 9th. E—Belle (1), DeMartinez (1), CpJones (1), Devereaux (1). LOB—Cleveland 9, Atlanta 7. 2B—DeMartinez (1). HR—JLopez (1) off De-Martinez; Murray (1) off Glavine. RBI—Murray 2 (2), CpJones (1), Justice (1), JLopez 2 (2). SB—Lofton 2 (4), Vizquel (1). SF—

(continued)

CpJones. GIDP—McGriff, Belliard. Runners left in scoring position—Cleveland 4 (Baerga 2, Belle, Thome); Atlanta 3 (Lemke, Klesko 2). Runners moved up—McGriff, Klesko. DP—Cleveland 2 (Baerga, Vizquel and Murray), (Vizquel, Baerga and Murray).

Cleveland	IP	H	R	ER	BB	SO	NP	ERA
Martinez L, 0–1	5 2/3	8	4	4	3	3	98	6.35
Embree	1/3	0	0	0	0	0	3	0.00
Poole	1	0	0	0	0	0	14	0.00
Tavarez	1	0	0	0	0	0	7	0.00
Atlanta								
Glavine W, 1–0	6	3	2	2	3	3	99	3.00
McMichael	2/3	1	1	0	1	1	19	0.00
APena	1	1	0	0	1	0	16	0.00
Wohlers S, 1	1 1/3	1	0	0	0	1	17	0.00

Inherited runners–scored—Embree 2–0, Wohlers 1–0, APena 2–0. HBP—by DeMartinez (Grissom), by Tavarez (JLopez). WP—Glavine, McMichael. T—3:17. A—51,877 (52,710).

3rd Game—Cleveland, Oct. 24
Cleveland 7, Atlanta 6

ATLANTA (N)	AB	R	H	RBI	CLEVELAND (A)	AB	R	H	RBI
Grissom cf	6	1	2	0	Lofton cf	3	3	3	0
Polonia lf	4	1	1	1	Vizquel ss	6	2	2	1
CpJones 3b	3	2	1	0	Baerga 2b	6	0	3	3
McGriff 1b	5	1	3	2	2–Espinoza pr	0	1	0	0
Justice rf	5	0	0	1	Belle lf	4	0	1	1
Klesko dh	3	1	2	1	Murray dh	6	0	1	1
b–Devereaux					Thome 3b	4	0	0	0
ph–dh	2	0	1	0	MRamirez rf	2	1	0	0
JLopez c	5	0	0	0	Sorrento 1b	4	0	1	0
Lemke 2b	5	0	2	0	1–Kirby pr	0	0	0	0
Belliard ss	2	0	0	0	HPerry 1b	1	0	0	0
a–DwSmith ph	1	0	0	0	SAlomar c	5	0	1	0
Mordecai ss	1	0	0	0					
Totals	**46**	**6**	**12**	**6**	**Totals**	**41**	**7**	**12**	**7**

Atlanta	100	001	130	00—	6	12	1
Cleveland	202	000	110	01—	7	12	2

No outs when winning run scored. a–grounded out for Belliard in the 7th. b–singled for Klesko in the 8th. 1–ran for Sorrento in the 8th. 2–ran for Baerga in the 11th. E—Belliard (2), Baerga (1), Sorrento (1). LOB—Atlanta 7, Cleveland 13. 2B—Grissom (1), CpJones (2), Lofton (1), Baerga (1), SAlomar (1). 3B—Vizquel (1). HR—McGriff(2) off Nagy; Klesko (1) off Nagy. RBI—Polonia (2), McGriff 2 (3), Justice (2), Klesko (1), Devereaux (1) Vizquel (1),Baerga 3 (4), Belle (1), Murray (1), SAlomar (1). SB—Polonia (1), McGriff (1), Lofton (5), MRamirez (1). CS—Grissom (1), Lofton (1). S—Mordecai. GIDP—Grissom, JLopez, MRamirez. Runners left in scoring position—Atlanta 4 (CpJones, JLopes 3); Cleveland 6 (Vizquel, Baerga 2, Murray, SAlomar 2). Runners moved up—McGriff, Vizquel, Baerga, SAlomar. DP—Atlanta 1 (Lemke and McGriff); Cleveland 2 (Baerga, Vizquel and Sorrento), (Baerga, Vizquel and HPerry).

Atlanta	IP	H	R	ER	BB	SO	NP	ERA
Smoltz	2 1/3	6	4	4	2	4	56	15.43
Clontz	2 1/3	1	0	0	0	1	32	0.00
Mercker	2	1	1	1	2	2	34	4.50
McMichael	2/3	1	1	1	1	1	17	6.75
Wohlers	2 2/3	0	0	0	2	4	32	0.00
APena L, 0–1	0	2	1	1	1	0	10	9.00
Cleveland								
Nagy	7	8	5	5	1	4	86	6.43
Assenmacher	1/3	0	1	1	1	0	10	27.00
Tavarez	2/3	0	0	0	0	0	3	0.00
Mesa W, 1–0	3	3	0	0	1	3	36	0.00

Nagy pitched to 2 batters in the 8th, APena pitched to 3 batters in the 11th. Inherited runners–scored—Clontz 3–0, Mercker 1–0, McMichael 2–0, Wohlers 2–1, Assenmacher 1–1, Tavarez 2–1. IBB—off Wohlers (Lofton) 2, off APena (Belle) 1. T—4:09. A—43,584 (42,865).

4th Game—Cleveland, Oct. 25
Atlanta 5, Cleveland 2

ATLANTA (N)	AB	R	H	RBI	CLEVELAND (A)	AB	R	H	RBI
Grissom cf	4	1	3	1	Lofton cf	5	0	0	0
Polonia lf	4	1	2	1	Vizquel ss	3	0	0	0
Devereaux lf	0	0	0	0	Baerga 2b	4	0	1	0
CpJones 3b	3	0	0	0	Belle lf	3	1	1	1
McGriff 1b	3	1	1	0	Murray dh	2	0	0	0
Justice rf	5	0	1	2	MRamirez rf	3	1	1	1
Klesko dh	3	1	1	1	HPerry 1b	3	0	0	0
b-Mordecai ph–dh	1	0	0	0	c-Sorrento ph	0	0	1	0
JLopez c	5	0	2	0	Espinoza 3b	2	0	1	0
Lemke 2b	5	0	1	0	a-Thome ph–3b	2	0	1	0
Belliard ss	4	1	0	0	SAlomar c	4	0	0	0
Totals	37	5	11	5	Totals	32	2	6	2

| Atlanta | 000 | 001 | 301 | — | 5 | 11 | 1 |
| Cleveland | 000 | 001 | 001 | — | 2 | 6 | 0 |

a–doubled for Espinoza in the 8th. b–lined out for Klesko in the 9th. c–doubled for Perry in the 9th. E—Lemke (1). LOB—Atlanta 12, Cleveland 8. 2B—Polonia (1), McGriff (1), JLopez 2 (2), Sorrento (1), Thome (1). HR—Belle (1) off Avery; MRamirez (1) off Wohlers; Klesko (2) off KHill. RBI—Polonia (3), Justice 2 (4), Klesko (2), JLopez (3), Belle (2), MRamirez (1). SB—Grissom 2 (2). CS—Ezpinoza (1). S—Belliard. Runners left in scoring position—Atlanta 7 (CpJones 2, McGriff, Justice 2, Lemke, Belliard); Cleveland 4 (Lofton, Vizquel, Murray, HPerry). Runners moved up—Polonia, CpJones 3, Lemke, SAlomar. DP—Atlanta 1 (Belliard, Lemke and McGriff).

Atlanta	IP	H	R	ER	BB	SO	NP	ERA
Avery W, 1–0	6	3	1	1	5	3	109	1.50
McMichael	2	1	0	0	0	0	15	2.70
Wohlers	0	2	1	1	0	0	10	2.25
Borbon S, 1	1	0	0	0	0	2	11	0.00
Cleveland								
KHill L, 0–1	6 1/3	6	3	3	4	1	94	4.26
Assenmacher	2/3	1	1	1	0	2	12	9.00
Tavarez	2/3	2	0	0	1	1	18	0.00
Embree	1 1/3	2	1	1	0	0	24	3.86

Wohlers pitched to 2 batters in the 9th. Inherited runners–scored—Borbon 1–0, Assenmacher 1–1, Embree 3–0. IBB—off Avery (MRamirez)1, off Assenmacher (CpJones) 1. PB—SAlomar. Balk—Avery. T—3:14. A—43,578 (42,865).

5th Game—Cleveland, Oct. 26
Cleveland 5, Atlanta 4

ATLANTA (N)	AB	R	H	RBI	CLEVELAND (A)	AB	R	H	RBI
Grissom cf	4	0	1	1	Lofton cf	4	0	0	0
Polonia lf	4	1	1	0	Vizquel ss	3	1	1	0
CpJones 3b	4	0	1	0	Baerga 2b	4	1	1	0
McGriff 1b	4	1	1	0	Belle lf	3	2	1	2
Justice rf	4	0	0	0	Murray dh	3	0	0	0
Klesko dh	4	2	2	2	Thome 3b	4	1	2	2
Lemke 2b	4	0	0	0	MRamirez rf	3	0	1	1
O'Brien c	1	0	0	0	HPerry 1b	1	0	0	0
b–JLopez ph–c	1	0	0	0	Sorrento 1b	3	0	0	0
Belliard ss	1	0	0	0	Kirby rf	0	0	0	0
a–DwSmith ph	0	0	0	0	SAlomar c	3	0	2	0
Mordecai ss	1	0	1	0					
Totals	32	4	7	4	Totals	31	5	8	5

| Atlanta | 000 | 110 | 002 | — | 4 | 7 | 0 |
| Cleveland | 200 | 002 | 01x | — | 5 | 8 | 1 |

a–was intentionally walked for Belliard in the 5th. b–grounded out for O'Brien in the 7th. E—Hershiser (1). LOB—Atlatna 3, Cleveland 5. 2B—CpJones (3), McGriff (2), Baerga (2), SAlomar (2). HR—Belle (2) off GMaddux; Thome (1) off Clontz; Polonia (1) off Hershiser; Klesko (3) off Mesa. RBI—Grissom (4), Klesko 2 (4), Belle 2 (4), Thome 2 (2). MRamirez (2). S—O'Brien. GIDP—Polonia. Runners left in scoring position—Atlanta 3 (Polonia 2, McGriff); Cleveland 2 (Lofton, Sorrento). Runners moved up—

Justice, Baerga, Murray. DP—Cleveland 2 (Vizquel, Baerga and Sorrento), (Hershiser and HPerry).

Atlanta	IP	H	R	ER	BB	SO	NP	ERA
GMaddux L, 1–1	7	7	4	4	3	4	98	2.25
Clontz	1	1	1	1	0	1	20	2.70
Cleveland								
Hershiser W, 1–1	8	5	2	1	1	6	100	2.57
Mesa S, 1	1	2	2	2	0	1	18	4.50

IBB—off GMaddux (Belle) 1, off Hershiser (DwSmith) 1. T—2:33. A—43,595 (42,865).

6th Game—Atlanta, Oct. 28
Atlanta 1, Cleveland 0

CLEVELAND (A)	AB	R	H	RBI	ATLANTA (N)	AB	R	H	RBI
Lofton cf	4	0	0	0	Grissom cf	4	0	1	0
Vizquel ss	3	0	0	0	Lemke 2b	2	0	1	0
b-Sorrento ph	1	0	0	0	CpJones 3b	3	0	2	0
Baerga 2b	4	0	0	0	McGriff 1b	4	0	0	0
Belle lf	4	0	0	0	Justice rf	2	1	2	1
Murray 1b	2	0	0	0	Klesko lf	1	0	0	0
MRamirez rf	3	0	0	0	Devereaux lf	1	0	0	0
Embree p	0	0	0	0	JLopez c	3	0	0	0
Tavarez p	0	0	0	0	Belliard ss	4	0	0	0
Assenmacher p	0	0	0	0	Glavine p	3	0	0	0
Thome 3b	3	0	0	0	a-Polonia ph	1	0	0	0
Pena c	3	0	1	0	Wohlers p	0	0	0	0
DeMartinez p	1	0	0	0					
Poole p	1	0	0	0					
KHill p	0	0	0	0					
Amaro rf	1	0	0	0					
Totals	27	0	1	0	Totals	28	1	6	1

| Cleveland | 000 | 000 | 000 | — | 0 | 1 | 1 |
| Atlanta | 000 | 001 | 00x | — | 1 | 6 | 0 |

a—struck out for Glavine in the 8th. b—flied out for Vizquel in the 9th. E—Thome (1). LOB—Cleveland 3, Atlanta 11. 2B—Justice (1). HR—Justice (1) off Poole. RBI—Justice (5). SB—Lofton (6), Grissom (3). CS—Belle (1), Lemke (1). S—Lemke. GIDP—Belliard. RLISP—Cleveland 1 (Vizquel); Atlanta 6 (McGriff, Devereaux 2, Belliard 3). DP—Cleveland 1 (Vizquel, Baerga and Murray).

Cleveland	IP	H	R	ER	BB	SO	NP	ERA
DeMartinez	4 2/3	4	0	0	5	2	78	3.48
Poole L, 0—1	1 1/3	1	1	1	0	0	25	3.86
KHill	1	0	0	0	0	0	5	4.26
Embree	1	0	0	0	2	0	9	2.70
Tavarez	2/3	0	0	0	0	1	15	0.00
Assenmacher	1/3	0	0	0	0	1	5	6.75
Atlanta								
Glavine W, 2-0	8	1	0	0	3	8	109	1.29
Wohlers S, 2	1	0	0	0	0	0	9	1.80

KHill pitched to 1 batter in the 7th. IRS—Embree 1—0, Poole 2—0. IBB—off Embree (CpJones) 1, off DeMartinez (Klesko) 1. Umpires—Home, Brinkman; First, Wendelstedt; Second, McKean; Third, Froemming; Left, Hirschbeck; Right, Pulli. T—3:02. A—51,875, (52,710).

SOFTBALL

Source: Amateur Softball Association.

AMATEUR CHAMPIONS

1959	Aurora (Ill.) Sealmasters	1974	Santa Rosa (Calif.)	1985	Pay 'n Pak, Bellevue, Wash.
1960	Clearwater (Fla.) Bombers	1975	Rising Sun Hotel, Reading, Pa.	1986	Pay 'n Pak, Bellevue, Wash.
1961	Aurora (Ill.) Sealmasters	1976	Raybestos Cardinals,	1987	Pay 'n Pak, Bellevue, Wash.
1962–63	Clearwater (Fla.) Bombers		Stratford, Conn.	1988	TransAire, Elkhart, Ind.
1964	Burch Gage & Tool, Detroit	1977	Billard Barbell, Reading, Pa.	1989	Penn Corp., Sioux City, Iowa
1965	Aurora (Ill.) Sealmasters	1978	Reading, Pa.	1990	Penn Corp., Sioux City, Iowa
1966	Clearwater (Fla.) Bombers	1979	Midland, Mich.	1991	Guanella Brothers, Rohnert
1967	Aurora (Ill.) Sealmasters	1980	Peterbilt Western, Seattle		Park, Calif.
1968	Clearwater (Fla.) Bombers	1981	Archer Daniels Midland,	1992	National Health Care, Sioux
1969–70	Raybestos Cardinals,		Decatur, Ill.		City, Iowa
	Stratford, Conn.	1982	Peterbilt Western, Seattle	1993	National Health Care, Sioux
1971	Welty Way, Cedar Rapids, Iowa	1983	Franklin Cardinals, West		City, Iowa
1972	Raybestos Cardinals, Stratford,		Haven, Conn.	1994	Decatur Pride, Decatur, Ill.
	Conn.	1984	California Coors Kings,	1995	Decatur Pride, Decatur, Ill.
1973	Clearwater (Fla.) Bombers		Merced, Calif.		

1995 AMATEUR SOFTBALL ASSOCIATION CHAMPIONS

Fast Pitch
Men's Major—Decatur, Ill. Pride
Men's Class A—Happy Chef, Mankato, Minn.
Men's Class B—California Earthquakes, Los Banos, Calif.
Women's Major—Redding, Calif. Rebels
Women's Class A—Hot Stuff, Torrance, Calif.
Women's Class B—Arizona Heat, Glendale, Ariz.
Women's Class C—Plate Burners, Lawrenceville, Ga.
Men's Class C—Cherokee Hosers, Tulsa, Okla.
Men's 40-Over—Knoll Lumber Legends, Snohomish, Wash.
Men's 45-Over—Southern Calif. Eagles, Apine, Calif.
Men's 23-Under—Hasvold Vending, South Dakota

Slow Pitch
Men's Super—Lighthouse/Worth, Stone Mountain, Ga.
Men's Major—Riveside Rams/TPS, Louisville, Ky.
Men's Class A—So Jern Travel, Cedarbrook, N.J.
Men's Major Industrial—Sikorsky, Stratford, Conn.
Men's Class A Industrial—Worthington Industries, Hilliard, Ohio
Men's 35-Over—Winchell Clinic, Evansville, Ind.
Men's 45-Over—Dan Smith Plastering, San Jose, Calif.
Men's 55-Over—Florida Legends, Fort Myers, Fla.
Men's 60-Over—Fairway Ford, Placentia, Calif.
Men's 65-Over—HW Sport, Fort Wright, Ky.
Men's Major Church—Houston First Baptist, Houston, Tenn.
Men's Class A Church—First United Pentecostal, Monroe, La.
Coed—Major—Stars, Jacksonvill, Fla.
Coed Class A—Keathley's/TPS, Villa Hills, Ky.
Women's Major—Armed Forces, Sacramento, Calif.
Women's 35-Over—California Connection, Redwood City, Calif.

Men's 40-Over—Harrison's, Portsmouth, Va.

Junior
Girls' Gold Fast Pitch—Orange County Batbusters, Santa Ana, Calif.
Girls' 18-Under Class A Fast Pitch—California Waves, Santa Barbara, Calif.
Girls' 16-Under Fast Pitch—Orange County Batbusters, Anaheim, Calif.
Girls' 14-Under Fast Pitch—California Cruisers, Irvine, Calif.
Girls' 12-Under Fast Pitch—Southern California Firecrackers, Santa Ana, Calif.
Boys' 16-Under Fast Pitch—KL Sports 18, Bountiful, Utah
Boys' 14-Under Fast Pitch—Norman's Surveying, Sioux Falls, S.D.
Boys' 12-Under Fast Pitch—South Sioux Kiwanis, Sioux Falls, S.D.
Boys' 18-Under Fast Pitch—Rees Development, Utah
Boys' 18-Under Slow Pitch—Chambers County, Lafayette, Ala.
Boys' 16-Under Slow Pitch—Dream Team, Roanoke, Ala.
Boys' 14-Under Slow Pitch—Al's Trophy Shop and Sporting Goods, Satellite Beach, Fla.
Boys' 12-Under Slow Pitch—Al's Trophy Shop and Sporting Goods, Satellite Beach, Fla.
Girls' 18-Under Slow Pitch—Lady Panthers, Lilburn, Ga.
Girls' 16-Under Slow Pitch—Oklahoma Renegades, Moore, Okla.
Girls' 14-Under Slow Pitch—Thrillers, West Palm Beach, Fla.
Girls' 12-Under Slow Pitch—Lady Magic, Greenbriar, Ariz.

Modified Pitch
Women's Major Modified—Roger's Renegades, Hookset, N.H.
Men's Major Modified Pitch—Brymile, Spokane, Wash.
Class A Modified Pitch—Jim's Gun Shop, Winslow, Me.

LITTLE LEAGUE WORLD SERIES CHAMPIONS

Year	Champion	Runner-up	Score	Year	Champion	Runner-up	Score
1947	Williamsport, Pa.	Lock Haven, Pa.	16–7	1972	Taipei, Taiwan	Hammond, Ind.	6–0
1948	Lock Haven, Pa.	St. Petersburg, Fla.	6–5	1973	Tainan City, Taiwan	Tuscon, Ariz.	12–0
1949	Hammonton, N.J.	Pensacola, Fla.	5–0	1974	Kao Hsiung, Taiwan	El Cajun, Calif.	7–2
1950	Houston, Tex.	Bridgeport, Conn.	2–1	1975	Lakewood, N.J.	Tampa, Fla.	4–3
1951	Stamford, Conn.	Austin, Tex.	3–0	1976	Tokyo, Japan	Campbell, Calif.	10–3
1952	Norwalk, Conn.	Monongahela, Pa.	4–3	1977	Kao Hsiung, Taiwan	El Cajun, Calif.	7–2
1953	Birmingham, Ala.	Schenectady, N.Y.	1–0	1978	Pin-Tung, Taiwan	Danville, Calif.	11–1
1954	Schenectady, N.Y.	Colton, Calif.	7–5	1979	Hsien, Taiwan	Campbell, Calif.	2–1
1955	Morrisville, Pa.	Merchantville, N.J.	4–3	1980	Hua Lian, Taiwan	Tampa, Fla.	4–3
1956	Roswell, N.M.	Merchantville, N.J.	3–1	1981	Tai-Chung, Taiwan	Tampa, Fla.	4–2
1957	Monterrey, Mex.	LaMesa, Calif.	4–0	1982	Kirkland, Wash.	Hsien, Taiwan	6–0
1958	Monterrey, Mex.	Kankakee, Ill.	10–1	1983	Marietta, Ga.	Barahona, D. Rep.	3–1
1959	Hamtramck, Mich.	Auburn, Calif.	12–0	1984	Seoul, S. Korea	Altamonte Springs, Fla.	6–2
1960	Levittown, Pa.	Ft. Worth, Tex.	5–0	1985	Seoul, S. Korea	Mexicali, Mex.	7–1
1961	El Cajon, Calif.	El Campo, Tex.	4–2	1986	Tainan Park, Taiwan	Tuscon, Ariz.	12–0
1962	San Jose, Calif.	Kankakee, Ill.	3–0	1987	Hua Lian, Taiwan	Irvine, Calif.	21–1
1963	Granada Hills, Calif.	Stratford, Conn.	2–1	1988	Tai-Chung, Taiwan	Pearl City, Haw.	10–0
1964	Staten Island, N.Y.	Monterrey, Mex.	4–0	1989	Trumbull, Conn.	Kaohsiung, Taiwan	5–2
1965	Windsor Locks, Conn.	Stoney Creek, Can.	3–1	1990	Taipei, Taiwan	Shippensburg, Pa.	9–0
1966	Houston, Tex.	W. New York, N.J.	8–2	1991	Tai-Chung, Taiwan	San Ramon Valley, Calif.	11–0
1967	West Tokyo, Japan	Chicago, Ill.	4–1	1992*	Long Beach, Calif.	Zamboanga, Phil.	6–0
1968	Osaka, Japan	Richmond, Va.	1–0	1993	Long Beach, Calif.	David Chiriqui, Pan.	3–2
1969	Taipei, Taiwan	Santa Clara, Calif.	5–0	1994	Maracaibo, Venezuela	Northridge, Calif.	4–3
1970	Wayne, N.J.	Campbell, Calif.	2–0	1995	Tainan, Taiwan	Spring, Texas	17–3
1971	Tainan, Taiwan	Gary, Ind.	12–3				

*Long Beach declared a 6–0 winner after the international tournament committee determined that Zamboanga City had used players that were not within its city limits.

MEDIA
(Courtesy of *Information Please Sports Almanac*.)

DAILY NEWSPAPER
USA Today
1000 Wilson Blvd., Arlington, Va. 22229
(703) 276-3400

WEEKLY MAGAZINE
Sports Illustrated
Time & Life Bldg., Rockefeller Ctr., New York, N.Y. 10020
(212) 586-1212

TELEVISION
ABC Sports
47 West 66th St., 13th Floor, New York, N.Y. 10023
(212) 887-4867

CBS Sports
51 West 52nd St., 30th Floor, New York, N.Y. 10019
(212) 975-5230

ESPN
ESPN Plaza, Bristol, Conn. 06010
(203) 585-2000

HBO Sports
1100 Ave. of the Americas, New York, N.Y. 10036
(212) 512-1000

NBC Sports
30 Rockefeller Plaza, New York, N.Y. 10112
(212) 664-4444

Prime Network
5251 Gulfton St., Houston, Texas 77081
(713) 661-0078

SportsChannel
3 Crossways Park West, Woodbury, N.Y. 11797
(516) 921-3764

Turner Sports
One CNN Center, Suite 1300, Atlanta, Ga. 30303
(404) 827-1735

USA Network
1230 Ave. of the Americas, New York, N.Y. 10020
(212) 408-8895

YACHTING

AMERICA'S CUP RECORD

First race in 1851 around Isle of Wight, Cowes, England. First defense and all others through 1920 held 30 miles off New York Bay. Races since 1930 held 30 miles off Newport, R.I. Conducted as one race only in 1851 and 1870; best four–of–seven basis, 1871; best two–of–three, 1876–1887; best three–of–five, 1893–1901; best four–of–seven, since 1930. Figures in parentheses indicate number of races won.

Year	Winner and owner	Loser and owner
1851	AMERICA (1), John C. Stevens, U.S.	AURORA, T. Le Marchant, England[1]
1870	MAGIC (1), Franklin Osgood, U.S.	CAMBRIA, James Ashbury, England[2]
1871	COLUMBIA (2), Franklin Osgood, U.S.[3]	LIVONIA (1), James Ashbury, England
	SAPPHO (2), William P. Douglas, U.S.	
1876	MADELEINE (2), John S. Dickerson, U.S.	COUNTESS OF DUFFERIN, Chas. Gifford, Canada
1881	MISCHIEF (2), J. R. Busk, U.S.	ATALANTA, Alexander Cuthbert, Canada
1885	PURITAN (2), J. M. Forbes–Gen. Charles Paine, U.S.	GENESTA, Sir Richard Sutton, England
1886	MAYFLOWER (2), Gen. Charles Paine, U.S.	GALATEA, Lt. William Henn, England
1887	VOLUNTEER (2), Gen. Charles Paine, U.S.	THISTLE, James Bell et al., Scotland
1893	VIGILANT (3), C. Oliver Iselin et al., U.S.	VALKYRIE II, Lord Dunraven, England
1895	DEFENDER (3), C. O. Iselin–W. K. Vanderbilt–E. D. Morgan, U.S	.VALKYRIE III, Lord Dunraven–Lord Lonsdale–Lord Wolverton, England
1899	COLUMBIA (3), J. P. Morgan–C. O. Iselin, U.S.	SHAMROCK I, Sir Thomas Lipton, Ireland
1901	COLUMBIA (3), Edwin D. Morgan, U.S.	SHAMROCK II, Sir Thomas Lipton, Ireland
1903	RELIANCE (3), Cornelius Vanderbilt et al., U.S.	SHAMROCK III, Sir Thomas Lipton, Ireland
1920	RESOLUTE (3), Henry Walters et al., U.S.	SHAMROCK IV (2), Sir Thomas Lipton, Ireland
1930	ENTERPRISE (4), Harold S. Vanderbilt et al., U.S.	SHAMROCK V, Sir Thomas Lipton, Ireland
1934	RAINBOW (4), Harold S. Vanderbilt, U.S.	ENDEAVOUR (2), T. O. M. Sopwith, England
1937	RANGER (4), Harold S. Vanderbilt, U.S.	ENDEAVOUR II, T. O. M. Sopwith, England
1958	COLUMBIA (4), Henry Sears et al., U.S.	SCEPTRE, Hugh Goodson et al., England
1962	WEATHERLY (4), Henry D. Mercer et al., U.S.	GRETEL I, Sir Frank Packer et al., Australia
1964	CONSTELLATION (4), New York Y.C. Syndicate, U.S.	SOVEREIGN (0), J. Anthony Bowden, England
1967	INTREPID (4), New York Y.C. Syndicate, U.S.	DAME PATTIE (0), Sydney (Aust.) Syndicate
1970	INTREPID (4), New York Y.C. Syndicate, U.S.	GRETEL II (1), Sydney (Aust.) Syndicate
1974	COURAGEOUS (4), New York, N.Y. Syndicate, U.S.	SOUTHERN CROSS (0), Sydney (Aust.) Syndicate
1977	COURAGEOUS (4), New York, N.Y. Syndicate, U.S.	AUSTRALIA (0), Sun City (Aust.) Syndicate
1980	FREEDOM (4), New York, N.Y. Syndicate, U.S.	AUSTRALIA (1), Alan Bond et al, Australia
1983	AUSTRALIA II (4) Alan Bond et al., Australia,	LIBERTY (3) New York, N.Y. Syndicate, U.S.
1987	STARS & STRIPES (4), Dennis Conner et al., United States	KOOKABURRA III (0), Iain Murray et al., Australia
1988[4]	STARS & STRIPES (4), Dennis Conner et al., United States	NEW ZEALAND Michael Fay, et al., New Zealand
1992	AMERICA 3, Bill Koch et al., United States	IL MORO DI VENEZIA, Paul Cayard, et al., Italy
1995	BLACK MAGIC, Peter Blake, et al., New Zealand	YOUNG AMERICA, Dennis Conner, et al., United States

1. Fourteen British yachts started against America; Aurora finished second. 2. Cambria sailed against 23 U.S. yachts and finished tenth. 3. Columbia was disabled in the third race, after winning the first two; Sappho substituted and won the fourth and fifth. 4. Shortly after Dennis Conner and his 60–foot, twin–hulled catamaran easily defeated the challenge of the New Zealand, a 133–foot, single–hulled yacht in the waters off San Diego in early September 1988, a New York State Supreme Court judge ruled that the Americans did not live up to the America's Cup Deed of Gift, which means competing boats must be similar. The judge ruled that the Americans had an unfair advantage over the monohulled ship, and awarded the Cup to New Zealand. However, an Appeal awarded the Cup to the United States.

CHESS

WORLD CHAMPIONS

Both the International Chess Federation (FIDE) and the breakaway Professional Chess Association (PCA) were to stage world championship matches in 1995. Azerbaijan's Garry Kasparov, 31, who was FIDE world champion until he quit to join the PCA, became the PCA's first world champion in 1993. He defended his title in the fall against Viswanathan Anand, 24, of India. Kasparov's old rival, Anatoly Karpov, who reclaimed the FIDE title in 1993, will also defend.

1894–1921	Emanuel Lasker, Germany
1921–27	Jose R. Capablanca, Cuba
1927–35	Alexander A. Alekhine, U.S.S.R.
1935–37	Dr. Max Euwe, Netherlands
1937–46	Alexander A. Alekhine, U.S.S.R.[1]
1948–57	Mikhail Botvinnik, U.S.S.R.
1957–58	Vassily Smyslov, U.S.S.R.
1958–60	Mikhail Botvinnik, U.S.S.R.
1960–61	Mikhail Tal, U.S.S.R.
1961–63	Mikhail Botvinnik, U.S.S.R.
1963–68	Tigran Petrosian, U.S.S.R.
1969–71	Boris Spassky, U.S.S.R.
1972–74	Bobby Fischer, Los Angeles
1975	Bobby Fischer[2], Anatoly Karpov, U.S.S.R.
1976–85	Anatoly Karpov, U.S.S.R.[3]
1985–	Gary Kasparov, Russia

1. Alekhine, a French citizen, died while champion. 2. Relinquished title. 3. In 1978, Karpov defeated Viktor Korchnoi 6 games to 5.

UNITED STATES CHAMPIONS

1909–36	Frank J. Marshall, New York
1936–44	Samuel Reshevsky, New York[1]
1944–46	Arnold S. Denker, New York
1946	Samuel Reshevsky, Boston
1948	Herman Steiner, Los Angeles
1951–52	Larry Evans, New York
1954–57	Arthur Bisguier, New York

1958–61	Bobby Fischer, Brooklyn, N.Y.
1962	Larry Evans, New York
1963–67	Bobby Fischer, New York
1968	Larry Evans, New York
1969–71	Samuel Reshevsky, Spring Valley, N.Y.
1972	Robert Byrne, Ossining, N.Y.
1973	Lubomir Kavelek, Washington; John Grefe, San Francisco
1974–77	Walter Browne, Berkeley, Calif.
1978–79	Lubomir Kavalek, New York
1980	Tie, Walter Browne, Berkeley, Calif. Larry Christiansen, Modesto, Calif. Larry Evans, Reno, Nev.
1981–82[2]	Tie, Walter Browne, Berkeley, Calif. Yasser Seirawan, Seattle, Wash.
1983	Tie, Walter Browne, Berkeley, Calif. Larry Christiansen, Los Angeles, Calif., Roman Dzindzichashvili, Corona, N.Y.
1984–85	Lev Alburt, New York City
1986	Yasser Seirawan, Seattle, Wash.
1987	Tie—Nick Defirmian, San Francisco, and Joel Benjamin, Brooklyn, N.Y.
1988	Michael Wilder, Princeton, N.J.
1989	Tie, Stuart Rachels, Birmingham, Ala. Yasser Seirawan, Seattle, Wash. Roman Dzindzichashvili, New York, N.Y.
1990–91	Lev Alburt, New York, N.Y.
1992	Gata Kamsky, Brooklyn, N.Y. Patrick Wolff, Summerville, Mass.
1993	Alexander Shabalov, Pittsburgh, Pa. and Alex Yermolinski, Edison, N.J.
1994	Boris Gulko, Fairlawn, N.J.

1. In 1942, Isaac I. Kashdan of New York was co-champion for a while because of a tie with Reshevsky in that year's tournament. Reshevsky won the play-off. 2. Championship not contested in 1982.

BILLIARDS

FINAL 1994 PRO TOUR TOP 20 RANKINGS

Points awareded at each event: 1st place—200 points; 2nd—160; 3rd & 4th—125; 5th & 6th—80; 7th & 8th—65; 9th–12th—50; 13th–16th—40; 17th–20th—30.

1. Nick Varner, Owensboro, Ky., 1,702 points; 2. Johnny Archer, Raleigh, N.C., 1,539; 3. Tony Ellin, Hollywood, S.C., 1,258; 4. Efren Reyes, Phillippines, 1,221; 5. Earl Strickland, Greensboro, N.C., 1,095;

6. Rafael Martinez, Mexico, 1,051; 7. Kim Davenport, Modesto, Calif., 930; 8. C.J. Wiley, Dallas, 875; 9. Tommy Kennedy, Orlando, 865; 10. George Breedlove, Indianapolis, 812;

11. Mike Sigel, Baltimore, 790; 12. Jeff Carter, Chicago, 760; 13. Buddy Hall, Metropolis, Ill., 685; 14. Howard Vickery, Columbus, Ohio, 682;

15. Allen Hopkins, Absecon, N.J., 660; 16. Jimmy Wetch, Minneapolis, 637; 17. Jim Rempe, Scranton, Pa., 625; 18. Dick Lane, Dallas, 620; 19. Danny Harriman, Springfield, Mo., 590; 20. Rodolfo Luat, Philippines, 582.

IDITAROD

23RD IDITAROD TRAIL SLED DOG RACE—1995
(Alaska, March 4–16, 1995)

The annual 1,159-mile race stretches from Anchorage to Nome, Alaska. Begun in 1973, the course follows an old frozen river route and is named after a deserted mining town along the way. The Iditarod also commemorates a famous midwinter emergency mission to get medical supplies to Nome during a 1925 diphtheria epidemic. Men and women mushers compete together.

Course: 1,159 miles, Anchorage to Nome.

1995 Champion—Doug Swingly became the first non-Alaskan to win, in record time of 9 days, 2 hours, 43 minutes, breaking last year's record set by Martin Buser.

Total purse: $350,000.

Winner's purse: $52,500.

Winning times since 1980: 1980, Joe May, 14 days–7 hours–11 minutes; 1981, Swenson, 12–8–45; 1982, Swenson, 16–4–40; 1983, Rick Mackey, 12–14–10; 1984, Dean Osmar, 12–15–7; 1985, Libby Riddles, 18–00–20; 1986, Butcher, 11–15–6; 1987, Butcher, 11–2–5; 1988, Butcher, 11–11–41; 1989, Joe Runyan, 11–5–24; 1990, Butcher, 11–1–53; 1991, Swenson, 12–16–34; 1992, Martin Buser, 10–19–17; 1993, Jeff King, 10–15–30; 1994, Martin Buser, 10–13–2; 1995, Doug Swingly, 9–2–43.

STANDARD MEASUREMENTS IN SPORTS

BASEBALL
Home plate to pitcher's box: 60 feet 6 inches.
Plate to second base: 127 feet 3 3/8 inches.
Distance from base to base (home plate included): 90 feet.
Size of bases: 15 inches by 15 inches.
Pitcher's plate: 24 inches by 6 inches.
Batter's box: 4 feet by 6 feet.
Home plate: Five–sided, 17 inches by 8 1/2 inches by 8 1/2 inches by 12 inches by 12 inches, cut to a point at rear.
Home plate to backstop: Not less than 60 feet (recommended).
Weight of ball: Not less than 5 ounces nor more than 5 1/4 ounces.
Circumference of ball: Not less than 9 inches nor more than 9 1/4 inches.
Bat: Must be one piece of solid wood, round, not over 2 3/4 inches in diameter at thickest part, nor more than 42 inches in length.070

BASKETBALL
(National Collegiate A.A. Men's Rules)
Playing court: College: 94 feet long by 50 feet wide (ideal dimensions). High School: 84 feet long by 50 feet wide (ideal inside dimensions).
Baskets: Rings 18 inches in inside diameter, with white cord 12–mesh nets, 15 to 18 inches in length. Each ring is made of metal, is not more than 5/8 of an inch in diameter, and is bright orange in color.
Height of basket: 10 feet (upper edge).
Weight of ball: Not less than 20 ounces nor more than 22.
Circumference of ball: Not greater than 30 inches and not less than 29 1/2.
Free–throw line: 15 feet from the face of the backboard, 2 inches wide.
Three–point field goal line: 19 feet, 9 inches from the center of the basket. In the National Basketball Association, the distance is 22 feet.

BOWLING
Lane dimensions: Overall length 62 feet 10 3/16 inches, measuring from foul line to pit (not including tail plank), with + or – 1/2 inch tolerance permitted. Foul line to center of No. 1 pinspot 60 feet, with + or – 1/2 inch tolerance permitted. Lane width, 41 1/2 inches with a tolerance of + or – 1/2 inch permitted. Approach, not less than 15 feet. Gutters, 9 5/16 inches wide with plus 3/16 inch or minus 5/16 inch tolerances permitted.
Ball: Circumference, not more than 27.002 inches. Weight, 16 pounds maximum.

BOXING
Ring: Professional matches take place in an area not less than 18 nor more than 24 feet square including apron. It is enclosed by four covered ropes, each not less than one inch in diameter. The floor has a 2–inch padding of Ensolite (or equivalent) underneath ring cover that extends at least 6 inches beyond the roped area in the case of elevated rings. For USA Boxing or Olympic-style boxing, not less than 16 nor more than 20 feet square within the ropes. The floor must extend beyond the ring ropes not less than 2 feet. The ring posts shall be connected to the four ring ropes with the extension not shorter than 18 inches and must be properly padded.

Gloves: In professional fights, not less than 8–ounce gloves generally are used. USA Boxing, 10 ounces for boxers 106 pounds through 156 pounds, 12–ounce for boxers 165 pounds through 201+ pounds; for international competition, 8 ounces for lighter classes, 10 ounces for heavier divisions.
Headguards: Mandatory in Olympic-style boxing.

FOOTBALL
(N.C.A.A.)
Length of field: 120 yards (including 10 yards of end zone at each end).
Width of field: 53 1/3 yards (160 feet).
Height of goal posts: At least 30 feet.
Height of crossbar: 10 feet.
Width of goal posts (above crossbar): 18 feet 6 inches, inside to inside.
Length of ball: 10 7/8 to 11 7/16 inches (long axis).
Circumference of ball: 20 3/4 to 21 1/4 inches (middle); 27 3/4 to 28 1/2 inches (long axis).

GOLF
Specifications of ball: Broadened to require that the ball be designed to perform as if it were spherically symmetrical. The weight of the ball shall not be greater than 1.620 ounces avoirdupois, and the size shall not be less than 1.680 inches in diameter.
Velocity of ball: Not greater than 250 feet per second when tested on U.S.G.A. apparatus, with 2 percent tolerance.
Hole: 4 1/4 inches in diameter and at least 4 inches deep.
Clubs: 14 is the maximum number permitted.
Overall distance standard: A brand of ball shall not exceed a distance of 280 yards plus 6% when tested on USGA apparatus under specified conditions, on an outdoor range at USGA Headquarters.

HOCKEY
Size of rink: 200 feet long by 85 feet wide surrounded by a wooden wall not less than 40 inches and not more than 48 inches above level of ice.
Size of goal: 6 feet wide by 4 feet in height.
Puck: 1 inch thick and 3 inches in diameter, made of vulcanized rubber; weight 5 1/2 to 6 ounces.
Length of stick: Not more than 60 inches from heel to end of shaft nor more than 12 1/2 inches from heel to end of blade. Blade should not be more than 3 inches in width but not less than 2 inches—except goal keeper's stick, which shall not exceed 3 1/2 inches in width except at the heel, where it must not exceed 4 1/2 inches, nor shall the goalkeeper's stick exceed 15 1/2 inches from the heel to the end of the blade.

TENNIS
Size of court: 120 feet long by 60 feet wide, with rectangle marked off at 78 feet long by 27 feet wide (singles) and 78 feet long by 36 feet wide (doubles).
Height of net: 3 feet in center, gradually rising to reach 3–foot 6–inch posts at a point 3 feet outside each side of court.
Ball: Shall be more than 2 1/2 inches and less than 2 5/8 inches in diameter and weigh more than 2 ounces and less than 2 1/16 ounces.
Service line: 21 feet from net.

SPORTS ORGANIZATIONS AND BUREAUS

(Note: Addresses are subject to change. An asterisk after a name indicates that no reply received to questionnaire.)

Amateur Athletic Union of the U.S. 3400 West 86th St., P.O. Box 68207, Indianapolis, Ind. 46268–0207

Amateur Softball Association/USA SOFTBALL.* 2801 N.E. 50th St., Oklahoma City, Okla. 73111

American Amateur Racquetball Association/International Racquetball Federation/Pan American Racquetball Confederation. 1685 West Uintah, Colorado Springs, Colo. 80904-2921

American Association of Professional Baseball Clubs. 6801 Miami Ave., Cincinnati, Ohio 45243

American Bowling Congress. 5301 South 76th St., Greendale, Wis. 53129–1127

American Hockey League. 425 Union St., West Springfield, Mass. 01089

American Horse Shows Association. 220 E. 42nd St., New York, N.Y. 10017–5876

American Kennel Club Inc. 51 Madison Ave., New York, N.Y. 10010

American League (baseball). 350 Park Ave., New York, N.Y. 10022

American Sportcasters Association, The. 5 Beekman St., New York, N.Y. 10038

Big Ten Conference, Inc. (1896). 1500 W. Higgins Rd., Park Ridge, Ill. 60068-6300

International Game Fish Association. 1301 E. Atlantic Blvd., Pompano Beach, Fla. 33060

International League of Professional Baseball Clubs, Inc. 55 S. High St., Ste. 202, Dublin, Ohio 43017

International Olympic Committee. Château de Vidy, Case Postale 356, 1001 Lausanne, Switzerland

International Tennis Hall of Fame. National Historic Landmark, Newport Casino, 194 Bellevue Ave., Newport, R.I. 02840

Little League Baseball. P.O. Box 3485, Williamsport, Pa. 17701

National Archery Association. One Olympic Plaza, Colorado Springs, Colo. 80909-5788

National Association for Stock Car Auto Racing. P.O. Box 2875, Daytona Beach, Fla. 32120-2875

National Association of Intercollegiate Athletics. 6120 South Yale Ave., Ste. 1450, Tulsa, Okla. 74136

National Baseball Congress. P.O. Box 1420, Wichita, Kan. 67201

National Baseball Hall of Fame. P.O. Box 590, Cooperstown, N.Y. 13326-0590

National Collegiate Athletic Association. 6201 College Blvd., Overland Park, Kan. 66211-2422

National Duckpin Bowling Congress. 4991 Fairview Ave., Linthicum, Md. 29090

National Field Archery Association. 31407 Outer I–10, Redlands, Calif. 92373

National Football Foundation and College Hall of Fame Inc. 1865 Palmer Ave., Suite 103, Larchmont, N.Y. 10538.

National Football League. 410 Park Ave., New York, N.Y. 10022

National Hockey League.* 75 International Blvd., Ste. 300, Rexdale, Ont., Canada M9W 6L9

National Horseshoe Pitchers Association.* Box 7927, Columbus, Ohio 43207-7927

National Hot Rod Association.* P.O. Box 5555, Glendora, Calif. 91740-0750

National Junior College Athletic Association. P.O. Box 7305, Colorado Springs, Colo. 80933-7305

National Rifle Association of America. 11250 Waples Mill Rd., Fairfax, Va. 22030

National Shuffleboard Association. *Summer:* 2508 Westmoor Rd., Findlay, Ohio 45840. *Winter:* 704 52nd Ave. Dr. W., Bradenton, Fla. 34207.

National Skeet Shooting Association. 5931 Roft Rd., San Antonio, Tex. 78253-9261

National Sporting Clays Association. 5931 Roft Rd., San Antonio, Tex. 78253-9261

New York Racing Association, Inc. P.O. Box 90, Jamaica, N.Y. 11417

New York State Athletic Commission* (boxing and wrestling). 270 Broadway, New York, N.Y. 10007

PGA TOUR, Inc.* 112 TPC Blvd., Sawgrass, Ponte Vedra, Fla. 32082

Pro Football Hall of Fame. 2121 George Halas Drive, N.W., Canton, Ohio 44708

Roller Skating Associations. 7301 Georgetown Rd., Ste. 123, Indianapolis, Ind. 46268

Thoroughbred Racing Assns. of N. America. 420 Fair Hill Dr., Ste. 1, Elkton, Md. 21921-2573

United States Amateur Boxing, Inc. One Olympic Plaza, Colorado Springs, Colo. 80909

United States Amateur Confederation of Roller Skating. P.O. Box 6579, Lincoln, Neb. 68506

United States Auto Club. 4910 West 16th St., Speedway, Ind. 46224

United States–International Professional Shuffleboard.* 1901 S.W. 87th Terrace, Fort Lauderdale, Fla. 33324

United States Sailing Association. P.O. Box 209, Newport, R.I. 02840-0209

USA Baseball. 2160 Greenwood Ave., Trenton, N.J. 08609

USA Basketball. 5465 Mark Dabling Blvd., Colorado Springs, Colo. 80918-3842

USA Gymnastics. Pan American Plaza, 201 S. Capitol, Ste. 300, Indianapolis, Ind. 46225

USA Hockey, Inc. 4965 N. 30th St., Colorado Springs, Colo. 80919

USA Track & Field. One Hoosier Dome, Ste. 140, Indianapolis, Ind. 46225.

U.S. Chess Federation. 186 Route 9W, New Windsor, N.Y. 12553

U.S. Cycling Federation.* One Olympic Plaza, Colorado Springs, Colo. 80909

U.S. Fencing Assn. One Olympic Plaza, Colorado Springs, Colo. 80909-5774

U.S. Figure Skating Association. 20 First St., Colorado Springs, Colo. 80906

U.S. Golf Association. Golf House, P.O. Box 708, Far Hills, N.J. 07931–0708

U.S. Handball Association. 2333 N. Tucson Blvd., Tucson, Ariz. 85716

U.S. Olympic Committee. One Olympic Plaza, Colorado Springs, Colo. 80909-5760

U.S. Orienteering Federation. Box 1444, Forest Park, Ga. 30051

U.S. Rowing Assn. Pan American Plaza, 201 S. Capitol Ave., Ste. 400, Indianapolis, Ind. 46225

U.S. Soccer Federation. 1801-1811 S. Prairie Ave., Chicago, Ill. 60616

U.S. Tennis Association. 70 W. Red Oak Lane, White Plains, N.Y. 10604

U.S. Trotting Association. 750 Michigan Ave., Columbus, Ohio 43215

Women's International Bowling Congress. 5301 S. 76th St., Greendale, Wis. 53129-1191

The New Welfare Reform Agenda

By Arthur P. Reed, Jr.

Welfare reform, a burning issue in Washington's political battles and partisan infighting, seemed to be moving closer to fulfillment in late 1995. The Senate acted on its own reform measure in early autumn; the House had earlier passed a more sweeping and stringent bill.

The issue seemed to have stalled when Congress left town for the late summer recess. The Senate Republican leadership appeared to have given up, at least for the time, their efforts to "end welfare as we know it," in the words of President Clinton's campaign pledge. The delay was a blow to the majority leader, Bob Dole of Kansas, his prestige caught in the crossfire of Democrats and ultra-conservative Republicans.

But the Senate, upon returning, approved with an overwhelming bipartisan vote a fundamental restructuring of the Federal antipoverty policy and guarantee of assistance to needy families. The vote was 87–12, with only eleven Democrats and one Republican opposed. Then the House–Senate conference committee faced a protracted battle over differences between the Senate measure and the conservative House version.

The Senate had made the many concessions that won over Democrats and Republican moderates. Thus there was a combination of forces and pressures—public discontent with the welfare system, political pressure for reform, and the strength of a coalition of Democrats and moderate Republicans in toning down some harsher provisions.

As Senate debate began, the bipartisan moderates deleted from the proposed legislation one of the most controversial items. This would have denied continued benefits to women who bore more children while on welfare. Then, on the same day, the Senate rejected a move to bar cash benefits to teen-agers who bore children out of wedlock. Also, moderate Republicans and Democrats voted to restore outlays for a $1-billion program to supply energy assistance to the poor.

Both Senate and House measures would replace many antipoverty programs with limited lump-sum payments to the states—block grants—and give the states broad authority over their own welfare programs. Estimates of the savings from the welfare reform measures varied. Mr. Dole estimated the seven-year savings from the Senate bill at more than $65 billion. The House leaders thought their measure would save somewhat more than $110 billion.

Both measures would abolish the present guarantees of Federal assistance, replacing it with block grants to the states. Both house and Senate would require recipients to work after two years. The House bill would prohibit aid to children born out of wedlock to mothers under 18. The House would deny aid to mothers who have more children while on welfare. The Senate leaves the policy to the states.

Actually there had been three attempts at rectifying the increasingly thorny welfare problem that crossed the lines not only of economics and budget-cutting but also bore heavily, for example, on morality (teen-age and unmarried mothers and the work ethic, with widespread distaste for what many viewed as idleness at the public's expense).

President Clinton, of course, had offered his own relatively moderate version of welfare reform. And comprehensive change has been among the Republicans' top priorities. Then there was the Senate leaders' measure, Senator Dole its chief sponsor. The extreme conservative wing had its own much tougher measure, spearheaded by Senator Phil Gramm of Tex-

as, Dole's probable rival for the G.O.P. Presidential nomination in 1996. The House of Representatives had passed its own harsh version several months earlier. Senators of both parties had drafted dozens of amendments to the Dole proposals.

Virtually all sides, in Congress and in the Administration, agreed that the nationwide welfare system must be changed. But there were sharp differences on the role of the Federal Government. This disagreement emerged most starkly and forcefully when Dole and Clinton presented their competing ideas of welfare reform at a meeting of the nation's governors in late July at Burlington, Vt.

Basically, the President, with Republicans and most Democrats, favors linking welfare to work requirements. At the Vermont gathering, Mr. Clinton clarified his stand by announcing that the Administration was moving quickly to approve state programs for putting welfare recipients to work, and to allow states to deny food stamp increases to those who lose welfare benefits for refusing to work. Thus, the President demonstrated the power of his office to act even during a Congressional deadlock.

His executive orders used a "waiver" policy under which states need Federal approval for experiments with welfare operations. The orders would direct the Health and Human Services Department to approve, within 30 days, such experiments by the states. One provision would require recipients to work but provide adequate child care. Another would require that minor mothers live at home and stay in school. The President also announced approval of welfare experiments in four new states.

Also, at the Vermont conference, Dole said the essence of his proposals was the principle that states should control welfare without seeking approval from Washington. In Congress, his compromise measure would give the states block grants with more discretion on using the appropriations. The Congressional Budget Office estimated that the savings from block grants would be $70 billion, or 10 percent of what would be spent in the next seven years, on Aid to Families With Dependent Children, food stamps, Supplemental Security income, and child nutrition programs.

In August, shortly before welfare debate was stopped in the Capitol, President Clinton said he opposed the Republican measure but a White House analysis suggested that major changes might make it acceptable. One Administration objection was that it would not guarantee child care for persons forced to work or seeking work. In its critical assessment, the White House study said of the Dole measure, "states will have to make tough choices providing child care, enforcing work, and insuring a safety net for poor families." But the Republican leaders said they believed the states could make better choices than could Washington. Although the President had proposed cutting off from the welfare rolls those refusing to work, he found the Republican bill too harsh. The Administration preferred the milder alternative Democratic measure.

The White House, however, seemed bent on achieving welfare reform; the President even made a personal appeal to President Dole to push for action in 1995. However, in a mid-August news conference, the President said the Senate legislation had come "wrapped up in Presidential politics."

So many currents and cross-currents! It was no wonder that welfare and many of its beneficiaries, deserving or not, became tossed in those eddies. ☐

The Congressional Scene

By Arthur P. Reed, Jr.

The Republican Party swept to a steamroller victory in the 1994 Congressional elections to win control of the Senate and House of Representatives for the first time in decades. The Republicans' battle cry, sounded by the new House Speaker, Newt Gingrich, was the "Contract for America," a blueprint for undoing many of the Federal Government programs since the New Deal of the 1930s and balancing the Federal budget by cutting it from $200 billion to zero over seven years—by 2002.

In the first tumultuous months of 1995, they achieved parts of their program. But others, such as welfare reform, were caught in a legislative tangle. The victors suffered one significant defeat: the drive for a balanced budget amendment to the Constitution sputtered out in the Senate by the narrowest of margins. There was a general feeling that the campaign for the amendment was tainted by what one editorialist called "a heavy dose of posturing." A proposal for a limit on terms of office also failed for the time being. Budget balancing emerged later as a key motif of regular measures for financing the Government.

By the time Congress returned after the summer recess, about half the Contract had come to a vote in both houses, but only two of its provisions had been signed into law. An early and uncontroversial measure in the Contract won prompt approval by both houses and the President's signature. This applied all Federal labor laws to Congress and its employees. Another approved measure restricted mandates to the states for programs without provision of funding.

Among other Contract provisions, welfare reform, although generally popular, was delayed by disputes over details. The Contract contained many other sections, generally of a right-wing nature. Key provisions called for tougher treatment of criminal offenders, cutting spending for peacekeeping operations, cutting taxes, and measures designed in general to reduce the role of the Federal Government in the activities of states and citizens.

In its first session in January, the House of Representatives adopted several immediate changes in rules and procedures. Among other actions, the Republicans abolished three standing committees and 25 subcommittees.

Thorny issues, many of them divisive even within the G.O.P., remained to be resolved when Congress returned from the late-summer recess. These included causes dear to the Republicans: Medicare and Medicaid reform, vague plans to cut taxes, and slashes in such politically and publicly sensitive programs as farm subsidies, public broadcasting, and heating assistance for the poor. Many liberals counted on the Senate to slow the swinging of the axe on matters vital to them.

One piece of legislation that had separately passed both houses faced an uncertain future later in the year. That aimed at overhauling the civil litigation system, described as tort reform. On this, there was general unwillingness for a House-Senate compromise.

Throughout the year, struggles with budget questions were the focus of most Congressional debate and infighting, with a balanced budget the persistent goal.

In early May, Republican Senators started out on the long journey by presenting a budget resolution as a concrete expression of how they proposed to balance the Federal books over the next seven years by reducing spending by nearly $1 trillion. Unusual haste had marked the approval of spending bills by the Senate Appropriations Committee. The panel approved the most controversial budget measure, a $263.8-billion outlay for the Departments of Labor, Education and Health and Human Services. The spending bills then went to the floor for debate and amendments that were discouraged by the Appropriations Committee. The program passed by a 57–42 vote.

The biggest reductions would come in Government health programs, Medicare, and Medicaid. The Democrats were critical of what they viewed as a glossing over of the specific curtailments that would be required.

The House of Representatives, in its own but broader program, also listed cuts in Medicare and Medicaid, and broad reductions in Cabinet and lesser Federal offices. This projected greater savings than the Senate's plan—between $1.1 trillion and $1.2 trillion over seven years. And the House had also to allow for the tax reductions it had approved earlier. The White House immediately denounced the tax cut proposals and said it would not negotiate spending reductions until they were abandoned.

Later in May, the House voted, 238–193, with a conservative Democrat joining the majority and one Republican voting nay, for the sweeping program to balance the budget. This bill called for $1.5 billion slashes in Federal spending through the year 2002. Some $350 billion of the package was allotted for the previously approved personal and business tax breaks.

Contrary to the House bill, the Senate voted for a $170-billion tax reduction over seven years if the Congressional Budget Office certified that this much could be saved in lower interest payments on Government bonds. And in the Senate, there were overtones of the rivalries building up for the 1996 Presidential nomination. Thus, Phil Gramm, Republican of Texas, sought to incorporate into the Senate budget much of the tax reduction that the House had approved in its own budget measure, including a tax reduction for most families of $500 per child. Mr. Gramm, a contender for the Presidential nomination in 1996, thought this would fulfill the party's campaign commitments.

However, the Senate rejected the Gramm proposal, 69–31, with 23 Republicans joining all 46 Democrats in voting against it. Bob Dole of Kansas, the majority leader and a 1996 rival of Senator Gramm, voted with the Texan for the tax cut. Many Republicans were divided over whether tax cuts or budget balancing should have precedence. Thus there were significant differences between the House and Senate proposals. In the pre-conference versions, the Senate proposals for deficit and tax reduction were appreciably lower than those in the House. But that was before the legislators had worked out the specifics of cuts in appropriations.

Hints of a general agreement on the budget emerged late in the session when President Clinton and Congressional leaders met and agreed to work for an accommodation. Neither side, however, indicated what concessions they might make. But the meeting was a step in what promised to be a protracted confrontation. As with all legislation, conference committees had to resolve differences between House and Senate versions.

In all the debates and negotiations, the question of reforming Medicare was predominant. Republican proposals, released in the House and Senate, aimed to reduce projected Medicare spending by $270 billion, or 14 percent, over the next seven years. The plans envisaged possible greater use of managed-care systems, payment vouchers, and other devices intended to cut costs. There was considerable uneasiness among organizations of the elderly, and President Clinton threatened a veto.

In the House, specific details of the Republican proposal for curbing Medicare costs began to emerge late in the year. Under this, the elderly would pay more, with the premium fore Part B coverage rising gradually to between $90 and $93 by 2002 from $60 under existing law. The Republicans would also limit payments to victims of medical malpractice and encourage the elderly to choose among various types of coverage—H.M.O.'s, medical savings accounts, and traditional fee for service. The Democrats vowed an immediate battle to slow these drastic changes.

Whatever the final version, the new budget is certain to have wide and deep effects on the populace in general. While Social Security is off limits, the elderly will feel the impact of limits on the growth of Medicare and Medicaid—together the biggest items in the budget after Social Security. Doctors and hospitals would also be affected. The poor will also suffer benefit reductions, although job opportunities are expected to increase. □

The International Scene

By Arthur P. Reed, Jr.

Warfare, brutal and savage beyond "civilized" standards, raged in Eastern Europe during most of 1995. Russia and former Yugoslavia were the scenes of carnage. Some observers likened the situation in Europe to the quagmire that Vietnam was for the United States. But in one hopeful move, the years-old ethnic conflict in areas of the former Yugoslavia showed some signs of abating toward the end of the year when the embattled rivals met in a conference at Geneva sponsored by the United States. In a first move toward peace, the Government of Bosnia and Herzegovina agreed on the establishment of a Serbian republic within Bosnia. But those talks followed a resumption of bombing by NATO forces after a breakdown of negotiations to end the Bosnian Serbs' 40-month siege of the Sarajevo capital. As a result, the Serbs agreed to pull their heavy guns out of range of Sarajevo. In August, there had been a new and unexpected escalation of the conflict when Croatian forces routed Serbian residents from their established homes.

In Russia, civil war raged in the province of Chechnya. There seemed to be no way for diplomacy to contain the spreading violence.

The seemingly brighter situation in Bosnia seemed to be the result of the new American approach to the President of Serbia, Slobodan Milosevic. For four years, since the breakup of the old Yugoslavia in 1991, the Bosnian Serbs had triumphed over Muslim and Croatian forces. They had wrought havoc on civilian areas. Their leaders had been denounced by the world as war criminals for abetting the atrocities of their troops.

But in August of 1995, the situation had changed, at least for the time, with continuing major movements of populations. The Croatian Government declared victory in a three-day campaign against rebel Serbs and the capture of their capital, Knin, in the Krajina region. Serb civilians charged the conquerors

with terrorism by shelling and by abuse of civilians during the battle. Croatian officials acknowledged that their forces had caused the deaths of three United Nations peacekeepers. The capital had been a Serbian town for centuries. For four years preceding the attack, it had been the headquarters of Serb nationalists, a symbol of their resistance to Croatian rule. The conquest was also a major setback for the Bosnian Serb forces.

Refugees in the tens of thousands fled from the Croatian onslaught, reversing the pattern of previous years when the Serbs themselves had carried out "ethnic cleansing" in the Muslim centers of Bosnia, forcing residents of opposing ethnic groups to flee.

The mass migrations forced by the conflict gave impetus to a new American peace approach. This was presented to the Serbian capital of Belgrade by Assistant Secretary of State Richard Holbrooke. The new peace initiative called for NATO air strikes on the Bosnian Serbs' positions if they returned to the offensive and spurned negotiations.

Earlier, the Serbs had mounted offensives against so-called U.N. "safe areas." The United States said it had photographs from spy planes and satellites of what appeared to be mass graves outside the Bosnian town of Srebenica. Refugees gave evidence that Serb troops had executed at least several hundred men and boys of military age.

In Russia, both sides suffered in the Chechnya warfare, and the political and moral cost to the Moscow Government was heavy, even though the fighting had died down by mid-year. The relatively brief eight-moth war took a heavy toll. Estimates of civilian deaths in the Russian province ranged as high as 40,000. The Russians reported that at least 2,000 soldiers had perished.

The Chechen capital, Grozny, was bombed and burned into a mass of ruins. The spark that ignited the war was the question of Chechnya's independence. In late summer, the leaders of both sides approved a broad agreement to end the fighting. The Russian Prime Minister declared the war over, with partial Russian withdrawal and disarmament of the rebels. There followed a political settlement on the status of the secessionist republic. Moscow insisted, however, that Chechnya must remain part of the Russian Federation.

A brighter note was Russia's progress in transforming the economy in the four years since the disintegration of the rigid Soviet system. In late 1994, there had been discouraging signs since the plunge of the ruble in October, which portended renewed inflation. This led to a shakeup of officials in economic affairs, an endeavor by President Boris Yeltsin to keep a balance between reformers and conservatives. By late 1995, market reforms were in place, accepted by a populace that had endured food shortages and rising unemployment. Inflation was checked. Parliament sought to rein in the deficit as a lure to foreign investors. And a middle class was slowly developing, with an increasingly sharp generation gap between younger entrepreneurs and their Communist-era parents.

Then, private TV networks sprang up to rival Government-controlled programs. In June, President Yeltsin narrowly escaped a parliamentary vote of no confidence that would have shaken the Government. As it was, a new political party formed by Yeltsin and his Prime Minister was trounced in an election in the President's home base of Sverdlovsk.

Internationally, Russia continued to play her part. In January, the U.S. Secretary of State, Warren Christopher, was assured of the nation's commitment to democracy and market reforms. And in June, Russia hesitantly agreed to take an active part in NATO's Partnership for Peace.

The spring summit meeting of Yeltsin and President Clinton was friendly but not conclusive. Yeltsin moved back on nuclear energy deals with Iran. After arguing over NATO expansion, they renewed their commitments to ratification of the 1992 nuclear-arms reduction treaty.

Elsewhere, Eastern Europe was continuing its awakening from the Communist-era nightmare, its economy growing in 1995 beyond the 3 percent rate of 1994. Hundreds of medium-sized companies are achieving commercial success in all the former nations of the Soviet bloc. Those companies are making and reinvesting their profits to improve life for workers and customers. A Polish shipyard at Szczecin has set the pace, with orders from the West and a record production speed. Earlier in the year, however, surveys had shown the Poles restive at Lech Walesa's program for economic reform.

Successful enterprises in Europe included a film developer and retailer in Hungary, a pharmaceutical company in Prague.

The three independent Baltic states signed accords with the European Union. In Bulgaria, a 35-year-old former Communist was Prime Minister after his Socialist party won an election in late 1994, and confronted serious economic and political problems. In two-year-old Slovakia, political freedoms were respected as she strove for political economy.

Western Europe

Unemployment was a major problem for the 15 nations of the European Union. Jobless rates were as high as 12 percent in France and Italy, 23 percent in Spain, and 9 percent in Germany—all the highest since the post-World War II recovery. Government leaders were under public pressure to reduce those levels.

In Britain and Northern Ireland, the prospects for peace in the North Ireland province of Ulster were brighter. The three governments involved—Britain, Ireland, and Ulster—began negotiations on ending the violence in the north and deciding on its political status. An extended cease-fire by the militant Irish Republican Army smoothed the way for talks.

Other Global Events

In the other nations of the world, the situation had calmed down somewhat from the horrors of 1994. But there was still a surfeit of death, suffering, and overall violent discontent.

In Africa, one bright spot was Liberia. There peace had returned after a devastating six-year civil war. In that conflict, the continent's bloodiest, teenage soldiers had slaughtered each other and countless innocent civilians. But in September, the leaders of the three main warring factions sat together at the Monrovia capital in a new six-member Council of State. As the nation, founded by freed American slaves, began to recover, the death toll, mainly civilian, was placed at 150,000 in a population of some two million. Huge crowds massed in the capital and heard the ceremony by radio. The peace had been brokered by Nigeria and Ghana.

Rwanda's refugee problem continued to escalate following the horrors of the previous year's killings. Prime Minister Faustin Twagiramungu resigned to protest reported killings by the army. Neighboring Zaire forced 3,500 from refugee camps to leave the country. Thousands of other Rwandans fled Zaire camps to avoid being forced to return home.

One trouble spot in Asia was the Korean peninsula, where North Korea was believed to be challenging the armistice in existence since the Korean War. The North's suspected nuclear-weapons program was also a factor in the uneasiness. There was also turbulence and wide protests over French plans for atomic weapons testing in the South Pacific.

Tensions in the Middle East eased late in the year with a major triumph for diplomacy after months of crises. The Israelis and the Palestinians concluded a last-minute agreement on transferring to its Arab residents control of much of the occupied West Bank.

In the Western Hemisphere, Cuba took steps to increase foreign investment. This action came as frustrated American enterprises increased their pressure on the Clinton Administration to lift the embargo on trade with Cuba. The Castro Government allowed foreign investors access to all economic sectors except defense, health care, and education.

In Haiti, President Jean-Bertrand Aristide remained popular a year after returning to power with the protection of the U.S. troops. He has restored calm to a nation wracked by three years of military rule and international isolation.

Another Latin nation, Suriname, on South America's northern coast, sought to grant several Asian countries the right to cull ancient trees from dense rain forests. □

CURRENT EVENTS

What Happened in 1995

Highlights of the important events of the year from January to October 1995, organized month by month, in three categories for easy reference. The Countries of the World section (starting on page 143) covers specific international events, country by country.

JANUARY 1995
International

Fighting Intense in Russian Attack on Chechnya (Jan. 4 et seq.): Hundreds dead in tank and infantry onslaught on Grozny, capital of secessionist republic. Clinton Administration accuses Moscow of violating international agreement and calls for end to attack. Yeltsin declares war at end (**Jan. 19**) and dismisses top defense officials. Russian troops hoist flag over Grozny presidential palace (**Jan. 19**).

Pope Tours Asia and Australia (Jan. 11 et seq.): Despite ill-health, John Paul II, 74, embarks on strenuous 11-day trip, longest in three years. Pontiff hailed by millions in Philippines, Papua New Guinea, Australia, and Sri Lanka. Buddhist monks in Sri Lanka refuse to meet with Pope, a diplomatic setback.

New Italian Prime Minister Named (Jan. 13): Lamberto Dini, 63, nonpolitical banker and international financier, to guide fiscal and ballot reforms.

Suicide Bomber Kills 19 in Israel (Jan. 22): Two blasts wound 61 at Nordiya bus stop crowded with Israeli soldiers. It was fifth major suicide bombing by Islamic radicals since April 1994. Shadow cast over Israeli-Palestinian peace negotiations.

New U.N. Commander Reaches Bosnia (Jan. 26): Lieut. Gen. Rupert Smith of Britain arrives in Sarajevo to replace Lieut. Gen. Sir Michael Rose.

Ceremonies Mark Auschwitz Liberation (Jan. 27): Dignitaries and death camp survivors retrace steps taken by Nazis' prisoners. Speakers recall suffering of more than a million from many nations, especially Jews, in the Holocaust.

U.S. and Vietnam Act to Renew Ties (Jan. 28): Diplomats sign agreement giving U.S. custody of building to house first Vietnam mission in 20 years.

Car Bomb Kills at Least 38 in Algiers (Jan. 30): Some 250 injured in explosion in crowded street. Security forces blame Islamic militant guerrillas.

Report Calls China Lax on Human Rights (Jan. 31): State Department study coincides with trade impasses.

National

Republicans Take Control of Congress (Jan. 4): Senate Majority Leader Dole says reining in Government is his mandate. House Speaker Gingrich is conciliatory toward Democrats. (**Jan. 5**): President and the two leaders proclaim truce after first White House meeting.

House Clears First G.O.P. Legislation (Jan. 17): Sends Clinton measure ending Congressional exemption from discrimination and workplace statutes.

Senate Democrats Block Mandates Vote (Jan. 19): Minority shows strength in procedural test in new Congress by delaying action on measure to limit unfunded requirements for action by states.

High Court Backs Employee in Bias Suit (Jan. 23): Rules unanimously that employees dismissed because of discrimination are entitled to back pay even if employer later discovers valid reason for firing.

President's State of the Union Message (Jan. 24): Clinton calls for sharing of responsibilities by Government and citizens. Urges crackdown on illegal immigration, campaign against teen-age pregnancy, and increase in minimum wage. Repeats call for tax break for middle class. He congratulates new members of G.O.P.-dominated Congress.

House Votes for Balanced Budget Amendment (Jan. 26): Vote is 300 to 132, 10 more than required two-thirds, for measure to prohibit Federal Government from spending more than it takes in. House rejects three-fifths vote requirement in both House and Senate for any tax increase.

Commerce Secretary Faces Accusations (Jan. 26): Republican Congressman charges Ronald H. Brown failed to report income in violation of Federal law.

Senate Votes Limit on Mandates to States (Jan. 27): Approves, 86–10, legislation to curb Congressional action requiring costly new programs without providing funds to pay for them, a key Republican goal.

Clinton Offers $20 Billion Aid to Mexico (Jan. 31): President uses emergency power to rescue Mexican economy and prevent default on Government bonds. Action sidesteps action by Congress.

General

Suspect in Abortion Clinic Killings Indicted (Jan. 4): U.S. jury in Boston charges John C. Salvi 3rd, 22, with carrying gun across state lines with intention of committing a felony in attacks in Massachusetts. (**Jan. 9**): Salvi pleads not guilty in Massachusetts court to charges of murder in clinic shootings.

Heavy Rains Inundate California (Jan. 9 et seq.): Eleven dead, damage estimated at over $300 million as major winter storm drives out of Pacific. Floods ravage roads, homes, businesses, and crops. Tens of thousands evacuate homes before rising waters and mudslides. More than half of state declared Federal disaster area after 10-day storm.

Agreement Reached in Hockey Strike (Jan. 11): Owners and players report accord giving management gains on salary limits and arbitration curbs.

Malcolm X's Daughter Charged in Plot (Jan. 12): U.S. accuses Qubilah Bahiyah Shabazz, 34, of trying to hire hit man to assassinate Louis Farrakhan, minister of Nation of Islam and a Malcolm X rival.

More Than 5,000 Dead in Japanese Earthquake (Jan. 17 et seq.): Thousands injured in 20-second catastrophe that heaved trains on sides in Kobe area of West Japan, toppled elevated highways, and felled buildings, leaving thousands homeless and without utilities. Sections of Kobe, city of 1.4 million, in ruins from shock and ensuing fires. World trade to Kobe port disrupted. City finally recovering, with factories and offices opening and everyone having food, shelter, and sanitation (Jan. 25).

Trial of O.J. Simpson Opens (Jan. 24): Prosecution, in opening statement, says blood clues link former football star to murder of former wife and friend. (**Jan. 29**): Defense tells Los Angeles jury Simpson is victim of "rush to judgment."

Terrorism Trial Begins in New York (Jan. 31): U.S. judge examines prospective jurors for trial of twelve, including Sheik Omar Abdel Rahman, in alleged plot to blow up key installations.

FEBRUARY 1995
International

Jews and Arabs Agree on Talks (Feb. 2): Israeli Prime Minister takes part in regional summit meeting at Cairo with heads of Arab states and P.L.O.

Dutch Return Home as Floods Recede (Feb. 5): Most of 250,000 evacuated return as dikes hold on major Netherlands rivers. Heavy rains and melting snow had caused flooding in Germany, France, and Belgium, with runoffs into Dutch rivers.

Muslims Admit Algerian Capital Bombing (Feb. 5): Radical group takes blame for suicide attack that killed 42 and wounded 256 in downtown Algiers.

Serb Official Charged With Genocide (Feb. 13): U.N. tribunal accuses Zeljko Meakic, commander of camp in northwest Bosnia, of "crimes against humanity." Others at camp also accused of war crimes.

Israel Drops Bar to Palestinian Workers (Feb. 16): Agrees to admit laborers from Gaza Strip and West Bank in move to revive Middle East peace talks.

Aristide Purges Haitian Armed Forces (Feb. 21): Government ousts virtually all senior officers.

Chechnya Death Toll Set at 24,000 (Feb. 21): Russian human rights commission estimates toll in attacks on rebel forces in separatist republic as fighting rages.

U.S. Rescues Mexico's Economy (Feb. 21): Nations agree on $20-billion aid program to keep private banks from collapsing as part of $50-billion loan package. Washington gets veto power over much of Mexican economy policy for next decade.

Yeltsin Bans Alcohol and Tobacco Advertising (Feb. 21): Acts to reduce Russia's death and illness rates.

Britain and Ireland Issue Peace Plan (Feb. 22): Campaign for peace in Ulster with proposals for talks between Protestant majority and Roman Catholic minority. Cross-border council is one suggestion.

At Least 95 Killed in Algerian Prison Riot (Feb. 22): Islamic militants slain as security forces crush revolt at jail after four guards had been killed.

France Accuses Five Americans of Spying (Feb. 23): Orders them out of country at once on charges of political and economic espionage. Former C.I.A. station chief and his deputy among those accused.

U.S. and Canada Drop Aviation Curbs (Feb. 24): For first time, broad treaty will allow airlines to fly to and from any point in the two countries.

Chinese Intellectuals Demand Inquiry Into Corruption (Feb. 25): Twelve petition parliamentary units for independent investigation of nation's leadership.

U.S. and China Settle Copyright Dispute (Feb. 26): Agree on measures to protect such intellectual property as movies, compact disks, and computer software. Pact averts trade war and aids U.S. investors.

National

Congress Votes Curb on U.S. Mandates (Feb. 1): House overwhelmingly approves restriction on unfunded requirements on states. Measure already approved by Senate and is backed by President Clinton.

Federal Reserve Raises Rates 7th Time in Year (Feb. 1): Increases interest half a point in further move to prevent resurgence of inflation.

President Submits Budget for 1996 (Feb. 2): Clinton plans $1.6-trillion outlay. He foresees deficits in $190-billion range a year for next decade. Budget reductions far short of G.O.P. demands.

Clinton Asks Rise in Minimum Wage (Feb. 3): Proposes 90-cent increase to $5.15 an hour over five years.

House Approves Line-Item Veto (Feb. 6): Votes to give President power to strike specific parts of spending and tax bills without vetoing entire measure.

Clinton Picks New C.I.A. Chief (Feb. 7): Plans to nominate retired Air Force general, Michael P.C. Carns, 57, as Director of Central Intelligence.

House Approves Easing of Evidence Rules (Feb. 8): Votes, 289–142, to allow Federal law officers more latitude in making searches without warrants.

Former Senator J. William Fulbright Dies (Feb. 9): Arkansas Democrat was a leading opponent of Vietnam War as head of Foreign Relations Committee. Founded Fulbright scholarships for international study.

House Republicans Lose in Vote on Missiles (Feb. 15): Two dozen bolt G.O.P. to back Democrats on setting priorities for ballistic missile defenses.

Supreme Court Eases Federal Ethics Law (Feb. 22): Voids restriction barring civil servants from accepting pay for speeches and articles.

House G.O.P. Drops Abolition of Food Stamps (Feb. 24): Decision is first setback in Republican campaign to trim Federal social welfare programs.

General

U.S. Shuttle Rendezvous With Russian Space Station (Feb. 3): *Discovery* orbits from Cape Canaveral on historic mission. First woman pilot one of crew of six. **(Feb. 6):** Shuttle approaches within 40 feet of space station *Mir*. Both craft speed above Earth at more than 17,000 miles an hour. **(Feb. 11):** *Discovery* lands at Kennedy Space Center guided by Comdr. James D. Wetherbee of Navy.

First Big Winter Storm Hits Northeast (Feb. 4): Snow blankets region 6 to 16 inches deep after weeks of mild weather. Travel and power disrupted, businesses closed, areas flooded, and all but emergency Government services shut down.

Bomb Plot Defendant Aids U.S. (Feb. 7): Siddig Ibrahim Siddig Ali, 34, pleads guilty and agrees to give damaging testimony against group accused in plot to bomb key New York buildings and tunnel.

Quake Kills More Than 40 in Colombia (Feb. 8): At least 230 injured in worst temblor in 12 years.

Jury Awards $5.2 Million for Breast Implant Leak (Feb. 15): Woman wins damages in Houston court in action against Dow Corning Corporation and its parent, Dow Chemical Company. Second woman loses suit.

Brain Difference by Sexes Reported (Feb. 15): Research at Yale, using new technique, finds men use area in left side of brain, women areas on both sides.

Four Army Rangers Die in Training Mishap (Feb. 15): Succumb to severely lowered body temperatures after immersion chest-deep in Florida swamp.

Suspect Convicted in Train Massacre (Feb. 17): Long Island, N.Y., jury finds Colin Ferguson guilty of murder on 93 murder charges in railroad shooting in 1993 that killed six and wounded 19. Ferguson had rejected insanity defense and defended himself.

N.A.A.C.P. Replaces Leader (Feb. 18): Board of rights organization ousts chairman, Dr. William F. Gibson. Board elects Myrlie Evers-Williams, widow of murdered N.A.A.C.P. official, to succeed him.

Balloonist First to Cross Pacific Alone (Feb. 21): Chicago stockbroker, 50, breaks distance record for balloon on 5,885-mile flight from South Korea to cross Canada. Heaters on craft had failed.

Chevron Settles Harassment Charges (Feb. 21): Agrees to pay $2.2 million in action brought by four female employees who said they had suffered offensive jokes and comments and other indignities.

Major British Investment House Fails (Feb. 26): Barings P.L.C. collapses after discovery that trader in its Singapore office had lost millions in gamble.

MARCH 1995
International

Last U.S. Marines Leave Somalia (March 3): Action means end of U.N. involvement. Mission to feed hungry remains. But civil strife continues.

Gunmen Kill Two Americans in Pakistan (March 8): Wound a third in ambush of van in Karachi. Top Pakistani officials pledge move to track down killers.

Mexico Adopts Tough New Economic Policy (March 9): Government's stabilization plan augurs recession, job losses, and personal hardships as only steps to recovery after peso falls to new lows.

Bomb and Gun Attack Kills 11 in Pakistan (March 10): Twenty-two wounded as bomb explodes outside mosque and masked gunmen storm smoke-filled courtyard.

Croatian President Accepts U.N. Troop Presence (March 12): Franjo Tudjman agrees to let peacekeeping force remain after diplomatic maneuver by U.S.

Britain Moving Troops From Ulster (March 14): Undertakes largest reduction in decade in move to speed peace talks in Northern Ireland.

Conoco Inc. Drops Deal With Iran (March 14): Cancels agreement to develop two large offshore oil fields after President moves to bar such transactions.

Iraq Sentences Two Americans (March 17): Two civilian workers in Kuwait arrested after apparently straying into Iraq by mistake. **(March 25:)** Iraqi court sentences pair after convicting them of illegal entry. White House condemns action.

Bosnian Army Breaks Truce With Attack (March 20): Government forces storm Serbian positions six weeks before U.N. cease-fire was scheduled to expire.

Nerve Gas Attacks Tokyo Subway (March 20): Eight dead and 4,700 are treated at hospitals after catastrophe at morning rush hour peak in busy system. **(March 21:)** Police tighten security. **(March 22:)** Thousands of police officers raid offices of religious sect linked to type of gas used in attack. Sect combines Hindu and Buddhist teachings. It denies making nerve gas and involvement in subway attack. Sect has been accused of kidnapping and other crimes.

Turks Attack Kurdish Rebels Across Iraq Border (March 20): Troops, tanks, and jet fighters pursue separatist forces seeking Kurdish homeland inside Turkey.

Guatemalan Officer Linked to C.I.A. (March 22): House member says man who ordered killing of American and guerrilla was on U.S. intelligence payroll.

Nelson Mandela Expels Wife From Cabinet (March 27): South African President accuses estranged spouse of insubordination. Bribery also alleged.

Pope Condemns "Culture of Death" (March 30): Encyclical attacks abortion and euthanasia as "crimes" and voices tough opposition to death penalty.

Russians Seize Last Chechnyan Urban Base (March 31): Secessionist forces withdraw under attack after three and a half months of war. Death toll stands at 20,000, with 25,000 refugees.

Clinton Cheered on Haiti Visit (March 31): Ends role of U.S. security forces and hands responsibility to U.N. Hails "triumph of freedom over fear."

National

G.O.P. Modifies Stand on Food Stamps (March 1): House leaders agree to let some states use food stamp money to feed poor people as officials wish.

Balanced-Budget Amendment Loses in Senate (March 2): Rejected by one vote in blow to Republicans.

House Votes to Limit Investors' Suits (March 8): Approves, 325–99, measure to restrict ability of stockholders and lawyers in actions charging fraud.

Clinton C.I.A. Nominee Withdraws (March 10): Michael P.C. Carns, retired Air Force general, acts after F.B.I. discloses possible personal irregularities. President then chooses John M. Deutch, Deputy Defense Secretary, as Central Intelligence head.

Sinn Fein Leader and Clinton Meet (March 16): President shakes hands with Gerry Adams, leader of Irish Republican Army, in unexpectedly warm greeting at St. Patrick's Day luncheon. House Speaker Newt Gingrich entertains Irish Prime Minister, John Bruton.

First Chicken Pox Vaccine Approved (March 17): F.D.A. officials sanction marketing of substance to prevent one of most contagious childhood diseases.

U.S. Trade Deficit Rises to Record $12.23 Billion (March 22): Nation's imbalance worsened by Mexico's plunge deeper into economic crisis.

Senate Votes Line-Item Veto for President (March 23): Bipartisan action approves power to reject specific spending proposals and some tax benefits. Senate and House versions must be resolved.

House Rejects Term Limit Plans (March 29): Begins to scrap proposals to limit members' service.

Senate Stresses Budget Reforms (March 29): Votes unanimously for amendment requiring $13.5 billion in spending cuts in current fiscal year be applied to reducing Federal budget not to reducing taxes.

Court Rejects Pentagon Policy on Homosexuals (March 30): Federal judge in New York brands new standard as unconstitutional and catering to prejudices.

General

Space Shuttle *Endeavour* Launched (March 3): Crew of five men and two women begin longest flight of shuttle program. Battery of telescopes aboard to study evolution and composition of stars and galaxies.

Judge Fines Two Simpson Lawyers (March 3): Imposes sanctions for withholding from prosecutors audio-taped interview with important defense witness.

New York State Restores Death Penalty (March 7): Gov. Pataki fulfills campaign pledge by signing bill making state 38th with capital punishment.

Dollar Plunges on Currency Markets (March 8): Four-day dive stemmed as Federal Reserve Chairman hints at increase in American interest rates.

C.I.A. Finds Serbs Guilty of War Crimes (March 8): Reports Serbs committed 90 percent of "ethnic cleansing" acts in Bosnia and that leading Serbian politicians almost certainly had role in crimes.

Storms Batter California (March 13): At least 12 dead in one of century's most disastrous systems. Over broad front, heavy rains over long period cause tens of millions of dollars damage to roads, homes, and businesses and ruins crops in rich farmland.

Russian Space Station Greets First American (March 14): Dr. Norman E. Thagard and two Russians aboard *Soyuz* spacecraft launched from Kazakhstan. **(March 16:)** Russians greet NASA astronaut warmly as he boards space station *Mir* after capsule docks on schedule.

Michael Jordan Returns to Basketball (March 19): Plays first game in 21 months with Chicago team.

Four Shot Dead in New Jersey Post Office (March 21): Fifth postal worker wounded in Montclair. **(March 22:)** Former postal employee arrested in killings.

Railroad Killer Sentenced to 200 Years (March 22): Colin Ferguson to spend life in prison for murder of six persons on Long Island Railroad in New York and attempted murder of 19 others. Victims and families cheer as judge hands gunman maximum sentence.

Popular Singer Slain in Texas (March 31): Selena, 23, Grammy-winning star of the Tejano Tex-Mex Spanish-language music industry, shot dead. Suspect held.

APRIL 1995

International

Bomb Accident Kills Eight in Gaza City (April 2): Members of militant Hamas Palestinian group blamed by police for explosion while preparing bomb.

Russia Adopts Drastic AIDS Testing Law (April 3): Requires examinations for almost all foreigners. Move reflects concern over possible epidemic.

Combat Flares Up Again in Northeast Bosnia (April 4): Fighting near Tuzla reaches most intense level since Muslim-led Government mounted offensive. **(April 17):** Killing of two French soldiers in Sarajevo divides French Conservative Party over policy on war.

Six Israelis Killed in Gaza Bombings (April 9): Arab militants wound at least 45 in two car explosions.

Palestinians Arrest 100 Militants (April 10): Seize members of groups claiming responsibility for anti-Israel bombing in Gaza Strip. Toll rises to eight with deaths of Israeli soldier and American student. Yasir Arafat's stand stiffens.

Japan Moves to Control Yen (April 14): Government moves to check sharp fall in dollar ratio and prevent economy from plunging into recession.

U.N. Council Votes Easier Sanctions for Iraq (April 14): Unanimously approves offer of easier terms for Baghdad to sell oil to meet emergency needs. **(April 15):** Iraqi Government denounces proposal.

Japanese Arrest High Official of Sect (April 19): Seize Kiyode Hayakawa, 45, chief of clandestine activities of group suspected in nerve-gas attack in subway.

French Honor Marie Curie (April 20): Ashes of famous scientist enshrined in Pantheon in Paris. Ceremony makes her first woman to be so honored.

U.S. and North Korea Break Off Talks (April 20): Berlin conference at impasse on nuclear reactor.

Death Toll 2,000 in Rwanda Massacre (April 22): Government forces open fire on makeshift camp of tens of thousands of ethnic Hutu displaced in civil war. Hundreds wounded as gun battle erupts between Hutu militiamen and Government troops. Many trampled to death in panic. **(April 23):** U.N. and Western diplomats see major setback to aid efforts.

Yeltsin Orders Halt to Chechnya Fighting (April 25): Fears prolonged warfare will mar Russia's celebration of Allied victory in World War II.

Turkey Winds Up Operations in Iraq (April 26): Army reports success in mission to destroy base camps, arms depots, and supply routes used by Kurdish separatist guerrilla forces.

Blast Kills More Than 100 in South Korea (April 28): Explosion at leaking gas main in Taegu comes during rush hour at subway construction site.

British Labor Scraps Nationalization (April 29): Party conference votes, 2–1, to abandon its 77-year-old commitment to state ownership of industry.

National

Man Convicted of Trying to Assassinate Clinton (April 4): U.S. jury finds Francisco Martin Duran, 26, guilty of attempt when he fired at White House.

House Speaker Celebrates 100 Days (April 7): Newt Gingrich marks G.O.P. achievement and outlines proposal for "new partnership with American people."

Clinton Threatens to Veto Major Bills (April 7): Refuses to compromise on House versions of measures including those dealing with legal system, Government regulation, use of U.S. troops in U.N. operations, and compensation for property owners.

Thousands Protest Attacks on Women (April 9): Rally near Capitol denounces rape and battering, also political assaults on welfare and abortion.

Clinton Outlines Three Legislative Priorities (April 15): Seeks passage of tax cuts linked to education, welfare reform that promotes work, and anti-crime measures keeping ban on assault-type weapons.

Clinton Overhauls U.S. Secrecy Rules (April 17): Orders that highly classified documents be made public after 25 years, with some exceptions.

High Court Backs Election Law Change (April 19): Justices rule, 7–2, that Constitution protects right to distribute anonymous campaign literature.

High Court Kills Law on School-Zone Guns (April 26): Justices, 5–4, rule Congress exceeded Constitutional authority in making it a Federal offense to possess a gun within 1,000 feet of a school. Verdict is blow to U.S. role in local law enforcement.

Clinton Maps Anti-Terrorism Strategy (April 26): Seeks 1,000 new Federal agents and easing of ban on use of military to investigate crimes involving chemical, biological, or nuclear weapons.

U.S. Opposes Microsoft on Merger (April 27): Files anti-trust lawsuit to block company's planned $2-billion acquisition of Intuit Inc., software producer.

General

Major League Baseball Strike Ends (April 2): Owners accept players' offer to return after 234-day stoppage, longest in professional sports history.

Romanian Air Crash Kills 60 (April 3): In-flight explosion blamed for felling Tarom Airlines A-310 shortly after takeoff from Bucharest.

Former United Way Head Convicted (April 3): U.S. Court in Virginia finds William Aramony guilty of stealing more than $600,000 from charity that provides services for local, independent fund drives.

Blunders Blamed in Crash of U.S. Air DC-9 (April 4): National Transportation Safety Board finds errors by controllers and crew in accident that killed 37 and injured 20 at Charleston, N.C., in July 1994.

Infants' Deaths Linked to Smoking by Mothers (April 12): Massachusetts researchers report 5,600 fatalities in U.S. yearly and 15,000 miscarriages.

Court Rebuffs Dr. King's Widow (April 13): Massachusetts tribunal rejects plea by Coretta Scott King to regain control of husband's papers from Boston University, to which he had bequeathed them.

Woman Upheld in Plea to Enter Citadel (April 13): U.S. Appeals Court panel, in 2–1 ruling, paves way for Shannon Faulkner to become first female cadet at Charleston, S.C., military college.

Strenuous Exercise Called Key to Longevity (April 18): Harvard study following 17,300 men finds that only vigorous activity reduced risk of dying.

Scores Killed in Oklahoma City Bombing: Death toll past 100 in what officials call worst act of terrorism in nation's history. **Chronicle: (April 19):** Car bomb tears away facade of nine-story, block-long Federal building. Many victims are children in daycare center. F.B.I. seeks to arrest "two white males." **(April 21):** Timothy McVeigh, 27, Army veteran, held as suspect after arrest on traffic charge. **(April 22):** Authorities hunt second suspect. Link right-wing paramilitary groups to bombing. **(April 25):** Two brothers charged with engaging in bomb-building plot with McVeigh. Crews continue digging into wreckage of building to seek survivors and remove bodies. Whole nation mourns.

Earth Day Anniversary Celebrated (April 22): Hundreds rally in Washington to mark 25th year of modern environmental movement. Volunteers perform ritual of hauling trash from polluted Anacostia River.

MAY 1995

International

Wives Visit American Captives in Iran (May 1): Have tearful reunion with pair sentenced to eight years in prison for entering country illegally.

Fighting Escalates in Bosnia and Croatia (May 1): Highlights: **(May 1):** Croatian forces storm across U.N. cease-fire lines to attack rebel Serbs. **(May 2):** Serbs fire rockets into center of Zagreb, Croatian capital, killing and injuring many. **(May 25):** NATO warplanes bomb ammunition dump near Serbs' political headquarters in town of Pale. **(May 26):** Serbs seize scores of U.N. hostages, chaining some as human shields near bombing targets. **(May 28):** Bosnian Foreign Minister killed when Serbs shoot down helicopter. They seize more hostages. **(May 30):** Allies resolve to expand U.N. operations. Serbs declare U.N. peacekeepers an enemy.

U.S. Reverses Policy on Cuban Refugees (May 2): After 35 years, announces it will start returning boat people when final group of about 20,000 being held at Guantánamo Bay Naval Station is admitted.

French Elect Conservative President (May 7): Jacques Chirac, Paris Mayor, wins 52 percent of mainland vote on this third electoral attempt.

Fiftieth Anniversary of V.E. Day Celebrated (May 8): In Berlin, leaders of United States, Britain, France, Russia, and Germany pledge to prevent another catastrophe such as World War II. **(May 9):** In Moscow, massive victory parade is reviewed by President Yeltsin atop Lenin's tomb. President Clinton stands at side of tomb in silent protest against Russian use of massive force against Chechnya.

Clinton and Yeltsin Agree on Some Issues (May 10): Announce partial accord on aspects of European security and spread of nuclear weapons. Still far apart on expansion of NATO, Russian nuclear sales to Iran, and war in secessionist Chechnya.

Curb on Atomic Weapons Made Permanent (May 11): More than 170 nations agree at U.N. conference to extend Treaty on the Nonproliferation of Nuclear Weapons despite earlier opposition of nonnuclear nations to monopoly by five major powers.

Iran Says It Plans No Nuclear Arms (May 13): Denies U.S. charges of weapons development and reveals plans for 10 nuclear power plants over 20 years.

Japanese Police Seize Cult Leader (May 18): Thousands of police in major operation arrest Shoko Asahara, guru of Aum Shinrikyo cult, on charges of organizing nerve gas attack on Tokyo subway system. Forty of followers also taken in raids.

Former East German Spies Get Amnesty (May 23): Highest German court rules, 5–3, that they could not be tried in reunited nation. Says convicted top espionage officials need not serve sentences.

Syria Makes Concession in Golan Talks (May 24): Agrees to discuss security arrangements on Heights based on troop principles demanded by Israel.

National

Bush Quits National Rifle Association (May 10): Former President angry over letter from N.R.A. official branding Federal law agents as "jackbooted thugs."

High Court Rejects Local Bars to Group Housing (May 15): Justices rule, 6–3, municipalities may not use single-family zoning to outlaw residences for disabled people, including recovering addicts.

White House Imposes Harsh Sanctions on Japan (May 16): Clamps 100 percent tariff on 13 luxury car models in trade dispute stemming from issues involving openness of Japanese market to U.S. cars and parts.

Ethics Panel Accuses Senator Packwood (May 17): Charges Oregon Republican, 62, with sexual misconduct, tampering with evidence, and seeking help from lobbyists to help wife get a job.

Budget Proposals Advance in Congress (May 18): House, 238–193, votes sweeping Republican measure to erase Federal deficit by year 2002. Bill emphasizes cuts in Medicare and Medicaid and would reduce Cabinet departments and eliminate many Federal offices. **(May 24):** Senate, 57–42, approves similar measure. Tax relief remains divisive issue, even among Republicans.

Traffic Barred in Front of White House (May 20): Clinton orders closing of Pennsylvania Avenue section to all but pedestrians to prevent potential attacks by bombs from cars or trucks. President heeds long-time warnings from Secret Service.

High Court Rejects Term Limit Laws (May 22): Rules, 5–4, only a constitutional amendment can allow Congress or states to end service of Congress members.

Senate Panel Clears Clinton Nominee (May 26): Dr. Henry W. Foster, Jr., assured vote by full Senate on his choice by President Clinton to be Surgeon General. Two Republicans cast swing vote in his favor.

General

Malcolm X Daughter Gets Probation (May 1): Qubilah Bahiya Shabazz agrees to "accept responsibility" for role in plot to kill Louis Farrakhan.

Bombed Oklahoma City Structure Razed (May 5): Hundreds of rescuers call off search of ruins of Federal Building. **(May 11):** Federal prosecutors hold Terry Lynn Nichols, 40, as accomplice in the explosion, with Timothy J. McVeigh, 27, also held. **(May 23):** Ruins of building blown up by explosives experts as thousands watch. **(May 29):** Three bodies taken from the wreckage, believed to be the last of terrorists' 169 victims.

More Than 100 Killed in South Africa Mine (May 11): Underground train in gold mine plunges down 7,000-foot shaft after control cables snap.

Floods Ravage New Orleans Area (May 13): Damage estimated past $3 billion after heavy rains.

Implant Maker Forced to Bankruptcy (May 15): Dow Corning Corporation seeks relief in Federal court after hundreds of thousands of women file injury claims over silicone breast device. Action halts new lawsuits and existing litigation.

Tornadoes Wreak Wide Destruction (May 19): At least six dead and hundreds injured in trail of destruction from Tennessee to Maryland, damaging scores of buildings. Late spring storm blamed.

Microsoft Drops $2-Billion Acquisition (May 20): Abandons plans to merge with Intuit Inc. after legal challenge from Department of Justice to what would have been largest deal in software industry.

Death Toll Near 2,000 in Russian Earthquake (May 28): Temblor destroys most of little oil town of Neftegorsk on remote Far East Sakhalin Island. Many missing and feared dead. Ruins to be sealed.

Tornado Ravages Massachusetts Town (May 29): Slashes destructive path through Great Barrington. At least three killed. Property damage is heavy.

Death Toll Set at 153 in Zaire Plague (May 30): U.N.'s World Health Organization increases report of total of fatalities from viral Ebola infection. Reports 205 suspected or confirmed cases. Scientists say epidemic is under control in African nation.

"Superman" Star Paralyzed After Riding Mishap (May 31): Christopher Reeve, 42, suffers two broken spinal bones after being thrown from horse.

JUNE 1995
International

Bosnian Serbs Hold U.S. Troops as Hostages (June 2): Release 121 of U.N. peacekeeping troops. **(June 3):** Warn they will not release remaining captives unless NATO formally renounces use of air strikes. **(June 18):** To get release of remaining 26, U.N. abandons attempt to protect Sarajevo from shell fire.

Clinton Renews Trade Privileges With China (June 2): Acts on advice of Secretary of State Warren Christopher despite critics of human rights record.

South Africa Abolishes Death Penalty (June 6): Supreme Court ends decades-long policy, ruling capital punishment unconstitutional. Practice had been used as weapon to enforce apartheid system.

Japanese Indict Cult Leader in Killing (June 6): Six members of Aum Shinrikyo also charged in deaths from nerve gas in Tokyo's subway system.

U.S. Pilot Rescued in Bosnian War Zone (June 8): Marines brave Serbian fire to save Capt. Scott F. O'Grady, 29, who had been shot down by Serbs and survived for six days in wooded highlands.

Russia and Ukraine Settle Black Sea Dispute (June 9): Leaders reach agreement on former Soviet fleet and naval base, an issue that had fanned nationalist tensions between the two major nations.

Colombia Seizes a Top Drug Ring Leader (June 9): Police raid captures Gilberto Rodriguez Orejuela, called a principal figure in Cali cocaine and heroin gang, reputed to be world's largest trafficker.

Baltic Nations Sign Accord With Europe (June 12): Estonia, Latvia, and Lithuania sign agreement on trade and cooperation that may lead to full membership in European Union. Other former Communist nations have already established joint relations.

Angry China Recalls Ambassador to U.S. (June 16): Charges Washington changed policy toward Beijing by admitting Taiwan President Lee Teng-hui for personal visit. Envoy summoned home in protest.

Chechnya Gunmen Release Hostages (June 20): Free last 123 hostages after terrorizing Russian town for five days and holding hundreds captive.

John Major Quits as Conservative Leader (June 22): He seeks to regain control over divided British party, charging divisions are undermining Government.

Egyptian President Survives Ambush (June 26): Hosni Mubarak unhurt in assassination attempt on motorcade carrying him to African summit meeting in Ethiopian capital to Addis Ababa. Two gunmen and two Ethiopian police officers are killed.

U.S. and Japan End Dispute on Automotive Trade (June 28): Reach accord in marathon negotiations on expanding U.S. access to Japanese markets. Clinton cancels threat of $5.9-billion tariffs on luxury cars.

Yeltsin Dismisses Three Ministers (June 30): Russian President removes Security, Interior, and Nationalities officials for failures in Chechnya hostage crisis. Acts to counter parliamentary challenge.

National

Clinton Vetoes Budget-Cutting Bill (June 7): In first such action, President strikes down measure to trim $16.4 billion from current spending. It is new phase in confrontation with G.O.P. in Congress.

Justices Cast Doubt on Desegregation Plan (June 12): High court rules, 5–4, that Lower tribunals erred in ordering Missouri to help pay for magnet schools. Orders review of Kansas City integration case.

Justices Raise Doubts on Affirmative Action (June 12): Supreme Court, 5–4, rules race-based programs must be subject to searching judicial inquiry and be "narrowly tailored" to meet "compelling government interest" to be constitutional.

President Offers Own Plan to Balance Budget (June 13): Clinton seeks reduction over next decade by cutting growth of Medicare spending less than G.O.P. wants and covering the difference with smaller income tax cuts and by reducing corporate subsidies.

Justices Uphold Homosexual Parade Ban (June 19): Supreme Court rules unanimously that private sponsors of Boston's St. Patrick's celebration have right to bar groups whose message they reject, including gay men and lesbians.

Air Officer Cleared in Helicopter Downings (June 20): Court-martial exonerates Capt. Jim Wang, 29, of causing 26 deaths in accidental shooting of two Army helicopters over Iraq in 1994.

Senate Rebuffs Surgeon General Nominee (June 22): Democrats fail in second attempt to end G.O.P.'s filibuster blocking vote on Dr. Henry W. Foster, Jr. He had been under attack from conservatives and groups critical of record on performing abortions.

Supreme Court Limits Race in Redistricting (June 29): In 5–4 decision, Justices rule that race as "predominant factor" in drawing lines is unconstitutional. Blacks could lose electoral gains.

Congress Votes G.O.P. Budget-Balancing Plan (June 29): Senate and House approve, on party lines, proposal for seven-year program of cutting taxes and limiting spending for Medicare and other social programs.

Court Backs Funding for Religious Publication (June 29): Ruling, 5–4, rejects University of Virginia claim that payment to student religious magazine violates constitutional separation of church and state.

General

U.S. Indicts Former Drug Prosecutors (June 5): Charges Florida lawyers with corruption in protecting Cali, Colombia, cocaine cartel they had attacked.

Toll 1,632 in Russian Earthquake (June 6): Final survivors located in remote oil town of Neftegorsk.

Philip Morris Nicotine Study Disclosed (June 7): Documents show company's researchers found nicotine affected body, brain, and behavior of smokers.

Bomb Kills 30 in Medellin, Colombia (June 11): More than 200 wounded by blast during music festival attended by thousands. Explosion comes barely 24 hours after arrest of Cali cocaine cartel, country's leading drug-trafficking organization.

Oklahoma Bombing Linked to Robbery (June 14): Federal agents report evidence implicates two suspects to hold-up of Arkansas gun dealer that may have financed destruction of Oklahoma City building.

Former United Way President Sentenced (June 23): William Aramony gets seven-year prison term in Federal Court for fraudulently diverting $1.2 million of charity's money. Two former associates also sentenced to prison terms and other penalties.

U.S. Shuttle Docks With Russian Space Station (June 27): Atlantis blasts into orbit at Cape Canaveral, Fla., with crew of five Americans and two Russians. **(June 29):** Craft joins Russians' station *Mir* in flawless docking, first coupling of U.S. and Russian space craft in two decades. Two crews greet joyously.

Mail Bomber Threatens to Blow Up Airliner (June 28): Self-styled anarchist, an active terrorist for 17 years, warns of plan to destroy aircraft leaving Los Angeles International Airport.

Building Collapse Kills at Least 37 in South Korea (June 29): More than 700 injured in Seoul department store crowded with shoppers. Many believed trapped in debris and imperiled by fire.

JULY 1995
International

Russian Parliament Fails in Anti-Yeltsin Move (July 1): Government averts showdown when vote of no-confidence fails. Prime Minister Chernomyrdin hails compromise as vindicating Government policies.

Violence Breaks Out in Northern Ireland (July 3): Disorders flare in Roman Catholic areas of Belfast and Londonderry for first time in 10 months. Crowds protest release of British soldier sentenced to life in killing of teen-aged Catholic girl.

British Conservatives Re-Elect John Major (July 4): Tory party assures survival as Prime Minister by two-thirds vote. His victory is not decisive.

Israel and P.L.O. Agree on Key Issues (July 4): Reach accord on Israeli troop withdrawals from West Bank paving way for Palestinian elections, transfers of civil authority, and release of prisoners.

Iraq Admits Germ Arsenal Production (July 5): Reveals for first time that it developed offensive biological weapons in 1989–90 on even of Gulf War.

French Navy Seizes Greenpeace Ship (July 9): Commandos thwart attempt to land protesters on South Pacific atoll where France plans nuclear tests.

Democratic Leader Freed in Burma (July 10): Government ends six years of house arrest for Daw Aung San Suu Kyu, 50, winner of Nobel Peace Prize.

U.S. Extends Vietnam Full Recognition (July 11): Clinton announces move 22 years after American withdrawal from divisive war. President says it is time "to bind up our own wounds." Decision draws support and criticism from legislators and veterans' groups.

Serbs Seize Bosnia "Safe Zones": NATO Allies United (July 12 et seq.): Srebrenica, last remaining U.N. stronghold in an eastern region "safe area," falls to invaders, who drive out Muslim population. (July 14): Serbs overrun besieged "safe area" of Zepa. (July 21): U.S., Britain, and France, after indecision, pledge sustained campaign of air strikes if Serbs attack Gorazde, U.N. protected enclave in Eastern Bosnia. (July 23): More than 800 British and French troops, with heavy equipment, sent to Sarajevo to secure supply line and counter Serbs.

Iraq Frees Two Imprisoned Americans (July 16): President Hussein releases pair held since accidentally crossing border from Kuwait. U.S. officials see effort to persuade U.N. to drop economic sanctions.

At Least Six Dead in Blast Near Tel Aviv (July 24): Palestinian suicide bomber attacks bus during rush hour. Many injured. Lull in terrorism broken on eve of expected Israeli-Arab self-rule agreement.

Russians and Chechens Sign Partial Accord (July 30): Negotiators say treaty will end seven months of war that has devastated much of Chechnya and hurt Russian reforms. But they fail to agree on status of southern region that seeks independence.

National

Federal Reserve Lowers Interest Rates (July 6): Lowers short-term level a quarter point in move to bolster economy. Discount rate left unchanged.

Clinton Attacks TV Violence (July 10): In address to conference on family and the media, President endorses requirement that set makers install computer chip to screen out programs coded as violent.

F.D.A. Moves to Regulate Tobacco (July 12): For first time, rules that nicotine is an addictive drug and submits limited restrictions to White House.

President Admits France's Guilt on Jews (July 16): Chirac recognizes nation's part in deporting thousands to Nazi death camps in World War II.

Senate Begins Whitewater Hearings (July 18 et seq.): Special committee opens examination of Arkansas transactions and personal finances of the President and Hillary Rodham Clinton. (July 26): Secret Service officer and Mrs. Clinton's top aide clash over possible removal of files from office of Vincent W. Foster, Jr. after his suicide.

Clinton Hails Goals of Affirmative Action (July 19): President says preferential programs based on race and sex have been good for nation. In speech at National Archives he says affirmative action should be retired "when the job is done."

Waco Siege Subject of Congressional Hearings (July 26): On sixth day, F.B.I. officials tell why they rejected Branch Davidian leader's surrender proposal. (July 31): White House and House Republicans trade charges about President's possible role in attack on cult.

Senate, 98–0, Votes Limits on Lobbyist's Gifts (July 28): Adopts strict rules forbidding members and aides to accept free trips, lunches, and other offerings.

Clinton and Dole Offer Welfare Programs (July 31): President and prospective 1996 rival give nation's governors competing versions of needed reforms.

Senate Panel Bars Packwood Hearings (July 31): Ethics Committee votes against public inquiry into allegations of sexual and official misconduct.

General

Prosecution Rests in Simpson Case (July 6): Finish presentation in double-slaying case after 92 days of testimony, 58 witnesses, 488 exhibits, 34,500 pages of transcript. Conclusion is low-key.

U.S.–Russian Space Link-Up Ends (July 7): U.S. astronaut, Dr. Norman E. Thagard, 51, returns to Earth after nearly four months aboard Russian space station *Mir*. With him aboard shuttle *Atlantis* as it lands at Cape Canaveral are two Russian colleagues and five U.S. astronauts who linked up with the space station.

Lawyers Begin Defense of O.J. Simpson (July 10): Portray former football star as grief-stricken and in shock after learning of former wife's murder.

Space Shuttle *Discovery* Begins Delayed Orbit (July 13): Blasts off at Cape Canaveral five weeks after woodpeckers bored holes in fuel tank covering. Crew comprises three men and two women. (July 22): *Discovery* lands at Cape Canaveral after nine-day mission to deploy communications satellite and conduct medical and military experiments.

N.A.A.C.P. Audit Faults Accounting (July 13): Report finds shortcomings by 28 top officers. Board, meeting at annual convention, releases summary of findings that have slowed civil rights struggle.

Seven Dead in Blast on Paris Train (July 25): Scores wounded as bomb explodes during rush hour near Notre Dame Cathedral. Terrorist gang suspected.

Hormone Found to Cause Weight Loss (July 26): Scientists discover possible therapy for obesity. Tests show rapid loss of body fat in overweight mice.

Three Big Unions Plan Merger (July 27): Five-year program announced by steel workers, automobile workers, and machinists. Other unions to be invited.

Defect Delays Space Shuttle Flight (July 28): Engineers seek how to prevent scorching of critical seals in booster rocket nozzles in launchings.

Susan Smith Gets Life for Double Killing (July 28): South Carolina jury rejects death penalty for mother, 23, convicted of drowning two young sons.

Two Entertainment Giants Merge (July 31): Walt Disney Company to acquire Capital Cities/ABC for $19 billion in second largest takeover ever made.

AUGUST 1995

International

China to Expel Two U.S. Officers (Aug. 2): Arrests Air Force men accused of spying while monitoring Chinese military exercises to learn intent.

Anniversary of Hiroshima Bombing (Aug. 6): World observes 50th anniversary of day first nuclear weapon was dropped on Japan with enormous death toll and intense suffering for thousands of civilians.

Cali Drug Cartel Leader Arrested (Aug. 6): Action by Colombian police hailed by Colombian and American officials as a final blow against largest network.

Two Top Iraqi Army Officers Defect (Aug. 10): Sons-in-law of President Saddam Hussein flee to Jordan with wives and several senior officers in severe internal blow to nation's regime.

Kashmiri Rebels Behead Tourist (Aug. 13): Body of Norwegian hostage found with name of separatist group Al Faran carved on chest. More deaths threatened.

Japanese Apology for Wartime Suffering (Aug. 15): Prime Minister offers first frank expressions of regret. Japanese and other Asians welcome apology.

U.S. Builds Up Persian Gulf Force (Aug. 17): Acts on Iraqi troop movements and warnings that Saddam Hussein considered attacking Kuwait and Saudi Arabia.

Three U.S. Diplomats Killed in Bosnia (Aug. 19): Vehicle crashes on rough winding mountain road on way to Sarajevo. Accident victims were part of delegations discussing U.S. peace initiatives.

Five Killed in Jerusalem Bus Bombing (Aug. 21): Suicide attacker kills four passengers and himself and wounds 100. Hamas, Islamic resistance body, takes responsibility. Incident sets off day-long protests against Israel Government negotiations with P.L.O.

Zaire Expels 3,500 Rwandan Refugees (Aug. 21): Thousands more flee camps in Zaire to avoid being forced to return home. Hundreds from Burundi expelled.

Israel Captures Gang Linked to Bombings (Aug. 23): Hamas group suspected of organizing two most recent attacks. Two leaders and 30 followers arrested.

China Expels American Rights Activist (Aug. 25): Harry Wu departs day after Chinese court found him guilty of spying and stealing state secrets and sentenced him to 15 years in prison. U.S. diplomats discern move to mend official relations with America.

NATO Planes Bomb Bosnian Serb Targets (Aug. 28): Two Serbian shells crash into Sarajevo's central market, killing at least 37 and wounding 80 in most devastating single attack in 18 months. **(Aug. 30):** NATO planes fly more than 200 sorties to pound Bosnian Serb targets with air strikes across country after 40 months of hesitation. Forty-eight U.S. aircraft join Western alliance's biggest operation since its establishment in 1949.

Liberians Hail Peace After Six-Year Civil War (Aug. 31): Thousands in battered capital, Monrovia, to welcome end of conflict and praise leaders who waged it. Coalition Government to rule after wartime with death toll estimated at 150,000.

National

Clinton File Index Missing in Foster Office (Aug. 1): Secretary to Vincent W. Foster, Jr. tells Senate Whitewater inquiry she could not find it when papers were searched after White House counsel's suicide. **(Aug. 2):** Former Deputy Attorney General tells panel White House compromised inquiry into Foster death.

House Votes to Ease Communications Rules (Aug. 4): Decides, 305 to 117, to reduce regulations on everything from cable television to local and long-distance telephone services.

President Spurs Toxic-Emission Rule (Aug. 8): Issues executive order to assure that companies doing business with Government meet Federal requirements.

Clinton Seeks Curb on Teen-Age Smoking (Aug. 11): Urges sweeping plan, including ban on vending machines and restrictions on advertising aimed at young.

F.B.I. Suspends Four in Idaho Siege Inquiry (Aug. 11): High-ranking officials are targets in Justice Department investigation of possible cover-up of events in deadly standoff with white separatist.

Clinton Urges Ban on All Nuclear Tests (Aug. 11): Calls for permanent move to prevent additional nations from developing atomic weapons.

Clinton Vetoes Bill to End Bosnia Arms Embargo (Aug. 11): Uses second rejection of term to block legislation to end United States participation with allies.

Perot Holds Three-Day National Convention (Aug. 11–13): Leading politicians of all parties attend Dallas conclave of United We Stand America. Ross Perot concludes major parties have not properly reformed political system. Leaves open his 1996 candidacy.

Air Force Grounds Five Pilots in Iraq Incident (Aug. 14): Disciplines officers accused in deaths of 26 when two Army helicopters were downed in error.

U.S. to Pay Separatist's Family $3.1 Million (Aug. 15): Settles claims resulting from deaths of wife and teen-age son in Idaho shootout three years previously.

Women Celebrate Suffrage Victory (Aug. 26): Group rallies in Washington to mark 75th anniversary of winning right to vote and honor leaders in battle.

General

U.S. Indicts Two in Oklahoma Bombing (Aug. 10): Charges Timothy McVeigh and Terry L. Nichols with explosion that wrecked Federal building with at least 167 deaths. Government to seek death penalty. **(Aug. 15):** McVeigh and Nichols plead not guilty.

"Jane Roe" of Abortion Test Case Changes Sides (Aug. 10): Texas woman whose fight led to landmark 1973 Supreme Court ruling joins antiabortion forces.

Woman Cadet Quits Citadel (Aug. 18): Shannon R. Faulkner says stress of long legal battle to enter all-male Virginia military academy had exhausted her.

Train Crash Kills 300 in Northern India (Aug. 20): More than 400 injured when speeding passenger train rams another stalled after hitting a cow.

Monica Seles Stages Tennis Comeback (Aug. 20): Player, 21, stabbed by fanatic in Germany in 1993, wins du Maurier Ltd. Open tennis tournament at Toronto.

ABC News Apologies for Tobacco Program (Aug. 21): Settles suits brought by Philip Morris and R.J. Reynolds over reports on nicotine levels.

Twenty-Seven Survive Georgia Plane Crash (Aug. 21): Two killed as Delta commuter craft plunges in flames into hayfield after losing engine in flight.

Merger to Create Nation's Biggest Bank (Aug. 29): Chemical Banking and Chase Manhattan agree to combine in deal estimated at nearly $10 billion.

Abortion Method Uses Two Drugs (Aug. 30): New study finds pregnancies can be ended safely and effectively in early stages by administering two prescription drugs that are already widely available.

Simpson Jurors to Hear Two Taped Epithets (Aug. 31): Judge Lance Ito rules jury can hear only two of 41 recorded instances of use of "nigger" by former Los Angeles Detective Mark Fuhrman. Further ruling also a blow to defense of football star on trial for murder of ex-wife and her friend.

SEPTEMBER 1995

International

Separatist Rebels Kill 13 in Kashmir (Sept. 4): Bomb wounds 25 in summer capital of Srinagar.

France Explodes Nuclear Device in Pacific (Sept. 5): Detonates device buried beneath remote atoll southeast of Tahiti. It was first in a series that has brought protests from governments and environmental organizations.

NATO Forces Hammer Serb Air Defenses (Sept. 10): Use cruise missiles and long-range bombs for first time after Bosnian Serbs defy Allied ultimatum to withdraw heavy weapons from around Sarajevo.

Two American Balloonists Slain Over Belarus (Sept. 12): Die when fire from ground troops ignites hydrogen-filled balloon after they had crossed border from Poland while competing in annual Gordon Bennett Balloon Race. Two other American-crewed balloons in race forced to land. Four taken prisoner.

Women's Conference Agrees on Goals (Sept. 15): Fourth World session, at Beijing, votes broad declaration calling on world governments to protect women from increasing levels of violence and to improve the status of girls throughout the world.

Hong Kong Voters Reject Pro-China Party (Sept. 17): Spurns pro-Beijing candidates in last legislative election under British rule.

Israeli-Palestinian Agreement Reached (Sept. 24): Both sides conclude major accord on transferring control of much of occupied West Bank to its Arab residents. Agreement follows months of negotiations. **(Sept. 28):** In Washington ceremony, Yitzhak Rabin, Prime Minister of Israel, and Yasir Arafat, chairman of Palestine Liberation Organization, sign the accord cementing the agreement for transferring control of much of West Bank to the Arabs.

China Cancels Iran Reactor Deal (Sept. 27): Informs U.S. it has decided to abandon contract for selling two nuclear power reactors.

NATO Outlines Plan for Expansion (Sept. 28): States proposals for Central European countries to join alliance. But it is unable to reassure Russia that expansion would not revive Cold War tensions.

Enemies in Bosnia Take Move Toward Peace (Sept. 28): Foreign ministers of Bosnia, Croatia, and Serbian-dominated Yugoslavia endorse two-page statement calling for a group presidency, a Parliament, and a constitutional court.

French Police Kill Suspect in Bombings (Sept. 29): Slay 24-year-old Algerian, object of nationwide manhunt after series of terrorist attacks.

National

Senator Bob Packwood Resigns Under Pressure (Sept. 6): Senate Ethics Committee votes unanimously that Oregon member be expelled on grounds of sexual and official misconduct. Senator vows to fight charges. **(Sept. 7):** Packwood resigns seat. Majority Leader Bob Dole proposes 90-day reprieve to allow Packwood to manage legislation as chairman of Senate Finance Committee. **(Sept. 8):** Dole forced to settle for three weeks instead.

Miss America Receives Crown (Sept. 16): Shawntel Smith from Muldrow, Okla., is the new titleholder.

Leaders Agree to Avert Federal Shutdown (Sept. 27): G.O.P. in Congress and White House settle on six-week grace period for appropriations period to prevent cessation for lack of funds.

Gov. Pete Wilson Drops Out of 1996 Race (Sept. 29): California Governor withdraws from G.O.P. Presidential competition because of low standing of polls and lack of financial support.

General

Hurricane Luis Wreaks Havoc in Caribbean (Sept. 6): Most powerful storm in six years skips across resort islands, flattening houses, damaging hospitals, closing airports, and grounding power and communication lines. Island of Antigua is worst hit.

Space Shuttle Launched After Delays (Sept. 7): *Endeavour* carries five astronauts on 11-day mission to study the Sun, experiment with vacuum-produced electronic materials, and test new pressure suits. **(Sept. 18):** Shuttle glides to landing at Cape Canaveral, Fla., after trouble with wobbly satellite and clogged toilet pipe. O-ring seals on solid-fuel booster rockets come back unscathed for first time in months.

Simpson Case Witness Keeps Silence (Sept. 8): Mark Fuhrman, former detective, invokes Fifth Amendment privilege against self-incrimination in refusing to answer defense questions. He asserted the privilege when questioned about truthfulness in previous testimony and about whether he had planted or manufactured evidence in case.

Mail Bomber's Manifesto Printed (Sept. 19): *Washington Post*, aided by *New York Times*, publishes 35,000-word manuscript from serial killer known as the Unabomber in hope of ending his 17-year campaign of murder through the mails, as he had offered.

A.T.T. Announces Voluntary Split-Up (Sept. 21): Discloses plan to divide its business into three companies: communication services, communications equipment, and computers. Chairman says company is responding to changes in technology and regulation.

Time Warner and Turner System to Merge (Sept. 22): Time Warner agrees to buy the 82 percent of Turner Broadcasting it does not already own in stock deal estimated at about $7.5 billion. Ted Turner to become vice chairman of Time Warner.

O.J. Simpson Breaks Long Silence at Trial (Sept. 22): Explains failure to testify and reiterates his innocence in slaying of former wife and her friend. When jury returns, Judge Ito explains law, and both prosecution and defense rest their cases.

Major Emmy Awards for TV, 1995

(Sept. 10, 1995)

Drama Series: *N.Y.P.D. Blue* (ABC)
  Actress: Kathy Baker, *Picket Fences* (CBS)
  Actor: Mandy Patinkin, *Chicago Hope* (CBS)
  Supporting actress: Julianna Margulies, *E.R.* (NBC)
  Supporting actor: Ray Walston, *Picket Fences* (CBS)
Comedy series: *Frasier* (NBC)
  Actress: Candice Bergen, *Murphy Brown* (CBS)
  Actor: Kelsey Grammer, *Frasier* (NBC)
  Supporting actress: Christine Baranski, *Cybill* (CBS)
  Supporting actor: David Hyde Pierce, *Frasier* (NBC)
Variety, Music or Comedy Series: *The Tonight Show with Jay Leno* (NBC)
Variety, Music or Comedy Special: *Barbra Streisand: The Concert* (HBO)
Miniseries or Special: *Joseph* (TNT)
  Actress: Glenn Close, *Serving in Silence: The Grethe Cammermeyer Story* (NBC)
  Actor: Raul Julia, *The Burning Season* (HBO)
  Supporting actress (tie): Judy Davis, *Serving in Silence: The Grethe Cammermeyer Story* (NBC) and Shirley Knight, *Indictment: The McMartin Trial* (HBO)
  Supporting actor: Donald Sutherland, *Citizen X* (HBO)
Made for TV Movie: *Indictment: The McMartin Trial* (HBO)
Individual Performance, Variety or Music Program: Barbra Streisand, *Barbra Streisand: The Concert* (HBO)

OCTOBER 1995
(Through October 16)

International

Nigeria Chief Commutes Death Sentences (Oct. 1): In an effort to defuse political tensions, Gen. Sani Abacha offers to lift the death sentences for as many as 40 opponents of his military government.

Macedonian President Falls Victim to Car-Bomb Attack (Oct. 3): President Kiro Gligorov is seriously wounded when a bomb explodes in a parked car close to the Parliament building where Mr. Gligorov was on his way to work. The explosion kills his driver and wounds three bystanders. **(Oct. 4):** Parliament names Speaker of Parliament Stojan Andov as interim President.

French Troops Invade Comoros (Oct. 4): French marines and Foreign Legion soldiers land, end six-day-old coup, and free captured President Said Mohammed Djohar.

Cease-Fire Set for Bosnia (Oct. 5): Warring parties agree to a cease-fire to be followed by negotiations in the United States aiming at a full-scale international peace conference. **(Oct. 12):** After a series of delays, the 60-day cease-fire goes into effect at one minute past midnight.

Israel Frees Prisoners and Withdraws (Oct. 10): Fulfilling terms of its agreement with the P.L.O., Israeli authorities release 900 Palestinian men and withdraw from four West Bank towns.

National

Senate Cuts Money for Broadcasts Abroad (Oct. 1): Radio Free Europe and Radio Liberty suffer budget cuts as Senate transfers $48 million of their $75-million budget to the Maritime Commission.

House Derails Terrorism Bill (Oct. 2): After passage by the Senate and approved by the House Judiciary Committee, the bill has run into opposition from conservative Republicans and libertarian Democrats. Both are wary of giving so much power to the F.B.I.

AMA Criticizes G.O.P. Medicare Proposals (Oct. 3): Cuts in payments to doctors would make the program unattractive to many doctors, driving them out of Medicare, according to AMA spokesman James H. Stacey. **(Oct. 10):** Back plan after being reassured on payment cuts.

Action on Term Limits Falters (Oct. 4): Conceding that they lack enough current support to win Senate approval of a constitutional amendment, freshman Republicans seek to postpone a vote on it until next spring.

Million Man March Draws Hundreds of Thousands (Oct. 16): An estimated 400,000 black men from across the country fill the capital's Mall and pledge to take responsibility for their lives and their communities.

General

Jury Finds Sheik and Followers Guilty (Oct. 1): Sheik Omar Abdel Rahman and nine others are found guilty of conspiring to carry out a terrorist campaign aimed at destroying the United Nations, New York City landmarks, and killing hundreds of people.

Earthquake Rocks Turkey (Oct. 1): A major quake hits the market town of Dinar in southwestern Turkey, killing 55 people, injuring 200, destroying 1,000 homes, and damaging 4,000 others. **(Oct. 3):** Death toll rises to 73 and the number injured to at least 242.

Jury Reaches Verdict in Simpson Trial (Oct. 2): After less than four hours of deliberation, the jury comes to a decision but Judge Ito delays announcing the result until the next day. **(Oct. 3):** Jury finds O.J. Simpson not guilty of murder charges against him.

Pope Arrives on Whirlwind U.S. Visit (Oct. 4): Meets with President Clinton and leads vespers at Sacred Heart Cathedral in Newark. **(Oct. 5):** In addressing the United Nations, Pope John Paul II calls on the nations to live up to their moral responsibilities. In the evening, celebrates Mass at Giants Stadium in New Jersey. **(Oct. 8):** Pope ends U.S. visit saying Mass in Baltimore's Camden Yards ball park.

Hurricane Opal Hits Florida Coast (Oct. 4): With winds gusting to more than 145 miles per hour, Opal strikes the Gulf Coast, causing one death and widespread flooding. **(Oct. 5):** Death toll rises to at least 15 in four states as the storm travels northward. Early estimates of damage stand at $1.8 billion.

Sabotage Causes Train Wreck (Oct. 9): The derailment of an Amtrak train in the Arizona desert is the work of a saboteur. One crew member is killed, about 100 people are injured.

Kasparov Retains Chess Title (Oct. 10): After 18 games, Gary Kasparov defeats Viswanathan Anand with a final score of 10 1/2 to 7 1/2.

1995 Nobel Prize Winners

Peace: Joseph Rotblat (British) and his organization, the Pugwash Conference on Science and World Affairs, for campaign to eliminate nuclear weapons. The Committee said it wanted to send a message of protest to France and China over nuclear weapons testing.

Literature: Seamus Heaney (Irish) poet "for works of lyrical beauty and ethical depth, which exalt everyday miracles and the living past."

Medicine: Dr. Edward B. Lewis and Dr. Eric F. Wieschaus (American) and Dr. Christiane Nüsslein-Volhard (German) for studies of the fruit fly. "Together, these three scientists have achieved a breakthrough that will help explain congenital malformations in man." Dr. Lewis is professor emeritus of the California Institute of Technology. Dr. Wieschaus is at Princeton University and Dr. Nüsslein-Volhard is at the Max Planck Institute, Tübingen, Germany.

Economics: Robert E. Lucas, Jr. (American), who is "the economist who has had the greatest influence on macroeconomic research since 1970." He is a professor at the University of Chicago.

Physics: Dr. Martin L. Perl and Dr. Frederick Reines (American) for their discoveries of "two of nature's most remarkable subatomic particles"—the tau and the neutrino. Dr. Perl is a researcher at the Stanford Linear Accelerator at Palo Alto, Calif., and Dr. Reines is an emeritus professor of physics at the University of California at Irvine.

Chemistry: Dr. F. Sherwood Rowland (American) and Dr. Mario Molina (American) and Dr. Paul Crutzen (Dutch) for their pioneering work in explaining the chemical processes that deplete the earth's ozone shield. Dr. Rowland is a chemistry professor at the University of California at Irvine. Dr. Molina is a professor in the department of earth, atmospheric, and planetary sciences at the Massachusetts Institute of Technology. Dr. Crutzen is a professor at the Max Planck Institute for Chemistry at Mainz, Germany.

Deaths in 1994–1995

Abbott, George, 103: Broadway legend since 1913. Was famed as playwright, director, actor, producer, and play doctor. Jan. 31, 1995.

Arnold, Danny, 70: TV writer and producer who was the creative force behind "Bewitched" and "Barney Miller." He received an Emmy for the latter. Aug. 19, 1995.

Aspin, Les, 56: veteran Wisconsin Congressman and Secretary of Defense in first 11 months of Clinton Administration. May 21, 1995.

Bernays, Edward L., 103: pioneer in developing new techniques of public relations. March 10, 1995.

Berry, Noah, Jr., 81: character actor whose career spanned six decades. He was best known for his work in the TV series, "The Rockford Files." Nov. 1, 1994.

Brazzi, Rossano, 78: Italian actor who starred in the movie "South Pacific" and other romantic roles during the 1950s and '60s. Dec. 24, 1994.

Brett, Jeremy, 59: British actor who won fame for his portrayal of Sherlock Holmes in the long-running "Mystery" series on PBS and had also played him on stage. His career included work on stage and in films. Sept. 12, 1995.

Brophy, Brigid, 66: novelist, critic, and essayist who gained notice with her first novel "Hackenfeller's Ape" before she was 30.

Burger, Warren E., 87: fifteenth Chief Justice of the United States. Served 17 years. Regarded as transitional figure. June 25, 1995.

Calloway, Cab (Cabell), 86: band leader, actor, and singer known as "Hi-de-ho" man of jazz. Nov. 18, 1994.

Cook, Peter, 57: British writer and performer noted for creation of a new irreverent style of comedy.

Cosell, Howard, 77: nation's best known and most outspoken sports broadcaster over 30-year career. April 23, 1995.

Djilas, Milovan, 83: Yugoslav writer, revolutionary, soldier, and political leader. Became early advocate of dissidents and anti-Communists. April 20, 1995.

Duke, Angier Biddle, 79: scion of powerful American family. Served as Ambassador to El Salvador, Denmark, Spain, and Morocco. Chief of protocol for two Presidents. April 30, 1995.

Durrell, Gerald M., 70: British conservationist and author. Created role for zoos in preserving endangered species. Jan. 30, 1995.

Eckert, John Presper, 76: co-inventor of huge Eniac computer in 1945, believed to be first electronic digital computer. June 3, 1995.

Eisenstaedt, Alfred, 96: photographer for *Life* magazine whose work set a standard for American photojournalism. His most famous photograph is of the V–J Day celebration in Times Square showing a sailor kissing a nurse. Aug. 23, 1995.

Farrar, David, 87: British actor who began his career on the stage achieved fame for his role in the film "Black Narcissus." Aug. 31, 1995.

Faubus, Orval E., 84: former Governor of Arkansas. Defied Federal desegregation order in 1957, leading to Little Rock school crisis. Dec. 14, 1994.

Fistoulari, Anatole, 88: conductor who made his debut at the age of seven and sent on to an international career including conducting at the Metropolitan Opera. Aug. 21, 1995.

Fulbright, J. William, 89: a leading Senator, Democrat of Arkansas, prominent opponent of Vietnam War as chairman of Foreign Relations Committee. Created Fulbright scholarships for international study. Feb. 9, 1995.

Gabor, Eva, 74: actress acclaimed on Broadway and on television. Best known for TV's "Green Acres." July 4, 1995.

Garcia, Jerry, 53: Rock 'n' Roll guitarist and singer prominent in the Grateful Dead band. Aug. 10, 1995.

Gingold, Josef, 85: prominent violinist who became one of nation's most influential teachers. Jan. 11, 1995.

Gonzalez, Richard (Pancho), 67: twice national tennis champion, known for competitive spirit. July 3, 1995.

Gordon, Gale, 89: TV actor most remembered for his roles opposite Lucille Ball in "Here's Lucy" and "Life With Lucy." He also appeared in films and in the 1950s had regular parts in seven weekly radio shows. Aug. 31, 1995.

Grace, J. Peter, 81: controversial industrialist. Long head of W.R. Grace Company. Served at helm of President Reagan's Private Sector Study on Cost Control in the Federal Government. April 19, 1995.

Griswold, Erwin N., 90: U.S. Solicitor General under two presidents and dean of Harvard Law School for 20 years. Known as champion of civil rights and enemy of McCarthyism. Nov. 19, 1994.

Guardino, Harry, 69: actor who appeared in the movies, on the Broadway stage, and on TV, including a stint on the "Perry Mason" series. July 17, 1995.

Harris, Phil, 91: band leader and radio comedian who became famous as Jack Benny's sidekick on the long-running radio show. This led to roles in films as well. Aug. 11, 1995.

Hawkins, Erick, 85: a major figure and innovator in modern American dance. Nov. 23, 1994.

Herriot, James (James Alfred Wight), 78: British author of "All Creatures Great and Small" and other books on animals and veterinarians. Feb. 23, 1995.

Hobby, Oveta Culp, 90: created women's Auxiliary Army Corps in World War II. Was first Secretary of Health, Education and Welfare. Longtime Houston newspaper executive. Aug. 16, 1995.

Hunter, Howard W., 87: head of Mormon Church for nine months and the denomination's 14th "prophet, seer and revelator." March 3, 1995.

Ives, Burl, 85: folk singer and actor. Won international fame in 1940s with ballads. Acting in 1950s won Academy Award. April 14, 1995.

Julia, Raul, 54: actor who won acclaim in classics on and off Broadway. Also starred in Hollywood movies. Oct. 24, 1994.

Kelly, Nancy, 73: Hollywood and Broadway actress, winning a Tony Award for her performance in "The Bad Seed." Jan. 2, 1995.

Kennedy, Rose Elizabeth Fitzgerald, 104: daughter of Congressman, wife of ambassador, and mother of a President and two U.S. Senators. Jan. 23, 1995.

Kingsley, Sidney, 88: playwright known for realistic dramas of mean city streets. Won Pulitzer Prize for first play, "Men in White." March 20, 1995.

Koch, Howard, 93: screen writer who won an Academy Award as one of the authors of the film "Casablanca." He also wrote plays and was the author of Orson Welles's radio adaptation of "The War of the Worlds." Aug. 17, 1995.

Kunstler, William, 76: radical lawyer who was well known for representing controversial clients. One of his early clients was Martin Luther King, Jr. and the last were the suspects in the World Trade Center bombing. Sept. 4, 1995.

Kurtz, Efrem, 94: orchestra conductor who held posts with orchestras in Europe and America. In later years as a freelance conductor he performed regularly with European orchestras and opera companies. June 29, 1995.

Lamont, Corliss, 93: author, teacher, and humanist philosopher who waged life-long fight for civil liberties and international understanding. April 26, 1995.

Lancaster, Burt, 80: rugged screen actor, once circus acrobat. Starred in some 70 films over 45 years. Oct. 20, 1994.

Lansing, Robert, 66: star of stage, screen, and television. Oct. 23, 1994.

Lundberg, Ferdinand, 92: social critic whose books denounced the wealthy and what he regarded as their grip on nation's economic life. March 1, 1995.

Lupino, Ida, 77: veteran film actress known for portrayals of worldly wise villainess. Aug. 2, 1995.

Mantle, Mickey, 63: rated as most powerful switch-hitter in baseball history, a successor to Babe Ruth and Joe DiMaggio. Aug. 13, 1995.

Mason, Admiral Redfield, 91: helped Navy break Japanese military code in World War II. Won national prominence by winning $100,000 on television quiz show with knowledge of ancient mythology. July 9, 1995..

May, Dr. Rollo, 85: innovative psychologist and psychotherapist whose writings made him well-known. He also was co-founder of the Association for Humanistic psychology. Oct. 22, 1994.

McClure, Doug, 59: actor noted for his roles in television westerns, especially "The Virginian." He also appeared in films. Feb. 5, 1995.

Montgomery, Elizabeth, 57: TV actress famous for her starring role in the long-running comedy series "Bewitched." May 18, 1995.

Morrison, Sterling, 53: rock guitarist who was a founding member of the experimental rock band Velvet Underground. Aug. 30, 1995.

Natwick, Mildred, 89: versatile actress who preferred Broadway to Hollywood but appeared in films and on television as well. Oct. 25, 1994.

Nelson, Harriet, 85: actress identified as the mother in the long-running television series "The Adventures of Ozzie and Harriet," which began as a radio show in 1944. Oct. 2, 1994.

Neumann, Vaclav, 74: conductor of the Czech Philharmonic for more than 20 years gained worldwide fame through recordings and guest appearances. Sept. 2, 1995.

Nizer, Louis, 92: noted trial lawyer with long career of representing famous people. Autobiography, "My Life in Court," was a best seller. Nov. 10, 1994.

Osborne, John, 65: British playwright whose "Look Back in Anger" changed course of London theater. Dec. 24, 1994.

Pleasence, Donald, 75: British actor who was equally at home on stage in London and New York is best remembered for his title role in Pinter's "The Caretaker," a role he also performed in the film version retitled "The Guest." Feb. 2, 1995.

Primus, Pearl, 74: pioneering dancer, choreographer, and teacher. Developed dance about black life as important part of American culture. Oct. 29, 1994.

Raye, Martha, 78: singer, dancer, and actress for decades on Broadway, in Hollywood, and on television. Oct. 19, 1994.

Rich, Charlie, 62: country singer and songwriter known as the Silver Fox was an originator of the "countrypolitan" sound. He also wrote music for films. July 25, 1995.

Roebling, Mary G., 89: first woman to head a major American bank and a former Governor of American Stock Exchange. Oct. 25, 1994.

Rogers, Ginger (Virginia Katherine McMath), 83: vivacious film actress and dancer. Starred with Fred Astaire in elegant romantic musical films. April 25, 1995.

Romney, George W., 88: automobile executive who served three terms as Governor of Michigan, was a Republican Presidential aspirant and a member of Nixon Cabinet. July 25, 1995.

Rozsa, Miklos, 88: composer of film music was the winner of three Academy Awards for his scores for "Spellbound," "A Double Life," and "Ben-Hur." July 27, 1995.

Rudolph, Wilma, 54: track star, unable to walk as sickly child, won three gold medals as sprinter in 1960 Olympics in Rome. Nov. 12, 1994.

Rusk, Dean, 85: Secretary of State under Presidents Kennedy and Johnson. Severely criticized for defense of U.S. involvement in Vietnam War. Dec. 20, 1994.

Salk, Dr. Jonas, 80: medical researcher who developed first successful vaccine against poliomyelitis, crippling viral disease once of epidemic proportions. June 23, 1995.

Sarton, May, 83: poet, novelist, writer of nonfiction whose career stretched from 1929 to 1994 was a noted individualist and a heroine to feminists. July 16, 1995.

Seldes, George, 104: author, journalists, and critic of the press who gained his reputation with the publication of "Lords of the Press" and "Freedom of the Press." July 21, 1995.

Smith, Margaret Chase, 97: independent Maine Republican, first woman to win election to both houses of Congress. May 29, 1995.

Spender, Sir Stephen, 86: British poet, critic and novelist. Insisted that poetry should be linked to social and political issues. July 16, 1995.

Stander, Lionel, 86: stage and screen actor. Long exiled from films under Hollywood blacklist. Nov. 30, 1994.

Steegmuller, Francis, 88: American novelist, biographer, and translator. Noted for works on French novelist Gustave Flaubert. Oct. 20, 1994.

Stennis, John, C. 93: retired Democratic Senator. Was influential voice in Congress on military affairs over more than 41 years. April 23, 1995.

Suomi, Verner, E., 79: meteorologist who developed weather forecasting technology. July 30, 1995.

Swayze, John Cameron, 89: one of television's first evening news anchors. A household name in early days of television. Aug. 14, 1995.

Turner, Lana, 75: movie star who gained fame as the "sweater girl."

U Nu, 87: Prime Minister of Burma during 12 of its first years of independence. Feb. 14, 1995.

Venuta, Benay, 84: actress, singer, dancer was active in the New York theater for more than 50 years. She also performed in films and on radio. Sept. 1, 1995.

Wayne, David, 81: actor who played roles on Broadway, in television, and in films was the first Tony Award recipient for his portrayal of a leprechaun in "Finian's Rainbow." Feb. 9, 1995.

Wiesner, Dr. Jerome B., 79: science adviser to President Kennedy and later president of Massachusetts Institute of Technology. Oct. 21, 1994.

Wigner, Eugene P., 92: physicist who helped usher in atomic age with fundamental advances in nuclear physics and quantum theory. Won Nobel Prize in Physics in 1963. Jan. 1, 1995.

Wilkins, William J. 98: jurist who was a member of the four-judge panel that convicted Nazi industrialists during the Nuremberg war crime trials. Sept. 9, 1995.

Wilson, Harold, 79: long-term Prime Minister in British Labour Party Governments. May 24, 1995.

Wolfman Jack, 57: rock-and-roll disk jockey whose radio show brought him cult-following fame as one of America's best-known radio personalities. July 1, 1995.

Wood, Evelyn, 86: founded the Evelyn Wood Reading Dynamics Institute which promoted her method of speed reading. Aug. 26, 1995.

POSTAL REGULATIONS

U.S. Postal Rates and Fees

Domestic Rates Effective January 1, 1995

First-Class Mail

Single-Piece Letter/Flat Rates

1st ounce	$0.32
Each additional ounce	0.23

Weight not over (oz.)		Weight not over (oz.)	
1*	$0.32	7	$1.70
2	0.55	8	1.93
3	0.78	9	2.16
4	1.01	10	2.39
5	1.24	11	2.62
6	1.47	Over 11 ounces, see Priority Mail.	

*Nonstandard surcharge may apply to pieces weighing 1 ounce or less based on size.

Card Rates

Single postal card sold by USPS	$0.20
Double postal card sold by USPS	0.40
Single postcard (commercial)	0.20

Postcard Dimensions: Not larger than 4-1/4 by 6 inches by 0.0095 inch thick. Not smaller than 3-1/2 by 5 inches by 0.007 thick.

Second-Class Mail

Only publishers and registered news agents approved for second-class mailing privileges may mail at second-class rates. Publications mailed by the public are charged at the applicable Express Mail, Priority Mail, or single-piece First-, third-, or fourth-class rate.

Third-Class Mail

Used primarily by retailers, catalogers, and other advertisers to promote products and services. See postmaster for details. **Use**—For mailing certain items—circulars, books, catalogs, other printed matter, merchandise, seeds, cuttings, bulbs, and plants—weighing less than 16 ounces.

Single-Piece Rates

Weight not over (oz.)		Weight not over (oz.)	
1	$0.32	8	$1.93
2	0.55	9	2.16
3	0.78	10	2.39
4	1.01	11	2.62
5	1.24	13	2.90
6	1.47	Over 13 but	
7	1.70	under 16	2.95

Express Mail

Express Mail is the Post Office's fastest service. Next day delivery by 12 noon to most destinations. Delivered 365 days a year with no extra charge for Saturday, Sunday, or holiday delivery. All packages must use an Express Mail label. Items may weigh up to 70 pounds and measure up to 108 inches in combined length and girth. Call 1–800–222–1811 for delivery information between ZIP Codes.

Features—Express Mail envelopes, labels, and boxes are available, at no additional charge, at post offices or by calling 1–800–222–1811.

Post Office to Addressee Service

Up to 8 ounces	$10.75
Over 8 ounces, up to 2 pounds	15.00
Up to 3 pounds	17.25
Up to 4 pounds	19.40
Up to 5 pounds	21.55
Up to 6 pounds	25.40
Up to 7 pounds	26.45
Over 7 pounds, see postmaster.	

Flat Rate Envelope—Post Office to Addressee Service

$15.00, regardless of weight or destination for matter sent in a flat rate envelope provided by the Postal Service.

Priority Mail

Priority Mail offers 2-day service to most domestic destinations. Items may weigh up to 70 pounds and measure up to 108 inches in combined length and girth.

Features—Priority Mail envelopes, labels, and boxes are available, at no additional charge, at post offices or by calling 1–800–222–1811.

Single-Piece Rates

Up to 2 pounds	$3.00
Up to 3 pounds	4.00
Up to 4 pounds	5.00
Up to 5 pounds	6.00
Over 5 pounds, see postmaster.	

Flat Rate Envelope

$3.00, regardless of weight or destination for matter sent in a flat rate envelope provided by the Postal Service.

Fourth-Class Mail

For mailing circulars, books, catalogs, other printed matter, and packages weighing 16 ounces or more. Enclosed or attached First-Class Mail is charged at First-Class rates. Packages may weigh up to 70 pounds and measure up to 108 inches in combined length and girth.

Parcel Post Zone Rates

For rates priced by distance and weight, see postmaster.

Special Services (Domestic Mail)

Certificate of Mailing

Proves that an item was mailed. Must be purchased at time of mailing. No record kept at the post office.

Fee, in addition to postage—$0.55

Certified Mail

Provides a mailing receipt, and a record is kept at the recipient's post office. A return receipt can also be purchased for an additional fee. Available only with First-Class and Priority Mail.

Fee, in addition to postage—$1.10

Insurance

Provides coverage against loss or damage. Coverage up to $600.00 for third- and fourth-class mail as well as third- and fourth-class matter mailed at Priority Mail or First-Class Mail rate. Insurance up to $25,000 can be purchased by using registered mail. Do not insure a package for more than its value.

Liability	Fee, in addition to postage
$ .01 to $50.00	$ .75
$ 50.01 to $100.00	1.60
$ 100.01 to $200.00	2.50
$ 200.01 to $300.00	3.40
$ 300.01 to $400.00	4.30
$ 400.01 to $500.00	5.20
$ 500.01 to $600.00	6.10

Money Orders

Provides safe transmission of money. Available in amounts up to $700.00.

Fee, in addition to postage—$0.85

Registered Mail

Provides maximum protection and security for valuables. Available only for Priority Mail and First-Class Mail. May be combined with COD, restricted delivery, or return receipt. Additional postal insurance available.

Value	Fee, in addition to postage	
	With postal insurance	Without postal insurance
$ 0.00 to $100.00	$4.95	$4.85
100.01 to 500.00	5.40	5.20
500.01 to 1,000.00	5.85	5.55
1,000.01 to 2,000.00	6.30	5.90

For higher values, consult your postmaster.

Restricted Delivery

Available only for certified mail, COD, insured mail for more than $50.00, or registered mail.

Fee, in addition to postage—$2.75

Return Receipt

Available only for Express Mail, certified mail, COD, insured mail for more than $50.00, or registered mail.

Requested at time of mailing
Showing to whom (signature) and date delivered—$1.10
Showing to whom (signature), date, and addressee's address—$1.50

Requested after mailing
Showing to whom (signature) and date delivered—$6.60

Special Delivery

Available for all classes except Express Mail. Provides preferential handling to the extent practicable in dispatch, transportation, and expedited delivery at the destination.

Class of mail	Fee, in addition to postage		
	2 lb. or less	Over 2 lb., but not over 10 lb.	Over 10 lb
First-class & Priority Mail	$ 9.95	$10.35	$11.15
Other classes	10.45	11.25	12.10

Collect on Delivery (COD)

Allows mailers to collect the price of goods and/or postage on merchandise ordered by addressee when it is delivered. Fees include insurance. Maximum amount $600.00; see postmaster for details.

Sizes for Domestic Mail

Mail must meet these standards:
- Thickness—No less than 0.007 inch thick. Pieces that are 1/4 inch thick or less must be at least 3-1/2 inches high, 5 inches long, and rectangular in shape.
- Combined length and girth—No more than 108 inches.
- Weight—No more than 70 pounds.

Keys and identification devices are exempted from these requirements.

Additional standards apply to bulk mail and mail addressed to APOs and FPOs.

The Mail Order Merchandise Rule

The mail order rule adopted by the Federal Trade Commission in October 1975 provides that when you order by mail:

You must receive the merchandise when the seller says you will.

If you are not promised delivery within a certain time period, the seller must ship the merchandise to you no later than 30 days after your order comes in.

If you don't receive it shortly after that 30-day period, you can cancel your order and get your money back.

How the Rule Works

The seller must notify you if the promised delivery date (or the 30-day limit) cannot be met. The seller must also tell you what the new shipping date will be and give you the option to cancel the order and receive a full refund or agree to the new shipping date. The seller must also give you a free way to send back your answer, such as a stamped envelope or a postage-paid postcard. *If you don't answer, it means that you agree to the shipping delay.*

The seller must tell you if the shipping delay is going to be more than 30 days. You then can agree to the delay or, if you do not agree, the seller must return your money by the end of the first 30 days of the delay.

If you cancel a prepaid order, the seller must mail you the refund within seven business days. Where there is a credit sale, the seller must adjust your account within one billing cycle.

It would be impossible, however, for one rule to apply uniformly to such a varied field as mail order merchandising. For example, the rule does not apply to mail order photo finishing, magazine subscriptions, and other serial deliveries (except for the initial shipment); to mail order seeds and growing plants; to COD orders; or to credit orders where the buyer's account is not charged prior to shipment of the merchandise.

International Rates Effective July, 1995

Letters and Letter Packages— Airmail Rates

All countries except Canada & Mexico

Weight not over (oz.)		Weight not over (oz.)	
0.5	$ 0.60	9.0	7.40
1.0	1.00	9.5	7.80
1.5	1.40	10.0	8.20
2.0	1.80	10.5	8.60
2.5	2.20	11.0	9.00
3.0	2.60	11.5	9.40
3.5	3.00	12.0	9.80
4.0	3.40	12.5	10.20
4.5	3.80	13.0	10.60
5.0	4.20	13.5	11.00
5.5	4.60	14.0	11.40
6.0	5.00	14.5	11.80
6.5	5.40	15.0	12.20
7.0	5.80	15.5	12.60
7.5	6.20	16.0	13.00
8.0	6.60	16.5	13.40
8.5	7.00		

See postmaster for weights up to 4 lb. Maximum weight: 64 ounces.

Aerogrammes

All countries—$0.50

Letters and Letter Packages

Weight not over (lbs)	(oz.)	Canada[1]	Mexico	Weight not over (lbs)	(oz.)	Canada[1]	Mexico
0	0.5	$.48	$.40	0	10	2.28	4.06
0	1	.52	.48	0	11	2.47	4.46
0	1.5	.64	.66	0	12	2.66	4.86
0	2	.72	.86	1	0	3.42	6.46
0	3	.95	1.26	1	8	4.30	9.66
0	4	1.14	1.66	2	0	5.18	12.86
0	5	1.33	2.06	2	8	6.06	16.06
0	6	1.52	2.46	3	0	6.94	19.26
0	7	1.71	2.86	3	8	7.82	22.46
0	8	1.90	3.26	4	0	8.70	25.66
0	9	2.09	3.66				

1. A 4-pound maximum applies except for registered items sent to Canada. Canada-bound registered items may weigh up to 66 pounds. For registered items weighing over 4 pounds, the rate is $1.76 for each additional pound up to the 66-pound limit.

Post Cards and Postal Rates

Canada—$0.40; Mexico—$0.35; All others—$0.50

How to Complain About a Postal Problem

When you have a problem with your mail service, complete a Consumer Service Card which is available from letter carriers and at post offices. This will help your postmaster respond to your problem. If you wish to telephone a complaint, a postal employee will fill out the card for you.

The Consumer Advocate represents consumers at the top management level in the Postal Service. If your postal problems cannot be solved by your local post office, then write to the Consumer Advocate. His staff stands ready to serve you.

Write to: The Consumer Advocate, U.S. Postal Service, Washington, D.C. 20260-6320. Or phone: 1-202-268-2284.

Authorized 2-Letter State Abbreviations

When the Post Office instituted the ZIP Code for mail in 1963, it also drew up a list of two-letter abbreviations for the states which would gradually replace the traditional ones in use. Following is the official list, including the District of Columbia, Guam, Puerto Rico, and the Virgin Islands (note that only capital letters are used):

Alabama	AL	Kentucky	KY	Ohio	OH
Alaska	AK	Louisiana	LA	Oklahoma	OK
Arizona	AZ	Maine	ME	Oregon	OR
Arkansas	AR	Maryland	MD	Pennsylvania	PA
California	CA	Massachusetts	MA	Puerto Rico	PR
Colorado	CO	Michigan	MI	Rhode Island	RI
Connecticut	CT	Minnesota	MN	South Carolina	SC
Delaware	DE	Mississippi	MS	South Dakota	SD
Dist. of Columbia	DC	Missouri	MO	Tennessee	TN
Florida	FL	Montana	MT	Texas	TX
Georgia	GA	Nebraska	NE	Utah	UT
Guam	GU	Nevada	NV	Vermont	VT
Hawaii	HI	New Hampshire	NH	Virginia	VA
Idaho	ID	New Jersey	NJ	Virgin Islands	VI
Illinois	IL	New Mexico	NM	Washington	WA
Indiana	IN	New York	NY	West Virginia	WV
Iowa	IA	North Carolina	NC	Wisconsin	WI
Kansas	KS	North Dakota	ND	Wyoming	WY